D0706768

Reader's Guide to

MUSIC

History, Theory, Criticism

EDITORIAL ADVISORY COMMITTEE

Joseph Auner
State University of New York, Stony Brook

Charles S. Brauner
Roosevelt University

A. Peter Brown
Indiana University

J. Peter Burkholder
Indiana University

Donald Burrows
Open University, Milton Keynes

Susan C. Cook
University of Wisconsin, Madison

Mary E. Cyr
University of Guelph

Lawrence M. Earp
University of Wisconsin, Madison

Sarah Fuller
State University of New York, Stony Brook

Standley Howell
Chicago Public Library

Donald W. Krummel
University of Illinois, Champaign-Urbana

Thomas J. Mathiesen
Indiana University

Benito Rivera
Indiana University

Richard Sherr
Smith College

Anne C. Shreffler
Universität Basel

Susan Youens
University of Notre Dame

Reader's Guide to

MUSIC

History, Theory, Criticism

Editor

MURRAY STEIB

FITZROY DEARBORN PUBLISHERS
CHICAGO AND LONDON

ELMHURST COLLEGE LIBRARY

JUN 2000

Copyright © 1999 by
FITZROY DEARBORN PUBLISHERS

All rights reserved including the right of reproduction in whole or in part in any form.
For information write to:

FITZROY DEARBORN PUBLISHERS
919 N. Michigan Avenue, Suite 760
Chicago, Illinois 60611
USA

or

FITZROY DEARBORN PUBLISHERS
310 Regent Street
London W1R 5AJ
England

British Library and Library of Congress Cataloging in Publication Data are available

ISBN 1-57958-143-9

First published in the USA and UK 1999

Index prepared by Between the Lines Indexing and Editorial Services, Chicago, Illinois
Typeset by Print Means Inc., New York, New York
Printed by Sheridan Books, Ann Arbor, Michigan
Cover design by Chicago Advertising and Design, Chicago, Illinois

CONTENTS

EDITOR'S NOTE

Aims, Scope, and Selection of Entries

The literature on music is vast and growing at an ever-increasing rate. The past few decades in particular have seen a burgeoning of publications as music scholars have begun to embrace new methodologies employed earlier in other fields. Alongside more traditional approaches to music, scholars have begun to raise such issues as gender, class, race, and ethnicity. Methodologies pioneered in other disciplines, such as literary criticism and semiotics, are now widely employed, and, while broadening their scope in general, writers on music have introduced a welter of new ideas and terminology, some of which assumes a prior knowledge of non-music literature. Although there are still a few books that deal with broad issues and are addressed to a wide audience, the majority of recent studies deal with very narrow topics and are addressed to a relatively restricted audience of specialists and graduate students. Frequently, these publications engage in debates on issues which, although fascinating and important in their own right, can be confusing or opaque to a wider audience.

The aim of the *Reader's Guide to Music: History, Theory, Criticism* is to provide some help to those who wish to explore the wealth of writing on music. Because a simple list of books is not sufficient for this purpose, the *Reader's Guide* consists of a series of essays that describe and evaluate the critical monographic literature in English on a wide variety of topics in music. This approach is designed to help readers at all levels: students at both the undergraduate and graduate level who are looking for help with written assignments or research papers, or who are studying for exams; teachers in schools, colleges, and universities, especially those who face the problem of preparing classes outside their own specialty; and general readers who have an interest in music and seek advice on which books to read.

Because of the nature of music and the literature about it, the scope of this *Reader's Guide* poses some special problems. It was originally conceived as a reference guide to the secondary literature on Western art music, but the question of whether to include non-Western and popular music soon arose. While our self-imposed restriction of including only entries for which there are published books in English (with occasional exceptions) narrows the field somewhat, the limitation of approximately 500 entries makes inclusion of all music topics and people impossible. The question, then, became, what topics would be the most useful to the audience of this volume?

Our solution to the problem of scope was to treat Western art music as the basis for the book and to include individual composer entries (covering books about composers and their works) and topic entries (covering books about genres, styles, performance practice, and so forth) but not to include entries on individual works. This arrangement allowed us to include the more important non-Western and popular music topics with the same type of subdivision found in genre entries. For example, the *Reader's Guide* contains entries on Jazz and Rock and Roll, each with chronological subdivisions in which the most significant books, whether about styles, individual composers, or related issues, are reviewed. Geographic areas, such as Africa, India, and Latin America, are included as well.

One aspect of the *Reader's Guide to Music* that will strike the reader is that there are some important people who are not included. For example, there are no entries for Georg Philipp Telemann or for most women composers before the 19th century. The reason for this is simple: there are still many important topics for which there is little or no monographic literature in English. All of the work on Telemann, for example, is either in German or appears in dissertations or journal articles. Although there are a few dissertations and journal articles in the *Reader's Guide,* we did not include any entry for which there were fewer than two books in English devoted to that topic.

Arrangement of Entries

Entries appear in alphabetical order; a complete list of these can be found in the Alphabetical List of Entries (p. **xv**). Where there are several entries sharing the same general heading (e.g., Chamber Music, Jazz, Opera, Symphony, and many of the composers), the order does not proceed alphabetically. In entries on genres or topics (e.g., Keyboard Music), the order is normally chronological. In the case of composers, the order proceeds as far as possible from the more general to the more particular, beginning with "Biography" and continuing in what seems the most logical and helpful manner.

Although the overall arrangement of entries is alphabetical, the *Reader's Guide to Music* contains various aids to facilitate access to its contents. These are:

1. Thematic List (p. **xxi**). This list should be consulted to see the full range of entries that relate to a particular subject area, such as African-American Music, Patronage, Performance Practice, or Women in Music.
2. Booklist Index (p. **799**). This lists, in alphabetical order, the authors of all books and articles discussed in the entries and can be used to locate discussions of the works of particular scholars.
3. General Index (p. **835**). This lists individuals, topics, and particular works mentioned in the entries. This index will be particularly useful for locating references to individuals or topics that have no entry of their own.
4. Cross References. At the end of numerous entries there are *See also* references that refer the reader to entries on related topics.

Format within Entries

Each entry begins with a list of the books or articles to be discussed in the essay. Complete publication details are provided, including dates of the first publication and, where appropriate, the most recent revised edition. Reprints and paperback editions are normally omitted unless the original publication is more than 50 years old. Each essay begins with a short introduction that either gives an overview of the subject or discusses the issues on which scholars have focused. In the text of each essay, the first significant mention of each publication is indicated by the appearance of the author's name in capital letters. In cases where more than one book by the same author is discussed in the same essay, each book is introduced by the author's name in capital letters followed by the date of publication in parentheses. Although the list of books in each entry proceeds in alphabetical order by author, the books are not normally discussed in that order in the text. It was left to the judgment of contributors to decide whether to discuss books in order of publication or, more often, according to the subject matter and emphasis of each book.

Acknowledgments

At the conclusion of a project such as this, it is a pleasure to finally be able to thank all of the people who helped in one way or another. First, I would like to thank the advisory board, who helped me shape the scope and character of this *Reader's Guide to Music.* I am equally grateful to all those who have written for this volume; I deeply appreciate their cooperation and generosity in writing for the *Reader's Guide*. Special thanks must go to those contributors who quickly wrote essays with very short notice during the final stages of production. Thanks also go to Rika Asai, Diane Clymer, and Jonathan Shull, my graduate assistants who helped enormously during various stages of the book; and to Joseph Auner, Ralph Locke, Marilyn McCoy, Greta Olson, and Elizabeth Seitz, who very kindly helped me connect with potential contributors. The resources of the University of Chicago Library and Indiana University Library have been invaluable. Finally, thanks must also go to several people at Fitzroy Dearborn Publishers: Gretchen Willenberg and Amber Forst, the editorial assistants who worked on the book and without whom this book could not possibly have been completed; Paul Schellinger, who was instrumental in getting the book started and was very supportive at critical moments along the way; and especially to Steve LaRue, who first got me involved with the project and whose patience and hard work has seen it through to publication.

Murray Steib

ADVISERS

Joseph Auner
Charles S. Brauner
A. Peter Brown
J. Peter Burkholder
Donald Burrows
Susan C. Cook
Mary E. Cyr
Lawrence M. Earp

Sarah Fuller
Standley Howell
Donald W. Krummel
Thomas J. Mathiesen
Benito Rivera
Richard Sherr
Anne C. Shreffler
Susan Youens

CONTRIBUTORS

Allsen, J. Michael
Amati-Camperi, Alexandra
Antokoletz, Elliott
Archetto, Maria
Attinello, Paul
Bailey, Candace Lee
Bain, Jennifer
Baker, Evan
Baker, James M.
Balensuela, C. Matthew
Barz, Gregory F.
Benson, Mark
Bergquist, Peter
Bisson, Noël
Black, Brian
Block, Geoffrey
Bloom, Peter
Bomberger, E. Douglas
Browner, Tara
Bryan, Karen
Buck, Charles
Bücker, Andreas
Burdette, Glenn

Caballero, Carlo
Cahn, Steven Joel
Calico, Joy Haslam
Carruthers, Glen
Cateforis, Theo
Champagne, Mario
Chang, Sangtae
Charry, Eric
Christensen, Thomas
Clark, Renée Chérie
Clark, Walter Aaron
Clifton, Keith E.
Cochran, Keith Harris
Coeyman, Barbara
Converse, Ralph D.
Cook, Susan C.
Coppola, Catherine
Cowgill, Rachel
Cramer, Alfred
Cramer, Eugene Casjen
Crittenden, Camille
Cross, Charlotte M.
Crowe, Barbara J.

Davidian, Teresa
Davis, Mary E.
Desmond, Karen
Di Grazia, Donna M.
Dirst, Matthew
Dragone, Luann
Dubowchik, Rosemary Thoonen
Erickson, Raymond
Fader, Don
Fairtile, Linda B.
Farahat, Martha
Faucett, Bill F.
Feurzeig, Lisa
Florea, Luminita
Flynn, Timothy S.
Frantz, Charles Frederick
Fromson, Michele
Gagné, David
Gallo, Denise
Garf, Nancy F.
Gentry, Theodore L.
Gibbs, Christopher H.
Giger, Andreas
Goldberg, Halina
Grave, Floyd K.
Gray, John Douglas
Green, Robert Anthony
Greenwald, Helen M.
Grier, James
Haas, David
Haines, John
Harley, Maria Anna
Harris-Warrick, Rebecca
Hart, Brian J.
Harwell Celenza, Anna H.
Harwood, Gregory W.
Hayes, Deborah
Headlam, Dave
Heimarck, Brita
Herzog, Silvia
Heuchemer, Dane
Heyer, John Hajdu
Hill, Camille Crunelle
Hisama, Ellie M.
Hong, Barbara J.
Hooker, Lynn
Horne, William
Houtchens, Alan
Howe, Sondra Wieland
Hubbert, Julie B.
Hung, Eric
Hurley, David Ross
Jacobson, Daniel
Joe, Jeongwon
Joyner, David
Karr, John
Katz, Mark
Kauffman, Deborah

Kearns, Andrew
Kinder, Keith
Kinderman, William
King, Richard G.
Kluge, Mark
Koenig, Laura J.
Korstvedt, Benjamin M.
Kreitner, Kenneth
Laki, Peter.
Lam, Joseph S.C.
Langford, Jeffrey
Leclair, Charmaine Fran
Lerner, Neil
Leve, James
Libin, Kathryn L. Shanks
Lindberg, John E.
Lindeman, Stephen
Lindsey, Roberta
Lodato, Suzanne M.
Lopes, Luiz Fernando Vallim
Lorimer, Nancy
Lowe, Melanie
Lowerre, Kathryn
Lynn, Donna L.
Magee, Jeffrey
Marissen, Michael
Marsh, Gordon
Martin, Margot
Marvin, Roberta M.
Mathers, Daniel E.
Mattis, Olivia
Mayer, Constance
Mayfield, Connie E.
McCachren, Renee
McClellan, Michael E.
mcclung, bruce d.
McCoy, Marilyn L.
McGrade, Michael
McLamore, Alyson
Meconi, Honey
Melamed, Daniel R.
Meyer, Stephen
Miller, Roark
Miller, Stephen R.
Miyakawa, Felicia M.
Mockus, Martha
Moran, John
Morrison, Julie Dorn
Morrow, Mary Sue
Moulsdale, Gary
Muir, Theresa
Murata, Margaret
Murphy, Sheryl Kathleen
Nadeau, Nils
Nealon, Michael A.
Neff, Lyle K.
Neff, Teresa M.
Nelson, Bernadette

Nikitopoulos, Alison Terbell
Nolan, Catherine
Noonan, Timothy
O'Connell, Jeremy
Ogasapian, John
Olǎani, Robert William
Oleskiewicz, Mary
Olin, Elinor
Olson, Greta J.
Onderdonk, Julian
Orchard, Joseph
Orr, N. Lee
Ossi, Massimo
Paige, Diane M.
Palmer, John R.
Palmer, Robert E.
Parks, Richard S.
Pershing, Drora
Platt, Heather
Portowitz, Adena
Reich, Nancy B.
Reindl, Dawn O'Neal
Renwick, William
Rio, Robin
Risinger, Mark
Rivest, Johanne
Roberge, Marc-André
Robinson, Kathleen E.
Rohling, Geraldine M.
Romanou, Ekaterini
Rosenblatt, Jay
Saloman, Ora Frishberg
Saunders, Steven
Schenbeck, Lawrence
Schiano, Michael Jude
Schulenberg, David
Sears, Ann
Seitz, Elizabeth
Self, Stephen

Sheinbaum, John J.
Sherwood, Gayle
Shinnick, Julia W.
Simms, Bryan R.
Sims, Michael
Sipe, Thomas
Smith, Jeremy L.
Sposato-Allen, Lorraine
Sprout, Leslie
Stayer, Jayme
Steib, Murray
Stempel, Larry
Strader, Nikola D.
Strempel, Eileen L.
Suchoff, Benjamin
Sullivan, Todd
Swenson-Eldridge, Joanne E.
Termini, Olga
Tiedge, Faun Tanenbaum
Toft, Robert
Vaughn, Michael
Verble, Charles R.
Vishio, Anton
von der Linn, Michael
Wagstaff, Grayson
Walden, Valerie
Warfield, Patrick
Warfield, Scott
Wasson, Jeffrey
Wiecki, Ron
Wile, Kip
Wilson Kimber, Marian
Wolf, Edward Christopher
Woodside, Mary S.
Wright, Lesley A.
Youmans, Charles
Zank, Stephen
Zimmerman, Dan
Zohn, Steven

ALPHABETICAL LIST OF ENTRIES

THEMATIC LIST

Entries by Category

African-American Music
Baroque Music
Classical Music
Countries
Criticism
Dance
Ethnomusicology
Genres
Instrumental Music: Chamber Music
Instrumental Music: Keyboard Music
Instrumental Music: Orchestral Music
Letters and Correspondence
Medieval Music
Opera

Patronage
Performance Practice
Popular Music
Renaissance Music
Romantic Music
Sacred Music
Theory
20th-Century Music
Vocal Music: Chanson
Vocal Music: Choral Music
Vocal Music: Lieder
Vocal Music: Motet
Vocal Music: Song
Women in Music

AFRICAN-AMERICAN MUSIC AND MUSICIANS

Africa
Blues
Conductors and Conducting
Ellington, Edward Kennedy "Duke"
Ethnomusicology: Theory and
    Method
Hymn
Instruments: Percussion
Jazz: Early
Jazz: Dixieland
Jazz: Swing

Jazz: Bebop
Jazz: Cool
Jazz: West Coast
Jazz: Free
Jazz: After 1960
Joplin, Scott
Performance Practice: Romantic
Ragtime
Rock and Roll: 1950s United States
Rock and Roll: 1980s United States
Still, William Grant

BAROQUE MUSIC

Affections, Doctrine of
Bach, Johann Sebastian
Ballet: French
Band Music
Baroque Music: General Studies
Baroque Music: Specialized Studies
Borrowing
Burney, Charles
Buxtehude, Dietrich
Caccini, Francesca

Caccini, Giulio
Cantata: French Baroque
Cantata: German Baroque
Cantata: Italian Baroque
Carissimi, Giacomo
Castrato
Cavalli, Pier Francesco
Chamber Music: Baroque
Charpentier, Marc-Antoine
Commedia dell'arte

Concerto: Baroque
Continuo
Convents
Corelli, Arcangelo
Counterpoint
Couperin, François
Dance: Baroque
Early Music Movement
France: General Studies
France: Musical Centers
Frescobaldi, Girolamo
Fugue
Fux, Johann Joseph
Great Britain: General Studies
Great Britain: Musical
  Centers
Handel, George Frideric
Keyboard Music: Baroque
Libretto
Lully, Jean-Baptiste
Manuscript Studies: Baroque
Marais, Marin
Masque
Mattheson, Johann
Monody
Monteverdi, Claudio

Opera: 17th-Century Italian
Opera: French to 1800
Opera: German to 1800
Opera: 18th-Century Italian
Oratorio
Ornamentation: Baroque
Passion Music
Performance Practice: Baroque
Pergolesi, Giovanni Battista
Publishing: To 1750
Purcell, Henry
Quantz, Johann Joachim
Rameau, Jean-Philippe
Rhetoric
Scarlatti, Alessandro
Scarlatti, Domenico
Schütz, Heinrich
Sonata: Baroque
Spain: General Studies
Spain: Musical Centers
Stradivari, Antonio
Theory and Theorists: 17th Century
Theory and Theorists: 18th Century
Tuning and Temperaments
Vivaldi, Antonio
Women in Music

CLASSICAL MUSIC

Aesthetics: Classical
Analysis: General
Analysis: Schenkerian
Analysis: Tonal
Bach, Carl Philipp Emanuel
Bach, Johann Christian
Ballet: French
Band Music
Beethoven, Ludwig van
Boccherini, Luigi
Burney, Charles
Castrato
Chamber Music: Classical
Classical Music: General Studies
Classical Music: Specialized
  Studies
Clementi, Muzio
Concerto: From 1750
Criticism: 18th and 19th Centuries
Dance: Classical
Form
France: General Studies
France: Musical Centers
Gluck, Christoph Willibald
Great Britain: General Studies
Great Britain: Musical Centers
Harmony: Theory

Hasse, Johann Adolf
Haydn, Franz Joseph
Keyboard Music: Classical
Lied: To 1800
Manuscript Studies: Baroque
Mozart, Leopold
Mozart, Wolfgang Amadeus
Opera: French to 1800
Opera: German to 1800
Opera: 18th-Century Italian
Ornamentation: Classical
Performance Practice: Classical
Pergolesi, Giovanni Battista
Publishing: From 1750
Quantz, Johann Joachim
Rhetoric
Salieri, Antonio
Scarlatti, Domenico
Sonata: Classical
Spain: General Studies
Spain: Musical Centers
Symphony: General
Symphony: 18th-Century French
Symphony: 18th-Century German
Symphony: 18th-Century Italian
Theory and Theorists: 18th Century
Women in Music

COUNTRIES

Africa
Australia
Canada
China
Eastern Europe
France: General Studies
France: Musical Centers
Great Britain: General Studies
Great Britain: Musical Centers
India
Indonesia

Italy: Musical Centers to 1600
Japan
Latin America
Middle East
Native North American Music
Portugal
Russia
Scandinavia
Spain: General Studies
Spain: Musical Centers

CRITICISM

Adorno, Theodor W.
Aesthetics
Affections, Doctrine of
Africa
Analysis: Tonal
Beethoven, Ludwig van
    3. Orchestral Music
    6. Influence
Bellini, Vincenzo
Borrowing
Burney, Charles
Byrd, William
Cage, John
Classical Music: Specialized Studies
Copland, Aaron
    2. Works
Criticism: 18th and 19th Centuries
Dahlhaus, Carl
Early Music Movement
France: General Studies
France: Musical Centers
Glass, Philip
Hanslick, Eduard
Hindemith, Paul
Hoffmann, E.T.A.

Indonesia
Ives, Charles
    1. Biography
Mozart, Wolfgang Amadeus
    7. Style
Musicology: Feminist
Musicology: Gay and Lesbian
Musicology: New Musicology
Musicology: Traditional
Neoclassicism
Opera: German to 1800
Partch, Harry
Performance Practice: Romantic
Philosophy of Music
Reich, Steve
Rhetoric
Schoenberg, Arnold
    3. Aesthetics
Schumann, Robert
    5. Piano Music
    6. Aesthetics and Writings
Sonata: Classical
Wagner, Richard
    6. Philosophy
Wolf, Hugo

DANCE

Africa
Ballet: French
Ballet: Russian
Ballet: United States
Chanson
Copland, Aaron
    2. Works
Dance: Medieval and Renaissance
Dance: Baroque
Dance: Classical
Dance: 19th Century
Dance: 20th Century

Flamenco
France: Musical Centers
Indonesia
Masque
Medieval Music: Specialized
    Studies
Monody
Mozart, Wolfgang Amadeus
    2. Chamber Music
    5. Orchestral Music
Native North American Music
Opera: Staging

Stravinsky, Igor
  2. Ballets
Tchaikovsky, Piotr Ilyich
  2. Ballets

Verdi, Giuseppe
  3. Operas: Middle Period
  5. Operas: Staging

ETHNOMUSICOLOGY

Africa
Australia
Bartók, Béla
  2. Ethnomusicology
Canada
Chant: Byzantine
China
Eastern Europe
Ethnomusicology: History
Ethnomusicology: Theory and Method
Flamenco

Folk Music
India
Indonesia
Japan
Kodály, Zoltán
Latin America
Middle East
Mode: Non-Western
Native North American Music
Notation: To 1600
Villa-Lobos, Heitor

GENRES

Bach, Johann Sebastian
  2. Cantatas
  3. Chamber Music
  4. Keyboard Music
  5. Orchestral Music
Ballet: French
Ballet: Russian
Ballet: United States
Band Music
Beethoven, Ludwig van
  2. Chamber Music
  3. Orchestral Music
  4. Piano Music
Berg, Alban
  2. Operas
Blues
Brahms, Johannes
  2. Chamber Music
  3. Orchestral Music
  4. Vocal Music
Britten, Benjamin
  2. Operas
Bruckner, Anton
  2. Symphonies
Cantata: French Baroque
Cantata: German Baroque
Cantata: Italian Baroque
Chamber Music: Baroque
Chamber Music: Classical
Chamber Music: 19th Century
Chamber Music: 20th Century
Chanson
Chant: Ambrosian
Chant: Byzantine
Chant: Gregorian

Chant: Other Western
Charpentier, Marc-Antoine
Chorale
Concerto: Baroque
Concerto: From 1750
Dance: Medieval and Renaissance
Dance: Baroque
Dance: Classical
Dance: 19th Century
Dance: 20th Century
Electronic Music
Film Music
Flamenco
Folk Music
Fugue
Handel, George Frideric
  2. Operas
  3. Oratorios
  4. Instrumental Music
Haydn, Franz Joseph
  2. Chamber Music
  3. Keyboard Music
  4. Orchestral Music
  5. Sacred Music
Hymn
Jazz: Early
Jazz: Dixieland
Jazz: Swing
Jazz: Bebop
Jazz: Cool
Jazz: West Coast
Jazz: Free
Jazz: After 1960
Keyboard Music: General
Keyboard Music: Renaissance

INSTRUMENTAL MUSIC: CHAMBER MUSIC

INSTRUMENTAL MUSIC: KEYBOARD MUSIC

INSTRUMENTAL MUSIC: ORCHESTRAL MUSIC

LETTERS AND CORRESPONDENCE

MEDIEVAL MUSIC

OPERA

PATRONAGE

PERFORMANCE PRACTICE

POPULAR MUSIC

RENAISSANCE MUSIC

ROMANTIC MUSIC

SACRED MUSIC

THEORY

20TH-CENTURY MUSIC

Jazz: Dixieland
Jazz: Swing
Jazz: Bebop
Jazz: Cool
Jazz: West Coast
Jazz: Free
Jazz: After 1960
Kern, Jerome
Keyboard Music: 20th Century
Kodály, Zoltán
Korngold, Erich Wolfgang
Ligeti, György
Lutosławski, Witold
Mahler, Gustav
Martinů, Bohuslav
Messiaen, Olivier
MIDI
Milhaud, Darius
Musical Comedy
Music Therapy
Nancarrow, Conlon
Neoclassicism
Nielsen, Carl
Notation: 20th Century
Oliveros, Pauline
Opera: 20th Century
Opera: English
Opera: Set Design
Orchestration
Paderewski, Jan Ignacy
Partch, Harry
Penderecki, Krzysztof
Philosophy of Music
Porter, Cole
Poulenc, Francis
Prokofiev, Sergei
Psychology of Music
Publishing: From 1750
Puccini, Giacomo

Rachmaninoff, Sergei
Ragtime
Ravel, Maurice
Reger, Max
Reich, Steve
Rhetoric
Rock and Roll
Rodgers, Richard
Rorem, Ned
Satie, Erik
Schoenberg, Arnold
Serialism
Set Theory
Shostakovich, Dmitri
Sibelius, Jean
Skryabin, Alexander
Sound Recording
Spain: General Studies
Spain: Musical Centers
Still, William Grant
Strauss, Richard
Stravinsky, Igor
Symphony: 20th Century
Theory and Theorists: 20th Century
Thomson, Virgil
Toscanini, Arturo
Tower, Joan
Tuning and Temperaments
20th-Century Music: General Studies
20th-Century Music: Specialized
    Studies
Varèse, Edgard
Vaughan Williams, Ralph
Villa-Lobos, Heitor
Walton, William
Webern, Anton
Weill, Kurt
Women in Music
Xenakis, Iannis

VOCAL MUSIC: CHANSON

Berlioz, Hector
  2. Works
Chanson
Du Fay, Guillaume
Machaut, Guillaume de
Manuscript Studies: Medieval
Manuscript Studies: Renaissance

Medieval Music: Specialized Studies
Performance Practice: Medieval
Poulenc, Francis
Renaissance Music: Specialized Studies
Sequence
Troubadours and Trouvères
Willaert, Adrian

VOCAL MUSIC: CHORAL MUSIC

Bach, Johann Sebastian
  2. Cantatas
Brahms, Johannes
  4. Vocal Music

Britten, Benjamin
  3. Other Works
Buxtehude, Dietrich
Byrd, William

VOCAL MUSIC: LIEDER

VOCAL MUSIC: MOTET

VOCAL MUSIC: SONG

WOMEN IN MUSIC

Crawford, Ruth Porter
Hensel, Fanny
Hildegard von Bingen
Instruments: Keyboard
  2. Piano
Musicology: Feminist
Musicology: Gay and Lesbian

Native North American Music
Oliveros, Pauline
Schumann, Clara
Sonata: General
Tower, Joan
20th-Century Music: Specialized Studies
Women in Music

A

Acoustics

Backus, John, *The Acoustical Foundations of Music*, New York: Norton, 1969; 2nd edition, 1977

Benade, Arthur H., *Fundamentals of Musical Acoustics*, New York: Oxford University Press, 1976; revised edition, New York: Dover, 1990

Butler, David, *The Musician's Guide to Perception and Cognition*, New York: Schirmer Books, 1992

Cook, Perry R., editor, *Music, Cognition, and Computerized Sound: An Introduction to Psychoacoustics*, Cambridge, Massachusetts: MIT Press, 1999

Deutsch, Diana, editor, *The Psychology of Music*, New York: Academic Press, 1982

Fletcher, Neville H., and Thomas D. Rossing, *The Physics of Musical Instruments*, New York: Springer Verlag, 1991; 2nd edition, 1998

Hall, Donald E., *Musical Acoustics*, Pacific Grove, California: Wadsworth, 1980; 2nd edition, Pacific Grove, California: Brooks/Cole, 1991

Helmholtz, Hermann von, *On the Sensations of Tone as a Physiological Basis for the Theory of Music*, translated by Alexander J. Ellis, London: Longmans, Green, 1875; 6th edition, New York: Smith, 1948

Hutchins, Carleen Maley, compiler, *The Physics of Music: Readings from Scientific American*, San Francisco: Freeman, 1978

Plomp, Reinier, *Aspects of Tone Sensation: A Psychophysical Study*, London: Academic Press, 1976

Roads, Curtis, *The Computer Music Tutorial*, Cambridge, Massachusetts: MIT Press, 1995

Roederer, Juan G., *The Physics and Psychophysics of Music: An Introduction*, New York: Springer Verlag, 1973; 3rd edition, 1995

Sundberg, Johan, *The Science of Musical Sounds*, San Diego, California: Academic Press, 1991

Musicians are often surprised to discover the extent to which the history of music—usually presented as the development of composers, compositions, styles, and performers—has a parallel track in the scientific study of tuning systems, the physics and acoustical properties of musical instruments, the storage and reproduction of sound, and the perception and cognition of music. This parallel history is generally given in books on musical acoustics, in which names of scientists such as Pythagoras, Fourier, and Helmholtz are found along with charts, graphs, equations, and theorems that can often be intimidating. Finding the right balance of scientific and musical information is the goal of most books on acoustics for musicians. Those wanting more information may find much more complete and complex presentations in books aimed at scientists and in materials from the Acoustical Society of America and its journal, which should be consulted for serious research into acoustics.

Most acoustics texts for musicians divide into the two broad, related topics of acoustics and psychoacoustics: the former is the study of acoustical properties of music-related sound sources, and the latter is the perception of those sounds. More emphasis on acoustics is found in books aimed at scientists, and a greater emphasis on psychoacoustics can be found in sources for psychologists or music cognition researchers. Typically, acoustics texts have chapters on the physics of simple harmonic motion and traditional musical sound sources; the frequency, dynamic, and timbral characteristics of musical sounds, as physical properties and in relation to human perception; acoustical environments, such as concert halls; studies of members of each of the musical instrument families; the electromagnetic and digital storage and reproduction of sound; and harmonic theory, the overtone series, and musical tuning systems. Along the way, enough information on trigonometry, geometry, logarithms, calculus, basic algebra, and other mathematical operations is given for readers to gain some appreciation for the values being presented. The best books cite many examples of practical musical effects pertaining to the properties and characteristics under discussion, in terms that musicians can understand.

The era of modern acoustics study begins with the work of HELMHOLTZ, who studied medicine, physics, the conservation of energy, electricity, hydrodynamics, atmospheric conditions, electrodynamics, and acoustics. His book on acoustics begins with a statement echoed in most subsequent writings: that the physical and physiological bases of acoustics and musical theory and aesthetics have an intimate relationship, and Helmholtz embodies this relationship in the idea of the sensation of musical tones. The three parts of his study define a blueprint for later books on the subject: the physics, frequency characteristics, and perception of vibration and musical tone; the interaction of tones in chords; and the physical basis for the musical scales and chords of tonality, with added elements of physics and mathematics given in appendices. In the course of his writing, Helmholtz summarizes a wealth of previous work on acoustics, and he provides a basis for studies of timbre in the presence and relationship of upper partials or overtones, an explanation of consonance and dissonance in the beats produced by tones and their partials, and a foundation for the acoustical principles of tonal musical composition.

A book close in spirit to that of Helmholtz is BENADE. The author has a particular talent for relating complex physical systems in terms of simple experiments, activities, and analogies that translate what might otherwise be esoteric concepts into experience and understanding. Each chapter ends with a section titled "Examples, Experiments, and Questions" that immeasurably aids in cementing and exploring aspects of the preceding material. In addition to clear presentations of the mechanics of simple harmonic motion, the real strength is his discussion of tone on brass instruments in terms of the regime of oscillation or the relative strength and presence of supporting harmonics; the related input impedance curves on woodwinds; and the effects of open tone holes in woodwinds on harmonic content, called the open-holes lattice cutoff frequency. The latter discussions prove to be of great relevance for performing musicians in understanding the often elusive nature of good tone, and Benade's emphasis on the mechanics of sound make the presentation clear and directly relevant.

Backus, Hall, Sundberg, and Roederer typify the contemporary acoustics textbook. All four authors cover the menu of items given above but in varying detail. BACKUS is quite good at integrating physics and mathematics clearly into his discussions, while HALL is extremely well set up for teaching, with summaries, terms, questions, and directions for further reading given at the ends of chapters, as well as appendices with more mathematical and musical subjects and a glossary. Hall's chapter on tuning and temperament is also particularly clear for a subject that can be confusing in its combination of ratios and cents but is clearly significant for music study. SUNDBERG similarly attempts to be comprehensive and yet basic enough to act as an introduction for those without previous experience. Although he covers many of the same topics, ROEDERER focuses on psychoacoustics, emphasizing the role of perception and cognition in apprehending the pitch, loudness, and timbral aspects of musical sounds in relation to the usual discussions of physical vibration systems. This topic opens up a whole area of cognitive research and brain studies (described below) in a field that has exploded recently and, like the more advanced topics such as Fourier series and wavelets, goes beyond the usual acoustics book menus.

An excellent supplement for the general acoustics text is HUTCHINS, a collection of articles from *Scientific American*. This collection, from authors Benade and Sundberg as well as others, includes sections on physics and music, the acoustics of the singing voice, the physics of the piano, woodwinds, brasses, violins, the bowed string, and architectural acoustics. The sections on the bowed string and violin by Hutchins are clear and engaging and present the source materials used in most texts. The articles are uniformly excellent, but a particularly clear presentation is on the piano, by E. Donnell Blackham. His contribution includes some discussion of perceptual tests on the timbre of the piano using synthesized sounds—a topic found in many articles in the *Journal of the Acoustical Society of America*. Each article relates the sound of the instrument to the physics behind the sound production and the way musicians perceive these sounds. Those who wish to pursue the subjects in more depth and have some background in mathematics and physics may turn to FLETCHER and ROSSING for detailed considerations of the sound mechanisms in the instrument families.

The emphasis on psychoacoustics found in Roederer is greatly amplified in Plomp, Butler, Deutsch, and Cook. Of the three characteristics of tone—pitch, dynamics, and timbre—the first two have been studied extensively, and it is the latter, timbre, that has shaped more recent research. PLOMP reflects research in the Netherlands and focuses on the ear and its perception and altering of physical signals in the apprehension of timbre and pitch. The non-linear nature of this apparatus—the ways in which the ear alters and augments the signal that it receives—is a topic throughout. BUTLER, DEUTSCH, and COOK reflect the emphasis on basic acoustical factors that is found in studies of cognition and perception of music and add other items of interest to psychologists. The related compositional and experimental control of musical parameters using computers is found in ROADS.

DAVE HEADLAM

Adorno, Theodor W. 1903–1969

German composer, philosopher, and critic

Adorno, Theodor W., *Alban Berg: Master of the Smallest Link*, translated by Juliane Brand and Christopher Hailey, Cambridge: Cambridge University Press, 1991

———, *In Search of Wagner*, translated by Rodney Livingstone, London: NLB, 1981

———, *Introduction to the Sociology of Music,* translated by E.B. Ashton, New York: Seabury Press, 1976

———, *Mahler: A Musical Physiognomy,* translated by Edmund Jephcott, Chicago: University of Chicago Press, 1992a

———, *Philosophy of Modern Music,* translated by Anne G. Mitchell and Wesley V. Blomster, New York: Seabury Press, and London: Sheed and Ward, 1973

———, *Prisms,* translated by Samuel Weber and Shierry Weber, London: Spearman, 1967

———, *Quasi una fantasia: Essays on Modern Music,* translated by Rodney Livingstone, London: Verso, 1992b

Cook, Deborah, *The Culture Industry Revisited: Theodor W. Adorno on Mass Culture,* Lanham, Maryland: Rowman and Littlefield, 1996

Hohendahl, Peter Uwe, *Prismatic Thought: Theodor W. Adorno,* Lincoln: University of Nebraska Press, 1995

Jay, Martin, *Adorno,* Cambridge, Massachusetts: Harvard University Press, 1984

Paddison, Max, *Adorno, Modernism and Mass Culture: Essays on Critical Theory and Music,* London: Kahn and Averill, 1996

———, *Adorno's Aesthetics of Music,* Cambridge: Cambridge University Press, 1993

Subotnik, Rose Rosengard, *Developing Variations: Style and Ideology in Western Music,* Minneapolis: University of Minnesota Press, 1991

Williams, Alastair, *New Music and the Claims of Modernity,* Aldershot, England: Ashgate, 1997

One of the most important social philosophers of the 20th century, Adorno had a special interest in the sociology of music. Half of his writings are devoted to musical topics; primary areas of inquiry include a discussion of the 19th-century Austro-German tradition, a spirited defense of difficult modern music rejected by the public, and a scathing critique of the musical products of mass popular culture. Like many intellectuals and artists of Jewish heritage at the time, Adorno emigrated from Nazi Germany, first to Oxford, then to New York and Los Angeles as a member of the exiled Frankfurt Institute for Social Research. In 1949 he returned to Frankfurt, later becoming director of the institute and professor at Frankfurt University.

Adorno's work is notoriously difficult to read: straightforward argument is eschewed in favor of suggestion, allusion, parataxis, and thoroughly dialectical reasoning, and his idiosyncratic use of his native German is known even in German-speaking countries as *Adorno-deutsch.* Much of the important literature on Adorno is in German, and it is only recently that English-language academics in general, and musicologists in particular, have published works about him. The 1980 *New Grove Dictionary of Music and Musicians,* for example, lists no sources in English in its Adorno bibliography.

JAY is in a unique position to have constructed a solid and straightforward introduction to Adorno, as he had previously written the first scholarly study of the Frankfurt Institute, *The Dialectical Imagination: A History of the Frankfurt School and the Institute of Social Research, 1923–1950* (1973). Jay discusses Adorno's life and philosophical background, from Marx and modernism to conservatism and Judaism, and explores the ways they influenced Adorno's analyses of society and culture. Unlike the other important early English-language monographs on Adorno, such as Susan Buck-Morss's *The Origin of Negative Dialectics: Theodor W. Adorno, Walter Benjamin, and the Frankfurt Institute* (1977) and Gillian Rose's *The Melancholy Science: An Introduction to the Thought of Theodor W. Adorno* (1978), Jay makes music central to his interpretation of Adorno's thought.

The Adorno chapters in SUBOTNIK's collection of essays were originally published as musicology journal articles during the 1970s, at a time when Adorno was largely unknown in American musicological circles; to the extent he was familiar, he was not considered a viable object of scholarship. These groundbreaking essays challenged then orthodox views of musicology as an ideology-free discipline. In Subotnik's reading, Adorno's theories are fueled by the paradox that, as Western art music as a whole seems to become more autonomous from society, individual works can be seen more and more to embody social tendencies. Beethoven's music springs from Enlightenment values, but his late style is a harbinger of the dissolution of those very values, a "symptom" of a "fatal condition" that will fully arrive in Schoenberg's music. In the aptly titled "Why Is Adorno's Music Criticism the Way It Is?" Subotnik argues that Adorno's critique of modern culture can be used to explain idiosyncrasies in his work, from his narrow choice of repertory to his difficult writing style and avoidance of pure musical analysis. Subotnik is willing to read Adorno "against himself," applying his concepts in other contexts, reaching different conclusions, and critiquing him from a framework outside his own.

PADDISON (1993) traces the use of key concepts in Adorno's writings over time, searching for an overarching method in Adorno as a whole. At its best this approach problematizes the solidity of Adornian concepts, arguing that Adorno operates by critiquing other philosophical systems rather than proposing his own system per se. Paddison's examination of the tensions between Adorno's conceptions of form, on the one hand, and musical material, on the other, is especially engaging. Rather than present a teleological picture of music history, Paddison argues, Adorno constructs a dialectic between an integration of formal levels and a disintegration and fragmentation of musical material. In his slimmer and more readable later volume PADDISON (1996) proposes a broad framework centered around Adorno's writings on both modernism and mass culture. Just as important, it allows English-speaking readers to understand the dialectical mode of thought essential to Austro-

German criticism in general and to the critical theory of the Frankfurt Institute in particular. This is a commendable introduction to Adorno's work: Paddison provides the background to read more challenging scholarship and interact more successfully with Adorno's writings themselves.

In light of the recent proliferation of secondary literature, one of HOHENDAHL's major contributions is his historiographical approach, which highlights the different ideological biases that inform Adorno scholarship. In his "tentative typology" Hohendahl asserts that much work on Adorno can be seen either as a political distancing, a poststructuralist reading, a critique from a postmodern perspective, or an attempt to construct an "authentic" Adorno. Equally important are Hohendahl's essays that explore largely unexamined periods of Adorno life: his U.S. exile and his return to postwar Germany. In his argument these contexts contribute to a more nuanced picture of Adorno's writings than is usually proposed; Adorno is never allowed to represent easy dialectical binaries. In this view Adorno is not a simple cultural elitist: upon his return to Frankfurt, he expressed ambivalent views toward "high" German culture, and his polemic against the products of mass culture is read as a critique of and warning against authoritarian societies. Although Hohendahl tends to assume much background knowledge, this monograph contributes important contextualized perspectives toward understanding Adorno's philosophies.

COOK concentrates on one aspect of Adorno's work: his theory of mass culture and the 20th-century "culture industry," the pervasive web of cultural products geared toward corporate profit making while exerting a powerful role in the lives of ordinary individuals. Cook's primary issues concern the production of culture when conceived as a commodity for a mass audience, the psychological techniques and effects of the culture industry, and the ideologies both of mass culture and Adorno's critique. Cook argues that, even in these postmodern times a generation after Adorno's death, his philosophy of the culture industry remains relevant. Although this book is not particularly focused on music, its perspectives are widely applicable to contemplating current music culture and the pervasiveness of popular music. Furthermore, in contrast to many monographs on Adorno, Cook is notable for her concentrated focus on a single area.

WILLIAMS does not so much attempt to explicate Adorno's theories as to use an Adornian perspective to analyze post–World War II art music, a repertory largely either outside Adorno's purview or subject to caustic criticism. For the bulk of this book Williams uses a modified version of Adorno's aesthetics, in which aesthetic response and a dialectical perspective continue to inform musical analysis, to discuss composers as diverse as Pierre Boulez, John Cage, and György Ligeti. Williams consistently cuts across the grain: Boulez's music is shown to often contradict its supposedly purely rational and systematic bases, and the supposed raw sound of Cage's structures is tempered by a controlling organization. This volume exhibits an interesting engagement with Adorno, although for the introductory reader it may not sufficiently explain the philosophical and musical background necessary for contemplating the diversity and complexity of postwar composition.

Of course, no reasonable picture of Adorno is possible without wading into Adorno's writings themselves, even with the inherently compromising nature of translations. Many of his texts on music are now available in English, and for those interested in his philosophies it is essential to become exposed to his fascinating, frustrating, and ultimately rewarding work. ADORNO (1967) was the first to be translated, and it includes Samuel Weber's introductory essay "Translating the Untranslatable." The essays on music include a stinging critique of jazz ("Anyone who allows the growing respectability of mass culture to seduce him into equating a popular song with modern art because of a few false notes squeaked by a clarinet . . . has already capitulated to barbarism"), a revisionist picture of Bach, and a warm portrait of Schoenberg, who had recently died. ADORNO (1973) presents a dialectical opposition between Schoenberg, seen as progressive, and Stravinsky, seen as reactionary. Thomas Mann leaned heavily on this volume for musical discussions in his 1948 novel *Doktor Faustus*. ADORNO (1976) consists of lectures, many that were originally radio broadcasts, that cover various genres (opera, chamber music, popular music) and societal topics (function of music, classes and social strata, and public opinion, among others). Five decades of writings are collected in ADORNO (1992); important entries include Adorno's 1960 Mahler Centenary Address given in Vienna and a spirited defense of his Stravinsky discussion in the *Philosophy of Modern Music* (translated 1973). Given the diverse origins of the entries, an introductory essay would be helpful, but Livingstone's translations are among the most readable.

Also worth exploration are the translations of Adorno's monographs on individual composers, where there is space for more detailed discussions and multiple perspectives. ADORNO (1981) presents essays written during his exile and critiques both Wagner's social character, as someone who was "inclined to despise . . . victims" and his "doomed" concept of music drama. In ADORNO (1991b) the writer's ability to compose powerful metaphorical descriptions of musical phenomena comes to the fore. No conventional analysis, for example, can describe the introduction to Mahler's Symphony no. 1 as well as Adorno's haunting image: "A thin curtain, threadbare but densely woven, it hangs from the sky like a pale gray cloud layer, similarly painful to sensitive eyes." For Adorno, Mahler's symphonies are like novels, where "pedestrian material" and "sublime execution" operate in a dialectical relationship between the naive and the sophisticated. Some of Adorno's most personal writings can be found in ADORNO (1991b), his reflections on his mentor, friend, and former composition teacher Alban Berg. An introductory essay and useful afterword of annotations to the text by the translators help frame Adorno's reminiscences and analyses of numerous major Berg compositions, including two contrasting essays, written 33 years apart, on the unfinished opera *Lulu*.

JOHN J. SHEINBAUM

Aesthetics: Classical

Draper, John William, *Eighteenth Century English Aesthetics: A Bibliography,* New York: Octagon Books, 1931

Hosler, Bellamy, *Changing Aesthetic Views of Instrumental Music in 18th Century Germany,* Ann Arbor, Michigan: UMI Research Press, 1981

Le Huray, Peter, and James Day, editors, *Music and Aesthetics in the Eighteenth and Early Nineteenth Centuries,* Cambridge: Cambridge University Press, 1981

Neubauer, John, *The Emancipation of Music from Language: Departure from Mimesis in Eighteenth-Century Aesthetics,* New Haven, Connecticut: Yale University Press, 1986

Schroeder, David P., *Haydn and the Enlightenment: The Late Symphonies and Their Audience,* Oxford: Clarendon Press, and New York: Oxford University Press, 1990

Steblin, Rita, *A History of Key Characteristics in the Eighteenth and Early Nineteenth Centuries,* Ann Arbor, Michigan: UMI Research Press, 1983

Sulzer, Johann Georg, *Aesthetics and the Art of Musical Composition in the German Enlightenment: Selected Writings of Johann Georg Sulzer and Heinrich Christoph Koch,* edited by Nancy Kovaleff Baker and Thomas Christensen, Cambridge: University of Cambridge Press, 1995

Thomas, Downing A., *Music and the Origins of Language: Theories from the French Enlightenment,* Cambridge: Cambridge University Press, 1995

Classical aesthetics is generally accepted as encompassing the mid-18th through the early 19th century. Students of the topic should beware, however, that the term *classical* has a variety of associations, including the theories of ancient Greece, the *Wiemarer Klassik* of Goethe, the Viennese period of Haydn, Mozart, and Beethoven, and even the whole of art music. Additionally, musicians and critics in the late 18th and early 19th centuries used the word *classical* loosely to describe Mozart and Haydn as well as Palestrina, Cimarosa, Handel, or Gluck. Many scholars avoid the *classical* label altogether, preferring to use either the specific dates or topic (i.e., the Enlightenment, rationalism) under consideration. To make matters more confusing, the boundaries with baroque and romantic aesthetics are blurred. Traditionally, scholars have oversimplified matters, classifying baroque aesthetics as concerned with the expression of passions or musical affects in primarily vocal music, romanticism as obsessed with the expressive power of pure instrumental or absolute music, and classicism as merely the transition. Indeed, the 18th century witnessed a shift from the aesthetic justification of vocal (music with words) over instrumental music to the acceptance of pure instrumental forms such as the symphony, concerto, and string quartet. Recently, more scholars are recognizing the importance of the classical period not only as a transition but for the development of independent musical aesthetics divorced from mandatory comparisons with other arts.

LE HURAY and DAY's excerpts offer the English-language reader an overview of musical aesthetics from Du Bos's *Réflexions critiques sur la poësie et sur la peinture* (1719) through Krüger's *Allgemeine musikalishe Zeitung* (1848). Classical authors represented include Kant, Schlegel, Staël, and Leclerc. The availability of primary sources is especially important to students of aesthetics, where the aesthetic biases of the scholar can overshadow those of the historical counterparts. It is beneficial to peruse the primary material to gain a general sense of an era before sifting through the opinions of other interpreters. In their introduction, Le Huray and Day are sensitive to the ambiguity of terms such as *classical* and *romantic* in discussing the aesthetic shift from vocal to instrumental music. Readers will gain familiarity with such key aesthetic terms as *imagination* and *invention* and the strong influence of Descartes, Locke, Leibniz, Hume, and Condillac on subsequent discourse. Each entry is prefaced with brief background accounts of author and commentary on the selected passage.

NEUBAUER's title speaks volumes: the classical period in his eyes is a transitory episode from an aesthetic of music bound to language to the acceptance of music as an autonomous art. As a result, specific theorists are pigeonholed into holding one of the two possible aesthetic opinions. According to Neubauer, theories of the affects and rhetorical models for music were passé by the 19th century. Although the author is extreme in his classification, this study is certainly thorough in its commentary on numerous writers of the classical period, offering sources for further study.

By analyzing medical and aesthetic texts concerned with music, THOMAS seeks to understand how changing theories in language and sensory perception engineered the shift from vocal to instrumental music. His efforts are particularly worthy as scholarship on 18th-century French aesthetics is weighted to earlier events—primarily, the "Querelle des Bouffons." Thomas's bibliography and clear citations mentioning both primary texts and secondary studies are excellent resources for further study. Thomas is critical of sweeping studies of 18th-century aesthetics (specifically Neubauer) and proposes a more "nuanced reading" of the literature. He argues, for example, that instead of undermining the importance of rhetorical models in music aesthetics, the move away from vocal music encouraged the musical applications of grammatical principles such as phrase structure, inflection, and punctuation.

DRAPER lists the titles of numerous primary sources from the whole of the 18th century, offering the names of British aesthetic treatises often overshadowed by the German and French philosophers of this period. The entries are organized by works dealing first with general aesthetic issues, then those falling loosely into the categories of painting, poetry, and music. Unfortunately, aesthetic texts of this period are often difficult to categorize; a chronological or alphabetical ordering would have been more useful. Nevertheless, Draper includes helpful dates of all treatise editions as well as annotations directing the reader to contemporaneous reviews and commentary.

HOSLER seeks connections between the concurrent rise of instrumental music and independent musical aesthetics in the late 18th century. After discussing the mixed reception in Germany of French theory, primarily that of Batteaux, Holser describes the growing acceptance of instrumental music in German aesthetics. Holser is thorough to the point of redundancy, with individual philosophers from Mattheson and Baumgarten to Sulzer and Forkel receiving in-depth analysis. Footnotes and references are excellent for encouraging further study, and all quotations appear in the body of the work in both original and translated language.

SULZER is a collection of writings by Sulzer and Koch, which are intended to show how Sulzer's aesthetic abstractions relate to Koch's "concrete" musical illustrations. In his introduction, Thomas Christensen discusses the growing importance of psychology and sensory perception in contrast to "rationalist neo-classical doctrines." Christensen translates articles from *General Theory of the Fine Arts* (1771–74), organizing them into categories of general aesthetics, artistic creation, and music. Nancy Kovaleff Baker's introduction outlines the influence of Sulzer on Koch, who, for example, shared Sulzer's belief that instrumental music was acceptable for military marches, festivals, or dances, but that words were necessary for true expression. As we learn in Baker's translation of *Introductory Essay to Composition, Volume 2, Part 1* (1787), Koch worried over the rise of virtuoso performances and feared composers were merely writing to receive audience approval.

SCHROEDER investigates the possible influence of contemporaneous aesthetic theories on Haydn's compositional process, specifically the composer's search for intelligibility in his pure instrumental music. According to Schroeder, Haydn's use of quotations from vocal music (e.g., folk songs or opera excerpts) in his instrumental works were influenced by his study of Shaftsbury. Unfortunately, Schroeder is perhaps too simplistic in his portrayal of the vocal to instrumental aesthetic shift, and his evidence is limited to sketchy accounts of Haydn in philosophical circles. Nevertheless, the author's efforts in allaying discrepancies between theory and practice are commendable.

STEBLIN's explorations of affects and key characteristics (the association of keys with specific emotions and meaning) provides in-depth analysis on a crucial aspect of classical and indeed all 18th-century aesthetics. After offering a history of the subject from ancient Greece through the Middle Ages and the Renaissance, Steblin compares and contrasts the viewpoints of 18th-century theorists such as Mattheson, Rameau, Rousseau, Marpurg, and Kirnberger. "Appendix A" is a catalog of "Characteristics Imputed to Keys from Jean Rousseau (1691) to Berlioz (1843)." Each entry takes a specific key and lists the opinions of various theorists (e.g., C major is "majestic" or "cheerful"). Steblin provides extensive notes and bibliography for further study. Appendices B and C present the original language of the plentiful quotes presented in translation throughout the text.

LAURA J. KOENIG

Aesthetics: Romantic

Bujic, Bojan, *Music in European Thought: 1851–1912,* Cambridge: Cambridge University Press, 1988

Dahlhaus, Carl, *Esthetics of Music,* translated by William A. Austin, Cambridge: Cambridge University Press, 1982

———, *The Idea of Absolute Music,* translated by Roger Lustig, Chicago: University of Chicago Press, 1989

Dahlhaus, Carl, and Ruth Katz, editors, *Contemplating Music: Source Readings in the Aesthetics of Music,* 4 vols., New York: Pendragon Press, 1987–93

Le Huray, Peter, and James Day, editors, *Music and Aesthetics in the Eighteenth and Early-Nineteenth Centuries,* Cambridge: Cambridge University Press, 1981

Lippman, Edward A., *A History of Western Musical Aesthetics,* Lincoln: University of Nebraska Press, 1992

———, *Musical Aesthetics: A Historical Reader,* 3 vols., Stuyvesant, New York: Pendragon Press, 1986–90

Strunk, W. Oliver, editor, *Source Readings in Music History: From Classical Antiquity through the Romantic Era,* New York: Norton, 1950; revised edition, edited by Leo Treitler, 1998

To some extent, the romantic movement in musical aesthetics defined itself in reaction to Enlightenment philosophy and in particular to the writings of Kant. Although Kant, in his *Critique of Judgment* (1790), included music in his hierarchy of arts, he hesitated over music's inherent abstractness. Because music could not be said to refer to or represent anything concretely, as would a visual art, Kant described music as having an "indeterminable content" and so assigned it to the lowest level of arts. Several authors and philosophers after Kant attempted to rescue music from its lowly place among the arts. In fact, it was precisely music's abstractness that caused romantic writers such as the poet Wackenroder and the philosopher Schopenhauer to venerate music and elevate it above the other arts. Schopenhauer's understanding of music was particularly influential:

> Music is by no means like the other arts, namely a copy of the Ideas, but a *copy of the will itself.* . . . For this reason the effect of music is so very much more powerful and penetrating than is that of the other arts, for these others speak only of the shadow, but music of the essence.

This new appreciation of music inspired romantic philosophers to scrutinize the musical work. Schelling and Hegel, for instance, devoted significant portions of their philosophical lectures on aesthetics to the discussion of music. But for the first time, the topic of musical aesthetics began to interest composers as well. Schumann, Liszt, Berlioz, and Wagner all contributed significant essays about various aspects of the musical work. Of paramount concern for both camps was the question of musical content. Now that music was considered the pinnacle of human expression, the question of what exactly it expressed, and the subsidiary question of how best to describe that content, became a central issue. Walter Pater's observation, that all the arts now aspired to the condition of music (not poetry), neatly sums up the romantic turn in musical aesthetics. A debatable endpoint to the romantic position was initiated by the music critic Hanslick, who in his essay *On the Musically Beautiful* (1854) denied music an emotional content by insisting on a meaning and content for music that was not emotional but, as he described it, "purely musical."

Research into romantic musical aesthetics has taken shape as two separate enterprises: (1) collecting, editing, and translating source materials and (2) criticism. These two pursuits are by no means separate. As many scholars have noted in the introductions to their collections of source materials, deciding which documents represent the romantic tradition in musical thought is a critical task itself. A critical viewpoint is implied by the excerpts each editor selects for his or her edition.

The first publication of its kind, and still perhaps the most widely consulted, is the volume of essays edited by STRUNK. Strunk first organizes his material chronologically by era and again chronologically within each stylistic period. As a result, his definition of romantic aesthetics begins with the writings of Wackenroder and ends with the essays of Wagner. Within those endpoints, Strunk organizes the excerpts into two groups, writers and composers. The writers include Jean Paul, Wackenroder, and E.T.A. Hoffman. The larger group of essays,

however, are those authored by composers: Weber, Berlioz, Schumann, Liszt, and Wagner. Strunk's collection is not comprehensive. His selections are limited by space (these essays are part of a larger project to represent aesthetics in all music history) and by proximity to the subject (he gives the composers' comments priority over the philosophers'). Many key arguments are represented in these excerpts, however, which makes this collection still valuable. The excerpts from the writers display a romantic style of commentary about music that is characteristically overdescriptive, highly personal, and emotionally overwrought. The composers continue this tradition of descriptive prose but address the problem of content more directly in their discussion of the viability of program music. Schumann, Berlioz, and Liszt all used written programs and titles to describe the content of their pieces, and they defended the practice against critics who eschewed such programs as extra- or nonmusical. Another romantic concern, the issue of music's origin, is addressed in the excerpt from Wagner's writings, in which the composer attempts to locate the origins of music in dance and poetry. The overall style of Strunk's edition of source readings, wherein each excerpt is introduced with a brief biographical profile of the writer, has been become a model for such collections.

DAHLHAUS and KATZ have also taken on the larger project of representing aesthetic thought throughout music history, and so their consideration of romantic writings is likewise limited. They depart from Strunk, however, in terms of organization. Here the essays are arranged topically, not chronologically, which leaves to the reader the task of determining where romanticism begins and ends. The critical emphasis in this collection is on the philosophical discussion of music, and to that end, Dahlhaus and Katz include a very different set of writings than Strunk. The romantic perspective on the ontology of the musical work is described by Schelling, Hegel, Schopenhauer, Herbart, and Hanslick. The discussion over the emotional content of music is again represented by Wackenroder, although the selection is different and arguably more relevant than Strunk's, and is followed by the observations of the philosopher Vischer and the influential German historians Lazarus and Ambros. The disadvantage of this collection is its organization. Because the romantic perspective is represented piecemeal throughout three large volumes and confined almost exclusively to the German tradition, it is difficult to gain a sense of the romantic attitude toward music as a whole. The aspect of the collection that recommends itself above all the others, however, is that the editors critically analyze and contextualize each excerpt with a lengthy introductory essay.

The aesthetics reader offered by the editors LE HURAY and DAY distinguishes itself by being devoted specifically to the topic of romantic aesthetics. As a result, the selections in this volume represent a more comprehensive picture of musical and general aesthetics of the 18th and 19th centuries. Indeed, the emphasis here, as the editors note in their preface, is on defining romanticism. Musical romanticism, they observe, is defined in relation to the romantic movement as a whole, an approach that stresses the similarity of intention between the separate arts. Thus, Le Huray and Day include an equal mix of entries from philosophers, poets, novelists, and composers, and their representation of English, French, Italian, and German traditions is admirable. Perhaps in their desire to be thorough, however, Le Huray and Day begin their discussion half a century earlier than the other editors, with the Enlightenment philosophy of Kant, Voltaire, and Rousseau and the musical commentary of Webb, Sulzer, Gluck, and Forkel. A contemporary introduction to romanticism in the arts is represented by selections from K.W.F. Schlegel, A.W. Schlegel, Schelling, Staël, Millin, Toreinx, Schilling, and Lamennais. Hegel and Schopenhauer weigh in on the philosophy of musical aesthetics, and the composer's perspective is covered by the writings of Schumann, Berlioz, and Liszt. The editors stop short of including Hanslick and Wagner on their list of romantics; have selected noticeably different excerpts than Strunk; and are the only ones to include such writers as Herder, Michaelis, Nägeli, Mazzini, Runge, and Krüger. This collection also gives voice to the growing tradition of concert reviewing by featuring articles from journals like the *Neue Zeitschrift für Musik* and *Revue musicale*. But the strength of this collection is also its shortcoming: the numerous excerpts are by necessity brief and often give the reader only a cursory glance at a specific author or idea.

LIPPMAN's (1986–90) historical reader is similar to Dahlhaus and Katz's in that he, too, favors the writings of philosophers over composers on the topic of 19th-century musical aesthetics. Only one composer, Wagner, is represented in the whole volume. Lippman also organizes 19th-century thought by category, although his descriptive titles of those categories are quite different. He separates the first half of the century into three subjects—"the romantic conception of feeling," "absolute realism," and "emotional realism"—with the usual list of authors being represented by Wackenroder, Schelling, Hegel, Schopenhauer, Kierkegaard, and Wagner. Some selections are different than Strunk's and Dahlhaus and Katz's, and almost all the excerpts included here are more extensive and lengthier than those in any of the other collections. The final three categories in Lippman's collection represent trends that are more specifically from the latter half of the century, but again his descriptive titles are unusual. Hanslick and Ambros address what Lippman calls the "specificity of music"; Wagner and Nietzsche offer an "alternative to rationalism"; and Spencer, Gurney, and Hausegger describe the "biological view of expression." Although Lippman does include a few British writers in his collection, his understanding of romantic musical aesthetics highlights almost exclusively the German tradition.

Because the romantic movement in music, like any general category of thought, is difficult to define, especially in terms of specific beginning and endpoints, BUJIC's collection of essays is particularly useful. By design, Bujic picks up where editors Le Huray and Day leave off, focusing on aesthetic thought from 1851 to 1912. As Bujic rightly points out in his preface, so many of these postromantic writings are extensions of arguments offered in the first half of the century that it is difficult to draw a firm line between the two halves of the 1800s. Considering, however, that these authors are more preoccupied with the nature of the musical work, and are interested in defining music from scientific and music-theoretical perspectives in addition to philosophical and composition perspectives, these authors do form a distinct and separate tradition. Bujic organizes the transition from romantic to postromantic according to topic. The argument in favor of defining music in terms of its emotional or expressive force is continued by Wagner, Ambros, Vischer, Nietzsche, and Kretschmar and opposed by formalists such as Hanslick and Zimmerman. The French and British versions of these arguments are represented by the authors Combarieu, Baudelaire, Mallarmé, Gurney, and others. A new interest in the quasi-scientific questions of acoustics and psychology is introduced by Helmholtz, Stumpf, Spencer, Gurney, and Darwin. The beginnings of modern criticism, music history, and music theory proper are suggested by pertinent excerpts from the writings of Chrysander, Adler, Riemann, and Schenker.

Only two authors have provided significant critical commentary to these source documents—commentary other than the introductions that have been used to preface individual excerpts. Perhaps the most definitive discussion of sources is to be found in DAHLHAUS (1982). Although the title suggests a broad scope, the term *aesthetic*, as the author himself points out, represents a phenomenon that took root specifically in the 19th century and the romantic movement. The author traces the term back to a popular essay of the same title by the early romantic philosopher Baumgartner (*Aesthetica*, 1750) and views the discipline of aesthetics as separate from philosophy. Dahlhaus's discussion of musical aesthetics, then, is essentially a critical examination of romantic aesthetics. In addition to the pivotal question of the role emotions play in music, he touches on several other romantic concerns—the emancipation of instrumental music, aesthetic judgment versus taste, genius and originality, musical affect versus musical idea, program music, and the relationship of words and music in opera.

In the companion volume to his source readings collection, LIPPMAN (1992) does not confine the examination of musical aesthetics to romantic and postromantic thought, as Dahlhaus (1982) does, but interprets the term *aesthetic* to include critical thought from all periods in music history. In the section on the 19th century, he organizes his commentary under four branches of thought: romantic aesthetics, emotional realism, formalism and autonomy, and the idealist tradition. In the first two categories, which cover romantic aesthetics proper, Lippman presents chronologically the usual list of authors managing to introduce a few new voices into the discussion. Schelling's successor, Solger, for instance, is mentioned for the first time, as are the seldom-discussed comments of Kierkegaard. The emphasis here, in contrast with Dahlhaus (1982), is on close, critical readings of specific essays and excerpts.

DAHLHAUS (1989), in yet another volume on romantic musical aesthetics, turns his attention to the same transitional period covered by Bujic's postromantic source readings. As the title suggests, Dahlhaus's concern here is the primary aesthetic that developed from the romantic preoccupation with musical content and meaning. If some music used programs and titles to describe the content of the composition, then instrumental or absolute music represented the opposite, a separate kind of music whose content was inexpressible in the sense that its meaning was already contained and related in the music itself. To the extent that written programs were considered unnecessary, even redundant, "absolute music" came to represent the opposite of program music and opera. Dahlhaus admirably traces the history of this overused term and its misinterpretation and examines several subsidiary aesthetic issues including the ideas of musical logic and musical prose. His style here is dense (he often moves quickly and without preparation through an encyclopedic range of topics and authors), but the end result is rewarding.

JULIE HUBBERT

Aesthetics: Modern

Adorno, Theodor W., *Philosophy of Modern Music*, translated by Anne G. Mitchell and Wesley V. Blomster, New York: Seabury Press, and London: Sheed and Ward, 1973
Alperson, Philip, editor, *Musical Worlds: New Directions in the Philosophy of Music*, University Park: Pennsylvania State University Press, 1998
————, editor, *What Is Music? An Introduction to the Philosophy of Music*, New York: Haven, 1987
Bowman, Wayne D., *Philosophical Perspectives on Music*, New York: Oxford University Press, 1998
Budd, Malcolm, *Music and the Emotions: The Philosophical Theories*, London: Routledge, 1985
Clifton, Thomas, *Music as Heard: A Study in Applied Phenomenology*, New Haven, Connecticut: Yale University Press, 1983
Davies, Stephen, *Musical Meaning and Expression*, Ithaca, New York: Cornell University Press, 1994
DeBellis, Mark Andrew, *Music and Conceptualization*, Cambridge: Cambridge University Press, 1995
Goehr, Lydia, *The Imaginary Museum of Musical Works: An Essay in the Philosophy of Music*, Oxford: Clarendon Press, and New York: Oxford University Press, 1992
Ingarden, Roman, *The Work of Music and the Problem of Its Identity*, translated by Adam Czeriawski, edited by Jean G. Harrell, Berkeley: University of California Press, and London: Macmillan, 1986
Kivy, Peter, *Sound and Semblance: Reflections on Musical Representation*, Princeton, New Jersey: Princeton University Press, 1984
————, *Sound Sentiment: An Essay on the Musical Emotions, Including the Complete Text of the Corded Shell*, Philadelphia, Pennsylvania: Temple University Press, 1989
Levinson, Jerrold, *Music, Art, and Metaphysics: Essays in Philosophical Aesthetics*, Ithaca, New York: Cornell University Press, 1990
————, *Music in the Moment*, Ithaca, New York: Cornell University Press, 1997
Lippman, Edward A., *A Humanistic Philosophy of Music*, New York: New York University Press, 1977
————, *Musical Aesthetics: A Historical Reader*, 3 vols., Stuyvesant, New York: Pendragon Press, 1986–90
Morgan, Robert P., editor, *Source Readings in Music History: 20th Century*, New York: Norton, 1997
Robinson, Jenefer, editor, *Music and Meaning*, Ithaca, New York: Cornell University Press, 1997
Scruton, Roger, *The Aesthetics of Music*, Oxford: Clarendon Press, 1997
Shusterman, Richard, *Pragmatist Aesthetics: Living Beauty, Rethinking Art*, Oxford: Blackwell, 1992
Smith, F. Joseph, editor, *Understanding the Musical Experience*, New York: Gordon and Breach, 1989

The history of aesthetics traces a path from the earliest metaphysics of beauty in classical Greece through the 18th-century theory of taste introduced by the British Empiricists, the 19th-century theories of expression and communication initiated by German romanticism, and the many 20th-century arguments concerning the nature and value of the work as object. These latter arguments were developed by positivists, neo-Kantians, phenomenologists, Marxists, and others working in both the analytic (Anglo-American) and hermeneutic (continental) traditions. Within music aesthetics, the most frequent themes are the ontology and the possibility of an epistemology of the musical work—that is, the extent to which representation, expression, emotion, feeling, communication, and so forth can be ascertained and analyzed. Even in the analytic tradition, the metaphysics of music appears to be alive and well. Only recently has the Western cultural paradigm of the fixed, notated work been problematized.

Taken in its entirety, the range of literature from the 20th century is truly staggering, and guidance through such a vast quantity and divergence of thought is highly problematic. Thus, with a few exceptions, the following books are all relatively recent. Many of the 20th century's landmarks (Suzanne Langer and Leonard Meyer being perhaps the most conspicuous) are only found here in anthologies and critical overviews. Still, while the list is not comprehensive, what follows should give the reader a direct path not only into the field as practiced today, but also to the wealth of ideas found throughout the 20th century. The entry focuses on the philosophy of music and thus excludes psychology, cognitive science, acoustics, semiotics, ethnomusicology, sociology, and gender studies—all of which contribute to modern aesthetics.

Any survey must begin with a distinction between modern aesthetics and modernism: the former indicates aesthetic philosophies developed during the modern era; the latter refers to a theory of art, and artistic theory is all too often conflated with aesthetics. Granted, compositional theories unfold within the purview of aesthetics and such theories rely on a compositional aesthetic, however fragile its philosophical underpinning. Strictly speaking, however, the study of musical aesthetics involves the reasoned, argued, and defended consideration of the nature and value of music qua music.

MORGAN is certainly one of the most complete single sources of excerpted writings on musical modernism. Although a student of particular composers and performers benefits from reading what the artists have to say about their craft, this material generally teaches more about the artists' relation to music than about the nature of music itself. Nietzsche dismissed the entire history of philosophy for this reason. Nonetheless, a volume such as Morgan's offers an important reference for anyone seeking grounding in modernist musical thought.

The student new to the philosophy of music will find an excellent introduction in BOWMAN. Each chapter concludes with discussion questions; as a textbook, it is best suited for a philosophy curriculum or a graduate program in academic music. As a text for such a course, one would want to augment it with a reader, but not all the material discussed is available in print. The book opens with an introduction to philosophizing on music, followed by philosophical and historical perspectives (music as imitation, as idea, as autonomous form, as symbol, as experienced, as social and political force), and concludes with an essentially postmodern chapter on feminism and pluralism. The conventional and the unconventional, the traditional and the anti-traditional, the conservative and the radical are presented here with equanimity and an eye to comparative criticism. An impressive collection of material and an important source of ideas, the book is free of Anglo-American bias and is highly recommended.

Another introduction to the field, ALPERSON (1987) ushers the reader directly into the fold of current Anglo-American music philosophy (including that of Philip Alperson, Arnold Berleant, Stephen Davies, Peter Kivy, Jerrold Levinson, Joseph Margolis, Jenefer Robinson, Roger Scruton, Francis Sparshott, and Nicholas Wolterstorrf). The book is augmented by contributions from one of the deans of music theory, Edward T. Cone, and the provocative cultural historian Rose Rosengard Subotnik. Alperson gives a historical overview from Aristotle to the present and introduces all the material contained in the book. The book contains essays on the nature of the musical work, musical form, and music as metaphor, as sign, as representation, and even as philosophy. Also found here are essays on historical and cultural values and performance (this last issue treated as a matter of ethics). However, the crux of the book is found in Sparshott's lead essay, a lengthy prolegomenon to which all the remaining essays are a response. Sparshott, a distinguished philosopher of art, offers a brilliant dissection of the possibility of a philosophy of music. Implicit throughout his essay is the need to question the limits imposed by Western ideology and by the cultural practices and prejudices held in place by modern institutions of music. Sparshott does not subject these institutions to any serious attack, however, nor does he offer any alternative vision; he simply sets the stage and outlines a scenario. The degree to which Sparshott's respondents meet his challenge cannot be addressed here, but the encounter is commended as an excellent and stimulating introduction to discourse in the field.

ALPERSON (1998), an outstanding collection of provocative pieces, a few of which are included in other anthologies, contains essays by a number of philosophers and musicologists, and presents rebuttals to some of their arguments (e.g., Sparshott's response to Budd). Alperson introduces the set of essays, and the discussion moves from expression and representation, to understanding and evaluation, and on to the avant-garde and less traditional musics and musicologies. The most important aspect of this book is probably its step away from the hermetic field of Western art music and the inclusion of musical categories usually excluded from such discourse: thus, it contains articles on rock music, political music, blues, feminist musicology, and ethnomusicology. This collection debates how changes in intellectual life have begun to affect the aesthetics of music: speculative theory and meta-narratives on music's autonomous being and meaning have begun to give way to pluralist narratives on the interdependence between music and society.

A good place to locate some difficult-to-find readings is LIPPMAN (1986–90). This is a strange collection, including writings by several composers (Anton Webern, Arnold Schoenberg, Igor Stravinsky, and John Cage), and some dated mid-20th-century work by French existential phenomenologists, including Gisèle Brelet (1949) and Jeanne Vial (1952). Furthermore, Lippman includes one of his own essays, which simply fails to distinguish itself as a historical artifact given the tenor of the collection. Lippman's philosophical approach is historical, and it is therefore not surprising that his anthology comprises the many quirks and wonders of modern aesthetics. For instance, the collection opens with the hermeneutics of Hermann Kretzschmar (1902 and 1905), followed by two examples of organicism, by August Halm (1913) and Heinrich Schenker (1930). Also included are selections from Suzanne Langer (1953), Arnold Schering (1935), and Max Dessoir (1906), all of whom propose sweeping (and sometimes vague) generalizations about the nature of music as symbol. This material will interest those studying these thinkers, but it adds very little to the aesthetics of today. Many aestheticians active during the mid century were caught up in the desire to create a universal science of art (Dessoir's work is a precursor). Thus, Charles Lalo (1939) and Nicolai Hartmann (1953) sought to situate music within the panoply of arts, defining and designating its ontology via categorical weights and measures. Other significant selections are an excerpt from Roman Ingarden's seminal work in the phenomenology of the work as stratified structure (1962), and the still-relevant work in the sociology of music produced by Adorno (1932, 1938, and 1962); furthermore, the book closes with a document of 1960s structuralism by Nicholas Ruwet (1966).

The reader unfamiliar with the philosophy of music might wish to start with a general style of philosophy, one that is global in its analysis and not overly systematic in its approach. LIPPMAN (1977) offers a solid example of this sort of work. Lippman, a contextualist, argues that the philosophy of music must be humanistic, by which he means rooted in human artifacts. His prose is simple and direct, and chapter headings indicate generalized topics. The discussions reflect an interactionist view: each successive chapter (material, form, meaning, style, permanence, composites, context, conception) builds on the previous one. Lippman considers the philosophy of art an exercise in weighing the interrelationships between sensory and conceptual forms; however, the reference to forms does not mean Platonic forms, but rather the wealth of man-made forms, which the author considers best addressed by an amalgam of psychology, sociology, and anthropology, rather than metaphysical speculation.

Like Lippman (1977), SCRUTON offers a general aesthetics of music. However, whereas Lippman stresses the contingency of such thought, Scruton seeks to establish criteria for judgments in musical aesthetics. Scruton, one of the most prolific aestheticians of the century, grounds his thought in Kant's notion of aesthetic judgment as a faculty of the mind. The significance of contingency in aesthetic discourse, be it Freudian or Marxian or otherwise, is something Scruton not only questions, but dismisses. He is an amateur composer himself and,

with due modesty, strives to demonstrate what separates his own efforts from those of the masters. Scruton covers a wide range of literature and weighs the value of contemporary thought on everything from music as sound object, as composed work, and as performance, to the importance of developing a cultural ethics (again, as a Kantian, Scruton argues along the moralistic lines of Kant's categorical imperative). Defiantly conservative, this book is not without its deep insights: no paean to the avant-garde, it will certainly comfort those who believe in the eternal truths of what is essentially a classic Western metaphysics of beauty.

Critical response and evaluation have placed LEVINSON (1990) at the forefront of the philosophy of music. One-half of the collection of essays concerns the concept of music and the identity of the musical work. In particular, Levinson seeks to establish necessary and sufficient conditions for the products and activities of musical culture. He considers both the paradigm case (the musical work of the Western canon) and the concept of music in general (applicable across cultures). An interesting outcome of Levinson's criteria for the musical work is his emphasis on the primacy of normally secondary parameters associated with performance means and practices (instrumentation, tempo, etc.). His discourse on the concept of music refutes those that regard music as organized sound and as an object of aesthetic appreciation. Levinson argues instead for a concept that combines soundingness, audibility, and temporal structure, on the one hand, with human-centered intentionality, purposiveness, and interactivity, on the other. In this way, Levinson hopes to arrive at a cross-cultural concept. Theorists and historians should find his analysis of truth in music quite interesting: in effect, he borrows from theories of representation to use the notion of correspondent truth (vis-à-vis musical emotion and feeling) as a criterion for evaluating truth in musical works. This provocative scheme bears strongly on the much-argued concept of meaning in music.

GOEHR offers a powerful thesis regarding the interaction between philosophical and musical thought. The example for Goehr's argument is taken from E.T.A. Hoffman; thus Goehr argues for a historical rather than analytical aesthetics. However, her version of a historical aesthetics is far more critically nuanced than Lippman's approach. Goehr's project is to analyze how the work-concept informs and controls what people think, say, and write about music. Thus, she opens with a critique of the analytical approach: specifically, the nominalist theory of Nelson Goodman and the neo-Platonist theory of Jerrold Levinson. While Goehr's argument relies on 19th-century thought and considers the music of Beethoven (via Hoffman) as central to the enforcement of the work-concept, she does conclude with a chapter on contemporary music and musical life. Goehr's point is that whatever is said about the nature of a musical work is necessarily determined by one's concept of music; this position also suggests that a musical work is the creation of a composer and, as such, exists as an objectified expression of the composer's thought. Goehr proposes a philosophy of music that rises above analytical ontology and strives instead for what she terms a cultural metaphysics, a genealogy or anthropology of music, an aesthetics that reveals music as a regulated, projected, and emergent concept—a product of cultural practice, not an absolute entity.

ROBINSON brings together significant recent contributions by philosophers, historians, and theorists. This anthology is one of the finest collections to appear and is of considerable value to the music student, especially the student in musical analysis. A response to Eduard Hanslick's classic *On the Musically Beautiful* (1854), this book contains a series of consistently eloquent testaments to the notion that music consists of more than mere form. Emergent expressive qualities, fictional or make-believe worlds, cognitively complex emotions, action and agency—these are argued for as identifiable elements in a musical work. In her introduction, Robinson makes some concessions to the role played by personal experience and 19th-century aesthetics in these essays; however, formal analyses are offered throughout as evidence of extramusical meaning. Indeed, she and her fellow contributors offer rich readings of specific musical works. The purpose of the collection is to provide examples of the belief that a deep, meaningful connection with music derives from the search for and discovery of human meaning in music.

One of the central questions in modern aesthetics is whether one can distinguish an aesthetic quality from a non-aesthetic one, and whether cognitive content can be correctly identified as distinctly aesthetic. In music, the question has often been argued with respect to emotion in music: can one distinguish specifically musical feelings and emotions evoked by musical dynamism from indefinite feelings and emotions suggested by music (sadness, happiness, etc.)— Another way of framing the argument is to contrast the notion of metaphoric description of what one might hear in a work with putatively literal descriptions of what one does (or ought to) hear. BUDD explores theories designed to dissociate music from the fixed, explicit reference to emotion. Such theories seek to frame musical emotion as something abstract and thus philosophically plausible: for example, ideal or embodied emotion as unconsummated symbol or as the expression of emotion. Budd also considers go-between theories that treat musical emotion as an object of communication and information theories (especially that of Meyer). According to Budd, a strong defense for the concept of emotion in music exists, but that defense does not once and for all establish the concept's power as a basis for music aesthetics. However, his conclusion—that none of these theories does justice to music—does not lead to

an alternative theory. This omission does not necessarily detract from the value of Budd's volume, for his overall evaluation deepens awareness of how central emotion is to a concept of the musical work.

Certainly the most prolific philosopher of music, Kivy has made a career of reviving and refining the ideas of the Enlightenment, especially those associated with feeling and emotion. The two volumes listed here form a pair and offer the fullest account of his brand of aesthetics. KIVY (1989) is a reprint of *The Corded Shell* (1980), to which he has added his responses to criticisms from the musical and philosophical communities. Kivy's purpose is to silence effectively proponents of the arousal theory of emotion in music, which holds that people perceive music as "sad" because they experience sadness, not because the music is itself sad. In modern aesthetics, the arousal theory became an accepted explanation for emotion and expressiveness in music, as it offered a way out of the quandaries posed by representation in music. Kivy argues that the views of the 17th and 18th centuries that held that the physiognomy of the music is what expresses sadness are correct, and that the arousal theory is but an unfortunate digression from the insight of an earlier age.

KIVY (1984) takes the reader on an investigative journey through the theories and repertoires of musical representation. A companion work to *The Corded Shell*, this book presents a plethora of examples from the Western canon, ranging from the score as representation of music to the representation of the world by music. While some will find Kivy's approach too conservative, grounded as it is in a critique of Enlightenment and Empiricist theories (and reliant as it is on standard concert repertoires), others will find its premise patently false: how can music represent anything? But it is exactly this question that Kivy answers with patience, humor, and vigor. One might dismiss Kivy's argument because he founds his discussion in the conventions of 18th-century thought. However, one might also find his perspective informative and stimulating: Kivy navigates a broad corpus of music and considers the question of how music has traditionally represented, depicted, expressed, and even narrated the world.

DAVIES is a study that will challenge even the most experienced reader. The author is a philosopher whose argument proceeds systematically through each and every preexistent argument, mapping out the terrain and methodically evaluating the applicability of each proposition. There are more than 500 sources cited in this text. (Davies's earlier book, *Definitions of Art* [1991], similarly presented, is dwarfed by the present work.) Davies seeks an adequate account of the expression of emotion in music that explains, in particular, how it is that music is understood to express emotion. He is especially interested in the work of contemporary philosophers—particularly Budd, Kivy, and Levinson—but he devotes considerable attention to landmark theses of Hanslick, Langer, Caroll Pratt, and Nelson Goodman. Throughout, Davies steers a middle path, suggesting that theories of musical meaning cannot escape the issues of cultural literacy and historical style. For the serious student interested in a detailed overview of the literature, this book offers perhaps the most thorough discussion of the topic.

Another work of specialization, certainly more restricted than Davies, is DeBELLIS. This book is intended for the professional philosopher and for the music theorist interested in questions of theoretical representation and conceptualization. Its goal is to establish the epistemological relation between hearing music with or without theoretical clarification. DeBellis distinguishes between strong and weak conceptual hearing, but his point is that the theoretical study of music and the aesthetic value of music are not independent, because a theory-laden hearing enhances the perception and understanding of value in music. A welcome argument for theorists and a problematic one for non-theorists, DeBellis asserts his point with clarity and rigor.

LEVINSON (1997) has been much discussed since its publication. A slight volume with a simple premise, it has incited debate because it calls into question the academic premise that understanding music requires knowledge of musical form. Levinson bases his argument on what he calls *concatenationism*, which he derives from a reading of Edmund Gurney's *The Power of Sound* (1880). According to Levinson, music analysis overreaches its capacity when it seeks to explain the listening experience. From Gurney, he derives the essential quality of listening as constituted by the moment-to-moment impression of connectedness, rather than the perception of large-scale connections. In effect, Levinson appears completely at odds with DeBellis: he argues that knowing the form of a musical work is not required for grasping the music, since a basic understanding of music is accomplished in the progressive unfolding of events and relations. Levinson's point is necessarily circumscribed (perhaps to the point of being trivial), and while the book can have little effect on the category of hearing articulated by DeBellis above, it is worth reading for its defense of moment-by-moment musical experience.

From a completely different perspective, SMITH offers the reader an anthology of eight essays in the phenomenology of music. Phenomenology relies on the theories of Edmund Husserl (1859–1938). Originally a mathematician, Husserl developed phenomenological analysis, a radical form of logic in which so-called pure essences are ascertained from a probing analysis of intentionality (as defined by psychologist Franz Brentano [1838–1917]). Phenomenology teaches that a deeper understanding of the world is reached if one's subjective relation to the world is analyzed; technical analysis must be suppressed, as it interferes with the immediacy of experience (of the thing in itself). According to the phe-nomenologists, truth is revealed in the grasp of immediate experience and is obscured by technical conceptions. Ironically, most phenomenology creates its own technical jargon, thus directing the reader to a world viewed through a phenomenological lens. The opening essay of this volume offers a useful explication of Husserl, and a perusal of the topics contained therein (Schoenberg, temporality in recent music, musical expression, Heidegger, etc.) will give the reader a sense for what it means to explore phenomenology in music.

A better example of phenomenological discourse is CLIFTON. The book is addressed to music theorists and argues for phenomenological description in music analysis. The criteria for such analysis include the importance of restricting discourse to the work as intentional object (as a content of consciousness), and the significance of excluding theoretical conceptualizations while focusing instead on the experience of the composition itself. Phenomenological description frames musical understanding as a grasp of the work's constitution in the meaning act of its perception. The aim of Clifton's theory of description is precision and relevance, but the author locates the intrinsic interest of music in its experiential meaning. In essence, such description faces head-on the problem of reconciling empirical fact with phenomenological experience. However jargonesque, there is much that is fresh and stimulating here. For instance, of value to analytical discourse are Clifton's discussion of what he calls temporal intercut, and the constitution of groups, with respect to Mozart, Debussy, Boulez, Bartók, Beethoven, and Mahler; and his notions of relief, depth, faceting, and ritual essence.

As an example of the impact of phenomenology on musical ontology, INGARDEN remains the classic monograph. The author begins by asking the thought-provoking question, Where is the musical work located? Is it in the score, the performance, or the recording? Is it in all of its recordings or all of its performances? Ingarden concludes that the work of music is found in the conception of the composer, which is itself a relational construct that is notated in the score and replicated in subsequent live or recorded (and real or imagined) performances. While this conclusion may not be very startling, the path by which it is reached has significance. The notion that the work exists as the intentional object of the composer's consciousness—that the work is, in fact, located in the mental act(s) of the composer—cuts to the core of the difference between phenomenological and analytical methods. Given that the work is commonly taken as a product of the composer's craft—and therefore as existing outside the composer (e.g., in score, in performance, in the tradition of all performances)—the notion that the work is metaphysically located in the composer's consciousness boasts considerable intellectual edge.

One of the landmarks of Marxist thought and a still relevant critique of music in the 20th century, ADORNO presents the author's dialectical analysis pitting the music of Arnold Schoenberg ("Schoenberg and Progress") against that of Igor Stravinsky ("Stravinsky and Restoration"). Originally published in 1948, this study aims to expose Stravinsky's neoclassical technique as evidence of cultural retrogression, while extolling Schoenberg's 12-tone language as cultural progression. Adorno's argument seeks to establish the historical necessity of 12-tone music on the one hand and the depravity of neoclassicism on the other. His dialectic is rigorously Hegelian, juxtaposing 12-tone and neoclassical music in order to illuminate an unfolding zeitgeist. In fact, it is a reading intended to expose public taste as the victim of industrialism. According to Adorno, the public is controlled and manipulated by the culture industry, which is one more manifestation of the totalizing concept of capital, the (Hegelian) phase or ideological situation in which modern-day humans find themselves. Confined within this totalizing ideology, the institutions of culture—the orchestra associations, recording industries, broadcast companies, and, in their reaction against the new, the music schools and conservatories—engender and support the reception of music as commodity. In Adorno's critique, the culture industry cannot produce any legitimate culture of its own; it merely enshrines the residues of past culture. This treatise is essential reading for anyone interested in the great cultural debates of the second half of the 20th century.

In contrast to Adorno, SHUSTERMAN offers a defense of music normally excluded from serious philosophical consideration. He begins by taking yet another look at the dominant theories of art: art as imitation, expression, form, play, and symbol. He suggests that, in response to Adorno's critique of the contemporary art scene, art needs to be redefined—a redefinition that will circumvent the subjectivity of aesthetics and art theory. By subjectivity, he refers to the notion of art works as self-satisfying unities or as trivialized objects of aesthetic pleasure—or simply notions that fail to face the limits of art. Shusterman claims to have found an answer in the pragmatic aesthetics of John Dewey. Dewey's radically experiential standard of aesthetic value is pitted against the claims for cultural primacy and intrinsic value made by modern (analytic or critical) aesthetics. In the second part of his book, following an argument for the value of Dewey's philosophy, Shusterman devotes a chapter each to rock and rap music and, indirectly, jazz. His examples are taken from musics that exist primarily in performance rather than in score—music connected with, and derived from, bodily experience. Shusterman's conclusion appropriates Wittgenstein's assertion that ethics and aesthetics are one, articulating a proposal for the postmodern aestheticization of ethics, a lived beauty, one that arises from the body rather than the mind—what Shusterman calls an embodied aesthetic.

GORDON MARSH

Affections, Doctrine of

Bartel, Dietrich, *Musica Poetica: Musical-Rhetorical Figures in German Baroque Music*, Lincoln, Nebraska: University of Nebraska Press, 1997

Burmeister, Joachim, *Musical Poetics*, translated by Benito V. Rivera, New Haven, Connecticut: Yale University Press, 1993

Lippman, Edward A., *A History of Western Musical Aesthetics*, Lincoln: University of Nebraska Press, 1992

———, *Musical Aesthetics: A Historical Reader*, 3 vols., Stuyvesant, New York: Pendragon Press, 1986–90

Mattheson, Johann, *Johann Mattheson's Der vollkommene Capellmeister: A Revised Translation with Critical Commentary*, translated by Ernest C. Harriss, Ann Arbor: UMI Research Press, 1981

Ratner, Leonard, *Classic Music: Expression, Form, Style*, New York: Schirmer Books, 1980

The doctrine of affections (Ger. *Affektenlehre*), a principle of Baroque musical aesthetics and compositional theory, traces its origins to Aristotelian poetics. Although suggested by Zarlino as early as 1558, it was Descartes who gave the doctrine its clearest articulation in 1618 and German music theorists who developed the idea most systematically. Essentially, the doctrine holds that music is capable of arousing specific passions in listeners such as love, anger, joy, or fear. Such affections are usually sustained through a given composition, often with the aid of various compositional figures inspired by classical rhetorical tropes.

Useful introductions to the history and philosophy of the doctrine of affections may be found in LIPPMAN (1992), who offers a general overview of the doctrine, placing it within the context of Baroque rhetorical theory and aesthetics. RATNER also offers a general discussion of the doctrine, although his focus is 18th-century writers, and his concern is less with the philosophical issues involved than compositional and stylistic ramifications.

The most useful compendium of musical figures is found in BARTEL, who has surveyed all important treatises on Baroque musical aesthetics in order to identify and enumerate over 150 individual figures (ranging from "Abruptio"—a kind of anticipation—to "Variatio"—the embellishment of a given melody through diminutions). All relevant definitions and descriptions drawn from 15 sources are given for each figure, including musical illustrations. In addition, an introductory essay summarizes the work of the 15 writers Bartel consulted (from Burmeister to Forkel), as well as overlapping appendices in which the various figures are categorized and cross-listed.

German treatises by BURMEISTER and MATTHESON containing substantial discussions of musical affect and figures available in English translations. Burmeister's treatise is one of the earliest sources for musical figures, and contains a famous analysis of a Lasus motet parsed into sections using rhetorical terminology. Mattheson's bulky *Vollkommene Capellmeister* is far less systematic than Burmeister's treatise in treatment of musical figures, although it offers more musical examples and illustrations. Relevant sections from Mattheson may be more conveniently found in LIPPMAN (1986–90).

THOMAS CHRISTENSEN

Africa

Agawu, V. Kofi, *African Rhythm: A Northern Ewe Perspective,* New York: Cambridge University Press, 1995

Bebey, Francis, *African Music: A People's Art,* translated by Josephine Bennett, Brooklyn, New York: Hill Books, 1975

Berliner, Paul, *The Soul of Mbira: Music and Traditions of the Shona People of Zimbabwe,* Berkeley: University of California Press, 1978

Chernoff, John Miller, *African Rhythm and African Sensibility: Aesthetics and Social Action in African Musical Idioms,* Chicago: University of Chicago Press, 1979

Danielson, Virginia, *The Voice of Egypt: Umm Kulthum, Arabic Song, and Egyptian Society in the Twentieth Century,* Chicago: University of Chicago Press, 1997

Erlmann, Veit, *Nightsong: Performance, Power, and Practice in South Africa,* Chicago: University of Chicago Press, 1996

Graham, Ronnie, *The Da Capo Guide to Contemporary African Music,* New York: Da Capo Press, 1988

———, *The World of African Music,* London: Pluto Press, and Chicago: Research Associates, 1992

Jones, A.M., *Studies in African Music,* 2 vols., London: Oxford University Press, 1959

Kirby, Percival Robson, *The Musical Instruments of the Native Races of South Africa,* London: Oxford University Press, 1934; 2nd edition, Johannesburg: Witwatersrand University Press, 1965

Kisliuk, Michelle, *Seize the Dance! BaAka Musical Life and the Ethnography of Performance,* New York: Oxford University Press, 1998

Locke, David, *Kpegisu: A War Drum of the Ewe,* Tempe, Arizona: White Cliffs Media, 1992

Nketia, J.H. Kwabena, *The Music of Africa,* New York: Norton, 1974

Stone, Ruth M., editor, *The Garland Encyclopedia of World Music,* vol. 1, Africa, New York: Garland, 1998

Tracey, Hugh, *Chopi Musicians: Their Music, Poetry, and Instruments,* London: Oxford University Press, 1948; reprinted with a new introduction, 1970

Waterman, Christopher Alan, *Jùjú: A Social History and Ethnography of an African Popular Music,* Chicago: University of Chicago Press, 1990

After more than five centuries of passing references to music in Africa primarily in Arabic, French, British, Portuguese, and German travel accounts, scholarly articles and monographs (e.g. Ankermann's *Die Afrikanischen Musikinstrumente,* 1901) began appearing in the first few decades of the 20th century. One of the legacies of the continent's colonial history is that there are few English-language books on music from francophone African countries (and vice versa). During the 20th century, rich and diverse bodies of specialized literature on all aspects of music-making in Africa developed. Broad surveys of the continent are bound to be disappointing due to the sheer number of unique musics that demand representation. The focus up to the 1980s was on detailed inquiries of traditional music in single societies. Each of the following references has broken new ground in African music research and continues to maintain its relevance. The following review proceeds chronologically in order to reflect the changes in the field.

Firmly within the early 20th-century comparative musicological tradition of Hornbostel, KIRBY focuses on music objects, documenting a wide array of instruments with descriptions of how they are played, transcriptions, and 73 photographic plates from a fertile musical region. Given that it was written in the 1940s, TRACEY's study of the Chopi xylophone orchestras of Mozambique is especially far-reaching. Discussing in turn the musicians, lyrics, dancers, and instruments, Tracey, the preeminent musicologist of southern Africa, treats the music holistically. His release of LP recordings of the music discussed in the book (he writes that "no description of music can replace the actual experience of the sound") established a practice that has since been followed by other scholars in the field. While one must, of course, read his analyses from a historiographical perspective, it is refreshing to read an early example of a now-in-vogue confessional approach.

Despite its many methodological and notational problems, JONES is an enormously influential wellspring of research into Ghanaian music, setting a standard for the next generation of scholars. Addressed "in the first place to musicians and, in the second, to those who . . . would wish to know what African music is like, and the social contexts in which it thrived," Jones primarily focuses on the Ewe people, grappling with difficult issues of representation that continue to be problematic in the field. The second volume, consisting exclusively of drum and vocal transcriptions, catalyzed what would become the richest body of technical literature dealing with the problem of transcribing African musics, much of it reworking the same Ghanaian traditions. Although many of Jones's broader comparative conclusions have been superseded by more recent research, he did anticipate many areas that would later figure prominently in the field. For example, referring to "neo-folk music," which "demands that the majority of people should be spectators and listeners rather than participants," as bland, he also recognized that "this neo-folk tradition is a vital one. It is a true fusion of Africa and the West."

Bebey and Nketia share much common ground: for two decades they stood as the only English-language surveys of the continent; they were written around the same time; they privilege traditional music over its more modern manifestations; and the authors are African. BEBEY is more a philosophy of African music than a survey of the sounds of the continent. Privileged by his position as head of the music division of the United Nations Educational, Scientific, and Cultural Organization (UNESCO) but hampered by a dearth of sources, he provides a good overview of the role of traditional music in African society. Southern and North Africa are neglected in favor of West Africa, but otherwise there is a fair balance in the coverage of the various instrumental traditions. NKETIA, who is one of the most prolific writers on African music and has produced several earlier, exquisitely detailed books on music in Ghana, takes a more musicological approach than Bebey. Nketia discusses technical aspects of the music and presents extensive transcriptions, making use of analytic taxonomies that were then standard (although now are dated) in ethnomusicological writing. All of Africa's regions are not equally represented here; most of the musical examples come from Ghana, a well-documented country (surely due to Nketia's work).

BERLINER's masterly ethnomusicological study of the *mbira* played by the Shona people of Zimbabwe remains one of the few books devoted to a single African musical instrument. Berliner covers all aspects of the instrument, including its origins, how it is tuned and played, how the music is constructed, playing styles and contexts, the social background of the music and its practitioners, and vocal music and poetry associated with the instrument. He even provides an appendix on how to build an mbira. Released in conjunction with two albums of music discussed in the book, Berliner has produced a compelling and enduring model of how to "help bridge the tremendous gap between words about music and the experience of live music itself."

CHERNOFF's deeply personal, interpretive account of his experiences as a drumming apprentice among the Ewe and Dagbamba of southern and northern Ghana, respectively, is probably the most widely read of the books reviewed here. Written from the viewpoint of a social scientist actively engaged in learning the tradition, Chernoff quotes liberally from his teachers, stressing the moral and aesthetic aspects of drumming in Ghana. Transcriptions occasionally illustrate his basic points about the relationships of drums in an ensemble, but his interest primarily lies in broader social meanings of drumming. Speaking to an interdisciplinary audience, Chernoff opened a new avenue for writing about African music, and his book has been one of the major sources of information on the field for a generation of students of African music.

GRAHAM (1988, 1992) filled a major void in African music studies with his two volumes that focus primarily on modern popular music south of the Sahara Desert. Organized according to large regions, Graham proceeds country by country, introducing some of the major trends, providing informative overviews of a variety of artists and groups as well as accompanying discographies. The scope of Graham's work is unprecedented, and these two works are major research tools for popular music studies, giving credibility to an under-researched and blossoming field of study.

Production of books on music in Africa greatly accelerated in the 1990s, with many picking up where Chernoff left off but, now under the growing influence of performance studies, often moving deeply into more popular musics marked by international influences. WATERMAN's treatment of a major popular music in Nigeria, Africa's most populous country, is "about the relationship of music, identity, and power in a modernizing African society." Waterman establishes a solid detailed history of the Yoruba-based Jùjú music in the urban centers Lagos and Ibadan and makes a serious case for the music as a metaphor of Yoruba and modern Nigerian social order. ERLMANN's study of *isicathamiya*, the century-old South African Zulu choral tradition whose most well-known exponent around the world is Ladysmith Black Mambazo, covers a great deal of territory. Integrating recent trends in performance theory and continental philosophy with finely detailed musicological scholarship, Erlmann provides multiple perspectives on a major African choral tradition and offers an unprecedented 100-page discography of the genre.

Ghana continues to enjoy a wealth of technical writing that builds on the earlier work of Nketia and Jones. On the side of practice, LOCKE has published several books with accompanying cassettes, CDs, and videotapes documenting various Ghanaian drumming traditions for the performer. On the theoretical side, AGAWU, a staunch proponent of applying European (especially Schenkerian) music theory to the study of African music, examines the musical language of Northern Ewe of Ghana with a native speaker's insight. Writing of the culture in which he grew up (although, like many African writers, lacking practical experience in some traditions due to social expectations), Agawu's musicologically and linguistically sophisticated analyses broach new issues in the relationship between language and music.

Due to a scholarly tradition that typically focused on communal aspects of music-making, biographies have only recently begun to appear. DANIELSON's full-length biography of Umm Kulthum is a rich study of the how the forces of Islam, Arab culture, early and mid-20th-century Egyptian society, gender, and personal charisma combined in the formation of one of the most popular singers in North and East Africa, not to mention the Arab world.

KISLIUK is perhaps the most personal ethnomusicological account of an African music culture. She explicitly advocates a performance ethnography, weaving her own experiences with those of the people with whom she lived and worked, aiming to "show what I learned by revealing how I learned it . . . to make the reader aware of the process of turning experience into text." The two superb accompanying CDs of her recordings of BaAka people in the Central African Republic bring her story to life.

Among the many edited collections of writings on African music, STONE is the most systematic and comprehensive, examining the whole continent with regional overviews followed by a variety of finely focused articles by a cross-section of scholars.

ERIC CHARRY

Albania *see* Eastern Europe

Albéniz, Isaac 1860–1909

Spanish composer

Baytelman, Pola, *Isaac Albéniz: Chronological List and Thematic Catalog of His Piano Works,* Warren, Michigan: Harmonie Park Press, 1993
Clark, Walter Aaron, *Isaac Albéniz: A Guide to Research,* New York: Garland, 1998
———, *Isaac Albéniz: Portrait of a Romantic,* Oxford: Clarendon Press, and New York: Oxford University Press, 1998

Albéniz is a major figure in the history of Spanish music and was one of the most outstanding pianist/composers of the 19th century. He was a child prodigy who, after completing his education at the Brussels Conservatory in 1879, took Europe by storm as a touring virtuoso. He also developed considerable craft in composition and after 1892 gradually gave up concertizing to devote himself to it. Up to that time, his works had been largely for solo piano, the most successful of them inspired by Spanish folk music and exotic locales in his homeland. Among these works are such popular collections as the *Suite española* (1886) and *Recuerdos de viaje* (1887). In the 1890s, however, he wrote increasingly for the stage. His operas and operettas from this period achieved only moderate success (his best opera is *Pepita Jiménez,* which premiered in 1896) and have not remained in the repertoire. This is due partly to the poor quality of the librettos, most of which were written by a wealthy Englishman, Francis Money-Coutts (1852–1923). Money-Coutts gave Albéniz a large income in exchange for setting the librettos to music. Most commentators have interpreted this arrangement negatively as a "Faustian pact," but it was not severely binding, and Money-

Coutts continued to give Albéniz generous support even after the composer was no longer productive in this area. In fact, Albéniz abandoned stage music entirely in 1905 and returned to piano composition. The result of this was *Iberia,* a collection of 12 solos of great technical difficulty as well as musical charm and sophistication. After completing this work in 1908, the composer's health declined, and he died of complications from kidney disease in May of the following year. Albéniz's blending of Spanish folklore with modern elements of form and harmony, especially under French influence, set an example for future Spanish composers. The most eminent of these were his friends Joaquín Turina and Manuel de Falla, who were inspired to write, as Albéniz put it, "Spanish music with a universal accent."

BAYTELMAN is the first thematic catalog of Albéniz's music ever published and the first monograph on him in English. It presents a summary of biographical issues, discusses stylistic periods and publishers, and offers a detailed examination of both the composition and publication of the piano music in chronological order. It concludes with a discography and several other appendices, including a chronology of his life and lists of piano works by collection and grade of difficulty. It contains many reproductions of cover designs from first editions.

CLARK (1998b) is the first biography of the composer in English and examines both his life and works. It begins with a history of Albéniz's biography and confronts the issue of Albéniz's prevarication about his early career and the inconsistencies and discrepancies that, as a result, plague all biographical accounts. The biography traces his family history and then attempts, on the basis of much new and previously overlooked documentation, to provide an accurate account of Albéniz's remarkable early career as a touring prodigy and his metamorphosis into a full-time composer of considerable importance. It includes a critical examination of his major compositions for piano, voice, orchestra, and the stage, with an emphasis on his handling of folkloric material. The study of his music's critical reception is supported by ample citation of press notices. Also extensively cited are letters to and from the composer and his own diary entries, which tell a great deal about his relationships and thoughts. The biography concludes with a critique of his legacy, his role in Spanish music history, and his status in Spain today. It contains a genealogical chart and work list, as well as numerous musical examples.

CLARK (1998a) is a valuable tool for quickly accessing information about sources, works, and recordings of Albéniz's music. It begins with a summary biography, discussion of his stylistic evolution, and the current state of research (with suggestions for further work on Albéniz and Spanish music in general). The bibliography is in three sections and covers primary and secondary sources, as well as reviews of his concerts and works, during and after his life. The guide continues with a complete work list, as well as a thorough discography, including arrangements and transcriptions. The summary chronology of Albéniz's life brings into sharp focus the major events in his illustrious career.

WALTER AARON CLARK

Aleatoric Music

Boulez, Pierre, *Orientations: Collected Writings,* edited by Jean-Jacques Nattiez, translated by Martin Cooper, Cambridge: Harvard University Press, and London: Faber, 1986

Cage, John, *Silence: Lectures and Writings,* Middletown, Connecticut: Wesleyan University Press, 1961

DeLio, Thomas, *Circumscribing the Open Universe,* Lanham, Maryland: University Press of America, 1984

Feldman, Morton, *Essays,* Kerpen: Beginner Press, 1985

Karkoschka, Erhard, *Notation in New Music: A Critical Guide to Interpretation and Realisation,* translated by Ruth Koenig, New York: Praeger Publishers, 1972

Morgan, Robert P, *Twentieth-Century Music: A History of Musical Style in Modern Europe and America,* New York: Norton, 1991

Xenakis, Iannis, *Formalized Music: Thought and Mathematics in Composition,* Bloomington: Indiana University, 1971; revised edition, Stuyvesant, New York: Pendragon Press, 1992

Music in which the composer incorporates elements of chance in the process of composition and/or in performance is defined as aleatoric music. This music is often called chance music or music of indeterminacy. Although major composers of the 18th century such as Mozart and Haydn were believed to practice dice music (an early example of chance music), it was not until the middle of the 20th century that chance operations emerged as an important compositional method.

Twentieth-century composers of aleatoric music have shown diverse approaches to chance operations. In his *Music of Changes* (1951), John Cage used the *I-Ching,* an ancient Chinese book that prescribes methods for arriving at random numbers, to determine several parameters of sound, such as duration, tempo, and dynamics. Because the results obtained from the *I-Ching* are fixed and notated in the traditional manner, the role of performers remains passive, as in nonaleatoric music. Pierre Boulez's *Piano Sonata no. 3* (1957), Karlheinz Stockhausen's *Klavierstück IX* (1956), and Earle Brown's *Available Forms II* (1962) exemplify another type of aleatoric music, one that is indeterminate with respect to its performance. In these works, the composers provided notated events, but their arrangements are left to be decided by the performer(s).

The use of nontraditional methods of notation such as graphic or verbal symbols yields a greater degree of indeterminacy. In notating *Intersection no. 2* (1951) for solo piano, Morton Feldman used coordinate paper; the squares viewed horizontally represent a time unit, and three vertical squares in each row suggest relative pitch levels—high, middle, and low. The score of Earle Brown's *December 1952* (1952) consists of lines and rectangles of various lengths and thicknesses that are meant to be read as implying pitch, direction, loudness, and duration. The first version of Cage's *4'33"* (1952) has only a verbal indication, which specifies broad aspects of the piece, such as the number of sections and the length of each section. Composers have practiced chance operations not only in instrumental music but also in opera. In Henri Pousseur's *Votre Faust* (1967), the audience is asked to take part in deciding the plot of the opera at the performance. In Cage's *Europeras* series (1987–92), singers are asked to choose their favorites from the set of arias that the composer selected from existing operas.

CAGE's book, a collection of the composer's lectures and articles on his musical philosophy, is a useful source to study the aesthetic and philosophical background of his advocacy of chance in music. Cage maintains that art is an imitation of nature in its manner of operation, which he believes is chaotic and noncausal. Influenced by oriental philosophies, particularly Zen Buddhism, Cage stresses the acceptance of nature. By analogy, he views composition as an act of acceptance of any sound regardless of its results. For Cage, there is no split between art and life. The purpose of composing music, he contends, is an "affirmation of life," not an attempt to bring order out of chaos. Accordingly, he exhorts composers to renounce the will to control and, instead, to let sounds be themselves. Cage demands a complete break with the past and in this respect is critical of European aleatoric music composers, including Boulez, Stockhausen, and Pousseur. Of their efforts to use chance operations within the tradition of Western music, Cage comments, "It will not be easy . . . for Europe to give up being Europe." Cage's book would be enjoyable to the general reader as well as music specialists.

XENAKIS, a trained mathematician and engineer, has been composing what he calls "stochastic music," a type of aleatoric music in which he uses mathematical laws of chance to determine the microscopic elements of a composition. Xenakis's book is an extensive study of his stochastic music. Defining chance as "an extreme case of *controlled* disorder," Xenakis opposes Cage's unlimited use of chance. In contrast to Cage, he claims that a composer should determine at least the macroscopic shape of a composition, leaving each microscopic detail to the determination of chance. Indicating two major problems, Xenakis produces polemics against the Cagean open-form compositions. First, when the composer accepts any sound events in performance, the performer is promoted to the rank of composer by the composer him- or herself. Second, despite the composer's desire to remove personal taste from the music, as Cage wished, the work cannot be entirely free from it; even if the composer could keep his habits and tastes out, the performers cannot do the same. Because Xenakis's book is laden with mathematical theories, it might be frustrating to those not well acquainted with mathematics.

First published in German, KARKOSCHKA's volume is a thorough investigation of music notated in nontraditional ways, many of which involve aleatoric elements. His study is divided into three parts. Part 1 is an introductory essay about the current phenomena in today's notation. In part 2, Karkoschka examines in detail new notation systems, grouping them into five types—exact, frame, indicative, graphic, and the notation of electronic music. Part 3 provides musical examples of these different types of notations, drawn from numerous works by various composers. Although Karkoschka's work may be a bit too technical for the reader without a strong background in musical terminology, the general reader will be able to understand the author's point at least at the conceptual level. In fact, most of the symbols used in new notations are easier to understand than traditional symbols, since the former, through their pictorial representation and verbal instruction, tend to be clearer in signifying musical parameters.

In his collection of five analytical essays, DeLIO closely examines five open-form works by five composers—Cage, Feldman, Christian Wolff, Robert Ashley, and Alvin Lucier. The author links these composers by their aesthetic credo that artwork is not a fixed entity but a process, not a "circumscribed object" but a "circumscribing event." Although DeLio's dichotomization of open and closed structures is not without controversy, his essays are among the most extensive and finest analyses of open-form works ever written. DeLio's book is one of the few monographs devoted entirely to aleatoric music.

FELDMAN's views on the aesthetic and technical aspects of aleatoric music appear scattered throughout his book. Like Cage, Feldman asserts that sounds should exist in themselves. Unlike Cage, however, he allows chance only to the extent that a composer's identity is preserved in the composition, so that he or she can call the work his or her own. Like Xenakis, Feldman observes a dilemma in aleatoric music—the dilemma that he encountered in his own *Intersection no. 2,* in which he used a graphic notation. Feldman deplores that, in this piece, he was not only allowing the sounds to be free but he was also giving the performer too much freedom.

First published in French, BOULEZ's book is the most extensive collection of the composer's writings. Some of the essays contrast with Cage's writings in terms of the two composers' concepts of chance and their chance operations. Boulez agrees with Xenakis in that he tries to control the role of chance and restrict performers' freedom in aleatoric works. In the essay "Sonate, que me veux-tu?" Boulez emphasizes the importance of system as well as indeterminacy in Mallarmé's poetry, which inspired Boulez's use of chance operations in his composition of the *Third Piano Sonata.* Boulez's interest in chance was motivated by his frustration that chance cannot be entirely avoided in composition and performance regardless of the composer's intention. Although his book is less focused on aleatoric music than Cage's, it is valuable for providing different views of chance in composition.

MORGAN's work is one of the best sources for a synoptic overview of the history of aleatoric music in the broader context of 20th-century music. His discussion of the contrasting yet parallel relationships between serialism and aleatorism is particularly illuminating. He argues, for instance, that, although these two compositional methods are situated at the extreme ends in terms of the degree of control, both have contributed to the blurring of the temporal direction. Chapters 17 and 18 are the most focused on aleatoric composition.

JEONGWON JOE

See also Cage, John

Analysis: Atonal

Forte, Allen, *The Structure of Atonal Music,* New Haven, Connecticut: Yale University Press, 1973

Lewin, David, *Generalized Musical Intervals and Transformations,* New Haven, Connecticut: Yale University Press, 1986

Morris, Robert D., *Composition with Pitch-Classes: A Theory of Compositional Design,* New Haven, Connecticut: Yale University Press, 1987

Perle, George, *Serial Composition and Atonality: An Introduction to the Music of Schoenberg, Berg, and Webern,* Berkeley: University of California Press, 1962; 6th edition, revised, 1991

Rahn, John, *Basic Atonal Theory,* New York: Longman, 1980

Simms, Bryan R., *Music of the Twentieth Century: Style and Structure,* New York: Schirmer Books, and London: Collier Macmillan, 1986; 2nd edition, 1996

Straus, Joseph N., *Introduction to Post-Tonal Theory,* Englewood Cliffs, New Jersey: Prentice Hall, 1990

Beyond its literal meaning, the term *atonal* has come to refer to two things: first, the repertoire of radical music that emerged early in the 20th century (especially that of the Second Viennese School) and second, analytical theories and techniques that focus on pitch materials and musical structures not associated with the traditional tonal repertoire. Allen Forte's evocative definition of the atonal repertory is useful: "The repertory of atonal music is characterized by the occurrence of pitches in novel combinations, as well as by the occurrence of familiar pitch combinations in unfamiliar environments." Another way to define the atonal repertoire is through association with its more prominent composers, which include, from the early 20th-century, the three Second Viennese composers for whom the term originally was coined, Schoenberg, Webern, and Berg, as well as Debussy, Skryabin, Ives, Ruggles, Bartók, Stravinsky, and Varèse. More recent atonal composers include Messiaen, Carter, Britten, Lutoslawski, and Crumb. To characterize their works as "not tonal" would be inaccurate and miss the point. Most, if not all, of the compositions that comprise this repertoire do exhibit features that are aptly described as tonal, without necessarily conforming to traditional practice. What distinguishes them is that one cannot formulate comprehensive structural descriptions of their pitch materials and structures by reference to tonal features alone, as is possible with tonal compositions of the 18th and 19th centuries.

Numerous theories have been advanced to identify and explain the special features of atonal compositions, ranging from the ad hoc and prosaic recitations of "devices" by Vincent Persichetti (*Twentieth-Century Harmony: Creative Aspects and Practice,* 1961) and Leon Dallin (*Twentieth Century Composition: A Guide to the Materials of Modern Music,* 1974) to the insightful if unsystematic discussion of complex and novel harmonies by Schoenberg (*Theory of Harmony,* 1978; see especially chapters 18–22) and the eccentric but pioneering harmonic catalogs of Paul Hindemith (*The Craft of Musical Composition,* Book 1, 1945) and Howard Hanson (*Harmonic Materials of Modern Music: Resources of the Tempered Scale,* 1960). What began with attempts to explain music that on its face seemed irrational and iconoclastic, compared with the advanced tonal idiom of the later 19th century, has evolved into explorations of the nature and limits of musical materials and relations. Beginning in the late 1950s, with articles by the U.S. composer Milton Babbitt (e.g., "Set Structure as a Compositional Determinant," *Journal of Music Theory* 5 [1961]), there emerged a body of music theory that appropriates principles and terms drawn from the theory of sets (a branch of Boolean algebra) and that has become the predominant basis for analytical approaches today. The sources listed at the head of this article all treat the analysis of atonal music from this mainstream perspective. In general, the literature is rather technical, and in some cases mathematicians who are also experienced musical amateurs will find it easier going than postgraduates in music theory whose programs did not include mathematics.

As its title implies, SIMMS is a survey, but it differs from most such works because, in addition to its excellent historical review, it treats general aspects of current theory and analysis. The author provides a solid overview of the analytical problems associated with the atonal repertoire and outlines in a general way the direction music theory has taken toward their solution. The language is nontechnical. For readers who wish to become acquainted with the repertoire's historical and social context, as well as the theory that has evolved to address it, this is a good place to start.

While PERLE is the first source to treat the atonal repertoire from a set-theoretical perspective, it is not a comprehensive treatise on pitch-set theory; rather, it seeks to explicate aspects of pitch structure in the atonal repertoire (especially works by the Second Viennese composers) by invoking some of set theory's concepts and terminology. Perle's premise is that early atonal compositions constitute an evolutionary step toward classical 12-tone serial composition, and he considers atonal pieces experimental and inferior to the serial compositions that followed, a position generally rejected today. Despite its age (the material remains much as in the original 1962 publication), the book remains provocative and insightful, if difficult owing to the author's unnecessarily turbid style.

Straus and Rahn are both textbooks intended for undergraduate music majors. STRAUS provides an excellent introduction to pitch-set theory, and mastery of this volume's materials will prepare readers for the more advanced literature treating the atonal and serial repertoires and equip them with the basic tools required for set-theoretical analysis. The book requires little background beyond facility in reading music notation, a modicum of conventional music theory, and some affinity for simple algebraic formalisms. The writing style is perspicuous.

RAHN evinces a strong compositional slant, which reflects the author's activities as a composer and composition teacher. Although readers need no mathematics beyond introductory high school algebra, the book's style of discourse is strongly mathematical and its structure is idiosyncratic. Theorists regard both Rahn and Straus highly, but the latter is more straightforward and comprehensive. Rahn's narrower and more technical orientation, however, offers detailed explanations of the math behind various operations as well as some wonderful analytic insights.

FORTE's book is the first comprehensive source devoted to pitch-set theory. Although others (especially Babbitt) had applied concepts drawn from mathematical set and group theory to the world of pitch relations, Forte is the first to explore systematically the notion of the pitch-class set in terms of each of its associated properties and operations, and he is the first to expound many of the principles, terms, ranges, and limits of phenomena associated with the theory and its repertoire. The book is divided into two parts: the first examines all of the basic aspects of set theory; the second presents Forte's theory of set complexes and several substantial analyses. Although some of the material is now quite dated, from an analytical standpoint this monograph is still the richest comprehensive source available, bountifully supplemented by the author's analytic insights gained through his considerable experience. Those new to pitch-set theory may find the work's technical content daunting, but the writing is clear and the material is logically and thoughtfully structured; the author keeps mathematical formalisms to a minimum. Forte's *The Harmonic Organization of the Rite of Spring* (1978) complements this work by demonstrating the efficacy of its analytical principles and techniques for exploring a large-scale atonal masterpiece.

MORRIS is another comprehensive source for pitch-set theory, more current than Forte and more exhaustive in its coverage of principles of pitch-set theory, which the author ties to the wider conceptual field of group theory. He also explores many aspects of 12-tone theory. Morris's innovative conceptions using the metaphors of contour space, pitch space, and pitch-class space are important advances. Although the writing style is often algorithmic and filled with formalisms, its demands do not exceed the scope of high school algebra. Because it is written from a composer's perspective rather than an analyst's, noncomposers may find its approach less congenial. Nonetheless, it is essential for anyone interested either in perusing advanced literature in the field or undertaking sophisticated set-theoretical analysis.

In its formulation of a true field theory, LEWIN constitutes an enormous advance in the realm of abstract musical relations. Strictly speaking, field theory's scope is not limited to the atonal and serial repertoires, although to date it has found the most application there, nor is it limited merely to pitch relations. Lewin's book actually presents two distinct but overlapping field theories: his theory of generalized musical interval systems allows relations among musical events of all kinds to be construed as values, which can be measured and compared, and his theory of transformational networks makes such events and relations subject to operations (as understood in group theory). Lewin's theories are inspired by the mathematics of Boolean algebra and group theory. Whereas the application of conventional pitch-set theory is limited primarily to pitch materials in the atonal repertoire, both of Lewin's theories may be applied to any aspect of music that is amenable to representation in values, including pitch, duration, register, instrumentation, texture, and form. The book is difficult due to its use of a discourse laden with formalisms. It is, however, one of the most important theoretical treatises of the 20th century, and theorists are just beginning to explore its myriad and exciting possibilities.

RICHARD S. PARKS

See also Atonality

Analysis: General

Ayrey, Craig, and Mark Everist, editors, *Analytical Strategies and Musical Interpretation: Essays on Nineteenth- and Twentieth-Century Music,* Cambridge: Cambridge University Press, 1996

Bent, Ian, and William Drabkin, *Analysis,* Basingstoke: Macmillan, and New York: Norton, 1987

Berry, Wallace, *Structural Functions in Music,* Englewood Cliffs, New Jersey: Prentice Hall, 1976

Clifton, Thomas, *Music as Heard: A Study in Applied Phenomenology,* New Haven, Connecticut: Yale University Press, 1983

Cook, Nicholas, *A Guide to Musical Analysis,* London: Dent, and New York: Braziller, 1987

Dunsby, Jonathan, and Arnold Whittall, *Music Analysis in Theory and Practice,* London: Faber, and New Haven, Connecticut: Yale University Press, 1988

Epstein, David, *Beyond Orpheus: Studies in Musical Structure,* Cambridge, Massachusetts: MIT Press, 1979

Forte, Allen, *The American Popular Ballad of the Golden Era, 1924–1950,* Princeton, New Jersey: Princeton University Press, 1995

LaRue, Jan, *Guidelines for Style Analysis,* New York: Norton, 1970; 2nd edition, Warren, Michigan: Harmonie Park Press, 1992

Lerdahl, Fred, and Ray S. Jackendoff, *A Generative Theory of Tonal Music,* Cambridge, Massachusetts: MIT Press, 1983

Lewin, David, *Musical Form and Transformation: 4 Analytic Essays,* New Haven, Connecticut: Yale University Press, 1993

Meyer, Leonard B., *Emotion and Meaning in Music,* Chicago: University of Chicago Press, 1956

Narmour, Eugene, *The Analysis and Cognition of Basic Melodic Structures: The Implication-Realization Model,* Chicago: University of Chicago Press, 1990

Nattiez, Jean-Jacques, *Music and Discourse: Toward a Semiology of Music,* translated by Carolyn Abbate, Princeton, New Jersey: Princeton University Press, 1990

Reti, Rudolph, *The Thematic Process in Music,* New York: Macmillan, 1951

Music analysis may be characterized as the experiential, practical dimension of a dichotomous endeavor for which music theory is the contemplative, idealistic counterpart. Neither element operates without the other; music analyses imply theories about musical events and relations, and music theories imply their verifiability through analysis. Thus, it is difficult to separate the terms *theory* and *analysis*, although here we focus on the latter.

Music analysis seeks chiefly to explore two kinds of questions: *How* does music work? and *How* do we hear music? (These questions are related to, but significantly different than, the questions *What* is music? and *What* do we hear in music?) It is essentially an empirical activity; that is, its practitioners proceed on the implicit premise that what we may "know" about the nature of music is that which we can experience, either by hearing (in actual performance or through mental audition) or by inference from notation seen in a score.

Within the modern literature of music analysis, we may discern two distinct perspectives. One is *theory-driven,* in that some theoretical issue provides the impetus for analysis. The other is *analysis-driven,* in that questions are framed in the context of particular compositions, with music analysis (and its results) serving as its own raison d'etre, while theory remains in the background. Theory-driven studies usually proceed by posing some relatively abstract question, explicating a theory that addresses it, and turning to analysis to demonstrate the theory's efficacy. Analysis-driven studies usually presume the applicability of some theory (such as pitch-set theory) and proceed to explore compositions by means of that analytical method, but the focus of study is primarily on the repertoire under consideration. Of the two emphases, North American literature tends to favor theory-driven studies, whereas British literature favors those that are analysis-driven. Perhaps not surprisingly, most of the more general books listed above are by British scholars, and the more specialized studies are by North American authors.

We may divide the music-analytical literature into books that address analytical theories of music versus extended studies that address specific repertoires or issues pertaining to those repertoires. Either way, pitch materials in tonal and post-tonal music have received and continue to receive by far the most analytical attention, although this situation changed during the last decade and a half of the 20th century because of an increasing interest in musical features other than pitch and because of interdisciplinary influences from the fields of phenomenology, feminist and minority studies, semiotics, narratology, and critical theory.

Of the books listed in the bibliography, those by Bent, Cook, Dunsby and Whittall, and LaRue are broad in scope, seeking to provide general introductions to techniques and theories of music analysis. The remainder are specialized and mainly theory-driven (Forte, and Ayrey and Everist are exceptions).

LaRUE considers how to examine a musical score systematically. He sets forth a comprehensive taxonomy of musical features divided into five main categories that align with the enduring musical parameters of sound (which encompasses texture, timbre, and more), harmony and counterpoint, melody, rhythm and meter, and what the author calls "growth" (which others might call "form"). The analytical method is simplistic and LaRue's explicatory goals are modest, but many performers and conductors practice the author's strategies and consider them essential to score preparation. Eschewing technical jargon and arcane theoretical concepts, this well-written book is accessible to nonmusicians as well as professionals and is a good starting point for the novice analyst.

Much more sophisticated are the works by Bent, Cook, and Dunsby and Whittall, which are comprehensive in their coverage of current analytical theories, although each evinces a decidedly different slant. COOK is by far the most comprehensive. He presents his own taxonomy of five approaches to analysis: "traditional," "Schenkerian," "psychological," "formalistic," and "comparative." Under the first paradigm he places Riemann and thorough-bass theories; the second division treats the work of Heinrich Schenker and his followers; under "psychological" Cook discusses Leonard Meyer's ideas and motivic analysts such as Rudolph Réti; the "formalistic" category embraces pitch-set theory, semiotics, and linguistics; and finally, by "comparative" the author refers to approaches that measure and compare some feature in a large number of compositions.

Cook's taxonomy is idiosyncratic and on some counts contestable. Schenkerian analyses are "psychological," for example, in much the way Meyer's are, insofar as both focus on the experience of music (although in markedly different ways). And Meyer's theories are also "formalistic," especially as developed by Narmour, whereas Nattiez's semiotic approach arguably is "comparative" as well as "formalistic." Nonetheless, the categories are a useful basis for sorting out the welter of theories and methodologies that underlie the diverse literature of modern analysis, and Cook's discussion does not trivialize or distort in order to enforce his taxonomic assignments. His descriptions of analytical methods are sufficient to inform readers of the essential qualities and purviews of each technique along with their sources of contention. Particularly valuable are his thoughtful comparisons of the many analytical approaches, which are full of insights and constructive criticisms. He captures very well essential differences among methods and aptly identifies the crucial issues that attend the approaches. The latter half of the book is a wide-ranging demonstration through analyses of several diverse pieces, which readers will find instructive and helpful. Of the books that survey methods of music analysis, this is the best.

BENT's book, an expansion of his important article of the same name that first appeared in the *New Grove Dictionary of Music and Musicians* (1980), is especially valuable for its excellent, comprehensive historical survey of music theorist-analysts and their contributions and works. Although less detailed than Cook, the survey of analytical theories and methods is more inclusive. For example, Bent's volume fills some of Cook's lacuna in its coverage of linguistics and cybernetics and its summary of Wallace Berry's theory of structural functions. The glossary by William Drabkin of terms used in analysis, which occupies the second half of the book, is wonderfully eclectic and quite useful. There is also an extensive bibliography.

Ostensibly similar to Cook, DUNSBY and WHITTALL is more succinct. It is organized around the two repertoires—tonal and post-tonal—that dominate concert programming and subdivided into various musical issues that arise within each. There is also a substantial chapter devoted to semiotics. Dunsby and Whittall is informative and engaging in a very different way from Cook; vis-à-vis the theorists it covers, it is more anecdotal and pointedly critical. Together, Cook, Bent, and Dunsby and Whittall provide an admirable view of the field by the end of the 1980s, its chief practitioners, and their works.

Each of the following books and authors exemplifies a distinct place within the diverse range of scholarship that characterizes the field of music analysis today.

EPSTEIN seeks to demonstrate complementarity between Schenkerian and Schoenbergian-motivic analyses by examining a limited number of large excerpts and whole compositions, mostly from the tonal repertoire. His book is narrower in scope and assumes more background than the studies discussed above and requires a significantly greater technical background in music theory and analysis. It addresses profound musical issues, however, and will reward the reader with many insights.

BERRY's volume is one of the most stimulating 20th-century treatises on theory and analysis. Interested particularly in the dynamic nature of musical experience, the author has developed a conceptual basis, terminology, and variety of analytical techniques by which to study that experience concretely. Comprehensive in its approach, this work addresses all elements of music, including texture and register as well as pitch and duration, and is applicable to music of any era. Although the book does not require an extensive background in music theory, Berry does impose a considerable body of his own terms and concepts, and his prose style is dauntingly turbid.

The 1987 publication of LEWIN's seminal treatise, *Generalized Musical Intervals and Transformations* (*GMIT*), was a signal event with immediate and profound implications for music analysis. However, the demands of its heavily formalistic language and reliance on mathematics, coupled with a sparsity of analytical examples, somewhat impeded the theory's dissemination. Hence, for a time its potential for uncovering abstract musical structures was circumscribed. Most welcome, therefore, was the book's sequel, discussed here, which is devoted to exploring the theory through analysis of four post-tonal compositions. In the introduction, Lewin states his intention "to make the essays accessible to a general reader interested in twentieth-century music, a reader who may not have read *GMIT* or even heard of it." Indeed, technical discussions are limited and largely consigned to footnotes, and although some acquaintance with mathematical logic and transformational theory is helpful, the book stands on its own. Its importance (and that of the 1987 volume) is its explication of a field theory that allows the analyst to infer abstract relations

within or among the domain(s) of any musical element or combination of elements. This is not a book for novices; knowledge of pitch-set and 12-tone theory is necessary for at least two of the essays. Diligent readers will be well rewarded, however, by Lewin's illuminating and eminently musical discoveries.

CLIFTON explores the philosophy of phenomenology, from Husserl onward, and its application to music analysis. The study is controversial and fundamentally contradictory. One of the author's main premises is that a listener should approach a composition naively, free of erudite preconceptions of musical style or structures; on the other hand, Clifton formulates a set of characteristic types of musical events, and his analytical method consists of identifying them in compositions, which implies that a listener versed in his typology and able to distinguish its types in analysis will thereby gain knowledge. Despite this and other weaknesses, Clifton's ideas are provocative and perspective-broadening. This work is not simply another analytical method concealed beneath a robe of iconoclasm. The author's insistence that we reflect on the nature and quality of experience when listening is genuinely different from most other approaches. He provides a starting place for those interested in the potential of the phenomenological point of view to inform our understanding of the nature of musical experience.

LERDAHL and JACKENDOFF apply principles drawn from Chomskian linguistics to the task of formulating an analytical method. Specifically, the authors present an approach that ties sets of "well-formedness rules" and "preference rules" to a "prolongational tree-structure" method of analytical reduction, which is used to parse tonal passages and compositions. Although the discourse is technical, most of the terminology is developed within the book. When published, this book attracted a great deal of attention and was widely embraced, especially by scholars from the fields of music psychology and music education. By the end of the 20th century, its impact seemed greatly diminished, as little scholarship built on its foundations. It stands, nevertheless, as a demonstration of fruitful interdisciplinary synthesis.

MEYER's concept of pattern perception lies at the center of his theory of musical relations and experience. NARMOUR, his student, developed his "implication-realization model" from Meyer. Together, these two books provide a starting point for exploring analysis grounded in principles of psychology and perception. Neither presents problems of accessibility, although Narmour does develop his own terminology to support his analytical methodology.

There is a large and growing body of literature devoted to semiotics (and semiology) in music. The translation of NATTIEZ is the most recent comprehensive work devoted to the application of this discipline to music. Readers will not find here a clear methodology for semiotic analysis of music. However, the author does set forth a theory of semiotics along with some sample analyses; discusses the work and influence of figures such as Umberto Eco, Charles S. Peirce, and Nicholas Ruwet; and provides an extensive bibliography.

RETI is perhaps the most influential proponent of the Schoenberg-derived concept of the *Grundgestalt* or "basic shape" as a basis for pitch structure in compositions, particularly those of Beethoven. The author proposes that pitch motives identified at the beginning of a composition could, with the aid of various kinds of melodic transformational operations, be demonstrated to provide the stuff of all that follows. His analyses are fundamentally flawed, on the one hand, by an absence of constraints on the range and kinds of admissible transformations and, on the other, by a capricious avoidance of comprehensiveness; they are nonetheless often intriguing, provocative, and informative. Furthermore, his ideas are important as precursors to pitch-set analysis.

FORTE's volume is an excellent demonstration of the adaptation of analytical techniques originally developed for the tonal repertoire of the 18th and 19th centuries to the analysis of 20th-century popular music. He uses modern analytical procedures to explore musical structures in the large repertoire of songs composed for musical theater in the United States and for the big bands, as well as Tin Pan Alley songs by songwriters such as Harold Arlen, Hoagy Carmichael, George Gershwin, Jerome Kern, and Cole Porter, with a view to demonstrating popular music's uniqueness and high artistic value. Potential readers would benefit from some exposure to Schenkerian theory.

The collection of essays edited by AYREY and EVERIST covers a wide variety of topics in music analysis, with emphasis on interdisciplinary influences, important areas of controversy, and exploring the nature and limits of the enterprise of music analysis. Imbued throughout with an iconoclastic freshness, the essays are divided into two categories, "transformations" and "rhetorics," which the editors use to underscore the interpretive character of all music analysis and to group the chapters according to common themes. The articles treat music from Schumann to Birtwhistle and discuss topics as diverse as defining the identity of a work, intertextual influences on composition, and the role and use of narratology in composition and analysis. These articles capture well the ambivalent flavor of current thinking in music theory and analysis. They are demanding, and readers will find a background in philosophy, letters, and recent literature in music analysis a distinct advantage.

RICHARD S. PARKS

See also Form

Analysis: Schenkerian

Forte, Allen, and Steven E. Gilbert, *Introduction to Schenkerian Analysis,* New York: Norton, 1982

Jonas, Oswald, *Introduction to the Theory of Heinrich Schenker: The Nature of the Musical Work of Art,* translated by John Rothgeb, New York: Longman, 1982

Salzer, Felix, *Structural Hearing: Tonal Coherence in Music,* 2 vols., New York: Charles Boni, 1952

Schenker, Heinrich, *Counterpoint,* 2 vols., translated by John Rothgeb and Jürgen Thym, New York: Schirmer Books, and London: Collier Macmillan, 1987

———, *Free Composition,* translated by Ernst Oster, New York: Longman, 1979

Snarrenberg, Robert, *Schenker's Interpretive Practice,* Cambridge: Cambridge University Press, 1997

———, *Harmony,* translated by Elisabeth Mann Borgese, edited by Oswald Jonas, Chicago: University of Chicago Press, 1954

Heinrich Schenker (1868–1935) was the most influential music theorist of the 20th century. He trained in Vienna and pursued a varied career as a pianist, accompanist, music critic, editor, private teacher, and composer. Beginning with the idea of developing artistic performances and interpretations based on intimate knowledge of the musical score and its implications, Schenker developed over his lifetime a powerful analytical method that draws out the network of interrelations that form the multilayered structure of a composition. Schenker took this notion further and, based on criteria of organic coherence, asserted a canon of great composers, the Austro-German masters of the common-practice period from Bach through Brahms, as the embodiment of creative genius in music. Schenker developed and set forth his theory in a series of three works, *Harmony, Counterpoint,* and *Free Composition,* collectively known as *New Musical Theories and Fantasies.* In addition to this theoretical contribution, he published many examples of applied musical analysis, including detailed analyses of keyboard and orchestral works by Bach, Beethoven, Chopin, Haydn, Mozart, Schubert, and others. Much of this material is now available in English translation.

Schenker's analytical method itself depends on considerable expertise at perceiving structural relationships among notes and in synthesizing underlying fundamental structures that demonstrate the organic connections by which musical artworks project coherence. Musical relationships are often represented through graphic notation that utilizes the symbols of traditional musical notation. SCHENKER (1954), originally published anonymously by "an artist," presents his basic approach to chord structures, chord progressions, and key relationships. A key element in his thinking is the functionality of harmonies within their contexts and over considerable expanses of time. Already at this early stage Schenker makes the distinction between the actual notes of a composition and the underlying structural basis of scale steps on which they are built.

SCHENKER (1987) represents a detailed reworking, expansion, and criticism of species counterpoint as set forth by J.J. Fux. Here, note-by-note relationships are considered in an abstract world of essential counterpoint. This work forms the foundation of his theory of voice leading as the underlying means by which coherence is achieved. Schenker includes frequent reference to the work of other theorists such as Riemann, Bellermann, Albrechtsberger, and Cherubini. In addition, Schenker often refers to brief excerpts of classical and romantic music that demonstrate the application of principals of strict counterpoint in a free context.

SCHENKER (1979), published posthumously, presents his fully developed theory of structural levels and musical organicism. Here for the first time he synthesizes and lays out his concept of musical structure in its entirety. Characterized by continual reference to short but pithy graphs of passages from the common-practice repertoire, *Free Composition* proceeds from the most general concept of the "Chord of Nature"—that is, the principal notes of the overtone series—to the concepts of "background" and "fundamental structure." It continues to the "middleground," where Schenker illustrates the composing-out of the background through various contrapuntal techniques such as interruption, mixture, neighboring notes, linear progressions, arpeggiations, unfolding, etc. The "foreground" is portrayed as specific arrangements of similar techniques at later structural levels, giving rise to the unique characteristics of individual compositions. At this level technical features such as obligatory register, cover tones, and diminutions come into prominence. Later chapters are brief but of utmost importance. "Meter and Rhythm" sets forth ideas of the role of pitch relationships in understanding rhythmic and metrical relations. "Form," as brief as it is, presents a digest of Schenker's view of the interrelationships between voice-leading structures and the articulation of formal plans such as binary, ternary, sonata, rondo, fugue, and variations. Ironically, this text presents Schenker's thought as an inductive theory while in its development it was always firmly deductive, based on the observations of the structure of many samples of music from the 18th and 19th centuries.

Schenker's challenging prose style hampered the widespread appreciation of his work but also prompted contributions from others. JONAS, a disciple of Schenker, proceeds from foreground phenomenon rather than background and bases much of his work on Schenker's *Harmony*. By minimizing the dependence on abstract notions, Jonas provides an introduction that is easily understood and appreciated. The appendix contains an illuminating discussion of the relationship of tonal structures to text.

SALZER, another disciple of Schenker, attempts a considerable systematization of Schenker's theories as well as of notational conventions. Salzer also seeks to broaden the scope of Schenkerian analysis by applying it to early music as well as to modern music, in examples ranging from Perotin through Bartók. One may feel that in systematizing Schenker's method, however, Salzer at the same time reduces the subtlety of the technique. His examples, in their attempt to be transparent and logical, at times lack sensitivity to the nuances of the music.

FORTE and GILBERT is a pedagogically oriented work based on a highly technical approach. Part 1 reviews basic musical elements such as counterpoint, harmony, and voice leading from a Schenkerian perspective. Part 2 presents Schenkerian structural notions in a progression from simple one-part forms through increasingly complex forms. Its dogmatic approach may be initially helpful to students but ultimately limits the depth to which the musical materials can be explicated in Schenkerian terms. The graphic notation differs in important respects from Schenker's, particularly in the frequent use of plain note heads and beams. Further, the book steers clear of the philosophical and polemical issues that inevitably surround Schenkerian analysis, issues that increasingly are seen as important in understanding the theory in its context.

In recent years, theorists have begun to deal with Schenker in a more critical manner. SNARRENBERG is particularly insightful in contextualizing Schenker's work within contemporary philosophical thought. This author eloquently discusses Schenker's basic concepts within broad topical perspectives of "Effects," "Intentions," "Synthesis," and "Participation," categories that allow Snarrenberg to consider Schenker's contribution in enlightening ways that are at once critical and sympathetic. At the same time, the author brings useful insights and perspectives into the discussion and revisits basic Schenkerian tenets with new and well-focused critical thought. For example, under the rubric of "effect," Snarrenberg places three basic genera—passing, delay, and entity—to which many specific Schenkerian notions relate as particular instances. In this sense Snarrenberg succeeds in creating a metatheory of Schenkerian theory that holds promise for further development and ultimately for defining the place of Schenkerian studies in the broader context of historical and theoretical reflection.

WILLIAM RENWICK

See also Fugue

Analysis: Serial

Babbitt, Milton, *Milton Babbitt: Words about Music,* edited by Stephen Dembski and Joseph N. Straus, Madison: University of Wisconsin Press, 1987

Bailey, Kathryn, *The Twelve-Note Music of Anton Webern: Old Forms in a New Language,* Cambridge: Cambridge University Press, 1991

Brindle, Reginal Smith, *Serial Composition,* London: Oxford University Press, 1966

Haimo, Ethan, *Schoenberg's Serial Odyssey: The Evolution of His Twelve-Tone Method, 1914–1928,* Oxford: Clarendon Press, and New York: Oxford University Press, 1990

Hyde, Martha M., *Schoenberg's Twelve-Tone Harmony: The Suite Op. 29 and the Compositional Sketches,* Ann Arbor, Michigan: UMI Research Press, 1982

Leibowitz, Rene, *Schoenberg and His School: The Contemporary Stage of the Language of Music,* translated by Dika Newlin, New York: Philosophical Library, 1949; reprint, New York: Da Capo, 1970

Mead, Andrew Washburn, *An Introduction to the Music of Milton Babbitt,* Princeton, New Jersey: Princeton University Press, 1994

Milstein, Silvina, *Arnold Schoenberg: Notes, Sets, Forms,* Cambridge: Cambridge University Press, 1992

Perle, George, *The Operas of Alban Berg,* 2 vols., Berkeley: University of California Press, 1980–85

————, *Serial Composition and Atonality: An Introduction to the Music of Schoenberg, Berg, and Webern,* Berkeley: University of California Press, 1962; 6th edition, revised, 1991

Rognoni, Luigi, *The Second Vienna School: Expressionism and Dodecaphony,* translated by Robert W. Mann, London: Calder: 1977

Rufer, Josef, *Composition with Twelve Tones Related Only to One Another,* translated by Humphrey Searle, London: Barrie and Jenkins, 1954; revised edition, 1970

Serialism refers to the compositional method developed by Arnold Schoenberg in the 1920s. It ultimately became the musical language of the so-called Second Viennese School, which consisted of Schoenberg and his two most celebrated pupils, Alban Berg and Anton Webern. The coherence of serial music (also known as 12-tone or 12-note music) depends in a fundamental way on a particular sequence of interval classes and its transformations. The term *serialism* also refers to later compositional systems (often called total, integral, or post–Webern serialism) that were inspired by Schoenberg's method (which is sometimes called classical serialism). The term *serial analysis* describes how serialism is at work in a particular musical composition. In order to follow (or construct) such an analysis, an understanding of Schoenberg's method is fundamental.

Several authors provide contemporary accounts of this method of composition. RUFER, a student of Schoenberg, illustrates the 12-tone method in a straightforward way. He subscribes to his teacher's view that the method represents a further step in the direction defined by the great German tradition: that is, great music consists of the continuous variation of a basic shape, and 12-tone music is Schoenberg's way of continuing this tradition, which began with Bach and continued through Brahms. Rufer's book includes 12-tone analyses of many passages by Schoenberg.

LIEBOWITZ was an influential exponent of the music of the Second Viennese School. His book, written at about the same time as Rufer's, traces the evolution of the school's various musical styles (from tonal through atonal to serial) largely through musical analysis. ROGNONI's book has the same aim but was written much later and in fact often refers to analyses and interpretations put forward by Rufer and Liebowitz.

The above writings make excellent introductions to the topic, as they mix historical perspectives with the basic musical principles and techniques of serialism. A more analytically oriented work is PERLE (1962), which not only demonstrates analytical methodologies that apply to the Second Viennese School but also addresses similar musical procedures in Scryabin, Bartók, and Stravinsky. BRINDLE also expands the repertory under consideration by turning briefly to such composers as Nono and Dallapiccola. Unlike Perle, however, this book is meant to instruct in the art of serial composition.

In the late 1950s and early 1960s, the first formal studies of the technique and theoretical implications of serialism began to appear; among them was a series of articles by Babbitt. These remain essential references for the serious student of serialism, and they continue to be cited in almost every book about the topic. They are notoriously difficult for many readers, however, because of their somewhat mathematical tone. While it is true that some of his ideas could have been presented more clearly, Babbitt's writing succeeds in demystifying some of the important tenets of serialism. His work has been a breath of fresh air for many readers yearning for precise and logical explanations. One can find several of these articles, as well as other similar writings by other authors from this stimulating period in music theory, reprinted in Benjamin Boretz and Edward T. Cone, editors, *Perspectives on Contemporary Music Theory* (1972) as well as Paul Henry Lang, editor, *Problems of Modern Music: The Princeton Seminar in Advanced Musical Studies* (1962).

One of the unfortunate by-products of the technical literature from the 1950s and 1960s is the spread of the notion that serial music is somehow a mathematical concoction, constructed rather than composed and analyzed rather than enjoyed. BABBITT is a response to this problem, an excellent book consisting of lectures given by the author at the University of Wisconsin, Madison, in 1983. It is not a book from which to learn the basics of serialism; rather, it illuminates (in a relaxed manner) some of the art of serialism. It makes many convincing connections between serial structure and musical comprehension and enjoyment.

Several books focus on the analysis of a particular serial composition or on the serial works of a single composer. These analyses illustrate clearly that the properties and character of 12-tone music come from the composer and not simply from the method. Each composer uses serialism in an individual way, and various issues are explored in different pieces.

BAILEY's comprehensive book discusses each of Webern's serial works. She leads the reader through every 12-tone movement, considering in detail the symmetries, canons, and formal structures that one often associates with the composer's music. Beginners will find the detailed readings fascinating, while experienced analysts may find the text a bit slow. The appendices include matrices and row counts for all the music discussed.

PERLE (1980–85) studies the formal design and serial, tonal, and dramatic structure of Berg's operas *Wozzeck* and *Lulu*. It compares the musical devices in *Lulu* and *Wozzeck* (Berg's earlier, atonal opera) and discusses the relationship between the libretto of *Lulu* and the plays by Frank Wedekind on which it is based. These topics, as well as Berg's keen interest in secret messages and musical codes, are intrinsic to the fruitful study of this composer's music.

Regarding Schoenberg's own serial technique, HAIMO reminds us that Schoenberg himself had to learn to be a 12-tone composer. The author traces the technique's development from its first sign of life (placed in 1914, with the oratorio *Die Jakobsleiter*) through the actual birth of the 12-tone idea (the music of the early 1920s) to the art of 12-tone composition, which is achieved, after refinement and experimentation, with the String Quartet no. 3, op. 30, and the *Variations*, op. 31 (1926–28). Haimo isolates and discusses those techniques that became Schoenberg's means of creating art from the 12-tone method.

Two other books on Schoenberg's serialism may be briefly noted here. HYDE's pioneering work shows the relationship between serial technique and Schoenberg's sketches for the Suite, op. 29, before mounting a detailed analysis of the harmonic structure of the piece. MILSTEIN constructs detailed serial maps of several late works but has been criticized for stopping short of drawing fruitful conclusions. This kind of problem, however, is nothing new to musical (not only serial) analysis, as curious readers often need to extend further published analyses in the direction where their interests lie.

Finally, MEAD discusses serialism in Babbitt's compositions, first explaining serial techniques that extend those of Schoenberg and Webern: the array, the superarray, and various rhythmic procedures. The author then shows how these techniques developed in Babbitt's music, from the early pieces in the 1940s through his grand synthesis (since 1981). Mead's prose is extraordinarily clear, and this book is an excellent introduction to a musical philosophy that is so easily misunderstood.

MICHAEL JUDE SCHIANO

See also Serialism

Analysis: Tonal

Bent, Ian, editor, *Music Analysis in the Nineteenth Century*, 2 vols., Cambridge: Cambridge University Press, 1994

Bent, Ian, and William Drabkin, *Analysis*, Basingstoke: Macmillan, and New York: Norton, 1987

Cook, Nicholas, *A Guide to Musical Analysis*, London: Dent, and New York: Braziller, 1987

Dunsby, Jonathan, and Arnold Whittall, *Music Analysis in Theory and Practice*, London: Faber, and New Haven, Connecticut: Yale University Press, 1988

Epstein, David, *Beyond Orpheus: Studies in Musical Structure*, Cambridge, Massachusetts: MIT Press, 1979

Lester, Joel, *Compositional Theory in the Eighteenth Century*, Cambridge, Massachusetts: Harvard University Press, 1992

Meyer, Leonard B., *Explaining Music: Essays and Explorations*, Berkeley: University of California Press, 1973

Reti, Rudolph, *Thematic Patterns in Sonatas of Beethoven*, edited by Deryck Cooke, London: Faber, and New York: Macmillan, 1967

———, *The Thematic Process in Music*, New York: Macmillan, 1951

Rosen, Charles, *The Classical Style: Haydn, Mozart, Beethoven*, London: Faber, and New York: Viking Press, 1971; expanded edition, New York: Norton, 1997

———, *The Romantic Generation*, Cambridge, Massachusetts: Harvard University Press, 1995

———, *Sonata Forms*, New York: Norton, 1980; revised edition, 1988

Salzer, Felix, *Structural Hearing: Tonal Coherence in Music*, New York: Dover, 1962

Schoenberg, Arnold, *Fundamentals of Musical Composition*, edited by Gerald Strang and Leonard Stein, London: Faber, and New York: St. Martin's Press, 1967

———, *The Musical Idea and the Logic, Technique and Art of Its Presentation*, edited and translated by Patricia Carpenter and Severine Neff, New York: Columbia University Press, 1995

Tovey, Donald Francis, *A Companion to Beethoven's Pianoforte Sonatas*, London: Associated Board of the Royal Schools of Music, 1931; reprint, New York: AMS Press, 1976

———, *Essays in Musical Analysis*, 6 vols., London: Oxford University Press, 1935–39

Walker, Alan, *An Anatomy of Musical Criticism*, Philadelphia: Chilton Books, 1968

———, *A Study in Musical Analysis*, London: Barrie and Rockliff, 1962

This article surveys books concerned with analytical methods employed in the study of music whose comprehensibility is, at least in part, based on the tonal language.

Three books survey contemporary methods of musical analysis. BENT and DRABKIN is a revision of the analysis article from the *New Grove Dictionary of Music and Musicians* (1980), and includes clear explanations, an extensive bibliography, and a fine glossary of analytical terms; DUNSBY and WHITTALL offers an insightful commentary on traditional analytical ideas. COOK constructs his own classification of analytical approaches (psychological, formal, and comparative). His tone is generally more critical, but he offers chapters on beginning an analysis, and on problem pieces (music particularly resistant to traditional analysis).

The most influential analytical methodology is that of Schenker. In fact, many feel that having a deep structure based on tonal voice-leading is a fruitful working definition for tonality. For many years, the English-speaking world relied on SALZER, which claimed to be an introduction to Schenker's work. The inaccuracy of that statement is now well known, but Salzer's contributions remain quite valuable. Rather than condemn music written before Bach and after Brahms (as Schenker did), Salzer tampered with Schenkerian techniques and terminology in order to create an analytical methodology that could fruitfully discuss that music.

Another Schenkerian approach was put forward by EPSTEIN, who attempted to accommodate Schoenberg's notion of Grundgestalt within the Schenkerian model. The ability to see an adapted, quasi-Schenkerian model in a composition is to see to what extent tonality operates in that composition.

The first to criticize Schenkerian analysis on formal grounds was Eugene Narmour (*Beyond Schenkerism*, 1977), who compares it unfavorably to the implication-realization model of Leonard B. Meyer. MEYER proposed that a melodic skip will create a tension that may resolve only when the scale steps making up that interval are traversed. His work is based on results from the behavioral sciences.

While these authors wrote for theorists and musicologists, Tovey's audience was the intelligent, educated amateur. TOVEY (1931, 1935–39) are concerned with many of the masterpieces that make up the core of the tonal repertory. His essays may at times seem informal, but they represent what has become the tradition in the analysis of tonal classical music: musical forms are seen as projections of tonal motion, and at the center is the organic metaphor (how all parts of a great work are cut from the same cloth, and how they work together in a complex system). ROSEN (1971) demonstrates this aesthetic, and it is perhaps this book that introduced tonal analysis to many of today's analysts. Generous examples from all classical genres are used to illustrate the various means by which this music achieves unity and expressivity. ROSEN (1995) similarly discusses works of romantic composers, from the cycles of Schubert to the operas of Bellini. Especially useful is the lengthy discussion of Chopin. Finally,

ROSEN (1980) focuses on the evolution and pliability of sonata allegro, a fundamental form in tonal music.

Another exponent of the organic tradition in tonal analysis was Rudolph Reti. His work focused on how a great work is unified through hidden repetitions in thematic structure. RETI (1951) demonstrates how apparently contrasting themes are often, in fact, different elaborations of a single idea. Even the key scheme of an extended composition may be a projection of the structure of the main theme. A wide variety of pieces serve as examples, including works by Bach, Schumann, Liszt, and Berlioz. RETI (1967) is devoted to the detailed, comprehensive discussion of the thematic processes in the Pathetique and Appassionata Sonatas. Reti's work is often criticized on the grounds that his analyses are ad hoc, and that he really offers no consistent methodology. One might argue, however, that studying the thematic parameter requires this kind of analytical flexibility.

Also in this thematic tradition are the books by WALKER (1962, 1968). However, he more often sees thematic unity in the function and appropriateness of successive passages and themes, rather than exclusively as hidden repetitions.

For much of his life, Schoenberg thought and wrote about how musical comprehensibility (in tonal works or otherwise) was the result of the endless variation of a basic musical idea, the basic shape, or the *Grundgestalt*. SCHOENBERG (1967, 1995) sheds light on these and other related concepts. Although he never tied them all together to propose a single analytical method, his ideas have provided great insight, and a groundwork for later analysts.

The history of tonal analysis is only beginning to be written. Eighteenth-century analyses of music are generally found in books on compositional technique or harmonic theory. LESTER discusses these books, and illustrates harmonic and melodic analyses by such 18th-century figures as Rameau, Mattheson, Kirnberger, Riepel, and Koch.

BENT is a compilation of 19th-century essays in analysis, which shows the diversity of approaches and variety of issues at that time. Included are essays on Mozart's Dissonant Quartet (1832), Beethoven's Quartet, op. 18, no. 2, and the uses of and Leitmotifs in *Tristan und Isolde*.

MICHAEL JUDE SCHIANO

Arabic Music *see* Middle East

Atonality

Crawford, John C., and Dorothy L., Crawford, *Expressionism in Twentieth-Century Music*, Bloomington: Indiana University Press, 1993

Dunsby, Jonathan, and Arnold Whittall, *Music Analysis in Theory and Practice,* London: Faber, and New Haven, Connecticut: Yale University Press, 1988

Forte, Allen, *The Structure of Atonal Music,* New Haven, Connecticut: Yale University Press, 1973

Kramer, Jonathan D., *The Time of Music: New Meanings, New Temporalities, New Listening Strategies,* New York: Schirmer Books, and London: Collier Macmillan, 1988

Lewin, David, *Generalized Musical Intervals and Transformations,* New Haven, Connecticut: Yale University Press, 1986

Morris, Robert D., *Composition with Pitch-Classes: A Theory of Compositional Design,* New Haven, Connecticut: Yale University Press, 1987

Perle, George, *Serial Composition and Atonality: An Introduction to the Music of Schoenberg, Berg, and Webern,* Berkeley: University of California Press, 1962; 6th edition, revised, 1991

Rahn, John, *Basic Atonal Theory,* New York: Longman, 1980

Samson, Jim, *Music in Transition: A Study of Tonal Expansion and Atonality, 1900–1920,* London: Dent, 1977

Watkins, Glenn, *Pyramids at the Louvre: Music Culture, and Collage from Stravinsky to the Postmodernists,* Cambridge, Massachusetts: Harvard University Press, 1994

The term *atonality* identifies 20th-century compositional practices intended to avoid or move beyond the principles of tonality. The term particularly denotes one such practice: the pre-12-tone music of Schoenberg, Webern, and Berg (sometimes designated *free atonality*). Some studies view atonality as the absence of musical system that resulted when tonality dissolved around the turn of the 20th century; others see atonality as a system in its own right. Analytical accounts of atonality as a system usually take the basic units of atonal music to be cells or sets of intervals. Historical studies tend either to trace the development of atonality in terms of musical structure and style or to interpret atonality as a piece of 20th-century culture.

SAMSON traces the early development of atonality in terms of declining tonality. The book's first part explores expansions and reinterpretations of tonality with attention to music of Liszt, Busoni, Debussy, Bartók, and Stravinsky. The second part addresses weakened tonality in music of Skryabin, Szymanowski, Schoenberg, Webern, and Berg. Part 3 treats atonality itself, in terms of vestigial tonal features, free elements, and unifying features such as reiterated interval cells, a device that led Schoenberg to 12-tone serialism.

PERLE takes the interval cell to be the basis of both atonal and 12-tone music. After elucidating overlaps and subtle differences between atonality and 12-tone music, he discusses atonality in music of Schoenberg, Webern, Berg, Skryabin, Debussy, Stravinsky, and Roslavetz. Later chapters devoted to 12-tone serialism emphasize one of the principal tenets of atonal theory: the notion that cells may be stated as harmonic simultaneities or as temporally unfolding melodies.

Because of the melodic/harmonic duality of atonality, it is often associated with a suspension of meter. KRAMER analyzes this nontraditional kind of temporal experience. Subjects include linear versus nonlinear perceptions of musical time, musical continuity, and the sensations of beginning and ending. Large analytic interludes are devoted to works by Beethoven, Schoenberg, Webern, and Stravinsky.

Understanding the coherence generated by interval cells (also called *pitch-class sets*) has been a central project of music theory for several decades. Most writings in this area make use of concepts borrowed from the mathematics of set theory. Thus, the field requires special introduction, which may be gained from RAHN's short textbook. Intended for readers with knowledge of high school-level mathematics and tonal music theory, its accessible and original exposition of these principles is interposed with some complete analyses of works by Webern and Schoenberg.

FORTE's book is in two parts. The first presents Forte's system for naming sets, now universally used by music theorists, as well as basic principles of pitch-class set theory. Much of this discussion overlaps with material presented by Rahn. The second part presents Forte's theory of the set complex, according to which coherence arises when many interval cells in a work are subsets of one large pitch-class set. This theory, once dominant in atonal analysis, has lately been overtaken by other accounts of relationships between sets.

Exemplifying such newer accounts, the mathematically sophisticated books by Morris and Lewin are aimed at the initiated reader. MORRIS makes a systematic attempt to lay out the set-theoretical possibilities available to the atonal composer. LEWIN seeks to give pitch-class set theory a complete mathematical grounding. His discussion culminates in musical analyses of common-practice and early 20th-century atonal music.

Because writers such as Forte, Morris, and Lewin do little to let the reader understand their purposes, DUNSBY and WHITTALL's book is valuable. Their discussions of atonal voice leading, symmetry, form, duration, and 12-tone composition constitute a valuable investigation of the objectives and problems of atonal analysis. The section devoted to atonality, the longest of the book's four parts, is closely tied to Forte's approach and thus cannot be considered a complete statement of atonal theory.

Pitch-class set theory is largely absent from historical accounts of atonality. Many historians argue that atonal practices arose as much for cultural, aesthetic, and extra-musical reasons as for purely musical ones. Many prefer, as Schoenberg did, not to use the term *atonality* at all. WATKINS rests a coherent account of almost all 20th-century music on just a few concepts, including orientalism, primitivism, and 20th-century conceptions of time, theatrical ritual, and collage. Watkins does not discuss atonality per se, and the reader not versed in atonal music will find it difficult to distinguish between atonal music and the other types of music under discussion. The book is otherwise accessible to nonspecialists, and its discussion bears directly on atonality.

The account of the aesthetics of early atonal music in CRAWFORD and CRAWFORD treats atonality not as a harmonic system but as part of an artistic movement, namely, expressionism. The authors pay close attention to musical devices in the music of Schoenberg, Webern, and Berg, as well as Richard Strauss, Mahler, Skryabin, and Ives. While this repertory could safely be called atonal, the Crawfords find the music's motivation to be the pursuit of an aesthetic doctrine rather than the development of a harmonic system.

ALFRED CRAMER

See also Analysis: Atonal

Australia

Bebbington, Warren, editor, *The Oxford Companion to Australian Music,* Melbourne: Oxford University Press, 1997

Chatwin, Bruce, *The Songlines,* London: Cape, and New York: Viking, 1987

Covell, Roger, *Australia's Music: Themes of a New Society,* Melbourne: Sun Books, 1967

Kaeppler, Adrienne Lois, and Jacob Wainwright Love, editors, *Australia and the Pacific Islands,* The Garland Encyclopedia of World Music, vol. 9, New York: Garland, 1998

Modern-day Australia is a cosmopolitan nation. Musics of the indigenous peoples, the Aborigines—inhabitants of the continent for at least 40,000 years—coexist with musics of subsequent settlers who have been arriving from overseas since the 18th century. Several recent books provide substantial introductions to Australian Aboriginal music; Australian classical music with its European, mainly British, roots; the influence of American and Asian genres in Australia—country music, popular urban styles—and folk and traditional musics of hundreds of transplanted cultures.

BEBBINGTON presents a wealth of information about Australian musical life in more than 2,000 alphabetical entries. Short articles on musicians, patrons, and organizations occupy about half of this volume; the other half consists of longer essays on general topics. Bibliographies at the end of almost every entry list the major scholarly literature. Photographs show leading musicians

and famous concert halls such as the Sydney Opera House and the Victorian Arts Centre in Melbourne. Aboriginal Music in traditional and contemporary cultures is discussed in a long essay. Smaller entries consider related topics such as the "Didgeridu," described as "perhaps Australia's most readily recognizable contribution to the world's music." An essay on the "Torres Strait Islands" discusses Australia's other main indigenous tradition. Western mainstream concert traditions are treated in many essays, including "History of European Music in Australia," "Composition in Australia," "Opera and Opera Companies," "Electronic Music," "Church Music," and "Concert Halls and Venues." There are also entries on "Waltzing Matilda" and "Reggae" and longer essays on "Country Music," "Jazz," "Migrant Music in Australia," "Eastern European Traditional Music," "Vietnamese Music," "Greek Music," and other musics of modern Australia.

CHATWIN's highly readable book is probably the best source for understanding the important connection between Aboriginal song and the Australian landscape. According to Aboriginal myth, Chatwin explains, the totemic ancestors of all species "sang their way all over the world," naming the rivers and ranges and sand dunes; they "wrapped the whole world in a web of song." Aboriginal chants are "songlines" or "dreaming tracks," which form the labyrinth of invisible pathways that were created by the ancestors as they sang the world into existence. The melodic contour of a song describes the nature of the land over which the song passes. Chatwin, an English art collector and writer, describes his travels in the Central Australian desert around Alice Springs and the people he encountered. Based on the Australian songlines and related ancient traditions elsewhere in the world, he hypothesizes that human beings are fundamentally nomadic people at home in the desert.

COVELL, a critic and historian, presents a history of art music in Australia through the mid-1960s, which he organizes around two themes: the attempts of composers and other musicians to "come to creative terms in music with a new country" and the steady growth of Australian musical institutions largely based on "the practice of wholly imported music." English and European settlers in the 18th and 19th centuries could not understand what was of value in songs of the Aborigines, probably because, Covell observes, European musical culture during that era was quite rigid about tonal forms and rhythm. The author discusses many traditions, including the genteel music of Australia's colonial period and the country's largely British folk tradition, that are imitative of European genres. When his book was published, Australia's composers had only recently achieved an Australian musical identity and substantial international recognition. (Bebbington brings the reader into the 1990s in the second part of the essay "Composition in Australia," headed "1960 to the present.")

Covell's history is extraordinarily well researched and well written, with extensive references to music and writings and many pages of musical examples. It is probably most suitable for readers who are already familiar with at least some aspect of Australian music. The author predicts that a rich, ethnically diverse music will develop in Australia because of its location in the Pacific and Asian regions.

KAEPPLER and LOVE comes with a compact disc so that readers may hear a sampling of what is being discussed. In accordance with the format of this Garland series, articles by international music authorities, summarizing major findings that have resulted from research since the 1960s, are grouped into three large parts. Part 1, an introduction to Australia and the Pacific Islands, its culture, and its music, includes an overview of Australian and Torres Strait Islanders' music and poetry and dance and the role of music in the lives, arts, and culture of the people. Although art music is mentioned, the emphasis is on traditional forms and popular music, including folk, country, pop, jazz, and rock; Aboriginal rock, one writer notes, is the Aboriginal music with the most widespread public exposure today. Part 2 reviews the major issues and processes that link the musics of the field. Sections on Australia and the Torres Strait Islands are included in essays on popular music, music and religion, music and gender, music and education, music and dance in the schools, and compositional processes. Information about women's roles in Aboriginal music, one writer explains, depends on sources published quite recently, since the 1970s. Part 3 provides detailed accounts of individual music cultures. The section on Australia includes sections titled "The Music and Dance of Australia" (an overview), "Traditional Australian Music," and "Traditional Australian Dance." Besides long lists of references for each chapter of the book, there is a major list of resources at the end of part 3: archival collections, recordings, films and videos, and books.

Owing to the format of the anthology that calls for three different but related approaches in the three parts, some material recurs in varied forms. Although the overall plan is carefully explained, the book's organization tends to be confusing enough to require the reader to refer continually to the table of contents in order to find related material.

DEBORAH HAYES

B

Babbitt, Milton b. 1916

United States composer

Babbitt, Milton, *Milton Babbitt: Words about Music,* edited by Stephen Dembski and Joseph N. Straus, Madison: University of Wisconsin Press, 1987

Boretz, Benjamin, editor, *Sounds and Words: A Critical Celebration of Milton Babbit at 60,* Annandale-on-Hudson, New York: Perspectives of New Music, 1977

Dubiel, Joseph, "Three Essays on Milton Babbitt," *Perspectives of New Music* 28 (1990), 29 (1991), and 30 (1992)

Mead, Andrew Washburn, *An Introduction to the Music of Milton Babbitt,* Princeton, New Jersey: Princeton University Press, 1994

Milton Babbitt is neither a composer who has done some theoretical writing nor an academic theorist who has done some composing; he is one of the foremost 20th-century composers and possibly the most important contemporary theorist. Professor emeritus of both music and mathematics at Princeton University, Babbitt has explored the realm of 12-tone music in both his compositions and his theoretical writings, embracing Schoenberg's dodecaphonic system but building upon and beyond it, extending the serial concept to the dimensions of time and structure, as well as to pitch. A compilation of Babbitt's many theoretical writings is long overdue. At present, they are scattered among various journals of contemporary music published over the past 40-some years.

BABBITT is known for density, both in his music and his theory. This book, however, is quite accessible and should be required reading for those interested in his work. It is a transcription of a series of lectures Babbitt gave at the University of Wisconsin–Madison during his two-week residency in the fall of 1983, and the author's manner is refreshingly chatty and approachable, making his points lucidly and offering many entertaining biographical asides (there is a charming reminiscence of Schoenberg in chapter 1). The lectures were geared to a broad-ranging audience, from undergraduate nonmusi-cians to graduate music students. The first and last chapters assume little or no formal training and provide, respectively, a prologue and a thought-provoking discussion of the present position and future of the contemporary composer. In addition, an analytical discourse on the professional theorists of the past 200 or so years and their influence is not highly technical.

The rest of the book embodies the crux of Babbitt's canon and requires a fundamental familiarity with 12-tone theory. Babbitt begins at the molecular level with the contrapuntal and harmonic properties of serial composition, including such basic elements as hexachord generation, Schoenbergian aggregate (12-pitch collection) creation, and the interrelationships of intervallic content and ordering. The next level is the building of structure and achievement of continuity, including the association between the harmonic and the contrapuntal. Finally, Babbitt brings all of the elements together to define the parameters of a piece, discussing the applications that go into the planning of a piece (precompositional decisions). Babbitt's points are copiously illustrated with examples from Schoenberg, Webern, and his own music. The editors have provided a convenient and succinct glossary.

BORETZ incorporates almost 30 articles, consisting primarily of personal remembrances and tributes, both verbal and musical, by composers and scholars, as well as score facsimiles and pictures. Diverse discussions treat various issues of serial composition, and there are several analyses of Babbitt pieces, including *Du* (song cycle, 1951) by John Rahn, String Quartet no. 2 (1954) by Mark Zuckerman, *Semi-Simple Variations* (1956) by Christopher Wintle, and String Quartet no. 3 (1970) by Stephen Arnold and Graham Hair. The work list and bibliography are exhaustive through 1977.

The three essays by DUBIEL pertain to Babbitt the composer rather than Babbitt the theorist (although the two are certainly intertwined). The first essay provides an introduction to the analysis of Babbitt's music, in which his compositional system is compared with Schoenberg's, from which it derives. There are some partial analyses, with musical examples, of Babbitt's construction and use of aggregates and arrays (uninterrupted compositional structures). The second essay makes a case for using one's awareness of the composer's precompositional planning as a standpoint for investigation, rather than as a model for listening. The second and third essays present lengthy analyses of Babbitt's *A Solo Requiem* (1977) and *Composition for Four Instruments* (1948), respectively, with consideration of how aggregates and arrays are constructed, used, and reinterpreted.

MEAD is a well-written if somewhat dense introduction to Babbitt's oeuvre. It opens by providing a synopsis of Schoenberg's system and Babbitt's extensions thereof. The primary thrust of the book is to identify and elaborate on Babbitt's three compositional periods. The first, 1947 to 1960, is characterized by the composer's use of trichordal arrays—shorter row segments that contain only three pitch classes, usually arranged in two blocks, the second the retrograde of the first. Mead's discussion of the mapping of trichordal arrays includes detailed examples from Babbitt's work of the period. The next period, 1961 to 1980, sees the emergence of the use of all-partition arrays, an extrapolation of the trichordal array, obtained by swapping pitch classes across aggregate boundaries to achieve varied horizontal-structure segments. Two middle-period works, *Post-Partitions* (1966) and *My Ends Are My Beginnings* (1978), are analyzed. Babbitt's latest period, from 1981 on, is identified by the use of super arrays, in which all-partition and/or trichordal arrays are assembled into larger contrapuntal networks. Because each period of composition is marked by Babbitt's addition of the new technique to his procedure, not the replacement of the old, Babbitt's mature style represents the synthesis of his prior mastery of the various techniques, resulting in an enrichment of his compositional practice. A good many late pieces are sampled, with frequent musical illustrations.

Babbitt's two basic rhythmic systems are also outlined in Mead. In duration rows the rhythmic row is based on duration, which is in turn based on the pitch-class ordering. Time point rows are based not on duration but on the location of units of equal length in the modulus (a fixed time span, analogous to a bar of music). (Of course, Babbitt's rhythmic procedure is not confined merely to these two systems.) The study concludes with a cursory outline of Babbitt's newest (at the time of publication) piece, a 20-minute work for three clarinets, three strings, and piano. A catalog of compositions is arranged chronologically; a section of charts map out a sampling of Babbitt's all-partition arrays from various pieces; and a discography is arranged alphabetically by title. The extensive bibliography embraces writings both by and about Babbitt plus related topics. This bibliography is the ideal source for locating Babbitt's extensive theoretical writings until such time as a compilation of his writings is published.

NANCY F. GARF

Bach, Carl Philipp Emanuel 1714–1788

German-born composer

Bach, Carl Philipp Emanuel, *Essay on the True Art of Playing Keyboard Instruments*, translated and edited by William J. Mitchell, New York: Norton, 1949

———, *The Letters of C.P.E. Bach*, edited by Stephen L. Clark, Oxford: Clarendon Press, and New York: Oxford University Press, 1997

Clark, Stephen L., editor, *C.P.E. Bach Studies*, Oxford: Clarendon Press, 1988

Helm, E. Eugene, *Thematic Catalogue of the Works of Carl Philipp Emanuel Bach*, New Haven, Connecticut: Yale University Press, 1989

Ottenberg, Hans-Günter, *C.P.E. Bach*, translated by Philip J. Whitmore, Oxford: Oxford University Press, 1987

Schulenberg, David, *The Instrumental Music of Carl Philipp Emanuel Bach*, Ann Arbor, Michigan: UMI Research Press, 1984

Wade, Rachel W., *The Keyboard Concertos of Carl Philipp Emanuel Bach*, Ann Arbor, Michigan: UMI Research Press, 1981

The most productive son of J.S. Bach and an acknowledged influence on Haydn, Mozart, and Beethoven, C.P.E. Bach has been noted since the 19th century for his important role in European music history; distinctive features of his music, especially his works for keyboard instruments, have been recognized and analyzed by critics since his own day. Musicological study of the composer and his works began with the biography by the German scholar Carl Herrmann Bitter (1868); around the turn of the 20th century, the German theorist Heinrich Schenker wrote several analytical essays and published an edition of selected keyboard pieces by the composer. Over the course of the 20th century, C.P.E. Bach was the subject of many articles as well as a number of books and dissertations. In addition, important research relevant to him and his works has appeared in publications whose primary concern has been the life and music of J.S. Bach.

The majority of studies about C.P.E. Bach are published in German and are not available in English. An upsurge of interest in the composer that took place during the 1970s, particularly in the United States, has produced most of the currently available English-language material. A project to issue the composer's complete musical works in a modern critical edition was commenced in the United States in the 1980s but was suspended after just four volumes. Nevertheless, a substantial portion of the composer's output has appeared in modern editions, many of which contain useful commentary.

OTTENBERG, originally published in German (1982), is the only recent biographical study. The English translation is accurate and accessible to the nonspecialist and includes an updated bibliography. This study provides a dependable outline of the composer's life and works, more complete and up-to-date than that found in encyclopedic reference works. Written in East Germany during the last years of the Communist regime, the book focuses on aspects of the music's social context, avoiding in-depth critical analysis of the biographical documents or of the music itself. The book is therefore most valuable as an introduction to the composer's cultural milieu, which included historically important intellectual and artistic circles in Berlin and Hamburg, the composer's two main cities of residence. Ottenberg's account of musical life in Leipzig and Berlin can be supplemented by the relevant chapters in Heinz Gärtner's *John Christian Bach: Mozart's Friend and Mentor* (1994), which draws on a broader range of sources but is sometimes inaccurate (for further discussion, see the entry on J.C. Bach).

More specialized and directed toward a more scholarly readership is the volume of essays edited by CLARK. Particularly important is Clark's own comprehensive bibliography of writings about the composer up to 1988. Significant biographical material is found in Darrell Berg's essay on the composer's "character" pieces for solo keyboard; other authors provide critical and analytical commentary on various pieces, especially the concertos, trio sonatas, and chamber works for flute or violin with keyboard (harpsichord or piano).

The most important subsequent English-language contribution to C.P.E. Bach scholarship is doubtless BACH (1997) translation of and commentary on the composer's letters. Because the letters tend to focus on business matters—especially sales of the composer's published musical scores during his Hamburg years (1768–88)—they appear at first glance to provide a very incomplete picture of the composer's life and personality. Indeed, they say almost nothing directly relevant to his compositions, their performance, or the composer's views of music or his contemporaries. Nevertheless, the volume contains clues to the composer's life and works that will be mined by scholars in future years. General readers will find that the letters shed light on the daily routine and concerns of a leading 18th-century musician.

Apart from Ottenberg, no author has attempted a survey of the composer's musical output as a whole, and even in the specialized scholarly literature, important areas, notably the vocal works, have been neglected. The chief reference work on the music is the HELM thematic catalog. Helm supersedes the 1905 catalog of Alfred Wotquenne, whose "W" or "Wq" numbers have been used (in place of opus numbers) for identifying individual works of the composer. Notable features of Helm include concordances to earlier catalogs, an annotated bibliography of 18th-century printed editions, and an index of proper names, including those of librettists and other figures associated with Bach's work—among them many of the leading German writers and intellec-

tuals of the day. Readers seeking information about specific works will find bibliographic references (through 1988) within the entries for individual compositions. Unfortunately, reviewers of Helm's catalog have found fault with its organization and questioned its accuracy concerning such matters as the content of manuscripts, dates of composition, and even the authorship of certain works. For this reason some scholars have not adopted the "H" numbers derived from Helm. Nevertheless, it remains an indispensable tool for researchers when used with caution.

WADE's book, a revised version of her dissertation, examines the surviving autograph manuscript scores of the composer's keyboard concertos in an effort to reconstruct the compositional process used to create these works. The concertos constitute one of the most important categories of his music, and the volume includes a thematic index of all such pieces attributed to C.P.E. Bach. Issues concerning the manuscripts themselves and their history and study are also discussed. A highly technical volume, it will primarily interest specialists.

SCHULENBERG's book, which also originated as a dissertation, is a study of selected stylistic features of C.P.E. Bach's instrumental music, including his distinctive approaches to melody, rhythm, and form. Although not a comprehensive survey, it offers analytical commentary on many of the sonatas and concertos for keyboard instruments, as well as a number of the symphonies and other works. There are also summaries of relevant 18th-century music theory and criticism, plus a detailed examination of two of the pieces for solo keyboard from the composer's famous collections that bear the subtitle *für Kenner und Liebhaber* (for connoisseurs and music lovers).

BACH (1949), originally published in two volumes (Berlin, 1753–62), is among the most important sources on 18th-century keyboard performance. It has been considered an authoritative text ever since its first appearance, used and praised by no less than Beethoven. Widely consulted today by specialists in historical performance practice, it is essential for anyone seriously interested in performing C.P.E. Bach's music or that of his contemporaries. The first volume is concerned with the elements of solo keyboard playing, especially fingering, ornamentation, and general matters of interpretation. Volume 2 chiefly concerns accompanying, especially the realization of figured bass, but it concludes with a well-known chapter on the improvisation of fantasias. The book is illustrated by numerous musical examples as well as a set of six special keyboard sonatas, known as the *Probestücke* (Examination Pieces), which are published separately in several modern editions. Mitchell's translation is highly readable, and at the time of its publication it represented a major contribution to the understanding of 18th-century music in the English-speaking world. Given the subsequent advances that have taken place in the scholarship of historical performance, this translation now occasionally seems imprecise; moreover, a number of errors in the musical examples have not been corrected despite the numerous reprintings of the translation. Nevertheless, the book successfully conveys both the author's lively musical personality and his teaching, which reflects in part the influence of his father.

DAVID SCHULENBERG

Bach, Johann Christian 1735–1782

German-born composer

Gärtner, Heinz, *John Christian Bach: Mozart's Friend and Mentor,* translated by Reinhard G. Pauly, Portland, Oregon: Amadeus Press, 1994

Roe, Stephen, *The Keyboard Music of J.C. Bach: Source Problems and Stylistic Development in the Solo and Ensemble Works,* New York: Garland, 1989

Terry, Charles Sanford, *John Christian Bach,* 2nd edition, edited by H. C. Robbins Landon, London: Oxford University Press, 1967

Warburton, Ernest, "Johann Christian Bach," in *The New Grove Bach Family,* edited by Christoph Wolff et al., London: Macmillan, and New York: Norton, 1983

Johann Christian Bach, the youngest son of J.S. Bach, was a major early classical composer of opera and instrumental music, becoming one of the most widely admired and imitated European composers during the last 20 years of his life, which he spent mainly in London. During the early 20th century he attracted attention particularly for his influence on the young Mozart, whom he befriended during the Mozart family's London visit of 1764–65. The relationship between the two composers remains the focus of recent writings for general readers, despite the existence of a small but growing body of more specialized scholarly works that consider J.C. Bach and his music in their own right.

Probably the most important recent contribution to the understanding of J.C. Bach and his music has been the publication of the composer's complete works in a collected edition (*The Collected Works,* edited by Ernest Warburton [1984]). Prefatory matter in the volumes of this series contains much material about individual works. In addition, recent years have seen numerous recordings of the composer's works, many of them accompanied by valuable program notes.

TERRY became the standard reference on the composer at the time of its first edition (1929) but is now seriously out of date. The text, unaltered in the second edition, is prefaced by a substantial "Corrigenda," which must be carefully consulted as one reads. This second edition is now also out of date; the detailed catalog of works, which occupies the latter half of the book, is especially unreliable and has been superseded by the work lists cited below. Yet scholars have continued to identify the composer's works by citing the page number in Terry's catalog on which each piece is listed, and the descriptive remarks about individual compositions in the main text (liberally illustrated with musical examples) remain of interest. Moreover, Terry gives complete texts for letters that are merely excerpted in other works and remains the sole published source for much other information as well. Hence, for serious research, Terry complements the works described below.

WARBURTON is a revised reprint of the author's article on the composer in the *New Grove Dictionary of Music and Musicians.* More than a cursory encyclopedia entry, it presents most of the known biographical data about the composer. But it is perhaps most valuable for its annotated list of compositions, which supersedes Terry's and is currently the most authoritative summary of the composer's works. (A complete thematic catalog is planned for publication as the final volume of the *Collected Works.*)

GÄRTNER is the translation of a work that originally appeared in German in 1989. Despite its subtitle, the book in fact does not dwell inappropriately on the composer's relationship to Mozart, which is the subject (in part) of only one chapter. Unlike Terry, the book focuses almost exclusively on the composer's biography—substantive discussions of the music are few—and includes substantial chapters on the composer's early years at Leipzig and Berlin, neglected by previous biographers. The lively, almost novelistic tone makes the book accessible to the general reader, and the author provides a great deal of material on the social and cultural background in each of the cities in which Bach worked, including many valuable illustrations. The book also pays considerable attention to the composer's patrons and acquaintances, including his older brother and teacher, C.P.E. Bach. In addition, it incorporates material on the composer's historical and cultural context taken from various 18th-century publications and other literary sources that are not cited by other authors. Unfortunately, the book is marred by numerous factual errors and a failure to acknowledge recent advances in scholarship. For example, Roe's dissertation, published in 1989, remains unmentioned in the English version, and thus several doubtful works are listed as Bach's own. More seriously, suppositions are not always distinguished from established facts. Thus, although it offers numerous attractive hypotheses (many of a psychological nature) about the composer and his associates, the book must be read with extreme caution and all facts checked against other sources.

The music of J.C. Bach has been the subject of several dissertations, but ROE appears to be the only such work in English to have reached publication. It goes well beyond the somewhat narrow focus suggested by its title. The "keyboard works" that form its subject include not only the sonatas and variations for solo harpsichord or piano but the numerous duos, trios, and larger works for keyboard and other instruments (including the piano duets and concertos) that comprise perhaps half of the composer's total instrumental output. A brief introduction critically surveys the literature on the composer. Two chapters on manuscripts and early printed editions of the composer's music, as well as a detailed thematic catalog, will be of interest primarily to scholars. Part 2, "A Critical Examination of J.C. Bach's Solo and Ensemble Works," includes a study of the composer's stylistic development applicable to his complete oeuvre and is thus valuable to anyone seriously concerned with the composer's music.

DAVID SCHULENBERG

Bach, Johann Sebastian 1685–1750

German organist and composer

1. Biography

Blume, Friedrich, "Outlines of a New Picture of Bach," in *Twentieth-Century Views of Music History,* edited by William Hays, New York: Scribner, 1972

Boyd, Malcolm, *Bach,* London: Dent, 1983; 2nd edition, 1990

David, Hans T., and Arthur Mendel, editors, *The New Bach Reader: A Life of Johann Sebastian Bach in Letters and Documents,* revised and enlarged by Christoph Wolff, New York: Norton, 1998

Forkel, Johann Nikolaus, *Johann Sebastian Bach; His Life, Art, and Work,* translated by Charles Sanford Terry, New York: Harcourt, Brace and Howe, and London: Constable, 1920; reprint, New York, Da Capo Press, 1970

Geiringer, Karl, and Irene Geiringer, *Johann Sebastian Bach: The Culmination of an Era,* New York: Oxford University Press, 1966

Spitta, Philipp, *Johann Sebastian Bach,* 3 vols., translated by Clara Bell and John Alexander Fuller-Maitland, London: Novello, 1884; reprint, New York, Dover, 1951

Terry, Charles Sanford, *Bach: A Biography,* London: Oxford University Press, 1928; 2nd edition, 1933; reprint, 1972

Wolff, Christoph, and Walter Emery, "Johann Sebastian Bach," in *The New Grove Bach Family,* edited by Christoph Wolff et al., London: Macmillan, and New York: Norton, 1983

The two earliest biographies of J.S. Bach—the obituary compiled by a son and a student of the composer and the pioneering volume by Forkel—were based on information from eyewitnesses to Bach's life and career and thus have a status somewhere between primary and secondary sources. The monumental biography by Spitta was the first to be based on a comprehensive study of documents and musical sources and is still the most important shaper of the modern view of Bach's life. Although many biographies of Bach have appeared since, only recently have they added anything to the material presented by Forkel and Spitta.

The first biographical treatment of J.S. Bach is the obituary notice by his son Carl Philipp Emanuel and his student Johann Friedrich Agricola, written in the year of Bach's death, published in 1754 in the journal of the learned musical society founded by another Bach student, Lorenz Mizler, and translated in David and Mendel. All biographical research on Bach is heavily indebted to the detailed information this source provides from members of Bach's closest circle. Many statements in the obituary have been the subject of intense scholarly scrutiny (especially the summary list of Bach's works); some are difficult to verify or to square with other information, but given that the authors had the closest possible relation to Bach, their claims cannot be dismissed easily.

The first extended study on Bach is that by FORKEL, a work based largely on information garnered from correspondence with Bach's sons Carl Philipp Emanuel and Wilhelm Friedemann. Forkel outlines Bach's ancestry and life, but this study is more a critical appreciation of Bach as an artist than a biography, treating his keyboard and organ playing, harmony, melody, teaching, character, musical works, and other topics. The study's tone clearly reflects both the German national sentiment of its day (its subtitle commends it to "patriotic admirers of true musical art") and Forkel's unabashed admiration for Bach. Like the obituary, some of this work's biographical details have since been corrected, but it is unmatched as an appreciation of Bach compiled from recent memories of the man himself.

The comprehensive biography by SPITTA, published in German between 1873 and 1880 and in English translation soon after, set standards (for Bach studies and for musical biography in general) for its thoroughness and for its foundation in the comprehensive study of documents and of musical sources. Spitta combines extensive original research into Bach's life and music with strong and brilliantly projected views about Bach as a musical figure. When the documentation does not provide answers to some important questions—for example, when Bach composed much of his music—Spitta has made educated guesses based on the thesis that Bach wrote most of his organ music while he was employed as an organist, instrumental music when working as a court musician, and church music while he was a cantor. Among other consequences, this method places the bulk of Bach's vocal church compositions in the later part of his life as a kind of theological culmination of his musical career. Some of Spitta's conclusions have been superseded and even overturned by research undertaken in the century since his biography was published, especially by the chronological studies of the 1950s, which radically redated much of Bach's church music. But Spitta's views of Bach's life and career are still influential and remain the starting point for much Bach research. Nothing approaching the scope of Spitta's book has since been attempted. Readers should be sure to notice Spitta's various appendices, supplementary materials, and lists of corrections, not all of which appear in the English version. The English version has its own scholarly value, however, as it contains some author's revisions that were not incorporated into subsequent printings of the German version.

The widely read studies by Albert Schweitzer (*J.S. Bach, le musicien-poète*, Leipzig, 1905, translated as *J.S. Bach* by Ernest Newman [1911]), André Pirro (*J.S. Bach*, Paris, 1906, translated by Mervyn Savill [1957]), and Charles Hubert Hastings Parry (*Johann Sebastian Bach: The Story of the Development of a Great Personality*, London, 1907; revised 1934) are all based on Spitta's research and add little that is factually new. All three are valuable as documents of Bach appreciation in their times and as reflections of the music outlooks of their authors. Also not strictly biographical but of great use is *J.S. Bach: Life, Times, Influence* (Kassel, 1977), edited by Barbara Schwendowivs and Wolfgang Dömling, a richly illustrated collection of essays on various aspects of the composer's life and his world.

The result of new archival research gleaned from the literature on Bach and undertaken by the author appears in TERRY's biography. Terry knew a great deal about Bach's music, especially the vocal works, although this biography is more strongly oriented to the documentation of Bach's life than to his music.

The biography by GEIRINGER and GEIRINGER is essentially an expansion of the chapter on J.S. Bach published in the authors' 1954 survey of the Bach family. It is aimed at the general reader and does not shrink from creative interpretation of Bach's works and the events of his life. Its narrative is meant to be satisfying to a nonspecialist audience.

Following upon the new chronological research of Alfred Dürr and Georg von Dadelsen in the 1950s, BLUME radically questions Spitta's image of Bach as pious Lutheran, now seeing the composer as a begrudging, impious church musician. The avalanche of protest that followed Blume's essay—essentially defending Spitta's view of Bach's character and musical and theological goals—is mostly unavailable in English.

There is no comprehensive biography in any language that takes into account the explosion in Bach research in the second half of the 20th century. The most readable and reliable short work in English is that by BOYD, which does a particularly nice job of combining the documentary evidence and facts of Bach's life with analytical and critical discussions of his music. It takes into account the most recent scholarship and treats problematic matters with admirable caution.

Somewhat less readable but extremely useful is WOLFF and EMERY, which compresses into a small space the state of knowledge about Bach's life. The article, mostly chronological, is the best place to see the events of Bach's life and his compositions outlined in order. Its work list is the best summary of Bach's output.

A useful resource for Bach biography is DAVID and MENDEL, a venerable collection of translated documents of Bach's life. Not a biography per se (except possibly in the sense of the 1960s genre of documentary biography), it presents annotated texts of most of the primary evidence of Bach's life, including letters and other writings, along with an early translation of Forkel's biography.

DANIEL R. MELAMED and MICHAEL MARISSEN

2. Cantatas

Bach, Johann Sebastian, *The Texts to Johann Sebastian Bach's Church Cantatas*, edited and translated by Z. Philip Ambrose, Neuhausen-Stuttgart: Hänssler-Verlag, 1984

Chafe, Eric, *Tonal Allegory in the Vocal Music of J.S. Bach*, Berkeley: University of California Press, 1991

Daw, Stephen, *The Music of Johann Sebastian Bach: The Choral Works*, Rutherford, New Jersey: Fairleigh Dickinson University Press, 1981

Marshall, Robert L., *The Compositional Process of J.S. Bach: A Study of the Autograph Scores of the Vocal Works*, 2 volumes, Princeton, New Jersey: Princeton University Press, 1972

Meyer, Ulrich, *Biblical Quotation and Allusion in the Cantata Libretti of Johann Sebastian Bach*, Lanham, Maryland: Scarecrow Press, 1997

Robertson, Alec, *The Church Cantatas of J.S. Bach*, New York: Praeger, and London: Cassell, 1972

Terry, Charles Sanford, *Joh. Seb. Bach Cantata Texts, Sacred and Secular: With a Reconstruction of the Leipzig Liturgy of His Period*, London: Constable, 1926; reprint, London: Holland Press, 1964

Unger, Melvin, *Handbook to Bach's Sacred Cantata Texts: An Interlinear Translation with Reference Guide to Biblical Quotations and Allusions*, Lanham, Maryland: Scarecrow Press, 1996

Whittaker, W.G., *The Cantatas of Johann Sebastian Bach, Sacred and Secular*, 2 volumes, Oxford: Oxford University Press, 1959

Wolff, Christoph, editor, *The World of the Bach Cantatas*, 3 vols., New York: Norton, 1997

Young, W. Murray, *The Cantatas of J.S. Bach: An Analytical Guide*, Jefferson, North Carolina: McFarland, 1989

In the cantata repertoire of J.S. Bach, one finds virtually every conceivable style of concerted music practiced in the early 18th century; Bach's works have come to define the genre itself. Composed in a wide variety of text types, ranging from newly created poetry to librettos that juxtapose biblical passages and chorale texts, the Bach cantatas are multi-movement works for variable numbers of singers and instrumentalists. Despite their fame, the cantatas have only recently become popular; their generic classification is similarly the invention of a later age. Their long obscurity (due mostly to their nature as occasional pieces composed for either specific liturgies or social events to accompany texts that speak to those occasions with some specificity) may well have prompted the founding members of the Bach Gesellschaft to begin their *Gesamtausgabe* (in 1851) with a volume of these works, which they called "Kantaten." (Bach referred to his own church pieces as concerto, motetto, or sometimes just music.) Although the standard reference work, Alfred Dürr's *Die Kantaten von Johann Sebastian Bach* (1971), will probably never be available in translation, there are numerous English-language studies and handbooks of the church cantatas especially, as well as reference books on the texts and their translations.

Addressing a broad range of Bach's music, CHAFE devotes six of 14 chapters in a large and challenging book to the cantatas. His principal concern throughout is with allegory, which he finds everywhere in compositions by Bach, from the most banal tonal progressions in the cantatas to the reception history of *The Art of Fugue*. Unfortunately, it is never clear whether Chafe uses the term *allegory* to refer to symbolism overlaid by narrative to indicate a kind of metaphorical reading of Bach's intentions, or to identify something else entirely. Compounding this problem, Chafe makes little attempt to ground his single-minded pursuit of (mostly theological) meaning in Bach in either Lutheran theology or the compositional theory of Bach's time, preferring more recent philosophy and critical theory (Walter Benjamin in particular). That said, Chafe's theories are not without merit: his discussion of BWV 106 (the "Actus Tragicus") in particular is a remarkable piece of imaginative criticism.

DAW is the only relatively recent English-language survey of Bach's concerted church music. Organized chronologically, the book devotes more attention to some of the best-known cantatas from Bach's Weimar and pre-Weimar periods; far fewer of the more numerous Leipzig cantatas are treated with much detail. While the author has a good command of the literature to 1981, readers should be aware that much has happened in Bach scholarship since this study was published. The title alone suggests how far opinion has changed: those who subscribe to more recent thinking on the likely constitution of Bach's ensemble no longer view the cantatas especially as choral works. Daw's 40-page discography is likewise out-of-date, although his perfunctory assessments of each recording make for a fascinating look at the state of the art in the 1970s.

MARSHALL's two-volume study, a model of its kind, contains much fascinating information on the genesis of the cantatas as well as many detailed insights into the music. Having examined virtually every autograph of the vocal music, Marshall deduces the ways in which Bach composed in a variety of contexts. The most important distinction is between Weimar, where the pace of cantata production was fairly leisurely, and Leipzig, where Bach initially had to be considerably more efficient in his working methods. Marshall confirms C.P.E. Bach's description of his father's standard operating procedure: as the autographs of the four-part chorales make plain, J.S. Bach commonly began with the melody, wrote a bass line to it, and only then turned to the inner voices. While the copious musical examples—including an entire volume of transcriptions of Bach's sketches and drafts—reinforce Marshall's major points, one will want to have handy a complete edition (preferably the *Neue Bach Ausgabe*) when consulting this seminal work.

WHITTAKER was written before the revolutionary findings of Alfred Dürr and Georg von Dadelson concerning the dating of the cantatas and hence does not reflect the latest thinking on this topic, as well as many other issues. The study nonetheless remains the only extended discussion in English of all the Bach cantatas. Although the translations now seem rather clumsy and the author's thoughts on performance practice hopelessly outdated, Whittaker's sheer industry and imagination make this two-volume set indispensable.

WOLFF brings together various experts in a three-volume series that serves as a companion to Ton Koopman's recordings of the complete cantatas on the Erato label. Clearly more than just introductory guides, these books stand on their own as the first to set the entire corpus of the Bach cantatas in a rich, multi-layered context that addresses not only the composer's milieu and the unique character of his work but also the world from which his cantatas sprang. Essays range from illuminating background studies ("Genres and Styles of Sacred Music around 1700") to close readings of the texts themselves ("Classical and Modern Myths in the Secular Cantatas") and discussions of pertinent issues in performance practice. The three volumes treat Bach's pre-Leipzig sacred cantatas, his secular cantatas, and his Leipzig church cantatas, respectively.

UNGER's useful book supplies, on one side of the page, a literal and a poetic translation for each of the church cantatas; in a facing column one finds a wide range of biblical passages that Unger uses as a kind of commentary on his reading of the librettos. This large reference work also includes many valuable indices: most helpful are those listing scriptural quotations and paraphrases, chorale texts, librettists, first performances, chronology, and liturgical ordering. Regrettably, Unger relies exclusively on the Revised Standard Version of the Bible for his copious scriptural allusions.

MEYER's more compact volume, on the other hand, uses Luther's German Bible throughout but provides no English translations of the biblical texts.

The translations found in BACH, adapted from the notes to Helmuth Rilling's recordings of the church cantatas, will appeal more to Christians familiar with the King James Bible than to serious students of the music. The volume is, moreover, curiously incomplete: translations of the cantatas comprising the "Christmas Oratorio" are missing entirely.

TERRY remains the only reference work to include translations of all the cantatas, both sacred and secular, although here again the English renderings will strike many as quaint. A further handicap for the reader hoping to find translations alongside the originals is the lack of the full German texts.

Intended as a companion to Terry, ROBERTSON is a handbook of the church cantatas arranged in liturgical order. The emphasis here is on the essentials: for each cantata Robertson supplies BWV numbers, dates (when known), the relevant Epistle and Gospel readings, instrumentation, librettist, and brief commentary.

Essentially an update of Robertson, YOUNG includes the secular cantatas as well. Despite the book's title, there is no musical analysis per se. Instead, Young proceeds chronologically through the sacred, then the secular cantatas, and for each he gives a summary description of the text setting in each movement. The writing is unexceptional, and many of the best insights are borrowed. As in Robertson's earlier effort, the bibliography occupies barely half a page; there are, in addition, numerous factual and typographical errors.

MATTHEW DIRST

See also Borrowing; Continuo

3. Chamber Music

David, Hans Theodore, *J.S. Bach's Musical Offering: History, Interpretation, and Analysis*, New York, Schirmer, 1945; reprint, New York: Dover Publications, 1972

Dreyfus, Laurence, *Bach and the Patterns of Invention*, Cambridge, Massachusetts: Harvard University Press, 1996

Marshall, Robert L., *The Music of Johann Sebastian Bach: The Sources, the Style, the Significance*, New York: Schirmer Books, 1989

Melamed, Daniel R., editor, *Bach Studies 2*, Cambridge: Cambridge University Press, 1995

Vogt, Hans, *Johann Sebastian Bach's Chamber Music: Background, Analyses, Individual Works*, translated by Kenn Johnson, Portland, Oregon: Amadeus Press, 1988

Wolff, Christoph, *Bach: Essays on His Life and Music*, Cambridge, Massachusetts: Harvard University Press, 1991

As with postwar Bach research in general, inquiries into the chamber music have tended to focus on issues of chronology and authenticity, frequently at the expense of investigations of musical style. In recent years, with many such issues seemingly resolved or unresolvable through source-critical research, scholars have begun to reexamine the music from a variety of perspectives, stressing Bach's ingenious manipulations of style and genre, his relationship to the music of his contemporaries, and the theological character of his compositions. To date, much attention has been paid to the flute sonatas and the *Musical Offering,* somewhat less to the violin and gamba sonatas, and surprisingly little to the unaccompanied works for violin and cello.

DAVID's volume, originally intended to accompany the author's edition for Schirmer of the *Musical Offering,* is the classic study of this work. After relating the familiar story of Bach's 1747 visit to Potsdam, he examines the theme and its variations in each of the canons, ricercars, and the sonata before considering both small- and large-scale musical structure. David's study of Bach's notation and the music leads him to suggest a number of possibilities for the scoring of individual movements or works; these suggestions tend to minimize or eliminate the role of a soloistic keyboard instrument in the canons and ricercars. A chapter on "Interpretation" contains useful discussions of tempo, articulation, and ornamentation, although David adheres to the now discredited notion of terraced dynamics and perhaps places too much emphasis on the bowing instructions of Georg Muffat, who mainly describes a practice from a time and place (France in the 1670s and 1680s) that is relatively far removed from the Berlin court of the 1740s. A chapter on "Sources and Editions" provides much valuable detail about the autograph manuscript of the *Ricercar a 6* and the production of the 1747 print, in addition to discussing solutions to the puzzle canons, 18th-century continuo realizations, and editions from the 19th and early 20th centuries. David's analytical chapter on the ricercars and sonata is insightful without resorting to overly technical language. The appendix discussing matters of textual criticism overturns some of Philipp Spitta's conclusions regarding the work.

Two essays in WOLFF examine Bach's chamber music. The essay "New Research on the Musical Offering," originally published in 1971, focuses on the layout of Bach's 1747 edition. Collating all 18 known copies of the print (Spitta, David, and other writers consulted only a few copies), Wolff discards the often convoluted solutions to the ordering of the work offered by previous scholars in favor of a much simpler one that reveals Bach's edition to have a "very smart and practical layout." Wolff also clarifies the production methods and chronology of the edition, suggests that the work is performable by the instrumental ensemble specified in the edition (flute, two violins, and continuo), and discounts the possibility that

Bach intended the entire *Musical Offering* to be performed as a cycle. A postscript summarizes the research of other scholars since the essay first appeared. In "Bach's Leipzig Chamber Music" (originally published in 1985) the author challenges the long-held notion that all or most of Bach's music for instrumental ensemble was composed during the Köthen period (1717–23). Pointing out that most of Bach's chamber music is transmitted in sources that are "certainly, or possibly, of Leipzig origin," and that his various activities in Leipzig, including the direction of the Collegium Musicum, would have presented him with many opportunities to write instrumental works, Wolff suggests that five works usually assigned to the Köthen years (BWV 1027, 1030, 1041, 1043, and 1067) may actually have been composed in Leipzig during the 1730s.

Building on his earlier thesis that the *Musical Offering* is arranged by genre (two fugues, one sonata, ten canons), Marissen, in his article "The Theological Character of J.S. Bach's *Musical Offering*" found in MELAMED, argues that the work "assumes an increasingly theological character as it moves from genre to genre." Although his musical arguments are not always convincing, the author is generally persuasive in connecting the ten canons to biblical law and detecting a theological significance in the work's preface and the inscriptions accompanying individual canons. Marissen also provides a rich historical context for the *Musical Offering* by exploring the somewhat contradictory musical aesthetics of Frederick the Great.

MARSHALL's essay "The Compositions for Solo Flute: A Reconsideration of Their Authenticity and Chronology," first published in 1979 and republished in the collection of essays under consideration here, combines source- and style-critical investigations with a reexamination of Bach's biography to provide a new chronology of the flute sonatas. He begins by considering three works often regarded as spurious: BWV 1020, 1031, and 1033. Although agreeing with previous writers that the first sonata is almost certainly by C.P.E. Bach, he argues that the second is an authentic work written during the early 1730s and that the third is at least partially authentic, Bach having originally conceived it as a work for unaccompanied flute (perhaps around 1718) and later assigning a composition student (probably C.P.E. Bach) to invent a bass for it. (With regard to BWV 1031 and 1033 Marshall's views have been partially called into question by Jeanne Swack in "Quantz and the Sonata in E-flat Major for Flute and Cembalo, BWV 1031" *Early Music* 23 [1995] and "On the Origins of the Sonate auf Concertenart," *Journal of the American Musicological Society* 46 [1993].) Marshall also suggests that the inspiration for BWV 1013 (around 1718) and 1030 (G minor version, ca. 1729; B minor version, ca. 1736) may have come from contact with the French flute virtuoso Pierre Gabriel Buffardin. He places BWV 1034

in the mid-1720s and BWV 1032 in the 1730s (C major version, ca. 1731; A major version, ca. 1736) and strengthens the case for assigning BWV 1035 to Bach's 1741 visit to Potsdam.

First published in German as *Johann Sebastian Bachs Kammermusik,* VOGT's study is not a piece of scholarly research but is intended as a guide for the professional and amateur musician. The first part of the book considers questions of chronology and authenticity, historical background, instruments, and historical performance practices, drawing on German scholarly literature published before 1980. Least valuable is Vogt's discussion of performance practice, which frequently oversimplifies or underinterprets the views of 18th-century writers; some of the author's views on period instruments will strike many as reactionary (e.g., "The flutes of Bach's time can hardly be played satisfactorily today"). In the second part of his study, Vogt examines various aspects of Bach's instrumental style (form, counterpoint, thematic and motivic invention and development, rhythm, sequence, and harmony). If some of the brief discussions of individual works in the book's third part are perfunctory, others contain a number of perceptive observations.

Jeanne Swack, in her article "J.S. Bach's A Major Flute Sonata Revisited" found in MELAMED, reopens the debate surrounding the fragmentary first movement of BWV 1032, closely examining the movement's texture and structure as a key to reconstructing its missing measures and offering an explanation of why Bach transposed the outer movements from C major to A major. Reading the first movement as a ritornello-form structure combining elements of the concerto and trio sonata, she proposes two possible formal plans for the entire movement, then speculates that the sonata was transposed to A major at the request of the Dresden flutist Johann Joachim Quantz, who probably could not have performed it in C major and whose own sonatas "auf Concertenart" may have inspired the composition of the first movement.

DREYFUS's chapter entitled "The Status of a Genre" is a revised and expanded version of an article published in 1987. In it he uses Bach's G minor sonata for viola da gamba and harpsichord, BWV 1029, to demonstrate how a single work "converses with a tacit code of genres that both enables its unique articulation and determines, as it were, its status." After identifying the first movement of this sonata as belonging to the subgenre of the "Sonate auf Concertenart," as defined by the 18th-century theorist Johann Adolph Scheibe, Dreyfus shows how the complexity of Bach's invention goes far beyond Scheibe's prescription to create something that "expands the horizons of both concerto and sonata." He reads Bach's second movement as a kind of struggle between a sarabande and an Italian adagio and finds unsettling reversals of affect in the third movement. Dreyfus's discussion of Bach's music perceptively identifies and evaluates the composer's manipulations of genre and style, offering in the process a methodology that should prove useful to future analysts of Bach's instrumental music.

STEVEN ZOHN

See also Borrowing; Continuo

4. Keyboard Music

Badura-Skoda, Paul, *Interpreting Bach at the Keyboard,* translated by Alfred Clayton, Oxford: Clarendon Press, and New York: Oxford University Press, 1993

Boyd, Malcolm, *Bach,* London: Dent, 1983; 2nd edition, 1990

Keller, Hermann, *The Organ Works of Bach: A Contribution to Their History, Form, Interpretation and Performance,* translated by Helen Hewitt, New York: Peters, 1967

————, *The Well-Tempered Clavier by Johann Sebastian Bach,* translated by Leigh Gerdine, London: Allen and Unwin, and New York: Norton, 1976

Schweitzer, Albert, *J.S. Bach,* 2 vols., translated by Ernest Newman, London: Breitkopf and Härtel, 1911; reprint, New York: Dover, 1966

Stauffer, George B., *The Organ Preludes of Johann Sebastian Bach,* Ann Arbor, Michigan: UMI Research Press, 1980

Stauffer, George B., and Ernest May, editors, *J.S. Bach as Organist: His Instruments, Music and Performance Practices,* London: Batsford, and Bloomington: Indiana University Press, 1986

Stinson, Russell, *Bach: The Orgelbüchlein,* New York: Schirmer Books, and London: Prentice Hall, 1996

Williams, Peter F., *The Organ Music of J.S. Bach,* 3 vols., Cambridge: Cambridge University Press, 1980–85

Many of Bach's musical scores, both autographs and copies, were scattered and eventually lost after the composer's death. As a result, scholars often overlook Bach's obvious importance to his son Carl Phillip Emmanuel, who refers to him in his famous *Versuch;* to Mozart, who, it is said, learned about Bach from Baron von Swieten; and to his students beyond his immediate family (especially Krebs). In fact, it now appears that Bach's keyboard works were not nearly as neglected as his works for larger ensembles; rather, they were used constantly by a small but devoted circle of students and admirers. This constant use is evident not only in the physical condition of the sources, but also in the number and type of variants found in them. Several recent studies of the keyboard works have decidedly altered notions about the popularity of Bach's music in the first decades after his death, and can be compared to the studies by Dürr and Dadelson on the cantatas, which altered the current view of Bach's compositional practice and the chronology of important parts of his oeuvre.

SCHWEITZER's experience in theology and philosophy as well as organ playing and scholarship (he edited Bach's complete works for organ) are evident in his legendary masterwork on Bach, the first volume of which is especially useful to keyboard players. The book begins as a study of the chorale preludes, one of the first explanations of Bach's pictorial and poetic devices. Later chapters address biography, performance practice, non-chorale-based keyboard works, chamber and orchestral works. Nevertheless, because of the great explosion of Bach research in the 1950s, no work on the composer written before that decade can be regarded as definitive or reliable in isolation from later sources.

BOYD is an excellent, more recent one-volume life-and-works study that shows the influence of later scholarship and examines "the unique connexion that exists between Bach's music and the circumstances in which it was written." Boyd departs from chronological exposition at times for extended surveys of genres. Relevant here are the chapters or subchapters relating to organ music, keyboard works, harpsichord concertos, the Clavier-Übung, and canons and counterpoints. The volume is quite useful to the nonspecialist because it avoids technical language.

The three-volume study (including free works, chorale-based works, and a historical volume) by WILLIAMS may already be considered a classic in this field. Each organ composition by Bach is treated individually in the first two volumes, with discussion of extant sources, original titles, and variants, followed by a review of formal matters and compositional techniques used. Williams gives ample references not only to modern scholars but also to theorists and critics contemporaneous with Bach. The study is thus an important reference work for organ scholars and music theorists, with valuable documentation, indices, a list of musical sources, a glossary, and a bibliography.

Among books devoted to particular genres within Bach's oeuvre, that of KELLER (1976) on the *Well-Tempered Clavier* must be mentioned. Keller brings his skills of musical analysis to bear on each of the preludes and fugues in both sets of the *Well-Tempered Clavier,* and, unlike other music theorists interested only in fugal techniques, he places equal emphasis on the preludes. A brief introduction gives general advice on various theoretical and performance practice topics, although Keller's remark that "Bach intended the preludes and fugues of the *Well-Tempered Clavier* for a single manual keyboard instrument" is unduly restrictive.

KELLER (1967) is devoted to the organ works and combines music analysis (the study's greatest strength) with subjective matters of performance practice and, in some cases, source criticism and textual transmission. The first section of the book consists of a series of brief essays addressing "The Culture of the Baroque," "The Organs of the Baroque," "Authenticity and Chronology," and similar introductory topics. The second section of the book provides a work-by-work analysis of Bach's organ works and presupposes a basic knowledge of the terminology of both music theory and organ literature. Keller's own musical sensibilities and the care he takes to place each work in its proper context are evinced in his suggestions for performance, although these suggestions might be considered dated.

The books by Stinson on the *Orgelbüchlein* and by Stauffer on the free preludes are especially authoritative and useful. STINSON easily integrates the work of previous *Orgelbüchlein* scholars into his own masterful analysis, thereby employing a variety of approaches and perspectives: his discussion of the motivic structure of the chorale preludes, for example, leads him to consider issues of text painting and the rhetorical figures cited by baroque theorists. He is equally adept in treating such issues as the reception history of the collection, in providing a list of some published transcriptions of the pieces, and in considering the Neumeister chorales, recently attributed to Bach. Stinson has also made a study of compositional processes at work, and proposes a compositional history or chronology divided into early (1708–12), middle (1712–13, 1715–16), late (1716–17), and Leipzig (after 1726) periods. The core of the book, however, is the section discussing each chorale in turn, which makes it an invaluable reference work for every organist.

STAUFFER is a study of all compositions that fulfill an introductory purpose, whether titled prelude, fantasia, toccata, or anything else. This book, like Stinson's study, is aimed at the serious organ student or teacher. Intrigued by the question of what purpose the pieces were intended to serve, Stauffer undertakes a complete study of all the manuscript evidence related to the preludes, such as their earliest sources and the manner of notation employed in them. Also taking into account the stylistic development of the composer, Stauffer proposes a new chronology for the preludes, and he surmises that the pieces were intended for organ recitals or for teaching. He traces Bach's establishment of the prelude and fugue pairing as a genre. Stauffer shows a thorough knowledge of preceding and contemporary organ composers, the context of Bach's own choral works, and the writings of relevant music theorists. There is ample material here on the topic of variants: the author contends that most of the variants, especially those involving musical refinement, are by Bach himself.

The collection of essays edited by STAUFFER and MAY are arranged in the tripartite structure to which the subtitle alludes. Especially useful in the first part of the book, titled "The Instruments Used by Bach," are essays by Ulrich Dähnert ("Organs Played and Tested by J. S. Bach") and Hartmut Haupt ("Bach Organs in Thuringia"). Among the essays in the second part are: "Bach's Organ Music" by Christoph Wolff, which draws attention to the role of Johann Adam Reinken in Bach's early career; several essays on chorale-based compo-

sitions; and several specialized essays on fugue types in the free organ works, the *Stylus Phantasticus*, and the concerted organ parts in Bach's cantatas. Among "Matters of Performance Practice," are essays titled "Organ or 'Klavier'? Instrumental Prescriptions in the Sources of Bach's Keyboard Works" (Robert L. Marshall), "French Influence in Bach's Organ Works" (Victoria Horn), and "The Snares and Delusions of Notation: Bach's Early Organ Works" (Peter Williams).

BADURA-SKODA provides a useful compendium of performance practice advice from an acknowledged authority, although the author does not aim for comprehensiveness. Nonetheless, the topics included are amply developed, well documented, and accompanied by musical examples. There are chapters on the rhythmic issues (inequality, assimilation of duple to triple rhythms, *tempo rubato*), tempo, articulation, and other features that are found in Bach's keyboard (excluding organ) works. A performer himself, Badura-Skoda is concerned not to "offer patent solutions, or 'predigested' instructions on how to perform the music but . . . to stimulate 're-creation' in future Bach interpretation." Badura-Skoda devotes considerable space to ornamentation, a topic that, he argues, most scholarship has grossly over simplified.

GLENN BURDETTE

See also Borrowing; Continuo

5. Orchestral Music

Boyd, Malcolm, *Bach*, London: Dent, 1983; 2nd edition, 1990

———, *Bach: The Brandenburg Concertos*, New York: Cambridge University Press, 1993

Breig, Werner, "The Instrumental Music," in *The Cambridge Companion to Bach*, edited by John Butt, Cambridge: Cambridge University Press, 1997

Butler, Gregory G., "J.S. Bach's Reception of Tomaso Albinoni's Mature Concertos," in *Bach Studies 2*, edited by Daniel R. Melamed, Cambridge: Cambridge University Press, 1995

Marissen, Michael, *The Social and Religious Designs of J.S. Bach's Brandenburg Concertos*, Princeton, New Jersey: Princeton University Press, 1995

Marshall, Robert L., *The Music of Johann Sebastian Bach: The Sources, the Style, the Significance*, New York: Schirmer Books, 1989

Wolff, Christoph, *Bach: Essays on His Life and Music*, Cambridge, Massachusetts: Harvard University Press, 1991

The vast bibliography on Bach includes general as well as specific studies and analytical as well as historical and biographical works; Daniel Melamed and Michael

Marissen's *Introduction to Bach Research* (1998) is a thorough and well-organized guide to this literature. There is relatively little in English about the orchestral music per se, however, and hardly anything about the orchestral suites. A picture of this body of Bach's work must therefore be developed largely from standard life-and-works biographies, general genre discussions, and journal articles.

The best review of the current scholarship in English can be found in BOYD (1983). The author integrates recent information concerning the dating of Bach's music into a smooth narrative that discusses the works by genre. His chapter on orchestral and instrumental music, although short, includes many bibliographic details in its survey of the concertos and orchestral suites. Like the symphony in the classical period, the concerto was the standard baroque work for larger instrumental ensemble. However, Boyd maintains (and Wolff agrees) that a distinction between chamber music and orchestral music was probably not made in Bach's own time. BREIG reflects this view, considering all of Bach's instrumental music in turn, from solo works to concertos and orchestral suites. In his discussion of Bach's Leipzig chamber music, WOLFF groups together all the instrumental ensemble pieces (except the Brandenburg concertos), terming all of them "Leipzig works for instrumental ensemble" and discussing all the categories in turn.

The characteristic feature of the baroque concerto, the ritornello form, captures the attention of most of the scholars cited in the bibliography cited for this entry. BUTLER discusses the importance of differing ritornello techniques in all of Bach's work, including cantata movements written in Leipzig.

BOYD (1993) goes into finer detail about the concertos than in his earlier biography of the composer, describing Bach's first acquaintance with the new Italian concerto style in Weimar in 1713, including *L'estro Harmonico* by Vivaldi. Bach immersed himself in these works, transcribing many of them for organ (16 solo concertos) and absorbing the characteristics of this new style for use in his own music. Far from being solely a careful examination of these famous pieces, this book includes a thorough and detailed background of Bach's instrumental ensemble music in general, in addition to a discussion of the six individual concertos, their ritornello techniques, varied instrumentation, and performance history.

A completely different perspective may be found in MARISSEN. The author combines manuscript studies and theoretical analyses with sociological and philosophical arguments to paint a picture of the Brandenburg concerto as a symbol of 18th-century hierarchy.

MARSHALL, the first American Bach scholar to examine the composer's compositional procedures, has produced a compendium of Bach essays. The author explains Bach's universal style as in great part the result of his artful integration of all the different national styles of his day. Elements of French dance, Italian concerto, and German counterpoint permeate all his music, sacred and secular, vocal and instrumental. To cite examples from the orchestral music, the first Brandenburg concerto ends with a minuet with three trios, one of them a polonaise; all three movements of the Concerto for Two Violins are in a fugal texture; and the B-minor Flute Suite (no. 2), in many ways a concerto itself, contains a saraband in canon. Marshall describes the last movement of the Brandenburg Concerto no. 5 as, at one and the same time, an (Italian) concerto, a (French) dance, and a (German) fugue, all within a (vocal) da capo aria form.

In contrast to these specific and general discussions of the concertos, the four orchestral suites (BWV 1066–1069) have seen little examination in the Bach literature. Breig briefly mentions the instrumentation of the works. Boyd's (1983) biography alludes to a "frenchified" German tradition, citing Telemann and Graupner as other composers of overture suites, and refers briefly to some formal details of the Bach pieces. Wolff points out the uncertain datings of the four works, calling the second suite (BWV 1067), with its conflation of genres, the latest and the greatest of the set.

DRORA PERSHING

See also Borrowing; Continuo

6. Performance Practice

Badura-Skoda, Paul, *Interpreting Bach at the Keyboard*, Oxford: Clarendon Press, and New York: Oxford University Press, 1993

Butt, John, *Bach Interpretation: Articulation Marks in Primary Sources of J.S. Bach*, Cambridge: Cambridge University Press, 1990

———, *Music Education and the Art of Performance in the German Baroque*, Cambridge: Cambridge University Press, 1994

David, Hans T., and Arthur Mendel, editors, *The New Bach Reader: A Life of Johann Sebastian Bach in Letters and Documents*, revised and enlarged by Christoph Wolff, New York: Norton, 1998

Dreyfus, Laurence, *Bach's Continuo Group: Players and Practices in His Vocal Works*, Cambridge, Massachusetts: Harvard University Press, 1987

Emery, Walter, *Bach's Ornaments*, London: Novello, 1953

Faulkner, Quentin, *J.S. Bach's Keyboard Technique: A Historical Introduction*, St. Louis, Missouri: Concordia, 1984

Little, Meredith, and Natalie Jenne, *Dance and the Music of J.S. Bach*, Bloomington: Indiana University Press, 1991

Melamed, Daniel R., and Michael Marissen, *An Introduction to Bach Studies*, New York: Oxford University Press, 1998

Neumann, Frederick, *Ornamentation in Baroque and Post-Baroque Music: With Special Emphasis on J.S. Bach*, Princeton, New Jersey: Princeton University Press, 1978

Stauffer, George, and Ernest May, editors, *J.S. Bach as Organist: His Instruments, Music and Performance Practices*, London: Batsford, and Bloomington: Indiana University Press, 1986

Williams, Peter F., *The Organ Music of J.S. Bach*, Cambridge: Cambridge University Press, 1984

Published advice on the proper performance of J.S. Bach's music first appeared in the early 19th century, as music editors and journalists began promoting a repertory that had formerly been the exclusive domain of connoisseurs. Amid a growing enthusiasm for both "early" music and historical performance practices in the early 20th century, the first English-language studies of Bach's instrumental music—the organ and keyboard works especially—began to appear. More recent writers address a variety of performance issues from virtually every corner of the Bach canon, in books that span the gamut from rigorous scholarship to highly personal readings of familiar works. The best of these books emphasize the lack of clear, unequivocal solutions to problems and encourage the reader to form his or her own conclusions from the available evidence and arguments. Interestingly, the field has now come full circle and has begun to interrogate itself: some of the most intriguing recent work looks into the ideology behind certain habits of 20th-century Bach performance.

BADURA-SKODA tailors his practical guide to the Bach keyboard works for those who play Bach on modern instruments, despite his predilection as a performer of historic pianos. The first half of his book examines "general problems of interpretation," and the second half presents a series of studies on various aspects of ornamentation—including essential background, Bach's ornaments, and some thoughts on improvised ornamentation in this music. Because of the multiplicity of chapters and concerns, there is much overlap (cross references abound); perhaps the most valuable parts of the text are the idiosyncratic yet insightful close readings of individual works.

Essential reading on the topic of articulation in Bach, BUTT (1990) proceeds from the idea that articulation is a means of subtle elaboration, not simply a matter of phrasing: dots and slurs decorate and define, making fundamental progressions interesting. Articulation, in his view, lies at the intersection of composition and performance. There is a mass of detail here, much of which serves to answer specific problems: How does one reconcile inconsistencies in the sources? Do slurs always indicate bowings? and so on. While some may find the musicological apparatus daunting (the substantial appendix of slur patterns in the concerted vocal works is not for the faint of heart), there is no better book on the subject.

BUTT (1994) examines the prevailing system of music education in the German baroque via the extant treatises and primers used in the Lutheran "Latin" schools (e.g., St. Thomas, Leipzig). This approach—Butt wants to know why young singers and instrumentalists did what they did—forces one to rethink a number of fundamentals: what does this music do, and how are we as performers to think about it? Pithily summarizing one major difference between modern and baroque attitudes and training, Butt notes that in the earlier period, "style was . . . the result rather than the aim of performance," the happy by-product of a curriculum that emphasized both rhetoric and the *Affekten*. On a more practical level, he teases out the fundamentals of good singing during the baroque era—"correct pronunciation, the avoidance of nasal singing, and the cultivation of a naturally balanced, flexible voice"—and examines the role of the conductor, the pitch levels in use during this time, and the size and disposition of the ensemble.

DAVID, MENDEL, and WOLFF is a welcome revision of a familiar reference work, in which one finds virtually all the important early sources of information on Bach and his milieu, including every extant piece of writing from the composer's hand. Of particular interest to the study of performance practice are payment and maintenance records, organ specifications, facsimiles of original sources, church service orders, concert announcements, various communiqués to and from employers (including a new translation of the often disputed 1730 *Entwurff*), advice on continuo playing, reports and reviews about Bach's music and his playing, and a smattering of documents on Bach performance in the late 18th and early 19th centuries.

DREYFUS takes on the central problems of continuo playing in the Bach vocal works—who plays what? when? and how?—and manages, from his thorough study of the original parts, definitive answers for some questions, and reasoned hypotheses for others. His conclusions about the use of melody instruments (cello, violone, and bassoon) are straightforward and make good musical sense; so too does his argument for short accompaniment in recitatives. More controversial is his advocacy of harpsichord and organ dual accompaniment in Bach, a concept for which Dreyfus produces plenty of evidence but few practical guidelines.

Drawing mainly on the keyboard and organ works, EMERY carefully considers every ornament sign found in Bach. The occasionally fervent language (the author refers to one of his own realizations as a "blameless alternative") and old-fashioned terminology ("imperfect shakes" and other strange tremors) might bring a smile, but the discussion is generally clear and untroubled by pedantry. The lack of a better, more recent study points to the difficulty of the enterprise: theorists often contradict one another on this topic, and the most essential element of performance practice—good taste—cannot be taught by book.

FAULKNER has decidedly modest aims; the ambitious title notwithstanding, its primary concern is organ playing, and fingering especially. Drawing attention to Bach's unusual use of the thumb, Faulkner presents, for the first time in a single source, all extant examples of explicit fingering from Bach and his circle.

LITTLE and JENNE argue for a bodily understanding of rhythm in Bach's dance music. They provide a concise introduction to baroque dance and separate chapters on each dance type found in Bach, with comparisons to the dance music and choreography of his contemporaries. One might wish for more help putting together the many insights offered about both music and gesture, but perhaps this omission is intentional, since Bach's dance music did not, as far as anyone knows, serve for actual dancing. Some familiarity with the notation and feel of baroque dance is helpful, though not absolutely necessary, for comprehending this study.

MELAMED and MARISSEN is a bibliographic guide to the extensive literature on Bach. Especially helpful are the citations in chapter nine ("Bach's Music in Performance") of seminal work on Bach's vocal and instrumental forces, the instruments of his time, and questions of ornamentation, tempo, dynamics, and pitch in his music.

NEUMANN's study makes two rather startling claims: that most of Bach's trills should begin on the main note and that many of his ornaments should be performed before—not on—the beat. Marshaling innumerable Italian, French, and German sources in support of his unconventional ideas, Neumann infuses his work with an evangelical fervor—perhaps not the most effective way to convince those brave enough to read his massive tome—while arguing against various tenets of modern orthodoxy. Although his conclusions remain controversial, the sheer amount of data is overwhelming and will ensure the book's usefulness, irrespective of its argument.

A collection of papers from various 1985 tercentenary symposia, STAUFFER and MAY offers essays on a wide range of organ-related topics. The categories announced in the subtitle are surely not exclusionary: one learns as much about performance practice from either Ulrich Dähnert on Bach organs or Harald Vogel on North German organ building as one does from Stauffer on Bach's organ registration or Peter Williams on "the snares and delusions of [organ] notation." Organology and source studies, as these authors know very well, can be just as helpful to the performer as advice from a treatise on how to trill.

WILLIAMS offers an abundance of riches: stop lists and discussions of all the Bach organs, thoughts on appropriate registration and temperaments, and a highly informative, cogent guide to fingering, ornamentation, and articulation in the organ and keyboard works. There is throughout a humane, musical reading of the evidence: Williams's sympathy for manual changes that are not indicated in the text or supported by theorists, for exam-

ple, comes from his feeling that the sound of an organ should never become tiresome. Typically, however, much is left for the reader to decide: "Only gradually can the player reach a climate in which to answer such questions," as this author is fond of saying.

MATTHEW DIRST

See also Borrowing; Continuo

Bali *see* Indonesia

Ballet: French

Arbeau, Thoinot, *Orchesography,* translated by Mary Stewart Evans, introduction by Julia Sutton, New York: Dover, 1967

Beaumont, Cyril W., *Five Centuries of Ballet Design,* London: Studio, 1939

Christout, Marie-Françoise, *The Ballet de Cour in the 17th Century,* Geneva: Minkoff, 1987

Danseurs et Ballet de l'Opéra de Paris depuis 1671, Paris: Archives nationales, 1988

Foster, Susan Leigh, *Choreography and Narrative: Ballet's Staging of Story and Desire,* Bloomington: Indiana University Press, 1996

Garafola, Lynn, editor, *Rethinking the Sylph: New Perspectives on the Romantic Ballet,* Hanover, New Hampshire: Wesleyan University Press, 1997

Guest, Ivor Forbes, *The Ballet of the Enlightenment: The Establishment of the Ballet d'Action in France 1770–1793,* London: Dance Books, 1996

———, *The Ballet of the Second Empire,* 2 vols., London: Adam and Charles Black, 1953–55; reprint as 1 vol., Middletown, Connecticut: Wesleyan University Press, 1974

———, *The Romantic Ballet in Paris,* Middletown, Connecticut: Wesleyan University Press, 1966; 2nd revised edition, London: Dance Books, 1980

Harris-Warrick, Rebecca, and Carol G. Marsh, *Musical Theatre at the Court of Louis XIV: Le Mariage de la Grosse Cathos,* Cambridge: Cambridge University Press, 1994

Hodson, Millicent, *Nijinsky's Crime against Grace: Reconstruction Score of the Original Choreography for Le Sacre du Printemps,* Stuyvesant, New York: Pendragon Press, 1996

Lawson, Joan, *A Ballet-Maker's Handbook: Sources, Vocabulary, Styles,* London: Black, and New York: Theatre Arts Books/Routledge, 1991

McGowan, Margaret M., *The Court Ballet of Louis XIII: A Collection of Working Designs for Costumes 1615–33,* London: Victoria and Albert Museum in association with Hobhouse and Morton Morris, 1986

Pitou, Spire, *The Paris Opéra: An Encyclopedia of Operas, Ballets, Composers, and Performers*, 3 vols., Westport, Connecticut: Greenwood Press, 1983–90

Rameau, Pierre, *The Dancing Master*, translated by Cyril W. Beaumont, Brooklyn, New York: Dance Horizons, 1970

Silin, Charles, *Benserade and His Ballets de Cour*, Baltimore: Johns Hopkins Press, 1940; reprint, New York: AMS Press, 1978

French style, technique, dancers, and repertoire have dominated ballet throughout its 400-year history. During these four centuries, French ballet has gone through significant evolution, but many common social and technical characteristics have united the dancing called *ballet,* which has been recorded by a variety of notational systems and written treatises. Early ballet developed primarily in the French court, where dancing was central to social identity. Theatrical ballet for the public emerged on the opera stage, centered at the Paris Opéra. Many innovative studies of French ballet in English have appeared within the past few decades. These examine technical content and social context, and many include translations of French treatises and other verbal descriptions of ballet. The above bibliography includes publications that address the entire 400 years of ballet history from various investigative approaches.

ARBEAU's treatise is a detailed account of 15th- and 16th-century ballroom dances, such as the allemande, *branle,* galliard, pavane, and *passamezzo.* Published in 1589 for the well-bred courtier following the first court ballet of 1581, Arbeau explains steps, with music, and social settings of the dance. Steps are technically uncomplicated and can be easily mastered from Arbeau's descriptions. This Dover edition also includes some of Arbeau's dances in labanotation.

Arbeau's Renaissance style evolved into baroque court ballet, filled with bizarre and fantastic characters. Costumes of this repertoire appear in McGOWAN's catalog of 188 designs from the workshop of Daniel Rabel used for court ballets under Louis XIII. Many plates are in color. Containing 181 images of costumes, as well as scenery, machinery, and dancers, CHRISTOUT's book complements McGowan's, depicting ballet in the courts of Louis XIII and Louis XIV and from English settings. Commentary in French and English summarizes the history of court ballet. SILIN's work on court ballets to texts by Benserade overlaps some of Christout's repertoire. Silin primarily examines literary content and dancing personnel.

HARRIS-WARRICK and MARSH address ballet as it evolved into theater dance by examining one court entertainment for Louis XIV, the score of which is historically significant because of its unique notation system documenting virtually all aspects of stage performance, including movement of dancers and musicians.

Containing the more familiar Feuillet notation, RAMEAU's treatise is the most explicit explanation of French ballet technique published up to 1725. Its many illustrations and detailed descriptions enabled students to learn dance at home. Rameau explains positions of arms and legs, social decorum such as bowing, and behavior at formal balls. The work quickly spread throughout Europe: it was published in English by 1728.

FOSTER amassed many sources for her history of French dramatic ballet in the 18th and 19th centuries. Theatrical ballet was initially dependent on opera for its dramatic content. Around 1750, however, through gesture, pantomime, and acting, ballet developed dramatic expression independent of opera. Foster addresses training of dancers, choreographers, institutions, and audience reception and focuses on the body and the increasing gendering of ballet and objectification of ballerinas. She includes many ballets texts, such as *La Sylphide* and *Giselle,* and illustrations.

The works of Ivor Guest, preeminent English-language historian of French and English ballet, collectively address dance from the 17th century to the present. Three of his more comprehensive books provide a detailed history of French ballet ca. 1770–1870. All three emphasize the significance of dancers. GUEST (1996) covers 1770–93, when ballet found independence from opera and became an autonomous dramatic theater art. Guest interprets this development in the context of the Enlightenment and focuses on influential dancers and choreographers: Vestris, Noverre, the Gardels, and Dauberval. GUEST (1966) addresses core repertoire of French classical ballet, when female dancers such as Marie Taglioni and Fanny Elssler, dressed in white, appeared in repertoire called *ballet blanc.* Guest's tables list dancers, ballets, opera divertissements, and other Paris theaters with dance. Finally, GUEST (1953–55) examines Second Empire ballet in two installments, covering 1847–58 and 1858–70. These volumes resemble his book on romantic ballet, addressing repertoire, choreographers, and dancers, with illustrations and lists of repertoire and personnel.

Exemplifying the spate of recent thinking about dance is GARAFOLA's anthology of well-researched essays. The volume offers new interpretations of 19th-century French ballet as a modern artistic genre that emerged in the 1830s and 1840s. The essays emphasize the centrality of music and iconography and discuss ballet's folk and national identity; the ballerina, gendering of ballet technique, and increasing feminization of ballet. Well-known ballets such as *Les Sylphides* and *Giselle* are discussed.

HODSON's volume is devoted to one of the most influential ballet's of the 20th century, *Le Sacre du Printemps (Rite of Spring)*, choreography by Nijinsky and music by Stravinsky. The ballet startled the French dance world at its Paris premiere in 1913. Its lost choreography was reconstructed by Hodson in the 1980s from surviving sketches of dancers and costumes, written notes, and memories of original dancers. The book, Hodson's written account of that reconstruction, includes the musical score and hundreds of drawings.

An illustrated handbook such as LAWSON offers a good introduction to ballet, especially for prospective ballet goers. The book covers more than French ballet, but French style is central. Readers can find a brief history of classical through modern ballet (19th and 20th centuries) and explanations of related components such as music and literature. The roles of solo and corps dancers and technical vocabulary of ballet are also explained. BEAUMONT's overview of ballet design provides a comparable introduction to visual aspects of the art in 275 images of scenery, stage settings, costumes, and dancers.

PITOU's four-volume dictionary is comprehensive, covering the Paris Opéra from 1671 to the 1970s. Pitou includes both ballet and opera, whose histories cannot be separated from one another. The dictionary discusses repertoire; choreographers, composers, and librettists; and performers. Its introduction summarizes the opera and opéra comique during the 300 years covered by the dictionary. The work is indispensable for study of Parisian ballet and opera.

In French, the catalog *DANSEURS ET BALLET DE L'OPÉRA DE PARIS DEPUIS 1671* also provides an overview of the Paris Opéra ballet's 300-year history. Accompanying an exhibit by the Musée de l'Histoire de France in 1988, the catalog includes costumes, dance notations, dancers, and scenery. Images illustrate title pages of texts, portraits of opera personnel, photos of ballet classes, and so on. Several time lines summarize French ballet history.

BARBARA COEYMAN

Ballet: Russian

Benois, Alexandre, *Reminiscences of the Russian Ballet,* translated by Mary Britnieva, London: Putnam, 1941; reprint, New York: Da Capo Press, 1977

Fokine, Michel, *Memoirs of a Ballet Master,* edited by Anatole Chujoy, translated by Vitale Fokine, Boston: Little, Brown, and London: Constable, 1961

Garafola, Lynn, *Diaghilev's Ballets Russes,* New York: Oxford University Press, 1989

Kshesinskaia, Matilda Feliksovna, *Dancing in Petersburg, the Memoirs of Kschessinska,* translated by Arnold Haskell, London: Gollancz, 1960

Levinson, Andre, *Ballet Old and New,* translated by Susan Cook Summer, New York: Dance Horizons, 1982

Lifar, Serge, *A History of Russian Ballet, from Its Origins to the Present Day,* translated by Arnold Haskell, New York: Roy Publishers, 1954

Petipa, Marius, *The Diaries of Marius Petipa,* edited and translated by Lynn Garafola, Pennington, New Jersey: Society of Dance History Scholars, 1992

———, *Russian Ballet Master: The Memoirs of Marius Petipa,* edited by Lillian Moore, translated by Helen Whittaker, London: Black, and New York: Macmillan, 1958

Roslavleva, Natalia Petrovna, *Era of the Russian Ballet,* New York: Dutton, and London: Gollancz, 1966

Slonimsky, Yury, *The Bolshoi Theatre Ballet Notes,* Moscow: Foreign Languages Publishing House, 1956

Slonimsky, Yury, editor, *Soviet Ballet,* New York: Philosophical Library, 1947

Souritz, Elizabeth, "Russia" in *The International Encyclopedia of Dance,* 6 vols., edited by Selma Jeanne Cohen, New York: Oxford University Press, 1998

Swift, Mary Grace, *The Art of Dance in the U.S.S.R.,* Notre Dame, Indiana: University of Notre Dame Press, 1968

Wiley, Roland John, *Tchaikovsky's Ballets: Swan Lake, Sleeping Beauty, Nutcracker,* Oxford: Clarendon Press, and New York: Oxford University Press, 1985

Wiley, Roland John, editor, *A Century of Russian Ballet: Documents and Eyewitness Accounts, 1810–1910,* Oxford: Clarendon Press, and New York: Oxford University Press, 1990

The history of Russian ballet is closely related to significant developments in music for dance. However, books on the subject are primarily written by dance critics, historians, and performers and mostly describe the visual elements of the ballets, along with the repertoire, cast, and production history. The two major ballet companies, the Maryinsky Ballet in St. Petersburg and the Bolshoi Ballet in Moscow, are a primary focus of attention.

Life-and-works studies of individual composers who wrote ballet music sometimes include a description and/or analysis of the music but typically do not present the work in the context of the dance. Nineteenth-century ballet music can also be traced through its connections with opera, as, for example, in the works of Mikhail Glinka. Much significant information is preserved in the archival materials from the Russian imperial theaters, including lists of librettos and production records. Of interest in this material are the generations of "specialist" or staff composers engaged to compose or arrange ballet music as specified by the ballet master or choreographer. For example, Cesare Pugni, official ballet composer at the Imperial Theater, wrote music for more than 300 ballets. Overall, however, only a small percentage of the thousands of works produced during imperial times survives today.

The *International Encyclopedia of Dance* includes an excellent article by SOURITZ on theatrical dance in Russia, with a broad historical overview and recent bibliography. The article includes a summary of publications in Russian on ballet history and criticism and outlines the history of Russian dance research and publication from the late 19th to the 20th centuries. Special mention is given to the work of Andre Levinson, Yuri Slonimsky, and Vera Krasovskaya. Souritz also cites several Russian musicologists who write about music and the ballet, in particular Irina Vershinina, who has written studies on Igor Stravinsky. Recent research reflects an interest in further exploring the history of ballet in Russia, especially in reevaluating the creative trends and developments of the early 20th century.

For books in English, early surveys describing Russian ballet were published in the 1930s and 1940s by British dance critics, including Cyril W. Beaumont (*A History of Ballet in Russia* [1930]), Arthur Haskell, Iris Morley, and Joan Lawson. Significant views from a first-hand perspective are available through several of the books of SLONIMSKY (1947, 1956) published in English translation. Slonimsky places a high value on the role of music for ballet, where music becomes the "third dimension," thereby making ballet the equal of drama. Slonimsky's work is distinguished by both a sociological and theoretical approach, often concerned with the differences between imperial and Soviet ballet. Also now available in English are the historical and analytical views of LEVINSON, in the translation of his *Stary e novy balet* (1918).

Strictly historical accounts are given by both Lifar and Roslavleva, whose history was the first in her country to be written in English. LIFAR, who became ballet master at the Paris Opéra, claims that, despite French and Italian influence, ballet in Russia was a Russian heritage. He states that "ballet in Russia was Russian not in its choreographic design, but in its interpretation." ROSLAVLEVA shows a steady emergence of creative Russian artists and traces the history through the major choreographers and their repertoire.

The memoirs of famous performers offer another view of the history of ballet in Russia. For example, the reminiscences of the imperial theater school by one such performer, the ballerina Matilda KSHESINSKAIA, are available in translation. Due in part to his famous collaborations with Tchaikovsky, there has always been an interest in the creative work of ballet master Marius Petipa. Petipa built on 19th-century conventions and established the high quality of the Russian school of ballet, creating more than 50 works for the imperial theaters. PETIPA (1958, 1992) includes instructions to the composers with whom he worked, which provide us with a view of the compositional process of music for ballet and frequent references to his assistant Lev Ivanov, but there is no book written yet dedicated to Petipa's contributions.

Other perspectives on events and collaborations are preserved in the writings of Fokine and Benois. FOKINE's reforms, outlined in his memoirs, greatly influenced the quality of music for dance. BENOIS's published memoirs include an organized index with detailed references to various composers and their works.

WILEY (1985) makes a unique contribution with his book on Tchaikovsky's ballets. The author presents a detailed musical analysis of *Swan Lake, Sleeping Beauty,* and the *Nutcracker.* In addition, he includes revealing documents that relate to the first productions of these works; he also includes translations of primary source materials of dance notation and performance scores. Wiley shows how Tchaikovsky set new standards for the role of music in classical ballet. By infusing "greater sophistication and art—especially in the realms of rhythm, orchestration, and tonal structure—[Tchaikovsky] took ballet music out of the hands of Minkus and delivered it into the hands of Stravinsky."

WILEY (1990) focuses mostly on documents relating to the imperial ballet in St. Petersburg. These include the recollections of Charles Didelot, the first ballet master at the Imperial Theater, the visits to Russia by Marie and Filippo Taglioni and Fanny Elssler and Jules Perrot, and the memoirs of 19th-century Russian dancers, including those of Nadezda Bogdanova.

There is substantial literature on the legendary circle of artists connected with Sergey Diaghilev and the Ballets Russes, as well as many specialized studies on the music of Igor Stravinsky, who composed for the Ballets Russes, from this time. GARAFOLA's study analyzes the impact of Diaghilev's company on its era from three different perspectives. She examines the sources and ideology of the choreographer's works, presents the Ballets Russes as an economic enterprise, and shows how the identity of the Ballets Russes reflected the social composition of its audience.

SWIFT studies the fate of ballet under the Soviet regime, examining the relationship of the art of ballet to the Soviet government and the question of censorship. A repertoire index from 1929 rates the ballets ideologically from "universally recommended for presentation" to works that were forbidden. The implications for music are quite interesting in furthering an understanding of which works were heard during the Soviet era. Swift describes the restrictions imposed on music at this time and shows how the Soviet Union used the stage for political and social purposes, assigning a very specific mission to Soviet ballet.

FAUN TANENBAUM TIEDGE

Ballet: United States

Amberg, George, *Ballet in America: The Emergence of an American Art,* New York: Duell, Sloan and Pearce, 1949; reprint, New York: Da Capo Press, 1983

Easton, Carol, *No Intermissions: The Life of Agnes de Mille,* Boston: Little, Brown, 1996

Goldner, Nancy, *The Stravinsky Festival of the New York City Ballet,* New York: Eakins Press, 1974

Moore, Lillian, *Echoes of American Ballet: A Collection of Seventeen Articles,* edited by Ivor Guest, Brooklyn, New York: Dance Horizons, 1976

Siegel, Marcia B., *The Shapes of Change: Images of American Dance,* Boston: Houghton Mifflin, 1979

Terry, Walter, *The Dance in America,* New York: Harper and Row, 1956; revised, 1971

The history of ballet in the United States has for the most part been documented as a living art, chronicled in reviews, biographies, interviews, repertory surveys, and as preserved on film. In recent decades, however, dance scholarship has rapidly grown as an academic discipline with the establishment of dance history archives, the publication of scholarly monographs, and the participation of dance specialists in interdisciplinary fields. From the mid-19th century onward, reviews of dance in the United States were a regular feature in contemporary journals, a reflection of the popularity of dance as entertainment. More specialized dance criticism dates from the 1920s, leading up to the eras of the first U.S. ballet companies. The roster of notable dance critics, as both advocates and educators, includes Mary F. Watkins, John Martin, Walter Terry, Edwin Denby, and Clive Barnes.

Popular books on dance, especially stories of the ballets and biographies of individual dancers, became readily available as audiences in the United States continued to grow. Magazines and journals devoted to dance include news, reviews, and significant articles on aspects of dance history. Among the many dictionaries of dance, special mention must be given to *The Dance Encyclopedia* (edited by Anatole Chujoy and P.W. Manchester, 1967) and Selma Jeanne Cohen's *International Encyclopedia of Dance* (1998).

EASTON's volume is a biography of one of the most important and influential figures of American ballet, Agnes de Mille. The author includes excerpts from many of de Mille's books, as well as other primary source information from people involved with de Mille's long career.

TERRY explores the "landscape" of dance in the United States through the stories of the dancers and choreographers who helped shaped the United States into the "dance capitol of the world." He names Anna Pavlova as the inspiration for the revival of U.S. interest in ballet during her tours there in the early part of the 20th century. Terry traces the history of the first ballet companies and shows the transition from Russian-trained U.S. dancers to the first U.S. choreographers. He defines ballet in the United States as a genre with European ancestors, but with the rhythm, accent, and color of a new land. Further, Terry asserts that ballet in the United States presents new works on American themes, with choreography using American idioms, and he shows that its leadership is committed to training American dancers. The author also describes the regional ballet movement, unique to the United States, which helped to decentralize the genre, increase local interest, and elevate artistic standards. In defining the U.S. ballet style, he cites the "speed, size, humanity, expansiveness, bravado, energy, friendliness, and athleticism of America."

Surveying the formative process of ballet as an American art, AMBERG describes two essential trends of development. One is an "affirmation of a new classicism as manifested in the works of Balanchine and his disciples." The other is represented by the integration of dramatic narrative and other expressive theatrical modes with the ballet, as in the works of Anthony Tudor, Agnes de Mille, and Jerome Robbins. As U.S. ballet artists have gained full artistic authority and present works that are a genuine reflection of the social, aesthetic, and creative climate in the United States, Amberg surmises that ballet has "become American." Much of the book is devoted to the development of the Ballet Russes, Kirstein and the New York City Ballet, and the American Ballet Theatre and its choreographers. The author names Willam Christensen, Catherine Littlefield, and Ruth Page as three pioneers who pursued dance company affiliations with the large opera houses outside of New York. In addition to the commercial companies, he also discusses smaller ensembles such as the Dance Players and Ballet International. This book includes an excellent collection of photos from the 1930s and 1940s, a chronology of dance events from 1767 to 1948, and charts showing the history and ballet repertories of the different companies covered in the text.

MOORE's writings, distinguished by a commitment to archival research combined with the perception of a dancer and teacher, provide information on theatrical dancing from colonial and revolutionary times through the 20th century. The 17 short articles collected for this volume include findings on ballet in Charleston, South Carolina, New York's first ballet season (1792), ballet music at the time of George Washington, the arrival in 1840 of the Viennese ballerina Fanny Elssler, and the Metropolitan Opera Ballet, from 1883 to 1951. Moore also charts the dance genealogies of Margot Fonteyn, Maria Tallchief, and Galina Ulanova.

A unique event in the history of ballet took place in 1972, when a festival was organized to celebrate the life and work of Igor Stravinsky. Conceived by Balanchine, the New York City Ballet performed 31 ballets (including 21 new works) to music by Stravinsky during the course of one week. GOLDNER's book documents this event from its planning and preparation through performance and includes relevant written excerpts by Stravinsky, Robert Craft, and Balanchine. The author richly captures the intensity and sentiment of the festival, which featured a new version of Stravinsky's *Pulcinella* by both Balanchine and Robbins, with the choreographers in cameo appearances. Each evening's program is given with the performance history of the works and a detailed description of the choreography and the dancers. The text is aided by an excellent collection of photos (mostly by Martha Swope) and includes reviews of the festival by seven major critics. Craft described the event as "seven one-man exhibitions seven days in a row."

SIEGEL traces the evolution of ballet and modern dance in the United States through a critical analysis of landmark works created by the most significant U.S. choreographers, dancers, and companies. The author describes the need for the dancers to "reshape the syntax" of the classical ballet vocabulary and explores the philosophical undercurrents that inspired the ballet works of Balanchine, Tudor, Robbins, Eliot Feld, and Twyla Tharp. Along with studying American themes, Siegel observes the flexibility of form in dance in the United States and the view that "American dance expresses people." Covering more than 40 works, the narrative helps to preserve an essential body of dance works from over five decades of performance. The work also includes a chronology of important first events in the development of dance in the United States.

The stories of the first U.S. ballet companies and their repertories are the subject of several books (Lincoln Kirstein [1973], Anatole Chujoy [1982], Nancy Reynolds [1977], Charles Payne [1978], and Sasha Anawalt [1996]). The principal U.S. ballet companies were independent of the established opera companies and developed with the support of private patrons rather than civic or state funding. Performance histories and photographs help preserve the essentials of the choreography and the artistry of the individual dancers. These books show the diversity of the various ballet organizations, from the New York City Ballet's pursuit of classic dance for its own sake to the Joffrey's aesthetic quest to create new American works based on a classical heritage but set in a modern context to appeal to wider audiences.

FAUN TANENBAUM TIEDGE

Band Music

Brand, Violet, and Geoffrey Brand, editors, *Brass Bands in the 20th Century,* Letchworth: Egon, 1979

Camus, Raoul F., *Military Music of the American Revolution,* Chapel Hill: University of North Carolina Press, 1976

Cipolla, Frank J., and Donald Hunsberger, editors, *The Wind Ensemble and Its Repertoire,* Rochester, New York: University of Rochester Press, 1994

Fennell, Frederick, *Time and the Winds: A Short History of the Use of Wind Instruments in the Orchestra, Band and the Wind Ensemble,* Kenosha, Wisconsin: Leblanc, 1954

Goldman, Richard Franko, *The Wind Band: Its Literature and Technique,* Boston: Allyn and Bacon, 1962

Rehrig, William H., *The Heritage Encyclopedia of Band Music: Composers and Their Music,* 3 vols., edited by Paul E. Bierley, Westerville, Ohio: Integrity Press, 1991–96

Whitwell, David, *Band Music of the French Revolution,* Tutzing: Schneider, 1979

———, *A Concise History of the Wind Band,* Northridge, California: WINDS, 1985

———, *The History and Literature of the Wind Band and Wind Ensemble,* 12 vols., Northridge, California: WINDS, 1984–91

———, *A New History of Wind Music,* Evanston, Illinois: Instrumentalist, 1972

Any discussion of bands and band music must inevitably begin by addressing the issues of what actually constitutes a band and what music should be considered as band music. At present, three quite different and equally vigorous ensembles exist. The large concert, symphonic, or military band is unique in its principle of permitting unrestricted doubling of all individual parts. The use of a single player on each part defines a second type of band, the wind ensemble. The brass band falls somewhere in between the concert band and the wind ensemble, permitting limited doubling in general usage and extensive doublings for ceremonial events. Wind-ensemble music encompasses a much wider range of styles than that for the concert or brass band and in modern parlance includes music written for the *Hautboisten* ensembles of the baroque, the *Harmoniemusik* ensembles of the 18th and 19th centuries, orchestral winds, large woodwind ensembles, brass and percussion ensembles, and works scored for full concert or brass-band instrumentation but played with one player per part. Since the middle of the 18th century concert/military bands and wind ensembles have developed simultaneously but separately, although a significant amount of cross-pollination between these two types of bands has always been present. Brass bands originated in the 19th century. Recently the term *wind band* has come into general usage and is understood to incorporate all of the ensembles mentioned above. This term represents a useful generalization and will be employed in this article.

For wind-music researchers, the pre-1750 time period presents a number of challenges. First, most of the instruments in use during the Middle Ages exhibit little or no resemblance to their modern equivalents. Tracing the lineage of wind instruments is difficult. Second, printed sources of wind-band music throughout much of this time were limited; by and large, only vocal music was written down. Wind instruments seem to have had primarily secular, functional associations, especially in military and dance music. The music performed in these contexts was learned by verbal/aural instruction rather than through published tutors or printed music. Third, until well into the baroque, composers did not specify instrumentation, raising legitimate questions about what actually constitutes wind-band music during the pre-1750 time period. Despite the number of unanswered questions, it is clear that the late Renaissance and baroque were crucial periods for the development of bands and their music. During the middle decades of the 16th century, new French oboes and bassoons, with much improved tone and intonation, led to the formation of the first standardized wind ensembles, the *Hautboisten*. These oboe bands stimulated the creation of an enormous amount of music. Over the next two centuries, the ensemble was expanded to include horns and occasionally flutes, trumpets, and drums, and the first great wind-band repertoire was born.

The most detailed studies of the wind band and its repertoire end at the year 1900. Information about the 20th century must be gleaned from a multitude of sources, including composer and genre studies, sharply focused examinations of particular individuals or music, and general histories. The definitive study of wind bands in the 20th century remains to be written.

WHITWELL (1984–91) is the most comprehensive study yet published and covers a vast historical time frame, from ancient times to 1900. Whitwell is the foremost wind-music researcher writing in English, and his publications are essential reading for all persons interested in the wind band and its repertoire. The structure of this multivolume work is unusual. Of the 12 volumes, the first five outline the history of the ensembles. Each of these five volume considers a particular stylistic period and addresses the different types of bands by country and by their societal function—at court, in the military, at civic functions, or in church. The historical background of wind-band music prior to 1750 is addressed in volumes 1, 2, and 3; the analogous repertoire appears in volumes 6, 7, and 10. The initial volume surveys wind music from ancient times to 1500 and draws on historical writings, anecdotal evidence, and iconographic representations to present a fascinating picture of the function of wind music in ancient and medieval society. Whitwell shows how these functions became specialized by the end of medieval times. Civic, court, and church bands were established and developed national identities. Volume 2 explains how these trends solidified during the Renaissance. Volume 6 presents the correlated repertoire for both these stylistic periods. The listings lack specified instrumentation, and much of the music includes text, showing that the works could either be played or sung. All of the pieces date from the late medieval and Renaissance periods. The baroque is explored in Whitwell's third volume. During that era, the organization of bands by function and country remained important, but the military band assumed a significant role. Works with unspecified instrumentation still appear in the analogous repertoire, discussed in volume 7, but also included are more than 1,500 compositions with wind-instrument designations, showing the impact of the *Hautboisten* ensembles. Volume 10 presents additional works from the Renaissance and baroque. Volumes 4 and 5 explore the classic period and the 19th century, respectively, and offer a detailed study that draws on a wide range of sources, including the standard music reference literature, published letters, the voluminous court records of the time, journalistic sources, and recently published research. Volumes 8, 9, and 10 present the correlated repertoire and are an essential complement to the historical volumes, if a thorough understanding of the importance of the wind band during this time period is desired. Volumes 1 through 9 present extensive lists of works that are organized by country/region and by composer and also provide publishers (for printed works) and/or libraries (with shelf numbers) for manuscripts, as well as instrumentation and melodic incipits for most entries. The final three volumes were published between 1990 and 1991, six years after the original nine. Volume 10 is a supplementary catalog organized by stylistic period; volume 11 is a name index to the previous ten volumes; and volume 12 is a listing of chamber music for winds. Although the research is authoritative and comprehensive, the writing style focuses on factual accuracy at the expense of fluidity, and the overall structure makes the use of these volumes unwieldy.

WHITWELL (1985) is a much-condensed single-volume version of his 12-volume study. It is intended as a textbook for university-level courses in wind literature and as a supplement to undergraduate music history courses, where "virtually no mention is made of wind bands." The first three chapters address bands and band music prior to 1750 and provide an excellent ready reference. The final two chapters address the classic period and the 19th century and provide a meticulous, if succinct, explication of the subject. However, readers with a consuming interest in this field will wish to explore the more exhaustive material in the 12-volume work.

WHITWELL (1972) is a compilation of articles written by the author between 1965 and 1969 for publication in *The Instrumentalist* magazine. Although much of the material in this book has been superseded by subsequent research, it presents details about specific compositions that do not appear in other sources. The chapters are ordered by stylistic period and further divided into subchapters that consider a single composer or distinctive group of composers. The exploration of the wind works of particular composers is facilitated by this arrangement. Whitwell's only book to investigate wind-band music in the 20th century, it examines most of the major composers of the first decades of the century.

CAMUS's book has a very specific purpose and a narrow focus. Although little precise discussion of music appears, the first two chapters trace the history of European wind bands and show how their traditions were transplanted into North America. These chapters provide an excellent overview of the development of the band from earliest times to the 18th century, and considerable reference is made to composers and works that are significant to that development. The writing style is fluid, and the research is meticulous.

The French Revolution had an enormous impact on the development of the military band. The frequent grandiose outdoor ceremonies involving thousands of spectators required an ensemble that could be heard at some distance in the open air. Bands grew to unprecedented sizes, and these large bands led directly to the modern military, symphonic, or concert band. WHITWELL (1979) traces the progress of the band during the tumultuous years of the Revolution and documents the composers and compositions associated with the advancement of the band during that period. Part 2 is a detailed list of more than 150 compositions written for Revolutionary bands between 1790 and 1800—the first and only such list ever compiled. Much of the historical material reappears in abbreviated form in volume 4 of Whitwell (1984–91).

GOLDMAN was a prominent band conductor, and the second and fourth parts of his book discuss pedagogical issues relating to performance. Part 1 traces the history of the wind band; although most of this material has been supplanted by the work of Whitwell, the chapter chronicling band music in the United States is the most comprehensive record published to date. Part 3 discusses the development of the repertoire and is particularly interesting because of its insights into 20th-century literature. The author and his father, Edwin Franko Goldman, were enthusiastic promoters of the band throughout the first half of the century and were at the center of the campaign to develop new repertoire. Goldman's comments are insightful and historically important.

FENNELL's study, essentially a pamphlet, was groundbreaking at the time of its publication. It purports to trace the history of wind music, but the centuries before 1750 receive a cursory review in a few pages. Subsequent research, particularly that of Whitwell, has overtaken this slim volume. However, Fennell's colorful writing style, his observations on the 20th-century repertoire, and his freely expressed personal opinions about the works discussed add considerably to our appreciation of this repertoire.

REHRIG's encyclopedia is organized by composer. Each listing consists of a short biography and a catalog of compositions. The biographies provide the only readily available source of information on many obscure figures. The work lists do not distinguish between original band compositions and transcriptions from other media and provide no information other than title and publisher. The appendices are invaluable and, in addition to an excellent bibliography and discography, include concise essays on the history of band music in the United States, U.S. publishing practices as they relate to band music, the history of the march, band journals, band-music publications in England, and adapting music of other countries for performance by bands in the United States. Few other sources exist for this information.

CIPOLLA and HUNSBERGER's book is a series of essays that consider the historical development of the wind band and its music, as well as studies of specific repertoire and surveys of the band movement in England, continental Europe, and Japan. Also included is a history of the Eastman Wind Ensemble, with complete repertoire lists and discography for the first 40 years of this famous wind band's existence. Historical essays aside, the primary focus of this publication is the 20th century. An excellent addition to the reference literature, it provides substantial information on, and insight into, a large body of repertoire that is inadequately represented in other sources.

Despite its inclusive title, the anthology edited by BRAND and BRAND concentrates almost exclusively on British traditions throughout the 19th and 20th centuries. Readers desiring a wider perspective may wish to consult Newsom's article on 19th-century U.S. brass bands in Cipolla and Hunsberger. In addition to historical aspects, the essays in the Brands's book explore the outstanding brass-band repertoire, largely intended for the National Championships and written by some of the most important British composers of the 20th century. Thoroughly researched and written in a pleasant, familiar style, this book adds significantly to the discourse about one of the most important contemporary band traditions.

KEITH KINDER

Barber, Samuel 1910–1981

United States composer

Broder, Nathan, *Samuel Barber*, New York: Schirmer, 1954

Cohn, Arthur, *The Collector's Twentieth Century Music in the Western Hemisphere*, Philadelphia, Pennsylvania: Lippincott, 1961

Gleason, Harold, and Warren Becker, *20th-Century American Composers*, Rochester, New York: Levis Music Store, 1969; 2nd edition, Bloomington, Indiana: Frangipani Press, 1980

Hennessee, Don, *Samuel Barber: A Bio-Bibliography*, Westport, Connecticut: Greenwood Press, 1985

Heyman, Barbara, *Samuel Barber: The Composer and His Music*, New York: Oxford University Press, 1992

Machlis, Joseph, *American Composers of Our Time*, New York: Crowell, 1963

Wittke, Paul, *Samuel Barber*, New York: Schirmer, 1994

At a time when those who wrote music usually needed additional jobs as a source of income, Samuel Barber's only employment was as a composer. His compositions were prized, and he never lacked for a commission—an indication of his high public esteem and critical success. His ability to reach a large audience was considered commercial by those envious of his talents. Yet Barber's music is a true reflection of the man. His lyrical melodies could only have been produced by one familiar with the human voice; Barber was a trained singer, well acquainted with the fragility of the voice. There is a timeless, cosmopolitan sound to Barber's music, which contains elements from the romantic period translated into a contemporary age. Each of the following sources illuminates this multifaceted artist.

HEYMAN has produced the definitive tome on Samuel Barber. In this book, Barber's life and music are intertwined, and the author relates the details of how Barber learned his craft and slowly built his career. She does not romanticize the composer's life or music but instead allows letters, sketchbooks, autograph manuscripts, and interviews from various colleagues and friends to speak for themselves. Her book, produced 11 years after Barber's death, is the most complete reference source available. As Heyman states in her preface, this study "traces Barber's career in relation to *all* his published and all but a few of his unpublished works" [emphasis added].

HENNESSEE's study of Barber was completed four years after the composer's death. The author provides a brief biography before dividing the book into works, discography, and bibliographic information. Although this book is not as extensive as Heyman's, it is an excellent beginning resource, furnishing the young scholar with basic tools to locate the diverse materials pertaining to a particular piece of music.

GLEASON and BECKER provide an excellent resource for the music historian and educator. The authors present the lives and works of 17 U.S. composers in outline form, beginning with Barber. His compositions are divided chronologically by performance medium. Detailed information concerning style, including compositional techniques and musical devices, are mentioned, with corresponding compositions serving as illustrations.

MACHLIS, in his chapter on Barber, furnishes the basic biographical information that can be found in numerous sources. When discussing various compositions by Barber, such as *Overture to the School for Scandal*, *Vanessa*, and *The Symphony Dedicated to the Army Air Forces*, the author provides detailed information, including musical analyses of portions of each works.

WITTKE's essay is an excellent and witty tribute. He elucidates the trials and tribulations Barber endured by being not only "a maverick romantic lyricist in a turbulent age" but also "a cosmopolitan when most composers were belligerently American, or took refuge in European techniques that have no relationship to the American psyche." Wittke portrays Barber as an erudite gentleman, one who was "truly cultivated, with an encyclopedic knowledge of art, literature, music, and more than a few other subjects," noting that the composer was fluent in French, German, Italian, Spanish, and other languages. The essay concludes with a detailed work list (arranged chronologically) compiled by Norman Ryan. Each entry contains the date, opus number (if any),

genre, instrumentation, and performance history. Providing an invaluable service, Ryan also provides information on the availability of scores for purchase.

BRODER's account of Barber is divided into two parts, "The Man" and "The Music." Broder follows Barber's life up to the time of publication in 1954, employing letters, Barber's journal entries, and reproductions of speeches to draw the reader into a more intimate knowledge of the composer. However, it is in part 2 that Broder's musical perception is demonstrated. This portion of the book is filled with musical examples that support the text. Following a general description of the various musical elements found in Barber's compositions, Broder focuses on specific genres. In every instance, any piece that was currently available is mentioned, sometimes with a musical example. Broder concludes his book with three appendices: a listing of Barber's published works with first performance information, a listing of recordings of Barber's music, and a brief bibliography of articles concerning the composer.

In the judgment of COHN, there are two types of composers:

Those who work on the definite principle brought to fruition by the previous generation . . . and those—a minority—who cast off, almost ruthlessly, the fetters of the past and strike out for richer newness (though . . . there is always some connection with the past).

So begins Cohn's chapter on Barber. Cohn states that Barber was a lyrical composer whose music remains true to its classical and romantic antecedents. Following a short introduction to Barber's musical roots, Cohn provides pithy analyses of Barber's major compositions, which he has divided by genre.

ROBERTA LINDSEY

Baroque Music: General Studies

Anthony, James R., *French Baroque Music from Beaujoyeulx to Rameau*, New York: Norton, 1978; revised edition, Portland, Oregon: Amadeus Press, 1997

Borroff, Edith, *The Music of the Baroque*, Dubuque, Iowa: Brown, 1970

Buelow, George J., editor, *The Late Baroque Era: From the 1680s to 1740*, Basingstoke: Macmillan, and Englewood Cliffs, New Jersey: Prentice Hall, 1993

Bukofzer, Manfred F., *Music in the Baroque Era: From Monteverdi to Bach*, New York: Norton, 1947

Palisca, Claude, *Baroque Music*, Englewood Cliffs, New Jersey: Prentice Hall, 1968; 3rd edition, 1991

Price, Curtis, editor, *The Early Baroque Era: From the Late 16th Century to the 1660s*, Basingstoke: Macmillan, and Englewood Cliffs, New Jersey: Prentice Hall, 1993

Sadie, Julie Anne, editor, *Companion to Baroque Music,*
London: Dent, 1990; New York: Schirmer, 1991

The term *baroque,* first employed in a pejorative context
when applied to music, has now come to identify an era
of musical history stretching from the very late 16th century to the mid-18th century. The era is marked by the
rise of the thoroughbass as a principal approach to accompany both instrumental and vocal music and the subsequent rise of proportional form in the sonatas and
symphonies of mid-18th-century composers, the arrival
of which marked the decline of baroque style. The composers of the baroque span the time from Monteverdi
(1567–1643) to the age of J.S. Bach (1685–1750) and
Handel (1685–1759). The richness of the music of this
era attracted a great quantity of scholarly writing in the
second half of the 20th century.

SADIE presents the most comprehensive volume of
detailed information on baroque music that is currently
available. The book has an unusual format that makes it
useful as a reference work as well as a series of readable
narratives. Organizing her work in three main divisions—
"Places and People," "Baroque Forces and Forms," and
"Performing Practice Issues"—Sadie isolates the traditions
of music making within a geographical system that elucidates the phenomenon of "centres of musical excellence"—violin making in Cremona, brass instrument
making in Nuremberg, organ building in North Germany,
music publishing in Amsterdam and London, etc. Essays
in the first section, each prepared by a specialist and written in a lively style, include Michael Talbot's "An Italian
Overview," Sadie's own "Paris and its Environs,"
Geoffrey Webber's "German Courts and Cities," Susan
Wollenberg's "The Austro-German Courts," Peter
Holman's "Private and Public Music" (in the British Isles),
and Louise Stein's "The Spanish and Portuguese
Heritage." The collection offers an exceptional array of
historical-geographical overviews. Biographical entries by
Sadie follow each essay and include the composers and
musicians who flourished in the appropriate region or city
during the period 1600 to 1750. The second section of the
volume offers three essays. One addresses "Voices," a subject enormously important to this period of great singing.
A second, on "Instruments," offers clear technical descriptions of baroque instruments and thereby makes a complicated subject accessible. The third, on "Forms and
Genres," deals exceptionally well with instrumental music
and its literature. The last section presents an overview of
"Performing Practice Issues," again in three essays, opening with Howard Schott on "National Styles"—a difficult
subject admirably covered. "Ornamentation" is addressed
by David Fuller with wit and expertise. A closing essay by
Stanley Sadie reflects on "The Idea of Authenticity."

PALISCA offers a concentrated history of the era in a
volume that is used widely as a college textbook. The
book opens with an excellent essay that addresses the history of the term *baroque.* The volume delineates the complete range of baroque genres (opera, sacred concerto,
cantata, oratorio, lute and keyboard music, sonata,
instrumental concerto, and sinfonia) and concentrates on
the major developments in Italy, Germany, England, and
France. The author provides passing discussion of specific
leading composers, except for Bach, to whom the final
chapter is devoted. Now in its third edition and written by
a leading authority on the history of baroque music, this
book is up-to-date on the latest research. The third edition adds chapters on French sacred music and English
church music and cites recently published items of importance in the bibliography. The book includes many musical examples.

BUKOFZER, writing the first major volume dedicated to the subject, presents a comprehensive history of
baroque styles in music, which he divides into three periods: early (1580–1630), middle (1630–80), and late
(1680–1730). These periods apply most clearly to
Italian music but also can be seen, somewhat later in
each case, to baroque music in other countries of
Europe. Within each period Bukofzer traces the development of specific styles, forms, techniques, and theories. Chapter 1 treats the baroque era as a whole and
distinguishes it from the music of the Renaissance.
Although each of the chapters 2 through 9 focuses on
the music of a specific country, they also consider the
music of other countries as needed to complete the discussion. The last three chapters (10–12) evaluate the
overall topics of form, thought, and sociology, respectively. The major shortcoming of Bukofzer's volume is
the shallowness of his treatment of French music, a subject for which Sadie and Anthony must be consulted.

BORROFF gives a brief and concise introduction to
the basic concepts and music of the baroque. In a few
sentences each, Borroff defines the most important
genres of music—the styles, forms, instruments, and
theory. This is not an in-depth history: specific composers and their music are mentioned sparingly only to
illustrate particular points. The importance of this book
emerges in Chapter 8, on baroque music in North
America, which addresses a topic not treated in other
books on the baroque. The brevity of the book limits its
usefulness to students, for whom more examples would
be helpful, and to scholars, who will find topics covered
in greater depth elsewhere.

ANTHONY's volume, now in a revised and expanded
edition, presents the most important work on French
music, an area of scholarship that until recent times drew
less attention than Italian and German baroque studies.
French scholars have questioned whether the term
baroque applies to music of the *grand siècle,* which was
in many respects the great age of French classicism, but
Anthony presents a rationale for using the term in this
context by relating French music to the Italian, German,
and English musical practices of the age. Rich in quota-

tions from early writers on the subject, the volume provides a revealing overview of French music from 1581 to 1733, including the music of the stage, church music, and vocal and instrumental chamber music, as well as music for lute, guitar, and keyboard.

PRICE and BUELOW each offer what has been described, perhaps because of their copious illustrations, as "coffee table" histories of music. These books are much more than that, however, for they present a comprehensive series of readable essays by a roster of leading scholars offering an informed overview of the era. Each volume opens with an essay on "Music, Style, and Society," which is followed by a series of essays on the principal geographic centers, ranging from North Italy to Mexico (in Price's early baroque volume) to Rome and St. Petersburg (in Buelow's late baroque collection). Informative and useful chronological tables comparing literature, arts, and sciences conclude each volume. Scholars may find some oversimplifications and omissions in these volumes, but the novice will enjoy them for their easy-to-read informative and communicative style.

JOHN HAJDU HEYER

Baroque Music: Specialized Studies

Anthony, James R., *French Baroque Music from Beaujoyeulx to Rameau*, New York: Norton, 1978; revised edition, Portland, Oregon: Amadeus Press, 1997

Ashbee, Andrew, and Peter Holman, editors, *John Jenkins and His Time: Studies in English Consort Music*, Oxford: Clarendon Press, and New York: Oxford University Press, 1996

Bartel, Dietrich, *Musica Poetica: Musical-Rhetorical Figures in German Baroque Music*, Lincoln: University of Nebraska Press, 1997

Butt, John, *Music Education and the Art of Performance in the German Baroque*, Cambridge: Cambridge University Press, 1994

Cowart, Georgia, editor, *French Musical Thought, 1600–1800*, Ann Arbor, Michigan: UMI Research Press, 1989

Hammond, Frederick, *Music and Spectacle in Baroque Rome*, New Haven, Connecticut: Yale University Press, 1994

Holman, Peter, *Four and Twenty Fiddlers: The Violin at the English Court, 1540–1690*, Oxford: Clarendon Press, and New York: Oxford University Press, 1993

Monson, Craig, *Voices and Viols in England, 1600–1650*, Ann Arbor, Michigan: UMI Research Press, 1982

Selfridge-Field, Eleanor, *Venetian Instrumental Music from Gabrieli to Vivaldi*, New York: Praeger, and Oxford: Blackwell, 1975; 3rd revised edition, New York: Dover, 1994

Smithers, Don L., *The Music and History of the Baroque Trumpet before 1721*, London, Dent, 1973; 2nd edition, Carbondale: Southern Illinois University Press, 1988

Walker, Paul, editor, *Church, Stage, and Studio: Music and Its Contexts in Seventeenth-Century Germany*, Ann Arbor, Michigan: UMI Research Press, 1990

Specialized studies in baroque music that are not genre specific or that do not have a particular composer as their focus tend to fall into examinations of specific repertoires, institutions, or geographic locations. Whereas earlier research tended to treat musical analysis, performance practice, and archival studies separately, recent research often combines these categories with each other as well as with a healthy dose of cultural studies.

HOLMAN concentrates specifically on the musical activities in the Tudor and Stuart courts in which the violin had a key role. He organizes his study according to the different string consorts in activity at the various royal courts; through an examination of extensive archival records, he ascertains the role the court played in the musical life of the times. He traces the development of musical forms from their inception at court and illustrates how musical influence was disseminated from the activities of the courts throughout England and Europe. Holman further interprets the archival records as a performance guide, considering such topics as the types of instruments used, the number of performers, and the occasions for performance. It is a fascinating study of musical development.

ASHBEE and HOLMAN is a series of essays exploring issues connected with Jenkins and/or English consort music. While John Jenkins is the main composer of focus, papers dealing with the works of other composers are also included. Topics include questions of semantics, cosmography, part reconstruction, manuscript studies, contextualization of pieces, and musical apprenticeship. The book is illustrated with photographic plates and several musical examples, and there is an extensive bibliography listing both music and books and articles.

MONSON presents a detailed study of a large body of British manuscripts containing music for voices and viols—that is, verse anthems and consort songs. He relies on a combination of musical analysis, repertory comparison, and scientific evidence—such as paleographic information and watermark data—to guide him in determining the origin and background of each manuscript studied. Besides recounting the date, history, and provenance of each manuscript, Monson also includes information on its contents, compiler(s), and physical construction. A concluding chapter suggests avenues for future study.

BUTT examines the role of music within the educational system of the Lutheran school and church. He reconstructs some of the rationale behind musical performance within this institution, bounding his study between the years of 1600 and 1750. As the basis of his study, Butt has examined an extensive number of primers and instruction/training manuals for young people that were published between 1530 and 1800. Although performance history is the main issue, this subject is approached through questions of various relationships such as those between composer and performer, between music and the art of rhetoric, and between notation and actual performance. Butt ties the theoretical works with examples from actual musical repertoire, making this work both an interesting cultural study and a helpful performance guide.

BARTEL examines musical-rhetorical figures as a part of musical syntax in German baroque music, exploring how composers applied rhetorical practices to musical composition. Bartel reviews the philosophy behind the concept of musical-rhetorical figures and discusses the musical-rhetorical figures (*Figurenlehren*) as they appear in 17th- and 18th-century treatises. He then presents an alphabetical listing of the various musical-rhetorical figures found in the various treatises. Each entry contains a general definition and explanation of the figure as it applies to music. Musical definitions of the figures are quoted from the treatises, with English translations appearing side by side with the original text. This section of the book forms a type of encyclopedic dictionary of musical-rhetorical figures and can function as an independent reference.

WALKER is a collection of essays by leading scholars in the field of 17th-century German music. The essays emphasize music's relationship to other aspects of German culture, including literature, theater, liturgy, and social structure. Part 1 explores different aspects of organ music; part 2 focuses on various topics concerning vocal music (sacred and secular); and part 3 centers on questions of theory and notation. Individually, each essay offers insight into specific areas of German baroque music. Combined, the essays increase one's depth and breadth of understanding of 17th-century German music.

HAMMOND investigates Barberini musical patronage in its various contexts: social, physical, and ideological. His study is founded on extensive archival material, such as letters, financial records, manuscript books and music, and works of art. He establishes the contexts of musical spectacles by examining the organization of the Barberini family, the running of the palace household, the ways of dispensing money on the arts, the magnitude of the amount spent, the physical context of musical performance, and the occasions of musical performance. Within this large-scale operational context, Hammond examines several individual works, which allows him to interpret the individual event as to its function, significance, and meaning. This fine blend of musicological and anthropological study gives the reader a depth of understanding not achieved through musical analysis alone.

SELFRIDGE-FIELD surveys a significant body of 17th-century Venetian instrumental music. She outlines instrumental musical activities at San Marco, including the organization of the *cappella*, the organs used, and the instrumental ensembles. She also discusses activities at other music centers in Venice, such as theaters, homes and palaces, and orphanages and conservatories. Selfridge-Field then examines the Venetian instrumental musical style as it developed throughout the 17th century, focusing on genres such as the toccata, ricercar, canzona, sonata, and concerto. The musical examples are drawn mainly from original prints and manuscripts, and an extensive bibliography lists both music in modern editions and music in original prints and manuscripts.

ANTHONY is a comprehensive survey of the music of the French baroque. It was a great pioneering work when it was first published in 1974, and today it still stands as the definitive work on French baroque music. The study contains sections on stage music; religious music; lute, guitar, and keyboard music; instrumental ensemble and solo music; and vocal chamber music. Anthony references early writers throughout the book as he considers various aspects of French baroque music. There are several plates of illustrations and musical examples, and an epilogue gives the author's thoughts on the performance of this music. An extensive bibliography serves as an excellent research resource.

COWART brings together a group of 11 essays by respected scholars that consider various aspects of French musical thought from the early 17th century to the late 18th century. The essays present a diversity of topics covering areas of opera, tuning, theory, language, philosophy, representation of passions, and political and social movements. Several of the essays consider the many quarrels that took place throughout these two centuries, illustrating the many opposing lines of thought regarding music that developed during the 17th and 18th centuries. The variety of methodologies contained within this collection combines to give the reader a more profound understanding of the many thought processes that governed musical composition during the French baroque.

SMITHERS examines the baroque trumpet and its accompanying repertoire, surveying a large cross section of the trumpet's repertoire found in France, England, Italy, Germany, and the Austro-Bohemian Empire. Discussions of the trumpet's development of its acoustics and construction are linked to an examination of the repertoire for the instrument. Smithers illustrates the connections between the physical properties of the trumpet and the types of music composed for the instrument; he also discusses the trumpet's use and place in society, showing how that, too, was reflected in the music written for the instrument. His work is based on archival sources that include treatises, guild records, musical manuscripts, and artistic representations. There are many photographic plates, and an appendix includes an inventory of musical sources for baroque trumpet.

MARGOT MARTIN

Bartók, Béla 1881–1945

Hungarian composer and ethnomusicologist

1. Biography

Antokoletz, Elliott, *Béla Bartók: A Guide to Research,* New York: Garland, 1988; 2nd edition, 1997

Bartók, Béla, *Béla Bartók Essays,* edited by Benjamin Suchoff, New York: St. Martin's Press, 1976; reprint, Lincoln: University of Nebraska Press, 1992

Chalmers, Kenneth, *Béla Bartók,* London: Phaidon Press, 1995

Demény, János, editor, *Béla Bartók Letters,* translated by Peter Balabán and István Farkas, New York: St. Martin's Press, 1971

Frigyesi, Judit, *Béla Bartók and Turn-of-the-Century Budapest,* Berkeley: University of California Press, 1998

Gillies, Malcolm, editor, *Bartók Remembered,* London: Faber, 1990; New York: Norton, 1991

Stevens, Halsey, *The Life and Music of Béla Bartók,* New York: Oxford University Press, 1953; 3rd edition, 1993

Tallián, Tibor, *Béla Bartók: The Man and His Work,* translated by Gyula Gulyás, Budapest: Corvina Press, 1981

Ujfalussy, József, *Béla Bartók,* translated by Ruth Pataki, Budapest: Corvina, 1971

The history of Bartók biography in English has long been hampered by barriers both of language and politics. The Hungarian language has acted as a forbidding wall for many Western scholars, and Cold War difficulties prevented some of them from examining the bulk of Bartók's papers in the depth they would have liked; meanwhile, items from the end of Bartók's life, which he spent in the United States, were not always freely available to Hungarian biographers. However, the partial political thaw that occurred in Hungary in the 1970s and 1980s affected Bartók studies positively, and the momentous changes of the post-1989 era promise even more interesting work to come. Despite the difficulties faced by earlier Bartók biographers, however, their efforts were by no means in vain. Taken together with the newer books, they offer a developing picture of the man as composer, performer, teacher, and scholar.

STEVENS was the first major biography of Bartók in English, and it remains an important resource decades after its original publication. It observes the tradition of dividing a biography into two sections, life and works. The "Biographical Study" takes up just over 100 pages; the author devotes the remaining two-thirds of the book to an analysis of Bartók's music. The brevity of Stevens's biography and the difficulties gaining access to Hungarian documents limit the depth with which he could delve into certain topics. Malcolm Gillies, who prepared the third edition of this biography, identifies the recognition of specific folk-music sources of Bartók's

music and the discussion of music with text as particular shortcomings of Stevens's book, but it remains a good introduction to Bartók's life. The reader especially interested in these other areas should consult the volumes in this list written by Tallián, Ujfalussy, and Frigyesi. Stevens's compact, accessible analyses provide the nontheorist with a good introduction to Bartók's music. In the third edition, Gillies has attached a thorough, revised chronological work list, with dates of composition, first performance, and publication, many of which are inaccurate in Stevens's first two editions and in the other listed biographies. A selected discography and bibliography are also attached, listing some 130 of the most important sources, emphasizing those readily available to English-language readers.

CHALMERS fleshes out Bartók's life more fully than does Stevens, while also adding some interesting reflections on Bartók's psyche. Still, the limits that this book's length places on the author prevent in-depth exploration of either his psychoanalytical comments or his study of the environment in which the composer worked. Some of Chalmers's side comments are curious, bordering on misleading: for instance, he refers to Kodály in 1907 as Bartók's mentor, although Bartók was the more recognized composer and performer and a year older than Kodály. The author's overall picture of Bartók as an ascetic, passionately musical nature lover is accurate. As in Ujfalussy's book, Chalmers's treatment of texts Bartók sets is more thorough than are his discussions of untexted music, and all of these discussions are accessible to the general audience. Chalmers's book also has the largest number of photographs and illustrations of any of the other books listed here, many of which are not generally available in any other source, English or not. These illustrations lend a welcome texture to the book.

UJFALUSSY emphasizes Bartók's interest in folk music and his relationship with Hungarian culture at greater length than the other conventional biographies, partly due to the author's effort to demonstrate the composer's progressive philosophies. The narrative at times becomes mired in explications of circumstances from an orthodox Marxist standpoint. This effort and emphasis are in keeping with the time in Hungary when the book was written, but political motivations do not invalidate Ujfalussy's point of view; also, the rich historical background the author paints, including lengthy discussions of history of Bartók reception and criticism, is an important addition to our understanding of Bartók's life.

TALLIÁN, by contrast with Ujfalussy, evokes Bartók's struggles and passions in much more personal language and treats his music more thoroughly, though without the use of musical examples and in less depth than Stevens; instead, Tallián concentrates on the events and emotions of Bartók's life. Tallián uses the language of romanticism whereas Ujfalussy uses that of Marx and

Chalmers uses that of psychoanalysis. These three books complement each other well, with Stevens as a compact summary. Of these four, only Tallián and Stevens include footnotes to assist the scholar interested in searching out primary sources.

The most recent and interesting contribution to Bartók biography is FRIGYESI. This book is not a conventional biography at all but rather an extended exploration of the cultural environment in which Bartók came of age as an artist and developed his aesthetic philosophy. This environment was not just or even primarily the villages in which he collected peasant tunes but rather the capital city of Budapest. The author grounds Bartók's aesthetic in the particularity of the Hungarian modernist movement, especially the poems of Endre Ady, and examines Bartók's *Duke Bluebeard's Castle* as a reflection of these ideals.

For the reader interested in primary sources, DEMÉNY's volume of correspondence and BARTÓK, an edition of essays selected from Bartók's voluminous prose output, are quite useful. The letters offer a view into Bartók's private life, including some opinions on music and dealings; the essays, meanwhile, show the breadth of his professional activities and his evolving thoughts on many issues. For an anecdotal and personal look at Bartók in his many roles, GILLIES provides recollections by those who knew him. Gillies also includes one of the more thorough published chronology tables of Bartók's life.

For the researcher planning further work on Bartók, an essential source is ANTOKOLETZ's mammoth annotated bibliography, which catalogs 1,200 items in a variety of media and languages, broken down by category, from writings and pieces by Bartók to biographical and historical studies, studies of Bartók's music, and discussions of archives and other sources.

LYNN HOOKER

2. Ethnomusicology

Bartók, Béla, *Béla Bartók Essays*, edited by Benjamin Suchoff, New York: St. Martin's Press, 1976a; reprint, Lincoln: University of Nebraska Press, 1992

———, *Béla Bartók Studies in Ethnomusicology*, edited by Benjamin Suchoff, Lincoln: University of Nebraska Press, 1997

———, *Hungarian Folk Music*, edited by Benjamin Suchoff, translated by M.D. Calvocoressi, London: Oxford University Press, 1931; reprinted as *The Hungarian Folk Song*, Albany: State University of New York Press, 1981

———, *Hungarian Folk Songs: Complete Collection*, Budapest: Akadémiai Kiadó, 1993

———, *Rumanian Folk Music*, edited by Benjamin Suchoff, 5 vols., The Hague: Martinus Nijhoff, 1967–75

———, *Turkish Folk Music from Asia Minor*, edited by Benjamin Suchoff, Princeton, New Jersey: Princeton University Press, 1976b

Bartók, Béla, and Albert B. Lord, *Yugoslav Folk Music*, edited by Benjamin Suchoff, 4 vols., Albany: State University of New York Press, 1978

Saygun, A. Adnan, *Béla Bartók's Folk Music Research in Turkey*, Budapest: Akadémiai Kiadó, 1976

Although Béla Bartók is widely recognized as a great composer, his pioneering achievements as one of the founding fathers of musical ethnography are unknown, unappreciated, or considered outdated by most scholars in the English-speaking ethnomusicological community. Bartók believed in a systematically scientific examination of the morphological aspects of folk music, and he developed a classification technique—described as the method of methods—for the study of East European, Arabic, and Turkish folk music. During his last years in the United States, following his brief investigation of collected American-English and British-English folk melodies, he declared that his analytical methods, appropriately modified, could be easily applied to the many thousands of those melodies as well as to collections of Western European folk-music material.

BARTÓK (1967–75) is a monumental anthology of 3,404 melodies Bartók collected in Transylvanian rural villages from 1908 to 1917. The evidence related to instrumental melodies includes dance genres together with line drawings of their choreography, pieces based on irregular bagpipe motives, alphorn music played by shepherds, and illustrated descriptions of peasant instruments. The material on vocal melodies consists of ceremonial and nonceremonial songs, mourning songs, and *colinde* (pagan carols and Christmas songs). Bartók discovered a unique genre, the *Hora lunga* (long-drawn song), consisting of a single melody and its variations, which shows Persian-Arabic influence. The collected material also reveals the influence of Hungarian rhythm and, along the southern tier of Transylvania, the use of certain Yugoslav scales.

BARTÓK (1976a) is a large volume of the composer's writings. Approximately half of the book is devoted to monographs, lectures, and articles on folk music, organized according to the following categories: (1) the investigation of musical folklore; (2) national folk music (American-British, Arabic, Bulgarian, Hungarian, Rumanian, Slovak, Turkish, and Yugoslav); (3) comparative music folklore; (4) book reviews and polemics; (5) musical instruments; and (6) the relationship between folk music and art music. The book is widely quoted as a primary source in Bartók studies.

BARTÓK (1997) contains those monographs and articles whose length, substantial number of music examples, and other factors prevented their inclusion in Bartók (1976a). Collected here for the first time and in English translation are "Arab Folk Music from the Biskra District," "Transylvanian Hungarians: Folk Songs," "Hungarian Folk Music and the Folk Music of

Neighboring Peoples," and the introductions to *Romanian Folk Songs from Bihor County* (1913) and *Slovak Folk Songs* (1959). The editorial preface examines Bartók's developing views on the folk-music traditions of Eastern Europe and the Arab world.

The first volume of BARTÓK (1978) is a reprint of *Serbo-Croatian Folk Songs* (1951); Bartók's introduction presents a comprehensive study of transcription methods and solutions to such problems as variants and ornamentation. Three editorial appendices provide additional materials: facsimiles of instrumental melodies, facsimiles of Serbian folk music collected by Bartók in the Banat region of southwestern Transylvania, and the holographic classification of Serbo-Croatian refrain texts. The second volume consists of Bartók's unique "Tabulation of Material," in which 3,524 previously published Yugoslav folk melodies are classified according to certain structural characteristics. The editorial appendix, "Thematic Index of the Tabulated Melodies," provides a supplemental method of locating and comparing individual melody sections. The third and fourth volumes contain autograph facsimiles of the published melodies, as classified in the second volume.

BARTÓK (1981) was originally published in Hungary (*A magyar népdal*, 1924), in a German edition (*Das ungarische Volkslied*, 1925), and in English translation of the German edition (*Hungarian Folk Music*, 1932). The edited reprint of the English edition contains five editorial appendices: "Addenda and Corrigenda" (with annotations by Zoltán Kodály), "Provisory List of Variants Published Elsewhere," "Tabulation of Material," "Index of Rhythm Schemata," "Thematic Index of the Tabulated Melodies," and "Index of First Lines." The editorial preface provides an ethnohistorical overview of the Hungarian people and an analysis of the differences between Bartók's systematization of Hungarian folk music and the classification methods of Kodály and his students.

BARTÓK (1993) is the first in a projected series of nine volumes that will include approximately 13,505 melodies collected by Bartók (2,834), Kodály (3,546), and other researchers. The classification method is essentially that of *The Hungarian Folk Song*, with certain modifications that Bartók developed for the grouping of his Slovak material (*Slovenské l'udové piesne*, 1959, 1970). The scholarly editorial apparatus includes more than 300 pages of introductory commentaries and supplementary appendices, facsimiles, and photographs. It should be noted that a substantial number of melodies from the mentioned collections appear in the ten volumes of *Corpus Musicae Popularis Hungaricae* (CMPH), published in Budapest between 1957 and 1992.

BARTÓK (1976b) presents his 1936 fieldwork among the nomadic tribes of Southern Turkey, which was motivated by his hypothesis that a comparison of old-style Hungarian folk-music material with tribal melodies collected in a remote region of Turkey might disclose variant relationships. After Bartók classified the collected material, he was elated to find that a part of the Turkish melodies was identical with or closely related to old-style Hungarian melodies, and he concluded that "[t]hese kinships point to a common western-central Asiatic origin of both Turkish and Hungarian materials and determine their age as being at least fifteen centuries."

SAYGUN, a Turkish composer, served as text translator and collected performers' data during Bartók's fieldwork. While *Turkish Folk Music from Asia Minor* was in preparation for publication, based on the complete fair copy Bartók had deposited at the Columbia University Music Library on 1 July 1944, Saygun used preliminary drafts that Bartók left behind when he emigrated to the United States in 1940 to reconstruct the melodies and revise the texts and translations, creating a holographic draft of the music, which appears in facsimile here as "Transcription of the Melodies." Notwithstanding the value of Saygun's other contributions in the book, comparison of his transcriptions and revisions with Bartók's work uncovers an enormous number of discrepancies—to the extent that the Saygun publication represents a disservice to Bartók's work.

BENJAMIN SUCHOFF

3. Works

Antokoletz, Elliott, *The Music of Béla Bartók: A Study of Tonality and Progression in Twentieth-Century Music*, Berkeley: University of California Press, 1984

Gillies, Malcolm, *Notation and Tonal Structure in Bartók's Later Works*, New York: Garland, 1989

Kárpáti, János, *Bartók's Chamber Music*, translated by Fred Macnicol and Mária Steiner, revised by Paul Merrick, Stuyvesant, New York: Pendragon Press, 1994

Lendvai, Erno, *Béla Bartók, An Analysis of His Music*, London: Kahn and Averill, 1971

Somfai, László, *Béla Bartók: Composition, Concepts, and Autograph Sources*, Berkeley: University of California Press, 1996

Suchoff, Benjamin, *Bartók: Concerto for Orchestra, Understanding Bartók's World*, New York: Schirmer, 1995

Wilson, Paul, *The Music of Béla Bartók*, New Haven, Connecticut: Yale University Press, 1992

Béla Bartók established himself during his lifetime not only as one of the most creative of 20th-century composers but also as a piano virtuoso, pedagogue, editor of a significant body of keyboard music, linguist, and humanitarian. In the field of folk-music research, he is recognized for his pioneering work in collecting, transcribing, analyzing, and classifying thousands of folk melodies from Eastern Europe, North Africa, and Turkey. Bartók's compositional career may be described as an evolution toward synthesis of divergent Eastern folk-music sources and Western art-music influences. From 1908 on he transformed the ultrachromatic idiom of German late romanticism, the pentatonic/diatonic and other modalities of Eastern European folk music and French impressionism, and the contrapuntal techniques of the Italian and German baroque into a highly systematic network of nontraditional pitch and rhythmic relations. The diversity of Bartók's activities both as composer and scholar has dictated the need for a more integrated scholarly approach to the field of Bartók research. Since the 1930s Bartók scholars have addressed his folk-music investigations, analyzed his musical compositions, and scrutinized his surviving sketches in great detail. Nevertheless, although his compositions form an essential part of the standard repertory, the basic principles of progression and the means by which a sense of tonality is established in his music have remained problematic. The principles that govern his musical structures have been given diverse and often contradictory interpretations. Such diversity may be due in part to geographical separation, which has prevented access to the folk sources as well as archival materials relevant to Bartók research. Language barriers have also contributed to the lack of an integrated scholarly approach and the fostering of distinct schools of theory and analysis. Equally significant to the problem of arriving at a full understanding of the Bartók idiom is the complexity and diversity of the musical language itself. As scholars continue to gain significant—though often isolated—insights into Bartók's musical language, aesthetics, compositional processes, and historical sources, it is evident that a proper understanding depends on a concerted effort toward a more integrated approach to the Bartók disciplines.

ANTOKOLETZ demonstrates that while Bartók turned to Eastern European folk music as source material for his compositions, it was his ability to transform these sources into an original musical language that accounts for the unique quality of his music. This pioneering study reveals stages of transformation from the folk modes to a highly integrated use of nontraditional pitch formations. These include Bartók's harmonization of authentic folk tunes, symmetrical transformation of both diatonic and nondiatonic folk modes, construction, development, and interaction of intervallic cells, tonal centricity based on axes of symmetry and modal-tonal centers, interactions of diatonic, octatonic, and whole-tone formations, and generation of the interval cycles. Analyses of several contemporary works in addition to Bartók's own compositions reveal the relevance of his compositional principles to a larger body of 20th-century music. The theoretical assumptions are supported by pertinent sketch studies. This work also explores symmetrical pitch relations as they had been emerging in music of the 19th and early 20th centuries.

GILLIES is the first to explore systematically the changing role of pitch notations in the course of Bartók's compositional development. The early works reveal a notation oriented toward a late-romantic chordal role. Between 1908 and the early 1920s, a competition and gradual shift occurs in the role of Bartók's notation, from a vertical to a horizontal emphasis. From 1926 these pitch notations became primarily horizontal, the consistency of this role permitting notation to serve as a useful tool for tonal analysis. Volume 1 ("Theory") outlines eight hypotheses regarding the relevance of notation in the tonal analysis of Bartók's later works. Volume 2 ("Analyses") is intended to support these hypotheses by analyzing *Music for Strings, Percussion, and Celesta*, the Violin Concerto, String Quartet no. 6, Sonata for Solo Violin, pieces from the *Forty-four Duos*, *Twenty-seven Choruses*, *Mikrokosmos*, and the first movement of String Quartet no. 5.

KÁRPÁTI expands his original study (*Bartók's String Quartets*, 1975) of the forms and styles of Bartók's string quartets to a broader selection of the major chamber works and places them in the larger context of Bartók's entire oeuvre. The first part of the book deals with Bartók's musical idiom and style, including discussions of the legacy of Beethoven, forerunners and contemporaries, the influence of folk music, monothematicism and variation, polymodal chromaticism, and tonality and polytonality—the phenomenon of mistuning. The second part of the book (analyses) includes discussions of selected early chamber works composed between 1895 and 1904, the two Sonatas for Violin and Piano (1921, 1922), the Sonata for Two Pianos and Percussion (1937) and the trio *Contrasts for Violin, Clarinet, and Piano* (1938), in addition to the six string quartets, which represent the core of this study.

LENDVAI is one of the first to have formulated an original theoretical approach intended to draw together the diversity of elements of Bartók's musical language into a larger system. Lendvai attempts to establish a direct connection between traditional tonal functions and the system based on equal subdivisions of the octave. He suggests that through tone substitution (i.e., based on the traditional relative-key substitutes), such key schemes as C, E, A-flat, C in the Sonata for Two Pianos and Percussion represent the traditional harmonic functions of tonic, dominant, subdominant, tonic. As illustrated in his polar-axis system, in which each of these three functions (tonic, dominant, subdominant) has four poles (as outlined in each of the minor-third cycles: C, E-flat, F-sharp, A [tonic], G, B-flat, C-sharp, E [dominant], and F, A-flat, B, D [subdominant]), he is suggesting that the tonic C, dominant E, and subdominant A-flat have the same functions as their tritone equivalents and minor thirds. He further shows that Bartók's music is integrated by interlocking tonal principles of his polar-axis system with chords and intervals derived from the Golden Section (chromatic system) and the acoustic (overtone) scale (diatonic system). While the application of his theoretical principles to Bartók's harmonic structures is somewhat problematic, his application of the Golden Section to formal proportions appears to be a significant contribution to Bartók studies.

SOMFAI provides the first comprehensive study of Bartók's compositional process based on all of the extant primary sources. Conclusions are based on the analysis of about 3,600 pages of sketches, drafts, and autograph manuscripts, as well as numerous documents that include corrections preserved on recordings of Bartók's performances of his own compositions. Chapters present documentation pertaining to the following: Bartók on composition, his concepts, and works; a survey of the sources, including a study of the existing sources, the function of different types of manuscripts, and reconstruction of the chain of sources; sketches and the plan of a work in successive stages of development; fragments and unrealized plans; paper studies and the microchronology of the composition; the draft as key manuscript; final copy, orchestration, reduction, arrangement; editing and correcting process; and a study of Bartók's notation and performing style.

SUCHOFF demonstrates that the Concerto for Orchestra, which embodies what one might refer to as the "total Bartók," is based on a thorough synthesis of Eastern European folk-music sources and Western art music techniques. He shows that the concerto is a kind of index to the multiplicity of musical sources that the composer absorbed and transformed throughout his evolution. The author's organizational approach in three large parts and the individual topics subsumed under them forms one of the most comprehensive and coherent views of Bartók's varied musical life and compositional activity. An overall historical survey of Bartók's musical language and style is presented in part 1; a systematic analytical overview of the concerto's melodic, harmonic, rhythmic, thematic, and formal dimensions follows in part 2; and a discussion of Bartók's legacy based on the impact of his music on composers in the post-World War II era (including Alberto Ginastera, Benjamin Britten, György Ligeti, George Crumb, Witold Lutosławski, and Olivier Messiaen) is presented in part 3.

Finally, WILSON provides a theoretic-analytical study of five works of Bartók, including the Sonata for Piano, String Quartet no. 3, and movements of the String Quartet no. 5, Sonata for Two Pianos and Percussion, and Concerto for Orchestra. It includes an introductory outline of the basic steps toward a theory, including a general overview of Bartók's sources, style, and tonality, and a synopsis of contrasting theoretical views of the music (Lendvai, the Hungarian Circle, Milton Babbitt and his successors, Elliott Antokoletz, Felix Salzer and Roy Travis, and other recent work). The first part of the book contains the theory in abstract terms, the second the analyses based on application of the theoretical ideas. Wilson's theory adopts the notion of a diverse amalgam of elements as the basis

for his analyses, in which he admits traditional harmonic principles based on contextual considerations along with the concepts and terminology derived from Allen Forte's atonal set theory. The work points to the philosophical similarities between Wilson's theory and the studies of David Lewin and Charles Taylor in the areas of perception and hermeneutics.

ELLIOTT ANTOKOLETZ

Beach, Mrs. H.H.A. (Amy) 1867–1944

United States composer

Beach, Amy, *Quartet for Strings (in One Movement)*, op. 89, edited by Adrienne Fried Block, Madison, Wisconsin: A-R Editions, 1994

Block, Adrienne Fried, *Amy Beach, Passionate Victorian: The Life and Work of an American Composer, 1867–1944*, New York: Oxford University Press, 1998

Brown, Jeanell Wise, *Amy Beach and Her Chamber Music: Biography, Documents, Style*, Metuchen, New Jersey: Scarecrow Press, 1994

Eden, Myrna G., *Energy and Individuality in the Art of Anna Huntington, Sculptor, and Amy Beach, Composer*, Metuchen, New Jersey: Scarecrow Press, 1987

Jenkins, Walter S., *The Remarkable Mrs. Beach, American Composer: A Biographical Account Based on Her Diaries, Letters, Newspaper Clippings, and Personal Reminiscences*, edited by John H. Baron, Warren, Michigan: Harmonie Park Press, 1994

Amy Beach, who preferred to use the title Mrs. H.H.A. Beach during a long career stretching from the 1880s to the 1940s, attracted a loyal following of enthusiastic admirers during her lifetime and after a hiatus of several decades, posthumously. Her charming personality and a significant body of very appealing music help to explain this ongoing fascination. In recent decades there has been a spate of recordings and new editions of her works, whose lush textures, chromatic harmonies, and occasional forays into impressionistic territory sound fresh in an age in which radical modernism is no longer the order of the day. More than any other member of the so-called Second New England School, she is being recognized as a major composer.

Along with the scores and recordings has come a growing body of literature on Beach's life and works. That the quality of this literature varies widely is due both to the varying backgrounds of the writers and to the strange history of the documentary sources. When Beach died, the papers in her Hillsborough, New Hampshire, apartment were taken to the Fuller Public Library, Hillsborough, which recognized the value of the materials but was ill equipped to catalog and preserve them.

Another significant collection of manuscripts, diaries, and scrapbooks was held by the Special Collections Library at the University of New Hampshire at Durham. A third group of materials was in the possession of Walter Jenkins, a composer and organist on the faculty of Tulane University. The archives of Beach's principal publisher, A.P. Schmidt, which contain numerous letters and musical manuscripts, are in the Library of Congress. A final collection of significant Beach materials is housed at the University of Missouri at Kansas City. These scattered sources were brought closer together by the University of New Hampshire's acquisition of the Jenkins materials after his death in 1990 and the Hillsborough materials in 1991.

JENKINS's loving account of the composer he had come to know during summers at the MacDowell Colony was completed by the mid-1960s. For a variety of reasons it was not published until after his death, when his former Tulane colleague John Baron edited the manuscript. Despite Baron's best efforts, the book is full of errors and has limited documentation. Jenkins, who was not a musicologist, freely mixes personal reminiscences with undocumented historical facts in a narrative that often defies chronology. Nevertheless, the book is important for Jenkins's recollections of the composer and her views, even if it is impossible to verify some of his statements.

BROWN is a performer, and the strength of her study lies in the detailed analyses of individual chamber works. She discusses 15 works for various chamber combinations, supporting her analytical insights with numerous musical examples. The biographical section is extensive but suffers from a lack of familiarity with the source materials. The general comments on musical style and the two work lists should be used with caution.

EDEN's study is a revised edition of her 1977 dissertation. Although the author had less access to sources than any of the other writers, she is careful to avoid unsubstantiated assertions, which gives her book an integrity that makes it worth reading more than two decades after it was written. The strength of her work is the interdisciplinary approach she applies to compare the works of a composer and of a sculptor from Gilded-Age Boston.

Quite apart from the foregoing books are those of BLOCK, whose decades of research and writing have made her name nearly synonymous with that of Beach. No scholar is as familiar with the sources and the music, and none has produced so many articles, conference papers, and reviews. Her long-awaited biography of the composer draws on all the available primary sources, and her edition of the quartet for strings sets a new standard for Beach analysis.

Block's biography attempts to do a number of things. First and foremost, it is a fastidiously documented account of the composer's life. Her thorough examination of the source materials and wide-ranging ancillary research are reflected in 70 pages of endnotes. Second, the author intersperses her biographical narrative with chapters devoted to analysis of the works. These discussions are supported by hundreds of musical examples, including a substantial number of reproductions from original manuscripts. Finally, Block discusses Beach's life and works in light of recent research on cultural studies, particularly feminist writings. This allows her to speculate on the inner life of a composer whose Victorian mind-set kept her from expressing frustrations and dissatisfaction as freely as a biographer might have wished. Particularly insightful are her thoughts on the effects on Beach's creative life of her parents' child-rearing techniques and her older husband's stipulations regarding her career.

Block's edition of BEACH's String Quartet, op. 89, is the sort of critical edition that has long been standard for the works of major European composers but is rarely seen for U.S. works. In an extensive introduction, the author gives a biographical sketch, traces the evolution of Beach's style, discusses the role of folk music in her works, and analyzes the quartet stylistically and structurally. The edition itself is exceptionally clear, with a full score, parts, and a detailed critical apparatus. An appendix presents a facsimile of the draft score with notes on the compositional process as reflected in that document.

E. DOUGLAS BOMBERGER

Beethoven, Ludwig van 1770–1827

German-born composer

1. Biography

Beethoven, Ludwig van, *The Letters of Beethoven*, 3 vols., edited and translated by Emily Anderson, New York: St. Martin's Press, 1961

Cooper, Martin, *Beethoven: The Last Decade, 1817–1827*, Oxford: Oxford University Press, 1970

Dahlhaus, Carl, *Ludwig van Beethoven: Approaches to His Music*, translated by Mary Whitall, Oxford: Clarendon Press, and New York: Oxford University Press, 1991

DeNora, Tia, *Beethoven and the Construction of Genius: Musical Politics in Vienna, 1792–1803*, Berkeley: University of California Press, 1995

Kerman, Joseph, and Alan Tyson, *The New Grove Beethoven*, London: Macmillan, and New York: Norton, 1983

Rolland, Romain, *Beethoven the Creator*, translated by Ernest Newman, New York: Harper, 1929

Schindler, Anton Felix, *Beethoven as I Knew Him*, edited by Donald MacArdle, translated by Constance S. Jolly, Chapel Hill: University of North Carolina Press, 1966

Solomon, Maynard, *Beethoven*, New York: Schirmer, 1977

———, "Beethoven's Tagebuch of 1812–1818," in *Beethoven Studies 3*, edited by Alan Tyson, Cambridge: Cambridge University Press, 1982

Thayer, Alexander Wheelock, *Thayer's Life of Beethoven*, 2 vols., edited by Elliot Forbes, Princeton, New Jersey: Princeton University Press, 1964

Wegeler, Franz Gerhard, and Ferdinand Ries, *Beethoven Remembered: The Biographical Notes of Franz Wegeler and Ferdinand Ries*, Arlington, Virginia: Great Ocean, 1987

Ludwig van Beethoven probably did more to shape the course of Western music than any other single individual. He lived at a time when music printing and music criticism allowed for easy dissemination of musical scores and aesthetic ideas. His style was at the same time accessible and uniquely challenging. He has been called a revolutionary, a magician, and a prophet. For years it was a commonplace that Beethoven had spilled his life's story into his music, and many biographers focused specifically on painting the common portrait of both. However, apart from the telling of an artist's story and all the difficulties in reconciling creativity with biography, Beethoven's life has confronted writers with three specific questions, none of which have been definitively answered to date. Perhaps they will never be explained to everyone's satisfaction. First, to what extent did the composer's deafness—which brought him to the brink of suicide—affect his life and work? Second, who was the "Immortal Beloved" to whom Beethoven addressed an uncharacteristically passionate love letter? Finally, what was the nature of Beethoven's relationship with his nephew that so obsessed him and thwarted his creativity in his later years? Specialized studies (not to mention fanciful fictitious accounts) have emerged on all these issues, as they have on virtually every provocative aspect of Beethoven's life. The legendary proportions to which Beethoven's life has been scaled unfortunately have frequently distorted the perception of many biographers, although the result is a glorious and inspiring myth of creativity to which modern composers and historians, with all their critical objectivity, are still occasionally susceptible. Primary biographical sources in Beethoven's own hand include letters, a short-lived diary, and the so-called conversation books that were used by the deaf composer to communicate with visitors in his last years (the surviving conversation books have not yet been translated completely). Even the most significant secondary sources are far too many to survey; those discussed here are generally characteristic of the most responsible scholarship and will easily lead the researcher to other studies.

BEETHOVEN's own letters are, of course, a primary source of information concerning his life and character. Emily Anderson's annotated translation is regarded as authoritative. It includes the famous Heiligenstadt Testament (6–10 October 1802), in which Beethoven admits suicidal thoughts brought on by increasing deafness, and the "Letter to the Immortal Beloved" (6–7 July 1812), which Anderson describes simply as to "An Unknown Woman." The correspondence is sparse for the early years but dense for the later ones, when Beethoven had already become famous.

Beethoven kept a diary (*Tagebuch*) from 1812 to 1818 that has been translated and edited by Maynard SOLOMON (1982). This was one of his least productive periods as a composer. The entries show that Beethoven read widely and deeply and reflected in writing on his situation as an artist and a human being. They reveal a philosophical and poetical bent in a man generally regarded as exclusively a musician. Solomon's article that accompanies the translation elucidates many of the enigmatic entries.

Both WEGELER and RIES knew the composer personally. Most of their anecdotes have been authenticated by biographers, and the colorful character of these brief accounts (usually no more than a page in length) help flesh out the composer's personality. One of the most famous of these is Ries's description of Beethoven's violent reaction to Napoleon's coronation as emperor and the corresponding destruction of the dedication of the *Eroica* symphony to Napoleon. Other anecdotes testify to Beethoven's haughty attitude toward his aristocratic patrons.

THAYER's biography of Beethoven is generally regarded as the most complete and informative. Thayer was a U.S. diplomat, historian, and musical enthusiast. Ironically, his original notes and the parts of his text that he completed in English are lost. Thayer did not feel comfortable enough writing German to publish in that language, but he recognized that the need for a good German-language biography was most pressing if further research was to be undertaken. Hermann Deiters, in close consultation with Thayer, published a German edition of Thayer's work in three volumes from 1866 to 1879. This biography breaks off in the year 1817—Thayer had not completed his work on the last ten years. He died after 40-some years of ill health in 1897, leaving his work on the last decade of Beethoven's life in notes. Deiters died before he could bring the biography past the year 1823. Hugo Riemann took up the task of revising and completing the biography on Deiters's death. It appeared in German in five volumes from 1907 to 1917. Meanwhile, interest in an English-language edition prompted Henry Edward Krehbiel to issue the original text in that language. Like Riemann, Krehbiel worked only from Thayer's notes in writing the biography of the last years. Elliot Forbes compared all these editions, correcting and updating them. Dieters, Krehbiel, Riemann, and Forbes all assimilated Thayer's painstaking attention to detail and historical accuracy. Some inaccuracies still exist in Forbes's edition, but these are relatively few.

Thayer's narrative is chronological, proceeding year by year, and he provides little or no interpretation of Beethoven's music. In his travels, Thayer met many of Beethoven's contemporaries, and he interrogated them about the master firsthand. Biographers in Germany such as Ludwig Nohl, who published an ardently nationalistic, multivolume biography of Beethoven contemporaneously with Thayer's first edition (Nohl's work has never been translated in its entirety), faulted him for scientific coldness and for neglecting the music. However, Thayer was the first biographer who really wanted to put an end to the many myths about Beethoven the man. His work is invaluable and should form a constant reference for any biographical research into Beethoven's life.

The other principal 19th-century biography is that of SCHINDLER. Schindler knew Beethoven and had attended to many of the composer's personal needs in the later years. The English translation of Schindler's first biography (1840) had originally prompted Thayer to do some research and set the record straight. It contains many inaccuracies and personal opinions clouded in the premises of objectivity and firsthand knowledge. The third edition (first published in 1860), far more detailed, has been carefully annotated by Donald MacArdle, who points out the contradictions and historical variances. Schindler established the categorization of Beethoven's life into three periods: an early period of adaptation to the Viennese classical style, a middle period brought on by deafness and leading to a revolt against that style, and a late period involving a retreat into his private world, in part due to the unpleasant fight for custody of his nephew. Most Beethoven scholars have accepted this division, even if they disagree about the specific dividing points. Because he knew Beethoven and lived closely with him (especially during the last years of the composer's life), Schindler's biography is still valuable. However, most recent biographers are generally unable to separate Schindler's enthusiasm for Beethoven—at times bordering on a public relations campaign—from the factual information that he provides. Most notoriously, Schindler is known to have destroyed many entries in the conversation books and altered or fabricated many others. The extent to which Schindler rewrote Beethoven's biography to suit his own agenda has yet to be determined.

ROLLAND's work is only one part of his series of books on Beethoven's life and music, and it deals only with a relatively short (but intensely productive) period of the composer's life—his middle (heroic) period. The book's significance lies not in its biographical accuracy (it is often inaccurate) but in Rolland's uncanny understanding of the music and his adroit interpretation of it as expressive of the composer's inner life. Effusively rhetorical and overtly literary, Rolland nevertheless manages to convince the scholarly world that Beethoven's heroic works were specific expressions of his personal triumph over his deafness. One wants to believe Rolland, even if sometimes the facts (i.e., the sketches, the chronologies, and so on) speak differently. Rolland's work is at the heart of Beethoven mythology.

Given the overwhelming amount of information in Thayer and Forbes concerning the last ten years of Beethoven's life, COOPER's contribution is a welcome biographical overview. Most of Cooper's book is devoted to the music of the late period, which is discussed separately from the biography. However, Cooper's study shows how modern biographers broke with romantic mythology and devoted serious research into the authentic historical facts of the 19th-century biographies, including more accurate medical evaluations (Beethoven's health, apart from his poor hearing, was consistently bad during his last ten years). Cooper's study is most noteworthy for its clarity of presentation, especially concerning the nephew issue. Although much more than a biographical sketch, it significantly compresses the Thayer and Schindler chronicles.

SOLOMON is *the* 20th-century Beethoven biographer. In his 1977 work, he tackles Beethoven's life with superb command of the facts and Beethoven's music with sensitive understanding of the style and musical language. His premise is controversial—he interprets Beethoven's life from a Freudian (or in any case, psychoanalytic) perspective. He focuses clearly on the Heiligenstadt Testament, the Riddle of the Immortal Beloved, and the nephew issue and brings to bear a wealth of insights culled from his broad psychological research. He claims to have identified the immortal beloved as Antonie Brentano (others have proposed Josephine von Brunswick, Beethoven's flame from a few years earlier, or Johanna von Beethoven, the mother of his nephew). Concerning Beethoven's obsession with his nephew, Solomon has coined the phrase "nobility pretense" and regards Beethoven's insistence on custody of the nephew as a working out of the composer's (delusional) conviction that he was—or had to be—of noble descent. Solomon must be commended for his fairness in representing the views of those with whom he disagrees, for his comprehensive study of the earlier sources, and for his historical accuracy, which has never seriously been questioned. However, his interpretation of Beethoven's character and music is clearly prejudiced toward his Freudian presuppositions—for example, he plainly regards Beethoven as oedipal and interprets some of the music accordingly. Had a historian of lesser caliber undertaken such research, it would have been immediately suspect. The greatest argument for Solomon's psychological approach is his own integrity as a scholar.

In distinction to Solomon's sometimes polemic or speculative treatment, KERMAN and TYSON provide a clear and concise biography and bibliography. The significance of Beethoven's major works is made clear with respect to the most recent scholarship, and one gains a general sense of Beethoven's life that can easily be lost in the details of the more lengthy biographies.

DAHLHAUS's life and work study has a deeply abstract, philosophical bent. As a critic, his gaze has consistently been set on aesthetic issues. For example, how does music relate to the culture that gave it birth? What role can biography play in demonstrating this relationship? How can theoretical analysis explicate this relationship? His Beethoven study shows how problems of biography can lead to more profound questions about the musical experience, questions that Dahlhaus answers in ways that do not always satisfy but that nevertheless nag at the conscience and force one into serious reflection.

DeNORA's work illustrates the most recent trend in Beethoven biography, which might simplistically be described as postmodern. In direct opposition to Rolland's romantic view of artistic creativity and Solomon's psychoanalytic, modern interpretations, DeNora argues that Beethoven's unique musical achievements as a performer and a composer were as much a function of his patrons' aesthetic goals as of his own creative drives. DeNora challenges the traditional view of Beethoven as an artist who rejected patronage for the sake of expressive integrity. She views Beethoven's success as a function of aesthetic conditioning by a Viennese social elite; she also regards Beethoven as a precursor of the modern superstar. Her case is somewhat exaggerated and sometimes involves distortion or neglect of counterevidence (including Beethoven's own letters), but it promises to elicit more careful studies of the relationships between Beethoven, his patrons, and his audiences.

THOMAS SIPE

2. Chamber Music

Abraham, Gerald, editor, *The Age of Beethoven, 1790–1830,* The New Oxford History of Music, vol. 8, London: Oxford University Press, 1982

Arnold, Denis, and Nigel Fortune, editors, *The Beethoven Companion,* London: Faber, 1971; as *The Beethoven Reader,* New York: Norton, 1971

Cooper, Barry, editor, *The Beethoven Compendium: A Guide to Beethoven's Life and Music,* London: Thames and Hudson, and Ann Arbor, Michigan: Borders Press, 1991

D'Indy, Vincent, "Beethoven," in *Cobbett's Cyclopedic Survey of Chamber Music,* edited by Walter Willson Cobbett, 2nd edition, edited by Colin Mason, 3 vols., London: Oxford University Press, 1963

Ferguson, Donald N., *Image and Structure in Chamber Music,* Minneapolis: University of Minnesota Press, 1964

Kerman, Joseph, *The Beethoven String Quartets,* New York: Knopf, and London: Oxford University Press, 1967

Radcliffe, Philip, *Beethoven's String Quartets,* London: Hutchinson, 1965; 2nd edition, Cambridge: Cambridge University Press, 1978

Schmidt-Görg, Joseph, and Hans Schmidt, editors, *Ludwig van Beethoven,* translated by the editorial department of the Deutsche Grammophon Gesellschaft, London: Pall Mall Press, and New York: Praeger, 1970

Smallman, Basil, *The Piano Trio: Its History, Technique, and Repertoire,* Oxford: Clarendon Press, and New York: Oxford University Press, 1990

Ulrich, Homer, *Chamber Music,* New York: Columbia University Press, 1948; 2nd edition, 1966

Winter, Robert, and Robert L. Martin, editors, *The Beethoven Quartet Companion,* Berkeley: University of California Press, 1994

Beethoven's chamber music has been explored from a variety of perspectives. These include descriptive analyses of the music, explanations of Beethoven's artistic development as reflected in his chamber music, examinations of his contributions to the chamber music idiom, and studies of the historical and social contexts within which Beethoven composed his chamber music. Beethoven's string quartets are among the most important contributions to music. The significance of the quartets is reflected in the number of books devoted exclusively to them beginning as early as the 19th century and continuing through the 20th century; only a few of those books are discussed here. Several surveys of chamber music, such as those by Cobbett, Ulrich, and Ferguson, contain chapters on Beethoven's works. Books consisting of collections of essays on his life and works also often include specialized treatment of the chamber music.

ABRAHAM's comprehensive overview of music in Europe around the turn of the 19th century includes a chapter on Beethoven's chamber music. Guided by the premise that the chamber music, more than any other sphere of his creative output, reveals Beethoven's full genius and the full scope of his professional contributions, Abraham traces the composer's work in that realm chronologically, from the youthful works of a Bonn teenager to the last quartets. The discussion not only outlines Beethoven's development as a composer but also reveals gradual changes in the chamber music idiom in general as reflected in these pieces. Other topics include performers, reception history, the chamber works' relation to sketches and other compositions, social circumstances surrounding his work, and the influences of Haydn and Mozart.

ARNOLD and FORTUNE coordinate a collection of articles by noted specialists into a symposium covering major aspects of Beethoven's creative work. Contributions include two articles on the chamber music: Nigel Fortune discusses chamber music with piano, while Robert Simpson presents the chamber music for strings. Both writers provide brief analytical descriptions of the works in chronological order, highlighting Beethoven's development as an artist. They also discuss the changes in chamber music media as a result of Beethoven's treatment. Because of their sensitivity to the historical and cultural contexts, both scholars help readers imagine the novelty and ingenuity of Beethoven's music perceived upon first hearing by audiences of his day.

COOPER summarizes a broad range of topics covering every significant aspect of Beethoven's life and music. Within the section entitled "The Music," Nicholas Marston contributes three essays on the chamber music, categorized according to the scoring. Each essay explains biographical contexts for the pieces, stylistic features in relation to Beethoven's other compositions, and the relation of Beethoven's works to those of Haydn and Mozart. Following each essay, a complete listing of the chamber music includes catalog numbers, key, tempo and meter indications for each movement, scoring, publication information, and dedications.

FERGUSON explores the notion of classicism and romanticism within social and artistic contexts, reviews the historical antecedents to chamber music, and describes the development of formal structures associated with chamber music, particularly sonata form. Rather than a complete history or comprehensive survey of the music, he provides a description of the more important works by significant composers. Within this context, Ferguson devotes an entire chapter to Beethoven's chamber music, including descriptive analyses and an overview of the general mood and character of each work, categorized by scoring.

D'INDY's article begins with a catalog of Beethoven's chamber music, including such information as title, key, scoring, catalog number, and date of composition. Arguing that the work of all great artists can be arranged according to three style periods, d'Indy organizes his essay based on three such periods for Beethoven: imitation, externalization, and reflection. For each of the three, he identifies the chamber music composed during that period, recounts contemporaneous historical circumstances, and suggests events in Beethoven's personal life that may have triggered the artistic characteristics associated with that period. D'Indy analyzes selected works that represent Beethoven's style within each period.

KERMAN discusses the string quartets, which he groups into chapters according to the works' stylistic parallels and chronological proximity. Through detailed descriptive analyses, he traces Beethoven's growth and development as a composer from his early foundation in the heritage of Haydn and Mozart to his exploration of new expressive realms in the late quartets. Kerman measures each quartet against other works by Beethoven, always striking a careful balance between considering the artistic integrity of an individual composition and evaluating the significance of that work within the composer's total output. Commentary includes such related issues as biographical details, the sketches, reception history, Beethoven's teachers, and his relations with patrons, performers, and publishers. The bibliography lists several other books devoted to the string quartets.

RADCLIFFE provides descriptive analyses of all the string quartets. His discussions include brief historical background for the pieces and commentary on Beethoven's stylistic development as reflected in the quartets. The author relates the quartets to other works by Beethoven, particularly the piano sonatas and other chamber music; Radcliffe also compares the quartets with those of other composers, especially Haydn and Mozart. Radcliffe closes by tracing the impact of Beethoven's artistic contributions on later generations of composers, extending through the 19th century and into the early 20th century.

SCHMIDT-GÖRG and SCHMIDT present firsthand evidence of the life and work of Beethoven through such available documents as Beethoven's own letters and memoranda, original sketches and manuscripts, conversation books, contemporary reports, and comments by critics of his time. Each chapter, prepared by a musicologist closely associated with the Beethoven-Archiv in Bonn, introduces an important area of Beethoven's creative activity. The five chapters devoted to chamber music chronicle the events in Beethoven's life surrounding the creation of those works; his relationships with patrons, publishers, and performers; and the reception of those works by his contemporaries. Reproductions of oil paintings and other illustrations throughout the book create an appropriate atmosphere for each of the chapters.

SMALLMAN traces the history and repertoire of the piano trio genre from the late 18th through the 20th century, providing a unified overview of the development of that medium, especially in relation to major style changes during those 200 years. Emphasizing accepted masterpieces of the genre, with some reference to lesser-known works, Smallman explains how Beethoven expanded the piano trio genre through the addition of a minuet or scherzo movement, the exploitation of the technical improvements in the instruments, the exploration of a broader range of key relationships, and the increasing breadth of artistic conception, particularly in development and recapitulation sections. Smallman places individual compositions in the context of Beethoven's biography and sketch history and frequently compares Beethoven's style with that of Haydn and Mozart.

ULRICH devotes the first section of his book to an overview of the historical development of chamber music before the late 18th century; subsequent chapters present major composers and literature since the time of Haydn. The chapter on Beethoven begins with a condensed biography and a survey of the chamber works; more detailed treatment of the chamber music is categorized according to scoring. Within each category, Ulrich describes the historical context, provides information on performances and dedications, and identifies general style features in relation to Beethoven's other music and in comparison with other composers.

WINTER and MARTIN identify two goals for their book: to develop a cultural context for understanding the quartets and to enhance the reader's listening experience. To accomplish the first goal, several scholars contribute essays addressing such issues as Beethoven's audiences; the social circumstances surrounding performances; the Viennese cultural, political, and intellectual climate; reception history; perspectives of classicism and romanticism; and performance issues. The second goal is fulfilled by Michael Steinberg's movement-by-movement descriptions of each quartet. A glossary at the end of the book provides handy reference for technical terms.

RENEE McCACHREN

3. Orchestral Music

Arnold, Denis, and Nigel Fortune, editors, *The Beethoven Companion,* London: Faber, 1971; as *The Beethoven Reader,* New York: Norton, 1971

Berlioz, Hector, *A Critical Study of Beethoven's Nine Symphonies,* translated by Edwin Evans, London: William Reeves, 1913

Fiske, Roger, *Beethoven Concertos and Overtures,* London: British Broadcasting Corporation, 1970; Seattle: University of Washington Press, 1971

Grove, George, *Beethoven and His Nine Symphonies,* London: Novello, 1903; 3rd edition, New York: Dover, 1962

Hopkins, Antony, *The Nine Symphonies of Beethoven,* London: Heinemann Educational Books, and Seattle: University of Washington Press, 1981; Brookfield, Vermont: Scolar Press, 1996

———, *The Seven Concertos of Beethoven,* Aldershot, England: Scolar Press, and Brookfield, Vermont: Ashgate, 1996

Saloman, Ora Frishberg, *Beethoven's Symphonies and J.S. Dwight: The Birth of American Music Criticism,* Boston: Northeastern University Press, 1995

Thayer, Alexander Wheelock, *Thayer's Life of Beethoven,* 2 vols., edited by Elliot Forbes, Princeton, New Jersey: Princeton University Press, 1964

Beethoven's music has occupied a central position in the canon of Western music for 200 years. In his own lifetime his orchestral works, especially his symphonies, received popular and critical acclaim. Composers throughout the 19th century, from Schubert to Wagner, expressed great appreciation for Beethoven's musical language, which was seen by artists and critics alike as an expression of romantic ideals. Subsequent scholarship has developed a broader view of Beethoven's accomplishments by showing his work as grounded in the forms and musical idioms of the classical era but reaching beyond that genre's conventions with the structural, harmonic, and orchestral innovations that earned Beethoven the praises of his successors. Beethoven's life has also attracted the interest of scholars who attempt to ground the composer's artistic achievements in the events of his tumultuous life.

One instance of this ongoing fascination with the relationship of art to life is FORBES's revised edition of Thayer's classic Beethoven biography, *Ludwig van Beethovens Leben* (originally published 1866–79), which in turn was indebted to the work of other biographers, including Arthur Schindler (*Biographie von Ludwig van Beethoven*). Forbes's book localizes Beethoven's works within their specific historical contexts. Excerpts from Beethoven's letters and personal diary provide the beginning student of Beethoven with interesting and often entertaining reading that lays the groundwork for further study. For easy reference the book contains an index of musical works discussed, including symphonies, overtures, and concertos.

Beethoven's symphonies became a landmark and point of comparison for the composers who succeeded him. BERLIOZ, himself a successful innovator of orchestration, acknowledges that Beethoven set the stage for 19th-century musical expression, and what Berlioz calls "modern" music, by charting new territory in his use of instrumentation, dynamics, and form. Berlioz, however, also suggests ways to improve areas in Beethoven's symphonies the author deems weak in content and expression. This book not only provides the student with an intriguing look at Beethoven's orchestral style but also gives insight into 19th-century musical aesthetics as influenced by Beethoven.

Even in the 19th century, Beethoven's works were not only known and revered on the European continent but had also found admirers in the United States. One of them, the music critic and editor J.S. Dwight—whose work on the *Journal of Music* has recently been examined by SALOMAN—communicated in his essays, concert reviews, and correspondence what he thought was the merit of Beethoven's symphonic music and how it could contribute to the moral and cultural ideas of U.S. culture. Dwight's essays reproduced in Saloman's study provide valuable information regarding the public reception of Beethoven's symphonies by 19th-century audiences in the United States. Saloman's own goal is to help today's U.S. listeners enjoy Beethoven's symphonies. To this end, he presents various philosophical and interpretive approaches to the music, providing a detailed discussion of the various movements from each work. Each chapter contains an extensive works-cited list, enabling students to conduct additional research on this subject.

A valuable aid designed for nonspecialists and amateur musicians studying Beethoven's orchestral music is GROVE's study of Beethoven's nine symphonies. At the start of each chapter, Grove establishes the historical background to the genesis of each work and provides a concise list of keys, orchestration, and publishing information about the symphony to be discussed. Grove then analyzes the symphonies, movement by movement, with regard to thematic, formal, and harmonic concerns and compares each work to similar music by Beethoven's contemporaries, taking care to avoid extremely technical jargon. Grove believes that a study of themes and musical structures allows the listener to make better sense out of the musical content. Grove also includes Beethoven's own thoughts about the public reaction to his symphonies. A translation of the famous *Heiligenstadt* Testament of 6 October 1802 yields insight into Beethoven's struggle with deafness, the shaping of his faith, and the crystallization of his philosophy on life, all of which played an important role in his compositional process.

HOPKINS (1981) represents a more recent trend in Beethoven studies that seeks to understand Beethoven's innovations in terms of the classical orchestral style of Haydn and Mozart. He discusses the symphonies in great detail, dividing them into five chronological groups in order to demonstrate the various influences that affected Beethoven's changing style and creative genius. Hopkins highlights Beethoven's penchant for heroism, his love of nature, but also what Hopkins calls the "creative demon" within. Students will learn not only about melody, harmony, and structure but will also delve into the mood and character of each work.

Beethoven's orchestral works also comprise a number of concertos and overtures. In his discussion of these works, FISKE first traces the evolution of both style and form of the classical concerto, distinguishing it from the earlier concertos of J.S. Bach and Handel. Armed with this information, the reader is led to appreciate the stylistic and structural innovations Beethoven brought to this genre. In order to trace this stylistic evolution, Fiske organizes his discussion of these works around the chronology of Beethoven's concertos and the solo instruments featured in them. He takes the same approach to the overtures, both incidental and dramatic, furnishing the reader with added understanding of the genesis, mood, and style of each work. For the operatic overtures, Fiske provides the dramatic context of important themes. Students will find his discussions concise and accessible.

HOPKINS (1996), using the same approach employed in his book on Beethoven's symphonies, presents his research on the concertos with the same attention to the details of structure, style, and performance conventions. Besides giving the reader the historical context of each work, Hopkins highlights musical themes and the relationships that exist between the solo and orchestral dialogue within the music. His discussion of performance practice provides insight into the treatment of solo lines and cadenzas during actual performance. It also invites the reader to contemplate the emotional dynamics of music in performance.

ARNOLD and FORTUNE can serve as a handbook to introduce the reader to Beethoven's life and works as well as to Beethoven scholarship. The various essays consider biographical issues, focus on the genres in which

Beethoven worked, and analyze different works in their historical context. In addition, the editors include information on a planned overture based on the name of Bach and on a proposed tenth symphony. The essays in part 6 concern the reception of Beethoven's music by his contemporaries and by posterity.

CHARLES R. VERBLE

4. Piano Music

Arnold, Denis, and Nigel Fortune, editors, *The Beethoven Companion*, London: Faber, 1971; as *The Beethoven Reader*, New York: Norton, 1971

Barth, George, *The Pianist as Orator: Beethoven and the Transformation of Keyboard Style*, Ithaca, New York: Cornell University Press, 1992

Blom, Eric, *Beethoven's Pianoforte Sonatas Discussed*, London: Dent, and New York: Dutton, 1938; reprint, New York: Da Capo, 1968

Czerny, Carl, *On the Proper Performance of All Beethoven's Works for the Piano*, London: Cocks, 1846; edited by Paul Badura-Skoda, Vienna: Universal, 1970

Drake, Kenneth, *The Sonatas of Beethoven: As He Played and Taught Them*, Cincinnati: Music Teachers National Association, 1972

Kinderman, William, *Beethoven*, Berkeley: University of California Press, 1995

Newman, William S., *Beethoven on Beethoven: Playing His Piano Music His Way*, New York: Norton, 1988

Rosen, Charles, *The Classical Style: Haydn, Mozart, Beethoven*, London: Faber, and New York: Viking Press, 1971; expanded edition, New York: Norton, 1997

Schindler, Anton, *Biographie von Ludwig van Beethoven*, Munster: Aschendorff, 1840; 3rd edition, 1860; *The Life of Beethoven* (translation of 1840 edition), edited by Ignaz Moscheles, London: Colburn, 1841; *Beethoven as I Knew Him* (annotated translation of 1860 edition), edited by Donald W. MacArdle and translated by Constance S. Jolly, London: Faber and Faber, 1966

Tovey, Donald Francis, *A Companion to Beethoven's Pianoforte Sonatas*, London: Associated Board of the Royal Schools of Music, 1931; reprint, New York: AMS Press, 1976

Beethoven wrote solo piano music (32 sonatas, 5 sonatinas, 20 sets of variations, and about 29 miscellaneous works) almost continuously from the age of 11 until a few years before his death. Perhaps not surprisingly, books on Beethoven's piano music focus almost exclusively on performance practices and analytical aspects of the sonatas. By the 1840s, Schindler and Czerny had offered the first of many studies designed to help pianists decide how to execute and interpret this literature. The complex controversies surrounding the seemingly incompatible stances taken by these two important contemporaries have themselves led to many diverse and rich interpretations, especially since the Beethoven bicentennial in 1970. Analytical surveys of some or all of the sonatas began to appear in English in the 1920s, most comprehensively and insightfully in Tovey and Blom. Surveys and more extended treatments of representative piano works figure prominently in countless books not primarily devoted to Beethoven's solo piano legacy. Two of these (Kinderman and Rosen) are singled out below.

SCHINDLER is undoubtedly the most controversial figure in Beethoven biography. Along with Czerny, he is also the most important source of information on performance practice issues related to Beethoven's piano music (see especially the "Musical Section" of the 1860 edition). Schindler bases his advocacy of tempo flexibility and a rhetorical style ("piano oratory") on his recollection that Beethoven's "playing was free of all constraint in respect to the beat," a view that directly contradicts Czerny, who insistently argues that the composer espoused metronomic regularity. Readers must decide to what degree the presence of numerous demonstrable factual errors and exaggerations in Schindler's biography of Beethoven and over 200 forgeries in the composer's conversation books affect the reliability of Schindler's often articulate and seemingly persuasive views—often supported by specific musical examples—on how the composer may have wished his piano music to be performed.

In some respects, CZERNY possesses unimpeachable credentials as an authority on the performance practices of Beethoven's piano music. A composer, piano virtuoso, and pedagogue, Czerny began his three-year period of studies with Beethoven in 1799. In subsequent years, he would sight-read Beethoven's new works in the composer's presence, and he was asked to play the debut of the fifth and final piano concerto in 1812 and to teach Beethoven's nephew Karl in 1816. Czerny also heard his teacher play on numerous occasions, certainly more than any other interpreter who published recollections of how Beethoven wanted his music performed. Although he allows for some flexibility under highly restricted conditions, Czerny, in stark contrast to Schindler, consistently advocates playing "strictly in time." Perhaps most controversially, Czerny himself on more than one future occasion would significantly alter the tempo markings he so scrupulously assigns to each of the numerous musical examples in his treatise in order to indicate "the time in which Beethoven himself performed his works."

TOVEY offers "a bar-to-bar analysis of all Beethoven's pianoforte sonatas from the first note to the last." For every sonata he provides comprehensive annotated commentary throughout each movement and each section within a movement. With systematic thoroughness, Tovey reliably identifies thematic, harmonic, and notable rhythmic and contrapuntal features. Considering the inherent constraints of the book's format, he also manages to incorporate a considerable amount of interpretative detail and a number of thoughtful digressions.

BLOM is distinctive as the first book-length survey in English that combines historical narrative and descriptive analytical commentary for each sonata. Although less systematic, detailed, and comprehensive than Tovey, Blom's reader-friendly analysis is considerably aided by more than 300 musical examples.

Essays by Truscott and Barford in ARNOLD and FORTUNE divide the sonatas into two extended essays. Truscott's survey (opp. 1–57) devotes extensive coverage to Muzio Clementi's (and to a lesser extent J.L. Dussek's) alleged influences on Beethoven's work up to 1801 (op. 28). Even readers who make distinctions between priority and influence may welcome the assemblage of musical examples by Beethoven's predecessors. Barford judiciously applies harmonic analysis as well as the principles of motivic analysis espoused in Rudolph Réti's once influential but now widely criticized *Thematic Patterns in Sonatas of Beethoven* (1967) to demonstrate an intricate but largely credible pattern of organic connection in several of Beethoven's piano sonatas composed after 1809.

Although ROSEN treats only three late sonatas in detail (opp. 106, 110, and 111), he nonetheless places his discussions of these and other sonatas within the context of Beethoven's overall development. He also forcefully articulates an approach to Beethoven that demonstrates the composer's originality as well as his allegiance to the principles and conventions of the classical style inherited from Haydn and Mozart. Rosen's discussions of the third relations throughout op. 106, the diminished seventh in the first movement of op. 111, and the "dramatic reworking, in the finale, of the most conventional elements of academic counterpoint" in op. 110 are lucid, penetrating, and compelling.

DRAKE uses Beethoven's known remarks and the recollections of his students, especially Czerny and Schindler, to approach tempo and modifications of tempo, dynamics, declamatory style, pedaling, and ornamentation. Drake's well-chosen and numerous musical illustrations are especially useful. For example, in treating tempo, Drake presents nearly 70 excerpts to support his view that, although "it is impossible to speak with any certainty about the degree of tempo modification which Beethoven's taste demanded in playing his works," the "scores in themselves provide excellent examples of tempo modifications and free performance."

NEWMAN offers the most comprehensive and well-documented exploration of Beethoven performance practice. The compendium of topics is thoughtfully organized into the following chapters: (1) "Orientations"; (2) "Source Manuscripts and Editions"; (3) "Beethoven and the Piano: His Options, Preferences, Pianism, and Playing"; (4) "Tempo: Rate and Flexibility"; (5) "Articulation: The Demarcation and Characterization of Beethoven's Musical Ideas"; (6) "The Incise and

Phrase as Guides to Rhythmic Grouping and Dynamic Direction"; (7) "Realizing Beethoven's Ornamentation"; (8) "Further Expressive Factors" (legato, pedaling, dynamics, and agogics); (9) "Some Broad, Structural Considerations"; and (10) "Keyboard Techniques as Both Clues and Consequences." Some of Newman's positions on long-debated issues, however well reasoned, have not gone unchallenged; for example, his view that Beethoven's trills for the most part begin on the main note in all phases of his career has been vigorously disputed by Robert S. Winter. A valuable additional source for performance issues explored in Newman can be found in Sandra P. Rosenblum's *Performance Practices in Classic Piano Music* (1988).

BARTH begins by establishing the background of the rhetorical tradition that Beethoven inherited from Johann Mattheson and Johann Philipp Kirnberger. In subsequent chapters he clarifies and refines the premises, contradictions, and points of reconciliation between Czerny and Schindler, even on the divisive issue of tempo modification. In contrast to Newman and others who place Beethoven's predilection for tempo modification exclusively in the composer's later years, Barth shows that the contrasting approaches of Czerny and Schindler were applied as early as op. 10 (1798). Most originally, Barth demonstrates that Czerny's modernizations were for the most part distortions of Beethoven's articulation, dynamic marks, and note values, which directly contradict Czerny's frequently invoked performance axiom that "the player may permit himself throughout no alteration of the composition, no addition, no abridgment." Despite the absence of systematization and the lack of the copious examples that prevail in Czerny, Drake, and Newman, Barth's small volume makes an indispensable contribution to the issues that frame our understanding of Beethoven performance.

KINDERMAN devotes approximately a third of his comprehensive survey of Beethoven's music to 22 of the piano sonatas (opp. 2/1–3, 10/1–3, 26, 28, 31/1–3, 53, 54, 57, 78, 81a, 90, 101, 106, and 109–11), the Diabelli Variations (an encapsulation of the author's important 1987 monograph devoted exclusively to this work), and the Bagatelles, op. 126. Although interspersed with discussion of works in other genres, the analytical commentary in this book represents an expansion of Kinderman's essay in *Nineteenth-Century Piano Music* (New York, 1990), edited by R. Larry Todd. The author argues that "Beethoven had already by the 1790s achieved a consummate mastery in the piano sonata" but reserves his highest praise for the accomplishments of the later works. Within his concise discussions, he isolates crucial local harmonic, rhythmic, or melodic details without losing sight of Beethoven's larger structural levels and meanings.

GEOFFREY BLOCK

5. Sketches

Brandenburg, Sieghard, editor, *Ludwig van Beethoven: Kesslersches Skizzenbuch,* 2 vols., Bonn: Beethoven-Haus, 1978

Cooper, Barry, *Beethoven and the Creative Process,* Oxford: Clarendon Press, and New York: Oxford University Press, 1990

Johnson, Douglas, *Beethoven's Early Sketches in the "Fischhof Miscellany:"Berlin Autograph 28,* 2 vols., Ann Arbor, Michigan: UMI Research Press, 1980

Johnson, Douglas, et al., editors, *The Beethoven Sketchbooks: History, Reconstruction, Inventory,* Berkeley: University of California Press, 1985

Kerman, Joseph, editor, *Ludwig van Beethoven: Autograph Miscellany from circa 1786 to 1799: British Museum Additional Mansucript 29801, ff. 39–162 (the "Kafka Sketchbook"),* 2 vols., London: British Museum, 1970

Kinderman, William, *Beethoven's Diabelli Variations,* Oxford: Clarendon Press, 1987

Kinderman, William, editor, *Beethoven's Compositional Process,* Lincoln: University of Nebraska Press, 1991

Kramer, Richard, editor, *Ludwig van Beethoven: A Sketchbook from the Summer of 1800,* 2 vols., Bonn: Beethoven-Haus, 1996

Lockwood, Lewis, *Beethoven: Studies in the Creative Process,* Cambridge, Massachusetts: Harvard University Press, 1992

Mies, Paul, *Beethoven's Sketches,* translated by Doris Mackinnon, London: Oxford University Press, 1929; reprint, New York: Dover, 1974

Nottebohm, Gustav, *Beethoveniana,* Leipzig: Reiter-Bidermann, 1872; reprint, 1970

————, *Ein Skizzenbuch von Beethoven,* Leipzig: Breitkopf und Härtel, 1865; English translation by Jonathan Katz in *Two Beethoven Sketchbooks,* London: Gollancz, 1979

————, *Ein Skizzenbuch von Beethoven aus dem Jahre 1803,* Leipzig: Breitkopf und Härtel, 1880; English translation by Jonathan Katz in *Two Beethoven Sketchbooks,* London: Gollancz, 1979

————, *Zweite Beethoveniana: Nachgelassene Aufsätze,* Leipzig: Reiter-Bidermann, 1887; reprint, 1970

Of all the major composers, none relied more on a process of painstaking revision than Beethoven. An astoundingly detailed record of Beethoven's creative process is preserved in about 8,000 pages of surviving musical sketches in various formats: more than 30 large-format sketchbooks; many loose pages and gatherings of leaves; and, from the later years of his life, a substantial number of sketches in score as well as many pocket sketchbooks that he carried with him on his outings. Beethoven's autograph scores also bear vivid witness to his creative struggles, as many of them are heavily revised. Where they are not, one often suspects that preliminary work took place in the form of sketches and drafts. The existing manuscript sources, though numerous, are by no means complete, and many more sketches and autographs must have been lost or discarded. The largest number of these sources is held at the Staatsbibliothek preussischer Kulturbesitz in Berlin, reunited since the fall of the Berlin Wall in 1989; other important collections are found at Bonn, Vienna, Paris, London, and Krakow, Poland.

There is mounting evidence that Beethoven's use of his sketchbooks was more flexible than is often assumed. Frequently these sources contain entries that predate their assembly as sketchbooks. Some sketchbooks seem to have come into existence as a housekeeping measure, with Beethoven gathering together many loose pages, some of which were already filled with work. The entries within the sketchbooks are not always made in chronological order, Beethoven sometimes dividing the books into distinct sections devoted to different projects. Especially during his later years he tended to employ multiple sketch formats simultaneously, with copious use of pocket sketch sources. Much research remains to be done, and many insights remain buried in this mainly unpublished material.

The distinguished 19th-century pioneer of Beethoven sketch studies was NOTTEBOHM, who surveyed most of the material available to him. Nottebohm published his work in many articles and two short monographs, offering revisions in the chronology of Beethoven's works and many glimpses into stages of their genesis. Nottebohm's work was pathbreaking but rarely definitive or exhaustive. For about a century, most scholars were content to rely unquestioningly on Nottebohm's findings and transcriptions. The interpretations of MIES, for instance, are based entirely on Nottebohm's work.

Not until the 1970s was a significantly more advanced position reached in the study of Beethoven's sketches. One landmark was the transcription and analysis, by KERMAN and JOHNSON (1980), of most of Beethoven's working papers used up to about 1799. The appearance of the edition of the "Kessler" sketchbook edited by BRANDENBURG signaled an advance in the program of the Bonn Beethovenhaus to issue complete sketchbooks in accurate transcription, but subsequent progress has been disappointing. During the entire decade of the 1980s no further editions were published by the Beethovenhaus.

One barrier to the study of Beethoven's sketchbooks has been the incomplete state of the sources. The need to "reconstruct" the sketchbooks, by conceptually restoring many surviving leaves that originally belonged in the books but that were removed by later collectors or by Beethoven himself, became widely recognized by the 1970s. In an important collaborative catalog published in 1985, JOHNSON et al. offered for the first time a proper overview of the inventory of sketchbooks and of the missing parts of these books that are preserved in various archives and private collections. Theirs was primarily a study of the condition rather than the content of the sketchbooks, and they did not consider the large number of loose sketch leaves never bound into books. Notwithstanding such limitations, their work brought the study of Beethoven's sketches to a new stage, offering a more solid context for interpretative studies of individual works.

A model study in the reconstruction of a specific source is KRAMER. This reconstructed sketchbook comprises a core of 20 leaves in the Berlin Manuscript 19e, to which no fewer than 14 leaves now held in ten different collections can be added. The reconstructed source offers insight into the genesis of works including the op. 18 string quartets, the Piano Sonata in B-flat major, op. 22, and the violin sonatas op. 23 and op. 24.

Since the 1980s, several attempts have been made to examine the content of Beethoven's sketches, with the aim of elucidating his working methods as well as aspects of his creative process. COOPER discusses some of Beethoven's characteristic working procedures, such as his long-term use of an ongoing portfolio of bagatelles for piano, some of which were rejected movements from larger forms such as sonatas, or his practice, in composing many works, of making a series of continuity drafts, which often gradually increase in length as progress is made toward the final, definitive version of the music. In general, Cooper's study focuses far more on the material basis for Beethoven's practices than on the specific artistic problems that confronted the composer.

Attempts to elucidate Beethoven's finished works through analysis of his sketches have been made by several scholars. A collection of several such studies, including a valuable assessment of the state of sketch research by Lewis Lockwood, is found in KINDERMAN (1991). In his study of the Diabelli variations, KINDERMAN (1987) demonstrates how Beethoven imposed a large-scale design on an earlier, pre-existing draft of the whole.

LOCKWOOD, in his studies of the "Eroica" Symphony, traces the manner in which Beethoven gradually developed the cyclic plan of the symphony, beginning with the finale, based as it was in turn on the model of the "Prometheus" Variations for piano, op. 35. Lockwood has pointed out various instances in which the sketching process did not in fact end when the autograph scores were begun, since Beethoven would often make extensive revisions at this point that required further use of the sketchbooks. The content of Beethoven's sketches is often only fully comprehensible in relation to other sources, such as rudimentary scores, drafts made on loose pages, or the autograph scores themselves.

WILLIAM KINDERMAN

6. Influence

Bouillon, Jean Paul, *Klimt: Beethoven: The Frieze for the Ninth Symphony,* translated by Michael Heron, New York: Skira/Rizzoli, 1987

Comini, Alessandra, *The Changing Image of Beethoven: A Study in Mythmaking*, New York: Rizzoli, 1987

Dennis, David B., *Beethoven in German Politics, 1870–1989*, New Haven, Connecticut: Yale University Press, 1996

Kropfinger, Klaus, *Wagner and Beethoven*, translated by Peter Palmer, Cambridge: Cambridge University Press, 1991

Marx, Adolf Bernhard, *Musical Form in the Age of Beethoven: Selected Writings on Theory and Method*, edited and translated by Scott Burnham, Cambridge: Cambridge University Press, 1997

Schrade, Leo, *Beethoven in France: The Growth of an Idea*, New Haven, Connecticut: Yale University Press, and London: Milford, 1942

Sipe, Thomas, "Interpreting Beethoven: History, Aesthetics, and Critical Reception," Ph. D. dissertation: University of Pennsylvania, 1992

Wallace, Robin, *Beethoven's Critics: Aesthetic Dilemmas and Resolutions during the Composer's Lifetime*, Cambridge: Cambridge University Press, 1986

Beethoven's influence, as pervasive as it has clearly been, has received only sporadic and unsystematic scholarly study. Two distinct types of influence can be seen: compositional (or musical) and ideological (or cultural). The two are not mutually exclusive, but they have rarely been treated together. Studies on compositional influence have been relatively scarce, partly because of its very conspicuousness. Beethoven unequivocally established the instrumental genres, and the symphony in particular, as the pinnacle of Western musical expression. Paradoxically, Wagner's wholehearted assimilation of Beethoven's heritage into his style of music drama ultimately weakened the vibrancy of pure instrumental genres based on classical forms despite the persistence of Brahms and his school. However, Wagner's exploitation of Beethoven's music was as much ideological as it was compositional. Beethoven's romantic spell over the 19th century—largely the product of literary-minded composers and critics, such as Berlioz and Schumann—was manipulated by Wagner into a propaganda campaign for his own artistic aims. The break with romanticism that was completed by the end of World War II recovered Beethoven as a classicist whose command of form assured him an influential position among both aestheticians concerned with spreading formalism as an artistic agenda and composers concerned with objectifying music from an increasingly sentimentalized audience. Throughout, Beethoven has been a veritable icon of compositional excellence and depth of musical expression.

Studies that deal with specific aspects of Beethoven's influence, musical or cultural, can be arranged chronologically, starting with Beethoven's contemporaries and ending with the present day. In addition, three studies in English (as well as several in German that have not been translated) have emerged that deal variously with what might more generally be called the history of Beethoven influence.

WALLACE treats Beethoven's reception in the critical press of the early 19th century. His work climaxes in a comparison of E.T.A. Hoffmann's enthusiastic paean to the Fifth Symphony with the writings of Berlioz and A.B. Marx on the same work. Thus, apart from his thorough treatment of much of the more mundane criticism produced during Beethoven's lifetime, Wallace is fundamentally concerned with Beethoven's influence on the romantic generation. He tries to reconcile the differing views of these critics with one another and with more recent trends in Beethoven interpretation (including theoretical Schenkerism and organicism). Historically, Wallace's study is valuable for bringing to light Beethoven's profound impact on music criticism; critics such as Hoffmann had to account for Beethoven's unusual musical procedures in terms that his contemporaries could readily understand, and to do so they invoked well-established principles of literary romanticism. However, Wallace's case that romantic and modern critics are basically in harmony over Beethoven's music is weak and highly problematic.

MARX presents both his fanciful interpretative criticism of Beethoven's music and selections from compositional textbooks that Marx largely based on the composer's works. The textbooks have been routinely criticized by critics and theorists—even up to the present—as stiff and dogmatic (and some of the excerpts from the textbooks translated here do indeed illustrate that problem). However, Marx's formal prescriptions cannot be separated from their somewhat Hegelian philosophical basis: the notion that form conveys spirit and that, although the former can be dryly codified, the latter is the province only of genius. This conviction becomes especially clear in his interpretation of the *Eroica*, translated in this collection. Thus, the two kinds of musical writing that Marx offers are meant to be complementary. Marx's approach, if not always his specific writings, conditions Beethoven's compositional influence over the more conservative romantics of the late 19th century (e.g., Brahms and Dvořák), who frequently imitated his formal procedures.

Wagner's progressive understanding of Beethoven is clearly conveyed by KROPFINGER. From his earliest, semi-autobiographical writings to his last compositions, Wagner adopted Beethoven as a spiritual predecessor. At times Wagner went even further, maintaining that he was the continuation of Beethoven's creative consciousness (by metempsychosis). The extent to which Wagner actually believed what he wrote is unclear; fiction and fact blended freely in Wagner's creativity. However, he managed to become so close to Beethoven's creative persona in his own mind—and the minds of his supporters—that some real conviction must have stood behind his claims. To Wagner, Beethoven's symphonies were akin to unfinished music dramas, lacking only the dramatic texts (thus the special significance of the Ninth Symphony). Kropfinger presents some purported instances of direct compositional influence, the most interesting of which involve Wagner's passion for Beethoven's late string quartets.

BOUILLON's study shows Beethoven's influence operating outside the sphere of music. Gustav Klimt's "Beethoven Frieze" was completed for the Fourteenth Viennese Secession on 15 April 1902. On the day of the opening, Gustav Mahler directed an arrangement for winds and brass of a passage from the finale of the Ninth Symphony. The frieze was derived from Wagner's program to the symphony (itself involving references to Goethe's *Faust*), but Klimt combined the program with a pervasive eroticism characteristic of the Secession movement's political and artistic agendas. Beethoven, the composer whose music overwhelms the senses and the emotions, became for the Secessionists the paradigmatic artist—hero, martyr, and redeemer of humankind. Bouillon writes, "Liberation and sublimation by art alone: that has become the primary meaning of the Ninth Symphony." This kind of psychologism is characteristic of the late romantics and expressionists.

DENNIS treats the political appropriation of Beethoven's music in Germany from the nation's formation as an independent state in 1870 to the fall of the Berlin Wall. As Dennis readily admits, his book is not about Beethoven's music. Rather, it is about his influence, as a man who has been made and remade by biographers and propagandists. Both the extreme right and the extreme left have tried to make Beethoven their own; neither, as Dennis points out, have confronted the reality of the composer's existence or work. Thankfully, Dennis refrains from a cynical conclusion that Beethoven can be anything that his critics desire. Rather, he is concerned to illustrate how genuinely symbolic Beethoven's life and work has been to the German national consciousness, however that consciousness has been defined politically.

None of the accounts of Beethoven's influence from a general historical perspective do justice to the immensity of the subject. SCHRADE shows that Beethoven's music eventually touched every significant aspect of French culture. In fact, by World War I, France could legitimately claim Beethoven as one of the nation's own. Schrade's book, finished in the middle of World War II has a very different intent than that of Dennis. Schrade intends to show that Beethoven's music succeeded in authentically transcending national consciousness. His language will strike the modern reader as obsolete, but it glows admirably with idealism.

COMINI's lengthy essay traces the history of what might be called the idea of Beethoven, even when it contradicts the facts. Thus the subtitle: *A Study in Mythmaking*. The book is amiably written, factually sound, and replete with pictures and plates, but it tends to wander into novelistic narrative. Comini does reveal a great deal of fascinating information about pictorial representations of Beethoven—art history is clearly her emphasis. Historically, Comini breaks off in 1902. She admits in the preface that the study grew to huge proportions (over 400 pages and well over 1,000 footnotes) as she was drawn deeper and deeper into the myriad of Beethoven's historical reception.

SIPE's dissertation forms a sharp contrast to Comini's book. Sipe addresses not Beethoven's image or reputation but his music as it has been understood by his critics. In contrast to Comini's eminent readability, Sipe's prose is sometimes dense and difficult and is consistently focused on organizing and categorizing the unwieldy amount of material relating to Beethoven reception. He identifies a historical succession of philosophical modes of critical reception. His aim is partly to enable scholars to investigate how criticism of Beethoven has conditioned the composer's historical influence on music and culture.

THOMAS SIPE

Bellini, Vincenzo 1801–1835

Italian composer

Lippmann, Friedrich, "Vincenzo Bellini," in *The New Grove Masters of Italian Opera,* London: Macmillan, and New York: Norton, 1983

Maguire, Simon, *Vincenzo Bellini and the Aesthetics of Early Nineteenth-Century Italian Opera,* New York: Garland, 1989

Orrey, Leslie, *Bellini,* London: Dent, and New York: Farrar, Straus and Giroux, 1969

Rosselli, John, *The Life of Bellini,* Cambridge: Cambridge University Press, 1996

Weinstock, Herbert, *Vincenzo Bellini: His Life and His Operas,* New York: Knopf, 1971

Compared to other early 19th-century Italian opera composers, Vincenzo Bellini was an anomaly. With his fair hair and delicate features, he did not resemble his colleagues, nor did he share their often harried approaches to composing. His appearance and attitude combined to add a distinct charisma to him in life; then, as witnessed by the numerous depictions of his "apotheosis," he was carried to the heights of artistic sainthood in death. Early commentaries about Bellini are more mythical tribute than real scholarship, and this inauspicious beginning has proved a challenge for those who later have tried to decipher the truth. Only recently have sources begun to present the composer as anything less than opera's ephemeral "Golden Boy."

The earliest notable biography of Vincenzo Bellini, *Vita di Vincenzo Bellini* (1859), written by Filippo Cicconetti, was published 25 years after the composer's death. Two others appeared in 1882: *Bellini: Memorie e lettere*, a volume of memoirs and personal correspondence collected and edited by Bellini's closest friend, Francesco Florimo (archivist/librarian at the Naples Conservatory, where both men had studied), and *Vincenzo Bellini: Note ameddotiche ecritiche*, a book of biographical anecdotes and musical criticism by Michele Scherillo. Although these works are of historical significance, they are rife with legend and falsities, especially Florimo's, in which Bellini's character and career are purposefully sterilized so as to erase many of his flaws. None of these three has been translated into English, yet their errors are perpetuated in biographies such as William A.C. Lloyd's, *Vincenzo Bellini: A Memoir* (1908), which at times is outright fiction. Although the centennial of Bellini's birth in 1935 occasioned a burst of scholarship, the majority of it—and of subsequent studies—is in Italian. Fresh perspectives on Bellini published recently in English can be found in musicological journals.

An elementary point of departure is ORREY's contribution to Bellini biographical studies. This slim volume, part of *The Master Musician Series*, gives an adequate account of the composer's youth in Sicily as well as his introduction to music studies and the theater in Naples. A chapter is devoted to Bellini and his affair with Giuditta Turina, an issue often omitted or glossed over in earlier versions of his life. Much of Orrey's information has been taken from the composer's letters (complete editions of which are available only in Italian); due to the limited scope of the work, however, the composer's complex character is only implied. A useful appendix contains an outline of major events in the composer's brief life. Those unfamiliar with Bellini's works should be aware that Orrey's discussion of them (lacking musical excerpts as support) often seems subjective. His stereotyping of the contemporary Italian theater world as a wasteland that Bellini then salvaged is unfair.

WEINSTOCK's detailed and well-documented volume is more substantial. It is in two parts, the first offering a chronological look at the composer's career and the second containing discussions of his music, including nonoperatic vocal pieces and sacred works as well as instrumental compositions. Weinstock presents a reasoned description of the world of 19th-century Italian opera, introducing Bellini's numerous colleagues and his often problematic relationships with them. Each of Bellini's operas merits its own section, complete with plot summary, information on premieres and original casts, autograph manuscripts and revisions, and commentary on the music (with examples from scores). A series of useful appendices includes information on such issues as variants of operas and accounts of the composer's final illness (including a translation of Bellini's autopsy report).

A new contribution to Bellini studies was provided recently by ROSSELLI, who explodes many of the myths that have survived over much of the 20th century. For example, he aptly demonstrates how Florimo posthumously molded Bellini's persona by editing, rewriting, and in some cases even inventing letters (many of which had been quoted in good faith in earlier research). Rosselli's forte is theater history; therefore, he not only provides an introduction to the composer's life but also paints a vivid picture of the milieu in which he and his colleagues worked. Unfortunately, his comments on the composer's music are not supported with examples from the scores. Also, although Rosselli offers a more realistic view of Bellini, he often fails to document the sources from which his facts are drawn; thus, while the book certainly could be read by students wishing an introduction to Bellini, it would be utilized more effectively by those with the skills to pursue the author's research.

LIPPMANN's analysis of Bellini's music (published in German) has long been considered a cornerstone study; a fair sampling of the author's work in English is available in his entry on Bellini. After a brief chapter on the composer's life, Lippmann presents an expert discussion of the origins of Bellini's style, his unique synthesis of melody and text, and his innovative developments to the traditional forms of contemporary Italian opera (supported by musical examples). Readers without a proficiency in music might select a more elementary discussion of Bellini's works. A thorough list of Bellini's compositions (operatic, sacred, vocal, and instrumental), with annotations on revisions, premieres, and manuscript sources, as well as an ample bibliography, conclude Lippmann's contribution to the volume.

For those seeking an advanced discussion of Bellini as bel canto composer, MAGUIRE presents a study of the aesthetics governing Italian opera just prior to and during Bellini's composition career. Deferring musical analysis to Lippmann, Maguire, supporting his argument with translated excerpts from contemporary treatises on music and poetry, first considers the artistic environment in which 19th-century opera thrived. Specific to Bellini are discussions of his *filosofia*, or his approach to setting librettos (with a useful explanation of Italian verse forms); his use of the orchestra for dramatic expression; and his construction of vocal lines (with musical examples).

DENISE GALLO

Berg, Alban 1885–1935

Austrian composer

1. Biography

Adorno, Theodor W., *Alban Berg: Master of the Smallest Link*, translated by Juliane Brand and Christopher Hailey, Cambridge: Cambridge University Press, 1991

Berg, Alban, *Alban Berg: Letters to His Wife*, edited and translated by Bernard Grun, New York: St. Martin's Press, 1971

——, *The Berg-Schoenberg Correspondence: Selected Letters*, edited by Juliane Brand, Christopher Hailey, and Donald Harris, New York: Norton, 1987

Carner, Mosco, *Alban Berg: The Man and the Work*, London: Duckworth, 1975; 2nd, revised edition, New York: Holmes and Meier, 1983

Jarman, Douglas, "'Man hat auch nur Fleisch und Blut': Towards a Berg Biography," in *Alban Berg: Historical and Analytical Perspectives*, edited by David Gable and Robert P. Morgan, Oxford: Clarendon Press, and New York: Oxford University Press, 1991

Jarman, Douglas, editor, *The Berg Companion*, Boston: Northeastern University Press, 1989

Monson, Karen, *Alban Berg*, Boston: Houghton Mifflin, 1979

Pople, Anthony, editor, *The Cambridge Companion to Berg*, Cambridge: Cambridge University Press, 1997

Redlich, Hans, *Alban Berg: The Man and His Music*, London: Calder, and New York: Abelard-Schuman, 1957

Reich, Willi, *Alban Berg*, translated by Cornelius Cardew, New York: Harcourt, Brace and World, 1965

No composer's posthumous biography has undergone so substantial a revision in the last 25 years as that of Alban Berg. Following the 1976 death of his widow, Helene, information about Berg's personal life has come to light that fundamentally affects the way scholars interpret his life and works. Despite these developments, no full-length, scholarly biography has been written in the intervening years about this extraordinary 20th-century composer. Perhaps because Berg's music itself richly rewards close study, more scholars have been compelled to examine it at the expense of attention to biographical details. Yet, especially in Berg's case, the most fruitful area of investigation often proves to be the intersection of work and biography.

The available Berg biographies fall into two categories: those by authors who knew the composer personally and those by scholars working from documentation left behind. Reich's, Redlich's, and Carner's biographies and Adorno fall into the first category. (German readers may also wish to consult Soma Morgenstern's *Alban Berg und seine Idole* and Eric Alban Berg's [the composer's nephew] *Der unverbesserliche Romantiker* and *Alban Berg: Leben und Werk*.) In the second category fall Monson's biography and articles in the "companion" volumes listed above. Collections of correspondence offer yet another category of biographical material. Fortunately for scholars, Berg was an avid correspondent, and valuable collections of letters to his wife and to his mentor, Arnold Schoenberg, are available in English translation. These personal documents complement the picture of Berg, the modernist composer, with scenes of his domestic life and intimate friendships.

Any Berg-related scholarship written before the death of his widow was closely vetted by her and omits mentioning one of Berg's most important relationships, that with Hannah Fuchs-Robettin. George Perle's scholarship on the *Lyric Suite* brought details of this relationship to light in 1977, in the *Newsletter of the International Alban Berg Society*, another source for up-to-date Berg research. As valuable as the early biographical sketches by Berg's students REICH and Adorno may be for their personal anecdotes, they do not serve as reliable or thorough accounts of Berg's life. REDLICH achieved a greater degree of distance from his subject, but his chapter on "The Life of Alban Berg" reaches fewer than 30 pages. CARNER's biography was substantially revised for the second edition, published in 1983, and provides a more thorough treatment of Berg's personal life than was possible when the composer's widow was still alive. Redlich's and Reich's books also include correspondence and essays by Berg, translated into English for the first time.

In his panegyric, ADORNO fondly recalls his teacher's personality. Despite its occasionally cloying tone, it offers a glimpse of Berg's life from an unparalleled perspective and gives a sense of Berg as a companion. Adorno recalls meals and concerts they shared, reveals details of Berg's reading habits, and recounts conversations with a variety of people. Comments such as "He liked giving me advice on how to adjust my typewriter, nor was he above discussing the question of shaving" offer the reader a flesh and blood feeling for the composer. These personal habits do not go unrelated to his music: "His patient attention to daily routine and his passionate attention to trivial activities became to no small degree a part of his music, the manic perfection of detail." Adorno's article, like Reich's biography, provides glimpses of Berg as a teacher, a valuable counterweight to his more famous role as a pupil.

JARMAN (1991) offers a useful point of departure for anyone surveying the landscape of Berg biography. He points out the deficiencies and omissions of most previous biographies and laments the false picture of Berg as the simple, happy husband that was propagated by his widow and close biographers, an image that contradicts what most of his music seems to express.

MONSON's biography, now 20 years old, is one of few attempts to integrate a discussion of Berg's life with a consideration of his work. She has written an accessible account, creating her narrative through interweaving passages of correspondence, biography, and musical assessment. Her work is geared toward a general audience and includes no critical apparatus. As devotedly as she recounts Berg's life and personality, she often has mistaken ideas about Berg's colleagues, especially Schoenberg, whom she makes out to be a stern modernist in every way. She writes, for example, "[In 1897] the overripe sonorities of Mahler and Strauss, issuing from oversized orchestras, seemed to Schoenberg every bit as dangerous as did Viennese society's compulsive reliance on layers of dusty *Kitsch*." In fact, all the composers of the Second Viennese School, with Schoenberg in the lead, had great regard for Mahler's works, and Schoenberg himself was yet to write *Gurrelieder*, a work requiring forces just as "oversized" as Mahler's "Symphony of a Thousand." Despite its breezy tone and questionable conclusions, Monson's biography stands as the only full-length, post-Helene biography to date.

Scholars have BERG (1987) to thank for the largest volume of Berg correspondence published in English, that between him and his teacher, Arnold Schoenberg. The fluidity and elegance of the editors' translation belies the fastidious attention devoted to every aspect of the correspondence. Although the collection is made up of selected letters, not a complete edition, extensive footnotes bridge any gaps in the chronology of events. Theirs is the most recent and most reliable translation of correspondence.

BERG (1971) is a collection of letters from Berg to his wife that has been translated and edited from the original German edition compiled by Helene in 1965. Although this volume, too, was carefully supervised by Helene, it improves on the original by including explanatory footnotes, a chronology of events, and maps of Vienna and Austria marked with Berg-related sites. The correspondence between Berg and Webern, as well as between Berg and other members of the Schoenberg circle, has yet to be published in German or English. These letters will be an essential complement to the existing published correspondence.

Several recent collections of essays have included articles pertinent to Berg's biography: JARMAN (1989) offers "Berg's Vienna" by Martin Esslin, "Between Instinct and Reflection: Berg and the Viennese Dichotomy" by Christopher Hailey, and "Berg's Character Remembered" by Joan Allen Smith. Smith conducted extensive interviews with many members of the Schoenberg circle and their students for her book *Schoenberg and His Circle: A Viennese Portrait* (1986), another book relevant to Berg's life as a student and member of the Schoenberg coterie. POPLE also includes an article by Hailey, "Defining Home: Berg's Life on the Periphery," as well as an article by Andrew Barker, "Battles of the Mind: Berg and the Cultural Politics of 'Vienna 1900,'" both of which describe the physical and intellectual atmosphere of the city in which Berg spent the majority of his life and which constituted an essential part of his personality and his music. Until a full-length critical biography appears (and none are on the horizon at the moment), these sources must serve as piecemeal contributions to our understanding and appreciation of this enigmatic figure, a leading composer of the 20th century.

CAMILLE CRITTENDEN

2. Operas

Berg, Alban, *Wozzeck,* London: Calder, and New York: Riverrun Press, 1990

Carner, Mosco, *Alban Berg: The Man and the Work,* London: Duckworth, 1975; 2nd, revised edition, New York: Holmes and Meier, 1983

Hall, Patricia, *A View of Berg's "Lulu" through the Autograph Sources,* Berkeley: University of California Press, 1996

Jarman, Douglas, *Alban Berg: Lulu,* Cambridge: Cambridge University Press, 1991

———, *Alban Berg: Wozzeck,* Cambridge: Cambridge University Press, 1989

Perle, George, *The Operas of Alban Berg,* 2 vols., Berkeley: University of California Press, 1980–85

Redlich, Hans, *Alban Berg: The Man and His Music,* London: Calder, and New York: Abelard-Schuman, 1957

Reich, Willi, *Alban Berg,* translated by Cornelius Cardew, New York: Harcourt, Brace and World, 1965

Schmalfeldt, Janet, *Berg's Wozzeck: Harmonic Language and Dramatic Design,* New Haven, Connecticut: Yale University Press, 1983

The immense literature that now exists on Berg's first opera, *Wozzeck,* began to amass even before the work received its 1925 premiere and well before Berg was generally acknowledged as a major composer. In several early articles written by Berg and others from his circle, the principal critical issues for future discussions of the opera were defined. The primary topic for debate would not be the work's modernistic features—its atonality, dissonance, new treatment of the voice, or the nihilism of its text—but instead its musical form. Berg stressed his use of compositional principles associated with instrumental music, which he said were necessary to give coherence to the author Georg Büchner's dramatic fragments. The result was, in Berg's view, an opera in which traditional musical designs far outweigh any revolutionary ideas about operatic form or expression.

Berg's appraisal of *Wozzeck* has persisted in both technical and general studies of the work even to the present day. It underlies JARMAN (1989), which is a good first choice for the nonspecialist reader. The author concisely analyzes the text, places the work in the context of Berg's larger compositional development, and explains aspects of its musical form and means of expression. Jarman also adds an informative survey of the work's performance history and critical reception. Nearly half of the book is devoted to a compilation of previously published documents, which are deftly chosen and include several articles available for the first time in English. Among these the reader should go first to Berg's own 1929 "Lecture on 'Wozzeck'," in which the composer persuasively argues that the opera is a work based on traditional musical forms.

BERG suffers in comparison with Jarman's guide. The volume is a hodgepodge of pictures and short articles by different authors, some new and others reprinted. Although not offering the depth of coverage found in Jarman, the short articles by Mark DeVoto, Kenneth Segar, and Theo Hirsbrunner are informative. The book also includes the complete text of the opera, both in German and in the 1952 English translation by Eric Blackall and Vida Harford.

Shorter discussions of *Wozzeck* geared to the nonspecialist can be found in all of the major studies of the composer's life and works. The earliest of these in English is by REDLICH, who analyzes *Wozzeck* in considerable detail. His book was followed by REICH's study. Reich, a student of Berg from 1927 until the composer's death in 1935, wished to advance the knowledge of his teacher's oeuvre in accordance with Berg's own conceptions, and he accounts for *Wozzeck* by way of an adaptation of Berg's own *Wozzeck* lecture. CARNER is less doctrinaire, using the author's considerable experience as a conductor, journalist, and musicologist to give a leisurely and personalized overview of both *Wozzeck* and *Lulu*, whose imaginative content concerns him more than the musical structure.

Among the studies of *Wozzeck* written for the specialist, PERLE has a preeminence that comes from the author's long involvement with Berg's music and the wide influence of Perle's ideas concerning its musical structure. The scope of this two-volume work goes beyond a mere description of two operas to embrace Berg's complete oeuvre and examine the composer's entire musical language. In volume 1, on *Wozzeck*, Perle deals in detail with Büchner's literary fragments and the overall design accorded them in Berg's opera. The central chapter, "The Musical Language of *Wozzeck*," elaborates upon a previously published article by Perle from 1967, in which the music of the work is explained as a conflation of many devices and techniques—pitch centers, pitch-class sets, interval cells, scalar manipulations, and symmetrical collections of tones, among others. These, Perle concludes, mirror the multiplicity of styles on the musical surface. The reader is presented not with a guide to the opera so much as a technical encyclopedia of Berg's atonal musical language, of which *Wozzeck* is the principal embodiment.

SCHMALFELDT, also for the specialist reader, presents *Wozzeck* as the outcome of a more unified musical thinking, which the author seeks to explain by using Allen Forte's theory of structure in atonal music. Schmalfeldt analyzes the pitch formations associated with the characters Wozzeck and Marie, identifying two families of interrelated pitch-class sets that characterize and distinguish the music of both figures. Her book begins with a lucid explanation of Forte's theory and its analytic relevance to Berg's opera.

Studies of *Lulu* are far less numerous than those of *Wozzeck*, and they have typically addressed different issues despite the many parallels that exist between the two works. The literature on Berg's second opera was stunted until 1978 by the unavailability of music for the third act; only a few books prior to this time (including those by Reich and Redlich) contain detailed information about the music in toto. Because Berg left no clearly formulated guidelines for interpreting or analyzing his second opera, as he had done for his first, the technical literature on *Lulu* has grown in a more fragmented form and has proven more susceptible to differing analytic viewpoints and conclusions than the literature on *Wozzeck*.

The volume on *Lulu* by Perle summarizes and extends the author's numerous earlier studies of the work. In *Lulu* Perle finds the same number-opera structure as in *Wozzeck*, and he again explains Berg's musical language as a great mixture of devices and techniques—some carried over from the atonal style of *Wozzeck*, others reflecting an idiosyncratic approach to 12-tone composition that owes relatively little to the ideas of Schoenberg. In this conclusion, Perle's account of *Lulu* differs sharply from that of Reich and probably even from Berg's own opinion that the underlying musical conception of the work is congruent with that of Schoenbergian serialism.

Berg's viewpoint is documented by HALL, who closely studies Berg's compositional manuscripts for *Lulu* and uses their contents to support an analysis intended to reveal the composer's own thinking about the work's dramatic symbolism and the 12-tone method of composition. She concludes that *Lulu* represents a systematic 12-tone work but in a sense that was unique to Berg.

JARMAN (1991) follows the same pattern as the author's earlier study of *Wozzeck*. Both books are intended for the general reader, although the author's discussion of musical language in *Lulu* may well be found impenetrable by those unfamiliar with Perle's ideas and terminology. Jarman's selection of source readings is much less apposite than those in the earlier volume. The most valuable document is an address concerning Wedekind's *Pandora's Box*, given by Karl Kraus in 1905 and well known to Berg, who was influenced by Kraus's ideas when he created the dramatic conception in *Lulu*.

BRYAN R. SIMMS

3. Other Works

Adorno, Theodor W., *Alban Berg: Master of the Smallest Link*, translated by Juliane Brand and Christopher Hailey, Cambridge: Cambridge University Press, 1991

DeVoto, Mark, "Alban Berg's Picture-Postcard Songs," Ph.D. dissertation: Princeton University, 1967

Gable, David, and Robert Morgan, editors, *Alban Berg: Historical and Analytical Perspectives*, Oxford: Clarendon Press, 1990; New York: Oxford University Press, 1991

Headlam, David John, *The Music of Alban Berg*, New Haven, Connecticut: Yale University Press, 1996

Jarman, Douglas, *The Music of Alban Berg,* London: Faber, and Berkeley: University of California Press, 1979

Jarman, Douglas, editor, *The Berg Companion,* Boston: Northeastern University Press, 1989

Perle, George, "Berg's Master Array of Interval Cycles," *Musical Quarterly* 63 (1977): 1–30

————, *Style and Idea in the Lyric Suite,* Stuyvesant, New York: Pendragon Press, 1995

Pople, Anthony, *Berg: Violin Concerto,* Cambridge: Cambridge University Press, 1991

Pople, Anthony, editor, *The Cambridge Companion to Berg,* Cambridge: Cambridge University Press, 1997

Rauchhaupt, Ursula von, compiler, *Schoenberg, Berg, Webern: The String Quartets; A Documentary Study,* translated by Eugene Hartzell, Munich: Ellermann, and Hamburg: Deutsche Grammophon Gesellschaft, 1971

Redlich, Hans, *Alban Berg: The Man and His Music,* London: Calder, and New York: Abelard-Schuman, 1957

Reich, Willi, *Alban Berg,* translated by Cornelius Cardew, New York: Harcourt, Brace, 1965

Simms, Bryan R., *Alban Berg: A Guide to Research,* New York: Garland, 1996

Berg's small number of works is deceptive, for his expressive language within each piece encompasses entire worlds of emotion and structure. The interaction of these two elements—emotion embodied in romantic gestures, tonal references, and symbolic programs that recall the 19th century, and structure found in complex, layered forms, a pervasive musical language based on motivic transformation, cycles, and, later, serial manipulations, and systematic uses of rhythm, tempo, and orchestration that foreshadow later developments in the 20th century—underlies most discussions of Berg's music.

Scholarly research into Berg's nonoperatic music falls into three eras. The first is characterized by writings by Berg himself and writers who knew him personally and who frequently cite his authority, among them Adorno and Reich. The second era commences with Redlich and features the establishment of a distinct analytical method for Berg's music in Perle (1977) and a study of Berg's complete oeuvre in Jarman. This era also sees the uncovering of autobiographical programs in Berg works by Perle, Douglass Green ("Berg's De Profundis: The Finale of the *Lyric Suite,*" *International Alban Berg Society Newsletter* 5 [1977]), Jarman, and others, as well as the detailing of sketch materials and other sources. The third era begins a vastly increased period of research, including Headlam's analyses of all of Berg's works and the collections by Jarman (1989), Gable and Morgan, and Pople (1997) reflecting the varied interests and contributions of many authors. Finally, a guide to Berg research may be found in SIMMS.

Berg's own writings form a significant and continuing source of inspiration and knowledge for scholarship on his music. Translations of many of the composer's writings on musical language and formal matters in *Wozzeck,* which contain clues to his preceding works (including the *Chamber Concerto* and *Lyric Suite*), are found in Redlich, Reich, and Rauchhaupt. These sources clearly demonstrate the composer's concern for complexity and elegance in form, an abiding fascination with the tonal tendencies of his materials, and a systematic thoroughness with regard to rhythm, tempo, and orchestration. REDLICH is valuable for its comparison of Berg's works with gestures and forms from the late 19th century, particularly in the music of Mahler. Redlich's discussion of motives and 12-tone procedures forms a basis, along with Berg's own writings, for much of the literature that follows. REICH, who was a pupil of Berg, presents notes that supplement Berg's own writings. RAUCHHAUPT uses Berg's writings as the basis for an incisive discussion of his quartets.

A companion volume from another Berg pupil is ADORNO. This excellent translation makes the author's subtle discussions accessible to English audiences. Woven throughout Adorno's considerations of Berg's works is the philosopher's concept of *kleinsten Übergangs,* translated as the smallest links. These links are part of a seemingly contradictory dialect in Berg's music between continual variation and dissolution of motivic linking materials, on the one hand, and highly structured forms, on the other. This paradox may be understood by modifying Adorno's dialect to assert that it is Berg's careful control over the *rate* of change in the variation of linking materials that allows for the creation of formal function. Thus, the clarity in formal structure of the String Quartet, op. 3 (sonata and variation form) and the continual motivic dissolution and formal ambiguity of the *Clarinet Pieces,* op. 5 may be accommodated within the work of the one composer.

It is only with the writings of Perle, which use a theory of symmetry and interval cycles, that analysis of Berg's music achieves the level found in studies of music by Schoenberg and Webern. In a seminal article, PERLE (1977) lays out the premises of his analytical method, supported by a letter from Berg to Schoenberg in which Berg writes out a complete set of interval cycles and adds comments on invariance as well as tonal implications. PERLE (1995) uses the compositional history of *Lyric Suite*—from sketches and drafts through the published score—as the basis for an analysis of the musical language and formal design of the piece. The author uses the annotations in the presentation copy that Berg gave to Hanna Fuchs-Robettin, as well as the text and context of the secret vocal part for the finale, to elucidate the secret program of the work. Readers interested in Perle's views may also wish to consult his two-volume study *The Operas of Alban Berg* (1980–85).

HEADLAM builds on Perle's theory and demonstrates how Berg's use of symmetry may be traced through the composer's complete output. The author argues that the change from tonal to atonal and 12-tone languages may be seen as surface-level style changes occurring over the foundation of symmetry. Headlam also applies some aspects of pitch-class set theory and 12-tone theory in his analyses of Berg's music.

A motivic approach is found in Jarman (1979) and DeVoto. DeVOTO's study of the hitherto virtually unknown *Altenberg Lieder* is a landmark in Berg studies and demonstrates the elaborate web of motives and motivic transformations found in these songs. JARMAN (1979) similarly discusses Berg's atonal and 12-tone works in the context of motivic and thematic transformation and adds chapters on rhythm and form that demonstrate for the first time Berg's systematic approach to these elements in the nonoperatic works. As Berg eschews recognizable motives and themes in only a few pieces (songs, op. 2, no. 4 and op. 4, no. 4, the *Clarinet Pieces*, op. 5, and the *Orchestra Piece*, op. 6, no. 3), a motivic approach is useful for analysis of his music. Jarman carries the approach into the realm of rhythm, demonstrating motivic transformations unique to rhythm, and even into form, where tempo and orchestration are themselves treated motivically.

The increased attention paid to Berg's music by scholars is manifest in the three collections of writings: Jarman (1989), Gable and Morgan, and Pople (1997). Aside from one article by Perle in the Jarman anthology, however, none of the articles in these collections follows Perle's approach. POPLE (1997), as in POPLE (1991), adds a few details in relation to the nonoperatic works but largely consists of summaries of work found in other writings on Berg's music.

JARMAN (1989) includes motivic-based studies by DeVoto, who revisits the *Altenberg Lieder*; Steven Kett, in a discussion of the op. 2 songs, with valuable background comments; Bruce Archibald, in a survey of Berg's instrumental works that includes some mention of symmetry; and Michael Taylor, who focuses on the intriguing form in the *Orchestra Piece*, op. 6, no. 1, where the piece slowly arises from the depths, develops briefly, then returns to the amorphous percussion noises of its beginning. In two landmark articles that follow, the revelation of the secret autobiographical program in the *Lyric Suite* uncovered by Perle and Green is continued by Brenda Dalen and Jarman, who present evidence for similar programs in the *Chamber Concerto* and the *Violin Concerto*. That Berg infused his systematic compositional style with great emotion has always been a hallmark of writings on the composer's music, and the unveiling of the symbolic associations of notes, rhythms, tempi, and forms adds to the emotional depth of these works.

GABLE and MORGAN's volume stems from papers given at a conference in Chicago in 1985 and includes an extremely interesting discussion of Berg's popularity, wherein Peter Burkholder explores Berg's masterful reworking of tonal forms, gestures, and harmonies in

his works and considers how these reminiscences gain meaning for audiences. Robert Morgan discusses the psychological and musical effects stemming from the symmetrical nature of many of Berg's forms, particularly those in the second movement of the *Chamber Concerto*, the third movement of the *Lyric Suite*, and the second song of *Der Wein*, in which the music goes forward to a point then reverses itself. Echoing an earlier study of Schoenberg's music, Janet Schmalfeldt details Berg's path to atonality in his Piano Sonata, op. 1, which begins tonally but continues motivically. She posits pitch-class set connections among these motives as the organizational force for extended passages. Schmalfeldt's combination of Schenkerian voice-leading graphs, Schoenbergian *Grundgestalt* motivic variation methods, and pitch-class set theory, along with other authors' uses of 12-tone theory and Perle's theory of symmetry and interval cycles, exemplifies the plurality of approaches to the analysis of Berg's music.

DAVE HEADLAM

Berio, Luciano b. 1925

Italian composer

Berio, Luciano, *Two Interviews, with Rossana Dalmonte and Bálint András Varga,* edited and translated by David Osmond-Smith, London: Boyers, 1985

Osmond-Smith, David, *Berio,* Oxford: Oxford University Press, 1991

———, *Playing on Words: A Guide to Luciano Berio's Sinfonia,* London: Royal Musical Association, 1985

Luciano Berio has built a reputation for reconciling innovation and convention. Even so, here is music that speaks strongest to an educated audience, for whom the composer's idiosyncratic style is not one more example of modernist extremes but is a product of historical imperative. According to David Osmond-Smith, who has accomplished more than anyone in furthering our understanding of Berio, it is Berio's approach to gesture that singles him out from the rest of the avant-garde. Berio's handling of gesture is not abstract in the way that a Webernian gesture is abstract (i.e., pure) but is rendered concrete in its dialogue with history, an intertextuality in which connectedness also takes the form of destructiveness. Thus, Berio's use of tradition involves not only a reference to a gesture's past but also a search for its future. As Osmond-Smith argues, Berio has succeeded at tempering the radically new with a love for the past, thus transforming the past (including his own past) into something new.

To explore the depth and range of Berio's artistic theory and aesthetics, one should turn to BERIO, a beautifully presented book of interviews translated by Osmond-Smith. Two sets of interviews are contained here. The first of these, the Dalmonte interviews, was originally produced for an Italian series in which an expert provided insight into a given field—in this case, Berio on music. A wide-ranging intellect, a literary musician, and an arch-modernist ("music is everything that one listens to with the intention of listening to music"), the composer worked the transcripts into a polished exposition of his thought, and this thought roams among philosophers (from Marx to Adorno to Bergson) and composers (from Beethoven to Schoenberg to Puccini) and musical forms (from serial to electronic to jazz). In the fifth part of this interview—Berio's workshop, as Dalmonte dubs it—the reader finds an essay on the composer's all-encompassing project of extending the parameters of the musical object. By contrast, the Varga interview is more conversational than the Dalmonte; however, in it one encounters details regarding Berio's collaborations with his friends Umberto Eco and Edoardo Sanguinetti—details explored in connection with the composer's lifelong love of literature.

One rarely finds a Berio compact disc for which the liner notes have not been written by Osmond-Smith, and, indeed, all three books in this listing are the handiwork of this one scholar. Although OSMOND-SMITH (1991) can cover Berio's output only to 1989, it is still the single most important work on Berio in English. For the general reader, it is a sophisticated book of analysis but will repay anyone willing to tackle it. In Osmond-Smith's narrative, Berio's vocal style is central to the study of both the music and its impact on other music. The analyses begin with two works, *Chamber Music* (1953) and the electronic *Thema (Omaggio a Joyce)*, and culminate with *Circles* (1960). This is then extended to *Sinfonia* (1968) and its two siblings, the vocal megaworks *Opera* (1970) and *Coro* (1976). (This is probably the only source for studying *Opera,* which is neither published nor recorded.) Of the book's extended analyses, perhaps the most brilliant are those that tackle what Osmond-Smith calls Berio's commentary technique (chapter 4). Here we find some of the finest prose analyses of 20th-century music available in English. Any student interested in the potential for language to communicate the form and meaning of avant-garde music should read these, especially the analysis of *Sequenza VI* for viola (1967) and two of the "self-commentaries," the *Chemin II* for viola and nine instruments (1967) and the *Chemin III* for viola, nine instruments, and orchestra (1968). Osmond-Smith's study traces several threads in Berio's career, but one of these stands out: the issue of compositional rigor. In discussing the roots of Berio's art in postwar dodecaphony, Osmond-Smith notes that Berio's precompositional plans are so fluid, and their implementation is so general (e.g., a gradual shift in nuance, be it harmonic or

timbral), that the word *plan* loses its very meaning—and yet there is no escaping the idea of plan in Berio. Thus, Berio's career unfolds the paradox of an iconoclast among iconoclasts, producing an avant-garde radicalism that denies the hegemony of the new.

The choice to focus on specific technical markers in Berio's development rather than to analyze in detail one work after another enables Osmond-Smith to use brief excerpts and examples throughout *Berio*. This frees the reader from the need for access to scores. However, this is definitely not the case with OSMOND-SMITH (1985), a monograph on *Sinfonia,* and it is difficult to imagine a reader following this stunning analysis without score in hand. Still, much can be gleaned from this book, for in it Berio's modernist aesthetic receives its most exhaustive exegesis. Osmond-Smith sheds light on the elaborate musical and literary complex that Berio pursued in this work, unpacking its many layered meanings between literary texts and musical texture and revealing the multiple techniques bound up in the composer's unique conception of musical time-space. Although possessing the score is to the reader's advantage, it is not essential for grasping the book's riches: reading with the score yields a thorough analysis of this seminal work; perusing it without the score will offer insight into how Berio produced an audacious masterpiece.

GORDON MARSH

Berlin, Irving [Israel Balin] 1888–1989

Russian-born composer

Barrett, Mary Ellin, *Irving Berlin: A Daughter's Memoir,* New York: Simon and Schuster, 1994

Bergreen, Laurence, *As Thousands Cheer: The Life of Irving Berlin,* New York: Viking Press, and London: Hodder and Stoughton, 1990

Berlin, Irving, *Early Songs,* edited by Charles Hamm, Madison, Wisconsin: A-R Editions, 1994

Freedland, Michael, *Irving Berlin,* London: Allen, and New York: Stein and Day, 1974

Furia, Philip, *Irving Berlin: A Life in Song,* New York: Schirmer Books, 1998

Hamm, Charles, *Irving Berlin: Songs from the Melting Pot: The Formative Years: 1907–1914,* New York: Oxford University Press, 1997

Hyland, William, *The Song Is Ended: Songwriters and American Music, 1900–1950,* New York: Oxford University Press, 1995

Whitcomb, Ian, *Irving Berlin and Ragtime America,* London: Century, 1987

Woollcott, Alexander, *The Story of Irving Berlin,* New York and London: Putnam, 1925; reprint, New York: Da Capo Press, 1983

As one of—if not the most—successful composers of American popular songs in the 20th century, Irving Berlin (born Israel Balin in Russia) occupies a central place in the musical history of his adopted land. The paucity of serious studies of Berlin's life and music is therefore more a reflection of U.S. musicology's long-standing disinterest in commercial forms than any judgement on the merits of Berlin's musical legacy. With over 1,500 songs to his credit—among them such widely popular tunes as "Alexander's Ragtime Band," "God Bless America," and "White Christmas"—and a reputation as a shrewd businessman, Berlin's career and output stand as a record of 20th-century American popular taste that begs for serious examination by qualified scholars. In some ways, Berlin himself contributed to this scholarly neglect by refusing to cooperate with most writers, but the real problem is that the field has been overrun by journalists and popular biographers, who have stressed such lesser matters as Berlin's inability to read music, his use of a transposing piano, his financial affairs, and his irascible personality while neglecting the songs that made Berlin's reputation and fortune. Only one capable scholar has dealt in any meaningful way with Berlin's music, and even Berlin's biography awaits a definitive scholarly study.

BERGREEN's biography, the first major study completed since Berlin's death, stands above similar publications, if only by default. Although by far the longest book available on Berlin, its contents are neither comprehensive nor entirely objective, and anyone who uses this book must do so with care. Writing with an eye toward the mass market and not as a scholar, Bergreen concentrates on Berlin as a public figure and popular celebrity. The author has sifted through a large mass of source material to add more details to the story of this life than has any previous writer. Unfortunately, Bergreen seems to have been personally offended by Berlin's refusal to cooperate in the preparation of this book, and thus he portrays Berlin in an unflattering light whenever possible. Paraphrased statements and secondhand quotations are presented as Berlin's own words; conversations have been invented; and any exculpatory evidence that might have created a more honest picture of Berlin is frequently ignored. Bergreen's lack of musical knowledge is everywhere evident in his commentary on Berlin's songs, which in any case forms only a modest portion of this book.

In contrast to Bergreen's biased effort, Berlin's daughter, BARRETT, sketches a remarkably honest portrait of her father. Tracing Berlin's life from 1924—the time of his first meeting with the woman who would soon become his second wife and Barrett's mother—until his death, Barrett admits to her father's difficult and often reclusive nature, especially in his final years. Writing from inside the family circle, Barrett reveals much about the private life and character of Berlin as well as details about his social and professional contacts. Information on Berlin's music is less abundant, although Barrett does supply a few facts on the genesis of several songs.

Theater critic WOOLLCOTT's biography of Berlin's first 36 years (up to 1924) offers a useful complement to Barrett's memoir. As a close personal friend of the songwriter and a member of the same New York literary and social circles, Woollcott's access to Berlin and the milieu in which he worked makes this biography of the composer (the first such publication) an important primary source. Many of the fundamental facts of Berlin's early life—including the story of his forebears, his work as a singing waiter in the immigrant culture of New York's Lower East Side, and his unschooled manner of song composition—are revealed by Woollcott for the first time. The general accuracy of these facts confirms the value of this book.

FREEDLAND, a writer who specializes in biographies of popular entertainers, covers Berlin's career to age 85 as well as anyone else writing for a general audience. The facts of his life are presented in an easily read chronology, but the lack of notes or even a basic bibliography demonstrates the book's limitations for serious readers.

HYLAND, a career diplomat and an amateur musician working chiefly from secondary sources, has written a credible history of American popular song in the first half of the 20th century. Only five chapters (or portions thereof) are devoted directly to Berlin's songs, but Hyland covers the familiar ground capably, while the remainder of the book provides background on Berlin's peers.

WHITCOMB limits his book to Berlin's music in the ragtime era, ending in about 1919. The author's prose reads more like a novel than a serious study, however, and the story of Berlin in particular is often neglected for pages at a time while Whitcomb explores some other element of the ragtime era.

In the most recent study to appear, FURIA concentrates ably on Berlin's work as a lyricist but says very little about the music. He does include some new material gleaned from newspapers and other contemporary sources, as well as some items from the Berlin family scrapbooks.

The works of Hamm stand apart from almost every other book on this topic, for his writings are the only genuinely scholarly studies of Berlin's music. In HAMM, the author deals only with Berlin's songs from the pre-World War I era, but his approach should be a model for the study of Berlin's later output. Organizing the songs by types, Hamm explores not only Berlin's tunes, but also the world that spawned them, which in turn reinforces the author's commentary on the music. The chapter on "Alexander's Ragtime Band" is impressive for its level of detail and serves as a reminder of how little others have delved into the circumstances and music of specific songs. BERLIN (which Hamm edited) is primarily a scholarly edition of the more than 190 songs discussed in the study by Hamm, but its 40-page preface tells more about the production of Berlin's songs as Tin Pan Alley wares than has any other publication to date.

SCOTT WARFIELD

Berlioz, Hector 1803–1869

French composer

1. Biography

Barzun, Jacques, *Berlioz and the Romantic Century,* 2 vols., Boston: Little, Brown, 1950; 3rd edition, New York: Columbia University Press, 1969; revised and abridged as *Berlioz and His Century: An Introduction to the Age of Romanticism,* Chicago: University of Chicago Press, 1982

Bloom, Peter, *The Life of Berlioz,* Cambridge: Cambridge University Press, 1998

Cairns, David, *Berlioz 1803–1832: The Making of an Artist,* London: Deutsch, 1989

Holoman, D. Kern, *Berlioz,* Cambridge, Massachusetts: Harvard University Press, 1989

Macdonald, Hugh, *Berlioz,* London: Dent, 1982

Raby, Peter, *Fair Ophelia: A Life of Harriet Smithson Berlioz,* Cambridge: Cambridge University Press, 1982

Hector Berlioz was born in 1803—one year before First Consul Napoléon Bonaparte had himself crowned as emperor—in the postrevolutionary period that saw the construction of a highly centralized administration whose ramifications were to mark French history for the next two centuries. Berlioz lived through the turmoil of the restoration of the Bourbon monarchy, the revolution of 1830 that established the "July Monarchy" of Louis-Philippe, and the revolution of 1848 that led, after the short-lived Second Republic, to the Second Empire of Napoléon I's nephew, Louis-Napoléon, who took the throne as Napoléon III. Berlioz died on 8 March 1869, 16 months before the outbreak of the Franco-Prussian War.

Accounts of Berlioz's life appeared before his death (by Eugène de Mirecourt, for example, in 1856), but the most important source of information comes from his own posthumously published *Mémoires* (1870), which has several times been translated into English, most convincingly by David Cairns (London: Cardinal, 1990). Early studies in French by Edmond Hippeau (1883), Adolphe Jullien (1888), Julien Tiersot (1904), and J.-G. Prod'homme (1905) were largely superseded by Adolphe Boschot's three-volume life-and-works of 1906. Impressive as a compendium of information but irritating in its curious admixture of criticism and praise, Boschot's book long remained authoritative in France.

BARZUN, the first edition of whose book appeared in 1950, when Berlioz's music was little available on recordings and widely reputed to be bombastic and excessively "literary" or autobiographical, set out to show the breadth of the composer's musical and intellectual gifts in the context of the French 19th century. Battling the curious belittling of the composer by Boschot (as well as the errors and misconceptions that tainted his and others' writings on the composer), Barzun completed two volumes of brilliantly lucid prose that treat matters of musical architectural and broad cultural history in such a way as firmly to establish Berlioz as the major composer of the era.

MACDONALD, writing to the specifications of the Master Musicians Series, provides a succinct treatment of the life and, separately, a concise appreciation of the work (with a calendar, personalia, and work list as back matter). This is a study by one who, as general editor of the New Berlioz Edition, knows the music intimately and who comments on it uninhibitedly. Macdonald's assertion that Berlioz's music can seem "strange" to one brought up on the German classics causes consternation for some who admire everything from the master's pen and for others who find eminently logical relationships just beneath the surface. Of particular interest is the chapter on "Berlioz's character," where, with a cool head that can boil the blood of those who still have Berlioz as a "cause," the author suggests that Berlioz's passions reflected both artistic principle and personal defiance in ways that we may applaud but that were not always welcomed at the time by listeners, readers, and those in power in the world of the arts.

HOLOMAN treats the life and the music in a single narrative whose pauses for musical analysis (designed for the reader with advanced training) show the hand of the practical conductor, the hat worn by the author when he is not practicing musicology. Holoman's notion that Berlioz often took to playing the role of the artist is readily supported both by the composer's prose writings and by his habit of injecting into his music facets of his private self. This book is the logical complement of the author's authoritative *Catalogue of the Works of Hector Berlioz* (1987). In the biography we find an especially useful list of all the major performances of Berlioz's works and concerts at which Berlioz conducted—in itself a demonstration of a central and sometimes underplayed aspect of his career.

CAIRNS gives us a lovingly detailed portrait of the composer's first three decades, profiting (as does Holoman) from the nearly completed edition of the composer's correspondence and from a wealth of further documentation gathered over many years, here gracefully translated and given in generous measure. Cairns's chronicle of Berlioz's youth is as accurate and detailed as any we are ever likely to have; his discussions of Berlioz's encounters with the women who illuminated the morning and early afternoon of his life—Estelle Duboeuf, Harriet Smithson, Camille Moke—are more penetrating than all that have gone before. The composer comes across as a highly complex individual whose difficult relationships with his parents, among other things, caused him to behave with what one might view as excessive passion, but always—in the view of this thoughtfully admiring biographer—with integrity. The book takes us only through December 1832; at this writing (1998) the volume that will take us to 1869 is forthcoming.

BLOOM contributes a succinct account of the biography (with brief musical commentary woven in) that emphasizes Berlioz's interactions with the political forces of the day: not only the revolutions of 1830 and 1848 that affected his work and career, but the individuals in places high and low—the rulers and the bureaucrats—whose decisions worked at times to his advantage, as when certain government commissions were to be had, and at times to his disadvantage, as when certain administrative and teaching posts were available at the Opéra and Conservatoire.

With particular emphasis on the little-known period of her apprenticeship, RABY brings to life Harriet Smithson—the gifted woman who for a brief, shining moment became a symbol of Shakespeare in France and thus a touchstone of the French romantic movement. And he brings to life the vulnerable woman who subsequently became the wife and companion of the fiery French composer for what was a short period of intense joy followed by long years of increasing unhappiness.

PETER BLOOM

2. Works

Barzun, Jacques, *Berlioz and the Romantic Century,* 2 vols., Boston: Little, Brown, 1950; 3rd edition, New York: Columbia University Press, 1969; revised and abridged as *Berlioz and His Century: An Introduction to the Age of Romanticism,* Chicago: University of Chicago Press, 1982

Cairns, David, *Berlioz 1803–1832: The Making of an Artist,* London: Deutsch, 1989

————, *Berlioz, 1832–1869,* London: Abacus, 1995

————, "Hector Berlioz (1803–69)," in *The Symphony,* edited by Robert Simpson, 2 vols., Baltimore, Maryland: Penguin Books, 1967

Holoman, D. Kern, *Berlioz,* Cambridge, Massachusetts: Harvard University Press, 1989

Holoman, D. Kern, editor, *The Nineteenth-Century Symphony,* New York: Schirmer Books, and London: Prentice Hall, 1997

Macdonald, Hugh, *Berlioz,* London: Dent, 1982

————, *Berlioz Orchestral Music,* London: British Broadcasting Corporation, and Seattle: University of Washington Press, 1969

Noske, Frits, *French Song from Berlioz to Duparc,* 2nd revised edition, translated Rita Benton, New York: Dover, and London: Constable, 1970

Primmer, Brian, *The Berlioz Style,* London: Oxford University Press, 1973

Rushton, Julian, *The Musical Language of Berlioz,* Cambridge: Cambridge University Press, 1983

There is no single book devoted exclusively to the works of Berlioz. A close approximation of such a book, however, *The Cambridge Companion to Berlioz,* edited by Peter Bloom, is soon to be released (projected date of publication, 1999). This book will present an overview of Berlioz's works in a collection of chapters divided by topic (usually genres). Intended for educated music lovers, it does not presuppose a high degree of theoretical knowledge. Each essay is written by a different scholar in the field and therefore offers the benefit of diverse points of view on the composer's works.

Aside from this single volume, discussions of Berlioz's works can be found only in books of a more general nature or in volumes that are more specialized and narrowly focused. These books fall into three broad categories. The first comprises general biographies (all, to some extent, life-and-works volumes), the second consists of books, or chapters in books, devoted to a limited segment of Berlioz's oeuvre (usually a single genre such as the symphonies), and the last is made up of books devoted to the analysis of the style of Berlioz's music in general.

In the first category are three major English biographies. The oldest, and in many ways the most individual, is BARZUN's 1950 biography. This book reflects the author's years of work as a cultural historian and is justly famous for its emphasis on the composer in relation to his cultural context. Barzun's discussion and analysis of major compositions is likewise infused with this cultural/historical bias. The book is therefore an excellent choice for those with no technical knowledge of music theory who want a more general, yet highly perceptive, analysis of Berlioz's music.

Two other excellent biographies of Berlioz are both newer works. HOLOMAN (1989) is excellent in its discussion and analysis of nearly every important work Berlioz ever wrote. Holoman is not only a musicologist but also a conductor; his treatment of Berlioz's works is therefore informed by his practical experience as a performer. Discussions are more technical than those found in Barzun, but not dauntingly so.

CAIRNS (1989, 1995) is devoted to Berlioz's life and works. This is a biography of lavish detail, but in terms of the music itself, the detail is spent almost exclusively on historical discussion. There are no musical examples in the book, and the treatment of each work is not theoretical.

One other biography, MACDONALD (1982), is also useful as a source of information on Berlioz's works.

The book is divided into two large sections: one devoted to Berlioz's life, the other to his works. This is a convenient arrangement for anyone interested only in information about the music itself. Macdonald's discussion effectively combines historical context with musical analysis and is divided into chronological periods. All major works and many lesser known works are covered here.

Another source of information on the music of Berlioz can be found in books that deal with the broad history of one genre, devoting a section to the contribution of Berlioz, or those books that limit their coverage to Berlioz's work within one or two genres only. The former category is represented by two large surveys of the symphony that offer collections of essays by various authors. The more recent of these includes a fine essay by HOLOMAN (1997), also the volume's editor, on the symphonies of Berlioz. Holoman considers the significance of programs in Berlioz's music, the composer's use of the orchestra, and the relationship of his symphonies to the mainstream tradition. This essay includes many musical examples but is not overly technical. CAIRNS's (1967) essay is also useful. It points to the importance of extended melody and "developing variation" in Berlioz's symphonies and argues that these works have a purely musical logic apart from any specific programmatic associations.

Also worthy of consideration among those books devoted to the study of a single genre is NOSKE's survey of French song. It traces the evolution of Berlioz's work in this genre from the early strophic *romance* to the more complex *mélodie*.

Among the specialized studies focused on a narrow segment of Berlioz's works, MACDONALD's (1969) short book on the orchestral music (part of the BBC Music Guides series) is especially good for the general reader and student. Its style and approach is similar to that found in his biography but is limited to instrumental genres such as overtures and symphonies.

Lastly, two important books approach the discussion of Berlioz's works through an analysis of different aspects of his compositional style. PRIMMER and RUSHTON are both excellent books, but they can be frustrating as sources of information on the works of Berlioz because the arrangement of the book is by theoretical topics such as "melody," "harmonic style," "formal structure," etc. The discussion of any particular work may therefore be divided among several different chapters. In addition, these books require a much greater knowledge of music theory than any of those mentioned previously. This technical detail can represent a valuable expansion of information one can gather elsewhere, but it may also become overwhelming for some readers.

JEFFREY LANGFORD

Bernstein, Leonard 1918–1990

United States composer and conductor

Burton, Humphrey, *Leonard Bernstein,* London: Faber, and New York: Doubleday, 1994

Burton, William Westbrook, editor, *Conversations about Bernstein,* New York: Oxford University Press, 1995

Chapin, Schuyler, *Leonard Bernstein: Notes from a Friend,* New York: Walker, 1992

Gradenwitz, Peter, *Leonard Bernstein: The Infinite Variety of a Musician,* Leamington Spa: Berg, and New York: St. Martin's Press, 1987

Myers, Paul, *Leonard Bernstein,* London: Phaidon Press, 1998

Peyser, Joan, *Bernstein: A Biography,* New York: Beech Tree, and London: Bantam, 1987; revised edition, New York: Billboard, 1998

Secrest, Meryle, *Leonard Bernstein: A Life,* New York: Knopf, 1994; London: Bloomsbury, 1995

Venezia, Mike, *Leonard Bernstein,* New York: Children's Press, 1998

One of the most versatile musicians of the 20th century, Leonard Bernstein won renown as a conductor, composer, and educator. He was the first American to conduct at La Scala and the first major conductor to achieve an international reputation despite being schooled entirely in the United States. He was largely responsible for bringing the music of Gustav Mahler to its current prominence, chiefly through his pioneering first complete recorded cycle of Mahler's symphonies.

Bernstein made his conducting debut with the New York Philharmonic in 1943. After musical studies under Fritz Reiner, Dmitri Mitropoulos, and Serge Koussevitzky, he was appointed music director of the New York City Symphony in 1945, succeeding Leopold Stokowski. Named joint principal conductor of the New York Philharmonic in 1957, he became its music director the following year, a position he retained until 1969, when he became its laureate conductor. Other major conducting engagements included the U.S. premiere of Benjamin Britten's *Peter Grimes* (in 1946) and numerous appearances with the Vienna Philharmonic (from 1966), the Metropolitan Opera, and the Vienna State Opera. Bernstein composed in a variety of genres, including symphonies, a ballet, an opera, Broadway musicals, and film music. As an educator, he is remembered for his Young People's Concerts with the New York Philharmonic, as well as his Charles Eliot Norton Lectures, given at Harvard University in 1973. Especially toward the end of his life, his flamboyant lifestyle, his embrace of controversial political causes, apparent egotism, and attention-getting behavior on the podium, including a propensity for extreme tempos, began to affect adversely his reputation in some circles. He was also sometimes criticized for his inability to choose between conducting and composing, or between the composition of classical and Broadway works.

PEYSER covers Bernstein's life and career through the Deutsche Grammophon recording of *West Side Story* in 1985. (The revised and updated edition adds a chapter on Bernstein's death and contains numerous tributes from colleagues.) The biography emphasizes Bernstein's personal side: his self-destructive behavior born of physical and emotional pain, his interpersonal relationships, and his flamboyant, charismatic public persona. It stresses the behavioral ramifications of his Jewishness and his homosexuality on his life and art. Much of the book deals with his love affairs, marriage, children, and treatment of colleagues and contemporaries, such as Aaron Copland and Dmitri Mitropoulos. The author dwells on the bacchanalian side of Bernstein's personality and the contrast between the adulation he received from the public and the private demons that Peyser feels pursued him throughout his life. The picture the author paints is that of a tortured genius, prone to being opportunistic, a showman as much as an artist. The book veers in the direction of tabloid journalism, setting Bernstein's life and career in the context of the music business in which he worked, and it contains numerous factual errors and other evidence of inadequate research.

GRADENWITZ offers a more objective, and far more scholarly, study of Bernstein's life and work, rejecting the psychological approach and taking the point of view that the anomalies of Bernstein's private life had no bearing on his importance as a conductor and composer. The book attempts to redress the damage done to Bernstein's reputation by the media's portrayal of him as a popular-culture hero rather than a serious musician. Gradenwitz pursues a scholarly course through Bernstein's achievements, finding that a close study of the musician's interpretations and writings reveal his breadth and depth. Bernstein's compositions are studied in detail, and the author spends a substantial portion of the book on a careful exploration of Bernstein's skill at interpreting the works of the symphonic and operatic repertoire. Appendices include a chronology of Bernstein's life, discography, filmography, and bibliography of works by and about Bernstein.

Several biographies were published after Bernstein's death in 1990. CHAPIN's book is a personal memoir, a fond, informal reminiscence by a close friend and colleague of more than 30 years. It relies on anecdotes to create a picture of Bernstein as a person rather than an icon and downplays the controversial facets of his life.

SECREST's psychological study serves in part to restore balance after Peyser's highly slanted approach, without slighting the contradictions of Bernstein's personality or their probable causes. Intended as an objective study, and largely dependent on lengthy quotations and reminiscences of Bernstein's colleagues, this volume portrays the seemingly conflicting sides of Bernstein's personality and career, contrasting, for example, the sacred *Kaddish* symphony with the profane Broadway *Mass*, the proponent of radical chic with the erudite scholar of the Norton lectures, the artist with the shrewd businessman. Beginning with a detailed study of Bernstein's Jewish roots, which instilled in him both a deep-seated religious faith and a strong social conscience, the monograph traces his youthful left-wing political activities, his close, if conflicted, personal relationships, and his musical training, suggesting how these influences contributed to the development of his complex nature. Secrest describes Bernstein's chameleon-like ability to reshape himself according to people's expectations, his use of his breadth and flexibility to ingratiate himself to fellow musicians and audiences, and his tendency to embroider (or selectively forget) incidents from his past in order to cultivate his image. Bernstein's close identification with Mahler—and the many similarities in their lives—is examined in the discussion of Bernstein's championing of Mahler's music, beginning with a performance of the latter's *Resurrection* symphony in 1948. A nontechnical study, more about the man than the music, the book includes extensive bibliographic notes, but no separate bibliography, discography, or other scholarly apparatus.

The most comprehensive of the Bernstein biographies is Humphrey BURTON. Culled from an exhaustive collection of newspaper articles and performance reviews, interviews, program notes, scripts of television appearances, letters, and the journals of Bernstein's family, the book provides, in an accessible style, a balanced view of the personal and professional sides of Bernstein, slighting neither his achievements nor the paradoxes of his character. Unlike Peyser, Burton reveals his admiration for Bernstein, allowing the facts to speak for themselves. Beginning with a look at Bernstein's Russian roots, the book traces his childhood in Massachusetts, the influence of his religious training on his life, his early musical education, his sexual orientation, his initial success as a conductor, his concentration on composing during the 1950s, his conducting activities through the late 1960s, his growing reputation as an educator, the controversies that arose out of his political activism and his increasingly flamboyant style, and the debilitating illness of his final years. It offers a detailed account of the conflicting demands of his compositional and conducting sides, as well as an encyclopedic study of the myriad factors—religion, politics, psychology, and interpersonal relationships—that influenced his achievements. The book includes a chronology of major events in Bernstein's life, copious notes, and an index.

William Westbrook BURTON consists of transcriptions of interviews with musicians in various fields, including opera singers Jerry Hadley, Christa Ludwig, and Frederica Von Stade; cellist and conductor Mstislav Rostropovich; music critic Harold Schonberg, conductors John Mauceri and Justin Brown (both Bernstein protégés); composers David Diamond and Lukas Foss; director Jonathan Miller; *West Side Story* original cast member

Carol Lawrence; record producer Paul Myers; and members of the New York, Vienna, and Israel Philharmonics; as well as Joan Peyser. Their reminiscences have a scholarly bent, although they are not technical. The author asks each of the participants the same questions, and the answers are generally well considered, often insightful, and sometimes moving. Among the topics covered are the compositions for which Bernstein will be best remembered, his conducting technique, and his sources of inspiration and motivation. The interviews combine to form a rounded portrait, more a tribute than a critical exposé.

VENEZIA's biography is a brief, nontechnical introduction aimed at young children, stressing Bernstein's early musical training and the televised Young People's Concerts and concentrating on the compositions rather than his conducting activities. Flashily produced and heavily illustrated with photographs, cartoons, and paintings, it tries, as do the other books in the series, to present classical music in a way that will attract the interest of the very young.

MYERS, a short, accessible biography written in highly readable style, is a good starting point for those interested in learning more about one of the major figures of 20th-century music and performing arts. Admiring without being adulatory, the book covers all sides of Bernstein's compositional legacy, although Myers sees Bernstein as a serious composer who only secondarily wrote lighter works, a man who pursued a lifelong quest to create a composition that would place him in the ranks of the great composers. Myers sets Bernstein's work in the context of the music world of his time, along with sufficient background information about his personal life to complete the picture.

MICHAEL SIMS

Bingen, Hildegard von

see Hildegard von Bingen

Bizet, Georges 1838–1875

French composer

Bizet, Georges, *Carmen,* London: Calder, and New York: Riverrun Press, 1982

Cooper, Martin, *Georges Bizet,* London: Oxford University Press, 1938; reprint, Westport, Connecticut: Greenwood Press, 1971

Curtiss, Mina, *Bizet and His World,* New York: Knopf, 1958; and London: Secker and Warburg, 1959

Dean, Winton, *Bizet,* London: Dent, 1948; 3rd edition, 1975

Lacombe, Herve, *Les Voies de l'opera français au XIXe siecle,* Paris: Fayard, 1997

McClary, Susan, *Georges Bizet, Carmen,* Cambridge: Cambridge University Press, 1992

Parker, Douglas Charles, *Georges Bizet, His Life and Works,* New York: Harper, and London: Paul, Trench, Trubner, 1926

Spies, Andre Michael, *Opera, State and Society in the Third Republic, 1875–1914,* New York: Lang, 1998

Georges Bizet was only 36 when he died in June 1875, exactly three months after the troubled premiere of *Carmen.* The press criticized the opera's mixture of musical styles, but the true controversy focused more on whether the subject—with its depiction of the all-too-believable interaction of working class characters and criminal outcasts with the forces of social order, not to mention Celestine Galli-Marie's sultry portrayal of the sexually liberated title character—was appropriate for the stage of the staid Opera-Comique. Outside Paris, *Carmen* quickly established itself as a favorite, and in the 1880s, its enormous success throughout the world helped resuscitate Bizet's other works. Although various anniversaries of Bizet's birth and death have brought forth publications, exhibitions, and concerts, only a few book-length studies in English exclusively examine this composer. Nonetheless, because Bizet was once perceived as a one-masterwork author (or maybe two, if one counts *L'Arelsienne*), library collections contain many guides and analyses of *Carmen,* as well as opera histories with a chapter focusing on this work.

PARKER, Bizet's first scholarly biographer in English and a friend of the composer's widow, does not credit Bizet with profundity, writing that "He had no residence above the snowline of sublime thought." Parker shows firm control of the principal publications that appeared during the first 50 years after the composer's death. Almost half the book, however, is concerned with the genesis and reception of *Carmen,* and Parker's fascination with this work precludes an in-depth discussion of any other pieces.

On the centennial of Bizet's birth in 1938, his second English biographer, COOPER, also maintains a certain disdain for his subject: "His gifts, even when fully developed, were unspectacular, for they were typically French and, for that very reason, easy to under-estimate." Cooper uses his narrative to prove that *Carmen* did not materialize from a void. One of the first scholars to mention Bizet's youthful masterpiece, Symphony in C (published in 1935), Cooper focuses mainly on tracing the evolution of Bizet's style in the stage works during the decade after *Les Pecheurs de perles* (1863).

CURTISS sets new standards for Bizet biography, and hers is one of the finest examples of musical biography of its time. Previous writers had depended largely on published letters and a small selection of memoirs by Bizet's contemporaries, but by acquiring the Bizet-Halevy family documents, Curtiss had access to hundreds of unpublished (or partially published) letters sent by Bizet to his family and letters addressed to him by family, collaborators, and other contemporaries. After eight years of research in private collections, archives, memoirs, and the press, the author answers many questions and tells Bizet's story in fascinating detail, drawing heavily on his own words and the comments of his contemporaries.

In her preface Curtiss gratefully acknowledges the work of DEAN, the other major Bizet scholar of the mid-20th century. Dean is the first to analyze seriously Bizet's entire oeuvre; he examines the manuscripts, compares editions of the printed scores, and traces Bizet's self-borrowings. The author's rigorous biographical accuracy and profound understanding of the music's stylistic development make his volume valuable still, although methods of operatic analysis have since changed under the influence of literary criticism and cultural studies. Dean's later editions incorporate references to Curtiss's biographical insights, Michel Poupet's discoveries in the Parisian archives, and Dean's own commentary on the flawed Oeser edition of *Carmen* in mid-1960s. He also adds information about Bizet's manuscripts and compositional process first brought to light in Lesley Wright's doctoral dissertation, "Bizet before *Carmen*" (1981).

LACOMBE has completed an important study of the contexts for French opera in the Second Empire. By focusing on Bizet's *Les pecheurs de perles,* he reveals the stylistic mobility of French opera at that time, explains the nature of German and Italian influences, and discusss topics as diverse as the elements of operatic production and orientalism. Informed by extensive reading in the musical press and familiarity with scores long forgotten, he provides a particularly rich historical context that is valuable for researchers and general readers alike.

Since the premiere of *Carmen,* opera appreciation guides and scholarly studies have turned to the score of the opera repeatedly. Both Cooper (1947) and Dean (1949) wrote accessible, high-quality introductions to the work, a niche now filled by BIZET. This guidebook features valuable brief essays on the genre of opera comique, the music, and the immediate cultural context as well as the full text of the libretto and a good English translation.

The largest recent study of *Carmen,* by feminist scholar McCLARY, has rejected a traditional interpretation that sees Carmen (the prototypical femme fatale) and Don Jose (her male victim) as colliding in a predestined, tragic fate. McClary challenges readers to examine with her the French attitudes toward orientalism and prostitution; reinterpret the music of *Carmen* as "playing along important faultlines of racial, class and gendered Otherness"; compare the opera's reception before and after its canonization; and interpret its recent film versions. This important book of thought-provoking originality has stimulated much discussion, but McClary seems to have depended largely on the works of Dean and Curtiss for data on the *Carmen* reception in 1875,

and she has picked up the old idea that Bizet is a one-work composer whose other pieces are only performed due to their authorial affiliation with *Carmen.*

SPIES has investigated an impressive body of archival material and periodical literature in his broad study of French politics and culture and their relationship to the social function of late-19th-century French opera. He uses the reception of *Carmen* as a starting point both for his analysis of the complex relationship of opera production and administration and for his discussion of the dynamics of public opinion management, a process that was cannily guided by the press and the Tout-Paris of the premieres. Because he bases his comments on an even more extensive list of sources than Curtiss, Spies adds new sophistication to an understanding of the initial reception and provides a needed historical counterbalance to McClary's conjectural, if intriguing, interpretation of the same subject.

LESLEY A. WRIGHT

Blues

Baker, Houston, *Blues, Ideology, and Afro-American Literature: A Vernacular Theory,* Chicago: University of Chicago Press, 1984

Davis, Angela Yvonne, *Blues Legacies and Black Feminism: Gertrude "Ma" Rainey, Bessie Smith, and Billie Holiday,* New York: Pantheon, 1998

Evans, David, *Big Road Blues: Tradition and Creativity in the Folk Blues,* Berkeley: University of California Press, 1982

Handy, W.C., *Father of the Blues: An Autobiography,* edited by Arna Wendell Bontemps, New York: Macmillan, 1941; reprint, New York: Da Capo Press, 1991

Jones, LeRoi, *Blues People: Negro Music in White America,* New York: Morrow, 1963

Keil, Charles, *Urban Blues,* Chicago: University of Chicago Press, 1966

Lieb, Sandra R., *Mother of the Blues: A Study of Ma Rainey,* Amherst: University of Massachusetts Press, 1981

Lomax, Alan, *The Land Where the Blues Began,* New York: Pantheon Book, and London: Methuen, 1993

Oliver, Paul, *Blues Fell This Morning: The Meaning of the Blues,* London: Cassell, and New York: Horizon Press, 1960; 2nd edition, Cambridge: Cambridge University Press, 1990

———, *The Story of the Blues,* Philadelphia: Chilton Books, and London: Barrie and Rockliff, 1969; 2nd edition, Boston: Northeastern University Press, 1998

Titon, Jeff Todd, *Early Downhome Blues: A Musical and Cultural Analysis,* Urbana: University of Illinois Press, 1977; 2nd edition, Chapel Hill: University of North Carolina Press, 1994

The blues is a musical genre that emerged from African-American improvisatory, secular song traditions of the rural southern United States. It retains such basic characteristics of African-American style as call-and-response improvisation, preaching, and bent, or blue, notes. Thus, the blues is an expression deeply rooted in African-American culture and is perhaps one of the most significant artistic expressions to emerge in the 20th century. The blues derives from multiple foreign sources, including Africa and Europe; the term *blue* was used in England to refer to a state of melancholy as early as the 17th century. Despite its presumed foreign roots, no African, European, or other diasporic music closely resembles the blues; since the turn of the 20th century, the blues has contributed significantly to many other forms of American popular musics.

BAKER provides an outline for the blues, suggesting that it is a historically expressive force among African-Americans that has prompted and documented many important elements of African-American cultural discourse. Although other forms of expressive culture now supersede the music of the blues as an aesthetic marker for many black communities, Baker argues that the blues, along with preaching styles and perhaps jazz, remains one of the most influential aspects of contemporary African-American expressive culture.

DAVIS locates the roots of a specific form of African-American feminism in the music, specifically within the lyrics, of three great early singers: Gertrude "Ma" Rainey, Bessie Smith, and Billie Holiday. In a series of essays, Davis traces the roles these women (among others) played in redefining gender politics through their recordings and performances, and by projecting a new identity for immigrant southern black populations in the North. In the song texts and performances of Rainey, Smith, and Holiday, Davis situates the "inchoate presence" of later social movements and the consequent transformation of gender, race, and class relations. Nearly half of the book is dedicated to documenting the song lyrics of these three performers. The song transcriptions are precise, and the meticulous attempt to document sentiment faithfully represents a monument to the sung traditions of these female singers.

EVANS traces creativity in black southern blues singing traditions by focusing on early methods used in the transmission of blues, including commercial recording efforts. The study is grounded in the field research experiences of the author, a performer/student in the tradition himself, and centers on his experiences in the local tradition of Drew, Mississippi, which is located in a region of the country that has been the subject of thorough documentation efforts. Evans outlines life histories of blues performers and devotes a significant portion of the book to the historical and contemporary compositional techniques of blues songs.

According to his autobiography, HANDY first heard the blues performed by rural black Mississippians in the first years of the 20th century; initially, he found the songs outside his own musical tradition. To Handy, the Mississippi blues traditions were strangely dissonant and monotonous, yet he quickly recognized the commercial possibilities for marketing the blues both as compositions and as recordings. He published his composition "Memphis Blues" in 1912, and his "St. Louis Blues," published in 1914, solidified his career as a composer and publisher and established his popular title, "Father of the Blues." Handy's blues style is often referred to as "classic" or "city" blues.

JONES attempts to locate the blues within a historical continuum that bridges the experiences of African-American slavery and contemporary culture. According to Jones, music often created links between African cultures and the foreign experiences of North America, and within these links—such as work songs—a series of cultural translations necessarily occurred. Although spirituals, work songs, and other earlier black musical genres also demonstrate features such as call-and-response interaction, a strong rhythmic drive, blue notes, and intense expressivity, the blues for Jones is nevertheless a distinct musical form and genre. Jones's study of that genre from city, classic, and country blues through rhythm and blues provides details for understanding the blues as a historical and ongoing phenomenon.

In his study of urban blues performance, KEIL contrasts the presumed lack of culture among urban African-Americans with actual examples of expressive culture, such as blues performance. Keil reclaims Africanisms in blues performance as specific West African retentions that have survived and even thrived on adversity. Urbanization began to affect the blues in the 1930s, as the electric guitar was becoming increasingly popular, and blues performers either adopted the instrument or rejected it. The blues performances of Muddy Waters, rooted in the Mississippi Delta, demonstrate the shift from rural roots to urban popular styles. Waters's later performances included electric guitar as well as other amplified accompanying instruments. In response to urbanization, very different styles were developed by T-Bone Walker and B.B. King, among others. Keil's study concludes with an annotated schematic outline of blues performance styles.

LIEB is an important biography of the first major American female blues singer, Gertrude "Ma" Rainey (1886–1939), an early singer of the so-called city or classic blues tradition. As early as 1902 Rainey was referred to as the "Mother of the Blues." As Lieb outlines, Rainey was the first professional female blues performer, and in her surviving recordings she remains the "strongest single link between folk blues and black show business."

LOMAX is a personal reflection on recording projects that began in the 1930s in the Delta region of the southern United States. Lomax argues that the blues functions as a response, albeit a satirical one, to what must surely be African retentions, "a creative deployment of African style in an American setting, the operation of African temperament in new surroundings." Lomax's ethnography of the blues begins in 1942 with a visit to Memphis's Beale Street; he ends his account in Arkansas in 1959, documenting his observations of change that occurred during the "Century of the Blues." He provides details of his relationships with such Delta blues singers as Big Bill Broonzy, Son House, Blind Lemon Jefferson, Robert Johnson, and Memphis Slim, among others, and explores the dominant themes of their blues lyrics, such as homelessness, social injustice, sexual conflict, and poverty.

OLIVER (1969) locates the blues within a sociohistorical context. One of the most intriguing aspects of this study is the inclusion of almost 200 historical photographs and illustrations that beautifully document early blues musicians and their performances. OLIVER (1960) is perhaps one of the best-known historical sources for chronicling the blues, specifically the recorded blues traditions.

Vocal blues were primarily recorded by female singers until the mid-1920s. As black audiences began to be targeted by recording labels, however, a different blues known as "downhome" emerged, according to TITON. Southern downhome blues contrasted with vaudeville blues in form, performance, and accompaniment; the form of the downhome blues was more irregular, the singing was often more shouted, and the accompaniment was usually just a guitar. An additional contrast was that downhome blues was a male-dominated singing tradition. Titon contends that, although many early downhome blues performances can be (and have been) interpreted as merely entertainment, they can also be understood as social rituals that "purg[ed] sadness from singer and audience alike." Prominent performers of early downhome blues included Charley Patton and Blind Lemon Jefferson.

GREGORY F. BARZ

Boccherini, Luigi 1743–1805

Italian composer

Gérard, Yves, *Thematic, Bibliographical, and Critical Catalogue of the Works of Boccherini,* translated by Andreas Mayor, London: Oxford University Press, 1969

Ophee, Matanya, *Luigi Boccherini's Guitar Quintets: New Evidence,* Boston: Orphée, 1981

Rothschild, Germaine Halphen, baronne de, *Luigi Boccherini: His Life and Work,* translated by Andreas Mayor, London: Oxford University Press, 1965

Luigi Boccherini enjoyed considerable popularity in his day both as composer and as virtuoso cellist, and recent decades have witnessed a resurgence of interest in his works. The earliest major stride in Boccherini scholarship was *Notice sur la vie et les ouvrages de Luigi Boccherini*

by Louis Picquot. The foundation for many subsequent studies of the composer, this book contains a transcription of the data included in the composer's autograph thematic catalog, a document of essential importance to Boccherini studies that was destroyed during the Spanish Civil War in 1936. The growth of popularity of Boccherini's music is due both to its distinctive and ingratiating character and to the considerable scholarly strides achieved by the authors of the present studies.

ROTHSCHILD is the only book-length biography of Boccherini in English. Originally published in French in 1962, it represents an attempt to draw together all available biographical material concerning the composer. The author cooperated with Yves Gérard, compiler of the thematic catalog discussed below, to create a complementary pair of books designed to clarify certain previously nebulous aspects of Boccherini's life and works. The biography is an admirable achievement for its time and remains an essential starting point for the music lover and performer of the composer's works. For the scholar, the book is unfortunately lacking in sufficient documentation; at times it makes statements that clearly call for a footnote, yet it does not provide the necessary citation. The text contains little discussion of the music, its style, and the circumstances of its composition. The book does, however, clarify some of the more problematic aspects of the composer's life. For instance, Rothschild concludes that Boccherini and Joseph Haydn never met or corresponded, despite a documented interest on the part of both men in contacting the other. The author also believes that Boccherini never visited Berlin or Potsdam during his period of employment by Friedrich Wilhelm II, long a point of controversy in Boccherini studies; recent scholarship has corroborated this view. The book includes useful supplementary material that complements the biography. The principal portraits of Boccherini are reproduced in black and white plates, and translations of the surviving letters of Boccherini are provided. The letters, dated in the period 1796–99, are directed to music publishers with whom the composer negotiated, particularly Ignaz Pleyel, a composer and pupil of Haydn who worked as a music publisher in Paris in this period. The letters reveal the kindly and manipulable Boccherini striving not to be cheated by the, at times, unscrupulous dealings of the publishers.

GÉRARD's thematic catalog, like Rothschild's biography, was originally published in French and then translated into English. The catalog makes it clear that the works of Boccherini that appear in the composer's autograph thematic catalog—to which he assigned opus numbers (1–64) and dates (1760–1804)—are by no means all the compositions that may securely be attributed to the composer. Apparently, Boccherini included only those works he intended for publication, excluding others without comment. These latter compositions include his sonatas and concertos for the cello, written as vehicles for his own performance, as well as the popular guitar quintets. Gérard's catalog organizes both these classes of works by performance medium (music for instrumental ensembles of increasing size, followed by vocal music), assigning a number (1–580) to each work.

One of the major contributions of Gérard's book is its sifting of the various contradictory opus numbers attached to many of Boccherini's works. In addition to the numbers given in the composer's catalog, publishers have often assigned their own numbers to the works they print; indeed, many recordings of Boccherini's music cite opus numbers that are not in accordance with the numbers the composer himself supplied. (Many recordings today cite opus numbers as well as "G" numbers derived from this catalog.) Boccherini's own opus numbers are indicative of the chronology of his works and should be preferred over publishers' numbers. While the autograph catalog is a tremendous aid in establishing the chronology of Boccherini's output, a substantial number of undated works remain, precluding organization of the catalog in chronological order (in the manner of, for example, the Köchel catalog of Mozart's works). In cases of questionable authenticity, Gérard discusses the evidence for and against Boccherini's authorship. He is also careful to point out the faulty editions of Boccherini's works that have been published, striving to correct a problem that in part gave rise to this catalog: musicians need to locate correct editions of the music in order to transmit Boccherini's ideas accurately to modern audiences. The bibliography and discography are, of course, dated, but there is a revised edition of the catalog, now in preparation.

OPHEE addresses a body of works by Boccherini that are among his most popular and widely recorded: his guitar quintets, scored for guitar and string quartet. Boccherini created these works in 1798 and 1799 by arranging his own preexisting works (especially the piano quintets opp. 56 and 57), and in some cases they consist of a recombination of individual movements from different works. Ophee has uncovered a group of five letters exchanged in 1847 and 1848 between Boccherini biographer Picquot and François de Fossa, a guitarist, composer, and retired officer in the French army. Fossa reported that he copied the guitar quintets in Madrid in 1811 directly from the original manuscripts. Picquot borrowed these copies from Fossa, apparently with no intention of returning them. Ophee notes that Picquot's dishonesty, ironically, resulted in the preservation of the copies: Fossa's library has since been entirely lost. The monograph concludes with additional material on Fossa, including a biography and work list. This book will be of interest both to guitarists studying this repertory and persons interested in pursuing a more in-depth treatment of the background of these works than is available in other studies.

TIMOTHY NOONAN

Borrowing

Burkholder, J. Peter, *All Made of Tunes: Charles Ives and the Uses of Musical Borrowing*, New Haven, Connecticut: Yale University Press, 1995

Carrell, Norman, *Bach the Borrower*, London: Allen and Unwin, 1967

Messing, Scott, *Neoclassicism in Music: From the Genesis of the Concept through the Schoenberg/Stravinsky Polemic*, Rochester, New York: University of Rochester Press, 1996

Rosen, Charles "Influence: Plagiarism and Inspiration," *19th-Century Music* 4 (1980): 87–100

Sparks, Edgar, *Cantus Firmus in Mass and Motet, 1420–1520*, Berkeley: University of California Press, 1963

Straus, Joseph N., *Remaking the Past: Musical Modernism and the Influence of the Tonal Tradition*, Cambridge, Massachusetts: Harvard University Press, 1990

Taylor, Sedley, *The Indebtedness of Handel to Works by Other Composers*, Cambridge: Cambridge University Press, 1906; reprint, New York: Da Capo Press, 1979

Wolff, Christoph, "Mozart's Messiah: 'The Spirit of Handel' from van Swieten's Hands," in *Music and Civilization: Essays in Honor of Paul Henry Lang*, edited by Edmond Strainchamps and Maria Rika Maniates, New York: Norton, 1984

Although the term *borrowing* comes specifically from 20th-century music criticism, the practice it describes is not limited to 20th-century music. Defined as the practice of using or recycling existing music or adapting material from another composer's work, borrowing has a long and varied history. Composers have made use of preexisting music in some fashion since the rise of polyphony, but the approaches of composers to the music of their predecessors, and critical and historical interpretations of these attitudes and procedures, have changed over time.

During the Renaissance, composers borrowed freely from one another with little distinction made between the new composition and the borrowed material. In this era and the following baroque period, borrowing was most likely perceived to be either a form of praise and homage to the original composer or an act of compositional convenience. It was not until the 18th and 19th centuries that the question of ownership and originality began to surface. In the 19th century in particular, composers began looking for new ways of describing the relationship between the new and borrowed material, in large part because the changes or additions from the new composer were beginning to be considered either to rival the importance of the original work or to be an encroachment on the initial composition. In the 20th century, as the preoccupation with compositional originality gave way to an overriding self-consciousness about the nature of composition, an enormous number of examples of borrowing—as well as an expanded range of critical descriptions—have surfaced.

Perhaps the oldest form of borrowing was a type of composition called a *contrafactum,* a technique used by medieval and Renaissance composers for setting a new text to an old melody. In the sacred music of the Renaissance, however, the most widely used borrowing practice involved the use of a *cantus firmus,* a fixed or preexisting melody upon which the composer based a new composition, usually a polyphonic Mass. In his comprehensive and thoughtful study of the *cantus firmus* technique, SPARKS not only describes what kinds of melodies and whole pieces were borrowed, but also evaluates how widespread the phenomenon of basing a new composition on preexisting music was during the Renaissance. Sparks's survey starts with Dunstable, Du Fay, and Ockeghem and ends with a final section devoted to the motets and Masses of Obrecht and Josquin. The book offers very useful, factual analyses of many specific works, including when, where, and how the borrowed material was used, as Sparks argues that the manner in which the original material was quoted reflects the compositional personality of the new composer.

In their respective books on Handel and Bach, both Taylor and Carrell detail some of the different borrowing methods used in the baroque era, when, for the first time, questions of plagiarism and originality began to surface in connection with the practice of borrowing. Some contemporary critics of Handel, for instance, accused him of pilfering music from other composers. TAYLOR never disputes these claims that Handel adapted, cut, arranged, or quoted the music of a vast and varied collection of composers from Josquin to Bach and Pergolesi. Instead, his analysis is limited to simply comparing several of Handel's works to their original source material. But the most striking part of his study is the final chapter, which is devoted to the question of whether such borrowings were morally justified, an inquiry that Taylor admits is wholly a concern of his own century and not Handel's.

CARRELL's study of Bach is far less preoccupied with the question of originality than is Taylor's. Instead, Carrell provides a kind of bibliographic listing of Bach's works that borrow material either from his own compositions or from the music of such composers as Legrenzi, Albinoni, Corelli, and Vivaldi. Each entry is accompanied by descriptive commentary and critical appraisal of Bach's borrowing methods. Carrell almost always interprets Bach's borrowing as instances of homage, whether or not Bach explicitly acknowledged the work of other composers. Bach recognized worthy pieces of the past, Carrell asserts, by incorporating them into his own compositions.

All of the borrowing practices reviewed above continued in the classical and romantic periods, although perhaps in different proportion. Haydn, Mozart, Beethoven, Brahms, and Liszt, for example, engaged in overt forms of borrowing, such as variations on preexisting themes. But the practice of a kind of uncredited borrowing flourished. The most influential study of these more subtle kinds of borrowing is ROSEN's article, which has had a profound effect on music criticism since its publication. His brief but provocative analysis of Brahms's allusions to the music of Beethoven and Chopin has not only sparked intense interest in investigating such relationships among composers; it has also inspired critics to create a vocabulary to accommodate these less superficial instances of borrowing. Rosen finds the term *influence* a more capable umbrella term than borrowing for describing all instances of creative exchange and inspiration among composers.

Many classical and romantic era composers continued the practice of making arrangements of previous composer's work, and the most famous example of this type of borrowing comes from Mozart, who arranged several works of Handel, including his famous oratorio the *Messiah.* Although many Handel scholars have deemed Mozart's cuts and revisions intrusive, even sacrilegious, WOLFF defends the changes as necessary for a performance in a much different physical space (a small court theater instead of a large public hall).

The practice of rewriting or rearranging a previous composer's works, and the controversy that surrounds it, continued into the 19th and 20th century. Examples range from Wagner's famous rearrangement of Beethoven's Ninth Symphony, which influenced Mahler and Schoenberg's recompositions of previous composer's works, through Hindemith's subtle evocation of Bach in his piano work, *LudusTonalis,* and Ravel's allusions to baroque clavichord music in *La Tombeau de Couperin,* to Berio's literal quotation of Mahler's Second Symphony in the *Sinfonia* and Stravinsky's re-harmonization of Pergolesi's music in *Pulcinella.* The profusion of borrowing examples and techniques in the 20th century has triggered an intense critical interest in this compositional trend. Many of the borrowings of this century have been described as a general kind of neoclassicism, and MESSING's book is useful on this topic, for the author offers an excellent history of the term *neoclassicism,* illustrating various applications of the term by different composers and in different national traditions.

Recently, however, another critical theory, introduced for the most part by STRAUS, has gained momentum. Drawing from the literary theory of Harold Bloom, Straus describes musical borrowing as the symptom of a kind of "anxiety of influence." Looking at the works of a variety of composers—including Schoenberg, Stravinsky, Webern, and Bartók—Straus interprets their references to the past, both overt and implied, as evidence of the composers' general awareness or self-consciousness of the history of musical composition.

Although BURKHOLDER's book is devoted to a single composer, his study of the composer Charles Ives illustrates the variety of techniques and labels that contemporary critics have developed for describing different types of borrowing employed in 20th-century composition. In this century, allusion, echo, homage, emulation, modeling, and general nostalgia for the music of the past have become frequent, if not ubiquitous tools for composition.

JULIE HUBBERT

Boulez, Pierre b. 1925

French-born composer

Born, Georgina, *Rationalizing Culture: IRCAM, Boulez, and the Institutionalization of the Musical Avant-Garde*, Berkeley: University of California Press, 1995

Boulez, Pierre, *The Boulez-Cage Correspondence*, edited by Jean-Jacques Nattiez et al., translated and edited by Robert Samuels, Cambridge: Cambridge University Press, 1993

————, *Boulez on Music Today*, translated by Susan Bradshaw and Richard Rodney Bennett, Cambridge, Massachusetts: Harvard University Press, and London: Faber, 1971

————, *Conversations with Célestin Deliège*, London: Eulenburg Books, 1976

————, *Orientations: Collected Writings*, edited by Jean-Jacques Nattiez, translated by Martin Cooper, Cambridge: Harvard University Press, and London: Faber, 1986

————, *Stocktakings from an Apprenticeship*, edited by Paule Thévenin, translated by Stephen Walsh, Oxford: Clarendon Press, and New York: Oxford University Press, 1991

Koblyakov, Lev, *Pierre Boulez: A World of Harmony*, Chur: Harwood, 1990

Pierre Boulez has become one of the most important figures in the history of Western European art music after World War II. As a composer, Boulez has ferociously advocated modernist aesthetics. While relentlessly criticizing his predecessors, he has readily opted for bold compositional alternatives in numerous works. Boulez has also contributed tremendously to disseminating 20th-century music by conducting internationally renowned orchestras (the Cleveland Orchestra, BBC Symphony Orchestra, New York Philharmonic Orchestra), teaching (the International Summer Courses for New Music at Darmstadt, the Basle Academy of Music, Harvard University), and directing performance and research institutions devoted to 20th-century music (the Domaine Musicale, Institut de Recherche et de Coordination Acoustique/Musique). Abundant primary sources for research on Boulez include the composer's own essays, interviews, lectures, and personal letters, most of which have been published and translated in English. Most autograph manuscripts for his entire oeuvre have been collected and conveniently housed at the Paul Sacher Foundation in Basle. Nonetheless, there are extremely few monograph-length studies in English on the composer's life or work except for unpublished dissertations. A reliable biography remains as yet unwritten in any language. Although a full-length, life-and-works biography was written by Dominique Jameux (1984) and translated in English (1991), it exhibits considerable shortcomings such as unwarranted anecdotes and superficial accounts of composition. For general information on Boulez's life and work, the reader must consult outdated articles in standard references such as *The New Grove Dictionary of Music and Musicians* (1980) and *Die Musik in Geschichte und Gegenwart* (1949). The lack of a comprehensive study on the composer means that the reader must plough through the composer's essays, interviews, lectures, and personal letters for a better understanding of Boulez—a daunting task that constantly requires discrete interpretation.

BORN's study of the Institut de Recherche et de Coordination Acoustique/Musique (IRCAM) exemplifies an interdisciplinary approach to examining a musical institution that aims to research, implement, and disseminate new technologies for composition. Adopting ethnographic methods, which involve the systematic analysis of firsthand fieldwork, this study identifies a paradox between the uncompromising ideology and the pragmatic practice of IRCAM. The volume's interdisciplinary nature requires the reader to be familiar with not only 20th-century music history but also current debates on postmodern criticism that span several disciplines, including anthropology, sociology, and cultural studies.

KOBLYAKOV's published dissertation presents a detailed and generally convincing analysis of one of the most celebrated works by Boulez, *Le Marteau sans maître*. This study is intended for specialists keenly interested in a theoretical framework of composition, and its minute analytical accounts require the reader to be able to generalize about the composition. The conclusion, which was written anew for publication and addresses the development of Western European art music after World War II, makes sweeping assertions, many of which remain as yet unsubstantiated. The appendix includes diagrams and portions of the score with analysis to support the claims made in the main text, but the reader will find these copious, hand-written examples are often difficult to follow.

Boulez's theory about serial composition culminates in BOULEZ (1971), which includes the first two chapters of an unfinished book based on his lectures given at the International Summer Courses for New Music in Darmstadt between 1959 and 1961. Intended for specialists in 20th-century music, this essay details theories about the series, musical space, and musical syntax. Boulez's analysis of his own works in this essay has compelled many scholars to investigate the composer's serial compositions. Unfortunately, many of these studies either did not develop into full-length monographs or are not available in English.

BOULEZ (1976) is a translation of a series of conversations between Boulez and the Belgian composer Célestin Deliège. Boulez concentrates on addressing

aesthetic and technical aspects of his own works ranging from the *Sonatine* for flute and piano (1946) to . . .
explosante-fixe . . . (1971–74). In so doing, he suggests
a complex relationship between his works and those of
his predecessors (Schoenberg, Webern, Berg, Debussy,
and Stravinsky) in a bid for historical legitimacy. One
hopes that Boulez's earlier interview with Antoine
Goléa (1958) will be translated in English in the near
future; a comparison of the two interviews, both of
which have a similar scope, would provide rare insights
into the state of Boulez's compositional perspectives
from the 1950s to the 1970s.

BOULEZ (1993) is a collection of select documents
and letters exchanged between Boulez and John Cage
from 1949 to 1962. The two composers express their
uncompromising criticism of contemporary musical
environment, keen interest in future development, and
bold compositional alternatives. Their vivid and intimate
accounts, which are not readily available in a third-person study, repeatedly compel one to reinterpret the life
and work of Boulez.

BOULEZ (1991) is a collection of essays originally
published between 1948 and 1962 together with articles
he wrote for the *Encyclopédie Fasquelle de la musique*
(1958–61). The essays and articles are grouped under
four large categories: "In Search of a Musical Aesthetics," "Towards a Technology," "A Few Squibs," and
"Entries for a Musical Encyclopedia." The essays under
the first three categories project, respectively, the state of
Boulez's aesthetic belief, his compositional technique,
and his personal response to tradition; the articles for the
encyclopedia synoptically represent his accumulated
understanding of musical concepts and his assessment of
his predecessors. The introduction to this collection, prepared by Robert Piencikowski, is especially informative
as it addresses the contexts within which Boulez wrote
these essays and articles.

BOULEZ (1986), a collection of his lectures, interviews, and essays, complements his 1991 volume. The
first six essays of this collection, derived from his lectures
at Darmstadt between 1960 and 1961, further complements his 1971 volume of lectures given between 1959
and 1961. This collection extensively covers virtually
everything written by Boulez from the 1950s through
1980 to which the editor had access, including unpublished texts. These writings are grouped in three large
parts: the first part addresses not only aesthetic and technical matters directly related to composition but also the
relationship between composing and teaching; the second part assesses Boulez's predecessors and their compositions; and the third part manifests his keen interest in
innovating musical institutions and, especially, coordinating research in new compositional techniques and
technologies with actual composition and performance.

SANGTAE CHANG

Brahms, Johannes 1833–1897

German composer

1. Biography

Brahms, Johannes, *Johannes Brahms: Life and Letters,*
    selected and annotated by Styra Avins, translated by Josef
    Eisinger and Styra Avins, Oxford: Oxford University Press,
    1997

Gál, Hans, *Johannes Brahms: His Work and Personality,*
    translated by Joseph Stein, New York: Knopf, 1971

Geiringer, Karl, *Brahms: His Life and Work,* London: Allen
    and Unwin, 1936; 3rd enlarged edition, New York: Da
    Capo Press, 1982

Keys, Ivor, *Johannes Brahms,* Portland, Oregon: Amadeus
    Press, 1989

May, Florence, *The Life of Johannes Brahms,* 2 vols., London:
    Arnold, 1905; enlarged and illustrated reprint of 2nd
    edition, Neptune City, New Jersey: Paganiniana
    Publications, 1981

MacDonald, Malcolm, *Brahms,* London: Dent, and New
    York: Schirmer Books, 1990

Niemann, Walter, *Brahms,* translated by Catherine Alison
    Phillips, New York: Knopf, 1929; reprint, New York:
    Cooper Square Publishers, 1969

Specht, Richard, *Johannes Brahms,* translated by Eric Blom,
    London: Dent, and New York: Dutton, 1930

Swafford, Jan, *Brahms: A Biography,* New York: Knopf, 1997

Biographies of Brahms may be divided into three groups:
those written by authors who knew the composer personally and moved in his circle of friends (May, Specht); those
written by later scholars and critics who still retained a
connection to his cultural milieu (Gál, Geiringer, Niemann); and more recent studies that incorporate modern
Brahms scholarship (Avins, Keys, MacDonald, Swafford).
All owe a significant debt to the four-volume study
Johannes Brahms, by the German critic, poet, translator,
and Brahms friend Max Kalbeck, which established the
biographical outline in detail, but which has never been
translated into English owing to its length and the prolix-
ity of its style. Brahms cultivated a wide group of friends
and musical associates, leaving behind a voluminous correspondence, much of which was published early in the
20th century by the German Brahms Society and by Clara
Schumann biographer Berthold Litzmann. These letters,
along with Clara Schumann's diaries as transmitted in
Litzmann's biography, and reminiscence literature by contemporaries such as J.V. Widmann, Albert Dietrich,
Gustav Jenner, George Henschel, Richard Heuberger, and
Eugenie Schumann form the primary-source backbone of
all Brahms biography. Additional primary sources have
continued to appear up to the present day and inform
more recent studies. (For a comprehensive overview of the
vast literature about Brahms and his music, see Thomas

Quigley, *Johannes Brahms: An Annotated Bibliography of the Literature through 1982* [1990], and *Johannes Brahms: An Annotated Bibliography of the Literature from 1982–1996* [1998].)

MAY studied piano with Brahms in 1871, and her personal contact with him continued intermittently through 1895. Her first-person accounts of Brahms as teacher, pianist, and personality are frequently cited in the Brahms literature. The first edition (1905) is the earliest comprehensive biography of Brahms and inevitably contains gaps in primary sources. The second edition (revised in the 1910s) takes Kalbeck into account as a corroborative source and contains expansions and corrections. Neither edition accesses Brahms's correspondence with Clara Schumann, which was closely held by the Schumann family until its publication in 1927. May follows the conventions of Victorian biography both in her reverence for her subject and in her fastidious silence about Brahms's sexuality, and thus it does not convey the balanced view of his personality that would be expected in a modern study. Nevertheless, her benign view of Brahms's early life, challenged by Kalbeck and others, has been increasingly validated by recent scholarship. May's writing is fundamentally reportorial and quite detached, considering her closeness to the subject. Her substantial quotations from a wide variety of correspondence give the biographical narrative great authenticity of tone but also tend to present Brahms as his friends and supporters saw him. May's discussion of the music is limited to major works and, like most Victorian music criticism, centers on their emotional content.

NIEMANN provides the first attempt at a critical biography of Brahms,—that is, one that considers his life and music from a perspective of detached evaluation—as well as the first major study to discuss his life and works separately. As part of his critical stance, Niemann eschews much direct quotation from primary sources, giving his text an interpretive rather than presentational quality. Niemann only partly achieves the critical detachment to which he aspires. His badly overdrawn picture of Brahms as a scion of sturdy, peasant stock, imbued with simple virtues and strength of character, is rooted in postwar Spenglerian pessimism and disillusionment with the Wilhelminian cultural milieu and also reflects a bias toward his own north German background. This image has, however, widely influenced later biographers. Niemann's study remains valuable as a snapshot of German Brahms reception at the close of the Wilhelminian era. His discussion of the works draws on the earliest university theses on Brahms's music, and his critical views echo in some later studies, for example, Reinhold Brinkmann's monograph on the second symphony (*Lute Ldyll: The Second Symphony of Johannes Brahms,* 1995).

SPECHT joined Brahms's circle of Viennese associates in the last decade of the composer's life, and the most compelling moments in his biography are his first-person accounts of Brahms. Writing in the casual style of the feuilleton, he assumes the reader's familiarity with Brahms's biography and music and with 19th-century European culture in general. The biographical narrative is almost devoid of specific time-and-place information. It is interlaced with three chapters on the works and a valuable essay on the members of Brahms's Viennese circle. Specht makes no pretensions of scholarly detachment, but writes from the contemporary critic's point of view, expressing strong opinions about Brahms's character and music. These are colored by his position in the "Brahms-Wagner controversy"—Specht was originally a Brahmsian but later adopted the New German view. The editorial tone of the work is, however, part of its intrinsic value, as it gives modern readers the flavor of the partisan journalism of Brahms's time. Despite its shortcomings as a reliable, well-organized biography, Specht's study remains important as a primary source for anecdotal information about Brahms's later years.

From 1930 to 1938 GEIRINGER was museum curator and librarian of the Gesellschaft der Musikfreunde in Vienna, the repository for most of Brahms's estate, including the composer's personal library and much of his correspondence. More than 1,000 letters in this collection were placed under seal at Brahms's death and were thus unavailable to the first generation of biographers. Geiringer's study made use of these materials for the first time, quoting, sometimes at length, from 168 previously unpublished letters. The concise narrative summarizes much biographical detail, allowing Geiringer to focus on new perspectives arising from the correspondence. Presentations of Brahms's early life and his relationship to his father, in particular, are refined. Geiringer is circumspect about Brahms's private life and skeptical about much of the anecdotal information that was by this time creeping into the biographical canon. Brahms had a long association with the Gesellschaft der Musikfreunde, and Geiringer's ruminations about the society's politics have the air of an insider's view. He divides Brahms's works into four style periods, a now dated approach influenced by contemporaneous Beethoven scholarship. Despite its age, Geiringer's study probably remains the best general introduction to Brahms's life and works.

GÁL assisted Eusebius Mandyczewski in editing the complete edition of Brahms's works published by Breitkopf und Härtel in 1926–27. (Gál is listed as editor of Brahms's chamber music and music for orchestra but, due to Mandyczewski's ill health, was deeply involved in other parts of the project as well.) Gál's writing is informed by his intimate acquaintance with Brahms's music, as well as by his closeness to Mandyczewski, who had been a friend and factotum to Brahms during the composer's later years. Gál's book is more a collection of essays about Brahms and his music than a conventional biography. (Its first chapter, a "biographical sketch," is as concise as a dictionary article.) Nevertheless, with well-chosen support from correspondence and reminiscence literature, the broad themes of Brahms's life are developed in chapters that focus on particular aspects of his personality and career. Gál does not break new ground here; his view of Brahms the man is informed but conventional. Furthermore, the scholarly underpinnings of his work are dated and betray a certain carelessness about details. His insightful commentary on Brahms's music, however, is of great value.

Drawing on a new resource—Margit McCorkle, *Johannes Brahms: Thematisch-Bibliographisches Werkverzeichnis* (1984), a massive thematic catalog thoroughly informed by modern Brahms scholarship—KEYS provides a spare factual litany of Brahms's movements from place to place, works he composed or performed, and professional positions he assumed. His selections from Brahms's correspondence are sometimes refreshingly unconventional, but his overreliance on British secondary sources betrays a myopic view of the Brahms literature. Although excellent for quick reference, Keys's study provides little context for or interpretation of the facts. He suggests Brahms's infatuation with Julie Schumann, for example, yet never hints at a connection between this and the composition of the Alto Rhapsody. Keys gives more information than usual about Brahms's connections to England. A separate, annotated catalog of Brahms's works is organized by genre, and within genres, by opus numbers. Despite occasional flashes of insight, the annotations mostly have the quality of program notes.

MacDONALD's well-balanced study reflects to some degree Arnold Schoenberg's influential view of Brahms as a progressive composer. (MacDonald is editor of *Tempo*, a British journal dedicated to reviewing modern music, and author of a study on Schoenberg.) His incorporation of secondary literature, while up-to-date, favors British scholarship. Organizationally, MacDonald moves between concise and rather conventional chapters of biographical narrative, much weightier analytical chapters on the music, and interpretive chapters that lay out the romantic underpinnings of Brahms's thinking, explore his reception of the past, and discuss the consequences of his music for the 20th century. He presents Brahms as a romantic historicist—as opposed to conservative—composer who was at the same time a "progressive" precursor of much important 20th-century compositional technique. This perspective reflects the dominant interpretive trends in late 20th-century Brahms scholarship and marks MacDonald's study as the first fundamentally modern English-language biography of Brahms. Discussions of Brahms's music are organized by genre, and chronologically by date of composition rather than date of publication, with the exception of pieces of obscure gestation, such as the first symphony. His analyses often focus on motivic relationships as an element of musical

coherence and are especially indebted to Musgrave, *The Music of Brahms* (1985).

BRAHMS is the closest thing to a documentary biography. Edited and annotated by Avins, this massive study presents 564 items of correspondence between Brahms and his family, friends, and colleagues, accompanied by explanatory memoranda and a sparse connecting tissue of biographical narrative. Avins's new translations, made in collaboration with Josef Eisinger, are based to some degree on firsthand examination of original sources. Avins carefully avoids the interpretive function of conventional biography, allowing Brahms to speak with his own voice, a goal that is greatly facilitated by her decision to include complete letters rather than excerpts. She has chosen letters that map Brahms's life and career clearly and that illuminate his music and character. Avins's study benefits from a command of the scholarly literature that is, in the field of Brahms biography, unparalleled in its breadth and currency. She is, for example, the first English-language biographer to dispute Kalbeck's conventional picture of Brahms's childhood as extremely impoverished or even abusive, a view that has been increasingly questioned by some scholars. The "Brief Biographies" in Appendix C—well over 200 in number—provide excellent background information about Brahms's correspondents and members of his circle. Analytical discussion of Brahms's music lies outside the scope of this study.

To read SWAFFORD is essentially to survey all the major English-language biographies from May to MacDonald, as his enormous text was compiled largely from them, as well as from Kalbeck, the standard primary-source literature, and a number of American, British, and German scholarly studies. (Swafford's discussion of Brahms's sexuality, however, is colored by relatively uncritical acceptance of Schauffler, *The Unknown Brahms* [1933], a source of controversial anecdotal information that has been received cautiously by many scholars.) The biography is shaped critically by Swafford's background as a composer. Brahms's strategies for developing and managing his career receive much attention, and his responses to musical, cultural, and personal issues are often interpreted from a composer's point of view. Discussion of the compositions is limited to major works and, although informed by recent trends in Brahms scholarship, is clearly aimed at the nonspecialist reader. Swafford's development of Brahms's personality is insightful, and his interpretation of the correspondence sensitive and persuasive. His explanations of the social and musical conventions of Brahms's time are especially helpful to the nonspecialist. Regrettably, the book's scholarly apparatus is severely flawed. Endnotes often do not correspond with their numbered references in the text, and some are simply left out.

WILLIAM HORNE

2. Chamber Music

Drinker, Henry Sandwith, *The Chamber Music of Johannes Brahms,* Philadelphia: Elkan-Vogel, 1932; reprint, Westport, Connecticut: Greenwood Press, 1974

Keys, Ivor, *Brahms Chamber Music,* London: British Broadcasting Corporation, and Seattle: University of Washington Press, 1974

Lawson, Colin, *Brahms: Clarinet Quintet,* Cambridge: Cambridge University Press, 1998

Mason, Daniel Gregory, *The Chamber Music of Brahms,* New York: Macmillan, 1933; reprint, New York: AMS Press, 1970

Musgrave, Michael, *The Music of Brahms,* London: Routledge and Paul, 1985; Oxford: Clarendon Press, 1994

Notley, Margaret, "Discourse and Allusion: The Chamber Music of Brahms," in *Nineteenth-Century Chamber Music,* edited by Stephen E. Hefling, New York: Schirmer Books, and London: Prentice Hall, 1998

Smallman, Basil, *The Piano Quartet and Quintet: Style, Structure, and Scoring,* Oxford: Clarendon Press, and New York: Oxford University Press, 1994

Tovey, Donald Francis, "Brahms," in *Cobbett's Cyclopedic Survey of Chamber Music,* edited by Walter Willson Cobbett, 2nd edition, edited by Colin Mason, 3 vols., London: Oxford University Press, 1963

Johannes Brahms initially made his mark as a composer of chamber music, and this fact has encouraged some critics to place him in the conservative, traditional German camp, opposite Liszt and Wagner. Oddly enough, it was also Brahms's inclination to write in a chamber-music style—with emphasis on counterpoint, thematic-motivic development, and logical forms—that earned him his reputation as a composer of brain music, the progenitor of young progressive composers such as Schoenberg. Traditional or innovative, chamber music remained an important part of Brahms's compositional output at every stage of his career, and writers have long noted its significance. Around the centenary of Brahms's birth (1933), several books devoted solely to his chamber music appeared. At least two of these have remained in circulation, while more recent analyses have for the most part been presented in the form of journal articles or essays within books that address more general topics. Broadly speaking, writers have emphasized the individuality of Brahms's chamber idiom and have looked inward at the structure and style of the music to discern wherein its power lies. Recently, writers have also focused on the historical context of Brahms's chamber music, investigating performance practices and drawing detailed comparisons between Brahms's music and that of other composers.

DRINKER prepared his small and engaging volume for a series of concerts in Philadelphia, given in celebration of the centenary of Brahms's birth. The composer's chamber music was performed in its entirety at these concerts, and Drinker provides a precis of each work (in the order of performance), along with anecdotes regarding that work's composition. He prefaces his notes with a sketch of Brahms's life and a summary of the distinguishing characteristics of his music, such as cross-rhythms, the dovetailing of voices, and motion by thirds or sixths.

KEYS organizes his survey of Brahms's chamber music according to the instrumental forces involved, making scarce mention of chronology, or, indeed, any other biographical facts. The descriptions of each opus are brief—rarely more than a paragraph per movement—and few examples are given. The only exception to this presentation format occurs in the treatment of the first piece discussed, the Piano Quintet in F Minor, op. 34, where Keys offers a considerable number of examples to illustrate Brahms's transformation of the melodic material. All told, this book is more useful as a listener's guide than as an academic handbook.

TOVEY wrote his essay as an entry in a chamber music encyclopedia, where it appeared along with two shorter entries: recollections of Brahms and of his close friend, the violinist Josef Joachim, by Fanny Davies and Frau Horowitz-Barnay, respectively. Davies's entry is of particular historical interest. A pupil of Clara Schumann, Davies gives a detailed report of a rehearsal she attended, in which Brahms, Joachim, and the cellist Robert Hausmann played Brahms's as yet unpublished C Minor Trio, op. 101 (Clara turned pages). Tovey's lengthy essay was later published separately within his collected *Essays and Lectures on Music* (Oxford: Oxford University Press, 1949). As a pianist, Tovey performed Brahms's chamber opuses many times, most often with Joachim, and his analyses are sprinkled with personal insights into the character and interpretation of the music. Furthermore, Tovey studied music from all ages, and he frequently digresses from the works at hand to offer his discerning historical perspective on how the composer dealt with form, texture, or the transformation of themes. His essay remains a touchstone of research on chamber music.

MASON's monograph is the only full-length study of Brahms's chamber music. Mason divides his book into four periods: youth, young manhood, mastership, and the last years, devoting a chapter within each period to each chamber opus. His analyses are rather outmoded but are noteworthy for his frank, often critical view of how the music progresses. Mason is most critical of the Piano Quartet in C Minor, op. 60, which he regards as an ungainly amalgamation of compositional styles and skill levels (evidence suggest that Brahms worked on the piece for as long as 20 years). Yet even here, Mason gives the music its analytical due, weighing, for example, the lack of rhythmic contrast against the masterly regrouping of harmonies before he concludes that the work is a noble failure.

In a study of Brahms's entire compositional output, MUSGRAVE offers two separate chapters on the chamber music, one from the composer's second period and one from his third period. He also considers separately the chamber works for clarinet within his chapter on the final period. Musgrave does a good job of relating the music for small ensemble to Brahms's other compositions. The author's analyses are quite detailed, although not overly technical. He is particularly interested in highlighting the qualities that lend each movement its distinctive style, showing how Brahms develops the character of a melody, rhythm, or texture.

NOTLEY also divides Brahms's chamber music into periods (four, counting the Piano Trio in B Major, op. 8, as a separate period) and goes further than either Mason or Musgrave in her attempt to identify the stylistic and expressive considerations that occupied the composer within each period. Notley demonstrates, for instance, how mode change and fugato concerned Brahms in the early chamber works (1860–65) as he grappled with finding his individual sound and aesthetic stance; in the chamber music of the mid-1870s, he shifted his focus to the logic of musical events. Especially compelling is Notley's analysis of how Brahms reimagined sonata form in his late chamber works. At times, perhaps out of space constraints, Notley goes beyond the demonstrable and makes claims regarding Brahms's compositional intent that cannot be verified. For example, Brahms wrote a theme that is reminiscent of a baroque folia theme for the variations in the second movement of his Sextet in B-flat Major, op. 18; furthermore, he used the baroque technique of rhythmic divisions in the first three variations. From these facts, Notley concludes that Brahms made "the collision of discourses the point of the movement: the set of variations is formed around the very opposition between latter-day subjectivity and the monumental, impersonal quality of both the Baroque theme and the technique of divisions." Notley provides no musical examples to illustrate this claim, leaving the readers to imagine (or performers to create) these opposing expressive aims. On the whole, however, Notley's analyses contribute significantly to an understanding of Brahms's compositional process and the special place chamber music held for him within his developing technique.

SMALLMAN's book on the history of piano quartets and quintets includes a chapter titled "The Ascendancy of Brahms." The author begins by analyzing Brahms's three piano quartets, focusing on issues such as scoring and the evolution of themes. In the remaining, larger portion of the chapter, Smallman offers a comparative account of several late-19th- and early-20th-century chamber works for piano by other composers. His most penetrating comparison is between Brahms's Piano Quintet in F Minor, op. 34 (1864), and a piano quintet in the same key by Cesar Franck (1879). The differences and similarities between these compositions are surprisingly far-reaching, and Smallman's treatment of them is essential reading for anyone wishing to grasp the uniqueness of Brahms's achievements.

LAWSON's monograph on Brahms's Clarinet Quintet, op. 115, is one of the most in-depth treatments to date of any single piece of chamber music. A bar-by-bar analysis of the structure and design of the Quintet is the heart of the monograph, but before this analysis, Lawson thoroughly investigates the history of clarinet chamber music prior to Brahms, the composer's own orchestral writing for the instrument, aspects of his chamber music style that may have had bearing on his conception of the role of the clarinet within small ensembles, and, of course, the genesis of the Quintet itself. After his structural analysis of the work, Lawson delves into performance practice issues and the question of Brahms's influence on later composers of chamber music with clarinet. This balanced, well-documented study sets a standard for future research on individual works within Brahms's chamber music oeuvre.

DONNA L. LYNN

3. Orchestral Music

Bozarth, George S., editor, *Brahms Studies: Analytical and Historical Perspectives,* Oxford: Clarendon Press, and New York: Oxford University Press, 1990

Brinkmann, Reinhold, *Late Idyll: The Second Symphony of Johannes Brahms,* translated by Peter Palmer, Cambridge, Massachusetts: Harvard University Press, 1995

Brodbeck, David, "Brahms," in *The Nineteenth-Century Symphony,* edited by D. Kern Holoman, New York: Schirmer Books, and London: Prentice Hall, 1997

———, *Brahms, Symphony no. 1,* Cambridge: Cambridge University Press, 1997

Brodbeck, David, editor, *Brahms Studies 2,* Lincoln: University of Nebraska Press, 1998

Frisch, Walter, *Brahms: The Four Symphonies,* New York: Schirmer Books, and London: Prentice Hall, 1996

Frisch, Walter, editor, *Brahms and His World,* Princeton, New Jersey: Princeton University Press, 1990

Harrison, Julius, *Brahms and His Four Symphonies,* London: Chapman and Hall, 1939; New York: Da Capo Press, 1971

Knapp, Raymond, *Brahms and the Challenge of the Symphony,* Stuyvesant, New York: Pendragon Press, 1997

Tovey, Donald Francis, *Essays in Musical Analysis,* 6 vols., London: Oxford University Press, 1935–39; vol. 5 published separately as *Concertos and Choral Works,* London: Oxford University Press, 1981

Brahms's orchestral output includes two serenades, four concertos (two for piano, one for violin, and a double concerto for violin and cello), two overtures (the *Tragic* and *Academic*), and four symphonies. Among these compositions, the symphonies have drawn by far the most attention, with books on the group of four as well as monographs devoted to individual works. Nevertheless, most of the books discussing these four pieces also make mention of the other orchestral works, especially the earlier compositions, which are viewed as training ground for the symphonies. The publications discussed below cover a wide range of approaches including structural analyses of individual movements as well as studies of historical concerns, such as the circumstances under which Brahms created the works and the reactions of early critics. Almost all of these publications assume that the readers have a copy of the music close at hand.

TOVEY covers all of Brahms's orchestral works, with essays on each work spread throughout this series: volume 1 includes essays on the symphonies and serenades; volumes 2 and 6 discuss the Haydn Variations and the overtures; and volume 3 considers the concertos. These essays were originally intended as program notes, and the articles on the four symphonies in particular are based on the notes that Tovey wrote for the 1902 London concerts of the Meiningen Orchestra—an orchestra that Brahms greatly admired and which premiered his Fourth Symphony. In typically eloquent prose, Tovey offers excellent introductions to these works, evocatively describing the structure of each movement, and locating and quoting each of the principal themes.

FRISCH (1996) offers the best general introduction to the symphonies, combining analyses with historical information in a manner that holds the interest of amateurs and professional musicians alike. He presents clear overviews of each movement's structure, drawing the reader's attention to special points of interest, such as noteworthy harmonic details, fascinating aspects of the phrase structure of some of the most important themes, and artful motivic manipulations (including the ways in which motives are used to connect the individual movements of each symphony). These analytical chapters are surrounded by ones dealing with historical matters. The first historical section investigates the events that led up to the composition of the First Symphony, considering the influence of contemporary symphonies by other composers as well as the importance of some of Brahms's earlier works, in which he developed the compositional techniques that enabled him to produce such an impressive symphony. Brahms honed his orchestration skills in the earlier works that employ orchestras, including the First Piano Concerto and *A German Requiem,* but it was in the chamber works, such as the Piano Quintet op. 34, that he mastered the handling of large-scale forms. The final chapters of the book concern the performance and initial reception of the works, although reception is such an enormously complicated issue (involving diverse topics and intersecting with the politics of the period) that Frisch can only give a sample of the relevant research possibilities in his brief discussion. Aside from noting how frequently each of the symphonies has been performed, he points out recurring critical debates, such as

comparisons of Brahms's compositions to those of Beethoven and to chamber music, and he samples various hermeneutic analyses from the 19th and 20th centuries. He concludes with an intriguing chapter on period performance, comparing recordings by prominent conductors, particularly those from the first half of the 20th century (including Stokowski and Weingartner), with reports of 19th-century performances.

HARRISON briefly describes Brahms's gradual approach to the genre of the symphony before launching into a study of the general characteristics of the symphonies, discussing such topics as the key relationships among movements, harmonies, motives, counterpoint, and style of orchestration. He devotes two chapters to this last topic, dealing with each of the symphonies in turn and evaluating how the instruments are effectively combined and highlighted. The majority of the book analyzes the movements of each work, emphasizing the themes and instrumentation. Harrison hopes to reach both the general public as well as the highly skilled musician, and these analyses can be followed by anyone with a score. The author's reverence for these works is readily apparent in his compelling prose.

KNAPP's book is a challenging, multifaceted approach intended for the reader who is already well acquainted with the symphonies. Like Frisch, Knapp investigates the background to these works, noting the scores of contemporary symphonies that Brahms owned. While describing Brahms's debt to past composers, the author also stresses the influence of Brahms's contemporary, Liszt. Knapp's interest in Brahms's relation to earlier works culminates in chapter 4, which depicts each of the symphonies as allusive webs that, through their use of earlier composers' works, synthesize past traditions and composers. There is much in this chapter that is worthy of very careful consideration, and readers should be prepared to make their own close study comparing Brahms's symphonies to the works that Knapp suggests are related to them. Chapter 5 offers an innovative interpretation of Brahms's much admired use of variation, demonstrating that many movements of the symphonies, including those in sonata form, make use of some type of variation technique. This chapter also explores the motivic relationships between the movements of each symphony, especially the Third and Fourth, a topic also treated in chapter 6, "The Quest for Unity." Knapp contends that orchestration and harmonies unify the movements of the First Symphony, but he tends to emphasize more narrative concerns for the other symphonies: for example, he describes the combination of pastoral, melancholy, and heroic themes in the Second Symphony. Finally, Knapp assesses the historical significance of these works, asserting that they do not quite serve the purpose that Brahms might have intended. Rather than forming a bridge between the works of Beethoven and those of the future, these compositions mark the end of the tradition that includes the major works of the classical and romantic symphonists from Haydn to Schumann.

BRODBECK (1997a) gives a concise introduction to the symphonies and serenades. In addition to pointing out the structural highlights of many of the movements, he places each symphony in its historical context by identifying the composers and pieces that may have influenced specific passages or compositional techniques, and by describing early critiques. These analytical and historical details are not entirely separate matters, and Brodbeck weaves them together, proposing that both types of information should inform one's appreciation of a piece.

Much of the discussion of Brahms's First Symphony concentrates on its tortured origins, an issue that BRODBECK (1997b) further explores. The first and final chapters of this book deal with the symphony's history, covering early performances, the publication process, and critical reception. In the inner chapters, Brodbeck analyzes the individual movements of the composition, focusing on the cyclic nature of the work and on the significance of its numerous allusions to precursor works. He interprets the first movement through its relationship with Schumann's *Manfred Overture* and evaluates the last movement in relation to Beethoven's Ninth Symphony and Bach's Cantata 106, as well as to works by Schubert and other compositions by Schumann.

Numerous commentators have observed the popularity of the Second Symphony, and they often ascribe the success of this work to its pastoral nature. BRINKMANN offers a far more sophisticated and insightful approach, arguing that the work is a blend of the idyllic and the melancholic (as these terms were understood in Brahms's time). This combination, as well as other aspects of the piece, are further elucidated when they are compared with turn-of-the-century works, including those of the painter Gustav Klimt and the writer Thomas Mann. Brinkmann's sensitive analyses of the symphony's individual movements are coordinated with a study of the manuscript sources and perceptive readings of the opinions of Brahms's contemporaries, especially those of the conductor Vincenz Lachner. Brinkmann also assesses the historical place of the symphony in relation to other 19th-century symphonic works and in particular in light of the influence of Beethoven.

BOZARTH contains papers delivered at the International Brahms Conference in Washington, D.C., in 1983. These articles, written by some of the most important Brahms scholars, encompass the entire gamut of Brahms studies, with many contributors making reference to the composer's orchestral works. Two essays focus on the Third Symphony: Robert Bailey's "Musical Language and Structure in the Third Symphony" and Robert Pascall's "The Publication of Brahms's Third Symphony: A Crisis in Dissemination." Bailey views the Third Symphony as a homage to two of the most influential composers of the preceding generation, Schumann and Wagner. He then

concentrates on the sonata-form structures of the first and last movements, particularly as they relate to the archetypes of the 18th and 19th centuries. Pascall focuses on the publication history of the same symphony, describing many of the types of errors that were introduced into the score during the copying and publication process. No doubt this type of research is primarily intended for the specialist, but Pascall's lucid prose makes it possible for lay readers to follow and thus to appreciate more fully the complicated history of this work. In addition to these essays, this volume contains a number of other studies that deal with the orchestral works, including Claudio Spies's "'Form' and the *Tragic Overture*: An Adjuration" and Margit L. McCorkle's "The Role of Trial Performances for Brahms's Orchestral and Large Choral Works: Sources and Circumstances." Two analytical articles by James Webster and Siegfried Kross concentrate on Brahms's use of sonata form but also make reference to some of his orchestral works.

BRODBECK (1998) includes two essays on the symphonies: Kenneth Hull's "Allusive Irony in Brahms's Fourth Symphony" and Frisch's "'Echt symphonisch': On the Historical Context of Brahms's Symphonies." Brahms's employment of allusions to and quotations from other composers' works is well known, and many of the above publications describe this part of his compositional technique. In his intriguing article, however, Hull does not just identify such borrowed material in the Fourth Symphony; he integrates this analysis into his programmatic interpretation of the piece. This symphony is quite unusual because it ends tragically, rather than with the more optimistic triumph over fate that occurs in many other symphonic works. Despite this emphasis on tragedy, Brahms alludes to two works in the Fourth Symphony that do express optimism: Beethoven's Fifth Symphony and Bach's Cantata 150. Frisch's article, incorporating information from chapters 1 and 3 of his book on the symphonies (Frisch [1996]), explores the cultural and musical understanding of the genre of the symphony that formed the backdrop to Brahms's struggle to compose his first symphonic work. After demonstrating that the audiences of the third quarter of the 19th century judged new symphonies against unusually high standards, Frisch asserts that Brahms was eventually able to deal with these demands—and indeed had something of an advantage—because he was already a well-respected composer when his First Symphony eventually premiered.

FRISCH (1990) publishes annotated translations of some early critical responses to Brahms's works, including those by two of the most influential writers of the late 19th century—Hermann Kretzschmar and Eduard Hanslick. Adolf Schubring discusses the First Piano Concerto (1862); Kretzschmar reviews the four symphonies (1887); and Hanslick evaluates the Double Concerto (1889). Schubring and Kretzschmar's reviews, while not comprehensive, offer overviews of each work's structures and still serve as great introductions for the novice. Hanslick's article is more impressionistic, describing a performance of the Double Concerto by Robert Hausmann and Joseph Joachim. Hanslick is not as positive as the other two critics, but his reservations are perhaps justifiable, for even today this work is not as popular as Brahms's symphonies. The anthology also contains a number of other articles by present-day historians, including Brodbeck's "Brahms, the Third Symphony, and the New German School," in which the author skillfully demonstrates that although Brahms had publicly opposed the members of the New German School, this symphony nevertheless echoes the works of the school's leaders, Liszt and Wagner.

HEATHER PLATT

4. Vocal Music

Bell, A. Craig, *Brahms—The Vocal Music,* Madison, New Jersey: Fairleigh Dickinson University Press, and London: Associated University Press, 1996

Evans, Edwin, *Historical, Descriptive and Analytical Account of the Entire Works of Johannes Brahms,* 4 vols., London: Reeves, and New York: Scribner, 1912; reprint, New York: Franklin, 1970

Friedländer, Max, *Brahms' Lieder: An Introduction to the Songs for One and Two Voices,* translated by C. Leonard Leese, London: Oxford University Press, 1928

Hancock, Virginia, *Brahms's Choral Compositions and His Library of Early Music,* Ann Arbor, Michigan: UMI Research Press, 1983

Musgrave, Michael, *Brahms: A German Requiem,* Cambridge: Cambridge University Press, 1996

Sams, Eric, *Brahms Songs,* London: British Broadcasting Corporation, and Seattle: Washington University Press, 1972

Stark, Lucien, *Brahms's Vocal Duets and Quartets with Piano: A Guide with Full Texts and Translations,* Bloomington: Indiana University Press, 1995

Stark, Lucien, *A Guide to the Solo Songs of Johannes Brahms,* Bloomington: Indiana University Press, 1995

Throughout his life Johannes Brahms wrote for the voice; indeed, his solo lieder, which total almost 200, span his entire compositional career. In addition to these solo works, he composed numerous unaccompanied and accompanied vocal ensembles (ranging from two to eight parts) as well as works for orchestra and chorus, the best known of which are *Ein deutsches Requiem* (*A German Requiem*) and the *Rhapsodie für eine Altstimme, Männerscor, und Orchester* (*Alto Rhapsody*); for alto, male chorus, and orchestra). During Brahms's lifetime many of these works attracted the attention of music critics, and this interest continued through the 20th century. Many of the resulting publications, however, are in German; although there are numerous U.S. and British dissertations and scholarly ar-

ticles on Brahms's vocal works, only a few English-language monographs have appeared. Furthermore, with the exception of the books by Bell and Evans, authors have separated the lieder from the choral works and for the most part have concentrated on the former.

Although published in 1912, EVANS remains the most comprehensive treatment of Brahms's vocal music. After four brief introductory essays on Brahms's life and work, this book examines the vocal music by opus number. Each piece (or movement) within an opus is briefly described, and an English translation of the text is provided. Although the commentary about the music occasionally includes insightful observations, for the most part it is quite superficial, usually making reference to a work's form, mood, and, in the case of the solo lieder, piano figuration. While helpful to the person who knows nothing about Brahms's vocal music, this book offers little to someone already familiar with the works.

BELL also deals with all of Brahms's vocal compositions, but he divides the works by genre and then discusses each group chronologically. Overall, he provides a general introduction for the student or amateur musician, and the book can easily be read from cover to cover. Bell's most interesting observations concern the solo songs, and he enthusiastically points out the composer's genius for conveying particularly heart wrenching or important moments in the texts. Despite the numerous musical examples, the descriptions of the ensemble and choral pieces are so short that they do not do the pieces justice; moreover, Bell seems not to be impressed by many of the ensembles.

First published in German in 1922, FRIEDLÄNDER remains the best introduction to Brahm's lieder; all of the solo lied and the duets, including the folksong arrangements, are covered. The author proceeds systematically through each opus number, giving extremely useful background information about when these works were composed and describing the reactions of Brahms's contemporaries (with numerous references to the letters of the composer and his friends). The manuscript sources for these works are not abundant, but occasionally Friedländer is able to document some of the changes that Brahms made in the final stages of composing specific songs as well as his alterations to the printer's proofs. Friedländer also describes the sources of Brahms's texts— sometimes identifying the exact editions of poetry that the composer used—and explains Brahm's alterations to the original poems. In many instances the author provides brief descriptions of the poets, and, where relevant, their relationship to Brahms. Although not intended as a comprehensive analytical guide, Friedländer does occasionally point to particularly affective passages of music.

STARK (1995a) is strongly influenced by Friedländer and includes much of the earlier author's information about Brahms's texts. In addition, Stark provides English translations of these texts and updated information regarding the origin of the songs and when they were first performed. After a sketchy overview of Brahms as a songwriter, Stark discusses each of the opus numbers. Each chapter begins with introductory remarks concerning the opus as a whole, including such details as when it was published, important contemporary events in Brahms's life, and, in some cases, observations about the possibility of treating the particular opus as a type of cycle. Discussions of individual songs cover such details as their form and harmonies. Stark's observations, which reveal his own deep reverence for the works, are often followed by remarks of Brahms's contemporaries (most frequently comments from Clara Schumann and Elizabeth von Herzogenberg). Setting his book apart from others, Stark specifically addresses performers, and he provides practical advice on tempo, dynamics, breathing (for the singer), and balance between the singer and pianist as well as comparisons of various editions.

SAMS is not as comprehensive as Friedländer or Stark, but it is nevertheless an informative source on Brahms's Lieder for those readers who do not need to know the details of every song. This book gives a general survey of Brahms's lieder and provides many provocative ideas. It also gives a clear sense of Brahms's overall style as a songwriter (including discussion of such topics as declamation, word painting, form, use of piano, and choice of poets) and explains how this style compares with those of the other great lieder composers Schubert, Schumann, and Wolf. As an author of books on the lieder of Schumann and Wolf, Sams is well placed to make such comparisons and cross references, and although it is obvious that Sams greatly values Brahms's work, he takes a more critical approach than the authors discussed above. After the overview of Brahms's style, the book treats the songs in six chronological groups. Within each chapter Sams jumps from one song to another, grouping together those with similar images, musical styles, or texts. Because many of the songs are not identified by opus number (and there is no index), one needs to have some familiarity with Brahms's works to be able to follow Sam's discussion. Aside from his analytical observations, Sams often attempts to place the works in the context of Brahms's life and particularly in relation to the composer's friendship with Clara Schumann—a topic on which Sams has also published a number of articles.

Brahms's music for vocal ensembles has attracted considerably less attention than the solo lieder. The principal monographs on these compositions tend to focus on small groups of works. STARK (1995b), for example, deals with the duets and quartets with piano. His volume follows the same format as his book on the solo lieder, and again he provides a mixture of historical information about the origins of each work as well as analytical observations that concentrate on Brahm's sensitive handling of his texts. Like Stark's other book, this volume concludes with brief biographical sketches of the poets and translators mentioned in the preceding entries. In addition, it also provides similar information for Brahms's friends and associates—a useful feature for those readers completely unfamiliar with Brahms.

Although concerned only with a single work, MUSGRAVE's volume on *A German Requiem* is one of the most informative and accessible English-language monographs on Brahm's choral works. This volume brilliantly combines a vast array of historical and analytical information about one of Brahms's most popular works. Aside from discussing the style, structure, and expressive properties of each movement, Musgrave describes the history of the work's composition, its early reception, and performances in the 19th and 20th centuries. Despite the technical nature of some of these subjects, Musgrave ensures that the nonspecialist is still able to grasp the information, and in so doing he introduces the reader not only to Brahms's masterpiece but also to the various topics that Brahms scholars are currently pursuing.

Whereas Musgrave and Stark are excellent introductions to some of Brahms's choral pieces, HANCOCK is intended for readers already familiar with these works, and it examines their relationship to Brahms's study of early music. Hancock first investigates Brahms's knowledge of early music, principally by examining the contents of the composer's library. This section not only includes a list of the volumes Brahms owned but also describes their contents, explains when Brahms might have acquired each, and notes whether they include any of Brahms's own annotations. The study also describes Brahms's handwritten copies of pieces by a wide variety of composers from the 16th to the 18th centuries (including Palestrina, G. Gabrieli, Schütz, and J.S. Bach) as well as numerous folksongs. These copies were made from approximately 1854 to 1877, and many of them seem to have aided Brahms in his study of the compositional techniques used by earlier composers. After an overview of Brahms's choral output, the final section of the book demonstrates how Brahm's study of these earlier compositions influenced specific passages in his own choral works.

HEATHER PLATT

Britten, Benjamin 1913–1976

English composer

1. Biography

Blyth, Alan, *Remembering Britten*, London: Hutchinson, 1981

Britten, Benjamin, *Letters from a Life: The Selected Letters and Diaries of Benjamin Britten, 1913–1976*, 2 vols., edited by Donald Mitchell and Philip Reed, Berkeley: University of California Press, and London: Faber, 1991

Britten, Beth, *My Brother Benjamin*, Abbotsbrook: Kensal Press, 1986

Carpenter, Humphrey, *Benjamin Britten: A Biography*, London: Faber, and New York: Scribner, 1992

Duncan, Ronald, *Working with Britten: A Personal Memoir*, Bideford: Rebel Press, 1981

Evans, John, et al., compilers, *A Britten Source Book*, Aldeburgh: Britten-Pears Library, 1987

Gishford, Anthony, editor, *Tribute to Benjamin Britten on His Fiftieth Birthday*, London: Faber, 1963

Headington, Christopher, *Britten*, London: Methuen, 1981; New York: Holmes and Meier, 1982

Holst, Imogen, *Britten*, London: Faber, 1966; 3rd edition, 1980

Kennedy, Michael, *Britten*, London: Dent, 1981; revised edition, 1993

Mitchell, Donald, *Britten and Auden in the Thirties: The Year 1936*, Seattle: University of Washington Press, and London: Faber, 1981

Mitchell, Donald, and John Evans, editors, *Benjamin Britten, 1913–1976: Pictures from a Life*, New York: Scribner, and London: Faber, 1978

Oliver, Michael, *Benjamin Britten*, London: Phaidon, 1996

Palmer, Christopher, editor, *The Britten Companion*, London: Faber, and Cambridge: Cambridge University Press, 1984

White, Eric Walter, *Benjamin Britten: His Life and Operas*, London: Faber, 1970; 2nd edition, edited by John Evans, Berkeley: University of California Press, 1983

Britten's life has been a matter of some public scrutiny since the success of *Peter Grimes* in 1945. Scholarly interest in his music developed quickly, with a collection of analytical essays, mainly by writers personally acquainted with Britten, appearing in 1952. Aspects of the composer's life, however, did not capture attention until shortly after the premiere of *War Requiem* ten years later in 1962. Such interest appears to have developed partly as a response by Britten scholars to understand more fully the influences on Britten's choice of topics and texts for his vocal works. With *War Requiem* in particular, it became apparent that Britten's personal beliefs and convictions formed a substantial context for his compositional genius, although various themes, such as the individual versus society, innocence and innocence lost, and sleep, had been recognized in his operas and other vocal works since *Peter Grimes*. After Britten's death in 1976, more attention has been given to his biography not only to gain a more complete picture of his life as a whole but also to shape and guide new interpretations of his music.

Although the first biographies of Britten appeared in the 1960s, it was after Britten's death that more intense investigations of his life, particularly his homosexuality, were undertaken. The Britten-Pears Library located in the composer's home in Aldeburgh, Suffolk, has been invaluable to those seeking to understand Britten. To that end, the volume compiled by EVANS et al., published to assist the public in learning about Britten's life, career, and music, is an ideal starting point, especially with its biographical outline and extensive bibliography.

Donald Mitchell, more than any other scholar, has cast much light on Britten's life. He was personally acquainted with Britten and was approved by the composer to be his official biographer. Mitchell has provided the public with a number of publications on Britten. MITCHELL is a book of lectures that illustrate Britten's collaboration with W.H. Auden in the 1930s; MITCHELL and EVANS is a collection of pictures that span Britten's life; and Benjamin BRITTEN provides a two-volume set of letters and diaries by Britten. The set of letters and diaries is particularly tantalizing because it covers only the time period from 1929 to 1945. These writings provide insight into the formative years of Britten's life; unfortunately, no similar collection is yet available to reveal the inner workings of Britten's mature years.

To help fill this gap, the biography published by CARPENTER provides considerable insight into post-*Peter Grimes* Britten. The early years are covered, but this book is particularly useful for the later periods, especially as relating to the operas. The reader should be aware, however, that Carpenter adopts a somewhat sensationalistic viewpoint by concentrating on Britten's sexuality. Such focus often obscures or ignores other important motivations and interpretations (including Britten's religious, social, and political views), and one must wonder what interesting tidbits have been left out. Carpenter makes no attempt to mention every piece that Britten composed, and those that have significant homosexual interpretations attached to them figure prominently. Despite the homosexual leaning, however, it is clear that Carpenter has taken full advantage of the material available in the Britten-Pears Library and elsewhere. The book is full of quotations from letters, diaries, interviews, newspapers, and other sources. Carpenter also makes use of publications written by those who worked with Britten on a daily basis and by a number of singers, instrumentalists, writers, visual artists, fellow composers, and scholars who were associated with him.

HOLST, who worked with Britten for almost 25 years, offers a concise overview of Britten's life and works in a manner possible only by someone who personally witnessed Britten's activities as a composer, conductor, and pianist. Holst, as well as Rosamund Strode who succeeded Holst as Britten's assistant, also describes working with Britten in an essay for the group of essays collected by PALMER. Although Palmer's collection concentrates on the music, the first section, "Perspectives," includes personal essays that elucidate Britten's personality as well as his musical abilities.

GISHFORD's edition was a publication put together in secret, intended to surprise Britten on his 50th birthday. It brings together a number of essays from other composers, singers, instrumentalists, writers, and personal friends of

Britten to pay him tribute for his contributions to music. From a biographical viewpoint, the persons included in the book shed light not only on Britten's music but also on who Britten knew and what they thought about working with him.

Working with Britten is the topic of DUNCAN's book. The librettist of Britten's first chamber opera, Duncan was a lifelong friend of Britten, and his book is a candid look at both what it was like to work with Britten and how their friendship survived over the years. The author relies on both his memory and the correspondence he kept, producing a straightforward book with an admittedly personal bias that makes little apology for the information, both positive and negative, that it contains.

BLYTH's collection in memory of Britten is an effort "to preserve the first-hand accounts of how a great composer lived, worked, and behaved." Many of Blyth's contributors are included in the earlier tribute put together by Gishford, but given their different purposes, the tones of the two books are considerably different.

Beth BRITTEN, a contributor to Blyth's collection, also put together her own biography of her younger brother. Her memoir is a poignantly personal account of her brother's life and offers a considerable amount of detail, particularly about his childhood and early years as a composer.

White, Kennedy, and Headington are all concerned with Britten's music within the context of his life. WHITE, with the assistance of John Evans, sketches out Britten's life as a backdrop specifically for the operas, while KENNEDY's biographical overview is intended to prime the reader for a chronological survey of Britten's entire musical output. HEADINGTON combines biographical and musical details to produce a concise study of Britten as man and musician.

OLIVER's volume is one of the newest Britten biographies available. Like Headington, he combines details of biography and music into one coherent text. Unlike Headington, and indeed almost everyone else who has concentrated on Britten's biography, he has the advantages of time and the resources and new interpretations that time brings. Oliver, however, is careful with his own interpretations, preferring to let the music, events, and others' interpretations stand on their own within the context he provides. Readers just beginning to look into Britten may want to start with this biography, as Oliver relies heavily on almost all of the sources listed here.

NIKOLA D. STRADER

2. Operas

Banks, Paul, editor, *Britten's Gloriana: Essays and Sources,* Woodbridge: Boydell Press, and Rochester, New York: Britten-Pears Library, 1993

Brett, Philip, compiler, *Benjamin Britten: Peter Grimes,* Cambridge: Cambridge University Press, 1983

Cooke, Mervyn, and Philip Reed, *Benjamin Britten: Billy Budd,* Cambridge: Cambridge University Press, 1993

Corse, Sandra, *Opera and the Uses of Language: Mozart, Verdi, and Britten,* Rutherford, New Jersey: Fairleigh Dickinson University Press, and London: Associated University Presses, 1987

Evans, Peter Angus, *The Music of Benjamin Britten,* London: Dent, and Minneapolis: University of Minnesota Press, 1979; 3rd edition, Oxford: Clarendon Press, and New York: Oxford University Press, 1996

Herbert, David, editor, *The Operas of Benjamin Britten: The Complete Librettos,* London: Hamilton, and New York: Columbia University Press, 1979; revised edition, London: Herbert Press, and New York: New Amsterdam, 1989

Howard, Patricia, editor, *Benjamin Britten: The Turn of the Screw,* Cambridge: Cambridge University Press, 1985

Mitchell, Donald, editor, *Benjamin Britten: Death in Venice,* Cambridge: Cambridge University Press, 1987

Mitchell, Donald, and Hans Keller, editors, *Benjamin Britten: A Commentary on His Works from a Group of Specialists,* London: Rockliff, 1952; New York: Philosophical Library, 1953

Palmer, Christopher, editor, *The Britten Companion,* London: Faber, and Cambridge: Cambridge University Press, 1984

White, Eric Walter, *Benjamin Britten: His Life and Operas,* London: Faber, 1970; 2nd edition, edited by John Evans, Berkeley: University of California Press, 1983

Interest in the music of Benjamin Britten has grown over the last 40 years of the 20th century, building on a small core of scholarly and critical works devoted primarily to introducing, analyzing, and often extolling Britten's genius as an English composer. A shift can be seen between the earlier writers of the 1950s and 1960s, many of whom personally knew and worked with Britten, and the newer scholars and critics, who had little or no opportunity to become personally acquainted with the composer. Early writers in the forefront of Britten studies focused on writing for the musical connoisseur and provided insights on most of Britten's works without becoming overly technical or analytical. After Britten's death and with several of his operas (most notably *Peter Grimes, Albert Herring, Billy Budd, The Turn of the Screw,* and *Death in Venice*) firmly placed in the repertory of opera companies worldwide, scholarly attention has increasingly focused on score and text analysis and biographical investigations that attempt to identify the personal and musical sources that underlie the genesis, development, and possible interpretations of the operas.

Among the earliest writers on Britten's operas, WHITE's intention is "simply to try to answer some of the more obvious questions an astute listener is likely to ask." To do so, he offers first a short biography of Britten, followed by essays on each of the operas that include a brief synopsis of the libretto, short but effective musical and textual analyses of selected scenes, information about the development of the opera, and a summary of the critical reception at each opera's premiere. The book is especially useful as an introduction to Britten's life and music in general as well as to the operas in particular.

Another early investigation of Britten's works, including the operas, is the collection edited by MITCHELL and KELLER. Although limited by its time of publication (1952), the essays on *Peter Grimes*, *The Rape of Lucretia*, *Albert Herring*, *Billy Budd*, and Britten's realizations of *The Beggar's Opera* and *Dido and Aeneas* are, together with White's book, among the earliest interpretations and analyses of these operas. Compared to later studies of the operas, these essays may appear somewhat limited in scope, but their identification and descriptions of musical themes and motives, literary themes, and relationships to the original literary sources paved the way for the more detailed analyses and divergent viewpoints that characterize the later interpretations.

EVANS's book is considered a classic in Britten studies and is one of the most comprehensive studies of Britten's music available. Evans covers Britten's entire output through critical analyses of what he considers important or interesting portions of the scores, usually devoting entire chapters to each of the operas, except for the Church Parables, which are grouped together. This volume is the main source for information related to the Church Parables (*Curlew River*, *The Burning Fiery Furnace*, and *The Prodigal Son*) and *Owen Wingrave*, and a critical resource for all other works. Almost all writers on Britten's music have relied on Evans's observations at some point, often quoting him to substantiate their own interpretations or, less frequently, to propose an alternative analysis.

PALMER's collection of writings forms another extensive resource on Britten's music that complements and expands upon the earlier sources in Mitchell and Keller, and Evans. Although not devoted strictly to the operas, the bulk of the essays deal with them. Some of the essays are reprints of older material, but most provide new insights especially for the Church Parables, *Owen Wingrave*, and *Death in Venice*.

The Cambridge Opera Handbooks edited by Brett, Cooke and Reed, Howard, and Mitchell each focus on a particular opera. Each handbook follows the general organization outlined for the series, bringing together a variety of essays that provide historical and literary backgrounds, analysis of one or more portions of the score, and critical views that address various—often conflicting—interpretations of the opera under discussion. BRETT's compilation of writings on *Peter Grimes* brings together writings of historical interest, such as E.M. Forster's essays on George Crabbe and Britten's own introduction, as well as newer essays including David Matthews's analysis of act 2, scene 1, and Brett's

own interpretations of Grimes's character in light of Britten's sexuality. Several of the essays provide conflicting interpretations of Grimes's character and form the basis for the prominent critical focus in Britten studies on Britten's homosexuality as an influence not only in the composition of *Peter Grimes* but in the shaping of his entire compositional output.

HOWARD's choice of essays on *The Turn of the Screw* offers a similar variety of interpretive views, beginning with insightful analyses of both Henry James's short story and Myfanwy Piper's reworking of the story as a libretto. Critical essays that examine the unusually tight musical and dramatic structure of the opera are well illustrated with musical examples, although a score is still necessary to follow the entire analysis. A brief look at the opera's performance history rounds out the collection of essays.

COOKE and REED follow the example of Brett and Howard by offering essays on *Billy Budd* that elucidate the literary background of the opera, its unusual compositional history, and its stage history and critical reception since its premiere. The dramatic and musical action of *Billy Budd* is examined as well, including a detailed musical analysis by Cooke of the tonal symbolism Britten used in the opera.

For Britten's last opera, *Death in Venice*, MITCHELL presents a collection of writings that includes firsthand accounts of the compositional history (libretto and music), the first production, and the critical reception at its premiere, along with examinations of Thomas Mann's novella as a source for opera and film and analyses of the music that illustrate its tonal and timbral ambiguities and influences. Mitchell himself offers to the reader his own recollections of conversations with Britten and notes of the opera's genesis and development that provide a unique view of Britten's compositional techniques and abilities.

CORSE concentrates on two of Britten's operas, *Owen Wingrave* and *Death in Venice*, along with operas by Mozart and Verdi, in a study that focuses on the relationship of language and music in opera. With Britten's operas, she is especially concerned with how language limits human perception and behavior and how music can exceed these limits by expressing the nonverbal aspects of human communication and meaning.

HERBERT's contribution to the literature surrounding Britten's operas emphasizes the librettos and the original stage productions. Chapters on "Working with Britten," "Designing for Britten," "Writing for Britten," and staging the first productions of each opera are written by those who were actually engaged in these activities. The complete librettos have been printed and are illustrated with original costume sketches and photographs of the first productions.

BANKS's edition of studies on *Gloriana* is the result of a course on this opera given at the Britten-Pears School for Advanced Musical Studies. The nature of the book's contents is similar to that of the Cambridge Opera Hand-books in that the text includes material on the cultural and historical background of the opera and its libretto, musical and textual analyses, and the critical reception at its premiere. These essays form the only extensive source of material available on this opera.

NIKOLA D. STRADER

3. Other Works

Cooke, Mervyn, *Britten: War Requiem*, New York: Cambridge University Press, 1996

Evans, John, et al., compilers, *A Britten Source Book*, Aldeburgh: Britten-Pears Library, 1987

Evans, Peter Angus, *The Music of Benjamin Britten*, London: Dent, and Minneapolis: University of Minnesota Press, 1979; 3rd edition, Oxford: Clarendon Press, and New York: Oxford University Press, 1996

Mark, Christopher, *Early Benjamin Britten: A Study of Stylistic and Technical Evolution*, New York: Garland, 1995

Mitchell, Donald, and Hans Keller, editors, *Benjamin Britten: A Commentary on His Works from a Group of Specialists*, London: Rockliff, 1952; New York: Philosophical Library, 1953

Palmer, Christopher, editor, *The Britten Companion*, London: Faber, and Cambridge: Cambridge University Press, 1984

Whittall, Arnold, *The Music of Britten and Tippett: Studies in Themes and Techniques*, Cambridge: Cambridge University Press, 1982; 2nd edition, 1990

The study of Benjamin Britten and his music has focused mainly on his life and his operas, but almost all Britten's music has been investigated to some degree by scholars and critics. It can be difficult, however, to find critical interpretations and analyses of most of the nonoperatic works. Except for *War Requiem*, none of the nonoperatic works by Britten has a book devoted to it. To find out more, one must go either to collections of essays devoted specifically to Britten's works as a whole or to books by individual authors who have taken up the task of investigating large bodies of compositions to draw specific conclusions about Britten's music.

The earliest investigation of Britten's works as a whole is the collection edited by MITCHELL and KELLER. Although dated, the essays, most of which were written by those who worked closely with Britten, offer an excellent introduction to the variety of genres in which Britten worked, including not only opera but also vocal music, choral music, chamber music, orchestral music, concertos, piano music, incidental music, and music for young people. None of these essays is overly technical or analytical, and some authors might appear to overexalt Britten's compositional abilities in their enthusiastic discussions of his works. In general, however, the identification, descrip-

tion, and critical interpretation of musical themes and motives, stylistic considerations, and reasons for composition provided in this collection have paved the way for the more detailed analyses and divergent viewpoints that characterize later writings on Britten's works.

EVANS's book, a "classic" in Britten studies, is one of the most comprehensive studies of Britten's music available. Evans covers Britten's entire output through critical analyses of what the author considers important portions of the scores, usually devoting entire chapters to each of the operas and grouping the remaining works by genre and chronology. The only nonoperatic works that receive extensive individual treatment are *The Prince of the Pagodas*, Britten's only ballet, and *War Requiem*, the most ambitious and successful choral-orchestral piece Britten produced. Evans is especially interested in the dramatic quality of Britten's music and develops almost all his analyses to illustrate this quality.

PALMER's edition of writings by several different scholars forms another extensive resource on Britten's music that complements and expands the earlier sources in Mitchell and Keller and the observations made by Evans. The bulk of the essays deal with the operas, but the sections on vocal and instrumental works that cover the song cycles, Purcell realizations, chamber works, orchestral works, and concertos are critical for developing interpretations of these works that take advantage of the research that has occurred since Mitchell and Keller was published.

WHITTALL's investigation is often viewed as both a complement and a supplement to Evans's study. The book offers musical and biographical comparisons of Britten and Michael Tippett, concentrating on compositional techniques, especially manipulations of melody, harmony, and structure, as found in works written by both composers during the same time periods. Although Whittall's analyses provide some additional insights into Britten's use of harmony and melody, the primary importance of the author's contribution comes in the juxtaposition of two contemporaries who illustrate highly individual yet simultaneous paths in the development of English music.

The primary purpose of EVANS et al. is to publicize the numerous sources of information available on Britten's career and compositions. The book comprises a brief chronology of Britten's life and works; a detailed catalog of the incidental music for film, theater, and radio; a list of Britten's recordings (as conductor, pianist, violist, and speaker); and an extensive bibliography covering every aspect of Britten's life and works. Limited only by its time of publication (1987), it is an ideal starting point for those interested in finding sources on the lesser-known works by Britten, including the nonoperatic vocal music, the instrumental works, and the incidental music.

MARK's book is the main source for information and analyses of Britten's music before *Peter Grimes*, providing a detailed, analytical history of the evolution of Britten's style and technique from his childhood, through his time at the Royal College of Music and his life in the United States, to his return to England. Mark focuses on Britten's techniques for achieving "enriched simplicity" through melodic, textual, harmonic, and rhythmic manipulations and adaptations. Although many of Mark's analyses rely on familiarity with Schenkerian analysis and Forte's set theory, much of the surrounding text includes pertinent biographical and compositional information that is accessible to most readers.

Unlike the other sources for most of the nonoperatic works by Britten, COOKE's handbook focuses on one composition, *War Requiem*. With the assistance of Philip Reed, Cooke provides details about Britten's lifelong pacifism and the effect of this pacifism on his choice of poems from the body of war poetry by Wilfred Owen; an analysis of the structure and musical language of *War Requiem*; and an account of the relationship of the work to Britten's output as a whole. A compositional history based on the correspondence and sketches held in the Britten-Pears Library in Aldeburgh and a survey of the varied critical reception of the work from its premier in 1962 to 1989 round out the discussion on *War Requiem*.

NIKOLA D. STRADER

Bruckner, Anton 1824–1896

Austrian composer

1. Biography

Cooke, Deryck, "Anton Bruckner," in *The New Grove Late Romantic Masters,* edited by Deryck Cooke et al., London: Macmillan, and New York: Norton, 1985

Doernberg, Erwin, *The Life and Symphonies of Anton Bruckner,* London: Barrie and Rockliff, 1960; reprint, New York: Dover, 1968

Floros, Constantin, "Anton Bruckner," in *Heritage of Music: The Nineteenth-Century Legacy,* edited by Michael Raeburn and Alan Kendall, Oxford: Oxford University Press, 1989

Neumayr, Anton, *Music and Medicine,* 3 vols., Bloomington, Illinois: Medi-Ed Press, 1994–97

Redlich, Hans, *Bruckner and Mahler,* London: Dent, and New York: Farrar, Straus, and Giroux, 1955; revised edition, 1963

Schönzeler, Hans-Hubert, *Bruckner,* London: Calder and Boyars, and New York: Grossman, 1970

Watson, Derek, *Bruckner,* London: Dent, 1975

Wolff, Werner, *Anton Bruckner, Rustic Genius,* New York: Dutton, 1942

Anton Bruckner has not always fared well with his biographers. To this day, no authoritative, thoroughly documented biography has been published in any language, and none of the works available in English is wholly ad-

equate. Biographers have traditionally tended to offer heavily filtered portrayals of Bruckner's life and character. Even before Bruckner's death, a stock image had begun to emerge: the composer was styled as a naive, mystical character whose cultural, social, and intellectual horizons were circumscribed by his provincial upbringing, his deep piety, and his psychological simplicity. Although not without some basis in fact, such portrayals at best are misleading and at worst verge on caricature. Moreover, many biographers have been too inclined to play the role of apologist or advocate. This tendency peaked in the middle decades of the 20th century, when writers eagerly adopted overtly partisan attitudes in discussing, among other things, Bruckner's negative reception by the important segment of Viennese musical society headed by Johannes Brahms and Eduard Hanslick and the reputedly manipulative behavior of Bruckner's students. These approaches began to wane only in the 1980s and 1990s as scholars grew increasingly willing to recognize Bruckner's personal sophistication, social ambition, and intellectual complexity as well as his provincial idiosyncrasies and profound religiosity. However, this new tendency has been slow to influence English-language writing and thought.

WOLFF's book is the first substantial biography in English. The author, who was a professional conductor, was born into a prominent musical family in Berlin in 1883 and as a boy met Bruckner. He offers an account of Bruckner's life that is personal, rather florid, and filled with many striking details. Although Wolff does not wholly escape the stereotypical images perpetuated by many biographers of Bruckner (as his subtitle implies, he saw Bruckner as a simple provincial soul), his work is relatively free from the aggrieved tone and partisan advocacy that were common at the time of the book's publication. In particular, Wolff is at pains to counter the hagiographic and mystifying impulse of other (German-speaking) biographers. This biography falls far short of modern standards of scholarship (it is rambling and poorly documented), but as a historical document in its own right, Wolff's picture of Bruckner is valuable for its freshness and historical proximity.

REDLICH's volume was published in the first Master Musicians series. Like Wolff's biography, Redlich's work represents a relatively early phase of Bruckner studies. His account of Bruckner's life is short and somewhat sketchy but is followed by a thoughtful discussion of Bruckner's personality that avoids easy simplifications. In particular, Redlich discusses the significance of the editions of Bruckner's works published during the composer's lifetime without resorting to the polemics and dogmatism that usually accompany the topic. The book is far from definitive, but it deserves attention as a corrective to the conventional wisdom of subsequent decades.

DOERNBERG's widely read book, which was written for the "wide circle of music lovers," typifies several important tendencies in postwar British and, to a slightly lesser extent, American reception of Bruckner. Doernberg takes a slightly peculiar, if characteristic, tack. He holds that Bruckner was socially and culturally isolated: "the whole bent of Bruckner's mind was out of keeping with the period in which he lived." Doernberg also posits an enigmatic schism between Bruckner's life and his music; the author refers to "the unaccountable capacity of this timid and apparently limited man to write music with an assurance which was totally absent from his daily life." Despite—or, more likely, because of—his obvious sympathy for Bruckner and his music, Doernberg emphasizes both the difficulties that Bruckner faced in establishing himself in Vienna and the harshly critical response that his symphonies attracted from some critics. Doernberg, along with Deryck Cooke, helped promulgate among English readers the belief that Bruckner was victimized by manipulative and unscrupulous editors and that, as a result, the editions published during his lifetime contain inauthentic, bowdlerized texts. (This position was taken over, probably quite unwittingly, from Nazi-era German criticism.) Despite its obvious partiality, Doernberg's book does contain some useful information, including a number of excerpts from Bruckner's letters (which are otherwise unavailable in English), and it is an important English source of a widespread, albeit questionable, attitude toward Bruckner's personality and life.

SCHÖNZELER's book contains the most extensive, reliable, and useful biographical account available in English. It concisely and often rather dryly outlines the essential facts of Bruckner's life. The text partakes of the same basic tradition that informs Doernberg's volume (e.g., they have similar views on Bruckner editions and his position in Viennese culture), but it avoids the excessive partisanship and hint of zealotry that weaken the earlier book. Schönzeler devotes a separate chapter to Bruckner's character that, like the rest of the book, is temperate and intelligent.

WATSON's book, which replaced Redlich's volume in the Master Musicians series, is competent and reliable enough but conventional in the bad sense. Watson seems to have leaned too heavily on secondary sources; as a result, his work lacks critical focus and does not present a distinctive point of view. The revised edition is little changed and does not take adequate account of work done in the two decades following the publication of the original edition.

COOKE's article on Bruckner is problematic. The author's understanding of Bruckner's character is marred by an uncritical acceptance of the image of Bruckner as an inspired naif who was beset by deep insecurity and intellectual simplicity. Cooke also makes too much of Bruckner's victimization by both his enemies and his "well-meaning, but misguided" allies. Cooke's discussion of the various versions of the symphonies has been quite influential (not surprisingly, considering its place-

ment in the most prestigious English-language musical reference work). Yet, Cooke's treatment of this topic is often frankly incorrect and does not reflect an adequate knowledge of the manuscript sources or the compositional history of the works in question.

The two most discerning biographical accounts currently available in English are both translated from German. FLOROS's concise essay is valuable because it reflects the newly emerging view of Bruckner as more astute and culturally engaged than critics previously believed. Floros deliberately sets out to clear away "many preconceptions about Bruckner," and, although he does not deny Bruckner's relative lack of philosophical and social sophistication, the author pointedly rejects any ascription of "naiveté, simple-mindedness or even childishness to him." Floros also briefly considers the implications of this biographical position for the interpretation of Bruckner's music.

Although it might seem an unlikely source, NEUMAYR's article is important. In about 100 pages, it provides a reasonably sustained and detailed account of Bruckner's life, which rejects the common belief that Bruckner was narrowly pietistic and estranged from the culture of his time and place. By discussing the scope of Bruckner's personal relationships, social connections, and (to a lesser extent) cultural and musical affiliations, Neumayr humanizes the composer and shows that he was more socially engaged and lived a fuller life than is often supposed. Not surprisingly, Neumayr gives due consideration to medical issues. More important is his attention to Bruckner's psychology. With a level of psychological awareness uncommon among Bruckner's biographers, he argues, for example, that Bruckner's inner life did not center exclusively on devotion and piety but was dominated by "conflict between his world of feelings and emotions, and his coolly calculating, rational mind." The author is also rather skeptical of the urge to depict Bruckner as a social and psychological enigma: as Neumayr writes, many of Bruckner's legendary personal oddities prove "on closer inspection, not to be so eccentric and peculiar after all." This stimulating article is a vivid and believable exposition of Bruckner's life.

BENJAMIN M. KORSTVEDT

2. Symphonies

Barford, Philip, *Bruckner Symphonies,* London: British Broadcasting Corporation, and Seattle: University of Washington Press, 1978

Cooke, Deryck, *Vindications: Essays on Romantic Music,* Cambridge: Cambridge University Press, and London: Faber, 1982

Doernberg, Erwin, *The Life and Symphonies of Anton Bruckner,* London: Barrie and Rockliff, 1960; reprint, New York: Dover, 1968

Engel, Gabriel, *The Symphonies of Anton Bruckner*, Iowa City, Iowa: Bruckner Society of America, 1955

Newlin, Dika, *Bruckner, Mahler, Schoenberg*, New York: King's Crown Press, 1947; revised edition, New York: Norton, 1978, and London: Marion Boyars, 1979

Redlich, Hans, *Bruckner and Mahler*, London: Dent, and New York: Farrar, Strauss, 1955; revised edition, 1963

Schönzeler, Hans-Hubert, *Bruckner*, London: Calder and Boyars, and New York: Grossman, 1970

Simpson, Robert, *The Essence of Bruckner*, London: Gollancz, and Philadelphia: Chilton, 1967; 2nd revised edition, London: Gollancz, 1992

Watson, Derek, *Bruckner*, London: Dent, 1975

Wolff, Werner, *Anton Bruckner, Rustic Genius*, New York: Dutton, 1942

Bruckner's symphonies represent a singular case in the standard symphonic repertoire. Critical and public reception alike remain colored by reactions to the composer's vast forms, his mania for multiple revisions of his works, and his reputedly naive and malleable character. There is mounting evidence that Bruckner was both more sophisticated and more resolute than previously thought, placing the presumed influence of his students and colleagues in a different light. Modern scholars may deplore his revisions as unnecessary, but the composer almost invariably regarded them as improvements that facilitated performance and increased his reputation. Much important research remains to be done on the genesis of Bruckner's symphonies. The available literature is dated in this respect; our understanding of these works within their historical context is limited, although individual writers may be proficient in outlining the compositions' thematic and harmonic structures. Too often, discussion centers on the divergent viewpoints of Bruckner's editors, including Robert Haas and Leopold Nowak. The reader is faced with consulting multiple sources, in particular for complete understanding of the symphonies' early versions that are just now beginning to find appreciation.

WOLFF's book contains the first extensive analysis of the symphonies in English. He presents a performer's viewpoint, primarily concerned with contrast, motivic shape, and orchestral color. His personal writing style speaks of his affection for the music, although the analyses are elementary. Wolff holds the advantage of historical proximity to a performing style unheard today. His discussion of the first publications and the (then newly published) critical editions treats them from the standpoint of a practical musician, providing insights into details of the early editions.

NEWLIN's approach to Bruckner analyzes only certain examples from symphonic movements to evaluate the development of the composer's treatment of principal theme, sonata form, adagio, scherzo, and finale. Although insightful and clearly written, the work is dated in many respects. The revised edition does little to update the discussion, ignoring, for instance, modern consensus that the D minor symphony known as *Die Nullte* postdated the First Symphony. Nevertheless, the treatment of Bruckner within the context of two other Viennese composers who struggled for acceptance provides an engaging perspective.

ENGEL's book was the first in English devoted entirely to Bruckner's symphonies. His idiosyncratic analysis depicts these works in pictorial, almost programmatic fashion. Various motives are presented as representing hope, awe, conflict, faith, consolation, etc. This attitude is carried over into Engel's own subtitles for the symphonies: the First is *Storm and Stress*, the Sixth, *Philosophic*, the Ninth, *Farewell*. The book reproduces its musical examples from Max Auer's biography of Bruckner (*Bruckner*, 1923), which predates the critical editions.

REDLICH provides complete thematic analysis of only the Third Symphony. The other symphonies are described primarily in stylistic terms, with special emphasis on Bruckner's self-quotations from his sacred works. Notable for the time is the author's thoughtful appraisal of the *Zero* Symphony in D Minor (*Die Nullte*). Redlich's discussion of versions and editions, while not accurate in every detail (e.g., he greatly overstates the differences between manuscript and first publication of the Sixth Symphony), is generally free of the heated rhetoric that often attends the subject. The revision updates the bibliography, which also facilitates his sparring with Doernberg over subsidiary details.

DOERNBERG devotes half of his book to "Notes to the Symphonies." His thematic and structural analysis is direct and useful. Doernberg is hardly objective on the matter of versions, polarizing the work of editors Haas and Nowak to the latter's detriment. This bias influenced a generation of later commentators, with two important results. Meaningful research on the genesis of the versions was averted (Haas presumably having done all that was necessary), and the eventual publications of first versions of Symphonies 3, 4, and 8 were slow to win advocacy for those works. Doernberg's musical analysis has merit, but the study must be viewed with caution.

SIMPSON offers the most thorough analytical discussion, which is also the most passionate and the most controversial. Simpson approaches Bruckner as a fellow composer and is far more concerned with a delightful harmonic turn than with modern musicological research. Therefore, he advocates the old Bruckner-as-victim stereotype. This paradigm spurs Simpson's insistence that passages he finds objectionable simply could not have originated with Bruckner. However, cited examples from Symphonies 1, 3, and 4 are all documented in the composer's hand. Simpson also advocates a cut in the slow movement of the Second Symphony that is universally decried elsewhere. The second edition adds an appendix addressing the then newly published scores of the first versions of the Fourth and Eighth Symphonies. The third edition incorporates that information, as well as an extensive analysis of the first version of the Third Symphony, within the main text. Portions of the book date from the 1940s and are outmoded. Nevertheless, this text is essential for serious study of Bruckner's symphonies.

COOKE attempts to characterize (in highly partisan fashion) the various versions of the symphonies and their printed editions in the essay, "The Bruckner Problem Simplified." Despite its influence and perceived authority, this article is essentially critical opinion, not a work of scholarly research. Cooke has consulted only secondary sources, not Bruckner's manuscripts, and the conclusions rely too often on the author's personal appraisal of internal score details; still, simple scrutiny of the available literature should have averted blunders such as his assertion that Haas published the 1872 first version of Bruckner's Second Symphony. The piece is marred by further errors and Cooke's arbitrary, unjustified terminology—"first definitive version"—which merely belittles the early versions as being without merit.

SCHÖNZELER provides a brief general discussion of the symphonies and does not analyze the individual works. This book has mainly supplementary value based on its inclusion of historical information and pertinent photographs. Schönzeler's treatment of versions and editions is also conspicuous for its probity and lack of partisanship.

WATSON replaces Redlich's earlier book in the Master Musician Series. His discussion of versions is generally influenced by Cooke and reflects the latter's limitations. The revision adds a brief treatment of the early versions but does not entirely shake off the old prejudices. Watson is generous with musical examples and avoids the trap of viewing the symphonies as variations on a typical construction; each work is presented on its own merits.

BARFORD's slender book borrows heavily on the previous work of Doernberg and Simpson, while adding little in the way of new insights. The author perpetuates some of the more egregious generalizations about the symphony versions and Bruckner's supposed victimization. Barford's analysis of the works is idiosyncratic, to say the least, conjuring up relationships both evident (Beethoven) and tenuous (Josef Lanner and Chopin).

MARK KLUGE

3. Other Works

Göllerich, August, and Max Auer, *Anton Bruckner, Ein Lebens-und Schaffens-Bild*, 4 vols., Regensburg: Bosse, 1922–37; reprint, 1974

Redlich, Hans, *Bruckner and Mahler*, London: Dent, and New York: Farrar, Straus, and Cudahy, 1955; revised edition, 1963

Schönzeler, Hans-Hubert, *Bruckner*, London: Calder and Boyars, and New York: Grossman, 1970

Watson, Derek, *Bruckner*, London: Dent, 1975; 2nd edition, New York: Oxford University Press, 1996

Surprisingly little has been written about Bruckner in English, despite his immense importance in the musical canon. The venerable German-language reference sources written by Ernst Kurth, Göllerich, and Auer have not been translated, and no comprehensive study of the life and works of this major figure has appeared in any language since the 1930s. Researchers concerned with Bruckner's works have concentrated their efforts on his symphonies, which justifiably are seen as his major contribution to the musical literature. Thus, readers interested in his other compositions must glean information from various sources. However, with the exception of the three great masses of the mid-1860s, the *Te deum*, and *Psalm 150*, these nonsymphonic works receive but a passing mention in most of the reference literature. A detailed study in English of all of Bruckner's music is long overdue.

GÖLLERICH and AUER is the standard reference source for all Bruckner research and is still the most comprehensive analysis of the composer's life and works. Begun by Göllerich and completed by Auer, this monumental work was published sequentially between 1924 and 1937. It was reissued in 1974 but has not been translated from German. Every known work by Bruckner is discussed in these four volumes. As in other sources, the symphonies and large choral works receive the most attention, but intriguing details about many lesser-known compositions also appear. Supplementary volumes include numerous complete scores, either printed or in facsimile, that still represent the only published editions of a number of compositions. Although more recent research has overtaken some of the details, no investigation of any of Bruckner's music can afford to ignore this historic publication.

WATSON has provided the best English-language source on Bruckner. His book first appeared in 1975 but was revised and expanded in 1996, during the centennial of Bruckner's death. A considerable part of the book is dedicated to biography and to analyses of the symphonies, but chapters dealing with the smaller works and the sacred choral music also appear. The large choral/orchestral works (the three Masses from the mid-1860s, the *Te deum*, and *Psalm 150*) and the String Quintet in F are examined in substantial detail in these chapters; these cogent studies furnish perceptive musical insights as well as historical details. The lesser works receive but a cursory mention. Appendices include a calendar of Bruckner's life, a catalog of works arranged chronologically by genre, and a list of persons associated with the composer. These supplements provide important information and are much easier to use than those previously published in Göllerich and Auer and in Redlich. For readers interested in Bruckner's complete oeuvre, Watson's book is an excellent entry point, but any thorough understanding of the non-symphonic music requires exploration of the complementary resources provided by Schönzeler and Redlich.

SCHÖNZELER's book could be considered a companion to Watson, as it employs a similar structure and considers essentially the same material. Biographical details absorb more than two-thirds of the text. Only one short chapter is specifically assigned to the music, but numerous insightful comments on individual works appear throughout the other chapters. Details about the early and lesser compositions complement the information found in Watson. Perhaps this book's major contributions to the literature are the author's wonderfully lyrical prose and the inclusion of many photographs of Bruckner and of people and places directly associated with the composer.

REDLICH's book was a significant addition to the literature at the time of its publication. More recent research has overtaken it, and some historical details are now known to be inaccurate. However, this study remains important for its selective musical analyses, which were heavily drawn upon, but not superseded, by Schönzeler and Watson. This book also pays considerable attention to Bruckner's often neglected early works and provides the most significant insights into them since Göllerich and Auer. In the biographical pages, Redlich carefully considers Bruckner's personal and professional relationships and the impact they had on his compositional activity. A calendar of the composer's life, a chronological catalog of his works organized by genre, and a list of persons associated with him are included as appendices. The calendar is complicated by the inclusion of Mahler's life, and the catalog of works and list of persons has been largely supplanted by Watson.

KEITH KINDER

Bulgaria *see* Eastern Europe

Burney, Charles 1726–1814

English organist, music historian, and chronicler

Burney, Charles, *Catalogue of the Music Library of Charles Burney, Sold in London, 8 August 1814*, introduction by Alec Hyatt King, Amsterdam: Knuf, 1973

————, *An Eighteenth-Century Musical Tour in Central Europe and the Netherlands*, edited by Percy A. Scholes, London: Oxford University Press, 1959a

————, *An Eighteenth-Century Musical Tour in France and Italy*, edited by Percy A. Scholes, London: Oxford University Press, 1959b

————, *A General History of Music from the Earliest Ages to the Present Period (1789)*, 2 vols., edited by Frank Mercer, New York: Harcourt Brace, 1935

————, *The Letters of Dr. Charles Burney*, edited by Alvaro Ribeiro, Oxford: Clarendon Press, 1991

————, *Memoirs of Dr. Charles Burney, 1726–1769*, edited by Slava Klima et al., Lincoln: University of Nebraska Press, 1988

————, *Music, Men, and Manners in France and Italy 1770, Being the Journal Written by Charles Burney . . .*, edited by H. Edmund Poole, London: Folio Society, 1969

Burney, Frances, *Memoirs of Doctor Burney, Arranged from His Own Manuscripts, from Family Papers, and from Personal Recollections by Madame d'Arblay*, 3 vols., London: Moxon, 1832; reprint, Farnborough: Gregg International, 1972

Grant, Kerry S., *Dr. Burney as Critic and Historian of Music*, Ann Arbor, Michigan: UMI Research Press, 1983

Lonsdale, Roger, *Dr. Charles Burney: A Literary Biography*, Oxford: Clarendon Press, 1965

Scholes, Percy A., *The Great Dr. Burney: His Life, His Travels, His Work, His Family, and His Friends*, 2 vols., London: Oxford University Press, 1948

In tracing the development of music historiography, it would be difficult to overestimate the significance of Dr. Charles Burney. His ambition to produce the first comprehensive history of music in his native tongue—and thus to "fill up a chasm of English literature"—inspired him to document the musical life of his age and of previous centuries with astonishing energy and tenacity. Despite his humble origins and hectic music-master's schedule, Burney achieved acclaim throughout Europe for his musical scholarship, and his writings still provide a rich source for scholars of 18th-century musical life.

Burney's crowning achievement was his four-volume *General History of Music* (1776–89), which, according to his estimate, took 30 years to research and write. Far from the bland survey suggested by its title, the *General History* is recounted from an engaging personal perspective: Burney speaks critically and authoritatively, condemning the harmonic "crudities" of the hapless John Blow, for example, while expressing boundless enthusiasm for Italian music and the music of Haydn—the "modern" music of his day. Burney's volume 4, which took his *General History* up to "the present time" (1789), is particularly recommended for readers with more than a passing interest in the Enlightenment period. MERCER has done much to render Burney's magnum opus accessible to 20th-century readers: an introduction, critical notes, and detailed index have been added to Burney's text, along with an appendix of letters published here for the first time.

Burney addressed a cultivated English readership in his *General History*, and in many ways his outlook was that of an 18th-century Englishman, but his discussion of music history was by no means insular. In order to collect materials for the *General History*, Burney undertook several European tours, publishing accounts of his musical travels in the early 1770s. Selections from these stories were published in 1927 by Cedric Howard Glover, but Percy Scholes later produced a complete edition of them with explanatory notes in BURNEY (1959a and 1959b). Volume 1 is a pragmatic conflation of Burney's manuscript travel journal and the two editions of his *Present State of Music in France and Italy* (1771); volume 2 is a reprint of the second edition of Burney's *Present State of Music in Germany, the Netherlands, and the United Provinces* (1773). Although Scholes intended his edition to be definitive, the first volume ultimately lacks authenticity. BURNEY (1969) addresses this shortcoming to some extent, as well as Scholes's apparent ambivalence toward the manuscript sources, by publishing a transcription of the original journal kept by Burney during his sojourn in France and Italy. As snapshots of continental musical life in the mid-18th century, these volumes are invaluable; Burney records with delight his encounters with the young Mozart and his father, Rousseau, Hasse, Gluck, Jomelli, Metastasio, and C.P.E. Bach, among others.

By the end of his career Burney had become one of the most well-connected gentlemen in London; in rank and eminence his social circles far exceeded those generally enjoyed by musicians of his day. He was on familiar terms with royalty, to the extent that George III engaged him as official chronicler of the Handel commemoration in 1784, and his opinion on musical matters held great sway. Understandably proud of his accomplishments and "connexions," Burney began to compile his autobiography, which he entrusted to his daughter Frances BURNEY, the novelist and diarist, just before his death: "A book of this kind," he predicted in the opening pages, "though it may mortify and offend a few persons of the present age, would be read with avidity at the distance of some centuries by antiquaries and lovers of anecdote." On taking up the project, however, Fanny censored her father's notebooks heavily, excising vast amounts of text with thick pencil or scissors whenever she judged his words unworthy of the Burney name—we can but speculate on the detailed first-hand accounts of musical events and figures such as Arne, Handel, Garrick, and Johnson, that may have been lost by this calculated act of editorial vandalism. The *Memoirs* eventually produced by Fanny in 1832 present a distorted and overblown account of her father's life, the tone ringing false where the sparkling wit and characteristic animation of Burney's original prose is stifled by his daughter's heavy-handedness.

No doubt sensing the inadequacy of Fanny Burney's work, SCHOLES published a full-length biography, although Burney's manuscript memoirs were not available to him; it was assumed that Fanny had destroyed them entirely. Illustrated with plates of significant people and places in Burney's life, Scholes's lively, well-crafted account explores its subject in contemporary social and musical contexts: hence, we find chapters on Burney's experience of the Gordon Riots and his interest in astronomy alongside discussion of his friendship with Haydn and his introduction to the music of J.S. Bach. Scholes's achievement was to register the importance of Burney as a figure in his own right—previous writers having mentioned him only in passing, as a member of the celebrated literary circle at Streatham or as the father of Madame d'Arblay.

During the 1950s several caches of Burney family papers came to light, which included the fragmentary memoirs. Rediscovery of this material necessitated a fresh assessment of Burney and his career, and it was LONSDALE who rose to the challenge. His is a "literary biography" in every sense of the word: in polished, elegant prose he argues convincingly that it was by seeking fame as "a scholar and a man of letters" rather than a "mere musician" that Burney was able to expand his horizons and climb the social ladder so dexterously, and that his example did much to raise the status of musicians in late 18th-century English society. Lonsdale is the first Burney biographer to make full use of the memoirs; indeed, a whole chapter is devoted to exposing and admonishing Fanny's treatment of the manuscript. Lonsdale marshals his sources masterfully, and a deep understanding of 18th-century life and culture is evident throughout this scholarly but immensely readable narrative.

More recently, Joyce Hemlow's pioneering work on the Burney family papers has been the inspiration for a series of scholarly editions of Burney's writings. In BURNEY (1988), the first volume of Burney's manuscript memoirs from over 100 surviving fragments scattered among archives on both sides of the Atlantic have been carefully reconstructed. Fanny's alterations have been expurgated, and stubborn gaps bridged sensibly with material from Burney's letters and other writings. The result is a coherent, well-indexed account of Burney's career up to 1769, furnished with copious annotations and a useful appendix of excerpts from Burney's articles for Rees's *Cyclopaedia*.

Burney's great prolificacy and prowess as a letter writer are celebrated in BURNEY (1991) an edition of his early correspondence—the first in a planned set of four volumes. Most of this material is collected and published chronologically here for the first time, and although the scars of Fanny's censorship are again in evidence, Ribeiro performs his task with sensitivity and careful judgment. From a blow-by-blow commentary of the writing of the *General History* to his thoughts on Captain Cook's voyages of discovery, Burney's letters are full of spontaneous observations on music, events, and people of consequence, all meticulously elucidated in the editorial notes. Once complete, this edition promises to be of inestimable value to the scholarly community.

Burney's significance as a collector of music and musical literature is highlighted by Charles BURNEY (1973), the sales catalog of his collection published in facsimile by Hyatt King. Although slight, this volume is crucial in establishing the basis on which Burney made his critical and historical judgments, the breadth of his musical experience, and the fate of rare or unusual items from his library listed among the 1,047 lots sold (the auctioneer's annotations recording the purchasers and prices paid are easily legible).

Amid this proliferation of accessible modern editions of Burneyana, one looks principally to GRANT for a scholarly assessment of Burney's powers as critic and historian. From a survey of Burney's writings, Grant defines the critic's aesthetic preoccupations and considers them in relation to his social and cultural milieu; Burney's predilection for Italian over German music, for example, can be seen as a reflection of the English love affair with Italy, ancient seat of civilization and favorite destination for the grand tour. Grant's survey also reveals intriguing discrepancies between Burney's public and private statements, many of which resulted from tensions between critical integrity and his desire for social elevation and recognition; his willingness to temper his published views on Handel's music so as not to fall out of favor with that arch-Handelian George III is the most striking example. Grant's intention is not to undermine Burney's achievements; indeed, he applauds Burney's remarkable foresightedness—Burney was among the first to recognize the great triumvirate of the classical era by linking the names of Haydn, Mozart, and Beethoven in his prose. Scholars will continue to consult Burney's writings as a unique index of 18th-century musical taste, but Grant's well-considered reassessment enables us to do so with greater understanding, insight, and critical awareness.

RACHEL COWGILL

Busoni, Ferruccio 1866–1924

Italian composer and critic

Beaumont, Antony, *Busoni the Composer,* London: Faber, and Bloomington: Indiana University Press, 1985

Busoni, Ferruccio, *Letters to His Wife,* translated by Rosamond Ley, London: Arnold, 1938; reprint, New York: Da Capo Press, 1975

———, *Selected Letters,* translated and edited by Antony Beaumont, New York: Columbia University Press, 1987

Dent, Edward J., *Ferruccio Busoni: A Biography,* London: Oxford University Press, 1933; reprint, Oxford, Clarendon Press, 1966

Levitz, Tamara, *Teaching New Classicality: Ferruccio Busoni's Master Class in Composition,* Frankfurt: Lang, 1996

Roberge, Marc-André, *Ferruccio Busoni: A Bio-Bibliography,* New York: Greenwood Press, 1991

Sitsky, Larry, *Busoni and the Piano: The Works, the Writings, and the Recordings,* New York: Greenwood Press, 1986

Ferruccio Busoni made his mark in Germany's musical life at the beginning of the 20th century in various ways: as pianist, composer, arranger, editor, writer, and teacher. He was an acclaimed virtuoso pianist, yet any time not spent composing was for him time lost. As a composer he began writing in the late 19th-century idiom before embracing new techniques of expression around 1907. His production comprises several works for his instrument in addition to operas (especially *Doktor Faust*), orchestral and chamber works, and songs. He was well known for his numerous arrangements and editions of works by other composers, especially Johann Sebastian Bach. His critical writings show his prophetic desire for musical expression not bound by the limitations of traditional tonality, temperament, and instruments. During the last years of his life he taught a selected group of composition students, including Kurt Weill, to whom he introduced his doctrine of "Young Classicism."

Up to the 1960s, research on Busoni consisted mainly of introductory and, too often, repetitious articles written to generate interest in his life and music. The centenary of his birth in 1966 led to the publication of a few doctoral dissertations, mostly dealing with the piano works written after 1907 and the operas. The scholarly literature has increased sharply in recent years, and Busoni is now considered an important transition figure at the beginning of the 20th century, worthy to be given some space in histories of music, rather than simply being reduced to a footnote, as has long been the case. Reprints of scores and recordings of previously unavailable works are now making possible a better assessment of his career. Vast areas of his life and compositional activity, however, remain almost uncharted territory. The most pressing task is the preparation of a new, critical biography based on unpublished sources, which would correct the more or less idealized image that his entourage has created.

Despite the existence of other, more recent, books in German and Italian, DENT's biography of Busoni remains the most complete narrative of the composer's life. Unfortunately, it no longer answers the needs of modern scholars who too often balk at the absence of footnotes, the undocumented statements, omission of names, occasional dialogues, and so on. Also problematic is that the author, a friend of the composer, was prevented from including certain information by Busoni's widow, who wanted to preserve the mythical image created and disseminated by his disciples.

BEAUMONT, an English musicologist and conductor, offers the only comprehensive book discussing in some detail a significant portion of Busoni's mature compositional output (from 1890 onward). His book, the result of extensive research in the Berlin Busoni collection, provides literary and aesthetic background data and nontechnical analyses of all of Busoni's mature works. Another book laid along the same lines is now needed to do justice to the 235 works written prior to 1890 (many of which are unpublished) as well as to the numerous transcriptions, editions, and cadenzas (approximately 115).

Beaumont also published a substantial collection of carefully annotated letters by BUSONI (1987) in English translation. These 352 letters to 40 correspondents, written from 1872 to 1924, provide insight into the composer's personality and attitude to his works and to various contemporaries. The important correspondence between Busoni and Arnold Schoenberg forms a substantial appendix. Beaumont's collection is a welcome supplement to the comprehensive selection from the 800-odd letters from BUSONI (1938) to his wife Gerda, which document the activities of the touring pianist away from home. Unfortunately, these unannotated letters contain countless omissions of personal matters that are nowadays considered essential to a comprehensive picture of the composer.

SITSKY, an Australian composer and pianist who studied with a disciple of Busoni, offers a detailed survey of the works for piano and for piano and orchestra, including the editions and transcriptions. His book includes several music examples in support of brief analyses of this important segment of the composer's output. Several original works and transcriptions are discussed here for the first time, at least in English and outside doctoral dissertations.

ROBERGE, a Canadian musicologist who has studied Busoni's relationships with the United States and France, offers an extensive reference work on the composer. His book comprises a biographical sketch followed by a list of works providing essential data such as identification number (using Jürgen Kindermann's numbers) and title, author of the text and initial line, date of composition, name of the dedicatee, instrumentation, publication information (including modern reprints), first performance data (when available), and arrangements. This is followed by an extensive retrospective discography that includes piano rolls and recordings by Busoni himself. The larger part of the book is an annotated bibliography of Busoni's writings and of the literature about him, comprising 1,325 detailed citations (with no limitation of language). The bibliography also features a guide to the contents of nine editions of Busoni's writings and a list of dates, casts, and reviews of the performances of his operas. The book concludes with an alphabetical list of works by genre and four indices.

LEVITZ, in a revised version of her Ph.D. dissertation, presents the best example of the type of research that can result from a detailed study of archival sources, chief among which is the extensive Busoni collection of the German National Library. With the help of unpublished sources, such as letters, official documents, and manuscripts, and the diary of Gottfried Galston, a friend of the composer, this Canadian musicologist documents the

workings of Busoni's composition class in Berlin from 1920 until his death and, in so doing, provides a much-needed new biography of the composer's final years.

Only a critical, objective study based on the numerous letters, the unpublished drafts and manuscripts, and other archival documents housed primarily in the German National Library will make it possible to present a clear and undistorted picture of Busoni. Recent research has covered in much detail his contacts with Finland, France, and the United States; it is now especially urgent to incorporate these findings into a new study that would do likewise with his relationships with Italy, Russia, and Switzerland as well as investigate his letters to and from countless correspondents never mentioned in the extant literature.

MARC-ANDRÉ ROBERGE

Buxtehude, Dietrich 1637–1707

Danish-born organist and composer

Snyder, Kerala J., "Buxtehude, Dietrich," in *The New Grove North European Baroque Masters*, edited by Joshua Rifkin et al., London: Macmillan, and New York: Norton, 1985
———, *Dietrich Buxtehude, Organist in Lübeck*, New York: Schirmer Books, and London: Macmillan, 1987
Webber, Geoffrey, *North German Church Music in the Age of Buxtehude*, Oxford: Oxford University Press, and New York: Clarendon Press, 1996

One of the most respected and influential composers of his time, Danish organist and composer Dieterich Buxtehude stands as the principal leading figure in German music between Heinrich Schütz and J.S. Bach. Buxtehude's style was an important formative influence on many young North German composers, and especially Bach, who took Buxtehude's sacred vocal and instrumental music as a model. Buxtehude wrote more than 120 sacred vocal pieces, including oratorios, cantatas, chorale settings, and arias. His most important and influential works are those for organ, which include toccatas, preludes, fugues, chaconnes, pieces based on chorales, and a passacaglia to which Bach's Passacaglia in C Minor is indebted. His organ works represent a fusion of the complex contrapuntal North German style and the brilliant keyboard style of Froberger.

SNYDER's (1987) monograph, recognized as the definitive and indispensable study, takes a comprehensive view of the composer's biography and musical output and is directed to a range of readers: listeners, performers, and scholars. The author addresses this task with a tightly organized presentation and a lucid, engaging prose style. The volume is organized in three parts. Part 1, "Buxtehude's World," addresses his Danish origins, career in Lübeck, connections to musicians elsewhere, and pupils. The four chapters of this section present an excellent synthesis of the biographical, historical, and social contexts from which Buxtehude's music emerged. Part 2 is devoted to the music in detail, addressing in turn the vocal music, works of learned counterpoint, keyboard works, and sonatas. Although the composer's fame derives primarily from his organ music, the largest portion of his oeuvre consists of vocal pieces. This volume offers the most penetrating analysis of this dimension of Buxtehude's music available. Part 3, in three chapters, is titled "Studies Pertaining to Buxtehude's Music." In this group of essays, the author addresses the sources, chronology, and performance of Buxtehude's music, including information derived from a consideration of watermarks and handwriting, theories about the changing temperament of the organ at St. Mary's Church, dated compositions, revisions of the composer's music, and elements of musical style. It outlines the limitations of the available criteria for assembling a chronology of Buxtehude's works and closes with a discussion of performance practices specific to the composer's music. Appendices offer a complete list of the composer's works, a list of his extant prose writings (letters, poems, and dedications of printed works), and the principal sources of his works.

SNYDER (1985) is an updated and slightly expanded version of the author's entry in the *New Grove Dictionary of Music and Musicians* (1980). Her discussion of Buxtehude here will be of interest to readers who seek a concise version of the basic information in the author's 1987 study. Prepared before the completion of her comprehensive study, this version offers up-to-date information without the detail or insight of the larger book. The essay is organized into sections addressing Buxtehude's life, vocal works, and instrumental works. A final section discusses sources, chronology, and literature and is followed by a work list and bibliography.

WEBBER, although not devoted strictly to Buxtehude, will interest those seeking information relating to the composer and his music because, as the author states, "The aim of this book is to examine the surviving repertoire of North German church music composed during Buxtehude's lifetime, . . . and to give due consideration to the context in which the music was composed and performed." Webber takes his readers a long way toward an understanding of Buxtehude and the church music of the latter half of the 17th century by addressing the role of music in religious thought and education; music in the Lutheran liturgy; the influence of Italian music; the contexts of composers in town and court; texts; scoring; compositional techniques and styles; and performance practice. The author, a professional organist as well as active scholar, traces changes in the treatment of rhythm and meter at the hands of German composers and considers the compositional implications of the growing acceptance of a tonal harmonic language. He gives the reader a balanced view of how these changes—many of them introduced by the pervasive Italian style—unfolded alongside the more conventional German techniques of polyphony, including techniques related to ostinato basses and the chorale-based cantus firmus.

JOHN HAJDU HEYER

Byrd, William 1543–1623

English composer

Andrews, H.K., *The Technique of Byrd's Vocal Polyphony,* London: Oxford University Press, 1966

Brown, Alan, and Richard Turbet, editors, *Byrd Studies,* Cambridge: Cambridge University Press, 1992

Fellowes, Edmund H., *William Byrd,* London: Oxford University Press, 1936; 2nd edition, 1948

Harley, John, *William Byrd: Gentleman of the Chapel Royal,* Aldershot: Scolar Press, and Brookfield, Vermont: Ashgate, 1997

Kerman, Joseph, *The Masses and Motets of William Byrd,* Berkeley: University of California Press, 1981

———, "William Byrd," in *The New Grove High Renaissance Masters,* edited by Gustave Reese et al., London: Macmillan, and New York: Norton, 1984

Neighbour, Oliver, *The Consort and Keyboard Music of William Byrd,* Berkeley: University of California Press, 1978

Turbet, Richard, *William Byrd: A Guide to Research,* New York: Garland, 1987

Widely recognized in his lifetime as the "father of English music," William Byrd's reputation has not only retained but has exceeded its former luster. Nineteenth-century commentators were content simply to assert that Byrd's music was equal to, or greater than, that of Giovanni Palestrina, the recognized continental "master" of the High Renaissance. In the 20th century, the aim seemed to be to provide a basis in fact and critical argument for this lofty claim.

Although Byrd himself controlled the music printing industry in England for a significant period, a substantial amount of his music survives only in manuscripts; consequently, there are many pieces that appear without (or with incorrect) attribution or date. Such omissions and errors have naturally led to a scholarly preoccupation with the issues of authenticity and chronology in Byrd studies. To solve these issues, as well as to gain an appreciation of the composer's art, scholars have relied to a great extent on the evidence of Byrd's evolving musical style. Given his long life, prolific output, and notable versatility, stylistic studies have, of necessity, reached an intensity that tends to bring a forbidding quality to their prose. Nonetheless, with so many basic findings attributable to this method of inquiry, it stands as the dominant thrust of Byrd scholarship. Studies of Byrd's personal life, particularly his dangerous yet steadfast commitment to the Catholic cause in officially Anglican England, provide a rich counterpoint to the many treatments of his style. The hypothesis that the composer used his musical skills rather often to express his religious views has understandably attracted great interest among Byrd scholars.

FELLOWES's study of Byrd's life and music was originally written for the tercentenary, in 1923, of the composer's death. Although outmoded in some respects, the revised version of the work that appeared in 1948 still serves as an excellent introduction to its subject. Fellowes treats aspects of Byrd's life and music separately, an approach that introduces an artificial distinction, but he manages nonetheless to bring forth a consistent view of the artist. Fellowes's comments stem from his intimate knowledge of the repertoire; he was responsible for the first modern editions of much of the music and includes in his text many musical examples illustrative of Byrd's style. This often-cited study is valuable especially for its breadth of coverage, touching, for example, on the legal troubles Byrd encountered with his rising fame and fortune and on the composer's relations with his fellow Catholics. Despite the objective tone of Fellowes's discussion of Byrd's religious views, Kerman, in particular, has argued that Fellowes was unable, or unwilling, to provide a full appreciation of the nonconformist aspect of Byrd's life.

NEIGHBOUR presents a volume on Byrd's keyboard and consort music as one of a series of three books entitled "The Music of William Byrd." The series includes the monograph by Kerman (1981) discussed below and Philip Brett's work on Byrd's songs, anthems, and services that is currently in preparation. The authors have set an ambitious critical agenda: a "searching appraisal" of the 500-plus works written by the composer. They also have provided enlightening discussions of authenticity and chronology in the Byrd canon. Neighbour is sharply focused on the music itself, and very often one must have the relevant musical score in hand to follow the author's points. Yet there are excellent, if brief, treatments of broader topics as well, including an informative history of consort music in England and a revelatory view of Byrd's ability to inspire progressive trends in his students' instrumental music despite his own conservatism as a composer. Perhaps most exciting is Neighbour's achievement in moderating the former view that Byrd was, at heart, a composer primarily of vocal music. Especially in his treatment of Byrd's pavans and galliards for keyboard, the author convincingly argues that Byrd poured "intelligence, energy, and certainty of purpose" into his instrumental music no less than into his vocal works.

KERMAN's (1981) work will surely stand for many generations as the outstanding monograph on Byrd's Latin-texted music. Its synthesis of up-to-date research and its masterful critical appraisal make this an indispensable volume for Byrd scholars. Like Neighbour, Kerman does not allow his focus to stray far from the notes Byrd wrote, tackling forthrightly the more problematic issues concerning the sources and purposes of Byrd's music while elucidating the essence of Byrd's stylistic growth. The author traces Byrd's treatment of the motet as a vehicle for musical experimentation, for the most intense personal expression, and for the specific liturgical needs of his fellow Catholics. Despite its focus on Masses and motets, this book captures well the essence of Byrd's musical thought and sets Byrd's contribution clearly apart from those of his contemporaries.

Although it was initially greeted with criticism, ANDREWS's intensive study of Byrd's compositional techniques in his vocal music may now be seen to fit rather well in the canon of Byrd scholarship. Unlike the subjectivity of critical studies, Andrews brings a measure of scientific rigor and objectivity to the study of Byrd's style. The author also appears to have had a strong didactic purpose. Andrews identifies and discusses rather small musical phenomena in Byrd's vocal works, ranging from short passages to such minutiae as the single dissonant interval between two notes. Although its computer-like coverage is exceptional, Andrews's work may otherwise be seen to present an English counterpart to Johann Fux's famous *Gradus ad Parnassum* (1725), which focuses with similar didactic intent on the music of Palestrina. Unlike Fux, however, Andrews includes copious and highly revealing excerpts from the works of 16th-century theorists in his text. This work is a welcome complement to the critical thrust of most other writings on Byrd.

The essays in BROWN and TURBET discuss sources of Byrd's music, the application of computer technology to the study of the composer's style, and Byrd's musical relations with his contemporaries, among other subjects. The volume also includes a valuable critical discography. For the most part, these essays tend to amplify and refine, rather than thoroughly revise, the findings of the recent past.

With his research guide, TURBET has provided a great service to all students of Byrd. It contains a listing, with commentary, of virtually everything written about Byrd that appeared before 1986 (several supplements cover more recent years). Turbet's scope is extraordinarily comprehensive, and his thorough commentary carries considerable authority. In his appendices, Turbet provides a hitherto unpublished report of the 1923 Byrd tercentenary and some valuable directions for future research.

HARLEY has taken on the daunting task of presenting another full-length study of Byrd's life and music. The author's announced aim is to summarize and supplement prior research. Like many other Byrd scholars, he casts a wide net in the search for relevant subjects and in so doing establishes some new findings: the date of 1540 for the composer's birth, for example. Like Fellowes, Harley separates his discussion of the composer's life from that of his music; because of Harley's extensive coverage of each topic, however, it is perhaps more difficult to gain from this presentation a satisfyingly complete view of the composer. Harley does benefit from, and contributes to, much productive work on the chronology of Byrd's music. It is with this book, in fact, that one encounters for the first time a full-length study of Byrd's complete works from a chronological perspective.

KERMAN's (1984) chapter on Byrd is relatively brief, but it provides a remarkably coherent view of the composer. Instead of separating Byrd's life from his music, as has become something of a tradition, Kerman integrates the two topics throughout. Drawing on his own prior work, Kerman presents the powerful argument that Byrd's music was closely affected by the events of his career path and his religious life. Enlivening his already engaging prose as he makes this case, Kerman exhibits the rare inclination in this field to venture into the realm of risky speculation. It is here, for example, that Kerman takes Fellowes to task for underestimating the effect of the most radical elements of Catholic thought on Byrd's creative output. Because it embraces controversy, yet summarizes well the best of recent research, this short and very readable exposition of Byrd's achievements stands as one of the most important studies in the realm of recent Byrd scholarship.

JEREMY L. SMITH

C

Caccini, Francesca 1587–ca. 1640

Italian composer

Bowers, Jane, and Judith Tick, editors, *Women Making Music: The Western Art Tradition, 1150–1950*, Urbana: University of Illinois, 1986

Cusick, Suzanne G., "Of Women, Music, and Power: A Model from Seicento Florence," in *Musicology and Difference: Gender and Sexuality in Music Scholarship*, edited by Ruth A. Solie, Berkeley: University of California Press, 1993a

———, "'Thinking from Women's Lives': Francesca Caccini after 1627," in *Rediscovering the Muses*, edited by Kimberly Marshall, Boston: Northeastern University Press, 1993b

Kirkendale, Warren, *The Court Musicians in Florence during the Principate of the Medici: With a Reconstruction of the Artistic Establishment*, Florence: Olschki, 1993

Raney, Carolyn, "Francesca Caccini, Musician to the Medici, and Her Primo Libro (1618)," Ph.D. dissertation: New York University, 1971

Francesca Caccini was one of the first professional female musicians to combine singing and composing in her career and to be internationally renowned. In early German musicological studies, she was both lavishly praised and severely criticized, perhaps because of her gender. Aspects of her life and works were the focus of several articles and one dissertation through the greater part of the 20th century. However, with the recent surge of interest in women in music, Caccini has become an important subject in musicological literature. She is mentioned in every book on women in music as a model example of an early woman composer, and she has proven a felicitous subject indeed for Cusick's explorations of gender relationships in 17th-century Florence, both within operatic plots and in Caccini's professional and personal life.

RANEY's dissertation, the only monograph on Caccini, presents a documentary study of Caccini's life and a stylistic analysis of her monodies in her *Primo libro delle musiche*. The author cites many documents from Florentine archives to portray Caccini's life and relationships with her family, colleagues, and court functionaries. The study is an expansive and readable account of Caccini's life, but many errors exist (as Kirkendale points out), and much additional documentary evidence has been located since by Kirkendale and Cusick. Raney's stylistic analysis of the monody publication is relatively lengthy and unimaginative. It includes a section on the texts in which the author discusses poetic form and meter; the section on musical analysis focuses on melody (emphasizing how well suited to the voice these monodies are and the high degree of coloratura they exhibit), but other aspects, such as harmony and harmonic rhythm, bass lines, dissonance, and word painting, are covered as well. The author's works list and discussion of lost works is helpful, as are the transcriptions of some of the monodies.

Jane Bowers's article "The Emergence of Women Composers in Italy, 1566–1700" in BOWERS and TICK traces Caccini's career briefly; however, more important is the context in which the author places Caccini's activities. Reading the chapter, one sees how exceptional were Caccini's accomplishments not only in relation to the activities of other women at the time (Bowers supplies simple statistics detailing the number of women composers and their compositional output) but also in the face of social opposition to professional women musicians and the scarcity of professional posts available to women at that time.

KIRKENDALE's 30-year study of 200 years of Medici musical patronage in Florence, painstakingly undertaken in archives and libraries across Italy, traces Caccini's life in Florence. Quotations from primary sources abound; indeed, the author states, "I aim at saying nothing which cannot be documented with a primary source." The author treats Caccini's life chronologically, with excellent documentation on her activities singing for her Medici patrons and her compositions for court festivities. There is a mass of detail in this book, and the author integrates his work with that of other secondary sources, supplying references to them in rebuttal or support of their statements. However, Kirkendale does not document Caccini's activities in Lucca in the late 1620s and in Florence during the

1630s, although she was actively singing for the grand duchesses. Furthermore, the untranslated quotations, some more than a page long and liberally interspersed with the author's commentary, make for very disjunct reading for those unfamiliar with Italian. Although the gist of Caccini's career and interactions with the Florentine court can be obtained by reading the author's commentary alone, many of Kirkendale's subtler observations about Caccini and her relationships with family and colleagues at court will be lost.

CUSICK (1993a) discusses the plot and analyzes scattered excerpts of music from *La liberazione di Ruggiero dall'isola d'Alcina*, the most significant musico-theatrical work by Caccini and one that was created for an important political event. Because the plots of such occasional works typically present allegories that affirm the ruling monarchy, because the work was written by a woman and sponsored by one of the ruling female regents of Florence, and because its plot involves two women antagonists (sorceresses) fighting for power over the male character Ruggiero, *La liberazione* represents a superb case study for Cusick to examine the ways in which women wielded, or were perceived as wielding, power in 17th-century Florence. The author supports her reading of the power struggle between the two sorceresses with musical examples that characterize the approaches taken by each woman in her quest for dominance over Ruggiero's action. Alcina uses chromaticism, an extended tonal range, and a reliance on musical rather than poetic form—displaying her "mastery over the formal and tonal means of musical pleasure"—in her futile attempt to influence Ruggiero. However, Melissa, in the male guise of Ruggiero's tutor, sings diatonic, firmly tonal music that remains faithful to word accent—"rational rather than . . . sensual in appeal"—and successfully influences Ruggiero's actions. According to the author, Caccini's musical portrayal of these characters and their relationship with Ruggiero—and, by extension, with all men—reveals an acceptable model, for that time, through which women can effectively rule: women must "speak and act from within the androcentric discourse of patriarchy, repressing what is feminine within them." Given limited space, Cusick's musical examples are short and few, but they support her argument well, and their discussion is easily followed.

CUSICK (1993b) refutes the traditional ending to Caccini's life story (that is, that she died from cancer of the mouth after remarrying and retiring from public life), which was relayed in successive musicological works from the late 1800s through Kirkendale. Cusick accomplishes this revisionist history through careful archival research inspired by a feminist methodology in which the author uses personal insights gained from her own experience as a woman musician to suggest alternative interpretations of "facts" from Caccini's life. In short, Cusick refused to believe that such a successful, professional musician would renounce her career on becoming a widow and remarrying, and she sought, successfully, to prove her contention. The author first traces the source relaying Caccini's death—a contemporary horoscope—and proceeds to document Caccini's activities after supposedly retiring. In reality, Caccini remarried a nobleman of Lucca who was also a musician, founder of a musical academy, and prominent in another academy whose presentation of musical *intermedii* coincided with Caccini's arrival in Lucca. Such coincidences lead the author to suggest that Caccini in reality had, on remarrying, entered into a contract with this nobleman, providing legitimacy to her new husband's heir (whether or not Caccini was the natural mother) and professional musical services. In return, Caccini greatly increased her social status; however, her position as wife of an aristocrat prevented public acknowledgment of these services. Cusick then traces Caccini's musical services on her return to Florence, where she was listed in payrolls of the grand duchesses not as a common musician but as lady-in-waiting supplying musical services; thus, through the course of her life, Caccini greatly changed her social fortune through her skill as a professional musician and adroit marriages. Cusick has written a fascinating history, personally charged with an explicit feminist agenda that makes the story even more compelling, of the end of Caccini's life.

ROARK MILLER

Caccini, Giulio 1551–1618

Italian singer and composer

Caccini, Giulio, *Le nuove musiche,* edited by H. Wiley Hitchcock, Madison, Wisconsin: A-R Editions, 1970

Carter, Tim, *Music in Late Renaissance and Early Baroque Italy,* London: Batsford, and Portland, Oregon: Amadeus Press, 1992

Hanning, Barbara Russano, *Of Poetry and Music's Power: Humanism and the Creation of Opera,* Ann Arbor, Michigan: UMI Research Press, 1980

Kirkendale, Warren, *The Court Musicians in Florence during the Principate of the Medici: With a Reconstruction of the Artistic Establishment,* Florence: Olschki, 1993

Palisca, Claude V., *The Florentine Camerata: Documentary Studies and Translations,* New Haven, Connecticut: Yale University Press, 1989

Pirrotta, Nino, and Elena Povoledo, *Music and Theatre from Poliziano to Monteverdi,* translated by Karen Eales, Cambridge: Cambridge University Press, 1982

Rosand, Ellen, editor, *Baroque Music. I: Seventeenth Century,* New York: Garland, 1985

Giulio Caccini is remembered as the earliest practitioner of Italian monody. His publication *Le nuove musiche* (1602) is one of the earliest printed sources for monody.

The characteristic musical texture of monody, a dominating melodic vocal line supported by a sustaining, slower-moving bass line (with harmonies implied but not written out), contrasts greatly with the imitative polyphonic textures that pervade much of the music of the 16th century. For this reason, scholars seized on Caccini and his "new musical pieces" as convenient markers in the shift from Renaissance to baroque musical epochs. However, scholarship has also focused on two other significant aspects of Caccini's career: his roles as vocal pedagogue and as composer of early opera. In his lengthy preface to *Le nuove musiche*, Caccini included instructions on how to sing his monodies that are invaluable for today's performers trying to re-create his music; no performance practice manual on baroque singing is complete without mention of this work. Finally, much scholarship has been devoted to untangling the roles that Caccini and his court rivals played in the development of opera, another new baroque genre that would eventually dominate musical capitals across Europe.

Despite Caccini's relatively prominent place in music history, there is no published English-language monograph devoted to him. The earliest scholarship on Caccini was published in Italian and German and is relatively inaccessible; only in the 1950s did he begin receiving treatment in English-language periodicals and unpublished theses. Fortunately, critical scholarship on Caccini is available in an assortment of books containing reprinted essays, chapters summarizing earlier research, or new research covering broader topics than a single musician.

As editor of Caccini's two published editions of monody, Hitchcock in CACCINI (1970) thoroughly examines the music written by Caccini, both published and in manuscript, and is well qualified to assess his stylistic innovations. In his edition of *Le nuove musiche*, Hitchcock carefully and separately displays the texts in their original poetic structure and provides translations—an important point given the careful consideration Caccini gave to the texts when setting them to music. Especially important, however, is Hitchcock's translation of Caccini's famous preface, in which he also includes Caccini's original musical examples, which are vital to understanding the points on vocal technique and practice made by Caccini. In addition, the ample annotations to the translation help clarify ambiguities inherent in Caccini's text.

ROSAND's anthology contains two important studies of Caccini. Nigel Fortune's groundbreaking work on "Italian Secular Monody from 1600 to 1635" was written in the mid-20th century and set the path for all future investigations of this genre. Although the scope of the article (a summary of his dissertation research) is extremely broad, investigation of Caccini's music receives an important place: Caccini is viewed as progenitor of Florentine monody as opposed to styles of monody that developed in other cities (Rome and Venice). A few short musical examples flesh out the simplistic stylistic comparisons between Caccini's monody and the monodies of his successors and contemporaries in other cities; the author also discusses texts used by the various composers. Fortune concludes that, despite Caccini's initial importance in the development and proliferation of monody throughout the peninsula, the specific style of Florentine monody eventually languished in comparison to the more vital styles of Venetian and Roman monody.

Also included in Rosand's collection is Hitchcock's stylistic assessment of the monodies of *Le nuove musiche*, which is based on a much more thorough (but easily comprehensible) analysis of the songs than had been done previously by Fortune. Fundamental to the author's approach is reconciling the seemingly paradoxical characteristics of Caccini as virtuoso singer and Caccini as reformer of vocal music who attempted to fulfill the goal of contemporary Florentine humanists to reassign primacy of text to vocal music by eliminating extravagant vocal display that interferes with text comprehension. Hitchcock shows that Caccini combined these varying tendencies by restricting his written-out ornamentation to strong syllables of the text (which would be emphasized in natural speech) and to texts with strongly affective content. The highly refined approach taken by Caccini in writing out previously improvised ornamentation is one of the features that makes this music "new."

KIRKENDALE's 30-year study of Medici musical patronage in Florence, painstakingly undertaken in archives and libraries across Italy, is the definitive biographical study on Caccini. Although the book is an exhaustive compendium covering 200 years of Medici patronage, Kirkendale devotes over 60 pages to tracing Caccini's life in Florence. Quotations from primary sources abound; indeed, the author states, that he aims "at saying nothing which cannot be documented with a primary source." Such careful scrutiny of documents allows Kirkendale to clarify biographical questions pertaining to Caccini's familial relations, and it also helps draw a very human picture of the musician, for we see Caccini in the unflattering light of various political intrigues as well as basking in the success of his horticultural endeavors. Kirkendale's account of Caccini's life is chronological, focusing mainly on the singer-composer's musical activities at court and on trips away from Florence as well as his relationships with other musicians both at court and abroad. There is a mass of detail in this book, and the author integrates his work with that of other secondary sources, supplying numerous references to them in rebuttal or support of their statements. A final section covers the tributes paid to Caccini by contemporaries and composers of the following generation, to which Kirkendale appends a thorough list of sources and editions of Caccini's music (more comprehensive than the list found in the *New Grove Dictionary of Music and Musicians*). Unfortunately, the untranslated quotations, liberally interspersed with the author's commentary, make for very disjointed reading for those unfamiliar with Italian (and some Latin). Although the gist of Caccini's career and interactions with the Florentine court can be obtained by reading the author's commentary alone, many of Kirkendale's subtler observations about Caccini and his relationships with other musicians of the period will be lost.

Pirrotta's seminal article, "Early Opera and Aria," in PIRROTTA and POVOLEDO, admirably explicates the confusing history of the earliest operas and the jealous rivalries of their creators: Caccini, Peri, and Cavalieri. The author also examines the musical styles of these composers, quoting liberally from statements actually made by them to help reinforce his observations, and he comes up with basic differences such as Peri's "dramatic" versus Caccini's "lyric" temperaments. Indeed, the literary quotations are perhaps more effective than the musical examples supplied by the author, which are not analyzed and are only briefly discussed. Furthermore, one is disappointed that Pirrotta compares musical examples of Peri's opera and Caccini's monodies—not Caccini's own opera on the same text.

HANNING actually compares the music of the two operas by Peri and Caccini and supplies generous musical examples and extensive analyses of them along with a thorough examination of the text and its structure (meter and rhyme scheme). The author reaches strong conclusions with regard to the individual composers' styles. In less affective sections of the libretto, for example, Caccini uses harmonic progressions and rhythms that follow a logic independent of text structure, whereas Peri relies heavily on rhyme schemes to organize his harmonic and melodic goals. In more affective textual passages, Peri includes rhythmic syncopation that creates harmonic and rhythmic tension over static bass harmonies, a much more dramatic effect than the lyric convention of melodic sequencing used by Caccini in setting the same passages. Although generally accessible to any motivated reader on the topic, the inclusion of numerous poetic extracts in Italian, lengthy musical examples, and diagrams mapping the harmonic rhythm in tandem with rhyme scheme can be intimidating.

PALISCA's volume on the Florentine camerata is important for understanding Caccini's relationship to the Florentine humanists in whose circles he traveled. The main contents consist of documents written by members of the camerata in the original language and in translation (side by side); by reading these documents we can see firsthand the ideas that might have influenced Caccini in his composition. (Palisca also supplies copious introductory notes for each document.) Also important in this volume is the author's introductory chapter, which details the history of the camerata; discusses its host, Bardi; and disentangles numerous secondary sources that have lumped together uncritically the activities of actu-

ally disparate societies and organizations all under the term "Florentine camerata."

In the chapter "The Florentine 'New Music'," CARTER provides an excellent summary of much of the above scholarship, complete with musical examples and excellent analyses that are easily accessible to any reader. The author makes an important point in this chapter when arguing the close relationship between the "new" monody and its not-so-distant cousin, the polyphonic madrigal. Carter's footnotes should be very helpful to the student, as they reference many important and more current articles available only in periodical format.

ROARK MILLER

Cage, John 1912–1993

United States composer

Cage, John, *I–VI*, Cambridge, Massachusetts: Harvard University Press, 1990
———, *For the Birds: John Cage in Conversation with Daniel Charles*, Boston, Boyars, 1981
———, *Empty Words: Writings '73–'78*, Middletown, Connecticut: Wesleyan University Press, 1979; London: Boyars, 1980
———, *M: Writings, '67–'72*, Middletown, Connecticut: Wesleyan University Press, and London: Calder and Boyars, 1973
———, *Silence: Lectures and Writings*, Middletown, Connecticut: Wesleyan University Press, 1961
———, *X: Writings '79–'82*, Middletown, Connecticut: Wesleyan University Press, 1983
———, *A Year From Monday: New Lectures and Writings*, Middletown, Connecticut: Wesleyan University Press, 1967
Gena, Peter, and Jonathan Brent, editors, *A John Cage Reader: In Celebration of His 70th Birthday*, New York: Peters, 1982
Griffiths, Paul, *Cage*, London: Oxford University Press, 1981
Kostelanetz, Richard, *Converging with Cage*, New York: Limelight Editions, 1988
Perloff, Marjorie, and Charles Junkerman, editors, *John Cage: Composed in America*, Chicago: University of Chicago Press, 1994
Pritchett, James, *The Music of John Cage*, Cambridge: Cambridge University Press, 1993
Revill, David, *The Roaring Silence: John Cage, A Life*, New York: Arcade, 1992

John Cage—variously called a composer, philosopher, charlatan, member of the avant-garde, and inventor—is one of the most difficult to characterize of the eclectic composers of the 20th century. This difficulty stems from his constant pushing of the boundaries of music and composition in order to "write the music [he hadn't] yet heard." Allegedly labeled "an inventor of genius" by Arnold Schoenberg, Cage devoted his life to writing music from a decidedly philosophical and ethical perspective. His oft-repeated dictum that music should just allow sounds to be themselves is often interpreted as license for anarchy. In reality his concern, especially after *4'33"* (the silent piece), was to strip hierarchy, not just harmonic or tonal, but also that of compositional hierarchy and choice, from the music he wrote.

Starting from a self-created dodecaphony and moving through a period of writing for the prepared piano, Cage's exploration of chance operations after his exposure to the Chinese *I Ching* or *Book of Changes* led him to create a new compositional path. Seeking new means of making and organizing sounds, while at the same time removing his own faculty of choice from those decisions, Cage wrote works such as *4'33"* and *Musicircus*. These works and many others try to create circumstances in which the sounds (or music) happen without Cage determining precisely what occurs, but with the composer reserving the right to select solutions that are beautiful. This last concern was important to Cage, because he felt that it was a matter of getting the question, or original premise, of a piece correct that caused the composition to be beautiful; beauty was not a function of his own compositional choices. Cage's engagement with sounds also led him eventually into the literary arts with his famous *Mesostics* and other word-play works.

The student of John Cage will find much to be learned from his own writings included in a half-dozen books: CAGE (1961), CAGE (1967), CAGE (1973), CAGE (1979), CAGE (1983), and CAGE (1990). None of these require any musical background, although musical training will sometimes be an asset in comprehending some of the discussions of the earlier works of Cage by other people. However, the reader is cautioned that to gain the most from these collections of works, lectures, articles, and miscellaneous writings, she or he will need patience and the ability to synthesize multiple lines of simultaneous discourse. Cage's own writings explain much about his thought process, but that process is evolutionary and sometimes apparent only in disparate bits of text. One can even retrace the path of his intellectual development by reading the texts he mentions as important or useful to him.

The works by PERLOFF and JUNKERMAN and by GENA and BRENT include articles by the composer, transcriptions of performance pieces, and lectures given by Cage in various venues. As with most self-created writings by composers, one must take these texts with a healthy dose of skepticism and remember to search for second-party corroboration of the facts Cage reports, for Cage himself cautions that he only remembers the interesting things in his past. The many anecdotes sprinkled through the volumes also illumine Cage's relationship with his friends and acquaintances.

CAGE (1981), a book of six interviews with Cage, provides a different avenue into Cage's thoughts and understandings of music. The interviews are augmented by other texts by or about Cage that have appeared in other sources, arranged in a more-or-less coherent sequence. This is also the pattern for KOSTELANETZ's volume, although he arranges the questions and answers from disparate sources into categories that cover topics such as Cage's music before 1970, his performances, aesthetics, precursors, successors, and so forth. Kostelanetz also provides an extensive bibliography, but many new books, articles, and pieces have appeared since this book was first published. These two volumes make a good combination, covering a total of some 25 years of Cage's experiences and writings. In both cases, Cage reviewed the materials, offering his emendations to earlier texts either in brackets or in notes.

REVILL is the best comprehensive source for the student of Cage. It has the advantages of covering all of Cage's life and reflecting the author's close interaction with the composer during the writing process. The prefatory material clearly outlines the process of how the book came to be and the scope of Cage's input into its writing. It is fully annotated and chronologically organized and also provides a detailed bibliography and a chronological work list (musical and visual). The nonmusician will gain much insight into John Cage, but the text does require familiarity with 20th-century music and composers, as their works and relationships to Cage form part of the story told in this volume. Although one can skip those references and still learn a great deal, it enriches the reader's experience to know who Henry Cowell was or what Stravinsky's *L'histoire du soldat* sounds like to appreciate the references throughout the book.

A good complement to Revill is PRITCHETT. This volume tries to address the act of composition, honoring both the composer and the completed compositions. This rather difficult task is carried out well by Pritchett, who provides the reader with a chronological narrative about Cage and his music. Drawing on his insights gained from retracing Cage's intellectual path through Zen, the *I Ching,* and modern music and art and from his engagement with both the music and the man (he spent much time with Cage and was granted access to many of Cage's papers), Pritchett analyzes the music, word art, and visual art of Cage by employing different methods proper to each kind of work. The text, gracefully written and informative, does demand from the reader moderate to advanced knowledge of musical notation and a fairly broad knowledge of the music of the 20th century. Pritchett also offers one of the best explanations available of Cage's chance procedures in composition.

GRIFFITHS is probably the most theoretically rigorous of the texts discussed here, presupposing that the reader recognizes more than the rudiments of 20th-century music theory and has an understanding of British musical terminology. The author groups Cage's works into periods that he calls "Chromatic Studies," "Rhythmic Systems," "Towards Silence," "Beyond Composing," and "Beyond Music (And Back Again)." In each section he describes the evolution of Cage's style by using specific pieces and suggesting potential models and influences. Griffiths also includes a work list and bibliography, both of which are good for the period they cover (through 1981).

MARIO CHAMPAGNE

Canada

Amtmann, Willy, *Music in Canada 1600–1800,* Montreal: Habitex Books, 1975

Bradley, Ian, *Twentieth Century Canadian Composers,* 2 vols., Agincourt, Ontario: GLC, 1977–82

Diamond, Beverly, and Robert Witmer, editors, *Canadian Music: Issues of Hegemony and Identity,* Toronto: Canadian Scholars' Press, 1994

Ford, Clifford, *Canada's Music: An Historical Survey,* Agincourt, Ontario: GLC, 1982

Kallmann, Helmut, *A History of Music in Canada 1534–1914,* reprinted with amendments, Toronto: University of Toronto Press, 1987

Kallmann, Helmut, et al., editors, *Encyclopedia of Music in Canada,* Toronto: University of Toronto Press, 1981; 2nd edition, 1992

McGee, Timothy J., *The Music of Canada,* New York: Norton, 1985

Morey, Carl, *Music in Canada: A Research and Information Guide,* New York: Garland, 1997

Proctor, George Alfred, *Canadian Music of the Twentieth Century,* Toronto: University of Toronto Press, 1980

The history of Canada, and therefore the history of its music, embraces two cultures—English and French. Although these cultures intersect often and at various levels, each has its own point of view and inner forces that affect its course. Generally speaking, the written history of music in Canada has concerned itself primarily with its European roots and has followed the European model in other ways as well: the creators of music and the music they have created, especially the music written in the forms and styles of their European ancestors, have been given priority. It is only recently that the music of aboriginal peoples, folk music, and popular music has received more than passing recognition. Only three histories of the music of Canada have been published, none recently. All are products of their time, approaching the subject from an English/French duality rather than an indigenous/immigrant or composition/folk song partition.

KALLMANN (1987) was the first of these histories to appear, and it not only set the tone for those that followed but also provided the information base for the parallel sections in the later histories. The author has opted for what he calls an "unorthodox approach." He states in his introduction: "The aim of this book is the description of music at various stages of Canadian history and of the meaning it held in the life of the Canadian people." To Kallmann, the available data indicated an approach that was concerned "more with social than with artistic aspects of music." These statements notwithstanding, the underlying historical view is one of progress (growth), and the narrative is as much centered on important individuals as it is on music making in a given city or region or of a given ethnic group. To his credit, Kallmann deals with sacred and secular music with an even hand throughout.

FORD also approaches the history of music in Canada from a sociological perspective in his work, which is intended as a textbook. The introduction to Ford's survey is an extensive explanation and justification of his thinking. Nevertheless, as he states in his postscript, he concentrates on "some of the achievements of Canadian musicians, from the first settlements through periods of crises and growth to the present day [early 1970s]." Thus, in spite of his intentions, Ford has written a rather traditional history and one that includes a modicum of analysis, especially in the final chapters. In this regard, it bears noting that the greater part of Ford's book is devoted to the post–World War I period and thus nicely complements Kallmann.

McGEE provides a traditional but compact musicohistorical survey. There are short, musical examples in every chapter, including the last, which briefly discusses the music of aboriginal Canadians. Many of the examples are provided with what McGee calls "analytical hints." The author also includes an anthology containing 13 works or sections thereof. Like Ford, McGee treats all aspects of the field equally only in the early periods. In the post-1945 period, composition is considered to be that aspect of musical life most worthy of study. However, because of space, only a few individuals and their works are examined. Although published later, McGee covers roughly the same time period as Ford.

PROCTOR has written a companion to the 20th-century sections of Ford and McGee. His aim is to inform the reader about the wealth of concert music written in Canada. He describes a very large number of works, but few of his commentaries are analytical in nature. Each time period, including a chapter on 1967, Canada's centennial year, is organized by genre (opera, song, orchestra, choral, piano, chamber, ballet, organ, electronic). Useful features include a chronological table of Canadian history, music, and other arts from 1900 to 1979 and the sources of the scores and recordings for the works discussed.

BRADLEY is a guide to 64 works—mostly instrumental—by 20 Canadian composers. The selection is well balanced: compositions by composers from the early part of the century (Willan, Champagne, and MacMillan), women composers (Coulthard, Pentland, and Archer), and Quebec composers (Papineau-Couture, Mercure, Garant, Tremblay, Mather, and Prévost) are discussed, as are works by some of the best-known composers from English Canada (Adaskin, Weinzweig, Turner, Freedman, Schafer, Morawetz, Ridout, and Somers). For each composer there is a brief, general introduction including biographical information and an overview of his or her works up to the date of publication. The compositions discussed are liberally illustrated with musical examples. The analyses, however, are not detailed. The writing and kind of information given is directed to the general reader, and a younger one at that. In this regard, Bradley is similar to the music appreciation books by Joseph Machlis, especially his *Introduction to Contemporary Music* (1961).

AMTMANN supplies the earliest and most thorough investigation of the music of French Canada. He is also the only writer to concentrate exclusively on the music of Quebec. The two versions of the book—one in English and one in French—although similar, are not the same. The French version, which has the more accurate title, is a translation of the English version with an added final chapter that extends the time period covered from 1800 to 1875 and numerous facsimiles of title pages, concert programs, advertisements, etc., as well as color plates that reproduce relevant works of art. Most of these illustrations, which form the basis for the historical narrative, are not found in the English version. Amtmann has done an admirable job of balancing the religious and secular aspects of life in Nouvelle-France—the former takes precedence in the discussion of the 17th and early 18th centuries, and the latter comes to the fore in the discussion of the late 18th and 19th centuries.

The DIAMOND and WITMER anthology is essential reading for those interested in this topic. In selecting and organizing the material to be included and in writing the essays that introduce each of the sections, the editors have sought to highlight some of the recent issues in musicology, ethnomusicology, Canadian studies, and postmodern theory. The introductory essay (by Diamond) is especially helpful in identifying and explaining the two primary issues: hegemony and identity. Students of Canadian music will find this book informative not only because it discusses the views of other disciplines but also because it provides a counterbalance to traditional thinking about music, whether that thinking has a positivistic or sociological bias. Many of the essays are also notable for their extensive bibliographies.

The second edition of KALLMANN (1981) is the primary source available to date for information on the quality and variety of music in Canada. The goal of the encyclopedia—to cover all kinds and all aspects of music—has for the most part been realized. The emphasis throughout, however, is on people—composers, educa-tors, performers, etc.—and many subjects, for example, popular music, are covered via discussions of the persons involved rather than in separate articles. Exceptions include the extensive essays on "Native North Americans in Canada," "Folk Music," and "Ethnomusicology." The discographies, excellent at the time of publication, are now out of date because of the explosion of recordings in the 1990s. The numerous pictures of people, places, programs, and music are a helpful feature. Because numerous entries in the first edition have been dropped (although some of the information in them has been incorporated into other articles), it might be useful to consult the earlier edition as well.

MOREY provides an annotated guide to most of the literature, past and present, on music in Canada. He has selected the most important sources of information on a variety of topics, including those that reflect the musicological thinking and interests of the people working in the field in the 1990s. Because much of the basic research on and writing about music in Canada is found not in books but in articles, and these are not always in journals indexed by the usual sources, the reader will find Morey to be an especially useful guide to further reading.

EUGENE CASJEN CRAMER

Cantata: French Baroque

Anthony, James R., *French Baroque Music from Beaujoyeulx to Rameau*, New York: Norton, 1978; revised edition, Portland, Oregon: Amadeus Press, 1997

Barthélemy, Maurice, *André Campra (1660–1744): Étude biographique et musicologique*, Paris: Picard, 1957; revised edition, Arles: Actes Sud, 1995

Girdlestone, Cuthbert, *Jean-Philippe Rameau: His Life and Work*, London: Cassel, 1957; revised edition, New York: Dover, 1969

Sloan, Lucinda Heck, *The Influence of Rhetoric on Jean-Philippe Rameau's Solo Vocal Cantatas and Treatise of 1722*, New York: Lang, 1990

Tunley, David, *The Eighteenth-Century French Cantata*, London: Dobson, 1974; 2nd edition, Oxford: Clarendon Press, 1997

Tunley, David, editor, *The Eighteenth-Century French Cantata*, New York: Garland, 1990–91

The story of the cantata in France is one in a series of tales that draw their theme from that country's ambivalent artistic relations with Italy. An Italian genre par excellence, cultivated in the only European land where Italian opera never gained a foothold and where the operas of Jean-Baptiste Lully served as the model of all that was noble in music, the cantata was a potentially revolutionary introduction indeed. Its aesthetic credibility was not helped by its low rank in the pantheon of literary genres inherited from the glorious Greco-Roman tradition, and its lack of a classical pedigree made it appropriate only for the entertainment of the idle and frivolous in the minds of many contemporary critics. Strangely enough, however, the great poet Jean-Baptiste Rousseau devoted himself to "Frenchifying" this Italian genre, and the first settings of his poetry by the circle of composers surrounding the duke of Orléans (the future regent under Louis XV) created something of a *succès de scandale*. The incongruity of this success, in view of the critical reception the cantata received, has intrigued a number of scholars, but many questions concerning the cultural roots of the cantata's popularity remain to be answered. Much of the history of the genre, as it has so far been told, concerns itself with the cantata's stylistic evolution, in answer to the question of how French composers adapted Italian models to please their countrymen's ears.

Recently revised and updated based on research published since its initial printing, TUNLEY (1974; 2nd edition, 1997) is the central general study of the genre. The introductory material contains an account of the social background and literary origins of the cantata as well as a cogent differentiation between the French and Italian stylistic traits employed by cantata composers of the period. In this discussion, Tunley casts a particularly penetrating light on the differences between the two styles' melodic structure and harmonic language. The rest of the book is divided into sections devoted to the cantatas of particular composers and is organized in approximate chronological order. These sections discuss each composer's individual style and musico-dramatic conception of the genre and are well documented by musical examples. A later chapter treats the "Decline of the Cantata," its miniaturization, and the influence of preclassical stylistic traits. A final chapter considers performance practice issues in the cantata, including a brief discussion of the flexibility of instrumental scoring in period chamber music.

TUNLEY's (1990–91) series of cantata-print facsimiles is an important contribution to the field and also a useful companion to his book. Each volume is devoted to the works of one or two composers and contains a brief preface on the music and its composer(s) as well as useful plot summaries. Tunley unfortunately includes no translations of the texts, which might otherwise be helpful to performers.

Two discussions in more general works, Anthony and Barthélemy, serve to balance Tunley's assertion that the French cantata cannot be considered "an opera in miniature"; while his point is well taken, Tunley's attempts to convince the reader lead him to downplay the many mutual influences between the two genres. ANTHONY, pointing out the operatic features of many composers' cantatas, notes that the clearest example of the interpenetration of the two genres occurs in the music of André Campra, arguably the most important composer of French opera in the late 1690s to the 1720s and also the author of three books of cantatas. BARTHÉLEMY likewise gives a good account of the Italian and cantata-like elements in Campra's operas that were likely to have influenced not only the new genre's stylistic evolution but its popularity with a wider Parisian audience as well.

Although the cantatas of Jean-Philippe Rameau did not have a particularly significant influence on the history of the genre or on Rameau's stature as a composer, his fame alone recommends these works, and a number of general studies on the composer fill the gap left by Tunley's rather terse treatment of the pieces. The study that is most accessible to English readers is GIRDLESTONE. His discussion of the sources is out-of-date, but the author does an admirable job of analyzing three cantatas. He also includes a translation of Rameau's famous letter recommending himself and his cantatas to the librettist Houdar de la Motte.

SLOAN is a specialized study of Rameau's cantatas in the context of his theoretical writings and of French thinking about rhetoric in general. The author shows how Rameau's wish to legitimize music on its own terms led the composer to adopt an ideology that was "both conservative and revolutionary." On the one hand, Rameau claimed as a theorist that the laws of music could be derived solely from the natural phenomena of sound and were not subject to the imposition of nonmusical rules, and, on the other hand, his music adhered to the traditional rhetorical conception of music as heightened speech and to certain formal and stylistic traits of the music of Jean-Baptiste Lully. The book presents an excellent discussion of French views of rhetoric's role in musical composition and sheds light on one of the major issues in the music history of this period. It founders somewhat, like many studies of its kind, when it tries to apply rhetorical principles to actual music, although it does present solid analyses of the composer's cantatas.

DON FADER

Cantata: German Baroque

Blume, Friedrich, *Protestant Church Music: A History,* New York: Norton, 1974

Kirwan-Mott, Anne, *The Small-Scale Sacred Concertato in the Early Seventeenth Century,* Ann Arbor, Michigan: UMI Research Press, 1981

Samuel, Harold, *The Cantata in Nuremberg during the Seventeenth Century,* Ann Arbor, Michigan: UMI Research Press, 1982

Spitta, Philipp, *Johann Sebastian Bach,* 3 vol., translated by Clara Bell and John Alexander Fuller-Maitland, London: Novello, 1884; reprint, New York, Dover, 1951

Unger, Melvin P., *The German Choral Church Compositions of Johann David Heinichen, 1683–1729,* New York: Lang, 1990

Wolff, Christoph, editor, *The World of the Bach Cantatas*, 3 vol., New York: Norton, 1997

The German baroque cantata is, in a sense, the invention of the 19th century; the term *cantata,* which formerly referred solely to a genre of secular Italian vocal music, was applied retrospectively to a large body of diverse Lutheran church works from the late 17th and early 18th centuries that carried various generic designations—"motetto," "concerto," "ode," occasionally "cantata," but more often just "church piece." Performed before (or around) the sermon on Sundays and on feast days, the typical German cantata is a multimovement work for voices and instruments on texts taken from various sources: the Bible (especially the Psalms), chorales, free poetry, even dialogues. The musical style of the cantata is similarly heterogeneous: in the Bach cantatas, for example, one finds older, motet-style settings of biblical passages alongside Italianate settings of the new, madrigalian poetry of ca. 1700. The repertory is almost entirely sacred, the lack of concern over the mixture of musical styles reflecting the Lutheran view that all music glorifies God. Major composers include Dietrich Buxtehude, Johann Pachelbel, and, above all, Johann Sebastian Bach, whose works define the genre.

BLUME's classic text offers a paradigmatic account of the genre and its principal composers, with primary emphasis on the church cantatas of J.S. Bach. Discussing the birth of the German cantata, Blume notes that it "combined in form and content what had previously been separated"—namely, music and preaching. Its mingling of diverse texts and musical styles led, in his view, first to greater systematization, then decline, in the age of rationalism. Although Blume's teleologic view of history is no longer fashionable, the broad reach of his book makes it essential reading.

KIRWAN-MOTT treats the genre's precursor: the 17th-century sacred concertato. Focusing on the earliest German contributions to this originally Italianate genre, she notes that few German composers used obbligato melody instruments in their sacred works before the 1640s; standard practice featured voices plus continuo only (this latter texture survived as the *stile antico* in Bach's day). The later, more colorful concertatos began to look very much like the typical German cantata: separate movements, each with different scoring. Kirwan-Mott's treatment of Protestant solo songs with dialogue-type texts provides particularly useful background for the earliest German cantatas.

SAMUEL is a detailed study of the cantata repertory of Nuremberg, one of the most important Lutheran cities in the 16th century (its churches were early to embrace the Reformation in 1524), whose gradual decline during the 17th century has long obscured the impressive work of its musicians. Bibliographic citations and short descriptions for nearly 400 extant works are given; the main text has detailed information on 94 cantatas by the Nuremberg composers, among whom Johann Erasmus Kindermann, Johann Philipp Krieger, and Pachelbel produced the finest work. The author includes a useful chapter on the use of musical-rhetorical figures in this repertory, even though the Nurembergers were not as adept as Heinrich Schütz in this respect (numerous problems of text declamation in the Nuremberg cantatas are noted). One major caveat: Samuel's discussion of performance practice seriously overestimates the size of the performing ensemble, which likely consisted of a single player or singer to a part.

Volume 1 of SPITTA includes a history of the German cantata, along with extended discussions of selected works of both Bach and Buxtehude. Dividing the repertory into "early" and "late" cantatas—the former including those based on biblical and chorale texts, the latter incorporating newly composed poetry set as recitatives and arias—Spitta provides the framework for virtually every subsequent discussion of the genre. His chronology of the Bach cantatas has been supplanted, but his insight into the music remains keen. For generations the most respected figure in Bach criticism, Spitta writes with engagement and persuasion (and occasional chauvinism); one is never left wondering what the author thinks about a particular issue or piece.

UNGER surveys the subgenres of the German cantata in the late 17th and early 18th centuries and notes how the combination of different kinds of texts (chorales, odes, biblical passages, newly composed poetry) and the increasing variety in texture (more voices, instruments) distinguish German cantatas from their Italian forebears. A cogent chapter on context likewise summarizes the salient features of turn-of-the-century Lutheran theology and liturgical practice. The discussion of Heinichen, though generous with detail, is fairly routine: Unger supplies a brief biography and information on the sources, then proceeds to examine various aspects of structure in the works themselves.

WOLFF brings together various experts in a three-volume series that serves as a companion to Ton Koopman's Bach cantata recordings. Much more than just introductory guides, these books stand on their own as the first to place the entire corpus of Bach cantatas in a rich, multilayered context that addresses not only the composer's milieu and the unique character of his work but also the world from which his cantatas sprang. Essays range from illuminating background studies ("Genres and Styles of Sacred Music around 1700") to close readings of the texts themselves ("Classical and Modern Myths in the Secular Cantatas") and discussion of pertinent issues in performance practice. While the three volumes are primarily devoted to Bach's pre-Leipzig sacred cantatas, secular cantatas, and his Leipzig church cantatas, respectively, there is no more comprehensive single source of information on the genre as a whole.

MATTHEW DIRST

Cantata: Italian Baroque

Bennett, Lawrence E., "The Italian Cantata in Vienna, 1700–1711: An Overview of Stylistic Traits," in *Antonio Caldara: Essays on His Life and Times,* edited by Brian Pritchard, Aldershot: Scolar Press, 1987

Burney, Charles, *A General History of Music from the Earliest Ages to the Present Period (1789),* edited by Frank Mercer, New York: Harcourt, Brace, 1935

Caluori, Eleanor, *The Cantatas of Luigi Rossi,* 2 vols., Ann Arbor, Michigan: UMI Research Press, 1981

Dixon, Graham, *Carissimi,* Oxford: Oxford University Press, 1986

Gianturco, Carolyn, *Alessandro Stradella, 1644–1682: His Life and Music,* Oxford: Clarendon Press, and New York: Oxford University Press, 1994

———, "The Italian Seventeenth-Century Cantata: A Textual Approach," in *The Well Enchanting Skill: Music, Poetry, and Drama in the Culture of the Renaissance,* edited by John Caldwell et al., Oxford: Clarendon Press, and New York: Oxford University Press, 1990

Hill, John Walter, *Roman Monody, Cantata, and Opera from the Circles around Cardinal Montalto,* 2 vols., Oxford: Clarendon Press, and New York: Oxford University Press, 1997

Jakoby, Richard, *The Cantata,* translated by Robert Kolben, Cologne: Volk, 1968

Rosand, Ellen, "The Voice of Barbara Strozzi," in *Women Making Music: The Western Art Tradition, 1150–1950,* edited by Jane Bowers and Judith Tick, Urbana: University of Illinois Press, 1987

The few thousand Italian cantatas that professional singers sang in palatial apartments and academic gatherings in the baroque era have yet to receive comprehensive treatment in English for either general or specialized readers. Apart from the standard music reference works and surveys, one can turn to sections or chapters in biographies of composers, introductions to scores (such as those to the 16 volumes of *The Italian Cantata in the Seventeenth Century,* 1985–86), or to specialized doctoral dissertations.

The use of the term before 1650 is scattered and of inconsistent designation; the word became common in titles of prints of solo vocal music only in the last quarter of the 17th century. For baroque music, modern usage employs *cantata* broadly, as a label for chamber or devotional works for one to five solo voices (or more) with figured bass accompaniment, with or without other instrumental parts, on texts with some literary pretension. They are often distinguished from straightforward strophic songs or *canzonettas* by their tone and musical variety, though they may use the same poetic forms. Typically set to music are poems with varied line lengths, in no fixed rhyme schemes, that display or describe a range of affections. These prompt varied and changing styles of melody and meter, resulting in compositions of contrasting sections or, in the late baroque, of contrasting arias separated by recitatives. Ensemble cantatas—for example, those intended for use in the oratories—often consist of solos, duets, and trios, typically concluding with a tutti ensemble often called a madrigal. Just as a musical work to be performed in an oratory (*oratorio* in Italian) came to be called an oratorio, an ensemble cantata written for an academy gathering came to be called an *accademia.* Another species of ensemble cantata was the *serenata.*

GIANTURCO (1990) usefully sets out the textual foundations for the musical variety of the classic Italian cantata of the 1650s to 1680s, with a brief background on the development of Italian poetry for music. She succinctly addresses a number of topics with regard to musical settings of text: recitative and aria, strophic and nonstrophic arias, passages in aria style (or ariosos), and word setting. An additional topic on refrains or texted ritornellos cites the contemporary term *intercalare* but not the synonymous *streviglio,* a presumed corruption of the Spanish *estribillo.*

The survey anthology by JAKOBY takes the widest possible definition of cantata—that of vocal chamber music. Of its eight Italian baroque examples, however, Gianturco would probably consider only three to be cantatas (the anonymous "Tra pellegrine piante" and the late examples by Alessandro Scarlatti and Antonio Caldara). The introduction includes a sketch of the development of this broad repertory from beginnings in Florentine monody and vocal pieces on ground basses, but the discussion overemphasizes those elements that anticipate the late baroque cantata (such as the da capo aria) and deflates its own purposes by noting a "decline in the artistic quality of the cantatas" at the end of the 17th century. Some statements are incorrect, for example, that "recitative was sung . . . in prose" or that Luigi Rossi (d. 1653) cultivated the da capo aria. Biographical material should be checked against more recent reference works.

BURNEY, writing in the 18th century, is circumspect, thoughtful, and evaluative in his chapter called "Cantatas or Narrative Chamber Music." He stops briefly to mention the sacred cantata and then concentrates on Giacomo Carissimi and Pietro (also known as Antonio) Cesti. He proceeds to other composers who are still considered among the primary masters of the genre: Rossi, Giovanni Legrenzi, Alessandro Scarlatti, and Giovanni Bononcini, among others. The only large section that has proved invalid is Burney's discussion of Salvator Rosa as a composer; the music that Burney attributes to Rosa is instead by various other composers, including Bononcini and Luigi Mancia. The chapter has numerous musical examples of passages that struck Burney's ear. His comments are apt and demonstrate his desire to persuade his readers of the delights he found in them.

HILL examines a set of scores traceable to local and Neapolitan musicians working in Rome from the late 16th century to the 1630s. He connects their manner of solo singing, which emphasized strophic variations and florid, virtuoso writing, to improvisational practices in Spain-dominated south. His study identifies a constellation of composers whose music is as important to the mid-century cantata as that of the Florentine monodists.

CALUORI's monograph, based on her doctoral dissertation of 1971, is the only work listed here entirely devoted to the cantata. Luigi Rossi worked for Roman patrons from about 1620 and was in his own time the first recognized master of the lyric style. The author discusses the texts in terms of the subjects they treat and describes four common formal designs found in the short ariettas that dominate Rossi's oeuvre. She then explores their textual and musical features "that are independent of the formal differences." Only in the introduction and in places in the later chapters does the book address Luigi's longer compositions—the 17 laments and 61 free forms made up of several sections. In this latter category, Caluori identifies a type she informally designates as series cantatas, which are also found in the repertory discussed by Hill.

The approximately 150 cantatas by Carissimi and 125 by Stradella are surveyed in the biographies of these two composers by Dixon and by Gianturco, respectively. DIXON gives numerous excerpts to illustrate the contrasts of style that delineate or reorder the musical forms. (His examples 30 and 31, however, come from a cantata whose composer is unknown, and his assessment that the famous *Vittoria, mio core* "is simply a da capo aria" ignores its intercalation of two strophes between three statements of the refrain, or *streviglio*.) GIANTURCO (1994) describes Stradella's varied procedures according to categories of scoring: general features of the solo cantatas, brief attention to the cantatas for two and three voices, followed by a more extended discussion of the cantatas, *accademie*, and *serenatas* with instruments in addition to those of the usual basso continuo ensemble. Her chapter closes with a section on Stradella's sacred and moral cantatas, which includes the cantata for the Christmas season, *Ah! troppo è ver*. No single cantata is discussed in its entirety, which, until more recordings or scores are available, leaves Stradella's music somewhat more abstract than the historical details about it.

ROSAND's chapter on Barbara Strozzi is a well-integrated examination of the musical compositions by and in the life of a professional singer. It offers a portrait of a performer of cantatas in Venetian society, emphasizing the lyric expressivity of Strozzi's settings, particularly in nonaria sections. According to Rosand, this lyricism is partly generated by a "dissociation of word and music," even while it remains text-inspired. This is perhaps the only essay discussed here that gives the reader some notion of the Italian cantata in performance and of its intended effects on its listeners.

Italians pursued musical careers outside of Italy throughout the baroque era. BENNETT provides a tidy survey of about 100 Italian cantatas by Carlo Badia, Giovanni and Antonio Maria Bononcini, Marc'Antonio Ziani, and Attilio Ariosti, who all worked in Vienna and wrote in the formalized patterns of the late baroque. The article summarizes the elements that make up their cantatas (formal design, scoring, dynamics, kinds of ariosos, key, tempo and meter, etc.) without discussing any interpretive or expressive aspects or examining any single cantata in its entirety.

MARGARET MURATA

Cantus Firmus

Bloxam, M. Jennifer, "Sacred Polyphony and Local Traditions of Liturgy and Plainsong: Reflections on Music by Jacob Obrecht," in *Plainsong in the Age of Polyphony*, edited by Thomas Forrest Kelly, Cambridge: Cambridge University Press, 1992

Le Huray, Peter, "Some Thoughts about Cantus Firmus Composition; And a Plea for Byrd's *Christus resurgens*," in *Byrd Studies*, edited by Alan Brown and Richard Turbet, Cambridge: Cambridge University Press, 1992

Lowinsky, Edward E., editor, *Josquin des Prez*, in collaboration with Bonnie J. Blackburn, London: Oxford University Press, 1976

Sparks, Edgar, *Cantus Firmus in Mass and Motet, 1420–1520*, Berkeley: University of California Press, 1963

The term *cantus firmus* is used with at least two meanings in the literature. In its most restrictive sense it refers to a preexistent melody borrowed as generative material for a new composition, as with a chant that provides the basis for a Mass setting. In this case the cantus firmus most often appears in a relatively pure, unembellished form at some point in the new composition. In its less restrictive sense the term refers to any previously determined material used in the creation of a new work. Under this latter meaning fall such instances as a series of notes based on the vowels of an honoree's name, a polyphonic complex used in its entirety or in part, or even a preexistent melodic line that never appears in easily recognizable form but is frequently present in the background as a generative element. Although either of these two meanings is possible, recent scholarship tends to prefer the former, substituting such expressions as *soggeto cavato*, imitation Mass, parody Mass, and paraphrase technique for other compositional procedures.

Discussions of cantus firmus procedure, regardless of the sense in which the term is understood, generally consider one of two issues: identification of the specific material borrowed and features of the way in which the borrowed material is applied throughout the new composition. Because so many cantus firmus works are labeled according to their borrowed material in manuscripts, identification is not often an issue. Tracing the cantus firmus as it is used in a specific work, however, is often a difficult task. Recent discussions have attempted to relate one composer's treatment of a cantus firmus to that of another composer, thus drawing parallels and suggesting spheres of influence. Much scholarship regarding cantus firmus treatment has focused on individual works or genres within a single composer's output, in which case they have been published as journal articles (see, for example, Richard Taruskin, "Antoine Busnoys and the *L'Homme armé* Tradition," *Journal of the American Musicological Society* 39 [1986]; R. Larry Todd, "Retrograde, Inversion, Retrograde-Inversion, and Related Techniques in the Masses of Obrecht," *Musical Quarterly* 64 [1978]; and Leeman Perkins, "The L'Homme Armé Masses of Busnoys and Okeghem: A Comparison," *Journal of Musicology* 3 [1985]).

The essential book-length resource for an introduction to cantus firmus procedures is SPARKS, who traces the development of the technique from some of its earliest appearances in early 15th-century English music through the major composers of the 15th and early 16th centuries. In its earliest manifestations the cantus firmus is applied in long values and in a single voice, but in later uses the borrowed material is more subtly integrated into the rhythmic and melodic fabric of the composition. Sparks's methodology is clear: he discusses only works that are identified as cantus firmus compositions in manuscripts of the period; therefore, he is prompted to consider works that some might consider paraphrase or imitation Masses. The author is generally conservative in approach, tending to note cantus firmus application only where it is clearly present; numerous musical examples confirm his carefulness.

Elder's essay in LOWINSKY applies the various procedures discussed by Sparks to a single composer, Josquin des Prez. Josquin's methods for adopting a chant for use in a polyphonic liturgical work are numerous: the amount of the chant, extent of embellishment, presence or lack of canon, and number of voices carrying the chant widely vary in the composer's output. Elders gives examples of each of these factors, citing several works from various genres. The author even suggests that cantus firmi may be so disguised in some works as to prevent definitive identification (as in Josquin's "Liber generationis"). Of particular value to those interested in observing the spectrum of cantus firmus procedures adopted by Josquin is a table identifying the composer's manner of cantus firmus deployment in works other than Masses.

The reader may wish to follow Elders's discussion with that of Reese, also found in LOWINSKY, who compares Josquin's *Missa de Beata Virgine* (considered by the theorist Glareanus so excellent that "finer music cannot be created") with those of Brumel, Isaac, Pierre de la Rue, Finck, and Compère, among others. Reese observes that, although several composers may label their Masses with the same "de Beata Virgine" title, the cantus firmi they employ are often distinct from one another. This is no doubt because composers employed cantus firmi that circulated within their own liturgical tradition and environment. A natural conclusion is that a cantus firmus work is not always an abstract compositional exercise but a personal statement of devotion and admiration.

BLOXAM uses Obrecht's deployment of cantus firmi in several Masses as a point of departure for considering cultural and social issues surrounding the composer's life. By comparing Obrecht's borrowed chant melodies with those same melodies as found in chant sources, Bloxam is able to suggest dating and geographic provenance of various works and thus offer biographical insight as well. In a particularly intriguing reversal on typical discussions of cantus firmus technique, the author suggests that the manner in which some cantus firmi are presented in Obrecht's Masses may inform the way in which they were expected to be performed as plainchant. That is, if a plainchant cantus firmus appears in a Mass in an unadorned manner and with its original text—thus reflecting its original manner of performance—perhaps the *rhythm* used for the chant in the Mass reflects that which would have been used in a plainsong performance.

LE HURAY focuses on a single composer, William Byrd, to note the potential difficulties a composer faced in using a cantus firmus. The author notes ways in which Byrd manipulates mode and harmonic implication in the creation of his cantus firmus motet *Christus resurgens*. In an intriguing prelude to his discussion of Byrd's motet, the author notes Thomas Morley's comments from *Plaine and Easie Introduction* (1597) regarding composition and considers their implications for cantus firmus writing. As Morley was a pupil of Byrd, Le Huray suggests that we may actually be reading the sentiments of Byrd when reading his pupil's writings. The essential considerations inherent in composition seem to Le Huray to reflect closely those of Byrd in his motet.

STEPHEN SELF

Carissimi, Giacomo 1605–1674

Italian composer

Bianchi, Lino, *Carissimi, Stradella, Scarlatti e l'oratorio musicale,* Rome: de Santis, 1969

Culley, Thomas D., *Jesuits and Music: A Study of the Musicians Connected with the German College in Rome during the 17th Century and of Their Activities in Northern Europe,* Rome: Jesuit Historical Institute, and St. Louis, Missouri: St. Louis University, 1970

Dixon, Graham, *Carissimi,* Oxford: Oxford University Press, 1986

Jones, Andrew V., *The Motets of Carissimi,* Ann Arbor, Michigan: UMI Research Press, 1982

Sartori, Claudio, *Giacomo Carissimi: Catalogo delle opere attribuite,* Milan: Finarte, 1975

Giacomo Carissimi is now mainly remembered for his oratorios, chief among them *Jephte,* although, as Gloria Rose demonstrates in her unpublished dissertation (Yale University, 1959), "a survey of his entire musical output shows this emphasis to be altogether misplaced." In fact, in addition to his 16 oratorios, he composed at least 14 Masses, 82 motets, four humorous compositions in Latin, and 146 cantatas (although the authenticity of many works attributed to Carissimi is dubious due to the lack of autograph manuscripts). Scholarship on Carissimi's life and work has been sporadic and often highly specialized (e.g., articles on a specific genre or work). In fact, the only book that deals with all aspects of the composer's life and works is the monograph by Dixon, which is unfortunately very short. Two of the major studies of Carissimi's music are unpublished (Rose's dissertation mentioned above and another by Lowell P. Beveridge [Harvard University, 1942] on the composer's life and his works based on Latin texts). A complete and comprehensive book has yet to be written.

CULLEY's book systematically examines the story of the Collegio Germanico e Ungarico in Rome and the musicians employed there, basing the investigation on previous scholarship and all documents available at the Collegio (about one-third of the volume is dedicated to the reproduction of relevant documents from the archives). The discussion is divided into three periods: 1573–1600, 1600–1630, and 1630–74. Within each period, the author considers all aspects of music at the college and the history and activities of each and every musician involved, from each *putto soprano* to the *maestro di cappella* and outside instrumentalists. In chapter 3 (1630–74), the author examines in detail Carissimi's role. He was *maestro di cappella* at the Collegio from 1629 until his death, despite several separate attempts by other institutions to hire him, including one by St. Mark in Venice (which wanted him to take the position made vacant by Monteverdi's death). Among the other topics discussed by Culley are Carissimi's reputation, his legacy, his influence on German music, his students, and the esteem accorded to him in royal circles (evidenced in letters and other documents).

JONES, after a review of Carissimi's biography and a study of the activities of some of his students in Rome and abroad, enters the topic of the motets. The second and third chapters deal in detail with the printed and manuscript sources of Carissimi's motets. For each source Jones addresses not only the contents but also his-tory, genesis, reliability, specific problems, testimony, and other miscellaneous commentary. When differing versions of a motet appear in the sources, Jones analyzes the variants. He also considers the problem of lost sources and the evidence for their existence. After surveying the sources, Jones offers an insightful and highly informed discussion of the difference between a Latin oratorio and a motet, especially in the formative years of the oratorio (ca. 1640–60), and he includes stylistic assessments of several compositions as case studies. One chapter attempts to determine the chronology of the motets as far as possible on the basis of objective external evidence—given the absence of autograph manuscripts, the author bases his hypotheses on publication and copying data, external evidence such as letters and diaries, and partly on stylistic grounds. The final two chapters closely examine the motets: the penultimate chapter compares the texts of the motets to their sources, and the last evaluates the style and technique of the pieces. In the latter section, the reader will find a wealth of musical examples relevant to the topics discussed (tonality, melody, rhythm and meter, harmony, instruments, counterpoint, structure, and so forth). The greater topics are subdivided in very manageable small sections that often include cross-references. A brief final section provides conclusions and a summary of Jones's work.

The second volume includes a few bibliographic appendices, such as a complete thematic and source catalog of all motets attributed to Carissimi, with musical incipit (which occupies one-quarter of the volume); a list of the printed sources arranged chronologically; a list of the manuscript sources in each individual library; and a transcription of 33 motets originally written in an often hard-to-read hand, with critical commentary.

With his relatively recent monograph, DIXON fills a remarkable gap, albeit succinctly. The author seeks to introduce the reader to Carissimi by discussing his musical style in a representative cross-section of his most securely attributed works. After discussing the specifics of musical style in Rome and the changes that took place between the time of Palestrina (who died in 1594) and that of Carissimi, Dixon explains in some detail how the latter composer did and did not change the music he inherited and how his music adheres to the general tenets of the baroque style. The following chapters discuss specific pieces by genre and function (i.e., respectively, liturgical music, music for oratories, and cantatas). The discussion of the individual pieces is detailed without being overly technical, and it includes, where appropriate, issues of text setting, instrumentation, attribution, and function, among other topics. The book concludes with a summary in which Carissimi is again placed in his historical context and compared with some of his contemporaries and disciples, and his influence is assessed.

BIANCHI's book, in Italian, begins with an overview of the oratorio as a genre and an institution, in particular the Oratorio del Crocifisso in Rome. The author then devotes the majority of the book to individual discussions of those oratorios that he attributes to Carissimi. (For a discussion of Bianchi's classification and attributions see Jones's book.) These discussions are basically superficial descriptions of the texts and main musical features.

SARTORI's catalog includes an interesting introduction with a summary of Carissimi's life and activities and an account of the scholarship on him, followed by a catalog of the works attributed to him with indication of the scoring, location, and condition of the extant sources. The catalog is divided into three sections: the editions in print, the music in manuscript form on Italian text (cantatas and arias), and that on Latin text (motets, Masses, and oratorios, including the two on Italian text). An appendix lists elaborations of Carissimi's music with English text, instrumental pieces, and doubtful compositions.

ALEXANDRA AMATI-CAMPERI

Carter, Elliott b. 1908

United States composer

Carter, Elliott, *Elliott Carter: Collected Essays and Lectures, 1937–1995*, edited by Jonathan W. Bernard, Rochester, New York: University of Rochester Press, 1997
———, *Elliott Carter: In Conversation with Enzo Restagno for Settembre Musica 1989*, translated by Katherine Silberblatt Wolfthal, Brooklyn, New York: Institute for Studies in American Music, 1991
———, *The Writings of Elliott Carter: An American Composer Looks at Modern Music*, edited by Else Stone and Kurt Stone, Bloomington: Indiana University Press, 1977
Edwards, Allen, *Flawed Words and Stubborn Sounds: A Conversation with Elliott Carter*, New York: Norton, 1971
Harvey, David I.H., *The Later Music of Elliott Carter: A Study in Music Theory and Analysis*, New York: Garland, 1989
Rosen, Charles, and Morgan Cundiff, *The Musical Languages of Elliott Carter, with a Guide to Elliott Carter Research Materials at the Library of Congress Music Division*, Washington, D.C.: Music Division, Research Services, Library of Congress, 1984
Schiff, David, *The Music of Elliott Carter*, London: Eulenburg Books, and New York: Da Capo Press, 1983; 2nd edition, Ithaca, New York: Cornell University Press, 1998

Elliott Carter's career as a composer has spanned more than a half-century and encompassed a wide variety of styles. This varied and lengthy career, coupled with the fact that Carter has written extensively on his own music as well as that of his colleagues, has made him a daunting subject for music theorists and historians alike. Recent years have seen a wealth of dissertations and articles examining individual compositions by Carter or tracing the development of specific techniques in his music; nevertheless, there have been relatively few general studies of this important American composer's work. The books discussed here reflect the two complementary facets of Carter's career: composition and musical scholarship.

EDWARDS is a "condensed, reordered, and partly rewritten" transcript of interviews between the author and Carter that took place between 1968 and 1970. The volume is divided into three sections, each written in question-and-answer format. The first section compares musical life in Europe and the United States and considers the place of serious music in U.S. culture. The second section discusses Carter's musical development and explores the influences of other musicians, including Nadia Boulanger, Richard Strauss, Edgard Varèse, Aleksandr Skryabin, and Charles Ives. The final section includes technical discussions of several of Carter's works, including the Piano Concerto, Concerto for Orchestra, and Double Concerto. Because none of these sections is titled, the book can be difficult to follow, but a thorough index helps make the material manageable.

CARTER (1977) contains 69 of Carter's essays dating from 1937 to 1976. The earliest of these, written while Carter was a regular reviewer for the magazine *Modern Music*, primarily discuss new music in New York City. The early, idealistic articles also include brief sketches of modern composers, such as Charles Ives, Walter Piston, and Roger Sessions. The later articles (1945–79) deal with a wider variety of subjects and include important program notes by Carter on his own music. The volume is arranged in chronological order, which allows the reader to follow not only Carter's personal development as a writer but also his changing aesthetics. Perhaps most interesting are the articles focusing on Charles Ives, which are spread across Carter's career. The collection's arrangement can make it difficult to follow Carter's changing attitudes on a single topic, but the editors have provided a detailed index that assists the reader in pulling together Carter's remarks on any subject. Carter's more recent essays are not included.

Published by the Library of Congress in honor of Carter's 70th and 75th birthdays, ROSEN and CUNDIFF includes two essays by Rosen. The first, originally given as a talk for a performance of the Piano Sonata, explores Carter's creation of a rhythmic and harmonic language based on the sonority of the piano. The second, "One Easy Piece," discusses the issues surrounding performing and listening to modern music, focusing on Carter's Double Concerto. In addition, the book contains Rosen's 1983 interview with Carter in which they discuss issues of sonority and rhythm, as well as Carter's idea of assigning personalities to various instruments and his use of programs. This brief volume also includes a guide by Cundiff to the Carter research materials housed at the Music Division of the Library of Congress.

HARVEY argues against the view that Carter is a composer whose music relies on systematic theoretical speculation. Rather, the author sees Carter's precompositional organization simply as serving to limit musical materials and provide a place for experimentation and play. This volume seeks to create a method of analysis that starts from a musical surface defined by register and time, proceeding to explain the perceived qualities of continuity and contrast in Carter's works in a way that other analytic techniques have not. After two chapters that summarize Carter's development prior to the 1950s, Harvey applies his method to the Second String Quartet, Double Concerto, and Concerto for Orchestra. As a result of these technically complex analyses, a view emerges of Carter as an empiricist who has distanced himself from the 20th-century mainstream of U.S. and European music.

CARTER (1991) is an English translation of Enzo Restagno's 1989 interviews with Carter. Restagno and Carter cover a variety of topics ranging from the composer's childhood through his compositions of the 1980s. While the book focuses on Carter's musical aesthetics, it also contains Carter's reactions to other composers and artists, including Edgard Varèse, Igor Stravinsky, Guillaume de Machaut, Charles Ives, Paul Valéry, Maurice Ravel, and John Cage. Restagno's writing is accessible to the nonspecialist, and Carter's candid responses help to place him within European and American modernism. Sadly, the work lacks both an index and a table of contents, which makes it unsuitable for easy reference.

CARTER (1997) duplicates many of the essays already published in Carter (1977), but it also contains a large number of previously unpublished essays from the Carter Collection at the Paul Sacher Foundation in Basel, mostly dating from the 1950s and 1960s. Instead of a chronological arrangement, the editor has opted to group the essays under six headings: "Surveying the Compositional Scene," "American Music," "Charles Ives," "Some Other Composers," "Life and Work," and "Philosophy, Criticism, and the Other Arts." This topical organization allows the reader to easily trace Carter's ideas on a single topic. The editor also includes a list of Carter's published writings not included in this volume. Because this collection does not include many of Carter's earliest essays for *Modern Music,* it cannot replace Carter (1977), but its focus on the author's longer and more recent essays makes it an important addition to the Carter literature.

SCHIFF, a former student of Carter at the Juilliard School, has created a very readable volume, covering virtually all of Carter's music from his student compositions until 1997. This is certainly the most comprehensive study of the composer's music to date; most of his works receive detailed discussions, including historical background and analysis. While the first edition treats the music chronologically, the second approaches it by genre. Chamber, vocal, piano, and orchestral music each receive a separate chapter, allowing the reader to see Carter's development through individual genres but obscuring the progression of his work as a whole. Schiff also offers an excellent chapter in which he situates Carter as an American and international composer, particularly in relationship to Henry James, Wallace Stevens, Charles Ives, Nadia Boulanger, and Aaron Copland. There is also a helpful glossary that clarifies the analytic terms applied to Carter's music. Schiff states that Carter's work is meant for listeners, performers, and composers, and to this end the author has avoided overly complex technical discussions in favor of analyses that are appropriate not only for the specialist but also for the educated general reader. John F. Link has added a selected bibliography of works by and about Carter, as well as a discography.

PATRICK WARFIELD

Castrato

Burney, Charles, *Music, Men, and Manners in France and Italy 1770, Being the Journal Written by Charles Burney,* edited by H. Edmund Poole, London: Folio Society, 1969

Heriot, Angus, *The Castrati in Opera,* London: Secker and Warburg, 1956

Rosselli, John, "The Castrati as a Professional Group and a Social Phenomenon, 1550–1850," *Acta Musicologica* 60 (1988): 143–79

A castrato was a male soprano or alto whose vocal register was produced by castration prior to the onset of puberty rather than through the use of falsetto. The operation arrested the development of a youth's vocal cords and ultimately coupled them with the lungs and chest of an adult male. The result was a powerful yet flexible voice that listeners prized as much for its unusual timbre as for its agility and exceptional range. The practice originated in Italy as a solution to the ecclesiastical ban on the singing of women within churches. Although choirboys made suitable treble singers, they required intensive training and lost their usefulness as sopranos or altos once their voices broke. A castrato, or *musico* (the term used for these singers in the 1700s), had the advantage of keeping his vocal range for a lifetime and enjoyed the benefit of a musical education uninterrupted by puberty. Although the majority of these men maintained close professional ties with religious establishments or music conservatories, the best-known castrati earned their fame as opera singers. Indeed, they are commonly remembered today in connection with opera seria, a genre that they dominated. Castrati flourished from the end of the 16th century through the beginning of the 19th century. The last known castrato died in 1922.

HERIOT's study of the castrati concentrates on the 18th century, when they still enjoyed great popularity. His work relies heavily on printed sources and includes much anecdotal information that is interesting, if not always reliable. He bases much of his discussion on contemporary descriptions of the castrati and their performances, creating a vivid impression of these men as seen by their colleagues, admirers, and detractors. Although he lavishes a great deal of attention on successful singers such as Carlo Broschi (better known as Farinelli) and Gaetano Majorano (called Caffarelli), Heriot also looks at the careers of less-illustrious figures and attempts, in doing so, to reconstruct the life of the average castrato. The book ends with biographical sketches of 33 well-known singers, including a summary and partial translation of the delightful verse autobiography of Filippo Balatri. The information contained in this final section of the book demonstrates the variety of career paths available to these men and is fascinating to read. Unfortunately, Heriot fails to examine the data he has assembled in a methodical manner. Furthermore, his discussion of the historical context in which the castrati thrived lacks nuance and depth. The result is a somewhat simplified view of the 18th century that disregards the enormous musical, social, and cultural changes taking place at that time. Although an influential work, this monograph is best used in conjunction with recent studies that examine many of the same sources but analyze them more rigorously.

BURNEY is one of the primary sources to which Heriot owes a debt. One of the first serious historians of music, Burney is still appreciated for his intelligent and perceptive comments about the music of his time. While traveling throughout continental Europe in 1770, Burney kept this journal as a daily record of his trip. In it, he carefully chronicled his meetings with several of the most famous musicians of the day, including a number of prominent castrati. The descriptions of Farinelli and Tommaso Guarducci are especially interesting for Burney's keen insights into the personalities of the two singers. Burney also mentions the growing discomfort that some Italians expressed over the use of castration to create high-voiced male singers, a change in outlook that would become much stronger in the 19th and 20th centuries. Because Burney intended this journal for personal use, not for publication, the text possesses a loose, episodic structure, which makes any attempt at systematic reading difficult. Nonetheless, the wealth of information conveyed makes Burney's writing an indispensable reference when studying the history of 18th-century music and musicians.

For the serious student, ROSSELLI's article remains the most thorough analysis of the primary and secondary sources concerning the castrati. His essay reviews the existing literature and responds to the many stereotypes and misconceptions that have developed around these singers. Roselli avoids the anecdotal treatment that weakens so many other studies of the castrati. Instead, he approaches the phenomenon by focusing on the cultural context that produced it. Carefully weighing what is known and what is unknown about this group of men, the author not only explains the origin of the practice but also accounts for its demise. In doing so, he explores the career patterns of the castrati and dispels many of the unsubstantiated myths associated with the singers. Furthermore, he addresses the embarrassment that is evident in so much writing about the castrati. Roselli suggests that the uneasy reaction of many authors to the very existence of castrated male singers began at the end of the 18th century. Previously, castration for musical reasons would not have been viewed as unjustified or undesirable. This outlook, which differs strikingly from our own, reflects a completely different set of social values. In the 17th century, castration may have made economic sense for impoverished families: a musically talented son might have offered the only promise of future financial security. In addition, Roselli suggests, Italian society may have understood the operation as a parallel to monastic vows of celibacy, a form of sexual renunciation. Given the prevalence of Christian asceticism in southern Europe at this time, the public could have accepted castration as one way of realizing a religious ideal. As the European economy improved and the standards of Western society started to shift, attitudes changed. By 1850, castrati no longer appeared on the operatic stage. The few remaining castrati, who lived until the end of the 19th and the beginning of the 20th centuries, worked primarily within church establishments.

MICHAEL E. MCCLELLAN

Cavalieri, Emilio de' 1550–1602

Italian composer

Abraham, Gerald, editor, *The Age of Humanism 1540–1630*, The New Oxford History of Music, vol. 4, London: Oxford University Press, 1968

Bianconi, Lorenzo, *Music in the Seventeenth Century*, translated by David Bryant, Cambridge: Cambridge University Press, 1987

Bukofzer, Manfred F., *Music in the Baroque Era: From Monteverdi to Bach*, New York: Norton, 1947

Cavalieri, Emilio de', *The Lamentations and Responsories of 1599 and 1600*, edited by Murray C. Bradshaw, N.p.: American Institute of Musicology, and Neuhausen-Stuttgart: Hanssler, 1990

Grout, Donald J., *A Short History of Opera*, New York, Columbia University Press, 1965; 3rd edition, 1988

Kirkendale, Warren, *The Court Musicians in Florence during the Principate of the Medici: With a Reconstruction of the Artistic Establishment*, Florence: Olschki, 1993

Massenkeil, Gunther, *The Oratorio*, translated by A.C. Howie, Cologne: Arno Volk, 1970

Palisca, Claude, *Baroque Music*, Englewood Cliffs, New Jersey: Prentice Hall, 1968; 3rd edition, 1991

———, *Studies in the History of Italian Music and Music Theory*, Oxford: Clarendon Press, and New York: Oxford University Press, 1994

Parry, C. Hubert H., *The Music of the Seventeenth Century*, The Oxford History of Music, vol. 3, Oxford: Clarendon Press, 1902; 2nd edition, 1938

Smither, Howard E., *A History of the Oratorio, Volume I, The Oratorio in the Baroque Era: Italy, Vienna, Paris*, Chapel Hill: University of North Carolina Press, 1977

Strunk, W. Oliver, editor, *Source Readings in Music History: From Classical Antiquity through the Romantic Era*, New York: Norton, 1950; revised edition, edited by Leo Treitler, 1998

Although Emilio de' Cavalieri was an important contributor to music and musical life in Italy in the late 16th and early 17th centuries, there does not yet exist a comprehensive study in English devoted solely to his life and works. Fortunately, several prominent European and U.S. musicologists have discussed Cavalieri and his compositions in books covering various topics in baroque music. Early 20th-century scholars viewed Cavalieri as a key figure in the development of baroque musical style, and his *Rappresentatione di Anima e di Corpo (Representation of the Soul and the Body)* was considered to be the first oratorio. By the 1930s and 1940s, this view was revised, and some considered *Rappresentatione di Anima e di Corpo* to be a hybrid form. Since the 1970s, the scholarly consensus has been to place the work in the tradition of the *sacra rappresentazione* of the Renaissance. In recent scholarship, Cavalieri's importance as a stylistic innovator for early baroque music remains unchallenged, and his influential role as superintendent of music at the Medici court has received serious attention.

PARRY considers Cavalieri to be "the strongest and most imaginative of the representatives of the *Nuove Musiche*" of the early 17th century and classifies *Rappresentatione di Anima e di Corpo* as the first surviving oratorio. Parry briefly describes the style of *Rappresentatione di Anima e di Corpo*, accompanying his discussion with a few musical examples, including excerpts from the opening sinfonia and two choruses.

Simon Towneley's chapter on early Italian opera in ABRAHAM includes a discussion of Cavalieri and his *Rappresentatione di Anima e di Corpo*. Towneley classifies the work as "neither laude . . . nor an oratorio," and he cites some performance instructions, including suggestions for instrumentation, given by the composer in the original edition. Edward J. Dent's chapter on music and drama in the same anthology places Cavalieri's contributions to the Florentine *intermedi* of 1589 in the context of late Renaissance drama. Dent cites Cavalieri's solo arias and his *ballo* of 1589 as influential in the development of such crucial baroque style features as strophic variation, concertato, and ritornello.

BUKOFZER also discusses Cavalieri and his work in relation to the new compositional forms of the early 17th century. He classifies *Rappresentatione di Anima e di Corpo* as a hybrid form with features of both opera and oratorio, and he cites Cavalieri as an early contributor to the development of the *stile recitativo*. Although he characterizes Cavalieri's recitatives as mediocre in quality, Bukofzer does recognize the importance of *Rappresentatione di Anima e di Corpo* for the history of the oratorio.

STRUNK provides carefully annotated English translations of the forewords to Jacopo Peri's *Euridice* and Claudio Monteverdi's *Quinto libro de' madrigali*, in which Cavalieri is cited as a major contributor to a new compositional style. Peri named him as the first composer of monody, and Monteverdi considered him as one of the originators of the second practice.

GROUT compares the style of *Rappresentatione di Anima e di Corpo* to that of the earliest operas. He considers the work as a forerunner of opera and also as one of the first sacred dramatic works to employ monody; he briefly summarizes its most important textual and musical features.

MASSENKEIL considers *Rappresentatione di Anima e di Corpo* as part of the prehistory of the oratorio because of its sacred, nonliturgical character, its presentation in a Roman oratory, and its text, which contains *laude* in dialogue form. He includes the music for the text "Anima mia che pensi," which is set in *stile recitativo*. Massenkeil contends that *Rappresentatione di Anima e di Corpo* cannot be considered an oratorio because it was staged; he instead classifies it as a *sacra rappresentazione*.

SMITHER discusses Cavalieri's biography and *Rappresentatione di Anima e di Corpo* in detail, including a summary of the plot and musical analysis. He posits Cavalieri as the primary transmitter of the ideas of the Florentine *Camerata* to the oratory of the *Chiesa Nuova* in Rome, where the oratorio genre had its origins. Smither stresses the importance of the performance of *Rappresentatione di Anima e di Corpo* at the oratory in 1600. He describes the earliest printed score and libretto of the work and includes several musical examples. He also discusses the librettist, Padre Agostino Manni, a disciple of Saint Philip Neri. Smither notes that the title and libretto of *Rappresentatione di Anima e di Corpo* links it to the genre of *sacra rappresentazione*, but he believes the work to be more closely related to opera because it was staged. Although he does not classify *Rappresentatione di Anima e di Corpo* as an oratorio, Smither considers it a part of the history of the oratorio because it was "performed in a Roman oratory" and it "exerted an influence on other works performed in oratories." He stresses that it was the first sacred dramatic presentation in an oratory featuring the recitative style that would later become "an essential element of the oratorio."

BIANCONI considers Cavalieri's music for the *ballo del granduca* from the Florentine *intermedi* of 1589 and *Rappresentatione di Anima e di Corpo* as models for later compositions; however, he downplays the importance of the latter for the history of the oratorio by naming other precursors for that genre.

Bradshaw's edition of the *Lamentations and Responsories,* a collection of sacred, liturgical pieces by CAVALIERI composed in 1599 and 1600, includes detailed historical, critical, and analytical commentary. Bradshaw argues that Cavalieri's place in the history of monody is more important than had been previously realized because the *Lamentations* are the first important extant collection of monodies whose performance predates the performances of *Rappresentatione di Anima e di Corpo* and the opera *Euridice.*

KIRKENDALE's comprehensive documentary study of musicians at the Medici court from 1543 to 1737 includes editions and discussions of a variety of documents relating to Cavalieri's life and work. These documents, many of which are published here for the first time, provide an invaluable context for the understanding of Cavalieri's life and music.

PALISCA (1994) includes a chapter on Cavalieri's diplomatic correspondence, with excerpts from Cavalieri's letters. Palisca discusses Cavalieri's work as a diplomat and administrator for the Medici court and notes that, although Cavalieri's correspondence is mainly concerned with affairs of state, it is a valuable source of commentary on music and musical life in Florence and Rome. Cavalieri's correspondence provides evidence about the musical world of the Medici and their court, and especially about Cavalieri's work as a composer, performer, choreographer, music instructor, and administrator of artistic events.

PALISCA (1968) includes excerpts from *Intermedio VI* of 1589 and the *Lamentations and Responsories.* He describes Cavalieri's procedure of embellishing a vocal line in the *intermedio* and discusses a passage from the *Lamentations* in relation to the ideas of Vincenzo Galilei. Although Palisca places Cavalieri's *Rappresentatione di Anima e di Corpo* outside the mainstream of the history of the oratorio, he cites it as an example of the early use of the figured bass.

MARIA ARCHETTO

Cavalli, Pier Francesco 1602–1676

Italian composer

Glover, Jane, *Cavalli*, New York: St. Martin's Press, and London: Batsford, 1978

Rosand, Ellen, *Opera in Seventeenth-Century Venice: The Creation of a Genre*, Berkeley: University of California Press, 1991

Pier Francesco Cavalli became one of the most revered musicians in 17th-century Venice. At the height of his career, he was virtually without peer in Italy as a singer, organist, and composer. Like his mentor Claudio Monteverdi, the esteemed *maestro di cappella* at San Marco, Cavalli moved effortlessly between the religious and profane musical spheres of the island republic. More than 30 operas and several dozen sacred compositions of his have survived. Nearing the age of 60, Cavalli ventured to Paris on the invitation of Cardinal Mazarin for productions of his operas in a newly built theater. This experience should have offered a triumphant climax to a distinguished career. Instead, Cavalli suffered his most dismal failure. Jean-Baptiste Lully, an Italian-born musician living in France, allegedly considered Cavalli a potential rival and sabotaged his productions by inserting superfluous, highly elaborate dance segments into the operas. After one-and-a-half years, the humiliated composer returned to Venice. Operatic tastes had shifted perceptibly in the meantime, and Cavalli soon left the theater to concentrate on sacred music.

GLOVER's authority as a Cavalli scholar rests on her threefold involvement as researcher, editor, and conductor, as well as her exceptional knowledge of his entire output. Combining previously known information with new facts gleaned from her own archival research, Glover constructs a detailed profile of the composer's life and career. Segments pertaining to the Caletti family and Cavalli's involvement in opera especially benefit from recently discovered documents. The second chapter focuses exclusively on the literary style and dramatic innovations of Cavalli's librettists, as well as the changing theatric conventions in Venice. An examination of the operas occupies the largest part of this study, as Glover discusses the manuscript sources, Cavalli's compositional methods, varieties of aria forms and recitative styles, character types, makeup and uses of the orchestra and chorus, and issues relating to performance practice. The chapter on sacred music addresses this often overlooked repertoire, and Glover concludes with contemporary appraisals of Cavalli and his music. Appendices provide valuable information about Cavalli and his music, including lists of his operas (authentic and doubtful) with performance dates, a catalog of known religious compositions, extracts from archival documents, and a brief inventory of modern editions.

Two decades of archival research in Venice, manuscript study, and assimilation of previous research have equipped ROSAND to construct this monumental study of opera in 17th-century Venice. The book adopts a topical organization, and references to Cavalli and his librettists are scattered throughout. Nonetheless, the author's perceptive analyses of musical style, structural conventions, changing literary trends, and local economics deepen our understanding of this formative period in opera. Cavalli, whom Rosand calls the most important Venetian composer of the mid-17th century and a bridge between the first generation of *seconda prattica* musicians and the next generation, naturally emerges as a central figure in this study. Rosand's discussions of certain works (*Giasone* is the prime example) convey an astounding amount of information. The book includes transcriptions of four archival documents relating to Cavalli, facsimiles of two manuscripts, and an invaluable collection of musical excerpts from more than one dozen operas.

TODD SULLIVAN

Chamber Music: Baroque

Allsop, Peter, *The Italian "Trio" Sonata: From Its Origins until Corelli,* Oxford: Clarendon Press, and New York: Oxford University Press, 1992

Apel, Willi, *Italian Violin Music of the Seventeenth Century,* edited by Thomas Binkley, Bloomington: Indiana University Press, 1990

Hogwood, Christopher, *The Trio Sonata,* London: British Broadcasting Corporation, 1979

Newman, William S., *The Sonata in the Baroque Era,* Chapel Hill: University of North Carolina Press, 1959; 4th edition, New York: Norton, 1983

Rowen, Ruth Halle, *Early Chamber Music,* New York: King's Crown Press, 1949; reprint, New York: Da Capo Press, 1974

Sadie, Julie Anne, *The Bass Viol in French Baroque Chamber Music,* Ann Arbor, Michigan: UMI Research Press, 1980

Sadie, Julie Anne, editor, *Companion to Baroque Music,* London: Dent, 1990; New York: Schirmer, 1991

Selfridge-Field, Eleanor, *Venetian Instrumental Music from Gabrieli to Vivaldi,* New York: Praegar, and Oxford: Blackwell, 1975; 3rd revised edition, New York: Dover, 1994

In discussing chamber music of the baroque period it is necessary to distinguish between current and earlier usage of the term *chamber music.* In the 17th and 18th centuries, the category of chamber music would not have referred to the size of the performing forces but rather to the social function of the music, broadly divided into music for church, chamber, or theater, so that even music for orchestral forces could have been considered chamber music, if it served that function. On the other hand, from a modern perspective much of the church music of the time, especially instrumental, is defined as chamber music. Most recent authors have sidestepped the difficulties of reconciling the modern concept of chamber music with baroque music by concentrating on more specific repertoires, often centering on a particular region or genre.

Although originally written more than a half century ago, ROWEN is the only broad survey of baroque chamber music. The author does a good job of laying a foundation for understanding the characteristics of baroque chamber music that set it apart from later chamber music, such as the use of basso continuo, the frequent interchangeability of instruments, and the sharply contrasted national schools. However, Rowen tends to view baroque chamber music as a historically necessary preparatory stage before classical chamber music rather than as a subject in its own right.

NEWMAN investigates the term *sonata* as it was used in the baroque and so includes in his discussion accompanied and unaccompanied solo sonatas, trio sonatas, and sonatas for four or more parts. However, this specific interest in sonatas means that much repertoire—consort music or instrumental suites, for example—is not considered in this survey. The treatment of French and English music, therefore, is mostly limited to somewhat later music written after the Italian manner. Nevertheless, within his stated scope Newman is particularly thorough. His clear prose and broad scope remain unsurpassed.

In the absence of any up-to-date monograph devoted to the chamber music of the baroque period, the best single-volume resource for material on the field is SADIE (1991). Each of the major national regions receives an essay by a different specialist, with six further essays, discussing topics such as forms and genres and instruments. Additionally, this work contains a detailed biographical dictionary arranged by local regions. Because of the important status of chamber music in the baroque era and the degree of detail in this volume, readers will find it an indispensable reference tool for the entire range of baroque chamber music.

HOGWOOD presents a concise, orderly account of the trio sonata, which is arguably the primary genre in baroque chamber music. Chapters are divided by national schools, giving the reader a good idea of why differentiation of national styles is important in the baroque, while providing a solid contextual overview of the repertoire. The coverage of France, German-speaking countries, and England are particularly useful because the chamber music of the these regions has only been treated in rather specialized texts that tend to focus on narrow issues. Hogwood's insights as both performer and scholar and his facility with language mean that this book has more to offer than its modest length would suggest.

APEL presents a broad range of information on an important body of baroque chamber music, 17th-century Italian violin music, making this book a useful resource. However, readers should be warned of the book's limitations. Apel restricts himself to music that was published in the 17th century, omitting mention of music that survives only in manuscript or of important works written by the composers under consideration just after 1700. Furthermore, although the German original was published as recently as 1983, a large portion of Apel's bibliography is drawn from the early decades of the 20th century, with few items published more recently than the 1960s. Unfortunately, the author does not take advantage of the wealth of more recent research that could have improved the overall quality of the book.

ALLSOP shares a substantial overlap in his repertoire with Apel, but the differences in the authors' approach are as important as the differences in their focus. Although published shortly after Apel, Allsop is plagued by none of the limitations of the earlier work. Allsop is more concerned than Apel with the context of the music, providing substantial consideration of the social function of this music and the possible links between composers, as well as careful consideration of regional differences and questions of instrumentation and continuo practice. This approach stands in sharp contrast to Apel's catalog-like arrangement of material.

SELFRIDGE-FIELD remains a model of how to address broadly a carefully focused repertoire so that it stands as a body of related works, while at the same time delineating different trends within that body. This book is an indispensable resource for anyone interested in Italian baroque music. It is to be hoped that eventually other scholars will produce similar studies for other regions such as Rome, Dresden, and Austria. In addition to a composer-by-composer survey, Selfridge-Field takes on issues of instrumental genres and Venetian institutions.

Although limited to music in which the viol features prominently, SADIE (1980) helps redress the serious lack of literature on French chamber music. The role of the viol in France was significant enough that much of the music covered is of importance beyond its interest for students of the viol. Additionally, Sadie's concentration on the viol allows her to consider specific pieces in some detail. The narrow scope of the book, in itself praiseworthy, is an eloquent reminder of the work still to be done in the field.

JOHN MORAN

Chamber Music: Classical

Cobbett, Walter Willson, *Cobbett's Cyclopedic Survey of Chamber Music*, 2nd edition, edited by Colin Mason, 3 vols., London: Oxford University Press, 1963

Cohn, Arthur, *Literature of Chamber Music*, 4 vols., Chapel Hill, North Carolina: Hinshaw Music, 1997

Downs, Philip G., *Classical Music: The Era of Haydn, Mozart, and Beethoven*, New York: Norton, 1992

Griffiths, Paul, *The String Quartet*, New York: Thames and Hudson, 1983

Kirkendale, Warren, *Fugue and Fugato in Rococo and Classical Chamber Music*, translated by Margaret Bent and Warren Kirkendale, Durham, North Carolina: Duke University Press, 1979

Robertson, Alec, editor, *Chamber Music*, Harmondsworth: Penguin Books, 1957

Rosen, Charles, *The Classical Style: Haydn, Mozart, Beethoven*, London: Faber, and New York: Viking Press, 1971; expanded edition, New York: Norton, 1997

Wolff, Christoph, and Robert Riggs, editors, *The String Quartets of Haydn, Mozart, and Beethoven: Studies of the Autograph Manuscripts*, Cambridge, Massachusetts: Harvard University Department of Music, 1980

The genre of chamber music in the classical era is primarily defined by the string quartets of Haydn, Mozart, and Beethoven. Because the quartets are often viewed as stylistic bridges between the three composers, it is profitable to turn to books on these three composers and their works to learn about chamber music in the classical era.

Beyond the quartets of these masters, there remains the problem of delimiting the repertoire. For this essay, I define it as including music played by two or more performers with one musician to a part. Chronologically, the period encompasses composers born between 1730 and 1770, parameters mostly determined by the lives of Haydn and Beethoven.

During this period, expectations for chamber music underwent a dramatic change. In 1750, it was viewed as a private genre, using modest performing forces and including vocal music. By the death of Haydn, quartets were considered on a par with public genres such as symphonies, concertos, and opera. Of course, there were also a number of different chamber genres and styles. Haydn's divertimenti, piano trios, and baryton trios are prominent in his output. Mozart's string quintets are frequently considered as important as his quartets; he also wrote a number of divertimenti in a chamber format; and his duo sonatas, flute quartets, piano quartets, piano and wind quintet, and clarinet quintet are all noteworthy compositions. Beethoven's duo sonatas, piano trios, piano wind quintet, and septet are also important. Different nations cultivated other genres, such as the *quatuor brilliant* and *quatuor concertant* found in Paris. The art of counterpoint was also a pivotal part of the development of chamber music during this period. All of these styles, although initially found in particular geographical areas, were heavily borrowed internationally, thus breaking down distinctions between national styles.

COBBETT is a reliable, although dated, source of information about chamber music in general. It contains entries for composers as well as articles about terminology, styles, performing organizations, and outstanding performers of chamber music. The quality of the articles on composers of the late 18th century varies from entry to entry. The shorter entries frequently refer the reader to other sources for more information, but the volumes remain a valuable point of departure. One of the prize entries of the collection is Donald Francis Tovey's essay on Haydn's chamber music.

ROBERTSON contains essays on Haydn, Boccherini, Mozart, and Beethoven, each by a different author, with additional considerations of these composers in separate chapters on duet sonatas without wind instruments and chamber works with wind instruments. The discussions are stylistic analyses, providing comments on the history and structure of works discussed.

ROSEN is the most prized overall treatment of the music of this period, mostly because of the author's thorough knowledge of the repertoire. Although one could argue about his overselectivity, his chapters devoted to Haydn's quartets and piano trios and to Mozart's string quintets contain important revelatory insights about the period as a whole. His comments are primarily analytical and are supported by a contextual grasp of biography and source material.

KIRKENDALE attempts to account thoroughly for the stylistic changes of the middle and late 18th century as manifested in chamber music. The volume continues to be recognized as the finest study of its kind and demonstrates the importance of fugue and fugal technique to the rise of chamber music in the classical period. The author's approach leads him to consider a vast number of composers of the period, with special attention to Haydn, Mozart, and Beethoven.

WOLFF and RIGGS's volume contains essays by some of the most outstanding scholars in the field of manuscript studies. It brings together several divergent topics: not only the music of the three master composers but also the views from musical historical, musical analytical, and performance perspectives. The reader will gain insight into the wide variety of recent scholarship on the string quartets of this period.

GRIFFITHS's survey of the string quartet should be used carefully. The author possesses an undeniable enthusiasm for his topic and manages to make insightful comments about a large number of works, but his comments can be a mixture of fact and opinion. The portion of Griffiths's volume embracing Haydn and Beethoven occupies roughly half the book; his chronological approach intertwines the works of Mozart and Haydn. Griffiths is not very interested in moving off the beaten path, as demonstrated by his criticisms of Haydn for his fugal endings and Mozart for his use of the *quatuor concertant* style. The book is not helpful for those seeking the precursors of the genre.

DOWNS is a broad survey of late 18th-century music, with four essays pertaining specifically to trends in chamber music. The first, "Music for Private Performance," discusses music from the end of the baroque period up to about 1760. It covers formal and stylistic predecessors to classicism. "Music in the Home" notes the passing of the continuo and the rise of significant chamber genres: string trio, string quartet, string quintet, and keyboard sonatas with optional accompaniment. A third essay discusses "Solo and Chamber Music" during the last two decades of the century, including accompanied keyboard sonatas and chamber music for strings. The final essay notes the arrival of "Chamber Music in the Concert Hall" in the early 19th century. Placed among the last three essays are discussions of Mozart, Haydn, and Beethoven, which treat the composers' works more specifically. Downs's approach tends to be statistical with no real insight. His discussion of the origin of the string quartet is an exception in this regard, and his comments are not limited to Vienna. Otherwise, his perspective tilts in favor of the piano.

COHN's multivolume work on chamber music, despite some disappointing aspects, has many rewarding features. The set is intended as an introductory guide to chamber music. The writing is facile with broad statements, some of which should never be repeated. The factual statements call attention to their accuracy, and there are interesting tidbits of information. The work is most successful for its breadth of coverage of the repertoire; it is possible to find references to composers not mentioned by either Cobbett or Kirkendale. The set, however, is much stronger on recent works than early chamber music. Every chamber piece listed is given a brief stylistic description, often with references to stylistic origins. Dates and places of composition are occasionally provided. Although he does not provide publication information for rare works, Cohn often cites the comments of a work's editor.

JOSEPH ORCHARD

Chamber Music: 19th Century

Abraham, Gerald, editor, *Romanticism (1830–1890)*, New Oxford History of Music, vol. 9, Oxford: Oxford University Press, 1990

Cobbett, Walter Willson, *Cobbett's Cyclopedic Survey of Chamber Music*, 2nd edition, edited by Colin Mason, 3 vols., London: Oxford University Press, 1963

Hefling, Stephen E., editor, *Nineteenth-Century Chamber Music*, New York: Schirmer Books, and London: Prentice Hall, 1998

Kerman, Joseph, *The Beethoven String Quartets*, New York: Knopf, and London: Oxford University Press, 1967

Smallman, Basil, *The Piano Quartet and Quintet: Style, Structure, and Scoring*, Oxford: Clarendon Press, and New York: Oxford University Press, 1994

———, *The Piano Trio: Its History, Technique, and Repertoire*, Oxford: Clarendon Press, and New York: Oxford University Press, 1990

Winter, Robert, and Robert L. Martin, editors, *The Beethoven Quartet Companion,* Berkeley: University of California Press, 1994

As with many genres in the 19th century, chamber music was most profoundly influenced by the music of Beethoven. Heir to a Viennese tradition stemming from Haydn and Mozart, Beethoven wrote chamber music throughout his career, and his chamber works—especially the string quartets—remain the foundation of the modern repertoire. Beethoven both enlarged the expressive scope of chamber music and, as one of the first composers to write works for professional performers, raised the level of technical proficiency required to perform it to unprecedented heights. Thus released from the exclusive preserve of amateur players in aristocratic salons, chamber music became increasingly important as public concert music in the 19th century.

The context in which Beethoven's career as quartet composer flourished is admirably assessed in a number of articles collected in WINTER and MARTIN. The contributors include noted Beethoven scholars Joseph Kerman (on musical style), Maynard Solomon (on aesthetics), Leon Botstein (on Viennese culture and society), and Winter (on reception in the 19th century). There is also a fascinating article by cellist Robert Martin on the process of preparing Beethoven's quartets for performance. The discussion of the individual quartets by Michael Steinberg, while often insightful, is written in the style of concert program notes.

For a sustained critical analysis of Beethoven's quartets, KERMAN's classic study is essential. He incorporates biography, historiography, sketch studies, and commentary by earlier critics (especially Donald Francis Tovey) to produce a richly textured discussion of the works and their significance in Beethoven's creative life. Kerman analyzes nearly every bar of every quartet, although not necessarily in the order they appear. His treatment of the late quartets is indicative of his approach: the first chapter devoted to them is entitled "Voice," in which Kerman treats what he calls "the vocal impulse" (an impulse to create expressive, songlike melodies) in five movements from four different quartets. His focus on topics such as this one creates opportunities for drawing connections between works, and more important, for illuminating Beethoven's broader compositional concerns. Kerman's method has become a model for much modern critical analysis. No one studying the quartets—indeed, Beethoven's music in general—can afford to ignore this monograph.

A good overview of chamber music after Beethoven is provided in two chapters of ABRAHAM. The first, "Chamber Music: 1830–1850," by John Horton, is more balanced in its focus than the latter. In addition to a critical discussion of works by Mendelssohn, Spohr, and Robert Schumann, the most significant composers of chamber music in modern eyes, Horton provides sympathetic coverage of secondary masters such as Franz Berwald, Johann Nepomuk Hummel, George Onslow, Niels Gade, and William Sterndale Bennett, noting that these were composers who were "able to amass a great body of work (whatever judgments may be made on its quality), to set fashions, and to control taste over many decades." Horton also touches on most of the important issues of the period as a whole, including performance practice, aesthetic and social conditions, the increased importance of the piano in chamber music composition, and the rise of professional chamber groups.

Chamber music in the latter part of the century is covered in the second half of Robert Pascal's chapter, entitled "Major Instrumental Forms: 1850–1890." Portions of this chapter cover Russian composers (with emphasis on Borodin and Tchaikovsky) and French composers (primarily Fauré), but the bulk of the attention is given to Brahms and Dvořák. Pascal's approach is more narrowly analytical and statistical (tabulations of numbers of chamber works, numbers of sonata-form or dance-inspired movements, etc.) than Horton's.

Although the number of performances of chamber music by professional musicians in public concerts increased significantly in the later 19th century, most performances were still given by accomplished amateurs in private circles. Amateur performers provided the main market for published music, and they frequently offered commissions for new works. The ability to perform, appreciate, and sponsor chamber music remained important in upper-class society throughout century. British businessman COBBETT was a particularly passionate devotee of this chamber music culture, and he became the compiler and editor of the most comprehensive reference work on chamber music. Written primarily for the art-loving community, *Cobbett's Cyclopedic Survey* was originally published in 1929; its second edition retains the original articles, supplemented with a new volume of corrections, additions, and updates. It remains indispensable as a source of information on composers who are now neglected, but whose music was still performed in the early part of the 20th century. In addition, it contains some classics of musical criticism, including Vincent d'Indy's article on Beethoven and Tovey's essay on Brahms. Other notable articles on 19th-century composers include the study on Fauré by his student Florent Schmitt, and the essay on Robert Schumann by Fanny Davies, who was a student of Clara Schumann.

Two recent books by British scholar Basil Smallman provide valuable introductions to their respective topics: SMALLMAN (1990) investigates piano trios, while SMALLMAN (1994) discusses piano quartets and quintets. Both are general histories of these media, but the bulk of both repertoires comes from the 19th century. Smallman attempts to delineate a mainstream tradition, but he does not neglect discussion of composers at the fringes of this tradition. Both books are well researched, and Smallman's descriptive analyses of major works are excellent.

HEFLING is a collection of nine articles by ten different authors that generally treats composers individually. Approaches vary, according to the amount and quality of previous critical attention on the topic. Thus, the discussions of Beethoven (by Kofi Agawu), Mendelssohn (by R. Larry Todd), Robert Schumann (by John Daverio), and Brahms (by Margaret Notley) seek to offer new critical interpretations and assume some prior knowledge of the music. The articles on Spohr and Weber (by Clive Brown), Smetana and Dvořák (by Derek Katz and Michael Beckerman), and French chamber music (by Joël-Marie Fauquet) are more in the nature of introductory surveys. Most extensive and wide ranging in critical approach is the article on Schubert by Hefling and David S. Tartakoff. The authors draw on biography, social and cultural history, and musical analysis to produce the most significant and well-balanced critical analysis of Schubert's chamber music to date. Another thought-provoking contribution is Daverio's article on the transformation of chamber music from a conservative, classicizing genre in the 19th century into a vehicle for modernism at the turn of the 20th century.

Each article in Hefling contains a select bibliography, an essential feature considering that monographs on this topic are almost nonexistent. Most of the criticism and analysis of 19th-century chamber music has been presented in monographs on individual composers, and in the periodical literature. Hefling's book, in addition to offering stimulating insights into the music, provides a very useful guide to this literature.

MARK BENSON

Chamber Music: 20th Century

Griffiths, Paul, *The String Quartet,* New York: Thames and Hudson, 1983

Kárpáti, János, *Bartók's Chamber Music,* translated by Fred Macnicol and Mária Steiner, revised by Paul Merrick, Stuyvesant, New York: Pendragon Press, 1994

McCalla, James, *Twentieth-Century Chamber Music,* New York: Schirmer Books, and London: Prentice Hall International, 1996

Simms, Bryan R., "Twentieth-Century Composers Return to the Small Ensemble," in *The Orchestra: Origins and Transformations,* edited by Joan Peyser, New York: Scribner, 1986

Smallman, Basil, *The Piano Quartet and Quintet: Style, Structure, and Scoring,* Oxford: Clarendon Press, and New York: Oxford University Press, 1994

———, *The Piano Trio: Its History, Technique, and Repertoire,* Oxford: Clarendon Press, and New York: Oxford University Press, 1990

Walsh, Stephen, *Bartók Chamber Music,* London: British Broadcasting Corporation, 1982

Whittall, Arnold, *Schoenberg Chamber Music,* London: British Broadcasting Corporation, and Seattle: University of Washington Press, 1972

Chamber music has played a vital role in the history of music written in the 20th century. Economic necessity, along with a new conception of sound based on independent lines and individual timbres, led composers in the early decades of the century to write music for small numbers of instruments. The influence of jazz musicians and folk- or ethnic-derived music, a renewed interest in baroque and early classical styles, and the growth of broadcast and recording industries contributed to the persistence of the chamber-music ideal. Finally, 20th-century composers increasingly had the opportunity to respond to direct calls for chamber music, either by commission or for a competition. The persistence and sheer variety of chamber music in the 20th century make it a certain topic for anyone writing about the era, and yet to date, only one author has devoted an entire book to the subject. Others have included the 20th century in their examination of a chamber genre that emerged in previous centuries. Just two 20th-century composers, Schoenberg and Bartók, have had full-length studies of their chamber music published.

McCALLA's is the only book devoted entirely to 20th-century chamber music. After an introductory chapter, he arranges his study by genre, devoting a chapter each to programmatic chamber music, vocal chamber music, music (without narrative) for new ensembles, the sonata, and the string quartet. McCalla believes that musical temporality, or the nature of time itself, has been an overarching concern of 20th-century composers and addresses this idea in each of his chapters. He also ties the book together by using single works to provide examples in more than one chapter. Thus, for instance, Schoenberg's *Pierrot lunaire,* op. 21, appears in the chapter on vocal chamber music as well as in the chapter on new ensembles. McCalla's analyses are not technically challenging. He focuses on poetic-musical correspondences, melodic material, and questions of form and does not neglect to consider the issue of performance practice. The value of this study lies in its scope. But of course, McCalla cannot address every piece written for chamber ensemble in the 20th century, and his criteria for choosing the pieces he discusses at length are at times questionable. For example, he analyzes all six of Bartók's string quartets but dismisses Shostakovich's 16 string quartets with scarcely a page. Similarly, in the chapter concerning new ensembles, he devotes one page to Stravinsky's *L'histoire du soldat,* then nearly seven pages to Debussy's Sonata for Flute, Viola, and Harp. Substantial references would be helpful, but only occasionally does a footnote direct readers to other published analyses of the music. All told, McCalla leans heavily on German, French, and U.S. music of the first two-thirds of the century. Important composers of other nationalities, such as Benjamin Britten (English), Luigi Dallapiccola (Italian), and Alberto Ginastera (Argentinean), go unmentioned, as does most of the "trend" chamber music of the last three or four decades of the 20th century: minimalist, new age, ethnic- and pop-influenced works that have made their way into classical concert halls.

GRIFFITHS's thorough knowledge of 20th-century music comes into play when he dedicates fully a third of his historical account of the string quartet to works written in this century. Griffiths organizes his study into four parts, corresponding to the four movements of a musical opus. Part 3 and Part 4 are essential reading for any student of the genre in the 20th century, up to about 1980. Although Griffiths's treatment of individual works is brief, his rich descriptive vocabulary and choice points of reference evoke a clear sense of the music. He avoids lengthy quotations by composers—a pitfall of authors writing on 20th-century topics—and partly as a consequence, his assessment of the expressive and technical tendencies of the string quartet in this century takes on a historical perspective, rather than being merely a report of the situation at hand. An appendix with annotated references for bibliographies, editions, and recordings of the music discussed is valuable, as is a second appendix in which Griffiths provides a chronological list of historically significant string quartets.

What Griffiths has done for the string quartet, Smallman has done for the piano trio and, in a subsequent study, the piano quartet and quintet. In SMALLMAN (1990), the author touches on recent examples of the genre in chapter 4. He then devotes an entire chapter (chapter 7) to the 20th century. Throughout, Smallman concentrates on aspects of the scoring, examining different ways in which composers have handled the unique textural and timbral possibilities of the piano trio. Closing in on the decade in which he completed his study (the 1980s), Smallman focuses on developments in Great Britain and the United States, although he is careful to point out the international character of the time.

SMALLMAN (1994) is much like his first book on chamber music but includes even more 20th-century examples, especially in the final chapter (chapter 7), which covers mixed-ensemble works with piano. Chapter 4 includes many examples from just after the turn of the century, and chapter 5 concerns the evolution of piano quartets and quintets up to the middle of the century. In chapter 6, Smallman offers a particularly valuable overview of the various approaches to orchestrating works for piano and small ensemble. His examples here are more analytical than elsewhere but still can be easily grasped by the musically educated reader.

SIMMS's essay on 20th-century chamber music is part of a book devoted to the history of orchestral music, and thus he approaches the subject differently than do Griffiths and Smallman, from the angle of the composer who conceives a symphony "scored small" rather than a traditional work for small ensemble. Simms offers an insightful summary of the circumstances and models for composers' turn to small orchestras at the beginning of the century and provides a detailed survey of the literature, organized by nationality, up to the mid-20th century.

WHITTALL's express object in examining Schoenberg's chamber music is to elucidate the relationship between radical and conservative elements in the composer's style. Early on, Whittall makes the apology, "It may often seem as if the discussion of these works as chamber music takes second place to a discussion of more general matters, but this is inevitable . . . where the medium . . . may be the most conventional, traditional feature." And indeed, Whittall proceeds essentially to ignore matters of texture and timbre, or the historical context of Schoenberg's choice to compose in a chamber-music style. Despite his irregular approach, Whittall's clear line of thinking and comprehensible (if technical) examples make this a valuable book for anyone interested in the inner workings of this revolutionary composer's music.

WALSH's guide to Bartók's chamber music is vivid and informative. He makes frequent reference to the context of Bartók's creative efforts, as well as to other published analyses of the works. His own analyses are nothing less than eloquent, with colorful descriptions and metaphors that neatly conceptualize the music. This book is an excellent resource for readers who are not already familiar with Bartók's chamber music style.

KÁRPÁTI's study of Bartók's chamber music is more involved than Walsh's. Kárpáti devotes the first half of his book to questions of musical idiom and style, including the historical time and place in which Bartók worked and the evolution of the composer's thematic structures, harmonic language, and formal preferences. Numerous examples allow the reader to follow Kárpáti's detailed theoretical explanations. The second half of the book comprises a no less detailed analysis of the individual numbers in the composer's chamber oeuvre. Kárpáti draws out pertinent information from the compositional history of each opus and frequently makes comparisons to other music, folk and classical. This is a brilliant study, not only of Bartók's chamber music, but also, more generally, of the technical resources and aesthetic goals of European composers in the first part of the 20th century.

DONNA L. LYNN

Chance Music *see* Aleatoric Music

Chanson

Aubrey, Elizabeth, *Music of the Troubadours*, Bloomington: Indiana University Press, 1996

Brothers, Thomas, *Chromatic Beauty in the Late Medieval Chanson: An Interpretation of Manuscript Accidentals*, Cambridge: Cambridge University Press, 1997

Brown, Howard Mayer, *Music in the French Secular Theater, 1400–1550*, Cambridge, Massachusetts: Harvard University Press, 1963

Jeffery, Brian, *Chanson Verse of the Early Renaissance*, 2 vols., Uttoxeter: Jeffery, 1971; and London: Tecla, 1976

Kemp, Walter H., *Burgundian Court Song in the Time of Binchois: The Anonymous Chansons of El Escorial, MS V.III.24*, Oxford: Clarendon Press, and New York: Oxford University Press, 1990

Stainer, J.F.R., and C. Stainer, editors, *Early Bodleian Music: Dufay and His Contemporaries*, London: Novello, and New York: Ewer, 1898

Stevens, John, *Words and Music in the Middle Ages: Song, Narrative, Dance, and Drama, 1050–1350*, Cambridge: Cambridge University Press, 1986

Werf, Hendrik van der, *The Chansons of the Troubadours and Trouvères: A Study of the Melodies and Their Relation to the Poems*, Utrecht: Oosthoek, 1972

In the most general sense, the term *chanson* signifies an art song written to a French vernacular text, for a single voice (monophonic chanson) or multiple voices (polyphonic chanson). Musicologists concur that the genre flourished from the late Middle Ages through the late Renaissance; there is some disagreement with regard to appropriate limitations of chronology and lexicology. Whereas some scholars extend the term into the 19th and 20th centuries to include the French *mélodie*, others limit the chanson to polyphonic songs of the 15th and 16th centuries that do not employ lyric poetry in one of the *formes fixes*: ballade, rondeau, or virelai. The term is also recognized as a genre of poetry. The bibliography above includes works that discuss three widely recognized periods of chanson development: (1) the monophonic chanson, which represents the principal genre of secular medieval music through the 13th century in the repertoires of the troubadours and trouvères; (2) the polyphonic chanson of the *ars nova* (14th and 15th centuries); and (3) the Renaissance chanson of the 16th century. A distinction is also made between the international usage of *chanson* and other French applications of the term, such as that for folk song (*chanson populaire*) or drinking song (*chanson pour boire*). In addition to the literature discussed here, the serious student of the chanson is directed to collected works editions of the chanson repertoire, published in series such as Corpus Mensurabilis Musicae and Polyphonic Music of the Fourteenth Century.

One of the earliest publications in English on the genre, STAINER's volume offers a history of the late medieval chanson as represented in a single manuscript, MS Canonici misc. 213, in the Bodleian Library at Oxford. Although portions of Stainer's volume discuss complex analytical issues, such as methods of rhythmic transcription, treatments of dissonance, and *musica ficta*, there is much for the general reader: facsimiles of the manuscript, biographical sketches on the most prominent composers, commentary on individual chansons—including subsequent use of these melodies by later composers—and transcriptions into modern notation of the chansons contained in the manuscript. Stainer's goal is to present an unfamiliar repertory to performing musicians; it is a valuable tool despite subsequent changes in musicological thought regarding methods of transcription and performance practice.

BROWN's work unapologetically gives detailed attention to discussion of the literary and performance contexts of 15th- and 16th-century chansons associated with the theater. In fact, the contextual positioning of this repertory is the great strength of this groundbreaking work in cultural musicology. The core of the book is devoted to the chansons themselves: their role and placement within the plays, performance practice, and definition of subgenres within the chanson repertory. It is thorough to the point of revealing difficulties associated with the genre. Textual references to improvised singing styles and to chansons that do not survive, and uncertain correlations between extant music and actual theatrical performance, make discussion of the music itself difficult. Yet Brown gives detailed consideration of surviving musical examples that is as valuable for its detective work as it is for its stylistic analysis. Included in the volume is a lengthy catalog of theatrical chansons and their sources.

As an ancillary to investigations of the musical genre, JEFFERY presents a complete edition of 12 extant printed collections of chanson verse from the early 16th century. Although the study is limited to poetry published without music, it is chanson verse that was employed by the most significant composers of the late 15th and early 16th centuries—often in musical collections that do not give the full poetic texts. Jeffery is critical of musicologists editing early chansons without "literary interest"; his study is intended as a tool to increase familiarity and competence with the topic of lyric poetry in France. A brief discussion of each of the 12 chanson verse collections precedes transcription of the poetry (without translation).

Attempting to bridge the gap between musicological and philological studies, WERF offers a general study that focuses on aspects of text-music relationships in the extant repertoire of troubadour and trouvère chansons rather than on details of musical analysis. As such, his survey offers a broad discussion of topics ranging from problems of oral versus written transmission to issues of rhythm and form concerning both poetry and melody. The substance of the book, however, is its presentation and discussion of 15 individual chansons; each is transcribed, with a comparison of multiple extant versions and a full translation of the poetry.

Continuing and expanding van der Werf's investigation of text-music relationships, STEVENS's work is a broad, comprehensive inquiry into that relationship as manifested in the art of melody in northern Europe, ca. 1050–1350. Although he discusses other monophonic genres, such as the Latin *conductus* and German narrative song, Stevens's treatment of the courtly chanson is both thorough and insightful. Stevens argues that medieval music was most of all a numerical art and that composing poetry was a musical art in the medieval sense as well. Reasoning that poetic rhythm was inextricably bound to the musical composition, Stevens advances a theory of isosyllabism: equal duration for the performance of each syllable in the chanson, no matter the number of corresponding pitches. Although this theory has been criticized in more recent studies, the contextual background to the argument is compelling, and the scope of the work is unsurpassed.

KEMP's volume, like the earlier work by Stainer, examines a category of chansons as they are represented in one manuscript: a *chansonnier* written at the 15th-century Burgundian court of Duke Philip the Good. Kemp concurs with Stainer's assessment of stylistic attributes and quality of prominent composers' works; Kemp's aim is to establish criteria through musical analysis by which unattributed chansons might be referenced. As such, analysis of specific chanson characteristics takes precedence, with a detailed rationale for aspects of performance practice and attribution of anonymous chansons to prominent composers. In his subsequent discussion of cultural context, Kemp takes issue with the great-man tradition used with national qualifiers by Stainer (and others) to classify music. Instead, he argues, this repertoire should be considered within the framework of chivalric humanism, which flourished at the court of Philip the Good. Kemp examines the lyric poetry of the chansons, although there are no translations given for the French texts.

AUBREY offers an exhaustive, yet highly readable study of all 315 extant chansons of the 12th- and 13th-century troubadours. Including biographies of the troubadours and a discussion of their social and political milieu, Aubrey's work examines medieval literary traditions as they were intertwined with music in the troubadour's art. The core of the study is an in-depth analysis of the forms and styles of these monophonic chansons, including translations of the poetry and a thorough discussion of the most controversial issue of performance practice: rhythm. Discounting theories of the modalists and of those in the isosyllabic camp, Aubrey argues that a close analysis of poetic and musical structure, style, and variants for each chanson must be considered rather than an overarching principle of interpretation.

This work is essential to a serious investigation of the troubadour chanson.

BROTHERS's volume presents a narrow topic within broad chronological boundaries: that of expressive chromaticism in both monophonic and polyphonic chansons of the late 13th century through the late 15th century. Brothers analyzes and interprets the beautiful use of chromatic inflection in the detail and overall design of these works. Like Aubrey on rhythm, Brothers approaches chromaticism as an issue of compositional practice in individual works rather than as a single theory of performance practice. He advances the self-proclaimed radical view that musical manuscripts (and the accidentals therein) can be taken at face value rather than as the result of an unnotated tradition that was obvious to medieval performers. Brothers's topic is detailed by nature and demands a close reading; his discussion of selected chansons is thorough and insightful.

ELINOR OLIN

Chant: Ambrosian

Bailey, Terence, *The Ambrosian Alleluias*, Egham: Plainsong and Medieval Music Society, 1983

———, *The Ambrosian Cantus*, Ottawa, Ontario: Institute of Medieval Music, 1987

———, *Antiphon and Psalm in the Ambrosian Office*, Ottawa, Ontario: Institute of Mediaeval Music, 1994

Bailey, Terence, and Paul Merkley, *The Antiphons of the Ambrosian Office*, Ottawa, Ontario: Institute of Medieval Music, 1989

Bailey, Terence, and Paul Merkley, editors, *The Melodic Tradition of the Ambrosian Office-Antiphons*, Ottawa, Ontario: Institute of Medieval Music, 1990

Hiley, David, *Western Plainchant: A Handbook*, Oxford: Clarendon Press, and New York: Oxford University Press, 1993

Jesson, Roy, "Ambrosian Chant," in *Gregorian Chant*, by Willi Apel, London: Burns and Oates, and Bloomington: Indiana University Press, 1958

Weakland, Rembert, "The Performance of Ambrosian Chant in the Twelfth Century," in *Aspects of Medieval and Renaissance Music: A Birthday Offering to Gustave Reese*, edited by Jan LaRue, New York: Norton, 1966

Ambrosian chant, also known as Milanese chant, is the repertory of sacred monophonic music used in the churches of Milan. It takes its name from the fourth-century bishop of that city, St. Ambrose, who was credited with revising the liturgy of Milan and introducing the practice of antiphonal psalmody, or singing psalms with alternating choirs. His role in this development is seriously doubted, however, and his connection to the music may be limited to the same symbolic relationship that links St. Gregory to the chant that bears his name. In the 11th and 12th centuries, the term *Ambrosian* was applied by southern Italian singers to the liturgical chant of Benevento, suggesting a link between their music and the melodies of the metropolitan north, but modern scholars use the term only to identify the Milanese rite. Ambrosian chant is the only sacred musical tradition of the Middle Ages that survived the imposition of Gregorian/Frankish chant in a notation we can accurately transcribe; the earliest sources with such notation were copied in the 12th century. Scholarly work on the repertory has focused primarily on analyzing the melodies and comparing them with their Roman, Beneventan, and Gregorian counterparts, although some important studies have pursued other lines of inquiry.

JESSON provides a concise overview of the Ambrosian repertory, but much of his work, particularly his melodic analyses, have been superseded or corrected by the specialized studies of Bailey. Jesson briefly describes the early history of the Milanese Church, lists the most important musical sources, and charts the progress of the liturgical day and year in the basilica. His discussion of the Mass is particularly illuminating because he provides a table that compares the formularies, or sequence of events, for Ambrosian and Gregorian Masses. Having discussed the liturgical aspects of this music, he reviews the salient melodic characteristics of various classes of chant—psalm tones, office and Mass propers, and so forth—and concludes his essay with a brief discussion of mode. Although still useful, Jesson's chapter should be used with caution and supplemented with the overview in Hiley's book.

Although it is more than 30 years old, WEAKLAND's essay remains an important contribution. He offers an excellent survey of the personnel who participated in the Milanese liturgy by drawing on the contents of a 12th-century ordinal, a book that describes the way religious observances ought to be carried out. Weakland delineates the duties of the different clerics in the cathedral and points out important performance directions in the ordinal. He concludes his essay by giving a detailed description of the way in which a Mass, divine office hours, and a procession would have been observed in Milan and urges other scholars to complement their analytical studies of the Ambrosian repertory with the information on performance contained in works such as this 12th-century ordinal.

BAILEY (1983) is the first of several studies in which the author provides historical background for a single Milanese chant genre, together with an edition of the music. In this volume, Bailey traces the early history of the Ambrosian Alleluia, discusses its particular development in Milan, and examines the melodic characteristics of the chants. Only about ten Alleluias were used in the Milanese rite, and Bailey devotes the last chapter of his essay to an exploration of their close melodic affiliation, as well as

their relationship to Alleluias in other repertories. He closes his discussion of the Alleluia melodies by examining the verses that were sung to each of the ten Alleluia types.

BAILEY (1987) presents a thorough study of the chant that was the Ambrosian counterpart of the Gregorian Tract. His study considers the vexed use of the word *Cantus* in the Milanese manuscripts, the liturgical assignment of these chants, and aspects of its performance in the early church. Bailey follows his historical and liturgical discussion with a detailed analysis of the melodies that highlights their close relationship. He uses his analytical findings to comment on the development of the Cantus chants and the repertory as a whole. The book closes with an edition of Cantus chants.

BAILEY and MERKLEY (1989), the first installment of a three-volume study, provides the reader with inventories and indices to the office antiphons of the Milanese rite. The chants are listed in four tables that arrange the antiphons in turns by feast, alphabetically, by psalm assignment, and by liturgical type (i.e., Benedictus antiphons, Magnificat antiphons, etc.). BAILEY and MERKLEY (1990), the second volume of this series, complements their inventories with an edition of the melodies.

HILEY briefly cites important scholarship on Ambrosian chant and then reviews some of the general features of the Milanese melodies, illustrating them with several examples. For a more complete overview of the liturgy, however, the reader should consult Jesson or the article "Ambrosian Rite" in *The New Grove Dictionary of Music and Musicians* (1980).

BAILEY (1994) concludes his three-volume investigation of the Milanese office antiphons by offering the reader a detailed discussion of the use of psalms and antiphons in the Milanese rite. His book begins with a survey of the early history of the church and continues with a valuable chapter on the nature of antiphonal psalmody and the misunderstandings that have surrounded it. After considering many late antique and early medieval comments on antiphonal singing, he clears up several misconceptions about the presence of divided choirs in Ambrose's church and doubts the role Ambrose played in bringing this practice to Milan. In the remaining chapters, Bailey examines the structure of the office hours in the Milanese liturgy and discusses the use and placement of psalms and antiphons during the liturgical year.

MICHAEL McGRADE

Chant: Byzantine

Conomos, Dimitri, *Byzantine Trisagia and Cheroubika of the Fourteenth and Fifteenth Centuries: A Study of Late Byzantine Liturgical Chant*, Thessaloniki: Patriarchal Institute for Patristic Studies, 1974

————, *The Late Byzantine and Slavonic Communion Cycle: Liturgy and Music,* Washington, D.C.: Dumbarton Oaks Research Library and Collection, 1985

Moran, Neil, *Singers in Late Byzantine and Slavonic Painting,* Leiden: Brill, 1986

Strunk, W. Oliver, *Essays on Music in the Byzantine World,* New York: Norton, 1977

Velimirovic, Milos, *Byzantine Elements in Early Slavic Chant: The Hirmologion,* 2 vols., Copenhagen: Munksgaard, 1960

Wellesz, Egon, *A History of Byzantine Music and Hymnography,* Oxford: Clarendon Press, 1949; 2nd, revised edition, 1961

The liturgical chant of the Byzantine Empire (ca. 330–1453) comprises a large repertory that survives in thousands of manuscripts dating predominately from the 12th to the 15th centuries. Scholarship in this field has focused on deciphering the unique system of Middle Byzantine musical notation, control of the sources, analysis of the formulaic structure and modal qualities of the music, and historical study of the relationships with other chant repertories, notably Latin chant and early Slavonic chant. A considerable amount of research has taken place under the auspices of the Monumenta Musica Byzantinae (MMB), which was founded in Copenhagen in 1931 by Egon Wellesz, H.J.W. Tillyard, and Carsten Høeg, and which has sponsored publication of manuscript facsimiles, musical transcriptions, historical studies, and most recently, editions of important theoretical treatises on music.

Many leading Greek scholars vehemently disagree with the historical views and policies for musical transcription that were developed by scholars associated with the MMB. The rift is a fundamental one, centered on the question of whether the performance tradition (in particular, the tuning system, use of the drone or *ison*, and ornamentation practice) extends in an unbroken line from the time of the Byzantine Empire to the present-day Greek Orthodox Church. Explicit evidence for certain aspects of performance is lacking in music manuscripts from the time of empire, but most scholars outside of Greece have been unwilling to endorse the assumption that these gaps can be filled by working backward from 18th- to 20th-century practices. Most European and U.S. scholars posit ruptures in the tradition during the aftermath of the Turkish conquest of Byzantium and again in the 19th century when Chrysanthos of Madytos led a reform of chanting. The bibliographical items cited in this article are the work of Western scholars, and the discussion that follows is limited to studies of Byzantine chant in the time of the Byzantine Empire and the century after its fall.

The most comprehensive and influential study of Byzantine chant, which has not yet been surpassed, is the classic history by WELLESZ. It contains an account of the decipherment of Byzantine Round notation and basic guidelines for transcription, an outline of the Byzantine liturgy that was the context of the surviving musical repertory, descriptions of the main genres of chant, analysis of the formulaic structure of Byzantine music, a discussion of the relationship between the melodies and texts, and a list of hymnographers. Although very little musical evidence survives from the early period of the Byzantine Empire, Wellesz stresses the continuity of Byzantine musical institutions with those of late antiquity and early Christianity and devotes much of his work to the major early genres, the *troparion, kontakion,* and *kanon,* which flourished before the end of the eighth century.

The collected essays of STRUNK are among the most elegant and penetrating studies of Byzantine music and epitomize the work of the generation that followed the decipherment of Round notation. These essays cover a wide range of difficult topics, including seminal studies of the paleobyzantine notation systems called "Chartres" and "Coislin." Central to many of Strunk's studies are questions concerning the use of relatively late Byzantine sources to recover music of earlier Byzantine periods, and the role of oral tradition, which is more prominent in the Byzantine chant system (with its use of hymns with borrowed melodies, called *prosomoia*) than in Latin chant. Strunk is also concerned with the relationship of Byzantine and Latin chant, not simply examining individual instances of borrowed chants, but also discussing more basic kinships of modality, psalm tones, and responsorial practices.

CONOMOS (1974), a scholar of Greek heritage who was a student of Wellesz at Oxford, shifts attention to music of the 14th and 15th centuries in a study devoted to two of the most important chants of the Byzantine liturgy, the *trisagion* and *cheroubikon.* During this later period (when, contrary to earlier practice, composers' names appear in music manuscripts), the texts of the liturgy remained unchanged, but the music was less bound by conventional formulaic melodies. Increasingly, the music was freely elaborated in *kalophonic* (literally, beautiful-sounding) style. This stylistic change in the music was accompanied by significant developments in musical notation, and the interplay between the structure of the melodies and the new notational features of later sources is a central theme in Conomos's study.

The comparative methods advocated by Strunk are put into practice in an exemplary study of the *koinonikon,* or communion chant, by CONOMOS (1985). By comparing all of the extant melodies for the 26 *koinonika* of the Byzantine cycle, not only in the *asmatikon* (cathedral) and the *akolouthiai* (monastic-urban) manuscript traditions, but also the Slavonic branch, Conomos demonstrates both continuity in the musical tradition and the intricate stylistic evolution of Byzantine chant.

The relationship between Byzantine chant and the music of the early Slavonic church is of great significance for Byzantine studies because the melodies of the Greek church were often retained even when the texts were translated. In a pathbreaking study, VELIMIROVIC demonstrates the modal affinities, reliance on Byzantine forms, and individual instances of borrowings in early Slavic sources. In addition, close analysis of chants in the D authentic mode leads Velimirovic to conclude that early Slavic notation might be transcribed through comparisons with parallel passages in Byzantine sources, a technique that has played a major role in subsequent investigations of early Slavonic melodies.

Finally, whereas most studies of Byzantine music have been concerned with the manuscript tradition and performance problems, MORAN has undertaken an investigation of the singers, or *psaltai,* as they are represented in art and literature. Moran has identified a few *cheironomic* (hand) gestures, most notably the *ison* and *oxeia,* in addition to unearthing considerable amounts of information about the number, physical position within the church, and vestments of singers during the liturgical ceremonies at Hagia Sophia in Constantinople and other major ecclesiastical centers in Byzantium.

ROSEMARY THOONEN DUBOWCHIK

Chant: Gregorian

Apel, Willi, *Gregorian Chant,* London, Burns and Oates, and Bloomington: Indiana University Press, 1958

Hiley, David, *Western Plainchant: A Handbook,* Oxford: Clarendon Press, and New York: Oxford University Press, 1993

Hughes, Andrew, *Medieval Manuscripts for Mass and Office: A Guide to Their Organization and Terminology,* Toronto: University of Toronto Press, 1982

Levy, Kenneth, *Gregorian Chant and the Carolingians,* Princeton, New Jersey: Princeton University Press, 1998

Treitler, Leo, "Homer and Gregory: The Transmission of Epic Poetry and Plainchant," *Musical Quarterly* 60 (1974)

Wagner, Peter, *Introduction to the Gregorian Melodies. Part 1, Origin and Development of the Forms of Liturgical Chant up to the End of the Middle Ages,* translated by Agnes Orme and E.G.P. Wyatt, 2nd edition, London: Plainsong and Medieval Music Society, 1901; reprint, New York: Da Capo Press, 1986

Strictly speaking, Gregorian chant is the repertory of texts and melodies that grew out of efforts to impose Roman chant on Northern European churches and monasteries during the reign of Charlemagne. The chant is a Carolingian transformation of music imported from the papal court in Rome. Thus the Gregorian repertory is a hybrid of late eighth-century Roman and Frankish chanting practices, but the precise nature of this relationship is not known. The earliest recorded reference to this repertory as Gregorian dates from the middle of the ninth century, and the allusion probably reflects an attempt to enhance the authority of the music, giving it a pedigree that reached back to the papal choirs established by Pope Gregory I. The prestige of this false attribution probably helped further the goals of liturgical reforms—the ongoing efforts to impose the chant throughout the Carolingian Empire and thus standardize liturgical observations—that had been underway since the late eighth century.

In common usage, the term *Gregorian chant* is often used to identify almost any monophonic Latin song. Scholars tend to apply it in the more narrow sense outlined above, distinguishing between the "Gregorian" Mass propers and Office chants—introits, graduals, offertories, responsories, etc.—preserved in the earliest notated liturgical manuscripts, and the "medieval" chants—sequences, tropes, hymns, and others—composed by ninth-century Frankish singers and the generations of European musicians who came after them. Scholarship in the field has followed several lines of inquiry, including paleographic and philological studies, stylistic analyses of the music, studies of performance practice, text-music relationships, the origins of musical notation, and the origins of the chant itself.

The first modern, comprehensive study of Gregorian chant is WAGNER's three-volume *Introduction to Gregorian Chant.* Only the first volume of this work has been translated into English. Wagner was motivated in part by pious impulses to restore the chant of the Catholic Church to its ancient state, and for a time he cooperated with the monks of the Abbey of Solesmes who first called for a reform of modern chanting practices. In the first volume of his study, Wagner delineates the formation of Gregorian chant, arguing that the liturgical function of the music played a key role in the development of the repertory. The second volume of his *Introduction* contains an extensive investigation of chant notation; the third volume is devoted to an analysis of the melodies. Many of Wagner's historical explanations have been superseded by more recent scholarship—he accepts at face value, for example, the myth that Pope Gregory I composed the repertory. Nevertheless, his work laid the foundation for much of the scholarship that followed. The breadth and depth of his study have not yet been surpassed.

APEL's book was the first successor to Wagner's and the first major study of Gregorian chant in English. It falls into three sections, roughly akin to the format of Wagner's study: the first is devoted to a survey of the liturgy, the second reviews the texts, notation, and modal system of the repertory, and the third presents analyses of the principal chant types. More than half of the book is devoted to analysis, with particular emphasis on formal musical matters. After discussing liturgical recitative, Apel turns to "free compositions," chants with distinctive melodies. He first surveys the general musical characteristics of this repertory and then gives specific information on each chant type, noting what musical phases are most common to the genre, how those phrases are deployed in a melody, and how the subgroups of a genre may differ. While Apel's observations here give us a detailed account of the melodic mechanics in each type, they suffer from two serious shortcomings. First, he explains their structure without any significant reference to the texts they set and thus leaves aside a compositional determinant of crucial importance. Second, all of his analyses are based on the heavily edited melodies anthologized in the *Liber Usualis*. Moreover, many of Apel's historical explanations—his remarks on the origin of neumes, for example—have been questioned or superseded by later work. Nevertheless, the book remains a useful resource.

TREITLER's article is a landmark in the scholarly study of Gregorian chant. By drawing on studies of human cognition and the oral performance of epic narrative, the author explores the mechanics of chant performance and transmission in the period before music was written down. His study prompts us to question simplistic notions of how music is performed from memory. He argues that remembering is a creative, reconstructive process and as such belongs in the same category as composition. Both remembering and composing were subject to the same stylistic constraints, and it was these limiting features—modal conventions, stereotyped melodic gestures, liturgical function, the structure of the text being sung, and so forth—that passed from singers to students in daily performances. Treitler warns the reader against equating the oral composition of chant with common ideas about improvisation that emphasize a spontaneous, stream-of-consciousness mode of performance, because this false connection obscures the aim of oral traditions to preserve valued repertories. Treitler has revised and refined his views in subsequent articles, particularly in those that focus on the role of early notations in chant transmission, but this essay remains one of the most important (and controversial) in the field. Among those who disagree with Treitler's views, Levy has mounted the most extended challenge (see below).

HUGHES's systematic account of how liturgical books are organized is an indispensable reference work. In the first part of his book, he lays out the details of the liturgical year and formulas for calculating liturgical time, outlines the textual and musical forms of the chant, and reviews the chants that comprise the Office and Mass observations. The remainder of the book examines the format and content of liturgical books in close detail. Twenty-eight plates, along with many small facsimiles, give the reader clear examples of the points he makes in his discussions, from the size and placement of rubrics to the relationship among initial capitals and different colored inks.

HILEY offers the most up-to-date general survey of medieval liturgical chant. Containing discussions of liturgy, notation, and musical characteristics, his book is modeled on those by Wagner and Apel but includes top-ics not covered by its antecedents, such as early medieval music treatises, liturgical dramas, and later medieval chant reforms. Hiley's discussion of the music does not adhere to a single, narrow analytical procedure; rather, he tries to convey the range of approaches that have been used to illuminate this repertory. The book has many excellent practical features: an extensive bibliography of scholarship through 1990, references to key literature at the head of each topic of study, beautifully clear, full-page photographic plates with commentary on the facing pages, and indices of chant incipits and manuscripts in addition to names and terms. In short, Hiley's book should be the starting point for anyone interested in studying Gregorian chant.

LEVY's book, a combination of previously published articles and newly written essays, is an inquiry into the early history of Gregorian chant. Levy considers how and when the chant repertory became the stable collection of melodies and texts preserved in the liturgical manuscripts of the tenth century. He argues that the music was committed to memory verbatim and that musical notation, by constraining singers' improvisational impulses, helped to fix the exact form of each melody. Because the earliest notated liturgical books agree to such a great extent, and because they preserve a repertory that appears stable, Levy posits the existence of a lost "authoritative neumatic edition" of Gregorian chant that would have been in use in the Carolingian realm by the year 800. This is perhaps his most controversial assertion. For contrasting viewpoints, the reader should refer to the articles by Treitler, Hucke, and van der Werf cited in Levy's notes.

MICHAEL McGRADE

Chant: Other Western

Boe, John, and Alejandro Planchart, editors, *Beneventanum Troporum Corpus II: Ordinary Chants and Tropes for the Mass from Southern Italy, A.D. 1000–1250*, 2 vols., Madison, Wisconsin: A-R Editions, 1990

Brockett, Clyde W., *Antiphons, Responsories, and Other Chants of the Mozarabic Rite*, Brooklyn, New York: Institute of Medieval Music, 1968

Cutter, Paul F., *Musical Sources of the Old-Roman Mass*, Neuhausen-Stuttgart: Hänssler-Verlag, 1979

Hiley, David, *Western Plainchant: A Handbook*, Oxford: Clarendon Press, and New York: Oxford University Press, 1993

Kelly, Thomas Forrest, *The Beneventan Chant*, Cambridge: Cambridge University Press, 1989

Levy, Kenneth, *Gregorian Chant and the Carolingians*, Princeton, New Jersey: Princeton University Press, 1998

Randel, Don M., *An Index to the Chant of the Mozarabic Rite*, Princeton, New Jersey: Princeton University Press, 1973

———, *The Responsorial Psalm Tones for the Mozarabic Office*, Princeton, New Jersey: Princeton University Press, 1969

Extra-Gregorian, or more properly, proto-Gregorian, plainchant repertories are not well represented by book-length efforts in English. Thus, two relatively Gregorian-oriented studies are included here (Hiley and Levy); interested readers can peruse their bibliographies for articles to complement the books discussed here. Only by pooling all of the resources of the chant scholar does a picture of proto-Gregorian plainchant begin to develop: the Old Italian repertories of Rome and Benevento (including the chant of Milan, known as Ambrosian chant), the Gallican repertory, and the Iberian Peninsula repertory originally misnamed Mozarabic and now variously known as Old Spanish, Old Hispanic, and, perhaps most satisfactorily, Hispano-Visigothic. Although traces of Gregorian chant's historical hegemony certainly remain in contemporary scholarship, proto-Gregorian resources have been assembled and research undertaken in the hope of a far richer picture of plainchant, a musical style even today making itself felt in classical, popular, and religious musical idioms.

HILEY treats extensively the forms, sources, and theory of Gregorian chant. However, this magisterial compendium of chant scholarship reviews each alternative plainchant repertory as well, suggesting further bibliography not confined to book-length studies. Hiley reviews the topics important in chant scholarship, such as liturgical setting, musical notation, and the ebb and flow of plainchant's centuries-long development.

In Hiley's bibliography are references to several dissertations dealing with the Old Italian repertory from Rome, notably those of Joseph Michael Murphy and Joseph Henry Dyer, as well as numerous articles. Books in English on this repertory must be confined to CUTTER, primarily a research tool consisting of an inventory of three Roman graduals with their entire texts printed in parallel. Cutter includes both the earliest Roman source, dated 1071, and the latest, dated in the 13th century, making it possible to track the changes in the chant texts both within the rite and between the Roman and Gregorian rites. A number of articles cited in Hiley have studied the Roman chant repertory by genre, drawing on Cutter and other editions.

Benevento is given critical as well as practical scholarly attention in KELLY, a thorough and articulate introduction to the entire repertory. It is replete with chant texts and attributions, a careful review of the surviving sources, commentary on Beneventan melodic style, and reproductions of various manuscript folios. Kelly reflects on the whole enterprise of investigating proto-Gregorian plainchant, suggesting that "[proto-Gregorian plainchant] gives a far richer picture of musical practice in early medieval Europe than was formerly known."

Supplementing Kelly's work with the Beneventan sources, BOE and PLANCHART have edited the texts and melodies of two Mass ordinary troped chant genres, the Kyrie and Gloria, from the nearby Benedictine monastery of Montecassino. Montecassino's plainchant tradition had much in common with Benevento's, and Boe and Planchart's manuscripts contribute to a broader understanding of the region's musical reaction to the encroachment of Gregorian chant as well as the high-medieval practice of troping ordinary chants.

Due to a dearth of surviving material, Gallican chant has garnered only articles as of yet. LEVY reprints among others the important article "Toledo, Rome, and the Legacy of Gaul," which makes interesting connections among the aforementioned proto-Gregorian repertories based on careful comparison between the texts and melodies of several nonpsalmic offertory chants now found in the Gregorian liturgy.

Hispano-Visigothic chant is discussed in two book-length studies in English as well as a comprehensive index of the surviving materials, the latter in RANDEL (1973). RANDEL (1969) reviews the particular nature of the responsory on the Iberian Peninsula; this study accomplishes Kelly's hope that any extra-Gregorian repertory "be understood on its own terms, where possible without holding it up to the Gregorian yardstick by which students of the chant almost invariably measure deviation."

BROCKETT is a more sweeping review of the various Hispano-Visigothic plainchant genres; he considers an ambitious range of topics much like Kelly, including the history of the liturgy and its sources, its notational practices, and the chant texts. Brockett joins most of these other studies of proto-Gregorian repertories in attempting to situate Hispano-Visigothic chant relative to its equally ancient neighboring traditions and to its omnipresent successor; in this case, the meager remains of the Gallican rite likely point to an intimate relationship with the plainchant of the Iberian Peninsula. Both repertories, however, also share the same dramatic fate: virtual abandonment in the face of their Gregorian heir.

NILS NADEAU

Charpentier, Marc-Antoine ca. 1645–1704

French composer

Anthony, James R., *French Baroque Music from Beaujoyeulx to Rameau*, New York: Norton, 1978; revised edition, Portland, Oregon: Amadeus Press, 1997

Cessac, Catherine, *Marc-Antoine Charpentier*, translated by E. Thomas Glasow, Portland, Oregon: Amadeus Press, 1995

Hitchcock, H. Wiley, *Marc-Antoine Charpentier*, Oxford: Oxford University Press, 1990

————, *Les Oeuvres de Marc-Antoine Charpentier: Catalogue Raisonné = The Works of Marc-Antoine Charpentier*, Paris: Picard, 1982

Smither, Howard E., *A History of the Oratorio, Volume I, The Oratorio in the Baroque Era: Italy, Vienna, Paris,* Chapel Hill: University of North Carolina Press, 1977

The music of Marc-Antoine Charpentier went almost entirely unpublished during his lifetime and is preserved largely in a 28-volume collection of autograph manuscripts. This collection slept virtually undisturbed on the shelves of the Bibliothèque Nationale in Paris for most of the 18th and 19th centuries. Its rediscovery easily rates as one of the major musicological finds of recent times and has prompted new reflections on the history and aesthetics of French music of the late 17th century, particularly in the field of sacred music, in which Charpentier excelled. The composer spent his career on the margins of musical influence, employed throughout his life by various figures of the nobility and Parisian churches rather than at the royal court at Versailles, whose institutional influence provided a springboard for the fame of Jean-Baptiste Lully and Michel-Richard Delalande. Charpentier's music is distinguished by its unique character, a mixture of the harmonically rich and contrapuntal Italian style he had studied in Rome under Carissimi and the French music of Lully with its emphasis on balance and simple expressivity. Although widespread public acceptance may have eluded Charpentier during his lifetime, his work seems to have been a harbinger of the enormous influence of Italian music on early 18th-century French composers, and many questions about his role in these later developments remain to be answered.

HITCHCOCK (1982) is the complete catalog of Charpentier's works and their sources. The introduction includes a brief biographical essay on the composer, which contains some now superseded material but a good discussion of the complex makeup and organization of Charpentier's manuscripts (the so-called *Mélanges*). The most provocative aspect of the introduction, however, is Hitchcock's dating of works in the collection. Charpentier himself ordered his manuscripts by numbering the various fascicles, and Hitchcock argues that this organizational system is in fact a chronological one. His dating is accomplished by using the position of compositions of known date in the *Mélanges* as guides for interpolating the relative dates of other works. The results have so far proved to be fairly accurate, but not entirely so; there are a number of compositions whose putative dates determined by other means do not agree with their position in the organization of the *Mélanges*. The catalog itself divides the composer's oeuvre by genre and lists works chronologically within each section. This organization occasionally causes confusion when works of different genres that belong together (e.g., instrumental preludes to vocal pieces), or works with the same text but different titles, are cataloged separately. Finding a particular piece in the catalog is sometimes made difficult due to the absence of a title index.

HITCHCOCK (1990) is the first book published on Charpentier's works in English. The brevity required by the Oxford series, which necessitates a certain amount of condensation of the material, makes it a fine introduction to the subject. The book is prefaced by a brief summary of the composer's life, and the main body divides the discussion of his works by genre, using much the same organization as Hitchcock's catalog. Within Hitchcock's discussion of each genre, he manages to address more general aspects of Charpentier's music: central characteristics of Charpentier's style (in particular, the relationships between French and Italian influences in his music), the composer's development over the course of his career, and his music's intellectual background (based on the composer's writings and those of his contemporaries). One of the book's strengths is the author's use of copious and lengthy musical examples to illustrate his points.

CESSAC, the most complete and in-depth study of Charpentier's life and music to date, brings together all of the scholarly work in the field up to the time of her writing (the book was originally published in French in 1988) and admirably organizes and integrates the information drawn from many different biographical, historical, and musical sources. The organization of the work, partly chronological and partly divided by genre, allows the author not only to draw conclusions about Charpentier's style and its influences but also to make connections between characteristics of his music and the complex network of patrons and institutions for whom he worked. Within this organization, Cessac discusses virtually all the known works of the composer, making the book an excellent reference tool as well. Another of the book's strengths is its usefulness as an accompanying reference guide to Hitchcock's catalog; the author includes a title index and an index of instrumental and vocal forces that are cross-referenced to the catalog and to the *Mélanges* and that also incorporate recent information and hypotheses concerning the dating of particular pieces.

In addition to these major studies devoted to Charpentier, two other works deserve mention for their discussions of the composer's contribution to the major genres in which he worked. The first is SMITHER, who includes a short chapter on Charpentier as part of his larger study of the oratorio. The chapter presents a structural comparison of Charpentier's *histoires sacrées* to the oratorios of his Italian contemporaries and to those of the generation of Carissimi, showing their resemblance to the latter. Stylistically, however, Charpentier's oratorios demonstrate the influence of his native land, and they make greater use of instrumental and choral music than do the Italians. A short analysis of the composer's *Judicium Salomonis* serves to demonstrate the author's claims.

The second general work to include important information about Charpentier's music is ANTHONY, who discusses Charpentier's motets at some length in the chapter entitled "The Motet from Du Mont to Delalande." He paints a clear picture of their harmonic audacities, illustrated by long musical extracts, and places the compositional style of Charpentier's motets in the context of his contemporaries.

DON FADER

China

DeWoskin, Kenneth J., *A Song for One or Two: Music and The Concept of Art in Early China,* Ann Arbor: Center for Chinese Studies, University of Michigan, 1982

Jones, Andrew F., *Like a Knife: Ideology and Genre in Contemporary Chinese Popular Music,* Ithaca, New York: East Asia Program, Cornell University, 1992

Jones, Steve, *Folk Music of China: Living Instrumental Traditions,* Oxford: Clarendon Press, and New York: Oxford University Press, 1995

Lam, Joseph S.C., *State Sacrifices and Music in Ming China: Orthodoxy, Creativity, and Expressiveness,* Albany: State University of New York Press, 1998

Liang, Ming-Yueh, *Music of the Billion: An Introduction to Chinese Music Culture,* New York: Heinrichshofen, 1985

Mackerras, Colin, *The Performing Arts in Contemporary China,* London: Routledge and Paul, 1981

Pian, Rulan Chao, *Sonq Dynasty Musical Sources and their Interpretation,* Cambridge, Massachusetts: Harvard University Press, 1967

Schimmelpenninck, Antoinet, *Chinese Folk Songs and Folk Singers: Shan'ge Traditions in Southern Jiangsu,* Leiden: CHIME Foundation, 1997

Witzleben, Larry, *"Silk and Bamboo" Music in Shanghai: The Jiangnan Sizhu Instrumental Ensemble Tradition,* Kent, Ohio: Kent State University Press, 1995

Yung, Bell, *Cantonese Opera: Performance as Creative Process,* Cambridge: Cambridge University Press, 1989

China is an old civilization/country that has been rapidly changing since the 1950s. Reflecting this history, Chinese music constitutes a conglomerate of not only millennia-old aesthetics and traditions but also cutting-edge forms and expressions. Its diverse genres range from Confucian ceremonial music performed on ancient instruments of bell chimes and stone chimes to multimedia operas that rely on traditional performance practices, to rock and other postmodern forms of popular music. As such, Chinese music makes a fascinating subject for music scholarship. In fact, Chinese scholars have produced a vast collection of specialized studies; since the 1980s, Chinese music scholarship has been particularly productive. Scholars in the West have also produced many monographs, dissertations, and journal articles written in English and other Western languages. The following samples, all unique studies of specific historical eras and/or genres of Chinese music, are representative.

LIANG's monograph is a basic survey of Chinese music for general readers in the West. It includes a summary of musical and cultural traits of Chinese music, a historical survey, and discussions of six selected topics. Written as a general text, the volume presents many fundamental and useful facts but lacks an overall theme and in-depth discussions. The historical survey, for example, gives a clear idea of the topics in Chinese music history but offers little explanation about its processes of continuity and change. Liang's volume underscores the fact that Western scholars have emphasized more synchronic than diachronic aspects of Chinese music.

There are more detailed studies on historical Chinese music than Liang. With copious citations from authentic documents, DeWOSKIN's monograph offers a concise discussion of early Chinese music thoughts and practices: topics include music as a means of governance and self-cultivation, music as expressions of private and public sentiments, the performance of music in ritual contexts, listening to music, the measurement of pitches, and so forth. The volume projects a vivid image of the sounds of ancient Chinese music but does not address specific works—no verifiable notation or performance records of ancient Chinese music exist.

The earliest notated samples of Chinese music that have verifiable geneses are the 84 tunes from Song China (960–1279), which are discussed in PIAN's monograph. Using a positivist methodology, Pian describes the sources, explains the notation and musical modes, and transcribes the music, providing a meticulous work that is distinguished, but also limited, by its focus on technical and bibliographic details.

Many sinological and musical studies written in English allude to Chinese court and ritual music, but only LAM's study of 323 Ming dynasty (1368–1644) state sacrificial songs addresses actual compositions, historical musicians, theorists, and their activities. Featuring an abundance of data collated from a variety of primary sources, the author discusses historical and cultural aspects of the music as much as its technical structures and sources and argues that creativity and expressiveness of ritual music operates within orthodox constraints. The volume does not contextualize the court ritual music with other sacred and secular genres of Ming dynasty music.

Unlike the above studies, the following monographs depict music in contemporary China, reflecting the authors' ethnomusicological and social approaches. MACKERRAS's book presents no technical discussions of musical works but explains the ways Chinese performing arts, including music, responded to various political events, such as the Great Leap Forward and the Cultural

Revolution, and underwent fundamental changes during the critical period 1949–80. The book includes many insightful reports about performances the author attended in China in the early 1960s and between 1977 and 1980, revealing an individual scholar's view of contemporary Chinese performance arts.

By incorporating many detailed ethnographic data about folk songs and singers in the southern region of Jiangsu province, and by citing many translated song texts, SCHIMMELPENNINCK projects a vivid picture of tenacious regional folk-song traditions. When used with the accompanying CD, which includes marvelous recordings, and when read critically, the volume, currently the only detailed English discussion of Chinese folk songs, offers needed information about a music that is little known in the West.

Chinese operas are better known but there are still only a few scholarly and musical monographs written in English. One of them is YUNG's sophisticated study of Cantonese opera. The author introduces the history and social context of Cantonese opera, describes its use of musical instruments and scripts, and analyzes its various music elements—the speech types, aria types, fixed tunes, narrative songs, and so forth. By theorizing performances as creative processes, and by explaining relationships between melodic and rhythmic structures with linguistic tones of the sung texts, Yung pinpoints fundamental and distinctive attributes of Chinese operas.

Among a number of Western studies of Chinese instrumental music, Stephen JONES's work is currently the most comprehensive. It registers valuable ethnographic and musical data—genres, musicians, terminology, and so forth—collected by the author and his colleagues in the Music Research Institute of Beijing. When used with a set of two CDs of Chinese instrumental music (Folk Instrumental Traditions, VDE CD-822) produced by the author, the wealth of factual details in this volume becomes more meaningful for readers unfamiliar with Chinese culture and music.

WITZLEBEN's monograph provides a user-friendly discussion of a specific genre of traditional Chinese instrumental music, namely the Silk and Bamboo Music (*Jiangnan sizhu*) of Shanghai. Organized according to historical context, repertory, form, and other musicological topics, the volume presents a wealth of data and interpretations in such a way that they can be easily understood even by general readers—the compartmentalized presentation, however, renders the author's individual voice more objective than it actually is. The volume also includes a translation of a set of regulations for members of the Chinese National Music Ensemble, revealing an insider's view of the music and efforts to adjust to a changing world.

Since China opened herself to global cultures in the early 1980s, Western popular music has gained a foothold there. As demonstrated by Andrew F. JONES's monograph, Chinese rock music has developed into an underground medium through which young people express their collective and individual voices amid those controlled by the authorities. By copiously citing interview data and translated song texts, Jones provides a cultural and social picture of popular music in China; the volume hardly discusses technical features of the music, however.

JOSEPH S.C. LAM

Chopin, Fryderyk 1810–1849

Polish-born composer

1. Biography

Atwood, William G., *Fryderyk Chopin Pianist from Warsaw,* New York: Columbia University Press, 1987

Eigeldinger, Jean-Jacques, *Chopin: Pianist and Teacher as Seen by His Pupils,* 3rd edition, edited by Roy Howat, translated by Naomi Shohet, Cambridge: Cambridge University Press, 1986

Harasowski, Adam, *The Skein of Legends around Chopin,* Glasgow: MacLellan, and Boston: Branden Press, 1967

Hedley, Arthur, *Chopin,* London: Dent, 1947; revised edition, edited by Maurice J. E. Brown, 1974

Karasowski, Maurycy, *Frederic Chopin: His Life and Letters,* translated by Emily Hill, London: Reeves, 1879; 3rd edition, 1938

Kobylańska, Krystyna, editor, *Chopin in His Own Land: Documents and Souvenirs,* Krakow: Polskie Wydawnictwo Muzyczne, 1955

Liszt, Franz, *Frederic Chopin,* translated by Edward N. Waters, New York: Free Press of Glencoe, 1963

Niecks, Frederick, *Frederick Chopin as a Man and Musician,* 2 vols., London: Novello, and New York: Ewer, 1888; 3rd edition, 1902; reprint, Neptune City, New Jersey: Paganiniana, 1980

Samson, Jim, *Chopin,* Oxford: Oxford University Press, 1996

Załuski, Iwo, and Pamela Załuski, *Chopin's Poland,* London: Owen, 1996

Zamoyski, Adam, *Chopin: A Biography,* London: Collins, 1979; as *Chopin: A New Biography,* New York: Doubleday, 1979

From the outset, biographies of Fryderyk Chopin have been plagued by legends, errors, and misrepresentations. The particulars of his life have habitually been distorted, and his music repeatedly appropriated to serve various aesthetic and political agendas. Romanticized images of the artist, the nationalist framework through which native culture was perceived in Chopin's homeland of Poland, and the communist doctrine imposed by the authorities in post-World War II Poland have all adversely shaped biographers' conclusions about the composer. Equally harmful was the marginalization of Polish culture by foreign writers, much of it caused by Poland's tragic political circumstances. In addition, the centuries-long cultural conflict between France and Germany contributed to both the neglect of the salon milieu and the perception of Chopin and his style as effeminate or androgynous. In light of these historiographic considerations, many of Chopin's biographies reveal more about the mindset of the particular biographer and his or her cultural and social framework than about the life of the great composer. Perhaps it is most telling that, with a few exceptions, the field of Chopin biography tends to be the domain of amateurs, some of whom are underqualified to deal with the subject.

LISZT is one of the earliest, most famous, and most nonchalantly inaccurate biographies of Chopin. Through lavish, metaphoric characterizations of the composer and his works, the author provides fascinating insights into the reception of Chopin's music by his contemporaries. However, Liszt's work cannot be used as a reliable biographic source: its author had neither assistance from the Chopin family nor access to important information, and he cared little about accuracy. It is also worth noting that much of the text was actually written not by Liszt but by Princess Carolyn von Sayn-Wittgenstein, who was Liszt's companion at the time.

One of the first biographies of Chopin written by a Polish author, KARASOWSKI has some merit and, unlike several other Polish texts, it is available in English. Chopin's relatives and acquaintances cooperated with Karasowski—most importantly, they permitted him access to various documents, particularly letters. Given this proximity to primary sources, it is unfortunate that Karasowski's study is so inaccurate. The volume includes unsubstantiated assertions, inexact quotations, and inaccurate translations. In spite of its faults, Karasowski's account of Chopin's life is a useful, if imperfect, report, which is especially valuable because many of the documents cited by Karasowski have subsequently perished.

NIECKS was the first conscientious biographer of Chopin. His monumental two-volume work represents more than a decade of careful research. Sources for the study include the press, correspondence, and interviews with Chopin's pupils, friends, and acquaintances. The book is now a century old, and subsequent research has rendered some of the information gathered by Niecks obsolete; especially weak is the discussion of the composer's early years in Poland. In fact, the author's unfamiliarity with Polish sources is the greatest shortcoming of the book.

The goal of HARASOWSKI is to dismantle myths and correct errors in Chopin literature. This collection of essays reviews several dozen works (including the notorious Liszt) and addresses their fallacies and biases. Because Harasowski is not a scholar, he does not provide proper documentation (given the focus of his investigation, one often would like to know more about his

sources); his assertions, however, are carefully researched and are by and large correct.

The updated HEDLEY and the ZAMOYSKI are both good English surveys of Chopin's life and works. Correcting errors (in particular updating and filling gaps in Niecks's knowledge) was Hedley's primary intent: the author thoroughly familiarized himself with the work of Chopin's Polish biographers and examined original sources from pre-World War II Poland. Hedley and Zamoyski's works are well written, and they capture Chopin's personality and the context of his life. Small inaccuracies notwithstanding, these books offer sober judgments about the composer and perceptive characterizations of his music. They are appropriate for musicians and general audiences alike.

For the more demanding reader, SAMSON offers the most up-to-date scholarship. This carefully documented, exhaustive study rectifies the fallacies and biases of older and less thorough biographies; gives appropriate attention to Chopin's Polish background; and situates his music in its specific cultural, historical, and biographical contexts. A volume such as this one was long overdue, and Samson is by far the best English-language work dealing with the life and oeuvre of Chopin.

A few specialized studies are worth mentioning. Two of them introduce the geographic and historic landscape of Chopin's Poland. ZAŁUSKI and ZAŁUSKI take the reader on an informative tour of Polish sites associated with Chopin. The volume contains lively descriptions of locations, historical background, and people and events associated with the composer's sojourn in each place. KOBYLAŃSKA's work is a superb documentary collection that permits firsthand acquaintance with Chopin's Polish environment. In addition to the typical illustrations of places and people associated with Chopin, the album contains facsimiles of selected letters and manuscripts, clippings from Polish newspapers and periodicals, posters, archival records, and early 19th-century prints. Unfortunately, English captions and translations are often insufficient, and the book's oversized format is unnecessary and cumbersome.

Two other specialized publications focus on Chopin's musical activities. ATWOOD presents Chopin's piano career in light of letters, memoirs, and press announcements. Where possible, the author describes performance venues, reconstructs concert programs, presents information on the instruments used in particular concerts, discusses coperformers, and even reports on Chopin's earnings. There are two very useful appendices: one lists all public concerts; the other contains concert reviews. EIGELDINGER is a compilation of quotations that presents a musical image of Chopin the composer, teacher, and pianist. The material comes from Chopin's own writings as well as reports written by his pupils, acquaintances, and contemporaries. The main text provides insights into Chopin's pianistic technique and his ideas on musical style, and gives clues regarding the interpretation of his works. The detailed notes, which occupy almost as much space as the main text, often contain additional vital information. The second half of the book includes data concerning those students of Chopin who are quoted in the first half; a list and descriptions of the specific contents of scores annotated by the composer; selected contemporary accounts of his playing; and a translation of Chopin's "Sketch for a Method." Eigeldinger's carefully researched and clearly presented study is an invaluable resource for the scholar and performer alike.

HALINA GOLDBERG

2. Works

Abraham, Gerald, *Chopin's Musical Style,* London: Oxford University Press, 1939

Kallberg, Jeffrey, *Chopin at the Boundaries: Sex, History, and Musical Genre,* Cambridge, Massachusetts: Harvard University Press, 1996

Rosen, Charles, *The Romantic Generation,* Cambridge, Massachusetts: Harvard University Press, 1995

Rink, John, and Jim Samson, editors, *Chopin Studies 2,* Cambridge: Cambridge University Press, 1994

Samson, Jim, The *Music of Chopin,* London: Routledge and Kegan Paul, 1985; Oxford: Clarendon Press, 1994

Samson, Jim, editor, *The Cambridge Companion to Chopin,* Cambridge: Cambridge University Press, 1992

———, editor, *Chopin Studies,* Cambridge: Cambridge University Press, 1988

Walker, Alan, editor, *The Chopin Companion: Profiles of the Man and the Musician,* New York: Norton, 1966

The greatest impediment to an adequate appraisal of Chopin's oeuvre has been its position at the boundaries of epochs and cultures. The 1878–80 publication of Chopin's collected works by Breitkopf und Härtel marked their official induction into the canon of German classical music. Breitkopf und Härtel's decision to include Chopin among German composers from Bach to Brahms validated his music in the German world and opened it for musicological investigation, but it also imposed on it aesthetic and analytic confines. Although the analytical methods used by the German-speaking scholars (mainly Hugo Leichtentritt and Heinrich Schenker) illuminated certain aspects of Chopin's style, they precipitated the neglect of qualities that were identified with French or Polish cultures. Only within the last two decades has an effort been made to create an all-inclusive picture of Chopin's style, one that accounts for the multiple aesthetic forces that shaped it.

ABRAHAM is among the earliest monographs devoted specifically to Chopin's works (although many early biographies address his music as well). Written for the practical musician, Abraham's volume maintains a descriptive, rather objective tone and contains many perceptive observations. Unfortunately, he often compares Chopin with Beethoven, an approach that disregards Chopin's intrinsic aesthetic qualities and lessens his merit.

In contrast, SAMSON (1985) is among the most recent books on the subject; it fills a lacuna in the study of Chopin's music by providing the most comprehensive, up-to-date examination of the composer's entire output. It also includes a work list and useful bibliography. Samson interlaces his own analytical conclusions with a critique of other writer's views on Chopin's music (an approach particularly discernible in the chapter on the preludes). Because the author is well acquainted not only with English writings but also with Polish- and German-language scholarship, this method is especially valuable. It is also notable that Samson attempts impartiality while introducing the reader to the different facets of Chopin scholarship—a commendable endeavor in a study of this kind. An unexpected outcome of the recent explosion in Chopin research is that some of Samson's conclusions need to be verified and updated against the information in his more current biography, *Chopin* (1996).

Surprisingly, in the nearly half a century between Abraham's monograph and Samson's 1985 volume, no other English book on Chopin's works appeared except for the modest volume of articles edited by WALKER. Walker purposefully chose essays written by and addressed to practical musicians. Undeniably, writers with this type of intimate knowledge of the music provide valuable insights; in this case, however, their unfamiliarity with sources and foreign-language writings results in many inaccuracies and gaps in knowledge.

In recent years, three more collections of articles have appeared: Samson (1988), Samson (1992), and Rink and Samson. These indispensable volumes cover a wide range of topics: from cultural context, performance practice, reception and influences to style criticism and analysis. Many research and analytical methods are also represented, including Schenkerian analysis, manuscript studies, gender studies, semiotic and narrative approaches, and computer analysis. Various levels of technical vocabulary and specialized methodology are offered; some articles are accessible to the general educated reader, others require familiarity with musical terminology, while others still are addressed to the music scholar.

On the whole, the articles in SAMSON (1992) are the most general and most accessible to the nonscholar. They are grouped into three subject areas: cultural and stylistic background, overviews of some genres, and reception history. Included also are a useful list of Chopin's works and a concise but informative bibliographical note. SAMSON (1988) and RINK and SAMSON tend to address more specific topics, such as certain aspects of Chopin's compositional technique, structural issues in individual compositions, and select historical questions.

In these three volumes, Samson has amassed some of the best, most carefully documented research and some of the most imaginative, thought-provoking ideas on Chopin's music and times. Some of these studies are available here for the first time to the English reader.

To these three compilations should be added KALL-BERG, a collection of articles by one of the foremost modern Chopin scholars. Although these articles have all appeared previously elsewhere, having them assembled into a book presents the reader with a coherent set of historiographic challenges stemming from social and ideological contexts. Kallberg's intimate knowledge of Chopin sources, enhanced by his familiarity with the early 19th-century milieu (including interdisciplinary research), elucidates our understanding of genre, meaning, and the compositional process in Chopin's music.

Although not dedicated exclusively to Chopin, ROSEN devotes three chapters (almost 200 pages) to this composer's music. The book is written from a pianist's perspective and includes a compact disc of Rosen playing some of the solo piano works discussed in the text. It is not Rosen's goal to include all genres: the volume is not intended as a comprehensive survey of early 19th-century music literature. The author informs us that he chose as illustrations pieces that he most enjoys "playing, listening to, and thinking about." Thus, one finds nothing on Chopin's songs and virtually nothing on his cello works or the waltzes. Rosen's thoughts on the works that he does include—not just large works such as the sonatas, ballades, and scherzos, but also instrumental miniatures, including the mazurkas, nocturnes, études, and preludes—are most informative and illuminating. Particularly remarkable and detailed is his engaging discussion of the mazurkas. The section on Chopin confirms the author's vast knowledge of 19th-century music and culture, as well as his familiarity with modern Chopin scholarship. This work will be useful for performers and scholars alike.

HALINA GOLDBERG

Chorale

Blume, Friedrich, *Protestant Church Music: A History*, New York: Norton, 1974

Riedel, Johannes, *The Lutheran Chorale: Its Basic Traditions*, Minneapolis, Minnesota: Augsburg, 1967

Schalk, Carl, editor, *Key Words in Church Music: Definition Essays on Concepts, Practices, and Movements of Thought in Church Music*, St. Louis, Missouri: Concordia Publishing House, 1978

Stulken, Marilyn Kay, *Hymnal Companion to the Lutheran Book of Worship*, Philadelphia, Pennsylvania: Fortress Press, 1981

Terry, Charles Sanford, *The Four-Part Chorals of J.S. Bach*, London: Oxford University Press, 1929; reprint 1964

Zahn, Johannes, *Die Melodien der deutschen evangelischen Kirchenlieder*, 6 vols., Gütersloh: Bertelsmann, 1889–93; reprint, Hildesheim: Olms, 1963

Chorales are the hymns or congregational songs of the German Evangelical (Lutheran) Church. The term itself derives from the German *choral*, which refers to the liturgical chant of the Roman Catholic Church. Like Gregorian chant, the first chorales were unison melodies that were constructed from melodic formulas related to both chant and old German folk or Latin hymns. Lutheran chorales are usually considered to be the progenitors of modern hymns, although both Latin and vernacular hymns did exist during the Middle Ages. During the Reformation, chorales were sung in unison by the congregation without instrumental accompaniment, but by 1600 it became increasingly customary to set chorales in four-part harmony with the melody in the soprano and with organ support. This arrangement, known as cantional style, is the standard way that hymn tunes are harmonized to the present day. Also, by the 17th century, the term *chorale* referred to the melodies and texts taken together and not only the tunes. Beginning with Johann Walter's settings in 1524 and continuing to the present, chorales have served as the source for a great body of church music, such as organ preludes, choral settings, cantatas, motets, oratorios, concertatos, and passions. Thus, the chorale is to Lutheran church music what Gregorian chant has been to Roman Catholic music. The chorale-based works of Johann Sebastian Bach stand as musical peaks in that genre that have never been surpassed.

BLUME has compiled the most comprehensive study of Lutheran and German Reformed church music that is available in English. A large portion of this book originally appeared in Germany as *Geschichte der evangelischen Kirchenmusik* (1964), and the English translation has been updated and enlarged to include chapters on the United States and England. Contributors, in addition to Blume, include Ludwig Finscher, Georg Feder, Adam Adrio, Walter Blankenburg, Torben Schousboe, Robert Stevenson, and Watkins Shaw. However, despite its attempt to embrace all Protestant church music, there is a decided emphasis on German and especially Lutheran developments. Consequently, one can find here a readily available and complete history of the chorale and its influence on music to the present day.

RIEDEL has compiled a relatively slim volume, but it provides a good introduction to the chorale, its basic development, and its use in Lutheran worship. This book is designed especially for readers who have more limited knowledge of the chorale and the influence that chorales have had on Christian hymnody. The text reads smoothly, and a brief glossary provides assistance for understanding some of the more technical terms.

SCHALK is editor of a reference book of short essays by recognized scholars in their respective fields on such topics as chorale, chorale vocal settings, organ chorale, hymnody, metrical psalmody, church music history, cantional style, German hymnody, alternation practice, and many similar topics related to the use of chorales. These essays are informative without being excessively technical and are intended for practicing church musicians or college students seeking information about aspects of church music. Consequently, the presentation is very useful for persons who are beginning study of the chorale and its development, especially as it relates to other music based on chorales. Each topic concludes with a short bibliography that gives suggestions for further, more detailed research.

STULKEN called on several leading scholars of Lutheran church music to assist in this compilation, which was one of the first companions for major denominational hymnals to appear during the last quarter of the 20th century. Because of its Lutheran orientation, the first 114 pages of historical essays include an emphasis on the development of the Lutheran chorale and its position in Protestant hymnody. The remainder of the volume contains individual studies of each chorale or hymn that is included in the *Lutheran Book of Worship* as well as short biographical accounts of the respective authors and composers.

TERRY has assembled the most complete publication of Bach chorales with texts in both German and English, and it is easily available. Although Bach himself composed very few chorales, his many settings are the standard by which all chorale settings tend to be judged today. Terry's collection contains over 400 four-part chorales and almost 100 other tunes with a continuo part, except for a few that are melodies only. The chorales are arranged in alphabetical order, and tunes with alternate names are indicated in an appendix for easy cross-reference. The great volume of Bach research in recent decades has uncovered many factual details that were unknown to Terry, however. Thus, although the volume remains an important resource for anyone seeking the music and texts for most standard chorales, some of the historical notes need updating and revision.

ZAHN has been the standard source that scholars have used to locate and identify chorale tunes since the late 19th century. Although it is a German-language publication, persons who cannot read German can still use it to locate specific chorales by name, meter, and musical notation. Zahn gives each chorale as it was notated in its earliest known version, the composer and origin of the melody, notation of major tune variants in later years, and subsequent chorale or hymnbooks in which the tune is found. The melodies are arranged by the number of lines and the metrical pattern of each chorale and its text. Thus, volume 1 begins with simple chorales of two lines in iambic meter, and Zahn proceeds successively to more complex tunes, ending with chorales of more than 20 lines and mixed or irregular meters in volume 5, which

includes additions and corrections that were discovered after the earlier volumes were printed and biographical information on the composers arranged both chronologically and with an alphabetical index. There is also an alphabetical index of the tunes. Volume 6 is a bibliography of both printed and manuscript sources that Zahn used in his massive study and comprises a final listing of additions for earlier volumes. This final volume has largely been superseded by Konrad Ameln, Markus Jenny, and Walther Lipphardt, editors of *Das deutsche Kirchenlied*, volume 1 (Kassel: Bärenreiter, 1975–80), which provides a detailed bibliography of printed sources of German hymns of all denominations (up to 1800) that contain at least one melody in musical notation. This bibliography is in series B, volume 8, parts 1 and 2, of the *International Inventory of Musical Sources*, usually identified by its French title, *Répertoire international des sources musicales* (RISM).

EDWARD CHRISTOPHER WOLF

Chromaticism

Baker, James, "Chromaticism in Classical Music," in *Music Theory and the Exploration of the Past*, edited by Christopher Hatch and David Bernstein, Chicago: University of Chicago Press, 1993

Boatwright, Howard, *Chromaticism: Theory and Practice*, Fayetteville, New York: Walnut Grove Press, 1994

Harrison, Daniel, *Harmonic Function in Chromatic Music: A Renewed Dualist Theory and an Account of Its Precedents*, Chicago: University of Chicago Press, 1994

Kurth, Ernst, *Ernst Kurth: Selected Writings*, edited and translated by Lee A. Rothfarb, Cambridge: Cambridge University Press, 1991

Proctor, Gregory, "Technical Bases of Nineteenth-Century Chromatic Tonality: A Study in Chromaticism," Ph.D. dissertation: Princeton University, 1978

Samson, Jim, *Music in Transition: A Study of Tonal Expansion and Atonality, 1900–1920*, London: Dent, 1977

The complete tonal palette of Western music has been reckoned at anywhere from 12 to 21 tones—in any case, more than the diatonic scale's 7 tones that normally enjoy conceptual priority. In tonal contexts, the use of pitches outside the governing diatonic scale imparts a measure of interest and variety; true to its etymology, chromaticism colors the normative diatonic style. Chromaticism—both its interaction with diatonicism and its use as a compositional principle in its own right—raises a host of theoretical and historiographical issues. Although a certain amount of scholarship has addressed chromaticism in pretonal music (Thomas Brothers, *Chromatic Beauty in the Late Medieval Chanson* [1997], Karol Berger, *Theories of Chromatic and Enharmonic Music in Late Sixteenth Cen-

tury Italy [1980], Edward Lowinsky, *Secret Chromatic Art in the Netherlands Motet* [1946]), the more common association of chromaticism is with tonal and post-tonal music, as represented by the sources discussed here. Finally, discussion of these theoretical and historical writings may be prefaced with mention of two textbooks appropriate for students in search of a more pragmatic treatment of the subject: Justine Shir-Cliff, et al., *Chromatic Harmony* (1965) and the relevant chapters of Edward Aldwell and Carl Schachter, *Harmony and Voice Leading* (1989).

KURTH's writings are only beginning to receive attention in the English-speaking world. Rothfarb's selected translations (along with his *Ernst Kurth as Theorist and Analyst* [1988]) provide an introduction to the theorist's views, many of which have made their way into Anglo-American musicological discourse only indirectly and anonymously. Kurth was among the first to treat chromaticism seriously from the perspectives of both theory and history. His theory of chromaticism involves the notion of "energetic harmony," whereby chromatic linear forces insinuate themselves into diatonic harmonic progressions. These forces result in various types of chordal alteration, from the most elementary of chromatic inflection, the secondary dominant, to advanced nonfunctional progressions. Depending on the composer's inclinations, chromaticism can work either constructively or destructively; according to Kurth's now commonplace historical interpretation, Wagner's *Tristan* signaled the onslaught of rampant destructive chromaticism and consequently, the beginning of the end of common-practice tonality.

SAMSON, less apocalyptic than Kurth, concerns himself at least in part with the various constructive trends that emerged in response to the tonal crisis of the early 20th century. Whereas the chromatic expansion epitomized by Wagner ultimately led to the rejection of tonality by Schoenberg and his circle, an equally important development, tracing a gradual "reinterpretation of the tonal principle," arose in the non-German traditions, from Mussorgsky to Debussy, Bartók, and Stravinsky. The tonal modification by the composers in this lineage derived from chromatic influences from without, for example, via exoticism and so-called empirical harmony. Samson reminds us that Schoenbergian atonality was only one avenue among many and implies that the emergence of new tonal styles such as Debussy's in fact commanded the greater influence on the music of the 20th century. As for atonality, some welcome attention is given here to the persistence of traditional elements in this music, as well as to the awakened interest in nonharmonic musical parameters such as rhythm and timbre. Samson does admirable justice to the importance of Liszt, Skryabin, and the Russian nationalists within the history of chromaticism, and he further challenges the reader to afford Busoni and Szymanowski a comparable status.

PROCTOR's dissertation introduces an explicitly theoretical account of 19th-century chromaticism and the fate of the tonal system. In his view there is no single common practice but rather two overlapping tonal eras: that of classical diatonic tonality and that of 19th-century chromatic tonality. The former system is essentially the one described by Schenker, who consistently regarded diatonicism as conceptually and hierarchically prior to chromaticism. (Proctor gives a particularly lucid exposition of this theory, which is largely contained in Schenker's *Harmony* and also treated in Salzer and Schachter, *Counterpoint in Composition* [1969].) In this classical view, chromaticism arises from two operations—tonicization and modal mixture—which produce all the familiar chromatic harmonies but which, in Proctor's opinion, fail to sufficiently account for the proliferation of techniques of the romantic style. Beginning with the music of Beethoven, Schubert, and Chopin, he argues, evidence of a related but qualitatively different system can be discerned whose pitch-space reduces to no less than the complete 12-tone chromatic universe. Equal temperament, both in theory and practice, is important here, and enharmonic equivalence becomes a structural reality, not just a notational exigency. From this follows the possibility of harmonic reinterpretation—for example, the augmented sixth chord as dominant seventh—as well as symmetrically divided tonal space and the literal (nontonal) sequence. Proctor's history is hence related to Kurth's but different in that here late romantic music is purported to resemble more the atonal style that follows than the diatonic style that precedes.

HARRISON is one of many contemporary theorists who is distrustful of Schenkerian-derived (linear) explanations of hyperchromatic music. Convinced of the ultimately harmonic genesis of chromaticism in the music of Reger, Pfitzner, and other analytically neglected modernists, Harrison proposes a revised version of Riemann's function theory in which the tonal function of any chord depends on the function of that chord's constituent scale degrees. Some unorthodox concepts result, such as a more liberal notion of dominantness and hence of cadence. Ironically, Harrison's chromatic speculations are most successful when they most resemble Schenker—his chromatic projections (for instance, the sharpened fourth degree in an augmented sixth chord, purported to mirror the flattened sixth degree) are in the end scarcely distinguishable from what Schenker would have called microtonicization. A portion of the book contains sample analyses in which chromatic technique is explored at varying depths of structure.

BAKER makes an inadvisable attempt to push the 12-tone threshold back into the 18th century. The main subject here is Mozart, whose chromatic usage is indeed imaginative and masterful. Baker goes too far, however, in attributing to Mozart the technique of strategic aggregate completion, an idea that, even if it were not absurdly anachronistic, is in any case exaggerated at best. This analytical zeal may be forgiven, as Baker astutely discusses the use of chromaticism as a rhetorical device in this music, as well as its role in period structure. Another redeeming feature of the essay is its survey of theories of chromaticism from Kirnberger to Schoenberg.

BOATWRIGHT's manual considers chromaticism as a material of modern composition; following the custom of treatises of old, the theory is illustrated by music of the author's own creation. In a manner reminiscent of his teacher Hindemith, Boatwright invokes acoustical criteria to formulate an elaborate measurement of any sonority's harmonic tension. Boatwright does not pretend that his somewhat idiosyncratic theory will pertain to any music other than his own (despite an intriguing prefatory claim: "Since no one has a patent on chromaticism . . . there must be resemblances between all chromatic music"). Hence, notwithstanding the inclusion of an enlightening history of tuning and the occasional psychoacoustical digression, this treatise may appear to the theorist little more than a curiosity. Composers on the other hand—at least those inclined toward compositional methods—may be better served, inasmuch as the book presents strategies of fully chromatic usage while also recognizing the need for control and balance between chromaticism and diatonicism.

JEREMY O'CONNELL

Ciconia, Johannes ca. 1370–1412

Liègeois composer and theorist

Ciconia, Johannes, *Nova Musica* and *De Proportionibus,*
    edited and translated by Oliver B. Ellsworth, Lincoln:
    University of Nebraska Press, 1993
——, *The Works of Johannes Ciconia,* edited by Margaret
    Bent and Anne Hallmark, Polyphonic Music of the
    Fourteenth Century, vol. 24, Monaco: Editions de
    l'Oiseau-Lyre, 1985

The composer and theorist Johannes Ciconia has suffered posthumously from a unusual biographical problem: Was there only one or were there two 14th-century musicians with this name? An accumulating body of research suggests two figures: one Johannes Ciconia, born about 1335, and (in all probability) his son by the same name, born about 1370. The latter, the subject of this essay, is one of the most significant musical figures of the late Middle Ages. Born in Liège, Ciconia spent his last years in Padua. He is especially noted for his work in both music theory and music composition. As a composer, his highly distinctive music embraced sacred and secular domains, and certain of his compositions display stylistic features of both the French *ars nova* and the Italian trecento. As a music theorist, Ciconia's work was largely speculative. (This

term refers variously to discussions of the function of music within the cosmos, religion, society, and aesthetics, as well as music's interrelations with other disciplines; the expression *speculative theory* contrasts with *practical theory,* which concerns music as it is composed and performed.) Ciconia's theoretical works, *Nova musica* and *De proportionibus,* address neither contemporary music nor performance—such as he himself had produced in his lifetime—but rather concern music from the early Middle Ages.

CICONIA (1985) is a fine scholarly edition of Ciconia's known works, and the editors have also provided at the beginning of the volume a biographical sketch of the composer, discussions of both his secular and sacred works, and a useful commentary on various aspects of the edition. The numerous problems associated with the transcription of medieval musical notation into modern notation are amply addressed by the editors. Such aspects as sources, provenance of notation, texts, textual underlay, vocal and instrumental performance practice, and *musica ficta* are discussed in detail, making this edition useful for both scholars and performers.

CICONIA (1993) contains Ciconia's monumental *Nova musica* (ca. 1403–10), his principal theoretical work, and *De proportionibus* (1411), a revision of the third book of *Nova musica.* Distinguished medieval scholar Oliver Ellsworth has edited and translated these treatises from the five surviving manuscript sources, providing meticulous translations and a useful introduction that touches on Ciconia's biography, the dating of his theoretical works, and the structural organization of *Nova musica.* Other features of the introduction include a listing of the numerous ancient, patristic, and medieval authors who are quoted and cited by Ciconia, and in-depth discussions of the four books comprising *Nova musica.* Of particular note is Ellsworth's evaluation of the significance and influence of Ciconia's theory. Of particular interest is Ciconia's associations to the literary arts, specifically grammatical principles and constructs. Throughout the Middle Ages, music was seen as a mathematical discipline, but with the growing interest in ancient Greek and Roman literature in the 14th and 15th centuries, music was increasingly allied with the literary arts. Ciconia appears to have been the first major music theorist to adopt certain of the humanistic impulses of what would later become known as the Renaissance.

JOHN DOUGLAS GRAY

Classical Music: General Studies

Blume, Friedrich, *Classic and Romantic Music: A
    Comprehensive Survey,* translated by M.D. Herter Norton,
    New York: Norton, 1970
Dahlhaus, Carl, *The Idea of Absolute Music,* translated by
    Roger Lustig, Chicago: University of Chicago Press, 1989

Downs, Philip G., *Classical Music: The Era of Haydn, Mozart, and Beethoven,* New York: Norton, 1992

Heartz, Daniel, *Haydn, Mozart, and the Viennese School, 1740–1780,* New York: Norton, 1995

Larsen, Jens Peter, *Handel, Haydn, and the Viennese Classical Style,* translated by Ulrich Kramer, Ann Arbor, Michigan: UMI Research Press, 1988

Ratner, Leonard, *Classic Music: Expression, Form, Style,* New York: Schirmer Books, 1980

Rosen, Charles, *The Classical Style: Haydn, Mozart, Beethoven,* London: Faber, and New York: Viking Press, 1971; expanded edition, New York: Norton, 1997

Zaslaw, Neal, editor, *The Classical Era: From the 1740s to the End of the 18th Century,* London: Macmillan, and Englewood Cliffs, New Jersey: Prentice Hall, 1989

Scholars who have attempted to define or circumscribe the classical style have taken three distinct routes: a philosophical approach that treats the very meaning of the term *classical* as applied to music; a purely historical approach that seeks to establish precise historical criteria for the style, involving evidence from the music and/or the social and cultural factors determining the music; and an interpretative approach that seeks to explain how the music works and what it says or means.

Philosophically, BLUME sets the stage in an article that originally appeared in the German encyclopedia *Die Musik in Geschichte und Gegenwart* in 1958. Blume writes, "In classicism the antinomies of individuality and historical currents are neutralized through the power of a creative personality in the convincing (and, one may add, unique) form of the work of art." *Form* is the key word here. Blume believes that in the works of Haydn, Mozart, and early Beethoven (who were grouped together even by their contemporaries as part of the same Viennese school), individuality vanished behind a kind of transcendental form, especially sonata form. Simple melody took precedence over "the highly intensified composing techniques of the waning Baroque." Blume's assessment has itself become classic despite his many contradictions (e.g., he regards classicism as universal but also uniquely German by virtue of its indebtedness to Haydn, Mozart, and Beethoven).

LARSEN's book is a collection of topical essays that frequently engage Blume's traditional approach: when Larsen calls for a "penetrating re-examination of those conceptions and methods of research that . . . have tacitly been accepted and passed on for generations," he means Blume's conceptions and methods of research. Larsen looks more deeply into the roots of Viennese classicism (in an essay titled "The Style Change in Austrian Music between the Baroque and Viennese Classicism"), examines alternative sources of style change ("On the Importance of the Mannheim School"), and reconsiders the almost sacred concept of sonata form ("Sonata Form Problems"). His humanistic spirit is contagious, and his essays are well worth reading even if they have been in part superseded by the research of his many disciples.

The voluminous collection of articles by DAHLHAUS on the subject of classicism in music aesthetics has unfortunately not yet been translated (*Klassische und romantische Musikästhetik* [*Classical and Romantic Music Aesthetics*], 1988—the very title suggests a certain indebtedness to Blume), but his abstract approach can be gleaned from his study on the idea of absolute music—the idea of music whose form *is* its meaning. Dahlhaus focuses on aesthetics and aestheticians, not on the music and its composers, and takes Blume's orthodoxy to task by demonstrating that not even musical form exists in an aesthetic vacuum. Still, he demonstrates that the notion of music for music's sake, however questionable its accuracy might be, both conditioned the development of the classical style and facilitated its understanding.

ZASLAW accounts for the Viennese classical style historically, politically, and geographically. The Habsburg Empire (centered in Vienna) encompassed the vocal culture of North Italy, the brilliant wind playing of Bohemia, and close political ties with France by virtue of Austrian control of part of the Low Countries and Marie Antoinette's marriage to Louis XVI (Marie Antoinette was the sister of Habsburg Emperor Joseph II). Zaslaw also points to the eclecticism of Austria's musical culture: especially the area around Vienna combined the urbane advancements of London and Paris with the more provincial musical cultures of smaller towns, noble estates, and monasteries. From this conglomeration of musical cultures emerged the so-called universal style that Haydn took successfully to London and Paris and that Mozart took throughout Europe.

The historical approach of DOWNS is more comprehensive and less centered in Vienna than Zaslaw. He reviews concert life in the principal European centers and notes the flourishing of music publication, the rise of the virtuoso, and the advent of music criticism all as formative on the development of the classical style. Concerning criticism especially, he notes that the Leipzig-based *Allgemeine musikalische Zeitung* "became a powerful force at the turn of the century, compelling music lovers to look back toward earlier models and inculcating the idea of an exemplary 'Classical' period of composition." He also treats subjects as diverse as the business and the institutions of music and music in the home. His study is refreshing for its look outside the specifically Viennese origins of musical classicism, although his treatment of various topics is sometimes rather cursory.

HEARTZ's lengthy historical study is more detailed than Zaslaw's work and more focused than that of Downs. He shows the importance of the neglected Viennese Court composers, especially Georg Christoph Wagenseil, on the formation of Haydn's style. Unlike many of his colleagues, Heartz takes the importance of opera seriously in the formation of the classical style.

Most notable here is his emphasis on the operas of Gluck and Galuppi and their contribution to the stylistic developments of Haydn and Mozart, which demonstrates how international cross-currents contributed to the composers' universal, Viennese style. Heartz is at home discussing both the music itself and the social conditions surrounding it.

ROSEN's interpretative book has been highly influential, sometimes to the chagrin of the more philosophically or historically minded. For him, the essence of the classical style is the drama of sonata form as it reconciles the opposition of tonic and dominant (or secondary) key areas. Himself a performer, Rosen took Blume's abstract emphasis on form and demonstrated convincingly how it generates the dramatic excitement that generally characterizes the instrumental music of Haydn, Mozart, and Beethoven. In effect, Rosen almost single-handedly changed the notion of classical form in music from a static, transcendental idea to a vibrant, dramatic concept. Analytically, Rosen stays well within traditional melodic/harmonic approaches (avoiding the theoretical excesses of Schenker or Reti), and this restraint has kept his book easily accessible and especially agreeable to critics and performers who like to refer to musical details as well as deeper levels of form.

RATNER's work presents an interpretative understanding of the classical style based largely on the writings of its contemporary theorists. He focuses on two key words: *expression* and *rhetoric*. Through these catchwords of late-18th-century music theory, Ratner shows how classical music can be understood. *Expression* is treated through what Ratner has coined topics—musical types, often identical with easily identifiable dance or theatrical genres of the period, that were conjoined in a combinatorial, mosaic-like fashion. *Rhetoric* in the eighteenth-century aesthetic aimed at coherence and eloquence. Ratner's work is more historically attentive than Rosen's and in many ways more convincing. The only difficulty is Ratner's insistence in treating almost every musical detail in terms of his "topics." Although late-eighteenth-century theorists did apply these types, they never did so as systematically—one might even say dogmatically—as Ratner. However, Ratner's attempt to understand the classical style in its own terms must be highly recommended. It discloses a playfulness—and sometimes a depth of meaning—in the music of this era that previous critics had been unable to address adequately.

THOMAS SIPE

Classical Music: Specialized Studies

Agawu, V. Kofi, *Playing with Signs: A Semiotic Interpretation of Classic Music*, Princeton, New Jersey: Princeton University Press, 1991

Allanbrook, Wye Jamison, *Rhythmic Gesture in Mozart: Le Nozze di Figaro and Don Giovanni*, Chicago: University of Chicago Press, 1983

Charlton, David, *Grétry and the Growth of Opéra-Comique*, Cambridge: Cambridge University Press, 1986

Kirkendale, Warren, *Fugue and Fugato in Rococo and Classical Chamber Music*, translated by Margaret Bent and Warren Kirkendale, Durham, North Carolina: Duke University Press, 1979

Lester, Joel, *Compositional Theory in the Eighteenth Century*, Cambridge, Massachusetts: Harvard University Press, 1992

Morrow, Mary Sue, *German Music Criticism in the Late Eighteenth Century: Aesthetic Issues in Instrumental Music*, Cambridge: Cambridge University Press, 1997

Steblin, Rita, *A History of Key Characteristics in the Eighteenth and Early Nineteenth Centuries*, Ann Arbor, Michigan: UMI Research Press, 1983

Webster, James, *Haydn's "Farewell" Symphony and the Idea of Classical Style: Through-Composition and Cyclic Integration in His Instrumental Music*, Cambridge: Cambridge University Press, 1991

Weimer, Eric, *Opera Seria and the Evolution of the Classical Style 1755–1772*, Ann Arbor, Michigan: UMI Research Press, 1984

This group of specialized studies in music of the classical period cannot claim to represent every significant contribution to this field; however, it does include several important studies that fill gaps in areas frequently neglected, represent recent analytical and historiographical approaches, or deliberately broaden their scope to examine important issues pertaining to the classical style and period.

CHARLTON provides a thorough study of André Grétry and his opéras comiques, an important composer and genre that have often been neglected in general studies despite their influence on the operas of both classical and early romantic composers. The major portion of the book contains detailed accounts of 25 opéras comiques by Grétry (including plot synopses, genesis and performing history, evolution of musical style in arias, act finales and orchestration, and comparison of different versions) interleaved with chapters on Grétry's life and career, the general development of Parisian opera and opéra comique between the 1760s and 1790s, and Grétry's development of overtures and entr'actes that were linked to the opera through such devices as general mood, shared musical material, and mimed stage action.

LESTER provides an excellent survey of compositional theory (as opposed to speculative theory, aesthetics, and performance theory) from the 1720s to the 1790s, detailing "what eighteenth-century writers on compositional theory said, when they said it, and what they meant in the context of their own time." The book is therefore a survey of the major ideas and issues in compositional theory that form an important part of the background to the music of Haydn, Mozart, and Beethoven. Lester, who is as concerned with the derivation and dissemination of ideas as much as summarizing them, identifies three theoretical traditions in the earlier 18th century: species counterpoint (exemplified by Fux's *Gradus ad parnassum*), thoroughbass treatises (especially those by Heinichen, Niedt, Campion, and C.P.E. Bach), and harmony (as codified by Rameau). A fourth tradition centering on melody and phrase structure emerges around 1730 in the works of Mattheson and is later developed by Riepel and Koch, whose *Versuch* also includes much from the other theoretical traditions in a comprehensive treatise on composition. The contributions of several other important theorists, particularly Marpurg and Kirnberger, are also discussed at length.

STEBLIN's book is an excellent history of the controversial issue of key characteristics as the topic appears in writings of the 18th and early 19th centuries. Although the idea that each key had a particular affective association was questioned by many musicians, many others believed in the phenomenon—including major composers such as Rameau and Beethoven. The author does not try to find a definitive answer as to whether key characteristics really exist. Rather, she shows what musicians believed those characteristics to be, how they explained the phenomenon, and the controversies between believers and nonbelievers. Three common explanations were advanced by the writers surveyed: unequal temperament of keyboard instruments, psychological associations of sharp and flat keys, and physical properties of certain instruments (such as the use of open or stopped strings on the violin). (While Steblin recognizes that several factors might be involved in perceiving key characteristics, this possibility was not considered by the vast majority of writers examined.) Lists of key characteristics from the earlier part of the 18th century seem to have been highly personal in inspiration, but Steblin shows that, by the late 18th century, there was a relatively high consistency in the attributes described on such lists, reflecting a rather widespread convention of which composers must have been aware, whether or not they agreed with it. Steblin presents many lists of key attributions within the discussion, as well as a comprehensive list arranged by key in an appendix. Key characteristics have not been a major factor in modern discussions and analyses of classical music, but this study shows the importance of the topic and provides the necessary background information for its further exploration.

The 18th-century idea of music as a mimetic art led several theorists of the period to speculate about the expressive role of characteristic figures and rhythms, which alluded to specific types and styles of music. These speculations were codified into a more substantial theory of topics as a means of explaining expression in Leonard Ratner's *Classic Music* (1980). ALLANBROOK provides an important follow-up and expansion of one category of topics, those based on rhythmic gestures derived from dance rhythms and the contrast between ecclesiastical and *galant* styles. The introduction and first part of the book present a clear discussion of musical topics and their relation to the theory of mimesis and explore in detail the metrical spectrum of time signatures, dance rhythms, and expressive associations employed by Mozart. In parts 2 and 3 of the book, *Le nozze di Figaro* and *Don Giovanni* are analyzed with regard to expressive topics, leading to many fresh insights and conclusions sometimes at variance with more conventional analyses.

For AGAWU, a fundamental question is "*how* (rather than *what*) does Classic music mean?" He is less concerned with deciphering the intended meanings of composers than how they communicate with their audiences through a variety of musical signs, which leads the author to apply the theory of semiotics—the study of signs and symbolism—to musical analysis. Agawu distinguishes two principal kinds of musical signs: topics (in the sense used by Ratner and Allanbrook) that allude to musical types and styles and therefore have expressive connotations, and structural signs associated with a Shenkerian-derived "beginning-middle-end paradigm." Neither form of discourse can be fully understood without consideration of the other, and the interaction between the two modes defines the author's concept of play, through which the attributes of individual works can be discerned. The introductory chapter clearly summarizes the concept of expressive topics as well as semiotic theory, and sets out the model of analysis followed in the book. In addition to chapters devoted to topics and structure, movements of works by Mozart, Haydn, and Beethoven are analyzed. The final chapters summarize the elements of a semiotic theory for the interpretation of classical music and discuss which aspects of such a theory might be applicable to romantic music.

In a fundamental study of fugue and fugato during the second half of the 18th century, KIRKENDALE elucidates the primarily Austrian tradition of fugal writing in chamber and orchestral music and examines the works of Haydn, Mozart, and Beethoven in relation to that tradition and to the influence of J.S. Bach. The first part of the book covers the rococo period (the author's term), investigating the fugal works of many mid-century composers active in Austria, Italy, England, North Germany, and the Palatinate; Austria remained a particularly important region for fugal writing because of the persistence of the *sonata da chiesa* tradition. Kirkendale discusses a variety of issues, including musical treatises and their relationship to the fugal writing of several prominent composers, circumstances of performance in church and chamber, genres of composition in which fugal writing is found, the form of fugal movements (including proper fugues and fugal binary movements), and the characteristics of fugue subjects. In the second part of the book, devoted primarily to the three Viennese masters, the author analyzes their accomplishments in the context of this tradition and their individual syntheses of formal and stylistic elements.

Music historians have tended to assume that the classical style reached full maturity in the music of Haydn and Mozart around 1780, although a few would push the date back a decade to 1770. WEIMER's study shows persuasively that ca. 1770 indeed marks a time of style change in the works of several composers and that several traits associated with the mature classicism of Haydn and Mozart are in fact fully evident in opera seria arias of that decade. Moreover, he shows that the achievement of these stylistic elements was not limited to the Austrian/German domain, as has been claimed, but occurred simultaneously in the music of composers working in Italy and London. The study is based on the analysis of opera arias by three primary composers, Johann Adolf Hasse, Niccolò Jommelli, and Johann Christian Bach, with reference to the works of many others. No attention is given to plot, character, music/text relationships (other than the origin of a common ABB phrase structure), or the interpretation of individual operas; rather, the evolution of a restricted group of stylistic features is analyzed over a broad repertory. These features include harmonic expansion (the gradual slowing of harmonic rhythm to which Weimer relates certain aspects of phrase and tonal structure), classical counterpoint (an English equivalent of *motivische Arbeit,* in which the accompaniment is made up of fragments, variants, and recombinations of motives often with a quasi-contrapuntal result), and the gradual expansion of the wind section of the orchestra and its development from ripieno doubling of string parts to the functional roles of sustaining a harmonic background and doubling fragments of string parts, both of which came to be used to articulate structure.

MORROW demonstrates that much 19th-century aesthetic theory pertaining to instrumental music had its origins in the music criticism of the 18th century. Examining 1,300 reviews of instrumental music published in nearly 50 German periodicals between 1760 and 1798, she shows how reviewers in that era were beginning to develop a vocabulary to evaluate instrumental music on its own terms, implicitly rejecting the theory of mimesis that had long dominated aesthetic thought and which placed instrumental music below vocal music in the aesthetic hierarchy. Rejecting current aesthetic standards, German reviewers of the 1760s adopted an anti-Italian rhetorical stance that sought to identify the style and superiority of German music. At the same time, reviewers came to regard correct compositional technique as a major aesthetic criterion in evaluating music. During the 1770s and 1780s, critics focused more on creative genius and originality as criteria and began to develop a concept of nonmimetic expressivity. In the final phase,

the late 1780s and 1790s, reviewers explored ideas of unity and order in a composition explained by purely musical means. Although it would be left for the thinkers of early 19th century to develop a full-blown aesthetic theory that placed instrumental music at the top of the hierarchy of musical expression, many of the concepts that ultimately made up that theory had been explored by 18th-century reviewers.

The entire concept of classical style is subjected to a thought-provoking examination in WEBSTER's book. He begins with a thorough analysis of the *Farewell* Symphony, drawing on a variety of techniques—"formal analysis, Schenkerian structural-tonal voice-leading, Schoenbergian 'developing variation,' phrase rhythm, instrumentation, and register"—in order to demonstrate the use of through-composition and cyclic integration in the work and to provide insight into the work's extramusical associations. In turn, the author's illustration of Haydn's use of through-composition (in the sense of dynamic and gestural phenomena such as run-on movements, recalls, unresolved instabilities, and lack of closure) and cyclic integration between movements (in the commonalities of material and tonal relations) opens a discussion on the use of these techniques in the composer's instrumental music (especially, but not limited to, the symphonies) and ultimately leads to a consideration of the concepts of classical style and classical period. For Webster, the conventional view of Haydn's development, including the assertion that the composer reached maturity about 1770 (or 1780, as some would have it) reflects the ideology of the classical style that has blinded musicologists to the mastery evident in Haydn's earlier works. The book thoroughly discusses techniques used to integrate an instrumental cycle, covering such topics as gesture and rhetoric, destabilization, through-composition, extramusical associations, cyclic form in 18th-century music, and tonal organization, and Webster demonstrates their use in several individual works by Haydn. Although largely directed at the specialist and advanced student, the fine chapter on extramusical associations and the concluding historiographic essay on the problematic concept of the classical style are accessible to most readers.

ANDREW KEARNS

Clementi, Muzio 1752–1832

Italian-born pianist and composer

Plantinga, Leon, *Clementi: His Life and Music,* London: Oxford University Press, 1977

Schonberg, Harold C., *The Great Pianists,* New York: Simon and Schuster, 1963

Spada, Pietro, *The Complete Symphonic Works of Muzio Clementi,* Milan: Edizioni Suvini Zerboni, 1977

Tyson, Alan, *Thematic Catalogue of the Works of Muzio Clementi*, Tutzing: Hans Schneider, 1967

Westerby, Herbert, *How to Study the Pianoforte Works of the Great Composers*, New York: Scribner, 1900

Williams, Peter, editor, *Bach, Handel, Scarlatti: Tercentenary Essays*, Cambridge: Cambridge University Press, 1985

A Roman by birth, Clementi spent most of his life in London, where he became eminent as a composer, performer and teacher of keyboard music, publisher, instrument manufacturer, and merchant. His fame diminished rapidly after his death.

Clementi's first biographies appeared in English music periodicals during his life. The earliest, published in the *Quarterly Musical Magazine and Review* in 1820, contains information almost certainly supplied by the composer. The first extensive biography, *Muzio Clementis Leben*, was written by Max Unger in 1914. In 1921, Giulio Cesare Paribeni published his *Muzio Clementi nella vita e nell'arte*.

Publishers in most European musical centers issued multiple editions of Clementi's works, numbering them arbitrarily. The resulting mess in the numbering of Clementi's published works delayed a universally accepted catalog of his compositions. This was bravely compiled by Alan Tyson, who adhered to the numbering of Clementi's English publishing firms (including his own) that generally printed the authentic publications. TYSON's catalog is divided into works with opus number and works without opus number. A work of doubtful authorship is also discussed. Appendix 1 includes works not published during Clementi's life. For each entry, Tyson gives a single-stave incipit of every movement, a description of the first edition, a reference to all other authentic editions, and information on the autograph.

PLATINGA is regarded as the standard book on Clementi's life and work. The study proceeds chronologically. Each chapter covers a period of Clementi's life, starting with his biography and ending with a discussion of the works produced. Clementi's music reflects the radical changes in Western music during the 50 years he was writing. Similarly, his many professional activities reflect the changing conditions in the dissemination of music. Combining shrewdness and a notorious avarice, he was highly successful in the musical profession's new profitable directions, based on the support and the exploitation of the bourgeois amateur. Clementi's activities and interests, and his connection with leading musicians and businessmen of his time, from London to St. Petersburg, Russia, offered Platinga the opportunity to transform this biography into a perceptive study of daily musical life in Europe.

Platinga shows that Clementi did not perform at the pianoforte during his first stay in London, at a time when the instrument was quite often played in public. In the 1780s, Clementi usually played the harpsichord. In fact, he played his sonatas of op. 2 (Platinga uses Tyson's numbering), famous for their novel pianistic virtuosity, before the London public on the harpsichord. Nevertheless, Platinga stresses the importance of Clementi's three-volume pedagogical work titled *Gradus ad Parnassum* (1817–26), consisting of 100 pieces composed over 45 years, representing all the styles and species of keyboard pieces written by Clementi. At the end of the book are the 27 most widely known 20th-century editions of Clementi's works, with cross-reference to each work in Tyson's catalog.

A number of myths dissolved by later writers do exist in WESTERBY's examination of sections from ten pianoforte sonatas by Clementi. Nonetheless, his discussion, illustrated with music examples, is very instructive, as Westerby—by frequent comparative reference to contemporary works—illuminates the trail of influences in the application of pianistic innovations.

In his small work of 45 pages, SPADA investigates Clementi's symphonic works (Clementi did not allow their publication, and their autographs were for a long time lost after his death). Spada maintains that Clementi was an able orchestrator and, in certain aspects, a forerunner of Schumann and Brahms. He attributes to the "mental laziness" of writers the distorted image of Clementi, projected for over a century, and pays tribute to the few exceptional researchers who did study Clementi's symphonic music (most notably, Alfredo Casella). In a *Thematic Catalog of Muzio Clementi's Complete Symphonic Works*, ten symphonic works and some fragments are listed (with single-stave incipits of all the movements). In the main text, Spada highlights the characteristics of four symphonies and three shorter works (whose autographs are kept in the British Museum, London, and the Library of Congress, Washington, D.C.), with the help of many musical examples.

In SCHONBERG's account of the development of piano playing from Mozart to Van Cliburn, a chapter is devoted to Clementi. Schonberg goes straight to the core of Clementi's pianism, relating what Mozart abhorred in his art: his "showmanship, the extravagance and technical brilliance of his piano music, his almost romantic modulations . . . all added up to something offensive." It was popularization of instrumental music that Mozart detected in Clementi—the star-system ingredients that 19th-century pianists inherited from 18th-century opera singers.

A neglected aspect of Clementi's significance is discussed in Stephen Daw's essay "Muzio Clementi as an Original Advocate, Collector, and Performer, in Particular of J.S. Bach and D. Scarlatti" in WILLIAMS; namely, the influence Clementi exerted on the Bach cult in England around 1800, and the interest in the old masters that characterized his times. Daw demonstrates Clementi's involvement with the music of Bach, Handel, and D. Scarlatti as a performer, collector of manuscripts, and publisher.

EKATERINI ROMANOU

Commedia dell'arte

Cairns, Christopher, editor, *The Commedia dell'arte from the Renaissance to Dario Fo*, Lewiston, New York: Mellon Press, 1988

Duchartre, Pierre-Louis, *The Italian Comedy; The Improvisation, Scenarios, Lives, Attributes, Portraits, and Masks of the Illustrious Characters of the Commedia dell'arte*, translated by Randolph T. Weaver, London: Harrap, 1921; reprint, with new pictorial supplement reproduced from the Recueil Fossard, New York: Dover, 1966

George, David J., and Christopher J. Gossip, editors, *Studies in the Commedia dell'arte*, Cardiff: University of Wales Press, 1993

Heck, Thomas F., *Commedia dell'arte: A Guide to the Primary and Secondary Literature*, New York: Garland, 1988

Lea, Kathleen Marguerite, *Italian Popular Comedy: A Study in the Commedia dell'arte, 1560–1620, with Special Reference to the English Stage*, 2 vols., Oxford: Clarendon Press, 1934; reprint, New York, Russell and Russell, 1962

Nicoll, Allardyce, *Masks, Mimes and Miracles: Studies in the Popular Theatre*, New York: Harcourt Brace, 1931; reprint, New York, Cooper Square, 1963

Oreglia, Giacomo, *The Commedia dell'arte*, translated by Lovett F. Edwards, New York: Hill and Wang, 1968

Richards, Kenneth, *The Commedia dell'arte: A Documentary History*, Oxford: Blackwell, 1990

Rudlin, John, *Commedia dell'arte: An Actor's Handbook*, London: Routledge, 1994

Scala, Flaminio, *Scenarios of the commedia dell'arte: Flaminio Scala's Il teatro delle favole rappresentative*, translated by Henry F. Salerno, New York: New York University Press, 1967

The commedia dell'arte is an improvised theatrical genre that originated in Italy in the early Renaissance and was performed by traveling troupes of players. Probably generated from even earlier dramatic sources, the commedia became enormously popular and eventually during the 17th and 18th centuries found its way into the rest of Europe and beyond, becoming an important influence on many dramatic forms, including the works of playwrights such as Shakespeare and of major operatic composers. Today, the commedia heritage is recognized as a principal foundation of comedy, especially the visual elements of "stage business." Music in the commedia dell'arte is a problematic issue because of the nature of the medium; the improvisatory nature of the drama makes it difficult to identify a body of music that was clearly used in performances, although we know that the comedians were also musicians and that many of the pictorial representations show musical instruments. Included in the works cited here are primary sources, all of which were originally published in languages other than English.

OREGLIA's concise work serves as an excellent introduction to the commedia dell'arte, outlining its history and origins as well as introducing the important masks and providing samples of the scenarios from which the staged dramas were drawn.

RICHARDS's volume is one of the best resources available in English. More comprehensive than Oreglia's study, it gives a good, basic understanding of the evolution and nature of the commedia, including references and translations of many of the most important documents, as well as a representative selection of pictorial images, the material from which much of our information comes. The book is organized chronologically, from the antecedents of commedia to the major companies and best-known performances, through a discussion of the nature of masks and improvisation and an introduction to the major players. It concludes with some of the more recent manifestations and a brief discussion of the dispersal of the technique throughout Europe and beyond. Within each section, the author includes translations of important supporting documents as well as bibliographic detail.

Unlike the other resources included here, RUDLIN's intent is to help performers to understand the commedia style well enough to be able to employ it in current productions. He includes a brief history of the origins of commedia, the use of masks, the players' style, and a more detailed description of the individual character masks, followed by an investigation of 20th-century attempts at reconstruction or performance in the commedia style. His work is most useful for practitioners whose goal is to produce either a commedia from an established scenario or a theatrical production in the commedia style. Unique among the studies is the author's clear recognition of the importance of music in a commedia production, although he admits that exactly how this inclusion should be realized is problematic. He specifically rejects the idea that commedia should be action and dialogue interspersed with song, but rather sees it as an inherently musical enterprise "constantly on the brink of tipping over into operetta." A brief bibliography is supplemented by notes to each section.

GEORGE and GOSSIP is a collection of essays that focuses on the outgrowths of the genre as it traveled beyond Italy to other countries, especially France. The book explores commedia elements in a wide range of settings from Shakespeare, Molière, and the Commedie Italienne in France, into the late 18th-century Spanish manifestations, as well as the works of Russian symbolists in the early 1900s. The early 20th-century music of Arnold Schoenberg is the subject of a discussion of recent commedia musical influences.

CAIRNS's recent collection includes essays on specific questions relating to the commedia dell'arte. Several of the essays specifically address musical issues, a problem in any commedia performance, because so many of the extant pictures show performers with instruments but we have very little music known to have been included in any specific commedia. Three of the 15 essays are in Italian and one is in French.

In a thoughtful and compelling fashion, NICOLL not only presents a description and analysis of the essential features of the commedia, but, unlike many other authors, he is also willing to speculate about many of the outstanding performance questions relating to the commedia dell'arte. His work surely has been the impetus for some of the more recent authors, including those in the George and Gossip and in the Cairns volumes, to examine these performance issues.

The translation of SCALA's scenarios provides the most comprehensive available English resource for these brief plot outlines that formed the basis for commedia dell'arte productions. This work and the DUCHARTRE edition of the Recueil Fossard's collection of iconographic data give researchers the primary tools from which to study and draw their own conclusions about what the commedia was and how it was performed. Duchartre, like many others, gives historical and descriptive observations of the masks, players, scenarios, and staging. The importance of this book, however, is primarily the extensive collection of pictorial evidence of masks and individual performers—some of whose identities are known—and the information these pictures give regarding the staging of commedias.

LEA's two-volume work parallels that of many others, providing perhaps more bibliographical material than some authors, with less insightful commentary. Her principal addition to commedia studies is her focus, in the second volume, on the influence of commedia dell'arte on the English stage.

HECK's work is a comprehensive bibliography for literature of and about the commedia dell'arte. He includes references for the primary sources, the scenarios, and historical studies of the commedia dell'arte. He also provides sections on the spread of the genre, works identified with particular actors, the masks, and improvisation, as well as sections on references for dance and music, revivals of the commedia in the 19th and 20th centuries, and references to iconographic sources. Most materials cited are in Italian, English, or French. There are a few sources in other languages.

MARTHA FARAHAT

Concerto: Baroque

Boyden, David, "When Is a Concerto not a Concerto?" in *Baroque Music I: Seventeenth Century,* edited by Ellen Rosand, New York: Garland, 1985

Drummond, Pippa, *The German Concerto: Five Eighteenth-Century Studies,* Oxford: Clarendon Press, New York: Oxford University Press, 1980

Everett, Paul, *The Manchester Concerto Partbooks,* 2 vols., New York: Garland, 1989

Hutchings, Arthur, *The Baroque Concerto,* London: Faber, 1961; 3rd revised edition, 1978

Selfridge-Field, Eleanor, *Venetian Instrumental Music from Gabrieli to Vivaldi,* New York: Praegar, and Oxford: Blackwell, 1975; 3rd revised edition, New York: Dover, 1994

Talbot, Michael, "The Concerto Allegro in the Early Eighteenth Century," *Music and Letters* 52 (1971)

Whitmore, Philip, *Unpremeditated Art: The Cadenza in the Classical Keyboard Concerto,* Oxford: Clarendon Press, and New York: Oxford University Press, 1991

Wolf, Eugene K., and Douglass M. Green, editors, *Antecedents of the Symphony,* New York: Garland, 1983

First appearing around 1680, the instrumental concerto eventually became the most widely cultivated genre of the late baroque period. (The era's other principal genre of orchestral music, the orchestral suite or *ouverture,* arose at about the same time but found relatively few adherents outside of Germany, its country of origin.) Recent investigations of the baroque concerto have demonstrated the great diversity in scoring, structure, and style in each stage of the genre's development while illuminating the important contributions made by Italians such as Corelli, Torelli, Albinoni, and Vivaldi in these areas before 1720. Ironically perhaps, rather less is presently understood about the concerto during the period 1720–40, except for the well-known works of J.S. Bach, Handel, and Vivaldi.

HUTCHINGS's volume remains the most significant, though a somewhat limited, survey of the baroque concerto in English. Following three chapters that summarize the principal figures and places associated with the early concerto, the uses of the terms *concerto* and *sinfonia,* and important stylistic features of the baroque concerto, the author organizes the bulk of his discussion according to schools of composition. He considers the school of St. Petronio in Bologna, the "First German (Austrian) School" (principally Muffat and Pez), the "Venetian School" (Albinoni, Vivaldi, and the Marcellos), the "Main German School" (Bach and Telemann), and "The English School" (Geminiani, Avison, and Stanley). Other chapters treat "Corelli and His Contemporaries" and "The Last Phase" (Barsanti, Sammartini, and Locatelli). This method of organization leads Hutchings to discuss some composers without reference to any school or group (Handel, Bonporti, and Leclair) and overlook the importance of others. Seemingly because "no French school can be justly grouped around Leclair's concertos," which Hutchings considers "the only great French baroque concertos," he barely mentions the many works published in France during the 1730s and 1740s. Perhaps the least informative chapter is that focusing on the German contemporaries of Bach and Telemann, territory that is still relatively unfamiliar. Hutchings's writing style is colorful and engaging, but his discussion of the music is on a very basic level and is illustrated with musical examples that are often inadequate in their brevity.

BOYDEN meticulously traces the etymology of the term *concerto* from the 16th to the early 18th century, concluding that, during the baroque period, concerto was understood "as one or two manners of setting, involving either the concept of 'joining together' or 'ensemble' of musical forces, or the idea of 'striving, contrast, and opposition.'" He demonstrates that this flexible usage of the term helps explain why the terms *concerto, sonata,* and *sinfonia* were often used interchangeably in late baroque instrumental music.

TALBOT's article explores the structure and style of fast concerto movements that display a periodic organization. Surveying Italian concertos composed between about 1680 and 1720, he focuses especially on Corelli, Torelli, and Albinoni, although significant attention is paid to Albicastro and Vivaldi as well. Talbot offers especially shrewd evaluations of each composer's musical innovations, strengths, and weaknesses.

Although SELFRIDGE-FIELD focuses her attention more on Venetian sonatas than on concertos, she includes extended discussions of concertos by Albinoni, Vivaldi, and the Marcellos, providing musical discussions that are sophisticated and engagingly written. Before discussing Albinoni, she considers the origins of the Venetian concerto grosso and solo concerto; after discussing the Marcellos, she surveys the outputs of Tessarini and other minor figures.

DRUMMOND's study takes the form of five lengthy essays surveying the concerto output of J.S. Bach, Handel, Telemann, Hasse, and C.P.E. Bach. Each essay addresses sources, chronology, historical background, instrumentation, and other pertinent issues (drawing on the most important secondary literature appearing before 1975) then devotes considerable space to the music itself. Drummond's discussions of the music are substantial and perceptive and for the concertos of Hasse and Telemann remain the most extended treatments in English. Although the concertos of the Bachs and Handel have been the subject of much scholarly attention since the appearance of this study, Drummond's chapters remain valuable introductions to these works.

WOLF and GREEN provides an excellent introduction to the Italian ripieno concerto, or concerto for string orchestra without soloist(s). He identifies two main types of ripieno concerto: the sonata type, similar in form and style to the *sonata da chiesa*; and the sinfonia type, with a three-movement structure also found in the opera overture, solo concerto, and early symphony. Concertos of the sinfonia type are often indistinguishable from the "concert symphony" of the 1720s and 1730s, and Wolf breaks with earlier writers in associating the ripieno concerto, not the opera overture, with the origins of the concert symphony. A survey of the most important ripieno concerto publications ca. 1690–1720 is followed by discussions of the individual works edited in the volume.

EVERETT examines a collection of early 18th-century Italian concertos, especially rich in works by Vivaldi, preserved at the Manchester Public Library in sets of part books belonging originally to Charles Jennens, Handel's friend, benefactor, and librettist. On the basis of a close study of paper types, stave rulings, and copyists' hands, the author traces the history of the collection and the Italian provenance of individual manuscripts in great detail; his second volume provides a detailed catalog of the collection with numerous illustrations of watermarks and handwriting. Everett's discussion of the sources is dense enough that only those with a serious interest in Vivaldi and his Italian contemporaries will be tempted to follow his arguments in all their detail. Such close examination of the manuscripts, however, sheds considerable light on Vivaldi's compositional process and the chronology of a number of his works. Everett also shows that the Manchester sources for Vivaldi's *Le quattro stagioni* are more accurate and authentic than the 1725 edition on which modern versions have been based. His discussions of musical style in chapters 5 and 7 are helpful, especially with regard to the concertos of Giuseppe Valentini.

Although mainly addressing the classical concerto repertory, WHITMORE discusses the late baroque cadenza in the first five chapters of his study. After tracing the origins of the cadenza, providing a definition of the term, and exploring the 18th-century performance of cadenzas, the author considers types of related improvisatory writing. Of particular interest is his discussion of the capriccio, an extended improvisatory insertion found in the concertos of Locatelli, Tartini, Vivaldi, and J.S. Bach (in the first movement of Brandenburg Concerto no. 5). Throughout these chapters, Whitmore devotes much attention to Quantz's 1752 discussion of the cadenza (*On Playing the Flute*) as well as to other important writers from the early 18th century. A chapter surveying the late baroque cadenza is largely concerned with the organ concertos of Handel and the harpsichord concertos of Bach.

STEVEN ZOHN

Concerto: From 1750

Emery, Frederic Barclay, *The Violin Concerto*, Chicago: Violin Literature, 1928; reprint, New York: Da Capo Press, 1969

Forman, Denis, *Mozart's Concerto Form*, New York: Praeger, and London: Hart-Davis, 1971

Girdlestone, Cuthbert Morton, *Mozart's Piano Concertos*, London: Cassell, 1948; 3rd edition, 1978

Harris, John M., *A History of Music for Harpsichord or Piano and Orchestra*, Lanham, Maryland: Scarecrow Press, 1997

Hill, Ralph, editor, *The Concerto*, London: Penguin Books, 1952

Layton, Robert, editor, *A Companion to the Concerto*, London: Helm, 1988

Milligan, Thomas B., *The Concerto and London's Musical Culture in the Late Eighteenth Century*, Ann Arbor, Michigan: UMI Research Press, and Epping: Bowker, 1983

Norris, Jeremy, *The Russian Piano Concerto*, Bloomington: Indiana University Press, 1994

Roeder, Michael Thomas, *A History of the Concerto*, Portland, Oregon: Amadeus Press, 1994

Veinus, Abraham, *The Concerto*, New York: Doubleday Doran, 1944; reprint, New York: Dover, 1964

White, Chappell, *From Vivaldi to Viotti: A History of the Early Classical Violin Concerto*, Philadelphia: Gordon and Breach, 1992

Zaslaw, Neal, editor, *Mozart's Piano Concertos: Text, Context, Interpretation*, Ann Arbor: University of Michigan Press, 1996

The concerto after 1750 evolved in a number of significant ways: an essentially intimate chamber genre became a popular entertainment for large, predominantly middle-class audiences; a group interaction featuring differentiated textures of tutti and soloists became an opposition between the mass and the solitary individual, with all the conflict and dialogue that implies; and the solo role itself served increasingly as a vehicle for virtuosity and display. Substantial chapters in the history of the concerto remain to be written; certain difficulties, such as the fact that thousands of 18th-century concertos survive only in manuscript parts, have hampered scholars in their efforts to survey and to understand the repertory. Thus, the literature on the concerto is not as extensive as one might expect for so important a genre. Apart from general studies of the concerto, which often describe its formal traits and provide lists of available works by various composers, there are also books that concentrate particularly on concertos for the two most popular instruments, piano and violin. A significant handful of studies focus even more specifically on the body of concertos by Mozart.

VEINUS provides one of the earlier overviews of concerto style and repertory, but the actual contents of the book are rather sketchy. In "The Classical Concerto," he discusses J.S. Bach's sons and Haydn in four pages and devotes the rest of the chapter to Mozart, with no hint of the dozens of other composers who contributed to the concerto's flowering after 1750. Veinus does not analyze the concertos but sets them in a chronological narrative alongside events in Mozart's life; his chapter on Beethoven is quite similar. The treatment of "The Romantic Concerto" hinges on the idea that "the development of the art [concerto] owes much to the virtuoso; so does its debasement." It is therefore odd to find an extended discussion of Berlioz's *Harold in Italy*, a symphony with obbligato viola in which virtuosity plays no role. The weakest portion of the book is a cursory summary of 20th-century concertos.

A simultaneously richer and more comprehensive survey of concertos by individual composers is found in HILL, which assembles short essays by leading scholars in the field. The general essay on the development of the concerto that opens the book may be considered old-fashioned today because it relies entirely on the sonata form model to analyze concerto first-movement form. Each following essay introduces the most important concertos by the composer in question, providing a brief historical background and a movement-by-movement description that includes examples of main themes and any special traits of the works (unusual orchestration, use of national dance styles or other folk elements, etc.). A student in search of information on English concertos will be gratified to discover essays on Elgar, Delius, Walton, and other composers normally neglected in such studies. Concertos by Bartók, Bloch, Berg, and Prokofiev also represent the 20th century.

LAYTON's book is also a collection of essays by various authors, but here the concertos are examined more contextually, both in terms of chronology and geography; thus, essays such as "The Concerto in Pre-Revolutionary Russia" or "Central Europe in the Twentieth Century" place concertos and their composers in their original time and place. The valuable approach to 19th-century concertos divides the genre into virtuosic and symphonic styles; here the solo-oriented achievements of the virtuoso performer-composers such as Hummel or Paganini are studied together, in contrast to the more symphonic texture and argument of concertos by Brahms, for example. Discussions of the concerto in the 20th century are especially extensive, with composers grouped together by nationality as well as style, and featuring considerable material on post-World War II developments.

ROEDER, of all the general studies, has most successfully combined analytical and contextual approaches to the concerto; this work would make an excellent textbook for a course surveying the development of the concerto. Roeder includes accessible graphs that illustrate changing formal types in concerto first movements; reflecting current scholarship, these analyses integrate sonata and ritornello-form principles for a more flexible and nuanced view of the style. The overview of composers is more comprehensive than those found in the other general studies, especially in the area of 20th-century music. Issues of performance practice, including instrumental types and techniques and the role of improvisation, are addressed more straightforwardly here than elsewhere; useful photographs of 18th-century wind instruments are found in the section on the classical concerto. The clear, engaging style of writing and the ample bibliography further enhance the book's value for classroom use.

Emery and White both survey the repertory of the violin concerto. The subtitle of EMERY's two-volume work gives a good indication of its contents: "Through a Period of Nearly 300 Years Covering about 3,300 Concertos with Brief Biographies of 1,000 Composers." Organized geographically, the entries for each composer are necessarily brief, but there is a certain fascination in the sheer number of obscure names, a reflection of the great demand for violin concertos over generations, as well as the diligence and creativity of composer-violinists. For important individual pieces, such as the Beethoven violin concerto, Emery provides a detailed descriptive analysis of the work along with a catalog of its many editions. WHITE takes a more in-depth and scholarly stance on the violin concerto, with chapters on its role in the musical culture of the 18th and 19th centuries, its texture and formal structures, the unique sonority of the violin, and performance practice issues. The author then undertakes a geographical survey of composers of violin concertos, with special emphasis on Italy and the Austro-German regions. White supplies considerably more information about composers and their works and has studied enough concertos to be able to make well-founded comparisons between, for example, the Mannheim and North German schools of concerto writing.

Harris and Norris each examine the piano concerto. HARRIS, which has a chronological framework that begins with J.S. Bach, includes concertos for harpsichord as well; the author has assembled lists of composers within various geographical areas and supplied brief sketches for most of them. Certain composers, such as Mozart, receive somewhat more attention, but most interesting and useful are the accounts of truly obscure composers from remote regions not generally covered at all in such surveys, such as Estonia and Guatemala. A substantial discography adds a valuable dimension to the book. NORRIS focuses on the piano concerto in Russia (this first volume covers the 19th century). Here, the concertos of Rubinstein and Tchaikovsky receive the detailed critical analysis that they deserve, alongside treatments of Rachmaninoff, Balakirev, Arensky, and others. Norris does not flinch from offering strong value judgments, which often make for colorful reading; but most important is his exploration of early-romantic influences from Europe—especially the "brilliant technique and rich sonorous tone" of John Field—in the formation of a Russian school of pianism and concerto writing. This book also contains a good discography.

MILLIGAN examines the concerto against the backdrop of the extraordinarily lively musical culture of late 18th-century London. His analysis of the concertos is organized by instrumental genre; the ubiquitous piano and violin naturally figure here, but concertos for harp and organ also flourished in London and thus receive an unusual amount of attention. Milligan's work is perhaps most important as a social history, showing the concerto's role in London's concert life and commercial spheres, especially the vigorous publishing industry.

Mozart's keyboard concertos have generated the most literature of any works in this genre. The now venerable GIRDLESTONE describes each concerto in loving detail, although he has comparatively little to say about Mozart's earlier concertos (K. 175 through K. 415) and thus neglects a critical stage in Mozart's development as a keyboard composer-performer. FORMAN analyzes the first movements of each concerto, dividing them into "galant," "melodic," and "symphonic" types; these descriptors do little to define Mozart's formal procedures but serve to differentiate among styles of thematic "character" that Forman discerns in given movements. ZASLAW presents an impressive collection of essays that originated in a festival-conference devoted to Mozart's keyboard concertos at the University of Michigan in 1989. Many of the best scholars in Mozart studies today are represented here: topics range widely, including Mozart's concerto manuscripts and other sources; humor and drama in the concertos; relationships between Mozart's concertos and operas; formal elements of the often neglected second and third movements; and performance practice issues, including improvisation, orchestral size, and aspects of the basso continuo.

KATHRYN L. SHANKS LIBIN

Conductors and Conducting

Blackman, Charles, *Behind the Baton,* New York: Charos Enterprises, 1964

Carse, Adam von Ahn, *The Orchestra from Beethoven to Berlioz,* Cambridge: Heffer, 1948

Davison, Archibald T., *Choral Conducting,* Cambridge, Massachusetts: Harvard University Press, 1940

Ewen, David, *The Man with the Baton,* New York: Crowell, 1936

Galkin, Elliott W., *A History of Orchestral Conducting: In Theory and Practice,* New York: Pendragon Press, 1988

Handy, D. Antoinette, *Black Conductors,* Metuchen, New Jersey: Scarecrow Press, 1995

Leinsdorf, Erich, *The Composer's Advocate: A Radical Orthodoxy for Musicians,* New Haven, Connecticut: Yale University Press, 1981

Matheopoulos, Helena, *Maestro: Encounters with Conductors of Today,* New York: Harper and Row, and London: Hutchinson, 1982

Rudolf, Max, *The Grammar of Conducting,* New York: Schirmer, 1950; 3rd edition, with the assistance of Michael Stern, 1995

Scherchen, Hermann, *Handbook of Conducting,* translated by M.D. Calvocoressi, London: Oxford University Press, 1933

Schuller, Gunther, *The Compleat Conductor,* New York: Oxford University Press, 1997

The necessity of leadership in musical groups is apparent from earliest times, and the role of musical leaders has been modified gradually as music's compositional style has changed. After 1600, it became common practice for the keyboard player or the leader of the violins to lead the ensemble while simultaneously performing, a practice, in the case of the violin, extending well into the 19th century and still sometimes used today. The role of conductor in the modern sense did not appear until the 19th century. Numerous sources describe the various aspects of a conductor's role, demystifying some requirements, such as thorough musical preparation, knowledge of the historical placement and style of the music being performed, organizational skills, and the ability to convey musical intent to performers and audiences alike. More esoteric characteristics, however, such as magnetism, projection of personality, and charisma, are also cited as essential to the success of a conductor. Fascinating and instructive remarks by renowned conductors can offer insight into the attitudes and inspirations that shape a conductor's approach and can help describe aspects of a conductor's unique role.

EWEN's well-organized volume provides a good starting point for a reader new to the topic of conducting. In chapters 2 and 3 of part 1 of his work, Ewen pinpoints some benchmarks of conducting history and helps define the practice of conducting in easily read prose. The thorough index guides the reader to specific topics, and a biographical guide provides brief synapses of the achievements of numerous conductors prominent before 1936. The introduction to Ewen's book features conductor Serge Koussevitzky's view of a conductor's important role as interpreter between composer and audience.

CARSE's extensive scholarly history of conducting has been a principal resource for subsequent writers. Carse portrays in detail the role of musical leaders and baton conductors from the 18th century to the mid-19th century. Topics specific to Germany, Austria, France, Italy, and England are discussed, and specific conductors and subjects related to conducting are clearly referenced in the index. Carse has produced an engagingly written work, densely packed with details.

GALKIN expands upon the research begun by Carse. All facets of the history of orchestral conducting are covered in Galkin's extremely thorough work. Galkin cites original sources throughout the study to add credence to the current understanding of conducting history. Part 3, "The Art of Conducting in Practice," delineates variations of musical leadership from audible time-beater to the baton conductor. The extensive lists of entries under "conductor" and "conducting" in the index not only assist the reader but also verify Galkin's scholarly approach. Also noteworthy are the many illustrations, caricatures, and photos—depictions that bring to life the voluminous text.

SCHERCHEN writes from a conductor's perspective in an instructive manner. Although the book is intended particularly for aspiring conductors, portions of it are useful for anyone intent on studying a conductor's insights.

There is a relatively extensive table of contents, but an index is not provided. Particularly useful sections are titled "Conducting," "Clarity of Conducting Gestures," "Representation of Works," The Performer's Standard," and "The Problems of Conducting."

In his introductory pages, throughout which a number of famous conductors are quoted, MATHEOPOULOS seeks to define the essence of conducting—those somewhat intangible qualities beyond stick technique and musical knowledge. Some essential attributes of a successful conductor are enumerated. The remainder of the volume portrays specific conductors; a perusal of the accompanying photographs proves interesting and in some cases informative.

BLACKMAN devotes almost an entire volume to a conductor's function and responsibilities, a topic addressed through direct quotations from 40 conductors, educators, and composers. Similarly, 21 professional instrumentalists discuss what orchestras expect of a conductor. A critical reading of Blackman's chapter titled "Psychology in Conducting" is particularly rewarding.

SCHULLER convincingly argues for careful analysis and examination of a composer's notations in order to remain true to the highest aspirations of a conductor's art—his or her creative interpretation. These ideas are set forth in part 1, "A Philosophy of Conducting."

RUDOLF's work primarily addresses the intricacies and complexities of conducting techniques. His preface and portions of his introduction as well as the foreword by conductor George Szell address the need for complete technical mastery in order to interpret music effectively.

LEINSDORF's chapter titled "Knowing the Conductor's Role" is a lengthy exposé on the conductor's image, authority, and tasks, but it does not discuss stick technique. In the brief "Finale," the author maintains that knowledge, imagination, and a modest personal character are attributes of a successful conductor.

One of HANDY's significant contributions is found in her introductory section, where she presents brief historical information about jazz orchestra conductors or leaders, women conductors, and black conductors, often overlooked groups that are important to the complete history of conducting.

Even though DAVISON's small book is intended primarily for choral conductors, its inclusion here is warranted because, like Handy's volume, it adds to a comprehensive view of conductors and conducting. The opening chapter, "The Conductor," is recommended; a clear outline of each chapter, found in the table of contents, provides easy access to further relevant information.

JOANNE E. SWENSON-ELDRIDGE

See also Toscanini, Arturo

Continuo

Arnold, Frank Thomas, *The Art of Accompaniment from a Thorough-Bass, As Practiced in the XVIIth and XVIIIth Centuries,* Oxford: Oxford University Press, 1931; reprint in 2 vols., with introduction by Denis Stevens, New York: Dover, 1965

Bach, Carl Philipp Emanuel, *Essay on the True Art of Playing Keyboard Instruments,* translated and edited by William J. Mitchell, New York: Norton, 1949

Bach, Johann Sebastian, *J.S. Bach's Precepts and Principles for Playing the Thorough-Bass or Accompanying in Four Parts,* translated and edited by Pamela L. Poulin, Oxford: Clarendon Press, 1994

Borgir, Tharald, *The Performance of the Basso Continuo in Italian Baroque Music,* Ann Arbor, Michigan: UMI Research Press, 1987

Buelow, George J, *Thorough-Bass Accompaniment According to Johann David Heinichen,* Berkeley: University of California Press, 1966; revised edition, Ann Arbor: UMI Research Press, 1986

Dreyfus, Laurence, *Bach's Continuo Group: Players and Practices in His Vocal Works,* Cambridge, Massachusetts: Harvard University Press, 1987

Keaney, Helen, *Figured Bass for Beginners,* Boston: Schirmer, 1981

Keller, Hermann, *Thoroughbass Method: With Excerpts from the Theoretical Works of Praetorius and Numerous Examples from the Literature of the 17th and 18th Centuries,* translated by Carl Parrish, New York: Norton, 1965

Ledbetter, David, *Continuo Playing According to Handel: His Figured Bass Exercises,* Oxford: Oxford University Press, 1990

Morris, R.O., *Figured Harmony at the Keyboard,* 2 vols., London: Oxford University Press, 1932

North, Nigel, *Continuo Playing on the Lute, Archlute, and Theorbo,* Bloomington: Indiana University Press, 1987

Rameau, Jean Philippe, *Treatise on Harmony,* translated by Philip Gossett, New York: Dover, 1971

Williams, Peter F., *Figured Bass Accompaniment,* 2 vols., Edinburgh: Edinburgh University Press, 1970

Most 17th- and 18th-century music for instrumental ensemble includes, on the lowest staff in the written score, a part referred to today variously as the continuo, basso continuo, or the like. The notation of such parts frequently includes numbers (figures) and other symbols; these indicate chords that were to be improvised above the bass line by one or more of the players of this part—hence, the term *figured bass* has been used for this type of notation (also known as thoroughbass). Invented around 1600, figured bass has continued to the present to be employed in the teaching of music theory, that is, harmony. But continuo playing in the historical sense—the improvised realization of the figured bass in performance—died out in the early 19th century; among the most recent compositions to use it are the masses of Schubert and the occasional so-called *secco* recitatives still found in early romantic opera. With the revival of historical performing practice in the 20th century, there has been renewed interest in the subject.

Publications on the subject include a large number of original treatises from the 17th and 18th centuries, many of which have been reissued in recent years in new editions and translations, as well as in facsimile editions. In addition, there is a large body of 20th-century writings, which can be divided between (1) scholarly reconstructions of the various historical practices associated with continuo parts and (2) practical manuals and guides intended to instruct modern players in continuo playing.

Writings about continuo are invariably technical works, largely inaccessible to those without some proficiency at a keyboard instrument. Most of the original treatises are in Italian, French, or German and are too specialized to serve as introductions to the subject. One monograph worth mentioning here, however, because of its widely known English translation and its heavy influence on later writers, is C.P.E. BACH. The author, a son of J.S. Bach and an important composer and keyboard player in his own right, includes a detailed study of continuo playing in the second volume of the original work (published in Berlin, 1762). The modern English translation, in one volume, is generally accurate and dependable, although on points of detail it occasionally now seems dated.

Another important historical source is the fourth and final section of the famous treatise on harmony by RAMEAU, the major French composer and music theorist of the 18th century. Frequently overlooked even by scholars, Rameau's chapters on accompaniment provide an account of figured-bass realization in the French late-baroque style, which differs in significant ways from the contemporary German practices described by C.P.E. Bach and a number of other writers of the period. Despite a somewhat confusing organization, the treatise is considerably more detailed than that of other French baroque writers and, like Bach's, provides essential material for performing the works of its author in period style. The translation is clear and accurate, as are the musical examples.

Substantial extracts from other historical treatises are given by ARNOLD in English translation. Reflecting early 20th-century views, Arnold tends to view the German 18th-century sources (especially C.P.E. Bach) as having achieved a perfection of theory and practice toward which other musicians had been striving. Today, most players and scholars recognize instead that earlier writings, as well as French and Italian contemporaries of Bach, represent distinct but equally valid traditions. Moreover, the revival of early performing techniques and instruments has rendered much of Arnold's commentary obsolete. Nevertheless, his volume remains a useful collection of some of the most important historical documents and the only source for English versions of a number of them.

More recent scholarly writings include detailed studies of continuo practices associated with particular composers, with emphasis on the German late baroque. BUELOW discusses in depth the teachings of Johann David Heinichen, whose two books on continuo playing reflect not only German practices but also those associated with Italian opera and sacred music in the early 18th century. LEDBETTER's similarly titled book is in fact quite differently conceived; it is an edition of several sets of exercises composed by Handel that provide advanced practice not only in continuo playing but in the related skills of improvised counterpoint and fugue. Ledbetter's commentary on the exercises is helpful even for those who will not make practical use of the exercises.

J.S. BACH similarly presents an annotated edition of 18th-century manuscript material. There is only weak evidence to connect the translated work directly to J.S. Bach; nevertheless, the book is valuable to scholars and reflects teachings with which Bach certainly would have been acquainted. Some of the examples will also provide continuo players with ideas for use in performing the music of Bach and his contemporaries.

Several recent scholarly works offer revisionist views on the instruments employed in the realization of baroque continuo parts. BORGIR shows that modern assumptions about the instrumentation of the continuo part in Italian baroque music have proved wrong; many performers have taken up his findings. DREYFUS surveys J.S. Bach's practices, but his arguments concerning so-called dual accompaniment—simultaneous use of harpsichord and organ in many of Bach's sacred vocal works—have not found full acceptance with scholars or performers. Both books are convenient sources for information about continuo parts and the instruments used for playing them in their respective repertories.

Those seeking instruction in continuo realization have traditionally turned to sets of exercises such as those mentioned above. In the 20th century, the exercises in MORRIS have proved popular in English-speaking countries. But although these consist in large part of extracts from J.S. Bach's works, Morris presupposes 19th-century concepts of harmony and performance that have been discarded by specialists in historical performance practice in favor of newly revived 17th- and 18th-century approaches.

KEANEY's primer represents an effort in the direction of 17th- and 18th-century performance practice, and its numerous elementary exercises have reportedly served beginners well, although it lacks substantial extracts from actual baroque music. The latter might be supplied in part from KELLER, which consists largely of brief extracts from historical treatises and compositions (and for this reason is too advanced for beginners). But Keller's almost exclusive limitation to German sources

(especially those of the 18th century) reflects the time and place of its original publication (Kassell, 1931); much of the author's commentary has also been superseded by more recent findings.

Probably the most valuable work of this type is that of WILLIAMS, which displays a much more generous chronological and geographical breadth in the sources for its musical and theoretical extracts than other comparable volumes do. The numerous and thoughtful hints on accompaniment are derived in part from the author's professional experience as a harpsichordist and organist as well as a music historian. The book includes a quick introduction to the rudiments of figured-bass realization, although beginners may require some preliminary preparation in keyboard harmony.

NORTH is intended as a comprehensive guide geared toward plucked string instruments such as the lute and guitar, which were neglected in all earlier treatments of the subject. It contains numerous extracts (including translations) from original sources concerning performance on those instruments, as well as musical examples; little of this material is readily available elsewhere, and for that reason the book is valuable to all musicians, not just players of plucked instruments. Reflecting its sources, it is oriented more toward the earlier than the later baroque.

DAVID SCHULENBERG

Convents

Kendrick, Robert, *Celestial Sirens: Nuns and Their Music in Early Modern Milan,* Oxford: Clarendon Press, and New York: Oxford University Press, 1996

Monson, Craig A., *Disembodied Voices: Music and Culture in an Early Modern Italian Convent,* Berkeley: University of California Press, 1995

Monson, Craig A., editor, *The Crannied Wall: Women, Religion, and the Arts in Early Modern Europe,* Ann Arbor: University of Michigan Press, 1992

Yardley, Anne Bagnall, "'Ful weel she soong the service dyvyne': The Cloistered Musician in the Middle Ages," in *Women Making Music: The Western Art Tradition, 1150–1950,* edited by Jane Bowers and Judith Tick, Urbana: University of Illinois Press, 1986

The tradition of female religious monasticism within the Catholic religion is an old one: the first convents of nuns were formed soon after the earliest Benedictine monasteries in the sixth century. Similarly, female convents associated with the Franciscan and Dominican orders formed in the 13th century. Because both monks and nuns were obligated under monastic rule to recite the Divine Office and Mass at prescribed times every day, the principal musical activity within both types of cloistered communities consisted of the singing of plainchant. Recent musicological research has centered on what other kinds of musical traditions were present within communities of nuns, focusing both on music written for nuns and by nuns. With the exception of scholarly work on the music of Hildegard von Bingen, research on the history of music in convents is in an early stage, with few books published. Monson (1995) and Kendrick are the most extensive studies available, each discussing the status of music in the female monastic houses of a different Italian city from the time of the Council of Trent (in the 16th century) to the 18th century.

The greater part of MONSON's (1995) book concentrates on one convent (Santa Cristina) and its primary nun composer, Lucrezia Orsina Vizzana, the only Bolognese nun to publish collections of her music. Monson offers a detailed history of post-Tridentine life at Santa Cristina (including details of a musical rivalry among the nuns that threatened the very existence of the convent), using this case study to describe convent women's culture in a more general sense. The most important aspect of the history of convent music in Bologna is how these religious houses maintained their musical traditions despite the strong and persistent opposition of the local episcopate. Monson devotes several chapters to the published works of Vizzana, analyzing the music and viewing their texts in the light of Vizzana's personal piety and the social dynamics of the crisis caused by musical rivalries among nuns. The book contains a number of lengthy musical examples, but the author makes an effort (not always successful) to keep the musical analyses nontechnical.

KENDRICK offers a detailed account of the surviving information about the post-Tridentine history of polyphonic music in the most prominent convents of Milan from the decade of the 1560s to 1706. Like Monson, he highlights the struggles between the nuns and a series of bishops over the constrictions of *clausura* (the enforced enclosure of nuns within their convent, allowing no contact with the outside world) on music making within the houses. Several composers among the nuns are given special attention, especially Chiara Margarita Cozzolani and, to a lesser extent, Rosa Giacinta Badalla, both of whose published music circulated in Germany, France, and Italy during their lifetimes. Kendrick also places the music of these nuns within the contemporary Milanese perspective, closely analyzing texts to a number of Cozzolani's and Badalla's motets, showing how they reflect the general spirituality of contemporary Milan as well as that of the nuns themselves. The last four chapters feature extensive musical analyses that will be difficult for readers not trained in music to follow.

While most of the contributions to MONSON (1992) deal with nonmusical subjects, three focus on convent music. The chapters by Monson ("Disembodied Voices: Music in the Nunneries of Bologna in the Midst of the Counter-Reformation") and Kendrick ("The Traditions of Milanese Convent Music and the Sacred Dialogues of Chiara Margarita Cozzolani") are both distillations of subject matter covered in their full-length book treatments of the same subjects. However, the information in Patrick Macey's chapter ("*Infiamma il mio cor*: Savonarolan *Laude* by and for Dominican Nuns in Tuscany") is published nowhere else. His work shows how *laude*, Italian-language spiritual texts sung to familiar strophic melodies, were an important part of the devotions of nuns in the area around Florence during the 16th century. A number of publications were intended for the use of nuns, and several were written by Caterina de' Ricci, an influential nun at San Vincenzo in Florence. Macey explains how some of the texts (subsequently suppressed by church authorities) exhibit the influence of the renegade priest Savonarola. The chapter is informative without being highly technical, and the use of musical examples is minimal.

YARDLEY's article provides important basic information and references for the history of chant singing in convents during the Middle Ages. She presents general discussions of the musical education of nuns, the organization of medieval monastic life, the requirements of the liturgy, the performance of liturgical drama and polyphony, and evidence of musical composition by nuns. Yardley keeps musical examples to a minimum and avoids the use of complex musical vocabularies.

DEBORAH KAUFFMAN

Copland, Aaron 1900–1990

United States composer, conductor, and writer

1. Biography

Berger, Arthur, *Aaron Copland*, New York: Oxford University Press, 1953

Butterworth, Neil, *The Music of Aaron Copland*, London: Toccata Press, 1985; New York: Universe Books, 1986

Copland, Aaron, *Our New Music: Leading Composers in Europe and America*, New York: McGraw-Hill, 1941; revised and enlarged as *The New Music, 1900–1960*, New York: Norton, and London: Macdonald, 1968

Copland, Aaron, and Vivian Perlis, *Copland: 1900 through 1942*, New York: St. Martin's Press/Marek, 1984

Copland, Aaron, and Vivian Perlis, *Copland: Since 1943*, New York: St. Martin's Press, 1989

Dobrin, Arnold, *Aaron Copland, His Life and Times*, New York: Crowell, 1967

Pollack, Howard, *Aaron Copland: The Life and Work of an Uncommon Man*, New York: Holt, 1999

Skowronski, JoAnn, *Aaron Copland: A Bio-Bibliography*, Westport, Connecticut: Greenwood Press, 1985

Smith, Julia, *Aaron Copland: His Work and Contribution to American Music*, New York: Dutton, 1955

Much of the extensive literature devoted to Aaron Copland regards him as the leading exponent of American art music during his era. Like many other composers, he matured when the creation of a characteristically American idiom of serious composition still meant separation from Europe. Yet well before his old age, Copland attained a breadth of achievement and recognition not only unprecedented in American music, but one which made him one of the most-discussed composers of the 20th century worldwide. Especially precipitating a wealth of articles, reviews, monographs, dissertations, and books were the following: Copland's compositional attempts to address a range of audiences encompassing lay listeners and cultivated publics alike; his vast organizational activities on behalf of numerous other American and contemporary composers, including for example, his involvement with the League of Composers and the American Composer's Alliance; his educational ventures at Tanglewood and elsewhere; and finally, his own prolific writings, which in many respects have given the literature on Copland its catchwords. By the late 1940s even critics abroad were perceiving in his accomplishments the heralding of American music's coming of age. In the 1950s the first full-length books solely about Copland also hailed his historical importance, although by that time musical trends were evolving further away from the Americanist aesthetic Copland had come to symbolize. Only recently has a marked resurgence of scholarly interest in Copland occurred. Much new scholarship now benefits from primary sources in the immense Aaron Copland Collection of the Library of Congress (the beneficiary of Copland's papers). Thus far, the tenor of this current research identifies previously neglected aspects of Copland's development without actually displacing the monopolizing effects nationalism and differences of compositional approach formerly had on research and writing in the field.

COPLAND includes a historically important chapter titled "Composer from Brooklyn: An Autobiographical Sketch." In its original version (reprinted in the original edition of this volume [1941] from a 1939 issue of the *Magazine of Art*), Copland outlines his development through mid-career, from musical beginnings to study with Nadia Boulanger in Paris (1921–24) to American repatriation and a subsequent interest in composing works identifiably American (first jazz-inspired and then intensely modernistic) to his emphasis on simplicity for the sake of reaching expanded audiences through increased compositional opportunities. Although citing the advent of new media (film, radio, and phonograph) and the importance of other functional demands (i.e., music for schools, dance, and theater), his statements regarding simplification in time proved controversial. The subsequent reprinting of this brief memoir (in the 1968 revised edition) adds a supplement from the perspective of 1967 both defending his original position and alluding to developments of his later career, including the adoption of serial techniques and his second livelihood from conducting.

Throughout the 1940s and beyond, Copland's "Autobiographical Sketch" provided the most salient and well-known articulations of his aims as a composer. As a mini-testament never disavowed, it was cited again and again by other writers seeking to characterize Copland's place in history.

Carefully prepared, SMITH's examination of Copland's life and works draws from her Ph.D. dissertation (1952), which seeks to determine the composer's position in American music and to assess his contributions. Her account remained the most thorough study until the 1980s, although it was somewhat criticized for its dry academic tone. Nevertheless, the categories she addresses—European versus American influences, issues of austerity and absolutism versus accessibility and referentialism, and the influences of audience and of media—persist as the standards by which Copland and his periodizations are typically judged. At times, Smith's presentation of biographical information is sufficiently detailed to rival that of later studies, as when she reports on Copland's travels. Her final chapter considers Copland's critical writings (from 1924 to 1955) and summarizes the composer's influence, although many readers of today may wince at the wisdom of arguing anyone is "the first definitive American composer."

Some of the most expert and incisive commentary on Copland comes from BERGER, whose first several pages address biographical matters, principally the composer's professional objectives. Berger himself maintained a long association with Copland, initially as a member of the Young Composer's Group, which Copland led in the early 1930s. Such firsthand knowledge and Berger's seeming ability to locate the musical quintessence of matters make this publication far more valuable and timeless than its short length and now dated discography and bibliography would suggest. Without any harm to his considerable technical sophistication, Berger avoids an abundance of detail that would make his text unreadable to nonmusicians.

Given the substantial music Copland composed for young people, the appearance of Copland biographies written specially for young readers seems highly appropriate. The work by DOBRIN for young people contains original information. Adult readers willing to overlook quaint evidence of humor and other limitations (owing to the genre and to a lack of specifically musical expertise) will find much of his writing richly suggestive and rewarding.

Details of time and place for Copland's compositional activity abound in BUTTERWORTH's introduction to the composer's music, although few other contextual and biographical references surface. The body of the text resembles superbly written program notes; the final chapter summarizes Copland's four books on music (*Copland on Music*, 1960; *Music and Imagination*, 1952; *What to Listen for in Music*, 1939, revised 1957; *Our New Music: Leading Composers in Europe and America*, 1941, revised and enlarged as *The New Music, 1900–1960*, 1968) in the order they were written. The book also reproduces an intriguing interview with Copland (by Leo Smit) on composing his piano music.

A modest biographical sketch opens the bio-bibliography by SKOWRONSKI, along with a chronological listing of Copland's compositions. Unfortunately, the work list repeats erroneous dates found elsewhere and reproduces similar omissions. Even so, other factors make this reference book indispensable: a vast discography; an annotated listing of most of Copland's published writings; and, finally, an annotated bibliography of over 1,000 sources about Copland and his music.

COPLAND and PERLIS (1984 and 1989) goes well beyond being autobiographical, for the two volumes array a variety of materials and perspectives into a multifaceted record of Copland's life. Sections in the first person (Copland's own autobiographical narratives) predominate, whereas sections in the third person (mainly connecting interludes by Perlis) contextualize and amplify Copland's discussion. Further commentary occurs in the form of recollections obtained from people close to Copland, who together comprise a roster of several luminaries. Copious facsimiles of photographs, letters, music manuscripts, and other documents also appear. Such devices create an imposing authoritativeness, as the first volume takes the reader from background on Copland's family and his early life to the time of his first duties at Tanglewood and the composition of his first intensely patriotic works, and as the second volume chronicles the continuation of his life in wartime United States to his eventual retirement in the 1970s (from composition) and 1980s (from conducting and making public appearances). A rarely discussed episode in Copland's life involving political troubles during the McCarthy era adds unusual spice to the second volume.

Unfortunately, as newspaper reports revealed around the time of his death, Copland suffered from Alzheimer's disease during the period in which work on the autobiography progressed. The two volumes thus ultimately owe their existence to the extraordinary intervention of their resourceful coauthor, who succeeds wonderfully in capturing a life without transmitting any hint of the dementia then affecting Copland. In view of the composer's illness, necessity rather than choice may have prompted many of the features that make the autobiography so unique and remarkable, including a heavy reliance by the authors both on interviews Perlis had obtained from Copland in the 1970s (for an oral history project in American music at Yale University) and on the composer's previous writings.

POLLACK's volume surveys Copland's complete works and examines virtually every significant critical topic circulating in Copland studies. Without slighting any main area of interest, whether aesthetic views, influences, personal characteristics, or professional activities, Pollack's main contribution to Copland biography may well be his unprecedented exploration of the composer's private life, going beyond familiar categories of identity, such as nationality and ethnicity (Jewishness), into sexuality. To some readers, a perspective so balanced and unapologetic might seem an impropriety. The book is not iconoclastic or irreverent, however, due to Pollack's sympathetic attitude and willingness to find musical significance in potentially every area of Copland's life. A full appreciation of the extraordinary richness of Copland's imagination and creativity marks Pollack's results. He cites an enormous amount of research and archival materials and, equally remarkably, assimilates their content for a wide readership. Finally, his catalog of Copland's compositions embodies one of the most complete lists yet to emerge.

DANIEL E. MATHERS

2. Works

Berger, Arthur, *Aaron Copland*, New York: Oxford University Press, 1953

Butterworth, Neil, *The Music of Aaron Copland*, London: Toccata Press, 1985; New York: Universe Books, 1986

Copland, Aaron, and Vivian Perlis, *Copland: 1900 through 1942*, New York: St. Martin's Press/Marek, 1984

———, *Copland: Since 1943*, New York: St. Martin's Press, 1989

Gleason, Harold, and Warren Becker, *20th Century American Composers*, 2nd edition, Bloomington, Indiana: Frangipani Press, 1980

Rosenfeld, Paul, *By Way of Art: Criticisms of Music, Literature, Painting, Sculpture, and the Dance*, New York: Coward-McCann, 1928

———, *An Hour with American Music*, Philadelphia, Pennsylvania: Lippincott, 1929

Skowronski, JoAnn, *Aaron Copland: A Bio-Bibliography*, Westport, Connecticut: Greenwood Press, 1985

Smith, Julia, *Aaron Copland: His Work and Contribution to American Music*, New York: Dutton, 1955

Thomson, Virgil, *American Music since 1910*, New York: Holt, Rinehart and Winston, 1971

To say that Aaron Copland's life consisted of composing, writing, and conducting would be an incredible understatement of this great composer's activities. He wrote more than 77 articles on music related topics from 1924 until 1964 and three books, including one that was substantially revised in the late 1960s. During his tenure as an active composer, Copland wrote the music for two operas, six ballets, and eight films, as well as numerous orchestral and chamber pieces, and keyboard, choral, and solo vocal works. According to the work list in the *New Grove Twentieth-Century American Masters* (1988), the number of compositions that comprise Copland's professional works totals over 100. The following review seeks to describe the multitudinous sources that in some fashion elucidate Copland's considerable accomplishments. There are many other sources available for those who wish to study his music; perhaps the best source is the composer's own letters and journals located in the Copland Archive at the Library of Congress.

Copland coauthored two semiautobiographical books with Yale oral historian Vivian Perlis. In both COPLAND and PERLIS (1984) and COPLAND and PERLIS (1989), Copland's recollections of events surrounding compositions and his numerous articles are interspersed with interviews from his colleagues and peers. Copland states of his 1948 Clarinet Concerto, for example, "I never would have thought of composing a clarinet concerto if Benny [Goodman] had not asked me for one. I can't play a single note on the instrument!"

Fellow composer BERGER's account of Copland's life and music is divided into two sections: the first contributes biographical information; the second examines Copland's development as a composer. Berger illustrates his point of view with musical examples from various compositions, including *Piano Variations, Billy the Kid,* and the *Short Symphony.* He includes a listing of Copland's juvenilia, recordings, and articles and books by Copland, as well as a select bibliography.

BUTTERWORTH's short book on Copland's music begins with a preface by André Previn. Butterworth succeeds in his goal to whet the appetite for Copland's works. He does not simply create a book full of musical examples that illustrate Copland's maturing musical style; he also pays attention to Copland the writer and discusses the books *What to Listen for in Music, Our New Music* and its revision as *The New Music, 1900–1960,* and *Music and Imagination.* Butterworth concludes with a conversation between Copland and Leo Smit concerning the piano music. There is also a list of compositions by genre, as well as chronologically.

SKOWRONSKI provides not only a listing of the known compositions and literary works but also a discography and bibliography of writings by and about Copland. She divides the works chronologically and includes performance and publication information.

SMITH's study of Copland's music is based on information gathered during work on her doctorate. Her contribution is exhaustive in its examination of all of the known compositions to 1955. Smith was among the first to state that Copland's music can be divided into clear-cut categories: French-Jazz, Abstract, American Folksong, and *Gebrauchsmusik* American Style.

THOMSON was Copland's friend and peer for almost 50 years and devotes the sixth chapter in his book to Copland. Thomson begins this section with a focus "on Copland as a colleague, a career man, and a mobilizer" because he considers Copland's contribution in those areas to be as remarkable as his music. Thomson follows Smith's lead in dividing the music into stylistic periods. He also notes that ballet was a major inspiration for Copland due to the excitement of conflicting rhythms that contrast in the dance genre with slow chantlike episodes. Thomson takes credit for steering Copland in the right direction by preparing the way with his own musical works.

GLEASON and BECKER provide an excellent resource for the music historian and educator. The lives and works of 17 U.S. composers are presented in outline form. After dividing Copland's compositions chronologically by performance medium, the authors provide detailed information concerning style, including compositional techniques and musical devices. The extensive bibliography contains general and specific references to Copland as well as the numerous articles by the composer.

Perhaps some of the most entertaining books that elucidate Copland's music are by his friend and critic, Paul Rosenfeld. In the chapter "Copland without the Jazz" in ROSENFELD (1928), the author likens Copland's musicianship to a young colt, "all legs, head and frisking hide." Each part of the "colt" illustrates a portion of Copland's musical style in the early stages of his career. In ROSENFELD (1929), the author compares Copland's music with that of Gershwin.

ROBERTA LINDSEY

Copyright

Bielefield, Arlene, and Lawrence Cheeseman, *Technology and Copyright Law: A Guidebook for the Library, Research, and Teaching Professions,* New York: Neal-Schuman, 1997

Brinson, J. Dianne, and Mark F. Radcliffe, *Multimedia Law and Business Handbook,* Menlo Park, California: Ladera Press, 1996

Bruwelheide, Janis H., *The Copyright Primer for Librarians and Educators,* Chicago: American Library Association, and Washington, D.C.: National Education Association, 1995

Crews, Kenneth D, *Copyright, Fair Use, and the Challenge for Universities: Promoting the Progress of Higher Education,* Chicago: University of Chicago Press, 1993

Gasaway, Laura N., and Sarah K. Wiant, *Libraries and Copyright: A Guide to Copyright Law in the 1990s,* Washington, D.C.: Special Libraries Association, 1994

Goldstein, Paul, *Copyright's Highway: From Gutenberg to the Celestial Jukebox,* New York: Hill and Wang, 1994

Jensen, Mary Brandt, *Does Your Project Have a Copyright Problem?: A Decision-Making Guide for Librarians*, Jefferson, North Carolina: McFarland, 1996

Patterson, L. Ray, and Stanley W. Lindberg, *The Nature of Copyright: A Law of Users' Rights*, Athens: University of Georgia Press, 1991

Shemel, Sidney, and M. William Krasilovsky, *This Business of Music*, New York: Billboard, 1964; 7th edition, 1995

Strong, William S., *The Copyright Book: A Practical Guide*, Cambridge, Massachusetts: MIT Press, 1981; 5th edition, 1999

The Copyright Act of 1976 (Title 17 U.S. Code) grants exclusive rights of reproduction, distribution, preparation of derivative works, performance, and display of "original works of authorship fixed in any tangible medium of expression" to copyright owners. Exceptions to these exclusive rights, the most notable of which is the fair use exception, were written into the law in order to promote the advancement of learning. Scholars, educators, performers, and librarians continue to struggle with interpreting the legal meaning of this balance between authors' and users' rights as the law applies to their roles as creators, users, and disseminators of intellectual property. Emerging new technologies, increasing globalization, and the legislative updates addressing issues related to copyright add further complexity to the topic.

This selection of books attempts to provide basic information about the nature of copyright and its application to the intellectual and artistic endeavors of people living in the United States today by offering snapshots of the topic from different perspectives. Copyright law is changing so rapidly that even relatively new monographs lack information on the most recent legislative developments; therefore, readers are encouraged to supplement their reading by referring to online resources such as the services provided by the Library of Congress.

STRONG provides a well-organized, general source for basic copyright questions. He examines the subject matter of copyright; copyright notice and registration; ownership and transfer of copyright; rights in copyrighted works; compulsory licenses; infringement and fair use; tax treatment of copyrights; and international copyright protection. Traditional media, as well as newer technologies such as computer programs, databases, and videotapes, are incorporated into the discussions. He also includes a chapter on interpreting copyright laws for works created before 1978.

Several of the general guides listed here cover the types of questions librarians and library users are likely to confront. BRUWELHEIDE is a standard primer that employs a question-and-answer format to address many of the issues of concern to librarians and educators. Sections on copying materials for use in schools and performance and to supplement the library-focused discussions

of photocopying, reserves, digitization, fair use, off-air recording, computer software, and databases.

After a brief historical overview of Anglo-American copyright law, GASAWAY and WIANT address copyright issues that most directly affect librarians and library users. Topics include a discussion of the application of Sections 107 and 108 of the Copyright Act of 1976 to library photocopying; licensing agencies and collectives; library duplication of audiovisual and non-print works; computer software and databases; unpublished works; and course reserves. Additional chapters address international copyright issues and the Public Lending Act.

JENSEN's goal is to provide a system for finding and analyzing copyright issues that can be used by librarians to assess more accurately potential copyright problems in their own projects. To that end, she has developed a series of ten flow charts, each of which serves as a step-by-step guide through a specific type of decision-making process. "Decision Chart 1," for example, enables the reader to decide whether or not a work is copyrighted; "Decision Chart 8" decides whether the use of a work is fair use. This book is not the best source for a quick answer to a specific copyright question, but it could be a valuable asset to the reader who is willing to invest some time in studying the process.

BIELEFIELD and CHEESEMAN add a focus on technology to a concise but comprehensive general source. In the first section, they summarize the historical and legal background of copyright and offer predictions for the future. A section on technology and copyright in libraries and classrooms includes an extensive discussion of fair use basics and applications; a consideration of Section 108, which enumerates special privileges for libraries and archives; and a chapter on licensing and other contractual agreements. In the last section, they examine the implications of copyright on distance learning and briefly discuss international copyright issues.

Although most sources discuss music and copyright at some level, the most complete coverage of issues related to intellectual property laws and printed music, sound recordings, and videos can often be found in books about the music industry. In a standard and frequently updated source for information on all aspects of the music business, SHEMEL and KRASILOVSKY present substantial information on relevant topics including copyright in sound recordings; music videos; record covers, labels, and liner notes; licensing of recordings for motion pictures; the nature of copyright in the United States; duration of copyright and limitation of grants; works for hire; performing rights organizations; foreign publishing; mechanical rights; arrangements and abridgements of music; co-ownership and joint administration of copyrights; uses and new versions of public domain music; infringements of copyrights; buying and selling copyrights; and international copyright protection. Discussions of related topics such as names and trademarks, protection of ideas and titles, and privacy and publicity rights also provide useful information.

BRINSON and RADCLIFFE address the legal issues involved in the development and distribution of multimedia in a source that will be valuable to anyone contemplating the development of either a commercial or an educational multimedia project. The authors survey the basics of intellectual property law; production relationships including work for hire and contractual agreements; use of preexisting works; and protection of the developer's intellectual property rights. A final section discusses online presentation, special exceptions for educators, and distance learning.

On a more philosophical level, GOLDSTEIN explores the influences of copyright optimists, copyright pessimists, and changing technologies on the evolution of copyright law from Gutenberg's time to the present. In a series of essays focusing on technological innovations such as the printing press, photography, sound recordings, photocopiers, VCRs, and personal computers, he shows how optimists, who assert the natural right of authors to full compensation for their labors, and pessimists, who believe creators should receive only as much payment as absolutely necessary to provide incentives to create new works, have tested their views in the courts with varying degrees of success. Describing his view of the future, Goldstein invokes the metaphor of a celestial jukebox from which information of all types will be available, at a price, to users on demand, allowing the optimists to reign.

PATTERSON and LINDBERG represent the "pessimist" point of view in a work that pushes the limits accepted by many writers on copyright. They outline the historical foundations of Anglo-American copyright, examine the nature of the law, and argue that copyright is fundamentally a grant of limited statutory monopoly, not a natural-law property right, and therefore the law protects a user's right as well as an author's right. Based on some of the ideas expressed in Patterson's earlier work, *Copyright in Historical Perspective* (1968), this argument takes the reader through various stages of copyright legislation including the Stationer's Copyright in 1557, the Statute of Anne in 1710, and the first U.S. copyright statute, the Copyright Act of 1790. Rather than providing a list of rules based on case precedents, the authors hope to lead readers to a better understanding of the basics of the law that will help users to make appropriate decisions and avoid giving away privileges that are rightfully theirs.

CREWS also encourages users, particularly those associated with research universities, to understand the right of fair use that Congress established and to be open to its opportunities for advancing the academic mission. In an empirical analysis of the copyright policies of 98 research universities across the United States, he found

that librarians and educators tended to employ unnecessarily restrictive guidelines regarding the educational use of copyrighted material.

CONSTANCE MAYER

Corelli, Arcangelo 1653–1713

Italian composer and violinist

Allsop, Peter, *Arcangelo Corelli: New Orpheus of Our Times*, Oxford: Clarendon Press, and New York: Oxford University Press, 1999
Apel, Willi, *Italian Violin Music of the Seventeenth Century*, edited by Thomas Binkley, Bloomington: Indiana University Press, 1990
Newman, William S., *The Sonata in the Baroque Era*, Chapel Hill: University of North Carolina Press, 1949; 4th edition, New York: Norton, 1983
Pincherle, Marc, *Corelli: His Life, His Work*, New York: Norton, 1956
Schwarz, Boris, *Great Masters of the Violin: From Corelli and Vivaldi to Stern, Zukerman, and Perlman*, New York: Simon and Schuster, 1983

The last half of the 20th century witnessed a proliferation of virtuosos and ensembles specializing in performances of baroque music and the widespread dissemination of diverse and inexpensive recordings of those performances, and, as a result, Arcangelo Corelli's name and his music have become better known than at any time since that of the composer himself. Nevertheless, surprisingly little is known of the composer's life, particularly about the years before he went to Rome, and surprisingly few authors have discussed musical influences on Corelli compared to the number who have discussed Corelli's influence on others.

The greatest step taken by a scholar to revive interest in Corelli was that of PINCHERLE, who published his French monograph in 1933. It is, unfortunately, too brief to be considered a complete study of the life and works of such a significant composer, performer, and teacher, unlike Mario Rinaldi's voluminous Italian monograph (*Arcangelo Corelli* [Milan, 1953]). Pincherle's undisguised disdain for Rinaldi's work, however, particularly for the biographical passages, prompted Pincherle to produce a "free reshaping" (more accurately, a retitled second edition) of his own work in 1954. The English-language version cited here is a translation of this second French edition and provides the best overview of Corelli's life and works currently available in English. The book is essential for anyone reading earlier sources, as it incorporates rigorous scholarship and careful documentation. The author takes great care to correct many erroneous notions about Corelli's life and musical career, some arising from simple confusion of names (misreading that of Cavalli or Torelli, for instance, for that of Corelli), and he discredits many cherished anecdotes that had masqueraded as biography since the 18th century. Pincherle discusses each collection of works separately, devoting approximately 30 pages to the trios of opp. 1–4, 35 to the solo sonatas of op. 5, and 20 to the concerti grossi, op. 6. An extensive musical bibliography, the first of its kind and still useful, lists editions of Corelli's works, original or arranged, and various spurious attributions.

Pincherle also brings to his work a broad understanding of the context of Corelli's work (he also wrote an authoritative monograph on Vivaldi), which shows especially in the chapter concerning Corelli's influence in Italy, France, England, and Germany. This understanding springs from a firsthand knowledge of musical sources. Moreover, Pincherle reports for the first time the existence of the Dubourg Manuscript, then owned by concert pianist Alfred Cortot, which has since shed much light on ornamentation practices of the time. Many of Pincherle's remarks are of general interest, ranging beyond the world of violinists alone. He shows, for example, how Corelli's own written-out ornamentation applies to fast as well as slow movements, how there was less difference in style between the *sonata da chiesa* and the *sonata da camera* than has been often supposed, and how performers were invited to choose some movements and omit others of multimovement sonatas. The author additionally contends that Corelli's music did not make great technical demands of the performers, but that his genius lay in his striving for "a constant perfection, a voluntary moderation, and an exemplary sense of proportion."

It is by these same two techniques—the critical evaluation of anecdotes and the use of primary documents, that ALLSOP contributes. His study of Corelli, much longer than that of Pincherle and incorporating many musical examples, uses "extensive archival research over recent years" to dispel "much of the anecdote and hearsay accumulated over the centuries," while providing "a more balanced evaluation of Corelli's true status in the development of the prime instrumental genres," each of which is considered in separate chapters.

NEWMAN observes that Corelli "standardized and internationalized the Italian sonata almost single-handedly." Newman covers much ground quickly and manages to put the composer and his music in historical context. He argues that the popularity of Corelli is proven by the great number of reprints of his music and compares in passing Corelli's compositional strengths and weaknesses with those of several contemporaries. The musical discussion is not highly technical; it chiefly concerns movement types or categories and the relative importance of those types within the total work of the composer. Newman's overall judgment echoes Pincherle, seeing in Corelli's music less stylistic or technical innovation than in that of certain contemporaries, but admiring

him for "a remarkable sense of balance in the concentration and direction of his musical forces."

The section devoted to Corelli in APEL is fuller than that found in Newman and makes greater use of technical language. Apel provides a useful survey of Corelli's work opus by opus, focusing particularly on formal elements and, to a lesser extent, on musical style and violinistic technique. The author's analysis of compositional techniques used by Corelli make this book the best choice for those seeking information on the music alone. Apel is uninterested in the composer's life: neither Cardinal Ottoboni nor Queen Christina of Sweden are mentioned. But where relevant, Apel draws comparisons to earlier or contemporary composers. A thorough list of first and other early editions is provided, keyed to the Répertoire international des sources musicales (RISM), which should be invaluable to many researchers. Writing in 1983, Apel was able to make use of the Corelli catalogue raisonné by Hans Joachim Marx, who referred in the volume *Werke ohne Opuszahl* (1976) to a particular sinfonia written in 1689 that proved that Corelli had indeed, as has been supposed by musicologists, "cultivated the concerto grosso long before the publication of Concerti grossi, Opus 6, in 1712."

SCHWARZ's brief account of Corelli is the most popular in nature of those listed here, and extensive musical knowledge is not presupposed of the reader. The basic movements of Corelli's career are mentioned, as are the important professional connections that shaped that career. Schwarz is less useful to those looking for insights into Corelli's music than to those seeking basic biographical information. It should be used in conjunction with other sources, however, as oft-repeated "traditions" concerning Corelli—that is, the anecdotes prevalent in earlier writing—are related without critical comment.

GLENN BURDETTE

Counterpoint

Fux, Johann Joseph, *The Study of Counterpoint from Johann Joseph Fux's Gradus ad Parnassum*, translated by Alfred Mann, New York: Norton, 1943; revised edition, 1971

Gauldin, Robert, *A Practical Approach to Eighteenth-Century Counterpoint*, Englewood Cliffs, New Jersey: Prentice Hall, 1988

———, *A Practical Approach to Sixteenth-Century Counterpoint*, Englewood Cliffs, New Jersey: Prentice Hall, 1985

Jeppesen, Knud, *Counterpoint: The Polyphonic Vocal Style of the Sixteenth Century*, translated by Glen Haydon, New York: Prentice-Hall, 1939; reprint, New York: Dover, 1992

Morley, Thomas, *A Plaine and Easie Introduction to Practicall Musick*, London, 1597; reprint, New York: Norton, 1963

Salzer, Felix, and Carl Schachter, *Counterpoint in Composition: The Study of Voice Leading*, New York: McGraw-Hill, 1969

Schenker, Heinrich, *Counterpoint*, 2 vols., translated by John Rothgeb and Jürgen Thym, New York: Schirmer Books, and London: Collier Macmillan, 1987

Tinctoris, Johannes, *The Art of Counterpoint*, translated by Albert Seay, [Rome]: American Institute of Musicology, 1961

Zarlino, Gioseffo, *The Art of Counterpoint: Part Three of Le Istitutioni harmoniche, 1558*, translated by Guy A. Marco and Claude V. Palisca, New Haven, Connecticut: Yale University Press, 1968

Counterpoint is the art of combining musical parts into polyphony. It respects principles of consonance and dissonance, of rhythmic coordination, and of style. In contrast to harmony, counterpoint addresses the linear relations among notes. Up to the end of the 16th century, counterpoint embodied the principles for composing in the polyphonic vocal style and represented the dominant mode of thinking about musical structure and composition. As harmonic and melodic thought exerted an increasing influence on musical thinking in the succeeding centuries, counterpoint adapted itself to the common-practice style as the art of voice leading. Jeppesen's chapter titled "Outline History of Contrapuntal Theory" summarizes the historical development of the study of counterpoint.

TINCTORIS was the first to postulate general rules of counterpoint as the basis of practical composition. Appearing at the beginning of the Renaissance period, the eight rules of Tinctoris are justly famous. Among them are technical points, such as the beginning and ending of a composition on perfect consonances, and general principles, such as "the parts should sound well together." Other parts of the work, which examine intervallic relations between paired voices in minute detail, reflect the thought of his predecessors, such as Ugolino of Orvieto.

Part 3 of ZARLINO's treatise is a thoroughgoing treatment of counterpoint and the first to present the principles of composition in a comprehensive manner. In addition to providing a clear and systematic presentation of the fundamentals of counterpoint, Zarlino devotes considerable attention to the arts of imitative and double (invertible) counterpoint. He includes a table that indicates the intervals that ought to be used in four-part counterpoint. An important aspect of this table is its illustration of an intervallic as opposed to a harmonic approach to multivoice counterpoint in the 16th century. Zarlino exerted considerable influence on a wide range of subsequent theorists, including Artusi, Tigrini, and Sweelinck.

MORLEY approaches the study of counterpoint from a practical point of view, beginning with the rudiments of singing and of the hexachords rather than modes and intervals. Part 2 sets out the principles of two-part counterpoint and has many illustrations, whereas part 3 discusses counterpoint for three and more voices. Morley focuses on practical techniques, such as adding descants and additional voices to existing plainchant. He does not concern himself with theoretical issues such as mode. Morley's claim that his treatise follows the method of his master, William Byrd, gives the volume considerable historical importance.

FUX extracts the core of his *Gradus ad Parnassum* (1725). Here, in presenting the five "species" of counterpoint on a cantus firmus, Fux establishes a new pedagogical approach. The first four species of counterpoint link rhythmic values with consonance and dissonance in a systematic manner. Written in the form of a dialogue between teacher and pupil, this work remains impeccable in form and content to this day and has to some degree influenced all subsequent studies of counterpoint. However, it is this work that first established the study of counterpoint as an abstract and historical discipline distinct from the study of composition. We attribute this development to the fact that Fux chose to work within the strict style of dissonance treatment characteristic of Renaissance music rather than the free style characteristic of the baroque.

Two centuries later, SCHENKER revisited the species counterpoint of Fux in exacting detail and at the same time commented on many exponents of Fux's work in the work of composers such as Bellermann, Albrechtsberger, and Cherubini, all of which follow Fux's method of strict counterpoint. Schenker's declared purpose is to study "pure" counterpoint without reference to harmony, and it is in this sense that Schenker's work takes counterpoint to a new level of abstraction. Nevertheless, Schenker remains surprisingly flexible in regard to the musical applications of counterpoint. For example, Schenker prohibits the *cambiata* in the strictest application of third species but recognizes its suitability to a freer context. In treating the problem of parallel fifths, Schenker suggests that the number of notes that must intervene to "hide" the fifths depends on context.

JEPPESEN represents a wholly new approach to the study of counterpoint that has become increasingly popular as historical musicology has developed. Growing especially from his analytical studies of the music of Palestrina, Jeppesen's approach emphasizes style rather than abstract principles while still retaining the species of Fux. Thus, counterpoint becomes a practical means for studying musical gestures and idioms.

SALZER and SCHACHTER is a textbook based on Schenker's work. The major differences are that two- and three-part counterpoint are considered together rather than sequentially, that harmonic function is integrated with counterpoint, and that an introduction to imitative techniques is included. The excellent examples from the literature include detailed analytical graphs. Thus, Salzer and Schachter represents a synthesis of Schenkerian contrapuntal and analytic theories. Schenker's theory is further clarified by explaining contrapuntal patterns in terms of motion and of tension and release rather than by referring to psychological interpretations. The final chapter contains an analytical anthology of polyphonic music ranging from Binchois through Scriabin.

GAULDIN's twin textbooks represent the best current work in counterpoint and include both technical and stylistic components presented in a systematic manner. In recognition of the stylistic aspects of counterpoint, Gauldin includes in his 16th-century study such topics as text setting, parody technique, and the "familiar" style. His 18th-century study includes such important topics as chromaticism, chorale preludes, fugue, and classical style, rounding out the study of counterpoint as a creative and reflective mastering of historical compositional styles and genres.

WILLIAM RENWICK

Couperin, François 1668–1733

French composer, harpsichordist, and pedagogue

Beaussant, Philippe, *François Couperin,* translated by
  Alexandra Land, Portland, Oregon: Amadeus Press, 1990
Brunold, Paul, *François Couperin,* translated by J.B. Hanson,
  Monaco: Lyrebird Press, 1949
Higginbottom, Edward, and Graham Sadler, "François
  Couperin," in *The New Grove French Baroque Masters,*
  edited by James R. Anthony et al., London: Macmillan, and
  New York: Norton, 1986
Mellers, Wilfrid, *François Couperin and the French Classical
  Tradition,* Durham: Dobson, 1950; new revised edition,
  London: Faber, 1987

Twentieth-century research on François Couperin took place in spurts rather than in a steady progression. There was a flowering of interest especially after World War II and another resurgence of Couperin scholarship in the late 1960s—probably due to the tercentenary of Couperin's birth. The early music revival has no doubt contributed to the more steady interest in Couperin's music of recent years, but large-scale English-language studies on Couperin still comprise only a handful of works.

In the preface to the first edition of his book, MELLERS states that it is the first book on Couperin in the English language. First published in 1950, it remained the only large-scale English-language study on Couperin for over three decades, even up to the publication of the revised expanded edition in 1987. The new version retains the original text with only minor revisions, with most of the new material presented in an added chapter and a series of addenda at the end of the book. Part 1 concentrates on the composer's life and times. Mellers not only gives a factual biography of the composer but also contextualizes Couperin's life experiences within the social milieu of the day—including the accompanying tastes and aesthetic values. In Part 2 the author gives a detailed descriptive analysis of all of Couperin's known works, examining each work by genre and also providing a brief account of the history and tradition of each genre. The analyses often include Mellers's own judgments of the particular work's merit in the overall repertoire as well as its significance in Couperin's compositional development. Part 3 deals with theory and practice, with commentary on the composer's *L'Art de toucher le clavecin* and suggestions for modern performance. The various appendices and addenda consider topics such as instruments, tuning systems, dance tempos, ornamentation, and the relationship of bowings and fingerings to musical phrasing. There is also a handbook to the harpsichord pieces that provides a gloss to the titles, people, and places attached to the individual pieces. This book is highly useful as an introduction or springboard for further research; however, it can also prove to be frustrating to English-only readers. Nearly all of the major quotations from primary sources (and there are many) are in untranslated French. Scholars may also be frustrated by the lack of clear references, as there are no footnotes to any of the quotations and only sketchy information about their sources.

Mellers's claim in 1950 that his was the first book in English on François Couperin was not entirely accurate, for in 1949 BRUNOLD published a short monograph on the subject. The introduction explains that the book derived from the author's collection of notes and observations on Couperin. After a brief overview of Couperin's life, Brunold presents his observations on an assortment of Couperin's works. The author discusses the pieces that he considers especially noteworthy, giving a brief description and examining them from the performer's point of view. Of special interest is the monograph's section of portraits and documents. It contains plates of four different portraits of Couperin and a facsimile of his signature. Those interested in historical recordings may also find the discography of some interest with its list of pre-1949 recordings.

BEAUSSANT's volume makes an interesting comparison with Mellers's. Whereas the latter weaves Couperin's biography into the tapestry of the 17th- and 18th-century French aesthetic, Beaussant presents Couperin's life mainly through the interpretation of legal deeds and official documents. He avoids, however, a dry rendition of facts and figures, injecting a great deal of warmth and human emotion into his rendering of Couperin's life and work. Whereas Mellers presents Couperin as an 18th-century man shrouded in a veil of nostalgia for the past of Louis XIII—someone who lived in his world but was not quite of his world—Beaussant presents Couperin as a man of his time and as a vital part of his world's everyday workings. Like Mellers, Beaussant undertakes an analysis of each of Couperin's known works but avoids theoretical analysis and focuses instead on providing the reader with an in-depth listener's guide. In his examination of the music, he often includes discussion on the historical background of the piece or the genre, as well as a description of the setting or occasion for which the music was used. He also uses his exploration of the music as a means to trace Couperin's development as a composer. Tables compare Couperin's activities with those of other harpsichord composers and also juxtapose events in his career with coinciding historical and artistic events. Readers may find the discography of some interest.

For a concise rendering (50 pages) of Couperin's life and works, readers may turn to HIGGINBOTTOM and SADLER. After providing a straightforward, factual chronicling of Couperin's life, the author offers a discussion on Couperin's works, dividing his examination into sections on style, organ music, instrumental chamber music, vocal music, harpsichord music, and theoretical works. He gives a brief general background on each of the works or genres and also sets forth a brief synopsis of the work with comments on scoring, stylistic and formal characteristics, and Couperin's development as a composer. At the end of the chapter is a work list and short bibliography.

MARGOT MARTIN

Cowell, Henry 1897–1965

United States-born composer

Cowell, Henry, *New Musical Resources*, with an essay by David Nicholls, Cambridge: Cambridge University Press, 1996

Lichtenwanger, William, *The Music of Henry Cowell: A Descriptive Catalog*, Brooklyn, New York: Institute for Studies in American Music, 1986

Manion, Martha L., *Writings about Henry Cowell: An Annotated Bibliography*, Brooklyn, New York: Institute for Studies in American Music, 1982

Nicholls, David, *American Experimental Music, 1890–1940*, Cambridge: Cambridge University Press, 1990

Rich, Alan, *American Pioneers: Ives to Cage and Beyond*, London: Phaidon, 1995

Saylor, Bruce, "Henry Cowell," in *The New Grove Twentieth-Century American Masters*, edited by John Kirkpatrick et al., London: Macmillan, and New York: Norton, 1988

———, *The Writings of Henry Cowell: A Descriptive Bibliography*, Brooklyn, New York: Institute for Studies in American Music, 1977

As of yet, a definitive biography of Henry Cowell remains to be published. In fact, despite Cowell's importance to American music as a composer, writer, and editor from the 1920s until his death in 1965, there is a relative paucity of published books on his life and music. The few published sources fall into two groups: reference sources and musical analyses. The three monographs (Lichtenwanger, Manion, and Saylor [1977]) published by the Institute for Studies of American Music provide crucial details about Cowell's music and published writings, as well as a bibliography of writings about Cowell. Both Nicholls and Rich place Cowell within the American experimental tradition through analyses and discussions of his music.

SAYLOR (1977) provides valuable descriptions of all of Cowell's published writings. The study is organized into three parts: books, articles and reviews, and score prefaces and recording liner notes. The last category includes substantial excerpts or complete texts. Saylor's commentary on each publication is succinct and pertinent, often including direct quotations to illustrate Cowell's ideas.

A complementary volume to Saylor (1977), MANION indices and annotates over 1,300 published writings about Cowell. These publications include periodical articles, encyclopedia entries, and newspaper reviews, dating between 1914 and 1975, that address Cowell's biography, published writings and lectures, performances, musical style, and recordings. Presenting this exhaustive collection of international sources, Manion compiles a survey of reactions to and opinions about Cowell from his childhood to ten years after his death. Her annotations identify the purpose of the published writing and often include extensive quotations from the primary sources. Annotations are in English, although most direct quotations from non-English sources are left untranslated.

Like Saylor (1977) and Manion, LICHTENWANGER is most valuable as a reference source. Lichtenwanger's catalog is the most comprehensive descriptive list of Cowell's compositions. The approximate chronological listing indices Cowell's complete oeuvre of almost 1,000 works, with information on dates, texts, instrumentation, premieres, manuscripts, publication, and general comments. The author integrates unique observations on everything from manuscript addenda to Cowell's and Cowell's wife's descriptions of the compositions. The introductory chapter, "Henry Cowell: Mind over Music," explores Cowell's intellectual disposition, focusing on Lewis M. Terman's study of Cowell as a boy. Although intriguing, the chapter digresses into a somewhat puzzling comparison of Cowell's musical approaches with the multiple intelligences theories of Howard Gardner.

An extension of the entry about Cowell in the *New Grove Dictionary of American Music* (1986), SAYLOR (1988) is a factual narrative of Cowell's life and major works. While helpful for the specialist, the analysis is at times advanced and includes specialized terms without explanation. Saylor also introduces other major musical figures without elaboration, which may prove frustrating for some. However, the chapter includes an excellent work list prepared by Lichtenwanger with Elizabeth A. Wright.

In his collection on experimental composers, RICH emphasizes the most progressive aspects of Cowell's music. The general biography is balanced by a stylistic overview of Cowell's extensive and varied output. Rich's examination of the diverse musical, aesthetic, and philosophical influences on Cowell reveal "both the eclectic genius of Cowell himself and the polyglot nature of his America." His descriptions of stylistic elements and approaches are intriguing and succinct: analyses of the major works are approachable and insightful. Unfamiliar terms are defined and other major musical figures are introduced. Although it lacks references, this is a meritorious volume that includes valuable reproductions of photographs and recital programs.

NICHOLLS presents a thorough overview of many of Cowell's most experimental works, including the String Quartet no. 1, *Ensemble,* and the *Quartet Romantic.* The author examines Cowell's style with an emphasis on progressive compositional techniques; the analyses are demanding and aimed at the specialist. Illustrated with numerous musical examples and structural charts, the chapter places Cowell's compositional experiments within the context of the composer's book *New Musical Resources,* published in 1930.

A complement to his earlier study, Nicholls's essay on *New Musical Resources* in COWELL is a more extensive investigation of Cowell's book. The author painstakingly retraces the history of the work's evolution by comparing extant manuscript sources. Further, Nicholls correlates Cowell's own music, the music of his contemporaries, and more contemporary music with the techniques discussed in the volume. Although the analysis is somewhat involved, the observations are pertinent, thoughtful, and timely.

GAYLE SHERWOOD

Crawford, Ruth Porter 1901–1953

United States composer

Gaume, Matilda, *Ruth Crawford Seeger: Memoirs, Memories, Music,* Metuchen, New Jersey: Scarecrow Press, 1986

Hisama, Ellie, "Gender, Politics, and Modernist Music: Analysis of Five Compositions by Ruth Crawford (1901–1953) and Marion Bauer (1887–1955)," Ph.D. dissertation: City University of New York, 1996

Nicholls, David, *American Experimental Music, 1890–1940,* Cambridge: Cambridge University Press, 1990

Straus, Joseph N., *The Music of Ruth Crawford,* Cambridge: Cambridge University Press, 1995

Tick, Judith, *Ruth Crawford Seeger: A Composer's Search for American Music,* New York: Oxford University Press, 1997

Since her death in 1953, interest in the composer Ruth Crawford has grown steadily, but the meteoric rise in Crawford scholarship over the last two decades alone has done even more to further her reputation. It has also helped to solidify her importance in the history of music in the United States. Although the approach to her music varies considerably, two themes commonly recur in the field: the innovative construction of her 1931 String Quartet and her application of Charles Seeger's theory of dissonant counterpoint. Beyond this, the writing on Crawford's music has ranged widely from mostly historical narratives to theoretically oriented studies.

GAUME is the author of the first full-length biography on Crawford. Her book divides into three parts. Part 1 is a generally solid discussion of the composer's life that is based on diverse sources. The primary materials include Crawford's letters and diaries (which are conserved in the Seeger Collection in the Music Division of The Library of Congress), contemporary newspaper and periodical reviews, and interviews with Crawford's family, friends, and colleagues. Part 2 begins with a brief sketch of Crawford's art music, moves to a summary of her folk music activities, and concludes with excerpts of Crawford's own writings (letters, "jottings," poems, stories, and articles). Among the most relevant information in part 3 is a catalog of Crawford's music. Given the wealth of information, there is something for everyone in Gaume's book. Despite its many strengths, however, Gaume's biography is neither as illuminating nor as broad as Tick's, and her descriptive musical analyses have been largely superseded by more recent analytic studies.

The most comprehensive book on Crawford to date is by TICK. It may also be classified as a biography, but the contents range far more broadly. Proceeding within a chronological format, she interweaves a well-documented biography with insightful analyses, drawing examples from virtually all of Crawford's music. In addition, she considers Crawford from several different perspectives—as a young composer operating within the male-dominated avant-garde circles in Chicago and New York during the 1920s and 1930s; as an enthusiastic participant in the American folk music revival and radical social movements of the 1930s; and as a mature woman struggling to balance the responsibilities of marriage, motherhood, and career. Particularly fascinating is Tick's discussion of the cast of characters who played a part in Crawford's life story. We meet not only famous composers but also less well known figures such as Madame Djane Lavoie Herz, Crawford's temperamental patron, and Imre Weisshaus (Paul Arma), her friend and rival in Berlin. In the two appendices, Tick includes Crawford's own analysis of the third and fourth movements of her famous string quartet as well as a chronological checklist of Crawford's compositions, folk song transcriptions, and folk song arrangements.

STRAUS's book is perhaps the most sophisticated analytic study of Crawford. To interpret her music, he not only invokes Seeger's theoretical approach but also relies on more recent concepts and techniques of atonal theory, drawing most heavily on pitch-class set theory. For readers unfamiliar with set theory, Straus's technical explanations may seem dense and formidable, but his writing style is always lucid and coherent. He essentially divides his book into three parts. In the first, he considers the basic elements of Crawford's style, organizing his discussion according to Seeger's compositional categories (including melody, register, and large-scale design). In the second part, he presents detailed analyses of six works, often finding fascinating dramatic associations in them. The demonstration works are two of the *Three Songs,* which set poems of Carl Sandburg, two movements of the String Quartet, and two movements of the Suite for Wind Quintet. In the final chapter, Straus contextualizes Crawford's music in light of her biography, the ultra-modern movement, and the history of women in music. He makes an important contribution to the current literature on Crawford, and readers cannot help but be impressed by his authoritative and penetrating analyses.

The only other sizable theoretical study on Crawford is by HISAMA, whose main concern is to show how gender and politics informed Crawford's musical thought. Specifically, she argues that the third and fourth movements of the String Quartet convey Crawford's own experience of discrimination against women composers; in her reading of the 1932 song "Chinaman, Laundryman," the author identifies a musical link to Crawford's leftist politics. In constructing her intensive analyses, Hisama relies heavily on aspects of contour theory and literary theory, and she also devises two analytic tools of her own ("contour deviance" and "degree of twist"). Readers will undoubtedly be impressed by her multivalent approach, but some might shy away from the purely technical aspects of her discussion (which are extensive). However, there is much good to be gleaned from Hisama's study. Above all, it ultimately takes us beyond a strictly musical context, thereby broadening our understanding of Crawford's ideas.

Within NICHOLLS's sweeping survey of experimental music in the United States are valuable analytic readings of Crawford's compositions, some of which have previously received only cursory attention. The author offers substantial coverage of the *Four Diaphonic Suites, Three Chants,* String Quartet, and *Three Songs.* Due to space limitations, Nicholls does not explore these works in great depth, but he succeeds in contributing an efficient introduction to Crawford's music. One of the more provocative features of his book are the musical connections he identifies between specific works of Crawford and younger experimental composers. Before the issue of her legacy can be addressed, however, Nicholls's brief and unnuanced observations demand further exploration.

TERESA DAVIDIAN

Criticism: 18th and 19th Centuries

Berlioz, Hector, *The Art of Music and Other Essays,* translated and edited by Elizabeth Csicsery-Rónay, Bloomington: Indiana University Press, 1994

Cowart, Georgia, *The Origins of Modern Musical Criticism: French and Italian Music, 1600–1750,* Ann Arbor, Michigan: UMI Research Press, 1981

Ellis, Katharine, *Music Criticism in Nineteenth-Century France: La Revue et Gazette musicale de Paris, 1834–1880,* Cambridge: Cambridge University Press, 1995

Graf, Max, *Composer and Critic: Two Hundred Years of Musical Criticism,* New York: Norton, 1946; London: Chapman and Hall, 1947

Hanslick, Eduard, *Music Criticisms, 1846–99,* translated and edited by Henry Pleasants, Baltimore, Maryland: Penguin, 1950; London: Gollancz, 1951

Haskell, Harry, editor, *The Attentive Listener: Three Centuries of Music Criticism,* London: Faber, 1995; Princeton, New Jersey: Princeton University Press, 1996

Hoffmann, E.T.A., *E.T.A. Hoffmann's Musical Writings: Kreisleriana, The Poet and the Composer, Music Criticism,* edited by David Charlton, translated by Martyn Clarke, Cambridge: Cambridge University Press, 1989

Morrow, Mary Sue, *German Music Criticism in the Late Eighteenth Century: Aesthetic Issues in Instrumental Music,* Cambridge: Cambridge University Press, 1997

Murphy, Kerry, *Hector Berlioz and the Development of French Music Criticism,* Ann Arbor, Michigan: UMI Research Press, 1988

Plantinga, Leon, *Schumann as Critic,* New Haven, Connecticut: Yale University Press, 1967

Saloman, Ora Frishberg, *Beethoven's Symphonies and J.S. Dwight: The Birth of American Music Criticism,* Boston: Northeastern University Press, 1995

Shaw, Bernard, *Shaw's Music: The Complete Musical Criticism,* 3 vols., edited by Dan H. Laurence, New York: Dodd, Mead, and London: Reinhardt, 1981; 2nd revised edition, 1989

Music criticism in the 18th and 19th centuries aesthetically evaluated musical works of art. Such criticism could reflect, challenge, interpret, or promote musical tastes and stylistic changes within historical and social contexts. Whatever the mix of scholarly criticism and journalism, the criteria for aesthetic judgment may have depended on the critic's predilections, the aims and affiliations of the critical document, and the readership to which it was directed, among other factors. The development of active public concert life in the 19th century increased awareness of criticism's potentially significant guiding role. Criticism has recently become an important field of musicological research, as musical works and the history of their critical receptions or changing performance practices are analyzed within broad cultural frameworks.

GRAF's history of music criticism in the 18th and 19th centuries is an early survey in English by a former practitioner. Although it has been superseded by recent scholarly books and dissertations that consider aspects of the subject in detail, it remains a serviceable general introduction. Placing criticism within the general development of ideas in history enables the author to integrate information about music critics and magazines in a clear and eminently readable presentation.

Among the available anthologies of journalistic criticism, HASKELL's recent compilation offers a welcome selection of translated excerpts extending beyond Western Europe. It is useful for those seeking a chronologically organized overview that takes into account, among other themes, operatic controversies of the 18th century and the growth of program music in the 19th century. The engaging selection and the editor's sympathetic view of the critic primarily as "the attentive listener" support a broadly inclusive approach.

COWART's work appropriately places national stylistic controversies of the 18th century, often called the Age of Criticism, within a larger framework of aesthetics resulting from an interaction of criticism and philosophy. She traces how the earlier opposition between "objective" preference for the style of the ancients and "subjective" preference for the modern Italian style tended toward reconciliation at mid-century in a French critical mode, also developed somewhat later by German critics, "based on rational, comparative analysis and tempered with the description of personal response and appreciation." As a revision of a doctoral thesis, this study is necessarily a detailed exposition.

MORROW describes the development of a practical aesthetic vocabulary for evaluating new instrumental music in late 18th-century Germany, using as her sources over 1,000 reviews of printed instrumental music appearing in German-language periodicals and newspapers between 1760 and 1798. She demonstrates how a "review collective" initially engaged technical problems of independent instrumental composition and then rejected the older mimetic doctrine of the imitation of nature as it considered genius and unity deriving from purely musical factors. Readers with a developed appreciation of musical issues in that era will find the material stimulating.

A rich selection of translated music criticism and imaginative writings invites the English-speaking reader into the world of HOFFMANN, the influential German music critic, composer, and author. Charlton's excellent introductions and notes provide context for Hoffmann's extraordinary essays, which represent issues and describe pieces characteristic of the transitional era spanning 18th-century classicism and early 19th-century romanticism. The volume contains primarily texts never previously translated into English or hitherto inaccessible in English as complete entities.

SALOMAN's book is the first to identify documentary connections between diverse European critical, literary, and musical sources, and early American critical responses to Ludwig van Beethoven's symphonies. Considering essays addressed to the literate public by John Sullivan Dwight, the first major U.S.-born critic of art music, the author traces the formation of his career from 1835 to 1846 and his role in setting a new standard for musical discourse. Saloman also places Dwight's conceptions of Beethoven in the context of New England transcendentalist thought and activities at Brook Farm, the utopian community in Massachusetts. This work contributes to an understanding of the development of mid-19th-century American musical culture.

PLANTINGA's volume on Robert Schumann's criticism in the *Neue Zeitschrift für Musik*, the music journal Schumann helped found in 1834 and edited from 1835 until 1844, is well organized and invites careful study or, for the curious music lover, profitable browsing. Extracts from Schumann's reviews are presented with insightful commentary and occasional musical excerpts. There are sections analyzing the journal's high goals, Schumann's role in it, and his views of music both historical and contemporary. Schumann's importance as a critic of 19th-century music and his musical tastes emerge clearly from this work.

MURPHY provides useful background for understanding French critical developments by examining the role of music criticism in early 19th-century journals and newspapers. Chapters on Hector Berlioz's critical position and contemporary critical practices are followed by an overview of his actual criticism written primarily between 1823 and 1837 and divided according to vocal and instrumental categories. Murphy's approach is thoughtful; by situating Berlioz's work "as part of a critical community, not as an isolated phenomenon," she underscores the importance of the critic's shared concerns with other writers even as she delineates reasons for the superiority of his music criticism.

A sampling of BERLIOZ's superb music criticism in French publications is available in Csicsery-Rónay's recent translation with notes. The volume contains essays and shorter extracts that the composer-critic had collected for republication in 1862 but which had initially appeared primarily in the *Gazette Musicale* and the *Journal des Débats*. Readers will find enjoyable and informative Berlioz's discerning commentaries about works by composers he admires, including Beethoven, Carl Maria von Weber, and Christoph Willibald Gluck, as well as his ironic appraisals of the state of performance in Paris.

ELLIS offers an admirable and detailed scholarly examination of an important French music periodical that was addressed to a limited, musically literate readership. She analyzes the mid-19th-century music criticism contained in that journal while positing a general reception history of works performed in France between 1834 and 1880 and assessing the underlying philosophical framework permeating the reviews. In the process, she considers how a musical canon took form and why tensions occurred between commercial interests and independent aesthetic judgments as the journal shifted its character from early modernism to later conservatism.

The selection of reviews and essays by HANSLICK, in Pleasants's translation, provides a fascinating glimpse of Vienna's varied concert life between 1846 and 1899, while enabling readers to learn about the contemporary music critic whom Richard Wagner caricatured. Hanslick challenged on aesthetic grounds those works he deemed highly significant but conceptually dominated by poetic material. Access to Hanslick's writings about many compositions and famous performers affords valuable and necessary perspective on his critical views.

The strong influence of music on SHAW can be detected in his novels and plays, but his impassioned convictions about it emerge clearly in his formal music criticism. Laurence's edition organizes this criticism in the following order: volume 1, 1876–90; volume 2, 1890–93; volume 3, 1893–1950. Whether appraising English musical traditions or the wide range of compositions and performances presented in London, Shaw's criticism remains inimitable, direct, and lively.

ORA FRISBERG SALOMAN

D

Dahlhaus, Carl 1928–1989

German musicologist, philosopher, critic, and editor

Dahlhaus, Carl, *Analysis and Value Judgment,* translated by Siegmund Levarie, New York: Pendragon Press, 1983
——, *Esthetics of Music,* translated by William A. Austin, Cambridge: Cambridge University Press, 1982
——, *Foundations of Music History,* translated by J.B. Robinson, Cambridge: Cambridge University Press, 1983
——, *The Idea of Absolute Music,* translated by Roger Lustig, Chicago: University of Chicago Press, 1989
——, *Ludwig van Beethoven: Approaches to His Music,* translated by Mary Whittall, Oxford: Clarendon Press, and New York: Oxford University Press, 1991
——, *Nineteenth-Century Music,* translated by J. Bradford Robinson, Berkeley: University of California Press, 1989
——, *Richard Wagner's Music Dramas,* translated by Mary Whittall, Cambridge: Cambridge University Press, 1979
——, *Schoenberg and the New Music: Essays,* translated by Derrick Puffett and Alfred Clayton, Cambridge: Cambridge University Press, 1987
Dahlhaus, Carl, and Ruth Katz, editors, *Contemplating Music: Source Readings in the Aesthetics of Music,* 4 vols., New York: Pendragon Press, 1987–93
Deathridge, John, and Carl Dahlhaus, *The New Grove Wagner,* London: Macmillan, and New York: Norton, 1984

Carl Dahlhaus was one of the most influential German musicologists of the 20th century. His writings cover a broad spectrum, from theory and analysis to music aesthetics and its history, and he played an important role in the revival of Wagner scholarship that began in the 1970s. A constant theme in Dahlhaus's writings is the conception of music and its place in the modern world. Dahlhaus viewed musicology as a comprehensive discipline that included not only the examination of compositions but also the investigation of their performance and reception. He was one of the first musicologists to embrace subcategories such as criticism, aesthetics, and musical sociology into the field, and his influence is still noticeable in the work of many young scholars. (Please note that because all of the books discussed in this essay were written, co-authored, or co-edited by Dahlhaus, citations are given by title rather than author.)

Foundations of Music History is a necessary introduction to Dahlhaus's methodology. In this small volume, Dahlhaus draws on the competing philosophies of history that have arisen throughout the ages and assesses the advantages and disadvantages of applying them to the special requirements of music history. For those interested in philosophical issues, this is an especially thought-provoking study, and J.B. Robinson's clear and accurate translation makes it accessible to both students and scholars.

As an introduction to the field of aesthetics, Dahlhaus's *Esthetics of Music* can hardly be surpassed. Arranged thematically, this text provides an account of developments in the field and in so doing illustrates the chronology and unity of essential aesthetic elements throughout history. In this intellectually challenging book, Dahlhaus's chief concern is to explore the manner in which diverse social, artistic, or philosophic interests led to the adoption of different aesthetic ideas. Chapters 1 through 4 contain historical sketches of the development of various aesthetic precepts, whereas chapters 5 through 9 deal successively with five individual writers: Kant, Wackenroder, Schopenhauer, Hegel, and Hanslick. Chapter 13 discusses the 20th-century phenomenology of music, and chapters 12 and 14 present Dahlhaus's own contemplations of two systemic issues: "Esthetics and History" and "Standards of Criticism."

For readers interested in a further exploration of musical aesthetics, *Contemplating Music: Source Readings in the Aesthetics of Music* is highly recommended. Divided into four volumes, this anthology takes on four separate themes—"Substance," "Import," "Essence," and "Community of Discourse"—and presents generous excerpts from the writings of 73 European philosophers and other philosophically inclined figures (e.g., Aristotle, Augustine, Busoni, Eco, Guido d'Arezzo, Vincenzo Galilei, Helmholtz, David Hume, Kivy, Leibniz, Plato, Wittgenstein, and Zhdannov). Each excerpt is preceded by an informative introduction, and the clear translations make this collection a useful source of serious writings for readers of all levels. The only drawback to this anthology is its abstract framework. The categorization of diverse philosophical essays under vague subject themes is confusing, and the general introductions to each volume do little to resolve this problem. However, when the systematic aspect of the anthology is overlooked, comparisons of the various excerpts soon reveal the relative importance of opposing intellectual concepts and their possible relationships with other ideas.

In *Analysis and Value Judgment,* Dahlhaus addresses various questions concerning analysis and its usefulness in determining musical value. Topics such as value judgment versus objective judgment, historical-philosophical categories of music, aesthetics, and reception history are discussed along with the work of various theorists (e.g., Koch, Adolph Bernhard Marx, Schenker, Halm, and Adorno). The book concludes with specific examples of Dahlhaus's own analysis and its application to works by J.S. Bach, Stamitz, Haydn, Schubert, Liszt, Mahler, and Schoenberg.

Dahlhaus's *Nineteenth-Century Music* is considered by many to be the most significant comprehensive study of the period. Arranged chronologically, this book combines the fields of music, aesthetics, and social history into a metahistorical exploration of topics such as classicism versus romanticism, the rise of the bourgeoisie, virtuosity and interpretation, the myth of Beethoven, musical nationalism, absolute music versus program music, music realism, exoticism, and folklore. Each chapter includes an extensive list of bibliographic references for those interested in further exploration of the topics discussed, and a glossary at the end of the book serves as an aid to readers new to the field. Specialists will also find the book useful, for it offers a wealth of interdisciplinary material rarely included in musicological studies. However, this study is not flawless. Little mention is made of women composers and performers, and various non-German composers, including Debussy, Elgar, and Grieg, are neglected. The translation is clear if not always accurate.

The Idea of Absolute Music is another study of 19th-century music. In this philosophical study, Dahlhaus suggests that the idea of absolute music arose in the 19th century as a response to changes in aesthetic thought. In short, he believes that the 18th-century conception of music as "a means of discourse about problems of morality" was superseded in the 19th century by the conviction that instrumental music expressed "the true nature of music by its very lack of concept, object, and purpose." To support this theory, Dahlhaus makes use of generous quotes from the works of numerous romantic writers and philosophers (e.g., Wagner, Hanslick, Hoffmann, Tieck, Schliermacher, Hegel, Forkel, and Nietzsche). His commentaries on these excerpts are both insightful and

convincing, and his ability to elucidate the often obscure meanings of romantic texts is commendable. For those interested in the philosophical context surrounding the idea of absolute music versus program music, this study is quite useful. Unfortunately, the complex structure of Dahlhaus's sentences makes conveying his thoughts in languages other than German quite difficult, and in this case the translation is only moderately readable.

Ludwig van Beethoven: Approaches to His Music is not a biography but a study of the critical reception of Beethoven's music. Dahlhaus examines Beethoven's works from various analytical and philosophical vantage points, making this a thought-provoking study for those interested in the use of music analysis as a tool for aesthetic interpretation. Typical of Dahlhaus's style, the book contains many interdisciplinary forays into German philosophy and literary history, and the author's critical interpretations of Beethoven's music are often based on aesthetic motives rather than historical circumstances. The translation is clear and accurate, making the complex structure of Dahlhaus's theories easily accessible to an English audience. However, readers should approach this work with a critical eye, for it is not a positivist essay of documented facts but a subjective interpretation of Beethoven's musical essence. Dahlhaus is at his best in this book, but his theories will go unappreciated if the reader is not already familiar with the general details of Beethoven's life and music.

For readers interested in the unique features of Wagner's *Gesamtkunstwerke* and his success in creating profoundly unified effects, *Richard Wagner's Music Dramas* is indispensable. The core of the text consists of a general chapter on *The Ring* and 11 brief but complex chapters on each of Wagner's "canonical" operas, ranging from *Der fliegende Hollander* to *Parsifal*. These insightful explorations of Wagner's works are supported by careful analysis, and topics such as the changing relations of musical phrase type, poetic structure, and motivic technique appear frequently. However, the reader should be aware that Dahlhaus (and his translator) occasionally makes use of technical jargon that could prove confusing for readers unacquainted with theoretical terminology. Also, it is advisable to refer to the appropriate scores when reading these analyses rather than relying on the occasional music examples that appear in the text. The book concludes with an epilogue on the staging of Wagner's operas.

A more general introduction to Wagner's life and works can be found in *The New Grove: Wagner.* Intended for college-level students and educated nonspecialists, this book presents a concise, detailed account of Wagner's life and a general discussion of his major compositions and the evolution of his musical style. A complete list of works is included as an appendix along with a select bibliography. However, the reader should be aware that although editions of this book appeared in

1984 and 1997, the greater part of the text originally appeared as an entry in the *New Grove Dictionary of Music and Musicians* published in 1980.

Schoenberg and the New Music: Essays by Carl Dahlhaus is a collection of 28 essays written over a period of approximately 20 years. Contrary to what the title might suggest, not all the essays in this volume deal specifically with Schoenberg—two are devoted to Webern, one to Schrecker, and one to Skryabin, whereas others address the broader idea of "new music" as defined by Adorno. Because these essays were originally prepared for a variety of sources (scholarly and semischolarly journals, Festschriften, congress reports, and exhibition catalogs), they do not present the reader with a continuous stream of thought as many of his monographs do. Rather, each chapter is presented as a self-contained whole. The brilliance of Dahlhaus's scholarship shines brightly in this book, but unfortunately the complexity of the translations makes reading it a challenge for both student and scholar.

ANNA H. HARWELL CELENZA

Dance: Medieval and Renaissance

Arbeau, Thoinot, *Orchesography,* translated by Mary Stewart Evans, introduction by Julia Sutton, New York: Dover, 1967

Bukofzer, Manfred F., *Studies in Medieval and Renaissance Music,* New York: Norton, 1950

Dolmetsch, Mabel, *Dances of England and France from 1450 to 1600: With Their Music and Authentic Manner of Performance,* London: Routledge and Paul, 1949; reprint, New York: Da Capo Press, 1975

———, *Dances of Spain and Italy from 1400 to 1600,* London: Routledge and Paul, 1954; reprint, New York: Da Capo Press, 1975

Hudson, Richard, *The Allemande, the Balletto, and the Tanz,* 2 vols. Cambridge: Cambridge University Press, 1986

Kinkeldey, Otto, "Dance Tunes of the Fifteenth Century," in *Instrumental Music: A Conference at the Isham Memorial Library, May 4, 1957,* edited by David G. Hughes, Cambridge, Massachusetts: Harvard University Press, 1959

McGee, Timothy J., *Medieval Instrumental Dances,* Bloomington: Indiana University Press, 1989

Wood, Melusine, *Historical Dances (Twelfth to Nineteenth Century): Their Manner of Performance and their Place in the Social Life of the Time,* London: Imperial Society of Teachers of Dancing, 1952

The dance music of the Middle Ages and Renaissance falls into three distinct chronological periods: the medieval period (the 14th century, beginning about 1325); the early Renaissance (15th century); and the later Renaissance (16th century). Interestingly, the medieval period is fairly easy to encompass. There are 47 extant dance works of this era, and their music is widely available. The period of the early Renaissance presents the greatest problems. There are only a few surviving pieces of dance music that date from the 15th century. These monophonic works are found in two primary sources in black notation. Some of these melodies have been identified, through polyphonic realizations found in other sources. Many of the recorded performances of these dances are conjectural reconstructions. The 16th century abounds with a vast number of musical dance compositions, due primarily to the invention and development of music printing. With later Renaissance dance works, it is difficult to grasp an overview of this extensive repertoire. Some sources are primarily about music; others mainly concern the dances but contain valuable information about the music.

Research has been in process on all three historic periods since the later 19th century, but much of the work has been fragmentary. The dances of the Middle Ages have received considerable attention, especially in foreign-language books and articles; recently, a major work by Timothy McGee has appeared in English. The problems surrounding the study of the 15th-century dances have been recognized for most of the 20th century. However, it was not until the 1940s and 1950s that serious efforts to go beyond defining the problems were initiated. This remains a highly conjectural area. The 16th-century material has been studied is smaller segments, sometime concentrating on a particular music printer or a specific genre, such as the pavane or galliard. Often these are dictionary or encyclopedia entries or articles published in journals. A considerable amount of printed material of the period, musical and literary, has been published and studied.

McGEE is the most comprehensive and most recent source about medieval dance music. The first part is a study of the music, which covers virtually every facet of the historical, theoretical, and practical aspects of the subject. McGee discusses "Dance in the Middle Ages: The Repertory of Textless Dances," such as the *estampie* and saltarello; "Dancing," including the round and carol and the *estampie*; and "Performance Practices." The text is well written and highly accessible to those unfamiliar with the subject. The second part of the volume is devoted to modern notation transcriptions of the 47 works that make up the medieval dance repertoire.

BUKOFZER outlines the problems related to studying the dance music of the 15th century in a chapter titled "A Polyphonic Basse Dance of the Renaissance." He also gives a brief summary of the research on the limited repertoire and some collaborating manuscript evidence. The next portion of the discussion examines a polyphonic version of the dance *La Spagna,* tracing the way in which the polyphonic version was found, and analyzing how the bass line matches one of the bass melodies in Michel de Toulouze's *L'art et instruction de bien dancer* (one of two primary sources of the more than 49 pieces in this repertoire). The last section considers the *basse danse* and the polyphonic chanson as well as some possible interrelationships between the two genres. This scholarly essay may also prove useful to the nonspecialist.

KINKELDEY covers a different part of the same period discussed by Bukofzer. In addition to the two major French and Flemish sources, Kinkeldey also reviews treatises about Italian dance. He cites lists of dances (with one- and two-word titles), but the music for these dances is mostly lost. He makes comparisons between the Italian and French/Flemish repertoire and introduces the "measures" of the choreography and the tempi of various kinds of dances. Mensural signs, clef and key signatures, and modern restorations are among other topics that are addressed. This scholarly essay is supplemented by a discussion of Kinkeldey's findings by a group of distinguished musicologists.

ARBEAU is an important period source of later Renaissance dances and music for dance. The English translation from the original French includes the engravings and notation from the original, displayed in much the same manner as found in the 1573 print. The majority of the book is a dance manual, which is written in the form of a dialogue between Capriol, the student, and Arbeau, the teacher. The pavane, galliard, *basse danse, tourdion,* various kinds of *branles,* and other less well known dances are discussed, with examples of music provided. The dance tunes are given only as monophonic melodies. Some are familiar and can be found in polyphonic versions in other sources, including those of Pierre Attaingnant, Adrian Le Roy, Claude Gervaise, Pierre Phalèse, Jacques Moderne, Michael Praetorius, and Tielman Susato.

HUDSON is in two volumes: the first is the written history and the second volume contains musical examples. Volume 1 is in three parts: "The Renaissance," "The Transition," and "The Baroque Period." It is mainly Part 1 that is of interest here. However, it should be understood that Renaissance-style music was still being composed and published into the 1600s. A good example of this genre is Michael Praetorius's *Dances from Terpschore* (1612). Hudson discusses the German dance for lute, cittern, and keyboard from 1540 to 1603; the *almande* (allemande) for lute, cittern, and instrumental ensemble in France and the Low Countries from 1546 to 1603; and the Italian *Balletto tedesco* for lute, keyboard, and ensemble from 1561 to 1615. Although this book is scholarly, it is exceptionally well organized, accessible to the reader, and illustrated with plates and musical examples.

DOLMETSCH (1949) is a book more about dance than music. This is a volume full of historical and practical information, with numerous music examples given in piano score. Caution is advised concerning several 15th-century examples and some monophonic examples from Arbeau's *Orchésographie*. In several instances, the polyphonic versions of these monophonic works have been arranged by either Mabel or Arnold Dolmetsch; however, there are also many polyphonic examples from authentic sources. The important dance types of the Renaissance are discussed, including the *basse danse, branle,* pavane, galliard, *volta,* and allemande. Some of the musical examples are underlaid with dance steps and/or movements. The book is based mainly on primary sources.

DOLMETSCH (1954) is also a book more about the dances themselves rather than the music. However, there is a considerable amount of important information in this volume and a large number of musical examples, in piano score. Two of the musical examples are keyed to the dance steps in an interesting arrangement in which the dance movements are underlaid to the measures of the printed music. There is a considerable amount of space given to the *bassa danza*. Other dance types that are discussed include the *bassa et alta, spagnoletto, villanos, pavaniglia* (Spanish pavane), *hachas, passomezzo,* and two types of *balletti*. The various dance movements are given in outline form. The order of the body's movements are given together with the kind and number of steps. In some cases, the number of beats or measures assigned to the movement pattern is included. The book is based mostly on primary sources.

WOOD is a widely known work that is primarily about dance, but it does include numerous musical examples. The book's chapters are arranged in chronological order, beginning with the 12th to the 14th century. Each historical period has at least two chapters devoted to it. The first chapter in each instance is titled "Historical Notes" and provides information about the kinds of dances and their cultural background, as well as some material about their musical content. The second chapter considers how the historic dances were performed. Here, the primary literary device is an elaborate outline with descriptive paragraphs interspersed throughout. The outlines usually include the measure numbers and the beat number keyed to the dance step or motion to be performed. These second chapters hold the musical examples, which are in piano score. Wood compiled a sequel to this book, titled *More Historical Dances* (1956).

JEFFREY WASSON

Dance: Baroque

Harris-Warrick, Rebecca, and Carol G. Marsh, *Musical Theatre at the Court of Louis XIV: Le Mariage de la Grosse Cathos,* Cambridge: Cambridge University Press, 1994

Hilton, Wendy, *Dance and Music of Court and Theater: Selected Writings of Wendy Hilton,* Stuyvesant, New York: Pendragon Press, 1997

Little, Meredith Ellis, and Carol G. Marsh, *La Danse Noble: An Inventory of Dances and Sources,* Williamstown, Massachusetts: Broude Brothers, 1992

Mather, Betty Bang, and Dean M. Karns, *Dance Rhythms of the French Baroque: A Handbook for Performance,* Bloomington: Indiana University Press, 1987

McCleave, Sarah, and Geoffrey Burgess, editors, *Dance and Music in French Baroque Theatre: Sources and Interpretations,* London: Institute of Advanced Musical Studies, King's College London, 1998

Ralph, Richard, *The Life and Works of John Weaver,* New York: Dance Horizons, and London: Dance Books, 1985

Rameau, Pierre, *The Dancing Master,* translated by Cyril W. Beaumont, Brooklyn, New York: Dance Horizons, 1970

Schwartz, Judith L., and Christena L. Schlundt, *French Court Dance and Dance Music: A Guide to Primary Source Writings, 1643–1789,* Stuyvesant, New York: Pendragon Press, 1987

Winter, Marian Hannah, *The Pre-Romantic Ballet,* London: Pitman Publishing, 1974; Brooklyn, New York: Dance Horizons, 1975

Witherell, Anne L., *Louis Pècour's 1700 Recueil de Danses,* Ann Arbor, Michigan: UMI Research Press, and Epping: Bowker, 1983

The term *baroque dance* is generally understood to encompass the style of dancing that developed in France starting in the mid–17th century and that gave rise to what is now known as ballet. Because of its connections to the court of Louis XIV, who was himself a proficient dancer, the style is sometimes called "court dance," even though it was also danced in the theater and even though this term can apply equally well to earlier periods. Whereas ballet histories (of which there are a substantial number) acknowledge the origins of the art in the 17th century, they tend to treat the baroque period superficially and all too often pass along half-truths or outright misinformation, much of which has regrettably gained currency simply from having been repeated numerous times. Musicologists have devoted quite a bit of attention to baroque dance music, although considerably more to the numerous suites and chamber sonatas composed for listening than to the music composed for actual dancing. This article focuses only on books that take the dance itself into account; most of the serious work of this type has been published within the last two decades. Although the field of baroque dance is still relatively small, readers should be aware that important books have been published in other languages, particularly French, and that a good deal of significant work has appeared in periodicals.

Among ballet histories, WINTER has the most to say about baroque dance. It covers the period from the early 17th century to 1830 by surveying an enormous amount of primary material—dance manuals, theoretical treatises, chronicles, diaries, archival documents—and by supplying an abundance of period illustrations. The book does not confine itself to France but covers Europe from England to Russia and from Italy to Sweden. Its organization is somewhat fanciful, but this is compensated by a very thorough index. A more serious weakness is the sometimes incomplete documentation or the occasional inaccuracy, especially in quotations. Although researchers are advised to check every citation, the book remains a wellspring of valuable information, presented with intelligence and enthusiasm.

HILTON's volume has become the bible for those wishing to learn how to perform baroque dance. It supersedes all previously published efforts at reconstruction through its meticulous reliance on 18th-century sources rather than on creative imagination. Part 1 gives an overview of the contexts in which dancing participated, the differences between court and theatrical styles, and the sources that tell us about the dances of the period. Part 2, the heart of the book, takes the reader through the rudiments of baroque technique and notation, building from individual movements to an entire minuet, with excursions in the direction of more complex dances along the way. The book is clearly organized and copiously illustrated. Although Hilton does not take into account alternative interpretations of how steps were performed, her conclusions are based on long experience as a dancer, reconstructor, and historian.

One indispensable source for Hilton and all other reconstructors is RAMEAU's *Maître à danser* (Paris, 1725), which was published in translation as *The Dancing Master* with a brief introduction by Cyril Beaumont; it describes how to perform many of the steps indicated only schematically in Raoul Auger Feuillet's groundbreaking compendium of dance notation, *Chorégraphie* (Paris, 1700). These two works and many other primary materials (a number of which are available in facsimile) are listed in SCHWARTZ and SCHLUNDT's extremely useful bibliography, which gives full references and substantive annotations for 116 writings pertaining to baroque dance from the 17th and 18th centuries. The book has three sections: writings on dance and dance notation; writings pertaining to dance music; and related writings on the performing arts.

An essential companion to this volume is the catalog of dance notations prepared by LITTLE and MARSH, which lists the approximately 330 choreographies preserved in Feuillet notation, along with the sources, both printed and manuscript, in which they are found. Each listing for a choreography includes an incipit of the music, the names of the choreographer and composer, the numbers of dancers involved, the dance type, and the sources of both choreography and music. There are useful indices of dance titles, choreographers, performers, dance types, musical sources, and tunes.

Three recent books incorporate facsimiles of important source material within a larger contextual study.

HARRIS-WARRICK and MARSH reproduce the choreography and music for an entire *mascarade* performed at Versailles in 1688, along with an extended study of the heretofore unknown dance notation (Favier notation), the music, the performers and creators, and the performance practices of late 17th-century French ballet. RALPH provides annotated facsimiles of all of the theoretical writings of John Weaver, the English choreographer who promoted independent pantomime ballets in London in the early 18th century, preceded by a thorough and meticulously documented study of Weaver's life and works. WITHERELL's study of the first published collection in Feuillet notation of ballroom choreographies focuses on the relationship between music and dance in these works and includes facsimiles of each of the nine dances.

MATHER attempts to provide practical help for performers of baroque music by summarizing information on such dance-related topics as the melodic and poetic rhythms of dance songs, dance steps, tempo, bowings, and articulation. She then discusses the rhythmic characteristics of 15 dance types, in alphabetical order from the allemande to the sarabande. Although she quotes many primary sources, she tends to overgeneralize and draw overly firm conclusions. The book contains much solid information, including an extensive bibliography, but it should be used with caution.

The anthology of five articles edited by McCLEAVE and BURGESS, selected from presentations at the 1996 conference "Dance for Kings," shows that, while research is of necessity still continuing on basic questions regarding the practice of baroque dance, more interpretive and critical efforts are now also underway.

REBECCA HARRIS-WARRICK

Dance: Classical

Dahms, Sibylle, "Ballet Reform in the Eighteenth Century and Ballet at the Mannheim Court," translated by Barbara Maria Verble, in *Ballet Music From the Mannheim Court,* edited by Floyd K. Grave, Madison, Wisconsin: A-R Editions, 1996
Hastings, Baird, *Choreographer and Composer,* Boston: Twayne, 1983
Landon, H.C. Robbins, editor, *The Mozart Compendium: A Guide to Mozart's Life and Music,* London: Thames and Hudson, and New York: Schirmer Books, 1990
Landon, H.C. Robbins, and Donald Mitchell, editors, *The Mozart Companion,* London: Rockliff, and New York: Oxford University Press, 1956
Lynham, Deryck, *The Chevalier Noverre: Father of Modern Ballet: A Biography,* London: Sylvan Press, and New York, British Book Centre, 1950
Nettl, Paul, *The Dance in Classical Music,* New York: Philosophical Library, 1963; London: Owen, 1964
Scherman, Thomas K., and Louis Biancolli, editors, *The Beethoven Companion,* Garden City, New York: Doubleday, 1972
Searle, Humphrey, *Ballet Music: An Introduction,* London: Cassell, 1958; 2nd ed., New York: Dover, 1973
Zaslaw, Neal, and William Cowdery, editors, *The Compleat Mozart: A Guide to the Musical Works of Wolfgang Amadeus Mozart,* New York: Mozart Bicentennial at Lincoln Center, Norton, 1990

The first distinction that should be made with regard to the category of classical dance concerns the different definitions of the words *classic* or *classical* when applied to dance and dance music. In music, the classical period is dated between about 1760 and about 1820. The three major composers of the period are Haydn, Mozart, and Beethoven; numerous other composers of importance during this era include Gluck, Boccerini, Clementi, and J.C. Bach. Among dancers, the term *classical ballet* refers to the important 19th-century standard repertoire including such well-know examples as Adam's *Giselle,* Dukas's *Sylvia,* and the three great ballets of Tchaikovsky. This article deals with the first definition of classical dance and dance music, not with classical ballet.

The most important development for dance in the classical era was the emergence of independent theatrical and professionally choreographed ballet, separate from other theatrical productions, particularly opera. Another important type of dance music from this era is that of the social dances, which include the contredanse, the Deutschertanz, the Ländler, the minuet, and the waltz. The third type of dance-related music from this era is the stylized dance, such as minuets found in symphonies and string quartets. The bibliography given here provides a sampling of the first two of these types, as well as references to various repertoires and major composers of dance music during the classical era.

NETTL's monograph is undoubtedly the most comprehensive book on the subject. It deals with ballet, social dances, ballet in opera, and the major composers of the era. The volume begins with a discussion of Handel and the role of ballet in his operas. It proceeds to an investigation of Gluck and his pivotal role and importance in the development of ballet, independent of opera. The choreographers Jean-Georges Noverre (1727–1810) and Franz Anton Christoph Hilverding (1710–68) are addressed, as are the idioms of French and Italian ballet. Social dances including the minuet, the contredanse, and German dances are included, as is a chapter on "Dance Halls." Mozart, Haydn, and Beethoven are discussed in their various roles as composers of social dances and ballets. The book is constructed as a series of brief chapters, each one concentrating on a specific aspect of dance in the classical period.

HASTINGS is a comprehensive book that emphasizes the role of choreography over that of music. Chapter 4,

"The Eighteenth Century: The Classical Age," covers the later part of the baroque era as well as the classical era. A discussion of the classical era of dance music is contained in a part of the chapter titled "The Impact of Noverre." Noverre was one of the first truly important choreographers and impresarios of dance, and this portion of the chapter discusses his collaborations with major composers of the era, including Gluck, Mozart, Jommelli, and others.

SEARLE is a survey of ballet music from the inception of professionally choreographed music in the late 1500s up through the 20th century. Although the majority of the volume is given over to repertoire from the 19th and 20th centuries, about half of the first chapter is devoted to music of the new pantomime ballet, beginning with Gluck's *Don Juan*. The ballets of Boccherini, Mozart, and Beethoven are also discussed. Some of the information contained here has been superseded by newer research, and the section on Mozart presents some questionable material. Nevertheless, this section is a valuable introduction to the beginnings of ballet as independent from opera. The lengthy chart at the conclusion of the volume, "Details of Some First Performances" is quite informative and highly useful for readers interested in the history of the ballet and its music.

DAHMS discusses a little-known repertoire of ballet music that originated in Mannheim, Germany. The orchestra of Mannheim and its repertoire is a fairly well-known part of the musical developments in the classical era. The works presented in these volumes, however, have only recently come to light as some of the earliest independent ballet music. The music featured in this edition was composed by three relatively obscure figures: Christian Cannabich (1731–89), Carl Joseph Toeschi (1731–88), and Georg Joseph Vogler (1749–1814). Their ballets presented in this volume all have French titles, including *Médée et Jason, L'enlèvement de Proserpine*, and *Le rendez-vous de chasse*. In addition to Dahms's introductory article, there is extensive prefatory material of other kinds, including discussions of ballet reform in the 18th century, commentary on ballet at the Mannheim court, sources of Mannheim ballets, and discussions of the ten edited ballets. Because this repertoire is virtually unknown, the introductory material, as well as the edited scores, is revelatory. The standards of scholarship are quite high, yet the writing and discussion of the music are accessible.

LYNHAM offers a book-length study of the most important figure in the development of 18th-century ballet, Noverre, who, in many ways, can be considered the "Diaghilev of the 18th century." This compact volume addresses his biography, as well as his various periods of creativity in Lyons, Stuttgart, Vienna, Paris, and London. Also discussed is the *Ballet d'action* before Noverre and the ballets of Noverre himself. The first appendix offers selected scenarios of his ballets; the second appendix is a listing of the known productions of Noverre. This latter appendix is generally quite helpful; however, in many cases the composer or composers of the music are either unknown or not listed.

Included in LANDON is David Wyn Jones's article, "Dance and Ballet," which is presented in two parts. First is a short introduction addressing Mozart's dances and ballets. This introduction is followed by a series of entries about each of the individual works, each approximately a paragraph in length and arranged in chronological order, by Köchel number. Most of the article is about the role of dance and dance music in Mozart's life and career; the material about the ballet music is limited. The work list gives pertinent information about the title, published location, date and places of composition, number of pieces or movements, and scoring, as well as a brief comment about each work.

In LANDON and MITCHELL, an article by H. Engel deals mainly with the three main types of dances on which Mozart focused. There are several pages devoted to each dance type: the minuet, German dances, and contredanses. Engel provides a more substantive analysis of these works than do other writers mentioned here. He employs musical examples, diagrams of formal construction, and references to harmonic writing to supplement basic information and historical contexts of the works.

Two chapters in ZASLAW provide information about each of Mozart's dance and ballet works. Cowdery's chapter on the "Dances" begins by giving some background and overview of the composer's dances and the categories into which they fit. The author then provides highlights of important information about each of the dances or sets of dances in chronological order of their composition. Smith's entry, "Ballets and Incidental Music," is very short. However, because there are fewer pieces to cover, some of the individual entries are longer and have more substance that those in Cowdery's chapter. This is a good quick reference source that provides basic information about Mozart's dances.

SCHERMAN and BIANCOLLI's volume about Beethoven contains several articles discussing the dance and ballet works. "*Ritterballet*, WoO1," J.-G. Prod'homme's brief article about Beethoven's first work, a little-known composition dating from 1791 and consisting of eight short pieces or movements, is one of the few discussions of the *Ritterballet* in the vast Beethoven literature. The article titled "Music for the Ballet: *The Creatures of Prometheus*" is written by several authors: S.W. Bennett, Andre Levinson, Felix Borowsky, and Scherman. The entry gives a substantive overview of the ballet's design, history and background; material about the first performance; the sources of the score; and a recounting of the plot with comments concerning the musical portrayal of the story. The final portion of this article, written by Bennett with additions by Scherman, is an account of the content of the ballet's 16 movements that follow the work's well-known overture. This chapter also includes seven entries that discuss the dances that Beethoven wrote for various performing media. Many of the discussions are by Scherman; others writers include Georg Kinsky and Sidney Finkelstein.

JEFFREY WASSON

See also Gluck, Christoph Willibald

Dance: 19th Century

Aldrich, Elizabeth, *From the Ballroom to Hell: Grace and Folly in Nineteenth-Century Dance*, Evanston, Illinois: Northwestern University Press, 1991

Balanchine, George, *Complete Stories of the Great Ballets*, edited by Francis Mason, Garden City, New York: Doubleday, 1954; revised and enlarged as *Balanchine's Complete Stories of the Great Ballets*, 1977

Brown, David, *Tchaikovsky: The Crisis Years, 1874–1878*, London: Gollancz, and New York: Norton, 1983

———, *Tchaikovsky: The Final Years, 1885–1893*, London: Gollancz, and New York: Norton, 1991

Carner, Mosco, *The Waltz*, London: Parrish, and New York: Chanticleer Press, 1948

Fantel, Hans, *Johann Strauss: Father and Son, and Their Era*, Newton Abbot: David and Charles, 1971; as *The Waltz Kings: Johann Strauss, Father and Son, and Their Romantic Age*, New York: Morrow, 1972

Franks, A.H., *Social Dance: A Short History*, London: Routledge and Kegan Paul, 1963

Guest, Ivor Forbes, *The Romantic Ballet in Paris*, Middletown, Connecticut: Wesleyan University Press, 1966; 2nd revised edition, London: Dance Books, 1980

Lawrence, Robert, *The Victor Book of Ballets and Ballet Music*, New York: Simon and Schuster, 1950

Searle, Humphrey, *Ballet Music: An Introduction*, London: Cassell, 1958; 2nd edition, New York: Dover, 1973

Studwell, William E., *Adolphe Adam and Léo Delibes: A Guide to Research*, New York: Garland, 1987

Terry, Walter, *Ballet Guide: Background, Listings, Credits, and Descriptions of More than Five Hundred of the World's Major Ballets*, Newton Abbot: David and Charles, and New York: Dodd, Mead, 1976; 2nd edition, Newton Abbot: David and Charles, 1979

Wiley, Roland John, *Tchaikovsky's Ballets: Swan Lake, Sleeping Beauty, Nutcracker*, Oxford: Clarendon Press, and New York: Oxford University Press, 1985

Warrack, John, *Tchaikovsky Ballet Music*, London: British Broadcasting Corporation, and Seattle: University of Washington Press, 1979

The three main categories of dance and dance music in the 19th century are social dances, independent theatrical ballet, and ballet as part of opera. This entry does not discuss the few 19th-century ballets that are part of the classical period, such as Beethoven's *Creatures of Prometheus*.

Social dance of the era centered about the enormously popular waltz. There were, however, numerous other popular social dances of the period including the cakewalk, country dance or *contra* dance, the galop, various kinds of marches, the polka, the quadrille, the square dance and the reel, and the two-step.

Independent theatrical ballet, which emerged in the 18th century, developed into an important musical idiom with the rudiments of a standard repertoire. In the dance profession, this standard 19th-century repertoire is sometimes referred to by the misnomer *classical ballet*. It is a fairly limited repertoire of major works that include Adolphe Adam's *Giselle*, Paul Dukas's *Coppélia* and *Sylvia*, the three great ballets of Tchaikovsky, and two ballets of Glazunov. There are less well remembered ballets composed by Scheitzhoeffer, Minkus, Gade and various partners, and other obscure composers.

The third category of dance music is that for theatrical presentation as part of opera. Much of this music was associated with productions of the Paris Opéra, which maintained a tradition of ballet in their productions. Composers from Gluck through Verdi added ballet scenes and music for Parisian productions of their works. There are also examples of this kind of music by composers Donizetti, Rossini, Verdi, Wagner, Berlioz, and Meyerbeer, who included ballet music in their operas.

ALDRICH includes over 100 excerpts from 19th-century etiquette, dance, beauty, and fashion manuals in her strangely titled volume. A large percentage of the book is not about music but rather is concerned with social background and customs, etiquette, and dancing. The last two sections of the book address "Music and Musicians" and "Dances and Party Games." Dances and music discussed include minuets, reels, country dances, early cotillions, quadrilles, mazurkas, marches, polkas, and waltzes. It is a quaint, often amusing collection of descriptions about the practice of social dancing in the 19th century. The book includes illustrations and music examples from a variety of North and South American and European sources. There is also a select bibliography and an annotated bibliography.

FRANKS is a comprehensive history of social dance from the 15th century through the 20th century. Chapter 6, on the 19th century, is titled "Revolutions and Scandals—and the Birth of a New Style." In addition to social and cultural background to the popular dances of the era, Franks provides a few paragraphs to most of the important social dances of the time. His work is a compilation of many sources and in effect provides a summarized overview of the way in which important composers and writers view the subject.

CARNER's small volume deals with the history and practice of the waltz. There are numerous illustrations encompassing historic prints of dancing to photographs of great waltz composers, as well as facsimiles of manuscript and title pages of famous waltzes. The author also includes several music examples. This volume surveys the antecedents of the waltz, the 19th-century emergence of the danced waltz and its music, and the Strausses and the Viennese waltz. Additionally, it contains a chapter about stylized waltzes intended for concert music, including orchestral movements, works by Chopin and Liszt for piano, and works with waltz-style foundations. The final chapter, titled "As in Opera, So in Ballet," shows the influence of the waltz in theatrical idioms.

FANTEL's biography of the Strausses is directed toward the general audience. There is considerable discussion of Viennese social and cultural history and how the two major composers of the waltz fit into this milieu. The author includes a chapter about the famous "Blue Danube" waltz and a chapter about the theatrical works written by Johann Strauss II. A listing of the compositions of each of the Strausses by opus number shows that they wrote other types of dances as well.

BALANCHINE is one of the best known of the books that describe the plots of the great ballets. The repertoire included is quite broad but tends to concentrate on ballets of the 20th century. The standard repertoire of 19th-century ballet is included, however. The individual entries are extensive and the plot summaries quite detailed. Each plot summary is preceded by a paragraph that provides fundamental information about the scenario. Some of the information includes composer, choreographer(s), source(s) of the plot, first performance particulars, and details about the history of other important productions, particularly those by the New York City Ballet. The plot summaries are fairly detailed.

TERRY's guide is similar to Balanchine's volume, providing a plot summary of the major works of the ballet repertoire. Works of the 18th and 20th centuries are included, as are the major ballets of the 19th century. In general, the plot summaries provided here are more concise than those in the Balanchine book. An introductory paragraph precedes each entry and provides the same type of fundamental information as in the Balanchine book. In most cases, the introductory material is more abbreviated than in the Balanchine counterpart.

LAWRENCE's volume is an earlier and somewhat different approach to the stories of the great ballets. It encompasses 18th-, 19th-, and 20th-century works. The most significant difference between this volume and those of Balanchine and Terry is the inclusion of brief musical examples scattered throughout the rendering of the ballet plots. Additionally, there are numerous photographs of dancers posed in specific ballets, which are coordinated with the verbal text.

SEARLE's book is a survey of ballet music from the inception of professionally choreographed music in the late 16th century up through the 20th century. The majority of the volume is given over to repertoire from the 19th and 20th centuries. The second chapter, titled "Ballet Music in Opera during the 19th Century," is one of the few discussions of this topic to be found in the literature. Most of the discussion centers about Paris Opéra productions of non-French operas by composers such as Rossini, Donizetti, Verdi, and Wagner; and French operas by composers such as Berlioz, Meyerbeer, Léo Delibes, Bizet, Massenet, and Gounod. There are also a few paragraphs concerning ballet in Russian and eastern European operas. The third chapter is about the "Grand Romantic Ballets" as independent theatrical works. It covers the major works of Adam, Delibes, Tchaikovsky, and Glazunov. The book includes plot summaries and in several instances analysis of movements and construction of ballets, especially those of Tchaikovsky. The lengthy chart at the conclusion of the volume, "Details of Some First Performances," is quite informative and useful for readers interested in the history of the ballet and its music.

GUEST is an important historian of the ballet and dance. He normally offers little about the music of the ballets of which he writes. His volume on Parisian romantic ballet does, however, include a small amount about music in the first chapter. More important is the intertwining of the history of the Paris Opéra and ballet that is distributed throughout the book. Guest has written other significant books about 19th-century ballet history that have little to say about music; however, these volumes do help complete the broader picture of ballet history. These include *The Ballet of the Second Empire, 1847–1858* (1955, revised 1972) and *The Romantic Ballet in England: Its Development, Fulfillment, and Decline* (1954, revised 1972).

STUDWELL's book on Adam and Delibes is one of a series of research guides published by Garland aimed at scholars as well as students and interested readers looking for further information on a specific composer. For each composer, Studwell provides an overview of the composer's life and music, a list of his musical works by type of composition, and an extensive bibliography segmented into various categories. There are also sections on "Ballets in General" and on "Individual Ballets." The information is up-to-date, extensive, and presented in an orderly fashion.

WILEY provides the most complete and thorough book about Tchaikovsky's ballets available. While the discussion of the music is the central premise of the volume, the author also provides information about the composer's relationship to the ballet master and other collaborations, the librettos, and the productions. The appendices include scenarios of the ballets and choreographic notation of *The Nutcracker* among other topics—both musical and nonmusical. The musical analysis is quite thorough, dealing with thematic unity, thematic variation and its uses within the scenarios of the ballets, harmonic writing, programmatic elements, rhythmic construction, and orchestration. There is one appendix on Tchaikovsky's harmony and another about metronomic markings in *Sleeping Beauty*. Even though a large amount of the musical analysis is technical in nature, the writing style makes the majority of the text accessible to a wide audience.

WARRACK's brief book about the ballet is part of the excellent BBC Music Guide series. The volumes as a whole are fairly limited in nature, being directed toward the interested listener. The series covers major works of the literature from Bach cantatas to Debussy orchestra music. After an introductory section, Warrack addresses the three Tchaikovsky ballets separately on a movement-by-movement (or scene-by-scene) basis. Necessary plot summaries are provided for the specific movement being discussed. There are notational examples of important themes and melodic ideas. Each ballet is preceded by a historical introduction.

BROWN (1983) and BROWN (1991) are volumes 2 and 4 of his extensive and scholarly 4 volume study of Tchaikovsky. Volume 2 (1983) includes a chapter on the Third String Quartet and *Swan Lake*; volume 4 (1991) devotes sections to *Sleeping Beauty* and *The Nutcracker*. Brown's approach is integrative, combining historical background of the ballets and their creation with plot summaries and musical analysis. The musical analysis pays particular attention to antecedents and contemporary examples of ballet and theatrical music, as well as addressing the standard components of formal construction, thematic use, tonality, chromaticism, and their relationship to the programmatic nature of the ballets.

JEFFREY WASSON

Dance: 20th Century

Balanchine, George, *Complete Stories of the Great Ballets*, edited by Francis Mason, Garden City, New York: Doubleday, 1954; revised and enlarged as *Balanchine's Complete Stories of the Great Ballets*, 1977

Benbow-Pfalzgraf, Taryn, and Glynis Benbow-Niemier, editors, *International Dictionary of Modern Dance*, Detroit, Michigan: St. James Press, 1998

Butterworth, Neil, *The Music of Aaron Copland*, London: Toccata Press, 1985; New York: Universe Books, 1986

Cox, David Vassall, *Debussy and Orchestral Music*, London: British Broadcasting Corporation, 1974; and Seattle: University of Washington Press, 1975

Gutman, David, *Prokofiev*, London: Alderman Press, 1988

Horst, Louis, and Carroll Russell, *Modern Dance Forms in Relation to the Other Modern Arts*, San Francisco: Impulse Publications, 1961

Lawrence, Robert, *The Victor Book of Ballets and Ballet Music*, New York: Simon and Schuster, 1950

Lederman, Minna, editor, *Stravinsky in the Theatre*, New York, Ballet Caravan, 1948

Orenstein, Arbie, *Ravel: Man and Musician*, New York: Columbia University Press, 1975

Percival, John, *The World of Diaghilev*, London: Studio Vista, and New York: Dutton, 1971; revised edition, London: Herbert Press, 1979

Searle, Humphrey, *Ballet Music: An Introduction*, London: Cassell, 1958; 2nd ed., New York: Dover, 1973

Stearns, Marshall Winslow, and Jean Stearns, *Jazz Dance: The Story of American Vernacular Dance*, New York: Macmillan, 1968

Stravinsky and the Dance: A Survey of Ballet Productions, 1910–1962, New York: Dance Collection of the New York Public Library, 1962

Teck, Katherine, *Music for the Dance: Reflections on a Collaborative Art*, New York: Greenwood Press, 1989

Terry, Walter, *Ballet Guide: Background, Listings, Credits, and Descriptions of More than Five Hundred of the Worlds Major Ballets*, Newton Abbot: David and Charles, and New York: Dodd and Mead, 1976; 2nd edition, Newton Abbot: David and Charles, 1979

White, Eric Walter, *Stravinsky: The Composer and His Works*, Berkeley: University of California Press, 1966; 2nd edition, 1979

Wachtel, Andrew, editor, *Petrushka: Sources and Contexts*, Evanston, Illinois: Northwestern University Press, 1998

The explosion of creativity, increased number of dance companies, expansion of dance repertoire, developments of new types of dance, and the changes these events brought to the relationship between music and dance are hallmarks of the 20th-century evolution in these disciplines. In addition to social dance, ballet within the context of opera, and independent theatrical ballet, a new idiom known as modern dance was also created. Much of the important developments of dance in the 20th century can be traced to the ideas and influence of Sergey Diaghilev (1872–1929). Contributions to the development of modern dance were made by performer/choreographers such as Isadora Duncan, Martha Graham, Merce Cunningham, Twila Tharp, Alvin Alley, and Paul Taylor.

The developments in social dance are more difficult to trace. Certain well-known dances such as the tango, Charleston, lindy hop, and jitterbug were associated with jazz through the big band era. Following World War II, however, only a few types of new dances can be identified and documented. Some of these include the rumba, bossa nova, twist, and various kinds of disco dances. In many cases these social dances do not align themselves with a particular type or style of music. The tango and most kinds of "swing" dance music are aligned with particular styles of music, as are several varieties of Latin dances. Many of the popular social dances of the 1950s through the 1990s are not, however, connected with specific musical styles or types.

The amount of ballet music associated with opera diminished during the 20th century, although some composers including Richard Strauss, Arnold Schoenberg, Anton Berg, Benjamin Britten, and Sergey Prokofiev did incorporate ballet music in their works. Theatrical dancing and choreography for vaudeville, the English music hall, Broadway musicals, motion picture musicals, and other idioms of popular entertainment became a new and major source of growth in the integrated arena of theater and dance. Most of these choreographed works are attached to particular songs, instrumental works, or scores for theatrical productions. This category of dance music is rarely discussed apart from its theatrical context. Two well-known exceptions are Agnes de Mille's ballet-style choreography for Rodgers and Hammerstein musicals and Jerome Robbins's choreography for the musicals of Leonard Bernstein. What we normally consider as "classical" ballet was most highly influenced by Diaghilev and the commissions for his Ballets Russes. Works written by Claude Debussy, Maurice Ravel, Erik Satie, Richard Strauss, Darius Milhaud, Prokofiev, Manuel de Falla, and most important, Igor Stravinsky changed the formal and musical status of ballet composition. Aaron Copland is also an important figure in 20th-century ballet music. While ballet music continues to be written, the most important works of the repertoire are from the first half of the century.

Choreography for music not written for or intended for dance began in earnest with Michel Fokine's idea and Diaghilev's commissioning the orchestration of Chopin piano works for the ballet *Les Sylphides* in 1909. This began a practice that has grown to virtually dominate the music for classical ballet and modern dance. In addition, the technological innovations in recording and sound reproduction have all but eliminated the use of live music for dance performances, except for the most important ballet companies. Because of the way in which modern dance has evolved, it is difficult to associate a large body of compositions originally written for modern dance performances. The collaborative efforts of John Cage and Merce Cunningham are a major exception.

Books about social dances in the 20th century tend to be "how-to" books, with pictures, charts, diagrams, and so on. There is little discussion of the trends, origins, life span, or music associated with social dancing. STEARNS and STEARNS is one of the few volumes to address these issues. It should be pointed out that a large amount of the book is devoted to theatrical dancing as a historical antecedent of modern social or "vernacular" dancing. The book is written in a conversational and defuse style that requires the reader to consult the index to find information about specific dances. At the conclusion of the book is labanotation for a broad array of vernacular dances. The table of contents for the diagrams is a useful list of 20th-century social dances.

There are numerous books about Diaghilev, including Richard Buckle's large biography, *Diaghilev* (1979), and Boris Kochno's *Diaghilev and the Ballets Russes* (1970), a pictorial view of the innovative repertoire associated with the company. However, relatively little writing is directed solely toward the music. PERCIVAL does include a short chapter with the title "His Composers," which includes numerous photographs and a basic text about the relationship between the composers associated with the great impresario.

SEARLE contains three chapters on 20th-century ballet: "The Impact of Diaghilev, 1909–1929," "Ballet Music, 1930–1957," and "Modern Developments, 1958–1972." The Diaghilev chapter spends considerable space tracing facts and separating them from legends that have grown up about Diaghilev. For example, the orchestration of the Chopin piano works for *Les Sylphides* was really Fokine's idea, not Diaghilev's; however, Diaghilev did encourage the practice of choreographing to music not originally intended for dance. Searle also spends a substantial amount of space discussing the compositions commissioned by Diaghilev, especially those by Stravinsky. Searle's chapter on ballet from 1930 to 1957 is organized by country, ballet company, major creators in the dance world, and music. The music covered includes preexistent music with added choreography and original ballet compositions. The British section mentions works by Ralph Vaughan Williams, William Walton, and Britten; the section on the United States discusses works by Stravinsky, Copland, Bernstein, and Paul Hindemith. There are briefer discussions about the dance repertoires of France, Italy, German, Scandinavia, and Eastern Europe. The final division is a survey of the original ballet music written in the Soviet Union by Shostakovich, Glière, Khatchaturian, and Prokofiev. The chapter on ballet from 1957 to 1972 takes much the same nationalistic approach as the previous chapter. Several different concepts are emphasized, including the widespread use of preexistent music as material for choreography. Indeed, few original ballet scores are mentioned. The section on the United States includes a considerable discussion about modern dance troupes and their repertoires, as well as material concerning ballet companies. The Cunningham-Cage collaboration is also addressed. After discussing Great Britain and the United States, the author treats other national-based trends and repertoires. This is one of the more important writings about the history of 20th-century dance.

WHITE's book about Stravinsky has been a standard resource for several decades. Following a comparatively brief biography, there is a "Register of Works," which in turn is followed by a discussion of each composition. The order is chronological, and discussions range from a few paragraphs to lengthy explorations of important works. The ballets fall into this latter category.

STRAVINSKY AND THE DANCE is a catalog of an exhibition held at the New York Public Library in 1962.

The important parts of the contents are an introductory essay "Stravinsky and the Muses" by Herbert Read, a group of photographic plates (both color and black and white) concerning the ballets, and a listing of "Ballet Productions 1910–1962" by Selma Jeanne Cohen. In this final part, the list of the vital information about each ballet's productions is preceded by a historical introduction to the ballet and its creation.

LEDERMAN's collection centers mostly on Stravinsky and ballet and includes essays by Ernest Ansermet, George Balanchine, Bernstein, Jean Cocteau, Copland, Craft, Kirstein, and others. Most of the first section, "Reminiscence," is about the ballet. "Studies of the Music," the second part, includes an essay by Arthur Berger entitled "Music for the Ballet" and a Balanchine article, "The Dance Element in the Music." Even though this book was compiled long before the end of Stravinsky's career, it is a valuable avenue for the study of the most important ballet composer of the century.

WACHTEL is a broadly based collection of essays about *Petrushka*. Wachtel himself contributes two essays: one on its context in modern Russian culture and the other on "The Ballet's Libretto." Tim Scholl writes about Fokine's concept of the ballet, while Janet Kennedy contributes "Shrovetide Revelry: Alexander Benois's Contribution to *Petrushka*." The last essay, "Stravinsky's *Petrushka*," is contributed by well-known Stravinsky scholar Richard Taruskin. This may be one of the few volumes devoted to a specific ballet.

Debussy wrote three complete ballets: *Khamma, Jeux*, and *La boîte à joujoux*. There are sketches for an incomplete work (*No-ja-li*) and the "hybrid" work *Prélude à l'après-midi d'un faune*, hybrid because it was not written as a ballet but was approved for choreography as a ballet by the composer. COX, in his compact volume, addresses the four complete works, each in a separate section. The author also provides historical background, information on the circumstances surrounding the composition, and musical analysis or observations for each work. *Prélude à l'après-midi d'un faune* and *Jeux* are given the most space.

ORENSTEIN is one of the most scholarly and well-organized monographs on Ravel. Part 1 is devoted to the biography and cultural background of the composer. Part 2 discusses his artistic and musical processes. A large percentage of chapter 8, "Ravel's Musical Language," is a chronological examination of each of Ravel's compositions, in which the major works, including the ballets, are given the most space. These entries provide background material as well as musical analyses of the individual works. Orenstein also discusses Ravel's practice of making multiple versions of the same piece. For example, *Ma Mère l'Oye* exists in three versions: piano four hands, an orchestral transcription, and a ballet adaptation. The book includes numerous photographic reproductions, including those of manuscripts and theatrical productions. Appendices include a detailed work list and a list of historical recordings, compiled by Jean Touzelet.

Although there are several good books about Copland, including the Copland and Perlis oral history (2 vols., 1984 and 1989), and Arthur Berger's book (1953), the nature of their construction and writing does not allow the reader to easily locate information about the ballets. BUTTERWORTH's volume is an exception, providing us with a well-organized view of Copland's compositions and an accessible discussion of the composer's five ballets, covered in chronological order in separate entries. For each, Butterworth includes a historical background, programmatic story line, and an overview of the musical substance. He also provides musical examples. Unfortunately, the book is not well indexed. Appendices do include useful lists of Copland's compositions.

GUTMAN takes a chronological approach to Prokofiev's life and works. Prokofiev composed eight or nine ballets (depending on how one counts), and each of these works may be traced via the index. For a particular ballet, the larger print text, written by Mr. Gutman, is interspersed with smaller print text taken from the words of the composer or from other identified sources. This approach emphasizes the historical rather than the analytical aspects of this volume, and it offers the reader an organized perspective that is reinforced by the thoughts of the music's creator and important figures in Prokofiev's life and the study of his works.

BALANCHINE, LAWRENCE, and TERRY are important sources for information on ballets, and their plots, that were created for music not intended for choreographic performance. In this widespread practice of marrying music and dance, the elements of theatrical presentation are conceived on a preexistent musical composition or compositions. This custom is so prevalent that it is difficult to grasp the breadth and content of this category of the dance repertoire and its music. These volumes provide a fundamental guide and documentation to this elusive element of 20th-century ballet.

BENBOW-PFALZGRAF and BENBOW-NIEMIER is a fairly traditional single-volume dictionary about modern dance. A section of moderate-length articles in alphabetical order covers dance companies and festivals, choreographers, individual dances and ballets by title, and overview articles about modern dance in specific countries. Each entry begins with "vital information" about the subject. Such things as a list of works, publications, films, and videotapes are given in chronological order. Then follows a section of historical background, critical appraisal, and analysis. Purposely or inadvertently, this volume emphasizes the secondary role of music in the creation of modern dance. For example, only one major composer, John Cage, is given an entry, and while *Einstein on the Beach* is given a separate article, its composer, Phillip Glass, is not.

HORST and RUSSELL's erudite volume is an impressive attempt to define modern dance and its practice. The authors accomplish this by comparison and analogy to other modern art idioms, particularly visual arts and music. On a different level, the volume is a fundamental handbook for dancers on the components of modern dance creation, especially in relationship to music. Structured in three sections, the book deals with "The Elements of Dance," including melody, space design, rhythm, and texture; "Background or Sources," encompassing primitivism, the archaic, and medievalism; and "The Immediacies of Modern Life," containing sections about expressionism, jazz, and impressionism. There are numerous musical examples by composers such as Lothar Windsperger, Satie, Béla Bartók, Aleksandr Scriabin, Ernst Toch, and Ravel. This is an exceptional book concerning a discipline difficult to comprehend.

The subtitle of TECK's book, "Reflections on a Collaborative Art," announces the emphasis of this original and unusual volume. It is a group of essays based on interviews with important figures in modern dance. Choreographers surveyed include Agnes de Mille, Paul Taylor, George Balanchine, Erick Hawkins, and others. Composers discussed include Louis Horst, Henry Cowell, William Schuman, Virgil Thomson, and Lou Harrison. Topics of essays or parts of essays include the collaboration between composers and choreographer, multitalented musicians associated with dance companies, orchestral performers, observations about ballet companies and their orchestras, conductors, and dancers, as well as other topics. This is a most valuable source in the study of the music and its interrelationship with modern dance and ballet.

JEFFREY WASSON

Debussy, Claude 1862–1918

French composer and critic

1. Biography

Briscoe, James R. *Claude Debussy: A Guide to Research,* New York: Garland Publishing, 1990

Debussy, Claude, *Debussy Letters,* edited by François Lesure, translated by Roger Nichols, Cambridge, Massachusetts: Harvard University Press, and London: Faber, 1987

——, *Debussy on Music,* translated by Richard Langham Smith, London: Secker and Warburg, and New York: Knopf, 1977

Dietschy, Marcel, *A Portrait of Claude Debussy,* edited and translated by William Ashbrook and Margaret G. Cobb, Oxford: Clarendon Press, 1990

Lockspeiser, Edward, *Debussy: His Life and Mind,* 2 vols., London: Cassell, and New York: Macmillan, 1962–65

Nichols, Roger, *Debussy Remembered,* Portland, Oregon: Amadeus Press, 1992

——, *The Life of Debussy,* Cambridge: Cambridge University Press, 1998

Vallas, Léon, *Claude Debussy: His Life and Works,* translated by Maire O'Brien and Grace O'Brien, London: Oxford University Press, 1933; reprint, 1972

The history of Debussy biography encompasses two major lines of inquiry. Earlier research, notably that of Léon Vallas, focused on an "impressionistic appreciation" of music and the "national identity" of the man (James R. Briscoe, *Claude Debussy: A Guide to Research,* 1990). By contrast, later biographies by Marcel Dietschy and Edward Lockspeiser have attempted a more profound contemplation of the man and the music. These works have stimulated further research of contemporary movements in literary and visual art. In the same vein, the most recent biography by Nichols further explores issues of cultural context. In addition, relatively recent translations of Debussy's letters and critical writings have contributed valuable information concerning the composer's interpersonal relationships and his unique aesthetic principles. Finally, an anthology of memoirs from Debussy's friends and colleagues reveals insight into his character.

VALLAS, in the earliest comprehensive biography translated into English, presents a poetic account of Debussy's innovative musical aesthetic. Consequently, he focuses on the mature works at the expense of earlier music. He quotes numerous sources that refer to critical reception of Debussy's music, especially *Pelléas et Mélisande*. A thematic catalog, included in the back of the book, needs updating. Despite much commendable scholarship, Vallas's treatment of Debussy's personal history and music is superficial. Psychological topics are not explored, and negative comments concerning personality are avoided. Although the musical analyses are vivid and colorful, they do not probe the music. The commentary is descriptive rather than analytic.

DIETSCHY's work concentrates on the composer's life and personality. He begins with comprehensive research into the composer's ancestry, parents, family, childhood, and adolescence. Information on the Conservatoire years is expanded far beyond Vallas. There are many quoted references to correspondence with friends, poets, and painters. Dietschy's portrait is both personal and sympathetic. His writing style is clear and poetic. In his treatment of the early reception history of *Pelléas et Mélisande*, Dietschy elucidates the significance of Debussy's musical revolution. In another section, he characterizes "Et la lune descend sur le temple qui fut," a solo piano work from *Images*, set 2, as "an evocation of nothingness, the icy, pale reflection of stellar spaces, where all pain is numbed." Although he does not focus on the music (at least from an analytical perspective), Dietschy does append a catalog of works at the end of the book;

information is given on genre, dates of composition, publication, and first performance, text (if vocal), dedication, orchestration, and location of autograph score.

LOCKSPEISER's biography achieves an "interpenetration" of Debussy's life and works from a background of contemporary movements in literature and painting. Proceeding from the assumption that Debussy's art cannot be approached as "an isolated musical phenomenon," Lockspeiser draws symbolist connections to Stéphane Mallarmé, Henri de Régnier, Jules Laforgue, Pierre Louÿs, Oscar Wilde, Edgar Allan Poe, and many others. In the visual arts, he traces links to art nouveau, the Pre-Raphaelites, impressionism, and orientalism in the work of Maurice Denis, Dante Gabriel Rossetti, J.M.W. Turner, Claude Monet, and Ando Hiroshige. In Lockspeiser's words, Debussy's aesthetic is "not merely a reflection of one aspect or another of his period. It is the period." He continues: "Music was at that time regarded as the quintessential, privileged art, and I see no other composer who so closely realized the musical ideals to which the writers and painters of his time openly aspired." Lockspeiser reveals Debussy's revolution from the perspective of this cultural milieu and provides an analytical interpretation of his music. At the end of the second volume, he contributes a penetrating overview of harmonic practice and musical form. He correctly declares that Debussy's most significant innovation is a formal procedure based on timbre—not thematic development and "musical discourse" of the older sonata form, but a structure that evolves from the sonority of exotic scales, modes, and parallel chords.

The collection of DEBUSSY's (1977) critical writings is an indispensable complement to the above-mentioned biographies. Debussy discusses the works of numerous composers (including Bach, Rameau, Beethoven, Dukas, Grieg, and Richard Strauss) in several important Parisian journals. The articles, written between the years 1901 and 1915, offer deep insight into Debussy's emerging aesthetic. The wit, descriptive writing style, and caustic remarks guarantee an enjoyable reading experience.

DEBUSSY (1987), selected letters from Debussy to his friends, fellow artists, and publishers, deepens the appreciation of the composer's character. This correspondence spans Debussy's entire adult life (1884 to 1918), which makes this primary source central to any in-depth biographical study. Remarks pertaining to art, literature, and contemporary aesthetics are found abundantly in the letters.

NICHOLS's (1992) collection of friends' memoirs penetrates Debussy's personality. Many aspects of the composer's life are reflected: his youth, Conservatoire years, return from Rome, composition and rehearsals of Pelléas, friendships, pianistic artistry, home life, tours abroad, and last years. Sources are given at the end of each memoir. In addition, a chronology of Debussy's life presents information on his compositions (completion dates and first performances), significant events (personal and professional), other artists' works, and contemporary historical events.

NICHOLS (1998) represents the latest addition to biographical scholarship. This book offers both a concise review of earlier biographies (Vallas, Dietschy, Lockspeiser) and fresh insights into Debussy's life and music. Consequently, Nichols's study presents an overall treatment of biographical details for the first-time reader and also deepens the perspective for connoisseurs of the composer and his music. For those who want to follow up references, many sources are included within the text. Nichols connects the mystery and richness of Debussy's music to the dualities or pluralities of his complex character: a "heartless treatment of at least one mistress and one wife" caused by "his greater fidelity to music," the "pull between privacy and publicity," the "struggle between simplicity and complication," and the "reluctance to engage reality" in an inner world of fantasy.

Finally, BRISCOE is an essential bibliographic source (up to 1990) for Debussy research. The scope is comprehensive with over 900 annotated entries. This material appears in the following categories: letters, critical writings and interviews, reference books, studies of Debussy's life, collective volumes and conferences, personal relationships, musical style and aesthetics, and studies of compositions. In addition, a chronology of life and works, a catalog of musical compositions, an index of letters, and a list of manuscript letters in libraries and private collections are included. Briscoe's monumental work is justified by his well-founded claim that "the compositions and ideas of Claude Debussy comprise one of the most pervasive achievements in Western music."

CHARLES FREDERICK FRANTZ

2. Works

Briscoe, James, editor, *Debussy in Performance*, New Haven, Connecticut: Yale University Press, 1999

Holloway, Robin, *Debussy and Wagner*, London: Eulenburg, 1979

Howat, Roy, *Debussy in Proportion: A Musical Analysis*, Cambridge: Cambridge University Press, 1983

Lenormand, René, *A Study of Twentieth-Century Harmony*, translated by Herbert Antcliffe, London: Williams, and Boston: Boston Music, 1915; reprint, New York: Da Capo Press, 1976

Lockspeiser, Edward, *Debussy: His Life and Mind*, 2 vols., London: Cassell, and New York: Macmillan, 1962–65

Nichols, Roger, and Richard Langham Smith, *Claude Debussy: Pelléas et Mélisande*, Cambridge: Cambridge University Press, 1989

Orledge, Robert, *Debussy and the Theatre*, Cambridge: Cambridge University Press, 1982

Parks, Richard S., *The Music of Claude Debussy,* New Haven, Connecticut: Yale University Press, 1989

Roberts, Paul, *Images: The Piano Music of Claude Debussy,* Portland, Oregon: Amadeus Press, 1996

Smith, Richard Langham, editor, *Debussy Studies,* Cambridge: Cambridge University Press, 1997

Vallas, Léon, *Claude Debussy: His Life and Works,* translated by Maire O'Brien and Grace O'Brien, London: Oxford University Press, 1933

The large and diverse literature devoted to Claude Debussy's music is extraordinarily rich, ranging from the superficially descriptive to the recondite and intensely technical, from comprehensive coverage of Debussy's oeuvre to monographs that focus on a single composition, and from single-issue studies to the eclectic. More recent studies reap the benefits of both the artifacts (e.g., letters and autograph scores) that have become available to scholars and the changing perspectives in musicology, theory, and performance. Diversity rather than contention characterizes Debussy scholarship, and there is an enormous, ever-increasing accumulation of estimable literature.

This literature review is organized by degree of selectivity in the coverage of compositions, beginning with sources that strive to treat all or most of Debussy's oeuvre. However, this scheme might obscure some trends in research. For example, early studies (e.g., Lenormand and Vallas) are preoccupied with the novelty of the composer's musical language and his role as iconoclast. These studies treat pitch and form as preeminent and objectify compositions embodied in musical scores. Studies from the 1950s, 1960s, and 1970s (e.g., Lockspeiser) continue to objectify Debussy's music while showing a much greater sophistication because of the burgeoning availability of primary materials, including autographs and letters, as well as the scholars' increased experience and better training in musicology. By this time, Debussy's central role in shaping the course of 20th-century music is taken for granted. Throughout the late 1970s and 1980s (e.g., Holloway, Howat, and Parks), empirical studies of Debussy's music embodied in artifacts (scores and autographs) culminate in sophisticated theoretical-analytical studies that postulate deep musical structures for form and pitch materials. The 1990s (e.g., Nichols and Langham Smith, Roberts, Smith, and Briscoe) witnesses the same shift toward holism and interdisciplinarity that characterizes other areas of inquiry in the arts and humanities along with an attitude that is less confidently objectivist.

LOCKSPEISER, still the only truly comprehensive study of Debussy in English, weaves copious, largely descriptive accounts of individual pieces throughout an excellent (although dated) historiographical account of the composer's life and times. The second volume concludes with a chapter titled "Debussy's Musical Language," in which Lockspeiser discusses a number of general stylistic features. This is an excellent first source both for readers broadly interested in the composer's works and for those wanting to investigate particular pieces.

VALLAS is mainly biographical and valuable for the author's contemporaneity to the composer and his milieu. The author discusses many individual works, albeit in very general terms. Similarly, Roger Nichols's concise *The Life of Debussy* (1998), which reflects recent scholarship, discusses many individual works in general terms.

PARKS is a comprehensive study of Debussy's musical language. It treats many compositions across all genres spanning the whole of Debussy's career. Although non-specialist readers might find abstruse the chapters that treat the nature of Debussy's harmonic vocabulary and relations using Schenkerian and pitch-set theory as analytical tools, other material—involving form, meter, register, and orchestration—requires only a modest knowledge of music theory.

ORLEDGE covers all of Debussy's stage works, from *Diane au bois* to *Le martyre de Saint Sébastien,* as well as all of the incomplete or aborted projects. The author describes in detail the extant sources and circumstances of composition surrounding each work, which he supports with some music analysis. Orledge eschews profound musical analysis and technical language in favor of wide accessibility. Although the author's discussions of individual works are necessarily succinct, this engaging work of exemplary scholarship conveys well the central role that stage works played in Debussy's career and compositional thinking.

A specialized work devoted exclusively to Debussy's compositions for piano, ROBERTS takes as his point of departure the premise that an acquaintance with contemporaneous national currents in the other arts, especially painting, poetry, and literature, is essential for understanding Debussy's music. Organized around the general artistic milieu that surrounded Debussy, Roberts's discussion of all of the piano pieces proceeds in a fashion that allows each work to emerge from this context most naturally. Roberts is well known as an accomplished interpreter of Debussy's music; as this book reveals, he is also quite knowledgeable about fin de siècle art, especially painting, for his observations about musical features and performance issues reflect the pieces' relations with the other arts. Although reminiscent in its concentration on piano repertoire of E. Robert Schmitz's book *The Piano Works of Claude Debussy* (1950), this volume by Roberts is far less technical in its discussion of both musical and pianistic details and far more synesthetic in its outlook.

HOLLOWAY's provocative book addresses a topic that has long been an issue in Debussy studies: the question of Wagnerian influence. The author claims that the project originated in a conceit: in the preface, he thanks "Egon Wellesz who by his contempt for the whole project first stirred me into thinking for myself." Holloway's thesis, supported copiously by examples, is that despite Debussy's inveterate denials of Wagnerian influence—there is his famous aphorism, "Wagner . . . was a beautiful sunset that often has been mistaken for a sunrise"—in fact, Wagner's influence can be seen throughout Debussy's oeuvre. It is blatantly obvious in relatively early works, such as the Baudelaire songs, and more subtly concealed in later pieces, such as *Le martyre de Saint Sébastien* and *Jeux*.

LENORMAND is one of the earliest scholarly attempts to come to terms with Debussy's and his younger contemporaries' new harmonic language. Despite its age, this study remains a good catalog of novelties, exoticisms, compositional devices, and bold extensions of 19th-century tonal practices found in Debussy's music, documented in many fascinating examples culled from the repertoire.

HOWAT is an intriguing exploration of the Golden Section as a means of proportional construction of asymmetrical formal structures. Howat carefully builds his case that the composer deliberately incorporated classical proportional schemes into many pieces. The author proposes formal schemes for works based on conventional musical cues that establish formal boundaries of small and large scale; he then calculates proportions reckoned spatiotemporally by counting bars and beats and constructing schema of the resultant durations. He concludes by discussing "external" evidence, such as the fin de siècle esoteric currents that characterized Debussy's milieu and influenced his circle of associates. The external evidence is hearsay, the internal evidence circumstantial; nonetheless, the author succeeds in framing a most interesting issue and making a persuasive (if not altogether compelling) case. Although theoretical in tone, this book is readily accessible to nonspecialists as well as to scholars.

BRISCOE's collection of 11 essays begins with chapters by Smith, Claude Abravanel, and Louis-Marc Suter that explore attitudes toward performance by Debussy and his milieu. Next, Briscoe, Cecilia Dunoyer, Stephanie Jordan, and Brooks Toliver each treat a different genre and consider, in light of historical sound recordings, the flexibility and range of values affecting such elements as performance sources, tempo, performance techniques, interpretive freedom, and the handling of expressive indications. Prominent Debussy interpreters Désiré-Emile Inghelbrecht (in a reprint of his 1933 essay) and Pierre Boulez (in an interview) provide firsthand accounts. The last two chapters by Parks and Jann Pasler are overtly analytical, focusing on musical structures within the domains of texture, timbre, voice leading, metric and phrase structure, and the musical arabesque in piano works and the chamber sonatas. Although all of these essays were written to be accessible

to nonspecialists, their authors' prominence and international standing should attract the interest of music scholar-specialists as well.

The SMITH congeries of nine essays is highly eclectic. Its authors are well-established scholars; many are involved with the critical edition of Debussy's complete works and bring that experience to bear in these papers. Using autograph sources and letters, Myriam Chimènes examines Debussy's process of orchestration as carried out for *Jeux* to shed light on the role that timbre and instrumentation played in his compositional thinking. David Grayson considers the treatment of psychological versus "real" time in *Pelléas et Mélisande*, emphasizing circularity and nonlinearity among dramatic events as factors contributing to the opera's dreamlike character. Denis Herlin's topic is the highly convoluted journey traversed by Debussy's *Nocturnes* from the Fromont edition of 1900 to the Jobert edition of 1930. The author vividly demonstrates the problems, all too common with Debussy's works, that plague editors of critical editions. Howat discusses issues that arise, in preparing performances of the piano works, from Debussy's notation and contemporaneous performance conventions. Jean-Michel Nectoux writes about Debussy's lesser-known artistic predilections, which included the painters Lerolle, Degas, and de Groux and the notorious sculptress Camille Claudel. Nichols's topic is Debussy reception in England from the mid-1890s to 1914, and Orledge explores Debussy's enduring and complex friendship with Eric Satie. Marie Rolf considers Debussy's settings of two of Stéphane Mallarmé's poems, "Apparition" and "Soupir," examining the poems' structures, symbols, and images and Debussy's musical treatment of them. Finally, Smith discusses Debussy's early opera (not performed during his lifetime) *Rodrigue et Chimène*, based on Catulle Mendès's libretto (itself based on *El Cid*). All articles are written for a wide audience of academics, students, and informed music lovers.

NICHOLS and SMITH is one of the Cambridge Opera Handbooks, a series of monographs, each devoted to a single opera, and intended for nonspecialists as well as music students and scholars. These seven essays cover various facets of Debussy's only published opera. The first of three chapters by Smith examines Maeterlinck's play, on which the opera is based. The second is devoted to Debussy's idiosyncratic treatment of musical motives and symbols and the third to the polar dramatic roles of "darkness" versus "light" and their associated key schemes. A chapter by David Grayson focuses on the opera's compositional history, autograph sketches, and publication sources while exposing conflicts among accounts of the circumstances of composition and inconsistencies among extant autograph and published sources. Readers attracted by this superb but compressed account might want to read the expanded version of the opera's compositional journey: Grayson's dissertation,

The Genesis of Debussy's Pelléas et Mélisande (1986). Three chapters by Nichols include a thorough précis of the opera that emphasizes Debussy's particular musical treatment of the text and its dramatic content and two studies of the work's performance history. One of the latter essays treats the circumstances of production, from the initial performance in 1902 through subsequent presentations to 1985. The other focuses on styles of interpretation and critical reception. In all, this is a fascinating, well-conceived, and informative collection.

RICHARD S. PARKS

de Falla, Manuel *see* Falla, Manuel de

Delius, Frederick 1862–1934

English composer

Carley, Lionel, *Delius: The Paris Years,* Rickmansworth: Triad Press, 1975

Carley, Lionel, editor, *Frederick Delius: Music, Art and Literature,* Aldershot: Ashgate, 1998

Delius, Clare, *Frederick Delius: Memories of My Brother,* London: Nicholson and Watson, 1935

Delius, Frederick, *Delius: A Life in Letters I 1862–1908,* edited by Lionel Carley, London: Scolar Press, 1983

————, *Delius: A Life in Letters II 1909–1934,* edited by Lionel Carley, Aldershot: Scolar Press, 1988

Fenby, Eric, *Delius as I Knew Him,* London: Bell, 1936

Heseltine, Philip, *Frederick Delius,* London: Bodley Head, 1923; revised edition, 1952

Hutchings, Arthur, *Delius,* London: Macmillan, 1948; reprint, Westport, Connecticut: Greenwood Press, 1970

Jefferson, Alan, *Delius,* London: Dent, and New York: Octagon Books, 1972

Jones, Philip, *The American Source of Delius' Style,* New York: Garland, 1989

Palmer, Christopher, *Delius: Portrait of a Cosmopolitan,* London: Duckworth, and New York: Holmes and Meier, 1976

Redwood, Christopher, editor, *A Delius Companion,* London: Calder, 1976; revised edition, 1980

Frederick Delius was an English composer of German descent who resided primarily in Grez-sur-Loing. Because he is part of our recent past, existing scholarship is for the most part biographical. Only in the last 25 years have writers started to take a critical look at Delius's music or its place within the artistic and cultural framework in which it was written.

HESELTINE is the first book-length study to appear about the life and work of Delius. Published 11 years prior to the death of the composer, it provides us with an early record written by a younger contemporary. Heseltine's book is the product of a 20-year friendship between subject and author and therefore includes a vast amount of information about Delius's memories, views, influences, and musical intentions, much of the time presented in the composer's own words, which are particularly important for material relating to the period before 1910, the year Heseltine was introduced to Delius. The book contains no letters (which is undoubtedly due to Heseltine's passing disregard for correspondence rather than to a notion of privacy) but does exhibit some of the finest musical criticism coming out of England in the first decades of the 20th century.

Clare DELIUS's book was not meant to be a complete biography, and, as she states in her introduction, it is written from the point of view of a sister rather than a music expert. This work provides a written illustration of the Delius household and their family life; intimate details of the composer's early years, his relationship to family members, and his everyday life; and a detailed description of the composer's relationship with their father. In this respect, Clare Delius's memoir provides a balance to the many accounts of the relationship between Frederick and his father found in later works (although her perspective is most likely due to her own familial connection). She includes a good deal of family genealogy and identifies spurious relationships for which she can find no evidence. While she makes no attempt at critical discussion of Delius's music, she does provide the reader with pertinent information that does not exist elsewhere.

The purpose of FENBY's book is to present an account of the author's decision to travel to Grez-sur-Loing and act as amanuensis to the (by then) severely ailing composer. Part 2, entitled "How He Worked," is perhaps the most important section of the book. Here Fenby details the process of composition that took place during his stay with Delius, as well as the day-to-day work of composing, by a man who was, at this time in his life, blind and virtually paralyzed.

HUTCHINGS's book is in two parts: a biographical study of the composer and a critical study of his music. The information found in the first section is similar to that found in other biographies, but the second section, while dated, is well worth reading. Hutchings groups Delius's works according to genre (opera, chamber music, song, etc.) and briefly examines each piece. He includes the history of the pieces, their critical reception, and compositional techniques, as well as word settings and literary counterparts (if applicable), all followed by musical examples.

JEFFERSON's study is part of the Master Musician series. The author emphasizes that his book is concerned "with Delius the man, especially as emphasis on his later life has generally led to a somewhat misleading impression of what he was really like." Jefferson goes into detail about the composer's early life as a bohemian, adventurer, and practical joker, and as a man eagerly sought after by women, in order to deflect the belief that developed during his later years that he was a man utterly devoid of humor and consideration for others.

CARLEY's (1975) study is meant to be a prelude to a more extended work. This chronological study focuses on Delius's more notable friendships, relationships with artists, and place within the European artistic culture of the day. Carley compares the musical techniques of a variety of Delius's works to the theories and artistic techniques of his painter friends. Presented here are references to manuscript sources, including letters from people such as Grieg, Molard, de Monfried, Sinding, de Mouvel, Calvé, Gaston-Donville, Fauré, Leblanc, Maddison, Moreau, Ouvré, Ravel, Schmitt, and de Séverac. This study breaks away from previous biographical writing by analyzing Delius's place within the artistic climate of the years surrounding the turn of the 20th century. Carley also includes facsimiles of manuscripts for two unpublished songs, *Chanson Fortunio* and *Nuages*.

PALMER takes Delius out of his usual classification as an English composer and places him within the wider framework of the historical, cultural, and cosmopolitan contexts in which he lived. The author uses these contexts as backgrounds for examining the composer's compositions, including textures, sonorities, color, melody, technique, form, and orchestration.

REDWOOD's edition is a collection of articles on Delius's life and music. The authors of the articles are drawn from a wide circle, including Delius himself, other composers, musicologists, music critics, music scholars, a conductor, musicians, a poet, a farming expert, and three Delius Trust archivists. The topics range from memoirs and studies of his personality and his wife, Jelka, to detailed studies of particular pieces.

DELIUS (1983) and DELIUS (1988) are seminal works in Delius studies and vital for research on his life or music. The two volumes include over 600 letters to and from Delius. The first volume covers the period from 1862 to 1908, the second, from 1909 to the composer's death in 1934. The letters are presented with footnotes and biographical data for each year. These volumes also contain Delius's memories of his childhood, his 1887 summer diary, his recollections of Grieg and Strindberg, and Jelka's memories of her husband.

JONES is a critical book-length study that seriously examines the role of the various types of American music with which Delius came into contact during the last quarter of the 19th century (such as African-American spirituals, black minstrelsy, white minstrelsy, and early strains of jazz). This book discusses these American influences and traces the origins of their influences in Delius's music back to his first visit to the United States. Jones examines particular works from 1887 to 1916. Also included here is a reconstruction of the tone poem *American Rhapsody for Orchestra*.

CARLEY (1998) is a collection of 12 articles authored by scholars from around the world. Carley's aim is to get away from a purely English standpoint on the composer because Delius was, in fact, a cosmopolitan composer. The articles included follow the trend in scholarship set up by the editor of this volume in his previous 1975 work: the articles focus on Delius's connection with contemporary art and literary movements, as well as reception and performance history.

RENÉE CHÉRIE CLARK

Dello Joio, Norman b. 1913

United States composer

Bumgardner, Thomas A., *Norman Dello Joio*, Boston: Twayne, 1986

Ewen, David, editor, *Composers since 1900: A Biographical and Critical Guide*, New York: Wilson, 1969

Hitchcock, H. Wiley, *Music in the United States: A Historical Introduction*, Englewood Cliffs, New Jersey: Prentice Hall, 1969; 4th edition, 1999

Machlis, Joseph, *American Composers of Our Time*, New York: Crowell, 1963

The diversity of compositional style in 20th-century American music is vast, but certain broad trends can be delineated. Those apparent during Norman Dello Joio's early years of composing (1937–50) were neoclassicism and the avant-garde. The former category was characterized by adherence to classical structure yet modern treatment of harmony, rhythm, and melody; experimentation and exploration of new ways to organize sound within a composition characterized the latter trend. Dello Joio's emphasis on melody and his retention of classical form while employing a moderately dissonant harmony clearly place his music during this time in the neoclassical genre. He enjoyed public acclaim and with it, awards and commissions.

After 1950, two new categories of compositional style, now expressed in terms of eclecticism and modernism, arose concurrently in American music. Dello Joio's belief that music should be accessible to more than the musically educated precluded his placement as a modernist, although in four works dating from the early 1960s and 1970s, he did experiment with serialism. His refinement of compositional technique and its application to scores for opera and television films or documentaries, rather than exploration of new means of musical expression, were his hallmarks. During the late 1950s and 1960s, when the younger modernist generation of composers emerged, tending toward Stravinsky's adoption of serialism and the newly exciting arena of electronic music, Dello Joio's music was considered passé.

Nonetheless, his mastery of compositional craft and his appeal to a broader audience have enabled him to fulfill a purpose that took root during his study with composer Paul Hindemith in the early 1940s—to compose music that is expertly crafted and reflects his personal inclinations and experience.

Since the mid-1970s, musical experimentation has continued, but the search for musical expression that has a more immediate appeal to the general public has also enjoyed a resurgence. Minimalism and looking to the distant past for appealing musical connections are prominent themes. Renewing or seeking acquaintance with music by respected composers of the recent past, including Dello Joio, enriched the musical spectrum at the close of the 20th century.

MACHLIS devotes individual chapters to 16 American composers, including Dello Joio. From his perspective as a contemporary musical colleague, Machlis reflects knowledgeably on Dello Joio's early life and the most publicly prominent years of his career. The readable, chronologically arranged text is enhanced by descriptions of compositions. Machlis discusses Dello Joio's attitudes toward and habits of composing, providing the reader with an excellent orientation to this composer, his works, and his compositional style. A helpful glossary of musical terms precedes the index.

BUMGARDNER's thoroughly researched and carefully organized biography reveals relevant personal details, addresses the scope of the composer's work, and shares insights into Dello Joio's attitudes and philosophy about life, music, and music education. A works list and discography enhance the volume. In addition to an opening chapter devoted to Dello Joio himself, there are chapters on his music, organized by category of composition: vocal music, orchestral works, concertos, chamber music, keyboard music, music for band, dramatic music (incidental theater music and television film scores), and operas. Bumgardner's selected bibliography cites primary sources; secondary sources, which he briefly annotates; and articles. He refers to Dello Joio's music as "easily comprehendible"; Bumgardner's writing about a composer he clearly respects and admires is likewise easily comprehensible.

The inclusion of HITCHCOCK's volume in this discussion is merited not because of the brief (but fitting) reference to Dello Joio, but because part 3 of the book provides an excellent survey of the multiplicity of musical styles and compositional currents in the United States during the 20th century. This discussion is necessary background for a more complete understanding of Dello Joio's placement within this context.

EWEN presents a straightforward biography of Dello Joio and interjects partial descriptions of some of his major compositions. The list of works contains no dates, and certain dates suggested for biographical events have been challenged in later scholarship (see Bumgardner or

The New Grove Dictionary of American Music), but quotations from several magazines and newspapers offer further insights into the life and works of Dello Joio.

JOANNE E. SWENSON-ELDRIDGE

Denmark *see* Scandinavia

des Prez, Josquin *see* Josquin des Prez

Divine Office *see* Liturgy: Divine Office

Donizetti, Gaetano 1797–1848

Italian composer

Allitt, John Stewart, *Donizetti: In Light of Romanticism and the Teaching of Johann Simon Mayr*, Shaftesbury: Elements, 1991

Ashbrook, William, *Donizetti and His Operas*, Cambridge: Cambridge University Press, 1982

Ashbrook, William, and Julian Budden, "Gaetano Donizetti," in *The New Grove Masters of Italian Opera*, edited by Philip Gossett et al., London: Macmillan, and New York: Norton, 1983

Black, John, *Donizetti's Operas in Naples: 1822–1848*, London: Donizetti Society, 1982

Gossett, Philip, *Anna Bolena and the Artistic Maturity of Gaetano Donizetti*, Oxford: Clarendon Press, 1985

Osborne, Charles, *The Bel Canto Operas of Rossini, Donizetti, and Bellini*, Portland, Oregon: Amadeus Press, and London: Methuen, 1994

Weinstock, Herbert, *Donizetti and the World of Opera in Italy, Paris, and Vienna in the First Half of the Nineteenth Century*, New York: Pantheon Books, and London: Methuen, 1963

The world of opera in 19th-century Italy was so competitive that, with the limited number of commissions to be had, composers often resorted to backroom bargaining and underhanded deals. One man succeeded in rising above all the pettiness and backbiting: Gaetano Donizetti. His letters (the bulk of which sadly remains untranslated) portray a kind and generous character who, exceptional for his time, wished his colleagues well. Only once, when goaded by Vincenzo Bellini, did Donizetti resort to an angry reply. Often called "Dozinetti" because of the dozens of scores which he penned, his life was riddled with sorrow, and after the deaths of his wife and children, scholars suggest, his music became tinged with melancholy. Donizetti's career ended tragically after he lost both physical and mental faculties due to complications caused by the final stage of syphilis. His operas, particularly the romantic masterpiece *Lucia di Lammermoor* and comic classics such as *Don Pasquale,* continue to assure him a place among the geniuses of Italian theater music. Although the majority of sources on Donizetti are in Italian, a commendable core of studies is available to English-speaking readers. Moreover, the Donizetti Society in London publishes a newsletter that features recent research on the composer as well as articles on other early 19th-century opera topics.

WEINSTOCK notes in his introduction that both he and Ashbrook, each unaware of the other's work, were compiling materials on Donizetti at about the same time. Fortuitously, each had taken a different direction. Weinstock takes a more historical approach and leaves musical discussion and analysis to Ashbrook. In a well-documented volume, Weinstock follows Donizetti from his birth in Bergamo in 1797 to his return there to die in 1848. Referring often on Zavadini's monumental study of the composer (Guido Zavadini, *Donizetti: Vita, musiche, epistolario* [1948]), Weinstock includes translations of sections of pertinent correspondence and personal documents; most useful is the author's adaptation of Zavadini's chronology of Donizetti's works, which offers information on premieres, original casts, and, when known, the location of autograph scores. Also listed are Donizetti's vast nonoperatic works, including sacred, orchestral, and chamber compositions. The generous appendix contains transcriptions of documents such as the composer's birth certificate, record of marriage, medical accounts of the composer's physical and mental conditions prior to his death, and an autopsy report. This volume offers a readable and respectable biography perfect for those beginning a study of Donizetti.

ASHBROOK, perhaps the most renowned authority on the works of Donizetti, begins his book with a biography, followed by an expert discussion of the operas. Although some general knowledge of music is necessary to understand the musical examples provided, Ashbrook's descriptions are not laden with complicated theoretical terms and can be comprehended by readers with a basic familiarity with the individual operas, their structures, and their musical numbers. In addition, the author traces and comments on the composer's artistic development; included as well is useful information on the librettists with whom Donizetti worked and their approaches to writing. While not recommended as a starting point for the novice, this volume offers an excellent introduction to the operatic world in which Donizetti's career took place; those with a basic understanding of Italian opera will benefit from the section on Donizetti's compositional approach, which includes the necessary vocabulary used for 19th-century Italian theater music.

Readers wishing to familiarize themselves with individual operas might investigate OSBORNE, which offers a capsulized history of and commentary on each work, as well as information on characters, plot settings, and premieres. Then, after listening to a recording or studying the score, one could make an easy transition to Ashbrook's volume.

Following a concise biography, with a brief section on the composer's character, ASHBROOK and BUDDEN survey the operas and comment on the melody, harmony, form, and orchestral and vocal writing. Donizetti's chamber, sacred, and instrumental compositions also merit commentary. The entry concludes with a work list and extensive bibliography.

BLACK deals specifically with productions of Donizetti's operas in Naples from 1822 until 1848, the year of the composer's death. Illustrated with reproductions of the covers of the printed librettos from the various productions, Black offers data and statistics rather than any interpretation or analysis. Gleaning his information from archival research, Zavadini, and announcements published in the *Giornale del Regno delle due Sicilie,* the author provides information on specific productions, as well as tables of statistics related to the city's various theaters and the performance history of Donizetti works. A noteworthy section explains the theatrical administration and the operatic calendar specific to Naples.

Those with significant musical knowledge will want to explore GOSSETT's fascinating study of Donizetti and *Anna Bolena.* The author, through a well-documented study of Donizetti's revisions to this score, has attempted to "catch [Donizetti] in the act of composition." With ample musical excerpts, Gossett demonstrates the composer's development and approach to form and melody. Topics covered include balance and proportion in the score, tonal closure, and the specific compositional practices Donizetti used in the setting of cabalettas. Gossett argues that, although Donizetti often tended to revert to Rossinian models when faced with decisions, he nevertheless still continued to press against the boundaries of those paradigms.

ALLITT presents a book of essays that consider Donizetti and his art. Topics include Donizetti's character, his work as a composer, his connections to romanticism and to religion, and Donizetti and the tradition of romantic love. The author also offers his views on the themes of six of the composer's operas—*Linda di Chamounix, Maria Stuarda, L'elisir d'amore, Lucia di Lammermoor, Poliuto,* and *Don Pasquale*—and he discusses the important link between Donizetti and his teacher Johann Simon Mayr, whose own role in the development of 19th-century opera is often overlooked. Because the book deals in interpretations of symbolism, it requires an intimate acquaintance with the operas discussed; therefore, this work is not suggested for those with little musical or literary background.

DENISE GALLO

Dowland, John 1563–1626

English (Irish?)-born composer

Doughtie, Edward, *English Renaissance Song,* Boston: Twayne, 1986

Fischlin, Daniel, *In Small Proportions: A Poetics of the English Ayre 1596–1622,* Detroit, Michigan: Wayne State University Press, 1998

Maynard, Winifred, *Elizabethan Lyric Poetry and Its Music,* Oxford: Clarendon Press, and New York: Oxford University Press, 1986

Poulton, Diana, *John Dowland,* London: Faber, and Berkeley: University of California Press, 1972; revised edition, 1982

Rooley, Anthony, "New Light on John Dowland's Songs of Darkness," *Early Music* 11 (1983)

———, *Performance: Revealing the Orpheus Within,* London: Dryad, 1988

Toft, Robert, *Tune Thy Musicke to Thy Hart: The Art of Eloquent Singing in England 1597–1622,* Toronto: University of Toronto Press, 1993

Ward, John M., "A Dowland Miscellany," *Journal of the Lute Society of America* 10 (1977)

John Dowland ranks as the preeminent composer of English lute music at the end of the 16th and beginning of the 17th centuries. As Poulton points out, "During his lifetime John Dowland was one of the few English composers whose fame spread throughout Europe." Dowland's life was filled with disappointment—he felt he did not receive the recognition, particularly from Elizabeth I—an amateur lutenist and musical patron—that he deserved. His inability to obtain a post at the English court has never been satisfactorily explained, although theories abound. Having a personality that all too easily offended possibly contributed to his failure, as did his flirtation with Catholicism. As a result, Dowland traveled widely, establishing himself in Northern European courts, where he received more than ample compensation for his musical abilities. Upon the death of Elizabeth and accession of James I, he finally obtained the long-sought-after court post.

POULTON may come as close to the definitive word as any composer's biography. She discusses all the surviving biographical evidence, only cautiously filling in the gaps and offering tentative solutions to the mysteries. Poulton analyzes both the lute music and songs (airs), laying out the rather complex background to the editions of the airs. WARD, as the title indicates, is a large collection of primary material revealing biographical information and musical sources. Although Poulton has incorporated material from this article in her revised edition, much remains in the article that is not included in her biography.

Much discussion in recent years has focused on the airs for solo voice and lute. What did these airs mean to the composer, the singer, and the audience? While this discussion considers the lute song in general, the music of Dowland is central to it and references to specific airs of his appear frequently. This literature is so extensive that only those works that deal extensively with Dowland are mentioned here. DOUGHTIE, whose edition of English lyrics is the basic source for identifying all the texts set by Dowland, is concerned with the changing relationship between poetry and music in the 16th and early 17th centuries and how they influenced each other. He emphasizes Dowland's sensitivity to the poetry in fashioning the melodies for his airs.

MAYNARD presents a straightforward survey of the lute song. The chapter devoted in part to Dowland addresses such questions as whether the airs or their versions for solo lute came first, the authorship of the lyrics, and the relationship between the voice and accompaniment.

ROOLEY (1983) argues that the lyrics of Dowland's melancholy airs, often interpreted as reflections of the composer's personality, were in fact collections of rhetorical devices in common use. To support his case, Rooley demonstrates Dowland's familiarity with the Italian madrigal composer Luca Marenzio, who used similar devices, and shows how Dowland incorporated passages from Marenzio's music into his airs.

ROOLEY (1988) approaches the lute song from the performer's point of view, asserting that singers should imagine themselves as Orpheus, the celebrated musician of antiquity, inspired to move the soul of the listener through their art. TOFT likewise approaches the songs from the perspective of the performer, describing in detail how certain passages should be rendered in order to bring out the meaning of the text. According to Toft, the singer should function in part as an actor, interpolating sobs and sighs, and changing vocal color to reflect the mood. The result seems a bit histrionic and represents an extreme approach to communicating the meaning of the text.

FISCHLIN is strongly at variance with both Rooley and Toft. For Fischlin, the airs represent a courtly dissimulation in an era when the honest expression of feelings was often dangerous, or even fatal. Further, he demonstrates that poets were always aware of the ultimate inability of language to express the true feelings of the composer, singer, or members of the audience. The interiority of these works argues against the outward performances suggested by Toft. This feature poses problems for the modern performer, who must present the music in a setting far different from that intended by the composer. Fischlin argues that, far from serving as a model, Orpheus represents the ultimate insincerity of his art in his failure to follow Euridice in death and instead to attempt to avoid the consequences of the very sentiments he expresses in his song. The author argues that the idea of moving the soul expressed in the literature of the period had no literal meaning and only rhetorical value. Fischlin seeks support for his arguments from a number of currently popular philosophical trends expressed in terminology familiar only to the initiate. While not denying the value of the author's insights, the supporting arguments are at times verbose and redundant.

ROBERT ANTHONY GREEN

Du Fay, Guillaume ca. 1397–1474

French-born composer

Atlas, Allan W., editor, *Papers Read at the Dufay Quincentenary Conference: Brooklyn College, December 6–7, 1974*, Brooklyn, New York: Department of Music, School of Performing Arts, Brooklyn College, CUNY, 1976

Fallows, David, *Dufay*, London: Dent, 1982; revised edition, 1987

———, *The Songs of Guillaume Dufay*, Neuhausen-Stuttgart: American Institute of Musicology and Hänssler-Verlag, 1995

Hamm, Charles E., *A Chronology of the Works of Guillaume Dufay, Based on a Study of Mensural Practice*, Princeton, New Jersey: Princeton University Press, 1964

Planchart, Alejandro Enrique, "Guillaume Du Fay's Benefices and His Relationship to the Court of Burgundy," *Early Music History* 8 (1988)

Perhaps the most important musician of his age, Guillaume Du Fay is represented by a huge number of surviving works—primarily sacred and occasional music, but also more than 80 secular songs. His 60-year musical career has been documented to an extent unmatched by that of any other contemporaneous composer. Hundreds of references to Du Fay's activities in Cambrai, northern Italy, and the Savoy court have been brought to light, and gaps in the documentary record are often filled in by the composer's own occasional works.

Although highly regarded by his contemporaries and by the succeeding generation of musicians, Du Fay remained largely forgotten until the late 19th century, when he was first mentioned in general histories of music. True Du Fay scholarship began with the publication of Jules Houdoy's history of Cambrai cathedral (1880), a monograph by F.X. Haberl (1885), and the publication of several of Du Fay's songs by Stainer (1898). Until the 1950s, works on Du Fay were usually published in German or French. Among the most influential of these publications were a monograph by Borren (1926), Andre Pirro's study of 15th- and 16th-century music (1940), and two works by Heinrich Besseler: his analytical study of 15th-century style (1951) and his article on Du Fay for *Die Musik in Geschichte und Gegenwart* (1954). A thorough assessment of Du Fay's music began in the late 1950s and 1960s with the publication of Besseler's six-volume complete edition of the works. At the same time, archi-val research began to yield a more complete picture of Du Fay's biography. Wright's investigation of the Cambrai archives (1975) and subsequent research by Craig Wright, Planchart, David Fallows, Barbara Haggh, and others have produced an amazingly complete picture of Du Fay's life.

FALLOWS (1982) provides the most comprehensive survey of the life and works of Du Fay. The book contains a detailed biography synthesizing an enormous amount of documentary and biographical literature into a readable narrative. The chapters dealing with individual genres offer both additional biographical information and musically sensitive analyses of the works. The appendices are also useful: a concise calendar of Du Fay's life, a works list, and a series of thumbnail sketches of all the people—nearly 100 in all—with documented connections to the composer's career. The bibliography is invaluable, although it contains references only through 1980 (1987 in the revised edition). While the original edition will be adequate for most purposes, the more recent edition includes corrections and additions that reflect discoveries of the early 1980s.

More recently, Fallows updated volume 6 of Besseler's edition (the secular songs) to reflect current scholarship. While FALLOWS (1995) is published as the critical apparatus to the revised edition, its usefulness goes well beyond that purpose. Fallows provides critical commentary for each of more than 90 songs (including dubious works), often including sources that were unknown at the publication of Besseler's edition. Entries also include extensive discussion of dating, texts, and musical style. The bibliography on the songs is more up-to-date than that in Fallows's biography.

HAMM was the first systematic study of Du Fay's musical works, and it has strongly influenced later research. Hamm places the works in nine chronological groupings based upon careful consideration of notation and mensural issues. In many cases, works that can be dated by other means, such as references in their texts, serve as chronological anchors for these groupings. Many of Hamm's conclusions regarding the dating of individual works have been proven wrong by later research, but the book is still useful for its insightful analyses of rhythm in Du Fay's music. Readers who are unfamiliar with mensural notation may find the book a bit daunting.

The 500th anniversary of Du Fay's death was marked in 1974 by a conference on his life and music. The proceedings of this conference, edited by ATLAS, are irregular with regard to subject matter and in the degree to which their findings have been revisited in later publications. However, at least three of the papers included in this anthology are fundamentally important pieces of Du Fay research. Lewis Lockwood's paper on Du Fay in Ferrara sheds light on a court that provided patronage to Du Fay and that was responsible for manuscripts that preserve many of his works. The paper by Planchart makes valuable conclusions regarding the dating and manuscript transmission of several of the Masses. In an analytical essay, Leo Treitler discusses the use of motives in the *Missa L'homme armé.*

There are several exemplary general studies that consider Du Fay in the broader context of 15th-century music. Gustave Reese wrote the first thorough English-language history of 15th- and 16th-century music, and it still stands as an impressive and useful piece of scholarship more than 40 years after it was written (Gustave Reese, *Music in the Renaissance,* 1959). His chapter titled "Age of Dufay" considers the composer's work as the standard by which early 15th-century music can be judged. Most of his musical observations are still valid, although the biography is now quite dated. There are several more recent college textbooks that provide easily comprehensible overviews of the period, but the text by Atlas is perhaps the best with regard to coverage of Du Fay (Allan Atlas, *Renaissance Music: Music in Western Europe, 1400–1600,* 1998). Like Reese, Atlas leans heavily on Du Fay's music to illustrate style and musical processes in the early 15th century and provides detailed analyses of several works (those included in the accompanying anthology). The study by Reinhard Strohm is the most valuable of all recent book-length studies regarding Du Fay (Reinhard Strohm, *The Rise of European Music, 1380–1500,* 1993). Strohm steps away from the great-artist viewpoint that colors Reese's treatment in order to discuss Du Fay against a wonderfully rich cultural and historical backdrop. Strohm discusses Du Fay's music in the context of the broader musical styles of Italy, England, and northern Europe, and provides detailed information about music by Du Fay's contemporaries.

While the biography by Fallows is relatively exhaustive, there has been an enormous amount of research since its publication. PLANCHART is a mere sample of the work published in the late 1980s and 1990s. The article, based on archival and historical discoveries and careful analysis of the works, presents fresh information about the composer's activities in Italy during the 1420s and outlines the connection between Du Fay and the court of Philip the Good. Planchart also makes a convincing case for Du Fay's authorship of a large body of Mass Proper settings—a significant addition to the composer's works. In subsequent articles, Planchart fills in several holes in the knowledge of Du Fay's life—including his date of birth, the dating and circumstances of several of the early works, and the context of some of his very last compositions. Several other scholars have made fundamental additions to the outline of Du Fay's career as laid out by Fallows. One of the most significant finds of the 1980s was Barbara Haggh's discovery that Du Fay was responsible for composing a large body of plainchant, the *Recollectio.*

J. Michael Allsen

Dunstaple, John ca. 1390–1453

English composer

Bent, Margaret, *Dunstaple,* London: Oxford University Press, 1981

——, "A New Canonic Gloria and the Changing Profile of Dunstaple," *Plainsong and Medieval Music* 5 (1996)

Dunstable, John, *Complete Works,* edited by Manfred Bukofzer, Musica Britannica, vol. 8, London: Stainer and Bell, 1953; 2nd, revised edition, edited by Margaret Bent et al., 1970

John Dunstaple was certainly the most important English musician of his generation, and his influence was also recognized on the Continent. Writing more than two decades after the composer's death, the Franco-Burgundian theorist Johannes Tinctoris still referred to Dunstaple as a leader of the English style that influenced composers such as Du Fay and Binchois in the early 15th century. Although a few secular songs are ascribed to Dunstaple, the vast majority of his works are devotional or liturgical in nature. Unlike his contemporary Du Fay, whose biography is relatively complete, Dunstaple remains, to some extent, a rather mysterious historical figure.

Dunstaple's name was known to English music historians of the 19th and early 20th centuries, but Manfred Bukofzer deserves the most credit for bringing Dunstaple and his works to light. Beginning in 1936 with a German-language article on Dunstaple's life and works, Bukofzer was responsible for a series of publications that culminated in his article on the composer for the dictionary *Die Musik in Geschichte und Gegenwart* (1954) and his edition of the *Complete Works,* DUNSTAPLE (1953). The introduction to the second revised edition (1970) of this collection is a fundamental source of information on the composer. The revised edition includes and discusses additional works and sources not known to Bukofzer in 1953. The widely available 1983 reprint of the second edition also includes a brief postscript by Brian Trowell detailing additional discoveries of the 1970s.

BENT (1981) is the best starting point for research on Dunstaple. This slim monograph summarizes the scant biographical details concerning Dunstaple and analyzes the musical works by genre in a series of chapters that are generously illustrated with musical examples. The chapter on isorhythmic motets is particularly useful and might serve as a good general introduction to this genre as it existed in the 15th century. The bibliography is complete through the late 1970s, and a cursory works-list also serves as an index to the musical examples.

Several general histories of music also contain significant information about Dunstaple and his works. Bukofzer's valuable chapter in the *New Oxford History of Music* describes the stylistic practices of English composers of the period, and his comments on Dunstaple relate the works to those practices (Anselm Hughes and Gerald Abraham, editors, *Ars Nova and the Renaissance, 1300–1540,* New Oxford History of Music, vol. 3, 1960). In his *Music in Medieval Britain,* Frank Harrison takes a similar approach to Dunstaple's music, although Harrison presents an even broader perspective than Bukofzer, placing Dunstaple in the context of English music of the 12th through 15th centuries. Harrison's references to the music are scattered throughout this book, but are generally quite good (Frank Harrison, *Music in Medieval Britain,* 4th edition, 1980). Virtually every textbook and general history of music in the medieval period contains a discussion of the influence of English music on Continental composers of the early 15th century, and Dunstaple and his music are usually addressed in such accounts. Among these accounts, Reinhard Strohm's discussion of English style and influence is particularly penetrating. Strohm's introduction to Dunstaple's style and role in the creation of the cyclic Mass is especially useful, and his general discussion of English influence—the so-called *contenance angloise*—is masterful (Reinhard Strohm, *The Rise of European Music, 1380–1500,* 1993).

The biographical information summarized by Bent (1981) is rather sketchy, but there have been several discoveries since the publication of that book that add important details to Dunstaple's biography. Most of this research is published in scholarly journals. A good entry point into this later research is BENT (1996). This publication not only describes a significant newly discovered work composed by Dunstaple but also provides a useful summary of scholarship published in the 1980s and 1990s.

J. MICHAEL ALLSEN

Dvořák, Antonín 1841–1904

Czech composer

1. Biography

Beckerman, Michael, editor, *Dvořák and His World,* Princeton, New Jersey: Princeton University Press, 1993

Butterworth, Neil, *Dvořák: His Life and Times,* Speldhurst: Midas Books, 1980; expanded edition, Neptune City, New Jersey: Paganiniana, 1981

Clapham, John, *Antonin Dvořák: Musician and Craftsman,* New York: St. Martin's Press, 1966

———, *Dvořák,* Newton Abbot: David and Charles, and New York: Norton, 1979

Dvořák, Antonín, *Korespondence a dokumenty,* edited by Milan Kuna et al., Prague: Supraphon, 1987–

———, *Letters and Reminiscences,* edited by Otakar Šourek, translated by Roberta Finlayson Samsour, Prague: Artia, 1954; reprint, New York, Da Capo Press, 1985

Dvořák, Otakar, *Antonín Dvořák, My Father,* edited by Paul J. Polansky, translated by Miroslav Nemec, Spillville, Iowa: Czech Historical Research Center, 1993

Ivanov, Miroslav, *In Dvořák's Footsteps: Musical Journeys in the New World,* translated by Stania Slahor, edited by Leon Karel, Kirksville, Missouri: Thomas Jefferson University Press, 1995

Robertson, Alec, *Dvořák,* London: Dent, 1945; revised edition, 1964

Schönzeler, Hans-Hubert, *Dvořák,* London: Boyars, 1984

Šourek, Otakar, *Antonín Dvořák: His Life and Works,* Prague: Orbis, 1952

Stefan, Paul, *Anton Dvořák,* translated by Y.W. Vance, New York: Greystone, 1941

Tibbetts, John C., editor, *Dvořák in America 1892–1895,* Portland, Oregon: Amadeus Press, 1993

The pioneer in scholarly research on Dvořák was Otakar Šourek (1883–1956), whose four-volume study—which appeared between the years 1916 and 1957 in as many as three revised editions depending on the volume (some undertaken after his untimely death by the next great Dvořák scholar, Jarmil Burghauser)—still remains the definitive biography of the composer. This study has never been translated from the Czech language, but a much smaller, more general biography by Šourek was published in English, and, although it may be out of date in places, this briefer work nevertheless serves its purpose and reflects the author's vast knowledge of his subject. Because STEFAN mainly used material supplied directly to him by Šourek, his book, too, is useful insofar as English readers can glean secondhand some of the insights found in Šourck's four-volume work.

After Šourek, Clapham may be regarded as the most thorough and intensely devoted biographer of the composer. CLAPHAM (1966) concentrates on describing the genesis and composition of Dvořák's works and discussing their stylistic and structural features. Although the author supplements and, wherever necessary, amends the discussions of the earlier volume in CLAPHAM (1979), his intention in the latter work is to focus on tracing as fully as possible the events and circumstances of Dvořák's life. This book provides the most substantial account in English.

The book by ROBERTSON contains some information that has been revised in light of recent research, but the analyses of the works appearing in the later chapters remain useful and accessible to readers with a rudimentary knowledge of music. Appendices include a calendar marking the birth and death dates of contemporary musicians alongside important events in Dvořák's life, a catalog of works, and a section containing brief biographical sketches of some of the persons who figure prominently in Dvořák's life or the reception history of his music. A new book for the series, written by Jan Smaczny, is forthcoming.

Although SCHÖNZELER occasionally presents new information or a viewpoint that is particularly insightful—he devotes some space comparing the artistic approaches of Dvořák and Anton Bruckner, for instance—inaccuracies are abundant in this book, and the author's descriptions ultimately prove to be too general to have any real impact or, in some cases, intelligibility. Apparently seeking to make the book acceptable for popular consumption—in itself a worthy endeavor—the author avoids musical terminology, limits himself to only three musical examples, and unnecessarily reverts to a chatty, sometimes colloquial style of writing.

BUTTERWORTH's effort is perhaps the least successful of the popular biographies, although it is replete with pictures. He has largely garnered material from previously published sources to write a narrative that is readable but sorely lacking in documentation.

IVANOV, an avid music lover but apparently not a trained musician, originally published his book in Czech in 1984 with the title *Novosvetská* (*From the New World*, after the subtitle of Dvořák's Symphony no. 9). The author sets out to document a personal pilgrimage, as he suggests on the dedication page, for the truth: the truth concerning not only Dvořák's activities during his sojourn in the United States but also the composer's aspirations, feelings, likes and dislikes; and the truth concerning American society in the 1980s—its spiritual strengths and weaknesses, its material riches. Although the truth sometimes eludes him, Ivanov conveys a sense of atmosphere in a thoroughly enjoyable narrative that unfolds in travelogue fashion, with chapters labeled "A" relating the events of Dvořák's sojourn alternating with chapters labeled "B" describing in an engaging manner the author's own odyssey as he searches for source materials and retraces the composer's comings and goings. The "B" chapters are clearly intended to provide a window through which readers—especially those readers who, like Ivanov himself, suffered (at the time of writing) from Communist censorship and restrictions on travel—can view American life through the author's wide-open eyes. As such, these parts of the book provide for American readers of the English edition a slice of history, a foreigner's take on their society and culture. The book is not documented in a scholarly manner, but it includes numerous direct quotations and insights gleaned from material that otherwise is not accessible to English readers; indeed, a few items cannot be found in any other published source.

Interest in reassessing Dvořák's life and work during the time he spent in the United States (1892–95) spawned two important collections of essays. TIBBETTS contributes eight essays to the volume he has edited, some of which are colorful, engagingly written, and richly illustrated vignettes capturing the atmosphere of places Dvořák visited. The other 18 articles are diverse in approach and perspective, having been written by people with wide-ranging professional interests. Consequently, parts of the book will appeal to specialists in the field while others will be appreciated most especially by the general public.

BECKERMAN's compilation is divided into two parts: a group of five essays by different contributors on various topics concerning Dvořák's life and works, and a collection of letters, critiques, and biographical details that heretofore have not been readily accessible (some translated from Czech by Tatiana Firkušný and from German by Susan Gillespie with critical annotations by Jarmil Burghauser). Emphasis is placed in the documents section on Dvořák's activities during his American sojourn; each item is appended with excellent annotations by the editor. In a separate essay, Beckerman considers what constitutes national and nationalistic styles in Dvořák's music, principally with regard to the Ninth Symphony. In the opening article, "Reversing the Critical Tradition: Innovation, Modernity, and Ideology in the Work and Career of Antonín Dvořák," Leon Botstein demonstrates his command of German-language writings on music and aesthetics. Beckerman and Botstein have pretensions to be both substantive and provocative, and once in a while they succeed, but, as Beckerman himself recognizes in his introduction, Dvořák remains an elusive figure, and we can allow for provocations and conjectures as long as they are not taken for fact. To round out the volume, Joseph Horowitz sets the stage for Dvořák's visit to New York in a brief essay, and David Beveridge and Jan Smaczny, both seasoned Dvořák scholars, contribute outstanding pieces. Beveridge traces Dvořák's associations with Johannes Brahms and raises some important, thought-provoking issues. In a brief essay, Smaczny manages to present an exemplary overview of Dvořák's operatic output within the context of contemporaneous trends in Bohemia. Both lay readers and specialists can especially appreciate Smaczny's discussion of the influence on Dvořák of Italian opera, French grand opera, operetta, and the works of Wagner.

Otakar DVOŘÁK was the composer's youngest son in a family that included six children who survived infancy. His memoir was written in 1961, within three months of his death (at age 75), which means that his first reminiscences—of events in the year 1891—were not put down on paper until 70 years later. The narrative is largely anecdotal, which makes for easy and enjoyable reading. A few interesting details emerge concerning the composer's working methods, hobbies, and personality traits, as well as his qualities as a father and family man, but in some ways the book provides more insight into the character and personality of Otakar himself. One must wonder how much has been lost (or gained) as a result of Polansky's editing: comparison of select passages appearing elsewhere reveal that he included or excluded material in a rather freewheeling fashion. A selection of letters to and from Dvořák is placed at the end; all may be found in other sources, most notably in the critical edition of Dvořák's correspondence.

The critical edition of DVOŘÁK's (1987–) correspondence and related documents is still in the process of being compiled. Milan Kuna and his team of editors have organized the vast amount of material in the following fashion: letters dispatched by Dvořák (vols. 1–4), letters sent to Dvořák (vols. 5–8), and other miscellaneous written documents, such as contracts, diplomas, personal certificates, and concert programs in which Dvořák participated as a performer or conductor (vols. 9–10). The sixth volume, which contains correspondence received by Dvořák during the years 1885 to 1892, is the most recent to appear in print. All documents are organized chronologically. Most of the correspondence is written in Czech or German, but beginning in 1884, Dvořák found it increasingly necessary to communicate with his English and American contacts in their language. The editors provide English synopses of the letters written in other languages, but these summaries are often much too brief and contain a frustratingly large number of mistranslations and unidiomatic phrases, especially in the earlier volumes. Readers unfamiliar with Czech are further hampered by the fact that the endnotes, which contain annotations and critical commentary reflecting the several editors' exhaustive research, are presented only in that language.

Until the last volume of Kuna's critical edition appears, a small book containing selections from DVOŘÁK's (1985) letters and from correspondence and reminiscences written by his acquaintances will continue to be useful. An index of proper names and titles of compositions was specially prepared for the Da Capo Press reprint.

ALAN HOUTCHENS

2. Works

Beveridge, David R., editor, *Rethinking Dvořák: Views from Five Countries,* Oxford: Clarendon Press, and New York: Oxford University Press, 1996

Brabcová, Jitka, and Jarmil Burghauser, editors, *Antonín Dvořák, the Dramatist,* Prague: Divadelní ústav, 1994

Burghauser, Jarmil, *Antonín Dvořák, Thematicý kcatalogue = Thematic Catalogue,* Prague: Bärenreiter Editio Supraphon, 1996

Clapham, John, *Antonín Dvořák, Musician and Craftsman,* London: Faber, and New York: St. Martin's Press, 1966

Dvořák, Antonín, *Korespondence a dokumenty = Correspondence and documents,* edited by Milan Kuna et al., Prague: Supraphon, 1987–

Fischl, Viktor, editor, *Antonín Dvořák: His Achievement,* London: Drummond, 1942

Hallová, Markéta, et al., editors, *Musical Dramatic Works by Antonín Dvořák,* Prague: Česká hudební společnost, 1989

Layton, Robert, *Dvořák Symphonies and Concertos,* London: British Broadcasting Corporation, and Seattle: University of Washington Press, 1978

Pospísil, Milan, and Marta Ottlová, editors, *Antonín Dvořák 1841–1991: Report of the International Musicological Congress Dobříš,* Prague: Ústav pro hudební vědu Akademie ved Ceské republiky, 1994

Sourek, Otakar, *The Chamber Music of Antonín Dvořák,* translated by Roberta Finlayson Samsour, Prague: Artia, [1956]

———, *The Orchestral Works of Antonín Dvořák,* translated by Roberta Finlayson Samsour, Prague: Artia, [1956]

Winter, Robert, *Antonín Dvořák Symphony no. 9 in E Minor: From the New World,* Irvington, New York: Voyager, 1994

Yoell, John H., editor, *Antonín Dvořák on Records,* New York: Greenwood Press, 1991

Perhaps because knowledge of the Czech language is not necessary to come to an understanding of Dvořák's instrumental compositions, these pieces have always received more attention than his vocal works outside of his native Bohemia, as have the details of his life. A new direction in research was sparked, however, by a series of several international conferences sponsored principally by the Antonín Dvořák Society in Czechoslovakia during the years leading up to the sesquicentennial of Dvořák's birth (he was born on 8 September 1841) and the 100th anniversary of his sojourn to the United States (1892–95). Each conference was dedicated to an aspect of Dvořák's compositional style or his life that was felt to demand more widespread consideration. Popísil and Ottlová's publication and the two books on Dvořák's dramatic works edited by Brabcová and Burghauser and by Hallová and associates essentially grew out of this initiative.

Many of the articles included in POPÍSIL and OTTLOVÁ seem to have been prepared in a rather slapdash fashion, but of the 13 written in English (out of a total of 25), those by Milan Kuna ("On the Unrealized Staging of Dvořák's *Rusalka* in Vienna"), Petr Wittlich ("A Message from the Depths: An Interpretation of Antonín Dvořák's Bust by Josef Mařatka"), Jan Smaczny ("Dvořák and the Seconda Pratica"), and Popísil (concerning the libretto of *Dimitrij*) deserve special mention. Three of the seven contributions in BRABCOVÁ and BURGHAUSER are written in English, two by Jan Smaczny (dealing with *Alfred* and *The King and the Charcoal Burner*) and one by Alan Houtchens (*Vanda*). These essays provide the most up-to-date and thorough discussions published to date of those particular works. The other four essays are in Czech, but fairly extensive summaries are provided in English. The majority of the contributions in HALLOVÁ are in German (no summaries in English are provided); the six written in English, however, offer important assessments of Dvořák's first three operas and *Rusalka*, and provide new information concerning the reception histories of Dvořák's operatic works in Vienna and Barcelona and in Britain and the United States.

The collection of articles edited by BEVERIDGE grew out of yet another festival and conference, this time in New Orleans, organized to celebrate the sesquicentennial of the composer's birth. Unlike some of the other commemorative compilations that have an international cast, all of the contributions in this volume are in English. Twenty-five articles are included, by nearly as many writers, on topics that mostly concern the geneses and composition of Dvořák's works and their stylistic features. The essays are arranged under the following headings: "The Unknown Dvořák: A Mini-Symposium on the Early Song Cycle, *Cypresses*," "The Unknown Dvořák: Operas," "Dvořák as a Czech Composer," "Dvořák as a Slavic Composer," "Dvořák as a European Composer," "The Impact of America on Dvořák," and "The Impact of Dvořák on America." This is a carefully edited volume, and the quality of the contributions is very high. As an appendix, Beveridge has reprinted with scholarly annotations two important but relatively inaccessible interviews with Dvořák that appeared in London newspapers during his visits to England in 1885 and 1886.

BURGHAUSER's completely revised edition of his thematic catalog, first published in 1960, is an essential reference source. Compositions are listed in chronological order by "B" numbers (standing for the surname of the author). Each entry includes incipits and information in three languages—Czech, German, and English—concerning dates of composition and first performance, location of primary source materials, and the more significant writings about that specific work. An exhaustive bibliography (prepared in collaboration with John Clapham) and a timeline of events in Dvořák's life are also included.

Burghauser did not include a discography in his new thematic catalog, as he had in the earlier edition, so YOELL undertook the unenviable task of preparing an updated list. He makes no claim to completeness, but he has chosen the entries carefully in accordance with their historical significance. At the end of each entry, Yoell appends a few brief remarks that are generally of a popular nature. Sometimes he relates relevant events in the composer's life or describes the genesis of a composition, but more frequently he offers a value judgment about the music or the excellence of the interpretation and execu-

tion (but not with regard to sound quality or standard of recording technology) that reflects his own particular interests and biases as an enthusiastic amateur collector. In an informative introductory essay, Yoell traces the interest shown by various singers, instrumentalists, and conductors during the first half century of recorded sound, up to just after the end of World War II.

The importance of CLAPHAM's contribution to research on Dvořák is beyond measure. This volume is chiefly devoted to providing detailed discussions of individual works. It includes analyses copiously illustrated by musical examples and, although incorporating specialized terminology, remains accessible to the nonspecialist. The work lists appearing at the back, arranged by genre and in order of composition, are useful for those who do not have access to Burghauser's catalog.

With considerable input from Michael Beckerman, WINTER has prepared a captivating interactive guide to one of Dvořák's most popular works, the New World Symphony. Regrettably, Winter subscribes to what has come to be known in disbelieving quarters as the "Hiawatha Myth," namely, that Dvořák's aim throughout the entire composition was to render into music parts of Longfellow's epic poem and to evoke the character of its hero. Winter nevertheless manages not only to provide a marvelously entertaining and informative examination of the music but to transport the computer user into the multilayered and multicolored milieu of New York City at the end of the 19th century and to weave a rich cultural tapestry around the composer's activities as director of the National Conservatory of Music of America.

Of the older books that still prove to be occasionally useful, LAYTON's booklet and ŠOUREK's separate studies of Dvořák's chamber and orchestral music should all be mentioned. Both authors provide background information concerning the genesis of each composition, along with perceptive analytical comments. In like manner, the volume of essays edited by FISCHL may still be recommended for the many insights into Dvořák's music offered by Gerald Abraham, Ernest Walker, H.C. Colles, and eight other contributors, even though research conducted since its publication inevitably has shed new or, at least, different light on certain aspects of Dvořák's creative activity.

ALAN HOUTCHENS

E

Early Music Movement

Campbell, Margaret, *Dolmetsch: The Man and His Work,* London: Hamilton, and Seattle: University of Washington Press, 1975

Cohen, Joel, and Herb Snitzer, *Reprise: The Extraordinary Revival of Early Music,* Boston: Little, Brown, 1985

Dreyfus, Laurence, "Early Music Defended against Its Devotees: A Theory of Historical Performance in the Twentieth Century," *Musical Quarterly* (1983)

Haskell, Harry, *The Early Music Revival: A History,* London: Thames and Hudson 1988

Kenyon, Nicholas, editor, *Authenticity and Early Music: A Symposium,* Oxford: Oxford University Press, 1988

Sherman, Bernard, *Inside Early Music: Conversations with Performers,* New York: Oxford University Press, 1997

Taruskin, Richard, *Text and Act: Essays on Music and Performance,* New York: Oxford University Press, 1995

The early music movement uses knowledge of historical performance practices and other historical tools as a springboard to reappraisals of music. The movement has variously been identified by terms such as *authenticity, original instruments,* and *historically informed performance.* Central to the movement has been the use of historically appropriate instruments, contemporaneous with the music being performed. This approach encourages clear delineations between different styles of music and specialization in particular repertoires. The term *early music* refers to the movement's original focus on music that predated what was then in the repertoire, particularly medieval, Renaissance, and early baroque music. Today, the revival of neglected music is still an important task of the early music movement, but the movement spans a spectrum of specialists devoted to all periods from the Middle Ages to the early 20th century. It is impossible to pinpoint the beginning of the early music movement. One can look back variously to the founding of the Academy of Vocal Music (1726) or the Academy of Ancient Music (ca. 1710) in London, Baron van Swieten's cultivation of interest in older music through the *Gesellschaft der Associierten Kavaliere* (from ca. 1780) in Vienna, Mendelssohn's revival of J.S. Bach's *St. Matthew Passion* (1829) in Berlin, or the *Concerts Historiques* presented by Fétis in both Paris (from 1832) and Berlin (from 1839). Current practitioners, however, trace their work more directly back to early 20th-century pioneers such as Arnold Dolmetsch, Wanda Landowska, and August Wenzinger. Since the late 1970s, the movement's popularity has been greatly aided by the recording industry, which has embraced the marketability of new interpretations of the standard repertoire.

Because the movement is still growing and changing and is relatively young, much of its history has not yet been written and can still only be gleaned from scattered reviews and articles. However, HASKELL has managed to put together a balanced overview of the movement's history through the mid-1980s. This book stands out for its universal view of the movement, covering many important but now neglected aspects such as the founding of the Bethlehem (Pennsylvania) Bach Choir or the attention given to early music by the BBC's Third Programme from 1946 on. Haskell is also more mindful than most commentators of the important role played by institutions in fostering an interest in early music, with discussions of the role of educational institutions, the press, and the music industry. This book provides the single best introduction to the evolution of the movement.

COHEN and SNITZER provide a more personal view of the early music movement than that found in Haskell. The first half of the volume presents Cohen's history of the movement, with special emphasis on the virtues of a few musicians of great importance, such as Noah Greenberg, Thomas Binkley, the Harnoncourts, the Kuijkens, and Alfred Deller. This treatment is more a tribute than an attempt at an objective overview of the field. The second half is a fascinating collection of captioned photographs taken by Snitzer. Most pictures were taken in rehearsals and have a candid immediacy that gives them special appeal. Although the selection of artists photographed is not as wide ranging as it could be, this is probably the biggest collection of pictures of musicians in the movement.

SHERMAN's interview format allows a sharp focus on details important to each interviewee, while the careful selection of performers interviewed ensures that an admirably broad and varied cross section of the movement is represented. The specializations of the artists range from medieval chant to romantic symphonies. Sherman's interview questions are well selected, demonstrating an awareness of the currently important issues across a diverse range of fields within the movement, and giving the reader a greater appreciation for the thoughts and research that lie behind early music performances. This book gives the best picture of the current state of diversity in the early music movement.

Although not without precursors, Dolmetsch is widely viewed as the progenitor of the 20th century's early music movement. CAMPBELL brings together a large body of material to present a sensitive portrait of this multifaceted man. Dolmetsch was probably the first to take seriously the value of using instruments of the sort that would have been used when the music was composed. As performer, instrument builder, and researcher of performance practice, he embodied three of the most important aspects of the movement and set standards that remained a benchmark long after his death.

The most heated debate surrounding the early music movement has revolved around the issue of authenticity, a term used by many into the mid-1980s to indicate the use of historical instruments and adherence to historical performance practices. Because of the term's obvious implications of superiority, its use has been problematic and sparked a lively debate. KENYON brings together enlightening essays by six different scholars on this topic, presenting the gamut of views within the movement on just what the aims of the movement are.

An important impetus for Kenyon's collection of essays was the work of DREYFUS, who goes far beyond the question of authenticity in establishing an outline for a philosophy behind the early music movement. Dreyfus cleverly points out that "Early Music" is a social phenomenon rather than the repertoire it takes as its object. He is an insider with an insider's knowledge who is yet unafraid to take seriously the criticisms of the movement's detractors.

TARUSKIN, probably the most outspoken critic of the early music movement, presents a collection of essays that includes a revised version of his essay in Kenyon. Although seemingly partial to many of the aims of the movement, Taruskin is highly critical of the polemics used by some prominent performers and by recording companies to validate the movement on pseudophilosophical rather than musical grounds. He is not actually a detractor of the movement as such; however, his deliberately provocative writing incenses many insiders who denounce him without fully comprehending his purposes.

JOHN MORAN

Eastern Europe

Abraham, Gerald, *On Russian Music,* London: Reeves, and New York, Scribner, 1939; reprint, New York: Johnson Reprint, 1970

Bartók, Béla, and Albert Bates Lord, *Serbo-Croatian Folk Songs: Texts and Transcriptions of Seventy-Five Folk Songs from the Milman Parry Collection and a Morphology of Serbo-Croatian Folk Melodies,* New York: Columbia University Press, 1951

Beregovski, Moshe, *Old Jewish Folk Music: The Collections and Writings of Moshe Beregovski,* edited and translated by Mark Slobin, Philadelphia: University of Pennsylvania Press, 1982

Brăiloiu, Constantin, *Problems of Ethnomusicology,* translated by A.L. Lloyd, Cambridge: Cambridge University Press, 1984

Czekanowska, Anna, *Polish Folk Music: Slavonic Heritage, Polish Tradition, Contemporary Trends,* Cambridge: Cambridge University Press, 1990

Frigyesi, Judit, *Béla Bartók and Turn-of-the-Century Budapest,* Berkeley: University of California Press, 1998

Lord, Albert Bates, *The Singer of Tales,* Cambridge, Massachusetts: Harvard University Press, 1960

Nixon, Paul, *Sociality, Music, Dance: Human Figurations in a Transylvanian Valley,* Göteborg: Göteborg University Institute of Musicology, 1998

Rice, Timothy, *May It Fill Your Soul: Experiencing Bulgarian Music,* Chicago: University of Chicago Press, 1994

Sárosi, Bálint, *Folk Music: Hungarian Musical Idiom,* translated by Maria Steiner, Budapest: Corvina, 1986

Slobin, Mark, editor, *Retuning Culture: Musical Changes in Central and Eastern Europe,* Durham, North Carolina: Duke University Press, 1996

Sugarman, Jane C., *Engendering Song: Singing and Subjectivity at Prespa Albanian Weddings,* Chicago: University of Chicago Press, 1997

Taruskin, Richard, *Defining Russia Musically: Historical and Hermeneutical Essays,* Princeton, New Jersey: Princeton University Press, 1997

The field of Eastern European studies in music is both difficult to define and geographically and culturally vast; thus, selecting only a handful of representative books on the subject is problematic. In the study of art music, scholarship has been focused on a few star composers. Some books concern themselves with several composers and/or a composer's role in the context of a specific nation in Eastern Europe; these are one concern of the present entry. Eastern Europe was in some ways the cradle of ethnomusicology, and important work continues in many parts of the region. The bibliography provides a few examples of classic works of Eastern European ethnomusicology as well as very recent ethnomusicological studies representing decades of work. The rise and fall of communist governments have led to interesting changes throughout this region, which are documented musically by these studies.

FRIGYESI addresses the cultural environment of Budapest, in which Bartók came of age as an artist and developed his aesthetic philosophy. The first four chapters contrast turn-of-the-century modernism in Vienna and Budapest and discuss the role of music as a reactionary Hungarian national symbol. Frigyesi grounds Bartók's aesthetic in Budapest's modernist movement. Of particular interest is the effort by Bartók and others to create a new ideal of national music, based on the previously unknown music of the Hungarian peasantry. Discussions of pieces (*Bluebeard's Castle,* First Piano Concerto) require musical literacy but are not overly technical.

TARUSKIN is a collection of essays organized around the role of Russian identity in the careers of Russian musicians and composers from Lvov and Glinka to Stravinsky and Shostakovich, as well as the reception of Russian music inside and outside Russia. The author decries the simplistic fetishizing of difference that has masqueraded as the celebration of nationalist composers. Taruskin's point is relevant not only to Russians but to any Eastern European artist: composers from outside the central countries of Germany, France, and Italy have traditionally been discussed largely on the basis of their degree of nationalism, particularly in the use of folk-song material. Historical accounts in this book effectively demonstrate composers's struggles with their environments and with the question of their identities as Russians. Some of the musical analyses may be difficult for a reader with no music theory background, but any interested reader will enjoy Taruskin's historical and polemical writings.

One of Taruskin's great predecessors in the study of Russian music is ABRAHAM, who wrote many essays on Russian art music. The collection listed here covers a variety of topics dealing with Russian composers from 1836 to 1910. Abraham offers a good and accessible introduction to specific pieces, as well as a historical perspective on some issues, such as oriental elements in Russian music and Liszt's influence on the Mighty Handful. Abraham is especially useful in his discussion of the content and history of Russian operas.

Both Lord and Bartók and Lord discuss work done in Bosnia-Herzegovina by Slavicist Milman Parry, with Lord as one of his assistants. LORD is a classic investigation of the way in which oral epic poets learn and compose their songs. Bartók transcribed and analyzed the women's songs collected by Parry and Lord during this project; this work was published in part 1 of BARTÓK and LORD after Bartók's death. Lord translated and discussed the texts and the mode of collection in part 2 of the book. This work is something of a pivot point in the history of ethnomusicology: Bartók always seeks objectivity and perfection in the transcription and classification of these songs even while he acknowledges the

impossibility of really achieving these aims, as folk music "shows an almost absolute variability." Bartók's nascent consciousness of methodological crisis is telling.

BRĂILOIU, one of the founders of ethnomusicology, explored this crisis in his essays on the field of musical folklore, chiefly using examples from his work in Romania. These essays, including the important 1931 "Outline of a Method of Musical Folklore," as well as his writings on specific topics such as rhythms and funeral laments, are collected in this volume. Brăiloiu's work is excellent in its teasing apart of the very problems Bartók was unable to confront and is recommended for any person interested in the music of Romania or issues in ethnomusicology in general.

BEREGOVSKI is a collection of essays that span decades of the author's work on Jewish music of Ukraine, from the 1930s to the 1960s. Whereas Bartók never quite gives up the idea of the authentic ur-folk song, Beregovski, like Brăiloiu, explicitly attacks this idea and includes in his collection works clearly inspired by recent events, such as workers' songs. Particularly in "Jewish Folk Songs" (1962), he also discusses the social context of these songs. Another of Beregovski's articles explicitly addresses the intermingling of Ukrainian and Jewish folk music in a way that was extremely rare at that time (1935) and is highly readable. The methods and discussion can give valuable insight into Jewish and Eastern European cultural studies.

CZEKANOWSKA focuses on the transitional nature of Polish folk music, seeing it as a struggle between Slavonic or Eastern traditions and influences and Polish (that is Catholic and Western European) ones. Czekanowska first defines what she means by this binary opposition; she then goes on to discuss transmission, musical structure, and the role of folk and music culture in contemporary Poland. The writing style is impersonal and scientific, making the book difficult to read; also, the opposition between Slavonic and Polish cultures seems problematic and ill-named. Still, this is the best available monograph in English on Polish folk musics.

SÁROSI is a collection of brief 1973 radio lectures on Hungarian folk music. Because of the original format, the author briefly presents topics for a general audience. Although this format limits the collection's sense of continuity, it also allows the reader to jump easily from topic to topic—from the history of ethnomusicology in Hungary and the role of music in certain events (work, weddings, burials) to types of songs and instruments. Sárosi treats music's role in urban as well as rural life, a scope which is particularly rare in books on Hungarian folk music. These features make this study an ideal introduction to Hungarian ethnomusicology and musical life.

RICE deals with the changes and tensions in Bulgarian musical life, from the mostly amateur days of pre–World War II village life to the professionalization and other drastic changes made as the new communist government used music as a tool—for cultural education and as a symbol of national(ist) purity and aesthetic power. Rice sets up the background of the aural tradition of prewar village music making rooted in social gatherings through personal accounts and the musical examples; he then addresses the implication of professional and institutional changes in the communist period. Rice alternates his focus from musicians' personal stories to more wide-angled historical accounts and thoughtful theoretical analyses, making for an enjoyable read.

SUGARMAN demonstrates ways in which traditional gender roles, patriarchal village social structures, and group identity are inscribed in Prespa Albanian polyphonic wedding singing and how performance practices reinscribe categories of identity on the members of the group. Vivid descriptions of rituals and events in the Prespa region and in the North American diaspora, assisted by sound examples on an accompanying compact disc, show both continuity with traditions on the one hand and the struggle of a small immigrant community to accommodate changes in economic conditions and family structures on the other. In her exploration of changing roles of women, Sugarman provides a nuanced view of the problems and possible conflicts created by gender identity and small-group ethnic identity.

For reflections on recent changes in the entire region, SLOBIN is a collection of essays on post–Soviet era musics from Poland to Yugoslavia, Czechoslovakia to Ukraine. This book provides a glimpse of the rich variety of practices in this region as well as within ethnically diverse nations, authored by "Western" as well as native scholars. Slobin's grouping of this broad spectrum of work offers an introduction to some of the issues at the fore in the academic and cultural politics of this region.

NIXON observes post-1989 changes in Romania. He links primary field experiences with Hungarian-speaking and Romanian-speaking Transylvanian villagers and with communities of settled Gypsies in 1979, under Ceausescu, with the less predictable circumstances of the postrevolutionary 1990s. Shifts in political and social dynamics are addressed, together with changes in community interactions; Nixon then shows in text, photographs, diagrams, and transcriptions how local idioms of music making and dance reflect these transformations.

LYNN HOOKER

Editing

Caldwell, John, *Editing Early Music,* Oxford: Clarendon Press, 1985; 2nd edition, 1995
Dart, Thurston, et al., *Editing Early Music: Notes on the Preparation of Printer's Copy,* N.p.: Novello, 1963
Emery, Walter, *Editions and Musicians,* London: Novello, 1957
Grier, James, *The Critical Editing of Music: History, Method, and Practice,* Cambridge: Cambridge University Press, 1996

The editing of music is its preparation for publication, performance, and study, usually by someone other than the composer. Editing is an act of interpretation, and as such requires the critical engagement of the editor at every step of the enterprise, from the choice of subject to the appearance of the final printed page. No edition, therefore, can claim to be definitive, and consequently, no two editors will edit the same piece in precisely the same way. Moreover, the creation of every piece of music is influenced by a unique combination of cultural, social, historical, and economic circumstances. An acknowledgement of those circumstances, and thus of the uniqueness of each creative product, affects the conception of all editorial projects: each piece, source, and edition presents a special case. This idea leads naturally to the corollary that different repertoires of music require different editorial methods and even that each edition calls for a unique approach. Hence any set of guidelines would fail to accommodate the plurality of solutions each editorial problem can engender. Every project generates the editorial procedures that best represent the editor's critical engagement with the subject of the edition and its sources.

EMERY emphasizes the importance of the factual evidence on which an edition is based. He condemns "aesthetic and stylistic criticism" and characterizes editing as "a quasi-science, and the more scientific it is, the better," based on "paleography and bibliography, and historical facts in general." Quite a few of the observations Emery makes, however, arise from subjective critical observations regarding musical style rather than objective bibliographic, paleographic, or historic facts. He presents an elaborate argument, for example, about the disposition of the voices in the A-flat major fugue in book two of the *Well-Tempered Clavier.* His reasoning is convincing, showing that Bach would most likely not have allowed the soprano to rest for 14 out of 50 bars, as one of the autograph sources reads. Emery's conclusion here depends on musical rather than bibliographic, issues, sharpened through a critical and even aesthetic sense; he shows that musical consideration is essential to scholarly editing. He observes that much of the interpretation of musical notation is reserved for performance, and for this reason editors should retain notational conventions and allow the performer scope for interpretation. Finally, he calls for a full, succinct, and attractive commentary.

DART et al. announces its program in the subtitle: it is primarily a guide to the preparation of clean copy for the benefit of music printers and is published cooperatively by three of the firms in the forefront of music publication in post–World War II England. The need for the book arose from the enthusiasm, principally in the British Isles, for the performance of early music. Its pragmatic approach takes as a point of departure the problem of creating clear, usable editions of old music originally written in notation no longer familiar to practicing musicians. These editors gave clear precedence to presentation over critical issues.

The first edition of CALDWELL's book (1985) was commissioned as a replacement for the volume by Dart, Emery, and Morris. As such, it too dispenses with critical issues in a brief introductory passage before turning to the more mechanical aspects of editing, such as problems of transcription and the preparation of the text for the printer. Drawing on his extensive experience as an editor of early music, and as one who has supervised the editing of music, Caldwell presents much sound guidance and provides a basic procedure for creating an edition. He organizes his guidelines around the particular problems that music from different repertoires and chronological periods present. The main text of the second edition (1995) remains unchanged from the first edition. Caldwell does add a postscript in which he provides updates on several mechanical issues covered in the main text. He also presents a brief discussion titled "Stemmatics and Textual Criticism" that touches on a number of matters, including the evidence for creating a stemma and the ramifications of oral transmission, without engaging the critical issues that lie behind them.

GRIER is the only comprehensive discussion in English of the critical aspects of editing music to date. It attempts to provide a generalized theory of music that can be applied to any editorial project in Western art music, most of which is closely linked with a written tradition. (Musics of other cultures, especially those in which an oral tradition predominates, pose different and equally important problems for the editor. Editors in ethnomusicology have developed conventions of their own, particularly in regard to the use of notation, that establish their work as an independent field.) The theory presented here, based on the writings of Jerome J. McGann in English philology, is rooted in the principle that the work of art is a social artifact; moreover, the act of transmitting the work to an audience is a fully integrated part of the creative process. By entering into this dialog, artists abandon their autonomy and inevitably shape the work somehow to accommodate and facilitate that act of communication. This conception of the work and its meaning transforms the process of editing from a psychological endeavor (in which the editor attempts to determine the author's intentions) into a historical undertaking. Under this principle, each source attests to a particular historical state of the work; the editor assesses the value of that evidence against the background of the larger historical context in which the piece was created; and the final edited text reflects the editor's conception of the piece as it existed in its historical and social environment. The work is organized around the various stages of the editorial project, from the location and inspection of the sources to the presentation of the edited text, raising and discussing the critical issues that affect each stage of the process; and it draws examples from the entire recorded history of Western art music from plainsong to late-20th-century compositions.

JAMES GRIER

Education: History

Birge, Edward Bailey, *History of Public School Music in the United States,* Boston: Ditson, 1928; revised edition, Philadelphia: Ditson, 1939; reprint, Reston, Virginia: Music Educators National Conference, 1988

Carpenter, Nan Cooke, *Music in the Medieval and Renaissance Universities,* Norman: University of Oklahoma Press, 1958

Cox, Gordon, *A History of Music Education in England 1872–1928,* Aldershot: Scholar Press, and Brookfield, Vermont: Ashgate Publishing, 1993

Green, James Paul, and Nancy F. Vogan, *Music Education in Canada: A Historical Account,* Toronto: University of Toronto Press, 1991

Keene, James A., *A History of Music Education in the United States,* Hanover, New Hampshire: University Press of New England, 1982

Mark, Michael L., *Contemporary Music Education,* New York: Schirmer Books, 1978; 3rd edition, New York: Schirmer Books, and London: Prentice Hall, 1996

———, *Sources Readings in Music Education History,* New York: Schirmer Books, and London: Collier Macmillan, 1982

Mark, Michael L., and Charles L. Gary, *A History of American Music Education,* New York: Schirmer Books, 1992

Rainbow, Bernarr, *Music in Educational Thought and Practice: A Survey from 800 B.C.,* Aberystwyth, Wales: Boethius Press, 1989

Sunderman, Lloyd Frederick, *Historical Foundations of Music Education in the United States,* Metuchen, New Jersey: Scarecrow Press, 1971

Tellstrom, A. Theodore, *Music in American Education: Past and Present,* New York: Holt, Rinehart and Winston, 1971

Ulrich, Homer, *A Centennial History of the Music Teachers National Association,* Cincinnati, Ohio: Music Teachers National Association, 1976

Scholars have described the history of music education in the United States as a history of public school music and the development of the Music Educators National Conference (MENC). Nineteenth-century topics include the introduction of music in the Boston public schools, the expansion of urban school systems, and the development of textbooks. Twentieth-century topics include the development of music organizations, expansion of band programs, and new trends in methodology including Orff and Kodály. Although there are doctoral dissertations on independent music teachers, conservatories, parochial schools, and ethnic minorities, this information is not included in the basic books on the history of music education. There are publications on British and Canadian music education, but little information on international organizations or the history of music education in other countries.

In the United States, the earliest history was written by BIRGE; it is often quoted, although it includes some factual errors. Birge describes the singing schools in colonial America, Lowell Mason and the Boston public schools, the development of music reading methods, and textbooks. He describes the growth of music associations including the Music Teachers National Association (MTNA), Music Section of the National Education Association (NEA), and the Music Supervisors' National Conference (MSNC). The book includes pictures of leading men and women in music education.

SUNDERMAN's book, based primarily on his 1939 dissertation, gives a historical account similar to Birge: music education from colonial days through the development of textbooks; and the growth of professional organizations in the early 20th century. He provides details on individual states and higher education, as well as an extensive bibliography.

TELLSTROM emphasizes philosophical movements that have influenced music education and describes music educators who have followed these philosophies, beginning with humanism and the common schools in the United States: the influence on Lowell Mason of the Enlightenment and Johann Heinrich Pestalozzi's principles; the development of textbooks and emphasis on note reading during the industrial age—an epoch of "utility" and science; child-centered schools featuring songs and active participation during the era of progressivism and the philosophies of Francis Wayland Parker and G. Stanley Hall—although some educators still favored more structured methods; and the importance of music tests and measurements during an age of experimentalism and an emphasis on psychology. Birge, Sunderman, and Tellstrom all cover the 19th century and the beginning of the 20th century.

ULRICH tells the history of the MTNA, an organization of independent music teachers, from 1876 to 1975. He gives an account of the organization's structure, constitution, convention papers, and the activities of each state. This is a valuable reference for readers interested in MTNA, but a comprehensive historical account of independent music teaching in the United States still needs to be written.

KEENE's book is refreshing because it includes topics not covered in earlier books: singing schools and tune books, private academies, and teacher education in the 19th century. He covers the influence of Pestalozzi, Johann Friedrich Herbart, and Herbert Spencer on U.S. education. Twentieth-century topics include music appreciation, choirs, and the growth of band music.

MARK and GARY is the major book on the history of music education. Clearly written and containing an extensive bibliography, it is the best overall view of the subject to date. After a brief survey of European music education from antiquity to the 17th century, the authors trace music education in the United States from colonial times through the 19th century, giving general historical background and describing specific educators. Twentieth-century topics include appreciation and the development of bands. There are descriptions of professional organizations (NEA, MTNA, MSNC) and a detailed account of MENC.

MARK (1978) gives a full account of music education since 1950. He describes the pivotal events organized by MENC: the Contemporary Music Project, Yale Seminar, Juilliard Repertory Project, Tanglewood Symposium, Goals and Objectives Project, and the National Standards for Arts Education. Mark also covers the major methods: Dalcroze, Orff, Kodály, Suzuki, Comprehensive Musicianship, and Gordon's learning theory. Issues relevant today include advocacy, multicultural music, technology, teacher training, and assessment. There is an extensive bibliography.

MARK (1982) provides readings of the European philosophies of education from Plato and Aristotle to Comenius, Locke, Pestalozzi, and Spencer. U.S. views are represented by Lowell Mason, Horace Mann, John Dewey, James Mursell, and excerpts from the Tanglewood Symposium. Contemporary accounts include James Bryant Conant and Charles E. Silverman. This book is useful for a course in the philosophy of education.

The two books by Mark complement the Mark and Gary history to provide an excellent account of music education in the United States, with an emphasis on activities of MENC. There is a need for publications that look at other aspects of teaching music: independent music teachers, teacher training, conservatories, community music, ethnic music, preschool music, and a more extensive account of the role of women in education.

The U.S. publications discuss the European roots of U.S. music education but do not mention music education outside of the United States in the 20th century. RAINBOW is an excellent survey of European music education to the middle of the 20th century. This is a chronological account from ancient times through the Middle Ages, Renaissance and Reformation, and the French and Industrial Revolutions. Rainbow discusses the competing teaching systems of note reading in the 19th century: Galin-Paris-Chevé, Wilhem, Hullah, Mainzer, and Curwen. The 20th century includes German reforms and English teaching of appreciation, Dalcroze eurhythmics, and the development of music organizations.

COX complements Rainbow by giving an account of music education in England from 1872 to 1928. He assesses the contributions of specific male music educators (Hadow, Hullah, McNaught, Sharp, Shaw, Somervell, Stainer, and Stanford) and Her/His Majesty's Inspectorate of Schools.

CARPENTER, in a 1958 publication based on her doctoral dissertation, covers music education in medieval and Renaissance universities in a detailed account with extensive footnotes. After a brief summary of music in the Greek and Roman rhetorical schools and the Christian *schola cantorum* (singing schools), she discusses the medieval universities to 1450 in Italy, France, England, Spain, Germany, and other countries. *Musica theoretica* was taught as part of the quadrivium along with arithmetic, geometry, and astronomy. *Musica practica* included music activities for religious services, university ceremonies, and informal secular music. In the Renaissance universities (1450–1600), music continued to be taught as part of mathematics and was performed at collegiate functions. There was a new interest in instrumental music and in integrating music with humanistic studies.

GREEN and VOGAN discuss the early days of music education and expansion of schools in the various sections of Canada: Quebec, Maritimes, Ontario, and the western provinces. They show how national institutions such as the Canadian Broadcasting Corporation, the Toronto Conservatory of Music, and the Canadian College of Organists were important in the expansion of music education. Twentieth-century topics include the development of vocal and instrumental music, private teaching, parochial schools, teaching training, and music teacher associations. The book focuses on music education until the 1960s. There is still a need for books on the history of music education in Canada and the United Kingdom in the second half of the 20th century.

SONDRA WIELAND HOWE

Education: Methodologies

Campbell, Patricia Shehan, *Lessons from the World: A Cross-Cultural Guide to Music Teaching and Learning,* New York: Schirmer Books, and Toronto: Macmillan, 1991

Choksy, Lois, *The Kodály Method: Comprehensive Music Education from Infant to Adult,* Englewood Cliffs, New Jersey: Prentice Hall, 1974; 3rd edition, 1999

Choksy, Lois, et al., *Teaching Music in the Twentieth Century,* Englewood Cliffs, New Jersey: Prentice Hall, 1986

Costanza, Peter, and Timothy Russell, "Methodologies in Music Education," in *Handbook of Research on Music Teaching and Learning,* edited by Richard Colwell, New York: Schirmer Books, and Toronto: Macmillan, 1992

Frazee, Jane, and Kent Kreuter, *Discovering Orff: A Curriculum for Music Teachers,* New York: Schott, 1987

Ghezzo, Marta Arkossy, *Solfège, Ear Training, Rhythm Dictation, and Music Theory: A Comprehensive Course,* Tuscaloosa: University of Alabama Press, 1980; 2nd edition, 1993

Gordon, Edwin, *Learning Sequences in Music: Skill, Content, and Patterns,* Chicago: G.I.A., 1980; new edition, 1997

Jaques-Dalcroze, Émile, *Eurhythmics, Art, and Education,* translated by Frederick Rothwell, edited by Cynthia Cox, New York: Barnes, and London: Chatto and Windus, 1930; reprint, New York: Arno Press, 1976

Landis, Beth, and Polly Carder, *The Eclectic Curriculum in American Music Education: Contributions of Dalcroze, Kodaly, and Orff,* Washington, D.C.: Music Educators National Conference, 1972; revised edition, edited by Polly Carder, Reston, Virginia: Music Educators National Conference, 1990

Suzuki, Shin'ichi, *Nurtured by Love: A New Approach to Education,* translated by Waltraud Suzuki, New York: Exposition Press, 1969; 2nd edition, Smithtown, New York: Exposition Press, 1983

Suzuki, Shin'ichi, et al., *The Suzuki Concept: An Introduction to a Successful Method for Early Music Education,* edited by Elizabeth Mills and Therese Cecile Murphy, Berkeley, California: Diablo Press, 1973

Warner, Brigitte, *Orff-Schulwerk: Applications for the Classroom,* Englewood Cliffs, New Jersey: Prentice Hall, 1991

A methodology for music education is a system of principles, practices, procedures, and curricula that explains how to teach music. Ideally, a methodology should be based on a philosophy and include a body of research, but most of the various methods for teaching music do not really meet this standard. Instead, most systems are very practical, emphasizing specific techniques and curriculum, and lack a philosophical foundation. Historically, music educators have promoted methods of reading notes, including solfège (fixed and movable do), tonic solfa, shape notes, song methods, interval approaches, and number notation. In the second half of the 20th century, international organizations developed to convey methods promoted by such charismatic music educators as Jaques-Dalcroze, Orff, Kodály, and Suzuki, and by followers of these methods. Although there are numerous individual methods for teaching keyboard and other specific instruments, this entry will be limited to general methodologies that are useful in school classrooms. Very little research comparing methodologies and evaluating the effectiveness of specific methods has been conducted, but there are useful books for the music student, parent, and teacher.

CHOKSY et al. (1986) is a college textbook. It summarizes the findings of major U.S. conferences in the second half of the 20th century that have influenced music teaching: Woods Hole Conference, Young Composers Project, Yale Seminar, Manhattanville Music Curriculum Program, Tanglewood Symposium, and Ann Arbor Symposium. Choksy covers the methodologies of Jaques-Dalcroze, Kodály, Orff, and Comprehensive Musicianship. Comprehensive Musicianship is a method developed in the United States that emphasizes the integration of all facets of music study as elements of music are experienced through performance, listening, composition, and improvisation. For each method, the text provides a clear description of the philosophy, lists of goals and objectives, and specific teaching suggestions and musical examples for instructing kindergarten through grade-12 students.

LANDIS and CARDER is an overview of the Jaques-Dalcroze, Kodály, and Orff approaches. The Swiss educator, Émile Jaques-Dalcroze (1865–1950), emphasized three areas of study: solfège with fixed do, improvisation with the piano, and eurhythmics (that is, the expression of musical concepts through body movements). The Hungarian composer, Zoltan Kodály (1882–1967), developed a method of musical literacy with solfège (movable do) and a progressive repertory of Hungarian folk songs. The method of the German composer, Carl Orff (1895–1982), emphasizes creativity and improvisation with groups of children singing and playing percussion instruments.

COSTANZA and RUSSELL discuss methodologies popular in 20th-century general music, choral, and instrumental education. They cite specific research assessing the effectiveness of various methodologies and conclude that there is a need for further studies. The bibliography is useful for research.

GHEZZO is a comprehensive analysis of solfège suitable for a college course on singing and theory. Solfège is a system of singing scales, intervals, and melodic exercises to solmization syllables: *do, re, mi, fa, sol, la, si (ti)*. The 51 lessons in Ghezzo cover tonal, chromatic, modal, and atonal music. Each lesson includes a theoretical explanation, exercises to improve intonation, rhythmic exercises, dictation to write, and short melodies in the treble clef to sing with solfège syllables. The appendix includes further work in C clefs.

The collection of JAQUES-DALCROZE's writings from 1922 to 1925 describes his system of eurhythmics with detailed diagrams. This method is best taught through participation in training classes, but the book is a good explanation of Jaques-Dalcroze's educational philosophy. There are sections on eurhythmics, rhythm in education, and art.

CHOKSY (1974) presents chapters on using the Kodály method with children in grades 1 through 6, with teaching charts, rhythmic dictation, songs, and diagrams with hand positions for solfège syllables. There is information on lesson planning and introducing songs, and the appendix includes additional songs. This is a practical book for the classroom teacher.

FRAZEE and KREUTER is a practical guide to the Orff method for the classroom teacher. The Orff approach includes speech activities, singing, the playing of recorders and percussion instruments, and listening, as students are led through a four-stage learning process of imitation, exploration, literacy, and improvisation. The book includes a sequence of skills and concepts for grades 1 through 5, with specific teaching ideas and many musical examples.

WARNER's textbook on the Orff method offers chapters on rhythm, melody and accompaniment, songs and instrumental pieces, pentatonic modes, recorder playing, and word and language. This book is designed to be used along with volumes of Orff songs in a teacher-training course.

GORDON's extensively researched philosophy states that the primary purpose of music education is to teach students to understand music. Students should be aware of the aural elements of tonality and meter, and audiate music (hear music silently) before they study verbal descriptions and attempt a theoretical understanding of music. A college text describing Gordon's method, this book covers sequences of tonal content and rhythm content and discusses the development of a course of study and the evaluation of musical achievement.

Suzuki (1898–1998) is known for his system of teaching the violin to young children through listening and by using a fixed sequential repertoire of European music. He was interested in developing character through music education, and his "mother tongue" approach to learning many subjects is described with personal anecdotes in SUZUKI (1969). SUZUKI (1973), a collection of articles by various authors, explains how the Suzuki approach works in various settings as a method for teaching stringed instruments and piano. These two books are useful for both parents and teachers.

CAMPBELL is an overview of methods of teaching music throughout the world, including Asia and Africa. Drawing from his extensive work on multicultural music education, Campbell explains methods of ear training and improvisation used throughout history; explores traditional music learning from various cultures, including Indonesian music and jazz; and describes various learning settings from the school classroom to the private studio.

SONDRA WIELAND HOWE

Egypt *see* Africa; Middle East

Electronic Music

Appleton, Jon H., and Ronald Perera, editors, *The Development and Practice of Electronic Music,* Englewood Cliffs, New Jersey: Prentice Hall, 1975

Baggi, Denis, editor, *Computer-Generated Music,* Los Alamitos, California: IEEE Computer Society Press, 1992

Chadabe, Joel, *Electric Sound: The Past and Promise of Electronic Music,* Upper Saddle River, New Jersey: Prentice Hall, 1997

Chávez, Carlos, *Toward a New Music: Music and Electricity,* translated by Herbert Weinstock, New York: Norton, 1937; reprint, New York: Da Capo Press, 1975

Emmerson, Simon, editor, *The Language of Electroacoustic Music,* London: Macmillan, and New York: Harwood Academic Publishers, 1986

Ernst, David, *The Evolution of Electronic Music,* New York: Schirmer Books, 1977

Griffiths, Paul, *A Guide to Electronic Music,* New York: Thames and Hudson, 1979

Heifetz, Robin Julian, editor, *On the Wires of Our Nerves: The Art of Electroacoustic Music,* Lewisburg, Pennsylvania: Bucknell University Press, and London: Associated University Presses, 1989

Hiller, Lejaren Arthur, and Leonard M. Isaacson, *Experimental Music: Composition with an Electronic Computer,* New York: McGraw-Hill, 1959

Judd, F.C., *Electronic Music and Musique Concrète,* London: Spearman, 1961

Manning, Peter, *Electronic and Computer Music,* Oxford: Clarendon Press, and New York: Oxford University Press, 1985; 2nd edition, 1993

Roads, Curtis, and John Strawn, editors, *Foundations of Computer Music,* Cambridge, Massachusetts: MIT Press, 1985

Russcol, Herbert, *The Liberation of Sound: An Introduction to Electronic Music,* Englewood Cliffs, New Jersey: Prentice Hall, 1972

Schwartz, Elliott, *Electronic Music: A Listener's Guide,* New York: Praeger, and London: Secker and Warburg, 1973; revised edition, New York: Praeger, 1975

The history of electronic music runs parallel to the development of electronic instruments and other devices in the 20th century. The aesthetic, technical, and compositional processes of electronic music are highly dependent on the type of equipment available to the composer. Most writings on this topic regard the two aspects, music and equipment, as inseparable. This style of music runs the gamut from tape music composition, to compositions actually written by a computer, to music created with synthesizers, to music that comes from a computer-based sound card manipulated through a programming language. Classical and popular composers alike have written electronic music, and some recent scholarship has mentioned the blurring of lines between art and pop music. Many writers have also made the point that despite the highly technical aspects of its creation, a listener need not be technically literate to appreciate electronic music.

One of the earliest written accounts of electronic music, CHÁVEZ provides a fascinating glimpse into the first published opinions on the subject. He discusses the impact of physical science on the world of music, citing the early methods of reproducing music including the tape recorder and the phonograph. He considers the use of music in film scores and on radios and speculates about where these developments might lead.

Another early book that describes a single project in electronic music is by HILLER. This book documents the process of producing one of the first computer-generated compositions, *The Illiac Suite*. The project began in 1955 and involved a variety of experiments, each designed to have the computer generate increasingly sophisticated music. This book documents the philosophy and rationale, as well as the entire technical process, for the project. There is also a significant discussion of man versus machine, dealing with musical aesthetics.

JUDD approaches the discussion of electronic music by exploring sound sources. As he describes the electrical signals that generate musical tones, he presents technical details about subjects such as analysis of sound waves. The author explains the compositional process for electronic music and musique concrète and examines a number of electronic compositions.

The discussion in RUSSCOL is composer-oriented. The author places electronic music in a historical context and describes the emergence of technology, which happened simultaneously with the decline of tonality in the 20th century. From the changes in music initiated in the romantic period, he traces a tradition of experimental music in the United States through composers such as Ives and Cowell, finally focusing on Varèse as one of the first electronic composers. The book includes a discussion of major electronic compositions, and each chapter has a listing of major figures in the field.

APPLETON presents a collection of essays dealing with a variety of aspects of this subject. These articles are suited for the lay person are were written by people intimately involved with electronic music, such as Otto Luening and Joel Chadabe. The topics include the historical context of electronic music, the perception of music, the tape studio, modular synthesis, programming languages, and live performance of electronic music.

"Music for Solo Tape," "Music for Performers and Tape," Live Electronics," and "Compositional Techniques" are the headings in ERNST. This genre-based study describes in nontechnical terms compositions that are available on commercial recordings. The book consists of essays that are similar to program notes, covering a wide variety of music and composers including Cage, Stockhausen, Frank Zappa, and the Beatles.

Another book that includes discussions of classical and popular electronic music is GRIFFITHS, who covers Boulez and Birtwistle, the Grateful Dead and Jimi Hendrix. He emphasizes that electronic music often consists of sounds rather than notes, as would be typical in more conventional styles. He also notes that the creation of electronic music is dependent on the means available at the time: an awareness of the development of electronic instruments is necessary to the understanding of electronic music, just as an awareness of the development of the piano is necessary to understand the differences between the piano styles of Mozart and Liszt.

ROADS presents a collection of essays dealing specifically with computer music. These articles are technical and offer a great deal of information that would be of use to engineers and programmers. The subjects include computer system architecture and microprogramming. The book also deals with the influence that computers have had on compositions and music literature.

EMMERSON's collection of essays seeks to "clarify the central issues surrounding technology-related composition." The essays were written by a wide variety of composers who work in the field of electronic music. The stated goal of the book is to "initiate a debate which will develop a long-term view of electronic music." The opening article, by Boulez, is a classic discussion of the transmission of ideas within the realm of electronic music and the gestures, shapes, and forms that are possible.

Geared toward non-musicians, SCHWARTZ is compelling and easy to read. He observes that "human choices govern electronic music," and he seeks to de-mystify electronic music on those grounds. He discusses the development of the major electronic studios such as Cologne Radio Studio and the Columbia-Princeton Electronic Music Center. His comparisons of figures such as John Lennon and Cage are interesting, and he contends that the future will see a blurring of the lines between popular music and art music.

HEIFETZ presents articles by significant figures in the world of electronic music including Appleton, Luening, and David Keane. One of the goals of the book is to reveal and promote the aesthetic ideals of composers who work in electronic media. The editor states that "electronic musicians hide behind masks," with the technical equipment often isolating the artists from the reality of society's aesthetic expectations. In one interesting imaginary discussion, a composer is asked, "What instrument do you play?" He responds, "The computer." "No, really, what instrument do you play?" "I play the computer." This dialog provides an interesting commentary on the extent to which technology has permeated the world of music.

An extremely dense and complex discussion of many issues in electronic music is found in BAGGI. These essays are highly technical and written for people with a background in electronics and programming. The contributors touch on a wide variety of issues and activities that are pertinent to electronic music, such as various programming languages, artificial intelligence programming for music composition, and a computer program that attempts to simulate a jazz rhythm section.

MANNING is an ambitious and serious book that deals with electronic music from both historical and technical perspectives. The author mentions a wide variety of other writings by inventors and innovators, including treatises and works on methodology. The chronological exploration starts with the background of electronic music up to 1945 and finishes with the digital revolution of recent years. Manning describes significant musical compositions that spurred the development of electronic music and breaks the process down country by country. Although there is a great deal of technical information, it is not really the central focus. The book contains an excellent discography.

One of the most recent contributions to the body of writings on electronic music is CHADABE. The book is largely a historical survey of the subject and is not highly technical. The author describes the 20th-century process of broadening the spectrum to embrace a wider variety of sounds than were acceptable or even possible in earlier generations. He discusses the computer program MAX and offers a good treatment of synthesizers and MIDI. Chadabe considers many of the people involved in the changing world of technology, and the final chapter—titled "Where Are We Going?"—speculates about the future of electronic music.

CONNIE E. MAYFIELD

Elgar, Edward 1857–1934

English composer

Anderson, Robert, *Elgar,* London: Dent, and New York: Schirmer Books, 1993

———, *Elgar in Manuscript,* Portland, Oregon: Amadeus Press, 1990

Elgar, Edward, *Edward Elgar: Letters of a Lifetime,* edited by Jerrold Northrop Moore, Oxford: Clarendon Press, and New York: Oxford University Press, 1990

Kennedy, Michael, *Portrait of Elgar,* London: Oxford University Press, 1968; 3rd edition, 1987

Kent, Christopher, *Edward Elgar: A Guide to Research,* New York: Garland, 1993

Monk, Raymond, editor, *Edward Elgar: Music and Literature,* Aldershot: Scolar Press, and Brookfield, Vermont: Ashgate Publishing, 1993

Monk, Raymond, editor, *Elgar Studies,* Aldershot: Scolar Press, and Brookfield, Vermont: Ashgate Publishing, 1990

Moore, Jerrold Northrop, *Edward Elgar: A Creative Life,* Oxford: Oxford University Press, 1984

———, *Elgar and His Publishers: Letters of a Creative Life,* Oxford: Clarendon Press, and New York: Oxford University Press, 1987

Redwood, Christopher, editor, *An Elgar Companion,* Ashbourne: Sequoia Publishing, 1982

Less than 50 years ago, at the centennial of his birth (1957), Elgar was still viewed in many quarters as a second-rate, late romantic composer, who might have been the best English composer since Purcell but who was far from the equal of his Continental contemporaries, Gustav Mahler and Richard Strauss. As more of Elgar's music has found its way into the international repertory, however, his stature has risen, and with it, the level of his bibliography. Initially, most writings on this enigmatic composer came from within Elgar's closest circle of friends, but although Elgar's early defenders had the virtues of proximity and access, much of their writing also suffered from a hero-worshiping myopia that failed to admit Elgar's complexities and flaws.

No one else has succeeded so admirably in illuminating the contradictions in Elgar's character as KENNEDY. At its initial publication, this work was hailed as "the most perceptive and the most distinguished study of Elgar that has yet appeared," and its latest edition retains currency through its acknowledgment of the latest research into Elgar's life and works. Although this book stands at the vanguard of the Elgar revival, it is chiefly a biography and not a study of his music: Kennedy selectively describes—rather than analyzing—most of Elgar's major works.

MOORE (1984) likewise focuses on Elgar's biography, but not at the expense of the music. For Moore, a composer's life is inextricably bound up with his works, and so this volume's narrative thread slips easily back and forth between Elgar's personal history and extended descriptive analyses of virtually every composition by him. The importance of this work lies in the mass of new details that the author has brought forth from 30 years of studying Elgar's letters and other primary documents. As a biographer, Moore has tried not to force his own interpretation on the evidence, and thus this book paints the most objective picture of Elgar possible. In dealing with the music, however, the author sometimes posits a closer link between some of the events of Elgar's life and his creative works than the evidence can clearly sustain. Nevertheless, this volume is a major achievement in musical biography, which will stand unchallenged for decades to come as the essential study of Elgar's life.

Moore's two collections of Elgar's letters—ELGAR, a more general collection, and MOORE (1987), the more particular volume—further substantiate his position as Elgar's greatest biographer. Both of these volumes have been prepared with meticulous care and therefore displace earlier editions of these letters. Moore's annotations and commentary are also exemplary, elevating these reference works nearly to the status of biographies that explain various aspects of Elgar's life. The correspondence with his publishers is especially important in that regard.

ANDERSON (1993), the third and latest volume on this composer in the Dent Master Musicians series, follows the tradition of that series by treating Elgar's life and works separately. The biographical sketch is comprehensive, if somewhat compressed, and balances an affection for Elgar's "quicksilver creative mind" with an honest appraisal of the composer's flawed character. Anderson's intimate knowledge of Elgar's working methods makes his discussion of the music this book's strong point, although his personal enthusiasm for individual works often colors his commentary. Supported by a calendar of Elgar's life, a work list, personalia, and an excellent short bibliography, this book is among the best introductions to Elgar for readers of almost any level.

In contrast to the general accessibility of his *Elgar*, ANDERSON (1990) is a book only for those who understand musical notation and have access to the scores of Elgar's compositions. The keen insight that Anderson—who claims to be no more than an observer of Elgar's working methods—acquired as the general editor of the new Elgar complete edition is evident throughout this volume. The topical rather than chronological organization of this work, however, obscures the evidence of Elgar's frequent practice of revisiting old sketches in subsequent projects.

Two recent collections of essays, both edited by Monk, offer a series of specialized studies by nearly every major expert on Elgar. Among the contents of MONK (1990) are "Elgar's Harmonic Language" by Ian Parrott, two reappraisals of works ("*King Olaf* and the English Choral Tradition" by Michael Pope and "Elgar and Falstaff" by Diana McVeagh), and a survey of recordings by Elgar and his contemporaries in "Some Elgar Interpreters" by Michael Kennedy. Other studies deal variously with Elgar's biography, personality, and specific compositions.

Brian Trowell's 150-page essay on "Elgar's Use of Literature" is the impressive centerpiece of MONK (1993). Trowell expands his topic to illuminate not only many of Elgar's texted works but also aspects of the composer's private life and personality. Robert Meikle's "'The True Foundation': The Symphonies," though scarcely one-fifth the length of Trowell's piece, is nearly as important for the rigor of its analyses of Elgar's major orchestral works. The remaining ten essays, covering issues that range from biography to analysis, are worthy companion pieces, if on more modest levels, although the highly technical language found in some essays in both of Monk's volumes may limit their potential readership. Many of the analytical essays, such as Meikle's, will be almost incomprehensible to readers who lack advanced training in music theory, whereas other pieces, such as Ronald Taylor's "Music in the Air: Elgar and the BBC" (in the 1993 collection), may be read with profit by almost anyone.

REDWOOD's book is a compilation of more than 40 well-chosen items, most of which were previously published elsewhere. These pieces range from early journalistic reviews of Elgar's music in the 1890s to a group of more critical essays on Elgar's music and musicianship. This collection also contains a large number of personal reminiscences of Elgar, several accounts of the disastrous premiere of *The Dream of Gerontius,* and five proposed solutions to the never-ending question of the identity of the "Enigma" Variations' unheard theme.

KENT's book is the single best source for information of all kinds on Elgar and his music. The catalog of compositions—which collates sketches with published scores, arrangements, and the like—is the most thorough listing of Elgar's music ever made. It stands, along with the listing of archival sources, as a tool primarily for advanced scholars. The selective, but extensive and well-annotated, bibliography will be useful to anyone interested in Elgar and his music.

SCOTT WARFIELD

Ellington, Edward Kennedy, "Duke" 1899–1974

United States composer, pianist, and bandleader

Collier, James Lincoln, *Duke Ellington,* New York: Oxford University Press, 1987

Ellington, Edward Kennedy, *Music Is My Mistress,* Garden City, New York: Doubleday, 1973

Hasse, John Edward, *Beyond Category: The Life and Genius of Duke Ellington,* New York: Simon and Schuster, 1993

Rattenbury, Ken, *Duke Ellington: Jazz Composer,* New Haven, Connecticut: Yale University Press, 1990

Schuller, Gunther, *Early Jazz: Its Roots and Musical Development,* New York: Oxford University Press, 1968

———, *The Swing Era: The Development of Jazz, 1930–1945,* New York: Oxford University Press, 1989

Stratemann, Klaus, *Duke Ellington: Day by Day and Film by Film,* Copenhagen: JazzMedia, 1992

Tucker, Mark, *Ellington: The Early Years,* Urbana: University of Illinois Press and Oxford: Bayou, 1991

Tucker, Mark, editor, *The Duke Ellington Reader,* New York: Oxford University Press, 1993

Ulanov, Barry, *Duke Ellington,* New York: Creative Age Press, 1945

As one of the most prolific of U.S. composers, Edward Kennedy "Duke" Ellington left a legacy of an estimated 1,500 compositions spanning a variety of genres and styles. His half-century career as the leader of one of the most successful dance (and later concert) jazz bands often kept Ellington on tour throughout the United States and abroad. His constant movement, huge and varied output, and closely guarded private life have created enormous difficulties for biographers. These difficulties forced early Ellington scholars to draw their information primarily from trade magazines and informal interviews and to write with a focus on the biography and character of Ellington the bandleader. Since 1988, how-

ever, writers have had access to the vast collection of Ellington scores, parts, sketches, business records, and other documents located at the Smithsonian's National Museum of American History. With the greater availability of Ellington sources, we have begun to see more scholarship that explores Ellington the composer's creative process and his work's place in the traditions of 20th-century popular and art music in the United States.

ULANOV, the first author to devote an entire study to Ellington's career, was writing during the peak of the band's fame and was faced with a subject who stated, "Biographies, like statues, are for dead men, aren't they?" Due to Ellington's lack of interest in the project, Ulanov's work relies primarily on interviews with band members and articles in the trade press, all of which are embellished by fictional dialogue. Although there is virtually no discussion of the music itself—and Ulanov's study was completed too early to include any of Ellington's important late works—this remains a useful source, providing an interesting look at the social and racial experiences of the Ellington band as understood by a mid-20th-century author.

SCHULLER (1968) devotes the final chapter of this volume to "The Ellington Style: Its Origins and Early Development," in which he examines Ellington's recorded output through the early 1930s. For Schuller, the band's tenure at the Cotton Club was a protracted workshop period, during which Ellington synthesized the regional musical characteristics of his players to develop his own musical language. Schuller's history is based almost solely on recordings, leading him to virtually ignore social and biographical issues but allowing for an impressive journey through recorded Ellington music. By the end of his survey, Schuller has identified five distinct types of Ellington compositions: dance tunes, Cotton Club production pieces—often in the "jungle style," "blue" or "mood" pieces, popular songs, and abstract compositions.

SCHULLER (1989) picks up the story of the Ellington band in 1932 and follows it through the early 1950s. Again, the focus is on the influence of the band's sidemen and their contribution to Ellington's compositional process. Especially important is the extended analysis of what Schuller considers one of Ellington's most successful large works, *Reminiscing in Tempo*. Schuller demonstrates his point that Ellington remained a modernist, while avoiding the lures of bop and modern jazz, through a detailed discussion of the composer's recordings.

ELLINGTON's autobiography is one of the most important primary sources on the composer and bandleader. Because of its informal organization and lack of an index, the volume can be a maze to the reader. Ellington casually reminisces on his career, providing memories of values learned in childhood, his first trips to New York, and early successes and failures, as well as essays outlining his musical aesthetics. Most interesting are the nearly 100 sketches on performers, teachers, friends, and family members, ranging from Sidney Bechet to Frank Sinatra. In addition, the book contains a generous supply of photographs and extensive supplementary matter listing honors and awards as well as compositions.

COLLIER's controversial biography, which focuses on the years prior to 1940, begins from the assumption that "Ellington's most important music came before he was fifty." The study then paints the second half of Ellington's career as a steady decline caused by the loss of several major soloists and what Collier sees as Ellington's less-successful emphasis on large-scale concert works. That Collier covers most of Ellington's career without technical musical discussion makes his work useful to the casual reader, but he has been roundly criticized for his historical errors and unsupported assumptions. The frequent use of anecdotal evidence to paint a picture of a bandleader who allegedly had no great talent for composition, but needed to control those around him, severely limits the effectiveness of the work.

RATTENBURY, like Schuller, focuses on Ellington's music rather than on his biography. The author takes a detailed look at five pieces written between 1939 and 1941, Ko-Ko, Mr. J.B. Blues, Concerto for Cootie, Junior Hop, and Subtle Slough. Each composition is transcribed into a full score and analyzed in terms of harmony, form, voicing, and tempo. Through this small sampling of pieces, the author demonstrates the extent to which Ellington used aspects of blues, ragtime, jazz, and Tin Pan Alley popular song to create an individual style. Rattenbury also includes brief discussions of Ellington's principal sidemen in an attempt to better define the so-called Ellington Effect. Rattenbury's transcriptions are not entirely accurate, and his desire to show how Ellington absorbed African American folk traditions often causes him to ignore other aspects of the composer's style.

While most Ellington scholarship has focused on the band's activities during the 1930s and 1940s, TUCKER (1991) explores Ellington's early biography and music in remarkable detail. Tucker, like Ulanov, believes that in order to understand Ellington's later accomplishments, we must first come to terms with the influences of the African American culture of Washington, D.C., on the young composer and also with Ellington's pre-Cotton Club experiences in New York City. Because Tucker limits himself to the years between 1899, Ellington's birth, and 1927, the beginning of his Cotton Club engagement, he is able to supply by far the most complete study of Ellington's early career. Of particular interest are the thorough examinations of Ellington's early masterworks. Pieces such as East St. Louis Toodle-Oo, Black and Tan Fantasy, and Creole Love Call, along with lesser-known works, receive careful technical discussions that help reveal how Ellington absorbed and synthesized a variety of musical styles, while explaining variations between recorded and published versions of his music. In short, Tucker's book, although limited to a small portion of Ellington's career, stands as one of the most important pieces of jazz scholarship to date.

STRATEMANN's work is an enormous repository of Ellington information. The focus of the study is the more than 60 films in which Ellington was involved as a composer or bandleader between 1929 and 1974. For each film Stratemann provides production information, cast lists, and reviews. In addition, he takes pains to place the films in cultural context, both in terms of Ellington's career and film history. Several "interludes" provide chronological lists detailing the band's day-to-day activities, including recording sessions, radio and television broadcasts, and live performances. Also included are nearly 400 photographs and illustrations, brief discussions of selected Ellington television appearances, and a month-by-month chart that lists the Ellington band's personnel. Although there is no central argument to this study, Stratemann has produced, by thoroughly examining articles in the trade press, one of the largest reference works on Ellington's daily professional activities.

HASSE, in what is no doubt the best complete biography, explores what Ellington called his "two careers," those of composer and bandleader. The chronological narrative is interspersed with brief sections that discuss social issues relevant to Ellington's career, such as the history of the Cotton Club. In addition, most chapters end with short, nontechnical descriptions of the music. Written in conjunction with the Smithsonian's exhibition, Beyond Category: The Musical Genius of Duke Ellington, Hasse's book assumes no prior knowledge of "music, jazz, or Ellington." The appendices contain brief guides to Ellington's musicians, recordings, and films. Although an important Ellington biography, Hasse's complex citation system and informal musical discussions make the work difficult to use as a scholarly source.

For the serious Ellington student, TUCKER (1993) is an indispensable tool. The author has carefully compiled over 100 articles spanning seven decades from 1923 to 1993, from record reviews in the popular press to technical discussions and reactions to Ellington's music. Each article is introduced by a brief description of Ellington's activities at the time, as well as biographical information on the article's author. In addition, Tucker has carefully annotated the articles themselves to provide corrections and clarifications. The two indices make this study easy to use as a reference work for those who wish to see how Ellington was viewed throughout his career and since his death.

PATRICK WARFIELD

See also Jazz: Swing

Ethnomusicology: History

Barz, Gregory F., and Timothy J. Cooley, editors, *Shadows in the Field: New Perspectives for Fieldwork in Ethnomusicology*, New York: Oxford University Press, 1997

Blum, Stephen, et al., editors, *Ethnomusicology and Modern Music History*, Urbana: University of Illinois Press, 1991

Merriam, Alan P., *The Anthropology of Music*, Evanston, Illinois: Northwestern University Press, 1964

Meyers, Helen, editor, *Ethnomusicology*, 2 vols., London: Macmillan, and New York: Norton, 1993

Nettl, Bruno, *The Study of Ethnomusicology: Twenty-Nine Issues and Concepts*, Urbana: University of Illinois Press, 1983

Nettl, Bruno, and Philip V. Bohlman, editors, *Comparative Musicology and Anthropology of Music: Essays on the History of Ethnomusicology*, Chicago: University of Chicago Press, 1991

Shelemay, Kay Kaufman, *Ethnomusicology: History Definitions, and Scope*, New York: Garland, 1992

The history of ethnomusicological scholarship has taken many different paths since the development of *vergleichende Musikwissenschaft* (comparative musicology) in the 1880s, although from its beginnings, ethnomusicology has generally resulted in studies of people making music. Such studies have not been limited to the study of non-Western music; European and North American folk, popular, and traditional musics have been foci since ethnomusicology's inception. The history of ethnomusicology is the history of what ethnomusicologists do and have done and the new directions they are taking. Texts devoted to the history of the academic discipline of ethnomusicology have increased considerably in the 1990s, as the following publications attest.

BARZ and COOLEY suggest that a major paradigm shift in ethnomusicological thought has occurred, embracing a new fieldwork that focuses more on the process of doing and understanding ethnomusicological fieldwork than on the representation of fieldwork. Ultimately, what ethnomusicologists do in the field is not totally separable from what they do out of the field, yet much of the focus in traditional ethnomusicological writing and teaching centered on analyses and ethnographic representations of musical cultures instead of the rather personal experience of understanding and conducting fieldwork that this volume addresses. Cooley's introduction provides an excellent historical overview of the role of fieldwork in ethnomusicology.

BLUM concerns ethnomusicology's position in modernity, specifically investigating its place within the relationship between modernity and music history. The book is divided into four sections. The first section includes articles that approach the position of history in several musi-cal traditions (e.g., Christopher Waterman's treatment of Nigerian *jùjú*) and the significance of historic music events (Ali Jihad Racy's article on the Cairo Conference of 1932). The second section concerns authority and interpretation. Essays include Regula Qureshi's outline of the spiritual lineage of sheikhs in sufism and Thomas Turino's study of the history of Peruvian panpipe traditions. The third section includes articles that focus on the relationship of the musical specialist to a greater community, as broker for or mediator of a musical tradition. The fourth section introduces the concepts of musical reproduction and renewal. Among articles in this section are a study of the chamber music of *Yekkes* in Israel by Philip Bohlman, and an examination of music in Felicity, Trinidad, by Helen Myers.

MERRIAM is a classic text devoted to locating musical performance within the center of cultural organization. In addition to providing an outline of methodological and theoretical issues concerning the study of music as a specific human behavior, Merriam's introductory chapter, "The Study of Ethnomusicology," details in particular the contributions of anthropology to developing strains of ethnomusicology. These contributions are traced from the early German efforts of the 1880s onward—through the salvage perspectives of Erich Moritz von Hornbostel, Hugh Tracey, and Curt Sachs in the first half of the 20th century, to the work of those who studied music's communicative powers (Mantle Hood, Charles Seeger, and George Herzog), and finally to broad-based studies of music, such as those by Nettl. Throughout the remaining chapters Merriam draws on historical materials, thus providing a valuable historical outline of the discipline as it was perceived in the 1960s.

MEYERS is a two-volume set. The first volume is a guidebook intended to provide the general reader with the basic tools needed to approach, engage, and examine the subject material of ethnomusicology. The collection of individually authored essays provides insight into subjects such as theories and methods, definitions, the roles of anthropology and musicology, organology, iconography, the music industry, biology, technology, dance, gender, ethics, and documentation and preservation. The bibliographies accompanying these articles are extremely broad-based and are thus useful for both the beginner and advanced reader. Concluding this volume is an essay by Nettl on recent directions in ethnomusicology. Nettl not only reflects on specific issues covered within the text, but also questions the effect ethnomusicology has had on contemporary musical experiences, both Western and non-Western. The volume includes several valuable reference aids focusing on research resources in ethnomusicology, major instrument collections, the Hornbostel/Sachs classification of musical instruments, pitch measurement, and national mains frequencies and voltages (television standards).

The second volume of Meyers's set is a collection of individually authored essays that provides a regional and historical overview of the study of the world's musics. The volume's introduction presents a historical survey of ethnomusicological contributions, reaching as far back as Jean-Jacques Rousseau (*Dictionnaire de musique*, 1768), moving through the seminal ethnographies of the 1970s and 1980s (A. Seeger, S. Feld, and P. Berliner, among others), and looking forward toward the year 2000. Meyers divides this volume into two parts. The first section is devoted to the early history of ethnomusicology and its roles in various parts of the world, covering the period up to World War II. The second section contains regional studies focusing on postwar research and scholarship. As in the first volume, the bibliographies provide a useful tool for further studies.

NETTL presents a valuable historical construction that approaches a comprehensive understanding of ethnomusicology. In a series of vignettes and reflections, Nettl positions ethnomusicological theory within the actions, products, scholarship, and field research of the main contributors to the diversified discipline. By focusing on many of the key issues of current and past ethnomusicological theory (universals, language, comparison, fieldwork, and folk music, among other topics), Nettl identifies a system of beliefs—a credo of sorts—within which ethnomusicologists approach the diversity of musics that exist in people's lives.

NETTL and BOHLMAN, a collection of essays, offers perspectives on the larger intellectual history of the contemporary discipline of ethnomusicology. Debating such topics as key historical players in ethnomusicology's formation (Hornbostel, Stumpf, and Merriam, among others), the role particular geographic areas have had on the discipline (Africa, China, Eastern Europe), and the relationship of ethnomusicology to other related disciplines and fields, the authors locate ethnomusicology as a discipline within a broad historical context. The authors collectively represent a cross-section of ethnomusicology, broadly defined, including historical musicologists, systematic musicologists, and anthropologists among the general ethnomusicologists. One result of these essays is that the value of a community of scholars in ethnomusicology is strongly asserted.

SHELEMAY is one volume of a seven-part series of anthologies of previously published articles from many sources that have contributed to the methodological and practical foundations of the academic discipline of ethnomusicology. Selections in this collection cover the history, definitions, and breadth of ethnomusicology. While the majority of these articles are from the 1960s and 1970s, texts from as early as 1909 are included, providing a depth of material concerning the history of the ethnomusicology.

GREGORY F. BARZ

Ethnomusicology: Theory and Method

Barz, Gregory F., and Timothy J. Cooley, editors, *Shadows in the Field: New Perspectives for Fieldwork in Ethnomusicology*, New York: Oxford University Press, 1997

Blacking, John, *How Musical Is Man?*, Seattle: University of Washington Press, 1973

Blum, Stephen, et al., editors, *Ethnomusicology and Modern Music History*, Urbana: University of Illinois Press, 1991

Feld, Steven, *Sound and Sentiment: Birds, Weeping, Poetics, and Song in Kaluli Expression*, Philadelphia: University of Pennsylvania Press, 1982; 2nd edition, 1990

Herndon, Marcia, and Norma McLeod, *Field Manual for Ethnomusicology*, Norwood, Pennsylvania: Norwood Editions, 1983

Hood, Mantle, *The Ethnomusicologist*, New York: McGraw-Hill, 1971; new edition, Kent, Ohio: Kent State University Press, 1982

Kartomi, Margaret J., *On Concepts and Classifications of Musical Instruments*, Chicago: University of Chicago Press, 1990

Keil, Charles, *Tiv Song*, Chicago: University of Chicago Press, 1979

Manuel, Peter Lamarche, *Popular Musics of the Non-Western World: An Introductory Survey*, New York: Oxford University Press, 1988

McLeod, Norma, and Marcia Herndon, editors, *The Ethnography of Musical Performance*, Norwood, Pennsylvania: Norwood Editions, 1980

Merriam, Alan P., *The Anthropology of Music*, Evanston, Illinois: Northwestern University Press, 1964

Myers, Helen, editor, *Ethnomusicology: An Introduction*, London: Macmillan, and New York: Norton, 1992

Nettl, Bruno, *Theory and Method in Ethnomusicology*, New York: Free Press of Glencoe, 1964

Nettl, Bruno, editor, *Eight Urban Musical Cultures: Tradition and Change*, Urbana: University of Illinois Press, 1978

Nettl, Bruno, and Philip V. Bohlman, editors, *Comparative Musicology and Anthropology of Music: Essays on the History of Ethnomusicology*, Chicago: University of Chicago Press, 1991

Roseman, Marina, *Healing Sounds from the Malaysian Rainforest: Temiar Music and Medicine*, Berkeley: University of California Press, 1991

Shelemay, Kay Kaufman, editor, *The Garland Library of Readings in Ethnomusicology: A Core Collection of Important Ethnomusicological Articles*, 7 vols., New York: Garland, 1990

Stone, Ruth M., *Let the Inside Be Sweet: The Interpretation of Music Event among the Kpelle of Liberia*, Bloomington: Indiana University Press, 1982

A vast amount of scholarship either discusses or demonstrates the theories and methods that make up the discipline of ethnomusicology. In this select bibliography, several works provide an overview of the theories underlying ethnomusicological scholarship and others clarify research methodologies, such as fieldwork techniques. Some scholars devise methods for transcribing, analyzing, or classifying the music of different areas, and others emphasize musical performance in its social and cultural context. In the early years, ethnomusicology was generally divided into two separate camps, musicological versus anthropological. Since the 1970s, many scholars have tried to address both concerns. There have been studies of tradition and change in countries undergoing modernization or Westernization, as well as historical or socio-historical studies and new approaches that emphasize reflexivity, experience, or dialogue. Further, there has been considerable interest in power relationships, popular music, issues of identity, and music and healing in different societies.

Other developments in the discipline include the emergence of a more evocative narrative style and an increase in collaborative work that gives greater recognition to indigenous performers and scholars. Many early theories used scientific methods—whether to analyze musical sound or to gather data on musical cultures—whereas more recent theoretical approaches have derived from structuralism, symbolic interactionism, linguistics, semiotics, anthropology, communications, gender studies, Marxism, hermeneutics, phenomenology, and discourse theory.

BARZ and COOLEY bring together exciting new perspectives in fieldwork, field relationships, and the field experience in ethnomusicology. Allowing for cultural relativism and ideological diversity, this collection explores feminist theories, phenomenology, reflexive and dialogic ethnography, and other approaches. By shifting the focus "from *representation* (text) toward *experience* (fieldwork)," they aim to emphasize the interactive role of the researcher engaged in postmodern, or post-postmodern, processes of doing fieldwork.

In an essay titled "Knowing Fieldwork," Titon traces different theories of knowledge prevalent in ethnomusicology and outlines four basic paradigms for this field. He advocates people making music as his paradigm case of musical "being-in-the-world." Cooley also provides a useful history of old and new perspectives for fieldwork or field research in ethnomusicology in his insightful introduction. Concerning theory and methodology, the article and epilogue by Barz suggests an intriguing, reflective use of fieldnotes and calls for creative diversification of ethnographic writing, including ethnography as a form of performative writing. Rice draws on phenomenological hermeneutics to explore the fieldworker's experience of a temporal arc that moves from understanding through explanation to new understandings. Babiracki gives a reflexive account of her fieldwork experiences in villages in India, which explores gender identity and its influence on research, both in terms of the researcher's gender identity and with regard to the gender roles of musicians in a particular community. She considers feminist and postmodern approaches as alternatives to the traditional social science paradigm of ethnographic research, and she critiques the potential of the new methods. These and other essays in this collection offer a valuable impetus for new directions in ethnomusicology.

BLACKING explores the social, musical, and cognitive processes involved in musical creativity as well as the human value of music. He considers music as a form of communication that is inextricably connected to a social situation. The author acknowledges the biological processes of aural perception as well as cognitive and physiological processes that may generate musical composition and performance. He emphasizes creative, informed, and structured listening and is concerned with what defines music, including musical meanings and music as a sign of human experience. Blacking personally upholds the value of music for all of humankind, and he relates music to creativity and dance, as well as broad social, biological, and psychological concerns.

BLUM et al. collect 15 essays concerning musical interpretations of history or historical interpretations of music and musical life. Each essay offers a historical case study of musical performance or discourse about music in specific cultures. Taken as a whole, these essays raise political concerns as well as issues of identity, gender, power, social order, authenticity, acculturation, appropriation, and explorations of modern performance genres. The prologue by Blum and the epilogue by Neuman are very useful both for their summaries of the articles and because they place the individual essays within a broader framework of paradigms and practices in ethnomusicology.

FELD has created a unique and rich ethnographic study of sound as a cultural system (i.e., a system of symbols) among the Kaluli people of Papua New Guinea. He interweaves poetics and linguistic analysis with discussions of bird sounds, modes and codes of sound communication, such as weeping, and social analysis in order to develop an understanding of Kaluli sound expressions as embodiments of the ethos of their society. This work is distinguished by Feld's interpretive, communications-based methodology that contributes substantially to ethno-poetics, aesthetic anthropology, and ethnomusicology.

HERNDON and McLEOD's book is a prescriptive guide for ethnomusicologists preparing to embark on their first field trips. The authors give numerous examples of questions to ask, equipment to bring, how to negotiate the initial and subsequent visits to the field, issues concerning participation and observation, record-keeping strategies, tape recording techniques, transcription, translation, and ethical responsibilities. This basic but useful introductory text offers straightforward explanations of many factors involved in ethnomusicological fieldwork. For actual fieldwork, this text would need to be supplemented by the latest information on audiovisual technologies, and the proposed fieldwork strategies should be adapted to address individual research needs.

HOOD is known for his emphasis on the study, performance, and analysis of music as fundamental to ethnomusicology. In this text, he draws upon examples from his fieldwork experiences in Indonesia and Africa in order to demonstrate what an ethnomusicologist actually does. Hood emphasizes musical literacy and discusses the music mode and the speech mode of discourse in his exploration of field methods (recording, photography, film); transcription and notation; organology; musical analysis; and the human equation. This text contains detailed analytical and ethnographic information written in a style that is more anecdotal and less prescriptive than that of other studies.

KARTOMI provides an in-depth investigation of the theory and methodology of classification for musical instruments and instrumental ensembles. She considers classification in societies oriented toward literary transmission (including China, India, Tibet, Java, Greece, Europe, the United States, and the Arab World) and in societies oriented toward oral transmission (Mandailing, Minangkabau, T'boli, West Africa, 'Are'are, and Finnish-Karelian). Further, she explores how the prevalent philosophies and ideologies of a particular culture ascribe meaning and significance to instruments. This book represents a broad-based exposition of taxonomical organology.

KEIL gives a self-deprecating, linguistically informed, materialist view of Tiv song and culture, which he contrasts with the elitist and hierarchical imperialism of anthropology and Western scholarship in general. This ethnography is interesting not only for its clarification of what Tiv song is but also for its ruthless critique of certain predominant approaches to ethnomusicology and anthropology. Keil's study represents a Marxist approach, and it raises some important and penetrating questions.

MANUEL has been instrumental in developing the study of popular music within ethnomusicology. This survey begins with theoretical perspectives and proceeds to cover a diverse collection of non-Western popular musics from Latin America and the Caribbean, Africa, Europe, the Middle East, South Asia, Southeast Asia, China, and the Pacific. Genres include film music, dance music, contemporary styles of traditional music, syncretic genres, indigenous pop music, and music that reflects a political ideology. Manuel successfully combines detailed musical information with discussions of conceptual concerns. Given the increasing interest in popular music in many music departments, this book is sure to be influential.

McLEOD and HERNDON have compiled seven ethnographic studies focused on musical performance. These introductory essays address diverse geographical areas; the authors aim to at develop an understanding of musical events through studies of the social or cultural context for performances, the exchange between audience and performer, and indigenous conceptions of performance, as well as other more philosophical or ideological concerns. Based on the ethnography-of-communications model, these essays incorporate ideas from sociolinguistics with ethnoscientific and ethnomethodological approaches to cultural analysis.

MERRIAM explores the anthropological approach to musical culture with the aim of providing a theoretical framework and methodology for the study of music as human behavior. He defines ethnomusicology as the study of music in culture, and he creates a three-part model for analytical studies, involving conceptualization about music, behavior in relation to music, and music sound itself. Musical behavior consists of physical behavior, social behavior, and verbal behavior. Merriam aims to approximate scientific methods based on hypothesis formulation and testing. He delineates six areas of inquiry for field research in ethnomusicology: musical material culture, song texts, categories of music, the musician, uses and functions of music in relation to other aspects of culture, and music as a creative cultural activity (which includes the concepts of music held in a given society as well as the compositional process). Merriam's structural functionalist, anthropological approach has exerted a strong influence on theory and method in ethnomusicology.

MYERS provides a clear and thorough introduction to the discipline of ethnomusicology. Eleven chapters in part 2 are devoted to theory and method with articles by various authors covering fieldwork, field technology, ethnography of music, transcription, notation, analysis of musical style, historical ethnomusicology, iconography, organology, the biology of music-making, and dance. This book introduces up-and-coming ethnomusicologists to the influential concepts in the field as a whole and to the scholarship in each area of research. Myers guides the reader from the requirements of a dissertation proposal through various methodologies prevalent in ethnomusicology (fieldwork, participant observation, recording, interviews, field records). Different styles of writing and different forms of analysis are also covered in depth. This book is essential reading material for those who are serious about pursuing ethnomusicology and are eager to understand its theories and methodologies in detail, although the most recent technological developments related to the discipline, such as digital recording equipment, are not discussed.

The collection of articles edited by NETTL and BOHLMAN places ethnomusicology in a historical perspective. This volume demonstrates diverse historical approaches to a wide range of musical traditions and provides an intellectual history of the discipline. The first section concerns the development of ethnomusicology in different regions of the world. The second section provides a critical discussion of intellectual paradigms, source material, and methodologies. Section 3 elucidates the diverse approaches used by early leaders in ethnomusicology. Finally, section 4 introduces issues such as recording technology, psychological theory, interdisciplinary approaches, and styles of musical ethnography. Bohlman's essay outlines some of the significant theories and methods used in ethnomusicological practices, including scientific observation, experimentation, fieldwork, and cultural critique, all of which bear on the broader issue of representation.

NETTL (1978) presents a significant set of ethnomusicological studies concerning traditional musics in cities from Asia, Africa, the Middle East, and the Americas. These studies explore the role of traditional music in the context of the cultural changes that occur when societies move toward a more modern, or Western, way of life. Nettl terms this area of study *urban ethnomusicology,* contrasting the concerns of this field to many earlier studies that concentrated on rural village traditions and avoided the contradictions and complex syntheses often found in urban environments. Nettl's collection contains a broad range of informative and thought-provoking studies, many of which develop from a historical or sociological approach, while others concentrate on musical style or genealogies.

NETTL (1964), on theory and method, outlines research methodologies for fieldwork, transcription, analysis or description of musical compositions, determination of style, and classification of instruments, and he explains different approaches to the study of music in culture. This work provides a useful introduction to many of the ongoing concerns in ethnomusicology.

ROSEMAN shows the close association of sound and healing in Temiar life and performances. Music is connected to the Temiar conceptual and cultural worlds and is capable of creating a transformative and healing experience. Drawing upon theories from interpretive anthropology, performance theory, medical ethnography, and ethnomusicology, Roseman explores the "configurations of meaning and power that inform Temiar curative performances."

SHELEMAY has compiled numerous core articles in ethnomusicology in seven volumes on select themes. Volume 2 concerns ethnomusicological theory and method and provides a wide spectrum of seminal articles in the field. Of particular interest are Feld's discussion of linguistic models in ethnomusicology, Nattiez's investigation of musical semiotics, Gourlay's critique of Merriam and call for the return of the missing ethnomusicologist, Rice's suggestions for remodeling ethnomusicology, Tunstall's overview of structuralism and musicology, Hood's discussion of bi-musicality (learning about a foreign musical tradition through performance), and Merriam's treatment of methods using music to study acculturation or to reconstruct culture history. Volume 4 contains detailed information on musical transcription. Volume 5 explores cross-cultural analysis and includes several articles on theory and method, such as Kaeppler's discussion of method and theory in analyzing dance structure, Powers's exposition on language models and musical analysis, Freeman and Merriam's application of anthropological methods of statistical classification to ethnomusicology, and Herndon's critique of previous methods of treating music and their underlying assumptions.

Volume 6 of Shelemay's work also contains articles related to theory and method in ethnomusicology, including Porter's survey of documentary recordings, Blacking's investigation of musical change, Stone and Stone's discussion of the use of research media in the study of music events (especially the feedback interview as a research technique), Nettl's model for the comparative study of repertoires (based on types of tradition and transmission), and Seeger's essay on sound archives. The seven volumes compiled by Shelemay make an impressive number of influential articles in ethnomusicology accessible to students and scholars.

STONE draws from musical and anthropological methods in a study focusing on a music event among the Kpelle of Liberia. She uses theories of symbolic interactionism and semiotic-cybernetic communication to build a methodology for this approach.

BRITA HEIMARCK

F

Falla, Manuel de 1876–1946

Spanish composer

Burnett, James, *Manuel de Falla and the Spanish Musical Renaissance,* London: Gollancz, 1979

Crichton, Ronald, *Falla,* London: British Broadcasting Corporation, 1982

Demarquez, Suzanne, *Manuel de Falla,* translated by Salvator Attanasio, Philadelphia, Pennsylvania: Chilton, 1968

Falla, Manuel de, *On Music and Musicians,* translated by David Urman and J.M. Thomson, London: Boyars, 1979

Harper, Nancy Lee, *Manuel de Falla: A Bio-Bibliography,* Westport, Connecticut: Greenwood Press, 1998

Pahissa, Jaime, *Manuel de Falla: His Life and Works,* translated by Jean Wagstaff, London: Museum Press, 1954

Manuel de Falla is without question the greatest of Spanish composers in modern times. It was he who brought the Spanish nationalist tradition of Albéniz and Granados to its highest level of development, in his opera *La vida breve* (The Short Life, 1913) and his ballets *El amor brujo* (Love, the Magician, 1915) and *El sombrero de tres picos* (The Three-Cornered Hat, 1919). He then ushered Spanish music fully into the 20th century with his embrace of neoclassicism, under the influence of Stravinsky, in the 1920s. From this decade came such masterpieces as the puppet-theater opera *El retablo de Maese Pedro* (Master Peter's Puppet Show, 1923), based on an episode from *Don Quixote,* and the Harpsichord Concerto (1926). These works break with his earlier reliance on Spanish folklore and reach back to the *siglo de oro* for their inspiration. Falla composed with great deliberation and was not prolific; he is remembered today for a relatively small number of pieces. But his craftsmanship was of the highest order, and the above works have gained a permanent place in the musical canon. Born in Cádiz, Falla first came to prominence in Madrid. But he matured as a composer only after a seven-year residence in Paris (1907–14), where he became acquainted with Debussy and adopted elements of impressionism in his style. He returned to Spain with the outbreak of war and there composed his greatest works. Falla fled the devastation of the Spanish Civil War, emigrating to Argentina in 1939, where he remained until his death. His final work, the scenic cantata *Atlántida,* was left incomplete at his death.

BURNETT's study begins with a brief overview of the development of Spanish music up to the time of Falla, in order to place his work in historical context. It continues with an examination of the most important type of Spanish theater music in modern times, the zarzuela, which alternates set musical numbers with spoken dialogue (rather than recitative) and was the chief occupation of most Spanish composers well into the 20th century. Falla essayed the genre in his early career without memorable results. However, discussion of Falla's zarzuelas forms the necessary backdrop for Burnett's treatment of *La vida breve,* which Falla composed in 1905 but which did not premiere until 1913. The two middle chapters explore the composer's most fruitful decade, to 1919, during which he composed his most famous works, all in a national style, followed by a discussion of the universalizing tendencies that characterize Falla's adoption of neoclassicism in the 1920s. Indeed, the neoclassical virtues of economy and precision were part of Falla's basic musical temperament, which may account for his painfully slow pace of composition and lack of creative fecundity. In the final chapter, Burnett surveys the achievements of Spanish composers after Falla, with emphasis on the fate of the nationalist style in Spain. Some composers, such as Joaquín Rodrigo, have continued in this vein and found new approaches to it. Others, such as Robert Gerhard, abandoned it for atonality. Although there are some outstanding composers in Spain today, there is no figure of Falla's stature.

CRICHTON is one of the leading authorities on Falla and presents a brief but insightful overview of the composer's life and works. The organization of the material is chronological, with discussion of the major works nested within the biographical narrative. This is a highly accessible introduction to the man and his music, illustrated with some musical examples.

DEMARQUEZ similarly provides a comprehensive overview of Falla's life and works, with ample discussion of the music within the context of the biography. The singular virtue of the author's approach is that she provides a capable examination of the folkloric sources of Falla's nationalist impulse. This area frequently gives many writers, especially non-Spaniards, great difficulty, and her insights are valuable.

FALLA wrote a number of essays after his return to Spain from Paris, many of them for publication in Spanish periodicals, which are presented here in English translation. Falla expresses his opinions on a wide variety of musical subjects and personalities, including contemporary Spanish music, Debussy, Granados, Pedrell, Stravinsky, Turina, and Wagner. Also appearing here are his thoughts on flamenco *cante jondo* (deep song) and its impact on European music. This is among the most important sources for understanding Falla's attitudes and opinions.

HARPER's bio-bibliography is the most up-to-date work on Falla available in English and should be the point of departure for anyone interested in the composer. It includes a summary biography as well as an annotated bibliography, list of works and performances, and selected discography. It also treats the holdings of the Archivo Manuel de Falla in Granada, where nearly all the primary sources are located.

PAHISSA became acquainted with Falla during the composer's tenure in Argentina. As a study of Falla's life and works, this book was the most comprehensive work up to the time of its first publication (1954). Although it has been superseded in this regard by the studies above, the text still contains a wealth of information from Pahissa's numerous conversations with Falla during the Argentine exile.

WALTER AARON CLARK

Fauré, Gabriel 1845–1924

French composer

Fauré, Gabriel, *Gabriel Fauré: His Life Through His Letters*, edited by Jean-Michel Nectoux, translated by J.A. Underwood, London: Boyars, 1984

———, *Gabriel Fauré: A Life in Letters*, edited and translated by J. Barrie Jones, London: Batsford, 1989

Nectoux, Jean-Michel, *Gabriel Fauré: A Musical Life*, translated by Roger Nichols, Cambridge: Cambridge University Press, 1991

Orledge, Robert, *Gabriel Fauré*, London: Eulenburg Books, 1979; revised edition, 1983

Suckling, Norman, *Fauré*, London: Dent, 1941

Tait, Robin, *The Musical Language of Gabriel Fauré*, New York: Garland, 1989

The philosopher Gabriel Marcel once marveled at the way Fauré's late works achieve the improbable union of purely abstract thought and intense sensibility. In Fauré's music, fantasy and reason, emotion and form are reconciled in a musical discourse of such extraordinary syntactic density that at times it seems to offer listeners no level stretches in which to pause and catch their breath. It is no surprise that a style that makes such demands on listeners and performers continues to challenge historians and analysts as well. Outside of France, Fauré's paradoxical qualities have, until recently, held back both the circulation of his music and its treatment in scholarly literature. The earliest monographs on Fauré were short biographies; the latest have been well-documented studies that take greater account of the substance of Fauré's musical style and the rich cultural history of the Third Republic.

The first book on Fauré in English was published only at the end of World War II. SUCKLING's work relies on the most important printed sources available to him: the monographs in French by Fauré-Fremiet (1929), Koechlin (1927), and Jankélévitch (1938). It also labors under the smoldering political resentments of 1946: anti-German, anti-Italian, and antiromantic feelings lead him to indulge in an overly polemical revision of musical history. But the prejudices are plain, and a careful reader can take them into account. The first chapter is a biography, but the bulk of the volume is devoted to studying Fauré's music in different media, with special attention to musical style. Suckling portrays Fauré as a key figure in the deliverance from "the aberrations of nineteenth-century romanticism" and supports this thesis—and others less contentious—with many musical examples. Remarks on the composer's harmony and counterpoint in the chapters on instrumental music draw attention to important points and quicken curiosity. Indeed, subsequent British writers have relied heavily on Suckling's observations. Slimmer and less demanding than the books by Nectoux and Orledge, this older study remains a concise, thought-provoking introduction to Fauré's art.

Shortly after his book on Fauré was published in 1979, ORLEDGE was criticized for borrowing too liberally from Nectoux's work, particularly the short biography entitled *Fauré* (1972). It is equally possible to show that Orledge relies overmuch on Fauré-Fremiet and Suckling for some of his formulations. His book nonetheless contains original contributions. He is especially concerned with details of Fauré's style and discusses compositional processes as illuminated by extant sketchbooks and manuscripts. Also of particular value is a chapter on Fauré's contemporary and posthumous artistic reputation, in which the author discusses his findings on Fauré's important musical activities in England. Orledge divides Fauré's work into three periods but unfortunately lends excessive force to this convention by using it to explain features of Fauré's music rather than the other way round. Each period receives a long chapter that is subdivided by musical media. The resulting text is a bit laborious to read and, more seriously, hedges an intensive, synthetic discussion of Fauré's style; however, the sectional organization of the book makes it easy to consult. Orledge delves into Fauré's compositional choices in the penultimate chapter, which discusses in detail the genesis of several works. "Fauré's Musical Techniques," the final chapter, seems hastily assembled and often superficial, but Orledge's explication of Fauré's modal practice is excellent. The three appendices to this book are useful: a catalog of works, based on a provisional redaction by Nectoux done in about 1975, which includes the location of original and copied manuscripts; a list of musical cross-references in Fauré's oeuvre; and an extensive bibliography. The second edition of this book is preferable to the first: it corrects minor errors, brings facts up to date (especially in the appendices), and eliminates references to two songs that Orledge had incorrectly attributed to Fauré. Unfortunately, the second edition had a very short print run and is more difficult to find than the first.

NECTOUX's monumental volume is the most important study of the composer published to date and is likely to remain so for some time. The author treats his topic with expansive historical knowledge and dazzling documentary control; the information here is the most accurate now available. This study integrates over 20 years of research during which Nectoux painstakingly established the facts of Fauré's life and the dating and genesis of his compositions. He offers a fine selection of primary materials for the reader's scrutiny, in particular excerpts from letters and interviews. Fauré's stylistic evolution is treated more subtly here than in any other study except Tait. Nectoux organizes the book along broadly chronological lines but fruitfully suspends the narrative from time to time with essays on topics of special importance, such as Fauré's projects for the theater, the genesis of *La bonne chanson,* his orchestration, and his influence as a teacher. A detailed chronology of Fauré's entire life is provided as an appendix. The vast back matter also includes a catalog of works and a massive bibliography. Unlike Orledge, Nectoux does not include the location of manuscripts, but otherwise this work list replaces all others, including Nectoux's own earlier one for the *New Grove Dictionary of Music and Musicians* (1980). Finally, Nectoux draws his readers into the world of Fauré's musical language, but here, as with Orledge, the analytical methods are loose, the analyses incomplete, and, indeed, some of the musical examples and prose descriptions inaccurate. A thorough appreciation of Nectoux's thinking and Fauré's music will thus, for more than the usual reasons, require all but casual readers to consult the original scores.

What the preceding authors provide in the way of musical analysis is suggestive rather than conclusive.

Nowhere, for example, does one find a harmonic analysis of a whole piece. It is therefore worth mentioning that a number of doctoral dissertations over the past 30 years have subjected works by Fauré to detailed analyses in the Schenkerian tradition. Among these is Taylor Greer's "Tonal Process in the Songs of Gabriel Fauré: Two Structural Features of the Whole-Tone Scale" (Yale University, 1986), which takes pride of place for its accuracy, analytical insights, and lucid presentation. For other facets of Fauré's achievement not treated intensively elsewhere in the literature, researchers will want to know about James Kidd's careful study of "Louis Niedermeyer's System for Gregorian Chant Accompaniment as a Compositional Source for Gabriel Fauré" (University of Chicago, 1973), Gail Hilson Woldu's "Gabriel Fauré as Director of the Conservatoire Nationale de Musique et de Déclamation, 1905–1920" (Yale University, 1983), and Carlo Caballero's "Fauré and French Musical Aesthetics" (University of Pennsylvania, 1996).

One dissertation that has been distributed commercially, but without revision, is TAIT. His study could be described as a book-length development of Orledge's final chapter on Fauré's techniques: the various musical parameters are examined in turn. Tait also continues Orledge's work on the sketches and manuscripts in an appendix that looks especially closely at the String Quartet, op. 121. In the chapter on melody, there are many examples of Fauré's "self-borrowing," but Tait often falls into the trap of taking raw material for characteristic material. He treats Fauré's harmony, modal techniques, melodic style, and harmonic rhythm in perceptive detail, and he isolates specific chordal structures for detailed study.

Two collections of the composer's letters appear in the above bibliography. Correspondence, even in translation, is invaluable evidence, and Fauré's letters also make for delightful reading that will have much to say to the student and amateur. The tenor of the two collections is different; although both provide excellent introductions for the layman, the one edited by Nectoux is the more intellectually focused and is geared toward musical historians. Of the 212 letters in FAURÉ (1984), all but 29 are by the composer. Groups of letters are thoughtfully introduced and, in the first part of the book, connected together through narrative biographical passages. In much of the volume, however, Nectoux's editorial presentation is so self-sustaining as to create a succession of short essays. For example, the chapter that treats the interaction of social life and creativity, and the connections between Fauré and Proust, is a true essay in which letters are simply furnished in evidence. Nectoux ends with an important essay, "Fauré the Innovator." He lays out his sources and methods of dating in the front and back matter.

The letters in FAURÉ (1989) are connected with linking passages of more modest dimensions. As with the earlier collection, this collection, edited by Jones, is conscientious, well translated, and thoroughly documented. Jones deliberately avoids overlap so that only 15 letters are common to his book and Nectoux's. Of the 312 letters presented, 62 are letters to Fauré from other correspondents. Besides editing previously unpublished manuscripts in the Bibliothèque Nationale, Jones draws the majority of his texts from two untranslated sources: an edition of selected letters from Fauré to his wife (Paris, 1951), and Nectoux's edition of letters between Fauré and Saint-Saëns (Paris, 1973).

CARLO CABALLERO

Fauxbourdon

Bradshaw, Murray C., *The Falsobordone: A Study in Renaissance and Baroque Music,* Rome: American Institute of Musicology, 1978

Kenney, Sylvia, *Walter Frye and the Contenance Angloise,* New Haven, Connecticut: Yale University Press, 1964

Moll, Kevin N., editor and translator, *Counterpoint and Compositional Process in the Time of Dufay: Perspectives from German Musicology,* New York: Garland, 1997

Park, Eulmee, *De Preceptis artis musicae of Guilielmus Monachus: A New Edition, Translation, and Commentary,* Ph.D. dissertation: Ohio State University, 1993

Trowell, Brian, "Faburden—New Sources, New Evidence: A Preliminary Study," in *Modern Musical Scholarship,* edited by Edward Olleson, Stocksfield and Boston: Oriel Press, 1978

Trumble, Ernest, *Fauxbourdon: An Historical Survey,* Brooklyn, New York: Institute of Medieval Music, 1959

Fauxbourdon can be loosely defined as a composition for three voices, two of which are completely written out, the third of which is improvised according to a formula that places it in the middle voice moving at the interval of a fourth beneath the uppermost voice. English *faburden* and Italian *falsobordone* are related to *fauxbourdon,* although the specific nature of the relationship has been the source of much of the debate.

The earliest studies from the 1930s to the 1950s were primarily by German scholars and focused on the origins of *fauxbourdon.* These studies reveal three main contentions: the origin and meaning of the term *fauxbourdon/faburden;* whether the practice of *fauxbourdon* was Continental or English in origin; and whether *fauxbourdon* represents tonal thinking or whether it was contrapuntal in nature, being the result of voice-leading formulas instead of chord progressions.

MOLL has collected and translated many of the influential German articles of this period, including two that are representative of the debate among German musicologists at that time. He also provides an outstanding overview of these critics' basic goals and methodologies and places the *fauxbourdon* debate among the larger issue of the time regarding triadic harmony and counterpoint. The first of the two important articles is Heinrich Besseler's "Dufay—Creator of Fauxbourdon" (1948), which was expanded upon and included in his seminal *Bourdon und Fauxbourdon* (1950). Besseler's main idea is that Dufay created the practice of *fauxbourdon* by taking the English "sound" and placing it into the framework of Continental contrapuntal technique. Besseler also contends that the term *fauxbourdon* was meant to describe a voice that could not be a harmony-bearing line (as opposed to a "bourdon," which could be). His belief in the existence of the "bourdon," for which no proof can currently be shown, is one of the major weaknesses of his study.

The second article preserved in Moll's anthology is Rudolf von Ficker's "Toward a History of the Genesis of Fauxbourdon" (1951), written to refute Besseler's *Bourdon und Fauxbourdon* of the previous year. Von Ficker asserts that the English tradition of discant and its specific practice of *faburden* was the ancestor from which sprang the Continental *fauxbourdon.* In contrast to Besseler, von Ficker argues that the term *fauxbourdon* represents a Continental misunderstanding of the English term *faburden.* Finally, von Ficker's writing represents the view that *fauxbourdon* and *faburden* emerge from within the context of contrapuntal duets and not from triadic harmony and emerging tonality as Besseler proposes. Criticism of von Ficker challenges his contention that musical proof of his theory may be found in Burgundian manuscripts lost since their copying in Dufay's time.

In the wake of these earlier German writings, later studies began to concentrate on the specific genres discussed by the Germans. Such is the case with KENNEY, whose focus was the transmission of the English musical tradition to the Continent during the early decades of the 15th century. The most important contribution she makes to the topic of *fauxbourdon* is her thorough examination of the tradition of English discant, including the improvised practice of "sighting," of which *faburden* represents one variety. Kenney argues that the English *faburden* emerged from a purely improvised tradition as opposed to the written tradition of *fauxbourdon* and therefore cannot have been received from the French as Besseler would insist. It is her view that *fauxbourdon* was created as the result of an attempt on the part of French musicians to experiment with the rich sound of the English tradition.

Some of these same sentiments are expressed by TROWELL. The leading focus of this study is that of proving the English preeminence in the creation of *fauxbourdon* by demonstrating the early existence of the English term *burdon* to designate a lower voice, and by demonstrating that the parallelism of *faburden* and later *fauxbourdon* existed in English music of the 14th century.

Although much was written about *fauxbourdon* in the 1950s, it is curious that in practically all instances the studies dealt only with the origins of *fauxbourdon* and its relationship to *faburden*. Not until TRUMBLE did anyone explore the history, style, and evolution of *fauxbourdon* after its creation. His monograph represents the only complete investigation of *fauxbourdon*. It includes a full discussion of the sources containing *fauxbourdon* and theoretical literature relating to it, an elaboration of an evolutionary model for *fauxbourdon* consisting of three style periods, and an in-depth analysis of the structure and mechanics of *fauxbourdon*. The problem with this work occurs when the author insists on a very narrow definition of "authentic" *fauxbourdon* but must then alter or ignore his narrow definition in order to maintain his equally rigid insistence on an evolutionary path, which has four-part *falsobordone* emerging directly from *fauxbourdon*.

If Trumble's monograph represents the only complete source on *fauxbourdon*, BRADSHAW represents the same for *falsobordone*. Contrary to Trumble's assertion that *falsobordone* emerges directly from *fauxbourdon*, Bradshaw suggests that the practice of *falsobordone* is in no way related to *fauxbourdon* but rather is created as the result of the application of late 15th-century cadences to the medieval psalm tones. Like Trumble, he also provides a path of development, which shows that *falsobordone* begins in the late 15th century, matures into a "classical" style in the 16th century, and later evolves into other forms in the 17th and subsequent centuries.

Guilielmus Monachus's *De preceptis artis musicae* represents the only 15th-century treatise to discuss practically how *fauxbourdon* should be performed. Most of the modern studies investigating *fauxbourdon*, *faburden*, and *falsobordone* discussed here draw heavily on this treatise, yet, until recently, no complete English translation was available. PARK has provided a critical edition and translation of this enormously important text.

JOHN KARR

Fétis, François-Joseph 1784–1871

Belgian music historian, theorist, and critic

Barzun, Jacques, *Berlioz and the Romantic Century,* 2 vols., Boston: Little, Brown, 1950; 3rd edition, New York: Columbia University Press, 1969; revised and abridged as *Berlioz and His Century: An Introduction to the Age of Romanticism,* Chicago: University of Chicago Press, 1982

Berlioz, Hector, *The Memoirs of Hector Berlioz from 1803 to 1865, Comprising His Travels in Germany, Italy, Russia, and England,* translated by Rachel Holmes and Eleanor Holmes, annotated and the translation revised by Ernest Newman, New York: Knopf, 1932; reprint, New York: Dover, 1966

Bloom, Peter, "François-Joseph Fétis and the *Revue Musicale* (1827–1835)," Ph.D. dissertation: University of Pennsylvania, 1972

Fétis, Joseph-François, *Equisse de l'Histoire de l'Harmonie: An English-Language Translation of the François-Joseph Fétis History of Harmony,* translated and edited by Mary I. Arlin, Stuyvesant, New York: Pendragon Press, 1994

———, *Music Explained to the World; or, How to Understand Music and Enjoy its Performance,* translated for the Boston Academy of Music, Boston: Perkins, 1842; reprint, with an introduction by Peter Bloom, New York: Da Capo Press, 1987

To most music students and musicians alike, the name of François-Joseph Fétis is virtually unknown. However, he made numerous important contributions to the field of music as a theorist, historian, encyclopedist, librarian, composer, and teacher. Due no doubt in part to his conservatism, there has been little research dedicated to this brilliant academician whose discoveries and theories made him one of the most respected scholars of his day. Among his many achievements, Fétis developed the discipline of comparative musicology. Despite this, the most important information today on Fétis comes from his own writings, most of which are in French, and the introductory materials included in modern editions of these works. Bloom's landmark dissertation is the only English-language monograph dedicated entirely to Fétis, and it is a virtual treasure trove of information on his life and career.

While he is perhaps best known for his *Biographie Universelle* and theoretical writings, one of FÉTIS's most popular books was *La Musique mise à la portée de tout le monde* (1830). The 1987 reprint of the 1842 English translation contains a valuable introduction by Bloom. A discussion of the general subject matter of the monograph, as well as enlightening material pertaining to its reception, subsequent editions, and various translations, is included in this reprint. This first music appreciation text is not a study in the great man approach so popular during the 19th century and so often the method employed by music appreciation textbooks of today. Instead, Fétis discusses the elements of music, including melody, harmony, and rhythm, as well as compositional techniques, such as imitation, canon, and fugue. In the course of discussing genres, the author enters into brief historical explanations; however, he does not become bogged down in technical or detailed information. Fétis also does not avoid giving his opinion. Various remarks make it clear that he is fond of more traditional and conservative musical styles, and his preference for the music of Mozart, Haydn, and Rossini, as well as his respect for Beethoven, is evident. Although some of his explanations may be arguable, the majority are straightforward and quite useful. Particularly interesting is the section on the formation of judgments at the conclusion of the book.

Here Fétis points out to the reader that it is necessary to listen deeply to music and pay attention to the details of melody, rhythm, and harmony. He indicates that being able to appreciate and understand how a musical work is composed takes a great deal of practice by means of repeated listening. But Fétis assures the reader that continual aural exercise will bear fruit. Whether his subject matter is the elements of music, musical instruments, instrumentation, or acoustics, Fétis's writing style is well organized and lucid, a testament to the popularity of this monograph, not only in the 19th century but into the 20th century as well.

FÉTIS (1994) is another important primary source, originally published in 1840, that has been translated into English. Mary Arlin includes an extremely welcome and concise biographical account of the author, in addition to an insightful explanation of his theoretical concepts, in the preface to her translation of Fétis's treatise. She chronicles the important contributions that Fétis made to music history and theory and identifies the crucial elements that influenced him, from his ability to memorize symphonies of Haydn and Mozart and then play them at the piano to his self-imposed, thorough study of German counterpoint. More personal biographic information is included, such as a detailed account of the occurrences that created his rift with Berlioz and a brief mention of the *Affaire Fétis* that caused his removal as the librarian of the Paris Conservatoire. Arlin identifies Fétis as arguably the inventor of the modern use of the term *harmony* and explains in her discussion of his basic harmonic concepts that, for Fétis, the scale was the "primary factor in the determination of tonality." She compares his approach to that of Schoenberg, who basically agrees with Fétis, and of Hindemith, who does not. This treatise of Fétis is "a chronicle of the theoretical tenets of harmony from Franco of Cologne to 1840" and consequently is not geared to the musical amateur. Its technical language and discussions of various theories and authors presumes more than a passing knowledge of music. Although the main body of the treatise is directed to the professional, the extremely important introductory material is accessible to anyone who is curious on the subject.

One of the many hats worn by Fétis was that of critic and founder of the journal the *Revue Musicale*. The study nonpareil on this aspect of his career is BLOOM. This extremely important contribution to Fétis studies is valuable not only for the light it sheds on Fétis the man and musician but also on the groundbreaking information Bloom offers regarding the founding of the *Revue Musicale* (which was written almost single-handedly by Fétis himself). Among the most fascinating portions of this monograph are Fétis's appreciation of Beethoven and his critiques of contemporaries, such as Berlioz, Meyerbeer, Rossini, and Liszt. In addition to the painstaking research, perhaps Bloom's greatest contribution is the chapter entitled "Fétis' Historical and Philosophical Notions about Music as Developed in the *Revue Musicale*." Here Bloom discusses Fétis's concept of the transformation versus the progress of music from epoch to epoch. Bloom indicates that Fétis did subscribe to the idea of the progress of music "of a sort," but more uniquely, he was an advocate of musical eclecticism, that is, an "amalgamation of the best aspects of music of the past." To support this assertion, Bloom quotes a lengthy passage of Fétis from the *Revue Musicale*. Fétis also wrote in the journal that he believed "the history of the arts is so closely allied with the history of people." This unique position made Fétis the first to relate musicology to anthropology, and consequently he became the founder of what is now known as comparative musicology. Bloom's landmark monograph is a must for any scholar or student intrigued by this Renaissance man of the 19th century or for anyone interested in 19th-century music history and the periodic press. A detailed and exacting study, this dissertation is not for the casual reader.

A primary source of limited but nevertheless valuable information on Fétis is BERLIOZ. Despite the rift in their relationship around 1832, Fétis was originally supportive of Berlioz, whose contempt for Fétis's alleged corrections of Beethoven's symphonies caused the hot-tempered composer to publicly humiliate the revered scholar. The account of this incident, as well as others, indicates the contempt in which Berlioz held Fétis, a man whom he regarded as a hopelessly conservative pedant. The irony is that Berlioz's indignation may have been provoked by nothing more than a misunderstanding. According to Bloom (in his dissertation noted above), Fétis made changes to the music believing that he was remedying mistakes made by another printer and that he was not attempting to correct Beethoven at all.

BARZUN is an important secondary source that chronicles the Berlioz-Fétis relationship. While many of the details from other sources are confirmed by Barzun, he also offers an account of the reconciliation between the two men who, although they differed greatly in their philosophies, still admired one another. Both the Berlioz and Barzun books are fascinating and can be enjoyed by a diverse readership. The *Memoirs* of Berlioz give the reader a vivid insight into the composer's personality and career, whereas Barzun's chronicle does the same with the added benefit of placing events and people in the context of the era.

The contributions Fétis made to the art of music cannot be overestimated. In addition to his monumental work as a music journalist, theorist, and historian, his efforts as a lexicographer must not be overlooked. The *Biographie Universelle* was his crowning achievement, and although this voluminous work does not appear in an English translation, its historical importance necessitates its inclusion here. This monumental work stands alongside *Die Musik in Geschichte und Gegenwart* and the *Grove Dictionary of Music and Musicians* while pre-dating them both. Unfortunately, it contains inaccuracies and mistakes, and the user must beware; however, it remains an extremely valuable resource for music scholar, serious student, and devotee.

TIMOTHY S. FLYNN

Film Music

Adorno, Theodor W., and Hanns Eisler, *Composing for the Films,* New York: Oxford University Press, 1947; London: Athlone Press, 1994

Bruce, Graham, *Bernard Herrmann: Film Music and Narrative,* Ann Arbor, Michigan: UMI Research Press, 1985

Flinn, Caryl, *Strains of Utopia: Gender, Nostalgia, and Hollywood Film Music,* Princeton, New Jersey: Princeton University Press, 1992

Gorbman, Claudia, *Unheard Melodies: Narrative Film Music,* Bloomington: Indiana University Press, and London: BFI, 1987

Kalinak, Kathryn Marie, *Settling the Score: Music and the Classical Hollywood Film,* Madison: University of Wisconsin Press, 1992

Marks, Martin Miller, *Music and the Silent Film: Contexts and Case Studies, 1895–1924,* New York: Oxford University Press, 1997

Palmer, Christopher, *Dimitri Tiomkin: A Portrait,* London: T.E. Books, 1984

Prendergast, Roy, *A Neglected Art: A Critical Study of Music in Films,* New York: New York University Press, 1977; as *Film Music: A Neglected Art: A Critical Study of Music in Films,* New York: Norton, 1977; 2nd Edition, 1992

Film music is divided into two types, diegetic and nondiegetic, which are sometimes distinguished as source and background music, or as realistic and functional music, respectively. The term *diegesis* denotes the fictional space and time implied by the narrative of a film. If the music is an integral part of the filmic narrative—for example, a song performed by a character—it is diegetic. The music is nondiegetic when it simply accompanies the image track outside the diegesis of a film. Accordingly, nondiegetic music is heard by spectators but not by on-screen characters.

The history of film music dates back to the era of silent film. Strictly speaking, motion pictures have never been really silent, as a presentation of a silent film was usually accompanied by either recorded or, more commonly, live music performed by a pianist or an orchestra. In the silent era, music was employed to mask the noise from the projector and to compensate for the lack of speech and sound effects. In sound film, too, music has been an essential component of film, supporting

visuals in various ways. Among the common functions of film music are embellishment and enhancement of emotions; indication of geographical and temporal setting of a film through music's well-established conventions associated with particular times and locations; creation of a sense of continuity and unity that the cinematic apparatus fundamentally lacks; and, like Wagnerian leitmotifs, signification of dramatic ideas, situations, characters, or places. However, despite its invaluable functions, film music has held a marginalized position within the discipline of film studies.

ADORNO and EISLER's book, which was first published under Eisler's name alone, is one of the earliest serious studies of film music. This study provides an ideological critique of Hollywood film music, especially its practice of synchronization, which attempts to establish a strong bond between music and image. Adorno and Eisler's virulent attack on the synchronization of music to visuals is deeply rooted in their Marxist critique of the culture industry. They argue that synchronous film music attempts to bind spectators to the fictive reality by creating a fictive unity between music and image at the expense of the autonomy of music. For Adorno and Eisler, this manipulative intent is a prime example of the culture industry's objectification of subjectivity. As opposed to synchronization, they strongly advocate the practice of counterpoint, in which music would unsettle visual meanings and in so doing prevent the spectator's hypnotic identification with the filmic fiction. Adorno and Eisler's book has initiated the critical discourse of film music. Yet this study remains a rather idiosyncratic and isolated work in the literature on film music, as it is much too laden with ideology.

PRENDERGAST's second edition consists of four parts. The first three parts, which are reprinted from the original edition without change except for the last 30 pages, deal with what the author conceives as the three major areas of film studies: history, aesthetics, and technique. The fourth part is an extension of part 3 and focuses on contemporary techniques, such as the use of digital and electronic instruments. Prendergast's original edition is known as one of the first comprehensive and critical studies of film music intended for the general reader. If the originality of Prendergast's work is marred by overdependence on earlier studies, it has the merit of integrating into a monograph previously fragmented discussions of the major aspects of film music.

PALMER's study, one of the finest biographical studies of a film composer, is divided into three parts. Part 1 is an entertaining biographical essay about Dimitri Tiomkin's life and his musical training. Part 2 discusses general characteristics of the composer's music, especially his Russian heritage, and compares them with the dominant styles of Hollywood film music at that time. Part 3 is devoted to the examination of what Palmer considers to be landmarks of Tiomkin's film scores, including *Lost Horizon,* the first full-score work by which Tiomkin was first recognized as a capable film composer; *The Alamo; High Noon;* and the Hitchcock trilogy, *Strangers on a Train, I Confess,* and *Dial M for Murder.* Palmer does use some technical terms in his musical description, but they are not too overwhelming for the general reader.

BRUCE's work is an outstanding study of Bernard Herrmann, one of the most accomplished composers in the genre of film music, who wrote the scores for many films, including Orson Welles's *Citizen Kane;* eight Hitchcock films, including *Psycho* and *Vertigo;* and, most recently, Martin Scorcese's *Taxi Driver.* Bruce's study is the first monograph that critically and extensively analyzes the works of a single film composer. Whereas previous studies on Herrmann and many other film composers combine biographical information with brief comments on their film scores, Bruce's work provides in-depth examination of Herrmann's film scores, emphasizing the ways in which music articulates the formal structure of a film and the ways in which musical parameters, such as orchestral color, harmony, and rhythm, are employed to represent particular narrative situations in film. Although Bruce's study focuses on a single composer, it is an exemplary work in the general study of the narrative and structural interplay between music and image in film. Replete with technical terms, Bruce's work is intended for the musically literate.

GORBMAN's book established the standard for technical discourse about film music and stimulated later theoretical studies in the field. In part 1, she explores the rationale for the existence of music in film from diverse theoretical perspectives. She finally settles on the two overarching roles of background music, which she characterizes as psychological sutur" and semiotic *anchrage,* based on Roland Barthes's notion of anchoring unstable meanings of visual signs. In part 2, Gorbman closely analyzes three films—*Zéro de conduite* (1933), *Sous les toits de Paris* (1930), and *Hangover Square* (1944)—and shows various kinds of the interplay between music and visuals in the construction of the narratives of these films.

FLINN's book is the most rigorous theoretical study of film music since Gorbman's work. Flinn examines, from the theoretical perspectives of semiotics, psychoanalysis, and Marxism, the utopian and nostalgic functions of film music that uphold a utopian conception of music as being related to an idealized lost past. She also raises important issues concerning the connection between music and femininity while exploring music's association with the lost maternal object, that is, with the sounds experienced by an infant during the prelinguistic, pre-oedipal stage of development (the stage that Julia Kristeva calls chora). Following her theoretical chapters, Flinn provides case studies of two films—the film noir classic *Detour* (1945) and the maternal melodrama *Penny Serenade* (1941)—and shows ways

in which music projects specific kinds of utopian visions. Many reviewers agree that the weakest point of Flinn's book is her analysis of music. Overall, her analytical chapters are outweighed by her theoretical explorations, which might be a bit too overwhelming for those who are not well acquainted with contemporary critical theory.

Unlike Flinn's work, KALINAK's study balances theory and analysis. It focuses on Hollywood film music during the so-called classical era of the 1930s and 1940s. In one of her theoretical chapters of part 1, Kalinak examines Western culture's cognitive tradition that privileges the visual over the aural and relates this tradition to the prevalent practice of film music, which demands the subordination of music to visuals. In part 2, Kalinak provides detailed analyses of four film scores as case studies to illustrate her theoretical exploration. On the basis of her comparative analyses of three scores from the Hollywood classical era and John Williams's more recent score from the 1980s, Kalinak argues that the classical model remains a dominant influence on Hollywood's film scoring today. Her analyses also reveal that although the 19th-century romantic style was the dominant musical language for the Hollywood classical score, idioms of popular music, especially jazz, were used to depict indecent female sexuality. Kalinak's book will be of particular use for those who are not conversant with technical musical terms, for she provides definitions of those terms in chapter 1.

MARKS's book is the first extensive study devoted entirely to the film music of the silent era. After the introductory chapter, which provides a pithy review of the literature on film music, Marks analyzes five scores chronologically, identifying the ways in which each score was created to solve the problems unique to a particular silent film. On the basis of his analyses, Marks argues that despite the differences in style, the two principal methods of film scoring during the silent era—compilation and original composition—were based largely on 19th-century musical traditions.

JEONGWON JOE

Finland *see* Scandinavia

Flamenco

Mitchell, Timothy, *Flamenco Deep Song,* New Haven, Connecticut: Yale University Press, 1994

Pohren, D.E., *The Art of Flamenco,* Jerez de la Frontera, Spain: Jerez Industrial, 1967; revised edition, Shaftesbury, England: Musical New Services, 1984

——, *Lives and Legends of Flamenco: A Biographical History,* Madrid: Society of Spanish Studies, 1988

Schreiner, Claus, editor, *Flamenco: Gypsy Dance and Music from Andalusia*, translated by Mollie Comerford Peters, Portland, Oregon: Amadeus Press, 1990

Washabaugh, William, *Flamenco: Passion, Politics, and Popular Culture*, Oxford: Berg, 1996

The precise origins of the word *flamenco* are unknown, but it is a term that refers to the folk music, poetry, and dance of southern Spain. Flamenco has exerted a powerful influence on the romantic imagination of Western Europe for the last 200 years and has achieved popularity around the world. Yet its rich history and complexity are often obscured by a haze of stereotypes. Only in recent times has a body of serious literature in English become available on this fascinating topic. The essence of flamenco is found in individual expression, principally through singing. Dancing and guitar playing achieved their present prominence only in the 19th century, when flamenco left the cradle of private performance and became public and commercial. Although the art is not the exclusive preserve of Gypsies, they have played a central role in its development. Other tributaries of influence have come from the Moors, Jews, central and northern Spain, and Latin America. There are many types of flamenco song and dance, grouped according to their rhythmic and melodic characteristics, as well as by their texts and regional associations. Some flamenco genres are light and carefree; others express a tragic fatalism. The most serious of flamenco songs belong to the *jondo* category, so named for its profound feeling. The greatest flamenco performers tap into a well of emotion known as *duende*, the rough equivalent of "soul" in the blues. *Duende*-rich *jondo* flamenco is out of fashion now, however, as the art has been transformed since the 1980s by the admixture of elements from rock and jazz. This "fusion" flamenco is popular among younger practitioners of the art and has been promoted by Paco de Lucia, the Gypsy Kings, and others. The more traditional style is fast disappearing as the older artists retire or die, and this decline has likely increased the sense of urgency in studying and recording this unique art form: both to preserve it for future generations and to improve our understanding of one of the great folk traditions of the world.

MITCHELL is among a new generation of scholars seeking to go beyond mere data gathering and description to analyze flamenco from an interdisciplinary, multicultural, postmodernist standpoint. He examines the ways in which class structure and ethnic relationships are reflected in the art and the roles that socioeconomic factors have played in the genre's history and journey from private to public performance spheres. He focuses on the *jondo* tradition of flamenco singing because it forms a revealing intersection of text and music and is the most powerfully expressive type of flamenco performance. This is perhaps a book to peruse after acquiring a fundamental understanding of the art through a more traditional approach, such as the one taken by Pohren.

Pohren is the leading authority in English on flamenco. He has acquired his knowledge through several decades of living in Spain and performing as a flamenco guitarist. His wife is a renowned flamenco dancer. He is a traditionalist, and some find his point of view out-of-date or snobbish. But there is no doubting his command of the subject, and his enthusiasm is infectious. POHREN (1984) is a landmark book that lays out the various aspects of flamenco performance (dancing, singing, guitar playing, and audience participation) in admirable detail. The introductory essay on the origins and true nature of flamenco, and on the Gypsies themselves, is revelatory. The second half of the book treats the various songs and dances in alphabetical order, with sample lyrics. The book includes many fascinating photographs and concludes with useful appendices, including one dealing with the flamenco guitar and its makers.

POHREN (1988) is the sequel to his earlier work and offers biographies of celebrated artists, past and present. Singers, dancers, and guitarists are all represented. The photographs of these performers often tell more than any biography, of any length, possibly could. This is a one-of-a-kind resource, indispensable to anyone interested in Spanish folklore.

SCHREINER, a German scholar who has distinguished himself in the area of Spanish and Brazilian music, has edited this volume of essays by a wide variety of specialists. His introduction furnishes the necessary background on Andalusia, the homeland of flamenco, and the Gypsies, who have played a leading role in flamenco's genesis. His explanation of the art form itself is highly accessible to the nonspecialist. Marion Papenbrok takes us through the sometimes uncertain terrain of flamenco's history, from its earliest phases to the modern era. The succeeding four chapters, by Christof Jung, Madeleine Claus, Bernhard-Friedrich Schulze, and Ehrenhard Skiera, treat the main subdivisions of flamenco performance: song (*cante*), dance (*baile*), guitar (*guitarra*), and group participation (*jaleo*). Several useful appendices guide the reader to other sources of information regarding performance venues, festivals, research centers, recordings, and guitar makers.

WASHABAUGH, like Mitchell, adopts a critical approach to the study of flamenco, utilizing the latest postmodern methodologies. He focuses, however, not on *jondo* singing but on the politics of flamenco, its role in popular culture, and especially on issues of gender and sexuality. Despite the similarity of approach, he takes exception to many of Mitchell's views; however, the two books point the way for future flamenco research and interpretation. The general reader will find the contentious disputation on ideological grounds bewildering and tiresome without a solid grounding in the history and basic components of the art form.

WALTER AARON CLARK

Folk Music

Bohlman, Philip V., *The Study of Folk Music in the Modern World,* Bloomington: Indiana University Press, 1988

Cantwell, Robert, *When We Were Good: The Folk Revival,* Cambridge, Massachusetts: Harvard University Press, 1996

Coffin, Tristram Potter, *The British Traditional Ballad in North America,* Philadelphia, Pennsylvania: American Folklore Society, 1950; revised edition, 1963

Cohen, Ronald D., editor, *"Wasn't That a Time!": Firsthand Accounts of the Folk Music Revival,* Metuchen, New Jersey: Scarecrow Press, 1995

Goldsmith, Peter David, *Making People's Music: Moe Asch and Folkways Records,* Washington, D.C.: Smithsonian Institution Press, 1998

Lornell, Kip, *Introducing American Folk Music,* Madison, Wisconsin: Brown and Benchmark, 1992

Nettl, Bruno, *Folk and Traditional Music of the Western Continents,* Englewood Cliffs, New Jersey: Prentice Hall, 1965; 3rd edition, 1990

Folk music is many things to many peoples. As a term, folk music has passed through various historical interpretations in a myriad of historical and cultural contexts. One culture's folk music might be another's traditional or even popular music. To present a cohesive musical tradition, the texts presented in this entry are, therefore, selected to cover the presence and influence of folk music traditions in only a particular geographic area: North America. In addition, several texts covered here present materials more specifically related to the folk music revival of the 1960s in the United States. Folk music in North America has had multiple functions and purposes in the past several hundred years. Among these functions have been the conservative preservation and portrayal of a culture and its past, the teaching of political ideology and revival of presumed folk traditions, an ongoing exchange between traditional and folk music, the translation and transportation of cultures, and the general education of folk music study. That there is no single definition of folk music embraced by the authors of the following texts will quickly be apparent. Typical definitions might once have restricted understanding to rural music culture, but this is no longer the case, as examples of the folk music revival challenge established notions. Thus, if there is such a thing as a canon in folk music scholarship, it surely embraces change and adaptation, transformation and stability.

BOHLMAN is a good starting point for any reader interested in the various historical and contemporary meanings and contexts of folk music, both Western and non-Western. In his opening chapters, Bohlman traces the origins of folk music traditions and also outlines the dialectical relationship between authenticity and change that has been omnipresent in folk music research. Subsequent chapters detail oral transmission of folk music traditions as well as the classificatory systems historically used to study, interpret, and understand folk music. Bohlman's finest contribution is his section on the folk musician. By contextualizing individual creativity within folk traditions, Bohlman attempts to break down the barriers surrounding the timeless quality of folk music. Bohlman points out that folk musicians have typically been portrayed as everymen and thus as representative of a collective unit, rather than as individual tradition-bearers. He suggests instead a focus on the performance of folk music in order to identify the role of the individual in folk music's change and stability. The final chapter, "Folk Music in the Modern World," is a significant reflection on folk music's response to modernization and urbanization.

CANTWELL focuses primarily on the cultural roots within which the North American folk music revival of the late 1950s and 1960s flourished, a short-lived response culminating in the Newport Folk Festival of 1965. For Cantwell the very idea of a folk culture is not a thing unto itself (nor are folksong, folklore, or folklife). Rather, folk is a perspective informed by the interdependence of various cultural relationships: race, class, and position within social strata. Cantwell outlines the way in which the folk revival was in many ways an attempt to locate an authentic folk-rooted voice for North America and for North American culture.

COFFIN functions as a guide to the study of ballad and story variation in traditional child ballads in North America. The volume includes two essays on ballad variation and the development of traditional ballads as a specific art form. Also included are a bibliography of studies pertaining to story variation and an annotated bibliographic guide to specific variations in traditional North American ballads.

COHEN is a collection of individually authored essays that focus on providing personalized overviews of the folk music revival, the various folk magazines that emerged from this scene, stories of performances, and the New York folk music scene. Particularly useful are the overviews provided by Joe Hickerson, John Cohen, and Neil Rosenberg. Hickerson provides suggestions for relevant topics that should be addressed when dealing with the folk music revival. Cohen, an original member of the New Lost City Ramblers, situates the role of traditional culture within the folk music revival in an attempt to understand the interdependence of the back-porch and commercial traditions. Rosenberg reflects on the more academic side of the folk music revival by drawing on his experience with the Indiana University Folk Song Club and the study of folklore at the university.

GOLDSMITH approaches the cultural milieu of the folk music revival by focusing on the life and influence of Moe Asch and more specifically on his creation of the institution of Folkways Records. Goldsmith argues convincingly for an understanding of the role of commercial recordings in the social processes involved with North America's cultural identification with the very idea of the folk.

LORNELL provides an excellent overview of the history and traditions of folk music in North America, focusing particularly on the roles and involvement of African-American contributions, including gospel and the blues. In addition to covering secular and sacred aspects of folk music, Lornell also demonstrates clearly the relationships that exist between contemporary popular music and their distinct folk roots. A final chapter, "Fieldwork in Postmodern America," is especially helpful.

While NETTL devotes individual chapters to the folk musics of Europe, sub-Saharan Africa, and Latin America, there are significant sections on African-American folk traditions in North America and ethnic folk music in contemporary North America. In addition, there are extremely useful introductory chapters on folk music and the study of folk music, including a discussion of transcription, analysis, research, and style. Nettl concludes by suggesting that all forms of folk music are constantly in a state of flux; that is, they respond to change by adapting, developing, and growing.

GREGORY F. BARZ

Form: General

Berry, Wallace, *Form in Music: An Examination of Traditional Techniques of Musical Form and Their Applications in Historical and Contemporary Styles,* Englewood Cliffs, New Jersey: Prentice Hall, 1966; 2nd edition, 1986

Cogan, Robert, and Pozzi Escot, *Sonic Design: The Nature of Sound and Music,* Englewood Cliffs, New Jersey: Prentice Hall, 1976

Cone, Edward T., *Musical Form and Musical Performance,* New York: Norton, 1968

Green, Douglass M., *Form in Tonal Music: An Introduction to Analysis,* New York: Holt, Rinehart, and Winston, 1965; 2nd edition, 1979

Kamien, Roger, *Music: An Appreciation,* New York: McGraw-Hill, 1976; 6th edition, 1996

LaRue, Jan, *Guidelines for Style Analysis,* New York: Norton, 1970; 2nd edition, Warren, Michigan: Harmonie Park Press, 1992

Leichtentritt, Hugo, *Musical Form,* Cambridge, Massachusetts: Harvard University Press, 1951

Stein, Leon, *Structure and Style: The Study and Analysis of Musical Forms,* Evanston, Illinois: Summy-Birchard, 1962; revised edition, Princeton, New Jersey: Summy-Birchard Music, 1979

Tovey, Donald Francis, *The Forms of Music: Musical Articles from the Encyclopedia Britannica,* London: Oxford University Press, 1944

There are three broad types of studies about form: philosophical, practical or formulaic, and revisionist approaches. In addition, there are four chronological categories of formal types: *formes fixes* and other strict forms of the Middle Ages and Renaissance; major-minor tonal instrumental music; major-minor tonal vocal music; and post-tonal forms dating mostly from post-1945. Finally, there are two major divisions of form: form at the level of the single movement (micro-form) such as the rondo or da capo aria; and larger multiple movement works (macro-forms), such as the symphony or Mass ordinary setting. Most of the bibliographical selections here take the practical/formulaic approach to music and emphasize single movements for instruments cast in major-minor tonality.

Although the philosophy of formal construction is not considered in this article, the reader may find the following selections helpful. The most accessible introduction to the philosophical aspects of form may be found in Arnold Whittall's article on "Form" in *The New Grove Dictionary of Music and Musicians* (London, 1980). Books about this aspect of form include Susan Lager's *Feeling and Form* (New York, 1953) and the entry on "Matter and Form" in Siegmund Levarie and Ernst Levy's *Musical Morphology: A Discourse and a Dictionary* (Kent, Ohio, 1983).

The practical or formulaic approach to form offers a series of "textbook" models. There are relatively few pure textbook models; however, it is possible to see how great composers such as Beethoven varied these models or shaped them in different ways to have the formal designs appear fresh and original.

The revisionists contend that the formulaic approach to form does not allow sufficient freedom for the varieties of structural designs found in well-known constructions, such as sonata form. Instead, they advocate a more subtle, less strict metamorphological process of composition, in which, to quote Louis Sullivan, "form follows function."

The concept of form as a branch of music theory seems to have originated in the late 19th century, in a series of books having the word *Formenlehre* in the title. One of the most influential of writers about musical form was the important German theorist Hugo Riemann. From 1900 to the 1960s, books and collegiate courses about form were fairly common. However, research in this area seems to have gone out of fashion in the last few decades; beginning in the 1970s, the books and courses on the subject appear to have diminished. Discussions of form in music prior to 1600 tend to be in the province of music history and can be found in books devoted to historical period studies; musical form in the 20th century is discussed also in period studies.

KAMIEN's volume is a widely used textbook in the area of music appreciation. It is a well-organized and well-written book for the beginner. Although the coverage is broad and includes various aspects of music, it tends to concentrate on the practical forms in major-minor tonal music (ca. 1600–ca. 1900). Kamien gives written and graphic illustrations of both standard vocal and instrumental forms and, most helpfully, provides well-ordered verbal listening outlines. There is also a brief section introducing form as a musical element. The author uses examples from the standard repertoire of classical music; there is a set of recordings that accompany the musical listening outlines.

STEIN provides the most comprehensive practical guide to musical forms. He begins with small units of form, including the phrase and the period. There are chapters on song form and single-movement instrumental forms such as rondo and variation. Contrapuntal forms or procedures are also addressed, including the canon, fugue, and chaconne. He then discusses macro or multi-movement works, including the sonata, concertos of various types, and the suite. Both smaller and larger sacred vocal types are considered in a loosely chronological order; these include sections on chant, the Mass, the motet, and other sacred vocal idioms. The section on secular vocal music begins with a brief discussion of opera and proceeds to smaller forms and styles of singing such as recitative, *Sprechstimme,* aria, arioso, and the ballad. Unlike many authors, Stein addresses the standard forms of music prior to 1600, including the rondeau, *lai,* virelai, ballade, *caccia, frottola,* and madrigal. Twentieth-century music is covered in two chapters. The first explores music up to 1950. Here, the author emphasizes styles and techniques of earlier 20th century music and only implies their formal properties. The chapter on music since 1950 is similar to its predecessor; however, the author devotes several pages to the creation and employment of form in later 20th-century works.

GREEN is a well-known and widely used volume about form in tonal music. Its main strengths are the well-chosen musical examples and the clear and orderly manner with which he explores this subject. The majority of the volume is devoted to single-movement instrumental forms. The volume also examines phrase structure and analytical method.

BERRY's work follows the standard approach to practical form largely drawn from tonal instrumental music. He begins by discussing the motive, phrase, and period, moves on to the simple forms (binary and ternary), and then devotes most of the remainder of the volume to single-movement instrumental forms, although he does include macro-forms of the sonata and concerto. The chapter concerning contrapuntal genres is particularly strong. The final chapter, "Form and Structure in Music," is an intriguing summary about the formal process that provides useful and thought provoking ideas.

TOVEY is a compilation of articles written for the 11th edition of the *Encyclopedia Britannica* (1906) and revised for the 14th edition (1929). Tovey was a great

figure in the study of music history, and this collection of 28 articles arranged alphabetically is a classic in the field. Both single-movement vocal and instrumental forms are discussed, as well as some of the macro-forms such as opera, oratorio, and symphonic poem. A few articles are only tangentially related to form, such as those on harmony, melody, and music. The articles are informative and written for a general readership; however, they are sufficiently substantial to warrant the attention of professional musicians.

LEICHTENTRITT states in his introduction that he views form using aesthetic principles as a basis. With this approach in mind, it may be valuable to read chapters 10 and 11 first, which deal with "Aesthetic Ideas as the Basis of Musical Styles and Form" and "Logic and Coherence in Music." Part 1 of the volume examines the standard formal designs, including vocal forms. Part 2, which begins with chapter 10, examines a wide range of topics, from the formal and stylistic significance of accompaniment to unusual types of monophonic music. The remainder of the second part re-examines selected forms discussed in part 1, using specific examples. A wide range of works are investigated, including Bruckner's Symphony no. 8 and Schoenberg's piano works opp. 11 and 19.

CONE's short volume consists of revised and expanded versions of lectures given at the Oberlin College Conservatory in January of 1967, and an added fourth essay. In these essays Cone straddles the lines dividing philosophical, practical, performing, and intellectual ideas about form. The essays are original and thought provoking. This is one of the earlier writings to begin moving toward revisionist ideas about the role of form.

Although LaRUE's book concerns style analysis, two major sections of the volume are devoted to form and formal procedures. Chapter 6 offers a series of revisionist concepts about the morphology, typology, and various dimensions of musical growth (or evolution). Chapter 7 is a practical approach to form. LaRue's volume, therefore, presents a mixture of revisionist thought and more traditional views of single-movement instrumental forms. The author has created his own series of symbols to aid in the analysis of standard formal designs, which some readers will find logical and clearly descriptive, while others may find cumbersome. This book is quite technical.

COGAN and ESCOT have devoted only a small section of their book to form, near the end of the volume in the section titled "Postlude." Their view of form is unequivocally revisionist. They discuss revisionist ideas of form and a differentiation of the term *structure.* Additionally, they provide a critical examination of the practical concepts of form. Although brief, this is a concise and useful summary of revisionist ideas about this issue.

JEFFREY WASSON

Form: Sonata Form

Berry, Wallace, *Form in Music: An Examination of Traditional Techniques of Musical Form and Their Applications in Historical and Contemporary Styles,* Englewood Cliffs, New Jersey: Prentice Hall, 1966; 2nd edition, 1986

Caplin, William Earl, *Classical Form: A Theory of Formal Functions for the Instrumental Music of Haydn, Mozart, and Beethoven,* New York: Oxford University Press, 1998

Green, Douglass M., *Form in Tonal Music: An Introduction to Analysis,* New York: Holt, Rinehart, and Winston, 1965; 2nd edition, 1979

Kohs, Ellis B., *Musical Form: Studies in Analysis and Synthesis,* Boston: Houghton Mifflin, 1976

Leichtentritt, Hugo, *Musical Form,* Cambridge, Massachusetts: Harvard University Press, 1951

Ratner, Leonard, *Classic Music: Expression, Form, Style,* New York: Schirmer Books, 1980

Rosen, Charles, *Sonata Forms,* New York: Norton, 1980; revised edition, 1988

Spink, Ian, *An Historical Approach to Musical Form,* London: Bell, 1967

Straus, Joseph N., *Remaking the Past: Musical Modernism and the Influence of the Tonal Tradition,* Cambridge, Massachusetts: Harvard University Press, 1990

Tovey, Donald Francis, *The Forms of Music: Musical Articles from the Encyclopedia Britannica,* London: Oxford University Press, 1944

There are several approaches to the study of sonata form. Most commonly, a chapter devoted to the topic appears within books covering musical form more generally. Some specialized studies address particular form-related issues during a specific time period. Others consider the historical perspective, discussing sonata form within the context of changing styles and artistic priorities. A.B. Marx, a 19th-century theorist, is credited with naming the sonata form and codifying its structure according to sections now referred to as exposition, development, and recapitulation. Theorists since Marx have offered two different fundamental approaches to sonata form: Some, such as Tovey, emphasize the tonal nature of its structure, describing a binary pattern characterized by departure from and return to a tonic key; others, such as Leichtentritt, focus on the thematic content of the form, thereby identifying a three-part structure that presents, develops, and restates those themes. In several journal articles dating from the mid-20th century, Ratner examines theoretical discussions of musical form predating those of Marx, which reveal that 18th-century theorists were preoccupied with an underlying tonal framework, a concern that accurately reflects 18th-century musical practice. Research since the mid-20th century tends to acknowledge both tonal binary and thematic ternary approaches to sonata form, with the historical context of

the discussion and the purpose of the study helping to determine the author's specific orientation.

BERRY discusses the most important categories of musical forms. In the chapter addressing sonata form, he describes the exposition, development, recapitulation, coda, and optional slow introduction, explaining the structural function served by each of these sections. Drawing illustrations from the 18th through the 20th centuries, Berry strikes a careful balance between identifying structural norms and observing the endless possibilities for creative individuality exhibited among various pieces.

CAPLIN bases his theory of musical form on the underlying premise that structural units within a composition serve a specific purpose in articulating the form. Focusing primarily on the instrumental music of Haydn, Mozart, and Beethoven ca. 1780 to 1810, the author's presentation of concepts arranged in order of increasing complexity culminates in his explanation of the functional roles served by exposition, development, recapitulation, and coda sections within a musical structure. Caplin applies his principles to several formal types, including sonata form. He acknowledges both the binary and ternary aspects of sonata form, explaining that his focus on formal function tends to emphasize its ternary nature.

GREEN's two chapters on sonata form begin with a historical overview of the term *sonata* and its uses to designate a genre, a multimovement cycle, and the form of an individual movement. He argues that the nature of sonata form is rooted in tonality, noting that the recapitulation completes a harmonic motion begun in the exposition and sustained through the development. He identifies the structural function served by each section of the form and describes techniques used by composers to achieve the desired result. Musical examples represent the 18th through the 20th centuries.

KOHS's chapter on sonata form explains the nature and general characteristics of the exposition, development, and recapitulation, as well as an optional slow introduction and coda. He considers the structure of sonata form to be ternary in nature, although he acknowledges the binary view held by other theorists. His detailed exploration of the form through analysis of six pieces covers a variety of genres by composers from the 18th through the 20th centuries.

LEICHTENTRITT contends that the motive provides the indispensable foundation of structure and form, and this assumption leads him to approach sonata form in terms of thematic content, characterizing the function of each section in relation to its treatment of themes. Drawing most of his examples from Beethoven and later composers, he discusses issues of cyclicism, thematic transformation, and leitmotif. Structural analyses focus on motivic unity and thematic continuity in sonata-form works from the 19th and early 20th centuries.

RATNER defines the compositional principles underlying music during the age of Haydn, Mozart, and Beethoven (approximately 1770 to 1800) by considering four broad topics: expression, rhetoric, form, and style. In the chapter devoted to sonata form, he evaluates both the thematic and harmonic approaches to that formal procedure. Because the harmonic approach prevails among theorists and composers during the era under consideration, Ratner discusses sonata form from this perspective, explaining the exposition, development, recapitulation, and coda in terms of their harmonic treatment and giving secondary consideration to the thematic content.

ROSEN presents sonata form as a compositional technique that integrates tonality, texture, themes, and cadential articulation into a structural process that pervades many genres, including symphony, chamber music, and solo sonatas. He stresses the functional role served by various musical elements in the articulation of the formal process and elaborates on the structural purpose of the exposition, development, recapitulation, and coda. In his historical treatment of the subject, Rosen traces sonata form from the early 18th century through the age of Haydn and Mozart, documenting its rise in prestige at the hands of Beethoven; he then demonstrates the form's transformation in Schubert's works. Rosen also examines the impact of Marx's theoretical codification of the form as well as an aesthetic shift toward greater emphasis on thematic content in the 19th century, before commenting briefly on the adaptation of sonata principles to compositional procedures of the 19th and 20th centuries.

SPINK chronicles the gradual growth, change, and development of musical forms from the early Christian era to the middle of the 20th century. For each time period, he presents the more prevalent genres in terms of their predominant unifying structural principles and the resulting forms that embody those principles, and his discussion of music since the 18th century treats sonata form as one of the major structural types. Spink explains how the predominance of tonality as the primary structural principle of the classical period resulted in an approach to sonata form as a tonal plan, and he documents Beethoven's dramatic intensification and expansion of sonata form, as well as the composer's exploration of the theme as a source of structural unity. Spink also investigates how the growing importance of such thematic processes as cyclicism and thematic transformation modified sonata form during the 19th century, and he notes how the increasing predominance of chromaticism and frequent modulation undermined the structural power of tonality. Additionally, he briefly discusses sonata form in relation to 20th-century compositional techniques.

STRAUS documents early 20th-century strategies of incorporating and reinterpreting musical elements from earlier traditions into a post-tonal idiom. He devotes an entire chapter to the treatment of sonata form, the most important formal paradigm of tonal music. After reviewing the 18th-century approach based on tonal polarity and the 19th-century practice based on thematic presentation and repetition, he demonstrates how 20th-century composers draw upon both traditions. Analyzing examples from Stravinsky, Bartók, and Schoenberg, Straus argues that during the 20th century, sonata form is not really revived but rather recreated according to post-tonal artistic priorities.

TOVEY's book contains a series of articles originally prepared for the *Encyclopedia Britannica*. In the essay "Sonata Forms," his reliance on harmonic closure as a structural priority leads the author to consider sonata form as originating in binary tonal types with no standard procedures for the distribution of themes. He emphasizes the dramatic nature of the form, concentrating on the widely contrasting treatment of details by such masters as Haydn, Mozart, and Beethoven. He briefly mentions treatment of sonata form by several 19th-century composers.

RENEE MCCACHREN

Foster, Stephen 1826–1864

United States composer

Austin, William W., *"Susanna," "Jeanie," and "The Old Folks at Home": The Songs of Stephen C. Foster from His Time to Ours,* New York: Macmillan, 1975; 2nd edition, Urbana: University of Illinois Press, 1987

Emerson, Ken, *Doo-dah!: Stephen Foster and the Rise of American Popular Culture,* New York: Simon and Schuster, 1997

Finson, Jon, *The Voices That Are Gone: Themes in Nineteenth-Century American Popular Song,* New York: Oxford University Press, 1994

Foster, Morrison, *Biography, Songs and Musical Compositions of Stephen Collins Foster,* Pittsburgh, Pennsylvania: Smith, 1896; reprint, New York: AMS Press, 1977

Hamm, Charles, *Yesterdays: Popular Song in America,* New York: Norton, 1979

Howard, John Tasker, *Stephen Foster: America's Troubadour,* New York: Crowell, 1934, revised edition, 1953

Morneweck, Evelyn Foster, *Chronicles of Stephen Foster's Family,* Pittsburgh, Pennsylvania: University of Pittsburgh Press, 1944

Saunders, Steven, and Deane L. Root, *The Music of Stephen C. Foster,* 2 vols., Washington: Smithsonian Institution Press, 1990

Tawa, Nicholas E., *Sweet Songs for Gentle Americans: The Parlor Song in America, 1790–1860,* Bowling Green, Ohio: Bowling Green University Popular Press, 1980

Despite Stephen Foster's unchallenged status as the United States' preeminent songwriter of the 19th century, the literature on the composer remains surprisingly meager. The crude racial stereotypes and offensive language in some of his minstrel songs have posed one obstacle to the serious study of Foster's works. Yet even several early songs, including "Nelly Was a Lady" (1849) and "Melinda May" (1851), contain sympathetic portrayals of African Americans. Indeed, by the early 1850s, Foster had made a conscious decision to abandon what he saw as "trashy and really offensive" themes in his minstrel songs, thereby creating a new hybrid song type, the "plantation melody," which blended elements of the genteel parlor ballad with blackface minstrelsy. In the best of these songs, such as "Old Folks at Home" (1851) and "My Old Kentucky Home, Good-Night" (1853), Foster used African American characters living under slavery to voice his most universal, genuine, and deeply felt sentiments. The musical simplicity of Foster's style and the often sentimental lyrics have provided additional obstacles to the serious treatment of his output. However, recent scholarship has shown how the parlor songs skillfully unite resonant poetic images with memorable melodies, drawing on both indigenous elements and on gestures appropriated from English and Irish song, Italian opera, and German lieder.

Morrison FOSTER's adulatory tribute to his younger brother was the first extensive biography. Based largely on personal recollections and family tradition, it is incomplete and in many respects untrustworthy, but it is nevertheless valuable for eyewitness accounts of events not documented elsewhere.

MORNEWECK provides another biographical contribution from a family member. Foster's niece furnishes copious genealogical information, but her work is most valuable for its enumeration of primary sources and its transcriptions of family letters and memorabilia.

HOWARD's seminal biography establishes the outlines of Foster's education, travels, career, and finances, relying on materials then in the possession of the Foster family and on the rich resources of Josiah K. Lilly's Foster Hall Collection (now part of the Center for American Music at the University of Pittsburgh). The basic chronology established in this dispassionate work—nearly a documentary biography—has not been seriously challenged or augmented. Howard debunks several myths surrounding the composer, revealing Foster's limited contact with the South and exposing the complexity of Foster's financial dealings with his publishers. However, Howard suppresses or de-emphasizes negative aspects of Foster's life—for example, his marital troubles and his drinking—and discusses Foster's music only in passing. Howard also perpetuates the image of the composer as an untutored genius, whose success as a songwriter is both mysterious and inexplicable.

EMERSON's breezy biography does little to alter the basic picture of Foster's career established by Howard more than 60 years earlier. This book's central importance is its forthright handling of biographical details

suppressed by Foster, Morneweck, and Howard, as well as the parallels it draws between Foster and his contemporaries. Emerson deals with William Foster's (Stephen's father) propensity to drink, his staggering lack of financial acumen, and his fathering a son out of wedlock. The author also discusses several previously suppressed letters concerning marital difficulties between Stephen Foster and his wife Jane from 1854 and deals frankly with the composer's alcoholism. Most revealing, Emerson provides a lyrical evocation of the upper-middle-class prosperity that the Foster family enjoyed and their subsequent fall from financial grace at around the time of Stephen's birth. He argues convincingly that the Foster family's precarious financial situation colored Foster's lyrics, which express a longing for a lost, idealized past, often made concrete as a desire for a distant, dimly imagined home. The book is marred, however, by specious parallels between Foster and 20th-century popular music figures, a rather heavy-handed psychoanalysis of the composer, and the author's lack of acquaintance with the 19th-century popular song repertoires.

AUSTIN's richly textured work is the first book by a music historian to offer a sustained examination of Foster's music. He formally divides of Foster's songs into three categories, yet his central concern is not merely taxonomy or formal analysis. Instead, Austin adopts a two-pronged approach to Foster's compositions, not only probing the original context and meanings of the songs (and showing brilliantly how Foster's works mirrored 19th-century cultural conditions), but also tracing the changing reception of Foster's music since its creation. He sketches the appropriation, adaptation, and reception of Foster's music by musicians as diverse as Charles Ives, Irving Berlin, Ray Charles, and Ornette Coleman. The network of connections that Austin forges is sometimes far flung, yet he succeeds in illuminating the central paradox surrounding Foster's music: that such seemingly simple and unassuming songs have never ceased to be vital and resonant with so many diverse groups of listeners.

The chapter about Foster by HAMM is the most thoughtful and original assessment of the composer's place in the history of U.S. popular music. Hamm rejects the conventional view of Foster as inspired but fundamentally incompetent, arguing that his music succeeds precisely because of the composer's skill at blending various ethnic songs styles (including Italian opera, German lieder, and Scotch-Irish melodies) into a polyglot, which remains widely accessible. The author also confronts the problematic texts of the minstrel songs, showing that Foster turned away from the coarse caricatures of African Americans found in most examples of this genre, eventually investing them with the same sentiments, particularly a world-weary nostalgia, that pervade the more elevated parlor songs.

TAWA is important because it places Foster's oeuvre within the broader context of the 19th-century parlor song repertoire. Although discussions of Foster's works are scattered throughout the book, Tawa provides insights into the typical structural features of the genres in which Foster wrote, as well as the types of texts current in the mid-19th century.

FINSON presents a comprehensive survey of the themes found in popular song lyrics from the 19th century, exploring the ways in which song texts mirror the attitudes, passions, and cultural predilections of the songs' creators and their audiences. The organization is topical: part 1 deals with themes central to 19th-century U.S. culture (love and courtship, protocols of dying, and technology); part 2 treats facets of race and ethnicity in the United States, including the blackface tradition. Foster's music naturally receives prominent treatment in both parts of this survey. The author shows adeptly how Foster's sentimental serenades emerged from a tradition of songs that employed elevated language; distant, fantastic settings; and the feigned medieval imagery enshrined in the works of Sir Walter Scott. Moreover, Finson's identification of three dominant uses of minstrel songs—as expressions of fascination with exotic or primitive aspects of things African, as somewhat ambivalent metaphors for a lost rural paradise, and as evocations of a carnivalesque alternative reality—provides a useful framework for reconsidering many of Foster's minstrel songs.

SAUNDERS and ROOT provides a complete critical edition of all of Foster's works, along with useful introductions to the composer, the dissemination of his works, performance practice, and musical style.

STEVEN SAUNDERS

France: General Studies

Anthony, James R., *French Baroque Music from Beaujoyeulx to Rameau,* New York: Norton, 1978; revised edition, Portland, Oregon: Amadeus Press, 1997

Cowart, Georgia, *The Origins of Modern Musical Criticism: French and Italian Music, 1600–1750,* Ann Arbor, Michigan: UMI Research Press, 1981

Cowart, Georgia, editor, *French Musical Thought, 1600–1800,* Ann Arbor, Michigan: UMI Research Press, 1989

Fulcher, Jane, *French Cultural Politics and Music: From the Dreyfus Affair to the First World War,* New York: Oxford University Press, 1999

Isherwood, Robert, *Music in the Service of the King: France in the Seventeenth Century,* Ithaca, New York: Cornell University Press, 1973

Johnson, James, *Listening in Paris: A Cultural History,* Berkeley: University of California Press, 1995

Mongrédien, Jean, *French Music from the Enlightenment to Romanticism: 1789–1830,* translated by Sylvain Frémaux, Portland, Oregon: Amadeus Press, 1996

Page, Christopher, *Discarding Images: Reflections on Music and Culture in Medieval France,* Oxford: Clarendon Press, and New York: Oxford University Press, 1993

———, *The Owl and the Nightingale: Musical Life and Ideas in France, 1100–1300,* London: Dent, and Berkeley: University of California Press, 1989

Verba, Cynthia, *Music and the French Enlightenment: Reconstruction of a Dialogue, 1750–1764,* Oxford: Clarendon Press, and New York: Oxford University Press, 1993

Watkins, Glenn, *Pyramids at the Louvre: Music Culture, and Collage from Stravinsky to the Postmodernists,* Cambridge, Massachusetts: Harvard University Press, 1994

Those in search of a comprehensive English-language overview of the history of French music will be frustrated to learn that such a volume does not yet exist. The classic French studies in this vein—including the 11-volume *Encyclopédie de la musique et Dictionnaire du Conservatoire* edited by Albert Lavignac and Lionel de La Laurencie, which appeared between 1913 and 1931, and the 2-volume *Histoire de la musique* edited by Roland-Manuel and published between 1960 and 1963—remain to be translated. Lacking such a source, and in lieu of studies devoted to particular composers or genres, the English speaker may rely instead on individual studies covering discrete topics and time periods in French history.

Medieval France is the subject for PAGE (1993), in which the author argues for a reconsideration of musical aesthetics, compositional process, and performance practice in the Middle Ages. Motivated, he states, by a desire to reconcile the sound of the music from this period with conventional assessments of it, Page's study undertakes a wide-ranging examination of music's situation in medieval culture and society. The book opens with a discussion of "cathedralism," which aims to deflate the widely held view of music from these years as an expression of the same intellectualizing and mathematical impulse that has been associated with Gothic architecture—an interpretation that Page questions in its own right. The motet, a locus for such architectonic analyses, is the subject of the two chapters that follow. Challenging the notion that the medieval motet was intended for an educated or elite audience, he demonstrates both that the materials for vernacular motets emanated from a much broader base than previously acknowledged and that the audience for these works was indeed diverse. In making this last point, he offers a fascinating new interpretation for a seminal 14th-century treatise that, while bearing directly on the motet, also has implications for music and cultural life generally. Subsequent chapters offer similarly bold considerations of the *ars nova*, which Page places in the context of the rise of arabic numerals and a decimal system in Europe, and the 20th-century view of the chanson as a genre of central importance to French tradition.

The focus for PAGE (1989) is the relationship of musical activity to the emergence of the French state in the 12th century, and the concomitant shift of focus away from the Church. He illuminates a fundamental paradox in this regard—namely, that even as the clerical literati became increasingly tolerant of secular music and musicians, the Church sought ever more intensely to impose authority on human interactions. Ultimately, Page demonstrates, the owl, symbol of Christian spirituality, is overcome by the nightingale, symbol of emergent humanism. Within this framework, he traces a number of major topics, including the rise of troubadours and trouvères, the elaboration of polyphony at the cathedral of Notre Dame, and the emergence of the literary romance, exploring professional and amateur music in both courtly and popular contexts. The theoretical writings of two Parisian musicians, flourishing at each end of the 12th century, provide a basis for Page's analytical evaluation of the changing role of secular music and musicians during these years, which notably included the development of a professional class of musicians.

ISHERWOOD considers music, politics, and society in the 17th century, devoting himself especially to the association of music and monarchy during the reign of Louis XIV. Musical aesthetics in France, which drew on Plato and Aristotle, as well as a succession of medieval and Renaissance authors, are shown to be integral to this enterprise, clearing the way for an explicit connection of traditional musical doctrines, such as the concept of universal harmony, with political ideas, such as the "harmony of the state." Opera, as Isherwood demonstrates, proved a particularly valuable expressive medium, uniting music and poetry to affect human temperament and moral conduct; more important, it served an ideological function, affirming the power of the king. The book traces the rise of French opera from its origins in musical spectacles under the Valois kings to its full realization in the *tragédies lyriques* of Lully and documents the genre's decline that followed his death in 1687.

In a newly expanded and revised version of his classic study, ANTHONY provides a culturally informed history of developments in French music from the 1580s through the mid-18th century. His extensive discussions encompass issues in dramatic and religious music, instrumental repertories, vocal chamber music, and performance practice; they also document the musical institutions and organizations of 17th-century France. The book paints the age in broad strokes while also providing historical and musical detail to convey a rich narrative connecting musical life and cultural practices. Coherent considerations of composers in shadow of Lully, Couperin, and Charpentier are made vivid through musical examples and contemporary commentary.

COWART (1989) presents a collection of 11 essays, extending chronologically from a study of the early 17th-century writings of Mersenne to a consideration of late 18th-century ideas of ecstasy and irrationality. Charting the shift in musical aesthetics in France in those years, other papers in the book illustrate aspects of the tension between the mimetic theories of Aristotle and the developing ideals of sensuous beauty, *galanterie*, and good taste. Two essays are devoted to these issues as reflected in French opera and its criticism; three illuminate topics in the history of music theory; and two mine contemporary commentary to illuminate aspects of terminology. Among these latter essays is Claude Palisca's reconstruction of the etymology of the term *baroque*, which is now recognized as a seminal discussion in French studies. Finally, two essays examine the relationship of musical aesthetics to the arts more broadly, drawing on iconographic evidence as well as treatises on painting and literature to demonstrate the change from rational, mimetic views of art to an outlook based on the senses. Reflecting a sensitivity to the range of issues raised in these years, the volume is notable for its depth of interdisciplinary scholarship.

COWART (1981) traces 17th-century quarrels over the relative values of French and Italian music to the cultural rivalry between France and Italy during the Renaissance and, more immediately, to the modern Italian style that dominated European music during the course of the century. She draws a parallel between these debates and the quarrels over ancient and modern music that arose from the larger European controversy between ancients and moderns in the 16th and 17th centuries. These two scholarly disputes, finally converging in the early 18th-century exchange between François Raguenet and Jean-Laurent Lecerf de la Viéville, signaled the growth of a modern critical outlook. Characterized by the formulation of critical standards through the juxtaposition of historical and national styles, this outlook influenced a new brand of musical criticism not only in France but also in Germany and Britain.

The musical controversies of the 18th-century French Enlightenment are VERBA's focus. She identifies three major events of the 1750s as catalysts for a long dialogue about music that took place over the remainder of the century—namely, Rameau's postulation of the fundamental bass; the publication of the *Encyclopédie*; and the "Querelle des Bouffons," the argument over the relative merits of the Italian comic opera and the French *tragédie lyrique*. Illuminating the interdisciplinary profile of music during this time, Verba demonstrates that music was viewed as both an art and a science and thus served as a locus for controversy over such issues as the nature of artistic expression and validity of scientific inquiry. The book provides an absorbing examination of music theory and aesthetics in the context of the broadest philosophical currents of the day and is particularly valuable for its appendices, which offer the first English translations of seven documents.

MONGRÉDIEN covers the half-century extending from 1780 to 1830, the interregnum between the

Enlightenment and romanticism. This is a period lacking apparent masterpieces or towering musical personalities, yet the book argues compellingly for its importance based on political considerations. In seven chapters Mongrédien demonstrates that, in the midst of revolution and widespread instability, music was a site of both innovation and organization. His initial discussions detail musical developments spurred by the French Revolution, including the founding of the conservatory in Paris in 1795 and the use of Revolutionary hymns and songs as instruments of propaganda. The book's longest chapter is given over to consideration of musical theater, encompassing productions at the Opéra, Opéra-comique, and Théâtre italien: censorship is the main concern here, although issues of staffing and repertory are also covered comprehensively. Sacred music, perhaps the arena in which the most explicit changes occurred after the Revolution, is also treated in detail, as the shifts in repertory at the Tuileries Chapel are used as a case study of the more widespread secularization in France. Changes in musical aesthetics, which Mongrédien also attributes to political currents, are considered as they are reflected in contemporary concert programming, as well as developments in French instrumental music. The book's final chapter is devoted to a study of the influence of German music in France, an issue with broad ramifications through the 19th and 20th centuries. Comprehensive in its approach and convincing in its effort to situate music in a political context, Mongrédien's book suffers only from its relative lack of musical examples.

JOHNSON presents a cultural history of music in France from the 1750s through the mid-19th century, structuring his discussions as an effort to explain the gradual acceptance of silence as proper audience behavior at musical events. Positing that political considerations and social codes motivated public responses to music, he argues that listening habits evolved as a response to a broad aesthetic shift, in which transcendent emotionalism ultimately supplanted pleasurable diversion as an artistic ideal. This argument is especially convincing because of his considerations of opera in the ancien régime and in the romantic era, which demonstrate that opera in the age of Louis XIV was a backdrop for noisy aristocratic social interaction and the reinforcement of political ideologies, but by the time of the genre's revival after the 1830 Revolution, it provided a milieu in which the high bourgeoisie sat silently, captivated by musical spectacle. Between these two poles, Johnson traces a history of the links among public attentiveness, musical practice, and social politics. Discussions of the harmonic innovations of Rameau and Gluck illuminate the fact that 18th-century France understood emotion as the essence of musical expression, while the Revolution, the author shows, identified music as a site for explicit political expression as well a vehicle for public instruction and edification. The post-Revolutionary return to luxury and entertainment is assessed as a rejection of the politicization of private life, a factor evident also in the reorientation of concerts from private entertainments to public events. Finally, Johnson contends that the rise of bourgeois politeness through the Empire and Restoration created both a more cultivated musical audience and one more prone to boredom, leading directly to the return of grandeur at the opera and the embrace of Beethoven in the concert hall.

FULCHER, focusing on the years from 1898 to 1914, argues that French musical meanings and values are best explained not in terms of contemporary artistic movements but rather in terms of political culture, which was undergoing subtle but profound transformation during this time as nationalist leagues enlarged the arena of political action. The author suggests that French music as a whole came to be viewed as a mechanism through which political values could be disseminated; thus, music criticism, education, and even performances accreted political significance. A discussion of the impact of this musical culture on composers such as d'Indy, Charpentier, Magnard, Debussy, and Satie constitutes the body of the study.

WATKINS, whose concern is French music in the 20th century, aims specifically to elucidate the significance of collage technique to compositional practice. Proposing that the techniques of juxtaposition, assemblage, and rearrangement—which are fundamental to collage in the visual arts—were also essential tools of modernism in music, the author makes a wide-ranging and eloquent argument for the importance of collage as an aesthetic in its own right. Although Stravinsky is the ostensible focus of the study, Watkins covers a breathtaking array of musicians, including all of the major composers of the 20th century, performers ranging from Josephine Baker to the Talking Heads, and a wealth of artists associated with the dada, futurist, and cubist projects, among others. Integrating close study of musical developments with an exploration of trends in literature and poetry as well as visual art, Watkins presents a cohesive interpretation of culture in the 20th century, suggesting a relocation of music from the margins to the mainstream.

MARY E. DAVIS

France: Musical Centers

Bloom, Peter, editor, *Music in Paris in the Eighteen-Thirties*, Stuyvesant, New York: Pendragon Press, 1987

Brody, Elaine, *Paris: The Musical Kaleidoscope 1870–1925*, New York: Braziller, 1987

Dobbins, Frank, *Music in Renaissance Lyons*, Oxford: Clarendon Press, and New York: Oxford University Press, 1992

Duhamel, Jean-Marie, *La Musique dans la Ville, de Lully à Rameau*, Lille: Presses Universitaires de Lille, 1994

Ellis, Katharine, *Music Criticism in Nineteenth-Century France: La Revue et Gazette Musicale de Paris, 1834–80,* Cambridge: Cambridge University Press, 1995

Johnson, James, *Listening in Paris: A Cultural History,* Berkeley: University of California Press, 1995

Pitou, Spire, *The Paris Opéra: An Encyclopedia of Operas, Ballets, Composers, and Performers,* 3 vols., Westport, Connecticut: Greenwood Press, 1983–90

Robertson, Anne Walters, *The Service Books of the Royal Abbey of Saint-Denis: Images of Ritual and Music in the Middle Ages,* Oxford: Clarendon Press, and New York: Oxford University Press, 1991

Tomasello, Andrew, *Music and Ritual at Papal Avignon 1309–1403,* Ann Arbor, Michigan: UMI Research Press, 1983

Wright, Craig, *Music and Ceremony at Notre Dame of Paris, 500–1500,* Cambridge: Cambridge University Press, 1989

————, *Music at the Court of Burgundy, 1364–1419: A Documentary History,* Henryville, Pennsylvania: Institute of Medieval Music, 1979

French music parallels other French cultural practices in that many important developments have been centered in France's largest city, Paris. Likewise, much of the available literature concerns music in Paris. There have been equally significant musical activities outside Paris, in provincial cities, courts, churches, and so on, but they have not been as widely written about, particularly in English-language publications. Most of the works listed here place the music within a social context: musical examples and technical analyses are minimal, and most books include visual illustrations. Most items are reasonably focused by topic and time period; together they offer a wider view of French musical life of the past.

WRIGHT (1989) has not attempted to write a comprehensive or chronological history of music of Notre Dame, site of Europe's musical avant-garde 1150–1250. Instead, he addresses several aspects of repertoire and musical life over a 1000-year period in essays that cross several musical style periods. His introduction to the church, clergy, and cloister emphasizes the role of the physical site of the church in his history. Other essays address chant and liturgy from early Gallican through late medieval repertoire; organs and organists; other personnel and institutions, such as choir boys; relation of church and court; repertoire, particularly the *Magnus Liber Organi*; composers such as Léonin, Pérotin, Vitry, and Ockeghem; and performance practice. Many illustrations enhance Wright's essays.

Opera is central to understanding Paris as a musical center. The books by Pitou and Johnson together offer a wide sweep of opera in Paris. PITOU's dictionary is comprehensive, covering both opera and ballet from the Paris Opéra's founding in 1671 to the 1970s. The work includes entries on repertoire, composers, librettists, choreographers, and performers. Entries of all subjects appear together, arranged alphabetically. The first volume's 125-page introduction summarizes the opera and opéra comique during the 300 years covered in the dictionary. Each volume contains a separate list of repertoire, singers, and dancers mentioned in its pages. Although not itself a history, the dictionary is indispensable for historical investigations of Parisian musical theater.

A cultural study of audience behavior at the Paris Opéra from the 1670s through the early 18th century, JOHNSON's book complements Pitou's. Johnson explains the repertoire of composers such as Auber, Beethoven, Berlioz, Gluck, Haydn, Rossini, and Rameau in the context of audience reception. He observes how Paris audiences in the public theater up to 1750 generally did not focus on the performed repertoire: only during the second half of the 18th century did audiences gradually become silent. The book includes many musical examples and images such as plans of theaters and paintings of concert and theater sites.

BLOOM's anthology consists of conference papers on music in Paris during the flowering of French romanticism, when music was central to social and cultural life. The book contains 22 essays, half of which are in English; those in French are summarized in English. The opening essay on the city of Paris in the 1830s by Jacques Barzun is followed by musical topics such as printing and instrument building, audiences, concert series, conductors, orchestras, and reviews of new musical theatrical repertoire.

ELLIS's work on music criticism in the 19th century reveals Paris's musical life as told by prominent critics. The book covers writings that appeared in various daily and periodical newspapers ca. 1834–80. The articles include critiques of repertoire, philosophical ideas pervading current musical thought, historical essays, composer biographies, and music theory. Ellis also discusses reviews of composers such as Gluck, Schubert, Chopin, and Brahms; repertoire, particularly to illustrate how the concert canon developed; and performance practice of old music.

BRODY was enamored with Paris at the turn of the 20th century, when the city was the musical capital of Europe. Consisting of chapters that can be read independently of one another, Brody discusses Wagner in Paris; music during the Great Expositions; music in café society, music halls, and cabarets; and music in conjunction with painting, dance, and literature. Of the many international composers and artists who reached Paris, Brody explores Russian, Spanish, oriental, and American connections. She includes easily readable descriptions of musical masterpieces by Debussy, Ravel, Satie, Bizet, and others.

The medieval duchy of Burgundy thrived under four rulers. WRIGHT's (1979) study investigates music under

Philip the Bold and John the Fearless. Most of Wright's information is taken from chronicles and account books. After historical background on Burgundy, he discusses rulers, court musicians, chapel and secular music, and manuscripts. The extensive bibliography includes sources of art, literature, and history of the period, as well as music.

TOMASELLO examines music in Avignon, site of one branch of the papacy during the great schism in the Catholic Church in the 14th century, from Pope Clement V to Benedict XIII. Connections between church musicians and secular poets and scholars contributed to a flourishing musical life in the papal court, in several magnificent palaces. The book discusses chapel musicians, leadership of the chapel, musical components of the liturgy, and polyphony and organ music. Tomasello also analyzes the Apt manuscript, an important primary source of polyphonic Mass ordinaries, hymns, and motets.

The coverage of ROBERTSON's musical center is one building, the pilgrimage church of Saint-Denis, burial site of French royals. Robertson's liturgical history of the church covers the years 250 to 1500. A relatively large body of surviving service books informs the author's interpretation of feasts and celebrations in the church year and their distinctive music and ritual. The book examines music's connection to art, architecture, and the political fabric of the church and contains detailed charts of liturgy and repertoire.

Reporting on music in this city central to the transmission of Renaissance culture by virtue of its position halfway between Paris and Rome, DOBBINS includes background on Lyon's trade, education, printing, and role in the Reformation. He discusses music in Lyonnais literature; Lyon's flourishing music printing business, led by printers such as Jacques Moderne; and the city's international repertoire, composers, and musical life. Several appendices include lists of musicians, instrument builders, publications, and patrons of music. The work contains nearly 100 pages of music from Lyon.

Several musical centers are included in DUHAMEL's cultural history of music in elite French society of the 18th century. In French, this work offers a comprehensive view of music in French culture: its organization is driven by physical locations and cultural entities, not by musical analysis. It considers musical life in urban centers of Paris, Marseilles, Lyon, Bordeaux, Lille, and Versailles. Coverage of musical institutions includes opera houses, concert halls, academies, salons, and churches, and the time frame of composers extends beyond Rameau, as suggested by the title, to Gretry and Mozart. Duhamel also examines issues such as the ancients versus the moderns and French versus Italian music, as these topics were distributed and debated throughout France in journals, memoirs, and letters.

BARBARA COEYMAN

Franck, César 1822–1890

Belgian-born composer

Archbold, Lawrence, and William J. Peterson, editors, *French Organ Music from the Revolution to Franck and Widor*, Rochester, New York: University of Rochester Press, 1995; revised edition, 1997

Davies, Laurence, *César Franck and His Circle*, London: Barrie and Jenkins, and Boston: Houghton Mifflin, 1970

———, *Franck*, London: Dent, and New York: Octagon Books, 1973

Demuth, Norman, *César Franck*, London: Dobson, and New York: Philosophical Library, 1949

Indy, Vincent d', *César Franck*, translated by Rosa Newmarch, London, Lane, 1910; reprint, New York: Dover, 1965

Smith, Rollin, *Playing the Organ Works of César Franck*, Stuyvesant, New York: Pendragon Press, 1997

———, *Toward an Authentic Interpretation of the Organ Works of César Franck*, New York: Pendragon Press, 1983

Vallas, Léon, *César Franck*, translated by Hubert Foss, New York: Oxford University Press, 1951

César Franck was one of the most polarizing figures in the history of French music. This gentle organist, teacher, and composer inspired fanatical disciples and equally impassioned enemies, and battles between the two factions raged for many years after his death. When examining literature on Franck, the reader will do well to consider the authors' biases—not only artistic, but also social, religious, and even political—because these often strongly inform writers' perspectives on the man and his music.

Franck remains controversial for today's scholars as well, if for more strictly musical reasons. An artist much written about but far less studied, many of his most famous compositions remain without detailed analyses to this day; discussions of his overall style usually restrict themselves to general and subjective observations. Some writers spend as much time complaining about the composer's perceived faults as they do praising his virtues; at times, they seem astonished that he wrote any good music at all. Books in English fall into two categories: biographies and studies of his organ music, the one body of Franck's compositions to have received serious attention in this language—and the only truly scholarly studies of Franck in English (none of the biographies qualify in this regard).

The best-known biography is by Franck's illustrious pupil INDY, an ardent apologist for his teacher's principles as he interpreted them. Indy famously romanticizes his subject. To him, Franck represents a latter-day saint, all of whose works are fundamentally Catholic in meaning; Indy ignores any person in Franck's life and profoundly reinterprets any composition that upset this paradigm. He presents Franck the teacher as a kindly soul martyred by a hostile and uncomprehending establishment, and Franck the composer as the only legitimate successor to Beethoven and Wagner. In so doing, he makes some opponents seem more antagonistic than they actually were, and he disregards the influence of other important composers on Franck, especially Schumann and Liszt. Once Indy's mythologizing is taken into account, his book can be read with much profit, and it remains the most authoritative study. He includes extended discussions of the oratorio *Les Béatitudes,* the Violin Sonata, and the Three Chorales for organ.

The original French title of VALLAS's biography, "The True Story of César Franck," gives an idea of its content. The author seeks to correct some of the more egregious distortions in Indy's biography. In contrast to Indy's deification of Franck, Vallas interprets the composer as a great secular artist, although he also misrepresents Franck by minimizing his genuine spirituality almost to extinction. Full of important—albeit undocumented—primary material and brief discussions of all of Franck's major compositions, Vallas's biography offers an essential complement to Indy's work.

DAVIES (1970) is the most significant modern source: the first half considers the life and works of Franck; the second concentrates on his pupils, some of whom have no other treatment in English. The book has liabilities, however. Although Davies provides a stylistic overview of Franck's music, his discussion of individual works can be superficial; further, one detects a patronizing attitude toward Franck and his pupils, which occasionally colors the author's comments; finally, although he explains the cultural context in which Franck and his circle lived (with almost no documentation), the picture Davies paints is not without oversimplifications and misunderstandings. Nevertheless, this book remains a valuable and rewarding source.

DAVIES (1973) studies the music itself in much more detail, although still not as much as one would like (due no doubt in part to limitations of space in books from the Master Musicians series). Nevertheless, this volume provides the most consistently in-depth analyses of Franck's significant nonorgan works in English.

DEMUTH's work is not important as a biography, but it often comments on the music in more detail than Vallas or even Davies. Like Vallas, Demuth received some of his material directly from surviving pupils of Franck, and for that reason alone, this book has real value. Demuth's musical observations contain numerous subjective and critical comments, which are not always explained or defended.

Smith has authored two important and complementary studies on Franck's organ music. In the introduction to SMITH (1983), which originated as his dissertation, the author points out that many false impressions and legends have arisen since Franck's day concerning his practice as an organist and organ composer. By examining primary documents relating to the organs Franck played,

accounts of his own performances, recordings of his music by his pupils (especially Charles Tournemire), and recollections of Franck as an organ teacher, the author strives to recover the "true" performer and composer.

SMITH (1997) devotes itself to a study of the works themselves; for each piece the author provides a composition history, analysis, practical performance advice, a comparison of variant editions and period recordings, and corrections to the standard Durand edition of 1956. An annotated bibliography brings that of Smith (1983) up-to-date. The author also includes a biography focusing on the churches in which Franck worked and the organs he played. Taken together, Smith's books offer a comprehensive view of Franck and the organ—the first giving the context for understanding his world, the second offering detailed information about every work. Both are important resources for the performer of this repertory.

Finally, ARCHBOLD and PETERSON present a collection of 11 essays about 19th-century organ music in France. Four concern Franck: Jesse Eschbach examines a manuscript in the Bibliothèque Nationale that provides clues about the registrations the composer used; Karen Hastings-Deans looks at discrepancies between the manuscript and published score of the Choral no. 1; Marie-Louise Jaquet-Langlais considers editorial and performance issues in each of Franck's organ works (her article resembles Smith [1997] in many ways and provides an equally vital source for organists to consult); and Daniel Roth compares Franck's playing to the tradition of the influential Belgian organist Lemmens.

BRIAN J. HART

Frescobaldi, Girolamo 1583–1643

Italian composer

Hammond, Frederick, *Girolamo Frescobaldi,* Cambridge, Massachusetts: Harvard University Press, 1983

———, *Girolamo Frescobaldi: A Guide to Research,* New York: Garland, 1988

Silbiger, Alexander, editor, *Frescobaldi Studies,* Durham, North Carolina: Duke University Press, 1987

———, editor, *Keyboard Music before 1700,* New York: Schirmer Books, and London: Prentice Hall, 1995

Few keyboard composers acquired as much fame during the 17th century as Girolamo Frescobaldi. He published an amazingly large number of compositions and held one of the most prominent positions available to organists during his day at St. Peter's (Rome). His lasting legacy includes directions on how to play his pieces, providing us with clues to his improvisational style and warning modern performers that there is much more to playing music of this period than that which is printed on the page. He wrote for several mediums, including voices and instrumental ensembles, but it is for his keyboard compositions that he is chiefly remembered today. The quatercentenary of his birth in 1983 kindled new interest in the composer. With his two books, the first published for the quatercentary, Hammond has led the field in publications about Frescobaldi, although several other writers have contributed substantially to Frescobaldi research.

Judd's essay on Italy in SILBIGER (1995) provides the best introduction to Frescobaldi's music, beginning with an overview of Italian keyboard music before Frescobaldi and a discussion of the context in which Italian music was originally heard (including helpful information on its use in the liturgy of the Roman Catholic Church). The author carefully lays out the musical landscape of Italy during this period and provides a road map for the local styles of individual areas. This background is especially useful for understanding the works of Frescobaldi, who relied on several traditions and culled various aspects of these styles into his own compositions. Judd explores Frescobaldi's music through careful analysis of various styles in order of publication. He also probes Frescobaldi's influence on later generations of keyboard composers. Some terminology may be unfamiliar, but it can be readily found in easily accessible music dictionaries or encyclopedias.

HAMMOND (1983) was the first scholar to summarize Frescobaldi's life and works comprehensively, and later authors almost always mention his contribution to the field. The biography is straightforward in its description of the composer's life and works and includes most available information known about the composer. Little attention is given to more subjective areas, and more thoroughgoing analysis of Frescobaldi's music—in particular, more emphasis on why the composer tackled certain compositional problems—is needed. For example, Frescobaldi clearly wrote in different styles in various genres, but his reasons for doing so are not explored here. Hammond's examination of the music—a daunting task considering the number of compostions—is not as easy to follow as the biographical section. He discusses the works in publication order, which makes the reading sometimes difficult and occasionally less exciting than it might be. Unsurprisingly, the keyboard music receives the bulk of the attention, and other music is only briefly discussed. Despite these detractions, any scrupulous investigation of Frescobaldi's music should include familiarity with this work.

HAMMOND (1988) should be consulted with his earlier work as the later volume includes corrections and additions. Furthermore, it provides a wealth of information on Frescobaldi's world, including such obscure items as 17th-century Italian currencies and postal systems. Particularly enlightening are discussions of Roman government, the pontifical household, and annotated lists of places and persons (including singers, patrons). The detail is astounding, and as a resource for Italian music

of the period, the text is remarkable. Hammond also evaluates the current state of Frescobaldi research, touching on the controversial topic of tempo/meter relationships brought forth by Etienne Darbellay. This reference work includes translations of the texts to Frescobaldi's publications, an extensive bibliography cross-referenced by topic, and a discography.

A 1983 conference on Frescobaldi held at the University of Wisconsin, Madison, celebrating the composer's quatercentenary yielded the collection edited by SILBIGER (1987). Silbiger's introduction to Frescobaldi adroitly begins the volume, providing an overview of the composer's various styles. Stylistic antecedents to the composer and the relationship of Frescobaldi's works to other Italian music of this period are considered in greater detail than in previous publications. Several of the essays analyze Frescobaldi's music for media other than keyboard and help balance the current state of research on the composer. New information is available here concerning Frescobaldi's time in Mantua (1615), patronage, and other biographical details (including an essay by Hammond). Of particular interest are the two essays by Etienne Darbellay and Margaret Murata, both of which deal with tempo, meter, and proportion. On the whole, the volume is aimed at a specialist audience, and the individual essays require a substantial understanding of music of the period.

CANDACE LEE BAILEY

Fugue

Bullivant, Roger, *Fugue,* London: Hutchinson, 1971

Gedalge, Andre, *Treatise on Fugue,* translated by A. Levin, Mattapan, Massachusetts: Gamut Music, 1964

Horsley, Imogene, *Fugue: History and Practice,* New York: Free Press, 1966

Mann, Alfred, *The Study of Fugue,* New Brunswick, New Jersey: Rutgers University Press, 1958

Nalden, Charles, *Fugal Answer,* Auckland: Auckland University Press, 1969

Prout, Ebenezer, *Fugue,* London: Augener, 1891; reprint, New York: Greenwood Press, 1969

Renwick, William, *Analyzing Fugue: A Schenkerian Approach,* Stuyvesant, New York: Pendragon Press, 1995

The genre of fugue developed from the instrumental canzona in the 16th century. Fugue typically features imitation of a subject or theme at the interval of the fifth or fourth. Indeed, the imitation of the fugue subject at the tonic and dominant levels was an important factor in the evolution of the common-practice tonal system in the 17th century. The genre reached its height in the music of Johann Sebastian Bach, whose exceptional fugue subjects were developed in highly imaginative ways. Bach contributed to the form of fugue by incorporating well-timed modulations and cadences as well as imaginative contrapuntal combinations. Fugues may include technical features such as invertible countersubjects, secondary subjects, stretto, augmentation, diminution, and inversion of the subject. Episodes, often sequential, in which the subject is not present, can provide relief from the main thematic material. Fugue remained a compositional technique throughout the 19th century, often incorporated as *fugato* within sonata and rondo forms. In the 20th century, composers as diverse as Bartók, Shostakovitch, and Hindemith continued to incorporate fugal techniques and forms while exploring alternative tonal systems.

MANN documents fugal theory with translated extracts of four of the principal historical texts, by Fux, Marpurg, Albrechtsberger, and Martini. The material is arranged pedagogically so as to cover the main topics of study: imitation in two, three, and four parts; double counterpoint; fugal form; choral fugue; canon; and fugue in up to eight parts. The prefatory chapters give an insightful historical overview of the evolution of fugue and of theoretical discussions of the genre.

Even over a century after it was written, PROUT's primer on fugue remains perhaps the single most useful pedagogical volume on the subject. Clearly presented, very musical, with excellent examples from the literature, it manages to give useful instruction while avoiding dogmatism. As is typical of the era, Prout views subject and answer structure in terms of key relationships and thus provides principles for creating real and tonal, modulating and nonmodulating answers. His discussions often focus on the musical issues surrounding the technical problems, and his examples are all extracted from the standard repertoire of instrumental and choral fugue.

GEDALGE represents the systematic instruction in fugue practiced in the French conservatories around 1900 (the *fugue d'ecole*). In the French tradition, Gedalge continues to use C clefs. He devotes considerable space to explaining the formation of correct fugal answers on the basis of key schemes but spends little time on the structure of subjects. He treats invertible counterpoint, the employment of countersubjects, stretto, and pedal point in great detail, using primarily examples drawn from his fugue classes rather than from the repertoire. His rigid formal structure has encountered criticism for not sufficiently responding to the formal possibilities that individual fugue subjects may suggest; this systematic approach to fugue marginalizes musical expression and creativity in preference to strict counterpoint and comprehensive design. Gedalge would argue that the *fugue d'ecole* is not so much composition per se as exercises in the development of musical technique.

HORSLEY, perhaps reacting against the formalism evident in the early 20th century, takes a comprehensive historical approach, spanning the point of imitation as developed by Josquin through the romantic products of Brahms. Horsley refers frequently to historical treatises and illustrates her points with musical examples from a wide range of composers. The discussion constantly turns on issues of historical and structural interest, such as how techniques developed and how they function in terms of the whole. This extensive and useful historical overview of fugal form with reference to many theorists and a variety of analyzed examples counterbalances the rigid formalism of Gedalge. Horsley successfully demonstrates that fugue should be regarded as a continually evolving process for exploring imitative possibilities in a polyphonic context.

BULLIVANT considers fugal technique from a historical perspective, giving an "account of the way in which fugues have been written since the type emerged in the early Baroque period." Like Horsley, he describes fugue as it is actually practiced, not as it appears through the lens of the theorist. His work is particularly useful for its discussion of 20th-century fugal style as seen in the music of Reger, Stravinsky, Bartók, and Shostakovitch, for example.

NALDEN is an unusual book because it focuses entirely on the problem of writing correct fugal answers. This circumscribed field is crucial, however, for it is in the nexus of subject and answer in which the whole structure of fugal imitation resides. The first part of the book gives an overview of fugal answer in historical music theory and practice. The second part contains a critical exploration of the problems inherent in creating "correct" answers for a wide variety of subject types. Naldin ultimately demonstrates the impossibility of devising a comprehensive set of rules by which correct fugal answers can be written.

RENWICK's highly analytical and technical study tackles the issue of tonal and voice-leading structure in fugue, taking as its starting point the structural theories of Heinrich Schenker. Following an introduction that illustrates a harmonic viewpoint toward the structure of fugue, the second chapter provides a detailed account of the tonal structure of fugue subjects. In contrast to most theorists, Renwick establishes three distinct categories of fugue subjects, based on their underlying harmonic structure: prolonging the tonic, moving from tonic to dominant, and modulating to the dominant. Through his comprehensive structural approach, the author challenges Naldin's view of the impossibility of developing a comprehensive theory of subject-answer structure. Subsequent chapters deal with the voice-leading characteristics of invertible counterpoint, fugal exposition, sequences, stretto, and inversion. Complete analyses of three fugues from Bach's *Well-Tempered Clavier* illustrate the application of Schenkerian structural theory to the fugue.

WILLIAM RENWICK

Fux, Johann Joseph 1660–1741

Austrian composer and theorist

Fux, Johann Joseph, *Gradus ad Parnassum,* Vienna, 1725; reprint, New York: Broude Brothers, 1966

————, *The Study of Counterpoint from Johann Joseph Fux's Gradus ad Parnassum,* translated by Alfred Mann, New York: Norton, 1965

Lester, Joel, *Compositional Theory in the Eighteenth Century,* Cambridge, Massachusetts: Harvard University Press, 1992

Mann, Alfred, *The Study of Fugue,* New Brunswick, New Jersey: Rutgers University Press, 1958

Wellesz, Egon, *Fux,* London: Oxford University Press, 1965

White, Harry, editor, *Johann Joseph Fux and the Music of the Austro-Italian Baroque,* Aldershot: Scolar Press, and Brookfield, Vermont: Ashgate, 1992

Johann Joseph Fux was the leading Austrian musician in the first part of the 18th century. His compositional output comprises mainly sacred music but also many oratorios, masses, motets, and miscellaneous choral music. He also wrote instrumental and keyboard works as well as several dozen operas, some of which achieved great success in the context of spectacles of the imperial court. Today, he is best known as a pedagogue.

Fux's theories, like his compositions, were for the most part conservative, whether in terms of mode, harmony, counterpoint, or style, and were in due course criticized by the more progressive north Germans, such as Mattheson and C.P.E. Bach. Nevertheless, his legacy lived on in the pedagogical tradition that he established, that was continued through the Viennese classicists (mainly Albrechtsberger and Haydn), and that strongly influenced subsequent generations of Viennese theorists, including Heinrich Schenker. Fux's compositional output has remained largely overshadowed, on the one hand, by the music of his towering contemporaries, Bach and Handel, and, on the other hand, by the successors to the Viennese classical school, which he was largely responsible for establishing. In contrast, FUX (1725), a comprehensive Latin guide to counterpoint, has maintained a central position since it was first published. "Liber Primus," the first part, reviews in summary fashion the basics of numerical proportions and relations employed in generating diatonic and chromatic intervals and ends with definitions of consonant intervals, musical motion, and finally the four rules that prohibit similar or parallel motion into a perfect consonance. "Liber Secundus," by far the larger part of the work, is written in the form of a dialogue between the teacher Aloysius, representing Fux's idol, Palestrina, and the student Josephus, representing the young Fux. *Gradus ad Parnassum* pursues the study of counterpoint in an unprecedented systematic manner, from the basic elements of two-part counterpoint (see Fux [1965]) through the complexities of many-voiced polyphony and fugue in the strict style (see Mann). Less familiar to English readers are the chapters on diminution, mode, musical taste and style, and recitative, chapters in which Fux sketches an aesthetic context for his theoretical work.

WELLESZ, an all-too-brief life and works, is the principal English study of Fux. The introduction documents the progress of Fux research, beginning with Köchel's biography of 1872. Wellesz portrays Fux as a diverse composer well versed in ancient music but also fully capable of working in modern instrumental styles. Many examples give a clear indication of the breadth and the limitations of Fux's style. Wellesz pays special attention to the musical content of Fux's operas, which contain many inventive and dramatic passages.

FUX (1965) is an excellent introduction to Fux's theoretical work. Mann has excerpted the core of Fux's teaching on the five species of counterpoint on a cantus firmus. First species, whole note against whole note, teaches the concepts of consonance and of part motion. Second species, two half notes against a given whole note, demonstrates the idea of the passing note. Third species, four quarter notes against a whole note, adds the notions of the auxiliary and the *cambiata.* Fourth species, comprising suspensions using half notes, teaches the preparation and resolution of accented dissonances. Fifth species unites the foregoing in free counterpoint. The later chapters, again based on species, explore the principles of three- and four-part counterpoint. In addition to the attractive dialogue, the work is compelling because of its continual reference to and reexploration of a single cantus firmus for each mode.

MANN contains further important extracts from *Gradus ad Parnassum*—the sections on imitation, fugue, and double (invertible) counterpoint. This material treats imitation at various intervals; constructing fugal answers according to mode and hexachord structure; fugue in two, three, and four parts; double counterpoint at the octave, tenth, and twelfth; inversion of themes; and fugues with more than one subject. The whole is beautifully organized from a pedagogical point of view, and the prose remains charming and lively.

LESTER provides an enlightening commentary on Fux's theoretical work, enabling us to view Fux's theories especially in relation to issues such as mode, triad, and key—issues that were at the forefront of theoretical thought in the early 18th century. Lester's particular strength is his ability to make comparative observations that define Fux's theoretical stance in relation to that of his contemporaries. Lester points out that although many aspects of *Gradus ad Parnassum* are already present in one or more of the earlier treatises of Diruta, Zacconi, Bononcini, and Berardi, "none was able to match Fux's achievement—the consolidation of the species approach into a comprehensive and convincing whole."

WHITE's collection of English and German essays documents current research on Fux: Mann's "Fux's Theoretical Writings" demonstrates the impact that Fux had on the young Haydn and later on Mozart. Wolfgang Suppan, "The Use of Wind Instruments in Fux's Music," surveys the breadth of Fux's instrumental output with respect to the evolving wind instruments. Herbert Siefert's "The Secular-Dramatic Compositions of Fux" examines the compositional history of Fux's operas and related works, emphasizing the circumstances surrounding the commission, casting, and staging. Fux's "sepulcro" oratorios—composed for performance at the replica of the Holy Sepulchre erected at the Imperial Court—are briefly considered by Erika Kanduth in "The Literary and Dramaturgical Aspects of the Viennese *Sepolcro* Oratorio." White explores the musical style and form of these works at length and with many musical examples in "The *Sepulcro* Oratorios of Fux." An extensive bibliography completes the volume.

WILLIAM RENWICK

G

Gabrieli, Andrea ca. 1510–1586

Italian composer

Arnold, Denis, *Giovanni Gabrieli and the Music of the Venetian High Renaissance,* Oxford: Oxford University Press, 1979

Benzoni, Gino, et al., editors, *Gli anni Andrea Gabrieli: Biografia e cronologia,* Milan: Ricordi, 1988

Bradshaw, Murray C., *The Origin of the Toccata,* N.p.: American Institute of Musicology, 1972

Carver, Anthony F., *Cori spezzati,* 2 vols., Cambridge: Cambridge University Press, 1988

Degrada, Francesco, editor, *Andrea Gabrieli e il suo tempo: Atti del Convegno internazionale (Venezia 16–18 Settembre 1985),* Florence: Olschki, 1987

Landon, H.C. Robbins, and John Julius Norwich, *Five Centuries of Music in Venice,* London: Thames and Hudson, and New York: Schirmer Books, 1991

Andrea Gabrieli, who spent the bulk of his career as second organist at San Marco Basilica in Venice, is regarded as among the leading performers, teachers, and composers of his day. Linked with the splendor of late 16th-century Venice, Andrea's impact on the music of his time cannot be ignored, and his compositions helped establish the style for which his nephew Giovanni Gabrieli ultimately gained great success. Although somewhat overshadowed by the work of his nephew, Andrea's influence as the younger Gabrieli's teacher is in itself worthy of note. Unfortunately, a complete English-language study of his life and works does not as yet exist, and the hit-and-miss nature of the English-language scholarly work available on Andrea Gabrieli is something of a hindrance to studying this very important musician. The available English-language scholarship does, however, yield a fair amount of information on his biography and specific areas of compositional activity. The titles listed here constitute a select representation of secondary sources for Andrea Gabrieli.

BENZONI et al. provides the most recent information available for the study of this composer. The work is in Italian, but the three main articles are summarized in English. Benzoni's "Venice at the Time of Andrea Gabrieli" concentrates on the political, religious, and social atmosphere of 16th-century Venice. "Music in Venice at the Time of Andrea Gabrieli," by David Bryant and Martin Morell, discusses the role of music in 16th-century Venetian ceremony. The musical activity sponsored by the *scuole grandi* is a primary topic, and there is also mention of music patronage by the city's elite. "Andrea Gabrieli: A Documentary Biography," by Bryant and Morell, includes revised information on the composer's life, much of it stemming from the study of recent archival discoveries. This most accurate biography of Andrea Gabrieli includes discussion of his popularity and his professional relationship with Orlando di Lasso. Although the remaining portions of this volume are not translated, the time line, lists of prints and manuscripts, and catalog of works should still be accessible. Forthcoming volumes of the series will include commentary on Andrea Gabrieli's compositional output. Gabrieli's compositions are being organized into two additional series, one for collections published during his lifetime and a second for posthumous prints, anthologies, and manuscript sources.

DEGRADA, the proceedings of a congress convened in Venice on 16–18 September 1985 to commemorate the 400th anniversary of the composer's death, is a collection of 16 essays, including seven in English. Unfortunately, no translations or summaries are provided for the nine Italian-language articles. The English-language articles include two essays, one each by Denis Arnold and Jerome Roche, on two collections of Andrea's single-choir motets published in 1565 and 1576. Arnold includes some discussion of individual works and connects these collections stylistically to Lasso. The author concludes that the 1565 collection was written for Munich and that these works were aimed at a "narrower, Venetian audience," particularly the confraternities and lesser-known Venetian churches. Roche, in his

"Liturgical Aspects of the Motets of Andrea Gabrieli Published in 1565 and 1576," also connects these works to Lasso but states that these collections were aimed at the broader north Italian market. Roche addresses each work with regards to its liturgical function. A. Tillman Merritt's "Apropos of Andrea Gabrieli's Madrigals" presents an overview of the composer's secular vocal output. According to Merritt, "the quantity and the variety of his secular vocal pieces hint strongly that his heart was especially in this area of composition." Merritt includes information on the composer's *greghesche* and *giustiniane,* wedding and battle songs, his interest in French secular music, and Giovanni's role in the publication of his uncle's secular works. In "Andrea Gabrieli and the Early History of the Toccata," Murray Bradshaw concludes that the composer's works "mirror the entire development of the 16th-century Venetian toccata from early, straightforward pieces to later, more sophisticated ones." Following an analysis of Andrea's eight extant examples, Bradshaw organizes the composer's toccata output into three eras. The author then uses his analysis to examine the entire 16th-century toccata repertoire. This essay is related to a larger, earlier work by Bradshaw, *The Origin of the Toccata,* discussed below. The remaining English-language essays are on topics that are largely nonspecific to Andrea Gabrieli. Rebecca Edwards contributes an essay, "An Expanded Musical and Social Context for Andrea Gabrieli: New Documents, New Perspectives," that discusses the importance of Venice in the Renaissance and the treatment of Venetian musicians. Jonathan Glixon's "Music at the Scuole in the Age of Andrea Gabrieli" considers Venetian centers of musical interest beyond the San Marco chapel. The 1571 Christian naval victory off Lepanto sparked annual celebrations for which composers (including Gabrieli) were commissioned to contribute special compositions—this is the subject of Iain Fenlon's essay, "The Victory of Lepanto in Sixteenth-Century Music and Letters." The Italian-language essays in this publication include a biography by Martin Morell and additional articles on Gabrieli's secular works and keyboard compositions.

BRADSHAW contains a considerable amount of information on Andrea's extant works in this genre. In addition to a discussion of the origins and development of the genre, an appendix includes transcriptions of eight of the composer's extant *intonatione* and four of his toccatas. Andrea and Giovanni Gabrieli are the focus of much of Bradshaw's attention, but works by many others are woven into the discussion.

Studies of Giovanni Gabrieli also contain information on Andrea. ARNOLD includes a substantial amount of information in the first chapter, "The Formative Years," discussing the relationship between Andrea and Lasso, Andrea's ceremonial music, and the relationship between uncle and nephew. In light of the more recent studies,

some of the information provided in this source should be regarded as dated.

Andrea Gabrieli is also discussed in CARVER, who credits the composer with the founding of the Venetian polychoral style. Like a number of authors mentioned previously, Carver discusses professional and stylistic links with Lasso. Separate sections in this chapter address the 1587 concerti, Lepanto motets, spatial writing in Andrea's polychoral music, cadential dissonance, psalm motets and the Magnificat, his mature antiphonal technique, and the Mass movements.

The opening chapter of LANDON and NORWICH includes a discussion of both Gabrielis and the role of music in 16th-century Venetian society and politics. Some of the information on Andrea is not reflective of more recent biographical research. In addition to a discussion of the ties between the Gabrielis and Lasso, there is a very brief general discussion of Andrea's music.

DANE HEUCHEMER

Gabrieli, Giovanni ca. 1554–1612

Italian composer

Arnold, Denis, *Giovanni Gabrieli and the Music of the Venetian High Renaissance,* London: Oxford University Press, 1979

Kenton, Egon, *Life and Works of Giovanni Gabrieli,* N.p.: American Institute of Musicology, 1967

Selfridge-Field, Eleanor, *Venetian Instrumental Music from Gabrieli to Vivaldi,* New York: Praegar, and Oxford: Blackwell, 1975; 3rd revised edition, New York: Dover, 1994

Giovanni Gabrieli, the nephew of Andrea Gabrieli, was one of the many great musicians that graced, enriched, and exalted Venetian music around the turn of the 17th century. He studied with his uncle and, after spending a few years at the Bavarian ducal court in Munich, was appointed organist at St. Mark's Basilica in Venice in 1585, a post he held until his death. The first study of Giovanni Gabrieli's music was by the German scholar Carl von Winterfeld (1784–1852), who transcribed by hand all of Gabrieli's music. Winterfeld's focus, however, was on the music for church and state, and he almost totally disregarded the works for instrumental ensemble and keyboard and the madrigals. The next comprehensive study, by Kenton, began as an attempt to translate Winterfeld's study, until Kenton realized that a new investigation was needed. After Kenton, Arnold began his decades-long series of writings on Gabrieli, most of which are in article form. A few unpublished dissertations, such as that by J.A. Flower titled "Giovanni Gabrieli's *Sacrae Symphoniae,* 1597" (University of Michigan, 1955) have also tackled the composer's repertoire. Kenton's book is the only one totally dedicated to Giovanni. The reason Gabrieli's music has been often disregarded or deemed unworthy of scholarly exegesis may be the unusual mixture of innovative and conservative facets in his works (as Arnold states, he was "a religious composer in a secular age and a purely instrumental one at a time when the most important genres are impure combinations of diverse arts"). Some recent manuscript discoveries and new attributions can be found in Richard Charteris's *Giovanni Gabrieli: A Thematic Catalogue of His Music with a Guide to the Source Materials and Translations of His Vocal Texts* (Pendragon Press, 1996).

ARNOLD is a comprehensive study of Gabrieli's life and music. The book is subdivided into chapters dealing with Gabrieli's life, his music, and his legacy as a teacher. The chapters dedicated to his music examine it by genre and in approximate chronological order: from the early organ works and the early music for Venice; through the grand ceremonial music, the early instrumental music, and that for the Scuola Grande di San Rocco; and finally to the madrigals and the later instrumental and church music. The book brings together newly discovered documents such as those from the account books of St. Mark's and those from the books of the Scuola Grande di S. Rocco; the discussion of Gabrieli's music for the confraternity of the Scuola Grande di S. Rocco is especially unique and enlightening.

In the chapters dedicated to Gabrieli's life, Arnold discusses the composer's biography within the framework of his predecessors, contemporaries, and the circumstances surrounding Gabrieli's life. For example, in the chapter dedicated to Gabrieli's service at St. Mark's, Arnold pays great attention to the position Gabrieli held and the duties associated with it; the author surveys all the ceremonies and occasions that demanded music (and identifies which kind of music was wanted), and he discusses Gabrieli's colleagues in the other positions at the basilica. Likewise, in the chapters dedicated to the composer's music, an assessment of the forces and instruments available, and of the techniques and traditions that affect music writing and making, precedes and accompanies the discussion of Gabrieli's compositions. For example, when analyzing the canzona, Arnold discusses first the genre in general, then addresses Merulo's and Andrea Gabrieli's canzonas, and finally, at greatest length, evaluates Giovanni's canzonas. Canzonas are again treated later in the book, feature by feature—virtuosity, concerto-like elements, formal design, and so forth.

KENTON's impressive tome places the music of Gabrieli in historical context and thus includes a discussion of Venice and St. Mark's music from their foundation. The author assesses then the life of Gabrieli and his reputation throughout the ages. The discussion is based first on existing documents and then on hypotheses based on existing sources. Kenton dedicates more than one-quarter of his book to a catalog of Gabrieli's works, comprising information about the early prints and manuscripts and the modern reprints, and a thematic index. The second half of the book is dedicated to a detailed review of Gabrieli's music, genre by genre—first the choral works, then the madrigals, and finally the instrumental works for organ and for ensembles. After a concluding discussion, four appendices list sources, names, subjects, and plates.

Kenton's treatment of the music is technical, but it is not so full of jargon as to alienate the average music enthusiast. In a fully accessible and yet accurate scholarly language, the author examines first the history of each genre up to the time when Gabrieli began composing in that mode and then describes Gabrieli's contribution by creating a typology and by analyzing representative pieces in each category. Considerable attention is also given to the texts of vocal compositions. The study is complemented with numerous musical examples. Kenton's concluding discussion of Gabrieli's historical role summarizes what the author sees as innovative and experimental in the composer's music, the formal aspects of his compositions, the chronological development of his style, and other elements, all placed in the larger historical and musical contexts.

Although SELFRIDGE-FIELD's book is not devoted entirely to Gabrieli, it includes a comprehensive if brief discussion of the composer's instrumental works and of their surroundings. The book is divided into two unequal parts. The shorter first section comprises two chapters on the history of instrumental music at St. Mark's and elsewhere in Venice, based on documentary evidence. The second section, titled "A History of Musical Style" and comprising 11 chapters, considers Venetian instrumental music before Gabrieli; Gabrieli's music itself; and finally, each genre as developed by different composers. Albinoni, Vivaldi, and the Marcellos are each discussed in individual chapters. The latest Dover edition of Selfridge-Field's book has an additional 40 pages addressing newer scholarship and additions since the book was first published. The discussion of Venetian instrumental music before Gabrieli draws on examples by both contemporary composers and theorists and outlines clearly the tradition in which Gabrieli began composing. The chapter on Gabrieli examines each separate genre in chronological order. The discussion is mostly descriptive and comparative rather than analytical. The only drawback to this study is that the author only identifies works by their numbers, often without musical examples, assuming easy accessibility to scores. Gabrieli's music is unfortunately not well known enough for people to know immediately the pieces to which Selfridge-Field refers. The points she makes, however, are clear even without looking at the music.

ALEXANDRA AMATI-CAMPERI

Gershwin, George 1898–1937

United States composer and pianist

Alpert, Hollis, *The Life and Times of Porgy and Bess: The Story of an American Classic,* New York: Knopf, 1990

Gershwin, Ira, *Lyrics on Several Occasions: A Selection of Stage and Screen Lyrics,* New York: Knopf, 1959

Gilbert, Steven E., *The Music of Gershwin,* New Haven, Connecticut: Yale University Press, 1995

Goldberg, Isaac, *George Gershwin: A Study in American Music,* New York: Simon and Schuster, 1931; new edition, New York: Ungar, 1958

Jablonski, Edward, *Gershwin,* New York: Doubleday, 1987

————, *Gershwin Remembered,* Portland, Oregon: Amadeus Press, 1992

Peyser, Joan, *The Memory of All That: The Life of George Gershwin,* New York: Simon and Schuster, 1993

Rosenberg, Deena, *Fascinating Rhythm: The Collaboration of George and Ira Gershwin,* New York: Dutton, 1991

Schiff, David, *Gershwin, Rhapsody in Blue,* Cambridge: Cambridge University Press, 1997

Schneider, Wayne Joseph, editor, *The Gershwin Style: New Looks at the Music of George Gershwin,* New York: Oxford University Press, 1999

Schwartz, Charles, *Gershwin: His Life and Music,* Indianapolis, Indiana: Bobbs-Merrill, 1973

Although George Gershwin has enjoyed an extraordinary amount of journalistic and other nonscholarly attention, as well as several important biographical treatments, the most substantial critical, source, and analytical studies (many on Gershwin's solitary opera, *Porgy and Bess*), which began to flourish in the 1970s and 1980s, have debuted in journals rather than books. A short list might include Richard Crawford on Gershwin's critical position in music history (*Yearbook for Inter-American Musical Research* [1972] and *Musical Quarterly* [1979]), Wayne Shirley on *Porgy and Bess* manuscripts (*Quarterly Journal of the Library of Congress* [1974; 1981]), Lawrence Starr on analysis and criticism of *Porgy and Bess* (*American Music* [1984] and *Musical Quarterly* [1986]), and Charles Hamm on the production history of *Porgy and Bess* (*Journal of the American Musicological Society* [1987]). Most of the major books on Gershwin's life and music did not appear until the late 1980s, and this interest will most likely continue in the wake of the centennial of the composer's birth.

GOLDBERG, who had considerable cooperation from his subject, including numerous conversations with George and "the untiring assistance" of Ira (George's brother and principal lyricist after 1924), offers a biographical portrait of a living composer that provides a repository of anecdotes and facts that set the tone for years to come. This first biography of Gershwin features descriptive and musically illustrated discussions of virtually all the instrumental works through the Second Rhapsody, including the then "underestimated and overlooked" Preludes, but it contains comparatively little on the musical shows. Goldberg died one year after Gershwin, and Edith Garson's posthumous supplementary summary of the years 1931 to 1937 did not appear until 1958.

Ira GERSHWIN's subtitle goes a long way toward capturing the topics and atmosphere of this famous book. His commentary provides privileged information about the historical and compositional genesis, practical and artistic goals, and priceless backstage anecdotes concerning dozens of songs he composed with his more famous brother. Lyrics for the verses and at least one full chorus are included with each discussion.

SCHWARTZ is the first comprehensive Gershwin biography and remains the most thoughtfully critical study of the composer's life, music, and personality. Other than some brief remarks in an appendix, however, the author focuses even less on the music than does Goldberg. Perhaps in reaction to earlier biographies such as Goldberg's, which tend toward hagiography, Schwartz depicts an overpraised composer and pianist lacking in both technique and substance and a composer whose "sophisticated handling of material" is "far outweighed by examples of musical crudities." Although not yet the monster described by Peyser, Schwartz's Gershwin is a man with deep and fundamental personal flaws, and this biographical treatment tends to dwell, perhaps excessively, on Gershwin's less desirable characteristics. Despite this bias, Schwartz's biography is thorough, well documented, and copiously annotated, and contains a comprehensive bibliography that has yet to be surpassed.

In contrast to both Goldberg and Schwartz, JABLONSKI (1987) takes a neutral position and instead allows the principal players to speak for themselves through liberal excerpts from contemporary conversations and printed documents, as well as family sources such as George's letters and Ira's diaries. The author adds considerably to Schwartz's earlier biographical portrait and offers a rich non-analytic compositional history of numerous works, especially *Porgy and Bess*. Perhaps most valuably, he concludes with an epilogue that surveys Ira's career throughout the 50 years that he survived his brother, first as a lyricist for the two decades following George's death and later as an active archivist and spokesman who helped formulate a potent Gershwin legend.

ALPERT's study of *Porgy and Bess* is notable as the first book-length treatment of a Gershwin work. A social survey that manages to eschew serious discussion of aesthetic and analytical issues explored by Crawford, Hamm, Shirley, and Starr, Alpert devotes considerable space to the origins of Gershwin's opera as a real-life incident involving a "crippled beggar" in 1924, and the evolution from DuBose Heyward's successful novel (1925) and play (written in collaboration with his wife Dorothy, 1927). Of undeniable importance is Alpert's extensive consideration of several important reincarnations of the opera after 1935, especially the Robert Breen-Blevins Davis world tour in the 1950s, the preproduction history of the Samuel Goldwyn film (1959), and the Metropolitan and Glyndebourne Opera productions in the late 1980s.

Unlike her predecessors, ROSENBERG devotes most of her attention to the songs George wrote with Ira between 1918 and 1937. Also more than previous authors, she examines the relationship between music and lyrics and the nature of collaboration. The accessible and frequently illustrated analytical discussions tend to emphasize the melodic connections from one song to another.

JABLONSKI (1992) presents arguably the most thoughtfully selected, well-organized, and helpfully annotated collection of reminiscences from Gershwin's contemporaries (and, in a short appendix, from Gershwin himself). Included among the nine chapters are topics ranging from "Boyhood and Musical Training" to "The Creation of Porgy and Bess" to "Gershwin and Art." Jablonski has also assembled a well-chosen, if not always generous, selection of contemporary critical assessments of individual works and, in "The Pundits: Pro and Con," of Gershwin's career as a whole.

PEYSER's unflattering psychobiography continues where Schwartz leaves off. Drawing for the first time on extensive interviews with George's last surviving sibling (Frances Godowsky), his valet and chauffeur, alleged illegitimate son, and descendants of Pauline Heifetz (Jascha's sister) and Kay Swift, among others, Peyser offers a plausible case that George did father at least one child out of wedlock and that the symptoms leading to Gershwin's inoperable brain tumor might have been detected soon enough to avoid a catastrophe. Despite her willingness to address and respond to difficult issue—for example, critical responses to Gershwin driven by anti-Semitism or Gershwin's own alleged racial insensitivity—Peyser rarely provides rigorous documentation or fully persuasive arguments to support her devastating portrait of Gershwin and most of his family.

GILBERT's study is the first book to address the major instrumental works (and several vocal works) in analytical detail. The technical language and numerous Schenkerian graphs will make this book inaccessible to many, especially when confronting the detailed dissections of songs. The most valuable portions of Gilbert's analysis are his overviews of Gershwin's larger concert works and Porgy and Bess. Here, in contrast to the minutiae that too often clouds the discussions of songs, detail enhances rather than overwhelms an often original and insightful approach to these works.

SCHIFF offers a brief but useful and exceptionally readable guide to Gershwin's best-known instrumental work. The author faces and sheds considerable light on the many controversies that surround Rhapsody in Blue,

including its identity and formal integrity in the face of multiple published versions, its stylistic classification and make-up, and its artistic merits. He also discusses Rhapsody in Blue in the context of the concert in which it premiered in 1924, surveys important interpretations of the work from Gershwin's own to jazz performances by Duke Ellington and Marcus Roberts, and traces the work's influence on Gershwin's subsequent pieces with orchestra and piano, and on Ravel's Piano Concerto in G, James P. Johnson's Yamekraw, and Ellington's Creole Rhapsody. Finally, Schiff thoughtfully examines the ideological framework behind the reception history of Gershwin's work from the composer's time to the 1990s.

SCHNEIDER is a varied anthology of 12 essays, the first such collection devoted to Gershwin. After a thoughtful introduction by Charles Hamm (reprinted from Putting Popular Music in Its Place [1995]), five established Gershwin scholars offer important and frequently insightful analyses and manuscript studies of individual works. There are essays on Porgy and Bess (Wayne Shirley) and Blue Monday (John Andrew Johnson), essays that explore the complex relationship between Gershwin's melodies and large-scale forms (Wayne Schneider's treatment of the operetta overtures and Larry Starr's comparative study of Rhapsody in Blue and An American in Paris), and an essay that scrutinizes the manuscript and stylistic issues in Gershwin's last songs (Steven E. Gilbert). The three essays on reception consider critical meanings and issues in the film biography Rhapsody in Blue (Charlotte Greenspan), Gershwin and popular music (Susan Richardson), and Gershwin and jazz (André Barbera). The volume concludes with Artis Wodehouse's historical and technical essay on Gershwin's piano rolls, Michael Montgomery's comprehensive piano rollography, and Edward Jablonski's revisitation of Ira Gershwin's creative life (including his subsequent professional use of his brother's unpublished songs).

GEOFFREY BLOCK

Gesualdo, Carlo ca. 1560–1613

Italian composer

Burney, Charles, A General History of Music from the Earliest Ages to the Present Period (1789), 2 vols., edited by Frank Mercer, New York: Harcourt Brace, 1935

Einstein, Alfred, The Italian Madrigal, 3 vols., translated by Alexander H. Krappe, et al., Princeton, New Jersey: Princeton University Press, 1949

Gray, Cecil, and Philip Heseltine, Carlo Gesualdo, Prince of Venosa, Musician and Murderer, London: Paul, Trench, Trubner, and New York: Dial Press, 1926; reprint, Westport, Connecticut: Greenwood Press, 1975

Maniates, Maria Rika, *Mannerism in Italian Music and Culture: 1530–1630,* Chapel Hill: University of North Carolina Press, and Manchester: Manchester University Press, 1979

Newcomb, Anthony, *The Madrigal at Ferrara: 1579–1597,* 2 vols., Princeton, New Jersey: Princeton University Press, 1978

Watkins, Glenn, *Gesualdo: The Man and His Music,* London: Oxford University Press, 1973; 2nd edition, Oxford: Clarendon Press, and New York: Oxford University Press, 1991

The music of Don Carlo Gesualdo maintains an interesting and controversial position in the history of Western music. Long famous for both the intensity and audacity of its expressive means, Gesualdo's style has elicited critical responses ranging from credit for creating "the sweetest modulations conceivable" to abrupt dismissals as "forced, affected, and disgusting." The reasons for this dichotomy of opinion are easy to identify. First, Gesualdo composed most of his music in the 1590s, a time now viewed as one of transition from the linear modal principles of the Renaissance to the harmonic practices of early baroque monody. Yet Gesualdo's music often seems to stand outside either style. Broad passages of chordal textures featuring dissonant, chromatic harmony stand side by side with passages of elegant, diatonic counterpoint. Second, Gesualdo's noble social status effectively forbade the open practice of any profession, including that of composer. Thus, he is sometimes dismissed as an inept amateur. Finally, the sensational story of his murder of his first wife and her lover in 1590, along with subsequent reports of erratic behavior, have made it all too easy to view Gesualdo's output as the product of an unbalanced mind. Analyses of his music and its significance have employed a variety of methods, and critical assessments have offered widely divergent conclusions.

Most of the important research and critical appraisal of Gesualdo's music has been presented in the periodical literature (much of it in Italian and German), in dissertations, and in short sections of broad surveys covering the madrigal and Italian Renaissance culture. There are only two scholarly, book-length studies in English; consequently, included here is a discussion of a few books that, while they treat Gesualdo only briefly, either provide important contexts for the study of his music or have had significant influence on its critical reception.

Gesualdo's music was almost universally admired by his contemporaries for both its technical perfection and its expressive qualities. The Gesualdo "controversy" was the product of a later age, apparently initiated by BURNEY in his late 18th-century history. Burney denies Gesualdo any praise for the effectiveness of his expression of the text, dismisses him as a an incompetent amateur, and furnishes a score of *Moro lasso* (still one of the madrigals most often discussed) in order to provide the reader with "a specimen of his . . . harsh, crude, and licentious modulation." Burney analyzes the first two chords only and finds their relationship "not only repugnant to every rule of transition at present established, but extremely shocking and disgusting to the ear." Burney's negative judgment is obviously based on his inability to reconcile Gesualdo's chord succession to the rules of tonal harmonic progression. His verdict has been echoed by analysts up to and including the 20th century, primarily by those who have attempted analyses according to the concepts of major/minor tonality.

GRAY and HESELTINE were the first to publish a book-length study of Gesualdo in English. In the biographical portion of the book, Gray presents for the first time many important documents, including four letters to the prince from the poet Torquato Tasso and court records from the inquiry into the murder. Clearly fascinated by this sensational story, Gray spends 30 pages of his 50-page biographical essay on this topic and adds another 12-page section analyzing the aesthetic merits of Gesualdo's performance as a murderer. In his discussion of the music, Heseltine spends much time providing historical justification for Gesualdo's style but concludes that Gesualdo's music is "the vivid and passionate expression of a strange personality." Gray and Heseltine's interpretation of Gesualdo's works as isolated products of a diseased mind has colored several critical evaluations, but it has also inspired scholars to search for a broader context for Gesualdo's style.

EINSTEIN's classic study of the Italian madrigal presents Gesualdo in the context of his time. Still valuable because of the quality of its insights, this work is the first modern, sustained analysis of the madrigals.

MANIATES attempts to place Gesualdo in the context of a broad "mannerist culture" that includes many 16th-century madrigalists, as well as poets such as Tasso and painters such as El Greco. Although her plea for a Mannerist musical period has gone largely unheeded, her research on Renaissance critical concepts such as *maniera* and *musica reservata* is quite valuable, as is her extensive bibliography.

NEWCOMB provides much information on musical life in the Este court at Ferrara, where Gesualdo spent time in 1594 in connection with his second marriage, and where he published his first four books of madrigals. In a chapter titled "The New Ferrarese Style of the 1590s," the author situates the new stylistic features seen in Gesualdo's third and fourth books of madrigals in the context of contemporary practices advanced by Luzzasco Luzzaschi and Giaches Wert.

The most extensive and balanced treatment of Gesualdo's life and works is WATKINS. His is a true "foundation biography," providing both a biographical and a cultural context for Gesualdo's music. Watkins's bibliography is comprehensive, containing all known primary sources and every significant secondary source published to 1990. The author analyzes all of the music, both sacred and secular, and takes into account the work of numerous scholars using many approaches. Summing up four centuries of criticism, Watkins concludes that it is too early to reach a final assessment of Gesualdo.

MARK BENSON

Gilbert, William Schwenck 1836–1911

and

Sullivan, Arthur 1842–1900

English librettist and writer/English composer

Baily, Leslie, *The Gilbert and Sullivan Book,* London: Cassell, 1952; revised edition London: Spring, 1966

Fischler, Alan, *Modified Rapture: Comedy in W.S. Gilbert's Savoy Operas,* Charlottesville: University Press of Virginia, 1991

Helyar, James, *Gilbert and Sullivan: Papers Presented at the International Conference,* Lawrence: University of Kansas Libraries, 1970

Hughes, Gervase, *The Music of Arthur Sullivan,* London: Macmillan, and New York: St. Martin's Press, 1960

Jacobs, Arthur, *Arthur Sullivan: A Victorian Musician,* Oxford: Oxford University Press, 1984; 2nd edition, Portland, Oregon: Amadeus Press, 1992

Stedman, Jane W., *W.S. Gilbert: A Classic Victorian and His Theatre,* Oxford: Oxford University Press, 1996

Traubner, Richard, *Operetta: A Theatrical History,* New York: Doubleday, 1983

Williamson, Audrey, *Gilbert and Sullivan Opera: A New Assessment,* London: Rockliff, and New York: Macmillan, 1953; revised edition, London: Boyars, 1982

Numerous books have been published about the works of Arthur Sullivan and William Schwenk Gilbert. They include concordances, bibliographies, and guides of all types. Most of them principally concern the 14 Savoy operas on which the two men collaborated between 1871 and 1896. However, as their contemporaries knew and an increasing number of 20th-century scholars are discovering, each man had an extensive and popularly acclaimed repertoire of work to his individual credit as well. Those interested in Gilbert's words are fortunate to have Ian Bradley's *The Complete Annotated Gilbert and Sullivan* (Oxford University Press, 1996) available to them (although it is sadly lacking the text to *Thespis,* the partners' first collaboration, for which almost no music survives). Most of Sullivan's music for the Savoy operas is readily available in piano-vocal scores, and there is a fine catalog of recordings. Unfortunately, the operas are not generally available in full scores suitable for careful study.

In her biography of Gilbert, STEDMAN seeks to "reconstruct the life of a nineteenth-century man of the theatre . . . a dramatist produced and stimulated by the Victorian theatre, but transcending it." Stedman draws on a range of documents penned by and about Gilbert, now scattered in various library collections, as well as contemporary newspapers. Her intent is to avoid repeating mistakes set down in earlier biographies, among them the humorous anecdotes attributed to Gilbert that had previously been attributed to H.J. Byron, the founding editor of the comic magazine *Fun* and Gilbert's employer in the 1860s. Gilbert's theatrical career is sufficiently varied and surprising without them, and Stedman's research provides plenty of telling details (including information about financial transactions, which were of course vitally important to those who had to earn a living amusing others). For those interested in biographical and autobiographical material about the original Savoyards, including leading actors Rutland Barrington and Jessie Bond, Stedman's bibliography lists many selections for further reading.

JACOBS's biography of Sullivan is equally painstaking, reproducing extensive passages from the composer's own diaries (often quoted only briefly elsewhere). In his complicated (and not always perfectly proper) life, Sullivan encountered many important figures in 19th-century European musical life, as well as the Prince of Wales and other members of the aristocracy, who admired both Sullivan's music and his personal charm. Sullivan's status as a composer has, as Jacobs notes, fluctuated enormously, with critics divided between appreciation of the Savoy operas and dismissal of them as empty amusements. Those seriously interested in Sullivan's music will want to consult the works list at the end of Jacobs's biography.

TRAUBNER's chapter on Gilbert and Sullivan is located at almost the exact center of the volume, and his account places the Savoy operas ("simply the best musical productions of the Victorian age") in their larger European context, following Jacques Offenbach's Parisian opéra bouffes. During his early stage career, Gilbert wrote comic "translations" of Offenbach numbers, and Sullivan knew the French composer's music well. A survey covering operetta from its apparent origins in 18th-century comic opera through its offspring the Broadway musical, Traubner's account provides a brief summary of each of the operas, together with illustrations drawn from various productions and bits of production history, although he is dismissive of Sullivan and Sullivan's other work. He attributes the Savoy operas' continued popularity to their "*intelligence* . . . musically and literarily."

For anecdotes, illustrations, and notes on performances of all types during the first half of the 20th century, BAILY is a treasure trove for the theater history buff. Those who are only familiar with fairly conventional performances of the operas will be intrigued by the "jazzed" versions performed in Berlin and New York and other very nontraditional productions.

WILLIAMSON's study of the Savoy operas includes a brief history of and commentary on each of the operas, including short musical examples and performance and production notes. Williamson's inclusion of musical examples and attention to performance details separates her assessment from the many guides to the operas that focus on explaining the plot and add a few good "First-Night-at-the-Savoy" anecdotes (although these other guides can also be fun, and many of them have beautiful illustrations, unlike Williamson's work, which has only a few).

In his introduction HUGHES complains of the lack of "full-length studies" of the composer's music. This comment was made in 1963. Were he to write today, however, he might well still complain. Hughes's work itself is not long, but his attempts to address Sullivan's music by examining basic elements including rhythm, text setting, harmony, counterpoint, melody, and orchestration (with musical examples) will be appreciated by those who have survived their first round of music theory courses. Hughes suggests reading through his work with the vocal scores of the operas at hand (one might add a piano as well, to play through the sections he excerpts for special mention). Throughout, Hughes alludes to the continental composers (including Mozart, Mendelssohn, Berlioz, Bizet, and Verdi) who may have inspired Sullivan's work and demonstrates the very real effect the composer's international training and experiences had on his music.

The collection of papers edited by HELYAR indicates some of the directions Gilbert and Sullivan scholarship has taken: Sullivan's hymn writing; Sullivan's overtures for the Savoy operas (some were written with the help of assistants who orchestrated Sullivan's sketches); collecting and editing the Bab Ballads (comic poems that were the original source for some of Gilbert's later Savoy plots); and Gilbert's techniques as a director (Gilbert not only wrote the Savoy operas, he drilled the company in rehearsal). Although these papers have been published by a university press, most Gilbert and Sullivan scholars do not take themselves too seriously, and as a result, several of the essays are witty, brief, and open-ended.

Part of a series titled "Victorian Literature and Culture," FISCHLER's work is the most overtly scholarly of the books cited here. Fischler argues that the Savoy operas represented a new approach to comedy for the Victorian theater in which "human law was established as a substitute for Providence . . . [and] meted out rewards and punishments in infallible accord with the duty-based morality that the middle class professed." The plot of any Savoy opera usually hangs somehow on a point of law—Fischler examines the whys and wherefores, as well as analyzing some of the explanations that have been previously offered for the Savoy operas' enduring popularity.

KATHRYN LOWERRE

Glass, Philip b. 1937

United States composer

Glass, Philip, *Music by Philip Glass,* edited by Robert T. Jones, New York: Harper and Row, 1987

Kostelanetz, Richard, and Robert Flemming, editors, *Writings on Glass: Essays, Interviews, Criticism,* New York: Schirmer Books, and London: Prentice Hall, 1997

Mertens, Wim, *American Minimal Music: La Monte Young, Terry Riley, Steve Reich, Philip Glass,* translated by J. Hautekiet, London: Kahn and Averill, and New York: Broude Brothers, 1983

Neveldine, Robert Burns, *Bodies at Risk: Unsafe Limits in Romanticism and Postmodernism,* Albany: State University of New York Press, 1998

Nyman, Michael, *Experimental Music: Cage and Beyond,* London: Studio Vista, and New York: Schirmer Books, 1974

Rockwell, John, *All American Music: Composition in the Late Twentieth Century,* New York: Knopf, 1983

Strickland, Edward, *Minimalism—Origins,* Bloomington: Indiana University Press, 1993

The 1960s musical movement known as minimalism—a designation that its practitioners have only grudgingly come to accept, and then only with qualifications—has attracted a wide audience, and Philip Glass in particular has enjoyed a level of recognition that bridges into popular mainstream culture. Regardless of the preferred signifier (early critics used terms such as *process music, trance music,* or even, somewhat cruelly, *stuck-record music*), these compositions share repetition as a major stylistic component. Compared to the amount of scholarly material published for other composers who are currently active, the output devoted to Glass and his music is unmatched by few, if any, figures from the contemporary music scene (within either concert hall or popular venues). In addition to being perhaps the most important American composer of opera of the last quarter of the 20th century, and thereby establishing his stature within elite musical culture, Glass also has a strong presence within vernacular culture. Coming to terms with Glass's output, then, often demands the careful consideration of complex aesthetic and cultural factors, and so one can find exegeses of Glass's work by cultural critics as well as the usual suspects of music critics, historians, and theorists.

NYMAN was one of the first writers to discuss the minimalist composers as a school unto themselves, chronicling the early works by the now-familiar tetrarchy of LaMonte Young, Terry Riley, Glass, and Steve Reich. An English composer of noteworthy film scores that demonstrate deep affinities for American minimalism, Nyman covers works from 1968 to 1971 in his chapter on minimal music and includes musical examples from *One + One* and *Music in Changing Parts.* His use of numbers to illustrate Glass's additive rhythm process in *Music in Fifths* is an especially clear way of describing that piece to the nonmusician.

ROCKWELL, a music critic, writes a mostly sympathetic account of Glass's rise to fame by the early 1980s, although he repeatedly makes the point, with the raised eyebrow of italics, that "people *like* this music." The highly accessible essay "The Orient, the Visual Arts, and the Evolution of Minimalism" effectively mixes biographical material with issues of aesthetics and reception. Some of Rockwell's terminology (e.g., "serious" music and "Oriental" music) has been problematized and rearticulated by later critics. This essay will prove valuable for anyone constructing a reception history of Glass and minimalism.

MERTENS's monograph on American minimalism contains numerous musical examples and insightful analytical remarks about Glass's music from *Strung Out* (1967) through *Satyagraha* (1980). The author attempts to trace the basic concepts of minimal music, focusing particularly on process as a compositional determinant. Mertens offers a historical model of 20th-century music that leads from Schoenberg to Webern to Stockhausen to Cage, ultimately culminating in minimalism. He also includes a succinct ideological analysis of minimalism that utilizes the critical writings of cultural commentators such as Adorno, Lyotard, Deleuze, Derrida, and Marcuse.

GLASS's own contribution to this list is an insightful book that focuses primarily on the three portrait operas, *Einstein on the Beach, Satyagraha,* and *Akhnaten.* He includes remarks about the compositions that led up to these operas and the works that follow them, up through 1987. The volume also contains the composer's recollections of the genesis of each opera, including glimpses into his collaborative methods. (Glass's career has been marked throughout by notable collaborations with some of the most fascinating and provocative creative minds in theater, opera, dance, literature, and film.) The book features selected musical examples, with commentary by Glass himself, along with photographs and complete librettos of the three focal operas. While some may wonder how much of this memoir came from the editor as opposed to the author, editor Jones assures the reader that, in this case, the text was "not 'ghost'-written, dictated, or 'told to'."

The term *minimalism* did not originate in music; instead, it came from the visual arts, and STRICKLAND's work reveals musical and visual minimalism's commonalities, blending art history, music history, and aesthetic and cultural criticism. Thoroughly researched, the study gives the history of the individuals, the works, and even the early reception history of minimalism (e.g., one chapter details how the term came to be applied to this music). Strickland's work is especially useful for situating Glass's output in the context of his fellow minimalist composers,

painters, and sculptors. The chapters are labeled with the progressing letters of the alphabet (minimalist art was earlier called "ABC Art"), and there is an index, which does not, unfortunately, contain references to specific works. The engaging, succinct prose will appeal to all levels of readers, and the bibliography is exhaustive.

The finest single book presently available on Glass's entire career to date, KOSTELANETZ and FLEMMING's collection consists of interviews and reprints of articles, reviews, and book chapters. After an opening overview section—containing Ev Grimes's interview on Glass's education, which Kostelanetz calls the fullest interview known to him—the anthology proceeds in approximate chronological order, often with articles addressing single works. This book is notable for its exceptional range of difficulty and tone, including both journalistic writing originally intended for a wide audience and more specialized and complex musical analyses (there are musical and analytical examples for the 1966 String Quartet, *Two Pages,* and *Akhnaten*). One of the nicer editorial touches is the placement of a negative review (of 1992's *The Voyage*) immediately after a positive article on the same work. An authoritative work list covers the years 1965–94, and the meticulous index includes specific works.

While some historians view minimalism as one of the final stages of high modernism (particularly in its more extreme, avant-garde manifestations from the 1960s), others see it as one of the first postmodern musical movements. NEVELDINE pursues such a postmodern reading of Glass's music. His section on Glass includes analyses of *Mishima, Akhnaten,* and a particularly fine reading of the film and score, *Koyaanisqatsi.* Neveldine's project does not include formal musical analysis, but those familiar with poststructural and postmodern criticism will find his prose accessible; his application of these methods to Glass's music is original and often persuasive.

NEIL LERNER

Glazunov, Alexander 1865–1936

Russian composer

Asaf'ev, Boris Vladimirovich, *Russian Music from the Beginning of the Nineteenth Century,* translated by Alfred J. Swan, Ann Arbor, Michigan: Edwards, 1953

Calvocoressi, Michel D., *A Survey of Russian Music,* Middlesex: Penguin Books, 1944; reprint, New York: Greenwood Press, 1974

Calvocoressi, Michel D., and Gerald Abraham, *Masters of Russian Music,* New York: Knopf, 1936

Mundy, Simon, *Alexander Glazunov: Russia's Great Musical Conciliator,* London: Thames, 1987

Rimsky-Korsakov, Nikolai Andreevich, *My Musical Life,* translated from the fifth revised Russian edition by Judah

A. Joffe; edited with an introduction by Carl van Vechten, New York: Knopf, 1923; 3rd American edition, 1989

Taruskin, Richard, *Stravinsky and the Russian Traditions: A Biography of the Works through Mavra*, 2 vols., Berkeley: University of California Press, 1996

Venturini, Donald J., *Alexander Glazunov: His Life and Works*, Delphos, Ohio: Aero, 1992

Alexander Glazunov's musical career unfolded in three different circumstances: in St. Petersburg during the last years of Imperial Russia, in the renamed city Leningrad of the early Soviet period, and, from 1928 on, in Paris. Proponents of the composer claim that both his life and works have been unjustly neglected and that the recent upsurge of recordings warrants new research. Half of the titles discussed here predate the awakening of scholarly interest for the composer among Soviet scholars in the 1950s. Such works represent a generation of Western European scholars that was more willing to assess Glazunov from an early 20th-century Western perspective than according to the standards of his own time and culture. That blinkered viewpoint can be corrected if careful attention is paid to Rimsky-Korsakov's memoirs, Asaf'ev's stylistic survey, Taruskin's chapter on the young Stravinsky's exposure to the music and teaching of Glazunov, and the two quite recent tentative reevaluations by Mundy and Venturini.

ASAF'EV's views on Glazunov emerge in his chapters on Russian orchestral and chamber music, which are indispensable, yet problematic for the non-Russian reader. The author's odd style and highly idiosyncratic vocabulary make for an especially awkward translation. Moreover, the book was written at a time when he was pressured to adapt his views and vocabulary to accord with Soviet Marxist ideology of the late 1920s, meaning that, in the case of Glazunov, the composer's alleged musical torpidity was linked with the plight of his social class in the late imperial period. However, if the reader can overlook the gratuitous sociological comments, she or he will find an illuminating view of Glazunov's music, in which praise for the composer's dazzling contrapuntal skill, harmonic experiments, and control of large-scale structure and pacing is tempered by misgivings about waterlogged textures and narrow emotional range. In addition Asaf'ev offers provocative insights into Glazunov's assimilation of musical styles and the composer's significance for his colleagues and students.

The essay on Glazunov in CALVOCORESSI and ABRAHAM provides a large amount of biographical material, such as family background, early influences, premieres, commissions, and honors. The essay in CALVOCORESSI presents the same general assessment of Glazunov's place in Russian music but differs in its emphases, discussing works and characterizing the composer's style. Representative symphonies, tone poems, and chamber works are identified by name and date of composition, then tagged with comments about stylistic

influences or affinities with other Russian or Western European music. A few technical points on matters of form and thematic development are clearly articulated and should be within reach of the general reader.

MUNDY's short and readable biography of Glazunov seems to be based entirely on English-language sources but succeeds well at placing the composer in various historical and musical contexts. Most musicians who are discussed are introduced with a capsule portrait or anecdote that illustrates how they behaved and how they were viewed by their contemporaries, yet without descending to the level of caricature and gossip, as often occurs in popular biography. Although the book lacks any extended consideration of musical style, many works are named and the important ones receive well-considered additional comments regarding their influences or significance for Glazunov's career. The work concludes with a short bibliography and chronological work list.

Despite the regret expressed by Anatoly Rimsky-Korsakov in his introduction, there is much of value on Glazunov in Nikolai RIMSKY-KORSAKOV's extensive memoirs, including information on nearly two dozen of Glazunov's works. The first entry dates from 1879, at which time 14-year-old Glazunov commenced his compositional study with the author, and it gives a clear idea of what was so impressive in the boy. Later entries chronicle Glazunov's evolution from Rimsky-Korsakov's student to his colleague in teaching, editing, and the promotion of concerts and composers. The activities of both men during and after the 1905 revolution are also discussed. The readability of Joffe's translation and the inclusion of the many detailed notes and appendices from the fourth and fifth Russian editions make this English edition especially valuable.

In his chronicle of Stravinsky's apprenticeship, TARUSKIN provides considerable information on the musical style and significance of Glazunov. In volume 1, the discussion of musical institutions and musical life in late 19th-century St. Petersburg emphasizes Glazunov's multiple roles as compositional figurehead, publisher's consultant to Mitrofan Belyayev, and colleague to Rimsky-Korsakov at the Conservatoire. Taruskin's extended commentary on the compositional process and influences on Stravinsky's Symphony in E-Flat, op. 1 makes repeated references to the symphonies and style of Glazunov; it can be considered the most detailed assessment in English of the Glazunov symphonic style.

VENTURINI's short monograph on Glazunov consists of a biography in seven chapters, a commentary on seven works, a work list, a discography (compiled by Saul Kruger), and several tributes from relatives and musicians committed to Glazunov's music. The biographical section depends heavily on earlier English-language texts but also incorporates personal letters, particularly from the composer's later years; neither category of sources inspires speculation on the man behind the music. The two ballets and five orchestral works chosen for commentary are described in general terms, with emphasis on the character of movements, tempi, and notable details of scoring. The book's most useful feature is its rich discography, which lists Russian and Western CDs, LPs, 78 rpm recordings, and, most unusual, works not yet recorded.

DAVID HAAS

Glinka, Mikhail 1804–1857

Russian composer

Abraham, Gerald, *On Russian Music,* London: Reeves, and New York: Scribner, 1939; reprint, New York: Johnson Reprint, 1970

———, *Studies in Russian Music,* London: Reeves, and New York: Scribner, 1936; reprint, 1969

Brown, David, *Mikhail Glinka: A Biographical and Critical Study,* London: Oxford University Press, 1973

Calvocoressi, Michel D., and Gerald Abraham, *Masters of Russian Music,* New York: Knopf, 1936

Campbell, Stuart, editor, *Russians on Russian Music, 1830–1880: An Anthology,* Cambridge: Cambridge University Press, 1994

Glinka, Mikhail Ivanovitch, *Memoirs,* translated by Richard B. Mudge, Norman: University of Oklahoma Press, 1963

Taruskin, Richard, *Defining Russia Musically: Historical and Hermeneutical Essays,* Princeton, New Jersey: Princeton University Press, 1997

Not surprisingly, the literature on Mikhail Glinka reveals the main preoccupations of each period in which it was written. GLINKA studiously avoids the controversial or the political, remaining within the confines of the composer's musical life. One would hardly know that the composer lived through tumultuous times, including the Napoleonic Wars, the burning of Moscow, the Decembrist Plot with its aftermath of exile and execution, and the expansionist war that saw the eventual annexation of the Caucasus to the Russian Empire. Maintaining this point of view, CALVOCORESSI, ABRAHAM (1936, 1939), and BROWN provide details of life and works without straying far beyond the personal and musical.

The treatments of Glinka's music seem confined as well. Most critical investigations of Glinka's works, such as Abraham, are focused on a few genres—the operas and, to a lesser extent, the later orchestral works. The accounts of Glinka and his music from the 1930s and 1940s, while presenting the necessary facts, take a curiously disparaging point of view. Glinka, along with other Russian composers, is compared with German composers in general and Beethoven in particular, regarded as the standards against which all other music should be measured.

Writing in the 1970s, Brown is not immune from this tendency and adds another curious angle. He seems always to be winnowing the truly Russian features from the contamination of Western characteristics in Glinka's music. Thus, the real Glinka emerges only when he is writing in Russian and only Russian when he is quoting or imitating folk music. Nonetheless, this is the best account of the composer's development, illustrated with generous musical examples and noting some of the copious Russian literature on the Father of Russian Music.

It is refreshing to read some of the contemporary criticism of Glinka's work—confined mainly to his operas—in CAMPBELL's fine collection of Russian musical commentary from the 19th century. We get genuine enthusiasm for the inventiveness of Glinka's music and an appreciation of its unique qualities. The writers saw that their culture's characteristics were not confined to ancient bards, folk choruses, and pagan rituals and that their music should not be so defined. Some of the ideas taken up by 20th century writers are already present in outline. For example, A.N. Serov wrote in 1859 about the role of a single motive throughout the opera *A Life for the Tsar,* a point developed by English-speaking writers only in the last part of the 20th century. Interesting too is Piotr Tchaikovsky's review of the 1872 revival of *Ruslan and Lyudmila.*

The change in musicology during the last decade or so can be read in the latest contributions to Glinkiana by TARUSKIN. Looking beyond the narrowly analytical to the broader implications of libretto and musical style, Taruskin sees orientalism in some of Glinka's works, expressions of a none-too-pleasant official nationalism in others. His work is extremely valuable in setting Glinka's works into the context of 19th-century Russian music. "How the Acorn Took Root," for example, presents a thorough account of *Kamarinskaya,* one of the three *Fantaisies pittoresques* written for orchestra, and the influence it had on later Russian composers, especially Balakirev.

Taruskin seems to see Glinka's contribution clearly, and makes no bones about his disdain for the convolutions of previous English-language writers. Here, for example, he upbraids Brown for failing to give true credit to Glinka's compositional control of the thematic principle in his music while ascribing this sign of greatness to unconscious inheritance from his Russian folk heritage. Taruskin set out to show the true artistry in Glinka's oeuvre and does so with the same enthusiasm as Russian 19th-century commentators.

Missing in all these works is a thorough account of the songs, according to some the best of the composer's output, and the religious music. A translation of Serov's treatment of the songs in his *Reminiscences of Mikhail Ivanovich Glinka* (1860) would be useful.

MARY S. WOODSIDE

Gluck, Christoph Willibald 1714–1787

German composer

Berlioz, Hector, *Gluck and His Operas: With an Account of Their Relation to Musical Art,* translated by Edwin Evans, London: Reeves, and New York: Scribner, 1914

Brown, Bruce Alan, *Gluck and the French Theatre in Vienna,* Oxford: Clarendon Press, and New York: Oxford University Press, 1991

Cooper, Martin, *Gluck,* New York: Oxford University Press, 1935; reprint, St. Clair Shores, Michigan: Scholarly Press, 1978

Einstein, Alfred, *Gluck,* translated by Eric Blom, London: Dent, and New York: Dutton, 1936

Gluck, Christoph Willibald, *The Collected Correspondence and Papers of Christoph Willibald Gluck,* edited by Hedwig Mueller von Asow and E.H. Mueller von Asow, translated by Stewart Thomson, London: Barrie and Rockliff, and New York: St. Martin's Press, 1962

Howard, Patricia, *Christoph Willibald Gluck: A Guide to Research,* New York: Garland, 1987

——, *Gluck: An Eighteenth-Century Portrait in Letters and Documents,* Oxford: Clarendon Press, and New York: Oxford University Press, 1995

——, *Gluck and the Birth of Modern Opera,* London: Barrie and Rockliff, and New York: St. Martin's Press, 1963

Howard, Patricia, editor, *C.W. von Gluck: Orfeo,* Cambridge: Cambridge University Press, 1981

Newman, Ernest, *Gluck and the Opera: A Study in Musical History,* London: Dobbell, 1895; reprint, New York: AMS Print, 1978

When Dr. Charles Burney took his leave of Christoph Willibald Gluck in Vienna in September 1772, the composer gave him scores of the operas *Alceste* and *Paride ed Elena* and of the ballet *Don Juan.* This acquisition can be taken as an emblem for much of the later Gluck scholarship; along with the score, Gluck gave Burney the preface to *Alceste,* which Burney excerpted at unusual length in his own history. For most of the two centuries since, the *Alceste* preface has been the focus of much Gluck scholarship, which generally views the composer as the hero of opera reform in Vienna and Paris in the 1760s and 1770s.

The centerpieces of BERLIOZ are reviews of *Orphée* and *Alceste* revivals at the Paris Opéra in 1860 and 1861, respectively, plus a long gloss on the *Alceste* score, other musical settings of the *Alceste* story, and the play by Euripides. In the *Orphée* and *Alceste* essays here, Berlioz is witty as always, even in translation. He addresses the apparently perennial problem of stylistic unevenness in Gluck—in this instance, what the author describes as the incongruous final chorus in *Alceste.* The *Alceste* commentary remains engaging when Berlioz discusses the musical score; the absence of musical examples does not weaken his observations. The additional material on other *Alceste* settings further showcases Berlioz's skill at literary comedy.

All 20th-century English-language biographies of Gluck have been superseded by Howard (1995), but NEWMAN is still useful in many aspects. Newman's book is interesting especially for its polemical frame, comprising an introduction in which he tries to create a comparative, scientific music criticism (as opposed to the abstract, metaphysical and Hegelian pseudohistory of music best represented by Wagner's writings) and his attempt in part 2 to situate Gluck in the history of ideas. Much of the biographical core of the book serves as a window onto 19th-century Gluck criticism, as many lengthy passages are borrowed from Schmid, Marx, and Desnoiresterres. In part 2, there are also large segments of the most famous 18th-century reform tracts, notably Marcello's *Il Teatro alla moda* and Algarotti's *Saggio sopra l'opera in musica.* Inconsistencies in Gluck's aesthetics interest Newman, as they interest nearly all writers after Newman, but his approach is unique. While his hostility for 18th-century Italian opera seria is unbridled, Newman is less critical than most commentators of Gluck's lapses into a prereform style; instead, Newman is attracted to moments of prophetic lyricism—in *Armide* and in *Paride ed Elena,* for example—where Gluck seems to forget that his principles oblige him to forget that he is a musician. For Newman, Gluck becomes in these moments a compelling protoromantic.

COOPER devotes more than half his book to long commentaries on the six reform operas, consisting of libretto synopses mingled with score annotations. Musical examples are numerous but brief and in short score. In the introductory and concluding sections, Cooper addresses a variety of topics of interest to the general reader in a manner consistent with the basic reform narrative, articulating Gluck's familiar place in the history of music. Gluck is generally viewed as being a member of a Neapolitan reform school comprised of Traetta, Jommelli, and Mozart. For Cooper, the fundamental reform designation of 1760 to 1762 (the years of *Don Juan* and *Orfeo*) as an aesthetic pivot point survived the 1920 challenge of German scholar Max Arend, whom Cooper credits with having been the first to identify reform antecedents in the little-known Italian operas Gluck wrote in the 1740s and 1750s. Cooper discards Gluck's ballets and the French opéras comiques of the 1750s as insignificant in music history; in place of any influence Gluck's work in these genres may have had, he prefers to speculate that Gluck may have met art historian and classicist Winckelmann in Rome around 1755 and that this meeting may have kindled an interest in Greek antiquity. French influence is only noted in the works composed during Gluck's years in Paris and in the context of coarse and mildly unfavorable (if unoriginal) ideas about national character. Cooper designates Gluck as one who envisaged a synthesis of national operatic styles but was unable to achieve that synthesis; in sum, Gluck was an Italian composer who lacked Italian lyricism.

Published in an English translation nearly 20 years before it was published in the original German, EINSTEIN poignantly seeks to negotiate the objective biographical facts about Gluck (such as his birthplace and nationality) in a study written at a time when central Europe was disintegrating and the author was in exile in England. As it does for other works, a strong adherence to the heroic reform narrative generates historiographic problems for this life and works biography. Both before and after *Orfeo,* single musical phrases, arias, and even whole operas can be identified that seem to defy any possibility of having been written by Gluck; the aesthetic lapses after *Orfeo,* which Cooper takes for a sign of a good business sense, Einstein finds utterly dismaying. An extreme romantic prejudice against florid singing is evident in this study, and Einstein's dismissive criticism of the forgotten opera seria works of Handel, Hasse, and Metastasio is scathing.

GLUCK served as a valuable collection of original materials in translation for more than 30 years—but it has been superseded by Howard (1995). The scholars who authored the annotations to the individual letters represent some of the most notable figures in Gluck studies, but Bruce Brown has recently called into question the accuracy of some of the translations. Letters and documents are presented only in English.

HOWARD (1963) is a frustrating work from the early part of the author's very important career. Part of the frustration stems from the nature of her project: committed to a broad historical account, she tries to paint Gluck as the leading figure in a second operatic era from 1760 to roughly 1900 by assessing his reforms in compositional subgenres of theatrical music: overture, ensemble, chorus, aria, and recitative. The plethora of bald aesthetic judgments makes this approach seem very old-fashioned, even if the prospect of a technical survey of Gluck's compositional habits is attractive. Unfortunately, while there are many musical examples, the number is inadequate to the task, and the examples included are poorly captioned and clumsily placed in the text. This book does not appear in the most recent scholarly bibliographies.

HOWARD (1981) is one of the earliest volumes in the important and accessible Cambridge Opera Handbook series—and the only volume to date devoted to a Gluck opera. Not a published libretto (as in the English National Opera guides), this anthology is mainly a reception history to which Howard and Eve Barsham are the chief contributors. Barsham presents a brief, clear survey of Berlioz's *Mémoires* and his treatise on organization with respect to the interest they display in Gluck's work. Regrettable, there is no companion piece on Wagner and his 1847 edition of *Iphigénie en Aulide.*

BROWN's meticulous work on the rise of the French theater in Vienna in the decade preceding *Orfeo* represents the most significant challenge to the simplicity of the enduring reform narrative and presents a potent contextual remedy—perhaps the only "thick description" English-language Gluck scholarship has to offer—for a period served poorly by surviving biographical material. In contrast to the tendency to assign credit for innovations either to Gluck or to Calzabigi, Brown illuminates the history of Viennese theatrical institutions from the establishment of the francophone "Lotharingian colony" in 1740 through the 1760s and portrays in lavish detail the culture engineered by Kaunitz and Durazzo (as well as the careers of the ballet producers and choreographers Hilverding and Angiolini). Newly available archival and manuscript sources—especially a chronicle of Viennese theaters in the years 1758 to 1763 compiled by the dancer Philipp Gumpenhuber and a collection of ballet scores once owned by Durazzo and now housed at the Biblioteca Nazionale in Turin—allow Brown to attribute dozens of ballet innovations to Gluck and to bolster Klaus Hortschansky's 1973 hypothesis about Gluck and pervasive self-borrowing. Where Newman, a century before, could only read Gluck and Calzabigi's prefaces against the background of other 18th-century reform tracts, Brown can show how the formal, tonal, and dramaturgical innovations of *Orfeo* are rooted in the ballets and *opéras comiques* of the 1750s. Musical excerpts are generous and ample in both short and full score; while German and Italian sources are translated, the abundant excerpts from French periodicals and private correspondences are not.

As indicated by its subtitle and in its introduction, HOWARD (1995) is not a life- and works-biography. Howard claims that the volume is not a biography at all, but rather an attempt to meet the more modest goal of publishing the surviving Gluck correspondence in readable translations, framed by contemporaneous public accounts of the composer in the international press, and private accounts in personal memoirs. Once again, letters and documents are not given in their original languages. In place of a contribution to style history, Howard offers something far more valuable: an austere documentary biography in the manner of Otto Deutsch, free of reform hagiography and the prejudices against Italian opera seria that Gluck the reformer cultivated and which became the legacies of the 19th century.

Finally, HOWARD (1987) offers information about the wider world of Gluck scholarship—periodical literature, non-English writings, and bibliographic tools available through 1987.

GARY MOULSDALE

Górecki, Henryk b. 1933

Polish composer

Jacobson, Bernard, *A Polish Renaissance,* London: Phaidon, 1996

Maciejewski, B.M., *H.M. Górecki: His Music and Our Times,* London: Allegro Press, 1994

Thomas, Adrian, *Górecki,* Oxford: Clarendon Press, and New York: Oxford University Press, 1997

More than 40 years after Henryk Górecki's 1958 concert in Katowice (the capital of his home province of Silesia, Poland), no book-length monographs about him were available in his native country. Of the three books published in English, one (by Maciejewski) is so seriously flawed that its mention might be only negatively justified, and one (by Jacobson) discusses Górecki along with his three contemporaries. There are several reasons for Górecki's late rise to fame and the resultant dearth of research material about him. The composer, born in Czernica, is a sincere Catholic who dedicated some of his works to the Pope (*Beatus Vir*) and to the victims of communist persecutions (*Miserere*) and who therefore was not favored by the socialist Polish government, which offered more support to others. Górecki's reticence also played a role in furthering his obscurity: for years he shunned publicity, avoided making public statements and appearances, and refused to give interviews and guest lectures. He also did not travel to conduct his works abroad; one could say that the more widespread recognition of Penderecki and Lutoslawski is partly due to the fact that both artists frequently engaged in these activities.

The situation changed in the 1980s. Following the phenomenal Western success of Górecki's Symphony no. 3 (*Symphony of Sorrowful Songs,* 1976), English-language research began, including an increasing number of theses and dissertations—for example, Luke Howard's doctoral dissertation "A Reluctant Requiem: The History and Reception of Henryk M. Górecki's Symphony No. 3 in Britain and the United States" (1997)—and one detailed monograph (by Thomas). In Polish, six master's theses have been written about Górecki since Krzysztof Droba's pioneering 1971 study of *Refrain and Canticum Graduum.* Droba's research articles (1977–86) opened the way for the scholarly recognition of Górecki's achievements.

MACIEJEWSKI is a good example of how not to write books about music; given its vacuous prose and puzzling content choices, it is clearly a text to be avoided. The book includes many snapshots of the author with various former and current celebrities as well as frequent digressions into unwelcome details of the personal life of the author; much less is said about Górecki.

In contrast, the volumes by Jacobson and Thomas have considerable merit, although each is designed for a different market. JACOBSON's volume about four composers, included in the popular series by Phaidon Press that could be dubbed "Great Composers of Our Times," is an engaging portrait of his subjects, replete with direct quotations and many photographs giving the readers an idea about the context of the composers' lives, not only their music. There is a photograph or two on almost every page, although it is difficult to find any musical examples. Obviously, one could enjoy the book even without knowing how to read music. The author presents an overview of the composers' lives and careers and only briefly mentions the music's technical aspects. The text is organized into two parts, the first focusing on the life and music of Panufnik and Lutoslawski and the second on Penderecki and Górecki. Both sections end with comparisons of the music by the two coupled subjects; this curious arrangement seems intended to lead one to believe that these men are direct competitors. The choice of cover photos, with Panufnik at the front and Górecki at the back cover, suggests a superiority of these two over their peers. Jacobson concludes his comparison of Penderecki and Górecki by declaring, "Whereas Penderecki's ceaseless search for new creative stimuli seems to have diminished his own artistic size, Górecki, by burrowing ever more deeply within himself, has grown to world stature." There are many quotations from interviews and recorded statements by Górecki and many photographs. The book provides a brief list of works, suggestions for further reading, and a selective discography (annotated) for each composer; there is also a useful index. In general, although the discussion of Górecki is not extensive, Jacobson's text provides a well-written introduction to his subject matter.

For a thorough study focused solely on Górecki's music, one needs to turn to THOMAS's monograph. The series in which it appeared does not permit massive volumes, which is a loss, considering the wealth of knowledge that Thomas imparts in the 150 pages allotted to the main text. The author knew the composer for years (he admits that his fascination with Górecki's music started in 1970); he also published many articles before summarizing his insights in this volume. The book consists of seven chapters, with titles borrowed from the composer's pieces—for example, "Collisions" (i.e., Scontri for orchestra, 1960), "Old Polish Music" (for brass and strings, 1969), "Sacred Songs" (two songs for baritone and piano, 1971), and "Quasi Una Fantasia" (String Quartet no. 2, 1991). These titles capture the evolution of the composer's style, from the dramatic sonorism of the early avant-garde years, through his turn to Polish early music (especially religious) and folklore (especially of the Tatra Mountains), through the deepening of the spiritual commitment and a simplification of language epitomized by Symphony no. 3, and to the creative freedom of the recent years. Thomas rightly points out that Górecki's innovations in the 1950s and 1960s preceded those of Penderecki; he also notes, for the first time, the extent of Górecki's involvement with 12-tone composition. The thoroughness of Thomas's research into the Polish background of his subject should embarrass his Polish colleagues: he identifies the scope of Górecki's musicological knowledge and its sources in obscure articles and finds musical quotations and allusions to folklore, early music, Beethoven, Chopin, and other influences in Górecki's compositions. One can only praise the precision of Thomas's analyses and the subtlety of his interpretations, which are often supported by statements from the composer. A detailed list of works contains the pertinent data about each of the compositions up to 1996, with its original title, name and dates for the author of the text, the facts about the first performance, and more. The many musical examples are well chosen and edited; the technical segments read smoothly, and the book is destined to be a must for all students of Górecki's music.

MARIA ANNA HARLEY

Gottschalk, Louis Moreau 1829–1869

United States composer and pianist

Chase, Gilbert, *America's Music: From the Pilgrims to the Present,* New York: McGraw-Hill, 1955; revised 3rd edition, Urbana: University of Illinois Press, 1987

Doyle, John G., *Louis Moreau Gottschalk 1829–1869: A Bibliographical Study and Catalog of Works,* Detroit: College Music Society, 1982

Gottschalk, Louis Moreau, *Notes of a Pianist,* edited by Jeanne Behrend, New York: Knopf, 1964

Loggins, Vernon, *Where the Word Ends: The Life of Louis Moreau Gottschalk,* Baton Rouge: Louisiana State University Press, 1958

Marrocco, W. Thomas, "America's First Nationalist Composer, Louis Moreau Gottschalk (1829–1869)," in *Scritti in onore di Luigi Ronga,* Milan: Ricciardi, 1973

Schonberg, Harold, *The Great Pianists,* New York: Simon and Schuster, 1963

Starr, S. Frederick, *Bamboula! The Life and Times of Louis Moreau Gottschalk,* New York: Oxford University Press, 1995

The majority of studies on Louis Moreau Gottschalk have been published only recently. Biographical studies of this famous 19th-century U.S. pianist and composer remain most popular, beginning with Loggins and culminating with Starr. Scholarship on Gottschalk's compositions is less common, although significant contributions have been made by Marrocco and Chase. Starr, Chase, Behrend, and Schonberg place Gottschalk

within a cultural context, relating his compositions, writings, and reception to both U.S. and international society of the period.

LOGGINS's volume is the earliest available English biography of Gottschalk. Loggins adopts a sentimental style that overly dramatizes accounts of the pianist's life, performances, and reputation. The lack of citations, and inclusion of unfounded and rumored events, places this account outside of more authoritative scholarship.

Behrend's introductory and concluding essays in GOTTSCHALK offer a basic biographical overview that presents the background for Gottschalk's memoirs. The opening essay examines generally Gottschalk's international reputation as a performer and more specifically his interactions with U.S. audiences, critics, and contemporaries. The closing essay includes a more detailed account of Gottschalk's last activities and death. In these two chapters, Behrend contextualizes the composer's descriptions of, and reactions to, his concert tours within both national and international societal frameworks.

MARROCCO advances the view of Gottschalk as one of the United States' first nationalist composers by identifying borrowings from folk sources in his major compositions. The author distinguishes between direct quotations and stylistic paraphrase, arguing that the identity and form of Gottschalk's folk borrowings were chosen for specific music and extramusical contexts. In extensive thematic analyses of *The Banjo, Night in the Tropics,* and several other works, Marrocco asserts that Gottschalk's use of patriotic tunes such as the *Star Spangled Banner* and *Yankee Doodle* illustrates a considerable sympathy toward the American vernacular. At the same time, general stylistic quotations of dance rhythms from the Caribbean and South America support Gottschalk's contemporary reputation as a cosmopolitan artist. Although not comprehensive, this article is a useful survey of Gottschalk's use of national and international folk sources.

Essentially a reference work, DOYLE's combined bibliography and catalog provides significant information on both primary and secondary sources concerning Gottschalk up to the early 1980s. The author lists contemporary and historical books, articles, encyclopedia entries, reviews of concerts, recital and concert programs, recordings, piano rolls, and music publishers' catalogs. Although inconsistent, his annotations of these items often include direct quotations and summarize relevant content. For those interested in archival sources, Doyle indices library collections of Gottschalk's musical manuscripts, letters, iconography, memorabilia, and early printed editions. Perhaps most important is the extensive descriptive catalog of all known Gottschalk compositions, which includes performing forces, dates, quotations of descriptions and performances by Gottschalk, early reception, and publisher information.

Doyle's brief outline of scholarship and his overall chronology of Gottschalk's life are surprisingly detailed, particularly in the account of Gottschalk's death.

Chase and Schonberg each devote one brief but illuminating chapter to Gottschalk. In the third edition of his landmark volume, CHASE uses quotations from reviewers, critics, and Gottschalk himself plus musical examples to position the composer within the late-romantic narrative of the exotic in the chapter "Exotic Romanticism." In contrast to Marrocco, Chase focuses on how Gottschalk's use of Hispanic and Afro-Caribbean musical materials, titles, and imagery appealed to 19th-century critics and audiences alike. Chase's interpretations of Gottschalk's descriptions of the Caribbean and South America are particularly perceptive and sympathetic.

In contrast, SCHONBERG's chapter "The First American," presents an unsympathetic and highly critical view of Gottschalk as performer. The author describes Gottschalk as a concertizing relic who was "content to tickle his audiences and titillate them with his salon pieces and his little tricks." The chapter includes many negative reviews concerning Gottschalk's performances and suggests that a lack of discipline limited his professional and artistic accomplishments. Schonberg dismisses Gottschalk as a composer with the statement, "A good deal of his output is bad." Schonberg's chapter is intriguing, however, for its comparison of Gottschalk's pianistic technique, reputation, and repertoire with other romantic virtuosos such as Thalberg, Chopin, and Liszt.

STARR's volume offers the most extensive biography of Gottschalk to date. This exhaustive account includes contemporary reviews from throughout Gottschalk's career. Starr's most valuable contribution was unearthing private letters and written firsthand accounts from archives in North and South America, Europe, and the Caribbean. Accounts of Gottschalk's interactions with the cultural elite of late 19th-century United States (particularly the Boston music critic, John Sullivan Dwight) continue and expand Behrend's and Chase's interpretations of Gottschalk as performer, composer, and individual within the cultural history of the time. Within this life-and-works format, Starr concentrates more on the circumstances surrounding the creation of Gottschalk's music than on the works themselves. Discussions of individual compositions focus on general stylistic elements, as well as accounts of the premieres, reception of the works, and Gottschalk's own descriptions. A history of scholarship on the subject (essentially an expansion of Doyle's outline) is also extremely helpful. Starr's landmark study is amply supplemented with reproductions of rare photographs, paintings, caricatures, manuscript pages, and other personal documents.

GAYLE SHERWOOD

Gounod, Charles 1818–1893

French composer

Bovet, Marie Anne de, *Charles Gounod: His Life and His Works,* London: Low, Marston, Searle and Rivington, 1891
Gounod, Charles, *Autobiographical Reminiscences, with Family Letters and Notes on Music,* translated by W. Hely Hutchinson, London: Heinemann, 1896; reprint, New York: Da Capo Press, 1970
Harding, James, *Gounod,* London: Allen and Unwin, 1973
Huebner, Steven, *The Operas of Charles Gounod,* Oxford: Clarendon Press, 1990

The state of research on Charles Gounod is surprisingly limited. In addition to numerous journal articles, there exist only a handful of monographic studies on this composer, who was a friend of Mendelssohn, a respected colleague of Berlioz, a teacher of Bizet, and a favorite of Queen Victoria. Gounod's influence on French music of the 19th century was great and should not be minimized despite the paucity of current research. Fortunately, Huebner recently made an invaluable contribution with his study of Gounod's operas and their place in the history and tradition of French grand opera. However, more waits to be done in the way of manuscript studies and research on Gounod's writings about music.

HUEBNER's volume is the most recent and also most scholarly monograph on Gounod. The introduction acquaints the reader with the operatic world of the composer by drawing upon many primary sources such as correspondence and periodic press reviews, as well as scholarly secondary sources. The main body of this groundbreaking study is divided into three sections: "Chronicle," "The Operas," and "Style." The first part is a well-documented and succinct narrative biography of Gounod and includes material never before mentioned, such as the composer's seemingly platonic relationship with the Duchess Castiglione Colonna (a sculptor whose pseudonym was Marcello). Huebner recounts Gounod's biography with a detailed and intimate knowledge of both primary and secondary sources, including correspondence held in private collections and evidence from a variety of the composer's musical manuscripts. Part 2 analyzes each opera in detail, focusing on *Faust, Mireille,* and *Roméo et Juliette.* Huebner does not limit his discussion to purely musical elements but includes insightful and important discussions of the literary sources for these operas. Especially illuminating is the information on the history of the Faust legend in France and the use of Shakespeare's play as a model for *Roméo et Juliette.* Huebner gives a meticulous reading of the differences between these literary works and the musical composition. He also chronicles and explains the changes and adaptations made at various stages in the composition and production of these operas, offering an extremely clear and well-documented history of the genesis and performance of these works.

The final section of Huebner's study deals with the melody, harmony, and formal design of Gounod's operas, offering the reader an in-depth analysis of Gounod's scores. The author likewise gives an invaluable account of the musical style and form of contemporary French opera, examining large-scale formal designs and individual solo numbers. This section of the book is an extremely important addition to the existing literature on French grand opera in general. The volume includes an appendix of plot summaries of the operas, which correspond to the first edition of the vocal scores.

HARDING's biography chronicles the growth and development of Gounod as an artist and as a person. Especially insightful are chapters pertaining to the composer's early career and his subsequent concentration on religious music and the priesthood. Although the information offered on Gounod's relationship with soprano Pauline Viardot and the Russian poet Turgenev is not as complete and well documented as Huebner's, Harding does give a substantial account of the composer's unconventional friendship with the eccentric Englishwoman Georgina Weldon and her husband, which Huebner does not discuss. Harding's discussions of specific compositions, such as *Faust* and *Roméo et Juliette,* are brief but nevertheless insightful. The author limits his commentaries to general descriptions of the drama and musical numbers of certain operas. Despite these limitations, he adeptly reveals specific elements that contribute to a greater understanding of Gounod's music, such as the composer's indebtedness to the music of Bach and Mozart. This short, enjoyable biography gives a vivid account of the life and times of Gounod. Harding's writing style is engrossing, and his ability to recount events and characterize people is truly captivating. However, the lack of documentation of sources can be disturbing. A useful appendix contains a work list that includes cast members of the operatic premieres and publication dates, as well as a list of Gounod's literary works.

BOVET's account of the composer and his music was written during Gounod's lifetime. The author begins with a lecture on hero worship, which leads the reader to wonder if Bovet's infatuation with the composer will enable her to give an objective rendering of his life and music. The elevated style of writing and the rather protective account of Gounod's biography and career indicate that Bovet is not totally impartial. For example, she defends Gounod's sermonizing and flowery tone of speech, with which he could take command of a conversation, as his idealistic and enthusiastic response to any intellectual topic. In addition, she makes no mention of the *Affaire Weldon.* This colorful, and important, episode in the composer's career is treated by the author as though it virtually did not occur. Reproduced in this book are some brief letters between Bovet and the composer. However, she does not make clear just how much of her material is taken directly from correspondence and personal contact with him. Bovet also incorporates quotations from contemporary reviews, as well as articles written by Gounod himself and material from his autobiography. She deals with the composer's life in a chronological fashion and includes four chapters that discuss the man and the artist. These chapters exhibit most clearly Bovet's fondness for the composer and offer some of Gounod's own thoughts on the art of music.

GOUNOD himself offers a number of honest accounts of his successes and failures in his autobiography. This is an English translation of his *Mémoires d'un Artiste,* published in Paris in 1896. In this brief book, the composer writes of the "most important events in his artistic life, of the marks left them on his personal existence, of their influence on his career and of the thoughts they have suggested to his mind." The majority of his stories are anecdotal, such as the recollections of his youth, his trip to Germany, and the premiere of his first opera *Sappho;* these tales do, however, reveal Gounod as a first-class raconteur. Gounod's writing style is characteristic of his honest and straightforward manner, as well as his rhapsodic and at times lavish poeticism, a duality noted by both Harding and Huebner.

Throughout this book are found traces of Gounod's philosophy on music and aesthetics; included at the end are a few of his letters from 1870 and 1871 and five miscellaneous essays that were published previously in other contexts. These articles remain some of the composer's most insightful writings. In his essay on Berlioz, for example, Gounod praised his senior colleague's originality in both musical composition and instrumentation. In the essay on Saint-Saëns and his opera *Henry VIII,* Gounod comments favorably on the work as well as the composer's overall musical style. The three remaining essays all offer important insights into Gounod's philosophy of music. "Nature and Art" is a pseudo-religious oration in which Gounod defines the role of the composer. Drawing on a theological paradigm, he identifies art as one of the members of the "trinity" of the ideal. In "The Academy of France at Rome," Gounod again makes some unique observations about the essence of art, asserting that immersion in the artistic life of Rome was important for the creation of a truly well-rounded musician. In "The Artist and Modern Society," Gounod laments the commercialization of the modern artist, complaining that society takes up too much of a composer's time with requests for auditions and endorsements of method books and the demands of people who desire autographs, mementos, and photographs. This volume is a rare, firsthand glimpse of Gounod's philosophy on music and his thoughts on contemporary composers, musical composition, and art in general. It is a valuable and accessible resource for anyone interested in French music of the 19th century or this important composer.

TIMOTHY S. FLYNN

Great Britain: General Studies

Caldwell, John, *The Oxford History of English Music,* Oxford: Clarendon Press, and New York: Oxford University Press, 1991

Mackerness, Eric David, *A Social History of English Music,* London: Routledge and Paul, and Toronto: University of Toronto Press, 1964; revised edition, Westport, Connecticut: Greenwood Press, 1976

Raynor, Henry, *Music in England,* London: Hale, 1980

Spink, Ian, editor, *The Blackwell History of Music in Britain,* 5 vols., Oxford: Blackwell, 1988–95

Walker, Ernest, *A History of Music in England,* Oxford: Clarendon Press, 1907; 3rd edition revised by J.A. Westrup, 1952

Young, Percy M., *A History of British Music,* London: Benn, and New York: Norton, 1967

Music in Great Britain is largely synonymous with music in England, as developments in Scotland, Wales, and Ireland have not had especially far-reaching or important influence. Thus, most studies, although perhaps including "British" or "Great Britain" in their titles, are limited to the centralized musical activity of England. There is no shortage of such studies, as many writers, beginning most notably with Pepys and Evelyn in the 17th century and continuing to the present day, have attempted to chronicle and analyze the music and musical life of the nation. Therein, one finds a variety of approaches, from social, chronological, and biographical histories to musical analysis and commentary.

One of the earliest and most successful attempts to provide a comprehensive survey of English music was made by WALKER, whose primary concern is the actual music rather than biography and historical research. Quoting from the author's preface, the book "has been designed from the standpoint of a musician rather than from that of an antiquarian." Each chapter begins with a brief survey of pertinent historical background and biography and then moves quickly to discussions of specific, representative compositions. Of special interest are a chapter on folk music and one dealing with the general characteristics of English music, in which the author draws attention to those traits and techniques that he sees as uniquely English, such as the use of false relations and a predilection for full sonorities. The major drawback of the volume is its age: the original edition provides no coverage of musicians born after 1860. Westrup's 1952 revision remedies the situation to some extent, although contemporary music is still given little attention.

A vastly different approach is taken by MACKERNESS, a professor of English rather than a musician. His thoroughly interesting and readable work shows music through and in relation to significant societal trends. Thus, musical analysis and even detailed discussions of musical works are all but absent. In their place is a rich narrative that places music into a larger cultural and social picture, reminding the reader that music does not exist in a vacuum but is a product and reflection of its surroundings.

Taking a middle road between the previous entries, YOUNG attempts to combine sociocultural history with biography and musical analysis. The former meets with somewhat more success, as the author infuses his chronological narrative with ample detail, admirably describing musical events, situations, and trends. For example, a chapter devoted to Handel nicely sets the scene by providing information about the music trade of the 18th century, foreign artists working in London, and the operatic climate of the country, so that the reader is prepared and has a context for Handel's arrival in England. Subsequent chapters deal with topics not often covered in other sources, such as music publishing, criticism and journalism, music societies, and music and mass culture. Ironically, this prolific detail is also one of the book's potential problems, as much of the text is encumbered with excess minutiae and Young's occasional tendency to focus on minor events and personalities. Additionally, musical analysis tends to be general, covering broad points of style rather than dealing with specific works.

RAYNOR offers one of the best shorter studies of English music. His book is nicely balanced between history and biography and musical discussion, the latter never becoming overly analytical or excessively technical. The chronological survey is readable while demonstrating thorough, accurate scholarship. One of the highlights of this work is the author's constant awareness of the topic: music *in* England. As a result, the reader is given a unique view of the Englishness of the events, composers, and music at hand instead of another nondescript historical survey.

A far more in-depth study of the actual music of England is provided by CALDWELL. Divided into two volumes (the second forthcoming), the work offers a tremendous amount of sophisticated musical analysis of both specific compositions and broader trends and styles. Biographical and historical information is brief, serving only to introduce the more important analytical discussions. Thus, the musically untrained reader will find the book somewhat difficult and technically challenging, although for the musician this is one of the finest comprehensive analytical surveys available. The author's findings are strengthened by his meticulous attention to detail and his use of an enormous amount of documentary source material.

By far, the most detailed, in-depth, and exhaustive examination of British music is found in the Blackwell History of Music in Britain series, edited by SPINK. The various volumes of the study cover the Middle Ages through the 20th centuries. Each volume has a different editor and contains contributions by eminent scholars writing in their respective areas of expertise. Contributors include such notable figures as Stanley Sadie on domestic music, Tim Carter on 16th-century vocal music, and Nicholas Temperley on 18th-century church and organ music. This multiple-volume format allows for extensive coverage of each historical period, although the study is not simply a chronological historical survey but tends toward a genre approach. For example, the 16th century is covered by chapters devoted to sacred music on Latin texts, English church music, secular vocal music, keyboard music, and ensemble music. Especially noteworthy is the volume devoted to the 20th century. This volume is one of the most thorough and up-to-date examinations of Britain's modern musical epoch and pays due attention to popular music. Throughout the series, one encounters a consistently high level of scholarship, the employment of current research methodologies and findings, and the liberal use and documentation of a wealth of primary and secondary source material. The work is indispensable to the serious student of English music.

MICHAEL VAUGHN

Great Britain: Musical Centers

Bruce, George, *Festival in the North: The Story of the Edinburgh Festival,* London: Hale, 1975

Corder, Frederick, *A History of the Royal Academy of Music, from 1822 to 1922,* London: Corder, 1922

Cox, David Vassall, *The Henry Wood Proms,* London: British Broadcasting Corporation, 1980

Fellowes, Edmund H., *English Cathedral Music,* London: Methuen, 1941; 5th edition, revised by Jack Westrup, 1969

Hughes, Spike, *Glyndebourne: A History of the Festival Opera Founded in 1934 by Audre and John Christe,* London: Methuen, and Boston: Crescendo, 1965; new edition, Newton Abbot: David and Charles, 1981

Kenyon, Nicholas, *The BBC Symphony Orchestra: The First Fifty Years, 1930–1980,* London: British Broadcasting Corporation, 1981

Long, Kenneth R., *Music of the English Church,* New York: St. Martin Press's, 1971; London: Hodder and Stoughton, 1972

Musgrave, Michael, *The Musical Life of the Crystal Palace,* Cambridge: Cambridge University Press, 1995

Temperley, Nicholas, *The Music of the English Parish Church,* 2 vols., Cambridge: Cambridge University Press, 1979

Thompson, Wendy, *Piano Competition: The Story of the Leeds,* London: Faber, 1990; updated edition, 1991

Wroth, Warwick, *The London Pleasure Gardens of the Eighteenth Century,* London: Macmillan, 1896; reprint, 1979

The term musical center is both all-inclusive and nebulous. A musical center can be a specific building, but it might also be an institution or a festival or competition that has become a point of musical activity around which other musical activities revolve. Accordingly, the books discussed cover a wide range: churches (often musical centers of their communities), institutions, festivals and competitions, performance venues, and performance groups. The books listed here will be discussed chronologically within those categories. There are, of course, many other texts dealing with the various musical centers of Great Britain, but presented here are those texts that have the most merit and can be used as a point of departure for other reading.

FELLOWS's book provides a chronological account of the music written for English cathedrals and for those churches and chapels in which professional choirs "have been established by ancient endowments for the performance of the daily choral service." He covers the period between the publication of the first prayer book in 1549 (during the reign of Edward VI) until the outbreak of World War I (during the reign of Edward VII). Fellows focuses exclusively on the two types of composition that were performed in the cathedrals and were exclusive to the Anglican Church: the service and the anthem. He discusses the tradition of cathedral music, includes musical examples, and provides a detailed history of the musicians, composers, performances, and important people involved. The fifth edition includes additional musical examples, references to modern publications, and a summary of the character of 20th-century church music in England.

LONG's book presents a history of the growth and development of the art of English liturgical music from the Renaissance through the early part of the 20th century, placing that history within the wider context of Western European musical culture. Here English church music is projected against a religious, political, economic, and social background. This text would be acceptable for the scholar but is more suitable for those interested in or connected with music of the church. There are detailed explanations of some relatively elementary musical techniques and terms as well as some in-depth studies of a few pieces and composers.

TEMPERLEY's book focuses exclusively on the music of the English parish church, which was for many years the only regular formal musical experience for perhaps half of the British population. He discusses the music history of an institution that was "sensitive to social and economic changes and to movements of popular opinion," while at the same time removed from the influence of certain theological, aesthetic, or political ideas that were rampant in the more aristocratic institutions (i.e., cathedrals). Temperley goes into detail about the various types of music in the parish churches of each period (Reformation through the first part of the 20th century), traces the changes in this music, and tries to explain why these changes occurred. Perhaps the most interesting and important aspect of this book is the author's description of musical practices that disappeared long ago. The book contains a bibliography of manuscript sources, printed collections of music, and other pertinent sources. An accompanying volume includes a collection of music to peruse, study, or perform. A good working knowledge of music and music history is helpful but not necessarily required.

CORDER's history of the Royal Academy is one of only two published histories of what is among the most important musical institutions of Great Britain. The author reproduces letters; refers to and reproduces the contents of contemporary articles that appeared in the major music journals of the day; and includes lists of students, teachers, board members, benefactors, and concert programs. This detailed and well-documented history covers the period from the Academy's conception to 1922.

HUGHES's book provides the most comprehensive account of the background of the Glyndebourne Festival Opera. He discusses in detail the festival's development and function in British society as an alternative for the opera-going public. This standard history is suitable for the educated nonspecialist reader.

BRUCE presents a thematic history of the Edinburgh Festival. The material is arranged chronologically within the various chapters, so there is some overlap. Bruce provides solid information about the beginnings and subsequent trials of what has become one of the most important international music festivals.

THOMPSON's book, written with the assistance of pianist Fanny Waterman, is a history of the Leeds International Piano Competition. This competition has become not only a center for piano music in Britain but also an important international center for piano music. The text includes detailed discussions of the competitions, sponsors, juries, and participants (the runners-up and finalists as well as the winners), and Thompson follows the participants' careers as much as possible. This book is particularly interesting for its analysis of the role of the media in shaping musical opinion. A hefty appendix provides lists of juries, repertoire, and various photo illustrations.

WROTH's book is a well-documented history of 64 of the pleasure gardens of London that had their heydays in the 18th century. These gardens were important centers of musical entertainment for all classes of society, and Wroth presents a detailed description of the activities that took place in each garden as well as a description of what the literati of the day thought of them.

COX's book includes a history of the Proms as well as an analysis of the financial aspects, music, audience, and program development of this important musical venue for the mass public in Britain. Cox discusses the changes that occurred to the Proms, both before and after both World Wars, and he discusses the media's influence on the audience and programming.

The Crystal Palace was one of the central venues for music in Britain in the 19th century and the music performed there was soon regarded as standard orchestral repertoire in England. MUSGRAVE's book reconstructs the musical life of the Crystal Palace as a whole, focusing on the original purpose of the building and its transformation into a musical center for a vast majority of the British public. The author also goes into great detail about the financial necessities of such a venue.

KENYON's book provides a comprehensive account of the first 50 years of the British Broadcasting Corporation's Symphony Orchestra. This study is primarily a historical account, but the author also analyzes the orchestra's dual role as a broadcast orchestra and a public concert-giving orchestra. His discussion provides an important outlook on the orchestra as a leader and stimulator of British taste in art music.

RENÉE CHÉRIE CLARK

Grieg, Edvard 1843–1907

Norwegian composer

Bailie, Eleanor, *Grieg: A Graded Practical Guide*, London: Valhalla, 1993

Benestad, Finn, editor, *International Edvard Grieg Symposium, Bergen*, an entire issue of *Studia musicologica Norvegica* 19 (1993)

Benestad, Finn, and Dag Schjelderup-Ebbe, *Edvard Grieg, Chamber Music: Nationalism, Universality, Individuality*, Oslo: Scandinavian University Press, and New York: Oxford University Press, 1993

Benestad, Finn, and Dag Schjelderup-Ebbe, *Edvard Grieg: The Man and the Artist*, translated by William H. Halverson and Leland B. Sateren, Lincoln: University of Nebraska Press, and Gloucester: Sutton, 1988

Foster, Beryl, *The Songs of Edvard Grieg*, Aldershot: Scolar Press, and Brookfield, Vermont: Gower, 1990

Grieg, Edvard, *Grieg and Delius: A Chronicle of Their Friendship in Letters*, translated by Lionel Carley, London: Boyars, 1993

Halverson, William H., editor, *Edvard Grieg Today: A Symposium*, Northfield, Minnesota: St. Olaf College, 1994

Kortsen, Bjarne, editor, *Grieg the Writer*, 2 vols. Bergen: Kortsen, 1972

Edvard Grieg was the first composer from Norway to earn an international reputation, and he is considered by many to be the foremost musician that country has ever produced. Signs of Grieg's musical talent appeared at an early age. As a teenager he was encouraged by the violinist Ole Bull to study at the Leipzig Conservatory. But Grieg was not happy there and after returning to Bergen in 1862 decided to go to Copenhagen and study with Niels W. Gade. In Copenhagen Grieg met the young composer Rikard Nordraak, an enthusiastic champion of Norwegian music, who introduced him to the rich heritage of folk music. Grieg became an advocate for Norwegian music: he evoked the character of his homeland's native music in his compositions, and as a performer he established himself as a leading figure in Norwegian music in the early 1870s. Throughout his career Grieg divided his time between composition and the vigorous life of a traveling virtuoso, playing and conducting his own music in Norway and abroad.

Since the early 1990s, interest in Grieg and his music has been growing steadily. In 1993 the final volume of an edition of his complete works (*Samlede Verker*, C.F. Peters, 1977–93) appeared. This edition has sparking renewed interest in Grieg among scholars and performers. Consequently, many recordings and several notable studies concerning the composer have appeared in recent years.

At the forefront of new research on Grieg is the definitive biography by BENESTAD and SCHJELDERUP-EBBE (1988). More than a translation of the original Norwegian publication (1980), the English version is an updated revision of the earlier work. The biography is organized chronologically with pertinent compositions, letters, and other materials placed in context. The narrative provides full descriptions of Grieg's compositional style, his contact with various musical organizations, his conducting and speaking engagements, and the cultural/political climate of his surroundings. Excerpts from various primary sources, (letters, journals, speeches, manuscripts, and program notes) are presented here for the first time, and the catalog of works compiled by the authors is the most comprehensive now available.

BENESTAD and SCHJELDERUP-EBBE (1993) is a response to the neglect Grieg's chamber music has received from scholars and performers in the past. According to the authors, Grieg's chamber works had a stronger influence on later composers than is generally acknowledged. To support this theory, the authors describe each work in great detail and discuss the relationship between Grieg's chamber works and the rise of national self-consciousness in 19th-century Norway. The authors' analyses are clear and amply illustrated with more than 100 music examples. For the general reader interested in the rise of Norwegian national music, this volume is an invaluable supplement to the authors' biography of Grieg. For music students and scholars, this book serves as a long-overdue corrective to the general assumption that Grieg did not succeed in the field of chamber music.

FOSTER serves as an addition to the scant materials available on the proper performance practice of Grieg's vocal works. The book begins with a brief discussion of the folk-music traditions that influenced Grieg's compositional process. This section is followed by a series of chapters centered around groups and/or sets of songs. The pieces are discussed in chronological order, and special attention is given to Grieg's literary associations and the cultural circumstances that prevailed during each stage of composition. Consideration is also given to the difficulty of translating Norwegian texts into singable English or German versions, and discussions of persons with historical relationships to the songs are included in the appendices. This book is clearly intended for advanced singers familiar with theoretical terminology and the art-song tradition, and it is valuable for those interested in exploring Norwegian song. Readers should be aware, however, that Foster's discussions are highly subjective, and her translations, although artistic, are not always accurate. In addition, Foster's discussion of available texts and translations omits references to two important editions by Bradley Ellingboe: *45 Grieg Songs* (1988) and *A Grieg Song Anthology* (1990).

Pianists interested in the music of Grieg should turn to BAILIE. It is one in a series of works by the author dedicated to helping "pianists find pieces suitable for their own styles and capabilities." This reference book provides detailed pedagogical investigations of every piano work by Grieg. A ten-page introduction discusses Grieg's personality and shows how "the circumstances of his life and times helped shape and characterize his style." The introduction is followed by a discussion of the general aspects of Grieg's keyboard style and a description of the various performance-practice techniques used in the playing of Grieg's music. For the sake of clarity, readers should familiarize themselves with the contents of this final section before moving on to the author's commentaries of each of Grieg's piano pieces. The book concludes with a discussion of Grieg's works without opus numbers and unpublished pieces.

Grieg's literary activities are addressed in two volumes edited by KORTSEN, which present essays and articles Grieg wrote about composers and music, as well as selections from his correspondence. The articles in the first volume include Grieg's perceptions of various composers (Schumann, Mozart, Wagner, Verdi, Dvořák, Kjerulf, Nordraak, Horneman, Brahms, Strauss, and Svendson). An autobiographical sketch of Grieg's youth, "My First Success," and a description of his study in Leipzig are also included. Volume two contains Grieg's letters to his best friend, Frants Beyer. In these letters Grieg relates his experiences as an aging composer and discusses the many illnesses that plagued him during his final years.

Another collection of Grieg's letters can be found in GRIEG. The collection contains 110 examples of the correspondence between Grieg and Delius, most of which appear here in print for the first time and in accurate translation. These letters shed new light on the relationship that developed between the two composers during the last two decades of Grieg's life. Delius's growth as a composer owed much to the influence of Grieg, and these letters show that Delius's admiration for Grieg embraced both Grieg's talent as a composer and his acumen as a critic.

Finally, no discussion of Grieg literature would be complete without mention of two important collections of articles: BENESTAD and HALVERSON. The collections are the outcome of two important conferences on Grieg that took place in 1993. Comprehensive in their coverage, these volumes offer something for everyone. Articles concerning Grieg's biography, composition style, repertoire, reception history, and activities as a performer and conductor are presented alongside articles concerning pedagogy, performance practice, and Norwegian history.

ANNA H. HARWELL CELENZA

Guillaume de Machaut
see Machaut, Guillaume de

H

Handel, George Frideric 1685–1759

German-born composer

1. Biography

Burney, Charles, *An Account of the Musical Performances . . . in Commemoration of Handel,* London: Payne, 1785; reprint, New York: Da Capo Press, 1979

Burrows, Donald, *Handel,* Oxford: Oxford University Press, and New York: Schirmer Books, 1994

Burrows, Donald, editor, *The Cambridge Companion to Handel,* Cambridge: Cambridge University Press, 1997

Chrysander, Friedrich, *G.F. Händel,* 3 vols., Leipzig: Breitkopf and Härtel, 1858–67; reprint, Hildesheim: Olms, 1966

Dean, Winton, and Anthony Hicks, *The New Grove Handel,* London: Macmillan, and New York: Norton, 1982

Deutsch, Otto Erich, *Handel: A Documentary Biography,* London: Black, and New York: Norton, 1955; revised as *Händel-Handbuch, vol. 4: Dokumente zu Leben und Schaffen,* Kassel: Bärenreiter, 1978

Hogwood, Christopher, *Handel,* London: Thames and Hudson, 1984

Lang, Paul Henry, *George Frideric Handel,* New York: Norton, 1966

Mainwaring, John, *Memoirs of the Life of the Late George Frederic Handel,* London: Dodsley, 1760; reprint, Amsterdam: Knuf, 1964

Mattheson, Johann, *Grundlage einer Ehren-Pforte,* Hamburg, 1740; reprint, Kassel: Bärenreiter, 1969

Parker-Hale, Mary Ann, *G.F. Handel: A Guide to Research,* New York: Garland, 1988

Schoelcher, Victor, *The Life of Handel,* London: Trübner, 1857; reprint, New York: Da Capo Press, 1979

Simon, Jacob, editor, *Handel: A Celebration of His Life and Times, 1685–1759,* London: National Portrait Gallery, 1985

Streatfeild, Richard A., *Handel,* London: Methuen, 1909; 2nd edition, 1910; reprint, Westport, Connecticut: Greenwood Press, 1978

Thomas, Gary C., "'Was George Frideric Handel Gay?' On Closet Questions and Cultural Politics," in *Queering the Pitch: The New Gay and Lesbian Musicology,* edited by Philip Brett, et al., New York: Routledge, 1994

Unlike J.S. Bach and Monteverdi, the two other greatest masters of the baroque era, George Frideric Handel and his music were never forgotten. Already in his own lifetime, he had become an English cultural institution, and his status was consecrated with the commemoration concerts at Westminster Abbey in 1784 and further solidified by the great Handel festivals of the 19th century. Nor was he forgotten in Austria and Germany, where composers such as Haydn, Mozart, Beethoven, and Mendelssohn arranged, edited, performed, admired, or were influenced by his music. As a result, the scholar of Handel's life and works must confront an enormous body of literature.

Of the themes that have persisted in the writing of Handel's life, four are perhaps worth special mention. First, there is the disparity between what is known about Handel the public figure and about Handel the man. As Donald Burrows once observed, we can document Handel's professional life with remarkable fullness: there are periods for which we can trace his movements day by day. The man himself, however, is largely a mystery. We know little about his private life and personal views. His letters are neither numerous nor very informative, and the public record concerning his opinions of contemporary persons and events is negligible. With little evidence to investigate, biographers turn to what has become something of a cliche: the place we shall find Handel the man is in his music. This answer takes us into that slippery region of the relationship between a composer's biography and his works, but in reverse order: rather than trying to understand the work through biography (the usual approach) critics attempt to see the composer's character through his music (which is probably an equally dicey strategy).

Many of Handel's biographers, particularly the early ones, have unabashedly worshiped the composer as a hero. There is certainly much to admire in Handel's character and achievement: his independence, his generosity and devotion to charity, his industriousness and dedication to his art as well as his refusal to ever compromise it, and his perseverance through adversity, particularly in the 1730s, are themes that surface again and again in the biographies.

A third prominent theme in Handelian biography, since at least the time of Schoelcher, is the lament that Handel's works are, or have been, grossly misunderstood. This topic has two facets, both of which reflect aspects of Handel's reception since his death. The first recurrent complaint is that Handel's music is hardly known; apart from a few oratorios such as *Messiah*, the vast majority of his works—particularly the operas, but also most of his oratorios and instrumental compositions—are forgotten. It is only in recent years that we have come to a more balanced appreciation of Handel's entire output. The paradox is that perhaps no composer has been so long and so steadily in the public's ears and hearts as Handel.

More recent literature also questions the common, particularly Victorian, image of Handel as a pious composer whose works were created in the service of religion. Partly a result of limited familiarity with Handel's output, and partly willful misunderstanding, this image resulted in, among other things, the adaptation of new sacred texts to Handel's secular Italian melodies. This process, which began shortly after Handel's death, eventually led one Victorian to observe that "all Handel's fine Italian [opera] airs are essentially of a sacred character."

Fourth, Handel's sexuality has been debated by recent scholars. The composer never married, and there is no reliable evidence that he became romantically involved with anyone of either sex. Some have construed the absence of information as an indication that Handel was probably gay. The only plausible proof for this speculation is John Hawkins's statement, "That [Handel] had no female attachments of another kind [i.e., sexual] may be ascribed to a better reason." The better reason that some choose to see is a preference for men, but of course the better reason might have been anything: physical problems, emotional ones, and so forth. Faced with such alternate interpretations, the most popular strategy of those who consider the composer a homosexual has been guilt by association: because Handel moved in gay circles, he must have been gay himself.

Important 18th-century biographical contributions came from Burney, Coxe, Mainwaring, and Mattheson; their works form the foundation of our knowledge of Handel's life. Handelian biography begins with MATTHESON's brief contribution, which is particularly valuable for details of Handel's time at Hamburg (1703–06), when he and Mattheson worked together at the opera house there. The reminiscences of one who knew Handel as a friend are of considerable value.

MAINWARING is the first full-length biography of any European composer to be published in any language and the most important of the early Handel biographies

not only because it is the most complete but because the information appears to have come ultimately from Handel himself through his amanuensis, John Christopher Smith the younger. The chronology is often incorrect, but where details of Mainwaring's anecdotes can be checked against other contemporary documents, they prove reliable. The book also reflects contemporary English views of Handel's music as a perfect expression of the sublime.

BURNEY, like Mattheson, knew Handel personally, and his biography is a rich source of firsthand information and anecdotes. (Handelian anecdotes are among the most numerous and entertaining of those for any composer.) Burney was under some pressure from George III and the conductor Joah Bates to produce a favorable picture of the composer: he once observed that "one key of Panegyric is all they want—fine!—very fine!—charming! exquisite! grand! Sublime!!! These are all the notes (a Hexachord) I must use." Still, the biography clearly reflects the author's love and admiration for Handel and his music.

The 19th century produced two biographies of nearly equal documentary significance to those from the 18th century. SCHOELCHER was the first biography of Handel to be based on solid documentary evidence, and the credit goes to Schoelcher for uncovering many significant sources. He had the good sense to use systematically contemporary newspapers to fix dates of Handel's compositions and performances, using them and a wide range of other contemporary sources to provide a rounded portrait not only of the composer but also of the social and musical worlds in which he moved. Of equal importance, Schoelcher was the first to carefully study Handel's manuscripts in an attempt to establish chronology and in particular the original forms and various revisions of Handel's compositions.

CHRYSANDER's three volumes are of equal or greater documentary wealth, and they benefit from the author's unrivaled knowledge of Handel's music. But the book is incomplete (ending at 1740), and it betrays a nationalistic bias that dictates that Handel be promoted as yet another example of German excellence, despite his international experiences, his mastery of all the national styles of his time, and his decades in England.

STREATFEILD offers a balanced and elegantly written biography notable for its original contributions on early periods of Handel's career and its discussion of the operas at a time when they were generally thought beyond resuscitation. The element of hero worship that the study evinces is common to many of the early biographies.

DEUTSCH's documentary biography, one of the fundamental tools of Handel research, is a chronological arrangement of contemporary documents (newspaper advertisements, letters, diary entries, etc.) accompanied by rich commentary. The documents cover the period 1683 through 1780 and are organized with Mainwaring's *Memoirs* as framework. As Deutsch observes in his preface, the presentation of all the facts in such an arrangement results in a "cumulative truth" rarely, if ever, seen in the more common narrative biography. Deutsch's book has been revised and supplemented as volume 4 of the *Händel Handbuch,* which presents all the documents in their original languages with commentary in German.

LANG's substantial biography is also a notable cultural history. The author is more interested in interpretation than documentation, and, indeed, he brings no new documentary evidence to the field and commits some factual errors. But his biography is notable for its attempt to wash away older views of Handel's works and to see the composer and his music afresh. Lang brings a rich understanding of the culture and critical thought of Handel's time to the field. He also provides one of the few serious discussions of Handelian biography, and while this essay is perhaps excessively critical, damning nearly all German and English efforts predating his own, he raises some significant issues.

DEAN provides a succinct and authoritative biography that contains much information in a format that makes quick reference possible. Its origin as a dictionary article dictates that this study is concerned more with facts than interpretation. The volume also includes the definitive work list, by Anthony Hicks, which provides data concerning the histories and sources of each work, as well as volume references to the two editions of Handel's complete works, making it easy to find scores of Handel's music.

Written in a clear and accessible style, HOGWOOD is based on a sound documentary foundation and includes numerous illustrations and a reliable chronology (by Hicks). Hogwood has a happy habit of supplying quotations at regular intervals throughout his text. Especially useful is an extended treatment of "Handel and Posterity," which outlines Handel's reception in England, Germany, Austria, France, and the United States from 1759 to 1984.

The National Portrait Gallery's 1985 Handel exhibit, accompanied by this sumptuous catalog edited by SIMON, was "an attempt to tell the story of Handel's life and of the creation of his music through the people and events of his time." A vast collection of documents and images, beautifully reproduced and accompanied by scholarly commentary of a high standard, the catalog more than succeeds in achieving that goal. It is particularly notable for its opening pictorial essay, an exploration of the many portraits of Handel. Also useful are two of the appendices: a discussion of Handel's library based on book and score subscription lists and a gathering of the various references to Handel as a collector of paintings, with a list of those paintings he is known to have owned. This is one of the richest and most reliable pictorial biographies of any composer ever produced.

PARKER-HALE's annotated bibliography of the Handel literature is sensibly divided into various subject categories and is a useful place for the beginner to start.

A remarkable amount of new research on Handel's life and works has been conducted in the last 40 years, and as a result, we now know much more about his life. This research is all incorporated into BURROWS (1994), a reliable and informative presentation of the composer's life and works. The book has been criticized for its organization, which periodically splits the life and works into separate sections; as a result, the reader often must look in many places to find information on any given work or period of the composer's life (a search aided by the index). Useful appendices include a chronology, a list of Handel's works, and a helpful personalia (brief biographies of contemporaries connected with Handel); there is also a fine select bibliography.

One of the most widely read and discussed articles in recent years is THOMAS, which has provoked no end of heated response. As a paper given at the American Musicological Society's 1990 conference, the essay was originally titled "Was George Frideric Handel Gay?—And Why the Question Matters." Reactions to the published version have stubbornly concentrated on the first of these two themes, when Thomas's point seems to have been more connected to the second issue. He does not seek to "out" Handel. Barring the discovery of written testimony, Handel's sexuality cannot be determined. The author's primary intention is to ask why scholars have avoided posing the very question and in asking that, to make some points about the way we write history.

BURROWS (1997) is particularly helpful from a biographical point of view for the first two essays in the collection, which outline the current state of research on Handel's education and apprenticeship as a youth in Germany and his crucial formative years in Italy.

RICHARD G. KING

2. Operas

Burrows, Donald, *Handel,* New York: Schirmer Books, 1994

Dean, Winton, *Handel and the Opera Seria,* Berkeley: University of California Press, 1969

Dean, Winton, and John Merrill Knapp, *Handel's Operas 1704–1726,* Oxford: Clarendon Press, and New York: Oxford University Press, 1987; revised edition 1995

Deutsch, Otto Erich, *Handel: A Documentary Biography,* New York: Norton, 1955

Harris, Ellen T., *Handel and the Pastoral Tradition,* London: Oxford University Press, 1980

Hogwood, Christopher, *Handel,* London: Thames and Hudson, 1984

Lang, Paul Henry, *George Frideric Handel,* New York: Norton, 1966

LaRue, C. Steven, *Handel and His Singers: The Creation of the Royal Academy Operas, 1720–1728,* Oxford: Clarendon Press, and New York: Oxford University Press, 1995

Strohm, Reinhard, *Dramma per Musica: Italian Opera Seria of the Eighteenth Century,* New Haven, Connecticut: Yale University Press, 1997

———, *Essays on Handel and Italian Opera,* Cambridge: Cambridge University Press, 1985

Young, Percy M., *Handel,* London: Dent, and New York: Dutton, 1947; revised edition, 1975

George Frideric Handel is accepted as one of the greatest composers in Western music history and is usually mentioned in one breath with Johann Sebastian Bach as the pinnacle of the musical baroque. In view of the general agreement of his "greatness," it is indeed surprising to find so little early research on his music. As late as 1962, Stanley Sadie could still state that this consensus about Handel is based "on the strength of one major untypical work." To be sure, there did not seem to be a necessity for a great "revival movement" comparable to the Bach revival in the 19th century. Friedrich Chrysander's work on Handel, the collected edition of his works and biography, dominated the research scene. In the early 20th century came the Göttingen Handel Festivals, with revivals of some of the operas beginning in 1920 with *Rodelinda.* Edward J. Dent, an important Handel scholar in the earlier 20th century, published a Handel biography in 1934 and an article ("Handel on Stage" in *Music and Letters*) the following year. Although dated in point of view, Dent's texts stand at the beginning of English-language studies on Handel in general and the operas in particular and are still worth reading. The towering figure of Handel research is no doubt Winton Dean. His seminal book *Handel's Dramatic Oratorios and Masques* (1959) was followed by extensive research on the opera autographs and manuscript copies, which he found largely uninvestigated at that time. Two major works resulted from this work: *Handel and the Opera Seria* (1969) and, in collaboration with J.M. Knapp, *Handel's Operas 1704–1726* (1987).

In the area of Handel biography, Deutsch's *Documentary Biography* (1955) was a milestone with its array of primary sources, much of it relating to various aspects of the opera productions throughout the composer's career. Most biographies incorporated the discussion of the operas into the account of the career. But the central interpretative problem concerning Handel's operas is connected to the nature of opera seria in his time. To shed light on this issue, Handel scholars have delved into many different aspects of specialized research on the operas, such as libretto studies and pasticcios (Strohm), Handel's borrowings (John H. Roberts), Handel and the pastoral genre (Harris), Handel's singers (LaRue), and stage and staging (Lowell Lindgren), to name a few. The 1980s and 1990s saw a veritable crescendo in English-language publications on Handel and his operas, ranging from very scholarly to more popular, but all with the implied objective of educating the music-loving public,

opera directors, and performers so that ultimately some of the masterpieces among Handel's operas will not only be performed with understanding but be accepted as part of the regular repertoire of major opera companies.

YOUNG wrote and published his Handel biography before the great proliferation of Handel research, but for a concentrated life-and-music approach it is still useful to read, as it lives up to its objective of presenting Handel and his music in the context of the period, society, and audiences. The first half (eight chapters) is devoted to the detail-packed biography, written in a succinct and witty style, with the trials of the opera productions coming vividly to life. The second half of the book takes up matters of Handel's style—especially melodic—and influences on it, as well as issues of orchestration and of characterization in the music—both of the composer and of the operatic characters. Although there is no discreet chapter on the operas, examples pervade the discussion. Young presents Handel as a nature- and life-loving realist who demonstrated these traits in life as well as in his music.

Although outdated today, the groundbreaking documentary biography by DEUTSCH is still a fascinating source of information on the operas. For each year, documents are quoted with commentary (with occasional errors), ranging from newspaper notices regarding opera and concert performances, critiques, reports, publications of music, notices of payments, correspondence, and cast lists to poems, either biting satire or glowing hymns of praise to the composer.

LANG's Handel biography is scholarly, detailed, and comprehensive, again reflecting the need to study "a Handel largely unknown," that is, the composer of operas and other dramatic works besides *Messiah.* The operas are discussed in the biographical context; their success or failure and reasons for either are evaluated; and the author's view of them is presented. In the seventh chapter, he pauses for a discussion of baroque opera in relation to Handel. Lang's arguments about what to do with the castrato parts for modern performance are certainly outdated now, but they throw light on the problem as well as some earlier 20th-century authors' belief that women in heroic parts, not to mention countertenors, would be unpalatable to modern audiences. In general, Lang's emphasis is on literary and musical traditions and trends of importance to Handel's stylistic development. Chapter 23 deals mainly with the operas from this point of view, exploring how the Italian tradition, especially as a "class art" applied to and was transformed in the English context. Chapter 24 proceeds to musical style, in both operas and oratorios, issues of aria and recitative, ensemble writing, as well as aesthetics, and Handel's relationship to the *Affektenlehre.*

In the earliest truly important study (1969) specifically on Handel's operas, DEAN corrects his own earlier view of opera seria and Handel's "sheer genius" for overcoming its limitations. Dean explains the "opera seria convention" in light of modern audience attitudes, including the 18th-century attitude toward the choice of voices for parts, which selected singers according to the voice range and quality, not to the sex of the character (a different approach from Lang). Dean stresses the concept of the Handel opera "as a whole," as drama with a planned tonal scheme, aria design, and organization all fitting into this whole. Important also is the author's analysis of the libretto and the adaptations for London, including those made for the sake of the available singers and those for the sake of the audiences, as demonstrated, for example, by the abbreviation of the recitatives.

Dean discusses Handel's operas in three broad categories: heroic, magic, and antiheroic. The first group bearing the Metastasio stamp inspired Handel to present the protagonists "in their strength and weakness as human beings grappling with the problems of life and death." In each group Dean gives striking examples illustrated by musical excerpts. Questions of theatrical craftsmanship, recitative and aria forms, orchestration, and the pitfalls of modern revivals are raised in the remainder of the book. (In a very concise form the author also addresses some of these issues in his Handel biography in the New Grove series [1980], which includes a detailed work list with references to sources and editions by Anthony Hicks.)

In her thorough, scholarly study, HARRIS explores the pastoral genre, beginning with the late Renaissance pastoral drama and its relationships to earlier literary genres such as the medieval romance. She describes the pastoral in the three countries where Handel lived and composed and examines the complexities of the genre in each national tradition. The earliest Italian operas were pastorals, up to about 1630, when the "Venetian pastoral" moved closer to heroic opera, only to decline after about 1650 until the Arcadian revival at the end of the 17th century.

Handel was familiar with the German pastoral tradition early on; his last opera for Hamburg—*Florinda and Daphne* (divided into two)—was a pastoral. In the section on Italy, Harris focuses on his cantatas with pastoral texts, analyzing arias to identify the musical counterpart to the literary genre. It was in Italy that Handel learned about lyricism and Arcadian tastes. His second opera for England, the pastoral *Il pastor fido* (1712), was unsuccessful; the operatic pastoral was not popular there. After his emphasis on mostly heroic operas in the 1720s, Handel entered a later pastoral phase with a new version of *Acis and Galatea* (1732), in which he synthesizes elements of the Italian, German, and English pastoral traditions. Harris calls the Ariosto operas such as *Orlando* and *Alcina* pastoral operas, not magical, as Dean does.

HOGWOOD's biography—he calls it a "documentary biography"—is in some ways similar to that of H.C. Robbins Landon (*Handel and His World,* 1984): both commemorate the tercentenary of Handel's birth year,

both emphasize the quotation of documents, and both profess their indebtedness to Deutsch's documentary biography, which they expand with by new material come to light. For example, both authors bring in new evidence relating to Handel's Italian sojourn, such as the Ruspoli documents and Valesio's diary. Both are aimed at the general reader, but Landon's book seems more popularized by its general layout and a greater profusion of pictorial illustrations. Hogwood's third and fourth chapters, covering the years 1710 to 1737, are of particular interest in their detailed documentation of the opera productions with ample quotations from Burney, Hawkins, Addison and Steele, Mainwaring, and many others, always evaluated in terms of their prejudices and errors.

The results of STROHM's (1985) extensive scholarly research on Italian baroque opera, originally published in German during the 1970s and 1980s, illumine a host of issues and research perspectives in relation to Handel and his important contemporaries. In the preface, Strohm makes the startling remark that the essays were originally meant to hold Handel's operas up against the "Italian operatic tradition"—a position he no longer defends. Handel was, of course, extremely familiar with Italian opera, but his operas are consciously different, not just "better" than those of his contemporaries. The chapter on Handel's Italian opera texts examines each libretto and its antecedents, warning at the outset of the importance of distinguishing between the sources Handel actually used and the mere existence of an earlier version. The fourth essay illustrates one of Handel's models among Italian opera composers, Franceco Gasparini, who during his Roman period formed part of a conservative circle and whose later operas Handel studied and emulated. The two composers' settings of *Faramondo* illustrate this comparison with examples of melodic and rhythmic parallels. Another group of works, Handel's *pasticci,* are scrutinized for information about sources of libretti and original contexts as well as Handel's reasons for undertaking them, which sometimes included simply the sheer necessity of time pressures or singer availability.

In 1987 DEAN and KNAPP published their monumental study on the early Handel operas (1704–26), based on extensive manuscript and libretto study as well as the use of modern research tools. The chronological limitation was necessitated by the sheer volume of material and information (volume 2 has yet to appear). Handel is presented as a masterful composer capable of creating musical and dramatic unity, memorable characters of a wide range, aria designs of subtle variety, boldly expressive accompanied recitatives, overtures that sometimes link up with the opening action, inventive uses of the orchestra, and exceptionally sensitive treatment of the solo voice, even individual singers' voices.

This treasure trove of a book treats each opera in chronological order and in great detail, offering an act-by-act synopsis; discussion of the source libretti and the various changes by Handel; discussion of the music; the history of the composition and the performances (including the changes made for subsequent performances and revivals); and extensive exploration of autographs, copies, libretti, and editions. The appendices are also valuable references, containing, for example, a list of borrowings and one of revivals up to 1984.

Handel research in the 1990s continued on all fronts. BURROWS's study is based on the notion that the outer biography is complemented by the "inner biography" of the composer's creative life. Therefore, the author adopts an unusual methodology: imbedded in the chronological discussion are chapters on the music for each subperiod, except the final years. Thus, the operas are treated in the context of the music chapters, especially in chapters 7 and 10. A few examples are selected for brief discussion, and *Giulio Cesare* is singled out for more detailed analysis. For a generalized view of the operas of a given period in Handel's career, such as the "Academy years," this text is a good point of departure, for the book is written in an accessible style and refers the reader to the relevant modern studies for further information. When discussing *Giulio Cesare,* Burrows adopts the device of following Caesar and Cleopatra through the plot and their musical expressions, emphasizing the arias, their structures, and their melodic and harmonic style, among other elements.

The domination of the singers in the 18th-century opera seria has often been described, but LaRUE goes further in his penetrating study of Handel's singers in relation to the composer's concept of the characters they are to portray. Concentrating on a limited period (1720–28), LaRue undertakes a detailed examination of the libretti and autograph scores to determine how Handel's compositional process was affected by particular singers, an especially revealing process when different versions or revisions of a score are extant. For example, in *Tamerlano* the changes made for Francesco Borosini in the part of Bajazet after completion of the score can be identified. LaRue concludes that in the earlier works the character tended to determine the arias, whereas in the later ones, the prevailing factors were the singer's abilities and specific vocal qualities.

STROHM (1997) compiles another group of essays on opera seria, representing essays from the late 1980s and early 1990s. He explores the contemporary reception of the genre in such cities as Rome, Venice, and Madrid, and debates such issues as the comparison of *dramma per musica* with its models and contemporary theories. The third group of essays is largely devoted to Handel. For instance, the opera *Tolomeo* is examined in light of the contemporary rules of tragedy, their conflicts with operatic practice, and Handel and Haym's solution of blending "play and ethos." By way of the discussion of *Arianna in Creta,* the roles of classical dramatic theory, rhetoric and allegory, and gesture and stage direction are reviewed, and *Ariodante* is seen as a moralist's juxta-

position of guilt and innocence couched in the pastoral ambiance and enhanced by choruses and dances.

OLGA TERMINI

3. Oratorios

Burrows, Donald, *Handel: Messiah,* Cambridge: Cambridge University Press, 1991

Dean, Winton, *Handel's Dramatic Oratorios and Masques,* London: Oxford University Press, 1959

Hurley, David Ross, *Handel's Muse: Patterns of Creation in the Oratorios and Musical Dramas, 1743–1751,* Oxford: Clarendon Press, 2000

Larsen, Jens Peter, *Handel's Messiah: Origins, Composition, Sources,* New York: Norton, 1957; 2nd edition, 1972

Shaw, Watkins, *A Textual and Historical Companion to Handel's Messiah,* London: Novello, 1965

Smith, Ruth, *Handel's Oratorios and Eighteenth-Century Thought,* Cambridge: Cambridge University Press, 1995

Smither, Howard E., *A History of the Oratorio,* Volume 2, *The Oratorio in the Baroque Era: Protestant Germany and England,* Chapel Hill: University of North Carolina Press, 1977

Tobin, John, *Handel at Work,* New York: St. Martin's Press, and London: Cassell, 1964

———, *Handel's Messiah: A Critical Account of the Manuscript Sources and Printed Editions,* New York: St. Martin's Press, and London: Cassell, 1969

Young, Percy M., *The Oratorios of Handel,* London: Dobson, 1949

George Frideric Handel seems to have created large-scale English oratorio by synthesizing a large number of sources: Latin oratorio (such as Carissimi's *Jephthe,* from which Handel borrowed in 1741), Italian *oratorio volgare* (Handel's *Il trionfo del tempo* and *La resurrezione* of 1707–08 are examples of this genre), Italian opera seria, the German oratorio, the choral style of his own Latin psalms and English anthems, and the masque. We owe the protracted existence of the English oratorio genre to a chain of circumstances: a successful revival of Handel's 1718 version of *Esther* by the Children of the Chapel Royal under Bernard Gates at the Crown and Anchor Tavern in February 1732, which was admired by the royal princess, encouraged Handel to revise *Esther* for performance before the general public. The fact that the Children of the Chapel Royal were forbidden to appear in staged theatrical performances, as well as the fact that it was unacceptable to present a staged sacred work in a public theater, may have pushed Handel to cultivate the oratorio as an unstaged genre, thereby influencing the choral element, and had it not been for the success of this production, Handel might not have continued to cultivate the genre as he did. Given the multifarious sources for English oratorio and the chance events that shaped it, it is no wonder that Handel's oratorios embrace diverse characteristics—so extreme, in fact, that scholars have disagreed about as basic a fact as which works belong to the genre.

There are certain broad characteristics that help to define Handel's oratorios—they are unstaged works in English, with stories often derived from the Old Testament; they consist largely of recitative, arias, and choruses (with a small number of other ensembles, such as duets and quartets); they differ from the Passion because they lack a narrator and from continental oratorio because they give the prominent role to the chorus. There are nonetheless a huge number of variable elements among works that have been admitted to the genre: *Semele* and *Hercules* among the dramatic oratorios have secular texts, while *Theodora* is based not on a biblical episode but a novel about a Christian martyr; the nonnarrative works *Alexander's Feast* and *L'Allegro, il Penseroso, ed il Moderato* are based on poems by Dryden and Milton; *Saul* has very few da capo arias and sometimes cuts intervening recitatives, while the later oratorios *Susanna, Theodora*, and *Jephtha* see a dramatic rise in da capo arias and for long stretches without choral intervention, resemble opera seria.

Aside from *Messiah,* which has been treated in a number of studies, the emphasis in Handel studies has been on the composer as dramatist (Dean) and more recently on the political and religious ramifications of his texts (Smith), which is most apparent in the dramatic works. Consequently, the nondramatic secular works, such as *Alexander's Feast,* are among the least-studied of Handel's unstaged vocal/choral works. The literature on Handel's oratorios falls roughly into two categories: works dealing with the entire body or a large group of oratorios and studies devoted to *Messiah.*

YOUNG, the first book devoted to the Handelian oratorio, omits the secular works from consideration. The book can no longer be regarded as an authoritative source; the reader should not rely on its information without consulting more recent works. Nonetheless, Young's then fashionable evaluative approach combined with a flowery writing style make for entertaining reading. Certain of the book's assertions must always have been difficult to swallow. Of *La Resurrezione,* for example, Young writes, "It is with the mind of a medieval that Handel looks at Lucifer: the technique of caricature which turns Lucifer into a gargoyle, with very human face, is a transmutation of medieval practice."

Appearing a decade after Young's book, DEAN's volume has established itself as the classic study of Handel's oratorios. The author's focus on Handel as musical dramatist leads him to include the secular works *Semele* and *Hercules* in his discussion. Part 1 includes seven chapters that provide a history of the oratorio before Handel, Handel's early works, style and performance of the oratorios, the librettos and autographs, and the ora-

torio and English taste. Part 2 consists of 19 chapters, each devoted to a single oratorio. These chapters include detailed information on the historical background; the librettist; a summary of the plot; an analysis of the music, including orchestration, history and text, which embraces performances in Handel's lifetime; insertions and changes for later performances; and summary of the editions, the librettos, and the autograph and sketches. Extensive appendices include detailed information on various issues, such as lists of borrowings and Handel's oratorio singers.

After 40 years, Dean's almost impeccable scholarship holds up remarkably well; even the extensive study of Handel's autographs by Donald Burrows and Martha Ronish, *A Catalogue of Handel's Musical Autographs* (1994), has for the most part done little more than alter details. Performance practices have changed radically since the 1950s, however, and Dean's discussion of matters relating to musical performance are not always applicable today. There are three issues involved here: first, Dean's enthusiasm for Handel's dramatic genius leads him to argue for theatrical staging of oratorios—a position with which performers concerned with historical accuracy will take issue; second, following mid–20th-century performance practices, Dean believes that the oratorios need to be cut to preserve their strengths, resulting in versions unknown to the composer—these suggestions, too, should be taken with a grain of salt by those interested in performing authentic versions; and finally, Dean offers evaluation of the quality of the oratorios. Whether he intended it, his judgments have unfortunately suppressed performances of some worthy music.

SMITHER's discussion of Handel's oratorio in the author's larger history of the oratorio presents no new material, although the book includes some analytical information not found in Dean; in particular, Smither discusses the forms of the non-da capo arias. He excludes all of the secular works from discussion, since the early sources indicate that the term *oratorio* was avoided for these works.

SMITH offers a fresh and original approach to the oratorios in her work, which is devoted to texts rather than music. Contemplating the gap between modern critical evaluations of the oratorios (particularly from Dean) and the opinions of Handel and his audiences, she attempts to re-create Handel's world by placing the librettos in the context of religious and political discussions of early 18th-century England. The result is a book of interest not only to Handelians but to anyone interested in the culture of early Georgian England. In part 1, "English Origins of English Oratorios," which includes, among other subjects, discussions on contemporary views on the purpose of art, the biblical sublime, and Christianity defended, Smith argues that Handel's oratorios may be read as anti-Deist tracts. Part 2, "The Patriot Libretto from the Excise Bill to the Jew Bill: Israelite

Oratorios and English Politics," offers thoroughly grounded historical readings of the political implications of the oratorios.

HURLEY attempts to broaden our view of composition in the early 18th century (largely constructed by studies of Bach) by examining Handel's creative acts up to the first-performance version. The author draws on Handel's sketches and drafts to construct models of aria composition in the period, includes discussion of recurring compositional revisions by type, addresses Handel's manipulation of texture in choruses, and compares Handel's practice to contemporary writings. The later chapters are devoted to extramusical matters that shed light on dramatic considerations, changes related to specific singers (especially Giulia Frasi), and Handel's musical imagery.

LARSEN's book on *Messiah* presents a broad array of important information on a number of topics relating to Handel's oratorios. The work begins with a chapter on the development of Handelian oratorio that divides the oratorios into types: the biblical oratorios embracing heroic, anthem, and narrative types, and the nonbiblical, comprising concert or cantata and mythological types. Although scholars may quibble with details, Larsen's attempt to identify oratorios by characteristics was overdue. Larsen offers technical information on aria and choral structure that goes far beyond Young's earlier oratorio book; he includes new information on the sources and Handel's singers; and his identification of Handel's copyists has provided a foundation for later studies of the autographs.

A number of books devoted to *Messiah* appeared during the 1960s. Although none of them possess the scope of Larsen's work, taken together they form a detailed and comprehensive survey of information relating to or derived from the sources. While TOBIN (1964) claims that his book was written for the musical amateur, his presentation of compositional revisions in *Messiah*, together with generally convincing musical reasons for the changes, offers material of interest to scholars investigating in compositional process.

SHAW's volume, essentially a detailed critical commentary for the author's edition of *Messiah*, is perhaps the most important study of *Messiah* published between Larsen and the 1990s. It contains more comprehensive and detailed information on the early autograph and printed sources than Larsen and includes discussion of performing versions and textual authority, as well as Shaw's editorial policies.

A less well-known work, TOBIN (1969), which appeared four years after Shaw's volume, was written in conjunction with a performance of *Messiah* "in scale and style such as the composer himself would accept." Following a discussion of sources, the chapters on harmonic structure and Handel's treatment of English offer material still of interest today, while the chapter on style in

performance discloses a thoughtfulness that today's performers would do well to emulate.

In a number of articles on *Messiah* written from the 1970s through the 1990s, BURROWS established himself as one of the leading experts on this oratorio. As a result, his volume, one of the Cambridge Music Handbook Series, while intended as a general account, contains a great deal of fresh information, revising previous notions of the chronology of different versions (moving the common-time version of "Rejoice Greatly" from 1749 to 1745), questioning whether *Messiah* was unambiguously intended for Dublin from the beginning, and making use of the recent discovery of the libretto from the first London performance of 1743.

DAVID ROSS HURLEY

4. Instrumental Music

Abraham, Gerald, editor, *Handel: A Symposium*, London: Oxford University Press, 1954
Drummond, Pippa, *The German Concerto: Five Eighteenth-Century Studies*, Oxford: Clarendon Press, New York: Oxford University Press, 1980
Mann, Alfred, *Handel: The Orchestral Music*, New York: Schirmer Books, and London: Prentice Hall, 1996
Sadie, Stanley, *Handel Concertos*, London: British Broadcasting Corporation, 1972; Seattle: University of Washington Press, 1973

A survey of the scholarly literature devoted to Handel's music reveals a topography remarkably similar to the presentation of his music in performance: the vocal and choral music—opera and oratorio—are emphasized over the instrumental works. Although two of Handel's sets of concerti grossi place him among the best of his contemporaries in the instrumental genre, his stature within the pantheon of musical greats would be considerably diminished if his reputation were based only his instrumental music. As a result, the publications devoted to this facet of his output tend toward shorter studies found in periodical journals and Festschriften; monographs on the subject are relatively few.

ABRAHAM's collection of ten essays by eight authors presents some useful studies on Handel's life and work. A benchmark in Handel scholarship from the early 1950s, the anthology divides the instrumental music into three classifications—orchestral, keyboard, and chamber—and devotes a separate essay to each. Abraham's agenda, stated clearly in his preface, is to familiarize the reading and listening public with those parts of Handel's oeuvre with which they were almost completely unfamiliar—in essence, virtually every work except *Messiah*.

In his essay about the op. 6 Concerti Grossi in Abraham's collection, Basil Lam takes up each of the concerti ad seriatim, highlighting especially those characteristics that are unique to Handel's work. Devoting only a paragraph to each concerto, Lam makes frequent references and comparisons to Handel's near-contemporaries—Corelli, Bach, and Vivaldi—in addition to supplying anecdotal information from Burney and other admirers of Handel's music in the 18th and 19th centuries. The author then proceeds in similar fashion through the other orchestral works, including the op. 3 Concerti, the concerto in *Alexander's Feast*, the *Water Music*, the *Music for the Royal Fireworks*, the concerti *a due Cori*, and, finally, the organ concerti.

Also in Abraham, Kathleen Dale's essay on "The Keyboard Music" begins by acknowledging that Handel's works for harpsichord are largely ignored by performers. She provides an overview of the various sets of pieces comparable to Lam's survey, emphasizing once again that the pieces in question "bear the impress of the universality of [Handel's] style." Near the end of her essay, Dale enumerates passages from Handel's keyboard works that recall the style of Domenico Scarlatti.

Finally, John Horton's essay on "The Chamber Music" covers the various types of sonata for solo instrument (primarily flute and oboe) and basso continuo. Horton's article is the only essay of the three to deal in any consistent fashion with the numerous borrowings from and correspondences with other works that one finds in Handel's instrumental compositions.

SADIE's slim volume reads like an extended set of concert program notes, which is exactly how the BBC Listening Guides were conceived and crafted. Sadie covers the same repertoire as does Lam, but Sadie takes up each group of pieces in chronological order. Thus, he divides his discussion of the organ concertos into two parts—"Early" and "Late"—with a section on the op. 6 Concerti Grossi in between. He reserves discussion of the *Water Music* and the *Fireworks Music* until the end, arguing that they are "not properly 'concertos'" but rather belong to a category of "outdoor music" of French origin. In his introduction, Sadie acknowledges the difficulty of speaking in terms of a definitive version of a work; in the sections that follow, he takes account of sources and their textual problems in detail. Sadie uses musical examples in the text sparingly, for the purpose of illustrating the structure of fugue subjects, highlighting unusual textures, and providing comparisons to other works that use similar material.

Although not devoted exclusively to the music of Handel, DRUMMOND's monumental study provides a thorough and informative account of Handel's works alongside those of J.S. Bach, Telemann, Hasse, and C.P.E. Bach. These works include the usual sets—op. 3, op. 6, the organ concerti, the concerto in *Alexander's Feast*, the concerti *a due Cori*, and miscellaneous instrumental concertos—but Drummond does not discuss the *Water Music* and *Fireworks Music*. In addition to providing a convenient summary of the bibliographic history of these works and cogent musical analysis (illustrated with 31 musical examples), Drummond offers one of the most balanced and well-reasoned views available of Handel's borrowing in his instrumental works. She traces the history of discussion of Handel's reuse of earlier works (both his own and those of other composers), suggesting that "he was always more concerned with the successful working-out and development of ideas than with the invention of new themes."

MANN provides much the same type of discussion as Sadie and covers exactly the same repertoire in nearly the same order, although with more extensive musical examples. Mann includes chapters titled "On Handel's Technique of Composition" and "Some Considerations of Performance Practice" as well as 12 pages of facsimile illustrations from the autograph manuscripts. The penultimate chapter includes a lengthy comparison of a movement from Handel's Organ Concerto op. 7, no. 2, with the piece on which it is based, an unpublished fugue by Gottlieb Muffat. Mann uses this comparative illustration to comment on Handel's approach to counterpoint, form, and texture, as well as to evaluate Handel's stature relative to one of his illustrious contemporaries. After fleshing out this discussion with examples from other works and comparisons to other composers, Mann concludes that "Handel's imagination was as unlimited as his interest in revising, improving, and experimenting." A bibliography of reference works, critical editions, and recent specialized studies rounds off this volume.

MARK RISINGER

Hanslick, Eduard 1825–1904

Austrian music critic and essayist

Abegg, Werner, *Musikästhetik und Musikkritik bei Eduard Hanslick*, Regensburg: Bosse, 1974

Gay, Peter, *Freud, Jews, and Other Germans: Masters and Victims in Modernist Culture*, New York: Oxford University Press, 1978

Hanslick, Eduard, *Aus dem Tagebuch eines Rezensenten*, edited by Peter Wapnewski, Kassel: Bärenreiter, 1989

———, *On the Musically Beautiful: A Contribution towards the Revision of the Aesthetics of Music*, translated by Geoffrey Payzant, Indianapolis, Indiana: Hackett Publishing, 1986

———, *Sämtliche Schriften*, edited by Dietmar Strauss, Vienna: Böhlau, 1993

———, *Vienna's Golden Years of Music, 1850–1900*, translated and edited by Henry Pleasants, New York: Simon and Schuster, 1950

Payzant, Geoffrey, *Eduard Hanslick and Ritter Berlioz in Prague: A Documentary Narrative*, Calgary: University of Calgary Press, 1991

Among 19th-century music critics, Eduard Hanslick stood as a figure to be either emulated and admired or derided and scorned but always as one to be confronted. His *Vom Musikalisch-Schönen* (*On the Musically Beautiful*), first published in 1854, appeared in ten editions during his lifetime, making it one of the most widely read, if not most widely accepted, musical treatises of the century. Hanslick contributed to public discourse not only as an aesthetician and philosopher of music but also as a chronicler of his age. With frequent music reviews for Vienna's *Neue Freie Presse,* his voice provided a pipeline of information and a filter for the musical experiences of countless Viennese.

Hanslick's views acquired notoriety in his day as the antipode to Wagner's theories of musical expression. Debates between those pro- and contra-Wagner quickly became polemical, and Hanslick's ideas were often regarded more as bludgeons in the battle than as theories worthy of investigation for their own merits and nuances. This tendency to paraphrase Hanslick rather than to explore his writings persisted into the 20th century as well, as the few modern editions and even fewer translations of his work attest. Secondary literature devoted to Hanslick is correspondingly scarce despite his prominence within 19th-century musical life.

Peter Gay's essay "For Beckmesser: Eduard Hanslick, Victim and Prophet" in GAY provides a useful overview and contextualization of Hanslick's original contributions to musical aesthetics. Hanslick's role became defined in his own lifetime and after his death as one solely that of a critic of Wagner, but, as Gay shows, Hanslick wrote and lectured (in his post as the first professor of music history at the University of Vienna) on a wide range of composers and genres. Gay concludes this essay, the final one in the collection, by aligning Hanlick with the modernist culture explored in the preceding essays. Although the conservative, traditionalist Hanslick is rarely counted among music's modernists, his emphasis on form and aesthetic autonomy over communication of feeling allies his work with a later generation of creative artists.

ABEGG's book offers the German reader an introduction to Hanslick's career. With subsections titled "Hanslick's Conception of Aesthetics and Its Relationship to History," "General Problems of Aesthetics and Criticism," "Special Problems of Individual Genres," and "Hanslick's Position toward Music History," Abegg covers the leading aesthetic questions with which Hanslick and other critics concerned themselves. The author highlights many of the contradictions and contingencies of value that colored Hanslick's musical opinions—for example, the aesthetic value of a work is unrelated to its historical position, yet music before Bach was beautiful only in its own day; music must be continuously progressive as well as connected to preceding traditions; and music has an obligation to be beautiful, for "ugly music is false music"—and other premises either stated explicitly or left unarticulated by Hanslick himself.

Hanslick wrote countless reviews over the course of his journalistic career, one that spanned more than a half-century, but only a slim volume of these is available to English speakers: HANSLICK (1950). The publication history of this volume over the last half of the 20th century indicates the demand for Hanslick's work in English. The editor has selected a variety of writings covering contemporary performers (Joseph Joachim and Clara Schumann) and performances of older works (*St. Matthew Passion* and *Missa Solemnis*) as well as new music. The translations are both accurate and readable; however, several of the selections have been silently abridged, limiting the scholarly use of this volume. Nonetheless, it provides a general reader with a flavor for Hanslick as a writer and for the musical life of his day.

For the German reader, HANSLICK (1989) edition is preferable to Hanslick (1950). The editor includes a few of the same essays but generally selects reviews of contemporary music rather than of performers or performances of older repertoire. The anthology also includes Hanslick's obituaries for his friends Johannes Brahms and Johann Strauss as well as his obituary for Richard Wagner. This volume presents the full text of Hanslick's essays in a modern font, an improvement over the Gothic script of Hanslick's original volumes.

The German reader will greet the publication of HANSLICK's (1993) *Sämtliche Schriften* (Complete Writings) with enthusiastic gratitude. Editor Dietmar Strauss has undertaken to publish all of Hanslick's essays and reviews as they originally appeared. (When Hanslick collected his writings for later publication, he often edited them from the original versions first published in newspapers.) This immense undertaking will surely take decades to complete, but the first two volumes—which include Hanlick's writings between 1844 and 1854 plus several essays, extensive commentary, and a bibliography—promise to aid musicological research in a number of areas.

For English speakers, HANSLICK (1986) laudably presents a new translation of the critic's most notable work, *On the Musically Beautiful*. Hanslick's prose does not easily lend itself to idiomatic translation, and, as Payzant points out in the accompanying essay ("Towards a Revised Reading of Hanslick"), the only previous English translation of this singular treatise was first published in 1891 by Gustav Cohen. The present translation marks a significant improvement not only in its more readable style but also in conveying Hanslick's ideas more lucidly. End notes and thorough indices of subjects and persons make the book highly usable for students, scholars, and interested lay readers.

PAYZANT has also written one of the few volumes of secondary literature in English devoted to Hanslick. The book's subtitle, *A Documentary Narrative,* indicates its style and substance, a presentation of translated and original documents relevant to Hector Berlioz's 1846 visit to Prague, Hanslick's hometown. Payzant's purpose in this book is to explain the abrupt change in Hanslick's musical aesthetic that allowed him to wax enthusiastic about Berlioz's music initially, only to criticize it just as heartily a year later. Using correspondence and published material by Berlioz, Hanslick, and Hanslick's mentor, August Wilhelm Ambros, Payzant knits the documents together into an engaging narrative. This book is useful also for the scholar, for it translates several essays in their entirety, offers the original German text of "Ritter Berlioz in Prag" as an appendix, and includes an extensive bibliography, facilitating further research. More specific case studies such as this, whether focusing on individual composers or on specific genres, would be a welcome contribution to expanding our understanding of Viennese musical life and the role that Hanslick played in shaping it.

CAMILLE CRITTENDEN

Hanson, Howard 1896–1981

United States composer

Cohn, Arthur, *The Collector's 20th Century Music in the Western Hemisphere,* Philadelphia, Pennsylvania: Lippincott, 1961

Gleason, Harold, and Warren Becker, *20th Century American Composers,* Rochester, New York: Levis Music Store, 1969; 2nd edition, Bloomington, Indiana: Frangipani Press, 1980

Hanson, Howard, with David Russell Williams, *Conversations with Howard Hanson,* Arkadelphia, Arkansas: Delta Publications, 1988

Howard, John Tasker, *Our Contemporary Composers: American Music in the Twentieth Century,* New York: Crowell, 1941

Machlis, Joseph, *American Composers of Our Time,* New York: Crowell, 1963

Perone, James E., *Howard Hanson: A Bio-Bibliography,* Westport, Connecticut: Greenwood Press, 1993

Plain, Marilyn, *Howard Hanson: A Comprehensive Catalog of the Manuscripts,* Rochester, New York: Eastman School of Music Press, 1997

Tuthill, Burnet, *Howard Hanson,* New York: Schirmer, 1936

University of Rochester, Institute of American Music, *American Composers' Concerts, and Festivals of American Music, 1925–1971: Cumulative Repertoire,* Rochester, New York: University of Rochester Press, 1972

Howard Hanson was a gifted musician, educator, educational administrator, and advocate for music of the United States. During his lifetime he composed symphonies, choral works, an opera, a ballet, numerous songs, and orchestral and band pieces. Frequently classified as a neoromantic composer by musicologists, theorists, and critics, Hanson's programmatic symphonies and tone poems continue the romantic music tradition in the 20th century. Hanson's abilities extended beyond his compositional prowess, however. Joseph Machlis felt that Hanson played an essential role in the advancement of U.S. music during the first half of the 20th century. Hanson is primarily recognized for his role as director of the Eastman School of Music in Rochester, New York. It was during his tenure at this august institution that he instigated a series of concerts featuring new compositions by U.S. composers to give young composers an opportunity to hear performances of their works and to promote their careers. Hanson's primary contribution was his outstanding leadership and his ability to educate others about music of the United States.

There exist a multitude of texts regarding music of the United States and the people who have had an impact in this musical arena. However, few specifically address Hanson in detail. One of the best overall sources of information about Hanson is PERONE's excellent resource, which employs a narrative description of the composer at the beginning of the book. In addition to discussing Hanson's life and his numerous roles, including conductor and performer, Perone provides a listing of recorded interviews with the composer in the extensive discography. The book is divided into sections: a biography; a comprehensive listing of Hanson's compositions including dates, performance history, and manuscript information; a discography; and a complete bibliography of articles and books by and about this composer.

Another encyclopedic entry on Hanson appears in GLEASON and BECKER, a wonderful educational and teaching reference source. The section on this multifaceted artist includes a biographical outline, a listing of Hanson's numerous compositions, and extensive bibliographic material.

Frequently quoted by other scholars, TUTHILL is a reprint of an article that originally appeared in 1936. Tuthill questions what makes American music American and then eloquently elucidates the salient characteristics found in Hanson's music and ably demonstrates the true national quality created by the assimilation of a multitude of cultural influences. Tuthill also examines Hanson's "absorbing interest in everything musical," as director of Eastman, founder of a series of concerts of U.S. music, performer, conductor, recording artist, national and international musical adviser, and leader in the realm of U.S. music education.

In 1978 at the age of 81, HANSON embarked on a series of interviews with David R. Williams. The result is a highly entertaining and enlightening publication containing Hanson's views on composition, analysis, and conducting. In the chapter containing his opinions, Hanson reveals his knowledge of composers such as

Stravinsky, Beethoven, and Hindemith, discusses musical styles including folk music, and surveys the vast repertoire of 20th-century music. In contrast with many great people who are emotionally reticent, Hanson's personal feelings infuse the interviews. Williams concludes the book by incorporating a chapter that contains letters from some of Hanson's former students.

The UNIVERSITY OF ROCHESTER, INSTITUTE OF AMERICAN MUSIC discourse on Hanson eloquently addresses his contribution as director of Eastman to the performance of U.S. music. The book presents a complete listing of compositions performed at the American Composers' Concerts and American Music Festivals, initiated by Hanson during his first year as director of the school. This fascinating list includes such well-known composers as Hanson and Aaron Copland, in addition to students, faculty, and graduates of the Eastman School.

PLAIN's catalog of Hanson's numerous compositions illuminates the vast manuscript collection housed in the Sibley Music Library at Eastman. Because, as Plain notes, Hanson usually did not assign opus numbers to his works, she arranges the compositions alphabetically by title. Each entry contains the name of the piece, opus number if available, instrumentation, date, script/text information as applicable, information about the first performance, manuscript types, additional titles, and condition of the scores.

"It is no exaggeration to say that during the 1920s and 1930s no one in the United States did more for the cause of American music than [Hanson]." So begins the sixth chapter of MACHLIS's book on American composers. From the brief and concise biography to the examination of *Songs from "Drum Taps,"* this chapter reviews the strides Hanson made promoting music of the United States.

COHN's chapter on Hanson is comprehensive for its time, noting that Hanson participated in all facets of musical life as an educator, writer, composer, conductor, lecturer, organizer, and one who concentrated on all areas "pertaining to the good of musical art." However, the majority of this chapter contains information about Hanson's musical compositions. Cohn divides the works by genre and provides brief synopses. Although Cohn's descriptive text abounds, there is little in-depth musical analysis.

HOWARD observes that Hanson's importance to music in the United States transcends any individual composition by, or activity of the composer. His remarkable accomplishments by age 45 are detailed in Howard's early entry into the scholarship about U.S. composers. The essay is relatively long when compared to the other chapters in the volume and provides an interesting portrayal of Hanson's opera, *Merry Mount*, without offering a musical analysis of the work.

ROBERTA LINDSEY

Harmony: Theory

Fétis, Joseph-François, *Equisse de l'Histoire de l'Harmonie: An English-Language Translation of the François-Joseph Fétis History of Harmony*, translated and edited by Mary I. Arlin, Stuyvesant, New York: Pendragon Press, 1994

Forte, Allen, *The Structure of Atonal Music*, New Haven, Connecticut: Yale University Press, 1973

Harrison, Daniel, *Harmonic Function in Chromatic Music: A Renewed Dualist Theory and an Account of Its Precedents*, Chicago: University of Chicago Press, 1994

Hauptmann, Moritz, *The Nature of Harmony and Meter*, translated and edited by W.E. Heathcote, London: Swan Sonnenschein, 1888; reprint, New York: Da Capo Press, 1991

Hindemith, Paul, *The Craft of Musical Composition*, 2 vols., translated by Arthur Mendel, New York: Schirmer, 1941–42

Mickelsen, William, *Hugo Riemann's Theory of Harmony: With a Translation of Die Harmonielehre, Book III of his History of Music Theory*, Lincoln, Nebraska: University of Nebraska Press, 1977

Persichetti, Vincent, *Twentieth-Century Harmony: Creative Aspects and Practice*, New York: Norton, 1961

Rameau, Jean Philippe, *Treatise on Harmony*, translated by Philip Gossett, New York: Dover, 1971

Riemann, Hugo, *Harmony Simplified; or, The Theory of the Tonal Functions of Chords*, translated by Henry Bewerunge, London: Augener, 1895; reprint, 1983

Schenker, Heinrich, *Harmony*, translated by Elisabeth Mann Borgese, edited by Oswald Jonas, Chicago: University of Chicago Press, 1954

Schoenberg, Arnold, *Theory of Harmony*, translated by Roy Carter, Berkeley: University of California Press, 1978

Shirlaw, Matthew, *The Theory of Harmony*, London: Novello, and New York: Gray, 1917; reprint, New York: Da Capo Press, 1969

Wason, Robert W., *Viennese Harmonic Theory from Albrechtsberger to Schenker and Schoenberg*, Ann Arbor, Michigan: UMI Research Press, 1985

When Zarlino introduced the concept of the triad in 1558, he was among the first theorists to reflect the advent of a profound development in Western musical practice: the emergence of harmony. Although polyphony had existed for some five centuries, it was generally understood contrapuntally, that is, as a succession of intervals between pairs of voices—hence, the often haphazard (if colorful) sonorities of medieval music. Whereas polyphony entails merely the sounding together of individual melodic lines, harmony implies more specifically a controlled system in which vertical relationships and progressions command at least as much attention as do the constituent melodies. Harmony, which many consider the greatest triumph of Western music, developed into an elaborate, ever-changing art, and to this day composers continue to explore its riches. The more than 800 harmony treatises (and many more secondary sources and reviews) listed in James Perone, *Harmony Theory: A Bibliography* (1997) give some indication of the importance the subject has assumed over the centuries.

Notwithstanding the occasional appeal to contemporary musical taste, RAMEAU is a veritable caricature of speculative theory—the nearly complete omission of real musical examples will no doubt baffle today's student. Indeed, the work's derivation of harmonic principles from mathematics reveals a theoretical pedigree extending back to Pythagoras. Nevertheless, Rameau synthesized the latest thought and developed a new theory, which laid the foundations for modern conceptions of harmony. The most enduring idea popularized by Rameau is the theory of chord inversion, according to which a chord's essential identity is preserved regardless of which tone sounds in the bass. A corollary of this notion is the "fundamental bass," an analytical construct that provides the successive roots of chords and governs chord progression, generally through motion by fifth. (A note of the fundamental bass may in fact be absent from the sounding music but is rather "supposed" theoretically.) Although not all of his rules of progression accord with musical practice, the notion that there are such rules is a central assumption of harmonic theory. The fundamental bass, tertial harmony, and other of Rameau's concepts, while not without value, are somewhat overemphasized by the theorist, as is his general insistence on the priority of harmony over melody.

Whereas for Rameau harmony ultimately resides in the triad, FÉTIS locates its source in the scale. In Fétis's view, the scale is inherently dynamic; the degrees of the scale and their intervals are endowed with properties of repose or attraction, forces that embody the law of tonality: "The composition of chords, the circumstances that modify them, and the laws of their succession are the indispensable results of this tonality." The *Esquisse* finds Fétis sparring with theorists throughout the ages, culminating in an exposition of his own theory of tonality and a history of music based on that theory. Mary Arlin's introduction to the English translation provides a valuable overview of Fétis's *Traité d'harmonie* as well.

HAUPTMANN's treatise will be equally interesting to both students of philosophy and of music, for it develops a comprehensive theory of music based entirely on Hegelian logic. Hauptmann considers the paradigm of the dialectic to suffuse art no less than any aspect of human activity. For him, then, the triad represents a synthesis arising from the opposition of the root and the fifth, reconciled and unified by the third. Harmonic issues such as cadential progression and modulatory strategy are likewise discussed under the constant aura of metaphysics.

RIEMANN, like Hauptmann, epitomizes a school of theory known as dualism, which is couched in conceptual polarities. Typically dualistic is Riemann's solution to the problem of deriving the minor mode—a perennial difficulty for acoustically minded theorists preoccupied with natural laws. He postulates an undertone series, an inverted counterpart to the overtone series that so captivated Helmholtz and other 19th-century theorists. In fact, such a system is acoustically untenable. But although it presents some dubious theoretical contrivances—for instance, the minor triad's upper fifth serving as root—it nonetheless succeeds in articulating a salient aspect of tonal music: the flatness (in terms of key signature and melodic behavior) of the parallel minor and the subdominant realm, as compared to the major mode and the dominant. Riemann's most famous contribution to 20th-century harmonic theory—one for which he acknowledged a partial debt to Rameau—was his reduction of the harmonic vocabulary into three categories of tonal function: tonic, subdominant, and dominant. Hence, Riemann, like Fétis, displayed a concern for how tonality is expressed through harmonic relations.

Although Riemann has been available in English for over a century, MICKELSEN's volume may be more widely available and of greater usefulness; it provides a handy exposé of Riemann's evolving thought, a primer on his elaborate and unfamiliar analytical notation, and a translation of his history of harmonic theory.

Modeled after the thinking of the harmonic dualists, HARRISON's new theory of hyper-romantic music is more than a revival. Indeed, enriched by a century's worth of hindsight, and a lucid, musically sensitive presentation, Harrison makes a more eloquent case for functionalism than Riemann ever could have. Harrison's improvement lies in his disassociation of *function* from *chord*. His more nuanced understanding regards chords as "assemblies of scale degrees," each of whose functions variously support or annul one another, contributing to the "harmonic attitude" of the whole. An exposition of the theory is accompanied by sample analyses and is followed by an extensive discussion of each of several representative theorists from the late 19th century; the book will thus be important to both theorist and historian.

Fétis, Hauptmann, and Riemann are but three representatives from a century (the 19th) that has been called the golden age of music theory, a century, moreover, that saw 18th-century figured-bass pedagogy more or less replaced with Rameauian harmonic thought. In conservative Vienna, however, music theory traced a different path. WASON's brief but impressively detailed survey explains how Vienna's more gradual and skeptical integration of Rameau's principles led to some influential currents that largely dominate the theoretical outlook even today. Finally, and again for the benefit of historians of theory, mention must be made of SHIRLAW, who provides a more general critique of the history of harmonic theory from Zarlino to Riemann, including a treatment of the English school.

Of the theorists mentioned here, SCHOENBERG may be the most pedagogically balanced, displaying at once a deeply felt reverence for the musical past as well as a healthy distrust of absolutes: "The laws of art consist mainly of exceptions." Schoenberg is quick to relativize the distinctions among overtones, whence follows his liberal tolerance of dissonance: "The expressions 'consonance' and 'dissonance,' which signify an antithesis, are false." Relativism informs much of his thought; for instance, he prophesizes that the major scale will prove to have been "a provisional stopping place" of compositional history. Even though many of the concepts and prophesies articulated by Schoenberg the writer were little more than thinly veiled pleas on behalf of Schoenberg the composer, the cynical reader will be amply reassured of the intellectual and artistic authority represented here. But Schoenberg's discussion of harmony may be *under-theorized*, and his actual musical observations—for instance his preposterous discovery of an eight-part chord in Bach—are of considerably less worth than his countless brilliant digressions and ruminations.

A common deficiency of most theorists from Rameau to Schoenberg is their conception of harmony as essentially a vertical phenomenon. SCHENKER, reacting against systems that he considers needlessly speculative and excessively chordal, offers a profound contribution to the theory of harmony through his systematic recognition of the interpenetration of harmony with counterpoint. Many of the ideas codified in his magnum opus, the posthumous *Der freie Satz* (1935, translated as *Free Composition* in 1979) can be detected in the earlier *Harmony*, albeit exposed alongside received notions of lesser value. Thus, even if the seventh chord is understood as a superimposition of triads (the mature Schenker would recognize the seventh as a contrapuntal phenomenon), Schenker's insights are many, including the hierarchic structure of harmony, the unfolding of harmony by melody, and the postulate of an idealized harmonic substratum ("scale-steps," or *Stufen*). Always imaginative, Schenker fills his prose with biological metaphor, supporting his conviction that tonal harmony is both natural and organic. To be sure, Schenker's theory has its share of regrettable speculation—for instance, appeals to the "magic number five"—but the book's inclusion of numerous illustrative examples from the previous 200 years recommends it as a refreshingly sincere work of practical music theory.

Although the avant-garde music of the Second Viennese School effected a momentous breach with common-practice tonality, harmony (in the broadest sense) was never entirely abandoned (at least until the experiments of the 1950s and 1960s). FORTE is a meticulous and lucid theory of the nonfunctional harmony associated with this atonal repertoire. The harmonic language in question can scarcely be described as syntactic, yet Forte succeeds in explaining the unmistakable coherence of works such as Schoenberg's *Five Pieces for Orchestra* via

principles associated with the "pitch-class set"—a generalized harmonic entity whose most salient quality is described in terms of its "interval vector," a tally of the intervals contained in the set. Set theory adds a crucial reductive assumption to the familiar equivalence relations of tonal harmony: the inversional equivalence of intervals, which entails a drastically decreased specificity for the system (both major and minor triads, for instance, are subsumed into the set 3–11). Analyzing both melody and harmony as conceptual equivalents, Forte's sometimes indiscriminate decisions regarding musical segmentation—on which a large measure of the analytical burden rests—highlight a significant problem in the application of set theory. Also at issue is the estimable aural challenge confronting even the most sympathetic listener, particularly as regards the sets' various combinatorial properties detailed in the second half of the book.

Forte's set theory chiefly addresses music that arose somewhat self-consciously among a tight-knit group of composers, and the success of the theory owes something to this fact. The large portion of 20th-century music, however, may be too stylistically eclectic to admit of any theory, even as regards harmony. PERSICHETTI's account of 20th-century harmony is first and foremost a compendium. Theoretical pretensions are generally avoided, but the interested student will find here a generous compilation of such harmonic devices as have been heard only in this century. On the other hand, HINDEMITH's proposition of universal harmonic principles is a bold one and derives from his firm allegiance to the triad and to tonality. Notwithstanding these conservative traits, Hindemith is equally committed to the chromatic scale as the foundation of music, and most of his formulations represent liberal expansions of traditional harmonic theory. The work ends with a series of analyses that includes Machaut, Bach, and Schoenberg.

JEREMY O'CONNELL

Harris, Roy 1898–1979

United States composer

Chase, Gilbert, "The Grand Tradition," in *America's Music: From the Pilgrims to the Present*, New York: McGraw-Hill, 1955; revised 3rd edition, Urbana: University of Illinois Press, 1987

Stehman, Dan, *Roy Harris: A Bio-Bibliography*, New York: Greenwood Press, 1991

———, *Roy Harris: An American Musical Pioneer*, Boston: Twayne, 1984

The legend of Roy Harris begins with his celebrated birth in a log cabin, on Abraham Lincoln's birthday, in Lincoln County, Oklahoma, which was then a far western, somewhat exotic area of the continent separated from "civilization" by the vast expanse of the Midwest. Harris's reputation as a composer ultimately built on these near-mythological beginnings, but his unique personality, penetrating artistic vision, and well-crafted and interesting music sealed his fame. Seizing upon opportunities to become musically educated but not wishing to inhibit his own desires and aesthetic, Harris eventually forged one of the most individualistic compositional styles of the century by utilizing a lithe, motoric sense of rhythm, weighty melodies that have themselves been compared to the wide plains of his boyhood, and powerful yet economical orchestrations. Despite Harris's considerable reputation as a composer during his own day and now, however, a large part of his music unfortunately remains unavailable, unrecorded, and unknown.

Detailed study of Harris's life and music has largely been left to musicologist Dan Stehman, whose two volumes provide sturdy foundations for all other research. STEHMAN (1984) is a thorough biography with good sections on the composer's upbringing, musical education, character, and compositions. Although the details of his earliest musical experiences are disappointingly brief, Stehman manages to impart to the reader some sense of Harris's Western heritage and the obstacles he had to overcome to reach his musical goals, given his rural background and family circumstances. Most topics in the book are considered under numerous subheadings, which do not advance the literary character of the book but nevertheless are useful for referencing information. Although the biography portion of the book is thorough and illuminating, Stehman's strength is his understanding of Harris's innovative compositional style. Stehman provides good explanations of Harris's melodies and their structure, the composer's "autogenetic principle," his use of harmonies and the evolution of his distinctive harmonic style, chord relationships, and rhythm. Separate chapters cover nearly every genre of music to which Harris contributed and include sections on his use of folk material, programmaticism, self-borrowing, and orchestration. Stehman's own aesthetic evaluations of Harris's music lend considerable value to the volume, and the book benefits from the inclusion of numerous music examples.

Stehman's later bio-bibliography (STEHMAN, 1991) is a magnificent research tool that in part resulted from his earlier labors. The biography section of this book is largely based on his previous volume, although it is presented here in abbreviated form. There follows a catalog of works and performances that includes separate sections for original compositions; withdrawn, incomplete, and unattributed works; transcriptions; and a listing of Harris's editions of works by other composers. This section provides invaluable information about manuscript locations, publisher and catalog numbers, performance timings, numbers of measures, textual sources, and instrumentation. Premieres are also noted, as are other selected performances. Stehman has included at the end of each listing a paragraph or two about some interesting or important aspect of the composition. It becomes obvious after reading a few of these entries that the author's knowledge of Harris's works—particularly the symphonies, chamber works, and major choral works—is comprehensive. An unusually complete bibliography contains separate sections for reference sources, scholarly writings, general writings, text sources, folk song sources, writings by Harris, and critical reviews of his music. The book is further enhanced by a discography, and three useful appendices provide a chronological listing of compositions, a listing of works grouped by medium, and a register of variant titles. Although the book does contain several numbering and cross-referencing errors, Stehman's comprehensive and generally reliable scholarship make this volume invaluable to further research on all aspects of Harris's life and music.

CHASE's portrayal of Harris is limited to a very brief exposition of his early life and a consideration of the "Americanist" characteristics of his music. Several of his works are mentioned, but Chase clearly regards Harris's numerous symphonies as his most important artistic contributions. Chase offers a few comments on each symphony and presents the details of their commissions and premieres. He is clearly a fan of Harris and is sympathetic to at least some of Harris's philosophy of musical democracy, but this survey account, which does not rely on information gleaned from Stehman's research, does not give a very complete view of Harris or his music. Nevertheless, readers will find it a well-written and accessible, if brief, introduction.

BILL F. FAUCETT

Harrison, Lou b. 1917

United States composer

Garland, Peter, editor, *A Lou Harrison Reader,* Santa Fe, New Mexico: Soundings Press, 1987

Leylan, Winston, editor, "Lou Harrison," *Gay Sunshine Interviews,* 2 vols., San Francisco: Gay Sunshine Press, 1978–82

Miller, Leta, and Fredric Lieberman, *Lou Harrison: Composing a World,* New York: Oxford University Press, 1998

Von Gunden, Heidi, *The Music of Lou Harrison,* Metuchen, New Jersey: Scarecrow Press, 1995

Composer Lou Harrison has worked with virtually every major figure in 20th-century American music. He studied with Arnold Schoenberg and Henry Cowell, collaborated with John Cage, and earned recognition for

Charles Ives by conducting the premiere of Ives's *Third Symphony*. Of primary importance to Harrison is the study and integration of Eastern, mainly Asian, musical techniques, scales, tunings, and instruments. For example, he is fascinated by Javanese music and has composed numerous works for gamelan ensemble. Harrison is also an outspoken advocate for gay rights, anti-violence, and pro-environmental issues.

As with any living subject, scholarship on Harrison is greatly slanted by personal bias. In the case of Harrison, authors are more promotional than critical of his work, presenting him as unusually unflawed. Unfortunately, flowery comments outweigh any constructive analysis in the two biographies and the one celebratory collage listed here. Leylan's interview is included in the hope that Harrison's own unfiltered words may speak more directly. The bibliographies of Von Gunden and Miller and Lieberman also point the interested reader to the numerous dissertations, articles, and interviews concerning Lou Harrison.

VON GUNDEN casts a glowing portrayal of both Harrison's music and character. Despite the obvious favorable bias, Von Gunden offers an overview of Harrison's changing stylistic periods organized chronologically with numerous musical examples. A bibliography, work list, discography, and biographical timeline prove useful resources. Von Gunden covers a large number of compositions, and as a result, her discussions of the pieces do not go into much detail. She also assumes a proficiency with music basics, and her definitions may be difficult for those who cannot read music.

The introduction to MILLER and LIEBERMAN provides a full outline of the contents of the book, with helpful page number references. The book is divided into two parts: part 1 is a biography of Harrison; part 2, which addresses the works, is organized by genre rather than chronology. Topics include Harrison's collaboration with dancers, his experimentation with tuning, temperament, and instrument construction, and his devotion to East Asian Music. The authors also address the infusion of Harrison's political and social views into his compositions, such as his use of homosexual themes. Appendices include a "List of Interviews" with Harrison and others, Harrison's reviews in the *New York Herald Tribune* (1944–47), and a catalog of the composer's works organized in three ways: alphabetically, according to their instrumentation, and chronologically. The authors only mention Von Gunden's study to correct a few factual details. The book is accompanied by a compact disc of 74 minutes of Harrison's music, ranging from a performance by the Royal Philharmonic Orchestra to a monaural home recording of a piece for tack piano, with Harrison introducing the tuning system. Although this volume is an excellent resource for information about Harrison's style and compositions, readers should be aware that

the authors are personal friends of Harrison and refer to him throughout by his first name.

LEYLAN's 1973 interview with Harrison and his partner Bill Colvig, originally published in *Gay Sunshine* 23 (1974), is reprinted in a collection of interviews with gay artists including William Burroughs, Allen Ginsberg, Gore Vidal, and Tennessee Williams. Describing homosexuality as "the only minority which is produced spontaneously by nature herself generation after generation," Harrison provides a personal account of being a gay composer. Additional topics include Harrison's interest in Esperanto (a proposed international language) and Buddhism. The entry on Harrison by Ned Rorem from *The New Grove Dictionary of Music and Musicians* (1980) prefaces the interview.

GARLAND is a patchwork collection of tributes, interviews, and musical works celebrating Harrison's 70th birthday. Garland opens with a brief "Biographical Perspective" on Harrison followed by facsimiles of correspondences to Harrison from Ives, Varèse, Cowell, and Schoenberg, as well as glowing congratulations from Virgil Thompson and Cage, among others. The book also includes a four-page discussion by Jody Dramond of Harrison's gamelan music and a reprint of much of the interview from *Gay Sunshine,* supplemented by more recent photographs of Harrison and Colvig. The volume concludes with several greatly varying examples of Harrison's music.

LAURA J. KOENIG

Hasse, Johann Adolf 1699–1783

German composer

Hansell, Sven Hostrup, *Works for Solo Voice of Johann Adolph Hasse, 1699–1783*, Detroit, Michigan: Information Coordinators, 1968
Millner, Frederick, *The Operas of Johann Adolf Hasse*, Ann Arbor, Michigan: UMI Research Press, and Epping: Bowker, 1979

Considering Johann Adolf Hasse's importance to the development of the classical style and his popularity in 18th-century Italy and Germany, it is striking how relatively unknown his music is today. Not only was he the most widely admired opera composer in the mid-18th century, he also wrote a wealth of sacred music and oratorios that received wide acclaim. He was instrumental in bringing to Germany the new Italian style of opera, which he learned mostly in Naples. It is also noteworthy that Hasse was Metastasio's favorite composer. Hasse dominated opera in Dresden, and yet his contemporary renown could not prevent the following generations from virtually forgetting him. It was not until 1965 that his autographs were even identified, thanks to Sven Hansell. Most of the published information concerning Hasse's life and his music has been published in German. Several important dissertations and recent articles have contributed to our knowledge of this 18th-century giant, but sadly, there are few monographs in English dedicated solely to Hasse.

MILLNER convincingly asserts that Hasse is the newly acknowledged founder of the classical style. Although some may argue that this is an overstatement, Millner proves Hasse's importance in the 18th century and our need to pursue the study of his music more aggressively. This book is invaluable to anyone interested in Hasse generally or his operas specifically. The book is extraordinarily informative and the only monograph in English of such breadth concerning Hasse. Millner discusses Hasse's life and career and then presents a detailed study of his operas, namely, the revisions of 14 of them. The operas are not treated comprehensively, however. Rather, Millner discusses various aspects of the composer, including a chapter on Hasse's compositional practice with an examination of his autograph sources. This chapter is one of only a few article-length discussions in English that examine issues of Italian autograph scores, handwriting, folios, and compositional practices. Chapter 5, "Hasse and the Neapolitans," contains various musical examples of arias by composers such as Alessandro Scarlatti, Niccolò Porpora, Francesco Feo, and Leonardo Vinci. In this chapter, Millner directly addresses the notion of classical style and demonstrates both its development and the musical changes that took place in the style of the early 18th-century Italian operas of the Neapolitans. Millner shows how Hasse took an active part in the development of this new style, refuting the long-held notion that he was a mere follower of Leo and Feo. In addition, the book contains many interesting plates, tables, and diagrams; appendices listing the operas alphabetically, chronologically, and geographically; and indices of Hasse's works and all of the names of his arias. The more importance of this monograph to the musicological field cannot be overstated. Not only is it the first work of its kind for Hasse, it is a strong foundation on which to build future research.

HANSELL's book begins with a discussion of the general features of Hasse's music for solo voice. The author argues in favor of Hasse's genius, reminding the reader of the fame and appreciation awarded the composer by his contemporaries. The book's introduction is concise and informative concerning the nature of Neapolitan musical style. The subject matter of Hasse's cantatas is then examined, followed by a more detailed and demanding account of various types of cantatas. Hansell then discusses the motets and antiphons, with an emphasis on textual considerations rather than the music. The author includes a helpful chart of the singers at the Incurabili (the church of the Venetian hospital) during Hasse's ten-

ure there. The thematic catalog, which constitutes the bulk of the publication, is an invaluable resource for the study of the sacred music of Hasse. The work is solid and presents itself as a cornerstone for future research. Students and scholars alike will find this catalog easy to use and the musical examples very helpful, as most of the music remains unpublished to this day. Taken from an appendix of Hansell's doctoral dissertation, this catalog is an invaluable source of these musical genres of Hasse.

SHERYL KATHLEEN MURPHY

Haydn, Franz Joseph 1732–1809

Austrian-born composer

1. Biography

Barbaud, Pierre, *Haydn,* translated by Kathrine Sorley Walker, New York: Grove Press, 1959

Brenet, Michel, *Haydn,* translated by C. Leonard Leese, with commentary by W.H. Hadow, London: Oxford University Press, 1926

Geiringer, Karl, and Irene Geiringer, *Haydn: A Creative Life in Music,* New York: Norton, 1946; 3rd edition, Berkeley: University of California Press, 1982

Gotwals, Vernon, editor, *Joseph Haydn: Eighteenth-Century Gentleman and Genius,* Madison: University of Wisconsin Press, 1963; as *Haydn: Two Contemporary Portraits,* Madison: University of Wisconsin Press, 1968

Hadden, J. Cuthbert, *Haydn,* London: Dent, 1902; revised edition, 1934; reprint, New York, AMS Press, 1977

Hadow, William H., *A Croatian Composer: Notes toward the Study of Joseph Haydn,* London: Seeley, 1897; reprint, Freeport, New York: Books for Libraries, 1972

Heartz, Daniel, *Haydn, Mozart and the Viennese School: 1740–1780,* New York: Norton, 1995

Hughes, Rosemary, *Haydn,* London: Dent, 1950; revised edition, 1978

Jacob, Heinrich Eduard, *Joseph Haydn: His Art, Times, and Glory,* translated by Richard Winston and Clara Winston, New York: Rinehart, 1950

Landon, H.C. Robbins, *Haydn: Chronicle and Works,* 5 vols., Bloomington: Indiana University Press, 1976–80

Landon, H.C. Robbins, and David Wyn Jones, *Haydn: His Life and Music,* Bloomington: Indiana University Press, 1988

Larsen, Jens Peter, and Georg Feder, *The New Grove Haydn,* London: Macmillan, and New York: Norton, 1982

Nohl, Ludwig, *Life of Haydn,* translated by George P. Upton, Chicago: Jansen, McClurg, 1883; reprint, St. Clair Shores, Michigan: Scholarly Press, 1970

Schroeder, David P., *Haydn and the Enlightenment: The Late Symphonies and Their Audience,* Oxford: Clarendon Press, and New York: Oxford University Press, 1990

Stendhal, *Lives of Haydn, Mozart, and Metastasio*, translated and edited by Richard N. Coe, London: Calder and Boyars, 1972

Contemporary admirers of Haydn's music, responding to the extraordinary fame earned by the composer during his lifetime, praised his inexhaustible invention, universality of appeal, and penchant for humor. Late in life, Haydn himself collaborated with two acquaintances, Albert Christoph Dies and Georg August Griesinger, in describing his ascent, by dint of hard work and good fortune, from rural poverty to international acclaim. Appropriated and embellished by later generations of biographers, this inspiring tale formed the basis for an idealized image of "Papa" Haydn as a model of wholesome simplicity, piety, and moral integrity.

Although the tenacity of this endearing myth helped save Haydn's name from total oblivion in the years following his death, it did little to inspire further appreciation of his music. Interest flagged among younger audiences whose tastes inclined toward high drama, sublime transport, or spiritual revelation, not the tiresome blend of quaint humor and old-fashioned optimism that they had come to associate with Haydn's musical legacy. Unglamorous as a subject for 19th-century biographers, his story lacked either the excitement of Beethoven's triumph over adversity or Mozart's paradoxical embodiment of artistic perfection and human frailty.

Partially in reaction to perceived excesses of late romanticism, Haydn enjoyed renewed attention in the early 20th century. Fresh interest in his life, times, and accomplishment was fueled by the efforts of the German scholar Carl Ferdinand Pohl, who had assembled a wealth of information from contemporary documents and previous biographical studies in his *Joseph Haydn* (3 vols.; 1875, 1882, 1927, prepared by Hugo Botstiber, using the deceased author's research notes). Despite Pohl's shortcomings—including limited knowledge of the musical sources, evident carelessness in evaluating the authenticity of available information, and limited success in distilling his facts and anecdotes into a convincing narrative—his study furnished a basis for his successors.

Major 20th-century achievements in Haydn research included the publication of a detailed, comprehensive catalog of his works, the rediscovery and reappraisal of many contemporary documents and musical sources, and the undertaking of a definitive complete edition, slowly nearing completion. In recent decades, much of the energy and enthusiasm driving Haydn studies has been furnished by the composer's preeminent champion, H.C. Robbins Landon, whose five-volume *Chronicle and Works* is a monumental accomplishment. Yet Landon, as argued by James Webster in "Prospects for Haydn Biography after Landon" (*Musical Quarterly* [1982]), has honored all too faithfully the Pohl tradition by collecting a mountain of raw material that falls regrettably short of

a coherent, perceptive "view of the man . . . compatible with his astonishing success in life, his fundamental historical importance, and the overwhelming genius of his music."

GOTWALS translates the famous early biographical documents by Dies and Griesinger, supplying an informative introduction and extensive notes on the texts. Dies, reporting on 30 visits to the aging composer between April 1805 and August 1808, vividly records incidents from Haydn's life and travels; portrays the composer as a simple, noble-spirited, fatherly figure; and emphasizes qualities of wit and humor in his artistic personality. In Griesinger's account, originally published in the *Allgemeine musikalische Zeitung* 11 (1808–9), major emphasis falls on the London period and Haydn's later years in Vienna. Identifying Haydn as the founder of an epoch in music, Griesinger furnishes a character portrayal that emphasizes the composer's piety, modesty, generosity of spirit, and humor. Griesinger also includes discussion of Haydn's work habits, aesthetic outlook, and assessments of other musicians.

In STENDHAL's volume (originally published in Paris, 1814), the portion devoted to Haydn derives from a florid, epistolary biography by Giuseppe Carpani (Milan, 1812), which reflects on the composer's life and creative achievement. Instructive comparisons are drawn to illustrious predecessors and contemporaries, including artists, poets, and philosophers as well as composers.

NOHL's book, among the earliest and most frequently reissued popular Haydn biographies, gives us a romantically colored portrait that draws largely on Dies's account for anecdotal material. Nohl identifies Haydn as the first composer to sound the "tenderer and deeper notes of the heart," celebrates him as a predecessor of Beethoven, assigns him leadership in the development of the quartet and symphony, and emphasizes his distinct German character.

HADOW draws on the folk-song research of F. Kuhac as a basis for speculating about Haydn's ethnic background. Citing numerous correspondences between Croatian melodies and music by Haydn, the author argues his case for Haydn's alleged Croatian origins and describes the composer as "the true embodiment of his own national spirit."

HADDEN's biography, originally published in 1902, transmits the customary image of Haydn as a modest, pious, methodical artist, unspoiled by success. The author concentrates on Haydn's life, with special emphasis on the London visits, and has very little to say about the music.

BRENET's portrayal of the man and his accomplishment, first published in Paris, 1909, exemplifies the traditional image: "Simplicity, kindness, and tranquil endurance" formed the basis of his character, and these qualities determined the uplifting moral content of his music. Treating his operatic and sacred works with condescension, Brenet characterizes Haydn as a writer of musical "prose" rather than "poetry" and identifies him as one of the greatest masters of pure music as well as of instrumental scene painting.

GEIRINGER's authoritative treatment of Haydn's life and works, for many years regarded as an indispensable (if not ideal) resource for nonspecialist readers as well as music scholars, first appeared in 1946 and was substantially revised and enlarged in the course of later editions (1968, 1982). Part 1 divides into ten chapters, representing stations of Haydn's career and his development as an artist. Part 2 offers an introductory essay on the Haydn sources, followed by five chapters corresponding to Geiringer's categorization of style periods: youth (1750–60); a phase of transition (1761–70); a romantic crisis (1771–80); maturity (1781–90); and consummate mastery (1791–1803). Adorned with a minimum of technical detail and few music examples, the author's descriptions of Haydn's compositions are admirably concise but often lacking in interpretive insight.

JACOB's rather leisurely, reflective, and verbose narrative traces the course of Haydn's career and attempts to show how he managed to preserve his artistic freedom while submitting to outward servitude. The author includes colorful portrayals of contemporary figures and locales, recounts numerous biographical anecdotes, and supplies background discussion of 18th-century musical customs.

HUGHES's concise, carefully researched biography, first published in 1950, has gone through several subsequent editions, each incorporating advances in Haydn research (1956, 1962, 1970, 1974, 1978). She provides a clear, factual overview of Haydn's career and a balanced summary of his compositional output, with chapters on nonoperatic vocal works, keyboard music, chamber music for strings, orchestral music, and opera. Helpful appendixes include a chronology, a summary catalog of works, and a list of important names.

BARBAUD's volume, originally published in Paris, 1957, was evidently designed to offer the musically knowledgeable amateur an assortment of biographical information as well as critical discussion of the music. The author incorporates brief sketches of contemporaries with whom Haydn was associated, chronological tables of the symphonies and string quartets, and illustrations pertinent to Haydn and his milieu, including contemporary engravings, portraits, and architectural landmarks.

LANDON's monumental study, dwarfing previous biographies, strives for comprehensive breadth in documenting Haydn's career and describing his musical oeuvre. The "Chronicle" chapters lead us in minute detail through the stages of Haydn's life, with an entertaining but enervating wealth of quotations from letters and other contemporary documents. Chapters devoted to the music offer substantial factual information on composi-

tions within all genres, giving far more attention to early works than any previous biographer. Although the discussion of individual pieces often rambles, with little consistency of method or critical insight, there are many revealing observations concerning resemblances among compositions by Haydn as well as stylistic connections between his works and those of his contemporaries. In addition, Landon offers new insight into the nature and scope of Haydn's influence through the examination of music by his pupils and imitators. The contents of each volume are described briefly below.

Volume 1, *Haydn: The Early Years, 1732–1765*, includes chapters on Austria in the early 18th century, Haydn's family, mid-century musical fashions in Vienna, and Eisenstadt and the Esterházys. Landon discusses the role of copyists, monasteries, and music publishers in Paris, Amsterdam, and London in the dissemination of Haydn's works. Treatment of the music emphasizes evidence of artistic and technical maturity in early compositions. J.G. Albrechtsberger and F.X. Dussek are identified as members of a "First Haydn School."

Volume 2, *Haydn at Eszterháza, 1766–1790*, encompasses discussion of the administrative organization of Eszterháza; Haydn's role as composer of vocal music (sacred and operatic); the Sturm und Drang movement; Pleyel as pupil of Haydn's; the "Second Haydn School," including Vanhal, Ordonez, and (for a brief period) Mozart; Haydn and Viennese society; the dissemination of Haydn's music abroad; and the "Third Haydn School," including Pietrowski, Wranizky, Gyrowetz, and Hayda.

Volume 3, *Haydn in England, 1791–1795*, draws on Haydn's correspondence and the London notebooks, documents pertaining to his association with Salomon and other acquaintances, newspaper announcements and critiques of concerts, and concert programs. Discussion of the works divides into three chapters—vocal music, chamber works, and orchestral works—and features extended commentary on the opera *L'anima del filosofo* and the London symphonies.

Volume 4, *The Years of "The Creation," 1796–1800*, identifies the late oratorio as Haydn's most outstanding accomplishment and one of the greatest products of the age. Material is organized by year (1795–1800), with extensive quotations from contemporary documents in the "Chronicle" chapters and extended commentary on the works completed in each year. Discussion of *The Creation* itself encompasses the libretto, sketches (reproduced in transcription), sources, and musical design, including aspects of key structure, symbolism, and orchestration.

Volume 5, *The Late Years, 1801–1809*, divides into alternating "Chronicle" and "Works" chapters for the years 1801 to 1803, with subsequent chapters devoted to the time-period 1804 to 1809. In addition to reproducing documents pertaining to early performances of *The Creation* and offering extended discussion of *The*

Seasons, Landon gives the contents of Haydn's first will and final will, the Elssler catalog of Haydn's music library, the catalog of his libretto collection, and the auction catalog of artistic effects. An appendix, "Haydn and Posterity: A Study in Changing Values," traces the eclipse of Haydn's reputation in the years following his death, with relevant quotations from writings by Mendelssohn, Schumann, and Hanslick.

LARSEN furnishes a densely factual, though easily readable, account of Haydn's life, a conventional but clearly presented portrayal of his personality, and a condensed summary of his musical accomplishment that seems too lacking in detail to offer much insight. The volume includes both a large bibliography and a comprehensive work list (prepared by Georg Feder).

The one-volume survey by LANDON and JONES incorporates material from Landon's *Haydn: Chronicle and Works* in greatly condensed form, with alternating chapters on Haydn's life and music for five chronological periods: to 1765, 1766 to 1780, 1781 to 1790, 1791 to 1795, and 1796 to 1803. Brief descriptions of individual works, many adorned with music examples, include information on scoring and salient features of melody, harmony, texture, and structure. Disappointingly, there are no illustrations.

Although SCHROEDER focuses mainly on the late symphonies, he also discusses operas, string quartets, and pre-London symphonies while drawing fresh connections between Haydn's life and his music—specifically examining 18th-century literary and philosophical currents that may have impinged on Haydn's aspirations as a composer. Challenging previous biographers' tendencies to depict Haydn as a musician of limited cultural horizons and intellectual interests, the author examines evidence of the composer's acquaintance with aestheticians and intellectual leaders both in central Europe and in England. Schroeder gives special attention to the writings and influence of the English philosopher Shaftesbury; ponders the connection Shaftesbury made between morality and aesthetics; and develops the argument that Haydn, acutely sensitive to the interests, intellectual capacities, and limitations of his audiences, succeeded in embodying both rhetorical persuasion and moral instruction in his late symphonies.

HEARTZ portrays Haydn as a figure of preeminent importance in the development of Viennese musical style in the second half of the 18th century, and his book offers a succinct, well-informed account of Haydn's life through the decade of the 1770s. Successfully integrating biographical narrative and commentary on the music (a rare feat among writers on Haydn), the author provides clear explanations of the circumstances under which compositions in various genres were created (with considerable attention to opera) and offers a wealth of information on relevant Austrian political history and cultural environment. In addition to two long chapters devoted

specifically to Haydn, another chapter, richly supplied with description of musical style, discusses Viennese composers with whom Haydn came into contact in the earlier phases of his career.

FLOYD K. GRAVE

2. Chamber Music

Barrett-Ayres, Reginald, *Joseph Haydn and the String Quartet,* New York: Schirmer Books, 1974

Fruehwald, Scott, *Authenticity Problems in Joseph Haydn's Early Instrumental Works: A Stylistic Investigation,* New York: Pendragon Press, 1988

Griffiths, Paul, *The String Quartet,* New York: Thames and Hudson, 1983

Hughes, Rosemary, *Haydn String Quartets,* [London]: British Broadcasting Corporation, 1966; Seattle: University of Washington Press, 1969

Keller, Hans, *The Great Haydn Quartets: Their Interpretation,* New York: Braziller, and London: Dent, 1986

Konold, Wulf, *The String Quartet: From Its Beginnings to Franz Schubert,* translated by Susan Hellauer, New York: Heinrichshofen Edition, 1983

Landon, H.C. Robbins, *Haydn: Chronicle and Works,* 5 vols., Bloomington: Indiana University Press, 1976–80

Rosen, Charles, *The Classical Style: Haydn, Mozart, Beethoven,* London: Faber, and New York: Viking Press, 1971; expanded edition, New York: Norton, 1997

Sondheimer, Robert, *Haydn: A Historical and Psychological Study Based on His Quartets,* London: Bernoulli, 1951

Sutcliffe, W. Dean, *Haydn: String Quartets, Op. 50,* Cambridge: Cambridge University Press, 1992

Tovey, Donald Francis, "Haydn, Franz Joseph, 1732–1809," in *Cobbett's Cyclopedic Survey of Chamber Music,* 2 vols., London: Oxford University Press, 1929–30; 2nd edition, 3 vols., 1963

Haydn's music for small instrumental ensembles encompasses not only string quartets, string trios, and piano trios, but also a bewildering array of lesser-known, mostly early and rarely performed compositions, including baryton trios, other works involving one or two barytons, *notturni* for two *lire organizzate,* divertimenti for four or more instruments (strings and winds, alone and in combination), and divertimenti for small ensembles with keyboard. In light of persisting problems of dating and authenticity—summarized in the work list prepared by Georg Feder for the article "Haydn, Joseph" in *The New Grove Dictionary of Music and Musicians* (1980) and reprinted in Jens Peter Larsen, *The New Grove Haydn* (1983)—it is not surprising that no author has ventured a comprehensive survey of this repertory.

The string quartets, generally recognized for their artistic value and profound historical importance, have earned more scholarly attention than Haydn's other chamber works; but while the dearth of writings on peripheral genres is understandable, the neglect of the piano trios—a substantial, musically significant oeuvre—is less easy to explain.

For descriptive summaries and relevant historical information on chamber-music categories and individual works, LANDON's multivolume study is indispensable, though not easy to use—in part because of its immense bulk, but also because of its diffuse organization, which separates biographical narrative and documents from musical commentary. Guided by the detailed indices provided for each volume, the reader must sift patiently through the text to find pertinent material.

FRUEHWALD's study, based on his doctoral dissertation, focuses on a diversity of questionably authentic chamber music, including accompanied keyboard divertimenti, string trios, and piano trios; the author also examines the inauthentic op. 3 string quartets. Although highly technical, the book offers clear summaries of authenticity problems and gives concrete descriptions of style traits for chamber genres scarcely mentioned elsewhere in the literature.

TOVEY's famously witty and influential account of Haydn's chamber music, first printed in 1929, treats the piano trios disparagingly, stressing texture at the expense of other elements, and otherwise concentrates on the string quartets. Although it conveys unique insight into Haydn's appropriation and transformation of 18th-century conventions for texture, harmony, and formal design, the essay proves dated in notable respects: it was written before the discovery that the op. 3 quartets are not authentic, and the author's tirades against contemporaries' inadequate theories of form are now tiresome rather than instructive. Moreover, the analytical treatment seems oddly unbalanced, discussing early quartets at length and leaving late works virtually unexamined.

Embedded within ROSEN's important book, first published in 1971, are discussions of Haydn's piano trios and string quartets that surpass all other surveys in terms of clarity, coherence, and analytical acuity. His chapter on the piano trios eloquently defends their apparent lack of textural interest as a virtue and praises these works as "the vehicle of some of [Haydn's] most imaginative and inspired conceptions." A highly selective treatment of the quartets focuses principally on examples from opp. 33 and 50, using carefully chosen excerpts to illustrate subtleties of texture and compositional strategy.

SONDHEIMER's investigation—fascinating, yet dense, often tedious, and occasionally difficult to comprehend—examines aspects of 18th-century style and changing modes of musical expression, contemplates ways in which Haydn may have been influenced by predecessors and contemporaries, and subjects the quartets to detailed inquiry as reflections of his artistic personality. Although he offers valuable analytical insights, the author draws strangely provocative conclusions. Stress-

ing Haydn's "supremacy of form over the emotional subject-matter," Sondheimer finds signs of an "ominous separation of art and life," deplores Haydn's "habit of adding superficial padding to his music," and asserts that the composer was "not yet capable of lending it philosophical significance."

HUGHES's admirably concise, clearly organized guide examines Haydn's development as a composer of string quartets against the backdrop of major events in his life. She delineates five groups representing origins (opp. 1, 2), emergence (opp. 9, 17, 20), establishment (opp. 33, 42, 50, 54, 55, 64), transitional stage (opp. 71, 74), and final maturity (opp. 76, 77, 103) and offers a descriptive account of highlights in each opus. There are numerous thematic quotations, some excerpts in score, and a helpful chronological list of the quartets.

In the only extended, essentially comprehensive survey of the quartets, BARRETT-AYRES attempts to explore the evolution of Haydn's approach to the medium, encompassing a brief discussion of his predecessors and a more extensive inquiry into the quartets of Mozart. Richly supplied with music examples, but exasperatingly haphazard and lacking in analytical coherence, the text often seems no more than a random assemblage of factual data and superficial description.

The first two chapters of GRIFFITHS's survey, though slightly marred by factual lapses and faulty generalizations, offer an engaging account of Haydn's contribution, placing his quartets in the context of Mozart and other contemporaries and devoting at least some attention to questions of medium, audience, and the role of 18th-century publishers. Although not very dense analytically, the book assumes technical knowledge of 18th-century tonality and form.

KONOLD's book, originally published in German (1980), is pithy and rich in critical insight but hampered by an awkward translation and a turgid, elliptical, sometimes mystifying prose style. Characterizing each opus in terms of outstanding traits and tendencies, the book offers much shrewd commentary despite a dearth of music examples and the limited space for specific discussion of individual works.

KELLER's study, brilliant but wordy and eccentric, intends to address the performer rather than the listener or scholar. Examining op. 9, no. 4 and all the quartets from op. 20 on, except for op. 33, no. 4, the author declares these works to be immeasurably greater than the composer's symphonies. Each quartet is treated separately, in a deliberately unsystematic way, with emphasis on matters of tempo, dynamics, phrasing, and details of performance style involving the articulation of thematic material and the interaction among performers in the ensemble.

SUTCLIFFE's central topic is the six quartets of op. 50, and he provides solid, up-to-date commentary on each work in this set. In addition, he traces the origins of the genre and includes supplementary chapters that place these works in the context of Haydn's milieu and his previous accomplishments.

FLOYD K. GRAVE

3. Keyboard Music

Badura-Skoda, Eva, "Haydn, Mozart and Their Contemporaries," in *Keyboard Music*, edited by Denis Matthews, Harmondsworth: Penguin, 1971

Brown, A. Peter, *Joseph Haydn's Keyboard Music: Sources and Style*, Bloomington: Indiana University Press, 1986

Kirby, F.E., *Music for Piano: A Short History*, Portland, Oregon: Amadeus Press, 1995

Maxwell, Carolyn, editor, *Haydn Solo Piano Literature: A Comprehensive Guide, Annotated and Evaluated with Thematics*, Boulder, Colorado: Maxwell Music Evaluation Books, 1983

Newman, William S., *The Sonata in the Classic Era*, Chapel Hill: University of North Carolina Press, 1961; 3rd edition, New York: Norton, 1983

Sisman, Elaine R., *Haydn and the Classical Variation*, Cambridge, Massachusetts: Harvard University Press, 1993

Somfai, László, *The Keyboard Sonatas of Joseph Haydn: Instruments and Performance Practice, Genres, and Styles*, translated by László Somfai and Charlotte Greenspan, Chicago: University of Chicago Press, 1995

Franz Josef Haydn was a prolific composer in many genres, including keyboard music. He wrote piano trios, accompanied sonatas for various instruments and piano, and a few sets of variations, of which the best known is the late set in F minor (1793). The most important of his keyboard music are the 52 solo piano sonatas, which fall into three groups: the first consists of early sonatas written in Vienna and Lukavec in the 1750s; the sonatas of the second group were written during Haydn's years in the service of the Esterházy family from the early 1760s to the early 1780s; the remaining late sonatas were written between 1784 and 1795. The early sonatas are generally in three movements and all in the same key, showing the influence of the Viennese suite. They employ a light *galant* style with singing lines and simple accompaniments. During the Esterházy period, Haydn continued the *galant* style but also experimented with new directions, composing serious works with more frequent use of the minor mode. The late sonatas balance the *galant* and the serious, while continuing Haydn's lifelong experimental approach to form. Very few of Haydn's sonatas throughout his compositional career show the usual formula of the classical sonata, that is three movements with standardized character and key relationships; and he often developed one thematic idea within a movement, particularly in the early works.

Scholarly studies of Haydn's music are surprisingly sparse for a composer who has been accepted as an important musical figure for many decades. Although biographies were published as early as 1809–10, Anthony van Hoboken's catalog of Haydn's works only appeared after World War II. The earliest significant work on Haydn's keyboard music was Karl Päsler's preface to the 1918 edition of the sonatas. Several important articles were published in the 1930s and 1940s, and another influential essay appeared in the Wiener Urtext edition of the solo sonatas edited by Christa Landon in 1963. Also in 1963, William S. Newman published his landmark volumes about the keyboard sonata, most notably *The Sonata in the Classic Era*, which contains substantial information about Haydn's sonatas. These works laid the foundation for the scholarly work produced in the 1970s: Eva Badura-Skoda's article, and A. Peter Brown's and Elaine Sisman's 1970s dissertations, which led to book-length studies of Haydn's keyboard music. Haydn scholarship now includes several important lengthy studies, the most recent appearing in the mid-1990s. Haydn's originality, his contribution to the development of sonata form, and his understanding of the evolving sound capabilities of the piano are now recognized as they should be: his sonatas are cornerstones of the repertoire.

BADURA-SKODA's article is an ideal place to begin reading about Haydn and his keyboard music. Her elegant description of the social, political, and musical world in which Haydn lived and worked is brief but illuminating. She discusses the instruments for which Haydn wrote, making the transition from the harpsichord approach of the early sonatas to the truly pianistic nature of the late sonatas very clear. She explains the regional styles that influenced Haydn: C.P.E. Bach and the expressive style, the Bohemian and Austrian composers whose work he knew, and the Italian rococo. Her explanation of the style periods of the sonatas and their characteristics is complete, concise, and comprehensible. NEWMAN's chapter on this subject, entitled "Haydn and Mozart," is longer than Badura-Skoda's treatment, as he addresses questions of sources for the sonatas as well as the ensemble sonatas and Haydn's place in sonata history. Both Badura-Skoda and Newman discuss Haydn along with Mozart. Newman points out that Haydn's long life and his longer compositional career allowed him both to influence and be influenced by Mozart; therefore evaluating the two composers side by side in a study is very effective.

MAXWELL's short guide to Haydn's keyboard music is a good accompaniment to the Badura-Skoda and Newman articles, and it is invaluable to performers. Following a short preface, Maxwell outlines categories of Haydn's keyboard music: authentic pieces (short works and variations), sonatas (including a table of the numbering systems in the five most commonly available editions), authentic transcriptions, transcriptions from other media, works of doubtful origin, and the works for musical clock. Each piece is identified by title, Hoboken number, key, level of difficulty, and currently available editions. A summary of technical and formal aspects of the piece follows each entry.

KIRBY's chapter on Haydn, Mozart, and Beethoven in his history of piano music provides a fine overview of Haydn's keyboard works. The author's organization of the three stylistic periods and their characteristics is the most concise and easily understood discussion of this subject available.

Three longer works complete the literature on Haydn's keyboard music. The most extensive and thorough is BROWN's study of all of Haydn's keyboard music. This book contains a series of ten essays on the solo sonatas, the trios, divertimentos, concertinos, concertos, and shorter piano pieces. Part 1 addresses sources of the keyboard music; part 2 considers issues of style. Brown shows that Haydn was himself a fine keyboard player and that Haydn not only composed music for all media at the keyboard but also composed solo keyboard music throughout his compositional life. This volume is packed with information: tables of chronology, genres, and types of instruments used, a wide-ranging bibliography, and the Hoboken index.

The two other specialized works address specific aspects of Haydn's keyboard music: Sisman's study of Haydn and the variation principle in the classical era and Somfai's study of the solo sonatas. Both volumes are superb pieces of scholarly writing. SISMAN's profoundly intellectual book addresses Haydn's approach to variation writing throughout his career in various media; she ends with two chapters devoted to Mozart and Beethoven and the changes in variation writing that occurred as the romantic era opened. She gives a compelling reading of variation form and its place in the music of the classical era. This is a challenging book that must be read and absorbed while working directly with the music under discussion.

More accessible than Sisman's study is SOMFAI's book on the solo sonatas: there are sections on keyboard instruments in Haydn's day, instrument choice for the present-day performer, reading ornament notation, touch and articulation, Haydn's notation of dynamics and accents, and tempo in Haydn's music. Somfai's volume contains useful catalogs of the sonatas, tables of ornaments, an extensive bibliography (much of it in German), and abundant musical examples. Although long and detailed, it is well written and beautifully translated, offering a high level of scholarship and musical analysis.

ANN SEARS

4. Orchestral Music

Geiringer, Karl, and Irene Geiringer, *Haydn: A Creative Life in Music*, New York: Norton, 1946; 3rd edition, Berkeley: University of California Press, 1982

Grim, William E., *Haydn's Sturm und Drang Symphonies: Form and Meaning*, Lewiston, New York: Mellen Press, 1990

Haimo, Ethan, *Haydn's Symphonic Forms: Essays in Compositional Logic*, Oxford: Clarendon Press, and New York: Oxford University Press, 1995

Hodgson, Antony, *The Music of Joseph Haydn: The Symphonies*, London: Tantivy Press, and Rutherford, New Jersey: Fairleigh Dickinson University Press, 1976

Landon, H.C. Robbins, *Haydn: Chronicle and Works*, 5 vols., Bloomington: Indiana University Press, 1976–80

———, *Haydn Symphonies*, London: British Broadcasting Corporation, 1966; and Seattle: University of Washington Press, 1969

———, *The Symphonies of Haydn*, London: Universal Edition, 1955

Sisman, Elaine R., *Haydn and the Classical Variation*, Cambridge, Massachusetts: Harvard University Press, 1993

Webster, James, *Haydn's "Farewell" Symphony and the Idea of Classical Style: Through-Composition and Cyclic Integration in His Instrumental Music*, Cambridge: Cambridge University Press, 1991

Wheelock, Gretchen A., *Haydn's Ingenious Jesting with Art: Contexts of Musical Wit and Humor*, New York: Schirmer Books, 1992

The music of Franz Joseph Haydn played a vital role in the growing importance and popularity of orchestral music as a genre in 18th-century Western Europe. Nearly 30 years of his career were spent under patronage of Princes Paul and Nicholas Esterházy, who claimed ownership over Haydn's music and prohibited him from traveling. Despite this handicap, Haydn's reputation as an innovator eventually spread throughout Europe, culminating in the performances of his orchestral works at prestigious concerts in London and Paris after his employment with the Esterházy family had ended. To bolster their own reputations, the Esterházys had demanded innovation and novelty in Haydn's music, giving the composer license to experiment with formal structure, melodic content, and orchestral timbres. In addition, Haydn's own penchant for injecting elements of humor into his compositions helped to magnify his popularity and endear him to his audiences. Because some of Haydn's contemporaries attempted to benefit from his success by placing his name on their own works, scholars such as Landon have had to take on the arduous task of authenticating all of the composer's works and establishing the evolution of his entertaining musical style.

Aimed at novices, HODGSON's book depicts the melody, form, and color of the orchestral sound popular in Haydn's day in order to set the stage for a discussion of Haydn's orchestral works. The author acknowledges the various historical and present-day attempts to authenticate and record the composer's music, pointing especially to Landon as the foremost 20th-century Haydn scholar.

As Hodgson has argued, Landon is an authority on Haydn and his music and one of the most prolific contributors to recent Haydn research. LANDON (1966) begins by analyzing Haydn's early orchestral works, which he composed while working under the patronage of Count Karl Joseph Franz Morzin. Landon then reviews Haydn's symphonic output, highlighting some of the more famous works, such as the *Surprise* Symphony, and placing these compositions within their historical context. This concise book has a narrative style that will appeal to any interested reader; the volume will particularly help to acquaint students with Haydn's methods of musical communication with his audiences and their reactions to his works.

Taking a more biographical approach to Haydn and his music, GEIRINGER and GEIRINGER discuss all of the composer's music, tracing relationships between the symphonies and concertos and other genres in which he composed. Readers encounter aspects of Haydn's character and developing creativity, while at the same time learning about his innovative use of orchestral color and articulation and his relationships with patrons and public audiences.

LANDON (1955) takes a different approach to Haydn's symphonies than that employed in his 1966 work. The book first examines score authenticity and provides information on manuscript sources. Subsequent chapters deal not only with the size and instrumental make-up of the orchestras available to Haydn, but also with such issues of performance practice as tempo interpretation, ornamentation, and dynamics. Landon organizes his text by time periods, beginning each section with a brief chronological discourse, succeeded by a contextual discussion of works that traces the character and trends common to specific types of movements and provides greater detail about the more prominent works of each period. Landon concludes by paying special attention to the *London* symphonies, offering descriptions of Haydn's visits to London and his collaboration with the impresario Johann Peter Salomon. The book contains many illustrations; an extensive index; a catalog of works attributed to Haydn that Landon considers authentic, spurious, and doubtful; and a lengthy bibliography.

HAIMO's discussion differs from Landon's, as Haimo attempts to "reconstruct Haydn's formal thought, trying to account for and explain specific details of the music." Based upon the premise that 18th-century audiences expected entertaining music filled with new ideas and novelty, Haimo's book begins by introducing basic principles of form as a foundation for the analysis and then examines nine representative works that illustrate the evolution of Haydn's formal musical structures. The author places the works discussed within their historical context, comparing them to works by later composers, and he emphasizes both Haydn's formal innovations and

his propensity to cater to public taste. Haimo recommends that persons refer to full orchestral scores while reading the book.

LANDON's (1976–80) more recent and comprehensive work can best be used as a reference text, for the author treats all of Haydn's music within a wider, more detailed biographical context than that presented in his other books, analyzing other orchestral works in addition to the symphonies. Especially helpful is the list of works presented at the end of each volume, which enables readers to focus on compositions of specific interest to them without having to weed through the entire text. The extensive bibliography of source readings and critical editions of scores proves very helpful for research and serious score study.

While looking at representative examples of 18th-century orchestral, keyboard, and chamber music, SISMAN focuses upon the variation techniques used by Haydn, Mozart, and Beethoven in the various classical genres. She begins by describing the musical rhetoric associated with variation form and traces the evolution of the form in its treatment by these three composers. Sisman highlights chronologically the rhetorical conventions and innovations that Haydn brought to variation form in order to satisfy audiences for his music. The appendices list variations by Haydn, Mozart, and Beethoven, and an extensive bibliography is invaluable for further research.

GRIM's book addresses the controversy of stylistic identification associated with Haydn's so-called *Sturm und Drang* Symphonies. In his evaluation of various definitions and analyses of the Sturm und Drang, Grim contends that those of Haydn's symphonies listed in this category do not display a radical stylistic shift. Instead, the author argues that these symphonies show evidence of a remarkable continuity in Haydn's symphonic works when compared to the *Fürnberg-Mozin* Symphonies (ca. 1757–61) and the *London* Symphonies (1791–95). For greater detailed analyses of the works in question, Grim refers the reader to Landon's *Critical Edition of the Complete Symphonies of Joseph Haydn*.

When embarking upon the study of Haydn's *Farewell* Symphony presented in WEBSTER'S intriguing book, the reader discovers that the analysis not only identifies the symphony's distinctive traits; it also becomes a launching point for a discussion of Haydn's instrumental works as a whole. Webster criticizes what he sees as a historiographical generalization, the argument that Haydn's earlier works lack the verve and sophistication displayed in what musicologists and theorists call "the mature classical style." Focusing upon Haydn's intentional disruption of conventional expectations and demonstrating the composer's concern for cyclical integration and through-composition in the *Farewell* Symphony, Webster concludes that a person who recognizes the presence of these elements, among others, in this composition will have a better understanding of Haydn's influence on

Beethoven's compositions and will more fully comprehend what Joseph Kerman and other critics describe as the "symphonic ideal" established in the 19th century. Following this analysis of the *Farewell* Symphony, Webster examines nine other instrumental works by Haydn that demonstrate these same traits. Webster concludes with a brief survey of 20th-century criticism debating Haydn's compositional maturity and his relationship to the classical style.

A review of Haydn's orchestral music should never conclude without considering his ability to insert wit and humor into his music. This ability contributed greatly to the delight of patrons and public audiences, helping to ensure Haydn's successful career. WHEELOCK addresses this interesting topic by first shedding light upon the concepts of wit and humor as understood by 18th-century listeners and critics. She then works to relate these concepts to the expectations of 20th-century listeners, offering excerpts from various instrumental works as examples of numerous techniques and musical strategies, such as distraction, deception, and gesturing, that Haydn used to entertain not only his audiences but also himself. Although Wheelock attempts to avoid technical language whenever possible, she assume that the reader is familiar with the classical style and its conventions.

CHARLES R. VERBLE

5. Sacred Music

Brown, A. Peter, *Performing Haydn's The Creation: Reconstructing the Earliest Renditions,* Bloomington: Indiana University Press, 1986

Landon, H.C. Robbins, *Haydn: Chronicle and Works,* 5 vols., Bloomington: Indiana University Press, 1976–80

Landon, H.C. Robbins, and David Wyn Jones, *Haydn: His Life and Music,* Bloomington: Indiana University Press, 1988

MacIntyre, Bruce C., *Haydn: The Creation,* New York: Schirmer, and London: Prentice Hall International, 1998

Rosen, Charles, *The Classical Style: Haydn, Mozart, Beethoven,* London: Faber, and New York: Viking Press, 1971; expanded edition, New York: Norton, 1997

Schenbeck, Lawrence, *Joseph Haydn and the Classical Choral Tradition,* Chapel Hill, North Carolina: Hinshaw Music, 1996

Temperley, Nicholas, *Haydn: The Creation,* Cambridge: Cambridge University Press, 1991

Tovey, Donald Francis, *Essays in Musical Analysis,* 6 vols., London: Oxford University Press, 1935–39; vol. 5 published separately as *Concertos and Choral Works,* London: Oxford University Press, 1981

Webster, James, "*The Creation,* Haydn's Late Vocal Music, and the Musical Sublime," in *Haydn and His World,* edited by Elaine Sisman, Princeton, New Jersey: Princeton University Press, 1997

Joseph Haydn is today regarded as the most important composer of sacred music from the Viennese classical era. Although sacred music in all its forms occupied Haydn throughout his career, scholarship in English focuses on *The Creation* and the last six Masses. Writers on his sacred music have also addressed performance practices, possible misattributions, and the accuracy of modern editions. Yet some topics fashionable in mainstream Haydn scholarship—e.g., the composer's use of wit, his formal innovation, his involvement with contemporary intellectual movements—seldom surface in relation to Haydn's church music. That may be due to its continuing, undeserved status as a tradition-bound genre outside the most active currents of 18th-century musical life.

The most complete guide to this area, as to so many other topics in Haydn scholarship, is LANDON's massive five-volume documentary biography. Besides providing exhaustive historical background and detailed stylistic and formal descriptions of each work, Landon introduces an enormous amount of primary source material: for example, volume 2 contains a 1771 letter to Haydn's patron Nikolaus I from a singer in the chapel choir, who laments the sad state of the Esterházy church-music establishment. More pertinent are the descriptions of performing forces, sites, and conditions for the first performances of most of Haydn's pieces. Beginning in the 1950s Landon edited a considerable number of Haydn's sacred works. Perhaps because of that, the author respects the special qualities of music routinely dismissed by others: see his remarks on the *Stabat mater* or the *Applausus* cantata, for instance. His accessible musical analyses place each work in proper stylistic context; there are also numerous music examples. LANDON and JONES, essentially a single-volume condensation of Landon's much longer opus, also includes material on the newly recovered *Missa Sunt bona mixta malis*.

Haydn's church music is the principal concern of SCHENBECK's survey of the choral works. It includes a chapter on performance practices specific to this repertoire and an annotated work list designed primarily for conductors. Students and general readers will also find this book helpful, as it avoids overly technical language while offering a readable synthesis of the relevant scholarship. The author establishes the theological, cultural, and historical context in which Haydn wrote church music, tracing the influence of the Counter Reformation, the Habsburgs, and Italianate musical style in particular. Earlier and lesser-known works are given generous space; music examples occupy a quarter of the book.

Three recent books have been devoted to one masterpiece, Haydn's oratorio *The Creation*. BROWN limits himself to a discussion of its earliest Vienna performances. By examining Haydn's working scores and parts along with other contemporary evidence, he obtains a more accurate picture of the composer's intent, at least insofar as the premieres of 1798–99 are concerned.

Brown's main purpose is to offer a historical baseline for authentic performance; in doing so, he casts doubt on the absolute authority of the first printed score, which differs in a number of details from the materials he surveys.

The Temperley and MacIntyre books are similar to each other in scope, treating both historical context and the music itself, but they differ somewhat in content and organization. Brevity and elegant design greatly strengthen TEMPERLEY's book. He offers an accessible, slightly Anglocentric overview of *The Creation* with two special features: a discussion of the oratorio's theological underpinnings and a chronologically arranged section of excerpts from important critical essays. The excerpts range from remarks by Haydn's contemporaries Zelter and Gardiner to those of Wolf, Schenker, Tovey, and Rosen.

MacINTYRE uses his monograph's greater length to offer a number-by-number description of the music. At times his approach may seem diffuse. Readers will undoubtedly value some of MacIntyre's expansiveness, however—for example, the attention paid to the performance history of the work in the United States. Both MacIntyre and Temperley offer remarks on performance practice and a comparative list of editions.

For ROSEN, "the classical style is at its most problematic in religious music." He illustrates the bases of those problems, concentrating on the Catholic Church's preference for archaism and that style's clash with the embarrassing incursions made by Italian comic-opera techniques. After presenting a frank critique of the stylistic incoherence in Haydn's late Masses, Rosen describes the means by which Haydn overcame some of those difficulties in the oratorios and offers a comparative glance at Mozart's and Beethoven's efforts. His essay is at once one of the more influential recent commentaries on Haydn's church style and a reminder of doubts that have been raised for nearly 200 years.

Since their first appearance in the 1930s, TOVEY's essays on the two late oratorios have attained the status of classics. Many of his forthright observations were echoed in later writings, and others probably should have been. Apropos of the libretto of *The Creation* and its musical treatment, Tovey suggests that "Haydn is much more likely to have heard of the Nebular Hypothesis [of Kant and Laplace] than to have read Milton. . . . [The composer's Chaos] has nothing to do with the fiery ocean into which the rebel angels fell." Much of Tovey's analysis of the Chaos movement is remarkably penetrating for its time, not least his notice of certain *Tristan*-like harmonies and what he called "the difficulties of achieving a sublime style."

WEBSTER probes deeply into this latter problem. Definitions of the sublime are traced from Longinus through Burke and Kant to Haydn's contemporaries Sulzer, Schulz, and Michaelis. The author then provides long lists of specific constructions in Haydn's music that evoke the sublime in its many categories; selected examples are also described in more detail. Thus, the expressive strategies of Haydn's late sacred music are seen as rooted in classical aesthetic philosophy while ushering in a new, romantic view of artistic discourse. In demonstrating these relationships, previously only noted in instrumental contexts, Webster also brings Haydn's sacred music into the mainstream of late 20th-century musical scholarship.

LAWRENCE SCHENBECK

Hensel, Fanny 1805–1847

German pianist and composer

Cai, Camilla, "Texture and Gender: New Prisms for Understanding Hensel's and Mendelssohn's Piano Pieces," in *Nineteenth-Century Piano Music: Essays in Performance and Analysis,* edited by David Witten, New York: Garland, 1997

Citron, Marcia J., "Fanny Hensel's Letters to Felix Mendelssohn in the Green-Books Collection at Oxford," in *Mendelssohn and Schumann: Essays on Their Music and Its Context,* edited by Jon W. Finson and R. Larry Todd, Durham, North Carolina: Duke University Press, 1984

Hensel, Fanny, *The Letters of Fanny Hensel to Felix Mendelssohn,* translated and edited by Marcia J. Citron, Stuyvesant: Pendragon Press, 1987

Hensel, Sebastian, *The Mendelssohn Family, (1729–1847) from Letters and Journals,* 2nd edition, translated by Carl Klingemann, New York: Harper and Brothers, 1882; reprint, New York: Haskell House, 1969

Reich, Nancy B., "The Power of Class: Fanny Hensel," in *Mendelssohn and His World,* edited by R. Larry Todd, Princeton, New Jersey: Princeton University Press, 1991

Tillard, Françoise, *Fanny Mendelssohn,* translated by Camille Naish, Portland, Oregon: Amadeus Press, 1996

Wilson Kimber, Marian, "Fanny Hensel: Biography and Reception," in *Ein Rufen nur aus Träumen?,* edited by Beatrix Borchard and Monika Schwarz-Danuser, Stuttgart: Metzler Verlag, 1999

German composer and pianist Fanny Mendelssohn Bartholdy Hensel was the sister of Felix Mendelssohn. Fanny was the eldest child of an upper-class Jewish family and the granddaughter of the philosopher, Moses Mendelssohn. Able to reconcile Enlightenment ideals with Christianity, her parents had their children baptized, adding "Bartholdy" to their name to signify the change.

A child prodigy, Fanny had a musical education similar to that of her brother, but her gender and upper-class status prevented her from having a professional career as a musician. Fanny married the painter Wilhelm Hensel in

1829; they had one son, Sebastian. Fanny remained in the Mendelssohn family home, where her brilliant salons, featuring her music and that of her brother and others, became important in the musical life of Berlin. Her 400-plus compositions include numerous lieder and piano works as well as chamber music, including an excellent piano trio, and choral works. Although a few compositions appeared earlier, Hensel only began to publish her works in succession late in her life. Many remain unpublished today.

The two-volume family history by Fanny's son, Sebastian HENSEL, includes extensive treatment of her life. It contains many of Fanny's letters to her brother as well as to other friends and family members. Unfortunately, the letters have been highly edited in typical 19th-century fashion. Sebastian Hensel's desire to present the story of a "good middle-class family" and to assure readers that his mother had no desire to step outside the appropriate feminine sphere by publishing her music presents a somewhat inaccurate and overly romanticized portrayal of both Hensel and the Mendelssohn family. Nonetheless, the book remains an essential source of information about Fanny Hensel. Most of volume 2 centers on her two trips to Italy, high points of her life. Here, Fanny's letters predominate, largely unencumbered by her son's narrative, providing vivid descriptions of her encounters with the art, landscape, and culture of Italy.

Fanny HENSEL's letters to her brother appear in a modern edition, translated and edited by Marcia Citron. The volume contains 150 letters dating from between 1821 and 1847 but only includes letters that concern musical matters. The book is copiously annotated, and readers unfamiliar with the lives and musical output of the Mendelssohns may rely on the substantial footnotes. Hensel's ideas about music, her intelligence, and her sometimes acerbic wit are revealed here, as is the depth of the musical interchange between the sibling composers. Citron has provided essays on Hensel and her relationship with her brother that successfully avoid the amateurish psychological and overly dramatized interpretations of some biographical writings.

CITRON's essay about the collection of Fanny Hensel's letters to her brother at Oxford is a brief overview of the scope and nature of the correspondence. Large excerpts from the letters provide Fanny's commentary on Felix's pieces, her ideas about prevailing musical fashions and musical life in Berlin, and her feelings about her own compositions.

REICH has added considerably to our understanding of the cultural restraints under which Hensel lived. She explains how class as much as gender kept Hensel from having a professional career and made it improper for her to perform in public or to accept money for her compositions. Reich also notes that the salons hosted by cultured female relatives such as the Mendelssohns' great aunts served as models for Fanny's musical life.

TILLIARD has written the first full-length biography of Fanny Hensel to appear in English. It includes a large number of period portraits of Fanny and her circle not widely available elsewhere. Hensel's compositions are not discussed; the emphasis is completely on her life. The book opens with the cultural context in which Hensel lived and incorporates the various primary sources recently published. However, lacking sufficient primary sources for some of the pivotal periods of Hensel's life, the narrative frequently lapses into conjecture about her thoughts and feelings. Despite its more modern understanding of the obstacles facing a 19th-century woman composer, this biography represents a popular consolidation of the available materials, rather than an entirely newly researched contribution.

CAI provides detailed comparisons of piano music by Hensel and Mendelssohn in an article aimed at musically sophisticated readers. The term *texture* is used rather loosely here, as the analysis also covers melody, rhythm, and form. The article furthers the understanding of Hensel's style; however, Cai's linking of musical characteristics with gender is somewhat less convincing.

WILSON KIMBER assesses Hensel's posthumous reputation and reveals that she was actually quite well known between 1847 and 1920. Hensel's compositions were typically overlooked in favor of her biography, which was sometimes constructed to tell a story that merely conformed to female stereotypes. On the other hand, Hensel was recognized as having unique intellectual and musical powers. This analysis suggests possible wider dissemination of the meager body of her available published compositions than might otherwise be assumed.

MARIAN WILSON KIMBER

Henze, Hans Werner b. 1926

German composer

Bokina, John, *Opera and Politics: From Monteverdi to Henze*, New Haven, Connecticut: Yale University Press, 1997

Henze, Hans Werner, *Hans Werner Henze: Ein Werkverzeichnis, 1946–1996 = A Catalog of Works, 1946–1996 = Un catalogo delle opere, 1946–1996*, Mainz, New York: Schott, 1996

———, *Music and Politics: Collected Writings, 1953–81*, translated by Peter Labanyi, Ithaca, New York: Cornell University Press, and London: Faber, 1982

Hines, Robert Stephan, editor, *The Orchestral Composer's Point of View: Essays on Twentieth-Century Music by Those Who Wrote It*, Norman: University of Oklahoma Press, 1970

Rickards, Guy, *Hindemith, Hartmann, and Henze*, London: Phaidon, 1995

The German-born Henze enjoys an international reputation based on a large body of work featuring standard, large-scale forms (opera and symphony) in a wide variety of styles. He is also known for his leftist political convictions, which have greatly influenced his life and music. After serving in World War II, he studied composition with René Leibowitz at Darmstadt and briefly endorsed serialism before finding his own voice. His musical style has been described as inclusively synthetic, as he avails himself of numerous styles and musical languages. As a committed socialist and open homosexual, Henze felt he could not live in either Germany after World War II and emigrated to Italy. He cultivated professional relationships with several politically committed composers in East Germany and acted as a corresponding member of the Akademie der Künste in East Berlin. Henze has since made peace with the reunified Germany, and his Ninth Symphony was premiered by the Berlin Philharmonic in 1997. His penchant for composing in the traditional large forms, particularly symphonies and operas, continues to set him apart from most composers of his generation. He has also written numerous essays about his politics and his music and edits a series of books on the theme *Neue Aspekte der musikalischen Ästhetik.*

Little has been written about Henze or his music in the English language, except for reviews of performances of his works in the United States and Great Britain. His ardent leftist politics contributed to his absence from the U.S. musical scene during the Cold War—although the Santa Fe Opera produced five of his operas during that time—and he experienced several controversial performances in Great Britain as well. The works cited here represent not only the most recent scholarship but virtually the only readily available research on Henze's music in English.

HENZE (1996) is a catalog of the composer's works that supersedes two previously published catalogs. It is presented in Italian, German, and English; each page is laid out in three columns, one in each language, and works are accompanied by the composer's descriptions in all three languages. (The translations are always serviceable, if not idiomatic.) The catalog lists all of Henze's published works, including authorized arrangements, some incomplete works that were still in progress at the time of publication, and his writings. Occasional pieces, unpublished political songs, and contributions to collaborative pieces are omitted. This work is valuable because it provides the only comprehensive overview of the composer's large oeuvre, and it is conveniently indexed by title, instrumentation, and poets and librettists.

BOKINA's book is a wide-ranging effort to trace contemporary political events and opinions in operas across the centuries. The literal definition of high politics employed by Bokina means that his readings are not always as nuanced as other analyses of politics and opera in the 1990s, but his interpretation of Henze's *The Bassarids* (1966) is insightful. The author devotes substantial space to a summary of Henze's political ideology (although Bokina does not take the opportunity to investigate the choice of the opera genre as a vehicle for leftwing, politically committed art). The specific political situation Bokina identifies in *The Bassarids* is the 1960s conflict between the establishment and the New Left, of which Henze was a proponent. In addition to an account of the genesis of the libretto, which is based on Euripides' tragedy *The Bacchae* and written by W.H. Auden and Chester Kallman, Bokina persuasively analyzes the conflict between Penthaus and Dionysius in that text as representative of that 1960s conflict between the establishment and the New Left, respectively. Because Bokina is a political scientist, not a musicologist, the music of the opera receives very little attention. Nevertheless, this essay is a significant contribution to Henze scholarship because it acknowledges his masterful contribution to the modern operatic repertoire.

Much of what is available to the English reader consists of essays written by the composer himself in German or Italian and subsequently translated. This is the case in HINES's collection of essays by 20th-century composers, in which Henze's article, originally published by Schott in 1964, is rendered into English by Willis J. Wager. Most of the essay is devoted to a philosophical discussion of how Henze views the composer's role in society and his own compositional process. According to Henze, a composer occupies a space between materialization and chaos, and Henze tries to achieve a balance between these polar extremes. He disavows the compositional trends of the period, primarily electronic music and serialism, and states that all music must maintain its ties to the music of the past. He gives examples from his own music in which he relied on traditional processes, such as the chaconne and ostinato patterns, to demonstrate how he preserved historical connections while working with contemporary musical language. He describes composing as "a process of selection, of decision. What, from the universe of immanent possibilities, do I adopt for the work?" This philosophy is reflected in his oeuvre, which exhibits an eclectic range of styles and forms. For Henze, all music, even symphonic music, is informed by the theater. There is a brief discussion of his symphonic works up to the early 1960s, but the bulk of the essay is philosophical and abstract, not technical.

HENZE (1982) is basically a translation of *Musik und Politik: Schriften und Gespräche 1955–1975*. The English version includes a few more recent essays, such as the insightful "German Music in the 1940s and 1950s." This volume provides a comprehensive overview of Henze's political views and compositional processes from the mid-1950s to the early 1980s. Its contents can be divided roughly into three categories: essays dedicated to individual works (*König Hirsch, Der Prinz von Homburg, Elegy for Young Lovers, The Raft of Medusa,* Second Piano Concerto), essays about other composers (Mahler, Britten, Dessau), and essays that specifically address the relationships between music and politics and the composer and society ("The Bourgeois Artist," "Music as a Means of Resistance," "Art and the Revolution," and "Does Music Have to Be Political?").

RICKARDS groups Hindemith, Hartmann, and Henze together as the subjects for his book because he sees them as the three German composers who "collectively have been central to the development of the tradition of German music inherited from the previous century." More specifically, they are part of the lineage of outstanding German symphonic composers. As the author notes, the three composers did not interact with one another; therefore, the book is actually three biographies interwoven together. Chapters are divided by time periods, and separate sections consider what each composer did during those years, with little effort to integrate their respective histories into a single story. Missing from the book are points of convergence and commonality beyond their German citizenship and contributions to the symphonic repertoire. Because Hartmann and Hindemith died in 1963 and Henze is still alive, the end of the book focuses on Henze. Rickards's style is accessible and engaging, but he frequently cites sources without documentation and includes no footnotes, making the work difficult to use for scholarly purposes. Nevertheless, he provides the only general biography of Henze in English, and for the reader who wishes to compare Henze's musical career and wartime experiences with those of two other important German symphonic composers, Rickards has written a useful and entertaining book.

JOY HASLAM CALICO

Hildegard von Bingen 1098–1179

German abbess, poet, mystic, and composer

Davidson, Audrey Ekdahl, editor, *The Ordo Virtutum of Hildegard of Bingen: Critical Studies,* Kalamazoo, Michigan: Medieval Institute, 1992

Dronke, Peter, *Poetic Individuality in the Middle Ages: New Departures in Poetry 1000–1150,* Oxford: Clarendon Press, 1970; 2nd edition, London: Westfield College, University of London Committee for Medieval Studies, 1986

Flanagan, Sabina, *Hildegard of Bingen, 1098–1179: A Visionary Life,* London: Routledge, 1989; 2nd edition, 1998

Hildegard of Bingen, *Symphonia: A Critical Edition of the Symphonia armonie celestium revelationum [Symphony of the Harmony of Celestial Revelations],* translated by Barbara Newman, Ithaca, New York: Cornell University Press, 1988; 2nd edition, 1998

Newman, Barbara, editor, *Voice of the Living Light: Hildegard of Bingen and Her World,* Berkeley: University of California Press, 1998

Pfau, Marianne Richert, "Hildegard von Bingen's Symphonia Armonie Celestium Revelationum: An Analysis of Musical Process, Modality, and Text-Music Relations," Ph.D. dissertation, State University of New York at Stony Brook, 1990

Composer, poet, and dramatist Hildegard von Bingen is unique among major composers because she is known to the general public less for her music than for her writings in theology, natural history, and medicine. In the nine centuries since her birth, her music has taken a back seat to her other creative achievements; publications on her compositions are few and far between in Werner Lauter's two-volume comprehensive *Hildegard Bibliographie* (1970, 1982), which covers material through 1982. Despite the bibliographical handicaps of being a female composer and that musical rarity, a named composer of chant, Hildegard has been the subject of musical scholarship since the late 19th century, with a facsimile edition of her works appearing as early as 1913. Until relatively recently, however, all material was in German, with Hildegard being invisible in English-language publications, even in the so-called comprehensive discussions of chant or medieval music. Her visibility has increased in the last few decades, initially as the result of the efforts of nonmusicological scholars who focused on the poetry that she wrote and then set to music.

DRONKE's extended essay on Hildegard in his larger study of medieval poetry was the first English-language publication to draw attention to her extraordinary poetic language and unique achievements in the context of medieval imagery. He also places Hildegard's morality play with music, *Ordo virtutum,* the first of its kind by more than a century, "at the summit of twelfth-century dramatic achievement" and provided a critical Latin edition of its text.

One of the products of Hildegard's recent nonacentennial was a newly revised edition of FLANAGAN's important life and works volume. In addition to providing the most complete coverage of the seer's life in English, the work contains lengthy chapters on each of Hildegard's main creative achievements, including her music (again concentrating on the poetic texts). Flanagan further supplies a detailed discussion of the interdict that marred Hildegard's closing years, during which the composer laid out most clearly her understanding of the purpose of music.

Another general volume from the nonacentennial year was edited by NEWMAN. The nine essays in the collection, each penned by a different specialist, cover the multitudinous roles Hildegard played. The biographical chapter, written by Newman, draws on the recently discovered *Vita* of Jutta, Hildegard's first teacher (Flanagan is less ready than Newman to draw inferences from this material). Newman also authors the essay on "Poet," discussing the poetry's formal features and idiosyncratic imagery while placing the lyrics within the context of the works of her medieval peers. The superb entry on Hildegard's music written by Margot Fassler uses the *Scivias* songs and *Ordo virtutum* to support Fassler's argument that the music was intended as an educational tool especially useful in elucidating the tree of Jesse. On the problematic question of the function of the songs, Fassler comes down unequivocally on the side of liturgical use, a position with which not all scholars will agree. Fassler also provides the first published discussion of Hildegard's use of musical borrowing and places her supposedly old-fashioned sequences in context by noting that no contemporaneous collections of sequences, whose style Hildegard was theoretically rejecting, could have been known to the composer.

Newman's praiseworthy edition of HILDEGARD's *Symphonia* was the first English-language volume devoted exclusively to Hildegard's musical cycle. The backbone of the book is a critical text of the 76 Latin songs of the cycle (Newman conflates eight Ursula antiphons for a slightly different total of 69 songs). These Latin songs are accompanied by both poetic and prose English translations, the latter newly redone for the second edition. Important though this central text is, the value of the book is dramatically increased by Newman's pathbreaking auxiliary material, which includes a listing of contemporary sources, a discussion of the two main musical manuscripts and the ramifications of their differences, a hypothetical chronology, explication of the links between Hildegard's theological writings and her song texts (brilliantly demonstrating Hildegard's holistic creativity), and a commentary for each song. Newman argues that the *Symphonia* was not conceived as an entity but rather evolved throughout her life as Hildegard continued to compose songs for different occasions. Newman is also the first to give a major role to the problematic "Miscellany" that contains texts but no music for 26 of the songs, using these to constitute the middle period of Hildegard's composing. The author also suggests that Hildegard wrote several song texts, included in the volume, for which the music no longer survives (if it were indeed ever written). An added bonus is the inclusion of an essay by Marianne Richert Pfau on the text/music relationship in several of the antiphons.

PFAU's dissertation, now readily available through University Microfilms, is a more expansive discussion than the previously cited studies of the relationship between text and music in the works of Hildegard. In contrast to earlier negative treatment of Hildegard's music in German-language scholarship, Pfau carefully and positively describes the text/music synthesis that lies behind Hildegard's songs. She also argues that, instead of composition by centonization—relying on a jumbled patchwork of short recurring motives—Hildegard drew instead on idiosyncratic modal templates to provide a coherent and readily discernable structure for her compositions.

The collection of essays on Hildegard's *Ordo virtutum* edited by DAVIDSON, again the first in English, is thinner fare than Pfau but has several worthwhile features, including Robert Potter's delineation of the numerous differences between Hildegard's creation and the later morality plays, and Pamela Sheingorn's hypothesis that *Ordo virtutum* was performed prior to the Mass that included the consecration of virgins, not (as is more frequently suggested) during the celebration of the reconsecration of the church at Rupertsberg in 1152. The volume also contains a useful facsimile of the drama as it appears in its most important musical source, the Riesenkodex.

HONEY MECONI

Hindemith, Paul 1895–1963

German-born composer

Hindemith, Paul, *A Composer's World: Horizons and Limitations,* Cambridge, Massachusetts: Harvard University Press, 1952

——, *The Craft of Musical Composition,* 2 vols., translated by Arthur Mendel, New York: Schirmer, 1941–42

——, *Selected Letters of Paul Hindemith,* edited and translated by Geoffrey Skelton, New Haven, Connecticut: Yale University Press, 1995

Hinton, Stephen, *The Idea of Gebrauchsmusik: A Study of Musical Aesthetics in the Weimar Republic (1919–1933) with Particular Reference to the Works of Paul Hindemith,* New York: Garland, 1989

Kemp, Ian, *Hindemith,* London: Oxford University Press, 1970

Neumeyer, David, *The Music of Paul Hindemith,* New Haven, Connecticut: Yale University Press, 1986

Skelton, Geoffrey, *Paul Hindemith: The Man Behind the Music,* London: Gollancz, 1975

Reception of Paul Hindemith's career has tended to reflect his changing status in 20th-century music. Writings from the early 1920s portray him as an iconoclastic *enfant terrible*. By 1923, he was seen as a pioneering reformer who had rescued music from the excesses of late romanticism. From the 1930s onward, Hindemith was considered a conservative figure devoted to the preservation of the tonal system. This attitude was reinforced by his theoretical writings and activities as a traditionally minded teacher at Yale University and the University of Zurich. During the 1950s, beliefs that serialism was the legitimate language of contemporary music turned this reputation into a liability. Although his professional career continued to flourish, Hindemith was no longer considered an important force in the development of contemporary music. Critical and scholarly attention declined accordingly. Although Hindemith's contributions continue to be overshadowed by the work of such composers as Schoenberg and Stravinsky, no one disputes his importance. Praise for the depth of his musical knowledge, craftsmanship, seriousness, and efforts to promote the status of contemporary music in public life can be found even among his detractors. Hindemith has always enjoyed the attention of first-rate musicians and scholars. The English-language bibliography, although rather small, contains several studies of high quality. Readers should also be aware of the annual *Hindemith-Jahrbuch,* which publishes contributions in German, English, and French.

In the introduction to his 1952 volume, the composer describes himself as a "sideline literate who rather preferred to write music." He was nevertheless the author of several books, essays, and letters. HINDEMITH (1941–42), his most influential publication, aims to assert the continued primacy of the tonal system by demonstrating its foundation in acoustical laws. All music, he argues, is ultimately organized according to tonal principles. This claim is supported by a group of analyses that range chronologically from chant to a serial composition by Schoenberg. Beyond its interest to music theorists, the volume is notable for its insights into Hindemith's compositional language. It is also interesting as a sophisticated argument for the continued relevance of tonality in 20th-century music.

HINDEMITH (1952) is a revised version of lectures delivered during his tenure as the Charles Eliot Norton professor at Harvard University and can be considered a philosophical counterpart to his 1941–42 volumes. This book is also his most comprehensive statement about the practice of composition and music's social significance. Hindemith believed that music had the ability to promote ethical behavior and that the composer therefore has a sacred duty to create works that inspire the listener to seek lofty goals. Hindemith does not restrict himself to philosophical topics; working methods, ideas about music pedagogy, and the future of contemporary music are also addressed.

Although Hindemith was reticent about expressing his personal feelings, his letters indicate a witty and incisive correspondent. These qualities are evident in HINDEMITH (1995), a collection of personal and business letters written between 1913 and 1963. This useful supplement to his formal writings is arranged chronologically, with commentary that links the letters together in a narrative fashion. Besides giving the reader a sense of Hindemith's day-to-day life as a composer and musician, this volume offers wonderful insights into his personality. The translations and commentary are excellent.

Hindemith portrayed himself as a well-adjusted individual with both feet on the ground, an attitude aimed to discredit romantic conceptions of the artist as a unique, otherworldly individual. Biographers have confirmed this self-image. A solid overview of Hindemith's life is offered in SKELTON. As the title suggests, this well-written book is essentially an intellectual biography; musical works are not considered in any detail. Readers will also find an introduction to Hindemith's 1941–42 work and a synopsis of his 1952 lectures. The chapter that deals with the composer's relationship with the Third Reich between 1933 and 1940 is especially good.

KEMP's concise yet detailed chronological survey is a superb introduction to Hindemith's music. General discussions about the development of the composer's stylistic language are supplemented with longer descriptions of selected works. The author's observations about Hindemith's early development as a composer are quite good. This brief study was conceived for a general reader who possesses a basic understanding of music terminology and theory.

NEUMEYER is the most detailed English-language account of Hindemith's music and theoretical writings. An overview of the composer's stylistic development is complemented by thorough analyses of representative works. The first three chapters are an exposition of the ideas contained in the composer's 1941–42 volume and other writings. Hindemith's theories are then used as a basis for the analyses that follow. The work is intended for individuals who possess a solid grounding in music theory. The descriptive nature of the analyses, however, ensures that general readers can grasp its main ideas. This book also includes an excellent bibliography and a detailed chronological works list.

Hindemith is often associated with the composition of *Gebrauchsmusik* for amateurs and mechanical instruments. This connection is so intimate, in fact, that he is often credited with the creation of the genre during the 1920s. HINTON demonstrates that Hindemith's activities were instead a response to contemporary research into the history of musical autonomy. The first section of this three-part monograph traces the origins of *Gebrauchsmusik*. The concept is then considered in relation to other concurrent trends in Weimar Germany. Themes outlined in parts 1 and 2 are then used to analyze selected works by the composer. Although Hinton's argument is somewhat superficial in places, this study is nevertheless highly recommended for its insights into the composer's aesthetics during the Weimar era.

MICHAEL VON DER LINN

Hoffmann, E.T.A. 1776–1822

German writer, composer, and librettist

Garlington, Aubrey S., "E.T.A. Hoffmann's 'Der Dichter und der Komponist' and the Creation of the German Romantic Opera," *Musical Quarterly* 65 (1979)

Hoffmann, E.T.A., *E.T.A. Hoffmann's Musical Writings: Kreisleriana, The Poet and the Composer, Music Criticism*, edited by David Charlton, translated by Martyn Clarke, Cambridge: Cambridge University Press, 1989

———, *Selected Letters of E.T.A. Hoffmann*, edited and translated by Johanna C. Sahlin, Chicago: University of Chicago Press, 1977

Moraal, Christine Cochrane, "The Life and Afterlife of Johannes Kreisler: Affinities Between E.T.A. Hoffmann and Carl Maria von Weber, Hector Berlioz, and Robert Schumann," Ph.D. dissertation, University of Michigan, 1994

Schafer, R. Murray, *E.T.A. Hoffmann and Music*, Toronto: University of Toronto Press, 1975

Taylor, Ronald, *Hoffmann*, London: Bowes, 1963

Musical romanticism, especially in its earliest form, derived largely from the interaction between music and literature. No single figure stood more at the crux of this interaction than Ernst Theodor Amadeus Hoffmann. Hoffmann was not content to let his devotion to music speak for itself in his work. He changed his very name to reflect it, adopting Mozart's middle name as one of his own (he was born Ernst Theodor Wilhelm Hoffmann). Saddled by one bureaucratic position after another, Hoffmann nevertheless saw music as his first calling. He wrote critical reviews for the prestigious *Allgemeine musikalische Zeitung* of Leipzig, composed large amounts of vocal and instrumental music (including an influential opera, *Undine*), and created a seminal body of literary fantasies (including novels and short stories) that eventually made their way into romantic operas throughout the 19th century. Most important, his fictional alter ego "Kapellmeister Johannes Kreisler"—an imaginary court musician—has been likened to such epochal fictional characters as Faust and Don Juan. Kreisler became the model for two generations of romantic composers, including Robert Schumann, Johannes Brahms, and Richard Wagner.

Hoffmann's strongest influence was on the character of romanticism as an artistic movement in general: he was a staunch enemy of the Philistines who regarded art as decorative rather than profound. His short stories, or *Tales,* filled with supernatural occurrences, made their way directly onto the operatic stage by way of Offenbach; they exerted a pervasive influence on romantic literature as well. Hoffmann's criticism, especially his reviews of Beethoven's music, changed forever the nature of musical interpretation; his review of Beethoven's Fifth Symphony is a classic in music criticism. His own music, although consistently unsuccessful during his lifetime, demonstrates a thorough understanding of composition. But because his music does not nearly match the powerful effect of his literary work, it continues to be largely, and unfairly, neglected.

TAYLOR presents a short, balanced account of Hoffmann's life and the importance of his work overall. Hoffmann constantly drew inspiration from the conditions of his own life, typically exaggerating his experiences and putting them into the lives of his characters. For instance, his struggles as a composer, and the bitterness those struggles entailed, make their way into the rebellious character of Kapellmeister Johannes Kreisler, who is a perfect paradigm of a misunderstood artist. The romantic longing Hoffmann felt for the ideal woman (in real life an adolescent girl named Julia Marc) also makes its way into his fiction. Most important, his sense of mysterious, supernatural clairvoyance, which was certainly inspired by his own experience of music, permeates his writings.

A later companion to Taylor, and probably the best single book on Hoffmann written in English to date, SCHAFER combines essays on Hoffmann's work with translations from his short stories, novels, and music criticism. Schafer's book was written in the mid-1970s, when talk about romanticism was considered passé or embarrassing. But both in his articles and in his translations, Schafer makes an eloquent case that Hoffmann's predilection for the bizarre and the supernatural was not only influential on subsequent writers and composers but intrinsically valuable. The centrality of music reception to Hoffmann's writings cannot be exaggerated. Hoffmann drew literary inspiration from music the same way that Robert Schumann would draw musical inspiration from Hoffmann's literature in his *Kreisleriana*. Together, the works of these two men illustrate the permeable boundaries between romantic music and literature.

Joanna Sahlin's edition and translation of many of HOFFMANN's (1977) letters is especially welcome, as the majority of studies on Hoffmann are in German. The letters show Hoffman to be lively, eccentric, and witty. He alternates freely between matter-of-factness and poetic effusions. Some letters, in particular those to the librettist of his opera *Undine*, Friedrich de la Motte Fouqué, are elaborate and eccentric; they are signed not "Hoffmann" but "Johannes Kreisler."

David Charlton's edition of HOFFMANN's (1989) complete musical writings includes a lengthy introduction and fairly extensive prefatory remarks to each essay. It also includes a lengthy bibliography. The translations are meant to be readable rather than literal, and occasionally some of the subtleties of Hoffmann's convoluted style are lost. Although highly informative, Charlton's work has as yet failed to rally a Hoffmann revival. The reason may be the interdependence of Hoffmann's musical writings with his other literary work. This study is highly informative. Perhaps when other studies emerge in English (there is no scarcity in German) that treat Hoffmann's artistic life more completely, and editions of his lesser musical works become more readily available, Charlton's contribution will be better appreciated.

GARLINGTON summarizes the positions Hoffmann took on romantic opera by way of his fictional characters and other writings. The author emphasizes Hoffmann's involvement in theater (Hoffmann wrote large quantities of incidental music) as "crucial to any discussion of his career as a writer." Ultimately, Garlington finds Hoffmann's views on romantic opera to have been too idealistic to have made any practical impact. He argues that the mainstream of German romantic opera, leading from Weber to Marschner to Wagner, took a different path than Hoffmann had laid out in *Undine*. Garlington totally neglects the figure of Johannes Kreisler and concentrates instead on statements in Hoffmann's writings directed specifically at the topic of opera. Philosophically, Garlington is right on the mark, and his article is worth reading for its clear presentation of Hoffmann's theory of romanticism. On the other hand, although Hoffmann did not affect opera musically or dramatically, he did affect it aesthetically by creating such attractive role models of romantic composers as Johannes Kreisler. Both Wagner and Berlioz lived out their lives in the shadow of Hoffmann's characters. This influence inevitably affected their decisions as operatic composers.

MORAAL addresses some of the questions of Hoffmann's influence on other musicians that are overlooked in Garlington's article. Schumann's identity as a composer was demonstrably formed by Hoffmann's literary characters (and Brahms signed many of his early works "Johannes Kreisler, Jr."). Although Moraal finds little evidence of any direct influence between Hoffmann and Weber, her case for the influence of Hoffmann (whose writings were quickly translated into French) on Berlioz is quite convincing and probably bears further research. She also presents many short summaries of the vast literature on Hoffmann in German.

THOMAS SIPE

Honegger, Arthur 1892–1955

Swiss-born composer

Arthur Honegger, Paris: Editions Salabert, 1959

Harding, James, *The Ox on the Roof: Scenes from Musical Life in Paris in the Twenties*, London: MacDonald, and New York: St. Martin's Press, 1972

Honegger, Arthur, *I Am a Composer*, translated by Wilson O. Clough, London: Faber, and New York: St. Martin's Press, 1966

Myers, Rollo H., *Modern French Music: Its Evolution and Cultural Background from 1900 to the Present Day*, Oxford: Blackwell, 1971

Spratt, Geoffrey K., *The Music of Arthur Honegger*, Cork: Cork University Press, 1985

Of the three most prominent members of Les Six— Francis Poulenc, Darius Milhaud, and Arthur Honegger —the latter remained only marginally aligned to the music-hall aesthetic embodied by Jean Cocteau and Erik Satie. Honegger's musical style was decidedly more traditional, influenced partly by his love of the music of J.S. Bach and also by a fondness for contrapuntal complexity. Although a great deal has been written concerning Honegger's most famous work, *Le Roi David* (1921), the literature in English is limited, as major studies have appeared almost invariably in French and German. Several dissertations written in the past two decades provide a great deal of information on diverse aspects of Honegger's large output, much of which is rarely heard in the concert hall or opera house. Almost 50 years after his death, there is still a great deal of research to be done on this important composer.

With surprising candor, HONEGGER (1966) himself discusses his works, musical influences, and the future of modern music in an English translation of the 1951 *Mon Métier*. The book showcases Honegger's rather biased views to good advantage in a lively collection of 12 essays. One of the most incisive sections is found in chapter 2 ("Complaints"), in which the composer chastises a fickle public who "doesn't want to hear anything but the successes" when they attend a concert and who create a hostile climate for new music by their refusal to support such works. The composer's comments are not limited to audiences, however, as he criticizes composers for writing music of exaggerated complexity, where a "rational means of notation" would be more appropriate. Even with its serious intent, the text is peppered with amusing aphoristic gems, such as when he encourages readers to be selective in their perusal of his book, because "a book is not a symphony which must be endured in its entirety." Those looking for the key to Honegger's music will likely be disappointed, since he is generally reticent concerning specific compositional influences or his own creative process. Rather, the monograph is valuable as an engaging portrait of a complex individual with a great deal to say concerning the business of music.

For general information on a wide range of composers, trends, and styles in French music, MYERS is essential. In addition to comments on the other members of Les Six, the author situates Honegger outside the mainstream of this group largely as a result of his "tastes and musical formations," which are mainly classical in their orientation. This is a useful way to consider Honegger's music, and the book provides the seeds that will likely germinate into more extensive studies concerning the influences on Honegger's musical language.

One of the most important monographs concerning the fertile years in early modern Paris is provided by HARDING. He discusses all members of Les Six, as well as Cocteau and Satie, and Honegger is mentioned frequently, with chapter 7 devoted in large part to *Le Roi David*. Useful for the general reader, and written in lively, engaging prose, Harding's book is concerned with the genesis and reception of selected works by these composers. In all, 34 of Honegger's compositions are discussed.

While there are several places to find listings of Honegger's works, the most compact and useful English source is simply titled *HONEGGER* (1959) (no author is given). Following a brief biographical sketch, the works are organized by category, including "Dramatic Works," "Ballets," and "Piano Solo." Entries include instrumentation, date and place of first performance, dedicatee, and duration. Less than 100 pages, this resource provides a great deal of information in a compact space.

The most significant monograph for serious scholars is the massive study by SPRATT, based on his doctoral dissertation. Given the biographical approach typical of the majority of Honegger studies, Spratt's book is striking for its clear emphasis on the music. The study focuses on Honegger's nine major dramatic works, including *Judith, Antigone,* and *Jeanne d'arc au bûcher,* discussed chronologically, with detailed accounts of the structure of each, including tonal language, form, and thematic correspondences between sections of the work. The analyses, clear and often quite astute, are intended for advanced readers with a strong background in both traditional harmony and 20th-century techniques. Useful features include the extensive work list, discography, and bibliography. The bibliography—divided into several sections, including "The Writings of Arthur Honegger" and "Articles in Music Journals Relating to the Life and Works of Arthur Honegger"—is the most comprehensive listing of sources currently available. In short, there is no other resource that matches the breadth of Spratt's monograph, and this book will serve as a cornerstone for all subsequent research concerning the composer.

KEITH E. CLIFTON

Hungary *see* Eastern Europe

Hymn

Benson, Louis F., *The Hymnody of the Christian Church,* New York: Doran, 1927

Diehl, Katharine Smith, *Hymns and Tunes: An Index,* New York: Scarecrow Press, 1966

Dreves, Guido Maria, et al., editors, *Analecta hymnica medii aevi,* 55 vols., Leipzig: Reisland, 1886–1922; reprint New York: Johnson Reprint Corporation, 1961

Ellinwood, Leonard Webster, editor, *Dictionary of American Hymnology: First Line Index,* New York: University Music Editions, 1984

Glover, Raymond F., editor, *The Hymnal 1982 Companion,* 4 vols., New York: Church Hymnal, 1990–94

Julian, John, editor, *A Dictionary of Hymnology: Setting Forth the Origin of Christian Hymns of all Ages and Nations,* London: Murray, 1891; revised, 1907; New York: Dover Publications, 1957; reprint in 2 vols., Grand Rapids, Michigan: Kregel Publications, 1985

Spencer, Jon Michael, *Black Hymnody: A Hymnological History of the African-American Church,* Knoxville: University of Tennessee Press, 1992

Temperley, Nicholas, *The Music of the English Parish Church,* 2 vols., Cambridge: Cambridge University Press, 1979

Wasson, D. DeWitt, *Hymntune Index and Related Hymn Materials,* 3 vols., Lanham, Maryland: Scarecrow Press, 1998

In its original Greek meaning, a hymn was a song in praise of gods or heroes, and since the time of St. Augustine, Christian hymnody has embraced three elements: song, praise, and God. Hymns are mentioned in the New Testament and are distinguished from psalms and spiritual songs, although history often blurs the distinctions. Monophonic Latin hymns were a part of the Divine Office (mainly Lauds and Vespers) during the Middle Ages, and both Latin and vernacular hymns were sung by the people in medieval religious processions. Modern hymnody traces its origin to Martin Luther and the Reformation. First came the Lutheran chorale, soon followed by Reformed settings of metrical psalmody, which were the basis for Anglican and Scottish hymnody. Technically, *hymn* refers to the text, whereas the *hymn tune* is the melody to which a text in a given meter can be sung. Modern practice identifies hymns by their first lines, whereas hymn tunes have specific names, which are usually indicated by being printed in uppercase letters.

Before the mid-19th century, hymnals normally were printed with texts only, and the meters or tunes were indicated above each text. Organists and choirs obtained the music from separate tune books. A vast scholarly literature exists on hymnody and its history, and this literature continues to expand, following the lead of such earlier 20th-century scholars as Frost, Benson, Routley, Blume, Ellinwood, and others. Recent decades have seen many new hymnals. A bibliography of the companions for these hymnals up to 1990 was compiled by Leaver in the December 1990 issue of *Notes,* the quarterly journal of the Music Library Association.

BENSON was one of the most authoritative scholars of hymnody during the early 20th century. Taken from a series of lectures he delivered at Princeton University, his book remains a classic for defining Christian hymnody in the European tradition. Benson divides his subject into six general areas: the apostolic ideal of hymnody, the relation of the hymn to Holy Scripture, the hymn as related to literature, hymn contents, hymn texts, and hymn singing. The concepts that Benson develops are essential for anyone seeking the philosophy and purpose of traditional Christian hymnody.

Although ELLINWOOD is not a book or series of volumes in the traditional sense, it is a major resource for scholars. Work on the dictionary began in 1956, and by 1978 texts from 4,834 hymnals representing 142 religious bodies and ten languages had been arranged alphabetically and chronologically. The entry for each hymn provides author, translator, date, title and refrains, and the hymnal collection or library in which it can be found. Currently, the vast first-line index is being prepared for electronic publication. A second part of the project will attempt to identify tunes, using guidelines developed by Nicholas Temperley for the *Hymn Tune Index* at the University of Illinois.

DIEHL's index is a standard reference both for first lines of texts and for hymn tunes. It classifies the contents of 78 official hymnals used in North America and Great Britain from about 1890 to 1965. The tune index is especially helpful when one remembers a tune but not the tune name or a text with which it is associated. By using sol-fa syllables, Diehl has developed a coded system that enables the tune to be found. An excellent system of cross-references enables one to begin a search from first lines, authors, composers, tune names, or the tune itself.

DREVES and the associate editors of the *Analecta hymnica* have compiled 55 volumes of the most comprehensive published source for medieval and Renaissance Latin hymnody available today. This massive study provides the principal foundation for a history and appreciation of Latin hymns, and it includes not only previously unedited and scattered materials that are otherwise difficult to access but also materials from published collections by other scholars of Latin hymnody. The editors include a critical apparatus that gives the origin, age, location of sources, and variants and that indicates whether uncertainty exists regarding the accuracy of this information. The *Analecta hymnica* concerns mainly hymn texts, but some information is given on the melodies for these texts, although more recent scholars have called attention to occasional errors in the transcriptions. A three-volume index edited by Dorothea Baumann and others was published in 1978 and provides access to this vast resource.

GLOVER has edited a valuable, three-volume companion for the Episcopal hymnal of 1982 that contains a wealth of information. Volume 1 comprises essays by recognized authorities on English-language church music, and volume 2 discusses service music and includes biographies of persons whose hymns are in the 1982 hymnal. Volume 3 comprises two thick parts, each discussing the individual hymns. This publication is an excellent, readable first source for anyone seeking more information on any of the hymns, composers, or authors in the 1982 hymnal and contains a good cross section of contemporary English hymnody.

JULIAN has been the standard English-language dictionary for hymn texts and their authors for over a century. As stated on the title page, its aim is "Setting forth the Origin and History of Christian Hymns of all Ages and Nations." Because most of today's hymns were written before 1900, Julian's monumental work remains a principal source for information on hymns and their authors, especially for lesser-known writers who are rarely found in modern hymnals.

SPENCER considers issues related to race that historically have been invisible to most white European-American students of hymnody but that have considerable relevance for North American hymnody today. Although some persons might question the author's viewpoints, this study is essential for anyone who is trying to understand the African-American viewpoint and especially how events since the civil rights movement of the 1960s, have influenced black hymnody. Spencer asserts that the two major concerns facing African-Americans are self identity and self determination. The postscript that he has appended to his study posits that these concerns are "not *reflected* in the hymnody; to a considerable degree the problem *is* the hymnody" [his emphasis]. Spencer views the black churches in the United States through a hymnological lens, and in doing so he has created a carefully researched and definitive history of African-American hymnody.

TEMPERLEY's detailed study considers all aspects of music in English parish churches from 1549 to 1965, and the author includes extensive sections on the musical practices of psalmody and hymnody. Anyone seeking the history and performance practices of English hymnody will find this book especially valuable. Most studies of Anglican music have concentrated on the English cathedral traditions, so this study of parish church music is especially welcome. A second volume provides an anthology of parish church music of all kinds, newly edited for study or performance.

WASSON has compiled a three-volume index that will largely replace the hymn-tune portion of Diehl's index because Wasson includes not only the material covered by Diehl but also the many hymnals that have appeared since the Diehl index was published in 1966. In addition to cataloging over 33,000 melodies sung worldwide, Wasson includes references to choral, organ, and other music based on hymn tunes. Like Diehl, Wasson uses a coding system to make it possible to reference this vast number of tunes. Because this index it is based on hymn tunes in modern use, it will complement the four-volume *Hymn Tune Index* edited by Nicholas Temperley (1998). This index is historically based and provides a census of English-language hymn tunes in printed sources from 1535 to 1820.

EDWARD CHRISTOPHER WOLF

I

Iconography

Bowles, Edmund A., *Musical Ensembles in Festival Books, 1500–1800: An Iconographical and Documentary Survey,* Ann Arbor, Michigan: UMI Research Press, 1989

Brown, Howard Mayer, and Joan Lascelle, *Musical Iconography: A Manual for Cataloguing Musical Subjects in Western Art before 1800,* Cambridge, Massachusetts: Harvard University Press, 1972

Comini, Alessandra, *The Changing Image of Beethoven: A Study in Mythmaking,* New York: Rizzoli, 1987

Connolly, Thomas, *Mourning into Joy: Music, Raphael, and Saint Cecilia,* New Haven, Connecticut: Yale University Press, 1994

Fischer, Pieter, *Music in Paintings of the Low Countries in the 16th and 17th Centuries,* translated by Ruth Koenig, Amsterdam: Swets and Zeitlinger, 1975

Knighton, Tess, and David Fallows, editors, *Companion to Medieval and Renaissance Music,* London: Dent, and New York: Schirmer, 1992

Leppert, Richard, *Music and Image: Domesticity, Ideology and Socio-Cultural Formation in Eighteenth-Century England,* Cambridge: Cambridge University Press, 1988

McKinnon, James, "Iconography," in *Musicology in the 1980s: Methods, Goals, Opportunities,* edited by D. Kern Holoman and Claude V. Palisca, New York, Da Capo Press, 1982

Winternitz, Emmanuel, *Musical Instruments and Their Symbolism in Western Art: Studies in Musical Iconology,* New York: Norton, and London: Faber, 1967; 2nd edition, New Haven, Connecticut: Yale University Press, 1979

The iconography of music is a relatively new branch of music history that involves the study and interpretation of musical subject matter in visual works of art. Art works offer music scholars a broad range of historical evidence often lacking in verbal descriptions or musical sources. For example, works of art supplement our knowledge about the lives of composers and the milieus in which they worked; they offer concrete evidence concerning the history and construction of musical instruments; they supplement our knowledge of playing positions, performance practice, and acoustical environ-ments; and they improve our understanding of the role of music in society, both culturally and intellectually. The value of art works as musicological evidence has been recognized for some time, and there is even a small body of scholarly work that demonstrates exemplary mastery of the discipline. In general, musical iconography remains an undeveloped field. Most research has appeared in articles and journals rather than books. One of the most prominent journals in musical iconography is *Imago Musicae,* which offers an annual, comprehensive bibliography of contributions to the field.

McKINNON provides a good introduction to the field of musical iconography. He begins by discussing the pitfalls of the discipline, concentrating mainly on various problems of methodology. In general, the first half of his essay is concerned with the history of the field. McKinnon cites specific examples from previous studies and, in doing so, gives a brief history of the field and its early methodological problems. In the second half of the essay, McKinnon offers research suggestions to scholars interested in the subject. Here, topics such as organology, intellectual history, and cultural history are discussed briefly.

The value of visual sources to the study of early music is assessed in two chapters in KNIGHTON and FALLOWS. In chapter 29, "Music and Pictures in the Middle Ages," Elizabeth Teviotdale discusses the symbolic meaning of musical figures in the pages of illuminated manuscripts. Clearly, she is an advocate of McKinnon's methodology, claiming that the value of art works as musicological sources can be judged only after "their integrity as pictures is considered." In chapter 30, Iain Fenlon continues the discussion with "Music in Italian Renaissance Paintings." He approaches the topic of musical iconography from the viewpoint of the artist, taking into consideration his or her cultural and social milieu, education, and probable inspiration. In this manner, Fenlon demonstrates a workable methodology for establishing the value of a painting's organological, symbolic, and/or cultural information.

WINTERNITZ is considered by many to be a monument in the field of musical iconography. First published in 1967, this book is a collection of previously published articles concerned with at least one of three basic themes: the construction of musical instruments, the evolution of musical instruments, and the symbolic meaning of musical instruments in works of art. Great use is made of a wide array of primary sources, including prints, paintings, sculpture, musical instruments, and early treatises. Although the book cannot be described as a comprehensive survey of musical imagery in Western art, it does serve as a valuable introduction to the wealth of information available to the musical iconographer. Unfortunately, Winternitz never revised the book after its second edition in 1979, but in recent years his methodology has been refined substantially by later scholars.

FISCHER investigates the frequent occurrence of notated music in Netherlandish paintings. He divides his study into two parts, "The South Netherlands, 1565–1620" and "The North Netherlands, 1600–1690," and discusses the different social climates of the two regions. He examines an impressive number of paintings with musical notation and explains how, in general, artists in the south used music as an optimistic symbol for praising God, whereas artists in the north made use of it in moralizing genres, such as the "Vanitas" and allegories of the five senses. Fischer's discussions of notated music (both real and imagined) in paintings and engravings are fascinating for specialists and general readers alike, and his approach to the topic is a fine example of sound methodology.

BOWLES provides an illuminating view of how visual art works—in this case, woodcuts and engravings—can serve as a valuable source for the study of early performance practice. Using over 100 festival books as his source material, Bowles presents descriptions, illustrations, and discussions of festivities associated with royal weddings, state visits, coronations, births, baptisms, funerals, and other official events. With each event, the reader is informed of the prevalent role played by music and musicians. The instruments and ensembles used for each event are described in detail, and a wealth of information concerning the social, political, and cultural contexts of each festival is provided.

LEPPERT is an exemplary model for the use of music in comparative studies. Here, upper-class amateur music performance in 18th-century England is analyzed through the interpretation of visual representations of music making. According to Leppert, images of musical performances do not simply reflect practice but moderate it, defining both power and weakness in social structure. Separate chapters are dedicated to the study of male and female images associated with music, and these two chapters provide a foundation for the succeeding discussion of the relation of music to marriage and family as a whole. Throughout the book, Leppert emphasizes the need to study gestures, objects, and settings in portraits involving music and musical instruments, and in later

chapters, he examines the familial functions of amateur performances as they appear in family portraits.

COMINI describes the gradual metamorphosis of Beethoven's image during the 19th century and, in doing so, elucidates, step by step, the making of a myth. She presents an unprecedented number of Beethoven images (drawings, lithographs, engravings, paintings, and sculptures), with the *terminus ad quem* being the Klinger-Klimt-Mahler installation of 1902. This study gives credence to the theory that it was not only the music but also the image of Beethoven that affected the work of later composers such as Schumann, Berlioz, Liszt, Chopin, Wagner, and Mahler.

CONNOLLY takes on the history of quite a different musical image, that of St. Cecilia. He investigates the origins of her musical character, analyzing works from both the visual and the literary arts. His goal is to reconstruct the relevant motifs of the culture in which the legend of St. Cecilia developed and to understand what she signified to those who founded and propagated her cult. Raphael's famous altarpiece *The Ecstasy of Saint Cecilia* serves as a framing device for the study, but countless other images, dating back from as early as the sixth century, are discussed in detail as well.

Finally, for readers interested in creating a database of art works containing musical subjects, the BROWN and LASCELLE work is highly recommended. Here, the authors present a brief introduction to the field of music iconography and an effective, ready-made system for cataloging musical images.

ANNA H. HARWELL CELENZA

Improvisation

Bailey, Derek, *Improvisation: Its Nature and Practice in Music,* Ashbourne, England: Moorland in association with Incus Records, and Englewood Cliffs, New Jersey: Prentice Hall, 1980; revised edition, London: British Library National Sound Archive, 1992

Berliner, Paul F., *Thinking in Jazz: The Infinite Art of Improvisation,* Chicago: University of Chicago Press, 1994

Byrnside, Ronald, "The Performer as Creator: Jazz Improvisation" in *Contemporary Music and Music Cultures,* by Charles Hamm et al., Englewood Cliffs, New Jersey: Prentice Hall, 1975

Chase, Mildred Portney, *Improvisation: Music from the Inside Out,* Berkeley, California: Creative Arts, 1988

Ferand, Ernest T., *Improvisation in Nine Centuries of Western Music: An Anthology With a Historical Introduction,* Cologne: Volk Verlag, 1961

Goldstein, Malcolm, *Sounding the Full Circle: Concerning Music Improvisation and Other Related Matters,* Sheffield, Vermont: Goldstein, 1988

Prévost, Eddie, editor, *Improvisation: History, Directions, Practice,* London: Association of Improvising Musicians, 1984

Improvisation has been considered a serious subject of investigation only in recent decades of Western musicology. Most of its advocates are practitioners of the genre, either from the classical musical sphere, contemporary music, or the jazz idiom. However, not every writer agrees about the definition of improvisation, its value, or its significance. For some thinkers, music making that is spontaneous because it does not arise from a written score is necessarily an improvisation. For others, the very notion of spontaneity is questionable, because music making always belongs to a culture and implies preset values and personal knowledge or practice.

FERAND's historical survey is the first major contribution to the subject. Covering nine centuries of musical practice, from the Middle Ages to the baroque era in Western cultures, Ferand shows how improvisation was a predominant and necessary feature from the very beginning. He associates the word *improvisation* with spontaneous musical expression, when there is no notation or when the actual notation is lacking in precision. He insists that notation is a fairly recent achievement, needed especially for ordering the increasing complexities of polyphony. However, many polyphonic genres have developed at the crossroad of both improvisation and composition; he states that it is often difficult to determine whether a given form derives from improvisation or whether improvisation modifies a fixed form of composition. The text discusses an interesting selection of musical examples that are provided in appendices.

BYRNSIDE's contribution is included in a book that deals with music in the contemporary world, as seen in a broader social and cultural context. Keeping this enlarged vision in mind, Byrnside goes beyond his informative description of jazz procedures. His reflection offers an overview of the improvisation phenomena in diverse cultural practices, from historical Western art music to the traditions of some non-Western cultures. Although he defines improvisation in opposition to what he calls fixed music, the author shows how both categories are not absolute, arguing, on the one hand, that an "improviser cannot escape his own musical habits, his previous musical experiences, his personal performance facility and compositional procedures" and, on the other hand, that "utterly and permanently fixed pieces are rare."

Because jazz improvisation is so influential in contemporary practices, it is interesting to try to understand how it functions. BERLINER, himself a jazz musician and an ethnomusicologist, presents a detailed, but quite accessible study. Constructed from a series of interviews with jazz practitioners, ranging from well-established musicians to lesser-known ones, the book offers a generous description of principles and practices from 1945 until now, with musical examples given in appendices.

PRÉVOST, chairman of the Association of Improvising Musicians (AIM), collects two serious reflections from the proceedings of a forum on improvisation held at the Institute of Contemporary Arts in London on 31 March 1984. "No Meanings without Rules," by Christopher Small, starts by comparing music to speech in their need of rules to function socially; he contends that there is no total spontaneity in improvisation because it is based on the acceptance of common rules. The flaw of this theory, however, lies in the difficulty in defining what these rules are in music, a definition that Small does not attempt to give. One can speculate that, if they really exist, the rules are different from one culture or practice to another. The second essay, "Improvisation: Arguments after the Fact" by Alan Durant, questions the significance of the word *improvisation* to find why it often has negative connotations. Moreover, Durant posits that improvisation should not be considered as a product, but as a process. Similarly, Small argues that the traditional notion of a work of art, seen more as an object than as an act, goes against improvisation and music in general, which takes place in a social context and has a social meaning. Prévost contributes a third essay drawn from some of the panel discussions (chaired by Keith Rowe, with Evan Parker, George Weigand, John Tilbury, and Christian Wolff). He concludes that improvisation is mobile, mediating (versus meditative as composition), and collective. Therefore, it demands understanding and generosity of spirit for its performance and appreciation.

BAILEY's book is important for its scope and the diversity of practices it includes. The author, a renowned guitarist in the field of free improvisation, investigates practicing musicians' "use of improvisation, its place in music and their speculations on its nature." This point of departure defines the subjects covered (Indian music, flamenco, baroque, organ, rock, jazz, free, etc.), for Bailey limits his study to the specialties of his interviewees. The interviews give interesting insights into what each practitioner considers the value of improvisation and how he or she defines the term. Bailey appropriately distinguishes idiomatic from nonidiomatic improvisations, the former referring to the expression of an idiom (jazz, flamenco, or others), the latter being free of any idiom. However, independent from its allegiance, he considers improvisation as a "celebration of the moment" that "invites complete involvement in the act of music-making."

GOLDSTEIN's book is a collection of his own previously published articles, personal journals, and other essays or scores that focus on improvisation. The engaging tone is at times political, philosophical, and poetic. Goldstein is a violinist, composer, and improviser. These last two activities are linked in Goldstein's approach, as the scores he produces always incorporate a large amount of improvisation within preestablished frameworks (structured-improvisation compositions). Because of its radical aesthetic and social implications, however, the concept of improvisation is the main focus of his thinking. Improvisation, for Goldstein, shakes the ground of our value systems: "What does improvisation ask of the performer that is so different from printed, through-composed pieces of music? . . . [P]erhaps, 'who are *you*? How do *you* think or feel about this moment/sounding?'"

CHASE is a classical pianist and teacher who has a humanistic approach to improvisation; she believes that everybody is able to improvise, if only they are open to what happens and are ready to practice, learning from their own trials and errors. She insists on relaxing every tension that could intervene, psychological (such as negativity) as well as physical. She gives some examples of exercises one can do to approach improvisation, including exploration of physical gesture and listening activities. Chase defines improvisation as "the imagination guiding an action in an unplanned way, allowing a multitude of split second adjustments." In saying so, she expresses an underlying and agreed-upon meaning for improvisation: an activity that unifies the time of thinking with the time of doing.

JOHANNE RIVEST

India

Massey, Reginald, and Jamila Massey, *The Music of India*, New York: Crescendo Publishing, and London: Kahn and Averill, 1976; revised edition, 1993

Meer, Wim van der, *Hindustani Music in the 20th Century*, The Hague: Nijhoff, 1980

Miner, Allyn, *Sitar and Sarod in the 18th and 19th Centuries*, Wilhelmshaven: Noetzel, and New York: Peters, 1993

Neuman, Daniel M., *The Life of Music in North India: The Organization of an Artistic Tradition*, Detroit, Michigan: Wayne State University Press, 1980

Perera, E.S., *The Origin and Development of Dhrupad and Its Bearing on Instrumental Music*, Calcutta: Bagchi, 1994

Powers, Harold, "The Background of the South Indian Raga-System," 3 vols., Ph.D. dissertation, Princeton University, 1958

Rowell, Lewis Eugene, *Music and Musical Thought in Early India*, Chicago: University of Chicago Press, 1992

Ruckert, George, *Introduction to the Classical Music of North India*, St. Louis, Missouri: East Bay Books, 1991

Wade, Bonnie C., *Music in India: The Classical Traditions*, Englewood Cliffs, New Jersey: Prentice Hall, 1979

A wealth of information concerning the classical music of India has been published in English during the last 20 years. India's music is enriched by a dynamic culture that is supported by the traditions of great beings, saints, sages, and revealed scriptures. The music has evolved through several languages, many religions, and a tumultuous political history. India itself is a vital entity, and its music reflects boundless potential in inspiration and creative outpouring. Most of the books discussed here are written by Westerners who have been personally touched by the profundity of the musical heritage of India. Their research was compelled not only by the authors' desire to share information but also by their longing to deepen their own understanding of the spiritual goal of India's classical music—to attain union with the Divine.

Several books present a general overview of Indian music, surveying the two canonic schools, Hindustani and Carnatic, with the stated purpose of familiarizing the Western listener with Indian music. The works by Khan, Wade, Neuman, Massey and Massey, and Miner successfully address the difficulty of this enormous task. To introduce a nonspecialist to Indian music is challenging because of the countless terms that cannot be translated, such as the names of musical instruments, the terms of the raga system, and the Sanskrit words from the text sources. Therefore, even the most basic text on Indian music is at an intermediate to advanced level for the average music enthusiast. Many of the more in-depth works are based on dissertations by students of Indian music. These focus on more specific topics and are intended for an advanced audience.

RUCKERT is a successful beginner's guide to the complex topic of Indian ragas. The author patiently leads the reader through simple information about Indian customs, such as why the student bows to the teacher, to more complicated concepts such as the *bhav*, or feeling of the *gharana* traditions. The book is a manual for learning to play basic ragas and *thekas* on the sitar, sarod, or tabla. A section of ragas and *bols* is presented in a user-friendly way. It is Khan himself who gives this book a wonderfully unique place in the literature, for he is a true master from a *gharana* lineage who has been teaching in the United States for over 30 years. Thus, he has a particular compassion and understanding of the Western student's state of mind as he or she embarks on the fascinating journey of exploring ragas.

WADE's book is to be highly commended for its thorough research, although it has a noticeably dry delivery. There are two striking omissions: the book lacks a glossary of terms, which is indispensable for this topic, and Wade presents an entire survey of classical Indian music without ever mentioning the *gharana*, or guru-disciple, system. This oral tradition is truly the heart of the culture of Indian music, and its absence here is curious. However, the author does an excellent job of comparing the Indian and Western musical systems. The text is formatted so that Indian musical terms such as *raga* or *tala* (in both the Hindustani and Carnatic systems) are presented on the right-hand page and the Western equivalent or corresponding term is presented on the facing page with a musical example. Wade includes this comparison, even though she does not favor this approach, for the sake of assisting the beginner.

NEUMAN, a student of a *gharana* master, explains this oral tradition of India. He speaks from a heartfelt experience, vividly portraying the affection that develops between the master and disciple. As to why gurus often refuse to share information about certain ragas to Western researchers, he explains that a guru would rather die with his knowledge left intact than to pass on his learning to a student who may never have correct understanding. Neuman points out that, if a guru would not share information with his most beloved disciple, why would he then share it with a foreign ethnomusicology student from Berkeley? Neuman's style is poetic and sincere, and he clearly portrays the level of devotion a true master has for music: the true guru always considers himself to be a student, with God as his patron.

MASSEY and MASSEY have taken a scholarly yet light-hearted approach to clarifying myths and misconceptions about Indian music. Anyone attempting to research the history of Indian music soon becomes frustrated with the lack of written documentation, which results in conflicting information. The authors wrote this survey with the intention to "dust off the fiction and leave the bare facts." It is easy to read, includes a good description of the Vedic tradition, and provides a list of prominent Indian musicians with short biographical sketches.

MINER, a disciple of Ali Akbar Khan, published her dissertation on the history of the sitar and sarod, two of the main melodic instruments of India. Because of the lack of written documentation, it is not clear how the instruments evolved and became part of the Indian culture. Miner painstakingly presents conflicting theories and weighs the evidence for each. She includes an excellent photo-history of the musical instruments and provides an impressive bibliography.

If you happen to be familiar with various ancient texts from India such as the Bhagavad Gita, the Rig-Veda, and Narada's Naradiyasiksha, or if you have texts by Abhinavagupta expounding on the philosophical system of Kashmir Shaivism sitting on your coffee table, then ROWELL will be relatively easy reading. Otherwise, it might not be obvious what a heroic effort Rowell exerted in order to compile a thesis encompassing the music of India from the ancient period to the 13th century. This is truly an impressive undertaking. Rowell explores the roots of modern Indian musical concepts and practices, emphasizing what Indian music was, rather than what it currently is. Not only does he research Indian art music, sacred chant, and theater, he also studies the ideology of Indian music in its entirety,

from exploring technical aspects of raga to the broad philosophical questions of what music means in the context of Indian culture. Due to the lack of manuscripts, Rowell accepts the fact that knowledge of early Indian music must come from two sources: the textual evidence in sources such as the Vedas and texts on Kashmir Shaivism, and current performance practices heard today. He admits that the concurrences and overlappings of the events in Indian history make for an unavoidably discontinuous format. In his book, Rowell teaches Indian musical, philosophical, and cultural concepts that are difficult to grasp for the Western student because there is little to compare them to in Western thought. For example, in the chapter on *Shastras*, he explains *karma* with the aid of quotations from the Bhagavad Gita that discuss *dharma* (right action). In the chapter on time, Rowell explains the functions of *tala* by exploring the five-fold function of Shiva (creation, sustenance, concealment, destruction, and revelation), as seen in the dancing form of the Shiva Nataraj.

POWERS is devoted solely to the Carnatic system of Southern India. His presentation of the theoretical foundation of the raga system is supported by insightful quotations from his Indian teachers that explain principles and technicalities of various aspects of raga. Another notable feature of his work is that he uses the details of phrase structure of the *svaras* to explain the raga system rather than the commonly accepted scale-theory approach. Powers's rendering is meticulous, and it is smooth reading through the unavoidable sea of definitions of nontranslatable terms. The second and third volumes are helpful transcriptions of the ragas that he learned during his research tenure. Powers comments that many of the ornamentations in the Carnatic style are at times incomprehensible, much less transcribable, but that he did his best. His thesis also includes a brief history of the notation of Indian music.

MEER contributes an exhaustive survey of the existing research on Indian music. He points out the flaws and omissions of previous researchers and attempts to fill the gaps and add his own interpretations. Noteworthy is Meer's discussion of the concept of *rasa*.

PERERA dives into the history of *dhrupad*, the musical form from which classical Indian music, both vocal and instrumental, seems to have its origin. After exploring the various definitions of the term, he analyzes the elements of the *dhrupad*. Perera then provides a convincing argument for the spiritual inspiration of the *dhrupad* with a satisfying background of its text sources: the Vedic scriptures, the Narada *bhakti sutras*, and the *bhajans* of the bhakti yogis of the medieval period.

CHARMAINE FRAN LECLAIR

See also Mode: Non-Western

Indeterminacy *see* Aleatoric Music

Indonesia

Becker, Judith O., *Traditional Music in Modern Java: Gamelan in a Changing Society,* Honolulu: University Press of Hawaii, 1980

———, *Gamelan Stories: Tantrism, Islam, and Aesthetics in Central Java,* Tempe: Program for Southeast Asian Studies, Arizona State University, 1993

Herbst, Edward, *Voices in Bali: Energies and Perceptions in Vocal Music and Dance Theater,* Hanover, New Hampshire: University Press of New England, 1997

Hood, Mantle, *The Evolution of Javanese Gamelan,* 3 vols., New York: Peters, 1980–88

Kunst, Jaap, *Indonesian Music and Dance: Traditional Music and Its Interaction with the West,* edited by Maya Frijn et al., translated by Sandra Reijnhart and Andrew Baxter, Amsterdam: Royal Tropical Institute and the University of Amsterdam, Ethnomusicology Centre "Jaap Kunst," 1994

———, *Hindu-Javanese Musical Instruments,* 2nd revised and enlarged edition, The Hague: Nijhoff, 1968

———, *Music in Java: Its History, Its Theory, and Its Technique,* 2 vols., translated by Emile van Loo, The Hague: Nijhoff, 1949; 3rd enlarged edition, edited by Ernst L. Heins, 1973

McPhee, Colin, *Music in Bali: A Study in Form and Instrumental Organization in Balinese Orchestral Music,* New Haven, Connecticut: Yale University Press, 1966

Miller, Terry E., and Sean Williams, editors, *Southeast Asia,* The Garland Encyclopedia of World Music, vol. 4, New York: Garland, 1998

Morgan, Stephanie, and Laurie Jo Sears, editors, *Aesthetic Tradition and Cultural Transition in Java and Bali,* Madison: Center for Southeast Asian Studies, University of Wisconsin, 1984

Schaareman, Danker, editor, *Balinese Music in Context: A Sixty-Fifth Birthday Tribute to Hans Oesch,* Winterthur: Amadeus, 1992

Sumarsam, *Gamelan: Cultural Interaction and Musical Development in Central Java,* Chicago: University of Chicago Press, 1995

Sutton, Richard Anderson, *Traditions of Gamelan Music in Java: Musical Pluralism and Regional Identity,* Cambridge: Cambridge University Press, 1991

Tenzer, Michael, *Balinese Music,* Berkeley: Periplus, 1991; revised edition, Hong Kong: Periplus, 1998

Zanten, Wim van, *Sundanese Music in the Cianjuran Style: Anthropological and Musicological Aspects of Tembang Sunda,* Dordrecht: Foris, 1989

Early ethnomusicological scholarship on Indonesia consists of largely positivist studies of the instruments, scales, musical structures, rhythms, and melody lines of Javanese music, with occasional studies on Bali or other islands in the archipelago. Many more recent authors have continued this positivist approach while expanding the focus of their studies to include style analysis and the exploration of cultural aspects. Several works published since 1980 break out of a synchronic approach to consider the changes occurring in Javanese arts as a result of modernization or Westernization, and the most recent literature is also the most innovative.

BECKER (1980) gives a clear introduction to the instruments, structure, and modes of Javanese *gamelan* while arguing that the changing role of Javanese music in the 20th century reflects broader changes occurring in Indonesian society. She discusses the transition from an oral to a written tradition in music, demonstrated by the use of notation at the arts colleges, and traces the debate concerning the role of music within Indonesian nationalism. She also examines Western influences and modernization by analyzing the work of two contemporary Javanese composers, Ki Wasitodipuro and Ki Nartosabdho.

BECKER (1993) concentrates on the esoteric importance of music as evident in Javanese and Balinese musical manuscripts, medieval Javanese spiritual practices, Javanese aesthetics, and musical terminology reflecting the mystical philosophies of Tantrism or Sufi Islam. Becker provides a much needed interpretive history of Tantric and Sufi mystical orders that continue to influence Javanese arts through the form of gamelan stories, which ascribe meanings to gamelan instruments, compositions, and the *bedhaya* court dance.

HERBST combines Balinese philosophy with concrete musical details concerning voice production and dramatic characterizations in Balinese theater to create a rich, reflective dialogue based on his own practical studies and discussions with Balinese performers of *arja* (sung dance-drama), *topeng* (masked dance theater), and *wayang* (the shadow play). At the same time, his evocative writing style entices the reader to participate in this discussion. The book is organized around the pervasive Balinese concept of *désa, kala, patra* (which translates as place, time, and context). Balinese performers rely upon this philosophy to determine the appropriateness of certain actions and events, and it therefore helps to shape the performing arts in practice. While the voices of Balinese performers are more present in this study than in most previous scholarship, they are still relayed through Herbst's narrative style, with only short terms and phrases cited directly. Inspired by John Cage, Herbst contrasts different sections of the text through his playful use of spacing and italics, which serve to enhance the contemplative space given to anecdotes, theoretical discussions, and reflections while separating these interludes from the author's more straightforward exposition of the process of learning and performing vocal music and dance theatre in Bali. Herbst has devised a detailed notational system to convey the vocal melodies known as *tembang,* and recordings are included on a CD that accompanies the text.

Hood is not only intrigued by musical details; he also aims in his trilogy to supply historical, sociological, and cultural information in order to consider the role of music within society and analyze changes occurring in Indonesian arts. HOOD (1980), the first of the three books, is written as a novel in which the author theorizes that gamelan may have originated from bronze drums and *gamelan munggang*. HOOD (1984), the middle volume, explores Javanese cultural history from the Hindu-Javanese period to the early 1980s. The final book, HOOD (1988), investigates the modes and performance practices of Javanese gamelan music as well as the effects of modernization. Hood is concerned about the decline of improvisation due to increased standardization of musical parts, the growing use of musical notation, and formal instruction in musical conservatories. He is the first Western author to include lengthy citations from interviews with a Javanese musician, namely Pak Tjokro.

KUNST (1949) describes the musical instruments and ensembles of Central and East Java, with a primary focus on the gamelan ensembles of Yogyakarta and Surakarta, and offers a basic introduction to Sundanese music of West Java. Kunst investigates tone-measurement and tone-systems, seeking to understand the origin of the *pélog* and *sléndro* scales. While Kunst (1949) gives extensive organological information, KUNST (1968) traces the history of each Hindu-Javanese instrument and includes musical references found in iconography and literature. Both publications contain valuable tables, charts, and photographs.

The more recent publication on Indonesian music and dance, KUNST (1994) contains both information on and articles by the distinguished scholar. The book delineates Kunst's contributions to the field of ethnomusicology, including his fieldwork in Indonesia, his field methods and recordings, and his research on the areas known during colonial times as the Outer Provinces and the Kai Islands. This collection also reproduces Kunst's seminal article "Musicologica" (1950), in which he introduces the term "ethnomusicology" to describe this discipline.

McPHEE offers the first classic text on the different musical ensembles in Bali, based on material collected in the 1930s. Part 1, "Music in Balinese Life," outlines the historical, courtly background of Balinese arts and describes their social and religious contexts. Part 2, "The Practice of Music," constitutes the majority of the text, in which McPhee provides extensive information on each ensemble, describing their instruments and giving transcriptions of their scales, musical compositions, and rhythmic interaction. He also relays the stories that underlie theatrical productions. McPhee's technical precision even extends to the bamboo flute fingerings used in *gambuh*. He analyzes the structural, tonal, metric, and thematic organization of characteristic pieces from each ensemble. Further, he explains the Balinese use of paired

tunings to create a wave, or *ombak*, and explicates the interaction of two essential parts, *polos* and *sangsih*, to create a range of textures such as unison melodies, interlocking parts, and four-part polyphony. McPhee's strong introduction to the music of Bali was unprecedented in its time and continues to hold an important place in the literature on Bali.

MILLER and WILLIAMS's extensive compilation of information on the various musical traditions in Indonesia is current, thorough, and descriptive. Each of the eight essays on Indonesia provides a long list of references that will lead interested students and scholars toward a broad range of relevant literature. This book is useful for its coverage of the musical instruments, genres, tuning, ensembles, musical structures, cultural history, and contemporary issues surrounding Indonesian music, and as a resource for additional scholarship.

MORGAN and SEARS have assembled an interesting collection with 11 articles on Javanese arts and culture and one article on language use in Bali. Several articles discuss the literary basis for the performing arts; five articles concern various Javanese arts in performance; and the last four articles explore issues of regional identities characterized by musical styles or linguistic practices.

SCHAAREMAN has collected 13 valuable essays that examine the connections between Balinese music and performing arts, on the one hand, and their social and cultural contexts, on the other. Abounding in foreign terms, the essays are detailed scholarly studies of such diverse topics as ritual, narrative, theatrical, geographical, political, theoretical, and textual concerns.

SUMARSAM breaks down monolithic perceptions of Javanese culture by emphasizing a heterogeneous, pluralistic history in which foreign influences have played a major part. The author considers the development of Javanese music—including music theories and scholarship—in relation to its social and cultural history. He examines both the role of Hindu, Buddhist, and Islamic elements and the significance of different ethnic groups (Javanese, European, Chinese, Eurasian) in the development of a "hybrid Javanese court culture of the nineteenth century." He also investigates the debate that took place among Indonesian nationalists concerning the type of music that would best represent Indonesian national culture. Finally, he explores the complexities of the compositional process in gamelan and the influence of European intellectual pursuits on Indonesian cultural developments.

SUTTON extends the discussion of Javanese gamelan music to include an in-depth, empirical study of different regional traditions in Java, which are examined in relation to musical aesthetics and regional cultural identities. He considers indigenous perspectives in order to elicit categories meaningful to the Javanese and acknowledges that modern institutions, contests and festivals, the inclinations of contemporary composers, and the public media all may lead to the redefinition or blurring of regional boundaries.

TENZER offers a concise overview of Balinese music, including the cultural history, the construction and tuning of instruments, and a description of the instruments used in the *gong kebyar* orchestra. He clarifies the structural principles, form, elaboration, and orchestration of gamelan music; briefly considers the role of music in Balinese society; and provides biographical information on several prominent performers. This book is particularly useful as an introduction to a wide range of Balinese gamelan ensembles and their repertoires.

ZANTEN provides needed information on the vocal music of West Java known as *tembang Sunda,* a type of sung poetry. He thoroughly describes Sundanese vocal genres and terminology; introduces the musicians and musical institutions; interprets the poetry used for *tembang;* recounts the historical background of the instruments; and discusses the tone systems, musical structures, ornamentation, and other stylistic features. Through this positivist investigation, Zanten aims to understand the social, intellectual, and musical patterns that underlie Sundanese culture.

BRITA HEIMARCK

Instrumental Music: Renaissance

Arnold, Denis, *Giovanni Gabrieli and the Music of the Venetian High Renaissance,* Oxford: Oxford University Press, 1979

Boydell, Barra, *The Crumhorn and Other Renaissance Windcap Instruments: A Contribution to Renaissance Organology,* Buren: Knuf, 1982

Boyden, David D., *The History of Violin Playing from Its Origins to 1761,* London: Oxford University Press, 1965

Brown, Howard Mayer, *Embellishing Sixteenth-Century Music,* London: Oxford University Press, 1976

———, *Instrumental Music Printed before 1600: A Bibliography,* Cambridge, Massachusetts: Harvard University Press, 1965

———, *Sixteenth-Century Instrumentation: The Music for the Florentine Intermedii,* [Dallas]: American Institute of Musicology, 1973

Holman, Peter, *Four and Twenty Fiddlers: The Violin at the English Court, 1540–1690,* Oxford: Clarendon Press, and New York: Oxford University Press, 1993

Kite-Powell, Jeffrey T., editor, *A Performer's Guide to Renaissance Music,* New York: Schirmer Books, 1994

Polk, Keith, *German Instrumental Music of the Late Middle Ages: Players, Patrons and Performance Practice,* Cambridge: Cambridge University Press, 1992

Selfridge-Field, Eleanor, *Venetian Instrumental Music from Gabrieli to Vivaldi,* New York: Praeger, and Oxford:

Blackwell, 1975; 3rd revised edition, New York: Dover, 1994

Thomson, John Mansfield, and Anthony Rowland-Jones, editors, *The Cambridge Companion to the Recorder,* Cambridge: Cambridge University Press, 1995

Whitwell, David, *The Renaissance Wind Band and Wind Ensemble,* Northridge, California: WINDS, 1982

Instrumental ensemble is a broadly inclusive term in the Renaissance: it can refer to such ad hoc practices as the performance of vocal music with instruments or the improvisation of dance music by ensembles of various kinds; or it can mean compositions specifically written for instruments, such as *bicinia,* ricercars, canzonas, sinfonias, ritornellos, and, late in the 16th century, sonatas. As the surviving record of publications suggests, books entirely dedicated to, or including, instrumental compositions gained increasing popularity in the second half of the 16th century. Until the 1580s, such music tended to be written for unspecified instrumental parts; as the surviving treatises on instrumental technique show, performers were expected to improvise ornaments and figurations idiomatic for their instruments, and the actual scoring of ensemble music was left to common practice and practicality. As a result, individual parts conform to a neutral, vocally inspired style. Toward the end of the century certain composers, such as Andrea and Giovanni Gabrieli, became increasingly explicit regarding the scoring of their works, initiating a trend toward a compositional style that exploits the particular idiomatic characteristics of individual instruments.

Like the repertory itself, the literature on the ensemble instrumental music is widely scattered in books and articles often not specifically about the subject itself; studies of music in individual cities, such as Ferrara, Mantua, Naples, and Venice, for example, often include information about players at court or in churches without necessarily treating instrumental music as a separate topic.

ARNOLD deals with Giovanni Gabrieli's instrumental music in two separate chapters, on the composer's early and late canzonas and sonatas. The author also considers to a lesser degree the instrumental music of Gabrieli's pupils and followers in a chapter devoted to them. Additional information on the composition and use of instrumental ensembles can be found throughout the book, so interested readers should look beyond those sections devoted specifically to the instrumental music.

SELFRIDGE-FIELD offers a survey of instrumental practices at St. Mark's and in Venice generally, and although the book is devoted largely to developments during the baroque, the author takes as her starting point the Renaissance origins of the tradition. Separate chapters deal with the various settings in which instrumentalists were employed, aspects of style before Giovanni Gabrieli, his works, and the music in the first decades of the 17th century; her appendices reach back into the mid-16th century in documenting the presence of instrumentalists at St. Mark's.

The most systematic surveys of instrumental music across the entire 16th century are those by Brown. BROWN (1965) gives access to Italian musical sources across the entire repertory, whereas BROWN (1973), focusing on the music of the Florentine *intermedii,* traces changes in instrumental practice in a well-documented and self-contained genre. From prose descriptions and other sources, Brown extrapolates general principles for scoring that, because they belong to the realm of ad hoc arrangements, do not survive in the musical sources themselves. The volume closes with several hypothetical reconstructions based on the specific information culled from documents. BROWN's (1976) study of ornamentation brings together information gathered from both vocal and instrumental treatises, showing how instrumentalists and singers would have elaborated the written line in solo and ensemble situations.

KITE-POWELL's survey of the problems posed by Renaissance music is not limited to the repertory for instrumental ensembles, but his collection of essays by specialists on the various aspects of Renaissance performance surveys systematically all the instruments, as well as questions of tuning and temperament, ornamentation, and scoring. It is a comprehensive practical guide aimed at performers.

Studies of individual instruments and their repertoires can also provide insights into their uses in ensembles. Perhaps most important among these instruments, at least from a scholarly standpoint, has been the violin. BOYDEN remains the principal broad survey of the violin's history, although the study's focus is necessarily on later repertoires and technical developments. HOLMAN, by contrast, focuses on the instrument in England. The first seven chapters treat the origins of the violin and its presence in string consorts at the Tudor and Elizabethan courts, including information on the repertoires, sources, composition of ensembles, and a chapter on music outside royal patronage.

THOMSON and ROWLAND-JONES's collection of essays focuses primarily on the recorder in the baroque, but the first two chapters, by Brown and Rowland-Jones, survey the instrument's uses and repertoires in the Middle Ages and Renaissance. BOYDELL treats the crumhorn from a largely organological perspective but also includes a discussion of the use of the instrument in Renaissance ensemble music. POLK covers instrumental practice in Germany between 1350 and 1520, including musical sources, documentary evidence, and aspects of performance practice. He treats *haut* and *bas* ensembles separately, considering their functions, composition, repertoires, and patronage, which he discusses in a separate chapter on the German courts. His discussion of the music falls into two broad areas: written instrumental polyphony and extemporaneous techniques. Finally,

WHITWELL systematically surveys the wind band throughout Europe and through the centuries (the Renaissance volume is the second in a series). The book is divided into three broad areas: court, civic, and church ensembles. Within each, separate sections discuss the repertories pertinent to individual countries.

MASSIMO OSSI

Instruments: General

Baines, Anthony, *European and American Musical Instruments,* London: Bratsford, and New York: Viking Press, 1966

Baines, Anthony, editor, *The Oxford Companion to Musical Instruments,* Oxford: Oxford University Press, 1992

Bragard, Roger, and Ferdinand J. de Hen, *Musical Instruments in Art and History,* translated by Bill Hopkins, New York: Viking Press, 1967

Brown, Howard Mayer, and Joan Lascelle, *Musical Iconography: A Manual for Cataloguing Musical Subjects in Western Art before 1800,* Cambridge, Massachusetts: Harvard University Press, 1972

Buonanni, Filippo, *Antique Musical Instruments and Their Players: 152 Plates from Bonanni's [sic] 18th Century "Gabinetto Armonico,"* edited by Frank L. Harrison and Joan Rimmer, New York: Dover, 1964

Diagram Group, *Musical Instruments of the World: An Illustrated Encyclopedia,* New York: Paddington Press, 1976

Donington, Robert, *The Instruments of Music,* London: Methuen, 1949; 3rd edition, 1962

————, *Music and Its Instruments,* London: Methuen, 1982

Galpin, Francis, *A Textbook of European Musical Instruments: Their Origin, History, and Character,* London: Benn, and New York: Graff, 1937

Marcuse, Sibyl, *Musical Instruments: A Comprehensive Dictionary,* Garden City, New York: Doubleday, 1964; corrected edition, New York: Norton, 1975

————, *A Survey of Musical Instruments,* New York: Harper and Row, and Newton Abbot: David and Charles, 1975

Praetorius, Michael, *Syntagma Musicum II, De Organographia: Parts I and II,* translated and edited by David Z. Crookes, Oxford: Clarendon Press, 1986

Sachs, Curt, *The History of Musical Instruments,* New York: Norton, 1940

Sadie, Stanley, editor, *The New Grove Dictionary of Musical Instruments,* 3 vols., London: Macmillan, 1984

Winternitz, Emmanuel, *Musical Instruments and Their Symbolism in Western Art: Studies in Musical Iconology,* New York: Norton, and London: Faber, 1967; 2nd edition, New Haven, Connecticut: Yale University Press, 1979

The study of musical instruments, or organology, is a relatively new and multifaceted field of scholarship. What qualifies a sounding mechanism to be a musical instrument? By what means are its sounds produced? How is it played? How has it been employed in social, performance, or compositional contexts, be they artistic or otherwise? Is there discernible development in the history of its construction or usage throughout the ages? Is it related to other musical instruments within or across cultural contexts? And what might be gleaned from secondary source renderings or descriptions of instruments, especially those for which no concrete models appear to be extant? Such broad lines of inquiry—definition, classification, historical evolution, performance practice, and iconography—underscore the multiplicity of specialized research areas within the field from its earliest inception in the late Renaissance to the most recent challenges faced by modern ethnomusicologists. Much of the literature is encyclopedic in nature, although sources vary considerably in scope and theme, discussing, for example, Western versus world instruments, classical versus folk instruments, or descriptive versus pictorial tools.

PRAETORIUS might well be considered the founding father of the study of musical instruments. His 17th-century work—didactic, systematic, and copiously illustrated—set standards of scholarship and completeness rarely achieved in the field before the 20th century. The treatise is invaluable for its contemporary descriptions of the great variety of musical instruments available to early baroque composers and performers alike, especially as they lend historical insight into the construction and playing of instruments in consort (related families of instruments). His in-depth treatment of the organ, and of keyboard instruments in general, reflects the growing importance of the continuo in composition and practice of the time. His methodology, although limited by comparison with those accepted today, nevertheless forms a viable basis for instrument classification by means of sound production.

BUONANNI, writing a century after Praetorius, has suffered considerable criticism from modern musicologists but presents an unusually broad pictorial survey of musical instruments in his *Gabinetto armonico* (1723). While his illustrations frequently turn to the fanciful, and sometimes depict unplayable instruments, they also serve to underscore the spirits of humanism and encyclopedism of his age. All instruments are shown in acts of performance, shedding light on how they might have been played. Healthy speculation and imagination draw the author into considerations of ancient, non-Western, and folk instruments, setting a course for later ethnomusicologists. Depictions of African, Turkish, Indian, Chinese, and even Native American instruments follow plates organized in groups of what today would be defined as aerophones (wind instruments), chordophones (string instruments), membranophones (drums), and idiophones (gongs, bells, cymbals, chimes, clappers, etc.).

Such modern terminology grew out of the pioneering and now universally accepted classification system developed by Curt Sachs and Erich von Hornbostel in 1914. A brief overview of this system is included in SACHS. Readable and well illustrated with photographs and drawings, this work presents a worldwide tour of musical instruments from geographical, chronological, and evolutionary perspectives. This work, although somewhat dated, evinces Sachs's genius for both systematic and historical thinking, as he builds on the vast knowledge of musical instruments first contained in his seminally important *Real-Lexikon* (1913). While many details of Sach's work have since been disputed, the value of his contributions, especially those aimed at global understandings of what defines a musical instrument, cannot be overestimated. Indeed, scholars have spoken in terms of pre- and post-Sachs periods of study in the field.

Marcuse proves herself a dedicated student of Sachs's science and methodology. MARCUSE (1964), alphabetical by entry, provides an expanded English-language alternative to Sachs's *Real-Lexikon,* supplying a most helpful reference tool. MARCUSE (1975), organized in accordance with Sachs's classification system, contains in-depth evaluations of musical instruments in detailed historical contexts. This volume assumes higher levels of experience and knowledge than Marcuse's earlier work, only occasionally incorporating illustrations. The 1975 book's scope is somewhat more global, and it also includes much useful information regarding instrument builders. The bibliography and indices in Marcuse (1975) are indispensable. Both works have established themselves as critical resources among music librarians.

GALPIN, after whom the British society for the study of musical instruments is named, offers a more succinct means of classification than Marcuse. This survey is focused largely on early Western instruments, many long since out of use. However, provocative attempts are made to understand the origins of various instrumental types. Historical profiles are significant in their abundant references to primary source materials and performance practices. Readers interested in the music of the Middle Ages and Renaissance will find this study a profitable starting point.

Donington, a founding member of the Galpin Society, takes different yet complementary paths in his two major works on the subject. Sound—its experience and its realization in the properties and uses of musical instruments—provides a common denominator. DONINGTON (1982), far from merely being a reworking of his own earlier monograph, sheds new light on the meaningful interrelationships that exist between the science of acoustics and the sensibility of hearing. This examination largely concentrates on modern instruments: those found among today's orchestras and within common-practice music making. Accounts of methods of sound production are followed by more detailed treatments of mechanics, openly admitting interesting considerations of electronics, technology, and even the human voice. Analytical discussions of instrumental ensembles and temperament found in DONINGTON (1949) remain quite helpful.

The DIAGRAM GROUP presents an innovative, graphically oriented and user-friendly reference volume. This immediately approachable tool brings together more than 1,000 illustrations with brief, accurate descriptions of instruments from around the globe and from every historical period. Schematic figures are clearly labeled, addressing the various components, mechanics, construction, tuning, and performance capabilities of many examples. Users will find it easy to relate instruments along both cross-cultural and chronological lines. Unlike many other works, this book features mechanical and electronic instruments, as well as special surveys considering instruments in geographical, historical, and ensemble contexts (e.g., orchestras, chamber groups, marching bands, popular bands, and combos). A brief aside to "Makers, Virtuosos and Writers" opens the door to further areas of study.

Other pictorial guides include BAINES (1966), with 824 plates, and BRAGARD and DE HEN, which includes approximately 200 plates and drawings. Both are virtually photographic museums; both focus primarily on Western musical instruments from Western historical perspectives; and both scrutinize details of invention, craftsmanship, provenance, and primary source writings. As such, both employ somewhat sophisticated systems of cross-referencing, necessitating frequent flipping among sections. Nevertheless, each work embraces its particular end with artistry and command. Baines, whose intended readership includes collectors and curators, is more thorough in his descriptions than Bragard and de Hen. Scope and space, however, require the exclusion from Baines of keyboard instruments altogether. Bragard and de Hen, whose chief aim is to place instruments within broader understandings of music history and compositional style, also touches on the related field of musical iconography.

BROWN and LASCELLE's volume focuses on the critical question: What can works of art teach us about music? The result is a complex yet eminently logical methodology for classifying musical instruments (real and imaginary) as represented in art works throughout history. This is a work for the specialist; yet even the student will gain considerable insight into the problems and interpretive solutions involving musical iconographers.

In the collected writings of WINTERNITZ, who was once curator of musical collections at New York's Metropolitan Museum of Art, the author's penetrating investigations forge interdisciplinary bridges between the study of musical instruments and music's sister arts. The breadth of his research progresses far beyond mere identification and description, unveiling symbolic and sociological meanings behind musical instruments portrayed in art works from around the world.

SADIE, in three extensive volumes, provides the most comprehensive coverage of musical instruments currently available in the English language. Contributors count among the most expert in their respective fields. The scope of the dictionary is enormous, and it is relevant to the novice and scholar alike. Pertinent information regarding all known classical and modern instruments is treated in almost exhaustive thoroughness. In its representation of global perspectives, containing over 10,000 entries on folk and non-Western instruments, this source is unparalleled. Likewise, readers will find abundant information regarding instrument makers and performance practices. Entry bibliographies provide points of departure for further research, while careful cross-referencing allows fecund opportunities for the exploration of the organological, historical, and cultural issues that are so much a part of this vast and growing area of study.

BAINES (1992) serves as an admirable and affordable desktop tool. Many of the entries here are directly culled from its parent source, the *New Oxford Companion to Music* (1983). Comprehensiveness is sacrificed to brevity, nontechnical language, and ease of use—perhaps this guide's greatest virtues for students. World musical instruments are included, but electronic instruments are excluded.

MICHAEL A. NEALON

Instruments: Brass

Bate, Philip, *The Trumpet and Trombone: An Outline of Their History, Development, and Construction,* London: Benn, and New York: Norton, 1966; 2nd edition, 1978

Bevan, Clifford, *The Tuba Family,* London: Faber, and New York: Scribner, 1978

Farkas, Philip, *The Art of Brass Playing,* New York: Wind Music, 1962

Hazen, Margaret Hindle, and Robert M. Hazen, *The Music Men: An Illustrated History of Brass Bands in America, 1800–1920,* Washington, D.C.: Smithsonian Institution Press, 1987

Herbert, Trevor, and John Wallace, editors, *The Cambridge Companion to Brass Instruments,* Cambridge: Cambridge University Press, 1997

Morley-Pegge, R., *The French Horn: Some Notes on the Evolution of the Instrument and Its Technique,* London: Benn, and New York: Philosophical Library, 1960; 2nd edition, London: Benn, and New York: Norton, 1973

Munrow, David, *Instruments of the Middle Ages and Renaissance,* London: Oxford University Press, 1976

Polk, Keith, *German Instrumental Music of the Late Middle Ages: Players, Patrons and Performance Practice,* Cambridge: Cambridge University Press, 1992

Smithers, Don L., *The Music and History of the Baroque Trumpet before 1721*, London, Dent, 1973; 2nd edition, Carbondale, Illinois: Southern Illinois University Press, 1988

The basic principle of brass instruments has been understood since antiquity; the entire history of brass instrument design and performance has been one of challenging the limitations of physics. Over the years, musicians have come up with five ways of maximizing the capabilities of brass instruments. First, it is possible to write music that uses only the notes in the harmonic series; bugle calls are the simplest and most familiar example of this music, but the whole baroque and classic trumpet repertoire essentially emphasizes the high clarino register where the available notes are closer together. Second, by stuffing a hand in the bell of a brass instrument, a player can raise the pitch somewhat, at the expense of the clearest possible tone; players of the natural horn achieved amazing results this way from Mozart's time through Brahms's. Third, uncovering and covering openings along an instrument's barrel, as on a recorder or clarinet, shortens or lengthens the vibrating column of air; this technique was the principle of the cornet, serpent, keyed bugle, and ophicleide. Fourth, a movable slide, as on a trombone, enables the player to lengthen or shorten the absolute length of the tube. Finally, a valve accomplishes the same effect as a slide by opening a small crook of extra tubing, as on a modern trumpet, horn, euphonium, or tuba.

The best historical overview of the whole world of brass instruments is HERBERT and WALLACE. They have gathered a collection of essays by distinguished performers and historians, most of them performer-historians, beginning with ancient history and physical principles and working through the various families of past and present brasses to their roles in the musics of today. The articles are uniformly well written and non-technical, with a judicious selection of illustrations and a fine up-to-date bibliography.

MUNROW introduces the early stages of European instrument design clearly and concisely with innumerable pictures from contemporary sources and photographs of surviving and reproduction instruments, and he writes with the authority of a practical musician who has read the sources and taught himself to play them all. Although this book covers all the families of musical instruments in use in the Middle Ages and Renaissance, it is particularly strong for the winds (Munrow himself was principally a woodwind player). The book was also issued in a boxed set with a pair of accompanying LP records, which can still be found in many libraries and which illustrate the narrative with some stupendous performances.

POLK, while concerned with loud and soft bands alike and not confining himself to brass instruments

specifically, is the fullest account yet available of the life and repertoire of the professional wind musician in the Middle Ages and Renaissance. The information was derived from a long process of patiently sifting through the German archives, and while portions of the text may as a result be somewhat dry, the author is never unclear or tedious.

SMITHERS focuses on the baroque trumpet, a natural instrument with no valves and a restricted (though extensive) repertoire. From organological description he moves to short discussion of the trumpet in the Renaissance and the early industry of trumpet-making, and then to a country-by-country account of the lives and repertoires of trumpet players in the 17th and 18th centuries. There is also an extensive appendix listing baroque trumpet music. Though perhaps a bit technical and detailed for the general reader, the book still gives a very vivid notion of the size and importance of this tradition despite the limitations of its instrument.

Bate, Morley-Pegge, and Bevan are the great triumvirate of the brass-instrument literature: written by Englishmen in the 1960s and 1970s, the books take on the three major categories of brass instruments in the orchestra today: BATE covers the trumpet and trombone (i.e., the cylindrical-bore instruments); MORLEY-PEGGE discusses the horn; and BEVAN addresses the conical-bore instruments such as the tuba and euphonium. All three books begin with early forms, have extensive discussions of the various mechanical developments that have been applied to the instruments over the years, and spend some time on the use to which the instruments have been put by composers and players. None of these volumes is dauntingly technical; of the three, Bate tends perhaps a bit more toward acoustic and mechanical details, Morley-Pegge toward the evolution of the French horn's technique, and Bevan toward repertoire and especially toward documenting the dazzling array of instruments among the tuba's relatives (including, for example, the family that includes bugles, serpents, and ophicleides; the cimbasso; and various eccentric sizes and shapes of instruments).

HAZEN and HAZEN discuss what may be the historical high point of the brass instruments' popularity: the amateur-band movement that swept through the United States between the 1830s and World War I. Their book is written for the nonspecialist but is informed by a rich array of primary sources: antique instruments, photographs, advertisements, programs, catalogs, newspaper accounts, minute books, and so forth. The authors give a thoughtful overview of the tradition and a great deal of detail on its paraphernalia, the industries that supported it, the music, and its perhaps surprisingly important place in the community. Especially fascinating is a chapter titled "Band Profiles," telling the stories of five individual bands, from various parts of the country, that had very different aspirations and histories.

Most of the technique of brass playing relies on the mouth and respiratory system and thus does not always lend itself to verbal description; a long line of instrumental tutors, beginning in the Renaissance and reaching a fever pitch in the 19th century with the method books of the European conservatories, have grappled with this technical task with more or, usually, less success. For most modern players, FARKAS holds a particularly revered position. His title may be misleading—the book is less about the art of brass playing than the practical means of achieving that art—but he does remarkably well at describing the nature of embouchure and breath control and outlining the most common problems and how to fix them, and he employs simple language. A series of other books have followed, based loosely on Farkas but adapting his general principles to the particular needs of specific instruments: Keith Johnson on the trumpet, Farkas himself on the horn, Edward Kleinhammer on the trombone, J. Kent Mason on the tuba. All of these texts are widely used by teachers and students today but are probably more valuable to players of the individual instruments than to the lay person.

KENNETH KREITNER

Instruments: Electronic

Brown, Robert Michael, and Mark Olsen, *Experimenting with Electronic Music,* Blue Ridge Summit, Pennsylvania: Tab Books, 1974

Crombie, David, *The Complete Synthesizer,* London: Omnibus Press, 1982

Darter, Tom, compiler, *The Art of Electronic Music,* New York: Quill, 1984

Dodge, Charles, and Thomas A. Jerse, *Computer Music: Synthesis, Composition, and Performance,* New York: Schirmer Books, 1985; 2nd edition, New York: Schirmer Books, and London: Prentice Hall, 1997

Drake, Russell, et al., *How to Make Electronic Music,* New York: Educational Audio Visual, 1975

Hammond, Ray, *The Musician and the Micro,* Poole: Blandford Press, 1983

Horn, Delton T., *Electronic Music Synthesizers,* Blue Ridge Summit, Pennsylvania: Tab Books, 1980

———, *Music Synthesizers: A Manual of Design and Construction,* Blue Ridge Summit, Pennsylvania: Tab Books, 1984

Jenkins, John, and Jon Smith, *Electric Music: A Practical Manual,* Newton Abbot: David and Charles, and Bloomington: Indiana University Press, 1975

Keane, David, *Tape Music Composition,* London: Oxford University Press, 1980

Mackay, Andy, *Electronic Music,* Minneapolis, Minnesota: Control Data Publishing, and Oxford: Phaidon, 1981

Newquist, H.P., *Music and Technology,* New York: Billboard Books, 1989

Trythall, H. Gilbert, *Principles and Practice of Electronic Music,* New York: Grosset and Dunlap, 1973

The history of the development of electronic musical instruments spans the entire 20th century. The earliest instruments include the Telharmonium, which was patented in the year 1899, followed within a few years by a variety of other large, cumbersome devices. The introduction of the transistor, electronic circuitry, and the computer revolutionized the development of electronic instruments. Today, most of them contain microprocessors that control all internal functions, and they bear more resemblance to personal computers than to their early 20th-century ancestors. In the second half of the 20th century, there was also a shift away from analog electronic instruments toward the realm of digital. Even the computer has become a musical instrument, with the use of advanced programming languages and sophisticated digital sound cards that can produce any sound to be imagined by a composer. Writings on this subject generally fall into three categories: narrative accounts that provide a historical explanation of the developments, technical manuals that provide users with specifications and other specialized knowledge about the devices, and how-to manuals that instruct readers on how to use or build electronic musical instruments.

TRYTHALL is a technical book that attempts to explain electronic instruments and circuitry in terms that can be understood easily by musicians. Basic acoustics, electronics, circuits, and components such as transistors and transducers are considered. The most valuable part of the book is its straightforward account of the function and operation of each component of a modular analog synthesizer. The book describes a classical analog electronic studio, which is quite different from today's digital, computer-based studios.

A similar book to Trythall is BROWN and OLSEN, which also deals with modular synthesizers such as the ARP 2500. This book is highly technical and contains a great deal of information on building electronic instruments such as organs, Theremin-like instruments, and mixers. Along with the technical diagrams for building these simple instruments, the authors present a mixture of facts on related topics such as signal generators and waveforms.

DRAKE et al. write primarily about tape music and synthesizers. This book describes a variety of tape recorders and specifications and includes step-by-step procedures on making tape music. Although tape music is now considered somewhat outdated as a means of producing electronic music, this book provides a historical perspective on the use of the tape recorder as one of the most significant electronic instruments of the century.

Another book that deals exclusively with tape recorders is KEANE. Tape recorder specifications are combined with a detailed description of all aspects of tape music. The book discusses a myriad of technical issues, including heads, transport mechanisms, reels, levels, VU meters, splicing, and signal noise, which makes it one of the most thorough and significant books on the subject. There is also information on how to set up a tape studio. The book avoids highly technical language.

JENKINS and SMITH evaluate a wide variety of electronic instruments and other electronic gear. The devices covered here include electric guitars, microphones, organs, electric pianos, and synthesizers. One of the most helpful discussions concerns amplifiers and loudspeakers, describing how they work and how a speaker is constructed. There is also a useful appendix on the physics of sound.

HORN (1980) is valuable for anyone interested in the specifications of the Moog modular systems. The book describes the technical aspects of synthesis including voltage controlled oscillators, filters, envelope generators, and keyboard controllers. There is also technical information on the MiniMoog, the ARP 2600, and a variety of other synthesizers such as those made by Oberheim and Odyssey. The second half of the book explains the construction of synthesizers. There are instructions and diagrams for simple devices, although, because the process is fairly technical, the reader is advised to have some background in electronics. A more recent book, HORN (1984), deals exclusively with the topic of building synthesizers and is even more technical.

MACKAY offers an in-depth history of electronic instruments, starting with the Telharmonium and the Hammond organ. He outlines the development of recording studios and tape composition from the 1950s and mentions famous compositions written using electronic instruments, such as the theme music from the television series, *Dr. Who*, produced by the BBC Radiophonic Workshop. This book also includes a discussion of electronic instruments in live performance settings, including classical and popular performers from John Cage to Frank Zappa.

Another historical perspective is provided by DARTER. This book begins with the oldest electronic instruments and moves forward chronologically to discuss the first synthesizers of the 1930s and 1940s. The second section of the book mentions many of the pioneers of the 1960s including Robert Moog and Don Buchla.

For anyone who wants specific information on using commercially available synthesizers, CROMBIE offers a great deal of valuable information. The book's introduction, "Understanding Sound," explains elements of sound, including frequency, waveforms, overtones, and various methods of synthesis such as additive and subtractive. The discussion is not highly technical. One of the unique aspects of this book is its advice on electronically synthesizing a variety of sounds from the world of traditional instruments, such as flute, violin, brass, human voice, and organ.

HAMMOND is one of the earliest books to deal specifically with the computer as a musical instrument. He starts by describing microprocessors and the evolution of the home-based personal computer, summarizes the creation of dedicated music computers such as the Fairlight CMI, and considers the impact of computers in the recording studio, through the automation of such functions as controlling faders levels on mixing consoles. The author also presents a good historical discussion of the use of computer chips in electronic instruments such as digital synthesizers.

A highly technical book on computer music is DODGE and JERSE, which deals with synthesis and composition on the computer. The authors discuss the scientific fundamentals of computer-based synthesis, which uses a variety of techniques, such as frequency modulation, subtractive synthesis, digitally reproduced reverb and delay, and speech synthesis. The book is filled with computer algorithms and mathematical formulas and is not for the faint of heart. A final chapter on multiple-synthesizer compositions and devices for live performances is valuable.

NEWQUIST investigates all aspects of music technology, including electronic instruments. Although the sections on software and computers are outdated, there are important discussions of sampling, electric guitars, signal processing, and a variety of instruments that can serve as MIDI controllers. Newquist supplies a brief history of electronic instruments that ends with today's digital synthesizers. The book is highly relevant to today's electronic music studios.

CONNIE E. MAYFIELD

Instruments: Harp

Rensch, Roslyn, *The Harp: Its History, Technique, and Repertoire*, London: Duckworth, and New York: Praeger, 1969

———, *Harps and Harpists*, Bloomington: Indiana University Press, 1989

Rimmer, Joan, *The Irish Harp*, Cork: Mercier Press, 1969; 3rd edition, 1984

Sanger, Keith, and Alison Kinnard, *Tree of Strings: Crann Nan Teud: A History of the Harp in Scotland*, Shillinghill: Kinmor Music, 1992

Schaik, Marinus Jan Hendrikus van, *The Harp in the Middle Ages: The Symbolism of a Musical Instrument*, Amsterdam: Rodopi, 1992

Schaik, Marinus Jan Hendrikus van, editor, *Aspects of the Historical Harp: Proceedings of the International Historical Harp Symposium, Utrecht 1992*, Utrecht: STIMU, 1994

Schechter, John Mendell, *The Indispensable Harp: Historical Development, Modern Roles, Configurations, and Performance Practices in Ecuador and Latin America*, Kent, Ohio: Kent State University Press, 1992

Zingel, Hans Joachim, *Harp Music in the Nineteenth Century*, translated and edited by Mark Palkovic, Bloomington: Indiana University Press, 1992

The concise definition of the harp is a cordophone in which the plane of the strings is perpendicular to the soundboard. However, the harp, one of the oldest instruments known and in possession of an almost mystical quality in physical appearance and sound, requires a unique research approach and an understanding far beyond the simple definition.

Our present-day knowledge of the early history of the harp stems entirely from artistic representations in early manuscripts, paintings, and carvings. The story of the Western harp in the ancient world probably begins in the Middle East, where bow-shaped harps—that is, harps lacking a column or fore-pillar—appear in carvings and paintings. The harp begins to appear more frequently in the manuscripts and art of the Middle Ages, the primitive design gradually supplanted by a triangular-shaped harp, incorporating the column. No authentic instruments survive from this time, and it is impossible to discern tuning or scales.

Descriptions of the harp begin to surface in technical treatises on music by the 16th and 17th centuries. Along with instructions on tuning, these treatises document attempts to achieve a greater tonal flexibility for the instrument by such methods as using double and triple rows of strings with alternate tunings and the introduction of a system of hooks and levers to raise or lower the pitch of individual strings. The early 18th-century harp, in which a mechanism operates the tuning levers with the feet, thereby liberating the player's hands, ultimately led to what we recognize today as the modern double-action orchestral instrument with seven pedals, each of which controls one tone of the diatonic scale, both raising and lowering all the strings of that pitch by a semitone. Parallel with the development of the Western harp we find rich harp traditions in the folk practices of Ireland, Spain, Latin America, Scotland, Africa, and elsewhere.

Harp research usually scrutinizes one or more of three broad, overlapping categories: historical iconography, which is the only confirmation of the existence of the harp in ancient times and is incorporated into most studies to a greater or lesser degree; examinations of the contemporary harp and its repertoire, encompassing musical compositions, performers, and performance practice; and ethnomusicological studies, which spotlight non-Western harp traditions and usually take an approach to their subjects similar to that used in studies falling within the prior two categories.

RENSCH (1969) makes a valiant attempt to summarize all aspects of this complex and varied topic. The first book to delve into the instrument, it provides a clear if cursory survey of Western harp history, gleaned from paintings and manuscript illuminations. Progressing to the modern pedal harp, the volume incorporates information on performance practice, performers, composers, compositions for harp, instructors, organizations of harpists, manufacturers, and construction. It includes such fundamentals as a diagram identifying all the parts of the harp and even demonstrates the proper way to knot a harp string. The appendix provides a list of graded compositions for use in programs.

RENSCH (1989), originally intended to be a revision of her 1969 volume, covers the history of the Western harp in much more comprehensive detail, beginning with ancient iconography, progressing through the point at which some music and instruments begin to survive, and concluding with the present-day state of the harp and harp world. An appendix records a selection of harp-related events that occurred between 1979 and 1985 as a demonstration of the wide range of ongoing harp activities at the present time. Master classes, performances, contests, grants and awards, and teaching and symphony posts are all listed. Both of Rensch's books include abundant illustrations.

RIMMER follows the Irish harp from antiquity to modernity in a slim, readable volume, published for the Cultural Relations Committee of the Government of Ireland.

Both SCHECHTER and the team of SANGER and KINNARD provide rigorous ethnomusicological studies, tracing harp history and development through the ages in their respective locations (Ecuador/Latin America and Scotland). Both begin with ancient pictorial representations, eventually considering harp usage in the modern era, with investigations of contemporary performance practice and the role and position of the instrument in folk tradition.

SCHAIK (1992) provides a meticulous study of the appearance of the harp in medieval representations and literature. Limited to the period spanning ca. 1000 to ca. 1400, the author approaches the medieval harp through the integration of iconography with theology, music studies, and history of art and literature. The focus is on five aspects: etymology, a survey of the relationship of the name "harpa" to the object we recognize as a harp; the harp and King David; the delta harp (named for its physical resemblance to the Greek letter); the appearance of harps in illuminations of psalm initials; and appearances of the theme of the ass with the harp. Each chapter closes with a concise summary of the findings. The appendix provides a compendium of manuscripts and other sources of visual representations of the harp.

SCHAIK (1994) is a collection of transcriptions of lectures presented during a 1992 Historical Harp

Symposium held in Utrecht. Articles on iconography, repertoire, ethnography, technique, and construction are included. A useful bibliography of historical harp literature from 1980 through 1993 is incorporated.

ZINGEL, a translation of a 1976 German work, concentrates on the state of the Western harp in the 19th century, a period when the harp established its own musical niche apart from the piano and lute. The rivalry among the various methods of harp design and manufacture, a result of attempts to achieve increased chromatic flexibility, was finally resolved by the triumph of the double-action harp. This newly perfected design changed harp-playing technique and endowed the instrument with increased musical scope. Harp compositions, both by virtuoso harpists and by nonharpist composers, are discussed, as are the harp concerto and the orchestral use of the harp. The thoroughness of the information makes one hope for the eventual translation of three other volumes in German by the same author, a discourse on the baroque harp, a study of the harp from the 16th to 18th centuries, and a harp lexicon.

NANCY F. GARF

Instruments: Keyboard

1. Organ

Bicknell, Stephen, *The History of the English Organ,* Cambridge: Cambridge University Press, 1996

Brunner, Raymond J., *That Ingenious Business: Pennsylvania German Organ Builders,* Birdsboro: Pennsylvania German Society, 1990

Ochse, Orpha Caroline, *The History of the Organ in the United States,* Bloomington: Indiana University Press, 1975

Ogasapian, John, *Organ Building in New York City, 1700–1900,* Braintree, Massachusetts: Organ Literature Foundation, 1977

Owen, Barbara, *The Organ in New England,* Raleigh, North Carolina: Sunbury Press, 1979

Thistlethwaite, Nicholas, *The Making of the Victorian Organ,* Cambridge: Cambridge University Press, 1990

Williams, Peter F., *The European Organ, 1450–1850,* London: Batsford, and Bloomington: Indiana University Press, 1966

———, *A New History of the Organ: From the Greeks to the Present Day,* London: Faber, and Bloomington: Indiana University Press, 1980

———, *The Organ in Western Culture, 750–1250,* Cambridge: Cambridge University Press, 1993

Williams, Peter F., and Barbara Owen, *The New Grove Organ,* London: Macmillan, and New York: Norton, 1988

The organ produces its tone by means of wind under pressure being admitted into the feet of tuned pipes, causing the column of air in those pipes to vibrate. Pitch is determined by the length of the pipe, and tone quality by its shape and construction. Pipes are of wood or metal (usually tin and lead). Most organs also contain reed pipes, wherein the tone is produced when wind causes a reed to vibrate against a slotted block. Pipes are grouped in ranks, or stops, one pipe per note. The stops, in turn, are grouped in discrete divisions, each played by its own manual keyboard or by the pedals. Stops are used alone as solo colors or combined into ensembles. The pipes stand on windchests, over valves that open to admit wind into their feet. The mechanism, or action, by which key and stop control is transmitted to the valves may be electrical or mechanical (also called a tracker organ). The wind is supplied to the chests at a steady pressure reservoir, a bellows-like box, which receives it from the blower, essentially an enclosed fan.

The roots of the organ go back to the hydraulus of antiquity, wherein water pressure was used to force air into the pipes. By the late Middle Ages or early Renaissance, the principles were established on which modern organs function. Similarly, the literature on organ construction extends back to works by Arnaut of Zwolle (ca. 1445–50) and Arnold Schlick (1511). More recent literature (apart from works on the music for the instrument) ranges from technical and historical studies for specialists to items easily accessible to the nonspecialist and readily available in most well-stocked public and academic libraries. The foregoing list is drawn from this latter group; however, the books discussed also include careful documentation that can serve to point the student who seeks more depth toward specialized items in the literature.

WILLIAMS and OWEN is the standard overview of the instrument and its history. The book builds on the material originally published in *The New Grove Dictionary of Musical Instruments* (1984). The main portion consists of Williams's history of the instrument, from antiquity to the present; there are also sections on the organ's construction, related instruments, and registration, a glossary of stops and list of builders, and a complete bibliography up through the time of its publication.

WILLIAMS (1966) and WILLIAMS (1980) antedate the Williams and Owen volume, but the research is solid and thorough, and surprisingly little beyond the bibliographies is in need of updating. Both books enhance the text with plates, drawings, and stop lists. Williams (1966) is surprisingly detailed for so broad a study. It provides examples of mixture composition and pipe construction, as well as instrument design. The book is organized geographically and contains a map of the area each section addresses.

WILLIAMS (1993) is the author's most recent work, and it is a definitive and distinctive study. He gathers and analyzes the extant original data on the organ from the Carolingian era to the 13th century around the question of why and how the organ came to be used in churches in western Europe. Williams argues convincingly from his sources that the instrument's development and adoption by churches in Europe is largely due to the Benedictine monks who during and after the Carolingian renaissance made other such musical advances as chant notation.

If there is any fault to be found with Williams's general historical approach, it is his lack of interest in and attention to the period after the mid–19th century. Williams (1966) breaks off at 1850 and Williams (1980) entitles its chapter on the period "Contributions to the Nadir of 1890–1910." Although he is British, Williams has little sympathy for English organs and organ building, and even less for organs in the United States. Accordingly, while his work constitutes the best source for information on continental European organs and organ building to 1850 or so, those interested in the British and American schools must look to another cluster of specialized studies.

BICKNELL is now the standard history of the organ in England, from the tenth century to the present. The book contains sample stop lists, numerous plates, a glossary of terms, and a selected but extensive bibliography. As its title indicates, THISTLETHWAITE is a concentrated and exhaustive study of British organs in the 19th century and as such fills one of the larger gaps left by Williams's studies. The text is systematic and critical and is accompanied by stop lists, plates, and diagrams. There is a good bit on particular builders of the period, as well as on mechanical and tonal innovations in organ building arising from the so-called industrial revolution.

OCHSE remains the standard history of the organ in the United States. The work is carefully researched, systematically laid out, and carefully written, with stop lists and photographs, and was a landmark work when it appeared. In fact, it inspired so much research in the years that followed that vast new ground has been broken since its publication nearly a quarter-century ago, and a considerable amount of the information contained in it has been superseded. Consequently, either a major revision or a whole new work is now in order, although the work is still valuable not only for its content (even where subject to revision) but especially for its exhaustive bibliography covering the years up to its publication.

Brunner, Ogasapian, and Owen are among the books that grew out of Ochse's work and superseded it in their respective areas. All are based on primary sources and contain sample stop lists. OWEN has a section of plates grouped together at the end of the book, and BRUNNER is well illustrated throughout. OGASAPIAN is valuable for its text and bibliography; however, the book, which was poorly produced by photo offset of the typescript, is in need of revision. Owen is also ready for a second edition. As they stand, however, each fills a niche in American organ history, and all three remain the definitive studies of particular geographic areas of significance in organ building in the United States.

JOHN OGASAPIAN

2. Piano

Clinkscale, Martha Novak, *Makers of the Piano, 1700–1820*, Oxford: Oxford University Press, 1993

Crombie, David, *Piano*, San Francisco: Freeman Books, 1995

Gill, Dominic, editor, *The Book of the Piano*, Oxford: Phaidon, and Ithaca, New York: Cornell University Press, 1981

Good, Edwin M., *Giraffes, Black Dragons, and Other Pianos: A Technological History from Cristofori to the Modern Concert Grand*, Stanford, California: Stanford University Press, 1982

Harding, Rosamund E.M., *The Piano-Forte: Its History Traced to the Great Exhibition of 1851*, Cambridge: Cambridge University Press, 1933; 2nd edition, Old Woking: Gresham Books, 1978

Lieberman, Richard K., *Steinway and Sons*, New Haven, Connecticut: Yale University Press, 1995

Loesser, Arthur, *Men, Women, and Pianos: A Social History*, New York: Simon and Schuster, 1954; reprint, New York: Dover, 1990

Michel, Norman Elwood, *Historical Pianos, Harpsichords, and Clavichords*, Pico Rivera, California: Michel, 1963

Ratcliffe, Ronald V., *Steinway and Sons*, San Francisco: Chronicle Books, 1989

Ripin, Edwin M., et al., editors, *Piano*, London: Macmillan, 1987; as *The New Grove Piano*, New York: Norton, 1988

Roell, Craig H., *The Piano in America, 1890–1940*, Chapel Hill: University of North Carolina Press, 1989

The piano, invented in the early 18th century by Bartolomeo Cristofori, had become by the mid-19th century arguably the most important musical instrument. Composers wrote some of their most characteristic pieces for it; virtuosi traveled around the world concertizing on it; and millions of amateurs had their most intimate contact with musical culture through it. With the advent of recorded sound, the piano's importance has waned, although it retains its prominence. The literature on the piano and its history is large and widely variable in both the expertise and viewpoints of the authors, as well as the intended audiences and levels of historical and technical accuracy. The range extends from books written by enthusiasts, filled with anecdotes and information of questionable value, to highly technical books by physicists and acousticians. However, since about 1975 the general revival of early music has resulted in deeper and more serious considerations of the history of the piano, not only from the technical side but also by examining the social aspects of that history, and in the best studies, the relationships among art, commerce, and technology.

MICHEL, a self-published example of the enthusiastic amateur category, is a volume of black-and-white plates showing literally hundreds of pianos. The only organization is found in sections devoted to pianos of the U.S. presidents (through Nixon), celebrities, and instruments owned by various institutions and individuals. Although the methodology is naive, and the text consists only of sketchy captions, many of the pianos have unique or artistic case designs or decorations or other significant details. Because it is likely that many of these pianos no longer exist, the visual documentation is invaluable. This book is useful when read in conjuction with more scholarly volumes.

GILL is a fine example of a volume aimed at a general readership, consisting of a series of essays by well-known scholars and musicians and lavishly illustrated with color and black-and-white plates. The essays explore the development of the piano through the centuries and focus on several specialized areas, including the piano in chamber music, jazz and popular piano styles, and piano makers. There is a chronology of prominent pianists, and several essays include discographies, which, given the date of the volume, list LPs exclusively.

More up-to-date than Gill and reflective of the better aspects of other books discussed here, CROMBIE synthesizes a wealth of information in a slim, though large-format, volume. The style of the book is that of a visual dictionary, with copious color plates, sidebars, and text geared to the illustrations for each entry. The book also has several foldout pages that allow more space for certain topics. For each piano illustrated there is a chart showing the instrument's specifications and a color plate. Many entries also include exploded or partially dismantled views, showing details of the action and construction. Illustrations of recordings made on the piano shown are also provided, with a short caption. If one wants a one-volume book on the piano, this is the best choice.

HARDING is perhaps the best book on the early piano. It is a detailed and thorough history, including discussion of the invention and spread of the piano as well as comments on the social history of the piano. In his discussion of the various sound modification devices invented during the early years of the 19th century, Harding includes examples of music written for some of these modifications. The book is especially useful because it offers numerous technical drawings of keyboard actions and details of case construction (drawn mostly by Harding) and because it presents a wealth of technical descriptions of such things as wood, wire gauges and alloy content, construction techniques, and tuning and temperament. Information from this book is generally reliable but should be compared to more recent research.

As a companion to Harding, CLINKSCALE is an exhaustive catalog of surviving pianos from approximately the first 100 years after the instrument's development. The bulk of the catalog is a listing by makers' names. Each entry includes information on the maker's dates of activity and on the maker's business, including information on mergers with other companies and extent of production. Known exemplars of the maker's instruments are also listed. The volume includes an extensive bibliography and a listing of collections by country.

Far ahead of its time in many ways, LOESSER looks at the history of the piano through the lens of social history. The writing is witty and sardonic, while still being historically informed and intensely focused on the subtle cultural changes affecting composers, the musical public, and the piano. The book also contains what must be one of the earliest uses of the term *politically correct*. Ultimately, the author sees the piano as a "feature in the physiognomy of a certain way of life," that of the moneyed bourgeoisie, whose cultural ideals were dominant in the Euro-American world for nearly 200 years.

RIPIN excerpts, with minor additions and changes, articles on the history of the piano, piano playing, and piano music from the *New Grove Dictionary* and the *New Grove Dictionary of Musical Instruments* and adds one new essay by Harold C. Schonberg. Schonberg's essay examines the most influential pianists since the mid-19th century. The main value of this book is that it presents, in one compact and inexpensive volume, a summary of the state of research on the piano and its history as of the mid-1980s, and includes a glossary, list of makers, and useful bibliography.

Among general histories of the piano, GOOD is the most engagingly written, and it is factually accurate. The author examines approximately a dozen pianos in some detail and works into the discussion wider issues at appropriate points. Particularly informative are Good's investigations into and speculations about (due to a spotty historical record) the interrelationships of the artistic needs of pianists and composers, the wider musical world of amateurs, and the technological and commercial developments that went into the development of the piano as we know it today. Good insists that invention does not imply immediate acceptance, and he argues that there was often a decades-long lag between the first prototype and industry-wide use of certain inventions. Therefore, the development of the piano should not be seen as a teleological progression toward the modern instrument but as a response to changing social and aesthetic needs. The pianos of earlier periods, then, are not inferior precursors to later instruments, but expressions of the sonic expectations of their time.

The role of the piano in the United States from the 1890s through the beginning of World War II is examined by ROELL. He describes how the piano-making industry that reached such heights that it could get itself declared an essential industry during World War I, yet within the next dozen years it shrank to a fraction of its former size as a result of the introduction of radio and the growth of consumer culture. The author shows how the piano industry at first abetted the trends toward technology through the introduction of the player piano but later fell victim to many decades of faulty marketing.

This is a valuable book on the changes in the musical culture of the first half of the 20th century.

Few piano makers have yet been studied in book-length monographs, and it is appropriate that among the first such studies is LIEBERMAN's examination of Steinway and Sons. From this study it is clear that the Steinway mystique and legacy were the result of care in manufacturing, effective marketing, and often hard-nosed business tactics. Although the picture drawn is sometimes unflattering, it is largely a story of continuing success through the shifting cultural fashions of a century and a half. The story continues up to the time of the book's publication, providing some insight into the very different business pressures acting on the piano industry during the 1970s and 1980s.

Complementing Lieberman's scholarly study, RATCLIFFE is a photographic history of the Steinway piano company. There are reproductions of numerous engravings, lithographs, and photographs showing various members of the Steinway family; views of the factory and production line from several periods; custom-made, or otherwise notable, instruments; and examples from the Steinway art collection, which primarily consists of renderings of important composers and Steinway associates created by more-or-less well-known artists and used in marketing campaigns through the years. The text incorporates some original research into the history of the firm, but the most useful sections of the book are those on "Steinway Artists" and "Steinway Art-Case Pianos." It is in these sections that readers get the best idea of Steinway as a force in the intertwining musical, commercial, and social worlds since the middle of the 19th century.

RON WIECKI

3. Other Keyboard

Boalch, Donald H., *Makers of the Harpsichord and Clavichord, 1440 to 1840,* London: Ronald, 1956; 3rd edition, edited by Charles Mould, Oxford: Clarendon Press, 1995

Bond, Ann, *A Guide to the Harpsichord,* Portland, Oregon: Amadeus Press, 1997

Hubbard, Frank, *Three Centuries of Harpsichord Making,* Cambridge, Massachusetts: Harvard University Press, 1965

Neupert, Hanns, *The Clavichord,* translated from the second German edition by Ann P.P. Feldberg, Kassel: Bärenreiter, 1965

Palmer, Larry, *Harpsichord in America: A Twentieth-Century Revival,* Bloomington: Indiana University Press, 1989

Paul, John, *Modern Harpsichord Makers,* London: Gollancz, 1981

Ripin, Edwin M., editor, *Keyboard Instruments: Studies in Keyboard Organology, 1500–1800,* Edinburgh: Edinburgh University Press, 1971; 2nd, revised edition, New York: Norton, 1977

Ripin, Edwin M., et al., editors, *The New Grove Early Keyboard Instruments,* London: Macmillan, and New York: Norton, 1989

Russell, Raymond, *The Harpsichord and Clavichord: An Introductory Study,* London: Faber, 1959; second edition, revised by Howard Schott, 1973

Schott, Howard, editor, *The Historical Harpsichord: A Monographic Series in Honor of Frank Hubbard,* 3 vols., Stuyvesant, New York: Pendragon Press, 1984–92

Zuckermann, Wolfgang, *The Modern Harpsichord: Twentieth-Century Instruments and Their Makers,* New York: October House, 1969

Scholarly publications concerning early keyboard instruments began to appear in the mid-20th century, following on the heels of pioneering efforts of builders and performers such as Arnold Dolmetsch and Wanda Landowska. The groundbreaking work of Boalch, Russell, and Hubbard established foundations for future studies and also instituted categories of inquiry that later scholars have continued to employ. Most studies fall into one of the following categories or are a combination of such: studies of makers and their instruments, studies of the history and development of a particular instrument, or studies of building and keyboard organology.

BOALCH chronicles the known makers of harpsichord, clavichord, virginal, and spinet who worked between 1440 and 1840. He presents a list of the makers, giving the time they flourished, a brief recounting of their lives, and a descriptive inventory of each of their surviving instruments. The descriptions of the instruments are standardized and include, among other things, maker, type of instrument, date of manufacture, and specifications and special features of the instrument. Also included are a glossary of technical terms in seven languages and a geographical and chronological conspectus of makers. The original 1956 edition contained 32 photographs of instruments, but these have been omitted in the updated volume.

RUSSELL outlines the history and development of the harpsichord, clavichord, spinet, and virginal. His survey develops along geographic lines as he discusses the major centers of keyboard building throughout Europe. He gives a brief summary of the notable builders and workshops in each center and provides some specifics on the types of instruments produced by the various makers. Russell uses the physical evidence of existing instruments as the foundation for his discussions. His conclusions are based on his personal examinations of hundreds of instruments and are supported by various historical documents such as guild records, workshop inventories, and personal letters and memoirs. There are over 100 photographs of instruments, and the appendices reprint pertinent historical documents.

HUBBARD focuses on the art of the instrument builder and devotes attention to the five schools of harpsichord making that were most important between the years 1500 and 1800. He outlines the history and traditions of building for each school and traces the evolution of the harpsichord through the use of historical documents and the examination of extant instruments. Hubbard's commentary also encompasses the other keyboard instruments that developed alongside the harpsichord. His primary sources include dictionaries, encyclopedias, guild records, music treatises, workshop inventories, and personal travelogues. Besides chronicling developments in harpsichord construction, Hubbard examines social fashions and business considerations that influenced the types of instruments that were produced. He also provides practical information for the construction of different instruments and gives the modern-day builder some sound historical evidence from which to proceed. The result is a study that is of interest to both historians and aspiring builders of historical keyboard instruments. The prose is clear and accessible to both the specialist and nonspecialist alike; he provides a glossary that explains specialized terminology.

RIPIN (1989) is a useful reference for those seeking a scholarly overview of the subject. It provides individual chapters on the harpsichord, clavichord, virginal, and spinet, as well as a chapter on other related instruments. The discussions provide descriptions of the physical properties of the various instruments, details on their construction (types of material used, tuning systems, decorations, etc.), and explanations of how the playing mechanisms of the instruments function. In many cases, a history of the instrument and its usage is also given. Illustrations show different instruments, playing mechanisms, building plans, and paintings of keyboard instruments. The final chapter outlines the known repertory for these instruments from the 14th to the 20th centuries. Appendices include a glossary of terms, an index of instrument makers, and a list of editions of early keyboard music.

RIPIN (1971) is a collection of specialized essays dealing with early keyboard instruments. Some essays focus on Italian harpsichords, examining their physical properties and their alterations over time. Others consider Flemish virginals and harpsichords and their unique characteristics. There are also studies on novelty keyboard instruments and an inventory of 15th-century keyboard instruments based on artistic representations (accompanied by illustrations). In addition to physical descriptions, most of the studies address the working mechanics of the instruments and discuss particulars of specifications. Most topics are approached in a scientific manner, and much of the vocabulary is technically oriented and filled with details of measurements and proportions.

NEUPERT presents a short monograph on the clavichord. With the aid of treatises and original documents, he traces the history and development of the instrument. He discusses the builders and their workshops,

details the physical properties of the instrument, reviews its repertory, comments on playing technique, and describes the special properties of sound unique to the clavichord. Although Neupert speaks of the clavichord in highly romanticized terms, he does draw support for this representation from accounts and treatises of the period such as Forkel's "On the true quality of clavichords," which is presented in the appendix. Final chapters discuss problems encountered by modern builders and address instrument maintenance. There are also several plates of illustrations.

PALMER focuses on the harpsichord revival in the United States, from about 1885 to 1960. He profiles the individuals who played a key role in bringing the harpsichord back to prominence from its 19th-century obscurity and details their pioneering efforts on behalf of early music. His subjects encompass instrument collectors, builders, and performers and include individuals such as Morris Steinert, Arnold Dolmetsch, Wanda Landowska, and Ralph Kirkpatrick. The biographies Palmer presents specify the individuals' early music activities in the United States and are drawn from reviews, interviews, records of concert and teaching activities, and other documents. Palmer does not use technical terms, and even the musically untrained can enjoy this book. It is a performance history rather than an organology study, and it is especially good for those wanting to know more about early music activity in the United States.

BOND's volume is intended for the harpsichord novice. The author's aim is "to steer those who are new to early music toward an understanding of its basic issues without foundering in complex argument." Consequently, scholarly references are kept to a minimum. Using simple terms, Bond describes the elementary mechanics and construction of the harpsichord and gives a brief historical summary of the different types of instruments that existed in the various schools of building. She explains practical aspects of playing the harpsichord, such as touch, fingering, and articulation, demonstrating application of these principles in several musical examples. She also addresses issues of historical performance, outlines beginning principles of ornamentation, and gives basics of continuo playing. Finally, Bond proffers advice on buying an instrument and provides tips on the care and tuning of the instrument.

ZUCKERMANN compares historical harpsichords with modern harpsichords and briefly traces the history of harpsichord making. He classifies the different types of harpsichords in (then) current production and offers a listing of modern makers, outlining the techniques of the various makers and the characteristics of their instruments, as well as discussing some of the problems encountered by modern makers. The reader should note, however, that this book was written at a time when the majority of the harpsichords being built were based on modified piano designs rather than on historical models. Consequently, much of the information comparing the features of historical instruments with modern instruments is dated. Still, this study is of value in documenting the development of the harpsichord in the 20th century.

PAUL examines the work of several British harpsichord makers to present an overview of present-day builders in Great Britain. He sets up a framework for discussing the work of modern builders by explaining the mechanics of the harpsichord and clarifying some differences among the instruments of various historical schools of building. He then profiles his selected builders, giving a biography of their building career and listing their innovations and contributions to the field of harpsichord making. Paul's sources include taped interviews, personal discussions, and autobiographies by the builders themselves. Photographs of the makers and their instruments are provided, as are several drawings of early keyboard instruments.

SCHOTT presents three volumes of essays on various aspects of the harpsichord. Subjects covered include authentication of instruments, studies in metallurgy, and inventories of instruments. There is also an essay by Frank Hubbard that offers his personal ruminations on constructing historical instruments. Photographs and illustrations abound, but some of the essays are highly scientific in nature and use a great deal of technical language. They are especially useful for active harpsichord builders and for those conducting advanced research on historical instruments, but they are probably too detailed and too in-depth to benefit novices in the subject.

MARGOT MARTIN

Instruments: Lute and Guitar

Coelho, Victor, editor, *Performance on Lute, Guitar, and Vihuela: Historical Practice and Modern Interpretation,* Cambridge: Cambridge University Press, 1997

Grunfeld, Frederic V., *The Art and Times of the Guitar,* New York: Macmillan, 1969

McCutcheon, Meredith, *Guitar and Vihuela: An Annotated Bibliography of the Literature on Their History,* New York: Pendragon Press, 1985

North, Nigel, *Continuo Playing on the Lute, Archlute, and Theorbo,* Bloomington: Indiana University Press, 1987

Schneider, John, *The Contemporary Guitar,* Berkeley: University of California Press, 1985

Spencer, Robert, "Chitarrone, Theorbo, and Archlute," *Early Music* 4 (1976)

Summerfield, Maurice J., *The Classical Guitar: Its Evolution and Its Players since 1800,* Gateshead: Mark, 1982; 4th edition, Newcastle-upon-Tyne: Mark, 1996

———, *The Jazz Guitar: Its Evolution and Its Players,* Gateshead: Mark, 1978; 3rd edition, 1980

Turnbull, Harvey, *The Guitar from the Renaissance to the Present Day,* New York: Scribner, and London: Batsford, 1974

Tyler, James, *The Early Guitar: A History and Handbook,* London: Oxford University Press, 1980

Wade, Graham, *Traditions of the Classical Guitar,* London: Calder, 1980

The lute is a descendant of a variety of Middle Eastern instruments, notably the *oud*, from which it derives its name. Until some time in the late 15th century, it was played with a plectrum, which limited its use to single melodic lines or melodic lines with a simple chordal accompaniment. Toward the end of the 15th century, playing with the fingers allowed the performance of polyphonic music, vastly increasing the possibilities of the instrument. Although the instrument began a decline in some countries in the 17th century, notably in France and England, its widespread use continued to the end of the 18th century, particularly in Germany.

The guitar emerged somewhat later, probably in the 16th century. Like the lute, it existed in a number of different forms until its standardization as a six-string, single-strung instrument in the early 19th century. Even after this standardization, its size and stringing continued to evolve into the 20th century. In addition, a number of ethnic forms of the guitar are found in Eastern Europe and Russia and in Central and South America.

COELHO presents a variety of essays on different repertories and periods associated with the lute and guitar. The anthology is not comprehensive, and the quality of the essays varies considerably. Of particular interest is "Lute Tablature Instructions in Italy: A Survey of the *Regole* from 1507 to 1759" by Dinko Fabris, which provides a comprehensive list of methods and summarizes their general principals. Kevin Mason's "Accompanying Italian Lute Song of the Late Sixteenth Century" deals in specific terms with the surviving evidence for accompanying polyphonic songs, such as madrigals, arranged as solo songs at the end of the Renaissance. One of the most valuable articles is Richard Savino's "Essential Issues in Performance Practices of the Classical Guitar," which summarizes the different technical approaches taken by Dionisio Aguado and Fernando Sor in the early 19th century, at the dawn of the standardization of the classical guitar.

NORTH has provided a thorough treatise on accompaniment during the 17th and 18th centuries for the instruments listed in the study's title. Of general interest is an overall view of the different types of lutes used during this period for accompanimental purposes, a complex subject with many potential confusions. SPENCER clarifies in more detail the different instruments used in the 17th century both for solo and accompanied playing.

Three surveys of the history of the guitar are noteworthy, each approaching the subject from a different point of view. GRUNFELD considers the subject in a cultural context, focusing on the iconography of the instrument and the message these pictorial representations tell us about attitudes toward the guitar in various periods. Although the account is frequently inaccurate, the excitement and enthusiasm with which he writes makes the book a pleasure to read. TURNBULL provides a brief, straightforward history of the instrument, placing the guitar in the context of music history. WADE presents a history of the lute and guitar repertory as it relates to the modern classical guitar. Rather than discussing lute music itself, he explains how guitarists became aware of its beauties and made it part of their repertory, while at the same time compromising its unique features through transcription. He emphasizes the development of a central tradition largely through the efforts of Andre Segovia and evaluates how it has evolved since Segovia's passing.

Summerfield's series presents a compendium of largely undigested information. SUMMERFIELD (1982) contains an essay on the history of the classical guitar, followed by descriptions and photos of players, composers, makers, and scholars. Each entry has a brief biography, and in the case of performers, a discography is included as well. There is also a section on the flamenco guitar with photos and discographies. There are several bibliographies, as well as lists of stores in various countries where one might go to buy recordings and music. SUMMERFIELD (1978) contains much the same type of information for the jazz guitar, including photos of over 120 players, biographies, and select discographies.

Two specialized studies deserve mention here. In an introduction to the guitar from its origins to the middle of the 18th century, TYLER provides a complete list of the musical sources and a brief discussion of the repertory, tunings, tablature, and ornaments. SCHNEIDER discusses the resources the guitar offers to the contemporary composer, examining a variety of techniques on both the acoustic and electric guitar.

McCUTCHEON is a useful bibliography organized by subject. The author offers critical comments concerning each entry and an index of reviews, including for each historical period specific articles on composers, theorists, performers, and performance practice. The section on construction covers publications about makers from different periods. This bibliography is limited to the classical guitar, and although dated, it provides a helpful guide for introductory research.

ROBERT ANTHONY GREEN

Instruments: Percussion

Bajzek, Dieter, *Percussion: An Annotated Bibliography with Special Emphasis on Contemporary Notation and Performance,* Metuchen, New Jersey: Scarecrow Press, 1988

Blades, James, *Percussion Instruments and Their History,* London: Faber, 1970; revised edition, 1984

Brincard, Marie-Thérèse, editor, *Sounding Forms: African Musical Instruments,* New York: American Federation of Arts, 1989

Brindle, Reginald Smith, *Contemporary Percussion,* London: Oxford University Press, 1970; 2nd edition, 1991

Diagram Group, *Musical Instruments of the World: An Illustrated Encyclopedia,* New York: Paddington Press, 1976

Peinkofer, Karl, and Fritz Tannigel, *Handbook of Percussion Instruments: Their Characteristics and Playing Techniques, with Musical Examples from the Literature,* translated by Kurt Stone and Else Stone, London: Schott, 1976

At the beginning of the 20th century, percussion instruments were used sparingly in Western concert music. Basic instruments such as timpani, snare and bass drums, and cymbals were common, but the role of percussion instruments was generally limited to producing military or other special effects. Early in the century, however, increased Western exposure to world cultures and the rise of popular dance music and jazz inspired composers of many styles of music to explore an increasing variety of percussion timbres in their music. Since World War II, both the number of instruments and the frequency of their use in concert music has increased tremendously. Percussion ensembles—both Western and non-Western—are common, and the sounds of Indian tabla, Caribbean steel drums, and the Indonesian gamelan are familiar to most musicians.

In the widely used Hornbostel and Sachs instrument classification system (first introduced in 1914), percussion instruments comprise two of the four basic categories. These are idiophones (instruments in which the vibrating medium is the body of the instrument itself, such as bells, cymbals, xylophones, etc.) and membranophones (instruments in which a membrane, or "drum head," is the vibrating medium). The books discussed below all use this system of classification to some degree.

The most comprehensive monograph on percussion instruments in English is that of BLADES. The author covers the history, construction, usage, and playing techniques of hundreds of percussion instruments from around the world. Line drawings of instruments and playing techniques are numerous throughout his narrative, and there are also 193 plates, a general index (primarily of instruments), and an index of names (primarily Western composers) and works. The first half of the book is devoted to percussion instruments in early Western history and in non-Western cultures. Citing a wide variety of sources, Blades provides an exhaustive amount information on materials, construction, playing techniques, and the social use of the instruments. Among his many topics are drum-making rituals in Ghana, the archaeological and pictorial evidence concerning instruments in ancient Greece, the history of

Chinese music, and the use of nakers in medieval and Renaissance Europe. The second half of the book is devoted to percussion instruments in Western concert music from the classical era to the present day. This portion is profusely illustrated with music examples from the standard orchestral literature. A professional percussionist for most of his life, Blades's knowledge of this literature is encyclopedic.

Because of the quality and scope of its factual material, Blades's book is the most authoritative source of information on percussion instruments in any language. The chapter bibliographies, which include books by historians, anthropologists, ethnologists, and colonial explorers, are indispensable. There is, however, a disturbing Eurocentric cultural bias in his treatment. This is announced quite blatantly in the two figures juxtaposed on the page that faces the very first page of the text: Figure 1, labeled "Primitive musician," shows a naked, African man beating sticks, while figure 2, labeled "Modern timpanist," displays a Caucasian, tuxedo-clad orchestral musician. This bias is also displayed in the organization of the book, which begins with Africa, proceeds through other non-Western cultures and early European music, and culminates in the discussion of modern concert music. To be fair, Blades seldom uses language that is condescending toward the cultures he discusses. Nevertheless, the word "primitive" rings as a negative value judgment in too many cases in the opening chapters.

BRINDLE is primarily a handbook on orchestration for the modern composer. The author discusses the origins, playing techniques, and contemporary usage of a wide variety of percussion instruments, and he provides many musical examples from scores by 20th-century composers who have used percussion instruments extensively. The composers most frequently cited are Bartók, Britten, Boulez, Stockhausen, Dallapiccola, and Varèse. Brindle also includes information on such practical topics as the layout of the percussion section, the acoustical properties of the instruments, and notation, including the modern symbolic notation for designating instruments.

A useful companion to Brindle is the handbook by PEINKOFER and TANNIGEL. Its focus is on a similar repertoire of 20th-century Western music, but the number of instruments (non-Western, in particular) included is much greater, and the discussion of the instruments is accompanied by photographs of each one. Historical Western instruments are included, and there is a useful section on mallets and beaters, a glossary of instrument names in English, French, German, and Italian, and a table of ranges for 23 instruments that produce definite pitches.

Two general instrument catalogs must also be mentioned for their interesting approaches to percussion instruments. The first, by the DIAGRAM GROUP, presents an unusually large number of percussion instruments, most of which come from non-Western cultures.

There are the expected (though unusually excellent) drawings and diagrams of the instruments themselves, but there are also illustrations showing native performers using the instruments. These give the reader an indication of the physical aspect of performance, as well as the social and cultural contexts in which the instruments are generally used.

BRINCARD's catalog also deserves mention for its presentation of African musical instruments as works of art containing a rich cultural significance. This significance is examined in ten brief articles contributed by noted anthropologists, ethnologists, art historians, and ethnomusicologists, each of whom provides a separate bibliography. Produced as an exhibition catalog, the book contains 149 plates, half of which show percussion instruments.

A useful guide to further information is the annotated bibliography of BAJZEK, which covers over 1,400 books, articles, and dissertations from 1965 to about 1985. The organization is topical, and despite its title, items covering historical instruments and non-Western cultures are listed.

MARK BENSON

Instruments: Strings

1. Violin

Applebaum, Samuel, et al., *The Way They Play,* 14 volumes, Neptune City, New Jersey: Paganiniana, 1972–86

Beament, James, *The Violin Explained: Components, Mechanism, and Sound,* Oxford: Clarendon Press, 1996

Boyden, David D., *The History of Violin Playing from Its Origins to 1761,* London: Oxford University Press, 1965

Boyden, David D., et al., *The New Grove Violin Family,* London: Macmillan, and New York: Norton, 1989

Flesch, Carl, *The Memoirs of Carl Flesch,* translated by Hans Keller, London: Rockliff, and New York: Macmillan, 1957

Kolneder, Walter, *The Amadeus Book of the Violin: Construction, History, and Music,* translated and edited by Reinhard G. Pauly, Portland, Oregon: Amadeus Press, 1998

Schwarz, Boris, *Great Masters of the Violin,* New York: Simon and Schuster, and London: Hale, 1983

Stowell, Robin, editor, *The Cambridge Companion to the Violin,* Cambridge: Cambridge University Press, 1992

The literature on the violin is vast, reaching back more than three centuries to the first treatises on violin playing. Since then, nearly every conceivable topic related to the instrument has received attention, from the acoustics of the violin to the medical problems of violinists. Today, the literature is best divided into four areas: the physical instrument, violin music, violinists, and violin playing. Boyden (1989), Kolneder, and Stowell are general works that survey each of these areas; Beaument's focus is the violin itself; Applebaum, Flesch, and Schwarz are concerned, in very different ways, with violinists and violin playing; and Boyden (1965) investigates the intersection of performance, music, and the development of the instrument. Readers interested in further information on any of these areas should consult the specialized journals, such as *Strad* or *Strings*, which cover string instruments generally, and the *Journal of the Violin Society of America*, which focuses on violin making.

Drawn from *The New Grove* series of music encyclopedias, the essays in BOYDEN (1989) survey all aspects of the violin family. The six chapters on the violin address construction, performance technique, repertoire, extra-European usage of the violin, acoustics, and the bow. One chapter each is also devoted to the viola, cello, and double bass. The numerous musical examples and illustrations, as well as the bibliography, glossary, and biographical index of violin and bow makers, help make this an excellent reference tool.

The 15 essays gathered by STOWELL also cover the main areas of violin scholarship. This collection is strong in its discussion of baroque violinists and its coverage of the repertoire generally; it is also notable for its treatment of the violin in jazz, violin technique in contemporary music, and the violin's role in chamber ensembles. A list of important treatises, a glossary of terms, and an extensive bibliography supplement the essays.

The translation of KOLNEDER's *Das Buch der Violine* should be welcomed by all English-reading violin enthusiasts. This is a remarkable work of scholarship, impressive in its discussion of all matters pertaining to the violin, from its origins to 20th-century pedagogy. The book is in three main parts: part 1 discusses the physical properties of the modern violin; part 2 covers the origin of the instrument and profiles important violin makers; and part 3 treats performance, pedagogy, and repertoire. The text is generously illustrated with diagrams, drawings, and musical examples. Reinhard Pauly acts both as translator and editor, rendering Kolneder's German into idiomatic English and updating the text with numerous editor's notes. For scholarly readers, the only notable weakness of this book is its inconsistent approach to documentation: there are no footnotes or endnotes, and not all quotations can be traced to the bibliography.

APPLEBAUM's 14-volume series comprises interviews with most of the important string players and teachers of the mid- and late 20th century. These volumes will interest performers, historians of modern violin technique, and biographers and admirers of this century's great violinists. Those featured include Dorothy DeLay, Mischa Elman, Ivan Galamian, Jascha Heifetz, Fritz Kreisler, Anne-Sophie Mutter, and Itzhak Perlman. The tone is informal, and discussions range from biographical matters to problems of technique and interpretation. The volumes are profusely illustrated with photographs and musical examples. The first volume is largely a reprint of earlier interviews published in Applebaum's *With the Artists* (1955). Volume 14 includes a cumulative index.

BEAMENT's purpose is to explain, without resorting to equations or technical language, how the violin produces sound and how humans perceive those sounds. In clear and engaging prose, he covers both theoretical concepts (e.g., the vibration of strings or the nature of sound perception) and practical matters (e.g., choosing and maintaining instruments for children or what a wolf note is). In the process, Beament disproves long-held myths and offers sound advice to performers and makers. Readers seeking the mathematical underpinnings of the phenomena Beament discusses should consult Lothar Cremer's *The Physics of the Violin*, translated by John S. Allen (1983).

BOYDEN's landmark work, the first of its kind in English, should be consulted by any serious student of the violin's early history. The author divides the years between 1520 and 1761 into four periods and examines not only violin technique but that technique's interrelationship with developments in violin music and violin construction. These three topics are covered for each of the four time periods, so that, although there is some redundancy, readers can easily trace the development of any given technique over time. A final chapter offers practical advice to modern violinists performing old music. The hardcover edition includes a phonorecord illustrating the differences in sound between old and modern violins, as well as a variety of technical matters. Although there has been no second edition of this work, the 1979 reprint contains numerous corrections and minor revisions.

For the student of 20th-century violin playing, FLESCH is indispensable. Hungarian born and German speaking, Flesch was one of the century's most influential violin pedagogues and a concert violinist of the first rank. His observations on violin performance practice, the violin repertoire, and his fellow violinists are detailed, insightful, and authoritative. Flesch's insistence on the posthumous publication of these memoirs also allows him a remarkable candor, particularly in his statements about his colleagues. The memoirs chronicle his life and times up to 1928. His son, C.F. Flesch, has added a chapter on the violinist's last 16 years.

SCHWARZ's survey of the great classical violinists of the past 350 years is well researched and a pleasure to read. The work proceeds chronologically, grouping violinists by nationality or school within each period. Schwarz also gives attention to the important violin teachers. Particularly strong are the chapters on 20th-century violinists (especially from the Russian and Soviet schools), many of whom Schwarz knew as colleagues and friends. For another fine survey of violinists, readers should consult Margaret Campbell's *The Great Violinists* (1980).

MARK KATZ

2. Other Strings

Barrett, Henry, *The Viola: Complete Guide for Teachers and Students,* Birmingham: University of Alabama Press, 1972; 2nd edition, 1978

Boyden, David D., editor, *The New Grove Violin Family,* London: Macmillan, and New York: Norton, 1989

Brun, Paul, *A History of the Double Bass,* translated by Lynn Morrel and Paul Brun, Chemin de la Flanerie, France: Brun, 1989

Cowling, Elizabeth, *The Cello,* New York: Scribner, 1975; 2nd edition, 1983

Danks, Harry, *The Viola D'Amore,* Halesowen: Bois de Boulogne, 1976; 2nd edition, Halesowen: Bonner, 1979

Ginzburg, Lev Solomonovich, *History of the Violoncello: Western Violoncello Art of the 19th and 20th Centuries, Excluding Russian and Soviet Schools,* edited by Herbert Axelrod, translated by Tanya Tchistyakova, Neptune City, New Jersey: Paganiniana Publications, 1983

Mersenne, Marin, *Harmonie Universelle: The Books on Instruments,* translated by Roger E. Chapman, The Hague: Nijhoff, 1957

Riley, Maurice W., *The History of the Viola,* 2 vols., Ann Arbor, Michigan: Braun-Brumfield, 1980–91; revised edition, 1993

Sachs, Curt, *The History of Musical Instruments,* New York: Norton, 1940

Stowell, Robin, editor, *Cambridge Companion to the Cello,* Cambridge: Cambridge University Press, 1999

Straeten, Edmund S.J. van der, *History of the Violoncello, the Viol Da Gamba, Their Precursors and Collateral Instruments,* London: Reeves, 1915; reprint, 1971

Walden, Valerie, *One Hundred Years of Violoncello: A History of Technique and Performance Practice, 1740–1840,* Cambridge: Cambridge University Press, 1998

Wasielewski, Wilhelm Joseph von, *The Violoncello and Its History,* translated by Isobella S.E. Stigand, London: Novello, 1894; reprint, New York: Da Capo Press, 1968

Woodfield, Ian, *The Early History of the Viol,* Cambridge: Cambridge University Press, 1984

Stringed-instrument research is subdivided into the following categories: organology; construction techniques; acoustical studies; history of use and performance practice; biographical profiles; teaching methodologies; and repertory analysis. Research materials consist of primary and secondary written sources, extant instruments, and iconography. Reflecting the evolving scientific methods of inquiry, investigation of the various families of instruments and their physical properties has generated scholarly writings from the early 16th century onward. The earliest pedagogical information also dates from the 16th century; as instrumental music making became increasingly independent from vocal performance, musicians devised and documented idiomatic performance practices. Ever-increasing playing complexities, continuous stylistic changes, and the desire for technical uniformity have necessitated continuous additions to this literature. The 19th century witnessed the codification of instrumental construction and performance techniques, simultaneous with the rise of European nationalism; consequently, interest in historic precedents induced the discipline of musicology, with concomitant research on historical stringed-instrument performers and repertoire. Twentieth-century studies of period performance practices have amplified these topics.

MERSENNE's *Harmonie Universelle* (1636), a primary source widely quoted by subsequent writers, is one of the earliest treatises to approach music using modern scientific principles. Roger Chapman has translated the seven books in which Mersenne classifies, with physical descriptions, 17th-century musical instruments. Book 4 details those that are bowed. Theoretical considerations for acoustics, proper stringing, and tuning take precedence, but the pleasure-giving qualities of each kind of instrument are recounted and compared through the author's philosophical assessments. Remarks about construction, sound production, and playing techniques support the scientific analysis, as do the iconographic representations frequently replicated in modern publications.

The identification and description of all stringed instruments known in the 20th century is encyclopedically presented by SACHS. Trained in art history and intimate with the varied instrumental collections of Europe's pre–World War II museums, the author was a founder of organology and ethnomusicology. In this English publication, which synthesizes much of the information presented in his numerous German writings, he differentiates the characteristics of all Eastern and Western plucked and bowed instruments, beginning with prehistory and continuing to the modern era. Usage within their parent culture is explained, as are tunings, basic playing techniques, and theories about each instrument's derivation. Sachs also details the full range of primary sources used in his research.

Both WASIELEWSKI and STRAETEN are required reading for historical researchers. Replete with gossip and personal opinions, these books summarize what was then known about 18th-century individuals and provide primary source information about 19th-century players, performances, repertoire, and pedagogical publications. Straeten additionally includes valuable iconography and, as a pioneer in the early music revival, lays the groundwork for subsequent studies through his research on the early viol and violin families. The caveat in using these books is that more recent investigations, especially for pre-19th-century subjects, should also be consulted for comparison.

Boyden and Stowell are collaborative volumes addressing all topics related to current stringed-instrument research. BOYDEN's book includes specific chapters on viola, cello, and double bass history; performers; performance practice; and repertoire, as well as general discussion of the bow, acoustics, and construction techniques for the violin family. In addition to books, the extensive bibliography identifies journal articles and dissertations. STOWELL presents the most comprehensive book on the cello to date. Specialists explain the origins and evolution of construction techniques for instrument and bow and analyze acoustical principles. Biographies, repertory, performance practice, and pedagogical sources for all stylistic periods to the present complete the survey.

WOODFIELD limits his examination to the viol family and its utility through the 16th century. This history is subdivided, as he considers medieval viols to be disassociated from those of the Renaissance. Summarizing the theories of previous scholars, his own research adds considerably to current knowledge about correlating instruments, and comparative analysis of the divergent origins of the viol and violin families convincingly separates each. For Renaissance viols, he delineates construction characteristics, tunings, historic playing methods, and repertory. More than 100 photographic plates illustrate extant instruments and iconography.

Further specialization is provided by DANKS, a modern scholar of the viola d'amore, which is cultivated most often as a second instrument by violists. The author offers a comprehensive overview of the instrument, including descriptions of the English violet. In addition to information about construction techniques, builders, performers, and repertoire, he translates historic performance instructions by Attilio Ariosti (ca. 1724), Joseph Majer (1732), J.P. Eisel (1738), and Dr. F.A. Weber (1788). The high-quality photographic plates of instruments and iconography are equally commendable.

The history of the viola is exhaustively presented by RILEY, who spent over 30 years compiling information on all of its aspects. Published in two volumes, the first addresses the viola's evolution from its beginnings to the present: construction practices for bows and instrument; performance practice; solo, chamber, and orchestral repertoire; schools of performance, including those of Eastern Europe, Israel, North America, and Argentina; and biographical profiles. The second volume is a collaborative issue updating select topics. Here, Riley examines luthiers on a regional basis, as well as historic and current viola performance practices. Contemporary interchange is recounted through the proceedings of international and national congresses for viola and viola d'amore, from 1980 to 1990.

BARRETT surveyed over 250 U.S. viola teachers regarding repertoire and contemporary pedagogy before writing his volume. In response to discerned teaching and playing difficulties, he formulated a compendium of teaching techniques and a complete listing of repertoire for the instrument. His technical recommendations separate viola from violin technique, and performing and study materials for all playing levels are listed. Supplementing the repertoire discussion is an appendix of music in print for viola and viola d'amore.

COWLING's research speciality is baroque cello repertoire, and her book chronicles the development of the 18th-century concerto and continuo sonata. In a comprehensible manner, she dissects the form of these works, their technical configurations, and their stylistic attributes. For those interested in manuscript and first-edition sources, she also names the libraries where such works are held. Her subject is broadened by a history of violoncello construction, profiles of respected luthiers, and discussion of modern usage, incorporating analysis of select 19th- and 20th-century compositions.

European regional variations in performance practice, with updated biographies and exacting detail about the playing characteristics of 18th- and 19th-century cellists, is WALDEN's province. Drawn from period tutors and solo repertoire, over 300 music examples illustrate written directions, which are complemented by excerpts from instructional sources, journal reports, and diary entries. Varying fingering and bowing methods, ornamentation, special effects, stylistic attributes, and accompanying skills are analyzed and compared, as are attendant changes in the construction techniques of solo and accompanying instruments.

GINZBURG wrote *Istoriia violonchel'nogo iskusstva* (1978), a three-volume history giving a complete synopsis of Russian and non-Russian cello playing. This translation covers 19th- and 20th-century non-Russian cellists. Although Soviet ideology is evident in his comparisons, the translation of Eastern European primary sources not generally available to Western scholars gives this book a range different from other contemporary publications. Biographies of eminent performers are documented, together with annotated commentary about each player's technical mannerisms, performance style, and cello compositions.

Originally published as *Histoire des contrebasses à cordes* (1983), BRUN provides information about the double bass as a classical instrument. Minimizing the double bass's early relationship with the viol family acknowledged in Boyden, the author considers the instrument to be the largest member of the violin family. This book's strength lies in Brun's insights concerning the solo skills of the 18th-century Viennese school and his coverage of evolving performance practices in an orchestral environment. The diagrams of 18th- and 19th-century orchestral seating charts are also useful, this information being relevant to all historical researchers. Brun evaluates the specialized issues of stringing and tuning, the development of fittings, and bow design and technique. The final chapter offers brief biographical sketches.

VALERIE WALDEN

See also Instruments: Lute and Guitar

Instruments: Wind

Baines, Anthony, *Woodwind Instruments and Their History,* London: Faber, and New York: Norton, 1957; 3rd edition, London: Faber, 1967

Bate, Philip, *The Oboe, An Outline of Its History, Development, and Construction,* London: Benn, and New York: Philosophical Library, 1956; 3rd edition, London: Benn, and New York: Norton, 1975

Brymer, Jack, *Clarinet,* London: Macdonald and Jane, 1976; revised edition, 1979

Galway, James, *Flute,* London: Macdonald, and New York: Schirmer Books, 1982

Goossens, Leon, and Edwin Roxburgh, *Oboe,* London: Macdonald and Jane, and New York: Schirmer, 1977; 2nd edition, London: Macdonald, 1980

Hunt, Edgar, *The Recorder and Its Music,* London: Jenkins, and New York: Norton, 1962; revised edition, London: Eulenberg Books, 1977

Jansen, Will, *The Bassoon: Its History, Construction, Makers, Players, and Music,* 5 vols., Buren: Knuf, 1978

Krell, John, *Kincaidiana,* Culver City, California: Trio Associates, 1973; 2nd edition, Santa Clarita, California: National Flute Association, 1997

Lawson, Colin, editor, *The Cambridge Companion to the Clarinet,* Cambridge: Cambridge University Press, 1995

Quantz, Johann Joachim, *On Playing the Flute,* translated by Edward R. Reilly, New York: Schirmer, and London: Faber, 1966; 2nd edition, 1985

Rice, Albert R., *The Baroque Clarinet,* Oxford: Clarendon Press, and New York: Oxford University Press, 1992

Thomson, John Mansfield, and Anthony Rowland-Jones, editors, *The Cambridge Companion to the Recorder,* Cambridge: Cambridge University Press, 1995

Timm, Everett L., *The Woodwinds: Performance and Instructional Techniques,* Boston: Allyn and Bacon, 1964; 2nd edition, 1971

Toff, Nancy, *The Flute Book: A Complete Guide for Students and Performers,* Newton Abbot: David and Charles, and New York: Scribner, 1985; 2nd edition, New York: Oxford University Press, 1996

Westphal, Frederick William, *Guide to Teaching Woodwinds,* Dubuque, Iowa: Brown, 1962; 5th edition, 1990

Woodwind Anthology: A Compendium from the Instrumentalist on the Woodwind Instruments, Evanston, Illinois: Instrumentalist, 1972

The literature on woodwind instruments, their development, construction, methods, and performance issues is so extensive that one can provide a guide to only a few of the most important studies. Evidence of the existence of wind instruments dates back at least to Pharaonic times, and their existence in the early cultures such as those of China and Greece is documented both iconographically and through written description. It is likely that primitive flutes were used in nearly every early society and that these are the predecessors of the other wind instruments. From the seventh-century Coptic archaeological sites in Egypt, we find a predecessor of the clarinet as well as some indications of a double-reed instrument.

By the beginning of the Renaissance in Europe, flutes, recorders, oboes, bassoons, and *chalemeaux* (precursors of the clarinet) were produced in various sizes ranging from high to low, and instrument makers, who were often also fine performers, were experimenting with design modifications, additional keys, and tuning systems. Early instruments were limited. Playing in tune was challenging, and the differing tone qualities between, for example, flutes and reed instruments, made mixed-ensemble performance problematic.

When in the mid-19th century Theobald Boehm accomplished a major reworking of the mechanical key system for the flute, an accomplishment that greatly eased fingering problems and vastly improved intonation, the other instruments quickly adopted similar modifications. Since that time there have been only relatively minor changes in the design of woodwind instruments. Two of the most significant are the dominant usage today of flutes made from metal (silver, nickel, gold, platinum), rather than wood, and the increased use of plastics for clarinets, oboes, and bassoons.

Since its first printing, BAINES's book has provided a good overview of the woodwind family. In addition to discussing their physical characteristics, history, and some musical considerations, he supplies a helpful first resource of bibliographical material.

Westphal and Timm cover all the woodwinds, for slightly differing audiences. TIMM writes for "person[s] oriented in music, with little knowledge of the woodwinds, [so that they] may learn to play and teach." He gives practical information on purchasing and maintaining instruments, brief summaries of playing techniques and common problems, and for each section, a brief bibliography.

WESTPHAL, addressing the needs of college students preparing for a career in instrumental teaching, includes graded instrumental literature, with sources for obtaining music and other teaching aids, such as checklists for hand position and assembly, in addition to descriptions and pictures of proper form. Like Timm, this work contains many illustrations and photographs.

The volumes by Thomson and Rowland-Jones and by Lawson, two works in a recent series from Cambridge University Press, are concise and very readable, and are organized as collections of essays by prominent musicians and musicologists. The anthology edited by THOMSON and ROWLAND-JONES covers the history, repertoire, and recent developments for the recorder and contains a review of instruction books. Particularly fascinating are the two essays on the revival of the recorder in the 19th and 20th centuries, the first of which documents the interest of George Bernard

Shaw in period instruments. Shaw, through his newspaper column, first savaged but later championed Arnold Dolmetsch's efforts to revive the performance of early music on period instruments. The final essay is a guide to further reading.

LAWSON is equally informative, examining the antecedents and early development of the clarinet, followed by discussions of the clarinet family from the basset horn and bass clarinet through the various species of high clarinet. Additional articles cover the repertoire, mechanics, teaching, prominent players and composers, and the contemporary topics of jazz performance and recording.

Goossens and Roxbough, Brymer, and Galway, authors of volumes in the Yehudi Menuhin Music Guides series on the clarinet, oboe, and flute, respectively, are written in a somewhat more popular style than the Cambridge Companions series but are nonetheless valuable resources as a first foray into the literature about these instruments. Each volume contains concise historical information, an overview of the instrumental family, general aspects of technique and performance, and some brief bibliographies and discographies. These volumes aim to convey the "warmth and adventure which music can give," guiding the reader through the history, technique, and literature of each instrument. These volumes contain many musical insights of value not only to players but to any music lover. GOOSSENS and ROXBURGH go into some detail on modern techniques of the oboe. The descriptions of maintenance and reed making, and the illustrations of correct embouchure and playing position, provide excellent models for aspiring amateurs. This volume also discusses performance of baroque music, underlining the differences between the early and the modern instruments and recognizing the difficulties of performing music "on a different instrument from the one for which the music was originally written."

BRYMER's volume treats similar topics for the clarinet and spends some time explaining the harmonic organization of the clarinet, which overblows at the interval of a 12th rather than the octave common to the flute and the oboe. He also explains clearly the phenomenon of the transposing instrument, its origins, and practical implications. A substantial section of Brymer's work addresses specifically pedagogical issues in teaching clarinet.

GALWAY, a superb performer, has long been one of the most high profile of classical artists. He writes with the same joie de vivre one hears in his performances, sharing his comprehensive knowledge of the flute and also often humorous comments on life as it affects a musician: "Don't . . . become so obsessed with practice that you stop developing as a person, and only develop as a practitioner of a D major scale in thirds." Although his style is informal, his content is practical and pertinent, worth reading by any aspiring flutist and accessible for anyone interested in music.

KRELL is a small but important book summarizing the lesson notes the author took during his flute study with William Kinkaid: "To a great degree, [Kinkaid] was responsible for developing a robust style that might be called the American school of flute playing." Written in an informal style, both pragmatic and at times poetic and metaphorical, Krell passes on to the reader insights on flute playing and musicianship. Kinkaid's sensitive musical understanding makes this book a valuable resource not only for flutists but for all musicians.

Although QUANTZ is an 18th-century treatise on the flute, its significance today is undiminished. Quantz's writings have influenced flutists since his day and are one of the principal sources of information about historical performance practice for all instrumentalists. Some of the advocated techniques are more appropriate for the baroque flute than the modern; however, many of the musical recommendations are our most complete resource for baroque music performance, cadenzas, accompanimental techniques, and ornamentation, among other topics. Because such a large part of flute repertoire stems from this period, this work is invaluable for any performer of this literature.

TOFF provides a comprehensive but pedestrian compendium of information on the flute. Nevertheless, her work is useful, incorporating practical information such as chapters on choosing an instrument, care and maintenance, an overview of the history of the instrument, discussion of recital planning and recording, the musical repertoire organized by period, a repertoire catalog, and valuable appendices with mundane but useful entries for fingering charts, flute manufacturers, repair shops, sources for music and books, periodicals, and organizations relevant to flutists.

BATE's book on the oboe is a standard source for the history, development, and construction of the instrument. Written for the serious instrument player, or possibly for composers who need to know the capabilities and limitations of the oboe, his work is informative and includes a good bibliography.

RICE, one of the most complete resources on the baroque clarinet, recounts the history of the physical instrument that became the clarinet and the concomitant expansion of the repertoire as the instrument's capabilities increased. Unlike other woodwinds, the fundamental acoustic system of this instrument altered to a wind that overblows at the interval of a 12th, from the original, more common, interval of an octave. Rice's work deals extensively with the wide-ranging techniques of performance on the early clarinet, such as articulation using variously the chest, throat, and tongue, for example. He includes a comprehensive bibliography for further reading.

JANSEN's five-volume work on the bassoon is a masterful and comprehensive work, opening with an introduction intended for the casual reader. Volume 1 covers the history of the bassoon. Volume 2 discusses the manufacture and maintenance of the instrument, reeds and specific sources for cane with the differing properties of each kind, fingering methods, orchestral works that feature the bassoon, musical excerpts from a variety of compositions, and the development of woodwind ensembles. Volume 3 is a bibliography of bassoon solo and ensemble literature. Volume 4 contains biographies of prominent bassoonists up to the time of his writing, and volume 5 consists of illustrations and photographs of bassoon, bassoonists, and art works that include bassoons or bassoon players, ending with a selected bibliography of sources.

The WOODWIND ANTHOLOGY is a collection of essays printed in the *Instrumentalist,* a magazine catering to band directors and music teachers and covering many issues of importance to wind players, from sample exercises and new tuning systems to reviews of method books and articles by noted teachers and performers. Although this collection is a good source for current and specific material, the quality of both the writing and the information is less consistently excellent.

Of the early woodwind instruments, the recorder is unique in that the instrument in use today varies little from the original of centuries ago. Because of the convenient size of the alto recorder and the modest cost of some plastic models, the recorder is often the first instrument to which children are introduced. HUNT's work is a short but detailed history of the instrument and its music, with some discussion of recorder technique. He concludes with a bibliography of articles and books about the recorder.

MARTHA FARAHAT

Instruments: Builders

Boalch, Donald H., *Makers of the Harpsichord and Clavichord, 1440 to 1840,* London: Ronald, 1956; 3rd edition, edited by Charles Mould, Oxford: Clarendon Press, 1995

Clinkscale, Martha Novak, *Makers of the Piano, 1700–1820,* Oxford: Oxford University Press, 1993

Gellerman, Robert F., *Gellerman's International Reed Organ Atlas,* Vestal, New York: Vestal Press, 1973; 2nd edition, Lanham: Vestal Press, 1998

Hill, W. Henry, et al., *Antonio Stradivari, His Life and Work (1644–1737),* London: Hill, 1889; 2nd edition, London: Macmillan, 1909; reprint, New York: Dover, 1963

———, et al., *The Violin Makers of the Guarneri Family (1626–1762): Their Life and Work,* London: Hill, 1931; reprint, New York: Dover, 1989

Jalovec, Karel, *Encyclopedia of Violin-Makers,* 2 vols., London: Hamlyn, 1968 (Includes material in translation by J. B. Kozak, from Willibald Leo Freiherr von Lütgendorff,

Die Geigen- und Lautenmacher vom Mittelalter bis zur Gegenwart, Frankfurt: Keller, 1904; 4th edition, 2 vols., 1922)

Langwill, Lyndesay Graham, *An Index of Musical Wind-Instrument Makers,* Edinburgh: Langwill, 1960; 6th edition, 1980

Lieberman, Richard K., *Steinway and Sons,* New Haven, Connecticut: Yale University Press, 1995

O'Brien, Grant, *Ruckers: A Harpsichord and Virginal Building Tradition,* Cambridge: Cambridge University Press, 1990

Waterhouse, William, *The New Langwill Index: A Dictionary of Musical Wind-Instrument Makers and Inventors,* London: Bingham, 1993

Young, Phillip T., *Twenty-Five Hundred Historical Woodwind Instruments: An Inventory of the Major Collections,* New York: Pendragon Press, 1982; 2nd edition, *4900 Historical Woodwind Instruments: An Inventory of 200 Makers in International Collections,* London: Bingham, 1993

Books in English about musical-instrument builders often take the form of encyclopedic reference works, which contain brief entries on a wide variety of different makers of either one instrument type (e.g., reed organs) or of an instrumental category (e.g., woodwinds). Such reference guides are generally updated and revised periodically, resulting in multiple editions. A smaller number of monographs devoted exclusively to the history and/or instruments of a single instrument maker generally treat only the best-known builders. There is a particular paucity of books on individual wind-instrument makers and modern makers of instruments generally. This survey focuses on historical makers.

The plethora of instrument types and the even greater number of individual makers make it possible to provide only a representative summary of literature, which is treated here according to subject: makers of keyboard instruments, stringed instruments, and wind instruments. Preference is given to single-volume standard reference materials, from which the reader may turn to additional literature. However, it should be noted that the best starting point for general inquiry on instrument makers, types of instruments, terminology, and bibliography are *The New Grove Dictionary of Musical Instruments* (1984) and *The New Grove Dictionary of Music and Musicians* (1980). The former contains some material from the latter set and provides useful bibliographies.

Because reference materials are often incomplete or even obsolete by the time they are published, the serious reader is strongly advised to consult additional recent scholarship on musical-instrument makers in journal articles. Some of the important journals in English are *The Journal of the American Musical Instrument Society (JAMIS), The Galpin Society Journal, Fellowship of Mak-*

ers and Researchers of Historical Instruments Quarterly (FoMRHI), The Organ Yearbook, The Early Keyboard Journal, and the Journal of the Violin Society of America. Others, such as Early Music, are not organology-specific but frequently contain articles about musical instruments that are accessible to the nonspecialist.

BOALCH remains the standard and most complete general reference on the harpsichord and clavichord. The third edition is divided into two parts: the first provides brief, alphabetical biographies of known harpsichord makers; the second part lists their surviving instruments, with summary descriptions, locations, and references. Appendices include genealogical tables for important families of makers, including Ruckers, Stein, and Silbermann, and a useful conspectus of makers, listed chronologically by the cities in which they worked. Technical terms used to describe the instruments are conveniently indexed with their equivalents in six foreign languages; however, a glossary is not provided.

CLINKSCALE's important treatment of the piano is closely modeled on that of Boalch, although with much less success. The volume is indispensable as a guide to hundreds of instruments and their locations but must be used with caution due to countless omissions and errors of fact. Unlike Boalch, Clinkscale does not provide geographical or chronological lists of makers.

O'BRIEN provides a thorough study based on the surviving instruments by Ruckers, the most influential makers of harpsichords and virginals in the late 17th and early 18th centuries. There is a good bibliography and a particularly informative section on performance practice. The book begins at a moderately advanced level; novices may want to turn to more basic references such as Boalch, Raymond Russel's The Harpsichord and Clavichord: An Introductory Study (1973), or Frank Hubbard's Three Centuries of Harpsichord Making (1965).

An in-depth social history of the piano makers Steinway and Sons is described by LIEBERMAN, but for information specific to the instruments they produced, one might turn to the highly illustrated volume by Ronald V. Ratcliffe, Steinway (1989).

GELLERMAN comprehensively references makers of reed organs (including harmoniums, melodeons, and other types of parlor organs) from the early 19th-century origins of the instrument to the present. It includes, where possible, brief histories of each maker, with serial numbers, numerous manufacturer's illustrations, and other information intended to help identify and date particular instruments. A geographical index of makers and an extensive bibliography for further reading are also provided.

JALOVEC, one of the standard dictionaries of all makers of bowed and plucked stringed instruments, includes information on both historical and recent makers worldwide. Makers are listed alphabetically with brief biographical entries and concise general descrip-

tions of their instruments, but inventories and locations of their surviving instruments are not provided. Numerous photographs of makers' labels are shown, along with some illustrations of instruments. Readers will find a glossary of instrument types, tunings, and technical terminology, although the information provided there is not altogether reliable.

Although now quite old, HILL et al. (1889) is the most widely available standard book on Stradivari. It covers the maker's violins, violas, and violoncellos, materials and varnish, and labels and construction, along with illustrations and biographical material. The revised reprint contains new supplementary indices and introduction. HILL et al. (1931), on the Guarneri family, is similar in format to the Stradivari volume; it has also been reprinted but without change.

The few standard references on historical wind-instrument builders (brass and woodwind) include WATERHOUSE, a volume that surveys makers of major Western mouth-blown wind instruments, excluding folk instruments, makers of reeds, keys, and valves. Although the original LANGWILL, only included entries of woodwind and brass makers' names and marks as transcribed from original instruments, the sixth edition has been revised to include documented makers whose names are not found on surviving instruments. The new edition emphasizes biographical detail, providing additional information about the locations of representative surviving instruments. Some entries suffer from omissions, errors of fact, or misleading typographical mistakes, and although brief literature lists are offered after each entry, adequate documentation is sometimes lacking. User-friendly features include a glossary of technical and foreign terms and an extensive bibliography.

YOUNG's indispensable book provides the largest survey of historical woodwind-instrument makers. The guide presents locations for the makers and handy, uniform, tabular descriptions of their surviving instruments, which are the emphasis of the volume. No biographical data is offered beyond the location and approximate period in which each maker (or family of makers) flourished. Included are handy lists of collections, collectors, photo sources, and lucid explanations of specialized terminology. The large number of makers represented span the period from ca. 1500 to ca. 1900, but Young does not attempt to be all-inclusive. In addition, the instrument inventories have been found to contain numerous omissions, but the volume nevertheless remains an excellent place to begin to locate a maker's known woodwind instruments and much more.

MARY OLESKIEWICZ

See also Stradivari, Antonio

Italy: Musical Centers to 1600

Atlas, Allan W., *Music at the Aragonese Court of Naples*, Cambridge: Cambridge University Press, 1985

Cummings, Anthony M., *The Politicized Muse: Music for Medici Festivals, 1512–1537*, Princeton, New Jersey: Princeton University Press, 1992

D'Accone, Frank A., *The Civic Muse: Music and Musicians in Siena During the Middle Ages and the Renaissance*, Chicago: University of Chicago Press, 1997

Fenlon, Iain, *Music and Patronage in Sixteenth-Century Mantua*, 2 vols., Cambridge: Cambridge University Press, 1980

Fenlon, Iain, editor, *The Renaissance: From the 1470s to the End of the 16th Century*, Englewood Cliffs, New Jersey: Prentice Hall, and London: Macmillan, 1989

Landon, H.C. Robbins, and John Julius Norwich, *Five Centuries of Music in Venice*, London: Thames and Hudson, and New York: Schirmer Books, 1991

Lockwood, Lewis, *Music in Renaissance Ferrara, 1400–1505*, Cambridge, Massachusetts: Harvard University Press, 1984

Reynolds, Christopher A., *Papal Patronage and the Music of St. Peter's, 1380–1513*, Berkeley: University of California Press, 1995

Wilson, Blake, *Music and Merchants: The Laudesi Companies of Republican Florence*, Oxford: Clarendon Press, and New York: Oxford University Press, 1992

Until recently, very little had been written about the various important musical centers in Renaissance Italy. However, many new studies focusing on the musical centers themselves, and less on genres and composers as in the past, emerged at the end of the 20th century. This shift could perhaps be the result of a trend in musicology toward more wholistic investigations of a city's cultural expressions, or it could perhaps reflect the effect on musicology from other fields of research, such as ethnomusicology and sociology. Whatever the cause, these new musicological studies cover the full range of musical expression in a particular city, including musical institutions, patterns of patronage, styles and types of music, people involved in music making, and the production of manuscripts and prints.

An invaluable source that can serve as a starting place in the investigation of musical centers in Renaissance Italy is FENLON (1989). This volume was published as part of a series of books, conceived in conjunction with the *Man and Music* documentary for television, whose intent was to focus on the social, historical, and intellectual context of the music in each of the time periods covered in the series. This volume contains four separate essays on Italian musical centers. Fenlon himself provides a long introductory essay titled "Music and Society," wherein he identifies key societal forces that he thinks most influenced the music of the Renaissance. He is also the author of the essay titled "Venice: Theatre of the World," which describes how music in Venice was directly linked to the "politics of prestige" and explains how music was an essential contributor to what he labels the "myth of Venice." He maintains that musical institutions, such as the chapel of St. Mark's or one of the many *scuole*, were guided by political considerations in such matters as performance practice and repertoire.

Christopher Reynolds contributes to Fenlon's edition the essay "Rome: A City of Rich Contrast," which focuses on the influence of the papacy and the Roman curia on the musical life of that city. After discussing the types and manners of patronage present, the kinds of music, and the methods of the music's performance, he initiates a discussion of whether a Roman style of composition existed and what that style might be. These ideas are developed further in REYNOLDS, in which the author also attempts to link certain composers to Rome by identifying style characteristics common to composers there. To further buttress his arguments, he adds an in-depth analysis of select compositions of Roman music from the period as well as information from another of his studies on the use of musical and textual allusion in composition, the latter of which he attributes to the influence of humanism in the Roman curia.

The third article in Fenlon's edition is William F. Prizer's "North Italian Courts, 1460–1540," which focuses on Mantua, Ferrara, and, to a lesser extent, Milan. Rather than depicting in detail each of the courts, Prizer mainly describes common patterns of music making in each of the cities, noting exceptions where applicable. His study limits itself to court musical institutions and does not deal with churches and their musical life. He identifies a "northern Italian style," which he claims emerges from these courts in the latter 15th and early 16th centuries, but he presents only a brief analysis to support this assertion. This study is apparently a distillation of two other, full-length studies mentioned below and an article on Milan by Prizer.

The first of the full-length studies drawn on by Prizer is that by LOCKWOOD, who examines the roles of the Este dukes on the musical life of Ferrara in the 15th century. The study traces the development of this important musical center under each of the dukes, beginning with Niccolò III and continuing until the apogee of the Ferrarese musical establishment under Ercole I. The book investigates such topics as important musicians and theorists, musical institutions (including the cathedral and court chapel), manuscripts, and types of music, as well as related items such as improvisatory traditions, the economics of music, and the recruitment of talent. Most of the book is devoted to music under the patronage of Ercole I, and it is in this investigation that the best musical analysis is to be found, along with in-depth discussions of various musical genre, styles, and repertory.

The second full-length study on which Prizer draws is FENLON (1980). This book, like Lockwood, focuses only on the court musical establishment, presuming that the most important music making in Mantua was linked to the court. The two main points are that music in Mantua reflects the reformist principles of 16th-century Europe and that it seems to reinforce the cultivation of a mythology surrounding the dukes. A second volume presents an edition of selected musical examples.

The final article in Fenlon (1989) is Atlas's "Aragonese Naples." This essay is a distillation of material presented in ATLAS, which focuses on the courts of Alfonso I and his son Ferrante during the 15th century. Most of the study deals with the Royal Chapel and the composers, singers, and other personae associated with it, including biographical sketches of the key figures in the court's musical life and a detailed list of singers. After a brief discussion of secular music, the author offers a more substantial investigation of the sources and repertory in use. The remainder of the book, roughly a third, presents an edition of selected musical examples.

LANDON and NORWICH contribute a study of the musical life of Venice from the 16th to the 20th century. This volume, like the *Man and Music* series, was originally conceived as a set of scripts for a television documentary. The first chapter is devoted to music in 16th-century Venice and is divided into two parts. The first (to about 1550) deals with the musical institutions and performing forces available and the main composers who helped set the stage for Venetian musical greatness. The second section (from about 1550) covers the realization of that greatness under the auspices of the Gabrielis. The strength of this book lies not so much with its scholarly detail as in the lavish visual element in the form of numerous black-and-white and color reproductions of artwork, portraits, documents, photographs, etc.

Currently, no complete study of music in Florence exists; however, two studies discuss different aspects of musical culture in this important musical center. The first, by CUMMINGS, is a very narrowly focused study of the use of music in the political context of the Medici restoration of the early 16th century. This study is formatted to present a chronologically ordered documentation of important musical events, linked only by a limited continuous narrative framework, which shows how musical spectacle was used to bolster the Medici political prestige and the image they wanted to portray to the world at large. The study attempts to draw on a synthesis of period artwork, literature, and primary documentary evidence to reproduce each spectacle for the modern reader.

The second study, by WILSON, focuses not on the music of the Medici court but on the music associated with the *laudesi* companies (musical/social lay religious associations) that were such an important part of Florentine life. He places the formation of these companies into the larger social context of lay devotion and shows how this devotion worked itself out in these companies. The

study examines the major companies; their membership, churches, and altars where they gathered; their organization; and special events for which music was performed.

If there is one example of a study that can be said to be complete, it would have to be that of D'ACCONE, who presents a full history of all facets of music in Siena from the 14th to the 16th century. The book is divided into three parts, each of which examines one aspect of Sienese musical life. The first part focuses on the cathedral with in-depth studies on the administration, organization, personnel, liturgy, and performances associated with it. This section also traces the development, evolution, and decline of the institution in different periods. The second part considers the music associated with the Palazzo Pubblico and the establishment and maintenance of the town's corps of trumpeters and its wind band. The third part delves into the everyday music of the people of Siena by investigating the role of music in the social life of the town and the activity of the professional musicians, dancing masters, instrument makers, and others who contributed to the rich musical life of Siena. Although this book is of such monumental size and of such depth that a casual reading of it is almost impossible, it is a most useful reference work.

JOHN KARR

Ives, Charles 1874–1954

United States composer

1. Biography

Block, Geoffrey, *Charles Ives: A Bio-Bibliography*, New York: Greenwood Press, 1988

Burkholder, J. Peter, editor, *Charles Ives and His World*, Princeton, New Jersey: Princeton University Press, 1996

Cowell, Henry, and Sidney Cowell, *Charles Ives and His Music*, London, Oxford, and New York: Oxford University Press, 1955; 2nd edition, 1969

Feder, Stuart, *Charles Ives, "My Father's Song:" A Psychoanalytic Biography*, New Haven, Connecticut: Yale University Press, 1992

Ives, Charles, *Essays before a Sonata and Other Writings*, edited by Howard Boatwright, New York: Norton, 1962; reprint as *Essays before a Sonata, The Majority, and Other Writings*, 1970

——, *Memos*, edited by John Kirkpatrick, New York: Norton, 1972

Perlis, Vivian, *Charles Ives Remembered: An Oral History*, New Haven, Connecticut: Yale University Press, 1974

Rossiter, Frank R., *Charles Ives and His America*, New York: Liveright, 1975; London: Gollancz, 1976

Swafford, Jan, *Charles Ives: A Life with Music*, New York: Norton, 1996

Charles Ives has been served well by biographers. Beginning with the first comprehensive account by Cowell and Cowell, which first appeared in 1955, Ives's life has been approached from a variety of perspectives ranging from traditional chronological narrative to psychoanalysis. Despite their methodological differences, all of these volumes use biography as a tool to locate the factors that led Ives to compose in his unique manner. Themes that have engaged each of these authors in pursuit of this question include Ives's relationship with his father, the difficulties he faced as a U.S. composer in a culture dominated by European art music, his parallel career as a businessman, his relationship with the world of music, and his political beliefs. As Swafford indicates, recent studies have opened new avenues by examining Ives's attitudes toward gender and the physical and mental factors that plagued him for most of his adult life.

Ives's writings are a good starting point for those who are interested in his biography. Although he was rather reticent in person, Ives expressed his thoughts freely and at length in print. One has an immediate sense of intimacy when reading Ives because his often idiosyncratic personality is clearly evident in his prose style. Some of these writings were motivated by a desire to leave a record of his ideas. Others arose from requests for information. A final group functioned as diary entries, recording his reactions to specific events. Overall, Ives's numerous published and unpublished writings offer unmatched insights into his character, thoughts, and attitudes.

IVES (1972), a compilation of (for the most part) unpublished memoirs written in the 1930s is especially illuminating. Topics addressed in this volume include his music, the music of other composers, composition, criticism, autobiography, and aesthetics. John Kirkpatrick's editorial contributions (including 21 appendices) are first rate; each memo, as Ives called them, is annotated copiously.

IVES (1962), an anthology of pieces written for publication, complements the aforementioned volume. Most of the topics covered in the 1972 anthology are also addressed, often with more detail, in this collection. This book is also interesting because it contains Ives's most important political and social writings.

The composer's personal testimony is complemented nicely by PERLIS, a collection of interviews with 58 people who knew Ives as a private individual, a musician, or as a businessman. Compiled between 1968 and 1971, this superb oral history is divided into four sections: "Youth and Yale Years"; "Insurance"; "Family, Friends, and Neighbors"; and "Music." The annotations in Perlis are first-rate. Reproductions of several important photographs and documents are also included.

BURKHOLDER offers a variety of well-chosen source materials, including a selection of Ives's correspondence, reviews of his music written between 1881 and 1952,

and contemporary accounts of the composer and his music. Five original essays were commissioned for this volume. Two of these address biographical topics. Mark Tucker's essay, "Of Men and Mountains: Ives in the Adirondacks," explores how stimuli Ives experienced during his annual vacations in New York's Adirondack mountains between 1896 and 1915 affected his personal, intellectual, and artistic development. Michael Broyles's contribution, "Charles Ives and the American Democratic Tradition," offers a fascinating revisionist view of the composer's political thought that rejects earlier claims that he embraced Populism or Progressivism.

An overview of the secondary literature is provided by BLOCK, a handy annotated guide that treats materials ranging from monographs to videocassettes. An introductory section offers a concise biography of the composer. This truly comprehensive bibliography considers aesthetic and stylistic studies as well as reviews and critical evaluations. Literature that deals with Ives's music and his relation to contemporary figures is also examined. The appendices include a worklist, data about first performances, and a list of Ives's writings.

The following formal biographies are notable for their unique viewpoints. Perhaps the most distinguished member of this group is the biographical section of COWELL and COWELL. Written for the most part by Sidney Cowell, this volume is notable for its promotion of Ives as a true American (iconoclastic, experimental, visionary, free from tradition), a Yankee composer (individual, skeptical, with a wry sense of humor), and a transcendentalist (concerned with morality and the spirit). Each of these themes are addressed in some way by the other biographies treated in this entry. Although this volume has been superseded in many respects, it still has much to offer contemporary readers. On a basic level, Cowell and Cowell offer a concise and accurate chronicle of Ives's life. The book is more important, however, as the record of a personal relationship between the authors and the composer that lasted nearly 30 years. This biography was written with Ives's cooperation (and active participation). It therefore projects a degree of intimacy that gives the reader a distinct sense of what Ives was like as a person. And as a composer deeply involved with Ives's music since the 1920s, Henry Cowell offers a vivid firsthand account of Ives's early reception history. An idea of Ives significance for younger composers in the United States is also conveyed. This work certainly demonstrates the authors' deepest admiration for Ives; this sentiment is reflected, unfortunately, in the Cowells' general tendency to portray things the way Ives perceived them. Their deference to the composer's viewpoint has resulted in a biography that is rather hagiographic.

ROSSITER was the first biography to question the image promoted by the Cowells, especially their claims about the composer's unique worldview. The author, a cultural historian, places Ives in a detailed historical context in order to demonstrate that he was a product of his environment. Rossiter's account of how Ives fought and accommodated himself to the world around him is especially interesting. This study offers superb discussions of life in Danbury, Connecticut, and the commercial, social, and cultural contexts that influenced Ives's music. His political ideas and business career are also considered in detail. Remarks about his music, which appear through this book, often seem overdetermined by the author's sociological perspective.

Ives was deeply attached to his father, George, a musician who introduced him to composition and performance and who died when Ives was 20. Throughout his adult life, Ives glorified his father's musical and intellectual gifts. More important, he claimed that his music was inspired by George Ives's example. FEDER, a psychoanalyst with musicological training, investigates George Ives's psychological influence on his son, emphasizing the trauma inflicted on Charles by his father's untimely death. The author also explores why Ives felt the need to promote his father's reputation. Feder claims that Ives was drawn to compose in order to work through the feelings caused by his father's death and in a larger sense to collaborate posthumously with his father. Some readers may object to Feder's Freudian perspective.

SWAFFORD is a warmly written, highly readable study that critically evaluates the other books discussed here. The author, a composer himself, offers a biography that reflects a composer's perspective. Although this volume contains several original insights, it is especially valuable for its synthesis of recent scholarship. This study is therefore a good starting point for an exploration of Ives literature. Along with a review of topics dating back to Cowell and Cowell, the reader will find up-to-date discussions of Ives's gender attitudes, social outlook, politics, psychology, and medical history. Although critical, Swafford is obviously fond of Ives, and his admiration for the composer is evident throughout this biography.

MICHAEL VON DER LINN

2. Works

Block, Geoffrey, and J. Peter Burkholder, editors, *Charles Ives and the Classical Tradition,* New Haven, Connecticut: Yale University Press, 1996

Burkholder, J. Peter, *All Made of Tunes: Charles Ives and the Uses of Musical Borrowing,* New Haven, Connecticut: Yale University Press, 1995

———, *Charles Ives: The Ideas Behind the Music,* New Haven, Connecticut: Yale University Press, 1985

Cowell, Henry, and Sidney Cowell, *Charles Ives and His Music,* London, Oxford, and New York: Oxford University Press, 1955; 2nd edition, 1969

Henderson, Clayton W., *The Charles Ives Tunebook,* Warren, Michigan: Harmonie Park Press, 1990

Hitchcock, H. Wiley, *Ives,* London: Oxford University Press, 1977; reprint with revisions as *Ives: A Survey of the Music,* Brooklyn, New York: Institute for Studies in American Music, 1980

Lambert, Philip, *The Music of Charles Ives,* New Haven, Connecticut: Yale University Press, 1997

Starr, Larry, *A Union of Diversities: Style in the Music of Charles Ives,* New York: Schirmer Books, 1992

Serious criticism of Ives's music began to appear during the 1920s. Early studies most often portrayed the composer as a pioneering innovator in musical technique. Ives was also considered the first composer to write in a distinctly American idiom. These writings also betray a nationalistic agenda in their attempts to demonstrate that a U.S. composer invented several techniques that would later be adopted by—and attributed to—such individuals as Schoenberg, Stravinsky, and Bartók. This nationalist image persisted into the 1980s, and it continues to influence popular reception of the composer. Although both claims about Ives's artistic primacy and the need to assert the United States' contribution to musical modernism have largely disappeared, these themes persist as a starting point for much contemporary research.

The landmark life-and-works study by COWELL and COWELL was the first book-length examination of the composer. It also offers the most comprehensive exposition of the "Ives legend" outlined above. Although contemporary research has changed attitudes toward Ives in many respects, this volume remains an essential text. The Cowells offer an excellent introduction to Ives's treatment of polyphony, harmony, melody, rhythm, form, instrumentation, and part writing. These general discussions are supplemented by analyses of *Paracelsus,* the *Concord Sonata,* and sketches from the *Universe Symphony.* The reader should keep in mind that the appended list of published works and recordings does not include materials issued after 1968.

HITCHCOCK is not concerned with establishing Ives as a modernist or an "American" composer. His brief study offers a straightforward analytical overview that is both detailed and concise. It is therefore an excellent introduction to Ives's music. As the title of the revised edition suggests, biographical and aesthetic aspects are considered only in passing. This survey is arrayed chronologically with an emphasis on Ives's contributions to the genres in which he worked: songs, choral music, compositions for keyboard, chamber works, and orchestral music. A number of pieces are treated at length. Hitchcock is an astute critic who clearly loves this music. His ability to demonstrate how each work relates to the emergence of Ives's unique compositional voice is especially good. Readers with a limited musical background should not be put off by the study's analytical orientation. Like the Cowells, Hitchcock supplements his technical observations with lucid descriptive prose.

The collection edited by BLOCK and BURKHOLDER disputes the venerable claim that Ives was a quintessentially American composer who rejected the musical techniques and aesthetics of 19th-century Europe. The seven essays in this volume demonstrate instead that he was committed to continuing the classical tradition exemplified by Bach, Beethoven, and Brahms. Ives's reception of the techniques and aesthetics of European art music is examined in the first three essays. The influence of U.S. composers working within the European tradition is also considered. Other contributions explore similarities between Ives and Mahler, Schoenberg, Berg, and Stravinsky. This collection ultimately suggests that the similarities between Ives and these composers reflect a shared musical heritage.

Although Ives is regarded as a modernist composer, his cultural outlook, intellectual tastes, and philosophy of music were rooted firmly in the 19th century. This fact is evident in BURKHOLDER's (1985) groundbreaking intellectual biography, which thoroughly examines Ives's aesthetics and the ideas that influenced them. The development of his thought is considered chronologically. Chapters discuss the intellectual tradition of his family and father, teachers at Yale University, and the influence of transcendentalism. Ives's *Essays before a Sonata* and other writings are analyzed in detail. Although this book does not engage in music analysis, it is recommended for its elucidation of the ideas that governed his compositional thought. Listeners will certainly appreciate the insights into the meaning of Ives's music offered by this engaging study.

One of the primary hallmarks of Ives's music is its extensive use of material adapted from other compositions. This feature is the subject of BURKHOLDER's (1995) study. More than a survey, this important book argues persuasively that an important key to understanding the nature of Ives's music lies in his various uses of borrowed material. This book also offers valuable observations about Ives's treatment of musical form and motivic development. The sections that trace Ives's attempts to integrate quotation with procedures inherited from the European classic-romantic tradition are especially interesting. Burkholder assumes a fairly solid musical background. General readers should not be put off, however, because one can follow his main ideas without the benefit of specialized technical knowledge.

HENDERSON offers the most detailed compilation of vernacular and art music sources used by Ives. This exhaustively researched book is both an indispensable resource and a useful supplement to Burkholder's 1995 volume. Each work, or "tune," is cross-indexed to the appropriate Ives composition. Readers can search by composition, title of quoted work, or melodic incipit. The measure where a quotation first appears clearly, and the instrument(s) that perform it, is indicated as well. Extensive notated examples are also included.

Many listeners are amazed by the plurality of musical styles that are combined in Ives's compositions. STARR uses this characteristic as the starting point for a general theory about the nature of Ives's music, emphasizing the underlying features that unify these different musical types. The author concludes that this eclectic musical collage *is* Ives's style. More important, this reconciliation of disparate genres aims to create a musical reflection of the complexity and ambiguity of life itself. The main argument of this study is complemented by a superb discussion of Ives's "layering" procedures. Starr hopes to address the general reader in this book. To this end, he keeps technical discussion to a minimum.

Ives explored unique compositional ideas throughout his career. LAMBERT explores this experimental side. Contending that this dimension of Ives's music has not been taken very seriously, Lambert seeks primarily to rehabilitate the composer as an innovative pioneer in the language of tonal music. This book combines general discussion of compositional practices with detailed analyses of "experimental" works created to examine specific compositional problems, such as *Tone Roads no. 1* and *Study no. 5*. In this respect, Lambert has done a great service by analyzing works that are usually overlooked. A note of caution, however: although Lambert's ideas are outlined clearly, the full extent of his analyses will be difficult to comprehend if the reader lacks a solid grounding in post-tonal theory.

MICHAEL VON DER LINN

J

Janáček, Leoš 1854–1928

Czech composer

Beckerman, Michael Brim, *Janáček as Theorist*, New York: Pendragon Press, 1994

Beckerman, Michael Brim, and Glen Bauer, editors, *Janáček and Czech Music: Proceedings of the International Conference (Saint Louis 1988)*, New York: Pendragon Press, 1995

Chisholm, Erik, *The Operas of Leoš Janáček*, Oxford: Pergamon Press, 1971

Ewans, Michael, *Janáček's Tragic Operas*, London: Faber, and Bloomington: Indiana University Press, 1977

Hollander, Hans, *Leoš Janáček; His Life and His Work*, translated by Paul Hamburger, London: Calder, and New York: St. Martin's Press, 1963

Janáček, Leoš, *Intimate Letters, Leoš Janáček to Kamila Stösslova*, London: Faber, and Princeton, New Jersey: Princeton University Press, 1994

———, *Janáček: Leaves from His Life*, edited and translated by Vilem Tausky and Margaret Tausky, London: Kahn and Averill, and New York: Taplinger, 1982

———, *Janáček's Uncollected Essays on Music*, edited and translated by Mirka Zemanova, London: Boyars, 1989

———, *Jenůfa; Katya Kabanova*, London: Calder, and New York: Riverrun Press, 1985

———, *Leoš Janáček: Letters and Reminiscences*, edited by Bohumir Stedron, Prague: Artia, 1955

Susskind, Charles, *Janáček and Brod*, New Haven, Connecticut: Yale University Press, 1985

Tyrrell, John, *Janáček's Operas, A Documentary Account*, London: Faber, and Princeton, New Jersey: Princeton University Press, 1992

Tyrrell, John, editor, *Kát'a Kabanová*, Cambridge: Cambridge University Press, 1982

Vogel, Jaroslav, *Leoš Janáček: His Life and Works*, translated by Gerladine Thomsen-Muchova, London: Hamlyn, 1962; revised edition, as *Leoš Janáček: A Biography*, edited by Karel Janovicky, New York: Norton, and London: Orbis, 1981

The life and works of the Czech composer Leoš Janáček are relatively unknown despite his importance to early 20th-century music. In addition to the language barrier, the composer's works have remained obscured from view because of the ways in which historians discuss music of the late 19th and early 20th centuries. His musical style eludes simple classification into one of the many "isms," such as postromanticism or atonalism, often used to define music of this period. Unlike his compatriots Antonin Dvořák and Bedřich Smetana, Janáček is not easily classified as a nationalist composer, although he wrote many works on Czech and Slavic subjects. Finally, unlike Schoenberg or Stravinsky, he was not part of any school or movement and left few pupils to continue his work.

The literature on Janáček in English consists of documentary materials, biographies, operatic studies and surveys, collections of essays, and specialized studies. While a majority of English-language works is of a documentary and biographical nature, increased study of the composer in both Great Britain and the United States, as well as greater access to archives in the Czech Republic, will undoubtedly produce more critical, analytical, and interpretative studies in the future.

The earliest collection of letters and reminiscences is JANÁČEK (1955), a useful compilation of selected excerpts translated into English from the original Czech. The activities of Janáček as an avid writer of feullitons for daily newspapers is chronicled in JANÁČEK (1982), which gives the reader a sense of the composer's idiosyncratic language and writing style. His ideas on speech-melody and other musical issues can also be gleaned from the documents presented in this anthology. A similar, but more diverse collection is JANÁČEK (1989), which presents a wide selection of the composer's prose writings. Included in the 47 essays are reviews of concerts and interviews conducted by Janáček, his thoughts on the arts and other composers, his travel impressions, and his analyses of speech and song. Both the 1982 and 1989 collections are well translated and capture the flavor of Janáček's stream-of-consciousness style and odd turns of phrase.

Undoubtedly, the most significant contributions in this category are those of British scholar John Tyrrell. TYRRELL (1992) offers details about the operas of Janáček, and it presents letters, reminiscences, and reviews that highlight the conception, creation, and production of the composer's nine operas. Additionally, JANÁČEK (1994), Tyrrell's edition and translation of the correspondence between the composer and his muse, Mrs. Kamila Stösslová, allows a view of the creative and private world of the couple through more than 600 letters. Tyrrell includes copious annotations to aid the reader not familiar with Janáček's milieu, as well as a glossary of personalities mentioned in the correspondence.

The most comprehensive and balanced view of the composer's life and works is found in VOGEL. This study is the only biography of Janáček that attempts to cover his entire oeuvre, rather than focusing primarily on those works known outside of the composer's homeland. Vogel's discussion is replete with musical examples and offers an excellent introduction to the composer and his works. The study by HOLLANDER is significant because it presents the composer and his works in a larger European context. Hollander's incisive comments on the nature and style of Janáček's works are excellent and well documented and generally tend to be more discerning than those of Vogel.

A more specialized biography is the study by SUSSKIND, which details the working relationship between the composer and Max Brod, who translated many of Janáček's operas for the German stage. The author also provides a good introduction to the mature operas of Janáček and the reputation his works have had outside the Czech lands. The relationship of the composer and Kamila Stösslová, and her effect on his compositions, figures prominently in this survey.

Full-length studies of the composer's oeuvre have focused mostly on his operatic works. The best and most detailed dramatic analysis of the five later tragic operas of Janáček is EWANS. The earlier survey by CHISHOLM contains discussions of all nine of the operas as well as an analysis of a scene from the last opera, *From the House of the Dead*. Unfortunately, Chisholm's observations are often marred by inaccuracies, and thus the book must therefore be used with caution.

Studies of individual dramatic vocal works include an introductory manual to the operas *Jenůfa* and *Kát'a Kabanová* by (JANÁČEK [1985]), which includes an excellent essay by Karel Brusak on *Jenůfa* as well as an informative review of early 20th-century Czech realism by Jan Smaczny. TYRELL (1982) offers a comprehensive study of *Kát'a Kabanová* and includes such topics as the genesis of the libretto and Janáček's interest in Russian culture, as well as a thorough musical analysis of the opera.

BECKERMAN and BAUER is a large collection of essays on Janáček drawn from the proceedings from the international conference held at Washington University, St. Louis, in 1988. All papers are in English and cover such topics as Janáček and Czech opera, problems of analysis, editing, and reception of the composer's works, and a substantial section on the unfinished Danube symphony.

Janáček's activities as a theorist have largely eluded scholars due to the composer's difficult prose style and his use of a highly idiomatic vocabulary. The only full-length study devoted to the topic of composer as theorist is BECKERMAN, which provides the aesthetic background to Janáček's musical thinking and illuminates the various theoretical terms used by the composer.

DIANE M. PAIGE

Japan

Adriaansz, Willem, *The Kumiuta and Danmono Traditions of Japanese Koto Music*, Berkeley: University of California Press, 1973

Brandon, James R., et al., *Studies in Kabuki: Its Acting, Music, and Historical Context*, Honolulu: University Press of Hawaii, 1979

Garfias, Robert, *Music of a Thousand Autumns: The Togaku Style of Japanese Court Music*, Berkeley: University of California Press, 1975

Gerstle, Andrew, et al., *Theater as Music: The Bunraku Play "Mt. Imo and Mt. Se, an Exemplary Tale of Womanly Virtue,"* Ann Arbor: Center for Japanese Studies, University of Michigan, 1990

Harich-Schneider, Eta, *A History of Japanese Music*, London: Oxford University Press, 1973

Kondo, Jo, and Jaoquim Bernitez, editors, *Flute and Shakuhachi*, an entire issue of *Contemporary Music Review* 8, Part 2 (1994)

Malm, William P., *Japanese Music and Musical Instruments*, Rutland, Vermont: Tuttle, 1959

Ortolani, Benito, *The Japanese Theatre: From Shamanistic Ritual to Contemporary Pluralism*, Leiden, Netherlands: Brill, 1990; revised edition, Princeton: New Jersey: Princeton University Press, 1995

Takahashi, Chikuzan, *The Autobiography of Takahashi Chikuzan: Adventures of a Tsugaru-Jamisen Musician*, translated by Gerald Groemer, Warren, Michigan: Harmonie Park Press, 1991

Tamba, Akira, *The Musical Structure of No*, Tokyo: Tokai University Press, 1981

Tokumaru, Yoshihiko, and Osamu Yamaguti, editors, *The Oral and the Literate in Music*, Tokyo: Academia Music, 1986

Japanese music culture is uniquely shaped by large-scale adoption of foreign musics, controlled transmission of music knowledge and repertory along institutionalized genealogies of musicians, conscientious preservation of cultural-musical heritage, and relentless pursuit of expressions through sounds. As a result, Japanese music culture features a number of self-contained traditions of musics that demand distinctive methods of study. Music historians, for example, trace the exemplars of *gagaku* (court music), which were imported to Japan from Tang China (618–907), or reconstruct the creative world of Zeami (1363–1443), the founder of traditional *noh* drama, while anthropologists and sociologists can examine the hierarchical communities of blind musicians who developed *koto* and *shamisen* music in Edo Japan (1603–1868) or decipher the meanings of love and double suicides that were dramatized on the *bunraku* (puppet theater) stage. Given such a diversity of scholars and research interests, it is no surprise that English works addressing Japanese music culture range from technical analyses of specific musical works to humanistic studies that include few references to the music's sounds.

Among general introductions, MALM is a modern classic. It begins with an overview of Japanese music culture and then offers nine chapters on specific genres or groups of related genres, such as *gagaku, noh, koto,* and *shamisen* music, describing their histories, instruments, stylistic features, and performance practices. The volume shows signs of aging but has not yet been superseded.

Among English accounts of Japanese music history, HARICH-SCHNEIDER is distinguished by its selective coverage and methodology. The bulk of this large tome is devoted to *gagaku* and other ancient and medieval genres, their documented evidence, and the introduction of Western music to Japan in modern times. For example, the 12th-century *Shinzei kogaku zu* (Shinzei's Illustration of Ancient Music) is discussed at length and its informative illustrations faithfully reproduced. In contrast, *shamisen* music, a representative type of traditional Japanese music since the Edo period, is only briefly discussed over several pages. Currently the only detailed English publication on sources of ancient Japanese music, the volume is an important reference, despite its limitations.

Among technical studies of specific genres written for specialists and connoisseurs, the following three titles are representative. GARFIAS analyzes *togaku*, a specific style/repertory in the Japanese court music of *gagaku*. After a brief historical introduction, the author introduces *togaku* by describing its instruments, theory, notation, and performance practices and by analyzing two representative works.

ADRIAANSZ offers an equally technical examination of the song cycles (*kumiuta*) and instrumental (*danmono*) repertories of *koto* music. After brief introductions to historical sources of the genre, the instrument, it tunings, notation, and playing techniques, he analyzes melodic, rhythmic, and formal structures and principles of the genre. The volume concludes with a convenient anthology of *koto* music transcribed into staff notation; English translations of sung texts of the vocal pieces are also included.

TAMBA is a technical study of the music of *noh* drama. After a brief chapter on the history of the genre, the author describes in great detail techniques of *noh* chanting, the two kinds of chants, organological features of the *noh* flute and drums, formulaic patterns of instrumental and vocal music, notation, and other musical elements. When supplemented with critical listening of the music being described, and contextualized with cultural and historical data, the technical discussions in these three volumes constitute solid foundations for in-depth understandings of Japanese music.

Much traditional Japanese music developed as a component of theater or other forms of multimedia performance arts. Reflecting this fact, many social and cultural studies of Japanese culture and theater make crucial reading for understanding Japanese musics in their contexts. Among these works, ORTOLANI's history of the Japanese theater, which the author defines broadly, is outstanding. It clearly explains historical developments of and interrelationships among all major forms of traditional Japanese performance arts, including, for example, the *kagura* ritual, the *bugaku* dances, and the theaters of *noh, kabuki,* and *bunraku*. In addition, the volume describes 20th-century genres, such as the *shingeki* (new drama) and the Takarazuka revue, and provides a sketch of Western scholarship on the topic. The lack of discussion about music in the volume is typical of social and cultural studies and does not render the information less relevant.

Realizing the limitation of cultural studies that avoid musical discussion, and vice versa, some scholars have produced interdisciplinary volumes, the following two of which are representative. BRANDON et al. offer concise and informative descriptions of the social environment of *kabuki*, acting practices and aesthetics, and narrative and offstage music of the theater. With many illustrations, musical examples, and selected bibliography, this volume makes a most informative introduction to the world of *kabuki*.

Similarly, the volume by GERSTLE et al. offers an interdisciplinary view of *bunraku* by presenting revealing descriptions and study materials for a representative play, *Mt. Imo and Mt. Se*. The book includes historical reviews of the genre, its performance tradition, playwrights, and performers; discussions of its musical conventions and notation; a full translation of the sung script of a central scene, "The Mountains Scene"; a cassette recording of a performance of the scene; and musical analysis and comments on the music as performed. Any reader who takes time to study the insightful descriptions and detailed study materials, which can be overwhelming, will be rewarded with an eye-opening experience with *bunraku*.

Four current English publications on Japanese music provide glimpses of insiders' understandings. TAKAHASHI's autobiography tells the *shamisen* player's life story, tracing his rise from a blind beggar musician in the 1930s to a popular star of traditional Japanese music in the 1970s. Typical of autobiographies, the narrative is personal and anecdotal, but it still furnishes many insights on the dynamics of traditional Japanese music. Takahashi's careful recounting of what he learned from his teachers, for example, underscores Japanese esteem of formal teaching and authentic sources. By describing the way in which he learned music from other musicians and recordings, Takahashi also reveals how individual musicians can creatively expand their repertories and styles.

TOKUMARU and YAMAGUTI is the result of an international music conference held in Tokyo in 1985. It includes articles by a number of leading Japanese scholars. Yamaguti's article discusses musical transformations during performances by examining various aspects of *koto* music, including, for example, bodily movements during performances and the learning/memorization of instrumental melodies using vocables (*shoka*). Tokumaru's article provides an insightful analysis of *shamisen* music by considering three interactions between musical thoughts and practices: the fingerboard of the musical instrument as an "ordered terrain of pitches," musicians' cognizance and use of melodic patterns in the music, and verbal terms with which musicians discuss their music. Tsuge's article offers an insider's explanation of how the sketchy notation of *koto* song cycles (*kumiuta*) not only served as effective memory aids for musicians but also allowed them to flexibly and creatively maintain fine details of vocal ornaments learned through oral transmission. Offering a wealth of technical details and embodying Japanese discussion strategies, these articles do not make easy readings, but they vividly demonstrate indigenous scholarship on Japanese music.

Under the editorship of KONDO and BERNITEZ, *Contemporary Music Review* brought out a special issue on the Japanese *shakuhachi*. Written by composers and scholars interested in Japanese and Western contemporary music, the collection shows *shakuhachi* music in a new light, demonstrating how it adjusts to a changing world and becomes a source and a means for contemporary expressions by both Japanese and non-Japanese composers. By presenting different types of essays, ranging from Takemitsu Toru's aesthetic statement to Ralph Samuelson's analysis of the *shakuhachi* and the American composer, the collection vividly projects the musical interface between Japan and the West.

JOSEPH S.C. LAM

See also Mode: Non-Western

Java *see* Indonesia; Mode: Non-Western

Jazz: Early

Armstrong, Louis, *Louis Armstrong: In His Own Words: Selected Writings,* edited by Thomas Brothers, New York: Oxford University Press, 1999

Bergreen, Laurence, *Louis Armstrong: An Extravagant Life,* New York: Broadway Books, and London: HarperCollins, 1997

Berrett, Joshua, editor, *The Louis Armstrong Companion: Eight Decades of Commentary,* New York: Schirmer Books, 1999

Bushell, Garvin, as told to Mark Tucker, *Jazz from the Beginning,* Ann Arbor: University of Michigan Press, 1988

Collier, James Lincoln, *Louis Armstrong: An American Genius,* New York: Oxford University Press, 1983

Giddins, Gary, *Satchmo,* New York: Doubleday, 1988

Hadlock, Richard, *Jazz Masters of the 20s,* New York: Macmillan, 1965

Hennessey, Thomas J., *From Jazz to Swing: African-American Jazz Musicians and Their Music, 1890–1935,* Detroit, Michigan: Wayne State University Press, 1994

Kennedy, Rick, *Jelly Roll, Bix, and Hoagy: Gennett Studios and the Birth of Recorded Jazz,* Bloomington: Indiana University Press, 1994

Kenney, William Howland, *Chicago Jazz: A Cultural History, 1904–1930,* New York: Oxford University Press, 1993

Lomax, Alan, *Mister Jelly Roll: The Fortunes of Jelly Roll Morton, New Orleans Creole and "Inventor of Jazz,"* New York: Grosset and Dunlap, 1950; 3rd edition, London: Cassell, 1955

Marquis, Donald M., *In Search of Buddy Bolden, First Man of Jazz,* Baton Rouge: Louisiana State University Press, 1978

Morton, Jelly Roll, *The Collected Piano Music,* edited by James Dapogny, Washington, D.C.: Smithsonian Institution Press, and New York: Schirmer Books, 1982

Ogren, Kathy L, *The Jazz Revolution: Twenties America and the Meaning of Jazz,* New York: Oxford University Press, 1989

Peretti, Burton W., *The Creation of Jazz: Music, Race, and Culture in Urban America,* Urbana: University of Illinois Press, 1992

Schuller, Gunther, *Early Jazz: Its Roots and Musical Development,* New York: Oxford University Press, 1968

Sudhalter, Richard M., *Lost Chords: White Musicians and Their Contribution to Jazz, 1915–1945,* New York: Oxford University Press, 1999

"Early Jazz"—the conventional term for jazz before 1930—emerged as a flourishing area of jazz studies in the 1960s, although widespread serious interest in and publications about the music have existed for much longer than that. The discipline has developed in several directions, including biographies of major figures; oral histories and autobiographies of leading, neglected, and obscure musicians; histories of musical style; and cultural history. Through the 1980s, much serious jazz history and criticism grew from the impulse to demonstrate the artistic worth and cultural legitimacy of jazz, thus the emphasis on identifying and describing canonical sound recordings and the styles of the musicians who made them. In the 1990s, cultural history became the leading subgenre of early jazz studies, thereby confirming that previous critics had successfully established a legitimate field of musical study while also drawing attention to topics those critics had largely neglected. Cultural historians have studied the ways in which forces such as migration, commerce, mass media, and racial interaction shaped jazz. They have analyzed contemporary writings about jazz and distilled larger themes that reveal currents in American culture in general. For the most part, however, they have not woven commentary on music into their interpretations. At this writing, then, an integrated history of early jazz—one that successfully combines cultural and musical analysis—has yet to be written.

SCHULLER's landmark text offers the first comprehensive analytical study of early jazz music. Inspired by a tradition of serious music criticism dating back to the 1930s, Schuller directed his book toward "the 'classically' trained musician or composer, who may never have concerned himself with jazz." A wealth of descriptive form diagrams and musical transcriptions from jazz recordings accompany Schuller's incisive analyses of the music of Louis Armstrong, Jelly Roll Morton, early Duke Ellington, and others. If the transcriptions now seem overly literal and complex, they reflect Schuller's strong impulse to demonstrate the musical sophistication of an idiom long neglected by serious, trained musicians. Also, his effort to claim legitimate artistry for jazz musicians leads him to be overly critical of commercial forces, concentrating solely on their negative effects on the music. Three decades of jazz research and autobiographies have changed the field, but Schuller stands out as a pioneer jazz historian whose musical insights remain fresh and useful.

Originally published in 1965, HADLOCK's book remains a useful guide by a knowledgeable critic to the music of several jazz musicians who flourished in the 1920s, including Louis Armstrong, Earl Hines, Bix Beiderbecke, Fats Waller, Fletcher Henderson, Bessie Smith, and others. Each chapter focuses on a single musician or group of musicians. Some of Hadlock's commentary has been supplanted by the tremendous growth of jazz studies, but the volume reflects a considered critical perspective on early jazz that was rare before the publication of Schuller's book.

At nearly 900 pages, SUDHALTER's work offers a powerful complement to standard histories of jazz that stress the innovations and artistry of African-American musicians. Included here are detailed, vivid discussions of white jazz musicians who exerted considerable influence in their own day only to be neglected by later generations. Sudhalter devotes entire chapters to such early jazz musicians as the New Orleans Rhythm Kings, Miff Mole, Red Nichols, Adrian Rollini, Bud Freeman, Frank Trumbauer, the Casa Loma Orchestra, and the bands of Jean Goldkette and Ben Pollack. A chapter titled "Bix Beiderbecke and Some of His Friends" offers fresh insights on Beiderbecke, about whom Sudhalter and Philip R. Evans published an excellent biography in 1974. Along the way, Sudhalter demonstrates a patient awareness of the racial and cultural ironies inherent in his subjects' lives and works.

OGREN analyzes the heated controversy surrounding jazz in the 1920s, when the music first reached a broad swath of Americans through its dissemination on sound recordings and the radio and in nightclubs and ballrooms. Her thorough investigation of printed sources such as newspapers, magazines, literature, and poetry allows her to demonstrate the complex and contradictory attitudes toward jazz held by whites and blacks alike. From the jazz controversy, she extrapolates a perspective on American culture in general, showing how "For many Americans, to argue about jazz was to argue about the nature of change itself."

PERETTI offers a cultural history with high ambitions: "to unite and redirect three major streams of jazz studies that have proven of limited use to cultural historians: musicology, social science fieldwork, and aficionado history." Toward that end, he places early jazz "within the great contexts of American culture—urbanization, race relations, individual development, professionalization, and capitalism." With such a broad scope, the book can offer no more than a survey of each theme, suggesting avenues for further research. Indeed, as Peretti concedes, "stronger sociological analyses can be made on a smaller scale." In particular, his perspectives on race tend to oversimplify a complex and far-from-monolithic field of activity and outlook. Reacting against the conventional demonization of commerce, Peretti accepts commerce as a fact and notes that "the musicians were not as nostalgic for a folklike past as some jazz historians might be today. . . . On the contrary, musicians found the power of the new broadcast technology stimulating" and experienced many benefits of the commodification of jazz through sound recording and radio.

Drawing from newspapers, trade papers, sound recordings, interviews, and autobiographies, KENNEY presents a detailed examination of the social history of jazz in a specific time and place: 1920s Chicago. That specific focus enables the author to present a cultural history of jazz with a more complex texture than Peretti's. Kenney depicts jazz musicians as crossing boundaries between entertainment and art and between jazz and other kinds of popular music, in a field where such boundaries were blurry at best and even nonexistent for many musicians and listeners. He concludes that "jazz in 1920s Chicago was neither just folk music, nor merely commercial entertainment, nor solely concert hall art, but instead it was a synthesis of these elements. In the process, it created an original, indigenous, richly varied musical form."

Distilled from a still-useful 1973 dissertation, HENNESSEY's book presents another cultural history of early jazz as "an art form and entertainment medium" that was a product of the transformation of the United States "from a rural, handmade, homemade culture to an urban, mass-produced, mass-consumed culture." In the process, jazz itself was transformed "from a primarily local music rooted in black folk traditions to the tightly managed product of a national industry controlled by white businessmen and aimed at a predominantly white mass market." Both a chronological and geographical survey, the book identifies the particular circumstances leading to the development of jazz in various cities and regions of the United States. The author considers issues such as the Great Migration of blacks from the rural South to the urban North, the rise of public dancing and ballrooms, and the impact of the phonograph and radio.

KENNEDY offers a unique and invaluable perspective on early jazz by focusing on the history of Gennett Records, "the small Indiana label . . . [that] released the debut recordings not only of Armstrong, Oliver, Beiderbecke, and Morton, but also of Hoagy Carmichael, Earl Hines, Muggsy Spanier, Johnny Dodds, Leon Roppolo, and other jazz pioneers." Kennedy traces Gennett's roots in the Starr Piano Company of Richmond, Indiana, and its development as a groundbreaking record company for jazz, blues, and country music in the 1920s. The book grew out of research begun when the author was a newspaper reporter in Richmond, and its compelling, well-written narrative weaves together a wealth of primary source material, including the company's daily recording ledgers, interviews of former Starr and Gennett employees, firsthand accounts by early jazz musicians, and the original 78-rpm records.

Three major biographies of Louis Armstrong were published in the 1980s and 1990s. COLLIER has written a compelling narrative of Armstrong's career. The book, however, seems intent on questioning the claim of genius stated in its subtitle; although Collier acknowledges Armstrong's extraordinary impact on 20th-century music, the author also characterizes the last two-thirds of Armstrong's career as a "bitter waste of his astonishing talent." GIDDINS, a long-time jazz critic for the *Village Voice,* offers an intelligent, concise, interpretive biography in the guise of a lavishly illustrated coffee-table book. The titles of the book's two halves—"The Entertainer as Artist" and "The Artist as Entertainer"—represent the complexity and contradictions Giddins finds in his subject. BERGREEN's book is a vividly written chronicle of Armstrong's life that draws extensively from Armstrong's own writings and from written and oral accounts of Armstrong by his contemporaries. The book's effectiveness is sometimes compromised by Bergreen's lack of musical background, which leads him to make several misstatements about music in general and jazz in particular.

Two collections of writings by and about Armstrong were issued in 1999. BERRETT offers an entry in Schirmer's companion series devoted to major jazz musicians. The volume features a few selected, excerpted writings by Armstrong and many essays about his life and music by other musicians, critics, and scholars. Each entry is preceded by a brief helpful summary placing the article and its author in context. ARMSTRONG focuses exclusively on Armstrong's own writings—including several texts that were previously unpublished—that shed new light on the major figure of early jazz. Included here are "The Armstrong Story," a section cut from the end of Armstrong's autobiography, *Satchmo: My Life in New Orleans* (1954); and "The Goffin Notebooks," which comprise material Armstrong sent to the French writer Robert Goffin during the preparation of the biography, *Horn of Plenty.* Beyond its inclusion of new material, the editor's thoughtful introductory essay develops the idea that "Armstrong saw himself as a writer" who sought to "master diverse verbal styles" in an attempt to offer a depiction of speech. The book may be read not only as a record of the life and values of a major American musician but also as a verbal analog to his playing and singing and as a memoir of a "central witness to the Great Migration" of African-Americans from the rural South to the urban North.

Based on recorded interviews conducted at the Library of Congress in 1938, LOMAX's book stands as a pioneering work in the oral history of jazz; Jelly Roll Morton, generally considered the first great jazz composer, tells the story of his life and of music in turn-of-the-century New Orleans. The story is related with an engaging, although sometimes tangled, mix of fact and legend, including Morton's famous claim to be the "inventor of jazz." Lomax, an important folklorist of African-American music, provides footnotes and interludes that expand upon Morton's own commentary. An extended appendix includes reprints of sheet-music versions of Morton's compositions and transcriptions of a few of the pieces he sang and played in the Library of Congress recordings.

MORTON's collection, another pioneering work, comprises the first scholarly edition of music by a jazz composer. The edition contains 40 pieces by Morton, most of them meticulously transcribed from sound recordings of the 1920s and 1930s. Several are presented in their original published version. A set of concise introductory essays considers Morton's compositions, piano playing, and colorful life. The edition also includes an explanation of editorial method (and the unique challenges of preparing a critical edition of a jazz musician) and a chronology of compositions—a much-needed feature for an edition on a musician who sometimes exaggerated his own importance in jazz history.

MARQUIS strips away the accretion of legend and sets the record straight on Buddy Bolden, the cornet player who became romanticized as the first tragic figure of jazz. Bolden's band was popular in turn-of-the-century New Orleans, and Bolden himself was renowned for his powerful, blues-tinged tone and for his rapid fall into alcoholism and mental illness. Using a vast range of primary sources—including vital statistical records from the city of New Orleans; certificates of birth, marriage, and death; police department records; letters; newspapers; and many other local history sources—Marquis manages to paint a vivid picture of Bolden and the city that nurtured jazz.

The 1980s and 1990s saw a burst of memoirs, autobiographies, and oral histories of early jazz musicians. Some of the most illuminating of these texts come from relatively obscure musicians who lived long lives. BUSHELL and TUCKER is one of these titles, and it is a model of the as-told-to autobiography. Bushell was a reed player who served as a sideman in the bands of Sam Wooding, Fletcher Henderson, Cab Calloway, and Chick Webb. Much later, he performed with modern jazz greats Eric Dolphy and John Coltrane. Tucker is a musicologist with a firm grasp of the historical import of Bushell's remarks. Thanks to Bushell's sharp memory, the book contains fascinating sketches of early jazz and blues musicians and insightful commentary on race and culture. It also includes two useful appendices: an annotated discography featuring complete recording information and Bushell's own commentary on the records he made from 1921 to 1964, and a listing of musicians and performers mentioned in the book.

JEFFREY MAGEE

Jazz: Dixieland

Berendt, Joachim E., *The Jazz Book: From Ragtime to Fusion and Beyond,* translated by H. Bredigkeit et al., Westport, Connecticut: Hill, 1982; 6th edition, Brooklyn, New York: Hill, 1992

Brunn, Harry O., *The Story of the Original Dixieland Jazz Band,* Baton Rogue: Louisiana State University Press, 1960

Collier, James Lincoln, *Jazz: The American Theme Song,* New York: Oxford University Press, 1993

Pasternak, Judith Mahoney, *Dixieland: The Birth of Jazz,* New York: Friedman/Fairfax, 1995

Schuller, Gunther, *Early Jazz: Its Roots and Musical Development,* New York, Oxford University Press, 1968

Smith, Charles Edward, "White New Orleans," in *Jazzmen,* edited by Frederic Ramsey and Charles Edward Smith, New York: Harcourt Brace, 1939

In the early 19th century, the mint in French New Orleans issued a $10 note called a *dix* (ten in French). American riverboatmen who traded their goods for this currency called it the *dixie;* hence, the term now generally associated with the South originally referred specifically to New Orleans. That Dixieland jazz originated in New Orleans is certain; beyond that, however, opinions on Dixieland differ. While the majority of sources define it as jazz of the early New Orleans school, some maintain that it was the idiom of white musicians influenced by or imitating the African American and Creole styles that permeated the city's musical culture. Others claim that the name was derived from Nick LaRocca's Original Dixieland Jazz Band, which, during its brief period of fame, set the pace for other groups, such as Jimmy Durante's Original New Orleans Jazz Band. Dixieland musicians have been linked to brass-band and ragtime traditions in New Orleans as well as to the musicians who entertained at the bordellos in Storeyville and the orchestral ensembles that played during Mardi Gras. All sources, however, agree that Dixieland is synonymous with traditional jazz, which, after its decline in the 1920s, enjoyed a revival in the 1940s and 1950s.

BRUNN's readable account of Nick LaRocca and the Original Dixieland Jazz Band, which the author credits as the first group of the white New Orleans "Jass" revolution, is based on personal interviews with LaRocca and on memorabilia gathered from him and other musicians involved in early Dixieland. Brunn documents the history of the band from its formation and early gigs to its bitter dissolution. Stylistically known for their frantically paced music and characteristic devices (such as the trombone roar highlighting the text "Hold that tiger!" in their hit "Tiger Rag"), the band traveled widely, even to England, creating a taste for jazz in Europe. Although it offers a colorful introduction to the milieu and cast of characters in one of the most important early Dixieland groups—indeed, the first to record the music—Brunn's book, as Schuller notes, aims at creating a legend and fails to acknowledge the band's debt to contemporary African-American groups.

Although SCHULLER devotes only 13 pages to Dixieland, he manages to trace its origins to the white New Orleans ragtime groups, such as those organized by drummer Jack "Papa" Laine, and discusses its development in Durante's band and other groups, such as the Famous Jazz Band and the Louisiana Five. Schuller also includes brief explanations of Dixieland's musical style, which he terms New Orleans polyphony.

SMITH also maintains that Dixieland's beginnings can be traced to musicians who played in groups founded by Laine. This cult of white jazzmen, originally ragtime players, developed a style of hot music produced by five- and six-piece ensembles. Their main influences, he maintains, were the local African-American bands, especially those ragtime groups popular in the first decade of the 20th century. BERENDT also describes Dixieland as hot or intense music; however, he credits its genesis to New Orleans' multiethnic heritage (African-American, Creole, and European). Berendt often speaks subjectively, however, especially when he characterizes Dixieland as less expressive than its African-American jazz counterpart. Yet he accurately concludes that the story of Dixieland is more than simply an issue of black music versus white music.

A more complete musical discussion can be found by searching through portions of COLLIER's book. The author explains how Dixieland players altered the marching-band texture by cutting back each section to a single instrument, with guitar and string bass often substituting for drums and tuba. The addition of the violin continued the string tradition begun in indoor dance ensembles. Mentioning the earliest recordings of Dixieland, Collier then follows its demise in the wake of new directions taken in the late 1920s by Duke Ellington, Louis Armstrong, and Bix Beiderbecke. He also discusses the Dixieland revival, which was particularly strong among white college audiences influenced by African-American jazz greats such as Armstrong. Collier, however, suggests that Dixieland, not unlike the symphonic jazz of Paul Whiteman, would not be classified as jazz based on today's definition of the term.

PASTERNAK's book blurs a strict discussion of Dixieland by including references to the music of the prewar South, indeed going as far back as the African diaspora and minstrelsy. Perhaps the book's subtitle best describes the author's intent, for she presents an elementary study of the birth of jazz in general with some references to the musical phenomenon known as Dixieland. Although not classifying as a true history of Dixieland, the book is a useful iconography, including photographs of all the major players and ensembles in both early Dixieland and its mid-century revival.

DENISE GALLO

Jazz: Swing

Collier, James Lincoln, *Benny Goodman and the Swing Era*, New York: Oxford University Press, 1989

Gridley, Mark C., *Jazz Styles: History and Analysis*, Englewood Cliffs, New Jersey: Prentice Hall, 1978; 6th edition, 1997

Korall, Burt, *Drummin' Men: The Heartbeat of Jazz, The Swing Years*, New York: Schirmer Books, 1990

Schuller, Gunther, *The Swing Era: The Development of Jazz, 1930–1945*, New York: Oxford University Press, 1989

Simon, George T., *The Big Bands*, New York: Macmillan, 1967; 4th edition, New York: Schirmer Books, and London: Collier Macmillan, 1981

Stowe, David W., *Swing Changes: Big Band Jazz in New Deal America*, Cambridge, Massachusetts: Harvard University Press, 1994

Tirro, Frank, *Jazz: A History*, New York: Norton, 1977; 2nd edition, 1993

Tucker, Mark, editor, *The Duke Ellington Reader*, New York: Oxford University Press, 1993

The term *swing* has two meanings: it can refer to a style of jazz performance (not discussed in this essay), or it can be defined as a chronological time period in which big bands dominated popular music in the United States. The big bands (which used multiple numbers of trumpets, trombones, and saxophones, resulting in groups of 13 to 18 or more players) were a progressive expansion of the small "traditional" or "Dixieland" jazz groups centered around New Orleans in the early 20th century. During the latter 1920s, instruments were gradually added to these small combos, and by the early 1930s, a new style emerged that became *the* popular music of its time. In contrast to the collective improvisational style prevalent in earlier jazz, swing used written arrangements that required each musician to play a specified part. Bands such as those led by Duke Ellington and Fletcher Henderson stressed improvisation within the framework of the band's arrangements. Other musicians (Glenn Miller, for example) emphasized the overall sound of the band and swing's appeal as dance music. Whatever the approach, the musicians of the swing era were, as a rule, more musically sophisticated and instrumentally proficient than their predecessors. The popularity of swing continues to the present but is confined to a much smaller audience (the current neo-swing movement notwithstanding) than it enjoyed during its peak of the 1930s and 1940s. Modern trends in jazz today play a large part in attracting young people to jazz performance. Big band jazz is routinely taught as part of the musical curriculum in most high schools in the United States and continues to flourish in colleges and universities throughout the world.

SIMON's was one of the first, and still one of the most complete, retrospectives on the swing era. Although its style is decidedly "folksy" and overtly nostalgic, the book is a wealth of information on big bands written by someone who knew many of the musicians and was a practitioner himself (Simon was the drummer in Glenn Miller's first band). A portion of the book concerns itself with many of the peripheral institutions surrounding the musicians (recording studios, the press, etc.), but the bulk of the volume is devoted to stories on, and photos of, the leaders and the sidemen who made up the big bands. Collectively, there are historical examinations of more than 70 of the major groups and capsule summaries on the achievements of some 200 others. What the book lacks in detail and scholarly erudition it makes up for in scope and breadth of coverage. It is essential reading for persons interested in the "flavor" of the swing era.

The work of SCHULLER is, without question, the most exhaustively detailed and scholarly work on the big bands yet written. Its main text is nearly 900 pages long; it has two appendices, an eight-page glossary, and an index of some 400 items. In addition, it contains more than 500 musical examples, including transcriptions of some of the finest jazz solos on record. Some of these examples allow the reader to make notational comparisons of the distinctive sounds achieved by many bands (for example, Duke Ellington's *Pickin's* with Glenn Miller's *Moonlight Serenade*). The depth of this study, however, goes beyond music and personalities to evaluate historical context; as Schuller notes, "No art or act of creativity stands in isolation, self-contained and uninfluenced by its times." To be sure, this study is not light reading (those well versed in music theory will appreciate the harmonic interrelational chart Schuller includes), but it is a rewarding experience for anyone seeking to understand the overall cultural experience of the 1930s and 1940s.

STOWE takes many of the social and cultural issues raised in Schuller to a deeper level by placing the music of the 1930s and early 1940s within the context of political, racial, and gender-sensitive issues of the period. Stowe provides a depth to this epoch lacking in other studies that focus on the music, musicians, and the popularity of swing. Although some of Stowe's conclusions are controversial (e.g. "the relationship between swing and the [Communist] left carried benefits for both sides"), the importance of the issues he raises is beyond reproach. Among the subjects covered are the relationship between Benny Goodman and the Communist party in the 1930s, the cultural pluralism of swing "ideology," racial discrimination at Carnegie Hall concerts and within the American Federation of Musicians, and the continuing expatriation of U.S. jazz musicians. In Stowe's view, the swing era assumes a pivotal role, musically and culturally, in jazz history.

Although COLLIER's work deals with all of Goodman's career, including bands formed between 1940 and his death in 1986, 18 of the book's 28 chapters concern the period from 1930 to 1940. The book furnishes the usual biographical information on Goodman and many of his major sidemen and provides descriptive analyses of significant recordings. Unlike Schuller, however, Collier does not supplement the descriptions with notational examples. The book is well researched, is written in an easy conversational style, and has an extensive index that lists individual issues, musicians, and tunes.

On the surface, KORALL's book might seem to be narrowly focused, centering on the drummers of the swing era, but this volume is actually a series of extensive quotes from an astoundingly wide array of musicians who collectively tell the story of the big bands. The views of nearly 200 individuals form the core of this oral narrative, which also includes a detailed index and an important discography on the 14 drummers profiled. In addition, the notes section is a valuable reference for those who want to go directly to the source of the information Korall provides in the text. To quote Max Roach, this book is "a brilliant account of a very important period in the history of American music."

TUCKER contains more than 100 articles on one of the United States' compositional icons, Duke Ellington. Included are interviews with, and essays by, Ellington, biographical profiles of many contemporary musicians, several pieces of musical analysis, and assorted critical commentaries. The volume presents a wealth of biographical and musical material on this influential jazz personality and his work. There are, for instance, 175 separate references in the general index on *Black, Brown, and Beige* and nearly 100 on Ellington's longtime baritone saxophonist Harry Carney. The essays range from the analytical (e.g., Gunther Schuller's series from *The Jazz Review)* to the anecdotal (e.g., Whitney Balliet's interview of Sonny Greer). This is an important source for students of popular music in the United States.

TIRRO has fashioned an extraordinarily rich and detailed account of the history of jazz. The chapter titled "The Swing Era" comprises some 80 pages of text, more than is given to any other single period. There are subsections on the major bands, arrangers, women instrumentalists, vocalists, and the "Territory Bands." Twenty listening guides accompany recordings of major works, including four from the swing period by Art Tatum, Duke Ellington, Count Basie, and Benny Goodman. The transcribed solos include one each by Coleman Hawkins and Lester Young. Aside from the text, perhaps the most unique and valuable features of the book are contained in the back matter. There is a "Synoptic Table" that places jazz events within a historical/cultural context; a 23-page annotated bibliography of publications arranged within subcategories, most of which are historical periods ("Swing" contains 48 items); a selected discography; a glossary; and four separate indices on recorded jazz anthologies, some of which are cross-referenced.

Of the 16 chapters in GRIDLEY's book, three are devoted to the swing era, including one each to Ellington and Count Basie. The author tackles many of the difficult questions surrounding jazz, so the book is replete with positions that invite debate (e.g., "the popular success of jazz bands during the swing era was partly a result of their appeal to the eyes and feet of fans instead of to the ears alone"). Much of the volume's success (it is a widely used text for jazz courses in U.S. colleges and universities) is undoubtedly attributable to its many supplementary features that include more than 20 listening guides (designed to be used with accompanying recordings) and hundreds of tables, illustrations, drawings and photographs of musicians, instruments common to jazz, and more. Among the several invaluable appendices are the "Elements of Music" (for those unfamiliar with musical notation), guides to "Album Buying" and "Jazz Videos," "Supplementary Reading," "Sources for Notated Jazz

Solos," and "For Musicians." The latter section will appeal to the individual familiar with basic notation but lacking a background in the musical elements unique to jazz. This is a fine book for those wanting a basic education in the fundamentals of swing (or jazz in general) written in an economical and readable style.

RALPH D. CONVERSE

Jazz: Bebop

DeVeaux, Scott, *The Birth of Bebop: A Social and Musical History,* Berkeley: University of California Press, 1997

De Wilde, Laurent, *Monk,* translated by Jonathan Dickinson, New York: Marlow, 1997

Fitterling, Thomas, *Thelonious Monk: His Life and Music,* revised edition, translated by Robert Dobbin, Berkeley, California: Berkeley Hills Books, 1997

Gillespie, Dizzy, *To Be or Not . . . to BOP: Memoirs,* Garden City, New York: Doubleday, 1979

Gitler, Ira, *Jazz Masters of the Forties,* New York: Macmillan, 1966

———, *Swing to Bop: An Oral History of the Transition in Jazz in the 1940s,* New York: Oxford University Press, 1985

Gourse, Leslie, *Straight, No Chaser: The Life and Genius of Thelonius Monk,* New York: Schirmer Books, 1997

Jones, LeRoi, *Blues People: Negro Music in White America,* New York: Morrow, 1963

Martin, Henry, *Charlie Parker and Thematic Improvisation,* Lanham, Maryland: Institute for Jazz Studies and Scarecrow Press, 1996

Owens, Thomas, *Bebop: The Music and the Players,* New York: Oxford University Press, 1995

Porter, Lewis, *John Coltrane: His Life and Music,* Ann Arbor: University of Michigan Press, 1998

Rosenthal, David, *Hard Bop: Jazz and Black Music, 1955–1965,* New York: Oxford University Press, 1992

Williams, Martin, *The Jazz Tradition,* New York: Oxford University Press, 1970; 2nd edition, 1993

Woideck, Carl, *Charlie Parker: His Music and Life,* Ann Arbor: University of Michigan Press, 1996

Woideck, Carl, editor, *The Charlie Parker Companion: Six Decades of Commentary,* New York: Schirmer Books, 1998

———, editor, *The John Coltrane Companion: Five Decades of Commentary,* New York: Schirmer Books, and London: Prentice Hall International, 1998

For writers seeking to discern an underlying continuity in the jazz tradition, bebop has been interpreted as a stylistic evolution with strong connections to swing. For other writers, bebop was above all a social revolution representing an effort by black musicians to achieve an artistic autonomy unavailable during the swing era. The 1990s witnessed the beginnings of a synthesis of those perspectives. In that decade, the literature on modern jazz, and bebop in particular, expanded dramatically on all fronts, including biography, oral history, musical analysis, and cultural history. Broad surveys of the music have synthesized the existing material, defined the terrain, and charted new territory. Excellent studies of the lives and artistry of individual musicians have deepened understanding of the entire jazz landscape; compilations of articles and interviews—published as readers or companions—have blossomed into a thriving subgenre of the literature.

OWENS offers a style history of bebop with particular focus on its major soloists. Owens's central chapters are devoted to the leading figures organized according to their instruments: alto saxophonists, tenor saxophonists, trumpeters, pianists, bassists and drummers, and other instrumentalists. "The Parker Style"—a chapter on Charlie Parker—precedes the survey of other players, emphasizing the primacy of Parker's place in bebop history. A later chapter on ensembles considers how the musicians worked together, and a final chapter titled "Younger Masters" discusses the leading bebop musicians of the 1980s and early 1990s. Owens's primary sources are sound recordings, and his book, which would be a useful text in a course on modern jazz for music majors, includes numerous transcriptions.

DeVEAUX delivers an unusually sophisticated blend of social and musical history in order to vivify "the complexity and ambiguity of lives lived in a particular historical moment"—the lives of the men who developed bebop in the early 1940s. By focusing on the common experiences of individual musicians, DeVeaux seeks to redirect the two master narratives of modern jazz, which tend to reduce the music to either a stylistic evolution or a social revolution. At every turn, DeVeaux's study offers a fresh spin on the economic, racial, and musical issues that have confronted jazz musicians and the historians and critics who interpret their work. "For the young black men who created bebop," DeVeaux argues, "musical and social issues were not warring abstractions, but conjoined elements of their adult identities."

GITLER (1966) is a well-written survey of the musicians who developed bebop. It remains a useful introduction to the subject for musicians and non-musicians alike, thanks to Gitler's knowledge of the musicians and the music, his fluent writing style, and his instinct for revealing biographical and musical detail. The book's nine chapters discuss the major musicians on each instrument, beginning with Charlie Parker and other saxophonists and proceeding through trumpeters, pianists, trombonists, bassists, drummers, and arrangers.

GITLER (1985) documents the transition from bigband swing to bebop through the testimony of more than 60 men and women who caused and/or witnessed this change. The chapters proceed chronologically and thematically, from "The Road" and "Roots and Seeds" (on the swing era) to "The Bop Era" and "End of an Era." Each chapter includes commentary by several interviewees, ranging from one sentence to five pages. Gitler's own commentary provides transitions and contexts for the observations of his subjects. The autobiographical introduction explains Gitler's growing awareness of bebop from the 1940s, when he was a student, to his professional fascination with the music as a New York journalist in the 1950s and beyond.

In the late 1990s, the University of Michigan Press issued two excellent books on the twin towers of modern jazz saxophone: alto saxophonist Charlie Parker and tenor saxophonist John Coltrane. WOIDECK (1996) offers a penetrating and well-written life-and-works study of Parker that likely will endure as the single most authoritive book on bebop's central figure. The biographical chapters document Parker's alternately inspiring and heartbreaking life with detail and clarity. The musical chapters, which Woideck modestly terms a guided tour of Parker's recorded legacy, present numerous fresh insights. Woideck distills general elements of Parker's style and proceeds to explain them in vivid prose that is firmly grounded in sensible analysis and numerous transcribed musical examples.

PORTER's book on Coltrane is likewise a commanding work on a central figure in jazz history. Representing nearly two decades of research, the book weaves substantial musical analysis into a compelling biographical narrative. Porter traces Coltrane's apprenticeship with bebop pioneers, such as Dizzy Gillespie, and his important collaboration with Miles Davis. Porter's exploration of the range of possible influences on Coltrane's classic "Giant Steps" demonstrates how sophisticated, wide-ranging musical knowledge and painstaking source research can illuminate the subject. An appendix includes a lengthy chronology listing all known public performances, recording sessions, and interviews with Coltrane.

WOIDECK (1998a) is a compilation of articles, interviews, and reviews about Parker and his music designed for musicians and non-musicians alike. The book is truly a companion, because it serves as an excellent supplement to Woideck's 1996 book. Organized thematically, the writings range chronologically from 1945 to 1997 and include essays on Parker by four leading jazz critics (Gary Giddins, Martin Williams, Ira Gitler, Stanley Crouch); commentary on Parker and his music in the jazz press (most notably by Leonard Feather); interviews with Parker (newly transcribed); reminiscences by musicians who knew and worked with Parker in Kansas City and New York; and reviews of public performances and sound recordings. The book also includes a descriptive chronology of Parker's life.

Like the Parker compilation, WOIDECK (1998b) is another true companion, published in the same year as Porter's authoritative life-and-works study of Coltrane. The articles range from a 1956 review claiming that "the tenor on the Rollins-Stitt kick is . . . out of tune" to more recent assessments of his legacy. The book includes several profiles and surveys of Coltrane's work by leading jazz critics spanning more than three decades, several interviews with Coltrane, and many critical assessments of his performances in nightclubs and concert halls, and on sound recording.

MARTIN's book is a dense, compact, technical study of Parker's improvisatory method. The study aims to go beyond existing models that demonstrate Parker's solos as chains of melodic formulas, and it challenges the conventional wisdom that Parker's solos ignore the original melodies on which they are based. The early and last chapters consider general issues of theory, style, and analysis. The three middle chapters are case studies of Parker's approach to his sources, namely popular song (especially rhythm changes such as those found in Gershwin's "I Got Rhythm"), and the blues. The discussion is amply illustrated with transcriptions and analytic distillations of melodic and formal patterns.

The year 1997 saw the publication of three useful biographies of composer-pianist Thelonius Monk. None of these books stands out as the most authoritative work, but all will undoubtedly inform more scholarly and comprehensive studies. GOURSE is a well-written chronicle of Monk's life incorporating fresh information gleaned from numerous interviews. Gourse's descriptive commentary on the music, as she acknowledges, must "await augmentation by a musicologist or musician." The book includes a list of Monk's compositions and a "Sessionography" of Monk's recordings. FITTERLING, a leading German jazz critic, offers a more sustained assessment of Monk's music in the form of a traditional life-and-works narrative. The book is divided into three parts: "Monk's Life" (the biography), "Monk's Music" (a general commentary on style), and "Monk's Catalogue" (a disc-by-disc commentary on Monk's records, with complete discographical information). DE WILDE, an American-born French jazz pianist, dispenses with all the apparatus of scholarship (footnotes, bibliography, discography, and index) and presents an eloquent biographical essay. Scholars accustomed to finding insight in a more formal guise should not be discouraged by de Wilde's intimate, conversational style. Among its many delightful surprises, the book includes a vivid disquisition on Monk's hands and a striking comparison of how Monk's saxophonists Johnny Griffin and Charlie Rouse played his music. With its blend of elegant writing, musical insight, and human understanding, the book represents a unique jazz biography.

GILLESPIE is a hybrid work combining elements of the as-told-to autobiography and a compilation of interviews. Besides the voice of its main subject—bebop's most innovative trumpet player and theorist—the book includes commentary gleaned from more than 150 interviews with other musicians, entertainers, critics, producers, friends, and family members. The book remains a central document in jazz history for its insight into a major American musician and bebop in general.

ROSENTHAL focuses on the lives and styles of musicians—including Horace Silver, Art Blakey, Cannonball Adderley, Lee Morgan, and Jackie McLean—who developed a brand of bebop powered by a strong beat, tinged with an earthy blues and gospel flavor, and less dependent on popular song styles and forms than earlier bop. Rosenthal has an engaging, somewhat breezy prose style that makes for an accessible introduction to the subject, although readers with little or no previous understanding of hard bop must read patiently to learn what the term connotes.

One of the most influential books on jazz, WILLIAMS defines a historical perspective on the music in 20 chronological chapters that assess the music of the men and women he deems the most significant, from the early New Orleans cornetist King Oliver to the modern jazz innovator Ornette Coleman. The book includes several chapters on musicians who played bebop, including Parker, Monk, Davis, Mingus, Coltrane, and others. The introduction explains how Williams arrived at his choices and articulates a theory of the fundamental importance of rhythmic innovation in the jazz tradition. The epilogue provides a thoughtful reflection on the meanings of jazz to its creators and listeners of all races. Each chapter is packed with observations and insights that jazz critics and scholars continue to mine, even as they question the work's unspoken assumptions about musical canons and masters.

Although he surveys the entire history of black music in the United States, JONES writes from a bebop sensibility, and his book has had a powerful impact on writers seeking to articulate the music's cultural resonance. His sharp, polemical analysis of spirituals, blues, and jazz strives to explain how music can be heard as an expression of African-American life struggles in particular historical circumstances. For Jones, the blues form the core of black music and constitute "the parent of all legitimate jazz." Bebop, in Jones's view, served the function of restoring jazz to its cultural distinctiveness after swing had commercialized and corrupted jazz. As a result, the final chapter, "The Modern Scene," appears as the culmination of the entire book.

JEFFREY MAGEE

Jazz: Cool

Collier, James Lincoln, *The Making of Jazz: A Comprehensive History,* Boston: Houghton Mifflin, 1978

Gridley, Mark C., *Jazz Styles: History and Analysis,* Englewood Cliffs, New Jersey: Prentice Hall, 1978; 6th edition, 1997

Hobsbawm, Eric, *The Jazz Scene,* London: MacGibbon and Kee, 1959; revised edition, New York: Pantheon Books, 1993

Porter, Lewis, et al., *Jazz: From Its Origins to the Present,* Englewood Cliffs, New Jersey: Prentice Hall, 1993

Rosenthal, David H., *Hard Bop,* New York: Oxford University Press, 1992

Shaw, Arnold, "A New Cool Generation" in *Esquire's World of Jazz,* New York: Crowell, 1975

Tirro, Frank, *Jazz: A History,* New York: Norton, 1977; 2nd edition, 1993

The cool-jazz period, by far the most problematic in jazz history for which to define a specific time span, is thought to encompass the years from 1946 to 1952, between the swing/Dixieland/bop era of the 1930s and 1940s and the hard-bop era of the late 1950s. Cool jazz reached its peak in 1949 with an album titled *The Birth of the Cool,* led by trumpeter Miles Davis. The album, although virtually ignored by record buyers, had a significant impact on contemporary jazz musicians and established a standard for the style of the era.

As a phenomenon, cool jazz denoted a more subtle, lighter-sounding, emotionally cool style of playing, compared to the passionate, "hot" style of the bebop players. It was more closely associated with classical music, becoming known as "chamber" jazz. Cool-jazz musicians used fewer overtones than bebop and little or no vibrato in their playing, and they achieved a lessening of the raucous, hard driving "bop" sound of the rhythm section; improvised counterpoint; and a more classically inspired approach to performance. In addition, the music of the cool period included instruments heretofore unused as solo, improvisational instruments in jazz, such as the French horn, bassoon, flute, and cello. Most historians agree that the main proponents of the movement were pianist Leonard Joseph "Lennie" Tristano, alto saxophonist Lee Konitz, tenor saxophonist Warne Marsh, and guitarist Billy Bauer, as well as composer-arrangers Gil Evans and Gerry Mulligan.

For PORTER et al., the term *cool jazz* refers to a style of playing that continued for some time throughout the 1950s. They describe the cool-jazz period as extending into what is commonly known as West Coast jazz, terms they find synonymous. They cite three distinct groups as innovators of the cool-jazz sound: first, the composers and musicians centered around Evans—whose sparse, ethereal arrangements had been influenced by bandleader Claude Thornhill—including Johnny Carisi, Mulligan, and John Lewis, who were the arrangers of the *Birth of the Cool* recording, as well as Davis, who emerged as the recording date's leader; second, the musicians centered around virtuoso pianist and teacher Tristano, including his students Marsh, Konitz, and Bauer; and third, a group consisting of three individuals who on their own were significant proponents of the cool-jazz sound—alto saxophonist Art Pepper, Stan Getz, and West Coast pianist Dave Brubeck.

HOBSBAWM argues that the term *cool jazz* is a paradox in itself because the very nature of "jazz" is "hot—

sensuous, emotional, [and] physical." He states that cool jazz "aimed at a hitherto irrelevant ideal of musical purity, at the complete reversal of most jazz values."

A chapter in GRIDLEY's excellent textbook is devoted exclusively to cool jazz. He does not define a specific cool-jazz period but instead considers cool jazz as a group of diverse styles throughout the postbop era, stemming from the influences of Davis, Count Basie, and Lester Young, as well as the East and West Coast schools. He recognizes that the term *cool* was primarily applied to jazz musicians whose sound was subdued and understated. He continues, however, that a "confusing aspect of 'cool' is that the term described an attitude more than a style of music." He cites Tristano as a "modern jazz alternative to bop in the late forties" and Konitz as single-handedly the most influential proponent of the cool style on the West Coast.

In his comprehensive historical study, COLLIER treats the emergence of the cool-jazz movement less as a reaction to the drive and intensity of the bop school and more as a pull toward the trend of "symphonic jazz" that had existed in jazz for some time. He notes that composers such as Scott Joplin, James P. Johnson, Paul Whitman, and George Gershwin were already successful at blending the sound of European classical music with jazz and that in the area of big bands, symphonic jazz was also being featured prominently, as seen in the bands of Stan Kenton, Woody Herman, and Thornhill. He relates how the collaboration of Thornhill and Evans shifted the emphasis of the big band from hard swing to sheer sound where melody, harmony, and rhythm moved at minimum speed, with an intent to create a "sound that hung like a cloud."

For the serious music student, TIRRO's text offers historical information as well as theory and analysis of a number of cool-jazz harmonies and melodies. Tirro defines the cool-jazz period as a development of bebop, not a reaction to it. Through analysis, he proves that the main proponents of the movement were schooled in the bop tradition and cites three musicians responsible for the trend to a cool-jazz sound: Getz, Tristano, and Davis. Tirro describes Tristano as a "radical thinker and an outspoken critic of contemporary musicians" who "explored the possibility of decreased redundancy and increased complexity" in his music through asymmetrical phrases, avoidance of clichés, constantly shifting accents, and pulsating harmonic rhythm. Tirro believes that the *Birth of the Cool* recording was the "birth of nothing." Instead, it was merely the product of some musicians from the Thornhill band getting together to test some new arrangements of Evans and Mulligan.

SHAW's depiction of the cool-jazz movement focuses on the musicians, whom he describes as uninterested in audience approval and, instead, who played for themselves. He laments the fact that they created music for listening rather than dancing. But he also describes the music as "soft, insinuating and tender, and usually cerebral," able to express many moods, including the pensive and meditative.

ROSENTHAL states that, "although some blacks—for example, Miles Davis and pianist John Lewis—were involved with the 'cool' movement, it was overwhelmingly a white phenomenon, both in its protagonists and in its audience." He contends that bebop had burnt itself out as a fad and, to some extent, as a school of jazz and argues that the cool-jazz movement as a whole "produced a great deal of forgettable 'chamber jazz' and preciosity of various sorts."

LUANN DRAGONE

Jazz: West Coast

Gioia, Ted, *West Coast Jazz: Modern Jazz in California, 1945–1960*, New York: Oxford University Press, 1992

Gordon, Robert, *Jazz West Coast: The Los Angeles Jazz Scene of the 1950s*, London: Quartet Books, 1986

Gridley, Mark C., *Jazz Styles: History and Analysis*, Englewood Cliffs, New Jersey: Prentice Hall, 1978; 6th edition, 1997

Klinkowitz, Jerome, *Listen, Gerry Mulligan: An Aural Narrative in Jazz*, New York: Schirmer Books, 1991

Lee, William F., *Stan Kenton: Artistry in Rhythm*, Los Angeles: Creative Press, 1980

Lees, Gene, *Leader of the Band: The Life of Woody Herman*, New York: Oxford University Press, 1995

Pepper, Art, and Laurie Pepper, *Straight Life: The Story of Art Pepper*, New York: Schirmer Books, 1979; updated edition, New York: Da Capo Press, 1994

"West Coast" is a label applied to a jazz performance style that flourished in California during the 1950s. This classification is controversial (some musicians and critics deny the existence of the genre), and a precise definition is elusive. Many observers acknowledge that "cool" and "West Coast" jazz describe a part of the same aesthetic. The difference is both geographical ("cool" being East Coast in origin) and, to some degree, racial. Most West Coast musicians who took a "cool" approach to their art in California were white. Furthermore, many of the musicians who performed in this style during the 1950s and early 1960s had played with big bands, particularly those of Woody Herman and Stan Kenton (hence the inclusion of books on those bands in the bibliography). Like the cool school that provided the original impetus, West Coast groups were mostly small ensembles of three to ten players. Unlike bop, the music was structured around tightly written arrangements of choruses and background riffs with ample room for solo improvisation. The writing emphasized contrapuntal lines and the occasional inclusion of unusual jazz instrumentation (tuba, oboe, bassoon, French horn, flute, etc.). The phenomenon was centered in southern California (the Lighthouse Cafe in Hermosa Beach was a favorite venue), but at least one prominent practitioner (Dave Brubeck) claimed roots in the northern part of the state. Many of the musicians were professional studio artists whose technical expertise and polished execution brought a new, more cerebral quality to jazz.

GIOIA's book is the quintessential reference on the subject. The index combines names, tunes, and performance venues. Extensive endnotes help direct the reader to further information, and the appendix lists 50 of the most representative West Coast jazz recordings from 1945 to 1960. Gioia's work is well organized and easily readable, interesting for both the musical neophyte and the well-informed listener. To his credit, the author recognizes a multiplicity of jazz types that existed in California during the 1950s, including bop along Central Avenue and the beginnings of "free jazz" with Ornette Coleman and Eric Dolphy. Extensive coverage is given to Brubeck, Art Pepper, Shelly Mann, Shorty Rogers, Chet Baker, and the big band influence on the West Coast style.

GORDON is closely akin to, and a predecessor of, Gioia. Like Gioia, Gordon contends that "the jazz scene of the fifties was more variegated than current jazz criticism would lead one to believe," and so he covers much of the same territory discussed in Gioia's text, including the mostly black bop bands (Gordon offers two chapters on Charlie Parker, Dizzy Gillespie, and the Central Avenue scene). This study also stresses the importance of the Lighthouse Cafe and the advent of free jazz. In addition, there are chapters on Rogers, Gerry Mulligan, and Pepper. Gordon helps the reader understand how West Coast jazz came to prominence by discussing the development of independent recording labels such as Pacific Jazz and Contemporary that sprang up in the 1950s, and details the historical importance of performances at Billy Berg's in Hollywood by Gillespie and his sextet for eight weeks in 1945. His discography is annotated but a bit overly selective.

GRIDLEY devotes a sizable portion of his 20-page chapter on cool jazz to the West Coast phenomenon, although he recognizes the difficulties encountered when appending descriptive labels: "A substantial amount of music called 'cool' is not distinguishable from bop." Much of this volume's appeal as a college and university text can be traced to its many supplementary features that guide both the musically informed and the uninitiated. There are hundreds of useful tables, illustrations, drawings, and photographs, as well as 20 listening guides to be used with the tapes (or compact discs) accompanying the text. The several appendices include "Elements of Music" (a guide to basic notation), "Album Buying," a list of "Jazz Videos," "Supplementary Reading," and, for the musically adept, "For Musicians" and "Sources for Notated Jazz Solos." The book is an excellent primer for anyone wanting a basic education in jazz generally or the West Coast style in particular.

As KLINKOWITZ's subtitle suggests, this volume focuses on recordings by Mulligan and a multitude of his cool/West Coast colleagues. In fact, there is a 53-page discography devoted solely to Mulligan's commercially recorded performances and arrangements. Among the values of the discography are the dating of all recording sessions and the rosters of personnel involved in each. A reader wanting a list of, for instance, all Chet Baker recordings with Mulligan would have only to consult the detailed index for discography page numbers where Baker's name occurs. Similarly, the index contains the tunes from all the recorded collections, and one could quickly determine that, for example, "I Remember April" is on three different Mulligan albums. The main text of the book deals with major musical events in Mulligan's career, including his involvement with *The Birth of the Cool* album, his work on both coasts, his connections to Brubeck, and his excursions into fusion.

PEPPER's autobiography is a stark and brutally honest assessment of one of the finest West Coast artists of the 1950s and 1960s and one of music's tragic figures. Pepper himself, in appraising *Straight Life*, wrote frankly of his addictions: "That's what I still am. And that's what I will die as—a junkie." The book covers many musical issues, but in the end, it is the personal story that provides the reader with a revealing account of the underside of jazz.

LEES is the one biography Herman asked be written in 1986, only months before the band leader's death. Lees draws on earlier work by other authors who started biographies but, for a variety of reasons, never finished them. His effort is the result of nearly a decade of research and interviews with musicians, friends, and family members. Musicians identified with the West Coast movement who spent time with the Herman band are chronicled near the back of the book in the "Woody Herman Alumni List." Lamentably, this volume does not include a discography, and the index lists people's names but not tunes or places. Apart from those oversights, the book is a comprehensive and eloquent story about one of the United State's enduring jazz personalities.

Finally, no West Coast sojourn would be complete without a look at the massive (700-plus pages of text) undertaking by LEE, which documents "the history of the life and professional activities of Stan Kenton and those who were fortunate enough to be touched by his . . . genius." The book is loosely organized into 13 chapters plus 5 appendices. Most chapters are titled for one of the major creative periods in the Kenton legacy (e.g., "New Concepts of Artistry in Rhythm," "Creative World," "Neophonic"). Although always interesting, the book has a feel of randomness and disorganization about it. At times the text degenerates into a seemingly endless and disconnected stream of quotes, news releases, and reminiscences about Kenton and his musicians. (Those wanting a more tightly constructed narrative might engage Carol Easton's *Straight Ahead: The Story of Stan Kenton* [1973].) For all of its flaws (the limited index has extensive names, few places, and no tunes), Lee's volume is certainly a monumental achievement. The five appendices include band personnel (a roster of West Coast who's who), film work by Kenton, arrangements and compositions by him, recordings available through Creative World, and a 59-page chronological discography. Perhaps more than any other leader, Kenton, with his cutting-edge approach, helped pave the way for the movement called West Coast jazz.

RALPH D. CONVERSE

Jazz: Free

Bruyninckx, Walter, *Progressive Jazz: Free—Third Stream Fusion*, 5 vols., Mechelen, Belgium: 60 Years of Recorded Jazz Team, 1984

Budds, Michael, *Jazz in the Sixties: The Expansion of Musical Resources and Techniques*, Iowa City: University of Iowa Press, 1978; expanded edition, 1990

Jones, LeRoi, *Black Music*, New York: Morrow, 1967

Jost, Ekkehard, *Free Jazz*, Graz: Universal Edition, 1974

Kofsky, Frank, *Black Nationalism and the Revolution in Music*, New York: Pathfinder, 1970; revised as *John Coltrane and the Jazz Revolution of the 1960s*, New York: Pathfinder, 1998

Litweiler, John, *The Freedom Principle: Jazz after 1958*, New York: Morrow, 1984

———, *Ornette Coleman: A Harmolodic Life*, New York: Morrow, 1992

Porter, Lewis, *John Coltrane: His Life and Music*, Ann Arbor: University of Michigan Press, 1998

Raben, Erik, *A Discography of Free Jazz: Albert Ayler, Don Cherry, Ornette Coleman, Pharaoh Sanders, Archie Shepp, Cecil Taylor*, Copenhagen: Knudsen, 1969

Radano, Ronald Michael, *New Musical Figurations: Anthony Braxton's Cultural Critique*, Chicago: University of Chicago Press, 1993

Spellman, A.B., *Four Lives in the Bebop Business*, New York: Pantheon Books, 1966

Szwed, John, *Space Is the Place: The Lives and Times of Sun Ra*, New York Pantheon Books, 1997

Wilmer, Valerie, *Jazz People*, London: Allison and Busby, 1970; 3rd edition, 1977

The title of Ornette Coleman's 1961 landmark album, *Free Jazz*, has come to symbolize the music of a community of predominantly African-American innovators active in the 1960s and 1970s. Convenient bookends to define the initial burst of creative activity are Coleman's New York performances and Atlantic label recordings in 1959 and John Coltrane's saxophone and drum duets recorded the year of Coltrane's death in 1967. This era saw the development of an increasingly radical and abstract language that moved beyond the harmonic, melodic, timbral, rhythmic, and structural conventions associated with the tradition for the previous half century. The music was much discussed in popular magazines such as *Down Beat*, and limited scholarly writing began to appear in the 1970s. A small number of listeners and critics embraced the music, but the vast majority were unprepared to appreciate the new direction and were consequently alienated by the inaccessible sounds that in some quarters were accompanied by a rhetoric of black nationalism. The aesthetic of free improvisation continued to be creatively explored through the 1970s, especially by members of the Chicago-based Association for the Advancement of Creative Musicians. The thin lines between scholarship, journalism, and criticism are evident in the relative plethora of biographical writing, ranging from surveys of the era to extended life stories. Discographies have also been an important scholarly focus. The least abundant and useful writing has been musical analysis; the tools inherited from earlier styles or from contemporary Western music theory have so far not been up to the task of analyzing free-jazz compositions.

JOST's outstanding volume is the classic in the field, an early effort yet to be surpassed. Beginning with the late 1950s and stopping around 1970, the author effectively surveys the initial decade, devoting separate chapters to the major players and forerunners: Coltrane, Coleman, Charles Mingus, Cecil Taylor, Archie Shepp, Albert Ayler, Don Cherry, the Association for the Advancement of Creative Musicians, and Sun Ra. Without the argumentative tone of other contemporaneous writing, Jost mixes sober biography, intense musical analysis, and discography, all in a solid scholarly tradition typical of Austro-Germanic jazz writing. Although some of his musical analyses may need revision, they at least gain entry into one of the most difficult musics to analyze of any genre. The discographies provide an essential listening list.

WILMER is unusual and effective primarily because of the author's personal contact with most of the musicians about whom she writes, communicating a deep sympathy for their personal lives and contexts in which they live. In a remarkable section entitled "Woman's Role," the author explores the psychology of relationships between the male musicians and the women in their lives, as well as the cold reception of female musicians. Concluding chapters covering the small labels that recorded the music and the economic future of the music are invaluable.

Writing about the new music while in the thick of it, SPELLMAN provides sympathetic and compelling biographies of the two most influential early innovators: Ornette Coleman and Cecil Taylor. The chapter on

Taylor, full of illuminating quotes, is especially valuable as one of the few extended pieces of writing on the elusive pianist. Spellman, who later moved on to major positions in the National Endowment for the Arts, is an eloquent spokesperson for an issue that was on the minds of many musicians of the day, criticizing "the gross indifference with which America received those aspects of Afro-American culture that are not 'entertaining.' Jazz's entertainment value has decreased as black artists have conscientiously moved out of the realm of folk art and into the realm of high art." The decidedly noncommercial appeal of free jazz pointed up inherent problems in referring to jazz as popular or dance music, leaving "art" as an option embraced by many players and critics.

JONES was also listening to, writing about, and championing the music as it initially appeared on the scene. His essays, culled from his *Down Beat* articles, record liner notes, and other sources from 1959 to 1967, not so subtly reveal the strained polemic that the new music brought to the forefront. Unapologetically opinionated, as criticism of the new music was apt to be, and disinterested in musicological viewpoints, his writing can be harsh, particularly when discussing the place of black musicians and jazz in American society, a consuming passion of the time.

Similarly sociological and polemical, KOFSKY primarily focuses on Coltrane's radical explorations of the mid-1960s, thus diverging from the other dozen or so books devoted to Coltrane that treat the whole career of the mainstream legend who only in the last several years of his life joined the ranks of his younger peers to become a widely admired leading figure in the new music. Kofsky's extended interview of Coltrane reveals much about the man, especially that he saw himself as a musical explorer rather than the social activist that others imagined him to be.

RADANO is perhaps the most interdisciplinary of the works reviewed here, examining from many perspectives a major figure in the immediate post-Coltrane extensions. In the tradition of Jost, but reflecting the subsequent two decades of critical developments, Radano's scholarly accounting of the music of Anthony Braxton and the critical and cultural climate from the time in which Braxton first appeared as a leader (late 1960s) to the height of his commercial celebrity (late 1970s) is unique in its breadth. Biography and discography combine with analysis, ranging from the musicological— replete with transcriptions, schematic diagrams, and manuscript reproductions—to the aesthetic, relating the music to larger issues of black expressive culture.

Other full-length biographies stand out. SZWED's expansive and meticulously researched study of Sun Ra, one of the more mysterious, influential, senior, and legendary figures, who had great longevity, is an eminently readable and scholarly investigation. In a similar nonmusicological tradition is LITWEILER's (1992) study of Ornette Coleman from childhood to the early 1990s. Although the author often quotes from published sources, some of his own interviews, including the one in which Gunther Schuller describes his contact with Coleman, are priceless. Several chapters in PORTER's authoritative musicological study of Coltrane are devoted to his important role in free jazz. The welcome intense musical analyses often illuminate but also occasionally reveal the limitations of the theoretical tools the author uses to show what "Coltrane is really attempting to create." The problematic idea that the author's (or any other) analysis "accurately represents Coltrane's intention" is not addressed. LITWEILER (1984), a survey of the era with chapters devoted to the major innovators as well as related subgenres, is a good introduction to the players and issues.

Recognizing the abundance of journalistic writing, BUDDS concentrates almost exclusively on technical aspects of the music. Treating innovations in distinct chapters with titles such as "Color and Instrumentation" and "Melody and Harmony," biography is eschewed in favor of discussions of technique and procedures. Unfortunately, these accounts are often either too general or too specific in peripheral areas to provide a real sense of what the core players were up to.

Jazz discography has been an important field of research, giving the reader great insight into some of the details of the creative life of an artist. Raben and Bruyninckx each provide essential discographies of the era, giving details of song titles, personnel, and recording dates. RABEN focuses exclusively on the careers of six major players. BRUYNINCKX, the premier jazz discographer, is typically comprehensive. His musician index (in volume 5) gives an impressive taste of the variety of musicians active in this area.

ERIC CHARRY

Jazz: After 1960

Coryell, Julie, and Laura Friedman, *Jazz-Rock Fusion: The People, The Music,* New York: Dell, and London: Boyars, 1978

Davis, Francis, *In the Moment: Jazz in the 1980s,* New York: Oxford University Press, 1986

Giddins, Gary, *Rhythm-a-ning: Jazz Tradition and Innovation in the 80's,* New York: Oxford University Press, 1985

Jost, Ekkehard, *Free Jazz,* Graz: Universal Edition, 1974

Nicholson, Stuart, *Jazz: The Modern Resurgence,* London: Simon and Schuster, 1990; revised as *Jazz: The 1980s Resurgence,* New York: Da Capo Press, 1995

———, *Jazz Rock: A History,* New York: Schirmer Books, 1998

Radano, Ronald Michael, *New Musical Figurations: Anthony Braxton's Cultural Critique,* Chicago: University of Chicago Press, 1993

Such, David Glen, *Avante-Garde Jazz Musicians: Performing "Out There,"* Iowa City: University of Iowa Press, 1993

Literature on jazz after 1960 has been relatively sparse compared to studies of the music before that time. This relative neglect has probably been due to prevailing negative historical opinions of free jazz and jazz-rock fusion, the dominant styles that emerged in the 1960s and 1970s, respectively. Jazz in the 1980s and 1990s may be neglected in the literature because many historians and critics have concluded that jazz has not developed in significant or original directions since the death of saxophonist John Coltrane in 1967. There seems to be no single style or musical figurehead that defines jazz from the last 20 years of the 20th century, indicating not a decline in the validity of jazz but rather a stylistic diversity that is not represented by any one individual.

At the beginning of the 1960s, free jazz was the dominant style of progressive musicians, particularly those in New York and Chicago. Although Ornette Coleman, Charles Mingus, and others had laid the groundwork in the late 1950s, it was clearly the free jazz explorations of John Coltrane in the mid-1960s that most influenced the jazz scene at the time. Observers of this spontaneous music, which was seemingly without form or logic, were at a loss as to how to analyze the recorded results of this musical process.

JOST, through schematic diagrams and innovative theoretical techniques, demonstrates that a coherent inner logic often did exist within free jazz improvisations, but he does not take into account the social/cultural context and meaning of the music. This omission probably occurs because his only sources are the recordings and literature. Nevertheless, Jost successfully offers a methodology for making better musicological sense of free jazz. Other books, particularly those by Valerie Wilmer, a photojournalist, explore the social context but with little regard for the musical content.

SUCH marries several scholarly disciplines including musicology, social sciences, and psychology, with his own experience as an active performer of the music to give a balanced analysis of the music. He prefers the term *out jazz,* meaning "out of this world" or "far out," to better capture the ideals of the musicians and the reaction by their audience.

Similarly, RADANO illuminates the need for interdisciplinary scholarship on free jazz. Using the life and career of composer and performer Anthony Braxton as a springboard, Radano reminds us that free jazz must properly be viewed as something defined beyond the linear development within jazz history itself because it is a musical development resembling other artistic developments in a postmodern culture. He also identifies Braxton and his contemporaries as those who "signalled the appearance of a dramatically new kind of musician: the *black experimentalist.*"

Although free jazz seemed the most liberating, artistic, and uncompromising approach to have developed in jazz, it was eventually abandoned by the majority of musicians, fans, and critics. The maturation of rock in the mid-1960s, led by musicians in Britain and the psychedelic stylists of the San Francisco area—particularly guitarist Jimi Hendrix—compelled some jazz musicians to incorporate rock rhythms and instrumentation as the new means for jazz stylistic innovation. Such musicians hoped to match rock's popularity and rectify jazz's increasing financial failure. The jazz world generally viewed this jazz/rock fusion as a corrupting force, however, and has historically considered fusion an artistic wrong turn in the history of jazz. Therefore, few authors have treated jazz/rock with empathy or given it serious investigation. CORYELL and FRIEDMAN was published toward the end of the 1970s when jazz/rock artists were realizing an unprecedented degree of commercial success, which the book depicts as a triumph for the music. This volume, a series of interviews, attempts to allow the musicians to defend their decision to reach a larger audience and please their record companies.

Twenty years later, NICHOLSON (1998) brought forth another book-length study of the development of jazz-rock, chronicling it to the end of the 20th century. Nicholson insists on distinguishing jazz-rock from fusion. The former he considers the sincere creative incorporation of rock elements by jazz musicians; the latter he relegates to the market-driven, easy-listening type of music typically played on light jazz radio stations. Nicholson casts the rise of jazz-rock within the context of rock developments in San Francisco and Britain and genealogically categorizes most of the artists and groups that have comprised the movement. In almost every case, he concludes that the demise of each artist and group came about when initial experimentation gave way to commercial compromise.

The 1980s have been viewed as a jazz renaissance. Characterized by trumpeter Wynton Marsalis, the decade saw a reaction to both the free jazz movement of the 1960s and the jazz/rock movement of the 1970s. It became fashionable among record companies to sign sartorially dressed young lions who specialized in reviving pre-1960 jazz styles. GIDDINS celebrates this return to "swing, melody, and beauty" from the expressionistic extremism of the 1960s, viewing the movement as a replenishing of older jazz traditions. DAVIS views this renaissance not as a retrogression in the development of jazz but rather as a part of jazz's postmodern, "tortuous search for its own forms," as musicians rationalize that "the past is one of the few places left to look." Both Giddins and Davis, in Davis's words, "do not share the fear . . . for the survival of jazz as an art form. The survival of individual jazz *musicians* is another matter, though." The 1980s are depicted as a bleak environment for jazz musicians, as most jazz clubs closed and the jazz recording industry suffered from a less-than-four-percent market share.

While Giddins and Davis were writing from the middle of the 1980s, NICHOLSON (1990) offers a more up-to-date critical assessment of the 1980s. Whereas Giddins and Davis offer a collection of vignettes on artists, Nicholson surveys the various existing genres of jazz practiced in the 1980s.

DAVID JOYNER

Joplin, Scott 1868–1917

United States pianist and composer

Berlin, Edward A., *King of Ragtime: Scott Joplin and His Era*, New York: Oxford University Press, 1994

Blesh, Rudi, and Harriet Janis, *They All Played Ragtime*, New York: Knopf, 1950; 4th edition, New York: Oak, 1971

Curtis, Susan, *Dancing to a Black Man's Tune: A Life of Scott Joplin*, Columbia: University of Missouri Press, l994

Gammond, Peter, *Scott Joplin and the Ragtime Era*, New York: St. Martin's Press, 1975

Hasse, John Edward, editor, *Ragtime: Its History, Composers, and Music*, New York: Schirmer Books, 1985

Ping-Robbins, Nancy R., *Scott Joplin: A Guide to Research*, New York: Garland, l998

Scott Joplin is one of the most important composers of the music that came to be known as ragtime, which first drew the attention of the general public when it was heard by large numbers of people at the Chicago World's Fair in 1893. First popular as ragtime songs, ragtime came to be the principal form of popular music in the 1890s to 1910s. By the 1920s and 1930s ragtime's popularity declined as jazz gradually became more prominent. The ragtime revival began in the 1940s when Rudi Blesh reissued some early ragtime recordings through his Circle Records and published his book *Shining Trumpets*. The publication of *They All Played Ragtime* in 1950 contributed to further interest in the genre. The civil rights movement of the 1960s and early 1970s and the United States' bicentennial celebration in 1976 prompted a search for the cultural heritage of African-Americans, and the discovery of Joplin's music was an important part of the general reworking of American musical history.

Joplin's biography is of necessity sketchy; documentation for him, as for many African-Americans who lived in the late 19th and early 20th centuries, is often lost or incomplete. He is thought to have been born in 1868 near Marshall, Texas, but the date and place of birth cannot be proved with certainty. He grew up in Texarkana and is known to have lived the life of an itinerant musician during his early years. He spent some years after 1894 in Sedalia, Missouri, and probably appeared at the 1893 Chicago World's Columbian Exposition. His life changed dramatically with his meeting with John Stark and the publication of his most famous piece, "Maple Leaf Rag," in 1899. The financial and musical success of "Maple Leaf Rag" led to Joplin's being christened the "King of Ragtime Writers" and provided him time to compose. In 1901 Joplin moved to St. Louis, then to New York in 1907. Although he continued to compose rags until late in his life, his mature compositional efforts focused on larger-scale pieces, including a lost opera, *A Guest of Honor* (1903), and *Treemonisha* (1911). Joplin tried valiantly to have *Treemonisha* premiered during his lifetime, but the single reading of the opera was a failure. Joplin died of dementia paralytica, or the late stages of syphilis, in 1917, never having seen his opera staged. When Joplin's rags were used as the soundtrack for the enormously successful motion picture *The Sting* in 1974, the ragtime revival intensified. *Treemonisha* was recorded; Joplin was awarded a posthumous Pulitzer Prize in 1976.

BLESH and JANIS is the earliest book-length study of Scott Joplin and the genre of ragtime. Much of their information comes from interviews with more than 100 people who had been involved in the ragtime era, making this work unique. However, much of the oral history is difficult to evaluate based on the authors' documentation. Elderly informants may have been unreliable, and it is difficult to determine sources from the format of the book. The appendices and photographs are still useful, as are the 16 piano rag scores reproduced in the book. The affection with which it is written and the vitality of the historical figures' own words make this volume an ideal starting place for anyone studying Joplin and ragtime.

HASSE's collection of essays on ragtime includes reprints of important early scholarship about Joplin, as well as helpful articles on ragtime's history and critical reception. The work is excellent for its understanding of the place of ragtime in the United States at the turn of the century.

GAMMOND presents an appealing biography of Joplin that has short chapters and little documentation; however, there are interesting illustrations and musical discussions geared to the musical amateur. While this volume may not satisfy the music specialist, it is a good choice for a less-experienced musician.

BERLIN offers the most thorough biographical study and most comprehensive analytical discussion of Joplin's music. The author's examination of contemporaneous newspapers, particularly those of the black community, is much more extensive than any other study, and the results are stunning. Berlin is the only biographer to have discovered Joplin's significant relationship with Freddie Alexander, the woman who was probably the inspiration for the figure of Treemonisha. The author has examined an enormous number of documents, allowing him to follow Joplin's professional life in the greatest possible detail. In addition to the music itself, Berlin explains the important currents in American music during Joplin's lifetime and Joplin's place in American music history. Berlin's elaboration of the ragtime song is illuminating, offering a compelling argument about early ragtime's controversial status in American musical circles. Berlin had written highly regarded articles and books about ragtime before this biography, and his mastery of the material makes this volume a very clear and valuable resource.

CURTIS approaches Joplin's life through the history of the era and the cultural and political context in which the music was created. She does not presume to be a musicologist, and any student of American music history will immediately note her use of the first edition of Eileen Southern's standard history, *The Music of Black American: A History* (1971), rather than the second edition (1983). Curtis accepts much biographical information concerning Joplin that Berlin has challenged, such as the birth date of 24 November 1868. However, her approach to Joplin's life through the historical events that framed his experience paints a vivid picture of the United States and the changes in American society at the turn of the century. Her discussion of race, ethnicity, and the Americanness of music is thought provoking and easily accessible to the general reader. She lucidly explains complicated sociological phenomena, such as the different cultural and political currents within the African-American community.

Both Berlin and Curtis tell convincing stories about Joplin. The serious researcher should read both works, as they complement each other extremely well. Few historical figures have two such fine biographies, so different and yet each so valuable.

For the reader who wishes to research ragtime and Scott Joplin further, PING-ROBBINS's recent publication is a virtual bonanza. It contains a lengthy introduction summing up the current state of Joplin research and the challenges that remain. The author lists all Joplin's compositions by copyright deposit date, musical anthologies of Joplin's compositions, collections of sheet music, memorials to Joplin, and many other resources that might interest a Joplin scholar. Sections on "Maple Leaf Rag" and *Treemonisha* are informative. The general bibliography is the most complete resource of its kind available about Joplin or ragtime, listing items from the 19th century through 1998. Clearly indexed and intelligently organized, this guide is an invaluable aid for every reader.

ANN SEARS

Josquin des Prez ca. 1450–1521

French-born composer

Charles, Sydney Robinson, *Josquin des Prez: A Guide to Research,* New York: Garland, 1983

Elders, Willem, editor, *Proceedings of the International Josquin Symposium, Utrecht 1986,* in collaboration with Fritz de Haven, Utrecht: Vereniging voor Nederlandse Muziekgeschiedenis

Lowinsky, Edward E., editor, *Josquin des Prez,* in collaboration with Bonnie J. Blackburn, London: Oxford University Press, 1976

Matthews, Lora, and Paul Merkley, "Iudochus de Picardia and Jossequin Leblotte dit Deprez: The Names of the Singer(s)," *Journal of Musicology* 16 (1998)

Osthoff, Helmut, *Josquin Desprez,* 2 vols., Tutzing: Schneider, 1962–65

Reese, Gustave, and Jeremy Noble, "Josquin des Prez," in *The New Grove High Renaissance Masters,* edited by Gustave Reese et al., London: Macmillan, and New York: Norton, 1984

The enormous amount of scholarship on Josquin des Prez consists primarily of journal articles rather than book-length studies. Scholars have focused on four main issues, all of which are interconnected at some level: Josquin's biography, the establishment of a canon of authentic works, the context for his music, and his style in general and its development during his career. There are still many gaps in Josquin's biography, and important new information—that Josquin des Prez was not the Josquin who worked in Milan from 1459 through the mid-1470s—has forced us to shift his birth date from ca. 1440 to sometime during the 1450s and thus to reconsider his early career. All of the books discussed here were published before this information was discovered. Many works by other composers were attributed to Josquin during the Renaissance, and scholars are still trying to determine which pieces are authentic and which are spurious. By determining where, when, and for whom individual pieces were written, scholars have been able to articulate plausible hypotheses concerning his biography, address issues of style and chronology, and fit his music into the cultural milieu in which it flowered. The new biographical information undoubtedly will have a strong impact on questions of style and chronology. Because scholars can no longer talk about a Milanese period in Josquin, they have begun to reexamine his early career, define his early style, and determine a new chronology.

CHARLES, a useful guide to the sources of and literature on Josquin up to 1981, is divided into five principal sections. The biographical section is not presented as a narrative but rather as a list of the 23 documents that concern Josquin and a summary of the hypotheses that scholars have built around these documents. Although the number of documents pertaining to Josquin has grown considerably since the publication of Charles's study, and although some of the documents listed here have subsequently been shown to refer not to Josquin des Prez but to other people named Josquin, this section is still useful both as a record of Josquin scholarship and as a study in methodology. The second section lists all of Josquin's works by genre and the literature that pertains to them. The third section is a listing of all known sources that contain music by Josquin. The sources are listed by type (manuscripts, prints, theoretical treatises, and intabulations) and are cross-referenced with the work list. The fourth and least useful section is a discography. It is here that the greatest number of mistakes occur and where the obsolescence of this research guide is most keenly felt. The last section is a bibliography of books, articles, and dissertations in English and many other languages. In short, this is an excellent introduction to pre-1981 Josquin scholarship, but readers should not neglect the more recent work.

OSTHOFF was the first life-and-works study of Josquin, but unfortunately it is only available in German. In this two-volume biography, the author has assembled all documents concerning Josquin known at the time of publication and attempts to place them in a coherent narrative; where gaps appear in documentation, Osthoff offers plausible speculation based on his extensive knowledge of the sources, music, and cultural milieu in which Josquin worked. The author then provides the most thorough discussion of Josquin's works available in a single source. Volume 1 contains the biography and discussion of the Masses; volume 2 contains the discussion of the motets and secular music, as well as several useful appendices (including a work list) and complete transcriptions of ten pieces.

For a similar treatment of Josquin's life and works in English, REESE and NOBLE provide a slightly more up-to-date overview of Josquin's biography and an introduction to his works. Here, the reader will find a much more succinct rendition of Josquin's biography (which does not, of course, take into account the discoveries of the mid-1990s) presented in a narrative format. This biography is followed by a discussion of his works, divided into four sections: chronology, motets, Masses, and secular music. Because the authors try to paint a broad picture, the essay is relatively jargon free and does not go into much detail about any single piece. Particularly useful is the work list (which replaces that of Osthoff) arranged by genre and the list of doubtful and misattributed works, also arranged by genre. The bibliography lists most of the important writings to the early 1980s.

LOWINSKY is a large and diverse collection of essays that resulted from the International Josquin Festival Conference that was held in 1971. This book contains 32 essays divided into six sections: biography, source studies, style and analysis, studies of genres, studies of individual works, and performance practice; in addition, there are three workshops on interpretation and a symposium on the problems of editing. Although a few of the essays have not aged well, the majority of them remain classics of clarity and models of methodology. Some of the essays are focused on very broad issues,

including those by Lowinsky, who looks carefully at the life of Ascanio Sforza in an attempt to better understand Josquin's biography and the chronology of his works; Lewis Lockwood, who presents archival documents from Ferrara that shed light on Josquin's relationship with the Este family; and Howard Brown, who examines keyboard and lute intabulations of Josquin's motets in order to understand ornamentation, the art of intabulation, and *musica ficta* in the 16th century. Other essays are more narrowly focused, such as those by Jacquelyn Mattfeld, who investigates the absence of Ambrosian melodies in Josquin's sacred music; Virginia Callahan, who resolves the riddle of the text of *Ut Phoebi radiis;* and Brian Jeffery, who discusses the sources and forms of the literary texts for Josquin's chansons. Accompanying this book are three seven-inch phonodiscs that include some of the music performed by various groups at the workshops in this conference. Although some of the recordings sound clunky by recent standards, these discs represent for a few of the pieces the only recordings available.

ELDERS is a collection of essays that address the question of authenticity and attribution. The opening essays deal with a variety of related issues. Wim van Dooren, for example, places the question of authenticity within the framework of Renaissance philosophy; Patrick Macey provides compelling evidence that the motet *Celi enarrant* is not by Josquin but rather by someone imitating his style; and Joshua Rifkin suggests that we need to reexamine Josquin's entire corpus—even those pieces that do not have conflicting attributions—in order to come to a better understanding of what is really by Josquin and what is not. As a case study, he examines the sources and style of *Absalon, fili mi* and suggests that this motet is not by Josquin but by Pierre de la Rue. The majority of the book is organized around a series of workshops that examine questions of conflicting attributions between Josquin and Verdelot, Brumel, La Rue, and Mouton. Most of the essays deal with both source evaluation and matters of style. One of the strengths of this book is the diversity of approaches that individual scholars bring to the debate over conflicting attributions. J. Evan Kreider is primarily concerned with source evaluations in his essay on the works attributed to Josquin and La Rue. Brown suggests that, rather than concentrating on stylistic details that may have been the work of a publisher or scribe, scholars should concentrate on broad issues of compositional planning in order to understand what one can expect in a general way in works from one composer that is seldom or never found in the music of another. The appendix includes a list of works, arranged by genre, that will appear in the *New Josquin Edition*.

There has been an enormous amount of research on Josquin since Elders. One of the more important articles is MATTHEWS and MERKLEY, which gives the details of their recent archival discovery that the person named

Josquin who worked in Milan from 1459 until the mid-1470s was not the composer Josquin des Prez but rather a singer with the same first name who died in 1498. The article presupposes a familiarity with the traditional view of Josquin's biography as summarized in Reese and Noble and elsewhere. Although many of the archival documents are given in English translation as well as in their original language, some are left untranslated. Despite these shortcomings, this essay has the excitement of a good mystery and more than repays the effort spent in reading it. The information it disseminates has already had a profound effect on Josquin studies and will continue to influence future research for a considerable time.

MURRAY STEIB

See also Cantus Firmus

K

Kern, Jerome 1885–1945

United States composer

Bordman, Gerald Martin, *Jerome Kern: His Life and Music,*
    New York: Oxford University Press, 1980

Davis, Lee, *Bolton and Wodehouse and Kern: The Men Who
    Made Musical Comedy,* New York: Heineman, 1993

Ewen, David, *The World of Jerome Kern: A Biography,* New
    York, Holt, 1960

Forte, Allen, *The American Popular Ballad of the Golden Era:
    1924–1950,* Princeton, New Jersey: Princeton University
    Press, 1995

Freedland, Michael, *Jerome Kern: A Biography,* London:
    Robson Books, 1978

Kreuger, Miles, *Show Boat: The Story of a Classic American
    Musical,* New York: Oxford University Press, 1977

Lamb, Andrew, *Jerome Kern in Edwardian London,*
    Littlehampton: Lamb, 1981; revised edition, Brooklyn,
    New York: Institute for Studies in American Music, 1985

Wilder, Alec, *American Popular Song: The Great Innovators,
    1900–1950,* New York: Oxford University Press, 1972

Had he composed nothing but *Show Boat,* Jerome Kern would still merit a place in the first rank of Broadway composers. Beyond that landmark work, however, none of Kern's musicals have been revived with much success, and thus his eminence today rests more on a body of superior songs—among them "All the Things You Are," "Smoke Gets in Your Eyes," and "The Way You Look Tonight"—that have outlived their theatrical and motion picture origins. In some ways, it is not completely inaccurate to classify Kern as primarily a song composer, as he began his career and achieved his first successes writing American songs for insertion into London shows brought to New York. In a series of Princess Theater productions around the time of World War I, Kern—in collaboration with P.G. Wodehouse and Guy Bolton—established a nascent form of musical comedy in which the songs actually contributed to, rather than disrupted, the plot. A decade later, Kern—now working with Oscar Hammerstein II—forever changed the American theater

with *Show Boat,* the first musical to attain classic status and secure a permanent place in the American repertoire. No other show by Kern ever equaled that success, although few genuinely failed. Kern spent his last decade in Hollywood, where he produced a number of significant songs. To this day, Kern's music is admired for the naturalness of its melodies, the sophistication of its harmonic language, and an elegance of style that is almost timeless. Despite the central place that his songs occupy in American popular music, the bibliography for Kern is not very deep, with the few serious studies outnumbered by anecdotal essays and memoirs.

The biography by BORDMAN is easily the most important study to date of Kern's life and music. The study deals honestly and objectively with the effects of the composer's sometimes nettlesome personality on his professional career and, to a lesser extent, his personal life. Although neither an exhaustive nor detailed study of the music, Bordman does cover nearly every show and motion picture on which Kern worked from its earliest tryouts to its final form, with much attention paid to the changes that occurred along the way. Practical information, such as plot synopses and cast lists for the first productions, make this book essential for anyone interested in Kern.

EWEN's biography remains a serviceable and evenhanded survey of Kern's life. Although lacking the detail of Bordman's study, this book retains some authority, particularly for Kern's later years, because Ewen was able to interview many of those closest to Kern only a short time after the composer's death. At the same, because he addresses a general audience, Ewen favors an anecdotal description of Kern's life over a more substantial examination. Ewen also fails to provide documentation of his facts, and there is no real commentary on Kern's music.

FREEDLAND offers another popular biography. Unlike Bordman and Ewen, however, Freedland takes an informal and almost cavalier approach that sometimes distorts the basic facts of Kern's life. For instance, the story of Kern's first heart attack in 1937 is told in quite different ways by these three biographers. While Bordman presents the incident in a matter-of-fact tone that amplifies Ewen's basic account, Freedland transforms the event into an overblown melodrama, without presenting evidence to support his version. As with Ewen, Freedland provides no documentation—not even a bibliography—and no real description of the music.

A lifelong obsession with Kern's greatest work led KREUGER to devote a single volume to *Show Boat*, and the result is an admirable record of the performance history of this American classic. This study is liberally illustrated, and an appendix provides detailed lists of the casts and crews of nearly every major stage and screen production from the 1927 premiere to a 1983 revival. Kreuger's commentary on the strengths and weaknesses of seven major productions of *Show Boat* is as important as the thorough documentation.

The significance of Kern's early professional experience in London is a generally accepted fact, but no one before LAMB had ever chronicled Kern's first years abroad. This brief but well-documented volume provides answers to numerous mysteries from that period of Kern's life, superceding even Bordman's work in this area. Several appendices provide such useful information as the most accurate list of Kern's English songs and the identities of the most important figures working in London theaters at the same time as Kern.

DAVIS focuses exclusively on Kern and his Princess Theater collaborators in a three-pronged biography that moves easily back and forth among the lives of the three principals. There are many segments of the book from which Kern is entirely absent, however, as Davis follows the careers of Wodehouse or Bolton in other directions. The accounts of this trio's work together are more detailed in this volume than in any other study, but only in terms of the events that led to the music and not in terms of the music itself.

Only one chapter of WILDER's highly idiosyncratic look at the American popular song is devoted to Kern, but those 60 pages represent one of the few serious published examinations of his music. Wilder makes no pretense of comprehensiveness or even complete objectivity in his personal tour of about three dozen of Kern's melodies. The author's admiration and criticism are always supported by specific musical references, however, making this chapter an excellent introduction to Kern's style for those who can read and understand the many musical illustrations.

FORTE's study of the American popular ballad takes this repertoire one step further than Wilder into the realm of advanced musical analysis. Although this book is intended to be accessible to readers beyond the academic community, only a small audience—those who are able to read music fluently and who are also conversant in the language of music theory—will be able to understand and appreciate these technical descriptions of six of Kern's best songs.

SCOTT WARFIELD

Keyboard Music: General

Apel, Willi, *The History of Keyboard Music to 1700*, translated by Hans Tischler, Bloomington: Indiana University Press, 1972

Arnold, Corliss Richard, *Organ Literature: A Comprehensive Survey*, 2 vols., Metuchen, New Jersey: Scarecrow Press, 1973; 3rd edition, 1995

Bond, Ann, *A Guide to the Harpsichord*, Portland, Oregon: Amadeus Press, 1997

Burge, David, *Twentieth-Century Piano Music*, New York: Schirmer Books, 1990

Friskin, James, and Irwin Freundlich, *Music for the Piano: A Handbook of Concert and Teaching Material from 1580 to 1952*, New York: Rinehart, 1954

Gillespie, John, *Five Centuries of Keyboard Music: An Historical Survey of Music for Harpsichord and Piano*, Belmont, California: Wadsworth, 1965

Gordon, Stewart, *A History of the Keyboard Literature: Music for the Piano and Its Forerunners*, New York: Schirmer Books, and London: Prentice Hall, 1996

Hinson, Maurice, *Guide to the Pianist's Repertoire*, Bloomington: Indiana University Press, 1973; 2nd edition, 1987

———, *Guide to the Pianist's Repertoire: Supplement*, Bloomington: Indiana University Press, 1979

Hutcheson, Ernest, *The Literature of the Piano: A Guide for Amateur and Student*, New York: Knopf, 1948; 3rd edition, revised by Rudolph Ganz, 1975

Kirby, F.E., *Music for Piano: A Short History*, Portland, Oregon: Amadeus Press, 1995

———, *A Short History of Keyboard Music*, New York: Schirmer Books, and London: Collier Macmillan, 1966

Kratzenstein, Marilou, *Survey of Organ Literature and Editions*, Ames: Iowa State University Press, 1980

Lukas, Viktor, *A Guide to Organ Music*, translated by Anne Wyburd from the 5th, revised and enlarged edition, Portland, Oregon: Amadeus Press, 1989

Marshall, Robert L., editor, *Eighteenth-Century Keyboard Music*, New York: Schirmer Books, 1994

Silbiger, Alexander, editor, *Keyboard Music before 1700*, New York: Schirmer Books, and London: Prentice Hall, 1995

Todd, R. Larry, editor, *Nineteenth-Century Piano Music*, New York: Schirmer Books, 1990

Wolff, Konrad, *Masters of the Keyboard*, Bloomington: Indiana University Press, 1983; enlarged edition, 1990

Studies of general keyboard music examine works for four families of instruments—organ, harpsichord, clavichord, and piano—dating from the 14th century to the present. Three different approaches have been taken in this field: comprehensive narratives documenting the historical development of styles and genres, discussions of selected works by significant composers, and catalogs of compositions. The earliest research in English in this field tends to be broad in scope and to include all, or most, keyboard families; among these, Apel and Kirby (1966) provide detailed narratives describing the historical development of styles and genres associated with keyboard music. Following these initial contributions, comprehensive catalogs of works for one instrument appear, often including lists of editions, publishers, collections, and anthologies. More recently, authors such as Kratzenstein, Bond, Todd, Burge, and Kirby (1995) have selected particular keyboard instruments for historical consideration. Books published during the 1990s generally include more information on women, minorities, and non-Western composers than previous studies did.

APEL's comprehensive coverage of compositions for keyboard instruments contributes to an appreciation of composers before 1700 as outstanding artists in their own right rather than mere precursors to J.S. Bach. Introductory chapters summarize the history of the instruments and explain notational conventions that delineate music for keyboard from that for other instruments. Arranged chronologically, the text explains the historical development of numerous types of keyboard pieces. Subdivision of the book according to geographic regions clarifies stylistic trends as they varied among different countries. The extensive bibliography of primary and secondary sources and the indices of composers and compositions contribute to this book's usefulness as a reference tool for both students and scholars.

ARNOLD organizes his survey of organ music from the 14th to the 20th centuries into two volumes. The first, arranged according to geographical regions, discusses historical background for significant composers, types of pieces, and original sources for the music. Volume 2, arranged alphabetically by composer, includes brief biographical data and a list of organ compositions for each composer. Volume 2 also provides a list of organ anthologies, directory of publishers, and list of German chorale titles with their English translations. Both volumes contain extensive bibliographies.

BOND's general handbook includes several chapters dedicated to music written for the harpsichord family. Organized according to geographic regions, these chapters identify significant composers, the types of pieces they wrote, original sources of literature, and general historical context. Chapters covering the harpsichord's use as a continuo instrument enhance the context for the review of the music. The book concludes with an appendix on 20th-century harpsichord music and a bibliography.

BURGE provides an overview of significant composers and repertoire for solo piano for the first nine decades of the 20th century. Organized according to four major time periods, the book discusses various styles and compositional techniques that characterize 20th-century piano music. It also incorporates performance and practice suggestions for some of the pieces. Burge includes a selected bibliography, chronological list of works and publishers, and discography.

FRISKIN and FREUNDLICH's catalog of piano music references the works of over 500 composers from the late 16th century until 1952. Entries for virtually every composition describe the form and character of the piece and identify the types of technical demands involved. Several brief critical commentaries address performance practice issues and general historical background. Discussions of available editions, collections, and anthologies appear throughout the book. In addition to solo piano works, this catalog includes works composed or arranged for two pianists and for piano and orchestra. Because pianists frequently perform music composed before the invention of the pianoforte, works of the late 16th and early 17th centuries originally intended for harpsichord, clavichord, or organ are included.

GILLESPIE surveys solo compositions for stringed keyboard instruments (harpsichord, clavichord, and piano) from the 14th century to the middle of the 20th century. The book is as valuable for its brief biographical information as for its treatment of the music. The breadth of coverage, nontechnical language, glossary, general bibliography, and list of the most important publishers of keyboard music make this book particularly useful for students and nonspecialists.

GORDON's survey covers the music of all keyboard instruments from the 14th century to the present with special emphasis on the repertoire studied and performed by pianists. Musical contributions by a broad spectrum of composers are described briefly; more comprehensive discussions of the most significant keyboard composers of the 18th, 19th, and early 20th centuries include biographical sketches followed by brief stylistic and analytical descriptions of many of their important pieces. Gordon provides lists of available anthologies, collections, and complete editions, as well as a bibliography.

HINSON (1973) is an extensive catalog of solo piano works organized alphabetically by composer. Each entry includes the composer's dates and national origin and a list of solo piano compositions with graded difficulty levels indicated. Including lists of anthologies and collections, an extensive bibliography, historical recital programs, and numerous indices, this guide is a valuable resource for students, performers, and teachers. HINSON (1979) is an update of the 1973 work. The supplement follows a similar format without duplicating information found in the original work. Its indices include references to electronic resources and prepared piano, and the bibliography is expanded.

HUTCHESON's general survey for the piano includes solo works as well as concertos and ensemble music. Primary emphasis begins with the music of J.S. Bach. In addition to descriptions of the compositions, Hutcheson critiques various editions and suggests guidelines for the selection, interpretation, practice, and performance of individual pieces. Ganz's revised, updated edition includes more recent developments in works for the piano, including concrete music, electronic music, and use of magnetic tape.

KIRBY (1966) provides a comprehensive interpretation of the historical development of keyboard music and its composers and genres beginning in the 14th century and extending to the mid-20th century and includes instruments for all four keyboard families. The focus is on solo works composed since 1750, although significant duets and two-piano works are included. Kirby establishes a context for the significance of keyboard music within given historical eras by relating that music to that composed for other instruments and by explaining the importance of keyboard pieces within individual composers' artistic output. Kirby also suggests social and political circumstances that have had an impact on the development of music. Because of its extensive list of editions, bibliography, and indices, this book is also a useful reference work.

KIRBY (1995) presents a comprehensive discussion of the historical development of compositions, styles, and genres for piano with primary focus on music composed after 1750. The brief overview of keyboard music before that date reveals the forms, styles, and techniques of earlier composers that influenced the development of piano music. Discussions of major composers incorporate lists of their principal compositions. In addition to solo works, Kirby also covers duet and two-piano pieces. An extensive bibliography contributes to this book's usefulness as a reference tool.

KRATZENSTEIN's book is a reprint of a series of her articles published from 1971 to 1977 in *The Diapason*, expanded to include a more thorough list of editions. Covering the time period from the 14th century to the middle of the 20th century, Kratzenstein provides a concise historical overview of the development of organ music according to geographical regions. The narrative for each country identifies significant composers and types of pieces written. Kratzenstein also discusses the organs themselves as they relate to the pieces developed for them. This book is particularly useful for its lists of editions and collections; it also includes an extensive bibliography.

LUKAS provides a catalog of organ music from the 15th century to the mid-20th century, arranged chronologically by composer. Entries include composers' dates, brief biographical data, editions, and a list of works with brief descriptions. The book concludes with a glossary and list of publishers.

MARSHALL covers keyboard music during a century that witnessed not only the major style shift from baroque to classical but also the development of a new keyboard instrument—the pianoforte. This collection of essays by specialists provides an overview of the keyboard literature organized according to the major composers of the 18th century. Each composer's chapter includes critical and historical analyses, descriptions of stylistic features, an overview of important genres, and an explanation of the historical context. Each chapter also lists editions and facsimiles and provides a selected bibliography. Introductory chapters describe the various keyboard instruments in use during the century and discuss performance practice issues.

SILBIGER's collection of essays by specialists provides an introduction and guide to music for all keyboard instruments before 1700. Rather than a continuous narrative on the historical development of keyboard music found in Apel's book covering the same time period, the contributors to this volume examine specific works they consider to have artistic interest and value. Organized according to national regions, this book places primary emphasis on the music itself; such issues as styles, textures, genres, original sources, notation, and performance practice receive treatment. Each chapter concludes with a guide to works and editions, bibliography, and list of manuscript short titles.

TODD coordinates this group of essays by noted specialists according to his premise that the piano held preeminent status during the 19th century, not only in its primary role as disseminator of musical culture, but also its central position in European society. Todd first establishes a context for the articles that follow by exploring the role of the instrument itself in 19th-century musical culture and by considering the piano's physical development and concurrent impact on the repertoire written for it throughout the century. Subsequent essays focus on contributions of the most significant composers and address the works through a variety of approaches—analytical, social, cultural, and historical. Each chapter concludes with a bibliography.

WOLFF focuses on the particular contributions of Bach, Haydn, Mozart, Beethoven, Schubert, Chopin, and Brahms, the latter two added in the 1990 edition. Discussions include concertos and ensemble music as well as solo compositions. Through analyses of individual works, Wolff illustrates style traits and compositional techniques characteristic of each composer.

RENEE MCCACHREN

Keyboard Music: Renaissance

Apel, Willi, *The History of Keyboard Music to 1700*, translated by Hans Tischler, Bloomington: Indiana University Press, 1972

Caldwell, John, *English Keyboard Music before the Nineteenth Century*, New York: Praeger, 1973

Cunningham, Walker, *The Keyboard Music of John Bull*, Ann Arbor, Michigan: UMI Research Press, and Epping: Bowker, 1984

Diruta, Girolamo, *Il Transilvano*, 2 vols., edited by Murray C. Bradshaw and Edward J. Soehnlen: Institute of Mediaeval Music, 1984

Harley, John, *British Harpsichord Music*, 2 vols., Aldershot: Scolar Press, and Brookfield, Vermont: Gower, 1992

Neighbour, Oliver, *The Consort and Keyboard Music of William Byrd*, Berkeley: University of California Press, 1978

Ripin, Edwin M., et al., editors, *The New Grove Early Keyboard Instruments*, London: Macmillan, and New York: Norton, 1989

Silbiger, Alexander, editor, *Keyboard Music before 1700*, New York: Schirmer Books, and London: Prentice Hall, 1995

Tomas de Santa Maria, *The Art of Playing the Fantasia*, edited by Almonte C. Howell and Warren E. Hultberg, Pittsburgh, Pennsylvania: Latin American Literary Review Press, 1991

Williams, Peter F., and Barbara Owen, *The New Grove Organ*, London: Macmillan, and New York: Norton, 1988

Keyboard music of the Renaissance (ca. 1450–1600) was a traditional subject of 20th-century European musicology. Standard textbooks, however, have tended to treat Renaissance keyboard music as secondary to contemporary vocal polyphony by such composers as Josquin des Prez and Giovanni Perluigi da Palestrina, despite the flowering of keyboard music during the period and its importance in European music culture. Moreover, current academic trends, especially in North America, have diverted scholars from the study of original music sources, performance practices, and instruments, so that a reader curious about Renaissance keyboard music is faced with a dearth of recent monographs or even articles in English. Thus, a serious student of the subject must often turn to unpublished dissertations and to older writings, many of them in foreign languages.

In addition, early keyboard music does not show the sharp chronological and stylistic boundaries suggested by the conventional division of music history into medieval, Renaissance, and baroque categories. Instead, one finds a smooth and steady evolution from the time of the earliest surviving keyboard instruments and notated keyboard scores in the late Middle Ages. The literature on keyboard music reflects this continuity; there are no books in English confined to any one of these periods, as authors prefer to draw chronological lines at points that more realistically reflect the nature of the surviving documents. The most important of these lines has been the division around 1700, which corresponds, very roughly, to a shift from a tradition in which keyboard playing was largely the domain of professional church organists to one in which secular professionals and amateurs played significant roles. Although there were important exceptions, keyboard playing before 1700 was in many ways an improvisatory art; notated music served primarily for instruction and was transmitted chiefly through manuscripts. Paradoxically, the disappearance of the older improvisation tradition and the limited survival of pre-1700 instruments and manuscripts has led histories of this music to focus on the relatively rare publications and

other documentary evidence that do remain but which may not represent the entire range of music.

This documentary focus is particularly true of APEL, a comprehensive study of pre-1700 keyboard music containing some 300 pages relevant to this topic. An updated translation of a German original published in 1967, this book remains the only source in English on much of the repertoire, particularly that from before 1550 and from outlying regions such as Eastern Europe. But Apel, although a pioneer in the study of historical performance practice, does not always convey the living nature of the traditions he describes, focusing instead on a systematic (and therefore sometimes dry) survey of the notation and formal aspects of the surviving musical scores. The same can be said of much other literature on the subject.

Fortunately, an indispensable exception is provided by SILBIGER, a superb collection of essays on the most important national traditions of keyboard music before 1700. Several of the individual contributors are distinguished keyboard players as well as scholars. A particularly valuable feature of this work is the attention paid to surviving keyboard instruments and their relationship to the music and its performance practice. Also useful is the guide to editions and literature included in each chapter. The book is organized by region; thus a reader interested in Renaissance music will consult the appropriate portions of the respective chapters on English, French, German, and Italian keyboard music. Because of the unbroken line of development from earlier music, it is important to read the editor's introduction as well as the portion of each chapter on the medieval tradition.

The other writings listed above treat more specialized topics. Not surprisingly, English-language publications have focused on English music, which shows a particularly rich development during the Elizabethan and Jacobean periods (1558–1625). HARLEY, although spanning the entire history of English keyboard music, provides a good introduction to this era. Volume 1 is a bibliographic study useful primarily to specialists, and volume 2 includes a survey of English Renaissance keyboard music as well as summaries of social settings, compositional approaches, and performance practices for English keyboard music in general. CALDWELL is an older work treating much the same material as Harley from a more traditional standpoint.

Neighbour and Cunningham provide in-depth studies of the keyboard music of the period's two most important English keyboard composers. The keyboard works of William Byrd occupy more than half of NEIGHBOUR, which is distinguished by its detailed analysis of and critical commentary on each composition. Neighbour's interpretations have not been universally accepted, and they must therefore be read with a critical eye, but his work remains the most magisterial critical study of any pre-baroque keyboard composer. CUNNINGHAM provides similar treatment for the works of John Bull, correcting some misunderstandings perpetuated by earlier literature.

For keyboard music of other regions and traditions there are virtually no English-language monographs (for other literature, see Apel and Silbiger). Recordings and modern editions of music sometimes include valuable commentaries, but older materials must be read with caution. Useful information about specific repertoires can be found in the introductions to several volumes containing keyboard music in the Recent Researches in the Music of the Renaissance series (Madison, Wisconsin: A-R Editions). Less informative are the often perfunctory prefaces to volumes in the Corpus of Early Keyboard Music series (American Institute of Musicology); an exception is Robert Judd's edition of works by the important Italian composer Claudio Merulo (Neuhausen-Stuttgart, 1991–).

Writings on instruments and performance practice, although not the focus of the present article, provide necessary background for study and analysis of the surviving scores. The volumes by RIPIN and by WILLIAMS and OWEN contain updated versions of previously published material on harpsichords, clavichords, and the organ. DIRUTA, originally published in two volumes (1593–1609) by a student of Merulo, is the principal source on Italian keyboard practice, shedding light not only on performance but on genres and conditions of keyboard composition during the late Renaissance; it is thus essential for serious study of the subject. The same is true of TOMAS DE SANTA MARIA, originally published in Spanish in 1565. Spanish keyboard music was of fundamental importance during the Renaissance; primarily a composition treatise, this work incorporates the earliest substantial commentary on clavichord playing. The translation, although idiosyncratic and hard to use because of its clumsy typography and format, conveys the substance of the original, whose relevance extends to much European keyboard music of the time.

DAVID SCHULENBERG

Keyboard Music: Baroque

Apel, Willi, *The History of Keyboard Music to 1700,* translated by Hans Tischler, Bloomington: Indiana University Press, 1972

Caldwell, John, *English Keyboard Music before the Nineteenth Century,* New York: Praeger, 1973

Harley, John, *British Harpsichord Music,* 2 vols., Aldershot: Scolar Press, and Brookfield, Vermont: Gower, 1992

Ledbetter, David, *Harpsichord and Lute Music in 17th-Century France,* Bloomington : Indiana University Press, 1987

Marshall, Robert L., editor, *Eighteenth-Century Keyboard Music,* New York: Schirmer Books, 1994

Silbiger, Alexander, *Italian Manuscript Sources of 17th Century Keyboard Music,* Ann Arbor, Michigan: UMI Research Press, 1980

Silbiger, Alexander, editor, *Keyboard Music before 1700,* New York: Schirmer Books, and London: Prentice Hall, 1995

Stauffer, George, and Ernest May, editors, *J.S. Bach as Organist: His Instruments, Music and Performance Practices,* London: Batsford, and Bloomington: Indiana University Press, 1986

Williams, Peter F., *The Organ Music of J.S. Bach,* 3 vols., Cambridge: Cambridge University Press, 1980–84

Williams, Peter F., editor, *Bach, Handel, Scarlatti: Tercentenary Essays,* Cambridge: Cambridge University Press, 1985

Music for organ, harpsichord, clavichord, and other keyboard instruments was composed throughout the baroque (ca. 1600–1750) and has figured prominently in historical studies of that period. Yet few books in English have been devoted specifically to this topic. Instead, one finds general histories of early keyboard music as well as studies of individual repertories from the baroque. General histories tend to focus on later periods and for this reason offer only cursory (and not always accurate) treatments of the topic. Prominent among more specialized studies are books on the keyboard music of J.S. Bach and of earlier German composers who have been viewed—not quite accurately—as his predecessors. The very distinct repertories of Italian, French, and English keyboard composers during the period have each been subjects of studies as well. Another important area of research has been the instruments themselves and the performance practices appropriate to each. The present entry is concerned primarily with writings about the musical compositions, their style, and its development. The emphasis is on books that survey the entire period or portions of it; also listed are several works that, although focusing on individual composers, include substantial material of more general interest.

APEL is a massive compendium of information about keyboard music up to 1700. It is indispensable for serious study of keyboard music from the 17th century, which takes up more than half of the volume's 878 pages. Ably translated from the German original published in 1967, the book includes biographical sketches of most of the composers, major and minor, as well as descriptions of their works and extensive bibliographic references. The text is well organized for ready reference: parts 3 and 4 discuss keyboard music from the first and the second halves of the 17th century, respectively, with individual chapters on music from the various regions of Western Europe. Unfortunately, much of Apel has become seriously out of date. Moreover, it tends to discuss the music through a dry, superficial type of formal analysis that ignores original performance contexts and practices. For this reason it must be supplemented by reference to more recent accounts, which are likely to be more accurate and more lively. Nevertheless, it remains the only true survey of the subject in English, and it provides coverage of subjects barely touched elsewhere (e.g., organ music of southern Germany). It is unfortunate that no comparable volume exists for baroque keyboard music after 1700.

Silbiger and Marshall have both edited volumes in a recent series on the history of keyboard music. Each book consists of essays by different authors on selected specialized repertories, surveying the principal composers and genres and thus updating the matter provided by Apel for those particular subjects. Although lacking Apel's comprehensive coverage, the writing in these volumes tends to be more accessible to the general reader while paying more attention to the historical and cultural context of the music. SILBIGER (1995), like Apel, provides coverage starting with the beginnings of keyboard music, arranged by country. Thus, only the latter portion of each of the last five chapters is relevant here (on England, France, Germany and the Netherlands, Italy, and Spain and Portugal, respectively). Nevertheless, these chapters will provide readers with the most up-to-date, concise introductions to early baroque keyboard music in each of these regions. MARSHALL provides more selective coverage within the 18th century. In addition to the editor's survey of the keyboard music of J.S. Bach, there are also essays on C.P.E. Bach, Domenico Scarlatti, and the later French harpsichord composers.

German keyboard music, especially that of J.S. Bach, has been the subject of numerous specialized studies. WILLIAMS (1984) is the third volume of a comprehensive study of Bach's organ music. Intended to furnish a background to the work's two preceding volumes on individual pieces by the composer, this volume can also be read independently as an introduction to German organ music and its performance during the late baroque. Williams is particularly interested in the actual duties and practice of organists—such things as the playing of hymns (chorales) in services and recitals—and how these activities were shaped by the instruments and by contemporary views of musical rhetoric and symbolism. Each of the major late-baroque German organ genres is discussed as well, including potential French and Italian influences. Throughout, one finds numerous incisive observations that frequently cast doubt on widely held assumptions about the music and its players.

STAUFFER and MAY is one of several anthologies published in connection with the Bach tercentenary (1985). It supplements Williams (1984) by providing 17 essays divided roughly evenly among Bach's instruments, the music itself, and performance practice. Most of the essays are fairly specialized, but together they provide a sampling of recent trends in Bach scholarship. Of particular note in the present context are essays by Ernest May, Werner Breig, and Christoph Wolff on the types and compositional histories of Bach's chorale settings; some

of the material is relevant to similar works by other composers as well.

Approximately half of the essays in WILLIAMS (1985), also published for the Bach (and Handel and Scarlatti) tercentenary, are concerned with keyboard works of Domenico Scarlatti, Handel, and J.S. Bach. The 19 essays range widely in subject; those on keyboard music tend toward matters relevant to practice and interpretation, such as articulation (Mark Lindley), tuning and temperament (Rudolf Rasch), and musical rhetoric (Williams). Also notable are essays by David Humphreys and Giorgio Pestelli concerning the origins of two keyboard works attributed to Bach.

LEDBETTER is a scholarly study of French harpsichord music, which is considered alongside the closely related repertory for the lute. The book surveys the two repertories and their sources (manuscripts and early editions), as well as the types of harpsichord that were in use. It then critically examines the relationship between the two repertories, long recognized by Apel and others, closely analyzing specific cases of both influence and divergence. Particularly interesting are stylistic analyses of the chief genres of keyboard piece, arranged by composer and demonstrating the relationship of each to earlier lute works.

SILBIGER (1980) is a study of the early manuscript sources of the Italian baroque repertory. Although the title suggests a narrow focus on dry bibliographic material, the book provides a searching consideration of general style and performance practice in this music, discussing, in particular, style and conflicting theories about authorship in works attributed to Frescobaldi, his teacher Ercole Pasquini, and the later composer Bernardo Pasquini (unrelated). The author has subsequently published a series of facsimile editions reproducing many of the sources discussed in this book (*Seventeenth-Century Keyboard Music: Sources Central to the Baroque,* 1987–89). Prefaces in these volumes provide essential updates to the material here.

Not surprisingly, English music has been the subject of a significant number of English-language writings, despite the relatively small size and peripheral nature of the English baroque keyboard repertory. Most treatments have covered the important pre-baroque periods as well, especially the late Renaissance (Elizabethan). CALDWELL surveys the best-known works through the 18th century; reasonably accessible to nonspecialists, it also summarizes matter pertaining to the sources and thus provides scholars as well with a dependable introduction to the subject. (Dedicated scholars will find additional material pertaining specifically to the English baroque repertory in Barry Cooper, *English Solo Keyboard Music of the Middle and Late Baroque,* New York: Garland, 1989, essentially a reprint of the author's 1974 dissertation.)

HARLEY is a more comprehensive and up-to-date treatment of much the same material as Caldwell (excluding organ music). Volume 1 is a detailed catalog of sources and thus of interest primarily to scholars. Volume 2, of more general interest, includes two substantial chapters on the history of baroque harpsichord music in England. In addition, part 2 of the volume contains chapters on the instruments, "The Social Setting," "The Composer's Materials," and notation and performance practice. Of these, the second chapter is particularly useful to general readers for contextualizing the music in its historical setting.

DAVID SCHULENBERG

Keyboard Music: Classical

Badura-Skoda, Eva, and Paul Badura-Skoda, *Interpreting Mozart on the Keyboard,* translated by Leo Black, London: Barrie and Rockliff, and New York: St. Martin's Press, 1962

Brown, A. Peter, *Joseph Haydn's Keyboard Music: Sources and Style,* Bloomington: Indiana University Press, 1986

Kirby, F.E., *A Short History of Keyboard Music,* New York: Schirmer Books, and London: Collier Macmillan, 1966

Komlos, Katalin, *Fortepianos and Their Music: Germany, Austria, and England, 1760–1800,* Oxford: Clarendon Press, and New York: Oxford University Press, 1995

Marshall, Robert L., editor, *Eighteenth-Century Keyboard Music,* New York: Schirmer Books, 1994

Newman, William S., *Beethoven on Beethoven: Playing His Piano Music His Way,* New York: Norton, 1988

————, *The Sonata in the Classic Era,* Chapel Hill: University of North Carolina Press, 1961; 3rd edition, New York: Norton, 1983

Rosenblum, Sandra P., *Performance Practices in Classic Piano Music: Their Principles and Applications,* Bloomington: Indiana University Press, 1988

Somfai, László, *The Keyboard Sonatas of Joseph Haydn: Instruments and Performance Practice, Genres, and Styles,* translated by the author and Charlotte Joyce Greenspan, Chicago: University of Chicago Press, 1995

Keyboard music in the second half of the 18th century gained an unprecedented importance as increasing numbers of amateur performers were drawn to the instruments, and the taste for solo and chamber works for keyboard developed. Organ music, however, with its own repertoire and traditions centered in the church, actually declined in this period and is not considered here. The gradual but phenomenal rise in popularity of the piano after 1750, driven by new demands for dynamic contrast and a more vocally oriented means of expression, transformed keyboard music in profound and enduring ways. In terms of scholarship, music for keyboard has not received nearly as much attention as the grander orchestral genres of the classical period, especially the symphony and concerto. However, the revival of interest in

early music on period instruments has made the sounds of the harpsichord, clavichord, and fortepiano nearly commonplace and has encouraged scholars to reexamine a repertoire long taken for granted. Thus, performance practice issues have received serious treatment in recent years, and studies devoted to repertoire and genre—especially in relation to Haydn, Mozart, and Beethoven—are also available.

BADURA-SKODA and BADURA-SKODA is one of the earliest and most influential books in the field. Though it addresses Mozart's works specifically, the issues raised here apply equally well to classical keyboard music in general. The authors' intent is to supply performers with a practical manual for understanding and interpreting Mozart's keyboard works, and the book combines extensive research with actual experience. Modeled along the lines of Carl Philipp Emanuel Bach's famous treatise on keyboard performance, this book provides comprehensive explanations of classical keyboard ornamentation, articulations, and continuo accompaniment, and illustrates them copiously with examples from Mozart's works. In a chapter titled "Mozart's Sound," the authors provide one of the earliest informed reflections on the use of historical instruments and discuss the types of instruments that Mozart used. Two chapters deal with the issue of improvisation in Mozart's works and offer numerous suggestions to the performer who wishes to embellish a melody or to devise a cadenza in Mozart's style. They even devote a chapter to advice on developing the technique necessary to play essential elements of Mozart's keyboard music, such as non-legato passages, scales and arpeggios, and broken octaves, among others.

A more recent study of performance practice is ROSENBLUM. This extraordinary book should be required reading for college-level courses on performance practice and classical piano style; it is by far the most comprehensive resource available on these topics. Rosenblum's discussion of such issues as dynamics, articulation, pedaling, tempo, and ornaments is thoroughly grounded in critical readings of 18th-century keyboard treatises, including many minor theorists as well as the celebrated essays by Carl Philipp Emanuel Bach and D.G. Türk; indeed, the author makes no performing suggestions that have not been sanctioned in contemporary documents, and she scrupulously cites every source. In keeping with recent scholarly trends, she offers background on keyboard music and rhetorical principles popular in the 18th century and also gives a detailed technical overview of the classical fortepiano. The thorny issues of tempo and metronome markings in Beethoven's music are tackled at length. In conclusion, Rosenblum offers a sample analysis of a Beethoven bagatelle, applying the historical performance practices explored throughout the book and demonstrating the insights that may be gained through such study.

NEWMAN (1988) also focuses largely on performance practice issues. He presents the most complete survey available of Beethoven's pianos, the differences between them, and what impact these differences would have on his music. Like the Rosenblum book, this study is founded on careful evaluation of contemporary documents; in this case, the writings of Beethoven and his circle and the manuscript sources for Beethoven's keyboard music. Newman's analysis of Beethoven's articulation markings, particularly slurs and staccato signs, is especially penetrating. The author has gathered much valuable data on Beethoven's own playing and technique, such as the significance and meanings of Beethoven's original fingerings. Questions of tempo and metronome markings are explored here in great depth, with a useful table correlating tempo markings and time signatures throughout the Beethoven sonatas. This book would be an excellent teaching tool, for it handles even quite technical analysis in an accessible style and is amply illustrated with musical examples.

KOMLOS addresses three main topics: fortepiano history and design, classical piano repertoire, and performance practice. However, because the book is quite short it must necessarily serve as an introduction rather than an in-depth investigation. The book is a comparative study that links the musical styles of various late-18th-century composers (such as Johann Christian Bach and Joseph Haydn) with the types of pianos for which they wrote (Broadwood in London or Schanz in Vienna, for example). The substantial differences between English and Viennese fortepianos during this period were reflected clearly in the textures and idiom of the music written for them, and Komlos provides numerous examples to illustrate such connections. The book concludes with a useful review of the important piano treatises of the period as well as a survey of playing techniques and styles of leading pianists in London and Vienna.

Surveys of keyboard repertoire are found in Kirby and Newman (1961). KIRBY features two substantial chapters on the subject of keyboard music in the classical era. "The Time of Change" (ca. 1720–90) is especially interesting because it discusses many lesser known musicians, including the last great school of Italian keyboard composers writing for both harpsichord and fortepiano, from Giustini and Platti through Alberti, Galuppi, and Sammartini. One does not find detailed analyses of keyboard works here, but the book outlines general trends and changes in style in a largely geographical context. NEWMAN (1961) is concerned with genre as well as repertoire, tracing the development of the sonata from about 1735 until the end of the 18th century. While the sonata was by no means exclusively a keyboard genre, the book demonstrates that the link between the genre and the instrument was an increasingly potent one; in fact the bulk of 18th-century

sonatas were intended for keyboard, whether solo or accompanied by another instrument, usually flute or violin. This work is a geographical survey that examines the composers and repertoire of Italy, Spain and Portugal, France, England, and Germany (especially major courts such as Mannheim and Dresden); the author also considers cities such as Stockholm and St. Petersburg that have been overlooked in most general studies but had flourishing keyboard schools in the 18th century.

Brown and Somfai, both devoted to the keyboard music of Joseph Haydn, represent the very best scholarship in this field. BROWN provides an exemplary study of sources and style in Haydn's keyboard music. The author examines in great detail such complex issues as questions of authenticity (a very large number of false attributions to Haydn have complicated the study of his music) and debates concerning which types of keyboard instruments are most appropriate for Haydn's various works. Brown's discussion of keyboard idiom is extremely intricate and subtle, and his analyses of Haydn's keyboard works demonstrate the composer's evolution as an architect in formal structures such as the sonata, revealing the most distinctive traits of his keyboard style. SOMFAI focuses on Haydn's keyboard sonatas, introducing the topic with a discussion of the keyboard instruments available at the time of composition. One of Somfai's specialties is the subject of Haydn's notation; here the author applies his highly refined expertise to the analysis of Haydn's keyboard markings (such as articulations and dynamic signs) and their interpretation. One will not find a more authoritative treatment of Haydn's musical language in the sonata form; individual chapters investigate each component of the structure (primary theme, development, etc.) in Haydn's hands and also examine movement types within the sonatas. Somfai provides a valuable catalog of the sonatas with the most up-to-date chronology and publication data available.

MARSHALL offers a very worthy collection of essays by prominent scholars on various aspects of 18th-century keyboard music (including the baroque era). Useful and clearly written summaries of keyboard instruments and performance practices may be found at the beginning of the book; essays on the second half of the century encompass Carl Philipp Emanuel Bach, Johann Christian Bach and the Italian keyboard school, Haydn's solo keyboard music, and early piano music by Beethoven. Particularly noteworthy are two articles by Robert D. Levin, "Mozart's Solo Keyboard Music" and "Mozart's Keyboard Concertos." Levin's analyses are insightful, colorfully written, and informed by a vast performance experience. This book would serve very well in the college classroom for courses on keyboard repertoire.

KATHRYN L. SHANKS LIBIN

Keyboard Music: Romantic

Arnold, Corliss Richard, *Organ Literature: A Comprehensive Survey*, 2 vols., Metuchen, New Jersey: Scarecrow Press, 1973; 3rd edition, 1995

Dale, Kathleen, *Nineteenth-Century Piano Music: A Handbook for Pianists*, London: Oxford University Press, 1954

Hildebrandt, Dieter, *Pianoforte: A Social History of the Piano*, translated by Harriet Goodman, New York: Braziller, 1988

Kirby, F.E., *Music for Piano: A Short History*, Portland, Oregon: Amadeus Press, 1995

Matthews, Denis, editor, *Keyboard Music*, New York: Praeger, 1972

Todd, R. Larry, editor, *Nineteenth-Century Piano Music*, New York: Schirmer Books, 1990

Studies of romantic keyboard music may be conveniently divided into two types: general surveys of the literature and interpretative or critical discussions. Surveys vary both in the depth of coverage and in the way they present the vast number of works. Interpretative or critical discussions go beyond the music and into the realm of meaning and implication. The piano was undoubtedly the single most dominant instrument of the romantic era. Significantly, the only composers to ignore it as a forum for their works were the operatic composers. The duality between Brahms and Wagner, so often held as characteristic of the romantic movement in music, demonstrates this perfectly. It would be too much to say that the piano was an alternative outlet for an operatic impetus—that the piano became an orchestra and a cast of singers for a 19th-century living room (although it is a commonplace to regard Chopin's lyricism, Schumann's drama, and Liszt's mass appeal all as operatic). But in general, the 19th century brought music to the general public in two main ways. Regular operatic productions in large opera houses for mass audiences were one avenue; the ubiquitousness of the keyboard as a vehicle for entertainment and education was the other.

DALE's survey is organized traditionally according to genres: the most extensive genres such as sonata and variations take precedence. Different contributions to the various genres are thus handily compared. At times judgments are based on formal preconceptions: for example, Dale writes that "Schumann did not conceive his sonatas as organic wholes," implying that the works suffer because of the composer's approach. But she is quick to defend these compositions nonetheless: "Schumann's long opening and closing movements are like great tapestries filled with incidents depicted in glowing colors." Of the surveys reviewed here, Dale's book is the most engagingly written, even if the tone is somewhat dated at times. The study includes a short preface by renowned pianist Dame Myra Hess. Dale's text is a clear introduction to the forms that dominate piano literature.

MATTHEWS titled his text *Keyboard Music* but is quick to point out that he excludes organ works. There are three lengthy chapters on 19th-century piano music: one on the Viennese tradition of Beethoven, Schubert, and Brahms; another entitled "The Romantic Tradition," which concentrates on the keyboard technicians such as Chopin and Liszt; and a third that traces "The Growth of National Schools." Whereas Dale concentrates on form, Matthews and his contributors concentrate on the great composers. In the chapter on the romantic tradition, John Ogdon argues that the stylistic workings of the later romantics almost always can be traced back to Chopin, Schumann, and Liszt. This assertion is clearly an overstatement, but the advantage of this approach is that it allows a coherent portrayal of the formal and technical idiosyncrasies of the great composers.

KIRBY nicely complements Dale and Matthews. The organization here is strictly chronological. Kirby follows the course of the well-known composers, but he includes many significant asides on lesser figures, including German composers such as Max Reger, who is neglected by Matthews. Kirby also includes lesser-known national schools such as Latin America and the United States, reflecting more recent, comprehensive trends in historical musicology. For instance, whereas Dale does not mention MacDowell and Matthews gives him one sentence, Kirby treats him equally with Grieg. To be fair, Grieg deserves more from Kirby, and a traditional Lisztian virtuoso like Henry Charles Litolff, highly influential in his day, is not even mentioned.

TODD's compendium includes detailed musicological contributions by leading scholars. Some of the articles, such as those on Beethoven, Schubert, and Liszt, are general stylistic discussions, written with the latest musicological issues and controversies in mind. On the other hand, the articles on Chopin, Schumann, and Brahms are directed at establishing a new historical point of view. By focusing specifically on music for the piano, this volume represents the current status of 19th-century musicology in general.

HILDEBRANDT's elegant, literary book consists of a series of creative essays that explore the importance of piano music for 19th-century European culture in general. Although he does not specifically discuss the music, he brings out the importance of the music for the culture. After reading this book, it would be difficult to think of piano music as a world in itself because the author connects the music with business, literature, exploration, and personality—almost every significant aspect of 19th-century Western civilization. This book is not about piano music itself but about where it came from, where it went, and how it got there (both geographically and intellectually).

ARNOLD reviews the neglected repertory of the organ in his two-volume comprehensive survey. The first volume is a historical survey with brief descriptions of the styles and output of the various composers, in the manner of an annotated catalog. Many of the works for the organ from the romantic period discussed here are virtually unknown to most scholars. The second volume includes a bibliography and an alphabetical work list.

THOMAS SIPE

Keyboard Music: 20th Century

Armbruster, Greg, editor, *The Art of Electronic Music,* New York: Morrow, 1984

Burge, David, *Twentieth-Century Piano Music,* New York: Schirmer Books, 1990

Chadabe, Joel, *Electric Sound: The Past and Promise of Electronic Music,* Upper Saddle River, New Jersey: Prentice Hall, 1997

Gordon, Stewart, *A History of the Keyboard Literature: Music for the Piano and Its Forerunners,* New York: Schirmer Books, and London: Prentice Hall, 1996

Hinson, Maurice, *Guide to the Pianist's Repertoire,* Bloomington: Indiana University Press, 1973; 2nd edition, 1987

Kirby, F.E., *Music for Piano: A Short History,* Portland, Oregon: Amadeus Press, 1995

Lyons, Len, *The Great Jazz Pianists: Speaking of Their Lives and Music,* New York: Morrow, 1983

Taylor, Billy, *Jazz Piano: History and Development,* Dubuque, Iowa: Brown, 1982

Keyboard music as a field has expanded rapidly over the course of the 20th century, both in the development of new genres and the invention of new keyboard instruments. General surveys of the Western classical repertoire concentrate on innovations of composers during the first half of the 20th century as the culmination of over 200 years of music for solo piano and, to a much lesser extent, the organ; Burge's focus on the piano in the 20th century encompasses the work of more recent composers in Asia and the United States as well as in Europe. Books on keyboard music in jazz, starting with American piano ragtime around the turn of the century, take a biographical approach more appropriate to the study of a genre for which improvisation in live performances and on recordings highlights the individuality of each performer. Although highly technical language dominates studies of electronic music and the new keyboard-based instruments constructed for much of its production—from the Hammond Organ and the Ondes Martenot in the 1930s to postwar arrivals such as the Moog synthesizer, the Yamaha DX7, and MIDI keyboards—Chadabe's history of this 20th-century phenomenon brings a specialist's insight to a general introduction to the field, while Armbruster's compilation demonstrates how electronic innovations have made keyboard instruments an integral part of experimental music, popular music, and film scoring in the second half of the 20th century.

KIRBY's survey of piano music since the 17th century is a substantial revision of his *A Short History of Keyboard Music* (1966), once a standard keyboard literature textbook that has long been out of print. Intended for piano students and teachers, this volume presents a chronological survey of composers active during the 20th century and their works for piano. Although much of the scholarship informing the text is out of date, the extensive bibliography is an excellent guide to books and articles on individual composers in both English and foreign languages. Those looking for a survey of the repertoire for organ to 1950 need to turn to the original 1966 version, in which Kirby makes particular mention of French organist-composers Jehan Alain and Olivier Messiaen.

HINSON's reference guide is a systematic list of the repertoire for solo piano, first by individual composer and then by anthologies and collections—including anthologies of contemporary music. Each listing provides brief annotations pertaining to style or biography, bibliographical entries, and a grading of the difficulty of representative works. The book includes many American and 20th-century composers and ends with an index of composers by nationality and a general bibliography.

GORDON's comprehensive survey of keyboard music features a well-researched discussion of music for piano in the 20th century that begins with a chapter on Debussy and then proceeds geographically through Europe, North America, and South America, with a brief chapter reserved for music of nontonal composers in Europe. The geographical organization allows Gordon to sidestep older debates about the extent of German influence—here Debussy is compared more to his compatriots at the Schola Cantorum than he is to Wagner—and the alleged superiority of composers using serial techniques after 1945. The most complete coverage is that of the early 20th-century composers at the core of most pianists' repertoires: Debussy, Ravel, Rachmaninoff, Prokofiev, Bartók. Nevertheless, Gordon provides a comprehensive picture of composition for piano in each country mentioned, complete with frequent musical examples of works by both little-known and more famous composers, making the text a useful overview of the 20th century.

As a performer and teacher who specializes in contemporary music, BURGE has written a scholarly guide to 20th-century solo piano music that contains invaluable practical advice on performance and interpretation. He explicitly discusses the composers and pieces that interest him most, referring those looking for a more complete list to Hinson's guide. While Burge's viewpoints and analyses of well-known pieces from the early 20th century are insightful, the unique merits of the book lie in his discussion of music composed more recently, especially from the 1970s and 1980s. Detailed explorations of the music of George Crumb and Frederic Rzewski, to cite two examples, join informative overviews of contemporary music from North America, Europe, and Asia; the entire study is complemented by many musical examples and a select discography of piano music written after 1945. The book is geared toward teachers and advanced pianists wary of this unfamiliar territory, but its hints on performance will interest informed listeners as well.

TAYLOR, a jazz pianist and educator, gives a highly personal account of the history of the piano and pianists in jazz. The book is in fact a beginner's introduction to jazz via the repertoire of jazz piano. With many musical examples of jazz styles from ragtime to neogospel, Taylor invites the nonspecialist to read the book at the piano, producing the sounds of typical chord voicings and figurations as one reads. His discussion is at its best in the sections on early jazz, bebop, and 1960s free jazz—the periods during which solo pianists were in the spotlight—and Taylor emphasizes many now-forgotten pianists whose innovations greatly influenced well-known figures. To supplement Taylor's account, look for LYONS's compilation of interviews with 27 jazz pianists, ranging from Teddy Wilson to McCoy Tyner. More recent biographies of jazz pianists, such as Edward Berlin's *King of Ragtime: Scott Joplin and His Era* (1994), provide up-to-date bibliographies of books on individual artists.

CHADABE's history of electronic music covers topics as wide ranging as the invention of various instruments, their multifarious uses by composers and performers, and the process by which electronic instruments came to be marketed on a vast scale. This is not a book about electronic keyboard music per se, for Chadabe states in his preface that "the electronic musical instrument, after all, can take any form," and here the keyboard figures merely as the form most frequently chosen. Consequently, information on keyboards is scattered throughout various chapters, most notably chapters 6 ("Synthesizers") and 7 ("The MIDI World"). While Chadabe's approach can makes it difficult to find specific information about electronic keyboard music, the reader benefits by seeing how the different uses of a keyboard interface fit into the larger history of electronic music.

For a more keyboard-centered account, ARMBRUSTER's compilation of materials originally published in *Keyboard Magazine* from 1975 to 1983 contains an illustrated history of early electronic instruments, followed by more than 30 interviews with inventors and artists involved in the diverse fields of academic music departments, experimental music, popular music, film soundtracks, and the electronic music industry.

LESLIE SPROUT

Kodály, Zoltán 1882–1967

Hungarian-born composer, ethnomusicologist, and pedagogue

Barron, John P., editor, *A Selected Bibliography of the Kodály Concept of Music Education*, Willowdale: Avondale Press, 1979

Breuer, János, *A Guide to Zoltán Kodály*, translated by Maria Steiner, Budapest: Corvina, 1990

Choksy, Lois, *The Kodály Method: Comprehensive Music Education from Infant to Adult*, Englewood Cliffs, New Jersey: Prentice Hall, 1974; 3rd edition, 1999

Eôsze, László, *Zoltán Kodály: His Life and Work*, translated by István Farkas and Gyula Gulyás, London: Collet, and Boston: Crescendo, 1962

Johnston, Richard, editor, *Zoltán Kodály in North America*, Willowdale: Avondale Press, 1986

Kecskeméti, István, *Kodály the Composer: Brief Studies on the First Half of Kodály's Oeuvre*, translated by Judit Pokoly, Kecskemét: Zoltán Kodály Pedagogical Institute of Music, 1986

Kodály, Zoltán, *Folk Music of Hungary*, translated by Ronald Tempest and Cynthia Jolly, London: Barry and Rockliff, 1960

———, *The Selected Writings of Zoltán Kodály*, edited by Ferenc Bónis, London: Boosey and Hawkes, 1974

Legányné Hegyi, Erzsébet, *Solfege According to the Kodály-Concept*, translated by Fred MacNicol, Kecskemét: Zoltán Kodály Pedagogical Institute of Music, 1975

Ránki, György, editor, *Bartók and Kodály Revisited*, Budapest: Akadémiai Kiadó, 1987

Young, Percy M., *Zoltán Kodály: A Hungarian Musician*, London: Benn, 1964

Zemke, Lorna, *The Kodály Concept: Its History, Philosophy, and Development*, Champaign, Illinois: Foster Music, 1977

In the various aspects of his career, Zoltán Kodály made an impact not only as a composer but also as a pioneering ethnomusicologist and educator. Perhaps his greatest impact in the West has been in the area of music pedagogy; of Kodály literature in English, writings on his contributions to this area are the most extensive, while there are proportionally fewer items analyzing his compositional or ethnomusicological work or historical role. The present entry encompasses the majority of monographs on Kodály the composer and ethnomusicologist, including some seriously flawed works; only a fraction of the important works on the Kodály method of music pedagogy are discussed, as most of them use Kodály only as a starting point.

In the realm of biography, there are two main choices, both written while Kodály was still alive. EÔSZE's brief work, translated from the 1956 Hungarian original, is divided into sections reflecting different aspects of Kodály's life: first, a biographical overview, followed by sections on "The Musicologist," "The Teacher," and "The Composer," and then a short epilogue and an appended list of musical and prose works. Eôsze introduces the events of Kodály's life up to the point of writing and summarizes his activities. The reader often gets the impression of Kodály's own voice intervening, which can be a problem, but the book's partisanship does not invalidate it. In fact, in some matters, such as the inquiry into Kodály's involvement in the Republic of Councils in 1919 and 1920, the author presents an exceptionally thorough exposition. However, overall, Eôsze espouses a dated and Hungaro- (and folk music-) centric version of 20th-century music history that must be taken with a grain of salt.

YOUNG's slightly longer biography is laid out in a more straightforward linear narrative format and is more anecdotal and readable in style than is Eôsze's. In other ways, however, Young's book is at least as problematic. The problem begins with the foreword, a letter to the author by Kodály himself, which gives an authorized-biography flavor to the work. In the body of the work, Young provides a Hungarian history that is biased in favor of the Hungarian side; the British author's references to British music may wear on the reader; and the value of "authentic Hungarian music" is taken as self-evident, in a fairly simplistic, nationalistic way. All of these problems can only be corrected with a more distanced, balanced perspective. Although Young's approach to the music and the sources he cites complement Eôsze's biography, the definitive Kodály biography remains unwritten.

BREUER's more recent volume, also translated from an earlier (1982) Hungarian original, offers an interesting alternative to Young and Eôsze: it is a guide for concertgoers to Kodály's life's work as a composer, the sphere that Breuer considers to be the central category of Kodály's career. Each of Kodály's major works is given a chapter that covers the genesis of a work, its reception, and a brief, readable analysis of the music. Similar chapters are dedicated to categories of smaller works, such as those for piano or chorus. This book is probably the best available introduction to Kodály's music, although it lacks the specificity that musical examples and measure numbers would have lent its analyses. It also lacks the biographic detail and comprehensive work lists of Eôsze and Young. Therefore, although those books are quite out of date, they retain their usefulness.

Another work centered around Kodály's musical output is KECSKEMÉTI, a set of essays that each take some element of Kodály's composition as a theme, such as recurring motives, procession music, role changing in songs, and analogues to works of other composers. In a balanced manner, Kecskeméti addresses Kodály's works influenced by ancient Hungarian folk song, his art songs, his use of the stereotypically Hungarian-gypsy *verbunkos* style, and his interest in French music. These analyses are straightforward enough for the nonspecial-

ist musician, yet extensive enough to engage the scholar interested in further exploring Kodály's work.

The volume of essays edited by RÁNKI forms an excellent overview of Kodály and Béla Bartók's cultural environment. Although the emphasis here is mainly on Bartók, the writings on the composers' common surroundings are applicable to both, and the comparison of the folk-song research methods used by the two men is quite useful.

The selection of works listed on the Kodály method of music education includes two general overviews, by Choksy and Zemke. ZEMKE's monograph is a very concise introduction, only 50 pages long. Its brevity is helpful for the reader wishing to discover what defines the Kodály method: its philosophy that music is for everyone; its emphasis on the importance of music in a person's development; its use of folk songs in the language of the pupils; its foundation of musical training in singing; and its use of a movable-do solfège system. Zemke also outlines of the application of this program in the Hungarian schools. CHOKSY thoroughly discusses Kodály's method both in Hungarian practice and as it may be applied in U.S. schools. In a more detailed discussion of the application of this method, LEGÁNYNÉ HEGYI offers a complete curriculum of solfège sight-singing exercises and lesson plan suggestions, translated from the material she published for use in Hungarian schools.

KODÁLY (1974) has selected some of the more significant of Kodály's many writings, offering an interested reader direct access to Kodály's views. JOHNSTON includes a translation of KODÁLY (1960) and reprints of interviews and lectures Kodály gave in a North American tour late in his life. These primary sources give a much more direct view of Kodály's public face than Young or Eôsze could.

Finally, for the researcher looking to dig further, either the bibliography given in Kecskeméti's book or BARRON's bibliography may act as a starting place. Kecskeméti's bibliography updates those of Young and Eôsze; Barron's book covers many of the same works cited by Kecskeméti but also gives a more extensive listing of the pedagogical literature, especially (though not exclusively) that in English.

LYNN HOOKER

Korngold, Erich Wolfgang 1897–1957

Austrian-born composer

Carroll, Brendan, *The Last Prodigy: A Biography of Erich Wolfgang Korngold*, Portland, Oregon: Amadeus Press, 1997

Duchen, Jessica, *Erich Wolfgang Korngold*, London: Phaidon, 1996

Kalinak, Kathryn Marie, *Settling the Score: Music and the Classical Hollywood Film,* Madison: University of Wisconsin Press, 1992

The fame of Erich Wolfgang Korngold, one of the most popular early 20th-century composers, began to decline as early as the mid-1930s. The reasons are manifold, including musical style, the rise of national socialism, the composer's association with Hollywood, and the role of his father Julius Korngold (the conservative and outspoken critic of the Viennese newspaper *Neue Freie Presse*), whose machinations led to retaliations against his son. Since the 1970s, when romantic tendencies became once again fashionable in Western art music, and especially since the late 1980s, Korngold's music has been successfully revived, and the past few years have seen an explosion of new recordings. Scholarship, however, is lagging far behind: it provides mainly superficial analyses of Korngold's works; good biographies have until very recently not been available. The present survey reviews only the most relevant writings.

The first full-length biography appeared in 1996. DUCHEN does not write primarily for the scholar. Footnotes are not provided, and the musical discussions are kept at a level easily understood by the amateur. Nevertheless, Duchen provides an ideal introduction to Korngold's career and appreciation of his music. Beautiful illustrations, concise discussions of cultural context, and short but informative descriptions of the music make this an attractive book.

Only one year after Duchen, CARROLL, president of the Erich Wolfgang Korngold Society and tireless promoter of the composer's work, published an extensive and thoroughly footnoted biography that provides a solid basis for future research. A wide range of sources, including letters, memoirs, interviews, and reviews (most of which have until now been nearly or totally inaccessible), make this the most important current study of Korngold. The book clearly attempts to draw attention to a hitherto neglected composer, and in doing so, it approaches his musical career perhaps a bit uncritically. For example, Carroll largely blames Julius Korngold for the decline of Erich's career, ignoring many of the other important factors cited above. Furthermore, he persistently praises the 1927 opera *Das Wunder der Heliane* as Korngold's greatest work, even though stylistic problems in the libretto and music—not to mention the work's reception—speak against such an assertion. Carroll also analyzes most of the composer's works. His observations, although generally more elaborate than Duchen's, are often more emotional than scholarly.

The best treatment of Korngold's film music remains KALINAK's study, even though her chapter on Korngold focuses on only one film score, *Captain Blood.* In an earlier chapter, the author provides a survey of theory of film music, implicitly unveiling how imperfect and thus largely irrelevant such theories have been. The analysis of *Captain Blood* does not follow the approach of most other books on Korngold's film scores that lead the reader through the film while subjectively pointing out how the music expresses the visual aspects. Rather, Kalinak approaches the music by topic (e.g., "Music and Structural Unity," "Music and Narrative Action," 'Music and Emotion'), occasionally referring to issues discussed in the chapter on film theory. Regularly drawing on standard cinematic terminology, the author provides not only an insightful study but also one that can serve as point of departure for future research.

ANDREAS GIGER

L

Lasso, Orlando di 1532–1594

Belgian-born composer

Bergquist, Peter, editor, *Orlando di Lasso Studies,* Cambridge: Cambridge University Press, 1999

Bergquist, Peter, et al., editors, *Orlando di Lasso: The Complete Motets,* Madison, Wisconsin: A-R Editions, 1995–

Boetticher, Wolfgang, *Orlando di Lasso und seine Zeit: 1532–1594,* 2 vols., Kassel: Bärenreiter, 1958

Bossuyt, Ignace, et al., editors, *Orlandus Lassus and His Time, Colloquium Proceedings, Antwerpen 24–26.08.1994,* Peer: Alamire Foundation, 1995

Crook, David, *Orlando di Lasso's Imitation Magnificats for Counter-Reformation Munich,* Princeton, New Jersey: Princeton University Press, 1994

Erb, James, *Orlando di Lasso: A Guide to Research,* New York: Garland, 1990

Haar, James, "Lassus [Lasso], Orlande," in *The New Grove High Renaissance Masters,* London: Macmillan, and New York: Norton, 1984

Leuchtmann, Horst, *Orlando di Lasso,* 2 vols., Wiesbaden: Breitkopf und Härtel, 1976

Luoma, Robert, *Music, Mode, and Words in Orlando di Lasso's Last Works,* Lewiston, New York: Mellen Press, 1989

Revue belge de musicologie, vol. 39–40 (1985–86), Brussels: Société Belge de Musicologie, 1986

Roche, Jerome, *Lassus,* London: Oxford University Press, 1982

Schmid, Bernhold, editor, *Orlando di Lasso in der Musikgeschichte, Bericht über das Symposion der Bayerische Akademie der Wissenschaften, München, 4.–6. Juli 1994,* Munich: Verlag der Bayerischen Akademie der Wissenschaften, 1996

Orlando di Lasso is probably one of the least known of the acknowledged great masters. The sheer size of his output has tended to defeat efforts to view it comprehensively, and in addition, a collected edition that includes all of his music was completed only in 1995, almost a century after it was begun. Until recently, studies of Lasso have been carried on mainly in Belgium, where he was born, and in Germany, where he spent most of his life in the service of the Dukes of Bavaria in Munich. Important work has also been done in France, as French was his native language. Lasso spent his formative years in Italy, where he adopted the Italian form of his name that he used throughout his life, but little scholarship has emanated from that region, or from English-speaking regions until relatively recently. Only after World War II did a new phase of Lasso study begin that now includes substantial contributions from the United States and Britain.

BOETTICHER provided the first and still the only full-scale life-and-works of Lasso. Despite the size of this book, the author's discussions of the music are necessarily brief, and his judgments have often been found questionable by others who have worked in the field; Boetticher's hypothetical chronology of posthumously published works is especially dubious. His biographical studies provide much detail but have been shown to be frequently mistaken in fact and interpretation. What remains most valuable in his book is its bibliography of Lasso sources. Even after more recent publications in the field such as the Répertoire internationale des sources musical, Boetticher is useful because it has compiled information about all known printed and manuscript sources of Lasso's music into a comprehensive list. This book must be used with great caution, but there is still nothing else like it available in any language.

LEUCHTMANN's biography of Lasso remains the standard work in the field. He painstakingly corrects Boetticher's numerous errors and has provided an unshakable documentary base for future Lasso studies. Some newly discovered material has added to the picture, but Leuchtmann's work has only been augmented, not superseded. The second volume of this study collects Lasso's letters and translates them into modern German. A few more letters have been discovered since Leuchtmann's publication.

HAAR is the best available overview in English of Lasso's life and work. It also has the best work list presently available, which includes the separate parts of multimovement motets, madrigals, chansons, and lieder. The work list is now slightly out of date due to research on Lasso since the study's publication.

ROCHE is another useful survey of the music, with only a few pages of biography. He discusses each genre in turn, beginning appropriately with the motets, Lasso's most extensive and greatest achievement, and continuing with the Masses and other liturgical music before moving on to the vernacular settings. Roche discusses each genre in chronological order so as to provide some sense of Lasso's development as a composer. The author's dependence on Boetticher's chronology occasionally leads him astray, but on the whole, he provides a useful picture of all of Lasso's output.

ERB's research guide is a comprehensive annotated bibliography of writings on Lasso in all languages up to the time of its publication. The coverage is complete, and the annotations give detailed information about the contents and usefulness of each entry. The ample index and frequent cross-references lead one easily to any useful item. The book also includes a biographical sketch drawn from Leuchtmann, a detailed list of modern editions of Lasso's music and their contents, and a comprehensive discography. Discographies quickly go out of date, but this one is nonetheless helpful as a guide to what has been recorded and what may be available in reference collections.

CROOK's study of Lasso's imitation (sometimes termed parody) Magnificats is the most detailed study in English of any part of Lasso's output. After a chapter that places Lasso's 101 Magnificats within the history of that genre's development in the Renaissance, the book has two main parts. The first section looks closely at liturgical practice in the Bavarian court before and during Lasso's tenure, focusing especially on the gradual supplanting of the local Use of Freising with the uniform liturgy promulgated by the Council of Trent. Related to these developments is the increase in Bavarian devotion to the Virgin Mary, which Crook traces in a succeeding chapter. The second part of the book examines Lasso's music itself, first examining the representation of psalm-tone categories in the imitation Magnificats, then considering the intertextuality of that music, that is, the relation of the imitation Magnificats to their polyphonic models. Among the appendices to the book is a lengthy compilation of correspondences between the imitation Magnificats and their models.

LUOMA provides a detailed analysis of Lasso's last published work, the spiritual madrigal cycle *Lagrime di San Pietro*. The study is based primarily on 16th-century music theory and the recent work of Bernhard Meier. Luoma's rejection of the findings of Harold Powers make the volume's conclusions suspect, as does its lack of reference to the work of Boetticher and Leuchtmann.

The Lasso 450th birth and 400th death anniversary years, 1982 and 1994, were the occasion for international conferences on his life and music. The published proceedings of these conferences include many papers in English in addition to those in German, French, and other languages. The 1985–86 issue of the *REVUE BELGE DE MUSICOLOGIE* was devoted mainly to articles from the 1982 conference held in Mons, Belgium, Lasso's birthplace. Papers in English include a study by Haar of Lasso's early madrigals that suggests that much if not all of Lasso's first three books of five-voice madrigals and his book of four-voice madrigals was composed in Italy, before he returned north. Kristine Forney looks carefully at one of Lasso's first publications, the *Quatoirieseme livre* of 1555, and its twin, *D'Orlando di Lassus il primo libro,* and revises the traditional view that the latter was published first. Karol Berger examines the theoretical background for the chromaticism of Lasso's *Prophetiae sibyllarum*, and Frank Dobbins explores the relationships between Lasso's chansons and those of his predecessors.

BOSSUYT and his coeditors present the papers given at the Antwerp conference of 1994. Eleven of the 20 papers and Bossuyt's introduction are in English. Among these contributions, special mention should be made of Donna Cardamone's study of Lasso's political allegiance during his Italian years. Her work here and elsewhere has greatly illuminated this obscure period in Lasso's life. Space does not permit listing all the articles in this volume; among the others in English, Bossuyt's introduction, Philip Weller's study of Lasso in the theater, and another study by Dobbins of the chansons are especially noteworthy.

SCHMID edited the proceedings of the Munich symposium held earlier in the same summer of 1994. Six of its 17 papers are in English, the rest in German or French. Among the papers in English, those by Bergquist and Powers consider aspects of mode and tonal center in Lasso's compositions. Bossuyt examines the chansons by Jean de Castro that are modeled on chansons by Lasso, and Crook documents a performance of Lasso's "secret" *Penitential Psalms* in 1580. M.A. Katritzky offers a most valuable study of Lasso's involvement with the commedia dell'arte, and Andrew McCredie explores relationships between Lasso's Munich and the Wurttemberg chapel at Stuttgart.

In the collection of Lasso studies edited by BERGQUIST (1999), 11 leading Lasso scholars explore various aspects of his life and work. Erb, Marie Louise Göllner, and Daniel Zager explore the liturgical music Lasso wrote for Munich, dealing respectively with the Magnificats, Masses, and polyphonic hymns. Papers by Cardamone, Mary Lewis, and Schmid consider the early circulation of Lasso's settings of Italian texts, the structure of one of Lasso's six-movement canzone settings, and the dissemination of one of Lasso's drinking songs on a Latin text. Three papers consider Lasso's relationships with other composers: Noel O'Regan comments on the impact of his sacred music in Rome, and Bossuyt and Haar discuss northern composers who reflect Lasso's influence. Bergquist examines how the contents of some Lasso prints represent the eight modes in numerical order, while Leuchtmann evaluates the relationship of verbal and musical stresses in Lasso's music and its implications for performance and scholarship.

The new edition of Lasso's motets with BERGQUIST (1995–) as general editor is mentioned here because of the introductions to each volume, which provide extensive commentary on individual motets as well as new information on their sources, dating, and purpose. Lasso's own prefaces to his motet books are reproduced in facsimile and in English translation.

PETER BERGQUIST

Latin America

Béhague, Gerard, *The Beginnings of Musical Nationalism in Brazil*, Detroit, Michigan: Information Coordinators, 1971

———, *Music in Latin America: An Introduction*, Englewood Cliffs, New Jersey: Prentice Hall, 1979

Béhague, Gerard, editor, *Music and Black Ethnicity: The Caribbean and South America*, Coral Gables, Florida: North-South Center Press, University of Miami, 1994

Manuel, Peter Lamarche, *Popular Musics of the Non-Western World: An Introductory Survey*, New York: Oxford University Press, 1988

Olsen, Dale A., and Daniel E. Sheehy, editors, *South America, Mexico, Central America, and the Caribbean*, The Garland Encyclopedia of World Music, vol. 2, New York: Garland, 1998

Parker, Robert, *Carlos Chávez: Mexico's Modern-Day Orpheus*, Boston, Massachusetts: Twayne, 1983

Seeger, Anthony, *Why Suyá Sing: A Musical Anthropology of an Amazonian People*, Cambridge: Cambridge University Press, 1981

Stevenson, Robert Murrell, *Music in Aztec and Inca Territory*, Berkeley: University of California Press, 1968

———, *Music in Mexico: A Historical Survey*, New York: Crowell, 1952

———, *The Music of Peru: Aboriginal and Viceroyal Epochs*, Washington, D.C.: Pan American Union, 1960

———, *Renaissance and Baroque Musical Sources in the Americas*, Washington, D.C.: General Secretariat, Organization of American States, 1970

Some of the most outstanding monographs dedicated to music in Latin America were published in English during the second half of the 20th century by American scholars, with Gerard Béhague and Robert Stevenson foremost among them. Even though much work remains to be done, the current state of research available in English provides a reasonably accurate and wide-ranging composite picture of the art-, folk-, and popular-music traditions of the region. One misses, however, first-rate studies dealing with music in individual countries such as Argentina, Brazil, Chile, and Venezuela, as well as monographs on the life and works of internationally successful composers such as Alberto Ginastera and Carlos Gomes. Heitor Villa-Lobos, about whom a healthy number of English-language monographs have been written, is an exception. The 19th century is perhaps the least-studied time period, and there are no comprehensive surveys of opera or musical institutions in Latin America during the romantic era or the 20th century, outside of unpublished dissertations. A critical assessment of art music in Latin America after 1945 is also needed because the best monographs are now at least 25 years old. Latin America's popular music is highly original and influential and rightly deserves a scholarly book solely devoted to the subject.

The first book-length overview of music in Latin America was published in the United States by Eleanor Hague (*Latin American Music: Past and Present*, [1934]). Also appearing during the times influenced by the good-neighbor policy of President Franklin Delano Roosevelt was Nicolas Slonimsky's reminiscences of his "Pan-American fishing trip" (*Music of Latin America*, 1945). These two pioneer studies, however, fail to do justice to their topic in great measure due to the incomplete state of research at the time. Especially lacking were annotated bibliographies, such as Gilbert Chase's *Guide to Latin American Music* (1945; 2nd edition, as *A Guide to the Music of Latin America* [1962]), which decisively contributed to the remarkable achievements of later scholars.

STEVENSON's (1952) survey of music in Mexico from ancient times to 1950 marked the beginning of his seminal studies of colonial art music in Hispanic America, all characterized by virtuosic command of bibliographical tools coupled with personal examination of musical and archival sources. This work is still is the only book in English on the topic and remains authoritative despite its age.

Even more significant for the advancement of the study of Latin American music was STEVENSON's (1960) book on music in Peru from the time of the Incas to 1821. It is the first monograph in any language on the topic and has uncovered the country's unsuspected wealth of colonial art music. Especially important are the chapters on cathedral music and opera, the latter one discussing the first such work written in the New World for which music is extant. A transcription of this opera along with an extended introductory essay can be found in Stevenson's edition of *La purpura de la rosa* (1973).

A few of the musical treasures held in Latin American archives are mapped in STEVENSON (1970), which is organized by city and includes many annotated entries of manuscripts and printed sources seen by the author. The importance of this reference work transcends the scope of its title, and readers interested in other time periods and geographical locations should consult it as well. This book provides a valuable panorama of music in Latin America and, although mostly dealing with Renaissance and baroque sources, it includes important items from the Middle Ages up to ca. 1870.

BÉHAGUE (1971) is a revision of a section of the author's doctoral dissertation. Although quite short, this monograph treats musical nationalism—a topic of great importance to all Latin American republics—with acute perception and insight. Moreover, it competently fills part of the gap in English-language publications on music in Brazil. (David Appleby's *The Music of Brazil* [1983] is unreliable and should be approached with caution by interested readers.)

The highest expectations of a scholarly history of art music in Latin America from colonial times to the 20th century are fulfilled by BÉHAGUE's (1979) far-reaching introductory survey. The book is marked by a remarkable synthesis of previous research and also evinces everywhere the careful judgment of the author's critical mind. The music is treated in detail with a profusion of musical examples. The survey is organized into three sections: "The Colonial Period," "The Rise of Nationalism," and "Cross-Currents in the Twentieth Century." Due to linguistic and historical reasons, the music in Brazil receives individual treatment within each section, while the music in Hispanic America is divided into sacred and secular genres in the first part, by large geographical areas in the second, and by decades in the third. Although it covers events only up to the mid-1970s, which were terra incognita at the time of publication, this introduction is still the single most important reference work on the subject.

PARKER is one of the few English-language studies devoted to a single Latin American art-music composer and is unique in covering Chávez's entire life span. The greater weight of the book, however, rests on a survey of the composer's works, with six out of the eight chapters devoted to specific genres. Parker's annotated bibliography is also to be recommended (*Carlos Chávez: A Guide to Research* [1998]). Peter Garland's *In Search of Silvestre Revueltas: Essays 1978–1990* (1991) places the composer within the context of 20th-century American art music and Mexican folk music and presents a refreshingly revisionist approach, marred somewhat by the liberal use of unqualified statements.

Any serious discussion of the art-music tradition in Latin America can hardly fail to mention the powerful mesh of indigenous, European, and African cultures in native soil. Furthermore, the rich folk- and popular-music traditions must be studied on their own in order to yield a balanced picture of Latin American music as a whole, as well as a proper understanding of its component parts. An authoritative overview of Latin American folk music and African-American music is found in Béhague's two concise chapters contributed to the second edition of Bruno Nettl's *Folk and Traditional Music of the Western Continents* (2nd edition, 1973; 3rd edition, 1990).

STEVENSON (1968) has compiled a unique ethnomusicological opus, dealing with the music of two of the world's greatest ancient civilizations. The book includes greatly revised and extended chapters on music in Mesoamerica and the Andean highlands previously published in Stevenson (1952) and (1960), as well as new material. Musical practices from ancient times and the complex process of acculturation following contact with the Europeans are traced up to 1800 and are reconstructed in this study that is based mostly on surviving musical instruments and eyewitness accounts from the 16th through the 18th centuries.

SEEGER has been widely received as a landmark in the field of ethnomusicology, even though its narrow scope may seem forbidding to the average reader. Written by a leading scholar and focusing on the Suyá Mouse Ceremony, the book makes a convincing case for "a study of society from the perspective of musical performance," enlarging and redefining Alan Merriam's highly influential work on the anthropology of music.

The widespread role of the African diaspora in various regions of Latin America is the focus of BÉHAGUE (1994). Written by established experts and emerging authorities, the essays cover the complex range of African survivals and interactions in Brazil, Colombia, Cuba, the Dominican Republic, Ecuador, Haiti, Panama, Peru, Puerto Rico, and Venezuela.

The outstanding achievement in the field of Latin American ethnomusicology is OLSEN and SHEEHY. Instead of alphabetically arranged entries, this handsomely illustrated encyclopedia has articles by a variety of knowledgeable specialists. Part 1 is a short introductory overview; part 2 contains a series of general cross-cultural surveys of musical instruments, the contextual role of music in the region, the music of Amerindians and immigrants, and brief discussions of popular and art music. The heart of this volume is found in part 3, which is devoted to individual essays on every nation and most major cultural groups of Latin America, including several Amerindian and some African-American populations.

A concise and scholarly survey of the popular music of Latin America and the Caribbean is found in chapter 2 of MANUEL, which includes individual sections on Argentina, Brazil, Colombia, Cuba, the Dominican Republic, the French Caribbean, Jamaica, Mexico, Puerto Rico, and Trinidad and Tobago. Brazil and Cuba arguably boast the most influential popular-music traditions south of Rio Grande and are covered in Chris McGowan and Ricardo Pessanha's *The Brazilian Sound: Samba, Bossa Nova, and the Popular Music of Brazil* (1991; new edition, 1998) and in *Caribbean Currents: Caribbean Music from Rumba to Reggae* (1995) by Manuel et al. The lack of scholarly apparatus and the frequent inadequacies of *The Brazilian Sound* are a small price to pay for a comprehensive discussion not found elsewhere.

Malena Kuss has published a useful annotated bibliography on *Latin America and the Caribbean* (1983), part of an ambitious and unfinished project titled *Music in the Life of Man: A World History.* Kuss's bibliography is a welcome update to Chase's guide, despite being less comprehensive. Its organization follows the pattern of individual topic areas and time periods found in the music section of the annual *Handbook of Latin American Studies* (1935–97), rather than Chase's division by country.

LUIZ FERNANDO VALLIM LOPES

Lauda

Anglès, Higinio, "The Music Notation and Rhythm of the Italian Laude," in *Essays in Musicology: A Birthday Offering to Willi Apel,* edited by Hans Tischler, Bloomington: Indiana University Press, 1968

Barr, Cyrilla, *The Monophonic Lauda and the Lay Religious Confraternities of Tuscany and Umbria in the Late Middle Ages,* Kalamazoo, Michigan: Medieval Institute Publications, 1988

Black, Christopher F., *Italian Confraternities in the Sixteenth Century,* Cambridge: Cambridge University Press, 1989

Kenney, Sylvia W., "In Praise of the Lauda," in *Aspects of Medieval and Renaissance Music: A Birthday Offering to Gustave Reese,* edited by Jan LaRue, New York: Norton, 1966

Wilson, Blake M., *Music and Merchants: The Laudesi Companies of Republican Florence,* Oxford: Clarendon Press, and New York: Oxford University Press, 1992

The *lauda* is best understood as nonliturgical sacred song from Italy. Its text is occasionally Latin but more frequently the vernacular language. It is documented as a monophonic genre as early as the 13th century and lasted in polyphonic guise into the 16th century; discussions of the *lauda* usually consider one or the other of these subtypes. *Laude* are first associated with Italian devotional fraternities of singers, *laudesi,* whose paraliturgical worship services included songs in the vernacular in praise of God and various saints, particularly the Virgin. The year 1260 witnessed the commencement of a wave of flagellant mania among the *laudesi,* a development that naturally affected the tone and texts of *laude.* In some modest measure, the monophonic *lauda* is also connected with the rise of religious drama. The polyphonic *lauda* may have arisen in the 14th century, but it experienced its greatest popularity in the late 15th and early 16th centuries. During the flourishing of the *frottola,* the polyphonic *lauda* also came into prominence; in fact, the musical settings for the two genres are virtually indistinguishable in many cases. These polyphonic *laude* were no longer so strongly associated with fraternities but could be used in monastic circles and paraliturgical services conducted by clerics. Petrucci published two collections of *laude,* the first entirely devoted to works by Innocentius Dammonis. Later *lauda* publications date from the second half of the 16th century. Much of the detailed scholarship on the *lauda,* particularly on the polyphonic variety, has been published in journal articles (see, for example, Frank A. D'Accone, "The Musical Chapels at the Florentine Cathedral and Baptistry during the First Half of the 16th Century," *Journal of the American Musicological Society* 24 [1971]; Jonathan Glixon, "The Polyphonic Laude of Innocentius Dammonis," *Journal of Musicology* 8 [1990]; and William F. Prizer, "Music at the Court of the Sforza: The Birth and Death of a Musical Center," *Musica disciplina* 43 [1989]).

An excellent starting point for exploration of the monophonic *lauda* is BARR's book-length study. The author distinguishes between *laudesi* and *disciplinati*—the latter being principally concerned with flagellation—because the *lauda* repertoire from these groups differs in several respects. Barr focuses on two manuscripts, Cortona 91 and Florence 122, the only complete sources to include musical settings for the *lauda* texts. The first of these has a Franciscan connection, and its dating from the mid-to-late 13th century is essentially unchallenged; Florence 122 is of Florentine provenance. The musical style of these *laude* is discussed at length, with particular attention given to the variety of formal organizations used: most *laude* from this period use *ballata*-related texts, thus calling for a bipartite musical setting. The settings in Florence 122 display an intriguing variety of musically sophisticated techniques: some employ partial or complete repetition of one section within another; and some use fioratura of such complexity that soloistic performance seems warranted. Finally, the liturgical rubrics given in the book offer precise information regarding the placement and use of the *lauda* repertoire within the ceremonies of some confraternities.

WILSON focuses on the Florentine *laudesi* companies, using primary sources to describe exhaustively the organization and activities of both the principal and minor companies. By tracing the archival records of various companies, the author reveals how *laudesi* responded to changes in general liturgical practice by employing organists and increasing numbers of singers. Of particular interest is the treatment of *lauda* performance: Wilson describes musical forces, the relationship of the *laude* to architectural features of the worship environment, and physical actions that may have accompanied the performance of these works. Readers interested in the *lauda*'s musical manuscript traditions will find the book's collated readings of several *laude* from various sources of particular use.

A complement to Barr's and Wilson's discussions of the medieval *laudesi* is BLACK's volume on 16th-century confraternities. The *lauda* had become polyphonic by this time and it had probably moved outside its original confraternity environment as well; consequently, vernacular music used by these late confraternities may well have been of the monophonic *lauda* type. That is, ceremonies of the confraternities—including pilgrimages, processions, and other devotional activities—would have been appropriate venues for continuation of this now old-fashioned style.

In an article published much earlier than the above volumes, ANGLÈS gives transcriptions of several monophonic *laude*. These readings are mensurally transcribed; to render them in this way, the author invokes the Spanish *cantiga* repertoire, which he believes to have been mensurally notated and, upon examination, notationally related to the *lauda* repertoire. However, these transcriptions have not been universally accepted and must remain dubious; the transcriptions found in Barr's and Wilson's volumes are probably more reliable.

Comprehensive studies of the polyphonic *lauda* are not readily available, perhaps because this genre was so closely related to the *frottola* in musical style and of minor import in relation to contemporaneous developments in the Mass and motet. However, an excellent introduction to one component of the polyphonic *lauda* is that of KENNEY. The author traces the sometimes confusing history of the Latin-texted *lauda* (an admittedly unusual subtype that seems to have flourished in the 15th century), noting its relation to the song motet, but also recognizing that it borrows some musical features from contemporaneous secular forms. This Latin *lauda* gradually merged with the motet.

STEPHEN SELF

Libretto

Fuld, James J., *The Book of World-Famous Libretti: The Musical Theater from 1598 to Today*, New York: Pendragon Press, 1984; revised edition, 1994

Groos, Arthur, and Roger Parker, editors, *Reading Opera*, Princeton, New Jersey: Princeton University Press, 1988

Smith, Patrick J., *The Tenth Muse: A Historical Study of the Opera Libretto*, New York: Knopf, 1970; London: Gollancz, 1971

Thomson, Virgil, *Music with Words: A Composer's View*, New Haven, Connecticut: Yale University Press, 1989

Weisstein, Ulrich, editor, *The Essence of Opera*, New York: Free Press of Glencoe, and London: Collier-Macmillan, 1964

The word *libretto* (Italian for "little book") describes both the complete text of an opera and the physical object in which that text is presented, the latter of which might be anything from a 17th-century manuscript to a booklet accompanying a compact disc recording. While the relative importance of an opera's text compared to that of its music has historically been a subject of intense debate, most 20th-century opera scholarship has tended to ignore libretto texts in favor of more exclusively musical discussion. Librettos were viewed as literature beneath contempt. However, because opera consists of a complex interplay of language, music, and drama, recent scholars have contended that it makes sense to approach its language aspect not as literature but as one of many systems of operatic communication. Today, libretto studies cover an enormous variety of subjects, including, but by no means limited to, prosody and versification, literary sources for librettos, social and political implications of libretto texts, and librettist-composer collaborations.

SMITH's monograph remains the only book-length history of the libretto in English. Amid the sea of more recent specialized libretto studies, this work is still an excellent introduction for those with a good general knowledge of opera but little background in its textual aspects. Smith limits his study to the librettos of Italy, France, and Germany. His approach is chronological, beginning with the birth of opera in Italy and continuing with its spread into France. German librettos are not introduced until well into the discussion of French and Italian librettos of the 19th century, primarily because a German vernacular operatic tradition started later and does not seem to have engendered the lively debates over the relative importance of words and music seen in France and Italy. Smith alternates general historical chapters with chapters on individual librettists, including Metastasio, Hofmannsthal, Boito, and Wagner.

Not confined exclusively to libretto discussion, WEISSTEIN provides wonderful insight into all aspects of operatic creation. He has compiled a marvelous collection of English translations of original writings by librettists and composers covering all four centuries of the existence of opera. Included are excerpts from well-known publications such as Wagner's *Opera and Drama* and Jean-Jacques Rousseau's *Dictionary of Music*; prefaces to operas ranging from Ottavio Rinuccini's *Euridice* in 1600 (music by Jacopo Peri) to Berlioz's *Damnation of Faust* to Richard Strauss's *Intermezzo*; letters between composers and librettists (e.g., Verdi-Boito and Puccini-Adami); and essays by philosophers such as Kierkegaard and Nietzsche, critics such as George Bernard Shaw, and numerous composers including Kurt Weill, Ferruccio Busoni, and Alban Berg. Weisstein provides essential historical and critical context to these excerpts in his linking commentaries.

One of the finest collections of essays devoted exclusively to the libretto is GROOS and PARKER. While the majority of contributors focus on German and Italian operas from the second half of the 19th century, the variety of approaches makes this collection truly valuable. Source studies—such as Hepokoski's analysis of librettist Arrigo Boito's annotated copy of F.-V. Hugo's French translation of Shakespeare's *Othello* (used in preparing the libretto for Verdi's *Otello*)—provide insight into the creative process of transforming a play into a libretto. Interdisciplinary work combines literary topics such as narrative (Abbate on Wagner) and deconstruction (Bergeron on Verdi) with more traditional musico-dramatic commentary on the libretto. An interesting genre study on Italian *Literaturoper* by Jürgen Maehder takes a closer look at plays that have been set directly to music with little or no adaptation. From a more personal perspective, Paul Robinson's essay "Deconstructive Postscript: Reading Libretti and Misreading Opera" argues persuasively that the operatic listening experience necessarily hinders understanding of the words via four "enemies of intelligibility": librettos in foreign languages, the incompatibility of operatic vocal technique (especially on high notes) with clear diction, ensembles in which many different words are sung simultaneously, and the orchestra. With its inclusion of such a diverse assortment of scholarly approaches and topics, this collection opens many doors for further libretto inquiry.

For those interested in the libretto as a physical object, FULD presents a wide-ranging collection of illustrations and descriptions of the title pages of more than 150 printed librettos. In most cases, Fuld tries to reproduce an exemplar of the "original libretto"—that is, one printed on the occasion of the opera's first premiere. Title pages of librettos can include a wealth of information: the title, composer, and librettist; the city, theater, and date of the given performance; and the publisher. Fuld furnishes further facts not included on the title page, such as a description of the libretto's size and color, information included on the verso of the title page, any dedications, and the library or private collection where one can consult the original. Although most of the information in this volume is easily accessible elsewhere, the large number of illustrations makes it a unique contribution to the field of libretto studies.

THOMSON wrote some of the most singable vocal music in the 20th century and is therefore an ideal author for a book on the process of setting of words to music. This volume is primarily a practical manual for composers, but it addresses such a wide variety of issues in such an accessible manner that it is of genuine value to anyone interested in the dynamic interaction of language and musical sound. Thomson describes the mechanics of phonetics, prosody, word groups, accent, rhyme, and versification, contextualizing their usage in English by constant comparison with that of other languages. He then gives practical instruction on the setting of different kinds of verse, providing examples from his own music as well as that of other composers. Of particular interest is his enumeration of all the different functions of a vocal line's accompaniment. It can enhance textual intelligibility, keep singers on pitch, create rhythmic variety, and evoke emotion, weather, or even different sociological, geographical, or historical references (using varying musical styles). The two chapters on opera contain much discussion of the importance of the libretto—the author urges that it be comprehensible, that it contain poetic language, and that composer and librettist work together as equal partners.

ALISON TERBELL NIKITOPOULOS

Lied: To 1800

Blume, Friedrich, *Protestant Church Music: A History,* New York: Norton, 1974

Kmetz, John, editor, *Music in the German Renaissance: Sources, Styles, and Contexts,* Cambridge: Cambridge University Press, 1994

Moser, Hans Joachim, *The German Song Solo and the Ballad,* Cologne: Arno Volk Verlag, 1958

Osthoff, Helmut, *German Part Song from the 16th Century to the Present Day,* translated by Hans-Hubert Schönzeler, Cologne: Arno Volk Verlag, 1955

Sayce, Olive, *The Medieval German Lyric 1150–1300: The Development of Its Themes and Forms in Their European Context,* Oxford: Clarendon Press, and New York: Oxford University Press, 1982

Smeed, J.W., *German Song and Its Poetry, 1740–1900,* London: Croon Helm, 1987

Stoljar, Margaret Mahony, *Poetry and Song in Late Eighteenth Century Germany: A Study in the Musical Sturm und Drang,* London: Croon Helm, 1985

Taylor, Ronald J., *The Art of the Minnesinger,* 2 vols., Cardiff: University of Wales Press, 1968

Thomas, R. Hinton, *Poetry and Song in the German Baroque: A Study of the Continuo Lied,* Oxford: Clarendon Press, 1963

The term *lied* has a threefold meaning: it refers to a German-texted poem that is intended to be set to music, the combination of such a poem with a melody, or a homophonic or polyphonic musical setting of a text/music combination. The text of a lied may be either secular or sacred. With such a broad definition, subcategories of lieder abound and are frequently identified by either text type or musical setting: the *Kunstlied* (art song), *Hoflied* (court song), *Volkslied* (folk song), *Kirchenlied* (sacred song), etc. English-language studies on the lied are scarce, and as might be expected with such a broad definition, there is no single work that provides a comprehensive overview of the lied before 1800.

The studies of OSTHOFF and MOSER appear as volumes 10 and 14, respectively, in the Anthology of Music series, which was first published in German as Das

Musikwerke. Both volumes are anthologies of lieder, with extensive prefaces that provide a good overview of the songs included. The English translations, it should be noted, are not always idiomatic. Osthoff focuses on the solo song, whether those songs are found in monophonic or homophonic settings; approximately one-half of the songs in the anthology date from before 1800. Moser presents polyphonic settings of German lyric poetry; over half of his anthology dates from before 1800 (12 pieces were first published in the 16th century). These volumes are excellent introductions to the development of the lied from the mid-16th century onward, with their combination of musical settings, translations of texts, and broad historical overviews by respected scholars.

SAYCE deals only with the texts of medieval lieder in her book, noting that manuscript sources frequently include no musical notation or they present musical notation that resists transcription into modern notation. She examines the structure of lyric poetry and its subject matter and compares German lyric poetry of the period to Italian and French poetry from the same era.

TAYLOR provides transcriptions into modern notation of several dozen 13th-century lieder by various composers and includes commentary on the transcriptions and musical settings. His discussion of *contrafacta* is notable, because one normally associates that technique with the music of later eras.

KMETZ's compilation includes two essays of particular interest to the student of the Renaissance lied: Martin Staehelin's "The Constitution of the 15th-century German Tenor Lied" is one of the few English-language studies of the music of the transitional period from the Middle Ages to the Renaissance; Ludwig Finscher's "Lied and Madrigal" explores the relationship between the musical cultures of Germany and Italy and demonstrates the influence of Italian music on German lieder publications at the end of the 16th century.

BLUME writes not only about lieder but also of other genres of music in Protestant churches from their beginnings in the 16th century through the late 20th century. His book, first published in 1964 in German as *Geschichte der evangelischen Kirchenmusik*, contains the most thorough survey of the sacred lied available in the English language. The majority of his text deals with music in the period before 1800, although he also discusses Protestant sacred music of the 19th and 20th centuries.

THOMAS gives a thorough description of the development of the continuo lied out of the Renaissance polyphonic lied. The focus of the book is the poetry of musical settings from the late 16th century to the mid-18th century. Particular attention is paid to the Italian origins of changes in lyric poetry in the early baroque era, and the ways in which composers wrote musical settings that increasingly took the meaning of the text into account.

STOLJAR is highly recommended as a resource on the lied as it developed from the late 1700s into the romantic art song of the 19th century. The author covers C.P.E. Bach and the First Berlin School and also provides information on the more obscure composers of this period. There is, however, relatively little discussion about the lieder of Haydn, Mozart, and Beethoven—one must search for that information in literature devoted specifically to those composers. Fortunately, the author provides a bibliography to assist the reader in locating those sources. SMEED, who provides coverage of the same period as Stoljar, fails to provide additional references and offers somewhat less thorough coverage. About half of his book deals with the period before 1800.

JOHN E. LINDBERG

Lied: 19th Century

Hall, James Husst, *The Art Song,* Norman: University of Oklahoma Press, 1953

Hallmark, Rufus, editor, *German Lieder in the Nineteenth Century,* New York: Schirmer Books, 1996

Kravitt, Edward F., *The Lied: Mirror of Late Romanticism,* New Haven, Connecticut: Yale University Press, 1996

Stein, Deborah, and Robert Spillman, *Poetry into Song: Performance and Analysis of Lieder,* New York: Oxford University Press, 1996

During the 19th century the lied became increasingly prominent as a genre both for composition and performance. One of the lied's most important characteristics is the enmeshing of text and music, and through analyses of both, writers exploring this genre usually attempt to show how composers grappled with this fusion. Recently, however, lieder scholars have also branched out to explore other relevant matters, including how these works were first performed and received by audiences and how they relate to broader cultural issues. Traditionally, it is the works of the four composers who dominate the 19th-century lied, Schubert, Schumann, Brahms, and Wolf, that hold central place in monographs of this genre, although composers at the end of the century, such as Strauss and Mahler, are normally included as well. More recently, female composers, especially Fanny Hensel, have been studied in books devoted to the lied.

HALLMARK has put together a collection of ten essays by acknowledged scholars of the lied. Each essay ends with a bibliography that provides the reader with reference to more specialized literature, much of which is written in English. There are essays devoted to the major composers (Schubert, Schumann, Brahms, Wolf, Mahler, and Strauss) as well as a single essay on some of the now less well known composers (Carl Loewe, Fanny Hensel, Franz Liszt, Robert Franz, and Peter Cornelius). The song cycle is treated to a separate essay in which

John Daverio describes some of the problems involved in defining and tracing a history of these collections. Songs in this chapter are discussed only in terms of their place within cycles, and in addition to discussing works by the composers given main essays, there is also a section on Wagner. The book begins with a brief overview of 19th-century German poetry in which the author, Harry Seelig, traces the styles and themes of the poets favored by lied composers (especially Goethe, but also Eichendorff, Heine, Mörike, Dehmel, and Hölderlin). The book ends with Robert Spillman's advice to performers, which concentrates on vocal technique.

The essays on the individual composers are structured in a variety of ways, although most group the songs chronologically. In addition to discussing the composers' songwriting techniques, the authors have included numerous other pieces of relevant information. For example, Christopher Lewis discusses the reaction of audiences and critics to the first performances of Mahler's songs. In her essay on Schubert, Susan Youens includes sections on Schubert's overall style, his choice of poets, and a description of the songs that exist in more than one version. Viginia Hancock takes a somewhat unusual approach; she divides Brahm's lieder by style, separating those that imitate folk song from the *Kunstlieder*, in which she claims Brahms expressed more personal feelings. Perhaps the most novel essay is Lawrence Kramer's "Hugo Wolf: Subjectivity in the Fin-de-Siècle Lied." Kramer uses oedipal theory not only to explore Wolf's relationship with his father but also to analyze four songs as well as to propose narrative structures for Wolf's songbooks. Moreover, he argues that the expressive ideal of Schubert's and Schumann's lieder is not followed by Wolf. According to Kramer, Wolf's independent piano parts "scrutinize" the texts, which are carefully declaimed by the voice. The resulting "marked separation of voice and piano, forms a further means of perpetuating the structure of oedipal dialogue."

Whereas most monographs on the 19th-century lied are heavily biased toward earlier composers, KRAVITT focuses exclusively on those at the end of the century, including Wolf, Mahler, Strauss, Hans Pfitzner, Max Reger, and the young Arnold Schoenberg. The works of these composers are examined in light of the most important cultural trends at the end of the 19th century, including naturalism, nationalism, and symbolism. This study includes penetrating musical analyses as well as detailed, well-documented discussions of the aesthetics and performance styles of the period—a topic not usually covered in other general discussions of the lied.

There are a number of other monographs in which one or two authors trace the development of the lied throughout the entire century. Although these books provide decent general introductions, the music analysis is sometimes too simplistic, and in many cases the texts of individual songs are not properly considered. Nevertheless, for the nonspecialist these works can provide a useful introduction to this genre, and HALL in particular gives a sound overview of the lied, including the major composers as well as Carl Loewe, Liszt, Felix Mendelssohn, and Franz.

STEIN and SPILLMAN offer a textbook on how to analyze lied, and as such their book is rather unusual in that it is structured around analytical topics rather than specific composers. This work provides students and nonspecialists with greater understanding of the technical ways text and music are combined, in addition to which singers are encouraged to use their analyses to influence performance decisions. The book begins with an excellent overview of the major themes in German romantic poetry. This initial chapter places the lied within 19th-century culture and gives the reader a good background to the images and themes that repeatedly appear in lieder. After a chapter on poetic devices and structures, there are chapters on performance and musical analysis, each of which includes numerous references to mainstream repertoire and analytical exercises. There are a few disadvantages to this pedagogical thrust, one of which is that there are only passing references to composers' individual styles. At least in part, this is compensated for by examining texts set by more than one composer, although this is somewhat problematic, particularly for Brahms, whose best songs use texts that were rarely set by others. Moreover, the conclusions that these analyses produce are so general that they could be found in any music history text. Thought-provoking analyses of other works by these same composers are, however, distributed throughout the preceding chapters, and they better demonstrate the authors' thorough understanding of the intricacies of the text-music relationships in this genre.

HEATHER PLATT

Ligeti, György b. 1923

Hungarian-born composer

Griffiths, Paul, *György Ligeti,* London: Robson Books, 1983; 2nd edition, 1997

Ligeti, György, *György Ligeti: In Conversation with Péter Várnai, Josef Häusler, Claude Samuel, and Himself,* translated by Gabor J. Schabert et al., London: Eulenburg, 1983

Richart, Robert W., *György Ligeti: A Bio-Bibliography,* New York: Greenwood Press, 1990

The composer György Ligeti has so far received little in the way of sustained critical commentary in English. Besides the brief descriptive analyses found in books on 20th-century music, there exists only one book-length introduction, plus a book of conversations, an annotated bibliography, and a published dissertation. This last item covers Ligeti's pre-1956 compositions and seeks to dispel the myth of a radical change in the composer's style following his escape to the West (Friedemann Sallis, "An Introduction to the Early Works of György Ligeti," [1996]). Indeed, the composer's life experiences as a Holocaust survivor, as a young composer in Stalinist Hungary, and as a refugee of the 1956 Russian invasion are central to understanding how this radical among radicals succeeded in producing one of the most significant bodies of work in the late 20th century. Nonetheless, the pre-1956 works arose in a musical culture cut off from the West's high modernism, and although Ligeti himself notes the continuity in his output, he also speaks of his musical rebirth after 1956. Equally significant is Ligeti's role in the postmodern story of an aging avant-garde. In point of fact, the composer's opera, *Le Grand Macabre,* begun in 1972 and premiered in 1978 (revised in 1996), offers a case study in the modernist's grappling with what some postmodern theorists have called "the return of the repressed," a shift away from autonomous expression and toward a new historicism. As an essay in meaning, both human and musical, the opera not only comprises an encyclopedia of Ligeti's expressive range (ironic, analytical, serious, comic, despairing, and optimistic) but also traces an encyclopedic, Borgesean narrative of identity. Indeed, Ligeti's music of the 1980s and 1990s further explores the nature of identity. In this music, one finds Caribbean and African polyrhythms, Southeast Asian tunings, and the algorithmic processes found in fractal mathematics: music epitomizing the notion of the postmodern containing the modern.

RICHART contains a brief biography of Ligeti that serves as introduction to an extensive annotated bibliography. The bibliography spans the years 1956 to 1989 and covers works and performances, writings by Ligeti, writings about Ligeti, and a discography. An appendix lists Ligeti's compositions by category and provides a select list of concerts and festivals devoted to Ligeti. Also useful is the index. In a field of study with less than a handful of book-length studies—and none of a suitably analytical nature—this book gives the Ligeti student a quick survey of past research in the field.

Readable, informative, and up-to-date, GRIFFITHS provides a tidy little narrative of Ligeti's output up to 1996. The book is divided into two parts. Part 1 ("East") contains one of the best accounts of the composer's extraordinary early life. Part 2 ("West") is basically a 15-chapter program note to the works composed between 1956 and 1995. Especially fine is the material narrating the shift from East to West, a source of insight into totalitarianism's effect on the arts and an excellent introduction to the postwar avant-garde. Although limited in its technical analyses (it contains only 12 musical examples), the book offers an excellent introduction to Ligeti's style. With several books on the postwar avant-garde to his

credit, Griffiths writes with insight into the music of the 1960s. For example, he articulates the difference between Ligeti's handling of the cluster and the way it is handled by Xenakis, Stockhausen, and Penderecki. Regarding the composer's first mature style, Griffiths suggests that the autonomous tone-color melody of *Apparitions, Atmosphères, Volumina,* and *Lontano* involves an erasing of content, for in these and other works Ligeti's micropolyphony suppresses gesture and event by systematically eliminating any motivic or thematic presence. As Griffiths puts it, this approach produces a music of absence: sounds come and go, commingle, and repel one another in what the composer himself has called the permeability of musical forms. All in all, although originally intended for the general reader as an incitement to listen to Ligeti's music (cf. 1983 ed.), this book also has value for those already familiar with the composer.

Some of the most interesting material in Griffiths is found in the quotes from the composer himself, and so it is recommended that one read LIGETI. This contains four interviews, arranged not chronologically but in terms of scope and nature. A three-day interview conducted by Várnai (1978) fills half of the book; it is followed by two shorter ones, conducted by Häusler (1968–69) and Samuel (1981), respectively, and a fourth one written by Ligeti (1971) as a question-and-answer session with himself. The book contains a number of widely disseminated anecdotes about Ligeti's childhood and development as a musician and composer. Várnai leads Ligeti through an examination of his career, including his aesthetics (Day 1), his compositional output (Day 2), and his work as a composition teacher (Day 3). Häusler's radio interview reveals Ligeti's way of conceptualizing his music as sound planes, light and illumination, radiance, and so on and gives locations in the scores of *Apparitions, Atmosphères, Volumina,* and *Lontano* heard in broadcast. Samuel interviews Ligeti following the premiere of *Le Grand Macabre* and includes Ligeti's thoughts on stylistic allusion, pastiche, and pop art. Finally, Ligeti's own piece provides a strikingly concentrated vision of his technique of musical composition, with topics including precompositional planning, harmony (and nonharmony), serialism, form, and method.

GORDON MARSH

Liszt, Franz 1811–1886

Hungarian-born composer, pianist, and conductor

1. Biography

Burger, Ernst, *Franz Liszt: A Chronicle of His Life in Pictures and Documents,* translated by Stewart Spencer, Princeton, New Jersey: Princeton University Press, 1989

Lachmund, Carl, *Living with Liszt: From the Diary of Carl Lachmund, an American Pupil of Liszt, 1882–1884,* edited by Alan Walker, Stuyvesant, New York: Pendragon Press, 1995

Legány, Dezsö, *Ferenc Liszt and His Country, 1874–1886,* translated by Elizabeth Smith-Csicsery Rónay, translation revised by Paul Merrick, Budapest: Occidental Press, 1992

Saffle, Michael, *Liszt in Germany, 1840–1845: A Study in Sources, Documents, and the History of Reception,* Stuyvesant, New York: Pendragon Press, 1994

Taylor, Ronald, *Franz Liszt: The Man and the Musician,* London: Grafton, 1986

Walker, Alan, *Franz Liszt,* revised edition, 3 vols., Ithaca, New York: Cornell University Press, 1987–97

———, *Liszt, Carolyne, and the Vatican: The Story of a Thwarted Marriage,* original church documents edited and translated by Gabriele Erasmi, Stuyvesant, New York: Pendragon Press, 1991

Watson, Derek, *Liszt,* New York: Schirmer, 1989

One of the most colorful, innovative, and influential musicians of Western history, Liszt has been the subject of numerous biographies. From the works of Lina Ramann and Marie Lipsius (La Mara) in the 19th century through studies by James Huneker, Peter Raabe, and Sacherevell Sitwell in the early 20th century to a host of others since, Liszt's life has not grown less interesting for being retold. In recent decades, however, the literature on Liszt has expanded rapidly, spurred by a resurgence of scholarship in Hungary, the activities of the British and American Liszt Societies, and the discovery of new sources in libraries, archives, and private collections. Among the many fine works of recent years, Walker and Burger stand out.

The first volume of WALKER's (1987–97) monumental biography begins with a chapter entitled "Liszt and the Literature," which discusses previous work on the composer, delineates the author's reasons for tackling such a project, and presents his views on the task of the biographer. The subsequent volumes, spaced out over more than a decade, reflect his conviction that "Liszt was the central figure in the Romantic century (Berlioz and Wagner notwithstanding) and that a book was needed to proclaim that fact." He succeeds in demonstrating the seminal role of Liszt in the 19th century with a combination of engaging writing and thorough scholarship. Walker points out that the documents available to the Liszt biographer are nearly overwhelming because of their volume and dispersion throughout the world. He successfully pulls together widely scattered documentary sources into a coherent narrative that is not slavishly chronological. The biography is distinguished by the author's ability to correct received notions of this often-misunderstood musician through the discovery of new source materials (notably on Liszt's childhood and on his thwarted marriage to Princess Carolyn von Sayn-Wittgenstein) and the correction of erroneous judgments

(the biases of Ramann and La Mara are discussed in depth). As befits a biography of such a fascinating figure, the prose style is engaging. Walker has the ability to tell a story in novelistic terms that constantly delight and only occasionally cross the boundary to sensationalism.

All three volumes appeared first in hardcover from Knopf (1983, 1989, 1996) . Especially in the case of the first volume, which has been substantially revised, it is important to use the later edition published by Cornell University Press. The documentation is thorough, with extensive footnotes and numerous source citations. The only criticism is the unwieldy system of abbreviations used to denote sources—the reader must constantly flip back and forth between the footnotes and the bibliography in order to decipher the often-illogical sigla. Although Walker is fastidious in citing primary sources, one wishes he had been a bit more generous in acknowledging the work of other scholars—recent secondary literature is almost entirely absent from his bibliography and footnotes.

BURGER's pictorial biography was originally published in German during the centennial of Liszt's death in 1986. The book is a chronology, tracing each year of the composer's life with a minimum of text and a maximum of photographic reproductions, many of them in color. The large format allows for some stunning visual images, not least of which is a color reproduction of the famous Danhauser painting of Liszt and his circle. There are hundreds of photographs, cartoons, letters, and scores—many of which are available nowhere else—that provide a context for Liszt's life and music.

Although Walker's biography is unrivaled in its depth and breadth, some readers will prefer something shorter. For the general reader, TAYLOR gives an overview in broad strokes that is noteworthy for its incorporation of contemporary historical and cultural observations. As a professor of German, the author not surprisingly emphasizes German source materials.

WATSON's book is a rare one-volume work that successfully combines historical narrative with stylistic analysis. Although not as detailed as Walker's biography, this work is reliable and comprehensive. Especially useful are appendices devoted to a chronology of the composer's life, a detailed work list categorized by genre, and a list of persons who appear in the biography, with dates and several sentences on the significance of each.

Numerous recent works explore specialized facets of Liszt's life. SAFFLE's examination of Liszt's *Glanzzeit* of the early 1840s has turned up fascinating new information and perspectives on the composer's reception in Germany. During this time he was constantly in the public eye and was the object of much publicity; nevertheless, Saffle has demonstrated, much was still to be discovered concerning Liszt's life and music.

LEGÁNY gives a detailed analysis of the composer's final years, with emphasis on his connections to his native Hungary. Although the book could have used a bit more proofreading (the author explains the difficult production problems in a preface), it makes interesting and informative reading.

WALKER (1991) tells the story of the marriage that almost was, which had remained a mystery to Liszt scholars until Walker's fortuitous discovery in the Vatican of the original documents on the case. His book on the subject centers on these documents, which are given in their original languages as well as in translation.

LACHMUND is a memoir by one of Liszt's most faithful students of the 1880s that had previously been available only in an inadequate German translation. Walker's edition allows modern readers to glimpse the day-to-day life of Liszt in Weimar during his declining years, when alcohol and health problems took their toll on his body but could not dull his musical acuity.

E. DOUGLAS BOMBERGER

2. Orchestral Music

Bonner, Andrew, "Liszt's *Les préludes* and *Les quatre éléments*: A Reinvestigation," *19th Century Music* 10 (1986)

Johns, Keith T., *The Symphonic Poems of Franz Liszt*, Stuyvesant, New York: Pendragon Press, 1997

Kaplan, Richard, "Sonata Form in the Orchestral Works of Liszt: The Revolutionary Reconsidered," *19th Century Music* 8 (1984)

Merrick, Paul, *Revolution and Religion in the Music of Liszt*, Cambridge: Cambridge University Press, 1987

Rosenblatt, Jay, "The Concerto as Crucible: Franz Liszt's Early Works for Piano and Orchestra," 2 vols., Ph.D. dissertation, University of Chicago, 1995

———, "Liszt's Piano and Orchestra Works," in *The Liszt Companion*, edited by C. Benjamin Arnold, Westport, Connecticut: Greenwood Press, 1999

Searle, Humphrey, *The Music of Liszt*, London: Williams and Norgate, 1954; 2nd revised edition, New York: Dover Publications, 1966

Walker, Alan, editor, *Franz Liszt: The Man and His Music*, London: Barrie and Jenkins, and New York: Taplinger, 1970

Watson, Derek, *Liszt*, London: Dent, and New York: Schirmer, 1989

Liszt's orchestral music is central to his development as a composer, both musically and chronologically. The great works from his Weimar Period (1848–61) include the Faust and Dante symphonies as well as 12 symphonic poems, in which Liszt pioneered new approaches to form and harmony. From the beginning, these works inspired musicians such as Richard Wagner and infuriated conservative critics such as Eduard Hanslick. Wagner himself was among the first to publish a spirit-

ed defense, and he stands at the head of a line of supporters, many from Liszt's intimate circle. The most prominent of these was Richard Pohl, whose articles discussed the symphonies, symphonic poems, and concertos in the *Neue Zeitschrift für Musik*. They were later collected in *Franz Liszt: Studien und Erinnerungen* (Leipzig: Bernhard Schlicke, 1883). Later in the century, Lina Ramann included comments on many of Liszt's important works in her biography, *Franz Liszt als Künstler und Mensch* (three volumes, Leipzig: Breitkopf und Härtel, 1880–94; volume 1 published in English translation as *Franz Liszt: Artist and Man*, trans. E. Cowdery, London: W.H. Allen, 1882). Scholarly assessment begins years after Liszt's death with the publications of Peter Raabe, especially his two-volume *Franz Liszt* (1931; rev. ed. by Felix Raabe, 1968). This was the first major study based on a wide array of primary sources, and the work list concluding the second volume in some ways remains unsurpassed. Raabe marks the true beginning of Liszt research.

SEARLE was among the first to provide a scholarly foundation for Liszt research in English. His contribution to the fifth edition of *Grove's Dictionary of Music and Musicians* (1954) was a considerable advance in depth and accuracy over previous editions, although his reliance on Raabe is clear, especially in the work list. Searle expanded this article to create *The Music of Liszt*. Within a broad chronological division ("The Early Years," "The Virtuoso Period," "The Weimar Years," "The Final Period"), virtually every composition is mentioned, with many receiving a brief discussion, including musical examples. Searle also deals with such subjects as Liszt's and Wagner's mutual influence and Liszt's development of chromatic harmony. He stumbles, however, over the issue of Liszt and orchestration. By borrowing selectively from Raabe, he arrives at the erroneous conclusion that Liszt did not know how to orchestrate prior to his arrival in Weimar. Nevertheless, Searle has produced a useful guide to the music. Revisions to the 1954 edition are limited to corrections and the inclusion of a handful of works.

WALKER contains important essays by Collet and Searle. Collet discusses seven of Liszt's works for piano and orchestra. He includes the lesser known *Grande Fantaisie Symphonique* and *Malédiction*, two works freely transcribed from solo piano originals (*Hungarian Fantasy* and *Fantasia on Motifs from Beethoven's "Ruins of Athens"*), the two concertos, and *Totentanz*. The essay begins with a consideration of Liszt's technique of thematic transformation, demonstrated with an example from Piano Concerto no. 2. Each work is examined with attention to transformations and their relationship to form, accompanied by copious musical examples. Collet also examined several manuscripts, including those of earlier versions, and he includes these observations. Although research plays a minor role in this essay, the discussion of each work is insightful, and the whole is a useful introduction to the repertory.

Searle's essay concentrates on the symphonic poems and the symphonies. He begins by again addressing the subject of Liszt and orchestration. Like Collet, Searle provides an example of thematic transformation, this one from *Les Préludes*. His discussion of the music is accompanied by musical examples. Since he has more space than in *The Music of Liszt*, he amplifies his previous insights. In this context, it is useful to mention Searle's final work, his contribution to the *New Grove Dictionary of Music and Musicians* (1980). Searle was woefully out of touch with recent scholarship, and important revisions to his article were necessary. These were made by Sharon Winklhofer and published as *The New Grove Early Romantic Masters I: Chopin, Schumann, Liszt* (1985).

A sympathetic appraisal of Liszt's sacred music has been long overdue. MERRICK structures his book in three sections, beginning with a revisionist review of Liszt's life from a religious standpoint and ending with an attempt to read sacred programs into his instrumental music. Although he intended the first and third parts to be the most provocative, it is the second and most substantial that leaves the greatest impression. Here we find an overview of this repertory, including two oratorios, five Masses, and various shorter pieces. For each composition, he provides historical background, performance history, and an analytical overview with musical examples. His research was current as of 1980 (despite the 1987 publication date), and he makes excellent use of Liszt's letters, for which he provided his own elegant translations. This is a fine introduction to a neglected portion of Liszt's output.

WATSON is an introduction to Liszt's life and works, with approximately half the book given over to a discussion of the works by genre. His chapters on the concertos and orchestral music are fine overviews. In his discussion of *Les préludes*, he includes a series of examples that illustrates Liszt's use of thematic transformation. Similar treatment is given to lesser known works. For *Die Ideale*, he offers a breakdown of the piece by measure number, taking into account both the musical form and the program. Once again, there is little original scholarship, but Watson's research was current.

Following Raabe's ground-breaking work, it has taken nearly 50 years for Liszt research to blossom. Much of this scholarship has not yet been incorporated in monograph form, although Watson makes some use of it, as does Alan Walker in his *Franz Liszt*. A comprehensive bibliography may be found in Michael Saffle, *Franz Liszt: A Guide to Research* (New York and London: Garland Publishing, 1991), but three articles are singled out here as excellent examples. KAPLAN is at pains to show the relationship that four of the symphonic poems and the *Faust* Symphony bear to sonata form. He is very convincing, but perhaps at the expense of downplaying their revolutionary nature (see, for example, Rey M. Longyear and Kate R. Covington, "Tonal and Harmonic Structure in Liszt's Faust Symphony," *Studia musicologica* 28 [1986]: 153-171). Nevertheless, his conclusions reinforce the purely musical coherence, providing a much-needed response to accusations of formlessness in Liszt's works.

BONNER is concerned with the history of *Les préludes*. He has examined all the surviving manuscripts and produced a plausible chronology that accounts for all extant versions. He discusses Liszt's compositional process, his use of programs, and the copyists who assisted him. His remarkable conclusion is that *Les préludes* was not associated with its well-known program or given its title until several years after it had been completed. In part, Bonner's work is a response to an article by Alexander Main ("Liszt after Lamartine: 'Les préludes,'" *Music and Letters* 60 [1979]), but it is a fascinating study in its own right and representative of such compositional process studies. Although both Kaplan and Bonner require a high degree of technical knowledge, the analytical portions, printed in smaller type, may be easily passed over.

ROSENBLATT (1995) concentrates on the concertos written before 1835, including the earliest version of Concerto no. 1 and *Malédiction*. It is the first study to take into account all surviving manuscripts, and his analysis of these documents allows him to provide precise dates, some of which challenge the currently accepted chronology. The first part is a comprehensive review of the literature concerning Liszt's complete concerto output, with chapters on secondary sources, primary sources, and an overview of Liszt's compositional process. In the second part, each of the early concertos receives extensive discussion, with a review of all primary sources, analysis of the score, and transcription of the sketches. Rosenblatt concludes that these works of the early 1830s served as a laboratory in which Liszt was able to work out and first apply his innovations of form, harmony, and thematic transformation. ROSENBLATT (1999) summarizes his research on the earlier concertos and adds commentary on all later works. Again, he provides a more precise chronology than has heretofore been available.

JOHNS is notable as the first monograph devoted to the symphonic poems. Unfortunately, he did not live to complete it, and though Michael Saffle prepared Johns's manuscript for publication, it is unclear how much of the book remained unfinished. For example, the analytical discussion of each work appears to be no more than an outline, in contrast to the extensive definition of terms that precedes it. The latter portion of the book appears to be more complete. The section on reception history is exhaustive, with translations of many performance reviews through 1861, and the discussion of chronology and manuscripts is very thorough. Johns was well aware of recent scholarship and deftly incorporated it. One particularly delightful example is the way he was able to reconcile the arguments of Bonner and Main. Thus the final sections are the most useful parts of the book and are a fine testament to his scholarship.

JAY ROSENBLATT

3. Piano Music

Hamilton, Kenneth, *Liszt, Sonata in B Minor,* Cambridge: Cambridge University Press, 1996

Liszt, Franz, *Klaviersonate H-moll: Faksimile nach dem im Eigentum von Mr. Robert Owen Lehman befindlichen Autograph,* Munich: Henle, 1973a

———, *The Liszt Studies: Essential Selections from the Original 12-Volume Set of Technical Studies for the Piano,* edited by Elyse Mach, New York: Associated Music, 1973b

Longyear, Rey M., "Liszt's B Minor Sonata: Precedents for a Structural Analysis," *Music Review* 34 (1973)

Searle, Humphrey, *The Music of Liszt,* London: Williams and Norgate, 1954; 2nd revised edition, New York: Dover Publications, 1966

Walker, Alan, editor, *Franz Liszt: The Man and His Music,* London: Barrie and Jenkins, and New York: Taplinger, 1970

Watson, Derek, *Liszt,* London: Dent, and New York: Schirmer, 1989

Westerby, Herbert, *Liszt, Composer, and His Piano Works: Descriptive Guide and Critical Analysis,* London: William Reeves, 1936; reprint, Westport, Connecticut: Greenwood Press, 1970

Winklhofer, Sharon, *Liszt's Sonata in B Minor: A Study of Autograph Sources and Documents,* Ann Arbor, Michigan: UMI Research Press, 1980

Liszt's piano music covers an astonishingly wide range of genres, from the original works, such as the Sonata in B Minor, to operatic paraphrases and transcriptions. He was the greatest virtuoso of his day, and, although he retired from the concert stage in 1847, his reputation was maintained through occasional charity performances and his many students. But while these students promoted their master's music through their concerts and teaching, few wrote about it in any detail. Comments on some of this repertoire appear throughout Lina Ramann's biography, *Franz Liszt als Künstler und Mensch* (three volumes, 1880–1894; volume one published in English as *Franz Liszt: Artist and Man,* trans. E. Cowdery, 1882), but it is not until the early 1930s, when the first wave of scholarship appeared in German, that we find detailed discussion of this music. Peter Raabe is among the first, with his two-volume *Franz Liszt* (1931; rev. ed. by Felix Raabe, 1968). In the second volume, *Liszts Schaffen,* he devotes a long chapter to the piano music. Working at about the same time, Rudolf Kókai discusses Liszt's music of the 1830s in *Franz Liszt in seinen frühen Klavierwerken* (1933). The earliest English-language authors were indebted to these studies, but by the 1980s there was a growing body of new scholarship.

WESTERBY harks back to a period of Liszt research when anecdote counted as scholarship. The first part of the book is a survey of Liszt's life, but from the first sentence the narrative contains so many factual errors it is unusable. More substantial is the second part, where the works are discussed under various headings ("Bravura Style, Etc.," "The Consolations, Sonata, Etc.," "The Song Transcriptions"). There are also chapters on "Piano Works with Orchestra" and "The Symphonic Poems and Symphonies." Westerby offers little more than musical description with occasional comments on the level of technical difficulty, and the few quotations from other authors generally lack bibliographic citation. The third part might hold some usefulness for the practicing pianist, devoted as it is to graded repertoire and possible recital programs, and the chapter devoted to "Memorabilia"—quotations by and about Liszt (again often without bibliographic citation)—could be used for program notes. Chapter 29, "Liszt Research," is only a list of various works with their publishers. The "concise and popular style" of the title should not have precluded accuracy and substance, but it does in this case.

SEARLE highlights the Sonata in B Minor, with musical examples of the principal themes and an overview of the form. The author also devotes attention to the important cycles, including the Transcendental Etudes, *Années de pèlerinage,* and *Harmonies poétiques et religieuses.* Liszt was an inveterate reviser of his own works, and Searle provides several examples that reveal the ways Liszt's conception changed. He also discusses many of the transcriptions and paraphrases, generally without musical examples. For the revised edition, he added comments on a few of the late works that had come to light since the 1954 edition. While Searle has done little original research, he has carefully examined this music and often provides valuable insights.

Kentner and Ogdon were both concert pianists whose repertoires contained many works by Liszt, and, in the anthology edited by WALKER, they divide the solo piano music. Their approach is to focus on the finest works in Liszt's large output, not necessarily in chronological order. Kentner covers Liszt's middle period (very little is said of the earlier years), and Ogdon covers the late period. Kentner begins with some of Liszt's finest works, including the Sonata in B Minor. His coverage is limited to the principal themes of each work as well as his own speculative programs. In the Sonata, he presents both the themes and their transformations. His next section deals with the concert etudes, followed by the cycles. He provides many musical examples but few musical insights. Ogdon takes a similar approach, but his discussion ultimately leaves the reader with a fine idea of Liszt's late style. Walker also devotes a chapter to the transcriptions and paraphrases by Wilde, following a similar format. He begins with Liszt's greatest achievement in the transcription medium, the Beethoven Symphonies, and he gives a very sympathetic appraisal of Liszt's work with many supporting musical examples.

The first attempt to analyze the Sonata in B Minor can be found in William S. Newman, *The Sonata Since Beethoven* (1969). His discussion is brief, but he was the first to describe this work as a sonata in one movement as well as a sonata in four interconnected movements. He was also the first to use the term "double function" to describe this approach. LONGYEAR wrote his article partially in response and gives considerable detail to his own viewpoint. He fully accepts Newman's double function but disagrees in the details. In addition, he is able to find several precedents for Liszt's approach. The result is a fine introduction to this complex piece, albeit one that should be read in conjunction with Newman's book. HAMILTON is a thorough and up-to-date study of the Sonata in B Minor and the music and ideas surrounding it. His knowledge of the primary and secondary sources allows him to write a lively narrative that covers a number of relevant topics, including Liszt's etudes, his approach to the piano, and, unexpectedly, his unfinished opera. The chapter on form casts an especially wide net, catching several contemporaries whose works anticipated Liszt's novel ideas. In his analysis of the Sonata, Hamilton weaves together the analyses by Newman, Longyear, and Winklhofer, while adding insights of his own. And like Winklhofer, he uses the autograph in his search for understanding. Rounding off the book is a performance history (including selected recordings), a discussion of pianos, and comments on works inspired by the Sonata. Hamilton should satisfy anyone seeking a state-of-the-art summary of Liszt research.

Among scholarly studies of Liszt's piano music, WINKLHOFER must be ranked among the finest. She brings to her work an extensive background with the primary sources, including firsthand knowledge of Liszt's manuscripts in Europe and the United States as well as a comprehensive sampling of Liszt's published letters. Her work also reveals a careful study of the secondary sources, both on Liszt and on compositional process. Part 1 presents the historical context of the Sonata in B Minor, beginning with the circumstances that led Liszt to Weimar, and ending with the first performances of the work in 1853. It is full of valuable insights into Liszt's career at this time, buttressed by numerous citations from the letters. Part 2 introduces the world of Liszt's autographs, including various aspects of his working habits from writing utensils to paper preferences. Part 3 applies the information from part 2 to the manuscript of the Sonata. In part 4, Winklhofer reviews the analyses of Newman and Longyear, reinforcing the double function aspect, but disagreeing in many details. She, too, is convincing. Using this analysis as a basis, she turns to the manuscript itself, discussing Liszt's many revisions in order to gain an understanding of his compositional process. In addition to many musical examples, she includes transcriptions of all earlier sketches and drafts from the autograph. Her entire study is superb and one of the landmarks of contemporary Liszt scholarship.

WATSON devotes two chapters to the piano music, "Original Piano Music" and "Transcriptions." This may seem odd, but a statistical glance at Liszt's output reveals nearly as many transcriptions as original works, the vast majority for piano. Watson views the transcriptions as acts of re-creation, with the result an original composition based on borrowed materials. He divides these works into two groups: free arrangements, as in the operatic paraphrases, and strict arrangements, as in the Beethoven symphony transcriptions and other "partitions de piano." As one example, he contrasts several measures of a transcription of Symphony no. 3 by Friedrich Kalkbrenner with that by Liszt, deftly pointing up the manner in which elements of the orchestration can be captured on the piano. The original works are discussed in chronological sequence. With a sure hand, Watson highlights many of Liszt's innovative compositions from all periods, even to the point of comparing different published versions. Another useful aspect is the division of Liszt's output into a Roman period (1861–67), offering attention to the years surrounding his taking of minor orders of the priesthood.

Two other publications are primary sources relevant to a survey of Liszt's piano music. Although several of Liszt's students left memoirs that include descriptions of his playing and his master classes, LISZT (1973b) must be singled out as in some ways the most revealing. This volume is largely devoted to a selection of Liszt's own exercises, but it is the extended introduction by Elyse Mach that is the main attraction. Here we find her complete translation of Madame Auguste Boissier, *Liszt pédagogue: Leçons de piano données par Liszt à Mademoiselle Valérie Boissier à Paris en 1832* (1923). Boissier's daughter was Liszt's student for several months in late 1831 and early 1832, and her mother observed the lessons. Her resulting diary has the immediacy of an event taking place while containing considerable detail. Aside from the insights into Liszt's teaching, Boissier reveals many details of his solutions to problems both musical and technical. The result is a unique snapshot of the pianist on the eve of his greatest accomplishments.

Finally, there is the color facsimile of the LISZT (1973a) autograph of the Sonata in B Minor, published in 1973 by Henle. (The original is in the Pierpont Morgan Library in New York.) Following the facsimile is a short essay, "Some Final Thoughts," written by Claudio Arrau. Liszt's written notation is very expressive, with countless subtle inflections, untranslatable into engraved music. Here one can also see the details mentioned by Rey M. Longyear ("The Text of Liszt's B Minor Sonata," *Musical*

Quarterly 60 [1974]), Winklhofer, and Hamilton. Unfortunately, the pasteovers ("collettes") that cover a number of passages are in place, but transcriptions of the music beneath them can be found in Winklhofer.

JAY ROSENBLATT

Liturgical Drama

Collins, Fletcher, *The Production of Medieval Church Music-Drama,* Charlottesville: University Press of Virginia, 1972

Crocker, Richard, and David Hiley, editors, *The Early Middle Ages to 1300,* New Oxford History of Music, vol. 2, Oxford: Oxford University Press, 1990

Rankin, Susan, *The Music of the Medieval Liturgical Drama in France and England,* 2 vols., New York: Garland, 1989

Smoldon, William L., *The Music of the Medieval Church Dramas,* edited by Cynthia Bourgeault, London: Oxford University Press, 1980

Young, Karl, *The Drama of the Medieval Church,* 2 vols., Oxford: Clarendon Press, 1933

At high festivals in many medieval churches from the tenth century on, clerics and canons performed semi-representational, wholly-sung dramas based on scenes from the Bible or liturgy. Given a variety of names (*representatio, officium, ludus, ordo,* etc.) in the original sources, these plays have been given the collective name of liturgical drama by modern musicologists and drama scholars.

Variations on the most widespread and oldest liturgical drama, known as the *Visitatio sepulchri,* were performed on Easter Day throughout much of Europe and in England from at least the tenth century on. The drama in its simplest form draws its music and text from a trope, *Quem quaeritis,* performed at Matins on Easter Day and first appears with music in a manuscript from Aquitaine from around 930. The text is a dialogue between the three Marys and the angel they encounter at the empty tomb of Christ, who informs them that Christ has risen. In many places, notably Winchester, the dialogue was augmented with other pre-existing antiphons based on biblical texts and the dramatic possibilities of the scene were emphasized with performance directions. A second early play, known as the *Officium stellae* or the Magi play, is less widespread in the sources. While based on an antiphon that also begins *Quem quaeritis,* the Magi play, unlike the *Visitatio,* first appeared outside the context of a liturgical ceremony, and even in its earliest sources, the Magi play includes newly-composed music and text alongside more traditional liturgical antiphons and chant.

These two plays remained popular for about 600 years. Different locations adapted the plays to their needs, local tastes, and practical considerations such as the architecture of their church, by adding, subtracting, or varying the texts. In many places, new dialogues were grafted onto the older ones to extend the play; in others, the original *Quem quaeritis* dialogue remained unchanged.

The 11th and 12th centuries saw an explosion in the diffusion and adaptations of liturgical drama, particularly in Normandy and northern France. Alongside the Easter and Magi plays, a number of other dramas appeared, including the *Officium pastorum,* the *Ordo peregrinus,* the *Ludus Danielis,* the four miracle plays of St. Nicholas, and the *Conversion of Saint Paul.* The *Officium pastorum* and the *Ordo peregrinus* were the most widely spread of these newer plays and have the strongest connection to the liturgy. The others are much more theatrical and independent of liturgical influences, and they appear in only a few sources. The *Conversion of Saint Paul* appears only in one manuscript, generally known as the Fleury Playbook, along with nine other liturgical dramas. Many of the plays in this unique collection, which probably originated in the student circles of Paris or Orleans, are extensively rubricated, with instructions about actions, props, and even costumes (beards were particularly popular). Also of note are the *Ordo virtutum,* by Hildegard von Bingen, the only known drama attributed to a single known author-composer.

Much of the research on liturgical drama has been conducted by drama scholars rather than musicologists, and as a result, little notice has been given to the music. Among the best discussions of liturgical drama is YOUNG's comprehensive study of all types of the genre, which includes transcriptions of all the variant texts he could find. This study has been corrected and critiqued over the years for its adherence to an evolutionary model of history, and its information about the location of source material is outdated, but these volumes nevertheless remain a basic reference work on liturgical drama. Young's major drawback for the reader interested in the music of the dramas is that he does not discuss the music at all, focusing only on texts and analyses of texts.

COLLINS approaches liturgical drama as the producer of a play or opera might. He analyzes the major episodes of the repertory of liturgical dramas for their dramatic content and discusses production questions such as appropriate physical actions, costumes, colors, and sets, drawing much of his evidence from stained glass and manuscript illuminations of the 12th and 13th centuries. His discussion of the music is limited, but he does emphasize its importance to the production as a whole. There are some short discussions about numbers of singers, rhythm, instruments, and the difficulties inherent in presenting the music as a cohesive whole. Although somewhat dated, Collins is a useful text for those considering producing liturgical dramas.

Unfinished at his death and completed by Cynthia Bourgeault, SMOLDON's study is the first book-length monograph to consider the music of liturgical drama. The volume is intended to serve as a complement to

Young's work, and Smoldon uses melodic comparison and analysis to trace the geographic origins and chronology of music and text in liturgical dramas. Unfortunately, his reliance on Young's questionable assertions about the dates of a number of manuscripts containing liturgical dramas renders some of Smoldon's conclusions unconvincing. (The editor's introduction notes that Smoldon himself intended to rewrite certain sections in light of new developments in chronology and research in the field.) Nevertheless, the text is a valuable contribution to the field, and it remains the best in-depth source for the general reader. Smoldon also offers his opinions about the performance of liturgical dramas, including critiques of plays produced by Noah Greenberg in the 1960s.

RANKIN, written before Smoldon was published, investigates the mixing of pre-existing material with new compositions in order to trace the diffusion and development of Easter, Magi, and *Peregrinus* plays. Rankin identifies the sources of texts and melodies (whether biblical, liturgical, or otherwise) and pinpoints the geographical region of origin for particular melodic and textual variants. She also analyzes the newly composed items and borrowings found in liturgical drama, as she aims to differentiate chronologically the various layers of composition, which may appear concurrently within one drama. She concludes that in the late 11th and 12th centuries, the *Pastorum* and *Peregrinus* plays were created when new scenes using music from a variety of sources were added to the *Visitatio*. In the later 12th and the 13th centuries, certain centers, particularly in the Norman areas of France, expanded these plays even further through the use of new metrical texts and original music and through the development of large-scale dramatic scenes. Rankin's work is important and groundbreaking for the musical study of liturgical drama, and her scholarship impeccable. It is a complex work, composed primarily of technical description, transcriptions, and tables, but the textual portions are very accessible.

In CROCKER and HILEY, Rankin summarizes many of her earlier conclusions in her essay "Liturgical Drama," and she extends the discussion to other plays in the repertory, particularly those of the Fleury Playbook. As part of a larger anthology on medieval music before 1300, Rankin's essay is necessarily a concise history and analysis of liturgical drama. However, it is the most current and most readable introduction to liturgical drama in a musical framework.

NANCY LORIMER

Liturgy: Introduction

Cabié, Robert, *The Eucharist,* translated by Matthew J. O'Connell, Collegeville, Minnesota: Liturgical Press, 1986; London: Chapman, 1987

Chupungco, Anscar J., editor, *Handbook for Liturgical Studies,* 2 vols., Collegeville, Minnesota: Liturgical Press, 1997

Dalmais, Irénée Henri, et al., *The Principles of the Liturgy,* translated by Matthew J. O'Connell, London: Chapman, and Collegeville, Minnesota: Liturgical Press, 1987

Harper, John, *The Forms and Orders of Western Liturgy from the Tenth to the Eighteenth Century,* Oxford: Clarendon Press, and New York: Oxford University Press, 1991

Hoppin, Richard H., *Medieval Music,* New York: Norton, 1978

Hughes, Andrew, *Medieval Manuscripts for Mass and Office: A Guide to Their Organization and Terminology,* Toronto: University of Toronto Press, 1982

Jones, Cheslyn, et al., editors, *The Study of Liturgy,* London: SPCK, and New York: Oxford University Press, 1978; revised edition, 1992

Jungmann, Joseph A., *The Mass of the Roman Rite: Its Origins and Development,* 2 vols., translated by Francis A. Brunner, New York: Benziger, 1951–55; new edition, revised by Charles K. Riepe, 1961

King, Archdale Arthur, *Rites of Western Christendom,* 4 vols., London: Longmans, Green, 1955–59

Lang, Jovian, *Dictionary of the Liturgy,* New York: Catholic Book Publishing, 1989

Quasten, Johannes, *Music and Worship in Pagan and Christian Antiquity,* translated by Boniface Ramsey, Washington, D.C.: National Association of Pastoral Musicians, 1983

Vogel, Cyrille, *Medieval Liturgy: An Introduction to the Sources,* translated by William Storey and Niels Krogh Rasmussen, Washington, D.C.: Pastoral Press, 1986

Wegman, Herman A.J., *Christian Worship in East and West: A Study Guide to Liturgical History,* translated by Gordon W. Lathrop, New York: Pueblo, 1985

Liturgy is the official corporate worship of the Church, the authorized physical coming together of a community of believers to worship God; it is distinguished from worship in the Church or that of public and private devotions. The liturgies of the Church are the Eucharist (also known as the Mass, the Lord's Supper, and the Divine Liturgy), the Hours (Divine Office), the sacraments (Rites of Christian Initiation, Penance, Ordination, Marriage, Anointing of the Sick), and those for various occasions (e.g., religious profession, the consecration of a church). The study of liturgy strives to present an overall view of the rite (the order and content of the service; what is said, sung, or done and when), the ceremony (those who perform the rite and how; the utilization of liturgical accessories, signs, symbols, and space), and its use (a regional, diocesan, or local variant of the rite). This is achieved through studies of a historical, theological, and pastoral nature that examine sources, prototypes, traditions, and cultural influences.

WEGMAN divides liturgical history into five periods from early Christianity to the Council of Trent and the

Counter Reformation, stressing the Roman Rite. One chapter is devoted to the development of the Byzantine liturgy after A.D. 610. Using the comparative school of liturgical study begun by the German liturgiologist Anton Baumstark, each chapter contains a historical and cultural overview; provides a survey of relevant liturgical sources; gives selections of primary sources both in the original language and in translation; and furnishes summaries of liturgical data on the liturgies of the Eucharist, the Hours, the sacraments, and on the liturgical calendar. Of particular quality is the chapter on the development of the Western liturgy from the time of Gregory the Great (A.D. 590–604) to that of Gregory VII (A.D. 1073–85). In his discussion of sources, Wegman enlists the scholarship of Cyrille Vogel. While there is occasional mention of music, a categorical commentary is lacking. Summaries of renewal efforts from the late 15th century to Vatican II are given in an appendix. The glossaries are helpful in understanding technical terms of the Western and Byzantine liturgies.

VOGEL's introduction to the sources of medieval liturgy (A.D. 590–1485) is fundamental in the study of the development of the Western or Roman and papal forms of worship, the manner in which these liturgies squeezed the older non-Roman rites out of Europe, and the reason for the strong emphasis on Roman liturgical texts. The study is specific to sources that were used in liturgy, and which were the basis for the late medieval liturgy and the standardized Roman or Tridentine Rite, in particular: the *ordines*, the complement to the sacramentary, which detail the execution of ritual actions; and the organization, origins, and contextual considerations of the Mass lectionaries. The revised section on the Frankish Gelasian and Gregorian sacramentaries and the private Mass introduce new material in light of new scholarship in the early 1980s. The use of manuscripts, many of which are available in reprint, facsimile, or critical editions, enhances the utility of the book. Terminology is well defined, and the bibliography is excellent. However, the discussion on the Office only "orients" the reader to sources on homilies and antiphonaries, and there is a general dearth of music sources.

The five-volume collection of multiauthored essays published by the Pontifical Liturgical Institute offers a thorough course of liturgical studies. The spectrum of worship from the early days of Christianity to the reforms of the 20th century is presented through an integration of materials from the East, the non-Roman West, and the Roman West. The first volume, edited by CHUPUNGCO, discusses the effects of information contained in liturgical books, history, tradition, and in the human sciences. The sections to be highlighted are "Liturgical Sources," which examines the literary genre, characteristics, actual use, and evolution of documents and books, and the "Interpretation of Liturgical Sources," which advocates the science of liturgy, which

"must be understood, taught, and learned under its theological, historical, spiritual, pastoral, and juridical aspects." Music sources are included. Although the individual interests and personal opinions of the authors are at times punctuated, the information presented is derived from solid liturgical sources and tradition. A superb select bibliography is provided for each essay.

The handbook by DALMAIS et al. explores a wide variety of worship forms, languages, and cultures. This book gives a comprehensive overview of the history of liturgy and the liturgies of the past. Referred to as a guided tour of the Church's ritual library, the work directs the reader to critical editions of texts and to classical studies, which are cited in the bibliographies and in the footnotes. Martimort's introductory chapter on "Definitions and Method" is an excellent preface to the study of liturgy. He defines the history of the word *liturgy*, explains the relationship between popular devotions and liturgy, and clearly summarizes the science of liturgy. The select bibliographies are weighted with French publications.

Another excellent starting point for readings in the main areas of liturgical study is JONES et al. A discussion of theology and rites serves as the prelude to the body of the work: the development of the liturgy. This section consists of the historical study, from scriptural origins to current changes and developments, of the five major elements of liturgy: Initiation, Eucharist, Ordination, Office, and the Calendar. The articles by various authors serve to show that the historical study of liturgy is not irrelevant to the liturgy of today. The recent use of human sciences is also included.

The definition of words and terms is often problematic in the study of liturgy. LANG's dictionary focuses on but is not exclusive to Roman Catholic tradition. It includes phonetic pronunciation, popular prayer texts not readily available, illustrations (which are at times outdated), explanations of the parts of the Mass, and the use and relationship of each book of the Bible to the liturgy. It is a good source when a quick and concise definition is wanted; it is more of a popular ready-reference tool than a scholarly one.

The early Christian disposition toward music and singing in worship, and its relationship within the context of the pagan cult, is explored by QUASTEN. Because music was very closely associated with pagan worship, the primitive Church refrained from complete musical embellishment of the liturgy, even though it was part of the Old Testament tradition. Thus, the Church forged a musical art that cultivated devotion rather than magic. Quasten considers the use of music in the pagan Greek and Roman cultic sacrifice and the mystery cults or rites of initiation, including the mystery dramas, music and mysticism, music in early Christian liturgy and private life, and music in the Christian and pagan cults of the dead. In light of the liturgical practices, laws, and reforms of the past and present, the discussion of the singing by women and young boys, the use of musical instruments, and the use of dance at worship is quite revealing. The bibliography and annotations are excellent reference tools. Although there have been scholarly advances on this topic since the book's initial publication in 1929, it remains the most extensive study of its kind.

HOPPIN believes that the first millennium in the history of Western music "must of necessity be a history of the Christian liturgy." Thus establishing the religious, sociopolitical, and geographical climate of the first Christian millennium, the author examines medieval music from the earliest days of the Church to the polyphony of the early 15th century. This is paralleled by a brief discussion of the non-Roman and Roman liturgies of the West, the liturgical year, and the chant (A.D. 800–1000). The core of this book is devoted to chant (music for the Office and the Mass), the development of tropes and sequences, and the growth of organum, motets, and polyphony (sacred and secular) during the 13th and 14th centuries. The book is for both the student and the scholar, is well illustrated, and includes music examples in addition to those of the anthology. For those looking to embark on a journey into the history of music in the Church, this is a good place to begin.

HARPER considers the structures and content of the mainstream Western liturgy (i.e., the Roman Rite) in its artistic, cultural, and architectural contexts from the 10th to the 18th centuries. The chapter on "Establishing the Order of a Latin Liturgical Celebration" is a guide for using resources and the four layers of the reconstruction process: text, music, ritual, and ceremony. The manuscripts studied introduce the reader to the organization of several surviving medieval sources, most of which are English in origin: Salisbury, Hereford, York, and the Roman Curia (secular churches); and Winchester, Westminster, St. Mary's at York, Norwich, Barking, Worcester, and Durham (monastic churches). Devotional and paraliturgical forms of worship such as processions, memorials, suffrages, liturgical dramas, and commemorations are also surveyed. The sketch of the liturgies for Triduum and Easter deals primarily with texts and music practices. The complexities of the liturgical calendar, the frequently used Latin choral texts (the English translations are not directly from the Latin but instead mainly adaptations from the Book of Common Prayer), and the Psalter are dealt with in the appendices. The author's borderline treatment of the Reformation in general, and the Tridentine reforms in particular, is an area of weakness. A knowledge of music is assumed.

HUGHES leads the reader through the intricacies and pitfalls of the medieval Mass and Office as found in manuscript sources of the 12th through the 16th centuries. Emphasis is on the Office. A summary of the development of the medieval Office and Mass, the latter of which is derived mainly from Jungmann, is useful for the average reader. Innovative and of particular interest is Hughes's method of using illuminated and capital letters as structural markers to deal with the format of liturgical books and manuscripts. This is fundamental in his study of individual services and books and is used in the detailed examination of the features, orderings, and disruptions of the usual sequence of materials in the *Graduale* and various Office books (antiphonals, breviaries, psalters, and hymnals). The reciprocal relationship between the Mass and the Office explored in this book is significant to the understanding of liturgy in general.

Fundamental to a comprehensive historical study of the theology, texts, sources, and ceremony of the Mass of the Roman rite is JUNGMANN's epochal work. The numerous footnotes are invaluable. The discussion of the nature and forms of the Mass (e.g., *Missa solemnis, Missa Cantata,* domestic Eucharist, private Mass) shows that the hybrid character of the Mass was the result of the low Mass appropriating features of the high Mass, the high Mass adopting elements from the low Mass, and the hybridization of both by medieval personal devotions and Gallican features. The detailed discussion of the ceremonies of the Mass comprises the major portion of these two volumes. The author's views on chant are moderate in terms of application and practice. There is also evidence of his support for congregational singing. The explanations or definitions of obscure terms such as *boxed Masses* (i.e., "one Mass sung up to the offertory or Sanctus, then continued as a low Mass while at another altar a second [sung] Mass was begun") are beneficial. This often cited work is a landmark in the study of liturgy and a must for every student of sacred music and liturgy.

KING presents a condensed study of various traditions and rites of the Mass. There is little or no mention of the Office. Volume 1 considers the Carthusians, Cistercians, Premonsratensians, Carmelites, and Dominicans. Each chapter briefly sketches the order; provides an account of the architectural styles, church ornamentations, and the vestments; describes the history, origins, development, liturgical year, and chant or music practices of each rite, and explains how they differ from the Roman rite. For example, if a Carthusian says Mass outside of the monastery, in order to avoid scandal, he may conform to Roman usage, such as saying the *Confiteor* before the altar, elevating the chalice, blessing the people at the end of Mass, etc. The appendices describe characteristics, obsolete rites, and ceremonies. Each chapter includes a bibliography. The illustrations are helpful and interesting.

What is to be gleaned from King's second volume is the description of "hieratic languages," ornaments of the Church (e.g., chalice, ciborium, pyx, monstrance, candles, etc.), vestments, the use of incense, liturgical books, and ceremonial, rubrics, and the liturgical year. The section that deals with the Mass itself is divided into "the Mass of the Catechumens" and "the Mass of the Faithful." The appendices offer information on some rather arcane terms, such as *Disciplina arcani* or "the discipline of the secret," which was used to indicate the withholding of knowledge of the sacraments from the unbaptized.

In volume 4 King speaks of the liturgies of the non-Roman West that are lost: Aquileia, Beneventan, Gallican, Celtic, medieval England, and Nidaros. It provides functional background reading on rites, ceremonies, and traditions that played an integral role in the history and transmission of chant.

CABIÉ's study of the Eucharist is not as comprehensive as that of Jungmann, nor is it meant to be. Keeping in mind that this text is a tour guide, the section on the development of the Mass prior to liturgical books is well presented and segues into that on the creation of formularies and the organization of rites. Each part of the Mass is described and an explanation of its development in various traditions is given. Comparisons are frequently made in parallel, for example, the discussion of the private prayers of the priest during the offertory of the Roman Missal of Pius V, the Lyons Missal, the Carthusian Missal, and the Dominican Missal. The Mass of Paul VI or the new Order is clearly defined in its final form. This section, when read in conjunction with Bugnini, is quite interesting. The book concludes with a look at concelebration, and communion and adoration of the Blessed Sacrament outside of Mass.

GERALDINE M. ROHLING

Liturgy: Divine Office

Dalmais, Irénée Henri, et al., *The Liturgy and Time,* translated by Matthew J. O'Connell, Collegeville, Minnesota: Liturgical Press, 1986

Hughes, Andrew, *Medieval Manuscripts for Mass and Office: A Guide to Their Organization and Terminology,* Toronto: University of Toronto Press, 1982

Jones, Cheslyn, et al., editors, *The Study of Liturgy,* London: SPCK, and New York: Oxford University Press, 1978; revised edition, 1992

Salmon, Pierre, *The Breviary through the Centuries,* Collegeville, Minnesota: Liturgical Press, 1962

Taft, Robert F., *The Liturgy of the Hours in East and West: The Origins of the Divine Office and Its Meaning for Today,* Collegeville, Minnesota: The Liturgical Press: 1986; 2nd revised edition, 1993

Van Dijk, Stephen Joseph Peter, and Joan Hazelden Walker, *The Origins of the Modern Roman Liturgy: The Liturgy of the Papal Court and the Franciscan Order in the Thirteenth Century,* Westminster, Maryland: Newman Press, 1960

The Divine Office is a series of nonsacramental services that are recited throughout the day and night, preferably in community. Communal prayer, an important activity of the primitive church, began to develop a structural form in the fourth century. These forms varied from place to place and were complicated by the differences between cathedral and monastic (to be distinguished from Benedictine) usages. The most familiar structure of the Hours is that of the Roman and Byzantine rites: seven-day Hours and a night Office. The Office became a clerical and monastic obligation, for which the laity substituted popular devotions. In 1568 the *Breviarium romanum* became mandatory for all secular clergy and all who could not verify a breviary of at least 200 years of age. The Tridentine breviary reduced the sanctorale and deleted the supplementary Offices and was essentially a restored classical monastic Office of the ancient Roman basilicas. Although it was intended to be definitive, papal additions and minor changes were made almost immediately. Major changes received only feeble attempts until the pontificate of Pius X. It is believed that this was the stimulus for the modern liturgical reform. In order to emphasize the injunction of the New Testament to "pray always," and the idea of consecrating time, the Divine Office (the name refers to the obligation) was renamed Liturgy of the Hours by Vatican II.

The standard work on the history of the Office is by TAFT. It focuses on the origins and development of the Office and how it can be traced through both Eastern and Western traditions. Fundamental to this are the cathedral and monastic usages, which were first defined by Anton Baumstark. Cathedral usage, or that of the secular churches, was a popular service at the bishop's church characterized by symbol and ceremony (light, incense, processions), chant (responsories, antiphons, hymns), diversity of ministries (bishop, presbyter, deacon, reader, psalmist, cantor, etc.), and psalmody that was limited and select. Monastic usage did not relate to a specific hour, day, or season and consisted of the recitation of the entire Psalter in its biblical numerical order. The author draws a distinction between those monastic traditions that added cathedral elements and those that began with cathedral usage and became monasticized. Taft also gives the first English outline of the structure of the liturgy of the hours in the various Eastern rites. The book is designed so that sections may be extracted without a loss in continuity.

VAN DIJK and WALKER is one of the more important works focusing on the advent of the curial Office and that of the Friars Minor from A.D. 1200 to 1244. During this period the Roman liturgy of the Hours began to evolve into the breviary. Crucial to this process was the adoption of the papal ordinal of Innocent III by the Friars Minor. In the mid-13th century, Haymo of Faversham revised the curial-type ordinal to regulate the usage of the existing Office books among the Friars. It is this revised usage that was adapted to local customs and was disseminated throughout Europe by the Franciscans. Van Dijk and Walker dispel the myth that the Franciscans invented the breviary. The original breviaries were not portable Office books for private recitation but an attempt to condense into one volume the various elements of the Office that up till then were scattered throughout several books. The prescription for what went where and when was governed by an ordinal. Such breviaries were in existence both before and after the reforms of Innocent III and their Franciscan adaptations.

HUGHES's exposition on the course of psalmody and matins is indispensable. Taken in conjunction with his discussion on the "Psalter and the Hymnal," a basic understanding of the medieval Office is achieved. The author states his purpose to be the examination of the "general method of the organization of various parts of the year and of the liturgical manuscripts" in order for the user to be able to identify the peculiarities of particular sources. Thus, by characterizing the ways in which the Office was celebrated in various locales, he secedes from the notion that a uniform ritual prevailed in the Roman West. Beginning with the antiphonal and ending with the "complete" breviary and antiphonal, Hughes presents a comprehensive study on this topic.

SALMON states that "the prayer of the Church is a positive datum, forming part of Tradition" and examines the development of the Latin Office, the course of Scripture in the Roman Office, and the Christian interpretation of the Psalms. He targets the past, present (i.e., the 1960s), and the future of the Office. The evolution of the Office is discussed pragmatically in order to instruct the clergy and religious in its formation, whereby they may better celebrate it. Salmon asserts that the perfect Office is in line with "the great Tradition, and corresponds best to actual conditions and needs of the Church and its ministers"; fidelity to tradition does not mean fixity. This book is not, nor was it planned to be, a definitive history of the breviary but instead more of a way station until a more complete study could be written. Nonetheless, Salmon's scholarship is of the first mark, and this book is a foundational stepping stone in the study of the Office.

The history of the Office in the West from the formative period (Cathedral and Monastic Offices) through the Middle Ages and into the Roman Rite of the 16th century is presented in essays in JONES et al. These narratives provide understandable abstracts for the complicated development of the Office.

DALMAIS et al. gives the other elements of the Hours equal time. Biblical canticles and the hymns are defined as a prolongation of the psalmody. The musical genres developed by other liturgies—troparia, antiphons, responses—are described as refrains for psalms or are sung independently. The presentation of the varied forms of the Hours in the East and West is a brief encounter. The explanation of the structure and spirituality of each Hour, however, is instructive particularly for those unfamiliar with the celebration of the Hours.

GERALDINE M. ROHLING

Liturgy: Mass

Butt, John, *Bach: Mass in B Minor*, Cambridge: Cambridge University Press, 1991

Drabkin, William, *Beethoven: Missa Solemnis*, Cambridge: Cambridge University Press, 1991

Hughes, Andrew, *Medieval Manuscripts for Mass and Office: A Guide to their Organization and Terminology*, Toronto: University of Toronto Press, 1982

Jungmann, Joseph A., *The Mass of the Roman Rite: Its Origins and Development*, 2 vols., translated by Francis A. Brunner, New York: Benziger, 1951–55; new edition, revised by Charles K. Riepe, 1961

Kerman, Joseph, *The Masses and Motets of William Byrd*, Berkeley: University of California Press, 1981

Kirkman, Andrew, *The Three-Voice Mass in the Later Fifteenth and Early Sixteenth Centuries: Style, Distribution and Case Studies,* New York: Garland, 1995

Leech-Wilkinson, Daniel, *Machaut's Mass: An Introduction,* Oxford: Clarendon Press, and New York: Oxford University Press, 1990

Lockwood, Lewis, *The Counter-Reformation and the Masses of Vincenzo Ruffo*, Vienna: Universal, 1970

Mac Intyre, Bruce C., *The Viennese Concerted Mass of the Early Classical Period,* Ann Arbor, Michigan: UMI Research Press, 1986

Palestrina, Giovanni Pierluigi da, *Pope Marcellus Mass: An Authoritative Score, Backgrounds and Sources, History and Analysis, Views and Comments,* edited by Lockwood Lewis, New York: Norton, 1975

Rilling, Helmuth, *Johann Sebastian Bach's B-Minor Mass,* translated by Gordon Paine, Princeton, New Jersey: Prestige, 1984

Sparks, Edgar, *Cantus Firmus in Mass and Motet, 1420–1520,* Berkeley: University of California Press, 1963

Stäblein-Harder, Hanna, *Fourteenth-Century Mass Music in France,* N.p.: American Institute of Musicology, 1962

Stauffer, George B., *Bach, The Mass in B Minor: The Great Catholic Mass,* New York: Schirmer Books, and London: Prentice Hall, 1997

The broadest definition of the term *Mass* designates the actions and ceremonies comprising the central rite of the Roman Church, the Eucharist. Musical settings of both Mass Proper (introit, gradual, alleluia, offertory, and communion) and Mass Ordinary (Kyrie, Gloria, Credo, Sanctus, Agnus Dei, and Ite missa est) texts were the main vehicle for compositional creativity during the Middle Ages when composers first concentrated on elaborate monophonic and polyphonic settings of individual Mass chants. Not until the 14th century did composers begin to group Ordinary chants as parts of a whole; the first Mass Ordinary recognized as a unit is Guillaume de Machaut's *Messe de Nostre Dame*. By the early Renaissance the term *Mass* was commonly used to designate particular polyphonic settings of the five main parts of the Ordinary wherein the Kyrie, Gloria, Credo, Sanctus and Agnus Dei settings contained shared motives, structure, or other unifying musical features. From the baroque to the present day, composers have continued to set these texts to music, producing not only Masses used in church liturgy but also Masses performed in court or public concerts, one of the most famous examples of the latter being Beethoven's symphonic Mass, the *Missa solemnis* in D major (1823).

First published in German in 1948 as *Missarum Sollemnia,* JUNGMANN's comprehensive book does not address specifically the music of the Mass; however, it is the definitive text to date on the Mass, providing a necessary grounding in the history and understanding of the Mass as liturgy and sacrament. Following an historical survey of the Mass as a whole, the author considers the different circumstances in which the Mass is celebrated. The main portion of the study presents in detail each of the Mass ceremonies from the entrance rite through the recession, describing liturgical actions and tracing individual historical developments of each separate part of the Mass.

HUGHES provides a much-needed resource addressing the difficulties of dealing with liturgical manuscripts, ca. 1200 to 1500, their internal organization, and the means of locating feasts, texts, chants, and so forth on the manuscript page itself. He discusses variants in terminology found in these sources and describes the structure and contents of these books, but he does not address the reading of medieval scripts. The introductory material on the liturgical seasons, feasts, and services and on the form of individual items such as the lessons of the Mass is invaluable for anyone pursuing research involving original manuscript sources.

In the first musicological, book-length examination of a single medieval composition, LEECH-WILKINSON presents a ground-breaking study of Machaut's famous Mass. From new supporting manuscript evidence, he convincingly argues that the Cathedral of Reims was the destination of the work. Closely analyzing Machaut's compositional process, the author offers persuasive evidence that Machaut conceived of the voice parts simultaneously and vertically, not successively and linearly. The edition appended to the analytical study (also published separately in score) contains perceptive and useful critical and performing notes.

STÄBLEIN-HARDER edits the extant corpus of 14th-century Mass compositions originating in or near Avignon; in the critical text companion volume she discusses the relationship of the pieces to the central French tradition in terms of categories of composition, the use made of liturgical melodies, harmony, and the interrelationship of the sources. These Mass pieces were modeled on secular forms and styles, most notably those of the isorhythmic motet, *discant* compositions, and *conductus.*

SPARKS focuses on cantus firmus use in Mass and motet compositions from 1420 to 1520, classifying procedures of cantus firmus use as either "structural" or "cantus firmus paraphrase." He contrasts Du Fay's "rational" cantus firmus technique and its planned and predictable patterns with Ockeghem's "irrational" technique. He also asserts a new importance for Busnoys's contribution to cantus firmus treatment and provides critical summaries of modern theories of cantus firmus usage. Detailed analyses of works of Obrecht and Josquin are presented in the third section. A serious omission is the neglect of English music after the death of Dunstable.

KIRKMAN addresses the style and distribution of the three-voice Mass in the late 15th and early 16th centuries. These Masses present a new type of three-part writing in which all voices occupy their own ranges in a stratified texture of contrapuntal equality. Distinct types within this body of works evidence quite different compositional approaches that had radical implications for 16th-century music, in which imitation came increasingly to infuse the entire texture.

LOCKWOOD (1970) examines the Masses of Vincenzo Ruffo, including those written both before and after he served as the *maestro di cappella* for the Tridentine reformer Cardinal Borromeo, Archbishop of Milan. Lockwood shows that Ruffo sought to follow the reformer's ideals by excluding secular material and ensuring the intelligibility of the words in the Mass. Indeed, Borromeo commissioned Ruffo to write a Mass "so that the numbers of the syllables and the voices and tones together should be clearly and distinctly understood and perceived by the pious listeners." The resulting simple, homophonic music, stripped of contrapuntal elaboration was a more radical solution to the cleric's proposed reforms than was Palestrina's famous *Missa Papae Marcelli,* but due to the lack of rapid communication and to the established style preferences of Rome and Venice, Ruffo and his followers were for the most part ignored in subsequent developments of the Mass.

In the material accompanying PALESTRINA, the definitive edition of the *Missa Papae Marcelli,* Lockwood has assembled a collection of background material, documents, and commentaries that shed much light on the controversy commonly associated with the Pope Marcellus Mass: the movement to reform polyphony in church music and to make the words more intelligible. Lockwood presents (in English translation) the sources of the legend that Palestrina "rescued polyphony" from the reforms of the Council of Trent and leaves it to the reader to discern what of the tale is fact or fiction.

KERMAN traces the development of Byrd's style as seen in his corpus of Latin sacred music. Acknowledging both Continental and English influences on Byrd, Kerman nonetheless holds Byrd to be a visionary among composers. The three Mass Ordinary settings—one each in three, four, and five voice parts—convey an intensely personal response to the text and appear to be freely composed, evidencing an organic growth in melodic ideas. In his thorough analysis of Byrd's *Gradualia*, Kerman does not attempt to match Mass Ordinaries to the 17 Mass Proper cycles contained in these two volumes, the composer's crowning work of sacred Latin music.

Three book-length studies on Bach's Mass in B Minor provide three levels of engagement with the work. BUTT's handbook, with summaries of the work's origins and reception history and chapters covering the forms, counterpoint, text-music interactions, and large-scale structuring, gives a good first introduction. STAUFFER delves more deeply into these topics and also treats performance practice and the issue of the work's performance goal in the light of Bach biography, concluding that Bach intended the Mass for the dedication of the new *Hofkirche* at Dresden. RILLING, whose book was first published in German as *Johann Sebastian Bachs h-Moll-Messe* (1979), is a choral conductor and is concerned with performance interpretation; his expository account of the events of each movement is grounded in an understanding of Bach's theology.

MAC INTYRE takes as his subject Masses composed in Vienna by 27 men and 1 woman during a 42-year period between 1741 and 1783, a time between the late-baroque and the high-classical periods. He considers historical background in the first part of the study, surveying the role and environment of church music during the period, stressing the large number of houses of worship hiring singers and instrumentalists in Vienna and its suburbs as well as the diversity of types of church music requiring these performing forces. The second part of the study addresses the music itself, with five chapters treating the five movements of the Mass Ordinary and focusing on overall structure and text treatment, but including such topics as mode, key, rhythm, tempo, texture, dynamics, and use of soloists and chorus. Throughout these chapters Mac Intyre traces the shift in style from baroque to classical, as seen in such characteristics as the growing use of sonata and/or rondo forms instead of the baroque ritornello in the Kyrie and Agnus Dei movements, and the transition away from the older "number" Mass with its multiple movements of Gloria and Credo towards fewer, more integrated settings or even single movements.

DRABKIN covers the compositional, performance, and publication history of Beethoven's *Missa solemnis* and presents an overview of the critical perspectives on the work. He provides a sophisticated analysis of the five movements, incorporating harmonic outlines with considerations of dynamics, orchestration, sketchbook evidence, music-text interactions, and form, concluding that, although Beethoven remained faithful to the basic design of the late 18th-century Austrian Mass, he achieved a balance of structural and programmatic elements, particularly in the Agnus Dei, with its "warmongering of the trumpets and timpani in a foreign key" integrated into the modified sonata form of the concluding "Dona nobis pacem."

JULIA W. SHINNICK

See also Machaut, Guillaume de

Lully, Jean-Baptiste 1632–1687

Italian-born composer

Anthony, James R., *French Baroque Music from Beaujoyeulx to Rameau,* New York: Norton, 1978; revised edition, Portland, Oregon: Amadeus Press, 1997

———, "Jean-Baptiste Lully," in *The New Grove French Baroque Masters,* edited by James R. Anthony et al., London: Macmillan, and New York: Norton, 1986

Benoit, Marcelle, "Paris, 1661–87: The Age of Lully," in *The Early Baroque Era: From the Late 16th Century to the 1660s,* edited by Curtis Price, Basingstoke: Macmillan, 1993

Heyer, John Hajdu, editor, *Jean-Baptiste Lully and the Music of the French Baroque: Essays in Honor of James R. Anthony,* Cambridge: Cambridge University Press, 1989

Isherwood, Robert, *Music in the Service of the King: France in the Seventeenth Century,* Ithaca, New York: Cornell University Press, 1973

La Gorce, Jérôme de, and Herbert Schneider, editors, *Jean-Baptiste Lully,* Laaber: Laaber-Verlag, 1990

Newman, Joyce, *Jean-Baptiste de Lully and His Tragédies Lyriques,* Ann Arbor, Michigan: UMI Research Press, and Epping: Bowker, 1979

Schmidt, Carl B., *The Livrets of Jean-Baptiste Lully's Tragédies Lyriques: A Catalogue Raisonné,* New York: Performers' Editions, 1995

Wood, Caroline, *Music and Drama in the Tragédie en Musique, 1673–1715,* New York: Garland, 1996

Literature on Lully focuses largely on his musical repertoire rather than on biographical information. There is little surviving firsthand information from the composer, such as personal writings or musical sources in his own hand; most of his biography is revealed through his repertoire. Lully served positions of leadership in the court of Louis XIV from the 1650s and the Paris Opéra from 1673 to his death in 1687. His more innovative and abundant works are for the stage, which include court ballets, *comédie ballets* (in collaboration with Molière), and particularly *tragédies en musiques* (also referred to as *tragédies lyriques*). His sacred music is less innovative, in the tradition of the established French motet. His operas remained well known throughout Europe until the end of the 18th century. Despite Lully's significance in French music history, research on the composer published prior to 1970 is largely anecdotal in nature and selective in coverage. In contrast, both his life and works have recently been the subject of rigorous research published in both French and English, comprehensive editing, and grand-scale performances in a historical style.

Lully is the principal musician in ISHERWOOD's study of music in the court of Louis XIV. This book is one of the earliest critical examinations in English of French baroque music, and it remains the best single evaluation of repertoire and musical life within a court political context. Isherwood explores music that supported the advancement of the king, the court, and the country. Musical examples are brief and discussions of repertoire largely descriptive. The book also provides a good overview of philosophical and aesthetic values during Louis XIV's reign.

Originally a doctoral dissertation, NEWMAN's book is one of the first studies in English of Lully's most important genre, his 13 *tragédies lyriques,* which constitute the bulk of his opera output. Prior to Newman's research, these operas had been studied largely as literary objects (most of the texts are by Philippe Quinault). The book serves well as a comprehensive reference tool on the operas, containing straightforward descriptions of textual and musical contents, summaries of plots, musical structures of each act, a brief biography of Lully, and nearly 100 pages of score.

ANTHONY (1997), first published in 1974 by Norton and significantly revised for the 1997 edition, was the first comprehensive study of French baroque music in any language. Like Isherwood's work, Anthony's book covers more than Lully, but he is the central composer, musician, and administrator of music. Lully's stage repertoire is the mark against which nearly all other French musicians and institutions of the period are evaluated. Anthony's encyclopedic command of repertoire and composers makes this book the best single reference work on French baroque music in any language, but the book provides only minimal information about the social and political context in which Lully worked.

ANTHONY's (1986) essay on Lully is an expansion of his article in the *New Grove Dictionary of Music and Musicians* (1980). The essay is in a life-and-works format. Repertoire discussed includes stage music (court ballet, *comédie ballet,* and opera), church music, and instrumental music. The concluding discussion of Lully's influence could be expanded. Typical of these *New Grove* handbooks, the essay contains a comprehensive, detailed work list and bibliography.

HEYER's anthology was inspired by the 1987 tercentenary of Lully's death. Dedicated to James Anthony, the volume complements the collection published by La Gorce and Schneider, but the Heyer essays are longer and contain more detailed investigations of particular topics in Lully studies. All 13 essays are in English, on subjects such as repertoire, including motets, Lully's orchestra, dance suites, court dance, and opera; other musicians and critics; Lully's residences in Paris; and Lully operas as seen from the 18th century.

LA GORCE and SCHNEIDER's collection of 35 essays first appeared as conference reports in an 1987 colloquium recognizing the tercentenary of Lully's death. The collection represents the single largest scholarly collaboration on the composer. Fifteen essays are in English; the remaining are in French or German. General subject areas include Lully's compositional style, critiques of his music by contemporaries, sources and interpretation of music and dance in performance, and the influence and diffusion of Lully's works. Most essays are quite focused and specific; together they provide a broad picture of Lully and at the time of publication represented a new era in critical research. The collection includes various musical examples and facsimiles.

BENOIT's view of Paris during the age of Lully covers 26 years of court and civic institutions. Other composers are generally described in relation to Lully. Benoit's expertise in court archival documents enhances her summary and interpretation of Lully and the court. She also covers civic institutions such as churches, street music, corporations, concert series, academies, and theaters. The bibliography is annotated.

Control of source material of Lully's music as represented by SCHMIDT's catalog is a relatively recent part of the scholarship on the composer. The complicated source situation is one reason that an edition of the collected works of Lully is only now under way. Schmidt amassed all known sources of librettos of Lully's tragedies. His information is presented in exemplary cataloging style. Primarily a reference tool about the librettos, the work also contains a wealth of other information about Lully's operas, such as lists of performers during the performance life of each work, facsimiles of title pages of scores and texts, references to related art works, information about dissemination of repertoire around Europe, and discussions of European printing devices.

WOOD's study first appeared as a doctoral thesis in 1981. Encompassing composers of *tragédies en musiques* from the entire reign of Louis XIV, the book uses Lully's repertoire as the basis for evaluating the works of Campra, Collasse, Destouches, Marais, and others. The first chapter presents a summary of the Académie Royale de Musique, of which Lully was the first significant composer and director. This chapter is followed by descriptions of repertoire by compositional types, including vocal music, ensemble works, choruses, divertissements, illustrated through copious musical examples. A chronological work list and lists of composers and librettists close the work.

BARBARA COEYMAN

Luther, Martin 1483–1546

German theologian and composer

Bainton, Roland H., *Here I Stand*, New York: Abingdon-Cokesbury Press, 1950

Blume, Friedrich, *Protestant Church Music: A History*, New York: Norton, 1974

Brecht, Martin, *Martin Luther*, 3 volumes, translated by James L. Schaaf, Philadelphia, Pennsylvania: Fortress Press, 1985–93

Buszin, Walter E., *Luther on Music*, Saint Paul, Minnesota: North Central, 1958

Lambert, James F., *Luther's Hymns*, Philadelphia, Pennsylvania: General Council Publication House, 1917

Luther, Martin, *Liturgy and Hymns*, edited by Ulrich S. Leupold, Philadelphia, Pennsylvania: Fortress Press, 1965

Marshall, Robert L., *Luther, Bach, and the Early Reformation Chorale*, Atlanta, Georgia: Pitts Theology Library, 1995

Nettl, Paul, *Luther and Music*, translated by Frida Best and Ralph Wood, Philadelphia, Pennsylvania: Muhlenberg Press, 1948

Riedel, Johannes, *The Lutheran Chorale: Its Basic Traditions*, Minneapolis, Minnesota: Augsburg, 1967

Schalk, Carl, *Luther on Music: Paradigms of Praise*, Saint Louis, Missouri: Concordia, 1988

Music held a significant place in the life of the religious reformer Martin Luther, who as a schoolboy in Eisenach sang in a group of *Kurrende* singers, earning a small stipend for singing at weddings and funerals of rich burghers of the town. Although his famous 95 theses (1517) called the Catholic Church to reform, Luther advocated continuity with tradition and retained great respect for the Latin Mass he had celebrated as an Augustinian priest-monk from his ordination in 1507. While calling for a vernacular German Mass (*Deutsche Messe*), he also advocated retaining the use of Latin in some circumstances. Luther's most famous contribution to music is in the genre of the chorale (the vernacular hymn of the German Protestant Church), a vehicle for congregational singing. Scholars today credit Luther with 35 different chorales; 15 of these are new hymns for which Luther very likely wrote both the text and the music. Drawing on medieval Roman Catholic plainchant, liturgical hymns for the Mass, and the native folk-hymn traditions of Germany, Switzerland, Holland, Poland, Hungary, and other nations, Luther contributed 20 other hymns: eight translations of Latin hymns and antiphons, four adaptations of German *Leisen*, five reworkings of secular and sacred folk songs, and three adaptations of known vernacular hymns (including one by John Huss and one from the tradition of the Bohemian Brethren). He also revised and set chant tones for the Latin litany and the German Agnus Dei, litany, Te Deum, Magnificat and Communion. Luther, like Augustine, viewed music as a gift from God. Unlike Augustine, how-

ever, he expressed no ambivalence nor suspicion toward the appropriateness of using music in worship, declaring that "*In summa,* next to the Word of God, the noble art of music is the greatest treasure in the world" and that "the devil flees from the voice of music just as he flees from the words of theology." Luther discoursed on music on many occasions, expressing well-established convictions that, taken together, form a theology of music. He stressed that music, God's gift, and an ideal and incomparable means of spreading the Gospel, should be used to enhance the worship of God as well as to promote joy, fellowship, and personal devotion in the secular realm of life.

BAINTON's book, probably the most popular biography of Martin Luther in English, is a good introduction to the life of the reformer. He includes mention of five of the hymns, the *Deutsche Messe*, and the liturgical reforms of Luther. A section on music surveys briefly Luther's use of the modes, his prescriptions for training musicians and choir, his reforms addressing congregational singing, and his thoughts on music as praise and gift of God.

Originally published in German in 1981, in connection with the 500th anniversary of Martin Luther's birth, BRECHT's masterful three-volume biography provides an up-to-date, scholarly presentation, based on the original sources and taking into account the wealth of recent Luther scholarship. Brecht treats neither Luther's thought on music nor his musical activities, but this is the most complete biography available in English.

Each section of the English-language edition of LUTHER's works includes a historical introduction, commentary, and extensive footnotes. All of Luther's writings on the liturgy and the prefaces to the hymnbooks are translated, as well as all of the liturgical chants and hymns and the four-voice motet "I Shall Not Die but Live." Notation is presented with all musical items. For the German texts of the musical items, however, one must go to the German edition of Luther's works.

LAMBERT presents a collection of Luther's hymns, with brief commentary on the history of hymnody, Luther's education, and quotations about Luther from Coleridge, Bacon, Melanchthon, and others. The volume includes full translations of Luther's prefaces to the hymnbooks. The 36 hymns of this collection are presented in approximate chronological order, with their music, the original German text (in Fraktur type), a rhymed English translation, and commentary on each hymn's history and reception during the Reformation and later. Reformation-era prints of three hymns (*Ein feste burg, Christ lag in Todesbanden,* and *Jesus Christus unser Heiland, der von uns*) show the original mensural notation.

NETTL not only surveys the life and thought of Martin Luther with respect to music but also gives a short outline of evangelical church music that considers theological and religious movements after the Reformation. He places Luther's music and thought on music in historical context, including chapters on the Passion, developments in Lutheran music from Luther to J.S. Bach, and a concluding chapter on the close kinship between Luther and Bach. Nettl does not look at Luther and music in great scholarly detail but provides an easily read, accurate survey of broad concepts and points of importance.

BUSZIN's study, a pamphlet reprint of an article that appeared in the January 1946 issue of the *Musical Quarterly,* is an excellent record of what Luther actually said about music. Arguing that Luther's understanding and love of music are the main reason that we possess a great body of German Protestant church music, Buszin proposes that Luther's discourses on music were not casual but were based on well-established convictions. He presents excellent and germane selections (in English translation) from Luther's writings on music, adding only a few remarks of clarification and historical identification to the source material. Thus, he allows Luther's words to speak for themselves.

SCHALK has three purposes for his short volume: to demonstrate the importance of music in general in shaping Luther's views on the role of music in Christian worship; to show how these views led him to become involved in the practical aspects of music; and to distinguish several ideas that dominated his understanding of the role music should play within the church. Schalk fulfills all three goals, providing quotations from Luther's discourses on music along with well-integrated commentary. The five paradigms of praise form the meat of the book and help integrate Luther's thought into historical context. Placing the reformer on the threshold between the Middle Ages and the Renaissance, Schalk points out that Luther's concept of music as a practical art that could be used for praise of the Creator and proclamation of the Word was truly reformative; it shifted the emphasis from the medieval view of music as a science and the proper object of speculation to one of music as a performed, practical art. Music, according to Luther, is God's gift, intended for proclamation and praise, and functioning within the historic liturgy in the song of the royal priesthood of all believers as a sign of continuity with the whole church.

RIEDEL treats the heritage of the Lutheran chorale, stressing that it has roots both in native European folk hymns and liturgical hymns of the Mass; furthermore, he asserts that there is no clear line of demarcation separating the eras of chorale production; therefore, what we find upon study of the chorale is an intertwined network of traditions and legacies. Riedel describes in chronological order the four basic traditions of the chorale: the medieval, Martin Luther (1483–1608), Johann Crueger (1600–60), and Freylinghausen (ca. 1644–1756) traditions. Introducing each with a brief description of its cultural period, he defines in detail the available compositional materials that each tradition used to create its chorales and shows the main trends in the evolu-

tion of the Lutheran chorale from ca. 1524 to ca. 1756. A chapter surveying German Lutheran hymnals for church and home concludes Riedel's study.

BLUME's study covers much more than Luther and music; indeed, only a quarter of the book treats music of the Reformation during the time of Luther. (Another quarter covers Lutheran music through the time of J.S. Bach.) Nonetheless, Blume is necessary reading on this subject because of the depth and comprehensive detail of his scholarship. He provides musical examples and facsimile photographs and organizes his discussion of Reformation music both by genre and chronologically.

MARSHALL focuses not on Luther but on J.S. Bach and his predominant use of Luther's chorale melodies in the organ chorales and cantatas. Including discussions of Luther's writings owned by Bach and Bach's compositional highlighting of Luther's melodies through placement and sheer force of numbers, Marshall makes a strong case that Bach not only venerated Luther but also felt a strong personal identification with the reformer. Bach, perhaps needing a credible model capable of inspiring emulation, turned to Luther, whose enthusiasm for music and its place in creation served to justify or even glorify Bach's existence as a musician, helping to define the composer's mission.

JULIA W. SHINNICK

Lutosławski, Witold 1913–1994

Polish composer

Kaczynski, Tadeusz, *Conversations with Witold Lutosławski,* translated by Yolanta May, London: Chester Music, 1984; 2nd edition, 1995
Rae, Charles Bodman, *The Music of Lutosławski,* London: Faber, 1994
Stucky, Steven, *Lutosławski and His Music,* New York: Cambridge University Press, 1981
Varga, Bálint András, *Lutosławski Profile: Witold Lutosławski in Conversation with Bálint András Varga,* London: Chester Music, 1976

Witold Lutosławski always insisted that his most significant accomplishment was his 12-tone harmony rather than his aleatoric counterpoint, and in every book listed here, the issue of Lutosławski's harmony features prominently. The composer was well aware of those who imitated his limited aleatory—the controlled chance that he first introduced in *Jeux Vénitiens* (1960)—without grasping the significance of his harmony, and whenever he encountered praise for his aleatorism, he would counter with an analysis of his harmony. Of course, it is exactly this—the sustained discussion of harmony—that is missing from the discussion of Lutosławski's music that one finds in general texts. However, the books reviewed in this essay tell the story of how Lutosławski fashioned his unique path through total chromatic harmony—a story of how exchanging the colorless sound (as he described it) of all-interval chords for limited-interval chords (chords of mainly one, two, or three intervals) can lead to a dynamic 12-tone language. A full appreciation of Lutosławski's craft derives from an analysis of pitch rather than rhythm. His use of these chord structures to direct pace and to shape tension provides the key to Lutosławski's teleological conception of form, and it is perhaps this teleology that most distinguishes his music not only from his fellow members of the Polish school but also from virtually the entire postwar avant-garde.

STUCKY was the first book to explain this harmonic system to the English-language world. It is here that Lutosławski's music received its first extended critical analysis in English. None of the works from the composer's final 15 years of output are included (the works catalog ends with the *Novellete* for orchestra [1979], a relatively lightweight work); however, access to this book can significantly increase anyone's understanding of the composer. In fact, Stucky's book will remain a landmark in Lutosławski studies, and the reader will certainly benefit from studying chapter 5, "Elements of the Late Style," and chapter 6, which explains how Lutosławski produced ten masterworks spanning a dozen years of creativity.

However, RAE has effectively eclipsed Stucky. A comprehensive study of virtually the entire Lutosławski oeuvre, Rae's offering contains the richest source of biographical, historical, and political details and articulates a relation between the man and his music not found in Stucky. The list of works covers the period 1934 to 1993 and includes a list of early works no longer extant; unpublished scores; and details of commissions, premieres, and recordings. (Rae also gives a key to Polish pronunciations: the composer's name is pronounced "Lootoswavski.") There is something very personal about this book, which is not surprising, once we learn that for a period of time the author lived with the Lutosławskis. Here is a thorough discussion of the composer's life and works, from the difficulties of postwar (totalitarian) musical life in 1940s Poland to the composer's late stylistic shift from texture music to a music of melody—music with a prominent instrumental line. One immediate difference between the two books, therefore, is that the music that Stucky calls "late" becomes, in Rae, a stage in the oeuvre's trajectory from mature to late. Yet, the differences do not result only from Rae's advantage of a decade, for Rae's approach to Lutosławski studies is several steps deeper than Stucky. He has, in effect, systematized Lutosławski's harmonic language. In chapter 3, "Sound Language and Harmony (1956–1960)," Rae introduces a classification of four-note chords (table 3) and their combinatoriality (table 4), and this classification is the first indication of Rae's synthetic

grasp of his subject. A second is his assignment of character labels to specific sections in the music, and a third is his ability to coordinate general terms of expression with specific technical features (e.g., the moods evoked by various interval pairings). This synthesis of analysis and interpretation not only communicates the meaningfulness of Lutosławski's language but also directs attention to Lutosławski's emphasis on communicative form, which was always the master's primary concern. Finally, the idea that links every chapter in Rae's book is the theme of artistic struggle.

This theme is found in Lutosławski's own narrative, which readers will encounter in the two books of conversations produced by Lutosławski's publisher, Chester Music. KACZYNSKI offers an exceptionally intelligent series of conversations. Perhaps most interesting are the discussions of formal matters. Kaczynski suggests analyses counter to Lutosławski's own, and the composer's responses offer insight not only into his own formal understanding but also into the general nature of such understanding. In these conversations, one learns of Lutosławski's struggle with harmonic flow, a struggle that he believed grew directly out of his decision to pursue aleatoric counterpoint. In these conversations, one finds a discussion not only of Lutosławski's trademark aleatory and harmony but also of traditional compositional matters, such as motive, rhythm, and harmony; choice of texts; questions of reference and representation; layout of the score; handling of contrast and unity; and choice of expression indications. Overall, this is an invaluable volume for anyone interested in the composer's thought.

VARGA, an earlier book, contains roughly ten hours of conversations first published in Hungarian but originally conducted in English, the language common to both Varga and Lutosławski. The composer reviewed the text, which is organized in the usual way from musical background to compositional technique to the issues of performance and teaching. It contains the main features of Lutosławski's aesthetic: for example, his notion of technique's relation to inspiration; his view of composing for instruments rather than scoring for them; his thoughts on the challenges faced in teaching orchestras to play ad libitum; and his perception of the necessity for a composer to turn within and become wrapped up in his or her own music. Lutosławski viewed his artistic heritage as a continuation of the great symphonic tradition, as a late 20th-century refiguring of Debussy, Bartók, Stravinsky, and Varèse, but there is much here on various contemporary media and on his individual approach to content and form. One will also find here a full account of that pivotal turning point in Lutosławski's career—the inciting moment for his pursuit of limited aleatorism—that took place as he listened to a 1960 radio broadcast of an excerpt from John Cage's *Piano Concerto*.

GORDON MARSH

M

MacDowell, Edward 1860–1908

United States composer

Gilman, Lawrence, *Edward MacDowell,* London: Lane, 1906

MacDowell, Edward, *Critical and Historical Essays: Lectures Delivered at Columbia University,* edited by W.J. Baltzell, Boston: Schmidt, 1912; reprint, New York: Da Capo Press, 1969

Page, Elizabeth Fry, *Edward MacDowell: His Work and Ideals,* New York: Dodge, 1910

Porte, John F., *Edward MacDowell: A Great American Tone Poet, His Life, and Music,* London: Paul, Trench, Trubner, and New York: Dutton, 1922; reprint, New York: Dutton, 1979

Edward MacDowell composed in the styles of his day, using the wide-ranging harmonic and tonal structures of late romanticism, notably chromatic harmony, rich textures, fluid modulations, and striking dramatic contrasts. MacDowell's mature works demonstrate the influence of Edward Grieg, with whom he shared a fascination for Celtic and Nordic myth. MacDowell, like Grieg, was a miniaturist, especially in his short, lyrical character pieces for piano (such as "To a Wild Rose" and "From Uncle Remus"), which proved to be his most successful compositions. Though works such as these evince a strong American style, earning MacDowell a reputation as "the great American composer," there is little identifiably nationalistic about his music. The composer's prominence in American music continued unabated into the 1940s, but by mid-century his works had largely disappeared from U.S. concert performances, with the exception of the Second Piano Concerto, *New England Idylls,* and a few other smaller pieces. The resurgence of interest in American music during the 1970s marked the restoration of his status as a major compositional figure.

GILMAN's short biography of MacDowell is marred by unqualified adulation and overblown romantic hyperbole. The author treats MacDowell's success at conveying musical imagery with almost mystic reverence, proclaiming that the composer's work captures the "authentic spirit of romance." The biographical portion of the study—nearly half of the book—rarely puts this theme aside for more balanced assessments. In the remainder of the volume, Gilman covers most of the compositions in a somewhat more objective, but superficial discussion. Even here, however, MacDowell's strongest pieces are subject to euphoric praise. An incomplete listing of MacDowell's works is included.

PORTE's study includes a section that details the basic facts about MacDowell's life, followed by chapters on MacDowell as a composer and man. In these latter two brief essays, the author lauds MacDowell for his dreamy, idealistic, and romantic nature, and for his scorn for high society and small talk. Porte portrays the composer as the epitome of the independent American male, whose artistic side rarely overshadowed his masculine identity. A concise history of the MacDowell Colony in Petersborough, New Hampshire, appears as well. The majority of the book is devoted to studies of all of MacDowell's compositions. The survey of the works is mainly descriptive and clearly meant for the appreciative amateur. The author expends little effort to place MacDowell's works into the context of other composers' music.

In her short monograph, PAGE does not discuss MacDowell's life or works in a critical fashion, preferring to portray him in a glowing romantic light as the great American tone poet, a musical prophet whose music exists in a mystic world unsullied by connections to common ideas or events. She compares him to Sidney Lanier, presenting both men as ennobled by their manly virility, poetic natures, and rare musical gifts. Also like Lanier, MacDowell had a deep love of literature, which is reflected in his music. Page's overblown prose and vague imagery drain the work of much value as a serious discussion of either MacDowell's music or the era in which he lived. The text concludes with poems by the author in praise of MacDowell.

In a posthumously published collection of essays, MacDOWELL reveals his thoughts on the early history of music, principally from the Greeks to the troubadours. The essays demonstrate his keen intellect and reveal his thoughts on the origins of Western music, although the selections say nothing about American music. Moreover, the fact that the writings were based on lecture notes precludes in-depth insights into the subjects under discussion. Unfortunately, as Irving Lowens's introduction to the reprint shows, the accuracy of the selections is in some doubt, due to Baltzell's careless editing.

N. Lee Orr

Machaut, Guillaume de ca. 1300–1377

French-born composer and poet

Earp, Lawrence M., *Guillaume de Machaut: A Guide to Research,* New York: Garland, 1995

Fuller, Sarah, "Guillaume de Machaut: *De toutes flours,*" in *Music before 1600,* edited by Mark Everist, Oxford: Blackwell, 1992

Huot, Sylvia, *From Song to Book: The Poetics of Writing in Old French Lyric and Lyrical Narrative Poetry,* Ithaca, New York: Cornell University Press, 1987

Leech-Wilkinson, Daniel, *Machaut's Mass: An Introduction,* Oxford: Clarendon Press, and New York: Oxford University Press, 1990

Levarie, Siegmund, *Guillaume de Machaut,* New York: Shed and Ward, 1954; reprint, New York: Da Capo, 1969

Machaut, Guillaume de, *Le Jugement du roy de Behaigne* and *Remede de Fortune,* edited by James I. Wimsatt et al., Athens: University of Georgia Press, 1988

———, *Le Livre dou Voir Dit,* translated by R. Barton Palmer, edited by Daniel Leech-Wilkinson, New York: Garland, 1998

Plumley, Yolanda, *The Grammar of 14th Century Melody: Tonal Organization and Compositional Process in the Chansons of Guillaume de Machaut and the Ars Subtilior,* New York: Garland, 1996

Reaney, Gilbert, *Guillaume de Machaut,* London: Oxford University Press, 1971

Switten, Margaret L., *The Medieval Lyric,* 4 vols., South Hadley, Massachusetts: The Medieval Lyric, 1988

The poet and composer Guillaume de Machaut has inspired a vast amount of research in the 20th century. In a move away from the anthology manuscripts of the 13th century, which contain the works of many different poets and composers, Machaut collected his own poetic and musical works and compiled them in large books. Machaut's preservation of his works has left scholars with an unusual wealth of material for a composer from the Middle Ages: five complete-works manuscripts representing a chronological development of his output. He composed polyphonic motets and a single polyphonic Mass dedicated to Our Lady, as well as monophonic and polyphonic chansons in fixed forms such as the ballade, virelai, rondeau, and *lai.* If popularity can be measured

by the number of recordings available, Machaut's *Messe de Nostre Dame* ranks as his most famous work. The motets and some movements of the Mass use preexistent chant melodies (or in the case of the motets, occasionally chansons) in the tenor parts, many of which are constructed isorhythmically, a technique associated with another 14th-century composer, Philippe de Vitry. In contrast, the chansons are not based on any preexistent music. Besides writing fixed-form lyrics, only some of which he set to music, Machaut also completed 14 narrative poems. The *Remede de Fortune* and *Le Voir Dit* are the most important of the narratives for musical studies: the former because it includes songs along with the narrative; the latter because it is arguably autobiographical and includes comments on the compositional process.

EARP is the single most important volume for Machaut research. Much more than simply an annotated bibliography, the strength of the work lies in its series of introductory essays that summarize the multifarious aspects of Machaut research and guide the reader to individual items in the bibliography. Essay topics include Machaut's biography (the most extensive available), his literary and musical legacy, and a discography of all recordings of the composer's music (listed by title of work as well as record company), with critical commentary on the performance of each individual work. The section specifically on Machaut's music will prove invaluable: Earp summarizes the arguments surrounding the chronology of Machaut's music and offers a historiography of musical studies covering topics such as 20th-century editions of Machaut's music, Machaut reception in the 20th century, and harmonic analysis and compositional procedure in the motets and chansons, again, with reference to specific studies in the bibliography. Furthermore, the author lists each work by title, giving detailed information about its location in manuscripts and modern editions, where translations of the text can be found, and where to locate literary and musical discussions of the work. The sheer amount of information in the volume may appear daunting at first glance, but careful perusal will aid, and indeed is essential for, all levels of research.

HUOT examines Machaut's self-perception as an author and as a compiler of his own works, as a new phenomenon in relation to 13th- and 14th-century French lyrical and narrative writing. Noting the paradox that "medieval literature is at once more oral and more visual than a modern printed book," Huot traces "a general shift of focus, in the later thirteenth and fourteenth centuries, from lyric performance to lyric composition." In chapters 7, 8, and 9, she demonstrates that Machaut's sense of himself as a writer is apparent even in his earliest manuscript (F-Pn 1586) in his compilation of different genres of composition (narratives, lyric poetry, and musical works), a feature not present in the 13th-century French anthology tradition. Furthermore, by comparing organizational features, texts, and illuminations in two manuscripts compiled 20 years apart during Machaut's lifetime, she identifies a growing sense of authorship on the part of Machaut.

REANEY, who from the 1950s until the early 1980s wrote prolifically on many issues surrounding 14th-century music, provides a concise study of the musical works of Machaut. Following a brief biography, the author describes Machaut's poetic forms and outlines stylistic features of his music. In the subsequent chapters, he focuses on each genre of work that Machaut composed and uses many musical examples to illustrate specific features. Although it is an excellent introduction to Machaut's musical style, Reaney's use of tonal terms such as *major* and *minor* is today considered anachronistic and inappropriate, and his views on performance practice—that the secular works are solo songs with instrumental accompaniment—have been contested by Christopher Page, who instead suggests that all parts should be sung.

LEVARIE stands out as the earliest book-length study in English about Machaut. This compact volume, aimed at educated readers who are novices in terms of musical and/or medieval studies, places Machaut's life in the context of the political and cultural world of the 14th century and then characterizes Machaut's Mass in very broad but useful terms. He describes first the Hundred Years' War, the plague, and the papal schism, as well as the historical importance of Boccacio, Dante, and Chaucer. Before dealing specifically with Machaut's Mass, Levarie considers the general "problems of a religious composer" over the last 500 years, an approach that perhaps leaps historical boundaries too easily, but which provides a basis for discussing compositional considerations in the setting of a Mass.

In contrast, LEECH-WILKINSON offers an edition of the Mass accompanied by extensive critical notes and performance information—such as the medieval French pronunciation of Latin—as well as detailed analytical commentary on the music. In response to some scholars' assertions that Machaut composed the Mass in individual movements over a period of time, Leech-Wilkinson states clearly that the Mass is not cyclic in the late 15th-century sense, but that it is consistent, indeed coherent, in its technique and style. Much of the discussion of Machaut's compositional process in general has centered on the issue of successive versus simultaneous conception of the different voices; Leech-Wilkinson argues emphatically for the simultaneous view, describing directed progressions and masterly dissonance control in the four-voice polyphony of the Mass.

PLUMLEY's study marks the first book-length analytical discussion published in English of Machaut's secular songs (several scholars have unpublished dissertations on this topic). Arguing for the successive composition theory, Plumley fleshes out a problematic

theory of tonal types put forward by Peter Lefferts (in "Signature-Systems and Tonal Types in the Fourteenth-Century French Chanson," *Plainsong and Medieval Music* 4 [1995]). This theory of tonal types places primacy on key signatures as well as on the *cantus* line of polyphonic works, particularly the final *cantus* note, as the propelling force in tonal organization. Plumley claims that the *cantus* in most cases was sketched out first and dictated the tonal structures of the other voices, a very different view of Machaut's compositional process than the one that Leech-Wilkinson puts forward.

In her chapter in *Music before 1600,* a useful collection of widely differing analytical approaches to medieval and Renaissance music, FULLER takes the reader through a model analysis of an individual secular song of Machaut, the ballade "De toutes flours." She considers the text and its musical setting, as well as the rhythmic and melodic organization of each voice and their implications for the overall sound of the work. A discussion of the contrapuntal fabric makes reference to 14th-century *contrapunctus* theories and focuses on the two-voice pairing of cantus and tenor before examining the tonal orientation of the three-voice texture. Fuller's clear prose and musical examples, if carefully studied, will prove indispensable to the analyst of Machaut's music.

MACHAUT (1988) provides French texts and English translations of two narrative poems, including the *Remede de Fortune,* which Wimsatt and Kibler describe as "probably the most important French love poem of the fourteenth century." The poem holds special interest for music scholars because of its song insertions, excellently transcribed by Baltzer in this edition. Baltzer includes critical notes (variants between manuscripts) and analytical commentary on each musical work. In their introductory material, Wimsatt and Kibler detail the didacticism of the *Remede de Fortune* in Machaut's use of medieval proverbs, in the composer's references to Boethius's *Consolation of Philosophy* and Guillaume de Lorris and Jean de Meun's *Romance of the Rose*, and in particular in his incorporation of each of the 14th-century fixed forms set to music. They furthermore trace Machaut's influence on Chaucer and include in the volume black-and-white facsimiles of the miniatures in Manuscript C.

SWITTEN's edition of the *Remede de Fortune* is a less scholarly approach but is more classroom friendly. Presenting excerpts from the 4,300-line poem, Switten includes editions of the musical inserts where they appear in the original, rather than at the end as a group as they occur in Machaut (1988). Furthermore, Switten's volume contains facsimiles of all the musical items from manuscript F-Pn 1586 and has an accompanying cassette of performances of the music (with instrumental accompaniment rather than a full vocal scoring). Baltzer's transcriptions, however, are to be preferred for accuracy and a closer approximation to the original in her use of signatures and accidentals.

A narrative poem in couplets, which contains prose insertions in the form of letters between a lover and his lady as well as lyric insertions in fixed forms written by both parties concerned, *Le Voir Dit* (the "True Story") has sparked controversy about the degree of its autobiographical content. Many scholars in recent years have claimed that the work is mostly fiction, but Palmer and Leech-Wilkinson, in their introductory essay to MACHAUT (1998), an edition and translation of *Le Voir Dit,* restore the case for the poem's autobiographical significance based on painstaking research into the historical accuracy of the events and time frame described and on a reordering of the letters within the manuscripts. For music scholars, the autobiographical nature of *Le Voir Dit* proves significant for the information it can provide about Machaut's compositional process. Consequential for many reasons, including the existence of a body of poetry within *Le Voir Dit* that can now be ascribed to a female poet of the 14th century, Palmer and Leech-Wilkinson's conclusions are far-reaching for all areas of Machaut research.

JENNIFER BAIN

Madrigal: England

Brown, David, *Thomas Weelkes: A Biographical and Critical Study,* London: Faber, 1969

———, *Wilbye,* London: Oxford University Press, 1974

Doughtie, Edward, *English Renaissance Song,* Boston: Twayne, 1986

Fellowes, Edmund H., *The English Madrigal Composers,* Oxford: Clarendon Press, 1921; 2d edition, 1948

Kerman, Joseph, *The Elizabethan Madrigal: A Comparative Study,* New York: American Musicological Society, 1962

Pattison, Bruce, *Music and Poetry of the English Renaissance,* London: Metheun, 1948; 2d edition, 1970

Teo, Kian-Seng, *Chromaticism in the English Madrigal,* New York: Garland, 1989

Once considered to be one of the great musical achievements of the Renaissance era in England, the English madrigal now holds a rather more confined historical position. Chiefly responsible for this change in its critical standing has been the acceptance of a more narrow definition of the genre itself. Formerly believed to include the complete secular vocal works of such composers as William Byrd and Orlando Gibbons, as well as the Italianate works of composers such as Thomas Morley, Thomas Weelkes, and John Wilbye, the English madrigal is now seen to encompass primarily the works of the latter group alone. Revision of the earlier formulation provides the student with a more accurate picture of the complexity of this rich era of English music.

The Elizabethan madrigal stemmed from an amateur enthusiasm among English aristocratic and merchant classes for singing Italian madrigals, an enthusiasm that was propelled forward in the late 1580s by the activities of a newly founded music press. The prototype was the "Englished" madrigal: a hybrid art form that presented precomposed Italian music nearly intact, but with English translations of the original texts. English madrigals themselves, which were directly influenced by this genre, were different from the Englished type for the simple but important reason that they featured original music by English composers. In this nascent period, English madrigals were the main preoccupation of the English music publishing trade, but they were not the only works then to appear in print. Later confusion seems to have derived from the efforts of Byrd and others to present a quite separate, native tradition of English consort song in prints that superficially resembled the madrigal publications. Careful analyses of both musical genres have uncovered a clear distinction between the Italianate style of the true madrigal and native traits of the song idiom, although many works show some influence of each style, revealing a newly found stylistic sophistication in both traditions.

FELLOWES provides the first full-length study of the English madrigal and its composers. His pioneering effort is based on extensive firsthand experience with the music itself, along with a wide-ranging, if somewhat haphazard, study of other relevant sources. To the author's great credit, he studied and put into score the entire range of madrigal works in editions that have been of great service to all students of the era. This particular book, however, has been justly seen by most later scholars to have serious limitations. Critics cite, for example, Fellowes's neglect of the importance and influence of the English madrigal's Italian progeny and conflation of the madrigal and the consort song. The book may be outmoded in significant aspects, but it retains enduring value nonetheless. Fellowes conveys his enthusiasm for his subject in an infectious manner, and the richly illustrated examples of the music he uses to highlight the repertoire stem from his rich experience as an indefatigable editor, providing material that evokes fullest appreciation of the genre.

The subtitle of KERMAN's book, "A Comparative Study," is a particularly apt description of his purpose as well as his critical method. Focusing almost exclusively on the music and texts of 16th-century English and Italian composers of madrigals, but founded on an astonishingly diverse knowledge of all periods of Western music history, music theory, and literary history, the book is well deserving of the vast praise it has received. It was designed for a reader with a musicological expertise, yet Kerman's elegant writing style makes it more accessible to a general readership than many works of its kind. His general purpose is twofold: first, to place the English madrigal within the context of England's contemporary Continental model, and second, to differentiate the madrigalesque musical style in England from England's native idiom of consort song. With his comparative methods, Kerman convincingly meets these goals, while supplying superb critical appraisals of the works at hand. Among the many other subjects for which Kerman brings forth revelatory findings are the specific musical and literary tastes of English madrigalists and their consumers; the important musical influences of Luca Marenzio and Alfonso Ferrabosco on younger madrigalists in England; Byrd's influence on the madrigal, despite his limited interest in the genre; Thomas Morley's pivotal role as the true founder of, and most prolific contributor to, the English school of madrigal writing; and the particular gifts of the finest writers of the style, Weelkes and Wilbye, both of whom Kerman evaluates with stunning acuity.

The monograph by TEO further explores the special nature of the English madrigal by following Kerman's comparative example. Focusing on chromaticism in music theory and practice—two issues of burgeoning importance in all Western music of the late 16th century—Teo reveals new information about developments in the late 16th-century stream of cultural exchange that ran from Italy to England. It may require a specialist's training to appreciate fully all of the nuances of Teo's arguments, but many of his most important points will be amply clear to the reader with basic music literacy thanks to the author's full and judicious use of musical examples. In addition to his findings on chromaticism itself, Teo notes hitherto unknown influences of John Dowland's lute songs on the English madrigalists, pinpoints the influence of specific Italian models of chromaticism in the works of English composers, provides a detailed study of the early sources of Italian madrigals in England, and offers some persuasive insights about the effect of Italian madrigals on English composers.

BROWN (1969) focuses on Weelkes, a notable English composer who was mainly, but not exclusively, a composer of madrigals. Every work by Weelkes is studied comprehensively from both an analytical and critical perspective. Benefiting from Kerman's overview, Brown identifies the dialectic influences of native and Italianate forces on Weelkes's music. By comparing Weelkes's music to that of Morley and Byrd, among others, the author finds not only distinguishable traces of both English and Italianate musical impulses but argues that Weelkes's special synthesis of the two may be seen as an essential feature of his style. Brown begins his study with a biographical sketch that is well researched, and he is careful to use caution where there are gaps in the record. The findings about the composer's personal life course, however—which show a downward progression from a youth of great promise to a troublesome, alcoholic failure at the end of his life—seem to darken unduly Brown's overall judgment about Weelkes's achievement as a composer.

BROWN (1974), a much shorter, but equally rigorous, study of Wilbye, benefits not only from Kerman's prior work but also from the author's own previous encounter with the music of Weelkes. As with Weelkes, Brown treats all of the musical works of Wilbye, but in this case he is able to focus even more sharply on the madrigal, for Wilbye produced little else of note. Perhaps of greatest value in this book are the conclusions Brown reaches in his comparisons of Wilbye and Weelkes, the two foremost composers of the genre. By comparing their styles, Brown effectively illustrates and contrasts the "mercurial brilliance" of Weelkes's approach to madrigal poetry with the "exquisite sensitivity" he considers to be a basic trait in the best music by Wilbye.

It is often noted that the age of Byrd and Dowland was also the age of Shakespeare and Johnson; thus it is not surprising that many scholars, such as PATTISON, have sought to mesh the musical and literary achievements of this rich period in their studies. Pattison's book is distinctive for its even-handed treatment of both arts. In the overview of the era, wherein the author considers the madrigal along with other, more elevated, poetry that was set to music, the volume's main purpose is to discover the "reciprocal" influences of the sister arts. Pattison is careful to explain the "poesia per musica" aspect of the madrigal genre and its consequent general lack of independent literary merit. Yet he argues well that credit must be given to madrigal poetry for "transforming impersonal techniques" of music in the prior age "into a medium of emotional expression."

DOUGHTIE's treatment covers similar ground to Pattison, but Doughtie's work naturally benefits from the use of later research findings. Although this work is geared more to students of literature than music historians, it provides two excellent chapters on the English madrigal that should be of interest to any student of the genre. Along with some detailed analysis of the ways in which various English composers handled the syntax of Italianate poetry, Doughtie provides a rich historical introduction to the features that drew poets as well as musicians to the Italian lyric, making this the best interdisciplinary guide to the events that led to the birth of the English madrigal.

JEREMY L. SMITH

Madrigal: Italy

Einstein, Alfred, *The Italian Madrigal,* 3 vols., translated by Alexander H. Krappe, et al., Princeton, New Jersey: Princeton University Press, 1949

Feldman, Martha, *City Culture and the Madrigal at Venice,* Berkeley: University of California Press, 1995

Fenlon, Iain, and James Haar, *The Italian Madrigal in the Early Sixteenth Century: Sources and Interpretation,* Cambridge: Cambridge University Press, 1988

Haar, James, *Essays on Italian Poetry and Music in the Renaissance, 1350–1600*, Berkeley: University of California Press, 1986

Newcomb, Anthony, *The Madrigal at Ferrara: 1579–1597*, 2 vols., Princeton, New Jersey: Princeton University Press, 1978

Roche, Jerome, *The Madrigal*, London: Hutchinson, and New York: Scribner's, 1972; 2nd edition, Oxford: Oxford University Press, 1990

Tomlinson, Gary, *Monteverdi and the End of the Renaissance*, Berkeley and Los Angeles: University of California Press, and Oxford: Clarendon Press, 1987

The term *madrigal* is used to refer to both the poetry and the music in secular settings of both the 14th and the 16th century, but aside from a parallel inclination toward lyricism, the two types reveal no connection. When the term was revived in the 16th century, the 14th-century genre had long disappeared from the musical landscape of Italy. In the 14th century, the madrigal was characterized by its setting of two or three three-line stanzas, usually with identical music for each stanza, followed by a one- or two-line ritornello in a florid style, which closes the setting. Appearing in manuscripts from the 1330s, the 14th-century genre reaches its height in the three-voiced madrigals of Jacopo da Bologna and Francesco Landini, which have become the defining examples of the genre. Studies of this genre are to be found in broader surveys of the Italian trecento.

Re-created in 16th-century Italy, the new madrigal grew out of a concurrent literary movement based on a desire among Italian humanists to elevate the Italian language to the heights of classical Latin literature. Under the influence of Cardinal Pietro Bembo, the literary movement known as *Petrarchismo* promoted the values of Francesco Petrarch's poetry, exalting the variety of accent, rhyme, and tone within his sonnets. Musicians were quick to respond to Bembo's analysis of the sound qualities of this poetry and began to set these poems in the most elevated polyphonic style of the day, borrowing from the Franco-Flemish composers of the north. The combination of elevated poetry and elevated compositional style created a secular genre as significant as the motets and Masses of the age.

A comprehensive study of the madrigal was done in 1949 by EINSTEIN, who, although he often views the madrigal in a progressivist way, offers the starting point for the madrigal scholar, as he provides references to numerous examples from within a large repertoire. Much new research has been conducted since Einstein's exhaustive three-volume study, but most of the more recent writers on the subject acknowledge him as an inspiration for their work.

HAAR brings to madrigal studies a method of inquiry that emphasizes the role of music as a "reader" of poetry, pointing out the ways in which musical gestures can interpret the meaning of words, not just in the sense of onomatopoeia or word painting but in terms of the rhetorical and syntactical intentions of larger sense units. With poetry as the starting point for his study, the author examines the Italian secular music tradition within a broader scope of time than one would expect to find in a study of the madrigal; thus, his examples are useful in considering the origins of the 16th-century madrigal. Particularly noteworthy is his essay exploring the curious paucity of Italian secular music in the 15th century, the period that creates a gap between the early and later versions of the madrigal. Chief among the causes cited for this paucity are the growing influence of French and Flemish composers and the problems of documenting a secular musical style during a period that relied largely on an unwritten tradition.

To see an emerging repertoire of madrigals in the 16th century, one should begin with FENLON and HAAR's study of the early years of the madrigal. The authors locate the origins of the genre in the 1520s in Rome and Florence, regions unfamiliar with the *frottole* of the Mantuan court, putting to rest a long-held idea that the madrigal grew out of the *frottole*. Thus, the authors have proposed a chronology and geography connected with the earliest school of madrigal composers—Arcadelt, Verdelot, and Festa—whose compositional style reveals the conflation of the French chanson, the Italian carnival song, and the Franco-Flemish motet, in the new genre of the madrigal.

By 1535 the center for madrigals shifted to Venice and to the music of Adrian Willaert, *maestro di capella* at San Marco. FELDMAN guides us through the cultural and literary climate of Willaert's Venice, examining his madrigals as musical models for Bembo's theories concerning the physical properties of sound including *numero*, *suono*, and *variazione*. Willaert's settings, according to Feldman, "consistently articulated syntactic structures with musical structure and rhetorical nuances with musical gestures and textures," and Feldman's sensitive musical analysis reveals intricate relationships between Renaissance literary theory and the compositional style of the madrigal.

A third stage for the Italian madrigal is examined in NEWCOMB's study of the madrigal in Ferrara. Focusing on Luzzaschi and Marenzio, this study offers an opportunity to consider the effect of performance practice on the madrigal. Ferrara was home to the famous *concerto delle donne*, women widely acknowledged for their virtuosic talents. For these women, including Laura Peverara, Anna Guarini, Livia d'Arco, and for a brief time, Tarquinia Molza, composers willingly adapted their style, composing in a noticeably high and agile range that favored soloistic writing. In this new texture, the singers, in elaborate contrapuntal and melismatic passage work, provide a block of sound in a higher-than-normal range, which is contrasted by the subordinated lower two voices, resulting in a treble/bass texture that would be fully explored only after the turn of the century.

Providing a view of the madrigal from the perspective of a single composer is TOMLINSON. He examines the madrigal output of Claudio Monteverdi, in whose musical style we can trace the evolution of the madrigal from the end of the Renaissance through the beginning of the baroque era—that is, from an equal-voiced polyphonic madrigal to the concertato madrigal, characterized by bold strokes of contrast and a basso continuo texture. Tomlinson outlines as well the shift in poetic taste in Italy, from Petrarch to Tasso and Guarini to Marino, Rinuccini, and Striggio, that seemed to encourage the shifting musical styles.

Finally, ROCHE provides a concise summary of the genre, tracing the madrigal beyond its secular origins in his discussion of the *madrigali spirituali*, and beyond the boundaries of Italy in a rare assessment of the German responses to the genre. His work sums up the scholarship of the last few decades, and his final chapter raises long-range questions that scholars continue to debate. Many have argued that the madrigal of the early 17th century, with its concern for expression and drama, diverges so significantly from the goals of the original madrigalists that it is impossible to conclude that there is any historical continuity between the two. Others see in the early baroque madrigal logical extensions of the goals of the Renaissance humanists.

SILVIA HERZOG

Mahler, Gustav 1860–1911

Austrian conductor and composer

1. Biography

Bauer-Lechner, Natalie, *Recollections of Gustav Mahler*, translated by Dika Newlin, edited by Peter Franklin, Cambridge: Cambridge University Press, 1980

Blaukopf, Kurt, *Gustav Mahler*, translated by Inge Goodwin, London: Lane, 1973

Blaukopf, Kurt, editor, *Mahler: A Documentary Study*, translated by Paul Baker et al., London: Thames and Hudson, and New York: Oxford University Press, 1976; revised as *Mahler: His Life, Work, and World*, London: Thames and Hudson, 1991

Carr, Jonathan, *Mahler: A Biography*, London: Constable, 1997; Woodstock, New York: Overlook Press, 1998

Franklin, Peter, *The Life of Mahler*, Cambridge: Cambridge University Press, 1997

Kennedy, Michael, *Mahler*, Dent, 1974; 2nd edition, 1990

La Grange, Henry-Louis de, *Mahler*, vol. 1, Garden City, New York: Doubleday, 1973; London: Gollancz, 1974; and *Gustav Mahler*, vol. 2, *Vienna: The Years of Challenge (1897–1904)*, Oxford: Oxford University Press, 1995

Mahler, Alma, *Gustav Mahler: Memories and Letters*, translated by Basil Creighton, London, Murray, and New York: Viking Press, 1946; 4th edition, London: Sphere Books, 1990

Reilly, Edward R., *Gustav Mahler and Guido Adler: Records of a Friendship*, Cambridge: Cambridge University Press, 1982

Walter, Bruno, *Gustav Mahler*, translated by James Galston, with a biographical essay by Ernst Krenek, New York: Greystone Press, 1941

In his lifetime, Gustav Mahler was acclaimed both in Europe and the United States primarily as a conductor. Only after his death did he receive similar recognition as a composer, largely through the advocacy of conductors who had been his colleagues. From the beginning, biographers have had to contend with the many complexities in Mahler's life and personality as they chart his path from his childhood in Bohemia through his compositional activities, various conducting posts, and ultimate achievements at the Vienna Court Opera and in New York. Early studies were often polemical efforts to validate Mahler in the face of musical conservatism and anti-Semitism rather than attempts at true biography; likewise, firsthand accounts of Mahler's life were generally limited in scope and anecdotal in nature. Large gaps initially existed in the available biographical documentation, particularly concerning Mahler's youth. Biographical opinions changed after the publication in 1940 of Alma Mahler's memoirs, which helped popularize the image of Mahler as a flawed and inevitably tragic figure. The surge in Mahler's popularity in the 1960s led to an explosion in research and the first generation of carefully documented biographies, which in many cases supported Alma's views. Some biographers, particularly those approaching the subject from a psychoanalytical bent, tended to perpetuate the perception of Mahler as neurotic and obsessed with death, an image that has consistently resonated with many devotees of his music. In recent years, however, as more documents have become available and the reliability of previous accounts has been reassessed, some biographers' opinions have again shifted away from focusing on Mahler's supposed neuroses in favor of viewing him as a misunderstood hero.

In REILLY, Guido Adler, who shared a 30-year friendship with Mahler and was himself one of the founders of modern musicology, offers a perspective on the composer that is both personal and marked by the detached objectivity of Adler's profession. Writing only three years after Mahler's death, Adler paints a succinct picture of his subject as seen through his work as composer and conductor. In his effort to place Mahler's work in the "gallery of history," Adler claims a scholarly approach that is "systematic and aesthetic"; he seeks to view Mahler from a "higher plane," eschewing personal anecdotes in favor of a selective discussion of the composer's personal and musical traits. Nevertheless, Adler's closeness to Mahler is clear in his many insights into the composer's character and musical style; his discussion of Mahler as a monotheistic "God-seeker" and "wrestler after truth" is a valuable early study of the composer's inner spiritual life. Reilly's accompanying commentary clarifies the relationship between the two men and addresses some of the factual errors found in Adler's study.

BAUER-LECHNER sketches a remarkable and highly personal portrait of Mahler and his daily life from 1890 until his marriage to Alma Schindler in 1902. As Mahler's close friend and confidante during these years, the author enjoyed unparalleled access to the working habits and lifestyle of the composer. Recognizing Mahler's future place in music history, she faithfully chronicled his words and activities in her diary, leaving an exceptionally detailed and discerning record of Mahler as man and musician. Especially fascinating are her glimpses into Mahler's compositional processes and her accounts of Mahler's opinions on musical interpretation.

WALTER, Mahler's best-known conducting protégé and one of the composer's greatest champions, writes from the multiple viewpoints of friend, colleague, and advocate. Writing in an era in which Mahler's music was still often excluded from concert programs (and after which the rise of National Socialism would in effect eliminate that music altogether), the author proclaims Mahler as personal hero, whose influence was "a blessing upon my entire life." Admitting his "Mahler worship," Walter is still able to provide a rich, if partisan, account of Mahler, particularly as conductor in Hamburg and Vienna. Confined in scope to the years of their acquaintance, Walter's study is most valuable for its illumination of Mahler's interpretive decisions. Walter's intimate knowledge of his subject compensates for limitations in biographical breadth and detail. Walter is among the first to describe Mahler as marked by "a profound world-sorrow," establishing a view of the composer and his music to be reiterated in many subsequent biographies.

Alma MAHLER's memoir of her husband and their ten-year marriage, accompanied by an edited selection of his letters to her, is an enthralling but not entirely reliable account that has been the root of many commonly held perceptions and misperceptions about Mahler. The volume is a source vital to our understanding of Mahler as man and artist, yet it should be read with caution. Published three decades after her husband's death, it also remains the most fascinating firsthand portrait of the composer available, and its lively style is as illuminating of its author as it is its subject. Nevertheless, the memoir is marked by inaccuracies and a lack of objectivity; her frequently one-sided depiction of Mahler as a suffering, sickly ascetic who often displayed "tyranny" throughout their tumultuous marriage set the stage for widely held assumptions about Mahler for many years. Recent scholars, notably de La Grange and Carr, have brought many of Alma Mahler's unpublished diaries and letters from her husband to light, providing a more balanced view of Mahler, Alma, and their life together. Approached with caution, Alma's memoir offers an immensely rewarding chronicle of Mahler as husband, father, and composer during the last decade of his life.

First published in German as *Gustav Mahler oder der Zeitgenosse der Zukunft* (*Gustav Mahler or the Contemporary of the Future*), BLAUKOPF's (1973) concise study was among the first full-length biographies written about Mahler. Published during the so-called Mahler Boom of the 1960s, it is a thoughtful and carefully researched volume that seeks to dispel some of the legends perpetuated by previous studies of the composer. The author rejects the notion, for example, that Mahler was persecuted and unhappy in his work as opera conductor in Vienna and New York. In particular, Blaukopf draws on primary sources to etch a finely detailed picture of Mahler's life and work as related to his social, cultural, and intellectual environment. Blaukopf takes a sociological approach that focuses on the "changing position of the work of art in its social context." In doing so, he intertwines biography, social commentary, and a clear, nontechnical discussion of Mahler's work in a way that is useful both for specialists and for those coming to Mahler for the first time.

The work of LA GRANGE represents the pinnacle of Mahler biography, and it is essential reading for anyone seriously interested in the composer. By far the most detailed and comprehensive account of Mahler's life available, this landmark biography draws from voluminous and often previously unpublished documents, including letters, reviews, diaries, and eyewitness accounts, to provide a carefully wrought portrayal of Mahler as seen from various angles: the singularly sensitive and individualistic composer; the relentless, perfection-driven conductor; and the emotionally, intellectually, and psychologically complex man. By exhaustively documenting Mahler's life and brilliantly illustrating his milieu, La Grange illuminates the many complexities and contradictions that define both Mahler's personality and his music. The first volume of this work, detailing Mahler's life from childhood to his marriage in 1902, is especially notable for its wealth of information on the composer's youth, an aspect of his life previously little addressed. A subsequent three-volume edition of the biography in French will be superseded by an expanded four-volume version in English; the second of these volumes, covering Mahler's early years in Vienna (1897–1904), appeared in 1995, with ensuing volumes forthcoming. In each case, La Grange provides a vibrant backdrop of the cultural climate of the times and striking portrayals of Mahler's contemporaries; the author's depiction of fin de siècle Vienna, with its environment of artistic ferment, bourgeois conservatism, and anti-Semitic under-pinnings, places Mahler in a perspective that further illustrates the paradoxes inherent in his personality. Noting that "detailed knowledge of Mahler's private and professional life" is "essential" for understanding his music, La Grange permits Mahler to emerge through a remarkably unbiased presentation of the biographical details. Concise musical analyses of works discussed are included, allowing for a complete picture of Mahler and his music.

KENNEDY offers an incisive examination of Mahler's life and works that is exceptionally balanced. Rejecting the trend toward "psychobiography," he provides a broad but clearly delineated overview of Mahler's life and a fairly in-depth yet accessible analysis of his compositions. The author resists the temptation to emphasize personality defects of the composer as transmitted by Alma Mahler's memoir and many subsequent studies and attempts to deflect the commonly held image of Mahler and his music as neurotic, self-indulgent, or decadent. The first part of the book, devoted to Mahler's biography, depicts Mahler from his childhood through each stage in his musical career. Kennedy dedicates the second part to a lucid discussion of Mahler's works, placing particular emphasis on defining the "Mahler sound." In his analysis the author avoids psychological or philosophical perspectives and cautions against spurious extramusical associations, reminding us that "it is Gustav Mahler who is in these symphonies in microcosm, not Western society and its political evolution and revolution."

BLAUKOPF (1976) has compiled a documentary biography that presents Mahler in his own words and through the eyes of his family, friends, colleagues, and critics. Not a conventional biography, the work draws from letters, diaries, reviews, and other contemporary documents pertaining to all stages of Mahler's life that, taken as a whole, create a compelling picture of the composer and his world. Blaukopf resists naming this work a biography, noting that the documentation provides the reader with the factual details of Mahler's life and encouraging the reader to "fit these pieces together to form their own Mahler portrait."

FRANKLIN's study ranks with the most recent generation of Mahler biographies, many of which aim to dispel mythology in an effort to confront the composer as an individual. This elegantly written study seeks to move beyond the accumulated images of Mahler as mythic hero, tyrannical director, cerebral artist, and modern neurotic, instead emphasizing the powerful (and often conflicting) political, philosophical, religious, literary, and intellectual forces that shaped Mahler and his music. Franklin suggests that the relationship between Mahler's life and his art was "intimate and ceaselessly dynamic" and recognizes external elements as critical to Mahler's music. The author convincingly places Mahler in the context of the highly politicized, fragmented world of the Austro-Hungarian Empire, with its concomitant move-ments of Pan-Germanism and anti-Semitism. Franklin also includes a thoughtful discussion of literary and philosophical influences ranging from German folklore to the writings of Nietzsche, Schopenhauer, and Dostoyevsky, all of which contributed to the "multiplicity of the stories of his music." Not for the uninitiated, Franklin assumes some prior knowledge of Mahler and his music; nevertheless, the author provides a fresh and well-considered view of his subject that is ultimately gratifying.

CARR has written a lively and somewhat controversial biography that claims to seek the "real Mahler": saint or devil, idealist or opportunist, naive introvert or worldly roué. The author's inevitable conclusion is that Mahler was all of these things and more, "brandishing his contradictions in music of stinging intensity and battling through to a synthesis time after time." Highly readable and animated in tone, Carr's study aims to present a balanced view of the composer. Relying on materials previously unavailable in English, including diaries and letters, Carr challenges many prevailing myths about Mahler, particularly those stemming from Alma Mahler's memoirs, noting that Alma did not merely make "chance mistakes" in her writings but deliberately "doctored the record." Interspersed with nontechnical but intelligent musical analyses, Carr's alternative portrait of Mahler offers an interesting counterpoint to more traditional studies of the composer.

JULIE DORN MORRISON

2. Works

Adorno, Theodor W., *Mahler: A Musical Physiognomy,* translated by Edmund Jephcott, Chicago: University of Chicago Press, 1992a

———, *Quasi una fantasia: Essays on Modern Music,* translated by Rodney Livingstone, London: Verso, 1992b

Bauer-Lechner, Natalie, *Recollections of Gustav Mahler,* translated by Dika Newlin, edited by Peter Franklin, Cambridge: Cambridge University Press, 1980

Cooke, Deryck, *Gustav Mahler: An Introduction to His Music,* Cambridge: Cambridge University Press, 1980; 2nd edition, 1988

Floros, Constantin, *Gustav Mahler: The Symphonies,* translated by Vernon Wicker, Aldershot: Scolar Press, and Portland, Oregon: Amadeus Press, 1993

Franklin, Peter, *Mahler: Symphony No. 3,* Cambridge: Cambridge University Press, 1991

Hefling, Stephen E., editor, *Mahler Studies,* Cambridge: Cambridge University Press, 1997

Lewis, Christopher, *Tonal Coherence in Mahler's Ninth Symphony,* Ann Arbor, Michigan: UMI Research Press, 1984

Mitchell, Donald, "Gustav Mahler," in *The New Grove Turn of the Century Masters,* London: Macmillan, and New York: Norton, 1985

———, *Gustav Mahler: The Early Years,* London: Rockcliff, 1958; revised and edited by Paul Banks and David Matthews, Berkeley: University of California Press, 1980

———, *Gustav Mahler: Songs and Symphonies of Life and Death: Interpretations and Annotations,* Berkeley: University of California Press, 1985

———, *Gustav Mahler: The Wunderhorn Years: Chronicles and Commentaries,* London: Faber, 1975

Morgan, Robert P., "Ives and Mahler: Mutual Responses at the End of an Era," *19th-Century Music* 2 (1978–79)

Newcomb, Anthony, "Narrative Archetypes and Mahler's Ninth Symphony," in *Music and Text: Critical Inquiries,* edited by Steven Paul Scher, Cambridge: Cambridge University Press, 1992

Redlich, Hans, *Bruckner and Mahler,* London: Dent, and New York: Farrar, Straus and Cudahy, 1955; revised edition, 1963

Reilly, Edward R., *Gustav Mahler and Guido Adler: Records of a Friendship,* Cambridge: Cambridge University Press, 1982

Walter, Bruno, *Gustav Mahler,* translated by James Galston, with a biographical essay by Ernst Krenek, New York: Greystone Press, 1941

Rebounding from near eclipse in the first half of the 20th century, the music of Gustav Mahler has grown increasingly popular in recent decades. At first glance, the copious Mahler commentary purports to view this repertoire through a profusion of interpretive prisms. But on closer examination, the apparent cornucopia collapses. Whether foiled by the complex compositions or titillated by programmatic gossip, many authors allow speculation about the music's hidden meanings to overshadow discussion of the music itself. Few, apparently, can resist the temptation to explain a Mahlerian symphonic movement in terms of either the vicissitudes of his life or the fin de siècle culture in which he lived. The items considered here, for the most part, stand out for their willingness to eschew the extramusical, choosing instead to articulate the specifically musical bases of an inimitable compositional language.

Unique among all the early memoirs, BAUER-LECHNER rightly earns its status as an aesthetic touchstone for works belonging to the first major flowering of Mahler's musical imagination. Between 1893 and 1902, the author, an attentive if worshipful admirer, recorded all that the composer had to say about his art. Because Mahler himself rarely addressed matters of craft in his correspondence, Bauer-Lechner's account regales with details that cannot be found anywhere else. Here we witness the *Wunderhorn* works taking shape in Mahler's mind, discover his sources of inspiration, and learn what he criticized and praised in other composers. One hopes that additional texts published in the most recent German edition will soon become available in an updated English edition of this book.

Two other members of Mahler's inner circle penned reminiscences that help magnify Bauer-Lechner's portrait.

Guido Adler, five years Mahler's senior and one of the founders of modern musicology, remained the composer's confidant and enthusiastic supporter for 30 years. Adler's 1914 Mahler monograph expertly evaluates the place of Mahler's works within the larger backdrop of music history, showing that they contain both dissonances with the past and portents of the future. REILLY's exquisite translation, outfitted with supporting essays and musical examples not included in the original, brings both partners of this friendship into revealing focus. WALTER, 16 years Mahler's junior, provides a conductor's counterpoint to the musicologist's view. Mahler's friend, protégé, and assistant for 17 years, Walter enjoyed unparalleled exposure to the creative and interpretive facets of the older man's personality. Despite the lack of references, musical examples, and close analyses, Walter's empathic identification with his mentor illuminates this psychologically riveting account.

Walter's book concluded the first, memoir-driven wave of Mahler commentary. The second wave, which commenced after World War II, was dominated by British-authored radio concert guides. REDLICH, one of the first and best of this genre, assays the Mahlerian repertoire in terms of the history of musical style. Musically astute, historically aware, and equipped with plentiful musical examples, the author's observations generally prove reliable, marred only slightly by his eagerness to find quotations from and allusions to other composers' music. The more recent concert guide by COOKE, the venerated Mahler expert who had the audacity to complete the Tenth Symphony, seems disappointing in comparison. Aside from his penetrating introductory essay, Cooke's treatment of the music tends to be superficial, consisting of vague mood readings without measure numbers or musical illustrations. One also rues Cooke's decision to employ quotations without indicating their sources. However, the volume is brief, easy to understand, covers all the works, and conveniently collects translations of all the songs in one place. For the complete novice, then, Cooke serves up a palatable first taste, but one too slight to satisfy the initiated.

At the opposite extreme from Cooke stands Adorno, the revered German critic. Even in translation, and even for the Mahler connoisseur, Adorno's convoluted arguments may seem barely penetrable. Yet his paradoxical vision of Mahler's symphonies as reflections of modern society and artistic tradition in turmoil hews close to the music's essence and deserves to be pondered. Readers would do well to follow Adorno's advice and attempt his essay from ADORNO (1992b) before tackling the more challenging ADORNO (1992a). Musical examples are sorely missed in both publications, but relevant score locations are at least indicated in the book.

MORGAN, an American critic who takes up where Adorno left off, offers an updated evaluation of Mahler's compositional technique and aesthetic, one perhaps more suited to our postmodern historical vantage point. The author lucidly describes how Mahler and Ives, against the avant-garde mainstream of their own time, propagated an alternate strain of modernism that has become influential only recently. Citing musical excerpts to corroborate each point, Morgan succinctly elaborates compositional features common to both composers, encouraging an enlightened reassessment of their contributions.

For books that revel in the particulars rather than the generalities of the Mahlerian repertoire, one looks to Donald Mitchell, who has long reigned as the preeminent English-language authority on Mahler's music. His three tomes cannot help but impress, and a fourth volume covering the five mature instrumental symphonies has been promised. Yet once the reader begins to wade through the hundreds of pages of material, admiration may soon give way to frustration. The books burst with information, but meandering narratives and confusing layers of footnotes tend to nullify their usefulness. Thus, Mitchell initiates are advised to consult the more concise and complete survey of works contained in MITCHELL (1985b) before grappling with his Mahler trilogy.

The problems of Mitchell's volumes, nevertheless, do not invalidate the worth of the many original contributions he has made to Mahler scholarship. MITCHELL (1958), which focuses on the previously understudied first 20 years of Mahler's life and work, brings many inconsistencies of earlier Mahler literature to light. In the process of clarifying those inconsistencies, the author not only identifies a large number of lost or incomplete juvenilia but also compiles the first list of extant autographs and sketches. Thus, while ostensibly biographical in focus, the book also has much to say about the music. Unfortunately, emendations and additions to this volume are not confined to its second 1978 edition, but also appear in part 2 of Mitchell (1975).

MITCHELL (1975) centers on the works of Mahler's "Wunderhorn" years (1880–1900), encompassing the *Lieder eines fahrenden Gesellen,* the first four symphonies, and the independent *Wunderhorn* settings. Here the author abandons biography in favor of two interlocking and monumental tasks. On the one hand, he illustrates how individual works evolved through reference to manuscript sources; on the other, he identifies general trends in Mahler's compositional development, attempting to trace them both backward and forward in time through all the works. Mitchell's effort to combine the microscopic perspective of sketch study with the macroscopic vision of style analysis has proved compelling to many succeeding generations of Mahler researchers.

MITCHELL (1985a) continues in the same vein as its predecessor, but on an augmented scale. Analytical dissection of the texts, manuscripts, and music of Mahler's late orchestral song cycle *Das Lied von der Erde* dominates the volume. Mitchell's investigation of the work's orientalism, particularly his rediscovery of Chinese, French, and German precedents for Mahler's texts, merits praise. The briefer introductory and concluding discussions of the *Fünf Lieder nach Rückert,* the *Kindertotenlieder,* and the Eighth Symphony are less convincing, perhaps because these works are not quite amenable to Mitchell's evolutionary scheme.

Those desiring an account of all the Mahler symphonies, including Cooke's version of the Tenth Symphony, should approach FLOROS, but with caution. Unlike many who believe Mahler divided his creative attention between programmatic and absolute musical genres, Floros is convinced that Mahler wrote *only* program music, the composer's claims to the contrary notwithstanding. The author's obsession with this issue lends the book an oddly forced tone, leading him to simply assert rather than demonstrate the validity of his claims. Still, with its scrupulous references, analytical charts, generous background information, and efficient coverage of all musical elements, the book outlines an introductory framework for the symphonies that both teachers and listeners will find helpful.

Turning to monographs that treat a single Mahler symphony, Franklin and Lewis aptly represent the hermeneutic divide within Mahler scholarship. FRANKLIN, who has chosen the avant-garde Third Symphony as his subject, advances a compendium of cultural-historical approaches appropriate to the work's many contradictions. The tools of reception and social history, mixed with sketch study, documentary prehistory, and programmatically motivated musical analysis, allow Franklin to read the Third Symphony as the embodiment of competing cultural currents in Vienna at the turn of the 20th century. LEWIS, who writes about the outwardly traditional Ninth Symphony, focuses on the surprisingly understudied topic of Mahler's mature harmonic practice. The author's elaboration of dueling dual-tonics in this symphony, a concept borrowed from his teacher Robert Bailey, leans heavily on Schenkerian analysis but unfolds with crystalline clarity. Even those unfamiliar with Schenker will have much to learn from Lewis's excellent musical examples, formal diagrams, and observations regarding the work's genesis.

Finally, readers in search of the most up-to-date and innovative work on Mahler's music should consult Hefling and Newcomb. HEFLING spans an assortment of topics, ranging from biographical and sketch studies to questions of musical influence to Schenkerian treatments of Mahlerian counterpoint and form. Although all the essays are commendable, Franklin's review of Adorno's thought, Feder's psychoanalytic survey of Mahler's relationships with women, Reilly's reassessment of the genesis of *Das klagende Lied,* and Agawu's exploration of the contrapuntal foundations of Mahler's late style are particularly engaging.

NEWCOMB, more than any other writer represented here, blazes a novel path in the interpretation of Mahler's music. One senses that the author has left no musical stone unturned in his struggle to discover narrative within Mahler's Ninth Symphony. Resisting a temptation indulged by all too many Mahlerian commentators, Newcomb refuses to blithely explain away musical, formal, and harmonic inconsistencies with hackneyed programmatic excuses. Instead, he continues to seek, and eventually finds, the answers to all such conundrums in the music itself, an exemplary methodological strategy that future Mahler scholars would do well to emulate.

MARILYN L. McCoy

Manuscript Studies: Medieval

Aubrey, Elizabeth, *Music of the Troubadours,* Bloomington: Indiana University Press, 1996

Baltzer, Rebecca A., "Thirteenth-Century Illuminated Miniatures and the Date of the Florence Manuscript," *Journal of the American Musicological Society* 25 (1972)

Hiley, David, *Western Plainchant: A Handbook,* Oxford: Clarendon Press, and New York: Oxford University Press, 1993

Hughes, Andrew, *Medieval Manuscripts for Mass and Office: A Guide to Their Organization and Terminology,* Toronto: University of Toronto Press, 1982

Karp, Theodore, *The Polyphony of Saint Martial and Santiago de Compostela,* 2 vols., Berkeley: University of California Press, 1992

Kelly, Thomas Forrest, *The Beneventan Chant,* Cambridge: Cambridge University Press, 1989

Paléographie musicale, 24 vols., Solesmes: Abbaye Saint-Pierre de Solesmes, and Tournai: Société Saint-Jean l'évangéliste, Desclée, 1889–1958; reprint, Berne: Lang, 1966–

Roesner, Edward, editor, *Le Magnus Liber Organi de Notre-Dame de Paris,* Monaco: Éditions de l'Oiseau-Lyre, 1993–

Roesner, Edward, et al., editors, *Le Roman de Fauvel in the Edition of Mesire Chaillou de Pesstain: A Reproduction in Facsimile of the Complete Manuscript Paris, Bibliothèque Nationale, fond français 146,* New York: Broude, 1990

Tischler, Hans, editor, *The Montpellier Codex,* 7 vols., Madison, Wisconsin: A-R Editions, 1978

Medieval music manuscripts fall into several distinct categories, including chant; secular monophonic music, which includes compositions in the traditions of the troubadours, trouvères, minnesingers, cantigas, and certain Latin and English language works; and polyphony (referred to as "organa" in its earliest form) which is a major source of music manuscripts. There are also seven important extant manuscripts that transmit the Parisian Notre Dame repertoire from the two-voice organa dupla through the earlier motet repertoire. Finally, later polyphony, beginning with the works of the ars nova and continuing up through Machaut, is an area in which

manuscript studies are more limited, owing to the relatively clearly defined notation found in the manuscripts and the concentration by scholars either on specific composers, such as Vitry, or on a particular genre, such as the isorhythmic motet or the *forms fixe.*

Many of the most important studies of medieval music sources are based on facsimiles or editions of the music. Several studies have been published in journals, in yearbooks, or as monograph chapters; there are only a few book-length works. Many of the most significant publications are in languages other than English, particularly French and German. A few of the most notable foreign-language titles have been included here. In the late 20th century, editions of the music with modern notation began to appear with substantial English-language commentaries.

Research on original sources of medieval music began in the late 19th century and progressed throughout the 20th century. The monks of Solesmes have been particularly instrumental in the study of chant manuscripts. Many early musicologists, such as Frederick Ludwig and Yvonne Rokseth, published works about the sources and repertoires of early polyphony. More recently, the works of Hiley, Karp, Roesner, and Tischler have reexamined the work of earlier generations of European scholars.

PALÉOGRAPHIE MUSICALE is a good starting point for the study of chant manuscripts. It is a 24-volume set of manuscript facsimiles and includes studies on specific chants. Most important for the reader, substantial and informative introductions are provided for each facsimile, although not always in the same volume as the manuscript itself. The introductions are in French.

HILEY's handbook is an important introductory source for the study of Western chant. Chapter 3, titled "Liturgical Books and Plainchant Sources," and chapter 4, on notation, are particularly useful. Hiley describes the different types of liturgical books and chant manuscripts and enumerates them by category, such as graduals and antiphoners. He includes brief references to specific manuscripts. Chapter 4 is a well-organized introduction to the various kinds of notation that characterize certain geographical regions; Hiley uses graphs to illustrate his findings.

HUGHES is devoted to the organization and contents of manuscripts for chants of both the Mass and the Offices, with or without musical notation. An enormous range of information is available in this volume. Hughes includes such topics as the liturgical year, textural and musical forms, the Offices, the Mass, and various kinds of liturgical books. There are nine appendices, the last of which contains many facsimiles.

KELLY focuses on Beneventan chant, which is closely related to many other Gregorian repertoires, such as Aquitanian manuscript repertoires. On the other hand, Beneventan chant is distinguished from other notational and geographical styles of Western chant by an independent and unique group of chants The second chapter of this book deals with the 86 manuscript sources of Beneventan chant. Kelly gives a brief overview of the problems and unique properties of the independent Beneventan repertoire and the sources in which it is contained.

AUBREY is a study of the secular monophonic music of southern France. It is a comprehensive study that deals with the broader issues of genre, form, style, and performance. In the second chapter, Aubrey discusses both the oral and written modes of transmission as well as the manuscript sources. She examines, in some detail, the four manuscripts that transmit the troubadour melodies. Charts of the manuscript contents are used to identify poets and composers and the number of extant melodies by these individuals in the manuscript. A group of sigla identifies the geographic region in which each troubadour worked.

KARP addresses the earliest repertoires of polyphony—the organa of Saint Martial and Santiago de Compostela. This two-volume work contains a study of critical commentary on the music in the first volume and an edition of the music in the second volume. Karp's ideas about vertical and rhythmic confluence are based on period concepts about consonance; his views have been employed in recent editions of the Paris-based repertoire of the *Magnus Liber.* Karp applies his theories to the earlier repertoires of organa and finds that the same principles appear to pertain to those compositions. This scholarly, detailed study is quite convincing. However, the topic of rhythmic alignment in early polyphony is still controversial, and diverse opinions have been expressed by reputable scholars.

ROESNER (1993) is a multi-volume edition of the organa contained in the "Great Book" described by the theorist Anonymous IV. The first and fifth volumes and two parts of the sixth have been issued to date. Each of these volumes contains introductory essays in both French and English. The introduction to volume 1 addresses the repertoire of the volume (three- and four-part organa) with commentary on the manuscript sources and discussion of the various components, editorial policies, and ideas about performance found in the edition. This clearly written scholarly work is accessible to most readers with some knowledge about the music of the Middle Ages.

TISCHLER is a modern edition of the sumptuous Montpelier codex manuscript. The preface to part 1 is very informative; it includes the contents and design (illustrated by several graphic figures of the types of page layouts in the manuscript), discussion of an earlier French-language edition by Yvonne Rokseth, performance concepts, pitch range, and the texts.

ROESNER (1990) is a facsimile of *Le Roman de Fauvel,* a later medieval source, that includes a substantial critical commentary discussing the manuscript, additions to the manuscript, texts, music contained in

the source, illuminations, and the creation of the manuscript. This scholarly and comprehensive discussion of this important source is followed by color plates and a black-and-white facsimile of the manuscript. It is a most impressive publication.

BALTZER's study draws from the disciplines of art history, paleography, general history, musical style, and manuscript history to propose an approximate date for the creation of the Florence Manuscript. She conjectures that it was created between the years 1245 and 1255. Baltzer is well acquainted with the historical and artistic information needed to make the kind of deductions that may be supported by complementary sources. An inscription on the final folio of the manuscript that places it in the library of Piero de' Medici enables Baltzer to cite two archival inventories of Medici's library; these documents help to establish that the manuscript was in his possession by 1464. This exemplary model of manuscript study shows that critical analysis of available information can be used to reach an enlightened conclusion. The article is approachable by readers who do not have a substantial technical background in manuscript analysis.

JEFFREY WASSON

Manuscript Studies: Renaissance

Brown, Howard Mayer, editor *A Florentine Chansonnier from the Time of Lorenzo the Magnificent,* 2 vols., Chicago: University of Chicago Press, 1983

Hughes, Andrew, and Margaret Bent, "The Old Hall Manuscript," *Musica Disciplina* 21 (1967)

Hughes, Andrew, and Margaret Bent, editors, *The Old Hall Manuscript,* 3 vols., N.p.: American Institute of Musicology, 1969

Lowinsky, Edward E., editor, *The Medici Codex of 1518,* 3 vols., Chicago: University of Chicago Press, 1968

Nádas, John, and Agostino Ziino, editors, *The Lucca Codex,* Lucca: Libreria Musicale Italiana, 1990

Picker, Martin, *The Chanson Albums of Marguerite of Austria: MSS 228 and 11239 of the Bibliothèque Royal de Belgique, Brussels,* Berkeley and Los Angeles: University of California Press, 1965

Perkins, Leeman L., and Howard Garey, editors, *The Mellon Chansonnier,* 2 vols., New Haven, Connecticut: Yale University Press, 1979

Pope, Isabel, and Masakata Kanazawa, editors, *The Musical Manuscript Montecassino 871,* Oxford: Clarendon Press, 1978

Renaissance manuscript studies may focus on any number of issues, including dating, provenance, intent, number of scribal contributors, layers of compilation, ordering of contents, and relationships with contemporaneous sources. Many studies provide a transcription of the contents, usually with the intent of incorporating evidence derived from the transcriptions into a larger discussion. With the understanding that some features of manuscript appearance cannot be represented easily in prose discussion, editors occasionally rely on facsimile reproductions of all or some folios, either with or without accompanying transcription into modern notation.

An excellent introduction to the field is that of BROWN, whose work will provide the reader with a clear understanding of the nature of this important manuscript and its relationship to the cultural and compositional milieu of its day. Brown addresses the question of the manuscript's intended recipient by methodically bringing into consideration biographical, cultural, and artistic features. The author also considers the rationale behind the choice of composers represented, again using biographical information to great advantage. This large-scale study provides transcriptions of the entire contents in an easily readable and performable format. Although Brown considers variants in concordant sources, he does not attempt to be exhaustive; rather, those variants judged to be most significant and/or pervasive are noted as annotations to the transcriptions, and the extent of texting in these concordances is provided in a brief critical apparatus. As the manuscript under consideration is a chansonnier, the author gives a particularly valuable treatment of the chanson's development, bringing into clear perspective the repertoire found in this manuscript.

The work of PERKINS and GAREY is of equal significance in that it gives a detailed and comprehensive treatment of the manuscript. A particularly notable feature among musical manuscript studies is Garey's contribution; this textual scholar is thorough in discussing apparent textual errors, variants, and aspects important to performers, including syllabification and mute letters. Overall, this study is impressive for the extent to which it establishes the manuscript's relationship to other sources. This task is accomplished in at least two ways: each of the concordant sources is discussed individually, with attention given to points of interrelationship; and variant readings are discussed in terms of divergent manuscript traditions. A separate chart providing information on mensuration and modality, complete with information on cleffing and range of rhythmic values, also contributes to the discussion of source relationships. The musical transcriptions are presented along with facsimile reproductions on facing pages; this format is not only visually pleasing but an invaluable aid because it focuses on issues of scribal error and idiosyncrasy.

POPE and KANAZAWA have also created an excellent treatment of an important manuscript. However, this manuscript has a unique background and diverse contents, both of which call for detailed attention to subtleties. The extant source is incomplete, so the authors use handwriting and arrangement of the repertoire to posit a reconstruction of the original, complete manuscript. Graphics that detail the various folio gatherings give a clear picture of the authors' argument. Pope and Kanazawa suggest that the source was created by and for use at a Benedictine monastery in the environs of Naples, arriving at their conclusion by means of references to Naples in the repertoire and the inclusion of three appropriate hymns. The manuscript includes works from several genres, including chansons, Spanish secular works, Italian secular works, and liturgical compositions. The authors' treatment of these genres is particularly noteworthy, as they consider historical perspective, formal distinctions within the larger genre, and textual subtleties. As with Brown's treatment of concordances, these authors consider only the most significant variants and list them as annotations to the transcriptions.

PICKER's study is particularly valuable for its discussion of the two manuscripts' place within the cultural milieu for which they were intended. In this case, the history of the manuscripts is well known; they were part of the musical library of Marguerite of Austria. As a result, Picker is afforded the luxury of giving a glimpse into the courtly environment that would have appreciated such repertoire. His delineation between subcategories of genres is quite valuable. For example, the song motet, canonic motet, and secular motet are all given separate treatments. Picker is exhaustive in listing variants in concordant readings, although his apparatus for doing so is not daunting.

LOWINSKY's edition should be coupled with his inventory and discussion of several years prior ("The Medici Codex: A Document of Music, Art, and Politics in the Renaissance," *Annales Musicologiques* 5 [1957]) in order to be most useful. The edition consists of three volumes: an introduction and commentary, a complete transcription, and a facsimile of the entire manuscript. Variants and corrections of both text and music are selectively listed. In his introductory discussion, Lowinsky offers extensive background on Lorenzo de Medici II, grandson of Lorenzo the Magnificent. This study is particularly valuable as a treatment of artistic features of the manuscript; various heraldic symbols, coloration, and other artistic depictions are all considered in light of their possible reference and homage to the Medici dynasty. Lowinsky even posits that Leonardo da Vinci assisted the illuminator in completing his task. Lowinsky's view that the manuscript was complied in France has been seriously challenged by recent scholarship, which suggests that it was produced in Italy. The author's discussion concludes with a thematic catalog that provides—in addition to incipits of all voices—information on concordances and texts.

NÁDAS and ZIINO are faced with a slightly different task than the above scholars, for an extensive treatment of their manuscript had already been completed by other musicologists prior to the discovery of several new leaves belonging to the manuscript. As expected, these new leaves call for a reconsideration of the entire source, including issues of original structure, layers of copying, and dating. This study does not attempt to provide exhaustive transcriptions, probably because so many of the works are already transcribed in other publications. However, this facsimile edition could be used quite effectively as a companion to published transcriptions in comparing notational nuances.

As with Picker, HUGHES and BENT (1969) have created an edition of the source's contents after having published a study of the source (HUGHES and BENT [1967]). The arrangement of the edition is slightly confusing, as the editors have provided in the first volume transcriptions of those works belonging to the original layer, and in the second volume, works of a subsequent layer. This ordering attempts to account for differences in style among generations of composers (the manuscript's contents may reflect as much as a 70-year span). The companion study is an excellent example of using manuscript contents to best advantage in determining provenance, for the authors consider biographical information on the contributors, coupled with observations on the cultural environments of various centers in England, to hypothesize that St. George's Chapel, Windsor was the locale of intended first use. The accompanying inventory is also excellent, as it contains information on, among other aspects, the presence of any borrowed chant material, the transposition of that material for use in the polyphonic composition, mensuration signs, and any accompanying rubrics affecting mensuration.

STEPHEN SELF

Manuscript Studies: Baroque

Best, Terence, editor, *Handel Collections and Their History,* Oxford: Clarendon Press, and New York: Oxford University Press, 1993

Brown, Howard Mayer, and Eric Weimer, editors, *Italian Opera 1640–1770: Major Unpublished Works in a Central Baroque and Early Classical Tradition,* 91 vols., New York: Garland, 1977–84

Burrows, Donald, and Martha J. Ronish, *A Catalogue of Handel's Musical Autographs,* Oxford: Clarendon Press, and New York: Oxford University Press, 1994

Cox, Geoffrey, *Organ Music in Restoration England: A Study of Sources, Styles, and Influences,* New York: Garland, 1989

Crawford, Tim, and Francois-Pierre Goy, editors, *The St. Petersburg "Swan" Manuscript: A Facsimile of MS O no. 124, Library of the St. Petersburg Academy of Sciences,* Columbus, Ohio: Editions Orphee, 1994

Gianturco, Carolyn, editor, *The Italian Cantata in the Seventeenth Century,* 16 vols., New York: Garland, 1985–86

Johnson, Joyce L., and Howard E. Smither, editors, *The Italian Oratorio 1650–1800: Works in a Central Baroque and Classic Tradition,* 31 vols., New York: Garland, 1986–87

Roberts, John H., editor, *Handel Sources: Materials for the Study of Handel's Borrowing,* 9 vols., New York: Garland, 1986–87

Silbiger, Alexander, *Italian Manuscript Sources of 17th Century Keyboard Music,* Ann Arbor, Michigan: UMI Research Press, 1980

Silbiger, Alexander, editor, *17th Century Keyboard Music: Sources Central to the Keyboard Art of the Baroque,* 24 vols., New York: Garland, 1987–89

Spink, Ian, *Restoration Cathedral Music, 1660–1714,* Oxford: Clarendon Press, and New York: Oxford University Press, 1995

Stinson, Russell, *The Bach Manuscripts of Johann Peter Kellner and His Circle: A Case Study in Reception History,* Durham, North Carolina: Duke University Press, 1990

A broad range of resources pertaining to manuscripts of the baroque era are available, including monographic surveys of selected repertoires, descriptive essays on manuscript collections, annotated catalogs, and manuscript facsimiles with commentary. Because there are relatively few monographs, a number of these alternative resources dealing with manuscripts deserve mention here.

STINSON's work on the manuscript copies made by Johann Peter Kellner of J.S. Bach's began as a dissertation, and Stinson later expanded it into a full-scale monograph. Kellner, an organ virtuoso and cantor, was among the most important copyists who preserved Bach's instrumental music, paying particular attention to the keyboard repertoire. As the author points out in his introduction, "in many instances a Kellner copy is the earliest extant source for a Bach work and in a few cases the only source." Thus Stinson justifies his focus on copies of Bach's manuscripts rather than actual autographs. Much of the information provided here is, of course, technical in nature, as the author traces the individual copyists constituting Kellner's circle by means of watermarks and handwriting analysis. The major works taken up for consideration include the sonatas and partitas for unaccompanied violin, three organ arrangements, and various other keyboard works. The final section of the book, titled "Miscellaneous Problems of Authenticity and Authorship," must be read with an awareness of the ongoing recovery of European sources from their World War II hiding places, such as Christoph Wolff's discovery of the Spitta collection in Poland in 1989. Many of these rediscoveries have changed or resolved questions of chronology and authorship that puzzled scholars for decades.

The manuscripts of Handel have received considerable scholarly attention as well, resulting in several very useful guides to their study. The collection of essays edited by BEST comprises the papers read at a conference in 1990. While the history of Handel's autograph scores is widely known and surprisingly uncomplicated, there are numerous significant collections of manuscript copies scattered throughout Britain and other parts of Europe, and these collections are the focus of the book. Each author is a senior scholar with a particular interest in the collection he undertakes to describe.

The most significant contribution to the study of Handel's manuscripts in decades, BURROWS and RONISH's work attempts to account for every extant page upon which Handel wrote music. The authors' achievement is staggering, since in addition to collation diagrams, rastral formats, and watermark tracings (actual size), they provide copious and detailed notes on marginalia, cancellations, and cross-references to other works.

Sacred music in England during the restoration is the focus of the monographs by Cox and Spink. COX's study of organ music is divided into two volumes. The first contains the text, including chapters on manuscript sources of organ music in England and in Europe, along with appendices that consist of a thematic index of music from these sources. Cox's second volume contains transcriptions and textual commentary.

SPINK's study of cathedral music describes not only the development of this repertoire through several generations of composers—centered around Blow and Purcell—but also traces the history of 26 cathedrals and collegiate foundations on a place-by-place basis. Reconstructing the history of musical activity at each of these locations naturally includes a lengthy discussion of the existing archival evidence; the book includes, therefore, not only the information conveyed regarding sacred music of the restoration but also a demonstration of how to utilize manuscript sources in constructing a historical narrative.

SILBIGER (1980) has effected another impressive transformation of dissertation into monograph in his study of Italian manuscripts of keyboard music. Divided into three sections, the book begins with a survey of the sources, including information on format, paper, notation, concordances, and provenance, in addition to the musical repertoire. The second part is an annotated catalog of the manuscripts, and the third section comprises individual studies of seven composers represented among the sources discussed in parts 1 and 2.

A number of scholars, including Silbiger, have assisted in the preparation of large, multivolume sets of manuscript facsimiles. These facsimiles include brief but scholarly introductions by the specialists who have selected the sources for presentation and who are best equipped to call attention to the most salient points of their study. Among these are the sets prepared and edited by BROWN and WEIMER, GIANTURCO, JOHNSON and SMITHER, ROBERTS, and SILBIGER (1987–89). Each of these works reproduces important sources that are not readily available in published form and, in the volumes of vocal music, includes transcriptions of the poetic texts or facsimile reproductions of the earliest extant libretti.

Similar to these publications but with a more substantial introduction, is the facsimile prepared by CRAWFORD and GOY. The editors describe this manuscript as "a substantial anthology of lute music in various tunings by French, German, English, and Italian composers." Its lengthy introduction includes sections on the compiler, the baryton, scribes, dating, tunings, the music, and an inventory and guide to concordances.

MARK RISINGER

Marais, Marin 1656–1728

French violist da gamba and composer of viol music

Bol, Hans, *La basse de viole du temps de Marin Marais et d'Antoine Forqueray,* Bilthoven: Creyghton, 1973

Marais, Marin, *The Instrumental Works,* 4 vols., edited by John Hsu, New York: Broude, 1980–98

Milliot, Sylvette, and Jérôme de la Gorce, *Marin Marais,* Paris: Fayard, 1991

Sadie, Julie Anne, *The Bass Viol in French Baroque Chamber Music,* Ann Arbor, Michigan: UMI Research Press, 1980

Teplow, Deborah A., *Performance Practice and Technique in Marin Marais' Pièces de viole,* Ann Arbor, Michigan: UMI Research Press, 1986

The life and works of the prolific composer Marin Marais is a field that is still very much open, especially when it comes to published book-length studies in English. A number of good but unpublished dissertations are important enough to the subject to list here: Clyde H. Thompson, "Marin Marais, 1656–1728," Ph.D. dissertation, University of Michigan, 1957; Margaret Urquhart, "Style and Technique in the *Pièces de violes* of Marin Marais," Ph.D. dissertation, University of Edinburgh, 1970; and Bonney McDowell, "Marais and Forqueray: A Historical and Analytical Study of Their Music for Solo *Basse de Viole*," Ph.D. dissertation, Columbia University, 1974. A number of important journal articles are available on Marais as well. The one topic concerning the composer that has attracted a number of published studies is performance practice, several authors having attempted to address the many thorny questions raised by Marais's demanding viol music.

The only published study of Marais's life and works, MILLIOT and LA GORCE, is available only in French. The work is really two books in one as the two authors divide the material according to their specialties—Milliot takes the composer's viol music, whereas la Gorce tackles his music for the stage—and the result is an unevenness of quality. The jointly written section on the composer's somewhat sketchily documented life is a fine discussion of the subject, although it, like the rest of the work, suffers from a lack of reference notes to guide readers interested in the often complex source details. Milliot's three chapters on the viola da gamba, on Marais's predecessors, and on the composer's music itself are something of a disappointment. These issues certainly hold the greatest interest for most Marais enthusiasts, and yet paradoxically the space devoted to them is by far the shortest. Milliot discusses some material here on the development of playing technique and musical form in the viol music of Marais and his predecessors but says almost nothing concerning the particularities of style that distinguished the composer. Furthermore, only a few of Marais's pieces—two *tombeaux* and the *Folies d'espagne*—are discussed in any detail. By contrast, la Gorce's section on Marais's operas is richly documented and replete with detailed information that sheds light on the often complex context of, and the stylistic influences on, the composer's stage works. One could only wish that more space were devoted to musical examples as Marais's operas are not generally available in print.

Two studies can serve as supplements to Milliot's and la Gorce's work. SADIE concerns herself with Marais's contributions to the technique of viol playing and his influence as a composer on the instrument's role in chamber music in a chapter titled "Reflections of Solo Viol Playing." She places Marais's music in the context of his predecessors and his contemporaries. MARAIS, the still-in-progress complete edition of the composer's instrumental music (of which the first three books of his *Pièces de violes* have appeared to date), is notable for pointing out the constant changes that the composer made to the printing plates of his works over the years. These alterations result in variations in the musical text between different print runs.

Among the works concerned with performance practice, BOL is an in-depth study that concentrates on technique and ornamentation in French viol music from 1650 to 1750. The book, unfortunately available only in French, is divided into two main sections. The first, introductory section deals with the construction of the viol family and its evolution, discusses the viol's repertoire in 17th- and 18th-century France (including a description of the Italian influence on French solo viol music), and presents general information on performance practice. The second, principal section details specific technical problems found in the repertoire and places performance practice issues raised by Marais's solo viol music in the context of the French tradition of viol playing as a whole. This section's three main topics are right-hand technique, left-hand technique, and ornamentation. Each part chronicles the development of and disagreements over viol playing, making liberal use of period documents and musical examples to illustrate the problems. Useful appendices contain transcriptions of a number of period writings on viol performance, including Marin Marais's prefaces to his works and the manuscript treatises of Du Buisson, Etienne Loulié, and Roland Marais.

TEPLOW presents a more hands-on approach to performance practice than Bol, tailoring her discussion to intermediate-level students of the viol and focusing exclusively on Marais. She includes an introductory chapter covering general aspects of technique in Marais's music; the remaining chapters focus on individual movements as studies exemplifying performance practice problems. Each chapter takes a common movement type from Marais's suites as its center (included are the menuet, *pièce de caractère,* prelude, allemande, gavotte, and gigue), progressing through increasing levels of technical difficulty. The lessons learned are then applied to "practice pieces," which allow performance practice issues encountered in other works by Marais to be considered.

DON FADER

Marenzio, Luca ca. 1553–1599

Italian composer

Arnold, Denis, *Marenzio,* London: Oxford University Press, 1965

Chater, James, *Luca Marenzio and the Italian Madrigal, 1577–1593,* 2 vols., Ann Arbor, Michigan: UMI Research Press, 1981

Einstein, Alfred, *The Italian Madrigal,* 3 vols., translated by Alexander H. Krappe, et al., Princeton, New Jersey: Princeton University Press, 1949

Luca Marenzio was one of the most prolific and versatile madrigal composers of the second half of the 16th century. His works display an emotionally charged style stemming from his careful choice of poetry (particularly that of Petrarch, Sannazaro, Tasso, and Guarini) and his ability to translate poetic figures into musical terms. Little information is available about his life, mostly due to the inaccessibility of the private archives of the Italian families with which Marenzio's career was associated. He worked for Cardinal Luigi d'Este in Rome (1578–86), the Grand Duke Ferdinando de' Medici in Florence (1589), and Virginio Orsini (1589–93) and Cardinal Cinzio Aldobrandini (after 1593), both in Rome. Other centers associated with Marenzio's musical activities are Mantua and Venice (where all but two of his madrigal books were printed). He was for a short while a member of the commission charged to appraise the work done toward revising the liturgical chant after Palestrina's death.

Marenzio's interpretation of poetry introduces a diversified collection of musical procedures that reinforce the formal organization of the text and highlight some of the more subtle semantic implications of individual words. The earlier books of madrigals are largely settings of pastoral poetry, light in character and employing an astounding variety of pictorial devices. Marenzio often elaborates on patterns already existing in madrigals by Cipriano da Rore, Marcantonio Ingegneri, Philippe de Monte, Giaches de Wert, and others. The later works, especially those composed after 1594, show the composer preoccupied with more serious subject matter; this preoccupation, for some authors, explains the dramatic change in Marenzio's style, with emphasis on the upper part against the harmonic background provided by the lower voices, unexpected harmonic changes, and use of harsh dissonances and chromaticism.

EINSTEIN's book, accessible to educated nonmusicians, devotes a lengthy chapter to the study of Marenzio's style, including numerous musical examples and a list of first editions. The author contends that Marenzio, Gesualdo, and Monteverdi are the three great virtuosi of the madrigal—an idea that permeates all later literature on the topic. Einstein gives abundant information about patrons, dedicatees, and audiences, along with descriptions of the probable circumstances in which individual pieces were composed and performed. He dispels the myth that Marenzio would have been a singer or organist in the papal chapel, and he asserts that Andrea Gabrieli and Marenzio are "the founders of the pastoral style that was to crystallize in the vocal and instrumental music of the 17th century as the *alla siciliana.*" In his detailed discussions of individual madrigals, Einstein focuses on striking text-setting techniques that set the tone for the music of each book; in addition, he compares works by Marenzio's contemporaries setting the same texts to Marenzio's treatments. With regard to the style change toward the end of Marenzio's life, Einstein believes that, in the sixth book of madrigals *a cinque* from 1594, "he becomes one of Monteverdi's immediate forerunners. Had he had the good fortune to survive the end of the century by a decade, history would perhaps need to consider him, with Monteverdi, as a composer of opera."

ARNOLD's short monograph addresses a readership that has some knowledge of the musical aspects of the madrigal but lacks skill in the Italian language: English translations are given for both short excerpts and entire poems set by Marenzio. Not a rigorous or systematic work, the book is nevertheless very readable and easy to follow. A chronological list of the published works of Marenzio is included, as well as lists of first printings and reprints. Arnold compares and contrasts the abstract style of Roman composers to the vividly pictorial style of Venetian composers; included are excerpts from works by Marenzio's contemporaries. The author argues that Marenzio's musical style was a consequence of his choice of poets, whereas the texture and number of voices was possibly determined by the level of the singers' musicianship. Arnold explains the change in Marenzio's style following his return from Poland by identifying the composer's contact with Florentine circles and ideas, especially Girolamo Mei's and Vincenzo Galilei's advocacy of monody. Unlike Einstein, Arnold concludes that, although Marenzio was acknowledged by Monteverdi as a modernist, he should probably be placed by the side of Palestrina as a classic composer.

CHATER's two-volume work is by far the most comprehensive and detailed published survey of Marenzio's works. It includes a chronology of Marenzio's entire output of madrigals and a comprehensive list of literary sources, reprints, arrangements, modern editions, and other settings of the same text by other composers. Volume 2 contains transcriptions and music examples. Like Einstein and Arnold, Chater believes that Marenzio's compositional techniques are on the whole subordinated to the requirements of expression. The author includes a chronological table of Marenzio's settings of Petrarchan poetry and classifies them into three groups: the first and the third show a preference for poems written after the death of Laura (Petrarch's beloved) (*in morte*), while the second group sets mostly those written before (*in vita*). Other Petrarchan metrical forms and their setting by Marenzio and other composers are discussed as well. Chater further considers problems of compositional decision (such as texture, mensuration, mode, voice combinations, register) and examines the treatment of the individual word, lines, and phrases, as well as whole sections. The chapter on the treatment of form is of particular interest to humanists of all specialties: it contains examples from settings of Petrarch, Sannazaro, Tasso, and Guarini and emphasizes rhetoric as the common preoccupation of the musician, orator, and poet in the 16th century. Chater views Marenzio's earlier style as "a network of multiple developments," while the later style is "a linear development." The growth and change in style ca. 1594, which the author describes as angular and including "frequent exclamatory figures" to convey "tension as in death, separation, deception, rape," is attributed to Marenzio's contact with the ideas developed in Florence in the 1570s and early 1580s by the members of the Camerata Bardi. Chater, like Einstein, posits that Monteverdi was influenced by Marenzio's late declamatory style.

LUMINITA FLOREA

Martinů, Bohuslav 1890–1959

Czech composer

Halbreich, Harry, *Bohuslav Martinů: Werkverzeichnis, Dokumentation, und Biographie,* Zürich: Atlantis, 1968

Large, Brian, *Martinů,* London: Duckworth, 1975; and New York: Holmes and Meier, 1976

Martinů, Charlotta, *My Life With Bohuslav Martinů,* translated by Diderik C.D. De Jong, Prague: Orbis Press, 1978

Šafránek, Miloš, *Bohuslav Martinů: His Life and Works,* translated by Roberta Finlayson-Samsourová, London: Wingate, 1962

———, *Bohuslav Martinů: The Man and His Music,*
translated by Božena Linhartová, New York: Knopf, 1944

One of the most prolific and eclectic composers of the 20th century, Bohuslav Martinů has sparked much recent interest among performers and audience members. The impossibly romantic story of his birth and childhood in the church tower of the Czech village of Polička and his subsequent career as an expatriate composer have added to the appeal of his substantial and varied outpouring of music. Most recent English-language studies have been in the form of journal articles and conference presentations rather than monographs, however, so the selection here is relatively thin compared to the research that has actually been done.

HALBREICH deserves mention here despite the fact that the text is in German, simply because this is the most comprehensive worklist to date. It can offer much assistance to anyone interested in tracking down a particular piece or obtaining information about its publication, first performance, dedications, the names of collaborators, or other details. This information is especially useful for Martinů, who had a curious lack of interest in cataloging or even publishing his own works. Halbreich also includes a short but thorough biography.

LARGE offers the most recent English-language biography of Martinů, the only biography not written by a close friend or relative of the composer. Martinů's life is divided into periods according to where he was living at the time (the United States, Polička, Prague, Paris, or elsewhere in Europe), and the book closely follows his compositional life. There are large sections in which the author basically proceeds from one composition to the next without much commentary about the composer's life beyond his work-table, but perhaps this format is only appropriate: Martinů composed quickly and nearly continually for most of his life. Large does gradually create a portrait of the man who was able to write everything from the simplest Czech folk-inspired choral music to large-scale works for film and radio to the orchestral pieces *Thunderbolt P-47* (in praise of North American World War II pilots) and *Memorial to Lidice.* The astonishing range of instrumental combinations and musical styles the composer employed in the creation of more than 400 works is very well described here. Large also makes an effort to secure a place for Martinů among the great composers of the 20th century; he compares Martinů most frequently to Prokofiev but maintains that Martinů's unique status comes from his identity as an expatriate Czech.

Large ultimately portrays Martinů as an eternal outsider and observer, someone who was keenly aware of and responsive to the musical developments and political events of his time, but also someone who felt more able to express himself with music than in any other way. His lifetime of shyness and the fact that he was forced to live far away from his family, friends, and childhood home make him the ideal onlooker, one who always saw things from a Czech perspective and never felt he quite belonged where he actually was. Large is delicate in his handling of the composer's private life and spends relatively little time on Martinů's relationships with important people such as his wife and Vítězslava Kaprálová. There are plentiful plates with photographs of the composer and his companions, his scores, and some of the many cartoonlike sketches the composer made.

The book by Charlotta MARTINŮ is important not only because of the personal view it gives of the composer but also because the author, who married the composer in 1931, was so instrumental in supporting his career and furthering the cause of his music after his death. She writes her memoirs with poignancy and personal feeling; the composer is always referred to as "Bohu" (a pet name), and her admiration for him borders on reverence. Martinů's long-suffering wife was a Frenchwoman who worked as a seamstress for years to support her husband and initially was intensely disliked by her Czech mother-in-law, who had always wanted her son to marry a Czech woman. In her humble way, Charlotta was a rock of support to Martinů throughout their married life. Her personal accounts of their travels, including their flight from France during the war, and her view of his work as a composer add depth to the understanding of his character.

Šafránek, a dear friend of the Martinůs, took it upon himself to promote the music and stature of the composer, whom the author felt was too modest to engage in self-promotion. The two men first met in Paris in 1927 and were later reunited in the United States, where Šafránek decided to pave the way for Martinů's arrival by a one-man publication blitz, including articles in *The New York Times, The Musical Quarterly,* and ŠAFRÁNEK (1944). This first book is marked as a product of its historical moment by its references to manuscripts the composer had left behind in France (some bits of music are recalled from memory by performers who knew him) and also the pervasive references to Czechoslovakia and the Czechoslovakian people. These references speak directly to the concerns of expatriate Czechs and Slovaks during World War II, who were doing their utmost to bring the plight of their people and their young nation to the attention of the U.S. government. The comments may speak less, however, of Martinů's own nationalistic feelings, considering that he was born in the Austria-Hungary of 1890 and left Czechoslovakia only a few years after its founding as a nation. He most certainly identified more with the people of his village and region than with the Czechoslovakian state.

ŠAFRÁNEK (1962) was authorized by the composer himself, who contributed materials and interviews to the author (albeit in a haphazard fashion). A sympathetic and complete portrait of the artist emerges from a combination of direct quotes, translations of letters and program notes, the author's recollections, and insightful discussion of the music and its meaning. Here Šafránek develops his idea of the unexpected composition, his name for those compositions that seemed to break with Martinů's previous development and stand out as different (one example is *Half-Time*). The opinions expressed in this biography are undoubtedly as much Šafránek's own as they are Martinů's—the author has even interpreted the composer's marginalia in literature he read—but the book nevertheless remains indispensable to readers seeking to know more about Martinů.

DAWN O'NEAL REINDL

Masque

Burden, Michael, *Garrick, Arne, and the Masque of Alfred: A Case Study in National, Theatrical, and Musical Politics*, Lewiston, New York: Edwin Mellen Press, 1994

Chan, Mary, *Music in the Theatre of Ben Jonson*, Oxford: Clarendon Press, and New York: Oxford University Press, 1980

Fiske, Roger, *English Theatre Music in the Eighteenth Century*, London: Oxford University Press, 1973; 2nd edition, 1986

Lindley, David, editor, *The Court Masque*, Manchester: Manchester University Press, 1984

Manifold, J.S., *Music in English Drama from Shakespeare to Purcell*, London: Rockliff, 1956

Orgel, Stephen, and Roy C. Strong, *Inigo Jones: The Theatre of the Stuart Court*, London: Sotheby Parke Bernet, and Berkeley: University of California Press, 1973

Sabol, Andrew J., editor, *Four Hundred Songs and Dances from the Stuart Masque*, Providence, Rhode Island: Brown University Press, 1978

Walls, Peter, *Music in the English Courtly Masque, 1604–1640*, Oxford: Clarendon Press, and New York: Oxford University Press, 1996

Welsford, Enid, *The Court Masque: A Study in the Relationship between Poetry and the Revels*, Cambridge: Cambridge University Press, 1927

Because of their many varied elements, English masques have drawn the attention of scholars of literature; political, theatrical, and social history; art history; dance; and music. The early 17th-century masques were spectacular combinations of elevated allegorical poetry and richly descriptive prose, elaborate instrumental music, singing and dancing with fantastic sets, special effects, and costumes. These earlier masques were often presented before the monarch at court. Those that came after the Commonwealth and Restoration were generally performed on the public stage, with somewhat less luxurious settings, although poetry, music, and dancing continued to be essential.

Books about the English masque and its music tend to focus either on the 18th-century theater masques or the 17th-century court ones. Some scholars insist that the two types are quite separate, whereas others have drawn attention to similarities between the two types and stressed the ways in which they overlap (noting, for example, the masques that appeared on the early 17th-century London stage, or the masques presented both at court and in the theaters during the later 17th century). Music historians have asserted that the English masque is the source for the later 17th-century dramatic operas (operas with spoken rather than sung dialogue, as in French and Italian operas), and the native "English Opera" tradition. Recent scholarly debate has focused on whether Henry Purcell's *Dido and Aeneas* (often called the first English opera) should be considered a court masque.

WELSFORD's work addresses a broad sweep of masque-related materials, from traditional festivals to Milton. The first half of the book is concerned with the origins of the 17th-century court masques, which the author traces from medieval pageants (the mummers) through the "disguisings" of the Tudor court. More recent accounts of the Stuart masques present the fruit of later research and historical insights, but Welsford's book remains a thoughtful account of the masque's origins, its early incarnations, and its collaborative artistic expression of humanistic principles.

ORGEL and STRONG present the most complete picture of the visual aspects of the early 17th-century court masques, including costumes, scenery, staging, and architecture. It contains complete texts for all of the masques Inigo Jones designed for the Stuart court; some selected contemporary comments about them; and prefatory essays about relevant theatrical and political history and philosophy, which provide enlightening context for these spectacular works. The authors describe the court masque as the "most ephemeral of Renaissance genres" and insist that, despite the attention previously given to masque texts, particularly those by famous playwright Ben Jonson, "most of a masque was not literature." Music, as one of the many extra-literary elements of the masque, is often mentioned but is not extensively discussed. Instead, Orgel and Strong offer essential background in the visual aspects of the entertainments, including all of Jones's fanciful drawings of the masquers and stage settings (reproduced here in facsimile). This is a handsome and massive work of scholarship (two oversize volumes, over 800 pages). For a brief and very readable introduction (90 pages, no footnotes) to the ideas in this classic work on masques (with a few of Jones's drawings), see Orgel's *The Illusion of Power* (1975).

MANIFOLD's chatty volume attempts to describe "the musical resources and the theatrical conventions of [the 17th century] . . . and the way the two things interact."

The author begins with chapters on the various sorts of music to be found in stage directions and dialogue from the beginning of the 17th century ("Shakespeare's Theatre") to its end ("Purcell's") and finishes by summarizing the surviving sources for theater music and suggesting music to be used in modern performances. This work serves well as a general introduction to the types of instruments used onstage during the 17th century and as a guide to many musical moments (often in masques) in the plays of Shakespeare, Beaumont and Fletcher, Dryden, Wycherley, and other dramatists of note. In its scope, breadth, and general readability on topics that are still (as Manifold noted in 1956) the domain of specialists, this text is a classic interdisciplinary work. Readers should be aware, however, that it is dated, and they are encouraged to follow up points of interest in more recent scholarly literature.

CHAN also combines music for the theater with music for the masque, linking the two through the work of the prolific author Ben Jonson. The section of the book devoted to masques is composed of three essays: the first on the courtly ideal, the other two on groups of Jonson's masques. Over 30 lengthy musical examples, mostly transcribed from contemporary sources, are included, though often with little by the way of commentary.

SABOL is an encyclopedic reference containing transcriptions of "virtually all the extant songs and a large number of dances" from the court masques presented between 1604 and 1640, with introductory material and notes on each piece. Readers interested in performance may wish to find a copy of Sabol's *Score for the Lords' Masque* (1993) the latest of his masque reconstructions, which arranges instrumental music by a variety of composers, as well as Campion's published songs, to provide appropriate pieces from the period for each musical moment in the text.

WALLS's work, the most recent book published on masque music, covers the same repertoire as Sabol's but addresses the "character and function of music in the masque" rather than cataloguing individual pieces. The opening chapters contain sections on musical and textual evidence about the music performed in masques; the use of vocal music in the masque (including that perennial source of scholarly debate, "The Origins of English Recitative"); and the performance and meaning of the dance and instrumental music, which he reconstructs and interprets differently from Sabol. References to the important poet-composer Thomas Campion are interwoven throughout. The chapters that follow are devoted to the masques of composer William Lawes, French influence on the Caroline masques of the 1630s, and masques presented in other venues than the court (including the famous masque by Milton); the work concludes with a chapter on masque realization. This will doubtless become the standard reference for masque music during this period. It is aimed at the scholar, and Walls assumes a certain amount of knowledge about 17th-century England in general and its music and musicians in particular.

LINDLEY contains a series of essays on subjects ranging from Thomas Nashe's Elizabethan entertainment *Summer's Last Will and Testament,* presented before the queen in 1592, to John Dryden's *Albion and Albanius* (an allegorical representation of Charles II and his brother James II), presented on the London stage in 1685. As can be seen by these examples, the definition of court masque used here is an inclusive one. The authors of the volume utilize a variety of approaches in their work on the masque, among which new historicism is perhaps the most evident. Like Walls, these authors assume some background in the period.

BURDEN's monograph explores a significant example of the less well-known 18th-century theater masque. Produced in London several times during the mid-18th century, *Alfred* was dedicated to the Prince of Wales (a royal connection that Burden sees as a continuation of the earlier masque tradition), set to music by Thomas Arne. The masque is, among other things, the original source of the musical setting of James Thomson's ode "When Britain first at heaven's command," which is instantly recognized today by its chorus, "Rule Britannia" (perhaps the best-known expression of British patriotic sentiment). Burden lays out the implications of the masque's story (pre-Norman King Alfred, inspired the by Spirit of England, defeats the Danes) and sorts out the tangled history of the masque, which was performed repeatedly in various versions, the final (1773) version including additions and emendations by the famous actor-manager David Garrick. Brief and well written, Burden's work is scholarly in tone (it is based on the author's doctoral dissertation), and the extensive apparatus of footnotes and appendices may seem a bit daunting.

FISKE's book presents an overview of musical productions including the masques and, masque-containing dramatic operas of Purcell's contemporaries (chapter 1) and, in "Masques and Pastorals 1734–1748" (chapter 5), a quick look at Arne's work in the genre, along with that of some of his contemporaries. The volume is a good introduction to the relevant works, composers, performers, and performing venues and includes brief musical examples.

KATHRYN LOWERRE

Mass *see* Liturgy: Mass

Massenet, Jules 1842–1912

French composer

Cooper, Martin, *French Music from the Death of Berlioz to the Death of Fauré,* London: Oxford University Press, 1951

Finck, Henry T., *Massenet and His Operas,* New York: Lane, 1910; reprint, New York: AMS Press, 1976

Irvine, Demar, *Massenet: A Chronicle of His Life and Times,* Portland, Oregon: Amadeus Press, 1994

Massenet, Jules, *My Recollections,* translated by Harry Villiers Barnett, Boston: Small, Maynard, 1919; reprint, New York; AMS Press, 1971

Salzer, Otto T., *The Massenet Compendium,* Fort Lee, New Jersey: Massenet Society, 1984

Having spent much of the 20th century relegated by scholars of music and other serious commentators to the status of a once-celebrated craftsman of operatic tunes, Jules Massenet has only recently been considered in a positive light by musicologists. Early commentator Arthur Hervey (1894) unwittingly perpetuated the composer's image as an ephemeral talent when he referred to "the feminine nature" of Massenet's music. Later, Martin Cooper (1980) accused the composer of having written mainly for the French public, who regarded opera "as one of the higher forms of hedonism rather than as a potential source of spiritual experience." Because Massenet's music has continually enjoyed wide popularity among opera lovers, many studies of the composer are popular in nature rather than scholarly critical assessments of repertoire and style. Nearly all the sources in English rely on the outline of Massenet's memoir; some go as far as adopting extensive portions of the composer's autobiography without citing a source. Although the issue of Massenet's gendered reception has yet to be undertaken, more critically objective studies of the composer and his music have recently begun to emerge, establishing the foundation for more focused approaches to Massenet scholarship.

FINCK's volume is the first of the full-length studies in English on Massenet, pre-dating many of the early French biographies of the composer. The work opens with a substantial biographic sketch, filled with anecdotes quoted from Massenet's autobiography and accounts by admiring contemporaries. The core of Finck's text is a presentation of 20 Massenet operas. As was customary in music criticism at the turn of the 20th century, Finck gives a fairly detailed synopsis of each opera libretto, highlighting several musical numbers and commending the singers. Although Finck's work is not the most objective, scholarly appraisal of Massenet's operas, it is a window to singing styles and audience reception during Massenet's lifetime. Included are a selective list of Massenet's compositions and a bibliographic note citing works in French and English to 1910.

MASSENET's memoir was first published in the year of his death as *Mes souvenirs (1848–1912).* Although the chronological details of Massenet's own account sometimes differ from those of the historical record, the composer's narrative is filled with gems: 19th-century life at the Paris Conservatory and his first impressions of works—such as those of Berlioz, conducted by the older composer—known to us only through jaded, postmodern ears. In sometimes flowery prose (exacerbated by translation from French to English), the composer portrayed himself as he wanted to be remembered. His dedication to long hours of compositional routine, careful regard for the consideration of others, extreme attention to details of performance, and an elevated sensitivity to criticism are evident in the language and the tone of the work. Music itself is rarely discussed by Massenet, but the memoir gives invaluable background to the genesis and reception of individual works.

Although not a source devoted exclusively to Massenet, COOPER's book remains the standard English-language survey of French music in the late 19th and early 20th centuries. Within a chronological overview of musical life in France between 1869 and 1924, Cooper discusses details of Massenet's life, his influence as a composer and teacher, and the genesis of selected works, with musical examples and a stylistic evaluation. Unlike the single-focus biographies and compendia, Cooper's assessment of Massenet is less than adulatory. The composer is cast as an opportunist who conformed to the style of the day—a "purveyor of the pretty" whose popularity was proportionate to the disdain of contemporary intellectuals. Cooper's work is written in an engaging style that is opinionated yet informative as it guides the reader through relationships among composers and works of this era.

SALZER's main concern is the rehabilitation of Massenet's operas in the face of negative, 20th-century criticism. Writing not from a musicologist's perspective but from "the vantage point of those for whom these operas were written," Salzer highlights dramatic and poetic elements of the libretti, augmented by anecdotes surrounding the genesis and reception of the works. The book is arranged chronologically, discussing 12 operas written before 1895. A substantial list of relevant facts is given for each opera, including librettist(s), date and place of premiere, original cast and conductor, length of first run, and first performance outside of France. Within the synopses of the operas, partial texts of selected arias are cited and translated into English. Salzer's work is weakened by its failure to include discussion of Massenet's music per se and the absence of any source material evidence. Nonetheless, the synopses given are more complete than those found in general opera compendia, and the book is a useful source for those interested in the singers for whom Massenet wrote his music.

By far the most comprehensive, scholarly work on Massenet, IRVINE's book is a highly readable study based on primary sources, rather than anecdotes and vignettes, with careful citations in the text. Irvine offers an objective, compelling response to critics of Massenet as a shallow, melodic portraitist of famous (and infamous) women. The scope of Irvine's biography ranges from a history of Massenet's family dating back to the early 18th century to cogent discussions of contemporary political events and literary movements. However, the stated goal of the study is to use Massenet as "the central theme for reanimating an era." Accordingly, Irvine gives invaluable background information on contemporary singers, conductors, poets, and critics—details that were assumed to be superfluous in turn-of-the-century biographies and that are overlooked in more recent sources on French music of the period. The listing of Massenet's works included as an appendix to the study is the most complete to date and is complemented by a discography of operas and other works. Massenet scholars, as well as students of 19th-century French music in general, will find the annotated index an indispensable tool for placing names and dates into the context of the era.

ELINOR OLIN

Mattheson, Johann 1681–1764

German composer, theorist, and lexicographer

Buelow, George J., "An Evaluation of Johann Mattheson's Opera *Cleopatra* (Hamburg, 1704)," in *Studies in Eighteenth-Century Music: A Tribute to Karl Geiringer on His Seventieth Birthday,* edited by H.C. Robbins Landon and Roger E. Chapman, London: Allen and Unwin, and New York: Oxford University Press, 1970

Buelow, George J., and Hans Joachim Marx, editors, *New Mattheson Studies,* Cambridge: Cambridge University Press, 1983

Cannon, Beekman C., *Johann Mattheson: Spectator in Music,* New Haven, Connecticut: Yale University Press, 1947

Mattheson, Johann, *Johann Mattheson's Der vollkommene Capellmeister: A Revised Translation with Critical Commentary,* translated by Ernest C. Harriss, Ann Arbor, Michigan: UMI Research Press, 1981

A contemporary of J.S. Bach and G.F. Handel, Johann Mattheson has been overshadowed by them in music history. His opinions and theories about music, especially those concerning the doctrine of affections, have been termed both brilliant and uninspired, and his musical tastes and aesthetics have been labeled both pro- and anti-French. The ideas of this controversial figure in music history incited many debates in his own time as well, the most contentious of those ideas being his view that allowing more dramatic musical expression (theater music) within the church service would halt the latter's decline. Mattheson remained in his native city of Hamburg his entire life, achieving notoriety as a performer and composer of both opera and sacred music while building a successful diplomatic career as secretary to the English Resident in Hamburg. Opera occupied his early days as a composer, and he claimed to have instructed Handel in

composing in this dramatic style. Mattheson turned his attention to sacred music later in his life, becoming director of music for the Domkirche. In his 20s, Mattheson noticed a problem with his hearing, which gradually worsened until 1728, when he resigned his church position due in part to deafness. His musical activities did not end then; he turned his energies to reflections on music and musical life in the 18th century. Among his many publications are *Critica Musica,* the first German musical periodical; *Grundlage einer Ehrenpforte,* a collection of 148 biographies of important musicians of his day; and *Der vollkommene Capellmeister,* a comprehensive guide of the skills that Mattheson felt were necessary to conduct a secular or sacred musical organization. While the investigations listed here are a good beginning for Mattheson studies, more work needs to be done in this area before his contributions to music history, both monographs and musical compositions, can be fully appreciated.

Harriss translated MATTHESON's *Der vollkommene Capellmeister* and provided some critical commentary as well. This translation, a revision of Harriss's 1969 dissertation, admirably retains the essence of Mattheson's original while offering the English speaker the opportunity to judge his aesthetic, theoretical, and practical musical ideas for themselves; Harriss asserts, however, that this work demonstrates Mattheson's pro-French and anti-Italian philosophy about music. Another unpublished dissertation (Harvey Phillips Reddick, "Johann Mattheson's Forty-Eight Thorough-Bass Test Pieces: Translations and Commentary," Ph.D. dissertation, University of Michigan, 1956) has translated another important Mattheson treatise, but there are no other published translations and commentaries of Mattheson's musical tracts. There is a great deal of work to be done in this area before a better understanding of Mattheson's contributions to music history and aesthetics can be ascertained.

BUELOW relates Mattheson's compositions to his musical opinions published in *Der vollkommene Capellmeister.* This study of Mattheson's third opera is particularly significant because most of his manuscripts were destroyed during World War II. Buelow notes the use of simple melodies that employ stepwise motion for expression and relates them to Mattheson's later plea for composers to write simple melodies that sound natural. Noting that Mattheson's opera is more French than Italian in character, Buelow views the composer as essentially pro-French but also critical of the harmonic theories of the famous 18th-century French composer and theorist Jean-Philippe Rameau, who believed that melodies were derived from harmony.

Although there are many journal articles, dissertations, and books about Mattheson's music, theories, and aesthetics written in German, studies in English are primarily articles or other works that are indebted to his ideas without engaging them fully or attempting to understand their historical background. The only full-length biography in English, CANNON remains the most comprehensive study of Mattheson and his times. The author carefully balances information available only from Mattheson's autobiography with facts that can be substantiated by other sources. The opening chapter on life in Hamburg in the 17th and 18th centuries provides an excellent backdrop for the rest of the monograph, which continually places Mattheson's life and works within his times. Also important is the critical bibliography of Mattheson's writings, both musical and literary. The appendix contains a continuation of Mattheson's autobiography, making that document more complete. Unfortunately, Cannon does not translate this material into English, supplying only a diplomatic transcription from papers found in the Hamburg Stadtbibliothek.

BUELOW and MARX present the proceedings of the First International Johann Mattheson Symposium held in Wolfenbüttel, Germany, in 1981. Containing papers in English and German, this anthology is the most recent treatment of Mattheson, his life, and works. Studies concerning Mattheson's relationship to other baroque composers, including his position as one of Handel's biographers and his potential influence on the fugues of J.S. Bach, as well as the discussion of his historical significance, are of particular interest to 18th-century studies. Because this work is a conference proceeding, it presents a variety of opinions about Mattheson.

TERESA M. NEFF

Medieval Music: General Studies

Cattin, Giulio, and F. Alberto Gallo, *Music of the Middle Ages,* 2 vols., translated by Stephen Botterill, Cambridge: Cambridge University Press, 1984–85

Crocker, Richard, and David Hiley, editors, *The Early Middle Ages to 1300,* New Oxford History of Music, vol. 2, Oxford: Oxford University Press, 1990

Hoppin, Richard, *Medieval Music,* New York: Norton, 1978

Hughes, Anselm, editor, *Early Medieval Music up to 1300,* New Oxford History of Music, vol. 2: London: Oxford University Press, 1954

Hughes, Anselm, and Gerald Abraham, editors, *Ars Nova and the Renaissance, 1300–1540,* New Oxford History of Music, vol. 3: London: Oxford University Press, 1960

McKinnon, James, editor, *Antiquity and the Middle Ages: From Ancient Greece to the 15th Century,* London: Macmillan, and Englewood Cliffs, New Jersey: Prentice Hall, 1990

Reese, Gustave, *Music in the Middle Ages: With an Introduction on the Music of Ancient Times,* New York: Norton, 1940

Wilson, David Fenwick, *Music of the Middle Ages: Style and Structure,* New York: Schirmer Books, 1990

Yudkin, Jeremy, *Music in Medieval Europe,* Englewood Cliffs, New Jersey: Prentice Hall, 1989

The writing of histories of medieval music, like the writing of music history in general, has been strongly influenced by an evolutionary model, in which music of earlier or other cultures is presented as the primitive state from which the more sophisticated Western music developed. Indeed, many medieval sources do claim a direct connection to music of the Greek and Roman empires, although historians have demonstrated that the relationship between ancient and medieval music is primarily a philosophical one, rather than evidence of the literal transmission of musical knowledge from one age to the next. Other recent works present Sumerian, Greek, Syrian Christian, Jewish, or Byzantine music as primitive ancestors of medieval Western music, despite their independent traditions.

Following the evolutionary paradigm, most discussions of medieval music begin with Gregorian chant, proceed to monophonic accretions to the liturgy and secular monophony, and then move to polyphony, which is usually divided into "early" and "later" genres. Although this analytic structure clearly displays the strong dependence of medieval musical composition on preexisting music, it de-emphasizes the fact that all the types of monophony and polyphony existed concurrently throughout much of the medieval period and beyond.

In one of the first textbook-style histories of medieval music in English, REESE follows the evolutionary model with some disclaimers. He begins with music of various ancient cultures, before proceeding to discuss Byzantine chant, Latin monody, and polyphony, suggesting a chronological movement from one genre to the other. The author concentrates on stylistic features, rather than any socio-cultural considerations, and the work is especially valuable for its critiques of contemporary scholarly debates, many of which still influence musicologists today. Of special interest in this text are Reese's discussions of the use of musical instruments, a topic many texts do not cover well, and his attempts to relate medieval musical style and performance to contemporary folk music traditions in Europe and Western Asia.

The two volumes on the Middle Ages in the *New Oxford History of Music* follow a similar scheme to that of Reese's text. HUGHES covers the early medieval period (to 1300) in greater depth than does Reese, placing more emphasis on accretions to the liturgy in the form of tropes, sequences, conductus, and liturgical drama, and reflecting the newly burgeoning studies in medieval chant. In their volume on the late medieval and early Renaissance era, HUGHES and ABRAHAM provide separate investigations of music in France, Italy, and England. These volumes lack any mention of instrumental music, a curious omission considering that they were published in the 1950s, when medieval instrumental performance was generally a popular subject.

CROCKER and HILEY's text claims to be a revised edition of Hughes and Abraham, but this is a misnomer, as the volume has been completely rewritten by different authors, who emphasize new themes. The book provides a fine, detailed introduction to the state of contemporary research in medieval music and is the most valuable up-to-date source available. Rather than following a strict chronological order, essays cover specific topics in medieval music, with a primary focus on medieval chant and polyphony. The essays are written by specialists, but most authors present their topics and research in a balanced manner. Unlike the earlier Hughes volume, a rather short essay on instrumental music is included in this edition, although its placement in the section on medieval polyphony is curious. This work also presents a exhaustive bibliography and list of original sources that will help the scholar.

HOPPIN is still the most in-depth textbook available on medieval music, although it is no longer used as the basic text in most undergraduate courses. Like Reese, Hoppin concentrates on musical style, but his major strength lies in his exhaustive discussion of musical forms and analysis. He also surveys important theorists, musical manuscripts, and the interpretation of medieval notations in an integrated and detailed manner not found in other histories. On the other hand, Hoppin does not evaluate instrumental music. Despite this shortcoming, his description of the music in the context of its culture, combined with his thorough descriptions of styles and particular manuscripts, is still unsurpassed. The text is accompanied by an anthology of music cited in the text, a useful list of material for further reading, and guides to manuscript facsimiles.

YUDKIN similarly emphasizes musical style, but this work is less detailed and more accessible to the general reader than Hoppin's study. Yudkin explains the cultural background of medieval music more fully than Hoppin does, and he places more weight on the philosophical roots of music, discussing the relationship of ancient philosophers to medieval theoretical ideas. The author places considerable stress on performance and dedicates more space to instruments and instrumental music than any other text on medieval music, giving his text a particularly balanced view of the world of medieval music. There is no accompanying anthology of music, but full-length musical examples are incorporated into the text, and performances are available on an accompanying cassette tape. Each chapter ends with a "Comments on notation and performance section," which presents short discussions of the problems in performance practice, as well as discographies and bibliographies. This integration of discussions of performance is another of Yudkin's important achievements in this work.

WILSON's short text, intended for undergraduate courses, comes with an accompanying anthology and CDs. The anthology is carefully designed: melodies from the section on chant reappear in conductus, motets, or Mass movements, clearly delineating the central compositional strategy of the medieval period. The author strongly emphasizes compositional and analytical techniques, notation, and source materials, and he offers student exercises in the analysis and composition of medieval music. These exercises are a unique addition to texts in medieval music and a good introduction to techniques of analysis of medieval composition.

McKINNON proffers a topical approach in a set of independent essays situating medieval music in its socio-cultural context. Beginning with Ancient Greece and ending with the 14th century, the text in fact follows the traditional paradigm for textbooks on medieval music, but its attention to the social and geographic context mutes any notion of an evolutionary model. Originally derived from a television series, the book is an eminently approachable and balanced introduction to medieval music written in non-technical language. For readers requiring more in-depth information, each essay is followed by an annotated bibliography with suggestions for further reading.

CATTIN is one of the few texts that concentrates exclusively on monophonic music in the medieval period, and this distinctive framework immediately challenges the evolutionary assumption that monophony is best understood as a precursor to polyphony. Using a contextual approach, Cattin places types of monophony in their cultural, ceremonial, or geographical milieu, while also stressing medieval commentators' views of the monophony of their time. The chant section, in particular, identifies the diversity of chant traditions in different geographical areas, effectively countering the popular notion of a monumental and unchanging repertory. The section about medieval commentators is supported by excerpts of their writings in an appendix. Another particular strength of this work is Cattin's thoughtful treatment of changing scholarly issues in medieval monophony, which includes problems of rhythm and interpretation and attends to political forces that have influenced scholarship. Few other books on medieval music so clearly demonstrate musicology at work. On the other hand, readers may find the brief text difficult, as terminology is not explained in the text itself. (There is a comprehensive glossary, however.) This is a fine book about both the history of medieval monophony and its study.

GALLO continues Cattin's work, concentrating mensural polyphony from the 13th to the early 15th centuries. His basic themes are the relationships of music and society, on the one hand, and music and literature, on the other. (This second topic refers to analogous literary and musical techniques, not correspondences between particular works.) Rather than analyzing specific musical compositions, Gallo primarily investigates close parallels between writings in music theory and texts on rhetoric and grammar in the Middle Ages, as well as the cultural milieu in which music was created. The book is divided into four sections: 13th-century France, 14th-century France, 14th-century Italy, and the 15th century in both countries, with each section subdivided into topical chapters. The second half of the book presents a collection of excerpted source readings from musical theorists and composers of the period.

NANCY LORIMER

Medieval Music: Specialized Studies

Crocker, Richard L., *The Early Medieval Sequence,* Berkeley: University of California Press, 1977

Evans, Paul, *The Early Trope Repertory of Saint Martial de Limoges,* Princeton, New Jersey: Princeton University Press, 1970

Everist, Mark, *French Motets in the Thirteenth Century: Music, Poetry, and Genre,* Cambridge: Cambridge University Press, 1994

Fassler, Margot, *Gothic Song: Victorine Sequences and Augustinian Reform in Twelfth-Century Paris,* Cambridge: Cambridge University Press, 1993

Harrison, Frank Llewellyn, *Music in Medieval Britain,* London: Routledge and Paul, 1958; 2nd edition, 1963

Huot, Sylvia, *From Song to Book: The Poetics of Writing in Old French Lyric and Lyrical Narrative Poetry,* Ithaca, New York: Cornell University Press, 1987

Jeffery, Peter, *Re-Envisioning Past Musical Cultures: Ethnomusicology in the Study of Gregorian Chant,* Chicago: University of Chicago Press, 1992

Kelly, Thomas Forrest, *The Beneventan Chant,* Cambridge: Cambridge University Press, 1989

Kelly, Thomas Forrest, editor, *Plainsong in the Age of Polyphony,* Cambridge: Cambridge University Press, 1992

McGee, Timothy J., *The Sound of Medieval Song: Ornamentation and Vocal Style According to the Treatises,* Oxford: Clarendon Press, and New York: Oxford University Press, 1998

Page, Christopher, *The Owl and the Nightingale: Musical Life and Ideas in France, 1100–1300,* London: Dent, and Berkeley: University of California Press, 1989

———, *Voices and Instruments of the Middle Ages: Instrumental Practice and Songs in France, 1100–1300,* Berkeley: University of California Press, 1986

Pesce, Dolores, editor, *Hearing the Motet: Essays on the Motet of the Middle Ages and Renaissance,* New York: Oxford University Press, 1997

Robertson, Anne Walters, *The Service Books of the Royal Abbey of Saint-Denis: Images of Ritual and Music in the Middle Ages,* Oxford: Clarendon Press, and New York: Oxford University Press, 1991

Stevens, John, *Words and Music in the Middle Ages: Song, Narrative, Dance, and Drama, 1050–1350,* Cambridge: Cambridge University Press, 1986

Wright, Craig, *Music and Ceremony at Notre Dame of Paris, 500–1500,* Cambridge: Cambridge University Press, 1989

Specialized monographic studies in medieval music have focused primarily on repertories and performance practice; these broad categories accommodate a wide range of approaches and scholarly interests. The study of musical repertories is an enduring pursuit in medieval music scholarship. The scope of these works ranges from the traditions of a single church to all of medieval monophonic song. In general, they offer the reader careful accounts of the primary source materials, musical analyses, discussions of genre, and assessments of music-historical significance.

EVANS introduces the reader to the basic trope repertory of the abbey of St. Martial in Limoges, France. Starting with a general discussion of tropes, Evans moves on to review the manuscript sources, texts, and musical structure of the works from St. Martial. His book concludes with a valuable transcription of the basic trope repertory.

CROCKER examines and describes early sequences to foster a deeper understanding of the style of these pieces. After drawing comparisons between East- and West-Frankish sequences of the ninth and tenth centuries, Crocker devotes most of the remainder of his book to careful investigations of melodic structures, connections between texts and their melodies, and the interrelationships of various *contrafacta*. He also discusses the liturgical function of the early sequence and comments on its place in the broader landscape of late-Carolingian culture. The book contains musical transcriptions of more than three dozen early sequences, including all of those mentioned by Notker of St. Gall.

KELLY (1989) gives an account of the Beneventan chant tradition. In addition to an extended discussion of musical style, the author surveys the historical events that influenced ecclesiastical and musical life in southern Italy. He provides a catalog of the manuscript sources containing Beneventan music and outlines the ritual practices and feasts that comprise the Beneventan liturgy. The book concludes with a study of the similarities and differences between the Beneventan rite and other liturgies.

STEVENS surveys the medieval repertory of monophonic song in its widest sense, from liturgical chant to secular chansons, and proposes a view of medieval aesthetics and composition that emphasizes the role of numerical patterns in music and poetry. His main argument is that words and music in medieval song are chiefly related by organizational structures that have their basis in numbers. Accordingly, compositional features such as the phrasing of melodies and the number of syllables in a text share underlying numerical patterns of design. Stevens's argument is controversial; his critics have especially questioned his dismissal of any general connections between melodic structures and the meaning of a text.

EVERIST begins by tracing the development of the motet, taking issue with oversimplified historical accounts that plot a linear, developmental course from the *discant clausula* to the two-voiced French motet. This linear model is symptomatic of the key problem Everist sets out to address: that of classification and genre. He examines classification systems founded purely on generalized musical characteristics and shows—by focusing on the interaction of music and poetry—how these systems can obscure rather than deepen our understanding of the repertory.

In contrast to the works discussed above, some repertorial studies integrate the findings of music-historical scholarship with research in the history of institutions, theology, politics, art history, and other fields relevant to the arguments the authors develop.

An early study that combines social history with a conspectus of musical styles is HARRISON's overview of music in England from the Normans to the Reformation. His book includes a full history of choirs and liturgical customs during the period under consideration. He also examines documentary records to learn about the lives and activities of musicians; these sources frequently provide information about performance practices. His book concludes with a collection of key sources in translation.

PAGE (1989) surveys a wide range of medieval texts—encyclopedias, sermons, romances, theological treatises, etc.—to shed light on the lives and activities of musicians in 12th- and 13th-century France. After considering evidence on a variety of music makers, he concludes by arguing that discourses on music in France changed focus during the two centuries covered by his study. Page proposes that music was viewed principally in terms of its use to the church in the early 12th century, but by the end of the 13th century, it was the role of music in the sphere of secular politics that was most emphasized.

WRIGHT traces the development of the liturgy at Notre Dame of Paris from 500 to 1500, and the information he gathers on the cathedral's personnel and ritual observances provides a foundation for the resolution of several long-standing scholarly problems. The two most significant results of Wright's study are the documentary identification of the 12th-century organum composer Léonin, whose very existence some scholars had questioned, and the author's proposition that Léonin's collection of two-part polyphonic compositions, the *Magnus liber organi,* was created solely for the cathedral of Notre Dame in Paris. Moreover, Wright argues that the three principal manuscripts containing 12th- and 13th-century Parisian polyphony do not bear witness to some kind of repertorial evolution, as had been suggested in earlier studies, but rather represent three independent renditions of the same repertory.

ROBERTSON's book is a comprehensive study of the music and liturgy at the Royal Abbey of St. Denis in Paris. The author presents a careful account of the annual cycle of religious celebrations at the abbey, noting important additions and deletions and identifying their impact on the musical and artistic life of the religious community. She also provides a catalog of all the extant service books from the abbey. From this foundation of sources, Robertson explores the ways in which architecture, royal politics, and music shaped religious life at the institution.

FASSLER studies the repertory of sequences associated with the Abbey of St. Victor in 12th-century Paris. In addition to reviewing the early history of the genre and tracing its development into the early 12th century, she argues that these chants contributed to the mystical theology developed by the monks of St. Victor.

Studies of performance practice have ranged in focus from those that consider the specific techniques of musical production to those that incorporate an explicit awareness and accounting of music as a performed medium into their analytical discussions.

HUOT examines the shift from the orally conceived vernacular poetry of the 13th century to the more writerly works of the 14th. She focuses on how writing and performance were treated as poetic themes, how the poet was characterized variously as a singer or a writer, and how individual authors responded to the new poetic currents. Her work is valuable to musicologists not only because of what it teaches about the poet/musician figure, but also because many of the poems she analyzes are drawn from musical settings of the period.

PAGE (1986) maintains that our use of instruments to accompany medieval secular monophony should be guided by a thorough understanding of musical genre. Consequently, the first part of his book is devoted to an exploration of musical genres in 12th- and 13th-century France. The second part of his book focuses on performance practices. Due to the nature of the evidence, Page limits his remarks to the use of stringed instruments. His book contains valuable appendices on instrument terminology, construction, and literary references to the use of stringed accompaniments in secular song.

JEFFERY calls for a new, broader approach to chant scholarship. Specifically, he advises musicologists to capitalize on the insights of ethnomusicology and ethnomusicological methods to enrich their research on historical questions. The author maintains that cross-cultural studies will shed new light on the history of Gregorian chant, especially the nature of its early transmission. The book includes Jeffery's reflections on current scholarship, a précis of relevant ethnomusicological issues, and general observations on features that have been associated with the music of oral cultures.

McGEE assembles a wide range of quotations from medieval theoretical treatises in order to challenge our notions about the sound of medieval music. He is critical of 20th-century performances of medieval music and argues that the melodic complexity known to medieval performers has been lost. He discusses a variety of melodic ornaments, inflections, and techniques that he believes are "required by medieval music," and he aims to show how these practices evolved into the ornamental conventions of Renaissance and baroque music. His arguments, especially those concerning the vocal sound of medieval singers, are controversial.

There are also several important collections of essays on medieval music. The book on the relationship between chant and polyphony edited by KELLY (1992) contains a landmark study by Robertson in which the provenance and liturgical use of Machaut's Mass is established. The volume edited by PESCE gathers together a series of articles that consider the motet from a variety of perspectives, from the implications of using borrowed material to the relationships among families of pieces related by common musical elements.

MICHAEL MCGRADE

Mendelssohn, Fanny *see* Hensel, Fanny

Mendelssohn, Felix 1809–1847

German composer

Devrient, Eduard, *My Recollections of Felix Mendelssohn-Bartholdy and His Letters to Me,* translated by Natalia Macfarren, London: Bentley, 1869; reprint, New York: Vienna House, 1972

Hensel, Sebastian, *The Mendelssohn Family (1729–1847) from Letters and Journals,* 2 vols., translated by Carl Klingemann, 2nd, revised edition, New York: Harper and Brothers, 1882, reprint, New York: Haskell House, 1969

Hiller, Ferdinand, *Mendelssohn: Letters and Recollections,* translated by M.E. von Glehn, London: Macmillan, and Cincinnati, Ohio: Church, 1874; reprint, New York: Vienna House, 1972

Jenkins, David, and Mark Visocchi, *Mendelssohn in Scotland,* London: Chappell, 1978

Köhler, Karl-Heinz, "Felix Mendelssohn," in *The New Grove: Early Romantic Masters: 2,* edited by John Warrack et al., London: Macmillan, and New York: Norton, 1985

Lampadius, Wilhelm Adolf, *Life of Felix Mendelssohn Bartholdy,* edited and translated by William Leonhard Gage, Boston: Ditson, 1865; reprint, Boston: Longwood Press, 1978

Mendelssohn-Bartholdy, Felix, *Felix Mendelssohn: A Life in Letters,* edited by Rudolf Elvers, translated by Craig Tomlinson, New York: Fromm International, 1986

———, *Felix Mendelssohn: Letters,* edited and translated by Gisella Selden-Goth, New York: Pantheon Books, 1945; London, Elek, 1946

———, *Letters of Felix Mendelssohn Bartholdy from Italy and Switzerland,* translated by Lady Wallace, Boston: Ditson, 1865; reprint, Freeport, New York: Books for Libraries Press, 1970

———, *Letters of Felix Mendelssohn to Ignaz and Charlotte Moscheles,* London: Trubner, and Boston: Ticknor, 1888; reprint, Freeport, New York: Books for Libraries Press, 1970

Petitpierre, Jacques, *The Romance of the Mendelssohns,* translated by G. Micholet-Coté, London: Dobson, 1947

Polko, Elise, *Reminiscences of Felix Mendelssohn-Bartholdy: A Social and Artistic Biography,* translated by Lady Wallace, New York: Laypoldt and Holt, and London: Longmans Green, 1869; reprint, Macomb, Illinois: Glenbridge, 1987

Radcliffe, Philip, *Mendelssohn,* New York: Dent, 1954; 3rd edition, edited by Peter Ward Jones, 1990

Todd, R. Larry, *Mendelssohn's Musical Education: A Study and Edition of His Exercises in Composition,* Cambridge: Cambridge University Press, 1983

Vitercik, Gregory John, *The Early Works of Felix Mendelssohn: A Study in the Romantic Sonata Style,* Philadelphia: Gordon and Breach, 1992

Werner, Eric, *Mendelssohn: A New Image of the Composer and His Age,* translated by Dika Newlin, New York: Free Press of Glencoe, 1963

As a leading figure in German music in the early 19th century and a child prodigy dead at age 38, Mendelssohn was frequently compared with Mozart, a comparison that hastened the production of a number of Mendelssohn biographies in the second half of the century. Moreover, Mendelssohn's ten visits to Great Britain engendered his adoption by the Victorian English as one of their own, in a manner similar to Handel, to whom Mendelssohn was also frequently compared. After his death in 1847, Mendelssohn's life was idealized (as the character Seraphael) in the fictional historical romance by Elizabeth Sheppard, *Charles Auchester* (1908), supposedly based on the life of violinist Joseph Joachim.

This reverence for Mendelssohn is apparent in POLKO. The author was an amateur singer who, having auditioned for Mendelssohn, knew him when she was a child in Leipzig. Polko describes her succinct book as an attempt "to furnish a kind of commentary on the precious legacy of Mendelssohn's letters, and likewise a sketch of his biography." (Polko bases some aspects of the biography on Lampadius' 1865 work.) She recounts her impressions of Mendelssohn's physical demeanor, his piano playing and conducting style, and aspects of performances in the Leipzig Gewandhaus. While not noting her sources, she includes descriptions of various meetings and performances not found in other books concerning Mendelssohn. However, there are many inaccuracies in her book.

The first substantial biography is by LAMPADIUS, a student at the Leipzig Conservatory who wrote from firsthand knowledge of Mendelssohn's piano performance style and manner of conducting as well as his coaching and teaching. Extensive accounts of particular performances are informative and interesting. The supplementary firsthand accounts by Benedict, Chorley, Rellstab (who describes one of Mendelssohn's visits with Goethe), and others are also of considerable interest.

Many studies of Mendelssohn are in the form of collections of letters, both to and from the composer, and recollections by his friends. Mendelssohn was a voluminous letter writer: more than 7,000 letters are preserved, although no complete collection of his correspondence has been published. This is one of the lacunae in modern Mendelssohn scholarship. Rudolph Elvers edited a collection of letters—MENDELSSOHN-BARTHOLDY (1986)—that reflects the highest level of critical research and documentation and contains letters from 1820 through 1847. Elvers uses Mendelssohn's letters to provide a biography of the composer, so his selection is diverse; other collections of letters have focused more narrowly on Mendelssohn's correspondence with certain individuals. MENDELSSOHN-BARTHOLDY (1888), a collection of the letters that the composer wrote to his close friend and colleague Ignaz Moscheles, focuses on the friendship of these two men, arguably two of the more famous pianist-composers of their time. MENDELSSOHN-BARTHOLDY (1865), edited by the composer's brother Paul, features letters from Felix Mendelssohn's grand tour of Germany, Austria, Italy, Switzerland, and France (1830–32). All of these letters were heavily edited to remove any references to then-living persons and any material deemed too personal. Finally, the letters found in MENDELSSOHN-BARTHOLDY (1945) are of considerable interest.

Eduard DEVRIENT was a trusted confidant and resource, especially concerning Mendelssohn's interest in finding a suitable text for an opera. Devrient's memoir provides many letters between the two and a firsthand account of Devrient's impressions of Mendelssohn's life, both as a child and a mature adult, and his relationship with members of his family and colleagues. Many insights not gained elsewhere abound concerning the composer's working habits, both musical and otherwise.

Born two years after Mendelssohn, in 1811, and in the same house in Hamburg, coincidentally, where Mendelssohn was born, composer, pianist, and conductor HILLER was also an especially close friend and colleague. Hiller's *Letters and Recollections*, with the 1972 edition prefaced with an excellent essay by Joel Sachs, is one of the best sources concerning Mendelssohn's personal life. The two roomed together at times, and Hiller's description of Mendelssohn's time in Paris is the most detailed record of that period. So impressed was George Grove with Hiller's account that he asked Hiller to provide the article on Mendelssohn for his dictionary (when Hiller declined, Grove wrote it himself). The letters date from 1822 through 1843, and Hiller interweaves descriptions of the various circumstances surrounding the letters.

One of the most influential biographical accounts of Mendelssohn's life is that of Sebastian HENSEL, the first nephew of Felix Mendelssohn, the son of Felix's sister, Fanny, and her husband, the painter Wilhelm Hensel. As a member of the close inner circle of those surrounding Mendelssohn, Hensel's biography is replete with a richness of detail and a ring of authenticity. His work provides much insight into the day-to-day life of the composer and his family. Hensel's first volume deals with Felix Mendelssohn's life through 1835, but is preceded by 75 pages concerned with the composer's ancestors. The first letters included are those of his grandmother, Leah Mendelssohn, Felix's mother. Unfortunately, Hensel's work is, in the words of Mendelssohn scholar Larry Todd, "marred by uncritical readings of the letters; many letters appear in a heavily edited form, and some are conflated, so that scholars are still compelled to consult the original autographs."

The foundation of modern Mendelssohn scholarship rests on George Grove's lengthy and comprehensive article in the first edition of his *Dictionary of Music and Musicians* (1890). Grove includes an in-depth discussion of Mendelssohn's childhood and home life, artistic development, and compositions. The author includes lengthy quotations of descriptions about Mendelssohn's physical appearance and personality, manner of performing, conducting, and teaching, and the article contains the first attempt at a comprehensive work list, incredibly accurate for the time. Grove prepared for the writing of his article by conducting research at the Berlin Royal Library (now the Deutsche Staatsbibliothek) and in Leipzig, examining Mendelssohn's autographs, and conducting interviews with members of the composer's family and friends.

RADCLIFFE's reliable biography attempts to present the composer's life "coloured neither by the exaggerated hero-worship by which they were first surrounded nor by the equally exaggerated denigration that followed."

The definitive biography is still that by WERNER, who has published a number of other articles and books concerned with the composer. Werner drew on extensive research of primary sources and documents largely unavailable to earlier biographers. He drew attention to a number of early, unpublished works by Mendelssohn, which he examined in the Deutsche Staatsbibliothek. One of Werner's primary goals is to analyze the conflict Mendelssohn felt between the German culture he was a part of and his Jewish ancestry.

KÖHLER offers the most up-to-date information, with a complete work list. TODD and VITERCIK both provide excellent views into the composer's workshop for those interested in Mendelssohn's compositional process.

Also deserving notice is a group of specialized biographies. PETITPIERRE is a descendant of Mendelssohn's wife, Cécile Jeanrenaud, and provides a portrayal of her ancestors and up-bringing. There are many illustrations, including watercolors and drawings by Felix and Cécile, and a description of the more domestic side of Mendelssohn's life. There is no index, but an extensive list of primary sources from the Jeanrenaud and Mendelssohn families. Robert Schumann's recollection is of particular interest to musicians.

JENKINS and VISOCCHI's book is replete with illustrations, including many of Mendelssohn's own watercolors and sketches, and engravings and images of Mendelssohn's family and circle by various other artists. The text, interspersed with many letters, begins with an account of the first 20 years of Mendelssohn's life, including information about his ancestors. The authors then concentrate on Mendelssohn's 1829 visit to York and Edinburgh, Abbotsford, the Highlands, Glasgow, and Loch Lomond. The book concludes with a brief discussion of the *Scottish* Symphony in A minor of 1842.

STEPHEN LINDEMAN

Messiaen, Olivier 1908–1992

French composer

Bell, Carla Huston, *Olivier Messiaen,* Boston: Twayne, 1984

Bruhn, Siglind, editor, *Messiaen's Language of Mystical Love,* New York: Garland, 1998

Griffiths, Paul, *Olivier Messiaen and the Music of Time,* Ithaca, New York: Cornell University Press, and London: Faber, 1985

Hill, Peter, editor, *The Messiaen Companion,* London: Faber, 1994; Portland, Oregon: Amadeus Press, 1995

Johnson, Robert Sherlaw, *Messiaen,* Berkeley: University of California Press, and London: Dent, 1975; new edition, 1989

Messiaen, Olivier, *Music and Color: Conversations with Claude Samuel,* translated by E. Thomas Glasow, Portland, Oregon: Amadeus Press, 1994

——, *Technique of My Musical Language,* translated by John Satterfield, Paris: Leduc, 1957

Nichols, Roger, *Messiaen,* London: Oxford University Press, 1975; 2nd edition, 1986

Rössler, Almut, *Contributions to the Spiritual World of Olivier Messiaen, with Original Texts by the Composer,* translated by Barbara Dagg and Nancy Poland, Duisberg: Gilles and Francke, 1986

Samuel, Claude, *Conversations with Olivier Messiaen,* translated by Felix Aprahamian, London: Stainer and Bell, 1976

Olivier Messiaen filled his compositions with his personal musical language and personal spiritual message. His musical language comprises nonmetrical rhythms of Hindu and Greek origin, his own symmetrical modes of limited transposition, bird-song transcriptions, and tone complexes that evoke visual color. His spiritual message centers on the mysteries of the Catholic faith and the dazzlement of God. Because Messiaen was earnest in explaining his musical techniques and religious symbols, other writers have built on his model.

MESSIAEN (1957) sets the tone for discussions of his music in a work originally published in French in 1944. The composer first assures the reader that his music is an act of faith and that his symmetrical rhythmic and modal constructions are explorations of the charm of impossibilities. Nonretrogradable rhythms (palindromes such as the Hindu *râgavardhana*), added values of a 16th note or a dot, and rhythmic pedals dominate the discussion. After he covers the traditional aspects of musical structure, from the phrase to the sonata form, Messiaen mentions his love of melodies based on plainchant and bird song. He concludes with an introduction to his seven modes of limited transposition, each illustrated by musical examples from his compositions of the 1930s. As if teaching his own students from the Paris Conservatory, Messiaen makes each aspect of his discussion accessible to the reader.

The first English-language works on Messiaen did not appear until 1975. The authors of the four biographies focus their analyses on the materials from Messiaen's *Technique of My Musical Language* as they follow the progress of the composer's works.

In each chapter of his brief biographical study, NICHOLS describes an era of Messiaen's musical development. The author uses *Banquet céleste* (1926) to illustrate modes of limited transposition and *La nativité du Seigneur* (1935) to explain added rhythms and Hindu talas. Nichols describes the fascination avant-garde composers in the 1950s expressed in the total serialism of *Mode de valeurs et d'intensités.* He also evaluates the criticism Messiaen received for turning from serial composition to the complex texture of bird-song transcriptions in *Chronochromie* (1960). Because Nichols's compact paragraphs combine description, technique, and critical citations, the reader will benefit from a previous knowledge of Messiaen's methods.

BELL reveals Messiaen's musical language by analyzing selected movements of works from 1926 to 1958. An opening survey of musical influences on Messiaen includes information on Greek and Hindu rhythms. The analytical essays trace the development of these rhythms as they are treated in symmetrical permutations. In analyzing the *Livre d'orgue* (1951), Bell describes Messiaen's technique of *personnages rythmiques,* in which one voice augments values, a second diminishes, and a third remains constant. Each analytical chapter includes descriptions of events in Messiaen's life at the time of the composition, as well as lists, charts, and formal outlines of the movement.

Johnson and Griffiths provide comprehensive biographies that also include explanations of Messiaen's techniques and analyses of his music. Writing from the point of view of a pianist who performs Messiaen's works, JOHNSON creates a method for the analysis of bird song found in the *Catalogue d'oiseaux*. After he classifies Messiaen's bird songs according to their complexity and patterns, the author provides elaborate charts of their interaction in every movement. Johnson includes a list of the Hindu talas and a catalog of Messiaen's bird songs in French, Latin, and English.

In his role as music critic and author of popular books on 20th-century music, GRIFFITHS makes his biographical and analytical monograph accessible to both music students and amateurs. Taking as his theme the music of time, the author ascertains that Messiaen's nonmetric rhythms, symmetrical modes, bird-song transcriptions, and the composer's longing for a heavenly eternity eliminate the traditional forward movement of Western music. Griffiths analyzes all major works to 1983. A list of works, with information on premieres and a discography, concludes the volume.

Two English translations of Samuel's interviews with Messiaen amplify the composer's earlier discussions of his musical language. Messiaen's responses demonstrate his personal warmth, the sincerity of his faith, and the meticulous care with which he analyzes his own works. In SAMUEL, Messiaen describes modes related to visual colors and bird-song transcriptions. In addition to discussing his own music, the composer assesses the importance of his teachers and such influential former students as Boulez. In MESSIAEN (1994), the composer supplies analyses of sound color, bird song, and the orchestral palette in *Sept haïkaï, Des canyons aux étoiles, La Transfiguration,* and *Saint François d'Assise*.

Like Johnson, RÖSSLER writes from the point of view of a performer, commenting on her interpretation and registration for Messiaen's organ works. The volume contains interviews with the composer and translations of lectures that Messiaen presented in the Netherlands (1971) and at Notre Dame Cathedral (1977). Focusing on the spiritual content of his music, Messiaen equates the perception of sound color with sacred dazzlement.

The two most recent of the ten volumes listed in the bibliography contain collections of articles on aspects of Messiaen's work. The essays in HILL survey works in chronological order, through the posthumous *Éclairs sur l'au-delà.* Several of the articles give advice to performers concerning Messiaen's style and the technical requirements of the songs, piano works, and organ works. Hill's interview with Yvonne Loriod contains Loriod's warm recollections of her meeting with her future husband when she was a Conservatory student, as well as with her

personal observations on their artistic life. The volume concludes with a work list and discography.

The articles in BRUHN focus on Messiaen's expression of his Catholic beliefs through the charm of impossibilities in his musical techniques. Authors explore the influence of surrealist poetry, the theology of Saint Thomas Aquinas, and Franciscan literature in Messiaen's own texts. Formal symmetry in *Vingt regards,* bird song in *Catalogue d'oiseaux,* sound color in *Saint François,* and communicable language in *Méditations* demonstrate Messiaen's search for sacred symbols and continue the themes of his *Technique of My Musical Language.* All writing about Messiaen remains faithful to the composer's goal of making his beliefs and his richly colored music accessible to musicians and audience.

CAMILLE CRUNELLE HILL

Meyerbeer, Giacomo 1791–1864

German composer

Armstrong, Alan, "Meyerbeer's Le Prophète: A History of Its Composition and Early Performances," 4 vols., Ph.D. dissertation, Ohio State University, 1990

Crosten, William L., *French Grand Opera: An Art and a Business,* New York: King's Crown Press, 1948

Dieren, Bernard van, *Down among the Dead Men and Other Essays,* London: Oxford University Press, 1935

Fulcher, Jane F., *The Nation's Image: French Grand Opera as Politics and Politicized Art,* Cambridge: Cambridge University Press, 1987

Meyerbeer, Giacomo, *Giacomo Meyerbeer: A Life in Letters,* edited by Heinz Becker and Gudrun Becker, translated by Mark Violette, Portland, Oregon: Amadeus Press, and London: Helm, 1989

Pendle, Karin, *Eugène Scribe and French Opera of the Nineteenth Century,* Ann Arbor, Michigan: UMI Research Press, and Epping: Bowker, 1979

Roberts, John Howell, "The Genesis of Meyerbeer's L'Africaine," Ph.D. dissertation, University of California, Berkeley, 1977

Wilberg, Rebecca S., "The Mise en scène at the Paris Opéra—Salle Le Peletier (1821–1873) and the Staging of the First French Grand Opéra: Meyerbeer's Robert le Diable," Ph.D. dissertation, Brigham Young University, 1990

The literature on Giacomo Meyerbeer reflects the changing fortunes in the composer's reputation. By the start of the 20th century, Meyerbeer's operas had already begun their steady decline in popularity, which eventually led to their banishment from the standard repertoire. Moreover, Wagner's negative assessment of Meyerbeer as a purveyor of effects without causes gained widespread acceptance. Consequently, Meyerbeer was generally deemed unworthy of investigation, and literature on the composer was sparse. Although still seldom performed, Meyerbeer's operas now receive more attention from scholars. His overwhelming importance for the history of opera is now recognized, even as debates about the artistic merit of his music continue. Not surprisingly, research on Meyerbeer has concentrated on his French operas, and comparatively little attention has been paid to his years in Germany and Italy.

The essay by DIEREN represents one of the earliest attempts to rehabilitate Meyerbeer's reputation. Its chief value for a reader today is the summary of charges commonly leveled against Meyerbeer at the time that Dieren wrote. As such, it provides a vivid picture of how Meyerbeer was viewed in the early 20th century. Among the criticisms addressed are the supposedly poor quality of Eugène Scribe's librettos and Meyerbeer's incorporation of elements from different nationalities in his style. Dieren's responses are still thought provoking; for instance, he sensibly questions whether the literary value of a libretto is crucial to the artistic merit of an opera. Meyerbeer's eclecticism is defended as a successful fusion of different styles, similar in kind (though not quality) to that achieved by Bach and Mozart.

The studies by Crosten and Fulcher place Meyerbeer's works within the context of the Paris Opéra and its relationship to the public. CROSTEN's study was influential for its focus on the business aspect of grand opera. He concentrates on a short period of the Paris Opéra, namely the directorship of Louis Véron from 1831 to 1835. Emphasis is placed on the ability of the Paris Opéra's administration to create a product desirable to the tastes of the Parisian public. Accordingly, chapters are devoted to the claque, staging and lighting, and the libretto. Crosten also includes a chapter on Meyerbeer that focuses on aspects of his style that contributed to his success. Features such as the heightened role of the chorus, his emphasis on ensembles over solo numbers, and his large-scale structural planning are seen as contributing factors to the grandeur of the composer's operas.

FULCHER presents a different picture of the relationship between the Paris Opéra and its public. She refutes Crosten's emphasis on grand opera merely as an institution pandering to bourgeois taste in order to ensure a profit at the box office. Instead, she draws attention to the continuous meddling by the French government in the administration of the Opéra. In her view, the state controlled the operatic repertoire as a means of promoting its political agenda to the public. Fulcher provides fascinating information on the genesis and reception of Meyerbeer's *Robert le diable*, *Les Huguenots*, and *Le Prophète*, in which the government's intervention and censorship are evident. A weakness of the book, however, is its tendency to ignore factors other than political ones that shaped the cre-

ation of these operas. Possible musical and aesthetic decisions made by Meyerbeer and Scribe in their works are rarely examined.

PENDLE considers grand opera from yet another perspective, that of the librettist Scribe. She includes chapters on *Robert le diable*, *Les Huguenots*, and *Le Prophète,* in each case outlining the genesis of the libretto and its relationship to historical or literary sources. Pendle also points out similarities and differences between these librettos and Scribe's endeavors in other genres. Scribe and Meyerbeer initially conceived *Robert le diable* as an opéra comique, for instance, and Pendle's discussion of the libretto's transformation into one for an opera is illuminating. Structural aspects of Scribe's librettos and their impact on Meyerbeer's construction of scenes and acts are also considered.

ROBERTS's dissertation on *L'Africaine* is the first in-depth study of the genesis of one of Meyerbeer's operas. Because Meyerbeer worked on this piece sporadically for 27 years and François-Joseph Fétis revised it after the composer's death, the opera's development is especially complex. Roberts was the first Meyerbeer scholar to use the extensive holdings of Scribe's papers (located in the Bibliothèque Nationale, Paris), which include numerous drafts of his librettos, unpublished letters, and other documents. With these materials at his disposal, Roberts not only carefully unravels the opera's tangled history, including the revision by Fétis, but also provides insights into Meyerbeer's art. One point of emphasis that clearly emerges is Meyerbeer's fascination with local color.

Following in Roberts's footsteps, ARMSTRONG gives an even more detailed study of *Le Prophète*. In addition to Scribe's papers, Armstrong also had access to the autograph score, which—along with those of *Robert le diable*, *Les Huguenots*, and *L'Africaine*—recently came to light in the Biblioteka Jagiellonska, Cracow. Armstrong describes the opera's evolution and demonstrates Meyerbeer's intense involvement with every aspect of its performance. Especially valuable are the appendices, which contain drafts of the libretto and hundreds of pages of music omitted from Meyerbeer's final version of the score.

WILBERG's study is part of the growing interest in the staging and other visual elements of grand opera. She provides a wealth of information on scenery, costumes, and stage design at the Paris Opéra in general and those used for *Robert le diable* in particular. As Wilberg points out, these elements were vital to the success of Meyerbeer's opera and were viewed by critics as one of the salient features of the work. The impact of the staging of this work on later productions at the Paris Opéra is also considered.

The Beckers' edition of MEYERBEER's letters is the only substantial collection of his correspondence available in English. As such, it is valuable, although it represents only a small portion of Meyerbeer's surviving correspondence. (The Beckers have also been working on an original-language edition that comprises four hefty volumes to date.) The editors helpfully place the letters in their historical contexts by providing commentary for each one. The selection of correspondence includes letters that shed light both on Meyerbeer's personality and family life and on the composition of his operas.

KEITH COCHRAN

Middle East

Al Faruqi, Lois Ibsen, *An Annotated Glossary of Arabic Musical Terms,* Westport, Connecticut: Greenwood Press, 1981

Danielson, Virginia, *The Voice of Egypt: Umm Kulthum, Arabic Song, and Egyptian Society in the Twentieth Century,* Chicago: University of Chicago Press, 1997

Jenkins, Jean L., and Poul Rovsing Olsen, *Music and Musical Instruments in the World of Islam,* London: World of Islam Festival, 1976

Manniche, Lise, *Music and Musicians in Ancient Egypt,* London: British Museum Press, 1991

Sawa, George, *Musical Performance Practice in the Early Abbasid Era 132–320 AH/750–932 AD,* Toronto: Pontifical Institute of Medieval Studies, 1989

Shiloah, Amnon, *Music in the World of Islam: A Socio-Cultural Study,* Aldershot: Scolar Press, 1994; Detroit, Michigan: Wayne State University Press, 1995

————, *The Theory of Music in Arabic Writings (ca. 900–1900): Descriptive Catalogue of Manuscripts in Libraries of Europe and the U.S.A.,* Munich: Henle, 1979

Touma, Habib, *The Music of the Arabs,* Portland, Oregon: Amadeus Press, 1996

Because the musical tradition of the Middle East was transmitted only aurally until early in the 20th century, and because our first documentation comes not from the written word but from recordings, it is, as Habib Touma notes, "difficult to ascertain the extent to which current living musical traditions are descended from early classical musical traditions." Access to many of the most important studies of Middle Eastern music is not easy unless one reads Arabic and French, compounding the problems for the English speaker.

An initial serious attempt to study this musical tradition was made by Henry Farmer, in *A History of Arabian Music* (1929), a work limited by the lack of available primary sources. His work continued with the convening of the first Congress of Arab Music in 1932, a scholarly meeting that sought to bring together Western musicologists and Middle Eastern musicians and scholars. That convention, the proceedings of which were published in Arabic and French, highlighted the need for primary source material, manuscripts that would broaden historical and cultural understanding of the musical traditions of the Arab world. In addition to the Arabs, the region of the Middle East encompasses other cultures, including Persian, Berber, Coptic, Hebrew, Turkish, and others. To some extent, each of these cultures has a distinct musical tradition, many of which are studied in detail only in dissertations covering very limited, specific musical repertoires.

SHILOAH (1994) provides an excellent introduction to the music of the Middle East. He studies both medieval Arabic writings and the living aural traditions of the 20th century and strives to make some links between the classical tradition and the music of today. Because, as he admits, "an analytical overview cannot possibly explore the multiple aspects of a topic of such magnitude," he includes an extensive bibliography. His historical view begins with pre-Islamic times, in which Middle Eastern music showed some similarities to that of surrounding regions. As Islam spread throughout the region, musical traditions blended and incorporated some of the characteristics of the wider territories. Shiloah describes the historical evolution of musical events and stylistic changes with respect to major historical and political situations. His last four chapters consider more specifically musical concepts: scales, modes, rhythms, forms, and genres.

TOUMA covers approximately the same subject matter as Shiloah, but after a brief historical overview, Touma emphasizes the technical aspects of the music. He describes the tonal system derived from the medieval writer al-Farabi, a system that divides the octave into 24 equal intervals, and contrasts that system with competing views of the tonal system proposed by other Arab theorists. Because all writings about aural traditions attempt to describe what already exists, differing experiences of the tradition result in differing descriptions. In Arab music, similar divergences occur in the documentation of standardized rhythmic patterns (*wazn*) and in genres that do not have regular rhythmic-temporal design. In his discussion of secular art music (*maqam, layali, mawwal,* and *taqsim* are among the most important), Touma details the interaction between vocal or instrumental soloists and supporting ensemble, particularly noting the way the parts participate in improvisation. His treatment of traditional instruments is complemented by excellent photographs. The religious music of non-Moslem Arabs has its roots in foreign musical cultures, and Touma therefore limits his comments to religious music of the Islamic Arabs, especially the reading of the Koran, and correctly points out that "[no] Moslem would ever use the word *singing* in reference to a recitation of the Koran." Touma's final chapters provide information on recent publications of Arabian music, a select discography, a useful glossary, and a bibliography.

DANIELSON's work concentrates on one Egyptian singer, Umm Kulthum, but the study is so well written, knowledgeable, and encompassing of many areas of culture and music that it may be the best available resource on popular (traditional) music of the Arab world. As Danielson asserts, "[Kulthum's] career, artistry, and dominant presence in the culture offer an impressive entree into Arab expressive culture." Danielson's research included every possible source, from personal music lessons to interviews with critics, journalists, writers, teachers, friends, and family of the artist, as well as discussions with shopkeepers, students, and others, almost all of whom acknowledge Kulthum as the most highly regarded of Arabic singers. Danielson's extensive documentation is supplemented by a companion videotape entitled *A Voice for Egypt.*

MANNICHE, a Danish Egyptologist, brings together research about music in Pharaonic times derived from representations of musicians and their instruments that survive through paintings, figurines, and relief and from existing instruments now residing in museums. Manniche gives a general survey and examines evidence pertaining to music in the courts of Nerfertiti and Akhenaten. She explores the antecedents of the divide between secular and sacred music, which for ancient Egypt manifested itself as a distinction between music for present life and music for the hereafter. Finally, Manniche draws some parallels between the ancient music and musical traditions and those that exist in modern times.

SAWA's study concentrates on the early period of Arabian music originating in the area that is now primarily Iraq and Iran. Treatises from the time document song texts, modes, rhythms, composers, and poets, as well as extensive descriptions and prescriptions for musical performance. Although music that has come down through the oral tradition has certainly been somewhat transformed, Sawa skillfully draws conclusions about similarities and differences between ancient and modern music.

AL FARUQI provides an glossary of terms relating to Middle Eastern music, useful for the casual inquirer or the scholar. Her work is most valuable as a supplementary resource, when context is confusing or inadequate.

JENKINS and OLSEN present pictures and descriptions of Islamic music and musical instruments. Stemming from museum exhibitions, their work is based on evidence similar to that used by Manniche but is derived from the later Islamic, as opposed to the Pharaonic, period.

An extensive resource and reference catalog for the serious scholar, SHILOAH (1979) provides additional links to the multitude of sources for writings on Arabic music that are found in many languages in libraries around the world.

MARTHA FARAHAT

MIDI

Anderton, Craig, *MIDI for Musicians*, New York, Amsco, 1986

Boom, Michael, *Music through MIDI: Using MIDI to Create Your Own Electronic Music System*, Redmond, Washington: Microsoft Press, 1987

Braut, Christian, *The Musician's Guide to MIDI*, translated by Heather Barbara Clifford, Paris: Sybex, 1994

Jacobs, Gabriel, and Panicos Georghiades, *Music and New Technology: The MIDI Connection*, London: Sigma Press, 1991

Rona, Jeffrey C., *MIDI: The Ins, Outs, and Thrus*, edited by Ronny Schiff, Milwaukee, Wisconsin: Leonard Books, 1987

Rothstein, Joseph, *MIDI: A Comprehensive Introduction*, Madison, Wisconsin: A-R Editions, and Oxford: Oxford University Press, 1992; 2nd edition, Madison, Wisconsin: A-R Editions, 1995

Rumsey, Francis, *MIDI Systems and Control*, London: Focal Press, 1990; 2nd edition, Oxford: Focal Press, 1994

Selfridge-Field, Eleanor, editor, *Beyond MIDI: The Handbook of Musical Codes*, Cambridge, Massachusetts: MIT Press, 1997

Turkel, Eric, *MIDI Gadgets*, London: Amsco, 1988

The Musical Instrument Digital Interface (MIDI) is a communications protocol and a set of specific messages that allow electronic devices to communicate with each other. These devices include, but are not limited to, computers, synthesizers, controller instruments, lights, mixers, and effects units. In its early days, MIDI was primarily used to control multiple sound sources from a single keyboard in live performance situations. Today it is most often used to control a synthesizer from a personal computer. A wide variety of MIDI software has been developed for use on personal computers. Most of this software allows extensive manipulation and editing of MIDI data in sequencing and music notation applications. Because MIDI was standardized and came into widespread use in the early 1980s, all the literature dealing with the subject is quite recent. Most of the books are written for users of MIDI and contain a great deal of advice for consumers who might be interested in purchasing their own equipment and setting up a MIDI studio.

In one of the earliest books to deal with the subject, ANDERTON provides a fairly sophisticated but easy-to-read discussion of the background and functions of MIDI. His approach is to describe a task that MIDI can perform, and then describe a product that can carry it out. The first chapter deals with an explanation of many aspects of MIDI, including serial transmission of data, modes, channels, cable pin configuration, synchronization, and clock rates. Although the information on products is outdated, the book includes a handy troubleshooting guide.

BOOM provides the most detailed account of the history of MIDI, listing the names of people and companies that developed it, and recounting how and why it was developed, when it was first tested, and how it has evolved. He describes a variety of uses for MIDI including live performances, work in schools and recording studios, and music in the home. One helpful feature of the book is its explanation of how MIDI information can be edited with a computer.

A great deal of information on the MIDI standard is contained in RONA, which is another of the earlier books on the subject. With pictures and a humorous approach, the author describes the technical details of MIDI for the novice. His account includes a discussion of why MIDI itself does not make sound, what happens inside a computer, and what kind of information is actually sent through the cables. The book also contains an excellent glossary.

TURKEL is characterized as a consumer guide for musicians interested in purchasing MIDI equipment. It is an excellent book with information about a lot of basic MIDI paraphernalia including keyboards, controllers, sync boxes, and effects units. Although some of the information on specific models is outdated, there is a helpful appendix listing names and addresses of manufacturers.

A book for those seeking technical information, RUMSEY provides information especially geared toward audio engineers and technically literate musicians and composers. This book is unique for the degree of sophistication with which it treats topics such as interface specifications and protocol, MIDI messages, samplers, mixer automation, and MIDI networks. The book does not refer to specific products because of the frequent rate of change in the manufacturing of MIDI devices.

JACOBS includes information on hooking up the components of a MIDI studio. His discussion of interfaces is somewhat outdated, but the book does contain information about software sequencing and notation programs. There is also a crash course in computer hardware for MIDI as well as information about microphones, sampling, analog synthesizers, mixers, and effects loops. Jacobs also addresses peripheral but practical issues such as keyboard specifications and buying equipment that has rack-mount capability.

An extremely serious and worthwhile book is ROTH-STEIN, which contains a wide variety of detailed and practical information. The book is not extremely technical, but it includes some enormously valuable advice about where to turn for help in all issues related to MIDI, including organizations, journals, user groups, online databases, and computer bulletin boards. There are sections on digital and analog sound, software, synchronization, programming for MIDI, and what is needed to build a studio. Copy protection and upgrade policies for software are also considered.

For highly technical information, BRAUT is an in-depth study of the MIDI standards and specifications. The beginning chapters review sound production and the development of synthesizers since the early 1980s. The specifications of the International MIDI Association are listed and the final chapters deal with MIDI-related software applications including sequencing, patch editors, and librarians. The book closes with a look at recent additions to the MIDI standard, such as general MIDI, and a list of MIDI identification codes for all major manufacturers. A MIDI implementation chart is also included, as well as test procedures and hidden functions for a variety of MIDI synthesizers.

One of the most recent additions to the body of writings on MIDI is SELFRIDGE-FIELD, a collection of essays describing various ways of representing music on a computer. Although the book is only partially about MIDI, it presents a series of proposed extensions to the MIDI standard that are intended to deal with the representation of many additional aspects of music, including expression, articulation, and enharmonic spellings. This significant collection of essays discusses diverse programming codes such as C Sound, Score, and Braille music notation. Information presented in this book relates to all the major computer operating systems, including DOS, Windows, Macintosh, OS2, NeXT, and UNIX.

CONNIE E. MAYFIELD

Milhaud, Darius 1892–1974

French composer

Collaer, Paul, *Darius Milhaud,* translated and edited by Jane Hohfeld Galante, San Francisco: San Francisco Press, 1988

Drake, Jeremy, *The Operas of Darius Milhaud,* New York: Garland, 1989

Milhaud, Darius, *My Happy Life,* translated by Donald Evans et al., London: Boyars, 1995

Nichols, Roger, *Conversations with Madeleine Milhaud,* London: Faber, 1996

Perloff, Nancy, *Art and the Everyday: Popular Entertainment and the Circle of Erik Satie,* Oxford: Clarendon Press, and New York: Oxford University Press, 1991

It is by now a commonplace to talk of neglect when reviewing Darius Milhaud's place in the English-language literature on French 20th-century music. His association with Jean Cocteau and Les Six in the 1920s was a decidedly mixed blessing, for it earned him—along with fellow composers Poulenc, Auric, Honegger, and Tailleferre—early fame that later transformed into enduring notoriety because of the frivolity and irreverence of his still well known scores, such as *La Création du monde, Salade,* and *Scaramouche.* Yet several books have recently appeared in English to dispel such a narrow view of this prolific composer who wrote some 450 works during a career that predated World War I and extended into the 1970s. The publication in English of Collaer's revised biography, a new translation of Milhaud's autobiography, and a collection of conversations with his wife have been joined by two recent studies focusing on diverse repertoires: the first on his operas and the second on the relationship of Milhaud's early works to the aesthetics of popular entertainment in Paris in the 1920s. Together, these volumes give a much more nuanced picture of an eclectic composer who was writing tonal music with full awareness of the work of Schoenberg and his followers, engaging with the popular musics of the New World as well as that of his native Provence, and actively negotiating his place in the musical heritage of France throughout much of the 20th century.

COLLAER, Milhaud's close friend for 50 years, wrote the first version of Milhaud's biography in 1939 and updated it in 1982 after the composer's death. This book is an excellent general introduction to Milhaud and his music. The preliminary chapters summarize Milhaud's life and works, providing an introduction to the composer's idiosyncratic use of melody, polyphony, and polytonality that will be useful for the nonspecialist. While Collaer presents a survey of nearly all of Milhaud's music, the author's strongest emphasis is on chamber music and the dramatic works; for the latter he gives informative concise summaries of the plot, musical style, first performance, and critical reactions, complete with copious musical examples of hard-to-find scores. The English edition does not rectify the original's weaknesses: there is no index, and quotes are frequently given without attribution. Translator Jane Galante, however, supplements Collaer's book with a valuable definitive catalog of works compiled by the composer's widow, Madeleine Milhaud; a discography of historical recordings featuring Milhaud as performer or conductor; and a bibliography of writings in English compiled by R. Wood Massi—many of the cited texts would otherwise be difficult to find.

DRAKE's study of Milhaud's operas is more specialized than Collaer's biography. The narrower subject, Milhaud's 16 operas from *La Brébis égarée* (1910–14) to *Saint-Louis, Roi de France* (1970), allows for more extensive musical analysis of each piece, and Drake incorporates useful information on manuscripts and sketches into his discussion when appropriate. His analyses convincingly refute Collaer's assertion that Milhaud's style "never varied from the day he first put pen to paper," for Drake discerns clear shifts in Milhaud's approach to texture, motivic development, and polytonality—which Drake prefers to call polymodality—during his 60 years of operatic composition. But Drake neglects questions of production and staging of the works, and nonspecialists may be frustrated by French quotations left untranslated and the

formal charts that take the place of musical examples. The book is best approached as a reference guide for each of Milhaud's operas.

MILHAUD initially wrote his memoirs before returning to France after his exile in the United States during World War II, and this first version appeared in an English translation by Donald Evans in 1952 as *Notes without Music*. Shortly before his death, Milhaud added seven chapters for a new complete autobiography, translated as *My Happy Life*. The valuable introduction by Christopher Palmer to the new English version highlights the contribution of this readable and entertaining book to studies of the composer: the memoir reveals his eclectic tastes, accomplishments as conductor and performer, and relationships to—and often strongly worded opinions of—colleagues as diverse as Satie and Stockhausen. Milhaud begins with the famous statement of his identity: "I am a Frenchman from Provence, and, by religion, a Jew." After an overview of his ancestry and childhood, fully half of the memoir concerns the fertile artistic activity of the interwar years in Europe. Milhaud provides details of his intense collaborations with writers and artists of his day, discussing both the genesis of his stage works and their often controversial productions across Europe and the United States, and thus fills the gaps in Drake's study. In a short chapter on "Music for the Theatre and the Cinema," the composer discusses works lost in the somewhat strict genre categories of Collaer's survey. The late chapters show Milhaud holding his ground in postwar aesthetic battles, refusing, for example, to let Hermann Scherchen replace sections of the original score with electronic music in the first complete performance of the *Orestie* trilogy in Berlin in 1963. A chronological list of works by Milhaud helps the reader follow the narrative when key dates are occasionally omitted from the text.

NICHOLS's 1991 conversations with Milhaud's widow were revised by her precisely to complement the information already available in *My Happy Life*. Like her husband, Madeleine Milhaud relates anecdotes about their families and childhood (they were first cousins), friends and colleagues, and performances in France and abroad. She briefly discusses her own career as well, as a teacher, actress, and recitant—often in her husband's own works. In addition, she offers unique insights into Milhaud's working methods and is often more forthright in her opinions of people and productions than he. The short book is illustrated by no fewer than 30 photographs, most not elsewhere in print.

PERLOFF focuses her study of Erik Satie and his circle on the composers' uses of popular music in their compositions between 1918 and 1924. While the first two chapters form an excellent introduction to the popular music and entertainment that captivated Paris after World War I, readers interested in Milhaud should turn to chapters 4 and 6. Chapter 4, "The Popular World of Cocteau,

Milhaud, Poulenc, and Auric," expands on Milhaud's own reminiscences as Perloff describes in detail the music Milhaud experienced in the Brazilian Carnival, the bars of Harlem, and the fairgrounds of Paris. In chapter 6, "Embracing a Popular Language," the author analyzes how these popular sounds made their way into Milhaud's works, including *Le Boeuf sur le toit,* a blend of play and revue for Fratelli and other clowns from the Cirque Médrano; *Le Train bleu,* a Diaghilev ballet with allusions to French operetta and Brazilian samba; and blues and jazz influences in the ballet *La Création du monde.* Perloff's parallel discussions of contemporaneous works by Satie, Poulenc, and Auric enriches our understanding of these well-known pieces by Milhaud while also exploring a rich tapestry of music at a time when American popular entertainment had its first decisive impact on European culture.

LESLIE SPROUT

Minimalism *see* Glass, Philip; Reich, Steve

Mode: Medieval

Apel, Willi, *Gregorian Chant,* London: Burns and Oates, and Bloomington: Indiana University Press, 1958

Bailey, Terence, *The Intonation Formulas of Western Chant,* Toronto: Pontifical Institute of Mediaeval Studies, 1974

Günther, Ursula, et al., editors, *Modality in the Music of the Fourteenth and Fifteenth Centuries,* Neuhausen-Stuttgart: American Institute of Musicology, Hänssler-Verlag, 1996

Hiley, David, *Western Plainchant: A Handbook,* Oxford: Clarendon Press, and New York: Oxford University Press, 1993

Hoppin, Richard, *Medieval Music,* New York: Norton, 1978

Reese, Gustave, *Music in the Middle Ages: With an Introduction on the Music of Ancient Times,* New York: Norton, 1940

Mode is a theoretical concept used by medieval theorists in their attempt to inventory and classify the chants of the Western church. *Modus, tonus,* and *tropus* were used interchangeably to refer to this concept. While much of the chant repertory fits well into a system of eight modes, there are individual chants that create problems with regard to their classification. Medieval modes are divided into four authentic (or principal) and four plagal (or secondary) modes. Theorists designate them by number (the odd-numbered ones are authentic, the even-numbered ones, plagal), by ancient Greek names (the authentics are Dorian, Phrygian, Lydian, and Mixolydian, respectively; in the case of plagal modes, the prefix *hypo* is added to these names), and by names associated with the Byzantine system of eight *echoi,* grouped in four *maneriae* (where

modes 1 and 2 form the *protus,* modes 3 and 4 are known as *deuterus,* modes 5 and 6 are *tritus,* and modes 7 and 8 are *tetrardus*). The criteria used in classifying modes as either authentic or plagal are the *finalis* (ending note—shared by modes 1 and 2, 3 and 4, and so on), *ambitus* (range or compass—higher in authentics, about a fourth lower in plagals) and *tenor* (a fifth above the finalis in authentics; a third below the tenor of the corresponding authentic in plagals). In modes 3 and 8, the tenor, which falls on B, is moved to C.

Closely related topics are solmization (the assigning of syllable names to notes, a procedure first associated with the Italian theorist Guido of Arezzo in the 11th century) and the hexachord system (the organization of the gamut into three six-note scales built on C [*naturale* or natural], G [*durum* or hard], and F [*molle* or soft, including B flat]).

REESE includes a chapter on the modal system of Gregorian chant, discussing mode in conjunction with Hebrew, Greek, Syrian, and Byzantine music. He stresses the differences between Western and Eastern (i.e., Byzantine) *maneriae* and uses the works of Boethius (based on Ptolemy), Cassiodorus, Isidore of Seville, Alcuin, Aurelian, Hermannus Contractus, and Aribo to expound on the adaptation of Greek nomenclature to the eight church modes. For Reese, the essence of a mode is contained in its "modal nucleus," comprised of the notes immediately above the final and various species of pentachords and tetrachords. He contends that the codification of various melody types/interval combinations that generate different modal scales was begun by the anonymous authors of *Alia musica.* Reese is a proponent of the pièn tone theory (applicable to Chinese music) in the analysis of Western chant; the major tenet of this theory is that, in each mode, there are two tones that are subordinate in nature to the other five. Reese maintains that solmization had been known to the ancient Greeks and was rediscovered in the 11th century, when it was attributed to Guido of Arezzo. Reese warns against referring to the tenor as "dominant" (which might cause confusion with the tonal system) and shows that different medieval writers believed that the tenor could fulfill the function of *finalis* (in that case, it is known as *confinalis, affinalis,* or *socialis*).

BAILEY addresses the question of the short melodic phrases included in medieval theoretical treatises and tonaries to "embody the essential characteristics of the eight classifications of chant." These melodic formulas are classified into three groups: Western *echemata*—or melodies on syllables such as *nonanoeane, noeagis,* etc., most likely of Eastern (Byzantine) origin, already known in the West in the ninth century and included in virtually all tonaries and treatises from the tenth century; textless characteristic melismas or *neumae,* introduced somewhat later than the *echemata*; and Latin mnemonic verses based on scriptural texts (*Primum querite regnum dei, Secundum autem simile est huic,* etc.), probably introduced in the mid-tenth century. Bailey presents a brief historical and theoretical essay on the concept and includes supporting evidence from contemporary texts. He maintains that such formulas had multiple functions: besides being of value in assigning a chant to a mode, these melodies were used as teaching aids in the West and served as preludes for the cantor in the East; some melodies were the basis for troping, and some provided the occasional tenor line for motets. Bailey provides examples of Byzantine and Western intonation formulas and discusses local variants. The comparative edition that follows this discussion is based on the study of 38 manuscripts and includes "only neumed sources which are clearly of the eleventh century or earlier," although the author has also consulted many manuscripts from the 12th century and later. The edition contains the Western *echemata*, the *neumae*, and the Latin formulas for each of the eight modes.

APEL's chapter on church modes is the classic exposition on the subject. He uses a historical approach and tonal analogies to explain modal characteristics and nomenclature, showing that the opening note or gesture of a chant plays an important role in its modal assignation. He dispels the myth that the authentics should be called Ambrosian and the plagals, Gregorian, and emphasizes the role of the Carolingian Renaissance in the process of classifying modes. In his discussion of modally significant melodic gestures, Apel differentiates between melody-type (which he does not find to be a relevant concept) and standard formula (a principle that he believes should be applied to special categories of chants). His table of modal distribution of chants and the accompanying commentary are based on a repertory of communion chants, which is used to study the relationship between mode as a theoretical construct and the melodies themselves. Apel discusses regular chants, chants with limited or excessive ranges, and transposed chants. He also examines modal ambiguity arising from the disagreement of modal assignations of chants found in different sources, such as theoretical treatises, tonaries, and liturgical books, and concludes that "what we have called 'modal ambiguity' could well be subsumed under the term 'transformation.'"

HOPPIN's textbook includes a chapter on the general characteristics of Gregorian chant. This chapter contains a systematic discussion of mode and related subjects (square notation, the solmization system proposed by Guido of Arezzo). Like Apel, Hoppin uses analogies (at times even referring to American popular tunes) to facilitate the understanding of classification and nomenclature. His definition of modes as "octave species characterized by different arrangements of whole and half steps around dominant and final notes" is also similar to Apel's concept. Hoppin describes the modes from the perspective of the listener and recommends practicing aural identification of modes based on listening to recorded chants. He speaks of an evolutionary development of the modal system and states that "it can be no accident that tonal organization went hand in hand with a concentration on the modes most nearly resembling our major and minor scales. What we are witnessing in fact is the beginning of a development that comes to full flower in the functional harmony of the eighteenth and nineteenth centuries."

HILEY devotes one chapter to the study of plainchant and early music theory and, like Apel, stresses the role of the Carolingian Renaissance in bringing together chant and chant theory. Hiley includes short biographies of relevant medieval theorists, along with descriptions of their works. He identifies a first phase in the development of modal theory, represented by people such as Aurelian of Reome, Johannes Scotus Eriugena, Remigius of Auxerre, and Hucbald of Saint-Amand, and treatises such as *Musica disciplina;* the second phase is represented by Regino of Prum and anonymous writings such as *Alia musica, Musica enchiriadis, Scolica enchiriadis,* and *Commemoratio brevis de tonis et psalmis modulandis.* The text contains tables of psalm-verse cadences and openings, comparative nomenclature, and chronological lists of writers on music theory.

GÜNTHER et al. is a collection of essays that were initially given as papers—in English and German—for the Fifth Neustift/Novacella Conference organized in 1993. While much of the material included is highly technical and many of the essays focus on the analysis of specific composers, works, and compositional techniques, some broader issues are also discussed. For example, one of the English-language essays discusses the modescape of medieval Europe (Shai Burstyn), and another assesses the relationship between consonance and mode (Keith Falconer). Burstyn coins the term *modescape,* which has obvious visual connotations, and proposes a realistic view of modal theories and their practical applications. The author asserts that microtones of Eastern origin were employed to a large extent in Western monophonic music and contends that some manuscripts reflect a transitional period in which both nondiastematic neumes and letter notation were used in "an attempt to capture microtonal appearances in the neumes." Burstyn also posits that the use of fixed-pitch notation on staff "must have led to the general acceptance of a diatonic melodic norm, and to the gradual disappearance of microtonal passages" and suggests that Western medieval theorists strove for the exclusion of these passages from the chant repertory—by stressing the move from melodic formula to scale, among other things. Falconer looks at music from a twofold perspective: that of the medieval theorist concerned with the mystical properties of number expressed in musical consonance, and that of the pre-14th-century musician whose practice was "to associate interval ratios chiefly with sounds produced by fixed-pitch instruments . . . and to encourage imitation of these intervals in vocal music," thus relating the concept of consonance to accurate tuning and good intonation. Falconer states that "consonances aided the transition from chant to polyphony and from there to mensural music."

This anthology also offers a detailed examination of several early 14th-century motets with middle-voice tenors, in which Virginia Newes summarizes recent trends among scholars dealing with the concept of late medieval mode. She demonstrates that Leo Treitler's study of Du Fay speaks of *tone system,* while Hendrik van der Werf (on troubadour and trouvère music) and Gilbert Reaney (on polyphonic songs of Machaut) independently propose the terms *medieval major* and *medieval minor,* and Jehoash Hirshberg employs the term *hexachord system* when referring to Machaut's music. Newes also shows that the *finalis* is "the only aspect of the modal system that seems to have been retained in the fourteenth-century concept of polyphonic tonality." Other contributions in this collection of essays pertain mostly to the music and music theory of the Renaissance. One of the best features of the volume is its large bibliography. Comprising some 450 titles, the list of works includes editions of scores and theoretical works, books, articles, Festschrift pieces, translations, transcriptions, and the like.

LUMINITA FLOREA

Mode: Renaissance

Everist, Mark, editor, *Music before 1600,* Oxford: Blackwell, 1992

Günther, Ursula, et al., editors, *Modality in the Music of the Fourteenth and Fifteenth Centuries,* Neuhausen-Stuttgart: American Institute of Musicology, Hänssler-Verlag, 1996

Lowinsky, Edward E., *Tonality and Atonality in Sixteenth-Century Music,* Berkeley: University of California Press, 1961

Meier, Bernhard, *The Modes of Classical Vocal Polyphony,* translated by Ellen S. Beebe, New York: Broude Brothers, 1988

Toft, Robert, *Aural Images of Lost Traditions: Sharps and Flats in the Sixteenth Century,* Toronto: University of Toronto Press, 1992

Scholars employ the term *mode* to represent the theoretical system within which Renaissance musicians operated. Many treatises describe the concepts of modality, and research on the subject divides into that which is contextual (remaining within the musical-theoretical culture of the period) and that which blends modern analytical approaches with Renaissance thought. The older view of modal music as some form of precursor to tonality has largely given way to the view of modes as a sophisticated system that served composers well. Nonetheless, some 16th-century theorists had difficulty in as-

signing individual pieces to specific modes, and this has led one scholar, Harold Powers, to doubt the existence of mode as a precompositional assumption (see especially his "Is Mode Real?" *Basler Jahrbuch für Historische Musikpraxis* 16 [1992]). However, the traditional eight-mode system was central to the activities of Renaissance composers, theorists, and performers, and no one has yet demonstrated convincingly that composers thought in a system other than the one described by their contemporaries. The literature is highly technical in nature and requires more than passing familiarity with Renaissance theoretical terminology.

MEIER's seminal study explores the relationship between modality and compositional practice in the 16th century. He considers both regular and irregular procedures with such thoroughness that one cannot help but be impressed by the comprehensiveness of the book. Meier first establishes the principles of modality in relation to the traditional eight-mode system of chant and then discusses various facets of modal procedure in polyphonic music (characteristic melodic patterns, cadences, as well as the authentic and plagal forms of the modes). The second part of the book treats mode as a means of word expression. For Meier, modal concepts determine compositional structure, especially in the choice of cadence notes and the shape of melodic lines, and throughout the study he meticulously links information in treatises to actual compositions.

LOWINSKY, on the other hand, writes of the "crisis of modality in sixteenth-century music." He concedes that most compositions were conceived within the traditional eight-mode system, but *frottole, villancicos, balletti,* lute ayres, and dances prefigure tonal or even atonal thinking. He describes the highly chromatic music of the second half of the 16th century as "triadic atonality" because it cannot be understood in terms of the older modality or the emerging tonality. The crisis of modality was caused by *musica ficta* (unnotated sharping or flatting of a pitch), which destroyed the purity of the modes, especially at cadences, and it is at these cadential points that the "cradle of tonality" can be found.

TOFT argues that the addition of unnotated sharps and flats and the concept of mode were interdependent in the 16th century. Modern notions of modal purity may have to be adjusted if one is willing to accept the idea of sharps and flats actually creating the sense of mode for Renaissance musicians rather than violating it. He relates hexachords to modes, introducing the concept of oscillation into the discussion of mode, and demonstrates in relation to several 16th-century works that no single concept of polyphonic modality existed for practicing musicians. Indeed, the notion of what constituted normal modal procedure varied widely among Renaissance performers.

GÜNTHER has edited a collection of fascinating essays addressing subjects as varied as modal transposition, species and mixture, the sound of the modes, and modal cadences. For the most part, the discussions remain within the musical-theoretical culture of the period. In the collection edited by EVERIST, some authors discuss specific works from both historical and modern perspectives. The composers treated range from Guillaume de Machaut to William Byrd, and reductive analytical graphs inform some of the writing.

ROBERT TOFT

Mode: Non-Western

Becker, Judith O., *Traditional Music in Modern Java: Gamelan in a Changing Society,* Honolulu: University Press of Hawaii, 1980

Farhat, Hormoz, *The Dastgah Concept in Persian Music,* Cambridge: Cambridge University Press, 1990

Garfias, Robert, *Music of a Thousand Autumns: The Togaku Style of Japanese Court Music,* Berkeley: University of California Press, 1975

Hood, Mantle, *The Nuclear Theme as a Determinant of Patet in Javanese Music,* Groningen: Wolters, 1954; reprint, New York: Da Capo Press, 1977

Jairazbhoy, N.A., *The Ragas of North Indian Music: Their Structure and Evolution,* London: Faber, and Middletown, Connecticut: Wesleyan University Press, 1971

Kaufmann, Walter, *The Ragas of North India,* Bloomington: Indiana University Press, 1968

————, *The Ragas of South India: A Catalogue of Scalar Material,* Bloomington: Indiana University Press, 1976

Kunst, Jaap, *Music in Java: Its History, Its Theory, and Its Technique,* 2 vols., translated by Emile van Loo, The Hague: Nijhoff, 1949; 3rd enlarged edition, edited by Ernst L. Heins, 1973

Malm, William P., *Music Cultures of the Pacific, the Near East, and Asia,* Englewood Cliffs, New Jersey: Prentice Hall, 1967; 3rd edition, Upper Saddle River, New Jersey: Prentice Hall, 1996

Nettl, Bruno, *The Radif of Persian Music: Studies of Structure and Cultural Context,* Champaign, Illinois: Elephant and Cat, 1987; revised edition, 1992

Pian, Rulan Chao, *Sonq Dynasty Musical Sources and Their Interpretation,* Cambridge, Massachusetts: Harvard University Press, 1967

Shiloah, Amnon, *The Dimension of Music in Islamic and Jewish Culture,* Aldershot: Variorum, 1993

Signell, Karl L., *Makam: Modal Practice in Turkish Art Music,* Seattle, Washington: Asian Music, 1977

Walton, Susan Pratt, *Mode in Javanese Music,* Athens: Ohio University Center for International Studies, 1987

Widdess, Richard, *The Ragas of Early Indian Music: Modes, Melodies, and Musical Notations from the Gupta Period to c. 1250,* Oxford: Clarendon Press, and New York: Oxford University Press, 1995

Wright, Owen, *The Modal System of Arab and Persian Music, A.D. 1250–1300,* Oxford: Oxford University Press, 1978

Zonis, Ella, *Classical Persian Music: An Introduction,* Cambridge, Massachusetts: Harvard University Press, 1973

In non-Western music, *mode* is a musicological concept for designating classes of melodies. More specific than a scale but less specific than a melody, mode implies both hierarchical relationships among pitches and particular arrangements of pitches in succession.

In East Asian and Southeast Asian musics, modal entities lie more toward the scale (or key, in a Western sense) end of the spectrum. The Chinese ideogram for *diaw-dieu-cho* represents mode throughout East Asia. *Diaw* is the Chinese term for mode. Chinese modes are, in essence, anhemitonic pentatonic octave species comprised of pitches from a set of 12 theoretically generated pitch classes. Each pentatonic scale has its own principal note.

Choshi is the Japanese term for mode in the *togaku* style of *gagaku* (Japanese court music). Like the Chinese modes from which they originate, Japanese modes are, in essence, anhemitonic pentatonic octave species, although in *choshi,* two of the scale degrees have alternative notes that may be substituted. In addition to pitch content, *choshi* are differentiated from each other by their tonic pitch, basic melodic shapes, distinct ranges, and characteristic accompanimental figures and instrumental timbres.

Dieu is the Vietnamese term for mode. There are two main modal systems, *bac* and *nam. Dieu bac* uses an anhemitonic pentatonic scale with two passing notes; *dieu nam* uses an irregular pentatonic scale, a tritonal scalar structure, or a scale with four main notes. In addition to the scalar differences, the two modes are distinguished by ornamentation, range of tempo, and expression or extramusical association.

In central Javanese *gamelan* music, there are two basic scales—the anhemitonic pentatonic *slendro* and the heptatonic *pelog.* For each scale there are three *patet,* the Javanese term for mode. The word *patet* means to curb, restrain, or limit. Melodic shapes, cadential formulas, and pitches both used and avoided as gong tones contribute to *patet* recognition.

In West Asian and South Asian musics, melodic aspects are at least as significant as scale composition in defining modal entities. The Arabic word *maqam,* which means place, is the general term for mode in Islamic West Asia. The word *naghmah,* which means tune and voice, is also used. The Persian term is *gusheh.* The scale is comprised of seven degrees from the general collection of 14 named pitches within one octave. Melodic units or motivic tags, cadential formulae, and final tones contribute to the identity of each mode.

The Sanskrit word *raga*—which means emotion, affect, or passion—is the South Asian term for mode. Above all, ragas are identified musically by clearly defined melodic units or motivic tags. These characteristic motives restrict how a performer may approach or leave a note or whether a note is omitted, resulting in both an ascending and descending form of the scale. The basic scale in Indian music is comprised of 7 notes out of 12 within an octave, each named according to its vocal solmization syllable. The note names identify the scale degree but do not imply a fixed pitch. Every raga has a tonic, called *sa*, the ground tone on which the scale begins. *Sa* has no octave equivalent. Further, one performer's pitch frequency for *sa* will be the same for each modal entity. The note *sa* therefore functions as the tonic of both a single mode and a system of modes. Finally, extramusical associations, such as times of the day or seasons, play a role in the identity of a raga.

MALM offers a general introduction to the musical cultures of Asia and Oceania and uses a variety of approaches to the subject: anthropological, historical, organological, and musical. For those musics in which the musicological concept of mode is operational, both musical manifestation and theoretical explanation contribute to the delineation of modal entities. Musical examples are transcribed into Western musical notation, allowing musically literate nonspecialists to grasp the music-theoretical essence of modal constructs. A cassette recording of many of the musical examples accompanies the text and compensates for much of the inevitable distortion and limitation of transcription of non-Western musics into Western notation.

PIAN includes chapters on mode in Chinese music. Using Sonq dynasty treatises as sources, the author describes the theoretical construction of classical and popular modes. Three tables present lists of modes in Western notation: the 84 theoretically possible classical modes as listed in two treatises from the close of the Sonq; the 28 popular modes as listed by a northern Sonq writer; and the 60 modes as generated by a radically different interpretation of modal construction and listed in one Sonq source. Discussion of the development and use of modes in the Sonq period follows.

Mode in Japanese court music is treated extensively in GARFIAS, with chapters dedicated to both theoretical and practical aspects. Several tables showing mode names, tone names, and pitch content support discussions of the three *togaku* modal systems and their relationships with the underlying Chinese theoretical system. Concerning modal practice, Garfias explains the tonal adjustments made for each *choshi* in *fue* and *hichiriki* technique and combines Western notation with a type of simple line graph (borrowed from the traditional notation of vocal music) to illustrate unnotated microtonal ornaments.

KUNST offers the most comprehensive source on Javanese music and dedicates nearly 100 pages to an intensive investigation of tone and scale systems. Although his theories of Javanese instrumental tunings have been dismissed, the author's inquiries into the origins and dissemination of *pelog* and *slendro,* as well as detailed descriptions of the *patet,* remain a most valuable source for students and scholars alike. Unlike Kunst, who considers the central tone of the basic scale as central in *patet* identity, HOOD proposes a nuclear theme (a principal melody) with specific cadential formulae playable on single-octave metallophones as integral in *patet* recognition. BECKER corroborates the melodic pattern (or melodic formula) as the most important aspect of *patet* and finds three interlocking factors to be the basis of *patet* recognition: the melodic pattern, formula, or contour; the pitch level of the pattern; and the position of the pattern within the formal structure of the piece. Further, she explains some of the extramusical associations of *patet,* such as time and mood, and links the emphasis on the range aspect of *patet* with the *dhalang,* the singer, actor, and priest of Javanese theater. Focusing on *sindhènan,* solo female singing associated with the *gamelan,* WALTON argues that there are two systems of *patet* operating simultaneously in the *gamelan,* one for vocal and vocally oriented melodies and one for instrumental melodies.

SHILOAH offers the best short introduction to the historical development of the Arabic concept of mode in a chapter devoted entirely to the subject. Following a critique of contemporary scholarship and a discussion of several treatises from the 13th through the 18th centuries, Shiloah compares the modal system described in theoretical treatises with the modal system of modern practice. WRIGHT, on the other hand, limits his study to 13th-century Arab and Persian musical theory. An exhaustive analysis of intervals, scales, and modes described by the systematist theorists supports the hypothesis that during this period Arab and Persian art music shared the same modal system. SIGNELL considers modal theory and practice in Turkish art music, focusing primarily on the Turkish *makam* system as a theoretical construct. ZONIS, FARHAT, and NETTL each consider modal theory and practice in Persian art music. All three present extensive tables, figures, and musical examples in Western notation to aid the reader in the analysis of intervallic, scalar, and motivic aspects of mode. In addition to their considerations of modal theory, Nettl analyzes a great many performances; Zonis delineates a theory of practice; and Farhat examines the contemporary tradition of the 12 *dastgah*s in composed pieces as well as the *radif.*

Dedicating one book each to Hindustani and Carnatic music, Kaufmann offers exhaustive descriptions of the scalar, melodic, and extramusical associations of North Indian and South Indian ragas. Following a thorough discussion of the term *raga* and a survey of important theoretical works, KAUFMANN (1968) resists generalization and delineates copious subtle musical details of hundreds of North Indian ragas. In discussing South Indian ragas, KAUFMANN (1976) focuses on scalar configuration in a survey of the 72 *melas* and their *janya* ragas. JAIRAZBHOY first explains the fundamental principles of raga structure and then explores subconscious processes that he hypothesizes have shaped North Indian ragas over many centuries. Limiting his study to written sources from the early first millennium through ca. 1250, WIDDESS traces general characteristics of modern ragas back to this period, revealing features of early Indian music present in contemporary Indian musical practice.

MELANIE LOWE

Monody

Aldrich, Putnam, *Rhythm in Seventeenth-Century Italian Monody, with an Anthology of Songs and Dances,* New York: Norton, 1966

Bianconi, Lorenzo, *Music in the Seventeenth Century,* translated by David Bryant, Cambridge: Cambridge University Press, 1987

Carter, Tim, *Jacopo Peri, 1561–1633: His Life and Works,* 2 vols., New York: Garland, 1989

————, *Music in Late Renaissance and Early Baroque Italy,* London: Batsford, and Portland, Oregon: Amadeus Press, 1992

Fenlon, Iain, and Tim Carter, editors, *Con che soavità: Studies in Italian Opera, Song and Dance, 1580–1740,* Oxford: Clarendon Press, and New York: Oxford University Press, 1995

Joyce, John J., *The Monodies of Sigismondo d'India,* Ann Arbor, Michigan: UMI Research Press, 1981

Maniates, Maria Rika, *Mannerism in Italian Music and Culture: 1530–1630,* Chapel Hill: University of North Carolina Press, and Manchester: Manchester University Press, 1979

Palisca, Claude, *Studies in the History of Italian Music and Music Theory,* Oxford: Clarendon Press, and New York: Oxford University Press, 1994

Tomlinson, Gary A., editor, *Italian Secular Song, 1606–1636: A Seven-Volume Reprint Collection,* New York: Garland, 1986

Monody, from the Greek words *mono* (one) and *oide* (song), refers in principle to all vocal music written for a single voice, but in general usage, it denotes mainly an Italian repertoire for voice and lute or keyboard accompaniment dating from the early 17th century. Various antecedents of this repertoire are found in the 16th century (intabulations of polyphonic madrigals, among others), but the genre flourished during the years between 1600 and 1635, when more than 200 monody collections were printed. Stylistically, this lyrical song repertoire is related to early opera and can be divided into two basic types: the aria, which has a fixed metric pattern and is often strophic in structure, and the solo madrigal, which is more freely structured and frequently incorporates recitative elements.

TOMLINSON is a comprehensive anthology of many of the most important monody collections. The seven-volume work reprints selections from 48 monody books by 41 different composers and one collection by different authors. The volumes are arranged according to geographical regions: Florence, Pisa and Siena, Rome and Naples, Northwestern Italy, Eastern Po Valley, and Venice (which is covered in two volumes). The extremely informative introductions provide biographical and analytical information on the mostly very little known composers and their music.

PALISCA collects this eminent scholar's most influential journal articles. Essays relevant to the study of monody include: "Vincenzo Galilei and Some Links Between 'Pseudo-Monody' and Monody," which lays to rest a spurious earlier distinction between those two notions; "Vincenzo Galilei's Arrangements for Voice and Lute," which relates monodic theory and practice, with the surviving music printed in the appendix; and "Peri and the Theory of Recitative," which evaluates contemporaneous descriptions and analyzes musical examples.

BIANCONI's comprehensive coverage of 17th-century music presents several chapters on monody. The author stresses the influence of such poets as Giambattista Marino and Gabriello Chiabrera on musical style and surveys the music of Sigismondo d'India, one of the finest composers of monody. Poetry and music are placed in a broad historical, political, and economic context. Separate chapters are devoted to the history of music printing and publishing and the social condition of the musician.

MANIATES includes an important chapter on "The Concerted Madrigal and Monody." The discussion of monody is mainly limited to the analysis of selected examples that are related to the concept of mannerism, which the author traces through a century of Italian literary, musical, and art history.

FENLON and CARTER present a collection of essays dedicated to Nigel Fortune, a pioneer in the study of monody. The essays of Barbara Russano Hanning and William V. Porter are particularly relevant to this topic, as Hanning analyzes depictions of singers and lute players in contemporaneous Italian painting and Porter takes his cue from Monteverdi's famous "Lamento d'Arianna," investigating monodies by various composers that were influenced by that famous operatic excerpt. Glenn Watkins compares several of d'India's works—both monodic to polyphonic—to treatments of the same lyrics by other composers. Giovanni Rovetta, whose work is represented in the seventh volume of Tomlinson's anthology, is the subject of a special study by John Whenham.

CARTER (1989) is a two-volume study of Jacopo Peri, whose fame rests on his operas but who also published an important collection of monodies. The book offers as complete a biography as the sources allow, plus an analysis and a reprint of Peri's music. CARTER (1992) covers monody in one chapter, evaluating in particular selected works by Caccini, Rasi, and d'India.

JOYCE is a monograph on d'India, who published five volumes of monodies (some of which also contain duets), in addition to polyphonic madrigals, villanellas, and sacred motets. Joyce discusses the melodic, harmonic, structural, and typological characteristics of the songs found in the monody books and relates the composer to the much-debated trend of mannerism. The appendix contains a representative sample of d'India's monodic output.

ALDRICH is still the only book-length study devoted exclusively to the performance of the monodic repertoire. Covering only the aria-type songs, the book describes the particularities of monodic notation, which was created during the transition from mensural notation to the modern system. Aldrich explains the relationships between the most frequent rhythmic patterns found in the songs and their corresponding dance movements (ballo, gagliarda, corrente), on the one hand, and poetic meters (five-, six-, seven- and eight-syllable lines), on the other. A short anthology of pieces is appended to the volume.

PETER LAKI

Monteverdi, Claudio 1567–1643

Italian composer

1. Biography

Fabbri, Paolo, *Monteverdi*, translated by Tim Carter, Cambridge: Cambridge University Press, 1994

Monteverdi, Claudio, *Lettere*, edited by Èva Lax, Florence: Olschki, 1994

———, *Lettere, dediche e prefazioni*, edited by Dominico De Paoli, Rome: De Santis, 1973

———, *The Letters of Claudio Monteverdi*, edited and translated by Denis Stevens, Oxford: Clarendon Press, and New York: Oxford University Press, 1980; revised edition, 1995

Prunières, Henry, *Monteverdi: His Life and Work*, translated by Marie D. Mackie, London: Dent, 1926; reprint, Westport, Connecticut: Greenwood Press, 1974

Schrade, Leo, *Monteverdi, Creator of Modern Music*, New York: Norton, and London: Gollancz, 1950

Monteverdi's biography poses relatively few problems or controversies. History has preserved a body of letters and documents from which to construct the basic outlines of his life and career, and with the exception of a few incidents—such as the circumstances and date of his hiring at the Mantuan court, the exact events surrounding his departure from there, and the lack of information re-

garding his visit to Rome as he was severing his ties to Mantua, his attempts to seek a position at the papal court, and the role that the *Vespro della Beata Virgine* (1610) may have played in that attempt—his biography has not generated a great deal of scholarly debate. Much of the information contained in both documents and letters pertains to his professional rather than personal life. That information illuminates the circumstances by which a composer of his stature conducted his business and is at times revealing of his aesthetic judgment and values, but it is lacking in the human dimension. We know little, for example, about his reactions to such key events as the death of the singer for whom he had intended the part of Arianna, his pupil Caterina Martinelli, or that of his wife Claudia Cattanei, or the plague that ravaged Venice in the early 1630s. But the difference in working conditions between Venice and Mantua is clearly shown by the composer's perspective in the letters, as is Monteverdi's continued contact with Mantua as composer of dramatic works. The documents also tell us about the relationship between the *maestro di cappella* of St. Mark's and his singers, as well as his relationship to his superiors. Finally, it must be noted that, due to the extensive body of surviving correspondence, Monteverdi's biography emerges as considerably more three-dimensional than those of the vast majority of his contemporaries.

All the major biographies of Monteverdi belong to the life-and-works genre. The principal differences among them result from the gradual accretion of information over the course of the past century and from the quantity of documents and details presented by each author rather than from significantly divergent views about Monteverdi's life. Where they differ, Monteverdi's biographers do so primarily as a result of their particular approaches to the music rather than to the life itself.

PRUNIÈRES emphasizes the progressive aspects of Monteverdi's output, focusing particularly on his dramatic works; in doing so, the author establishes a powerful and lasting view of the composer's historical position. Monteverdi's life until age 40 and the discussion of the first five books of his madrigals and the *Scherzi musicali* (1607) occupy a mere 50 pages, about the same amount of space devoted to *Orfeo*, *Arianna*, and Monteverdi's last years at Mantua, which total approximately five years. Despite his one-sided view of the composer, however, Prunières marks an important point in Monteverdi historiography, establishing a systematic approach to the documents of the composer's life as well as to his works: in the appendices, for example, the author catalogs all the known correspondence, translates significant letters, and lists all known published and unpublished compositions.

As his title implies, SCHRADE expands on Prunières's view of Monteverdi as pioneer of baroque genres and aesthetics. In the wake of Einstein's *The Italian Madrigal* (1949), however, Schrade devotes considerable space to the Renaissance background of the composer's technique, even if the historical context is viewed as a burden against which Monteverdi must struggle for his independence. In addition, Schrade gives greater space to Monteverdi as the *maestro di cappella* at St. Mark's. Thus, Schrade's creator of modern music emerges as an increasingly multifaceted figure set in a broader context—intellectual, historical, and biographical—than previous scholars had emphasized.

The most recent biographical study, FABBRI's volume makes by far the most comprehensive presentation of materials pertaining to the composer's life and professional activities. Each stage in Monteverdi's life and career is documented in great detail, often with extensive excerpts from contemporaneous sources; Fabbri relies heavily on documents original both to Monteverdi himself (for example, his letters) and to the period (such as contemporary reactions to his music). The range of scholarship is extremely wide, from treatments of historical details to references to literary theory, poetry, and aesthetics, as well as studies of musical sources. Thus, not only are the composer and his work the objects of a detailed portrait, but so are his life and that of the cities and courts that employed him. At the same time, however, Fabbri's monograph is the most neutral interpretation of the composer's career in broad historical terms. It is no accident that the book is without a subtitle: all aspects of Monteverdi's life and career are treated in an even-handed manner, so that the composer emerges as both a person living at the end of the Renaissance and a creator of modern music.

The editions of the letters reflect the incremental improvement of scholarship since the early 1970s. In MONTEVERDI (1973), Dominico De Paoli presents a fairly rough edition of the original Italian texts with minimal commentary and no translations. MONTEVERDI (1980) offers extensively annotated translations with introductions to each letter; editor and translator Denis Stevens does not, however, reproduce the originals. His annotations provide an invaluable background to the works and the historical figures to which the letters refer; however, the reader should consult the published reviews of this book before accepting the editor's suggestions for interpreting the correspondence. Finally, Èva Lax offers a new edition of the original Italian in MONTEVERDI (1994); editorial errors identified by Stevens in De Paoli's edition are corrected by Lax. Hers is now the standard edition.

MASSIMO OSSI

2. Madrigals

Arnold, Denis, and Nigel Fortune, editors, *The New Monteverdi Companion*, London: Faber, 1985

Besutti, Paola, et al., editors, *Claudio Monteverdi: Studi e prospettive*, Florence: Olschki, 1998

Chafe, Eric, *Monteverdi's Tonal Language*, New York: Schirmer Books, 1992

Einstein, Alfred, *The Italian Madrigal*, 3 vols., translated by Alexander H. Krappe et al., Princeton, New Jersey: Princeton University Press, 1949

Fenlon, Iain, and Peter N. Miller, *The Song of the Soul: Understanding Poppea*, London: Royal Musical Association, 1992

Leopold, Silke, *Monteverdi: Music in Transition*, translated by Anne Smith, Oxford: Clarendon Press, 1990

Leopold, Silke, and Joachim Steinheuer, editors, *Claudio Monteverdi und die Folgen*, Kassel: Bärenreiter, 1998

Monterosso, Raffaello, editor, *Claudio Monteverdi e il suo tempo*, Verona: Valdonega, 1969

Prunières, Henry, *Monteverdi: His Life and Work*, translated by Marie D. Mackie, London: Dent, 1926; reprint, Westport, Connecticut: Greenwood Press, 1974

Schrade, Leo, *Monteverdi, Creator of Modern Music*, New York: Norton, and London: Gollancz, 1950

Tomlinson, Gary, *Monteverdi and the End of the Renaissance*, Berkeley: University of California Press, and Oxford: Clarendon Press, 1987

Most books about Monteverdi are life-and-works surveys. In the biographical overviews, the music is treated in varying degrees of detail, ranging from the interpretative approaches of Prunières and Schrade, who seek evidence of forward-looking trends in the music, to the extensive but nonanalytical descriptions found in Paolo Fabbri's *Monteverdi* (translated by Tim Carter, Cambridge: Cambridge University Press, 1994). Because his career spanned more than half a century and bridged the transition from late Renaissance to early baroque aesthetics, Monteverdi's output has always been approached from opposing historiographic perspectives: thus, Schrade regards him as the creator of modern music while Tomlinson identifies him with the end of the Renaissance. Both views yield valuable insights about his music, but they come into conflict when interpreting those works that follow the fifth book of madrigals (1605). These pieces are viewed by some scholars as forerunners of baroque developments (as in Schrade's view of the *Scherzi musicali* of 1607, which foreshadow trio sonata and ritornello principles, and in Prunières's emphasis on the later books). Other scholars contend, however, that in these works Monteverdi abandoned the high aesthetic principles of the Renaissance in favor of a more superficial rhetoric of Marinist origin, which was clever (even brilliant) but ultimately hollow, a view that can be traced to Einstein's *The Italian Madrigal*.

PRUNIÈRES views Monteverdi as an entirely progressive composer, emphasizing his secular and dramatic output. The author treats both the early biography and first five books of madrigals in a cursory manner; only when he reaches the *Scherzi musicali* of 1607 does Prunières focus on the music, and then to identify it as having strong

French origins. Similarly, he relegates Monteverdi's tenure at St. Mark's in Venice, together with his sacred music, to a secondary role. Prunières does not give any of the church music collections, including the 1610 *Vespro della Beata Virgine,* separate treatment, and the entire topic is quickly dismissed. Conversely, the madrigals after the sixth book, Monteverdi's dramatic compositions between 1615 and 1638, and the last operas constitute the central core of the book. In keeping with his view of Monteverdi as an innovator, Prunières portrays the composer as forging a developmental path from the madrigal to the cantata, contending that the *Combattimento di Tancredi e Clorinda* heralds the arrival of the latter genre in the eighth book (1638).

In contrast to Prunières's emphasis on the later works, EINSTEIN makes short shrift of Monteverdi's works after the fifth book of madrigals. Despite being a broad survey of the entire genre, this study plays an important role (equal to that of Prunières) in defining the main trends of Monteverdi criticism. Approaching the composer not as a predecessor of the baroque but from the point of view of Renaissance aesthetics, the author regards the the first five books as crowning achievements of the 16th century and fully grounds Monteverdi in the *prima prattica.* In doing so, Einstein balances Prunières's perspective, but he also passes a negative judgment on the composer's later publications that still fuels much of the critical debate swirling around those works.

SCHRADE's study does much to establish a more evenhanded view of Monteverdi's production, although it clearly emphasizes the composer's role as an innovator rather than as a Renaissance master gone astray in the aesthetic turmoil of the new century. Well over half the book is devoted to the Renaissance background from which Monteverdi emerged and to his madrigals through the fifth book, although the author's treatment of the early works as a struggle with the past resembles the heroic construction of Beethoven's biography, down to the division of the composer's life into three main periods (the struggle, the establishment of the new, and the fulfillment of his maturity). Schrade's historiography represents a refinement of the basic themes laid out by Prunières, and his view is also considerably richer than that of any of his predecessors: he fills in the outlines of the composer's life with a great deal of contextual material, and even Monteverdi's role as a church musician is given more space than granted in previous biographies.

Writing some 35 years after Schrade and Einstein, TOMLINSON returns to some of the themes sounded in Einstein's volume. The early chapters on the madrigals and the poetry up to 1614 trace Monteverdi's increasingly refined treatment of the classic Renaissance madrigal, particularly in the economical settings of Guarini's epigrammatic poetry; in these chapters, as in much of the book, Tomlinson is indebted to Pirrotta's seminal work on Monteverdi's poetic choices. For Tomlinson, the modern works of the sixth, seventh, and eighth books, however, suffer in comparison with their Renaissance predecessors. After the aesthetic trough of the 1610s through the 1630s, the author argues that the quality of Monteverdi's works crested once again in the late operas, which fulfill the promise of his Renaissance masterpieces.

Prunières, Schrade, Fabbri, Tomlinson, and Chafe all take a chronological approach to Monteverdi's published works; LEOPOLD favors a genre- and technique-determined organization. As her title makes clear, the author emphasizes the progressive aspects of Monteverdi's works, focusing on new techniques (e.g., ostinatos), new genres (the lament), and poetic fashion (pastoral themes). She also places the composer in his social context and devotes an entire chapter to framing one of the thorniest problems in Monteverdi scholarship, the dating of individual works. In highlighting the question of chronology, she precedes Tomlinson, who proposes style-based dates for individual madrigals in the third (1592), fourth (1603), and fifth (1605) books.

The view of Monteverdi as a transitional figure is also evident in CHAFE's study, which focuses on the emergence of tonal principles in Monteverdi's opus. The author traces in detail the progressive shift from modal to tonal harmonic practices, beginning with the fourth book and culminating in the complex use of tonal areas as the underpinning for the dramatic structures of *Ulisse* (1640) and *Poppea* (1642). Chafe is the only commentator to develop a consistent theoretical methodology based on a hierarchy of tonal areas through which a composition can move and to interpret both localized harmonic events and large-scale trends in terms of that hierarchy.

The divergent interpretations of Monteverdi's career are generally reconciled in discussions focusing on *L'Incoronazione di Poppea.* The composer's last opera is unanimously regarded as the crowning example of his mature art, brilliantly drawing together Renaissance attention to the details of the text with the composer's interest in characterization and drama. Chafe argues for the coherence of the opera's tonal architecture, which functions as the allegorical subtext to the libretto. FENLON and MILLER put forth an interpretation, heavily influenced by Ellen Rosand's work, of *Poppea* as expressing the ideals of the Venetian *Accademia degli Incogniti* and provide an introduction to the neo-Stoic and Tacitist background of the academy's ideas. This line of interpretation goes a long way toward elucidating the moral ambiguity of the libretto.

Four volumes of essays gather important contributions to a variety of problems in Monteverdi scholarship. ARNOLD and FORTUNE is an entry-level collection surveying general aspects of the composer's output. MONTEROSSO brings together a wide-ranging sample of problems in Monteverdi scholarship from a conference held on the quatercentenary of his birth (1967).

BESUTTI et al. update the picture to the 350th anniversary of the composer's death (1993), also collecting papers presented at an international conference. LEOPOLD and STEINHEUER, which contains papers from another conference proceeding, focuses on Monteverdi and his influence and reception abroad.

MASSIMO OSSI

3. Operas

Arnold, Denis, *Monteverdi,* London: Dent, and New York: Farrar, Straus, 1969; 3rd edition, revised by Tim Carter, London: Dent, 1990

Arnold, Denis, and Nigel Fortune, editors, *The New Monteverdi Companion*, London: Faber, 1985

Donington, Robert, *The Rise of Opera,* New York: Scribner, and London: Faber, 1981

Fabbri, Paolo, *Monteverdi,* translated by Tim Carter, Cambridge: Cambridge University Press, 1994

Pirrotta, Nino, *Music and Culture in Italy from the Middle Ages to the Baroque: A Collection of Essays,* Cambridge, Massachusetts: Harvard University Press, 1984

Schrade, Leo, *Monteverdi: Creator of Modern Music,* New York: Norton, and London: Gollancz, 1950

Tomlinson, Gary, *Monteverdi and the End of the Renaissance,* Berkeley: University of California Press, and Oxford: Clarendon Press, 1987

Whenham, John, editor, *Claudio Monteverdi: Orfeo,* Cambridge: Cambridge University Press, 1986

Although forgotten for about two and a half centuries, the music of Claudio Monteverdi, including the operas, has made an astonishing comeback so that performances of *Orfeo* and *L'incoronazione di Poppea* are relatively frequent today. This development was spearheaded by the enormous amount of research on the composer and his operas conducted throughout the 20th century. At the century's beginning, pioneers such as Vogel, Heuss, Goldschmidt, Kretzschmar, Parry, and Prunières produced both biographies and specialized studies on aspects of these operas. Eitner's edition of the *Orfeo* score, although not suitable for performance, was published as early as 1881. Prunières in particular devotes a substantial discussion to the stage works for Mantua as well as Venice in the context of the composer's early biography (*Monteverdi: His Life and Work,* translated by Marie Mackie, 1926).

A wave of Monteverdi studies appeared in midcentury with books on life and works by Schrade, Redlich, Sartori, and the first thorough study of the stage works by Abert (*Claudio Monteverdi und das musikalische Drama,* 1954). Subsequently, most specialized studies appeared as scholarly articles, for example, on Monteverdi's opera orchestra (Westrup, Beat, and

Glover), on his *Orfeo* (Pirrotta, Donington, Fenlon, Whenham, and others), on the recitative in this opera (R. Muller), on aspects of *Il ritorno d'Ulisse in patria* and *L'incoronazione di Poppea* (Rosand), and on source problems of these two works (Osthoff). Although every historical survey and every opera history devotes some space to Monteverdi's stage works, full-length studies on them are rare. However, taken together, this extensive research reflects the drastic change of the operas' fortune from neglect to rediscovery, to renewed appreciation and intensified study, and finally to viable performance experience.

Almost half a century ago, SCHRADE wrote his admirable book in which he strove to integrate the then known facts of Monteverdi's life into the artistic process. The title reflects the author's viewpoint: Monteverdi as the "creator of modern music." Schrade's scene-by-scene description of *Orfeo,* with detailed analysis and a few musical examples, emphasizes the dramatic power of words and music in the context of the first production, its patrons, and its singers, all of which he also describes for Monteverdi's final Venetian operas. However, Schrade does not neglect the plans and commissions for dramatic works for which no or little music is extant, reconstructing the circumstances from documents and correspondence.

ARNOLD clearly aims his book at the general reader who might have limited knowledge of 17th-century Italian music. He also softens the view of the revolutionary Monteverdi to that of the moderate and progressive. After a relatively brief account of the composer's life, Arnold devotes several chapters to a discussion of the works, beginning with two on the madrigals, which he considers to be the heart of Monteverdi's music. In the chapter on the stage works, the author first gives the reader a general understanding of the genres that the composer was familiar with, such as the pastoral in relation to *Orfeo,* and then discusses the opera itself. An overview of the subsequent dramatic works is followed by a fine, largely nontechnical introduction to the last operas, a good starting point for the informed reader even today.

DONINGTON brings his neoplatonic interpretation of early opera to his study of Monteverdi's *Orfeo,* from the "golden lyre" of *La Musica* in the prologue to the altered ending, which is different from both Rinuccini's *Euridice* and Striggio's separately published poem. In his treatment of the Venetian stage works, Donington presents interesting comparisons of plots and characters with their models, noting, for example, Busenello's and Monteverdi's reshaping of the historical Nero, Ottavia, Seneca, and Poppea.

Among many other important essays and articles on early opera and its intellectual background, PIRROTTA includes two pieces on Monteverdi's operas in the collection listed here. In the first essay, he points out

Monteverdi's indebtedness to and parallelisms with the Florentine operas of 1600, thereby establishing a more balanced judgment instead of merely asserting Monteverdi's superiority. In the second essay, Pirrotta investigates the actual theaters or halls functioning as such (in Mantua) in which Monteverdi's works were performed and the implications for the stagings. Pirrotta suggests, for example, that *Il Ritorno d'Ulisse* was first performed in Bologna (1639) and subsequently at San Giovanni e Paolo in Venice. A third essay, on Monteverdi's poetic choices, focuses mainly on the madrigals.

ARNOLD and FORTUNE is an important collection of essays on Monteverdi, only a few of which deal with his operas. Jane Glover begins her essay on the Venetian operas with a general overview of the striking differences between those operas and *Orfeo*. The libretto and music of each of the works are discussed in a concise, clear, and largely nontechnical manner. The author emphasizes Monteverdi's mastery not only in the characterization of emotional responses of the protagonists but also in the musical shaping of scenes, and she suggests the influence of these late operas on the composer's successors. Iain Fenlon ("The Mantuan Stage Works") discusses Monteverdi's relationship to the Gonzaga court in Mantua.

WHENHAM, a collection of nine essays by a variety of early baroque specialists, deals in depth with various aspects of *Orfeo*. For example, Fenlon ("The Mantuan *Orfeo*") supplies interesting details about the first performance of *Orfeo* by publishing and analyzing correspondence between Francesco and Ferdinando Gonzaga revolving around the participation of Giovanni Gualberto (Magli), soprano castrato, and revealing aspects of rehearsal and performance. (The letters are transcribed and translated in appendix 1.)

Yet another point of view is TOMLINSON's, which presents Monteverdi as the last representative of a dying Renaissance humanism and depicts the composer himself gradually changing his approach to early ideals without ever totally abandoning them. The operas are discussed in the chronological context of the secular works, whose changing poetic styles are studied, as are the composer's responses to them. *Orfeo* is compared to the extant fragment of *Arianna,* and both works are compared to their respective antecedents, clearly showing the humanist goal of dramatized speech in music. However, the librettists of the last operas were steeped in Marinism as opposed to Petrarchian humanism, and, according to Tomlinson, Monteverdi's last operas reflect his attempt to synthesize these two modes, albeit not wholly successfully.

In his Monteverdi biography, revised for the recent English translation, FABBRI brings together an especially rich array of documentation, both biographical and bibliographical, and a variety of factual information on life and works, although without musical examples.

The operas are discussed relatively briefly in the biographical context. Thus, the first performances of *Orfeo* are described vividly, partly through the contemporary witnesses' words, including the known singers and the locales of the performances, the questions of the different endings, the structure of the libretto, and the genre it belongs to. Likewise, a similar emphasis in treatment of the late Venetian operas gives only generalized attention to the music but much valuable information on sources and publications of texts and scores.

OLGA TERMINI

4. Sacred Music

Arnold, Denis, *Monteverdi Church Music,* London: British Broadcasting Corporation, 1982

Kurtzman, Jeffrey G., *Essays on the Monteverdi Mass and Vespers of 1610,* Houston, Texas: Rice University, 1978

Stevens, Denis, *Monteverdi: Sacred, Secular, and Occasional Music,* Rutherford, New Jersey: Fairleigh Dickinson University Press, 1978

Whenham, John, *Monteverdi: Vespers (1610),* Cambridge: Cambridge University Press, 1997

Although Monteverdi is known primarily for his madrigals and operas, his extant sacred music reveals additional areas of compositional mastery. His sacred works range from the most conservative to the thoroughly innovative, and a single collection can display a considerable variety of old and new techniques. Most of Monteverdi's sacred music was printed in four collections: *Sacrae Cantiunculae* (1582), *Sanctissimae Virgini missa . . . Vespere . . .* (1610 Vespers), *Selve morale e spirituale* (1641), and *Messa . . . salmi . . . concerttati* (1650). In 1613 Monteverdi was appointed *Maestro di cappella* of the San Marco chapel in Venice. Although he delegated much of the responsibility for new sacred music to subordinates, Monteverdi likely composed for major events. The 1641 and 1650 publications cannot account for all of this activity, and much of his later sacred output is apparently lost.

Most of the books published about Monteverdi's sacred music are relatively concise, and much of the scholarly attention has been focused on the 1610 Vespers. An in-depth publication regarding Monteverdi's complete sacred output is not available. Although the books listed above vary in content and depth, their authors are acknowledged experts in this field. Important issues include chronology, performance practice, and style—most notably Monteverdi's use of older compositional styles in addition to more innovative techniques taken from secular music. Regarding the 1610 Vespers, additional topics include the composer's motivations, the role of the motets, and the concept of the collection as a unified work. The flexibility that Monteverdi provided to chapel masters, such as creating a variety of works suitable to a variety of available talent, is also commonly emphasized.

For an introductory overview of Monteverdi's sacred works, ARNOLD is the logical starting point. The author provides a general introduction to each collection, presented in chronological order, and then discusses specific works and styles, employing historical background and conjecture as appropriate. Arnold never loses sight of Monteverdi's overall style, personality, and approach to composition. Unfortunately, this work lacks a bibliography, and footnotes are sparse. In his introduction, Arnold addresses the state of religious music in Monteverdi's era and its transition to baroque aesthetics. On the impact of secular trends on Monteverdi's sacred works, Arnold argues that the composer approached religious music as he would any other genre, employing whatever techniques he felt best-suited to the text at hand. Chapter 3 focuses on the 1610 collection, which the author concludes was composed for Mantuan resources. In addition, Arnold argues that the entire collection was constructed as a unified work. In his chapter on Monteverdi's later collections, individual works are discussed briefly, with commentary largely limited to their general nature and individual innovations. This chapter, unfortunately, lacks a listing of works included in Monteverdi's 1641 and 1650 collections, something Arnold provided in his discussion of the 1610 Vespers.

Although not dedicated exclusively to Monteverdi's sacred works, STEVENS presents a significant discussion of these compositions, organized by genre. Like Arnold, Stevens offers a general overview of Monteverdi's complete sacred output. The book includes a bibliography of selected sources, and the index is superior to Arnold's, listing people as well as works. In the introduction to the sacred music section, Stevens provides a chronological list of published collections and printed anthologies that contain sacred works by Monteverdi. Although his chapter organization—each genre discussed in a two- to five-page span—makes a chronological understanding of Monteverdi's works more difficult, it allows for an easier comparison of works within genres. Individual works are treated briefly, with some noteworthy compositions considered in more detail.

For those interested in a complete overview of the 1610 Vespers collection, WHENHAM is the best choice. The author discusses the general nature of the Vespers and issues surrounding the collection in chapter 1. Departing slightly from Arnold's view of the print as a unified whole, Whenham contends that the 1610 Vespers is not one work but a collection of compositions, not necessarily composed within a single time frame. Whenham gives an explanation of the Vespers rite in chapter 2, including information regarding its plainsong and polyphonic traditions. In chapter 3, Whenham states that this collection may have been published in response to critics and presents a number of other interesting theories regarding Monteverdi's motivations.

Chapter 4 is dedicated largely to the motets, which are also commonly referred to as sacred concertos. Each work is discussed in considerable detail, touching on liturgical function, sources, and theoretical background. Chapter 5 concentrates on the psalm settings and Magnificats in a like manner. Whenham's work regarding the nature of the text settings is of particular value. Much of his chapter on performance practice discusses techniques employed in previously released audio recordings of the collection. Whenham includes as appendices a listing of texts for the Second Vespers of the Blessed Virgin and the plainsongs, with texts and translations, relevant to Monteverdi's collection. This section is followed by endnotes, a select bibliography, a discography, and an index.

KURTZMAN's volume is a collection of articles, largely revisions of previous research. The introduction provides some illumination about the goals of each essay and also furnishes some information on the construction of the 1610 collection. Kurtzman views the collection as a unified artistic unit that allows much flexibility for performers. The first essay evaluates three sources containing music from the 1610 Vespers. Through an examination of notation and performance practice issues, Kurtzman addresses transposition and chronology. In "A Critical Commentary on the *Missa in Illo Tempore*," Kurtzman provides a general overview of this Mass, an example of Monteverdi's ultraconservative approach to sacred composition. Composed in an academic, antiquarian style, this work has a special place in Monteverdi's compositional output. Kurtzman concludes that the work is an overwhelming exhibition of compositional technique, which emphasizes the older contrapuntal style as a response to his critics, especially Artusi. Monteverdi likely composed this work in part to display his flexibility and talent to prospective church employers.

In other essays, Kurtzman touches on a variety of topics, including an analytical discussion of Monteverdi's use of variation and development of unity and a brief treatment of the motet *Nigra sum*. The final essay, "Some Historical Perspectives on the Monteverdi *Vespers*," provides a review of the 1610 collection and the state of research, and it examines the collection's impact on subsequent composers. Kurtzman's impressive knowledge of 16th- and 17th-century vespers music helps place Monteverdi's collection in historical perspective. Ultimately, Kurtzman concludes that the 1610 Vespers was an isolated masterpiece, not representative of the mainstream music of its era. Kurtzman is currently working on a updated and enlarged edition of this work.

Dane Heuchemer

Morley, Thomas ca. 1557–1602

English composer

Fellowes, Edmund H., *English Cathedral Music,* London: Methuen, 1941; 5th edition, revised by Jack Westrup, 1969
————, *The English Madrigal Composers,* London: Oxford University Press, 1921; 2nd edition, 1948
Foster, Myles B., *Anthems and Anthem Composers,* London: Novello, 1901; reprint, New York: Da Capo Press, 1970
Kerman, Joseph, *The Elizabethan Madrigal: A Comparative Study,* New York: American Musicological Society, 1962
Le Huray, Peter, *Music and the Reformation in England, 1549–1660,* London: Jenkins, and New York: Oxford University Press, 1967
Long, Kenneth R., *Music of the English Church,* New York: St. Martin's Press, 1971; London: Hodder and Stoughton, 1972
Morley, Thomas, *A Plaine and Easie Introduction to Practicall Musick,* London, 1597; reprint, New York: Norton, 1963
Northcote, Sydney, *Byrd to Britten: A Survey of English Song,* London: Baker, and New York: Roy, 1966
Roche, Jerome, *The Madrigal,* London: Hutchinson, and New York: Scribner, 1972; 2nd edition, Oxford: Oxford University Press, 1990
Spink, Ian, *English Song from Dowland to Purcell,* London: Batsford, and New York: Scribner, 1974
Teo, Kian-Seng, *Chromaticism in the English Madrigal,* New York: Garland, 1989

Thomas Morley is one of the most significant figures in Elizabethan music. He composed nearly 150 works in a wide variety of genres, including Catholic and Anglican church music (services, anthems, psalm settings, motets), secular vocal works (English and Italian madrigals, canzonets, and balletts and solo ayres with lute accompaniment), keyboard music, and instrumental consort dances and fantasies. He also controlled the monopoly on music printing in London from 1598 until his death. Despite Morley's pivotal position, there has never been a book-length study of his life and works. To further complicate matters, much of the published material on Morley is at least 30 years old, and much of this is based on studies originally undertaken by Edmund Fellowes in the 1920s.

MORLEY himself wrote a 322-page treatise that was originally published in 1597. This landmark of English Renaissance theory is written as a clever dialogue between a master teacher (Morley himself) and two pupils: Philomathes (earnest and apologetic) and Polymathes (flashy and argumentative). The book is divided into three parts. The first part considers the rudiments of music (notes, clefs, the hexachord system, ligatures, time signatures, and so on); the second part discusses the arts of counterpoint and canon, including 56 examples of two—and three—voice descant, all written over the same fixed melody (canto fermo) as well as 14 canons written over a single canto fermo; and the third part explores the rules for composing polyphony in three or more parts. Within the lively dialogue, Morley discusses more than 90 composers and provides thorough definitions of the leading genres of his day. In addition, Dart's foreword to Norton's edition of this treatise is the most comprehensive commentary on Morley's life and works. It provides background on English music from ca. 1530 to 1610, explains the socioreligious circumstances that influenced English music under the Tudor family monarchs from Henry VIII to Elizabeth I, and reviews the history of music publishing in England and the effects of the music printing monopoly held successively by Thomas East, William Byrd, and Thomas Morley. It also offers brief descriptions of each of Morley's major madrigalian collections, a compelling three—page biographical sketch on Morley, and an eight-page in-depth summary and critique of Morley's *Plaine and Easie Introduction.*

The remaining selected sources present focused coverage of Morley's music within specific compositional categories, such as his madrigals (Fellowes [1921], Kerman, Roche, and Teo), church music (Fellowes [1941], Foster, Le Huray, and Long), and lute songs (Northcote and Spink).

FELLOWES (1921) is the groundbreaking work on Morley's madrigals. Although references to Morley are found on more than 50 pages in this book, Fellowes's most comprehensive coverage of Morley is contained in chapter 14, in which the author offers a two-page biographical introduction on the composer followed by a brief chronological discussion of Morley's madrigalian publications. Representative songs from each collection are highlighted by interpretive commentary and notated musical examples. Fellowes's chart "The Madrigalian Publications of Thomas Morley" provides a convenient itemized list of the individual songs contained in each of Morley's eight major madrigal collections.

The most extensive investigation of Morley's madrigals is found in chapter 5 of KERMAN's outstanding book. The author begins by detailing the critical relationship of Morley to the Italian madrigal tradition and then carefully compares Morley's compositional approach to the ballett, canzonet, and light madrigal to his theoretical descriptions of those genres or forms given in his treatise. (For readers who might be unfamiliar with the madrigal repertory, a ballett is a multiverse song with a fa-la refrain; a canzonet is a multiverse song with a repetitive musical structure, such as AABCC; and a madrigal is a more substantial, nonrepetitive (through-composed) song setting. Although Kerman's musical and poetic analysis at times exceeds the grasp of general readers, his work is extremely valuable and, for the most part, accessible to all levels.

Readers seeking a quick overview of Morley's madrigals should consult ROCHE. His commentary is general in focus, but there is still much useful information here, highlighted by brief musical examples. On the other end of the spectrum is TEO's intricate discussion of Morley. Despite the highly specific scope of Teo's study, the level of the material is surprisingly accessible for all levels of readers. On the basis of his thorough investigation of Morley's madrigals, canzonets, and balletts, Teo refutes the view that these compositions are lacking in chromatic effects, chromatic harmony, and word painting by stating that "in relation to his main [Italian] models: Vecchi, Anerio, Croce, Ferretti, and Gastoldi . . . Morley matches and often outstrips his models in chromatics . . . [and] also in expressive intensity."

It should also be noted that almost every commentator on the English madrigal lambastes Morley because, paradoxically, his actual madrigals do not appear to conform with his own theoretical descriptions of those forms or genres. However, in my investigation of Morley's works ("Thomas Morley and the Italian Madrigal Tradition: A New Perspective," *Journal of Musicology* 14 [1996]), I found quite the opposite to be true. Ninety-six percent of Morley's settings clearly adhere to his theoretical criteria of either a ballett, canzonet, or light madrigal; thus, the apparent paradox has resulted from Morley's intentional marketing decision to include more than one type of madrigal in each of his collections (e.g., his *Book of Balletts* [1595] contains not only balletts but a few canzonets and madrigals as well). In the final analysis, Morley consistently labeled each of his collections by the dominant song type in each volume.

Regarding Morley's church music, LONG is the best source. His coverage of Morley features an overview of the composer's life and works (including evidence concerning the possible friendship or acquaintance between Morley and Shakespeare) followed by specific coverage of Morley's Burial Service setting, motets, psalm settings, and anthems. The author's rigorous commentary is augmented by more than a dozen clearly organized musical examples. In Long's estimation, "Morley wrote little for the church and it is to be regretted that, with few exceptions, the standard of his church music falls well below that of his best secular pieces." The most notable exception to this assessment is Morley's verse anthem "Out of the Deepe" (for tenor or countertenor solo and five-part choir), which Long believes puts Morley "at one with the Restoration composers of a century later." LE HURAY's intricate account of Morley's church music concentrates on the verse structures, cadential formulas, and formal designs of his anthems and Services, with detailed discussion of his Magnificat from his Short Service. FELLOWES (1941) briefly touches on two of Morley's anthems and his four known Services (including the Burial Service).

Because Morley published only one set of lute songs (1600), he is given only passing coverage by both SPINK and NORTHCOTE. According to Spink, Morley's *First Booke of Ayres* (1600) "comes as close as any single volume to encompassing the complete range of expression found in the lutesong repertoire." Both Spink and Northcote cite Morley's delightful "Lover and His Lass" (based on a text from Shakespeare's *As You Like It*) as his best work in this genre.

DANIEL JACOBSON

Motet: Medieval

Allsen, J. Michael, "Style and Intertextuality in the Isorhythmic Motet 1400–1440," Ph.D. dissertation, University of Wisconsin-Madison, 1992

Bent, Margaret, "The Fourteenth-Century Italian Motet," in *L'Ars nova italiana del Trecento VI: Atti del congresso internazionale l'Europa e la musica del Trecento,* edited by Giulio Cattin and Patrizia Della Vecchia, Certaldo Edizioni Polis, 1992

Earp, Lawrence M., *Guillaume de Machaut: A Guide to Research,* New York: Garland, 1995

Everist, Mark, *French Motets in the Thirteenth Century: Music, Poetry, and Genre,* Cambridge: Cambridge University Press, 1994

Leech-Wilkinson, Daniel, *Compositional Techniques in the Four-Part Isorhythmic Motets of Philippe de Vitry and His Contemporaries,* 2 vols., New York: Garland, 1989

Lefferts, Peter M., *The Motet in England in the Fourteenth Century,* Ann Arbor, Michigan: UMI Research Press, 1986

Sanders, Ernest H., "The Medieval Motet," in *Gattungen der Musik in Einzeldarstellen: Gedenkschrift Leo Schrade,* edited by Wulf Arlt et al, Berne: Francke, 1973

Tischler, Hans, *The Style and Evolution of the Earliest Motets (to circa 1270),* 3 vols., Henryville, Pennsylvania: Institute of Mediaeval Music, 1985

The motet stands as the single most important polyphonic genre of the late Middle Ages—it was the form in which composers displayed both poetic and musical learning, and the form most often used to mark important political and ceremonial events. It had its beginnings in the late 12th century, with composers of the Notre Dame School, and the essential elements of the genre—a stratified polyphonic framework based upon a plainchant tenor, rhythmic repetition in the tenor (and later the upper voices), and polytextual upper voices—remained largely constant until the late motets of Du Fay in the 1440s.

The motet was a major research topic for musicologists throughout the 20th century. Early studies focused on cataloging, editing, and interpreting the notation of the huge repertoire of surviving motets, and the most recent studies have focused increasingly on issues of analysis, compositional procedure, intertextuality, and social context. As a result, there is a vast amount of literature on the motet, beginning early in the 20th century with the first scholarly edition by Pierre Aubry of 13th-century motets (1908) and important studies by Friedrich Ludwig (especially his monumental *Repertorium;* volume 1: 1910; volume 2: 1978, published posthumously) and by Heinrich Besseler (*Archiv für Musikwissenschaft,* 1926). Gradually, beginning in the 1930s, most of the major sources of the 12th and 13th centuries were issued in facsimile or in transcriptions. Motets of the 14th and 15th centuries also became generally available, beginning with Ludwig's publication of Machaut's works (1926–43).

SANDERS is the first English-language study that attempts to outline the entire history of the motet genre, and the essay departs from the earlier works by Ludwig and Besseler in its extensive coverage of English works. Sanders's treatment of early motets is generally more complete than his comments on works of the 14th century, but the article is still invaluable and has served as the basis for many later discussions of the motet.

The researcher will find several general histories of medieval music useful in obtaining an overall summary of the medieval motet. James McKinnon's anthology contains chapters by various authors, several of which contain valuable information on the motet. Daniel Leech-Wilkinson's chapter on the development of polyphony in the late 13th and 14th centuries is especially useful, as is the chapter by Lefferts on medieval England (James McKinnon, editor, *Antiquity and the Middle Ages: From Ancient Greece to the 15th century,* 1990). There are several college-level textbooks on medieval music available; most of these books provide a serviceable overview of the motet. The text by David F. Wilson is one of the most readily accessible historical surveys of the motet as a musical form, although the reader will find relatively little information in this work on the poetic or cultural aspects of the genre (David Fenwick Wilson, *Music of the Middle Ages: Style and Structure,* 1990). A similar text by Jeremy Yudkin provides more fragmented coverage of the motet as a genre but is somewhat stronger in its treatment of the motet's social milieu (Jeremy Yudkin, *Music in Medieval Europe,* 1989). Both Wilson and Yudkin present relatively balanced views of the French and English repertoires, and both volumes are accompanied by musical anthologies. The most thorough consideration of the cultural background of the genre in medieval France is by Christopher Page, who brings an amazing amount of historical, philosophical, poetic, and mathematical information to bear on the motet in an attempt to break down the conventional views on the history of the genre (Christopher Page, *Discarding Images: Reflections on Music and Culture in Medieval France,* 1993). Page's views have been controversial, however, and are not universally accepted by the musicological community.

Most of the works cited in the above bibliography are particularly useful for research into specific motet repertoires. TISCHLER's three-volume study is intended as a companion to his edition of the earliest motets (1982).

Tischler's catalog, designed in part as a continuation of the work of Ludwig, is exceptionally complete with respect to all motet sources and genres prior to 1270. However, many of Tischler's conclusions have been superceded by subsequent research into the early motet—despite its publication date, much of the text presented reflects research of some 20 or 30 years earlier. The nonspecialist reader may find this book rather daunting.

More engaging coverage of the early motet is provided by EVERIST, who puts forth revisionist views on the development of the form, challenging the picture of the motet's evolution presented by Ludwig, Besseler, Tischler, and others. Everist examines the development of the motet in relation to other contemporary musical and poetic forms and draws a revised picture of the genres and subgenres present in the early motet repertoire. The book also focuses on the direct musical, poetic, and structural interrelationships found among many early motets.

The early 14th century saw a new style of motet composition in France, connected to the development of ars nova notation—this new style, generally referred to as the isorhythmic motet, remained a dominant form of motet composition for some 125 years. LEECH-WILKINSON provides an excellent overview of previous research on the motet and on Philippe de Vitry, the figure most closely connected to the establishment of ars nova notation and motet style. The study focuses particularly on the four-voice motets of Vitry and Machaut and on several anonymous French works, discussing issues of text-music relations and compositional process.

EARP's resource guide is an exemplary piece of scholarship that should be the first resort for any research into the motets of Machaut. Citations of individual motets include extensive textual and musical analysis, a complete annotated bibliography, and a discography. Earp's study is also useful for any general research into the 14th-century motet. Taken together, this work and Leech-Wilkinson's book flesh out the still-useful overview of the motet in 14th-century France published by Virsula Günther more than 40 years ago (*Musica Disciplina,* 1958).

The book by LEFFERTS builds upon the work of Sanders and Harrison to deal comprehensively with the English motet of the 14th century. Lefferts approaches systematically this large and diverse repertoire, identifying and illustrating musical subgenres, exploring problems of notation, and discussing motet texts. The appendix lists and describes more than 130 motets found in English sources from this period.

BENT's seminal article on the Italian motet completes the international picture of the genre in the late Middle Ages. Although a small repertoire in comparison to the body of 14th-century motets that survive from France and England, the Italian motet was a vital tradition that was stylistically distinct and had a strong influence on motet traditions of the next century.

By the early 15th century, the motet as a genre encompassed a wide variety of styles, but a fundamentally medieval form—the isorhythmic motet—was still cultivated until mid-century. ALLSEN is the only comprehensive survey of this late repertoire. The study discusses systematically the surviving motets from three distinct cultural milieus: France, Burgundy, and Cyprus; northern Italy; and England. Allsen provides a complete outline of the development of the isorhythmic motet after approximately 1400 and discusses several cases in which motets were based upon other motets. The appendix includes a complete list of surviving works (134 motets) and a bibliography.

J. MICHAEL ALLSEN

Motet: Renaissance

Dunning, Albert, *Die Staatsmotette 1480–1555*, Utrecht: Oosthoek, 1970

Lowinsky, Edward E., *Secret Chromatic Art in the Netherlands Motet*, New York: Columbia University Press, 1946

———, *Music in the Culture of the Renaissance and Other Essays*, 2 vols., edited by Bonnie J. Blackburn, Chicago: University of Chicago Press, 1989

Pesce, Dolores, editor, *Hearing the Motet: Essays on the Motet of the Middle Ages and Renaissance*, New York: Oxford University Press, 1997

Sparks, Edgar, *Cantus Firmus in Mass and Motet, 1420–1520*, Berkeley: University of California Press, 1963

The motet is one of the most important genres of the Renaissance, for it represents a type of sacred composition that, unlike the Mass, was not strictly tied to the liturgy. This genre allowed the composer more freedom to experiment with compositions that were not necessarily dependent on a preexisting melody (cantus firmus) and with nonliturgical texts. The Renaissance motet often showed composers at their most creative, and for this reason much study has been directed toward it. Unfortunately, most of these studies have appeared only as journal articles, many in languages other than English. To date, no complete overview of the Renaissance motet has appeared in English.

Several sources present brief glimpses into the subject of the Renaissance motet. These are generally grouped into two broad categories: studies related to issues of compositional style, either of a single composer/school or of the genre in general, and studies focused on a single motet, most often motets written for specific occasions or persons. This second category is of special importance because many motets were written to commemorate special events; because many of these events can be dated with some degree of certainty, the motets written for them can be an aid in retrieving valuable biographical data on their composers.

A study of commemorative motets created for specific state or political celebrations has been undertaken by DUNNING but unfortunately exists only in German. It provides an overview of the use of these motets by examining specific motets from different periods, composers, and places. The book is divided into two parts covering the late 15th century and the first half of the 16th century. Within these two parts are specific sections devoted to individual countries and courts and the state motets existing for each. Dunning can be useful in tracing certain motets to the occasions for which they were composed, as well as the manner in which state motets were used in different times and places. One limitation to the work is that it only deals with a subspecies of motet, which, while admittedly a large one, does not represent the motet in general. Its other limitation is its self-stated inability to distinguish between motets known to have been written for specific state occasions and those that appear to have been written for a liturgical use but which may have also been linked to a state occasion.

SPARKS's book is an example of a study focused on issues related to style in the motet. He delineates two different ways that cantus firmi are used in motets: in an ornamented form, which he describes as representing an irrational, fanciful tendency, and in an unornamented framework, which he claims represents a more rational, formalistic tendency. His examination covers three periods of composition: that of Du Fay and his contemporaries, that of Ockeghem, and that of Josquin. This work presents some problems for the nonspecialist, however, as it uses terms to designate various types of motets but does not always define those terms and because the writing and analysis are quite technical. Because this study only deals with compositions based on preexisting melodies, a large number of freely composed pieces from the same period are not addressed.

Like Sparks, LOWINSKY (1946) also uses the motet to analyze issues of style. He contends that composers working in the Netherlands in the later 16th century began writing compositions with a greater use of chromaticism in their motets, much of which was implied but not written (hence, secret). The music therefore presented an acceptable diatonic face to the uninitiated listener that could also, through the secret arrangement of sharps and flats, offer a different sound to a select few. Lowinsky holds that this chromatic art was necessarily secret because it was linked to proscribed Reformationist thinking and because composers encountered church bans on new devices in music. Criticism has been directed against Lowinsky's work, however, because his analysis proceeds from the standpoint of major and minor tonality, which some modern scholars feel to be an anachronism.

LOWINSKY (1989) is a collection of the author's most influential writings. Included are two studies that represent the two broad categories of scholarly writings discussed above. One, "Orlando di Lasso's Antwerp Motet Book and Its Relationship to the Contemporary Netherlandish Motet," which grew out of Lowinsky's dissertation, is a stylistic study of one collection of motets by a specific composer. The essay examines Lasso's synthesis of the southern sound of Venice, with its rich harmonic style and text-dominated melodic idiom, and the northern style of the Netherlands, with its polyphonic tradition and blossoming sense of realistic expression through dissonance (the secret chromatic art discussed above) and religious sincerity. The other article, "Cipriano de Rore's Venus Motet: Its Poetic and Pictorial Sources," focuses on a specific motet. In this article Lowinsky demonstrates that the text of a motet by Rore was based on a poem by Girolamo Falletti, which, in turn, was based on a painting by Girolamo da Carpi, perhaps in homage to Ana d'Este. This essay is a wonderful interdisciplinary study linking art, poetry, and music, but it is only nominally about Rore's motet.

Perhaps the most complete examination of the motet grew out of a 1994 conference on the genre, the papers of which were edited for publication by PESCE. Within this anthology are various types of studies on the motet, which use different methodologies to investigate how the motet would have been heard by the listeners of particular times and places. One approach examines the sociohistorical context behind the creation of a specific motet or motets, as in Robert Nosow's "Dufay and the Cultures of Renaissance Florence," which demonstrates how two motets by Du Fay can be heard from the two different perspectives of humanism and lay piety. Another approach attempts to discover the performance context and liturgical function of a particular motet. Robert C. Wegman's "For Whom the Bell Tolls: Reading and Hearing Busnoy's *Anthoni usque limina*," for example, shows that Busnoy's motet was most likely a votive offering to his name saint composed during a time of distress. A third approach examines texts to uncover multiple meanings. For example, Richard Sherr's "Conflicting Levels of Meaning and Understanding in Josquin's *O admirabile commercium* Motet Cycle" explains how Josquin's use of text admits both a Marian and a Christological interpretation.

The fourth approach represented in Pesce's collection turns to studies on style in general and attempts to show how the music used by composers in their motets may have been perceived as new or innovative by contemporary listeners. David Crook's "Tonal Compass in the Motets of Orlando di Lasso" follows this path, positing that Lasso expanded upon the older traditions of composition by creating "meaningful tonal excursions" in his motets. The last approach considers how music and text work together to create music-poetic creations. For example, M. Jennifer Bloxam's "Obrecht as Exegete: Reading *Factus orbis* as a Christmas Sermon," traces how Obrecht used the model of a medieval thematic ser-

mon in his motet to help interpret the text. Although this anthology does not give a complete overview of the history and styles of the motet, its selection of the various types of studies being done on the motet provides enough information on the Renaissance motet to give the reader an accurate picture of the genre, its composers, and its audiences. For this reason, Pesce's collection is as close to an essential source on the subject of the motet as the reader will most likely encounter.

JOHN KARR

Mozart, Leopold 1719–1787

German composer

Eisen, Cliff, "The Symphonies of Leopold Mozart and Their Relationship to the Early Symphonies of Wolfgang Amadeus Mozart: A Bibliographical and Stylistic Study," Ph.D. dissertation, Cornell University, 1986

Halliwell, Ruth, *The Mozart Family: Four Lives in a Social Context,* Oxford: Clarendon Press, 1998

Mozart, Leopold, *A Treatise on the Fundamental Principles of Violin Playing,* translated by Editha Knocker, Oxford: Oxford University Press, 1948; 2nd edition, 1951

[Mozart, Leopold,] "Report on the Present State of the Musical Establishment at the Court of His Serene Highness the Archbishop of Salzburg in the Year 1757," in *Mozart's Symphonies: Context, Performance Practice, Reception,* edited by Neal Zaslaw, Oxford: Clarendon Press, and New York: Oxford University Press, 1989

Mozart, Wolfgang Amadeus, *The Letters of Mozart and His Family,* 3 vols., edited by Emily Anderson, London: Macmillan, 1938; 3rd edition, London: Macmillan, and New York: Norton, 1985

Solomon, Maynard, *Mozart: A Life,* New York: HarperCollins, and London: Hutchinson, 1995

Stowell, Robin, "Leopold Mozart Revised: Articulation in Violin Playing During the Second Half of the Eighteenth Century," in *Perspectives on Mozart Performance,* edited by R. Larry Todd and Peter Williams, Cambridge: Cambridge University Press, 1991

Leopold Mozart was a capable composer and the author of an influential treatise on violin playing. Yet he is remembered in the literature mainly—and not always favorably—as the father of Wolfgang Amadeus Mozart. Fortunately, scholarship is beginning to move beyond the romantic era's superficial image of Leopold. His musical influence on Wolfgang was probably greater than previously imagined, and new biographical perspectives urge a more balanced, objective view of Mozart the father as well.

No proper biography of Leopold exists. Serious students should begin with Wolfgang Amadeus MOZART, a translation and edition of the family letters that remains a touchstone of early 20th-century Mozart scholarship. Leopold's checkered personality—loving husband, anxious and demanding parent, cosmopolitan musician, and scholar—bursts vividly forth from the pages. The editor, Anderson, traces four distinct periods in Leopold's correspondence: early travel accounts; letters from Italy, which concentrate on music and social conditions there; letters to Wolfgang, who had gone job hunting without his father in Mannheim, Paris, and Munich; and letters to Nannerl (Leopold's daughter) after her marriage. Unfortunately, Anderson omits large portions of Leopold's letters from the first and fourth periods.

Another primary source, the "Report on . . . the Musical Establishment . . . at Salzburg," appeared without attribution in Marpurg's Historisch-Kritische Beyträge (1757) but was undoubtedly submitted by Leopold MOZART (1989). This brief document is valuable not only for statistics on the court's musical forces and the musicians' backgrounds and capabilities but also as evidence of Leopold's aptitude for self-promotion. His own biographical sketch is twice the length of that of any other musician, including those of his organizational superiors. And his assessments can be impolitically frank.

SOLOMON's penetrating study of Leopold forms the core of his biography of Wolfgang. By grounding his methodology in (but not limiting it to) psychoanalytic theory, the author has produced a convincing portrait of a father and son at first united and then forever at odds. Solomon begins by examining Leopold's own imperfect youth (he was expelled from university and essentially disowned by his mother), his early years in Salzburg, and his marriage. As his talented children developed, Leopold conceived a "family enterprise" in which the combined efforts of father, mother, daughter, and son could free them from a life of genteel poverty and lesser status at a provincial court.

> [Leopold's] career, financial health, and hunger for recognition came to depend on his son, particularly when he began to neglect his duties as deputy kapellmeister . . . and abandoned his activities as a composer and litterateur. . . . Not surprisingly, then, Leopold came to fear that Mozart would grow up.

Despite his father's greatest efforts, Wolfgang did eventually demand freedom and his own life. After Wolfgang's move to Vienna, Solomon continues to track Leopold, now bitter, old, and increasingly isolated in Salzburg, seeking other potential prodigies with which to restart the enterprise.

HALLIWELL's monograph covers roughly the same ground as Solomon's biography but with rather different results. Whereas Solomon emphasizes the psychopathology of family life, Halliwell stresses its internal logic and social determinants. As she strives to reveal the underlying ordinariness of an extraordinary family, she also rehabilitates Leopold. The author's pedestrian narrative (relying on the family letters but bleaching away their vitality) is especially useful: events are properly ordered, gaps in documentation smoothed over, and data added on contemporary attitudes and practices. Halliwell usually avoids interpreting her characters' actions and motives except to offer a bit of commonsense explication. She does, however, take issue with feminist critiques of Nannerl's upbringing, and she disagrees profoundly with some of Solomon's arguments. As for the father-son relationship, Halliwell firmly believes that Leopold's point of view has too often been misrepresented. She finds his actions logical, his values congruent with the time and place. This perspective does not prevent her from introducing new anachronisms, as when she notes with apparent surprise that Leopold was prolific between 1747 and 1756 despite the "domestic burdens" caused by his wife's pregnancies. But more often, Halliwell's evenhandedness pays off: she so carefully marshals the evidence surrounding Leopold's will and the disposition of his property, for example, that Solomon's explanation of the same events seems far less credible.

Leopold MOZART's treatise on the violin (1948), which originally appeared shortly after the birth of his surviving son, was immediately and highly successful, enlarged and reprinted in 1769 and 1787, and consulted well into the 19th century. It is probably the first comprehensive, systematic treatment of its subject. Like its author, the Violinschule cannily balanced the ideal and the practical. Stressing the importance of proper Affekt (feeling), Leopold recommends an acquaintance with literature and especially poetry, as the art of phrasing was akin to the science of rhetoric. As a practical violinist writing for his colleagues, he avoids undue emphasis on virtuosity. Instead, he exhorts his readers always to strive for the effect of fine singing. In various asides and footnotes, Leopold's prickly character surfaces, as well.

STOWELL does not survey the many revisions and reworkings of the Violinschule that followed its first publication. Instead, he summarizes its central precepts and examines their comparative influence throughout Europe. What he finds remarkable is not that other violinists differed in their approach, but how widely Leopold's principles were adopted and how little they were altered over time, especially in Germany and Austria.

EISEN makes the first comprehensive attempt to describe Leopold Mozart's symphonies and to evaluate relationships between those compositions and Wolfgang's earliest symphonies. Much of the study is devoted to issues of authenticity, attribution, and source evaluation; these are especially significant to a body of works in which authorship has so often been contested. (Many earlier writers routinely assigned the better pieces to Wolfgang simply on the basis of his superior reputation.) Through a close stylistic analysis of the symphony K. 42a (76), possibly by Leopold, Eisen demonstrates the folly of those attitudes. A concluding chapter reconstructs the repertory of Salzburg orchestral music, 1740 to 1780, suggesting that some features of Wolfgang's earliest works may derive from music by his father and other Salzburgers.

LAWRENCE SCHENBECK

Mozart, Wolfgang Amadeus 1756–1791

German-born composer

1. Biography

Braunbehrens, Volkmar, *Mozart in Vienna, 1781–1791,* translated by Timothy Bell, New York: Grove Weidenfeld, and London: Deutsch, 1990

Deutsch, Otto Erich, *Mozart, A Documentary Biography,* translated by Eric Blom et al., Stanford, California: Stanford University Press, and London: Black, 1965; 2nd edition, 1966

Einstein, Alfred, *Mozart: His Character, His Work,* translated by Arthur Mendel and Nathan Broder, New York: Oxford University Press, 1945

Eisen, Cliff, *New Mozart Documents: A Supplement to O.E. Deutsch's Documentary Biography,* Stanford, California: Stanford University Press, and London: Macmillan, 1991

Hutchings, Arthur, *Mozart: The Man, the Musician,* New York: Schirmer Books, and London: Thames and Hudson, 1976

Knepler, Georg, *Wolfgang Amadé Mozart,* translated by J. Bradford Robinson, Cambridge: Cambridge University Press, 1994

Köchel, Ludwig, Ritter von, *Chronologisch-thematisches Verzeichnis sämtlicher Tonwerke Wolfgang Amadé Mozarts,* Leipzig: Breitkopf und Härtel, 1862; 8th edition, edited by Franz Giegling et al., 1983

Kupferberg, Herbert, *Amadeus: A Mozart Mosaic,* New York: McGraw Hill, 1986; London: Robson, 1987

Landon, H.C. Robbins, *Mozart: The Golden Years, 1781–1791,* London: Thames and Hudson, and New York: Schirmer Books, 1989

———, *1791: Mozart's Last Year,* London: Thames and Hudson, and New York: Schirmer Books, 1988

Morris, James M., editor, *On Mozart,* Washington, D.C.: Woodrow Wilson Center Press and Cambridge: Cambridge University Press, 1994

Mozart, Wolfgang Amadeus, *The Letters of Mozart and His Family,* 3 vols., edited by Emily Anderson, London: Macmillan, 1938; 3rd edition, London: Macmillan, and New York: Norton, 1985

———, *Mozart Speaks: Views on Music, Musicians, and the World,* edited by Robert L. Marshall, New York: Schirmer Books, 1991

Ottaway, Hugh, *Mozart,* London: Orbis, 1979; Detroit, Michigan: Wayne State University Press, 1980

Sadie, Stanley, *Mozart,* London: Calder and Boyars, and New York: Vienna House, 1965

———, *The New Grove Mozart,* London: Macmillan, 1982; New York: Norton, 1983

Solomon, Maynard, *Mozart: A Life,* New York: HarperCollins, and London: Hutchinson, 1995

The life of composer Wolfgang Amadeus Mozart is the subject of a large number of books that vary greatly in scope and purpose. Biographies can be general or can concentrate on one period of his life, some presenting historical documents and letters and others describing the cultural and political milieu in which he lived. We are thus offered different perspectives on this extraordinary man both as a human being and as a composer. The bicentennial of Mozart's death in 1991 and especially the popularity of the film *Amadeus* inspired the publication of many new books.

Anderson's translation of the numerous letters that MOZART (1938) exchanged with his family remains the best complete edition in English of this correspondence. The letters began during his childhood concert tours with his sister Nannerl and continued later in life as he traveled in search of employment and finally settled in Vienna. A major source of information about Mozart's life, these fascinating letters provide great insight into his character and personality and his close relationships with other members of his family. The third edition corrects some minor errors and includes findings of recent research.

BRAUNBEHRENS has written a biography that, in many ways, complements Mozart's letters. The author considers Vienna during the historical period in which Mozart lived from 1781 to his death in 1791, and the lively discussion of living conditions, political conflicts, the economic and social balance of power, and other aspects of Viennese society create a vivid impression of the city. Thus, Mozart's environment, not a technical and aesthetic analysis of individual works, is the focus of the book, which provides a valuable context in which to understand and appreciate the composer's creative maturity.

DEUTSCH presents documents and contemporaneous information that form a year-by-year chronicle of Mozart's life. In contrast to biographical descriptions, we find here the actual historical records on which biographies are based. These records include dates of concerts and lists of works performed, contemporary criticism and commentary, and information about published works. The volume contains all the available documents relevant to Mozart's life, with the exception of his letters, which are available elsewhere (see Mozart [1938] and Mozart [1991]). Some events, such as the details of Mozart's journeys, which are established through the letters and journals but could not be indicated through other documents, have been inserted in chronological order. Collectively, the documents evoke a vivid sense of time and place, giving us a view into the actual world in which Mozart lived and composed (see also Eisen).

Since it first appeared in translation in 1945, EINSTEIN's biography has gained wide respect for its perceptive discussion of Mozart's life and relations with others. It also explores his music in depth, unlike many other Mozart biographies that discuss the music briefly, if at all. Sections on Mozart the musician, the instrumental works, the vocal works, and opera are enlightening for musicians and nonmusicians alike. This book lacks the abundant photographs that might be included in larger and more glossy formats, but it is still regarded as one of the best Mozart biographies available.

EISEN has supplemented Deutsch by examining a number of previously overlooked sources, such as 18th-century newspapers and other periodicals, books, catalogs, and archives. New documents and information have been uncovered, including advertisements about Mozart's music and its performance and contemporaneous remarks. The 241 additions provide valuable new information about Mozart's life as both a child and an adult.

HUTCHINGS's biography is lengthy and contains many illustrations in both color and black and white. One of the largest books on Mozart in English, it is intended for the general reader. It is divided into two parts—"Mozart: The Man" and "Mozart: The Musician"—as suggested by the title. This division results in some duplication of information, and the book has other flaws, such as the lack of a bibliography. Nevertheless, the wealth of illustrations and the extensive text will make the volume attractive to many readers.

KNEPLER views Mozart from the perspectives of his creative psyche, his political leanings, his relation to the thoughts and currents of the Enlightenment, and the underlying basis of his musical expression. This intellectual reconsideration of the composer and his music examines the family correspondence, his travels, the social and political context of the 1780s, his involvement with the Masonic Order, and other facets of Mozart's world and thought. By considering the composer's development in relation to intellectual development and cultural influences, the author provides many fresh and stimulating insights into the composer and his music.

KÖCHEL's thematic catalog of all Mozart's works is the source of the familiar "K" numbers that identify Mozart's compositions. The catalog gives detailed biographical information for each work, together with "incipits" of the first several measures of the theme for each movement to facilitate identification. In the sixth edition, the editors renumbered some compositions in accordance with new research findings; however, the musical community is familiar with the old numbers and often retains them instead of or in addition to the new ones. This major reference work is a cornerstone of Mozart studies and a valuable guide to Mozart's complete output.

KUPFERBERG has written a popular biography, as suggested by the title's reference to Peter Schaffer's play and the subsequent film. The book avoids the sensational, however, and is highly recommended because of its careful research, up-to-date scholarship, and clear literary style. Organized chronologically, it draws heavily on the published family correspondence to narrate the composer's life and describe his personality. This introductory biography is concise, interesting, and readable.

LANDON (1989), best known as a Haydn scholar, has also written several books about Mozart. He has directed these to a broad audience in an effort to fill "the ever-widening gap between the general reader and the specialist." Landon's study of Mozart's years in Vienna, which the author appropriately terms "the golden years," achieves this goal with mastery. The biography's illustrations and elegantly written text make it very appealing to the general reader. At the same time, it provides new archival information and is founded on authoritative scholarship. This book thus finds its middle way and is highly recommended.

LANDON (1988) focuses on 1791, the year of Mozart's death. Because many of Mozart's greatest works were composed near the end of his life, his final years are of particular interest. Adopting a limited time frame makes it possible for Landon to examine different facets of this single year in depth and in relationship to one another. As a result, this book puts the music into the full social and historical context of its creation. Quoting passages from letters, diaries, and various other papers, the author has written a book that evokes sights, sounds, and the atmosphere of the period. Old myths are reexamined, including that of Salieri's reputed hostility to the composer; Constanze's character and actions are also reevaluated. An excellent appendix by Else Radant proposes a new reconstruction of Mozart's apartment in Vienna. These stimulating and lucid essays incorporate old and new material in a comprehensive view of Mozart's final year.

MOZART (1991) adopts an approach to the words of the composer that is different than the more standard chronological organization of family correspondence. This book, drawn from both Mozart's letters and contemporary observations of his life, consists of selected quotations organized topically so that various aspects of Mozart's thought and personality emerge with clarity. In each of the three main parts—"Self Portrait with Landscape," "On Music," and "On Musicians"—entries are organized under topics and subheadings ranging from "instrumental music" and "church music" to "personal affairs" and "amusements and pastimes." The selections clearly document the combination of gaiety, humor, and deep sadness that was so characteristic of the composer. Statements on composition, performance, and dramaturgy illustrate his gifts as well as the difficulty he had when confronting the everyday problems of life. This book facilitates access to Mozart's thoughts both for informal reading and for a survey by topic.

MORRIS has edited a series of papers from several different fields that discuss Mozart from various perspectives. These include psychology and psychobiography, economics, literature, and movie criticism. Most of the papers originated in a symposium that took place in December 1991 at the Woodrow Wilson Center in Washington, D.C. This gathering, one of many conferences associated with the bicentennial of the composer's death in that year, was notable for the diversity of its participants and the breadth of its concerns. Among the contributors to this volume are the noted musicologists Wye J. Allenbrook, Joseph Kerman, Christopf Wolff, and Neal Zaslaw; historian Leon Botstein; psychobiographer Maynard Solomon; and movie critic Stanley Kauffmann, who considers three movie versions of Mozart's operas. The authors seek to present Mozart in the context of real life and to pursue a general inquiry into the nature of creativity as a point of departure for exploring Mozart's genius. Although interdisciplinary exchanges are not a feature of these essays, they address a broad range of subjects in terms that are accessible to the general reader.

OTTAWAY's biography can be recommended for its lively and attractive narrative. It is amply illustrated with 43 full-page illustrations, most in color, and 46 partial-page illustrations in black and white. The book was written primarily for nonspecialist music lovers and contains few musical examples or unexplained musical terms. Despite some errors in information and the somewhat arbitrary selection of works discussed, the book is written with insight and affection and will serve as a good introduction to the composer.

SADIE's (1965) biography is also written in a non-technical style that is both readable and interesting. This noted Mozart scholar's approach to the composer's life is illuminating, and the numerous black-and-white illustrations convey a vivid impression of Mozart's world. The book includes an extended discussion of Mozart's music in terms that will be accessible to most readers. Complementing this discussion is an appended list of works by genre and a table of works arranged by year. Other appendices include a four-page chronology of Mozart's life, a select bibliography, and an index of people and places. Although not as extensive as some biographies, this book can serve as an excellent introduction to the composer. It contains original ideas about style, correlations between events in Mozart's life and works that he composed, and consideration of outside influences on the composer.

SADIE (1983) differs somewhat from Sadie (1965); the later publication is shorter, contains fewer illustrations, and uses a more compressed literary style. It also reflects more recent research. Like other *New Grove*

composer biographies, it contains extensive appended listings, including a complete list of the composer's works organized by genre and an extensive bibliography that covers books and articles about Mozart and his music written up to the date of the volume's publication. A stylistic examination of his works is also incorporated in the biographical narrative.

SOLOMON explores Mozart's life from a psychological perspective. Rather than following a chronological narrative, the book examines different facets of the composer's life and states of mind. The result is a perceptive and illuminating series of commentaries about the composer as an individual and a creative artist. The author, who is known for his penetrating psychological studies of composers, has written a book based on solid scholarship.

DAVID GAGNÉ

2. Chamber Music

Abert, Hermann, "Mozart, Wolfgang Amadeus [Johann Chrysostomus Wolfgang Gottlich], 1756–1791," in *Cobbett's Cyclopedia Survey of Chamber Music,* compiled and edited by Walter Willson Cobbett, London: Oxford University Press, 1930; 2nd edition, edited by Colin Mason, 3 vols., London: Oxford University Press, 1963

Blom, Eric, "Wolfgang Amadeus Mozart (1756–1791)," in *Chamber Music,* edited by Alec Robertson, Harmondsworth: Penguin, 1957

Dunhill, Thomas F., *Mozart's String Quartets,* 2 vols., London: Oxford University Press, 1927; reprint, 2 volumes in 1, Westport, Connecticut: Greenwood Press, 1970

Einstein, Alfred, *Mozart: His Character, His Work,* translated by Arthur Mendel and Nathan Broder, New York: Oxford University Press, 1945

Ferguson, Donald N., *Image and Structure in Chamber Music,* Minneapolis: University of Minnesota Press, 1964

Irving, John, *Mozart, the "Haydn" Quartets,* Cambridge: Cambridge University Press, 1998

King, Alec Hyatt, *Mozart Chamber Music,* London: British Broadcasting Corporation, and Seattle: University of Washington Press, 1968

Landon, H.C. Robbins, and Donald Mitchell, editors, *The Mozart Companion,* London: Rockliff, and New York: Norton, 1956

Loft, Abram, *Violin and Keyboard: The Duo Repertoire,* 2 vols., New York: Grossman, 1973

Smith, Erik, *Mozart: Serenades, Divertimenti, and Dances,* London: British Broadcasting Corporation, 1982

Ulrich, Homer, *Chamber Music,* New York: Columbia University Press, 1948; 2nd edition, 1966

Mozart's chamber music includes duos, trios, quartets, quintets, sonatas for piano and violin, most of the composer's divertimenti and serenades, and a handful of works with individual labels for which only one person plays on a part. The images of Mozart that emerge in the studies of his chamber music range from the "Eternal Child" to the prefiguration of Beethoven—a pre-romantic artistic hero. The views become most territorial in the discussions and interpretations of Mozart's last ten string quartets, beginning with the six dedicated to Joseph Haydn. There is much evidence to support Mozart's claim that the works were difficult to compose. The music itself, which is unparalleled in his oeuvre, argues for this difficulty. The last three quartets, known as the "Prussian" quartets because of the traditional belief that they were written for the King of Prussia, are variously viewed as "retrograde," "pathetic," and "troublesome." The string quartets as a whole are also a favorite arena for stylistic comparisons between Mozart and Haydn, because the composers seemed to carry on a stylistic dialogue through these pieces. In surveys of the complete body of Mozart's chamber works, the quartets typically form the kernel of the discussion. The studies available in English do not address the recent interest in historical performance practice issues. The musical analysis in these studies will not intimidate readers with a basic musical knowledge.

DUNHILL sees Mozart as a "guardian of tradition" and defends the purity of his music. The author provides a summary of each of the string quartets, accompanied by examples of significant themes and commentary on the main musical themes and important rhetorical moments. Dunhill contends that early quintet, K. 174, rather than the quartets, portends later style developments in Mozart's chamber music. The later works receive more extensive treatment than do the earlier compositions.

ABERT begins with a thorough list of all the chamber works. He uses the music to portray Mozart as a proto-Beethoven: a stormy genius whose unsettled spirit is expressed through his art, although it is often suppressed because of the alleged impoverished taste of his audience. The biography is now out of date. The author makes some insightful points about the problems of distinguishing Mozart's chamber works from other genres, recognizing that the distinction did not exist in Mozart's mind. Abert's analysis primarily consists of keys and forms. The article concludes with a polite disclaimer from Cobbett.

EINSTEIN remains one of the most rewarding books in the literature on the composer. Eight years before this book, the author revised a catalog of the complete works of Mozart, and his comprehensive knowledge of the repertoire is a constant presence in the volume listed here. Einstein not only demonstrates his familiarity with particular pieces but also expresses insightful convictions regarding the goals of chamber music. The writing is both concise and rich, with worthwhile detail and colorful commentary. The author appreciates the early works both for the way in which they foreshadow later works and for

their inherent value. Although Einstein conveys a biased enthusiasm for Mozart's music—at times the author promulgates the "Eternal Child" image of the composer—he also supplies a healthy skepticism toward unsubstantiated stories. Still, his conjectural observations on social contexts need scholarly fine-tuning.

LANDON and MITCHELL contains two essays on Mozart's chamber music. Most of the repertoire is covered by Hans Keller, while Mitchell writes about serenades for wind band. Keller's text is directed at the chamber musician and includes some detailed performance suggestions. Seeking to demonstrate the unity of the works he discusses, the author attempts to map the development of motivic cells, an analytical approach used by Rudolph Réti. References by Keller to the undefined "greatness" of particular works are confusing, and the occasional sour tone of the writing may come across as pompous. The coverage of the repertoire is relatively thorough, but the chamber works with keyboard receive only cursory commentary. Mitchell's essay is a relatively generous, detailed study of three wind serenades: K. 361, 375, and 388. The analysis is thematic and rhythmic. The commentary, which includes brief quotes from Einstein, is limited to the music.

BLOM's discussion is divided into topics: contrapuntal devices, melody, originality, rhythm, harmony, technique, form, use of modes, and treatment of instruments. He notes Mozart's tendency to enrich elements such as accompaniments that might have been handled more simply. The study is firmly focused on the music, with some historical background. The author makes comparisons to other composers and works, both contemporaneous and otherwise. He examines problems raised by K. 387: tensions between chamber and symphonic style and the lack of an emphatic closure to any of the movements. In addition to discussion of the "Haydn" Quartets, Blom points to possible influences of Mozart's piano trios on Beethoven.

ULRICH calls attention to Mozart's extensive travels as a crucial influence on his music. The survey is weak with regard to early works but still tries to divine motivations for unexplained compositions—where evidence of commissions is lacking, inner reasons will do. Ulrich calls special attention to the role of the piano in chamber music. His occasional reliance on Einstein is consistent with the overall laudatory tone of this volume, although Ulrich does not fall into Mozart idolatry. The reader should be wary of the author's attempt to reduce Mozart's stylistic growth to a narrative.

The chapter on Mozart in FERGUSON regards Mozart's music as an "unconscious biography." The study tends toward the poetic in its broad statements, with frivolous references to the "bounds of beauty" and the "delight of creation." The treatments of specific works vary widely, but the author provides a brief history and sketchy analysis for most of the compositions, usually with an emphasis on first movements. The treatment of the "Haydn" Quartets is among the more extensive. Many of the earlier works are ignored.

KING is the most thorough consideration of Mozart's chamber music since Abert's work, although King excludes the divertimenti and the serenades (pieces discussed in Smith). The writing is less convivial than that in Einstein's study, but King's book is more detailed both historically and analytically. The survey is valuable for its even examination of all the movements of any particular work; the coverage of the "Haydn" Quartets—including their background and their substance—is particularly exhaustive. Much of the commentary and many of the narrative descriptions seem at first to be vain attempts to translate the music into a series of discursive events. But for those who know this repertoire, the observations challenge the reader either to confirm the comments or to refute them.

LOFT addresses performers who want to know more about the violin sonatas and how to approach them. The study lists the piano-violin music that is available, assesses the difficulty of the works, highlights points of interest, and suggests ways in which to approach a given work in performance. The writer, a violinist, is careful to say only what he knows, based on seasoned performance experience. In the historical background sketches, Loft quotes freely from Mozart's letters. The discussion of the music assumes the reader has some acquaintance with the works under consideration. Period performance practice issues and problems with editions are not confronted.

SMITH provides information on divertimenti and serenades, chamber works not covered in King's volume. Smith discusses chronology and authenticity, but he does not include footnotes or a bibliography. The musical discussions are brief, but incisive, compressing helpful analytical information into concise sections. His conjectures on possible social contexts of performances of this primarily outdoor repertoire are nuanced by a humorous disposition.

Three German books—*Studien zur Geschichte des Streichquartetts,* by Ludwig Finscher (1974); *Mozarts Streichquintette: Beitrage zum musikalischen Satz, zum Gattungskontext und zu Quellenfragen,* edited by Cliff Eisen and Wolf-Dieter Seiffert (1994); and *Mozarts frühe Streichquartette,* by Wolf-Dieter Seiffert (1992)—fill the 30-year gap since the last study in English dedicated to Mozart's chamber music was published; in addition, there are numerous chapters or articles scattered about in monographs, Festschrifts, and journals. Much research on this repertoire has recently been done in the areas of source studies, rhetoric, stylistic analysis, and performance practice; a new survey in English is in order.

IRVING is a brief but informative guide to the first six of Mozart's later quartets. In addition to covering the historical backgrounds of the works, Irving discusses the reception of the repertoire and current analytical trends, including several prominent references to rhetorical topics in the music. The limited size of the volume restricts the depth of the writing, but Irving identifies a number of approaches pursued by scholars and critics in both the 19th and 20th centuries.

JOSEPH ORCHARD

3. Keyboard Music

Levin, Robert D., "Mozart's Solo Keyboard Music," in *Eighteenth-Century Keyboard Music,* edited by Robert L. Marshall New York: Schirmer Books, 1994

Mercado, Mario Raymond, *The Evolution of Mozart's Pianistic Style,* Carbondale: Southern Illinois University Press, 1992

Wolff, Konrad, *Masters of the Keyboard,* Bloomington: Indiana University Press, 1983; enlarged edition, 1990

The keyboard works of Wolfgang Amadeus Mozart display an exceptional variety of compositional techniques and, like all his other works, reflect the evolution of the composer's style from the simplicity and galantness of his earlier pieces to the mature, controlled complexity of his later works. Most authors classify the keyboard works into several distinct groups. The compositions of the early 1760s include minuets, miniatures, and sonatas with violin accompaniment or with ad libitum violin, flute, or cello; their scores show signs of having been revised by Mozart's father, Leopold. The next group includes the six sonatas K. 279–284 composed in 1775 in Munich; these are followed by the two sonatas from Mannheim, composed in 1777 and 1778. The five sonatas K. 330–333 and 457 and the Fantasia K. 475 belong in the middle period (1783–84), while the threshold to the compositions of the last period is represented by three rondos, K. 485 and 494 (both of 1786) and 511 (1787). Finally, the four sonatas K. 533, 545, 570, and 576 and the Adagio K. 540 are usually considered to be the late piano compositions. Of these, K. 570, published by Artaria in 1796 with violin accompaniment, was until recently included with the sonatas for piano and violin.

LEVIN discusses Mozart's solo works from the perspectives of both a music theorist/historian and a piano performer. Levin's study is well informed, and his writing style is clear—scholarly but not pedantic, technical yet eloquent and expressive. An abundance of musical examples, chosen mainly from the piano sonatas, supplements the text, which is organized into several sections. The first examines the fundamentals of Mozart's compositional process (improvisation and variation); the remaining sections represent a chronological and stylistic investigation of Mozart's piano works. Levin examines each sonata in terms of formal design, harmonic and key relationships, rhythmic patterns, meter, tempo indications, texture, character, and the like, and finds that many of these features recur in Mozart's piano concertos as well. Levin argues that the operatic element was present—although mostly as rhetorical color—in the earlier sonatas; he posits that K. 457 is a work of "irascible angularity," and that K. 533 emphasizes the contrapuntal process as its expressive goal; he concludes, however, that in K. 576 "all of the threads of [Mozart's] prior styles reached a synthesis." A brief but competent bibliography of the available editions of the keyboard works is followed by notes and a short bibliography of studies about the composer himself.

WOLFF's declared intention is "to fill a gap for today's piano students"; the book as a whole achieves that goal. The chapter on Mozart's piano works, written from the perspective of the performer, is very useful: the language—although not entirely devoid of technical terms—is accessible, the concepts are discussed in light of their practical applicability, and the material for discussion is taken mostly from Mozart's piano sonatas, with occasional reference to fantasias or chamber music with piano. Wolff describes his own work as a scholarly book based on the study of the scores themselves and states that for that reason, he "refrained from giving concrete playing suggestions." One might, however, disagree with the latter statement, as many suggestions are in fact included, especially toward the end of the chapter.

Wolff divides the chapter into two sections, first examining the enlargement of instrumental style and then exploring realization of the possibilities of the pianoforte. In the first section, he notes Mozart's emphasis on the vocal character of instrumental melodies and shows that Mozart's lines can be "aria-like" or "recitative-like," especially in slow movements. Unlike Levin, Wolff contends that Mozart's use of the Alberti bass (as well as the use of pedal) introduces a suggestion of orchestral color. Wolff notes Mozart's avoidance of mechanical repetition, even when formal sections (such as the recapitulation of sonata form) could easily accommodate it. Wolff introduces the term "the locus principle," used to refer to Mozart's inclination to reserve certain musical techniques for specific points within the form (for instance, the use of sharp dissonance and modulation to remote keys in the developments of slow movements). With regard to fantasias, Wolff makes the intriguing argument that "the challenge for Mozart was in achieving cohesion without the three usual quasi-Aristotelian unities of time signature, key signature, and monothematic structure," and the author goes on to trace parallels between similar principles used in the French classicizing literature of the 17th century and in the forging of the classical style in the music of the 18th century. Two fantasias, C Major K. 394 and C Minor K. 475, are examined in some detail from this perspective.

In the second section of the chapter, analyzing Mozart's exploitation of the possibilities of the pianoforte, Wolff maintains that the vitality of melody comes from several factors, including the contrast between diatonic and chromatic lines, the centering of the melody around the fifth tone of the scale, the use of wide leaps conveying great intensity, and so on. Wolff's book includes notes, a bibliography for each chapter, and an index of persons (composers, performers, and publishers) and works.

MERCADO's study provides an excellent starting point for those interested in Mozart's piano works; detailed discussions of individual piano sonatas and fantasias are interspersed with analyses of piano concertos and chamber music that includes the piano. In a chapter on Mozart and the transformation of keyboard practice, Mercado highlights Mozart's enthusiasm for Stein's pianos and the composer's marked interest in playing the organ (Mozart's early performances on this instrument are characterized by the author as "spectacular"). Unlike Levin, who identifies the Fantasia in C Minor K. 475 as romantic, Mercado seems to agree with those who emphasize the baroque qualities of the piece and who argue that the fantasia was originally conceived as an introduction to an organ fugue.

A valuable feature of Mercado's book is its index of Mozart's keyboard compositions, classified by solo works (sonatas, variations, individual minuets, rondos, preludes, fantasias, allegros, adagios, and the collection known as *Finger Exercise*); chamber music (including four-hand works for two pianos, keyboard works with violin, and piano trios, quartets, and quintets); concerto arrangements; concertos for piano and orchestra; and cadenzas. The book also features a rather substantial bibliography, notes, a plethora of musical examples, excerpts from Mozart's letters, and writings by Mozart's contemporaries.

LUMINITA FLOREA

4. Operas

Allanbrook, Wye Jamison, *Rhythmic Gesture in Mozart: Le Nozze di Figaro and Don Giovanni*, Chicago: University of Chicago Press, 1983

Angermüller, Rudolph, *Mozart's Operas*, New York: Rizzoli, 1988

Benn, Frederick Christopher, *Mozart on the Stage*, New York: Coward-McCann, 1945

Brophy, Brigid, *Mozart the Dramatist*, London: Faber, and New York: Harcourt, Brace and World, 1964

Dent, Edward Joseph, *Mozart's Operas: A Critical Study*, London: Chatto and Windus, 1913; 2nd edition, London: Oxford University Press, 1947

Ford, Charles, *Cosi?: Sexual Politics in Mozart's Operas*, Manchester: Manchester University Press, 1991

Gianturco, Carolyn, *Mozart's Early Operas*, London: Batsford, 1981

Goldovsky, Boris, *The Adult Mozart: A Personal Perspective*, 4 vols., N.p.: National Opera Association, 1991

Heartz, Daniel, *Mozart's Operas*, Berkeley: University of California Press, 1990

Mann, William, *The Operas of Mozart*, New York: Oxford University Press, and London: Cassell, 1977

Mozart, Wolfgang Amadeus, *The Great Operas of Mozart*, edited by Nathan Broder, New York: Norton, 1962

Noske, Frits, *The Signifier and the Signified: Studies in the Operas of Mozart and Verdi*, Oxford: Oxford University Press, and The Hague: Nijhoff, 1977

Osborne, Charles, *The Complete Operas of Mozart: A Critical Guide*, London: Gollancz, and New York: Atheneum, 1978

Steptoe, Andrew, *The Mozart-Da Ponte Operas: The Cultural and Musical Background to Le Nozze di Figaro, Don Giovanni, and Così fan tutte*, Oxford: Clarendon Press, 1988

Till, Nicholas, *Mozart and the Enlightenment: Truth, Virtue, and Beauty in Mozart's Operas*, London: Faber, 1991; New York, Norton, 1993

Mozart composed 23 theatrical works; however, it is difficult to determine how many of these are "operas" because scholars disagree on how to classify many of them. In general, Mozart's theatrical works may be divided into the following types: opera seria, opera buffa, *dramma giocoso*, singspiel, and miscellaneous types of theatrical music (written primarily during Mozart's teen years) referred to by terms such *as festa teatrale, serenata, dramma per musica, play with music*, and *sacred drama*.

There are numerous general studies in English on Mozart's life and music, and all of them mention his theatrical music on at least a basic level. Although these types of books are not the recommended medium for finding opera-specific information, two such references are worth noting: Julian Rushton's entry on Mozart in *The New Grove Dictionary of Opera* (1992) and the section on "Operas" in *The Mozart Compendium* (1990), coauthored by Amanda Holden and John Stone. In his overview, Rushton traces Mozart's operatic career and style development, and the author highlights his account with quotes from the composer, notated musical excerpts, and brief analytical commentaries. He also includes an exhaustive bibliography and a chronological work list that provides critical information on each opera, including genre, number of acts, author of the opera's libretto, date of composition/first performance, orchestral scoring, page/volume location of the full musical score in Mozart's Complete Works editions, and the "K" number of the work (in reference to Köchel's well-known catalog of Mozart's work). In *The Mozart Compendium*, Stone summarizes Mozart's contributions to the operatic genre in five concise commentaries entitled "The Early Operas," "Idomeneo," "Die Entführung aus dem Serail," "The Da Ponte operas" (*Le nozze di Figaro, Don Giovanni*, and *Così fan tutte*—all based on librettos by Lorenzo Da Ponte), and "*Die Zauberflöte* and *La Clemenza di Tito*." Holden's anno-

tated "List of Works" provides the same information as Rushton, as well as character descriptions, brief plot synopses, critical notes on each work, and information on where to locate the libretto and musical score.

In addition to these general summaries, there are approximately two dozen book-length studies in English devoted specifically to Mozart's operas. This body of literature falls into four basic categories: (1) large-scale surveys and synopses of Mozart's theatrical works, (2) historical/analytical studies of his operas, (3) interpretive studies of dramatic symbolism in his operas, and (4) comprehensive studies of individual operas.

For general readers, the most direct and compelling large-scale survey is ANGERMÜLLER. This book offers an extensive discussion of 22 stage works, each covered in an individual chapter that provides sociohistorical background on the work and its genre; a discussion of the opera's libretto; how, when, and where Mozart composed the work; a list and description of the characters; a synopsis of the plot; basic analytical commentary on important aspects of the opera's internal structure; a wide range of vivid illustrations and photographs of performances, sets and costume designs, opera posters, etc.; and information on performances, critical reception, and printed editions of the work. Angermüller also includes an exhaustive bibliography of several hundred sources, arranged in relation to each individual opera.

Another excellent large-scale survey, OSBORNE covers 21 stage works in chronological sequence, using a biographical-historical approach that includes basic dramatic and structural analyses of each work, with cross-references to Mozart's analogous nonoperatic works. Although Osborne offers relatively few illustrations, he includes brief notated musical examples for major moments in each opera.

MANN is the most comprehensive survey of this topic, with individual, chronologically ordered chapters on 22 works. Each chapter begins with general background on a particular work, followed by a scene-by-scene description of the opera (including a full English translation of each aria and brief notated musical examples), and ending with an interpretive discussion of the work's significance. In addition, Mann includes commentaries on "Mozart's Choice of Keys," "Mozart and the Opera Seria," "Waiting for Idomeneo," and "Italian Comic Opera."

MOZART is an excellent source of concise and critical information for five major operas: *Die Entführung aus dem Serail, Le nozze di Figaro, Don Giovanni, Così fan tutte*, and *Die Zauberflöte*. It begins with a short overview on "Mozart and the Opera," followed by a section on each opera that includes a brief introduction to the work, its cast of characters, a synopsis of the plot, and the complete libretto (with the original language and the English translation set side-by-side). BENN offers charming scene-by-scene synopses for *Le nozze di*

Figaro, Don Giovanni, Così fan tutte, and *Die Zauber-flöte.* Both of these books are especially good introductions for readers preparing to attend a performance or listen to a recording, or as resources for compiling basic program notes or synopses for these operas.

DENT established the scholarly standard for this topic, and it is still a good overall source. The author begins with an introduction on "Mozart as a Classic" and then devotes a single chapter to Mozart's early operas before commencing with the main focus of the book—the seven mature operas: *Idomeneo, Die Entführung aus dem Serail, Le nozze di Figaro, Don Giovanni, Così fan tutte, Die Zauberflöte,* and *La Clemenza di Tito.* Nearly three-fourths of the book is devoted to *Le nozze di Figaro, Don Giovanni,* and *Die Zauberflöte.* Although the content is highly detailed, Dent's writing style is accessible to general readers.

HEARTZ is an outstanding recent musicological study of the same seven "master operas" discussed by Dent. Heartz and contributing author Thomas Bauman offer extensive historical background on the events surrounding the genesis of each work (illustrated by quotes from Mozart and his contemporaries), detailed analyses of the melodic, harmonic, and dramatic structures of these works, and intensive essays on "Mozart's Tragic Muse," "The Poet as Stage Director," and "Mozart and His Italian Contemporaries." The book also includes an excellent bibliography. Despite the richness of the book's content, the writing style will pose problems for general readers.

GIANTURCO's book provides detailed musicological coverage for Mozart's first 12 theatrical works—from the sacred singspiel *Die Schuldigkeit des ersten Gebotes* (1767) to *Zaide* (1779–80). Each work is covered in an individual chapter, each of which begins with extensive historical/biographical narrative (highlighted with contemporaneous quotes) followed by a scene-by-scene description and analysis of the opera.

GOLDOVSKY devotes nearly half of its pages to Mozart's last ten operas—*Die Entführung aus dem Serail* (1783) to *La clemenza di Tito* (1791). Goldovsky's insights are thoroughly researched and rich in content, offering something for everyone: fascinating and unusual details on the genesis, symbolism, scenarios, structure, and alternative versions/performances of these operas, presented within the personalized context of Mozart's life, opinions, and relationships. This study is a must-read for any lover of Mozart's music.

STEPTOE's volume offers cultural and musical perspectives on *Le nozze di Figaro, Don Giovanni,* and *Così fan tutte.* The first half of the book provides background on late 18th-century social and musical currents (such as "The Social Context: Vienna and Her Ruler" and "Musicians, Opera, and Audience in Mozart's Time") and a section on Mozart's personal circle of friends and supporters (including da Ponte) and his working life in

Vienna. The last half of the book traces how the magnificent collaboration between Mozart and da Ponte gradually transformed comic opera into a highly sophisticated idiom with a new sense of drama and musical form that surpassed opera seria in many ways.

ALLANBROOK's work is an intense theoretical discourse that is not intended for general readers. The author demonstrates that the rhythmic structures in particular arias, scenes, and acts of *Le nozze di Figaro* and *Don Giovanni* are based on 18th-century dances that make specific symbolic social references to the upper and lower classes. Allanbrook also shows how Mozart's ingenious musical settings intensify the portrayal of various characters by either contradicting, questioning, interpolating, or reinterpreting da Ponte's words.

The sources on interpretation and symbolism in Mozart's operas offer a wide range of perspectives. TILL explains how Mozart's operas from *La finta giardiniera* (1775) to *Die Zauberflöte* (1791) were impacted by the intellectual and social issues of late 18th-century Vienna and considers how these works, in turn, were a catalyst in the evolving philosophy of the Enlightenment. More important, Till demonstrates how issues related to the Enlightenment help to explain notorious performance problems in many of Mozart's operas—especially *Die Zauberflöte.*

A psychological study on the Enlightenment is found in FORD, as evidenced in such chapters as "Anglo-French Subjectivism," "The Dialectic of the Rococo," "The Amorality of Individualism," "Vulnerability, Dependency, Hysteria," and "Sexual Antagonism as Moral Resolution." Both Till and Ford assume the reader's familiarity with Mozart's operas—and to a lesser extent, the Enlightenment itself.

BROPHY provides a brilliant and refreshingly unorthodox account of why Mozart's music is so important and why opera is the idiom that best demonstrates his genius. She describes Mozart as "a creative psychologist whose characters deserve the serious and searching affection—passion, even—we give to Shakespeare's." Throughout the book, she boldly psychoanalyzes the composer, his stage music, and the era itself in chapters such as "Women and Opera," "Singing and Theology," "Anarchy, Impotence, and Classicism," "Hell, Love, and Society," "Seduction in Mozart's Operas (with a Note on *Who* Is Cherubino, *What* Is He?)," "Don Giovanni and Hamlet," and "*Die Zauberflöte* Solved."

NOSKE focuses on interpretative symbolism in Mozart's operas, as revealed through structural analysis (which the author describes as being more concerned with the factors of opera such as "relationship," "coherence," and "continuity" than with the formal analysis of elements contained in the musical object itself). The main strength of this book is the way that it connects the classic dramatic approaches of Mozart to those of the great master of Italian romantic opera, Giuseppe

Verdi—particularly in comparisons of Mozart's *Don Giovanni* to Verdi's *Otello* and *Don Carlos*. Although this book is clearly aimed at music scholars who have significant knowledge of this repertory, general readers who are willing to brave the specilized terminology will find the appended essay on "Semiotic Devices in Musical Drama" to be particularly informative regarding the inherent musico-dramatic "sign language" of opera.

Readers seeking comprehensive coverage of a specific Mozart opera should consult the *Cambridge Opera Handbooks* series, which so far includes seven individual book-length studies on the following Mozart operas: *Idomeneo* (Julian Rushton), *Die Entführung aus dem Serail* (Thomas Bauman), *Le nozze di Figaro* (Tim Carter), *Don Giovanni* (Julian Rushton), *Così fan tutte* (Bruce Alan Brown), *Die Zauberflöte* (Peter Branscombe), and *La clemenza di Tito* (John A. Rice). These are excellent resources; however, general readers should be aware that each study is aimed at "the serious opera-goer or record collector, as well as the student or scholar" and is designed with a three-fold purpose: (1) to describe the historical genesis of the work (its sources, literary prototypes, collaboration between the composer and the librettist, and information on the premiere, important performances, and the critical reception of the work; (2) to provide a full synopsis that includes a detailed dramatic and musical analysis of the work, highlighted by substantial notated musical examples; and (3) to discuss various interpretative accounts of the opera (via "classic statements" as well as newly commissioned essays). The appendix of each volume includes an extensive "Notes" section with further information cross-referenced to each chapter, as well as a select bibliography and discography.

DANIEL JACOBSON

5. Orchestral Music

Forman, Denis, *Mozart's Concerto Form*, New York: Praeger, and London: Hart-Davis, 1971

Girdlestone, Cuthbert Morton, *Mozart and His Piano Concertos*, Norman: University of Oklahoma Press, 1952

Landon, H.C. Robbins, editor, *The Mozart Compendium: A Guide to Mozart's Life and Music*, London: Thames and Hudson, and New York: Schirmer Books, 1990

Hutchings, Arthur, *A Companion to Mozart's Piano Concertos*, London: Oxford University Press, 1948; 2nd edition, 1950

King, Alec Hyatt, *Mozart's Wind and String Concertos*, London: British Broadcasting Corporation, and Seattle: University of Washington Press, 1978

Lawson, Colin, *Mozart Clarinet Concerto*, New York: Cambridge University Press, 1996

Levin, Robert D., *Who Wrote the Mozart Four-Wind Concertante?* Stuyvesant, New York: Pendragon Press, 1988

Mozart, Wolfgang Amadeus, *Piano Concerto in C major, K. 503*, edited by Joseph Kerman, New York: Norton, 1970

———, *Symphony in G minor, K. 550*, edited by Nathan Broder, New York: Norton, 1967

Neumann, Frederick, *Ornamentation and Improvisation in Mozart*, Princeton, New Jersey: Princeton University Press, 1986

Sadie, Stanley, *Mozart Symphonies*, London: Ariel Music, 1986

———, *The New Grove Mozart*, London: Macmillan, 1982; New York: Norton, 1983

Sadie, Stanley, editor, *Wolfgang Amadè Mozart: Essays on His Life and His Music*, Oxford: Clarendon Press, and New York: Oxford University Press, 1996

Saint-Foix, Georges de, *The Symphonies of Mozart*, translated by Leslie Orrey, London: Dobson, 1947

Sisman, Elaine, *Mozart: The "Jupiter" Symphony*, Cambridge: Cambridge University Press, 1993

Smith, Erik, *Mozart: Serenades, Divertimenti, and Dances*, London: British Broadcasting Corporation, 1982

Tovey, Donald Francis, *Essays in Musical Analysis*, 6 vols., London: Oxford University Press, 1935–39

Zaslaw, Neal, *Mozart's Symphonies: Context, Performance Practice, Reception*, Oxford: Clarendon Press, and New York: Oxford University Press, 1989

Zaslaw, Neal, editor, *Mozart's Piano Concertos: Text, Context, Interpretation*, Ann Arbor: University of Michigan Press, 1996

Interest in Mozart and his work grew immensely between the bicentennials commemorating the composer's birth, in 1956, and death, in 1991. The books reviewed here, mostly published during these years, pertain to Mozart's symphonies, miscellaneous orchestral works (serenades, cassation, divertimentos, and marches), and concertos.

The Sadie (1982) and Landon volumes offer convenient starting points for any inquiry into Mozart. SADIE (1982) intertwines the events of Mozart's life with a review of his works, enabling the reader to study the orchestral compositions within the context of Mozart's career. The book concludes with an exhaustive list of works that is cross-referenced to the text and a bibliography organized according to topic. LANDON contains informative articles by many important Mozart scholars covering the entire range of Mozart studies. Articles by Cliff Eisen, Robert Levin, and David Wyn Jones are devoted to Mozart's orchestral pieces, summarizing prominent stylistic traits and featuring chronological listings, including dates of composition, movement-tempos, orchestration, and the sources for the modern editions.

MOZART (1967) includes a reliable and clear reprint of the text of the *New Mozart Edition* of the Symphony in G Minor, K. 550. The volume also provides a historical background, analyses that focus on the music's most distinguishing characteristics (the minor mode and the repeated descending minor second), and critical reviews. Written during the 19th and 20th centuries, these reviews mirror how changing aesthetic values affected the reception of the symphony. Thus, while most critics acknowledged the sorrowful affect of the music, some 19th-century writers also sensed affects of grace, joy, and animation.

SADIE (1996) arose from the Royal Musical Association Mozart Bicentenary Conference held in London in 1991. Including 25 of the nearly 50 papers delivered at the conference, the book is subdivided into three broad topics: "Composer and Context," "Instrumental Music," and "Mozart and the Theater." László Somfai deals with the sketches for Symphony no. 38 and Piano Concerto K. 414; Dexter Edge recounts Mozart in performance, 1787 to 1791; William Drabkin suggests guidelines for the construction of cadenzas; and Cliff Eisen contends that the orchestral works written in Salzburg were socially and musically unacceptable, reflecting Mozart's rebellion against Salzburg and the archbishop.

Despite the fact that SAINT-FOIX was written more than 50 years ago, it remains pertinent as the first study of a complete instrumental genre. In addition to surveying the symphonies, the author focuses on Mozart's changing orchestral writing as a mirror of his developing style. Placing the works within a historic context, Saint-Foix compares these symphonies to those of Mozart's contemporaries and emphasizes Mozart's special relationship with Haydn.

SISMAN, a handbook on Mozart's last and most celebrated symphony, the *Jupiter*, K. 551, correlates the structure of the symphony with its expressive content. The book opens with discussions of the classical symphony in Vienna and the aesthetic context of 18th-century expression. Defining the grand style and the sublime, Sisman explains how both of these affects are essential to an understanding of Mozart's late symphonies. Following a review of the state of Mozart's life in 1788 and the composition and reception of the *Jupiter*, Sisman analyzes each of the symphony's four movements, coordinating the structural events with the expressive content of the music.

Sadie (1986) and Smith each address an audience of intelligent, non-professional musicians. Mozart composed serenades and other lighter works throughout his lifetime, and SMITH discusses the social functions for which these genres were intended. SADIE (1986) traces Mozart's growth as a symphonist and deals briefly but authoritatively with problems of chronology and authenticity.

The volumes in TOVEY devoted to orchestral works and concertos offer detailed analyses of representative works. These articles, originally written as program notes, offer much insight for general audiences as well as musicians. Tovey was the most perceptive English-language writer on music of his time. Orchestral works

analyzed include the Haffner Serenade; the Paris, Linz, and final three symphonies; operatic overtures; and orchestral dances. Concertos analyzed include selected piano concertos; concertos for the flute, clarinet, and flute and harp; and the last two violin concertos.

ZASLAW (1989) is the most authoritative study of Mozart's orchestral oeuvre published to date. Applying the full rigor of modern musicological methods, it examines nearly 100 works (symphonies, overtures used as symphonies, symphonic sections of Salzburg serenades, several lost symphonies, and dubious works) associated with Mozart, and establishes criteria for authenticity. The discussions, arranged chronologically, review the circumstances of composition as well as the dissemination, performance, and reception of each work. The sections devoted to the musical centers in which the symphonies were composed—Salzburg, Paris and Mannheim, London, and Vienna—also shed light on the development of the classical symphony during the 18th century. While the book does not offer stylistic analyses, the concluding chapters expand on issues of performance practice and possible meanings for the symphonies. Six appendices summarize valuable information, including the status of the 98 symphonies discussed in the book, the various systems of numbering Mozart's symphonies, a report of the state of the musical establishment in Salzburg in 1757, a brief history of the Köchel catalog, and an extensive bibliography.

FORMAN deals with the first movements of the piano concertos. An introductory chapter sites C.P.E. Bach and J.C. Bach as precursors of Mozart's concerto style. In part 1, Forman organizes the concertos in three groups: the galant concertos, the melodic concertos, and the symphonic concertos. In part 2, he provides chronological analyses of each of the movements. Forman's discussion differs from traditional analyses in that he bases first-movement concerto form on aria types rather than on modified versions of sonata form.

Girdlestone's and Hutchings's surveys, while somewhat dated, remain basic references for studies of the piano concertos. Both emphasize the historical events surrounding each of the concertos. Part 1 in GIRDLESTONE outlines guidelines for his ensuing survey, underlining the crucial role of structure and the piano-orchestra relationship. The introductory chapters in HUTCHINGS—"Mozart and the Concerto" and "The Mozartian Conception"—summarize the formal plans of the first, second, and third movements, and their relation to parallel opera forms. While the chapter "Keyboard Concertos before Mozart" reviews possible models for Mozart's concertos among the works of his predecessors, Hutchings concludes that Mozart's own works constitute the main sources for the development of his style. The above discussions are informative mainly with regard to their formal analysis. The discussions of expression, however, rely too heavily on subjective impressions.

MOZART (1970) provides a critically edited score of the Piano Concerto in C Major, K. 503, from the *New Mozart Edition,* as well as historical and analytical essays aimed at facilitating study. Two of the articles are historical: Einstein compares Mozart's concertos to those of his contemporaries, and he also compares K. 503 to Mozart's other concertos. Tovey presents a comprehensive survey of the classical concerto, focusing on its principles and form. Taken from his *Essays in Musical Analysis,* Tovey's study marks a turning point in the 20th century's evaluation of Mozart's works. Articles by Girdlestone and Keller are analytical; Girdlestone's essay is taken from his book, while Keller's contribution demonstrates means of unifying the contrasting themes of the concerto.

KING discusses all of the non-piano concertos (violin, horn, flute, clarinet, and sinfonie concertantes for violin and viola and for flute and harp). He places these works within the context of the composer's life and deals with problems of authenticity and uncompleted concertos. Most important, King highlights the variety and artistic excellence of these concertos, indicating the creativity of Mozart's compositions for instruments other than the piano.

LAWSON provides an ideal summary of pertinent information relating to the context and style of the Clarinet Concerto. The book's opening chapters present the historical background (including the origin and development) of the clarinet; Mozart's special relationship with the clarinetist Anton Stadler; and the genesis and reception of the concerto. Lawson continues with professional discussions of textual problems, analyses of the three movements, and recommendations regarding performance practice.

LEVIN traces the problems of authenticity regarding the well-known Symphonie Concertante in E-flat Major for oboe, clarinet, horn, bassoon, and orchestra, K. Anh. C 14.01 (297b). He concludes that the solo parts are based on Mozart's original composition, whereas the orchestral parts are not by Mozart. While some of the chapters deal with statistics and the relative proportions of the subsections in comparison with Mozart's other concertos, others reflect lively detective work substantiating Levin's position.

ZASLAW (1996) on the piano concertos contains the conference-proceedings from the Michigan MozartFest held at the University of Michigan in 1989. The conference combined concerts and lectures, encouraging an exchange of ideas between performers and scholars. The articles, written by leading scholars reflect these goals as they deal with the text, context, and interpretation (analysis and performance practice) of the piano concertos. This is the most significant collection of recent studies on the piano concertos.

ADENA PORTOWITZ

6. Sacred Music

Blume, Friedrich, "Requiem But No Peace," in *The Creative World of Mozart,* edited by Paul Henry Lang, New York: Norton, 1963

Einstein, Alfred, *Mozart: His Character, His Work,* translated by Arthur Mendel and Nathan Broder, New York: Oxford University Press, 1945

Heartz, Daniel, *Haydn, Mozart, and the Viennese School, 1740–1780,* New York: Norton, 1995

Humphreys, David, "Sacred Music," in *The Mozart Compendium: A Guide to Mozart's Life and Music,* edited by H.C. Robbins Landon, New York: Schirmer Books, and London: Thames and Hudson, 1990

Jahn, Otto, *The Life of Mozart,* translated by Pauline D. Townsend, 3 vols., London: Novello, Ewer, 1882; reprint, New York: Cooper Square, 1970

Landon, H.C. Robbins, *The Mozart Essays,* New York: Thames and Hudson, 1995

Maunder, C.R.F., *Mozart's Requiem: On Preparing a New Edition,* Oxford: Clarendon Press, and New York: Oxford University Press, 1988

Wolff, Christoph, *Mozart's Requiem: Historical and Analytical Studies, Documents, Score,* translated by Mary Whittall with revisions and additions by the author, Berkeley: University of California Press, and Oxford: Clarendon Press, 1994

The greatest share of Mozart's sacred music was written in his youth and while he served at the archbishop's court in Salzburg. Its reception has suffered on those accounts. It is true that some works were written as exercises; and it is also true that others seem perfunctory, mere chores from a maturing artist who yearned for freedom and a larger canvas. But much of his sacred music deserves more respect. That the two great works of Mozart's adult years, the Mass in C Minor, K. 427, and the Requiem, should both have remained unfinished is also unfortunate. But their very nature as fragments—tragic reminders of their composer's promise—has if anything increased scholars' interest in them over the years.

The first modern biographer of Mozart, JAHN must be also credited as the founder of a more balanced, historically objective view of Mozart's church music. In providing the first comprehensive discussion of the Requiem controversy, he avoids any polemicism regarding the work's authenticity while also stripping away some of the romantic myths surrounding its commission and creation. Jahn does not neglect Mozart's earlier efforts: his discussion of influence offers a comparison of the *Misericordias,* K. 222, and its probable model, a *Benedixisti Domine* by the Salzburg master Johann Ernst Eberlin. Above all, Jahn refutes the notion that Mozart's church style was too frivolous and operatic to be pious.

In the years since it first appeared, BLUME's essay on problems of authenticity in the Requiem has encountered no fundamental challenges. Dividing the topic into three components, Blume argues that Mozart did indeed compose most of the work himself, effectively limiting his assistants Eybler and Süssmayr to the task of filling out what he had already conceived in sketches and communicated in long conversations with Süssmayr in particular; that Süssmayr bears responsibility for the instrumentation, which would explain its monotonous and inappropriate consistency; and that the work can indeed be dated from the last year in Mozart's life, although questions will remain as to when he wrote various parts of the composition. The fact that Blume does not attempt to provide clear-cut answers to every issue is but one indication of his unbiased, thorough approach.

WOLFF's book on the Requiem does not claim to be an exhaustive study, but in fact it fills several roles: as an update to Blume's work (and that of Jahn before him); as a stylistic study situating the Requiem among certain works that indicate a new direction for their composer; as a documentary history of the work's genesis and attempted completion; and as one more attempt at discerning an urtext. Wolff has appended what he calls "Mozart's fragmentary score . . . supplemented by crucial excerpts from Süssmayr's . . . completion." Wolff believes that for Mozart the Requiem's musical substance was focused almost entirely in its four-part vocal score. In that regard Süssmayr followed Mozart's lead, and thus a score that focuses attention primarily on the vocal lines will enable a better comparison of what Mozart left with what Süssmayr added. The most valuable part of the book, however, may be Wolff's analytical chapter. Beginning with a detailed nod to Mozart's probable influences, which include Handel's *Funeral Anthem for Queen Caroline,* he offers convincing discussions of instrumentation, texture, and—most especially—harmonic design.

Because MAUNDER's book is mainly a defense of his controversial edition of the Requiem (in which he excised those sections of the score connected with Süssmayr), it will be less useful to the general reader than the studies reviewed above. But parts of his careful study should be consulted in any case, for instance the brief chapter on Mozart's counterpoint. A knowledge of music theory is needed.

For many years EINSTEIN's monograph was the standard one-volume treatment in English of Mozart's life and work; even today its discussion of the church music is useful. Here Einstein avoids the romantic metaphors that elsewhere give his discussions a nostalgic quality. As the advocate for an unprejudiced view of Mozart's church music (with which he grouped the Masonic music), he considers it his duty to sweep away 19th-century misconceptions.

HEARTZ, who in 1995 did not have to argue for the legitimacy of Mozart's sacred music, is able to devote more space to sophisticated commentary on its form and style. He uses it, in fact, to portray the development of a "master craftsman" up to 1780 and the Munich *Kyrie,* K. 341.

HUMPHREYS prefaces each of his annotated work lists of the Masses, Requiem, miscellaneous sacred music, and oratorios with a masterfully concise essay that discusses the originating circumstances, authenticity, and style of nearly every work in the list. In a very brief discussion he is able, for example, to balance the legends of Archbishop Colloredo's philistine demand for brevity and his "ban on fugues" with the fact that, often enough, Mass settings by Mozart's Salzburg predecessors also observed such limits. Likewise, Humphreys's Requiem essay admirably lays out the historical controversies and compares the most recent additions/editions by Beyer, Maunder, and Landon.

LANDON includes major discussions of the Masonic music, Requiem, oratorios, and the rest of the Latin church music in his collection; the essay on the oratorios and Latin church music is most valuable of these articles. There Landon reports on fundamental changes in scholarly opinion concerning the authenticity and chronology of Mozart's church music. Most of these revisions stem from Monika Holl's editing and related commentary on single movements and late-period drafts that appeared in 1990 as part of the Neue Mozart-Ausgabe. The chronological catalog attached to this essay thus updates Humphreys's 1990 work. Landon fashions his narrative with his customary, almost novelistic skill, enriching his descriptions of these works and their history with a collector's passion for detail. He notes, for example, that although the autograph of the *Missa longa,* K. 262, contains no timpani part, there exists at the Holy Cross Abbey in Augsburg a timpani part written in Mozart's own hand when he was an adolescent—but even that transcription lacks the Credo, which the composer probably thought he would get around to writing at a later date.

LAWRENCE SCHENBECK

7. Style

Allanbrook, Wye Jamison, *Rhythmic Gesture in Mozart: Le Nozze di Figaro and Don Giovanni,* Chicago: University of Chicago Press, 1983

Blume, Friedrich, *Classic and Romantic Music: A Comprehensive Survey,* translated by M.D. Herter Norton, New York: Norton, 1970

Eisen, Cliff, editor, *Mozart Studies,* Oxford: Clarendon Press, and New York, Oxford University Press, 1991

Küster, Konrad, *Mozart: A Musical Biography,* translated by Mary Whittall, Oxford: Clarendon Press, and New York, Oxford University Press, 1996

Lang, Paul Henry, editor, *The Creative World of Mozart,* New York: Norton, 1963

Ratner, Leonard, *Classic Music: Expression, Form, Style,* New York: Schirmer, 1980

Rosen, Charles, *The Classical Style: Haydn, Mozart, Beethoven,* London: Faber, and New York: Viking Press, 1971; expanded edition, New York: Norton, 1997

Zaslaw, Neal, and William Cowdery, editors, *The Compleat Mozart: A Guide to the Musical Works of Wolfgang Amadeus Mozart,* New York: Norton, 1990

Mozart's compositional style may be discussed in many different ways, ranging from the general and descriptive to the specific and technical. Overviews of classical style, which often focus on Haydn, Mozart, and Beethoven, are valuable because they establish a general context in which Mozart's music may be understood and interpreted. Some authors take a historical approach; others concentrate primarily on musical characteristics; still others present essays on Mozart's individual compositions, sometimes relating them to events in the composer's life. More specialized articles typically appear in collections that examine different aspects of Mozart's music and the circumstances surrounding their creation. Such texts usually go into greater depth about a particular topic—such as rhythm, performance, or genre studies of, for example, arias, songs, keyboard music, or symphonies—and may or may not be technical. They offer the reader a scholar's perspective on style and related subjects.

In her approach to two of Mozart's operas, ALLANBROOK invokes rhetorical concepts derived from different musical styles that Mozart would have known. Dance rhythms, patterns with specific associations such as hunting horns, and other expressive figures serve as the basis for investigating aspects of his compositional style. Rhythm and meter, in particular, become a means for interpreting stylistic origins and meaning.

BLUME presents a view of classical style in general terms. His book is highly recommended for its lucid exposition of topics such as rhythm, meter and tempo, harmony and tonality, motive and theme, and genres and forms. He also considers historical context, national styles, the classical orchestra, and the social position of music. The discussion of classicism as an historical concept is provocative and calls traditional categories into question. This book provides a foundation for the exploration of Mozart's style that is valuable for specialists and nonspecialists alike.

EISEN's collection of essays, published for the bicentenary of Mozart's death, represents a cross section of scholarly research. Webster examines Mozart's arias from a stylistic and analytical perspective, while Wolff revisits questions concerning the composition and completion of Mozart's *Requiem.* Schachter offers a comparison of Mozart's last and Beethoven's first symphonies utilizing the techniques of Schenkerian analysis. Additional essays consider Leopold Mozart's treatise on violin playing, the Mozarts' Salzburg copyists, and issues of authenticity in early Mozart biography. The articles, all by noted scholars, vary both in length and in the level of knowledge assumed, but all readers will find much that is of interest.

KÜSTER has not written a conventional biography. Rather, he traces the development of Mozart's compositional style over his lifetime. The author seeks to show how the circumstances of the composer's life, and the artistic environment in which he lived, helped to shape his music. A large number of works are discussed in the context of Mozart's life, illuminating many aspects of his compositional style. Issues such as Mozart's way of solving compositional problems, his approach to orchestration, and the influence of other musicians are considered, and the impact of these factors on Mozart's style is discussed. In this fascinating series of essays, Mozart's life and intellectual growth are interpreted in order to better understand his artistic development.

LANG has edited a group of essays, originally written for the *Musical Quarterly,* that address many aspects of Mozart's style with insight and wisdom. The composer's creative process, often a subject of speculation and wonder, is examined by Hertzmann Lowinsky compares aspects of rhythm in Mozart's music with that of Johann Christian Bach, Haydn, and other composers, concentrating on symmetry, development, phrase structure, and form. Key relationships and tonality in the composer's musical language are discussed in an insightful essay by Broder, who discusses Mozart's music for keyboard instruments in the context of his musical world and the instruments that he knew—the harpsichord, clavichord, and piano. Schmitt compares the lives of Mozart and Haydn and makes insightful observations about their stylistic influence on one another. Blume discusses complex issues associated with the composition of the *Requiem,* and Sternfeld considers the sources of Papageno's familiar song from *The Magic Flute.* The volume also includes Broder's description of an early guide to performance of Mozart's piano concertos, as well as Deutsch's discussion of some errors in Mozart biography. Now a classic, this collection of essays by noted scholars of the mid-20th century continues to be one of the best discussions of Mozart's music.

RATNER presents an original and intriguing perspective on classical style, drawing on theoretical writings of that period in order to define how 18th-century music was composed. Central to his idea of classical style is the notion of musical rhetoric, a concept that baroque and classic theorists derived from oratory. This notion involves musical figures, or "topics," that are related to characteristic pieces such as dances. Rhythm, melody, texture, and phrase structure are described as components of musical discourse that establish coherence and promote eloquence. Historical context, seen by Ratner as a continuum from the baroque era, becomes a basic for understanding expression, form, and style. The book is organized topically, rather than chronologically or by composer, but Mozart is frequently discussed. The volume is clearly written and presents a fresh perspective on the composer's music in the context of related musical styles.

As his title suggests, ROSEN has written a book on the nature of style in the classical era, especially in the music of Haydn, Mozart, and Beethoven. He examines the elements that are specific to classical style and to the music of each composer. The approach is not historical; rather, Rosen seeks to analyze and elucidate the fundamental principles that govern the music itself. Beginning with an overview of late 18th-century musical language, its stylistic origins, and theories of form, he proceeds to discuss elements of the language itself in detail. Sections on Haydn, Mozart, and Beethoven form the core of the book; a concluding epilogue discusses the influence of classical style on romantic composers such as Schubert and Robert Schumann. The section on Mozart, like those on Haydn and Beethoven, focuses on genres in which his compositional style is especially clear: concerto, string quartet, and comic opera. The author's critical perspective is brilliant and deeply personal, reflecting his deep knowledge of the period, its music, and especially the three great composers. He sees classical style as a living language and is articulate in describing its attributes.

Zaslaw, a noted Mozart scholar, organized performances of all of Mozart's compositions on the occasion of the bicentenary of the composer's death (1991) at New York's Lincoln Center for the Performing Arts. As part of the festival's production, program notes were prepared for all the works. These essays have been collected and published as a complete set in ZASLAW and COWDERY. Well researched and incisively written, the entries place each work in historical and stylistic context. Because of its completeness, the book serves as a good general guide to Mozart's music.

DAVID GAGNÉ

Musica ficta

Berger, Karol, *Musica ficta: Theories of Accidental Inflections in Vocal Polyphony from Marchetto da Padova to Gioseffo Zarlino,* Cambridge: Cambridge University Press, 1987

Hughes, Andrew, *Manuscript Accidentals: Ficta in Focus, 1350–1450,* N.p.: American Institute of Musicology, 1972

Lowinsky, Edward E., *Secret Chromatic Art in the Netherlands Motet,* New York: Columbia University Press, 1946

Toft, Robert, *Aural Images of Lost Traditions: Sharps and Flats in the Sixteenth Century,* Toronto: University of Toronto Press, 1992

In the Middle Ages and Renaissance, sharps and flats were largely left unspecified in vocal sources. Singers were expected to be familiar with the principles govern-

ing the application of unnotated sharps and flats and to make the appropriate alterations at the time of performance; consequently, certain details of composers' intentions were never recorded. The problem of ambiguous notation concerned Renaissance theorists such as Pietro Aaron (ca. 1480–ca. 1550), and it remains a concern today. Three types of documents bear on the problem: vocal sources, writings of theorists, and in the 16th century, intabulations of vocal music (instrumental versions of vocal music that specify pitches unambiguously). Modern scholarship on the subject has focused primarily on the first two types of documents, but one major study takes a balanced look at all three categories. *Musica ficta* is the term most often used to refer to unnotated sharps and flats. The literature is highly technical in nature and requires familiarity with theoretical terminology of the later Middle Ages and Renaissance.

BERGER provides a comprehensive review of theoretical treatises written between the early 14th and mid-16th centuries. However, the rather early terminal date of his study (1558) has left important later theorists untapped, and this has led to the occasional questionable conclusion, especially with regard to the use of dissonant octaves. Theorists that the author feels represent the most enlightened musical opinion of the period figure prominently in the study, and conclusions are often drawn from sources widely separated chronologically. Berger rightly places the term *musica ficta* in its proper context, distinguishing it from *musica vera*, before discussing the functions and uses of sharps and flats. Signatures are seen as either producing modal transposition, if the same signature appears in all of the voices, or providing an automatic insurance against vertical imperfect fifths, if the signatures in the voices differ. The prohibition of the tritone in both horizontal and vertical contexts had a number of exceptions, and Berger concludes that flats were used more frequently than sharps in the correction of dissonance. The application of sharps and flats at cadences is discussed in relation to mode, and the issue of accidental inflections in canon and imitation is derived mainly from the theorist Gioseffo Zarlino.

Through a comparative study of vocal sources, intabulations of vocal music, and theoretical treatises, TOFT documents the range of theoretical possibilities open to 16th-century performers and indicates which sharps and flats practicing musicians incorporated in their performances. The study establishes the spectrum of practices in relation to the intabulations of Josquin des Prez's motets, reveals nationalistic customs in German sources, and identifies the various traditions of pitch-content associated with five works by Josquin des Prez, Clemens non Papa, and Alexander Agricola. Toft views the three types of surviving documents as equally important and believes that intabulations may very well be a reliable guide to the sound of vocal music. He demonstrates that both singers and instrumentalists worked within the same theoretical tradition, a tradition that embraced widely divergent approaches to the application of sharps and flats. He not only documents the boundaries of the style in this regard but also discusses the Renaissance penchant for dissonance, particularly false relations involving fourths, fifths, and octaves. All of the discussions are placed in a modal context.

LOWINSKY's dislike of false relations and his rigid interpretation of what he calls ostinato motives led him to invent a theory of secret chromaticism for the 16th-century motet, and a storm of controversy has followed his proposition from the outset. In Lowinsky's view, singers maintained the intervallic integrity of repeated melodic figures, altering notes as necessary, and removed false relations when they occurred, even if this meant introducing a downward spiraling chain of flats. For example, if an e-flat (the "code note") was either notated or required by ostinato-like repetition, then an adjacent a would have to be lowered to a-flat, and if this were followed by a d, it too would be lowered, and so on. Objections to Lowinsky's theory have centered mainly on his speculative argumentation, for he cites no documentary evidence to substantiate his notion that ostinato-like figures must remain identical on each recurrence or that a code note exists. Both Berger and Toft reject the notion of secret chromaticism.

HUGHES focuses on the period 1350 to 1450, particularly on the English source known today as the Old Hall manuscript (copied ca. 1410–20), and derives much of his discussion from the writings of the Italian theorist Ugolino of Orvieto (fl. ca. 1430). Hughes places the "accidentals" found in Old Hall within Ugolino's concept of *musica recta* and *musica ficta* and makes a large number of practical suggestions for editors. His discussion of key signatures, which he believes indicate a transposition of the normal hexachord order, seems to suit the music in Old Hall but may not be applicable to later repertories.

ROBERT TOFT

Musical Comedy

Banfield, Stephen, *Sondheim's Broadway Musicals*, Ann Arbor: University of Michigan Press, 1993

Bordman, Gerald M., *American Musical Theatre: A Chronicle*, New York: Oxford University Press, 1978; 2nd edition, 1992

Engel, Lehman, *The American Musical Theater*, revised edition, New York: Macmillan, 1975

Smith, Cecil M., *Musical Comedy in America*, New York: Theatre Arts Books, 1950; 2nd edition, expanded by Glenn Litton, 1981

Swain, Joseph P., *The Broadway Musical: A Critical and Musical Survey*, New York: Oxford University Press, 1990

Although its origins may be traced to 19th-century British commercial theater, musical comedy is widely held to be a 20th-century and preeminently American form of entertainment that variously combines aspects of song, dance, speech, and spectacle. The term is elusive. It can refer ambiguously either to a type of production on the spectrum of light musical stage entertainments or to the spectrum itself as a whole. Moreover, recent writing on the subject favors the more inclusive term *musical theater* (and the even less restrictive *musical*) to accommodate developments both heavier and darker than the term *comedy* suggests. Scholarship has been relatively late to recognize musical comedy in its broadest sense as a subject fit for study, and journalistic writing dominates the field. Neither scholars or journalists, however, have paid much systematic attention to the performative aspects of the medium. Scholars, who tend to emphasize its value as art more than entertainment, have approached the medium mainly through textual analyses, drawing for their purposes on the methods of other more-or-less established disciplines—for example, theater history and literary criticism—to gauge musical comedy's development in terms of drama, musicology, and music theory and demonstrate its relationship to opera. However valuable, such work underscores the difficulty of developing scholarly methods for the study of musical comedy/theater that do not lose sight of the medium's own phenomenology of presentation and its distinguishing characteristics as a form of popular, indeed middle-brow culture.

SMITH is the first extended work to survey the history of the popular musical stage both as an autonomous domain, worthy of study apart from other forms of theater, and as an American art, though limited mainly to Broadway. The book describes and evaluates key works in the development of musical comedy and allied forms from *The Black Crook* (1866) to *South Pacific* (1949). The basis for most later writing in the field, this study remains a valuable repository of certain historical discourses even if much of its information has been superseded by subsequent scholarship. Smith, in fact, subverts traditional cultural values, prizing musicals precisely because they are entertainments and not operas, which (Smith contends) are "conceived unequivocally as art objects, and only secondarily as entertainments." Moreover, as Smith was writing when the work of Rodgers and Hammerstein was new, his book exudes a confidence in the development of the Broadway medium lacking in Litton's update of some 30 years later, which generally adopts Smith's methods but not his point of view. The difference between the two editions reveals much about the historiography of musical comedy in the interim. Litton brings an almost postlapsarian sensibility to a subject he now views with guarded optimism as musical theater, depicting a more self-consciously artistic, and infinitely more troubled, domain than that which is portrayed in Smith's book.

ENGEL's chief concern is to establish aesthetic standards for the study of musical theater. He offers a taxonomy of what he calls "working principles . . . imposed by the nature of the genre," which are actually derived from 11 shows (15 in the revised edition) that he considers models of excellence in themselves and avatars of the American musical theater "in its most complete and mature state." For Engel, these shows comprise a canon limited not just in number but time: originally including only works created between *Pal Joey* (1940) and *West Side Story* (1957). Because he values the shows as musical plays more than musicals as such, his study focuses on their librettos—the scripted scaffolds characteristically integrated into shows of this period, but not frequently employed before or since. Engel's aesthetic thus rests on a reductive reading of musical theater history, his canon providing a ready model for later accounts of the medium that center nostalgically on a golden age. Yet the book remains useful as an empirical study of the postwar Broadway musical by one of its respected conductors and musical directors. Engel uses the authority of behind-the-scenes experience not for anecdotal purposes but to probe Broadway aesthetics, identifying the patterns of dramatic structure that underlie many of the most successful shows of the era. (He treats the subject further in *Words with Music: The Broadway Musical Libretto* [1972].)

BORDMAN is an indispensable one-volume reference book unlike any other of its kind in English (save for Kurt Gänzl's two-volume *The British Musical Theatre* [1986]). It surpasses Smith and Litton, which progresses thematically, by proceeding systematically with a detailed account of virtually every Broadway production of a musical nature from 1866 to 1990, compiled in opening-night order, on a season-by-season basis. The book is comprehensive, indeed definitive as a chronicle, and it only falters when Bordman goes beyond the chronicle's documentary function to suggest a more historical project often based on rather speculative grounds. Thus, for example, he not only posits a golden age of the American musical, but he places it in the period 1924 to 1937, largely because of that era's "enthralling outpouring of magnificent melody" in show songs possessed of "the most brilliant lyrics the American Musical Theatre has ever known."

SWAIN gives primary importance to the musical element in Broadway musicals, but he is less concerned with the intrinsic quality of a show's songs than with the dramatic function of its score. His is a critical study set on demonstrating how "the music of a good musical play informs the drama that contains it." To that end, he offers incisive analyses of musical relationships in the scores to some 15 musical plays ranging from *Show Boat* (1927) to *Sweeney Todd* (1979). Swain's critical standards for what constitutes quality in musical plays, however, are not empirically derived from the shows he examines. Nor are his verdicts on a play's value dependent on box-office success: for example, he gives failing grades to *A Chorus Line,* accolades to *Porgy and Bess.* Swain's aesthetic criteria are those more conventionally applied to opera and are admittedly commandeered largely from Joseph Kerman's *Opera as Drama* (1956; new and revised edition, 1988). Indeed, Swain applies to Broadway musicals Kerman's tenet that in opera the dramatist is the composer, a method that transfers well enough to the extent that musicals and operas intersect as music dramas—the case Swain makes most convincingly concerns *West Side Story,* which fairly lends itself for the occasion. But the author fails to address the rather more complicated issues of dramatization in musicals in which music tends to negotiate its sway with other modes of dramatic representation (rather than retaining an exclusive hold on the dramatic viewpoint as traditionally in opera) and in instances in which music is also apt to position itself ironically or at least self-consciously *as* music.

It is with the aim of addressing precisely such concerns that BANFIELD brings the combined perspectives of critical theory and musicology to bear on the study of musical theater. His immediate focus, however, is on the work of Stephen Sondheim, specifically the ten Broadway shows for which Sondheim wrote the music and lyrics, from *A Funny Thing Happened on the Way to the Forum* (1962) to *Into the Woods* (1987). For these shows he pursues a broad agenda of topics that emphasizes the musical issues specific to each show, and he makes free use of Sondheim's early sketches and drafts to shed light on compositional processes. Musically, in fact, Banfield is the first full-length critical study of a Broadway songwriter/composer's creative oeuvre—in Sondheim's case, a rich and varied body of work of particular interest for the resistance it offers to the governing commercial ethos of the very medium it embraces. Yet Banfield acknowledges the limits of a purely musical approach to his subject. For example, he finds in *Sweeny Todd,* a show of seemingly operatic ambition, that the nonmusical ending of the plot demonstrates "even if by [Sondheim's] authorial default . . . the dramatic potency and rightness of music's self-denial in this genre that is not opera"; Banfield then proceeds to probe the character of the genre itself. Indeed, his study is all the more valuable as he regularly uses the occasion of his engagement with Sondheim's shows to examine the norms of the metier in and against which Sondheim has chosen to work. Banfield thus includes the musical comedy/theater medium as such in the project of what he terms humanistic scholarship. His book brims with extensive technical analyses of music, and it does not wear its erudition lightly. It is meant, in short, for the serious student of musical comedy.

LARRY STEMPEL

Musicology: Feminist

Block, Adrienne Fried, *Amy Beach, Passionate Victorian: The Life and Work of an American Composer, 1867–1944,* New York: Oxford University Press, 1998

Bowers, Jane, and Judith Tick, editors, *Women Making Music: The Western Art Tradition, 1150–1950,* Urbana: University of Illinois, 1986

Brett, Philip, et al., editors, *Queering the Pitch: The New Gay and Lesbian Musicology,* New York: Routledge Press, 1994

Citron, Marcia J., *Gender and the Musical Canon,* Cambridge: Cambridge University Press, 1993

Cook, Susan C., and Judy S. Tsou, editors, *Cecilia Reclaimed: Feminist Perspectives on Gender and Music,* Urbana: University of Illinois Press, 1993

McClary, Susan, *Feminine Endings: Music, Gender, and Sexuality,* Minneapolis: University of Minnesota Press, 1991

Neuls-Bates, Carol, editor, *Women in Music: An Anthology of Source Readings from the Middle Ages to the Present,* New York: Harper and Row, 1982; revised edition, Boston: Northeastern University Press, 1996

Solie, Ruth, editor, *Musicology and Difference: Gender and Sexuality in Music Scholarship,* Berkeley: University of California Press, 1993

Tick, Judith, *Ruth Crawford Seeger: A Composer's Search for American Music,* New York: Oxford University Press, 1997

Since the 1970s, when a few pioneering scholars energetically assumed the task of recovering the history of women in music, feminist musicology has taken some remarkable turns. Informed by writings in other disciplines, feminist music scholars have begun to record the collective history of women in music as performers, composers, and patrons; presented critical readings of canonical compositions; reinterpreted traditional theories of music; and analyzed instrumental and dramatic works by both female and male composers. These studies have galvanized the field of musicology and its branch disciplines of ethnomusicology and music theory, resulting in a profusion of books that will continue to enrich and transform the discipline as a whole over the coming years.

NEULS-BATES culls a fascinating set of documents that chronicles the musical lives of women as singers, instrumental performers, composers, pedagogues, and patrons. Presented in first-person accounts drawn from diaries, letters, autobiographies, concert reviews, interviews, and essays, these writings make for an informative portrait of women in music from the Middle Ages to the present.

Another significant early contribution to feminist music scholarship is BOWERS and TICK's answer to the question occasioned by the title of John Blacking's famous study "How Musical is Woman?" Concentrating on the Western art-music tradition, the 13 essays in Bowers and Tick's collection present valuable information about a diversity of topics, including the *jougleresses* and *trobairitz* of medieval France, women singers in 15th-century Italy, 19th-century female composers of lieder, and women's orchestras in the United States during the first half of the 20th century.

A lively and engaging introduction to feminist musicology, McCLARY's book is indispensable for anyone interested in exploring the discipline. This stimulating collection of criticism has inspired many younger scholars to challenge traditional assumptions and to examine music using new paradigms. Traversing the terrain of both classical music (Monteverdi, Bizet, Tchaikovsky, Beethoven, Donizetti, Strauss) and popular music (Laurie Anderson and Madonna) with equal ease, McClary poses questions crucial to a feminist rethinking of music while displaying an awesome command of the relevant literature both inside and outside of music. Her deeply held belief that music is a social discourse undergirds her finely wrought readings of specific compositions; it also accounts for the fact that McClary's work has been fiercely contested in some arenas by those who would be loath to accept her contention that "music is always a political activity, and to inhibit criticism of its effects for any reason is likewise a political act."

CITRON considers the important issue of why compositions by women have been excluded from the canon of Western art music by examining the politics behind canon formation and analyzing Cecile Chaminade's Piano Sonata, op. 21. Particularly useful is Citron's inclusion of primary source material about Clara Schumann's insecurity about composing despite her obvious musical talent. Citron succeeds in complicating the discourse around the reductive question of whether there have been any great women composers, an issue that all too frequently plagues discussions in unsympathetic quarters of whether music by women constitutes a legitimate category of scholarship.

COOK and TSOU's collection presents a variety of topics and approaches to the burgeoning field of feminist musicology. Articles that examine depictions of women in 17th-century French music, images of females in U.S. rap music, and the upbringing of a woman composer in New England all rub shoulders in this variegated collection. One of the most incisive contributions is Cook's own essay, which critically examines North American balladry as a discourse "that privileges the male voices and experiences of the community while muting, or even silencing, its women."

SOLIE's ensemble of essays likewise surveys a variety of topics, which are gathered around the theme of difference within the categories of gender, sexuality, class, and race. By locating issues of difference "in the formulation of the most basic questions about what pieces of music can express or reflect of the people who make and use them, and thus of the differences between and among those people," this groundbreaking book demonstrates the ways in which ideology operates, often undetected, in the study of music. Certain essays further uncover how ideological biases about music can be traced to beliefs held in society at large. For example, Philip Brett explores Britten's operas in relation to his sexual identity and to the cultural conditions within which he worked; Gretchen Wheelock examines Mozart's operas in relation to gendered conceptions about the minor mode in the 18th century, the affect of specific arias, and representations of ethnic Others as exotic; and Elizabeth Wood connects the prose writings, compositions, and sexuality of the British composer Ethel Smyth.

BRETT et al. is an outstanding collection under the rubric of sexuality and music. One of its most striking contributions is Suzanne Cusick's extraordinary meditation on the relationships between lesbian sexuality and music making and listening. Martha Mockus's affectionate study of country music singer k.d. lang and exploration of country's gay and lesbian fan base provides a fine example of how feminism can give fresh perspectives to popular-music scholarship.

TICK's biography of the U.S. composer Ruth Crawford Seeger, is an exemplary work of feminist scholarship. The composer's musical brilliance, warmth of character, and love of her family all emerge in a nuanced portrait of one of the 20th century's most interesting and gifted composers. Impeccably researched, gracefully written, and handsomely produced, this study of a fascinating female modernist sets a new standard for feminist music scholarship.

As in the case of Seeger, one cannot fully understand either the music or the life of the U.S. composer Amy Beach if the compositions and biography are separated from one another, or considered apart from the politics of gender. In her biography of Beach, BLOCK presents a complex portrait of a composer who redefined the role of women in music. Although women might still choose to be the muse for a man's creativity, "they had in Beach an alternative, a model for realizing their own" creative voices. Block's meticulous and dignified portrait of this uncommon composer will surely serve as a model of feminist musical biography for years to come.

ELLIE M. HISAMA

Musicology: Gay and Lesbian

Blackmer, Corinne E., and Patricia Juliana Smith, editors, *En Travesti: Women, Gender Subversion, Opera*, New York: Columbia University Press, 1995

Brett, Philip, et al., editors, *Queering the Pitch: The New Gay and Lesbian Musicology*, New York: Routledge Press, 1994

Koestenbaum, Wayne, *The Queen's Throat: Opera, Homosexuality, and the Mystery of Desire*, New York: Poseidon Press, and London: GMP, 1993

Kopelson, Kevin, *Beethoven's Kiss: Pianism, Perversion, and the Mastery of Desire*, Stanford, California: Stanford University Press, 1996

19th Century Music 17, no. 1 (1993), *Schubert: Music, Sexuality, Culture*

Sedgwick, Eve Kosofsky, *Epistemology of the Closet*, Berkeley: University of California Press, 1990

Solie, Ruth, editor, *Musicology and Difference: Gender and Sexuality in Music Scholarship*, Berkeley: University of California Press, 1993

Since the early 1980s musicology, a fundamentally conservative discipline, has been engaged with a new, and to some a disturbing, area of study: that of lesbian and gay enquiry. With increased exposure to parallel research by literary and cultural critics addressing issues of embodiment, sexuality, and gender, musicologists began applying these techniques and insights to music. (One early example is Susan McClary's *Feminine Endings: Music, Gender, and Sexuality* [1991].) Part of the impetus for this new interest in sexuality and specifically gay and lesbian scholarship in music comes from the increasing number of openly identified lesbian and gay scholars who find that their responses (and increasingly their students' responses) to music (both to individual works and to composers) are different from those of their nonhomosexual peers. These scholars have also increasingly explored and sought to rectify the lacunae in the biographical record, especially regarding living or recently deceased homosexual composers whose authorized biographies omitted information available in other, nonacademic sources.

One practical result of the disparate origins of the field is that it is not possible to speak of only one lesbian and gay musicology. Instead, there exist a number of gay and lesbian musicologies that adapt and utilize different methods and strive for different goals. These various approaches fall broadly into two camps: traditional musicology, with its emphasis on objectivity and structures of (factual) evidence, and a more subjective type of musicology that privileges the experience and reaction of the author to the music or musician. This division of labor is also apparent in the published work in the field. Those scholars using the traditional paradigm depend heavily on prior knowledge of music and literary criticism, while those using the more subjective mode require less specialized knowledge and include much work by nonmusicians. The best gay and lesbian musicological writing finds a productive balance between these two methods of research. The most serious publications are anthologies of essays gathered into what might be considered primers for lesbian and gay musicology. The few monographs available are either biographical studies of a single composer (Britten, Tchaikovsky) or extended explorations of the subjective perceptions of a single author loosely organized around one thematic thread (popular music, opera). There is a bias in recent work toward explorations of opera (e.g., *The Work of Opera: Genre, Nationhood, and Sexual Difference,* edited by Richard Dellamora and Daniel Fischlin [1997]) as inherently queer, a term used to encompass in one concept the terms *gay, lesbian, bisexual,* and *transgendered;* to create space for unlabeled discourse; and to access the perverse.

Lest the reader think that this subsection of musical research is merely a new way to discredit particular genres or works of music or reveal the private lives and desires of certain composers, it should be noted that this emerging part of the discipline is not primarily about uncovering lesbian and gay composers in the historical record, although that endeavor is certainly an important part of the ongoing work. Rather, gay and lesbian musicology is more profoundly interested in addressing questions that musicology usually fails to explore: how people listen to music, how they perform it, how they compose it, and how they react to it. (One notable exception to the general neglect of such issues in mainstream musicology includes some of the work done at Princeton University by Peter Westergaard, Edward T. Cone, Leonard B. Meyers, and others.)

An individual interested in studying gay and lesbian musicology will quickly discover that much of the research in this field is indebted to the work of 20th-century French literary and cultural theorists, such as Derrida, Foucault, Barthes, Cixous, and Irigaray. One resource that can be used to learn the basics of literary theory is Terry Eagleton's *Literary Theory: An Introduction* (1983). One can also learn much of the theoretical underpinnings of gay and lesbian musicology from SEDGWICK. This dense work, concerned with homosexuality, homoeroticism, and homosociality as it is expressed in some of the masterworks of Western literature, amply repays the effort required to understand it fully. Sedgwick points the way for the excavation of texts from the past and, by adapting her methods, one can approach and engage a type of text that is even more resistant to study than literature: music.

The 15 essays and introduction in SOLIE provide a variety of different methods and goals for applying and adapting these critical models to music. This work is a wonderful resource for either the novice or the experienced musicologist examining the questions and issues surrounding gender and music. The experienced reader will find the interrogation of these ideas to be revelatory, challenging, and thought provoking. The novice will find in the footnotes an extensive survey of the major articles and books published in the field before 1993. These essays, however, often presuppose a prior knowledge on the reader's part of literary criticism and such methods as deconstruction, as well as knowledge of a wide variety of music from the Renaissance to the present.

BRETT et al. is an anthology of essays that also presupposes a familiarity with the musical repertoire and enough musical training to follow the examples necessary for the arguments presented. This volume contains one of the best examples of gay and lesbian musicology from a traditional musicological perspective: Gary Thomas's "'Was George Frideric Handel Gay?': Closet Questions and Cultural Politics." In this comprehensive essay, Thomas reexamines the primary sources of Handel biography. He pieces together a coherent understanding of Handel's life that takes into account the probability that the composer was indeed homosexual. By not requiring a simple yes-or-no answer to the question of Handel's homosexuality, however, Thomas allows Handel to become more fully human than heretofore had been shown. This book also contains the dense but rewarding essay by Suzanne Cusick, "On a Lesbian Relationship with Music: A Serious Effort Not to Think Straight." Using a subjective point of view, she explores the deceptively simple question of how the various portions of the self responsible for musicality and sexuality relate to each other and reports the complexities of her findings in an enlightening way.

While Solie and Brett form a complementary set of highly recommended books and a comprehensive introduction to lesbian and gay musicology, another substantive collection of essays elucidates the ongoing debate about gay and lesbian musicology in relation to traditional musicology. These appear in a special issue of *19TH CENTURY MUSIC* and form a response to the seminal article published by Maynard Solomon in the same journal in 1989 entitled "Franz Schubert and the Peacocks of Benvenuto Cellini." The arguments, counterarguments, and rebuttals in these articles and the ensuing commentaries make explicit both points of contention and the intensity of the debate around the issue of the relevance of homosexuality to our views of canonical composers. These articles require a high level of musical knowledge but are revealing and highly recommended for those interested in how the arguments and methods of lesbian and gay musicology are deployed and rebutted.

The subjective point of view—using anecdotes from one's life to articulate an argument—has been revalued and recovered in gay and lesbian musicology (as in Cusick's essay in Brett). Two books that explore their topics from the perspectives of gay men provide a good introduction to this mode of gay/lesbian musicology. KOESTENBAUM explores his reactions to opera and specifically to the voice of the diva Maria Callas. The text is accessible to anyone who has an interest in opera, but it will resonate more deeply with the reader who is familiar not only with opera but also with its various performers. Somewhat less successfully, KOPELSON focuses on the piano as the locus of his argument, sharing his formative experiences with the instrument and explaining how his perceptions of the relation of other artists to the piano either as performers or composers are filtered and enriched through his gay sensibility.

A set of essays in BLACKMER and SMITH offers lesbian standpoints on musicology and opera, combining both the traditional and the subjective styles. These 12 essays explore history, performance, and cross-dressing (mostly female to male). Cross-dressing in opera is a result both of the disappearance of castrati—male sopranos who sang operatic leads—and of composed cross-dressing roles, such as are found in Richard Strauss's *Der Rosenkavalier*. Some of these essays require specialized musical knowledge, but most do not.

One final major resource on this topic, but beyond the purview of this article, is the *GLSG Newsletter,* the publication of the Gay and Lesbian Studies Group of the American Musicological Society. Consisting of short articles, reports, one or two feature articles, and a comprehensive bibliography, this semiannual newsletter has for almost a decade provided a forum for the ongoing discussion of gay and lesbian musicology. It is highly recommended for both the student and the professional interested in current developments in the field.

MARIO CHAMPAGNE

Musicology: New Musicology

Attali, Jacques, *Noise: The Political Economy of Music,* translated by Brian Massumi, Minneapolis: University of Minnesota Press, and Manchester: Manchester University Press, 1985

Kerman, Joseph, *Contemplating Music: Challenges to Musicology,* Cambridge, Massachusetts: Harvard University Press, 1985

Kramer, Lawrence, *Classical Music and Postmodern Knowledge,* Berkeley: University of California Press, 1995

Leppert, Richard, and Susan McClary, editors, *Music and Society: The Politics of Composition, Performance, and Reception,* Cambridge: Cambridge University Press, 1987

Subotnik, Rose Rosengard, *Deconstructive Variations: Music and Reason in Western Society,* Minneapolis: University of Minnesota Press, 1996

———, *Developing Variations: Style and Ideology in Western Music,* Minneapolis: University of Minnesota Press, 1991

Taruskin, Richard, *Text and Act: Essays on Music and Performance,* New York: Oxford University Press, 1995

Treitler, Leo, *Music and the Historical Imagination,* Cambridge, Massachusetts: Harvard University Press, 1989

Van den Toorn, Pieter C., *Music, Politics, and the Academy,* Berkeley: University of California Press, 1995

The new musicology is distinguished from traditional musicology in that the former is primarily concerned with exploration of the extra-musical meanings of musical works, whereas the latter focuses on analyzing and researching the technical aspects of music. The defenders of the new musicology challenge positivism, formalism, and the autonomy of music, positions that they associate with traditional musicology. From the viewpoints of the new musicologists, traditional musicology has promoted the autonomy of music by treating musical works primarily as aesthetic objects with universal and timeless values that transcend historical and social reality. Traditional musicology is regarded as formalistic because it focuses on technical analysis of musical parameters, form, and structure. Traditional musicology is also viewed as positivistic because its primary values are authenticity, accuracy, and objectivity, which (traditionalists assume) can be proved by documentary and archival materials such as composers' manuscripts, sketches, and diaries.

Opposing positivistic, formalistic forms of musicology, the new musicology treats musical works as culturally and socio-politically conditioned and constructed products rather than autonomous masterpieces. New musicologists have aimed to contextualize their musical analyses in broader cultural, social, and political discourses. This pursuit has inevitably invited interdisciplinary inquiries, as scholars borrow theories from diverse disciplines such as sociology, literary criticism, cultural theories, and psychoanalysis. The controversy between positivism and the new musicology is primarily an Anglo-American phenomenon. Some advocates of the new musicology have contrasted Anglo-American musicology with European musicology, which has a long history of interdisciplinary studies, and have accused Anglo-American traditionalists of having an empirical and positivistic orientation that is too rigid.

The formation of the new musicology can be traced to the mid-1960s, when Joseph Kerman and Leo Treitler made two inaugural attacks on positivistic musicology. In "A Profile for American Musicology," published in the 1965 issue of the *Journal of the American Musicological Society,* Kerman expressed strong dissatisfaction with the positivistic position advocated by a group of musicologists led by Claude Palisca. In a series of essays beginning with "Music Analysis in a Historical Context," published in the fall 1966 issue of the *College Music Symposium,* Treitler showed his anti-positivism by attacking deterministic historiography represented by Arthur Mendel's essay "Evidence and Explanation," published in the *Report of the Eighth Congress of the International Musicological Society* in 1962.

The new musicology is often called "postmodern musicology." In fact, the emergence of the new musicology coincided with the advent of postmodernism in the 1960s. Ideologically as well as chronologically, the new musicology shares much with the ethos of postmodernism. For instance, the new musicology's rejection of positivism is deeply rooted in a postmodernist skepticism about the presumed objectivity and absolutism of historical knowledge, on which positivism was founded. For many postmodern historians, historical facts are not stable but elusive: history is not an absolute truth but a construct.

History, they contend, is a form of story-telling, in which historians (like all story tellers) inevitably silence and exclude certain past events and people as they create their chronicles. To illustrate this process of silencing and exclusion, postmodern historians indicate the absence of the voices of the Other—usually construed in terms of the politics of class, race, gender, and sexual orientation—in the formation of historical knowledge. The postmodern exploration of traces of the Other has been a powerful impetus for the development of feminist musicology and gay and lesbian musicology, which are specialized branches of the new musicology. In spite of strong resistance from many music theorists and traditional musicologists, the new musicology has grown to become an influential force in recent musicological discourse.

KERMAN's book provides a lucid overview of the development of the new musicology up to the mid-1980s. It systematically traces the ideological, philosophical, and methodological conflicts between the new musicology and traditional musicology. Kerman also compares the new musicology with music theory represented by Heinrich Schenker and Rudolph Réti, who shared, in Kerman's words, a "fetish . . . about music's unity." This fetishism, Kerman contends, stemmed from the positivistic mind that mistrusts interpretive criticism and is obsessed with the absolutism of analytical facts. As an advocate of the new musicology, Kerman urges musicologists and music theorists to move from producing editions and chronologies or disentangling the syntactical aspects of musical works toward a more interpretive, contextual, and interdisciplinary approach. Kerman's book examines major writings by both defenders and detractors of the new musicology and thus serves as a good historiographical perspective on the controversy surrounding the new musicology.

ATTALI, a professional economist who served as an advisor to the late President Mitterand of France, produced a provocative example of the new musicology. His book examines the reciprocal interaction between economy and music, between the base and the superstructure, from the Middle Ages to the present. Attali attempts to show how the evolution of musical style can reflect as well as foreshadow social and political changes. Attali's writing is framed by the foreword written by Fredric Jameson, one of the most authoritative scholars on postmodernism, and the afterword by Susan McClary. Both Jameson's and McClary's short essays serve as good introductions to Attali and to the new musicology in general. Some of Attali's analyses of musical phenomena are far-fetched and too weak to support his argument, but his study has suggested a new perspective for musicological research. Devoid of technical jargon, his book can be enjoyed by the general reader.

LEPPERT and McCLARY's collection is another stimulating example of the new musicology. It begins with an introduction, written by Janet Wolff, that epitomizes the political agenda of the collection, namely, dismantling the ideology of aesthetic autonomy. The six essays in the collection (three deal with classical music; the others deal with popular music) are case studies exploring how a musical work can be socially grounded and ideologically charged. Like Attali's book, Leppert and McClary's collection contains some far-fetched socio-political interpretations of musical analyses. One of the most convincing studies is Leppert's essay devoted to the study of the iconography of music. This essay explores how musical objects in 18th-century colonial portraiture were used to validate an imperialist ideology.

TREITLER, a collection of ten essays written between 1966 and 1988, consists of critical readings of works by several composers from diverse periods—Du Fay, Mozart, Beethoven, and Berg—as well as a few polemical essays concerning methodological issues in musicology. In his polemical essays, Treitler reveals his position—much less aggressively than the authors in the Leppert and McClary collection—as an advocate of the new musicology by criticizing formalistic analysis as being too narrow and limiting to supply satisfactory insights. In his analytical essays, Treitler aims to demonstrate what he calls historical criticism as opposed to formalistic analysis. In his discussion of Berg's opera Wozzeck, for instance, Treiter first examines how the Enlightenment belief in the inevitable progress of humanity toward the ascendancy of reason is subverted and parodied in Büchner's original play, and he then shows how these qualities of the play are presented in the intricate motivic structures of Berg's opera.

TARUSKIN expands the anti-positivist critique to the realm of performance practice. His volume, consisting of 20 articles previously published in diverse sources, focuses on his criticism of the notion of the historically authentic performance. Taruskin denies the possibility of unmediated access to the past. All pasts, he claims, are reconstructed in the present. Arguing that creating a critical edition requires many conscious interpretive decisions linked to the process of evaluating multiple sources, Taruskin states, "Editing is interpretation. Period." Taruskin's critique of authenticity seems to be primarily ideological and political. He is not against the actual results of authentic performance, but he disdains the ideology behind the authenticity movement, which he traces to the purism and elitism of modernists who insist on precision and uniformity. Taruskin problematizes the arrogance and hypocrisy of the authenticists, who overlook or silence embarrassing information when it conflicts with their modernist aesthetic. Most of Taruskin's essays are accessible to the general reader. Some of the essays previously appeared in popular sources such as the New York Times and Opus, a record review magazine.

One of the most extensive counterattacks on the new musicology critique of positivistic music analysis has been produced by music theorist VAN DEN TOORN.

His argument focuses particularly on the views of McClary and Treitler. Van den Toorn's book consists of four chapters of polemical rebuttal and three of analytical demonstration and examples. In the first two chapters, Van den Toorn argues that the new musicology is not a liberatory project, as its proponents claim. Instead, it confines musicological research into another prison— namely, the prison of evaluating music based on that music's ideological and socio-political values. In chapter 4, a rebuttal to Treitler's anti-Schenkerian reading of Beethoven's 9th Symphony, Van den Toorn reassesses Schenker's organicist analysis, striving to demonstrate that it is not a positivistic cul-de-sac. Van den Toorn's analytical chapters renounce polemics and instead seek to persuade the reader with musical examples by analyzing works by Stravinsky, Debussy, Beethoven, and Bartók, among others. These analytical chapters are too technical to be enjoyed by nonspecialists.

Subotnik is known as one of the best commentators on Theodor Adorno, who examined composers and their music first and foremost in social and political terms and who has thus strongly influenced the new musicology. Subotnik's two collections of essays aim to save music from its technical isolation and to reintegrate it into a broader socio-cultural context. SUBOTNIK (1991) is primarily concerned with the elucidation of the complex relationships between musical and social structures in the classic and romantic periods. Using Adorno and Kant as a theoretical framework, she argues that the structural certitude found in classic music reflects the Enlightenment belief in the absolutism of reason, whereas romantic music, replete with arbitrary structural juxtaposition and the assemblage of fragments, manifests post-Kantian relativism emphasizing contingency. Subotnik patiently and systematically explicates her complicated arguments. Her discussion of the principles of deconstructionist theory in the second essay of SUBOTNIK (1996) is one of the best summaries of the theory. However, both of Subotnik's collections are demanding reading for the general reader and music specialists alike because of the complex concepts the author tackles.

The first chapter of KRAMER's volume serves as an excellent manifesto of the new musicology, which he identifies with postmodern musicology. Kramer's postmodern inquiry focuses on the reception of music rather than its composition or performance, for he sees the interaction between music and its listener as critical in determining the meaning of music. To pursue his inquiry, Kramer draws on Lacanian psychoanalytic theory and poststructuralist theories developed by Julia Kristeva and Jacques Derrida. As opposed to what he calls the logic of alterity, which separates self from other and divides subjects (such as listeners) from objects (such as music), Kramer proposes a theory of performative listening, a postmodern way of listening, which acknowledges music's function of mirroring the identity of the self. In six case studies, Kramer applies his

theory to the analysis of works by Haydn, Mendelssohn, Ives, and Ravel, among others, and discusses various issues in musical aesthetics, including representation, narrative, and expressivity. Although Kramer states that his volume intends to reach nonspecialist as well as specialist readers, his ideas are often impenetrable to the lay reader.

JEONGWON JOE

Musicology: Traditional

Adler, Guido, "Umfang, Methode und Ziel der Musikwissenschaft," *Vierteljahrsschrift für Musikwissenschaft* 1 (1885)

Bergeron, Katherine, and Philip V. Bohlman, editors, *Disciplining Music: Musicology and Its Canons*, Chicago: University of Chicago Press, 1992

Citron, Marcia J., *Gender and the Musical Canon*, Cambridge: Cambridge University Press, 1993

Forkel, Johann Nicolaus, *Über die Theorie der Musik insofern sie Liebhabern und Kennern nothwendig und nützlich ist*, Göttingen: Vanderhück, 1777

Harrison, Frank Llewellyn, et al., editors, *Musicology*, Englewood Cliffs, New Jersey: Prentice Hall, 1963

Haydon, Glen, *Introduction to Musicology*, Chapel Hill: University of North Carolina Press, 1941

Kerman, Joseph, *Contemplating Music: Challenges to Musicology*, Cambridge, Massachusetts: Harvard University Press, 1985

Kramer, Lawrence, *Classical Music and Postmodern Knowledge*, Berkeley: University of California Press, 1995

Leppert, Richard, and Susan McClary, editors, *Music and Society: The Politics of Composition, Performance, and Reception*, Cambridge: Cambridge University Press, 1987

Solie, Ruth, editor, *Musicology and Difference: Gender and Sexuality in Music Scholarship*, Berkeley: University of California Press, 1993

Treitler, Leo, *Music and the Historical Imagination*, Cambridge, Massachusetts: Harvard University Press, 1989

Musicology as a formalized discipline dates from the early 19th century and was firmly established as an independent area of scholarly study by the 1860s. Its founders saw it as a form of scientific inquiry, whereby objective techniques of analysis were to be applied to individual compositions. Early divisions were simple; classifications became more complex and detailed as the discipline evolved. Through the 20th century, the definition of musicology developed in such a way that two distinct areas became important: (1) the study of the musical work as an isolated phenomenon and (2) the study of the musician and his or her product as the result of cultural and sociological context. The relationship of the two areas has at times been close, at other times remote, and debate over the relative merits of each continues.

At its inception musicology existed as a broad field of study. All tools necessary for the examination and analysis of a composition were included in the definition formulated by early scholars, including theoretical concerns, physical properties of music, and a general aesthetic of the art of music. Historical considerations were included among these areas, but the historical placement of a work of art was secondary to the analysis of its physical properties.

By the middle of the 19th century, scholars still emphasized theoretical concerns, but they also gave more importance to the historical study of music. The result was a twofold division that continues to exist in many views of the discipline. FORKEL, although never specifically using the terms *musicology* or *Musikwissenschaft,* divides "musical science" into five categories, laying the foundation for future classifications. His labels for these divisions are historical (chronological) and systematic (or topical, including theory, acoustics, and pedagogy). ADLER broadens Forkel's divisions and declares the aim of musicology to be the illumination of unfamiliar repertories of music, making the individual work of art the focus of research and analysis. Biographical studies were to be a necessary part of this study because of the contributions such studies made to the historical placement of the piece of music. Adler and those who followed placed great emphasis on the discovery and editing of historically significant works, particularly from the distant past.

As a result of this early emphasis on objective, "scientific" examination of compositions and composers, a significant amount of scholarly activity in the 20th century has been positivist in nature: musicology very quickly became a process of stylistic examination and of placing musical compositions into a continuous historical fabric. Scholars focused on bringing to light less accessible repertories, translating the works when necessary into a notation and format readily accessible to modern scholars and performers. Criticism, to the extent that it played any part in this process, became a part of the descriptive process whereby "mistakes" or lacunae were filled by editors and scholars. Musicologists produced numerous editions dedicated either to single composers or to specific repertoires, rarely including anything more critical than a list of editorial changes for the works included in the publication. Their goal, instead, was to discover and to provide technical analyses and scholarly, critical editions. Musicological literature from most of the 20th century reflects this trend. There are descriptions of styles and repertoires, of historical eras and individual works, and of composers and national schools. There are volumes dedicated to the interpretation of early notations, as well as numerous archival and source studies. Texts in this vein emphasize the chronological approach to music history and comprise details that underscored musical history as a continuous process.

In the examination of the discipline itself, 20th-century scholars, with few exceptions, have used the divisions created by the early German scholars as a foundation for their own classifications within musicology. HAYDON, like Adler, divides the discipline into historical and systematic branches. In Haydon's definition the historical classification incorporates a more descriptive analysis of the work, including matters of style and chronological placement. The systematic branch includes a subordinate, "scientific" treatment that incorporates methodologies commonly found in anthropological studies.

HARRISON et al. represents a view of musicology, particularly American musicology in the 1960s, in which the role of the discipline is more narrow, confined primarily to objective scholarship and to the production of definitions and verifiable facts. Palisca defines the musicologist as historian; the scholar should concentrate on the role of critical texts and editions. He minimizes the role of criticism and evaluation, regarding the descriptive process as complete unto itself. The essays by Harrison and Hood clearly delineate the divisions between the approaches of the musicologist and of the ethnomusicologist, formalizing a distinction within comparative studies that becomes more clearly drawn with later scholars.

In many later studies the techniques of literary criticism and the methodologies of the social sciences have been incorporated into musicological investigations, and musicologists have begun to change their approach to the study of music. Although many writers continue to emphasize the role of positivism—and academic programs are generally structured to encourage this tradition—many scholars have expanded their scope of inquiry, turning to speculative and critical examinations of music. Those writers discussing the discipline itself have called for a broader, more subjective approach as well. They identify music as a cultural phenomenon, incorporating into their research not only the creators of the work of art but also those who receive it and who influence its creation within society.

KERMAN calls for studies following the precepts of literary criticism, in which the goal of the scholar becomes the evaluation and interpretation of the work of art rather than the establishment of a chronological continuum. The composition is still the foundation of investigation, but evaluative judgments should be made concerning its place in the repertory and the culture. TREITLER also argues for a more critical approach, incorporating into his philosophy issues of social and cultural relativism that inform the perception of musical works. Continuing this trend, KRAMER considers the place of the musical work in the larger musicological context and advocates the importance of criticism in the description of that work.

In recent decades the traditional view of music history in terms of set periods and geographical boundaries is changing. More often, scholars engage in research that transcends geographical and chronological restrictions and include more than simply the work of art and its creator. Current social issues and movements have shaped scholarship in musicology as well, with ethnic and gender studies especially prominent. CITRON argues that this inclusion became possible because of the critical work of Kerman and others. Musicologists have expanded their studies to include performers, critics, patrons, and audiences to give a complete view of the musical work and its creation and the evaluation of the role played by each of these agents. The articles in LEPPERT and McCLARY are examples of this approach. The essays found in BERGERON and BOHLMAN also expand the scope of musical inquiry, challenging more traditional views of the musical repertoire. A similar expansion in the area of gender studies is found in SOLIE.

KAREN BRYAN

Music Therapy

Alvin, Juliette, and Auriel Warwick, *Music Therapy for the Autistic Child,* London: Oxford University Press, 1967; 2nd edition, 1991

Bonny, Helen L., and Louis M. Savary, *Music and Your Mind: Listening with a New Consciousness,* New York: Harper and Row, 1973; revised edition, Barrytown, New York: Station Hill Press, 1990

Boxill, Edith Hillman, *Music Therapy for the Developmentally Disabled,* Austin, Texas: Pro-ed, 1985

Bright, Ruth, *Grieving: A Handbook for Those Who Care,* St. Louis, Missouri: MMB Music, 1986

Bruscia, Kenneth E., editor, *Case Studies in Music Therapy,* Phoenixville, Pennsylvania: Barcelona, 1991

Gaston, E. Thayer, editor, *Music in Therapy,* New York: Macmillan, 1968

Kenny, Carolyn Bereznak, *The Field of Play: A Guide for the Theory and Practice of Music Therapy,* Atascadero, California: Ridgeview, 1989

Nordoff, Paul, and Clive Robbins, *Creative Music Therapy: Individualized Treatment for the Handicapped Child,* New York: Day, 1977

Priestley, Mary, *Music Therapy in Action,* London: Constable, and New York: St. Martin's Press, 1975; 2nd edition, St. Louis, Missouri: MMB Music, 1985

Tyson, Florence, *Psychiatric Music Therapy,* New York: Creative Arts Rehabilitation Center, 1981

Wheeler, Barbara L., editor, *Music Therapy Research: Quantitative and Qualitative Perspectives,* Phoenixville, Pennsylvania: Barcelona, 1995

Since music therapy became an organized profession in the mid-20th century, many books introducing the techniques and processes of the field and providing descriptions of the clients receiving treatment have been produced. With such an abundance of meritorious literature, selecting a small survey is challenging. Most authors who are represented here have contributed more volumes of work than can be reviewed in the space allowed; therefore, this essay represents only a sample of the rapidly growing body of literature.

ALVIN and WARWICK presents a descriptive account of Alvin's music therapy philosophy and her techniques for working with autistic children. The discussion explains the responses of children to Alvin and the role of parents in music therapy sessions. Extensive use of case material enlivens the work. For example, one chapter focuses on Alvin's work with a school-age boy, while the second edition adds three chapters of more recent research by Warwick.

BONNY and SAVARY are responsible for developing the music therapy specialty called Guided Imagery and Music (GIM). Their method involves the use of recorded music to unlock the unconscious, as images that are invoked while listening to music are interpreted through an approach that resembles closely analytical methods used by Jungian psychologists. The authors take the reader through a series of exercises for relaxation and concentration intended to assist in the self-exploration of levels of consciousness. A list of musical selections are categorized according to the mood states that they reflect and induce. An emotionally healthy person who wants to become more aware of his/her own altered states of consciousness may find this a helpful manual, but the text should not be considered a self-help course for practicing therapy on one's own. It is important to consult a trained professional when engaging in GIM for therapy and personal growth.

BOXILL offers a clear, organized, and practical book appropriate for musical therapy students and professionals in related fields. The author begins with a survey of the profession, before defending her conviction that music therapy can serve as a primary treatment modality for the developmentally disabled, rather than as an ancillary or adjunct therapy. This text supplies information regarding clinical practice, resource materials, and organization of a music therapy program, and it includes an extensive glossary.

An expert on aging, BRIGHT investigates many important musical therapy topics related to the special needs of the elderly, as well as the often neglected issue of the needs of caregivers. Recognizing that elderly clients are often difficult to understand and manage and that their problems can be emotionally draining for friends, family, and care providers, the author addresses the issues that have an impact on the person providing assistance. Nursing-home and healthcare workers, as well as others who have cared for an elder or experienced any profound loss, can benefit from Bright's expertise and wisdom.

One of the most influential figures in music therapy publishing, education, and politics, BRUSCIA has written and edited many important contributions to the field, including this outstanding collection of 42 case studies by eminent clinicians, which provides a well-rounded and mature survey of schools of thought and treatment approaches in music therapy. Each contributor uses a personal documentation style to describe therapy experiences and offer his or her unique perspective on treatment. The case studies are organized according to client age and type: children, adolescents, adults, adults in psychiatric treatment, and adults in medical treatment. Clients' needs are as diverse as the authors' experiences; the subjects suffer from problems such as AIDS, autism, multiple personalities, abuse, dementia, and learning disabilities. Each author provides a reference and glossary section.

GASTON's behaviorally oriented text book is the first such work of its kind. Authored by 59 pioneers in music therapy, the chapters are organized according to client type. The book's emphasis on behaviorism as the primary psychological school of thought accurately reflects the perspective of the majority of clinicians during this period (the late 1960s). Although the scope of practice may seem narrow compared with the diversity of approaches used by later therapists, the text offers keen insight into the origins and development of the profession.

KENNY offers a thought-provoking and insightful journey into the complex topic of music therapy theory and philosophy. The introductory chapters give a historical overview of the fragmented theories of earlier therapists, who often relied heavily on theoretical frameworks of other closely related disciplines, such as psychology, education, and medicine. Kenny advocates the creation of a safe place for music making and interaction between the therapist and client. Once trust has been established, the participants may travel beyond what they have known previously, taking risks and creating new prototypes for expression. When this symbolic door opens, clients have entered the "field of play," where music acts as a metaphor for life.

PRIESTLEY is highly skilled in the use of music therapy with psychiatric patients, and this book profiles her experience bringing music into the lives of the many emotionally disturbed people with whom she has practiced. Analytical music therapy, improvisation, and the therapeutic music-lesson methods are discussed, and individual and group case studies are presented throughout.

NORDOFF and ROBBINS, a composer and a music therapist, respectively, are the developers of a specialized program of music therapy practice known as Creative Music Therapy. Nordoff and Robbins identify the "music child" as the musicality innate in each individual, regardless of handicap. A cassette tape with corresponding case material from actual sessions accompanies the volume. This guide to the improvisational model of child-centered music therapy is a valuable tool for students and professionals looking to incorporate the method into their work.

TYSON recounts her experiences as founder of the Creative Arts Rehabilitation Center in New York City, where she developed a program for mentally ill clients living in the community. The center uses music and other creative arts to foster the expression of emotion and emphasizes psychodynamic principles.

WHEELER is a comprehensive anthology of research approaches in music therapy. The authors, including Wheeler herself, explain various research methods and offer instruction on how to implement research. Key words and associated jargon are frequently defined in context. Additionally, a complete glossary, as well as name and subject indices, is provided, and a list of references follows each chapter. This is an invaluable resource, appropriate for students and clinicians at all levels of study.

ROBIN RIO

Mussorgsky, Modest 1839–1881

Russian composer

Brown, Malcolm Hamrick, editor, *Musorgsky: In Memoriam, 1881–1981,* Ann Arbor, Michigan: UMI Research Press, 1982

Calvocoressi, Michel-Dimitri, *Modest Mussorgsky: His Life and Works,* London: Rockliff, and Boston: Crescendo, 1956

————, *Mussorgsky,* edited by Gerald Abraham, London: Dent, 1946; revised edition, 1974

Emerson, Caryl, *The Life of Musorgsky,* New York: Cambridge University Press, 1999

Emerson, Caryl, and Robert William Oldani, *Modest Musorgsky and Boris Godunov: Myths, Realities, Reconsiderations,* Cambridge: Cambridge University Press, 1994

Leyda, Jay, and Sergei Bertensson, editors, *The Musorgsky Reader: A Life of Modeste Petrovich Musorgsky in Letters and Documents,* New York: Norton, 1947; reprint; New York, Da Capo Press, 1970

Orlova, Alexandra Anatolevna, *Musorgsky's Works and Days: A Biography in Documents,* translated by Roy J. Guenther, Ann Arbor, Michigan: UMI Research Press, and Epping: Bowker, 1983

Orlova, Alexandra Anatolevna, editor, *Musorgsky Remembered,* translated by Veronique Zaytzeff and Frederick Morrison, Bloomington: Indiana University Press, 1991

Russ, Michael, *Musorgsky, Pictures at an Exhibition,* Cambridge: Cambridge University Press, 1992

Taruskin, Richard, *Musorgsky: Eight Essays and an Epilogue,* Princeton, New Jersey: Princeton University Press, 1993

The literature on Mussorgsky falls roughly into three large categories: sources written before 1928 (when the first collected edition of his work was launched), which are concerned largely with his "musical realism" and technical competence; sources published in the wake of the collected edition, still rehearsing the question of competence while quietly accepting the nationalist view of the composer's work advanced by his friend Vladimir Stasov, or the more intense Soviet formulation of that view; and recent revisionist literature, questioning both late-imperial and Soviet perspectives and setting aside the question of competence in favor of a more thorough examination of the composer's style.

The earliest view of Mussorgsky (meagerly represented in English-language studies of book length) was that he was brilliant but inept, an amateur who disdained the technical studies that would have enabled him to realize his ideas and whose music therefore was flawed—splendidly conceived but poorly executed. This view originated in his own circle, was commonly accepted in Russia after his death, and found its best expression in the editions of Mussorgsky's music by Nikolai Rimsky-Korsakov, who introduced wholesale changes into the music in the name of correcting errors. In France, by contrast, the generation of Debussy and Ravel saw Mussorgsky as an innovator who had transcended mere textbook rules and breathed new life into his art, vividly portraying specific human types in music through a naturalistic setting of their words.

The modernist perspective exemplified by Debussy's and Ravel's admiration for the composer gained ground after World War I and is perhaps best exemplified in the work of Calvocoressi. This author wrote three books on Mussorgsky, of which CALVOCORESSI (1956), completed in 1938 but not published until two decades later, is the most extensive. (CALVOCORESSI [1946], unfinished at the author's death and completed by Gerald Abraham, condenses many of the bigger book's perspectives into the smaller space of a volume in the Master Musicians series.) Calvocoressi's narrative of the composer's life traces its point of view to Mussorgsky's first biographer, Vladimir Stasov. To fill in details, Calvocoressi relies on Soviet scholars of the Stalinist 1920s and 1930s. Discussing the composer's music, the author steadfastly defends the superiority of Mussorgsky's own scores to those of his editors, argues for performing the music in authorial editions, and seeks to prove the composer's technical competence, still at issue, through a close examination of details of his style. Many of the perspectives of Mussorgsky that, until recently, were current in the West trace their authority to Calvocoressi and, through him, to Stasov and the early Soviets. Although his work has now been superseded, he remains the most important and most influential scholar of Mussorgsky in the period between World War I and World War II.

BROWN, a collection of 15 essays published to commemorate the centenary of the composer's death, appeared near the beginning of a revisionist phase in Mussorgsky studies, and several of its contributors break new ground. Noteworthy here are the essays by Taruskin (correcting a misconception by Calvocoressi), Wiley (suggesting influences on Mussorgsky other than those acknowledged by Russian and Soviet critics), Oldani (disentangling the various versions of the opera *Boris Godunov*), and Reilly (discussing Mussorgsky's most important orchestral work, *Night on Bald Mountain*). Other contributors, although writing within a more conventional framework of interpretation, nonetheless provide useful synoptic information in English. Among these are essays by Basmajian (surveying a group of little-known songs), Garden (discussing Balakirev's influence on Mussorgsky), and Hoops (interpreting Mussorgsky as a populist, with translations of essays by Stasov).

RUSS provides a thorough guide to Mussorgsky's most famous piece, *Pictures at an Exhibition*. The author discusses the work's place in 19th-century Russian piano music, the circumstances surrounding its composition, and its musical language. Of particular value is the chapter on harmony, scales, tonality, and voice leading. The book concludes with a brief chapter on 11 orchestrations of the piece, including the most well-known one, by Ravel.

TARUSKIN's book is basic to all present-day Mussorgsky studies, strongly influencing current scholarship in both Russia and the West. The author reexamines Mussorgsky's historical and artistic image, debunking the conclusions of both Stasov and the Soviet and Western scholars who accepted Stasov's views uncritically. Taruskin documents the extent to which Mussorgsky, in *The Marriage*, was stimulated by the mimetic theory of word-tone relations that he had found in Georg Gervinus's book *Händel und Shakespeare*. The author argues persuasively that Mussorgsky's revision of *Boris Godunov* was undertaken for artistic reasons, not for the reasons of expediency advanced by Calvocoressi and others. Taruskin interprets *Khovanshchina* not as a populist folk-music drama but as an aristocratic tragedy. Even *Sorochintsy Fair* is seen in a new light, as the work that might have inaugurated Mussorgsky's full entry into his nation's musical life, had not death cut him off. The book ends with a chapter on views of Mussorgsky in the age of glasnost.

EMERSON and OLDANI take a new and comprehensive look at *Boris Godunov*, correcting along the way several oft-met errors in Mussorgsky scholarship. Emerson, a literary specialist, begins with an account of Tsar Boris's reign (1598–1605), then—drawing on Mikhail Bakhtin's theories of narrative—discusses Mussorgsky's literary sources for the story and his innovations as a librettist. Oldani, a music historian, discusses the composition and revision of the opera, together with its first productions in Russia and the West, and provides a detailed musical analysis. Translations of censorship documents and classic essays in the opera's reception history, plus a discography, are noteworthy features; the book ends with a chapter (by Emerson) speculating on the role that the Boris tale may have played in recent Russian cultural history.

EMERSON's biography is a culturally informed narrative of events in the composer's life; it treats with compelling conviction the texts, subjects, literary themes, and ideas that animated this most word-oriented of all the great Russian composers. In keeping with the editorial policy of the series, technical discussion of the music is minimal; here it is confined to a single brief, yet insightful, musical interlude by David Geppert. A common theme in much of this recent literature is that Mussorgsky was a highly intellectual, if unconventional, composer, and by no means an inept dilettante.

The principal documentary collections in English are by Leyda and Bertensson and by Orlova. LEYDA and BERTENSSON present translations of nearly all of Mussorgsky's letters, letters by others addressed to him, and extracts from memoirs and other documents. ORLOVA's (1983) documentary biography provides excerpts (some lengthy) from primary source materials—letters, documents, memoirs—arranged chronologically in the format of an appointment book. ORLOVA (1991) offers idiomatic translations of 36 full memoirs or extracts, together with commentary that remains committed to Soviet perspectives and interpretations.

ROBERT WILLIAM OLDANI

N

Nancarrow, Conlon 1912–1997

United States composer

Carlsen, Philip, *The Player-Piano Music of Conlon Nancarrow: An Analysis of Selected Studies,* New York: Institute for Studies in American Music, 1988

Gann, Kyle, *The Music of Conlon Nancarrow,* Cambridge: Cambridge University Press, 1995

Academic interest in the composer Conlon Nancarrow accelerated in the late 1970s, when Peter Garland, editor of the music journal *Soundings,* began to publish Nancarrow's works. In 1977 Garland published the first major overview of Nancarrow's work, which included the scores of eight of his studies for player piano as well as five brief articles, among them the first attempted overview of Nancarrow's compositions, by James Tenney. With this volume of *Soundings,* titled *Conlon Nancarrow: Selected Studies for Player Piano,* Nancarrow studies commenced.

By the early 1980s Nancarrow had begun to emerge from decades of self-imposed isolation, appearing at select performances of his early, nonmechanical works. Throughout this decade his public prominence increased, due in part to his positions as composer-in-residence at several U.S. and European music festivals, as well as to his brief tenure as a professor at Mills College. His place in the avant-garde was secured with composer György Ligeti's 1981 declaration that Nancarrow's music was "the greatest discovery since Webern and Ives"; a more mainstream acknowledgment arrived in 1982 when Nancarrow received the prestigious MacArthur Foundation prize. Scholarship lagged behind: the first short monograph devoted to Nancarrow appeared in 1988, while the first comprehensive analytical study of his work was not published until 1995.

CARLSEN's study of Nancarrow, developed from the author's doctoral thesis, is one of a series of analyses published under the auspices of the Institute for Studies in American Music at the City College of New York. A composer, conductor, and cellist, Carlsen makes modest claims for what he calls his "essay," noting that for reasons of practicality he has limited himself to discussion of only five of the studies for player piano (Studies no. 8, 19, 23, 35, and 36). In fact, this brief book contains a considerable amount of additional information, including a concise biography of the composer and a brief but cogent summary of Nancarrow's involvement with the player piano. Although Carlsen's detailed discussion of Nancarrow's compositions is limited, he has carefully selected works that span a number of years (although none of Nancarrow's works is dated, Carlsen correctly believed them to have been completed in roughly numerical order) and that illuminate a range of compositional issues and approaches fundamental to Nancarrow's aesthetic. By including many score facsimiles and musical examples, Carlsen gives the reader a sense of this musical sound; his analytical discussions are clear and sensible, although at times he struggles for a terminology capable of capturing Nancarrow's radically new compositional explorations. Above all, however, this study is limited by Carlsen's apparent lack of access to the composer: the book is based on perceptions gleaned through analysis of scores and recordings, relying on secondary sources for other information.

In contrast, GANN, a composer and music historian, clearly spent considerable time with Nancarrow. His book is remarkable not only for its sense of Nancarrow's own voice but for its intelligently comprehensive approach to the composer's works. Noting in the preface that he intends the study to serve "primarily [as] a groundwork for analysis of Nancarrow's music, secondarily as an introduction to his work for the general contemporary music lover," Gann nevertheless manages to couch detailed discussions of Nancarrow's seemingly impenetrable compositions in elegant and comprehensible language. The core of book is devoted, naturally enough, to analyses of the studies for player piano, and here Gann especially shines: he has devised a set of analytical tools that allow access into the music and has coined a number of terms to describe some of the compositions' salient features. Among his achievements is the organization of Nancarrow's work into sensible categories based on compositional technique; the studies are thus identified as influenced by blues or as exploring iso-rhythm, canon, acceleration, or sound-mass. Gann gives thorough consideration as well to the early and late works composed for live performers and provides the most comprehensive biography of the composer to date. The discography and extensive bibliography are invaluable tools for future Nancarrow scholarship, an area that will certainly be invigorated by this breakthrough study.

MARY E. DAVIS

Native North American Music

Densmore, Frances, *Teton Sioux Music,* Washington, D.C.: Government Printing Office, 1918; reprint, New York: Da Capo Press, 1972

Fletcher, Alice C., and Francis La Flesche, *A Study of Omaha Indian Music,* Cambridge, Massachusetts: Peabody Museum of American Archaeology and Ethnology, 1893; reprint, Lincoln: University of Nebraska Press, 1994

Howard, James H., and Victoria Lindsay Levine, *Choctaw Music and Dance,* Norman: University of Oklahoma Press, 1990

McAllester, David Park, *Peyote Music,* edited by Ralph Linton, New York: Viking Fund, 1949

Nettl, Bruno, *North American Indian Styles,* Philadelphia, Pennsylvania: American Folklore Society, 1954

Vander, Judith, *Shoshone Ghost Dance Religion: Poetry Songs and Great Basin Context,* Urbana: University of Illinois Press, 1997

————, *Songprints: The Musical Experience of Five Shoshone Women,* Urbana: University of Illinois Press, 1988

Vennum, Thomas, *The Ojibwa Dance Drum: Its History and Construction,* Washington, D.C.: Smithsonian Institution Press, 1982

Young Bear, Severt, and R.D. Theisz, *Standing in the Light: A Lakota Way of Seeing,* Lincoln: University of Nebraska Press, 1994

Until recently, scholarship about Native American music has been dominated by anthropologists, most of whom regarded music as just one out of many elements of expressive culture rather than a distinct and meaningful area of study. With a few notable exceptions, these scholars were non-Indians, and in addition to limited knowledge of Native American languages, few had more than minimal training in musical notation and transcription. Until the mid-1930s, a documentation-oriented methodology (termed *salvage-ethnology* by later scholars) was the norm, with fieldwork centering around the remnants of pre-European-contact Indian musical life, while hybrid and contemporary musical genres were generally ignored. Since the late 1940s, however, with the development of ethnomusicology as a distinct discipline, studies

of Native North American musical expression in present-day life have become more common.

Fletcher was an assistant in ethnography at Harvard University's Peabody Museum and held the museum's prestigious Thaw Fellowship during the early 1890s, enabling her to spend a significant amount of time in the field. Together, FLETCHER and LA FLESCHE (her adopted son and a member of the Omaha nation) produced one of the earliest and most complete studies of a Native American musical repertoire based on systematic research and fieldwork. An advocate of the "Indianist" movement among composers, Fletcher hoped that by making Omaha songs and melodies available to the greater U.S. public, Indian music would be more appreciated as the United States' first native music, with the goodwill generated by this understanding assisting in the assimilation of Indian peoples into the dominant society.

Inspired by Fletcher, DENSMORE went out among the Ojibwa (Chippewa) in her home state of Minnesota and in 1910 produced a study of the tribe that was the first of more than a dozen works on native music and culture for the Bureau of American Ethnology of the Smithsonian Institution. Her later two-volume work surveying the musical culture of the Teton (Lakota Sioux) people of South Dakota is considered the definitive study of that repertoire. Densmore's methodology, a blend of ethnology and formalistic musical analysis, is considered dated today. The sheer amount of information presented, however, combined with a skillful use of native-language translators (many Lakota of the era did not speak English) have made the volumes invaluable sources of information on cultural practice, oral tradition, and song texts.

McALLESTER's study of the ongoing pan-Indian religious movement known as the Native American Church, or the Peyote Way, is an early example of research on Indian music organized by a genre rather than by a tribal group or culture area, as was the common practice prior to the 1940s. Although brief, McAllester's writing style is lively and engaging, and his blend of transcribed oral narrative with textual and musical analysis is effective. A weakness of the work is its exclusively Southwestern orientation and lack of information on Native American Church practices among such groups as the Yanktonai (Sioux) and Winnebago.

NETTL's monograph is a synthesis of earlier works, primarily by anthropologists George Herzog and Helen Roberts. An early but still valuable reference work, it illustrates Indian musical styles and assigns them to various "culture areas" based on a preexisting musical taxonomy constructed from such musical elements as form, range, singing style, and rhythm.

VENNUM is renowned for blending meticulous historical research with ongoing fieldwork. His specialty is music of the Great Lakes region, most specifically of the Ojibwa people. Although technically devoted to the origin and spread of the Dream Dance society through the upper Midwest and eastern Canada, this work backtracks into the beginnings of the Grass Dance on the Great Plains. In doing so, Vennum relies too much on turn-of-the-20th-century research without engaging in a meaningful critique, allowing such outdated anthropological theories as diffusionism to creep into the text.

HOWARD and LINDSAY LEVINE is a straightforward documentation of social music and dance in contemporary Mississippi Choctaw society. Focusing on the cultural and musical revivals taking place since the early 1970s in Mississippi, the authors contrast contemporary Choctaw musical life to that recorded by Densmore in the early 1940s. Other areas discussed include the role of the Mississippi Choctaw as the preservers of traditional Choctaw music and language, and mechanisms of cultural transference from Mississippi to the Oklahoma Choctaw. Although brief and at times not entirely accurate, Howard and Lindsay Levine is one of the few available texts on Southeastern Indian music.

While doing field work on the Wind River Shoshone reservation in Wyoming during the early 1980s, VANDER (1988, 1997) forged relationships with two elderly sisters, Emily Hill and Dorothy Tappay, who would serve as Vander's primary consultants for much of her work. Vander's focus, unlike earlier scholarship about Indian music, engages predominantly with Native American women's repertoires. The author's Great Basin orientation stresses the connections between Shoshone life and their *Naraya* ceremony, principal precursor to the pan-Indian Ghost Dance. Vander's focus on a single division (Western) of a single tribal group, combined with an emphasis on song poetics, differs remarkably from any of the previous Ghost Dance studies. The core text is organized according to a Shoshone cosmology of song contexts, with five core chapters on water, mountains, animals (including spirits), plants, and beings that "inhabit the sky."

YOUNG BEAR and THEISZ sang together in the renowned Lakota Drum group the Porcupine Singers for more than 20 years, performing at powwows across the United States and Canada. This volume is essentially an autobiography of Young Bear organized and edited by Theisz; their collaboration represents the incipient realization by scholars that Indians are the foremost experts on Indian music and musical life. Theisz, a professor of English and American Indian Studies, does not fill the work with song transcriptions and analysis. Instead, Young Bear and Theisz synthesize an Oglala Lakota oral text into written form, using the history of the Young Bear family as an organizing framework for the non-Indian reader, who might have a difficult time with the circularity of most traditional Indian narratives.

TARA BROWNER

Neoclassicism

Lippman, Edward A., *A History of Western Musical Aesthetics,* Lincoln: University of Nebraska Press, 1992

Messing, Scott, *Neoclassicism in Music: From the Genesis of the Concept through the Schoenberg/Stravinsky Polemic,* Rochester, New York: University of Rochester Press, 1996

Morgan, Robert P., *Twentieth-Century Music: A History of Musical Style in Modern Europe and America,* New York: Norton, 1991

Salzman, Eric, *Twentieth-Century Music: An Introduction,* Englewood Cliffs, New Jersey: Prentice Hall, 1967; 3rd edition, 1988

Watkins, Glenn, *Soundings: Music in the Twentieth Century,* New York: Schirmer, and London: Collier Macmillan, 1988

Music historians apply the term *neoclassical* in an unconventional manner. Art historians originally coined the term in reference to late-18th-century painters and sculptors who emulated the order and symmetry of ancient Greek and Roman art. Because these artists revered the aesthetic values of an idealized classical past, scholars labeled their style *neoclassical*. Composers of the late 18th century showed a similar concern for balance and regularity within their music, but no suitable ancient models existed for them. Thus, the music of the late 18th century became known as classical rather than neoclassical. Later, musicologists applied the term *neoclassical* to 20th-century composers who self-consciously employed historical models—especially those of the 18th century—in their music. The stylistic attributes associated with these compositions include clear textures and emotional restraint, in addition to the use of historical forms. The label is applied most often to the works of Stravinsky that date from the early 1920s through the middle of the 20th century.

MESSING has written the only English-language monograph exclusively devoted to the question of neoclassicism in music. He focuses on the evolution of the term itself. Prior to the 1920s, neoclassicism and related categories such as *nouveau classicisme* and *Neue Klassizität* were employed in a loose and often contradictory fashion. The authors, artists, and musicians who used these terms emphasized the value of reviving forms and procedures of the 18th century, often with a sense of nostalgia. A change in outlook occurred between 1910 and 1920. According to Messing, the experience of World War I produced a sense of historical cynicism among Europeans that was coupled with a dread of chaos and disorder. Within this context, musicians sought a means of reconciling their creative freedom and innovation with an order and tradition derived from a more distant past. The result altered the meaning of neoclassicism.

Throughout the 1910s, several critics—including the poet Jean Cocteau—reacted against the extravagant art of the late 19th century. At this time, Cocteau became a champion of the composer Satie, whose austere stylistic simplicity matched Cocteau's insistence on naiveté and youthful disdain as fundamental artistic values. The aesthetic alternative offered by Cocteau and Satie eventually attracted the attention of Stravinsky and prompted him to experiment with transparent textures within his own compositions. Stravinsky stressed his break with the recent past by publicly declaring objectivity to be the main characteristic of his music. Thus, he presented his ballet *Pulcinella* (1920), a pastiche of 18th-century music, as an ironic invocation of the past rather than a sentimental return to the classical era. For Stravinsky and other young composers active in France, the resurgence of interest in 18th-century models involved a simultaneous rejection of romanticism and a supercilious scorn for German music of the 19th century. Messing has determined that by 1923 a stable definition of neoclassicism had emerged. It was based on four stylistic features that had appeared in the previous decade: simplicity, youth, objectivity, and an anti-German cultural elitism. This last characteristic was the primary reason for an acrimonious rift between Stravinsky and Schoenberg, who considered his own music to be a direct continuation of 19th-century German traditions. By the end of the 1920s, neoclassicism had become a category that not only identified Stravinsky's style, but also distinguished it from that of Schoenberg.

WATKINS defines neoclassicism more broadly than Messing, whose monograph focuses on the meaning of this term during the 1920s. Watkins argues that a new form of historical awareness developed in the late 19th and early 20th centuries and that this awareness created a cultural context in which the neoclassical aesthetic thrived. The establishment of the field of musicology, the popularization of older repertoires by performers such as Wanda Landowska, and the presence of classical textures and forms in the music of Debussy and Ravel contributed to an increasing fascination with music from the 18th century. For Watkins, concern with history is the defining characteristic of neoclassicism. To illustrate his point, he demonstrates how the aesthetic values associated with neoclassicism extend beyond the historical use of the term itself. To that end, he explores the music of Schoenberg, perhaps the harshest critic of neoclassical composers, and suggests ways in which Schoenberg's own compositions embody certain values typically associated with neoclassicism. For example, Schoenberg's use in the 1920s of clearly defined forms and procedures derived from 18th- and 19th-century practice parallels the neoclassicists' interest in historical models as a source of order. Of course, Watkins does not dismiss the differences between composers such as Schoenberg and Stravinsky, but he insists that they share an interest in many of the same compositional problems.

Like Watkins, MORGAN writes for a general audience rather than the specialist and incorporates his discussion of neoclassicism within a survey of 20th-century music. His attitude toward this aesthetic category, however, differs from that of Watkins. Although Morgan discusses the music of Poulenc, Mihaud, and Bartók in his chapter on neoclassicism, he reserves the term *neoclassical* for those compositions by Stravinsky that self-consciously invoke historical comparisons. Despite his narrow application of the term itself, Morgan recognizes that other qualities associated with neoclassicism, such as simplicity and clarity, informed much of the music produced between 1920 and 1940.

In his discussion of neoclassicism, SALZMAN focuses on strictly compositional techniques to arrive at his own definition of the term. Indeed, he argues that a better label for the phenomenon would be *neotonality*. In doing so, Salzman avoids issues pertaining to aesthetics and simplifies the question of what constitutes neoclassicism. Thus, he is able to apply the label *neoclassical* to the works of composers outside France without a problem. For example, Hindemith's attempt to create a new, theoretically coherent approach to tonality easily fits Salzman's definition of neoclassicism despite the substantial differences between Hindemith's music and that of Stravinsky.

LIPPMANN's approach contrasts significantly with those of the previous authors. He studies the contexts and aesthetic foundations that gave rise to specific styles rather than producing a history of style. Thus, his book introduces the concept of neoclassicism within a chapter that focuses on objectivity. Other stylistics features of neoclassicism are mentioned only in passing. Lippmann identifies neoclassicism as one of several manifestations of broader cultural and aesthetic trends that are dominated by the spirit of objectivity.

MICHAEL E. McCLELLAN

Nielsen, Carl 1865–1931

Danish composer

Balzer, Jürgen, editor, *Carl Nielsen: Centenary Essays,* London: Dobson, 1965

Fanning, David, *Nielsen, Symphony No. 5,* Cambridge: Cambridge University Press, 1997

Lawson, Jack, *Carl Nielsen,* London: Phaidon, 1997

Miller, Mina F., *Carl Nielsen: A Guide to Research,* New York: Garland, 1987

Miller, Mina F., editor, *The Nielsen Companion,* London: Faber, 1994; Portland, Oregon: Amadeus Press, 1995

Nielsen, Carl, *Living Music,* translated by Reginald Spink, London: Hutchinson, 1953a

———, *My Childhood,* translated by Reginald Spink, London: Hutchinson, 1953b

Simpson, Robert, *Carl Nielsen: Symphonist, 1865–1931,* London: Dent, 1952; revised edition, as *Carl Nielsen: Symphonist,* London: Kahn and Averill, and New York: Taplinger, 1979

Since the mid-20th century, Carl Nielsen's reputation has grown considerably. Once an obscure name in music textbooks, he is now a composer whose music is widely performed throughout Western Europe and North America. The fact that there are now approximately 30 commercial recordings of his two most well-known works—the Fourth ("Inextinguishable") and Fifth Symphonies—shows the extent to which Nielsen is canonized.

The marked increase in the number of performances and recordings of Nielsen's music, however, has not translated into a substantial body of English-language scholarship on the composer. This situation can be attributed mainly to two factors. One is the language problem. Few English-speaking scholars know Danish, and many of the most important primary documents (e.g., Nielsen's diaries and correspondence) have not been translated into English. It is hoped that we may some day see translations not only of these primary sources but also of the three most important biographies of Nielsen: Torben Meyer and Frede Schandorf Petersen's *Carl Nielsen: Kunstneren og mennesket* (1947–48; Carl Nielsen: The Artist and the Man), Ludvig Dolleris's *Carl Nielsen: En musikografi* (1949; Carl Nielsen: A Musical Biography), and Jørgen I. Jensen's *Carl Nielsen: Danskeren* (1991; Carl Nielsen: The Dane). The other major reason for the paucity of scholarship on Nielsen and his music is the admission policy of the Carl Nielsen Archive in Copenhagen. Until recently, gaining access to the primary source materials in this valuable collection was almost impossible. Consequently, there are numerous holes in the English-language scholarship on Nielsen and his music. In particular, a comprehensive life-and-works biography has not been written, and discussions of his two operas, *Maskarade* and *Saul og David,* are almost nonexistent.

To date, there have been three waves of scholarly interest on Nielsen in English-speaking countries. The first took place during the early 1950s. At that time, the Danish Radio Symphony Orchestra under the direction of Erik Tuxen toured Great Britain and introduced the symphonies of Carl Nielsen to British concertgoers. These performances shocked numerous people, and many writers still discuss the profound effects that these concerts had on them.

These performances, along with some early recordings, kindled interest in Nielsen's music and led to the publication of three important monographs in English. The first is SIMPSON, a life-and-works biography that focuses primarily on the six symphonies. This book contains two hypotheses that have been a source of controversy among Nielsen scholars in Denmark and in the English-speaking world. The first is the author's contention that Nielsen's greatest achievement lies in his use of progressive tonality. The other is Simpson's division of the composer's career into four periods: (1) earliest works to 1902–3; (2) *Sleep* (1904) to *Sinfonia espansiva* (1911); (3) Violin Sonata no. 2 (1912) to Symphony no. 5 (1922); and (4) the final years (1923–31). Also of interest in this volume is the appendix: a translation of a short biographical sketch by Torben Meyer, the coauthor of the most comprehensive biography of Nielsen. A quarter of a century later, Simpson produced a revised edition of his pioneering study (1979). This later edition presents a significantly different and much more positive view of the Sixth Symphony, as well as a new concluding chapter, which compares the symphonic styles of Nielsen and his Finnish contemporary, Jean Sibelius.

The other two books published during this initial wave are translations of Nielsen's writings. NIELSEN (1953a) contains eight essays on the aesthetics of music. Originally published in Danish on the occasion of the composer's 60th birthday, this widely read and highly regarded collection influenced numerous Danish musicians during the course of the 20th century. It helps to place Nielsen in the context of early 20th-century modernism. Some of the main themes in this volume are the rejection of program music, the importance of organicism in rhythm and polyphony, and the autonomous nature of music. NIELSEN (1953b) is a vivid portrait of the composer's first 18 years. Unfortunately, this entertaining volume has led biographers to overstate the importance of Nielsen's (or Nielsen's interpretation of his own) childhood for his mature music. This tendency is exemplified by Torben Meyer, who begins his biographical sketch of Nielsen (published in Simpson) by stating that, to gain understanding of Nielsen's music, one needs especially to consider the composer's childhood "in a poor labourer's cottage on the fertile island of Fyn, his struggle to get on in life, and his ceaseless search for knowledge." This common and overly simplistic view of Nielsen as a simple farm boy who overcame all obstacles to become Denmark's greatest composer is in large part rooted in some biographers' tendency to give undue weight to the composer's autobiography. Both volumes by Nielsen are translated into very readable English by Reginald Spink.

The second wave of scholarly interest in Nielsen occurred during the mid-1960s—the years surrounding the centenary of the composer's birth. This wave saw the publication of Johannes Fabricius's *Carl Nielsen, 1865–1931: A Pictorial Biography* (1965) and BALZER, the first English-language book that emphasizes Nielsen's nonsymphonic output. Balzer, published simultaneously in Danish and English, contains essays by eight Danish scholars. The first article, by Thorvald Nielsen (no relation to Carl), is an anecdotal account of the author's friendship with and view of the composer. The remaining seven essays are genre studies. Each chronologically surveys Nielsen's entire output in the given genre. There are also brief analyses of most of the larger works.

In the two decades after the centenary, Nielsen's music continued to gain converts in concert halls and record stores. In terms of English-language scholarship, however, these 20 years were fairly dry. With the exception of the revised edition of Simpson, no significant English-language monograph on the composer was published until MILLER (1987). This excellent bibliography contains more than 400 entries of materials in nine languages. Her annotations are generally accurate and frequently extensive.

Miller was instrumental in sparking the third wave of scholarly interest in Nielsen in English-speaking countries. Her Garland bibliography made research on the composer much less time consuming. Moreover, she organized a session on the composer for the 1991 Society of Music Theory conference, which was the starting point for MILLER (1994). This highly provocative but somewhat uneven collection of essays shows the growing diversity of musicological work on Nielsen. Its contents can be grouped into three categories. First, there are a number of articles of relatively narrow topics, such as Nielsen's compositional procedures, performance history, Nielsen's writings, and Nielsen's Danishness. Second are in-depth analyses of seminal works, such as the Fifth and Sixth Symphonies, the early songs, the string quartets, the violin sonatas, and the wind quintet. Finally, there are essays that examine Nielsen's tonal, formal, and thematic techniques. Unfortunately, this volume is almost completely silent with regard to Nielsen's operas. Of special interest are translations of a selection of Nielsen's letters and of two important articles written during the early 1930s (Tom Kristensen on Nielsen's writings and Povl Hamburger on the issue of form in *Sinfonia espansiva*).

While Miller (1994) is likely to interest listeners and performers who are well-acquainted with Nielsen's oeuvre, two recent books serve as good introductions to the composer and his music. LAWSON, the first book-length biography of Nielsen in English, includes an impressive number of illustrations, such as concert posters, portraits, art works that inspired the composer, and photographs of manuscripts. Lawson also extensively discusses the early reception of Nielsen's music and includes a large number of quotations from primary sources, such as Nielsen's letters, diaries, and early concert reviews. The discussion of Nielsen's music, however, is rather superficial and extremely brief.

The other excellent introduction to Nielsen is FANNING. This slim volume opens with a chapter that places Nielsen's Fifth Symphony in the context of the symphonic tradition and Nielsen's career, and it closes with an extended discussion of the 20-odd recordings of the work. The bulk of the book, however, is devoted to an extremely detailed analysis of the Fifth Symphony.

ERIC HUNG

Norway *see* Scandinavia

Notation: To 1600

Apel, Willi, *The Notation of Polyphonic Music 900–1600*, Cambridge, Massachusetts: Mediaeval Academy of America, 1942; 5th revised edition, 1953

Berger, Anna Maria Busse, *Mensuration and Proportion Signs: Origins and Evolution*, Oxford, Clarendon Press, and New York: Oxford University Press, 1990

Berger, Karol, *Musica ficta: Theories of Accidental Inflections in Vocal Polyphony from Marchetto da Padova to Gioseffo Zarlino*, Cambridge: Cambridge University Press, 1987

Cardine, Eugene, *Gregorian Semiology*, translated by Robert M. Fowells, Sablé-sur-Sarthe: Abbaye Saint-Pierre de Solesmes, 1982

Jeffery, Peter, *Re-Envisioning Past Musical Cultures: Ethnomusicology in the Study of Gregorian Chant*, Chicago: University of Chicago Press, 1992

Karp, Theodore, *The Polyphony of Saint Martial and Santiago de Compostela*, 2 vols., Berkeley: University of California Press, 1992

Mathiesen, Thomas, "Rhythm and Meter in Ancient Greek Music," *Music Theory Spectrum* 7 (1985)

Santosuosso, Alma Colk, *Letter Notations in the Middle Ages*, Ottawa: Institute of Mediaeval Music, 1989

The notation of music in western Europe prior to 1600 demonstrates the remarkable adaptability and invention of the musicians who documented and recorded the evolving styles of monophonic and polyphonic music. Although the pitch notation of the ancient Greek musicians was transmitted to the early Christian Church through music theory texts, the rhythmic notation of the Greeks apparently was not. Early chant books of the liturgy of the Church are annotated with a variety of symbols apparently indicating voice inflection, but there is considerable debate among scholars as to what these symbols represent. The ambiguity of early chant notation has led to a host of questions regarding the role of memorization in the transmission of chant and the possible use of improvisation in performances of the liturgy. The development of staff notation by the 11th century greatly clarified the notation of pitch. Two questions of pitch notation, however, remain for scholars of the music throughout this period: the division of the whole step into smaller intervals and the use of *musica ficta*—non-notated chromatic alterations.

Scholars are still divided on the appropriate rhythmic interpretation for much early medieval music. Interpreting rhythm becomes more certain for music notated after note shapes (or neumes) used in chant were adapted to form specific rhythmic patterns known as the rhythmic modes in the Notre Dame School of the late 12th century. By the late 13th century, musicians such as Franco of Cologne began to make distinctions among individual note shapes to indicate specific rhythmic durations. Symbols for the regular division of time in music (similar to the modern concept of time signatures) were used by the early 14th century. From that point onward, the development of rhythmic notation was mostly a matter of adding ever finer distinctions to the note shapes (such as stems, flags, and color) to produce increasingly precise distinctions of rhythm.

APEL's text has remained a standard introduction to the topic for over 50 years. The author derives general rules for interpreting the notation from a variety of theorists and applies these principles to a wide body of manuscript sources. The text includes 88 facsimiles of early manuscripts and provides sample transcriptions into modern notation. Although its longevity is a credit to Apel's ability to explain the intricacies of the subject, not all of his conclusions are currently considered valid. As can be expected of an introductory text on such a broad topic, general rules are stressed at the sacrifice of local variants and unique insights of individual theorists.

A basic introduction to chant notation can be found in CARDINE. As a publication of the Solesmes monastery, the book represents the interpretation of Gregorian notation promoted by the Catholic Church. The book introduces each basic neume, providing various examples from early chant sources, and describes its interpretation. The work is detailed, and a basic knowledge of chant notation and history is assumed by the author.

JEFFERY represents one of the most recent monographs on the transmission of chant. The author presents a brief review of the major theories in chant transmission of such scholars as Helmut Hucke, Leo Treitler, and Kenneth Levy. (The scholarly debate on early chant notation and transmission has taken place primarily in journals, and the interested student will need to consult articles by these writers for a full view on the topic.) Jeffery suggests that traditional methods of studying chant can be supplemented using the methods of ethnomusicology to investigate such questions as the interrelationships between chant and folk music. The book is brief for such a broad pursuit but contains an excellent bibliography on recent scholarship.

Anna Maria Busse BERGER gives a history of the various mensuration symbols developed in the 14th century, which are roughly equivalent to modern time signatures; a few of these symbols have remained in our notation system today. She documents the various ways musicians used these signs to create complex proportional relationships within their works. The book is intended for a specialist, but an introductory reader will gain a great deal from the first portions of the text in which the author recounts the early history of these symbols; the extensive bibliography and annotations are also very useful.

Musica ficta refers to the chromatic alterations of music that are not notated in the sources. The modern student will often see accidentals written above the staff of a modern edition of early music, indicating where the editor believes the addition of *ficta* is appropriate. Theo-

ries about what constitutes the correct application of *musica ficta* have varied from scholar to scholar; such debates explain why many recordings and modern editions of early music do not agree with one another. Karol BERGER's book gives a detailed history of *ficta*. Although the study is intended for an advanced student, a reader with a moderate degree of knowledge can gain a great deal from it. The work includes an extensive bibliography and is well annotated.

The polyphonic repertoire of Saint Martial and Santiago de Compostela provides an interesting test case in notation. Scholars have debated how to interpret the rhythm of these works and how these rhythmic interpretations might be related to the rhythm of the Notre Dame composers in Paris. KARP is the latest scholar to address the question of transcribing these works into modern notation. The first volume discusses the issues related to transcription; the second provides modern editions of the pieces. Karp gives a history of earlier transcriptions of these works and addresses such issues as the interpretation of basic note shapes, the interaction between the text and the pitches, theories of consonance and dissonance, and the role that ornaments played in the music.

MATHIESEN describes the rhythmic notation found in Greek manuscripts and explains his interpretation of it in light of Greek ideas of rhythm and meter. The work cites several Greek theorists and gives annotated examples. The article is written for a sophisticated student, but much of the arguments can be grasped by any interested reader.

SANTOSUOSSO thoroughly examines various letter notations employed by theorists of the early Middle Ages. These notations, derived from the pitch notations used by ancient Greek theorists, demonstrate the close relationship between theory and practice as they were subsequently employed to notate both monophonic and polyphonic music in the early Middle Ages. This volume contains numerous illustrations of the manuscripts and an extensive bibliography.

C. MATTHEW BALENSUELA

Notation: 20th Century

Bajzek, Dieter, *Percussion: An Annotated Bibliography with Special Emphasis on Contemporary Notation and Performance,* Metuchen, New Jersey: Scarecrow Press, 1988

Cage, John, editor, *Notations,* New York: Something Else Press, 1969

Cole, Hugo, *Sounds and Signs: Aspects of Musical Notation,* London: Oxford University Press, 1974

Elias, William Y., *Grapes: Practical Notation for Clusters and Special Effects for Piano and Other Keyboards,* 2nd edition, revised, Tel Aviv: Elias, and New York: Pendragon Press, 1984

Karkoschka, Erhard, *Notation in New Music: A Critical Guide to Interpretation and Realisation,* translated by Ruth Koenig, New York: Praeger, 1972

Read, Gardner, *Contemporary Instrumental Techniques,* New York: Schirmer Books, 1976

———, *Modern Rhythmic Notation,* Bloomington: Indiana University Press, 1978; London: Gollancz, 1980

———, *20th-Century Microtonal Notation,* New York: Greenwood Press, 1990

Risatti, Howard, *New Music Vocabulary: A Guide to Notational Signs for Contemporary Music,* Urbana: University of Illinois Press, 1974

Stone, Kurt, *Music Notation in the Twentieth Century: A Practical Guidebook,* New York: Norton, 1980

The most important and dramatic innovations in musical notation in the 20th century have largely appeared in the scores themselves. Books on this topic generally attempt either to illustrate the wide range of possibilities or to organize disparate symbols into consistent systems. Some books also take on the difficult project of creating a scientific notation that is more logically structured than traditional music notation; most of these attempts have met with little success, but the Chroma Foundation (in Canada and Switzerland) continues transcribing Bach and Schoenberg in its frequent but brief publications.

Many of the books reviewed here focus on the post–World War II years to the mid-1970s, centering especially on composers associated with Darmstadt or with John Cage's New York School, probably because those composers were so productive in notational experiments. Some examples also suggest links with literature (especially concrete poetry), drama (especially performance art), and various visual experiments with light or staging.

KARKOSCHKA, whether in English translation or the original German, is a classic guide to modern notation. Karkoschka presents the following: a study of notational reform systems (he decides that equitone is the most successful); a reference listing of symbols used by different composers (intelligently classified and cross-referenced); and a beautiful collection of score pages, mostly by European composers with a smattering of pages from American composers associated with Cage. This last section is perhaps the most useful published collection of its kind, especially as Karkoschka analyzes each experiment with intelligence and critical enthusiasm.

CAGE assembles his own collection from pages given to him by other composers; the book is similar to the third section of Karkoschka's work, but lacks explanations. A number of American composers of the 1960s, some of whom are now forgotten, are represented, resulting in an exciting and open-ended collection of ideas.

STONE is a textbook of contemporary notational practice, aimed at creating an approach to 20th-century techniques that is consistent with historical notation. His focus is chiefly on specific symbols that can be included on traditional staves, and he generally ignores more radical experiments.

RISATTI has written an extended reference list, most of which consists of isolated symbols and their interpretations organized by instrument and effect, with little discussion. This book might be used as an addendum to those listed above.

Read, a master of musical notation, has among his various books at least three that focus on the 20th century. READ (1976) analyzes both notation and physical technique and is referenced by instrument. READ (1980) is more sophisticated and thoughtful than the author's 1976 study; the relatively mathematical nature of the subject allows him to analyze meticulously the success or failure of different systems. READ (1990) is similarly intelligent and exact, presenting explanations of the tuning systems involved. In all of Read's books, including those on general notation, he makes it clear that he values logical consistency; it is not, however, particularly useful to go to his works for discussion of the more experimental graphic scores, as he often dismisses them out of hand.

ELIAS manages to assemble a remarkable range of symbols and effects, although this study is limited to notation for keyboards. A carefully organized book with numerous subtly differentiated examples, its only real flaw is that such a range of symbols and techniques could hardly be remembered by any performer. However, the logic and precision of this work make it a useful model.

BAJZEK is a reference bibliography, an extensive and meticulous listing of existing writings on contemporary percussion notation. Bajzek's careful descriptions of each cited text and separation of writings into topics make this guide required reading for percussionists.

COLE manages the remarkable and highly valuable feat of reflecting philosophically on the limits and possibilities of notation, especially contemporary variations and innovations. Fusing various periods in one complex, sophisticated argument, he has created one of the most interesting discussions of the topic. In fact, despite the usefulness of the Karkoschka and Read books, this brief, reflective study is certainly the most searching and imaginative book on this list. It deserves to be used as an introduction to the topic, with the other books used chiefly for reference.

PAUL G. ATTINELLO

Notre Dame Polyphony

Everist, Mark, *Polyphonic Music in Thirteenth-Century France: Aspects of Sources and Distribution,* New York: Garland, 1989

Falck, Robert, *The Notre Dame Conductus: A Study of the Repertory,* Henryville, Pennsylvania: Institute of Mediaeval Music, 1981

Knapp, Janet, "Polyphony at Notre Dame of Paris," in *The Early Middle Ages to 1300*, edited by Richard L. Crocker and David Hiley, The New Oxford History of Music, vol. 2, Oxford: Oxford University Press, 1990

Losseff, Nicky, *The Best Concords: Polyphonic Music in Thirteenth-Century Britain*, New York: Garland, 1994

Page, Christopher, *The Owl and the Nightingale: Musical Life and Ideas in France, 1100–1300*, London: Dent, and Berkeley: University of California Press, 1989

Wright, Craig, *Music and Ceremony at Notre Dame of Paris, 500–1550*, Cambridge: Cambridge University Press, 1989

Notre Dame polyphony refers to a repertory of polyphonic music that flourished from the latter half of the 12th century through the first half of the 13th century, comprising mainly the categories *organum, conductus,* and motet and associated with the cathedral of Notre Dame. The primary extant musical sources (known by the sigla W1, F, W2) date from 1230 to 1250, although the repertory is traditionally thought to have been created in the second half of the 12th century. It is the first polyphonic repertory for which we have named composers: according to the English music theorist Anonymous IV, Léonin (fl. 1150s–1201) created a great book of polyphony, the *Magnus liber*, which was then added to and edited by Pérotin (fl. 1190s–1238). This polyphony was quickly disseminated throughout Europe, probably by students returning home from their studies at the University of Paris. Research on Notre Dame polyphony was dominated at the beginning of the 20th century by German scholars, who were concerned mainly with identifying the sources and cataloging the repertory and with demonstrating an evolution of musical style. Recent research has concentrated on providing institutional and cultural contexts (Wright and Page), codicological analysis of the sources (Everist), and reassessing the relationship between the so-called central Parisian repertory and its transmission to peripheral centers (Losseff and Falck).

For a concise and relatively recent introduction to the topic, see the contribution by KNAPP. In this chapter, Knapp summarizes, in a very straightforward fashion, research on this topic up to the 1980s. The chapter is divided into several sections. In the initial sections, Knapp dispenses first with the manuscript sources and then deals with the definitions and techniques of *organum purum,* modal rhythm, and *copula,* as described by 13th-century music theorists. Her descriptions of these compositional techniques are clear, but it is unfortunate that she does not provide more illustrative musical examples. The final sections do contain more musical examples and treat the various genres of this repertory: polyphony for Mass and Office in two, three, and four parts; the *conductus;* and, briefly, the motet. Knapp's introduction is useful, if somewhat dry.

WRIGHT is the only full-length book study in English on the music of Notre Dame and the most important book on this list. An expert on the institutional history of this musical center, he covers the years between 500 and 1550, but the focal point of his narrative is the flourishing of the soloistic and virtuosic repertory of Léonin and Pérotin. Chapters 7 through 9 treat our topic directly, but the rest of the book, dealing with historical, institutional, and liturgical topics, is relevant as well. Because Wright has opted for a topical rather than a chronological approach, all nine chapters contain information on the later medieval period. The central issue of chapter 7, gothic polyphony, is Wright's hypothesis (developed against Husmann's) that the central core of the Notre Dame repertory, as represented by F, was liturgically appropriate for (and therefore originated at) the cathedral of Notre Dame. Chapter 8 adds considerable detail to the biography of Léonin, whom Wright has identified with a poet and canon of the cathedral; the author has less success identifying Pérotin, concluding that the most likely candidate is Petrus, succentor of the cathedral from ca. 1207 to 1238. Chapter 9 deals with the traditions of musical performance, including improvisation, which must have played some role in the creation and re-creation of this music.

PAGE presents a view of the musical life of the 12th and 13th centuries seen through the eyes of contemporary writers. The selections, apparently chosen at random from various literary genres, deal with minstrel music, courtly song and the carol, polyphony, and plainchant, but chapter 6, "Organum," is the most relevant to our topic. Several issues are addressed here. He briefly discusses the Cistercian movement of the 12th and 13th centuries and reviews how the movement's aesthetics of simplicity in all artistic endeavor might have affected attitudes toward the individualistic and virtuosic style of the new Notre Dame polyphony. His suggestion that the singers, being poorly paid, probably rented out their voices at various forms of secular entertainment is interesting (he suggests that they sang vernacular motets), but he offers no hard evidence to back up this claim. In the midst of this chapter, he also examines whether polyphony was ever studied at the University of Paris and concludes (quite rightly) that no solid evidence suggests that it was. Page's study is important in its presentation of some valuable new material, and although his writing style might irk some in its flowery and somewhat romantic tone, it certainly provokes reaction and maintains the reader's attention.

Although LOSSEFF is mainly a study of polyphony in England during the 13th century, it does discuss the repertory of Notre Dame in some detail. The author's repertorial focus is the insular *conductus* repertory of England, but to isolate this repertory, she needs to ask questions about the so-called central Parisian repertory. Her first chapter, "The Myth of Notre Dame," is important and thought provoking, encouraging us to rethink our perceptions of the central repertory. Urging a debunking of this myth, she emphasizes that although little doubt exists that the *organum purum* repertory was written for Notre Dame, little evidence shows that the *conductus* repertory was exclusively associated with Paris. Instead, she suggests that the *conductus* preserved in the central sources (e.g., F) had attained the status of a classical repertory but that this fact does not necessarily imply anything in terms of geographical or institutional origin. She discusses traits of this classical repertory, which she prefers to call the common repertory, in chapter 6. It is always important to keep in mind the strong connections between France and England at the time: chapter 3, "East Is East . . . and West Is West," elaborates on the theory that continental compositions were cultivated in the southeastern region of Britain, whereas the musical style of the western region remained more insular.

FALCK also concentrates on the *conductus* repertory. Mainly a study of concordance patterns, his book might make rather dry reading for nonspecialists. The book comprises four chapters and is followed by what is essentially a catalog of the 390 *conductus* that are preserved in the primary sources. This is probably the most useful section of this book for anyone embarking on detailed study of these compositions. The book begins with an introductory chapter, which is followed by three chapters that deal with three-part, two-part, and monophonic *conductus*, respectively. The discussion in each chapter is divided into two parts. Falck first considers the unique and peripheral repertory and then the central repertory. The evidence that he uses to come up with these layers of repertory are manuscript concordances, texts referring to contemporary persons or events, and the internal evidence of the music itself (i.e., stylistic traits).

EVERIST's analysis of the dissemination of Notre Dame polyphony is considerably better than Falck's, and he goes beyond the *conductus* repertory. Mainly a study of the physical aspects of the sources (chapters 2 through 5), he also has much to say about the distribution of this music, including the relationship between Paris and the provinces, (chapters 6 and 7). However, because of the very technical language and content of this book, I would recommend it only to specialists.

KAREN DESMOND

O

Obrecht, Jacob ca. 1457–1505

Belgian?-born composer

Lockwood, Lewis, *Music in Renaissance Ferrara, 1400–1505,* Cambridge, Massachusetts: Harvard University Press, 1984

Picker, Martin, *Johannes Ockeghem and Jacob Obrecht: A Guide to Research,* New York: Garland, 1988

Strohm, Reinhard, *Music in Late Medieval Bruges,* Oxford: Clarendon Press, 1985; revised edition, Oxford: Clarendon Press, and New York: Oxford University Press, 1990

Wegman, Rob C., *Born for the Muses: The Life and Masses of Jacob Obrecht,* Oxford: Clarendon Press, and New York: Oxford University Press, 1994

The Flemish musician Jacob Obrecht was one of the most admired yet enigmatic figures of the late 15th century. His preeminence as a composer, renowned particularly for a remarkable body of 30-odd polyphonic Mass cycles, remained undisputed and virtually unsurpassed for many years. Other aspects of his professional life merited considerably less praise. Obrecht never remained in any position for long but moved frequently among religious institutions within a short distance of his native Ghent. He twice accepted employment in Italy, where he succumbed to the plague in 1505. Several reasons may have accounted for his professional restlessness: bungled administrative responsibilities, alleged mismanagement or embezzlement of church funds, and neglect of choirboys under his care, among other possibilities. However, no malfeasance could diminish his stellar creative achievements.

LOCKWOOD, in his magnificent study of music under the Este family, examines Obrecht's activities during two brief sojourns in Ferrara (1487–88, although some scholars question whether Obrecht ever went to Italy at this time, and 1504–5). Duke Ercole I greatly admired the Flemish composer's music and employed every means within his power and influence to lure Obrecht to the Ferrarese court. Lockwood cites numerous archival documents, including correspondence from the first period and a later recommendation written by Ferrante d'Este on behalf of Obrecht, who was dismissed from the court by Alfonso d'Este following the death of Ercole I in 1505. An overview of the second period includes a discussion of manuscript Alpha M. 1.2, which contains Masses by Obrecht, Josquin Desprez, and Johannes Ockeghem.

As the subtitle implies, PICKER has assembled sundry information necessary to conduct research on Obrecht. These meticulously compiled materials include a biographical synopsis; an annotated work list containing information about durations, major subdivisions of the large-scale compositions, and cross-references to modern editions; an index of primary sources (manuscripts and prints); a bibliography of secondary literature with standard Library of Congress catalog numbers; and an extensive discography.

Obrecht served as *succentor* at the Collegiate Church of St. Donatian in Bruges, a thriving merchant town in Flanders, for eight checkered years (1485–91 and again in 1498–1500). STROHM details the requirements of the St. Donatian *succentor* and the condition of the choir at the time of Obrecht's arrival from Cambrai. From the beginning, the new *succentor* seemed inadequate to the task of administering the choir and training the choirboys. His absence two years later, presumably to visit Ferrara and Bergen op Zoom, did not improve relations with St. Donatian. The chapter dismissed Obrecht from his duties in 1491. This action did not completely sever the composer's ties with the church, for Obrecht afterward composed the *Missa de Sancto Martino* for services endowed by Pierre Basin. Strohm devotes the final section of his narrative to a discussion of Obrecht's sacred works (the *Missa de Sancto Donatiano* and four motets) and Flemish secular songs clearly conceived for Bruges. The author speculates that several other Masses, based on their stylistic affinity to the above-mentioned works, might also belong to the Bruges years.

Despite Obrecht's tremendous contemporary reputation, his life and works did not receive book-length treatment in English until WEGMAN's recent volume, an expanded version of the author's doctoral dissertation at the University of Amsterdam. Several persistent difficulties in Obrecht research explain the long period of scholarly neglect: insufficient documentary evidence to construct a comprehensive biography, particularly in the early years; an obscure chronology of his compositions; and the unfortunate tendency among many scholars to view Obrecht as a second-tier musician after Josquin. Wegman overcame these difficulties through extensive archival research and penetrating stylistic analysis. Biographical and interpretive strands intertwine throughout his book's three major subdivisions: the formative years (1457/58–85), evolution of the mature style (1485–91), and the progressive period (1491–1505). One fortuitous recent discovery by an art historian—an authentic Obrecht portrait by Hans Memling or an unknown Flemish master bearing the presumed date of completion (1496) and a reference to the subject's age (38)—shifted theories about the composer's birth date to 1457 or 1458, much later than the traditional time frame. Wegman fills other gaps in Obrecht's family background and early years in Ghent with some 50 previously unknown documents, reproduced in an appendix. This clearer picture of the early years remains one of this book's most significant contributions.

As impressive, although certainly more contentious, are the author's detailed musical analyses and their contributions toward a hypothetical chronology of Obrecht's works. Lacking any firm dating for most works, Wegman proposes a straight-line stylistic development from the early plainchant cantus firmus Masses inspired by Busnoys and Ockeghem to the middle-period consolidation of diverse compositional techniques and culminating in a rhetorical style more suited to the motet than the Mass. This proposed evolution, described in elegant prose and bolstered by the author's intimate, analytic familiarity with Obrecht's entire oeuvre, will spark debate for decades to come.

TODD SULLIVAN

See also Cantus Firmus

Ockeghem, Johannes ca. 1410–1497

Belgian?-born composer

Fitch, Fabrice, *Johannes Ockeghem: Masses and Models,* Paris: Champion, 1997

Günther, Ursula, et al., editors, *Modality in the Music of the Fourteenth and Fifteenth Centuries,* Neuhausen-Stuttgart: American Institute of Musicology, Hanssler-Verlag, 1996

Picker, Martin, *Johannes Ockeghem and Jacob Obrecht: A Guide to Research,* New York: Garland, 1988

Sparks, Edgar, *Cantus Firmus in Mass and Motet, 1420–1520,* Berkeley: University of California Press, 1963

Tijdschrift van de Koninklijke Vereniging voor Nederlandse Muziekgeschiedenis 47 (1997)

Johannes Ockeghem, a Franco-Flemish composer, was probably born in the early 1410s. He began as a singer in Antwerp and at the chapel of Charles I, Duke of Bourbon, but he spent most of his professional career, beginning in 1450, in the service of the French court, successively under the employ of Charles VII, Louis XI, and Charles VIII. He died on 6 February 1497. Ockeghem enjoyed a distinguished reputation during and just after his lifetime: for example, Tinctoris dedicated a theoretical treatise to him and elsewhere places him first among the great composers of his time. Furthermore, the lament that Jean Molinet wrote for Ockeghem's death was set to music by Josquin Des Prez. Research to date has focused on the production of a complete modern edition of Ockeghem's works and on studies of his compositional style. Also, at the end of the 20th century, there was renewed interest in the composer's biography.

PICKER's book is a guide to research on Ockeghem and Obrecht. He surveys the lives and works of the two composers separately, pointing the reader toward the relevant literature, and then presents an annotated bibliography and discography at the end of the book, complete for both composers. His biography of Ockeghem is particularly useful, as it summarizes the most recent research. There follows a discussion of the historical/analytical literature on Ockeghem's compositions, and a complete work list, including information on the sources of the Masses, motets, and secular works.

The only scholarly monograph on Ockeghem in English is FITCH's study of Ockeghem's Masses. Chapter 1 examines the reliability of the important Ockeghem manuscript source, the Chigi Codex: 14 Masses have been attributed to the composer, but the author excludes the two so-called speculative Masses, *Missa cuiusvis toni* and *Missa prolationum,* and the three-voice *Missa sine nomine,* because of its disputed authenticity. The following five chapters investigate the compositional procedures and the manipulation of preexistent material in the remaining 11 Masses, according to loosely chronological criteria—the chronology is based on Fitch's understanding of the stylistic affinities among these compositions. In the final chapter, on Ockeghem's *Requiem,* Fitch presents a case for the cyclical integrity of this Mass. The author concludes that Ockeghem's compositions exhibit much greater stylistic consistency than critics previously recognized. Thus, Fitch hopes that we will now assess Ockeghem's individuality in positive rather than negative terms.

SPARKS's classic book contains a comprehensive treatment of 15th- and early 16th-century examples of *cantus firmus* technique, in which preexistent material is used as the basis for a new composition. Chapters 6 and 7 analyze the Mass and motet from 1450 to 1485 and focus on the works of Du Fay and Ockeghem. The chapters present a consideration of structural types and procedures, which is followed by a discussion of individual works. Sparks's discussion is somewhat dry, concentrating on form rather than style, but it is useful because it includes extensive musical examples.

In 1997, the Dutch journal *TIJDSCHRIFT VAN DE KONINKLIJKE VERENIGING VOOR NEDER-LANDSE MUZIEKGESCHIEDENIS* published an issue devoted to Ockeghem, commemorating the 400th anniversary of the composer's death. Of the nine articles included in this volume, the essays by Donald Grieg and Rebecca Stewart consider Ockeghem's compositions from the performer's perspective; Rokus de Groot's contribution explores Ockeghem's influence on composers of the 20th century; and Jaap van Benthem's brief essay introduces his new edition of Ockeghem's Masses. More important to music historians are Richard Wexler's study of Ockeghem's political environment, proposing a number of new hypotheses about the composer's biography; and Barbara Haggh's essay on an ordinal of the Sainte-Chapelle created around the time that Ockeghem was active, in which Haggh provides an extensive outline of the performance directions found within this liturgical book, some of which may relate to the performance of polyphony. Scholars will be equally interested in Eugeen Schreurs's essay on some fragments from Tongeren that preserve two chansons by Ockeghem; and the articles by Peter Urquhart and van Benthem that analyze the pitch implications and modal manipulations of Ockeghem's *Prenez sur moy* and *Missa cuiusvis toni.*

Related to the topic of mode and polyphony, GÜNTHER et al. present two essays on Ockeghem: van Benthem examines the *Missa caput,* and Jeffery Dean authors an important study of "Ockeghem's attitude toward modality." Noting Ockeghem's unique position as the only 15th-century composer who is known to have given tonal titles to his Masses (*Missa cuiusvis toni* and *Missa quinti toni*), Dean addresses the conceptual understanding of pitch relationships in the 15th century, and he investigates what tonality meant specifically to Ockeghem. Through a comprehensive (and, by necessity, a very technical) overview of the relevant music theory—which addresses questions of *ficta*, key signatures, and *species*, as well as analyses of the two abovementioned Masses—Dean highlights the static aspect he perceives in Ockeghem's approach to tonality.

Given the paucity of books in English devoted specifically to Ockeghem, the reader may find it useful to explore the treatment of Ockeghem in the survey histories of Renaissance music. The most sophisticated of these general histories is certainly Reinhard Strohm's *The Rise of European Music, 1380–1500* (Cambridge and New York: Cambridge University Press, 1993). However, due to the layout of the text (loosely organized according to geographic/chronological criteria),

and Strohm's philosophy concerning musical traditions in Europe during this time, the reader searching for a detailed treatment of Ockeghem's life and works will be disappointed. The chapter "France and the Low Countries: The Invention of the Masterwork" is relevant, however, as Strohm integrates his discussion of the works of the great composers (Du Fay, Ockeghem) with analyses of works by lesser-known composers, such as Pullois, Barbingant, and Domarto, and works by anonymous composers. There is much valuable material here, including Strohm's examination of Ockeghem's secular songs, which are often given short shrift in the evaluation of Ockeghem's achievements.

For a more traditional historical/great composer approach, try Gustave Reese's *Music in the Renaissance* (New York: Norton, 1954). In chapter 3, the author evaluates Ockeghem's Mass composition techniques, including his use of *cantus firmus.* Chapter 3 of Howard Brown's *Music in the Renaissance* (Englewood Cliffs, New Jersey: Prentice-Hall, 1976) includes a briefer treatment of Ockeghem than Reese, which nevertheless is useful as the author includes several long musical examples and discusses the relationship of text and music in the Masses. Unfortunately, the *chansons* are given short shrift: there is only a one-paragraph discussion of these compositions, which Brown views as the simpler and more traditional side to Ockeghem's musical personality.

KAREN DESMOND

Offenbach, Jacques 1819–1880

German composer

Faris, Alex, *Jacques Offenbach,* London: Faber, 1980

Harding, James, *Jacques Offenbach: A Biography,* London: Calder, and New York: Riverrun Press, 1980

Kracauer, Siegfried, *Orpheus in Paris, Offenbach and the Paris of His Time,* translated by Gwenda David and Eric Mosbacher, New York: Knopf, 1938; reprint, New York, Vienna House, 1972

Offenbach, Jacques, *Orpheus in America: Offenbach's Diary of His Journey in the New World,* translated by Lander MacClintock, Bloomington: Indiana University Press, 1957

Despite the enormous popularity of the music and person of Jacques Offenbach during his lifetime, his compositions have suffered neglect and fallen out of favor. This is no doubt because much of his music was written for the day. The parody, humor, and considerable wit contained in his theatrical diversions would not have the same effect on modern audiences as they did on concertgoers in the late 19th century. It is also plausible that the lightness, carefree spirit, and humor of his musical style prevents him from being taken seriously by today's music historians. These facts not withstanding, little research has been done on this composer who was the toast of France, Germany, England, and the United States, and whose music influenced countless composers. The research that exists is primarily biographic in nature, and only Alex Faris's monograph offers an analytical approach to the composer's music.

In 1980, the centenary of Jacques Offenbach's death, two major biographies of the composer appeared, one by James Harding and another by Alex Faris. Although both monographs successfully discuss the composer's music and paint a colorful portrait of Paris during the Second Empire of Napoleon III, there are some fundamental differences between them. HARDING's biography is teeming with stories and anecdotes that bring Offenbach and the period in which he lived to life. However, none of Harding's primary source material is substantiated by footnotes, and the biography by Faris (discussed below) does not always corroborate some of these accounts. Harding gives no musical analysis; rather, he limits his discussions of Offenbach's major compositions to comments about their reception by the public, the content of their plots, and an occasional description of important arias, choruses, or instrumental movements. However, the author has a gift for insightful readings of the composer's operettas in the context of the social mores of the time. And whenever a new person is introduced into Offenbach's life or career, Harding always offers a thorough introduction and background, which gives the reader a more complete understanding. This book is an admirable character study of the composer. The author delves into Offenbach's personality to examine what motivated him, inspired him, and formed him into the extremely successful composer he was. Although this particular biography would not be considered scholarly by some academic writers, it is nevertheless an illuminating look into the methodical development of Offenbach from a salon cello virtuoso—half Liberace, half Victor Borge—to the most popular and beloved composer of operetta during the Second Empire. Harding includes a list of all Offenbach's major vocal and instrumental compositions that were published. He indicates that a more detailed listing of early and/or unpublished works can be found in *Offenbach Mon Grandpère* (1940) by Jacques Brindejont-Offenbach and Anton Henseler's *Jakob Offenbach* (1930).

In contrast to Harding's monograph, FARIS is full of musical examples used to support his analytical approach to the music of Offenbach. Drawing on a wide variety of primary and secondary sources carefully documented in footnotes, Faris gives a balanced account of the life and musical career of the composer. He offers a vivid depiction of the social, political, and artistic life of Paris and other major cities that Offenbach visited and also gives the reader a reasonably in-depth discussion of the music. While Harding makes an important assertion

that Offenbach's impact on German operetta was great, Faris actually demonstrates how the composer influenced others, such as Tchaikovsky and Gilbert and Sullivan, with the aid of musical examples. Faris's intimate knowledge of Offenbach's music as a conductor may account for his desire to look more deeply into the individual operettas. Faris's inclusion of a lengthy chapter devoted to the composer's final work, *Les Contes d'Hoffmann,* helps make this work an important addition to the limited monographs on Offenbach. The author gives an extremely helpful history of the literary inspiration for the composition, without which no truly complete understanding of the opera can be achieved. He not only offers important biographical information on Hoffmann but also discusses the play of Michel Carré and Jules Barbier in relation to the original writings of Hoffmann on which it is based. Also included in this chapter are a brief history of the fate of the unfinished score and a discussion of the challenges of achieving an authentic performance of the opera. Faris's examination of *Les Contes d'Hoffmann* is replete with copious musical examples that support his opinion that this opera is a unique and dramatic achievement for a composer who had previously made his money and name in the theater with parodies, comedies, and biting wit.

Included at the conclusion of Faris's biography are two appendices. The first discusses others who have claimed credit for having the original idea of the Orpheus parody (*Orphée aux Enfers*), and the second briefly considers the cause of Offenbach's death and is written by the author's sister, who is a medical doctor. Faris also offers what he considers to be a complete listing of the composer's stage works in a tabular form that gives the year, title, description of the work given by Offenbach himself (such as vaudeville, opéra comique, and *bouffonnerie*), number of acts, librettist(s), theater where it played, date of production (month and day), German title (when applicable), and English title (when applicable). As many of Offenbach's works were written or revised for productions in Bad Ems, Vienna, or London, some editions appear in German or English as well as in French. Faris also includes a listing of unpublished works and various vocal and instrumental compositions.

One of the first major 20th-century biographies of Offenbach was written in German by KRACAUER in 1937 and entitled *Jacques Offenbach und da Paris seiner Zeit*; an English-language translation appeared in 1972. This lengthy monograph is a highly readable and entertaining account of the life and times of the composer. Many of the incidents mentioned by Kracauer are recounted by both Harding and Faris. However, Faris is the only one of the three who always informs the reader of the original source of the material. Although this study deals only superficially with Offenbach's music, Kracauer gives an insightful glimpse into the heart and soul of 19th-century Parisian society. There is no critical analysis of musical style or compositional process; however, there is an admirable account of the theatrical life of the composer and the city during the reign of Napoleon III. Kracauer concentrates heavily on descriptions of the plots and librettos of Offenbach's operettas (as does Harding) and often gives a brief reception history of a composition. He confines his analysis mainly to aspects of parody or satire found in various works, an approach that does not escape other writers but upon which a work cannot alone be judged. To place Offenbach in time and history, Kracauer attempts to show him in light of his lesser-known contemporaries, such as Charles Lecocq and Florimond Hervé, whose struggles for fame and fortune were not unlike Offenbach's. While this monograph remains a standard in the repertory of Offenbach studies, its style is closer to that of historical biography than scholarly analysis.

Finally, OFFENBACH himself gives a brief account of his visit to New York City, Niagara Falls, and Philadelphia that he made in 1876. This diary, as he calls it, is a charming chronicle of his crossing, various concert performances, visits to restaurants, and short trips, recounted with keen observation and unique wit. It also offers insights into U.S. culture and practice as viewed by a sophisticated and well-traveled foreigner. This short narrative is likewise valuable for its description of some U.S. institutions during the time, such as the theaters in New York City and the press. Especially delightful is Offenbach's explanation of the sleeping car on his train trip from Niagara Falls to New York, and the U.S. custom of acquiring autographs of celebrities.

TIMOTHY S. FLYNN

Office *see* Liturgy: Divine Office

Oliveros, Pauline b. 1932

United States composer

Duckworth, William, *Talking Music: Conversations with John Cage, Philip Glass, Laurie Anderson, and Five Generations of American Experimental Composers,* New York: Schirmer Books, and London: Prentice Hall, 1995

Fuller, Sophie, *The Pandora Guide to Women Composers: Britain and the United States, 1629–Present,* London: Pandora, 1994

Gagne, Cole, editor, *Soundpieces 2: Interviews With American Composers,* Metuchen, New Jersey: Scarecrow Press, 1993

Oliveros, Pauline, *Software for People: Collected Writings 1963–80,* Baltimore, Maryland: Smith, 1984

Rycenga, Jennifer, "The Uncovering of Ontology in Music: Speculative and Conceptual Feminist Music," *Repercussions* 3 (1994)

Von Gunden, Heidi, *The Music of Pauline Oliveros,* Metuchen, New Jersey: Scarecrow Press, 1983

Oliveros is consistently regarded as one of the most successful women composers of her time. The above list includes works about Oliveros and her music by historians, composers, feminist scholars, and Oliveros herself. Her challenging body of work as composer, improviser, accordionist, writer, feminist, and teacher clearly sits at odds with most traditions of Western art music.

VON GUNDEN's wide-ranging survey of Oliveros's music is somewhat dated but nevertheless functions as the most useful reference work on the subject. It remains the only book-length study of Oliveros. In addition to providing extensive biographical information, Gunden discusses every major composition up to 1980 in chapters organized by genre: improvisation, electronic music, theater pieces, consciousness studies, sonic meditations, and ceremonial mandala pieces. The volume also includes an annotated catalog of compositions, discography, bibliography, and index. The chapter on the *Sonic Meditations,* arguably Oliveros's best-known pieces, discusses the author's firsthand experience with practicing these pieces and ranks their difficulty for those wishing to perform them. Although far-reaching in scope, Gunden's analyses of specific works are often superficial and contain many technical errors. Similarly, her contextual discussions of improvisation, feminism, meditation, and creativity also lack depth and clarity. However, her book is a helpful introduction to those unfamiliar with Oliveros's music and ideas.

OLIVEROS's collection of 26 essays covers roughly the same time period as Gunden's book and features the composer's ideas on a myriad of subjects in her own words. Several essays reflect Oliveros's characteristic sensitivity to different kinds of sound—musical, environmental, bodily, remembered, and imagined—and are written in a personal, engaging style that does not assume musical training. Other pieces trace the historical path of her work as a composer and dwell on the concepts behind many of her compositions from the 1970s. Oliveros's work as a feminist is also well documented here in articles addressing the marginalization of women in music as well as the gender bias found in much traditional thinking about music. The most unusual essays are nonlinear combinations of journal entries, letters, interviews, concert reviews, dreams, philosophical questions, and diagrams of psychological theory. Oliveros borrows from a wide variety of discourses to explore fundamental questions of music, musicianship, and musicality as they are inflected by history, pedagogy, and social life in the 20th century. In these explorations she asks her readers to ponder musical questions along with her and playfully encourages them to reach their own conclusions.

FULLER presents an updated summary of Oliveros's compositions contextualized by an excellent brief history of women in Western art music. The author pays close attention to class, race, and geographical location in her outline of both the opportunities and limits for women who have sought a profession in music and composition. She traces the long tradition of formal and informal networks that women musicians have formed to support one another. Thus, her essay on Oliveros differs markedly from many other authors who work from the assumption that Oliveros is one of many "descendants" of John Cage and inadvertently ignore her position as a woman in the music profession. Furthermore, Fuller offers a unique view of Oliveros's work alongside that of her diverse women contemporaries such as Barbara Kolb, Tania Léon, Nancy Van de Vate, Thea Musgrave, and Julia Perry. Fuller discusses Oliveros's recordings after 1980 (*The Wanderer, The Well and the Gentle,* and *Deep Listening*), as well as some of her intriguing compact discs from the 1990s, such as *The Ready Made Boomerang* and *Troglodyte's Delight.* She also draws attention to *Njinga,* an elaborate music theater piece created in collaboration with playwright and author Ione, which is certainly Oliveros's most important work of the 1990s.

DUCKWORTH's interview with Oliveros dwells on her interest in the accordion as a child and the ways in which this instrument shaped her music education. Oliveros discusses the peculiar phenomenon of combination tones on the accordion as well as the kinds of repertoire she enjoyed playing as a youngster. Her early experiences as a composer are defined as attempts to realize powerful "sonic images" in her imagination and the subsequent challenge of finding appropriate forms in which to bring these images to life as music. The discussion of form leads into her work with meditation; she clarifies the all-important distinction between religious meditation and sonic meditation, which she states is absolutely nonsectarian. Moreover, she claims that her move away from traditional forms in music toward her own experimentation and revision is directly related to her primary concern with sound as human interaction—with oneself, with others, with the environment—and the pleasurable revelations of the experience of the moment.

GAGNE engages Oliveros in an excellent discussion of tape music, especially her studio composition *I of IV* (1966). In user-friendly language, the composer elaborates on the technological background of this piece and her aesthetic concern with improvisation, or composing in real time. Gagne also inquires about Oliveros's technological interests of the 1980s, and she describes her work with the expanded accordion. Her use of digital delay processors on her accordion creates an interactive sonic environment with which she improvises, alone or with other performers. She retuned her accordion to just intonation and explains her preference for this tuning. She also discusses her long-standing interest in untrained musicians, particularly her inclusion of the audience in many of her pieces. Gagne's interview is extremely valuable for its list of Oliveros's compositions from 1951 to 1992, as well as its list of publishers.

RYCENGA's rigorous and densely written essay connects radical feminism to the worldview suggested by Oliveros's music. A scholar of religious studies, Rycenga assumes a basic familiarity with philosophical concepts and feminist theory. She moves away from an understanding of music as an object requiring power and control and favors the idea of music as a set of relations: with people, sound, environment, and oneself. To support her thesis she calls on the writings of Monique Wittig, Sally Gearhart, Toni Morrison, and Joanna Russ, who profess similar ideas about women making sound/music together, outside of traditional music-making formats. The author analyzes one of the *Sonic Meditations*—"Teach Yourself to Fly"—in detail, and elaborates on Oliveros's own gloss of this piece, underscoring its feminist ideas: nondualism, nonhierarchic structure, acknowledging the importance of material reality, listening and giving attention to the voices of women, dialogic nature, and respect for the agency and limitations of others. Rycenga is one of the only writers who treats Oliveros's lesbianism seriously. Her challenging and interdisciplinary essay contains a wealth of ideas to consider in conjunction with many other Oliveros compositions.

MARTHA MOCKUS

Opera: 17th-Century Italian

Bianconi, Lorenzo, *Music in the Seventeenth Century,* translated by David Bryant, Cambridge: Cambridge University Press, 1987

Bukofzer, Manfred F., *Music in the Baroque Era: From Monteverdi to Bach,* New York: Norton, 1947

Donington, Robert, *The Rise of Opera,* London: Faber, 1981

Grout, Donald J., *A Short History of Opera,* New York, Columbia University Press, 1965; 3rd edition, 1988

Pirrotta, Nino, and Elena Povoledo, *Music and Theatre from Poliziano to Monteverdi,* translated by Karen Eales, Cambridge: Cambridge University Press, 1982

Robinson, Michael F., *Opera before Mozart,* London: Hutchinson, 1966; 3rd edition, 1978

Rosand, Ellen, *Opera in Seventeenth-Century Venice: The Creation of a Genre,* Berkeley: University of California Press, 1991

Wolff, Hellmuth C., "Italian Opera from the Later Monteverdi to Scarlatti," in *Opera and Church Music, 1630–1750,* edited by Anthony Lewis and Nigel Fortune, London: Oxford University Press, 1975

Worsthorne, Simon Towneley, *Venetian Opera in the Seventeenth Century,* Oxford: Clarendon Press, 1954

Research on 17th-century Italian opera has a long history. Antonio Groppo's catalog of Venetian operas (1637–1745) dates back to the beginning of the 18th century (*Catalogo di tutti i drammi per musica* [1745]), and early 20th-century scholars such as Angelo Solerti and Federico Ghisi cast light on the precursors and earliest examples of Florentine pastoral opera publishing texts and other primary materials, as in Solerti's *Gli Albori del melodramma* (1903). German and French scholars did pioneering work in the exploration of Florentine and early Venetian opera, especially the works of Monteverdi, Cavalli, and Cesti. H.C. Wolff studied Venetian opera of the second half of the century, earlier considered part of the so-called decadent period of Italian baroque opera (*Die venezianische Oper in der zweiten Halfte des 17. Jahrhunderts* [1975]). More recently, the field has expanded with many specialized studies on topics such as theaters, opera houses, recitative, and opera revisions, or *rifacimenti,* to name a few. Studies of composers have branched out and deepened, including scholarship on Cavalli, Cesti, Stradella, Alessandro Scarlatti, and many other less prominent composers. Libretto studies include work on the reform librettist Frigimelica-Roberti, Antonio Ottoboni, and libretto reform beginning in the late 17th century. Florentine opera (1590–1750) and Roman operas for the Papal Court (1631–68) have also been the subject of specialized studies. Several significant texts emphasize social history, and sources such as the Venetian journal *Pallade Veneta* provide rich text and contemporary perspectives.

The quantity, variety, and depth of opera research are impressive, but few English-language studies of Italian 17th-century opera as a whole have been conducted. In his now dated but still important comprehensive book on the baroque era, BUKOFZER weaves his discussion of the rise of opera in the early baroque musical context together with the emergence of monody and the transformation of the madrigal, emphasizing Monteverdi in comparison to Peri and Caccini. Likewise, opera in Venice is part of the middle baroque, whereas opera seria and opera buffa are part of the late baroque Neapolitan School. The latter term is not accepted today, but the discussion still gives a balanced overall view of the genre.

WORSTHORNE undertook the first comprehensive study of Venetian opera in English. He presents the background of the new genre in Venetian society with its social and economic implications and then considers the stage practices prevalent in Italy, before proceeding to a survey of the theaters in Venice and a description of the stage spectacle in the era of the machine-opera. The music is discussed in chapters on the aria, the concerted music, and the orchestra. Observations on the relationship between composer and librettist and on the aesthetics of the period touch upon some of the issues that have continued to concern later students of operatic history, such as the relationship between drama and music and the functions of recitative and aria. This book still gives a fine overview of the various aspects of Venetian opera.

ROBINSON provides a compact description of opera from its beginnings as court entertainment to opera "for the populace," that is, Venetian opera, which the author faults for the large stylistic gulf between recitative and aria. In Robinson's view, composers, as well as singers and audiences, neglected the former and emphasized the latter, and this imbalance led to the "concert opera" of the 18th century.

WOLFF picks up the thread of Italian opera history from about 1630 (volume 4 of the New Oxford History of Music ends with Worsthorne's account of the first decades of the 17th century, including Monteverdi's *Orfeo*). Wolff believes that recitative and its expressive declamation remained important in the 17th century precisely because the libretto and the interpretation of the action also remained important. He therefore rejects the label *concert opera* for the operas of this period and stresses, for example, the dramatic power of Monteverdi's *L'Incoronazione di Poppea* and of Cavalli's *Pompeo Magno*. Wolff briefly discusses and presents musical examples for a variety of composers, including Cesti, Sartorio, Legrenzi, P.A. Ziani, Pallavicino, Melani, Stradella, C.F. Pollarolo, Steffani, and A. Scarlatti. Some of these composers' flair for comedy is brought out, whether in the treatment of "serious" plots, in comic scenes, or in comic operas. Needless to say, Wolff's range of composers exceeds the strictly Venetian scene and includes 17th-century Italian opera as a whole.

DONINGTON approaches the beginnings of opera from a philosophical vantage point, namely, Renaissance neoplatonism and its symbolism in poetry prior to and leading up to the first pastorals on the Orpheus myth. He explores the various reciting styles and their blend in early opera; the contributions of Peri, Caccini, and Cavalieri; and the Orpheus librettos of Rinuccini and Striggio in their respective settings. Italian opera in Rome and Venice in the following decades is treated rather briefly, depicted as "a very practical working compromise."

A similar range of topics, revolving around the Orpheus versions by Poliziano and Monteverdi, is explored in PIRROTTA and POVOLEDO. Pirrotta describes the earliest operas, librettos, and scores in fascinating detail, giving a vivid picture of the competing composer personalities (Peri and Caccini). In the early decades of Roman and Venetian opera, the beginnings of lament, prayer, and incantation, as well as comic aria, take shape. Part 2 of the book, by Povoledo, deals with the scenography of the Florentine *intermedi* and early operas, another important aspect of operatic production during this period.

BIANCONI gives a highly informative, balanced account of early Italian opera. More than other authors, he includes source material on the subject, evaluates the economic and artistic aspects of operatic production in the

Venetian theaters, and describes the geographic spread of opera throughout Italy and to German-speaking centers such as Vienna and Hamburg. His discussion of poetic structure, meter, rhythm, and imagery of the aria is instructive but lacks musical examples.

GROUT is both a specialist in early Italian opera and an admirable generalist. The third edition of his lengthy opera history is clear, well organized, and accessible. The antecedents of opera (e.g., *intermedio*, madrigal comedy, and pastoral) and the Florentine and Mantuan works are discussed, and interesting comparisons are made between them. Monteverdi's *Orfeo* is described in vocal and instrumental style, and a table outlines his instrumentation in relation to that of earlier works. Grout identifies in the late Monteverdi in Venice as the supreme interpreter of human character and passion and views Cesti as the catalyst for the shift toward the domination of music over drama, or aria over recitative. Grout has a chapter on Italian opera in Germany, touching on centers such as Vienna, Dresden, and Munich, among others. One of the virtues of this book is its enormous bibliography, which is organized by century; parts 1 and 2 are relevant to this topic.

Finally, ROSAND's excellent work presents a comprehensive yet specialized scholarly study of opera in Venice from 1637 to 1678, the opening dates of two major opera houses in the city. This period covers what Rosand calls the first of the cycles that shaped the development of opera. The wide-ranging history characterizes early opera in many respects before describing the rise of public opera in Venice, the theaters, librettos and librettists, impresarios and their competition, the subject matter in relation to the Venetian political situation, the staging, and the singers. Rosand provides a fascinating discussion of recitative and aria, explaining how they were shaped by librettists and the composers who set their texts, especially Monteverdi and Cavalli. She also describes the beginning of aria forms and the dramatic situations that gave rise to them as well as the variety of treatments within these forms. Examples of the conventions of the *dramma per musica* include aria types, such as the comic aria and the trumpet aria, as well as scene types, such as the sleep scene, the mad scene, and the incantation scene. The book is enhanced by many musical examples, some extensive, and by the painstaking documentation and specialized bibliography.

OLGA TERMINI

Opera: French to 1800

Anthony, James R., *French Baroque Music from Beaujoyeulx to Rameau,* New York: Norton, 1978; revised edition, Portland, Oregon: Amadeus Press, 1997

Carlson, Marvin, *The Theatre of the French Revolution,* Ithaca, New York: Cornell University Press, 1966

Charlton, David, *Grétry and the Growth of Opéra-Comique,* Cambridge: Cambridge University Press, 1986

Dill, Charles William, *Monstrous Opera: Rameau and the Tragic Tradition,* Princeton, New Jersey: Princeton University Press, 1998

Isherwood, Robert, *Music in the Service of the King: France in the Seventeenth Century,* Ithaca, New York: Cornell University Press, 1973

Johnson, James, *Listening in Paris: A Cultural History,* Berkeley: University of California Press, 1995

The institutional history of French opera began on 28 June 1669, when Louis XIV granted the composer Pierre Perrin a monopoly for the creation of operas in France. Of course, there were attempts to introduce opera at court prior to this date; six Italian operas were performed in France between 1645 and 1662. These works, however, failed to generate sustained enthusiasm for the genre or to prompt French imitations. It was not until the composer Jean-Baptiste Lully succeeded Perrin and produced his own operas of the 1670s and 1680s that a stable, indigenous operatic tradition emerged. With the librettist Philippe Quinault, Lully established many of the conventions that would dominate serious French opera until 1800. These conventions include a distinctive style of recitative (designed to complement the peculiarities of the French language), a high standard of poetic verse for the libretto, a large amount of visual spectacle, and the incorporation of dance and chorus.

French comic operas, by way of contrast, originated as ephemeral entertainments at seasonal fairs in Paris. The music for these plays was limited to simple melodies with improvised accompaniments. Typically the tunes were borrowed from popular sources and given new lyrics to suit the dramatic situation. From these modest beginnings, the tradition of opéra comique, with its characteristic alternation of spoken dialog and musical numbers, developed. By the end of the 18th century, French comic opera had matured, becoming a diverse, substantial genre with newly composed music that incorporated sentimental, romantic, and even heroic themes within their librettos.

ANTHONY's survey devotes considerable space to the development of opera in France. He begins with a thorough examination of the antecedents that contributed to the growth of *tragédie en musique*, as serious French opera was then known. The formal and stylistic changes that occurred in French opera from the 17th to the mid-18th century receive careful attention. In particular, Anthony offers a detailed account of the so-called *preramiste* composers, who wrote operas after the death of Lully but before Jean Philippe Rameau began composing for the stage. This generation of musicians greatly expanded the French musical palette and prepared the way for Rameau's advancement of the genre. Anthony also discusses the many operatic subgenres that developed in reaction to the *tragédie en musique*, making this book a useful reference tool. The volume is a straightforward introduction to the origins of French opera and its subsequent development during the baroque, and readers who are exploring this area for the first time will find Anthony's overview especially informative.

ISHERWOOD's influential study of the reign of Louis XIV has served as a model of historical scholarship since it first appeared. The author examines a monarchy that deliberately manipulated cultural products, such as music, in support of its social and political goals. Although the book considers all genres of music performed at the court of Louis XIV, a large portion of this monograph focuses on the creation of French opera and the relationship of operatic culture to the needs of the state. The book is not primarily concerned with musical style. Rather, it focuses on the socio-political function of opera and examines the reception of the genre.

Unlike Anthony and Isherwood, DILL concentrates on the musical tragedies of a single composer, Rameau. Much of this book concerns the extensive alterations that Rameau made to his operas following their premieres. In his examination of these revisions, Dill explains how music theory, Enlightenment aesthetics, and operatic conventions converge within the music of this composer. In doing so, the author not only demonstrates Rameau's extraordinary ability to interpret text musically but also shows the composer's willingness to accommodate popular taste. The result is a subtle reassessment of Rameau's operas within the context of 18th-century musical culture.

In his study of audience behavior, JOHNSON conveys a vivid impression of an average operagoer's experience in 18th-century Paris. The book successfully chronicles the change in habits of listening that characterized this period. Johnson, who is a historian and not a musicologist, demonstrates more interest in social and cultural issues than in questions of purely musical significance. Nonetheless, he makes a concerted effort to incorporate musical evidence within his analysis and to relate matters of musical style to larger cultural developments. At its best, this book offers new insights into musical culture that have been overlooked in other music histories.

CHARLTON tackles the topic of comic opera in France. To that end, his book focuses on André-Ernest-Modeste Grétry, the composer responsible for establishing the mature form of opéra comique. Before discussing the achievements of Grétry, however, Charlton reviews the origins of this genre. He traces its development from a lighthearted mode of entertainment associated with Parisian fair theaters to a privileged dramatic spectacle institutionalized as the Comédie Italienne. Having provided this useful introduction to the genre, Charlton proceeds to analyze each of Grétry's works, paying special attention to their innovations. This informative and well-written book has become an indispensable reference for the study of 18th-century comic opera.

CARLSON considers French comic and serious opera in connection with spoken drama produced during the 1790s. This approach proves to be one of the greatest strengths of the book. Carlson explains the close relationships among the various Parisian theatrical communities and demonstrates how developments in one genre affected another. Albeit anecdotal, the book synthesizes a large body of secondary literature that is unavailable in English. Moreover, by means of a strict chronological arrangement, Carlson confers a sense of order on the rapid changes that affected music and drama at this time. He offers readers who are unfamiliar with the theater of the French Revolution a lively introduction to an exciting period in the history of opera.

MICHAEL E. MCCLELLAN

Opera: German to 1800

Bauman, Thomas, *North German Opera in the Age of Goethe*, Cambridge: Cambridge University Press, 1985

Buelow, George J., editor, *The Late Baroque Era: From the 1680s to 1740*, Basingstoke: Macmillan, and Englewood Cliffs, New Jersey: Prentice Hall, 1993

Flaherty, Gloria, *Opera in the Development of German Critical Thought*, Princeton, New Jersey: Princeton University Press, 1978

Konold, Wulf, *German Opera, Then and Now*, Basel: Bärenreiter, 1980

The topic of German opera before 1800 presents the researcher and reader with at least three interrelated problems of definition. The first problem is determining the boundaries of Germany itself. In its most limited sense, the topic might refer only to those operas composed in the German language within the boundaries of the modern German nation. However, the very concept of "Germany" was fluid in the 17th and 18th centuries and might refer instead to all German-speaking lands (including Austria). The second, more important problem arises from the question of language. Eigteenth-century German courts were important centers for Italian opera seria, and serious composers from the German lands were naturally drawn to this sophisticated musical style. Many of them, such as Handel and Hasse, spent large parts of their careers in other countries. Furthermore, many important Italian composers (e.g., Nicolo Jommelli) made their homes in 18th-century Germany. Should the topic of German opera before 1800 embrace these composers and their works even though their operas were based on Italian librettos? Does "German opera" refer to language or only to country of origin? The third problem concerns the issue of genre. Few musico-dramatic works in German written before 1800 were called "operas"; instead, a wide variety of terms (*Singspiel, Operette, Lustspiel,* and *Lustposse*) were used.

There was no hard-and-fast distinction between "plays with music" and "operas," for nearly every work included both dialogue and music.

If the definition of 17th- and 18th-century German opera is a problem for the modern reader, it was also a central concern of 17th- and 18th-century composers and critics themselves. Indeed, for much of the 17th and 18th centuries, German opera was less a compositional practice than a theoretical issue—the topic of opera generated a rich body of criticism that was to have an important influence on succeeding generations. It is this critical debate that forms the subject of FLAHERTY's book. The author clearly summarizes the operatic criticism of famous thinkers such as Mattheson, Lessing, and Wieland, but her book is also valuable for the attention that it pays to less well-known figures, such as Krause and Möser. She includes lengthy quotations from these authors both in the original German and in English translation. Flaherty organizes her chapters, however, not so much around particular figures as around certain issues—such as the relationship between text and music, the relative value of foreign works as models for the German opera, and the idea of opera as a revival of ancient Greek tragedy—that were central to the development of opera in Germany. Her work should be of interest to students of philosophy, literature, and rhetoric, as well as musicians.

Although BAUMAN also discusses these types of theoretical issues, he is much more concerned with the music itself and the social environment in which it was created and performed. He begins by limiting his study to northern and central Germany; indeed, a key idea in his book is that important cultural differences set this region apart from German-speaking lands in the south. Bauman identifies seven stages of north German opera in the "Age of Goethe," which he defines as the period 1766–99. Few musicians know the operas of Hiller, Seydelmann, Reichardt, and Dittersdorf that appear in this work, and Bauman opens up a surprisingly diverse and complex area of operatic history. The book explores not only the musical style of these works but also the economic, social, and cultural environment in which they were produced. Bauman is especially interested in the institutional history of the many opera companies that operated during this period. Exhaustively researched, his work includes many musical examples and a catalog of north German operas that should prove invaluable to the scholarly specialist.

KONOLD's work will probably be most useful to the reader interested in a general background to the subject. Much of this brief book concerns German opera in the 19th and 20th centuries, but Kunold also includes chapters on two of the most important centers of 18th-century German opera: Hamburg and Dresden. The illustrations of opera houses, set designs, and performers that Kunold includes as an appendix help make the rich history of German opera come alive.

Many of the numerous biographies of Mozart and other 18th-century German composers contain useful information about 18th-century German opera, but they lie beyond the purview of this article. The topic of 18th-century German opera, of course, is also addressed in more broadly defined works, such as Donald Grout's *A Short History of Opera* or series such as *The New Oxford History of Music*. Of these, BUELOW includes chapters by a variety of writers on specific cities or countries. This format enables this book to explore a central fact of 18th-century German opera, namely, its cultural and stylistic diversity. The two chapters that are concerned with German opera, "Hamburg and Lübeck" and "Dresden in the Age of Absolutism," are by Buelow himself. In these chapters, Buelow incorporates some of the ideas about rhetoric in music that he has developed in other publications. His chapters are also significant for the ways in which they explore economic and cultural differences between commercial cities and court centers and the ways in which these differences stimulated the development of different types of opera.

STEPHEN MEYER

Opera: 18th-Century Italian

Dean, Winton, and Anthony Hicks, *The New Grove Handel,* London: Macmillan, and New York: Norton, 1982

Dent, Edward Joseph, *Alessandro Scarlatti: His Life and Works,* London: Arnold, 1905; reprint, 1960

Freeman, Robert S., *Opera without Drama: Currents of Change in Italian Opera, 1675–1725,* Ann Arbor, Michigan: UMI Research Press, 1981

Hunt, Jno Leland, *Giovanni Paisiello: His Life as an Opera Composer,* N.p.: National Opera Association, 1975

Hunter, Mary Kathleen, and James Webster, editors, *Opera buffa in Mozart's Vienna,* Cambridge: Cambridge University Press, 1997

McClymonds, Marita P., *Niccolò Jommelli: The Last Years, 1769–1774,* Ann Arbor, Michigan: UMI Research Press, 1980

Petty, Frederick C., *Italian Opera in London: 1760–1800,* Ann Arbor, Michigan: UMI Research Press, 1980

Price, Curtis, et al., *Italian Opera in Late Eighteenth-Century London,* Oxford: Clarendon Press, and New York: Oxford University Press, 1995

Robinson, Michael F., *Naples and Neapolitan Opera,* Oxford: Clarendon Press, 1972

Rosselli, John, *The Opera Industry in Italy from Cimarosa to Verdi: The Role of the Impresario,* Cambridge: Cambridge University Press, 1984

———, *Singers of Italian Opera: The History of a Profession,* Cambridge: Cambridge University Press, 1992

Steptoe, Andrew, *The Mozart-Da Ponte Operas: The Cultural and Musical Background to Le nozze di Figaro,*

Don Giovanni, and Così fan tutte, Oxford: Clarendon Press, 1988

Strohm, Reinhard, *Dramma per Musica: Italian Opera Seria of the Eighteenth Century,* New Haven, Connecticut: Yale University Press, 1997

————, *Essays on Handel and Italian Opera,* Cambridge: Cambridge University Press, 1985

Talbot, Michael, *Vivaldi,* London: Dent, 1978; 2nd edition, 1993

A study of Italian opera in the 18th century can take many paths. One, for example, examines the subgenres of Italian musical theater: opera seria, opera buffa, and the new, popular intermezzo. Another investigates the composers and theatrical centers within Italy itself. In order to grasp the full impact of Italy's greatest musical export of the 18th century, one must also study composers—including Niccolò Jommelli, Antonio Salieri, and Giovanni Paisiello—who took their art abroad. In addition to composers, foreign centers of Italian opera also attracted librettists such as Pietro Metastasio and Lorenzo da Ponte, singers such as Faustina Bordoni and Carlo Broschi (the famed castrato Farinelli), and impresarios, a role often played by Antonio Vivaldi. Finally, such popular and profitable entertainment inspired non-Italians. Therefore, a look at 18th-century Italian opera is incomplete without mentioning its place in the canons of composers such as George Frideric Handel, Johann Hasse, Franz Josef Haydn, and Wolfgang Amadeus Mozart.

FREEMAN presents a general introduction to the period that also includes a substantial discussion of the reforms of Apostolo Zeno and commentary on the librettos of Zeno and Metastasio. Although novices can glean much from the book, only those with strong musical and historical backgrounds may wish to attempt to tackle the series of charts on formal elements and the theoretically dense discussion of the compositional techniques of Antonio Caldara.

STROHM (1997) traces the roots of opera seria to classical drama. He also discusses the libretto as poetry, demonstrating the contrasting means of expression found in recitative and aria. Including historical information on other topics such as opera in the courts and in the cities, his research touches on the careers of Alessandro Scarlatti, Hasse, Handel, and Vivaldi.

An informative, though by now dated, life of Scarlatti is presented by DENT; readers need a knowledge of both musical terminology and some analysis to interpret the musical examples. For those wishing a thorough discussion of Vivaldi as composer and impresario, TALBOT presents a readable biography that also includes a section on the composer's style, supported with musical examples.

Perhaps the greatest center of opera in 18th-century Italy was Naples, where the likes of Nicola Porpora, Giovanni Battista Pergolesi, and Jommelli were nurtured. In the most comprehensive English-language study of the Neapolitan arena published to date, ROBINSON portrays this creative environment both from the viewpoint of the artists and from that of the Neapolitan audiences, whose reactions alternated between inattention and frenzy. Robinson also chronicles Metastasio's formative years in Naples and explains the methods of setting librettos in the Neapolitan style. In addition to covering opera seria, the author discusses buffa works and the intermezzo.

STROHM (1985) offers a look at the Italian musical world from the outside as he considers the foreign composers who studied in Italy and their introduction to the culture that gave birth to opera. In addition to essays on Handel's librettos and *pasticci,* there are discussions of Vivaldi as a producer and a reexamination of Scarlatti's place in the early 18th-century opera history and repertory.

Londoners proved to be among the most intriguing hosts to Italian opera. A worthwhile starting point is DEAN's study of Handel, which begins with the composer's training in Italy and moves on to his exploits with the Royal Academy and the Second Academy. PETTY chronicles the post-Handelian theatrical milieu, detailing the repertory at the King's Theatre and offering information on the importation of Italian artists such as the castrati to England. Included are samples of the views of the English, at one and the same time Italian opera's severest critics and most avid fans. PRICE also examines the King's Theatre, presenting a thorough explanation of the production of Italian opera in London, a chapter on Haydn's 1791 commission for *L'anima del filosofo,* and is significant information on the Italian opera industry in England.

A more general discussion of opera as business is offered by ROSSELLI (1984), which presents Italian musical theater through the eyes of the impresario and is replete with useful facts, statistics, and entertaining anecdotes. Helpful charts document the rise of singing as a profession and the growth of the theater orchestra. ROSSELLI (1992) is dedicated to the professional performers and their role in opera throughout the 18th and into the 19th century.

McCLYMONDS offers a portrait of Jommelli in his final post at the Portuguese court. Following a biographical account, she considers his music, both operatic and sacred, and his role in theatrical productions in Lisbon, one of the most active (but often ignored) foreign centers of Italian opera. Although the subject is fairly specialized, sections on librettos and on the Metastasian prescription for opera seria will prove useful to those seeking a general background.

HUNT's biography of Paisiello documents the composer's years as *maestro di cappella* at the Russian court of Catherine the Great, painting an informative picture of the life of an imported composer. A brief section considers Paisiello's early years at the Conservatory in

Naples, and appendices furnish selections from the composer's correspondence and a catalog of his works.

HUNTER and WEBSTER have compiled a volume about the popularity of opera buffa in Vienna in the second half of the 18th century. Although the essays deal primarily with Mozart's relationship to the genre, some chapters consider other issues such as how buffa works were influenced by the French tradition. Composers such as Salieri, Paisiello, Haydn, Hasse, Domenico Cimarosa, and Vicente Martín y Soler fall within the scope of this research. In a more complete explanation of Mozart's place in the Italian opera tradition, STEPTOE portrays the composer's collaborations with Da Ponte, offering a cultural and artistic look at the origins of the librettos, the cultural aesthetics that inspired them, and the audiences who applauded them.

DENISE GALLO

Opera: 19th-Century French

Crosten, William L., *French Grand Opera: An Art and a Business,* New York: King's Crown Press, 1948

Fulcher, Jane F., *The Nation's Image: French Grand Opera as Politics and Politicized Art,* Cambridge: Cambridge University Press, 1987

Gerhard, Anselm, *The Urbanization of Opera: Music Theater in Paris in the Nineteenth Century,* translated by Mary Whittall, Chicago: University of Chicago Press, 1997

Johnson, James, *Listening in Paris: A Cultural History,* Berkeley: University of California Press, 1995

Lacombe, Herve, *Les Voies de l'opera français au XIXe siècle,* Paris: Fayard, 1997

Pendle, Karin, *Eugène Scribe and French Opera of the Nineteenth Century,* Ann Arbor, Michigan: UMI Research Press, and Epping: Bowker, 1979

Spies, Andre Michael, *Opera, State and Society in the Third Republic, 1875–1914,* New York: Lang, 1998

Walsh, T.J., *Second Empire Opera: The Theatre Lyrique, Paris 1851–70,* London: Calder, and New York: Riverrun Press, 1981

There are three main genres of 19th-century French opera: grand opera, opera comique, and lyric opera. The latter refers to works produced later in the century that fused characteristics of the first two genres. Literature on 19th-century French opera tends to focus on these genres and on the three principal institutions that presented French-language opera in Paris—the Opera, the Opera-Comique, and the Theatre-Lyrique. Some specialized publications illuminate specific aspects of French opera history, such as surveys of operas by one composer, or an in-depth examination of a single opera. In addition, general opera history surveys usually include at least one chapter on 19th-century French opera.

For many years CROSTEN served as the standard reference work for grand opera. He succinctly introduces the principal characters who established this genre during the directorship of Veron (1831–35). From a sociological perspective, Crosten views grand opera as the product of capitalist enterprise, an eclectic and sometimes tasteless patchwork that pandered to a bourgeoisie who shunned challenges to their beliefs. A relatively weak discussion of Meyerbeer's contributions to French grand opera is confined to just one chapter.

PENDLE examines the structure and style of Eugene Scribe's voluminous output during the mid-19th century in an attempt to understand the impact of this most sought-after librettist on the history of libretti and French theater. She acknowledges flaws in Scribe's language and the sometimes formulaic way he constructed characters and plot, but Pendle treats her subject thoroughly and respectfully. Although few of Scribe's works are still performed, this study remains important for its insights into the development of French opera.

The Theatre-Lyrique (1851–70), which premiered such works as Bizet's *Les pecheurs de perles* (1863) and Gounod's *Faust* (1859) and *Romeo et Juliette* (1867), was the only mid-19th-century opera house to challenge the hegemony of the Opera-Comique and the Opera in French-language productions. Because most of the administrative documents of the Theatre-Lyrique have disappeared, WALSH's study of this institution depends heavily on documentation drawn from contemporaneous newspapers. His pleasantly written, strictly chronological account of the theater's activities avoids analysis of the repertoire and references to contemporary culture; it does, however, provide valuable information in the appendices as well as precious details within the text itself.

FULCHER has led the way among music historians in approaching the Opera's repertoire as the product of a dynamic cultural and political process. For the periods encompassing the July Monarchy and the Second Empire, she has studied the institution, its repertoire, its audience, and various politically motivated interventions in its affairs. Supported by extensive reading of the press, archival work, and exhaustive investigation into administrative history, Fulcher directly challenges Crosten's thesis that grand opera was simply a passive reflection of bourgeois tastes. She proposes instead that the music emerged from a provocative dialogue of political, artistic, and theatrical concerns and from public and private debates that shaped both the principal works and reception of them. This influential study maintains a fairly narrow focus and eschews dimensions of opera production.

JOHNSON, a cultural historian, investigates the instability and historical contingencies of listening in Paris. He attempts to explain the movement of the audience for opera and concerts from active involvement in the late 18th century to quasi-religious silence in the early 19th century. Ambitious and somewhat conjectural, this refreshing attempt to explain and document changes both in audience expectations of the conditions of performance and in the act of listening makes use of diverse sources such as memoirs, etiquette books, travel guides, music criticism, and fictional accounts.

SPIES, influenced by Fulcher's approach, concentrates on opera during the Third Republic to draw conclusions about the social functions of French opera. He explores the administration's strategies and actions, the backgrounds of the audiences and other participants in the theatrical world, and the sociopolitical mechanisms that controlled reception, and he substantiates his assertions by referring to numerous 19th-century sources. Spies has also analyzed the ideological content of some 138 full-length librettos and culled ten to 15 reviews for each of the 17 operas whose reception he examines in more detail. This fascinating study, sometimes more convincing in its examination of theatrical events and processes than in its investigation of political control, has inherent limitations, which are acknowledged by Spies, who chose not to engage the meanings and power of the music itself.

Two of the most recent publications on 19th-century French opera, by Gerhard and Lacombe, approach their subjects as both cultural products and musical subjects; both authors use multiple perspectives, in every case supported by virtuoso familiarity with sources and repertoire. GERHARD deals with the period 1826 to 1859 and discusses grand operas by composers such as Rossini, Auber, Meyerbeer, and Verdi. He identifies significant moments in eight scores, gives information about the genesis and initial reception of the opera, and then places these traditional topics of historical discussion in the context of changing modes of perception in that era. Gerhard attributes such changes in the expectations of audiences to the urbanization that increased the pace of daily life and introduced new socioeconomic and political forces. Interestingly, he has chosen to ignore some masterworks in order to discuss two operas not traditionally covered in books on grand opera: an intriguing failure, Louise Bertin's *La Esmeralda*, and Verdi's Italian opera, *Un Ballo in Maschera*.

LACOMBE explores opera of the Second Empire (1850–70). Although Second Empire operas have often been dismissed as inferior in quality, Lacombe points out dynamic elements in their stylistic inclusiveness and formal development. His musical focus is Bizet's *Les pecheurs de perles,* but the author uses sociological, aesthetic, and literary approaches to comment insightfully on such diverse issues as exoticism, construction of drama, poetic expression, stage space, decor, costumes, and the music itself (including orchestration, genesis, performance, and reception). This volume is the first book of real insight and scholarly depth to concentrate solely on the opera and cultural milieu of Second Empire France.

LESLEY A. WRIGHT

Opera: 19th-Century German

Chorley, Henry Fothergill, *Modern German Music,* 2 vols., London: Smith, Elder, 1854; reprint, 2 vols. in 1, New York: Da Capo Press, 1963

———, *Music and Manners in France and Germany,* 3 vols., London: Longman, 1841–44, reprint, New York: Da Capo Press, 1984

———, *Thirty Years' Musical Recollections,* 2 vols., London: Hurst and Blackett, 1862; reprint, New York: Da Capo Press, 1984

Dean, Winton, "German Opera," in *The Age of Beethoven,* edited by Gerald Abraham, The New Oxford History of Music, vol. 8, London: Oxford University Press, 1982

Garlington, Aubrey S., "German Romantic Opera and the Problem of Origins," *Musical Quarterly* 63 (1977)

———, "Mega-Text, Mega-Music: A Crucial Dilemma for German Romantic Opera," in *Musical Humanism and Its Legacy: Essays in Honor of Claude V. Palisca,* edited by Nancy Kovaleff Baker and Barbara Russano Hanning, Stuyvesant, New York: Pendragon Press, 1992

Goslich, Siegfried, *Die deutsche romantische Oper,* Tutzing: Schneider, 1975

Palmer, A. Dean, *Heinrich August Marschner 1795–1861: His Life and Stage Works,* Ann Arbor, Michigan: UMI Research Press, 1980

Warrack, John, "Romantic Opera: Germany and Austria," in *History of Opera,* edited by Stanley Sadie, Basingstoke: Macmillan, 1989; New York: Norton, 1990

There are few books in English devoted exclusively to the history of German opera, let alone German opera in the 19th century. The topic falls between two large fields of scholarship. On the one hand, there are studies on more specific topics (such as Beethoven's *Fidelio* or the life and works of Wagner or Weber); on the other hand, there are broad surveys of the history of opera in which the subject has only a subsidiary role. This essay considers information about 19th-century German opera contained in books about more general subjects as well as books and articles on composers and topics that are treated only tangentially in the Weber and Wagner literature. Because the history of German opera in the second half of the 19th century is dominated by Wagner, the literature discussed herein focuses on the period between 1800 and 1850. A description of even the most important works that have concerned themselves with 19th-century German opera would exceed the scope of this entry—my goal is rather to draw attention to aspects of the topic often neglected by standard reference works and biographies.

Readers interested in the history of German opera in the 19th century will find many valuable insights in well-known works such as Donald Grout's *A Short History of Opera* (1947) or Carl Dahlhaus's *Nineteenth-Century Music* (1989). The best short introduction to the specific topic of 19th-century German opera, however, is probably WARRACK. The author integrates his discussion of Weber and Wagner into a more general history of German operatic style, illuminating the connections between these composers and figures such as Marschner, Cornelius, and Humperdink. Researchers interested in the social history of opera or the history of operatic institutions would be better served by other sources.

A more comprehensive account of early 19th-century German opera is found in DEAN. The author covers the period from the death of Mozart through the operas of Weber, admirably illuminating the conflicting and competing strands of development that characterize German opera during that time. Apart from *Fidelio*, few operas from this period have found more than the most marginal place in the modern repertoire, but the ideas and institutions of the century's first decades had a lasting influence on the work of Weber and Wagner. Dean draws particular attention to the tremendous influence of French opera on German works during this period—not only rescue operas such as Cherubini's *Lodoïska* but also the later operas of Spontini and Méhul. Researchers interested in composers such as Weigl or Winter from the generation between Mozart and Weber will find Dean's work invaluable. The social and institutional history of German opera during this period was by no means monolithic, and Dean also describes some of the diverse and complex economic and cultural situations that conditioned the development of the genre.

Chorley was an English critic who traveled extensively in France and Germany during the 1830s and 1840s, and his goal as an author seems less to analyze than to entertain; his books are closer in style and content to the works of Burney than to modern musical scholarship. CHORLEY (1854) reprints much of the material from CHORLEY (1841–44) and resembles a travel diary, in which the author devotes one or two chapters to each of the most important musical centers in Germany. These works are not exclusively devoted to opera; Chorley not only describes other types of musical events but also gives entertaining accounts of the travelling conditions and the people that he encountered on his journeys. CHORLEY (1862) is a chronology, with individual chapters devoted to each year. Much of the material in this book only addresses tangentially the subject of German opera, but Chorley's comments on German singers, companies, and opera production make fascinating reading. His works provide invaluable insights into the musical life of the period.

GOSLICH is one of the foremost authorities on German opera from this period. The clear organization and encyclopedic scope of his volume make the work useful even for those readers with limited knowledge of German. The book covers the period between 1815 and 1848 and contains information on composers such as Wolfram and Reissiger that is not readily available in other works. Goslich also dedicates considerable space to the development of the German operatic libretto, a subject often neglected by other authors. He focuses on the development of operatic style rather than the broader social and cultural context for 19th-century German opera.

PALMER is the most important English-language source on the life and works of Heinrich August Marschner, who forms an important link between Weber and Wagner. Three of Marschner's operas, *Der Vampyr, Der Templer und die Jüdin,* and *Hans Heiling,* enjoyed enormous success in the 19th century and had an important influence on Wagner. Palmer's book contains a short biography of the composer as well as a comprehensive guide to his operas. For each of these works, Palmer provides a plot summary, description of the music, and short account of the composition's performance history.

GARLINGTON (1977 and 1992) is less concerned with concrete facts about composers or their works than with the ideology of the period. His articles provide an excellent introduction to the history of operatic theory in early 19th-century Germany, a theory that is perhaps even more important than the operas with which it is associated. Garlington concentrates on the dilemma of how to reconcile the demands of text and music that plagued early 19th-century German opera composers. This dilemma was, of course, one of Wagner's central concerns and constitutes perhaps the most important tension not only in the history of 19th-century German opera but in the entire history of the genre.

STEPHEN MEYER

See also Hoffmann, E.T.A.

Opera: 19th-Century Italian

Ashbrook, William, *Donizetti and His Opera,* Cambridge: Cambridge University Press, 1982

Black, John, *The Italian Romantic Libretto: A Study of Salvadore Cammarano,* Edinburgh: University Press, 1984

Budden, Julian, *The Operas of Verdi,* 3 vols., New York: Oxford University Press, 1973–81; revised edition, Oxford: Clarendon Press, 1992

Carner, Mosco, *Puccini: A Critical Biography,* London: Duckworth, 1958; New York: Knopf, 1959; 3rd edition, London: Duckworth, and New York: Homes and Meier, 1992

Gossett, Philip, et al., *The New Grove Masters of Italian Opera,* London: Macmillan, and New York: Norton, 1983

Nicolaisen, Jay, *Italian Opera in Transition: 1871–1893,* Ann Arbor, Michigan: UMI Research Press, 1980

Osborne, Charles, *The Bel Canto Operas of Rossini, Donizetti, and Bellini,* Protland, Oregon: Amadeus Press, and London: Methuen, 1994

Osborne, Richard, *Rossini*, London: Dent, 1986; revised edition, 1993

Pistone, Danièle, *Nineteenth-Century Italian Opera from Rossini to Puccini*, translated by E. Thomas Glasow, Portland, Oregon: Amadeus Press, 1995

Rosselli, John, *Music and Musicians in Nineteenth-Century Italy*, London: Batsford, and Portland, Oregon: Amadeus Press, 1991

——, *The Opera Industry in Italy from Cimarosa to Verdi: The Role of the Impresario*, Cambridge: Cambridge University Press, 1984

——, *Singers of Italian Opera: The History of a Profession*, Cambridge: Cambridge University Press, 1992

Weaver, William, *The Golden Century of Italian Opera from Rossini to Puccini*, New York: Thames and Hudson, 1980

Weaver, William, and Simonetta Puccini, editors, *The Puccini Companion*, New York and London: Norton, 1994

Weinstock, Herbert, *Donzietti and the World of Opera in Italy, Paris, and Vienna in the First Half of the Nineteenth Century*, New York: Pantheon Books, and London: Methuen, 1963

——, *Rossini: A Biography*, London: Oxford University Press, and New York: Knopf, 1968

——, *Vincenzo Bellini: His Life and His Operas*, New York: Knopf, 1971

Traditionally, 19th-century Italian opera history has been constructed around the careers of five composers: Gioacchino Rossini, Vincenzo Bellini, Gaetano Donizetti, Giuseppe Verdi, and Giacomo Puccini. Because most scholarship has deemed the rest of the period a wasteland in comparison, other composers (although highly successful in their day) have been ignored or mentioned only in passing. Such has been the fate of Carlo Coccia, Federico and Luigi Ricci, Achille Peri, Errico Petrella, Francesco Cilea, and Carlos Gomes, to name but a few. Early 19th-century composers better recognized for their significant roles are Saverio Mercadante and Giovanni Pacini; more noted still are the late 19th-century composers Ruggero Leoncavallo, Pietro Mascagni, and Amilcare Ponchielli, whose works (*I pagliacci, Cavalleria rusticana,* and *La gioconda,* respectively) are performed frequently. At present, however, no one study fairly represents this incredibly rich and prolific century in any serious depth.

WEAVER's book serves as an example of the traditional picture of this period, skewed in favor of the five "kings of Italian opera." Dismissing the century's earliest composers as "nonentities," he states that opera, then in decline, was saved by Rossini, Bellini, Donizetti, and Verdi, with the torch later passing to Puccini. Although this book, which was written as an introduction to the period, represents a narrow view, it does offer beginners an opportunity to meet a good sampling of the personages of 19th-century opera, including lesser-known composers, impresarios, singers, and librettists. A fine feature of the book is its illustrations (some color plates), including such items as contemporary portraits and photographs, costume designs, diagrams of theaters, and facsimile prints of autograph scores and correspondence.

A more inclusive introduction is PISTONE's overview of the era. Divided into three sections ("The Librettos," "The Music," and "Performance"), the volume covers issues such as choices of subjects and literary sources; stylistic evolution; politics, society, and censorship; vocal style; the period orchestra; musical language; theatrical administration; and audience tastes. Pistone also includes a fair number of minor composers. This work could be appropriate for those beginning a study of 19th-century Italian opera; those at a more advanced level will undoubtedly find it superficial.

The contribution of GOSSETT offers an advanced presentation of the traditional 19th-century repertoire. As always, the New Grove Masters volume features eminent scholars (Philip Gossett on Rossini, William Ashbrook and Julian Budden on Donizetti, Friedrich Lippmann on Bellini, Andrew Porter on Verdi, and Mosco Carner on Puccini) who have compiled biographical research on each composer, comments on their music (supported with musical examples), and annotated works lists. Those facing more advanced research projects will find the bibliographies that conclude each section quite useful.

In lieu of an adequate single-volume history, experienced researches may choose to investigate the general milieu of opera in the 1800s (or *ottocento*) in individual studies of the masters. BUDDEN, for example, begins the first book of his three-volume study of Verdi's operas with a chapter on the world in which the composer learned his trade. Richard OSBORNE offers similar material about Rossini's early training as well as depicting the composer in the Italian and Parisian opera arenas in which he worked. WEINSTOCK's volumes on Donizetti (1963), Rossini (1968), and Bellini (1971) are as much artistic and cultural studies as they are strict biographies. ASHBROOK, too, places his subject, Donizetti, in the theatrical world in which he composed, in addition to discussing contemporary operatic forms and conventions. CARNER examines the aesthetics of Italian opera in the second half of the century and considers the concept of realism, or *verismo,* with which Puccini's name is connected. In addition, editors WEAVER and PUCCINI (the composer's granddaughter) have included a chapter by Budden on the Italian opera milieu in which the young Puccini entered at the beginning of his career.

NICOLAISEN examines the second half of the century and the transition from "number" opera to seamless music drama; however, he limits his study by including only composers with "at least one major success" in theaters in Rome and northern Italy and by excluding comic opera. Nevertheless, the book presents a solid overview of stylistic trends, supported by materials gleaned from contemporary newspapers and correspondence (in translation), and serves as an introduction to the works of composers such as Francesco Cilea, Alberto Franchetti, and Umberto Giordano. Part 1 is a general look at the opera from 1871 to 1893, with particular emphasis on Verdi. Part 2 offers insights into the works of Ponchielli, Arrigo Boito, Alfredo Catalani, Puccini, and others of Puccini's generation. A well-constructed chapter on poetry and the shape of music drama and a cautious discussion of verismo (realism) also are included.

BLACK provides a different perspective on romantic opera in his book on Salvadore Cammarano, librettist of such works as *Il trovatore* and *Lucia di Lammermoor*. After a biographical introduction, Black considers Cammarano's collaborations with the major composers of the day, including Verdi, Donizetti, Mercadante, Pacini, and Ricci, as well as the poet's personal involvement in theatrical productions. This book also is a useful source for those seeking information about the literary sources for romantic operas, the framing of action into musical drama, and the poetic structure of a libretto.

Readers interested in the bel canto repertoire might begin with Charles OSBORNE's basic guide to the operas of Rossini, Bellini, and Donizetti. Each work receives its own section, which includes general information on genre (such as opera seria, *melodramma*, *farsa*, etc.), a list of characters and their vocal ranges, librettist, setting, premiere, and original cast followed by relevant historical data and brief—and at times subjective—commentary on the music (without musical examples). Because of the number of new recordings and rereleases of productions of the bel canto repertoire, Osborne's discography, while useful, is outdated.

Theater-historian ROSSELLI documents the history of 19th-century Italian opera from a novel perspective—backstage. His three books, on impresarios (1984), musicians (1991), and singers (1992), present a colorful view of production and performance history. Supported by tables of archival data, Rosselli explains the workings of the *ottocento* theater industry with information such as singers' salaries, subscription prices for boxes at major theaters, and total costs of operatic season expenses. Although the volumes will best serve someone who already has a fair amount of knowledge about the period, the anecdotes and illustrations featured in the books certainly will engage even the novice.

DENISE GALLO

See also Verdi, Giuseppe

Opera: 19th-Century Russian

Abraham, Gerald, *On Russian Music,* London: Reeves, and New York, Scribner, 1939; reprint, New York: Johnson Reprint, 1970

———, *Studies in Russian Music,* London: Reeves, and New York: Scribner, 1936; reprint, 1969

Asaf'ev, Boris Vladimirovich, *Russian Music from the Beginning of the Nineteenth Century,* translated by Alfred J. Swan, Ann Arbor, Michigan: Edwards, 1953

Campbell, Stuart, editor, *Russians on Russian Music, 1830–1880: An Anthology,* Cambridge: Cambridge University Press, 1994

Newmarch, Rosa, *The Russian Opera,* New York: Dutton, and London: Jenkins, 1914; reprint, Westport, Connecticut: Greenwood Press, 1972

Seaman, Gerald R., *History of Russian Music, Volume I: From Its Origins to Dargomyzhsky,* New York: Praeger, and Oxford: Blackwell, 1967

Stasov, Vladimir Vasilevich, *Selected Essays on Music,* translated by Florence Jonas, London: Barrie and Rockliff, and London: Praeger, 1968

Taruskin, Richard, *Defining Russia Musically: Historical and Hermeneutical Essays,* Princeton, New Jersey: Princeton University Press, 1997

———, *Opera and Drama in Russia as Preached and Practiced in the 1860s,* Ann Arbor, Michigan: UMI Research Press, and Epping: Bowker, 1981

Although one might think that any opera by a Russian composer would of necessity be Russian, there has always been disagreement over what constitutes truly Russian qualities in an opera. The appetite for Western European opera at the court theaters of the czars from the 17th through the 19th centuries meant that foreign operas were prized above those of Russian origin. It took a determined effort on the part of 19th-century Russian composers to overcome this obstacle. As a result, two main schools of thought developed during the 19th century: those who favored Russian composers who wrote in the international style of the day and those who favored the cultivation of a uniquely Russian compositional style. Which features were considered truly Russian and which were not provides a perennial plot for essays on Russian music in general, and Russian opera in particular.

NEWMARCH presents a rambling account of the development of the Russian genre from its beginnings to the end of the 19th century. Her work is valuable for its descriptions of the plots of several operas as well as its informally presented details of the biographies and social milieu of composers from the pre-Glinka period through the time of Rachmaninoff. The book is dedicated to Shaliapin in memory of Vladimir Stasov and reflects the opinions of the latter in portraying the political and aesthetic divisions among 19th-century Russian composers. Thus, Newmarch contends that only the nationalist composers, principally the Mighty Five (Balakirev, Borodin, Cui, Mussorgsky, and Rimsky-Korsakov), deserve to be regarded as truly Russian, while those with Western leanings have no legitimate place in Russian national opera.

Gerald Abraham can be considered one of the foremost English-language writers on Russian music, having written several books on Russian topics. Both ABRAHAM (1936) and ABRAHAM (1939) are collections of essays, many of them on operatic subjects. The value of Abraham's writing in these and other books is that he treats each opera in detail. Unfortunately, he takes a condescending tone against which Taruskin, for one, rails. For example, Abrahams posits that "The Russian musical mind is . . . childlike in many other respects than its love of bright primary orchestral colors." That assumption is merely objectionable, but another of Abraham's arguments is misleading and is the progenitor of many a similar statement in English writing on Russian music. After stating that Glinka could not avoid "Italianism in opera," Abraham adds, "But . . . it was almost inevitable that at first some foreign matter should mingle with the pure metal [of Russian musical thought]." The assumption that an Italian influence on Glinka's compositions detracts from their Russian character is bound to the preconception that Russian music should be entirely different from Western music. The challenge for the reader first approaching Russian opera is that the best introductory books are apt to convey this attitude, while the more thoughtful works that do not make such assumptions are not introductory.

Taruskin has recently dominated the field of Russian opera. He has contributed all the entries on Russian topics in *The New Grove Dictionary of Opera* and has written several books. The earliest of these, TARUSKIN (1981), is a revision of the author's thesis, in which the operas of Glinka, Serov, Dargomizhsky, and Cui are examined. Each of the chapters illustrates the complexity and gravity of discussion on operatic topics in Russia: "Art was and is a moral issue to the Russian mind; nowhere else on earth has *ars gratia artis* [art for art's sake] been held in such contempt." Already in this book the author's intention to grapple *de novo* with Russian operatic history while exposing the prejudices of previous writers is apparent. Newmarch's book, for example, is dismissed as "little more than a mirror of the prejudices of [her] acknowledged mentor, Vladimir Stasov, surely one of the most partisan and biased historians of art that ever lived."

The same attitude permeates TARUSKIN (1997). Several chapters present a wealth of detail about operas and their political and cultural background. They also provide a very sophisticated deconstruction of previous scholarship on Russian music. Taruskin makes blunt assessments of studies that he rightly claims to have consigned Russian music to a second-rate ghetto.

For readers who wish to know more about the Russian or Soviet point of view, the books by Asaf'ev, Campbell, Stasov, and Seaman are enlightening. ASAF'EV was a prominent Soviet scholar whose later life was affected by Soviet politics, but this book was published well before the infamous Zhdanov decree that forbade the linking of Russian music to any foreign influence. (Details of the Soviet control over music scholarship can be learned from Boris Schwarz, *Music and Musical Life in Soviet Russia*, enlarged edition, 1983, especially in chapter 10, "Musicologists on Trial.") In chapter 1, "Opera in Russia," Asaf'ev gives a brief overview of the development of 19th-century Russian opera from a Russian point of view. The chapter includes concise discussions of the operatic output of major and minor composers from Cavos and Verstovsky through to Serov and Taneiev. He offers valuable insights on the development of Russian opera without presenting details of plots, making his work increasingly useful as one's knowledge of Russian opera develops.

CAMPBELL presents translations of important critical writing on opera from 1830 to 1880. A brief preface and introduction warn of the difficulties of translating certain Russian terms and set forth the conditions of musical composition, performance, and criticism in the period under discussion. Four chapters are devoted to opera, each introduced by useful background. Chapters 1 and 4 highlight the importance of Glinka's founding operas as evidenced by the sheer amount of critical attention paid them both on their initial appearance and later in the century. The relative merits of these works as models for the development of Russian opera were frequently the focus of critical discussion. Chapter 5 includes critiques of operas not often treated in English literature: Dargomizhsky's *Rusalka* and *The Stone Guest*; Serov's *Judith, Rogneda,* and *The Power of the Fiend*; and Tchaikovsky's *The Voyevoda*. Chapter 7 deals with the popular operas of the 1870s: Rimsky-Korsakov's *The Maid of Pskov,* Mussorgsky's *Boris Godunov,* and Tchaikovsky's *The Oprichnik* and *Eugene Onegin.* Although primarily about instrumental music, chapter 8 includes an evaluation of the work of Mussorgsky by the critic and fellow kuchkist Cui, including his famously derogatory opinion of (but also grudging admiration for) *Boris Godunov.* All of these critical writings are valuable both in themselves and as the sources of many quotations chosen by 20th-century critics to support a particular point of view.

Readers who wish to investigate the views of Newmarch's master for themselves can do so with STASOV, which includes one essay devoted to opera: "Twenty-Five Years of Russian Art: Our Music." Stasov was a dominant figure in 19th-century Russian music whose agenda was the development of a unique national voice, separate from Western European music. He favored the Mighty Five and encouraged them to base their music on folk and historical traditions. His opposition to the founding of the Western-style conservatories and to the critic and composer Serov (who was, among other things, an avid Wagnerian) are legendary; together Stasov and Serov laid down the ideological template that so many writers seem unable to resist when evaluating Russian music.

Finally, SEAMAN treats opera in the course of writing a general history of Russian music up to the time of Glinka. This study is roundly criticized for its reliance on a single Soviet textbook account, but it is exactly this characteristic that allows the reader to glimpse the blinkered view of Russian music history held (possibly under duress) by Soviet-period historiographers. The result is an account truly fixated on the theme of Russian nationalism in music, as though Soviet hands had picked up the torch of Stasov. In this volume, as in all the literature discussed here, the challenge for the reader is to recognize the ideological point of view; never was the advice of historian E.H. Carr more appropriate: "To know the history, know first the historian."

MARY S. WOODSIDE

Opera: 20th Century

Boyden, Matthew, *Opera: The Rough Guide,* London: Rough Guides, 1997

Grout, Donald J., *A Short History of Opera,* New York: Columbia University Press, 1965; 3rd edition, 1988

Kobbé, Gustav, *The Complete Opera Book,* New York: Putnam, 1922; 11th edition, as *The New Kobbé's Opera Book,* edited by George Henry Hubert Lascelles, Earl of Harewood and Antony Peattie, 1997

Martin, George Whitney, *The Opera Companion to Twentieth-Century Opera,* New York: Dodd, Mead, 1979; 2nd edition, as *Twentieth-Century Opera: A Guide,* New York: Limelight Editions, 1999

Mordden, Ethan, *Opera in the Twentieth Century: Sacred, Profane, Godot,* New York: Oxford University Press, 1978

Parker, Roger, editor, *The Oxford Illustrated History of Opera,* Oxford: Oxford University Press, 1994

Sadie, Stanley, editor, *History of Opera,* Basingstoke: Macmillan, 1989; New York: Norton, 1990

At the dawn of the 20th century, opera composition continued late 19th-century traditions: Puccini followed the verismo style, and Richard Strauss's expressionist operas, *Salome* (1905) and *Electra* (1908), were an extension of Wagnerian practice. Beginning in the 1920s, however, a wide range of operatic developments began to emerge, incorporating newly developed compositional techniques and aesthetics of the time. Berg explored atonality in *Wozzeck* (1925) and 12-tone technique in *Lulu* (posthumously premiered in 1937). As a reaction to the complexity of serial composition and the exuberant emotions of late romanticism, neoclassical operas tried to revive the musical lightness and formal clarity of the 18th-century number opera, and the influence of the neoclassical movement can be found in such works as Hindemith's *Cardillac* (1926), Strauss's *Capriccio* (1943), and Stravinsky's *The Rake's Progress* (1951).

Opera was extended in innovative and iconoclastic ways during the second half of the 20th century. Music theater, developed primarily by Peter Maxwell Davies and Luciano Berio, rejected a rigid distinction between instrumental music and opera and instead explored new possibilities of more flexible combinations of music and drama on a smaller scale than traditional opera. Some operas, such as Bernd Alois Zimmermann's *Die Soldaten* (1964) and Hans Werner Henze's *We Come to the River* (1976), challenged the narrative continuity and temporal linearity of conventional opera by employing multiple stages, in which different actions or events were simultaneously presented. Philip Glass's *Einstein on the Beach* (1976) and John Cage's *Europeras* series (1987–92) went one step further in that they completely rejected narrative opera: in *Einstein,* traditional narrative is replaced by images evoked in the manner of stream of consciousness, while in Cage's work, aleatoric elements and extensive quotations obviate traditional narrative. Multimedia exploration was another growing influence in the second half of the 20th century. By utilizing multimedia forces, most notably cinematic techniques, composers tried to generate various dramatic effects that cannot be achieved in conventional opera theater.

In addition to the unprecedentedly diverse and radical experiments in opera, however, the traditional style of composition also flourished throughout the century. Most operas by Benjamin Britten, one of the most prolific and successful 20th-century composers of opera, exemplify a conservative side (although in relative terms) of 20th-century opera composition.

The current monograph studies of 20th-century opera focus on individual composers or individual operas rather than the general trend of the genre. The volumes on opera's general history serve as the best sources for historical survey and the general development of 20th-century opera. Some general guides to opera are also useful sources of basic information such as plot-summaries and compositional facts. In such sources, the space given to the 20th-century repertoire has been rapidly expanding for the past few decades. The number of book-length studies devoted entirely to 20th-century opera, however, is extremely limited.

MORDDEN, a former editor of *Opera News,* produced the first substantial monograph study of 20th-century opera. The 15-page introduction is a condensed survey of the previous history of opera up to Wagner. Mordden's discussion of 20th-century opera is organized chronologically, starting from Charpentier's *Luise,* which was composed exactly at the beginning of the 20th century. Mordden tries to trace 20th-century operatic innovations in the wider context of concurrent aesthetic, stylistic, and technological developments in other arts. Without much technical jargon and entirely devoid of musical examples, Mordden's book is straightforward enough to be enjoyed by the general reader. However, the author's flowery literary mannerisms might be annoying, especially to academics. A more scholarly and updated book-length study focusing on 20th-century opera, however, is yet to be written.

GROUT's book has been acknowledged as a classic in the general study of the history of opera. In the most recent edition, the section on the 20th century is completely reorganized and greatly expanded. Grout's description of music is much more technical than Mordden's but is not too overwhelming for the general reader. Considering that Grout mentions many obscure operas (although most often simply in passing), it is puzzling that Birtwistle, Kagel, and even Berio are ignored. Another problematic feature of Grout's study is that his treatment of nationalism and political opera is a bit too simplistic.

SADIE is a volume comparable to Grout. The part devoted to the 20th century is divided into nine chapters—seven geographically classified studies and two topical chapters on operetta and staging. Since each geographical chapter is written by a different regional specialist, the focal point of Sadie's volume is its geographical coverage, which is sophisticated in content and extensive in scope, encompassing less-represented countries in opera study, such as Finland, Belgium, Australia, and Spain. Like Grout, Sadie contains a fair number of illustrations, but unlike Grout, it is completely devoid of musical examples. Both volumes are well provided with bibliographical information for further study. In addition, Sadie includes a fairly extensive glossary of terms.

PARKER is a collection of 12 essays on opera, two of which are devoted to the 20th century, both by Paul Griffiths, one of the most authoritative commentators on 20th-century music. Griffiths uses the end of World War II as a chronological demarcation for his two essays. These essays are particularly informative concerning innovative operatic explorations, of which Griffiths has been a great defender and promoter. Like other chapters in the collection, Griffiths's chapters are entirely devoid of musical examples but replete with illustrations, some of which are in color. Although they are accessible to the general reader, Griffiths's essays are more oriented toward music specialists, requiring some background on the works and composers he discusses.

Although it is a general guide to opera, BOYDEN has a surprisingly extensive coverage of 20th-century opera—147 operas by more than 70 composers, including those composers who are marginalized or completely omitted in most of the general opera history books (such as Michael Nyman, Aulis Sallinen, Alfred Schnittke, Mark-Anthony Turnage, and Judith Weir. Boyden's guide is a particularly plot-oriented reference book. Three chapters out of eight are devoted to the 20th-century repertoire. Within each chapter, the composers are arranged in chronological order with concise biographical sketches for most of them. Each work is provided with compositional facts, a synopsis, and some additional information and comments. For those operas that are well represented in recordings, a selected and lightly annotated discography is also included. In addition, directories of singers and opera houses and a rudimentary glossary of operatic terms are provided at the end of the book. With this practical information, Boyden's book is a useful consumer guide for opera fans.

When HAREWOOD and PEATTIE's first edition was published in 1922 under a different name, it was hailed as a pioneering general guide to opera. The most recent edition is completely redesigned and enormously expanded, with the addition of nearly 200 new operas, most of which are from the 20th-century repertoire. Harewood and Peattie's inclusion of the 20th-century works exceeds Boyden's already extensive converge, encompassing more recent composers, such as Thomas Adés (b. 1971) and Oliver Knussen (b. 1952), and more recent operas, such as Birtwistle's *The Second Mrs. Kong* (1994). Although Harewood and Peattie's volume is basically a plot-focused reference guide with a minimum discussion of music (often supported by musical examples), it is a critical source for initiating the study of the most recent 20th-century operas.

MARTIN's volume, a reworking of his 1979 edition of *The Opera Companion to Twentieth Century Opera*, is the most up-to-date reference book focusing on 20th-century opera. It is divided into three parts. The second part is devoted to synopses of 90 operas by 30 composers, selected primarily on the basis of their popularity in performance and recording. Part 1 consists of six introductory essays: four biographical essays on Janacek, Puccini, Stravinsky, and Prokofiev, framed by two survey essays on the historical development of 20th-century opera. These chapters discuss many works in a wider historical context than is considered in the synopses part, and in so doing, complement the volume's relatively small coverage of the repertoire. Part 3 provides a glossary of composers, operatic terminology, and others topics, including some significant opera directors (for example, Patrice Chéreau and Wieland Wagner) and a number of librettists. While Martin's coverage of the repertoire is not as extensive as Boyden's or Harewood and Peattie's, Martin's synopses are much more detailed than other reference books of this kind and more sophisticated for their inclusion of the historical backgrounds of each opera and accessible technical discussions of the music (particularly its dramatic functions, which are often supported by musical examples and excerpts from the librettos). Martin's two most serious defects are weak coverage of more experimental operas (such as Berio's) and a lack of consistency and systematic criteria in his selection process: the arbitrariness in the choice of the four composers for the focused biographical essays in Part 1; the inclusion of such marginally operatic work as Stravinsky's *Histoire du Soldat* in Part 2 but no further selection of kindred works of instrumental theater; the synopses of complete operas for Britten but the omission of *Elektra* and *Salome* for Strauss; and finally, the surprising inclusion of Theodor Adorno in the glossary but no mention of John Adams and Philip Glass in spite of the inclusion of their operas in the synopsis part.

JEONGWON JOE

Opera: English

Banfield, Stephen, editor, *The Twentieth Century,* The Blackwell History of Music in Britain, vol. 6, Oxford: Blackwell, 1995

Biddlecombe, George, *English Opera from 1834 to 1864, with Particular Reference to the Works of Michael Balfe,* New York: Garland, 1994

Dent, Edward J., *Foundations of English Opera: A Study of Musical Drama in England during the Seventeenth Century,* Cambridge: Cambridge University Press, 1928; reprint, New York: Da Capo Press, 1965

Fenner, Theodore, *Opera in London: Views of the Press, 1785–1830,* Carbondale: Southern Illinois University Press, 1994

Fiske, Roger, *English Theatre Music in the Eighteenth Century,* London: Oxford University Press, 1973; 2nd edition, 1986

Girdham, Jane, *English Opera in Late Eighteenth-Century London: Stephen Storace at Drury Lane,* Oxford: Clarendon Press, and New York: Oxford University Press, 1997

Johnstone, H. Diack, and Roger Fiske, editors, *The Eighteenth Century,* The Blackwell History of Music in Britain, vol. 4, Oxford: Blackwell, 1990

Spink, Ian, editor, *The Seventeenth Century,* The Blackwell History of Music in Britain, vol. 3, Oxford: Blackwell, 1992

Temperley, Nicholas, editor, *The Romantic Age, 1800–1914,* The Blackwell History of Music in Britain, vol. 5, London: Athlone, 1981; Oxford: Blackwell, 1988

White, Eric Walter, *A History of English Opera,* London: Faber, 1983

————, *The Rise of English Opera,* London: Lehmann, and New York: Philosophical Library, 1951

White, Eric Walter, editor, *A Register of First Performances of English Operas and Semi-Operas from the 16th Century to 1980,* London: Society for Theatre Research, 1983

The critical and historical study of the tradition of English opera has, until recently, been largely neglected. The specter of "das Land ohne Musik" (the belief that the English language is inelegant when sung), suspicions that English composers were not as serious about their craft as their Continental counterparts, and the sheer bewildering variety of musical entertainments that have at some time passed as "English opera" have all contributed to this oversight. Purcell and Handel scholars have sought to establish a vernacular theatrical context for their studies, but English opera composers rediscovered in this manner have tended to be valued only for the light they shed on their more illustrious contemporaries. This present discussion, therefore, is concerned with scholarship that focuses primarily on the phenomenon of English opera—defined broadly here as English-language musical drama originating in the British Isles.

DENT's study of English opera from the masques of Ben Johnson to Purcell's semi-operas was begun in 1914, during preparations for a Cambridge performance of Purcell's *Fairy Queen.* Notwithstanding his pioneering revivals of this repertory, Dent baldly states that the history of English opera is "the record of three centuries of failure," though he marvels at the persistence of attempts to launch the genre. The allegiance of the English public to the spoken drama, he argues, has been too deep-seated for them to accept the central tenet of opera, that music can itself be an agent of the drama: "Shakespeare and his contemporaries never show us speech intensified into song under stress of emotion, but only the emotional effect produced by music on the characters represented." At this juncture, it is worth remembering that Dent's viewpoint predates by 20 years the premiere of Benjamin Britten's *Peter Grimes* (1945), the work considered by most to have established almost overnight the credibility of English opera as a serious genre. Dent's volume is more than a period piece, however. He traces the origins of early English opera back to the masque and discusses at length William Davenant's *Siege of Rhodes* (1656) as the first attempt at a genuine English opera, although the score itself has been lost. Dent is the first commentator to recognize the merits of John Blow's *Venus and Adonis* and its links with Purcell's *Dido and Aeneas,* and he makes a fruitful distinction between amateur and professional enterprises in the development of English opera. His extensive knowledge of opera enables him to illuminate parallels between the English and Continental traditions, and a particular strength of this study is his intuitive understanding of the art form as a collaboration between librettist, composer, designer, producer, and performer. Although it lacks detailed references and a bibliography, this work is rich in critical insight and stylish in presentation and therefore remains an excellent starting point for study.

The postwar renaissance of English opera, spearheaded by Britten, coincided with a flourishing of interest in the genre's history, as though the international success of the modern works validated the scholarly pursuit of their predecessors. These developments, combined with the nationalistic euphoria of the late 1940s, inspired WHITE (1951) to produce a study of English operas written since World War II for the 1951 Festival of Britain. White soon realized the need to view this revival in its proper perspective, however, extending the scope of the volume to incorporate a survey of three centuries of activity, culminating in Britten's *Billy Budd* (1951). Britten himself set the tone for the book, penning an impassioned endorsement of English opera—"the Cinderella of the arts"—for the introduction. White's main theme is the changing nature of the operatic industry in England, as reflected in the roles of organizations, management, librettists, and composers. Hence, there are interesting sidelights on the abortive national opera schemes of the 19th century, the touring Carl Rosa company, and the significance of regional opera festivals, among others. White clearly believes that his is the golden age of English opera, and part 2 of the book is a thought-provoking discussion of the conditions that made that age possible, along with practical suggestions for the revival of earlier works.

WHITE (1983a) later expanded and updated his book, producing a substantial basic history of the genre. The text is particularly useful for those interested in the pre-1900 period; in the later narrative there are unexplained imbalances that, for example, seem to favor Rutland Boughton at the expense of Ralph Vaughan Williams, and it is disappointing that White limits his discussion of developments since 1945 to Britten and Michael Tippett. A drawback throughout is the lack of detailed aesthetic evaluation of the works themselves: unlike Dent, White does not summarize libretti and analyze scores, and rather than presenting his own critical assessments, he prefers to quote or paraphrase the views of earlier commentators. However, as a source of data on the development and reception of English opera over the centuries, this ambitious volume remains a classic, and the accompanying volume (WHITE 1983b) is an indispensable research tool for scholars working in this field.

In a history that is narrower and sharper in focus than White's books, FISKE picks up the story of English opera where Dent leaves off, providing an exhaustive, in-depth exploration of music produced for London theaters between the deaths of Purcell (1695) and Storace (1796). Striking an effective compromise between a reference work and a book for general reading, the author presents a veritable gold mine of new discoveries and perceptive evaluations of the works themselves. For some, his cursory treatment of Handel and the Italian opera may come dangerously close to distorting the picture—indeed, he states categorically that the influx of Italian opera was "damaging" to the English genre—but this perspective results from his eagerness to document fully the achievements of native composers and changing theatrical conditions of 18th-century London. The book is structured by period and genre and is well indexed, and the appendices are especially valuable for the serious student of English opera: Fiske lists performers, works, surviving sources, borrowings, and so on—a fitting testament to years of painstaking archival research.

Just as meticulously, FENNER chronicles the operatic scene of Georgian London through the views of the press, producing a reference work that reflects current musico-logical interest in reception and criticism. Part 1 comprises an overview of opera coverage in newspapers and journals of the day, identifying individual critics where possible and discussing their work against the background of English romanticism. The book then bifurcates into sections on "The Italian Opera" (part 2) and "The English Opera" (part 3)—an arrangement that enables connections to be drawn between both sides of London's operatic life. Short essays on the theaters, audiences, operas, and performances provide helpful summaries, but the real substance of Fenner's work comes in the encyclopedic appendices—comprehensive listings of performances, reviews, premieres, librettists, composers, dramatists, adaptors, and singers. For anyone seeking orientation in the confusing world of opera production in Georgian London, this is a vital and welcome compass.

Research into the tradition of English opera has entailed the recovery of many forgotten works, which scholars are increasingly able to view in their proper contexts. The operas of Stephen Storace are the main focus of GIRDHAM's excellent study: her perceptive discussions make a strong case for the works' revival and highlight Storace's ambition to bring English opera closer to Italian principles. Through these works the author also explores questions of genre, copyright, and publishing practices in late 18th-century London; her investigation of borrowings, which have done much to undermine the reputation of English opera composers of Storace's generation, is particularly illuminating and is based on a thorough knowledge of the scores and their sources.

BIDDLECOMBE views early Victorian opera through the music of Michael Balfe and five of his contemporaries: Barnett, Benedict, Loder, Macfarren, and Wallace. The author defines and accounts for the characteristic features of English 19th-century opera, outlining the theatrical conditions and cultural factors that helped to shape both libretto and score. From his adept discussion of selected works, it becomes clear that Italian and German influences abounded far more than French and that, in some cases, the native tradition was represented only by the inclusion of a ballad or glee. The composer-by-composer layout of this volume makes the narrative a bit predictable, but the discussion is insightful and does much to encourage reassessment of a neglected repertory.

Brief mention should be made of both SPINK and TEMPERLEY, volumes in the Blackwell History of Music in Britain series. Following the operatic thread through each of these highly readable volumes yields a rich blend of historical account and aesthetic evaluation, which draws on the talents of some of the finest scholars of English music. The series helps to plug the gaps left by existing studies, and because of its broad contextual basis, many potentially fruitful avenues are opened up for future study.

RACHEL COWGILL

Opera: Set Design

Appia, Adolphe, *Essays, Scenarios, and Designs,* translated by Walther R. Volbach, edited by Richard C. Beacham, Ann Arbor, Michigan: UMI Press, 1989

———, *Music and the Art of the Theatre,* translated by Robert W. Corrigan and Mary Douglas Dirks, edited by Barnard Hewitt, Coral Gables, Florida: University of Miami Press, 1962

———, *Staging Wagnerian Drama,* translated by Michael Peter Loeffler, Basel: Birkhäuser, 1982

Aronson, Arnold, "Postmodern Design," *Theatre Journal* 43 (1991)

Baker, Evan, "The Scene Designs for the First Performance of Bizet's *Carmen,*" *Nineteenth Century Music* 13 (1990)

Bergman, Gösta Mauritz, *Lighting in the Theatre,* Stockholm: Almquist and Wiksell, and Totowa, New Jersey: Rowman and Littlefield, 1977

Bjurström, Per, *Giacomo Torelli and Baroque Stage Design,* Stockholm: Nationalmuseum, and Stockholm: Almquist and Wiksell, 1961; 2nd edition, 1962

Carini Motta, Fabricio, *The Theatrical Writings of Fabrizio Carini Motta,* translated by Orville K. Larson, Carbondale: Southern Illinois University Press, 1987

Durand, Carroll, "The Apogee of Perspective in the Theatre: Ferdinando Bibiena's 'Scena per angolo,'" *Theatre Research International* 13 (1988)

Friedman, Martin L., *Hockney Paints the Stage,* Minneapolis, Minnesota: Walker Art Center, and New York: Abbeville Press, 1983

Hewitt, Barnard, editor, *The Renaissance Stage: Documents of Serlio, Sabbattini, and Furttenbach,* Coral Gables, Florida: University of Miami Press, 1958

Oenslager, Donald, *Stage Design: Four Centuries of Scenic Invention,* London: Thames and Hudson, and New York: Viking Press, 1975

Ogden, Dunbar H., editor, *The Italian Baroque Stage,* Berkeley: University of California Press, 1978

Radice, Mark A., editor, *Opera in Context: Essays on Historical Staging from the Late Renaissance to the Time of Puccini,* Portland, Oregon: Amadeus Press, 1998

Wolff, Hellmut Christian: *Oper: Szene und Darstellung von 1600 bis 1900,* Leipzig: Deutscher Verlag für Musik, 1968; 2nd edition, 1979

The study of stage design specifically for opera is a unique and difficult field of research. Documentation is primarily visual and ephemeral, based chiefly on numerous reproductions of scene designs and production photographs. Due to the high costs of reproducing good quality photographs, published detailed studies on the history of stage design and its diverse styles are rare and expensive. Elaborately illustrated coffee table books containing general surveys of opera with numerous photographs of general stage designs usually have little or no analysis of production values. Although there is a large number of publications in German, French, and Italian that offer more detailed study, few scholarly or detailed surveys in English of stage design are specifically aimed at opera.

Both practical knowledge and aesthetic understanding of the rich and diverse styles in the history of operatic production involve four issues. First, one must have the means to study numerous reproductions of scene designs specifically for opera. Second, documentation, as well as iconography, of the development of theatrical architecture and stage machinery must be available. Third, one must study basic works on the theory and methods of stage design. Finally, one must have access to source materials related to the aesthetics and culture of the times and places where the designs were created and brought onto the stage. The requirements of scenic design are necessarily linked to the drama of the music, and it is rare that the designer has fully understood that connection, particularly in context of the available theater space and machinery. Unfortunately, because the areas of investigation are so rich and diverse, there does not exist any series of publications—particularly in English—that take into account all of the four cited areas. Moreover, few studies have been written by practitioners of the craft with a well-rounded knowledge of the history of the genre.

OENSLAGER, a prominent designer for Broadway and opera, as well as distinguished collector, offers the best available overview of the history of the scenic arts, particularly for the opera. The greatest assets of the book are the variety of designs reproduced (more than 200 designs appear in black and white along with 30 in color from the author's extensive personal collection) and the survey of different scenic styles up to 1975. Oenslager's commentary, although it contains occasional errors of fact, offers useful information from the perspective of a practicing designer. His collection can now be seen at the Pierpont Morgan Library, New York. Another valuable survey by WOLFF, albeit in German and also with some errors, is greatly valuable for its wide selection of reproductions of designs exclusively for opera. BAKER corrects a major error of attribution by Wolff concerning the designs of the first production of *Carmen,* reprinting the original designs and presenting documentation of little-known sources. Included in Baker are useful references to individual designers as well as additional illustrations and an extensive bibliography. The latter is especially useful for references to specialist publications in German, French, and Italian.

Over the centuries, theatrical spaces have been expanded to accommodate larger audiences (both physically and in numbers), and backstage machinery and lighting have developed to incorporate the latest technology. A collection of essays edited by RADICE examines a number of theaters (including the Haymarket, London; Teatro la Fenice, Venice; Opéra, Paris; Schauspielhaus,

Berlin; Wagner Festspielhaus, Bayreuth) and explains how the physical edifices of the particular venues influenced stage design and production of opera for the 18th and 19th centuries.

Several technical developments had a profound influence on the evolution of scene design for opera. The most prominent example was the application of stage lighting powered by controlled flames from natural gas. Its first use for the operatic stage was at the Paris Opéra with the production of *Aladin ou le lampe merveilleux* in 1821. Lighting again played a profoundly important role when electricity supplanted gas as a source of energy. Surprisingly, extensive histories of theatrical lighting are rare; the best is BERGMAN's survey—filled with documents and illustrations—of lighting from candlelight to electricity for both the stage and auditorium.

It was not until the acknowledgment and application of the theories of Adolphe Appia by the iconoclastic designer and director Wieland Wagner—grandson of Richard Wagner—that lighting truly became an integral part of the design and dramatic aesthetic in the production of opera. Two of Appia's works are of fundamental importance. His first major work, APPIA (1982), is perhaps the easiest to read (and accompanied by an excellent introduction). APPIA (1962) is his greatest work; among the major reforms advocated is the clearing the stage of unnecessary or superfluous scenery. He also contends that stage lighting must be a critical part of any operatic production. Beacham gives translations of other documents and essays by the designer, with important introductory material, in APPIA (1989).

Seventeenth-century theories of design and perspective, as well as a discourse on theatrical machinery, are available in HEWITT's collection of documents by Sebastiano Serlio, Niccolo Sabbattini, and Josef Furttenbach. Of these, Serlio's theoretical treatise is important for its discussion of the perspective; Sabbattini deals with stage machinery. In another anthology, Orville K. Larson provides the translation of a text dealing with theater architecture and machinery by another important Italian stage machinist, Fabrizio CARINI MOTTA. Giacomo Torelli is credited with the invention in 1641 of a mechanical method for changing scenery that became a standard for all theaters. BJURSTRÖM provides a fascinating study of Torelli's accomplishments, with ample illustrations of the designs for the earliest public operas in Venice.

Ferdinando Galli-Bibiena penned one of the most important treatises on stage design in 1711, and OGDEN performed a true service by translating and commenting on Bibiena's theories of perspective and the *scena d'angolo* (scenes viewed at an angle). As a bonus, additional translations of Troili, Pozzo, and Orsini are included. DURAND, in a valuable essay, provides a practical explanation of perspective with photographs of a stage model based on one of Bibiena's designs.

One monograph about a later 20th-century designer is FRIEDMAN's work about David Hockney. It is useful for an examination not only of Hockney's styles of design but also of the working methods of the artist and his collaborations with various stage directors and institutions such as Glyndebourne, Covent Garden, Scala, and the Metropolitan.

ARONSON covers postmodern design in one of the clearest essays ever written on the genre. Although he analyzes some of the more recent works for the spoken theater, the author's methodologies can be applied equally to opera. Aronson acknowledges Appia and Edward Gordon Craig—who was active at the beginning of the 20th century—as extremely important innovators while at the same time giving the current designers their due. Aronson notes that "Postmodern design virtually reeks with the presence of the past, and it often pastes together a collage of stylistic imitations that function not as style but as semiotic code." Such observations of scenic styles from the past and present will greatly assist the student striving to understand the possible applications of difficult theoretical concepts such as deconstruction and semiotics to the analysis of late 20th-century opera stage design.

EVAN BAKER

Opera: Staging

Bianconi, Lorenzo, and Giorgio Pestelli, editors, *Opera Production and Its Resources,* translated by Lydia G. Cochrane, Chicago: University of Chicago Press, 1998

Busch, Hans, editor, *Verdi's Otello and Simon Boccanegra in Letters and Documents,* 2 vols., Oxford: Clarendon Press, and New York: Oxford University Press, 1988

Carlson, Marvin, "French Stage Composition from Hugo to Zola," *Educational Theatre Journal* 23 (1971)

Carlson, Marvin, "Hernani's Revolt from the Tradition of French Stage Composition," *Theatre Survey* 1 (1972)

Coe, Doug, "The Original Production Book for *Otello*: An Introduction," *19th Century Music* 2 (1978)

Cohen, H. Robert, "On the Reconstruction of the Visual Elements of French Grand Opera: Unexplored Sources in Parisian Collections," in *Report of the Twelfth International Musicological Congress, Berkeley 1977,* edited by Daniel Heartz and Bonnie Wade, Kassel: Bärenreiter, 1981

———, *The Original Staging Manuals for Ten Parisian Operatic Premières, 1824–1843,* Stuyvesant, New York: Pendragon Press, 1998

———, *The Original Staging Manuals for Twelve Parisian Operatic Premières,* Stuyvesant, New York: Pendragon Press, 1990

Hartmann, Rudolf, *Richard Strauss: The Staging of His Operas and Ballets,* New York: Oxford University Press, 1981

Heartz, Daniel, and Thomas Bauman, editors, *Mozart's Operas,* Berkeley: University of California Press, 1990

Hewitt, Barnard, editor, *The Renaissance Stage: Documents of Serlio, Sabbattini, and Furttenbach,* Coral Gables, Florida: University of Miami Press, 1958

Parker, Roger, editor, *The Oxford Illustrated History of Opera,* Oxford: Oxford University Press, 1994

Radice, Mark A., editor, *Opera in Context: Essays on Historical Staging from the Late Renaissance to the Time of Puccini,* Portland, Oregon: Amadeus Press, 1998

Rosen, David: "The Staging of Verdi's Operas: An Introduction to the Ricordi *Disposizione sceniche,"* in *Report of the Twelfth International Musicological Congress, Berkeley 1977,* edited by Daniel Heartz and Bonnie Wade, Kassel: Bärenreiter, 1981

Rosselli, John, *The Opera Industry in Italy from Cimarosa to Verdi: The Role of the Impresario,* Cambridge: Cambridge University Press, 1984

Savage, Roger, and Matteo Sansone, "*Il Corago* and the Staging of Early Opera: Four Chapters from an Anonymous Treatise circa 1630," *Early Music* 17 (1989)

Sutcliffe, Tom, *Believing in Opera,* Princeton, New Jersey: Princeton University Press, and London: Faber, 1996

To study seriously any history of theatrical production in any form, one must have not only documentation—letters, essays, manuscripts, etc.—but also the means to view reproductions of the designs and photographs (if available) of the actual staging itself. Short of being present at the actual production, research must focus on the iconography of opera in order to obtain a greater understanding of the diverse aspects of operatic staging.

To produce an opera, there must be the means to assemble all of theatrical and musical elements of the staging—music, text, singing, scenery, costuming, and lighting—into a coherent whole. That means resides in the person of the stage director. Such a position, however, did not formally exist until the beginning of the 19th century. Previously, the composer or the librettist (if present), the impresario, theater director, or a leading singer or actor may have been the one to pull together all of the disparate aspects of the production. Documentation in English of 17th-century techniques of theatrical production is, with several notable exceptions, rare, simply because the documentation is ephemeral and much of it lost. The later periods, however, provide more resources for study.

For the 18th century there exists more documentation related to staging and production. The most notable documents are the published letters from Pietro Metastasio—such as those to the castrato Carlo Broschi (Farinelli) and the composer Johann Adolf Hasse—which are filled with exact instructions for staging and positioning of the singers and suggestions for dramatic interpretation of different roles. The letters are examined in HEARTZ and provide an excellent context for late 18th-century operatic stagings, particularly for the operas of Mozart. Iconographic documentation for this time, however, is less plentiful; particularly scarce are references to specific productions, outside of some prints or paintings depicting generic scenes of an opera. Early librettos occasionally reproduce an idealized version of several scenes in the opera, but again, they are only generic and do not refer to any particular staging.

Since the early 1980s, there has been a growing interest in the history of opera staging. The best brief historical overview of operatic production is by Roger Savage in PARKER. An extant 17th-century Italian staging manual for the precursor of the modern stage director, *Il Corago,* has been translated in part into English by SAVAGE and SANSONE. Among its highlights are instructions that archers should be stationed with their crossbows in the wings, ready to shoot any actor who peers out from the wings into the auditorium. Among the most important theatrical publications of the early 17th century is Niccolo Sabbattini's *Manual for Constructing Theatrical Scenes and Machines.* Sabbattini was among the first theater practitioners to elucidate the methods of production and stage machinery in a readable form that would travel throughout Europe. HEWITT presents excellent translations of not only Sabbattini's treatise but also those of Sebastiano Serlio and Josef Furttenbach.

Archival sources have revealed a richness of documentation and iconography from the beginning of the 19th century to the present day. Some scholars' interest in staging has focused on the rich resources of the Parisian libraries—chiefly the Bibliothèque de l'Opéra—and the archives of the Opéra in the Archives Nationales. A wealth of production material is found in the staging manuals that codified the blocking of the performers on the stage—that is, the positions where the singers stood, where they entered, and where they exited the stage, as well as additional directions for the chorus and scene designers. Stage directing of opera began to be codified with staging manuals (*livrets de mise-en-scene*) in 1820 at the Paris Opéra with the production of Auber's *La muette di Portici.* The manuals were published and either sold or rented to other theaters, especially in the French provinces. COHEN (1981) has pioneered the research for this field, publishing a report of his investigations of the Paris sources related to the grand coronation scene of the fourth act of Meyerbeer's *Le Prophète.* His article is a model of clarity and outstanding research.

CARLSON (1971), a theater historian, reports on similar staging manuals found in the archives of the Comédie-Française. In another exemplary article, CARLSON (1972) analyzes the spatial relationships of the stage blocking used in the theater settings in Paris during the first decades of the 19th century. Both essays—which include illustrations—provide a clear picture of the practices of the spoken theater that carried over in part into the lyric theater. Facsimiles of staging manuals for the Paris Opéra published by COHEN (1990, 1998) provide a unique insight into the staging practices of the most important center of opera production for the first half of the 19th century.

Italian staging manuals (*disposizione scenica*) are systematically investigated and discussed by ROSEN. His commentary is an illustrated overview of the manuals published by Ricordi for the operas of Verdi and Puccini. COE has analyzed one staging manual that was specifically created for Verdi's *Otello*. Both essays present valuable reproductions from the manuals themselves, but the impact of the studies is somewhat lessened by the lack of illustrations of the original stage settings. Recently, however, Ricordi has published complete facsimiles of the original manuals and set and costume designs, accompanied by essays, for Verdi's *Otello* and *Simon Boccanegra*, and Boito's *Mefistofeles*. Translations for the *Otello* manual are found in BUSCH (these texts are not free from errors).

For a greater understanding of the environment in which the operas were produced in 19th-century Italy, two publications stand out. ROSSELLI provides, with excellent documentation, a magnificent overview of the period from the perspective of the 19th-century Italian impresario. Drawing on mostly unpublished material, particularly the correspondence and business records of the Florentine impresario Alessandro Lanari, Rosselli depicts the working conditions not only for the singers and composers but also for the backstage personnel, a topic that still remains to be adequately researched. The first volume in translation of a series edited by BIANCONI and PESTELLI presents essays by distinguished musicologist and theater historians—carefully researched, documented, and accompanied by copious bibliographies—of the theatrical, social, and cultural conditions in which opera was presented in Italy from the its beginnings through the 20th century. Aspects of design, production, ballet, and dramaturgy are to be examined in later volumes.

Detailed works in English on opera production for Germany are still sparse, although the essays in RADICE indicate that the situation is slowly improving. One of the most important 19th-century German productions was that of Weber's *Der Freischütz* in Berlin in 1821, which is surveyed in an essay by E. Douglas Bomberger. Schinkel designed the theater in which *Der Freischütz* was premiered, and Bomberger examines how the new architectural design influenced staging of the opera. Also in Radice's collection, Evan analyzes the first staging of *Parsifal* and the construction of Wagner's Festspielhaus and notes the theatrical reforms instituted by the composer, which had a resounding influence on operatic staging, particularly after World War II. Rudolf, one of the more distinguished postwar German opera directors, discusses stagings—accompanied by a rich selection of illustrations—during the 1960s and early 1970s, most notably the productions of Jean-Pierre Ponnelle and Götz

Friedrich. HARTMANN also surveys the Strauss operas from the first performances to the 1980s.

For a broad overview of diverse productions of the last several decades, there exists no standard work, and one must examine reviews in journals, such as *Opera News* and the English *Opera* magazines. SUTCLIFFE has recently attempted to remedy this situation with the publication of a collection of his reviews, many of which center on production. Unfortunately, due to the lack of an extensive selection of illustrations of the works under discussion, this book is a wasted effort. Merely reading about a production—no matter how good the writing—is a poor substitute for being able to see at least some aspect of the staging.

EVAN BAKER

Oratorio: French to 1750

Anthony, James R., *French Baroque Music from Beaujoyeulx to Rameau*, New York: Norton, 1978; revised edition, Portland, Oregon: Amadeus Press, 1997

Cessac, Catherine, *Marc-Antoine Charpentier*, translated by E. Thomas Glasow, Portland, Oregon: Amadeus Press, 1995

Hitchcock, H. Wiley, *Marc-Antoine Charpentier*, Oxford: Oxford University Press, 1990

Smither, Howard E., *A History of the Oratorio*, Volume 1, *The Oratorio in the Baroque Era: Italy, Vienna, Paris*, Chapel Hill: University of North Carolina Press, 1977

French composers, unlike their Italian counterparts, demonstrated almost no interest in the oratorio prior to 1750. This indifference reflects, in part, French aesthetic chauvinism, which resisted the adoption of foreign genres in favor of what were perceived to be native forms and traditions. Throughout the baroque era, French composers of sacred music preferred the grand motet, a genre closely associated with the rarefied taste of the French court. Marc-Antoine Charpentier, however, stands apart from his contemporaries. As a young man, the composer spent several years in Italy, where he studied with Giacomo Carissimi, a distinguished composer of oratorios, who influenced his pupil's compositional style significantly. After returning to France, Charpentier composed some 34 sacred works on Latin texts that many scholars now identify as oratorios. Despite the high musical quality of these works, they attracted little attention and failed to establish an oratorio tradition in France. Between Charpentier's death in 1704 and 1750, only a handful of other composers approached the genre. During this period, Sébastien de Brossard, Louis-Nicholas Clérambault, and Jacques-François Lochon composed one oratorio each. A fourth French oratorio from this time is anonymous. The paucity of French oratorios prior to 1750 has led some scholars to contest the categorization of the 34 pieces by Charpentier as examples of the genre. While there is general agreement that Charpentier introduced many elements associated with the Italian oratorio into these vocal works, subtle arguments over musical style and liturgical function have led some authors to reject the term *oratorio* and to suggest alternative classifications when discussing the compositions.

SMITHER examines the development of the French oratorio within a general history of the genre. One of his goals is to clarify the formal boundaries of the oratorio and to generate a clear set of historically appropriate and accurate terms to use when discussing the genre. To this end, Smither considers any substantial work of unstaged sacred music that possesses a dramatically organized text with dialogue or narration to be an oratorio. The fact that Charpentier never used the term *oratorio* to describe his works does not affect Smither's decision to identify them as such. On the basis of his criteria and the clear stylistic influence of Carissimi on Charpentier's compositions, the author treats 22 of Charpentier's 34 pieces as oratorios. The remaining compositions are dismissed on the basis of their brevity. The strength of this study is that it places the oratorios, and Charpentier himself, within a broad, international context. The author compares Charpentier's compositions with those of his Italian contemporaries in order to illustrate their stylistic innovation. Smither ends his study with an analysis of *Judicium Salomonis* (*The Judgment of Solomon*), one of Charpentier's more impressive oratorios.

In general, ANTHONY agrees with Smither and classifies these vocal works of Charpentier as oratorios as well. Anthony recognizes the fact that the oratorio did not have a tradition in France immediately before or after Charpentier but argues that the stylistic similarities with earlier Italian oratorios justify his use of this category. To a large extent, the author adopts this position out of practical considerations. He believes that these works fit our modern-day perceptions of what constitutes an oratorio and therefore will be understood as oratorios regardless of the term employed. Like Smither, Anthony focuses his attention on the longest of these compositions and emphasizes their resemblance to the oratorios of Carissimi. In a concise and straightforward manner, the author describes Charpentier's style and draws the reader's attention to relevant scholarly literature.

HITCHCOCK disagrees with the decision to categorize these works by Charpentier as oratorios. An expert on the music of the French baroque in general and an authority on the music of Charpentier in particular, Hitchcock has extensively studied the sources, function, and contexts associated with Charpentier's sacred music. He eschews the term *oratorio* in favor of a new classification, *dramatic motet*, when discussing this repertoire. He bases his decision on a careful consideration of the function rather than the style of the music. Italian oratorios of the late 17th century, he points out, were not used during the Mass, the central worship service of Roman Catholi-

cism. Rather, they were performed at less formally organized prayer meetings, providing a form of devotional entertainment within a paraliturgical setting. Charpentier, however, most likely intended his works for performance as part of the Mass. In this respect, these so-called oratorios served the same function as the grand and petit motets, which were regularly performed during the Mass as service music. Although recognizing the dramatic nature of these works, Hitchcock does not believe these features warrant the use of the label *oratorio*. In his opinion, the liturgical role of this music in combination with its unusual position within the history of French sacred music seriously distinguishes it from the genre of oratorio.

In her study of Charpentier's life and work, CESSAC offers an extended discussion of the composer's oratorios. Although deeply indebted to the scholarship of Hitchcock, Cessac refers to the works in question as Latin oratorios. The issue of liturgical function that Hitchcock raises is not addressed here; Cessac makes no distinction between music composed expressly for the Mass and that intended for use within paraliturgical religious services. From her perspective, the musical similarities between Charpentier's music and the oratorios of Carissimi provide ample justification for the classification. Cessac argues for a close identification of Charpentier's Latin oratorios with those composed by Charpentier's one-time teacher, and she takes care to highlight the musical similarities between the works of both men. Cessac concludes her review of Charpentier's oratorios with a detailed analysis of individual works. Like Smither and Anthony, she focuses her attention on the longer, more substantial pieces.

MICHAEL E. MCCLELLAN

Oratorio: German to 1750

Boyd, Malcolm, *Bach*, London: Dent, 1983; 2nd edition, 1990

Daw, Stephen, *The Music of Johann Sebastian Bach: The Choral Works*, Rutherford, New Jersey: Fairleigh Dickinson University Press, 1981

Moser, Hans Joachim, *Heinrich Schütz: His Life and Works*, translated by Carl F. Pfatteicher, St. Louis, Missouri: Concordia, 1959

Pahlen, Kurtum, et al., *The World of the Oratorio: Oratorio, Mass, Requiem, Te Deum, Stabat Mater, and Large Cantatas*, translated by Judith Schaeffer, Portland, Oregon: Amadeus Press, and Aldershot: Scolar Press, 1990

Smither, Howard E., *A History of the Oratorio*, Volume 2, *The Oratorio in the Baroque Era: Protestant Germany and England*, Chapel Hill: University of North Carolina Press, 1977

Steinitz, Paul, "German Church Music," in *Opera and Church Music 1630–1750*, edited by Anthony Lewis and Nigel Fortune, New Oxford History of Music, vol. 5, London: Oxford University Press, 1975

Walker, Diane Parr, and Paul Walker, *German Sacred Polyphonic Vocal Music between Schütz and Bach: Sources and Critical Editions*, Warren, Michigan: Harmonie Park Press, 1992

The oratorio began to emerge in Germany as early as the mid-17th century, but its development was slow, and only in the 18th century did a somewhat clearly defined genre take hold and find its place in German musical life. Even then, the term *oratorium* seems to have been applied to a number of different musical settings and types, including the *historia*, Passion, sacred dramatic dialogue, and a number of other semidramatic vocal forms. As cultivated by such notable composers as Schütz, Buxtehude, and J.S. Bach, the German oratorio remained a loosely defined form, characterized by only the broadest of techniques and styles. Consequently, modern scholarship is marked by a variety of interpretations of and approaches to the genre: some compare the German oratorio to Italian models, others trace its uniquely Germanic ancestry through the *historia*, Passions, and other forms, while still others dismiss the form with few words. Any present attempt to derive a definitive picture of this unique genre from existing literature is likely to be met with certain amounts of frustration and confusion. The situation would be tremendously improved by the publication of a full-length study of the topic but, to date, none has been forthcoming. The student is forced to rely, then, on research contained within a number of volumes not necessarily devoted primarily to the topic at hand.

By far, the most important and complete investigation of the German oratorio is found in the second volume of SMITHER's authoritative study. Smither's approach is laudable because it aims to present a complete picture of the German oratorio in the baroque era, beginning with a study of antecedent forms such as the *historia* and culminating with an examination of the contributions of J.S. Bach. Indeed, the author's broad survey of the development of the genre in Germanic regions is superior to any other, leading the reader through a smooth, clearly presented contextual and chronological overview. The use of musical examples and analytical descriptions of the works under discussion should be welcomed by the more advanced student, although they may render portions of the text less comprehensible to general readers. Nonetheless, the narrative remains clear, immensely readable, and logically organized, and it is supported by thorough research reflecting sound scholarship. Until such time as a more thorough or up-to-date study emerges, Smither's volume stands as the best single source for information on the topic.

A less thorough, but still useful, discussion of the oratorio is found in STEINITZ, a chapter devoted to German church music. Its primary value is in the relative brevity and manageable scope of the article, which is structured as a short chronological survey of the repertory from Schütz to Bach. The oratorio is but one of the genres considered in this essay, which allows the reader to place this form in context of the broad scope of German religious music, including the Passion, Mass, motet, and cantata. The author has not engaged in musical analysis or discussion; thus, there is little to be learned of the actual music or even musical style. As a short historical survey of the German oratorio and contemporary forms, however, the article has merit.

Also useful as sources of information, although usually somewhat more restricted than general surveys, are studies devoted to individual composers, several of which have chapters or discussions devoted to the topic at hand. Among the earliest of German oratorio composers was Heinrich Schütz, whose life and works have been masterfully documented by MOSER. Although dated, this volume remains, the finest study of the composer and his vocal music available. The author gives considerable attention to Schütz's so-called *Easter Oratorio, Christmas Oratorio,* the three Passions (antecedents of the oratorio), and four additional works identified as oratorio-like. Additionally, Moser considers works such as *Musikalische Exequien,* which, he contends, move toward the oratorio tradition and include elements related to the genre. Each composition is treated with extensive, in-depth musical analysis and commentary. The entire text presupposes a fairly thorough acquaintance with the genre and its history, often referring to earlier works, styles, compositional techniques, and the like. Therefore, although the novice would be advised to avoid this book, for the serious student it is an indispensable examination of the early German oratorio in the hands of its first true master.

From its beginnings with Schütz, the German oratorio underwent various stages of development before reaching its first zenith at the hands of J.S. Bach, whose three contributions to the genre draw on the long tradition of Lutheran religious music. BOYD's biography of the composer provides a smooth and concise survey of Bach's Easter, Christmas, and Ascension oratorios, as well as other related vocal forms cultivated by the composer. Although not an in-depth discussion and lacking in musical analysis, the treatment of Bach's oratorios is, nonetheless, quite readable and easily understood by the nonspecialist. It is, therefore, a useful introduction to Bach's oratorio offerings.

More extensive coverage of Bach's oratorios is found in DAW's survey of the composer's choral works. This narrowly focused volume, one of the only works in English addressing Bach's choral output, is somewhat brief and its treatment of individual works rather cursory. Organized in chronological fashion, this survey shows, to some extent, the development of Bach's choral style and allows the reader to place compositions in the context of the composer's oeuvre. However, the author has not attempted to provide analytical or historical commentary and has geared his work to nonspecialists with the intent of acquainting them with the characteristic sound of Bach's choral repertory. The oratorios are discussed in some detail, although the text is primarily concerned with issues of performance practice, vocal requirements, and related topics. Its treatment of the oratorios in their chronological position among Bach's compositions is valuable for the musical amateur, as is the focus on the uniquely Bachian elements of the music.

Mention should also be made of two works of a reference nature. WALKER and WALKER attempts to list all extant German sacred vocal music for three or more voices dating from 1650 to 1700, covering the often neglected repertory between Schütz and Bach. The book provides titles together with information on texts, scoring, and the sources for a large body of music. PAHLEN's volume is not limited to German music, nor is it limited to the oratorio, also covers the Mass, Requiem Mass, Te Deum, Stabat Mater, and cantatas. The text is arranged alphabetically by composers, with major works then treated individually. After a brief biographical sketch, each entry provides information concerning the text, language, dates of composition, dates of performance, form/structure, scoring, and personnel. A short discussion of the plot and general historical comments follow. Although more extensive coverage of German oratorios is to be found in items discussed earlier, Pahlen brings together, in an easy-to-use format, much information not readily accessible elsewhere.

MICHAEL VAUGHN

Oratorio: Italian to 1750

Arnold, Denis, and Elsie Arnold, *The Oratorio in Venice*, London: Royal Musical Association, 1986

Crowther, Victor, *The Oratorio in Modena*, Oxford: Clarendon Press, 1992

Massenkeil, Gunther, *The Oratorio*, translated by A.C. Howie, Cologne: Arno Volk Verlag, 1970

Smither, Howard E., *A History of the Oratorio, Volume 1, The Oratorio in the Baroque Era: Italy, Vienna, Paris*, Chapel Hill: University of North Carolina Press, 1977

The oratorio has been defined traditionally as an unstaged, sacred musical work with either a dramatic text or a text that combines narrative and dramatic elements. The terminology for this genre has been problematic because such works were called by many different names in the first century after the genre's inception. The earliest monographs on this subject were written by Italian and German scholars; indeed, Arnold Schering's *Geschichte des Oratoriums* (1911) served as the standard work on the oratorio until the late 1970s, when publication of Smither's three-volume study commenced. One of

Smither's goals in publishing his extensive work was to point out the numerous remaining gaps in our knowledge of the genre and to encourage further investigation. The subsequent studies by the Arnolds and by Crowther, each focusing on a specific Italian city, demonstrate a specialized approach to research on this topic; the authors' narrow focus on Venice and Modena, respectively, flesh out the sparse coverage given these cities by Smither.

In his anthology of oratorio works, MASSENKEIL provides a succinct overview of the history of the oratorio from its inception to the 20th century. He introduces problems associated with terminology and discusses forerunners of style and genre that influenced the early development of oratorio, such as monodic singing styles in early opera and the *lauda*, simple strophic songs on sacred subjects. He then proceeds to identify the distinctive qualities of the Latin and Italian oratorios and names composers associated with each type of oratorio. He describes basic stylistic traits associated with these composers or schools of composers, illustrating these characteristics with copious musical excerpts. The translation reads poorly at times, tending toward wordiness and even occasionally contradicting itself, but the compilation of oratorio excerpts that comprises the bulk of this work is excellent; indeed, the musical anthology portion is the feature that makes this book useful for the student of the oratorio.

SMITHER's three-volume work on the history of the oratorio, which combines comprehensive coverage of secondary sources with extensive research of primary source materials, is the definitive work on this subject. The topic is vast, however, and, as the author points out, the study remains general in scope; no attempt is made to create comprehensive lists of particular composers' outputs or to offer an exact record of the number of composers of oratorios working in a given city during a specific time period. Rather, Smither has selected composers and their musical compositions based on "previous research, historical significance, inherent musical significance, and the importance of works in today's performing repertory." He begins by addressing the issue of terminology, deferring to baroque concepts of the genre when formulating his definition of the oratorio. He carefully describes the social context in which the oratorio developed in Rome (amid the 16th-century fervor of the Counter Reformation) and provides details about the paraliturgical functions of both oratorios and their antecedents (*laude*, sacred dialogues) in the new oratories (prayer halls of a new religious order, the Oratorians) of Rome. In subsequent chapters ("Mid-Century Rome I: The Oratorio Volgare," "Mid-Century Rome II: Carissimi and the Oratorio Latino," "The Later Baroque I: Social Contexts, Patrons, Composers, Poets," and "The Later Baroque II: The Libretto and Music"), Smither continues describing the development of the oratorio with numerous musical examples that demonstrate his points;

for instance, his discussion of Carissimi includes many examples illustrating this composer's reliance on musical-rhetorical figures. The author is also careful to provide some social context for the continuing development of the oratorio as the 17th century progressed, including discussions of important patrons and performance halls, as well as translations of primary sources that provide accounts of performances. Because the oratorio in Italy after 1720 shows strong pre-Classical tendencies, Smither continues coverage of the oratorio in Italy between 1720 and 1750 in the third volume of this set; his approach in that discussion remains the same as in the first volume. This history is geared to the music student; basic knowledge of music history and theory will suffice in order to grasp the author's points. Due to the sheer size of its scope and its date of publication, the book has limitations. For specialized topics, such as the music of a particular composer or geographic locale, the reader will need to consult other, more tightly focused studies. The bibliography, while thorough, is now outdated. Furthermore, the author concentrates on the development of the oratory in Rome obscuring similar musical developments in other cities that were not necessarily associated with the religious order of the Oratorian.

ARNOLD and ARNOLD's slender monograph on the oratorio in Venice is highly specialized. The authors focus on the period between 1660 and 1777, examining the music at five different institutions: the oratory church of the Fava and the four charitable institutions (*ospedali*) known today as conservatories. They provide a thorough account of the oratorios performed in Venice gleaned from firsthand research of primary materials that are amply cited. A fair number of musical examples are presented throughout the text; however, the authors offer little discussion and no analysis of these examples. Most helpful to scholars is the appendix, a compilation of all oratorios that can be documented as having been performed in Venice between 1662 and 1809. The 75 pages of text that describe the arrival and development of the oratorio in Venice are certainly helpful to scholars of Venetian musical history but may be off-putting to other readers. Numerous translations of primary source documents replete with unfamiliar monetary values, place names, and unknown musicians are inserted in the commentary; untranslated Italian and Latin words also pepper the text. The reader is expected to know what an oratorio is and be familiar with its basic history, and must also be familiar with Venetian musical history. For example, the Arnolds do not explain how the four Venetian conservatories functioned in that society; only a slight paragraph serves to remind the reader of the origins of the genre.

CROWTHER's work on the oratorio at Modena is an exemplary specialized study of this genre. The initial chapter discusses both the establishment of the Este dynasty in Modena and the important religious order devoted to Catholic reform, the Theatines. Each of these institutions, influenced by the other, exerted great influence on the development of the oratorio, making Modena one of the most important centers for this genre in the last quarter of the 17th century. In subsequent chapters, the author divides the development of the oratorio into three phases, 1674 to 1681, 1682 to 1686, and 1686 to 1702. In each of these chapters, Crowther provides background on the important composers of oratorio, describes the oratorio seasons and the general types of oratorios performed, and discusses developments within the court that affected the oratorio seasons. In the remaining ten chapters, the author selects ten oratorios by ten different composers from the three phases for in-depth examination. He follows the same formula for each chapter. First, he briefly considers the libretto, including the source of its derivation, a summation of its literary style, and an outline of the dramatic structure. Crowther then examines the music, describing the breakdown of the work into discrete musical numbers and identifying their type (e.g., continuo aria). He assesses the stylistic approaches of the different composers to the various arias and recitative sections they set to music and provides ample excerpts from the works (most of this repertory does not yet exist in modern edition). Musical examples are discussed to some extent, but the author's points are not indicated in the music; the reader should be familiar with basic theoretical concepts and elements of baroque musical style. Its specialized topic makes this book of limited use to those interested in the general history of the oratorio, but it does provide an excellent example of the kind of work that still needs to be undertaken for various geographic locales as researchers seek to develop a more comprehensive view of the Italian oratorio in the 17th and early 18th centuries.

ROARK MILLER

Orchestration

Becker, Heinz, *History of Instrumentation,* translated by Robert Kolben, Cologne: Volk, 1964

Berlioz, Hector, *A Treatise upon Modern Instrumentation and Orchestration,* translated by Mary Cowden Clarke, London: Novello, 1858

Berlioz, Hector, and Richard Strauss, *Treatise on Instrumentation,* translated by Theodore Front, New York: Kalmus, 1948

Carse, Adam von Ahn, *The History of Orchestration,* London: Kegan, Paul, Trench, Trubner, 1925; corrected edition, New York: Dover, 1964

Del Mar, Norman, *Anatomy of the Orchestra,* Berkeley: University of California Press, and London: Faber, 1981

Forsyth, Cecil, *Orchestration,* London: Macmillan, 1914; 2nd edition, 1936

Kennan, Kent, and Donald Grantham, *The Technique of Orchestration,* New York: Prentice Hall, 1952; 5th edition, Upper Saddle River, New Jersey: Prentice Hall, 1997

Koechlin, Charles, *Traité de l'orchestration,* 4 vols., Paris: Eschig, 1954–59

Perone, James E., *Orchestration Theory: A Bibliography,* Westport, Connecticut: Greenwood Press, 1996

Piston, Walter, *Orchestration,* New York: Norton, and London: Gollancz, 1955

Read, Gardner, *Style and Orchestration,* New York: Schirmer Books, 1979

Rimsky-Korsakov, Nicolai, *Principles of Orchestration,* 2 vols., edited by Maximilian Steinberg, translated by Edward Agate, Berlin, Edition russe de musique, 1912; reprint, 2 vols. in 1, New York: Dover, 1964

Stiller, Andrew, *Handbook of Instrumentation,* Berkeley: University of California Press, 1985; 2nd edition, Philadelphia, Pennsylvania: Kallisti Music Press, 1994

Orchestration is a word begging its root: interpretations of its meaning over time have varied according to assumptions about what might or might not have constituted an orchestra, and although the word may indeed be traced to dance, orchestration from the common-practice period through the late 20th century has generally been understood to be the discriminating mastery of combining different instrumental sounds. *Instrumentation,* hence, is a companion term to orchestration, although of wider purview.

The literature on orchestration is vast, comprising specialized studies pertaining to instruments, genres, and composers of virtually every period, as well as numerous texts for performers, composers, and listeners alike, which, especially in the 20th century, evince evolving interpretations of the word *orchestration* (e.g., orchestration for theater and school groups, wind ensembles, jazz bands of different sizes, dance, radio, music for the film, etc.).

PERONE traces much of this diversity in his bibliography, but not all entries are annotated, and many refer to reviews, academic theses, and related materials. His separate listings of band-related and jazz-arranging studies, the chronological list of treatises, and the general bibliography, however, are very helpful.

For a fine idiosyncratic introduction, see DEL MAR, an explanation of the intricacies of modern orchestras, instrumentation, and related matters by instrumental family (seating arrangements, repertories, technical devices and peculiarities, and the like). Conceived for a late 20th-century composer (Thea Musgrave), Del Mar nonetheless writes for a wide and diverse audience of listeners.

Histories of orchestration do not abound, but Carse, Becker, and Read each survey particular eras or themes. CARSE, although dated, begins with illustrations of 16th- and 17th-century instruments drawn from early sources (Mersenne, Praetorius) and outlines the emerging string orchestras of Lully, Purcell, and Scarlatti. The author sees the evolution of orchestras and orchestration as falling into two eras divided by the deaths of J.S. Bach and Handel. A transitional time of C.P.E. Bach, Gluck, and Hasse gives way to a second era from Haydn and Mozart forward to Strauss, Debussy, and Elgar.

BECKER's study pairs a persuasive but sweeping historical survey (with Wagner at its apex) with elegantly reproduced, full-score musical examples from the 17th through 20th centuries that underpin the author's historical convictions. Becker also provides a valuable chronology of instrumental treatises written between 1794 and 1959.

READ introduces complex issues of style in separate chapters devoted to what he defines as the principal historical categories (preclassical and classical forward to exotic and avant-garde orchestras). Each chapter describes changing instrumentation, prominent composers, and contemporary repertories with short examples in score.

Emphasizing practical concerns, FORSYTH offers some historical background to his discussions of instrumental families and venues but concentrates on the mechanics of orchestration: he covers pitch ranges, transpositions, and appropriate scoring and offers technical insights and specific advice (e.g., why string players must play in position—as opposed to keyboard players—and why their figuration must be conceived accordingly).

Many primary sources are accessible. BERLIOZ's statement near the end of his essential 19th-century study still provides the departure point for most useful discourse: "The orchestra may be considered as *a large instrument* capable of uttering at once or successively a multitude of sounds of different kinds." Among many compelling reasons for reading Berlioz is the author's humor: descriptions of the contemporary ranges, transpositions, and subtleties of all instruments are accompanied by an engaging and running commentary. Considerable space is devoted to new instruments (members of the saxophone family, various percussion instruments, etc.), and extended musical examples (drawn most often from Gluck, Spontini, Meyerbeer, Beethoven, and Mozart) offer a window on the active orchestral repertory of the time that were the inspirations for Berlioz's codification of orchestration practices. Discussions of vocal forces and the relatively new role of the conductor (with extensive technical advice on how to beat time and lead an ensemble) conclude his remarkable study. Other handbooks and instrumental manuals anticipated Berlioz, but his was the first truly systematic and comprehensive work. Its influence was tremendous, as evidenced in elaborations by composers such as Richard Strauss and Widor.

BERLIOZ and STRAUSS represents Strauss's effort to revise Berlioz and to close certain gaps in orchestration practices in the wake of Wagner, whose scores—Strauss freely admits in his pungent introduction (1904)—"are the alpha and omega of my additions to this work; they embody the only important progress in the art of instrumentation since Berlioz." Berlioz's original text remains (save for the organ chapter), but Strauss inserts running glosses and contemporary musical examples (works from Wagner, as well as his own compositions). As Berlioz had looked to Gluck (among others), Strauss sees Wagner as the inspiration for his newly modern orchestra. Wagner, despite enormous contributions, unfortunately left no organized study of orchestration and contradictions in his prose essays.

Although RIMSKY-KORSAKOV's highly original treatise preceded Strauss's study, it remained unpublished in the West until after the latter was published. Rimsky-Korsakov collapsed Berlioz's mechanics of instrumentation into one chapter, treating separately melody, harmony (voicing and part writing), the sharing and movement of materials between instruments, and voice (solo, ensembles, chorus, and orchestra). Musical examples are drawn from Rimsky-Korsakov's own works and are presented in a separate volume.

Subsequent 20th-century studies have followed Berlioz's model to a considerable degree. Ravel once considered writing a treatise, but it was his close friend KOECHLIN who succeeded. His magnificent four-volume work is divided between instrumentation proper and the subtleties of 20th-century orchestration (chamber and opera scoring, keyboard transcriptions, jazz, polytonal/atonal scoring, and more). Moreover, Koechlin uses numerous 20th-century musical examples (from Stravinsky, Debussy, Ravel, Bartók, and his own works). The sheer scope of his musical thought and supporting materials dwarfs other studies.

Various works from the mid-20th century forward have proven practically successful, among them PISTON, which is far less comprehensive than others and curiously dedicated to classical-era principles of instrumental combination. STILLER is quite fascinating because it offers no scored examples (the work is in memory of Praetorius), yet it includes scrupulous illustrations and information for all instruments in current use, as well as those reconstructed and/or reintroduced for historical performance purposes. Stiller's vocal section provides copious material concerning registers, paired-vowel ranges, the international phonetic alphabet, and even a section on whistling. KENNAN and GRANTHAM is adapted to recent requirements such as school-orchestra scoring while trying to retain the comprehensive ideals of Berlioz. Such a distillation is not easy, but Kennan and Grantham's book is exemplary in offering organized assignments, listening examples, and many scoring exercises.

STEPHEN ZANK

Organum

Crocker, Richard, and David Hiley, editors, *The Early Middle Ages to 1300,* New Oxford History of Music, vol. 2, Oxford: Oxford University Press, 1990

Erickson, Raymond, editor, *Musica Enchiriadis and Scholica Enchiriadis,* New Haven, Connecticut: Yale University Press, 1995

Karp, Theodore, *The Polyphony of Saint Martial and Santiago de Compostela,* 2 vols., Berkeley: University of California Press, 1992

Palisca, Claude V., editor, *Hucbald, Guido, and John on Music: Three Medieval Treatises,* translated by Warren Babb, New Haven, Connecticut: Yale University Press, 1978

Planchart, Alejandro Enrique, *The Repertory of Tropes at Winchester,* 2 vols., Princeton, New Jersey: Princeton University Press, 1977

Rankin, Susan, and David Hiley, editors, *Music in the Medieval English Liturgy: Plainsong and Mediaeval Music Society Centennial Essays,* Oxford: Clarendon Press, 1993

Roesner, Edward, et al., editors, *Le Magnus Liber Organi de Notre-Dame de Paris,* Monaco: Éditions de l'Oiseau-Lyre, 1993–

Waite, William, *The Rhythm of Twelfth-Century Polyphony: Its Theory and Practice,* Westport, Connecticut: Greenwood, 1954

Wright, Craig, *Music and Ceremony at Notre Dame of Paris, 500–1500,* Cambridge: Cambridge University Press, 1989

The word *organum* carried many meanings in the Middle Ages. Rooted in the Greek word for an apparatus or instrument, the Latin term often denoted musical instruments, the organ in particular. Organum was also used to mean a song of praise, a psalm, or even the entire Psalter. In its adjectival form, it denoted qualities of precise measure and proportion as well as an instrumental quality of sound. Its application to polyphony grew out of this latter sense and was applied not only to the sonorous note-against-note texture described in the ninth-century didactic treatise *Musica Enchiriadis,* but also to the florid melodies that decorated the slow-moving chant notes in the Aquitanian and early Parisian repertories of polyphony.

Readers can find the basic rules of composing early polyphony in a number of medieval music theory treatises edited by PALISCA and by ERICKSON. Each translation in this series is prefaced by a brief introduction that outlines the historical context and salient contributions of the treatise at hand. Illustrative examples in the texts are rendered both in modern musical notation and, where appropriate, in reproductions of the figures as they appear in the manuscript sources. The treatises in these volumes document three centuries of changing musical practices and pedagogy and offer students of this period an indispensable resource.

In addition to offering the first extensive collection of transcriptions of Parisian two-voiced organum, WAITE's book contains a historical overview of the Notre Dame school of polyphony as well as a detailed exposition of the groundbreaking notational developments that characterize the repertory. Waite argues that the two-part organum composed by Léonin can be interpreted according to the principles of modal rhythm. In this system, note heads are grouped to form patterns of ligatures that in turn denote repeating stereotyped patterns of long and short notes. The applicability of modal rhythm to this repertory has been a point of much scholarly debate, with opinions ranging from Waite's modal interpretation to more recent assertions that the ligatures in Léonin's organum contain no rhythmic information at all, or at least no recoverable information. Current opinion remains divided. Although much of Waite's work has been refined and in some cases overturned by more recent scholarship, it remains a seminal study.

The first large-scale collection of polyphonic music in Europe, dating to about the year 1000, is the cycle of polyphonic chants preserved in the Winchester Tropers, composed for use in Winchester Cathedral. This music receives its most comprehensive treatment in the two-volume repertorial study by PLANCHART. Following a brief historical overview of late tenth- and early 11th-century England, Planchart gives detailed descriptions of the principal sources of this music, including inventories and remarks on dates, origins, and the interrelationship of the manuscripts. The author's main goal is to trace the development of the repertory by studying individual tropes and their concordances. From this investigation, Planchart discerns a growing concern among copyists, a concern that suggests a search for authoritative versions of the pieces. While such conclusions are open to question, Planchart's work remains an important starting point for studies of this musical tradition.

WRIGHT's book is among the most important contributions to the study of Parisian polyphony since the publication of Waite's volume 35 years earlier. Wright traces the development of the liturgy at Notre Dame Cathedral of Paris from 500 to 1500, and the detailed information he gathers on the personnel and ritual observances of this church provides an unsurpassed foundation for the investigation of several long-standing scholarly problems. The two most significant results of Wright's study are the documentary identification of the composer Léonin, whose very existence some scholars had questioned, and the author's proposition that Léonin's collection of two-part polyphonic compositions, the *Magnus liber organi,* was created solely for the cathedral of Notre Dame in Paris. Moreover, Wright argues that the three principal surviving manuscripts do not bear witness to some kind of repertorial evolution, as had been suggested by scholars in earlier studies, but rather represent three independent renditions of the same repertory.

CROCKER and HILEY's anthology includes two relevant essays. Sarah Fuller's "Early Polyphony" offers the best historical overview of early polyphony currently available. Fuller surveys the theory and musical compositions that survive from the mid-ninth to the mid-12th century. After reviewing arguments on the origins of organum and presenting the numerous semantic uses of the word, she traces the stylistic developments of polyphonic music composed from ca. 850 to ca. 1150. For the first two centuries of this time period, her study is rooted in a careful discussion of theoretical treatises, the sources of the earliest surviving polyphony. Her treatment of the subject is notably holistic; considerations of theoretical principles and analyses of musical works are presented in complementary, illuminating ways. Two comparative tables provide the reader with synoptic views of the major organum treatises, outlining their dates, pedagogical aims, and theoretical contributions.

Janet Knapp's overview, "Polyphony at Notre Dame of Paris," in the same collection covers the period ranging from the middle of the 12th century through the first third of the 13th century. The focal point of her essay is a discussion of the compositional traits of Parisian polyphony, but she also includes comments on the principal sources and a survey of modal rhythm. Although her evaluation of the music is sound and useful, some aspects of her historical account have been superseded—in particular, her remarks on the origins of the earliest manuscript of Parisian polyphony (known as W1) and on our knowledge of Léonin's life and activity (for the most up-to-date discussion of this topic, see Wright).

KARP offers the reader an edition of and commentary on the entire polyphonic repertory preserved in Aquitanian sources and the Codex Calixtinus. In the first volume of this two-volume work, the author gives a detailed explanation and justification of his editorial choices, which are guided chiefly by controversial ideas on the structural role of consonance in this music. He postulates an underlying metrical framework that consists of alternating strong and weak beats, and his decisions about the rhythm, text declamation, and alignment of voices all derive from a belief that consonant sonorities must occur on strong beats. The lack of evidence for such a rhythmic framework and the unusual readings that the system necessitates have prevented this edition from being widely accepted.

Janet Rankin's essay "Winchester Polyphony: The Early Theory and Practices of Organum" in RANKIN and HILEY is similar to Fuller's chapter in Crocker and Hiley in its holistic approach. Rankin's aim is to move away from "theory-dominated" accounts of early polyphony because such views often leave little room for the judgment and creativity of the performer. Two polyphonic responsories from the repertory of Winchester organum form the heart of her discussion. She identifies points of similarity and disagreement between these works and contemporaneous theoretical writings. Her discussion of the points of disagreement shows that performance practices were far more sensitive to the exigencies of the text and the musical structure of the chant than any written principles would suggest. Rankin also examines a range of polyphonic realizations of common chant phrases to demonstrate that singers did use standard patterns, but with a flexibility that served the articulation of the chant. Rankin's treatment of this repertory is the best to date; its more general contribution to our understanding of the performance of polyphony in this period is likewise seminal.

The new edition of Parisian polyphony being published under ROESNER's purview aims to provide scholars and performers with readings informed by the most recent musicological research. The volumes containing the two-part organum in the manuscript W2 (edited by Thomas B. Payne) and the three- and four-part organum (edited by Roesner) follow a similar format. Introductory comments by the editors address the nature of the repertory and its relationship to the liturgy at Notre Dame of Paris; the editors also include inventories of concordant sources and remarks on performance practices. Payne's edition of two-part organum contains an excellent essay on the interpretation of rhythm.

MICHAEL MCGRADE

Ornamentation: Renaissance

Brown, Howard Mayer, *Embellishing Sixteenth-Century Music,* London: Oxford University Press, 1976

Conforti, Giovanni Luca, *The Joy of Ornamentation,* White Plains, New York: Pro/Am Music Resources, 1989

Ganassi, Sylvestro, *Opera Intitulata Fontegara Venice 1535; A Treatise on the Art of Playing the Recorder and of Free Ornamentation,* edited by Hildemarie Peter, translated by Dorothy Swainson, Berlin-Lichterfelde: Lienau, 1959

One of the most important topics relating to the performance of Renaissance music, and one much discussed then and now, is ornamentation. Ornamentation was, however, essentially a matter of improvisation and hence is poorly documented. However, the three volumes discussed here, taken together, provide both general and specific information regarding the topic; two are important instruction books of the period, and one provides a broad, synthetic historical perspective on the subject.

BROWN, in its mere 77 pages, provides the best introduction to the subject at hand. It offers a comprehensive overview of 16th-century practices of ornamentation, especially in Italy, at a time when Italy assumed the leadership of European music. In his introduction, the author reviews the sources for his study: ten Italian instruction books on ornamentation by nine authors; three comprehensive music treatises with relevant material; keyboard instruction books from Germany, Italy, and Spain; and

the corpus of 16th-century lute and keyboard music (which preserves versions of pieces with written-out embellishments). The main body of the book treats in separate chapters ornaments on single notes ("graces"), fast-note passage work replacing intervallic progressions (*passaggi* or "divisions"), extant pieces with ornaments provided by Renaissance musicians, different conventions of ornamentation for solo and ensemble performance, and similarities and differences between voices and instruments in matters of ornamentation. Although the approach is topical rather than chronological, the reader obtains a clear picture of chronological development in the style of ornamentation; for example, the later decades of the century see the element of virtuosity becoming, in many instances, an end in itself—a subject treated in the last chapter as well as in various places throughout the book. This book is essentially a musicological analysis and comparison of primary documents, but the author, for many years a collegium musicum director, occasionally provides ideas and notated examples of how the modern performer of Renaissance music might apply period practices. The book, which is accessible to the general reader but also useful to the specialist, thus combines in an exemplary way the virtues of careful scholarship and musical imagination.

GANASSI is the first of a series of instruction manuals on ornamentation published during the Renaissance and hence is of particular historical value. The treatise is aimed primarily at amateur players of the recorder (indeed, it is the only recorder manual of the 16th century), with much information about fingering and articulation (tonguing). The material on ornamentation, presented in a systematic way, is also applicable to the voice and all melody instruments, although the author's concerns do not include ornaments on single notes but are focused entirely on division, which he describes in terms of three factors: note value(s), proportion (meter), and melodic shape, each of which can be simple or compound. Thus, a division is compound in its note values, when more than one note value is used; compound in proportion when the meter or proportion changes in a division; compound in melodic shape (translated here as "melodic development") when successive motives within a division, or successive divisions, are not the same. There are further refinements of this classification as well. Most of the book is taken up with notated examples of divisions that represent ornamented versions of simple intervals and such intervals with one interpolated ornamental note; for each of these there can be up to ten divisions, thus generating hundreds of model examples that can be absorbed by the student and employed spontaneously in performance. There are also examples of divisions utilizing different meters or proportions (e.g., five notes in the time of four)—a laborious but concrete way of suggesting the rhythmic and inventive freedom possessed by the Renaissance musician. Indeed, Ganassi's stated purpose is to demonstrate to the student "every imaginable" option "so that you may have the possibility of making music entirely to your taste." The volume contains, in addition to the *Fontegara,* an appendix giving 175 examples of how a single cadential melodic phrase might be embellished.

CONFORTI, the shortest book of the three discussed here, represents Renaissance ornamentation at the point it began to be incorporated into the early baroque style. It consists mainly of musical examples and complements Ganassi both by showing the style of ornamentation characteristic of the late Renaissance and by being aimed primarily at singers—Conforti was a Roman virtuoso singer—while also presenting itself as useful to instrumentalists. Furthermore, comparison with Ganassi is facilitated by a fairly similar manner of representation, with numerous examples of *passaggi* ordered systematically by basic intervallic progression: each interval is given in long note values, then is immediately followed by a series of *passaggi* that are ornamented versions of the interval, first in duple meter, then in triple meter. This particular edition, essentially a facsimile edition of the musical examples, suffers from the lack of a translation of Conforti's preface, although Denis Stevens's introduction summarizes much of the material and opinions expressed in it. Conforti includes, along with examples of *passaggi,* certain ornaments that were not in use in Ganassi's time but that are characteristic of the late Renaissance and early baroque period. These include the *trillo* (rapid repetition on a single note) and *groppo* (trill). Unusual is Conforti's short-hand way of suggesting melodic variants of a given *passaggio*: he indicates various pitch options at a given point as a chord of two or more notes, the singer being able to choose any one of these notes in any given rendition of the *passaggio.* Therefore, a single three-note chord in the course of a single *passaggio* represents three possibilities; one three-note chord and one two-note chord would represent six possibilites, and so on. Conforti also regards his examples as independent of any specific clef, thus further increasing the efficiency of his notation.

RAYMOND ERICKSON

Ornamentation: Baroque

Brown, Howard Mayer, and Stanley Sadie, editors, *Performance Practice: Music after 1600,* London: Macmillan, 1989; and New York: Norton, 1990

Cyr, Mary, *Performing Baroque Music,* Portland, Oregon: Amadeus Press, and Aldershot: Scolar Press, 1992

Mather, Betty Bang, *The Interpretation of French Music from 1675 to 1775 for Woodwind and Other Performers,* New York: McGinnis and Marx, 1973

Mather, Betty Bang, and David Lasocki, *Free Ornamentation in Woodwind Music, 1700–1775: An Anthology with Introduction,* New York: McGinnis and Marx Music, 1976

Neumann, Frederick, *Ornamentation in Baroque and Post-Baroque Music,* Princeton, New Jersey: Princeton University Press, 1978

Quantz, Johann Joachim, *On Playing the Flute,* translated by Edward R. Reilly, New York: Schirmer, and London: Faber, 1966; 2nd edition, 1985

Tosi, Pier Francesco, *Observations on the Florid Song,* translated by John Ernest Galliard, edited with additional notes by Michael Pilkington, London: Stainer and Bell, 1987

Music of the early baroque period gradually evolved from modal harmonies into clearly tonal music, developing the newly popular style consisting of one melodic line together with a single bass line and harmonic chordal indications, referred to as *monody.* The scores often contained yet-to-be-standardized symbols for ornaments, and composers frequently included a list of appropriate realizations for those symbols. Theorists of the day wrote extensively about these graces—their appropriateness, their musical function, how to play them in various settings, and other related topics of concern. Because of the quasi-improvisatory nature of the music and because of the lack of conformity in a style that was still evolving, as musicians traveled between (primarily) Italy, France, Germany, and England, ornamentation practice changed during the 17th and 18th centuries. Composers tried to retain some control by including realization guidelines, and they gradually began to write more precisely the intended notes and rhythms. Nonetheless, because of the great diversity found in early sources and because of its rapid evolution, baroque ornamentation remains an area of great discussion and interest.

Evident in the literature are two distinct avenues of approach to the subject. On the one hand, primary sources, such as the numerous treatises by composers and theorists together with the examples included therein, give direct evidence of the practice of ornamentation at one time and place. Examples of these include writings of Francesca Caccini and Monteverdi, among the earliest, through Hotteterre, Corelli, Tartini, Montéclair, François Couperin, Telemann, C.P.E. Bach, Geminiani, and Leopold Mozart, to mention only a few of the most prominent.

On the other hand, there are extensive compendium studies that attempt to compile and organize the information gleaned from those primary documents. Two of the most complete modern sources are those by Neumann and Mather. NEUMANN is the contemporary authority on baroque ornamentation; his prolific output covers nearly all the important issues, and this massive book has elicited a lively dialogue in scholarly journals since its publication. Some of that discussion appears in his subsequent books of essays on baroque performance practice. In the text listed here, Neumann traces the development of ornamentation styles by country and date, dividing the baroque era into at least three time periods. Each point he makes is meticulously annotated and correlated to musical examples. This work is for the serious scholar.

MATHER directs her book to the performer. This volume contains musical examples and exercises with theoretical excerpts from primary sources and lucid explanations of those quotations. Mather includes a comprehensive table of symbols used for ornaments by different composers and points out how, where, and when the usage changed. She correlates suggestions for practice and short examples with each type of ornament. MATHER and LASOCKI present two sets of examples—one French and the other Italian, English, and German—that appear in both unadorned and ornamented versions. In most cases the ornamented version is provided by the original composer; occasionally it is the work of a contemporary to the composer. Through careful study of these scores, the authors have discerned some principles of ornamentation in the free style. Mather gives brief outlines of these principles for different types of movements and recommends to the performer several ways to learn the technique of free ornamentation. Both works include bibliographies for further research and study.

In her chapter on ornamentation CYR provides a concise outline of the principal issues of ornamentation in a manner accessible to the uninitiated, while at the same time giving references for further study of most points. As an initial source for understanding ornamentation questions, her book is valuable, but by highlighting two of the many possible tables of ornaments, she may wrongly lead the reader to undervalue the importance of what is not included.

As a first resource for serious inquiry, BROWN and SADIE's book gives a brief history and extremely clear description of the issues of baroque ornamentation practice, supplemented by well-chosen examples. In the chapter titled "The Performer as Composer," David Fuller gives an excellent annotated bibliography for additional sources on ornamentation. He summarizes contemporary research and provides references for further study.

Among primary sources, QUANTZ's treatise stands out for its clarity and completeness. Writing in 1752, at the end of the baroque period, Quantz addresses the teacher, the student, and the performer with guidelines for playing all types of music. He gives the most complete listing of ornaments to be found anywhere in primary sources, with indications of how those ornaments should be realized. For free ornamentation, he includes dozens of sample patterns that can be used as blueprints for ornamenting similar melodic fragments. Each chapter contains admonitions to the musician to apply these embellishments with good taste, a concept that Quantz attempts to make specific; exactly what level of ornamenting is tasteful continues to be an area for heated discussion.

Much of the scholarly discussion of baroque ornamentation centers on instrumental music, but the baroque era began with the new fashion of monody and the singing style outlined by Caccini in *Le nuove musiche*. TOSI presents ornamentation guidelines for singers. In a brief preface, Michael Pilkington points out that by the 1730s, the style of singing and ornamentation described by Tosi was outmoded and that the treatise "should be regarded as an authoritative guide to the late 17th and early 18th centuries in all matters of embellishment and interpretation: to the baroque style proper." Like many other early treatises, Tosi addresses a section to the teacher, then systematically examines particular ornaments such as the appoggiatura, the shake, and divisions, including those that are not specifically notated.

MARTHA FARAHAT

Ornamentation: Classical

Neumann, Frederick, *Ornamentation and Improvisation in Mozart,* Princeton, New Jersey: Princeton University Press, 1986

Newman, William S., *Beethoven on Beethoven: Playing His Piano Music His Way,* New York: Norton, 1988

Rosenblum, Sandra P., *Performance Practices in Classic Piano Music: Their Principles and Applications,* Bloomington: Indiana University Press, 1988

Stowell, Robin, *Violin Technique and Performance Practices in the Late Eighteenth and Early Nineteenth Centuries,* Cambridge: Cambridge University Press, 1985

Walden, Valerie, *One Hundred Years of Violoncello: A History of Technique and Performance Practice, 1740–1840,* Cambridge: Cambridge University Press, 1998

Although the subject of very few major studies thus far, ornamentation practices in the classical period are currently subject to passionately argued debate among scholars and performers alike. Disputed issues range from the proper way to execute notated or specified ornaments to the appropriateness of adding free ornamentation and improvising cadenzas. While there is some agreement about the proper use of ornamentation for baroque music, considerably less consensus exists regarding when and how to ornament in classical music. Even such basic issues as whether trills should begin from the upper neighbor or the main note and whether they should include terminations are in contention. A lively debate on the performance of free ornamentation in classical instrumental music has been conducted in the pages of the journal *Early Music* since 1997, with contributions to the debate appearing as articles, reviews of recordings, and letters.

There is no lack of relevant source material. In fact, the many unresolved issues in classical ornamentation arise from an overabundance of relevant documents, combined with disagreement among scholars regarding the appropriate application of firsthand sources. C.P.E.

Bach, Clementi, Czerny, Hiller, Hummel, Leopold Mozart, Pleyel, and Türk are among the more prominent authors of treatises from the classical period that deal with ornamentation. The wide range of views found in such sources shows that, within what is now considered the classical period, many divergent and conflicting practices coexisted. The composers of the period whose music is of greatest interest to current performers and audiences—Haydn, Mozart, Beethoven, and Schubert—left little in the way of specific instructions on the ornamentation of their music. Even when the meaning behind a treatise is understood—for example, specific instructions not to do something might well be strong evidence that most people were doing it—it can still be difficult to find agreement on the extent to which the instructions of a given treatise are applicable to a particular composer or piece of music. Czerny, for example, was a student of Beethoven and wrote in detail on the performance of virtually all of Beethoven's piano music, but it is clear that the two men were not always in full agreement, so it is not easy to determine in all cases how closely Czerny's suggestions reflect Beethoven's wishes.

NEUMANN provides the most ambitious and, to date, most comprehensive treatment of classical ornamentation. By focusing on a single composer, Neumann indicates his own awareness of the multiplicity of approaches and offers what he sees as the best practical solutions, making this book extremely useful to performers of Mozart. Although his research is thorough and his argumentation is convincing, he sometimes is forced to rely on sources, such as C.P.E. Bach, whose direct bearing on Mozart is tenuous, so prescriptions are not always the last word on a given topic. Because of the book's organization by type of ornamentation, it serves as a good starting point for persons who wish to compare what various sources might have to say about a given topic.

NEWMAN, along with Robin Stowell's *Performing Beethoven* (1994), is one of the few more recent books devoted to performance practices surrounding Beethoven. It devotes one chapter specifically to ornamentation. Newman is less doctrinaire than Neumann in his approach, presenting his sources together with explanations of how he reached his conclusions, which invites readers to think for themselves and seek their own solutions. Having set for himself the agenda of learning as much as possible from Beethoven's music and writings about how the music is to be performed, Newman is not interested here in comparing opinions of different treatises. Instead, he reads Beethoven very closely and, using detective-like induction, finds important clues to the execution of ornamentation in fingerings, articulation marks, and other places that are not immediately obvious. Newman is as valuable for his conclusions as for his effective demonstration of creative problem solving.

As a relatively recent contribution to the field, ROSENBLUM's extensive chapter on ornamentation is informative beyond the field of piano music. She makes a point of differentiating between composers and periods within the classical era in a way that sensitively addresses the application of various practices. At the same time, however, she is rather conservative in her views of what is permissible. She is ready to accept Mozart's and Beethoven's complaints about performers taking too many liberties with their scores as a prohibition on adding ornamentation, without acknowledging that these complaints are also evidence of elaborate ornamentation practices, which might not have always satisfied the composers' tastes but which were nonetheless expected. In the case of improvised cadenzas and *Eingänge*, Rosenblum takes the view that, if a composer has written a cadenza for his own work, he has done so to prevent others from inventing their own, and the composer's cadenza is then the only appropriate one to perform.

STOWELL presents one of the few recent overviews of classical ornamentation with an orientation toward performance by a melody instrument. Two chapters divide the topic into the specific ornaments generally indicated with signs and the freely added ornaments and improvisation added at the performer's discretion. On specific ornamentation, the author presents views of a wide variety of sources, giving a good idea of diversity but not attempting to draw many conclusions about which sources might most profitably be applied to what music. His survey of improvisation, which includes significant extracts from Baillot's (1834) unprecedented coverage of the subject, provides a good starting point for those interested in the classical violin cadenza.

WALDEN's chapter "Rules of Ornamentation" is ironic in light of her recognition of the important role taste played in matters of ornamentation. Nevertheless, she draws together an excellent selection of materials, mostly drawn from the literature of cello pedagogy, which have not been collected and presented together in previous studies. Comparison of her sources with the better known keyboard and violin sources tends to confirm the impression that each author had his own idea of rules; she identifies more areas of disagreement than are comfortable for scholars intent on finding easy answers to questions about how things were done.

JOHN MORAN

Ornamentation: Romantic

Czerny, Carl, *A Systematic Introduction to Improvisation on the Pianoforte*, translated by Alice L. Mitchell, New York: Longman, 1983

Dannreuther, Edward, *Musical Ornamentation*, 2 vols., London: Novello, 1893–95; 2nd edition, 1900; reprint, New York: Kalmus, 1960

Dunn, John Petrie, *Ornamentation in the Works of Frederick Chopin*, London: Novello, and New York: Gray, 1921; reprint, New York: Da Capo Press, 1971

Garcia, Manuel, *Treatise on the Art of Singing*, edited and translated by Donald V. Paschke, New York: Da Capo Press, 1975

Hamilton, Clarence Grant, *Ornaments in Classical and Modern Music*, Boston: Ditson, 1929; reprint, New York: AMS Press, 1976

Hummel, Johann Nepomuk, *A Complete Theoretical and Practical Course of Instructions on the Art of Playing the Pianoforte*, London: Boosey, 1828

Spohr, Louis, *Violin School from the Original German, Dedicated to Professors of the Violin*, London: Wessel, 1833

When dealing with Romantic ornamentation, one must be alert to some boundary issues. First, one needs to approach the Classic/Romantic division with great caution, for, in the matter of ornamentation, there is a continuity of tradition from Leopold Mozart to Baillot and Spohr, or from C.P.E. Bach and Türk to Hummel. This essay will only address the music after Beethoven. Second, the boundary between written and improvised music must be considered. One must keep in mind that for a 19th century musician, ornamentation was inseparable from improvisation. Thus, the period sources deal with both the classification and execution of written embellishments, as well as teaching the art of elaborating melody extempore.

Romantic ornamentation has not received comprehensive treatment in any major source. Dannreuther and Hamilton, the only English-language books that address the topic at large, devote only brief sections to ornamentation after Beethoven. In addition, there is Dunn on Chopin's embellishments. These two titles represent the entire monograph literature on this topic and they all are over 70 years old. Newer research addressing Romantic ornamentation comes in the form of dissertations and articles.

The oldest and by far the most extensive study of ornamentation in Western music is DANNREUTHER. The chronological organization, with cultural centers and instrumental idiom identified, is very useful in discerning stylistic differences. Equally useful is the index, which contains names of composers and theorists, as well as classes of ornaments and related musical terms. However, the section on Romantic period, beginning with Beethoven's contemporaries, Weber and Schubert, and closing with Wagner (no Brahms included), occupies only some 50 pages of this two–volume survey. Consequently, many important issues are overlooked and those included are often sketchy.

DUNN's investigation is, in the author's own words, "based only on internal evidence" of Chopin's music. Either by necessity or by choice, he does not consider the testimony that came down to us through the writings of Lenz, Kleczyński, Mikuli, and Koczalski and through scores annotated by Chopin. Nor does he compare his findings to information published by composers and performers who influenced Chopin. Dunn's study is not only a record of internal evidence, it is also a reflection of the author's own pianistic aesthetic.

The most recent of these monographs, HAMILTON relies heavily on both Dannreuther and Dunn. A subject of this range cannot be given justice in a 75-page essay. The book gives a quick historical overview, but does not have an index, which makes locating practical information on the execution of a specific ornament very difficult. This task is further complicated since Hamilton does not have chronological divisions. It is organized by classes of ornaments.

In the absence of reliable modern studies of Romantic ornamentation, the 19th century treatises in English translation are invaluable. The most indispensable sources are CZERNY, published in 1829 (there is also some helpful information in his op. 500), SPOHR, which first appeared in 1832, and HUMMEL. GARCIA, originally published in 1840 in French, is the most significant contemporary discussion of vocal ornamentation, and it sheds considerable light on 19th-century improvisational practice.

There are many other period textbooks, often not available in English. For instance, Austin Caswell's article on Mme. Cinti-Damoreau's didactic works deals with her published Method of 1849 and the seven extant manuscript books, which contain ornaments and cadenzas written by Damoreau, who was the leading soprano of Italian Opera in Paris during the 1820s and 1830s (see Caswell, *Journal of the American Musicological Society* 27 [1975]). This collection attests to the continuous importance of the art of melodic improvisation in the 19th century.

Even more unexpected is the source evidence that supports improvisation in Schubert's Lieder. On the testimony of annotations written into his Singbücher by Johann Michael Vogl and comments by other friends of Schubert, Walther Dürr maintains that Schubert approved of adding subtle embellishments to his songs, in order to bring out the sentiment (see Dürr, *19th Century Music* 3 [1979]).

The least researched area of ornamentation aesthetics is the late 19th century. There exist some praiseworthy efforts to open up this avenue of investigation. For instance, Jon Finson seeks to define the use of vibrato and portamento in Brahms as ornamentation used tastefully for expression only (Finson, *Musical Quarterly* 70 [1984]). Finson confirms that there are volumes of information to be gathered from published Methods and sound recordings of late 19th-century violinists (Carl Flesch, Leopold Auer, and Joseph Joachim). The same, of course, goes for pianists, singers, etc., but the research remains to be done.

HALINA GOLDBERG

P

Paderewski, Jan Ignacy 1866–1941

Polish composer

Drozdowski, Marian Marek, *Ignacy Jan Paderewski: A Political Biography in Outline,* translated by Stanislaw Tarnowski, Warsaw: Interpress, 1981

Landau, Rom, *Ignace Paderewski: Musician and Statesman,* New York: Crowell, 1934

Paderewski, Ignace Jan, and Mary Lawton, *The Paderewski Memoirs,* New York: Scribner, 1938

Phillips, Charles, *Paderewski: The Story of a Modern Immortal,* New York: Macmillan, 1933

Strakacz, Aniela, *Paderewski as I Knew Him,* translated by Halina Chybowska, New Brunswick, New Jersey: Rutgers University Press, 1949

Zamoyski, Adam, *Paderewski,* New York: Atheneum, 1982

Paderewski is a unique figure in 20th-century music history because of his importance as a politician and statesman as well as his extraordinarily long career as a virtuoso pianist. The three aspects of his life that have received the most consideration are his virtuosity, his role as an advocate for and leader of Poland, and his compositions. There was so much interest in him during his own lifetime that numerous articles and books about him—in addition to his own authorized memoirs—appeared before his death in 1941. Since that time there have been fewer book-length publications about him, but the two biographies by Drozdowski and Zamoyski provide some historical perspective and new insights into Paderewski's life and achievement.

DROZDOWSKI bases his book upon extensive research in archival sources both in the United States and Poland. His primary focus is on the ties between Polish-Americans (Polonia) and Paderewski, who was instrumental in motivating many Polish-American organizations to give aid and assistance to the Polish cause. The quotations from Polish-language newspapers published in the United States are especially useful for non-Polish readers, because translations may not be found elsewhere. Also of interest are the numerous illustrations, including many photographs and reproductions of cartoons, war posters, recital programs, and other documents. This book contains more specific information about Paderewski's day-to-day business, correspondence, colleagues, and especially the U.S. organizations that supported him than any of the other books here reviewed. It does not always read smoothly; the translation is sometimes a bit awkward, and there are often long lists of names, monetary figures, or other data that interrupt the flow of the narrative. On the other hand, the information is presented in strict chronological order, so one can go directly to the periods or events of greatest interest, such as the chapter devoted to 1919, the year in which Paderewski served as prime minister of the newly independent Poland.

LANDAU claims to have produced the first English-language biography of Paderewski, a claim also made by Phillips. Landau's aim is to combine Paderewski's personal, musical, and political life, and he thus divides his book into three parts, each dealing with one of these aspects. His primary concern with Paderewski's musicianship is his virtuosity, and there are many stirring accounts of the pianist bringing his audiences to their feet in thunderous applause. Landau provides some revealing commentary on the nature of virtuosity, asserting that the locus of musical genius had moved from the composer (Beethoven and Chopin) to the performer (Liszt, Rubenstein, and Paderewski) by the end of the 19th century. His account of Paderewski's political involvement is the only contemporary source to include a map (albeit small and general), demonstrating the importance of Paderewski's influence in the formation of independent Poland following World War I. The third section gives an almost worshipful account of the great man's generosity and nobility of spirit, using many personal anecdotes to illustrate these characteristics.

PADEREWSKI and LAWTON, the composer/performer's memoirs, serves as an important source for all of his later biographers; it is also well worth reading on its own. Written in a conversational style, it gives the reader access to Paderewski's charming and charismatic personality. Many of his statements about important people and events are quoted in Drozdowski and Zamoyski, but there are many delightful stories and tidbits found only here, such as his discussion of three "colossal" things that particularly impressed him in the United States: Niagara Falls, the Grand Canyon, and Chicago. These memoirs make clear that, at least at the time of publication, Paderewski saw himself first and foremost as a performer; most of his stories are about traveling and performing. He always maintains a modest attitude about his political influence, although he is not shy about discussing his encounters with U.S. presidents and other world leaders.

PHILLIPS offers a lengthy and poetic account, aiming to present his subject in as clear a light as possible. He relies on many of the same sources as Landau (including personal interviews), but Phillips divides his topic into two parts: he portrays Paderewski as two men, the great musician and the great statesmen. Accordingly, he organizes the book as two consecutive chronological biographies. In the musical biography much attention is given to Paderewski's compositions, more so than in most other accounts. The author also includes a work list and discography. Typical of biographies written at the time, much of the text reads more like a novel than a scholarly biography, and it can be difficult to keep straight the time span and specific circumstances surrounding events. It is noteworthy that Paderewski's good friend, Colonel Edward House, endorsed this book by writing its introduction.

STRAKACZ provides another look at the Paderewski household, this time from an insider's perspective. The author, wife of Paderewski's personal secretary, Sylwin Strakacz, kept a diary of her years with the family (1919–41). Not all of her recollections center on the pianist himself; she also has much to say about his wife, Helena, and his sister, who ran their estate in Riond-Bosson, Switzerland. There are occasional clarifying notes written by her husband sprinkled into the diary entries, usually with regard to political events she did not understand. These notes are tantalizing enough to make one wish that Sylwin himself had published some memoirs in English, because he was very closely associated with all of Paderewski's dealings from 1919 onward.

ZAMOYSKI's very readable and well-researched biography is the place to start if one wants a balanced approach to Paderewski. The author incorporates all the earlier biographical information with new archival material, to create an engaging portrait with a lot of substance. The description of Paderewski's political accomplishments is clear and accessible. There are details regarding Paderewski's personal life, such as his relationships with Rachel Brancovan and Helena Gorska (previous to Gorska and Paderewski's marriage in 1899), that appear nowhere else. The appendices contain a work list, discography, and an intriguing list of Paderewski's performance repertoire. The author man-

ages to debunk some of the overly sentimentalized attitudes toward Paderewski's "immortality" while still helping to explain why so many of his contemporaries did consider him a genius.

DAWN O'NEAL REINDL

Paganini, Niccolò 1782–1840

Italian violinist and composer

Borer, Philippe, *The Twenty-four Caprices of Niccolò Paganini: Their Significance for the History of Violin Playing and the Music of the Romantic Era*, Zurich: Stiftung Zentralstelle der Studentenschaft der Universität Zürich, 1997

Courcy, Geraldine I.C. de, *Chronology of Nicolo Paganini's Life*, Wiesbaden: Erdmann Musikverlag, 1961

———, *Paganini, the Genoese*, 2 vols., Norman: University of Oklahoma Press, 1957

Moretti, Maria Rosa, and Anna Sorrento, *Catalogo Tematico delle Musiche di Niccolò Paganini*, Genoa: Comune di Genova, 1982

Pulver, Jeffrey, *Paganini, the Romantic Virtuoso*, London: Joseph, 1936; reprint, New York: Da Capo Press, 1970

Roth, Henry, *Violin Virtuosos from Paganini to the 21st Century*, Los Angeles: California Classic Books, 1997

Sheppard, Leslie, and Herbert R. Axelrod, *Paganini*, Neptune City, New Jersey: Paganiniana Publications, 1979

Niccolò Paganini has received less scholarly attention than his fame would seem to warrant. The archetypal romantic virtuoso, rumor preceded and scandal followed him on his tours throughout Europe. To this day he remains a popular romantic figure, but he is neglected as an object of serious research in English. His fame rested largely on his performance of his own compositions rather than the pieces themselves. His music can be less interesting compositionally than for its violinistic effects, so most serious research has dealt primarily with his contribution to the evolution and expansion of violin technique. A serious attempt to reconstruct his performance practices in detail, which could shed tremendous light on his real contributions to the development of violin playing, is sorely lacking in the Paganini literature.

The one major work in English that goes beyond the above general criticism is BORER's study of the *Caprices*. It is the most significant new work on Paganini published in English in many years. Borer approaches Paganini on the composer's own terms, exploring the aspects of the *Caprices* that are most interesting without complaining about supposed musical deficiencies. Borer is also careful to place Paganini in the appropriate historical context as an heir to virtuosi such as Locatelli and Nardini, so that Paganini is not, as is often the case, portrayed as a unique artist without violinistic roots who sprouted from nowhere. Borer goes to great lengths, using iconography, written accounts, and Paganini's music itself, to analyze and reconstruct Paganini's violin technique in a historically plausible manner.

COURCY's (1957) biography is the best overview available of the violinist's life. Unlike much writing on Paganini, Courcy's text is objective, and her careful study of extensive source material is well documented. The author includes English translations of the biographical sketches related by Paganini to Lichtenthal and Schottky and, perhaps even more usefully, includes a list of his instruments and an appendix on the extensive iconography. The only serious shortcoming of the study is its age: besides obviously not being able to take into consideration the interesting studies in Italian and German of the last four decades, the positivist approach fails to raise questions that might interest current readers, such as the issues relating to the social implications of Paganini's popularity or a serious consideration of his actual manner of performance.

COURCY's (1961) volume provides a quick way to trace the activities and whereabouts of the virtuoso. Over the course of his life the frequency of entries increases, so that for his later years there are entries nearly on a daily basis. Entries are brief, with little analytical commentary. Although sources are not given for most entries, Courcy's standards, as demonstrated in her 1957 book, are high, making this chronology reliable. The chronology is arranged in two columns to allow for parallel English and German texts. Unfortunately, it is not indexed and can only be searched by date.

PULVER's biography, superseded by the work of Courcy in terms of sheer volume of information, remains relevant for its vivid personification of Paganini. Although he includes no footnotes, Pulver presents many contemporaneous accounts of Paganini and his playing. Pulver is more interested than Courcy in understanding Paganini as a cultural phenomenon and as a violinist. The biography is useful to the reader interested in a general understanding of Paganini's significance, while Courcy is better as a detailed documentation of his life.

SHEPPARD and AXELROD's biography is of uneven quality. It makes no pretense at being scholarly: it is devoid of notes and bibliography. Yet this book has much to offer. It brings together and reproduces the largest possible body of Paganini iconography, including many pages of color reproductions of the Paganiniana in the Library of Congress, as well as a brief discussion of this collection. A facsimile of the 24 *Caprices* appears as an appendix. A somewhat out-of-date but nevertheless extensive discography of recordings of Paganini's works will be useful to many readers. The text includes extensive quotes from firsthand sources.

ROTH's treatment of Paganini in the context of violin virtuosos in general is necessarily limited and is mentioned here as a cautionary example of some of the prejudices that still beset Paganini research. Roth cannot examine Paganini in his own historical context without asking whether Paganini was actually "the greatest violinist who ever lived." Using an outmoded idea of absolute progress, Roth answers his own question with a resounding "no," offering as one piece of proof the fact that Paganini did not cultivate the type of continuous vibrato that is the hallmark of most late 20th-century playing and which Roth believes is essential to a beautiful tone.

Although not in English, MORETTI and SORRENTO's thematic catalog is an essential resource for readers in any language. It is well organized and easy to use, dividing the surviving works into datable and undatable categories. Its value, however, goes far beyond that of a thematic catalog. It contains an exhaustive bibliography of the essential literature as well as a systematic index of nonmusical sources such as letters, diaries, account books, newspapers, and programs.

JOHN MORAN

Palestrina, Giovanni Pierluigi da
ca. 1525–1594

Italian composer

Baini, Giuseppe, *Memorie storico-critiche della vita e delle opere di Giovanni Pierluigi da Palestrina*, 2 vols., Rome: Società Tipografica, 1828; reprint, 1967

Bianchi, Lino, and Giancarlo Rostirolla, editors, *Iconografia palestriniana: Giovanni Pierluigi da Palestrina, il suo tempo e la sua fortuna nelle immagini*, Lucca: Libreria Musicale Italiana, 1994

Coates, Henry, *Palestrina*, London: Dent, 1938

Early Music 22, no. 4 (1994)

Jeppesen, Knud, *The Style of Palestrina and the Dissonance*, translated by Margaret W. Hamerik, Copenhagen: Levin and Munksgaard, and London: Oxford University Press, 1927; 2nd edition, 1946; reprint, New York: Dover, 1970

Palestrina, Giovanni Pierluigi da, *Pope Marcellus Mass: An Authoritative Score, Backgrounds and Sources, History and Analysis, Views and Comments,* edited by Lewis Lockwood, New York: Norton, 1975

———, *Three Pieces for Triple Choir*, edited by Noel O'Regan, Edinburgh: Edinburgh Music Imprint, 1994

Roche, Jerome, *Palestrina*, London: Oxford University Press, 1971

Sherr, Richard, editor, *Papal Music and Musicians in Late Medieval and Renaissance Rome*, Oxford: Clarendon Press in association with Library of Congress, Washington, and New York: Oxford University Press, 1998

The preeminent Catholic composer in the period following the Council of Trent, Palestrina is important in a number of music historical arenas. He was one of the first composers to receive extensive attention from music historians, and theorists have scrutinized his style more closely than that of any other composer. Although it would now be difficult to claim him as the quintessential composer of the Renaissance era (as has often been done in the past), scholars and audiences alike continue to acknowledge him as one of the most significant figures in the autumn of the musical Renaissance.

The changing nature of Palestrina studies through the years has produced a bibliography weighted toward older works. We may delineate several distinct eras of Palestrina research, marked initially by large-scale studies motivated by a kind of hero worship, continuing with an antiromantic reaction focused on the objective and scientific aspects of Palestrina's style, and culminating in recent years with shorter studies that explore the various stylistic, historical, social, and religious contexts of Palestrina and his works.

Within a few years of his death, a legend grew up about Palestrina that he had personally rescued choral polyphony from possible banishment within the Catholic liturgy. In conjunction with the Council of Trent (1545–63), so the story went, some zealous church officials aimed to eradicate abuses in church music by requiring choirs to sing only plainchant in Roman Catholic churches. Summoned before a panel that was considering such possibilities, Palestrina composed the eminently intelligible *Pope Marcellus Mass,* which convinced the committee that the "errors had lain not with music but with the musicians" and that polyphonic choral music should be retained for liturgical services. Palestrina's role in this debate—and indeed the debate itself—is largely mythical; PALESTRINA (1975) presents the relevant documents along with the text of the Marcellus Mass. Nonetheless, for several centuries Palestrina was virtually regarded as the patron saint of church musicians. As a result the early biographies focus narrowly on the person of Palestrina and his achievements on behalf of the church against philistine forces opposed to choral polyphony.

BAINI in many ways established this pattern but can hardly be dismissed as a hagiographic tract: it is among the first biographies dedicated to a single composer and is easily the most extensive of its time. The author was able to collect many of the sources that bear on Palestrina's life and works, even though he sometimes elaborates them in fanciful ways. Published originally in Italian and later translated into German, Baini served as the foundation for nearly a century of derivative accounts preoccupied with Palestrina's role in the salvation of church music. For one such example in English, see Charles Angoff, *Palestrina: Savior of Church Music* (1944). Similar prejudices persist in Zoë Kendrick Pyne, *Giovanni Pierluigi da Palestrina: His Life and Times* (1922), but that book does take account of some later research. (For English translation of one section of Baini, see Ian Bent, *Music Analysis in the Nineteenth Century* [1994].)

COATES is a much more balanced treatment, recognizing Palestrina's various secular occupations. It takes full advantage of biographical finds made by several Italian researchers in the late 19th and early 20th centuries and is less dated than Pyne in its consideration of Palestrina's style. Both Pyne and Coates, however, are necessarily unaware of important discoveries made about Palestrina in the 1940s and 1950s, especially details of the part-polyphony, part-plainchant Masses Palestrina composed for St. Barbara's at Mantua. Unfortunately, this material has yet to appear as part of a book-length treatment of Palestrina in English.

Researchers in the next several generations focused more narrowly on Palestrina's style. Considered the apex of the Renaissance idiom, Palestrina's works were closely inspected to find their generative principles. For centuries, theorists had recognized Palestrina's counterpoint and treatment of dissonance as exceptionally well crafted, and from at least the time of Fux's *Gradus ad Parnassum* (1725), composition students had taken an idealized form of Palestrina's music as their guide for learning species counterpoint. In the 20th century, scholars began more precisely to identify various elements of his style. JEPPESEN succeeds most spectacularly at this task by isolating essential aspects of Palestrina's melodic construction. The author also raises the study of dissonance to a new level, showing how Palestrina occasionally contravenes conventional contrapuntal rules but always within certain specific, predictable situations. H.K. Andrews, *An Introduction to the Technique of Palestrina* (1958) and Malcolm Boyd, *Palestrina's Style: A Practical Introduction* (1973) are practical, student-oriented texts that profit from these findings. The latter is particularly useful, because it takes a fresh look at a broader array of stylistic parameters, including modal organization, rhythm, and texture.

A common assumption in efforts to identify Palestrina's style is that Palestrina's works changed little through his career and that they represent an *ars perfecta.* By comparison to the works of a contemporary such as Lassus, who explored a great variety of styles, the works by Palestrina do appear remarkably consistent. But recent studies demonstrate the extent to which Palestrina, no less than any other Renaissance composer, must be interpreted within various contexts, especially a historical paradigm that allows for stylistic change and development. ROCHE constitutes one of the first studies to challenge the monolithic view of Palestrina's style. Although it is too short on biographical information to tie the composer's life and works together, it does recognize the ways in which Palestrina's approach changed later in his career. It distinguishes, for instance, the rhetorically sure technique of the mature Song of Songs settings from Palestrina's earlier motets. PALESTRINA (1994) is an edition (with a brief introduction) that illustrates another progressive aspect of

Palestrina's repertory, namely, the increasing interest in polychoral music in Rome after the Council of Trent.

SHERR, written for a specialized audience, offers recent research into other contexts relevant to Palestrina, including the organization of the papal choir (of which Palestrina was at one time a member) and the nature of his compositional process (which may have included use of a lute). *EARLY MUSIC* comprises a number of important articles that investigate other aspects of the composer's life and works, such as his connection with the incipient basso continuo practice, the way he managed his finances and found freelance employment, and the fortunes of posthumous publications of his music. This volume and the visually richly BIANCHI (a rich compendium of reproductions and photographs of places, engravings, documents, and musical sources) both had their genesis in the quatercentenary of Palestrina's death.

STEPHEN R. MILLER

Partch, Harry 1901–1974

United States composer, performer, and instrument builder

Blackburn, Philip, *Harry Partch,* Saint Paul, Minnesota: American Composers Forum, 1997

Gilmore, Bob, *Harry Partch: A Biography,* New Haven, Connecticut: Yale University Press, 1998

McGeary, Thomas, *The Music of Harry Partch: A Descriptive Catalog,* Brooklyn, New York: Institute for Studies in American Music, 1991

Partch, Harry, *Bitter Music: Collected Journals, Essays, Introductions, and Librettos,* edited and with an introduction by Thomas McGeary, Urbana: University of Illinois Press, 1991

———, *Genesis of a Music,* Madison: University of Wisconsin Press, 1949; as *Genesis of a Music: An Account of a Creative Work, Its Roots and Its Fulfillments,* 2nd edition, enlarged, New York: Da Capo Press, 1974

Harry Partch, a largely self-taught composer, instrument maker, and theoretician, was one of the most individualistic and original composers of the 20th century. Born to parents who had spent time in China as missionaries, Partch grew up in the southwestern United States, and he was as familiar with the music of China, the Yaqui people living near his home, and the songs of the transient railroad workers who befriended him as he was with music in the art music tradition. After encountering Hermann Helmholtz's *On the Sensation of Tone* in the mid-1920s, Partch burned all his early compositions and embarked on a remarkable artistic and intellectual journey that culminated in the publication of his book *Genesis of a Music,* in 1949, and the composition of a se-

ries of large-scale music theater works during the ensuing two decades that brought his music and ideas to a wide audience. In the course of the 40-odd years of this quest, he spent time during the Depression as a hobo, later held research positions at the University of Wisconsin and University of Illinois, and attracted the support of prominent patrons. While living this itinerant life, Partch designed and built an orchestra of original instruments to perform the music that he wrote, using a 43-tone scale, also worked out by him, using just intonation.

PARTCH (1949) was first conceived in the early 1930s and went through several drafts before reaching its published form. By turns thought-provoking, hilarious, dense, and exasperating, the book presents a complete historical and theoretical grounding for Partch's musical poetics. Part 1 introduces Partch's basic aesthetic position, which sees music divided between two tendencies—the corporeal and the abstract. Corporeal music is music that stays close to the body, especially the voice, as a source of authenticity. In abstract music, on the other hand, as represented by most Western music since the Renaissance, formalism is increasingly the driving force. Parts 2 and 3 are the core of the book, in which just intonation is explained, Partch elaborates his extrapolations of the basic theory, and he describes the instruments designed to make the theory come to life. These sections are highly technical and require close reading. Finally, although Partch was untrained as a scholar, his survey of the history of intonation part 4, from the time of the Greeks and ancient Chinese through the developments of the Renaissance to the immediate precursors of his own explorations, is among the best summaries of the topic. While this book is one of the major documents of 20th-century music, copies of it are extremely rare.

Genesis is better known through the revised second edition (1974), which was reworked by Partch during the final years of his life and published posthumously. Although this edition retains most of the text of the first published version, careful comparison shows numerous instances of deletion and addition of material. Most of the cut material relates to instruments later abandoned or superseded by Partch. Descriptions of instruments designed by Partch after 1950 are the main additions, along with four new appendices providing information on Partch's performances, films, and recordings. The appearance of this book rode the crest of the growing appreciation of Partch during the last decade of his life and has since helped sustain interest in his work.

Most of Partch's occasional writings throughout his career appeared in various small journals and were quite difficult to find before the appearance of PARTCH (1991). This volume collects several of Partch's most important essays, excerpts from unpublished diaries, and scenarios and librettos of the major theater works. The most valuable portions of this book are the two journals, "Bitter Music" and "End Littoral," the first of which recounts some of Partch's exploits in work camps in California in the months after returning from his 1934 through 1935 trip to Europe, with flashbacks to his experiences while in Europe. An entertaining story, it is illustrated with musical transcriptions of the spoken words of many of Partch's interlocutors. "End Littoral" is a more somber account of a hiking trip along the Pacific coast north of San Francisco in the fall of 1947. The essays, while often curmudgeonly, are frequently entertaining and occasionally prophetic.

McGEARY was the first attempt to approach Partch's legacy from a thoroughly scholarly point of view. The volume is mainly a bibliographic catalog of Partch's compositions, with entries giving details of circumstances of composition, instrumentation, status of manuscripts, and other similar information. The chronology was among the first published to bring together the known facts of Partch's life. The book also includes a comprehensive bibliography of writings about Partch from 1930 through 1974 and a discography up to 1991.

An invaluable source, BLACKBURN is a sumptuously produced volume of facsimile reproductions of material from scrapbooks assembled by Partch throughout his career. The book is the centerpiece of a series of publications that make available a large corpus of Partch's work, including two videotapes of films and two multidisk sets of recordings. This volume is invaluable for providing so much primary source material in facsimile, providing a glimpse into Partch's life from the public side, through clippings, programs, and performance material, to the very personal, in the pages from diaries, letters, and informal photographs.

Building on research regarding Partch and his career that has appeared since the 1980s, GILMORE presents the first complete biography of Partch. The biographical facts of Partch's life have been so shrouded in myth and legend that it is welcome finally to have an objectively researched biography of this important figure in 20th-century music and musical aesthetics. This book is particularly valuable for the light it sheds on Partch's early years, until now mainly known through Partch's elliptical references throughout his writings. Partch's career after about 1930, when his theoretical position had been basically set, is the story of alternating successes and failures, periods of intense progress and debilitating backtracking, all of which are carefully described. From this volume, one gets the feeling that Partch, with his attractive musico-theatrical ideas and iconoclastic stance, could have had a career as successful as his colleagues John Cage or Lou Harrison if he had only had a less volatile personality. Gilmore's passionate account of Partch's life is a fitting memorial to this original and uncompromising, yet tragically flawed, composer/theoretician.

RON WIECKI

Passion Music

Fischer, Kurt von, *Essays in Musicology,* New York: Graduate School and University Center, City University of New York, 1989

Leaver, Robin A., *J.S. Bach as Preacher: His Passions and Music in Worship,* St. Louis, Missouri: Concordia Publishing House, 1984

Smallman, Basil, *The Background of Passion Music: J.S. Bach and His Predecessors,* London: SCM Press, 1957; 2nd edition, New York: Dover, 1970

Steinitz, Paul, *Bach's Passions,* New York: Scribner, 1978; London: Elek, 1979

Terry, Charles Sanford, *Bach: The Passions,* 2 vols., London: Oxford University Press, 1926; reprint, Westport, Connecticut: Greenwood Press, 1970

The story of Jesus' Passion—his betrayal and death—forms a fundamental part of Christian theology and is retold as part of Holy Week services. The main personages of Christ, the narrator, and the crowd are usually represented in slightly different manners; even in 13th-century settings one finds instructions requesting different voice types, timbres, or physical actions for the various parts, which were sung in plainsong. In the Renaissance, polyphony was introduced, usually for sections assigned to the crowd, although in some settings polyphony was used for Christ's words or even the entire text. Over time, recitatives and arias were added to the choral sections, modernizing the textual and dramatic content of the work. Beginning in the second half of the 18th century, very few composers set the entire Passion, a trend that continued into the 20th century. The materials included below encompass studies that focus on the early polyphonic settings, 17th-century German settings, the relationship of text and liturgy, and text and music in J.S. Bach's Passions. A full-length book in English surveying the entire development of the Passion has yet to be written, and so the reader is urged to seek articles, essays, and doctoral dissertations on specific works or composers.

Beginning with the introduction of the Passion texts into the liturgy, FISCHER comprehensively analyzes the development of early monophonic and polyphonic settings of the four Gospel texts in the essay "The Passion from Its Beginnings until the Sixteenth Century." His chief concern is exploring the changing musical styles and textures used to set important words or phrases. He also highlights specific innovations and changes in the differing traditions of the Protestant and Catholic churches that became models for future settings. This essay is particularly insightful when it traces developments into 16th-century England, Germany, and Italy; it also contains brief references to the trends in France and Iberia. Originally published in German in 1973, this essay is an early version of the author's article in the *New Grove Dictionary of Music and Musicians* (1980);

more current information is contained in the author's *Die Passion Musik* (1997).

SMALLMAN provides a brief stylistic introduction to the Passion, concentrating on the techniques and forms used in settings prior to Bach. After sketching the main musical trends of the medieval and Renaissance periods, the author provides a survey of the genre in 17th-century Germany. He divides his study according to theatrical and musical topics, including sections on "The Drama," "The Dramatis Personae," and "The Role of the Orchestra," selecting examples from the works of Schütz, Vulpius, and others as illustrations. In the appendices, he offers a more detailed glimpse of works by F. Funcke, J. Meder, Bach, and Telemann, along with selections from the medieval and Renaissance periods. Although not detailed in scope, this book is a valuable introduction to lesser-known examples of the repertory.

In a revised series of BBC radio lectures, LEAVER reviews the theological significance of the Passion in Bach's settings. To support his view that Bach's Passions were "indeed sermons in sound," the author draws on various aspects of the music as well as on the fact that these Passions were intended for Good Friday vespers, a service that would not contain a sermon. The role of the Passion in the Lutheran liturgy, pietism and its effects on Bach and his Passions, the parallel in rhetorical structures found in Lutheran sermons of the time and Bach's Passions, and aspects of the performance and musical treatment of well-known hymns are discussed in a general and nontechnical manner.

In his examination of two of Bach's Passions, STEINITZ addresses the general music devotee, choral singer, and probable performer of these compositions, avoiding structural and overly technical analyses. After providing a brief chronology of the Passion prior to Bach, Steinitz highlights aspects of performance practice and instrumental usage of the period. The sources and history of the texts used in Bach's Passions (based in part upon Terry) are discussed, and brief comments about each section of Bach's St. John and St. Matthew Passions draw together the narrative and its musical portrayal. Steinitz's presentation is general, although he touches upon the palindromic structure of portions of the St. John Passion and aspects of the key structure of both Passions. Given the explosion of knowledge about baroque music and Bach's music in particular, the material is somewhat dated and cursory, but it still provides a useful introduction to these two masterpieces.

In his pioneering effort, TERRY considers the relationship between the librettos and the music of Bach's Passions. Catalogs of Bach's works made shortly after the composer's death list not two but five Passions, which Terry addresses in chronological order. In the first volume, Terry discusses the St. John Passion of 1723, followed by a synopsis of the text of Picander's rhymed Passion libretto of 1725 (which Bach might have set but

for which no music remains). In the second volume, the author considers the St. Matthew Passion and offers an outline of the pasticcio, the St. Mark Passion (libretto by Picander and using musical sections from Bach's *Trauer-Ode* of 1727). Terry argues against considering the final Passion, ostensibly on a text from St. Luke, authentic, even though it was included by Spitta in the 1898 Bach-Gesellschaft. Although musical motives or themes are occasionally quoted by Terry, the focus is on how the music enhances the meaning or emotions of the text used by Bach. Terry's background research into the texts and their history remains the basis for many writers.

GRETA J. OLSON

Penderecki, Krzysztof b. 1933

Polish composer

Penderecki, Krzysztof, *Labyrinth of Time: Five Addresses for the End of the Millennium*, edited by Ray Robinson, translated by William Brand, Chapel Hill, North Carolina: Hinshaw Music, 1998

Robinson, Ray, and Allen Winold, *A Study of the Penderecki St. Luke Passion*, Celle: Moeck Verlag, 1983

Schwinger, Wolfram, *Krzysztof Penderecki, His Life and Work: Encounters, Biography, and Musical Commentary*, translated by William Mann, London: Schott, 1989

There are three varieties of English-language books on Penderecki: studies of individual works or of aspects of his compositional technique, mostly in the form of dissertations (which may be considered equivalent to books but will not be individually reviewed here); survey books addressed to wider audiences, including those by Penderecki and Schwinger listed here; and collections of articles, such as the new yearbook *Studies in Penderecki* (Prestige, 1998–), which Regina Chlopicka and Ray Robinson initiated to overcome the Polish-English language barrier.

Many important studies of Penderecki's life and work (including interviews) are available only in Polish. The list of such works includes books by Krzysztof Lisicki, Ludwik Erhardt, Mieczyslaw Tomaszewski, and various conference proceedings, especially from Krakow, which is, at present, the strongest center for Penderecki studies. The Polish school focuses on hermeneutics and cultural-context studies; only Danuta Mirka has brought a new approach of Tarasti-style semiotics to the field. Numerous dissertations on Penderecki have appeared in Germany, France, and the United States, but evidence does not seem to indicate an emergence of many devoted Penderecki scholars.

Of the books under review, the most impressive in size, scope, and physical appearance is SCHWINGER. It is interesting to note that this work has been issued by the publisher of Penderecki's music, especially because the author presents a highly positive image of the composer. The expanded English text consists of "Encounters and Biography" (in six sections) and "Musical Commentary" (in which works are grouped by genre and discussed individually, with photographs and musical examples where necessary). The text is followed by two postscripts, one to the first edition and one to the English edition, and a series of appendices (list of works, selected recordings, indices). The biography includes such trivia as a copy of a letter from Ronald Reagan, but the author does not include an impartial examination of the composer's political involvement with the communist government of the Polish People's Republic (which permitted Penderecki's international career to flourish, sanctioned huge domestic festivals of his music in 1980 and 1988, and allowed the composer to accumulate an unusual—for socialist Poland—degree of wealth). The composer's places of residence, dates of premieres, and travel itineraries are dutifully noted. The most useful aspect of the book is its detailed, straightforward (although somewhat superficial) account of Penderecki's works. Written by a music critic, these descriptions are suitable for a general reader who is enticed to delve into the unfamiliar musical territory. There are some typographic or spelling errors in Polish names and mistakes in the index; on the whole, however, the volume is handsomely produced and edited.

Schwinger's book, despite its shortcomings, is much more useful than Ray Robinson's *Krzysztof Penderecki: A Guide to His Works*, compiled to celebrate Penderecki's 50th birthday. This short brochure consists of a biographical sketch, description of style periods until 1983, a list of works, a list of first performances, discography, chronology, and bibliography.

ROBINSON is intended for "both musical amateurs and professional musicians." The book consists of seven chapters outlining the general context of *St. Luke Passion*, its compositional and performance history, and many analytical details. Chapter 1 contains an overview of the composer's life as well as the genesis and reception of his work. Chapter 2 presents the history of the passion as a genre; the discussion of Penderecki's text in chapter 3 is followed in chapter 4 by a general account of the music and descriptions of individual movements in chapter 5. Chapter 6 addresses some theoretical issues: the use of quotation; the pitch set and motives derived from it; and serial and non-serial aspects of pitch organization. Chapter 7 compares the *St. Luke Passion* with other works. The book also includes a discography of and a bibliography (both are completely outdated by now). The text is clearly written, with sufficient references to musical details; the book provides a good introduction to one of the major pieces of the 20th-century choral repertoire.

Robinson also served as the editor for PENDERECKI, which presents English versions of four addresses the composer gave when receiving honorary degrees (1993–96)

accompanied by an additional essay; the texts for *Dies Irae, Cosmogony,* and *Seven Gates of Jerusalem;* a brief biography; and an interview of Penderecki by Robinson. The original Polish edition of this book appeared in 1997 and was greeted with abundant praise by Polish musicologists, music critics, and culture historians; Penderecki undoubtedly has had a profound impact on the intellectual life of that nation. This volume is important for all Penderecki scholars as it explains, in the composer's own words, his aesthetic views and philosophical stance. The sections of the book bear titles referring to nature and spirituality (with Judeo-Christian overtones): "The Tree Inside," "The Artist in the Labyrinth," "The End of the Century Does Not Mean the End of Art," "Elegy for a Dying Forest," and "The Ark." The author's tone is both polemical and self-referential; the composer criticizes chaos of modern ideas and proposes a solution—his personal "musical ark" of the genre of the symphony (drawing inspiration from Mahler). Penderecki refutes his critics and gives reasons for his personal evolution, which had been perceived by some as a betrayal of the avant-garde. The interview illuminates many interesting details about Penderecki's works and aesthetic stance, connecting traditional elements of musical language with modern innovations.

MARIA ANNA HARLEY

Performance Practice: General

Boyden, David D., *The History of Violin Playing from Its Origins to 1761,* London: Oxford University Press, 1965

Brown, Howard Mayer, and Stanley Sadie, editors, *Performance Practice,* 2 vols., London: Macmillan, 1989, New York: Norton, 1990

Dorian, Frederick, *The History of Music in Performance: The Art of Musical Interpretation from the Renaissance to Our Day,* New York: Norton, 1942

Ferguson, Howard, *Keyboard Interpretation from the 14th to the 19th Century: An Introduction,* New York: Oxford University Press, 1975

Le Huray, Peter, *Authenticity in Performance: Eighteenth-Century Case Studies,* Cambridge: Cambridge University Press, 1990

MacClintock, Carol, editor and translator, *Readings in the History of Music in Performance,* Bloomington: Indiana University Press, 1979

Sherman, Bernard D., *Inside Early Music: Conversations with Performers,* New York: Oxford University Press, 1997

The aspect of music known as performance practice revolves around the study of original sources and scores in an attempt to uncover aspects of musical performance that were associated with a particular work or genre at the time of its composition. The subject covers a wide variety of details of performance: the types of instruments or voices appropriate for a particular work or historical period, styles of bowing and articulation, the interpretation of notation, suitable ornamentation, and even how and when the performer might be expected to make extemporaneous additions to a score. This branch of musical study was initially undertaken in earnest in the first half of the 20th century in German universities and later in U.S. universities. The first modern study of performance practices was Arnold Dolmetsch's *The Interpretation of the Music of the XVII and XVIII Centuries* (1915), which focuses on the music of the baroque, offering a summary of the issues of phrasing, bowing, articulation, and ornamentation in music of that period. Most of the earliest publications on performance practice center on the music of the 17th and 18th centuries, while later works highlight the medieval and Renaissance periods. It is only more recently that scholarly attention has turned to the classical and romantic eras, which were previously thought to be close enough to our own era as not to warrant any further investigation.

The essential universal guide to performance practices is BROWN and SADIE. Its two volumes (divided into discussions on music before and after 1600) contain 36 essays by important scholars covering the major performing issues, instruments, and genres from the Middle Ages to the 20th century. Perhaps as informative as the essays is the work's scholarly apparatus; extended footnotes and bibliographies of primary sources (mostly treatises from each major period of music history) direct the reader to even more information than can be covered in each essay. Many of the essays go well beyond basic issues of ornamentation to deal with tempos (and fluctuations within them), timbres, voice types, and instrument development, as well as the sizes and makeup of musical ensembles. Because this is a scholarly work intended primarily for practicing musicians and music scholars, those with limited musical training are likely to have considerable difficulty with much of the material. Even students of music will find wading through discussions of Renaissance *musica ficta* and baroque tunings no easy affair.

DORIAN intended his book for a wider audience than Brown and Sadie, so those with only a general knowledge of music will be able to grasp the material more easily. On the other hand, Dorian does not go into the same depth as Brown and Sadie. Because it is one of the earlier books on performance practices, Dorian reflects an activist point of view against the prevailing performance style (particularly orchestral) of the first half of the 20th century. The author argues against the overemphasis of the role of the performer as interpreter, calling for loyalty to the score within the practical limits of notation. He offers quotations from earlier composers and theorists from the Renaissance to the 19th century to buttress his discussions of earlier performing styles and presents musical practices that are often not reflected in notation (e.g., size

of orchestras, rhythmic conventions, ornamentation, phrasing, and dynamics). Although his scholarship is not as up-to-date as that of Brown and Sadie, Dorian provides a basic introduction to the topic for the nonmusician.

MacCLINTOCK presents a representative selection of the original written sources from the Middle Ages to the early romantic period that form the core of performance practice scholarship. The sources divide into two general types: personal accounts of performances and performers and musical treatises on how to perform or compose. Within the second category can also be included introductions to published musical works that provide information from the composer on how the work might be (or should be) performed. Some of the most important and widely known authors are represented, including Frescobaldi, Praetorius, C.P.E. Bach, Quantz, Leopold Mozart, Türk, and Tosi, although MacClintock relies rather heavily on treatises about singing and keyboard playing. The disadvantage to this collection is its lack of information about how influential or widely held the views of the various authors were at the time of their writing.

Part of the recent history of the historical performance movement has been an ongoing debate over whether such performances are actually authentic or if reconstructing early musical practices is an impossibility or, worse, a sham. The introduction to SHERMAN offers an excellent summary of the often moral and political viewpoints held by those on either side of the issue. The book itself is a collection of interviews with acclaimed performers in the historical performance field, from Marcel Pérès discussing the performance of medieval plainchant to John Eliot Gardiner on Berloiz and Brahms. Each performer provides general information about the performance practice issues within his or her own specialty, as well as offering explanations of his or her own viewpoints and performance philosophies. The book is aimed at the general reader and concertgoer and should delight early music enthusiasts, while providing a good deal of general information for the uninitiated.

A number of books are intended as practical performance guides to specific instruments or works. LE HURAY includes ten different works representing major musical genres from the baroque and classical periods and discusses each in terms of performance issues and questions that they present. The book is targeted primarily at performers and demonstrates the kind of scholarship and original sources that can be used to apply principles of performance practices to other musical works. Although the moderate number of musical examples is beyond the knowledge of the general reader, other kinds of information about performing forces and styles may assist those with limited musical knowledge.

Like Le Huray, FERGUSON's book is a practical performance guide, specifically for players of keyboard instruments. Covering basic topics regarding types of keyboard instruments, musical forms, tempo, phrasing and articulation, fingering, rhythmic conventions, and ornamentation, Ferguson concisely summarizes the information available and offers several sets of questions intended to help the performer make necessary decisions about specifics of performance. Particularly helpful is his index of ornaments (designed to identify differing interpretations of the same symbol), as well as the bibliographies of original sources, facsimile scores, and scholarly editions that are available in modern publications.

Although BOYDEN also limits his topic to a single instrument—the violin—his book is not a practical guide to performers but a scholarly effort to document the history of the development of violin making, violin technique and style, violin music, and the interaction of these factors. The author examines and discusses music and musical treatises from four 50-year periods from the historical beginnings of the instrument to the year 1761, presenting a detailed account of the important aspects of violin playing of each era: grip, fingering, bowings, vibrato, multiple stops, articulation, phrasing, and ornamentation. As an important scholarly resource, it may be overwhelming to the nonviolinist.

DEBORAH KAUFFMAN

Performance Practice: Medieval

Brown, Howard Mayer, and Stanley Sadie, editors, *Performance Practice: Music before 1600,* Basingstoke: Macmillan Press, 1989; and New York: Norton, 1990

Dart, Thurston, *The Interpretation of Music,* London: Hutchinson, 1954

McGee, Timothy J., *Medieval and Renaissance Music: A Performer's Guide,* Toronto: University of Toronto Press, 1985

————, *The Sound of Medieval Song: Ornamentation and Vocal Style According to the Treatises,* Oxford: Clarendon Press, and New York: Oxford University Press, 1998

Munrow, David, *Instruments of the Middle Ages and Renaissance,* London: Oxford University Press, 1976

Page, Christopher, *Music and Instruments of the Middle Ages: Studies on Texts and Performance,* Aldershot, and Brookfield, Vermont: Variorum, 1997

————, *The Owl and the Nightingale: Musical Life and Ideas in France, 1100–1300,* London: Dent, and Berkeley: University of California Press, 1989

————, *Voices and Instruments of the Middle Ages: Instrumental Practice and Songs in France, 1100–1300,* Berkeley: University of California Press, 1986

Rayburn, John, *Gregorian Chant: A History of the Controversy Concerning Its Rhythm,* New York: Rayburn, 1961; reprint, Westport, Connecticut: Greenwood Press, 1981

Stevens, John, *Words and Music in the Middle Ages: Song, Narrative, Dance, and Drama, 1050–1350,* Cambridge: Cambridge University Press, 1986

Werf, Hendrik van der, *The Extant Troubadour Melodies: Transcriptions and Essays for Performers and Scholars,* Rochester, New York: Werf, 1984

Written music of the Middle Ages gives little indication, if any, about how the composition was to be performed. The number of performers required or expected, whether instruments were to be used, the appropriate occasion or location for performance, the vocal quality and style expected, and whether the musical lines were to be embellished are almost never explicitly noted. Even basic issues, such as correct text underlay, correct interpretation of rhythm, and even the actual pitches can be open to question. To supplement the meager evidence of the actual notated music, researchers turn to secondary sources—including musical iconography, theoretical and literary texts, and liturgical manuscripts—for hints about the performance of this music. Because it was not the prime consideration of these sources to describe accurate musical performances, such documents at best offer fragmentary and ambiguous evidence about performance practice in the Middle Ages. Some researchers therefore explore the living traditions of folk cultures in Europe and the Middle East for clues about medieval performances. This practice has produced some beautiful recordings but offers little substantive evidence of the validity of present-day cultures as resources for information about the performance of medieval music.

With the rise of groups performing medieval music in the 1950s, medieval musical performance came to be strongly associated with the eclectic use of musical instruments. Beginning in the late 1970s, a group of mostly British performers challenged this stance and began to explore a more vocally oriented performance practice. The most partisan defender of what came to be called the "English *a cappella* heresy" is Christopher Page, an English scholar and performer. Although the conclusions of Page and others subscribing to the so-called heresy are still controversial, their work has strongly influenced current research in performance practice as well as the actual performance of medieval music.

DART focuses primarily on the 17th and 18th centuries, but his chapter on the Middle Ages influenced the styles assumed by groups performing medieval music in the 1950s and beyond. Strongly emphasizing the medieval technique of successive composition of polyphonic lines, Dart encourages performers always to delineate the main melodic line, keeping other lines strictly subordinate. He also discusses musical instruments and appropriate venues for their use. Most of Dart's work is informed primarily by writings of the later 15th century, rather than by strictly medieval sources, and thus his conclusions about performance in the Middle Ages must be approached cautiously.

MUNROW, the central force behind the medieval performing groups of the 1960s and 1970s, discusses the instruments of the Middle Ages and Renaissance. Intended for a general audience, this heavily illustrated text gives a historical and technical description of the various classes of instruments, comparing them to modern folk instruments when applicable. Although he concentrates mostly on how the instrument was physically played, Munrow also gives some suggestions about performance practice.

McGEE (1985) introduces the potential performer of early music to the basics of interpreting early editions in a historically accurate manner, and he offers pragmatic advice for actual performances. His discussions of music for different sizes and types of performing groups emphasize issues such as text underlay, vocal style and timbre, phrasing, and the appropriate use of instruments. This general coverage is complemented by more detailed discussions of ornamentation and improvisation, although the emphasis here is more on Renaissance music than on medieval. This is a good practical introduction to medieval performance practice, although now somewhat dated.

McGEE (1998) further explores medieval vocal style through evidence presented in medieval theoretical treatises. He suggests that complex embellishment of the melodic line, through ornamentation, melodic inflections, and other techniques, was integral to the vocal style of the Middle Ages, something that is not reflected in present-day performances. His assertion that the singing traditions of the Middle East and India most closely resemble medieval vocal style is likely to be controversial.

BROWN and SADIE is a collection of essays by a number of authors on performance practice in both the Middle Ages and the Renaissance. Brown's introduction to the section on the Middle Ages is an excellent and concise overview of the problems and pitfalls of sources for the study of medieval performance practice and of the history of research in the area in general. The articles on music of the Middle Ages discuss performance of chant and secular monophony and polyphony to 1400, review past and present research in the area, and investigate problems specific to that repertory. Chapters on *musica ficta* and tempo and proportion cover both the Middle Ages and Renaissance, adding valuable detail about these complex topics. This is the best overall text on performance practice in the Middle Ages; most of it is immensely readable.

STEVENS focuses on the interaction of words and music in all types of monophonic song. He concludes that the aesthetic of number was of primary importance in the theory of medieval song and that the words and music are related through numerical structures. In order to maintain the emphasis on number and still achieve a balance between words and music, the rhythm of monophonic song should, according to Stevens, be given an isosyllabic interpretation and performers should not try to relate the text directly to the music. Stevens's conclusions in this complex and highly technical work are controversial.

PAGE (1986) investigates references to medieval song and instruments in contemporaneous literary sources, particularly French-language romances, psalm commentaries, and sermons. Surveying descriptions of medieval musical genres in the first part of the text and instruments in the second half, Page concludes that the role of accompanying stringed instruments in medieval song was determined primarily by musical genre and cannot easily be generalized further. The reliability of Page's sources is controversial, but this volume and his further studies have been influential among both performing groups and scholars.

PAGE (1989) is an extension of his earlier book, looking at a larger group of French repertories from 1100 to 1300, particularly in Paris. He discusses the cultural milieu of a number of medieval musical genres, including the carole, courtly song, plainchant, and Parisian polyphony. A highly readable text, the emphasis is less on practical lessons in performance practice than on placing medieval music in the context of cultural life of urban Paris.

PAGE (1997) is a collection of the author's journal articles, the majority of which discuss medieval performance. The subject matter is wide ranging, including instrument makers, instrument terminology, editions of theoretical works, the presence of music in chilvaric fiction, and the performance of specific musical genres. As a whole, this collection illustrates Page's dedication to gaining a holistic view of performance practice through contemporaneous source materials.

WERF is primarily a critical edition of troubadour melodies, but the introduction delves into the problems of interpreting the written sources in performance. Werf includes detailed and thoughtful discussions of chromatic alterations, the relationship of the text and music, and the difficulties of establishing practical performing editions. The emphasis on the relationship between scholarly editions and performance is enlightening, but the technical detail is perhaps too involved for the general reader.

RAYBURN proffers a history of the study of the rhythm of chant, an account of the numerous theories on the "correct" interpretation of rhythm in chant posited by scholars from the 19th to the mid-20th century. Fascinating in the variety of interpretations suggested for a single musical genre, this work is also notable because it reveals how politics, whether national or religious in origin, can influence what is accepted as authentic performance.

NANCY LORIMER

Performance Practice: Renaissance

Berger, Anna Maria Busse, *Mensuration and Proportion Signs: Origins and Evolution,* Oxford: Clarendon Press, and New York: Oxford University Press, 1990

Berger, Karol, *Musica ficta: Theories of Accidental Inflections in Vocal Polyphony from Marchetto da Padova to Gioseffo Zarlino*, Cambridge: Cambridge University Press, 1987

Brown, Howard Mayer, and Stanley Sadie, editors, *Performance Practice: Music before 1600*, Basingstoke: Macmillan Press, 1989; and New York: Norton, 1990

Kite-Powell, Jeffrey T., editor, *A Performer's Guide to Renaissance Music,* New York: Schirmer Books, 1994

McGee, Timothy J., *Medieval and Renaissance Music: A Performer's Guide,* Toronto: University of Toronto Press, 1985

Musicological research into performing practices of Western music of past ages became increasingly important in the course of the 20th century; there are even several relatively new scholarly journals devoted to the subject. Earlier in the century the main task was to make available to performers and scholars the raw materials for such study: the extant music itself (in scholarly editions), as well as editions and translations of theoretical and practical writings—activities that continue today. The second half of the 20th century also saw instrument makers creating precise modern copies of historical instruments and musicians relearning lost performing techniques; these techniques have been employed increasingly in both amateur and professional circles and are well documented in recordings. At universities, the collegium musicum movement has done much to acquaint students with the repertory, instruments, and performing techniques of early music. The books discussed below reflect the recent and growing interest in performing practices of music before 1600; two of them are addressed directly to the student performer or aspiring director of an early music ensemble (yet will also be very useful to the professional), and three are geared to the professional scholar or scholar-performer.

McGEE was the first and still quite useful effort to distill a wide range of information about performing medieval and Renaissance music in a form easily comprehensible to the nonspecialist performer. Divided into four parts, the book first introduces the reader to basic issues such as differences between original notation and modern editions, musical flow, and how one can deal practically with such problems as text underlay, tempo, *musica ficta,* singing technique, and instrumental scoring. The second part surveys the repertory based on performing forces (including such issues as instrumental doubling or replacement of vocal lines). The third treats ornamentation, improvisation, and articulation. The final part deals with practical considerations such as programming, program notes, and balance within an early music ensemble. There are also abbreviated bibliographies of music and secondary literature concerning virtually every topic taken up in the book.

McGee writes clearly and with an understanding of real-world conditions under which the modern performer must operate. On occasion he suggests performance options for which he adduces no evidence, but otherwise the limitations and liberties he sets forth are historically sound. His advocacy of improvised counterpoint is especially welcome, inasmuch as most music of the period was in fact improvised. (Indeed, it is not clear that instrumentalists needed to be able to read music, since they learned their craft by rote.) The usefulness of the book is enhanced by dozens of musical examples, 11 tables, a chronological chart showing the use of various musical instruments, and a fairly extensive bibliography.

KITE-POWELL lacks the synthetic perspective of a single-authored book such as McGee's, but its 31 chapters by 21 authors provide much more detailed and specialized information on many topics. There is, however, a qualitative difference among the chapters; a few authors have relatively little musicological training (being primarily performers), although most are recognized as leading scholarly authorities on their subjects. Similarly, whereas McGee's book focuses on which instruments ought to be employed in specific repertories, performance situations, and decisions to be made about instrumentation, repetition of sections, tempo, ornamentation, etc., Kite-Powell's volume is more concerned with the instruments themselves (15 chapters), for which one finds not only historical treatments but also practical information on modern makers, hints on performing technique, and so on. There is less about musical style and repertory than in McGee's book, but there are more detailed treatments of topics such as tuning and temperament, pitch and transposition, and pronunciation of text. Furthermore, while both books offer practical considerations, Kite-Powell alone offers a summary of Renaissance theory as well as an introduction to Renaissance dance. Finally, bibliographies and suggestions of recordings (where relevant) follow each chapter.

BROWN and SADIE, a book of musicological essays by noted scholars, is more technical and academic than the previous two books, focusing entirely on the evidence of the sources and issues of performance practice in the medieval and Renaissance periods, without much consideration of problems of performing such music today. Its two main parts ("The Middle Ages" and "The Renaissance") are separated by an "Interlude." The first part contains an introduction and chapter on instruments by Brown and essays on "Chant" by David Hiley (which includes a section "From the Middle Ages to the Present"), "Secular Monophony" by Wulf Arlt, and "Polyphony before 1400" by Christopher Page. The second part consists of an introduction and chapters on instruments by Brown, followed by essays on sacred polyphony by Christopher A. Reynolds, secular polyphony of the 15th and 16th centuries by David Fallows and Anthony Newman (respectively), and "Monophony and the Unwritten Tradition" by James Haar. The interlude confronts two of the principal issues of Renaissance performing practice with essays on "Musica Ficta" by Karol Berger and "Tempo and Proportions" by Alejandro Planchart. There are extensive end notes, a useful bibliography of sources to 1600, and a good index.

In addition to the more general books, two specialized musicological studies of music theorists of the late Middle Ages and Renaissance deserve mention, as they deal with fundamental issues related to performance practice, namely, pitch and the temporal aspects of Renaissance music. Neither book provides simple answers or a single, broadly applicable conclusion (nor could there likely be such a generalization), but both clarify the positions of individual writers and the various conventions of different times and places. Karol BERGER is the now standard study of *musica ficta*, the alteration in performance under certain circumstances of written pitches in manuscripts and early prints according to conventions of the period; the approach here is a systematic and thorough study of music-theoretic writings from the 14th through the 16th century on the subject; the study does not, by intention, deal much with the evidence of preserved music.

Anna Maria Busse BERGER takes a similar approach to the issue of the relationship of various note values in the Renaissance system of mensural notation and proportions. The author compares mensuration signs and the strokes and other figures that modify them to other methods of measuring time from the 13th to the 16th century. The relationships between perfect and imperfect time and between major and minor prolation are explored in some detail, as is the use of cut signs and proportions. This is not a book for the beginner, but it is the most thorough study of its kind.

RAYMOND ERICKSON

Performance Practice: Baroque

Borgir, Tharald, *The Performance of the Basso Continuo in Italian Baroque Music,* Ann Arbor, Michigan: UMI Research Press, 1987

Brown, Howard Mayer, and Stanley Sadie, editors, *Performance Practice: Music after 1600,* London: Macmillan, 1989; and New York: Norton, 1990

Butt, John, *Music Education and the Art of Performance in the German Baroque,* Cambridge: Cambridge University Press, 1994

Carter, Stewart, editor, *A Performer's Guide to Seventeenth-Century Music,* New York: Schirmer Books, 1997

Cohen, Joel, and Herb Snitzer, *Reprise: The Extraordinary Revival of Early Music,* Boston: Little Brown, 1985

Cyr, Mary, *Performing Baroque Music,* Portland, Oregon: Amadeus Press, and Aldershot: Scolar Press, 1992

Leppard, Raymond, *Authenticity in Music,* London: Faber, and Portland, Oregon: Amadeus Press, 1988

Mather, Betty Bang, *The Interpretation of French Music from 1675 to 1775 for Woodwind and Other Performers,* New York: McGinnis and Marx, 1973

Mather, Betty Bang, and David Lasocki, *Free Ornamentation in Woodwind Music, 1700–1775: An Anthology with Introduction,* New York: McGinnis and Marx, 1976

Neumann, Frederick, *Ornamentation in Baroque and Post-Baroque Music: With Special Emphasis on J.S. Bach,* Princeton, New Jersey: Princeton University Press, 1978

———, *Performance Practices of the Seventeenth and Eighteenth Centuries,* New York: Schirmer Books, 1993

Quantz, Johann Joachim, *On Playing the Flute,* translated by Edward R. Reilly, New York: Schirmer, and London: Faber, 1966; 2nd edition, 1985

Rice, Albert R., *The Baroque Clarinet,* Oxford: Clarendon Press, and New York: Oxford University Press, 1992

Today we take for granted that music of earlier periods will be played regularly and with some attention to details of authenticity, whether performed on original instruments or played with knowledge of improvisational and embellishing techniques of the time in which the composition was written, but the availability of such music is a relatively recent development. Before World War I, the works of Vivaldi were rarely heard, and much of Monteverdi's music was unavailable in print until 1942, to mention only two of many such examples.

The exploration into realms of music previously unknown or rediscovered, spurred by the enthusiasm of Arnold Dolmetsch for playing compositions on the instruments for which the pieces were written, flourished in the 20th century. Research into how musicians expected their music to be played, interest in publishing accurate texts, and the examination of the social and cultural milieu that gave birth to a particular body of music all complement the explosion of performances on original instruments.

Early treatises are often specific to the work of one composer, or to one carefully limited repertoire. Scholars today, led by Frederick Neumann, examine these early works and attempt to explain in more contemporary language the intent and application of the performance requirements. As interest in historically informed performance has grown, studies have proliferated and the interest of performers has expanded correspondingly.

LEPPARD's small volume presents a good introduction to the issues of authenticity in performance. He outlines the history of the inquiry and recognizes that these questions provide "a never-ending revision of the probabilities and possibilities" of the performance of early music.

Another source for a casual reader is COHEN and SNITZER, which examines the achievements of the musicians and scholars who have brought early music from the avant-garde to the musical mainstream. Through their work the reader understands more clearly the motivations and rewards of the enterprise of reconstruction and rediscovery of early music. Snitzer's annotated photographs of performers and instruments illustrate vividly the vigor and liveliness of the people who perform on early instruments.

CYR's volume is a concise guide to the performance of baroque music. Touching on topics such as tempo, sound, spirit, dynamics, pitch and temperament, the basso continuo, articulation, rhythm and notation, and ornamentation, the work functions well as an introduction for listeners and college students. It is less adequate for the performer, who may need the more systematically practical approach of Mather. Cyr includes good bibliographical notes at the end of each section to aid further study.

An indispensable book for a comprehensive understanding of the issues involved in a study of historical performance practice is the collection edited by BROWN and SADIE. The introduction provides valuable insight into questions about the relationship between the venue and the music, particularly the dichotomy between what was politically inspired and that which was motivated by artistic concerns. More fully than in other references, sources of information are outlined, from the theoretical to the practical, and from journals, diaries, and personnel records to iconographic evidence and surviving instruments. With essays detailing important performance questions for specific instruments, and others addressing more universal problems such as tuning, intonation, and articulation, to mention only a few, this book presents the most readable, yet scholarly work available. The second half of the book follows the progression of performance practices into the classical period and beyond.

MATHER and MATHER and LASOCKI, in their respective volumes examining performance practice of the French baroque and free ornamentation, as well as in other publications, offer guidance to the practicing musician. They extensively examine the original sources and present small exercises aimed at training a performer in the nuances of style relative to specific time periods, locales, and composers. In every case, the sources of both theoretical and musical material are clearly presented, allowing further independent examination. Clearly and concisely written, these books are invaluable for learning the appropriate application of theoretical maxims and for allowing them to become part of a musician's practical repertoire.

For the scholar, Neumann's prolific output is indispensable. NEUMANN (1978), a voluminous work, begins with an overview of categories of musical ornaments and then examines individual ornaments, especially as they occur in the music of J.S. Bach. In later chapters, Neumann presents exhaustive examples of nearly every ornament, categorized by time frame and country of origin, citing original sources, and giving musical examples, with written out realizations. This book elicited many comments and responses from other scholars, creating a lively dialogue primarily in journal

articles. Neumann replies to many of the topics of that debate in his *Essays in Performance Practice* (1982) and *New Essays in Performance Practice* (1989).

NEUMANN (1993) addresses his most recent work not to scholars but primarily to "performers and students of performance." This book relies heavily on his earlier work but is geared more to the practitioner and takes into account the extensive print dialogue that ensued between the publication of his first book and this one. The introduction to the work gives a concise, critical review of important literature and attempts to offer "a foundation of historical insights as a basis for making artistic decisions."

BUTT's study offers an unusual and valuable look at music education during the German baroque, an era notable for the rise of Protestant (especially Lutheran) singing style. Like the other works considered here, Butt examines applied performance practice. His emphasis focuses more strongly than other studies on the cultural, social, and political influences that produced these musical results.

BORGIR examines performance issues for the basso continuo in the Italian baroque, problems that arise in part from the fact that bass lines are mere outlines for what is to be played and in part from notations made by composers that offer options for realization on quite disparate instruments, from plucked or bowed strings to winds and to keyboard. Borgir's work is invaluable for any serious performer of this repertoire. While not offering definitive answers to all questions, he raises most of the relevant concerns and offers avenues for exploring solutions.

Because the clarinet first evolved during the baroque period, and because the repertoire for this instrument is limited, few studies address the particular problems and issues surrounding the clarinet. After a review of the clarinet's development, RICE gathers nearly all the written information concerning playing techniques for the early prototypes and offers insights into performance difficulties as well as possibilities. He follows this discussion with a presentation of the extant baroque musical sources for clarinet, astutely commenting on performance problems and solutions. Rice concludes with an extensive bibliography for further reading and research.

No student of baroque performance practice can ignore the work of QUANTZ. Through his translation of this treatise, Reilly gives us access to Quantz's seminal work. Although specifically addressed to flute playing, much of Quantz's treatise is applicable to all musical enterprise, and many of his comments that are relevant only for the music of the particular period in which he wrote can be applied to other instrumentalists and vocalists. Quantz covers topics as broad as aesthetics and musicality ("those who would dedicate themselves to music"), and as specific as how to hold the instrument. He discusses playing the allegro, improvisations, cadenzas, musical signs, graces, breathing, and the role of an accompanist, among other topics. Many observations are supported by musical examples.

Using contributions by many prominent scholars, CARTER systematically examines questions of style for vocalists (arranged both by country—France, England, Italy, and Germany—and by size of ensemble), instrumental issues (organized by general classification—woodwind, brass, and string), and finally performance practice (including ornamentation in early 17th-century music, questions of meter and tempo, the basso continuo, tuning, temperament, pitch, and concluding with dance and theatrical productions).

MARTHA FARAHAT

Performance Practice: Classical

Brown, A. Peter, *Performing Haydn's The Creation: Reconstructing the Earliest Renditions,* Bloomington: Indiana University Press, 1986

Brown, Howard Mayer, and Stanley Sadie, editors, *Performance Practice: Music after 1600,* London: Macmillan, 1989; and New York: Norton, 1990

Rosenblum, Sandra P., *Performance Practices in Classic Piano Music: Their Principles and Applications,* Bloomington: Indiana University Press, 1988

Stowell, Robin, *Violin Technique and Performance Practices in the Late Eighteenth and Early Nineteenth Centuries,* Cambridge: Cambridge University Press, 1985

Tosi, Pier Francesco, *Introduction to the Art of Singing, by Johann Friedrich Agricola,* edited and translated by Julianne Baird, Cambridge: Cambridge University Press, 1995

Zaslaw, Neal, *Mozart's Symphonies: Context, Performance Practice, Reception,* Oxford: Clarendon Press, and New York: Oxford University Press, 1989

The notion of a classical period of music history sandwiched between the baroque and romantic eras and embracing the second half of the 18th century is dubious although widely employed. In music, unlike in the fine arts, architecture, drama, poetry, or literature, there are no close parallels to be drawn between the 18th-century classical style of music and that of classical antiquity. Therefore, it is difficult to define a period or style of music as classical, and the definitions that do exist are enormously varied and complicated, with most limiting the term to refer to music falling within certain chronological boundaries, containing particular cultural elements, or expressing a set of overarching stylistic characteristics. The books reviewed below represent a general survey; specialized studies of voice, violin, and fortepiano music; and an in-depth study of a major work by a classical composer; taken together, they reflect the ambiguity of the notion of classical music.

For an excellent survey of most of the principal issues, one need go no farther than the section devoted to the classical era in BROWN and SADIE. Following a wide-ranging introduction by Zaslaw that does not substantially duplicate the other essays, four authors treat their own areas of expertise. Malcolm Bilson focuses on compositional style in its relationship to the historical development of the piano, arguing, for example, that certain passages in the *Pathétique* Sonata do not suit the modern piano as well as they suited the instruments Beethoven knew. He also challenges modern pedaling and basic playing technique, which is so different from techniques of the classical period. Stowell's essay on the playing of stringed instruments is primarily concerned with violin playing, although some attention is also paid to viola, cello, and contrabass. David Charlton studies a variety of woodwind and brass instruments—flute, oboe, clarinet, lower-pitched clarinets (e.g., basset-clarinet), bassoon, horn, trumpet, and trombone—dealing with classical ideals of tone, tonguing and articulation, vibrato, reeds, and special effects. Robert Levin, who improvises cadenzas in his piano concerto performances, brings that expertise to bear on "Instrumental Ornamentation, Improvisation, and Cadenzas," offering general guidelines and examples of embellishments, a list of contexts in Mozart's piano concertos where "the notated text may be incomplete," guidelines for cadenza improvisation (in the process comparing Türk's rules with Mozart's written-out cadenzas), fermata embellishments, free fantasies, and the use of continuo in keyboard concertos. Finally, Will Crutchfield tackles the most difficult area of all: vocal music. He argues that vocal teachings of both the classical and present-day eras are typically concerned only with "Italian music, principally operatic," but "many Classical practices are impossible to achieve" with the modern vocal technique used by most present-day "early music singers." He also analyzes singing treatises; voice types; technical aspects of classical vocalism; recitative; what he calls "the prosodic appoggiatura"; the aria, cantabile, and allegro styles (and their relationship to ornamentation, cadenzas and fermatas); and (briefly) non-Italian vocal music.

TOSI is a useful English translation by Julianne Baird of J.F. Agricola's *Anleitung zur Singkunst,* a 1757 German translation of, and gloss on, the *Opinioni de' cantori antichi e moderni* (1723), the most important 18th-century treatise on the Italian style of singing, which was authored by the famous castrato, Pier Francesco Tosi. Agricola's work, reflecting practices at the court of Frederick the Great, continued to be influential in Germany throughout the 18th century, affecting, for example, Türk's treatise on keyboard playing, the *Clavierschule,* and Johann Adam Hiller's important singing treatise, *Anweisung zum musikalische-zierlichen Gesange* (1780).

The introduction by Baird conveys the value and limits of Agricola's work. She explains that Agricola's extensive commentaries on Tosi's text update the original

Italian baroque perspectives, but she also makes clear that Agricola's point of view is that of a musician working under the authoritarian Frederick the Great, who forbade his musicians and singers to deviate from the written notation. Thus, Agricola could not use the kind of *improvised* ornamentation that was common elsewhere throughout the entire 18th century—including, one might add, in performances of Mozart's opera and even (later and on a more restrained scale) in Schubert's *Lieder.* Therefore, one of the chief values of the book resides in the discussion of *notated* examples of ornaments, which the modern singer can use as stylistic models for improvised ornamentation for music of the late baroque and classical eras.

Of Tosi's ten chapters, three offer general remarks aimed at singing teachers, music students, and professional singers, and seven treat appoggiaturas, trills, divisions, recitative, arias, cadenzas (i.e., treatment of cadences), and improvised variations of melodies, respectively. Agricola's commentary is sometimes very extensive and far removed from Tosi's more focused concerns. For example, in the first chapter, Tosi's advice to singing teachers is dwarfed by Agricola's excursus into solmization and the physiology of the voice. There is also an encyclopedic range of detail regarding musical performance at the time that Mozart was born and Haydn was gaining his stride.

STOWELL covers the period when the orchestra developed into a relatively standard symphonic ensemble dominated by members of the string family; at the same time, these instruments were themselves undergoing considerable changes, partly in response to new conditions of performance created by the growth of public concerts in large halls. In this context, Stowell treats a number of major trends relating specifically to the performance history of string, mainly violin, instruments. (Such trends are paralleled in other types of instruments, as well.) He regards the gradual ascendancy of the French school of violin playing over the Italian in the course of the 18th century as critically important. Ironically, this transformation was abetted greatly by the Italian G.B. Viotti, who trained a large number of the major violinists in France during the late classical and early romantic periods. Equally significant is the new style of bow associated with François Tourte, which has had an enormous impact on string technique as it has developed from about 1790 to the present. Finally, Stowell evaluates the pan-European influence of the Paris Conservatory (established 1795) and its relatively consistent style of training.

Stowell derives tangible evidence from a dozen important violin tutors published between 1760 and 1840. Following a brief historical overview, the chapters cover the development of violin and bow; playing posture; basic and advanced bowing techniques; basic and advanced left-hand techniques; pitch, tuning, and intonation; general remarks on expression; style; phrasing and accentuation; notation of ornaments; and improvi-

sation. There is also a comprehensive appendix listing chronologically by country nearly 200 publications on violin playing published between ca. 1760 and ca. 1840, as well as a glossary of ornaments, a useful index, and a comprehensive bibliography.

ROSENBLUM is "written for serious piano students, for performers—professional and amateur, for piano and fortepiano teachers, for students of performance practices and as a resource for scholars." The author sensibly states that she sees the classical period "as having evolved gradually from the late Baroque and early Classic styles rather than as a premature and incomplete version of nineteenth-century Romantic pianism." Focusing primarily on the "mature Classic period" (beginning ca. 1775), she closely ties classical performance practices to the development of the piano itself at a time that this instrument emerged as a major vehicle for artistic expression.

The introductory chapter surveys the early history of the piano and its ultimate triumph over the harpsichord and clavichord and discusses issues of music aesthetics (music and rhetoric, *Empfindsamkeit*, Sturm und Drang); changes in notational conventions; and the relationships of Haydn, Mozart, Clementi, and Beethoven to the piano. In the following chapters, the author takes up individual aspects of the subject, including the construction and popularity of the fortepiano between 1780 and 1820; "Dynamics and Accentuation"; and a comparison of the use of pedals in the 18th and 20th centuries. The chapter titled "Articulation and Touch" traces the gradual shift from the non-legato touch basic toward the use of more legato after 1790, as well as other keyboard touches and slurs dot/stroke/wedge marks, while "Historical Technique and Fingering" evaluates quiet hand/arm, finger-oriented technique, staccato touches, and Clementi's and Beethoven's fingerings. Other topics include ornaments (such as improvised ornamentation); "Mixed Meters and Dotted Rhythms" (the assimilation of duple notation to ternary meters, two-against three, over- and double dotting); and numerous issues related to tempo and rhythm. The final chapter, "Performing Beethoven's Bagatelle Op. 126, No.5," demonstrates "the application of historically founded performances to one piece."

This book is useful for practitioner and scholar alike. Performers will be comfortable with the fact that the author is first and foremost a pianist and piano teacher, who is intimately familiar with the repertory and with historical and modern pianos and the performance problems both types of instruments present. But she is also a serious scholar, familiar with all the sources, from composers' sketches to recent secondary literature, who emphasizes the importance of viewing classical piano music in historical context but does not advocate the abandonment of the modern piano for this music.

BROWN focuses on performance issues in Haydn's famous oratorio, *The Creation,* a work performed in more than 40 times in Vienna alone between 1798 and 1810. (The author summarizes the Viennese venues and participants in a chart.) As he assesses the several scores, sets of parts, and first edition contemporary with these performances, Brown demonstrates that "historical authenticity" is a chimerical concept, for some performances of *The Creation* during Haydn's life involved more than 1,000 participants while other involved as few as 32. Still, the author's careful research does reveal certain norms: the orchestra was generally about twice the size of the chorus, and string sections did not bow together; boys originally sang the soprano and alto parts; Haydn used three (rather than today's customary five) soloists—and these sang along in the choruses; the composer did not expect or want much embellishment, but was most tolerant of sopranos in this respect, and he liked fast tempos. (In particular, the instrumental introduction, "The Representation of Chaos," was likely played much faster than the norm today.)

Brown adheres to a more strictly musicological approach than the other books reviewed here: this volume is essentially a study of sources, especially manuscripts, which will interest conductors and musicologists more than it will singers or instrumentalists (except for the remarks on vocal ornamentation). The one facet of the monograph that might be questioned concerns the author's suggested bowings, as he does not consider historical bowing or discuss the natural qualities of the new Tourte bow and the degree to which it may have influenced string playing in Vienna at the turn of the 19th century.

ZASLAW is not primarily a performance practice book, but, in addition to remarks concerning the earliest performances of specific Mozart symphonies, it presents a substantial chapter on performance practice, containing especially valuable information on the varied composition and seating of the various orchestras that premiered Mozart's symphonies and a useful chart summarizing this material. In addition, Zaslaw offers summary coverage of such matters as articulation, tempo, and the question of repeats.

RAYMOND ERICKSON

Performance Practice: Romantic

Brown, Howard Mayer, and Stanley Sadie, editors, *Performance Practice: Music after 1600*, London: Macmillan, 1989; and New York: Norton, 1990

Jackson, Roland John, *Performance Practice, Medieval to Contemporary: A Bibliographic Guide*, New York: Garland, 1988

Keck, George Russell, and Sherrill V. Martin, editors, *Feel the Spirit: Studies in Nineteenth-Century Afro-American Music*, Westport, Connecticut: Greenwood Press, 1988

Kenyon, Nicholas, editor, *Authenticity and Early Music: A Symposium*, Oxford: Oxford University Press, 1988

Kivy, Peter, *Authenticities: Philosophical Reflections on Musical Performance*, Ithaca, New York: Cornell University Press, 1995

Kravitt, Edward F., *The Lied: Mirror of Late Romanticism*, New Haven, Connecticut: Yale University Press, 1996

Millington, Barry, and Stewart Spencer, editors, *Wagner in Performance*, New Haven, Connecticut: Yale University Press, 1992

Newman, William S., *Beethoven on Beethoven: Playing His Piano Music His Way*, New York: Norton, 1988

Rink, John, editor, *The Practice of Performance: Studies in Musical Interpretation*, Cambridge: Cambridge University Press, 1995

Smith, Rollin, *Toward an Authentic Interpretation of the Organ Works of César Franck*, New York: Pendragon Press, 1983

Stowell, Robin, *Violin Technique and Performance Practices in the Late Eighteenth and Early Nineteenth Centuries*, Cambridge: Cambridge University Press, 1985

Todd, R. Larry, editor, *Nineteenth-Century Piano Music*, New York: Schirmer Books, 1990

Walden, Valerie, *One Hundred Years of Violoncello: A History of Technique and Performance Practice, 1740–1840*, Cambridge: Cambridge University Press, 1998

Studies of performance practice in 19th-century music have flourished in recent times, perhaps in part because of their historical proximity to present-day concert life.

The most reliable starting point remains BROWN and SADIE. Touching upon principal institutions and events of 19th-century music history, Holomon's introduction makes the deceptively simple yet elegant point that "negotiating the compromise between past and present is as necessary for 19th-century music as it is for that of the Middle Ages." Subsequent chapters are devoted to groups of instruments—keyboards, organ, strings, woodwind and brass, and voices. The chapters vary in detail and number of musical examples according to the number and range of venues discussed, but each contains representative bibliographical references. The source bibliography at the end of the volume is extensive and chronological and again is arranged by instruments (the largest segment, keyboards, is subdivided), with supplementary sections on pitch and tuning.

JACKSON is useful for its bibliographies and references to specialized topics, but it is somewhat awkwardly arranged by general categories, then by centuries, and is further subdivided by composer, media, tempo, added and altered notes, and the like. Readers may also wish to consult Répertoire international de Littérature musicale (RILM) and bibliographies in *Basler Jahrbuch*, which appear periodically.

Controversies have descended from arguments over authenticity and have developed with special intensity since KENYON. Crutchfield's short address and Taruskin's extended essay in this anthology raise both practical and philosophical issues, such as performers' hostility toward (and occasional ignorance of) performance practice—regardless of the potential career consequences—and performance implications of the myriad interpretations of authenticity (i.e., are notational systems inadequate?).

Different notions of authenticity are enthusiastically pursued by KIVY. Lamenting the lack of a philosophical past for the topic, he divides his study in two sections, the first illuminating abstract assessments and the second exploring individual performers' responsibilities to composers' intentions. He argues for "authenticities in the plural" (philosophically) and—especially in view of wide historical precedence—personal authenticities of performance that transcend archetypes indebted to linguistic models of the 18th century.

Such enthusiasm is echoed in RINK, which focuses on the activity of performers. Rink divides this activity into three categories: fundamentals, structure, and performance as process. Howat immediately sets the tone for the anthology: performers must knowledgeably re-edit in performance in order to compensate for inadequacies of notation. Other topics include musical motion versus natural motion; tempi in Furtwängler recordings of Beethoven's Ninth Symphony; choosing tempi critically in Schubert and Chopin; and the importance of synthetic analyses, ambiguity, and historical awareness to performing practice.

TODD presents a collection of essays about the significance of the piano in 19th-century social history. Especially useful are the introduction and Plantinga's essay illuminating the roles of the instrument in everyday musical life (utility instrument, machine, etc.) and its powers of persuasion and influence upon literature. Winter addresses issues surrounding performance practice (changing audiences, performance traditions, methods of transmission), as well as matters more directly related to the topic, such as shifting interpretations of color in performance; what Winter perceives to be diminishing interpretative ranges; and—in a survey of recorded performances spanning 50 years—wildly varying tempi in recorded performances of conventional repertoire.

NEWMAN offers a highly organized, scholarly approach to Beethoven's piano and piano chamber music, although the author does not devote much time to the evolution of the instruments themselves. Important chapters discuss manuscripts and editions, tempi, articulation (i.e., expressive accents and ambiguity of staccato signs), phrasing (such as rhythmic groupings and dynamic direction), ornamentation, expressive means (such as pedaling, legato, tone quality), and idiomatic questions of style (such as fingerings). Chapters and sections are most often grounded in original sources with good musical examples; the bibliography is useful as well.

SMITH gives due consideration to the 19th-century organ. He seeks to advance authentic interpretation of César Franck's music through a compilation of contemporary testimonials discussing the composer as student, performer, and teacher, along with a study of the Cavaillé-Coll organs and their influence. Smith also illuminates the discourse, performance instructions, and recordings of Franck's distinguished student Tournemire. The author provides appendices of examination pieces played by Franck's students, harmonized plainchant examples, instrumental specifications, and personal reminiscences from Pierné, Busser, and others.

Stowell and Walden treat many issues related to string practice until approximately the middle of the 19th century. STOWELL traces the ascendancy of the French over Italian violin schools, specific developments in bowing, changing public performance and publishing venues, and the rise of touring virtuosos in the wake of Paganini. Pianists would do well to read the final chapter on ornamentation with its four-part division of the issue and treatise examples. Also useful are the appendix of primary sources between 1760 and ca. 1840 and the glossary of specific ornaments culled from these documents.

WALDEN's more recent study is similarly thorough, tracing performance issues regionally while outlining the development of the violoncello, its notations, fingerings, and ornamentation, and discussing related historical and aesthetic matters that contributed to what the author sees as an unacknowledged diversity of styles. For instance, the art of accompanying is described in dual terms for section (tutti) players, as opposed to principals or leaders (recitative). Musical examples, bibliography, and illustrations are excellent.

Central parts of the study about the lied by KRAVITT repay close reading. Chapters concerning declamation and description deal with many freshly conceived topics, such as the gray area between singing and speaking in the wake of naturalism; the ensuing dialectic between singer and actor; subsequent implications for solo and accompaniment writing; revivals of melodrama; and much more. Kravitt's conclusion that the late 19th century saw "the peak in performance of expressive aesthetics" and that these aesthetics remain largely lost in current performing practices deserves further inquiry.

MILLINGTON and SPENCER address performance practice and Wagner. Specific instructions (orchestral seating, balance, tempi, dynamics, vibrato, etc.) are examined by Brown, who begins by noting the increasing importance to Wagner in his maturity of reforms in performing practice and "a particular style of performance." Ashman and Carnegy question the authority of music versus that of stage directors. Other important chapters include a discussion of prominent conductors in the light of such stage/theatrical influences, a study of Wagner's unprecedented vocal demands and the attempts that were made to meet them by subsequent casts and artists, and an examination of changing vocal styles captured by recordings of Wagner's operas.

KECK and MARTIN make an important contribution to rectifying the current lack of understanding about performance practices of African-American musicians in the 19th century. Contributors illuminate the Civil War years, the dim but emerging outlines of solo keyboard music, and the celebrated Fisk Jubilee Singers. Other essays sketch the careers of male and female solo concert singers and address aspects of urban concert management pertaining to African-American virtuosos whose careers, for disconsolate reasons, have yet to be rediscovered.

STEPHEN ZANK

Pergolesi, Giovanni Battista 1710–1736

Italian composer

Degrada, Francesco, editor, *Pergolesi Studies I—Studi Pergolesiani,* Florence: La Nuova Italia, and New York: Pendragon Press, 1986

————, editor, *Pergolesi Studies II—Studi Pergolesiani II,* Florence: La Nuova Italia, 1988

Paymer, Marvin E., *Giovanni Battista Pergolesi, 1710–1736: A Thematic Catalogue of the Opera Omnia,* New York: Pendragon Press, 1977

Paymer, Marvin E., and Hermine W. Williams, *Giovanni Battista Pergolesi: A Guide to Research,* New York: Garland, 1989

Research concerning Giovanni Battista Pergolesi's life and his works has seen a resurgence since the 1960s. His life and early death were romanticized by writers in the 1750s and again in the early 20th century, and his musical contribution has been exaggerated. A more accurate perception of Pergolesi has recently emerged, however, as researchers have discovered that he composed approximately 40 works, instead of the 400 pieces once attributed to him. As research continues and manuscripts are identified, more information about his musical style and contribution will be available.

PAYMER and WILLIAMS's book provides an invaluable source of information for the student and scholar. The bibliography provides an annotation of literature about Pergolesi from the 18th century to 1989, listing almost 500 entries, including dissertations, books, and articles in English and foreign languages. The introduction provides a brief overview of the various issues of authenticity, sources, and Pergolesi's posthumous fame. The list of Pergolesi's works includes those that still need to be investigated, modern editions, and forgeries of Tobia Nicotra. An interesting section in the bibliography, "Literary and Musical Works Based on Pergolesi's Life," can prove useful to scholars and students of literature.

PAYMER (1977) is an invaluable listing that sets the record straight concerning the problems of misattributions, doubtful and spurious works, and omitted works. The *opera omnia* had misattributed many works to Pergolesi and omitted several authentic works. Although an explanation of the usage of the catalog is included, the treatment is confusing at first glance. The work, however, is invaluable to anyone interested in pursuing Pergolesi research because it addresses the huge previous confusion regarding his repertoire.

DEGRADA (1986) is an important collection of essays, and the editor's foreword introduces the reader to the volume and to the Pergolesi Research Center in New York, founded by Barry Brook in 1977. These essays are drawn from the proceedings of the international symposium held in 1983. The essays in English are the most current published information that we have concerning Pergolesi. The first article, by Brook, lays out the state of research and the various needs for progress. Paymer offers an article on Pergolesi's autographs and gives the reader the first authoritative account of the composer's notation by presenting Pergolesi's handwriting in tables. In the next English article, John Rice examines the notion that Pergolesi's opera *Ricimero* was mostly likely the opera *Il prigionier superbo* instead. Dale Monson's article "The Last Word: The Cadence in *Recitativo Semplice* of Italian Opera Seria" throws new light on current performances of recitative and actual 18th-century practices. This article is important for any musician who performs 18th-century vocal music. The next article, also by Monson, shows that labeling *recitativo semplice* and *recitativo secco* as synonymous is an imposition of German theory on Italian music. Hubert Beckwith's article, "Text and Harmony in Pergolesi's Recitatives for Stage and Chamber," discusses the correlation between text and harmonic progression. Gordana Lazarevich's article, "From Naples to Paris: Transformations of Pergolesi's Intermezzo *Livietta e Tracollo* by Contemporary Buffo Singers," is a concise and interesting account of 18th-century singers that reviews their changes to and performances of this intermezzo by Pergolesi. The anthology ends with an interim report on the current knowledge of Pergolesi's authentic sources. Paymer is the expert, and this report serves as an up-to-date overview of the state of the manuscripts in 1983.

DEGRADA (1988) is a continuation of research drawn from the next international Pergolesi conference held in 1986. Barry Brook's article, "Recent Developments in Pergolesi Research, Performance, and Publication," gives a summary of the recent achievements in Pergolesi research and an update concerning what is known about the manuscripts. Dale Monson offers an article titled "Evidence for Pergolesi's Compositional Method for the Stage: The *Faminio* Autograph." This is only one of two detailed discussions of Pergolesi's compositional process and manner of notation. Examples of the composer's handwriting are presented as invaluable benefits for anyone interested in primary sources involving Pergolesi's music. Roger Covell's article, "Purpose, Consistency, and Integration in Pergolesi's *San Guglielmo*," explains the source of the topic for Pergolesi's sacred drama *La conversione e morte di San Guglielmo* and the political and religious circumstances surrounding Guglielmo, who ruled as a duke of Aquitaine from 1127 to 1137. In the next English article, Paymer discusses seven problems associated with the much-needed study of Pergolesi's sinfonias, and his observations are relevant to much unexplored 18th-century music. Dennis Libby's article addresses some issues with which performers are presented when interpreting an 18th-century score. Sven Hansell also addresses performance practice issues concerning our notion of the ornament, the *acciaccatura*, as a possible misinterpretation of Gasparini's description. Hubert Beckwith offers an ongoing examination of Pergolesi's four posthumously published chamber cantatas. Hanns-Bertold Dietz's article is important for anyone interested in Neapolitan composers. He explores the reasons for the misattributions and sets the record straight for several works through a close examination of the manuscripts. Hermine Williams compares and contrasts the *Stabat Mater* by Alessandro Scarlatti and the *Stabat Mater* by Pergolesi; both works were commissioned by the same group. Bernard Toscani addresses the specific plots and the stock character, the maid-mistress, in Pergolesi's *La serva padrona*, in Jacopo Angelo Nelli's play *La serva padrona* and in Albinoni's *Pimpinone*. In the article "Pergolesi and the *Guerre des Bouffons*," Gordana Lazarevich discusses Pergolesi's posthumous reputation that developed in the Parisian-Italian controversy of 1752 to 1754. Evan Owens's study traces the various performances of *La serva padrona* in London from 1750 to 1783, including changes made to the libretto. In the last article in the volume, Libby examines the information that we have concerning Giuseppe Sigismondo's life and significance as a musician, librarian, and historian. This article contains important information for all who are involved with 18th-century music. Both volumes of *Pergolesi Studies* offer invaluable research for students and scholars.

Sheryl Kathleen Murphy

Persia *see* Mode: Non-Western

Petrucci, Ottaviano dei 1466–1539

Italian music publisher

Fenlon, Iain, *Music, Print and Culture in Early Sixteenth-Century Italy*, London: British Library, 1995

King, A. Hyatt, *Four Hundred Years of Music Printing*, London: Trustees of the British Museum, 1964; 2nd edition, 1968

Krummel, Donald W., *The Literature of Music Bibliography: An Account of the Writings on the History of Music Printing and Publishing*, Berkeley, California: Fallen Leaf Press, 1992

Krummel, Donald W., and Stanley Sadie, editors, *Music Printing and Publishing*, Basingstoke: Macmillan, and New York: Norton, 1990

Petrucci, Ottaviano, *Harmonice musices Odhecaton A*, edited by Helen Hewitt and Isabel Pope, Cambridge, Massachusetts: Mediaevel Academy of America, 1942

The first significant printer and publisher of polyphonic music, Ottaviano dei Petrucci centered his trade in Venice just before 1500, establishing Italian dominance in the production of printed music for next 20 years and more. His importance may be seen in the striking fact that, as Stanley Boorman has noted, in terms of overall production, Petrucci's editions account for "a major portion of surviving music in each of the genres he covered." His innovations contributed to the broadening of musical culture in general and, more specifically, began the widespread circulation of polyphonic music in a variety of genres. After 1511, Petrucci's operations were based in his hometown of Fossombrone. His workshop there produced reprints of Venetian editions, nonmusical works, and some new editions, notably, the series *Motetti de la corona* (1514–19). After about 1515, the quality of Petrucci's work deteriorated markedly, which may indicate that he was no longer in charge of the house himself. His last print appeared in 1520.

Petrucci adapted existing print technology to produce the elements of mensural notation and organ and lute tablature by means of multiple impressions. The results were editions of fine detail, remarkable beauty, and undoubtedly, great expense. This last point has led to speculation regarding Petrucci's intended audience for these volumes. The early prints, at least, may have been planned for professional performers, perhaps as reference works, although any given edition surely reached a far larger audience than was possible (or intended) with manuscripts. In any case, Petrucci's editions initially maintained a place in a specialized market, with apparently selective distribution. His volumes were issued in oblong quarto format, first laid out as choir books. Beginning in 1502, Petrucci introduced a new format for ensemble music consisting of sets of part books. Each book of the set contained the music for only a single vocal or instrumental part of each composition, making it necessary to own the entire set. As with other details of Petrucci's editions, this arrangement became standard practice for printed ensemble music throughout the 16th century.

Despite his importance in the development of music printing, the enormous amount of material he published, and the generally high quality of his publications, there have been no book-length studies in English devoted to Petrucci. Most of the scholarship on Petrucci appears in books devoted to music printing in general. Some work has been done in Italian, the most important of which is Claudio Sartori, *Bibliografia delle opere musicali stanpate da Ottaviano Petrucci* (Florence, 1948), which lists the complete contents of every volume that Petrucci published.

Hewitt and Pope's edition of PETRUCCI's groundbreaking first print, *Harmonice Musices Odhecaton A* (Venice, 1501), presents its contents, mostly French chansons, in modern notation with extensive commentary and bibliographic material. Although dated in some aspects, the commentary on the musical and literary background of the pieces is a valuable introduction to the repertory of the *Odhecaton*. The editions themselves are sound and provide immediate access to Petrucci's important anthology. Hewitt's discussion of Petrucci and his print methods has been largely superseded, however. Now essential for any study of the *Odhecaton,* its compilation, and publication history is Stanley Boorman, "The 'First' Edition of the *Odhecaton A,*" *Journal of the American Musicological Society* 30 (1977).

KING introduces the early history of music printing in a brief, highly readable account. It is also a source for good facsimile pages from several early printers. King's elegant descriptions of Petrucci's printing methods bring the process to life with clarity and detail. Similarly, the author is careful to place Petrucci's work in the tradition of the incunable printers upon whose techniques he plainly drew.

FENLON's book brings together his 1994 Panizzi Lectures at the British Library. These treat the broad social aspects of music publishing in the 16th century, during which the "reproduction of music" moved from the "copyist's desk to the printer's workshop." Petrucci figures prominently in the first section, wherein Fenlon focuses on the impact of the early editions on urban musical practice and the development and growth of a commercial market for printed music up to about 1550.

Two important surveys of the history of music printing and publishing contain much information on the Petrucci prints, their production, distribution, and significance for music history. KRUMMEL presents a broad overview of the historiography of music printing. Arranged by topic, annotated entries cover a variety of areas, including "Venice," which lists several studies dealing with Petrucci.

KRUMMEL and SADIE, a specialized handbook, outlines the history of music printing from early times and traces the music publishing trade from 1501 (the date of Petrucci's *Odhecaton*) to the present. Especially valuable is the biographical dictionary of music publishers and printers. These sections are revisions and enlargements of items that originally appeared in the *New Grove Dictionary of Music and Musicians* (1980). Also included here is an extensive glossary of technical terms useful for the study of music printing and publishing, as well as a classified bibliography. Stanley Boorman's article in this volume is the most recent and extensive survey of Petrucci's life and career. His discussion of the printer's output is detailed and clearly organized. Boorman, who has produced a number of specialized studies of Petrucci's editions, manages to discuss complicated editorial and transmission issues in his general text smoothly and efficiently. The bibliography included here is the standard reference point for work on Petrucci.

ROBERT E. PALMER

Philippe de Vitry *see* Vitry, Philippe de

Philosophy of Music

Bowman, Wayne D., *Philosophical Perspectives on Music,* New York: Oxford University Press, 1998

Bujic, Bojan, *Music in European Thought: 1851–1912,* Cambridge: Cambridge University Press, 1988

Dahlhaus, Carl, *Esthetics of Music,* translated by William A. Austin, Cambridge: Cambridge University Press, 1982

Hanslick, Eduard, *The Beautiful in Music,* edited by Morris Weitz, translated by Gustav Cohen, Indianapolis, Indiana: Bobbs-Merril, 1957

Hegel, Georg Wilhelm Friedrich, *The Philosophy of Fine Art,* 4 vols., translated by F.P.B. Osmaston, London: Bell, 1920

Kivy, Peter, *The Corded Shell: Reflections on Musical Experience,* Princeton, New Jersey: Princeton University Press, 1980

Langer, Susanne K., *Philosophy in a New Key,* Cambridge, Massachusetts: Harvard University Press, 1942; 3rd edition, 1957

Le Huray, Peter, and James Day, editors, *Music and Aesthetics in the Eighteenth and Early-Nineteenth Centuries,* Cambridge: Cambridge University Press, 1981

Strunk, W. Oliver, editor, *Source Readings in Music History: From Classical Antiquity through the Romantic Era,* New York: Norton, 1950; revised edition, edited by Leo Treitler, 1998

By the 18th century the systematic study of the philosophy of the meaning and value of music gradually came to be identified as the *aesthetics of music.* Musical aesthetics has existed as a distinct field for a relatively short time. The questions that concern the discipline, however, have been raised and pondered for centuries, such as the following: What is the nature of musical experience? What is the essence of sound? How does one analyze the meaning of music? Does music exist in time or does it allow one to perceive time? Treatises and essays on these types of inquiries are included in a variety of sources, often as part of a study devoted to music or to the philosophy and history of art, education, and culture in general. Not only have philosophers and musicians written on the subject, but so have critics, analysts, historians, intellectuals, and even serious students. Although the context may differ, and the level of musical experience may vary widely among the authors, they all share a common desire to establish a rational basis for the enjoyment and/or the evaluation of music. In his book *Esthetics of Music,* Dahlhaus aptly summarizes the quandary of defining the scope of the topic: "To do justice to this phenomenon [of musical aesthetics] requires recognizing that it is not so much a distinct discipline with a firmly limited object of inquiry, as, rather, a vaporous, far-flung quintessence of problems and points of view that no one before the eighteenth century could have imagined ever coalescing into a complex with its own name."

In a concise book that gives a general overview of the discipline, DAHLHAUS prefaces each chapter with one of various viewpoints of musical aesthetics, such as those of Kant and Schopenhauer. He then endeavors to rectify prevailing misunderstandings of these men's theories that may have resulted over the years from a poor translation of the original source, a lack of understanding of the context in which it was written, or merely ignorance of the subject.

In the same vein as Dahlhaus, BOWMAN attempts "to demystify the puzzling world of music philosophy." He candidly describes the task before him by admitting that "philosophical issues in music often seem remote and abstract, of little immediate relevance or consequence." Yet Bowman manages to do a superb job of simplifying the perplexities of the field by categorizing the issues as follows: music and philosophy, music as imitation, music as idea, music as autonomous form, music as symbol, music as experienced, music as a social and political force, and contemporary pluralist perspectives. These categories are then presented in chronological order. Several authors have written general overviews of the philosophy of music, including Lippman, Portnoy, and Scruton. Bowman's work is exceptional, however, in that it devotes significant space to the feminist perspective. Given that musical aesthetics has been completely male dominated until recent times, it is refreshing to see the feminist perspective acknowledged and analyzed. Also noteworthy are the excellent discussion questions at the end of each chapter.

LE HURAY and DAY's volume provides commentaries to the original sources, unlike many anthologies that merely furnish translations. It is in the anthologies of musical aesthetics that one can see that much of the creative essays in the field are produced by musicians and music enthusiasts in the course of their everyday work: performers defending or attacking novelties of musical practice, critics upholding their critiques, historians explaining why this or that had to happen the way it

did, and analysts of music substantiating their analytic procedures. Represented in this anthology are authors such as Rousseau, Burney, Schumann, and Liszt discussing the heated arguments of the day about such matters as romanticism in music, musical expression, and the nature of aesthetic experience. Each entry begins with a brief biographical description, continues to an excerpt from their most significant source, and ends with a commentary. According to the editors, the entries are organized only chronologically to avoid arbitrary categorization.

BUJIC, a companion anthology to le Huray and Day's, surveys the principal contributions from Germany, France, and England. Some authors represented are Nietzsche, Wagner, Berlioz, and Edmund Gurney. The entries follow the same format as le Huray and Day's with a brief biographical statement at the beginning before the excerpt from an original source, which is then followed by a commentary. The fourth chapter focuses on the gap between music theory and philosophy by bringing together musicological essays formulated by the German school of thought. Bujic observes that "the more the answer to the question of what music is slips through the net of general philosophical theories, the more a systematic study of music comes into its own." He argues that the systematic philosophers of the German mold of musicology fail to answer the question of what music is, going so far to state that they "disappoint, despite various persistent efforts to overcome it."

STRUNK is an indispensable text that has recently been updated to include writings from the 20th century. This is a collection of pedagogical treatises, opinions of critics, historical and descriptive writings, and commentaries by people of various vocations including composers, theorists, performing musicians, and philosophers from the age of antiquity to the present. The essays are penned by people such as Plato, Franco of Cologne, William Byrd, Claudio Monteverdi, Leopold Mozart, Robert Schumann, and Arnold Schoenberg, and they discuss how music should be composed, performed, listened to, and understood. The book is available in one volume or individually as seven separate volumes divided chronologically into seven periods. As one reads this book, it becomes evident that it is often the composers themselves who provide the most remarkable historical and philological findings.

Certainly one of the most provocative treatises on musical aesthetics is HANSLICK. He took an unwavering purist stance that music does not express or represent human emotion. Instead, he asserts, "the truly musical mode of engagement is strictly auditory, the pleasure that is properly musical consists in the mental alertness associated with such hearing, not some emotional experience." Although Hanslick's arguments are lively and were certainly influential to his opponents, they do not stand up to close philosophical analysis and have since become notably outdated, for example, Hanslick's assertion that women are incapable of intellectual powers due to their emotional nature.

HEGEL is not inhibited about reflecting on questions of the soul and the human spirit. In the last chapter of the third volume, he argues that art assumes a place of honor alongside religion and philosophy, whose common purpose is to bring to consciousness "the deepest interests of humanity, and the most comprehensive truths of the mind. It is in works of art that nations have deposited the profoundest intuitions and ideas of the hearts." Hegel believes that music has essentially to do with feeling and the spiritual side of human nature. He is also keen to elaborate on the profound insight that the mind is not merely intellect, but also spirit.

LANGER develops a comprehensive theory of music as symbol. She writes, "Music has all the earmarks of a true symbolism, except one: the existence of an assigned connotation." Langer's conviction that music is a means by which humans construct their conceptions of reality inspires her to theorize that music is a special kind of intelligence—that music as symbol is a vehicle to gain profoundly important human insights, attainable in no other way and that these insights can lead to a deeper understanding of the nature of human feeling.

Finally, KIVY's welcome sense of humor provides a breath of fresh air into the otherwise stilted pedantry of most philosophical essays. The author defines the scope of his study by stating, "whatever interest [there] may hold for the biographer or psychologist, it holds little [interest] for the listener or critic. That is a large question in the philosophy of [music] criticism." Kivy takes on the hypothetical role of a music critic to discover why it is so challenging to describe music in words. His work is based on the argument that the expressive properties of music are not trivial. Using the writings of Donald Tovey as his allies, he leads us to the conclusion that music does not express feeling, but rather that music is expressive *of* feeling. Therefore, a music critic can justifiably use the language of emotion to describe music. Anyone who has written about music, particularly program notes and reviews, may enjoy Kivy's witty evaluation of the music critic. He observes that music critics "may not have the patent on nonsense; but they have been mighty busy during the last two hundred years churning out more than their share of it." He then defends the critic's "nonsense" by declaring that "it is *useful* nonsense." Kivy devotes the last chapter of his study to explaining how one can describe music with emotive terminology and still "maintain . . . respectability."

CHARMAINE FRAN LECLAIR

Poland *see* Eastern Europe

Porter, Cole 1891–1964

United States composer

Eells, George, *The Life that Late He Led: A Biography of Cole Porter,* New York: Putnam, and London: Allen, 1967

Ewen, David, *The Cole Porter Story,* New York: Holt, Rinehart and Winston, 1965

Forte, Allen, *The American Popular Ballad of the Golden Era: 1924–1950,* Princeton, New Jersey: Princeton University Press, 1995

McBrien, William, *Cole Porter: A Biography,* New York: Knopf, 1998; as *Cole Porter: The Definitive Biography,* London: HarperCollins, 1998

Morella, Joseph, and George Mazzei, *Genius and Lust: The Creativity and Sexuality of Cole Porter and Noel Coward,* New York: Carroll and Graf, 1995

Schwartz, Charles, *Cole Porter: A Biography,* New York: Dial Press, 1977

Wilder, Alec, *American Popular Song: The Great Innovators, 1900–1950,* New York: Oxford University Press, 1972

Cole Porter composed songs for more than 40 stage and film musicals. He stands out from most other Broadway composers of the pre-*Oklahoma!* era for having written both words and music. Whereas most of the best-known Broadway composers and lyricists at the time were from New York City and Jewish by birth, Porter was born in the Midwest (Indiana) of a wealthy Episcopalian family. His mother, Katie, insisted that he receive the best education possible, which included music lessons. She sent Cole to Worcester Academy, a boarding school in the East. After graduating, Porter toured Europe and then attended Yale and Harvard Universities, where he cultivated his musical interests. Perhaps to avoid his domineering maternal grandfather, James Omar Cole, who strongly disapproved of his musical studies, Porter rarely returned to Indiana during this period. His first complete Broadway musical score was for *See America First* in 1916. The following year Porter went to Paris, where he lived into the 1920s as an expatriate. Although he was homosexual, he married the wealthy socialite Linda Lee Thomas, who was his elder by eight years. They spent the early period of their marriage in Paris and Venice, throwing lavish parties and hobnobbing with nobility. While in Europe, Porter continued to write songs for musicals produced in both New York and London. In 1937 he suffered a crippling horse-riding accident, which caused him tremendous pain for the rest of his life. Following a relatively unsuccessful period, in 1948 Porter wrote *Kiss Me Kate,* his greatest artistic achievement. A string of other hit musicals followed. After his wife's death in 1954, Porter became increasingly reclusive, and he stopped composing after his right leg was amputated in 1958. He died in Santa Monica, California in 1964. Most studies of Porter emphasize the urbane wit and innovative melodic features of his songs, attributing both in part to his upper-class lifestyle and world travels. Until the 1970s, biographers completely ignored Porter's homosexuality and the contradiction between his public and private lives, which seems to have been a source of inspiration for some of his songs.

EWEN divides Porter's career into four decades, which determine the four main sections of his book: "The Roaring Twenties," "The Somber Thirties," "The Historic Forties," and "The Apprehensive Fifties." By providing a historical context and describing the ambiance of each period, he shows that Porter's life and career did not always reflect the prevailing spirit of the times. For example, after the stock-market crash in 1929, Porter continued to live as extravagantly as he had during the 1920s, sometimes attracting criticism for his public displays of frivolous consumption. Like most historians, Ewen considers *Kiss Me Kate* to be Porter's greatest triumph and spends considerable time describing it. In his discussion of Porter's songs, the author notes the use of minor keys, Eastern-European melodies building toward a climax, insistent rhythms, and clever rhymes.

EELLS bases his biography on information from private interviews he conducted with the composer and primary sources, including diaries and letters. He reproduces many of these materials, including Porter's lengthy diary entry documenting the genesis of the film *Born to Dance* (1935). Using the 1937 riding accident as a turning point, the author divides Porter's life into two parts. In his review of the early years, he focuses on Porter's peripatetic existence, social activities, and growing professional recognition. Eells strongly contrasts this period with the last two-and-a-half decades of Porter's life, which were filled with artistic insecurity, physical and emotional suffering, and personal loss. It is not clear from Eells's discussion of the stage musicals whether Porter took an active role in shaping the dramatic structure of his works, as did Rodgers, Hart, and Hammerstein. The author occasionally digresses from his chronological narrative in order to describe the important people in Porter's life or to explore a particular aspect of his personality, such as the type of spoken drama he preferred.

Although not a great fan of Porter, WILDER recognizes his ingenuity and contribution to the popular-song tradition, the main topic of this study. The author claims that Porter is better known for his lyrics than for his music, but Wilder minimizes the quality of the lyrics and suggest that they were written mostly "for the special amusement of his social set." Wilder does admit, however, that Porter's music adds warmth to his words. Surveying about 55 of Porter's songs from 1915 to 1953, Wilder concludes that the best ones are from the 1930s. One of the features he admires is the use of chromaticism in the melodic lines and harmonies. He notes the unconventional formal designs but is sometimes critical of this

aspect of the music; he also makes disparaging remarks about Porter's song endings, verses, and rhythmic ideas. Wilder claims that Porter declined artistically after his riding accident, an assertion that contradicts most other assessments of Porter's music after 1937.

SCHWARTZ sets out to correct much of the fallacious information contained in earlier biographies. He covers all of Porter's stage and film musicals, as well as his single attempt at serious music (the ballet *Within the Quota*). The author also addresses issues related to Porter's homosexuality. In his treatment of Porter's music, Schwartz frequently refers to a remark the composer once made to Richard Rodgers: Porter claimed that to compose hit songs he would write "Jewish tunes." Schwartz offers numerous examples as proof that Porter was serious when he made this statement, contending that it might also have reflected latent anti-Semitic sentiments. He draws much attention to the nonformulaic formal designs and atypically long lengths of the songs. Like many other writers, he suggests that many of Porter's ideas for lyrics derived from his travels abroad and upper-class surroundings. In addition to addressing Porter's sexual orientation, Schwartz also considers other previously unexplored personality traits, such as Porter's tendency to control his public image through distortion of the real facts. One example Schwartz gives of this tendency is Porter's choice of Cary Grant to portray him in his movie biography *Night and Day*.

MORELLA and MAZZEI, in a study on the link between sexuality and creativity, compare the lives and careers of Porter and Noel Coward, illustrating the differences between the ways the two artists expressed their homosexuality in their art and private lives. According to the authors, Porter, unlike Coward, isolated his homosexual relationships from the rest of his personal life. For his sexual partners Porter preferred men of lower social standing, often paying for their services with money or gifts. There are reports that Porter liked to be degraded in the sex act and engaged in sadomasochistic behavior. Having described these aspects of Porter's sexuality, the authors examine how his attitudes toward sex, gender, and love are reflected in his songs, such as "Love for Sale." They also explore Porter's marriage, Hollywood sojourns, and strong aversion to boredom. Porter's marriage to Thomas was clearly one of convenience (for both parties), affording the composer the comforts he desired and allowing him to maintain the semblance of a heterosexual existence. It was Hollywood that brought his homosexuality out into the open, which caused his wife to leave him, only to return after the 1937 riding accident. The authors suggest that the songs Porter composed after her death, such as "True Love," indicate that he knew not only sexual love but also spiritual love, even if, for him, the two were not necessarily connected.

FORTE, a fervent Porter enthusiast, begins by pointing out that most writers use the adjective "sophisticated" to describe Porter's music but that the word can also apply to the songs of many other composers. The author's purpose in analyzing Porter's songs is to reveal what it is about them that continues to elicit widespread admiration. Forte provides detailed analytical reductions of six of Porter's songs written between 1932 and 1948. Although Forte makes no attempt to evaluate how these songs function dramatically within the musicals, he does comment on the connection between musical details and text expression. Forte's selection of songs allows him the opportunity to focus on the musical features most central to Porter's style. Readers will require some theoretical background in order to fully appreciate Forte's discussion of the music. Incorporating Schenkerian analytical concepts and techniques, he examines Porter's use of linear progressions, melodic elaboration, melodic substitution, and unconventional formal designs. In this way, Forte succeeds in explaining the intrinsically sophisticated nature of Porter's music.

McBRIEN has done an impressive amount of research. Unfortunately, he does not sift through the copious details he has gathered with a strong sense of purpose. He does provide a lot of valuable information, however, some of which throws new light on various aspects of Porter's life. Recently recovered notebooks from Porter's years at Yale reveal his views on some of the poets he studied, such as Tennyson, Byron, and Wordsworth. Personal correspondence proves that Porter had a number of serious homosexual relations, not just casual trysts with men well outside his social sphere, as was once believed. For example, in one collection of letters Porter expresses strong romantic feelings for Boris Kochno (who was professionally and intimately connected to Diaghilev). McBrien's discussion of Porter's musicals amounts to no more than a recounting of the backstage intrigue. The author practically ignores Porter's melodic gift, focusing on his poetic talent. McBrien quotes numerous lyrics, suggesting that many of them convey sentiments that Porter could not express openly in his public life.

JAMES LEVE

Portugal

Brito, Manuel Carlos de, *Opera in Portugal in the Eighteenth Century,* Cambridge: Cambridge University Press, 1989

Luper, Albert T., "Portuguese Polyphony in the Sixteenth and Early Seventeenth Centuries," *Journal of the American Musicological Society* 3 (1950)

Nelson, Bernadette, "Philip II and the Portuguese Royal Chapel, 1580–98," *Leading Notes* 8 (1998)

Nery, Rui Vieira, "The Music Manuscripts in the Library of King D. Joao IV of Portugal (1604–1656)," Ph.D. dissertation, University of Texas at Austin, 1990

Nery, Rui Vieira, and Paulo Ferreira de Castro, *A History of Music,* Lisbon: Imprensa Nacional-Casa da Moeda, 1991

Rees, Owen, *Polyphony in Portugal, c. 1530–c. 1620: Sources from the Monastery of Santa Cruz, Coimbra,* New York: Garland, 1995

Prior to the 1990s, few studies of Portuguese music were available in English. Significant contributions to musicological research were published in Portugal, however, from the late 19th century onward, and these studies have provided an important basis for most subsequent scholarship and remain indispensable sources of reference. Only recently have surviving repertoires of Portuguese music been made available in published editions, and this development has considerably facilitated further historical and musicological studies. Francisco Marques de Sousa Viterbo, Manuel Joaquim, Macario Santiago Kastner, Gerhard Doderer, and José Augusto Alegria are among the historians and musicologists who have compiled studies on source material, institutions, vocal and instrumental music, and composers.

NERY and CASTRO present a general account of the history of Portuguese music from the medieval period to the 20th century. (It succeeds João de Freitas Branco's 1959 study in Portuguese.) This book is a short and useful survey of the principal aspects of Portuguese musical repertoires and style, taking into account the role of music in both sacred and secular contexts (opera in particular) and focusing on select key institutions, such as the royal chapel and the Evora Cathedral. Nery and Castro divide the book into five broad historical sections, each of which is further divided into a number of subsections. There is no list of primary sources, but titles of works and references to other documentation are scattered throughout the book. Nery and Castro derive much information from earlier published studies, and they supply the appropriate bibliographical references. The book's coverage is broad, although its organization is not always easy to follow, and it is completely lacking in musical examples that would provide greater clarity. Readers in search of specialized material are advised to look elsewhere and also to consult Manuel Carlos de Brito and Luísa Cymbron, *História da música portuguesa* (1992).

Luper's seminal article on Portuguese polyphony and Rees's study of manuscript sources from the royal monastery of Santa Cruz in Coimbra provide excellent perspectives on repertoires of sacred vocal polyphony and musical style in the Renaissance. Although dated, LUPER is a good starting point for study of the history and scope of vocal music in Portugal from the medieval period onward, and it is supported by copious references to musical studies and editions both general and specific in nature. Luper outlines the main genres and developments of Portuguese music up to the time of King João IV (1604–56), taking into account the main contributions of such composers as Manuel Cardoso,

Duarte Lobo, Filipe de Magalhães, and others working in Coimbra, Evora, Vila Viçosa, and Lisbon.

REES's book focuses on the important series of prints and manuscripts preserved in the University of Coimbra dating from the 16th and early 17th centuries, rather than presenting a stylistic history of Portuguese music as a whole from this period as its title implies. The study is divided into two parts: "The Repertories in Their Context" and "Manuscript Sources," the latter comprising detailed descriptions and inventories of primarily vocal sources from the monastery of Santa Cruz in Coimbra. This manuscript collection is unparalleled in Portugal, and Rees's work is the first systematic musicological study to place it within a national and international context. Both the monastery and the University of Coimbra were among the leading cultural and musical institutions in medieval and Renaissance Portugal. Part 1 of Rees's book presents a survey of the contributions of the institutions from the perspective of the musical repertoires, particularly with regard to the earliest items of polyphony, which provide evidence about the importation of foreign printed books of music and of the so-called Spanish court repertories from the time of Ferdinand and Isabella. Part 1 also includes discussion of music composed for the Jesuit neo-Latin theater. In addition to providing physical descriptions and inventories of the selected 22 manuscripts from the university collection, Rees carefully contextualizes each piece: he offers information about the functions and origins of the repertoires represented, details of the copying and compilation of the sources, and explanations of concordance research. He also provides biographical details of some of the composers associated with Santa Cruz, including Heliodoro de Paiva, António Carreira, Francisco de Santa Maria, and Pedro de Cristo.

King João IV was probably one of the most active and acquisitive patrons of music and other arts in the Iberian peninsula, second only to the Habsburg monarchs (in particular Philip II and Philip IV of Spain). NERY's dissertation on the music manuscripts of João IV's library is based on the famous 1649 printed index of the first half of this enormous collection of prints and manuscripts (housed in the royal palace in Lisbon until the 1755 earthquake that destroyed the center of the city). There is no record of the proposed second half of this index. In this very specialized study, Nery focuses on the contents of the library and the information the manuscript collection provides on musical practice in Portugal and, to some extent, the Iberian peninsula as a whole. Part 1 of the book, "Historical Background," contains a comprehensive introduction to the House of the Dukes of Braganza (João was eighth Duke of Braganza) and the cultural and musical ambiance surrounding young João when he was living at the ducal court in Vila Viçosa prior to his accession to the restored Portuguese throne in 1640. Nery devotes part 2 to the music manuscripts of the royal library, and part 3 considers aspects of the repertoire. Nery's book is a significant contribution to patronage and music collecting and also provides extensive information and documentation relating to arguably the most important music library of 17th-century Europe.

NELSON uses available documentation to consider the extent to which Philip II (d. 1598) supported and patronized musical activities in the Lisbon royal chapel during the early decades of Spanish rule in Portugal. Relevant sources include the letters Philip wrote to his daughters during his visit to Lisbon from 1581 to 1583, and the set of statutes drawn up for the royal chapel at his instigation in early 1592, which provides information on the number of musical officers to be employed and their respective salaries.

Opera and theatrical entertainment became vital expressions of cultural life in 18th-century Lisbon and, to a lesser extent, in Oporto. BRITO's book is the first detailed documentary history of opera in Portugal. It is a chronological study that considers opera and other musical entertainment both for the public theater and for the royal court, and it provides a solid foundation for those readers who seek to comprehend musical currents prevalent in Portugal at that time and the extent to which these currents were dependent on Italian forms and influences. One of the most famous musicians associated with this development was Niccolò Jommelli. While the author includes copious references to musical works and performances, he has chosen not to supply detailed studies of the repertoire and its sources. Following the main text is a chronology listing all documented productions of operas and other musical compositions between 1708 and 1793. There is also an appendix of documentary material and an extensive bibliography.

BERNADETTE NELSON

Poulenc, Francis 1899–1963

French composer

Bernac, Pierre, *Francis Poulenc: The Man and His Songs,* translated by Winifred Radford, New York: Norton, and London: Gollancz, 1977

Daniel, Keith W., *Francis Poulenc: His Artistic Development and Musical Style,* Ann Arbor, Michigan: UMI Research Press, 1982

Hell, Henri, *Francis Poulenc,* translated by Edward Lockspeiser, London: Calder, 1959

Keck, George R., *Francis Poulenc: A Bio-Bibliography,* New York: Greenwood Press, 1990

Mellers, Wilfrid, *Francis Poulenc,* Oxford: Oxford University Press, 1993

Poulenc, Francis, *Diary of My Songs,* translated by Winifred Radford, London: Gollancz, 1985

————, *Selected Correspondence, 1915–1963: Echo and Source,* translated and edited by Sidney Buckland, London: Gollancz, 1991

Schmidt, Carl B., *The Music of Francis Poulenc (1899–1963): A Catalogue,* Oxford: Clarendon Press, and New York: Oxford University Press, 1995

As one of the most popular members of Les Six, a loosely organized group of French composers affiliated briefly with Jean Cocteau in the first two decades of the 20th century, Francis Poulenc has emerged as an important figure in modern music. This was not always the case, as his works have frequently been viewed with skepticism and disdain because of the overt use of music-hall and dance idioms deemed by some critics as inappropriate for serious classical music; as a result, full-length studies in English were rare before the 1980s. In the past two decades, however, Poulenc scholarship has blossomed, with a number of important monographs appearing. The sources considered below exemplify the diverse approaches that have characterized Poulenc scholarship since about 1960.

The first major biography of the composer, an important source to this day, was written by HELL. Organized chronologically, with useful comments on the history, reception, and background of a select group of works, this monograph is especially appropriate for general readers who wish to acquire a substantial amount of information in a small package. In keeping with its broad scope, musical analysis is limited to elementary observations.

Because of his lengthy association with Poulenc as recital partner, confidant, and close friend, BERNAC provides insight into Poulenc's prodigious song output that simply cannot be found elsewhere. Following the introductory material, which includes a complete list of songs with vocal ranges as well as useful comments on various aspects of interpretation—such as tempo, legato, and piano accompaniments—the majority of the study is arranged by poet, from the most significant in Poulenc's oeuvre (Apollinaire and Eluard) to the lesser writers. Entries include the complete song texts as well as interpretive comments from both Bernac and the composer himself, and the compact biographies of each poet are particularly useful. As Sir Lennox Berkeley notes in his preface, Bernac's book is "essential reading for singers who wish to include some Poulenc in their programmes."

The most extensive contribution to date concerning the analysis of Poulenc's music is DANIEL's study, a reprint of his doctoral dissertation. Following an ample biographical sketch in the opening five chapters, Daniel devotes much of his attention to the works, organized by genre, with chapter 11 focusing on the songs. Here Daniel's comments are especially effective, as he divides the vocal works into distinct categories such as "patter songs" and "songs with a popular flavor." Frequent musical exam-

ples amplify the text, although the quality of the reproductions are often mediocre. Chapter 6 ("Style") is particularly useful for a summary of Poulenc's use of harmony, form, and orchestration as well as the manner in which he created a distinct musical personality by borrowing "chord structures and progressions from diverse composers." Because much of the study is devoted to analytical issues, readers will need a strong grounding in music theory to fully appreciate Daniel's comments, but for serious students of Poulenc, this study is essential.

Fortunately, many of the definitive statements concerning his very best work, namely, the song output, were made by POULENC (1985) himself, and Radford's edition of the *Journal de mes mélodies* should be required reading for singers of French music. Poulenc provides useful interpretive suggestions, elucidates his relationship with the poets, and critiques the songs, even the less-successful ones. Radford effectively captures the spirit of Poulenc's colorful prose in her translation.

The purpose of KECK's bio-bibliography is to organize and annotate the vast secondary material related to the composer. The works, divided by genre, are assigned W numbers to facilitate easy reference throughout the text, with most discussed in the extensive bibliography. Encompassing about 500 entries, most with appropriate quotations and explanations of the methodology, usefulness, and scope of the source, the bibliography alone is a major contribution to the Poulenc literature. The highly selective discography is arranged alphabetically by D numbers.

Although a portion of Poulenc's correspondence had been selected and published after his death by Hélène de Wendel, this 1967 book has long been out of print. In an attempt to remedy the situation, POULENC (1991) includes substantially more letters than the original edition, all presented in complete form, whereas Wendel's monograph often contains omissions. This is an indispensable resource, as the volume includes some 350 letters, 102 of which have never been previously published. To better manage the material, Buckland divides the correspondence into three broad categories: 1915–35, 1936–53, and 1953–63. Entries are amply documented with valuable information on Poulenc's correspondents and the works themselves. The brief biographies of each correspondent at the end of the book are particularly useful.

According to MELLERS, his recent monograph is not intended to be comprehensive but rather focuses "on a number of works that seem to me to be not only representative, but also good." Compositions from each period of Poulenc's career are discussed, with chapters grouped by genre (such as "Piano Works of the 1930s"). As with Daniel's study, musical analysis is at the intermediate or advanced level, and general readers may find the discussions overly specialized. The works included are well chosen, although analytical comments tend to be somewhat brief, leaving one wishing for more extensive comments on a smaller group of pieces.

In the preface material, SCHMIDT refers to his recent monograph as the "first comprehensive attempt to list the wealth of sources that can be located" concerning Poulenc, supplying "as detailed biographical information for each as is currently available." The majority of the book is devoted to a chronological catalog of works, each given an FP number. Entries include date and place of composition, textual incipits (if any), and most important, the location of holographs, proof sheets, and other primary sources. Since Poulenc source material is divided between several libraries in Europe and the United States, their locations will prove immensely beneficial to scholars. This is a massive, scrupulously researched work, not likely to be superseded in the foreseeable future. Even with its large scope, Schmidt's resource is surprisingly efficient in its organization.

KEITH E. CLIFTON

Prokofiev, Sergei 1891–1953

Russian composer

Bass, W. Richard, "Prokofiev's Technique of Chromatic Displacement," *Music Analysis* 7 (1988)

Minturn, Neil, *The Music of Sergei Prokofiev*, New Haven, Connecticut: Yale University Press, 1997

Nestyev, Israel V., *Prokofiev*, translated by Florence Jonas, Stanford, California: Stanford University Press, 1961

Prokofiev, Sergei, *Prokofiev by Prokofiev: A Composer's Memoir*, edited by David H. Appel, translated by Guy Daniels, Garden City, New York: Doubleday, and London: Macdonald and Jane's, 1979

———, *Sergei Prokofiev: Materials, Articles, Interviews*, compiled by Vladimir Blok, Progress, 1978

———, *Soviet Diary 1927 and Other Writings*, edited and translated by Oleg Prokofiev, London: Faber, 1991; Boston: Northeastern University Press, 1992

Roberts, Peter Deane, *Modernism in Russian Piano Music: Skriabin, Prokofiev, and Their Russian Contemporaries*, 2 vols., Bloomington: Indiana University Press, 1993

Robinson, Harlow, *Sergei Prokofiev: A Biography*, New York: Viking, and London: Hale, 1987

Seroff, Victor, *Sergei Prokofiev: A Soviet Tragedy*, New York: Funk and Wagnalls, 1968

Shlifstein, Semen I., editor, *S. Prokofiev: Autobiography, Articles, Reminiscences*, translated by Rose Prokofieva, Moscow: Foreign Languages Publishing House, n.d.

Taruskin, Richard, "Tone, Style, and Form in Prokofiev's Soviet Operas: Some Preliminary Observations," in *Music and Drama*, Studies in the History of Music, vol. 2, New York: Broude Brothers, 1988

When he was 13 years old, Sergei Prokofiev left an agrarian estate in the Ukraine to train as a composer and pianist at the St. Petersburg Conservatory. Even before he graduated from the conservatory in 1914, he had gained a reputation as an enfant terrible with propulsive, dissonant works such as the Second Piano Concerto. In 1918, as the Russian Civil War was heating up, Prokofiev left the country on what he supposed would be only a tour of the United States. But Russia soon became a dangerous and desperate place—certainly not a promising environment for the pursuit of a musical career. Prokofiev stayed in the West, primarily in Paris, and did not even visit the Soviet Union again until 1927. About that time, he began to soften and simplify his style somewhat so that when he finally moved to Moscow permanently in 1935, his music was more in line with socialist realism, the conservative, propagandistic aesthetic dictated by Stalin's regime. In the Soviet Union, Prokofiev composed, among many other beautiful works, a good deal of appallingly sycophantic musical propaganda in support of that regime. Nevertheless, his music and the music of his greatest Soviet contemporaries—Shostakovich, Khachaturyan, and others—was officially denounced in 1948.

Encapsulated in this biographical sketch are the issues that primarily concerned Prokofiev commentators during the Cold War: Did Prokofiev's music gain or lose value as it became more conservative? Was Prokofiev inspired to greater heights by the Soviet experiment, or was his return a tragic mistake that constricted his creativity and indirectly contributed to his death? Why did Prokofiev decide to return to his homeland just as the full dimensions of Stalinist terror were becoming evident? This last question is still hotly debated today.

Soviet writer NESTYEV wrote the first full-scale biographies of Prokofiev. These studies inevitably reflect Soviet prejudices, especially the second biography, listed here, which was written after the official denunciation of musicologists in 1949. Virtually all important musicologists were censured then, and those, such as Nestyev, who were linked to sanctioned composers, were particularly threatened. Thus, Nestyev's value judgments in the second volume are swayed by the simple-minded aesthetics of socialist realism: conservative, tonal music is valued over experimental, dissonant music, and almost all consideration of the darker side of human experience, and of sexuality, is rejected. Also, artworks created in the Soviet Union receive bonus points. Nestyev's discussion of any particular work by the composer is dominated by these few factors, resulting in obviously skewed ratings of Prokofiev's output. Still, if one can read around the propaganda, Nestyev has many perceptive general points to make about Prokofiev's musical style.

SEROFF's biography, as might be predicted from its title, takes the opposite tack. Seroff, a Russian émigré, sees Prokofiev's homecoming as a capitulation to totalitarianism and a harbinger of his destruction. The composer is depicted as a courageous man savagely victimized by the Soviet regime.

ROBINSON's biography is the most accurate and complete source on Prokofiev's life yet written. Some have felt that Robinson, in his effort to be fair to Prokofiev, fails to censure inexcusable behavior such as Prokofiev's abandonment of his wife, Lina, for another woman. (As a nonnative, Lina was automatically viewed with suspicion by the Soviet authorities; Prokofiev's abandonment almost certainly opened the way for her eventual arrest and imprisonment in a Siberian labor camp.) Still, Robinson's book provides a welcome corrective to earlier one-sided approaches. For those who do not read Russian, Robinson's scholarly apparatus—notes, bibliography, catalog of works, and brief chronology of Prokofiev's life—will be invaluable. Describing music is not Robinson's area of expertise, but his book is very helpful in many other respects.

As a chronicler of his own life, Prokofiev should be ranked with Berlioz for sheer entertainment value. Although he could be insufferable in person, Prokofiev's energy, intelligence, self-knowledge, and dry wit are evident throughout his two autobiographies and the diary of his 1927 trip to the Soviet Union. Written in the late 1930s and late 1940s and based on his early letters and diaries, PROKOFIEV's (1979) longer autobiography deals solely with his rural childhood and urban adolescence. It provides fascinating glimpses of the Russian middle class at the turn of the century. The English translation, edited by Appel, has been somewhat abridged.

Prokofiev's shorter autobiography was written in 1941 and covers his life through 1936. The first English translation appears in SHLIFSTEIN, which also includes a selection of articles by Prokofiev on various musical topics and reminiscences of Prokofiev by some of his most prestigious Soviet colleagues. Film director Sergei Eisenstein's well-known essay on his working relationship with Prokofiev is here as well. Despite a fair amount of candor on the part of Prokofiev and the other authors represented in the Shlifstein collection, it is absolutely essential to read these articles critically with the contemporary political situation in mind. No Soviet citizen could be expected to tell the whole truth in the 1940s and 1950s, and these essays are clearly constrained by self-censorship.

The same could be said of the mixed bag of articles and reminiscences printed in BLOK, several of which originally appeared in Shlifstein. Particularly telling is Nestyev's transcription of Prokofiev's notes for a speech to the Composers' Union in 1937, a year and a few months after the infamous official attack on Shostakovich's Lady Macbeth. Here, Prokofiev mounts a necessarily circumspect yet surprisingly daring defense of musical innovation. "We must not try to get away with cheap music, because the masses are allegedly not cultured enough," warns the composer. "It is better to write a little bit harder than a little bit easier."

The composer's 1927 travel diary, PROKOFIEV (1991), on the other hand, was clearly not intended for public consumption. With complete candor, Prokofiev chronicles his successful concert tour of the Soviet Union, his emotional reunions with old friends, and his attempts to influence the Soviet authorities to free a cousin who was then being held as a political prisoner. Prokofiev's elder son, Oleg, discovered the diary among his mother's papers after her death in 1989. The volume Oleg edited and translated also includes several of Prokofiev's odd short stories and story fragments and another version of Prokofiev's shorter autobiography. Despite the claim that it is "extensively revised and corrected," this version very nearly duplicates the Rose Prokofieva translation that appears in Shlifstein.

Until recently, Prokofiev's work has been largely neglected by music analysts and theorists. The central issue confronting analysts has been the extent to which tonal conventions shape the music and, thus, the extent to which analytic tools designed for tonal music can and ought to be applied. MINTURN confronts this issue directly in the first monograph in a Western language to focus exclusively on Prokofiev analysis. The author tends to de-emphasize tonal interpretations, a stance that would likely elevate Prokofiev's standing among those who prize modernist innovation. Minturn focuses on Prokofiev's "wrong notes"—unexpected pitches that stand out from otherwise conventional surroundings—and combines them with other pitches to generate "structural sets," which the author uses to develop interesting set-theoretic analyses. A fairly thorough knowledge of set theory is a prerequisite for understanding most of this book, and certain analyses presuppose acquaintance with Schenkerian and Lewinian transformational theory as well.

BASS is the only writer to date who has developed an analytical apparatus specifically designed to handle Prokofiev's music, with its celebrated unexpected chromatic shifts. He suggests that listeners hear chromatic substitutions, which could range from individual pitches to whole phrases, as versions of implicit diatonic "shadows." One hears two sets of musical relationships, one generated by the displacing music and one implied by the displaced music. This fascinating idea grows out of Schenkerian theory. Bass's graphing technique is also Schenkerian: shadows are notated as boxed areas within multilayered Schenkerian graphs that indicate the various implied versions of the music.

ROBERTS views Prokofiev as the leading practitioner of a style that flourished in Russia in the second and third decades of the 20th century. His book has been justly praised for its second volume, which brings to light extended examples of unpublished and previously unavailable works by composers such as Lourié, Mosolov, and Roslavetz. (These three composed music considerably more dissonant than Prokofiev's.) Roberts's text is both interesting and maddening. His chapter on Prokofiev mixes genuine technical insights with misleading generalizations and with observations that could apply to much 20th-century music or Western music in general.

TARUSKIN is the essential source on declamation in Prokofiev's vocal works and dramaturgy in his Soviet operas. This impressive article suggests that Prokofiev's ideal of prose recitative opera, which renounces set pieces, was derived from Mussorgsky's *Marriage,* yet not slavishly so. For instance, Prokofiev introduced "melodic molds," musical phrases that are repeated with different texts fitted to them. Such repetition allows purely musical considerations to trump the libretto in a way Mussorgsky's *Marriage* disallows. Taruskin then shows how Prokofiev's ideals were partially compromised by socialist realist demands for accessible, optimistic opera. In recent years, Taruskin has become one of Prokofiev's most vocal critics, depicting the composer as a shallow narcissist whose middle-period scores are only superficially modernist and who nonchalantly supplied his share of Stalinist propaganda in exchange for special privileges. Taruskin is, however, considerably less harsh in this evaluation of Prokofiev's operatic career. For instance, he praises Prokofiev's innovative introduction of the cinematic techniques of flashback and montage into his late Soviet opera, *The Story of a Real Man,* and urges us to regard the work as "more than a concession to the rigors of totalitarian discipline."

DAN ZIMMERMAN

Psalmody: American

Billings, William, *Complete Works,* 4 vols., edited by Hans Nathan and Karl Kroeger, Boston: American Musicological Society and Colonial Society of Massachusetts: 1977–90

Crawford, Richard, *The American Musical Landscape,* Berkeley: University of California Press, 1993

————, "Introduction," in *American Sacred Music Imprints, 1698–1810: A Bibliography* by Allen Perdue Britton and Irving Lowens, completed by Richard Crawford, Worcester, Massachusetts: American Antiquarian Society, 1989

————, "Massachusetts Musicians and the Core Repertory of Early American Psalmody," in *Music in Colonial Massachusetts 1630–1820,* edited by Barbara Lambert, Boston: Colonial Society of Massachusetts, 1985

Crawford, Richard, et al., editors, *A Celebration of American Music: Words and Music in Honor of H. Wiley Hitchcock,* Ann Arbor: University of Michigan Press, 1990

Gould, Nathaniel D., *Church Music in America,* Boston, Johnson, 1853; reprint, New York: AMS Press, 1972

Hood, George, *A History of Music in New England,* Boston: Wilkins and Carter, 1846; reprint, New York: Johnson Reprint, 1970

Metcalf, Frank, *American Psalmody or Titles of Books Containing Tunes Printed in America from 1721 to 1820,* New York: Heartman, 1917; reprint, New York: Da Capo Press, 1968

Psalmody in the North American colonies provided the choral music for the singing of metrical versions of the Psalms in religious, recreational, and educational settings. The first American collections of psalmody appeared in tune books and reflected the styles and practices of the English parish church of the 18th century. Set syllabically, a typical psalm tune appeared in open score and was composed for four-part chorus, with the melody in the tenor voice. Most American tunes of the period contain enough notes to set a single stanza of text; the tune could then be repeated as needed for each of the successive stanzas. The tunes were cast in the same frequently used meters of the stanzas: common meter, 8.6.8.6; long meter, 8.8.8.8.; and short meter, 6.6.8.6. Known by proper names, the tunes often appeared without text and could be used for any psalm of the same meter. Many collections of the psalms, called word books, or psalters, contained no tunes. A congregational song leader could choose any tune in the appropriate meter for the psalms sung during a particular meeting. This peculiarly loose combination of words and music characterized the psalmody of England and Scotland and the English colonies, distinguishing it from the practice in France, Germany, and Holland, where tunes appeared in a greater variety of meters and were known by the first lines of the text, with which they often became associated. Absent from congregational psalmody of the English-speaking world was the historical intimacy between words and music that was so much a part of the continental heritage of sacred music.

During the latter half of the 18th century, interest in a wider repertory of more complex music emerged, resulting largely from the growing popularity of the singing school. American composers, publishing their own tune books for the first time after 1760, began to show greater rhythmic flexibility and more variety in their texture. From 1770, the collections by native composers increased, forming what some historians have called the first school of New England composers. By the 1780s, this movement showed a new sensitivity to the text, which led to a decrease in the number of tunes without texts. Some composers, notably William Billings, began selecting texts from a much wider range of sources and even set poetry by Americans. Tune-book production rose considerably, and by 1811 more than 7,500 different compositions had appeared. During the first decades of the 19th century, New Englanders traveled southward and westward through New York, Pennsylvania, Maryland, and the Carolinas, selling their books and leading singing schools and transforming their regional music into a national music.

HOOD published the first critical study of American psalmody, a musical heritage in which he himself was a participant. He begins the work by explaining, "The history of music in New England, for the first two centuries, is the history of Psalmody alone." He surveys the transplanting of English psalmody in the colonies, the controversy over regular singing, and the establishment of singing schools and choirs. His work continues to be a central source for study of psalmody, owing to his careful research into the original sources. In the first 150 pages, he frequently quotes 17th- and 18th-century musicians and divines. He discusses the important psalm books imported from England and the first collections by American composers. Included as well is a chronological listing of American sacred tune books derived from Hood's own collection and that of Lowell Mason.

GOULD's narrative, which is a loose collection of personal reminiscences from his own half century of work in sacred music, follows Hood's by seven years. Gould's primary concern is with the corruption that crept into sacred music during the second half of the 18th century. He shows little interest in historical research, as he states in discussing psalmody since 1770: "We now leave the traditional history of church music, and enter a field where, for the last fifty years or more, we are enabled, from experience, observation and information, to vouch for the facts we relate." For Gould, the main function for psalmody was as an aid to divine worship. He discusses at length all the foibles that can distract from the sacred purpose of music in worship: status-conscious singers, antagonistic clergymen, sleeping choristers, obstinate teachers, and critical parishioners. Gould's basic complaint centered on the increased presence of American compositions in the tune books from 1770 to 1800, which gave rise to a secular rather than a sacred spirit. However, by 1810, after vigorous debate, European music had outpaced American compositions. Gould describes the revival of ancient music in the early 19th century, a repertoire that was seen as an antidote to secularization: "publications . . . such as Village Harmony, Bridgewater and Worcester Collections, and soon many others . . . began to expunge some of the trash on their pages, and substitute ancient tunes in their stead." Soon the reckless spirit of dark age psalmody yielded to the more proper and reverent atmosphere of music firmly planted in the European tradition. Gould spends the remainder of his history surveying the recent 50 years of music education in America, musical instruments, concerts, and music's place in the divine service.

METCALF presents the first bibliography listing the short titles and library locations of more than 200 books containing sacred music that were published in America in the 18th and early 19th centuries. Although the work has been eclipsed by *American Sacred Music Imprints,* it proved an important contribution to American music and was the only published bibliography of American tune books until 1990.

In four different essays, Crawford offers an essential survey of the music of American psalmody, its place in 18th-century American culture, its dissemination, and its gradual displacement by European music after 1810. CRAWFORD (1989) places psalmody in the cultural context of early American life. He briefly chronicles the earliest psalm books, congregations, and singing schools, followed by the emergence of choirs and the first tune books in the United States. He then explains how the tune book and its music were physically conceived, composed, compiled, taught, performed, published, and sold. Pulling together more than 150 years of scholarship, the essay offers a stimulating narrative about how the tune book became a cultural icon, reflecting the rough, handmade quality of American craftsmanship as well as the deep and abiding religious faith that gave rise to the enduring presence of psalmody in American life. CRAWFORD (1990) on the Europeanizing of American psalmody, offers an outstanding account of Americans intentionally turning away from the music of native American composers toward that of European musicians. He points out that this development was a quick shift that occurred between 1801 and 1805 as a result of an appeal to religious ideals. Musicians and clergy around 1800 felt that American music, with its crude technique and boisterous performance, had become so secularized that it fostered an irreverent rather than a sacred spirit in worship. As a result, between 1806 and 1810, the number of American compositions published in the United States declined while European works more than doubled, and the number of tune books far exceeded the number printed in the previous five years. By 1810, European music had gained the upper hand. In CRAWFORD (1985), the author explains how he came to assemble a core repertory of the 101 sacred pieces most frequently printed in America between 1698 and 1810 out of about 7,200 sacred compositions published in the colonies and United States. Of that total, about 4,600, or two-thirds, can be traced to musicians who lived and worked in America. In CRAWFORD (1993), the author uses a core group of compositions by Billings to write a "bibliographical adventure" depicting how psalm tunes were disseminated throughout the colonies and the young republic. After analyzing why these tunes constitute an impressively well-balanced cross section of Anglo-American psalmody, he traces the reprinting of 25 works in Simon Jocelin's *The Chorister's Companion* (1782–83). This collection played a decisive role in determining which of Billings's pieces remained popular after his death.

BILLINGS was the greatest of the Yankee tunesmiths, and Kroeger—one of the two editors of this four-volume collection of Billings's works—provides a stimulating portrait of the origins and distinctiveness of the composer. He traces the roots of Billings's musical style in the Anglo-American sacred music, which dated from the Renaissance. Metrical psalm tunes first appeared in Calvin's psalters, were passed through English psalters (most popularly through the psalters of John Playford in the second half of the 17th century), and then reproduced in various forms in American collections. By the early 18th century, American composers began composing original psalm tunes embellished in a more lively and spiritual style than the old melodies. Billings appeared just as this rich tradition began flowering. With the publication of his first psalm book, *The New England Psalm Singer* (1770), Kroeger observes, Billings produced "the first American tunebook devoted to the compositions of one composer, the first to consist entirely of American compositions, and the tunebook responsible for introducing a new spirit into American psalmody."

N. LEE ORR

Psalmody: British

Long, Kenneth R., *Music of the English Church*, New York: St. Martin's Press, 1971; London: Hodder and Stoughton, 1972

Patrick, Millar, *Four Centuries of Scottish Psalmody*, London: Oxford University Press, 1949

Temperley, Nicholas, *The Music of the English Parish Church*, 2 vols., Cambridge: Cambridge University Press, 1979

Wilson, Ruth M., *Anglican Chant and Chanting in England, Scotland, and America, 1660 to 1820*, Oxford: Clarendon Press, and New York: Oxford University Press, 1996

The term *British psalmody* is somewhat ambiguous in meaning because it can be used to refer to several methods of psalm singing. Perhaps the oldest is the singing of psalms to Gregorian tones, this ancient practice having been retained, to some extent and in altered form, even after the establishment of the English Rite and lingering far into the 17th century. A reawakening of interest in pre-Reformation practices in the 19th century led to the appearance of several updated Gregorian psalters and a revival of psalm singing to Gregorian tones. Metrical psalms—rhymed, vernacular paraphrases intended for congregational singing and thus useful in parish churches—became quite popular in England after Thomas Sternhold issued his first metrical psalter in 1549. Their prevalence continued into the 19th century when choirs began to adopt fully choral services based on cathedral tradition. However, the most widely recognized and indigenous form of British psalmody is the so-called Anglican chant, a harmonized version of prose psalms. Early examples were often based on Gregorian melodies, with the psalm tone placed in the tenor, although by the 18th century, when memories of plainsong singing had passed, the melody was moved to the treble part.

Although a multifaceted topic of some complexity, British psalmody has only recently, with few exceptions, attracted the attention of scholars. Thus, a dearth of full-length studies exists. Those accounts that are accessible tend to address fairly specific topics rather than the whole of British psalmody. Such is the case with PATRICK's examination of Scottish psalmody. His book is largely a chronicle of the development of psalmody in Scotland, concentrating on the psalters of 1564 and 1650. As a historical conspectus the work is satisfying, presenting in one volume a wealth of information on the pedigree of Scottish psalmody as well as the genesis and growth of its most important psalters. The study, though dated, is the most important on the topic. Its shortcomings are a complete lack of musical examples, particularly noticed as regards the actual psalm tunes, and little information on specific tunes.

An extremely short yet adequate overview of English psalm singing is provided by LONG, a well-known authority on British music. His remarks, although somewhat generalized and sometimes biased, are mostly reliable. He divides psalm singing into four different categories (metrical psalm singing, Gregorian psalm tones, Anglican chants, and the Gelineau method), briefly discussing the history of each. The brevity of coverage and the author's outline-like approach to the topic, make this a useful introduction for the uninitiated reader.

Perhaps the best examination of psalmody in the parish church is TEMPERLEY's chapter devoted to country psalmody from 1685 to 1830. Tracing the development of psalm singing in country parishes, the author examines such issues as performance practice, stylistic traits, and accompaniments, as well as composers and editions of psalm tunes. Largely a historical account rather than musical analysis or commentary, the author nonetheless gives useful information about the development of psalm tunes and their typical musical characteristics. Temperley's research is exhaustive, and his authority on the subject is widely acknowledged and largely unchallenged, yet his scholarship is immensely comprehensible and reader friendly. This study is a must for anyone interested in psalmody outside the cathedral tradition.

An assessment of psalm singing in cathedrals and the repertoire that has come to be known as Anglican chant, WILSON's recent work is a welcome contribution to the existing scholarship that emerges as the finest full-length study of its kind. Mainly concerned with the choral service in the cathedral and limited in coverage to the years 1660 to 1820, the book does extend its scope to include chant in the parish church, as well as chant in Scotland and colonial America, providing a wealth of information on the evolution of chanting and the chant tune. One of the most commendable features of this study is the combination of historical survey with musical analysis. In addition to excellent archival information on the period and institutions in question, the author also provides detailed examinations of the repertoire from stylistic and theoretical perspectives.

MICHAEL VAUGHN

Psychology of Music

Critchley, Macdonald, and Ronald Alfred Hensen, editors, *Music and the Brain: Studies in the Neurology of Music,* Springfield, Illinois: Thomas, 1977

Deutsch, Diana, editor, *The Psychology of Music,* New York: Academic Press, 1982

Farnsworth, Paul, *The Social Psychology of Music,* New York: Dryden Press, 1958; 2nd edition, Ames: Iowa State University Press, 1969

Helmholtz, Hermann von, *On the Sensations of Tone as a Physiological Basis for the Theory of Music,* translated by Alexander J. Ellis, London: Longman, 1875; 6th edition: New York: Smith, 1948

Hodges, Donald A., *Handbook of Music Psychology,* Lawrence, Kansas: National Association for Music Therapy, 1980; 2nd edition, San Antonio, Texas: IMR Press, 1996

Lundin, Robert, *An Objective Psychology of Music,* New York: Ronald Press, 1953; 3rd edition, Malabar, Florida: Krieger, 1985

Mursell, James, *The Psychology of Music,* New York: Norton, 1937; reprint, Westport, Connecticut: Greenwood Press, 1971

Radocy, Rudolf E., and J. David Boyle, *Psychological Foundations of Musical Behavior,* Springfield, Illinois: Thomas, 1979; 3rd edition, 1997

Seashore, Carl E., *Psychology of Music,* New York: McGraw-Hill, 1938

——, *The Psychology of Musical Talent,* Boston: Silver Burdett, 1919

Wallin, Nils Lennart, *Biomusicology: Neurophysiological, Neuropsychological, and Evolutionary Perspectives on the Origins and Purposes of Music,* Stuyvesant, New York: Pendragon Press, 1991

Psychology of music is the study of the human behaviors collectively known as *music,* which can be defined as the organization of sound and silence over time for the purpose of human communication. By definition, studying psychology of music involves a vast array of human functions, behaviors, and reactions. These include psychoacoustics (the study of sound perception) and the closely aligned study of the neuroanatomical and neurophysiological basis of musical behavior. Psychology of music also involves investigation of musical behaviors, including performance and composition; study of the effects of music on human behavior such as emotional response, aesthetics, physiological response; and exploration of the influence of music on behavior. Additionally, psychology of music has included study of its social functions, nonaesthetic uses (e.g., work songs, music for therapy, uses in ceremony and religious expression), and, predominately, the factors that constitute musical talent. The books published on this subject over the last 150 years vary in the topics included. Some emphasize one approach, such as the neurological structures responsible for musical behavior. Others encompass many of the topics mentioned above, emphasizing reviews of current research. All place particular importance on the investigation of the constituent factors in musical aptitude or talent. The study of psychology of music has moved from its early roots in acoustics through a mentalist belief that all musical behavior and response is genetically and neurologically predetermined to a true psychological research basis. The early writers in psychology of music were physicists. The field was then dominated until the 1970s by research psychologists, shifting in the later part of the 20th century to researchers who were musicians, music educators, and music therapists.

The history of psychology of music begins with early studies in acoustics, the physics of sound. HELMHOLTZ was a physicist who wrote at length about acoustical principles and developed the first theory of psychoacoustics. His book is a classic work of general acoustics and the perception of single and combined tones. Other topics in the traditional study of psychology of music are not addressed. This work is important as the first publication in what is now psychology of music. Many of the basic principles set forth by the author are still valid today, although extensive research since its publication has modified or elaborated on many conclusions in this work.

Many works on acoustics after the Helmholtz book address psychoacoustical topics, but the first true publication in psychology of music was by SEASHORE (1919). Seashore, a psychologist, is considered the father of psychology of music and was the first to apply research methodology to its study. This work focuses on the factors involved in musical talent and their measurement. Seashore here holds a mentalist viewpoint, stating that nothing, including musical ability, is learned or gained from interaction with the environment. He postulates that a person with musical ability has a genetically determined musical mind, involving five testable factors: musical sensitivity, musical action, musical memory and imagination, musical intellect, and musical feeling. From this work, Seashore developed the first test of musical aptitude, the Seashore Measure of Musical Talent, a predictive assessment of musical success.

SEASHORE (1938) is a more general treatise on the broad topics of psychology of music and reflects a softening of the mentalist viewpoint. This book includes most of the material from the previous work but also addresses topics in psychoacoustics such as pitch and loudness perception; consonance and dissonance judgments; learning music; performance considerations in violin, piano, and voice; and aesthetics researched in Seashore's own laboratory. Both books make important contributions to psychology of music, setting the standard for scientific investigations of this topic. Much of Seashore's basic work is still used today and is partially substantiated by research. Neither book contains a comprehensive overview of topics in psychology of music. The mentalist approach seems dated by present-day standards and is often in conflict with current beliefs concerning the basis of human behavior.

Contemporary with Seashore, MURSELL retains a mentalist approach but disagrees with the former's belief in the inheritability of musical talent. Mursell postulates that musical behavior and reactions to music are indeed innate reactions, but they also are natural outgrowths of brain structure and functioning. He addresses three areas of psychology of music: the psychology of tonal and rhythmic forms; the psychology of musical functions including listening, performance, and composition; and musical ability and musical personality. The discussion on musical functions is an important contribution. Although superseded by more current research, this book offers a unique perspective and was the first study to look seriously at neuroanatomical basis of musical behavior.

A major shift in approach occurred with the publication of LUNDIN. Providing a direct counter to the mentalist approach, Lundin bases his ideas on interbehaviorism and offers an admittedly biased review of research literature to date. This book makes a major contribution in its organization of the wide-ranging topics in psychology of music and its comprehensive research bibliography. Similarly, FARNSWORTH directly confronts the mentalist viewpoint. A social psychologist, Farnsworth addresses the cultural determinants of musical behavior, reaction, and function. He believes there are no musical absolutes, writing extensively, for example, to disprove the adage "Music is the universal language." Both Lundin and Farnsworth provide comprehensive overviews of topics in psychology of music and offer unique perspectives. Although now outdated in many aspects, both texts make important contributions to the subject.

In the early 1980s, two publications appeared that provided comprehensive surveys of psychology of music topics. Both are notable as the first publications in psychology of music to be written or edited by musician researchers. HODGES covers a wide range of psychology of music topics in essays written by the most notable musician researchers in the field at that time. The book is a thorough review of literature, drawing conclusions based on findings in subjects ranging from psychoacoustics to learning theory and music. The first edition of RADOCY and BOYLE appeared one year after Hodges and is also a comprehensive summary of pertinent topics in psychology of music. Both books are well written and make difficult topics in diverse areas of investigation easy to understand. The third edition of Radocy and Boyle is the current standard text in psychology of music courses.

In addition to books providing comprehensive overviews of the subject, three notable publications have focused on specific aspects of psychology of music. DEUTSCH is a collection that summarizes extensive and detailed psychological research in psychoacoustical topics including perception and cognition in music. This book contains important and minutely detailed information on these topics but is often difficult to read because of extensive scientific language and scholarly rhetoric.

CRITCHLEY and HENSEN's compilation addresses the neurological aspects of musical experience. The authors in this collection are laboratory researchers in anatomy, physiology, pathology, psychology, and otology. This is the first book since Mursell to address brain structure and function as they relate to musical behavior. Although highly scientific in its language, the volume offers much valuable information on this aspect of psychology of music.

WALLIN is the most current overview of the neurobiological basis of musical behavior and reaction. It provides the most detailed treatment of the intricacies involved in the neurological mediation of all aspects of musical functioning. The explanation of the physiology involved in the human behavior of music in all its dimensions is invaluable, but the book is difficult to read and understand. Its language is unnecessarily complex and requires an understanding of neuroanatomical terminology.

BARBARA J. CROWE

Publishing: To 1750

Bernstein, Jane A., *Music Printing in Renaissance Venice: The Scotto Press, 1539–1572*, New York: Oxford University Press, 1998

Fenlon, Iain, *Music, Print, and Culture in Early Sixteenth-Century Italy*, London: British Library, 1995

Heartz, Daniel, *Pierre Attaingnant, Royal Printer of Music: A Historical Study and Bibliographical Catalogue*, Berkeley: University of California Press, 1969

Kidson, Frank, *British Music Publishers, Printers, and Engravers*, London: Hill, 1900; reprint, New York: Blom, 1967

Krummel, Donald W., *English Music Printing, 1553–1700*, London: Bibliographical Society, 1975

Krummel, Donald W., and Stanley Sadie, editors, *Music Printing and Publishing*, Basingstoke: Macmillan, and New York: Norton, 1990

Lenneberg, Hans, editor, *The Dissemination of Music: Studies in the History of Music Publishing*, Lausanne: Gordon and Breach, 1994

Lewis, Mary S., *Antonio Gardano, Venetian Music Printer, 1538–1569: A Descriptive Bibliography and Historical Study,* 2 vols., New York: Garland, 1988–97

Smith, William C., *A Bibliography of the Musical Works Published by John Walsh during the Years 1695–1720,* London: Bibliographical Society, 1948

Smith, William C., and Charles Humphries, *A Bibliography of the Musical Works Published by John Walsh during the Years 1721–1766,* London: Bibliographical Society, 1968

The history of music publishing before 1750 is inextricably tied to the history of music printing, but the precise moment when printed music began to fuel commercial opportunities for music publishers is difficult to establish with complete certainty. In its earliest stages, the aristocracy viewed printing as a magnificent invention, and ownership of a printing press was a status symbol. It is reputed that in the late 15th century, a certain Italian nobleman purchased a press and printing staff to produce single copies of books to fill his personal library. Only when technology was joined to capitalism did the industry of publishing begin to flourish.

The use of the new printing technology for music, however, lagged behind the application of that technology to text. Well after Gerardus of Lisa published Tinctoris's *Diffinitorum musicae* in 1494, music manuscripts, printed music, and published music continued to coexist in a variety of ways. Some music was printed but not published as, for example, the earliest copies of *Parthenia* (London, 1613) which were printed as limited-edition collectibles. Well in to the 19th century, hand-copied manuscripts continued to be distributed in the same manner as printed music. It was often argued that copyists could provide a musical score that simply looked better than a printed score.

Considering the overlapping developments in printing and publishing, any study of music publishing before 1750 should begin with KRUMMEL and SADIE. This volume presents an expanded version of the article "Music Printing and Publishing" from the *New Grove Dictionary of Music and Musicians* (1980). In addition, the editors have collected and updated all other related articles from the *New Grove Dictionary,* including approximately 650 entries dealing with specific publishers, printers, and techniques. Particularly useful is a glossary of technical terms associated with the printing and publishing industry.

Although Krummel and Sadie provide a useful overview of the key contributors to the history of publishing, their work does not deal extensively with issues concerning the role of printed and published music in shaping the social history of music. Contributors to the collection of essays edited by LENNEBERG address some of these questions by discussing publishing as a means of effecting a shift in musical taste in Europe; exploring the various roles of composers, editors, and publishers in the dissemination of specific works; and considering new legal issues raised by the publishing industry, such as copyright infringement.

FENLON's survey of the publishing business documents existing volumes, contemporary bibliographies, and other records that might provide clues concerning the distribution and use of music produced by the earliest leaders in the field—Ottaviano Petrucci, Andrea Antico, the Giunta family, Valerio Dorico, and Antonio Gardano. Petrucci's method for printing music was complicated and exacting, involving multiple-impression techniques. In this system, music was produced by running a page through three different presses—once to print the staff lines, once to place the note heads, and a third time to place the texts, initial letters, signatures, and page numbers. The resulting print was truly beautiful, with its elegant elongated notation and precise placement of noteheads. This method, however, was not cost-effective and was therefore short-lived.

Pierre Attaingnant solved the problems faced by Petrucci when he devised a technique of single-impression printing. His activities have been well documented by HEARTZ, whose study of Attaingnant's career traces the political problems faced by the music publisher, who was initially protected by Francis I but was later destroyed by Henry II. Heartz's discussion of Attaingnant suggests that the relationships among patrons, printers, and publishers were complex, and that the next generation of publishers necessarily sought to remove the limitations imposed by monarchical authority. Throughout Europe, Attaingnant's system proved most profitable for successful businessmen of this new industry, such as Jacques Moderne, George Rhau, Antonio Gardano, Girolamo Scotto, Tylman Susato, and Pierre Phalese.

The commercial publishing industry was particularly successful in Venice, and this history is well addressed by Lewis and Bernstein. LEWIS has completed the first two volumes of a projected four-volume study documenting the rich history of the firm of Antonio Gardano. The first three volumes are to provide a descriptive bibliography of each of the nearly 450 collections of sacred and secular music published by Gardano between 1538 and 1569. Each entry provides a transcription of the title page, format, pagination, texts of any dedications, concordances of pieces in other sources, and locations of individual copies. The first volume contains a brief survey of the history of music printing, a biography of Gardano, and a discussion of the economics, production methods, and repertoire of this massive enterprise. Volume 2 includes analyses of the style, structure, and genres of the collection.

Modeled after Lewis's thorough methodology, BERNSTEIN chronicles the works of Gardano's greatest rival, Girolamo Scotto, who in his 36 years of operation nearly matched the output of Gardano, producing approximately 400 editions of similarly Italian-dominated motets and madrigals. Bernstein is meticulous in her documentation of each edition, adding a listing of modern editions when available. The historical background that Bernstein provides emphasizes the socioeconomic aspect of the music publishing business in relationship to other printing industries.

Lewis and Bernstein agree that printers in Venice enjoyed a unique position of autonomy and privilege during the fledgling years of music publishing, a privilege not present elsewhere in Europe. Kidson and Krummel assess the history of music printing and publishing in England. There, Queen Elizabeth I exercised complete control over her craftsmen, granting an exclusive monopoly for printing to William Byrd and Thomas Tallis in 1575. The legacy of Tallis and Byrd was followed by the artistically fallow period of the Commonwealth; the Restoration period at the end of the 17th century finally eliminated the monopoly in this industry.

Although the works by KIDSON and KRUMMEL overlap in many areas, both should be consulted for a historical discussion of the variety of participants in the bustling trade spawned by John Playford and expanded by John Walsh. Particularly important to their studies are extensive technical discussions of the development of engraving as a less expensive alternative to the single-impression system in use since Attaingnant. While both Kidson and Krummel provide excellent reproductions of early examples of engraving, Krummel emphasizes the work of Walsh, who was notably zealous in his attempt to displace Playford and any other competitors by employing an inelegant but cost-effective engraving style. Krummel describes how Walsh swept through the major cities of the continent, including Rome, Paris, and Amsterdam, bringing back to London a wide assortment of sheet music, which he promptly pirated and sold through his own firm, making him perhaps the greatest success story in the business. Walsh's business, which is the subject of a two-volume study by SMITH and by SMITH and HUMPHRIES, continued its success while in the hands of his son, in part because of the strong partnership that the firm formed with Handel, who granted Walsh's son sole licensing rights to this most lucrative collection of music. Smith and Humphries is particularly useful for its descriptive catalog of each of Walsh's publications, providing title page information as well as locations of prints.

Culminating in the extravagant commercialism of Walsh, the history of music publishing to 1750 reveals a difficult and colorful struggle among composers, patrons, businessmen, and audiences. Furthermore, a consideration of the process of presenting music, from original conception to manuscript, to print, and to buyer, forces reconsideration of the notion of an authentic text.

SILVIA HERZOG

Publishing: From 1750

Barksdale, A. Beverly, *The Printed Note, 500 Years of Music Printing and Engraving*, New York: Da Capo Press, 1981

Benton, Rita, and Jeanne Halley, *Pleyel as Music Publisher: A Documentary Sourcebook of Early 19th-Century Music*, Stuyvesant, New York: Pendragon Press, 1990

Calderisi, Maria, *Music Publishing in the Canadas, 1800–1867*, Ottawa: National Library of Canada, 1981

Epstein, Dena J., *Music Publishing in Chicago before 1871: The Firm of Root and Cady, 1858–1871*, Detroit, Michigan: Information Coordinators, 1969

Hopkinson, Cecil, *A Bibliography of the Musical and Literary Works of Hector Berlioz 1803–1869, with Histories of the French Music Publishers Concerned*, Edinburgh: Edinburgh Bibliographical Society, 1951; 2nd edition, Tunbridge Wells: Macnutt, 1980

Humphries, Charles, and William Charles Smith, *Music Publishing in the British Isles, from the Earliest Times to the Middle of the Nineteenth Century*, London: Cassell, 1954; 2nd edition, Oxford: Blackwell, and New York: Barnes and Noble, 1970

Hunter, David, editor, *Music Publishing and Collecting: Essays in Honor of Donald W. Krummel*, Urbana: University of Illinois, 1994

Hurd, Michael, *Vincent Novello—and Company*, London: Granada, 1981

Johansson, Cari, *French Music Publishers' Catalogues of the Second Half of the Eighteenth Century*, Stockholm: Royal Swedish Academy of Music, 1955

Krummel, Donald W., *The Literature of Music Bibliography: An Account of the Writings on the History of Music Printing and Publishing*, Berkeley, California: Fallen Leaf Press, 1992

Krummel, Donald W., and Stanley Sadie, editors, *Music Printing and Publishing*, Basingstoke: Macmillan, and New York: Norton, 1990

Lenneberg, Hans, editor, *The Dissemination of Music: Studies in the History of Music Publishing*, Lausanne: Gordon and Breach, 1994

Ross, Ted, *The Art of Engraving and Processing*, Miami, Florida: Hansen Books, 1970

Roth, Ernst, *The Business of Music: Reflections of a Music Publisher*, New York: Oxford University Press, 1964

Music printing is the production of many copies of a piece of music. Although there have been numerous printing methods over the centuries, today most music is typeset electronically using computers. Music publishing involves the production of musical editions consisting primarily of musical notation. The publisher's activities include financing the printing, promoting, advertising, and distribution of musical works. The histories of music printing and music publishing are closely related (music publishers often did their own printing), but the two terms should not be confused: studies of music printing are commonly concerned with the history of technology, while studies of music publishing involve the dissemination of music and its effect on society and commerce.

The history of publishing and printing since 1750 can be divided into three overlapping periods: the age of engraving, the age of offset printing, and the age of computer-generated printing (desk-top publishing). The most thorough introduction to the fields of printing and publishing is KRUMMEL and SADIE. Part 1 presents detailed, up-to-date histories of music printing and publishing. The second part is a dictionary of music printers and publishers. This book is an excellent resource.

For readers interested in the fields of publishing and printing, KRUMMEL is an excellent place to start. This annotated bibliography examines historical surveys of music printing, studies on musical commerce and property, reference books, and other sources related to the history of publishing. There is a list of exhibition catalogs dedicated to printed music as a graphic art.

ROSS is a manual for readers interested in preparing music for reproduction and print. This is a good source for the guidelines and rules of proper notation. However, many of the printing processes discussed have been replaced by the computer.

BARKSDALE, first published in 1957, contains over 100 facsimiles of early music printing. This is an invaluable source for tracing the evolution of print types in Europe and America. The brief commentaries accompanying each facsimile are especially helpful.

The field of music publishing has gained more attention from scholars in recent years than music printing. HUNTER is a collection of nine essays honoring Donald Krummel, a scholar who has dedicated the majority of his career to music bibliography. A list of Krummel's own studies appear in a bibliography, and the essays reflect many of his interests, notably music publishing and collecting. Unfortunately, the field in which Krummel made some of his most important contributions, music printing, is not represented. Three studies deal specifically with the history of music publishing: James Coover's survey of the five-generation London bookselling and publishing business of William Reeves (which dates to 1825); William Lichtenwanger's detailed summary of the history of music copyright in the United States; and Mark McKnight's analysis of 19th-century American instrumental sheet music.

In LENNEBERG, three essays concern publishing since 1750: "International Dissemination of Printed Music during the Second Half of the Eighteenth Century," by Sarah Adams; "Copyists and Publishers in Italy between 1770 and 1830," by Bianca Maria Antolini; and "The Business Affairs of Gabriel Fauré," by Lisa Feurzeig.

Studies of music publishing can also be divided along cultural/geographical lines. HURD presents an in-depth history of the English publishing firm Novello. Special attention is given to the careers of the men responsible

for Novello's success, notably Vincent Novello, J. Alfred Novello, Henry Littleton, and Harold Littleton Brooke. As Hurd's study shows, this group exerted a widespread and stimulating influence on 19th-century England's taste and musical practice.

HUMPHRIES and SMITH is a directory of engravers, printers, publishers and music sellers in the British Isles that serves as a useful reference. A brief history of British printing and publishing is included, but this history has not been updated since the first edition in 1954.

JOHANSSON was published in two volumes in 1955. Volume 1 serves as an encyclopedia of French publishers and begins with a brief introduction to the dating of French printed music. Volume 2 contains facsimiles of the publishers' catalogs discussed in volume 1.

A brief introduction to 19th-century publishing in France serves as an appendix to HOPKINSON, reflecting the variety of publishing opportunities available to French composers during the first half of the century.

BENTON and HALLEY is a catalog of all the works published by Ignaz Pleyel. Although of little use to students and general readers, the 11-page introduction presents a fascinating account of Pleyel's entry into music publishing.

Readers interested in North American publishing should consult EPSTEIN and CALDERISI. Both look at the effect of music publishing on 19th-century society. While Epstein focuses on a single publisher, Root and Cady of Chicago, Calderisi presents a comprehensive study of Canadian publishers and their interests.

ROTH examines the vast changes that took place in the dissemination of both popular and serious music in the 1960s and 1970s. Issues such as copyrights and performing rights are discussed in depth, and various problems confronting composers and performers are addressed through personal reminiscences about 20th-century composers, from Richard Strauss to Karlheinz Stockhausen.

ANNA H. HARWELL CELENZA

Puccini, Giacomo 1858–1924

Italian composer

Ashbrook, William, *The Operas of Puccini*, New York: Oxford University Press, 1968; corrected edition, 1985

Ashbrook, William, and Harold Powers, *Puccini's Turandot: The End of the Great Tradition*, Princeton, New Jersey: Princeton University Press, 1991

Carner, Mosco, *Puccini: A Critical Biography*, London: Duckworth, 1958; New York: Knopf, 1959; 3rd edition, London: Duckworth, and New York: Homes and Meier, 1992

———, *Giacomo Puccini: Tosca*, Cambridge: Cambridge University Press, 1985

Greenwald, Helen M., "Recent Puccini Research," *Acta Musicologica* 65 (1993)

Groos, Arthur, and Roger Parker, *Giacomo Puccini: La bohème,* Cambridge: Cambridge University Press, 1986

Nicolaisen, Jay, *Italian Opera in Transition, 1871–1893,* Ann Arbor, Michigan: UMI Research Press, 1980

Weaver, William, and Simonetta Puccini, editors, *The Puccini Companion,* New York: Norton, 1994

Giacomo Puccini composed some of the best-loved works in the operatic repertoire even though his career spanned a volatile era in the history of Italian opera and Western art music in general. On the one hand, Puccini was caught in the ideological and practical maelstrom of a system of musical precepts under fire (in particular, the tonal system), and on the other, he, more than Verdi, had to cope with the dissolution of the conventions of early 19th-century (or *primo ottocento*) Italian opera, which increasingly gave way to Wagnerism and the demands for more realistic presentation of music and staging. Faced with the crumbling dictatorship of Italian prosody that had governed Italian opera for most of the century, and always feeling the burden of Verdi's shadow, Puccini developed his own musical and dramatic profile. His works are defined by subjects that are set against colorful locales (bohemian Paris, Nagasaki at the turn of the 20th century, post-Napoleonic Rome, mythical Beijing, for example) and explore the intimacies of human relationships, often within the context of family or friends. This focus is in stark contrast to the more global issues that characterized Verdi's often politically motivated music dramas. Contrary to popular myth, however, Puccini was not really a composer of verismo operas in the spirit of Pietro Mascagni (*Cavalleria rusticana*) or Ruggiero Leoncavallo (*Pagliacci*), who explored the raw emotions of the lower classes caught in the vise of economic depression and deprivation-fueled emotions. In this sense, only *Il Tabarro* fits comfortably within this particular trend in Italian opera at the end of the 19th century.

CARNER's (1958) book still stands as the definitive English-language life-and-works biography of Puccini. Written for the centenary of the composer's birth, it is the most comprehensive chronological narrative of his life, laced with letters, illustrations of family and residences, excerpts from youthful works, and a few of Puccini's own cartoons. The second part of the book is devoted to a discussion of the aesthetics of Puccini's art, his relationship to Verdi, and his dramaturgy and musical style. The third and final part of the book devotes a chapter to each work, followed by appendices, including a genealogical tree of the Puccini family, plot synopses, and a catalog of works that lists Puccini's librettists and the date and place of first productions. Unfortunate—but also a reflection of scholarly views and tastes that are beginning to wane—is Carner's tendency to apologize for what the author views as the composer's less worthy goals and the absence of profundity in his music.

ASHBROOK's volume on the operas is mainly a discussion of the works, but it is not devoid of biographical material, particularly as such information pertains to issues of revision and production. In addition to discussing the music of each work, the author comments on details of the Puccini autographs housed at the Ricordi publishing company in Milan as well as on the actions and interactions surrounding first performances.

NICOLAISEN takes a detailed look at what happened to the structure of Italian opera in the era following Verdi's *Aida.* The author's goal is to fill the void around Verdi, contending that he not only exerted influence but was himself influenced by his contemporaries. This book provides an excellent study of Puccini, the subject of two chapters. Nicolaisen begins with Ponchielli, who was one of Puccini's teachers at the Milan Conservatory, and follows up with chapters on Boito, Catalani, Puccini, and Puccini's contemporaries. Most significant is Nicolaisen's discussion of *Le villi* and *Edgar,* two works that enjoy little attention elsewhere. Even though both Carner and Ashbrook discuss these works, Nicolaisen puts them in a unique and important context—that is, the changing values of Italian opera at the end of the 19th century.

Both GROOS and PARKER, on *La bohème,* and CARNER (1985), on *Tosca,* are richly detailed volumes. In the tradition of the Cambridge Opera Handbook series, both volumes begin with the literary sources from which these operas were generated, and both also include essays by outside authors. The Carner volume includes an analytical essay by Roger Parker and an interpretive one by the late renowned bass-baritone, Tito Gobbi. The Groos and Parker volume includes essays by William Drabkin, Ashbrook, Jerrold Siegel, and Regina Psaki on such subjects as musical language, stage history, Bohemia, and the lost "Cortile" act of *La bohème.* Standard features of both volumes are synopses, genesis, analysis, bibliography, stage history, and discography.

ASHBROOK and POWERS's book on *Turandot* goes beyond the Cambridge series in its scope and is distinguished mainly by its fascinating and detailed musical-analytical sections. There is an extensive explanation of what Ashbrook and Powers call the "Four Colors" of *Turandot*: Chinoiserie (authentic Chinese sources), pentatonicism, dissonances and half-steps, and Persian versus Chinese exoticism. All of this discussion is pitted against the authors' study of the "Puccinian Norm." The book ends with an examination of staging, critical reaction, and performance history.

GREENWALD's article is an extensive critical annotated bibliography of scholarly works on Puccini published mainly after 1970. After a preface outlining past issues and problems in Puccini research, publications are organized into such categories as bibliographical studies and editions, life and works, source-critical studies, reception, contextual studies, analytical/interpretive studies, collections of essays, and studies of individual works. An additional section includes some conference papers, dissertations, and works in progress. About 300 items are listed and discussed.

The volume edited by WEAVER and Simonetta PUCCINI contains an interesting collection of essays on a range of topics from the Puccini family to the genesis of *Madama Butterfly* to 20th-century aesthetics and early Puccini performances. The book is enhanced by various appendices that address bibliography, first performances, chronology, and a valuable dramatis personae, or "who's who" of people in Puccini's orbit.

HELEN M. GREENWALD

Purcell, Henry 1659–1695

English composer

1. Biography

Burden, Michael, *Purcell Remembered,* Portland, Oregon: Amadeus Press, and London: Faber, 1995a

Burden, Michael, editor, *The Purcell Companion,* Portland, Oregon: Amadeus Press, and London: Faber, 1995b

Campbell, Margaret, *Henry Purcell: Glory of His Age,* London: Hutchinson, 1993

Cummings, William, *Purcell,* London: Low, Marston, Searle and Rivington, 1881

Dupre, Henri, *Purcell,* translated by Catherine Alison Phillips and Agnes Bedford, New York: Knopf, 1928; reprint, New York: AMS Press, 1978

Keates, Jonathan, *Purcell: A Biography,* Boston: Northeastern University Press, and London: Chatto and Windus, 1995

King, Robert, *Henry Purcell,* New York: Thames and Hudson, 1994

Price, Curtis, editor, *Purcell Studies,* Cambridge: Cambridge University Press, 1995

Westrup, J.A., *Purcell,* London: Dent, 1937; 8th edition, 1980

Zimmerman, Franklin B., *Henry Purcell, 1659–1695: His Life and Times,* London: Macmillan, and New York, St. Martin's Press, 1967; 2nd revised edition, Philadelphia: University of Pennsylvania Press, 1983

———, *Henry Purcell: A Guide to Research,* New York: Garland, 1989

The 1995 tercentenary of Henry Purcell's birth rejuvenated an interest in Purcell scholarship and gave rise to the appearance of several fine biographical and works studies that have largely superseded much of the existing early literature on the composer. Indeed, the proliferation of recent scholarship counteracts the relative neglect accorded to Purcell throughout much of the 20th century. Thus, the student of England's baroque genius notices an

uneven distribution of full-length studies; works from the opening and closing years of the century are more plentiful than those from the fallow years in between.

One of the earliest examinations of Purcell's life is to be found in CUMMINGS. Taking the approach of a chronological survey, the author gives little attention to the composer's compositional output but concentrates, instead, on his other musical activities. Purcell's life and career are chronicled in straightforward fashion, and the author's conclusions are supported with a surprising amount of documentary source material. Herein lies the strength of this brief study: although much of its information has been reproduced more recently elsewhere and discussed in greater detail, Cummings methodically and efficiently surveys Purcell's life and surrounding milieu without introducing musical analysis or commentary. The result is an intimate, familiar portrait of the composer and the environment in which he lived and worked. Besides its age, the main disadvantage to this volume is its lack of chapter partitions or other textual divisions, rendering quick location and retrieval of information difficult.

First published in French, DUPRE's work appeared at a time when the composer was little known outside of musical circles; therefore, this book is aimed largely at uninitiated amateurs with the purpose of making Purcell more widely known. In this capacity Dupre attempts to introduce the reader to the English musical scene of the 17th century, with particular attention given to English music prior to Purcell as well as to the artistic environment and institutions of the day. The author's style is simple and straightforward, unfettered by the use of complex musical terminology. Consequently, here is an immensely readable study that, although it may have been supplanted by more recent scholarship, still serves as a useful initial introduction to the life and works of the composer.

For many years WESTRUP's work was the most thoroughly documented and complete investigation into the life and music of Purcell and was traditionally viewed as the classic, standard biography. The book, now in its eighth edition, still stands as a model of informed yet accessible scholarship. Basing his findings on virtually all of the primary and secondary source material available at the time, the author presents a convincingly authoritative study of Purcell's life and music. The text is equally divided: eight chapters are devoted primarily to biography, while the remaining eight address the composer's musical output, style, and other compositional issues. Even in the analytical portions of the text, the writing remains clear and understandable to the general reader at whom the work is aimed. Subsequent revisions have not altered Westrup's original opinions.

The focus of CAMPBELL's work is, in her own words, "to discover something about the man and the times in which he lived, and, where possible, the effect his music had on his contemporaries." Thus, musical analysis is limited, and specific compositions are discussed only in as much as they impact and are relevant to biographical issues. The author pays particularly close attention to Purcell's early years as a child in the Chapel Royal and provides a wonderfully detailed account of his development as a composer and royal musician. She also offers evidence of the social, religious, and cultural timbre of the age, thus placing Purcell and his music within a contemporary context.

Like Campbell, KING places Purcell within a wider historical picture. His lavishly illustrated volume investigates the institutions, events, and circumstances of the composer's life and career, with particular importance attributed to the royal establishments. Indeed, the author largely views Purcell's life as defined and circumscribed by royal service and, therefore, divides his study accordingly, with chapters devoted to the Restoration, and the reigns of Charles II, James II, and William and Mary, respectively.

Contending that a traditional biography of Purcell is impossible to compile owing to the dearth of information regarding the composer's personal life, KEATES attempts to provide a context for the composition, performance, and acceptance of Purcell's works during his lifetime by describing the conditions, surroundings, and circumstances in which Purcell's music was conceived and heard. This unique approach is the book's strength, for while it is not a concise, chronological biography, no other works so thoroughly details the social, cultural, and religious milieu in which the composer functioned. The descriptive commentary and musical analysis of particular compositions is broad and nonspecific and, by the author's own admission, often reflective of personal preference. However, the detail given about the backgrounds of the selected compositions compensates for a lack of theoretical discussion.

Also unique in its approach is BURDEN's (1995a) volume, which is comprised entirely of documentary material. Through this collection of diary entries by figures such as Pepys and North, letters to and from the composer's contemporaries, payment accounts, court documents, prefaces to publications, and the like, the author has pieced together an unusual record of Purcell's activities that is useful to the serious scholar and, for the most part, fascinating reading for the nonexpert.

BURDEN (1995b) has assembled a collection of essays by noted scholars on a variety of Purcellian topics. Although most are devoted to the music and its performance, several articles address biographical issues. Such is the case with the contributions of Jonathan Wainwright and Michael Burden, which explore the English baroque and Purcell's contemporaries, respectively, providing a fresh look at the climate in which Purcell functioned. Graham Dixon examines the Italian influence on Purcell, including his familiarity with a number of Italian musicians, while Andrew Pinnock assesses Purcell's place in English music history and the legacy he left behind.

Another anthology of essays has been prepared by PRICE, who has selected topics not often addressed in other studies. For example, Bruce Wood's assessment of the relationship between Purcell and Blow provides new insights into an area that has often been mentioned but rarely explored in such authoritative detail. Robert Shay meticulously examines Purcell's personal collection of old anthems as evidence of his interest in and familiarity with the music of his forefathers. Robert Thompson deals with the confusing aggregation of Purcell autographs in an essay focusing on the physical make-up of the volumes, including issues such as handwriting and paper analysis. For the specialized topics these essays address, they are unparalleled in scholarship and up-to-date research.

ZIMMERMAN (1967) is a full-length biography and is, perhaps, one of the most complete and detailed studies of the composer available. The author gives much attention to historical and sociological background, placing Purcell and his music in the perspective of 17th-century English life. The details of the composer's life and activities have largely been drawn from appropriate 17th- and 18th-century documents, thus rendering the study most accurate and convincing. Though intended for a general readership, the proliferation of references to primary source materials, the extensive, in-depth detail of the narrative, and the author's general penchant toward wordiness might render the book somewhat cumbersome for the lay reader. For the serious student of Purcell, however, it is indispensable. Mention should also be made here of ZIMMERMAN (1989), a volume that contains, among other things, a complete works list, extensive bibliography, concise biographical sketch, and a compilation of unpublished prefaces and dedications. The latter is of particular interest as such texts often provide points of human and historical interest and show the music within the context of its composer's life and times.

MICHAEL VAUGHN

2. Dido and Aeneas

Adams, Martin, *Henry Purcell: The Origins and Development of His Musical Style,* Cambridge: Cambridge University Press, 1995

Burden, Michael, editor, *Performing the Music of Henry Purcell,* Oxford: Clarendon Press, and New York: Oxford University Press, 1996

——, editor, *The Purcell Companion,* Portland, Oregon: Amadeus Press, and London: Faber, 1995

Harris, Ellen, *Henry Purcell's Dido and Aeneas,* Oxford: Clarendon Press, and New York: Oxford University Press, 1987

Holst, Imogen, editor, *Henry Purcell, 1659–1695: Essays on His Music,* London: Oxford University Press, 1959

Price, Curtis, *Henry Purcell and the London Stage,* Cambridge: Cambridge University Press, 1984

Price, Curtis, editor, *Purcell Studies,* Cambridge: Cambridge University Press, 1995

Purcell, Henry, *Dido and Aeneas: An Opera,* edited by Curtis Price, New York: Norton, 1986

White, Eric Walter, *A History of English Opera,* London: Faber, 1983

Dido and Aeneas is the best known and most often performed of Purcell's dramatic works. Its musical appeal and modest requirements for casting, musicians, and staging have made it a staple of local (particularly university-related) groups since the early 20th century. It is unique among Purcell's compositions in that it is the only dramatic work set entirely to music, unlike the isolated songs, entertainments, and sets of instrumental music written for plays or his later semi-operas—*Dioclesian, King Arthur, The Fairy Queen,* and *The Indian Queen*—which all have spoken dialogue between the musical scenes. Both the fact that the first known performance of *Dido and Aeneas,* in 1689, was held at a girls' school run by choreographer Josias Priest (rather than at court or in a theater) and the lack of a manuscript of the music from the 17th century (the earliest extant score is from the later 18th century) also make the history of this work unusual.

Scholars of Purcell's music encouraged the first revivals of *Dido and Aeneas* after two centuries of obscurity, around the turn of the 20th century; later nationalist interest in English music in the 1920s and 1930s and the tercentenary of Purcell's birth in 1959 produced further scholarship on *Dido and Aeneas.* Interest in the work during the 1980s culminated in the tricentennial celebration of its first known performance, producing new editions, performances, and recordings. It continued to be the subject of scholarly debate in the 1990s.

WHITE fits *Dido and Aeneas* into the slot traditionally assigned to it by earlier scholars, as the first major breakthrough in the history of English opera. A revision of his earlier work, White's study is a thorough and accessible chronicle of English opera (which he defines as "a stage action with vocal and instrumental music written by a British composer to a libretto in English") from the 17th through the 20th century.

An influential earlier essay by White, "New Light on 'Dido and Aeneas,'" appears in the HOLST volume commemorating the tercentenary of the composer's birth in 1959. In this essay, White discusses the relationship of the 1689 production to the first performance of Purcell's work in a public theater in 1700, when it was performed between the acts of a revised version of Shakespeare's play *Measure for Measure.*

In PURCELL, the Norton Critical Score to this opera and a useful standard reference, essays by Curtis Price and Margaret Laurie preface the libretto and music. Price's essay is a revision of the material he published on *Dido and Aeneas* in Price (1984) (see below). Laurie's essay places *Dido and Aeneas* firmly in the English masque tra-

dition, referring, as does Price, to the similarities between *Dido and Aeneas* and John Blow's masque *Venus and Adonis.* The essay includes material from Laurie's 1962 dissertation (which is otherwise difficult to access). Following the libretto and score for the opera, the final section of the volume presents brief segments of criticism and analysis from the 1880s through the 1980s, including excerpts from classic works on Purcell and English opera by Edward Dent.

PRICE (1984) surveys the music Purcell wrote that was performed in the London theaters during the 1680s and 1690s. The author discusses the music's theatrical connections, from Nahum Tate's 1678 tragedy *Brutus of Alba* (originally titled *Dido and Aeneas*) to the 1700 production of *Measure for Measure,* and suggests possible allegorical readings (as he does for some of Purcell's other operatic works) with reference to the English monarchy. Although Price considers some scholarly concerns (such as conflicting musical sources), his overviews of the productions Purcell contributed to and general information about the performers (complete with contemporary portraits) are highly readable.

HARRIS attempts to give a comprehensive view of the work, although she quickly disposes of questions of text and context and the hotly debated first performance (presented in the opening section, "Background to the Music"). Harris argues that the allegorical readings of Purcell's work by John Buttrey and Price are strained and emphasizes instead the relationship between the text and that of *Brutus of Alba,* also modeled on the appropriate passages in Virgil's *Aeneid.* Harris's brief sections on the principal manuscript source (Tenbury), structure, declamation, and ground-bass techniques can be followed up in other Purcell scholarship. Of interest to those concerned with reception history and performances, the third section of Harris's book surveys the performance history following its revival at the London Academy of Ancient Music in the 1770s, while the appendix offers a listing of premieres, editions, and recordings. In the 1990s the number of recordings increased (especially around the tercentenary of Purcell's death in 1995), but the catalog of early recordings will be of interest to opera lovers.

ADAMS presents a chronological survey of Purcell's development and influences followed by a lengthier section of essays addressing particular genres. Material on *Dido and Aeneas* can be found in the chapter "Backgrounds and Beginning: Dramatic Music to 1689." Adams offers a detailed musical analysis, using Schenkerian techniques, of the opening of Act II ("The Witches' Scene"), which he praises for its musico-dramatic consistency, and further comments on the closing scenes and specific songs from earlier in the opera. In chapter 4 of his opening style survey, Adams provides a concise summary of the eclectic fusion of musical elements related to Italian opera, French *tragédie lyrique,* and the English masque tradition. He also makes reference to the heated debate over the dating of *Dido and Aeneas* carried out in the pages of *Early Music,* 1992 to 1994, which hinged on questions of style analysis and contemporary practices, specifically the possibility of a performance preceding the famous one at Josias Priest's school in 1689.

The two collections of essays edited by Burden contain only a single essay focused specifically on *Dido and Aeneas,* but other articles provide much of interest concerning performance issues, allegorical interpretation, and dancing. The final three essays in BURDEN (1994) (aimed at nonspecialists) are an overview of Purcell's theater music by Roger Savage, notes on "Performing Purcell" that refer to contemporary 17th-century practice by Andrew Parrott, and a new revision by Savage of his 1976 *Early Music* article on producing *Dido and Aeneas* (previously revised and published in the Norton Critical Score). BURDEN (1996) is a more scholarly assortment of articles on more specific topics (drawn from papers presented at the Oxford University conference of the same title in 1993), which assumes a general knowledge of Purcell's life and works. Andrew R. Walkling's "Performance and Political Allegory" argues for the importance of allegorical readings of 17th-century works and presents a flexible set of guidelines drawn from the work of scholars of literature, with reference to his *Music and Letters* article on "Political Allegory in Purcell's *Dido and Aeneas*" (another important strand of the 1992 to 1994 *Early Music* debate). Less controversial is Richard Semmens's "Dancing and Dance Music in Purcell's Operas," which makes repeated reference to *Dido and Aeneas* and gives some perspective (and useful references) for those interested in choreographer and schoolmaster Josias Priest.

PRICE (1995) is a collection of scholarly pieces, none of which is specifically concerned with *Dido and Aeneas.* However, Laurie's contribution to this volume, "Continuity and Tempo in Purcell's Vocal Works," and Katherine T. Rohrer's "Poetic Metre, Musical Metre, and the Dance in Purcell's Songs" both use extensive excerpts from *Dido and Aeneas* in their discussions of musical structure and text setting.

A recent collection of essays, BURDEN (1998) contains a useful interdisciplinary array of materials ideal for the study of Purcell's most famous work. Roger Savage's opening essay, "Dido Dies Again," provides general background concisely and amusingly. The essays in the third section, "Reinterpretations: Dido on the Stage (and Elsewhere)," are of particular interest, as they include representations of Dido in the visual arts, Christopher Marlowe's play *Dido, Queen of Carthage,* and Wendy Heller's reading of Francesco Cavalli's opera *Didone.* Burden's contribution, "'Great Minds against Themselves Conspire': Purcell's Dido as Conspiracy Theorist," summarizes differing scholarly conceptions of *Dido and Aeneas,* documents the latest thrusts and parries in the

Dido debates, and offers his own (stage-tested) interpretation in which Dido's tragic flaw is not her sexuality but her refusal to trust her love for Aeneas.

KATHRYN LOWERRE

3. Other Works

Adams, Martin, *Henry Purcell: The Origins and Development of His Musical Style,* Cambridge: Cambridge University Press, 1995

Burden, Michael, editor, *The Purcell Companion,* Portland, Oregon: Amadeus Press, and London: Faber, 1995

Holman, Peter, *Henry Purcell,* Oxford: Oxford University Press, 1994

Price, Curtis, editor, *Purcell Studies,* Cambridge: Cambridge University Press, 1995

Westrup, J.A., *Purcell,* London: Dent, 1937; 8th edition, 1980

Zimmerman, Franklin B., *Henry Purcell, 1659–1695: His Life and Times,* London: Macmillan, and New York, St. Martin's Press, 1967; 2nd revised edition, Philadelphia: University of Pennsylvania Press, 1983

The tercentenary of Henry Purcell's death sparked a renewed interest in the composer's music, and it is no coincidence that several of the books discussed here were published in or around 1995. Although none of these books on Purcell is devoted to a single genre, each contains essays or analyses that contribute to a greater understanding of his individual genres and works. In addition to these volumes, numerous journal articles consider different types of music by the composer and aspects of his style, and prefaces to various editions also prove most useful when delving into Purcell's works. Each of the books reviewed here contains pertinent bibliographies that can assist in further research.

The major genres covered in this survey are the odes, anthems, and other religious music; consort music; theater music (other than *Dido and Aeneas*); and keyboard music. Most of the authors analyze the same pieces, with the result that many examples in these books are roughly identical. Vocal music composed by Purcell in an official royal capacity, such as birthday odes or large-scale anthems, provides interesting avenues of investigation, because much of this music can be accurately dated, and several of the essays described below follow this path. Purcell's vocal music also offers an engaging comparison with similar works by John Blow, the other major composer in England at this time. Most modern authors focus heavily on the relationship between the music of the two composers and often compare their use of Italianate features. Much of Purcell's theater music was written during the 1680s, and it represents other facets of his talent. Among the current issues being investigated in his theater music are the relationship between text and music (and Purcell's use of various authors), his treatment of time and meter (both musical and poetic), and cohesion in the structure of these works. Purcell seemed to concern himself with keyboard music only a little, and the tercentenary studies likewise devote scarcely any space to these works. The consort music is perhaps more inviting to scholars because it reliably presents opportunities to view Purcell's connection to older English composers and because, like the odes and anthems, it offers the opportunity to gauge Purcell's compositional development. Unfortunately, most descriptions require an intimate knowledge of English instrumental music of the mid-17th century.

WESTRUP's groundbreaking biography appeared over 60 years ago, but it remains a major secondary source for Purcell's music. Many writers continue to incorporate Westrup's comments on various aspects of the composer and his music into their studies, a fact that speaks to this biography's pertinence and usefulness. The author's insight is remarkable considering the state of research in 1937, and his cues should be pursued with sincerity.

A much-needed updated biography when it was originally published, ZIMMERMAN has received a substantial amount of negative criticism, particularly from British authors, for assumptions and undocumented conclusions drawn about the composer's life and works. Nonetheless, most writers acknowledge the volume in one way or another, justifying its use if only as a reference point for different approaches. That Purcell works are now identified by Z numbers (for "Zimmerman") further shows the relevance of the author's contribution to the field. Zimmerman must be read with caution, and any research on Purcell needs to delve further than this single biography. As the author acknowledges, the second edition of Zimmerman contains relatively few changes from the first.

HOLMAN is the best introduction to the music of Purcell, written in a clear and concise style, which makes it useful to readers at every level. After a brief discussion of Purcell's biography, Holman reviews each major genre: domestic vocal music, instrumental music, church music, odes, and theater music. He concludes with an extensive bibliography and an index of Purcell's works (including the corresponding page numbers in Holman's text). Uncommon for such a general book, Holman's narrative goes deeper than a surface discussion of style. Drawing on his thorough knowledge of English music of this period, he treats such matters as Purcell's interest in writing fantasias at a time when viol consorts were rare. Holman also questions Purcell's relationship with theater music and introduces several of his major compositions. The text requires only a passing knowledge of the repertory, although some of the examples require familiarity with Restoration music.

BURDEN incorporates the expertise of several different authors to discuss particular aspects of Purcell's music. Essays by Andrew Pinnock, Jonathan Wainwright, Graham Dixon, and Burden provide background into Purcell's life and environment in the introduction and first section of the book. The remainder of the volume divides into three parts: "A Composer for the Church and Chamber," "Purcell and the Theatre," and "Purcell in Performance." Among the essays therein is Peter Holman's piece on the consort works—the most valuable commentary on these works as a whole to date. Bruce Wood contributes a substantial article on the odes, another underrepresented genre in Purcell's oeuvre that deserves more attention. Eric van Tassel provides a useful essay on the anthems and services. In the section on the theater, Edward Langhans gives practical details on the theatrical background, while Roger Savage deals more with the music itself.

PRICE includes three of the same contributors (different essays) as does Burden, resulting in substantial overlap in content between the two volumes, particularly in the essays on the odes. That said, other factors recommend the volume, such as the information on Purcell autographs provided by Robert Thompson and Robert Shay, as well as the essay on Purcell's revisions by Rebecca Herissione. Price himself is one of the few authors in any source to consider Purcell's keyboard music; his contribution on that subject here is limited to a single newly discovered autograph. Katherine Rohrer's essay on poetic and musical meter and dance involves sophisticated analysis of Purcell's vocal music in terms of poetic meters. The two pieces on *King Arthur* are refreshing looks at this "Dramatick Opera." Rather than taking Dryden's word on the subject as final, Pinnock investigates outside influences on the 1691 production of *King Arthur* and addresses adaptations made by another author. Ellen Harris investigates 18th-century revisions of the work.

ADAMS's approach differs somewhat from the other volumes discussed here; he begins by treating Purcell's stylistic development as a whole, later breaking down the specific genres in the second (longer) part. He employs some of the same examples as Burden and Price, making some overlap inevitable. Analyses form a greater part of Adams's narrative, and they often lead to interesting conclusions, contending that Purcell was a greater composer than, say, Matthew Locke (who influenced Purcell particularly in his instrumental music). Unlike most authors, Adams discusses his examples in some detail. Unfortunately, one has to often hunt down examples throughout the volume (e.g., example 2 and example 34 are discussed simultaneously), making the book a bit inconvenient at times. This is not a text for the casual reader, requiring a working knowledge of 17th-century English music and also of analysis. The author's work, however, opens the door for deeper inquiry into Purcell's style and that of his contemporaries.

CANDACE LEE BAILEY

Q

Quantz, Johann Joachim 1697–1773

German flutist, writer on music, and composer

Burney, Charles, *An Eighteenth-Century Musical Tour in Central Europe and the Netherlands,* edited by Percy A. Scholes, London: Oxford University Press, 1959

Hefling, Stephen E., *Rhythmic Alteration in Seventeenth- and Eighteenth-Century Music: Notes Inégales and Overdotting,* New York: Schirmer Books, 1993

Helm, E. Eugene, *Music at the Court of Frederick the Great,* Norman: University of Oklahoma Press, 1960

Quantz, Johann Joachim, "The Life of Herr Johann Joachim Quantz, as Sketched by Himself," in *Forgotten Musicians,* translated and edited by Paul Nettl, New York: Philosophical Library, 1951

———, *On Playing the Flute,* translated by Edward R. Reilly, New York: Schirmer, and London: Faber, 1966; 2nd edition, 1985

Reilly, Edward R., *Quantz and His Versuch: Three Studies,* New York: American Musicological Society, 1971

Regarded as one of the most renowned musicians and teachers of the 18th century, Johann Joachim Quantz made contributions to musical history that are threefold: as the most significant virtuoso flutist of his day; as a composer of a vast literature of more than 500 works for the flute; and most important, as the author of the preeminent treatise on baroque music instruction, *Versuch einer Anweisung die Flöte traversiere zu spielen (On Playing the Flute).* In his lifetime, Quantz enjoyed considerable fame, first as flutist in the *Kapelle* at the Dresden court and later as composer, teacher, and flute maker for King Frederick the Great of Prussia. Early accounts of the composer understandably focus on the 32 years Quantz spent in the service of Frederick, and the inevitable association of the composer with the king led to the long-held assumption that the majority of Quantz's works were composed during that time. More recent studies, however, have argued that Quantz was, in fact, equally productive during his earlier years in Dresden. Moreover, while earlier studies tend to treat the work of

Quantz and Frederick as one and the same, more recent scholars have recognized Quantz for his individual musical characteristics. As more of his works have come to light, Quantz's reputation as a composer has begun to approach his stature as author, flutist, and pedagogue.

QUANTZ (1951) himself provided the autobiographical sketch that formed the basis of subsequent studies of the musician. Written in 1754, more than a decade into his tenure in the service of Frederick the Great, Quantz's sketch is a straightforward chronological telling of the details of his life, from his earliest musical training at the hands of his uncle in Meresburg through his long and productive years in Dresden, his many travels throughout Europe, and finally his engagement as teacher and musician at the Prussian Court. Particularly absorbing are Quantz's accounts of his encounters with famous musicians of the day, including Alessandro Scarlatti, Hasse, Blavet, Weiss, Handel, and the famous castrato with the "fluent throat," Farinelli. Above all, one gains a sense of Quantz as a working performer, who realized that "the mere playing of the notes as set down by the composer was far from being the greatest merit of a musician."

BURNEY's well-known narrative about musical life in 18th-century Europe offers a sweeping portrait of the artistic landscape as viewed by the musically literate traveler. Published not long after Quantz's death, Burney's musical travelogue brilliantly depicts musical activities as they took place at artistic centers throughout Europe, including Frederick's court in Berlin and Potsdam. The author expresses great desire to attend the court of the ruler, who is as renowned for his cultivation of the arts as for his military prowess. By the time of Burney's visit in 1772, however, Frederick's court had stagnated musically; Frederick performed works Quantz had written 40 years before, and Quantz continued to compose in the outdated style of the late baroque, in no small part to please his patron. Recounting a concert in which Frederick performed works by Quantz, Burney admitted that many passages "are now become common and old . . . it is with music as with delicate wines, which not only become flat and insipid, when exposed to the air, but are injured by time, however *well-kept.*" Despite his evaluation of

Quantz's music as somewhat simplistic and old-fashioned, Burney's account displays admiration for the composer, particularly for his diligence, pedagogical skills, and performing capabilities. The author provides an extended biographical sketch of Quantz (based on the composer's autobiography) and offers a thoughtful description of a visit with the elderly composer. While clearly stating his preference for modern music, Burney concludes, after all, that Quantz's works "have stood their ground very well."

HELM, in his detailed study of music at the court of Frederick the Great, examines the unique environment in which Quantz lived and worked. The author paints clear portraits of Frederick as ruler and as musician, including contemporary reports, both favorable and unfavorable, of the monarch's flute playing. Helm's lucid discussion of Frederick's own works sheds light on Quantz's role as composer and tutor to the king; Frederick's sonatas and concerti evince a homophonic simplicity and studied "schematicism" that were both absorbed from models given him by Quantz and indicative of the style the monarch preferred and expected from his teacher. Helm's discussion of Quantz's music is more limited; his conclusions that Quantz's harmonies and melodies are "innocuous, if not monotonous," and that "a single unchanging ideal is followed from year to year, from composition to composition," demand a more detailed study of the music than Helm provides. Rather, the author emphasizes Quantz's importance to the codification of performance practice through his treatise and to the development of the flute and its literature. Helm also considers the contributions of other important musical figures who were influenced by Frederick's patronage and were therefore part of Quantz's circle, including C.P.E. Bach, Benda, and the brothers Carl Heinrich and Johann Gottlieb Graun.

Originally published in 1752, QUANTZ's (1966) treatise on playing the flute remains a classic instructional text. Far more than simply a flute method, Quantz's text offers a vivid and thought-provoking depiction of 18th-century performance practice and musical opinion that is useful to all musicians. Quantz devotes the first portion of his treatise to the history, structure, and mechanics of the flute: fingering, embouchure, tonguing, and breathing, as well as the basic elements of ornamentation. The chapters that follow provide a universally applicable discussion of matters of style and interpretation directed toward the more advanced musician. A chapter on performing in public concerts, including advice on tuning, playing with accompanists, adjusting for acoustics and handling nerves is, for the most part, astonishingly current. Likewise, Quantz's chapter delineating the duties of accompanying musicians is equally applicable to all instruments. Most

indicative of Quantz's era is the concluding portion on contemporary forms, styles, and national traits in both composition and performing. As a whole, the treatise represents both an exceptional instructional manual and a tremendously detailed guide to 18th-century music and performing styles. Reilly's introduction provides valuable insights into the history of the treatise and its reception.

Intended for those who want more detailed information about Quantz and his treatise, REILLY's concise collection of essays should be viewed as a companion piece to the treatise itself. He first considers Quantz's compositions in light of more recent research, providing one of the best discussions of the composer's works available. Unlike earlier studies, which emphasize Quantz's association with Frederick the Great, Reilly suggests that at least half of Quantz's work were written during his earlier years in Dresden. Moreover, although the author admits that Quantz was not a "profoundly original" composer, he maintains that the composer was somewhat more progressive in his work than is often acknowledged; while working within prescribed forms (such as ritornello form), Quantz was inventive in varying thematic material and displayed "unparalleled understanding" of the special qualities for the flute. While recognizing Quantz's compositional weaknesses of redundancy and dependence on formulas, Reilly also notes that those weaknesses "are implicit in his expressed attitudes and in the conditions under which he works." In addition to discussing Quantz's compositions, Reilly examines the dissemination of the composer's treatise throughout Germany, Holland, England, France, and Italy and elaborates upon several points in the treatise concerning matters of interpretation, such as ornamentation, tempo, and dynamics.

HEFLING presents a judicious source study of the 17th- and 18th-century musical practice of rhythmic alteration, including the primarily French practice of *notes inégales* (performing pairs of notes unevenly, despite their written value) and overdotting (performing dotted rhythms longer than is notated). He examines and compares discussions of both practices in numerous treatises, including Quantz's *Versuch,* which the author deems one of the most influential sources on the matter. Hefling notes that Quantz had encountered a mixture of French and Italian styles during his 20 years in Dresden and thus absorbed the French practice of rhythmic inequality. For the serious student of performance practice, this highly detailed study of the origins and transmission of these forms of rhythmic alteration will be particularly rewarding.

JULIE DORN MORRISON

R

Rachmaninoff, Sergei 1873–1943

Russian pianist and composer

Bertensson, Sergei, and Jay Leyda, *Sergei Rachmaninoff: A Lifetime in Music,* New York: New York University Press, 1956

Culshaw, John, *Sergei Rachmaninov,* London: Dobson, 1949; as *Rachmaninov: The Man and His Music,* New York: Oxford University Press, 1950

Martyn, Barrie, *Rachmaninoff: Composer, Pianist, Conductor,* Aldershot: Scolar Press, and Brookfield, Vermont: Gower, 1990

Norris, Geoffrey, *Rachmaninov,* London: Dent, 1976

Riesemann, Oskar von, *Rachmaninoff's Recollections,* London: Allen and Unwin, and New York: Macmillan, 1934

Seroff, Victor Ilyitch, *Rachmaninoff,* New York: Simon and Schuster, 1950

Four factors have contributed to the inadequacy of literature in English on Rachmaninoff. First among these was Rachmininoff's reluctance to discuss his own life or works. Even his well-known article "My Prelude in C-sharp Minor," which first appeared in *Delineator* in February 1910, and the half-dozen interviews that appeared in *Etude* between 1910 and 1941 are astonishingly uninformative. Second, appraisals of Rachmaninoff's music have rarely been balanced. Eric Blom's opinion, stated in the fifth edition of *Grove's Dictionary of Music and Musicians,* that Rachmaninoff's music "is monotonous in texture, which consists in essence mainly of artificial and gushing tunes accompanied by a variety of figures derived from arpeggios" is typical of critical appraisals from the 1950s and 1960s. Alternatively, Rachmaninoff's supporters tended toward hyperbole, without benefit of critical distance. Third, Rachmaninoff was as out of step with the musical current of his time as he was in step with the tastes of his public. Considered an anachronism, Rachmaninoff long remained outside the mainstream of scholarly study. Finally, the lack of reliable sources translated into English has meant that many writers have relied on material of questionable provenance. Scholars often made do with secondhand sources when primary sources would naturally have been preferred or have overlooked Rachmaninoff in favor of subjects more accurately and thoroughly documented in English.

Despite these limitations, there are several sources that, when taken together, provide an overview of the composer's life and works. The situation has also improved in recent years with the excellent book by Barrie Martyn and the extensive bibliography in Robert Palmieri's *Sergei Vasil'evich Rachmaninoff: A Guide to Research* (1985).

BERTENSSON and LEYDA trace Rachmaninoff's life and career year by year, providing detailed biographical data and mentioning most of his important works. This biography remains, after more than 40 years, a trove of information, whose authenticity and accuracy is for the most part unassailable. This quality is owing largely to the cooperation of the composer's cousin and sister-in-law Sophia Satin. Given Rachmaninoff's reticence to discuss his own life, and in the absence of much useful primary source material beyond a voluminous but as yet mostly untranslated correspondence, Satin's reminiscences are as close to Rachmaninoff's own thoughts and recollections as we are likely to get (but see Riesemann below). This biography is further enhanced by often-lengthy quotations from Rachmaninoff's letters, many of which appear here in translation for the first time. The work list at the end of the book records not only dates and places of composition but also completion dates, dedicatees, publishing data, and details of first performances.

As Bertensson and Leyda were assisted by Sophia Satin, so CULSHAW benefits from the cooperation of Rachmaninoff's longtime friends Nicolas and Madame Medtner and of Rachmaninoff's widow, Natalie. But whereas Bertensson and Leyda's focus is Rachmaninoff's life, Culshaw's concern is Rachmaninoff's music. A 30-page biography is followed by an assessment of the composer's style: its Russian roots, the composer's fatalism and its bearing on his music, the indelible mark of Rachmaninoff the pianist, and the melodic strengths and stylistic weaknesses that characterize his music. In the remainder of the book, Culshaw surveys Rachmaninoff's output, devoting a chapter to each genre and singling out the most popular works for analysis, illustrated by musical examples. The author does not regard Rachmaninoff's music with unwavering enthusiasm; Culshaw's premise that "Rachmaninoff's music has probably suffered more from the wild claims of some of its enthusiasts than from the severest critical judgements" sets the tone for a refreshingly balanced overview of the composer's sizable output. While conceding that Rachmaninoff's music is not inherently great, Culshaw acknowledges that it is historically significant, representing nearly the end point of the Russian romantic musical tradition, and as such warrants careful if not uncritical scrutiny. Culshaw has since admitted to having been unduly influenced by the tenor of his times, and he has recently adopted a more favorable view of Rachmaninoff's worth as a composer.

MARTYN is unquestionably the most important reference work on Rachmaninoff in English. This nearly 600-page volume is divided into three sections, dealing with Rachmaninoff as composer, pianist, and conductor. The first section traces Rachmaninoff's career from his student days in Russia to his years in the United States, but its greatest value lies in the careful consideration given, at the appropriate junctures in the unfolding biography, to every one of Rachmaninoff's works. The origin and genesis of each work is presented, followed by an analysis, often enhanced by musical examples. In the section on Rachmaninoff the pianist, concert statistics are provided season by season, every work Rachmaninoff played publicly is listed, and a complete discography and catalog of piano rolls is provided. These various lists are cross-referenced, making this book easy to use as a research tool. Similar detailed lists are provided in the final section, on Rachmaninoff the conductor. The whole study is framed by a thoughtful overview of Rachmaninoff's place in Russian musical history and by two indices, one of Rachmaninoff's works and the other of persons and works mentioned in the text. The "Pedagogical Genealogy of the Most Famous Russian Pianists," which appears at the outset of the section on Rachmaninoff the pianist, provides much food for thought. Rachmaninoff is one of only four Russian pianists discussed here whose pianistic lineage stems from Hummel; the 25 or so other pianists all stem from Beethoven.

NORRIS is laid out in the same manner as the other volumes in the Master Musicians series; the first half is a biography, the second half a review of works by genre. The biography is serviceable, but Rachmaninoff's works are more described than assessed. A calendar of the composer's life and works serves as an appendix, and the accompanying table of birth and death dates of other musicians helps place Rachmaninoff in a wider perspective; it also gives credence to Rachmaninoff's belief that he was born a generation or two too late. A concise annotated list of personalia will be welcomed by readers not versed in the music and musicians of Russia. This is not a profound book, but it does provide in a single volume an introduction to the composer and his works that lays the foundation for further reading.

RIESEMANN is included here because it is one of the most frequently encountered of all sources on Rachmaninoff. The unwary reader is apt to accept its text as gospel due to the description on the title page: "Rachmaninoff's Recollections as told to Oskar von Riesemann." Culshaw maintains that inaccuracies in the English-language edition stem from a poor translation (from the original German), but this weakness is clearly only part of the problem. As Norris explains, the title "clearly implied that Rachmaninoff had dictated his reminiscences," which was not the case. Rachmaninoff did review the proofs and paid for revisions before the book appeared in print, but as Martyn notes, Rachmaninoff, "at least privately, throughout the rest of his life disowned the work." Publicly, he gave it a grudging endorsement. Despite the controversy surrounding this work, Riesemann was indeed a friend of Rachmaninoff who discussed with him a wide range of personal and musical topics over a period of many years. While the title is misleading, Riesemann has written an lively book that gives Rachmaninoff's own thoughts a voice, if not verbatim, at least in spirit. No less an authority than Martyn makes frequent reference to Riesemann, and if the quoted material is understood to be paraphrased, the book remains a significant if not unblemished resource.

SEROFF, although written less than a decade after Rachmaninoff's death, it still today the most readable and engaging of the composer's biographies. Musical analysis is eschewed in favor of a relaxed narrative style, making this book accessible to lay readers. Seroff's Russian heritage serves him well, and the book's strongest chapters describe Rachmaninoff's early years, prior to leaving Russia in 1917, and the Soviet censure and subsequent rehabilitation of his music. Seroff has the advantage of having known Rachmaninoff personally and of having interviewed him for this book on several occasions. There emerges a portrait of a complex and intensely private man, whose success was based solely on his musical achievements. It is clear that he rejected the cult of personality that helped shaped the careers of many of his colleagues. This is not to suggest that Rachmaninoff was in any way bland and uninteresting. As Seroff's sympathetic account makes clear, Rachmaninoff was a figure "of strength and weakness, timidity and courage, surrender and persistence, in other words, an artist and a man." Quotations from many of Rachmaninoff's letters, a detailed work list by genre, and a bibliography (borrowed from another source), predictably strong in Russian sources, round out this landmark biography.

GLEN CARRUTHERS

Ragtime

Badger, Reid, *A Life in Ragtime: A Biography of James Reese Europe*, New York: Oxford University Press, 1995

Berlin, Edward A., *Ragtime: A Musical and Cultural History*, Berkeley: University of California Press, 1984

———, *Reflections and Research on Ragtime*, Brooklyn, New York: Institute for Studies in American Music, 1987

———, *King of Ragtime: Scott Joplin and His Era*, New York: Oxford University Press, 1994

Blesh, Rudi, and Harriet Janis, *They All Played Ragtime*, New York: Knopf, 1950; 4th edition, New York: Oak, 1971

Curtis, Susan, *Dancing to a Black Man's Tune: A Life of Scott Joplin*, Columbia: University of Missouri Press, 1994

Gammond, Peter, *Scott Joplin and the Ragtime Era*, New York: St. Martin's Press, 1975

Hamm, Charles, *Irving Berlin: Songs from the Melting Pot: The Formative Years: 1907–1914*, New York: Oxford University Press, 1997

Hasse, John Edward, editor, *Ragtime: Its History, Composers, and Music*, New York: Schirmer Books, 1985

The music called ragtime, which some consider to be the first truly national music of the United States, flourished between the late 19th century and the outbreak of World War I. Probably derived from the polyrhythms of traditional West African music, classic ragtime may be traced to plantation songs played on the banjo and fiddle, the so-called shouting style characteristic of the post–Civil War period, and dance forms such as the cakewalk. Ragtime originated in the bordellos of post-Reconstruction Sedalia and St. Louis, Missouri, and was carried from town to town by such African-American musicians as Scott Joplin, Blind Boone, Arthur Marshall, Scott Hayden, James Scott, Louis Chauvin, Joe Jordan, Charley Thompson, Tom Turpin, Artie Matthews, and forgotten itinerant pianists playing "jig piano," in which the "stomping" and "patting" left hand played against the right hand's syncopated melodies. The 1893 Colombian Exposition in Chicago, where many black musicians performed, brought ragtime to the attention of a wider audience. Scott Joplin's "Maple Leaf Rag" of 1899 sold more than one million copies of sheet music and signaled the entrance of ragtime into the mainstream, and the genre was picked up by Tin Pan Alley songwriters, including Irving Berlin, Charles L. Johnson, Joe Lamb, and Percy Wenrich. Presented on the stages of U.S. vaudeville theaters by performers such as May Irwin, Ed Morton, and the team of Bert Williams and George Walker, ragtime was further popularized through sales of sheet music and recordings, which were boosted by the increasing popularity of the piano in the parlors of the United States and the growth of the phonograph as the primary medium for home entertainment. Ragtime helped feed, and was in turn fed by, the dance craze that swept the nation in the years preceding World War I. It influenced such classical composers as Debussy, Satie, Stravinsky, and Ives; some ragtime composers, in turn, wrote pieces in such "serious" genres as opera and ballet, including Scott Joplin's ragtime opera, *Treemonisha*.

Books about ragtime can be divided into several categories. First, there are the histories devoted to the subject. Second are books that trace the history of American popular music, or specifically black American music, and devote substantial coverage to ragtime. Finally, there are the biographies and critical studies of musicians, both ragtime composers and performers and the Tin Pan Alley composers who wrote ragtime songs during some period of their lives.

BLESH and JANIS's pioneering work purports to be the first history of ragtime and includes the most comprehensive study of the early classic ragtime composers. It divides ragtime musicians into the "authentic" pioneers of "classic ragtime"—those of Sedalia and St. Louis—and the imitative songwriters of Tin Pan Alley, who integrated syncopation into the American song tradition. The authors see the piano rag as the pure form of ragtime, considering the term *ragtime song* of Tin Pan Alley an oxymoron. The authors' enthusiasm for classic ragtime is evident in their entertaining interviews with surviving pioneers of the genre. The book is poorly documented, however, with much unsubstantiated information, and it depends too much on the memories of the interviewees, who embellish their stories almost to the point of fiction. The haphazard organization of the book is also a disadvantage. Although the authors rely heavily on the notion of "classic ragtime" for their argument, the term is not consistently defined throughout the book. Despite these shortcomings, this study is the seminal work on the subject. Appendices include lists of musical compositions by composer and title, piano rolls, and selected recordings (78s and LPs). In addition to numerous photographs of composers, performers, and significant places, the book contains piano scores for 16 rags, including both classic works and pieces dating from the ragtime revival after World War II, in which Rudi Blesh played a significant part.

HASSE, a scholarly reaction to Blesh and Janis's book, is an edited collection with contributions by several prominent U.S. musicologists. Although the anthology contains much technical detail, its clear, accessible writing makes it suitable for the general reader. Hasse identifies four types of ragtime: instrumental rags, ragtime songs, ragtime waltzes, and the "ragging" of existing music (adding syncopation to existing pieces), which may have been the original manifestation of ragtime. He describes the spread of ragtime from Missouri through Chicago to New York, where it entered the mainstream in the songs of Tin Pan Alley. Contributors examine major figures of both ragtime's heyday and the ragtime revival that began in the 1940s, including Scott Joplin,

James Scott, May Aufderheide, James P. Johnson, and Rudi Blesh, and the volume offers analytical studies of the music and its influences on American culture. Appendices include a checklist of compositions, a bibliography including folios and method books, an LP discography, a list of ragtime compositions by women, and a register of ragtime organizations. The volume is illustrated with photographs and musical examples.

BERLIN (1987) is divided into two sections: the first covers familiar historical territory, embellished by numerous musical examples; the second focuses on the ragtime community of New York City, which Berlin feels was at least as important a site for the development of the music as Missouri had been. This brief study is carefully documented and includes a bibliography and discography of recordings cited.

A more substantial work than his 1987 volume, BERLIN (1984) relies heavily on excerpts from previously published books and articles as well as statistical analyses of numerous original sources (including more than 1,000 piano scores) to create a detailed, comprehensive study of the evolution of ragtime. This scrupulously documented study discusses what ragtime represented to the society of the time, how this music reflected what was happening in the United States, and the cultural, political, and aesthetic influences that shaped the music. Berlin attempts to devise a definition of ragtime that encompasses works that only exhibit some of the criteria usually attributed to ragtime but were considered to be ragtime pieces by contemporaries. He shows how the definition has varied through time as well and discusses the perspectives of the different types of musicians who composed and performed music to which they applied the name ragtime. The book includes a survey of the major works on the subject that compares the definition each author employs and an appendix that lists piano rags appearing in published anthologies.

Among the biographies of major ragtime composers and performers is BADGER's study of James Reese Europe. Born in Mobile, Alabama, in 1880 and raised in Washington, D.C., in the time when that city was becoming a cultural and intellectual center for African-Americans, Europe was a bandleader and composer of concert music and parlor songs, usually in the Victorian style. He worked with famed dancers Vernon and Irene Castle, introducing them to black-influenced dances from which they created several of the United States's pre–World War I dance crazes, such as the fox-trot, and he is also credited with helping jazz emerge from its ragtime roots. Europe was later famous as the first African-American officer to lead troops in combat during World War I. At the age of 39, Europe was murdered by one of the members of his band in 1919. Badger's carefully researched study covers the rise of the dance bands, the first American dance craze, and the changing American taste in popular music. The book includes a chronological list of composers during the ragtime era and a discography of original recordings by Europe's Society Orchestra, 369th Infantry Band, and Singing Serenaders.

GAMMOND's biography of Scott Joplin provides a solid, if brief, study of the composer and the context in which he worked. The book is especially valuable for its extensive appendices, which include bibliographies of books on American musical history, collections of ragtime composers' works, recordings on piano rolls, early records reissued on LP, modern recordings of ragtime and classical works influenced by that music, and a list of Joplin's works that indicates which have been published and which have appeared on piano rolls. Numerous illustrations include photographs and lithographs showing contemporary scenes, dances, vaudeville performers, classical composers influenced by ragtime, and important jazz musicians and composers of popular music.

CURTIS's biography of Joplin treats the composer as a catalyst in the breaking down of racial barriers in the United States at the turn of the century. She considers the importance of two factors in the rise of ragtime in the white consciousness: the 1893 Colombian Exposition in Chicago, which introduced Americans to a variety of exotic musical and other cultural forms, and a severe economic depression, which led to a rethinking of their way of life and cultural identity. Joplin had come to Chicago in search of work, where he was exposed to numerous other ragtime pioneers. The book traces the incorporation of ragtime into the mainstream through the medium of the piano; Joplin's encouragement of other black musicians, such as James Scott; Joplin's concentration on his opera *Treemonisha;* and his death and legacy. This well-researched and extensively documented study is illustrated with photographs and facsimiles of sheet music covers.

Employing recent research and documentary information unavailable to earlier biographers, BERLIN (1994) has compiled a detailed and well-documented study of Joplin that traces the composer's life from his childhood in Sedalia and St. Louis through his escape from poverty with the wildly successful publication of the "Maple Leaf Rag" and other compositions to his last years in New York, including his attempts to get *Treemonisha* staged. Newly discovered materials were consulted to fill in several gaps found in earlier biographies, including information about Joplin's relationship with Irving Berlin, and Joplin's second marriage. Appendices include a work list and scores for three songs not included in *The Complete Works of Scott Joplin* ("Good-bye Old Girl Good-bye," "Snoring Sampson," and "Lovin' Babe").

HAMM's scholarly study of Irving Berlin concentrates on his compositions in the 1907–14 period, when ragtime-inspired popular songs were at their height of popularity. The author compares ragtime songs with other ethnic novelty songs, songs for the vaudeville stage, and works in the minstrel tradition. A valuable feature of this work is a comprehensive list of period recordings of Irving Berlin's songs of this era, as well as a list of his published and unpublished songs from before 1915. Hamm lists the defining elements of these pieces, including an apparent connection with African-American culture, the use of particular stylistic mannerisms, certain relationships between the keys of sections of the songs, and characteristic rhythmic patterns. Many of Berlin's songs exhibit all of these elements; others, such as "International Rag," "Ragtime Soldier Man," and "Ragtime Violin," have no obvious African-American connection. One may argue that "Alexander's Ragtime Band" is not a ragtime song, as syncopation is found only in its opening lines, "Come on and hear," and, oddly, in its quotation from Foster's "Old Folks at Home." Yet the public perceived these songs, as they were performed at the time, as ragtime. It is this form of ragtime that swept across the United States until the new aesthetic of jazz and the new attitudes that emerged in the wake of World War I again changed the landscape of popular music.

MICHAEL SIMS

Rameau, Jean-Philippe 1683–1764

French composer and theorist

Christensen, Thomas, *Rameau and Musical Thought in the Enlightenment,* Cambridge: Cambridge University Press, 1993

Dill, Charles William, *Monstrous Opera: Rameau and the Tragic Tradition,* Princeton, New Jersey: Princeton University Press, 1998

Foster, Donald H., *Jean-Philippe Rameau: A Guide to Research,* New York: Garland, 1989

Girdlestone, Cuthbert, *Jean-Philippe Rameau: His Life and Work,* London: Cassel, 1957; revised edition, New York: Dover, 1969

Sadler, Graham, "Jean-Philippe Rameau," in *The New Grove French Baroque Masters,* edited by James R. Anthony et al., London: Macmillan, and New York: Norton, 1986

Sloan, Lucinda Heck, *The Influence of Rhetoric on Jean-Philippe Rameau's Solo Vocal Cantatas and Treatise of 1722,* New York: Lang, 1990

Initially, scholarship about Jean-Philippe Rameau tended to branch off into two different directions—studies of his life and works, on the one hand, and investigations of his theoretical writings, on the other. Recent studies, however, have used a more integrated approach and combine examinations of Rameau as composer, theoretician, and historical personage. Scholars have also begun to focus on the cultural and social issues surrounding Rameau in order to determine what influence these issues exerted upon him and, consequently, his works. Although Rameau scholarship is quite active, and interest in his music remains high, English-language books on Rameau are still relatively few.

GIRDLESTONE first published his groundbreaking biography on Rameau in the 1950s, and today it still remains the standard English-language survey of Rameau's life and works. The author spends the first chapter constructing the first 50 years of Rameau's life and then most of the remaining chapters discussing each of Rameau's works in detail, presenting the works by genre rather than chronologically. Girdlestone gives a brief history of each genre up to Rameau's time in order to establish the tradition from which Rameau's compositions grew and then undertakes a detailed analysis of each of the works in question. His discussions include detailed harmonic analysis as well as blow-by-blow descriptions of musical events. As this book was written before the advent of the early music revival, Girdlestone's assessment of the music is a bit dated, and it seems at times as if he is trying to fit the music into a 19th-century romantic mold. After his examination of Rameau's works, Girdlestone returns to a biography of Rameau's later years, followed by a brief discussion of Rameau's theories.

Readers will want to supplement Girdlestone's biography with SADLER, which gives Rameau's biography in a straightforward accounting that chronicles the main events and publications of his life. The chapter on Rameau's works is a brief but thorough overview of Rameau's compositional output, and a final chapter summarizes the main tenets of his theoretical ideas.

DILL delineates the conflict that arose from Rameau's artistic conception of the lyric tragedy as a musical drama and the public's unrelenting perception of the lyric tragedy as a poetic genre. Through detailed musical analysis, the author illustrates how Rameau worked to elevate the importance of music within the lyric tragedy and how Rameau strove to create a dramatic musical language equal to that of the poetry by following what he perceived to be the natural laws of harmony. Dill argues that the public, however, regarded such innovations as transgressing the "natural" laws of the lyric tragedy in which the poetry was to be supreme. The resulting paradox was that Rameau, who endeavored to compose according to natural principles, was accused of creating works that were distortions of nature, in other words, monstrous. Against the backdrop of 18th-century aesthetics, Dill evaluates Rameau's operatic revisions and shows how the changes in the composer's operas responded to public criticism. He asserts that the revisions were not reflective of changes in musical style, but reflective of Rameau's efforts to make his operas more accessible and acceptable to the public. They were the composer's attempts to reconcile artistic conception and public reception.

CHRISTENSEN presents an insightful look into Rameau's development as a theorist, illustrating how Rameau's theories were as much a product of Enlightenment philosophies as they were of his own imagination. The author systematically takes the reader through the development of each of Rameau's theoretical concepts and situates each stage of development within the realm of the philosophies and the scientific trends in vogue at the time. He shows that Rameau readily absorbed the most current scientific and philosophical advancements into his own thought processes and adapted a corresponding style of rhetoric for the exposition of his own theories. Christensen also notes the discrepancies inherent in Rameau's theories and illustrates how Rameau struggled to reconcile those discrepancies as his thoughts matured. In addition, he highlights the conflicting demands upon Rameau as he mediated between the worlds of practical composition and theoretical abstraction. Christensen's text is well written and highly readable, but readers should be prepared to spend some time dealing with theoretical prose and analysis.

SLOAN looks as a small body of Rameau's work, his six vocal cantatas and treatise of 1722, to demonstrate how the tradition of rhetoric played a part in the conception and development of these works. After discussing the rhetorical principles and tradition of rhetoric that existed in the 17th and 18th centuries, she then illustrates how corresponding rhetorical principles are found in these particular works of Rameau. Readers should note that the discussions offered here are of the most basic sort, and most of the quotations are taken from secondary and not primary sources. The discussions serve mainly as a springboard for more in-depth scholastic studies.

There are a large number of articles and dissertations dealing with various aspects of Rameau's music and/or theoretical writings. FOSTER provides an excellent guide for those wishing to explore this vast array of literature. This book is an exhaustive annotated bibliography of research works before 1987 that in some way pertain to Rameau. It includes categories covering general background and biography, specialized studies of Rameau's music, and specialized studies of his theoretical writings.

MARGOT MARTIN

Ravel, Maurice 1875–1937

French composer

Davies, Laurence, *Ravel Orchestral Music,* London: British Broadcasting Corporation, 1970; Seattle: University of Washington Press, 1971

Goss, Madeleine, *Bolero, The Life of Maurice Ravel,* New York, Holt, 1940

Jankélévitch, Vladimir, *Ravel,* translated by Margaret Crosland, New York, Grove Press, 1959

Myers, Rollo, *Modern French Music from Fauré to Boulez,* New York, Praeger, 1971; as *Modern French Music: Its Evolution and Cultural Background from 1900 to the Present Day,* Oxford, Blackwell, 1971

——, *Ravel: Life and Works,* London: Duckworth, 1960

Nichols, Roger, *Ravel Remembered,* New York, Norton, and London: Faber, 1987

Orenstein, Arbie, *Ravel: Man and Musician,* New York: Columbia University Press, 1975

Orenstein, Arbie, editor, *A Ravel Reader: Correspondence, Articles, Interviews,* New York, Columbia University Press, 1990

Stuckenschmidt, Hans Heinz, *Maurice Ravel: Variations on His Life and Work,* translated by Samuel R. Rosenbaum, Philadelphia: Chilton, 1968

The Ravel bibliography for the English speaker is slender although steadily growing. Many of the books currently available in English are biographies, with only a few requiring specialized musical knowledge. This lacuna in scholarly materials is slowly being filled as Ravel and his oeuvre are increasingly being studied. In many ways, Ravel's music embodies characteristics many of his contemporaries considered central to French music: clarity, linearity, and the art of making or organizing beautiful objects. Ravel, however, has suffered from being overshadowed by another prominent French composer of the turn of the 20th century, Claude Debussy. Two lines of thought exist that require comment: first, the supposed antagonism between these two men, and second, the grouping of many turn-of-the-century French composers in a general, undifferentiated musical impressionist category. The former notion seems to stem from the antipathy of one specific critic, Pierre Lalo, to Ravel and his music. This supposed friction between Debussy and Ravel has been discussed many times (including in some of the volumes listed here) and should now be laid to rest. The monolithic grouping of composers also has been under attack and revision and is finally yielding a wealth of new studies and articles devoted to these composers as individuals. Ravel has benefited from this reassessment.

GOSS is the first English-language biography of Ravel. Begun in 1938, less than a year after Ravel's death, its strength and value depend heavily on the many interviews with Ravel's brother, Edouard, and members of Maurice's close circle of friends and acquaintances, such as Ricardo Viñes, Marguerite Long, and Ravel's housekeeper, among others. As a result, this biography is rich with anecdotes, comments, observations, and other tidbits, as well as a work list and discography, making it a good introductory volume to Ravel for any level of reader. However, this book provides very little in the way of detailed or technical analysis of Ravel's music and lacks any substantial annotation for the sources used.

STUCKENSCHMIDT is an early biography of Ravel that consults many of the sources found in Goss but differs from that book in structure—each of the multiple sections is organized by period and then coordinated with the works written in that period. This presentation helps provide reference points for the reader between biographical details and musical compositions. As such, this book requires more knowledge of the whole period and is recommended for the advanced beginner with no special musical training.

In his full-length study, MYERS (1960) provides a book for both the casual reader without specialized musical knowledge and the one who has some musical background. The first section, "Life," is tightly written and interweaves biographical facts with pertinent works, anecdotes, and quotations. The "Works" section requires more musical knowledge for full appreciation, as it rehearses the so-called Debussy/Ravel controversy in detail and discusses Ravel's contemporaries as well. Myers also provides an annotated work list for those seeking more information about specific works. The most comprehensive portion of this list covers Ravel's vocal works and includes not only the title and date of each song but also the dedication, publisher, and the complete texts of the poems set. Other useful aspects of this volume include a chronological work list, a projected work list, and a good, if now somewhat dated, bibliography and discography.

MYERS (1971) includes a chapter on Ravel, Satie, and "Les Six" that provides an excellent, concise summary of the biographical details of Ravel's life, his works and musical language, and how he both influenced others and was influenced by them. Myers also provides the reader the context for understanding Ravel and his music, demonstrating Ravel's place within this period of French music.

NICHOLS is a completely different kind of book. Beginning with an extensive chronology that includes the important surrounding cultural, social, and scientific activities, it proceeds to a series of recollections by Ravel and of him by his friends and acquaintances. This material makes the volume a useful primary resource and does not require much musical knowledge.

The first section of ORENSTEIN (1990) is a partial condensation of his earlier book, recapitulating Ravel's biography and musical thought. The succeeding sections reproduce selected excerpts from Ravel's correspondence (chosen for their connection to Ravel's musical composition or performance), followed by articles published about him or by him during his lifetime, and concluding with transcriptions of interviews given by Ravel. This volume is a useful source of some primary documents that are only otherwise available in French sources; the reader will profit greatly by using this volume in conjunction with Orenstein (1975).

ORENSTEIN (1975) is one of the best studies available in English on Ravel, combining biographical details with discussions of the works in chronological order. Divided into three parts, Orenstein's text covers the biographical and cultural background, discusses the art of Ravel, and provides a comprehensive work list with dedications, first performance venues, and first performers, together with a discography. The biography is dense and fully annotated, providing a wealth of information for both the curious amateur and the scholar. The "Art" section includes discussions of Ravel's aesthetics, his creative process (with a few sketch studies), and an examination of Ravel's musical language that provides a brief analysis of the salient points of each of his pieces. This part of the text requires musical training for fullest understanding but will only whet scholarly appetites for further examination of the scores themselves.

JANKÉLÉVITCH provides a cultural context for understanding Ravel, with rich descriptions of the music, but he is one of the more difficult writers to follow in either French or English. The author presupposes a great familiarity not only with Ravel's music but also with that of all his contemporaries, French and otherwise. Jankélévitch first presents a biographical section, entitled "Evolution," where he traces Ravel's development, for example deriving Ravel's lineage from the "sensuous melodic lines" of Jules Massenet, the "gentle road" of Gabriel Fauré, and the "pleasure of music unconnected to literature" of Emmanuel Chabrier, statements wrapped in a thick layer of subjectivity. The following is another example of an interpretive statement: "Ravel . . . toyed with scandal and harsh friction; the provocation of bitonality was a kind of wager for him." The next section, "Works," is subdivided into musical disciplines, such as virtuosic instrumentation, counterpoint, and rhythms. In each subsection, Jankélévitch discusses pertinent examples not in enough depth to satisfy the scholar, but too deeply for the uninitiated to follow. In the final, most difficult, and most subjective section, "Heart," Jankélévitch addresses three facets of Ravel—"masks," "sensuality," and "vehemence"—trying to tease out the sense of the man, drawing an extended character sketch and analysis. This idiosyncratic text makes a useful adjunct to other analytic studies of Ravel and his music, but it is not easily accessible to the nonmusician.

DAVIES's volume focuses exclusively on Ravel's orchestral output, including his transcriptions. This volume assumes that the reader has either detailed knowledge of the music or the scores at hand for reference. The most useful section of this book is the last, which discusses Ravel's transcriptions and focuses mostly on the transcription of Mussorgsky's *Pictures at an Exhibition*.

MARIO CHAMPAGNE

Reger, Max 1873–1916

German composer

Brauss, Helmut, *Max Reger's Music for Solo Piano: An Introduction,* Edmonton: University of Alberta Press, 1994

Grim, William E., *Max Reger: A Bio-Bibliography,* New York: Greenwood Press, 1988

Popp, Susanne, and Susanne Shigihara, editors, *Max Reger: At the Turning Point to Modernism: An Illustrated Volume with Documents from the Collection of the Max Reger Institute,* Bonn: Bouvier, 1988

German composer Johann Baptist Joseph Maximilian (Max) Reger remains relatively unappreciated outside of Germany, despite the international recognition accorded to him during his lifetime as composer, conductor, pianist, teacher, and music critic. Reger is remembered for his enormous compositional output—146 works with opus numbers plus approximately 250 unnumbered works within a short career of around 27 years (1889–1916)—but his speed and prolific production have often prompted accusations that his music is overly mannered, technical, or mechanical. Critical writing on Reger's works emphasizes the combination of baroque and classical formal schemes with modernistic techniques. Reger considered himself to be an heir to J.S. Bach, Beethoven, and Brahms, yet he admired and emulated aspects of the music of Wagner and Liszt. Bach's influence is seen in the thick contrapuntal texture found in many of his works, which contain fugues, canons, and nonimitative counterpoint. Although the harmonic basis of his musical style is tonal, it is nevertheless highly chromatic, and his works are noted for their rapid and frequent modulations to distantly related keys. They are also recognized for such modernist traits as asymmetrical melodic structures and intensely emotional, expressionistic content. During his own lifetime, conservative critics took issue with the dense chromaticism and frequent modulations that characterized his musical style, while modernist commentators found both the organ and chamber music genres in which Reger excelled, and the classical and baroque forms that he employed, to be too reactionary. After his death, a number of political and social factors precipitated the decline in his reputation, and interest in Reger only began to revive internationally within the last 25 years. Only Reger's organ works continue to be played regularly today. Despite the admiration he inspired during his career, commentators have made almost no attempt to determine Reger's influence on other composers. Because the scope and significance of Reger's music is rarely acknowledged outside of Germany, only a few books on Reger have been published in English. A book-length biography as well as a book-length overview of his musical style in English are sorely needed.

GRIM serves as a comprehensive guide to resources concerning Reger that have been published from the late 19th century through the late 1980s. After a short biography and critical assessment, the guide presents lists of works, performances, and publishers; an undated discography of commercial recordings; a partially annotated bibliography of written works by and about Reger; and appendices of Reger's works organized chronologically and by genre. The bibliography includes articles; bibliographies; biographies; general books; discographies; dissertations; encyclopedia and dictionary entries; Festschriften; monographs; Reger's writings and letters; reviews; and fictional works (novels and poems) in which Reger is mentioned. Although this work provides an excellent starting point for research on Reger, it fails to list the locations and contents of manuscript collections.

Despite the somewhat awkward English translation from the original German, POPP and SHIGIHARA serves as an invaluable introduction to Reger iconography and manuscripts located, for the most part, at the Max Reger Institute (founded in 1947) in Bonn. The book focuses on illustrations of manuscripts, correspondence, concert programs, photographs, paintings, and caricatures from the collection. The accompanying commentary begins with a short year-by-year biography, followed by a chapter on Reger's compositional technique that discusses sketches and drafts, which reveal much about Reger's compositional process and provide insights into the interpretation of his works. By examining several manuscript drafts, the editors show that, once Reger had set down the essential voices that carried major themes or motives, he filled in ornamental and contrapuntal parts section-by-section or page-by-page, with few changes. The editors also find that Reger's deletions of entire blocks of measures with only minor amounts of recomposition to bridge the resulting musical gaps indicate not an organic conception but rather a "dynamic-energetic" one, in which phrases, instead of being developed, undergo processes of variation, "exchange, combination and elimination," a technique akin to "composing with scissors." The rather substantial chapter on reception traces the 20th-century social and political events that eventually led to widespread negative reception of Reger's music. The period of the New Realism (*Neue Sachlichkeit*) movement spawned the organ revival of the 1920s, during which the baroque organ was promoted as the ideal. This revival resulted in a problematic assessment of Reger's organ works, as his organ music was designed for 19th-century instruments, which had the capacity for crescendo and diminuendo as well as a sound that was orchestral in character. Another highly significant factor in the change in Reger reception was the adoption by the National Socialists of patriotic works that Reger wrote during World War I to fulfill their own propagandistic goals. This identification with National Socialism later resulted in a post–World War II rejection of Reger. The editors note that the maintenance of the Reger Archives in Meiningen and the founding of the Max Reger Institute in Bonn prevented Reger's works from becoming totally forgotten during the 20th century. While Popp and Shigihara attribute increased musicological interest in Reger beginning in 1968 to "overall social developments" in Germany, they do not elaborate on precisely which factors there caused the renewed attention to Reger's music. They do propose that the increase in international scholarly research on Reger since the late 1970s coincides with the emergence of postmodernism, which has resulted in a reevaluation of late 19th- and early 20th-century German music. Nevertheless, the editors find that, despite renewed interest in Reger's works, his music still resists analysis by methods suitable for both tonal and post-tonal music.

BRAUSS introduces professional pianists, piano teachers, and piano students to the solo piano works of Reger. Because Reger's large output of piano works remains virtually unknown, and because this oeuvre is of uneven quality, Brauss limits discussion to works of high artistic caliber that are suited for concert performance or for pedagogical purposes. The book, which contains ample musical illustrations, surveys general stylistic characteristics, interpretive problems, levels of technical difficulty, and pedagogical issues. Unfortunately, it eschews musical analysis. The opening chapters provide basic biographical information and a summary of Reger's piano style. Subsequent chapters contain brief descriptions, arranged by opus number, of over 50 piano pieces, most of which were written for solo piano. Appendices include lists of Reger's solo piano works, both with and without opus numbers; a selected discography; and a selected bibliography. A separate chapter discusses the interpretation of Reger's piano works by focusing on Reger's own recordings, which show that Reger's approach to his own notation, including his abundant expressive markings, was highly flexible. Reger himself declared that his metronome markings indicated only maximum tempi, and he did not adhere to strict tempi in his own playing. He was also noted for his subtle dynamics and articulation; his highlighting of important harmonic or thematic material within his densely written textures; and his preference for softer-voiced grand pianos such as the Ibach and Blüthner, which were decidedly less percussive than today's pianos. Brauss contends that, because Reger himself did not follow precisely the score when he himself played, it is evident that only the kind of interpretive flexibility that the composer himself practiced will bring out the expressive potential in his solo piano works.

SUZANNE M. LODATO

Reich, Steve b. 1936

United States composer

Duckworth, William, *Talking Music: Conversations with John Cage, Philip Glass, Laurie Anderson, and Five Generations of American Experimental Composers,* New York: Schirmer Books, and London: Prentice Hall, 1995

Gagne, Cole, and Tracy Caras, *Soundpieces: Interviews with American Composers,* Metuchen, New Jersey: Scarecrow Press, 1982

Johnson, Tom, *The Voice of New Music: New York City, 1972–1982,* Eindhoven: Het Apollohuis, 1989

Kostelanetz, Richard, and Robert Flemming, editors, *Writings on Glass: Essays, Interviews, Criticism,* New York: Schirmer Books, and London: Prentice Hall, 1997

Mertens, Wim, *American Minimal Music: La Monte Young, Terry Riley, Steve Reich, Philip Glass,* translated by J. Hautekiet, London: Kahn and Averill, and New York: Broude, 1983

Nyman, Michael, *Experimental Music: Cage and Beyond,* New York: Schirmer Books, and London: Studio Vista, 1974; 2nd edition, Cambridge: Cambridge University Press, 1999

Reich, Steve, *Writings about Music,* Halifax: Press of the Nova Scotia College of Art and Design, and New York: New York University Press, 1974

Reich, Steve, and Beryl Korot, *The Cave,* London: Hendon Music, Boosey and Hawkes, 1993

Schaefer, John, *New Sounds: A Listener's Guide to New Music,* New York: Harper and Row, 1987

Schwarz, K. Robert, *Minimalists,* London: Phaidon, 1996

Smith, Geoff, and Nicola Walker Smith, *American Originals: Interviews with 25 Contemporary Composers,* London: Faber, 1994; as *New Voices: American Composers Talk About Their Music,* Portland, Oregon: Amadeus Press, 1995

Strickland, Edward, *American Composers: Dialogues on Contemporary Music,* Bloomington: Indiana University Press, 1991

———, *Minimalism—Origins,* Bloomington: Indiana University Press, 1993

Steve Reich is one of the leading so-called minimalist composers and, for many critics, the most musically accomplished of these composers. The convenient label *minimalist,* borrowed from the visual arts, is most frequently applied to four innovative U.S. composers, all born in the mid-1930s, who came to prominence in the 1960s: La Monte Young, Terry Riley, Reich, and Philip Glass. The literature on Reich, including his own brief volume of essays, tends to focus primarily on compositions from the 1970s, for which the term *minimalist* captures the composer's concentration on a bare minimum of musical materials, usually presented in a repetitive manner. By the 1980s, however, Reich's music had become so rich and varied, and his musical concerns so much broader than they had been previously, that earlier categories such as minimalist, phase music, process music, and pulse music no longer seemed to describe adequately his work.

Most available studies on Reich are not only dated but also limited in scope and detail. In addition to his own writings, numerous published interviews give insights into Reich's background, influences, and compositions. Although Reich is discussed in most surveys of 20th-century music, especially those emphasizing recent trends, the treatment is usually fairly brief, superficial, and once again restricted to early compositions. A few particularly important studies, discussed below, specifically examine minimalism or experimental music in the United States and dedicate at least one chapter to Reich.

REICH writes extremely well about music. This small book includes 11 essays, some systematically developed, others more in the nature of scattered notes; many pictures and musical examples are included as well. Particularly important is the famous opening essay, "Music as Gradual Process" (1968), which served as a manifesto for Reich's early period. This volume must be supplemented by the liner notes and program notes that Reich has provided for his later works, most of which are available on recordings he has made of his own music. (A French translation, *Écrits et entretiens sur la musique* [1981] includes notes on later works, as well as five important interviews.)

REICH and KOROT is a program book for the composer's longest and most ambitious work to date, the video opera *The Cave* (1993), which Reich conceived and developed with his wife, Beryl Korot. The book contains excellent essays by K. Robert Schwarz and William D. Judson, an interview with the creators by Jonathan Cott, synopsis, libretto, and biographies.

Specialized studies of minimalist music tend to concentrate on Reich and Glass. MERTENS's book, first published in Belgium in 1980, opens with brief chapters on Young, Riley, Reich, and Glass. The second part of the book attempts to place minimalist music within a larger trajectory of the 20th century, specifically linking the so-called Second Viennese School, Karlheinz Stockhausen, and John Cage. Part 3, entitled "Ideology," considers the philosophical, social, and aesthetic place of minimalism with reference to the theories of T.W. Adorno and the French post-structuralists Gilles Deleuze and Jean-François Lyotard. Although the ambition of this short book is impressive, the results are disappointing. The treatment of the music in the opening chapters is descriptive rather than revealing, and the historical survey runs counter to most discussions of minimalist music in the United States by unconvincingly emphasizing peripheral figures while virtually ignoring the importance of non-Western and popular music, jazz, and the U.S. experimental tradition.

STRICKLAND's (1993) excellent examination of the minimalist aesthetic is not limited to music but also discusses painters and sculptors such as Ad Reinhardt, Richard Serra, Sol LeWitt, Donald Judd, and Frank Stella. The book offers a sophisticated and detailed investigation of the genesis of musical minimalism and connects that history with broader cultural and artistic trends. There are no musical examples and the level of technical discussion of specific pieces is not too demanding. The book is divided into sections on "Paint," "Sound," and "Space." Discussion of Reich alternates with that of Riley, Young, and Glass, which means that the book, or at least the part on music, is best read straight through. (One minor drawback: The index lists only persons' names, not individual works.)

SCHWARZ's superb study of minimalism is part of the handsomely illustrated Phaidon series devoted to 20th-century composers. A perceptive critic who has written widely on minimalism and Reich for nearly two decades, Schwarz covers a broad and representative selection of pieces. The study opens with an excellent chapter on Young and Riley that provides essential background for anyone interested in Reich's music. The next two chapters examine Reich, first as a minimalist and then as a maximalist whose more recent works go well beyond his original aesthetic. Schwarz employs a similar minimal and maximal approach for the next two chapters on Glass and concludes with two chapters on later U.S. and European composers influenced by the original minimalists: John Adams, Meredith Monk, Michael Nyman, Louis Andriessen, Arvo Pärt, and others. These chapters give useful insight into the importance of Reich's music for recent compositional trends.

NYMAN is himself a composer (perhaps best known for his score to the motion picture film *The Piano*) who wrote an early study of experimental music. The final chapter, "Minimal Music, Determinacy, and the New Tonality," is interesting because it shows how Reich was regarded in 1974. The early phase pieces get the most attention.

SCHAEFER's guide to new music (what Nyman might have called experimental) is based on a popular radio program that Schaefer hosted on National Public Radio. The chapter "Meet the Minimalists" traces the background and aesthetics of the movement and gives an annotated discography of minimalist works. The latter helpfully identifies younger composers who were influenced by Reich.

Both Reich and Glass are New York composers, often labeled as downtown because they have mainly lived and composed in that part of the city and also because most of their 1960s and 1970s works premiered there. JOHNSON gives a good idea of the state of the music scene in New York City at the time. Originally written as reviews for the *Village Voice*, the city's well-known alternative downtown weekly newspaper, the selections cover the musical scene and give a glimpse at the context in which Reich came to prominence. There are six featured reviews of Reich's music from the 1970s, as well as many passing references in other articles.

Further context is provided by KOSTELANETZ. Although this book is primarily devoted to Glass, the first third of the book contains essays and criticism relevant to Reich as well and includes a rare joint interview with critic Tim Page from 1980.

Unfortunately, there has neither been a book-length interview with Reich alone nor a comparable compilation of the many interviews he has given over the years that are scattered among a wide variety of newspapers, magazines, journals, and books. Some interviews are difficult to locate because they appeared in rather obscure forums, while those in the most accessible sources are not always revealing or historically valuable as they only trace the general development of Reich's career. Three particular volumes of interviews can be useful, however, for placing Reich in historical context. Duckworth and Strickland both interview all four founding minimalists, as well as other pivotal figures. Smith and Smith include other experimental composers, while Gagne and Caras's collection presents a much wider range of U.S. composers working in all styles. These collections offer valuable perspectives on alternatives to serialism, mainstream conservative Americana, and so forth.

The interview with DUCKWORTH charts Reich's compositional career particularly well up through *Tehillim* (1981) and includes some valuable remarks about his very earliest compositional experiments. The focus throughout is on specific compositions. The 1980 interview published in GAGNE and CARAS concentrates on Reich's training, influences on his musical development, and trends in contemporary music. The somewhat disjointed conversation does not explore his compositions in much detail. STRICKLAND (1991) offers an interview from January 1987 that provides the most detailed discussion of *The Desert Music* (1984). Although some of the interview is rather technical, it is also one of the most substantive discussions with Reich. The interview in SMITH and SMITH dates from the early 1990s. In addition to another summary of Reich's compositional development, there are especially interesting comments on non-Western influences. Reich's remarks on the profound shift that came with *Different Trains* ("[It] is a line in the sand") and the massive *Cave* project on which he was working at the time provide useful information about his recent interests and compositional directions.

CHRISTOPHER H. GIBBS

Renaissance Music: General Studies

Abraham, Gerald, editor, *The Age of Humanism, 1540–1630,* London: Oxford University Press, 1968

Atlas, Allan W., *Renaissance Music: Music in Western Europe, 1400–1600,* New York: Norton, 1998

Blume, Friedrich, *Renaissance and Baroque Music: A Comprehensive Survey,* translated by M.D. Herter Norton, New York: Norton, 1967

Brown, Howard M., *Music in the Renaissance,* Englewood Cliffs, New Jersey: Prentice Hall, 1976; 2nd edition, with Louise K. Stein, 1999

Hughes, Dom Anselm, and Gerald Abraham, editors, *Ars Nova and the Renaissance, 1300–1540,* London: Oxford University Press, 1960

Knighton, Tess, and David Fallows, editors, *Companion to Medieval and Renaissance Music,* New York: Schirmer Books, 1992

Palisca, Claude V., *Humanism in Italian Renaissance Musical Thought,* New Haven, Connecticut: Yale University Press, 1985

Perkins, Leeman L., *Music in the Age of the Renaissance,* New York: Norton, 1999

Reese, Gustave, *Music in the Renaissance,* New York: Norton, 1954; revised edition, 1959

Strohm, Reinhard, *The Rise of European Music, 1380–1500,* Cambridge: Cambridge University Press, 1993

Historical awareness has been a persistent concern of Western musicians. Medieval writers justified musical phenomena by expounding upon that phenomena's divine nature as defined by a centuries-old rationalist tradition bound to the quadrivium (arithmetic, music, geometry, and astronomy). Innovations in melody, harmony, rhythm, modal practice, and genre all fell subject to the analytic scrutiny and practices of this accumulated past authority. For example, modern chant types (sequences, tropes, and liturgical dramas) developed as embellishments of older sacred melodies, and composers began constructing most polyphonic genres by placing a preexisting chant melody in one voice.

This allegiance to historical continuity ended with the emergence of humanistic attitudes in the Renaissance. The theorist and composer Tinctoris boldly stated that no music written before Dunstable, Dufay, and Binchois (i.e., the early 15th century) was worth hearing. New was in, old was out. Historical consciousness did not disappear, however. It merely shifted from the preceding age to the glories of Greek and Roman antiquity more than a millennium earlier. This rebirth or revival of antiquity—formally christened the Renaissance during the 19th century—occurred first in Italian visual and literary arts during the 14th century, then spread throughout Europe.

Because music lacked the concrete sound artifacts of these past civilizations, its rebirth lagged behind the other arts. Ancient authors fortunately left a substantial archive of philosophic, aesthetic, literary, and theoretic writings upon which Renaissance musicians reconceived the distant past in modern terms. Humanistic endeavors, such as the elevation of learning based on the trivium (grammar, rhetoric, and logic) and the recovery and translation of ancient Greek texts, fueled the excitement of this new age. Music assumed new importance and meaning quite separate from its sterile medieval functionality—sound became a sensual medium as valid as stone, canvas, or quill on paper.

REESE constructs what has become the traditional paradigm of Renaissance music historiography: a central musical language first emerged in northern Europe (France and the Low Countries), migrated to Italy, and then radiated outward to the Iberian peninsula, German and eastern European countries, and England in a series of local dialects. The development of musical style forms the central thrust of this book; social, cultural, and political conditions only occasionally enter the narrative. Individual chapters focus on particular regions, genres, or countries, while subchapters highlight dominant figures followed by rosters of lesser contemporaries. The author details aspects of musicians' lives and careers, examines individual compositions (this dense text contains numerous short excerpts) for personal style traits, and locates these figures within their historical context. Reese has arguably been the most influential figure in American scholarship on Renaissance music, both as a teacher and author. His period history, although outdated in many respects, is a classic study worthy of regular consultation.

The monumental, 11-volume New Oxford History of Music series, with its companion recordings *The History of Music in Sound,* remains the most comprehensive music history in the English language. The team of editors states the primary objective of the series in a general introduction: "to present music, not as an isolated phenomenon or the work of a few outstanding composers, but as an art developing in constant association with every form of human culture and activity." Each chapter, defined either by genre or time, is the work of a different scholar of international stature. There is little uniformity of coverage or perspective beyond this primary level, however. Some authors firmly adhere to the concept of major-versus-minor composers, while others examine compositional trends from a broader cultural vantage point. One notable feature of this series is its unconventional chronological subdivision. Information relating to the Renaissance spans the third and fourth volumes. HUGHES and ABRAHAM view the period 1330 to 1540 as a continuous stylistic progression beginning with the rhythmic innovations and breakdown of medieval mysticism during the *ars nova* and culminating in the triumph of the human spirit in the Renaissance. Several points underlie their argument: many compositional forms, such as the rondeau, occupied musicians throughout this period; the alliance between music and mathematics, both from a theoretical and practical standpoint, exerted constant influence; and most musical innovations emanated from northern Europe. ABRAHAM defines the subsequent historic period (1540–1630) from

the beginning of polyphony's golden age until just after the first generation of opera composers. Italy—where humanistic thought deepened music's relationship to poetry—emerges as the driving artistic force. Although vocal music occupies the largest portion of both volumes, instrumental forms receive substantial consideration. Particularly interesting are the chapters devoted to the instruments themselves, their construction, and their representation in artwork and literature.

BLUME originally published his Renaissance and baroque articles in the multivolume German music encyclopedia *Die Musik in Geschicht und Gegenwart* (1949), for which he served as general editor. Norton's translation makes available these valuable essays to a wider English-speaking audiences. Blume intentionally shuns "preconceived ideas of music history," meaning musical developments determined according to their own formal and stylistic conventions. Instead, he advances a viewpoint that sets music against its cultural backdrop. The Renaissance article proceeds through five stages: general concepts behind the term *Renaissance,* how theorists of the period described music's function, the chronological and stylistic boundaries of the Renaissance period in music, an overview of stylistic developments in the northern and southern regions of Europe, and a summary of musical accomplishments during the Renaissance.

Like others volumes in the Prentice Hall History of Music Series, BROWN's modestly sized book is geared toward college students and informed lovers of music history. He emphasizes major (or great) figures, in contrast to the focus on genre and lesser masters found in many other music histories. Although certainly not conceived for commercial purposes, this approach understandably appeals to a general readership. Furthermore, Brown elaborates upon the multitudinous societal forces that influenced musical creation. The engaging and authoritative writing, generously embellished with musical examples and visual illustrations, brings life to the composers and their creations. Perceptive analyses of individual compositions are one of this book's strongest features. Sadly, Brown died before completing the second edition. Louise Stein, already collaborating with the author on the revision, continued the task by updating some factual information, adding examples, expanding bibliographies, and describing areas of recent or continued controversy.

PALISCA begins his imposing study by pondering an inherent contradiction in Renaissance history: although humanistic thought took root in Italy, northern Europe generally receives credit for inaugurating the musical Renaissance. Palisca takes an unequivocal stand on this subject, arguing that, together with the other arts, the movement in music traditionally called the Renaissance also began in Italy, taking as its chief source of inspiration the revival of antiquity. The author draws on a vast body of supporting evidence from well-known and obscure Renaissance theorists; many extended quotations with English translations are published here for the first time. Beginning with the recovery of theoretical sources in the early 15th century, Palisca traces the infiltration of ancient ideologies into modern musical thought, culminating in the theories of dramatic music articulated by the Florentine Camerata.

KNIGHTON and FALLOWS designed their volume not as a chronological survey of medieval and Renaissance music but as a printed forum for important issues related to the modern study of early music. Forty-nine scholars and performers have contributed articles on diverse subjects organized under six general headings. The initial essays address sundry, and in some cases misguided, assumptions about authentic performance practice, such as the subjective valuation of compositions, the history of a cappella performance, and trends in early music recordings and concert programming. The second section confronts the function of music in everyday life and ritual contexts, the social status of musicians, and the place of women musicians in medieval and Renaissance history. The editors devote more space to the brief essays on stylistic and formal conventions of various vocal and instrumental genres and techniques of composition than any other segment of this anthology. Remaining chapters suggest how iconographic evidence, improvisational techniques, archival documents, editorial considerations, pitch and rhythmic theory, and text conventions might influence the modern performance of medieval and Renaissance music. The book concludes with a chronology of musical and general historic events, along with a glossary of terms and brief biographical sketches.

STROHM traces the history of musical practice from the time of the Great Schism through the end of the 15th century, with emphasis on polyphonic developments. He rejects any linkage between this period and the concept of a musical Renaissance ("a consciously created sociocultural environment, not a style characteristic of music") and liberates the 15th century from its subordinate role as a preliminary phase to the High Renaissance. Part 1, which addresses the period of upheaval in the Catholic Church, illustrates the author's main historical thrust: a chronological orientation overlaid, as near as possible in written communication, with a geographical dissemination of style via north-south (central) and east-west (lateral) axes. Extensive discussions of composers, individual works, genres, manuscript sources, patronage, and performance contexts follow. A similar pattern holds in part 2 for the examination of the age of Dufay and Dunstable. The third part breaks from this chronological-geographic track to examine the function of music in various ecclesiastic, monastic, university, public, court, and private settings and to survey developments in chant, simple polyphonic traditions, and instrumental music. Strohm devotes the last segment (and nearly half of this admirable study) to music after 1450 in four major regions: Britain, France and the Low Countries, central Europe, and Italy and Spain. A valuable list of music manuscripts and their common informal titles and abbreviations precedes the extensive bibliography.

ATLAS intends his Renaissance history and companion anthology of musical scores, part of the Norton Introduction to Music History series, for use as a textbook. Several other features distinguish this book from most period histories. The "intermedii"—glimpses into aspects of the nonmusical world—appear throughout the text. The author also guides students through the interpretation of primary documents and the editing of a chanson in four stages (notation; *musica ficta*, text underlay, and barring; listing sources; and compiling a critical report). Perhaps the most delightful aspect of the text is its witty and engaging writing style. However, the scholarly component is anything but lightweight, as Atlas offers a tremendous amount of factual information and analytic insight. The book partitions the two centuries (1400–1600) into six segments, each of which is 30 to 50 years long. Although the basic orientation of the study is chronological, the focus shifts from geography, genre, and patronage to broader themes including music printing and "music in the service of words."

PERKIN's immense volume scrutinizes music's institutional, religious, social, cultural, and intellectual milieus. After discussing general concepts of the Renaissance and their realization in music, the author explains the internal workings of the institutional patrons of music: church, secular court, and urban organizations. There follows an overview of manuscript and print production, nicely illustrated with facsimiles of primary sources. Parts 2 and 3 consider 15th- and 16th-century music, respectively. Discussion of the music proceeds chronologically according to genre, although the author willingly pursues interesting tangents such as aesthetics, performance practice, or manuscript sources whenever the opportunity arises. Reflecting Perkin's meticulous approach to scholarship, this book conveys an impressive wealth of knowledge supported by countless musical excerpts, political maps, paintings, engravings, and other illustrations. This comprehensive book is justifiably considered the successor to Reese's masterwork.

TODD SULLIVAN

Renaissance Music: Specialized Studies

Cummings, Anthony M., *The Politicized Muse: Music for Medici Festivals, 1512–1537*, Princeton, New Jersey: Princeton University Press, 1992

Elders, Willem, *Symbolic Scores: Studies in the Music of the Renaissance*, Leiden: Brill, 1994

Everist, Mark, editor, *Music before 1600,* Oxford: Blackwell, 1992

Fallows, David, *Songs and Musicians in the Fifteenth Century,* Aldershot: Variorum, and Brookfield, Vermont: Ashgate, 1996

Günther, Ursula, et al., editors, *Modality in the Music of the Fourteenth and Fifteenth Centuries,* Neuhausen-Stuttgart: American Institute of Musicology, Hänssler-Verlag, 1996

Kirkman, Andrew, *The Three-Voice Mass in the Later Fifteenth and Early Sixteenth Centuries: Style, Distribution and Case Studies,* New York: Garland, 1995

Owens, Jessie Ann, *Composers at Work: The Craft of Musical Composition 1450–1600,* New York: Oxford University Press, 1997

Prizer, William F., *Courtly Pastimes: The Frottole of Marchetto Cara,* Ann Arbor, Michigan: UMI Research Press, 1980

Reynolds, Christopher A., *Papal Patronage and the Music of St. Peter's, 1380–1513,* Berkeley: University of California Press, 1995

The face of musical scholarship for the years 1400 to 1600 has changed greatly in the years since Gustave Reese produced his synoptic study of *Music in the Renaissance* (1954). The proper sense in which the term Renaissance itself should be applied is now far from clear—most scholars have come to recognize the limitations of periodization in general, and the resistance of these centuries in particular to coalesce as an autonomous historical entity. Recent studies have taken this lack of cohesion as a virtue, attempting to isolate musical strands in the tapestry of the Renaissance in order to better articulate the distinct principles of musical thought that gave rise to compositions and to understand the social structures that lay behind musical performance.

Renaissance polyphony has traditionally been examined in terms of the compositional technique exhibited and the structural devices and formal patterns employed, resulting in stylistic generalities and identification of compositional trends that are usually centered around schools of composers and headed by a major historical figure. Such analyses, while valuable, tell us little about the nature of musical thought and practice in the period and the ideas that informed them. Over the past 20 years, especially, a number of fresh strategies for analysis and study of Renaissance music emerged. Taking into account historical issues, religious and social parameters, questions of audience and reception, as well as specialized musical questions, these accounts place the specific musical materials, compositions, and repertories they investigate into broad contexts (musical and historical) appropriate to the time and places in which such music was produced. The studies mentioned here represent recent trends in Renaissance music scholarship and are among the most influential works in their areas, although they are necessarily only a small sampling of the studies now available. In each case, the authors provide bibliographies useful for further research.

ELDERS provides analyses based on various aspects of musical symbolism for works ranging from Guillaume Dufay to William Byrd. He evaluates the symbolic functions of structural devices in terms of numerology in cantus firmus and ostinato structures and canonic and imitative passages, as well as the (potential) symbolic content of *fauxbourdon.* Additionally, aspects of Marian symbolism are related to compositional devices found in a group of Masses and motets. While Elders's conclusions have been met with skepticism on some fronts, his analyses are rich, provocative, and point to the perceptual distance at which this music stands from modern thought.

EVERIST presents an extensive collection of analytical essays that examine individual compositions and groups of works dating from the early 13th century to the late 16th century. The authors employ a wide range of systematic approaches and historical viewpoints, including Schenkerian graphic analysis, text-musical analysis, and cultural-contextual interpretations. Each essay includes a newly prepared or specially revised edition of the work in question. The approaches offered in this volume are among the most important analytical work currently being done in music from the period and, although quite specialized, are useful in suggesting possible strategies for embarking on the study of Renaissance musical forms and vocabulary. Combining the perspectives of historian and analyst, Cristle Collins Judd, for example, contributes an especially rich view of Josquin des Prez's five-voice *Salve regina.* Her essay covers aspects of voice leading, melodic/modal functions of individual contrapuntal lines, and overall tonal coherence. The emphasis on text-music relations relative to the formal organization of Josquin's motet is particularly persuasive.

GÜNTHER likewise draws together a diverse collection of essays (some in German) on aspects of modal theory and its practical applications for both late-medieval plainchant and polyphonic compositions. This is a stimulating volume, often dealing with specialized research but useful in understanding the current range of approaches to the issue of modality and its function in analysis. In particular, Sean Gallagher's examination of the structural role assigned to the tenor line, and its peculiar modal manipulation in motets of Johannes Regis, affords a valuable new perspective for the study of cantus firmus applications.

One of the most noteworthy directions of recent years explores the nature of the creative process and technical apparatus of Renaissance composition and the role of composers in late-medieval and early modern society. OWENS brings a rich background in manuscript study to bear on her investigation of compositional process between 1450 and 1600. She is concerned here specifically with the genesis of musical ideas and the technical (written) procedures by which composers produced their works during the period. Her study is based on surviving documentary evidence of all kinds, including theoretical treatises, composers' letters, iconographical evidence, and manuscript fragments and "sketches." Additionally, she makes clear that manuscripts themselves may contain evidence of compositional activity from a variety of stages in a work's history. Owens's examination includes case studies, deduced from surviving documents, detailing the working methods of four Renaissance composers—Isaac, Rore, Palestrina, and Corteccia. Her study of Isaac's work on a motet, for example, shows how much information may be recovered from a careful reading of a single manuscript source, including particulars pertaining to his setting of chant melody and cantus firmus layout, text underlay, and eventual revisions of the composition. Owens's conclusions provide deep insights into both the process by which mensural music was composed and the complex nature of the sources in which it is preserved.

Many studies of Renaissance music focus on particular local and national repertories, or repertories and genres seen in terms of their distinct musical and social contexts. FALLOWS is a convenient collection of previously published essays (with updates and revisions) on 15th-century polyphonic secular song and matters of performance practice. The first section of Fallows's book is devoted to writings on 15th-century English song repertories, including those of John Dunstable, John Bedyngham, and a collection found in the Oporto manuscript. Stretching back to 1977, these articles form a series of the most influential recent studies on all aspects of English polyphonic song (style, transmission, sources, and attributions).

KIRKMAN is an incisive study of a neglected repertory of Mass settings from the late 15th and early 16th centuries, though its analytical approach has broader implications for the period in question. Considering aspects of texture, cleffing, and range, Kirkman establishes a typology of characteristic ranges for each voice part (and their resulting combinations) in the three-voice textures found in the repertory at hand. He goes on to investigate the opportunities for "non-hierarchic texture" and "shared contrapuntal interest" inherent in these structures. His conclusions are significant for the history of the development of 16th-century musical style, particularly for the four-voice writing and imitative texture that came to predominate the period. The second part of Kirkman's study comprises three case studies dealing with issues of style and transmission in works of Walter Frye, Johannes Ockeghem, and an anonymous English Mass from approximately 1450.

PRIZER surveys the development and cultivation of the *frottola* at the court of Mantua in the late 15th to early 16th centuries and its principal composer, Marchetto Cara. The study is centered on the patronage of Isabella d'Este, vital to the transformation of the form into a written genre, and demonstrates a broad, sociohis-

torical approach to a particular (and often misunderstood) repertory. Included in Prizer's study are editions of 49 of Cara's works.

Similarly, REYNOLDS centers his study of sacred music on works associated with the basilica of Saint Peter in Rome. The second part of Reynolds's study concentrates on the repertory of a 15th-century manuscript belonging to the choir of St. Peter's. This discussion includes a valuable consideration of the stylistic phenomenon of musical allusion, current in the later 15th century. This technique involves borrowings and quotations among two or more works that may point to further relationships among the compositions themselves, the models on which they may be based, and the careers of the various composers. Of particular interest, though not uncontroversial, is Reynolds's detailed survey of the components of attributive research (laid out in studies of a group of anonymous 15th-century Masses contained in the St. Peter's choirbook) and their value in establishing general patterns of "musical association," as opposed to (in his view) "authorial relationships."

Finally, CUMMINGS examines the role of music (along with works of art and literature) in Florentine political life of the early 16th century. He investigates accounts of civic festivals, religious feasts, and ceremonies celebrated publicly by the Medicis and the music that may have accompanied these events (few of the pieces demonstrably performed have survived). His methodology, drawing on Florentine narratives of the period, will provide a useful model for any study of the contexts in which Renaissance music was performed. Cummings's study helps clarify the relationship between context and musical language and points to the importance of understanding the broadest possible range of interactions between Renaissance music and the culture in which it was created.

ROBERT E. PALMER

Rhetoric

Agawu, V. Kofi, *Playing with Signs: A Semiotic Interpretation of Classic Music,* Princeton, New Jersey: Princeton University Press, 1991

Barth, George, *The Pianist as Orator: Beethoven and the Transformation of Keyboard Style,* Ithaca, New York: Cornell University Press, 1992

Bonds, Mark Evans, *Wordless Rhetoric: Musical Form and the Metaphor of the Oration,* Cambridge, Massachusetts: Harvard University Press, 1991

Burmeister, Joachim, *Musical Poetics,* translated by Benito V. Rivera, New Haven, Connecticut: Yale University Press, 1993

Haar, James, *Essays on Italian Poetry and Music in the Renaissance, 1350–1600,* Berkeley: University of California Press, 1986

Johnson, James, *Listening in Paris: A Cultural History,* Berkeley: University of California Press, 1995

Mattheson, Johann, *Johann Mattheson's Der vollkommene Capellmeister: A Revised Translation with Critical Commentary,* translated by Ernest C. Harriss, Ann Arbor, Michigan: UMI Research Press, 1981

Webster, James, *Haydn's "Farewell" Symphony and the Idea of Classical Style: Through-Composition and Cyclic Integration in His Instrumental Music,* Cambridge: Cambridge University Press, 1991

That music is a rhetorical art has been noted at least as far back as the Greek philosophers. In its broadest sense, the relationship between rhetoric and music subsumes any understanding of music as a communicative or persuasive act and all the elements pertaining thereto: the composer, the performer, the listener, the composition (as text or performance), and the composition's occasion, purpose, and technical makeup. Even if classically derived rhetorical terminology is not on view, a sense of music as a rhetorical act is still an underlying theme of any discussion of audience expectations, generic conventions, cultural context, text setting, performance practice, the tropes and figures of a musical language, instrumental or vocal idioms, historical or nationalist styles, and so forth. The animating question that unites such various lines of inquiry under the heading of rhetoric could be summarized as follows: how do composers or performers communicate to their audiences? Construed in this way, the rhetoric of music may seem to be so inclusive as to be virtually synonymous with the analysis of music. Indeed, it was during the Renaissance when the first fruitful intersection of rhetoric and music gave birth to modern music analysis. So, whereas all music can be said to be rhetorical, it is only since the late 16th century that musical commentators have explicitly mobilized the field of rhetoric—with the exception of delivery—in any systematic way. Since then, the European tradition of rhetorical education has influenced composers, theorists, and historians with varying degrees of intensity and with large shifts in meaning and emphasis.

With the advent of humanism, many Renaissance theorists and practitioners busily set about forging interdisciplinary links between music and rhetoric—then the most comprehensive field of the communicative arts—in order to account for the newly expressive practices of music, which were fast outstripping their mathematical roots in the quadrivium, and which fell outside the bounds of contrapuntal rules. Originally published in 1606 as the third version of an evolving treatise, BURMEISTER contains the first systematic exploration of music and rhetoric. A lengthy chapter that adapts rhetorical terminology to musical devices abounds with examples and shows Burmeister concerned with that narrow aspect of rhetoric termed *elocutio,* or style, that deals with figures, tropes, and ornamentation. Burmeister is also concerned, albeit more briefly, with *dispositio*—the arrangement of an oration—and its applications to the compositional structure of music and to its analysis. Rivera's edition provides the original Latin with the translation opposite and includes a lucid apparatus of explanatory footnotes and appendices.

Over a century of theorizing later—including, not incidentally, the flowering of richly expressive baroque music—MATTHESON's conception of rhetoric is at once broader and more specific than Burmeister's. Published in 1739 as a handbook for the "complete" *Cappellmeister,* this text addresses with vast erudition a range of issues affecting a music director. Mattheson's discussion of composition makes liberal use of the rhetorical tradition: his chapter on the "Art of Creating a Good Melody" invokes *inventio;* another chapter, the "Disposition, Elaboration, and Ornamentation of Melody," deals first with the arrangement (*dispositio*) of a musical composition according to the six parts of the classical oration (*exordium, narratio, propositio, confirmatio, confutatio,* and *peroratio*) and then explores the devices of *elaboratio* and *decoratio.* Another chapter on gesticulation invokes *hypocrisis,* or delivery. In this text can also be found a description and endorsement of the Doctrine of the Affections, that set of *topoi* that supposedly codified musical gestures and their corresponding emotive responses in the listener. From the nuts and bolts of composition, to the science of vocal pedagogy, to the proper temperament for earning a choir's respect, and the politics of producing a concert, Mattheson reveals a nimble mind intent on teaching his readers how to communicate effectively in every aspect of music making, and an intelligence steeped in a soon-to-be-displaced rhetorical education.

BONDS's analytical study is concerned with the relation between rhetoric and the movement-length instrumental forms of the late 18th and early 19th centuries. Bonds is particularly interested in what he identifies as the paradox of form. One current usage of the term treats form as an abstract convention, or a pattern shared with other works; another defines form as a generative process, or a pattern unique to each composition. Bonds argues that formal ordering, for composers of the 18th century, was not simply a matter of obeying abstract generic patterns or harmonic plans, so much as it was a function of the listener. Like the orator, the composer sought to communicate to the listener through an ordered succession of thoughts. Bonds's rhetorical approach to this paradox understands form as both a process and a plan, or as a process that can be made more intelligible through the application of certain conventional plans. Despite the lack of a sustained application of rhetorical concepts to music in late 18th-century thought, Bonds succeeds in showing that a rhetorical understanding of form was nonetheless pervasive as he identifies overlapping ways in which 18th-century writers approached the topics of rhetoric, music, and form. In Bonds's telling, rhetoric—whose metaphor of oration suffered a sea change to the metaphor of organism—continued to exert a considerable influence on accounts of form until well into the 19th century. In a concluding chapter, Bonds suggests how the 18th century's rhetorical concepts of form provide the historical foundation for current approaches to form that are similarly listener-oriented.

WEBSTER approaches the Farewell Symphony from a number of different analytical angles in order to illuminate the through-compositional nature of that work and others by Haydn. In the fifth chapter in particular, Webster explains certain gestural aspects (unstable openings, weak structural cadences, compromised closures) as typical elements that Haydn uses to maintain momentum within a movement or to relate separate movements. Hence, similar to Bond, Webster sees Haydn's through-compositional approach to form as essentially rhetorical: form as serving the function of communication and persuasion. This working out of a musical idea, in Haydn's case in general and in the Farewell in particular, leads to the cyclic integration of the work and the consequent blurring of formal boundaries. For Webster, the rhetorical aspects of Haydn's Farewell Symphony lie not only in its extramusical aspects but in its functioning "within a context of genre, *Affekt,* and 'topoi.'"

A learned study of the declamatory and rhetorical aspects of musical settings of poetry in the Italian Renaissance, HAAR's text presumes of its readers a working knowledge of the Italian language and the aesthetic battles of trecento and quattrocento Italy. Though not limited to a discussion of the madrigal, Haar concentrates on the historical context of this genre as well as on the effect of the improvisatory tradition and the Counter-Reformation on its evolution. In spite of the peculiar twists and turns of the Renaissance, Haar successfully pursues an argument, cast in rhetorical terms, about that era's "continuing desire to make a piece of vocal music a genuine meeting of word and tone." Musical examples are lumped together in a lengthy appendix.

Within the rhetorical tradition, BARTH is mainly interested in delivery but also evaluates the use of delivery for articulating musical structure. Specifically, Barth explores the shift from classical keyboard style to Beethoven's uniquely dramatic rhetoric. The author does not try to summarize neatly what the declamatory, or "choppy" (the romantics' pejorative term), style was, or what exactly it became in Beethoven's hands, so much as he usefully points to the interrelated factors that impinged on the transformation of that style: Beethoven's interest in legato, his phrasings that violated the bar line, and his familiarity with the rhetorical traditions of Mattheson and others. Barth queries Beethoven's problematic relationship to the newly popularized metronome in some depth, arguing that the rise of the metronomic tradition eclipsed that more familiar rhetorical tradition: thus,

accents, for example, that were measured prosodically came to be measured in this new style only in terms of dynamic stress. Barth's discussions serve as the framework for the analyses of tempo, gesture, and articulation in two Beethoven works. While Barth's prose is generally clear, the direction of his argument can sometimes be difficult to decipher.

Although JOHNSON's book is not peppered with rhetorical terminology, his project—in its overarching thesis and varied details—is profoundly rhetorical. A work of impressive scholarship, it explores how and why Parisian audiences evolved from the raucous, heterogeneous mobs of the reign of Lully into the quietly respectful bourgeoisie of the romantic era. Johnson draws on a wide array of historical artifacts—letters to the editor, diaries, correspondence, musical scores, eyewitness accounts, architectural plans, and police files—to document his argument. He shows how, in the Old Regime, where music was an adornment of the state, the behavior of Parisian audiences was a map of etiquette codes and hence of the invisible power structure. With the arrival of Gluck (1774), Paris saw the rise of bourgeois *sensibilité,* in which passion and emotion were understood as functions of domestic spaces, outside the scope of political control; the once-orderly division of classes fell apart, and audiences began to pay less attention to etiquette and more to the stage. Finally, Johnson moves to the romantic era, in which the professional critic served as judge of music's significance, further contributing to audience silence by preying on bourgeois fears of inferiority; also, the indeterminately expressive and intensely subjective nature of the "absolute" music of this era presumed a passive listening stance from its audience. Although it is subtitled "A Cultural History," Johnson's text, with its emphasis on the ways in which music reflects the social, historical, and class identities of its listeners, can be understood as a cultural history whose guiding principle is rhetorical.

Given the protean nature of rhetorical analysis, if a cultural history can be rhetorical, then it follows that a more theoretical treatise can be rhetorical as well. AGAWU uses semiotics (a field that studies how signs communicate meaning) to engage differing but related concepts within a philosophically consistent scheme: music and language, and more particularly, expression and structure. Agawu deploys semiotics as a rhetorical theory rather than as a purely epistemological one. Concentrating on the language of Haydn, Mozart, and Beethoven (examining a string quartet movement from each), Agawu employs the rhetorical concept of *topoi* (topic) to give a reading of classical era music as historically and socioculturally specific. Agawu's judicious use of semiotic terminology is well explained and should not deter the serious music student.

JAYME STAYER

Rimsky-Korsakov, Nikolai 1844–1908

Russian composer

Abraham, Gerald, *Rimsky-Korsakov: A Short Biography*, London: Duckworth, 1945; reprint, New York: AMS Press, 1976

Cook, Peter, *The Golden Cockerel: A Realisation in Music*, London: Cook, 1985

Griffiths, Steven, *A Critical Study of the Music of Rimsky-Korsakov, 1844–1890*, New York: Garland, 1989

Iastrebtsev, Vasilii Vasil'evich, *Reminiscences of Rimsky-Korsakov*, edited and translated by Florence Jonas, New York: Columbia University Press, 1985

Montagu-Nathan, Montagu, *Rimsky-Korsakof*, London: Constable, 1916

Rimsky-Korsakov, Nikolai Andreevich, *My Musical Life*, translated from the 5th revised Russian edition by Judah A. Joffe; edited with an introduction by Carl van Vechten, New York: Knopf, 1923; 3rd U.S. edition, 1989

Seaman, Gerald R., *Nikolai Andreevich Rimsky-Korsakov: A Guide to Research*, New York: Garland, 1988

Taylor, Philip, *Gogolian Interludes: Gogol's Story "Christmas Eve" as the Subject of Operas by Tchaikovsky and Rimsky-Korsakov*, London: Collet's, 1984

Despite the importance of Rimsky-Korsakov in the history of Russian music as both composer and educator, his long popularity in orchestral concerts and recent growing interest in his operas in the West, and the early interest in Russian music by British authors, who long dominated English-language publications in the area, there are relatively few monograph-length studies in English for either the general audience or the music specialist on his life and work outside of unpublished dissertations. There is not even a full-length third-person study of the composer in English comparable to those on Balakirev, Borodin, Musorgsky, and Tchaikovsky—none of whom, admittedly, left a document comparable to Rimsky-Korsakov's autobiography. Thus, the reader must consult brief accounts, biographies of others (especially the "Mighty Five"), histories of Russian music, and scattered articles on topics from Rimsky-Korsakov's teaching technique to his naval visit to the United States in the 1860s in order to find much on the composer in English. In lieu of an original, English-language study of the composer's life, work, and legacy, one hopes that the five-volume biography by the composer's musicologist son Andrei, entitled *N.A. Rimskii-Korsakov: zhizn' i tvorchestvo* (1933–46; Life and Work), and A.A. Orlova and V.A. Rimsky-Korsakov's four-volume *Stranitsy zhizni N.A. Rimskogo-Korsakova: letopis' zhizni i tvorchestva.* (1969–73; Pages from Rimsky-Korsakov's Life: Chronicle of Life and Work) might be made available in English in the near future, as well as the complete Iastrebtsev reminiscences and the several volumes of letters published already in Russian.

RIMSKY-KORSAKOV's posthumously published autobiography constitutes the single most important document available on the composer, not only as a personal account but also as a fascinating glimpse into Russian musical life from the 1860s to 1906. That said, the memoirs have some inaccuracies, are "badly written," according to van Vechten, and give "no exhaustive conception of their author's living personality," according to the composer's son. The English edition includes Andrei Rimsky-Korsakov's annotations and added chronicle of the last months (September 1906–June 1908), as well as additional material by the editor and translator.

IASTREBTSEV, Rimsky-Korsakov's Boswell, kept a running diary—with conversations—of his idolizing acquaintance with the composer from 1886 to the composer's death. These reminiscences, entitled *Nikolai Andreevich Rimskii-Korsakov. Vospominaniia V.V. Iastrebtseva*, were not published in full until 1959–60. The translation, intended for both the general reader and the scholar, is heavily abridged and seeks "to be faithful to the author while at the same time enriching his style" and omitting passages "of negligible interest." Russian vocal texts in musical excerpts are left untranslated.

MONTAGU-NATHAN's slim biography, quite dated now (e.g., Rimsky-Korsakov is referred to as "the Petrograd composer"; English titles of some works have a different form today) was produced before an English translation of the composer's autobiography was published. The biography proper is followed by an interesting discussion of the operas, comments on the instrumental music and the other vocal music, and plot summaries for all 15 operas.

Both Montagu-Nathan's volume and ABRAHAM's account of the composer, as old as it is and likewise based on the composer's memoirs, were published before certain material was available, such as the vast corpus of letters and the complete Iastrebtsev. (Compare Abraham's more recent biographical sketch, with work list, in *New Grove Russian Masters 2* [1986].) For Abraham, as for Montagu-Nathan and others, the operas stand as Rimsky-Korsakov's primary achievements, juxtaposing lyrical realism with artificial fantasy in brilliantly scored music, albeit virtually devoid of emotional or psychological depth. The interested reader should consult Abraham's more original writings on Rimsky-Korsakov, that is, the many articles concerning the composer's works (mostly operas) included in the collections *Studies in Russian Music* (1935), *On Russian Music* (1939), *Slavonic and Romantic Music: Essays and Studies* (1969), and *Essays on Russian and East European Music* (1985).

In contrast to Abraham's biography and miscellaneous essays, a more sustained attempt at examining Rimsky-Korsakov's works in detail, albeit closing with 1890, is GRIFFITHS's published dissertation, which divides the music roughly chronologically into several periods, each culminating in an opera. The copious musical excerpts are all printed separately from the detailed verbal analysis in the text, making the discussion difficult to follow, even for a specialist. Whereas musical analysis and comparison is expressly emphasized here above biography, one wonders for what reason—other than, possibly, availability—many Russian-language studies of Rimsky-Korsakov's works seem not to have been considered, as they are absent from the bibliographic citations.

The pair of books devoted to specific works appropriately consider Rimsky-Korsakov's most important works, the operas. COOK, in his tome on the composer's last opera, which has had the strongest staying power in the West, analyzes the various literary sources for Belsky's cohesive libretto in order to explain "most of the mystery and puzzlement about the meaning of the work" and recounts the opera's troubled early life. The libretto is included in transliteration and translation with some musical excerpts.

TAYLOR's study of the operas of the "objective" Rimsky-Korsakov and the "subjective" Tchaikovsky that derive from the same source seeks to expose the fundamental differences between the two composers. Besides containing original articles, it acts as a rich compendium with transliterations (unversified) and translations of the librettos, musical excerpts, and numerous translated supplementary documents, including Gogol's story and contemporaneous critical reviews.

SEAMAN's bibliography of over 1,300 sources and studies on the composer in major European languages, though now a decade out of date and by the compiler's admission necessarily incomplete, remains nevertheless quite indispensable as the only volume of its type in English. Its copious annotations allow for an excellent overview of the research (including dissertations) that has been done, especially as the vast majority of the items cited are in Russian. Seaman, like others, stresses the prime importance of the operatic output but also points out Rimsky-Korsakov's significance as a liturgical composer, propagandist of Russian music, communicator of ideas, and teacher.

LYLE K. NEFF

Rock and Roll: 1950s United States

Aquila, Richard, *That Old Time Rock and Roll: A Chronicle of an Era, 1954–1963,* New York: Schirmer; London: Collier Macmillan, 1989

Belz, Carl, *The Story of Rock,* New York: Oxford University Press, 1969; 2nd edition, 1972

Friedlander, Paul, *Rock and Roll: A Social History,* Boulder, Colorado: Westview Press, 1996

Gass, Glenn, *A History of Rock Music: The Rock and Roll Era,* New York: McGraw-Hill, 1994

Gillett, Charlie, *The Sound of the City: The Rise of Rock and Roll,* New York: Outerbridge and Dienstfrey, 1970; London: Souvenir Press, 1971; revised edition, 1983

Rubin, Nathan, *Rock and Roll: Art and Anti-Art,* Dubuque, Iowa: Kendall/Hunt, 1993

Stuessy, Joe, *Rock and Roll: Its History and Stylistic Development,* Englewood Cliffs, New Jersey: Prentice Hall, 1990; 3rd edition, 1999

The most useful treatments of early rock are found not in monographs but in rock magazines of the era. Monographs on rock and roll usually include a discussion of rock in the 1950s as part of a larger survey of rock in general and therefore have little detailed information about this particular era. The best of these sources typically have a single agenda or focus that sets them apart from other studies.

Most monograph sources on rock are relatively recent, but BELZ attempted to write about rock while the music was still in its infancy. Without the perspective of several decades, Belz's account has both advantages and disadvantages in comparison with more recent studies. He mentions several styles of music that influenced early rock (e.g., skiffle and calypso) that since have been forgotten. However, he cannot see a larger time line of development. For example, his attempts to sum up Elvis Presley's career while Presley was still making movies certainly do not give us a full picture of Presley. In his introduction, Belz emphasizes music, not sociology. Nevertheless, he spends a significant amount of time establishing that rock is essentially a folk music, a position hardly considered in later sources.

Although written in 1970, GILLETT's description of early rock and roll remains one of the most significant. His concern is the industry of rock, focusing specifically on the actions of the major and independent labels. His overview of the labels is exhaustive, as is his examination of musical styles and performers that influenced early rock. Gillett also discusses cover records (in which African-American performers cut a record for an independent label, and then a major label hired white performers to make a "cover" version so the song could be safely marketed to a white audience), but he is more interested in the role of the record companies and performers in producing the covers than in the covers themselves. Despite its age, Gillett's landmark research is still fresh and valuable.

AQUILA's survey is presented in three parts: a historical account of the rise of rock; a discussion of themes, topics, and hit records; and a survey of performers listed in alphabetical order. One of the most interesting aspects of Aquila's historical approach is the attention he gives to the relationship between the baby-boom generation and the rise of rock, for he links the boomers' demands for new musical styles with major historical events, noting for example Americans' disenchantment with syrupy pop after the assassination of President Kennedy. Aquila also spends a significant amount of time discussing those who worked behind the scenes to further the rise of rock, such as Alan Freed and Dick Clark.

FRIEDLANDER's book is intended for the musically uninitiated. The first chapter describes terminology to be used in the following chapters and describes useful ways to think about and listen to the music. Because of the intended pedagogical focus, the tone is sometimes pedantic, but the background Friedlander provides about the beginnings of rock and roll is useful. His three chapters on rock and roll of the 1950s are divided into an examination of first-generation (Buddy Holly and Chuck Berry) and second-generation (Presley) rockers and the doo-wop groups of the late 1950s.

STUESSY's book is also intended for the musical amateur; the introduction acquaints the reader with basic musical terminology and music theory. Stuessy identifies three main trends in 1950s rock (mainstream rock, rockabilly, and soft rock) and gives musical examples by representative performers for each trend. Each chapter also includes a "musical close-up" in which Stuessy introduces the reader to a dilemma of the music industry or a musical point of interest. These close-ups also offer him an opportunity to analyze specific pieces in more depth. Because this source is meant to introduce the reader to rock, the language is accessible, but the content is survey-like and lacks depth.

GASS limits himself to only the 1950s (what he terms the "rock and roll era"), and his study is therefore by far the most detailed, including discussions of performers and styles not mentioned in most of the other available sources. Although he is concerned with the historical background of this era, his study is most valuable for its musical insights. Gass describes the music from a sociological point of view but also in theoretical terms, providing a concrete description of several landmark recordings.

RUBIN's study is primarily a historical account of rock and roll. He begins by outlining the charges against rock and roll made by angry parents and teachers at rock's inception and then defends the music against these charges by comparing aspects of rock to similar ideas found in avant-garde art music. His consistent comparison between rock and art music is the most significant aspect of his book. Rubin does not attempt to validate rock by endowing it with the respectability of art music; rather, his comparisons are intended to show the similarity of musical impulses between the two. His language is somewhat technical at times, but a glossary is provided.

FELICIA M. MIYAKAWA

Rock and Roll: 1960s United States

Christgau, Robert, *Any Old Way You Choose It: Rock and Other Pop Music, 1967–1973*, Baltimore, Maryland: Penguin Books, 1973

Eisen, Jonathan, editor, *The Age of Rock: Sounds of the American Cultural Revolution: A Reader*, New York: Random House, 1969

Ennis, Philip H., *The Seventh Stream: The Emergence of Rocknroll in American Popular Music*, Middletown, Connecticut: Wesleyan University Press, and Hanover, New Hampshire: University Press of New England, 1992

Marcus, Greil, *Invisible Republic: Bob Dylan's Basement Tapes*, New York: Holt, and London: Picador, 1997

———, *Mystery Train: Images of America in Rock 'n' Roll Music*, New York: Dutton, 1975; 4th revised edition, New York: Plume, 1997

Pichaske, David, *A Generation in Motion: Popular Music and Culture in the Sixties*, New York: Schirmer Books, 1979

Santelli, Robert, *Sixties Rock: A Listener's Guide*, Chicago: Contemporary Books, 1985

It is perhaps axiomatic that rock achieved sentience in the 1960s as an enterprise essentially different from pop music. Scholars and critics therefore greet the music of this decade with a well-warranted enthusiasm. Many great songs remained to be written, of course, but the sense of musical adventure that drove the artists of the 1960s was in many ways unique to that time.

For an overview of this period, and for its wise and graceful prose, ENNIS is unrivaled in the literature of popular music. The Harvard-trained sociologist chronicles the stream of rocknroll that grew from a trickle to a torrent in the decades following World War II. In the chapter entitled "Continuum," he wryly observes,

> Such formerly despised arts as the cartoon, the comic book, graffiti, the circus, and commercial advertising, not to speak of rock, have refreshed and enlivened the other arts. It has been a long trek from 1959 when ASCAP's highbrow composers told the Congress that rocknroll had to be fumigated from the ranks of American music.

Ennis follows that trek through the 1960s in rigorous detail. Throughout the study, he weaves passion into the facts and provides a perspective on popular music that we come to realize is the result of an enviable and unassailable faith in rock and roll.

Equally full of musical faith, the idiosyncratic but effective cultural critic and scholar, Greil Marcus must be consulted in any investigation of rock music in the United States. Fortunately, he writes extensively on the 1960s. MARCUS (1975) is an epochal piece of rock and social criticism that features sprawling ruminations on The Band, Sly Stone, Randy Newman, and Elvis Presley. MARCUS (1997) revisits these considerations of the 1960s via a little-known set of basement tapes Bob Dylan recorded in 1967 with The Band. In the earlier book, Marcus observes of mid-20th-century writers of U.S. history, and of himself as well, that they were all "exhilarated . . . by something we can only call patriotism, and humbled by it too." It is a tribute to Marcus's abilities that his revolutionary zeal in uncovering the nation's foibles is constantly refracted through his love for his scarred but never beaten subject, the United States itself: Marcus (1975) is "an attempt to broaden the context in which music is heard; to deal with rock 'n' roll not as youth culture, or counterculture, but simply as American culture."

Whereas faith in music generally animates Ennis's and Marcus's work, faith in the 1960s revolutionary spirit animates PICHASKE, and this decade is in some ways particularly suited to his insider's perspective. His detail is convincingly immediate if his drama is somewhat predictable; to the extent that the 1960s represent an identifiable worldview, he captures what it sounds like in prose.

EISEN ventures directly into the purview of contemporaneous writers, offering a wide selection of music and social criticism by the likes of Ned Rorem, Jon Landau, Robert Christgau, Richard Meltzer, Tom Wolfe, and Joan Didion, among many others. In the introduction to the collection, Eisen remarks of the 1960s, "Now we seem to be back in the days of Chaucer—in a more verbal era when poetry and music are back in the hands of the people." The range of writers represented here reflects the fact that criticism had likewise undergone this democratic revolution.

Although CHRISTGAU deals chiefly with the late 1960s and its fallout in the early 1970s, he is a preeminent rock critic with a good deal to say about music, culture, and criticism. In his almost painfully self-conscious introduction, "A Counter in Search of a Culture," he avers, "But I did come to understand that popular art was not inferior to high art, and decided that popular art achieved a vitality of both integrity and outreach that high art had unfortunately abandoned." In relation to music, Christgau validates this claim on every page of this collection of his essays.

As with any listener's guide, SANTELLI is necessarily subjective; regardless of whether one agrees with his sentiments, however, he covers an enormous amount of music and complements the above scholarship and criticism with a sourcebook for the music itself. (He does not confine himself to U.S. releases.) Note, too, that various chronological series of record guides, which usually commit one of their issues to the 1960s, are still being produced with abandon, reflecting the collectors' ongoing penchant for doting upon their collecting.

NILS NADEAU

Rock and Roll: 1960s England

Bradley, Dick, *Understanding Rock 'n' Roll: Popular Music in Britain 1955–1964,* Milton Keynes: Open University Press, 1992

Brunning, Bob, *Blues: The British Connection,* Poole: Blandford Press, 1986

Davies, Hunter, *The Beatles,* New York: McGraw-Hill, 1978

Davies, Ray, *X-Ray,* London: Viking Press, 1994; Woodstock, New York: Overlook Press, 1995

DeCurtis, Anthony, and James Henke, editors, *The Rolling Stone Illustrated History of Rock and Roll,* New York: Random House, 1992

Gillett, Charlie, *The Sound of the City: The Rise of Rock and Roll,* New York: Outerbridge and Dienstfrey, 1970; London: Souvenir Press, 1971; revised edition, 1983

Giuliano, Geoffrey, *Behind Blue Eyes: The Life of Pete Townshend,* New York: Dutton, and London: Hodder and Stoughton, 1996

Hertsgaard, Mark, *A Day in the Life: The Music and Artistry of the Beatles,* London: Macmillan, and New York: Delacorte Press, 1995

Moore, Allan F., *The Beatles: Sgt. Pepper's Lonely Hearts Club Band,* Cambridge: Cambridge University Press, 1997

Norman, Philip, *The Stones,* London: Elm Tree, 1984

Schaffner, Nicholas, *The British Invasion: From the First Wave to the New Wave,* New York: McGraw-Hill, 1982

Wyman, Bill, and Ray Coleman, *Bill Wyman, Stone Alone: The Story of a Rock 'n' Roll Band,* London: Viking Press, 1990

The musical roots of 1960s English rock and roll lie in three popular musical phenomena of the mid- to late 1950s: American rock and roll, skiffle (rhythm and blues mixed with American folk song played by amateurs on homemade instruments), and trad (British Dixieland, a tame recreation of New Orleans jazz). The main social force behind English rock was the underground British youth culture. Working-class postwar baby boomers faced with economic depression formed rival gangs: the greased-up, leather-wearing rockers—an update of the 1950s teddy boys—and the pilled-up, fashion-conscious mods. The rockers remained loyal to American rock and roll of the 1950s; the mods favored new English rock.

Out of the skiffle craze and the rocker scene came the beat groups, the most famous of which is the Beatles. Modeling their sound on American rock-and-roll artists, the Beatles, like many other beat groups, began their career playing skiffle and covering American rhythm-and-blues and rock-and-roll hits in Liverpool clubs. Between 1962 and 1965, such beat groups as the Beatles, Gerry and the Pacemakers, and the Dave Clark Five topped the British charts.

While the rocker identity was closely tied to music, the mod movement was defined mostly by fashion. But when The Who, originally a rhythm-and-blues cover group, consciously adopted a mod image and began playing their own less blue-oriented compositions, the mods secured a musical identity as well. The lyric of the band's 1966 hit "My Generation" captured both the rebelliousness and image-consciousness of the mod movement, and the song became a mod anthem. The group's stage violence, volume, and ear-splitting feedback reflected the mods' anger and violent tendencies. The Who became mod heroes.

The Rolling Stones were neither rockers nor mods; their music is more a product of their musical models and tastes than of any particular social force. Many covers of American rhythm-and-blues songs appear on their early (1963–64) albums, but it was their hard-rocking originals (1965 and after) that were most commercially successful. This harder sound fit their raunchy, offensive image. The Rolling Stones became symbols of rebellion for English and eventually American youth.

DeCURTIS and HENKE include essays on most of the English groups mentioned above as well as on the British invasion and the blues revival. Each essay is written by a different popular music critic and includes as much opinion as historical fact. In addition to judgments of aesthetic and musical quality, each author considers the impact of commercial success or failure on the overall historical significance of an artist. Each essay concludes with a selective discography of albums and singles, indicating the original label, release date, and highest place on the *Billboard* charts.

In his single-volume history of rock and roll, GILLETT devotes two chapters to British rock in the 1960s. In "Transatlantic Echoes," Gillett explains that because England had neither specialist radio stations nor innovative record producers, live performance was the primary means of communication between rock performers and their audiences. After discussing the British fascination with African-American music, particularly jazz and blues, Gillett suggests that British pop (the Beatles), British rhythm and blues (the Rolling Stones, the Animals), and British rock (The Who, the Kinks) as distinct musical phenomena with a common influence— American rhythm and blues. In "Electric White Orchestras: British Rock Progresses," Gillett proposes three musical idioms as sources for post–British invasion rock: the blues for Cream, the Jeff Beck group, Led Zeppelin, and Fleetwood Mac; gospel for Traffic, Procol Harum, and Joe Cocker; and folk, at least in part, for Pink Floyd and David Bowie.

BRUNNING, a founding member of Fleetwood Mac, offers little discussion of music-stylistic features of British blues, but he provides historical facts, biographical details, and colorful anecdotes about nearly 30 blues bands. The many quotations from new interviews as well as more than 50 black-and-white photographs, a few of which depict the author with different bands, attest to Brunning's personal involvement with his subject. SCHAFFNER is also a testament to a deep personal involvement with British rock, but in this case from the perspective of a loyal American fan. A virtual encyclopedia of British bands, this book on the British invasion claims to be "the most extensive collection of Anglo-rock

photographs and lore ever published." Comprehensive histories of the Beatles, the Rolling Stones, the Kinks, The Who, Pink Floyd, T. Rex, and David Bowie complement shorter but detailed histories of 100 British artists written by different authors and critics. Each entry includes a list of U.S. hit singles, U.S. hit LPs, and U.K. hit singles.

Rather than focusing on particular bands and music-stylistic developments, BRADLEY considers British rock and roll as cultural practice. He argues that for the British youth culture of the late 1950s and early 1960s, American rock and roll defined a communal phenomenon that functioned as a central part of rituals of resistance. Bradley suggests that British youths played skiffle, British rhythm and blues, and beat music to reproduce the communality and resistance they found in American music, thereby solidifying, intensifying, and spreading their own youth culture. In its methodology and political ideology, Bradley's book is a clear product of Birmingham University's Centre for Contemporary Cultural Studies.

Based on interviews and information gathered during 18 months spent with the Beatles during 1966 and 1967, Hunter DAVIES offers a deeply personal and richly detailed biography of the Beatles from their respective childhoods through 1968. The introduction acknowledges the few changes Davies made to the manuscript at the request of various people—from George Harrison to John Lennon's aunt Mimi. The postscript considers reasons for the Beatles' split. Although Davies believes that Yoko Ono's presence in Lennon's life was the primary cause, he traces back to 1966 key events that contributed to the band's break-up.

HERTSGAARD's book concentrates on the Beatles' music more than the band's biography and discusses in varying degrees of detail the composition, recording process, and significant musical features of nearly every Beatles song. Particularly valuable are the extensive notes, in which Hertsgaard meticulously acknowledges his numerous sources. MOORE provides an intensive musical analysis of a single Beatles album, *Sgt. Pepper's Lonely Hearts Club Band*, framed by discussions of the album's inception and reception.

WYMAN's autobiography is also a history of the Rolling Stones. He acknowledges American electric blues artists Muddy Waters, Howlin' Wolf, and John Lee Hooker, along with rock-and-rollers Chuck Berry and Bo Diddley, as the Rolling Stones' first sources of inspiration. Wyman also sheds light on the friendly relationship between the Stones and the Beatles. Explaining that as early as 1963 the British press was looking to pit the good and clean Beatles against the bad and dirty Stones, Wyman insists that Andrew Oldham, manager of the Stones, did not construct the band's bad boy image. Rather, he claims, "that came later, completely accidentally . . . Andrew simply exploited it exhaustively." After relating the drug addictions and tensions among band members, Wyman concludes his story of the Rolling Stones with the death of guitarist Brian Jones.

NORMAN covers the same territory as Wyman, but Norman exposes the epoch (the 1960s) as much as the band. Based on countless interviews and access to the Rolling Stones during their 1981–82 concert tour, Norman's chronicle is told in a most entertaining way—full of compelling vignettes and character studies that often reveal the darker side of both the people and the times.

Part chronicle and part psychoanalysis, GIULIANO's biography of Pete Townshend is a fascinating and sympathetic portrait of The Who's lead guitarist and dominant creative force. Exploring everything from childhood anxieties and teenage violence to politics, drug addiction, spirituality, and bisexuality, Giuliano reveals Townshend as a tremendously complex and contradictory character.

Ray DAVIES's autobiography, cleverly fashioned as a biography of the Kinks' lead singer, is likewise a reflection on the age. Although at times it is difficult to sort out fact from fiction, Davies tells a thrilling tale of both the highs and the horrors of life as a rock star—with special guest appearances by the Beatles, the Rolling Stones, The Who, and other rock icons from the 1960s.

MELANIE LOWE

Rock and Roll: 1970s United States

Curtis, James M., *Rock Eras: Interpretations of Music and Society, 1954–1984,* Bowling Green, Ohio: Bowling Green State University Popular Press, 1987
Henry, Tricia, *Break All Rules! Punk Rock and the Making of a Style,* Ann Arbor, Michigan: UMI Research Press, 1989
Martin, Linda, and Kerry Segrave, *Anti-Rock: The Opposition to Rock 'n' Roll,* Hamden, Connecticut: Archon, 1988
Rubin, Nathan, *Rock and Roll: Art and Anti-Art,* Dubuque, Iowa: Kendall/Hunt, 1993
Stuessy, Joe, *Rock and Roll: Its History and Stylistic Development,* Englewood Cliffs, New Jersey: Prentice Hall, 1990; 3rd edition, 1999
Weinstein, Deena, *Heavy Metal: A Cultural Sociology,* New York: Lexington, and Toronto: Maxwell Macmillan Canada, 1991

Very few sources treat exclusively rock music of the 1970s. Most useful information on the subject is found either in surveys of rock music in general, in which typically a few chapters will be devoted to the 1970s, or in genre-specific studies, such as monographs on punk, disco, and heavy metal. Few authors limit their discussions to either British rock or American rock; in fact, most sources spend a significant amount of time establishing connections between British heavy metal and its American counterpart or comparing the British punk movement with its American cous-

in. Existing material on rock music tends to fall into three categories: documentary studies, which list and categorize hits or do little more than highlight important dates in rock and roll history; sociological studies of rock; and musical studies of rock. The sources described here fall under the latter two categories.

STUESSY's study, which identifies the 1970s as a decade of fragmentation, reaction, and continuation, is a comprehensive account of the many styles that proliferated in the 1970s. His focus is musical, and for that reason he spends much of his time identifying and categorizing rock genres of the 1970s, such as art rock/progressive rock, punk/new wave, heavy metal, disco, country rock, glitter rock, jazz rock, glam rock, soft rock, and black rock. However, Stuessy is also interested in the relationship between society and music. He points out that because the record industry was so fragmented in the 1970s, no single performer or group could again capture the attention of the public as had Elvis Presley and the Beatles in the 1950s and 1960s, respectively. Stuessy's study is intended for the musical amateur (and as such he includes an explanation of basic terms and music theory in the introduction) and is a useful survey of this complicated decade.

CURTIS's focus is more sociological than Stuessy's. He, too, identifies a plurality of styles in the 1970s but focuses on single artists or groups as representative of each style. Each chapter is therefore a self-contained study of a particular issue or performer; the book is not an attempt at a cohesive narrative history. Rather than discussing specific musical examples, Curtis links musical trends and styles with historical or sociological developments. He presents disco, for example, as the antidote to the Watergate scandal for a confused and disenchanted nation.

MARTIN and SEGRAVE also take a sociological approach. They focus on the often strong reactions against the newly emerging musical styles of the 1970s. By extension, they also discuss how the musicians in individual cases address their detractors through their art. Martin and Segrave limit their discussion to disco, metal, and punk, the three most controversial genres of the decade.

RUBIN is a musical study, but the author's approach is unique in that he consistently compares movements in rock with movements in art music. Especially interesting is his chapter on art rock, in which he attempts to identify which musical elements are necessary to qualify rock as art rock. Central to the concept of art rock is emulation of the classical tradition, but as Rubin points out this emulation can take several forms, such as style, borrowing, or instrumentation. He compares art rock with a similar movement in 20th-century art music, that of neoclassicism, but also suggests that, in borrowing from the Western art tradition, rock music loses some of its fundamental rebelliousness. His discussion of heavy metal begins with a brief review of Schoenberg's turn to atonality, contending that one must consistently move further away from tradition to shock an audience. Rubin also provides interesting links between the avant-garde of art music, as represented by John Cage, and the avant-garde of rock, as represented by the Velvet Underground.

Weinstein and Henry fall into the second category of sources in this bibliography: monographs that focus on a specific genre. Like Curtis's and Martin and Segrave's studies, WEINSTEIN's book is sociological. She locates heavy metal within a sociological framework and identifies the many codes (e.g., fashion, posturing, volume, and spectacle) within which heavy metal operates. She not only discusses the relationship between the music and the audience but also describes how metal events, such as concert venues, contribute to the entire metal environment. She provides extensive historical background to the heavy metal genre, locating it securely within the rock tradition, and also explains her terminology in the first chapter.

HENRY's study of punk is thorough and scholarly. She begins with the New York scene of the late 1960s and early 1970s with Lou Reed, the Velvet Underground, and Andy Warhol's *Exploding Plastic Inevitable*. Instead of offering a narrative about the history of the genre, she incorporates primary sources from the musicians and journalists of the 1970s for a more detailed look at the issues involved in the punk movement. Most of her study is limited to the American punk scene, although a single chapter on the Sex Pistols allows her to draw connections between the New York and London versions of this genre. She includes transcriptions of four punk "standards."

FELICIA M. MIYAKAWA

Rock and Roll: 1970s England

Covach, John R., and Graeme M. Boone, editors, *Understanding Rock: Essays in Musical Analysis,* New York: Oxford University Press, 1997

Curtis, James M., *Rock Eras: Interpretations of Music and Society, 1954–1984,* Bowling Green, Ohio: Bowling Green State University Popular Press, 1987

Hebdige, Dick, *Subculture: The Meaning of Style,* London: Methuen, 1979

Macan, Edward, *Rocking the Classics: English Progressive Rock and the Counterculture,* New York: Oxford University Press, 1996

Moore, Allan F., *Rock: The Primary Text: Developing a Musicology of Rock,* Buckingham: Open University Press, 1993

Stump, Paul, *The Music's All that Matters: A History of Progressive Rock,* London: Quartet Books, 1997

The study of an era still fresh in the collective memory is often hindered by a lack of critical distance. Over 20 years separate the publication of most of the scholarly studies of British 1970s rock and the release of the recordings the authors consider. Consequently, readers will find perspectives in these studies that are quite different from those of most contemporaneous commentaries. Although cultural studies of rock and roll have been available almost since Chuck Berry released his first recordings, recent, if reluctant, academic acceptance of popular music research has created an atmosphere conducive to the musicological study of rock, and three types of academic literature are available to the reader: cultural analysis, musical analysis, or a combination of these. Usually bypassing the most popular artists, such as Elton John, Peter Frampton, or Rod Stewart, scholarly publications on 1970s English rock have been concerned with either punk or what has come to be called progressive rock and the subcultures associated with each of these genres. Conventional wisdom has held that the appearance of punk was the meteor that caused the extinction of the progressive-rock dinosaur, but numerous observers suggest that these were most likely unrelated developments.

Using the works of writer Jean Genet as a model for the construction of style as subculture, HEBDIGE's book on the symbolic meaning of punk-rock style requires no education in music on the part of the reader. Defining subculture as "the expressive forms and rituals of those subordinate groups . . . who are alternately dismissed, denounced and canonized," the author combines semiotics, the sociology of deviance, Marxism, and structuralism to uncover the meanings behind the fashionable exteriors of Mod, skinhead, punk, and other British subcultures. Hebdige describes the subcultures precipitating punk style as "mediated responses to the presence in Britain of a sizeable black community." A comparison between this conclusion and Stump's assessment of the apparent rejection of black immigrant culture and its music by preprogressives a decade earlier should inform any discussion of the differences between British rock of the late 1960s and the late 1970s. Having appropriated elements of black immigrant styles to create a visual, behavioral shibboleth, punks adopted the language of crisis that permeated the media, creating a rhetoric that contrasted with that of the prevailing rock establishment, particularly glam rock. Hebdige acknowledges his debt to Roland Barthes, who especially influences Hebdige's consideration of the conscious construction and degrees of fabrication of subcultural style.

Although CURTIS's main concern is neither the 1970s nor British rock, he encapsulates and contextualizes events and trends that set the stage for the creation and reception of British rock of the 1970s. He notes the admixture of popular culture and high culture in British society during the 1960s, which was partly attributable to the existence of art schools in Britain. The cultural background of audiences educated in this social context made them receptive to The Who's *Tommy*—a synthesis of high and popular culture—and these same audiences would respond favorably to the musical experiments in rock of the late 1960s and early 1970s. Describing the 1970s as "the most complicated decade in the history of popular music," Curtis stresses the growing importance of the recording studio, as well as the diversity of styles that characterized the decade. When he discusses briefly what he calls art rock (labeled progressive by Macan and Stump), Curtis disappoints and finds only the standard, superficial connection between British progressive rock and high culture—arrangements of classical works by rock bands. More perceptively, Curtis contrasts American and British punk, noting that, unlike its U.S. predecessor, punk emanating from London was full of passion and lacked irony. He closes his comments on punk by devoting several pages to The Clash, calling them "one of the great bands of the seventies." In a revealing statement, he asserts that, while The Clash began as a punk band, as evinced by their first album, they soon "transcended their milieu" and produced fine albums with songs in diverse styles.

For the serious student of rock style, MOORE is essential. His ambitious book opens with a discussion of methods thus far employed in the study of rock. Citing Simon Frith as a prime example, Moore declares, "The problem is that a commentary that does not have a sound theoretical underpinning is liable to be of uncertain quality at best." While conceding that a musical text is produced by musicians working in social contexts, Moore insists that any attempt to answer an aesthetic question about that text "has to begin from the sounds, because *until we cognize the sounds . . . we have no musical entity to care about,* or to which to give value." Thus, the music itself, in the form of recorded sound, constitutes the primary text and should be given primary consideration in the study of musical style. Moore selects recordings from 1963 to 1967 as models that show how elements of music interact in rock, thereby establishing the analytical method and criteria he applies to 1970s British rock. Detailed analyses and a wide frame of reference contribute to a compelling presentation of how particular bands tested the limits of the received rock style. Although Moore calls these bands progressive, he insists that the term "encompasses distinctive, contemporaneous styles." Asserting that "[p]unk was a short-lived movement whose historical importance may prove to be very limited," Moore contends that punk's most notable feature was its experimentalism, not its antielitism. Moore's work is musicologically sophisticated, and training in music theory, or at least the ability to read music, is necessary to appreciate his intellectual rigor and analytical insight.

MACAN, like Stump, seems to have an ax to grind concerning popular commentary on progressive rock. After exposing the flawed logic of most rock commentators concerning progressive styles, Macan invokes Moore and questions the concept of blues-based authen-

ticity in rock music. A recurring theme in this study concerns the appropriation of elements of European art music by rock composers. Macan asserts that "progressive rock musicians drew on symphonic music and the Anglican/Catholic choral tradition because it was part of their cultural heritage as middle-class Europeans, and it made perfect sense for them to do so." However, a predilection for analyzing rock songs within the framework of sonata form may betray an unconscious, and unnecessary, attempt to legitimize or elevate the pieces by assessing them with methods traditionally applied to European classical music. Although there are no music examples, Macan assumes at least a superficial knowledge of musical terminology and music theory on the part of the reader. His sections on the visual aspects of progressive rock and the utopian, quasi-religious tendencies of the lyrics are thought provoking.

STUMP's study differs from Macan's work on the same subject in two important ways. First, Stump is not a musicologist and makes this fact clear to the reader early in the book. What musical terminology we find in this study is usually quoted from other sources. Second, Stump briefly summarizes the careers and describes the styles of progressive bands who did not achieve supergroup status, especially Henry Cow. By the end of the volume, Stump's assertion that progressive rock was "blasted into outer darkness by punk" remains unconvincing. Such an assertion is difficult to support, for, as Stump himself points out, numerous progressive bands produced successful albums after the appearance (and disappearance) of punk, and new bands who deliberately imitated the style of 1970s British progressive groups appeared in the early 1980s. More telling, however, are Stump's observations that the 1960s idealism on which progressive music fed had dissipated by the late 1970s, and record companies' overheads for punk and new-wave bands were lower than those for progressive bands. He also asserts that progressive's demise was certain in the mid-1970s when utopia fell out of style. Before closing with a survey of progressive rock in the 1990s, Stump devotes a chapter to the careers and styles of four figures associated with 1970s English rock: Robert Fripp, Anthony Phillips, Peter Hammill, and Mike Oldfield.

Of the seven articles in COVACH and BOONE's collection, only one concerns British rock of the 1970s: Covach's "Progressive Rock, 'Close to the Edge,' and the Boundaries of Style." Like Moore, Covach treats the music as the primary text in his essay addressing the internal logic of Yes's immense piece "Close to the Edge." Unlike Moore, he incorporates consideration of portions of the song text, providing conclusions about an entire aesthetic experience. Through analysis, Covach reveals that "Close to the Edge" combines features of Western art music and early 1970s rock at both surface and structural levels. The emphasis on the musical architecture of the work, illuminated by accurate transcriptions, makes the essay one of the best available discussions of a piece of progressive rock, demonstrating what is possibly the most fruitful method of study. Numerous lengthy footnotes give scholars suggestions for further research.

JOHN R. PALMER

Rock and Roll: 1980s United States

Carducci, Joe, *Rock and the Pop Narcotic: Testament for the Electric Church,* Chicago: Redoubt, 1990; 2nd edition, Los Angeles: 2.13.61, 1994

Gaines, Donna, *Teenage Wasteland: Suburbia's Dead End Kids,* New York: Pantheon Books, 1991

Garofalo, Reebee, *Rockin' Out: Popular Music in the USA,* Boston: Allyn and Bacon, 1997

Goodwin, Andrew, *Dancing in the Distraction Factory: Music Television and Popular Culture,* Minneapolis: University of Minnesota Press, 1992

Kaplan, E. Ann, *Rocking around the Clock: Music Television, Postmodernism, and Consumer Culture,* New York: Methuen, 1987; London: Routledge, 1988

Rose, Tricia, *Black Noise: Rap Music and Black Culture in Contemporary America,* Hanover, New Hampshire: University Press of New England, 1994

Schwichtenberg, Cathy, editor, *The Madonna Connection: Representational Politics, Subcultural Identities, and Cultural Theory,* Boulder, Colorado: Westview Press, 1993

Walser, Robert, *Running with The Devil: Power, Gender, and Madness in Heavy Metal Music,* Hanover, New Hampshire: University Press of New England, 1993

The American popular music recording industry limped into the 1980s, having suffered in 1979 a devastating recession—its first ever. In the 1980s, however, various technological developments, superstar performers, and newly popular genres emerged to lift the industry out of its slump. The most dramatic turn in the industry's course occurred in 1981 with the premiere of the 24-hour music video cable channel, Music Television (MTV). At first, the channel featured a significant rotation of largely unknown British "new pop" artists, but by the mid-1980s MTV had become a major catalyst in the mammoth sales of most American rock and pop stars, such as Michael Jackson, Prince, and Madonna. With such high visibility, it is little surprise that the greatest wealth of scholarly literature on popular music from the 1980s is devoted to MTV. In 1985, heavy metal, one of the genres in frequent rotation on MTV, came under attack in a congressional hearing spearheaded by the Parents Music Resource Center (PMRC), an influential group based in Washington, D.C., that wanted to regulate and restrict rock's allegedly violent and sexist imagery. Along with rap, heavy metal seemed to generate endless controversy throughout the 1980s, raising once more the specter of censorship that has always haunted the popular music industry. Because these two genres brought so dramatically to the surface contentious issues of youth, subcultures, race, and "musical value," they have attracted considerable academic attention, and one finds many writings on them. Conversely, there is a noticeable paucity of literature detailing the scores of 1980s punk, noise rock, and underground artists who traveled less visible pathways, releasing records on tiny independent labels and receiving support mostly from college radio stations, club gigs, and small local scenes. Any account of rock and roll in the 1980s must duly recognize these bands, whose collective efforts precipitated the flood of "alternative rock" music that would come to dominate the 1990s American popular recording industry.

Of the many books attempting a grand narrative of rock history, GAROFALO's provides the best overview of the 1980s American music industry. A long-standing member of the International Association for Popular Music Studies (IASPM), Garofalo draws liberally from much of the work published by his colleagues within that organization. Garofalo is especially interested in rock music's political dimensions; this concern bubbles to the surface most forcefully in his lengthy critique (and equally positive appraisal) of the many superstar "mega-events" (e.g., Live Aid and U.S.A. For Africa's "We Are The World") that during the 1980s found rock's corporate sponsorship mixing uneasily with humanistic charity causes. The entire book, including a chapter devoted especially to "youth and censorship" in 1980s heavy metal and rap, is meticulously detailed and thick with footnotes and bibliographic references that open onto dozens of other research avenues.

KAPLAN's pathbreaking book was the first extensive analysis to appear of MTV's videos of the early to mid-1980s. As an academic who is well versed in film studies, Kaplan is quick to recognize the various structures of narrative and address used in videos and how they allude to cinematic history and avant-garde film technique. This approach is both the book's blessing and its curse. To the extent that she can fit the videos into typical narrative "schemas," Kaplan convincingly characterizes some of their dominant tropes. Unfortunately, because her textual critiques privilege visual elements to the almost total exclusion of the videos' audio soundtrack, she fails to link the images with adequate music stylistic readings. In addition, given Kaplan's limited familiarity with the music at hand, the reader encounters descriptions of popular music performers and styles (on "nihilist" videos, "drums often roar, while the electric guitars are made to screech and scream and wail") that are too simplistic or dismissive to be of any real insight.

Much better is GOODWIN's study, which largely abandons Kaplan's restrictive models of cinematic narrative "realism" in favor of a more rounded approach. The author emphasizes that videos are but one integrated part of the music industry's "star machinery" and as such feature images of performers that draw on the conventional iconography of live performance spectacles, magazine spreads, posters, and other components designed to promote artists and sell recordings. As Goodwin points out, where critics such as Kaplan might find certain videos to be examples of disorienting, "postmodern" narrative perspectives, the visuals most often are organized specifically around both the music's rhythms and its stylistic nuances as well as various facets of the performer's persona and ongoing career. Simply put, Goodwin believes that videos should not be read as singular objects; they are always contextualized within the process of consumption and demand. With many examples and a detailed reading of George Michael's "Father Figure" video, Goodwin offers what will likely remain the definitive word on 1980s MTV.

Of all the artists who rose to prominence through MTV, none has garnered more attention among academics than Madonna. The superstar's multiple performative trajectories and subversive identity politics serve as the locus for SCHWICHTENBERG's edited anthology, a collection of generally provocative interdisciplinary essays that examine Madonna in relation to issues of race, audience reception, queer theory, feminist theory, and commodity culture. For all the time spent dissecting Madonna's savvy image and media manipulation, there is distressingly little consideration of her music. Nonetheless, this book is a fair representation of how popular music most often entered into cultural studies at the close of the 1980s.

WALSER's landmark book is a true rarity: an incisive musicological analysis of popular music style that deftly draws on contemporary cultural theory debates. Walser redefines the role of music historian, bringing his own experience as a practicing musician, his interviews with metal fans, and the discourse of metal performers to bear on an explication of heavy metal style. Much of Walser's rhetoric is aimed at disarming misguided attacks on metal from music critics, academics, religious groups, and the much-publicized PMRC. Where metal has been denounced as musically crude, misogynist, and insidiously linked with the occult, Walser reveals the genre's complex relationship with classical music traditions, its foregrounding of gender anxieties, and its manifestations of horror and mythology as reflective of unstable social, economic, and political realities. Walser keeps hidden much of his ethnographic data and reinscribes the very music analytical methodology that he finds wanting, but these are ultimately minor complaints. This brilliant book is essential reading for any student of popular music studies.

GAINES's sociological study gives a face to heavy metal's fans as she paints a compelling portrait of New Jersey "turnpike" teenage subcults. Basing her fieldwork on a community that had recently endured a tragic teenage suicide pact, Gaines presents a sympathetic view of "burnout" youths. She shows how, in a world where they have been discluded and institutionally ousted, music acts for them as important social glue, as their "religion." Gaines communicates her observations in a lively journalistic style that makes this book accessible to readers of virtually any level.

There are many writings on rap music, but none attend to the genre's historical and social context with as much penetrating insight as ROSE's study. Most commentators are content to focus on rap for its extremities of violence or sexism. Rose, however, eschews sensationalism in favor of exploring "the day-to-day cultural forces that enter into hip hop's vast dialogue." It would be easy, for example, to simply demonize male rappers as sexist, but Rose chooses to invoke the dynamic works of female rappers to show how sexism is embroiled in dialogic constructions through which participants of both genders are constantly negotiating patriarchal issues of female power and male vulnerability. Elsewhere, she extends her critique to the economically deprived conditions and technological advancements that are intertwined with rap's explicit orality. The result is a fascinating study of one of the most influential genres of the 1980s.

CARDUCCI's book is a wildly opinionated treatment of the aesthetics of rock that reads more like an epic fanzine editorial than any academic tome. The author's unchecked (and at times inflammatory) polemics are understandable given the cynical callus that Carducci developed working for the premier American underground rock label of the 1980s, SST. The intermittent references Carducci makes to SST and the travails of that label's legendary hardcore punk band, Black Flag, provide an interesting subtext that runs throughout the book's lengthy chapters. When Carducci details the rise of 1980s indie labels and distributors and expounds on the stylistic varieties of "alternative" bands, he gives a glimpse of the American music industry largely ignored in other popular music books.

THEO CATEFORIS

Rock and Roll: 1980s England

Cohen, Sara, *Rock Culture in Liverpool: Popular Music in the Making,* Oxford: Clarendon Press, and New York: Oxford University Press, 1991

Frith, Simon, and Howard Horne, *Art into Pop,* London: Methuen, 1987

Marcus, Greil, *Ranters and Crowd Pleasers: Punk in Pop Music, 1977–92,* New York: Doubleday, 1993

McRobbie, Angela, editor, *Zoot Suits and Second-Hand Dresses: An Anthology of Fashion and Music,* Boston: Unwin Hyman, 1988; Basingstoke: Macmillan, 1989

Redhead, Steve, *The End-of-the-Century Party: Youth and Pop towards 2000*, Manchester: Manchester University Press, 1990

Reynolds, Simon, *Blissed Out: The Raptures of Rock,* London: Serpent's Tail, 1990

Rimmer, Dave, *Like Punk Never Happened: Culture Club and the New Pop,* London: Faber, 1985

Savage, Jon, *Time Travel: Pop, Media, and Sexuality 1976–96,* London: Chatto and Windus, 1996

More than anything else, the course of rock and pop music in 1980s England bears the lasting marks of the late-1970s punk explosion. This legacy is twofold. First, during the 1980s an entire legion of musicians applied punk's do-it-yourself (DIY) ethos and subversive performance tactics to fashion a vast array of experimental hybrid styles. So pervasive were the remnants of punk's politics of style that the early 1980s in England are often simply referred to as the "postpunk" era. Second, following the lead of 1970s scholars such as Dick Hebdige of the Birmingham Centre for Contemporary Cultural Studies, who analyzed punk as a distinct subculture, academics and journalists alike began theorizing in-depth about the significance and signification of every unfolding nuance in the contemporary pop music landscape. Not only the weekly music papers such as *New Musical Express, Melody Maker* and *Sounds* but also politico-cultural organs such as *New Statesman, New Society,* and *Artforum* and style magazines such as *The Face* began to feature regularly the most adventurous and sophisticated viewpoints in British popular music criticism. In the 1990s, the best of these music critics published their collected journalistic writings, presenting their original observations on 1980s pop "as it happened." Of the many musical trends that attracted the critics' attention, three in particular stand out. First, writers in the early 1980s christened the dawn of "new pop": bands such as Culture Club and Duran Duran enjoyed tremendous chart success and made pop stardom, glamour, and glitz once again fashionable. Second, in the mid- to late 1980s a small cluster of critics, in search of alternatives to what they saw as a moribund pop/rock mainstream, began eagerly heralding the vital musical contributions of bands and artists on independent labels, including Creation, 4AD, and Rough Trade. At the same time, a third development dramatically transformed the shape of music in England: a "rave" scene emerged, making issues of drug excess and uninhibited youthful dancing and partying the concern of the nation's major press and tabloids. In the 1990s, this ever-expanding dance culture would prove to be the most prominent and controversial force in British music.

McROBBIE's anthology positions side-by-side a vast range of 1980s music critical approaches. Academic articles, heavy with footnotes, from scholars such as Richard Dyer and Dave Laing nestle with more polemi-cal pieces from journalists such as Paul Oldfield and David Stubbs. Many of the essayists confront the pervasive (and at times, problematic) presence of the past in contemporary style; as Stubbs notes, "every gesture groans under the weight of its several precedents." Such issues figured prominently in 1980s postmodern debates, as shown by the abundant references to postmodern theorists and theories strewn throughout the book's pages. Although bereft of musicological contributions, McRobbie's collection otherwise serves as a good introduction to the variegated theoretical slants of British popular music criticism.

SAVAGE's collection is a scrapbook overview of the 1980s, comprised of brief readings (few run over five pages) on pop music taken from a variety of newsstand publications. Savage began his career as a music journalist at the dawn of the punk explosion, and his fascination with the genre casts a long shadow over the book's middle section: "Style 1980–88." Many punk supporters dismissed progressive and hard-rock styles as irrelevant, and Savage follows suit, ignoring these genres in favor of readings on the construction of pop celebrities, such as Soft Cell and Culture Club, and the music's connection with sexual politics and fashion trends. By no means does Savage provide a complete picture of 1980s music. But his efforts to contextualize pop music, both as part of the larger spectrum of media production and within the chronicles of cultural history, make for engaging, critical reading.

Similar to Savage's anthology, MARCUS's collection compiles the author's journalistic snapshot views of 1980s popular music. Marcus, one of the United States' foremost rock critics, traces punk's 1970s tremors into early-1980s postpunk England in two general directions. First, he details the "postpunk pop avant garde" mindset and deconstructive musical settings of influential bands such as Gang of Four and P.I.L. Second, he gives considerable space to the numerous all-female and mixed-gender bands, such as, the Raincoats, Delta 5, and the Au Pairs, who through their music making addressed the social construction of gender roles. One lengthy article in particular—"It's Fab, It's Passionate, It's Wild, It's Intelligent! It's the Hot New Sound of England Today!"—remains among the most lucid accounts of early British postpunk ever published.

FRITH and HORNE base their book around a simple premise: There is an intimate bond between the British art-school experience and popular music. Although the authors devote much of their heavily detailed study to how the 1960s "rock bohemians" and 1970s "pop situationists" reconciled creativity and commerce in their pop music productions, they also include an important (albeit limited) discussion of 1980s pop music trends that plays off this historical perspective. Pop musicians in the 1980s, the authors argue, differ from their predecessors in that many of the 1980s performers sought not to make explicitly difficult or outrageous music but instead to weave a thoroughgoing, stealthy form of subversion into the normally unquestioned "act of consumption." As with Frith's many other writings, the book eschews text-based analyses and emphasizes instead the marketplace processes by which music becomes text.

As a writer for the largest-selling 1980s British pop magazine, *Smash Hits*, RIMMER was afforded close access to the bands who comprised the New Pop scene. This book is partly a loose biography of one of the New Pop's signature bands, Culture Club. But it is also a probing account of the New Pop vis-à-vis the changing music industry, tracing how the new stars extended punk's DIY credo at the same time as they rejected postpunk's "dour, gloomy" stylistics. Rather than recounting Culture Club's story in a strictly linear manner, Rimmer effortlessly weaves the group's saga in and out of more analytical discussions of the New Pop obsession with fashion, fame, gender politics, and African-American music styles. The result is an always intelligent, if not fully theorized, period study of British pop music up to 1985.

COHEN's influential study takes as its topic an element often missing from popular music writing: the role of music making as a social, culturally bound activity. In sharp contrast to Rimmer's portrayal of international pop celebrities, Cohen depicts the struggles of two aspiring, unsigned bands within the bleak economic locality of Liverpool. Based on her 1985 and 1986 fieldwork in Liverpool, she reveals the importance of community, gender relationships, and the intricacies of the music industry as they relate to the life functions of Britain's numerous small, regionally based rock bands. Most of all, however, this book stands as the keystone in Cohen's continuing advocacy for ethnographic detail in popular music studies, a clarion call that other academics have since adopted with ever-increasing frequency.

REYNOLDS's book is as much about the writing of rock criticism as it is about the various strands of late 1980s alternative rock music to which he finds himself drawn. As he states, he is seeking an "ideal" journalistic style: one that combines the erudition of literary and cultural studies with the giddy illogical prose that rock's most epiphanic, blissful moments can inspire. At times the results veer toward effusive poetry, spiced with occasional references to French intellectual thought. By the author's own admission, his borrowings of "high" criticism arise more from caprice than from any penetrating philosophical insights. That said, nobody has written as descriptively about the "discordant chaos" of late 1980s popular music as has Reynolds. For this reason, his book continues to be an important document.

REDHEAD's book takes as its starting point the media frenzy surrounding the 1988 explosion of "Acid House" music but soon branches out to more broad discussions. His general thesis is that "the myths of youth culture were all but exhausted by the late 1980s"; thus, he believes we are confronted not with genuine 1980s subcultures but with cultural theorists (and theories) in search of subcultures. Looking for some more coherent approach to 1980s music, Redhead proposes the categories "political pop" and "post-political pop" as a means of encompassing the renewed interest in folk and protest music. Although Redhead makes many sound arguments, his constant recourse to undigested British pop-music lingo and postmodern theories can make for needlessly muddled reading. As a result, those not conversant with the genres under discussion and unfamiliar with general British rock-music history will find this book daunting.

THEO CATEFORIS

Rodgers, Richard 1902–1979

United States composer

Engel, Lehman, *The American Musical Theater,* revised edition, New York: Macmillan, 1975

Ewen, David, *Richard Rodgers,* New York: Holt, 1957

————, *With a Song in His Heart: The Story of Richard Rodgers,* New York: Holt, Rinehart and Winston, 1963

Forte, Allen, *The American Popular Ballad of the Golden Era, 1924–1950,* Princeton, New Jersey: Princeton University Press, 1995

Green, Stanley, *The Rodgers and Hammerstein Story,* New York: Day, and London: Allen, 1963

Hyland, William, *Richard Rodgers,* New Haven, Connecticut: Yale University Press, 1998

Marx, Samuel, and Jan Clayton, *Rodgers and Hart: Bewitched, Bothered, and Bedeviled,* New York: Putnam, and London: Allen, 1976

Mordden, Ethan, *Rodgers and Hammerstein,* New York: Abrams, 1992

Nolan, Frederick, *The Sound of Their Music: The Story of Rodgers and Hammerstein,* New York: Walker, and London: Dent, 1978

Rodgers, Richard, *Musical Stages: An Autobiography,* New York: Random House, 1975

Wilder, Alec, *American Popular Song: The Great Innovators, 1900–1950,* New York: Oxford University Press, 1972

Richard Rodgers was the foremost composer of musical theater in the United States in the 20th century. He wrote over 50 works for stage and screen, from which derive numerous standard popular songs. His career falls into three distinct periods, the first two delineated by his two famous long-term collaborations: with the lyricist Lorenz Hart from 1919 to 1943, and with Oscar Hammerstein from 1943 to 1960. The third period, which lasted until his death in 1979, is marked by short-term collaborations with various lyricists, including Stephen Sondheim. Rodgers stands out from most other Broadway composers for his firm commitment to the advancement of musical theater. During his 20s and 30s, he and Hart sought to foster an indigenous American musical theater, avoiding the formulas of the three dominant types of musicals at the time, the European-based operetta, the loosely constructed musical comedy, and the plotless musical revue. Hart's alcoholism, which eventually killed him, and professional inertia led to the end of their 24-year partnership. In 1943 Rodgers joined with Hammerstein to write *Oklahoma!*, which established the musical play as the principal type of musical for the next three decades. After Hammerstein's death, Rodgers did not significantly deviate from the type of musical that he was accustomed to writing, even as younger writers were experimenting with new forms. Books on Rodgers are either general biographies or individual studies of his collaboration with Hart or Hammerstein. Drawing on many of the same sources, these volumes contain much of the same anecdotal information. No writer deals thoroughly with the years 1960 to 1979. While reaffirming Rodgers's tremendous contribution to the American musical, the more recent authors probe into certain negative aspects of his character. Most of the musical discussion in this literature tends to be vague or equivocal. For students with a background in musical theory, studies specifically on the American popular song are much better than the studies listed here for a deep understanding of Rodgers's music.

In the earliest biography of Rodgers, EWEN (1957) documents the key events in the composer's life and provides a brief background of his musicals and nonvocal compositions up to and including 1957. The sections dealing with Hart and Hammerstein contain useful factual information about the lyricists. Ewen does not attempt to analyze the musicals from a historical standpoint. He discusses the source material for the plots, the people involved, and the reception history. By disregarding the theatrical milieu in which Rodgers wrote, however, the author fails to explain the specific reasons why many of the composer's musicals were so innovative.

EWEN (1963) is a revision of his first biography. Although much abridged, it adds the three musicals Rodgers wrote in the interim. In the new closing section, the author describes Rodgers as immaculate, businesslike, affectionate, and philanthropic. Betraying Ewen's close personal relationship with the composer, this biased depiction may have influenced the tendency of many subsequent biographers to portray Rodgers in exaggeratedly positive terms.

GREEN, the first author to focus specifically on Rodgers and Hammerstein's collaboration, offers little new information. While describing the composer and lyricist's careers before 1943, Green emphasizes the fact that they both sought to write integrated musicals even before working together. Turning to the 11 musicals of their collaboration, Green draws attention to the undercurrent of Hammerstein's idealist life philosophy in the plots. He argues that Rodgers shared Hammerstein's optimism and that their works sprang from a collective positive feeling about human nature. Later authors contradict this notion and make stronger distinctions between Rodgers's and Hammerstein's personalities.

WILDER, in a study of American popular song up to 1950, surveys over 100 of Rodgers's songs, mostly from the Hart years, and is entirely dismissive of the music from Rodgers and Hammerstein's musicals. Wilder identifies the devices that best characterize Rodgers's early melodic style, such as that of returning to the same pitch or pitches within an ascending or descending sequential melodic segment. Other salient features include stepwise motion, successive fourths, lively rhythms, and a close thematic relationship between verse and chorus. Unfortunately, the reader is expected to be familiar with the songs, and the printed musical examples are fragmentary and devoid of lyrics.

In a historical overview of American musical theater, ENGEL includes a separate chapter ("The Contemporary Musical") on the book musical. Based on what he considers the 15 most representative examples of this genre, five of which are by Rodgers, Engel offers a methodical exegesis of the dramaturgical, poetic, musical, and stylistic conventions of the book musical. In his discussion of the libretto, he considers plot, subplot, character, source material, dramatic unity, and act structure. He also comments on the individual elements of a musical: the opening, lyric placement, musical scene, comedic invention, musical program, layout, and style. Engel is a valuable resource for any student of musical theater in general and of Rodgers and Hammerstein's musicals in particular.

RODGERS provides little new information. Even when recalling the evolution of some of his most famous songs, he offers no particularly fresh insights. The autobiography (apparently written with much assistance from Green) is interesting if only for its selectivity. The composer dwells most on the first period of his career; the section on Hammerstein is surprisingly brief. Of the six musicals Rodgers composed during the third period, he has the most to say about *No Strings*, the first of two musicals for which he himself supplied the lyrics. Rodgers's daughter Mary, herself a successful Broadway composer, wrote an introduction for the 1995 reprint. Like many other recent writers, she is critical of her father's aloof nature. She reaffirms his all-consuming devotion to musical theater, which, she asserts, took precedence over everything else in his life.

Examining Rodgers's first collaboration, MARX and CLAYTON are particularly sympathetic to Hart. Most of the people they interviewed recall the lyricist fondly, describing him as likable, gregarious, generous, but also self-effacing. Contributing to Hart's downfall was his inability to deal with his lack of height, his alcoholism, and his homosexuality. Rodgers, in contrast, has his detractors; he is remembered as being aggressive and singular in his artistic drive. For example, the book describes his intent pursuit of a new lyricist when he could no longer cajole Hart into working.

NOLAN sets out to examine Rodgers's collaboration with Hammerstein but includes an extensive section on the Hart years and a cursory examination of the composer's musicals after Hammerstein's death, not including *I Remember Mama*, which opened in 1979 shortly before Rodgers died. Of particular historic interest in this study is the reproduction of Howard Lindsay's and Russel Crouse's notes on the scenic production for *The Sound of Music*, located in the Lincoln Center archives. Nolan suggests that Rodgers and Hammerstein temporarily broke off their collaboration after *The King and I*. Based on Joshua Logan's recollection, the author reports that Hammerstein was crushed by his partner's noncommittal approbation of "Hello Young Lovers," which had taken Hammerstein weeks to complete and which he considered to be one of his best song lyrics. This event might have precipitated the alleged split between the collaborators, which, if it really did occur, lasted only a brief time. In order to provide a historical context for the chronology in the appendix, Nolan includes narrative annotations with useful relevant information.

MORDDEN, who brings a rich historical knowledge to bear on the study of Rodgers and Hammerstein's musicals, explores the unique dramatic and stylistic features of each work. Comparing *Oklahoma!* with Cole Porter's *Something for the Boys* from the same year, the author draws a strong distinction between the musical play and the musical comedy. He reevaluates Rodgers and Hammerstein's lesser-known works, such as *Allegro*, offering some interesting new insights. His musical discussions are cursory and not always entirely accurate. Each chapter includes stunning reproductions of black-and-white and color photographs, including some of original poster and sheet music.

For readers interested in American popular-song styles, FORTE is essential. His chapter on Rodgers contains detailed analytical reductions of six songs written between 1927 and 1937. (Like Wilder, he is not interested in the songs Rodgers composed with Hammerstein, as they signal a new style.) Readers will require some theoretical background in order to fully appreciate Forte's discussion of the music. Incorporating Schenkerian analytical concepts, the author examines the most unique melodic, harmonic, and rhythmic features of Rodgers's early song style, such as the use of ragtime and dance rhythms. One of Forte's many insightful observations concerns the close connection between the melodic and harmonious structures in some of the songs. Such a relationship is found in "Thou Swell," in which the closing bass line comprises the pitches of the identical pentatonic scale on which the main theme is based.

HYLAND has gathered plenty of pertinent information, but he relies too heavily on previously published accounts. Even though he had access to various archival sources, including some musical sketches, he offers few new details regarding the musicals, with the exception of those from the third period of Rodgers's career. The author probes into the composer's drinking, womanizing, homophobia, depression, and insularity. Hyland fails, however, to synthesize these personality traits into his portrait of the composer. The reader is left desiring a better explanation of the contradiction between Rodgers the man and the sentimental nature of the musicals he composed.

JAMES LEVE

Romantic Music: General Studies

Abraham, Gerald, editor, *Romanticism (1830–1890)*, The New Oxford History of Music, vol. 9, Oxford: Oxford University Press, 1990

Bent, Ian, editor, *Music Theory in the Age of Romanticism*, Cambridge: Cambridge University Press, 1996

Dahlhaus, Carl, *Nineteenth-Century Music*, translated by J. Bradford Robinson, Berkeley: University of California Press, 1989

Longyear, Rey M., *Nineteenth-Century Romanticism in Music*, Englewood Cliffs, New Jersey: Prentice Hall, 1969; 3rd edition 1988

Meyer, Leonard B., *Style and Music: Theory, History, and Ideology*, Philadelphia: University of Pennsylvania Press, 1989

Plantinga, Leon, *Romantic Music: A History of Musical Style in Nineteenth-Century Europe*, New York: Norton, 1984

Ringer, Alexander L., editor, *The Early Romantic Era: Between Revolutions, 1789–1848*, Basingstoke: Macmillan, 1990; Englewood Cliffs, New Jersey: Prentice Hall, 1991

Samson, Jim, editor, *The Late Romantic Era: From the Mid-19th Century to World War I*, London: Macmillan, and Englewood Cliffs, New Jersey: Prentice Hall, 1991

Whittall, Arnold, *Romantic Music: A Concise History from Schubert to Sibelius*, London: Thames and Hudson, 1987

Beginning in the 19th century the term *romanticism* was used to describe a new movement that embraced the arts, philosophy, politics, and even the sciences. Romanticism grew in different countries at different times and was never a cohesive movement; it embraced various ideas and included a number of contradictory strains. Yet in all its manifestations, romanticism emphasized the clear domination of emotion over reason. New value was given to novelty and sensation, technical innovation and experiment, and the cross-fertilization of ideas between different disciplines. The romantic period is generally defined as extending from the closing years of the 18th century to the early years of the 20th, but as the works in this bibliography reveal, scholars often disagree about the period's exact chronological boundaries.

WHITTALL presents a brief and engaging introduction for general readers new to the topic. The author begins with a discussion of the word *romantic,* describing its origins, history, and various connotations. He describes the romantic period as a time of great musical diversity, and to clarify this point, he divides his book into discussions of various regional and/or national practices: Germany, Italy, France, Eastern Europe and Scandinavia, Britain, and North America. Discussions of specific compositions are brief and accessible to those unfamiliar with theoretical terminology. Good use is made of contemporary sources and commentaries, but unfortunately, references for these are not included. A selected bibliography including both books and articles serves as a good starting point for further reading.

LONGYEAR also offers an introduction to the period, but this study is intended for readers with a basic background in music theory. The third edition has been substantially expanded from the original, and it is often used as a textbook for undergraduate music history courses. Longyear views the romantic period as an era of pronounced individuality. For this reason, he divides his book into discussions organized around the careers of composers rather than genres or locales. Approximately 150 composers are mentioned in the text and at least 20 are discussed at length. Brief descriptions of prominent compositions occur throughout the book and are enhanced by the use of music examples. Unfortunately, the music of Eastern Europe, England, and Scandinavia is relegated to a single chapter, and little attention is given to intellectual and social movements of the period. Each chapter concludes with a selective bibliography emphasizing works in English published since 1978.

ABRAHAM offers the most comprehensive survey of the period, and its large size makes it a useful source of information. The book is divided into two parts, the early romantic period (1830–50) and the late romantic period (1850–90), and the various chapters are arranged according to genre. Each chapter is written by a specialist in the field. Most essays discuss regional practices or the works of prominent composers. On the whole, this book offers an excellent survey of the breadth and variety of musical output in the 19th century; both major and minor composers are discussed in detail, and peripheral areas such as Scandinavia, Eastern Europe, and the United States are given adequate attention. However, little mention is made of music aesthetics. The book's fastidious layout facilitates its use as a reference tool for music students rather than a historical narrative for the general reader.

DAHLHAUS is considered by many to be the most significant study of the period. Arranged chronologically, this book combines the fields of music, aesthetics, and social history into a broad exploration of topics such as classicism versus romanticism, the rise of the bourgeoisie, virtuosity and interpretation, the myth of Beethoven, musical nationalism, absolute music versus program music, music realism, exoticism, and folklore. Each chapter includes an extensive list of bibliographic references for those interested in further exploration of the topics discussed, and a glossary at the end of the book will aid readers new to the field. Specialists will also find the book useful, for it offers a wealth of interdisciplinary material rarely included in musicological studies. But this study is not flawless: little mention is made of women composers and performers, and various non-German composers, including Debussy, Elgar, and Grieg, are neglected.

RINGER and SAMSON are both part of the Man and Music series originally conceived in conjunction with the British television series by the same name. Written with the educated nonspecialist in mind, these books offer an engaging view of European and U.S. musical culture. The chronological boundaries for the romantic period are defined rather broadly in these books: Ringer examines the period 1789 to 1848, and Samson discusses musical culture from the mid-19th century to World War I. The format for both books is the same: they do not attempt to treat music history comprehensively; instead they examine how music responded to social, economic, and political circumstances at various times and in various locations. Each chapter is written by a leading scholar in the field and examines the musical culture of a particular city or geographic region. Few musical examples are given, but details about each area's social, cultural, and intellectual forces are discussed in connection to their effect on musical practice. Detailed notes and extensive bibliographies are included at the end of each chapter.

The chronological boundaries of PLANTINGA are roughly 1790 to 1900. The author makes a few modest forays into the social and intellectual history of the period, but for the most part, he focuses his discussion on the music itself. Extensive analyses of individual compositions dominate many chapters and are facilitated by the volume of scores, *Anthology of Romantic Music* (1984), published as a companion to the book. The primary limitation of the book is its tendency to concentrate on the music of a small group of German composers. Full chapters are dedicated to the works of Beethoven, Schubert, Schumann, and Wagner, while composers such as Chopin, Liszt, Rossini, Verdi, and Berlioz are relegated to only a few pages. Likewise, discussions of the music tend to gravitate toward large stage and concert works. Little mention is made of program music, and discussions of chamber music and sacred works are generally avoided.

MEYER approaches 19th-century style from a different point of view. Borrowing methodologies from cultural anthropology and social psychology, the author examines the "culturally qualified behavior of human beings in specific historical/cultural circumstances." He discusses the compositional choices made by various musicians and shows how these choices create musical styles. According to Meyer, music histories are constructed from these changes in choice. The book is divided into three parts: parts 1 and 2 present a broad discussion of the nature of style and style history, while part 3 explains how the ideological beliefs of the 19th century were "translated into musical constraints" for many composers. This is a conceptually intricate book, filled with thought-provoking concepts and hypotheses rather than a positivist presentation of facts.

The various articles in BENT combine to form a cohesive exploration of theoretical thought and practice in the 19th century. The volume is divided into three broad topics. Part 1, "Cultural and Philosophical Frameworks," looks at how contemporary philosophical and intellectual ideas informed and conditioned the work of music theorists; part 2, "Hermeneutics, Analysis, Criticism," examines 19th-century music criticism; and part 3, "Rhetoric, Metaphor, Musical Perception," explores the use of metaphor and meaning in the concepts and linguistics of several 19th-century theorists. In general, the contributors to this volume are part of a new generation in the field of musicology. Their work is quite diverse in character, and each is well versed in both the positivistic methodologies of earlier generations and newer approaches that show the influence of literary criticism, hermeneutics, gender studies, and new advancements in music cognition.

ANNA H. HARWELL CELENZA

Romantic Music: Specialized Studies

Abbate, Carolyn, *Unsung Voices: Opera and Musical Narrative in the Nineteenth Century,* Princeton, New Jersey: Princeton University Press, 1991

Bergeron, Katherine, *Decadent Enchantments: The Revival of Gregorian Chant at Solesmes,* Berkeley: University of California Press, 1998

Bonds, Mark Evan, *After Beethoven: Imperatives of Originality in the Symphony,* Cambridge, Massachusetts: Harvard University Press, 1996

Burnham, Scott G., *Beethoven Hero,* Princeton, New Jersey: Princeton University Press, 1995

Daverio, John, *Nineteenth-Century Music and the German Romantic Ideology,* New York: Schirmer Books, 1993

Fay, Amy, *Music Study in Germany: The Classic Memoir of the Romantic Era,* Chicago: McClurg, 1880; reprint, New York: Dover, 1965

Gerhard, Anselm, *The Urbanization of Opera: Music Theater in Paris in the Nineteenth Century,* translated by Mary Whittall, Chicago: University of Chicago Press, 1997

Johnson, James, *Listening in Paris: A Cultural History,* Berkeley: University of California Press, 1995

Kinderman, William, and Harald Krebs, editors, *The Second Practice of Nineteenth-Century Tonality,* Lincoln: University of Nebraska Press, 1996

Kramer, Lawrence, *Music as Cultural Practice, 1800–1900,* Berkeley: University of California Press, 1990

Rosen, Charles, *The Romantic Generation,* Cambridge, Massachusetts: Harvard University Press, 1995

Taruskin, Richard, *Defining Russia Musically: Historical and Hermeneutical Essays,* Princeton, New Jersey: Princeton University Press, 1997

Before the late 1970s, monograph-length studies of romantic music tended to fall into two categories: general surveys (e.g., music appreciation textbooks, overviews of a particular genre) and in-depth examinations of single composers. Among more recent publications, one finds additionally a third kind of book on romantic music: specialized studies, or books that try to answer a specific question or set of questions about Western music in the 19th century. The scope of this article does not allow for a discussion of all of the excellent specialized studies of romantic music. Hence, the books discussed here are chosen not only for their quality but also because they collectively demonstrate the diversity of methodologies used and questions asked by musicologists in the last two decades of the 20th century.

After years of neglect, 19th-century opera has now become one of the most active and fruitful fields of research in musicology. One of the most interesting specialized studies in this area is GERHARD, whose subject is the much-maligned genre of French grand opera. According to Gerhard, the development of grand opera is closely related to new modes of perception and new aesthetic expectations that arose as a result of the rapid expansion and urbanization of Paris during the early 19th century. The book focuses on eight operas by Auber, Bertin, Meyerbeer, Rossini, and Verdi. Because several of these works are rarely performed today, the book's excellent plot summaries and lists of recommended recordings are extremely useful.

JOHNSON, another ambitious book on French opera, asks the following question: why did Parisian opera audiences, who went to performances to socialize during the 1750s, become silent and attentive by the 1840s? For Johnson, the answer lies in changes in political and social ideologies, the gradual decline of the notion that music is primarily a mimetic art, and innovations in music by such composers as Gluck, Haydn, Rossini, and Beethoven. The volume is very accessible and includes numerous quotes and illustrations from contemporary sources.

ABBATE is one of several musicologists who have questioned the traditional assumption that great musical works are coherent and organically unified. In this extremely rich but difficult text, she argues that 19th-century operas often contain brief moments of disjunction. In such moments, one frequently hears a voice—a storyteller who wants to tell the audience something. Abbate writes,

> I will interpret music as *narrating* only rarely. It is not narrative, but it possesses moments of narration, moments that can be identified by their bizarre and disruptive effect. Such moments seem like voices from elsewhere, speaking (singing) in a fashion we recognize precisely because it is idiosyncratic.

In her book, Abbate tries to uncover what storytellers in specific pieces are trying to say. She believes that her analysis of voice and narration can be extended to some 19th-century instrumental music. Her chapters on Dukas's "The Sorcerer's Apprentice" and the first movement of Mahler's Second Symphony are, however, less convincing and more problematic than her masterful and provocative reading of sections from Wagner's Ring.

Nationalism and exoticism (especially orientalism) are two central topics in 19th-century music studies. Of the numerous specialized studies that focus on these issues, the most substantial and provocative is TARUSKIN. In this book, he argues that since the mid-18th century, all of the constructions of Russian national identity (both from within Russia and from the West) have shared one constant: the myth of otherness—Russia is neither fully a part of the East nor fully a part of the West. Taruskin believes that this myth of otherness is best illustrated through an examination of Russian music from the late 18th century to the present. Although readers who are primarily interested in 19th-century music might want to concentrate on chapters 8 through 12, they would be ill-advised to skip the preface.

KRAMER, one of the first writers to apply late 20th-century literary theories to music, aims to show how musical forms and processes participate in the continual production and reproduction of culture. Of the five case studies that form the core of this volume, the most provocative are the discussion of sexuality in music by Wagner and Wolf and the analysis of gender construction in Liszt's *Faust* Symphony. The other chapters—on Beethoven's two-movement sonatas, Chopin's A-minor Prelude, and Beethoven's La Malinconia Quartet—are less convincing. One major asset of this book is Kramer's clear and concise presentation of recent literary theories.

Two specialized studies that examine the legacy of Beethoven in the romantic era are Bonds and Burnham. BONDS applies elements of Harold Bloom's controversial Anxiety of Influence theory to the 19th-century symphony. Bond argues that by 1830, the shadow of Beethoven and the increasing emphasis on originality led to a sense of crisis about the future of the symphony as a genre. He further contends that in order to get out of this crisis, composers had to confront Beethoven's legacy by misreading him (i.e., alluding to Beethoven's works and then veering away from them). The volume includes in-depth analyses of Berlioz's *Harold in Italy,* Mendelssohn's *Lobgesang,* Schumann's Fourth Symphony, Brahms's First Symphony, and Mahler's Fourth Symphony.

BURNHAM, one of the most engaging reception histories of music to date, asks why Beethoven's heroic works have had such a great impact upon the way people thought about all music during the 19th and 20th centuries. For Burnham, the unique valuation of Beethoven's heroic works rests upon three factors: the phenomenological experience of Beethoven's music, the fact that the technical characteristics of the heroic style formed the basis of analytic systems developed by four prominent theorists (A.B. Marx, Riemann, Schenker, and Réte), and the connection between Beethoven's music and the heroic concept of self.

Another important topic that has received a large amount of scholarly attention in recent years concerns the connections among romantic philosophy, aesthetics, and music. A good general introduction to this issue is DAVERIO, which examines how romantic ideas are embedded in 19th-century musical works, and explains how interpreting these works as commentaries on romantic ideas enhances an understanding of the music. Although Daverio overemphasizes the importance of Friedrich Schlegel's ideas in the second half of the 19th century, the book—especially the chapters on Schumann—provides numerous insights.

One of most widely-read books on romantic music is ROSEN. After an opening chapter that deals primarily with changes in piano technique and sound during the first half of the 19th century, Rosen spends two chapters on Schumann. Here, he expands upon some of the central ideas of the early chapters of Daverio's book, such as ruins, legends, and fragments. The center of this tome is an impressive study of mostly formal issues in Chopin's music. Rosen also includes single chapters on Liszt, Berlioz, Mendelssohn, and romantic opera.

BERGERON demonstrates the connection between romantic aesthetics and one of the most significant phenomena in the history of 19th-century music: the revival of Gregorian chant at Solesmes. Readers who wish to understand romantic composers' deep interest in myths, ruins, and early music and those who want to grasp evolving notions of the musical text, will find this volume essential reading.

A large amount of recent scholarship on romantic music focuses on cultural and philosophical aspects of music, but studies that concentrate on more technical elements—such as second part of Rosen—have continued to appear. One of the most significant recent monographs in this area is KINDERMAN and KREBS. This volume, containing essays by seven authors, discusses 19th-century works that do not seem to have one ultimate tonal center. Of particular interest in this book are the nonmusical parallels that are invoked to clarify arguments (e.g., Patrick McCreless borrows ideas developed by Stephen Jay Gould; Christopher Lewis discusses procedures in fiction and film; and Kevin Korsyn uses recent literary theories).

Although the forementioned specialized studies are extremely well-researched and contain the latest findings, readers who want to learn about romantic music should not neglect the vast amount of primary sources that are now available in English. One of the most informative and entertaining primary sources is the memoir by FAY, an American pianist who studied in Germany from 1869 to 1875. The volume—a book of letters edited by her sister Melusina Fay Pierce—was first published in 1880 and has since appeared in more than 25 editions. In addition to Fay's observations about musical life in Germany, the book offers fascinating glimpses of her lessons with Carl Tausig, Theodore Kullak, Franz Liszt, and Ludwig Deppe.

ERIC HUNG

Rore, Cipriano de ca. 1515–1565

Dutch-born composer

Einstein, Alfred, *The Italian Madrigal*, 3 vols., translated by Alexander H. Krappe et al., Princeton, New Jersey: Princeton University Press, 1949

Feldman, Martha, *City Culture and the Madrigal at Venice*, Berkeley: University of California Press, 1995

Lowinsky, Edward E., *Cipriano de Rore's Venus Motet: Its Poetic and Pictorial Sources*, [Provo, Utah]: Brigham Young University, 1986

———, *Music in the Culture of the Renaissance and Other Essays*, 2 vols., edited by Bonnie J. Blackburn, Chicago: University of Chicago Press, 1989

Meier, Bernhard, *The Modes of Classical Vocal Polyphony*, translated by Ellen S. Beebe, New York: Broude Brothers, 1988

Owens, Jessie Ann, *Composers at Work: The Craft of Musical Composition 1450–1600*, New York: Oxford University Press, 1997

Rore, Cipriano de, *Cipriano Rore: Opera Omnia*, edited by Bernhard Meier, [Rome]: American Institute of Musicology, 1959–77

Cipriano de Rore was one of the most important and innovative composers of his time. Fluent in the contrapuntal intricacies of his native Franco-Flemish musical heritage, Rore is perhaps more widely remembered for his leading role in the development of the Italian madrigal. Claudio Monteverdi himself cited Rore as the wellspring of a *seconda prattica*, one that placed music at the service of poetical or emotional conceits. Since then, Rore has assumed a pivotal position in music history. By

Einstein's assessment, "all madrigal music of the Sixteenth Century that lays claim to serious dignity is dependent upon Rore . . . [who] holds the key to the whole development of the Italian madrigal after 1550." Nevertheless, no comprehensive study of Cipriano de Rore's life and works has been undertaken, in any language, up through the present day. Perhaps in due recognition of the uniqueness of the composer's ingenuity, the bulk of Rore scholarship has unfolded in a series of highly specialized articles and conference papers addressing such issues as word-tone relationships, music in society, iconography, and the modes. Much can also be gleaned from the following unpublished dissertations, each of which amplifies significant aspects of Rore's creative output: Alvin H. Johnson, "The Liturgical Music of Cipriano de Rore" (Yale University, 1967); Stefano La Via, "Cipriano de Rore as Reader and as Read: A Literary-Musical Study of Madrigals from Rore's Later Collections (1557–1566)" (Princeton University, 1991); Louis Dean Nuernberger, "The Five Voice Madrigals of Cipriano de Rore" (University of Michigan, 1963); and Jessie Ann Owens, "An Illuminated Manuscript of Motets by Cipriano de Rore (München, Bayerische Staatsbibliothek, MUS. MS. B)" (Princeton University, 1979).

RORE, a modern edition of the composer's complete works, provides an invaluable resource and starting point for Rore scholarship. Contents of the eight-volume set are arranged by genre. Unfortunately, a promised volume of critical notes, frequently referenced in the forewords to each of the volumes, has yet to be released. Collectively, however, the editor's prefatory essays offer an engaging, informative, and often provocative introduction to the scope of Rore's creative genius.

Rore's imaginative use of word painting, musical texture, dissonance, notational practices, and modality for the purposes of poetic expression account for a large part of such analytical discussions. Musical examples are referenced to precise measure numbers from the editor's own careful transcriptions. No less significant are Meier's insightful readings of the poetic texts themselves, which often enable the editor to decipher the specific occasions for which Rore composed many of his works. Such information immeasurably advances clues to the composer's otherwise sketchy biography. Considerations also include Rore's attraction to cyclic compositional procedures (especially evident in his famous setting of Petrarch's *Vergine-Canzone*); his part in the origin of the *note nere* madrigal; and the vogue, even during Rore's lifetime, for quoting, paraphrasing, and arranging many of the composer's most popular vocal works. Footnotes direct the reader to pertinent primary and secondary sources. Illustrations include the several known portraits of the composer.

EINSTEIN's monumental study has long stood at the center of madrigal research, inspiring younger generations of musicologists to undertake deeper, more detailed examinations of the genre and its practitioners, masters and amateurs alike. For Einstein, as previously noted, Rore occupies a critical place in the madrigal's history, especially in what the author calls the "post-classic" style. Rore is seen as the singular champion and successor of Adrian Willaert. Indeed, all other composers active during the period are assembled as either being "contemporaries of Willaert and Rore" or as comprising an "immediate Venetian circle" about them.

Einstein weaves together the most readily available picture of Rore's life and career, largely drawing on contemporary accounts, the dedications to Rore's published collections, and assessments of the composer by 16th-century theorists and critics, as well as interpretive readings of the texts that Rore set to music. English translations are only sometimes provided (although readers will find them for the handful of representative works given in volume 3). Most examples employ older clefs, but this does not impede the otherwise clear and understandable survey of Rore's musical style. Einstein also explores the composer's literary choices and the changing tastes of mid-16th-century Italian poetry. In this respect, he paved the way for more recent avenues of musicological inquiry, upholding Rore as a worthy model.

FELDMAN sets a new exemplar for the investigation of madrigal literature, both musical and poetical, within broader cultural and sociological settings. Again, Rore figures in a seminal role (chapter 8). Feldman examines the composer's literary choices as they either relate to or stand outside of a Petrarchan tradition, as they function as a result of Willaert's impact on madrigalian style, and more significant, as they reflect the complex sharing and shaping of Venetian culture fostered by learned academies and the practices of musical anthologists. This is a highly specialized study, requiring considerable knowledge of modern analytical techniques, comparative methodologies, the subtleties of linguistics, and music history. Still, it presents even to the novice a true appreciation for the sheer depth of Rore's own vast learning, as well as that of the audiences for whom he composed.

LOWINSKY's (1989) interests in Rore and his music spanned a lifelong career of amazing interdisciplinary and multidimensional scholarly pursuits, only a cross-section of which is represented in part 5 of the author's collected essays ("Cipriano de Rore as Court Composer: Ferrara and Munich"). Of the four essays in this section, "Cipriano de Rore's Venus Motet" is also available as a monograph (LOWINSKY [1986]), complete with full-color reproductions of corresponding artworks. At once both speculative and convincing, this study unites the arts of music, poetry, and painting in a manner most revealing of the humanistic intellect embodied by Rore and the spirit of his time. The other essays in the 1989 collection shed light on Rore's influences beyond the Venetian orbit. Lowinsky offers alternative views of the composer's works for and rela-

tionships with the Bavarian court ("Rore's Gift to Albrecht V"), calling Owens's earlier findings into question. He also posits new interpretations of the unusually scored motet "Calami sonum ferentes" and of compositions addressed to the powerful Este family of Ferrara. While demanding in technical detail, Lowinsky's conclusions draw attention to relatively untapped parameters of Rore's musical legacy.

OWENS's pioneering study unveils systematic strategies, methods, and materials employed by Renaissance composers. Comparing published and manuscript sources with what appear to be copies of works in progress, Owens counters Lowinsky's claim that polyphonic composition was largely an additive process. Newly discovered drafts, including several of Rore's (chapter 9), imply nascent understandings of vertical sonority and careful harmonic planning. Other alterations in Rore's sketches support the composer's concerns both for correct counterpoint and for the genuinely musical and expressive setting of his chosen texts.

MEIER considers Rore's musical language throughout his study of the modes in polyphonic composition. No fewer than 128 of the composer's works are evaluated in support of Meier's theories: that modal principles not only guided the organization of many of Rore's published collections but also served as a most evocative and sophisticated means for text expression. The time appears ripe for a complete appraisal of the life and works of Cipriano de Rore.

MICHAEL A. NEALON

Rorem, Ned b. 1923

United States composer, pianist, and writer

Bowles, Paul, *Dear Paul, Dear Ned: The Correspondence of Paul Bowles and Ned Rorem,* N.p.: Elysium Press, 1997

Mass, Lawrence D., "A Conversation with Ned Rorem," in *Queering the Pitch: The New Gay and Lesbian Musicology,* edited by Philip Brett et al., New York: Routledge, 1994

McDonald, Arlys L., *Ned Rorem: A Bio-Bibliography,* New York: Greenwood Press, 1989

Rorem, Ned, *The Paris Diary and the New York Diary, 1951–1961,* San Francisco: North Point Press, 1983

———, *Knowing When to Stop: A Memoir,* New York: Simon and Schuster, 1994

———, *Other Entertainment: Collected Pieces,* New York: Simon and Schuster, 1996

Ned Rorem has secured his position in music history as a composer of exceptionally beautiful and well-crafted art songs. His extensive knowledge of literature and affinity for the written word are apparent not only in his songs but also in his many published essays and diaries. He grew up in Chicago, studied at the Curtis Institute and the Juilliard School of Music, and took composition lessons from Virgil Thomson and David Diamond. Rorem then lived in Paris and Morocco for many years before settling in New York. His written accounts of the musical and literary circles in which he moved, while mildly scandalous, are important primary documents chronicling the landscape of high culture in the mid-20th century. In addition to his many songs and song cycles, Rorem also composes instrumental works and won the Pulitzer Prize in 1976 for his orchestral composition *Air Music*.

There has been little published scholarly research devoted to Rorem's music. Most of what is available is written by the composer himself and takes the form of letters, memoirs, diaries, and essays. This literature is entertaining and often insightful, but the reader interested in learning about the music itself may be frustrated by the effort necessary to cull such information from personal reminiscences. Rorem is a Quaker and thus a pacifist. He was also one of the first composers of his generation to publicly identify himself as homosexual. As gay and lesbian studies move into the mainstream of academia and the press at large, an audience exists today that knows Rorem primarily as an openly homosexual author who also happens to be a composer. Nevertheless, Rorem maintains that his sexual orientation is not relevant to his music, a position for which he has been taken to task by many in a younger generation of musicians, scholars, and activists.

The bio-bibliography by McDONALD features a brief, perfunctory biography based largely on correspondence with the composer and Rorem's own previously published writings. Perhaps owing to its relatively early publication date (1989), McDonald omits any reference to Rorem's homosexuality and describes the composer's partner James Holmes as simply "a friend." The bibliographical section of the book is exhaustive and includes work lists (alphabetical and chronological), selected performances, a discography, and an annotated bibliography of writings by and about the composer. McDonald even catalogs such ephemeral items as Rorem's letters to the editor and liner notes from recordings. This volume must be considered the definitive reference work in Rorem scholarship to date.

Rorem is considered by many to be the best writer among living American composers and is either author or coauthor of the remaining items on the reading list. They are his most recent publications and comprise a representative sampling of the composer's primary literary works in his favorite forms of essays, correspondence, diaries, memoirs, and interviews. ROREM (1996) is his latest assemblage of critical writings on music and literature. Others include *Settling the Score: Essays on Music* (1988) and *Setting the Tone: Essays and a Diary* (1983). His assessments of musical value and style are couched in personal reflections and as such do not represent a methodical critical analysis, but rather demonstrate his unabashedly personal albeit uniquely knowledgeable perspective.

The correspondence between Rorem and BOWLES spans half a century and covers the lives and work of many composers and literary figures since the end of World War II. Although they rarely saw one another and corresponded only sporadically, their letters reveal many commonalities and several mutual friends, including Truman Capote, Gore Vidal, Leonard Bernstein, and William S. Burroughs.

The reissue of 1950s diaries in ROREM (1983) suggests that gossip about famous figures from that almost mythical golden age of high culture remains as titillating as ever. These were the first of Rorem's half dozen published diaries, and the strengths and weaknesses of these journals characterize the later ones as well: he is frequently self-absorbed to a fault, but to his credit he does not attempt to make himself look better than those around him. When he does take note of his colleagues and the music and literature to which he is exposed, his critical assessments are incisive and, reading them with the benefit of decades of hindsight, often deadly accurate. Rorem subjected himself and his own music to the same unflinching scrutiny he cast upon others.

ROREM (1994) recounts his youth in even greater detail than that found in the diaries of the same period, although this volume reaches back to his childhood in Chicago and includes the more ordinary friends and family who do not people his later journals. It also introduces the reader to some of the tropes that recur throughout his writings, such as the notion that there are two aesthetics in the universe, French and German, and everything falls in either one or the other paradigm. Rorem begins this partial autobiography with the deaths of his parents in the 1980s and then returns to his childhood to reconstruct the first part of his life in relation to theirs.

Rorem's interview with Larry MASS was first published in Mass's book *Homosexuality as Behavior and Identity: Dialogues of the Sexual Revolution, Volume 2* (1990). Rorem has repeatedly stated that his homosexuality is no more or less relevant to his music than another composer's heterosexuality. For him, sexual orientation is only interesting as a political subject, and he remains an avid gay activist. In the course of their wide-ranging discussion, which covers contemporary opera, music criticism, and music and politics, Mass points up their generational differences of opinion on such issues as outing other composers and the possible existence of "gay music."

JOY HASLAM CALICO

Rossini, Gioachino 1792–1868

Italian composer

Edwards, H. Sutherland, *Rossini and His School,* London: Low, Marston, Searle, Rivington, 1881; 2nd edition 1888

Gossett, Philip, "Gioachino Rossini," in *The New Grove Masters of Italian Opera,* edited by Stanley Sadie, New York: Norton, 1983

Osborne, Richard, *The Bel Canto Operas of Rossini, Donizetti, and Bellini,* Portland, Oregon: Amadeus Press, and London: Methuen, 1994

————, *Rossini,* London: Dent, 1986; revised edition, 1993

Stendhal, *Life of Rossini,* translated by Richard N. Coe, New York: Orion Press, and London: Calder and Boyars, 1970; new edition, London: Calder, and New York: Riverrun Press, 1985

Toye, Francis, *Rossini, a Study in Tragi-Comedy,* London: Heinemann, and New York: Knopf, 1934; reprint, New York: Dover, 1987

Weinstock, Herbert, *Rossini: A Biography,* New York: Knopf, and London: Oxford University Press, 1968

Rossini's contribution to opera has been well documented in numerous books published during the past century and a half. Nonoperatic works, such as his chamber music and sacred compositions, have received comparatively little attention. Most Rossini scholarship has been published in Italian; Radiciotti, Bonaccorsi, and Rognoni are among the many writers who have contributed to the literature. Only a small number of such works have been translated into English. Fortunately, Gossett, Osborne, and Weinstock have produced valuable studies in English. Their numerous books and articles provide illuminating analyses of the composer, and the accuracy of their scholarship often clarifies earlier research.

First published in French as *Vie de Rossini* (1824), STENDHAL's biography is an important early contribution to Rossini literature that was written when Rossini was only 32. Translated into English by Richard N. Coe, the book provides a fascinating account by a Rossini contemporary, although the biographical material is often marred by fanciful anecdotes and inaccurate information. The importance of the book rests on the author's critical analysis of Rossini's music and of musical life in Europe. Stendhal's penetrating insights are often simultaneously humorous and thought provoking. Coe corrects the most egregious errors in his well-written notes at the end of the book.

EDWARDS, in one of the earliest English accounts of Rossini's life, provides a brief examination and evaluation the composer from a 19th-century perspective. The slim volume also critically discusses Donizetti and Bellini. As can be expected of a study from this era, the book contains a number of mistakes, including incorrect dates for Rossini's birth and death. Although Rossini scholarship has made great strides since this book, it nevertheless provides an insight into early bel canto studies from a period when Verdi and Wagner were still active. Although hardly objective, it grants the reader a concise overview of Italian opera from a contemporary critic.

TOYE's pioneering English-language biography of Rossini provides a brief and easily readable account of the composer's life and music. Toye's skills as a critic are evident throughout the book. At the time the book was written, Rossini was still generally regarded as a second-rate composer who wrote only one or two outstanding works. Toye spiritedly rejects this perception. Therefore, objective scholarship often yields to a polemical defense of Rossini's value. Although some of the author's strong opinions may be questionable, they do not detract from the overall value of the biography. More recent biographies correct some of his misinformation. The list of compositions is incomplete but may be sufficient for the casual reader.

GOSSETT's critical biography credits Rossini for the establishment of 19th-century operatic conventions and singing style. Gossett argues that the overwhelming popularity of Rossini's comedic work explains why scholars have undervalued his overall importance in music history. Much of Gossett's work supports this contention in an objective and scholarly style. His study of Rossini comprises the first section of a broader book that examines the five most important Italian opera composers of the 19th century. Several musical examples effectively illustrate various points. A knowledge of music theory will help the reader to follow the argument. Brief discussions of Rossini's nonoperatic compositions are enlightening, especially the pages devoted to the short piano pieces. The work list and bibliography are excellent.

OSBORNE (1986) traces Rossini's operatic career chronologically. Separate chapters deal with overtures, sacred music, and vocal and piano works, and numerous musical examples provide insights for readers unfamiliar with the scores. Discussions of specific operas include synopses, contemporary evaluations, and casting. The appendices are particularly useful. The first appendix is a fairly detailed calendar of the composer's life that includes a parallel sequence of contemporaneous events. The work list includes editions and is divided by genre. The third appendix contains an intriguing list of 70 people who are either directly or indirectly connected to Rossini.

The first seven chapters of OSBORNE (1994) are devoted to Rossini's operas. Each entry lists the cast of characters and vocal types, the librettist, and premiere data. Discussion of each opera commences with a brief biographical essay describing the composer's life at that point in his career, often presenting background information on the formation of the opera being discussed. This essay is followed by a brief synopsis and limited critical evaluation of the work. Osborne incorporates some interesting anecdotes and brief translations of original sources. A selective discography and limited bibliography conclude the Rossini section of this volume.

WEINSTOCK's substantial biography is one of the most important Rossini volumes in English. Access to original sources, including dozens of the composer's letters, adds value and credibility often absent from other biographies. The author liberally quotes from these letters as well as from contemporary accounts, which are presented in readable English translations. In keeping with Weinstock's emphasis on biographical detail, the book is well illustrated with portraits and photographs but lacks musical examples. The reader does not need knowledge of music theory to understand this study because the author focuses on constructing a portrait of the composer without offering detailed analysis of the music itself. The composer's musical style, however, is vividly communicated, and Rossini's place in music history is evaluated with a fair degree of objectivity. The valuable work list is divided by genre and includes performance histories and publishers. An extensive bibliography contains important Italian citations.

THEODORE L. GENTRY

Russia

Beliaev, Viktor M. *Central Asian Music: Essays in the History of the Music of the Peoples of the U.S.S.R.*, translated by Mark Slobin and Greta Slobin, edited by Mark Slobin, Middletown, Connecticut: Wesleyan University Press, 1975

Brown, Malcolm Hamrick, editor, *A Collection of Russian Folk Songs by Nikolai Lvov and Ivan Prach*, Ann Arbor, Michigan: UMI Research Press, 1987

——, editor, *Russian and Soviet Music: Essays for Boris Schwarz*, Ann Arbor, Michigan: UMI Research Press, 1984

Brown, Malcolm Hamrick, and Roland John Wiley, editors, *Slavonic and Western Music: Essays for Gerald Abraham*, Ann Arbor, Michigan: UMI Research Press, 1985

Fanning, David, "Russia: East Meets West," in *Music and Society: The Late Romantic Era*, edited by Jim Samson, Englewood Cliffs, New Jersey: Prentice Hall, 1991

Malia, Martin E., *Russia under Western Eyes: From the Bronze Horseman to the Lenin Mausoleum*, Cambridge, Massachusetts: Harvard University Press, 1999

Olkhovsky, Yuri, *Vladimir Stasov and Russian National Culture*, Ann Arbor, Michigan: UMI Research Press, and Epping: Bowker, 1983

Ridenour, Robert C., *Nationalism, Modernism, and Personal Rivalry in Nineteenth-Century Russian Music*, Ann Arbor, Michigan: UMI Research Press, 1981

Schwarz, Boris, *Music and Musical Life in Soviet Russia, 1917–1970*, London: Barrie and Jenkins, and New York: Norton, 1972; enlarged edition, as *Music and Musical Life in Soviet Russia, 1917–1981*, Bloomington: Indiana University Press, 1983

Seaman, Gerald, "Moscow and St. Petersburg," in *Music and Society: The Early Romantic Era, between Revolutions, 1789 and 1848*, edited by Alexander L. Ringer, Englewood Cliffs, New Jersey: Prentice Hall, 1990

Swan, Alfred J., *Russian Music and Its Sources in Chant and Folk-Song*, London: Baker, and New York: Norton, 1973

Taruskin, Richard, *Defining Russia Musically: Historical and Hermeneutical Essays*, Princeton, New Jersey: Princeton University Press, 1997

The study of a particular composer or genre is a typical point of entry for scholarship on Russian music. Equally important is the historical context for that compositional activity. This essay includes books that deal with important musical sources of Russian music—its folk song, its Eastern element, and its sacred chant; works placing Russian musical life in various eras within the context of the general cultural milieu or political life; and collections of essays that investigate narrower topics.

The center of a mighty empire, European Russia (the area around Moscow and St. Petersburg) has functioned as a cultural center much like any other, attracting artists and drawing from influences from the surrounding areas in a process that allows for cross-fertilization and synthesis. The works by Brown and by Beliaev emphasize Russia's dual role as both a Slavic nation and a polycultural empire. BROWN (1987) presents a facsimile edition of part of the famous folksong collection that first appeared in five editions between 1790 and 1955. Reproducing the second of these editions (originally published in 1806 and containing 150 songs), this book is valuable both for the folksongs themselves and for its introduction by ethnomusicologist Margarita Mazo, which provides context for the collection. Mazo discusses the genres of *Rossiiskaia Pesnia* (Russian art songs) and *Kanty* (mainly psalm settings); identifies other 18th-century collections; and provides a detailed description of each of the categories of folksong contained in Lvov and Prach's collection. There are several appendices, one of which lists folksongs from this collection that have been used by composers, both Russian and non-Russian, in their music.

BELIAEV focuses on the central Asian areas of the Soviet Union. This volume presents a translation of the first of three books of essays on the music of the Soviet Union and includes discussion of the musical culture of Kirghizia, Kazakhstan, Turkmenia, Tajikstan, and Uzbekistan. In each case, Beliaev outlines very basic theoretical background, the genres of folksong, composers and performers, and the music of the period following annexation to Russia. Mark Slobin's introduction and notes on bibliography put Beliaev's work into perspective. Although at the turn of the 21st century Central Asia is no longer part of either the Russian or Soviet empires, it is still important for students of Russian music to have some acquaintance with the musical source material of the so-called Russian East. Nineteenth-century Russian composers from Verstovsky through Rimsky-Korsakov made use of this source material in their compositions, and its exotic character has therefore come to signify Russianness to many Western writers and listeners. Beliaev insightfully refers to the use of Asian melodies in works by Russian composers, although the lack of an index makes these references hard to find.

A third important basic source of Russian music is the sacred tradition. Because of the Soviet interdiction on scholarship on religious topics, there are few recent books on this subject. SWAN, an English-language authority on both Russian folksong and church chant, has argued that these genres are closely related, and material from his scholarly articles on these subjects is included in this collection. Although published posthumously and apparently in an unfinished state, this book is nonetheless valuable for the chapters on chant and folksong because it introduces these topics to the general reader. More scholarly readers can follow the suggested references to the work of Kenneth Levy and Miloš Velimirović. Written in the style of a memoir, Swan's book also introduces the main personalities in the pursuit of Russian folksong and presents some interesting photographs (including one of a white-bearded Vladimir Stasov earnestly lecturing the young Maxim Gorky). Appendix 3 contains the text of a folk wedding rite found by Swan himself in the Pskov region in 1936, complete with musical examples. The book does not mention that the sound recording of Swan's collection is now in the Library of Congress.

Because the arts in Russia are so intertwined with political currents, students of Russian music must have some knowledge of the country's history. A recent treatment is presented by MALIA. This book is also a useful touchstone for much of the scholarship on Russian music. Taking as his main thesis the idea that there is no "polarity *between* Russia and Europe" but rather that Russia has a place "*within* Europe," Malia counters "habitual essentialist thinking" to present "geographic Europe not as two cultural zones—a West and an East—but as a spectrum of zones graded in level of development from the former to the latter." This view is a valuable perspective to maintain as one approaches the frequently polemical accounts of Russian music, especially when these accounts take a turn to the mystical.

Introductions to the history of musical institutions in 19th-century Russia are provided by Fanning and by Seaman. The intention of the Music and Society series is to describe, in chronological order, the context in which musical genres and forms developed, whether that context is political, religious, or intellectual. Thus, SEAMAN describes the organization of Russian society, its musical institutions, publishers, theaters, concert life, and domestic music-making to the mid-19th cen-

tury. FANNING fits his discussion of the major musical composers and works into a narrative that outlines Russia's imperial conquests, social stratification, education, foreign influences, and political and literary movements. Both authors provide a wealth of information in endnotes and annotated bibliographies.

RIDENOUR is a detailed account of mid-19th-century musical life that focuses specifically on St. Petersburg from roughly 1850 to 1875, the period of the founding of the Russian Musical Society and the St. Petersburg Conservatory by Anton Rubinstein and, in response, the rival Free Music School by the Balakirev Circle. Going beyond the traditional dichotomy of Slavic and Western adherents, Ridenour deals with the personalities of composers and critics and assesses the practical considerations of competition for position, career, and financial success. In addition, Ridenour includes details of the organization of opera troupes, the makeup of theater audiences, and the logistics of patronage in what was an ancien régime as compared with the rest of Europe. This study is a thoroughly scholarly yet readable account, serving as an excellent foil for studies of individual composers.

SCHWARZ is an intensive work dealing with the 20th century. The expanded 1983 edition includes the period from 1917 to 1981 and is especially interesting for its treatment of the decade of "Soviet consent and dissent," in which "the Soviet Union had to acknowledge the existence of a protest movement." Schwarz researched the book while visiting the Soviet Union in 1930, 1960, and 1962, and he covers in great detail the musical life (as opposed to analyzing specific musical compositions) from as far back as 1905 through almost the whole of the Soviet experiment. Particularly fascinating is the account of the period of regimentation (1932–53), during which musicologists as well as composers were constrained by the infamous Zhdanov decree that forbade the linking of Russian music to any foreign influence. The music of the whole of the 20th century can only be understood against the backdrop of the political conditions described by Schwarz.

Among studies of individual figures and specialized topics, OLKHOVSKY has produced a portrait of Vladimir Stasov, the influential music critic and supporter of the New Russian School (the Mighty Five—Balakirev, Borodin, Cui, Mussorgsky, and Rimsky-Korsakov). Olkhovsky presents the polemics that surrounded Russian music of the mid-19th century from the personal perspective of his subject: "Stasov loved struggle and he considered polemics a very serious part of his cause . . . Yet for tactical reasons, Stasov would never publicly acknowledge either his errors or the weaknesses of the new Russian School." According to Olkhovsky, this characteristic grew out of Stasov's personality and did not prevent him from maintaining close friendships. The critic's relationships with Tolstoy, Turgenev, Balakirev, and Serov are discussed, and the author emphasizes agreements and oppositions between Stasov and these figures. In addition to personalizing the history of musical life, this book also gives interesting details of the development and daily workings of some of the principal musical institutions of the capitol.

The anthology edited by BROWN and WILEY contains several narrowly focused studies of Russian music topics, although the focus of the collection is not exclusively Russian. Articles on Kandoshkin, Serov and Mussorgsky, Tchaikovsky's ballets, Tchaikovsky and Chekhov, and Skryabin will be of interest to both specialists and more general readers. Two articles deal with important correspondence: letters to Alfred Swan from Soviet composer of church music Pavel Chesnokov, and Prokofiev's correspondence with Stravinsky and Shostakovich. The first of these two essays, giving details of Swan's own biography and the difficulties faced by a composer of sacred music in 1930s Moscow, add richness of detail to the books by Swan and Schwarz already described. All 19 articles in the BROWN (1984) deal with Russian topics and count among their authors such scholars of Russian and Soviet music as Taruskin, Gerald Abraham, Miloš Velimirović, Lev Ginzburg, and Laurel

Fay. Topics range from the ninth through the 20th centuries, from the historical to the analytical.

The most sophisticated treatment of Russian music by far is that found in TARUSKIN. Written as a series of articles, the book provides a vertiable history of Russian music through detailed examinations of individual topics. This approach allows Taruskin to bring a wealth of philosophical, cultural, and political background to the case in hand, be it the composer Fomin and folk music or Shostakovich and the Soviet regime. Several of the 14 chapters deal prinicipally with opera; others address instrumental music, such as ballet or symphony; still others focus more on composers than genres. The emphasis is always on understanding Russia through its music, avoiding the pitfalls of essentialism while retaining the close textual analysis that has been out of fashion of late. Taruskin puts up a brilliant defense against what he regards as false history, refusing to be constrained by the scholarly fads of the present or by the ineptitudes of the past.

MARY S. WOODSIDE

See also Opera: 19th-Century Russian; Stravinsky, Igor

S

Saint-Saëns, Camille 1835–1921

French composer

Fallon, Daniel Martin, "The Symphonies and Symphonic Poems of Camille Saint-Saëns," 2 vols., Ph.D. dissertation, Yale University, 1973

Harding, James, *Saint-Saëns and His Circle,* London: Chapman and Hall, 1965

Hervey, Arthur, *Saint-Saëns,* London: Lane, 1921; New York: Dodd, Mead, 1922; reprint, Westport, Connecticut: Greenwood Press, 1970

Lyle, Watson, *Camille Saint-Saëns: His Life and Art,* London: Kegan Paul, Trench, Truber, and New York: Dutton, 1923; reprint, Westport, Connecticut: Greenwood Press, 1976

Saint-Saëns, Camille, *Musical Memories,* translated by Edwin Gile Rich, Boston: Small, Maynard, 1919; reprint, AMS Press, 1971

———, *Outspoken Essays on Music,* translated by Fred Rothwell, New York: Dutton, and London: Kegan Paul, Trench, Truber, 1923; reprint, Westport, Connecticut: Greenwood Press, 1970

Smith, Rollin, *Saint-Saëns and the Organ,* Stuyvesant, New York: Pendragon Press, 1992

Stegemann, Michael, *Camille Saint-Saëns and the French Solo Concerto from 1850 to 1920,* translated by Ann C. Sherwin, Portland, Oregon: Amadeus Press, and Aldershot: Scolar Press, 1991

Although Camille Saint-Saëns occupied a central place in the French musical world of his day, history has not treated him kindly. In the 1870s he was a revolutionary: a staunch defender of Berlioz, Wagner, and Liszt before that stance was professionally prudent; the first to compose symphonic poems in France (and later the earliest prominent creator of a film score); and a cofounder of the Société Nationale de Musique, the principal base for instrumental music in France after the Franco-Prussian War. From the 1880s on, however, his unrelenting hostility to the prevailing trends in French music—the music of César Franck and his followers, the French Wagnerians, and especially Debussy—in favor of an art in which well-built forms took precedence over personal expression, earned him a reputation as a bitter reactionary who composed music of superlative craftsmanship but lifeless content. This misleading characterization has survived both in the concert hall and in scholarship: few works from his sizable output regularly receive performances, while serious studies of the composer are rare, even in French (although this is beginning to change).

HERVEY authored the first important book on Saint-Saëns in English. Based both on the composer's own writings and on information provided by his personal secretary, Jean Bonnerot, Hervey offers a brief biography, an overview of Saint-Saëns's artistic principles, and a discussion of his works by genre, concentrating on the operas and orchestral music. Written shortly before Saint-Saëns's death, Hervey's respectful monograph bypasses controversial issues, such as the composer's numerous quarrels with other musicians and his separation from his wife, who is not even mentioned. The musical analyses are essentially program notes, and the book provides no documentation. Because of the author's access to primary material, however, it continues to be a valuable source.

LYLE's study, which appeared in the year following Saint-Saëns's death, bears many similarities to Hervey's in format and organization. Lyle focuses more on the instrumental works than on the operas, and although his discussions of the compositions remain largely superficial, they are more detailed than Hervey's and even venture to criticize at times. Lyle also considers Saint-Saëns's style in general, which Hervey does not. On the other hand, he is less well informed about French music and culture and, like Hervey, is willing to overlook or even distort biographical incidents that are not to Saint-Saëns's credit.

HARDING's biography, the only one to appear since Saint-Saëns's time, draws from many primary sources and provides valuable anecdotal and contextual material for understanding the composer and his world. Like Hervey and Lyle, Harding offers neither analytical discussions nor documentation. In addition to lacking footnotes, the book contains erroneous or at least misleading statements—for example, the incorrect but oft-repeated assertion that Saint-Saëns composed his Third Symphony as a memorial to Liszt. Although it is written in an accessible and engaging manner, the reader should not rely on information in this book without secondary verification, which can be difficult to obtain in English.

FALLON's dissertation is invaluable for its in-depth critical studies of the composer's five symphonies and four symphonic poems. This amply documented source presents a composition history and analysis for each piece. Fallon lays particular stress on Saint-Saëns's experiments with form and orchestration. Although the analyses are at times more detailed than the reader might desire, this resource remains the most perceptive study of these compositions in any language and the only one available in English. At the end, Fallon includes a brief discussion of Saint-Saëns's aesthetics.

STEGEMANN's monograph also originated as a dissertation. He has two goals: to examine Saint-Saëns's style as found in his concerti and one-movement concerted pieces for solo instrument and orchestra, and to provide a history of the concerto in Saint-Saëns's France. He does not analyze each work individually, but his findings regarding the composer's style are quite detailed and apply equally to all of his oeuvre. Despite the dense prose and hermetic graphs that frequently confront the reader, the subject matter of this book recommends itself. Stegemann begins with a brief but detailed biography designed to correct errors in previous books (especially Harding's) and closes with a thematic catalog of Saint-Saëns's concertante works.

SMITH devotes himself to a little-studied area: Saint-Saëns and the organ. The author organizes his subject around a biography based primarily on Bonnerot and provides a thematic catalog of the pieces for organ and harmonium but no analyses. With many rare photographs and detailed appendices on various topics relating to Saint-Saëns as organist and organ composer, this book fills an important gap for anyone interested in 19th-century organ music. A knowledge of organ terminology is helpful but not essential.

Saint-Saëns wrote several books of essays, none of which are available in English. In the years immediately following World War I, however, two collections of excerpts from these volumes appeared: SAINT-SAËNS (1919) and SAINT-SAËNS (1923). The most substantial contribution, found in the latter collection, is "The Ideas of M. Vincent d'Indy," a late treatise (1919) in which Saint-Saëns summarizes his artistic philosophy. Other essays include autobiographical recollections, reminiscences of great artists he knew—including Rossini, Liszt, and Victor Hugo—reviews, and assorted miscellaneous writings. As a historian Saint-Saëns can be jaded and self-serving, but his writings serve as important primary sources for musical life in mid-19th-century France. Regrettably, neither book provides the reader with the locations of the original French versions of the essays.

BRIAN J. HART

Salieri, Antonio 1750–1825

Italian composer

Braunbehrens, Volkmar, *Maligned Master: The Real Story of Antonio Salieri,* translated by Eveline L. Kanes, New York: Fromm, 1992

Rice, John A., *Antonio Salieri and Viennese Opera,* Chicago: University of Chicago Press, 1998

Thayer, Alexander Wheelock, *Salieri: Rival of Mozart,* edited by Theodore Albrecht, Kansas City, Missouri: Philharmonia of Greater Kansas City, 1989

The importance of Antonio Salieri as a musician is overwhelmed by the significance of the era during which he flourished. Salieri came of age in the Vienna of the Enlightenment, deriving his musical language from the teachings of Gassmann and the reform opera movement inaugurated by Gluck. A firsthand witness to the musical genius of Mozart, Salieri ultimately reigned as teacher to many composers of the succeeding musical generation, including Beethoven, Schubert, Czerny, Liszt, and others. Because late 18th-century Vienna is best remembered as the city of Mozart and Beethoven, one is prone to ignore the *Kleinmeisters,* the sizable number of talented but anonymous musicians making their living in the artistically fecund arena of this epoch. Salieri, nevertheless, survives with a recognizable name, albeit for the wrong reason. As a consequence of Pushkin's play of 1830, *Mozart and Salieri,* which was subsequently set to music by Rimsky-Korsakov, and, later, Peter Schaffer's play *Amadeus* (1980), which was made into a motion picture, Salieri endures in folklore as the ostensible murderer of Mozart.

Salieri enjoyed great professional acclaim in his own time and was much more successful a composer than Mozart during their respective lives. Salieri served the Viennese court for more than 50 years, 36 of them as kapellmeister (1788–1824), composing more than 40 operas, the quality ranging from rousing successes (e.g., *Tarare* [1787], the biggest box-office success at the Paris Opéra for decades) to dismal failures (e.g., *Il mondo alla rovescia* [1795]). Certainly Salieri and Mozart were rivals; Mozart, who spent his last decade (1781–91) in Vienna, may well have coveted Salieri's position with the emperor because he was beneath Salieri in the court hierarchy. However, by 1820, when Salieri's operas were already outmoded, Mozart's posthumous reputation was blossoming. The aging Salieri found that public interest in him was now confined only to the fact that he had actually been acquainted with the great Mozart. Salieri's life ended in confusion, derangement, and depression in a hospital in Vienna. It was said that he had both confessed to Mozart's poisoning and denied it. The rumor of his supposed confession swept Vienna and caught the imagination of Pushkin.

THAYER, the noted 19th-century authority on Beethoven, also wrote a biography of Salieri, originally serialized in *Dwight's Journal of Music* (Boston) from December 1863 to November 1864, that is now available in book form. Penned in the flowery language and intimate style of the 19th century, the book relies heavily on an even earlier biography written by a friend of Salieri with access to his papers, Ignaz Franz von Mosel (*Über das Leben und die Werke des Anton Salieri* [1827]). Salieri's life story follows an opening chapter that examines the history of opera in Vienna during the 100 years preceding the arrival of Salieri. Much of the information from this early monograph has been incorporated into the modern biographies discussed here. The appendices contain several interesting essays, including a testament from the two medical attendants who cared for the dying Salieri declaring that they never heard him confess to poisoning Mozart.

BRAUNBEHRENS provides an exacting chronological journey through the life of Salieri. Preceded by an introduction that tries to make order out of the chaos of rumors surrounding Mozart's death and how Salieri came to be implicated, the book weaves all known details of Salieri's life into the narrative, displaying a valiant effort to leave nothing out. In addition, detailed background on most of Salieri's operas is interspersed without pause in the text, making the prose choppy and creating a volume that is cumbersome for readers seeking a specific opera or incident. For example, Salieri enjoyed a close personal friendship with Beaumarchais, author of *Le Barbier de Séville*, with whom the composer resided briefly in Paris while they collaborated on an opera. At this point in the biography, the discourse on Salieri pauses while the author devotes several pages to Beaumarchais's various literary projects and business dealings. Presently, Salieri's life resumes but with no delineation to separate the various trains of thought. The bibliography is thorough, but a work list is lacking.

RICE uses the life of Salieri as a canvas on which to paint the history of opera in Vienna during the last third of the 18th century. Salieri proves to be the logical choice as he is possibly the only composer, and surely the most successful, to have been present and active in Vienna during the entire period. The dual subjects of Salieri's life and Viennese opera receive rigorous scrutiny with copious documentation from primary sources, many pictures, and frequent musical examples. Also investigated are the changing political climate in the Viennese court throughout the era and the impact of court politics on opera composition and presentation.

The book's focus is really threefold. In addition to being a biography of Salieri up to the end of his opera career in 1804 and a history of Viennese opera, the volume also presents painstaking analyses of the music and drama of the operas themselves. Operas by composers other than Salieri are examined as well. Rice provides a chronological list of Salieri's operas, as well as a separate index referencing works by the composer. The bibliography lists primary as well as secondary sources. Of possible interest to some readers is an unpublished dissertation on Salieri (Edward Elmgrer Swenson, "Antonio Salieri: A Documentary Biography" [Cornell University, 1974]) that Rice frequently cites as an abundant source of information on the subject.

NANCY F. GARF

Satie, Erik 1866–1925

French composer

Gillmor, Alan, *Erik Satie,* Boston: Twayne, 1988

Orledge, Robert, *Satie Remembered,* London: Faber, and Portland, Oregon: Amadeus Press, 1995

———, *Satie the Composer,* Cambridge: Cambridge University Press, 1990

Perloff, Nancy, *Art and the Everyday: Popular Entertainment and the Circle of Erik Satie,* Oxford: Clarendon Press, and New York: Oxford University Press, 1991

Shattuck, Roger, *The Banquet Years: The Origins of the Avant Garde in France, 1885 to World War I,* London: Faber, 1959; revised edition, New York: Vintage Books, 1968; first published under the title, *The Banquet Years: The Arts in France, 1885–1918: Alfred Jarry, Henri Rousseau, Erik Satie, Guillaume Appolinaire,* London: Faber, 1958

Templier, Pierre-Daniel, *Erik Satie,* translated by Elena French and David French, Cambridge, Massachusetts: MIT Press, 1969

Volta, Ornella, *Erik Satie,* translated by Simon Pleasance, Paris: Hazan, 1997

Volta, Ornella, editor, *Satie Seen through His Letters,* translated by Michael Bullock, London: Boyars, 1988

Weiss, Jeffrey, *The Popular Culture of Modern Art: Picasso, Duchamp, and Avant-Gardism,* New Haven, Connecticut: Yale University Press, 1994

Whiting, Steven Moore, *Satie the Bohemian,* Oxford: Clarendon Press, and New York: Oxford University Press, 1998

French composer Erik Satie left a legacy that includes literature and visual art as well as musical scores and that encompasses stylistic approaches ranging from fin de siècle mysticism to jazz-age irreverence. Best known today for his early, ethereal *Gymnopédies* (1888), Satie was described by contemporaries as a "musical humorist" and gravitated toward the small forms and sparse textures that allowed an expression of his incisive wit. These qualities, as well as his adherence to the musical values of brevity, clarity, and simplicity, led Jean Cocteau to proclaim Satie the representative of a new French musical modernism in 1918. That year, in his manifesto *Le Coq et l'arlequin*, Cocteau cited Satie's thoroughgoing integration of elements of high art and vernacular culture as quintessentially modern, thus laying the groundwork for future studies of the composer. As Cocteau noted, Satie's biography provides one source for this mingling of high and low, as from the late 1880s through the 1900s he was at home equally in the elite musical circles as well as the popular entertainment venues of Paris; more important, however, Satie was part of a shifting circle of artists engrossed in the exploration of the same dialectic of high and low art in the early part of the 20th century, which included the cubists Georges Braque and Pablo Picasso, as well as the poet Guillaume Apollinaire.

Not only the breadth of Satie's activity but also his light touch and overt humor deterred critics and analysts, particularly in the years immediately following his death. John Cage began to introduce Satie to a new audience in the 1950s, inaugurating a resurgence of enthusiasm for the composer on multiple fronts. Publication and performance of Satie's music in the 1960s and 1970s sparked a wave of scholarly interest that continues to gain momentum. Appropriately enough for a composer whose own enigmatic work resists easy categorization, the literature that makes him its subject is rich and varied.

GILLMOR presents a comprehensive, chronological, and contextually detailed portrait of Satie. His opening chapter, which recounts the history of the Société Nationale de Musique (founded by César Franck and others in the wake of the Franco-Prussian War) provides an illuminating backdrop for consideration of Satie's compositional aesthetic. The remainder of the book organizes Satie's career into nine thematically defined chapters, each providing a mix of commentary, historical information, and musical analysis. Commendable for its effort to incorporate discussion of relevant contemporary issues in literature and the visual arts, the carefully annotated book is equally useful as an introduction to Satie's work and as a tool for more specialized research. The book includes a chronology, bibliography, catalog of works, and discography, all of which remain valuable.

ORLEDGE (1990) offers a breakthrough book, the first full-length study devoted exclusively to Satie's compositional practice. As he explains in his preface, Orledge's aim is to investigate both how and why Satie composed, and to this end he synthesizes evidence ranging from testimony of friends and collaborators to Satie's own musical, visual, and literary work. The book's 12 chapters focus on broad topics, such as Satie's relationship with Debussy and his interactions with other artists, as well as the more technical issues of orchestration, counterpoint, parody, and compositional design. Framing these discussions are considerations of various historical interpretations of Satie's career and place in the "wider world." Consistently focused on the music, the book is especially valuable for its lucid analysis of Satie's scores, explicated both in prose and musical examples and enlivened by the inclusion of numerous sketch and manuscripts facsimiles. Thorough and thoughtful annotations, a detailed chronology, and an eclectic bibliography provide useful and accessible information. Among the book's most important contributions is the chronological catalog of Satie's compositions, the first list of his works to amalgamate description; dates of composition, publication, and premieres; and information about manuscript sources. A giant leap forward in Satie scholarship, this book is an essential resource.

ORLEDGE (1995) presents a collection of reminiscences and commentaries about Satie recorded by a variety of the composer's friends, acquaintances, collaborators, and critics. In selected excerpts, more than half of which appear here in English translation for the first time, a cross-section of Satie's contemporaries provide accounts of the composer's eccentric habits and personality and discuss his influence and impact. Chronologically arranged to correspond to 11 phases of Satie's life, these recollections are individually illuminating and collectively add depth to the current views of the composer. Among the artists heard from are Cocteau, Stravinsky, Fernand Léger, Blaise Cendrars, Man Ray, Constantin Brancusi, Francis Picabia, and members of Les Six. A collection of photographs and a chronology complete the study.

PERLOFF considers Satie's music in relation to "everyday" art, a term never defined in her text but apparently intended as a reference to the entertainments of the Parisian cabaret, circus, fair, and music hall. She posits that Satie, seeking a style antithetical to musical impressionism, modeled his own compositions on music characteristic of these venues, attracting a small group of adherents—namely, Cocteau, Georges Auric, Francis Poulenc, and Darius Milhaud. The book's first two chapters provide background, summarizing information about the institutions, genres, and celebrities of popular entertainment in early 20th-century Paris. Also general in nature are chapters devoted to discussion of Satie's tenure as a cabaret pianist and the engagement of his circle with popular entertainments; more analytical approaches to the music are found in chapters focusing on Satie's *Parade* and on post-*Parade* works of the other composers. Skimming the surface of her topic, Perloff rarely touches on the social or political issues implicated in the composer's turn toward popular sources, nor does she attempt a synthetic discussion of the relationship of this musical project to parallel contemporary efforts in literature or the visual arts. Still, while simplifying the subject matter, the book can serve as an introduction to this important facet of Satie's compositional aesthetic.

SHATTUCK's classic study, which catapulted Satie into the consciousness of nonspecialists in the United States and Europe, identifies the composer as one of a quartet of figures responsible for the creation of the avant-garde in Paris before World War I. Shattuck contends that Satie, like Guillaume Apollinaire, Alfred Jarry, and Henri Rousseau, embodied four characteristics that defined modernity: childlike naïveté, absurd humor, devotion to the dream state, and an embrace of ambiguity. Against this backdrop, the author presents an insightful, enlightening, and unfailingly entertaining portrait of Satie and his work, accounting for his literary and visual art works as well as his musical compositions.

TEMPLIER, who befriended Satie in Arcueil, the Parisian suburb where the composer lived after 1898, authored the first book-length study of Satie in 1932. Completed with the help of Satie's brother Conrad, it has been the most comprehensive source of documentation concerning the composer's early life. The monograph is divided into two broad sections, covering Satie's biography and discussing individual musical works, though not in analytical detail. The English translation does not capture the elegance of the original French edition, but it includes the same rare photographs and facsimiles.

Volta, director of the Fondation Satie in Paris, has edited and fastidiously annotated Satie's writings—which run the gamut from aphorisms scrawled in sketchbooks to full-length essays published in contemporary magazines—and is completing an edition of his correspondence. Her volume *Satie: Ecrits* (1990) has provided a foundation for recent Satie scholarship, and although this work, like the bulk of Satie's writings, remains unavailable in English translation, Volta has produced two remarkable books that shed light on the composer for English audiences. In SATIE, Volta artfully weaves selections from the composer's letters into a biographical narrative to convey details of both his personal and professional life. Including correspondence with Debussy, Ravel, and Stravinsky, among many others, the volume is illustrated with line drawings by Cocteau, René Magritte, Picasso, and other contemporaries, as well as by Satie. Beautifully presented, at once charming and substantive, the book is evocative of Satie himself.

The commentary in VOLTA is concise; the pocket-size picture book is devoted to the presentation of images of the composer—paintings, drawings, caricatures, and photographs—as well as facsimiles of his manuscripts, artistic representations capturing performances of his works, posters, publicity, and a wide range of ephemera. Chronologically organized, and including many previously unpublished materials, the illuminating book provides visual documentation of Satie's life and work.

WEISS, an art historian, explores the relationship of avant-garde visual art to popular contemporary entertainments in the early part of the 20th century. Focusing on Picasso's cubist collages and Marcel Duchamp's readymades, the author convincingly argues for a connection between the aesthetic of modernist visual art and music-hall shows. His chapter "Le Spectacle intérieur" provides a compelling and original analysis of *Parade*, identifying the ballet's sources in the music-hall revue and demonstrating that the work was designed to serve as a vehicle for the popularization of cubism. Although technical discussion of Satie's musical score is limited, Weiss offers an articulate contextual analysis based largely on significant and heretofore overlooked period commentary. His argument as a whole offers a new framework for considering Satie's position among vanguard artists and suggests a revised reading not only of *Parade* but Satie's work in general.

WHITING offers yet another contextual perspective, illuminating Satie's work against the background of his involvement in the bohemian subculture of Montmartre at the turn of the 19th century. The book is by far the longest study of Satie to date, and its aim—to demonstrate a unifying theme for Satie's works as a whole—may qualify it as the most ambitious. Working from the thesis that Satie's aesthetic views and compositional strategies were shaped in fin de siècle popular entertainment venues, including the *café-concert*, music hall, and cabaret, Whiting devotes his initial chapters to a thorough examination of these milieux in general. He documents Satie's specific associations with a number of these establishments and offers an analytical examination of the songs, waltzes, and other popular music Satie composed or arranged for performance in these environments. Moving chronologically through Satie's work, Whiting then argues persuasively for a connection between the everyday idioms of the cabaret and music hall and the composer's later avant-garde style. His interpretation is fresh and soundly crafted, suggesting a plausible new approach to Satie's eclectic life and work.

MARY E. DAVIS

Scandinavia

Grinde, Nils, *Contemporary Norwegian Music 1920–1980*, translated by Sandra Hamilton, Oslo: Universitetsforlaget, and Irvington-on-Hudson, New York, Columbia University Press, 1981

Grinde, Nils, *A History of Norwegian Music*, translated by William H. Halverson and Leland Sateren, Lincoln: University of Nebraska Press, 1991

Hillila, Ruth-Esther, and Barbara Blanchard Hong, *Historical Dictionary of the Music and Musicians of Finland*, Westport, Connecticut: Greenwood Press, 1997

Hodgson, Antony, *Scandinavian Music: Finland and Sweden,* Rutherford, New Jersey: Fairleigh Dickinson University Press, and London: Associated University Presses, 1984

Horton, John, *Scandinavian Music: A Short History,* London: Faber, 1963

Ketting, Knud, editor, *Music in Denmark,* Copenhagen: Danish Cultural Institute, 1987

Lange, Kristian, *Norwegian Music: A Survey,* Oslo: Tanum, 1971

Schönfelder, Gerd, and Hans Astrand, *Contemporary Swedish Music through the Telescopic Sight,* [Sweden]: Edition Reimers, 1993

Searle, Humphrey, and Robert Layton, *Britain, Scandinavia, and the Netherlands,* New York: Holt, Rinehart and Winston, 1972

Yoell, John H., *The Nordic Sound: Explorations into the Music of Denmark, Norway, Sweden,* Boston: Crescendo, 1974

The boundaries of Scandinavia have been defined by scholars in various ways. Geographically, Scandinavia refers to the Scandinavian peninsula, occupied by Norway and Sweden, and the neighboring nation of Denmark. Inhabited by related peoples who speak similar languages and whose cultures and histories have always been closely connected, these three nations comprise the essential Scandinavia. However, Finland, a neighbor of Sweden and Norway, can also be included. Geographically, Finland is a part of the region, although its language and mythology are unrelated to those of Denmark, Norway, and Sweden. Setting geographical proximity aside, Scandinavia can also include the islands that for centuries have served as Scandinavian outposts: the Faeroe Islands and Greenland, which are still in union with Denmark, and Iceland, an independent republic since 1944. Scandinavia has a rich musical heritage dating back to the age of the Vikings, but unfortunately only a small part of this heritage is presently accessible to readers unfamiliar with Scandinavian languages. Few studies concerning Scandinavian music have been published in English, and those that have appeared offer little more than general information.

HORTON's work is the most comprehensive introduction to the topic. Here the musical heritage of Norway, Sweden, Denmark, and Finland is discussed in a clear, straightforward manner intended for general readers with little knowledge of Scandinavian history. (Iceland is mentioned briefly in the chapters on early music, but no discussion of the island's musical heritage is included.) The book is arranged chronologically, beginning with the pre-Christian and medieval periods and ending around 1950. Discussions focus on the contributions of prominent composers and their most popular works. General, albeit brief, biographies are included sporadically, and many musical examples, manuscript facsimiles, and photographs facilitate the author's discussions of compositions and common performance practices. Horton treats Scandinavian music

as a unified whole; only in discussions of 19th- and 20th-century music are readers exposed to the distinctive musical traits of each Scandinavian country.

YOELL's work is not a historical survey but a reference book supplying general information about compositions written in Denmark, Norway, and Sweden since the 17th century. The book is divided into two parts. Part 1, "Historical Perspectives," gives a brief but accurate survey of Scandinavian music history from antiquity to the 1960s. Part 2, "Composers Gallery," describes in moderate detail the most popular works of prominent composers from the baroque era to the 1960s. Yoell supplies brief biographies for every composer discussed in part 2, but unfortunately his choice of composers is governed by the availability of their music on phonograph recordings.

LANGE contends that the history of Norwegian art music began in the 19th century and that the music played in the courts and concert halls prior to that time was not part of the Norwegian tradition but a poor imitation of genteel music belonging to other European cultures. For this reason, the author does not discuss art music prior to the 19th century. Instead, he examines the key components of Norway's folk music tradition and attempts to illustrate how it generated a corpus of Norwegian art music in the mid-19th century. Chapters are dedicated to Grieg and his followers, and music after World War II is discussed in some detail. Unfortunately, Lange's discussions of Norwegian music and its relation to the music of other European nations are often colored by obvious nationalistic prejudices.

KETTING gives a more balanced view of a single nation's musical tradition and the influence of other nations. This book is not limited to an investigation of art music; rather, it presents a broad description of Denmark's complete musical tradition. Folk music, art music, jazz, rock, and music education are given equal weight in chapters written by noted scholars in the fields. An extensive bibliography of books and articles in English is included at the end of the volume, as are the names and addresses of Denmark's musical organizations and institutions. The breadth of this book leaves little room for detailed discussions of each topic, but it still serves as a good starting point for readers interested in Denmark's growing musical culture.

The title of HODGSON is somewhat misleading, for the book is limited to a discussion of Finland and Sweden. As Hodgson explains, the cultures of both countries were closely linked from 1582 until 1809, causing an overlap in their musical histories. However, when Russia took over Finland in the beginning of the 19th century, changes in Finnish culture occurred rapidly. Hodgson attempts to trace these changes. He charts the growth of both Swedish and Finnish musical life since the 1400s and describes the characteristic differences that have emerged over the 19th and 20th centuries. Much attention is given to political and linguistic influences, and the effect of separate folk traditions is discussed in detail. A substantial discography is included as an appendix to the book, and a brief bibliography of books in English is supplied for readers interested in exploring the topic further.

The lack of easily available information on Finnish music makes HILLILA and HONG an indispensable resource for both students and scholars. Each entry is written by a top scholar in the field and includes extensive bibliographies containing sources in various languages. In addition, appendices contain geographical information about Finland and chronological overviews of Finnish political and musical histories.

A good introduction to contemporary Scandinavian music is volume 2 of SEARLE and LAYTON. The authors present a general overview of art music by 20th-century composers in Britain, the Netherlands, and Scandinavia. Only the final chapters deal with music from Scandinavia: chapter 9 discusses the symphonists Sibelius and Nielsen, and chapter 10 presents an overview of works by composers in Finland, Denmark, Sweden, and Norway since Sibelius. In both chapters, Searle and Layton investigate the national characteristics particular to each Scandinavian country, using descriptions of specific well-known compositions as primary evidence. No music examples are included, and discussions are easily accessible to readers unfamiliar with theoretical terminology.

SCHÖNFELDER and ÅSTRAND present nine analytical studies of key compositions by contemporary composers: Hilding Rosenberg, Sven-Erik Bäck, Ingvar Lidholm, Jan Carlstedt, Lars-Gunnar Bodin, Eskil Hemberg, Daniel Börtz, Anders Eliasson, and Karin Rehnqvist. Chapter 1 is a thought-provoking essay on the nature of analysis and its various purposes. This essay is followed by nine lengthy and very detailed analytical studies. This book is clearly intended for readers well versed in theoretical terminology, and those who read it will quickly discover the wealth and diversity of Sweden's contemporary music culture.

GRINDE (1981) presents an accurate survey of the various music trends that have arisen in Norway since World War I. He begins this study with a discussion of nationalism and European influence, describing how Norwegian art music in the first half of the 20th century was characterized to a great degree by nationalistic tendencies. However, in the second half of the century, the influence of international modernistic tendencies caused something of a revolution in Norwegian art music. According to Grinde, this revolution was largely due to the influence of serialism and the impact of American jazz. This book is based on the last two chapters of Grinde's *Norsk musikkhistorie*.

No doubt the success of Grinde (1981) led to the full translation of *Norsk musikkhistorie* in GRINDE (1991). However, this book is more than a simple translation. Grinde has revised the text twice since its original publication, and the English translation has been updated by Grinde to include the most recent Norwegian musicians and compositions. This book traces the history of Norwegian music from antiquity to the present. It is the definitive study of Norwegian music and the finest book on Scandinavian music available in English.

ANNA H. HARWELL CELENZA

Scarlatti, Alessandro 1660–1725

Italian composer

D'Accone, Frank A., *The History of a Baroque Opera: Alessandro Scarlatti's Gli equivoci nel sembiante,* New York: Pendragon Press, 1985

Dent, Edward Joseph, *Alessandro Scarlatti: His Life and Works,* London: Arnold, 1905; reprint, St. Clair Shores, Michigan: Scholarly Press, 1976

Grout, Donald Jay, *Alessandro Scarlatti: An Introduction to His Operas,* Berkeley: University of California Press, 1979

Grout, Donald Jay, et al., "Alessandro Scarlatti," *The New Grove Italian Baroque Masters,* edited by Denis Arnold et al., London: Macmillan, and New York: Norton, 1984

Holmes, William, *La Statira by Pietro Ottoboni and Alessandro Scarlatti: The Textual Sources, with a Documentary Postscript,* New York: Pendragon Press, 1983

Vidali, Carole Franklin, *Alessandro and Domenico Scarlatti: A Guide to Research,* New York: Garland, 1993

Alessandro Scarlatti was perhaps the most important Italian composer of the late baroque. His works span from 1679 to 1725 and are of tremendous quality and quantity. He was the first of a new generation of Italian opera composers and is often referred to as the founder of the Neapolitan school of 18th-century opera. However, rather than advocating a newer classic style, as many of his students did, his pieces are the embodiment of the end of the baroque style. He brought enormous wealth to the world of music, including perhaps as many as 114 operas, some gaining great popularity as far away as London, of which we have only a surviving remnant. His importance in the education of a new generation of musicians cannot be overstated. He was a father figure, both in reputation and in musical style, to many of the composers who followed him. Scarlatti was not an innovator, although one can find in his music glimpses of the newer style, but rather a cornerstone for the world of music, on which the 18th century built its strong and impressive repertoire of Italian opera.

Interest in and research on Scarlatti and his music continue today, but most new studies appear in the form of articles and dissertations, and often in Italian. For this reason VIDALI is an important point of departure. It is a helpful, up-to-date work that contains a detailed annotated bibliography of English and foreign-language books, articles, and dissertations on Alessandro and Domenico Scarlatti. The first two-thirds of the book are dedicated to Alessandro. The work contains bibliographic entries on Scarlatti's life and works—including subdivisions on "Biographies," "Letters and Documents," "Scarlatti's Family," "Cultural and Aesthetic Background," and "Scarlatti's Relationship to Handel and Other Composers." There are also bibliographic entries for specific genres, performance-practice issues, and modern performance reviews, as well as a list of modern editions and facsimiles and a discography of in-print and out-of-print recordings. Vidali is an invaluable tool for any student or scholar interested in Scarlatti and his music.

DENT's musicological work is the only comprehensive monograph in English concerning Alessandro Scarlatti's life and works. First published in 1905, the book is organized chronologically, focusing on biographical issues and featuring discussions of Scarlatti's works within the biographical context. The newer edition of the book, presented here, features updated information such as corrected dates of events in the lives of Scarlatti and his relatives and information about newly found or identified manuscripts. The additional notes are an important source for the Scarlatti scholar and student. Both versions of Dent's book include a catalog of the extant works that designates the locations of the manuscripts. Dent supplies ample musical examples and provides insightful discussions about Scarlatti's musical style, including comparisons with such composers as Handel and Corelli. Although we now are discovering new information about the 18th century and music identified as Neapolitan in style, Dent's invaluable work is still the best comprehensive source in English.

GROUT's monograph is the only study of all of Scarlatti's operas. The introductory discussion of the *dramma per musica* in Scarlatti's time is both informative and interesting. The book is arranged chronologically, tracing important operatic works and pointing out notable musical characteristics of particular operas, arias, and librettos. The closing chapter addresses the forms of Scarlatti's operas, including discussions on aria forms and the composer's musical style. The appendix contains musical examples from six arias, two each from his three operas *La principessa fedele, Mitridate Eupatore,* and *Tigrane.* The details of Neapolitan society and the individuals with whom Scarlatti interacted make the reading of this text enjoyable. The only thing lacking is a complete list of operas. Grout's study on Scarlatti's operas is relevant for the music student of 18th-century opera, for the specialist looking for specific information about Scarlatti's operas, and for the general reader interested in details of 18th-century opera or Scarlatti.

GROUT (1984) is the most concise and up-to-date biography that we have. The work list by Boyd contains the most current research. The authors discuss biography, musical style, and related issues. This research is highly useful for students of all types and scholars wishing to verify information concerning Scarlatti or his music.

D'ACCONE's exhaustive study of Scarlatti's first opera, *Gli equivoci nel sembiante,* is well organized, well written, and extremely informative. The author surveys the circumstances of various performances and the reception of this 1679 opera. Following a description of the Roman carnival season and papal policy, D'Accone traces the opera's first performances in Rome using primary accounts. He then summarizes the libretto content and correlating arias. Chapter 3 discusses the music and 18th-century performance practice before considering other performances and examining the principal musical sources and their locations. This work is based on solid musicological research and will enlighten both the Scarlatti student and scholar.

HOLMES's monograph lives up to the promise of its subtitle. Divided into three sections, "Introduction," "The Sources Compared," and "A Documentary Postscript," the book is intended for the specialist and serious student of Scarlatti's operas. Pietro Ottoboni was the grandnephew of Pope Alexander VIII and cardinal and vice chancellor of the church. At age 22, Ottoboni commissioned Scarlatti to set a libretto that Ottoboni wrote himself, *La Statira.* Holmes discusses the four surviving orchestral scores, their whereabouts, and their format. A detailed comparison of the sources then ensues. The documentary postscript offers accounts of and letters about the performances of the opera.

SHERYL KATHLEEN MURPHY

Scarlatti, Domenico 1685–1757

Italian-born composer

Boyd, Malcolm, *Domenico Scarlatti: Master of Music,* London: Weidenfeld and Nicolson, and New York: Schirmer Books, 1986

Hammond, Frederick, "Domenico Scarlatti," in *Eighteenth-Century Keyboard Music,* edited by Robert L. Marshall, New York: Schirmer Books, 1994

Kirkpatrick, Ralph, *Domenico Scarlatti,* Princeton, New Jersey: Princeton University Press, 1953; revised edition, 1970

Vidali, Carole Franklin, *Alessandro and Domenico Scarlatti: A Guide to Research,* New York: Garland, 1993

Williams, Peter F., editor, *Bach, Handel, Scarlatti: Tercentenary Essays,* Cambridge: Cambridge University Press, 1985

In his youth, Domenico Scarlatti, son of Alessandro Scarlatti, followed his father's steps as a composer of vocal music in Naples, Venice, and Rome. He later enjoyed a quiet life in Lisbon and Madrid, devoted to his patroness, the musical Maria Barbara, infanta and queen, for whom he composed more than 555 keyboard pieces. These pieces were acknowledged by Chopin, among many others, as creations of originality, human ardor, and imaginative colors, demonstrating all the earthy vitality and amorous spirit of Iberia's folk music and dance. The greatest portion of those pieces (now kept in the Marciana library in Venice) were taken to Italy by the famous castratto Farinelli. Farinelli's account of Scarlatti related by Dr. Charles Burney in his *General History of Music* (London, 1776–89) was an important early source. An entire century had to pass before new information was provided, in Edward J. Dent's *Alessandro Scarlatti: His Life and Works*, (London, 1905). Then, in 1913, Alessandro Longo published in Naples his pioneer study *Domenico Scarlatti e la sua figura nella storia della musica*. Important contributions followed by Ulisse Prota-Giurleo and Sacheverell Sitwell, whose *A Background for Domenico Scarlatti* (London, 1935) was the first English book on Scarlatti. After Kirkpatrick's monograph, Hermann Keller, Giorgio Pestelli, Roberto Pagano, Joel Sheveloff, Malcom Boyd, and others have added to the unfolding of Scarlatti's scantly documented life.

The complete absence of autographs has led to the compilation of three catalogs. Scarlatti's sonatas were preserved in beautiful manuscripts by an anonymous copyist, that failed to have even a hint of their chronological order. The Italian pianist and composer Alessandro Longo published what he considered the complete works for harpsichord by Scarlatti, and compiled the first catalog of his keyboard works in 1906–10. Longo grouped the sonatas into suites with the sole criterion being their tonalities, resulting in chronological disorder.

In his capacity as a harpsichordist, researcher, editor, and author as well as the compiler of one of the three existing catalogs of Scarlatti's keyboard music, Ralph KIRKPATRICK is acknowledged as the main advocate of Scarlatti's keyboard music. Observing that a large number of the sonatas formed pairs, as was the custom with Italian keyboard music of the time, Kirkpatrick gives a catalog whose chronological order is not much disputed. This catalog, with cross references to the Longo catalog, is preceded by a bibliography, 44 illustrations, and a series of valuable appendices: a documented Scarlatti family tree, documents concerning the instruments at Scarlatti's disposal, a discussion on the ornamentation of Scarlatti's keyboard music, and a description of all the sources where Scarlatti's works have been preserved. Kirkpatrick's writing reflects his love and admiration for Scarlatti's music, and his own elegant humor and charm. His observations on the influence of traditional Spanish music on Scarlatti's sonatas radically transformed the interpretation of his music. For these reasons, Kirkpatrick is still considered a standard book on Scarlatti, despite the fact that certain theses have been refuted. Giorgio Pestelli's 1967 catalog does not seem to have replaced Kirkpatrick's, due to its debatable subjective criteria of Scarlatti's stylistic development. However, Joel Sheveloff, in "The Keyboard Music of Domenico Scarlatti: A Reevaluation of the Present State of Knowledge in the Light of the Sources," (Ph.D. dissertation, Brandeis University, 1970), includes evidence that Scarlatti did not write his sonatas in his late 60s and early 70s, as Kirkpatrick proposes.

VIDALI, published in one volume in the valuable Garland series, is divided into life and works of Domenico Scarlatti; studies of the music, subdivided into vocal music and keyboard sonatas and violin/continuo pieces; performance background; modern performances; sources, and modern editions or facsimiles, including the most important catalogs of Scarlatti's works, as well as a list of his works.

The most important English book on Scarlatti after Kirkpatrick, is BOYD, which offers a novel picture of the development of Scarlatti's general style. Scarlatti's vocal music, neglected by Kirkpatrick, is extensively presented. Boyd describes and evaluates all documents at hand, including the scores of three recently discovered operas (two are mentioned in Kirkpatrick's additions of 1963). In Boyd's chapter on Scarlatti's keyboard works, the premises of recently discovered manuscript copies or questionably "new" works are scrutinized.

Boyd discusses some arrangements by other composers, gives a translation of Scarlatti's will (also given by Kirkpatrick), and produces the first edition of two sonatas found in the Real Conservatorio Superior de Música of Madrid. A valuable list of compositions is divided into operas, the oratorios, the chamber cantatas, the serenatas, the sacred music, and the keyboard works. He indicates the location of manuscript sources for each work, except for the keyboard works discussed in the text. The catalog of keyboard works follows the Kirkpatrick numbers, with cross references to the Longo and Pestelli catalogs, as well as to the numbering in Emilia Fadini's edition of Scarlatti's harpsichord sonatas.

WILLIAMS compares aspects of Scarlatti's music to those of his contemporaries. Such is the case with the editor's own "*Figurae* in the Keyboard Works of Scarlatti, Handel, and Bach: An Introduction," where he traces the use of specific figures (motives described in theoretical works) by the three masters, discusses their possible connection to techniques inherent in the instruments or the voice, and observes that the study of figures in Scarlatti's keyboard music could contribute to the establishment of its chronology. A related subject, the use of consistently dotted melodies in vocal or instrumental pieces, is discussed by David Fuller in "The 'Dotted Style' in Bach, Handel, and Scarlatti." Giorgio Pestelli's "Bach, Handel, D. Scarlatti, and the Toccata of the Late Baroque" describes how each of the composers born in 1685 made use of the late toccata (the perpetuum mobile type, imitating the virtuosity of Italian violin masters).

Mark Lindley, in "Keyboard Technique and Articulation: Evidence for the Performance Practices of Bach, Handel, and Scarlatti" bases his discussion on fingering indications by 18th century performers and proposes the various possibilities in the execution of typical passages. Lindley believes Scarlatti actually favored excessive handcrossing. Kirkpatrick had questioned that, attributing its notation to the manuals of Scarlatti's instruments.

Luigi Ferdinando Tagliavini discusses the three Scarlatti sonatas doubtless written for the organ, deducing a description of the instrument for which they were conceived.

HAMMOND incorporates the latest research in a concise text. He discusses in detail the keyboard instruments for which Scarlatti may have written his sonatas as well as the meaning of his ornaments, taking into account both Kirkpatrick's study and its dispute by Frederick Neumann in *Ornamentation in Baroque and Post–Baroque Music. With Special Emphasis on J.S. Bach* (Princeton, 1987).

EKATERINI ROMANOU

Schoenberg, Arnold 1874–1951

Austrian-born composer

1. Biography

Brand, Juliane, and Christopher Hailey, editors, *Constructive Dissonance: Arnold Schoenberg and the Transformations of Twentieth-Century Culture,* Berkeley: University of California Press, 1997

Newlin, Dika, *Schoenberg Remembered: Diaries and Recollections (1938–76),* New York: Pendragon Press, 1980

Reich, Willi, *Schoenberg: A Critical Biography,* translated by Leo Black, London: Longman, and New York: Praeger, 1971

Ringer, Alexander L., *Arnold Schoenberg: The Composer as Jew,* Oxford: Clarendon Press, and New York: Oxford University Press, 1990

Schoenberg, Arnold, *Arnold Schoenberg-Wassily Kandinsky: Letters, Pictures and Documents,* edited by Jelena Hahl-Koch, translated by John C. Crawford, London: Faber, 1984

Smith, Joan Allen, *Schoenberg and His Circle: A Viennese Portrait,* London: Collier Macmillan, and New York: Schirmer Books, 1986

Stuckenschmidt, Hans Heinz, *Schoenberg: His Life, World, and Work,* translated by Humphrey Searle, London: Calder, and New York: Schirmer Books, 1978

Wellesz, Egon, *Arnold Schoenberg,* translated by W.H. Kerridge, London: Dent, 1925; reprint, New York: Da Capo Press, 1969

Biographies of the Austrian composer Arnold Schoenberg are complicated by three factors. First, his primary biographers knew him personally, and thus their accounts, like memoirs, are influenced to some degree by the strength of his personality and by his own idea of what his biography should contain. Second, and partly as a consequence of his influence, the facts about Schoenberg's life are so intimately bound up with his creative efforts that biographers have tended to measure the external circumstances of his life, especially the first half, according to their effect on his compositional style. Third, Schoenberg's life story is, in a word, complicated. Over the course of his life, he established homes in three different nations—Austria, Germany, and the United States—and had two separate families (after his first wife, a mother of two, died, he remarried and had three children with his second wife). He traveled extensively, taught in several different capacities, wrote copiously on many different subjects, and saved everything. Early scholars who wrote full-length biographies of Schoenberg attempted to tie together all that they knew of his life. Generally, later scholars have been both more focused and more eclectic than earlier scholars, addressing just one or another facet of Schoenberg's biography and using both inside (the composer's own) and outside (cultural or political) sources. These later scholars for the most part have published in journals; there is, in fact, a journal devoted entirely to Schoenberg and his *Nachlass, The Journal of the Arnold Schoenberg Institute.*

WELLESZ, the earliest biography of Schoenberg, was written in 1920, when the composer was not yet 50 years old. As Schoenberg's student, Wellesz witnessed the scandal surrounding the composer's abandonment of traditional tonality in the first decade of the 20th century. Later, the author participated in the private performance society that Schoenberg organized after World War I. His firsthand account, written under the master's watchful eye, is imbued with what Wellesz calls "the spiritual atmosphere in which Schönberg lived and worked." The bulk of Wellesz's account is taken up with his descriptions of Schoenberg's published works (up to op. 22; information on opp. 23 to 25 was added by the editor when the book was published in English in 1925). Wellesz's descriptions remain useful, if limited, because we can assume that his view of the music was guided by the composer.

Like Wellesz, REICH came into the Schoenberg circle early in his career and his biography seeks to evoke the "spiritual atmosphere in which Schoenberg's creative work was conducted" and, furthermore, "to bear witness . . . to the fact that Schoenberg's entire career, as man and artist, was ruled by a[n] . . . ineluctable compulsion, rooted in the individual ego, that leads to musical expression." Writing after the composer's death, Reich structures his account around the several, major creative periods of Schoenberg's life, quoting extensively from periodicals and reports of the time as well as from Schoenberg's own writings and correspondence. In the appendices, Reich also reproduces several complete documents that are not widely available in print: Schoenberg's "self-analysis" of his compositional process, written in response to a questionnaire made up by the German psychologist Julius Bahle in 1931; a 1933 interview with the composer concerning the transmission of modern music on the radio; Oskar Adler's contribution to a commemorative volume published on Schoenberg's 60th birthday (1934); and a preface to Reich's biography of Alban Berg, which Schoenberg drafted (but did not release) in 1936. Despite his biased account, the abundance of primary source material makes Reich's biography relevant for present-day scholars.

STUCKENSCHMIDT, who met Schoenberg in 1924 and maintained contact with him until his death, was the first to attempt an impartial biography of the composer. In preparation, he read through Schoenberg's papers, communicated with all manner of his relatives and acquaintances, and consulted many libraries, schools, churches, and other sites where documents pertaining to the composer were preserved (several documents appear in the appendix). Stuckenschmidt writes in a narrative-descriptive style, paying special attention to Schoenberg's contacts with other historically significant figures, such as Mahler and Richard Strauss. At times, and especially toward the end, his coverage of the dates and documents resembles a year-by-year, month-by-month news report. This book is valuable for readers interested in a multitude of details concerning Schoenberg's life without much critical commentary.

SMITH's study of the cultural-historical milieu in which Schoenberg lived as he developed the 12-tone method is not a biography per se but an oral history based on the author's interviews with 25 people who worked with the composer in Vienna and Berlin. Smith provides some explanatory and historical commentary, then pieces together and reproduces her interviews practically verbatim. Her approach is significant for the testimony it offers as to the strength of Schoenberg's character, which clearly continued to impress his students and friends long after his death. Smith also contributes a unique look, through the eyes of the persons interviewed, at the relationship between Schoenberg and three other creative luminaries in Vienna: Karl Kraus, Adolf Loos, and Oscar Kokoschka.

NEWLIN's diaries, written when she was Schoenberg's student in Los Angeles, preserve a fresh, unedited image of the composer that includes a good bit of levity and everyday fun. Newlin's experiences also bring home the point that, whether consciously or not, Schoenberg required emotional and intellectual dependency from his students. Newlin reflects,

> A majority of Schoenberg pupils looked up to him as a super-Father-Figure—maybe even quasi-divine? They were overawed by him, while often resentful of the "thought control" which he exercised over them.

(See also Newlin's article "Why Is Schoenberg's Biography So Difficult to Write?" *Perspectives of New Music* 12, nos. 1–2 [1973–74].)

RINGER is a thoughtful, well-documented study of Schoenberg's religious beliefs. The author devotes considerable space to the history of Jews in Austria and Germany and brings a substantial amount of biographical material, as well as the writings of numerous contemporary authors and poets, to bear on his proposal that Schoenberg's religious-ethical persuasions fundamentally shaped his evolution as a composer. At times, Ringer's zeal to find a connection between religious influence and music requires an imaginative stretch or a disregard for other possible influences, as, for example, when he rhetorically asks,

> What else but this deep-seated cultural trait [the nonmetrical prayers sung in Jewish homes] could have induced [Schoenberg] as early as 1911 to conclude his *Harmonielehre,* . . . with an outlook on "tone-colour melody"?

On the whole, however, Ringer provides a discerning inquiry into an important facet of Schoenberg's aesthetic outlook.

SCHOENBERG documents the friendship between Schoenberg and the Russian painter Wassily Kandinsky, publishing for the first time their complete catalog of exchanged letters as well as relevant texts that they independently wrote. Hahl-Koch (the editor) and Crawford (the translator) add chapters on Schoenberg's artistic development to 1911 and on the stages and common points of reference in the relationship between the two revolutionary masters. This excellent study provides a balanced assessment of Schoenberg's painterly talent and the role of Expressionist ideals in his compositions.

BRAND and HAILEY have assembled an interdisciplinary collection of essays on the historical, aesthetic, and intellectual issues surrounding Schoenberg's creative efforts. The opening section of the book, "Contexts," contains essays relevant to Schoenberg's biography, emphasizing his identity as an outsider, first as a Jew in Europe and later as an immigrant in the United States.

DONNA L. LYNN

2. Music

Bailey, Walter B., *Programmatic Elements in the Works of Schoenberg,* Ann Arbor, Michigan: UMI Research Press, and Epping; Bowker, 1984

Frisch, Walter, *The Early Works of Arnold Schoenberg,* Berkeley: University of California Press, 1993

Haimo, Ethan, *Schoenberg's Serial Odyssey: The Evolution of His Twelve-Tone Method, 1914–1928,* Oxford: Clarendon Press, and New York: Oxford University Press, 1990

Hyde, Martha M., *Schoenberg's Twelve-Tone Harmony: The Suite Op. 29 and the Compositional Sketches,* Ann Arbor, Michigan: UMI Research Press, 1982

Lessem, Alan Philip, *Music and Text in the Works of Arnold Schoenberg: The Critical Years, 1908–1922,* Ann Arbor, Michigan: UMI Research Press, 1979

Leibowitz, Rene, *Schoenberg and His School: The Contemporary Stage of the Language of Music,* translated by Dika Newlin, New York: Philosophical Library, 1949; reprint, New York: Da Capo, 1970

Milstein, Silvina, *Arnold Schoenberg: Notes, Sets, Forms,* Cambridge: Cambridge University Press, 1992

Perle, George, *Serial Composition and Atonality: An Introduction to the Music of Schoenberg, Berg, and Webern,* Berkeley: University of California Press, 1962; 6th edition, revised, 1991

Rognoni, Luigi, *The Second Vienna School: Expressionism and Dodecaphony,* translated by Robert W. Mann, London: Calder, 1977

Rufer, Josef, *Composition with Twelve Tones Related Only to One Another,* translated by Humphrey Searle, London: Barrie and Jenkins, 1954; revised edition, 1970

Stein, Erwin, *Orpheus in New Guises,* London: Rockliff, 1953

Arnold Schoenberg's music is of great interest from a number of perspectives. Above all, it is studied for its intrinsic beauty and masterful structure. It is also music of great historical interest, as it continues to play a crucial role in the development of musical thought. Finally, Schoenberg's compositional style evolved in a fascinating, complex way, and this evolution, too, has been an area of fruitful discussion. Although the categorization is a misleading simplification, commentators often refer to Schoenberg's three successive periods of musical composition as tonal, atonal, and serial.

FRISCH is concerned with the technique and language of Schoenberg's earliest music through the Second String Quartet, op. 10. These works are all tonal music, and they are divided into three stages: music heavily influenced by Brahms (1893–97), music that mixes Brahmsian techniques with Wagnerian chromaticism (1899–1903), and, finally, Schoenberg's wholly individual synthesis of these ideas (1904–8).

Discussions of Schoenberg's atonal music tend to be found in books that describe analytical tools appropriate for music by the Second Viennese School (Schoenberg, Berg, and Webern). PERLE's landmark book presents a methodology and aesthetic for analyzing music of the Second Viennese School. Perle refines the complex theory of pitch sets, which provide the means to analyze nontonal music in nearly as much depth as we can analyze tonal music. The examples by Schoenberg used in this study are largely piano pieces (Opp. 11, 23, and 33a), although other compositions are also cited.

LEIBOWITZ assesses the stylistic evolution of the Second Viennese School music, and presents analyses and commentaries on Schoenberg's music in this context. Liebowitz wrote during Schoenberg's lifetime, and he did not have access to modern terminology. The author maintains that each piece by Schoenberg is part of a logical series of artistic experiments and consolidations.

Like Leibowitz, ROGNONI treats Schoenberg's musical development as logical. His study emphasizes serialism as a culmination of Schoenberg's earlier compositional aesthetics and stresses the later music. At the time the book was written (early 1960s), serialism had a reputation of being mechanical and mathematical, but Rognoni's analyses emphasize the lyrical, humanistic, and dramatic properties of the music. His most extensive analyses are of serial operas, *Von Heute auf Morgen, Moses und Aron,* and the oratorio *Die Jakobsleiter.*

Concerning Schoenberg's serial music, one can either consider each piece on its own or show how Schoenberg's serial technique developed. HAIMO reminds us that the composer himself had to learn to be a 12-tone composer. The author traces the development of the technique from its first sign of life (placed in 1914, with *Die Jakobsleiter*) through the actual birth of the 12-tone idea (the music of the early 1920s), and, after refinement and experimentation, to the art of 12-tone composition, which is achieved with the Third String Quartet, op. 30, and the Variations, op. 31 (1926–28). Haimo isolates and discusses those techniques that became Schoenberg's means of creating art from the 12-tone method, including hexachord inversional combinatoriality, aggregate formation, and types of row partitioning.

This period of stylistic development also includes the Suite, op. 29, and HYDE's pioneering work is solely devoted to this piece. Hyde evaluates the relationship between serial technique and Schoenberg's sketches for the suite, and proceeds to show that the harmonic structure is also regulated by the row.

MILSTEIN is less concerned with Schoenberg's development as a serial composer than Haimo or Hyde, focusing instead on the integrity of the serial works themselves. The manner in which each piece is discussed is determined by the work's particular characteristics. For example, Milstein examines the Ode to Napoleon Buonaparte, op. 40, in terms of the relationship between serialism and pitch prolongation. Her analysis of the Largo from the Fourth String Quartet, op. 37, supports her hypothesis that a Beethoven quartet movement (op. 59, no. 1, third movement) may have served as the archetypal model. The serial structure of the String Trio, op. 45, and the Suite, op. 29, are also discussed.

The purpose of RUFER is twofold. First, it is meant as an exposition of Schoenberg's serial method of composition. Second, it aims to show how serialism is Schoenberg's logical continuation of the great tradition of building a composition from a single, basic shape.

These ideas lie behind the author's analyses of several works by Schoenberg, including the Wind Quintet, op. 26, and the Violin Phantasy, op. 46.

STEIN is a collection of essays, some of which concern Schoenberg's music. Among these essays is "New Formal Principles" (1924), which was written before the distinction between atonal and serial became standard. Stein therefore treats the recently composed opp. 23, 24, and 25 as a distinct, stylistic group, rather than as music leading from the atonal period to the serial period.

Finally, two works dealing with programmatic elements and text in Schoenberg's music are worthy of consideration. BAILEY identifies three classes of works: compositions (finished and unfinished) known to be based on programs, and pieces that were inspired by secret programs (the first three string quartets; Five Pieces for Orchestra, op. 16; the Suite, op. 29; the Piano Concerto, op. 42; and the String Trio, op. 45). LESSEM traces the crucial role that music with text played in Schoenberg's artistic development, both in terms of technical musical devices, and considering Schoenberg's own need to communicate his feelings with his audience.

MICHAEL JUDE SCHIANO

3. Aesthetics

Cooper-White, Pamela, Schoenberg and the God-Idea: The Opera Moses und Aron, Ann Arbor, Michigan: UMI Research Press, 1985

Crawford, John C., and Dorothy L. Crawford, Expressionism in Twentieth-Century Music, Bloomington: Indiana University Press, 1993

Dahlhaus, Carl, Schoenberg and the New Music: Essays, translated by Derrick Puffett and Alfred Clayton, Cambridge: Cambridge University Press, 1987

Ringer, Alexander L., Arnold Schoenberg: The Composer as Jew, Oxford: Clarendon Press, and New York: Oxford University Press, 1990

Rognoni, Luigi, The Second Vienna School: Expressionism and Dodecaphony, translated by Robert W. Mann, London: Calder: 1977

Rufer, Josef, Composition with Twelve Tones Related Only to One Another, translated by Humphrey Searle, London: Barrie and Jenkins, 1954; revised edition, 1970

Schoenberg, Arnold, The Musical Idea and the Logic, Technique and Art of Its Presentation, edited, translated, and with commentary by Patricia Carpenter and Severine Neff, New York: Columbia University Press, 1995

Webern, Anton, The Path to the New Music, edited by Willi Reich, translated by Leo Black, Bryn Mawr, Pennsylvania: Presser, 1963

Schoenberg never presented his aesthetics systematically. Up through the 1930s, his ideas evolved in conjunction with his compositional development and theoretical reflections as well as in response to his changing sociopolitical and cultural circumstances. Schoenberg gradually integrated his aesthetic into his philosophical and religious thinking, especially his vision of Judaism.

No book deals specifically with Schoenberg's aesthetics, which are generally discussed in connection with other issues, as this article will make clear. Webern, Rufer, and more recently Carpenter and Neff function mainly as spokespersons for Schoenberg. The Europeans Rognoni and Dahlhaus worked from a Hegelian conception of history and a fascination with Theodor Adorno's views of Schoenberg. For Ringer, Judaism is the ultimate source of Schoenberg's thought, whereas White's concern is Schoenberg's mature synthesis of his musical, philosophical, and religious views in his masterpiece Moses und Aron. The Crawfords present Schoenberg as the major figure in musical expressionism. Recent publications of Schoenberg's key theoretical treatises have helped pave the way for a book-length study.

WEBERN originated as lectures the author delivered in Vienna in 1932 and 1933. These lectures reflect Webern's intense concern for Schoenberg's fate as the Nazis assumed power in Central Europe. Webern indicates that many of the ideas he presents (e.g., the concept of new music, the harmonic theory) are Schoenberg's. Webern asserts that the issue underlying Schoenberg's approach to composition is moral rather than aesthetic (he draws a comparison with Karl Kraus's view of language). Webern seeks to reveal the hidden natural laws that composers throughout history have obeyed instinctively. The highest law is what Schoenberg called comprehensibility, that is, the need for clarity and unity in the presentation of musical ideas. Twelve-note music represented the temporary summit of music's evolution. Webern offers an eyewitness account of how Schoenberg arrived at his 12-note method as he intuitively followed the hidden laws. Webern simplified theoretical issues without compromising their profundity, making the book useful to readers of all levels.

RUFER's aim is to explicate "Schoenberg's method of composition [with 12 notes] and its development as an organic part of his general theory of composition." The author quotes frequently from Schoenberg's comments, both written and oral, as well as from his compositions. Although technical characteristics of Schoenberg's method are an important part of Rufer's exposition, Rufer also reveals the method's aesthetic significance to Schoenberg by relating it to Schoenberg's belief that "the idea and its realisation are ... the indispensable prerequisite of artistic composition." The author reiterates throughout the book that the music Schoenberg composed using his method is the result of inspired artistic creation and in this regard does not differ from other good music. Rufer explains that Schoenberg's method served the same purpose in composition as did tonality, to which it is frequently compared. In Schoenberg's own words, his method provided "a precisely definable aesthetic control," a "law" that determines the entire composition while allowing the composer freedom of imagination.

The main difficulty ROGNONI poses to English-speaking readers is his historical-philosophical outlook, which is largely Hegelian. Adorno and Husserl's influence are also evident. The discussion is peppered with the terminology of these philosophers. Rognoni regards expressionism, of which Schoenberg, Berg, and Webern were the main musical representatives, as a stage in the dialectic of the spirit that has always run through German art and culture. With respect to Schoenberg, Rognoni believes that the composer maintained the expressive immediacy that he achieved with his atonal works for the remainder of his career. However, his aim in his later years was not intense subjective expression for its own sake; rather, the search for the innermost ground of being became an ethical-religious quest. Rognoni emphatically disagrees with Adorno's view that Schoenberg ended the dialectical process. There are detailed discussions of most of Schoenberg's works, including a brilliant interpretation of *Moses und Aron*.

DAHLHAUS works from a profound knowledge of the German philosophical tradition, of aesthetics and its history, of Adorno's thought, and of Schoenberg's thought and music. Although difficult to comprehend, his essays on Schoenberg, produced from the mid-1960s through the mid-1980s, have been highly influential. Dahlhaus exposes the substrata of Schoenberg's thinking, whether it be the beliefs that motivated his compositional decisions or its roots in earlier religious, philosophical, and musical traditions. In "Schoenberg and Programme Music," the author reconciles Schoenberg's belief in the metaphysics of absolute music derived from Schopenhauer with his belief in self-expression and establishes criteria for determining which of Schoenberg's works are truly programmatic. In "Schoenberg's Poetics of Music," Dahlhaus outlines a method for investigating the prehistory of dodecaphony using Schoenberg's poetics, which Dahlhaus derives from the aesthetic and technical aspects of Schoenberg's basic categories (e.g., idea and consequence) In "Schoenberg's Aesthetic Theology," the author links Schoenberg to the tradition of art religion, which, with the metaphysics of instrumental music, is traceable to early romantic thinkers. Ultimately, Dahlhaus believes that Schoenberg's aesthetic is rooted in medieval Jewish mysticism. The composer's key decisions (e.g., the break with tonality) defy rational justification and can be explained only by his religious pathos, an energy that was also the essence of the musical idea.

RINGER's book is a collection of his articles, most of which were published separately from the early 1970s through the late 1980s. Ringer believes that the motivations behind Schoenberg's life work were as much religious and philosophical as aesthetic. Schoenberg synthesized these elements into a new view of music as the "prophetic conscience of modern man," a notion that Ringer discusses in "Prophecy and Solitude." Schoenberg is portrayed as a man and artist who remained faithful to a mission, which Ringer maintains is grounded in Old Testament notions. The author views Schoenberg's aesthetics, theories, and stylistic features of his music as reflective of Schoenberg's fundamentally Jewish mode of thinking. For non-Jewish readers, one of the books greatest contributions is the author's clear explanations of Jewish ideas (e.g., the notions of the unknowable God, man as made in the image of God, and history as a dialectic of freedom and constraint).

The expression "God-Idea" in COOPER-WHITE's title is the key notion of Schoenberg's mature aesthetic, which was an integral part of his philosophical and religious thought. Schoenberg came closest to realizing his vision in his opera *Moses und Aron*. Cooper-White draws copiously from primary sources (e.g., Schoenberg's sketches, writings, and personal library) to probe deeply into all aspects of Schoenberg's opera, including its genesis, the development of Schoenberg's religious thinking into the unique vision for the Jewish people expressed in the libretto, and relationships between the text and the music. The 12-tone method is shown as the primary means of providing unity and coherence in the music, which is itself an embodiment of the God-Idea. Chapter 2 can be read independently for a comprehensive overview of the interrelationships between Schoenberg's religious, philosophical, and aesthetic ideas from the 1890s through the early 1930s. Most important are the discussions of Schopenhauer, Kraus, and Schoenberg and Judaism.

CRAWFORD and CRAWFORD regard expressionism as an international phenomenon extending to as diverse a group as Bartók, Stravinsky, Shostakovich, Ives, Ruggles, Kirchner, and others. Still, Schoenberg is the book's protagonist, figuring prominently in the definition of expressionism and in the chapters on Berg and Webern and in the one titled "Synthesis of the Arts." Throughout the volume, the Crawfords examine musical expressionism within its psychological, biographical and cultural context. In the chapter on Schoenberg, they discuss personal crises that he experienced (e.g., his wife's affair with Richard Gerstl), his contact with radical intellectuals from various fields (e.g., Kraus and Kandinsky), the sociopolitical ambience of Vienna, and musical influences (e.g., Wagner, Strauss, and Mahler) as factors that helped Schoenberg to achieve his ideal of giving direct expression to extreme emotions, which the Crawfords believe is the hallmark of expressionism. The Crawfords briefly discuss almost every work of what they consider to be Schoenberg's expressionist period (1907–22), showing ways in which the expressive content, which ranges from anxiety and suffering to spiritual transcendence, is made manifest by specific musical techniques and symbols.

Predicating their views on SCHOENBERG's own penchant for organic wholeness, the editors, Carpenter and Neff, synthesize Schoenberg's pronouncements on art and music into a coherent statement centered on his notion of the musical idea. Beginning with his views of art (e.g., his belief that art gives expression to ideas and his theory of organic form), the editors move to his more specific aims as a music theorist and finally to his attempts, which were never entirely successful, to define the musical idea. Also part of the book's synthesis are Schoenberg's subsidiary theoretical concepts (e.g., coherence, comprehensibility, *Grundgestalt,* and theme). Carpenter and Neff flesh out Schoenberg's analysis of Brahms's Piano Quartet, op. 60, in which Schoenberg aimed to show the work's idea. They relate Schoenberg's thought to the German philosophical tradition of the late 18th and early 19th centuries, most notably Goethe, Kant, and Schopenhauer, and find affinities with Platonic and Aristotelian aesthetics as well as with Aquinas and da Vinci. Despite the nod to history, there is little regard for the historical nature of Schoenberg's thought.

CHARLOTTE M. CROSS

4. Writings

Armitage, Merle, editor, *Schoenberg,* New York: Schirmer, 1937; reprint, Westport, Connecticut: Greenwood Press, 1977

Berg, Alban, *The Berg-Schoenberg Correspondence: Selected Letters,* edited by Julianne Brand et al., Basingstoke: Macmillan, and New York: Norton, 1987

Schoenberg, Arnold, "Analysis of the Four Orchestral Songs, Op. 22," translated by Claudio Spies, in *Perspectives on Schoenberg and Stravinsky,* edited by Benjamin Boretz, Princeton, New Jersey, Princeton University Press, 1968; revised edition, New York: Norton, 1972

———, *Arnold Schoenberg Correspondence: A Collection of Translated and Annotated Letters Exchanged with Guido Adler, Pablo Casals, Emanuel Feuermann, and Olin Downes,* edited by Egbert Ennulat, Metuchen, New Jersey: Scarecrow Press, 1991

———, *Arnold Schoenberg Self-Portrait: A Collection of Articles, Program Notes, and Letters by the Composer about His Own Works,* Pacific Palisades, California: Belmont Music, 1988

———, *Arnold Schoenberg, Wassily Kandinsky: Letters, Pictures, and Documents,* edited by Jelena Hahl-Koch, translated by John C. Crawford, London: Faber, 1984

———, *Coherence, Counterpoint, Instrumentation, Instruction in Form,* edited by Severine Neff, translated by Charlotte M. Cross and Severine Neff, Lincoln: University of Nebraska Press, 1994

———, *Fundamentals of Musical Composition,* edited by Gerald Strang and Leonard Stein, London: Faber, and New York: St. Martin's Press, 1967

———, *Letters,* edited by Erwin Stein, translated by Eithne Wilkins and Ernst Kaiser, London: Faber, 1964

———, *Models for Beginners in Composition,* New York: Schirmer, 1943; revised edition, Los Angeles: Belmont Music, 1972

———, *Moses und Aron, Libretto,* translated by Allen Forte, Pacific Palisades, California: Belmont Music, 1990

———, *The Musical Idea and the Logic, Technique, and Art of Its Presentation,* edited and translated by Patricia Carpenter and Severine Neff, New York: Columbia University Press, 1995

———, *Preliminary Exercises in Counterpoint,* edited by Leonard Stein, London: Faber, 1963

———, *Structural Functions of Harmony,* edited by Leonard Stein, New York: Norton, and London: Williams and Norgate, 1954; revised edition, 1969

———, *Style and Idea,* edited by Leonard Stein, translated by Leo Black, New York: St. Martin's Press, 1975

———, *Theory of Harmony,* translated by Roy E. Carter, Berkeley: University of California Press, 1978

Arnold Schoenberg wrote as a polemicist and pedagogue, librettist and playwright, political activist, and in his later years, even as a psalmist. Echoing Schoenberg's musical compositions and paintings, the writings hum with an intense energy generated from his direct engagement with urgent issues in the arts, history, science, religion, and politics as he details his often precarious position as musician, intellectual, and Jew. A wealth of published material now exists in English that discloses the many facets of Schoenberg's thought, and ought to dispel any notion of Schoenberg as an artist in isolation. For Schoenberg, no human endeavor could remain oblivious of the upheavals in another—everything was interrelated.

Schoenberg emulated the style of Karl Kraus (1874–1936) whom he knew personally. Kraus, perhaps the most influential journalist in his time, was a prolific writer of intricate, crystal-clear prose. Schoenberg's proclivity for word play is reminiscent of his compositional predecessors, notably Beethoven and Brahms. Schoenberg's writings reflect philosophical ideas stemming from Kant, Hegel, Schopenhauer and Nietzsche along with religious or mystical ideas stemming from the Bible, August Strindberg, Rainer Maria Rilke, and Emanuel Swedenborg, all refracted through the values of the Viennese-Jewish subculture in which he was raised.

Three themes deserve to be highlighted. One occurs in essays from 1909, in which Schoenberg argues that receptivity to a musical work depends on the creativity of the listener's imagination. Another theme is the phenomenology of creative experience that pertains to how the totality of a compositional idea seizes the composer, how the details then must be worked out, and how, even after the composition is completed, musical relationships that were never consciously intended may disclose themselves to the composer. This view of creativity, so concerned with the relation of the pure idea and its material representation, informs questions of unity and variety in his own works as well as those of his predecessors. A third theme is resonant in Schoenberg's historical consciousness. While not pessimistic, Schoenberg's autobiographical writing has a persistently lachrymose cast adopted from the language of Jewish history and its tone of anguish and lamentation. It is at times offset by a tone of prophetic consolation.

The most comprehensive collection of Schoenberg's prose, rich in all of these themes, is SCHOENBERG (1975), a collection of essays and lectures written between 1909 and 1950 on a wide variety of topics concerning composition, performance, teaching, and social and political matters. Its origins date to 1944 when the Philosophical Library proposed a volume of Schoenberg essays to be published under the title *Music of Tomorrow,* a title with a decided Wagnerian ring that Schoenberg rejected. In 1950, that volume was published as *Style and Idea,* edited by Dika Newlin. The volume under consideration here is a greatly expanded collection, and includes essays such as "My Evolution," "Brahms the Progressive" and "New Music, Outmoded Music, Style and Idea."

ARMITAGE contains essays and interviews gathered with art works and essays by such prominent contemporary figures as Roger Sessions, Ernst Krenek, and Franz Werfel. SCHOENBERG (1988) contains abridged source materials geared for the lay reader interested in such works as the four string quartets, the Variations for Orchestra, *Pelleas und Melisande* or the Four Orchestral Songs. Schoenberg makes an excellent teacher and guide.

Due to the fragmentary state of the European works, and the condensed form of the American texts, the earliest book, SCHOENBERG (1978), the translation of *Harmonielehre,* is the most indispensable for serious musicians. *Harmonielehre* (1911, rev. 1922) abjures any impulse to present instruction in composition as a systematic theory grounded in eternal laws. While the book asserts new conceptualizations of harmony, rhythm, and timbre, it preserves leading concepts in the most conservative tradition of Viennese theory. In no other publication will a reader find as careful and logical an explanation of the unalterability of chordal roots, the cadential six-four, ninth chords, diminished-seventh chords, the Neapolitan sixth or the augmented six-five chords. Without this background, a reader might seriously misinterpret passages in the later books.

SCHOENBERG (1994), begun in 1917, was among several ongoing projects that followed *Harmonielehre.* This edition presents facing pages of transcription and translation of the often fragmentary text. An extensive introduction by the editor compensates.

SCHOENBERG (1995) is a compilation of manuscripts written between 1923 and 1936 presented in facing pages of transcription and translation. A substantial and authoritative commentary makes an excellent intro-

duction to Schoenberg's analytic technique. Among the works discussed are the Brahms Piano Quartet, op. 60 and Schoenberg's opp. 9 and 26. SCHOENBERG (1968) is an excellent introduction to Schoenberg's variation technique. The first song of op. 22, "Seraphita," receives particular attention.

From the American years, four books are branches of a common enterprise begun in 1936 to provide texts for American universities. SCHOENBERG (1963) offers a species approach in conjunction with chapters on compositional applications. Numerous possibilities are presented and evaluated. The technique of generating possibilities is fundamental to Schoenberg's teaching method. SCHOENBERG (1943), largely a collection of musical examples, ranges in scope from the smallest motives to the construction of sentences, periods, minuets, and scherzos. Concise explanations and a glossary provide key points that are further elaborated in the companion volumes. SCHOENBERG (1967) covers themes, small and large forms with an emphasis on asymmetrical construction. There are copious musical examples drawn from the German tradition. An unusual chapter called "Advice for Self-Criticism" is concerned with sketching and changing methods of variation, and typifies Schoenberg's approach. SCHOENBERG (1954) is perhaps the best known and widely applied of Schoenberg's pedagogical works. Concepts pertaining to tonal regions and the relative strength or proximity of tonal progressions have been regarded as emblematic of Schoenberg's approach to questions of harmonic relations with respect to form.

Schoenberg's libretto for the opera *Moses und Aron* (1930–32) is among his most important writings and may be found in SCHOENBERG (1990). Considered a modern *midrash* or commentary on verses from the books of Exodus and Numbers, the text unfolds largely as a philosophical argument between Moses and Aaron over the purity of the idea and the distortion of the idea in material representation.

There are four volumes of translated correspondence. The letters collected in SCHOENBERG (1964) enhance all the other writings. Letters to associates, students and publishers written between 1910 and 1950 are collected within particular time frames. Four letters to Mahler complete the book.

Spanning 1911 to 1935, the correspondence between Alban Berg (1885–1935) and Schoenberg collected in BERG traces the evolution of a relationship from teacher-student to friend and colleague. The letters are generously annotated so that the scores of names in the letters are clearly identified. Editor Julianne Brand provides crucial documentation concerning the Berg's guide to Schoenberg's *Gurre-Lieder,* the founding of the Society for Private Musical Performances and the periods during which Schoenberg composed *Pierrot Lunaire, Moses und Aron* and Berg composed *Wozzeck.*

SCHOENBERG (1984) is an extraordinary record of correspondence between two major figures best known for their achievements in two different arts, painting and music. The book is enhanced with much art work, plus essays in conjunction with the correspondence. One interested in expressionism in general or *The Blaue Reiter Almanac* in particular will find discussions of aesthetic issues. Important letters by Schoenberg include one from 1911 when he avers: "Art belongs to the unconscious," and in 1923, Schoenberg voices his dread over the situation of European Jewry, and his disgust with anti-Semitism.

SCHOENBERG (1991) comprises streams of polemical exchanges over matters of criticism and performance practice with an informative *hommage* to Schoenberg by Josef Rufer and a preface by the composer and Schoenberg's amanuensis Richard Hoffmann that is priceless. Included is a reproduction of Schoenberg's *basso continuo* realizations written between 1903 and 1913 at the behest of Guido Adler. These realizations are themselves the source of polemical exchanges in this work.

STEVE JOEL CAHN

Schubert, Franz 1797–1828

Austrian composer

1. Biography and Social Circle

Abraham, Gerald, editor, *Schubert: A Symposium,* London: Drummond, 1946; London: Oxford, 1952

Brown, Maurice, *Essays on Schubert,* London: Macmillan, and New York: St. Martin's Press, 1966

———, *The New Grove Schubert,* London: Macmillan, 1982; New York: Norton, 1983

———, *Schubert: A Critical Biography,* London: Macmillan, and New York: St. Martin's Press, 1958

Clive, H.P., *Schubert and His World: A Biographical Dictionary,* Oxford: Clarendon Press, and New York: Oxford University Press, 1997

Deutsch, Otto Erich, editor, *Schubert: A Documentary Biography,* translated by Eric Blom, London: Dent, 1946; as *A Schubert Reader,* New York: Norton, 1947

———, editor, *Schubert: Memoirs by His Friends,* translated by Rosamond Ley and John Nowell, New York: Macmillan, and London: Black, 1958

Einstein, Alfred, *Schubert: A Musical Portrait,* translated by David Ascoli, New York: Oxford University Press, 1951

Erickson, Raymond, editor, *Schubert's Vienna,* New Haven, Connecticut: Yale University Press, 1997

Flower, Newman, *Franz Schubert: The Man and His Circle,* New York: Stokes, 1928; revised edition, London: Cassell, 1949

Gibbs, Christopher H., editor, *The Cambridge Companion to Schubert,* Cambridge: Cambridge University Press, 1997

Grove, George, *Beethoven, Schubert, Mendelssohn,* London: Macmillan, 1951

Hilmar, Ernst, *Franz Schubert in His Time,* translated by Reinhard G. Pauly, Portland, Oregon: Amadeus Press, 1988

Kreissle von Hellborn, Heinrich, *The Life of Franz Schubert,* 2 vols., translated by Arthur Duke Coleridge, London: Longmans, Green, 1869; reprint, New York: Vienna House, 1972

McKay, Elisabeth Norman, *Franz Schubert: A Biography,* Oxford: Clarendon Press, and New York: Oxford University Press, 1996

Newbould, Brian, *Schubert: The Music and the Man,* Berkeley: University of California Press, and London: Gollancz, 1997

Reed, John, *Schubert,* London: Dent, 1987; 2nd edition, New York: Oxford University Press, 1997

———, *Schubert: The Final Years,* London: Faber, and New York: St. Martin's Press, 1972

Solomon, Maynard, "Franz Schubert and the Peacocks of Benvenuto Cellini," *19th-Century Music* 12 (1989)

Two remarkable documentary volumes compiled and edited by Otto Erich Deutsch are the foundation of all modern biographical work on Schubert. This diligent scholar devoted much of his career to discovering evidence concerning Schubert's life and to cataloging the composer's works (for which he earned some immortality through the Deutsch numbers that identify each of Schubert's compositions). Deutsch's first Schubert collections began to appear in German early in the 20th century; translations and revised editions of his books have continued to appear long after his death in 1967.

DEUTSCH (1946) chronologically assembles all known documents from Schubert's lifetime—including birth and death certificates, all known letters written by Schubert (as well as many letters to him), diary entries, reviews, and so forth. Most selections are accompanied by Deutsch's helpful commentary. Although some new materials, especially letters and reviews, have surfaced in the last 50 years, the collection is nevertheless remarkably complete. Both the interpretation of these documents and the understanding of Schubert's cultural and personal situation have evolved throughout the 20th century, however, which makes Deutsch's commentary somewhat out-of-date and requires one to exercise some caution against taking all explanations at face value.

DEUTSCH (1958) includes most of the more reliable reminiscences written by individuals who knew Schubert personally, beginning with the first memorial tributes of 1828–29 and extending to the late 19th century. Deutsch's commentary is once again extremely useful. This volume must be used with more care than the earlier one, because once Schubert died at age 31 in 1828, the process of mythologizing and romanticizing his life began, and by mid-century especially, many memories were wildly exaggerated.

KREISSLE VON HELLBORN wrote the first substantial biography of Schubert in German in 1865, and it soon appeared in two English translations. (The one cited here by Coleridge is fairly complete, while another [Wilberforce, 1866] is heavily abridged.) Because this biography had such an impact on later studies, it is still worth consulting for its historical interest, though it is not always factual. The same value and difficulties arise from GROVE, which was originally included in the first edition of his famous dictionary of music.

After Deutsch began to publish his documentary collections, more serious biographies were possible. While Deutsch pursued an objective approach to Schubert's biography, BROWN (1958), who worked closely with Deutsch, wrote a critical biography that gives narrative shape to the great mass of information in the documentary collections. For nearly 40 years this book provided the most responsible and well-informed overview of Schubert's life and works available in English and even now continues to offer a serious view. Brown's observations about the music are useful and not overly technical.

BROWN (1966) also wrote a volume of essays on Schubert that explore the most famous Schubert iconography, the composer's relationship with the Kärntnertor Theater in Vienna, the lives of four of the first great Schubert scholars, the release of his music after his death, and some individual compositions. BROWN (1983) was the author's last work on Schubert. As might be expected in this type of formal encyclopedia presentation, Schubert's life and career are explained in a broad and reliable overview with a minimum of explicit opinion and criticism. Particularly useful is the complete work list that gives all of Schubert's compositions, grouped by genre and including information about the date of composition, publication, Deutsch number, and remarks. Finally, an excellent bibliography lists most important writings until 1982 on Schubert in English and other languages.

After Brown's critical biography appeared there was little biographical study of Schubert in English for decades, except for several popular and ill-informed books. Near the end of the 20th century, however, Schubert's life sparked considerable interest. Some of the most provocative work is presented in a series of articles by SOLOMON, an important biographer of Beethoven and Mozart. Solomon suggests that Schubert, as well as some in his circle of friends, probably engaged in homosexual activities. The author's argument is based entirely on documents that had been available in Deutsch's collections for many decades, but through subtle, perceptive, and often persuasive readings of material long in full public view, Solomon devises new interpretations that challenge the traditional perception of Schubert. Solomon's articles have elicited exceptionally intense reactions, responses, and counter-responses that often carry not-so-hidden personal and political agendas. *Nineteenth-Century Music* (volume 17, no. 1 [1993]) devoted an entire issue to the issue of Schubert's sexuality, which opens with an article by musicologist Rita Steblin challenging Solomon's original article on many details and pointing to some questionable translations. Solomon responds to her objections, and further articles and essays in the same issue of the journal examine the controversy and its larger implications in more detail. The matter is certainly not resolved, although most U.S. scholars seem to have accepted Solomon's basic conclusions concerning Schubert's possible homosexual orientation and compulsive hedonism.

The 1997 bicentennial celebration of Schubert's birth prompted several important new books, as well as noteworthy reissues. These works are particularly welcome given the flurry of activity in Schubert scholarship during the preceding two decades. REED's (1987) admirable biography was revised for the Oxford reissue. Reed continues to build on Deutsch and Brown, while offering new interpretations and discoveries concerning both Schubert's life and works. The volume contains a helpful chronology, a work list divided by genre, a "personalia" that gives a brief description of the most important people in Schubert's life, and a good bibliography. REED (1972), on Schubert's final years (October 1825 to November 1828), is one of the best treatments of the late music and is particularly noteworthy for its discussion of the dating of the Great C Major Symphony. Both these books contain musical examples, although the level of technical discussion is not difficult.

Two major bicentennial studies complement one another more than they compete. McKay concentrates on the composer's life, while Newbould lives up to its title by focusing on the music. McKAY gives the most thorough and well-informed biographical survey now available in English. The most noteworthy reassessment she offers of Schubert is the suggestion that he was mildly manic-depressive (cyclothymic), addicted to both alcohol and nicotine, and that he may have occasionally smoked opium. Many clues help support these claims, and as with Solomon's revisionism, all the relevant documents have long been available. Once again, Schubert remains somewhat resistant to posthumous diagnoses, although much of the author's argument seems compelling. McKay pays careful attention to Schubert's general health and the cause of his early death. She incorporates many findings of recent scholarship and goes into considerable detail about the lives of Schubert's family and friends. She is careful to distinguish between evidence dating from Schubert's lifetime and reminiscences that appeared decades later. The tone of the book is serious and expertly informed, if somewhat dry.

NEWBOULD uses McKay's investigations, among others, as the basis for the brief biographical discussions in his book, as he is much more interested in surveying the music. (Newbould has made fine performing editions of Schubert's unfinished symphonies.) While McKay's book contains just one musical example, Newbould provides a generous selection. The study is sensibly organized so that the biographical discussion of a given span of years precedes consideration of music from that period. The music is treated by genre, with individual chapters about the early songs, early orchestral music, early keyboard music, and so forth. (The operas and four-hand piano music are treated in extended discrete chapters.) The advantage of this approach is that one can consult specific chapters, such as those on songs or symphonies, and thereby get a self-contained overview of Schubert's development in those genres. Newbould's observations about the music are perceptive and informative, yet not technically intimidating.

EINSTEIN takes a chronological approach in presenting a survey of Schubert's entire output and does so without offering much biographical comment or context. This fairly strict ordering can sometimes become confusing and unwieldy, although the index allows one to locate discussions of specific pieces. Einstein makes some brilliant observations, even though he is frequently highly opinionated and often dismissive of compositions, especially of Schubert's more social music.

Two anthologies survey Schubert's music by genre. ABRAHAM's symposium opens with a brief chapter on "Schubert the Man" written by Deutsch—a rare instance in which the great scholar explicitly interprets Schubert's life. There are individual chapters of uneven quality devoted to all the major genres, presented in a straightforward critical manner. Some musical examples are given at the back of the book and there are few footnotes. The book is quite outdated, although some musical insights remain compelling.

GIBBS takes a wider and more up-to-date approach than Abraham. Two chapters by Gibbs consider myths and legends about Schubert's life and the difficulty in classifying his musical achievement. Leon Botstein provides a fascinating look at the cultural, political, and daily realities of Schubert's Vienna. David Gramit, author of a seminal dissertation on Schubert's early circle of friends, contributes a chapter that traces Schubert's relationships with a remarkable assortment of contemporary poets, painters, and other intimates. Susan Youens's chapter examines the more than 100 poets that Schubert used in his lieder, while Charles Rosen considers the fingerprints of Schubert's musical style. There follow individual chapters on each of the genres in which Schubert composed, complete with musical examples and recent bibliographic citations given in the notes. The volume concludes with a discussion of the reception of Schubert's music in German-speaking countries, in England, and in France. The final chapter traces issues of historical performance practice relevant to Schubert's music.

Although the title is promising, FLOWER's biography is largely outdated, uncritical, and tends to perpetuate legends about the composer. For a better understanding of Schubert's cultural context and circle of friends, one must look to McKay's biography and Gramit's chapter in Gibbs. CLIVE's biographical dictionary provides entries on almost all of Schubert's family and friends, as well as poets whose texts he set, critics, and other important figures. This reference work is generally reliable and provides useful bibliographical references for further study.

HILMAR's book is not a biography of Schubert in the conventional sense but rather a study of specific areas of his life and cultural circumstances. One chapter examines the phenomenon of Schubertiades, the intimate domestic evenings devoted to Schubert's music; another considers public concert life at the time. Included are explorations of Vienna's theatrical and literary culture, as well as of Schubert's dance music and his relationship with publishers. This brief book contains information not readily available elsewhere but should be used after gaining knowledge of the basic biographical facts of Schubert's life elsewhere.

ERICKSON's collection of essays began as an Aston Magna Academy at Rutgers University in June 1993. This sumptuously produced and illustrated volume contains 11 essays by U.S. and European scholars on a wide range of cultural, political, and musical issues. Essays by Leon Plantinga, Alice Hanson, and Elizabeth Aldrich consider music and dance in early 19th-century Vienna. Many of the other contributors are experts in fields other than music history. Thus, for example, the distinguished historian Enno Kraehe writes about the political climate in which Schubert came to maturity during the time of the Congress of Vienna. Art, architectural, theater, and literary historians (including Thomas DaCosta Kaufmann, Gerbert Frodl, Simon Williams, and Jane K. Brown) likewise consider activities in Vienna during the composer's lifetime. Although occasional mistakes about Schubert arise from this arrangement, there also emerge new perspectives not found elsewhere in the musicological literature on Schubert.

CHRISTOPHER H. GIBBS

2. Chamber Music

Chusid, Martin, "Concerning Orchestral Style in Schubert's Earliest Chamber Music for Strings," in *Music in Performance and Society: Essays in Honor of Roland Jackson*, edited by Malcolm Cole and John Koegel, Warren, Michigan: Harmonie Park Press, 1997a

———, "Schubert's Chamber Music: Before and after Beethoven," in *The Cambridge Companion to Schubert*, edited by Christopher H. Gibbs, Cambridge: Cambridge University Press, 1997b

Dahlhaus, Carl, "Sonata Form in Schubert: The First Movement of the G-Major String Quartet, op. 161 (D. 887)," translated by Thilo Reinhard, in *Schubert: Critical and Analytical Studies,* edited by Walter Frisch, 1–12, Lincoln: University of Nebraska Press, 1986

McKay, Elizabeth Norman, "Schubert's String and Piano Duos in Context," in *Schubert Studies,* edited by Brian Newbould, Aldershot: Ashgate, 1998

Newbould, Brian, *Schubert: The Music and the Man,* Berkeley: University of California Press, and London: Gollancz, 1997

Schubert, Franz, *Complete Chamber Music in Three Volumes,* Kassel: Bärenreiter, 1996

Westrup, J.A., *Schubert Chamber Music,* London: British Broadcasting Corporation, and Seattle: University of Washington Press, 1969

Schubert's chamber music has received less critical attention than his songs in the century and a half since his death. In fact, no major book devoted exclusively to this music has yet appeared in English, despite the popularity of such masterpieces as the String Quartet in D Minor, D. 810, "Death and the Maiden," or the two Piano Trios. The reasons for this situation can be traced back to the reception of Schubert's music during the 19th century. While his genius as a song composer was recognized even in his lifetime, his achievements in instrumental music were consistently undervalued because his style diverged so markedly from that of Beethoven, whose works became the formal and expressive model for subsequent generations of composers. Such an attitude colors most of the discussions of Schubert's chamber music up to the 1970s. In the last two decades of the 20th century, however, a new appreciation of the uniqueness and validity of Schubert's instrumental writing emerged, particularly with regard to his mature chamber music.

SCHUBERT reprints all the chamber music from the new collected edition of Schubert's work edited by Walter Dürr and associates. The introductory essays, which have been translated into English, are a major source of up-to-date information, ranging from accounts of the biographical circumstances surrounding the creation of individual works to discussions of the autograph scores. The footnotes also provide useful leads to further reading and research. The musical text of Schubert is important in itself, because it corrects the numerous errors of the first collected edition of Schubert's work (*F. Schuberts Werke: Kritische durchgesehene Gesammtausgabe,* published by Breitkopf und Härtel between 1884 and 1897 and since reissued by Dover). Furthermore, the Dürr edition contains fragments, drafts, and even full movements that were previously unavailable. In short, this publication serves as the best starting point for research into Schubert's chamber music.

WESTRUP, the equivalent to a good collection of program notes with musical examples, makes only modest demands on the reader's knowledge of music theory. A movement-by-movement description and some background material is provided for the major chamber works, while lesser works, such as the early string quartets, receive a more general treatment. In both the detailed and general sections, however, Westrup exhibits the negative bias toward Schubert's chamber music that prevailed before the 1970s. The chief criticism he levels against many of the works is that their tone and style are inconsistent due to the intrusions of popular idioms or the use of trivial material. In fact, he declares that only two examples of the mature chamber music (the D Minor and G Major String Quartets, D. 810 and D. 887) are completely satisfying and that even these works have their occasional weaknesses.

CHUSID (1997b) is less detailed than Westrup but is free of the latter's judgmental stance. The individual works are discussed under two broad headings: "Schubert's Chamber Music for Strings" and "Schubert's Chamber Music with Piano," with a final section devoted entirely to the Octet in F Major, D. 803. Unfortunately there are few musical illustrations, and some pieces, such as the violin sonatinas, are only briefly mentioned on or are omitted entirely, as is the case with the Arpeggione Sonata, D. 821. As the article's title suggests, Chusid argues that Schubert passed from the apprenticeship of his early chamber works to the mastery of his late works due in large part to his contact with musicians from the Beethoven circle and his desire to emulate Beethoven's example.

CHUSID (1997a) gives details on the stylistic and formal influence of orchestral music on Schubert's early string quartets and the String Quintet in C Minor, D. 8. These works exhibit such an orchestral influence most obviously in the many instances of direct quotations from the symphonies and overtures of Haydn, Mozart, and Beethoven; in the orchestral style of the string writing; and in certain formal traits peculiar to overtures of the period. The article is well illustrated musically and requires only a moderate grasp of music theory.

NEWBOULD's recent biography of Schubert contains a good, but limited, survey of Schubert's chamber music aimed at the general reader. The subject is divided between two chapters, "The Early Chamber Music" (up to and including the "Trout" Quintet) and the "Late Chamber Music" (from the *Quartettsatz,* D. 703, on). The author's commentary offers observations on specific features of individual works rather than a bar-by-bar description of the form of each movement. More detailed treatment is reserved for some of the late works, the place of honor being awarded to the Piano Trio in E-flat Major, D. 929, which Newbould recognizes as "one of the great masterpieces of the trio repertoire." A comparison of his discussion of this last work with Westrup's discussion reveals how profoundly attitudes toward Schubert's chamber music changed in the last 30 years of the 20th century.

McKAY deals in some depth with a neglected area of Schubert's chamber music. Although the duos, particularly the violin sonatinas, are quite popular among amateur musicians and students, they are often ignored or denigrated in the critical literature. The article consists of two parts. The first, "The String Duos in the Context of the Viennese Musical Scene," provides useful information on public and private music-making in Schubert's Vienna, situating the works in their proper historical and social milieu. The second part, "The String Duos in the Context of Schubert's Chamber Music," is largely devoted to detailed descriptions of the individual works; here, a moderate to good knowledge of classical form is required. The background to some of the formal developments in the duos is supplied at certain points by analyses of other instrumental works from preceding periods in Schubert's career. Particular emphasis is placed on Schubert's treatment of rondo forms.

The analyses, although quite dry, are well illustrated by musical diagrams and examples. Unfortunately, the descriptions of the early duos undermine McKay's conclusion that in the period from 1816 to 1827, "Schubert developed from a young composer of the late classical period into a mature composer of increasingly romantic persuasion." Some of these duos are so far-removed from classical structural norms that Charles Rosen has presented the first movement of the Violin Sonatina in G Minor, D 408, as proof that Schubert's break with classical procedures was "particularly striking in [his] early period" (*Sonata Forms*, 1980).

DAHLHAUS eloquently defends Schubert's lyrical approach to sonata form. Dahlhaus implicitly answers an influential article by the Schenkerian theorist Felix Salzer ("Die Sonatenform bei Franz Schubert," *Studien zur Musikwissenschaft* 15 [1928]) in which Salzer asserts that Schubert's sonata form runs counter to the main line of development extending from C.P.E. Bach to Beethoven, because Schubert's lyrical expansions seriously weaken what Salzer considers the form's essential quality—its forward-driving energy. Dahlhaus argues, to the contrary, that the first movement of the G Major String Quartet stands within the tradition of sonata form but is distinct from the Beethovenian model because a web of logical connections exists among the various parts of Schubert's form without the necessity of a constantly striving dynamism. From this observation he concludes that:

Schubert's G-Major Quartet shows that consistent musical logic—the weaving of a tight fabric of motivic relationships—is quite reconcilable with a relaxed pace and a musical attitude that . . . remains devoid of pathos. Although the concept of a thematic process normally calls to mind the homogeneous image of both insistent energy and compelling logic, these two characteristics are in fact separable.

Such an assertion marks an important turning point in the critical approach to Schubert's instrumental music, for it establishes the validity of Schubert's unique handling of sonata form while calling into question the relevance of the Beethovenian model as a universal standard. Although the article is difficult, it rewards careful study.

BRIAN BLACK

3. Lieder

Capell, Richard, *Schubert's Songs,* London: Benn, 1928; 3rd edition, London: Duckworth, 1973

Fischer-Dieskau, Dietrich, *Schubert's Songs: A Biographical Study,* translated by Kenneth S. Whitton, New York: Knopf, 1977

Frisch, Walter, editor, *Schubert: Critical and Analytical Studies,* Lincoln: University of Nebraska Press, 1986

Hirsch, Marjorie Wing, *Schubert's Dramatic Lieder,* Cambridge: Cambridge University Press, 1993

Kramer, Lawrence, *Franz Schubert: Sexuality, Subjectivity, Song,* Cambridge: Cambridge University Press, 1998

Kramer, Richard, *Distant Cycles: Schubert and the Conceiving of Song,* Chicago: University of Chicago Press, 1994

Porter, E.G., *Schubert's Song Technique,* London: Dobson, 1961

Reed, John, *The Schubert Song Companion,* Manchester: Manchester University Press, and New York: Universe Books, 1985

Schubert, Franz, *The Hyperion Schubert Edition: Complete Songs,* edited by Graham Johnson, London: Hyperion, 1997

Youens, Susan, *Schubert's Poets and the Making of Lieder,* Cambridge: Cambridge University Press, 1996

Schubert composed more than 600 songs, and these pieces have long been recognized as some of his most significant musical contributions. Writings on the songs can be divided into three categories: surveys of the entire repertoire; discussions of Schubert's two song cycles—*Die schöne Müllerin* (The Beautiful Miller Maid) and *Winterreise* (Winter Journey); and works that treat the songs more selectively, either by considering Schubert's general musical practices in songwriting or by addressing individual songs or groups of songs.

Four of the sources covered here are comprehensive works that survey Schubert's songs. CAPELL, a chronological survey, was the first English-language book to tackle the entire Schubert song repertoire, and the volume is still widely in use; however, it suffers from serious flaws. While it may provide a useful overview, the study is based on an outdated view of Schubert's personality that has been changed by recent research. Capell tends to present his judgments and ratings of the songs as self-evident truths, but they must be taken with a grain of salt.

FISCHER-DIESKAU also takes a chronological approach but includes much more biographical information, supplemented with quotations from important letters and other documents, than does Capell. The author's commentaries on particular songs are informed by his experience as a distinguished performer who has recorded most of Schubert's songs. In the same spirit, Fischer-Dieskau devotes one of his concluding chapters to a history of the most important performers of this repertory.

REED is an extremely helpful reference work. It begins with an alphabetical catalog of the songs that provides the following information for each piece: incipits of the piano and voice parts, poet's name, Deutsch number, date of composition, where the song can be found in published editions, and where it is discussed in other books. Reed also provides English prose translations (by Norma Deane and Celia Larner) and brief descriptions that may include biographical, musical, or textual commentary. Part 2 surveys the poets of Schubert's songs, providing a biography and a list of settings for each poet. The book concludes with a series of appendices, including a list of all the songs organized by key, a chronological table, opus numbers and dates of first publication, and English translations for German musical terms used in the songs.

Pianist Graham Johnson, in collaboration with numerous singers, has issued a set of compact discs covering all of SCHUBERT's songs. These recordings on the Hyperion label come with Johnson's extensive program notes, which combine historical and biographical background with the informed musical observations of a sensitive performer. Johnson's familiarity with the latest research and writing on Schubert makes these notes particularly valuable.

Among the books that treat Schubert songs more eclectically are studies concerned with technical, expressive, and biographical aspects of the songs. Of course, these categories can never be completely separated, and every one of the books reviewed below frequently shifts between these topics. In the following discussion, these publications are described in an order that moves gradually from techniques to expression to biography.

Porter and Hirsch are both concerned primarily with technical issues. PORTER considers the musical categories of phrasing and form, key, harmony, modulation, expression marks and grace notes, and, as a kind of summation, the Schubert idiom. For each category, he makes general observations, which he supports with numerous examples drawn from a large number of songs. As these examples are often stated very briefly, this book is most effectively used when scores or recordings are readily available. As a frame, Porter includes chapters on particular groups of songs; he opens with an interesting discussion of the first 24 songs composed by Schubert, comparing them with passages from other lieder of the time, and concludes with chapters on songs of death, songs to texts by Johann Mayrhofer, and the songs of *Schwanengesang*. Porter's sweeping view of the reper-

toire is most useful for a reader already familiar with many Schubert songs; a general reader may get lost amid the references to individual songs.

HIRSCH is concerned with issues of genre, in particular with distinctions between the lyric, to which art song is usually supposed to belong, and the dramatic, on which Schubert drew heavily in many of his songs. She considers three types of pieces: dramatic scenes, dramatic ballads, and mixed-genre lieder that combine aspects of lyric and dramatic. She discusses the historical background for each type and then moves on to discuss particular songs as case studies. Her detailed commentaries on six songs include many music examples. Compared to Porter, she discusses far fewer works but takes a much more concentrated approach to the songs she does examine.

Many of the articles collected in FRISCH concern Schubert's songs, approaching them from various music theoretical perspectives. Particularly valuable is the essay by Thrasybulos Georgiades, a translated chapter from his book-length German study of Schubert songs. This chapter, a painstaking analysis of the Goethe setting "Wanderers Nachtlied," persuasively conveys Georgiades's argument that Schubert had an intuitive understanding of the German language that guided him to restructure poems in the process of transforming them into songs. Two seminal articles on the song "Auf dem Flusse" from *Winterreise* are also reprinted here: David Lewin's sensitive interpretation of how the music and text are linked and a thoughtful response by Anthony Newcomb.

Richard KRAMER takes a unique approach to Schubert's songs by considering various groups of songs as potential song cycles. He suggests that Schubert had cyclical relationships in mind more often than the published versions of his songs reveal. Kramer examines collections of songs with a single poet, the poets being Ludwig Rellstab, Heinrich Heine, Johann Wolfgang von Goethe, and Friedrich Schlegel. The author also devotes chapters to *Winterreise* and to issues of revision and recomposition, treating the last topic by comparing Schubert's four settings of Friedrich Schiller's poem "Der Jüngling am Bache." One particularly interesting technique introduced here is the method of comparing the end of one song with the beginning of another, seeking connections that would make the compositions appropriate neighbors in a song cycle. The argument of this book is complex and is best suited for readers with a high level of familiarity with the songs.

Positing that the meaning of individuality, or subjectivity, was in the process of being defined during Schubert's lifetime, Lawrence KRAMER considers how particular songs and groups of songs reflect this development, with special attention to issues of sexuality and gender. For example, the chapter on "Die Forelle" compares that poem and song to other literature involving a fish that can be transformed into or take on the role of a woman. Kramer's insightful commentaries intertwine critical theory with musical and poetic analysis.

YOUENS presents four moving, interpretive studies of selected Schubert poets and of Schubert's musical settings of each poet's work. The poets are Gabriele von Baumberg, Theodor Körner, Mayrhofer, and Ernst Schulze. Each chapter begins with a thorough and well-documented biographical section on the poet and then considers selected songs. The historical, personal, and psychological details presented in the biographical portions of this book are a treasure in themselves. The relationships among biography, poetry, and musical settings are different in each case, as Schubert's connections to these poets varied. In each case, however, Youens demonstrates significant relationships between the poet's ideas and the composer's responses. Most powerful, perhaps, is her argument that Schulze's obsession with a woman who did not love him influenced Schubert's settings of that poet's work, creating songs that reflect the composer's intuitive understanding that these poems represent a poisoned form of love.

LISA FEURZEIG

4. Song Cycles

Feil, Arnold, *Franz Schubert, Die schöne Müllerin, Winterreise,* translated by Ann C. Sherwin, Portland, Oregon: Amadeus Press, 1988

Moore, Gerald, *The Schubert Song Cycles, with Thoughts on Performance,* London: Hamilton, 1975

Youens, Susan, *Retracing a Winter's Journey, Schubert's Winterreise,* Ithaca, New York: Cornell University Press, 1991

————, *Schubert, Müller, and Die schöne Müllerin,* Cambridge: Cambridge University Press, 1997

————, *Schubert: Die schöne Müllerin,* Cambridge: Cambridge University Press, 1992

The song cycle, defined as a collection of songs linked by some unifying factor, was refined and perfected by Franz Schubert. The form emerged with the late 18th-century German poetic renaissance and came to fruition in the private salons (social gatherings of creative artists) of Vienna. Schubert's two celebrated cycles are *Die schöne Müllerin* (The Beautiful Miller-Maiden, D795, 1823) and *Winterreise* (Winter Journey, D911, 1928), which both set the poetry of Wilhelm Müller. In addition, 14 of Schubert's late songs, which he never intended to be a cycle, were published together after his death, under the title *Schwanengesang* (Swan Song, D957).

Die schöne Müllerin includes 20 songs that appeared originally in five booklets, which resemble five acts of a play. This *Liederspiele* (song-play) tells the tale of a wayfaring young man who falls in love with a miller's daughter. She returns his affections briefly but ultimately rejects him and falls in love with a hunter. The young man, left heartbroken and desolate, drowns himself. The cycle is presumed to have been written soon after Schubert discovered that he was afflicted with syphilis; the resulting fears of his own precarious mortality and possibility of an early, tragic death are reflected in the young man's plight. *Winterreise,* 24 songs in two sets of 12, is a monodrama (told by a single narrator) like *Die schöne Müllerin,* but without plot. Presenting a series of somber vignettes from a winter's journey, it is fraught with unrequited love, melancholy, and isolation. Schubert's labor of composing *Winterreise,* written shortly before his death, is thought by many to have contributed to his demise. Although *Schwanengesang*'s 14 songs include many virtuoso examples of the composer's late style, it lacks the central unifying link to classify it as a true cycle.

FEIL, translated from the 1975 German edition, presents a song-by-song analysis of both cycles and is liberally sprinkled with musical examples, using as its primary analytical focal point the relevance of rhythm and meter to the text. The poetry appears in the original German without translation. The introduction gives the reader an insight into the cultural and historical origins of the two cycles; a concluding essay by Rolf Vollmann, "Wilhelm Müller and Romanticism," examines the poet against the background of German romanticism and in comparison with the German romantic poet Heinrich Heine.

MOORE, similar to Feil, also furnishes a song-by-song analysis, but the focus is on performance issues, mostly from the point of view of the accompanist. It covers not only Schubert's two legitimate cycles but *Schwanengesang* as well.

YOUENS (1991) presents a thorough, in-depth portrayal of all aspects of *Winterreise.* The poet, Müller, who was underrated in the 20th century, is placed in the context of his own time. His painstaking revision and reordering of the poetry is well documented, as are Schubert's considerable musical reworkings. Other known musical settings of Müller's cycle (e.g., Kreutzer's) are considered, along with performance history and the initial critical reception of the Schubert setting. The poetry is examined at great length from a psychological as well as a symbolic point of view. A survey of the music covers form, speech style, piano writing, and dynamics; useful tables summarize tonal plan, tempo, and poetic rhythm vis-à-vis musical meter. Analyses of each song first examine the text and then factor in the musical setting, discussing particular elements pertinent to the song (melody, rhythm, meter, mode, tonality, use of repetition, and interplay between voice and piano), with some musical examples inserted. Each song is identified by a musical incipit; the text is quoted in German along with a summary translation.

YOUENS's (1992) Cambridge Handbook on *Die schöne Müllerin* skillfully fulfills the stated goal of that series, providing an accessible introduction to the cycle, presenting information on historical and musical context, composition, performance, reception, and critical discussion of the work. Every pertinent aspect is briefly summarized, including the genesis of the poetic cycle, earlier versions of the poetry, biographical background, and more. A brief explication of each poem in the cycle follows, considering meter, key, English translations, as well as a musical analysis of each song from the standpoint of poetic context and musical form.

YOUENS (1997) came about as the result of the requisite brevity of her 1992 volume. The author imparts a vast amount of background research here. The origin of the *Liederspiele*, a narrative in verse and song, is exhaustively explored. Rather than discussing *Die schöne Müllerin* itself, more than half the book examines the intricacies of the cycle's prototypes. The folk legend of the miller's daughter was ubiquitous in the poetry of its time. Much of this earlier, unknown poetry is introduced here, often quoted at length with English translation. Other composers' settings of Müller's cycle and/or of individual poems, both before and after Schubert's, are also taken into account. Finally, Youens considers biographical issues from both Schubert and Müller in light of the cycle, including a discussion of those poems that Schubert discarded from his setting. The bibliography is quite comprehensive.

NANCY F. GARF

5. Piano Music

Badura-Skoda, Eva, "The Piano Works of Schubert," in
  Nineteenth-Century Piano Music, edited by R. Larry Todd,
  New York: Schirmer Books, 1990
Gibbs, Christopher H., editor, *The Cambridge Companion to
  Schubert,* Cambridge: Cambridge University Press, 1997
Newbould, Brian, *Schubert: The Music and the Man,* Berkeley:
  University of California Press, and London: Gollancz, 1997
Radcliffe, Philip, *Schubert Piano Sonatas,* London: British
  Broadcasting Corporation, 1967
Weekley, Dallas A., and Nancy Arganbright, *Schubert's Music
  for Piano Four-Hands: A Comprehensive Guide to
  Performing and Listening to the Dances, Fantasies, Marches,
  Polonaises, Sonatas, Variations, and Other Duets,* White
  Plains, New York: Pro/Am Music Resources, 1990
Wolff, Konrad, *Masters of the Keyboard,* Bloomington:
  Indiana University Press, 1983; enlarged edition, 1990

Piano music accounts for a substantial portion of Schubert's compositional output. He composed for the piano dances and other music for social gatherings; fantasies and short concert pieces, which Schubert assembled in collections such as the *Moments musicaux,* op. 94 (D780); multimovement sonatas in the tradition of Haydn, Mozart, and Beethoven; and encompassing all these genres but deserving recognition of their own, some

70 piano duets, more than any other major composer. Despite the evident significance piano music held for Schubert, however, many of his compositions for this instrument were not published during his lifetime but appeared sporadically over the decades—some more than a century—after his death, and hence the piano music was slow to enter the concert repertoire and even slower to become a topic for researchers and analysts. Only in the second half of the 20th century were the number, order, and grouping of movements in the early sonatas established, for instance. Schubert's approach to piano composition has only recently begun to be examined on its own terms, rather than in terms derived solely from comparison to his other compositions or to Beethoven's solo piano music. Similarly, writers have just recently begun to address the historical value of Schubert's so-called social genres, for which he was well known in his lifetime but which were all but forgotten after his death. Most of the sources regarding Schubert's piano music appear within larger publications: biographies or collected essays. Two books devoted entirely to the subject are Radcliffe's slim volume on the solo sonatas and Weekley and Arganbright's comprehensive guide to the duet music.

NEWBOULD's critical biography of Schubert offers four excellent chapters on the piano music: "The Early Piano Music," "Four Hands at One Piano," "The Late Piano Sonatas," and "Other Late Piano Works." The author includes pertinent biographical and source manuscript information in each chapter and addresses some wide-ranging analytical issues—for example, why Schubert's unfinished pieces are significant and why Schubert frequently begins the recapitulation of a movement in sonata form with the primary theme in the subdominant. Newbould frequently draws comparisons between the piano music and other works by Schubert, Beethoven, and other composers who preceded or followed Schubert, and he is careful to spell out in what sense he finds these comparisons valid. There are relatively few musical examples in the text, and the examples given do not include headings or measure numbers. To follow Newbould's discussion closely, the reader needs to have a copy of the music at hand. On the whole, however, this is one of the most substantial studies of Schubert's piano music available.

One of the valuable essays in GIBBS is Margaret Notley's "Schubert's Social Music: the 'Forgotten Genres'." It is the first study devoted entirely to Schubert's social genres, covering the dances and piano duets, in addition to the part-songs. The composer wrote down approximately 500 dances, inspired by social gatherings at which he was pianist. These little pieces stand somewhere between improvisations and autonomous aesthetic works, and Notley considers examples from both ends of the spectrum. Her discussion would be enhanced by particulars regarding Viennese dance traditions (for instance, see Elizabeth Aldrich, "Social Dancing in Schubert's

World," in *Schubert's Vienna,* edited by Raymond Erickson, 1997). Notley concludes that Schubert's sets of dances are "loosely strung gems," and that it remained for the next generation of composers—Schumann, Liszt, Brahms, Ravel—to turn dances into glittering concert pieces. Schubert's music for piano four-hands, Notley argues, falls into a genre of its own. When considering the characteristics of the genre, she emphasizes its social qualities, the "divertimento aesthetic," but points out that the duets also often inhabit the more serious expressive universe of Schubert's chamber music with piano. Notley views this juxtaposition of the entertaining and the elevated as the unique achievement of the symbiotic relationship created between the duo-pianists.

A second essay from Gibbs is William Kinderman's "Schubert's Piano Music: Probing the Human Condition." The author opens his essay with mention of the rightful place of Schubert's piano compositions beside Beethoven's legacy. He goes on to ascribe the idiosyncrasy of Schubert's music to its looseness of organization, or the shifts in perspective, caused by stark thematic contrast, major-minor juxtaposition, abrupt modulation, and so forth. Kinderman proposes that these compositional tactics "embody a latent psychological symbolism," the perspective of the romantic wanderer. This is a provocative thesis, which Kinderman unfortunately does not develop with a close analysis of one or two pieces. Instead, he addresses nearly all of Schubert's solo piano music, plus a good number of the duets. Although he does draw upon German-romantic terminology, he is unable in the brief space he devotes to each piece to demonstrate specifically how the Wanderer analogy operates. The essay might well provide a springboard for an entire book—and new historical slant—on Schubert's achievement. As it stands, it is one of the most insightful surveys of the piano music available.

WOLFF devotes one chapter in his book to Schubert's piano music. He does not delve into historical or analytical issues but instead examines issues of performance: technical matters, such as quick jumps and repeated chords, as well as interpretive matters, such as the articulation of melodic lines and pacing of formal sections. No single piece receives thorough attention, however, and with its limitations, the chapter is primarily interesting for Wolff's personal anecdotes, drawn from his long career as a pianist.

Like Wolff's chapter, WEEKLEY and ARGANBRIGHT's book on Schubert's music for piano four-hands is written from the performers' point of view, but this study is intended for a much larger audience. The authors discuss every one of the duets, in chronological order, including information about the compositional history, manuscript(s), and publication history of the music, along with an incipit and brief description of each movement. Throughout the study they pay special attention to performance issues. The appendix offers a critical mosaic, a potpourri of quotations from writers across the centuries regarding Schubert's duets. Altogether, this book is a superb example of Schubert research and an indispensable resource for anyone pursuing their own study of the composer's piano duets.

RADCLIFFE was the first to publish a book solely on Schubert's piano music, in this instance the solo sonatas. The author proposes that Schubert found himself in his keyboard works, and the description of the sonatas focuses accordingly on the temperament of the music and how it reflects Schubert's personality or frame of mind. Thus, for example, Radcliffe claims that, in the first movement of the Sonata in D Major, op. 53 (D850), "for all its powerful rhetoric and masterly construction, . . . Schubert gives us least of his most individual qualities." The second movement "retains something of the grand manner, but tempered by a rich glow of lyricism." And "during the rest of the work Schubert moves with increasing happiness in the direction of friendly relaxation." Radcliffe implies in these statements and throughout the book that geniality and serenity are Schubert's truest forms of musical expression and that majestic or stormy sounding passages must ultimately give way to spacious repose. The author's point of view is outdated; nonetheless the book remains valuable for its early attempt to treat Schubert's sonatas as an independent accomplishment, on equal ground with the piano sonatas of other great composers.

BADURA-SKODA opens her essay defending the claim that Schubert's piano music ranks in importance with that of Beethoven. She traces the development of Schubert's idiomatic style of composing for the piano to the evolution of his song accompaniments, then goes on to discuss Schubert's solo piano music: the sonatas, fantasies, and shorter piano pieces (but not the social genres). Badura-Skoda's clarification of the manuscript sources for the sonatas is particularly valuable. She provides many fine musical examples to illustrate her observations about Schubert's harmonic and melodic language, although at times she could be technically more precise. For instance, the series of harmonic shocks in example 4.2 outlines a whole-tone descent. Considering its scope, however, this essay provides a well-balanced introduction to Schubert's solo piano music.

DONNA L. LYNN

6. Symphonies

Carner, Mosco, "The Orchestral Music," in *The Music of Schubert,* edited by Gerald Abraham, London: Drummond, 1946; New York: Norton, 1947

Brown, Maurice, *The New Grove Schubert,* London: Macmillan, 1982; New York: Norton, 1983

———, *Schubert Symphonies,* London: British Broadcasting Corporation, and Seattle: University of Washington Press, 1970

Griffel, L. Michael, "Schubert's Orchestral Music," in *The Cambridge Companion to Schubert*, edited by Christopher H. Gibbs, Cambridge: Cambridge University Press, 1997

Hutchings, Arthur, *Schubert*, London: Dent, 1945; 4th edition, 1973

Newbould, Brian, *Schubert: The Music and the Man*, Berkeley: University of California Press, and London: Gollancz, 1997

———, *Schubert and the Symphony: A New Perspective*, Surbiton: Toccata Press, 1992

Winter, Robert, "Paper Studies and the Future of Schubert Research," in *Schubert Studies: Problems of Style and Chronology*, edited by Eva Badura-Skoda and Peter Branscombe, Cambridge: Cambridge University Press, 1982

Like much of Schubert's output, his symphonies have an uncertain chronology. Even with the great strides made by researchers since 1970, some confusion still exists over their proper order and numeration; thus, to make sense of the related scholarship, general readers should be familiar with some of the major issues. Today, most scholars agree that Schubert's symphonic catalog includes ten symphonies, only seven of which were completed, and a handful of incomplete sketches and fragments. The first six symphonies (Nos. 1–6, written from 1813 to 1816) are complete four-movement works strongly influenced by Haydn, Mozart, and, to a lesser degree, Beethoven. For many years, Schubert's only other known symphony was the "Great" C major (D. 944, June–September 1825; discovered by Robert Schumann in 1839); thus, it became widely known as "Symphony no. 7." After the manuscript for the "Unfinished" Symphony in B minor (D. 759, October 1822) was brought to light in the 1860s, it received the label "Symphony no. 8" despite being written at least two years before the "Great" C major. This numbering system was firmly established when Breitkopf and Härtel published all of Schubert's known symphonies in 1884 and 1885. Over time, Sir George Grove and others became disturbed by the chronological inconsistency of this numbering system, so they began to call the "Great" C major "Symphony no. 9," leaving the seventh slot for Schubert's orchestral-score sketch in E minor/E major (D. 729, August 1821). This numeration/chronology for Schubert's symphonies persevered until 1978, when the editors of the New Schubert Edition decided to relabel the "Unfinished" no. 7 and the "Great" no. 8, eliminating the D. 729 sketch from the group. (It should be noted that none of the current studies employs the New Schubert Edition's numbering system.) Because certain European scores still list the "Great" as no. 7, three different numbering systems are presently in use. To add to the confusion, it was believed that yet another Schubert symphony once existed: the "Gmunden-Gastein" symphony (D. 849, composed June–September 1825), which is mentioned in Schubert's letters but for which the manuscript was apparently lost.

In 1978, paper/manuscript studies by WINTER determined that this "Gmunden-Gastein" symphony is actually the "Great" C major symphony. Also in the late 1970s, a three-movement Schubert symphony (D. 936A in D, September–October 1828) was reconstructed from piano-score sketches that were once thought to be fragments of three separate early works. (Winter's paper/watermark evidence substantiates this reconstruction.) Winter's article, although quite scholarly and detailed, is still within the grasp of general readers. (His specific evidence for the dating of the "Great" C major is presented on pp. 257–69, with illustrations of the watermarks on pp. 270–75.)

Most of the scholarship on Schubert's symphonies has been published as either journal articles or chapters in comprehensive studies of his life and work. NEWBOULD (1992) offers the first (and only) truly complete book-length study of Schubert's symphonies. This outstanding work presents a well-balanced blend of biographical information, analytical description, and the latest scholarly findings situated within a chronological framework. Newbould includes all the critical information as well as an introductory chapter explaining why symphonic composition was so important to Schubert, a discussion of Schubert's early symphonic training, an overview of the symphonic tradition Schubert inherited, and a full-chapter discussion of each symphony. Each of these symphonic chapters gives biographical background for the particular work's genesis and a comprehensive theme-by-theme discussion of each movement (with musical examples provided). Six valuable appendices provide a chronology of Schubert's symphonies, the proper numeration of the symphonies, a discussion of whether the "Entr'acte in B minor" from Rosamunde is actually the finale of the "Unfinished" Symphony, a description of how the Tenth Symphony was identified, a list of autographs and performing editions of the symphonies, and an exhaustive bibliography. Clearly, this book is the definitive resource on Schubert's symphonies.

In the bicentennial of Schubert's birth year, NEWBOULD (1997) released his comprehensive monograph on Schubert's life and music. Unlike other such biographies, Newbould's volume devotes complete chapters to the symphonies divided by style period. The book is engaging with a flowing, biographical focus, yet Newbould manages to interweave significant details about the musical content of each work.

The only other book dedicated to Schubert's symphonies is BROWN (1970), which, despite its brevity, is a good source for gaining a quick overview of Schubert's symphonies. After a short introductory chapter, the eight commonly known symphonies and two of his symphonic fragments are outlined chapter by chapter (the volume generally dedicates two to four pages per symphony with musical examples of the main themes and short comments from various critics). The discussions of the "Unfinished" and the "Great" C Major symphonies are more substantial. Some of the details have been superceded by recent research.

BROWN (1983), an updated reprint of his entry in the *New Grove Dictionary of Music and Musicians* (1980), reiterates some material from Brown (1970). This is an excellent study of Schubert's life and complete works; however, its biographical/chronological format scatters symphonic-specific information throughout the commentary. The book's most useful feature regarding the symphonies is Eric Sam's "Work-List," which was updated in 1982 to take into account Winter's new paper-based datings. Sam lists the Deutsch ("D.") catalog number for each symphony/sketch, the date of composition/publication, page references for locating the musical scores in the old and new Schubert editions, and the specific pages on which each symphony is discussed in Brown (1983).

An even more concise and current introduction to Schubert symphonies is GRIFFEL's assessment. Despite its brevity, this discussion of the symphonies is highly informative and would be an excellent place for the general reader to begin. Griffel intersperses compelling biographical information, including quotes from the composer's letters, musical commentary, and notated examples; an annotated/chronological list of Schubert's orchestral works; and a note on the numbering of the symphonies. The volume as a whole is one of the finest, most up-to-date resources available on the composer and his music.

Although CARNER's essay is devoted to all of Schubert's orchestral music, his specific coverage of the symphonies is substantial. Like Brown (1970), Carner gives a quick overview of each work, providing only a paragraph or two of general commentary for each movement. Beyond that, the author provides a useful summary of Schubert's general style traits, the musical forms he employed, his thematic/harmonic approaches, and his manner of orchestration. The book also includes a wonderfully crafted chronological list of Schubert's compositions divided by genre and opus number, as well as an extensive bibliography by A. Hyatt King.

HUTCHINGS's general study of Schubert was first published in 1945 and added little new information in its 1973 revised edition beyond the expected basic discussion of the rhythmic figurations. Unfortunately, some critical information remains outdated even in the revised edition. For example, he still describes the supposedly lost "Gmunden-Gastein" symphony as being different from the "Great" C major.

DANIEL JACOBSON

Schumann, Clara 1819–1896

German pianist and composer

Burk, John N., *Clara Schumann: A Romantic Biography*, New York: Random House, 1940

Chissell, Joan, *Clara Schumann, A Dedicated Spirit: A Study of her Life and Work*, London: Hamilton, and New York: Taplinger, 1983

Lindeman, Stephan D., *Structural Novelty and Tradition in the Early Romantic Piano Concerto*, Stuyvesant, New York: Pendragon Press, 1999

Litzmann, Berthold, editor, *Clara Schumann: An Artist's Life, Based on Material Found in Diaries and Letters*, translated by Grace E. Hadow, London: Macmillan, and Leipzig: Breitkopf and Härtel, 1913; reprint, New York, Da Capo Press, 1979

May, Florence, *The Girlhood of Clara Schumann (Clara Wieck and Her Time)*, London: Arnold, and New York: Longmans, Green, 1912

Reich, Nancy B., *Clara Schumann: The Artist and the Woman*, Ithaca, New York: Cornell University Press, and London: Gollancz, 1985

Schumann, Clara, *The Complete Correspondence of Clara and Robert Schumann*, 2 vols., edited by Eva Weissweiler, translated by Hildegard Fritsch and Ronald L. Crawford, New York: Lang, 1994

———, *Letters of Clara Schumann and Johannes Brahms 1853–1896*, edited by Berthold Litzmann, London: Arnold, and New York: Longmans, Green, 1927; reprint, Westport, Connecticut: Hyperion Press, 1979

Schumann, Eugenie, *The Schumanns and Johannes Brahms; The Memoirs of Eugenie Schumann*, New York: Dial Press, 1927; as *The Memoirs of Eugenie Schumann*, translated by Marie Busch, London: Heinemann, 1927

Schumann, Robert, *The Marriage Diaries of Robert and Clara Schumann: From Their Wedding Day through the Russia Trip*, edited by Gerd Nauhaus, translated by Peter Ostwald, Boston: Northeastern University Press, 1993

Wieck, Friedrich, *Piano and Song (Didactic and Polemical): The Collected Writings of Clara Schumann's Father and Only Teacher*, translated by Henry Pleasants, Stuyvesant, New York: Pendragon Press, 1988

Clara Schumann (née Wieck) was considered one of the greatest pianists of the 19th century, yet during her lifetime and for some years after her death, articles and books about her focused on the male figures in her life: her father and sole teacher, Friedrich Wieck (1785–1873); her husband, Robert Schumann (1810–56); and her close friend Johannes Brahms (1833–97). In the first full-length biography published after her death (Litzmann), Schumann is finally seen as the central figure rather than the woman pianist subsidiary to the men in her life. Since the 1970s, many studies of her manifold activities—as a virtuoso pianist, a wife and mother, a teacher and editor, and above all, an accomplished composer—have appeared. Most of these publications are in German, but a number of English-language dissertations, articles, plays, and even movies about her have been produced with some frequency. Discussion of Clara Schumann's life and work also can be found in almost every biography of Robert Schumann or Johannes Brahms.

LITZMANN's three-volume, family-authorized, fully documented biography of Clara Schumann, published in Germany between 1902 and 1908, is the recognized authority on which almost all subsequent books are based. Litzmann, who had access to the pianist's diaries and correspondence, gives Clara Schumann her full due as concert artist and "noble woman" but provides little information about her compositions or her activities as teacher and mother. Sifting through thousands of documents, he excises portions of letters and documents, partly to avoid giving offense, partly in the interests of length. His tome was not translated into English until 1913; the Grace Hadow translation, although accurate, is severely abridged—cut from 1,471 to 921 pages. Nevertheless, many English-language books and dramatized versions of Clara Schumann's life are founded on the Hadow translation.

Hadow's translation of Litzmann's edition of the correspondence of Clara Schumann and Johannes Brahms (Clara SCHUMANN [1927]) is a faultless translation but also abridged. Still, this shortened English version (1,271 pages reduced to 599) has shaped views of the relationship between the two musicians for many years.

In the first English-language book about the pianist, MAY, who studied piano with Clara Schumann and Johannes Brahms and wrote an acclaimed biography of Brahms, not only examines the girlhood years and family history of Clara Wieck but endeavors to write "from the standpoint of musical history." May's major sources are volume 1 of Litzmann's biography and Robert Schumann's letters. The language is dated, and the author's attitudes toward women and women's roles reflect her English Victorian background, but the volume is still a valuable document because of May's personal contacts with Clara Wieck Schumann and her family.

BURK uses Litzmann's biography, the Clara Schumann-Johannes Brahms correspondence, and selected Robert Schumann letters to create a "romantic biography." Burk works directly from German-language accounts; his translations of Litzmann and other German sources are accurate and read well. This fictionalized publication without documentation was popular in its time but has been superseded by more serious studies.

Eugenie SCHUMANN, the youngest of the four Schumann daughters, wrote her reminiscences in 1925, long after the death of her mother. Utterly candid, forthright, and moving, this book is the most authentic portrait of the personal life of Clara Schumann available. Eugenie Schumann lived and taught in England for a number of years and knew English well. Presumably, she had a hand in the translation, although the London edition attributes the translation to Marie Busch.

CHISSELL's work presents a new view of the great pianist. She shows us the extent of Clara Schumann's dedication to her art, whereas earlier biographers emphasized her dedication to her husband. Chissell delivers a life and works in a readable style aimed at the music lover rather than the scholar. Unfortunately, the author relies mainly on Hadow's translations of Litzmann for information on the life. Chissell studied the autographs and program collection related to Clara Schumann's activities as concert artist and composer found in the Schumann archives in Zwickau, Robert Schumann's birthplace, and she provides illuminating insights into Clara Schumann's compositions based on this archival research. Surprisingly, Chissell's monograph is not fully documented, as quotations from diaries and letters are given without citations.

The biography by REICH is the first to grapple with the many facets of Clara Schumann's life. The book is organized into two sections. The first is a biography, and the second takes up many of the themes of Schumann's life: her life as mother, teacher, editor, friend, and composer. Consistent with the work's subtitle, *The Artist and the Woman,* Reich deals with tensions between these two roles, pointing out many of the problems faced by this single mother who was endeavoring to raise a family of seven children and maintain an international concert career. Reich returns to the original German sources, many of which were previously consulted only by Litzmann, and reexamines and translates material from the family records, letters, diaries, music autographs and prints, program collection, and other primary sources, permitting a fresh assessment of Clara Schumann.

Hildegard Fritsch and Ronald Crawford are to be thanked for an exemplary and complete translation of the first two volumes (1832–38 and 1839) of Eva Weissweiler's critical German edition of the correspondence of Clara and Robert Schumann (Clara SCHUMANN [1994]). Although Weissweiler and her publishers have promised a third volume to complete the correspondence and, most important, to supply a critical and historical commentary, this has not yet been published. Presumably, the third volume would also include a general index and an index of musical compositions. Without this critical apparatus, the German edition is seriously limited. In their English translation, Fritsch and Crawford attempt to correct this problem with brief (and necessarily skimpy) end notes of their own for many of the letters—mostly identifying people and places mentioned in the text—and they also provide indices for each volume, including one of musical works mentioned in the letters.

Peter Ostwald's translation of the *The Marriage Diaries* in Robert SCHUMANN, edited by Gerd Nauhaus, is the only complete translation of this important document, which previously had appeared only in excerpts in Hadow's translation and in a journal article (*Music and Letters*, 1934). Although not as felicitous a translation as the Fritsch and Crawford translation of the correspondence, the edition does reproduce all of Nauhaus's meticulous notes, the biographical directory, and the index. The diaries, which are joint records kept by Clara and Robert Schumann for the first four years of their marriage, chronicle their personal and professional lives and major journeys undertaken by the couple.

WIECK's treatise, first published in 1853, has been translated into English three times. The most recent and, by far, the best of these translations is the publication by Henry Pleasants, who has added an informative introduction and enlightening annotations. Wieck, a master teacher and an acerbic character, describes the surprisingly modern pedagogic methods that turned his daughter into a world-class musician and makes trenchant comments on the German musical world of the early 19th century.

Finally, LINDEMAN's discussion of the early romantic piano concerto devotes a chapter to Clara Wieck's Piano Concerto, op. 7. Originally a dissertation, Lindeman's study, which deals with the concertos of Mendelssohn, Chopin, Liszt, and Robert Schumann (among others), gives a history and analysis of the young pianist-composer's opus and points to it as "evidence of her creativity and bold conception."

NANCY B. REICH

Schumann, Robert 1810–1856

German composer, writer on music, and critic

1. Biography

Abraham, Gerald, "Robert Schumann," *Early Romantic Masters I: Chopin, Schumann, Liszt,* edited by Nicholas Temperley et al., London: Macmillan, and New York: Norton, 1985

Daverio, John, *Robert Schumann: Herald of a "New Poetic Age,"* New York: Oxford University Press, 1997

Fischer-Dieskau, Dietrich, *Robert Schumann, Words and Music: The Vocal Compositions,* translated by Reinhard G. Pauly, Portland, Oregon: Amadeus Press, 1988

Ostwald, Peter F., *Schumann: The Inner Voices of a Musical Genius,* Boston: Northeastern University Press, 1985

Schumann, Robert, *On Music and Musicians,* edited by Konrad Wolff, translated by Paul Rosenfeld, New York: Norton, 1946

Taylor, Ronald, *Robert Schumann: His Life and Work,* New York: Universe Books, and London: Granada, 1982

Todd, R. Larry, editor, *Schumann and His World,* Princeton, New Jersey: Princeton University Press, 1994

Wasielewski, Wilhelm Joseph von, *Life of Robert Schumann,* translated by Abby Langdon Alger, Boston: Ditson, 1871; reprint, Detroit, Michigan: Detroit Reprints in Music, Information Coordinators, 1975

The study of Robert Schumann benefits greatly from the wealth of surviving primary source material, including regular, detailed, and often meticulous notes about events and ideas found in his diaries and household journals (*Tagebücher and Haushaltbücher*); his correspondence with family, friends, and associates; and his critical writings preserved especially in the pages of the *Neue Zeitschrift für Musik*, the journal he founded in 1833 and edited for ten years. There are also numerous writings on Schumann by contemporaries and eyewitness accounts by his wife Clara and his protégé Johannes Brahms.

Prior to the end of World War II, the most noteworthy biographies of Robert Schumann were those by Wasielewski, Philipp Spitta (1882), and Wolfgang Boetticher (1941). Of these, only Wasielewski's biography is covered here. It has been selected because an adequate and available English translation for it exists and because it occupies a privileged place in Schumann scholarship. Wasielewski was a violinist who played under Schumann and knew him as a colleague and sometime confidant in the last decade of his life. This closeness to the composer, often as actual observer, has given his biography a certain cachet, and he is still read and quoted by musicians, critics, and scholars today.

Schumann scholarship suffered some setback and confusion after World War II, when many primary documents were lost or scattered. German historians and musicologists worked in the succeeding decades to recover or, in some cases, to reconstruct this material, and specialists in more recent decades have reexamined at and transcribed the sources. New biographies in English based on this research considerably advance our understanding and perception of the composer. Although each biographer purports to correct the errors of earlier accounts, each study is primarily distinguished by the angle or emphasis the author takes. And, not surprisingly, all of the authors reviewed here venture their own opinions on how Schumann really died—syphilis or otherwise.

WASIELEWSKI, appearing just a year after the composer's death, emphasizes both the author's firsthand knowledge of Schumann, the Schumann family, and the composer's associates, as well as the first publication of the composer's letters, many of which are quoted or reprinted in the book. An enduring—at times, annoying—feature is Wasielewski's occasional interjection of personal observations, reminiscences, and judgments about Schumann and his music, which have largely shaped popular perceptions to this day. Because he is close to Schumann, the author sometimes exercises caution, even self-censorship, ostensibly to avoid disparaging the man or embarrassing the family. In a discussion of Schumann's premarital relationship with Ernestine von Fricken, Wasielewski maintains that the couple's breakup was desirable. Why? For "reasons which cannot be given," he writes. On the other hand, few besides Wasielewski can offer a trustworthy eyewitness description of Schumann's physical appearance, demeanor, and habits. This description is one of the more interesting portions of the book to read. Although most early biographies are difficult to find today, this one, in both the German original and its English translation of 1871, can be readily obtained—an effort well worth taking for a work that is as interesting to read for its own sake as it is for its subject's.

FISCHER-DIESKAU, best known for his performances and recordings as a baritone, writes from his unique vantage point as one who has sung and recorded nearly all of Schumann's lieder. The biography emphasizes in particular Schumann's musical setting of poetic texts in the songs and vocal works and offers brief biographical sketches of many of the poets. Fischer-Dieskau explores the age-old questions concerning words and music (i.e., How do they relate to one another? Which has primacy?), and he attempts to explain, somewhat unconvincingly, Schumann's views on these issues. But the strength of this biography is the author's practical familiarity with the vocal works and his descriptive analyses of texts and melodies.

TAYLOR, a scholar of German romanticism who has written on E.T.A. Hoffmann and Richard Wagner, seeks to reconstruct Schumann's life as a series of causes and effects. Like other biographers, the author takes his own look at the documentary sources and fleshes out the details with context and background. Although informative and interesting, his account is uneven. On the one hand, Taylor offers more details than most readers need or want, such as telling us, for example, that a grand piano arrived at Schumann's residence and, furthermore, that the piano was a Streicher. On the other hand, important details are left unexplored, such as Schumann's brief interest in the ideas of Anton Justus Thibaut, who championed the music of Palestrina, Handel, and Bach, and Schumann's own fugue and counterpoint studies, which had a great influence on his manner of composition in his later years. Taylor's careful reading of the primary sources will be appreciated by most general readers, but the lack of documentation weakens the book overall.

ABRAHAM, a music historian and critic, offers a fair and reasonable biographical account with a minimum of commentary and criticism. Originally appearing as an article in the *New Grove Dictionary of Music and Musicians* (1980), the biography was updated with corrections in 1985. Without implying any cause and effect, Abraham weaves the events and facts of Schumann's life with his musical compositions. The account presents a somewhat flat rendering of the person but is on the whole accurate and informative. Most

helpful are the work list and bibliographies, which, although now dated, are still an invaluable reference to scholars and musicians alike.

OSTWALD, a medical doctor, professor of psychiatry, and accomplished amateur musician, presents an original and compelling look at the composer. Using his psychiatric background and musical knowledge, Ostwald interprets the primary sources and relates a psychobiographical account of Schumann's life and works. Although the book received wide acclaim, it has also been rightly criticized for at times reading a bit much into Schumann's letters and diaries. For example, Schumann appears in this biography to be a man obsessed with sex and troubled by homosexual urges, premature ejaculation, oedipal rivalry, sexual conflicts, and constant infatuations. (See Daverio's response, below.) Nevertheless, Ostwald's credentials as a medical doctor and musician allow him to paint a richly hued picture of a tormented genius and brilliant composer. Most informative are his summary of the historical explanations of Schumann's illness and death and the analysis of the original autopsy report from the perspective of modern medicine.

TODD edited his volume on Schumann and his works on the occasion of the Bard Music Festival (New York) in 1994, which was dedicated that year to the works of the composer and his contemporaries. The essays by Schumann scholars are perhaps beyond the interest and ability of the nontechnical reader, but the translations of articles and criticisms by Schumann's contemporaries provide a glimpse of both the milieu in which Schumann lived and the kind of reception he was accorded. Especially interesting are the reminiscences by Richard Pohl, at one point Schumann's librettist; Franz Liszt's generous criticism of Schumann; and Eduard Hanslick's summary of Schumann's last two years spent in Endenich, where the composer died.

DAVERIO on the whole offers a convincing account of the musician-as-litterateur. The author's emphasis is literature, which, he argues, is the source of Schumann's creative energy and inspiration. Daverio traces Schumann's appreciation of and love for the written word from his readings as a youth and shows how his affection for literature continued nearly to the end of his life. Readers familiar with romantic writers and literature will find this biography most satisfying, for Daverio presents detailed excurses into the images and ideas expounded in the literature Schumann read. Literature also provides, Daverio contends, a more plausible explanation for the sexual overtones in Schumann's letters and diaries than does Ostwald's psychological approach. Seen in context, Schumann's sexual entries are just minor details interspersed among the wide-ranging observations of a fastidious author, "as if he were collecting notes for a novel." Daverio writes for both musicians and nonmusicians alike, although his musical analyses require some technical competence.

Finally, the only sure way to achieve as complete an understanding of Schumann as possible is to read the primary source material for oneself. Unfortunately, most of it is only available in German and in Schumann's sometimes indecipherable hand. For English-only readers, SCHUMANN must suffice. This collection of excerpts from the composer's *Gesammelte Schriften* (Collected Writings) suffers from weak translations, but the variety and overall quality of the materials selected give a good sense of Schumann's writing style and musical thoughts. Read with any of the above biographies, one readily perceives the utter complexity and sheer creativity of the man and musician.

CHARLES BUCK

2. Chamber Music

Abraham, Gerald, editor, *Schumann: A Symposium,* London: Oxford University Press, 1952

Daverio, John, *Robert Schumann: Herald of a "New Poetic Age,"* New York: Oxford University Press, 1997

Fuller-Maitland, J.A., *Schumann's Concerted Chamber Music,* London: Oxford University Press, 1929

Hefling, Stephen E., editor, *Nineteenth-Century Chamber Music,* New York: Schirmer, and London: Prentice Hall, 1998

Hüschen, Heinrich, and Dietz-Rüdiger Moser, editors, *Convivium musicorum: Festschrift Wolfgang Boetticher zum sechzigsten Geburtstag am 19. August 1974,* Berlin: Verlag Merseburger, 1974

Kohlhase, Hans, *Die Kammermusik Robert Schumanns: Stilistische Untersuchungen,* 3 vols., Hamburg: Wagner, 1979

Robertson, Alec, editor, *Chamber Music,* Harmondsworth: Penguin, 1957

Walker, Alan, editor, *Robert Schumann: The Man and His Music,* London: Barrie and Jenkins, 1972

Over time, Schumann's chamber works have enjoyed less popularity than his piano works, songs, and symphonies. A few chamber pieces, such as the piano quintet, are performed with some frequency; these selected works have also received the most attention in the secondary literature. Other large-scale works that occupied a major place in Schumann's compositional activity, such as the string quartets, however, remain little performed and little studied despite the sweeping reevaluation of Schumann's music and his career that has taken place over the last several decades. Only the most recent books listed above overcome earlier biases against the chamber works as an overall group and against pieces composed during the last decade or so of the composer's life. As is the case with other areas of Schumann's music, some of the most important contributions in the secondary literature fall outside the scope of this bibliographic essay, located in

journal articles, dissertations, and in German publications. In particular, readers who have access to a large research library will find a substantial discussion of this repertory in dissertations.

Most writing about Schumann's chamber works in English-language books takes the form of surveys encapsulated in larger studies of the composer's works or of chamber music in general. Of these, John Daverio's chapter, "'Beautiful and Abstruse Conversations': The Chamber Music of Schumann," in HEFLING's volume represents the most thorough and scholarly investigation. Incorporating recent scholarship, Daverio excels at assessing the place of the chambers works within Schumann's entire compositional production and clarifying the context of individual chamber works within the several main periods of the composer's life. Daverio traces Schumann's early interest in chamber genres, beginning with his early, unpublished Piano Quartet in C Minor and its roots in the music of Franz Schubert. The author points to the late string quartets of Beethoven as a particular influence in Schumann's initial turn toward the string quartet in the late 1830s and explains how the composer's intense study of counterpoint influenced the piano quintet and piano quartet. Daverio examines the shift in Schumann's composing process that occurred in the mid-1840s as well as the composer's turn toward *Hausmusik* later in that decade, showing how both of these events affected the chamber works from that period. Finally, the author connects the last group of chamber music from the 1850s to both an aesthetic synthesis of earlier styles and inspiration from new acquaintances of the Düsseldorf years: Joseph Joachim, Johannes Brahms, Ferdinand David, and Wilhelm Joseph von Wasielewski. Readers who wish to explore the biographical and aesthetic background of individual chamber works should also review DAVERIO's recent book-length study of Schumann's life and works.

KOHLHASE provides the most extensive and detailed survey to date of Schumann's chamber music. His three-volume study, only available in German, reviews the history of individual chamber works, considering their place as a group in Schumann's oeuvre but focusing on analytical details—particularly formal structure—and evidence about compositional process from the composer's drafts, sketches, and autograph scores. The second volume supplies a detailed examination of 12 chamber compositions in traditional genres, including the early, unpublished Piano Quartet in C Minor, op. 5; the three string quartets; the piano quintet and piano quartet; the three piano trios; and the three violin sonatas. The first two volumes include numerous short transcriptions, tables, and charts, while the final volume provides facsimile reproductions and transcriptions of longer passages from continuity drafts and autograph scores. Kohlhase's important study also includes a list of manuscript sources and an extensive bibliography of materials published through the mid-1970s.

ABRAHAM's volume contains a chapter by A.E.F. Dickinson on Schumann's chamber music. This survey provides brief descriptions of each movement from each of the chamber works, with a substantial number of illustrative musical examples. The author lavishes greatest detail on the early chamber works: the string quartets, piano quintet, and piano quartet, emphasizing their relationship, both in general and in some specific details, to Beethoven's chamber music. Dickinson argues that Schumann's interest in chamber music arose from a desire to work in historically significant genres rather than from an innate interest in chamber music itself. The volume contains a list of musical compositions and a substantial bibliography, although the latter is considerably out of date.

John Gardner provides a chapter on Schumann's chamber music in WALKER's collection. In addition to a general discussion of formal and stylistic features of individual works, the chapter offers an assessment of the place of Schumann's chamber works in music history, drawing connections in the past to Mendelssohn, Bach, and Beethoven, and in the future to Tchaikovsky, Smetana, Grieg, and Fauré. Despite this broad view of the works' influence, older prejudices toward Schumann's music still surface. Like many earlier writers, Gardner is apologetic about the later chamber works; he even cautiously endorses Harold Bauer's bowdlerized reworkings of the violin sonatas.

FULLER-MAITLAND contributes a small monograph devoted entirely to the chamber music of Schumann. The work is organized into chapters titled "Duets," "Trios," "Quartets," and "Quintet," the duet chapter including both works for piano duet and compositions for solo instrument with piano accompaniment. Commentary typically includes a general, descriptive overview of each work coupled with a few comments about the piece's history. In the case of the string quartets, piano quartet, and piano quintet, Fuller-Maitland proffers brief analytical comments about each of the movements. The volume includes a few musical examples, mainly in the more detailed discussion of the larger works.

ROBERTSON's survey of chamber music includes a short chapter by Joan Chissell devoted entire to Schumann. It offers brief descriptive remarks about each of the works with a few musical examples but lacks footnotes or references. Unfortunately, this essay exhibits a particularly strong bias against the string quartets.

HÜSCHEN and DIETZ-RÜDIGER contains a brief article in English by Jack Westrup describing Schumann's continuity draft for the piano quintet. While not offering nearly as detailed a discussion of the draft as that provided by Kohlhase, the article does point to some of the most significant changes the composer made during the course of writing the work. It includes a few illustrative fragmentary transcriptions from the continuity draft.

GREGORY W. HARWOOD

3. Lieder

Cooper, Martin, "The Songs," in *Schumann: A Symposium*, edited by Gerald Abraham, London: Oxford University Press, 1952

Desmond, Astra, *Schumann Songs*, London: British Broadcasting Corporation, and Seattle: University of Washington Press, 1972

Fischer-Dieskau, Dietrich, *Robert Schumann, Words and Music: The Vocal Compositions*, translated by Reinhard G. Pauly, Portland, Oregon: Amadeus Press, 1988

Moore, Gerald, *Poet's Love: The Songs and Cycles of Schumann*, London: Hamilton, and New York: Taplinger, 1981

Sams, Eric, *The Songs of Robert Schumann*, London: Methuen, and New York: Norton, 1969; 3rd edition, Bloomington: Indiana University Press, and London: Faber, 1993

Schumann, Robert, *Dichterliebe*, edited by Arthur Komar, New York: Norton, 1971

The songs of Robert Schumann, while representing only a small portion of his compositional output, hold a celebrated position within his own oeuvre as well as among 19th-century German lieder. The unique character of his songs owes much to the imprint of Schumann the pianist, and the significance of these pieces is inextricably linked to the events in his life surrounding their composition: most of the songs were composed in 1840, the same year in which Schumann finally received consent to marry Clara Wieck. This romantic tale gives credibility to the interpretation of the songs as the passionate effusions of a young composer in love. The period during which they were composed is commonly dubbed "the year of song" in most biographies of the composer, despite the fact that his burst of activity in this realm extended well into 1841.

COOPER, the earliest and most concise survey covered here, provides both a narrative of Schumann's activities as a song composer and a wide-ranging analysis of texts and their musical settings. Although he uses musical examples sparingly, Cooper avoids the temptation only to praise Schumann's creations. Instead, the author aims to provide a balanced view of Schumann's achievement, illustrating deficiencies as well as virtues (particularly when noting "the most unfortunate of [Schumann's] natural tendencies, rambling and divagation"). Cooper makes distinctions of type and function among the songs, designating ballads, romances, nocturnes, and others. He judges Schumann alongside other composers—particularly Hugo Wolf—by comparing multiple settings of the same text, primarily with the aim of demonstrating Schumann's inability to manage large-scale structures as a lieder composer.

In contrast to the comprehensive scope of Cooper's essay, Arthur Komar presents a volume devoted to the study of a single cycle of SCHUMANN. Like the other volumes in the Norton series, this edition offers an immensely helpful set of materials for understanding multiple facets of its subject in a concise format. An introductory essay on historical background precedes the songs, for which Komar prints both the score and the freestanding texts accompanied by parallel translations. Also included are four songs originally composed as part of the cycle by Schumann but removed prior to publication of the first edition. Following the songs, the second part of the volume comprises analytical essays by the editor and by distinguished theorists Heinrich Schenker, Allen Forte, and Felix Salzer. The final section, titled "Commentary," furnishes the reader with both 19th- and 20th-century views of Schumann's lieder, including excerpts from letters and published articles by the composer himself.

DESMOND divides the text of his slim volume into sections that provide a chronological account of Schumann's activity as a lieder composer. The author begins with a brief biographical note and proceeds to the first section, titled, "The Wonderful Year Begins." Four of the five central sections focus on the major cycles; the fifth is devoted to "Songs by Various Poets." Two concluding sections, "The Songs of 1849" and "The Last Years," assess Schumann's status as a song composer. In individual sections, Desmond comments briefly on each song in a cycle ad seriatim, offering occasional musical illustrations that tend to focus on text painting.

As a pianist, MOORE gave thousands of performances of Schumann's songs with some of the most renowned singers of the 20th century. His guide to the songs is a detailed and informative guide to performance for both singer and pianist. He considers songs from all of Schumann's major collections, not just from *Dichterliebe*. Proceeding song-by-song through the cycles, Moore offers interpretive commentary on the poems and advises performers on everything from tempi to fingering, pedaling, and dynamics, writing in a highly personable tone. In addition to the chapters on individual cycles, he includes two chapters titled "A Miscellany of Songs." These two sections correspond to the songs in the Peters edition, volumes 2 and 3, respectively.

Legendary baritone FISCHER-DIESKAU has contributed much to the study of lieder, including an extensive anthology of lieder texts that are annotated as to the composers who have set them. The volume listed here is an English translation of a work originally published in German. More generous in size and format than any of the other guides mentioned thus far, the book is rich in pictorial and musical illustrations. It provides a detailed narrative of Schumann's career and places it in the wider context of the literature, painting, and music of 19th-century romanticism. One particularly attractive and useful feature of the book is the inclusion of sidebar biographies, with accompanying portraits, of the poets who wrote the texts of Schumann's songs. Other illustrations include facsimiles of Schumann's manuscripts, portraits

of family members, and the title pages of many of his publications. While Fischer-Dieskau's comments on individual songs reflect the interpretive insights he amassed through many years of performance, the purpose of that commentary remains considerably less practical and didactic than that offered by Moore.

Regarded by most commentators as the definitive guide in terms of textual and musical analysis, SAMS has undergone two revisions and expansions. Originally published in 1969, Sams offers a format similar to that used by Moore, although Sams writes in a far less subjective tone. Where Moore intends to instruct and inspire the performers of Schumann's songs, Sams systematically annotates the 246 songs of the Peters edition with practical information, including translation, original key, vocal range, compositional process, and musical and thematic correspondences to other pieces (both Schumann's and those of other composers). The result is by far the most scholarly and systematic reference work available on the major corpus of Schumann's songs.

MARK RISINGER

4. Orchestral Music

Abraham, Gerald, editor, *Schumann: A Symposium*, London: Oxford University Press, 1952

Daverio, John, *Robert Schumann: Herald of a "New Poetic Age,"* New York: Oxford University Press, 1997

Finson, Jon W., *Robert Schumann and the Study of Orchestral Composition: The Genesis of the First Symphony, Op. 38*, Oxford: Clarendon Press, and New York: Oxford University Press, 1989

Finson, Jon W., and R. Larry Todd, editors, *Mendelssohn and Schumann: Essays on Their Music and Its Context*, Durham, North Carolina: Duke University Press, 1994

Holoman, D. Kern, editor, *The Nineteenth-Century Symphony*, New York: Schirmer Books, and London: Prentice Hall, 1997

Kapp, Reinhard, *Studien zum Spätwerk Robert Schumanns*, Tutzing: Schneider, 1984

Kross, Siegfied, and Marie Luise Maintz, editors, *Probleme der symphonischen Tradition im 19. Jahrhundert: Kongreßbericht des Internationalen Musikwissenschaftliches Colloquium, Bonn 1989*, Tutzing: Schneider, 1990

Mayeda, Akio, *Schumanns Weg zur Symphonie*, Zurich: Atlantis, and Mainz: Schott, 1992

Todd, R. Larry, editor, *Schumann and His World*, Princeton, New Jersey: Princeton University Press, 1994

Walker, Alan, editor, *Robert Schumann: The Man and His Music*, London: Barrie and Jenkins, 1972

Readers studying the four symphonies of Schumann will find widely varying accounts and appraisals of these works. Older studies generally regard the symphonies as weak compositions with scattered great moments, tolerated to a certain extent because their composer also wrote great piano music. They often judge Schumann to be out of his league in the symphonic genre, unskilled at orchestration and, in general, pushed and prodded by others (notably Clara) into working in a genre with which he had little affinity. It is not without irony that investigations of Schumann's relationship to the symphony were what, in large part, led to the recent wholesale reevaluation of his entire career as a composer.

The two grand pioneering studies by KAPP and MAYEDA are both written in German and are included here because of their significance. Both scholars furnish detailed, comprehensive reappraisals of Schumann's entire oeuvre, placing the symphonies at its very core. Both draw extensively on documentary material from the composer's diaries, sketchbooks, and letters to argue that the symphony was not an afterthought in his compositional plans or reaction to pressure from others, but rather the central focus of it from his youth. They propose that Schumann ultimately used his early piano works as studies to develop his technique in handling form and texture, progressing gradually to larger multimovement forms and richer, symphonic textures. In this view, the four published symphonies represent the culmination of many years of planning and preparation. Kapp offers a relatively concise account of this process, but his dense writing style will present difficulties for many readers without solid fluency in academic German. Mayeda's longer volume features many illustrations, including a facsimile reproduction of the entire continuity draft for Symphony no. 1 and many other manuscript pages.

General surveys of Schumann's symphonies clearly show the shift in attitude toward the works that has taken place during the last several decades. The most recent, contributed by Linda Correll Roesner in HOLOMON, focuses on three main topics. She first explores how the composer unified the individual movements of each symphony through musical, poetic, and programmatic ideas. Roesner argues that, while overt thematic cross-references through motto themes provide an obvious sense of unity in Symphonies no. 1 and 4 (the first two actually composed), Symphonies no. 2 and 3 are even more tightly woven, each deriving the thematic material for the entire work in a subtle manner from the opening of their respective first movements. (An accompanying chart shows the relationship of thematic material in all five movements of Symphony no. 3.) Second, Roesner examines the overall form of each symphony, drawing attention to how Symphonies no. 2 and 3 shift the overall balance toward the final movement by placing a slow, highly expressive movement in the penultimate position. The third main topic is programmatic/poetic associations in the symphonies, focusing on overt references and subtle allusions to Clara in Symphonies no. 1, 2, and 4. This important survey includes extensive footnotes and a thorough bibliography.

WALKER's collective volume, published over two decades earlier than Holomon, betrays a more negative attitude toward the composer's symphonies in Brian Schlotel's chapter on Schumann's orchestral music. Schlotel provides a descriptive analysis of each symphony, touching briefly on the concert overtures. He attributes Schumann's desire to write symphonies to pressure from Clara, holding with earlier writers that this turn was not altogether positive in terms of his personal development as a composer. A section entitled "Problems of Interpretation" lists specific criticism about Schumann's orchestration and discusses, with examples, general principles used in Gustav Mahler's reorchestrations of them.

Moving back yet another two decades to the survey by Mosco Carner in ABRAHAM, we find the older biases stated even more overtly: Schumann's handling of both form and orchestration is clumsy and uneven, the works require extramusical stimuli to hold themselves together, and symphonic conception went against Schumann's nature as a lyrical miniaturist. Carner, like Schlotel, provides fairly detailed descriptions of each work. He touches more extensively than Schlotel on Schumann's other orchestral music, such as the concert overtures and the Overture, Scherzo, and Finale.

Of the four symphonies, only the first is addressed by a full-scale monograph in English. FINSON's study, based in part on his doctoral dissertation, provides an impressive evaluation of Schumann's creative process in this symphony. Finson analyzes the composer's continuity draft and sketches for the work, discusses how Schumann adapted his ideas to fit standard formal schemes, and examines thematic interconnections across individual movements. Subsequent chapters consider the initial scoring of the work and details of its first performance, an analysis of changes in scoring and other features made after the premiere, the reception of the Symphony no. 1 in subsequent performances throughout the composer's lifetime, and additional refinements in the work's second edition. Beyond providing a solid study of Schumann's compositional process in this symphony, the volume makes two very significant contributions. One is the initial chapter, which places the composer's first symphony in the context of his earlier attempts to write symphonic music, dating as much as a decade earlier. It includes a discussion of Schumann's sketches for symphonies in E major and C minor and the more fully completed *Jugendsymphonie* in G minor, as well as the development of the composer's aesthetic viewpoints about the symphony as seen in his critical writings from the later 1830s. The other important contribution, found in the epilogue to the last chapter, is Finson's assessment of the negative reception accorded Schumann's scoring during the last 100 years. After reviewing the care Schumann lavished on the process of orchestration, Finson demonstrates that the work's scoring was well received during the composer's lifetime and argues that the onset of criticism related directly to the substantial alterations in the size and balance of the orchestra during the later 19th century. This elegant monograph contains a detailed bibliography and a useful index, primarily of names.

Several collective volumes incorporate important new scholarship about Schumann's symphonies. The volume edited by FINSON and TODD includes a fine article by Rufus Hallmark entitled "A Sketch-Leaf for Schumann's D Minor Symphony." Hallmark identifies three fragmentary sketches for the symphony written on a single sheet now located in the Bibliothèque Nationale, Paris. Based on details in the sketches, he suggests that these date from the original 1841 composition of the work, not its revision in 1853. One fragment shows an early version of the main allegro theme for the first movement; the other fragments show Schumann experimenting with canonic treatment of the main lyrical theme. These sketches show that Schumann perceived a relationship between the lyrical theme and the transitional theme played by the trombones that analysts have traditionally overlooked. The sketches are reproduced in both facsimile and transcription.

The volume of the proceedings from the 1989 international colloquium devoted to the 19th-century symphony and edited by KROSS and MAINTZ features an important section of seven articles that address Schumann's symphonies, only one of them, however, in English. Linda Correll Roesner's "Tonal Strategy and Poetic Content in Schumann's C-Major Symphony, Op. 61" offers a detailed analysis of the formal (especially tonal) structure of the work, with particular emphasis on the much-debated structure of the final movement. Roesner argues that programmatic associations with Clara can explain the many unconventional features of this movement. Other articles in this collection include Arnfried Edler's discussion of character and cyclicism in Schumann's symphonies (focusing on the sketches for an unrealized C-Minor Symphony and the Symphony no. 2); Reinhold Dusella's analysis of sketches for symphonic material found in the early sketchbooks; a discussion by Maintz about Schubert's influence on Schumann's symphonies; an appraisal by Michael Struck of the relationship between Schumann's concert overtures and his symphonies; Siegfried Oechsle's evaluation of Schubert, Schumann, and the symphony after Beethoven; and a study by Gerd Nauhaus about Schumann's symphonic finales (this article was later published in English translation in Todd, discussed below).

TODD includes two articles about the symphonies. "Schumann's Symphonic Finales," by Gerd Nauhaus, is an English translation of an article that first appeared in Kross and Maintz. It considers ways in which Schumann attempted to place more emphasis on the final movement as a culmination of the entire symphonic structure in the four numbered symphonies, as well as the G-minor *Jugendsymphonie*, symphonic fragments in C Minor dating from 1840–41, and the Overture, Scherzo, and Finale. Nauhaus argues that Schumann occupies a transitional position between composers such as Mozart, Beethoven, and Schubert, who began to struggle with the issue of the finale as a culminating gesture, and later romantics, such as Brahms, Bruckner, and Mahler, who viewed the finale as a "summarizing apotheosis" of all that went before. The book also provides a translation of comments by conductor Felix Weingartner critiquing Schumann's orchestration, including specific suggestions for revising the orchestration of the first movement exposition of Symphony no. 3.

GREGORY W. HARWOOD

5. Piano Music

Abraham, Gerald, editor, *Schumann: A Symposium*, London: Oxford University Press, 1952

Brown, Thomas Alan, *The Aesthetics of Robert Schumann*, New York: Philosophical Library, 1968

Chissell, Joan, *Schumann Piano Music*, London: British Broadcasting Corporation, and Seattle: University of Washington Press, 1972

Daverio, John, *Nineteenth-Century Music and the German Romantic Ideology*, New York: Schirmer Books, 1993

————, *Robert Schumann: Herald of a "New Poetic Age,"* New York: Oxford University Press, 1997

Finson, Jon W., and R. Larry Todd, editors, *Mendelssohn and Schumann: Essays on Their Music and Its Context*, Durham, North Carolina: Duke University Press, 1994

Fuller-Maitland, J.A., *Schumann's Pianoforte Works*, London: Oxford University Press, 1927; reprint, St. Clair Shores, Michigan: Scholarly Press, 1978

Marston, Nicholas, *Schumann, Fantasie, Op. 17*, Cambridge: Cambridge University Press, 1992

Maxwell, Carolyn, and William DeVan, editors, *Schumann Solo Piano Literature: A Comprehensive Guide, Annotated and Evaluated with Thematics*, Boulder, Colorado: Maxwell Music Evaluation, 1984

Rosen, Charles, *The Romantic Generation*, Cambridge, Massachusetts: Harvard University Press, 1995

Todd, R. Larry, editor, *Nineteenth-Century Piano Music*, New York: Schirmer Books, 1990

————, editor, *Schumann and His World*, Princeton, New Jersey: Princeton University Press, 1994

Walker, Alan, editor, *Robert Schumann: The Man and His Music*, London: Barrie and Jenkins, 1972

Although Schumann's piano works have long enjoyed perennial popularity among performers and audiences, few book-length studies about them have appeared in English. This paucity is all the more surprising because recent research has led to a substantial reevaluation of the place of the piano works in Schumann's musical career. Older studies frequently assert that the piano was

Schumann's true love and that the early piano works, together with his songs, constituted his only truly successful works. These studies typically denigrate Schumann's later piano works, suggesting that his creative inspiration waned as he grew older. In the last several decades, however, some scholars have adopted a fundamentally different viewpoint, arguing that the composer used his early piano works to work systematically through compositional problems involving form and texture before tackling his ultimate goal, orchestral writing. Scholars have also begun to examine Schumann's later works in greater detail, demonstrating that they were not fundamentally flawed pieces, but that their change in style represented a shift in aesthetic principles engendered by general cultural and musical trends. This reevaluation has grown, in part, out of intensive study of important primary source documents that were recently made available, including diaries, notebooks, and early compositional sketches, as well as new readings of the composer's correspondence and critical writings. Much of the revisionary thinking about the piano works has been presented in journal articles, dissertations, and in German publications, all of which fall outside the scope of this discussion. Dissertations, in particular, have been a major forum for writing about the piano works, and readers with access to them will find a veritable gold mine of information.

Anthony Newcomb's "Schumann and the Marketplace: From Butterflies to *Hausmusik*," a chapter in TODD (1990), offers a useful up-to-date historical overview of Schumann's piano works. Newcomb argues that Schumann's compositional and aesthetic goals responded to changing cultural and social demands of the marketplace in mid-19th-century Germany. While his division of the piano works into the three categories of early pieces, polyphonic studies, and *Hausmusik* is not original, he is one of only a few authors to consider the later *Hausmusik* as a serious compositional venture. Some readers will be surprised by the evidence that these later works were more successful economically during the composer's lifetime than his earlier works, which are now popular but were then considered bizarre and difficult to perform and comprehend. Newcomb also examines the substantial problems faced by modern editors and performers in choosing among conflicting versions of the same piece and, on a smaller scale, discrepancies in tempo designations and other expressive markings even within a single version of a piano work. Compositions discussed in greatest detail include the "Quasi variazioni" movement of the Piano Sonata in F Minor and the first movement of the Piano Sonata in G Minor—discussions based largely on studies of compositional process in those works by Linda Correll Roesner—as well as the first movement of the *Fantasie* and the *Novellettes*. The chapter includes a useful tabular overview of Schumann's piano works.

The chapter by Kathleen Dale in ABRAHAM's volume contains the finest older survey in English of Schumann's piano music. Written in a more integrative manner than Chissell's volume discussed below, the author considers individual works in a broadly chronological fashion, frequently grouping together similar types of pieces, such as variations, sonatas and pieces using sonata form, and contrapuntal works. Dale includes information (as it was known at that time) about some of the early, unpublished works preceding the op. 1, as well as compositions for piano duet or two pianos, most notably the Andante and Variations, op. 46. The article contains sporadic musical examples. A weakness of this survey is its bias against the later works.

WALKER's anthology includes two chapters that survey Schumann's piano music. The first, by Yonty Solomon, examines the piano sonatas and the *Fantasie*. It provides descriptive analyses of the works but offers little information on their compositional history. Bálint Vázsonyi's chapter considers the cycles of short piano pieces. Rather than systematically examining individual pieces, it focuses on the general issues of Schumann's cyclic use of melodic ideas and on his innovations in pianistic technique. Both chapters contain a large number of musical illustrations; facsimile reproductions of pages from Schumann's manuscripts are interspersed throughout the volume. Walker includes a useful index of works, a brief bibliography and name dictionary, and information about Schumann's piano works (and other compositions) presented in tabular form.

CHISSELL's small study offers a brief but solid survey of Schumann's piano music. Writing for a general audience, the author provides a short descriptive analysis of each work, together with some details about its compositional history. She also discusses the later revisions the composer made in some of his earlier piano works. This volume provides occasional musical examples and quotations from Schumann's correspondence, but there are very few footnotes documenting sources of information and no bibliography.

FULLER-MAITLAND's survey uses a similar approach to Chissell, but with less detail in both historical background and descriptions of the works. Works that have been less popular (generally from Schumann's later period) receive very terse descriptions. There are no footnotes, references, or bibliography.

MAXWELL and DeVAN's study is intended as a handbook for piano teachers and students of piano music. It provides a brief historical overview of each of the works, a list of available editions, a thematic incipit for each movement or section, and information about tempo, length, and technique requirements.

ROSEN's chapter entitled "Schumann: Triumph and Failure of the Romantic Ideal" concludes his broad survey of romanticism. Although the author does not offer a systematic overview of the piano works, most of his examples are drawn from the piano literature, emphasizing themes such as Schumann's idiosyncratic treatment of rhythm, meter, and form, and unusual pianistic effects related to texture and pedaling. (The opening chapters of the book provide additional examples of these themes in a number of Schumann's piano works, particularly the *Fantasie*.) The *Impromptus on a Theme by Clara Wieck* receive special attention in the final chapter, which particularly emphasizes their relationship to Beethoven's *Eroica* Variations and Schumann's substantive later revision of the work. A substantial passage in this final chapter is also devoted to *Kreisleriana*. Musical examples are reproduced from first or early editions, and the author points out many important details in notation that were often obfuscated in later editions. Despite Rosen's many brilliant observations about this repertory, he retains some old-fashioned biases about the composer and remains somewhat aloof from recent documentary research.

Although the subject of BROWN's monograph is Schumann's aesthetics, the discussion focuses almost entirely on the piano works. Brown offers a wide range of analytical comments about the piano compositions, including a particularly detailed discussion of the composer's use of extramusical and programmatic elements. The volume contains numerous musical examples.

MARSTON's monograph on Schumann's *Fantasie* represents the only monograph in English devoted to a single piano work by the composer. The volume includes a detailed examination of the *Fantasie*'s compositional history as seen in letters and diaries, sketches, the autograph manuscript, and the engraver's score. Other chapters consider the issue of the work's genre and title (which Schumann altered several times during its gestation), the composer's use of allusion and quotation, a detailed analysis of each movement's formal structure and the issue of thematic unity, and a study of the work's reception and performance history. An exemplary index and a substantial bibliography make this volume an invaluable source.

The volume edited by TODD (1994) contains several articles relevant to Schumann's piano music. Todd himself contributes a chapter entitled "On Quotation in Schumann's Music," an exemplary inquiry into the composer's penchant for quotation and self-quotation. The majority of examples are drawn from the piano compositions, complementing Brown's earlier discussion of this topic. Bernhard R. Appel contributes "'Actually, Taken Directly from Family Life': Robert Schumann's *Album für die Jugend*." He examines the *Album*'s genesis as a pedagogical tool for teaching Schumann's daughter Marie, later expanded conceptually as part of an anthology of works, and finally scaled back to its present form. Appel explores how individual pieces in the set represent events from the life of the Schumann family and offers an iconographic study of the title page for the first edition, designed by Ludwig Richter. A table graphically presents the organization of the work through the different stages of its compositional genesis. A final contribution of this volume is Carl Kossmaly's

review and assessment of Schumann's early piano works, "On Robert Schumann's Piano Compositions," first published in the *Allgemeine musikalische Zeitung* in 1844 and presented here in English translation by Susan Gillespie. This historically important essay offers significant insights into the reception of the early piano works during the composer's lifetime.

The Mendelssohn-Schumann volume edited by FINSON and TODD contains an article by Linda Correll Roesner that has important ramifications for the study of all of the composer's early piano works: "The Sources for Schumann's *Davidsbündlertänze*, Op. 6: Composition, Textural Problems, and the Role of the Composer as Editor." Roesner examines the work's history as seen in its only surviving manuscript, a copy used to engrave the first edition. This manuscript, however, actually consists of a mixture of early working drafts interspersed with a fair copy of the work. She concludes that in this work (and undoubtedly in others), Schumann proofread not by using the manuscript as a definitive version but rather by rereading the work in a new and creative way, substantially altering details of dynamics, accents, phrasing, pedaling, etc. Consequently, the act of editing became not merely a check for errors, but an additional stage in his compositional process. Although several writers have suggested that some of the variant readings in articulation, phrasing, and other details are intentional, Roesner proposes that many of these variations may be casual reinterpretations resulting from Schumann's creative approach to proofreading.

DAVERIO (1993) contains two lengthy essays on Schumann's piano music, both based on earlier journal articles and both incorporated, in lesser detail, into the biography by the author discussed below. "Schumann's Opus 17 *Fantasie* and the *Arabeske*" relates Friedrich Schlegel's formal category of the arabesque to structural features of the *Fantasie*, particularly its first and final movements. "Schumann's Systems of Musical Fragments and *Witz*" examines the romantic notions of quotation, humor, wit, and the fragment in Schumann's early piano works with particular emphasis on the *Fantasiestücke* and *Kreisleriana*. Both articles feature a large number of illustrative musical examples.

DAVERIO's (1997) landmark biography is the first major study in English to incorporate systematically the wide breadth of new research about the composer and to dispel past biases against the later works. This volume, both a biography and a compositional history of Schumann's works, offers the English-speaking reader many fresh interpretations, either original or based on recent scholarship, about the piano works and their place in Schumann's oeuvre as a whole. Readers will also find many important and interesting details about the genesis of individual compositions.

GREGORY W. HARWOOD

6. Aesthetics and Writings

Botstein, Leon, "History, Rhetoric, and the Self: Robert Schumann and Music Making in German-Speaking Europe, 1800–1860," in *Schumann and His World,* edited by R. Larry Todd, Princeton, New Jersey: Princeton University Press, 1994

Brown, Thomas Alan, *The Aesthetics of Robert Schumann,* New York: Philosophical Library, 1968

Chissell, Joan, *Schumann,* London: Dent, 1948; 5th edition, 1989

Daverio, John, *Robert Schumann: Herald of a "New Poetic Age,"* New York: Oxford University Press, 1997

Plantinga, Leon, *Schumann as Critic,* New Haven, Connecticut: Yale University Press, 1967

Schumann, Robert, *The Musical World of Robert Schumann,* edited and translated by Henry Pleasants, London: Gollancz, and New York, St. Martin's Press, 1965

———, *On Music and Musicians,* edited by Konrad Wolff, translated by Paul Rosenfeld, New York: Norton, 1946

Taylor, Ronald, *Robert Schumann: His Life and Work,* New York: Universe Books, and London: Granada, 1982

From an early age, Schumann was immersed in poetry, literature, and the arts. As a young man, his first career choice, to become a lawyer, was a reflection of his literary education and inclinations. After finishing a rather uninspired year of studying law in Leipzig, however, Schumann left the university to pursue what had become a growing passion for him: music. Despite Schumann's lack of early training, his teacher Friedrich Wieck encouraged him to pursue a career as a concert pianist. But when an injury left his right hand partially paralyzed, Schumann began to focus on musical composition and music criticism, a pursuit that drew on his earlier literary interests. In 1831 he published his first piece of music criticism, a review of Chopin's variations for piano and orchestra on a theme from *Don Giovanni*. The critique appeared in the well-known journal *Allgemeine musikalische Zeitung.*

Schumann adopted a personal and emotional writing style similar to his idol Jean Paul (Jean Paul Richter); his review of Chopin's variations was written as if it were a novel. In fact, Schumann wrote much of his criticism from the perspective of three fictional characters named Florestan, Eusebius, and Master Raro, each with a defining personality: Florestan was quick and passionate, Eusebius careful and introspective, and Raro mediated between the two extremes.

In his second published article, Schumann described these imaginary characters as members of *Der Davidsbündler* (The League of David) like the biblical David doing battle with the Philistines of music criticism. Schumann soon began to see *Allgemeine musikalische Zeitung* as the representation of that Philistine establishment. When the journal declined to publish more of his essays, Schumann rebelled by starting his own journal, the *Neue Zeitschrift für Musik,* which he did with the help of several colleagues in 1834. One of the goals of the new journal was to stem the flow of French and Italian music that had begun to dominate the concert and opera stages in Germany. The new journal tried to reverse this trend by promoting the works of new composers and native German composers.

For nearly ten years, Schumann presided over the *Neue Zeitschrift für Musik* as its general editor, contributing close to a thousand pages of text. Eventually his unusual novelistic descriptions gave way to a more conventional style of criticism, and his essays frequently turned to more aesthetic matters.

Schumann published a collection of his own essays and reviews in 1854. Although not the first translation of Schumann's writings into English, Rosenfeld's edition is the earliest version of SCHUMANN (1946) that is still readily available today. Rosenfeld, however, tampers with Schumann's original edition by rearranging the entries by topic rather than chronologically, as Schumann had preferred. This is the strength of Rosenfeld's edition, that one can read all the essays and reviews Schumann wrote about Beethoven, for instance, together in one place. Rosenfeld also includes a whole chapter of interesting and previously unpublished comments by Schumann that predate his tenure at the *Neue Zeitschrift für Musik.*

Rosenfeld's liberties with the organization of Schumann's essays is precisely the mistake that Pleasants hopes to correct in his edition of SCHUMANN (1965). Pleasants returns the presentation of material to its original order, arranging the essays chronologically, as Schumann did. Restoring the original arrangement, Pleasants asserts, gives the reader a better sense of the development of Schumann's thought as editor of the journal. The result is a collection of essays quite different in scope from Rosenfeld's. The reviews are presented unabridged and represent a much wider range of composers, including reviews of lesser-knowns such as Hummel, Spohr, Döhler, Bennett, and Thalberg. Pleasants's extensive footnotes and annotations are a further welcome and helpful addition to Schumann's text.

PLANTINGA presents the most comprehensive overview and analysis of both Schumann's aesthetics and his writings. This book bears the mark of extensive and detailed research into German music journalism, criticism and general musical culture of the early to mid-19th century. The author begins by chronicling the founding of the *Neue Zeitschrift für Musik.* The later chapters are aimed at contextualizing Schumann's aesthetic thought in relation to the larger romantic preoccupations with originality and history. Plantinga also covers the romantic discussion of programs and musical reference and in conclusion tackles an impressive number of Schumann's reviews, uniquely organized into the categories of old contemporaries, young contemporaries, virtuosi, and the romantic composers.

The first three chapters of DAVERIO's exhaustive critical biography are worth mentioning. Drawing on such additional material as diary entries and letters, Daverio describes Schumann's early fascination with the writer Jean Paul and the formation of the composer's musico-literary sensibilities. The author highlights the fact that as an endpoint to Schumann's interest in literature, *Neue Zeitschrift für Musik* was meant to depart from the current examples of criticism, to offer "music criticism in a new key," as Schumann himself described it. In the most notable chapter in his study, "Music as Literature," Daverio describes in great detail the intimate relationship between Schumann's literary aspirations, his aesthetic viewpoint, and musical works—many of which were composed during his years at the journal.

Two other biographies of Schumann devote chapters to Schumann's writing career and his years at the *Neue Zeitschrift für Musik*, but neither is as detailed as Daverio's study of the composer. In a chapter of his biography entitled "Literature and Music," TAYLOR writes a remarkably broad and readable account of Schumann's criticism and the influences that inspired it. While not covering any new ground, the author does summarize his point rather neatly, that Schumann's writings about music are not a corollary but an organic extension of his whole creative musical process. The abbreviated length and scope of CHISSELL'S chapter on "Schumann as Critic" makes it a perfect introduction to the topic. This short overview weaves commentary with many quotations from Schumann's criticism and letters.

BROWN's study of Schumann's writings is unique in its devotion not to reviews and journal articles but to Schumann's more strictly philosophical essays on music aesthetics. The author is the only author to focus exclusively on Schumann's unfinished treatise on music aesthetics, and on three other aesthetic fragments, all of which are included in the German edition of Schumann's complete writings. In addition to providing a close reading of these texts, Brown prepares his discussion by reminding the reader of the milieu of romantic writers in which Schumann had immersed himself. More important, Brown shows how influential Schumann's aesthetic explorations were to the formation of his criticism and composition, especially the practice of writing program music and the philosophical arguments it engendered.

The value of BOTSTEIN'S essay in understanding Schumann's aesthetics is contained in his introductory remarks. "No composer in the European tradition," Botstein asserts, "was so actively engaged in the public area with literature and, indirectly, aesthetic philosophy." The thrust of Botstein's discussion centers on the influence of German romantics on Schumann's musical aesthetics. The closeness between Schumann's intellectual life and work, his writings and his compositions, bears the mark of both Jean Paul Richter and Wolfgang Menzel. Menzel, Botstein argues, not only inspired Schumann's antithetical language, he provided the ideological framework from which Schumann formed his unique aesthetic position. While perhaps less easy to trace, the influence of Schlegel, according to Botstein, is also visible. The value of Botstein's essay, however, is in his introductory section, in which the author demonstrates how remarkably progressive Schumann's 19th-century aesthetic really was.

JULIE B. HUBBERT

Schütz, Heinrich 1585–1672

German composer

Blume, Friedrich, *Protestant Church Music: A History*, New York: Norton, 1974

Geier, Martin, *Music in the Service of the Church: The Funeral Sermon for Heinrich Schütz*, edited and translated by Robin A. Leaver, St. Louis, Missouri: Concordia, 1984

Miller, D. Douglas, and Anne L. Highsmith, *Heinrich Schütz: A Bibliography of the Collected Works and Performing Editions*, New York: Greenwood Press, 1986

Moser, Hans Joachim, *Heinrich Schütz: A Short Account of His Life and Works*, translated and edited by Derek McCulloch, New York: St. Martin's Press, and London: Faber, 1967

——, *Heinrich Schütz: His Life and Works*, translated by Carl F. Pfatteicher, St. Louis, Missouri: Concordia, 1959

Rifkin, Joshua, and Colin Timms, "Heinrich Schütz," in *The New Grove North European Baroque Masters*, edited by Joshua Rifkin et al., London: Macmillan, and New York: Norton, 1985

Schütz, Heinrich, *Letters and Documents of Heinrich Schütz, 1656–1672; An Annotated Translation*, edited by Gina Spagnoli, Ann Arbor, Michigan: UMI Research Press, 1990

Skei, Allen B., *Heinrich Schütz: A Guide to Research*, New York,: Garland, 1981

Smallman, Basil, *The Music of Heinrich Schütz, 1585–1672*, Leeds: Mayflower, 1985

Spagnoli, Gina, "Dresden at the Time of Heinrich Schütz," in *The Early Baroque Era*, edited by Curtis Price, London: Macmillan, 1993; Englewood Cliffs, New Jersey: Prentice Hall, 1994

Generally regarded as the most important German composer before J.S. Bach, Heinrich Schütz was widely acclaimed in his own day as "the father of German music," and "the most excellent musician of his age." His adaptation of 17th-century Italian styles to native German forms and his highly expressive settings of German sacred texts are counted among the highest musical achievements of the period. References to Schütz occur in a number of important 18th-century music dictionaries and histories, although they are largely restricted to biographical accounts. The real history of Schütz scholarship is closely linked to the rise, in 19th-century Germany, of musicology as an academic discipline and the concurrent revival of interest in performing music of the past. Schütz's music was first available in modern editions beginning in the 1830s, and a complete edition (*Sämtliche Werke,* edited by Philipp Spitta) was undertaken in 1858. Schütz research continued through the 20th century to be a mostly German enterprise. In broad terms, scholars have tended to treat the topic in either of two areas; music-historical research or socioreligious inquiry. Both areas are represented in the general studies of Schütz available in English.

MOSER (1959), in one of the most authoritative life-and-works studies in the field, has produced an exhaustive account of his subject, stretching to over 700 pages. His study first appeared in German (as *Heinrich Schütz: Sein Leben und Werk*) in 1936, with a substantial revision in 1954. (Carl Pfatteicher's English translation, cited here, is of the revised edition.) Moser's text set the tone for nearly all subsequent studies and, though dated and of a particular viewpoint, remains basic for any serious work on Schütz. A clear aim of his book is to interpret Schütz's importance for the history of German music, although the influence of Italian composers and musical styles—seen throughout Schütz's career—is taken into account. The extensive discussion of the composer's music is roughly chronological, arranged around works with published opus numbers, and it includes translations for most of the German texts. The book is generously supplied with music examples, plates, and an index of the musical works discussed.

MOSER (1967) prepared a generalized and highly condensed version (lacking musical examples) of the biography in 1940, appearing as *Kleines Heinrich-Schütz-Buch,* with a second edition in 1941. Derek McCulloch's English translation supplies a good introduction to the composer, although there is little of the detailed musical analysis that marks the complete study. McCulloch supplements Moser's brief edition with a few musical examples and a useful series of appendices covering geography, a works chronology, and a short glossary of German musical terms (many of which remained in German in Pfatteicher's translation).

BLUME surveys Schütz's major works in a generous section within part 2 ("The Age of Confessionalism") of his study on Protestant church music. This valuable assessment focuses on the relationship of Schütz's music to that of the composer's German contemporaries, the music's association with developments in 17th-century Lutheranism, and musical considerations arising from the religious wars of the period.

GEIER provides an excellent starting point for those wishing to utilize contemporary biographical accounts. As was the custom, the sermon delivered by Geier at Schütz's funeral included a lengthy biographical section, outlining the composer's life and work. It is extremely valuable for the light it sheds on Schütz's reputation in his own day and on the role of music in 17th-century Lutheran thought. Geier's sermon was published in 1672 and served as a primary source of information about Schütz throughout the 18th century. This edition includes historical and bibliographical material, information on the preacher and the funeral itself, as well as the English translation (prepared by Martin Franzmann) of the sermon and biographical oration.

RIFKIN is a substantial modification of his article on Schütz for the *New Grove Dictionary of Music and Musicians* (1980). The text here might be considered a supplement to that important article. The original discussion of the Schütz's music (prepared by Kurt Gudewill) has been replaced with a new text by Colin Timms, surveying the works in chronological order. The work list itself has been updated by Rifkin, as has the discussion of Schütz portraits. This generally reliable study is the most recent overall account available in English.

SMALLMAN's survey of Schütz's music, written for the 400th anniversary in 1985 of the composer's birth, is confined to details of style and technique and specifically directed to "the needs of the English student," as opposed to the discussions in Moser (1959). Avoiding the usual chronological scheme, Smallman divides his discussion into the areas of "polyphonic works," pieces written in the "concerto style," and "biblical dramas," examining a number of important works assigned to each area. This approach, while useful, tends to obscure the long path of stylistic development so interesting in Schütz's career, and the author's designations of some pieces are not always obvious. Discussions of technical musical points are usually sound, although there are occasional errors of historical fact in the text.

SPAGNOLI discusses musical life at the Lutheran court in Dresden during Schütz's time. Her study of court correspondence, chapel personnel lists, music catalogs, contracts, and account books provides an illuminating picture of the composer and his particular working environment. The "Bibliographical Note" includes useful annotations, pointing to broader musical and biographical studies.

SCHÜTZ is a thorough investigation of the important archival material pertaining to the composer's later life, especially his relation to changing musical tastes in Dresden, his role as advisor to other German courts, and the general duties of court musicians during the period. Spagnoli's translations of some 45 letters and documents (arranged to correspond with her introductory study) provide vivid primary information on Schütz, as well as the general practice of music in 17th-century Germany.

Two bibliographical guides bear mention. SKEI, aimed at serious researchers, presents a categorized guide to scholarly literature on Schütz (confined, in most cases, to that published before 1979). MILLER and HIGHSMITH is useful for persons navigating the often confusing trail of Schütz's some 500 compositions published in the three series of collected works, assorted sets, and various performing editions.

ROBERT E. PALMER

Seeger, Ruth Crawford
see Crawford, Ruth Porter

Semiotics *see* Rhetoric

Sequence

Crocker, Richard L., *The Early Medieval Sequence,* Berkeley: University of California Press, 1977
————, *Studies in Medieval Music Theory and the Early Sequence,* Brookfield, Vermont: Variorum, 1997
Fassler, Margot, *Gothic Song: Victorine Sequences and Augustinian Reform in Twelfth-Century Paris,* Cambridge: Cambridge University Press, 1993
Goede, N. de, editor, *The Utrecht Prosarium,* Amsterdam: Vereniging voor Nederlandse Muziekgeschedenis, 1965
Hiley, David, *Western Plainchant: A Handbook,* Oxford: Clarendon Press, and New York: Oxford University Press, 1993
Stevens, John, *Words and Music in the Middle Ages: Song, Narrative, Dance, and Drama, 1050– 1350,* Cambridge: Cambridge University Press, 1986

The sequence is a medieval chant for the Mass that was sung immediately after the Alleluia on important feast days. Some of the earliest extant sequences were composed late in the ninth century by Notker, a monk at the monastery of St. Gall in what is now Switzerland. In the preface to his collection of these chants, the *Liber hymnorum,* Notker tells us he learned how to compose sequences from "a certain monk of Jumièges" who had fled to St. Gall seeking refuge from marauding Vikings, an anecdote that points to the West-Frankish origin of these compositions.

Generally speaking, sequences are characterized by a double versicle structure in which the melody setting the first line of a text couplet is repeated to accommodate the words of the second line. Each pair of lines typically has its own shared melody, but not all sequences have paired lines throughout the composition. In some instances a single line opens or closes the chant; in others, particularly in early sequences, an unpaired versicle can appear anywhere. Sequence texts are most often syllabically set—that is, each syllable of text is assigned one note of the melody. Modest flourishes of melody

are usually reserved for the ends of lines and other significant points of articulation.

Musicologists tend to divide sequences into two or three stylistic periods. Sequences of the first period, composed from the late ninth to the early 11th century, are typified by highly crafted prose texts that rely on assonance and parallels in syllable disposition, syntax, and word division for their design. The number of syllables per line varies from couplet to couplet, often with impressive artistic effect. Sequences of the second period, composed from the late tenth to early 12th century, have texts that incorporate elements of rhyming, metrical poetry. There is a new regularity in the lengths of the lines, with careful attention paid to the placement of stressed and unstressed syllables. While some scholars consider the sequences composed from the ninth through the 11th century as a single epoch, all recognize a significant stylistic change around 1100. In this final period, the late 11th and 12th centuries, a relatively small number of verse schemes with uniform line lengths, regular accentual patterns, and prominent rhymes became standard and widespread. These verse forms dominated sequence composition from the 12th to the middle of the 16th century.

DE GOEDE's book is a transcription and commentary on sequences in the *Utrecht Prosarium,* the oldest known collection of sequences from the Netherlands, probably compiled sometime during the 13th century. This important collection offers the reader a compendium of sequence styles that ranges from works composed by Notker of St. Gall to Parisian sequences of the 12th century. The pieces are transcribed into modern square-note notation on four-line staves. Much of the lengthy introduction has been superseded by more recent scholarship, particularly the author's historical account of the early sequence.

The most extensive musical study of the early sequence is by CROCKER (1977). Although he warns that his book is merely preliminary and provisional, he offers his readers detailed analyses of more than three dozen compositions, including all those mentioned by Notker in his *Liber hymnorum.* Crocker's primary goal is to accumulate a set of stylistic observations that can serve as a point of reference for formulating and perhaps solving questions about critical versions of these chants. He begins by reviewing the relationships between Notker's sequences and those of West-Frankish provenance, a discussion that outlines the source-critical problems that have frustrated previous efforts to establish definitive renditions of these works. The body of the book is devoted to careful investigations of melodic structures, connections between texts and their melodies, and the interrelationship of various contrafacta. He also discusses the liturgical function of the early sequence and comments on its place in the broader landscape of late-Carolingian culture. Although many scholars now find in Crocker's pursuit of definitive readings a decidedly anachronistic imposition of modern academic values on this repertory, his sensitive and perspicacious analytical observations, particularly those focusing on musical style and text-music interactions, deserve to be valued.

STEVENS gives a broad overview of the sequence, surveying each of the three periods of sequence composition as part of a broader study on the role of numbers in medieval music and poetry. He closely examines three works, one from each stylistic epoch, presenting the reader with a short explication of each text and an analytical description of the melodies. The main argument of his discussion, indeed of the entire book, is that words and music in medieval song are chiefly related by congruent patterns of structure that have their basis in numbers. Accordingly, compositional features such as the phrasing of melodies and the number of syllables in a text follow underlying numerical patterns of design. Stevens also considers the organizational role of accent in the sequence repertory. As a result of this inquiry, he proposes that the verbal and musical patterns in early sequences could work against one another, with consequent tensions being reconciled in performance, but that in later pieces the words and music followed a common structural foundation built out of patterns of accents. Stevens's argument is controversial. The most important critics question his dismissal of any general connections between melodic structures and the meaning of a text.

FASSLER's work is simultaneously the most comprehensive study of the late sequence and the most thorough interdisciplinary account of a sequence repertory in a historical context. In her opening chapter she presents a model for the study of liturgical change that will guide the rest of her book. She reviews the history of the early sequence and traces the development of the genre through the early 12th century. The focus of her book is the role the 12th-century sequence played in formulating and disseminating the mystical theology developed by monks at the Abbey of St. Victor in Paris. Because much of the Victorine sequence repertory is based on a small number of verse forms, the chants have not attracted the interest of many scholars. Fassler has shown, however, that the sequence texts participated in a musical exegesis by virtue of the melodies they shared. Rather than being symptoms of imaginative indigence, the small number of standard verse forms highlights the importance placed on contrafacting and the ability to connect a given text to a larger exegetical scheme. Although Fassler has been criticized for being overly speculative, her book remains one of the most insightful studies of medieval music available.

An excellent, succinct discussion of the sequence appears in HILEY's general study of plainchant. His discussion is noteworthy not only for its clear outline of the formal changes that took place in the genre but also for its useful references to scholarly writings on the subject. He also includes notes on important facsimiles and editions.

Although many of his early writings on the sequence were incorporated into his book, CROCKER's (1997) collected essays contain several important articles, most notably "The Troping Hypothesis," that did not become part of his larger work. In this essay he not only calls into question once-common notions about the nature and value of tropes but also argues against viewing the sequence as a species of trope.

MICHAEL MCGRADE

Serbo-Croatia *see* Eastern Europe

Serialism

Babbitt, Milton, *Milton Babbitt: Words about Music*, edited by Stephen Dembski and Joseph N. Straus, Madison: University of Wisconsin Press, 1987

Griffiths, Paul, *Modern Music: A Concise History from Debussy to Boulez*, New York: Thames and Hudson, 1978; revised edition, 1994

Haimo, Ethan, *Schoenberg's Serial Odyssey: The Evolution of His Twelve-Tone Method, 1914–1928*, Oxford: Clarendon Press, and New York: Oxford University Press, 1990

Koblyakov, Lev, *Pierre Boulez: A World of Harmony*, Chur: Harwood Academic, 1990

Mead, Andrew Washburn, *An Introduction to the Music of Milton Babbitt*, Princeton, New Jersey: Princeton University Press, 1994

Perle, George, *Serial Composition and Atonality: An Introduction to the Music of Schoenberg, Berg, and Webern*, Berkeley: University of California Press, 1962; 6th edition, revised, 1991

———, *Twelve-Tone Tonality*, Berkeley and London: University of California Press, 1977; 2nd edition, revised and expanded, 1996

Rufer, Josef, *Composition with Twelve Tones Related Only to One Another*, translated by Humphrey Searle, London: Barrie and Jenkins, 1954; revised edition, 1970

Wuorinen, Charles, *Simple Composition*, New York: Schirmer Books, and London: Collier Macmillan, 1979

If serialism represents something more than an agglomeration of compositional techniques, it represents something less—far less—than a prescribed sound world. The question of just what, if anything, serial pieces have in common by virtue of their being serial is one that haunts writing on the subject. Many of the best writings on serial music focus on the music and techniques of a single composer, and there have been few attempts at a synthetic view of the various serial traditions. It is best to think of serialism as a family of compositional stances. The most basic of these stances is that a precompositionally determined, ordered succession of musical materials—commonly but not exclusively a series of all 12 pitch classes, the 12-tone row—provides a basis for context and continuity in a composition. But even this stance is filtered through a spectrum of attitudes. Some composers of serial music treat order flexibly; some allow other bases for musical coherence, including forms of tonality, to influence a serial work. The degree to which a series permeates a musical texture can also vary considerably, depending on how many other musical parameters are governed by it.

Schoenberg himself supplied RUFER with the title of his book. The work presents Schoenberg's oeuvre largely in concepts—and often quotations—emanating from the composer himself. The 12-tone series is taken for the *idea* of a composition, and much is made of how the row is the analog of the theme or motive in tonal music. Thus the two halves (hexachords) of the row are divided into antecedent and consequent, in conformity with traditional thematic theory. The row itself is held to grow out of melodies that gradually incorporate more and more of the 12 tones. The motivic play of Brahms and especially Beethoven is claimed to be the antecedent of row technique. The book emphasizes the myriad shapes the row can assume in the course of a work.

Rufer notes how much variety is available once a series is selected. Exploring one solution, Rufer sets out the constructive nature of rhythm in Schoenberg's compositions. The author provides a valuable appendix, which contains discussions of 12-tone issues by several major composers—among them Dallapiccola, Gerhard, Krenek, and Seiber—who belong to a much-neglected second serial generation. However, the book is marred by an uncritical approach to Schoenberg's explanations. For instance, the analogy to tonal practice is almost wholly unsuccessful, trading as it does on a confusion between materials and system: the motive in tonal music exists in a particular harmonic context, whereas the row is the datum out of which musical contexts are constructed. Most unfortunately, the "series-as-motive" fallacy has been a pesky red herring. Too many critics of serialism have confused the fallacy with the music, erroneously thinking that to deny the former is to invalidate the latter.

A better introduction to what is often referred to as "classical" serialism—the work of Schoenberg together with his pupils Webern and Berg—is provided by PERLE (1962). The book provides a clear and informal introduction to the basic tools of serial composition that is not limited to the use of a set as motive (Perle's discussion is more nuanced than Rufer's) and the basic operations performed on it—transposition, retrograde, inversion, and retrograde inversion—but that also extends to deeper structural properties, such as hexachordal combinatoriality (the combination of halves of different set forms to create aggregates, structures with all 12 pitch classes uniquely represented), invariance (the exploiting of similarities in different set forms), derived sets (sets constructed out of transformations of a smaller pitch class

unit), and inversional symmetry. A particular strength of the book is its placement of dodecaphonic music at one end of a continuum from "free" atonal music. Perle's analyses show ways in which a pitch class unit—a "basic cell"—in a freely atonal piece can take on momentary structural significance, while a serial piece can proceed by the setting into play of relatively unordered elements not derivable from the set itself. Perle follows the development of serialism through early works by Babbitt. Unfortunately, the various revisions to the text have mostly not taken into account developments in nontonal and 12-tone theory and analysis since the first edition, other than important work carried out by Perle himself.

HAIMO's book explores Schoenberg's compositional thought at the crucial period in which the 12-tone system crystallized. The author is particularly strong in tracing the genesis of Schoenberg's serial thinking, with excellent analyses of the earlier, protoserial pieces of *Fünf Klavierstücke,* op. 23, as well a discussion of sketches of incomplete works in which the composer experimented with serial ideas. Against the tendency to assign all serial compositions to a single category, Haimo points out that even within Schoenberg's 12-tone corpus there is considerable development. Haimo demonstrates that aspects of Schoenberg's mature style began to appear in the Orchestra Variations op. 31. Haimo emphasizes means devised by the composer for organizing sets to maximize regularity, from using aggregates as regular temporal segments, to different row forms partitioned in the same way, to formal schemes of paired row hexachords. Although Haimo's exposition is technical, the explanations are clear, and the references provide a way into recent issues in classical serial theory.

Since the end of World War II, serialism in Europe and serialism in the United States have had very different fates. In the United States, forms of serialism continue to be practiced in various corners, while in Europe, centered around Darmstadt, Germany, serial activity began to decline by the mid-1960s. The approaches to serialism on the two sides of the Atlantic have also been quite different from one another in the post-war era, and there has been little dialogue to bridge the gap. Generally, writings on this period tend to favor serialism from one continent or the other, leaving off the discussion of the rival at the point of near-simultaneous development of a notion of "total" or "integral" serialism, the serialism of as many musical parameters as possible, by Babbitt in the United States and Boulez and Stockhausen in Europe. GRIFFITHS is one of the few surveys of the period to buck this trend, although even he falls short of providing a thorough account. His discussion of American serialism is largely confined to early Babbitt, and one does not get the sense of the very different ways Martino, Wuorinen, and many others developed indigenous serial vocabulaies. This criticism aside, the book is the best introduction in English to the

European scene, as the author largely dispenses with technicalities. An extensive bibliography and a discography are provided. Griffiths points out that, slogans aside, the achievement of total serialism in Europe was limited to a few works in the early 1950s. He recounts the interesting history of the development of total serialism, drawing on writings by Richard Toop. Later works by Stockhausen, Nono, and their colleagues displayed a preoccupation with inventing formal constraints that were not necessarily serial in nature, while Barraque, Boulez, and others stretched the notion of a single series underlying a composition to the breaking point. The book is not primarily about serialism, but it effectively documents ways in which the serial experience continued to mold musical developments after World War II. The sense of "Beginning Again" that prevailed in postwar European musical circles led to a cycle of innovation and even more radical breaks from the just-distant past. Eventually, Griffiths notes, European serial composers came to the realization that "the ideal of starting music again from scratch could not be so easily accomplished." American serial composers on the other hand have tended to pursue continuity rather than disruption.

KOBLYAKOV's demanding book is one of the very few works in English wholly devoted to European serialism. It is primarily an extended discussion of Boulez's *Le Marteau sans maître*, one of the hallmarks of European serial composition. The author assesses a technique used in that piece, *multiplication*, an operation that, in its simplest form, places copies of one pitch-class fragment beginning at each of the notes of another pitch-class fragment, a procedure strikingly similar to the compositional practice of Bartók, among others. In *Le Marteau*, Boulez divides his row into fragments, and applies multiplication to them. His approach could be termed *meta-serial*: the 12-tone series becomes a source of material that is then ordered in other ways. The reader will see in the helpful, copious charts tracing Boulez's compositional choices a very different conception of serial workings from classical methods.

In addition, Koblyakov provides a wealth of information on other serial techniques devised or adapted by Boulez for use in this composition and some other works contemporaneous with it, and the author includes a guide to the serialization of dynamics and durations that the composer uses in other parts of the work. The writing is frequently obscure. Koblyakov revisits the "series-as-motive" fallacy by confusing Boulez's precompositional methods with the music itself. An examination of score fragments analyzed by the author makes it clear that his analysis does not fully explain the composition's success, although the techniques Koblyakov evaluates remain of intrinsic interest. The book closes with a disappointing chapter comparing Boulez and Stockhausen; while there are some valuable insights, most of which contrast Stockhausen's

tendency to be more integrative with Boulez's desire to create techniques to maximize conflict, Koblyakov invokes a naive evolutionist historicism, which leads him to a number of questionable assertions.

In a transcript of lectures given at the University of Wisconsin, BABBITT provides an accessible discussion of the foundations of American serial thought from the first author to give them something like their present form. The lectures often traverse material found in the composer's more technical published articles, but these topics are now couched in Babbitt's fluent speaking style. Analyses of Schoenberg, Webern, and serial Stravinsky show how various properties of row structure profoundly shape the choices available to the serial composer. This text is the best introduction to the role of contextual thought in music generally, including tonal music. Babbitt also offers insights into how his understanding of serialism has informed his own compositional practice.

Although the most recent printing of WUORINEN contains a note by the author denying that he intended to create a textbook about serial composition, his book remains a very useful introduction to composing with various 12-tone techniques by a prolific and highly regarded serial composer. Encouraging the student to examine the compositional process through a variety of exercises, the work serves as a reminder of the variety of choices confronting the composer who decides to use a series. The book explores Babbitt's timepoint system, as well as techniques of extending a 12-tone row to govern temporal proportions of the work, in the large and in the small. Significant also is Wuorinen's philosophy of composition: "When a piece has reached, through application of the method, a sufficient degree of completeness, it will begin to assert its own rights and needs." Such thinking helps to dispel the baleful notion that a serial composer's technique somehow produces a composition, and this philosophy points to a more realistic dialectic between piece and process that actually guides much compositional activity, serial and otherwise.

A different sort of serial system is presented in PERLE (1977). Drawing on precedents primarily in Berg and Bartók, Perle establishes criteria for a 12-tone harmonic language, opposing that language to what he finds arbitrary in the verticalization of set segments in Schoenbergian practice. By exploiting in a variety of ways the properties of pitch-class sums (where equal sums lead to a common inversional center) and pitch-class differences (where equal differences mean a common interval), he builds a system in which motion through an ordered symmetrical array becomes the basis for progression through a piece of music. Numerous examples from Perle's compositions that make use of such progressions are provided. An interesting aspect of the book is the way it shows how the technique has developed over several decades, and how that development has influenced Perle's understanding of his own compositions. The book is not easy reading, and its critique of harmony in classical serialism seems misplaced, as the application of serialism has always been more flexible than its image has suggested. Nevertheless, Perle has extended the reach of 12-tone thinking in a creative direction.

MEAD's survey of Babbitt's compositional practice is recommended as a guide to the state of the serial art, documenting Babbitt's seemingly inexhaustible delight in inventing new ways for a series to order different dimensions of musical experience. If, as Babbitt remarks in *Words about Music,* "it pleased Schoenberg (and Stravinsky, too, when he saw the light) to write 12-tone pieces," one can imagine the pleasure that can be derived from contemplating the diversity of Babbitt's contributions. Mead deals with technical matters in a clear and level-headed way, taking the reader through Babbitt's generalizations about the techniques of Schoenberg and Webern, through Babbitt's various solutions to the problem of rhythm in serial music, to his ideas of extending combinatoriality to larger assemblages of rows called arrays and to the form of the composition. The book is best treated as a manual for compositional exploration, providing ample material for several more generations of serial composers.

ANTON VISHIO

See also Analysis: Serial

Set Theory

Forte, Allen, *The Structure of Atonal Music,* New Haven, Connecticut: Yale University Press, 1973

Perle, George, *Serial Composition and Atonality: An Introduction to the Music of Schoenberg, Berg, and Webern,* Berkeley: University of California Press, 1962; 6th revised edition, 1991

Rahn, John, *Basic Atonal Theory,* New York: Longman, 1980

Schmalfeldt, Janet, *Berg's Wozzeck: Harmonic Language and Dramatic Design,* New Haven, Connecticut: Yale University Press, 1983

Straus, Joseph N., *Introduction to Post-Tonal Theory,* Englewood Cliffs, New Jersey: Prentice Hall, 1990

Set theory (also referred to as pitch-class set theory, atonal music theory, and 12-tone theory) may be defined as a theory of pitch relations that informs the analysis of 20th-century music. The field originated with Milton Babbitt's unpublished work at Princeton University during the 1940s. It was Babbitt who first used mathematical set theory as a way of analyzing

atonal music; he formulated other essential concepts and terms as well, including integer notation, normal form, and pitch-class set. Babbitt's ideas have been extraordinarily influential. Subsequent to the publication of his articles in the 1950s and 1960s, other composers and theorists began to demonstrate the scope of his theory while filling in many of the details. At first, Babbitt and his followers (the so-called Princeton school) focused on the 12-tone music of Schoenberg, Berg, and Webern while Allen Forte and his followers (the Yale school) concentrated on the pre-12-tone music of these composers and their contemporaries. In the 1980s and 1990s, however, writers demonstrated, with varying degrees of success, the relevance of set theory to the music of Alexander Skryabin, Claude Debussy, Ruth Crawford, and Ornette Coleman, to mention only a few composers. They combined components of set theory with those of Schenkerian or literary theory. And they moved on to newer areas of concern, such as voice leading, rhythm, contour, timbre, and syntax.

PERLE's book is an essential starting place for any discussion of set theory. Prior to the appearance of his book, there were few publications in English that dealt with the analysis of 20th-century music. After studying the writings and teachings of Babbitt and examining an impressive body of works, Perle advanced a number of unprecedented ideas, including that of separate categories of atonal music: nonserial (free) atonal compositions, nondodecaphonic serial compositions (e.g., the third movement of Schoenberg's Five Piano Pieces, op. 23, which is built mainly on a five-note series), and dodecaphonic (or 12-tone) compositions. Within the second category, Perle discerned further stylistic subdivisions, hence his use of the term *free.* Some later theorists have attacked him, most notably for failing to relate pitch-class sets to larger levels of structure, but others find his book easy to read, inherently musical, and full of brilliant insight.

FORTE holds the distinction of writing the first full-length study of pitch-class set theory. His book is still the most widely used reference on the subject. In the first half, he offers a systematic presentation of fundamental material and concepts, including those he is generally credited with inventing or naming (e.g., interval vector, inclusion relationships, invariants, basic interval pattern [BIP], complementation). In the second half he introduces a more elaborate notion, the set complex, which he integrates with highly detailed analyses of musical excerpts. In an appendix he presents a list of 232 set types. Critics argue that his criteria for determining sets (the process of segmentation and music groupings) are arbitrary and that his analyses are incomplete because they do not incorporate tonal features that may occur in the very same piece. These and other shortcomings should not stop readers from using Forte's work as a classroom textbook as well as a source for their own analytic inquiries. This book is not really introductory in nature and is more difficult than some other textbooks currently available.

For readers seeking a clear introduction to set theory and to more advanced studies, RAHN's book is an excellent choice. Teachers will appreciate the great lengths to which the author will go to help students understand basic concepts without resorting to oversimplification. He avoids academic jargon, includes exercises (with answers) to reinforce comprehension, and tries to encourage students to listen to atonal music in imaginative ways. Consider his instructions for one particular exercise: "Listen several times to Schoenberg's *Pierrot Lunaire* op. 21.... Then listen to it again, preferably late at night with all the lights off." Rahn's book is much more than just a classroom textbook, however. Indeed, his book is generally recognized as one of the three standard references on the topic (the other two are by Perle and Forte). To this day, in matters of terminology and expressions, Rahn's are sometimes preferred over Forte's.

STRAUS has also written a textbook that is an excellent introduction to the techniques of atonal set theory. His ordering and presentation of topics are usually lucid and consistent. In each of the six chapters he includes a discussion of technical fundamentals, substantial exercises and drills, two separate bibliographies (one for the sources of his technical discussions, the other for the analyses), and fairly lengthy analyses of two atonal works. All told he presents 12 separate analyses, a reflection of his concern with the practical application of set theory and of his pragmatic approach in general. To be sure, Straus has a flair for getting abstract concepts across to students, as in the way he draws specific connections between set theory and tonal theory: "In some ways, the normal form of a pitch-class set is similar to the root position of a triad. Both are simple, compressed ways of representing sonorities that can occur in many positions and spacings."

Within the opening section of her book on Berg's *Wozzeck*, SCHMALFELDT offers a rare historical perspective of set theory. This is essentially a concise but comprehensive survey of the major theorists and composers who played a role in the early development of the field (notably Babbitt, Howard Hanson, Perle, and Forte) as well as a critique of their respective achievements. Among other things, readers learn that Babbitt was the first to transfer the mathematical concept of group to a musical domain and that Hanson made the initial list of pitch-class collections. During the course of her survey, Schmalfeldt includes some definitions of terms and techniques, ostensibly to provide the requisite background for the analytic chapters that follow. However, clearer and more comprehensive discussions of the basic theoretical material can be found elsewhere.

TERESA DAVIDIAN

Shakespeare and Music

Charlton, Andrew, *Music in the Plays of Shakespeare: A Practicum*, New York: Garland, 1991

Gooch, Bryan N., and David Thatcher, editors, *A Shakespeare Music Catalogue*, 5 vols., Oxford: Clarendon Press, 1990–91

Hartnoll, Phyllis, editor, *Shakespeare in Music*, London: Macmillan, and New York: St. Martin's Press, 1964

Long, John H., *Shakespeare's Use of Music*, 3 vols., Gainesville: University of Florida Press, 1955–71

Schmidgall, Gary, *Shakespeare and Opera*, New York: Oxford University Press, 1990

Seng, Peter J., *The Vocal Songs in the Plays of Shakespeare: A Critical History*, Cambridge, Massachusetts: Harvard University Press, 1967

Scholarship on the topic of Shakespeare and music may be divided into several categories. First, there is Shakespeare's own dramatic and poetic use of music, including not only musical performance called for in stage directions or in the texts of the plays, but also the numerous musical metaphors and symbols scattered throughout the works. Second, there is the identification of music used in conjunction with actual performances of the plays in and since the time of Shakespeare and the establishment of reliable performance editions. The third area concerns music inspired by or based on Shakespeare's works but intended as concert or chamber pieces independent from performances of the plays. Many scholars combine these areas to provide a wider context for a given dramaturgical or poetic technique or performance practice.

Extended essays by John Stevens, Charles Cudworth, Winton Dean, and Roger Fiske in HARTNOLL effectively introduce the reader to many of the relevant issues, problems, and topics. The insights of Stevens and Dean, particularly, retain their value even in the light of more current research. Stevens's "Shakespeare and the Music of the Elizabethan Stage" focuses on the performance history of various musical genres used or alluded to by Shakespeare, explaining how the traditions of the medieval mystery cycle, the court masque, the chronicle play, the dumb show, and Plautine comedy communicated to the Shakespearean audience. He argues that Shakespeare drew from both medieval and Renaissance philosophies of music, variously employing music in its symbolic or sacramental function and for human-centered, expressive purposes. He illustrates how Shakespeare used vocal, military, and other instrumental music to imitate everyday life, emphasize dramatic irony, or add to characterization. Dean's excellent essay on "Shakespeare and Opera" examines structural affinities between the plays and 19th-century (primarily Italian) operas and describes some of the difficulties encountered when adapting the complex plots and characters of the plays to the operatic stage. Shakespearean operas from the current and previous centuries are discussed in detail, with valuable critical insights and factual information concerning plot alterations, musical influences, the quality and nature of libretti, and the overall effectiveness of the operas. The appendix contains a catalog of musical works based on the plays of Shakespeare.

GOOCH and THATCHER have created an outstanding research tool in their five-volume catalog, which can serve as a point of departure for most modern studies. The goal of the editors was to achieve comprehensiveness and a level of detailed documentation beyond that of previous compilations of Shakespeare-related music; the more than 21,000 compositions listed here, compared to the approximately 3,000 in the most complete previous catalog published in Hartnoll in 1964, attest to their achievement. The catalog includes both published and unpublished music related to Shakespeare's work, concentrating on music performed in major cities, by major companies, or by Shakespearean, university, or college companies. Also included are works that were only projected, such as operas based on *King Lear* by Verdi and Britten and *The Tempest* by Mozart, and unfinished works, such as an opera of *As You Like It* by Debussy and *Macbeth* by Beethoven. Misattributions are noted in cases where a Shakespearean source has been erroneously credited. In volumes 1 through 3, the plays are arranged in alphabetical order by title; volume 3 also contains the sonnets (listed numerically, 1–154), and music for commemorative occasions, music based on apocryphal texts, and a chronological listing of anthologies of Shakespeare's music. As a practical guide for the composer or director, each play's title is followed by the pertinent stage directions and a description of its musical requirements, including references to works suggesting appropriate music for the stage directions. The music for all of the entries is listed in the order of incidental music, operas and related music, nontheatrical vocal music, nontheatrical instrumental music, settings of combined and unidentified texts, obliquely related works, and misattributions. Volume 4 consists of indices to the catalog by titles and lines from Shakespeare's plays; titles of musical works; and names of composers, arrangers, editors, librettists, and writers. Entries are well cross-referenced in these indices; for example, Brahms's *Ophelia Lieder* can be accessed through the composer index, or under Shakespeare's title *Hamlet* as incidental music (because it was commissioned for, and used in, an actual performance of the play), or under "Non-Theatrical Vocal Music" by the first lines of the individual songs and again by the title "Five Songs of Ophelia." Volume 5 is a selected bibliography divided into useful categories. One drawback to this impressive compilation is that chronological and geographical indices are conspicuously absent, making access to the enormous amount of information contained here unnecessarily difficult for certain types of research.

LONG's three-volume study examines the dramatic functions served by instrumental and vocal music in Shakespeare's plays. Asserting that music is an integral part of the dramatic structure, the author examines its use in intensifying the language, forwarding the action, and delineating character and setting, as well as its practical applications as a suggestion of passing time or as a bridge between scenes. Long establishes a broad historical context, explaining the social and literal musical meaning of such directives as "flourish," "sennet," and "French March," and describes how Shakespeare was able to use music as an effective dramatic device because of his keen awareness of the associations his audiences made with certain types of music. For study or performance, a large number of musical examples from contemporary or near-contemporary sources are provided in the body of the text and in an appendix to volume 3. The dramatic functions of the art and lute songs in the comedies, of well-known popular songs and ballad fragments in the tragedies, and of musical anachronism are discussed in detail, as well as the atmospheric, comic, and ironic use of instrumental ensembles. Each of the three volumes has a substantial bibliography, and another appendix to volume 3 contains facsimiles and modern transcriptions of military and ceremonial signal music.

SENG limits his study to those lyric passages in the plays that were originally intended to be sung onstage by an actor and identified as such by a stage direction or a clear textual reference. This limitation is a strength, because it allows Seng to be unusually thorough in assembling all of the relevant material on the songs, providing musicians and directors with many resources and performance insights, and scholars with a succinct review of the critical literature. This work is a scholarly, yet very accessible, chronological history of textual and analytical criticism of the songs, and it includes information about original or early musical settings and an examination of their dramatic functions within the plays. The entries include the text of the songs, source of the text, its location in early and modern editions, information about the source's typography, and accompanying stage directions, followed by critical commentary arranged by date, along with textual commentary and information about the music itself. Many 16th- and 17th-century editions are listed in the bibliography, as well as complete editions since 1709 and individual editions of the plays or poems.

SCHMIDGALL expands on Dean's premise that operas and the plays of Shakespeare are dramaturgically similar. He compares the two dramatic arts in terms of style, dramaturgy, and performance, giving individual attention to the members of a selected group of Shakespearean operas at the end of the book. Similarities include the choice and character of protagonists, the establishing and disruption of rhythm, the use of rhetoric, the focus on virtuosity, the sustaining of theatrical illusion, the condensation of plot, the juxtaposition of modes of expression, and the dependence on aural sensation. There are also surprising structural similarities: for example, some of Shakespeare's scenes fit into 19th-century opera's recitative-cavatina-cabaletta format astonishingly well. Music scholars will recognize a definite bias toward the aesthetic of Verdi and Boito and wince at the facile dismissal of the opinions of Joseph Kerman, but Schmidgall is, nonetheless, thoroughly successful in establishing the dramatic connection he intended.

Finally, CHARLTON has made a significant contribution to modern Shakespeare production by compiling all of the music needed for performing each of the plays. Intended as a source for directors and performers, the book's contents are arranged according to the practical needs of the theater. The musical selections represent a broad range of styles from the art and folk traditions of the 16th and 17th centuries. The plays are listed alphabetically, with all pertinent musical information arranged according to act, scene, and line of occurrence, with cue numbers and estimated timings, together with an indication of whether the music is specifically indicated in the stage directions or suggested by Elizabethan theatrical convention. The songs and song fragments are provided with optional period-style accompaniments and can be found under the heading of the appropriate play. To allow for maximum flexibility in performance, Charlton has included a wide variety of ceremonial, incidental, and other special music. Editorial decisions and performance options are discussed in the introduction, and a glossary explains terms that may be unfamiliar to the modern musician or director.

LORRAINE SPOSATO-ALLEN

Shostakovich, Dmitri 1906–1975

Russian composer

Fanning, David, *The Breath of the Symphonist: Shostakovich's Tenth,* London: Royal Music Association, 1988

Fanning, David, editor, *Shostakovich Studies,* Cambridge: Cambridge University Press, 1995

Haas, David, *Leningrad's Modernists: Studies in Composition and Musical Thought, 1917–1932,* New York: Lang, 1998

Hulme, Derek C., *Dmitri Shostakovich: A Catalogue, Bibliography, and Discography,* Muir of Ord: Kyle and Glen Music, 1982; 2nd edition, Oxford: Clarendon Press, 1990

Longman, Richard M., *Expression and Structure: Processes of Integration in the Large-Scale Instrumental Music of Dmitri Shostakovich,* 2 vols., New York: Garland, 1989

MacDonald, Ian, *The New Shostakovich,* London: Fourth Estate, and Boston: Northeastern University Press, 1990

Martynov, Ivan, *Dmitri Shostakovich: The Man and His Work,* translated by T. Guralsky, New York: Philosophical Library, 1947

Norris, Christopher, editor, *Shostakovich: The Man and the Music,* Boston: Boyars, and London: Lawrence and Wishart, 1982

Ottaway, Hugh, *Shostakovich Symphonies,* London: British Broadcasting Corporation, and Seattle: University of Washington Press, 1978

Roseberry, Eric, *Ideology, Style, Content, and Thematic Process in the Symphonies, Cello Concertos, and String Quartets of Shostakovich,* New York: Garland, 1989

Schwarz, Boris, *Music and Musical Life in the Soviet Union, 1917–1981,* Bloomington: Indiana University Press, 1983

Shostakovich, Dmitrii Dmitrievich, *Dmitry Shostakovich, about Himself and His Times,* edited by Lev Grigorievich Grigoriev and Yakov Moiseyevich Platek, translated by Angus Roxburgh and Neilian Roxburgh, Moscow: Progress, 1980

————, *Testimony: The Memoirs of Dmitri Shostakovich,* edited by Solomon Volkov, translated by Antonina W. Bouis, London: Hamilton, and New York: Harper and Row, 1979

Sollertinsky, Dmitri, and Ludmilla Sollertinsky, *Pages from the Life of Dmitri Shostakovich,* translated by Graham Hobbs and Charles Midgley, New York: Harcourt Brace Jovanovich, 1980

Taruskin, Richard, *Defining Russia Musically: Historical and Hermeneutical Essays,* Princeton, New Jersey: Princeton University Press, 1997

Wilson, Elizabeth, *Shostakovich: A Life Remembered,* Princeton, New Jersey: Princeton University Press, 1994

Dmitri Shostakovich's ever-increasing popularity both within and beyond the former Soviet Union has created a growing need for books focused on the many unanswered questions about his life, opinions, music, and the interplay between all these factors. Since the publication of Shostakovich's memoirs in 1979, much effort has gone into identifying and resolving contradictions between the public persona of the office-holding and prize-winning Soviet artist and the tormented inner man who, before the memoirs, had chosen never to reveal the depth of his private anguish in print, rarely in conversation, and often ambiguously in his richly allusive musical works. Whereas earlier studies tend to be superficial and noncommittal on the thorny issues, more recent writing indicates a trend of facing the problems head on, with arguments substantiated by corroborating documents where possible or by speculative trains of thought where confirmation is unavailable. In the continued absence of full access to letters and other primary sources, the recent trend toward deeper engagement with the structure, style, and intertextual associations of the music is likely to continue.

SHOSTAKOVICH (1979) was introduced to the West as Shostakovich's memoirs, transmitted via interviews conducted in the early 1970s, transcribed by Solomon

Volkov, and signed by the composer as testament of their authenticity. The integrity of the transcription process has been questioned by a number of scholars, however, first on account of a resemblance between a significant number of passages in this work and previously published material and second because the editor has withheld the manuscript from scholarly scrutiny. The volume is divided into eight sections, which, in Antonina Bouis's highly readable translation, do suggest oral transmission. Because the doubts as to authenticity, in part or as a whole, may never be resolved, readers are cautioned from treating the work as a genuine autobiographical statement but are encouraged to mine it for invaluable clues and insights into the significant people, events, harrowing experiences, and coping mechanisms employed by Shostakovich and others of his generation.

SHOSTAKOVICH (1980) is an anthology of articles and excerpts signed by the composer and published throughout his career. Little of a personal nature is revealed, and nothing at all is reprinted that would suggest that he was anything but a loyal Soviet citizen. Apart from the obvious inadequacy of the volume's viewpoint, there are problems with the presentation of the materials—specifically, the book lacks a consideration of the role of ghost writers and collaborators in Shostakovich's articles and speeches, and it follows an unfortunate pattern of abridging hard-to-find articles, such as, for example, published statements on the fifth and later symphonies. Despite the problems, these published statements are necessary to a comprehensive study of the music's Soviet reception.

Two Soviet-period biographies intended for a general audience are included in the above list. MARTYNOV discusses both the life and works through 1945 in a book completed just after the close of World War II. The biographical coverage is cursory and carefully skirts controversial issues. More attention is given to musical works: the symphonies through the ninth, the two operas, the piano concerto, and chamber works. Most interesting for the time are the balanced views of the still-banned *Lady Macbeth* and the already-controversial Symphony no. 8.

SOLLERTINSKY and SOLLERTINSKY were relatives of the composer's close friend Ivan Sollertinsky and consequently could incorporate material from private letters and reminiscences into their chronological narrative. The book provides glimpses into the composer's day-to-day routines at various times as well as anecdotes concerning the composition of major works.

WILSON's compendium of reminiscences about Shostakovich is clearly organized through chronological ordering, logical chapter titles, and her own running commentary. As a result, it is less a set of haphazard and unrelated recollections and more a uniquely designed biographical project, related in a polyphony of voices and literary styles. All sources are thoroughly documented, and all contributors are identified in an appendix of biographical notes. Wilson's book surpasses all previous biographies in English, both in the level of detail and the degree of insight into the character, career, and tragedy of Shostakovich.

FANNING's (1988) exemplary monograph on Shostakovich's Symphony no. 10 combines rigorous technical analysis with lucid description of the sound of the work and cautious speculation as to its extramusical meanings. Each movement receives a chapter, illustrated with copious musical examples and charts outlining formal structures and processes. The analysis shows an unprecedented sophistication with respect to harmonic events and interthematic links. The charts are helpful in elucidating the composer's elaborate coordinations and contrasts of themes, meter, dynamics, instrumentation, and harmony. Both a score and a recording are necessary to follow Fanning's detailed argument and to appreciate the subtlety of his concluding points about the composer's achievement of doublespeak in an untexted work. Three useful appendices offer a translation of Shostakovich's comments on the work, a summary of the thematic allusions, and errata in the various published editions.

FANNING (1995) has collected a series of studies on issues of compositional process, reception, theory, and interpretation, written by an international set of scholars, most of whom aspire to the same deep (and often complex) engagement with their chosen issues that Fanning advocates in his introductory essay. Collectively, the chapters represent nearly all of the most innovative and significant research paths of the 1990s. The Russian scholar Yuriy Kholopov and the U.S. scholar Ellon Carpenter discuss relevant theoretical backgrounds for Shostakovich's modifications to 19th-century instrumental forms and his employment of modes and hybrid scales, respectively. Specific works receiving detailed theoretical discussion in the volume include the Symphony no. 5 (by Fanning, Richard Taruskin, and Kholopov), the Piano Sonata no. 2 (Kholopov), the Piano Trio no. 2 (McCreless), and *Lady Macbeth* (Fanning). Other chapters on *Lady Macbeth* (Fay), *The Golden Age* (Yakubov), and the song cycles (Redepenning) are concerned with the revision process, reception, and relationship of text and music. Finally, two essays continue the tradition of relating Shostakovich to other composers, here to Benjamin Britten and Alfred Schnittke.

HAAS's cycle of essays on the achievements of three modernist composers (Shostakovich, Vladimir Shcherbachyov, and Gavriil Popov) and the musicologist-critic Boris Asaf'ev, all of whom were active in Leningrad during the 1920s, gives special insight into the early reception of Shostakovich's music. Four chapters provide background information on musical institutions, societies, musical thought, and the propagation of modernist music in Shostakovich's native city. The essays on Shostakovich's Symphonies no. 1 and 2 include prose analyses of style and structure, together with evaluations of the scores' modernist qualities according to the broad-based conceptualization of form, melodic line, and style developed by Asaf'ev and Shcherbachyov.

The second thoroughly reworked and expanded edition of HULME's catalog of works is an indispensable aid to all English-language texts on Shostakovich, containing considerable factual information on both major and minor works. The author admits to organizing his catalog in accordance with the last Soviet work list, published by Grigoriev in 1976. Each work bearing an opus number receives an individual entry, with detailed information on the instrumentation, publication, premieres, and miscellaneous other topics. In Hulme's system, works without opus numbers are assigned single alphabetical letters and inserted in appropriate chronological order. Sketches and works of disputed authorship are placed at the end. The extensive discographies are properly placed underneath the individual work entries; work studies, however, are placed in the general bibliography.

The monographs of Longman and Roseberry share significant similarities: they are each reprints of dissertations, contain discussions of Symphony no. 4, and feature taxonomies of the composer's techniques of thematic and motivic transformation. Prior knowledge of the music and of conventional terminology of formal analysis are required for both. LONGMAN surveys a large number of symphonies and quartets, singling out Symphonies no. 13 and 14 to represent the late style. A lengthy middle part examines issues of form and content. ROSEBERRY turns from Symphony no. 4 to the two cello concerti. His introductory chapter and appendices provide sources and commentary related to actual and potential interpretive methodologies for the composer's instrumental works.

MacDONALD's book on Shostakovich is a true anomaly, perhaps the most sustained polemic in English on any musical topic. Its threefold purpose is to establish the essential authenticity of Shostakovich's (1979) memoir, to castigate and ridicule dissenting viewpoints, and finally, to promote the author's personal experience of the music, which owes much to the persona presented in the memoir. Both the narrative and the bibliography give evidence that the author has read broadly in the literature, literary memoirs, and history of the Soviet era; this knowledge allows him to provide useful contextual backgrounds to the biographical sections. Readers should not mistake the hyperbolic tone of MacDonald's numerous work interpretations for a literary approximation of Shostakovich's style. Too often, the author's voice blocks paths to the music's subtleties and, if taken literally, can diminish the experience of the music. The author's peculiar achievement is not the definitive interpretation of the musical content but the characterization of a widespread manner of experiencing the works in the late 20th century.

NORRIS's volume serves as a concert companion suitable for the musically literate general reader. Separate chapters are devoted to the string quartets, the sympho-

nies (through no. 12), the piano music, the operas, and the late works using voices. Most valuable in the set is the chapter on the quartets, in which Christopher Rowland and Alan George of the Fitzwilliam String Quartet offer insights gained from their intimate experience with performing the cycle of quartets. In the remaining chapters, three scholars and a composer assess Shostakovich in wider 20th-century musical and political contexts, two of these authors including cautious references to Volkov.

OTTAWAY's short concert companion to the 15 symphonies provides perceptive program notes on each work, which highlight the characters of movements and themes and relate the individual works to other music. The combination of technically accurate yet vivid general descriptions, numerous insights into the specifics of scoring, and thoughtful remarks on the main issues of symphonic composition makes this volume the best of its type.

Shostakovich figures as a main character in SCHWARZ's still-unsurpassed one-volume history of Soviet music. Schwarz strives for a multifaceted view of music and musical life and avoids both pro- and anti-Soviet extremes in interpreting the symphonies. These and other works are discussed in relation to works composed by Prokofiev and other lesser-known figures in the Soviet era. The volume includes a brief interview with Shostakovich's son Maxim, in which Maxim challenges the portrayal of his father as Soviet apologist and acknowledges the penning of certain of Shostakovich's articles by others.

TARUSKIN's three essays on Shostakovich are concerned with patterns in the reception and interpretation of such key works as *Lady Macbeth* and Symphonies no. 5 and 7. In each case the author challenges one-sided readings by Soviet, post-Soviet Russian, Western European, and U.S. writers and explains why the works are inherently polysemic, that is, susceptible to multiple conflicting interpretations. As a countertheme, the author raises questions as to the veracity of Shostakovich's memoir and various other attempts to portray Shostakovich as a lifelong dissident. The *Lady Macbeth* essay, the shortest and most accessible to the general reader, is also the most controversial because it hints that the musical caricatures of the murdered victims parallel Soviet propaganda techniques used to justify the liquidation of the kulak farmers under Stalin.

DAVID HAAS

Sibelius, Jean 1865–1957

Finnish composer

Abraham, Gerald, editor, *Sibelius: A Symposium*, London: Drummond, 1947; as *The Music of Sibelius*, New York: Norton, 1947

Blum, Fred, *Jean Sibelius: An International Bibliography on the Occasion of the Centennial Celebrations, 1965*, Detroit, Michigan: Information Service, 1965

Dahlström, Fabian, *The Works of Jean Sibelius*, Helsinki: Sibelius Seura, 1987

Goss, Glenda Dawn, *Jean Sibelius: A Guide to Research*, New York: Garland, 1998

Goss, Glenda Dawn, editor, *The Sibelius Companion*, Westport, Connecticut: Greenwood Press, 1996

Kilpeläinen, Kari, *The Jean Sibelius Musical Manuscripts at Helsinki University Library*, Wiesbaden: Breitkopf and Härtel, 1991

Tawaststjerna, Eric T., *Sibelius*, 3 vols., translated by Robert Layton, London: Faber, 1976–97

The first book-length study of Jean Sibelius's life and works, *Jean Sibelius, His Tone Poetry and Features of His Life*, (1916, available only in Swedish and Finnish) was written by Erik Furuhjelm, a violinist, teacher, and music journalist. Intended for the composer's 50th-birthday celebration in 1915, the book presents biographical information and a study of the works through the Fifth Symphony with emphasis on the early unpublished music. Karl Ekman's book, published on the occasion of the composer's 70th birthday, *Jean Sibelius: His Life and Personality* (1935; translated into English and published in London in 1936), was written in close collaboration with the composer and is considered authorized. Biographies with various points of view were written over the next few decades. Cecil Gray's insightful analyses in *Sibelius* (1931) are colored by the author's enthusiasm for Sibelius as "the greatest master of the symphony since Beethoven." Gerald Abraham's still useful work *Sibelius: A Symposium* (1947) examines the rising fame of the composer by covering the various genres of Sibelius's output in essays by various authors. By the mid-1950s, the height of interest in Sibelius had passed and a reaction set in, as seen in the title of René Leibowitz's book, *Sibelius: The Worst Composer in the World* (1955, in French). In 1959, a U.S. Fulbright scholar in Finland, Harold E. Johnson, produced a biography, *Sibelius*, which offended the Finns with its critical portrayal of the composer. By the time of Fred Blum's 1965 bibliography, *Jean Sibelius: An International Bibliography on the Occasion of the Centennial Celebrations, 1965,* published books, articles, and reviews had expanded to over 1,400 items. Finland's foremost musicologist, Erik Tawaststjerna, then began an exhaustive biography and discussion of the works, resulting in his five landmark volumes published over a 23-year period, 1965–88. Fortunately, these volumes are now available in a condensed English edition, translated by Robert Layton, who had also published his own independent biography in 1965 (4th ed., 1992).

In the late 1980s several important scholarly studies were published in Finland: a preliminary list of works that is part of a larger project of creating a thematic catalog (Dahlström); a short biography and detailed chronology of Sibelius's life (Erkki Salmenhaara, *Jean Sibelius* [1984], available only in Finnish); and a catalog of the largest collection of Sibelius manuscripts, those in the Helsinki University library (Kilpeläinen). In addition, plans were made for a definitive complete edition of works under the direction of Dahlström. Two international Sibelius congresses were held in Helsinki in the 1990s, the first in 1990 and the second in 1995. The proceedings of the first were published in 1995, with papers on a wide range of topics by a noted international group of scholars. In 1993 Finnish-American musicologist James Hepokoski produced a highly technical study of the Fifth Symphony for the Cambridge Music Handbook series, dealing with the sketches and revisions of the score. In the early 1990s, a U.S. musicologist, Glenda Dawn Goss, contributed four new books on Sibelius: an edition of Sibelius's correspondence with American critic Olin Downes, an edition of previously unknown Sibelius letters from his youth, a collection of essays by various scholars (Goss [1996]), and, most outstanding, an annotated bibliography of more than 700 items (Goss [1998]). In 1997 Englishman Guy Rickards published yet another biography, *Jean Sibelius*, which includes recent findings but paints an unattractive picture of the man. The anticipated thematic catalog and the complete edition, begun in 1996 and expected to run to 45 volumes, will make enormous contributions to Sibelius research.

ABRAHAM, though dating from 1947, provides a still-useful introduction to the whole output of Sibelius for the general reader. The anthology concentrates on the music, with authoritative contributions from various British authors on the symphonies, selected orchestral and theater works, chamber music, piano works, songs, choral works, and general style.

BLUM's extensive bibliography of writings about Sibelius lists 1,429 entries, plus more citations in an addenda, making it the most complete bibliography of Sibelius to that date. A valuable introduction discusses significant aspects of many of the entries, giving an overview of Sibelius research. Besides listing books and dissertations concerning Sibelius, Blum gives information on books partially devoted to Sibelius, short articles in both music and nonmusic publications, and reviews of concerts. Most entries include concise annotation. Although this work has been superseded by Goss (1998), it contains many items not found in the later work.

DAHLSTRÖM's chronological catalog appeared as a preliminary part of a larger thematic-bibliographic catalog to be published by Breitkopf und Härtel. The 1987 work, though now somewhat out-dated by the 1991 manuscript dating work of Kari Kilpeläinen, contains much valuable information: the opus number usually given to works known by various numbers, titles of works in their original language as well as in other later translations, performing forces, year of composition, dedication, date of first performance if known, and details about the publisher. Until such time as the thematic-bibliographic catalog is available, Dahlström's chronological catalog and the 1991 Kilpeläinen manuscript studies remain the predominant references for dating the Sibelius works.

GOSS (1998) is an annotated bibliography of some 730 items, covering published material up to 1994. This work updates that of Blum but excludes reviews of concerts and recordings. Goss's lengthy and pithy remarks on each item describe the content of the work and often note the author's bias and the reason for it. Among the works reviewed are studies in English, Finnish, Swedish, Danish, Norwegian, German, French, Italian, Czech, Hungarian, Portuguese, and Romanian. The English descriptions provide a great service by opening this material to a wider readership. The range of works offers a wealth of material not only on Sibelius but on the whole panorama of Finnish music and culture. The results are highly commendable, and the bibliography should be a researcher's first stop.

GOSS (1996) compiles 13 essays by recognized scholars, including some authors from Finland whose writings are often not available in English. Between the essays, Goss has inserted short biographical interludes with copious documentation at the end of each. She has also contributed a chronology of the works of Sibelius, which is based on the research of Dahlström and Kilpeläinen, and a register of names, giving background information on significant people in Sibelius's circle. Other chapters deal with Sibelius's study in Vienna, Wagner influences, Sibelius's interest in the Finnish epic *The Kalevala*, the Second Symphony, *Luonnotar* and creation myths, the violin concerto, solo songs, choral music, the reception of Sibelius's works in England, the Seventh Symphony, and a summary of Sibelius research. The essays represent the most current research on Sibelius and may be a starting point for reading the earlier writings of the individual authors.

KILPELÄINEN's catalog of the extensive Sibelius manuscript scores in the University of Helsinki library, the largest collection in the world, has revealed previously unknown material, some of which has been recently performed and recorded. In 1982 the composer's family donated many autograph scores to the library, with the stipulation that they be cataloged. Examining the papers, handwriting, inks, and watermarks, Kilpeläinen has been able to date works more accurately than ever before. He also has established connections between early works previously considered independent. The manuscripts include fair copies and works at various stages. Kilpeläinen's study provides the first reliable list of Sibelius autographs along with a wealth of additional information, such as performing forces, opus numbers, sketches, and student works.

TAWASTSTJERNA, originally published in Swedish as a five-volume study of the composer's life and works, is the most definitive study of Sibelius. Tawaststjerna had unrestricted access to a large body of correspondence, the composer's diaries (now closed to researchers until 2019), unpublished student manuscripts, and the composer himself, then in his final decade of life. The work gives extensive background information and analyses for a large number of compositions. It has been translated from the original Swedish into Finnish, Russian, German, and English. In 1989 Tawaststjerna received the annual Finlandia Prize for Literature for this work, the first nonfiction work to be so honored. In Layton's English translation, the condensed Tawaststjerna material appears without the original documentation in three volumes. The third volume, covering the years 1914 to 1957, has been criticized for omitting the analyses of works found in the original Swedish edition. However, this study remains the most important biographical source on Sibelius for English-language readers, as well as a pleasure to read. Revealing excerpts from diaries and letters depict the man as having been subject to human frailties and self-doubts, not the towering hero as painted by some writers.

BARBARA J. HONG

Skryabin, Alexander 1872–1915

Russian composer and mystic

Abraham, Gerald, "Alexander Scriabin," in *Masters of Russian Music*, edited by Michel D. Calvocoressi and Gerald Abraham, New York: Knopf, 1936

Baker, James M., *The Music of Alexander Scriabin*, New Haven, Connecticut: Yale University Press, 1986

Bowers, Faubion, *The New Scriabin: Enigma and Answers*, New York: St. Martin's Press, 1973

———, *Scriabin: A Biography of the Russian Composer, 1871–1915*, 2 vols., Tokyo: Kodansha International, 1969

Guenther, Roy James, "Varvara Dernova's 'Garmoniia Skriabina': A Translation and Critical Commentary," Ph.D. dissertation, Catholic University of America, 1979

Hull, A. Eaglefield, *A Great Russian Tone-Poet: Scriabin*, London: Paul, Trench, Trubner, 1916; 2nd edition, 1927

Macdonald, Hugh, *Skryabin*, London: Oxford University Press, 1978

Pople, Anthony, *Skryabin and Stravinsky, 1908–1914: Studies in Theory and Analysis*, New York: Garland, 1989

Roberts, Peter Deane, *Modernism in Russian Piano Music: Skriabin, Prokofiev, and Their Russian Contemporaries*, 2 vols., Bloomington: Indiana University Press, 1993

Rudakova, E.N., and A.I. Kandinsky, *Scriabin*, translated by Tatyana Chistyakova, Neptune City, New Jersey: Paganiniana, 1984

Sabaneev, Leonid Leonidovich, *Modern Russian Composers*, translated by Judah Achilles Joffe, New York: International, 1927; reprint, New York: Da Capo Press, 1975

Schloezer, Boris de, *Scriabin: Artist and Mystic,* translated by Nicolas Slonimsky, Berkeley: University of California Press, 1987

Swan, Alfred Julius, *Scriabin,* London: Lane, 1923; reprint, New York: Da Capo Press, 1969

Taruskin, Richard, *Defining Russia Musically: Historical and Hermeneutical Essays,* Princeton, New Jersey: Princeton University Press, 1997

Alexander Skryabin was educated at the Moscow Conservatory and pursued a career as a composer-pianist. His earlier music strongly reflects the influence of Western European romantics, especially Chopin, Liszt, and Wagner. By 1910, however, he had developed a highly original style and harmonic language that borders on atonality.

In the West, Skryabin was recognized during his lifetime as one of the leading "ultra-modernists," along with Schoenberg and Stravinsky. In the 1920s several studies of his music, life, and mystical and aesthetic philosophies appeared in English, based for the most part on previous Russian scholarship. Thereafter, the number of English-language publications on the subject waned until the approach of the centenary of the composer's birth, marked by the appearance of Bowers's massive biography in 1969. Analytical studies of Skryabin's music, generally highly technical, soon began to appear in English. Several articles appeared in the late 1990s relating musical structure to the composer's declared mystical objectives.

Although SCHLOEZER's biography did not appear in English until 1987, it deserves first mention, because the author, Skryabin's brother-in-law, was intimately familiar with the composer's life and beliefs and thus has been an important source for most subsequent studies. The English edition contains Nicolas Slonimsky's translations of the biography, written in 1919, and articles from 1953 and 1970, along with an astrological study by Skryabin's daughter, Marina, from 1958. The book also contains a brief introduction by Marina, a biographical sketch, and a work list. Schloezer's aim is to describe Skryabin's artistic personality and creative inner life and to assess his place in modern culture; thus, the book is short on biographical detail. The study is in three parts: "Thinker," "Artist," and "Mystic." Throughout, Schloezer recollects conversations and makes pronouncements about Skryabin's beliefs with a tone of absolute conviction and authority that speaks of a lack of critical distance and perhaps a hidden familial agenda that does not inspire confidence in all he reports. His remarks about other critics, in particular Sabaneev, are at times partisan and polemical. Schloezer focuses not on the completed works but rather on Skryabin's barely begun *Mysterium,* which he regards as the "logical and psychological acme of romantic culture." He speaks in evangelical tones about the composer's beliefs as if they comprised a body of dogma. Schloezer's writings, although central—especially for capturing the hothouse spiritual atmosphere that enveloped the composer and his circle—must be carefully measured against other musicological and analytical data.

SABANEEV, also a close associate of Skryabin, was a Russian critic, composer, and biographer of Skryabin who emigrated to the West in 1926. He includes a chapter on the composer in his book on modern Russian composers, written for a Western readership and designed to introduce the author as an expert on Russian music. He regards Skryabin as more romantic than modern and speaks of the art of performing the composer's works as already lost in 1927. He portrays the composer as a megalomaniac and as a man of contradictions—mystic yet rationalist, romantic yet academic—and characterizes the mood of Skryabin's music as one of exaltation teetering on the brink of despair. The style throughout is anecdotal, with no scholarly documentation or close analysis, and the author's perspective provides a good counterbalance to Schloezer.

HULL was an extremely knowledgeable devotee of Russian music and an early champion of Skryabin as the instigator of an "artistic revolution unequaled in the whole history of the arts." He regards Skryabin as part of a direct lineage from Bach, Beethoven, Brahms, and Liszt. Hull's book was the first full study of Skryabin's music in English and is remarkable in many ways. Part 1 is a biography culled from Gunst's study in Russian as well as newspaper articles and reviews. (Many programs and reviews are reprinted here.) In part 2 Hull offers a summary of the works and provides many brief musical excerpts to demonstrate characteristic stylistic features. In a chapter on the mystic chord, the author derives the focal harmony from the upper overtones and analyzes two short pieces (opp. 52/1 and 59/2) from this point of view. Elsewhere he offers thematic analyses of all ten sonatas and five symphonies. Hull is not afraid to record his personal responses to the music; nor does he shy away from criticizing aspects of the music that he considers flawed. The book is well indexed, and Hull provides a work list annotated with his highly personal observations.

SWAN's brief two-part study contains a biography (based largely on Engel's biography of 1915–16) followed by a survey of musical works, which appears to be based on Hull, supplemented by a list of published works. Swan's observations on the music are quite apt, though not technical; there are no musical examples. The tone is adulatory throughout. The author regards Skryabin as a "Messiah among men" and presents an evolutionary view of the composer's career, directed toward the *Mysterium,* the "one supreme idea dominating the composer." Swan focuses on the mystic chord and emphasizes the diabolical element. This book is a useful digest of previous studies with some original criticism.

ABRAHAM's essay offers a capsule summary of the composer's life and career but does not delve into character or philosophy. There is scant commentary on the music. Abraham ultimately regards the music as a failure and the composer's story as an instance of the "decline and fall of a remarkable talent through uninhibited egotism." This essay may well reflect the general status of Skryabin's music in the West in the 1940s.

BOWERS's (1969) two-volume biography is the most comprehensive source of information on Skryabin in the English language, drawing on all previous sources in Russian as well as memoirs of innumerable associates and relatives of the composer. As such it is a valuable resource, especially for the translations of extended passages from the composer's correspondence, notebooks, and poetic texts. A number of wonderful photographs are reprinted here as well. The book is not without significant problems, however. Although filled with information, the data seldom coalesce into a coherent picture, as Bowers's style is somewhat rambling. Discussion of musical compositions amounts to florid description of little analytical value; documentation is almost totally lacking; the narrative is relentlessly chronological, down to the day and hour; and the index is so general and spotty that it is difficult to locate a particular item of information that one remembers having read. Beyond the problems of organization and documentation, Bowers's critical stance is off balance. He often delves pruriently (and seldom convincingly) into analysis of the composer's sexuality. More important, his attitude toward the composer's mystical aspirations is ambiguous. He fails to provide a clear explanation of Skryabin's place in the culture of the Silver Age in Russia.

BOWERS (1973) is an attempt to remedy the faults of the earlier study and to include materials previously unknown or unavailable to the author, in particular the work of certain Russian scholars. Chapter 1 delves into the complex personality of the composer by describing conflicting scholarly views. Four chapters comprise a compact biography and are particularly good at conveying a sense of cultural milieu. Six chapters are devoted to aspects of Skryabin's creative life. The most useful is chapter 8, wherein the harmonic theories of Yavorsky and Dernova are sketched. (A full translation of Dernova's treatise is provided in Roy James Guenther's doctoral dissertation, "Varvara Dernova's 'Garmoniia Skriabina': A Translation and Critical Commentary," Catholic University of America, 1979.) Unfortunately, Bowers's second study suffers from the same problems as the first: a rambling, anecdotal style and a lack of scholarly documentation.

MACDONALD provides a very brief overview of Skryabin's career and works. There is a useful outline of his stylistic evolution, with a good account of his idiosyncratic use of tonal harmony (including an analysis of op. 52/3). Macdonald's understanding of the composer's relation to cultural trends in Russia is weak, however.

RUDAKOVA and KANDINSKY is a fascinating volume, reprinting a valuable collection of photographs, programs, and the like. The preface is a translation of a politically biased Soviet essay, reflecting the scholarly attitudes toward the composer during the Brezhnev era. The many quotations from scholars, critics, and acquaintances of the composer paint a vivid portrait.

All of the preceding works are accessible to the general reader. The 1980s saw the publication of analytical studies that assume a degree of familiarity with tonal harmony as well as various analytical approaches to post-tonal music.

BAKER is a theoretical treatise on musical structure that explores Skryabin's transition from conventional tonality to atonality. It is the most comprehensive study of Skryabin's music to date, analyzing a sizable sample of short pieces from both the transitional period (1905–10) and the atonal period (1911–14). Many analyses of complete pieces are presented, including the Pianos Sonatas nos. 4, 5, and 10, the *Poem of Ecstasy,* and *Prometheus.* Baker employs a combination of Schenkerian analysis and pitch-class-set theory to demonstrate the interpenetration of tonal and post-tonal structures and devises an original statistical method to survey types of harmonies in use in various phases of Skryabin's career. In addition to graphic sketches of musical structure showing levels from the surface to middleground and background, more conventional formal outlines are presented that will be useful to the lay reader.

POPLE's book is a reprint of his 1984 doctoral dissertation, combining aspects Schenkerian and pitch-class-set analysis as well as semiotics in a flexible, ad hoc approach to selected works by Skryabin and Stravinsky. Three small pieces by Skryabin (the Albumleaf op. 58, and Preludes opp. 67/1 and 74/4) are analyzed in-depth, as are passages from *Prometheus.* (Works by Stravinsky, treated in separate chapters, include *Zvezdoliki* and portions of *Le Sacre du printemps.*) Pople shows normative sets, including the octatonic scale, governing deeper-level structure and attempts an explanation of the syntax involved in the usage of the mystic chord in *Prometheus.* This book concentrates on analytical methodology and will be rough going for nonspecialists.

ROBERTS rejects the approaches of Baker and Pople, as well as Dernova's concept of dual modality, insisting on the need for an approach that will "allow the music to suggest the form of analysis that should be applied." Unfortunately, the bases for his analytical decision making are often unsubstantiated. At times he offers quasi-Schenkerian reductions; at other times description is purely verbal with excerpts of scores as examples. Roberts's authoritative tone and sweeping generalizations belie the lack of discipline and grounding of his analyses. He presents an admirably broad sample of modernist composition in Russia, but the relatively brief length of the book is far too short to do justice to his attempt to trace crosscurrents of influence emanating from Skryabin's later music.

Except for the work of Hull, biographical and analytical research on Skryabin remained separate from one another through most of the 20th century. One recent study, however, attempts to demonstrate the relation of aspects of technique and structure in Skryabin's music to his mystical beliefs and to Russian culture in general. TARUSKIN traces the evolution of Skryabin's harmonic practice from whole-tone to octatonic to full chromatic and integrates this progression with a formulation of the composer's vision set forth in 1919 by the composer's close friend, the poet Ivanov.

JAMES M. BAKER

Smetana, Bedřich 1824–1884

Czech composer

Bennett, John Reginald, *Smetana on 3000 Records,* [Blandford]: Oakwood Press, 1974

Clapham, John, *Smetana,* London: Dent, and New York: Octagon Books, 1972

Karásek, Bohumil, *Bedřich Smetana,* translated by Joy Kadecková, Prague: Supraphon, 1967

Large, Brian, *Smetana,* New York: Praeger, and London: Duckworth, 1970

Malý, Miloslav, *Bedřich Smetana,* Prague: Orbis, 1976

Mojžísová, Olga, editor, *Bedřich Smetana: Time, Life, Work,* translated by Michaela Freemanová and Zoja Joachimová, Prague: Národní muzeum, 1998

Mojžísová, Olga, and Marta Ottlová, editors, *Bedřich Smetana, 1824–1884,* Prague: Muzeum Bedřicha Smetany, 1995

Smetana, Bedřich, *Bedřich Smetana: Letters and Reminiscences,* edited by František Bartoš, translated by Daphne Rusbridge, Prague: Artia, 1955

Suermondt, R.P., *Smetana and Dvořák,* Stockholm: Continental Book, 1940

Thörnqvist, Clara, *Smetana in Göteborg, 1856–1862,* Göteborg: Universitetsbiblioteket, 1967

Judging from commentaries proffered in most music appreciation books, the only details of Smetana's life worth noting are that he championed the nationalistic aspirations of his fellow Czechs and that he suffered total deafness during the last ten years of his life; likewise, the only works worth hearing are those few pieces that have captured the (mostly pictorial) imagination of the general public, namely the tone poem *Vltava* (named for the great river that courses through Bohemia, which, most unfortunately, is generally known in England and the United States only by the German name *Moldau*), the String Quartet no. 1 in E minor (with its captivating subtitle "From My Life"), and at least the overture, if not the whole, of *Prodaná nevěsta* (*The Bartered Bride*). The biographies by Clapham and Large discussed below pro-

vide much richer and substantial views of Smetana, to the extent that any newer assessment, though it certainly would incorporate some interesting details and discoveries noted in recent periodical literature, would not substantially alter our knowledge or understanding of his activities, motivations, and interpersonal relationships. Nevertheless, the imperative still remains to publish monographs in English that treat his individual works in a thorough and systematic manner. Beyond those few compositions that have garnered public attention lie unknown treasures in a variety of genres: songs, part songs, and choruses; solo piano pieces; chamber music; overtures, dances, and other occasional instrumental works; the overlooked orchestral tone poems, not the least of which are the five parts in addition to *Vltava* that belong to the cycle *Má vlast* (*My Homeland*); and finally, the seven operas besides *The Bartered Bride*. Similarly, it is almost shameful, given the important place Smetana holds in the history of Czech music—and, indeed, in 19th-century music as a whole—that the majority of his letters and memoirs, sketchbooks, and other primary source materials have not been published, even in German, the language he felt most comfortable using.

Fortunately, SMETANA contains English translations of selections from Smetana's own writings (including essays and journal articles) and from letters and recollections of the composer by his pupils, friends, and other acquaintances. The selections were chosen with the aim of providing a more personal, intimate view of the Smetana the man. For example, we learn that, constantly suffering the irritation of having his last name mispronounced by German speakers, who tend to stress the penultimate syllable instead of the first, Smetana used to inform them of the correct way by singing the first four measures of Beethoven's *Fidelio* overture to the words "Sme'-ta-na, Sme'-ta-na, Sme'-ta-na sprich aus!"

LARGE, whose volume is one of only two (together with Clapham) full-length studies of the composer in English, presents a chronological narrative in which informed discussions of social, political, and cultural events and trends are integrated with biographical details and astute analyses of Smetana's works. His book is generously illustrated with photographs of the composer, important friends, family, and associates, and also reproductions of playbills, set designs, autograph manuscripts, and other significant documents. Useful appendices include synopses of the operas, lists of works organized chronologically and by genre, Smetana's family tree, selections from the correspondence between the composer and Eliška Krásnohorská (librettist of three of Smetana's completed operas and another left uncompleted), a catalog of the many character pieces for piano titled *Album Leaves*, and charts outlining the various versions of *The Bartered Bride* and *The Two Widows*. Large's book is bountifully documented, yet frequently the reader is left wanting more extended extracts from the letters. The appendix containing snippets from Krásnohorská and Smetana's correspondence, for example, is much too slim, considering the rather large number of letters that have survived and, in fact, previously been published by Mirko Očadlík (1940). That much of Large's research relies on secondary sources does not, in any case, detract from his study's comprehensiveness and his ability to tie loose ends together. His book remains the most valuable single volume that has been published in English, especially because it has been reprinted.

CLAPHAM's study was completed before, but published after, Large's book. Clapham is a slimmer volume than Large, but no less consequential. By organizing his chapters so that the earlier ones focus on the political, social, economic, and cultural milieu in Bohemia leading up to Smetana's time and on the details of Smetana's life and the later ones examine individual works (with each chapter devoted to a particular genre), Clapham has made it easy to find information concerning a specific topic or individual composition. The author also provides a useful guide to Czech pronunciation at the front of the book and, at the back, a calendar marking the birth and death dates of contemporary musicians alongside important events in Smetana's life. Other appendices include a personalia containing brief entries for 39 persons who figure prominently in Smetana's biography or the reception history of his music, and an English translation of the composer's autopsy report, for those readers interested in knowing how severely his body became ravaged by syphilis.

A recent publication edited by MOJŽÍSOVÁ, who is director of the Bedřich Smetana Museum in Prague, contains 12 articles in English and 13 others in German. Most focus on Smetana's compositional processes or on the genesis and composition of individual works. In a well-written and engaging essay, for example, Kenneth DeLong considers Franz Liszt's influence on Smetana, citing especially the similarities in approach and structure between their respective symphonic poems *Tasso* and *Richard III*. Jaroslav Jiranek and Jiri Berkovec offer their own assessments concerning the originality and "Czechness" of Smetana's music, while Milan Pospisil reveals the changeable, often self-serving, and sometimes duplicitous way in which, over the years, Eliška Krásnohorská characterized her dealings with the composer. Reading Jarmil Burghauser's essay, "Smetana's Influence on Dvořák's Creative Evolution," is particularly rewarding: in addition to addressing the topic suggested by the title, the author devotes considerable attention to the political and cultural milieu of the time and reevaluates the role played by Otakar Hostinsky, an influential Czech musicologist, teacher, and critic, in the reception history of the two composers' works.

A recent book edited by MOJŽÍSOVÁ and OTTLOVÁ is specifically intended to appeal to the general public. Sections listing Smetana's compositions and the most important events that took place in Prague during his lifetime serve as supplements to Radmila Habanova's thumbnail account of his life, Michaela Freemanova's overview of the political and cultural milieu in Prague (including concert and operatic life and the important music schools and institutions), and Zdenek Hojda's essay tracing the growth and development of Prague during Smetana's lifetime. Readers who are already familiar with the layout of the city and its architectural monuments will perhaps benefit most from Hojda's enlightening exposé: he carefully traces the efforts made during the 19th century to modernize the city's infrastructure, describes the changes in demographics and local and provincial government, and discusses the most significant and cultural initiatives. The entire volume is sumptuously illustrated with images, many in color, of important persons and places, concert and operatic posters, and cover pages of first editions of Smetana's compositions.

In her detailed, practically day-by-day chronicle of Smetana's activities during the years he spent in Sweden, THÖRNQVIST integrates some very interesting extracts from concert announcements, critiques, municipal records, and letters, diaries, and recollections of Smetana and others. She also includes a large number of well-chosen illustrations.

Starting from the turn of the 20th century, BENNETT offers a survey of recorded performances by listing recordings of entire compositions, as well as (for the operas and choral works) individual arias, duets, choruses, instrumental numbers, and so on, and (for instrumental and smaller-scale vocal works) individual pieces or movements. Compositions are listed chronologically within categories defined by genre. In an enlightening introductory essay, Bennett provides historical background concerning the various recording companies inventoried in the main catalog. For each of Smetana's most frequently recorded works, the author provides a brief discussion of its genesis and composition, then proceeds to describe the work from beginning to end, incorporating musical examples outlining the principal themes and offering intelligent personal insights and historical commentary along the way, rather in the tradition of popular guides to opera and orchestral or chamber music, but with many more examples than is customary for such books. Bennett seems to be most interested in opera; in a later section of the book, he provides biographical sketches of the singers who have recorded works by Smetana and, under the heading for each singer, lists the recordings made by that singer. In a second register, the specific operatic selections recorded by each singer are inventoried. Additionally, at the end of the main entry for each opera, Bennett lists the number of times that individual singers performed specific operatic roles at the principal theaters in the Czech lands (but primarily in Prague) beginning, presumably, with the advent of recorded sound up to the 1947–48 season. This section is patently gratuitous: its accuracy is suspect and its purview too narrow in terms of locale and time period. This one anomaly aside, Bennett's book is an important source for considering one aspect of the reception history of Smetana's works, and it serves as an excellent popular guide to Smetana's most-performed music.

For the sake of completeness, mention should be made of three other items, which are biographical sketches intended for young or amateur enthusiasts. SUERMONDT discusses Smetana and Dvořák separately, not in relation to each other, as the title might suggest. Twenty-three of the 59 pages are devoted specifically to Smetana. The book is written in a simple and direct style and provides a nice, if occasionally outdated, basic testament about the composer's life and work. The books by KARÁSEK and MALÝ, originally written in Czech, have been translated into several languages and most likely were widely distributed primarily for propagandistic purposes at a time when Smetana was championed by Czech authorities above all other composers, especially above Dvořák, as being a spokesperson for the proletariat. Karásek's biography is interesting, perhaps, only for the occasional interpretive nuances reflecting the socialist bent of the author, who held prestigious editorial and administrative positions during the period of communist rule in Czechoslovakia. Malý, who was also well placed in Communist Party circles and served as director of the Bedřich Smetana Museum in Prague, manages to be less doctrinaire.

ALAN HOUTCHENS

Sonata: General

Glickman, Sylvia, and Martha Furman Schleifer, editors, *Women Composers: Music through the Ages,* 3 vols., New York: Hall, 1995–

Mellers, Wilfrid, *The Sonata Principle,* London: Rockliff, 1957; revised edition, London: Barrie and Jenkins, 1988

Newman, William S., *The Sonata in the Baroque Era,* Chapel Hill: University of North Carolina Press, 1949; 4th edition, New York: Norton, 1983

———, *The Sonata in the Classic Era,* Chapel Hill: University of North Carolina Press, 1961; 3rd edition, New York: Norton, 1983

———, *The Sonata since Beethoven,* Chapel Hill: University of North Carolina Press, 1969; 3rd edition, New York: Norton, 1983

Ratner, Leonard, *Classic Music: Expression, Form, Style,* New York: Schirmer Books, 1980

Rosen, Charles, *Sonata Forms,* New York: Norton, 1980; revised edition, 1988

Tovey, Donald Francis, *The Forms of Music: Musical Articles from the Encyclopedia Britannica,* London: Oxford University Press, 1944

A sonata is a work for one or more solo instruments, usually in several movements. The word comes from the Italian, a *sonata* being, since the beginning of the 17th century, a sounded piece, played on instruments, as opposed to a *cantata* or sung piece; similar terms (*sonade, sennet, sonnet, sonada*) were also used to denote instrumental music. At times the term *sonata* has been used for instrumental works that include a part for voice, and even for an ensemble of solo voices that sound without singing words. The term *sonata* can be ambiguous, referring to a style, character, texture, or form, as well as a genre. *Sonata form* is the form of a single movement in most music written from about 1770 and 1820, the classical era, and it remained a standard musical form for at least 100 years. As described in the early 19th century, it consists of (1) an exposition of themes and motives in a main key and then in a second key, usually the dominant; (2) a development of themes and exploration of contrasting keys; and (3) a recapitulation of the material from the exposition that now remains in the home key, resolving the harmonic tension created in the exposition by the second key.

Books about the sonata generally examine its forms and instrumentations; readers are assumed to have scores and recordings at hand. Some writers refer to a sonata principle or sonata style in music by Viennese classical composers—Mozart, Haydn, and Beethoven. The term *sonata form* is used metaphorically in other arts to describe a novel or poem or even a painting that seems to have three parts that function as exposition, development, and recapitulation.

Newman began to write "A History of the Sonata Idea," but it became instead a descriptive catalog and history of sonatas in three indispensable volumes. NEWMAN (1949) covers the period from about 1600 through 1750. Typical compositions of this time are trio sonatas for two violins with basso continuo; related titles include *ordre,* partita, suite, canzona, and toccata. NEWMAN (1961) begins with solo keyboard sonatas from the 1740s and goes through the 1820s. Classical sonatas are sometimes also titled lessons, *esercizi, divertimenti,* or *pièces de clavecin.* NEWMAN (1969) covers the romantic era from the 1820s through the early decades of the 20th century when sonatas become virtuosic concert works.

In each volume, after an introductory chapter on methodology, chapters are grouped into two large parts. Part 1, "The Nature of the (Baroque, Classical, Romantic) Sonata," is an overview of styles, structures, composers, regions and schools, instruments, settings, social functions, theorists, critics, philosophers, audiences, and publications. Part 2 gives details of "The Composers and Their Sonatas," arranged chronologically and geographically. Although their titles may suggest a narrow range, these volumes in many respects present a broad history of Western music. The clear arrangement of material and the splendid bibliographies make them invaluable reference works for information on any particular sonata, with advice for further investigation.

TOVEY, in his article "Sonata," sketches the history of the genre mainly in the 18th century, citing Corelli (trio sonatas), Domenico Scarlatti (harpsichord sonatas), Clementi (piano sonatas), and Mozart (piano and violin sonatas). Other material about sonatas is found in his articles on "Sonata Forms," "Chamber Music," "Instrumentation," "Rhythm," "Harmony," "Melody," and "Music." The true sonata is in several movements, he comments, as individual sonata movements "raise emotional issues which each movement is unable to satisfy without the others."

MELLERS uses the term sonata principle to describe a way of composing sonatas and other instrumental music in the second half of the 18th century that grew out of a particular set of social and philosophical circumstances. For Mellers, music conveys human experience in the relation between musical forms and the phenomena of the external world. The sonata principle or sonata idiom in music of the classical composers represents a conflict of tradition and revolution. Viennese classical composers achieved a balance between tradition and revolution by using sonata form to give revolutionary popular musical styles an artistic sensitivity and dramatic order. Mellers finds this sonata principle in classical opera and other vocal music as well. Generalizing even further on the tonal and dramatic possibilities of this principle, he devotes the second part of his book to "a new kind of opera" in the 19th century.

RATNER examines sonatas and sonata forms in 18th-century music through the ears of 18th-century musicians and critics by using terms and concepts from their writings. He looks back beyond 19th-century descriptions to see that classical musicians perceived form as a two-part tonal drama: (1) movement away from the tonic or home key in the first part of the movement (19th-century writers' exposition) and (2) return to the home key in the second part (development and recapitulation). Ratner describes popular or commonplace sources of sonatas, including dance music and traditional textures, that would have had social and philosophical associations for 18th-century listeners; these are the topics of musical discourse.

ROSEN rejects 18th-century descriptions in favor of direct examination of the music itself. He describes the various ways sonatas and other pieces, mainly from the 18th century, are constructed. His analysis of procedures, movement by movement and section by section, reveals sometimes unexpected comparisons and contrasts.

While it is generally recognized that the accomplished amateur keyboardists for whom 18th-century sonatas were written and published were typically women, only in the 1990s did books first appear about the sonatas that women themselves composed. The 12-volume anthology edited by GLICKMAN and SCHLEIFER contains extensive essays and bibliographies with new editions of the music. Of the volumes published so far, three contain information about sonatas: volume 2, *Composers Born 1600–1699* (1996); volume 3, *Composers Born 1700–1799: Keyboard Music* (1998); and volume 5, *Composers Born 1700–1799: Large and Small Instrumental Ensembles* (1998).

DEBORAH HAYES

Sonata: Baroque

Allsop, Peter, *The Italian "Trio" Sonata: From Its Origins until Corelli,* Oxford: Clarendon Press, and New York: Oxford University Press, 1992

Anthony, James R., *French Baroque Music from Beaujoyeulx to Rameau,* New York: Norton, 1978; revised edition, Portland, Oregon: Amadeus Press, 1997

Apel, Willi, *Italian Violin Music of the Seventeenth Century,* edited by Thomas Binkley, Bloomington: Indiana University Press, 1990

Bonta, Stephen, "The Uses of the 'Sonata da chiesa,'" in *Baroque Music I: Seventeenth Century,* Garland Library of the History of Western Music, vol. 5, edited by Ellen Rosand, New York: Garland, 1985

Jensen, Niels Martin, "Solo Sonata, Duo Sonata and Trio Sonata: Some Problems of Terminology and Genre in 17th-Century Italian Instrumental Music," in *Festskrift Jens Peter Larsen,* edited by Nils Schiørring et al., Copenhagen: Hansen, 1972

Newman, William S., *The Sonata in the Baroque Era,* Chapel Hill: University of North Carolina Press, 1959; 4th edition, New York: Norton, 1983

Selfridge-Field, Eleanor, *Venetian Instrumental Music from Gabrieli to Vivaldi,* New York: Praeger, and Oxford: Blackwell, 1975; 3rd revised edition, New York: Dover, 1994

Swack, Jeanne, "On the Origins of the Sonate auf Concertenart," *Journal of the American Musicological Society* 46 (1993)

Zohn, Steven, "When Is a Quartet not a Quartet?: Relationships between Scoring and Genre in the German Quadro, ca. 1715–40," in *Johann Friedrich Fasch und sein Wirken für Zerbst,* edited by Konstanze Musketa and Barbara M. Reul, Dessau: Anhaltische Verlagsgesellschaft, 1997

Some of the most valuable recent research on the baroque sonata has concentrated on 17th-century Italy. What had been terra incognita (with the important exception of Corelli) just a few decades ago has been covered with admirable thoroughness by several writers. By contrast, studies of the 18th-century Italian sonata remain centered on a few important figures, especially

Albinoni and Vivaldi. As a repertory, the German baroque sonata has been underrepresented in the English-language literature, much of the important work having focused on the music of individual composers, particularly Biber, Buxtehude, Telemann, J.S. Bach, and C.P.E. Bach. If somewhat more general research has been undertaken on the sonata and suite in late 17th-century and early 18th-century France, it has also tended to concentrate on major figures such as François Couperin and Leclair; to date, no English-language study has come close to displacing Lionel de La Laurencie's monumental *L'École française de violon, de Lully à Viotti* (Paris, 1922–24).

NEWMAN's volume is the classic study of the baroque sonata, still valuable 40 years after its first appearance owing to its exceptionally broad scope. While including a consideration of "every composer of demonstrable significance to the sonata in the Baroque Era," Newman restricts his discussion to works with the title "Sonata," effectively excluding a large portion of the 17th-century repertory. Following five chapters that address contemporary uses and definitions of the term *sonata*, the sociological functions and dissemination of the genre, instrumentation, and formal structures, Newman discusses the sonatas of individual composers in sections arranged according to geography and chronology. His writing style is engaging, and he does not shy away from stating his opinions of the music, often formed on the basis of modern editions available during the 1950s. He devotes up to several pages to each of the more major figures; many of these discussions have been superseded by more recent specialized studies. But in some cases the single paragraphs devoted to lesser composers remain the best (or only) available summary of their sonata output. Particularly valuable is Newman's meticulous listing of modern editions and secondary literature.

BONTA explores the employment of the *sonata da chiesa* in the Roman Rite during the second half of the 17th century. After demonstrating that free instrumental music was used principally in connection with the Mass Proper (the liturgical function determining the type of piece used), he shows that the *sonata da chiesa* was occasionally used in its entirety for the Gradual, Communion, and Deo Gratias, but probably not at the Offertory or Elevation. Sonatas also appear to have been used as antiphon substitutes for both Vesper psalms and the Magnificat. Bonta adduces some evidence to suggest that sometimes only one or two movements/sections of a sonata may have been heard, a practice that is well documented for the 18th century.

JENSEN argues that the 18th-century terms *solo sonata* and *trio sonata* have misleadingly been applied to 17th-century repertories. Whereas in the 18th century the continuo was included in the count of voices ("solo" meant a scoring of one melody instrument and continuo; "trio" designated two melody instruments and continuo),

in the 17th century only the melody instruments were included in the reckoning. Thus "sonata a une" meant a sonata for one melody instrument and continuo, "sonata a due" a sonata for two melody instruments and continuo, and so forth. Jensen downplays the role of the continuo in the 17th-century sonata, viewing it as "primarily an accompaniment to a texture which is determined by linear factors" rather than a "governing element of the composition by reason of its harmonic function."

In her throrough study of Venetian instrumental music, SELFRIDGE-FIELD devotes more attention to the sonata than any other instrumental genre. After providing a valuable survey of instrumental music at the Basilica of San Marco and other musical venues (parish and monastic churches, confraternities, theaters, orphanage-conservatories, academies, homes and palaces, and dances), she devotes most of four chapters to the sonatas of individual composers. The sonatas of Giovanni Gabrieli, Albinoni, Vivaldi, and Alessandro and Benedetto Marcello are treated in individual chapters. Selfridge-Field's discussions of the music are as comprehensive as they are clear.

First published in German as *Die italienische Violinmusik im 17. Jahrhundert*, APEL's study examines the published sonatas of 61 Italian composers active during the 17th century. For each composer, he provides a brief biographical sketch, list of sources, and a discussion of the music that may range in length from a few paragraphs to a substantial essay, often richly illustrated with musical examples. His well-informed discussions provide much useful information about the publications and musical style. The volume is best used as a reference, for there is little attempt to provide an overall narrative to trace musical developments within or across regional boundaries during the long period covered by the study, despite the roughly chronological organization of the material.

ALLSOP takes a different approach than Apel to much the same repertory. Focusing on the genre of the Italian trio during the first three quarters of the 17th century, Allsop's work is a contextual study in which the achievements of individual composers are related to larger regional trends. The four chapters comprising the first part of the study "present the sonata and its composers in the widest historical context as a social and cultural phenomenon" through a survey of Italian cities and regions and their most important sonata composers and through a consideration of various issues surrounding "the instrumental ensemble," the meaning of the term *sonata*, the functions of the genre, and the social position of the composer in 17th-century Italy. The following chapters treat individual composers in the context of the city or region in which they worked. Musical examples are abundant, and the discussion is on a sophisticated level. By consistently relating one composer's sonatas to those of his predecessors and contemporaries, Allsop portrays the repertory as an intricate web of stylistic relationships and syntheses. Especially valuable is the final chapter, which examines Corelli's sonatas within the context of his Bolognese and Roman predecessors. Allsop finds that there are precedents for most of Corelli's compositional techniques in the works of composers of the Bolognese and/or Roman schools and concludes that "his originality lay in the novel reformulation of the former and unique synthesis with the latter."

ZOHN examines the generic status of the obbligato bass quartet (scored for two trebles, obbligato bass, and continuo, or treble, two obbligato basses, and continuo) in early 18th-century Germany. Drawing on a repertory of more than 60 such works by a number of composers, he shows that the classic definitions of the quartet by Scheibe and Quantz actually apply to only a small portion of surviving works: quartets or quartet movements "in which the obbligato bass is mostly independent of the continuo line and functions as the thematic equal of the other concertante parts . . . are in a distinct minority." The shifting function of the obbligato bass among doubling the continuo, playing diminutions of the continuo line (closely related to an improvisatory variation tradition), and engaging in imitative dialogue with the upper voices ally the obbligato bass quartet with the 17th-century *sonata a tre*. The fine line between trio and quartet is further demonstrated by some composers' addition of obbligato bass lines to pre-existing trios.

SWACK illuminates the history of a subgenre previously thought to have been invented by J.S. Bach, the concerted sonata. Following a close reading of Scheibe's definition of the *Sonate auf Concertenart*, the author demonstrates that German composers in Thuringia and Saxony (particularly at the Dresden court) began composing sonata movements in ritornello form during the 1710s. The apparent model for these works were the chamber concertos and conventionally scored concertos of Vivaldi. In discussing the music, Swack shows that composers frequently set up a clear distinction between "solo" and "tutti" material in the beginning of the movement, only to obscure it later by having the "soloist" and "orchestra" switch roles or engage in imitation more characteristic of the sonata than the concerto. Such generic interplay, she argues, inspired the more complex concerted sonatas of Bach.

Finally, an excellent introduction to the French baroque sonata—one that is more up-to-date than the relevant chapters in Newman—is provided by ANTHONY. He neatly summarizes the output of the most important composers of ensemble suites and sonatas and suites for solo instruments, with works of the latter category discussed by instrumentation (violin, flute, violoncello, viol, and "rustic instruments"). Especially useful are the extended discussions of works by Couperin, Leclair, and Marais.

STEVEN ZOHN

Sonata: Classical

Barford, Philip, *The Keyboard Music of C.P.E. Bach Considered in Relation to His Musical Aesthetic and the Rise of the Sonata Principle*, London: Barrie and Rockliff, 1965

Berger, Melvin, *Guide to Sonatas: Music for One or Two Instruments*, New York: Anchor Books, 1991

Loft, Abram, *Violin and Keyboard: The Duo Repertoire*, 2 vols., New York: Grossman, 1973

Newman, William S., *The Sonata in the Classic Era*, Chapel Hill: University of North Carolina Press, 1961; 3rd edition, New York: Norton, 1983

Rosen, Charles, *The Classical Style: Haydn, Mozart, Beethoven*, London: Faber, and New York: Viking Press, 1971; expanded edition, New York: Norton, 1997

———, *Sonata Forms*, New York: Norton, 1980; revised edition, 1988

Shedlock, John S., *The Pianoforte Sonata: Its Origin and Development*, London: Methuen, 1895; reprint, with foreword by William S. Newman, New York: Da Capo Press, 1964

By the classical period, the meaning of the word *sonata* (as an instrumental genre for one or more solo instruments) was far more well-defined than it had been in the baroque, when it also occasionally denoted works including voices for an orchestra. However, in the classical period, the word also came to be used for a form (sonata form) in addition to its genre indication. By the 1740s, the prominent type of sonata was that for keyboard instrument, and within the classical period the most frequent sequence of movements became the one that had been championed by C.P.E. Bach: fast-slow-fast. On the subject of classical sonata, scholarly books have concerned themselves mainly with the output of a single composer. Exceptions include the early book by Shedlock and the outstanding contemporary efforts of Rosen and Newman. The interested reader will find even more information in the monographs dedicated to single composers. This information could not be included here.

BARFORD's monograph presents C.P.E. Bach's keyboard music in a theoretical context and is specifically intended for performers of these works. In the preliminary discussion, the author relates the "growth of the sonata-principle to a metaphysical attitude which seems particularly congenial to the German mind." He then evaluates the individual works from both a philosophical and a theoretical and analytical standpoint.

LOFT's book discusses violin sonatas of composers from the early 17th-century (Cima, Marini, and Fontana) through Mozart's last sonatas. The book is "aimed at players—students, amateurs, professionals—who want to know about music that they can read, rehearse, and perform . . . and . . . for those who want some guidance as to the type of music in question, its difficulty, what particular points of interest it has, and how it can be approached in performance." Thus, the book limits itself to music available in modern, in-print editions (as of 1973). The choice of sonatas for inclusion is a personal one of the author and is based mostly on his preferences and on the importance of the work. For the preclassical and classical periods, the composers considered include Veracini, Tartini, Locatelli, Leclair, Schobert, C.P.E. Bach, J.C. Bach, Boccherini, Schulz, Hummel, Viotti, Dittersdorf, Kimmel, Benda, and Mozart (the study of Mozart's sonatas takes up close to one-quarter of the book). In each case, the author provides a general discussion of the composer and his repertoire and then offers either a short or an extended commentary of the sonatas themselves, with some analytical elements and a few performance suggestions.

The gigantic work of NEWMAN on the sonata throughout history, a work that he published in three volumes under the collective title *A History of the Sonata Idea,* affords us the most complete work in the field. In all three volumes, the main focus is on the "changing meanings and uses that the term 'sonata' itself underwent." The present volume is subdivided into an introductory historical chapter followed by two parts of uneven length. The introduction examines the problems related to the scope, style, methodologies, sources, and period, which he defines as "the crucial period of about eighty-five years from the first real flowering of the solo keyboard sonata, starting shortly before 1740, to the last sonatas of Beethoven and Clementi, completed shortly after 1820." Part 1 "offers a summary, overall view of the Classic sonata, organized in terms of its meanings, uses, spread, settings, and forms." Among the issues considered are the use of the term *sonata* as a title and its definition in contemporary theoretical writings, the social function of such compositions, the position in society of their composers, and the sonata in homes, churches, and public concert places. Newman then discusses at some length the main centers in which the sonata was cultivated or transmitted (and printed) and explains why some composers are considered part of one center or the other, regardless of where they were born and trained. After a chapter examining the various instrumental settings of sonatas, Newman devotes an all-important chapter to the problem of style(s) and form(s) in the sonata, with the sonatas by Haydn, Mozart, and Beethoven as constant points of reference (these works are thus skipped in the chapters devoted to the composers in part 2). Part 2, which is four times longer than part 1, explores more than 400 composers and their sonatas according to chronology, geographical location, "schools," and occasionally further considerations (e.g., instrumental medium): in this section he discusses the different kinds of sonatas in several countries up to the time of Haydn and Mozart, and then he devotes a chapter to the latter two composers and a chapter to Beethoven. The book is illustrated with many musical

examples drawn mainly from unpublished materials. The tone of the discussion is scholarly and technical, although not overly so. The study makes for very interesting reading for both the musicologist and theorist and the interested music lover. A monumental bibliography and an index conclude the book.

Rosen's books mix interesting and highly informed scholarly discourse with entertaining prose, all generously seasoned with excursions into other domains, both musical and literary, and a number of "high-level pronouncements incapable of proof or disproof" (Newman). ROSEN (1980) is lavishly endowed with musical examples that support the author's examination of the several possible forms of a movement or composition in sonata form. At the beginning, Rosen offers a summary of the history of the definition of sonata form and explains why they do not work well for the 18th century. He then studies the social function of several genres, both those using and those not using sonata form, and links some of these genres together (e.g., he emphasizes the common function of vocal aria and concerto, in both of which the solo performer counted more than the composer and the execution more than the work). He argues the important point that sonata form made it possible for instrumental genres, such as the symphony, to "take over from drama not only the expression of sentiment but the narrative effect of dramatic action, of intrigue and resolution" by providing a climax and a denouement, a closure in which everything is resolved. The next chapters explore forms related to sonata style: ternary and binary form, aria, and concerto and then sonata forms themselves in great detail (six chapters are devoted to this topic). The last two chapters explore sonata forms in Beethoven and Schubert's music and then after Beethoven. The book will please both the scholar and the amateur, for despite the technical language, all points are expressed clearly, convincingly, and tantalizingly. There is no bibliography (Rosen refers the reader to the excellent one in Newman's book), but the reader will find an extremely detailed index.

ROSEN (1971) (which in its latest edition is accompanied by a CD on which the author plays some examples at the piano) includes several sections pertinent to our subject, but these are embedded in a larger, more general discussion of the classical style. A very detailed index will help the reader find the relevant passages. Worth singling out are the discussions of the origins of the classical style and the coherence of the classical musical language; these parts of the text consider most of the elements of classical sonatas and present some particular examples of such compositions. A huge section on Beethoven's *Hammerklavier* sonata adds to the picture of the composer's freedom within the genre. This book is worth reading cover to cover.

SHEDLOCK's book has the advantages and disadvantages of being a pioneer work. It was the first attempt at a general view of the sonata. Newman oversaw its reprint in facsimile and added an extensive introduction. The errors and shortcomings are comparatively few. However, readers should be aware that the book predates important advances in bibliographic and historical research and that the study reflects outmoded historical views (the author, like most people at the time, was concerned mainly with tracing the evolution of sonata form). The sonatas that he takes into account are relatively few and reflect a personal choice. However, Shedlock richly illustrates his analyses with music and translations of contemporary sources and inscriptions, and he never shies away from giving his opinion of a work. In Newman's words, "Shedlock's book remains a worthwhile, highly readable account."

ALEXANDRA AMATI-CAMPERI

Sonata: Romantic

Dale, Kathleen, *Nineteenth-Century Piano Music: A Handbook for Pianists,* London: Oxford University Press, 1954

Kirby, F.E., *Music for Piano: A Short History,* Portland, Oregon: Amadeus Press, 1995

Newman, William S., *The Sonata since Beethoven,* Chapel Hill: University of North Carolina Press, 1969; 3rd edition, New York: Norton, 1983

Rosen, Charles, *The Romantic Generation,* Cambridge, Massachusetts: Harvard University Press, 1995

————, *Sonata Forms,* New York: Norton, 1980; revised edition, 1988

Todd, R. Larry, editor, *Nineteenth-Century Piano Music,* New York: Schirmer Books, 1990

Although the sonata is identified largely with the 18th century and was considered an anachronism by progressive 19th-century composers, it is encountered frequently in the romantic era, transmogrified in a panoply of ingenious ways. Indeed, the first dilemma encountered in researching the sonata in the 19th century is one of nomenclature. The conundrum dates at least back to Beethoven, whose two piano sonatas, op. 27, are marked "quasi una fantasia"; literally, sonatas that resemble fantasies. Liszt called one of his major piano works, *Après une lecture du Dante,* "fantasia quasi sonata," but curiously, this work has become known as the *Dante Sonata,* not the *Dante Fantasia.* Schubert unambiguously calls one of his finest works the *Wanderer Fantasy,* but it is in four distinct movements and is, in its external trappings, a sonata. Schumann's Fantasy in C major, op. 17, is in three movements and is a sonata in all but name, and his Piano Sonata in F minor, op. 14, which assuredly is a sonata, he subtitled "Concerto without Orchestra." Although this is not the place to decide what is and is not a sonata, readers should be aware that research into the romantic sonata inevitably entails works that fail to subscribe to the textbook notion of what a sonata is or should be.

Readers should also be cautioned that many books on the sonata, including three of those discussed below, deal only with the piano sonata. This should not be taken to imply that sonatas for other instruments are unimportant, but to point to the paucity of writings on the sonata per se, especially in its 19th-century forms. Monographs on individual composers, especially Beethoven, Schubert, Chopin, Schumann, Liszt, and Brahms, include discussions of sonatas.

Given the importance in the romantic era of shorter works, including dances, studies, and character pieces, it is somewhat surprising that DALE devotes 4 of 12 chapters to the sonata. She gives two full chapters to Beethoven, one to Weber and Schubert, and one to later 19th-century composers: Mendelssohn (whose three piano sonatas rarely receive much attention), Chopin, Schumann, Brahms, Liszt, and Grieg. Dale addresses a wealth of forms and styles, from works that are not "so unusual in shape to be unrecognizable" as sonatas to Liszt's Sonata in B minor, which comprises "within its scope some of the distinguishing characteristics of traditional movements, the structural principles of first-movement form and the elements of variation and fugue." Dale's book is intended primarily for the amateur pianist, but it neatly encapsulates the history of the sonata in the 19th century and serves as a practical introduction to the topic.

KIRBY devotes three chapters of his detailed survey of the history of keyboard music to the romantic era. He dispenses summarily with Weber and Mendelssohn, but Schubert receives careful attention. A chronological listing of Schubert's piano sonatas is broken down into five periods, and the general features and distinguishing characteristics of the form and structure of the works of each period are identified. Schumann's unsuccessful early attempts at writing sonatas are attributed, in part, "to the preference for the small form at the time and the general decline of the large form." Kirby considers Chopin's piano sonatas as continuing the 18th-century sonata tradition inherited by way of Beethoven and Schubert, but Liszt's *Dante Sonata* is viewed, reasonably, as a symphonic poem for solo instrument "that in size and scope corresponds to a sonata." The focus of the discussion of Liszt's Sonata in B minor is its reliance on thematic transformation for formal unity; the four principal themes are given in musical examples so that the work's cyclical form can be easily apprehended. Again, a parallel is established between this work and the composer's orchestral tone poems. Kirby notes that Brahms, like Schumann, wrote sonatas early in his career before developing a preference for small-scale forms. Brahms's three piano sonatas are considered rather extreme works in which overall unity is of utmost concern. Kirby takes pains, using musical examples, to elucidate the larger structural issues with which Brahms grapples, leading to an unlikely alliance, in this one regard, between Brahms and Liszt. In the chapter on the later 19th century, Kirby surveys piano music by country of origin, mentioning, for example, in the section on the Germanic countries, the piano sonatas of such lesser-known figures as Adolf Jensen, Julius Reubke, Robert Fuchs, and Felix Draeseke. In short, Kirby's overview of the 19th-century piano sonata is quite comprehensive, even though its context is a general survey of piano literature from the early 18th century to the present day.

NEWMAN's study of the sonata since Beethoven is as valuable as his volumes on the sonata in the baroque and classical eras. Although published over 30 years ago, this book remains the most exhaustive investigation of the romantic sonata to date. After defining the parameters of his study, which makes for good reading in itself, Newman explores the romantic concept of the sonata and its role in 19th-century society, the instruments and performance practices of the romantic era, and the form, structure, and style of the sonata in the early, high, and late romantic periods. Only then does he embark on a tour of the sonata in Germany and Austria, France and the Low Countries, Great Britain and Scandinavia, the Iberian Peninsula, Central Europe, Russia, and the United States. He analyzes the works of major composers and cites those of countless others to arrive at an account of the genre that is meticulous yet panoramic in scope. The breadth of Newman's study enables the reader to grasp the romantic sonata as a whole, while its scholarship is rigorous enough to engage the most jaded reader. The bibliography, running to almost 60 pages, lists sources embracing virtually every aspect of the romantic sonata; its only shortcoming is that it is now dated.

Had ROSEN (1980) considered sonata forms in isolation, independent of the contexts in which they occur, his book would have had only partial relevance to the romantic sonata. He is concerned not with the sonata as a three- or four-movement structure but with sonata form, found in the first and, less frequently, in the other movements of a variety of musical genres from the 18th century onward. He does, however, consider sonata forms—he prefers the plural—in the context of several different genres, including the aria, the concerto, and the sonata proper, and at the close of the book he turns his attention to sonata forms in the 19th century. Rosen probes the form of the first movement of Schubert's Sonata for Piano and Violin in G minor, D. 408, because it "represents a break with classical procedure," and explores the first-movement development sections of Schubert's last two piano sonatas, D. 959 and D. 960, citing the "oscillation between two tonal levels" as "perhaps the greatest of all" Schubert's innovations in sonata form. In the final chapter, which concerns sonata forms after Beethoven, Rosen points out that Hummel, in the finale of his Piano Sonata in F minor, op. 20, quotes Mozart and that Brahms, in the opening of his Piano Sonata in C major, op. 1, quotes Beethoven, as if to acknowledge that these works, and perhaps sonatas in general, are rooted a priori in the classical era. While Brahms found 18th-century genres congenial, other composers believed that the premises that make large-scale structures, including sonatas, appropriate vehicles for sonata form, were no longer viable after the first quarter of the 19th century. To support this view, Rosen scrutinizes key relationships in Schumann's Piano Sonata in F-sharp minor, op. 11, providing a detailed comparison of its exposition and recapitulation. Rosen's approach here and elsewhere is analytical, and his focus on specific issues makes his book of interest to those who have a broad understanding of the sonata's form and structure. Yet his premise that "there are many sonatas more closely related to concertos, arias, and even fugues than to other sonatas" and his probing analyses of several works help to explain if not resolve the ambiguities that arise from the romantic reinterpretation of a classical form that Schumann himself had once pronounced dead.

ROSEN (1995) sets the stage for a discussion of the principal composers of the romantic era from the death of Beethoven (1827) to the death of Chopin (1849) by examining correlatives between 19th-century musical form and the literary fragment, and between music and nature. In subsequent chapters, he considers the music of individual composers, and in the first two of three chapters on Chopin, and in the chapters on Liszt, Mendelssohn, and Schumann, he brings his critical acumen to bear on the sonata in the romantic era. Of special importance is his discussion of Chopin's Piano Sonata in B-flat minor, op. 35, which begins by noting that most editions have the repeat of the exposition commencing in the wrong measure. Because this misprint "has gone not only uncorrected but seemingly unnoticed for more than a century," Rosen reasons that we should "give very little weight to the standard critical opinion that Chopin's treatment of sonata form is uninteresting." Rosen's appraisal of Liszt is no less novel than his view of Chopin; he pronounces Liszt's Sonata in B minor seriously flawed and, in any event, not truly representative of its composer. He identifies Liszt's sources for the sonata as musical (Beethoven and Schubert), literary (Byron, Gothic novels, and Lamartine's religious poetry), and even pictorial (the Sainte-Suplice style of religious art). Rosen concludes that the association of sonatas and other large-scale 19th-century genres with the sublime is unwarranted, because shorter works such as etudes and character pieces may actually come much closer to the mark.

TODD brings together leading scholars of 19th-century music to consider, each in a separate chapter, the piano music of Beethoven, Schubert, Weber, Mendelssohn, Chopin, Schumann, Brahms, and Liszt. Although each of these composers contributed significant works to the sonata repertoire, the piano sonatas of Beethoven and Schubert receive particular attention in the chapters by William Kinderman and Eva Badura-Skoda, respectively. Kinderman deals with Beethoven's early, middle, and late sonatas, drawing numerous parallels with Beethoven's other major works. He also delves into Beethoven's innovations in form and structure, comparing one work against another in a clear and thoughtful manner. The bulk of Badura-Skoda's essay on Schubert is devoted to the sonatas, which she first surveys and then discusses individually, providing numerous musical examples to elucidate the text. This article is perhaps the most interesting short survey of Schubert's sonatas and is a good starting point for further research. Other chapters discuss sonatas in less detail, but the entire book helps to place the romantic sonata in the broader context of 19th-century repertoire. A number of insights about the sonata are scattered throughout the book, which help to distinguish 18th-century from 19th-century contributions to the genre. Performance practices are also discussed, and readers may find interesting Robert S. Winter's chapter on "Orthodoxies, Paradoxes, and Contradictions," which includes a table comparing the tempi, variation by variation, of 16 different recordings of the second movement of Beethoven's last piano sonata. This book should be read cover to cover, because much of relevance to the 19th-century sonata is embedded in intelligent discussions of other topics. Each chapter concludes with a selected bibliography current to 1990.

GLEN CARRUTHERS

Song: England

Banfield, Stephen, *Sensibility and English Song: Critical Studies of the Early 20th Century*, Cambridge: Cambridge University Press, 1985

Banfield, Stephen, editor, *The Twentieth Century*, The Blackwell History of Music in Britain, vol. 6, Oxford: Blackwell, 1995

Bray, Roger, editor, *The Sixteenth Century*, The Blackwell History of Music in Britain, vol. 2, Oxford: Blackwell, 1995

Johnstone, H. Diack, and Roger Fiske, editors, *The Eighteenth Century*, The Blackwell History of Music in Britain, vol. 4, Oxford: Blackwell, 1990

Karolyi, Otto, *Modern British Music: The Second British Musical Renaissance: From Elgar to P. Maxwell Davies*, Rutherford, New Jersey: Fairleigh Dickinson University Press, and London: Associated University Presses, 1994

Northcote, Sydney, *Byrd to Britten: A Survey of English Song*, London: Baker, and New York: Roy, 1966

Spink, Ian, *English Song from Dowland to Purcell*, London: Batsford, and New York: Scribner, 1974

Spink, Ian, editor, *The Seventeenth Century*, The Blackwell History of Music in Britain, vol. 3, Oxford: Blackwell, 1992

Stevens, Denis, editor, *A History of Song*, London: Hutchinson, 1960; New York: Norton, 1961

Temperley, Nicholas, editor, *The Romantic Age, 1800–1914*, The Blackwell History of Music in Britain, vol. 5, London: Athlone, 1981; Oxford: Blackwell, 1988

Students and researchers interested in English Song have their choice between one-volume general histories, such as Northcote or Stevens, and works that specialize in particular chronological periods, such as Banfield or Karolyi. In addition, the six volumes of *The Blackwell History of Music in Britain* contain well-researched sections on vocal music that make the studies invaluable for the more sophisticated student. The series, edited by Spink, is roughly broken down by century. Each volume deals separately with various genres; individual sections on the repertoire of English song begin with the second volume.

BRAY's work on the 16th century includes Tim Carter's extensive essay concerning secular vocal music. Carter examines the heavy Burgundian influences on the fledgling English solo song, placing the origins in a social and political context. This emphasis on historical background is complimented with musical examples and discussion of their manuscript sources. Carter also considers the song texts, especially those of the "new" Italiante poets of the 1580s.

SPINK's (1992) volume on the 17th century begins with a 66-page essay by Spink, "Music and Society," that gives a historical framework for ensuing musical developments. "Vocal Music I: Up to 1660" by David Greer covers composers from Thomas Morley through Robert Ramsey and John Hilton, while Spink's "Vocal Music II: From 1660" discusses John Banister through Purcell. Biographical details are included, but the emphasis remains on song literature and how it reflects its social context. Performers should note the helpful attention given to performance practice issues such as "gracing" (ornamentation) and appropriate figured bass realization.

JOHNSTONE and FISKE's concern with 18th-century musical life in Britain begins with examination of the social context by Fiske: "Music and Society." Secular songs are treated in two divisions: 1700 to 1760 and 1760 to 1800. This separation corresponds to the stylistic shifts that occurred as the galant style grew in popularity throughout England. Few of the vast numbers of art songs published during the 18th century are well-known today, but many largely neglected song composers are discussed in this anthology: Richard Leveridge, Henry Caney, Eccles, Weldong, Maurice Green, Croft, Hayes, through Boyce and Arne. The lesser attention given to English song in this century reflects the British preference throughout the century for music from Italy in this genre as well as others.

TEMPERLEY begins with a valuable discussion of "Music in Society" before launching into specific genres. Ballad and art song are covered separately. Temperley discusses the assertion of national character along with other stylistic characteristics in ballads, and he clarifies his arguments with various popular examples by Bishop, Balfe, Hullah, Sullivan, and Clay. Temperley's clear writing and carefully selected illustrations make this volume a valuable reference. Geoffrey Bush's section on the art song ranges from Mozart's pupil, Thomas Attwood, through the Germanic influences of Sterndale Bennet and Henry Pierson to the later romantics: Arthur Sullivan, Parry, and Stanford, and, more tangentially, Elgar and Delius. Lesser-known composers are noted, and the writing is succinct and well-illustrated with musical examples. Because the emphasis is on musical trends and historical context, those wishing more biographical information will have to go elsewhere.

BANFIELD (1995) divides the discussion into two categories: popular and art music. Patrick O'Connor discusses popular song along with its various influences: American musical comedies, European operettas, and music halls. Banfield covers the songs of Ivor Novello, Noel Coward, Vivian Ellis, Noel Gay, Lionel Bart, and Andrew Lloyd Webber, while providing pertinent musical examples. This brief section provides an overview but lacks the in-depth coverage characteristic of the series' more valuable sections. Stephen Banfield writes a persuasive essay on vocal music with an extensive portion on the outpourings of solo song that flourished along with post-Victorian poetry of Housman, Hardy, and Yeats. Banfield first addresses composers of the pre-World War II era: Gurney, Warlock, Vaughan Williams, Holst, Moeran, Grainger, Butterworth, Quilter, Ireland, and Finzi. The author presents Britten effectively by juxtaposing his works to the works of other composers and offering well-chosen examples. After the section on Britten, the discussion is less focused and less compelling.

BANFIELD (1985) gives a valuable overview of English song in 1900 before he examines the most notable 20th-century composers of English song. The first volume of this two-volume work is concerned with the emergence of "sensibility" and its relevance to romantic song in the works of Victorian, post-Victorian, and Edwardian composers. This volume also explores the impact of World War I as well as the "lyrical impulse between the wars" as exemplified by Ivor Gurney, Gerald Finzi, and the poetry of Housman. The second volume relates the slow decline of "sensibility" and the rise of modernism in the songs of Vaughan Williams, Rubbra, Holst, Bridge, Goosens, Warlock, and Britten. The exhaustive song lists for more than 50 British composers add to the usefulness of this book.

SPINK's (1974) critical examination of English Song in the 17th century outlines the shift from the lute songs and continuo songs of John Dowland to the songs of Henry Purcell and John Blow. Spink's work can be seen as a companion to his study of English songs in the *Musica Britannica* series, as he places more emphasis on discussing the songs than biographical details of the composers.

NORTHCOTE provides a good overview for the beginning student of song literature. Northcote confines his discussion to a few composers in each period. The lack of depth limits the usefulness of this resource for more advanced students.

STEVENS traces the development of song literature from the Middle Ages through the modern era, with a concluding essay on the genre by composer Michael Tippett. The concise coverage of English song by Arthur Jacobs provides a convenient overview of the history of song, although those concerned with composers working after 1950 are best served elsewhere.

KAROLYI finds its most valuable niche in the post–1950 realm. Proponents of music of the later half of the 20th century will appreciate information on composers ranging from Roberto Gerhard, Egon Wellesz, Mátyás Seiber, Elizabeth Lutyens, Humphrey Searle, Thea Musgrave, and others, including Michael Tippet and Peter Maxwell Davies. The entries on each composer are introductory in nature and lack any musical examples, but the wealth of information on more contemporary music, especially works by women composers, makes this resource valuable.

EILEEN L. STREMPEL

Sound Recording

Eisenberg, Evan, *The Recording Angel: Explorations in Phonography,* New York: McGraw-Hill, 1987
Gaisberg, Fred W. *The Music Goes Round,* New York: Macmillan, 1942; as *Music on Record,* London: Hale, 1946
Gelatt, Roland, *The Fabulous Phonograph,* Philadelphia, Pennsylvania: Lippincott, 1955; 2nd revised edition, New York: Macmillan, 1977
Harvith, John, and Susan Edwards Harvith, editors, *Edison, Musicians, and the Phonograph: A Century in Retrospect,* New York: Greenwood Press, 1987
Millard, A.J., *America on Record: A History of Recorded Sound,* Cambridge: Cambridge University Press, 1995
Philip, Robert, *Early Recordings and Musical Style: Changing Tastes in Instrumental Performance, 1900–1950,* Cambridge: Cambridge University Press, 1992
Read, Oliver, and Walter Leslie Welch, *From Tin Foil to Stereo: Evolution of the Phonograph,* Indianapolis: Sams, 1959; 2nd edition, 1976; as *From Tin Foil to Stereo: The Acoustic Years of the Recording Industry 1877–1929,* edited by Leah Brodbeck Stenzel Burt, Gainesville: University Press of Florida, 1994

Sound recording has fascinated writers since its near-mythic creation in the workshop of Thomas Edison in 1877. Early works on the subject typically served as guides to the use and maintenance of the machinery. Later, surveys of phonographic history as well as biographies and memoirs of important figures in recording became the staple of the literature; Gelatt and Gaisberg are early examples. More recently, writers such as Eisenberg and Philip have begun exploring new areas. Readers seeking further information on sound recording (particularly on historical and technical matters) should consult the specialized journals, including *Recorded Sound* (1961–84) and the *ARSC Journal* (1982–).

GAISBERG was an influential figure in early recording history. His memoirs begin in the United States in the 1890s, when he was an assistant to Emile Berliner, the inventor of disk recording. Later chapters cover his work in London with His Master's Voice (later the Gramophone Company), where he worked closely with such musical luminaries as Enrico Caruso, Edward Elgar, Fritz Kreisler, Ignace Paderewski, and Adelina Patti. Gaisberg's autobiography is valuable as a first-hand account of the development of recording technology and the recorded music industry. More information on Gaisberg and his times may be found in Jerrold Moore's biography, *A Matter of Records* (1977).

GELATT's entertaining and well-written survey of recording history was the first of its kind in English. He devotes chapters to the scientific, business, and musical aspects of recording, although his attention is most closely drawn to the musical side, particularly classical music. In this respect, Gelatt's work may be contrasted with Read and Welch's more technically minded survey. For the revised edition Gelatt adds three chapters covering stereo and popular music. The text of the earlier editions remains for the most part untouched.

READ and WELCH's text remains the standard work on the business and science of early sound recording. The authors provide not only a richly detailed history but a valuable sourcebook, generously reprinting technical drawings, patent applications, and countless photographs of early machines. The density of detail and occasional technical language, however, may make difficult reading for the uninitiated. Readers should also be aware of the authors' advocacy of Thomas Edison, which at times threatens the work's objectivity. The first edition chronicles the phonograph's history to 1959; the 1976 edition covers later developments but leaves the earlier chapters largely unaltered. The revised 1994 edition is essentially a different book—it treats only the period between 1877 and 1929, expanding on the earlier chapters of the previous editions.

EISENBERG focuses on the phenomenon of record collecting and the transformation of music through its capture and preservation on disk. The former he documents through anecdotal case studies of record enthusiasts, such as Clarence, who lives in squalor with his world-class collection, or Tomàs, a fan of opera recordings who expounds on the virtues of solitary listening.

The latter he examines in philosophical ruminations on the nature of recording and its influence on musical life. The journalistic style and discursive narrative are part of the charm of this provocative book, which questions the long-held assumption that recordings simply preserve music.

HARVITH and HARVITH offer a document of unique importance to the history of sound recording. The book collects more than 40 interviews with notable musicians, composers, record producers, and scholars about the impact of recording on musical life. The detailed and candid responses the authors draw from their subjects reveal a number of surprising insights. Many of the interviewees, for example, question the musical and documentary value of recordings; others argue that the demands of recording significantly affect the way musicians perform, both in the studio and in concert. An informative introduction identifies recurring themes and points of difference among the interviews.

PHILIP argues that recordings provide a largely untapped source of evidence about the performance of classical music in the early 20th century. Based on his study of countless recordings and the practices they reveal, he documents changes in approaches to rhythm, vibrato, and portamento in instrumental performance. For each of these developments, Philip surveys writings on the particular practice and analyzes recordings for evidence of trends. He comes to two main conclusions: that what is prescribed in the pedagogical literature and what is heard on recordings are often at odds; and that there has been a general trend over the 20th century toward more precise, consistent, and less idiosyncratic recordings. Although Philip's analyses are convincing and his conclusions compelling, he may be faulted for taking the documentary value of recordings at face value. His claim that "early recordings . . . present us with real history" ignores evidence that the exigencies of recording have in fact influenced performance styles (as demonstrated in Harvith and Harvith). Nevertheless, this is an important book and a seminal work in a growing area of musical scholarship.

MILLARD's survey of sound recording in the United States is intended for college students but is suitable for all readers. His scope is broad, spanning the acoustic, electronic, and digital eras of recording. This work's strong points include its coverage of popular music; its attention to the role of various communication technologies (the telegraph, telephone, radio, and film) in the development of recording; and its treatment of the recorded sound industry, from manufacturing to marketing. Millard presents his observations and arguments in clear, readable prose. The annotated bibliography and discography, as well as the multiple indices, are valuable resources for the reader.

MARK KATZ

Sousa, John Philip 1854–1932

United States composer and bandleader

Bierley, Paul E., *John Philip Sousa, American Phenomenon*, revised edition, Columbus, Ohio: Integrity Press, 1986
———, *The Works of John Philip Sousa*, Columbus, Ohio: Integrity Press, 1984
Chase, Gilbert, "Music for the Millions," in *America's Music: From the Pilgrims to the Present*, revised 3rd edition, Urbana: University of Illinois Press, 1987
Newsom, Jon, editor, *Perspectives on John Philip Sousa*, Washington, D.C.: Library of Congress, 1983
Sousa, John Philip, *Marching Along: Recollections of Men, Women, and Music*, Boston: Hale, Cushman and Flint, 1928

These days it is difficult to imagine that a military bandleader could rank among a nation's finest musicians, and, indeed, be favorably considered alongside the most eminent entertainers of his era, but that is precisely what John Philip Sousa was able to accomplish during his years as the director of the United States Marine Band and as leader of his own renowned Sousa Band. Today we know Sousa almost exclusively by virtue of a number of his marches that have evolved from their former status as mere popular ditties of a bygone day to their current positions as monuments of American music, compositions that are inextricably linked to their period and to the collective American musical experience. Sousa's incredible output in a number genres other than his famous marches, his common-sense managerial abilities, and his partly realized literary aspirations are little known to most of us. Sousa's life and music are, however, surprisingly complex, and only recently have writers and scholars begun to take seriously the challenge of interpreting his considerable musical and cultural contributions to the nation.

CHASE's brief consideration of Sousa is a fine starting point for discovering the impact that the "March King" had on music in the United States and on U.S. society at large. Chase discusses Sousa's upbringing in a musical family and his subsequent membership in the United States Marine Band, noting along the way Sousa's increasing interest in composition. Chase also mentions the best-known members of Sousa's bands and discusses Sousa's most important compositions. Interesting passages address the popularity of Sousa's music in various arrangements for unusual instruments and his flirtations with the recording industry.

NEWSOM's engaging volume comprises a mixed bag of essays and includes the editor's own introduction and seven articles by various authors as well as an extended photo section. The essays include scholarly and analytical contributions as well as personal reminiscences. Several contributions are particularly noteworthy: U.S. composer William Schuman's "Semper Fidelis" remarks on the Sousa mystique on the occasion of Sousa's posthumous enshrinement into the Hall of Fame for Great Americans, and renowned bandmaster Frederick Fennell writes "The Sousa March: A Personal View," his often penetrating analysis and appreciation of Sousa's compositions, generously peppered with musical examples. Other contributions include Neil Harris's "John Philip Sousa and the Culture of Reassurance"; James R. Smart's "Genesis of a March: The Stars and Stripes Forever"; Margaret L. Brown's "David Blakely, Manager of Sousa's Band"; Pauline Norton's "Nineteenth Century American March Music and John Philip Sousa"; and "A Few Observations and Memories," by John Philip Sousa III. Although a few of the essays will be most appropriate for musicians, musicologists, and bandmasters, the interested reader can learn a great deal about Sousa and his music, as well as his considerable significance in his own era.

SOUSA's autobiography is an engagingly written work that provides details and anecdotes from his first years until the late 1920s. Sousa provides fascinating and often humorous insights into his earliest musical experiences, family life, his escapades with the Marine Band and his resulting working relationships with five presidents, and, of course, information about his own band and his subsequent fame and fortune. The book contains some documentary information, including often extensive newspaper reviews of his band's performances, passages from various letters written to him and by him, and a number of seldom-seen photos. Readers will especially appreciate Sousa's enthralling tales of his life on the road and his insights into the characters of the many people he encountered during his travels around the world.

BIERLEY (1984) is an updated version of his earlier reference book, *John Philip Sousa: A Descriptive Catalog of His Works* (1973). This revision is a thorough consideration of Sousa's works, with complete listings of all Sousa's music in all genres. Listings, categorized by genre, are prefaced by often lengthy essays that attempt to place Sousa's music in a cultural context. In addition, each work listed is accompanied by remarks and anecdotes regarding its genesis, first performance, dedication information, manuscript location, and publication information. The section on Sousa's operettas includes casting requirements and synopses, and Sousa's literary works are summarized with commentary. The book also contains numerous photos and plates. Although this book is written primarily for performers and researchers, the lay reader will glean much from Bierley's comprehensive knowledge of Sousa's music and his engaging, conversational writing style.

BIERLEY (1986), an entertaining and informative biography, is the standard source of information about the composer. Not structured in the same manner as the typical life-and-works volume, this book is cast in six sections and does not follow a chronological order. Rather, it begins with an assessment of Sousa's impact on his own times and the music of his day and is then followed by a brief biography section that gives the basic facts of his life. An engrossing essay on Sousa's character and his hobbies follows, and an important chapter, "Sousa's Philosophy of Music," includes a summation of the composer's thoughts about composing, conducting, programming, instrumentation, and the future of music in the United States. Sousa's own legendary band is thoroughly discussed, and the book closes with four appendices that list Sousa's compositions, residences, family members, and the highlights of his military career. Bierley's often penetrating remarks and encyclopedic knowledge of the events of Sousa's life make this a fascinating and invaluable volume.

BILL F. FAUCETT

South Africa *see* Africa

Spain: General Studies

Bussey, William M., *French and Italian Influence on the Zarzuela 1700–1770*, Ann Arbor, Michigan: UMI Research Press, 1982

Chase, Gilbert, *The Music of Spain*, New York: Norton, 1941; 2nd edition, New York: Dover, 1959

Laird, Paul R., *Towards a History of the Spanish Villancico*, Warren, Michigan: Harmonie Park Press, 1997

Livermore, Ann, *A Short History of Spanish Music*, London: Duckworth, and New York: Vienna House, 1972

Marco, Tomás, *Spanish Music in the Twentieth Century*, translated by Cola Franzen, Cambridge, Massachusetts: Harvard University Press, 1993

Starkie, Walter, *Spain: A Musician's Journey through Time and Space*, 3 vols., Geneva: Edisli, 1958

Stevenson, Robert Murrell, *Spanish Cathedral Music in the Golden Age*, Berkeley: University of California Press, 1961
———, *Spanish Music in the Age of Columbus*, The Hague: Nijhoff, 1964

Trend, J.B., *The Music of Spanish History to 1600*, London: Oxford University Press, 1926; reprint, 1964

The works included in the above list complement each other in rather unexpected ways. The unique relationships of Arabic music and folk music to Spanish art music are important elements in the earlier studies. With the general expansion of musical knowledge, studies of music history in particular time periods have been superseded by books on specific topics in Spanish music, such as the *villancico*.

The books by Trend, Chase, Starkie, and Livermore are introductory guides to the music of Spain. TREND, writing in 1926, introduces music up to the death of Tomás Luis de Victoria in 1611. He concentrates on early Spanish monophonic and polyphonic songs and offers some thoughts about the music sung by the Arabs living in Spain during this period. Although CHASE devotes a substantial portion of his book to music from the Renaissance and baroque periods, he also highlights composers such as Domenico Scarlatti, Albéniz, Granados, and Falla. Folk song and dance music in Spain and the New World, along with the music of Portugal, constitute important elements in his understanding of Spanish music. Liberally illustrated with printed musical examples, color plates, and black-and-white reproductions of woodcuts, STARKIE brings the history and culture of Spain alive in a nontechnical manner. His charismatic storytelling abilities frame the discussions of the music, creating vignettes of time and place as he enlivens the chronological data presented in the first volume. The second volume deals with folk music from more than a dozen regions of Spain, concentrating on the music of Andalusia; Starkie concludes with a summary of music by Spanish composers in the first half of the 20th century. By weaving references to folk music into the body of her text, LIVERMORE hints that folk traditions were perhaps more strongly integrated into the life and the art music of Spain than in other areas. Covering many of the same topics as Chase, Livermore adds a number of 20th-century Latin American composers to her overview.

Stevenson's studies of Spanish liturgical music during the Renaissance have influenced almost all subsequent publications on this aspect of music history. Archival, historical, and contextual information frame his analysis of the compositions and musical styles. The majority of STEVENSON (1961) examines the life and contributions of Cristóbal Morales, Francisco Guerrero, and Victoria. Shorter sections on Juan Navarro, Alonso Lobo, Sebastián de Vivanco, and Juan Esquivel, among others, round out the author's picture of liturgical music. Stevenson admits that his discussion of this rich repertory is inherently limited by his decision to focus on music from only a few composers, but he suggests that perhaps the selected figures should really be seen more as "mere peaks in a chain of Alps." STEVENSON (1964) surveys medieval music, early Spanish theorists, and sacred and secular music of the 15th century. Most unusual is his section on the early printed Spanish liturgical books (missals, manuals, and processionals), which often contain melodies particular to the Spanish church and used by local composers. Both books provide a wealth of information and remain the starting point for many subsequent researchers. Stevenson's publications are designed for the advanced student and sometimes involve technical descriptions of the music.

BUSSEY outlines the multidimensional influences that Italian and French music and culture had on Spanish life and its native theatrical musical form, the zarzuela. Aspects of foreign influence on the music, its style, Spanish music theory, culture, and local politics are discussed chronologically. The author reviews valuable information about the zarzuela actors and singers, the libretto plots, and the financing of selected productions. Those with a general interest in the zarzuela will benefit from his simple explanation of poetic terminology and the glossary of Spanish terms. The appendices, especially those listing known zarzuelas and others describing the contents of the documents and manuscripts consulted may assist researchers.

The role of Spanish composers is often overlooked in 20th-century music histories. MARCO tackles this topic with breadth and understanding, identifying the composers, their training, and musical directions and explaining changes in financial support and community and national involvement. He classifies the composers in different categories, sometimes borrowing terms from Spanish literature or the other arts to identify various shades of nationalism (for example, *alhambrismo* or *casticista*). Although the majority of the presentation is chronological, there are separate chapters on influential individuals, as well as on groups of composers specializing in church music or the zarzuela. In the latter two cases, special attention is paid to the effects of political, social, or ecclesiastical actions on the compositional environment. Marcos introduces many new or little-known composers to the reader and may thus inspire interest in hearing or performing works by these artists. He discusses certain composers or generations of composers with perception and thoughtfulness, synthesizing their style in a manner easily understood by the reader, but this approach is not uniformly applied.

In the first full-length English-language survey of the *villancico,* LAIRD outlines the musical development of the genre from the polyphonic beginnings in the mid–15th century to about 1800. Admitting the genre remains understudied with thousands of untranscribed examples still in archives, he has chosen the title of his book carefully, trying to demonstrate "an observable, continuous history." His frequent musical examples are taken from the main *cancioneros musicales* or the works of composers from Pedro Ruimonte (Rimonte) to Antonio Soler. In the process, the author demonstrates the shift in the Renaissance *villancico* from a popular form of entertainment to the serious contrapuntal work of the later 16th century. A consideration of features of the harmony, texture, and form in *villancicos* from the 17th and 18th centuries highlight how this highly popular form integrated new musical styles. Although Laird focuses on musical rather than poetical analyses, understanding the content, authorship, and transmission of the poetic texts (sometimes published in collections or as *pliegros sueltos*) constitute an important facet in the scholarship on the cross-fertilization of the genre. The dissemination of poetic texts underscores the circles of *villancico* composers and their methods of exchanging ideas and music.

GRETA J. OLSON

See also Flamenco

Spain: Musical Centers

Knighton, Tess, "Ritual and Regulations: The Organization of the Castilian Royal Chapel during the Reign of the Catholic Monarchs," in *De musica hispana et aliis: Miscelánea en honor al Prof. Dr. José López-Calo, S.J. en su 65 compleaños,* edited by Emilio Casares and Carlos Villanueva, 291–320, Santiago de Compostela: Universidade de Santiago de Compostela, 1990
Nelson, Kathleen E., *Medieval Liturgical Music of Zamora,* Ottawa: Institute of Mediaeval Music, 1996
Noone, Michael J., *Music and Musicians in the Escorial Liturgy under the Habsburgs, 1563–1700,* Rochester, New York: University of Rochester Press, 1998
Stein, Louise K., *Songs of Mortals, Dialogues of the Gods: Music and Theatre in Seventeenth-Century Spain,* Oxford: Clarendon Press, and New York: Oxford University Press, 1993

Spain's rich musical traditions emerged in a number of active musical centers often patronized by the church, nobility, and general populace. Some of these centers featured music that was largely traditional or imported into Spain and are not considered in the present essay. Other areas of musical activity were strongly influenced by political or religious figures, as outlined by the writers discussed below. Although Spain continues to be an important musical center, studies of the institutions that supported music after the 17th century have not yet appeared in English.

The body of NELSON's study transcribes and analyzes monophonic and polyphonic musical fragments based on the Roman rite originating from the 12th to possibly the early 16th century. Most of the primary musical sources Nelson uses were recovered from book bindings currently housed in church archives in Zamora (a community in western Spain). However, the author indicates that "there is no immediate evidence in any of the fragments to say that their liturgical content was for the use of the Church of Zamora or of monastic or other religious establishments within the region of Zamora." Briefly and cogently, Nelson summarizes local and national changes in the liturgy from the 9th to the 12th centuries, along with selected information drawn from the surrounding monastic and collegiate communities. Chant notation discussed in Spanish theoretical works from the 15th and early 16th centuries is reviewed and subdivided according to the theorist's approach to the rhythmic interpretation of the notation (e.g., the equalist approach seen in the works of such authors as Domingo Marcos Durán or Gonzalo Martínez de Bizcargui, or the nonequalist approach of Guillermo de Podio and Juan Bermudo, among others). The music in this study includes not only various chants for the Mass Ordinary but also 5 *prosae* and 2 responsory *prosae,* 17 hymns, and 5 short polyphonic examples. The subsequent detailed analysis of the music and its notation may be beyond the grasp of most undergraduates, but the first several chapters of this book will enlighten the student interested in the monophonic and early polyphonic music of Spain.

KNIGHTON explores one of the important royal musical institutions, the Castilian royal chapel under the aegis of the Catholic monarchs Juan II, Enrique IV, Ferdinand and Isabella, Charles V, and Philip II. The constitutions governing the royal chapel are of a general nature, often dealing with a code of behavior that by 1504 would regulate the conduct of the nearly 150 adult members of the chapel. These constitutions provide a glimpse of the structure and activities (both musical and liturgical) of chapel members, which included the musicians Juan de Ancieta and Francisco de Peñalosa. Because the constitutions, as internal administrative documents, were not intended to explain or describe fully the system they encompassed, the author also draws on contemporary descriptions of the chapel to enhance our image of the musicians' routines and responsibilities. The picture, however, still remains fragmented. Nonetheless, Knighton advances our understanding of the activities and environment for liturgical music making in the Castilian royal court. Although this article does not contain technical musical terms, some ecclesiastical terminology is used, and readers will benefit if they have had an introduction to music making in monastic or cathedral settings.

NOONE explains how changes in patronage affected the music performed and produced by the members of the royal monastery San Lorenzo de El Escorial. The construction of the Escorial began in 1563, the author posits because Spain's most Catholic King, Philip II, sought a physical manifestation for his religious ideology. During his reign generous funding and meticulous attention were given not only to the palace construction and ornaments but also to the monastery's chapel, liturgy, and music so that elements conformed to a pious, austere, and Tridentine attitude. Only plainsong was initially permitted in the liturgy. But later in the 16th century, reports of the performance of polyphony in nonchapel locations appeared, and other statements suggest that improvised contrapuntal lines around the plainsong were condoned. During the reigns of subsequent monarchs, increasing freedom in the musical styles and performance practices of liturgical and devotional music at the Escorial were noted. In fact, during the reign of Philip III, music by Morales, Palestrina, Rogier, and others was included in the repertory. The transferral of various religious relics to the Escorial in 1684 and 1690 provided an opportunity for elaborate ceremonies involving the young King Charles II. These events were later recorded in commemorative literary and artistic works, complementing our knowledge of the music in the monastery and demonstrating the

degree to which the musical life in this institution changed during the 17th century.

Theatrical music, and especially operatic music, occupies a major segment of most surveys of music history, yet operatic music in 17th-century Spain has often been omitted or portrayed as less than enthusiastically received. STEIN refines our perception of early Spanish theatrical music, stating that "the seventeenth-century Spanish 'failure' . . . to replicate Italian opera was due to the deliberate refusal to cultivate it." Certainly, there were issues of class and national identity associated with the importation and patronage of Italian opera. However, Stein points out that long-standing and highly developed Spanish literary and theatrical conventions brought with them expectations for the use of some types of music or for certain types of texts to be associated with certain musical forms or styles. Some of these traditions extended back into the 16th century and continued through the 17th century. Masques, spectacle plays, semi-operas, operas, and zarzuelas were popular at the courts of Philip III, Philip IV, and Charles II. The argument developed by Stein relies on an examination of the extant music, librettos and plays, pertinent literary theories, and other relevant documents. Extensive discussions of the events leading up to the creation of the extant operas and a number of the stage works are combined with detailed analyses of plots and music. Also very useful are the numerous and sometimes lengthy musical examples, the tables of musical references found in the plays of Cervantes and Lope de Vega, and catalogs of court productions and known 17th-century Spanish theatrical songs.

GRETA J. OLSON

Spohr, Louis 1784–1859

German composer, violinist, and conductor

Berrett, Joshua, "Characteristic Conventions of Style in Selected Instrumental Works of Louis Spohr," Ph.D. dissertation, University of Michigan, 1974
Brown, Clive, *Louis Spohr: A Critical Biography*, Cambridge: Cambridge University Press, 1984
Spohr, Louis, *Louis Spohr's Autobiography*, London: Longman, 1865; reprint, New York: Da Capo Press, 1969
———, *The Musical Journeys of Louis Spohr*, edited by Henry Pleasants, Norman: University of Oklahoma Press, 1961

Any discussion of the publications by or about Louis Spohr inevitably centers on the composer's autobiography, which paints a vivid picture of musical life in the early 19th century. A talented violinist, conductor, and composer, Spohr toured throughout Europe, and in his autobiography, he incorporated comments from his diaries made during these trips. Particularly revealing are his observations on tastes and attitudes in foreign countries, especially Italy. The autobiography also records his opinions on the music of his contemporaries and his veneration for Mozart.

Although Spohr worked sporadically on his autobiography over a period of 12 years, it was unfinished at the time of his death in 1859. Because he had covered events only up to 1838, his family prepared a final chapter that dealt with the remaining years of his life. The autobiography was first published in German as *Louis Spohr's Selbstbiographie* (2 vols.) in 1860 and 1861. Two translations in English, neither complete, are available. The first, SPOHR (1865), is only slightly abridged, but the anonymous translation is marred by inaccuracies. Musical terminology in particular is often mistranslated. SPOHR (1961) concentrates on the composer's concert tours between 1801 and 1821. Consequently, Henry Pleasants's annotations are more felicitous, extensive, and helpful than the few notes in the anonymous translation.

BERRETT is valuable for its emphasis on Spohr's use of various compositional models from the late 18th century. The author shows how Spohr adapted elements of style and formal structure from figures such as Cherubini and Mozart, as well as the French violinists and composers, Rodolphe Kreutzer, Jacques Pierre Rode, and Pierre Baillot. Berrett also considers Spohr's relationship to later composers. Spohr's harmonic language and fondness for chromaticism, for instance, anticipate the music of Liszt and Wagner.

BROWN is the only comprehensive treatment in English of this composer. Brown approaches his subject in a straightforward manner. While drawing attention to Spohr's popularity during his lifetime and subsequent decline in critical estimation, Brown wisely refrains from making extravagant claims for his subject. Indeed, Brown's primary justification for this book is not to rehabilitate Spohr's reputation but rather to assess his importance in music history. Brown presents a sober evaluation of Spohr's music, often comparing it with that of the composer's contemporaries, and he points to pieces deserving a modest place in the repertoire.

KEITH HARRIS COCHRAN

Still, William Grant 1895–1978

United States composer

Arvey, Verna, *In One Lifetime*, Fayetteville: University of Arkansas Press, 1984

Detels, Claire Janice, editor, *William Grant Still Studies at the University of Arkansas: A 1984 Congress Report*, Fayetteville: University of Arkansas, 1985

Floyd, Samuel A., editor, *Black Music in the Harlem Renaissance: A Collection of Essays*, New York: Greenwood Press, 1990

Haas, Robert B., editor, *William Grant Still and the Fusion of Cultures in American Music*, Los Angeles: Black Sparrow Press, 1972

Smith, Catherine Parsons, *"A Study in Contradictions": Toward a Biography of William Grant Still*, Berkeley: University of California Press, 1999

Spencer, Jon Michael, *The New Negroes and Their Music: The Success of the Harlem Renaissance*, Knoxville: University of Tennessee Press, 1997

Spencer, Jon Michael, editor, *The William Grant Still Reader: Essays on American Music*, Durham, North Carolina: Duke University Press, 1992

Still, Judith Anne, editor, *William Grant Still and the Fusion of Cultures in American Music: Second Edition Revised for the 100th Anniversary of William Grant Still*, Flagstaff, Arizona: Master-Player Library, 1995

Still, Judith Anne, et al., editors, *William Grant Still: A Bio-Bibliography*, Westport, Connecticut: Greenwood Press, 1996

In a career marked by innumerable "firsts" that demonstrated the triumph of talent over racial prejudice, William Grant Still established himself as one of the most significant U.S. composers of the middle decades of the 20th century. His unofficial title, "Dean of Afro-American Composers," acknowledges Still's importance in breaking down artificial barriers and opening doors for subsequent black American composers in the field of serious art music. At the same time, Still's extensive work in popular and commercial music, his generally conservative musical language, and even his anti-Communist political beliefs have hindered the composer's acceptance by many into the first rank of recent U.S. composers. During his lifetime the chief writings on his music were journalistic, and as interest in Still's music declined in the last decades of his life, so did any sort of writing on him. It was only in the years after Still's death, prompted primarily through the diligent promotion of his music by his daughter, Judith Anne, that serious attention was once again focused on the composer's life and music. At present, the study of Still and his music is in its initial stages, and much work remains to be done before an honest portrait of the man and his art will emerge.

ARVEY's book, the only full-length publication on the composer's life, is both an important and a seriously flawed document. Written by Still's second wife, the daughter of Russian Jewish immigrants, and published from a poorly edited manuscript, this book offers an intimate view of Still's personal life. At the same time, the volume lacks any pretense of objectivity. Arvey views the world exclusively through the prism of her interracial marriage and blames every perceived slight or setback in Still's professional life on racial prejudice. Although there is no doubt that Still was frequently subjected to bigotry, Arvey points only to secondhand comments, rumors, and unverifiable or unidentified sources for her evidence. This book lacks even the most rudimentary documentation for the events Arvey describes, and she frequently invents dialogue for conversations she cannot possibly have heard. Despite its importance as a primary source, this book must be read more as a personal reminiscence of Still and not as an impartial biography.

HAAS's volume marked an important first step on the road to a more objective consideration of Still's life and works. Written to celebrate the composer's 75th birthday, the book includes a number of useful essays about Still's music, a few of his own writings, and a preliminary catalog of his music. Just over two decades later, nearly the entire contents of Haas's book were reissued in a second edition edited by Judith Anne STILL (1995). All of the descriptive essays from the first edition are retained without change, and ten new essays that expand coverage to genres not discussed in the earlier volume have been added. Another virtue of this new edition is its revised catalog of Still's music. In short, the Haas edition remains useful, but the Still edition is preferable for the wider range of its coverage and for its more accurate work list.

DETELS's brief book records the events from a William Grant Still festival held at the University of Arkansas in 1984, and the contents of this collective volume range from general introductory remarks that preceded concerts of Still's music to more substantial scholarly presentations. Eileen Southern's essay on Still's early years, based in part on her conversations with the composer, is the most valuable item here; other pieces by Thomas Warburton and Ruth Friedberg are competent introductions to Still's operas and songs, respectively.

Judith Anne STILL et al. (1996) is a reference work that reflects the current state of Still scholarship. Among its chief values are an annotated work list, an extensive bibliography, a nearly complete list of writings by Still and his wife, and a discography. Although this volume does not always meet the highest scholarly standards, it does strive for an objective presentation of its materials. The arrangement of the work list makes it difficult to use, and there are errors in several entries; the bibliography is also cluttered with many items of only minimal value. On the other hand, the writings by Still and his wife are well annotated, and the list includes numerous items heretofore unknown in the literature on Still. The brief "Biographical Sketch of William Grant Still" by Quin presents an impartial view of Still's life, with numerous references to sources, including the Still/Arvey papers now at the University of Arkansas, that will interest serious scholars.

SPENCER (1992) brings together 35 of Still's most important writings, making this book an essential primary source. Equally important is Spencer's introductory essay, which mixes biography with an appraisal of Still's attitudes and responses to prejudice.

The volume by FLOYD is only partly concerned with Still yet is important for helping to place Still in the context of political and social movements in the 1920s and 1930s. Rae Linda Brown's essay demonstrates how Still's use of African-American elements within European forms in his *Afro-American Symphony* is consistent with the intellectual aims of the Harlem Renaissance.

As with Floyd, SPENCER (1997) is helpful for placing Still in historical context. Spencer's primary goal is the refutation of the views of writers such as Nathan Huggins and David L. Lewis who labeled the Harlem Renaissance a failure. In contrast, Spencer views the artistic achievements of Still and numerous other serious black musicians as "de-essentializing" the line between the races. Through their art, black culture was validated, which contributed to the success of the Harlem Renaissance.

SMITH offers the first serious examination of Still in the 1930s, shortly after his move from New York to Los Angeles. In biographical sketches of Still, Arvey, and Still's Los Angeles collaborator, Harold Bruce Forsythe, Smith reveals the previously unknown triangle they formed and examines how it affected Still's music. She also investigates Still's strong anti-Communist beliefs and offers an analysis of the *Afro-American Symphony*. Essays by two other writers and a number of sources from the 1930s round out this important book.

SCOTT WARFIELD

Stradivari, Antonio ca. 1644–1737

Italian instrument maker

Doring, Ernest N., *How Many Strads? Our Heritage from the Master,* Chicago: Lewis, 1945

Fétis, François-Joseph, *Notice of Anthony Stradivari, the Celebrated Violin-Maker, Known by the Name of Stradivarius,* translated by John Bishop, London, Reeves, 1864; reprint, 1964

Goodkind, Herbert K., *Violin Iconography of Antonio Stradivari, 1644–1737: Treatises on the Life and Work of the Patriarch of the Violinmakers,* Larchmont, New York: Goodkind, 1972

Hart, George, *The Violin: Its Famous Makers and Their Imitators,* London: Dalau, 1875; reprint, Boston: Longwood Press, 1977

Hill, W. Henry, et al., *Antonio Stradivari, His Life and Work (1644–1737),* London: Hill, 1889; 2nd edition, London: Macmillan, 1909; reprint, New York: Dover, 1963

Sacconi, Simone F., *The Secrets of Stradivari: With the Catalogue of the Stradivarian Relics Contained in the Civic Museum Ala Ponzone of Cremona,* translated by Andrew Dipper and Cristina Rivaroli, Cremona: Liberia del Convegno, 1979

Vigdorchik, Isaak, *The Acoustical Systems of the Violins of Stradivarius and Other Cremona Makers*, Westbury, New York: About Face Press, 1982

The beauty and value of Antonio Stradivari's instruments have led to the luthier's virtual canonization, even by those who know little about music. Public appreciation for the superior quality of his craftsmanship was first stimulated by the performing attainments of renowned virtuosos who played his instruments. The 18th-century violinist J.B. Viotti is a likely candidate for having initiated the player/instrument relationship, and research and comment on Stradivari begins concurrently with journal articles and treatises, their focus being primarily on construction methodology. The earliest topical books were published in the second half of the 19th century. These detail the venturesome acoustical experiments and imitative workmanship fostered by the ever-increasing popularity of Stradivari's instruments among 19th-century performers. By the end of the century, wealthy amateurs had become enamored with the investment potential of historic instruments, necessitating additional monographs to catalog, appraise, and profile Stradivari's works. Twentieth-century writings seek to provide answers for all facets of Stradivari research: biographical information; cataloging of instruments, ownership, and prices; and scientific and operative analysis of Stradivari's construction practices.

Both Fétis and Hart are informative for those tracing the lineage of Stradivari scholarship. FÉTIS, an inaugural champion of historic research and performance, first published this earliest of books on Stradivari in France in 1856. Although much of the content is a tribute to the research, theories, and conjecture of Félix Savart and J.-B. Vuillaume, at this juncture, Fétis inexorably conjoins the instruments of Stradivari with the bows of François Tourte as the criterion against which all other instruments and bows have since been judged.

HART synthesizes 19th-century findings concerning Stradivari's life and comparatively appraises the craftsman's achievements. The numerous printings of this book issued between 1875 and 1909 attest to its popularity until such time as Hart's information was superseded by the investigations of the Hill family.

The preeminent book on Stradivari remains that of the HILL brothers. As builders and restorers of stringed instruments, the Hill workshop has been charged with appraising and repairing many historic instruments. Research, critical analysis, and personal experiences from the latter part of the 19th century are recounted in this publication. Oriented toward the lay reader, the anecdotal writing style conveys a wealth of detail concerning Stradivari's family heritage, training, and life, in addition to occupational facts. His development as a craftsman is chronicled through the descriptions of the instruments he made, a corollary theme being the more general evolution of stringed-instrument design, especially concerning body dimensions and fittings. Each instrument type is examined in a separate chapter, as are the individual components of instrument making: wood, form, varnish, and the mechanics of assembly. Final chapters assess the number of instruments existing at the time of publication and their appreciation in value.

SACCONI's treatise, originally published in 1972 as *I segreti di Stradivari*, is a specialist's handbook on Stradivari's construction practices. The author, renowned for the perfection of his restorations, repaired 350 of Stradivari's instruments, making exacting notes about the characteristics of each. He was also given access to the luthier's extant design patterns and templates, and these, together with tools, are itemized as a guide to the Stradivari holdings of the Civic Museum Ala Ponzone of Cremona. Practical knowledge from these hands-on experiences is supplemented by scientific and mathematical analysis. From the dimensions of the instruments, which are meticulously illustrated and explained, Sacconi derived the geometrical formulas that he considers Stradivari to have reached by inductive reasoning. "The intuitions of Stradivari," the author writes, "which to-day we see are related to precise principles of acoustic physics and chemistry, represent practical experiments with natural phenomena, a patrimony of an ancient knowledge of the ways of nature." From this point, the reader is guided through a step-by-step instruction manual for instrument making. Historical background places each of Stradivari's procedures in perspective, and detailed illustrations and photographs clarify the construction process. Of particular importance is the historical analysis of varnishes, for Sacconi's findings dispel many of the myths surrounding this subject. The comprehensiveness of the bibliography adds to the importance of this book as a research tool.

The verification and cataloging of Stradivari instruments have been attempted numerous times. DORING makes a significant contribution toward the completion of these tasks, verifying 501 instruments and furnishing precise details about 392 of them. Each is listed chronologically by construction date, and a synopsis of previous writings is used to cover Stradivari's biography and the physical descriptions of the instruments. The most compelling aspect of this book is the romantic, anecdotal narrative of each instrument's history, which is, in turn, an account of the dealers, professional soloists, and wealthy amateurs who have owned them.

GOODKIND completes Doring's catalog by documenting 712 extant Stradivari instruments, each indexed and its ownership updated. The bulk of this catalog is the 415 photographic plates, showing each portrayed instrument from the front, side, and back for a total of 1,503 views. Select close-ups show construction details of scrolls, f-holes, and interior elements. Supplementary material includes the republication of rare, historical

Stradivari journal articles, as well as auction prices and complementary iconography.

Although not without self-aggrandizement, the work of the Soviet-trained VIGDORCHIK is singular. He explains the acoustical tuning of violin plates, the history of the procedure, and the methodology of determining pitch by the tapping of the top and back plates. Rendered in uncomplicated prose and amply illustrated, the differing acoustical systems of historically prominent luthiers are dissected and their individual pitch systems compared through analysis of wood composition, thickness, and pitch distribution. Believing that "it was the achievement of Stradivari that brought the art of violin making to its apogee," the author demonstrates that it is "Stradivari's system of acoustical construction and principle of transverse distribution of flexibility that made possible the increase in projection and the dramatic soprano timbre that is the hallmark of the Stradivari sound." Recommendations for the modern tuning of bass bar, soundpost, and bridge broaden the primary topic. For those unfamiliar with the research of Russian/Soviet acousticians, the references to these authorities may be of additional interest.

VALERIE WALDEN

Strauss, Richard 1864–1949

German-born composer

Adorno, Theodor W., "Richard Strauss: Born June 11, 1864," translated by Samuel Weber and Shierry Weber, *Perspectives of New Music* 4, no. 1 (1965); no. 2 (1966)

Del Mar, Norman, *Richard Strauss: A Critical Commentary on His Life and Work,* 3 vols., London: Barrie and Rockliff, 1962–72

Finck, Henry T., *Richard Strauss: The Man and His Works,* Boston: Little Brown, 1917

Gilliam, Bryan Randolph, *Richard Strauss's Elektra,* Oxford: Clarendon Press, and New York: Oxford University Press, 1991

Gilliam, Bryan Randolph, editor, *Richard Strauss and His World,* Princeton, New Jersey: Princeton University Press, 1992a

———, editor, *Richard Strauss: New Perspectives on the Composer and His Work,* Durham, North Carolina: Duke University Press, 1992b

Newman, Ernest, *Richard Strauss,* London: Lane, 1908; reprint, Westport, Connecticut: Greenwood Press, 1970

Puffett, Derrick, editor, *Richard Strauss: Elektra,* Cambridge: Cambridge University Press, 1989a

———, editor, *Richard Strauss: Salome,* Cambridge: Cambridge University Press, 1989b

Schuh, Willi, *Richard Strauss: A Chronicle of the Early Years, 1864–1898,* translated by Mary Whittall, Cambridge: Cambridge University Press, 1982

Although the music of Richard Strauss has enjoyed remarkable popularity for over a century, the body of scholarly literature it has elicited during that time is modest at best. Interesting biographical and critical writings have been produced all along, but only within the last decade or two have musicologists begun to take Strauss seriously as a topic of study—even, and indeed especially, in Germany. English-speaking scholars have taken the lead in this new development, organizing the first international conference on the composer (Duke University, 1990), taking stock of the considerable surviving documentary evidence (sketches, manuscripts, correspondence, etc.), and drawing Strauss studies into the center of debates surrounding the New Musicology. Central areas of inquiry in the literature include Strauss's position relative to various avant-garde schools of composition in the late 19th and early 20th centuries; genre-specific questions regarding tone poem, opera, and lieder; new models of harmonic and formal organization; and the composer's varied roles as a political figure.

Although not involved in the more recent debates, DEL MAR's magisterial biography remains a center of gravity, thanks to its thorough, reliable coverage of the basic facts; its patient, guidebook-style accounts of every major work; and its evenhandedness in a lamentably partisan field. That Del Mar's image of Strauss's career is unaffected by popular opinion is shown by the division of works among the three volumes; *Der Rosenkavalier* (1912), the acknowledged apex of the composer's career, is properly placed at the end of the first volume (earlier than one might expect), and the National Socialist era and its aftermath receive an entire book. The series is weakened somewhat by outdated concepts—e.g., the notion of *Salome* (1905) and *Elektra* (1909) as "stage tone poems"—but as a comprehensive treatment in English of Strauss's life and works, this work still has no peer.

A richer work, at least in documentary evidence, is SCHUH's study of Strauss's first 34 years. Schuh, a Swiss whose long personal involvement with the composer intensified during Strauss's exile in Zurich after World War II, had virtually unlimited access to the Strauss archives, and his book is a treasure trove of factual information. Its failures in scholarly method—identification of sources is the exception rather than the rule—will frustrate those hoping to retrace the author's steps, and readers looking for discussion of music will find little in the way of analysis. For sheer density of biographical detail, however, the book is an inexhaustible mine.

The books of Finck and Newman both come from the early years of the 20th century, when Strauss reigned as the undisputed leader of European musical culture, and offer early glimpses of the ambivalence that has come to define Strauss reception. NEWMAN's loosely analytical work moves between admiration and disgust, marveling at a composer who could attempt *Zarathustra* and recoiling from one who could sink to the level of a grandiose *Domestic Symphony*. FINCK presents "everything tangible and elucidating I know about Strauss's compositions" (a considerable amount), including numerous biographical anecdotes unduplicated in the literature. This study gains an air of objectivity from Finck's undisguised bewilderment at the phenomenon of a master German composer/metaphysician.

ADORNO, perhaps the most commanding intellectual figure to have worked in musicology during the 20th century, launches an all-out attack on Strauss on the 100th anniversary of his birth, condemning the composer for using music to conceal the plight of the individual in late capitalist society. The caricature of Strauss as a wealthy anti-intellectual is no longer sustained by the historical record, and the vitriol of Adorno's assault indicates he may have suspected that Strauss represented an intellectually grounded opposing position. In any case, the essay raises issues of a different scholarly order than those found in any other work on Strauss and thus demonstrates that this art had a place in the most profound aesthetic debates of the 20th century.

The three contributions of Gilliam have solidified his position as the leader of English-language scholarship on Strauss. The study of *Elektra*, GILLIAM (1991), contains a useful survey of the work's early reception, a meticulous account of its compositional history (with interesting insights into the Strauss-Hofmannsthal relationship, and a description of the opera's surviving sketches), and detailed musical analysis informed by Strauss's own ways of thinking about his music. Perhaps more important for the field in general, however, have been two collections of essays that direct scholars of various nationalities and diverse approaches toward this intellectually undervalued repertoire. GILLIAM (1992b) presents the finest offerings from the 1990 international Strauss conference at Duke University, including analytical treatments of *Don Juan*, *Metamorphosen*, *Der Rosenkavalier*, and *Intermezzo*, as well as discussions of Strauss and Italian opera, Mahler, National Socialism, and early 19th-century romanticism. (Of particular interest is James Hepokoski's discussion of the structural and programmatic implications of "modernism" as a category within which to consider *Don Juan*.) GILLIAM (1992a) contains Leon Botstein's seminal treatment of Strauss as an early musical postmodernist, along with articles on *Daphne*, *Macbeth*, and the orchestral songs; it also provides original English translations of correspondence, memoirs, and early critical essays.

Two collections offered by Puffett divide the scholarly labor (libretto, dramatic structure, tonal organization, orchestration, critical reception) among a remarkably heterogeneous group of writers, leading to fragmented but provocative views of two central works, *Salome* and *Elektra*. The contributions to PUFFETT (1989b), on *Salome*, range from a brilliant discussion by Mario Praz of Salome as a theme of French decadent literature, to

Tethys Carpenter's painstaking investigation of connections between tonality and drama, to an overstated critique of Straussian kitsch by Robin Holloway. More even in quality is PUFFETT (1989a), on *Elektra*, particularly with the insightful analytical overview supplied by Arnold Whittall; Carolyn Abbate provides qualitatively superior provocation with a convincing extension to Strauss of her ideas regarding musical subversion of dramatic processes in Wagnerian opera.

CHARLES YOUMANS

Stravinsky, Igor 1882–1971

Russian-born composer

1. Biography

Asaf'ev, Boris Vladimirovich, *A Book about Stravinsky*, translated by Richard F. French, Ann Arbor, Michigan: UMI Research Press, and Epping: Bowker, 1982

Craft, Robert, *Stravinsky: Glimpses of a Life*, London: Lime Tree, 1991; New York: St. Martin's Press, 1992

——, *Stravinsky: Chronicle of a Friendship, 1948–1971*, New York: Knopf, and London: Gollancz, 1972; revised edition, Nashville, Tennessee: Vanderbilt University Press, 1994

Druskin, Mikhail Semenovich, *Igor Stravinsky: His Life, Works, and Views*, translated by Martin Cooper, Cambridge: Cambridge University Press, 1983

Griffiths, Paul, *Stravinsky*, London: Dent, and New York: Schirmer Books, 1992

Oliver, Michael, *Igor Stravinsky*, London: Phaidon, 1995

Routh, Francis, *Stravinsky*, London: Dent, 1975

Stravinsky, Igor, *Stravinsky, Selected Correspondence*, 3 vols., edited and translated by Robert Craft, New York: Knopf, 1982–85

Stravinsky, Vera, and Robert Craft, *Stravinsky in Pictures and Documents*, New York: Simon and Schuster, 1978; London: Hutchinson, 1979

Taruskin, Richard, *Stravinsky and the Russian Traditions: A Biography of the Works through Mavra*, 2 vols., Berkeley: University of California Press, 1996

van den Toorn, Pieter C., *The Music of Igor Stravinsky*, New Haven, Connecticut: Yale University Press, 1983

Walsh, Stephen, *The Music of Stravinsky*, London: Routledge, 1988

White, Eric Walter, *Stravinsky: The Composer and His Works*, Berkeley: University of California Press, and London: Faber, 1966; 2nd edition, 1979

Igor Stravinsky was one of the most influential and important composers of the 20th century. During his long career, he participated in, and in some cases pioneered, the most significant musical trends and developments of his era.

Stravinsky's compositions are usually divided into three stylistic periods. The first, called the Russian Period, was heavily influenced by Russian traditions and culminates in the three great ballets written for Serge Diaghilev and the Ballet Russes, *The Fire Bird* (1910), *Petrushka* (1911), and *Le Sacre du printemps* (1913). In the 1920s, Stravinsky drastically changed his compositional style and turned toward neoclassicism, a term that refers to music that incorporates stylistic features of the past, generally the 17th and 18th centuries. Stravinsky's first important foray into neoclassicism is considered to be the ballet *Pulcinella* (1920), also written for Serge Diaghilev and the Ballet Russes. *Pulcinella* is an arrangement of the 18th-century composer Pergolesi's music to accompany a commedia dell'arte scenario. While remaining faithful to Pergolesi's model, Stravinsky incorporated some of his own 20th-century compositional devices into the work. Perhaps his greatest contributions to neoclassicism are the Symphony in C (1940) and the Symphony in Three Movements (1945). While living in the United States during the late 1940s, Stravinsky became friends with Robert Craft, a young composer and conductor. Craft became Stravinsky's musical assistant and close friend until the composer's death and helped inspire Stravinsky to take a more focused interest in many of the newer trends in music, particularly those of the dodecaphonists. In the early 1950s, Stravinsky gradually turned away from neoclassicism toward the more contrapuntal and serial techniques associated with Arnold Schoenberg. The first piece by Stravinsky to depend wholly on serial techniques is his song for tenor, string quartet, and four trombones, *In memoriam Dylan Thomas* (1954). Other works from this third stylistic period in the composer's career include the ballet *Agon* (1957), *Threni* (1958), and *Requiem Canticles* (1965). Stravinsky remained a powerful force in musical circles. As the 20th century drew to a close, his music was still debated and critiqued as vigorously as ever. Each year there is a flood of new biographies, analyses, and scholarly articles about his work; these publications range in level from the easy-to-read to the highly analytical.

For readers seeking a quick overview, OLIVER presents Stravinsky's biography in a clear, concise manner, including many quotations from Stravinsky's prolific correspondence and his personal documents, and presenting many pictures of the composer and his acquaintances. Oliver is particularly good at placing Stravinsky within the musical establishment of his time. Other good overviews include WALSH and GRIFFITHS's biographies, both of which contain more musical examples than Oliver and attempt to analyze some of the pieces on a basic level.

Craft has published a great deal about Stravinsky's life and works. Some of the books were written in conjunction with either Stravinsky himself or the composer's second wife, Vera. A particularly beautiful book, filled with color photos and copies of Stravinsky's sketches and manuscripts is the volume compiled by Vera STRAVINSKY and CRAFT. Chronological in approach, this book examines many personal moments through quotations from letters and photographs. It is filled with primary sources and includes a brief section discussing how Stravinsky composed. CRAFT (1992) incorporates both basic biography and musical commentary. In the second half of the book, Craft examines several important pieces and offers a deeply personal account of specific performances and the discussions he had with Stravinsky during their friendship. Of particular note is his discussion of *Symphonies of Wind Instruments,* because Craft began his long association with the composer by writing him a letter about a performance of that piece.

Invaluable for biographical research is STRAVINSKY, a three-volume compilation of selected correspondence, edited by Craft, who provides some commentary during the course of the books. Volume 1 contains the complete correspondence of the composer with artists such as Jean Cocteau, Maurice Delage, Nadia Boulanger, and Craft himself. Volume 2 includes correspondence with Manuel de Falla, Serge Diaghilev, Pierre Boulez, and Alfredo Casella, among others. There is also a large section surrounding the publication of *The Fire Bird*. In volume 3, letters from Claude Debussy, Maurice Ravel, Erik Satie, Francis Poulenc, and Albert Camus are among the documents included, along with a large section of Stravinsky's letters to various publishers. Through these letters, Stravinsky, the composer and the man, emerges. His concerns about art, music, performances, and publications are brought to life in his correspondence.

CRAFT (1994) provides a particularly good discussion of the last 20 years of Stravinsky's life. The biography begins in 1948 when Craft and Stravinsky met. It contains selections of Craft's diaries, correspondence, and transcriptions of conversations he had with Stravinsky until the composer's death in 1971. There is a small postlude, in which Craft attempts to place Stravinsky's output in historical perspective.

For a more scholarly approach to Stravinsky's life and works than that found in Craft's memoirs, WHITE's detailed book is invaluable. Part 1 presents a concise biography of the composer; part 2 contains a register of his works in chronological order. Each work is considered, as White addresses the genesis, first performance, publication history, and any revisions made during the composer's lifetime. However, there are no detailed analyses of the works. The appendices, including a list of the manuscripts in Stravinsky's possession are useful.

As an analytical approach, which attempts to combine the biographical aspects of Stravinsky's life and his musical output, ROUTH is particularly important. The first section presents Stravinsky's biography; the next part traces the composer's views of art, and the book concludes with a section of stylistic analysis of a few of the most important works.

Even early in his career, Stravinsky's works were often controversial and much was written about his music. ASAF'EV's monograph, in Russian, was one of the earliest attempts to assess the composer's work; it was completed in 1926 and published in 1929. The English-language version of the monograph was translated by Richard French and contains a brief introduction by Craft. Asaf'ev's work was almost immediately suppressed in Stravinsky's native country and was for a long time the only attempt by a Russian to come to terms with the composer's music. The book presents a series of analyses of the early Russian pieces through the Concert Suite from the ballet *Pulcinella* for violin and piano (1925). Along with detailed analyses, the author supplies a basic biography of Stravinsky. Another particularly enlightening biography, which was originally published in Russian in 1979, DRUSKIN is less analytical than Asaf'ev's monograph. However, Druskin thoroughly explores the Russian elements in Stravinsky's music, including the later works, which have usually not been associated with the Russian features of his early stylistic period.

Important biographies that contain advanced analysis of the works include VAN DEN TOORN, which contains a significant discussion of the more advanced aspects of Stravinsky's musical language. This book is only accessible to those with an advanced grasp of harmony and theory. Van den Toorn's work is invaluable for its study of Stravinsky's unique harmony and pitch organization.

Finally, the most important study of Stravinsky in recent years is TARUSKIN's exhaustive two-volume work, dealing mainly with the first 20 years of Stravinsky's output. In more than 1,600 pages, Taruskin evaluates the growth of Stravinsky's art from early student exercises through the great ballets for Diaghilev and then into the 1920s. Taruskin provides detailed analyses, illustrations, photographs, terms, a Russian pronunciation guide, and an all-inclusive bibliography. The analyses are perhaps the best feature of the book and are intended for advanced musicians. Taruskin, a master analyst, affords each piece the attention and time required to delve deeply into aspects of form, function, theory, and harmony. Taruskin's discussion of *Svadebka* (*Les Noces*), for instance, is more than 100 pages long.

ELIZABETH SEITZ

See also Neoclassicism

2. Ballets

Lederman, Minna, editor, *Stravinsky in the Theatre,* New York, Ballet Caravan, 1948

Pasler, Jann, editor, *Confronting Stravinsky: Man, Musician, Modernist,* Berkeley: University of California Press, 1986

Stravinsky, Igor, *Petrushka: An Authoritative Score of the Original Version, Backgrounds, Analysis, Essays, Views, and Comments,* edited by Charles Hamm, New York: Norton, 1967

Taruskin, Richard, *Stravinsky and the Russian Traditions: A Biography of the Works through Mavra,* 2 vols., Berkeley: University of California Press, 1996

van den Toorn, Pieter C., *The Music of Igor Stravinsky,* New Haven, Connecticut: Yale University Press, 1983

———, *Stravinsky and The Rite of Spring: The Beginnings of a Musical Language,* Berkeley: University of California Press, and Oxford: Oxford University Press, 1987

Walsh, Stephen, *The Music of Stravinsky,* London: Routledge, 1988

White, Eric Walter, *Stravinsky: The Composer and His Works,* Berkeley: University of California Press, and London: Faber, 1966; 2nd edition, 1979

Although a great deal of attention has been focused on the three early ballets that Stravinsky composed for Diaghilev's Ballets Russes (*The Firebird* [1909–10], *Petrushka* [1910–11], and *The Rite of Spring* [1911–13]), this focus on these early compositions should not obscure the fact that the ballet continued to occupy a central position in the composer's output throughout his long and distinguished career. Indeed, Stravinsky expanded the boundaries of the genre, producing a series of hybrid forms, such as *Renard* (1915–16), a "burlesque" in which singers perform with an onstage orchestra while dancers depict the action; and *Les noces* (1914–17; 1921–23), a "dance cantata," which, like *Renard,* avoids a strict correspondence between the singers and characters. Yet, because the three early ballets have been emphasized with respect to both performance (they are often performed in concert versions) and scholarship, extended discussion of the later ballets is less frequent and is usually confined to studies surveying many or all of the composer's works.

Among writings concentrating on the early ballets, VAN DEN TOORN's (1987) multifaceted treatment of *The Rite of Spring* is especially noteworthy. Van den Toorn approaches *The Rite of Spring* from several perspectives (of varying degrees of complexity), consistently relating his findings to the more general characteristics of Stravinsky's compositional language. The aesthetic underpinnings of the work are explored, particularly the significance of its conception as a ballet as opposed to subsequent performances (and Stravinsky's apparent preference for it) as concert music. The genesis of *The Rite of Spring* is then considered from the standpoint of the composer's correspondence, a newly discovered sketchbook, and subsequent revisions. Of particular interest are the chapters devoted to metric and rhythmic structure, in which van den Toorn examines conflicts between irregular patterns and fixed "periodicity" (the latter sometimes concealed beneath seemingly asymmetrical surface organization) and demonstrates the presence of such conflicts in *The Rite of Spring* as well as additional works by Stravinsky. In the final two chapters, which are concerned with pitch structure, the author explores Stravinsky's usages of octatonic and diatonic materials, focusing on certain characteristic "routines" symptomatic of the composer's "Russian" period in general.

Also valuable is STRAVINSKY, a critical edition of *Petrushka*. The historical introduction by editor Charles Hamm provides an essential background to Stravinsky's collaborations involving the Ballets Russes and *Petrushka* in particular. Hamm's analysis, although lacking the technical accomplishment of more recent efforts such as van den Toorn's, offers a lucid guide to the action of the ballet and its musical realization. Contemporary critical reactions to *Petrushka* are also provided, including, most notably, Cyril Beaumont's remarkable description of the Nijinsky choreography.

PASLER's important collection of essays, culled from the International Stravinsky Symposium commemorating the centenary of the composer's birth in 1982, presents specialized studies, several of which focus on the ballet music of Stravinsky's early "Russian" period. In the opening essay, Simon Karlinsky draws correspondences between these works (including less frequently discussed ballets such as *Renard, Les noces,* and *L'histoire du soldat* [1918] and various forms of Russian "preliterate" theater—i.e., dramatized rituals and folk entertainments of the 17th century). In the next entry, Taruskin traces the roots of the composer's "Russian" aesthetic in the "neonationalist" resurgence of folk art that Stravinsky encountered in Diaghilev's circle. Pasler then discusses the composer's rapid development between *Petrushka* and *The Rite of Spring* from the perspective of his increasingly successful fusion of music with the companion art forms. The collection also includes two detailed theoretical studies that address the early ballets. Allen Forte contributes pitch-class set analysis of Stravinsky's early harmony and voice leading, and van den Toorn, anticipating his later studies, presents an analysis of octatonic pitch structure in *The Rite of Spring*.

The entire "Russian" period is the subject of TARUSKIN's encyclopedic two-volume study. Taruskin, versed in the most current theoretical approaches to Stravinsky, and one of the foremost musicologists in the area of 19th- and 20th-century Russian music, furnishes a singularly "contextual" approach to Stravinsky's music, blending source study, history, aesthetics, and analysis. The result is perhaps the most penetrating and insightful account of Stravinsky's compositional process to date. The author's broad outlook is established from the outset through introductory chapters dealing with Stravinsky's intricate relationship with his Russian heritage as well as the equally complex musical climate in which he matured. As part of the latter study, influential music by Rimsky-Korsakov, Glazunov, Mussorgsky, and others is analyzed in addition to Stravinsky's own works. Each of the "Russian" ballets (as well as two subsequent productions, *Pulcinella* [1919–20] and *Le baiser de la fée* [1928]) is then subjected to Taruskin's historical, aesthetic, and analytical considerations.

Of the more comprehensive studies of Stravinsky's music, VAN DEN TOORN's (1983) volume is the most technically sophisticated. The author summarizes and expands upon the discoveries of octatonic and diatonic pitch structure put forth in Arthur Berger's pathbreaking article "Problems of Pitch Organization in Stravinsky" (*Perspectives of New Music,* 1963) and extends these discoveries to Stravinsky's oeuvre in general. Thus, one of van den Toorn's principal accomplishments is his successful identification of characteristic "routines" of pitch organization that not only distinguish each of the composer's three major style periods (the "Russian," "neoclassical," and "serial") but also unify his entire output on a theoretical basis to a greater extent than previously been suspected. The ballet music discussed by van den Toorn includes the "Russian" pieces as well as such later works as the *Danses Concertantes* (1942), *Orpheus* (1947), and *Agon* (1953–57).

Since its initial publication in 1966, WHITE's monograph has provided a standard guide to Stravinsky's life and works. Supplementing the author's concise biography is a "Register of Works" describing the historical background, style, and essential features of each composition. Although superseded in certain respects (particularly with the subsequent discovery of Stravinsky's widespread use of the octatonic scale), White's volume is one of the few book-length studies containing extended treatment of all of Stravinsky's ballets.

WALSH's survey also includes much informative discussion of the ballets. Although up-to-date in theoretical matters, the author's approach contains less detailed analysis than van den Toorn's and is therefore more immediately accessible. Walsh combines history, aesthetics, and analysis into a compelling account of the composer's evolving style. Several less frequently discussed ballets are examined, such as *Apollon musagète* (1927–28), *Persephone* (1933–34), and *Jeu de cartes* (1936).

The anthology of essays gathered by LEDERMAN, although outdated in certain respects (the collection originated with a 1948 Stravinsky issue of *Dance Index*), provides an important assessment of Stravinsky from the standpoint of his "unique theatre dimension." Organized into "Reminiscences," "Studies of the Music," and "Appreciations," the essays present valuable source readings by such key figures as Stravinsky, Jean Cocteau, George Balanchine, Robert Craft, Arthur Berger, and Aaron Copland.

KIP WILE

3. Other Music

Boretz, Benjamin, and Edward T. Cone, editors, *Perspectives on Schoenberg and Stravinsky,* Princeton, New Jersey: Princeton University Press, 1968; revised edition, New York: Norton, 1972

Griffiths, Paul, *Igor Stravinsky: The Rake's Progress,* Cambridge: Cambridge University Press, 1982

Joseph, Charles M., *Stravinsky and the Piano,* Ann Arbor, Michigan: UMI Research Press, and Epping: Bowker, 1983

Taruskin, Richard, *Stravinsky and the Russian Traditions: A Biography of the Works through Mavra,* 2 vols., Berkeley: University of California Press, 1996

van den Toorn, Pieter C., *The Music of Igor Stravinsky,* New Haven, Connecticut: Yale University Press, 1983

Walsh, Stephen, *The Music of Stravinsky,* London: Routledge, 1988

———, *Stravinsky: Oedipus Rex,* Cambridge: Cambridge University Press, 1993

White, Eric Walter, *Stravinsky: The Composer and His Works,* Berkeley: University of California Press, and London: Faber, 1966; 2nd edition, 1979

Having attracted the limelight early in his career with his Ballets Russes triumphs, Stravinsky was in the unenviable position of having his subsequent works compared to these ballets; hence, many early supporters and advocates were confused or even disappointed when Stravinsky's style or interests changed. With the perspective of time, however, modern commentators now agree that Stravinsky's seemingly radical shifts in style—reflected in the traditional periodization of his works into "Russian," "neoclassical," and "serial" periods and their myriad subcategories and styles—belie a fundamentally consistent composer and compositional method. Scholars do not agree, however, on what makes such stylistically divergent pieces recognizably "Stravinskian."

The BORETZ and CONE volume offers reprints of articles originally published in the 1960s in the journal *Perspectives of New Music;* consequently, there is a hit-or-miss quality to the collection as a whole, but the dense articles reward close scrutiny, as they represent some of the first attempts to give a coherent theoretical overview of the Stravinsky oeuvre, particularly in light of the composer's then recent conversion to serial composition. An important article by Arthur Berger, "Problems of Pitch Organization in Stravinsky," discusses nonfunctionally tonic diatonic writing, the use of the octatonic scale, and the interaction of the diatonic and octatonic in Stravinsky's preserial works. Cone's "Stravinsky: The Progress of a Method" focuses on "the apparent discontinuities that so often interrupt the musical flow" in Stravinsky's music. Cone's identification of processes of "stratification, interlock, and synthesis" is worked out through a close reading of *Symphonies of Wind Instruments,* although he also shows the relevance of this method to other Stravinsky works, including 12-tone pieces. Following these essays are Milton Babbitt's general remarks on Stravinsky's serial method and Claudio Spies's readings of specific late works: *Abraham and Isaac, Variations, Introitus,* and *Requiem Canticles.*

VAN DEN TOORN rejects all tonally derived methods of analysis ("wrong-note" theories, bitonality, polytonality, pandiatonicism, etc.) and their often ill-defined use and haphazard application to Stravinsky's music. The author expands on Berger's classification system, developing a coherent, "binding" system of three pitch-class collections, and their use and interaction in 20 of Stravinsky's works from different points in the composer's career. Sitting squarely in the domain of analytical theory, van den Toorn discusses Stravinsky's identity within historically based, external frames of reference. This text is the first full-length, theoretically detailed picture of the consistency of Stravinsky's work. Thorough, well-written, and sufficiently cautious of the limits of this kind of study, this book is nonetheless dense and long, interesting only to the determined music theorist.

WHITE remains the standard and most easily accessible introduction to the works of Stravinsky. The largest portion of the text is devoted to a discussion, chronologically arranged, of each piece in isolation: White gives the scoring, premiere, and publication data, as well as lengthier notes on the composition and treatment, dealing with the genesis and formal makeup of each piece and noting any revisions later made by Stravinsky. White's tendency to take the composer's notoriously polemical pronouncements at face value is distracting; the author's reliance on key relationships to describe formal matters has its limitations as well. But the useful appendices, thorough index, full scope, and clear organization make this text ideal for the student who wants to learn quickly the basics of a specific work by Stravinsky.

Like White's volume, WALSH (1988) also addresses all of Stravinsky's works, but Walsh embeds the discussion of individual pieces in a biographical narrative. Making use of the more recent theoretical work by van den Toorn and other scholars, Walsh's volume is a more sophisticated and coherent approach to the entire oeuvre than White's, and it avoids the imposing density of van den Toorn's text. The narrative style allows Walsh to address other composers and stylistic influences on the works he discusses, although no one work is examined in exhaustive detail.

The piano was essential to Stravinsky's life as a composer and concert pianist, yet it is startling to see how little he actually composed for the instrument and how his piano music is often dismissed as colorless and unidiomatic. In his study of this paradox, JOSEPH discusses the piano music as a barometer of Stravinsky's compositional evolution and architectural experimentation, specifically arguing for the piano as a "vehicle for testing new ideas." Although the genesis of such chords as the

Symphony of Psalms pillars and the *Rite of Spring*'s "Augurs chord" can be traced to the physical shape of the human hand and keyboard spacings, Joseph's thesis shows more broadly how the tactile sensation of the keyboard anchored Stravinsky's compositional changes. Of particular interest to Joseph are the pianistic underpinnings of many orchestral works, the orchestral nature of the solo piano works, and the murky compositional ground occupied by Stravinskian transcriptions and reductions and their uneasy relationship to "original" scores. Because Joseph's focus is on the piano as fulcrum of Stravinsky's compositional changes, there are no full-length analyses of the piano works themselves. Another disadvantage to this study is that other theoretical discussions of Stravinsky's identity are more compelling than Joseph's. Yet this book is the fullest study of the piano works to date, its unique angle providing an important corrective to both the purely theoretical and broadly historical explanations of Stravinsky's work.

Oedipus Rex and *The Rake's Progress* represent milestones in Stravinsky's neoclassical thinking: the operas are, respectively, the first and last masterpieces of his middle period. Both Griffiths and Walsh, in their books on these operas, take up the vexed issue of neoclassicism: how each work functions with respect to the tonal and generic traditions on which the pieces rely. WALSH (1993), in particular, takes up that neoclassical bugbear—the scope and use of allusion. Both texts have the concertgoer and student in mind, including brief, accessible overviews (or at the very least, references) to other critical or production issues, in discussions only as weighty as the space limitations of the Cambridge Music Handbooks allow. GRIFFITHS's study of *The Rake's Progress* offers historical notes on the work's genesis and performance history and includes a detailed synopsis (no libretto), noting the key relationships of the separate numbers, as well as an extended reading of the Graveyard scene. Walsh's study of *Oedipus Rex* includes the libretto and, gratifying to the interested reader, devotes considerable space to the musical and dramatic unfolding of this problematic hybrid—an "opera-oratorio."

TARUSKIN brings the tools of a meticulous musicological understanding, broad historical sense, and sophisticated level of theory to bear on his massive study of the roots of Stravinsky's Russian style. Taruskin's thesis—quite different from other published views—is that the key to Stravinsky's coherence as an artist lies in his early Russian phase, which, the author argues, Stravinsky never really left behind. Early in his career, Taruskin contends, Stravinsky "deliberately retained that which was most characteristically and exclusively Russian in his musical training and combined it with stylistic elements abstracted from Russian folklore in a conscious effort to excrete from his style all that was 'European.'" This early synthesis, which was a rejection of Rimsky-Korsakov's tutelage and the "provincial, denationalized Russian art

music" of that circle, retained its mark on Stravinsky throughout his career, despite the composer's perceived breaks and concomitant sloganeering to the contrary. The better part of these volumes is devoted to a retelling of the musical, political, personal, and aesthetic issues affecting the young composer and to close readings of all of the works up through the opera *Mavra*. Because the trajectory of the thesis points to the end of Stravinsky's career, Taruskin applies his claims to later works, including the quasi-serial *Requiem Canticles*, in the final hundred pages. Despite the scope of his project and prodigious contextual detail, Taruskin's work remains eminently readable: he is a good storyteller with an eye for colorful detail and an instinct for pacing. The sheer ponderousness of the volumes may scare away the novice Stravinskian, but this text will not soon be displaced as the definitive contribution to Stravinsky studies.

JAYME STAYER

Sullivan, Arthur *see* Gilbert, William Schwenck and Sullivan, Arthur

Sweden *see* Scandinavia

Sweelinck, Jan Pieterszoon 1562–1621

Dutch composer

Curtis, Alan, *Sweelinck's Keyboard Music: A Study of English Elements in Seventeenth-Century Dutch Composition,* Leiden: University Press, and London: Oxford University Press, 1969; 3rd edition, Leiden: Brill, 1987

Noske, Frits, *Sweelinck,* Oxford: Oxford University Press, 1988

Tusler, Robert L., *The Organ Music of Jan Pieterszoon Sweelinck,* 2 vols., Bilthoven: Creyghton, 1958

Jan Sweelinck was a Dutch composer, keyboard performer, and church musician who spent the majority of his professional life employed at the *Oude Kerk* (Old Church) in Amsterdam. He was a well-known teacher, with several students who achieved prominence. During his lengthy career, he composed an extensive number of vocal and choral works, including collections of psalms and canticles, secular French chansons, Italian madrigals, and various Latin works and canons. About 70 authentic keyboard works of Sweelinck have survived. These include fantasias, echo fantasias, toccatas, a praeludium and a ricercar, sacred chorale-based works (usually in some type of partita or variation form), and a group of variation sets based on secular melodies. Research and writing about Sweelinck have been in process since the late 19th century. A large percentage has been done by Dutch scholars and published in the periodical *Tijdschrift van de Vereniging voor Nederlandse Muziekgeschiedenis*. In the last few decades, many of these articles have been published in English. In fact, the more recent scholarship on Sweelinck is usually found in English. Book-length studies have been fewer (either in English, Dutch, or other languages) than articles. There are two complete editions of the music of this Dutch master. Most interest has focused on Sweelinck's keyboard music, with the vocal and choral music neglected to some extent.

TUSLER seeks to situate Sweelinck and his organ music in the broader tradition of European organ literature. In the first volume (which contains the verbal commentary), the author addresses the subjects of "Sweelinck and His Milieu," providing a historical, cultural, and biographical background of the composer and his time. The organs of the period are studied, with stop lists and other descriptive material given. Sweelinck's important predecessors are also discussed. There is a fairly substantial overview of earlier organ music from German countries, England, Spain, France, Italy, and the Netherlands. In the section on works based on borrowed melodies, Tusler introduces a graphic diagram to indicate structural sections. The portion of the book concerning Sweelinck's predecessors also addresses the abstract-style compositions, including the ricercars, fantasias, and toccatas. Here, the treatment is more verbal than graphic. The next major section of the book studies Sweelinck and his contemporaries and explores the composer's stylistic traits, with comparisons made mostly to English composers. This discussion is the core of the study, providing substantial detail about Sweelinck's works, their construction, and style. The final part of volume 1 deals with "Sweelinck and His Immediate Successors." Comparisons are made with the music of the French organist Jehan Titelouze, the Italian composer Frescobaldi, Frescobaldi's German student Samuel Scheidt, and other lesser-known composers. Volume 1 concludes with three appendices and a bibliography. The second volume presents photographs, drawings, and graphic representations of a wide range of organs from the Sweelinck era. The remainder of the volume contains musical examples from a wide variety of composers discussed in volume 1.

CURTIS provides a study of rigorous scholarship that includes many important ideas and discoveries, which he puts forth in a most readable monograph. As the subtitle indicates, one of the focuses of the study is the English influences upon Dutch and particularly Sweelinck's compositions in the 17th century. The book begins with a cultural and biographical chapter titled "The Orpheus of Amsterdam." There follows a chapter devoted to documenting the English musicians who visited the Netherlands and who may have made the acquaintance of Sweelinck. Keyboard music of the Netherlands prior to Sweelinck is examined, focusing mainly on surviving manuscript collections rather than individual composers. Curtis concludes that at this time Italian, and not English, influences were most prominent. New sources of Sweelinck's keyboard music and problems of authentication are also addressed, as Curtis examines the manuscript sources in detail and provides a rigorous stylistic analysis in order to distinguish authentic from spurious works. He also attempts to determine a chronology of Sweelinck's keyboard compositions. This is a difficult task, and Curtis's conclusions are speculative but well considered. The core of the book examines in detail the style of Sweelinck's keyboard music. It is divided into sections dealing with "Works Based on English Pavans," "Variations on English Tunes," "English Figural Techniques," and "Chromatic Fantasies and Meantone Tuning." As the titles of these sections indicate, the English elements in Sweelinck's style are the main emphasis in this extensive and well-wrought analysis. The volume concludes with six appendices that deal with instruments Sweelinck played, ornament symbols, portraits of the composer, and a comparison of the contents of the 1943 and 1968, editions of Sweelinck's keyboard compositions. There is also a select bibliography and index.

NOSKE is important as the only English-language monograph to treat Sweelinck's vocal music. The volume begins with a biography of Sweelinck set in the culture of Amsterdam. This treatment is more extensive than most Sweelinck biographies and is eminently readable. The author then considers the vocal music, first discussing the secular vocal music, by category: chansons, madrigals, *rimes,* and nuptial songs and canons. There are brief musical examples, and poetic texts, some with translations, are provided. Noske gives an enlightened discussion of the texts and musical relationships, as well as their historical framework. Most of the discussion of the sacred vocal works is devoted to Sweelinck's 153 settings of texts from the Geneva Psalter and considers their melodic background and publication history, as well as providing analytical observations regarding Sweelinck's polyphonic techniques. The latter portion of the sacred music discussion considers Sweelinck's Latin motets, which were published in a collection titled *Cantiones sacrae* (Antwerp, 1619). There is much speculation about the appearance of the Catholic works in the Calvinist Netherlands. This section also includes numerous musical examples. Noske studies the instrumental music in the final portion of the book, covering Sweelinck's keyboard instruments, his stylistic characteristics, the various types of keyboard music, and lute music. Overall, this is the most comprehensive, well researched, and clearly written study about Sweelinck.

JEFFREY WASSON

Symphony: General

Berry, Wallace, *Form in Music: An Examination of Traditional Techniques of Musical Form and Their Applications in Historical and Contemporary Styles*, Englewood Cliffs, New Jersey: Prentice Hall, 1966; 2nd edition, 1986

Bonds, Mark Evan, *After Beethoven: Imperatives of Originality in the Symphony*, Cambridge, Massachusetts: Harvard University Press, 1996

Cuyler, Louise, *The Symphony*, New York: Harcourt Brace, 1973; 2nd edition, Warren, Michigan: Harmonie Park Press, 1995

Holoman, D. Kern, editor, *The Nineteenth-Century Symphony*, New York: Schirmer Books, and London: Prentice Hall, 1997

Lang, Paul Henry, editor, *The Symphony, 1800–1900*, New York: Norton, 1969

Pauly, Reinhard G., *Music in the Classic Period*, Englewood Cliffs, New Jersey: Prentice Hall, 1965; 3rd edition, 1988

Simpson, Robert, editor, *The Symphony: Haydn to Dvořák*, Baltimore, Maryland: Penguin Books, 1966

Ulrich, Homer, *Symphonic Music: Its Evolution since the Renaissance*, New York: Columbia University Press, 1952

The term *symphony,* which literally means sounding together, is used to refer to an extended multimovement or sectional single-movement composition for orchestra. Prominent in the late 18th century, the symphony came to be regarded as the most exalted genre of orchestral music from the time of Beethoven. Normally absolute and nonreferential in content, some 18th-, 19th-, and 20th-century symphonies are associated with a descriptive program, and examples with solo voice or chorus exist in the repertoire. Many authors confronted with writing about the symphony turn to the descriptive analysis of symphonies throughout the past 265 years. While accurate depiction of the symphony necessitates placement within a historical context with some reference to composers, a number of sources successfully focus more, at least initially or in part, on definition and historical context than on specific composers and their symphonic works.

CUYLER, in the most recent topical volume pertaining to the symphony, initially details the historical genesis of the symphony in the 18th century and in later chapters, surveys its alterations throughout the following centuries. Especially valuable are the concise descriptions related to symphonic content that appear at the beginnings of each chapter. Cuyler's writing style is direct, unencumbered by excessive detail, and factually accurate; ease of reading makes the search for pertinent information pleasurable.

As editor for a collection of single-author essays about symphonic composers from Haydn to Dvořák, SIMPSON contextualizes the symphony topic. The origin of the symphony, in terms of a new attitude toward tonality, is high-

lighted. Of considerable importance are the opening seven pages of Harold Truscott's essay on Haydn and the rise of the classical symphony, here viewed historically from a harmonic perspective. Tonal conflict is seen as the root of sonata form, which in turn became the classical symphony's basis. Although densely written, the insights in this anthology are significant.

HOLOMAN, editor of a recent collection of essays on 19th-century symphony composers, briefly prefaces the writings with a summary of symphonic evolution in that century, revealing the societal and other developments that influenced changes in the symphony. In this volume, 15 authors, including Holoman, convey the diverse scope of 19th-century symphonies. Extensive detail about specific composers' works is presented in the essays, and the opening pages of each are useful for a general understanding of the symphonic changes that occurred during the period.

PAULY's volume is perhaps the best source for the uninitiated because of its engaging and clearly written authoritative information. The author explains he historical and cultural setting during the classic era, and he elucidates the importance of the symphony in that period. The concise yet accurate description of sonata form found in chapter three under the heading sonata form is especially pertinent.

In the earliest of the sources cited, ULRICH intermingles the historical, analytical, biographical, and critical aspects of symphonic music in his review of its evolution since the Renaissance. The integrated approach requires some sorting, but a thorough index directs readers to relevant information, and the writing style encourages reading beyond the scope of the general symphony topic.

LANG prefaces the full scores of symphonies by nine representative composers with a cursory survey of the symphony in the 19th century. Although more recent scholarship adds considerable depth to the topic, Lang's summary provides a basic introduction. He portrays the classic symphonists as interested less in the sensuous quality of music than in the possibilities of manipulating motives derived from thematic ideas, and he contends that romantic symphonists emphasize expressive power over the architectural logic of their predecessors. Also clearly stated is the importance of viewing musical forms, apparent in symphonic movements, as following certain principles rather than establishing strict patterns of composition. Changes in the hierarchy of movements within a symphony and the expanding number and capabilities of various orchestral instruments are outlined. Some scanning is necessary, because relevant information is intermingled with observations about specific composers' general compositional style, and the brevity of the volume's text negates an index.

BONDS addresses the symphony topic through the historical perspective of 19th-century critics, aestheticians, and composers as they grappled with diminished expectations after Beethoven's symphonies. Questions of musical progress and originality, such as the conflict between the failure of intentional originality and spontaneity suffering from reflection, are representative of the self-consciousness of the era. This thought-provoking volume offers a welcome dimension to the customary symphony discourse, and the index refers the reader to the most appropriate pages.

Although music dictionaries are available for definitions of unfamiliar terms that arise in writings about the symphony, BERRY's comprehensive book on musical forms not only provides an in-depth discussion of various forms found in symphonic movements, but also cites numerous musical examples, many of which direct the reader to works most representative of the particular form. Of special significance to the symphony topic is the section on single-movement sonata form found in chapter 6.

JOANNE E. SWENSON-ELDRIDGE

Symphony: 18th-Century French

Carse, Adam, *18th-Century Symphonies*, London: Augener, 1951; reprint, Westport, Connecticut, Hyperion Press, 1979
Mongrédien, Jean, *French Music from the Enlightenment to Romanticism: 1789–1830,* translated by Sylvain Frémaux, Portland, Oregon: Amadeus Press, 1996
———, "Paris: The End of the Ancien Régime," in *The Classical Era: From the 1740s to the End of the 18th Century,* edited by Neal Zaslaw, London: Macmillan, and Englewood Cliffs, New Jersey: Prentice Hall, 1989
Schwarz, Boris, *French Instrumental Music between the Revolutions (1789–1830),* New York: Da Capo Press, 1987

Interest in the history of opera has greatly overshadowed the study of instrumental music from 18th-century France. To a large extent, this imbalance reflects a long-standing French aesthetic bias that privileged language over music. Thus, vocal genres received more critical attention than instrumental ones. Nevertheless, an enormous amount of instrumental music was composed and performed in France throughout the 1700s, including a large number of symphonies. The center of French symphonic composition and performance was Paris. The capital boasted a number of prominent performance venues, which included subscription concerts, private orchestral entertainments at the homes of wealthy patrons, and even outdoor performances in pleasure gardens. This abundance of performance opportunities, in conjunction with the presence of several music publishers, attracted composers to Paris. Over the course of the 18th century, the city became an increasingly cosmopolitan center where musicians from all over Europe vied to have their symphonies performed and published.

CARSE provides a general survey of the 18th-century symphony and examines French orchestral traditions within a broad European context. This approach has many advantages because diverse foreign influences played a large role in the early development of the French symphony. Carse pays particular attention to the years 1754 and 1755 when Johann Stamitz, one of the foremost early symphonists, resided in Paris. During this period, symphonies by Stamitz appeared on programs of the Concerts Spirituels, perhaps the most prestigious concert series of the 18th century. These performances, as Carse points out, attracted considerable attention, and composers such as François-Joseph Gossec began to model their own works on the symphonies of Stamitz. Although Carse's history of the symphony is basically accurate, some of his recommendations concerning the editing and performing of this repertoire are no longer relevant, as they are based on the assumption that present-day performances of these symphonies would employ modern instruments played without the support of a continuo. Today, however, early music ensembles that use original instruments are more likely to program and record these symphonies than are large symphony orchestras. Contemporary concern with historically sensitive performance practice, therefore, makes his suggestions for rewriting inner voices and for filling out the harmonies inappropriate. Although our knowledge of this repertoire has grown significantly since Carse wrote this study, it remains a useful introduction to the topic of the 18th-century symphony.

MONGRÉDIEN (1989) updates and expands many issues that Carse introduces in his book. Mongrédien begins by analyzing the musical culture of prerevolutionary France in order to place this music within its historical context. Like Carse, he argues that the numerous Parisian concert venues profoundly influenced the development of the French symphony by exposing native composers to important works by their German contemporaries. Mongrédien also addresses the problems of classification and terminology that beset studies of the 18th-century symphony. The French, he demonstrates, employed the term symphony to refer to a wide array of instrumental music. The *symphonie concertante,* a genre that was enormously popular in France from 1770 to 1820, is an example of this imprecise usage. The typical *symphonie concertante* consists of two movements, both in major keys, with two or more dominant solo parts. Although these works are often included with symphonies in published collections and thematic catalogs, Mongrédien argues that the genre is more accurately classified as a type of concerto. Its name simply reflects the fluid use of the term symphony that was typical of France at this time.

SCHWARZ provides a basic outline of the effects that the French Revolution had on musical culture in France. He argues that the Revolution ended the demand for symphonic composition by forcing the wealthy patrons of instrumental music into exile. Without this audience, private concerts disappeared and revered institutions such as the Concerts Spirituels folded. As a result, composers interested in the further development of orchestral composition turned their attention to opera, in which they expanded the role played by instrumental music. To demonstrate this fact, Schwarz analyzes a number of substantial opera overtures by such composers as Luigi Cherubini and Etienne-Nicolas Méhul that incorporate symphonic forms and procedures. Unfortunately, Schwarz's interpretation of the French Revolution reflects an outdated view of that event and overemphasizes the break with previous traditions. While it is true that the number of symphonies composed in France during the last decade of the 18th century decreased, the reasons for this decline are somewhat more varied and complex than those presented here. Nonetheless, Schwarz's discussion of instrumental music in this period reflects his extensive knowledge of the extant repertoire and offers many perceptive insights for those unfamiliar with it.

MONGRÉDIEN's (1996) monograph covers the same period as Schwarz's book, but it examines a broader range of musical activities and genres. In addition, Mongrédien offers a thorough analysis of the conflicting sociopolitical forces at work during the revolutionary decade, assessing their impact on French musical culture. Like Schwarz, Mongrédien chronicles the waning of symphonic production at the century's close, but he attributes the reduction in the number of symphonies to several overlapping factors, including the persistence of the traditional aesthetic bias that favored vocal music. He also shows that orchestral music did not completely disappear during the Revolution but that other symphonic genres took the place of the three- or four-movement symphony. To that end, he discusses the popularity of so-called battle symphonies, which blended patriotic programs with picturesque musical effects to create a suitably revolutionary genre. Mongrédien places the music of the 1790s within an intellectual and cultural framework that explains why the French symphony entered a brief period of decline.

MICHAEL E. MCCLELLAN

Symphony: 18th-Century German

Heartz, Daniel, *Haydn, Mozart, and the Viennese School, 1740–1780*, New York: Norton, 1995

Landon, H.C. Robbins, *The Symphonies of Haydn*, London: Universal Edition, 1955

Wellesz, Egon, and Frederick Sternfeld, "The Early Symphony," in *The Age of Enlightenment, 1745–1790*, New Oxford History of Music, vol. 7, London: Oxford University Press, 1973

Wolf, Eugene K., *The Symphonies of Johann Stamitz: A Study in the Formation of the Classic Style*, Utrecht: Bohn, Scheltema and Holkema, and Boston: Nijhoff, 1981

Zaslaw, Neal, *Mozart's Symphonies: Context, Performance Practice, Reception*, Oxford: Clarendon Press, and New York: Oxford University Press, 1989

Studies of the German/Austrian symphony of the 18th century have tended to focus on the origins of the genre in Vienna and Mannheim and the development of the mature symphonic styles of Haydn and Mozart. Three minor controversies are reflected in the literature: First, the debate earlier in the 20th century over the primacy of Vienna or Mannheim in the development of the symphonic form has given way to a more flexible position, in which the contributions of both centers are assessed and their indebtedness to Italy is recognized. Second, the use of the term *sinfonia da chiesa*, or "church sonata symphony," by some scholars (including Landon) to describe a type of early Haydn symphony beginning with a slow movement has generated debate as to whether this term has any meaning beyond designating a formal type and raises the more meaningful issue of the use of symphonies in the church (see Zaslaw). Finally, whereas the term *Sturm und Drang* was applied earlier in the 20th century to the minor-key symphonies by Viennese composers appearing in the late 1760s and 1770s by scholars who perceived a "romantic crisis" or a musical analogue to the literary movement (the latter sense affects Landon's discussion), a more balanced view has emerged recently, in which the term is understood more as a style used in some, but not all, works of the period—although there is still no consensus on the ultimate significance of the style. Aside from the main focus on the early Viennese and Mannheim schools and the later works of Haydn and Mozart, both the composers of North Germany, especially C.P.E. Bach, and the second generation of Mannheim symphonists have also received some attention.

Although out of date in some respects, WELLESZ and STERNFELD provide a useful introductory survey of the 18th-century symphony, excluding the works of Haydn and Mozart. Nevertheless, the scope of the chapter is somewhat broader than its title suggests, for it does include several other major symphonists of the later 18th century. Other relevant parts of the chapter cover North Germany, Vienna (with special attention to Wagenseil, Gassmann, and Hofmann), and Mannheim (with most space devoted to Johann Stamitz). The authors are concerned with features that contribute to the evolving classical style as well as influences of one center on another. While a progressivist stance is sometimes evident, where "regressive" features are singled out for criticism, at other times there is a willingness to explore the music on its own terms, as in a fine discussion of C.P.E. Bach emphasizing the baroque, classical, and preromantic aspects of his style.

HEARTZ integrates his discussion of the symphony as a genre within his larger work on the development of the Viennese school. Although thoroughly up-to-date in its methodology and analytical apparatus, the book is written in an engaging style accessible to the general reader and contains many fresh insights. Heartz contributes valuable information on concert life and the use of symphonies in Vienna during the 1750s and 1760s, which, among other things, saw the emergence of a type of *concertante* symphony. Modern and regressive features of the symphonies of Monn and Wagenseil are discussed, with Wagenseil emerging as the more important and forward-looking of the two. The development of Haydn's symphonic style to about 1780 is examined and put in the context of the Viennese tradition. Thus, octave doublings are found to derive from Viennese dance music, and the famous trilogy of *concertante* symphonies, nos. 6, 7, and 8, are seen as a kind of catalog of current styles and genres. Heartz explores the issue of the "church symphony" as it relates to the emergence of the slow introduction and finds a corollary for the minor-mode Sturm und Drang symphonies in Haydn's church music of the period. In his discussion of Mozart's symphonies before 1780, Heartz stresses their operatic roots and the folk element in the Salzburg finale. The symphonies of Gassmann, Dittersdorf, Vanhal, Hofmann, and Ordonez are also briefly discussed.

WOLF's definitive study of Stamitz's symphonies is geared more toward advanced students and specialists, but there is also information of use to general readers, including a short biography. The author's aim is to "develop an accurate and comprehensive analysis of Stamitz's symphonic style, its evolution, and its historical position." Several of the innovations previously attributed to Stamitz are traced to the Italian opera overture, which Stamitz adapted and further developed into an imaginative symphonic style. A thorough examination of the sources in relation to authenticity and chronology precedes several analytical chapters on the structure of the multimovement cycle, the phrase, and individual movements, forming the basis of an analysis of the early, middle, and late symphonies with summaries of their stylistic features. The organization of the book is clear, making it useful for the analyst seeking information on stylistic evolution during this period. A thematic catalog of all of the authenticated Stamitz symphonies as well as a selection of lost and questionable works is included.

LANDON's pioneering work on Haydn's symphonies is still useful, even if several aspects of his study (including details of chronology and sources, the church-sonata symphony, Sturm und Drang, and the extent of the use of C-alto horns) have been superseded by more recent scholarship. Particularly useful are extracts from many important documents, in English translation, and a large number of notices, reviews, and concert programs pertaining to the London symphonies. Landon discusses the

symphonies in five chronological groups, examining a number of individual symphonies and movements in some detail. An evolutionary perspective is evident in the tendency to measure each period against the overall development of Haydn's symphonic style (for Landon, Haydn reaches "full maturity" around 1771), although this paradigm does not blind Landon to the quality of some of the earlier works.

Having its origins in program notes for an acclaimed series of recordings, ZASLAW's book on Mozart's symphonies retains a writing style and level of musical analysis accessible to the general reader while still containing much information of interest to the specialist. Mozart's symphonies were written for several localities, each with its own performance traditions, and the author includes important information on the cultural context and performance traditions of symphonies in London, Holland, Italy, Salzburg, and Vienna. Added to this analysis are insightful treatments of the "church symphony," the Sturm und Drang style, and numerous aspects of performance practice, as well as a chapter exploring what Mozart's symphonies may have meant to his contemporaries.

ANDREW KEARNS

Symphony: 18th-Century Italian

Brook, Barry S., and Barbara B. Heyman, editors, *The Symphony, 1720–1840, Series A: Italy*, 8 vols., New York: Garland, 1979–85
Wellesz, Egon, and Frederick Sternfeld, *The Age of Enlightenment, 1745–1790*, New Oxford History of Music, Volume 7, London: Oxford University Press, 1973

In his introduction to volume 8 of Brook and Heyman, Rey M. Longyear observes that the "Italian symphony of the High Classic and early Romantic periods has not received the attention given to the German, Austro-Bohemian, or French symphonies of the time." One could expand his observation to include the early classical period as well, for no book-length treatment in English of the Italian symphony (in any century) has yet appeared in print. The work that has been done lies buried in unpublished dissertations and a sprinkling of specialized articles; a synthesis of the research remains to be written. Interested readers will even have a difficult time finding a basic overview, for most one-volume histories of the genre generally relegate Italy to a few pages in the section on the early symphony, then shift their attention northward, across the Alps, and never look back.

This gap in the scholarly literature (which is particularly odd, considering that the symphony as a genre originated in early 18th-century Italy) has resulted from a confluence of factors, chief among them the musicological myopia that, until recently, led scholars of the

18th century to focus almost entirely on Haydn, Mozart, and Beethoven. Moreover, our understanding of the subject has been hampered by the relative inaccessibility of the music, most of which survives only in the form of individual parts, requiring any research to begin with the tedious and time-consuming task of reconstructing the full score. Because Italian scholars have not shown much interest in so recovering their nation's symphonic past (unlike the Germans, who—in collections such as *Denkmäler der deutschen Tonkunst*—have resurrected legions of Teutonic symphonists), the Italian story has remained largely untold. Not until Churgin's dissertation on Sammartini in the 1960s did the research trend begin to turn (Bathia Churgin, "The Symphonies of G.B. Sammartini," Ph.D. Dissertation, Harvard University, 1963). Even the recent spate of articles and dissertations, however, has failed to dismantle a longstanding perception that continues to hobble further serious inquiry—a perception expressing lingering doubts about the quality of the Italian contribution. For example, Antonio de Almeida makes the startling declaration (in volume 4 of Brook and Heyman) that Boccherini "would probably have been a symphonist of the first rank had he not been Italian." That may well be true, but until we have a fuller exploration of the music and the cultural context of the 18th-century Italian symphony, we cannot hope to explain why.

In the meantime, a cohesive introduction to the subject can be found in WELLESZ and STERNFELD, which devotes its first 18 pages of the chapter "The Early Symphony" to Italy. The authors divide the material into sections on the opera overture, "Sammartini and the Symphony," and later Italian symphonists, proffering clear and pertinent (although not always flattering) observations about Italian style, illustrated with numerous musical examples. The discussion presumes an understanding of basic music theory concepts and a familiarity with the finer points of sonata-allegro form. Readers should remember, however, that the volume predates the recent flurry of scholarly activity, so that some of the authors' data has been superseded (e.g., the number of extant symphonies from the period has now risen well above 7,000). In addition, later scholars have expanded and refined explanations of the genre's early history, identifying antecedents in addition to the opera overture. Despite these shortcomings, a perusal of these pages will establish a scholarly context and make recent discussions more intelligible.

The main purpose of BROOK and HEYMAN is the presentation of forgotten and otherwise inaccessible symphonic scores. However, each volume also contains accompanying essays that, although brief and fragmented, provide the best and most current information on the subject in book format. The eight volumes of Series A are devoted to Italy and are edited by various specialists in the field. In the first volume, Eugene K.

Wolf proposes the ripieno concerto as the most likely progenitor of the symphony, and Gordana Lazarevich and Douglass M. Green discuss the cultural context and style of the Neapolitan overture and its relation to the early symphony. Their general observations are then followed by specific discussions of each score. Bathia Churgin's introduction to the second volume takes issue with the ripieno-concerto-as-single-progenitor theory and restricts any influence from the overture to a later period in the genre's development. Instead, she emphasizes the contributions made by the trio sonata, orchestral suite, and concerto in general, before concluding with an analysis of the music, in this case ten symphonies of Giovanni Battista Sammartini. The essays to volumes 3, 4, 5, and 8 (volumes 6 and 7 are concerned with the early 19th century) have a somewhat narrower scope, focusing on the individual biographies and musical styles of later 18th-century Italian symphonies, including A. Brioschi, F. Chelleri, A. Sacchini, G. Pugnani, G.B. Martini, G.B. Lampugnani, P. Anfossi, L. Boccherini, G. Brunetti, S. Mattei, and N. Zingarelli. The absence of a larger critical perspective in these discussions does not stem from any scholarly weakness or dereliction of duty but merely reflects the relatively recent attention paid to the post-Sammartini generations of Italian composers. We can hope that this music and information will help fuel a broader inquiry into the trajectory taken by the Italian symphony after its promising beginnings.

MARY SUE MORROW

Symphony: 19th-Century German

Bonds, Mark Evan, *After Beethoven: Imperatives of Originality in the Symphony,* Cambridge, Massachusetts: Harvard University Press, 1996

Dahlhaus, Carl, *Nineteenth-Century Music,* translated by J. Bradford Robinson, Berkeley: University of California Press, 1989

Einstein, Alfred, *Music in the Romantic Era,* New York: Norton, and London: Dent, 1947

Holoman, D. Kern, editor, *The Nineteenth-Century Symphony,* New York: Schirmer Books, and London, Prentice Hall, 1997

Stedman, Preston, *The Symphony,* Englewood Cliffs, New Jersey: Prentice Hall, 1979; 2nd edition, 1992

Tovey, Donald Francis, *Essays in Musical Analysis,* 6 vols., London: Oxford University Press, 1935–39

Weber, William, *Music and the Middle Class: The Social Structure of Concert Life in London, Paris, and Vienna,* London: Croom Helm, and New York: Holmes and Meier, 1975

Weingartner, Felix, *The Post-Beethoven Symphonists: Symphony Writers since Beethoven,* translated by Arthur De Bles, New York: Scribner, 1906; London: Reeves, 1907

In German-speaking countries during the 19th century, the symphony underwent distinct transformations. Many composers attempted to withdraw from their traditional roles as court servants and entertainers and became independent artists whose fortunes were tied to the tastes of a growing middle class. For the first time, symphonies became the most important items in a concert; by the latter part of the century, many concert halls designed expressly for serious orchestral music were constructed. As the tastes of the public both shaped and were shaped by the music, a delicate balance was negotiated between the formal demands of the genre and a romantic lyricism full of original, memorable melodies.

In many ways, the history of the 19th-century symphony is the history of composing in the shadow of Beethoven. Thus, the symphonic ideal became one of monumental struggles, interconnections across movements, and grand culminations. On the other hand, as in much mid- to late-19th-century music, a self-consciousness pervaded the genre, imbuing each work with a sense that it was not only *a* symphony but also *about* the symphony and concerned with whether it was still possible to compose symphonies at all.

One of the most important conductors around 1900, WEINGARTNER provides a fascinating, often unmediated view of symphonists after Beethoven. He maintains a conversational tone and offers ample personal ruminations; more contemporary historical scholarship rarely matches the spirit of his discussions about the reputations of figures such as Brahms, Strauss, and Mahler, whose works were still new. Weingartner's reflections on the symphonic landscape, echoing a view held through much of the 19th century, take on an aura of nostalgia: "So does a light feeling of melancholy creep over me, when, knowing the greatness of Beethoven, . . . I think of the many composers, who after him, have undertaken and still undertake to write symphonies . . . such an attempt seems almost as absurd as to wish to climb higher than the summit of a mountain." Thus, a figure such as Mendelssohn, although considered a "Master from Heaven," is said to have never fully developed his gifts, and Schumann is dismissed as not fully at home in the larger genres. However, Weingartner does have an optimistic view of the future and concludes by suggesting that one can imagine a new symphonic genius, a figure whose music will both be ideal and universal.

TOVEY's program notes, first collected in many volumes during the 1930s, cover individual works from many composers and periods, including many examples of the 19th-century German symphonic repertory. All the Beethoven and Brahms symphonies are treated, and many works by Schubert, Mendelssohn, Schumann, Bruckner, and Mahler are discussed as well. In a useful introductory essay, Tovey defines and discusses with characteristic sharpness and wit the few technical terms he uses, such as *key relations, tonality, tonic and dominant,* and various formal structures. For example, in attempting to describe the psychological differences between key areas, Tovey admits that this effort is "like trying to describe the taste of a peach; and, as a person with no pretensions to an expert palate, I doubt whether my most thorough researches in tonality can approach the august indefinables and incommunicables of the expert wine-taster." However, although Tovey practices the traditionally British avocation of amateur musicology, always keeping in mind the nongenius listener, these essays are masterful. They are straightforward and readable, and they exhibit a consistent level of musical insight that is much deeper than the program-note genre implies. Notwithstanding the facts that Tovey presents no "complete system of criticism" and that his essays are limited to the individual works treated, this is an important companion for this repertory.

The first part of EINSTEIN's overview of 19th-century music develops a conceptual framework; individual chapters cover such topics as contrasts, individual and society, contradictions, universal and national music, and forms and content. Part 2 explores individual genres and includes a chapter on symphonic and chamber music, and the final section describes the philosophy and aesthetics of the era. Despite romanticism's origins as a literary and poetic movement, wordless instrumental music reigned supreme in the 19th century because it could best express the wondrous and the ineffable. In Einstein's view, even the popularity of song and opera confirm this supposition, for the instrumental accompaniment took on an importance of its own—as a commentary on and a psychological reaction to the text. Readers should be aware that this book, as a product of its time, pervasively uses a paradigm of musical unity that is now often thought outdated. For example, Beethoven's symphonies are said to contain "not a single measure" outside musical logic, and, with respect to Schubert's lengthy Ninth Symphony, "every cut mutilates the unified structure."

The 19th century saw the development of concerts in a form that we would recognize today. WEBER is not interested as much in the music that was performed as in questions of who attended these concerts; what sorts of groups formed this public; and how this audience, which constituted the first consumers of the 19th-century German symphony, shaped the music world. As such, this book is a history of the rising middle class that constituted the core of this public and an exploration of society's influence on music. Weber compares members of different professions, genders, and citizens of national capitals such as London, Paris, and Vienna to problematize the notion of a unified middle class. In addition, he explores the musical tastes for popular as well as classical genres in both the upper and the lower middle classes. Weber's sociological approach strongly relies on empirical data: many tables in the back of the book categorize such items as different kinds of concerts, ticket prices, the makeup of concert series subscribers, and the occupations of members in amateur music groups.

Originally published in German in 1980, DAHLHAUS's influential survey of 19th-century music contains provocative discussions of the aesthetic problems facing the genre during that century. In Dahlhaus's view, the history of the 19th-century symphony is one of discontinuities. There is a "yawning chasm" between the first generation of post-Beethoven composers and the "second age" of the symphony during the final decades of the century. Further, no continuous chain of development during the century can be discerned; each composer, regardless of historical distance, operated in direct relation to Beethoven, with few interrelationships with one another. Dahlhaus argues that two aesthetic problems dominate the 19th-century symphony: "how to integrate contemplative lyricism . . . into a symphony without causing the form to disintegrate or to function as a mere framework for a potpourri of melodies" and, in the latter part of the century, how "the grand style fundamental to the genre" could exist when "split into a monumentality that remains a decorative façade" and an internal form that "can be dramatized only by applying a thick layer of pathos." Although his overall focus is broad, Dahlhaus presents a stimulating framework in which to understand the symphony and its history in the 19th century.

STEDMAN covers the entire history of the genre, from its baroque antecedents to avant-garde contemporary pieces. However, the book includes a chapter on the Beethoven symphonies and a long chapter on the 19th-century symphony, both of which are addressed to non-experts interested in acquainting themselves with this repertory. For each composer, Stedman presents an overview of stylistic features and a description of each symphony with a chart containing such information as key, date, and the formal type of each movement. These passages are best considered as the beginnings of inquiry and not as answers per se. Subsequently, however, Stedman provides expanded discussion of "examples for study," a movement-by-movement listening guide with many musical examples and helpful charts that plot the course of each movement. No strikingly new perspectives are found here, but the book is a useful way into the repertory.

BONDS's starting point is a paradox: successful 19th-century symphonies were supposed to be creatively original works, yet at the same time they often seem to make conspicuous references to Beethoven's symphonies. Through an analysis of individual works by Berlioz, Mendelssohn, Schumann, Brahms, and Mahler, Bonds argues that these references to Beethoven do not suggest a lack of originality but are conscious choices that demonstrate an anxiety of influence with respect to Beethoven (Bonds borrows the phrase from literary critic

Harold Bloom) by which the new work confronts Beethoven's legacy and misreads the old master's work in order to make room for the creation of new symphonies. For example, a theme in the finale of Brahms's First Symphony might resemble the Ode to Joy theme from the finale of Beethoven's Ninth, but in Bonds's argument what is interesting is that the theme becomes less important over the course of the finale and ultimately loses its battle for prominence with the movement's other themes. Bonds does not strictly adopt Bloom's model of artistic influence but sensibly develops the theory's main concept, suggesting that we consider musical influence not as part of a historically inevitable evolution but as a series of active and sudden transformations.

The chapters on individual post-Beethoven symphonists in the volume edited by HOLOMAN, part of Schirmer's continuing Studies in Musical Genres and Repertories series, are written by experts in their respective fields. Most of the essays cover Austro-German composers: Schubert, Weber and Spohr, Schumann, Mendelssohn, Bruckner, Brahms, the Strauss tone poem, and the first four symphonies of Mahler. Treatments of canonic works dominate, but discussions of lesser-known portions of a composer's oeuvre are often included. For example, Newbould's chapter on Schubert reviews both the earlier symphonies and the incomplete piano sketch for a tenth symphony; Todd's essay on Mendelssohn examines the early string symphonies; and Brodbeck's chapter on Brahms considers the Serenades and aborted attempts that pre-date the First Symphony. Some of the most interesting passages concern the philosophical background that affected a composer's symphonic output, as in Roesner's chapter on Schumann and in Hefling's essay on Mahler. Readers will also find useful the bibliographies that conclude each essay. In general, this volume contains not in-depth analyses but overviews of individual composers' symphonic works and the interconnections between these pieces and the genre as a whole.

JOHN J. SHEINBAUM

Symphony: 19th-Century Russian

Asaf'ev, Boris Vladimirovich, *Russian Music from the Beginning of the Nineteenth Century,* translated by Alfred J. Swan, Ann Arbor, Michigan: Edwards, 1953

Bakst, James, *A History of Russian-Soviet Music,* New York: Dodd, Mead, 1966

Brown, David, "Russia before the Revolution," in *A Companion to the Symphony,* edited by Robert Layton, New York: Simon and Schuster, 1991

Calvocoressi, Michel D., *A Survey of Russian Music,* Middlesex: Penguin Books, 1944; reprint, New York: Greenwood Press, 1974

Field, Corey, editor, *The Musician's Guide to Symphonic Music,* Mainz: Schott, 1997

Taruskin, Richard, *Defining Russia Musically: Historical and Hermeneutical Essays,* Princeton, New Jersey: Princeton University Press, 1997

The development of Russian symphonic music in the 19th century is intertwined with parallel and anticipatory trends in Russian opera, programmatic music, the collection of folk music, and the development of art music as a whole. Most English-language sources skirt the complexities of this history by addressing the contributions of each symphonist separately, flanked by considerations of the composer's other works. Consequently, significant continuities from Glinka to the end of the century unique to orchestral music are lost. Few of the surveys offer a level of detail beyond that of ordinary program notes. On the other hand, several essays or parts of essays that are not confined to the symphony proper provide illuminating detail of great relevance to the tradition. Beyond these, the reader is urged to consult materials listed in the bibliographic essays on individual composers.

ASAF'EV's important survey on Russian instrumental music of the prerevolutionary period begins with a brief commentary on conditions before Glinka and ends with a discussion of the early careers of Stravinsky, Prokofiev, Shostakovich, and several of their lesser-known contemporaries. The main concern of the chapter titled "Instrumental Music" is the symphonic repertoire, with separate treatments of orchestral suites, overtures, and concertos following. As Asaf'ev discusses individual careers in roughly chronological order, he emphasizes the assimilation of native and foreign musical elements, providing numerous leads to obscure figures in music and the other arts. Often, the comparisons of the composers succeed in conveying the distinctions of the individual styles. Asaf'ev's idiosyncratic vocabulary and richly allusive descriptions are not always adequately rendered in Swan's translation. However, several hundred explanatory endnotes (from Asaf'ev and the translator) often provide necessary background to obscure points. The special effort required to read Asaf'ev is justified, for his is the only survey in English, other than Bakst's, in which the achievements of both Tchaikovsky and the Mighty Five are evaluated on their own merits and Russian music is properly presented as a confluence of styles, none of which can be accepted as the dominant or true path.

BAKST divides his survey of Russian composers and musical trends into prerevolutionary and postrevolutionary eras, somehow omitting Stravinsky altogether. All of the major figures in 19th-century music are assigned individual chapters, with Tchaikovsky and Rimsky-Korsakov receiving the two longest treatments. In each case, the biographical treatment is brief, with emphasis instead given to aesthetics, stories of operas and programmatic works, and descriptions of music. Bakst's descriptions of instrumental works are accessible to the general reader but often contain insights of use to specialists as well. Particularly valuable are his summaries of Tchaikovsky's instrumental forms, movement types, and aesthetics and his cogent assessments of the style and significance of lesser-known figures such as Anton Rubinstein, Anatoly Lyadov, and Sergey Taneyev.

BROWN's survey of prerevolutionary Russian symphonies belongs to the category of the "critical evaluation" of a designated topic. The author traces the genre from Glinka's aborted symphonic projects and orchestral fantasies through the symphonies of Sergey Taneyev's most talented pupils: Skryabin and Rachmaninov. Brown's doctrinaire Germanocentric aesthetic of the symphony leads him to some questionable assertions about inherent flaws in the Russian approach to the symphony—for example, he contends that Russian creativity is decorative, not dynamic and that Russian symphonies "rarely achieve [a] total identity of form and content." However, the methodical discussions of each composer's style and works, the musical examples, and the comments on historical context give the general reader a sufficient amount of information on familiar and lesser-known works.

The coverage of Russian orchestral music in CALVO-CORESSI, while brief, is often insightful, particularly on Balakirev and the others of the Mighty Five. The chapter on "Special Features of Russian Music" explains typical aspects of Russian folk song, harmony, mode, and meter both plainly and precisely. The chapters on composers give a general idea of the main trends, genres, and representative works in Russian orchestral music. However, because the author maintains a bias against the composers he identifies as non-nationalists (e.g., Rubinstein, Tchaikovsky, Glazunov, Rachmaninov), the coverage is uneven and the comments on their style and significance misleading. Consequently, one comes away without any sense of Tchaikovsky's characteristic musical idioms or of Anton Rubinstein's importance in the development of the Russian symphony.

FIELD's collection of program notes reproduced from Eulenberg pocket scores includes comments on the symphonies and orchestral works of Balakirev, Borodin, Glinka, Mussorgsky, Rimsky-Korsakov, and Tchaikovsky, most of which were written by Gerald Abraham and David Lloyd-Jones. Priority in all cases is given to providing background on the circumstances of composition, translated excerpts from the literary works that inspired the music, and a sampling of early critical opinion. The reprinted note for Russian works rarely contain thematic incipits or thematic or harmonic analyses. Nevertheless, the essays on Borodin, Mussorgsky, and on Tchaikovsky's six numbered symphonies, Manfred Symphony, concertos, and other works are noteworthy for their rich documentation of the compositional process.

TARUSKIN's essay "How the Acorn Took Root" focuses on the rich legacy of a work celebrated by Tchaikovsky as the acorn or seed from which sprouted the full Russian symphonic tradition: Glinka's orchestral fantasy on a Russian wedding song and a dance song, titled *Kamarinskaya*. After examining in detail its folk sources, harmony, and form, the author compares the work with the two Russian overtures of Balakirev, leader of the Mighty Five. Taruskin concludes that Balakirev and his followers deviate from Glinka's model in their incorporation of sonata schemes and a more Germanic approach to thematic development. However, he also notes Balakirev's folk-inspired harmonic devices, which deviate from Glinka by having less to do with Western European common practice. The essay concludes with brief comments on Balakirev's shifting programmatic comments and on further extensions of the *Kamarinskaya* influence on the orchestral works of Borodin and Rimsky-Korsakov.

DAVID HAAS

Symphony: 20th Century

Austin, William W., *Music in the 20th Century: From Debussy through Stravinsky,* New York: Norton, and London: Dent, 1966

Ballantine, Christopher John, *Twentieth Century Symphony,* London, Dobson, 1983

Griffiths, Paul, *Modern Music: A Concise History from Debussy to Boulez,* New York: Thames and Hudson, 1978; revised edition, 1994

Kostelanetz, Richard, and Joseph Darby, editors, *Classic Essays on Twentieth-Century Music: A Continuing Symposium,* New York: Schirmer, and London: Prentice Hall International, 1996

Stedman, Preston, *The Symphony,* Englewood Cliffs, New Jersey: Prentice Hall, 1979; 2nd edition, 1992

Straus, Joseph N., *Remaking the Past: Musical Modernism and the Influence of the Tonal Tradition,* Cambridge, Massachusetts: Harvard University Press, 1990

Watkins, Glenn, *Soundings: Music in the Twentieth Century,* New York: Schirmer, and London: Collier Macmillan, 1988

From a strict evolutionary standpoint, the symphony is a problematic genre in the 20th century. Because it is viewed as tied to the classical-romantic tonal tradition in which it developed and flourished, the symphony in the 20th century is often considered to be looking back, rather than forward; furthermore, as global wars undermined confidence in moral and social absolutes, the symphony's status as a cultural symbol eroded. Indeed, most histories of 20th-century music treat the symphony as a marginal phenomenon, with the most important compositional developments occurring in other genres.

In addition, much of the century's symphonic activity came not from the traditional Austro-German states but from places such as Russia, France, Scandinavia, England, Eastern Europe, and the United States. However, there are numerous important examples of symphonies in the 20th century. Many of them have participated in contemporary trends, and audiences and composers alike still view the genre as one of the chief areas for grand musical statements. In recent years, the postmodern questioning of a linear view of history and the relaxation of battle lines separating high and low culture, as well as those separating tonality and avant-garde trends in music, have led to a resurgence of interest in the symphony, as composers once again turn to the genre, but with less of a sense of the immense weight of the past.

AUSTIN's classic survey of 20th-century music begins by exploring Debussy and his contemporaries, then turns to Schoenberg, Bartók, and Stravinsky as modern music's prime movers, and lastly investigates styles coming after and connected to those figures, including Webern, Hindemith, and Prokofiev. One of the most important chapters critically discusses many of the catchwords and issues in 20th-century music, including impressionism, expressionism, romanticism and anti-romanticism, and neoclassicism. Although the symphony as a genre is not a real focus for Austin, there are numerous comments on orchestration and occasional in-depth analyses, as with Webern's *Symphonie,* op. 21. The author asserts that the genre is important more as a contextual than a purely musical phenomenon: in Russia, for example, where socialist leaders loved Beethoven and nurtured the notion that symphonies could promote nationalism, a "continuity of musical tradition unusual in the 20th century" could be achieved.

BALLANTINE's monograph is organized into three large sections. Part 1 is a survey of concepts, categories, and the evolution of the pre-20th-century symphony that serves as a frame of reference for the discussion of the contemporary pieces that follows. Part 2 explores conservative and radical innovations in form, and part 3 considers innovations in content. Ballantine's approach is too dependent on binary oppositions that occasionally contradict the details of his analyses; form is considered in opposition to content, and an artificial dividing line is constructed between conservative and radical innovations. However, such recourse to polar models is related to his thesis that dualism represents the "essence of the symphony," a dualism that stems from the rise of Hegelian dialectical thought and democratic principles of argument and debate in the 18th and 19th centuries. Ballantine asserts that the genre in the 20th century continues to be based on notions of dualistic symphonic conflict but is redefined away from the traditional opposition of themes and key areas. Thus, for example, methods that Ballantine labels self-opposition and immanent dualism are used to enable motivic cells within a single theme to function against one another and organize an entire movement without explicit connection to sonata form procedures.

In his discussion of uses of the past in recent composition, WATKINS agrees with Ballantine: contemporary composers of pieces labeled with the title symphony are not interested in exhuming the standard symphonic forms and procedures. However, by citing examples from some of the most familiar 20th-century composers, such as Davies, Carter, Lutoslawski, and Penderecki, the author argues that the resurrection of the genre since the 1970s is related less to the desire to work with new compositional issues than to the rise of commissions allowing for the showcasing of contemporary music culture through the familiar orchestral institutions. Although Watkins's survey does not have a special focus on the symphony, the reader can follow throughout his history a strand of 20th-century symphonic thought stemming from Mahler and often find in symphony examples the locus classicus of numerous important compositional procedures. This book is an excellent resource for an in-depth, lengthy exploration of 20th-century music without a greatly politicized point of view; Watkins focuses on reporting, with little attempt to impose a simple picture on the proliferation of styles and directions.

Whereas the conventional view of music in the first half of the 20th century posits opposing progressive and neoclassic trends, STRAUS argues that a "more fundamental unity" underlies these repertories—namely, the development of common strategies to grapple with the weight of the tonal tradition, through the use and reinterpretation of traditional elements in a post-tonal context. Thus, Straus sees the music of Stravinsky, Bartók, and the Second Viennese School as rife with allusions to the music of previous centuries, and he proposes that concepts related to an anxiety of influence (derived from the work of literary critic Harold Bloom) can help describe and explain such pieces. From this perspective, 20th-century composers evoke and then deny aspects of earlier composition. For example, even if emphasis is placed on a tonal sound such as a triad, that sound may "retain its sonorous identity but not its structural power." In Straus's view, 20th-century sonata form constructions are an important place to view these tensions, for while a harmonic organization is utilized, in the absence of operating tonal relations, a recreation of the form often results. Although Straus relies too heavily on Bloom's influence, and too often emphasizes only those aspects of pieces that fit his overall thesis, his argument is a fascinating one, which forces a fresh examination of these influential composers.

STEDMAN's text covers the entire history of the symphony, but almost half of his book is dedicated to the genre in the 20th century, including separate chapters devoted to the contemporary symphony in the United States and symphonists not discussed in the main body of the survey. He considers individual composers in roughly chronological order, with descriptions of stylistic traits, charts of information, and thumbnail accounts of each movement of each piece, as well as expanded examples for listening and study. The overriding picture is an eclectic one: Stedman sees the genre as supporting both neoclassicists and atonal revolutionaries, both antiexpressiveness and neoromanticism, and both traditional techniques and experiments with electronic, aleatory, and minimalist elements. He poses the important question of what the label symphony actually means, as the genre can fit almost any style of musical rhetoric. Too often, the author relies on easy descriptions and labels (the final chapter, on other 20th-century symphonists, is not much more than lists, organized by country, of more recent composers with the number of symphonies they have composed), but the novice will find the listening guides useful, as they present clearly themes and formal outlines that can help one to explore a new piece in an unfamiliar style.

The symphony does not loom large in GRIFFITHS's survey of 20th-century music, but there are numerous individual discussions of representative pieces, often with a provocative perspective. The riotous interpolations of American folk tunes in Ives's symphonies are seen as symptomatic of a turn-of-the-century nationalism—a nationalism also observable in Hungarian, Czech, and Spanish examples—that was interested in breaking with traditional Germanic uses of folk music. Messiaen's *Turangalîla* symphony is interpreted as a welding of a quasi-gamelan orchestration to non-Balinese rhythms and harmonies, resulting in an unmistakable example of the composer's stylistic traits, such as the symmetrical use of the chromatic scale known as modes of limited transposition. In Griffiths's view, the symphony is inherently connected to the tonal tradition. He describes Schoenberg's first chamber symphony as written in a tonal style and points out that the composer completed the second chamber symphony only in the 1930s, a period when he occasionally returned to composing tonal works. Further, Stravinsky's neoclassical symphonies are seen as problematic pieces because, in Griffiths's reading, they use the anachronistic procedures of tonality without implying a sense of irony. Indeed, for Griffiths, it is only armed with the recent (and still controversial) understanding of a subtext of refutation and refusal in Shostakovich's symphonies that the "most apparently reactionary music . . . might indeed be, on a different level, [his] most forward-looking." This book also includes a wealth of interesting visual matter, including photographs of autograph manuscripts and composer portraits.

KOSTELANETZ and DARBY's volume consists of a compilation of primary documents on 20th-century music. Such documents are consistently fascinating because they often present a very different point of view from the conventional wisdom reproduced in surveys and textbooks and as such are a valuable companion. Although there are no selections that comment on the

20th-century symphony per se, these essays force a rethinking of the genre as it operates in 20th-century lives and for 20th-century ears. Virgil Thomson's essay, "Why Composers Write How" (1939, revised 1962), for example, argues that 20th-century notions of musical beauty and authority are largely limited to the symphonic repertory of the romantic era. In Thomson's words, "A strange thing this symphonic repertory. From Tokyo to Lisbon, from Tel Aviv to Seattle, ninety percent of it is the same fifty pieces." Thomson also argues against notions of music as pure art devoid of societal connections, showing how economic factors such as commissions, teaching, and royalties can affect musical style. A Glenn Gould essay on "The Prospects of Recording" (1966) explores the relationships between the sound contemporary listeners expect from orchestras both on recordings and in the concert hall. In Gould's view, early symphonic recordings tried to reproduce the acoustics of the hall, resulting in a cathedral-like sound that reinforced notions of a religious-like devotion to music. Now that listeners are very familiar with recordings and the potential intimacy of even large orchestral pieces, he asserts, the desired sound of the concert hall is becoming too objective and studio-like. Echoing the controversy over his own piano recordings, Gould discusses the issue of recordings made up of splices as compared to whole symphony movements recorded in a single take and argues that the concert experience should be different from the experience of recorded music.

JOHN J. SHEINBAUM

T

Tablatures

Apel, Willi, *The Notation of Polyphonic Music 900–1600,* Cambridge, Massachusetts: Mediaeval Academy of America, 1942; 5th revised edition, 1953

Fabris, Dinko, "Lute Tablature Instructions in Italy: A Survey of the regole from 1507 to 1759," in *Performance on Lute, Guitar, and Vihuela: Historical Practice and Modern Interpretation,* edited by Victor Coelho, Cambridge: Cambridge University Press, 1997

Göllner, Marie Louise, "On the Process of Lute Intabulation in the Sixteenth Century," in *Ars Iocundissima: Festschrift für Kurt Dorfmüller zum 60. Geburtstag,* edited by Horst Leuchtmann and Robert Münster, Tutzing: Schneider, 1984

Poulton, Diana, *An Introduction to Lute Playing,* London: Schott, 1961

Rastall, Richard, *The Notation of Western Music,* New York: St. Martin's Press, 1982; London: Dent, 1983

Traficante, Frank, "Lyra Viol Tunings: 'All the Ways Have Been Tryed to Do It,'" *Acta Musicologica* 42 (1970)

Tyler, James, *The Early Guitar: A History and Handbook,* London: Oxford University Press, 1980

Tablature is a type of musical notation that emphasizes the placement of the player's fingers over the actual pitch of the notes. A number of different types of tablature notation were used for the music of keyboard, plucked, and bowed instruments through the 17th century. Although it disappeared from keyboard music in the 18th century, tablature notation is still used in popular guitar music to notate chords. It is particularly useful in those cases in which multiple tunings might be used, for example, in lute and viol music of the 17th century, and the player's ability to read the music is separated from the actual pitch of the notes. Tablature makes possible the notation of certain effects that may not be apparent in pitch-oriented notation; the choice of open or stopped string may have considerable effect on the overall sonority. Transcription of tablature into pitch-oriented notation is often controversial, notably for plucked instruments. The length of time a note vibrates, particularly as an open string, is not notated clearly in tablature notation. How this problem is handled becomes particularly acute where polyphonic lines are implied. The transcriber is faced with the decision whether to make these explicit by lengthening note values beyond those indicated in the tablature in order to make the connections between the notes of the "imaginary" melodic lines.

APEL provides a description of most types of tablature used for lute and plucked instruments through the 17th century. These types include German and Spanish keyboard tablatures, as well as Spanish, Italian, French, and German lute tablatures. He outlines the differences among the tablatures of the various countries. For example, French tablature uses a letter notation (a, b, c, etc.) to indicate frets, and the highest-pitch string is indicated as the top of six lines. Italian notation, on the other hand, uses numbers (1, 2, 3, etc.), and the bottom line indicates the highest string (as the instrument is held). Intended as a textbook for the teaching of transcription of early notations, the book provides facsimiles and exercises, the completion of which is left to the student. In transcribing tablature, it is crucial to know the tuning of the instrument. Here Apel has made a serious error. He interprets the remarks of Hans Judenkunig describing the tuning for the piece *Der Judentanz* to indicate that the top string should be tuned to F-sharp rather than G. In transcribing *Der Judentanz,* Apel produces a melody a half-step lower than what is in fact notated. He explains the resulting "bitonality" as cacophonous satire aimed at the Jews. Apel takes a rigorous view of tablature transcription, using only the rhythmic values notated in the tablature, not taking into account the length of time a string might in fact vibrate. He does not examine tablature associated with bowed strings.

RASTALL provides a historical overview, which is less detailed than Apel, because Restall does not intend his book to be a textbook on transcription, but he includes a number of tablatures omitted from Apel, such as lyra viol, guitar, ukulele, and flageolet.

A number of sources treat in detail tablatures for specific instruments. All lute instruction books, for example, include practical instructions on the reading of tablature for that instrument. POULTON has been included here as one source of many. An appendix include explanations of French, Italian, and German 16th-century lute tablatures, as well as a brief discussion of ornamental signs used in conjunction with the tablature. Poulton provides no musical examples of Italian and German tablatures. Other manuals are more or less complete in their explanations and examples, as well as their discussion of ornamental signs.

Intabulation—the process of transcribing a polyphonic vocal work, such as a madrigal or Mass movement, into tablature so that it could be played on a solo lute—was a common procedure in the 16th century. A number of instruction books and other sources provide evidence as to exactly how intabulation was done. Because polyphonic music was copied into individual part books, rather than in score, each voice was transcribed individually. This process is of general interest for scholars of 16th-century music because accidentals not notated in the vocal parts are often included in the tablature. Also, the lute versions are often highly ornamented, providing some evidence of improvisational technique. GÖLLNER explains procedures used for the intabulation of vocal music and cites the surviving examples of the process. FABRIS, while reiterating the rules given in instruction manuals for the intabulation process, offers a complete list of all the manuals that discuss the subject.

The music for lyra viol was developed in 17th-century England in imitation of the lute. It involves often complex chordal writing for the viol and is notated in a way resembling French lute tablature. TRAFICANTE provides a thorough discussion of the tablature and tunings associated with this music. He attempts to answer five questions: How many tunings were there? What were their characteristics? How are they notated in the sources? Can pitch names, if not actual pitches themselves be determined in each case? and Why did such variability arise?

The guitar did not develop its modern shape, tuning, notation, or stringing until the 19th century. From the late 16th through the 18th centuries, the five-course guitar was used. It had its own tablature notation and ornamental signs and a number of different tunings. TYLER thoroughly explains this notation together with the ornamental signs and their execution. His description includes a number of facsimiles.

ROBERT ANTHONY GREEN

Tallis, Thomas ca. 1505–1585

English composer

Benham, Hugh, *Latin Church Music in England, ca. 1460–1575*, London: Barrie and Jenkins, 1977
Doe, Paul, *Tallis*, London: Oxford University Press, 1968; 2nd edition, 1976
Harrison, Frank Llewellyn, *Music in Medieval Britain*, London: Routledge and Paul, 1958; 2nd edition, 1963
Le Huray, Peter, *Music and the Reformation in England, 1549–1660*, London: Jenkins, and New York: Oxford University Press, 1967

Thomas Tallis was one of the most prominent and influential composers of sacred music in England during the 16th century. Employed at several important churches in southern England, including Canterbury Cathedral, he was also for much of his life affiliated with the royal household, serving under Henry VIII, Edward VI, Mary I, and Elizabeth I. He seems to have begun full-time service as Gentleman of the Chapel Royal by 1543. Tallis's career spanned the tumultuous years of the English Reformation, and his music reflects the changing liturgical requirements during those years. The dating of his Latin polyphony has been a matter of some debate among scholars; not all of these pieces necessarily pre-date the Reformation as the Catholic rite was briefly revived under Mary Tudor, and new pieces setting Latin texts were commissioned at that time.

DOE's work, a short but in-depth study, remains the main monograph on Tallis. It presents an excellent overview of Tallis's works, with helpful musical examples for the reader who does not have access to editions of all of the pieces. There is also a useful work list included. Several recent articles and dissertations, focusing on specific aspects of the composer's career and music, augment the current assessment of Tallis's life and works, but Doe's work lays the groundwork for dating much of Tallis's repertoire. The book is not a biography; it looks instead at Tallis's music, supplying approximate dates for most the pieces and assigning them to liturgical categories. Doe focuses on providing a chronology for the pieces and uses this timeline to help define the various musical styles that the composer explored over the course of his long career. Although Doe cautions that no piece by Tallis can be dated with absolute certainty, he sees a trend in the composer's move from a highly melismatic style in the early years to a more succinct and refined style later on. This view is largely supported by more recent scholarship. Doe's work reflects the highly versatile nature of Tallis's composition. Not only did the composer write in a variety of musical styles, but he also wrote for almost every liturgical genre. Each of the chapters offers insightful summaries of the liturgical practices of the old Sarum rite and the new Anglican rite as it developed under Edward VI and Elizabeth I. Tallis's music is analyzed as a reflection of the liturgical requirements of the time in which it was written.

The rest of the studies listed here do not focus exclusively on Tallis but view his life and works within a larger context of English religious music from the 16th century. HARRISON's seminal study is chief among these books. Revolutionary in its approach at the time it was written, his examination of Tudor music as a product of the institutions that employed the musicians has opened new avenues of research for later scholars. The book is a model of careful archival research, and the appendices provide transcriptions and translations of several documents that shed light on the place of music within the framework of royal, collegiate, and monastic foundations as well as parish churches and cathedrals. Tallis is discussed in passing throughout the book, but his music becomes a focal point in the last few chapters. The last three chapters of Harrison's book divide the various genres of English church music into three groups: Mass and motet, votive antiphon and Magnificat, and other ritual forms including the carol. Several of Tallis's pieces are analyzed here and compared to the works of other Tudor composers. These chapters are especially useful for anyone interested in seeing how Tallis's works fit into the progression of musical style during the early part of the 16th century. Tallis's late works, and particularly those that set English texts, do not appear in this book, however.

LE HURAY's book picks up where Harrison's leaves off: its period of focus is the years 1549 to 1660. In other respects, however, this book is quite different from Harrison's. Rather than looking at the musical institutions and using this context as a prism through which to view the music, Le Huray's focus is more on the liturgical shifts of the time and their reflection in the music that was written for the ever-changing religious practices that define this period of English church history. Nevertheless, Le Huray's first chapter gives a pithy assessment of the musical changes in the religious establishments of the time and provides several useful charts detailing the musical capabilities (size of choir, date of establishment) of the new choral foundations at the start of the Reformation. Also in the first chapter is a comparison of the new and old liturgical forms in the first years of the Reformation. A later chapter, "The Elizabethan Settlement," looks closely at the makeup of the Royal Chapel at the time of Elizabeth's accession. Tallis's biography and his music figure strongly in the first chapters of this book. Only his later music is examined in detail, however; a list of all of Tallis's compositions setting English texts is found in chapter 7, "Edwardian and Early Elizabethan Church Music." Tallis's partnership with William Byrd in the publication of the *Cantiones Sacrae* is considered at various points in the book as well. Throughout the book, Le Huray discusses the various manuscript and printed sources for music from this period, summarizing the main sources containing Tallis's later works.

BENHAM's study is a good introduction to English church music from the period ca. 1460 to 1575. Examining only settings in Latin, this work finishes with a look at Tallis and Byrd's publication of the *Cantiones Sacrae* in 1575. Tallis's music is discussed in Chapter 11 along with the works of John Sheppard and Christopher Tye.

These three composers' careers began before the Reformation, and all three men had to adapt to the changing liturgical requirements of the new rite. Benham's grouping of these composers (along with some lesser composers mentioned at the end of the chapter) provides a useful means of comparing changing musical styles during the tumultuous time between Henry VIII's last years and the beginning of the reign of Elizabeth I. The analysis of individual pieces by Tallis tends to be brief, but the overall discussion is helpful for anyone looking for a general summary of Tallis's output.

NOËL BISSON

Taverner, John ca. 1495–1545

English composer

Benham, Hugh, *Latin Church Music in England, ca. 1460–1575,* London: Barrie and Jenkins, 1977

Flood, William Henry Grattan, *Early Tudor Composers,* London: Oxford University Press, 1925

Hand, Colin, *John Taverner: His Life and Music,* London: Eulenburg Books, 1978

Harrison, Frank Llewellyn, *Music in Medieval Britain,* London: Routledge and Paul, 1958; 2nd edition, 1963

Josephson, David S., *John Taverner: Tudor Composer,* Ann Arbor, Michigan: UMI Research Press, and Epping: Bowker, 1979

John Taverner was the most influential English composer of the first part of the 16th century and is best known for his sacred music. Despite the importance of his music and his fame both during his lifetime and today, the path of his career has been a matter of much debate among scholars, and his biographers have disagreed about several aspects of his career. Some of the most serious contention has arisen concerning the last decade or so of Taverner's life. More than a generation after Taverner's death, John Foxe, Protestant martyrologist, asserted in his *Acts and Monuments of Matters Special and Memorable Happening in the Church* (published 1563) that the composer became so involved with Protestant doctrine that he came to regret writing music for the Catholic rite and that at this point he gave up composition altogether. It seems now that there is little evidence to support this idea. Further allegations that late in his life Taverner became an agent for Thomas Cromwell and participated in the dissolution of religious foundations and the persecution of Catholics are also largely exaggerated or false. Several of the authors listed here have done much to dispel the myths about Taverner's later years.

FLOOD was the first of a group of early 20th-century scholars in England to rediscover Taverner's music after several centuries of neglect. His biography of the composer, however, has been substantially revised by later scholars. The author bases some of his work on archival sources that he did not wish to identify, and for this reason, proving some of his assertions has been problematic. Still, this biography became the foundation for later scholars and is an interesting example of early scholarship on Tudor music.

JOSEPHSON provides the most comprehensive coverage of Taverner's life and music; the book is particularly valuable for its reworking of the composer's biography. Part 1 deals entirely with Taverner's life and career; part 2 assesses the music, looking first at the source situation for the sacred music, then the sacred music itself, and, finally, the secular songs. Several appendices provide translations and transcriptions of a number of documents important to the understanding of Taverner's career. Josephson is not the first scholar to try to untangle the myths from the facts in Flood's biography of Taverner, but his work is the most recent and offers a new assessment of Taverner's life in light of new archival sources, while pointing out the holes that still remain in the biography. His reinterpretation of Taverner's later years is widely acknowledged now to be the correct reading of the sources. Josephson's analysis of Taverner's music is also comprehensive. His chapter on the church music examines all the genres of Taverner's composition: Masses, antiphons, and Magnificats. The section on the Masses is particularly thorough. The chapter on Taverner's secular songs is one of very few studies to deal with this portion of the composer's output.

HAND's study, like Josephson's, deals first with Taverner's life and then with his music. In addition, it includes a third section on Taverner's musical style. The biographical portion of this book is much shorter than Josephson's and has less original research, but like Josephson, Hand discounts the common acceptance of Foxe's controversial statements about Taverner's last years. This assessment of Taverner's life is a good, quick overview but gives less coverage than Josephson. Hand's musical analysis is a bit more detailed than his biographical chapter. He provides a lengthy discussion of the Masses, dividing them into the categories of "festal" and "non-festal" settings, but only brief mention is made of the secular songs. The short final chapter on the composer's musical style makes mostly very general comments about Taverner's part-writing, and his use of imitation, harmony, text setting, and form.

The remaining books discussed here are not devoted exclusively to Taverner and his music but are instead larger studies. All of them, however, contribute to the field of Taverner studies. No mention of scholarship on Tudor composers can be made without reference to HARRISON's landmark work. In addition to its useful summaries of the careers of Tudor composers and their music, it also provides a careful analysis of the institutions that employed these composers. Harrison's focus on the musical establishments of pre-Reformation England spawned a whole generation of English musicological work on the connection between composers and their places of work as well as a new way of looking at the music that was written to be performed by the choirs of specific cathedrals, parish churches, or collegiate, monastic, and royal foundations. Harrison discusses Taverner's music within this context, examining the types of pieces the composer wrote and the choirs for which the pieces were written. By tracing English sacred music in its institutional context up to the eve of the Reformation, Harrison shows how Taverner's music fits within a larger framework of a growing musical tradition in pre-Reformation England. The main focus of the book is late 15th- and early 16th-century music, and several works by Taverner are discussed in great detail.

BENHAM's book is also a survey, but his focus is later than Harrison's, beginning in 1460 and ending in 1575, and spans the period of the Reformation. Benham limits his study by considering music only in Latin, thus excluding pieces in English which were written for the new Anglican rite. This limitation is not a problem for anyone studying Taverner's church music, however, for he set only Latin texts in these pieces. In the first four chapters, Benham addresses the topics of style and character of the sacred music from this period, explaining general issues of performance (for instance, scoring, notation, and tempo), and then turns to the topics of musical form and structure. The remainder of the book is devoted to the works of specific composers. After a brief synopsis of Taverner's life, Benham provides a quick survey of all of the composer's sacred music, emphasizing a few choice pieces. His summaries are sufficient for a quick introduction to the material, but most of the analyses merely scratch the surface. Nevertheless, this is a useful book for understanding Taverner's music within the greater context of Tudor music both before and after the Reformation.

NOËL BISSON

Tchaikovsky, Piotr Ilyich 1840–1893

Russian-born composer

1. Biography

Brown, David, *Tchaikovsky: A Biographical and Critical Study*, 4 vols., London: Gollancz, 1983–91

———, *Tchaikovsky Remembered*, London: Faber, 1993; Portland, Oregon: Amadeus, 1994

Poznansky, Alexander, *Tchaikovsky's Last Days: A Documentary Study*, Oxford: Clarendon Press, and New York: Oxford University Press, 1996

Tchaikovsky, Peter Ilyich, *Letters to His Family: An Autobiography*, translated by Galina von Meck, New York: Stein and Day, and London: Dobson, 1981

———, *To My Best Friend: Correspondence between Tchaikovsky and Nadezhda von Meck, 1876–1878*, translated by Galina von Meck, Oxford: Clarendon Press, 1993

Tchaikovsky is one of the most lavishly documented composers in music history; his letters, his autobiographical texts, and his articles in the press are numerous, as are the accounts of those who were associated with him in Russia and in the West. Between 1940 and 1971, the Soviet state publishing house issued, as part of the publication of his complete works, a number of volumes of those documents, the majority of which were kept in the Tchaikovsky archives in Klin.

Among these documents, the most important for Tchaikovsky's biography are (1) Modest Tchaikovsky's work in three volumes, *Zhizn P.I. Chaykovskovo* (Tchaikovsky's life) (1900–1902); (2) Tchaikovsky's *Dnevniki* (Diaries) (1923); (3) his *Perepiska s N.F. von Meck* (Correspondence with N. F. von Meck), in three volumes, (1934–36); (4) his *Pisma k bliskim* (Letters to his Family) (1955); (5) the *Vospominaniya o P.I. Chaykovskom* (Reminiscences of Tchaikovsky) edited by Protopopov (1962, 1973, 1979, 1980). In addition, Peter Jürgenson, Tchaikovsky's editor in Moscow, issued a *Catalogue thématique des oeuvres de P. Tschaikowsky* in 1897 (it was reedited in London, 1965). These editions have been a generous help to scholars and have permitted the propagation of knowledge about Tchaikovsky. Well-documented English books on Tchaikovsky appeared throughout the 20th century, and today the study of Tchaikovsky's life and work is revivified, as is the case with the entire history of Russian music.

BROWN (1983–91) is a monumental critical study and the standard book on Tchaikovsky. Aptly, the discussion of his music, inseparable from the man, is interwoven in the biography. Characteristics of the music are exhibited with the help of numerous examples, but the discussion rarely leads to complicated technical analyses. Brown shows how important and representative of Tchaikovsky's creativity are works that have not gained popularity in the West, most notably the greatest part of his operas. The author elucidates Tchechov's belief that Tchaikovsky was the greater Russian artist after Tolstoy, and Stravinsky's judgement that Tchaikovsky's music, with all its refinement and mastery, is more Russian than the music of the "Five," whose works were artificial reconstructions of popular melodies that had been strongly Germanized. Brown supplies information on Tchaikovsky's interest in and contribution to the music of the Russian Orthodox Church, a subject silenced by the Soviets (their "complete" edition of Tchaikovsky's work does not include his church music) and ignored by Westerners; Brown discusses Tchaikovsky's own church music, his *Short Manual of Harmony Adapted to the Study of Religious Music in Russia*, a request of the

Russian Synod, as well as his editing of Bortnyansky's complete church music in ten volumes. Brown describes Tchaikovsky's death, a subject of fervent debate among researchers, considering both the documents supporting the officially reported cause of cholera and the evidence published by Alexandra Orlova in 1981 (*Music and Letters*), which discloses the allegedly common secret among Russians that Tchaikovsky was forced to commit suicide for reasons relevant to his homosexuality. Brown seems to close the subject in a state of pure uncertainty.

The main source for BROWN (1993) is *Vospominaniya o P.I. Chaykovskom*, cited above. More than 80 people (correspondents, journalists, and memoirists) are quoted in a comprehensive characterization of the relative, the friend, the student, the teacher, the public personality, and the composer. The documents are laid out in chronological order and are preceded by short informative comments. An introductory chronology gives the most important dates of Tchaikovsky's life as well as the political and cultural events that influenced him. In a chapter entitled "How Did Tchaikovsky Die?" the subject of the composer's death is treated more extensively than in Brown (1983–91), but by 1993 (and subsequent to Orlova's report), all possible theories concerning the cause of Tchaikovsky's death had been explored.

TCHAIKOVSKY (1981) consists of 681 letters by the composer written between 1861 and 1893, which are preceded by short explanatory notes. The frequency of the letters' succession creates an autobiography from Tchaikovsky's student years on. It is fascinating reading, attesting to the composer's affectionate feelings for his close family and friends, his inner sentiments and weaknesses, his humor, his opinion on others, and his ideas on matters of music, society, culture, and politics. The translator, Galina von Meck, is the daughter of Tchaikovsky's niece, Anna Davydova, and Nikolay (Kolia) von Meck, son of the composer's patroness, Nadezda von Meck, whom Tchaikovsky contacted by correspondence only. Meck's annotations, written together with Percy M. Young, are efficacious, as is the biographical index, disclosing information on the less popular among the persons mentioned in the letters.

TCHAIKOVSKY (1993) is a translation of the first volume of *Perepiska s N.F. von Meck* (cited above), the correspondence with the composer's famous associates, in which the composer elaborates extensively on his creative process (the first four symphonies, the piano and violin concertos, the opera *Eugene Onegin*, and other famous works are discussed in this volume), his musical tastes, his outlook on music, love, and other topics. The editors provide a context for the events discussed in the 276 letters, and they append extracts from letters by Antonina Miliukova, the unfortunate heroine of Tchaikovsky's catastrophic marriage.

POZNANSKY refutes all theories and gossip that attribute Tchaikovsky's death to any cause other than cholera, using sound reasoning and sources never before published to support his case. Recovering all previously censored passages in Tchaikovsky's correspondence, Poznansky dismisses any unflattering picture of the composer. Thus, although he blames Western scholars for having misinterpreted Tchaikovsky's Russian soul as morbid, one can hardly find a more extensive and exclusive text on the morbid side of Tchaikovsky than the author's introduction. In short, Poznansky gives a partial picture of the composer but effectively refutes the debates on Tchaikovsky's death.

EKATERINI ROMANOU

2. Ballets

Warrack, John, *Tchaikovsky Ballet Music,* London: British Broadcasting Corporation, and Seattle: University of Washington Press, 1979

Wiley, Roland John, *The Life and Ballets of Lev Ivanov: Choreographer of The Nutcracker and Swan Lake,* Oxford: Clarendon Press, and New York: Oxford University Press, 1997

———, *Tchaikovsky's Ballets: Swan Lake, Sleeping Beauty, Nutcracker,* Oxford: Clarendon Press, and New York: Oxford University Press, 1985

Wiley, Roland John, editor, *A Century of Russian Ballet: Documents and Eyewitness Accounts, 1810–1910,* Oxford: Clarendon Press, and New York: Oxford University Press, 1990

Zajaczkowski, Henry, *Tchaikovsky's Musical Style,* Ann Arbor, Michigan: UMI Research Press, 1987

The glaring gap in English-language writing on the ballets of Tchaikovsky has been filled single-handedly by Roland John Wiley. His major contribution, Wiley (1985), is a full-length study that illuminates the social and artistic milieu of the imperial ballet by documenting productions and collaborations with choreographers and by offering musical analyses. Wiley has recently supplemented his fundamental study with translations of source documents and a biography of Tchaikovsky's lesser-known choreographer. The need to which Wiley responds is evidenced in Warrack's writing, which resembles program notes and is intended as a brief listener's guide. Zajaczkowski's references to the ballets are few, but they show how Tchaikovsky's procedures in the ballets relate to the composer's general practice.

WARRACK introduces three broad issues: the ballets' relation to Tchaikovsky's symphonic style, Russian influence, and interrelations between drama and music. Responding to the well-known paradox that critics sometimes find the ballet music too symphonic and the symphonic music too balletic, Warrack suggests that the use of a lyrical idea as the basis for extended dance movements is the source of the symphonic quality of the ballets.

He traces the Russian influence to Glinka's practice of developing a tune by varied repetition and combination. Musico-dramatic relations are especially strong in *Swan Lake,* for which Warrack identifies the tonal unity provided by a central dramatic idea and shows how the action is related by key to this area. The balance of the guide treats each of the three ballets individually, with brief plot descriptions accompanied by musical examples. Supplementing the descriptions are pithy observations on key areas and motivic development as they reinforce the dramatic high points (*Swan Lake*); dramatic and choreographic connections, conflicting themes for main characters, and large-scale tonal plan (*Sleeping Beauty*); and orchestral color, melody, and Hoffmanesque character (*Nutcracker*). The commentary is geared to readers with no technical background. The reader should be aware of recent alternatives to Warrack's presumption that the music reflects the composer's homosexual torment, notably those views expressed in Alexander Poznansky's *Tchaikovsky: The Quest for the Inner Man* (1991).

WILEY (1990) offers translations of selected documents. Of particular interest is the chapter on the 1890s, which includes four documents relevant to *Sleeping Beauty:* the libretto by Vsevolozhsky and articles by three persons who were present at early performances. Scant portions of Konstantin Skalkovsky's review of the premiere appeared in Wiley's earlier study (1985), but they are better translated here and gain much in the context of the entire review. The same is true of the early review by Tchaikovsky's friend German Laroche. The full citation illuminates Laroche's concern with the meanings of national identity, genre, and fairy tale. The third article is a reminiscence by Alexandre Nikolaevich Benois, an elderly artist who recalls the *Sleeping Beauty* of his youth. Interestingly, Benois bases his passion least on lyrico-melodious elements and most on fantasy-like qualities. He finds profound meaning in the fable and makes a historical connection between *Sleeping Beauty* and the work of the Diaghilev circle.

WILEY (1997) provides further context with his biography of Lev Ivanov, choreographer of *Nutcracker* and *Swan Lake.* Arguing for a reassessment of Ivanov, he disputes the imperial and Soviet views that the choreographer was mistreated by the foreigner Petipa and that the theater directorship discriminated against him. Instead, Wiley emphasizes the fact that Ivanov was the younger assistant to the established choreographer, Petipa. And if Ivanov were held in as low esteem as the imperial histories and Soviet writers suggest, Wiley questions why the theater director would give the assistant choreographer responsibility for two grand ballets. The first section begins with a translation of Ivanov's memoirs. A biographical reconstruction follows, drawing on eyewitness accounts, contracts, correspondence, and reviews. The second section deals with Ivanov's ballets. Some of this material will seem redundant to the reader of Wiley

(1985) but it is necessary to round out the picture of Ivanov. And Wiley adds an exploration of the collaboration between Petipa and Ivanov to ascertain who actually did what in *Nutcracker.* Similarly, he looks at Petipa's sketches to sort out each man's role in the revival of *Swan Lake.* Wiley places these two ballets in the context of Ivanov's life and career amid the inner workings of the imperial theater.

WILEY (1985), the author's seminal study, is the first full-length book on the topic. The introduction centers on performing traditions—particularly the collaboration of choreographer and composer, which encompassed varying degrees of reworking—and the role of the ballet audience. Instead of relying on present-day revivals that, as Wiley suggests, can produce false assumptions, he supplies copious documentary evidence from the imperial period: holograph scores, *répétiteurs* (rehearsal reductions), choreographic notation, librettos, reviews, and eyewitness accounts. While Russian writers claim a continuity of tradition, Wiley considers evolving performance traditions. He broaches enticing ontological questions that invite fuller investigation: Is a ballet defined by the score, the libretto, and/or the choreography? Do changes in performance create a new identity?

Wiley's chapter on the Moscow production of *Swan Lake* focuses on the libretto, composition, collaboration, cast, and production. He addresses several controversial issues: he finds no evidence to support Modeste Tchaikovsky's supposition regarding the uncertain authorship of the libretto; he shows that the holograph score shows differences between the composer's remarks in that score and the libretto; he reveals that press documents contradict historical assumptions of extensive cuts; and he posits that two sets of the choreographer Petipa's instructions to Tchaikovsky must be distinguished from each other and from the choreographer's plan (a widely published third set). For Wiley, one should not measure Tchaikovsky's work against symphonic composers—as Soviet writers have done—but against the ballet specialist composers whom he eclipsed. For instance, in *Swan Lake,* Wiley identifies sophisticated uses of tonality in both an association with a character or circumstance and in a particular progression that intensifies critical points in the narrative. Despite their depth, such discussions of tonality, melody, and orchestration remain accessible to the general reader.

The middle three chapters on *Sleeping Beauty* address Vsevolozhsky's theater reform in St. Petersburg; relations between the theater director, choreographer, and composer; documentation of the first production; and such musical issues as thematic unity (on which Wiley places more emphasis than does Warrack), rhythm (attributing complaints that the music was not suitable for dancing to the contrapuntal activity and metric displacement that obscure the pulse), sonority, classical variation, and tonality (advancing a tonal-dramatic interpretation). On comparing the score with Petipa's instructions, Wiley disputes the notion that Petipa supplied Tchaikovsky with detailed instructions, which the composer simply fulfilled.

The next chapter examines the first production of *Nutcracker* in light of the source documents. As do most writers, Wiley emphasizes sonority and melody in this work, but he also traces tonal connections to the story, particularly surprise changes of key. His final chapter on the St. Petersburg revival of *Swan Lake* documents the extensive cuts and revisions. Several useful appendices provide source material: scenarios translated from first editions of the librettos, poster of the first performance of *Swan Lake* in English translation, Petipa's scenarios for *Sleeping Beauty* and for *Nutcracker,* metronome markings in the holograph score of *Sleeping Beauty,* choreographic notation for the "Waltz of the Snowflakes," and a comparison of the St. Petersburg performance scores of *Sleeping Beauty* and *Swan Lake.*

ZAJACZKOWSKI is the main analytical English-language source on the music of Tchaikovsky. The author's brief references to the ballets are situated in the larger context of the major works, helping the reader connect the composer's procedures in the ballets to the balance of the repertoire—primarily the symphonies. For example, in considering Tchaikovsky's humor, the author compares the scherzo of the Fourth Symphony to the transformation of the love theme in the vision sequence of *Sleeping Beauty.* For Zajaczkowski, *Nutcracker* has been unfairly maligned by musicologists who treat it as an exercise in orchestral color rather than a work marked by emotional intensity. He supports this view with a comparison to the Sixth Symphony, in which he notes some Nutcracker-like material within a portentous context.

Beyond the observations made by Warrack and Wiley, Zajaczkowski addresses specific harmonic techniques. For instance, in the meeting of Siegfried and Odette in the final scene of *Swan Lake,* he connects the use of the augmented triad to the dramatic meaning of the scene. Adding to that meaning, he identifies a type of successive dissonance that forestalls the expected resolution.

CATHERINE COPPOLA

3. Operas

Abraham, Gerald, *Tchaikovsky: A Symposium,* London: Drummond, 1946

Brown, David, *Tchaikovsky: A Biographical and Critical Study,* 4 vols., London: Gollancz, 1983–91

Campbell, Stuart, editor, *Russians on Russian Music, 1830–1880: An Anthology,* Cambridge: Cambridge University Press, 1994

Kearney, Leslie, editor, *Tchaikovsky and His World,* Princeton, New Jersey: Princeton University Press, 1998

Taruskin, Richard, *Defining Russia Musically: Historical and Hermeneutical Essays*, Princeton, New Jersey: Princeton University Press, 1997

Zajaczkowski, Henry, *Tchaikovsky's Musical Style*, Ann Arbor, Michigan: UMI Research Press, 1987

More than any other composer, with the possible exception of Wagner, Tchaikovsky has suffered the misfortune of having his music judged through the filter of his personal life. In part because rumors of his homosexuality circulated outside Russia around the same time as the Oscar Wilde trial of 1895, critical reception of his music in the West turned from very favorable to intensely disapproving. Literature on the operas, only two of which are well known outside his own country, reflects the general opinion that Tchaikovksy's music is overly sentimental, poorly organized, and even in some way pathological. With recent changes in social attitudes, a more dispassionate judgment of his operas has emerged, but it is still a rare occurrence for a study of the music to omit discussion of Tchaikovsky's biography altogether.

ABRAHAM's book is a suitable place to begin an acquaintance with Tchaikovsky's ten operas. The author starts with the composer's general attitude toward opera: Tchaikovsky believed that opera was the most effective way to speak to the general public rather than a handful of connoisseurs and that the music must deal in deep human emotion. He also suggested that one predominant, broad, and simple motive must be coupled with living characters and strong, swift action. Tchaikovsky was more interested in the Italian opera of his day than in the Russian experiment in realism (which, he contended, led to the complete negation of opera) or the music drama of Wagner; he was not interested in stories from distant places, times, or levels of reality. The rest of the chapter on the composer's operas addresses each opera in turn, including the circumstances of each work's composition and performance, and showing that the most successful ones—*Eugene Onegin* and *The Queen of Spades*—are precisely those that follow Tchaikovsky's own strictures. The other eight operas, rarely discussed, are treated to Abraham's acute commentary, in which he notes such features as their use of Russian folk song or their affinity with the composer's instrumental works.

BROWN combines biography with musical commentary in his four-volume work on Tchaikovsky. The discussion of each opera is therefore found in its chronological place: *The Voyevoda, Undine, The Oprichnik,* and *Cherevichki (Vakula the Smith)* in volume 1; *Eugene Onegin* in volume 2; *The Maid of Orleans* and *Mazepa* in volume 3; and *The Enchantress, The Queen of Spades,* and *Iolanta* in volume 4. Brown follows the creation of each opera from first conception through the process of composition to performance and reception. A detailed plot summary and a scene-by-scene description of the musical treatment are provided in the main entry for each opera, and each work is mentioned elsewhere in the text where appropriate. At the end of volume 4, in lieu of an overall summary of the composer's style, Brown attempts to show some of the Russianness of Tchaikovsky's music. Together with "A Note on the Russianness of *Eugene Onegin*" in volume 2, this conclusion is essential reading if one is to understand Brown's vision of Russianness and hence the reaction of other writers to the author's work.

Chief among these writers is TARUSKIN, who argues against Brown's radical view of Russianness, according to which a Russian composer *must* be nationalist in order to be taken seriously, and yet Russians are excluded from the critical and academic canon for the very same reason. In his chapter "P.I. Tchaikovsky and the Ghetto," Taruskin examines the 19th-century polemics in both Russia and France that led to present-day attempts to vindicate Tchaikovsky as a nationalist. Taruskin specifically targets Brown's discussion of Russianness, showing that Brown posits that Russian nationalism requires the use of folk song, peasant lore, and music that springs straight from the Russian unconscious. Thus, Brown assumes that any use of Western technique is an adulteration of Russian purity, but the failure to use it is the badge of inferiority. After arguing against this view of Russianness, Taruskin moves on to an admirable explication of Tchaikovsky's music for *Eugene Onegin,* defending it eloquently from all manner of critics and criticism.

As KEARNEY states in her introduction to the group of essays she has edited, "Russian arts are not only inseparable from their social and political environment, but are also intensely interconnected." This statement could be extended in the case of Tchaikovsky to the connections between the composer's personal life and his music, including the critical assessments of both his biography and his music by Russian and Western writers. The curiously backhanded admiration of many Western critics for all of Russian music is amplified in the case of Tchaikovsky by the tendency of those critics to see his music in terms of their distaste for his personal life. Thus, Alexander Poznansky's essay "Tchaikovsky: A Life Reconsidered" is helpful because it represents the most recent scholarship on the composer's biography. Other essays in this book deal with particular characters in *Eugene Onegin*. The anthology also contains two views of *The Maid of Orleans:* one is by the critic for the *Moskovskie vedomosti* (Moscow News) in 1899, and the other is Kearney's convincing proposal that the heroine Joan is presented by Tchaikovsky as someone who, like the composer himself, stood outside the norms of society.

ZAJACZKOWSKI's book is not confined to the operas but is useful nonetheless for its detailed examination of Tchaikovsky's musical style. The author allows ample space for the discussion of structure, harmony, and orchestration; a wealth of examples include some from the operas, all ten of which are mentioned in the text. In addition, Tchaikovsky's style is set in the context of other Russian composers with minimal references to the sometimes tiresome polemics on Russianness and personal life of the composer. The book is a refreshing tonic for those who want to learn more about the music, which Zajaczkowski aims to deliver from the "musicological pantomime of derision that has passed for serious critical assessment . . . for so many years." The tone is objective, the admiration genuine, and the judgment reliable.

Tchaikovsky's own critical journalism is represented in CAMPBELL's anthology by his assessments of *Ruslan and Lyudmila* and Dargomizhsky's *Rusalka* and *The Stone Guest*. In the reviews by Laroche and Cui of three of his early operas, *The Voyevoda, The Oprichnik,* and *Eugene Onegin,* we see some of the same criticisms that are still alive today. It is worth remembering that, by the end of his lifetime in 1893, Tchaikovsky was considered a national treasure. Having passed through the critical fire of the last century, perhaps we have almost come full circle in our appreciation of this composer.

MARY S. WOODSIDE

4. Orchestral Music

Abraham, Gerald, editor, *Tchaikovsky,* London: Duckworth, 1944; as *The Music of Tchaikovsky,* New York: Norton, 1946

Asaf'ev, Boris Vladimirovich, *Russian Music from the Beginning of the Nineteenth Century,* translated by Alfred J. Swan, Ann Arbor, Michigan: Edwards, 1953

Brown, David, *Tchaikovsky: A Biographical and Critical Study,* 4 vols., London: Gollancz, 1983–91

Keller, Hans, "Peter Ilyich Tchaikovsky," in *The Symphony,* vol. 1: *Haydn to Dvorak,* edited by Robert Simpson, Hammondsworth: Penguin Books, 1966

Kraus, Joseph Charles, "Tonal Conflict and Resolution in Tchaikovsky's Symphony No. 5 in E Minor," *Music Theory Spectrum* 13 (1991)

Norris, Jeremy, *The Russian Piano Concerto,* Bloomington: Indiana University Press, 1994

Taruskin, Richard, *Defining Russia Musically: Historical and Hermeneutical Essays,* Princeton, New Jersey: Princeton University Press, 1997

Warrack, John, *Tchaikovsky: Symphonies and Concertos,* London: British Broadcasting Corporation, 1969; 2nd edition, 1974

Zajaczkowski, Henry, *Tchaikovsky's Musical Style,* Ann Arbor, Michigan: UMI Research Press, 1987

Zhitomirsky, Daniel, "[Tchaikovsky's] Symphonies," in *Russian Symphony: Thoughts About Tchaikovsky,* by Dmitri Shostakovich et al., New York: Philosophical Library, 1947

Tchaikovsky's original works for orchestra include six numbered symphonies, the programmatic *Manfred* Symphony, five concerti, more than a dozen overtures and tone poems, four orchestral suites, and miscellaneous smaller works. Despite the sizable output and the overwhelming popularity of perhaps a dozen pieces, there is no book-length study on the orchestral music and only a single recent study of the composer's musical style. Therefore, the interested listener must assemble an understanding from essays on Tchaikovsky in edited volumes and the program notes or work descriptions that appear episodically in biographical studies. Of the biographies, Brown's exceeds all the others in its attention to matters of style and composition.

ABRAHAM identifies the contributors to his Tchaikovsky handbook as prominent music critics, and indeed, their essays do emphasize the composer's strengths and weaknesses. Three chapters are devoted to orchestral music not originally belonging to stage works. Martin Cooper's essay on the symphonies is organized around general aspects of the style and such issues as Lisztian cyclic form, the problem of Tchaikovsky's themes, and the incorporation of native Russian material. Eric Blom champions the Piano Concerto no. 1 but faults aspects of the design of its first movement. In his chapter on the remaining orchestral works, Ralph Wood decides that *Francesca da Rimini* is the most successful and the 1812 Overture the least. His descriptions provide a good basic knowledge on what is traditional and what is unusual in the composer's formal designs, instrumentation, and programmatic evocation.

ASAF'EV's one-volume history of Russian music contains three chapters on orchestral music from the late 18th century through the beginning of the 20th century. Swan's translation of this major scholar's idiosyncratic style is occasionally awkward but still serviceable. From Asaf'ev one gains a unique perspective on the place of Tchaikovsky's symphonies in the general development of the symphony in Russia. The author's allusive style and endnotes provide the Western reader with considerable information on musical influences, affinities, and distinctions among the works of Tchaikovsky, Western Europeans, and other Russians. The argument positing a Tchaikovskian "lyrico-dramatic" symphonic type versus an epic, panoramic type in Borodin and others is a mainstay of much Russian writing on the symphony.

Each of the four volumes in BROWN's life-and-works study contains discussion of numerous compositions. Special attention is given to Symphonies no. 1 and 2 and early shorter works in the first volume; Symphonies no. 3 and 4, the B-flat Minor Piano Concerto, and Violin Concerto in the second volume; the orchestral suites in the third volume; and Symphonies no. 5 and 6 in the last. Much space in the work commentaries is devoted to interpretation and criticism, both drawing on the author's knowledge of published letters and other documents. In the analysis of featured works, priority is given to the ordering of themes, the main key areas, and the interthematic motivic links. Brown's chart of motives for the B-flat Minor Piano Concerto establishes plausible links between the soaring introductory theme and later themes distributed throughout three movements. The interpretations of the three last symphonies are perhaps too strongly tied to the author's overriding speculative views on the composer's psyche and character.

KELLER spares the reader from the typical evaluation of Tchaikovsky's symphonies in accordance with Germanic norms, instead providing insight into the works' salient qualities and intriguing speculations as to their significance for later symphonists. Keller regards Symphony no. 4 as the finest of the lot, and it receives the most attention. Keller's lucid commentary is useful both for his analysis of the novel yet logical harmonic plan and for his perceptions on the thematic character, contrasts, growth, and interactions.

KRAUS's study of Symphony no. 5 constitutes the most extensive harmonic analysis to date of a full-length work by Tchaikovsky and is also an intriguing first attempt at interpreting this famous work's programmatic/emotional content on the basis of a thorough and nonpartisan consideration of the composer's treatment of harmony. Using the voice-leading reductive techniques of the Austrian theorist Heinrich Schenker, Kraus interprets large-scale harmonic events within individual movements and then extends the ideas of Schenker to investigate a long-range strategy involving the opposition of the keys of E minor and D major that is unique to this symphony. This exemplary analysis is indispensable reading for theorists and for all other scholars and audiences interested in substantiating their intuitions as to programmatic content on the basis of closely observed harmonic as well as thematic events.

NORRIS devotes a lengthy chapter to the piano concerti and other concert works of Tchaikovsky, replete with musical examples and analytical diagrams. Much of his commentary concerns the pianistic idiom and the modifications to the Piano Concerto no. 1 suggested by the first generation of performers. The analysis is confined to a matching of themes with keys and a somewhat more ambitious identification of interthematic links derived largely from the work of David Brown.

TARUSKIN's polemical essay "Chaikovsky and the Human: A Centennial Essay" is necessary reading for anyone seriously interested in aesthetic, social, and stylistic contexts for Tchaikovsky's orchestral music. Intending to promote a wholesale reappraisal of the composer's achievement, the author touches on a wide range of works and topics. At the center of the essay is an extended consideration of four oft-neglected works, the four nonballetic orchestral suites. The descriptions of individual movements offer a wealth of detail on Tchaikovsky's compositional craft and collectively substantiate a characterization of the composer as a producer of nonconfessional, absolute music in the tradition of his idol, Mozart. The juxtaposition of melancholic waltz and triumphal polonaise in the Orchestral Suite no. 3, however, inspires a reflection on the two dances' discrete connotations in the Symphony no. 4 and other works.

WARRACK's slim volume consists of a compendium of program notes on the individual symphonies and concerti preceded by an exposition of several global issues. Discussing Tchaikovsky's consideration of the lyrical aspect of the 19th-century symphony, Warrack concludes that the composer is speaking of melodic ideas. In the work discussions, the author's focus is on the presentation and transformation of important themes.

ZAJACZKOWSKI's uniquely designed study of Tchaikovsky's compositional style contains no work-by-work survey, but rather a global consideration of motivic linking procedures, developmental procedures, harmony, and orchestration. This short but valuable book is distinguished first by its consistently high level of technical detail and second by the author's willingness to engage the many facets of Tchaikovsky's style independently of Germanic or other aesthetic norms. No analytical technique is systematically applied; instead, the author imparts a sense of Tchaikovsky's idiosyncratic compositional system by building it up, component by component, with lucid descriptions of representative passages from works, many of them accompanied by musical examples in short score.

The admirable anonymous translation of ZHITOMIRSKY's essay introduces an English-language readership to an important Soviet-era scholar on 19th-century music. Zhitomirsky rightly interprets Tchaikovsky's conception of the symphony as a lyrical form as a linkage with the poetic lyric and not as a self-limitation to lyrical themes. Much of the essay is concerned with defining emotional and philosophical content on the basis of thematic character. The thematic affinities with the music of other composers help substantiate Zhitomirsky's terse characterizations and facilitate interpretations of the music. The author's profile of the prototypical forms and genres of the late Tchaikovsky symphonic cycle is clearly phrased. After finishing with the symphonies, he then comments on the programmatic works and suites.

DAVID HAAS

Theory and Theorists: General

Bent, Ian, and William Drabkin, *Analysis*, Basingstoke: Macmillan, and New York: Norton, 1987

Cook, Nicholas, *A Guide to Music Analysis*, London: Dent, and New York: Braziller, 1987

Dahlhaus, Carl, *Studies on the Origin of Harmonic Tonality*, translated by Robert Gjerdingen, Princeton, New Jersey: Princeton University Press, 1990

Damschroder, David, and David R. Williams, *Music Theory from Zarlino to Schenker: A Bibliography and Guide,* Stuyvesant, New York: Pendragon Press, 1990

Dunsby, Jonathan, and Arnold Whittall, *Music Analysis in Theory and Practice,* London: Faber, and New Haven, Connecticut: Yale University Press, 1988

Lester, Joel, *Compositional Theory in the Eighteenth Century,* Cambridge, Massachusetts: Harvard University Press, 1992

Riemann, Hugo, *History of Music Theory, Books I and II: Polyphonic Theory to the Sixteenth Century,* edited and translated by Raymond H. Haggh, Lincoln: University of Nebraska Press, 1962

Shirlaw, Matthew, *The Theory of Harmony,* London: Novello, and New York: Gray, 1917; reprint, New York: Da Capo Press, 1969

Music theory is one of the oldest as well as one of the most recent disciplines of musicology. On the one hand, an extensive and varied literature may be identified that extends virtually without interruption back to the ancient Greeks. On the other hand, as a specific area of scholarly research, music theory is of relatively recent origin. Etymologically, *musica theorica* constitutes the contemplation of music. This notion has been historically interpreted in many ways, including abstract speculations about musical materials, practical writings concerning the regulation of tonal material and systems, and models for the analysis of individual pieces of music. Today, the methods of music theorists are particularly rich and varied, intersecting such fields as mathematics, linguistics, psychology, semiotics, and literary criticism.

The first real history of Western music theory was written by RIEMANN. Extending from the early medieval period to his own day, Riemann offers a broad overview of theoretical topics that still has some value as a resource, although his scholarship has in most cases been superseded and must be used with caution. Moreover, Riemann's scholarly perspective is almost fatally skewed by his obsession to uncover theoretical premonitions of harmonic tonality and his own theory of harmonic functions and dualism.

The bibliographic guide by DAMSCHRODER and WILLIAMS concentrates on music theorists active in the common practice period, roughly from 1600 to 1900. The bulk of the volume consists of an alphabetical listing of approximately 100 major theorists. Each entry consists of a short introductory essay followed by an exhaustive and meticulous list of primary and secondary literature cross-indexed to other entries. In addition, there is a literature supplement and other bibliographic supplements. While the introductory essays vary widely in scope and quality, the dictionary is an invaluable resource.

BENT is essentially an expanded and updated version of the eponymous article he authored for the *New Grove Dictionary of Music and Musicians* (1980). The book offers a wide-ranging historical overview of music analysis, richly illustrated with examples. Bent approaches his topic from both diachronic and synchronic perspectives, thus allowing himself to consider certain theorists from both historical and conceptual angles.

A user-friendly introduction to theoretical analysis is found in COOK. In lively and accessible prose, Cook walks the reader through several prominent analytic paradigms: Schenkerian theory, set theory, serial analysis, psychological theories of analysis, and semiotics. The book concludes with several chapters that help the student start his or her own analysis, along with a few model examples. The volume can hardly be considered an authoritative scholarly resource, but its individual essays will be useful introductions to students unfamiliar with the topics. Some may, however, find Cook's approach a bit too simplistic and his prose overly didactic.

DUNSBY and WHITTAL offer an interesting complement to Cook. While there is a good deal of overlap between the two studies—including chapters on Schenker, set theory, and semiotics—Dunsby and Whittal's text is far denser and more conceptually challenging than Cook's volume. Dunsby and Whittal is a work aiming to explore many critical and methodological issues rather than offering an introductory overview of models of music analysis.

For a conceptually dense but lucid historical study of harmonic tonality as a critical framing theoretical concept for Western music, DAHLHAUS is invaluable. Although not properly a history of music theory, Dahlhaus discusses a wide number of theorists and theoretical problems that cut across some 500 years of theoretical/musical thought.

LESTER is a systematically organized study that focuses upon the harmonic, contrapuntal, and melodic theories of numerous 18th-century writers, including Rameau, Mattheson, Fux, Kirnberger, Riepel, and Koch. SHIRLAW, is valuable as a history of harmonic thought, particularly its discussion of Rameau, despite its dated research.

THOMAS CHRISTENSEN

Theory and Theorists: Ancient

Anderson, Warren D., *Ethos and Education in Greek Music,* Cambridge, Massachusetts: Harvard University Press, 1966

Barbera, André, editor, *Music Theory and Its Sources: Antiquity and the Middle Ages,* Notre Dame, Indiana: University of Notre Dame Press, 1990

Barker, Andrew, *Greek Musical Writings I: The Musician and His Art,* Cambridge: Cambridge University Press, 1984

————, *Greek Musical Writings II: Harmonic and Acoustic Theory,* Cambridge: Cambridge University Press, 1989

Boethius, *The Fundamentals of Music,* edited and translated by Calvin M. Bower, New Haven, Connecticut: Yale University Press, 1989

Lippman, Edward A., *Musical Thought in Ancient Greece,*
New York: Columbia University Press, 1964

Wiora, Walter, *The Four Ages of Music,* translated by M.D.
Herter Norton, New York: Norton, 1965; London: Dent,
1966

Most ancient cultures, including India, China, and other countries in the Far East, have developed music theories. Scholars, however, have devoted their studies primarily to ancient Greek music theory and theorists from the sixth century B.C. to the end of antiquity—the most influential strain of thought on music in the West. These studies, mainly historical and interpretative in nature, focus in large part on the three different aspects of the Greek way of theorizing about music. The first aspect, speculation about the essence of music based on numerical ratios, is demonstrated mainly in the writings of the Pythagoreans and the Neoplatonists such as Ptolemy or Nicomachos of Geresa. A second aspect is the investigation of ethical and educational implications of music and musical modes, areas described by Plato and prominent Greek poets. The last aspect comprises the analysis of tonal and tuning systems—such as the "great system" (*systema teleion*) and the Greek modes—on a scientific basis, for which Aristoxenos is the most prominent example. Each of these facets, however, are interlinked and hence difficult to consider in isolation.

Scholars have also begun to focus on the theory of both Roman and late antiquity, where Greek ideas were acknowledged and integrated—mainly by the Roman thinker Boethius (A.D. 480–524)—into the curriculum of the seven liberal arts. The works of Boethius were chiefly responsible for the transmission of ancient music theory to the early Middle Ages and beyond, giving it a continued relevance.

In his classical study, WIORA takes a universal viewpoint in dividing the world history of music into four characteristic ages. He distinguishes a prehistoric period, a period of ancient and high civilizations, a period in which Western music held a special position, and a period of global industrial culture. From a contemporary standpoint, however, the concept of a universal history of music, with all its teleological implications, needs to be treated with care. Nonetheless, this book is distinguished by its comparative approach, which provides the reader with an overview of the music theories of less prominent ancient cultures, including those of Egypt and Asia.

The central issue of LIPPMAN's book is a concise study of the principle of *harmoneia* (harmony) in music. He begins with a detailed description of how the view of music as a mathematical-philosophical discipline developed. Harmony is achieved through and metaphysically founded in numerical ratios that underlie sounds. The main authors of this idealist and abstract position are Platonists and Pythagoreans. This is then juxtaposed with an opposing concept, expressed in Aristoxenos's theoretical writings. Lippman demonstrates convincingly that harmony for Aristoxenos "has no transcendental status" anymore but is "found in physics and mathematics and in the practical and productive sciences." It may be difficult for the philosophically inexperienced to follow all the arguments, but there is no work yet which can replace this fundamental study.

ANDERSON's book is entirely devoted to the concept of ethos in Greek musical thinking and is the most concise publication on the topic. Ethos is understood to comprise the real or supposed effects that music or musical modes have on the human soul. He examines the writings of Greek poets and philosophers, including Aristophanes, Plato, and Aristotle, chronologically and in great detail. In contrast to earlier studies, Anderson finds a high degree of diversity in the way these writers describe the associative, religious, and technical effects of music and modes.

The different shades of Greek music theory can often only be fully grasped by reading the actual theorist's texts. BARKER's (1984, 1989) two volumes of Greek musical writings present a plethora of new and authoritative translations of primary sources. In addition, Barker offers excellent introductions to each group of sources, providing the reader with invaluable insights that in many cases go beyond those of Lippman and Anderson. The first volume deals with passages describing either actual music making or texts on the social, psychological, and moral functions (in education) of music. The second book offers one of the best introductions of the Greek tonal system (the *systema teleion*) and tuning and contains texts on ancient harmonics and on acoustic theory, together with careful interpretations.

Ancient music theory in the West is a product of Greek thinking. Roman culture inherited that knowledge, and Roman scholars read, translated, and commented on the works of the Greeks. This acquisition reached its peak in Anicius Manlius Severinus BOETHIUS's work "Fundamentals of Music," which depends greatly on Neoplatonic thought. Bower has produced an excellently annotated translation of this most important and influential treatise on music of late antiquity. He also includes an illuminating introduction to the work, which places it in its context as one of the main texts for the educational system of the so-called seven liberal arts.

The collection of articles edited by BARBERA engages the music theory of both antiquity and the Middle Ages. The general scope of the questions raised in these studies is very broad and up-to-date. It ranges from the significance of codicology for textual sources of music by Thomas J. Mathiesen, via an examination of the characteristics of ancient music treatises by Barbera himself, to a consideration of individual sources, including Byzantine and Greek texts, by Jon Solomon. A brilliant article by Nancy Philips examines the influence of classical and late Latin authors, such as Augustine, Cassiodorus, and

Isidore of Seville, on music theory in the ninth century. This study highlights crucial aspects of ancient theory and its reception in the early Middle Ages.

ANDREAS BÜCKER

Theory and Theorists: Early Medieval

Babb, Warren, translator, *Hucbald, Guido, and John on Music: Three Medieval Treatises*, New Haven, Connecticut: Yale University Press, 1978

Barbera, Andrè, editor, *Music Theory and Its Sources: Antiquity and the Middle Ages,* Notre Dame, Indiana: University of Notre Dame Press, 1990

Boethius, *The Fundamentals of Music,* edited and translated by Calvin M. Bower, New Haven, Connecticut: Yale Univeristy Press, 1989

Erickson, Raymond, editor, *Musica Enchiriadis and Scholica Enchiriadis,* New Haven, Connecticut: Yale University Press, 1995

Riemann, Hugo, *History of Music Theory, Books I and II: Polyphonic Theory to the Sixteenth Century,* edited and translated by Raymond H. Haggh, Lincoln: University of Nebraska Press, 1962

Strunk, W. Oliver, editor, *Source Readings in Music History: From Classical Antiquity through the Romantic Era,* New York: Norton, 1950; revised edition of vol. 2, *The Early Christian Period and the Latin Middle Ages,* edited by James McKinnon, 1998

Yudkin, Jeremy, editor, *The Music Treatise of Anonymous IV: A New Translation*. Neuhausen-Stuttgart: Hänssler, 1985

Music theorists of the early Middle Ages addressed the profound conceptual and organizational developments in musical styles from the start of the Christian era to the late 13th century. These writers, many of them anonymous, synthesized the ideas of ancient Greek and Byzantine theory into Western musical thought, developed a terminology and notation for individual pitches, described consonant and dissonant intervals, and codified the modal system for the chants of the Christian liturgy. In addition to developing a theoretical language for the linear organization of the chant, medieval theorists also transformed these ideas to grapple with the increasingly vertical structures of polyphony; they established a new vocabulary to describe the new polyphonic works and created the basis of rhythmic notation based on differentiated note shapes. In addition to these purely technical developments, early medieval theorists also discussed music's relationship to other disciplines and its role as a metaphor for creation and reality. Early theoretical texts abound in references to mathematics, moral law, Scripture, and physics.

The theoretical developments in music of this time are often discussed in introductory texts to medieval music in general. Another concise source is Claude V. Palisca's article "Theory, Theorists" in *The New Grove Dictionary of Music and Musicians* (1980). As many of these medieval treatises are relatively brief, significant work on this topic has appeared in journals (rather than monographs), and a thorough investigation of the topic would necessitate a review of these sources as well. In the absence of a recent, concise, English text on this topic, the interested reader is best served by reading the theorists themselves in translation. Medieval music treatises do not usually present a complete picture of musical practice of the time; these works are not exactly parallel to a modern textbook on harmony. Instead, these writers sought to explain specific issues and ideas, assuming the reader was able to fit the contents of a particular treatise into a larger framework of knowledge. Therefore, the reader must be prepared to integrate a specific text into a wider knowledge of medieval musical practice.

BABB presents three complete treatises from important writers on chant in clear translations: Hucbald's *De harmonica institutione*, Guido of Arezzo's *Micrologus*, and the *De musica* of John of Cotton (also called John of Afflighem). As a whole, these writers touch on the formation of the gamut (or the entire range of notes), the formation of the church modes, and the earliest developments of polyphony. The famous "Guidonian Hand," however, does not appear in the *Micrologus*. The volume is notable for its clear musical examples and figures, extensive indices, and detailed introductions to each work.

BARBERA's book is a collection of essays that were first presented as papers at a conference on medieval theory. Although the articles are intended for the advanced student, an introductory reader can gain a great deal from these essays, which demonstrates the diversity of research possibilities in medieval theory, such as manuscript studies, codicology, the context of music in medieval learning, and the transmission of Greek and Arabic music theory. Unlike many conference reports, this work includes a bibliography and several indices (manuscripts, treatises, and topics).

BOETHIUS's text stands as probably the most important treatise of early medieval theory because it preserved in the West the basic ideas of such Greek writers as Pythagorus, Aristoxenus, and Ptolemy. It served as the cornerstone of medieval theory and is probably the work most often cited by later medieval theorists. Bowers presents a lucid English translation of the text along with an insightful introduction and thorough annotations. When examining the text for the first time, a reader will be struck by the mathematical conception the early theorists had of music.

ERICKSON has translated and edited the *Musica enchiriadis* and *Scolica enchiriadis*—two related texts that discuss the earliest type of polyphony, known as organum. The works mark an important point in Western music theory, as writers attempted to explain the relationship between two simultaneous voices, a fundamentally different structure than the chants of the Christian liturgy. The works employ a unique type of notation referred to as *daseian* notation. In addition to an English translation of the texts, Erickson provides an introduction and annotations, which an introductory student will find as useful as the translations themselves.

A classic collection of excerpts on all aspects of musical thought was first collected by the famous musicologist Oliver STRUNK. The work has recently been revised with separate editors for each period of music; James McKinnon was responsible for the medieval era. Leo Treitler served as the general editor for the entire revision, which is also available in a one-volume edition. McKinnon's volume contains 27 selections from medieval writers on music. This collection probably provides the best, one-volume overview of medieval music theory in English translation. The work excerpts texts on chant, early polyphony, and mensural theory; it also includes a complete translation of the *Ars cantus mensurabilis* of Franco of Cologne, an important treatise that formulated the basic rhythmic interpretation of music in the late Middle Ages.

RIEMANN's original *Geschichte der Musiktheorie im IX–XIX Jahrhundert* (first published in German in 1898) has had a tremendous influence on the discussion of music theory, as it is one of the few monographs devoted to a detailed history of music theory. Haggh's translation of the first two books (the third deals with music from ca. 1600 to Riemann's own time) provides one of the few book-length surveys of music theory through the Renaissance. Although not all of Riemann's ideas are currently valid, his work has formed the basis of much further research, and he is often referred to in the modern literature (if only to clarify or refute his conclusions).

After Boethius, probably the best-known early medieval theorist is the writer commonly referred to as Anonymous 4. YUDKIN provides an English translation of the text along with a selected bibliography. Anonymous 4 mentions two of the earliest known writers of polyphony (Léonin and Pérotin) and several of their works while describing the so-called Notre Dame school of polyphony.

C. MATTHEW BALENSUELA

Theory and Theorists: 14th Century

Ars Cantus Mensurabilis Mensurata per Modos Iuris (The Art of Mensurable Song Measured by the Modes of Law), edited and translated by C. Matthew Balensuela, Lincoln: University of Nebraska Press, 1994

Berger, Anna Maria Busse, *Mensuration and Proportion Signs: Origins and Evolution,* Oxford, Clarendon Press, and New York: Oxford University Press, 1990

Berger, Karol, *Musica ficta: Theories of Accidental Inflections in Vocal Polyphony from Marchetto da Padova to Gioseffo Zarlino,* Cambridge: Cambridge University Press, 1987

The Berkeley Manuscript, University of California Music Library, MS. 744 (olim Phillipps 4450), edited and translated by Oliver B. Ellsworth, Lincoln: University of Nebraska Press, 1984

Crocker, Richard L., *Studies in Medieval Music Theory and the Early Sequence,* Brookfield, Vermont: Variorum, 1997

Johannes de Grocheo, *Concerning Music (De Musica),* translated by Albert Seay, Colorado Springs: Colorado College Music Press, 1967, 2nd edition, 1974

Marchetto da Padova, *The Lucidarium of Marchetto of Padua: A Critical Edition, Translation, and Commentary,* edited and translated by Jan W. Herlinger, Chicago: University of Chicago Press, 1985

Odington, Walter, *De Speculatione Musicae, Part VI,* translated by Jay A. Huff, N.p.: American Institute of Musicology, 1973

Riemann, Hugo, *History of Music Theory, Books I and II: Polyphonic Theory to the Sixteenth Century,* edited and translated by Raymond H. Haggh, Lincoln: University of Nebraska Press, 1962

Robertus de Handlo, and Johannes Hanboys, *Regule (The Rules) and Summa (The Summa),* edited and translated by Peter M. Lefferts, Lincoln: University of Nebraska Press, 1991

Smith, F. Joseph, *Jacobi Leodiensis Speculum Musicae: A Commentary,* 3 vols., Brooklyn, New York: Institute of Mediaeval Music, 1966–83

Strunk, W. Oliver, editor, *Source Readings in Music History: From Classical Antiquity through the Romantic Era,* New York: Norton, 1950; revised edition, edited by Leo Treitler, 1998

Fourteenth-century music theorists as a group represent a wide array of geographical regions and equally diverse musical and intellectual traditions. In order to interpret or apply the information in medieval treatises, Lawrence Gushee proposes that each treatise be assessed in terms of its intellectual style, the institution for which it was written or the audience for which it was intended, and the type of music it considers ("Questions of Genre in Medieval Treatises on Music," in *Gattungen der Musik in Einzeldarstellungen,* 1973). Taking into account Gushee's recommendations, readers will find it useful to read commentary on 14th-century theory as well as translations of the treatises themselves. The introductions to the translations usually provide biographical information about the theorist, if any is known, and often cogent information about the possible origins of the treatise (choir school, monastery, or university) and the particular historical contributions of the work. Some 14th-century treatises include topics still relevant to chant performance, such as how to categorize plainchant modally and how to sing organum; others incorporate topics relevant to sacred polyphonic works such as masses and motets, as well as to secular song. They describe the rules of note-against-note counterpoint, explain the new developments in rhythmic notation (known generally under the term *ars nova*), and provide theoretical explanations for the newly available chromatic pitches. The critical, yet vexed, topic of performer's accidentals—the application of chromatic inflections not notated in the music (frequently, and often incorrectly, referred to as *musica ficta*) but thought to be part of performance traditions—surfaces sometimes in plainchant treatises in the discussion of hexachordal theory and also in counterpoint treatises in the description of appropriate intervals and kinds of progressions.

RIEMANN, which first appeared in German in 1898, remains the only critical study to date to cover the spectrum of 14th-century theory in a single volume, with chapters on mensural theory, counterpoint, and *musica ficta*. Haggh, in his 1962 translation and commentary, revises some of Riemann's attributions, discusses Riemann's ideas and emphases in the context of late 19th-century music writing, and provides references to more recent scholarship. Valuable for historiographical reasons, the many quotations of theorists in English and the breadth of coverage make the work an excellent point of departure for studies in 14th-century theory.

Karol BERGER's volume on *musica ficta* surveys treatises from the 14th through the 16th century that touch on the topic of *musica ficta* or *musica falsa* to varying degrees. Pointedly focusing on the treatises rather than on manuscripts of the music, Berger quotes extensively in English (with Latin in the endnotes) from the theorists. With a goal of finding consensus in the treatises in order to provide a practical approach to *ficta* usage, Berger sometimes overgeneralizes and applies, for instance, 16th-century conventions to 14th-century music. Because of the dense material and Berger's emphasis, the reader may find it difficult to keep straight chronological and regional differences among the treatises discussed, but the concise chapter summaries will prove very useful.

CROCKER's seminal article, "Discant, Counterpoint, and Harmony," on *discant* treatises and counterpoint (originally published in 1962) offers terminology and a conceptual framework for the discussion of vertical sonorities and their relationship to each other in music ranging from the 13th through the 16th century. To counter a then-prevalent, purely linear approach to medieval polyphony, Crocker provides a historical survey of *discant* authors, tracing the shifts in terminology and descriptions of contrapuntal rules from one century to the next. Crocker defines *discant* as "a system of teaching two-part composition," which

> shows how to combine one (and only one) note with each note of a given melodic progression by the application of two basic principles. The first principle deals with the kinds of sonority to be used, the second with the order in which sonorities may appear.

Crocker asserts that in the 14th century there surfaces an important concern for the progression between intervals and that certain progressions "acquire the force of necessity: their conclusion becomes obligatory." Two other essays in the volume will interest readers: Crocker's review of John Stevens's *Words and Music in the Middle Ages,* which draws on medieval theoretical treatises, and "A New Source for Medieval Music Theory," which discusses the 14th-century *Berkeley Manuscript,* described below.

Anna Maria Busse BERGER assumes that readers already understand the basic principles of the mensural system and leads them through the complex web of mensuration and proportion signs, principally as explained by theorists from the 14th through the 16th century, but with reference to manuscripts of the late 14th and early 15th centuries. She sets out to provide a precise meaning, vertically and horizontally, for each mensuration or proportion sign described by a theorist and to make a clear distinction between uncommon views and those shared by several theorists. Although it is a complicated topic, the many charts and headings throughout the book make the subject accessible, and the chapter on the mathematical origin of the signs themselves renders a compelling intellectual context for the appearance of specific kinds of signs.

Perhaps the most famous treatise of the 14th century, the so-called *Ars nova* by the Parisian Phillipe de Vitry, does not appear in English in any book-length study. However, the late 14th-century treatise, the *BERKELEY MANUSCRIPT,* comes from Paris, or at least northern France, and represents northern French teaching traditions well. Translator and editor Oliver Ellsworth offers a Latin edition with facing-page English translation of the *Berkeley Manuscript,* replete with lengthy footnotes offering commentary and noting variants between manuscript versions. Known in recent years for its theory of *coniuncta,* a theory that explains the new appearance of chromatic pitches, the *Berkeley Manuscript* is a compilation of five treatises, with the first on chant, the second on counterpoint, the third on notation, the fourth on tuning, and the fifth on speculative matters; each treatise survives in at least one other source, but no other manuscript contains all of the material. The first and second treatises on *discant* and mensuration, respectively, rely heavily on the works attributed to Jean de Muris; Ellsworth discusses those attributions, as well as the authorship of the *Berkeley Manuscript,* in his introduction to the edition.

Herlinger provides an edition and translation of the *Lucidarium,* a plainchant treatise from northern Italy by MARCHETTO DA PADOVA, a theorist famous for his unorthodox division of the whole tone into five parts. An excerpt from Marchetto's treatise on notation and mensuration, the *Pomerium,* can be found in Strunk, discussed below. Although the *Lucidarium* presents all of the customary topics found in a plainchant treatise, they are not in their usual elementary pedagogical order (for instance, although musical examples fill the treatise for the purpose of elucidating Marchetto's arguments, the fundamental topic of clefs appears only at the end of the work). Implicitly scholastic in style, the *Lucidarium* aims more to persuade its reader of a new understanding of chant, in both the construction and classification of melody, than to teach the rudiments of chant. Herlinger provides excellent commentary in his introduction, and in marginal notes throughout the translation he identifies Marchetto's sources and clarifies his meaning.

Where the *Lucidarium* is implicitly scholastic, the *ARS CANTUS MENSURABILIS MENSURATA PER MODOS IURIS* is explicitly so. This late 14th-century work, most likely from Florence, sets out to counter the "various opinions and diverse fallacies of the multitudes," by providing the correct rules of French mensural notation as the author understands them. Balensuela provides a facing-page translation with copious notes and a substantial introduction, in which he asserts that the *Ars cantus mensurabilis* would have been inadequate as an introductory guide; rather, the anonymous author was writing probably for a clerical audience already familiar with the mensural system and uses legal maxims as well as scholastic methodologies and vocabulary to justify and take to its extreme limits a system already accepted.

For an introduction to mensural theory, STRUNK is an excellent resource (although the serious student of notation should also consult the standard notation manuals by Parrish, *The Notation of Medieval Music* [1978], and Apel, *The Notation of Polyphonic Music 900–1600* [1953]). A collection of documents and excerpts relating to music from antiquity to the 20th century, Strunk includes Franco of Cologne's late 13th-century *Ars cantus mensurabilis* and excerpts from the 14th-century treatises *Pomerium in arte musicae mensuratae*, by Marchetto of Padua, *Notitia artis musicae*, by Jehan des Murs (Jean de Muris), and *Speculum musicae*, by Jacques of Liège. Franco explains the basic features of mensural notation, including imperfection and alteration, but only as they relate to divisions by three. Jehan des Murs articulates the hallmark of the innovations of *ars nova* notation: the possible division of every note value into two or three, and the proportional relationships between all levels of mensural values (the maxima long can comprise two or three longs, the long two or three breves, the breve two or three semibreves, the semibreve two or three minims). Marchetto details the differences between the Italian and the French mensural systems, and the *Speculum musicae* excerpt features Jacques of Liège's famous tirade against the new art and defense of the old.

SMITH offers a three-volume commentary on the monumental *Speculum musicae* of Jacobus Leodiensis, or Jacques of Liège. Jacques of Liège began the work to admonish the moderns but decided instead to offer a complete encyclopedia of music. Smith, however, revises the antimodern reputation that Jacques still has, stating that "there are passages which mitigate his apparent reactionism," and focuses instead on his discussions of the nature of consonances and on the nature of modes or tones, which form the bulk of the treatise. Some readers will find Smith's in-depth account of the most comprehensive medieval treatise on music difficult because of the lengthy quotes in Latin from the treatise itself.

JOHANNES DE GROCHEO's *De musica* stands in direct contrast to Jacques of Liège's *Speculum musicae*. Where Jacques intellectualizes the details of, for instance, musical proportions or the arrangement of tetrachords and aims to discuss every theoretical element of music, Johannes de Grocheo describes the social and functional aspects of music. Although Johannes begins with topics such as the consonances and the staff, his complete avoidance of musical examples and his generalized discussions set the tone of a tract for music appreciation. A valuable witness to the cultural context of 14th-century music around Paris, Johannes names different genres of music and explains whether they are played or sung, by whom, and for whom. Seay's translation is very readable; a brief introduction accompanies the work.

The sixth part of Walter ODINGTON's *De speculatione musicae* offers the "only contemporaneous discussion of English mensural polyphony in the late 13th and early 14th centuries." Huff offers just a brief introduction and cursory, but insightful, notes throughout. The strength of the volume comes from the plentiful examples that Odington provides, and which Huff presents in both original and modern notation.

Finally, Lefferts provides access to later English traditions, with editions and translations of treatises by ROBERTUS DE HANDLO and JOHANNES HANBOYS, who wrote in 1326 and ca. 1370, respectively. The substantial introduction considers the contributions of each theorist. Though writing in 1326, Robertus describes 13th-century mensural theory, using Franco's *Ars cantus mensurabilis* as a base text, rather than the "radical innovations of Parisian *ars nova* theory of the previous decade." Handlo draws on other works as well, always naming his authority before quoting or paraphrasing. Hanboys, on the other hand, is "emphatic about his modernity." Although he makes no explicit references to French theorists, Hanboys adopts *ars nova* practices and offers some of his own formulations; Lefferts also traces several generations of English theorists and their notational systems, including Handlo, as well as Johannes Torkesey and Robertus de Brunham.

JENNIFER BAIN

Theory and Theorists: 15th Century

Ciconia, Johannes, *Nova Musica and De Proportionibus,* edited and translated by Oliver B. Ellsworth, Lincoln: University of Nebraska Press, 1993

Gaffurius, Franchinus, *The Theory of Music,* translated by Walter Kurt Kreyzig, edited by Claude V. Palisca, New Haven, Connecticut: Yale University Press, 1993

Moll, Kevin N., editor and translator, *Counterpoint and Compositional Process in the Time of Dufay: Perspectives from German Musicology,* New York: Garland, 1997

Prosdocimus de Beldomandis, *Contrapunctus,* edited and translated by Jan Herlinger, Lincoln: University of Nebraska Press, 1984

Ramos de Pareja, Bartolomeo, *Musica practica,* translated by Clement A. Miller, Neuhausen-Stuttgart: American Institute of Musicology and Hänssler-Verlag, 1993

Tinctoris, Johannes, *The Art of Counterpoint,* translated and edited by Albert Seay, n.p.: American Institute of Musicology, 1961

———, *Dictionary of Musical Terms,* edited and translated by Carl Parrish, New York: Free Press of Glencoe, 1963

By the beginning of the Renaissance, explanations of music's structure as articulated by medieval theorists such as Boethius, Guido, and other venerated masters no longer explained the music being written by composers such as Du Fay. As a result, theorists of the 15th century found themselves reconsidering almost every aspect of musical structure and theory. For example, consonance and dissonance had previously been explained on the basis of mathematical proportions, but in the 15th century, thirds and sixths (mathematically dissonant intervals) were increasingly considered consonant. As a result, theorists of the century had to reexamine such basic concepts as consonance and dissonance, the church modes (and how they affected polyphonic composition), counterpoint, tuning and the division of the monochord, *musica ficta,* and notation.

The 15th century witnessed the advent of the printing press, and the treatises of 15th-century musicians were more widely disseminated than the writings of previous theorists. Fifteenth-century writers also had extensive knowledge of earlier theorists (such as Boethius, Guido, and Johannes de Muris) who continued to hold considerable influence on musical thought throughout the century. For example, many of the extant sources for the famous *Libellus cantus mensurabilis,* attributed to the 14th-century theorist Johannes de Muris, actually date from the 15th century. As a result of this knowledge, 15th-century music theorists wrote in a lively and argumentative style either to support or refute the ideas of previous or contemporary theorists.

Although there are few sources specifically devoted to early Renaissance theory, an interested reader can get a general grasp of 15th-century theory through music history texts on the Renaissance in general. An excellent concise source is Claude V. Palisca's article "Theory, Theorists" in *The New Grove Dictionary of Music and Musicians* (1980). A significant amount of research in 15th-century theory (such as studies of specific terms as well as entire shorter treatises) has appeared in journals rather than monographs, and an interested student will need to investigate these sources for a full understanding of the subject. The best way to get the sense of the era is by reading widely from various writers and treatises.

MOLL translates 12 articles by German scholars published between 1948 and 1967 on such topics as *fauxbourdon,* cantus firmus technique, counterpoint, and the origins of major-minor tonality. Moll's edition provides an extensive background essay and includes a wide-ranging bibliography; his translations make these seminal articles available to the non-German-speaking reader. A reader unfamiliar with the field can learn how various issues of music history are subject to changing interpretations over time.

CICONIA's theoretical works provide a excellent example of music theory from the earliest part of the 15th century. The *Nova musica,* his major work, is a large, speculative treatise in the tradition of works of the previous century and is notable for the several literary and grammatical sources cited in the text. While the large dimensions of the work may overwhelm a first-time reader, Ellsworth's concise introduction to Ciconia and his theoretical works, the clear translation, and ample documentation provide a student with sufficient support. As with many modern translations, a student may find the appendices of great help in searching for specific terms, ideas, concepts, and people.

GAFFURIUS's *Theorica musice* (translated as *The Theory of Music*)—another speculative treatise—is one of several works from this prolific theorist. Reconsidering the musical ideas of Boethius and earlier writers, Gaffurius provides lengthy explanations of the mathematical foundations of music in the tradition of these earlier writers. Although the novice may be a bit intimated by the mathematical content of the work, the reader can gain a tremendous insight into how Gaffurius developed these earlier ideas in Kreyzig's concise introduction to Gaffurius and his treatise and the careful documentation throughout the work.

The brief treatment of counterpoint by PROSDOCIMUS DE BELDOMANIS is an example of counterpoint treatises from the beginning of the century. Prosdocimus's terse text gives six basic counterpoint rules common to 14th- and 15th-century texts and provides justification for these rules. His one musical example has been controversial for its use of accidentals. Herlinger's text includes an explanatory essay, facing-page translation of the text, and helpful appendices. It is interesting to compare this work with the much longer treatment of the same subject by Tinctoris written toward the end of the century.

In his major work, RAMOS DE PAREJA reconsiders the inherited traditions of theory in light of the practical music of his time. As a result, he suggests changing, modifying, or simply doing away with those theories and constructs that no long suit the contemporary styles. In particular, he rejects the teachings of Guido and those who follow them. The *Musica practica* was a touchstone for some of the great debates in music theory—Ramos's ideas were issues for theorists well into the following century. The work provides an excellent example of theoretical thought of the time.

Tinctoris was one of the most prolific theorists of the century. In a series of works, he comments upon almost every aspect of musical practice of the age. TINCTORIS (1961), his *Liber de arte contrapuncti* (translated as *The Art of Counterpoint*), is one of the most often cited works of the time. In book 2 of the treatise, Tinctoris contrasts written counterpoint (which he describes as *res facta,* or "the thing made") with counterpoint, which is *cantare super librum,* or "sung above the book"—implying improvised harmony. These phrases and Tinctoris's possible meanings have been greatly discussed in the writings on Renaissance music. The counterpoint book also includes examples of numerous works by the best-known composers of the time (including Ockeghem and Busnoys). Seay's edition is not well documented or indexed, however, and a reader interested in specific works or terms will need to search the text carefully.

TINCTORIS's (1963) *Terminorum musicae diffinitorium* (translated as *Dictionary of Musical Terms*) is one of the earliest examples of a musical dictionary. In approximately 300 entries, he defines terms related to pitch, rhythm and meter, specific genres, intervals, and compositional techniques. These definitions show modern students how musicians of the time described, explained, and understood their own music.

C. MATTHEW BALENSUELA

Theory and Theorists: 16th Century

Glarean, Heinrich, *Dodecachordon,* 2 vols., edited and translated by Clement A. Miller, N.p.: American Institute of Musicology, 1965

Lowinsky, Edward E., *Tonality and Atonality in Sixteenth-Century Music,* Berkeley: University of California Press, 1961

Meier, Bernhard, *The Modes of Classical Vocal Polyphony,* translated by Ellen S. Beebe, New York: Broude Brothers, 1988

Palisca, Claude V., *The Florentine Camerata: Documentary Studies and Translations,* New Haven, Connecticut: Yale University Press, 1989

——, *Humanism in Italian Renaissance Musical Thought,* New Haven, Connecticut: Yale University Press, 1985

Vicentino, Nicola, *Ancient Music Adapted to Modern Practice,* translated by Maria Rika Maniates, edited by Claude V. Palisca, New Haven, Connecticut: Yale University Press, 1996

Zarlino, Gioseffo, *The Art of Counterpoint; Part Three of Le Istitutioni harmoniche, 1558,* translated by Guy A. Marco and Claude V. Palisca, New Haven, Connecticut: Yale University Press, 1968

The end of the Renaissance witnessed profound changes in music associated with the new chromatic musical style of the era. The best-known theorists were Italians who benefited from the revival of ancient learning taking place throughout the 16th century across the Italian peninsula. In seeking to describe the music of composers such as da Rore and Willaert, these writers expanded the traditional explanations of musical structure inherited from the previous centuries, especially in the areas of mode and chromaticism.

The new sources of Greek thinking brought about a reconsideration of musical structures. Theorists such as Heinrich Glarean and Gioseffo Zarlino augmented the eight modes of earlier Western theory by the addition of pairs of modes on the pitches A and C, creating 12 modes in all. The investigation of modal structure and its possible relation to the polyphonic music of the late Renaissance has been a topic of keen and varied discussion in musicology, leading one scholar to ask "Is mode real?" in relation to polyphonic composition. Much of the research on this issue (called "tonal coherence" by some writers) has been published in journal and encyclopedia articles by scholars such as Harold Powers, Leo Treitler, and Cristle Collins Judd.

While the definitions of modal structure were expanding, composers of the 16th century were writing increasingly chromatic music, especially in the evolving genre of the madrigal. These chromaticisms would seemingly contradict any possible modal influence on the polyphonic structure. Theorists had to rationalize the increasingly chromatic musical style in contrapuntal compositions.

Toward the end of the century, musicians began to experiment with the new musical texture of the monodic style (a single singer declaiming a text to music), which they conceived as being the true conception of ancient Greek music. Thus, theorists such as V. Galieli found renewed influences from antiquity and helped prepare the way for a new genre, opera, and a new era, the baroque.

LOWINSKY was one of the most influential musicologists of his time. In his study of chromaticism in the 16th century, which includes an introduction by Igor Stravinsky, Lowinsky argues that excessively chromatic music led to the demise of modal theory in the 16th century and stimulated the development of tonal theory based on major and minor scales. Lowinsky presents a unique interpretation of the role of chromaticism in musical developments of the time, and his views have been widely circulated and debated among scholars. His work has fueled continued scholarly interest in mode and chromaticism in the late Renaissance, as seen in studies by Meier and other authors.

The first theorist to posit a 12-mode system was GLAREAN. Glarean not only presents his explanations for the recognition of the additional modes, but also cites numerous examples of their size from both chant and polyphony. His system was widely accepted by later theorists (most notably Zarlino, although without acknowledgment) and composers who referred to these modes in their works. Clement Miller's two-volume edition presents a lengthy introduction, and it contains extensive indices of the musical examples cited by Glarean.

MEIER's study is divided into two large sections. The first, titled "Principles," reviews the structural characteristics of the modes, such as range, finals, and cadences, drawn from various 16th-century theorists, most notably Glarean and Zarlino. The second section, titled "Expression," examines how composers deviated from the principles outlined by the theorists to highlight the specific meaning of the text. Meier's work contains an extensive index of works discussed, a bibliography, and numerous musical examples. Although not universally accepted, Meier's ideas represent a large-scale synthesis of the both the theoretical and musical sources of the time.

Palisca's work on Renaissance and baroque theory is central to current conceptions of these eras. Any student who wishes to understand the theory of the 16th and early 17th centuries must read and understand Palisca's works, only two of which are cited here. PALISCA (1985) concerns the transformation of musical thought in the Renaissance that coincided with the revival of ancient learning. The work is an original analysis of many treatises, both famous and obscure, and contains extensive documentation in the form of notes, figures, and bibliographic information. PALISCA (1989) assembles seven brief works by such writers as Mei, Bardi, and V. Galilei. Palisca provides an introduction to each source and facing page translations with the original Italian. The work offers excellent insight into the thinking of those writers and musicians who forged the new monodic style at the close of the Renaissance.

ZARLINO was one of the most important theorists of his age. In this monumental work, he reviews the inherited knowledge of music theory before discussing at length counterpoint (book 3) and the modes (book 4). Zarlino's work on counterpoint progresses from a review of basic intervals to three-part and four-part writing. He includes the basic rules that have appeared in previous counterpoint manuals, such as beginning and ending with consonances and avoiding parallel perfect consonances. Zarlino also notes that the basic material for a work of music is not abstract counterpoint, but a musical subject. The translation by Marco and Palisca is clear and direct; the numerous examples are transcribed into modern notation. Book 4 of Zarlino's work has been translated by Vered Cohen.

One of the most comprehensive attempts to establish a theoretical basis for the new chromatic style of the mid-16th century was proposed by VICENTINO. By using the chromatic and enharmonic tetrachords (the "ancient" music of his title), he was able to find theoretical justification for the highly chromatic music of his day. Maria Maniates's edition is notable for its lengthy introduction and clear annotations, documenting Vicentino's reliance on earlier theorists and writers. Although his ideas on chromaticism were not widely adopted, they demonstrate the vitality of ancient theory for the thinkers of the 16th century.

C. MATTHEW BALENSUELA

Theory and Theorists: 17th Century

Brett, Ursula, *Music and Ideas in Seventeenth-Century Italy: The Cazzati-Arresti Polemic,* New York: Garland, 1989

Lester, Joel, *Between Modes and Keys: German Theory 1592–1802,* Stuyvesant, New York: Pendragon Press, 1989

Mathiesen, Thomas J., and Benito V. Rivera, *Festa Musicologica: Essays in Honor of George J. Buelow,* Stuyvesant, New York: Pendragon Press, 1995

Playford, John, *Introduction to the Skill of Musick,* London, 1674; reprint, Ridgewood, New Jersey: Gregg Press, 1966

Rivera, Benito V., *German Music Theory in the Early 17th Century: The Treatises of Johannes Lippius,* Ann Arbor, Michigan: UMI Research Press, 1980

Saint-Lambert, Michel de, *A New Treatise on Accompaniment,* edited and translated by John S. Powell, Bloomington: Indiana University Press, 1991

The books surveyed here convey a good deal about the state of research on 17th-century music theory and theorists: very little work has been published in book form. While the centuries flanking the 17th century have received a substantial amount of attention, scholars have been hesitant to investigate theory of this period. Part of the reason for this hesitancy no doubt lies in the potential minefields: is the century characterized by tonality or modality, or some combination of the two? The 17th century has long been recognized as the period in which many aspects of modern functional tonality developed, and the need for more comprehensive research on its dynamic harmonic/tonal language is great. For example, no inclusive English-language study of English music theory exists in book form, yet scholars often point to England as a place where tonality was worked out early.

The six works discussed below illustrate some of the different types of sources available. Lester's monumental study covers an extended period with more detail than can be found in any other comparable examination of

17th-century theory. Brett is less comprehensive, choosing instead to investigate practices in a specific time and place. The same is true of Rivera, whose investigation into the works of Lippius was naturally limited by that theorist's death at age 27. The articles in Mathiesen and Rivera provide additional information on particular topics and people. Powell's translation of Saint-Lambert illustrates yet another important aspect of theory that is sometimes overlooked: figured-bass treatises. Playford is a facsimile of the original but is quite easily read and understood. It also represents a common place where theory in the 17th century was discussed: tutors.

LESTER begins his study with Calvisius and takes it to 1802, a remarkable feat and one that certainly provides the best overview of changes in music theory available to date. Unfortunately, Lester mostly limits his study to German theory, with a few forays into other areas. His lengthy appendices include translations of works by Janowka, Fux, Walther, and Mattheson's tuning system. To these, Lester adds appropriate examples and annotations. Much of the book deals with the 17th century and includes some discussion of contemporary English, French, and Italian writers, especially noting their relevance to German theorists. Of particular interest are chapters entitled "Toward Twenty-Four Keys" and "Twenty-Four Keys." Typical of the information included here are Lester's observations that Werckmeister struggled to understand the evolution of modes into major and minor keys and that the German theorists' use of church keys gradually increased the number of keys formally recognized. (Indeed, Mattheson used church keys as the first 8 in his list of 24.) A significant point made by Lester concerning late 17th-century theory is the difference between the evolution of major/minor keys, which cannot be known, and the recognition of major/minor keys, for which a definitive history is possible. An excellent contribution to our understanding of the complex history of theory in the 17th century, Lester is neither too difficult nor too elementary.

Even though he died in 1612 at age 27, Johannes Lippius's ideas on music as presented in his *Synopsis musicae novae* were formed out of a desire to make practical music (*musica practica*) composition meld with *musica theorica* and *poetica*. In Rivera's words, "to view music as a totality and to show precisely how its many individual aspects fitted into a coherent system." RIVERA examines the scant biographical details available concerning the author, reviews his treatises, and then takes the better part of the study to examine Lippius's conception of how music fits together. Rivera notes the significance in Lippius's understanding of the triad, intervallic and triadic inversion, rhetorical principles in musical composition, and the establishment of the bass as "the starting point of polyphony," all of which constitute some of the most innovative ideas in early 17th-century theoretical treatises. The book itself is a slight revision of Rivera's dissertation, but this fact does not detract from its usefulness. Like the ideas treated in several other works reviewed in this entry, the concepts are advanced and require some knowledge of 16th-century theory and theorists.

BRETT's book differs significantly from Lester's, treating a debate that took place in Bologna during the mid–17th century. Although the polemic seems localized, it relates to broader issues of 17th-century theory. The two main topics involve the shift from modality to tonality and the application of modern ideas to sacred music, that is the *prima prattica* versus the *seconda prattica* in church music. The polemic has traditionally been viewed as an argument between Don Mauritio Cazzati and Giulio Cesare Arresti. The musical items in question are Cazzati's *Messa,* op. 17 (the first Kyrie), from which Arresti in turn composed his *Messa,* op. 1. (Also discussed are Cazzati's psalm settings, op. 35, and Arresti's *Gare musicali.*) Among the contributions that Brett makes is his suggestion of the possibility that Arresti is not the author of the *Dialogo fatto tra un maestro et un discepolo,* that Lorenzo Perti was involved in this polemic, and that Arresti did not initiate the debate. She also notes that Cazzati's *Riposta* is styled after a common Italian academic response. This book is extremely useful in examining Italian theory of the 17th century. It is intended for an educated reader and requires an in-depth understanding of relevant issues of this period.

SAINT-LAMBERT was originally published in Paris in 1707, following an earlier treatise by the same author (*Les Principles du clavecin,* 1702). The first book deals with rudimentary aspects of music; the second continues where the first left off. Thoroughbass treatises appeared in France from the 1660s, and Saint-Lambert was praised by the likes of Rameau and Heinichen. Saint-Lambert provides a more extensive discussion of harmony than his predecessors, especially in the final three chapters. The editor, John Powell, notes that, although he published in the 18th century, Saint-Lambert shows himself to be a "conservative musician rooted in the musical style of the latter part of the seventeenth century." This book is useful both as a beginning reference for figured-bass accompaniment and for providing a foundation of 17th-century theory.

MATHIESEN and RIVERA contains three English-language articles related to 17th-century theory and theorists: "Rule-Breaking as a Rhetorical Sign" by J. Peter Burkholder, "Jehan Titelouze as Music Theorist" by Albert Cohen, and "Another Critic Named Samber" by Lowell Lindgren. Additionally, Frederick Neumann's "Ornamentation and Forbidden Parallels" includes discussion of the 17th century along with periods before and after it. Burkholder's essay takes as its starting point the Monteverdi-Artusi debate over traditional theory and "innovative rhetorical practice," extending the discussion much further in history and concluding with comparisons to similar notions of rhetoric in music as examined by

Susan McClary. Cohen's piece is even more 17th-century specific in that he limits his discussion to the works of Titelouze. Cohen provides a glimpse of Titelouze as teacher and theorist by interpreting his prefaces to publications of 1623 and 1626. Among the topics discussed are expression and structure, mode, acoustics, tuning, intervals, and notation. Lindgren's subject is chronologically beyond the scope of this topic, based as it is on a 1728 book; however, a good deal of the article considers earlier events. This essay deals primarily with operatic practices, or at least with music for the stage. These articles are not beyond the scope of undergraduate-level students and are easy to follow.

PLAYFORD was the chief music publisher in England during the second half of the 17th century and brought forth many excellent volumes intended for amateur musicians. Immensely popular during the 17th century, Playford contains many basic elements of composition and, as such, provides an elementary lesson in music theory for this period. Playford (1674) is not the first edition but the seventh; the first was published in 1654. The seventh edition contains sections by Thomas Campion (rather remarkable considering that Campion's work dates from ca. 1613) and Christopher Simpson (as well as some information taken from Edward Lowe, though not acknowledged as such). The 12th edition, published in 1694, was "corrected and amended" by Purcell. As interesting for what it does not contain as for what it does, Playford completely avoids the discussion of mode in most editions (omitting it in editions between 1662 and 1670), only incorporating Simpson's offhand comments on mode in the 1672 edition. By the 1683 edition, mode was abandoned altogether. Perhaps the most significant theoretical distinction between the 1674 and 1694 editions is that Purcell notes that there are only two keys, one with a minor third above the keynote and the other with a major third. The 1674 edition (listed above) is available as a facsimile; the 1694 edition includes an extensive preface by Franklin Zimmerman.

CANDACE LEE BAILEY

Theory and Theorists: 18th Century

Arnold, Frank Thomas, *The Art of Accompaniment from a Thorough-Bass, As Practiced in the XVIIth and XVIIIth Centuries,* Oxford: Oxford University Press, 1931; reprint in 2 vols., with introduction by Denis Stevens, New York: Dover, 1965

Christensen, Thomas, *Rameau and Musical Thought in the Enlightenment,* Cambridge: Cambridge University Press, 1993

Damschroder, David, *Music Theory from Zarlino to Schenker: A Bibliography and Guide,* Stuyvesant, New York: Pendragon Press, 1990

Lester, Joel, *Compositional Theory in the Eighteenth Century,* Cambridge, Massachusetts: Harvard University Press, 1992

Parker, Mary Ann, editor, *Eighteenth-Century Music in Theory and Practice: Essays in Honor of Alfred Mann,* Stuyvesant, New York: Pendragon Press, 1994

Until the middle of the 18th century, the thoroughbass method (the use of numerical figures under the bass to indicate upper voices) was firmly entrenched in music composition. Although discussions of major and minor keys were starting to be formulated before this time, it was not until the efforts of Jean-Philippe Rameau (1683–1764) that theorists began to write in terms of tonal centers and harmonic progression. Rameau sought natural explanations for music principles. This rationalistic approach to music theory is common throughout the century, and many theorists considered themselves more scientist than musician. In fact, music theory in the 18th century was far from our present-day version, which hinges on music analysis. Instead, theoretical concerns were addressed by performers, composers, scientists, historians, and even dilettantes who were not only interested in the form, melody, or rhythm of a work but also issues of taste and music aesthetics, the latter becoming an independent field by the end of the century. It is therefore difficult to differentiate clear boundaries between 18th-century music theory and other 18th-century musical concerns.

Recent years have witnessed an increased interest in 18th-century theory, fueled by the rise of historical performance. Scholarship on 18th-century theory and theorists has taken off to the degree that a bibliographic guide must either tighten the ranks to propose a starting point for research or cite hundreds of references. The five books discussed below present the reader with both an overview of the topic and bibliographic information for further study.

LESTER succeeds in capturing the complexity of 18th-century theory by relating the diversity of opinions held by contemporary theorists. For example, by taking issue with scholars who describe Johann Joseph Fux's *Gradus ad parnassum* (1725) as reactionary, Lester reminds us that musical style does not progress linearly; older and newer practices often exist side by side. Lester's philosophy for historical scholarship is first to establish definitions of important concepts and terms from the perspective of the original author. He notes, for example, that *modulation* in the 18th century did not necessarily signify a change of key. After introducing various devices of composition such as voice leading, dissonance, cadence, and text setting, Lester launches into discussions of theoretical works from Rameau to Koch, touching on major 18th-century issues including counterpoint, realization of thoroughbass, natural harmonic succession, and the argument over melody and harmony. The result is an exemplary handbook of 18th-century theory and theorists representing a number of nations and ideologies.

For information on specific 18th-century theorists, DAMSCHRODER offers an excellent resource. He prefaces each of his alphabetically organized entries with biographical information and commentary on the works and philosophy of the particular theorist. This preface is followed by a two-part bibliography. The first section lists the publications by the theorists, with annotations about editions, including modern facsimiles. The second provides a multilingual listing of secondary sources on the theorist and his work.

PARKER's 14 essays selected in honor of Alfred Mann's long and esteemed career in 18th-century studies cover a wide base of theoretical topics, including harmonic patterns in Handel, Fux and temperament, the influence of harmonic theory on counterpoint, the importance of rhetoric models, and musical forms. The contributing authors are well-respected scholars in the field, and the collection provides a general sense of many aspects of 18th-century theory as well as the importance of theory for performing baroque and classical music.

A working knowledge of throroughbass is essential to understanding trends in 18th-century theory. ARNOLD offers this knowledge and much more in his large tome. When first published in 1931, the concept of historical performance practice (the striving for historical authenticity in style and interpretation) was at best limited. As Arnold discusses in his preface, editions at that time were heavily altered, and realizations of figured bass were typically carried out with modern harmonizations and piano technique in mind. Arnold's goal is to make figures accessible to performers. Of significance is the second chapter, in which Arnold surveys the principal treatises from the 18th century, comparing and contrasting guidelines for thoroughbass. Authors reviewed include Mattheson, Telemann, C.P.E. Bach, Kirnberger, and Türk. Although Arnold emphasizes German treatises, he also addresses theoretical works from France, Italy, and to a lesser extent, England. Rameau is mentioned in passing. The bulk of this book is organized by triad quality or figure with a comprehensive discussion of possible musical applications. Music examples permeate the text.

Of all 18th-century theorists, Rameau is undeniably the most influential to both his contemporaries and future generations. CHRISTENSEN succeeds in capturing the complexities of the man and his theories. According to Christensen, it is impossible to easily summarize Rameau's theories, as many of his ideas were reshaped or disavowed over the course of his career. For this reason, theorists with conflicting opinions can often claim affiliation with Rameau—or at least the Rameau of one given publication. This book is admirable in sorting the various strains of Rameau's evolving ideas and placing them in the broader context of Enlightenment thought.

LAURA J. KOENIG

See also Mattheson, Johann; Quantz, Johann Joachim

Theory and Theorists: 19th Century

Bent, Ian, editor, *Music Analysis in the Nineteenth Century,* 2 vols., Cambridge: Cambridge University Press, 1994

————, editor, *Music Theory in the Age of Romanticism,* Cambridge: Cambridge University Press, 1996

Bent, Ian, and William Drabkin, *Analysis,* Basingstoke: Macmillan, and New York: Norton, 1987

Damschroder, David, *Music Theory from Zarlino to Schenker: A Bibliography and Guide,* Stuyvesant, New York: Pendragon Press, 1990

Grave, Floyd K., and Margaret G. Grave, *In Praise of Harmony: The Teachings of Abbé Georg Joseph Vogler,* Lincoln: University of Nebraska Press, 1987

Harrison, Daniel, *Harmonic Function in Chromatic Music: A Renewed Dualist Theory and an Account of Its Precedents,* Chicago: University of Chicago Press, 1994

Jorgenson, Dale A., *Moritz Hauptmann of Leipzig,* Lewiston, New York: Mellen Press, 1986

Marx, Adolf Bernhard, *Musical Form in the Age of Beethoven: Selected Writings on Theory and Method,* edited and translated by Scott Burnham, Cambridge: Cambridge University Press, 1997

Mickelsen, William, *Hugo Riemann's Theory of Harmony: With a Translation of Die Harmonielehre, Book III of His History of Music Theory,* Lincoln: University of Nebraska Press, 1977

Shirlaw, Matthew, *The Theory of Harmony,* London: Novello, and New York: Gray, 1917; reprint, New York: Da Capo Press, 1969

Thompson, David M., *A History of Harmonic Theory in the United States,* Kent, Ohio: Kent State University Press, 1979

Wason, Robert W., *Viennese Harmonic Theory from Albrechtsberger to Schenker and Schoenberg,* Ann Arbor, Michigan: UMI Research Press, 1985

Whatley, Larry G., "Music Theory," in *Music in Britain: The Romantic Age: 1800–1914,* edited by Nicholas Temperley, London: Athlone, 1981

Nineteenth-century theorists treated a wide variety of subjects, including harmony, melody, form, counterpoint, rhythm and meter, and analysis. Scholars have approached the topic from several perspectives. These include historical overviews of one or a group of related theorists, surveys of the treatment of a particular topic, translations with accompanying commentary, and extensive bibliographic presentations with commentary. The only books on the topic available during the first half of the 20th century were those by Shirlaw and Riemann (*Geschichte der Musiktheorie,* 1898). More recent scholarship has focused heavily on 19th-century treatment of harmony, with other topics gradually receiving more attention. An extensive bibliography by Damschroder and Williams includes an overview of work by major 19th-century theorists. At present, 19th-century history of theory is a rapidly growing research area; consequently, much information on this topic found in journals, dissertations, and other scholarly formats is not yet available in book-length works.

BENT and DRABKIN is a revised and expanded version of Bent's article by the same title in *The New Grove Dictionary of Music and Musicians* (1980). Bent explains the nature of analysis, surveys historical approaches to analysis from the Middle Ages to the present, and discusses a variety of analytical systems currently in use. Regarding the 19th century, he summarizes contributions of theorists dealing with issues of phrase structure, formal models, harmony, rhythm, and organic growth and development. Within this overview, Bent identifies points of controversy and differences in approach and emphasis among theorists. A glossary of analytical terms prepared by Drabkin and an extensive bibliography are included.

BENT (1994) contains translations of analytical writings by some of the most important theorists and critics of the 19th century. Each translation is supplemented by a detailed introductory commentary and by supporting information provided in footnotes that help clarify the ideas presented within the selection. Bibliographical essays summarize sources and the current state of research for each of the writers and topics considered. Volume 1 contains writings related to fugue, form, and style; the selections in volume 2 are more metaphorical in approach. Some of the translated analyses are technical in nature.

BENT (1996) proposes to examine 19th-century theory on its own terms rather than as a mere extension of 18th-century ideas or as an anticipation of 20th-century approaches. The 11 essays by various scholars encompass three broad issues. Several address the relationship between the work of music theorists and contemporaneous philosophical and intellectual ideas. Another group of essays treats theory, criticism, and analysis within 19th-century cultural contexts. The final essays consider rhetoric, metaphor, and musical perception as intellectual models that can enrich our understanding of music theory.

Scott Burnham translates, with extensive commentary, excerpts from several major works by the German theorist MARX. The editor discloses Marx's progressive pedagogical views that emphasized the spiritual nature of artistic education and related education to the cultural well-being of the nation. Burnham also presents Marx's ideas on musical form that led to his recognition as the theorist responsible for naming and codifying sonata form. Finally, Burnham reveals the primacy of Beethoven's music for Marx.

DAMSCHRODER provides the most important reference work for the history of theory from the 16th to the early 20th century. More than 200 theorists are cited alphabetically. Each entry begins with a concise narrative explaining that theorist's concerns and contributions. Then follows a list of known writings and treatises, along with information about original manuscripts or prints and the availability of reproductions, facsimiles, modern editions, and translations. An extensive bibliography closes each article. Indices include a chronological list of theorists and treatises and a list of theoretical topics of concern during the time period covered. This book can serve as a useful introduction to the field and as a valuable resource for experienced scholars.

GRAVE and GRAVE interpret the theoretical writings of Vogler as an important link between the Enlightenment and early 19th-century romanticism. By contrasting Vogler's concepts with those of fundamental-bass and figured-bass theorists, the authors explain Vogler's reliance on the scale as his underlying premise. Such a foundation accommodates his system of Roman numerals for scale-degree triads and provides the background for his concept of tonal organization based on a single prevailing tonic.

HARRISON's attempt to develop a system for understanding late 19th-century chromatic harmony from a contemporaneous viewpoint leads him to explore and engage ideas of Hugo Riemann. The first part of the book presents Harrison's own theoretical ideas developed from those of Riemann; the second part summarizes and critiques harmonic theories of several German theorists, including Hauptmann, Helmholtz, Oettingen, and Riemann. Such concepts as dialects, empiricism, harmonic dualism, and harmonic function are treated in Harrison's discourse. Familiarity with the concepts of dualism and dialectics will provide a useful background for appreciating Harrison's work.

JORGENSON provides biographical background and an overview of the theoretical, pedagogical, and critical contributions of Hauptmann. Jorgenson clarifies the relation of Hauptmann's theories of harmony and rhythm to the dialectical method of Hegel and other German philosophers, as well as to the writings of such later German theorists as Helmholtz, Oettingen, and Riemann. Some understanding of Hauptmann's explanation of dialectics as the foundation for harmony and rhythm is helpful for an appreciation of Jorgenson's contributions.

MICKELSEN's book contains two major sections. Part 1 provides an overview of Riemann's theory of harmony, particularly his concepts of dualism and chord function. By organizing Riemann's work chronologically according to early, middle, and late periods, Mickelsen traces the growth and maturation of the theorist's ideas. Part 2 is a translation of Riemann's *Die Harmonielehre*, book 3 of *Geschichte der Musiktheorie* (*History of Music Theory*). Mickelsen's work complements that of Haggh, who translated books 1 and 2 of Riemann's *Geschichte der Musiktheorie* in 1962.

SHIRLAW constitutes the earliest English-language historical overview of theories of harmony. Although somewhat outdated, it still provides a good introduction to historical approaches to harmony. Beginning with 13th-century contrapuntalists and extending to the end of the 19th century, Shirlaw surveys various harmonic systems, explains their underlying foundations, and identifies particular strengths and shortcomings of each. For the 19th century, he discusses the French writer Fétis; the Germans Hauptmann, Helmholtz, Oettingen, and Riemann; and the English theorists Day, Macfarren, Ouseley, Stainer, and Prout.

THOMPSON traces the development of harmonic theory in the United States beginning with American editions of 19th-century European harmony treatises, continuing through the writings of Goetschius and his contemporaries, and culminating in the work of Piston, McHose, and Forte. Concerning 19th-century theories, Thompson's opening presentation on American editions of European treatises summarizes and critiques harmonic theories of the Germans Weber, Richter, and Faisst and the Victorians Day, Ouseley, and Prout. Thompson describes the impact of Europeans and Goetschius on American theorists during the first quarter of the 20th century.

WASON provides a critical survey of harmony treatises by Viennese theorists from the late 18th to the early 20th century. Through his study of the primary sources, as well as German and Austrian scholarship, Wason reveals fundamental-bass thinking as the foundation of Viennese harmonic theory; he traces this line of thought through the century to Schenker and Schoenberg. Although numerous theorists are discussed, primary attention falls on the contributions of Simon Sechter.

WHATLEY traces two lines of thought among 19th-century British theorists. The first follows the development of speculative theories of harmony, while the other focuses on the practical aspects of counterpoint, orchestration, melody construction, and form analysis.

RENEE MCCACHREN

Theory and Theorists: 20th Century

Baker, James, et al., editors, *Music Theory in Concept and Practice,* Rochester, New York: University of Rochester Press, 1997

Berry, Wallace, *Structural Functions in Music,* Englewood Cliffs, New Jersey: Prentice Hall, 1976

Forte, Allen, *The Structure of Atonal Music,* New Haven, Connecticut: Yale University Press, 1973

Hatch, Christopher, and David W. Bernstein, editors, *Music Theory and the Exploration of the Past,* Chicago: University of Chicago Press, 1993

Lewin, David, *Generalized Musical Intervals and Transformations,* New Haven, Connecticut: Yale University Press, 1987

———, *Musical Form and Transformation: 4 Analytic Essays,* New Haven, Connecticut: Yale University Press, 1993

Marvin, Elizabeth West, and Richard Hermann, editors, *Concert Music, Rock, and Jazz since 1945: Essays and Analytical Studies,* Rochester, New York: University of Rochester Press, 1995

Morris, Robert D., *Composition with Pitch-Classes: A Theory of Compositional Design,* New Haven, Connecticut: Yale University Press, 1987

Perle, George, *Serial Composition and Atonality: An Introduction to the Music of Schoenberg, Berg, and Webern,* Berkeley: University of California Press, 1962; 6th edition, revised, 1991

Pople, Anthony, editor, *Theory, Analysis, and Meaning in Music,* Cambridge: Cambridge University Press, 1994

Rahn, John, *Basic Atonal Theory,* New York: Longman, 1980

Schenker, Heinrich, *Free Composition,* translated by Ernst Oster, New York: Longman, 1979

Schoenberg, Arnold, *Theory of Harmony,* translated by Roy Carter, Berkeley: University of California Press, 1978

Straus, Joseph N., *Introduction to Post-Tonal Theory,* Englewood Cliffs, New Jersey: Prentice Hall, 1990

———, *Remaking the Past: Musical Modernism and the Influence of the Tonal Tradition,* Cambridge, Massachusetts: Harvard University Press, 1990

Wuorinen, Charles, *Simple Composition,* New York: Schirmer Books, and London: Collier Macmillan, 1979

The discipline of music theory in the 20th century has achieved an unprecedented degree of intellectual independence from pedagogy, composition, and music history, while still maintaining important associations with each of those disciplines. This independence emerged early in the century, notably in the writings of the Austrian theorist Heinrich Schenker, but the discipline began to be characterized as independent only after World War II, when Schenker's writings began to circulate in North America. In the 1950s and 1960s, growing interest in the theoretical premises of Schenker's thought and the ensconcing of composition (particularly serial composition) into university music curricula conspired to carry music theory into the academy as an independent research area. Theoretical writings in the 20th century reflect the challenge of formulating theories to account for the radical change in music from a well-defined, tonal harmonic language to a diverse range of atonal languages. The antithetical positions expressed in the writings of Schenker and Schoenberg provide a point of departure in the present essay for the discussion of the post–World War II writings to follow. Most music theories can be classified as analytical compositional, reflecting structural properties of pitch materials in a particular repertoire or style; the books by Perle, Forte, Rahn, Straus (1990a),

Wuorinen, and Morris fall into this category. But some theories are of such a general nature, deriving from their broad epistemological or mathematical foundations, that they imply no particular harmonic language or compositional style and remain ultimately speculative; the books by Lewin and Berry fall into this category. In the late 20th century, nourished by postmodernist and interdisciplinary currents of contemporary thought, a number of critical investigations of the nature of the music-theoretical enterprise and its discourse emerged; these are discussed at the end of this essay.

SCHENKER's retrospective theory reveres and demonstrates organic unity in tonal music from Bach to Brahms and responds to what the theorist perceives as the decadence of contemporary music in early 20th-century Vienna. His mature theory (albeit in incomplete form upon its publication in *Free Composition* [*Der freie Satz*] in 1935, the year of his death) is imbued with the philosophy of organicism and is predicated on his original concepts of the fundamental structure (*Ursatz*), structural levels (foreground, middleground, background), and prolongation. Schenker's theory did not circulate far beyond his immediate circle of admirers during his lifetime, but in the years following World War II, it captured the interest of North American theorists because of its theoretical depth and coherence. All of Schenker's major theoretical writings are now available in English translation.

SCHOENBERG presents a highly unconventional theory of harmony, whose goal is diametrically opposed to Schenker's: to explicate rational means of extending the harmonic resources of tonality by obfuscating the distinction between consonance and dissonance through denial of the existence of nonharmonic tones and by examining the status of harmonies formed by intervals other than successions of thirds. Schoenberg regards the tonal system as convention rather than destiny and considered the extensions he explored to be inevitable.

PERLE's study takes the position that preserial atonal works by Schoenberg, Berg, Webern, and other composers are generally free of traditional thematic procedures and are integrated by intervallic cells that can be manipulated as melodic successions or verticalities, that may be ordered or unordered, and that may be transformed by rigorous operations or by systematic voice-leading motions. Although the author supplies numerous analyses of fragments from a wide range of atonal compositions, he offers only general guidelines, rather than a comprehensive approach to analysis of atonal music. Perle presents the basic principles of the classical 12-tone (serial) method as defined by Schoenberg and explores not only the transformations of the row that form a work's substructure but also the derivation from the row of melodic and harmonic elements of a work in a wide variety of works.

Inspired by American composer and theorist Milton Babbitt's demonstrations of the mathematical underpin-

nings of the system of 12 pitch classes, FORTE, in his seminal work, sets out to demonstrate a general theoretical framework for the analysis of atonal music. Drawing directly on mathematical set theory, he establishes what is now widely known as pitch-class set theory. The pitch-class set—an abstraction by octave and enharmonic equivalence of any combination of pitches represented as integers from 0 to 11—is the basic unit of the theory. Forte examines relations between sets on the basis of interval and pitch-class content and defines equivalence of sets on the basis of transposition or inversion. In part 1, he systematically describes significant relations other than equivalence, such as the Z-relation, invariance, complementation, inclusion, and similarity. In addition to systematic theoretical formulations, Forte offers a wealth of analytical demonstrations of the components that make up the theory. In part 2, he offers a general structural model for atonal music, the set-complex.

RAHN uses formal mathematics to reformulate the principles of part 1 of Forte's treatise and extends the treatment of pitch relations into the study of 12-tone music through the appropriate interconnection of hexachordal inversional combinatoriality. Rahn distinguishes between operations on pitches and on pitch classes, and in the same vein, he distinguishes three types of set equivalence: equivalence based on transposition or inversion (as in Forte), on transposition alone, and on multiplication of pitch-class integers by 5. Although the analytical implications of each of Rahn's extensions of principles presented in Forte are not always explained in detail, Rahn's work is significant for its generalization of the properties of the system.

STRAUS (1990a) offers a lucid, pedagogically driven introduction to pitch-class set relations based on Forte's work, but incorporating a number of Rahn's extensions. The author avoids overt discussions of mathematics while still maintaining a remarkable level of clarity and precision. His engaging analyses at the end of each chapter relate new concepts to analytical practice. A unique feature is the chapter devoted to the study of music exhibiting the property of centricity, in which a pitch class or pitch-class set assumes a focal role in a composition.

WUORINEN introduces novice composers in a practical manner to the basic principles of 12-tone composition with a minimum of mathematics, while still addressing some relatively complex issues such as row derivation, combinatoriality, and partitioning. He also examines rhythmic organization through serial procedures using the time-point system and explores correlations of musical pitch and time.

MORRIS explains a comprehensive theory of pitch and pitch-class relations, which involves a good deal of mathematics. The technical challenge is greatly assisted by Morris's glossary and his recommendations of specific mathematics textbooks. He demonstrates the power and elegance of mathematical group theory for modeling operations and relations between sets of pitches and pitch classes, and he presents the group properties as primitives of the system, independent of whether the composition at hand is a 12-tone or a free atonal work. Like Rahn, Morris includes formal definitions and theorems for precision in establishing a secure foundation for the concepts being developed. He extends Forte's and Rahn's introductions to order relations and surveys a number of similarity relations to suggest methods for comparing nonequivalent sets. Notwithstanding the highly technical nature of his book, Morris emphasizes the importance of hearing, or attempting to hear, the relations under discussion. Little attention is given to analytical demonstration throughout the book, as its ultimate purpose, as indicated in its subtitle, is to formulate a theory of compositional design. Nevertheless, the book is a rich resource of theoretical formulations for analysis of 20th-century music.

Compared to Morris, LEWIN (1987) adopts an even more explicitly abstract presentation in his far-reaching theory of generalized musical intervals and transformational networks, necessitating an unabatedly mathematical conception and approach. In Lewin's theory, an interval is any quantity that can be measured between any pair of objects; the objects in question are not necessarily pitches or pitch classes but may be time points, ratios, serial transformations, or may represent any parameter to which some value may be associated. The formidable power of this work may be difficult for some readers to grasp because of its extreme level of abstraction. As a practical demonstration of selected applications of the theory, LEWIN (1993) offers four in-depth analyses of 20th-century works in which he demonstrates transformational networks in large-scale formal organization. Success in comprehending the analyses does not, however, depend on foreknowledge of Lewin's earlier work. Moreover, Lewin (1993) does not indicate that his theory applies only to 20th-century music; the theoretical formulations are not intrinsically attached to any particular repertoire or style. Lewin (1987) and Lewin (1993) are mutually beneficial for a reader familiar with or motivated to study both books, but each is also self-sufficient.

BERRY sets out to explore elements of structure in pitch relations, as well as in relations involving the non-pitch parameters most significant in their interrelations with pitch: texture, rhythm, and meter. His explorations of textural and rhythmic structures are particularly original. Throughout the book, Berry expresses his belief in the possibility of analysis of the musical experience through rational inquiry and, particularly in the chapter on texture, attempts to portray parallel quantitative and qualitative data. Although not successful in demonstrating unequivocally that theory is capable of modeling perception as well as it can model conception of musical structures, Berry's work is important for the boldness of

the questions it poses and for its intersections with ideas still current and active in music-theoretical inquiry.

The essays in HATCH and BERNSTEIN confront the circumscription and isolation of the discipline of music theory by exploring various modes of intersection between theoretical and historical research. The essays range from studies of historical music theories to analytical studies from a number of historical periods and to philosophical studies of the interaction of music theory with history and aesthetics.

BAKER et al. have gathered another diverse group of essays that reinforce the principal areas of music-theoretical research since World War II. At the same time, the essays reveal the enormous growth of the discipline in the 50 years following the war by offering new perspectives on the history of theory in the 20th century, extensions to familiar theoretical formulations from pitch-class set theory and transformations, and a variety of analytical studies of tonal and 20th-century works.

The essays in POPLE explore the nature and interrelations of music theory and music analysis, and the ways in which each discipline engages musical meaning. Theory and analysis are considered from perspectives informed by literary criticism, philosophy, and linguistics. The traditional concerns of music theory—explanatory power, objectivity, and coherence—are placed in a wider context that embraces other issues, including ambiguity and metaphor. Similarly, music analysis is also associated with narrative and metaphor. The use of strategic language by theorists and analysts is scrutinized in relation to meaning accrued by the status of their enterprise as text. The general bibliography is particularly relevant.

STRAUS (1990b) proposes a theory of musical influence that is adapted from literary critic Harold Bloom's theory of poetic influence. Straus asserts that the major composers of the early 20th century—Stravinsky, Schoenberg, Bartók, Webern, and Berg—shared common strategies for coming to terms with their rich and tenacious musical heritage and for revising structural aspects of pitch and formal organization. Straus's close analyses reveal a dynamic conflict between traditional elements and structures, on the one hand, and the will to subvert these in favor of modern practices, on the other.

The assemblage of essays in MARVIN and HERMANN includes a number of analytical studies of repertoires not conventionally represented in publications or professional conferences: post-World War II concert music, as well as rock and jazz. The collection celebrates diversity not only in the choice of repertoire but also in the range of approaches to understanding the works. In addition to the analytical studies, the collection includes several essays on the cultural contexts of the various repertoires of post-World War II music, the well-traveled aesthetic notions of unity and disunity, and the distinction between modernism and postmodernism. These more general essays orient the reader to the larger issues addressed in the book and join the various threads of the analytical essays.

CATHERINE NOLAN

Thomson, Virgil 1896–1989

United States composer

Hoover, Kathleen, and John Cage, *Virgil Thomson: His Life and Music,* New York: Yoseloff, 1959

Meckna, Michael, *Virgil Thomson: A Bio-Bibliography,* New York: Greenwood Press, 1986

Thomson, Virgil, *Selected Letters of Virgil Thomson,* edited by Tim Page and Vanessa Weeks Page, New York: Summit Books, 1988

————, *Virgil Thomson,* New York: Knopf, 1966

Tommasini, Anthony, *Virgil Thomson: Composer on the Aisle,* New York: Norton, 1997

Virgil Thomson occupies a unique position in United States art music in the 20th century. He was a Pulitzer Prize–winning composer of usually accessible, well-wrought music that often garners praise from experts and laymen alike. But, perhaps more importantly, he was the most eloquent and learned music critic of his time, an effective and opinionated spokesman for music, whose writings added an important and distinctive facet to New York City's intellectual life in the mid-20th century.

Thomson's life can best be described as kaleidoscopic. From his discovery of music at an early age to his adventures in World War I to his associations in Paris with some of the most riveting musical minds of the era to his storming the U.S. musical scene with important forays into opera and film, Thomson's life and career rarely lacked interest. Like so many American composers of his day, however, Thomson's most fervent wish was to have his music performed by professionals and given a fair hearing before the public. Of course, Thomson got his wish far too infrequently and today is known for but a handful of works. Although over the years several writers have taken up his cause, his catalog of currently available recordings is slim, and the outlook for a Thomson renaissance looks rather bleak at this time.

TOMMASINI's biography is the most important and comprehensive book presently available on Thomson. Written in a lucid, accessible style (Tommasini is a music critic for the *New York Times*), the book presents Thomson's story in detail, presenting the basic facts of his life and lending considerable insight into his artistic mission and sometimes peevish manner. Tommasini provides excellent essays on Thomson's family history, his earliest musical experiences, and his first true musical mentor, Robert Leigh Murray. "A Lovely War" chronicles a neglected aspect of Thomson's life, his experiences in World War I. Tommasini writes eloquently of Thomson's first experiences as a music critic in Paris, gives a fine overview of his 14-year tenure with the New York *Herald Tribune,* and includes excerpts from several of his most important and interesting reviews. Chapters or sections devoted to Thomson's many companions and acquaintances illuminate his fascinating personal life and add to our understanding of his professional life. Tommasini gives a good overview of Thomson's numerous collaborations, with especially important accounts of his work with Gertrude Stein on *Four Saints in Three Acts,* his work with John Houseman and Orson Welles on the groundbreaking production of Shakespeare's *Macbeth,* and his collaboration with Jack Larson on *Lord Byron.* Throughout the book Tommasini engages the reader with details of Thomson's homosexuality, from his initial recognition of it until his eventual acceptance of the lifestyle. Tommasini inserts himself into the narrative at the point in which he entered Thomson's sphere, 1979, and offers an up-close tale of the composer's growing dismay at having been forgotten by the public, his increasing cantankerousness, and his final days. The book also includes several valuable photo sections.

HOOVER and CAGE's monograph, the earliest attempt at a book-length, comprehensive study of Thomson, is divided into two sections that discuss his life and music, respectively. Hoover's 100-page biography, prepared with Thomson's assistance, presents a largely friendly and sympathetic portrait of the composer; these chapters include Thomson's early years, his experiences at Harvard and in Paris, and his "mature" years, the 1950s. Hoover's account is engagingly written and includes a good basic foundation for further study of his early life. Hoover's insightful report on Thomson and Harvard documents Thomson's varied activities in Boston, his broad interests, and his refusal to succumb to "academicism." Further, her chronicle of Thomson's Parisian period presents a lucid discussion of his attraction to French culture and his awakening to the field of music criticism. Cage's assessment of Thomson's music is based on a detailed familiarity with the scores, including numerous unpublished manuscripts. Like Hoover, Cage was assisted in his efforts by Thomson's own helpful insights and access to private, commercially unavailable recordings. The discussion is aimed at the advanced reader and includes numerous music examples and detailed discussions of harmony, form, and other musical parameters. While this portion of the book is most appropriate for knowledgeable musicians, Cage's enthusiastic delivery also includes many interesting details for the layman.

THOMSON's (1966) autobiography is a beautifully written work focused largely on his composing career and his many musical acquaintances. Thomson omits mention of the most intimate details of his life but illuminates his personal musical aesthetic, which lies somewhere between a disdain for the ultramodern school of composition (Boulez, Cage) and a mild resentment of the continued popularity of composers whose works comprise the standard orchestral repertoire (Mozart, Beethoven). Perhaps most intriguing is Thomson's final chapter, "A Distaste for Music," wherein he lists several vital needs for music's future success in the United States. These include "a genius of the lyric stage" (i.e., an important opera composer), a high-quality and perceptive music magazine, a clarification of music's role in U.S. civilization, and "the preservation, examination, and confrontation" of the music of other societies.

MECKNA's book includes a brief biography section based mostly on Hoover and Cage and Thomson's autobiography, with emphasis on his major compositions and the basic facts of his life. Most valuable is the catalog of Thomson's works and their performances, a discography, and two bibliographies, the first of writings by Thomson, the second of writings about him. The works catalog includes a complete listing of Thomson's compositions, their dates of composition, publication information, and the dates of premieres. Meckna's discography will help to locate recorded performances of Thomson's compositions. Although this research guide is intended to lead the reader to more advanced study, properly used it can provide valuable information to the novice.

Page and Weeks make a significant contribution to our knowledge of the composer with THOMSON (1988), an exquisitely annotated work that includes letters written from 1917 to 1985. Thomson's letters present his vivid life in his own unedited words. Selected from a wide variety of his letters to readers of his music criticism, eminent composers and performers, and various friends and acquaintances, his private writings inform the reader of the major events of his life with clarity and succinctness. The correspondence effectively illuminates his varied personal relationships, his compositions and his efforts to have them performed, and his numerous personal peeves and preferences. Thomson's legendary literary writing style is apparent throughout this valuable and engaging collection.

BILL F. FAUCETT

Toscanini, Arturo 1867–1957

Italian-born conductor

Antek, Samuel, *This Was Toscanini*, New York: Vanguard Press, 1963

Haggin, B.H., *Conversations with Toscanini*, Garden City, New York: Doubleday, 1959; 2nd edition, New York: Horizon Press, 1979

———, *The Toscanini Musicians Knew*, New York: Horizon Press, 1967; 2nd edition, 1980

Horowitz, Joseph, *Understanding Toscanini: How He Became an American Culture-God and Helped Create a New Audience for Old Music*, New York: Knopf, and London: Faber, 1987

Sachs, Harvey, *Toscanini*, London: Weidenfeld and Nicolson, and Philadelphia, Pennsylvania: Lippincott, 1978

———, *Reflections on Toscanini*, New York: Grove Weidenfeld, 1991; London: Robson, 1992

Over 40 years after his final concert appearance, Arturo Toscanini remains a controversial figure. Some rank him among history's greatest conductors; others dismiss his musical interpretations as inflexible and idiosyncratic. Books about Toscanini that were published during his lifetime are often factually incorrect and tend toward extremes, portraying him as either an ascetic seeker of truth or a childish and self-absorbed tyrant. The popular press, particularly in the United States, made Toscanini into a cultural icon whose name became synonymous with great music. After his death, more nuanced considerations began to appear. The recollections of colleagues, as well as the fruits of scholarly research, have led to complex characterizations of Toscanini's life and art. Although his name continues to be associated with strict discipline, with the passage of time it is now possible to weigh both the personal costs and artistic benefits of that quality.

HAGGIN (1959), the cantankerous music critic of *The Nation*, was one of the few journalists whose opinion Toscanini respected. During their nine-year friendship, he and Toscanini met to discuss recordings, composers, conductors, and other aspects of musical performance. Through Haggin's published recollections, the conductor emerges as a relentless perfectionist, whose ideals often clashed with the realities of performance. The author employs technical language to describe Toscanini's interpretations, weaving memories of rehearsals, private meetings, and musicians' observations into his story. The 1979 revision includes an account of Toscanini's resignation from the NBC Symphony Orchestra, record reviews (focusing on technical rather than artistic details), and a largely negative evaluation of other authors' writing about the conductor.

ANTEK, a violinist with the NBC Symphony during Toscanini's entire 17-year tenure, offers his fond memories of the conductor, who was affectionately nicknamed the "Old Man" by his orchestra. While Antek's recollections of private conversations, rehearsals, performances, and the NBC Symphony's 1950 cross-country tour may seem effusive, his affection for his subject appears genuine. Furthermore, he does not overlook Toscanini's weaknesses, which included a violent temper and limited baton technique. Although Antek sometimes engages in specialized musical discussion, especially when he explains how Toscanini conducted certain compositions, he also offers the nonmusician a glimpse of life in the Old

Man's orchestra. Robert Hupka's accompanying photographs of Toscanini in rehearsal effectively capture his personal style.

HAGGIN (1967) is an exceptionally honest portrait consisting of interviews with 17 performers—orchestral musicians, singers, and solo instrumentalists—who had worked with Toscanini at various points in his career. Although each musician contributes a unique perspective, most maintain that the conductor's sometimes unorthodox interpretations gave them a new appreciation for compositions that had become too familiar. Toscanini's strengths, such as his vitality, dedication, and scholarship, are contrasted with his counterproductive emotional outbursts and lack of success with certain types of music. More than once, Haggin skillfully conveys an informant's discomfort when revealing a negative opinion about the conductor. Technical musical references can be found in most chapters, although they are not essential to an understanding of the effect that Toscanini had on those who worked with him.

SACHS's (1978) authoritative biography substitutes meticulous research for recollection. Realizing that many readers are, like himself, familiar with Toscanini only through the recordings made late in his life, Sachs pays special attention to his subject's youth and middle age. A conductor in his own right, the author nonetheless favors biographical detail over technical discussion. Toscanini's family background and cultural milieu are examined at length, as is his legendary conducting debut at the age of 19 in Rio de Janeiro. Excerpts from newspaper reviews, correspondence, and published interviews document Toscanini's rapid rise to international prominence and demonstrate the lax performance standards against which he battled. Sachs does not neglect the conductor's political activities, which included active opposition to both Hitler and Mussolini as well as support for the fledgling Palestine Symphony Orchestra. Despite his obvious admiration for his subject, Sachs offers an evenhanded portrayal, often presenting important episodes from multiple viewpoints. He also addresses perceived biases in Toscanini criticism and offers a repertoire list and a register of casts for Toscanini's opera performances.

The subject of HOROWITZ's study is less Toscanini than it is the publicity machine that made the conductor's name a household word. After tracing the trajectory of cultural aspirations in the 19th-century United States—from Mark Twain through P.T. Barnum, and on to the ambitions of German immigrants—Horowitz arrives, not altogether convincingly, at Toscanini's first New York appearances in 1908. Despite its simplistic conclusion that Toscanini and his handlers laid the groundwork for many of today's cultural excesses, this controversial book effectively chronicles the adulation that accompanied the conductor's U.S. career. It becomes clear that although publicity did not "make" Toscanini, it did exert an influence on both the constitution and expectations of his audience. This book, which has been severely criticized by many of Toscanini's supporters, raises some thought-provoking questions.

Finally, SACHS (1991) is a collection of essays and articles, many of which first appeared in Italian periodicals. Several chapters shed new light on biographical episodes, such as Toscanini's youth, his early successes in Turin, and his well-documented opposition to Hitler and Mussolini. Sachs also offers an analysis of Toscanini's conducting gestures, based on an examination of videotaped performances. Perhaps most notable, he draws important conclusions about Toscanini's musical aesthetic from his recordings.

LINDA B. FAIRTILE

Tower, Joan b. 1938

United States composer

Briscoe, James R., editor, *Contemporary Anthology of Music by Women,* Bloomington: Indiana University Press, 1997

LePage, Jane Weiner, *Women Composers, Conductors, and Musicians of the Twentieth Century: Selected Biographies,* 3 vols., Metuchen, New Jersey: Scarecrow Press, 1988

Neuls-Bates, Carol, editor, *Women in Music: An Anthology of Source Readings from the Middle Ages to the Present,* New York: Harper and Row, 1982; revised edition, Boston: Northeastern University Press, 1996

Nichols, Janet, *Women Music Makers: An Introduction to Women Composers,* New York: Walker, 1992

Rischin, Rebecca, "Master Class: 'Wings' by Joan Tower," *Clarinet* 26 (1999)

As a pianist and founding member of the award-winning Da Capo Chamber Players, Joan Tower initially composed chamber music, often for specific players or ensembles. Her distinctive compositional voice, which she claims did not come into being until she was in her 30s, has never spoken to any "school" or easily labeled "ism" but has remained faithful to her abiding interests in timbral color, rhythmic vitality, and taking risks. Although Tower has more recently written successful works for orchestra (*Silver Ladders* won the prestigious 1990 Grawemeyer Award) and has become one of the most popular contemporary music composers with audiences and performers alike, the secondary literature on her remains limited, perhaps because of her early chamber inclinations and her unwillingness to subscribe to or promote any one compositional process. Tower has been an eloquent spokesperson for greater visibility for both women composers and new music in general, and all of the published work on her is largely a result of the growing interest in women in music and a more inclusive music history.

LePAGE includes a chapter on Tower in this multi-volume series. The chapter is largely descriptive, covering the composer's early work in the Da Capo Chamber Players and ending at the start of Tower's residency with the St. Louis Symphony in 1985, following the success of her first orchestral work, *Sequoia* (1981). LePage quotes extensively from interviews with Tower as well as from published critical reviews. The discography, although dated, is useful for material available on LP.

Tower emerges as an articulate composer, thoughtful musician, and creative woman in the revised edition of NEULS-BATES's groundbreaking anthology. Neuls-Bates asks straightforward questions and allows the composer to answer at length. Tower discusses her childhood in South America and considers how the music making within her family affected her as she became more proficient as a pianist. Tower learned to speak several languages and participated in dance and music rituals that instilled a lifelong love for rhythm and percussion. She describes her turn to composition as a student at Bennington College, her protracted graduate studies at Columbia University, and her initial participation in the so-called uptown composition scene loosely based around Milton Babbitt. The composer identifies *Black Topaz* (1976) as her breakthrough composition in which she shed serial techniques in favor of going her own way.

Tower also discusses her work as a founding member of the Da Capo Chamber Players, with whom she played until 1985, after which composition became her priority. Her articulation of the differences between the "tactile experience" of writing for such an ensemble and the "guesswork" of composing for orchestra is especially illuminating because it reflects her experience during her residency with the St. Louis Symphony from 1985 to 1987, where she honed her orchestral technique through direct work with symphony players and composed her monumental *Silver Ladders* (1986). Tower also discusses the role gender has played in her life and her own recent education regarding the missing history of women composers. Tower now actively supports younger and older women composers in whatever ways she can and remains optimistic about the future for women composers.

Briscoe and Rischin both focus on specific compositions, providing material of particular interest to performers. BRISCOE includes the musical score for Tower's single-movement work for string quartet, *Night Fields,* which has also been recorded. As preparation for listening to the work itself, Briscoe provides a good overview of Tower's life and work and a helpful introduction to the composition. This introduction includes quotations from the composer about her aims and responses from music critics. Tower's 1981 solo composition *Wings,* written for Da Capo Chamber Players clarinetist Laura Flax, has become a contemporary standard not only for clarinet but also in the composer's transcription for saxophone. RISCHIN's article treats issues related to the performance of this work, combining Tower's perspectives about the composition, including her overall fondness for the clarinet, with practical advice and approaches from clarinetists, such as Rischin herself, who have performed the work.

An unusual addition to the bibliography of works about Tower is the chapter on her by NICHOLS. The book is intended for young readers, especially girls who might be looking for role models or anyone desiring a more equitable view of the significance of women in music history, and Nichols's tone is accessible without being patronizing. Her material is factually accurate and warrants attention, especially as much of the narrative is in Tower's own words. Given her intended audience, it is unsurprising that Nichols stresses Tower's childhood, her time in South America, her early piano studies, the influence of her parents (especially her violin-playing father), and her abiding interest in Beethoven. This chapter contains biographical material not found elsewhere. Nichols presents Tower's turn to composition and her discovery of an individual voice in a compelling way, and the author's descriptions of particular works are commendable.

SUSAN C. COOK

Trope

Corpus Troporum, 8 vols. to date, Stockholm: Almqvist and Wiksell, 1975–

Crocker, Richard, "The Troping Hypothesis," *Musical Quarterly* 52 (1966)

Evans, Paul, *The Early Trope Repertory of Saint Martial de Limoges,* Princeton, New Jersey: Princeton University Press, 1970

Falconer, Keith, *Some Early Tropes to the Gloria,* Modena: Mucchi, 1993

Frere, Walter, *The Winchester Troper: From Mss. of the Xth and XIth Centuries,* London: Harrison, 1894; reprint, New York: AMS Press, 1973

Liturgische Tropen: Referate zweier Colloquien des Corpus Troporum in München (1983) und Canterbury (1984), Munich: Arbeo-Gesellschaft, 1985

Planchart, Alejandro Enrique, *The Repertory of Tropes at Winchester,* 2 vols., Princeton, New Jersey: Princeton University Press, 1977

Scholars of medieval music have only recently reached a consensus regarding the definition of the term *trope.* Today the word is taken to refer to newly composed text, along with its newly composed music, added to a preexisting liturgical chant. A *prosula,* on the other hand, is defined as text added to a preexisting melisma. As such, both types of additions constitute interpolations or introductions that expand the meaning of a chant and perhaps relate the chant more clearly to a particular feast. Almost all chants of the Mass Ordinary (Kyrie, Gloria, Credo, Sanctus, Agnus Dei, and Ite missa est) have been troped, as have many of the chants of the Proper, particularly the Introit, Offertory, and Communion. The most frequently troped chant of the Mass Proper is the Introit; of the Mass Ordinary, the Gloria is most frequently troped, and the Credo the least. Tropes (beginning with the line *Quem queritis*) to the Introit *Resurrexi* for Easter morning are considered to be the origin of medieval drama, for the *Quem queritis* tropes involve dialogue, and manuscript versions of the troped Introit exist that include primitive stage directions for the monks taking the roles of the three Marys and the angel at the tomb. Tropes to the Epistles are called *farsa* (*farses*), from the Latin, meaning "stuffed." The most frequently troped chants of the Office were the *Benedicamus domino* and Responsory. Troping began presumably in the ninth-century Frankish territories, and the earliest tropers (liturgical books of tropes) appeared in the early tenth century. By the mid-11th century, the art of troping was no longer a viable creative outlet for composers, who had turned their efforts to the *prosa*.

An early article by CROCKER is important for its defense of tropes as a viable art form against the implicit claims of the troping hypothesis formulated by a previous generation of scholars. The troping hypothesis sprang from the desire for a single, clear definition of tropes and led to the idea that tropes lack originality and are artistically inferior to their parent chants. Crocker argues that troping practice is much too varied to pin down with a single definition and that in many instances it is difficult to distinguish trope from original chant, as the two often share the same degree of originality and artistry.

EVANS surveys the early trope repertory of Saint Martial with the aim of making available in transcription this basic repertory from one of the most important centers of troping activity. Five chapters of commentary precede his transcriptions and cover the meaning of trope, its historical position, texts, and musical structure, as well as the particular manuscripts—the Saint Martial tropers. He concludes that tropes are usually a unique combination of music and text and are frequently neumatic in style—in contrast to the syllabic *prosas* and *prosulae*—that the intense but brief life of the trope had its high point in the tenth century, and that the nine tropers of Saint Martial varied in content in relation to the functions of the manuscripts within liturgical use. Furthermore, he argues that the great majority of trope texts were written in quantitative verse and that it is unlikely that the poet and composer were the same individual because the two worked according to completely different principles. Various formal schemes had to be adapted to the elements of fitting trope to chant, and composers probably eventually found the structure of the trope too restrictive to allow full development of musical ideas; this limitation led, understandably, to tropes falling out of favor and to composers turning to other forms by the 11th century.

The eight out of a projected nine volumes of the *CORPUS TROPORUM* are an invaluable resource for carefully edited trope texts and manuscript concordances and variants. Commentary for all except volume 9 (the volumes have been published out of sequence) is in French, but the major value of the bulk of these studies lies in their function as reference works wherein one can locate all manuscript variants of a particular trope text. Volume 9 provides an edition of liturgical tropes to the Mass Propers of the four feasts of the Blessed Virgin Mary: the Purification, Annunciation, Assumption, and feast of the Nativity of the Virgin. Based on 101 European manuscripts dating from the tenth to the 15th centuries, the edition is supplemented by an introduction and commentary in English. The editor notes that Marian tropes differ in character depending on the feast to which they belong and that regional differences occur in style and content; Italian manuscripts present a greater emphasis on the Virgin than German manuscripts, for example.

LITURGISCHE TROPEN, consisting of contributions from the 1983 and 1984 colloquium meetings of *Corpus troporum* scholars, contains 15 essays, eight of which are in English. Of these, three stand out as useful sources for general material on tropes and troping. Peter Dronke's "Types of Poetic Art in Tropes" is indispensable for an understanding of the verbal artistry of trope texts and the idea that the poetic art of troping lies in the whole range of interactions between tropes and liturgical texts. This chapter also posits an eighth-century, south German origin of the tropes. Susan Rankin, in "Musical and Ritual Aspects of *Quem queritis,*" revisits the background arguments for the *Quem queritis* dialogue as a trope, finding seven different versions of the sentences following the initial *Quem queritis* line and using close musical analysis to support the five-sentence dialogue form as the original. Leo Treitler's "Speaking of Jesus" examines melodic versions of a particular trope verse that both include and do not include the name of Jesus and concludes that the sources containing the name are later works, reflecting a change toward a more human and personal Christ, part of a major shift in cultural values and mentalities that took place during the 12th century.

FRERE is useful chiefly as a reference source for textual transcriptions of the tropes of the famous Winchester troper manuscripts. Although superseded by Planchart, the introduction is still a helpful orientation.

PLANCHART provides a repertorial and liturgical study of the Winchester tropers, limiting the repertory he addresses to Proper and Ordinary tropes and Kyrie *prosulae*. He links two of the Winchester tropers to the period of Aethelwoldean reform at Winchester, part of the tenth-century monastic revival in England, evidenced in the strong English corpus of unique pieces that use the elaborate poetry of the Anglo-Latin poets of the school of Aethelwold. Planchart points out relationships between the Winchester repertory and that of other centers and includes a musical edition of the Christmas tropes. Volume 2 contains complete inventories and catalogs of Proper and Ordinary tropes in the extant Anglo-Saxon tropers.

FALCONER, studying four particular tropes to the "Gloria in excelsis dei," one of the oldest hymns of the church, disagrees with Crocker's idea that the melodies for trope and Gloria were simultaneously composed. Tracing the four tropes through the sources and centuries, he finds them to be of diverse origin and links these tropes with the effort by Charlemagne to impose a standard liturgy and thus suppress the Gallican rite. These four tropes and perhaps many others, Falconer believes, are an attempt to preserve older Gallican material by interpolating it as tropes.

JULIA W. SHINNICK

Troubadours and Trouvères

Aubrey, Elizabeth, *Music of the Troubadours*, Bloomington: Indiana University Press, 1996

Aubry, Pierre, *Trouvères and Troubadours: A Popular Treatise*, translated by Claude Aveling, New York: Schirmer, 1914; reprint, New York: Cooper Square Publishers, 1969

Beck, Jean, "The Music of the Troubadours," translated by Timothy Wardell, in *The Music of the Troubadours*, edited by Peter Whigham, Santa Barbara, California: Ross-Erikson, 1979

Rosenberg, Samuel, et al., *Songs of the Troubadours and Trouvères: An Anthology of Poems and Melodies*, New York: Garland, 1998

Tischler, Hans, *Trouvère Lyrics with Melodies: Complete Comparative Edition*, 15 vols., Neuhausen: American Institute of Musicology; Hänssler-Verlag, 1997–

Werf, Hendrik van der, *The Chansons of the Troubadours and Trouvères: A Study of the Melodies and Their Relation to the Poems*, Utrecht: Oosthoek, 1972

———, *The Extant Troubadour Melodies: Transcriptions and Essays for Performers and Scholars*, Rochester, New York: Werf, 1984

The troubadours and trouvères were the lyric poets of medieval France and the inaugurators of the Western courtly love tradition. Guilhem de Poiters, the first known troubadour, lived about 1100 and composed songs in the southern French dialect of Old Occitan. Later poets, such as Bernart de Ventadorn and Folquet de Marseilla, flour-

ished in the late 12th century during the height of troubadour art, or *art de trobar*. Following the Albigensian Crusade (1209–29), the thriving culture that had given birth to the troubadours was all but eliminated, and the *art de trobar* found its last great representative in Guiraut Riquier. Meanwhile, troubadour song had already traveled north. Early exponents, such as the Châtelain de Coucy and Gace Brulé, composed their poetry in the northern dialect of Old French and were called trouvères. By the 13th century, a strong trouvère tradition was established in the work of such skilled poets as Thibaut de Navarre and Colin Muset, and the tradition did not wane until the death of Adam de la Halle at century's end. In general, trouvère melodies are more predictable in form and straightforward in tonality than their southern counterparts. For the over 2,500 extant troubadour poems, only about 300 melodies survive. Many more trouvère melodies have been transmitted: most of their 2,000 or so extant poems have a musical setting.

Although scholarly interest in the poetry of the troubadours and trouvères flourished in the latter half of the 19th century, it was not until AUBRY's publication that the music of these repertoires received its first book-length study. Writing for a lay audience, Aubry surveys primary genres and poets, enlivening his discussion with musical examples. His book's final chapter offers a method for discovering the rhythm of the melodies, most of which are found in a notation that does not indicate duration.

Aubry's rhythmic solution was soon challenged by BECK, who disagrees with Aubry's methods. Furthermore, Beck denounces Aubry as having plagiarized Beck's own ideas. His book is an effort to make his authorship of the "modal interpretation" public. Contrary to what the title would suggest, the author deals with both troubadours and trouvères. Beginning with an explanation of medieval notation, the first half of the book provides an explanation of the modal interpretation, the idea that the modal rhythms of medieval polyphony could be read into monophonic melodies. This conception is based on selective evidence from prosody and later musical readings. Thus, the Beck-Aubry debate launches the musicological study of these repertoires as a notational riddle, that is, how to translate nonmensural monophony into measured modern notation. Most musical studies prior to 1950 continued to emphasize this aspect, notably, the many writings of German scholar Friedrich Gennrich (see the bibliography in Werf [1972]).

In the mid-1960s, Werf offered a solution to the riddle, later expanded in WERF (1972). According to him, these repertoires were declaimed rather than sung and so could not be bound within the confines of modern notation. Thus, his musical editions use the "neutral" stemless notes common in plainchant. Werf also studies a given melody's manuscript variants, which he views as manifesting the preliterate, oral character of the original repertoires. Although most of Werf's innovations had precedents in the work of such scholars as Appel and Sachs, he deserves credit for developing these areas for the troubadours and trouvères. WERF (1984), an edition of the troubadour repertoire, presents all variants of a given tune in stemless notes, with each version aligned for comparison.

Later studies have followed Werf's lead in steering clear of the rhythm controversy. However, one notable exception is TISCHLER's monumental edition of the trouvère corpus. Its first 13 volumes contain over 1,200 songs, with the lais and rondeaus reserved for the last four volumes. Most melodies are edited in rhythmicized readings. Tischler's edition illustrates the editorial creativity required to create rhythmic transcriptions from nonmensural melodies, but these choices rely in part on incontrovertible evidence pointed out by Aubry at the beginning of the century: the use of trouvère melodies in some motets and the presence in certain manuscripts of monophonic and polyphonic repertoires written by the same hand.

AUBREY's book is the most thorough study to date on the troubadour repertoire. Focusing on the 300-odd extant melodic versions, Aubrey deals evenly with such issues as genre and style. Of particular note are the chapter on transmission (for its detailed description of the manuscript sources) and the chapter on form (for its discussion of both text and melody). Other chapters attest both to the postwar increase of musicological studies and to changing emphases since Aubry and Beck. For example, the cautious tone of Aubrey's discussion on rhythm contrasts with Beck's bold statements nearly 80 years earlier.

ROSENBERG et al. offer a more general anthology of the trouvères and troubadours. It, too, is the product of nearly a century's concerted labor of literary and musical scholarship. For example, the canon of poets includes several *trobairitz* (women troubadours) and one *trouveuse* not mentioned in Aubry's handbook. Whereas Aubry offers only 15 musical examples, over 100 melodies are edited and analyzed in this anthology, providing the reader with a sampling of primary genres and styles. With its updated bibliography and three introductory essays, it is an ideal introduction to the art of the lyric poets of medieval France.

JOHN HAINES

Tuning and Temperaments

Barbour, J. Murray, *Tuning and Temperament: A Historical Survey,* East Lansing: Michigan State College Press, 1951; 2nd edition, 1953

Blackwood, Easley, *The Structure of Recognizable Diatonic Tunings,* Princeton, New Jersey: Princeton University Press, 1985

Bosanquet, R.H.M., *An Elementary Treatise on Musical Intervals and Temperament,* London: Macmillan, 1876; reprint, Utrecht: Diapson Press, 1987

Danielou, Alain, *Introduction to the Study of Musical Scales,* London: India Society, 1943; reprint, New Delhi: Oriental Books, 1979

Ellis, Alexander J., and Arthur Mendel, *Studies in the History of Musical Pitch,* Amsterdam: Fritz Knuf, and New York: Da Capo Press, 1968

Jorgensen, Owen, *The Equal-Beating Temperaments: A Handbook for Tuning Harpsichords and Forte-Pianos, with Tuning Techniques and Tables of Fifteen Historical Temperaments,* Raleigh, North Carolina: Sunbury Press, 1981

——, *Tuning the Historical Temperaments by Ear,* Marquette: Northern Michigan University Press, 1977

Lindley, Mark, *Lutes, Viols, and Temperaments,* Cambridge: Cambridge University Press, 1984

Link, John W., *Theory and Tuning: Aron's Meantone Temperament and Marpurg's Temperament I,* Boston: Tuners Supply, 1963

Lloyd, Llewelyn S., and Hugh Boyle, *Intervals, Scales, and Temperaments,* London: MacDonald, and New York: St. Martin's Press, 1963; 2nd edition, 1978

Moore, F. Richard, *Elements of Computer Music,* Englewood Cliffs, New Jersey: Prentice Hall, 1990

Partch, Harry, *Genesis of a Music,* Madison: University of Wisconsin Press, 1949; as *Genesis of a Music: An Account of a Creative Work, Its Roots and Its Fulfillments,* 2nd edition, enlarged, New York: Da Capo Press, 1974

White, William Braid, *Piano Tuning and Allied Arts,* Boston: Tuners Supply, 1917; 5th edition, 1946

Before performing, an ensemble generally tunes, that is, establishes an overall group pitch by changing, for example, the length of tubing or amount of string tension on an instrument. Tuning is also the adjustment of intervals within a desired harmonic or melodic context. A tuning, however, is a system based on nonbeating or "just" intervals, which can be expressed as the ratio of two integers. A Pythagorean tuning, for example, is based on pure fifths. By contrast, a temperament is a system in which the purity of some or all of the intervals is sacrificed, their ratios containing radical numbers, in order to create set scales for fixed (i.e., keyboard) instruments. In equal temperament, the 12-note system used in common modern practice, all intervals are adjusted and therefore slightly "impure." Much of the literature on tuning and temperament has been motivated by a distaste for equal temperament and a desire to educate the reader about the advantages of alternative systems. The personal biases of the author should therefore be considered, whether the text be historical, pedagogical, or the promotion of an individual's experimentation with instrument or scale construction.

Appendix C, "Tuning," of MOORE provides a coherent and concise introduction to the technical language of tuning and temperaments. The author carefully organizes his material into an easy-to-follow sequence from the harmonic series and the derivation of ratios to specific tunings and temperaments. His goal is not to present a history but the basic concepts, and the reader should be aware that some of his statements about the history of temperaments are incorrect; for example, mean-tone temperament was in practice well before Moore's stated 19th-century beginnings. He raises interesting issues regarding the computer's role in tuning. According to Moore, the computer has "neutrality on questions of tuning" because it is not a fixed keyboard but offers more precision than other instruments. It is therefore more accurate in context-dependent tuning.

BARBOUR remains the most comprehensive guide to both the history and mechanics of tuning and temperament from Greek theory to mean-tone and equal temperaments, but it demands careful reading, including the preface for those unfamiliar with ratios and logarithms, which are necessary to understand the main text and tables. A glossary provides quick definitions of terms, and the section "From Theory to Practice" considers temperament and tuning for specific lute, keyboard, and choral compositions. Barbour believes that just intonation, a system based on pure octaves, fifths, and thirds, is the superior tuning method. He is one of the first scholars to question the notion that J.S. Bach embraced equal temperament.

LLOYD and BOYLE, in separate sections of their volume, both emphasize that tuning nonkeyboard or nonfixed instruments requires a flexible scale dependent on context. Lloyd criticizes both equal temperament and just intonation, taking every opportunity to disparage them throughout the text and promote mean-tone temperament as the ultimate compromise. Lloyd's history is less detailed than Barbour's, but to be fair, Lloyd omits Greek theory for fear of perpetuating uncertain and misleading interpretations. His style is more conversational and less technical than Barbour's. Chapter 6, "Temperaments without Tears," for example, presents the mathematics of ratios in a manner that could be understood by a child "who has mastered addition and subtraction in algebra." Lloyd's essay is paired with Boyle's examination of mostly acoustical issues such as sound waves and frequency, but Boyle's less-biting tone makes his discussion of ratios and scale derivation more objective.

BLACKWOOD looks more like a mathematics treatise than a music treatise. Logarithms and complex theorems gloss nearly every page. The author assumes a layman's knowledge of musical notation and basic algebra. Although his descriptions are clear and the book as a whole is well organized with headings and numbered subsections, this is not a book to be skimmed and is not recommended for those seeking merely an introduction to the topic.

BOSANQUET covers the basics of calculating beats per second, difference tones, and various tuning systems in only 76 pages. In addition to showing how little has

changed in tuning and temperament scholarship, this treatise is valuable for the promotion of the 53-note octave division realized in Bosanquet's enharmonic keyboards. Rasch's introduction presents an overview of keyboard experimentation from Bosanquet's and Thompson's enharmonic organs of the 19th century to George Secor's Scalatron, an electronic keyboard created for microtonal music in the 1970s.

JORGENSEN (1977) describes his volume as a "manual of eighty-nine methods for tuning fifty-one scales on the harpsichord, piano, and other keyboard instruments." In his introduction, he surveys the history of keyboard tuning and construction, describing just tuning as the antonym of temperament. The main body of the book is divided into tuning systems such as just, mean-tone, Pythagorean, and equal temperament. The author provides a clear description, history, and tuning procedure for each scale within the various section headings. Jorgensen has created what he calls a "temperament recital," designed around several differently tuned historical keyboards. The performer moves from instrument to instrument, realizing a specific composition in the temperament in which it might have initially been conceived.

Whereas his earlier volume outlines "theoretically correct temperaments that are practical by ear" (that is by beat speeds), JORGENSEN (1981) presents the probably more historically correct "intuitive method" of equal-beating intervals. Encouraging performers to tune their own instruments, Jorgensen offers detailed information on tools and procedures for tuning single- and double-manual instruments. In contrast to his first text, this smaller volume only allots two pages per each tuning and serves essentially as an appendix to his earlier publication.

LINK gives detailed accounts of two historical temperaments: a system of mean-tone first described in Pietro Aron's *Toscanello in musica* (1523) and Friedrich Wilhelm Marpurg's 18th-century temperament. Link describes the latter as very close to but not as flawed as equal temperament. His discussion of each temperament and its tuning procedure is clear, and he includes helpful charts and a glossary.

LINDLEY addresses the difficulty of "imposing a theoretical scheme" on fretted instruments such as the lute and viol, where slight variations in finger pressure can alter pitch. Thus, even though he describes the fret placement on these instruments as most often producing equal semitones, he also explores the use of Pythagorean and mean-tone temperaments, as well as just intonation—especially in situations where lutes and viols perform with keyboard instruments. Lindley constantly reminds the reader that the ear is the final judge for determining the tuning system for a specific piece, and he is openly judgmental of the criteria for a good or bad performance choice. Dense technical terms are balanced with numerous suggestions for further reading. Lengthy quotations appear helpfully in both original language of the treatise and English translation, and the numerous examples are found in both modern notation and tablature. The latter is explained in one of four appendices that follow the 94 pages of main text. The other appendices present pertinent music not composed for fretted instruments, geometrical devises for determining fret placement, and an essay on "Lute Design and the Art of Proportion" by Gerhard C. Söhne. A cassette tape accompanying the book offers examples from various baroque composers, performed twice on lutes with different fretting schemes.

With WHITE's practical advice on everything from the mechanical aspects of piano tuning to repairing broken mechanisms, all that a prospective tuner needs is a keyboard and a little courage. The author briefly discusses the mechanics of the musical scale and the physics of string vibration, but his goal is to present a how-to guide to tuning the piano in equal temperament without delving into historical or ethical considerations. The book contains a glossary and detailed diagrams of the piano action.

Although PARTCH provides a comprehensive guide to tuning and temperament and a glossary of important terms, his discussion of tuning experimentation in the 20th century is particularly valuable. Much of this discussion is autobiographical, with descriptions of his own creations, such as the adapted viola (with stops marked in ratios on a longer-than-usual fingerboard), Kithara, Harmonic canon, and Diamond marimba. His commentary on various colleagues reads as an in-depth annotated bibliography of 20th-century experimentalist composers, including Henry Cowell, Wilfred Perret, Joseph Yasser, and Kathleen Schlesinger.

DANIELOU is not only critical of equal temperament, but he is also openly hostile to what he views as a misrepresentation of ancient and Eastern music by Westerners who insist on interpreting such works through equal temperament. Despite his defensive tone, Danielou presents important information on Eastern tuning systems—especially those of China, Persia, and India.

For a tuning or temperament to move from theory to application, a general or starting pitch must be set. The essays by ELLIS and MENDEL reveal the complexity of pitch in historical scholarship. Until the standardization attempts of the mid-19th century, pitch varied not only from country or court but also between church organs only a few miles apart. Ellis is worth reading to learn about scholarship in the 19th century, while Mendel is especially thorough in his three essays on pitch in the 16th and 17th centuries, organ transposition, and pitch in Bach's time. Mendel also contributes an introduction to the collection, summarizing the history of pitch from 1500 to the present day.

LAURA J. KOENIG

Turkey *see* Mode: Non-Western

20th-Century Music: General Studies

Griffiths, Paul, *The Thames and Hudson Encyclopaedia of 20th-Century Music,* London: Thames and Hudson, 1986

Károlyi, Ottó, *Introducing Modern Music,* London: Penguin Books, 1995

Morgan, Robert P., *Twentieth-Century Music: A History of Musical Style in Modern Europe and America,* New York: Norton, 1991

Salzman, Eric, *Twentieth-Century Music: An Introduction,* Englewood Cliffs, New Jersey: Prentice Hall, 1967; 3rd edition, 1988

Simms, Bryan R., *Music of the Twentieth Century: Style and Structure,* New York: Schirmer Books, and London: Collier Macmillan, 1986; 2nd edition, 1996

Slonimsky, Nicolas, *Music since 1900,* New York: Norton, 1937; 5th edition, New York: Schirmer Books, 1994

Watkins, Glenn, *Soundings: Music in the Twentieth Century,* New York: Schirmer Books, and London: Collier Macmillan, 1988

Yates, Peter, *Twentieth Century Music: Its Evolution from the End of the Harmonic Era into the Present Era of Sound,* New York: Pantheon Books, and London: Allen and Unwin, 1967

Books on 20th-century music have been appearing since the 1920s. The history of scholarship on 20th-century music includes efforts to root the repertoire in the aesthetic currents and debates of the romantic era; to chronicle the unfolding series of events; and to identify major figures and trends. In many books, particularly the earlier ones, the century's music is portrayed as a dialectic between Schoenberg and Stravinsky, while more recent books seek to find places of honor for Ives, Varèse, Cage, and other previously neglected figures. Some authors shy away entirely from the depiction of music history as the story of great artists in favor of a broad analysis of trends and tendencies.

YATES is a classic. Intended for the interested lay reader, it stakes out a historical position in its subtitle. A fervent champion of the U.S. experimental tradition, to which he devotes two chapters, and the founder of the famous Evenings on the Roof chamber concert series in Los Angeles, Yates strongly believes that music has entered a new paradigm based on sound rather than harmony. He advances this hypothesis in his first chapter, "Music and Sound." This book is a very engaging and readable series of essays, rather than a classroom-oriented text.

GRIFFITHS is a handy gazetteer that is recommended as a companion to the survey books. It contains 1,044 entries, including short biographies of composers and other important figures, as well as extended definitions of such terms and movements as Black Mountain College, heterophony, Neue Sachlichkeit, and third stream. A helpful chronology provides dates of premieres of important pieces from 1901 to 1985.

WATKINS is the most ambitious book discussed here. It seeks to place the major composers and their music in an aesthetic and historical context that includes not only other composers and pieces but also synchronous aesthetic movements and credos in literature and the visual arts. "History rarely provides answers, only good questions which are relevant to the age," Watkins writes insightfully. The book is filled with thought-provoking questions and comparisons that encourage the reader to view musical phenomena such as serialism and neoclassicism within a larger historical framework. The visual presentation is as rich and engaging as the discussion, featuring historical photographs and illustrated works of cubist, futurist, expressionist, and abstract art. Each chapter ends with two helpful features: a repertoire, containing a list of works that fall under the category of discussion in that chapter, and a helpful bibliography on the subject.

SALZMAN, now in its third edition, is intended for the college classroom. An excellent introductory chapter, "Twentieth-Century Music and the Past," situates the aesthetic debates of modern music in the context of historical antecedents, including the notion of the composer as solitary cultural hero, the back to Bach movement, the discovery of non-Western music, and many other trends. The remaining chapters are short, with each one focused on a specific concept or trend such as "The Diffusion of Twelve-Tone Music" and "Technological Culture and Electronic Music."

Likewise, MORGAN is a textbook. As part of Norton's helpful series of surveys of each era in Western music history, this volume presupposes a certain level of musical literacy. Its bibliography is extensive and effectively organized. A companion anthology of major 20th-century scores is available but lacks a set of recordings. Morgan was one of the first scholars to suggest a place for Ives and Varèse in the musical pantheon on a par with the status accorded to Schoenberg and Stravinsky. Like Salzman's book, Morgan's study begins with a chapter discussing 19th-century antecedents to 20th-century musical trends. He highlights factors such as the breakdown of classical forms, the rise of nationalism, and the collapse of church and court patronage, and he advances the argument that these and other factors resulted in increased freedom of artistic expression for the composer. The remainder of the book is divided into three equal parts covering the pre–World War I years, the interwar period, and the post–World War II era. The result is a treatment that is weighted more heavily toward the first half of the 20th century.

SLONIMSKY, a classic now in its fifth edition, is a chronological presentation of events in music history from 1900 to 1991. The author, who was one of modern music's greatest champions, recounts events to which he was in many cases a witness or a participant. The book contains two singular appendices: a fascinating "Letters and Documents" section in which various documents are reproduced, and a "Dictionary of Terms." The latter includes such neologisms of Slonimsky as "kaleidophonia," defined as "a musical composition derived from multiple mirror-like reflections of a central subject," and "Wagneromorphism," defined as the "mass genuflection and humicubation before the unquestionable genius of Wagner."

KÁROLYI, a theoretical overview intended for beginners, is pedagogically oriented, with terms presented at the head of each chapter and defined as they arise. This volume seeks "to provide the reader with some technical awareness of what happens when a 20th-century composition is being performed." A basic knowledge of music notation is presumed, but the reader is led through concepts such as atonality, microtones, and metric modulation in a step-by-step, easy-to-follow manner. The historical presentation of movements and trends is condensed into a somewhat sketchy final chapter titled "Isms and Styles."

SIMMS is another book intended for the college classroom, although it presupposes less musical and cultural sophistication than Morgan, Salzman, or Watkins. A well-selected anthology of music scores and a companion set of recordings, both of which could be used in conjunction with any of the more rigorous texts, are available as well. The Simms volume includes short profiles of individual composers with their picture and a list of works. The book is divided into three sections, with the first devoted to structural principles and the other two to a chronological examination of trends and movements spanning the century.

OLIVIA MATTIS

20th-Century Music: Specialized Studies

Crawford, John C., and Dorothy L. Crawford, *Expressionism in Twentieth-Century Music*, Bloomington: Indiana University Press, 1993

Hertz, David Michael, *The Tuning of the Word: The Musico-Literary Poetics of the Symbolist Movement*, Carbondale: Southern Illinois University Press, 1987

Locke, Ralph P., and Cyrilla Barr, editors, *Cultivating Music in America: Women Patrons and Activists since 1860*, Berkeley: University of California Press, 1997

Messing, Scott, *Neoclassicism in Music: From the Genesis of the Concept through the Schoenberg/Stravinsky Polemic*, Rochester, New York: University of Rochester Press, 1996

Morgan, Robert P., *Modern Times: From World War I to the Present*, Basingstoke: Macmillan, and Englewood Cliffs, New Jersey: Prentice Hall, 1993

Nyman, Michael, *Experimental Music: Cage and Beyond,* New York: Schirmer Books, and London: Studio Vista, 1974; 2nd edition, Cambridge: Cambridge University Press, 1999

Perloff, Nancy, *Art and the Everyday: Popular Entertainment and the Circle of Erik Satie,* Oxford: Clarendon Press, and New York: Oxford University Press, 1991

Rosenstiel, Léonie, *Nadia Boulanger: A Life in Music,* New York: Norton, 1982

Watkins, Glenn, *Pyramids at the Louvre: Music Culture, and Collage from Stravinsky to the Postmodernists,* Cambridge, Massachusetts: Harvard University Press, 1994

Scholarly and critical examination of 20th-century music is a work in progress. In many areas, there is not enough perspective for more than provisional interpretation of the historical record, at least in part because that record is as yet incomplete. Throughout the 20th century, there has been a steady stream of publications on contemporary music, but until fairly recently, most of the literature has originated with composers or their partisans and, as such, must be evaluated through comparison with other primary source material. For composers active in the first half of the century, collections of documents are slowly becoming available as they are bequeathed to archives, and the historical record is being fleshed out as a result of this new information. In certain cases, access to such information has led to the wholesale rewriting of the history of certain periods, as, for instance, in the cases of Ives and Crawford, composers little-known in the period of their greatest creativity. Second, the century witnessed a split of composers into two main camps with a fertile, although anarchic, no-man's-land between them. This ideological confrontation was temporarily dominated at mid-century by the formalists following the lead of Schoenberg, who espoused a teleological view of artistic progress. All composers who did not fit into this rather narrow viewpoint were neglected, or worse, and scholarship has only recently begun to rectify the distortions caused by this interpretation of the century's music.

MORGAN is a wide-ranging, geographic survey of the main trends in 20th-century music, which are assessed in essays by specialists in the areas covered. The volume is divided into two chronological sections covering roughly the period between the two world wars and the period since 1945, respectively, so that most geographic areas are covered twice. While this format results in a somewhat encyclopedic superficiality of narrative in nearly every essay, it also reflects the diversity of musical production in this century. Those interested in digging deeper are well served by the helpful bibliographic entries at the end of each chapter. One important aspect of this volume is that it gauges the decline by the early 1990s of the formalist position in the historiography of 20th-century music. Not only does the book include chapters on areas once considered peripheral, such as

Latin America and Scandinavia, but in later chapters it also begins probing popular and non-Western music as objects of music historical study.

WATKINS, on the other hand, synthesizes a wealth of previous studies, using the idea of collage as a metaphor for composers' responses to popular and non-Western music as well as canonic music materials that are incorporated into new musical compositions. Beginning with an examination of the influences of exoticism and primitivism on French composers early in the century, the theme of collage gradually appears in part as a renewal of long-standing tendencies in composition and also as the beginning of a new viewpoint that has resulted in the ascendance of the critical position of vernacular musical genres. Stravinsky's works and artistic development serve as the core of the discussion, which ranges from Josephine Baker to the late works Alfred Schnittke.

The source of some of the most fertile and provocative developments in 20th-century music and art in general, the symbolist movement in the last decade of the 19th century and the first decade of the 20th is explored in HERTZ. At the end of the 19th century, musicians and poets, in interrelated developments, broke away from the symmetrical formal structures that had characterized the development of their arts to that point and began to explore structures built around asymmetry and syntactical disjunction. Concentrating on Debussy and Schoenberg, the author shows the importance of symbolist poets Stéphane Mallarmé and Stefan George, respectively, in the composers' move away from traditional musical syntax into a more flexible practice in which emotional, coloristic, and symbolic elements determine the structure of the work.

Complementing this study of the esoteric aesthetic of symbolism, PERLOFF examines the importance of popular music on composers in Paris in the decades between 1890 and 1930. As the focus of the study, Satie's career from his days as a cabaret pianist to his establishment as a central figure in the postwar avant garde of the early 1920s is thoroughly explored, and the interaction between vernacular and cultivated styles in Satie's compositions is especially emphasized. Also important is the discussion of the influence of American popular music on Parisian composers through Poulenc and Milhaud. Unfortunately, the reactionary elements of the aesthetic position associated with Cocteau are barely mentioned in this otherwise excellent study that aims to present Satie and his compatriots as heroes of multiculturalism.

The first survey of musical expressionism, CRAWFORD and CRAWFORD synthesizes earlier studies of this important 20th-century aesthetic position. The expressionist impulse is portrayed here as being as much an attitude as a style. Several common stylistic features of expressionist music are identified, including: the idea that form is the embodiment of content; the use of intervallic cells and abrupt shifts in register and dynamic; irregular rhythmic constructions; an interest in orchestral color as an end in itself; and a deep conviction of the symbolic value of music. The first half of the volume concentrates on Schoenberg and his students Anton Webern and Alban Berg and on their forerunners. Chapters on Stravinsky, Bartók, and surprisingly, Ives follow. While Stravinsky and Bartók wrote clearly expressionist works and to some extent participated in the milieu of the European movement, it is a stretch to include Ives, whose music, while superficially similar to expressionism, contains none of the cynicism and Weltschmerz of the Europeans' music, instead being based on an idealist position. Closing chapters on the legacy of expressionism discuss composers such as Weill, Krenek, and Ruggles. The historical and analytical aspects of this study are undercut somewhat by the authors' omission of any attempt at a critical approach to the ideological and cultural positions of expressionist composers.

An important clarification of an often misunderstood term, MESSING analyzes the various ways in which the term *neoclassicism* was used during the early decades of the 20th century. In turn-of-the-century France, the term stood for a nationalist anti-German stance that resented the German establishment of the Viennese masters as a classical musical style. Among the Germans, the term only appeared in the years prior to World War I as a pejorative reference to French academicism. After the war, however, the term was appropriated by Cocteau and others as a description of their program to discredit prewar experimentation in favor of a return to an ideal of simplicity, of which Stravinsky became the most prominent exponent. Messing's untangling of these various usages is a fine piece of scholarship.

Nadia Boulanger was one of the movers of neoclassicism and arguably the most important woman in 20th-century music; she receives a sympathetic treatment in ROSENSTIEL. Boulanger was long seen mostly as a legendary *eminence grise,* and this study first brought the full extent of her career into scholarly focus. The book is especially valuable for the light it sheds on the years up to her emergence into prominence (in the later 1920s) as the teacher of an entire generation of American composers. The study is slightly flawed by the author's hagiographical approach to her subject.

While most mid-century music awaits thorough scholarly treatment, the experimental music movement of the 1950s and 1960s is explored in NYMAN, a rare example of a historically based examination by a participant in a movement that was still developing. Beginning with an examination of the idea of experimental music—defined as anti-psychological music, that is, music interested more in sound as sonic event than as reification of the composer's psychology—the book provides the first serious analysis of John Cage's influence on music in this period. This analysis is followed by valuable chapters on the Fluxus movement, indeterminacy, and early live electronic music. The appearance of this volume arguably provided an important impetus to the emergence of minimalism into the general cultural consciousness, seen clearly in this study as growing out of a coherent aesthetic position with a tradition going back at least 25 years.

Recent research into the importance of patronage to composers during the 20th-century is brought into focus in the volume edited by LOCKE and BARR. All the studies in this volume are indebted to the emergence of cultural studies in musicology, here in the service of legitimate historical inquiry. The patrons examined are all female and are almost evenly divided between those who could be considered conservative, through their support of mainstream Euro-American art music, and those more interested in supporting less traditional composers. In addition to the fine essays by several prominent scholars, the editors' introduction to the volume and Locke's final summation provide important theoretical considerations of the role of women in art music during the past century, as well as of the place of that music within American society. The editors argue that persons involved in supporting art music were motivated by something more complex than any elitist hegemony of cultural production, a complexity that includes a strong element of the aesthetic. The essays in this volume take a big step toward addressing this complexity.

RON WIECKI

V

Varèse, Edgard 1883–1965

French-born composer

Bernard, Jonathan W., *The Music of Edgard Varèse,* New Haven, Connecticut: Yale University Press, 1987

Garland, Peter, editor, *Soundings: Ives, Ruggles, Varèse,* N.p.: Soundings, 1974

De la Motte-Haber, Helga, editor, *Edgard Varèse: Die Befreiung des Klangs,* Hofheim: Wolke, 1992

Ouellette, Fernand, *Edgard Varèse,* translated by Derek Coltman, New York: Orion Press, 1968

Peyser, Joan, *New Music: The Sense behind the Sound,* New York: Delacorte Press, 1971

Rich, Alan, *American Pioneers: Ives to Cage and Beyond,* London: Phaidon, 1995

Varèse, Louise, *Varèse, A Looking-Glass Diary,* New York: Norton, 1972

Edgard Varèse's music has just recently entered the mainstream of the 20th-century musical canon. Long considered "ultramodern" or "futurist," his music is now seen as squarely representative of its time. Varèse was one of the pioneers of what is now called the American experimental tradition.

OUELLETTE is a sympathetic biography written by one of Canada's leading poets with the help and encouragement of the composer and his wife. A revised edition was published in France in 1989 but has not yet been translated. The most notable feature of the revision is a tremendously useful 100-page bibliography and discography compiled by Canadian musicologist Louise Hirbour.

PEYSER was one of the first attempts to break the Schoenberg-Stravinsky dialectic as the paradigm for modern music. The book is organized into three sections: "Schoenberg, Webern, and the Austro-German Tradition," "Stravinsky and the Franco-Russian Style," and "Varèse and Other Musical Currents." The author's hypothesis is that the music of the 20th century can be understood as the history of three currents: the emancipation of dissonance, the emancipation of rhythm, and the liberation of sound.

VARÈSE is a profile of the composer's early years (1883–1928) written by his second wife, a professional writer and translator. It is based on documents such as letters, programs, and press reviews, in addition to personal reminiscences. This volume is helpful for raising the reader's awareness of the composer's state of mind during various periods, as well as of the people and places that were significant in the couple's life. The book contains a few misremembered names, such as Samuel Barber for Samuel Barlow and "the Irishes" for French illustrator Paul Iribe and his actress wife, Jeanne Dyris.

GARLAND, long out of print, is a fascinating series of documents and tributes concerning Charles Ives, Carl Ruggles, and Varèse assembled by their younger followers. The section on Varèse includes tributes by Peter Garland and James Tenney, a composition (*Sirens for Edgard Varèse*) by Malcolm Goldstein, an analysis of *Density 21.5* by Philip Corner, and an essay about all three composers by Lou Harrison. Photos of the composer, provided by Louise Varèse, complete the section.

BERNARD is the first full-length theoretical treatment of Varèse's music. Part of Yale's theoretically oriented books on 20th-century composers edited by Allen Forte, this volume uses Forte's set-theory method of analysis as the basis of its methodology. Bernard adapts Forte's theory to Varèse's music by incorporating the composer's concept of octave nonequivalence. Therefore, pitch register becomes an added and essential parameter as the basis of pitch analysis. The analytical chapters are preceded by a helpful and readable survey of Varèse's interactions with artistic movement of his time. A work list including dates of first performance is another useful feature.

DE LA MOTTE-HABER is a series of essays deriving from a September 1991 symposium on Varèse that took place in Hamburg, Germany. One of the essays (by Olivia Mattis) is in English; the others (by De la Motte-Haber, Hermann Danuser, Klaus Angermann, and ten others) are in German. Topics range from Varèse's use of melody to his concept of musical space to espousal of nationalist agendas. Photographs published here for the first time include a series depicting Varèse and toddler

Claude walking through the streets of Berlin and another depicting Louise Norton (later Varèse) and her infant son Michael. Both of these children would be abandoned within a year of these pictures being taken, so the images are not only fresh but poignant.

RICH, a volume in the 20th-Century Composers series by art publisher Phaidon, is a highly readable and attractive examination of four of the major figures of the American experimental tradition: Ives, Varèse, Cowell, and Cage. The images illustrated are mostly reproductions of images from books by Louise Varèse and French composer and author Odile Vivier, but the volume also includes fresh images of Busoni, d'Indy, and other figures in Varèse's life. Rich, an English music critic, is most in his element when comparing music critics of the era and explaining their backgrounds and points of view. The book contains some errors of fact, including misstatements that Frank Zappa studied with Varèse (they never met) and that Varèse destroyed *Bourgogne* in the 1930s (it was actually in the 1960s), as well as the misidentification of a mustachioed thereminist as being Leon Theremin himself.

OLIVIA MATTIS

Vaughan Williams, Ralph 1872–1958

English composer

Dickinson, Alan Edgar Frederic, *Vaughan Williams,* London: Faber, 1963

Foss, Hubert J., *Ralph Vaughan Williams: A Study,* London: Harrap, and New York: Oxford University Press, 1950

Frogley, Alain, editor, *Vaughan Williams Studies,* Cambridge: Cambridge University Press, 1996

Kennedy, Michael, *The Works of Ralph Vaughan Williams,* London: Oxford University Press, 1964; 2nd edition, 1980

Mellers, Wilfred, *Vaughan Williams and the Vision of Albion,* London: Barrie and Jenkins, 1989; revised edition, Illminster: Albion Music, 1997

Stradling, R.A., and Meirion Hughes, *The English Musical Renaissance 1860–1940: Construction and Deconstruction,* London: Routledge, 1993

Vaughan Williams, Ralph, *National Music and Other Essays,* London: Oxford University Press, 1963; 2nd edition, Oxford: Oxford University Press, 1987

Vaughan Williams, Ralph, and Roy Douglas, *Working with Vaughan Williams: The Correspondence of Ralph Vaughan Williams and Roy Douglas,* London: British Library, 1988

Vaughan Williams, Ursula, *R.V.W.: A Biography of Ralph Vaughan Williams,* London: Oxford University Press, 1964

Young, Percy, *Vaughan Williams,* London: Dobson, 1953

Ralph Vaughan Williams is usually regarded as the quintessential 20th-century nationalist composer. A pio-

neer in the collection and editing of English folk songs and hymn tunes, he took artistic inspiration from these and other indigenous sources to forge a compositional style that was at once deeply personal and demonstrably "English." He also dedicated himself to the national musical life, serving as teacher and administrator, championing the musical amateur, and contributing music for all manner of public and ceremonial occasions. But while this "nationalist" label has clear basis in reality, it has also obscured awareness of the composer's wider musical associations. Vaughan Williams studied with Max Bruch and Maurice Ravel and was strongly influenced by the 18th- and 19th-century German masters and by the harmonic and formal innovations of the modern French school. Far from withdrawing into an exclusively English world of church music and bucolic rhapsodies, he worked in widely recognized genres such as symphony and opera and evolved an eclectic musical and harmonic language that owed much to contemporaneous European models.

Unfortunately, the second half of this picture has generally been ignored. With notable exceptions, commentators have stressed his English orientation to the near exclusion of his continental interests and influences. Although some of the confusion is doubtless due to the composer's own writings and public statements, which almost invariably argue for national roots, there can be little doubt that the blinkered chauvinism of much 20th-century English music criticism has served to promote the simplification. As a consequence, Vaughan Williams has been marginalized in mainstream accounts of music history. The richness and variety of his works have often been overlooked, and he has undeservedly been characterized as a provincial composer musically and emotionally out of touch with the 20th century.

For this reason, then, studies of Vaughan Williams must be approached with special caution. The biases informing the accepted image of the composer should be kept well in view if the above books are to be of real use. This caution does not imply that the literature as a whole lacks interest or instruction for the curious reader. In recent years, appreciation of Vaughan Williams's compositional range has widened, while the more chauvinistic readings do address the important question of his nationalist beliefs and activities. Used judiciously, the existing studies can provide a balanced account.

FOSS offers the archetypal reading of the composer's exclusive "Englishness." Arguing that the music embodies such aspects of the "national character" as reticence and sincerity of expression, Foss set the pattern for studies that systematically ignore Vaughan Williams's wider interests and influences. However, while the author's analysis clearly relates more to the national tensions of the 1940s than to the composer's own compositional qualities, it may be that on some level Vaughan Williams was himself influenced by these same tensions. He evidently sanctioned Foss's study and specifically wrote his prose "Musical Autobiography" for the book.

YOUNG substantially repeats the Englishness theme, although in a more restrained manner than Foss. This monograph is particularly strong on the cultural and moral dimensions of Vaughan Williams's English associations and relates the composer's democratic and humanitarian beliefs to the reforming emphasis of the late Victorian and Edwardian periods. Like Foss, Young gears his study to the nonspecialized reader, although music examples and rudimentary analyses are included.

MELLERS posits the central "doubleness" of Vaughan Williams's artistic vision, arguing that his music exemplifies Carl Jung's theory of complementary opposites. Examining selected works in detail, Mellers suggests that the composer typically charts an existential journey from divisiveness to wholeness. But while the approach of this book is new, the underlying assumptions on which it is based are not. For all his breadth of reference, Mellers's study is fundamentally indebted to the Englishness tradition established by Foss and Young. The volume does offer a first-rate discussion of the composer's literary influences.

STRADLING and HUGHES employ the deconstructive methods of postmodern theory and cast a severely critical eye on Vaughan Williams and other composers of the English revival, whom they dismiss as representatives of an inherently conservative "musical establishment." The authors thus radically depart from other commentators who invariably assert the positive achievements of the 20th-century renaissance. And yet, even Stradling and Hughes's passionate iconoclasm cannot escape the influence of received tradition. They accept uncritically the idea of Vaughan Williams's supposed "English" exclusiveness and differ from other authors only in seeing this nationalism as a liability rather than as a strength. With respect to other topics, however, their book is refreshingly skeptical—if opinionated—discussing cultural and political aspects of Vaughan Williams's nationalism found nowhere else.

DICKINSON marks the earliest attempt to acknowledge the composer's non-English associations. Wagner and Debussy are openly admitted as influences, and Vaughan Williams's sophisticated use of dissonance and counterpoint is finally given its due. But even this advance is somewhat vitiated by the familiar focus on folk song and English hymnody as the "formative substance" of his style. Nonetheless, Dickinson stands out as one of the most thoroughgoing commentators on Vaughan Williams's music. The insights of the author's considerable analytical method are sometimes obscured, however, by a turgid and abstruse prose style.

KENNEDY offers what is probably the best all-round—and certainly the best introductory—study of the composer. Less technical than Dickinson, Kennedy's musical analyses give adequate attention to major works, and his discussion of Vaughan Williams's musical surroundings is unmatched. Drawing on press reviews and an impressive knowledge of the British music scene, Kennedy erects an effective framework that he uses to chart the composer's intellectual and stylistic development. Although generally inclined to accept the Englishness thesis, the author does achieve a balance by acknowledging Vaughan Williams's wider musical influences.

Ursula VAUGHAN WILLIAMS published her biography as a companion volume to Kennedy; together, the two books make up a life-and-works study. A close acquaintance, and later second wife of the composer, the author is uniquely situated to record the principal events of Vaughan Williams's life. This work is not a critical biography but rather a solid and elegantly written portrait of the composer and the musical and social world in which he lived.

Ralph VAUGHAN WILLIAMS and DOUGLAS is valuable for the firsthand information it provides about Vaughan Williams's working methods. Douglas served as musical assistant for the composer from 1947 to 1958— Vaughan Williams's last creative period, when he produced some of his most interesting, and least overtly "English," music. The book is organized around the letters Vaughan Williams wrote to Douglas about specific works in progress, and these texts show the composer to be restless, even anxious in his pursuit of perfection. As such, they conclusively belie the accepted image of him as technically inadequate and artistically complacent.

FROGLEY is notable for its head-on confrontation with the central issues of the Vaughan Williams scholarship outlined in this review. The ten essays (each written by a different author) examine aspects of the Englishness problem in both its musical and cultural dimensions. Frogley sets the agenda in his introductory discussion of the cultural politics underlying the composer's simplified "English" reputation. Four essays complement Frogley's efforts by demonstrating in stimulating analytical detail the sophistication and breadth of Vaughan Williams's musical language. Other contributions explore the specifically English orientation of his work but seek— through examinations of his letters, folk-song collecting, wartime film music, and biblical sources—to challenge the limitations previously associated with this designation. Altogether, the volume stands out as the single most balanced account of Vaughan Williams's achievement— a necessary corrective to all preceding publications.

Finally, Ralph VAUGHAN WILLIAMS is essential reading for any discussion of the composer. Despite an outspokenness that undoubtedly has contributed to some of the misconceptions described above, the essays indicate a subtlety of message not usually credited to the composer. Indeed, a close reading of the text suggests that nationalism, for him, was a means to the appreciation and acceptance of *all* nations and cultures. This breadth and spirit of inclusion—rather than a narrow exclusivity—is arguably the real message of Vaughan Williams's nationalist vision, one that may provide the ultimate connection to his wider, non-English interests and influences.

JULIAN ONDERDONK

Verdi, Giuseppe 1813–1901

Italian composer

1. Biography

Bonavia, Ferruccio, *Verdi,* London: Oxford University Press, 1930

Budden, Julian, *Verdi,* London: Dent, 1985; revised edition, 1993; corrected revised edition, New York: Schirmer, 1996

Conati, Marcello, editor, *Interviews and Encounters with Verdi,* translated by Richard Stokes, London: Gollancz, 1984; as *Encounters with Verdi,* Ithaca, New York: Cornell University Press, 1984

Crowest, Frederick J., *Verdi, Man and Musician: His Biography with Especial Reference to His English Experiences,* London: Milne, and New York: Scribner, 1897; reprint, New York: AMS Press, 1978

Gatti, Carlo, *Verdi: The Man and His Music,* translated by Elisabeth Abbott, New York: Putnam, and London: Gollancz, 1955

Hussey, Dyneley, *Verdi,* London: Dent, 1940; 5th edition, revised by Charles Osborne, 1974

Martin, George, *Aspects of Verdi,* New York: Dodd, Mead, 1988

Osborne, Charles, *Verdi,* London: Macmillan, 1978
———, *Verdi: A Life in the Theater,* London: Weidenfeld and Nicolson, and New York: Knopf, 1987

Parker, Roger, *Studies in Early Verdi, 1832–1844: New Information and Perspectives on the Milanese Musical Milieu and the Operas from Oberto to Ernani,* New York: Garland, 1989

Phillips-Matz, Mary Jane, *Verdi: A Biography,* Oxford: Oxford University Press, 1993

Pougin, Arthur, *Verdi: An Anecdotic History of His Life and Works,* translated by James E. Matthew, London: Grevel, and New York: Scribner, 1887

Toye, Francis, *Giuseppe Verdi: His Life and Works,* New York: Knopf, and London: Heinemann, 1931

Walker, Frank, *The Man Verdi,* London: Dent, and New York: Knopf, 1962

Weaver, William, editor, *Verdi: A Documentary Study,* London: Thames and Hudson, 1977

Weaver, William, and Martin Chusid, editors, *The Verdi Companion,* New York: Norton, 1979

Wechsberg, Joseph, *Verdi,* London: Weidenfeld and Nicolson, and New York: Putnam, 1974

Biographical accounts of Verdi's life began to appear as early as the 1840s, at first mostly in important music periodicals published on the Italian peninsula. By the time of the composer's death at the beginning of the 20th century, his enormous prestige as the foremost composer of Italian opera had led to an enormous number of publications, which have continued to grow at an ever increasing pace, particularly during the last three decades of the 20th century. The publication of selections from Verdi's voluminous correspondence, which began in earnest with Gaetano Cesari's and Alessandro Luzio's 1913 edition of the *Copialettere,* provided valuable new primary source material for biographers. Unfortunately, the *Copialettere,* as well as other early editions of his correspondence, contains many erroneous readings and inconsistencies that have entered into subsequent biographical studies. Scholarly and more comprehensive editions of the letters have recently started to appear and will no doubt make important contributions to future studies of the composer's life. While some important early biographies of the composer were translated into English and some important later ones were originally written in English, a number of significant studies, such as Franco Abbiati's magisterial four-volume set (*Giuseppe Verdi*; Milan, 1959) and Massimo Mila's examination of the young Verdi's life and works (*La giovinezza di Verdi*; Turin, 1974; 2nd edition, 1978) still remain inaccessible to English-speaking readers.

Considered by many to be the first important biography of the composer, POUGIN's volume is also among the earliest book-length accounts to be translated into English. He first published his material in short selections in the Parisian journal *Le Ménestrel* during 1878. At this point, it seemed to many that Verdi had reached the apex of his career, having recently completed *Aida* and the Requiem and publicly professing retirement. The public's great interest in the composer's life and the success of Pougin's biography is corroborated by the ensuing publication of the articles in German, Spanish, and English periodicals and thereafter in book format in Italian, French, English, and German. Today, Pougin's anecdotal approach still makes fascinating reading. It is noteworthy that much of the material came directly from Verdi's close associates or from the composer himself. Of special interest are Verdi's own reminiscences about his early career, dictated to his publisher Giulio Ricordi in 1879, which James Matthew incorporated into chapter 5 of his English translation. On the negative side, many anecdotes present a substantially biased picture of Verdi as a totally self-made man, rising to eminence from a peasant background of economic, educational, and social disadvantage through genius and arduous toil. Verdi himself fostered this viewpoint (as, for example, in his autobiographical reminiscences), and it dominates not only this volume, but most biographical studies of the next generations.

CROWEST's biography, published only a few years before the composer's death, is the first book-length popular biography of Verdi originally written in English. Much of the material, particularly relating to Verdi's early life, comes directly from Pougin. This volume's strength, as seen in the title, is its consideration of the early reception of Verdi's operas in England. The final chapter, which reviews 19th-century writings with a special emphasis on English publications, is also a valuable source for studies in reception history.

Most Verdi scholars consider GATTI to have produced the first "modern" biography of the composer; it remained the most significant treatment of Verdi's life and works until the publication of Abbiati's four-volume biography in 1959. Gatti's original two-volume set, published in 1931, is far longer and more detailed than any previous biography; but most important, Gatti had access to important primary source materials at Verdi's estate that were unavailable to earlier biographers. The most significant contribution of his biography is its incorporation of new primary material, as well as extensive citations from previously published documentary materials. Gatti's narrative creates a particularly vivid and sympathetic portrait of the composer, delineated with greater depth and detail than Pougin. Elizabeth Abbott based her English translation on a substantially abridged single-volume Italian edition that first appeared in 1951 rather than the more expansive original edition.

BONAVIA's short, readable biography is based largely on the *Copialettere* and other previously published material. Unfortunately, the extensive quotations in the body of the text lack references to their sources. Two particularly interesting chapters discuss the composer's soulmate and second wife, Giuseppina Strepponi, and Verdi's character and genius.

HUSSEY's volume, first issued as part of the *Master Musician* series, was once considered the standard biography of Verdi in English. The volume is heavily slanted toward the period of *Aida* and after (nearly half the book). Hussey's approach, especially for later operas, is to trace the compositional history through the composer's correspondence, relying heavily on the *Copialettere* and the early volumes of *Carteggi verdiani*. Although the author is sympathetic toward the composer and his works, his account is biased toward stage drama (particularly Shakespeare) as superior to opera. Appendices include a chronology, a list of works, and a list of people associated with Verdi.

At the time of its first publication, TOYE offered one of the more reliable accounts of Verdi's life: the author has carefully pruned out some errors consistently repeated by many earlier biographies. Toye divides his volume into two main sections. The first consists of the biography proper, while the second focuses on individual compositions. The concluding chapter, entitled "Verdi the Musician," is particularly noteworthy, furnishing a lucid assessment of the composer's position in music history.

BUDDEN prepared the Verdi volume for Dent's new *Master Musicians* series. It offers a much stronger and better balanced biographical study than Hussey's volume in the older series and offers an excellent starting point for readers who are unfamiliar with details of Verdi's life and works. Like Toye, Budden divides the volume into halves, the first presenting a biography of the composer, the second describing individual compositions. Budden's treatment is concise but accurate and incorporates significant recent research about the composer. A series of appendices present in a nutshell much useful reference material, including a chronology of Verdi's life, a list of works, a short biographical dictionary of the composer's friends and associates, a selective bibliography, and a glossary of 19th-century operatic terms frequently found in writings about the composer. The 1996 reprinting contains a few minor corrections and additions to the bibliography.

OSBORNE (1978) presents a concise, well-illustrated biography written for the general reader rather than the Verdi specialist, with emphasis on the history surrounding the genesis and reception of individual compositions.

OSBORNE (1987) provides a more expansive treatment, integrating the essence of the earlier biography with material from two other works by Osborne, *The Complete Operas of Verdi* (London, 1969; New York, 1970) and *Letters of Giuseppe Verdi* (London, 1971), a translation of nearly 300 letters from the *Copialettere*. The incorporation of many citations from the letters gives this biography a tone that is more detailed and academic than the author's earlier work; however, the extensive quotations from letters and documents replicate some errors in translation and commentary from Osborne's edition of the letters.

MARTIN integrates biography with a brief discussion of each of the operas. This volume excels at placing the composer's life and works within the context of the cultural and political milieu of 19th-century Italy. Useful appendices list family trees of the Habsburg rulers, the Dukes of Parma, and the House of Savoy; Verdi's works, noting librettists and information about the first performances; and a concise annotated bibliography that includes Verdi studies as well as general studies about politics, history, and literature in 19th-century Italy.

One of the most historically significant and thought-provoking biographies of the composer is WALKER. Charging that traditional, chronologically organized surveys of the composer's life and works do not readily reveal many fundamental aspects of Verdi's character, Walker adopts an unorthodox approach to biography. He organizes his book as a series of essays that focus on the composer's relationships with other people including, among others, Strepponi, Muzio, Mariani, Boito, Merelli, and Stolz. What emerges is a strong, sympathetic, and vibrant portrait of the composer that has been matched by few other books. Walker's writing has an explicitly revisionary tone: he states that one of his main concerns is to use careful documentary research to correct misinformation and fictitious legends about Verdi's life that had crept into much of the earlier secondary literature. Walker's rewriting of history is perhaps most apparent in the first chapter, which examines Verdi's early life in Busseto and his student years in Milan. The volume incorporates information from many sources that had not been published at that time (and some that have still not been published), including Strepponi's *Copialettere*, her letters to the impresario Lanari, and Verdi's correspondence with Boito, Stolz, and Mariani.

PARKER includes a significant study of the composer's early student years and the start of his career in Milan based on newly studied documentary material. Specifically, one chapter examines writings in the *Gazzetta privilegiata di Milano* that refer to Verdi's early career as a composer and conductor, while another assesses Verdi's exposure to Viennese classical music during his student years and its effect on the development of his musical style.

WECHSBERG presents a brief, but beautifully illustrated popular biography directed to a general audience. Much of the material derives from the work of Gatti, Wechsberg's mentor, updated with material from the writings of Walker, Martin, and others. The volume contains a useful detailed index of names, places, and compositions.

Several recent publications offer fine documentary biographies of the composer. WEAVER is a particularly handsome volume. Its first main section presents a lavish pictorial biography of the composer through 287 plates, some in full color. The second part consists of excerpts from letters and other documents (a few previously unpublished, but mostly from secondary sources) arranged in chronological order. The entire volume is prefaced by a reprint of Verdi's autobiographical narrative to Giulio Ricordi, first published in Pougin.

CONATI offers a fascinating anthology of 50 selected, short articles describing interviews or meetings with the composer that were originally published in European newspapers or periodicals between 1845 and 1900. Most materials concern the last three decades of Verdi's life and cover a variety of topics, such as descriptions of Verdi as a conductor, his views on singers and other composers, and his ideals about singing style. A short preface precedes each individual article, and all items contain annotations that clarify and fill out details as well as provide cross references to other literature. The list of sources and works consulted is a treasure trove of about 250 items, many of which are relatively little known.

PHILLIPS-MATZ has written the most recent major biography of the composer. This massive work incorporates many new details about Verdi's life from a wide range of archives and little-known sources. Her narrative is especially detailed in the area of Verdi's family background, his early years, and particulars of his

business affairs, such as the management of his estate at St. Agata; the author also proposes new ideas about the composer's relationships with Strepponi and Stolz. Verdi's compositions and musical development receive relatively scant attention. The biography is not as strong as some others in conjuring up a vivid characterization of the composer, assessing Verdi's rich and complex relationship to his musical and cultural milieu, or establishing a sense of his historical position.

Although not a traditional biography, WEAVER and CHUSID's volume presents an invaluable collection of general essays covering Verdi's musical and cultural milieu, relationships with librettists and publishers, performance practice, and musical style. Particularly useful features include a substantial name dictionary of people associated with Verdi; a list of major works by date of first performance; a chronology of Verdi's life, with references to secondary literature; and (in the hardbound edition) a reproduction of Verdi's family tree.

GREGORY W. HARWOOD

2. Operas: Early Period

Baldini, Gabriele, *The Story of Giuseppe Verdi: Oberto to Un ballo in maschera,* edited and translated by Roger Parker, Cambridge: Cambridge University Press, 1980

Basevi, Abramo, *Studio sulle opere di G. Verdi,* Florence: Tofani, 1859; reprint, Bologna: Antiquae Musicae Italicae Studiosi, 1978

Budden, Julian, *The Operas of Verdi,* 3 vols., New York: Oxford University Press, 1973–81; revised edition, Oxford: Clarendon Press, 1992

Godefroy, Vincent, *The Dramatic Genius of Verdi: Studies of Selected Operas,* 2 vols., London: Gollancz, and New York: St. Martin's Press, 1975–77

Kimbell, David R.B., *Verdi in the Age of Italian Romanticism,* Cambridge: Cambridge University Press, 1981

Parker, Roger, *Leonora's Last Act: Essays in Verdian Discourse,* Princeton, New Jersey: Princeton University Press, 1997

———, *Studies in Early Verdi, 1832–1844: New Information and Perspectives on the Milanese Musical Milieu and the Operas from Oberto to Ernani,* New York: Garland, 1989

Petrobelli, Pierluigi, *Music in the Theater: Essays on Verdi and Other Composers,* translated by Roger Parker, Princeton, New Jersey: Princeton University Press, 1994

Petrobelli, Pierluigi, et al., editors, *Ernani Yesterday and Today: Proceedings of the International Congress, Modena, Teatro San Carlo, 9/10 December 1984,* Parma: Istituto Nazionale di Studi Verdiani, 1989

Rosen, David, and Andrew Porter, editors, *Verdi's Macbeth: A Sourcebook,* New York: Norton, and London: Cambridge University Press, 1984

Verdi, Giuseppe, *Macbeth,* English National Opera Guides 41, London: Calder, and New York: Riverrun Press, 1990

Basevi, a music critic who was a contemporary of Verdi, was the first notable writer to establish the notion of dividing the composer's operas into distinctive stylistic periods (although at the time that Basevi wrote, Verdi's career was far from ending). Basevi's demarcation of a stylistic division between *La battaglia di Legnano* and *Luisa Miller*, both of which premiered in 1849, has long been accepted by most Verdi scholars. While previous writers integrated discussion of the 14 operas before *Luisa Miller* into general studies dealing with Verdi's life and works, scholars have recently paid more detailed attention to these early compositions. Many new studies, mostly articles published in periodicals or conference reports, have aided scholars in reconstructing an increasingly detailed and refined picture of Verdi's compositional development as a young composer.

Individual chapters in BASEVI's study explore each of the early operas beginning with *Nabucco*. This volume provides very important background for any study of Verdi's early and middle operas, mostly because some scholars have used it extensively as a philosophical foundation for their analytical discussion. Although this work has been relatively inaccessible due to its rarity (even in the 1978 reprint edition), the English translation recently announced by the University of Chicago Press will soon make this important work available to many more students and scholars.

The first book in BUDDEN's three-volume survey of Verdi's operas has become the most widely used and probably the most highly regarded English study of these works. As with Basevi, Budden's volumes have acquired particular importance as a standard point of departure by Verdi specialists in their own writings. Chapters devoted to individual operas detail the historical background and genesis of each work, as well as providing a descriptive analysis of the opera's plot and music. Additional chapters interspersed throughout the first volume provide useful information about the general cultural and artistic milieu in Italy at the outset of Verdi's career and on the main features of Verdi's early style. Budden's writing, especially in his description of the individual operas, never becomes so technical that it exceeds the reach of the knowledgeable musical connoisseur, yet it has enough substance not to be superficial.

KIMBELL offers one of the most sophisticated studies of the formation of Verdi's early style available to English-speaking readers. His volume is particularly valuable for drawing connections between the style of the composer's early operas and literary, social, and political aspects of the romantic movement in Italy and throughout Europe. The opening section surveys Verdi's political, social, and cultural milieu; provides a useful overview of the business and cultural aspects of staging operas in early 19th-century Italy; and examines general dramatic and formal principles used by composers and librettists in creating their works. Drawing on the com-

poser's own correspondence, the second part traces the history of the early and middle operas and the establishment of Verdi's career, while the third furnishes a complementary appraisal of the development of the composer's musical language. The final section presents a critical study of selected (including some of the more neglected) operas from Verdi's early period: *Nabucco, Ernani, I due Foscari, Il corsaro, Macbeth, La battaglia di Legnano*, and *I masnadieri*.

BALDINI offers a broad survey of Verdi's life and the operas through *La forza del destino*; about half of the book, however, concerns the composer's early operas, with special emphasis on *Ernani* and *Macbeth*. Baldini's interest in Verdi's earlier works results in part from the author's view of the composer as the last, culminating figure in a grand tradition of opera that viewed musical structure as the generative force that produced the drama and in which the dramatic structure existed primarily within musical means. Much of his discussion therefore focuses on the composer's dramaturgical development. While Baldini clearly reveres Verdi as a composer, he is highly critical of Verdi's orchestration and accuses him of indifference to some of his literary material, a charge that some other scholars would challenge. Roger Parker's English translation contains his own preface assessing the contribution of Baldini to Verdi scholarship.

GODEFROY presents a series of chapters devoted to selected early operas, focusing on descriptive analysis, dramaturgy, and early reception, although his treatment is not as comprehensive, imaginative, or up-to-date as Budden's. Operas from Verdi's early period discussed include *Nabucco, I due Foscari, Giovanna d'Arco, Attila, Macbeth*, and *I masnadieri*.

Each chapter in PARKER (1989) examines a specialized topic relating to the composer's early career and compositions. One broadly based essay examines the influence of the singer in Verdi's early operas. Other chapters explore individual operas, providing a detailed assessment of the compositional history of *Oberto* based on evidence from the autograph full score; an evaluation of Verdi's dramaturgical approach in *Un giorno di regno*, which focuses on differences between Romani's libretto and the text found in Verdi's score; an account of the reception of *Nabucco* in foreign lands during the years immediately following its premiere; and an analytical study of levels of motivic definition in *Ernani*.

PARKER (1997) contains two additional essays that are relevant to the early operas. "'Insolite forme,' or Basevi's Garden Path" assesses the modern reception of Basevi's *Studio sulle opere di G. Verdi*, particularly as seen in recent writings that invoke normative expectations of form and genre as an analytical tool. "'Va pensiero' and the Insidious Mastery of Song" offers a preview from a forthcoming volume by Parker entitled *"Sull'ali dorate": The Verdian Patriotic Chorus in the 1840s*. Here, Parker analyzes the famous chorus from *Nabucco*, shows its musical and dramatic dependence on the following "Profezia" of Zaccaria, and explores the way in which the chorus acquired stature as a great artistic symbol of the risorgimento movement.

The collection of articles by PETROBELLI (1994) contains several important essays about Verdi's early operas. "From Rossini's *Mosé* to Verdi's *Nabucco*," first published in 1967, is a seminal study of Verdi's early work, suggesting that the young composer used Rossini's older classic as a model for both dramatic characterization and musical approach. "Verdi's Musical Thought: An Example from *Macbeth*" analyzes Verdi's use of simple gestures—pitch levels, rhythmic figures, and instrumental timbres—to unify the key dramatic points of the plot and to establish inner coherence. The two other essays discuss Verdi's compositional process as seen in his sketches for several early works. "Thoughts for *Alzira*," one of the few serious studies written about the work, analyzes the young Verdi's revisions in the final chorus of the Prologue and "Remarks on Verdi's Composing Process" includes a discussion of the composer's earliest known composing sketch, which contains material from the conclusion of *I due Foscari*.

Only two of Verdi's most popular operas from his early period, *Macbeth* and *Ernani*, are represented by individual book-length works in English. *Macbeth*, Verdi's first interaction with a libretto based on Shakespeare, is well represented by ROSEN and PORTER. This magnificent volume offers selected reports from the Fifth International Verdi Conference, held in 1977, covering a wide range of topics such as the work's compositional genesis; staging and performance practice; reception; and aspects of dramaturgy and musical style, such as form, tonality, and key symbolism. The volume also reproduces a vast amount of invaluable documentation related to the opera, including, among other things, a chronological reproduction (in both the original language and English translation) of surviving letters and documents relating to the opera; English translations of reviews and other published commentary relating to early productions of the opera; reproductions of costume designs for the original production with historical commentary; a list of autographs, manuscript copies, and selected editions of both versions and their locations; and a discussion of scores, arrangements, and performance materials for *Macbeth* that have been published by Ricordi. The volume also contains transcriptions of the "Scala" libretto in Verdi's hand with revisions by Andrea Maffei, and of draft fragments for the 1865 libretto in Verdi's hand, as well as a facsimile reproduction of the original 1847 libretto.

VERDI, the English National Opera Guide for *Macbeth*, also contains several items of special interest: an introductory essay by Giorgio Melchiori discussing the general history of the opera and the major changes Verdi made for the Paris revision; an informative and thought-provoking reconstruction by Harold Powers of

Verdi's creative process in conceptualizing the opera; and several translations by Andrew Porter, including August Wilhelm Schlegel's "Nota al *Macbeth*," published in Carlo Rusconi's 19th-century Italian translation of the play, the standard preface published in the Ricordi libretto for the opera, and Piave's intended preface for the 1847 libretto.

PETROBELLI et al. (1989) contains the proceedings of an international conference devoted to *Ernani* and offers the most valuable single collection of research published to date about this early work. Essays consider the opera's genesis and compositional history, the history of the libretto, the intervention of censors, stylistic evaluations of the music, and issues surrounding performance practice, including staging. The volume also includes a complete discography of full and partial recordings of the opera to date together with a historical essay about the recordings.

GREGORY W. HARWOOD

3. Operas: Middle Period

Budden, Julian, *The Operas of Verdi*, 3 vols., New York: Oxford University Press, 1973–81; revised edition, Oxford: Clarendon Press, 1992

Chusid, Martin, editor, *Verdi's Middle Period, 1849–1859: Source Studies, Analysis, and Performance Practice*, Chicago: University of Chicago Press, 1997

Cordell, Albert O., "The Orchestration of Verdi: A Study of the Growth of Verdi's Orchestral Technique as Reflected in the Two Versions of Simon Boccanegra," Ph.D. dissertation, Catholic University of America, 1991

Crutchfield, Will, "Vocal Ornamentation in Verdi: The Phonographic Evidence," *19th Century Music* 7 (1983)

Jürgensen, Knud Arne, *The Verdi Ballets*, Parma: Istituto Nazionale di Studi Verdiani, 1995

Moreen, Robert Anthony, "Integration of Text Forms and Musical Forms in Verdi's Early Operas," Ph.D. dissertation, Princeton University, 1975

Parker, Roger, *Leonora's Last Act: Essays in Verdian Discourse*, Princeton, New Jersey: Princeton University Press, 1997

Verdi, Giuseppe, *The Works of Giuseppe Verdi*, edited by Philip Gossett et al., Chicago: University of Chicago Press, and Milan: Ricordi, 1983–

Verdi's middle-period operas, considered here to include the works from *Luisa Miller* through *La forza del destino*, count among the composer's most popular works. Despite their popularity, it was not until the 1970s that they began to attract consistent scholarly attention. Approaches have diversified and now include aspects of versification, performance practice, instrumentation, sociology, ballet, sketches (beyond the *L'Abbozzo del* Rigoletto *di Giuseppe Verdi* [1941]), gender studies, and staging—all in addition to the previous practices of editing letters and outlining the composer's dramatic progress.

Reflecting this diversification, Ricordi and the University of Chicago Press under the general editorship of Philip Gossett are in the process of publishing a critical edition of VERDI's works that goes far beyond a new edition of the musical text: the eight volumes to date offer extended introductions that shed light on the compositional history (including censorship, the libretto, unpublished letters, and sketches) and performance practice. Both the scores and their introductions must now form the primary basis for all further endeavors in Verdi research.

Recent scholarship has relied on two seminal studies by Robert Moreen and Julian Budden, both works of lasting importance. MOREEN provides an excellent introduction to the terminology of early 19th-century librettos and musical forms—including versification, textures, and scene structure—and an extensive discussion of text-music relationships. Although unpublished, Moreen's dissertation laid the foundation for a new and considerably more methodological approach to analyzing Verdi's operas than had previously been possible.

BUDDEN offers a comprehensive treatment of Verdi's operas, not only by essentially incorporating all previous significant research but also by adding a wealth of new information. In addition, Budden's extensive knowledge of 19th-century opera in general allows him to place Verdi in context, through chapters on "Verdi and the World of the *Primo Ottocento*," "The Collapse of a Tradition," and "A Problem of Identity (Italian Opera 1870–90)." The author occasionally engages in too much subjectivity by making sometimes obscure stylistic reference to other composers and passing value judgments on aspects of Verdi's operas better left to the reader, at least in a standard work as this one. The study allocates a chapter to each opera, discussing its gestation by drawing on the composer's correspondence and evaluating where relevant the libretto's relationship to the original source. This background information is followed by musical and dramatic analyses, focusing on whatever aspects strike the author as most important.

CHUSID, a significant recent book, contains a number of essays on a wide range of topics, including autograph and sketch studies, musical and dramaturgical analyses, gender studies, and performance practice. The quality of the contributions varies considerably, but they provide a good overview of traditional and newer analytical approaches. Earlier research is incorporated either in summary or by reference through the extensive bibliographical apparatus. Chusid's excellent introduction convincingly defines the meaning of Verdi's middle-period operas and elegantly integrates previews of the subsequent essays. Among the essays, Philip Gossett and Kathleen Hansell's research on the newly discovered manuscript sources of *Stiffelio* raises interesting questions about Verdi's compo-

sitional process. Due to the scarcity of available Verdi sketches, their findings are of particular importance. Chusid's discussion of dramaturgy in *Il trovatore* offers a paradigmatic analysis of the role played by tonality, while David Rosen introduces an interesting new approach to the concept of *tinta* (a term referring to one or more musical traits that unify an opera and lend it an unmistakable character) by drawing on the 3/8 meter and related parameters. Among the essays on performance practice, Linda Fairtile's contribution offers a noteworthy discussion of the scores prepared for the *primo violino direttore d'orchestra* (the orchestra leader), shedding light on the ways in which 19th-century Italian opera orchestras were rehearsed and conducted.

PARKER comprises a loose collection of essays with the explicit goal of incorporating new musicological trends into Verdi research, intending to interpret Verdi's operas in a new light by emphasizing multiple texts (i.e., multiple interpretations), none of which is necessarily definitive. The essays include criticism ("Reaching the Beguiled Shore" and the chapters on *La forza del destino* and *Il trovatore*), gender studies (the chapters on *Stiffelio* and *Rigoletto*), and staging ("Reading the *livrets*"), as well as more positivistic essays, such as one that attempts to put in perspective Abramo Basevi's phrase *solita forma* (the standard form of operatic numbers in general and duets in particular) and thus to warn of its unqualified use. Although the criticism-oriented chapters are at times heavily subjective and seemingly directionless in their discussion of the sources, they include an abundance of interesting and stimulating observations that merit further exploration. The general absence of jargon combined with Parker's awareness of the subjectivity of many of his points, not to mention his vast knowledge of Verdi's music, adds to the significance of this collection of essays.

Verdi research increasingly explores areas that have long been considered marginal. CORDELL, for example, investigates Verdi's orchestration, covering more than just the differences of the two *Boccanegra* versions mentioned in the dissertation's title. He discusses the distribution of instruments in chords, customary coupling of wind instruments, and instrument-specific detail concerning the three-stringed double bass and the *cimbasso*. In addition, he synthesizes a wealth of previous scholarship (perhaps overusing direct quotation), correcting mistakes where necessary. The bulk of the study consists of a scene-by-scene comparison of the *Boccanegra* revisions with meticulous listings of all the differences, sometimes providing musical and dramatic interpretation, other times leaving it up to the reader.

In the field of vocal performance practice, CRUTCHFIELD's study of vocal ornamentation based on early recordings should be singled out. The author transcribed some 200 phonographic excerpts, investigating them with regard to embellishments in internal and final cadenzas, melodic variants, strophic variation in cabalettas, facilitations, and variants in recitatives. He mentions 19th-century theoretical sources (such as Manuel Garcia's *Traité complet du l'art de chant* [1847], Laure Cinti-Damoreau's *Méthode de chant* [1849], and Luigi Ricci's *Variazioni, Cadenze, Tradizioni* [no date]. One wishes Crutchfield's study would have discussed these sources (if only for comparison), especially as he states that "[t]hese, and numerous scattered examples of cadenzas attributed to various other singers of the day, confirm that what we hear on early recordings does not by any means represent some latter-day flowering of soloistic liberty, but rather a stage in its diminution. What might be found surprising is just how gradual that diminution was." Crutchfield hypothesizes that, in general, Verdi was probably not against such variants, even though this article offers little supporting evidence.

With his 1995 study, JÜRGENSEN introduces a thorough study of a Verdian genre that had long been neglected. Drawing on choreographers' production notes, notation of original choreography, costume specifications, contemporary reviews, and passages from discarded music (many of these sources published for the first time), the author discusses not only the actual ballet but also other choreographed numbers (such as the *choeur dansé* in *Jérusalem* and the *tarantelle* in *Les vêpres siciliennes*). Although a more complete explanation of ballet-related terminology (a problem highlighted by the many untranslated quotations) and more extensive analyses and interpretation of the music (clearly the weakest part of the book) would have been helpful, Jürgensen introduces each opera containing a ballet with a general description of the ballet, following it with a survey of the music (including a complete set of incipits) and the choreographic sources with critical annotations.

ANDREAS GIGER

4. Operas: Late Period

Budden, Julian, *The Operas of Verdi*, 3 vols., New York: Oxford University Press, 1973–81; revised edition, Oxford: Clarendon Press, 1992

Busch, Hans, editor and translator, *Verdi's Otello and Simon Boccanegra (Revised Version) in Letters and Documents*, 2 vols., Oxford: Clarendon Press, and New York: Oxford University Press, 1988

Hepokoski, James A., *Giuseppe Verdi: Falstaff*, Cambridge: Cambridge University Press, 1983

———, *Giuseppe Verdi: Otello*, Cambridge: Cambridge University Press, 1987

Verdi, Giuseppe, *The Verdi-Boito Correspondence*, edited by Marcello Conati and Mario Medici, translated by William Weaver, Chicago: University of Chicago Press, 1994

Despite the tremendous popular success of *Aida* in 1872, Giuseppe Verdi was ready to retire from composition. He

was disheartened by some critics who had labeled his latest opera "Wagnerian," and he felt that Italian music was moving in a new direction, leaving him behind. If Verdi's publisher, Guilio Ricordi, had not gently nudged the composer into collaboration with the younger composer and librettist Arrigo Boito, Verdi may never have written another opera. After a reluctant beginning, however, this collaboration not only produced two masterpieces but also an extraordinarily close friendship between the two artists.

This so-called final period of composition produced what many consider to be Verdi's finest works: *Otello* and *Falstaff*. Boito and Verdi began working together in 1879, during a transitional time in Italian opera. The middle of the century had witnessed Verdi's music not only dominating Italian theatrical life but also taking on an important political role, as patriotic choruses from operas such as *Nabucco* and *Ernani* were used to champion the cause of Italian freedom during the Risorgimento. By the 1870s, however, a now unified Italy was ready to look outside itself for sources of entertainment. French operas by composers such as Gounod and Meyerbeer became standard fare, and even Wagner's operas gained modest popularity—despite his prominent use of the orchestra and his lack of overtly melodious vocal lines, characteristics that had previously been the antithesis of Italian musical taste. Furthermore, audiences began flocking toward concerts of purely instrumental music, as major cities began to establish societies for the string quartet and the orchestra. Through his collaboration with Boito, however, Verdi succeeded in reasserting his dominant position in Italy's operatic life and also in creating a new, modern, yet nevertheless distinctly Verdian style.

Because Verdi spent most of his free time at his country estate in St. Agata, he conducted most of his business affairs by letter. Much of the Verdi-Boito collaboration is therefore chronicled in their voluminous correspondence, which has been collected in VERDI from a wide variety of published and unpublished sources. The volume, which contains all of the known letters between the two men, is superbly edited and translated and includes informative annotations that provide crucial clarifying background information. Marcello Conati's excellent introductory essay describes the rather rocky beginnings of what eventually became a close working and personal relationship. This book provides an extraordinary glimpse into the workshop of late 19th-century Italian opera: from the creation of the librettos (the necessary transformation of Shakespeare into operatically viable Italian verse) to descriptions of staging, acting, and singing styles and even the collaborators' opinions on audience behavior, politics, operas by other composers, and other aspects of theatrical life.

BUSCH has also collected numerous documents and letters relating to both the creation of *Otello* and to Verdi and Boito's collaboration on a revision of Verdi's earlier opera *Simon Boccanegra*. The first version had premiered unsuccessfully in 1857, but when La Scala suggested a revival, Boito and Verdi interrupted preliminary work on *Otello* to revise substantially *Boccanegra* for the 1880–81 season. The result was a great success, raising Verdi's opinion of Boito's talent as a truly gifted librettist and sweeping away any last doubts about their continued collaboration. Busch's work is perhaps better suited for those with a solid knowledge of the two operas than for novices. The meticulously annotated letters are presented in chronological order, regardless of author and recipient, which can become confusing for readers who lack a firm grasp on the chronology of events. Additionally, many letters are included that, while revealing interesting facets of Verdi's personality (such as his dedication to farming), are not pertinent to the operas in question. However, these difficulties are mitigated by the wealth of useful information, including translations of the directorial stage books that were supervised by Verdi, biographical information on all relevant persons, source information for the two operas' subjects, and even an American journalist's reflections on the *Otello* premiere in Milan.

For thorough musical descriptions of all Verdi's operas, BUDDEN is the first place to which the interested reader should turn. (The late operas are included in volume 3.) Budden's familiarity not only with every note in each of Verdi's operas but also with virtually the entire 19th-century Italian operatic repertoire makes his observations invaluable. Although the large number of printed musical examples might initially deter the nonmusician, Budden's eminently readable descriptions of each opera's preparation, staging, and final revisions make these volumes accessible to musician and nonmusician alike. The third chapter of volume 3, "A Problem of Identity (Italian Opera 1870–90)," provides an excellent overview of the historical, musical, and personal circumstances that precipitated the creation of Verdi's late operas.

HEPOKOSKI's (1983, 1987) monographs on *Falstaff* and *Otello* come from the superb series of Opera Handbooks published by Cambridge University Press. Hepokoski examines the operas from all angles—poetic, musical, historical, critical, and interpretative. The synopsis chapter on each opera provides a detailed description of the action, punctuated throughout by textual quotations and astute musical observations. Also included are thoroughly researched and clearly presented chronologies of each opera's creation, in which, happily, construction and composition of both libretto and music are given equal weight. Each volume offers detailed musical analyses, production histories (including explanations of the survival of different versions of each opera), descriptions of contemporary singing styles, and multifarious critical assessments. As with all of the monographs in this series, these volumes represent the single most useful resource on each individual opera.

ALISON TERBELL NIKITOPOULOS

5. Operas: Staging

Busch, Hans, editor, *Verdi's Aida: The History of an Opera in Letters and Documents,* Minneapolis: University of Minnesota Press, 1978

———, *Verdi's Otello and Simon Boccanegra in Letters and Documents,* 2 vols., Oxford: Clarendon Press, and New York: Oxford University Press, 1988

Cohen, Robert, *The Original Staging Manuals for Twelve Parisian Operatic Premieres,* Stuyvesant, New York: Pendragon Press, 1991

Conati, Marcello, and Natalia Grilli, *Simon Boccanegra di Giuseppe Verdi,* Milan: Ricordi, 1983

Hepokoski, James, and Mercedes Viale Ferrero, *Otello di Giuseppe Verdi,* Milan: Ricordi, 1990

Jurgensen, Knud Arne, *The Verdi Ballets,* Parma: Istituto Nazionale di Studi Verdiani, 1995

Petrobelli, Pierluigi, and Fabrizio Della Seta, editors, *La realizzazione scenica dello spettacolo verdiano: Atti del Congresso internazionale di studi, Parma, Teatro Regio-Conservatorio di musica "A. Boito," 28–30 settembre 1994,* Parma: Istituto Nazionale di Studi Verdiani, 1996

Petrobelli, Pierluigi, et al., editors, *"Sorgete! Ombre serene!" L'aspetto visivo dello spettacolo verdiano,* Parma: Istituto Nazionale di Studi Verdiani, 1994

Verdi considered his operas to be theatrical events, works in which musical, verbal, and visual elements worked together in the service of the whole. The visual elements essential to the dramaturgical concept included staging, scenic designs, props, costumes, and to some extent dance. Yet, despite Verdi's attention to and involvement with these components in his operas, until recently serious study of the visual aspects of his works has been largely neglected. However, several publications concerning topics directly related to the staging of Verdi's operas have been issued recently by the Istituto Nazionale di Studi Verdiani (National Institute for Verdi Studies) in Parma, Italy. Two of these books were the products of the first conference (organized in 1994 by the institute), which was devoted solely to scenic elements in Verdi's operas. These books constitute the major literature issued to date on the subject of the staging of the composer's works during his lifetime. As scholars turn their attention toward the scenic requirements of these works and the possibilities inherent in modern-day staging, as well as the questions posed by filming operas, more works on these important topics will undoubtedly be published.

PETROBELLI and DELLA SETA have assembled the papers that were originally presented at the conference by Italian, French, German, Dutch, Russian, U.S., and British scholars into a fine collection of 18 essays intended for the serious scholar of Verdi's music. Each essay, published in the language in which it was delivered (Italian, English, French, or German), presents a study of a different facet of the staging of the operas.

Among the topics treated are the following: a summary of Verdi's ideas concerning staging of his operas, studies of scenic design and staging details in specific operas (*Otello* and *Falstaff, Aida,* and *La forza del destino*), discussions of the work of individual scenographers for some of Verdi's works (Andreas Roller, Giuseppe Bertoja, Alessandro Prampolini, and Girolamo Magnani), surveys of staging practices in certain theaters (the Teatro la Fenice in Venice, the Paris Opéra and the popular theaters of Paris, and the Teatro alla Scala in Milan), and the role of dance in the staging of the operas. The volume contains plates reproducing many scenic designs, either in color or in black and white, as well as various documents related to the staging of these works. The book presents the most comprehensive treatment of staging in Verdi's operas to date.

Another book issued by the National Institute for Verdi Studies is the catalog edited by PETROBELLI et al. for the exhibit mounted in conjunction with the 1994 Parma conference. The catalog contains beautifully printed full-color reproductions of 19th-century scenic designs for Italian productions of *Aida, Attila, Don Carlo, Falstaff, La forza del destino, Macbeth, Otello, Rigoletto, Simon Boccanegra,* and *Il trovatore* as well as a few photographs of modern productions and drawings for selected costumes and props from the 19th century. In the back of the volume are commentaries about and bibliographical references for each item in the exhibit.

Dance is an important visual aspect in many of Verdi's operas. Yet, until the appearance of JURGENSEN's *The Verdi Ballets,* no detailed treatment of ballet in Verdi's works had been undertaken. Using choreographic notations, costume specifications, director's notes, contemporary newspaper reviews, various types of illustrations, and passages of discarded music, Jurgensen devotes one chapter to the role and nature of dance in each of the following operas: *Jérusalem* (Paris, 1847), *Nabucodonosor* (Brussels, 1848), *Les Vêpres siciliennes* (Paris, 1855), *Le Trouvre* (Paris, 1857), *Macbeth* (Paris, 1865), *Don Carlos* (Paris, 1865), *Aida* (Paris, 1871–80), and *Othello* (Paris, 1894). The book is lavishly illustrated.

Before the appearance of these volumes, published information concerning the staging of Verdi's operas in the 19th century consisted mainly of isolated transcriptions or facsimiles of production books or *disposizioni sceniche:* BUSCH's (1978, 1988) English translations of the production books issued by the publisher Ricordi for *Aida,* the revised version of *Simon Boccanegra,* and *Otello;* CONATI and GRILLI's edition of the Italian production book for *Simon Boccanegra* and HEPOKOSKI and FERRERO's similar publication for *Otello;* and COHEN's facsimiles of the staging manuals (*livrets scèniques*), published by Palianti for 19th-century Parisian productions of *Le trouvre* and *Les Vêpres siciliennes.*

ROBERTA M. MARVIN

Victoria, Tomás Luis de 1548–1611

Spanish composer

Anglés, Higini, "Latin Church Music on the Continent 3: Spain and Portugal," in *The Age of Humanism 1540–1630,* edited by Abraham, Gerald, The New Oxford History of Music, vol. 4, London: Oxford University Press, 1968

———, "Problemas que presenta la nueva edición de las obras de Morales y de Victoria" in *Renaissance-Muziek 1400–1600: Donum Natalicium René Bernard Lenaerts,* edited by Josef Robijns, Leuven: Katholieke Universiteit, Seminarie voor Muziekwetenschap, 1969

Cramer, Eugene Casjen, "Some Elements of the Early Baroque in the Music of Victoria," in *De música hispana et aliis,* 2 vols., edited by Emilio Casares and Carlos Villanueva, Santiago de Compostela: Universidade de Santiago de Compostela, 1990

———, *Tomás Luis de Victoria: A Guide to Research,* New York: Garland, 1998

Rubio, Samuel, *Historia de la música española 2: Desde el "ars nova" hasta 1600,* Madrid: Alianza, 1983

Stevenson, Robert Murrell, *Spanish Cathedral Music in the Golden Age,* Berkeley: University of California Press, 1961

———, "Tomás Luis de Victoria," in *The New Grove High Renaissance Masters,* edited by Gustave Reese et al., London: Macmillan, and New York: Norton, 1984

Victoria, Tomás Luis de, *Officium hebdomadae sanctae,* edited by Samuel Rubio, Cuenca: Instituto de Música Religiosa, 1977

The music of Victoria includes some of the most moving Latin sacred works of the late 16th century. Victoria was born in the vicinity of Avila in Castile and spent much of his life in Rome, where he worked from 1565 until he returned to Spain in about 1586. He died in Madrid. Along with the works of prolific Italian composer Giovanni Pierluigi da Palestrina, the music by Victoria is viewed as most fully representing the goals and proclamations of the reformers of the Council of Trent in what became known as the Counter-Reformation. More so than Palestrina, Victoria was able to balance the intelligibility of the text with obvious expressive effects of, for example, harmony and contrasts of texture. His music has been consistently praised for its emotional content.

Victoria was a master of all genres of traditional Latin sacred music, including the Mass ordinary; motets or occasional pieces that could be added to a Mass or other ceremony; and specific items for the divine offices. This third group includes hymns, passions, and items in honor of the Virgin Mary, such as Magnificats and the so-called Marian antiphons. Victoria composed four settings of *Salve Regina*—the most popular Marian text in Spain. He is perhaps best known today for his works from the Liturgy for the Dead. The second of Victoria's two Requiems, a Mass for six voices that he published in 1605, is considered one of the most moving examples of this genre written in either the late 16th or early 17th century.

Of the recent authors dealing with Victoria's works in general, the two most important are Stevenson and Cramer. The seminal research of STEVENSON (1961, updated in *Inter-American Music Review* 12, no.1 [1991]; and 1984) defines modern scholarship on Victoria's life and work. Stevenson groups Victoria with Cristóbal de Morales and Francisco Guerrero as the three greats of the Spanish Golden Age of sacred music, and the author presents much of the relevant biographical information. He discusses examples of each genre of Victoria's compositional oeuvre and examines the differences between Victoria's works and those of his contemporaries, both Spanish and Italian. In addition, Stevenson provides many insightful opinions regarding Victoria's compositional approaches; these hypotheses have been probed by later scholars and in general prove true. Significantly, Stevenson's research places Victoria in the line of the great Spanish Renaissance tradition represented by Morales and Guerrero; Victoria's work, therefore, can be understood within the context of his Spanish background, and the author's interpretation is not distorted by discussing Victoria only in conjunction with Palestrina in the Roman milieu. STEVENSON (1984) is the best brief introduction to Victoria's life and compositions.

While Stevenson's work defines modern scholarship on the life of Victoria, the scholarship of Cramer provides a unique tool for understanding all the facets of evidence related to Victoria's compositions. CRAMER (1998) is the most effective tool available for locating specific extant pieces, the different kinds of sources for Victoria's music, or published studies covering all aspects of the composer's life, compositional practices, and importance. This wealth of data is a boon to all interested parties, as this volume can be used to find basic information as well as for more advanced investigation. Cramer also includes an outline of significant events in Victoria's life.

Among Spanish authors, both the prolific scholar Samuel Rubio and the researcher Higini Anglés have produced scholarly studies of Victoria's music. Anglés was the primary editor of Victoria's works and perhaps knew those compositions better than any scholar in his generation. ANGLÉS (1968) uses this knowledge to examine a number of pieces by Victoria. In a discussion of the problems of editing Victoria's works for modern performances, ANGLÉS (1969) contrasts such problems with the much more serious ambiguities encountered in Morales's works.

Rubio has contributed both editions and specific studies of Victoria's music. VICTORIA includes an overview by Rubio of Victoria's life and works. More importantly, Rubio extensively examines the composi-tional techniques found in the *Officium hebdomadae sanctae* and pays particular attention to the use of chant material, a fundamental aspect of Victoria's method of composition. In his survey of Spanish music history, RUBIO contrasts Victoria's pieces to the works of Palestrina, thus employing a different approach to analysis than that used by Stevenson. Rubio also emphasizes the evolution of Victoria's works over the course of the composer's lifetime.

There have been a number of studies published in English about specific aspects of Victoria's music. Most of these have been in journals and therefore are not suitable for this survey. CRAMER (1990) is very important because it examines the characteristics of Victoria's music that are more closely related to the emerging baroque style than to the high Renaissance style in which Victoria is usually associated. Cramer discusses the fact that many aspects of Victoria's music parallel techniques used by Giovanni Gabrielli in Venice. These parallels include aspects of scoring, such as the use of larger ensembles, different varieties of vocal combinations, and an independent organ part—one that does not play the same material as the voice parts. Cramer also stresses the care that Victoria took to establish the clear declamation of the texts by using such techniques as falsobordone, a very simple presentation of the text in what were later called chords.

GRAYSON WAGSTAFF

Villa-Lobos, Heitor 1887–1959

Brazilian composer

Appleby, David P., *Heitor Villa-Lobos: A Bio-Bibliography,* New York: Greenwood Press, 1988

Béhague, Gerard, *Heitor Villa-Lobos: The Search for Brazil's Musical Soul,* Austin, Texas: Institute of Latin American Studies, 1994

Maríz, Vasco, *Heitor Villa-Lobos: Brazilian Composer,* Gainesville: University of Florida Press, 1963; 2nd edition, as *Heitor Villa-Lobos: Life and Work of the Brazilian Composer,* Washington, D.C.: Brazilian American Cultural Institute, 1970

Peppercorn, L.M., *Villa-Lobos,* New York: Omnibus Press, 1989

——, *Villa-Lobos: The Music: An Analysis of His Style,* London: Kahn and Averill, 1991

Wright, Simon, *Villa-Lobos,* Oxford: Oxford University Press, 1992

Brazilian Heitor Villa-Lobos was one of the most prolific 20th-century composers and was both reviled and revered throughout his career. His critics frowned at his modern innovations; his supporters applauded his revolutionary art and considered him a voice for the Brazilian people. Villa-Lobos was a flamboyant man who worked tirelessly, writing, conducting, directing, and promoting several projects to improve the musical education of Brazil's children. Beginning during the presidency of Getúlio Dornelles Vargas (1930–45), he worked as an unofficial ambassador of art.

The bibliography of Villa-Lobos is extensive and in several languages, mostly Portuguese. Fortunately, five authors have written books in English on his life and works. They all agree on certain details, such as the diminished creativity of Villa-Lobos's compositions during the last 12 years of his life, which they attribute to his busy conducting and recording schedule. Villa-Lobos took on extra work in part to pay for the medical treatment of his cancer, which eventually took his life at the age of 72. The authors also comment that the sheer vastness of Villa-Lobos's output (more than 1,000 completed compositions and several incomplete scores) makes it difficult to categorize his works. Appleby explains further that people have been including pieces in Villa-Lobos's catalog that were never actually composed.

MARÍZ is the first musicologist to publish a book in English devoted solely to the life and works of Villa-Lobos. It is an easy-to-read introduction to this topic, although it contains some outdated, politically incorrect descriptions. His book does not include any musical examples, but he is the only author besides Appleby to attempt to include a complete list of works, although there are inaccuracies. Maríz's research is the first to provide concrete evidence for the correct birthdate of Villa-Lobos, which neither the composer nor his mother could remember.

Swiss musicologist Peppercorn's thesis, originally written in German in 1972, was published in English as two separate volumes. Peppercorn knew Villa-Lobos during the last 20 years of the composer's life. Her work is presented in coffee-table book format with photographs and images. PEPPERCORN (1989) focuses on Villa-Lobos's biography and is filled with fascinating information, but it does not include footnotes, and the endnotes are not numbered or categorized. PEPPERCORN (1991) does not include a list of works, but the chronology of Villa-Lobos's life is useful. The author analyzes several of Villa-Lobos's works, such as Choro no. 7, to show the influence of Brazilian folk music on his style. Peppercorn's primary argument is that Villa-Lobos quotes himself frequently by using the same thematic material in several different pieces. Although Peppercorn presents a valid hypothesis, she defends her statement by comparing musical examples that have little or no similarity.

WRIGHT admits that in his book, the categorization of works is arbitrary, confessing that he chose which works to analyze based merely on personal preference. Wright's arguments lean toward the 19th-century tendency to romanticize Villa-Lobos's personality. In his dis-

cussion of the opera Yerma, Wright makes an interesting comparison between the life of Villa-Lobos and that of the Spanish poet Federico García Lorca. Rather than including a list of works, Wright refers the reader to other sources for this information.

APPLEBY is to be commended for undertaking the seemingly impossible task of compiling a list of works. He qualifies his catalog by calling it a representative list, not a complete one, suggesting that a complete list is an unrealistic project for many reasons. Appleby's work is the most reliable source for information about Villa-Lobos's music, and he also presents an impressive discography and performance history.

BÉHAGUE has no list of works, but it has the best bibliography next to that of Appleby. It is well documented and displays the deepest understanding of Villa-Lobos, his music, and his musical nationalism. The influence of Brazilian native and folk music on the creative output of Villa-Lobos, along with his role as music nationalist, is a complex issue that is difficult to elaborate without oversimplifying the matter. Béhague is the only author to tackle the topic of musical nationalism, and he presents an excellent in-depth discussion. His discourse is useful for understanding Villa-Lobos and, for that matter, most Latin American composers from the first half of the 20th century. The author avoids overgeneralizations and assumptions.

CHARMAINE FRAN LECLAIR

Vitry, Philippe de 1291–1361

French-born composer, poet, and theorist

Fuller, Sarah, "A Phantom Treatise of the Fourteenth Century? The Ars nova," Journal of Musicology 4 (1985–86)

Leech-Wilkinson, Daniel, Compositional Techniques in the Four-Part Isorhythmic Motets of Philippe de Vitry and His Contemporaries, 2 vols., New York: Garland, 1989

Robertson, Anne Walters, "Which Vitry? The Witness of the Trinity Motet from the Roman de Fauvel," in Hearing the Motet: Essays on the Motet of the Middle Ages and Renaissance, edited by Dolores Pesce, New York: Oxford University Press, 1997

Roesner, Edward, et al., editors, Le Roman de Fauvel in the Edition of Mesire Chaillou de Pesstain: A Reproduction in Facsimile of the Complete Manuscript Paris, Bibliothèque Nationale, fond français 146, New York: Broude, 1990

Vitry, Philippe de, Philippi de Vitriaco Ars Nova, edited by Gilbert Reaney et al., N.p.: American Institute of Musicology, 1964

The French composer, poet, mathematician, diplomat, philosopher, clergyman, and music theorist Philippe de Vitry was probably born in Vitry-en-Artois on 31 October 1291, and died in Paris, 9 June 1361. During his lifetime, Vitry achieved distinction in many disciplines and was frequently the beneficiary of the highest praise. He served three crowns of France in various capacities, enjoyed the friendship of Petrarch (who called him "the one real poet of France"), and in 1351, he was elevated to Bishop of Meaux by Pope Clement VI. Today Vitry is especially celebrated for his motets, which extensively cultivated the procedures of isorhythm. But he is perhaps best known for a music treatise long purported to be of his authorship, the *Ars nova*, a work that not only codified the innovative rhythmic practices of the first quarter of the 14th century, but also has since bequeathed its name to the music of 14th-century France. However, current knowledge of this great polymath's life and achievements is much less certain than the dates of his birth and death. Indeed, many aspects of documents long thought to be his have proven to be highly elusive: mathematical treatises attributed to him seem not to have survived; the authorship of many motets ascribed to him has not been irrefutably determined; and Vitry's most famous monument, the *Ars nova,* as it is represented in surviving manuscripts, may not have originally come from his own pen, although concepts therein are very possibly of his formulation. Thus, the legacy of Vitry demands much further scholarly documentation.

In the early 14th century, isorhythmic motets evidenced an unprecedented structural and rhythmic complexity. The *Ars nova* codified the innovations of rhythm and notation found in motets written and performed in Parisian musical circles during the first quarter of the 14th century. Addressed principally to contemporary singers, the treatise explicated such early 14th-century innovations as time signatures, small note values, and binary mensuration. But considerably more problematic than the actual content of the treatise are the circumstances surrounding the origin and dissemination of the *Ars nova* itself. The treatise today survives in several manuscript sources in various libraries throughout Europe, but these sources (all of which are incomplete) differ greatly, and because the extant treatise is in such diverse fragments, the origin and integrity of the work have been seriously questioned. Did Vitry himself in fact write the text? Is the treatise the work of a disciple of Vitry? Or is it perhaps a written record (or records) of oral discussions delivered by Vitry? FULLER questions many of the assumptions concerning *Ars nova* historiography and Vitry's presumed authorship. More than any scholar before her, she incisively stresses the divergences found among the extant fragments and determines that several manuscripts previously thought to be *Ars nova* treatises are textually unrelated to what may be called the central documents, which bear among them close textual parallels. The three central *Ars nova* treatises are Vatican, Barbarini 307; Paris, Bibliothèque Nationale 14741; and Paris, Bibliothèque Nationale 7378A. Bear-

ing striking textual relationships to these are two treatises, Coussemaker III, Anonymous IV and Anonymous III, found in the same manuscript: Paris, Bibliothèque Nationale 15128. If Vitry did not write the *Ars nova,* it was in all probability written by a disciple closely associated with him: Vitry's name is mentioned in the explicit of the Vatican manuscript and the explicit found in Paris 7378A. Vitry's name is also found in the incipit of Anonymous III, a source that problematically bears both striking textual similarities and differences with its manuscript companion Anonymous IV. Anonymous IV reveals frequent textual parallels with Paris 7378A, but more importantly it also provides material to which both the Vatican treatise and Paris 7378A allude but do not contain in their surviving fragmented state.

VITRY is the most thorough edition of the *Ars nova.* This multilingual compendium includes an English commentary, a critical Latin text, and a French translation of the *Ars nova.* The critical text is based principally on the *Ars nova* source found in Vatican, Barbarini 307, and Paris, Bibliothèque Nationale, 14741. In addition, commentaries in both English and French and editions of four other late-medieval manuscripts are included. Edited separately (not collated with the Vatican treatise) are Paris, Bibliothèque Nationale, 7378A, and Paris, Bibliothèque Nationale, 15128, Anonymous III. Reaney also provides editions of the treatises found in London, British Library, Additional 21455, and Siena, Biblioteca Comunale, L.V. 30. However, Fuller has shown these last two texts to be textually unrelated to the central *Ars nova* treatises cited above. ("Philippe de Vitry's Ars Nova: a Translation" is an excellent English translation by Leon Plantinga and may be found in *Journal of Music Theory* 5 [1961]).

As a composer, Vitry has been closely associated with a most curious literary and musical satire, the *Roman de Fauvel* (1310–14), which both parodied and lamented the corruption of the Catholic Church and the French court under King Philippe IV (1268–1314). Of the dozen surviving manuscripts of the *Roman,* by far the most important is a spectacular manuscript housed in the Bibliothèque Nationale in Paris. This manuscript was supplemented by 167 13th- and 14th-century musical interpolations provided by Chaillou de Pesstain in 1316, including isorhythmic motets attributed to Vitry. ROESNER is an indispensable edition of this work. Extensive commentaries by François Avril (who examines the illustration of the manuscript), Nancy Freeman Regalado (who discusses its literary context), and Roesner (who explicates the musical background of the manuscript), precede a black-and-white facsimile edition. Roesner's discussions of early 14th-century French mensural theory and musical sources are perhaps the best and most lucid in the English language.

LEECH-WILKINSON is a most useful source investigating 14th-century four-part isorhythmic motets by Vitry and contemporaneous composers. This work is particularly important because of the depth and breadth of its written and graphic explications of the arcane technique of isorhythm. Volume 1 analyzes three four-part motets of Vitry, four motets by his illustrious contemporary, Guillaume de Machaut (1300–1377), and six motets from the Ivrea codex. The work provides meticulous coverage of such elements as text, rhythm, phrase lengths, talea, color, and harmonic structure as they are represented in these motets. In volume 2, an extensive array of diagrams—isorhythmic charts, harmonic reductions, and graphs illustrating the structuring of rhythmic values—both supplements and further coheres the detail of volume 1.

As noted above, biographical material concerning Vitry is strikingly sparse, and until recently, even his very origins were unknown. ROBERTSON is an investigation into Vitry's place of birth, using a motet probably written by Vitry as a source of inquiry. The surname "de Vitry" suggests that Philippe's birth place was, in fact, a town of that name. In the 14th century, however, there were at least 13 towns in France bearing the name Vitry; it therefore is uncertain which site was the composer's town of origin. An isorhythmic motet, *Firmissime fidem/Adesto sancta trinitas/Alleluia Benedictus es,* is mentioned in two versions of the *Ars nova* treatise, which suggests that the motet is by Vitry. The tenor of the motet—based upon the chant *Alleluia Benedictus es*—corresponds note-for-note to two chant sources from the Abbey of Saint Vaast in Arras, northwest of Paris. And a short distance to the east of Arras is the town of Vitry-en-Artois. Not only has Robertson discovered the most probable locale of Vitry's origin, but in so doing, she has provided a new foundation for further research into his biography. Robertson's painstaking research and facility with primary sources provide models for future scholarship.

JOHN DOUGLAS GRAY

See also Motet: Medieval

Vivaldi, Antonio 1678–1741

Italian composer, violinist, and pedagogue

Everett, Paul, *Vivaldi: The Four Seasons and Other Concertos, Op. 8,* Cambridge: Cambridge University Press, 1996

Heller, Karl, *Antonio Vivaldi: The Red Priest of Venice,* translated by David Marinelli, Portland, Oregon: Amadeus Press, 1997

Kolneder, Walter, *Antonio Vivaldi: His Life and Work,* translated by Bill Hopkins, London: Faber, and Berkeley: University of California Press, 1970

Landon, H.C. Robbins, *Vivaldi: Voice of the Baroque,* New York: Thames and Hudson, 1993

Pincherle, Marc, *Vivaldi: Genius of the Baroque,* translated by Christopher Hatch, New York: Norton, and London: Gollancz, 1957

Selfridge-Field, Eleanor, *Venetian Instrumental Music from Gabrieli to Vivaldi,* New York: Praegar, and Oxford: Blackwell, 1975; 3rd revised edition, New York: Dover, 1994

Talbot, Michael, *Antonio Vivaldi: A Guide to Research,* New York, Garland, 1988

———, *The Sacred Vocal Music of Antonio Vivaldi,* Florence: Olschki, 1995

———, *Vivaldi,* London: Dent, 1978; 2nd edition, 1993

The popular recognition of Antonio Vivaldi in the 20th century is a unique tribute to a once forgotten composer. An influential model to J.S. Bach, Vivaldi's music was first investigated in Germany by scholars of the Bach revival. Then in Italy in the 1920s, Vivaldi's personal collection of musical scores was rediscovered. This find resulted in a series of special performances of unknown Vivaldi works. In 1947 the founding of the *Istituto Italiano Antonio Vivaldi* initiated the publication (with Ricordi) of the first complete edition of Vivaldi's instrumental works. The rise of professional chamber orchestras at this time also helped to bring Vivaldi's music to new audiences via concerts and recordings. Two major studies on Vivaldi were written in the 1940s: Mario Rinaldi's *Vivaldi* (in Italian, 1943) and Marc Pincherle's highly influential *Antonio Vivaldi et la musique instrumentale* (1948). In the next decade, the Austrian scholar Walter Kolneder made significant contributions to an understanding of Vivaldi's musical style and performance practice. Remo Giazotto published a biography in 1965 that brought attention to the many significant original documents relating to Vivaldi's life and music in Venetian archives. In the 1970s, Peter Ryom published his study on Vivaldi's autograph manuscripts and provided a new catalog of Vivaldi's works. Ryom's catalog (*Verzeichnis der Werke Antonio Vivaldis,* Leipzig, 1974, revised 1979) has become the standard system used for listing Vivaldi's works (RV numbers). Since the 1978 tercentenary of Vivaldi's birth, an immense amount of new information on Vivaldi has become available. A new critical edition by Ricordi of Vivaldi's complete works was begun in 1982 (*Nuova edizione critica delle opere di Antonio Vivaldi*).

While earlier studies focus primarily on Vivaldi's more than 500 concertos, research in the 1980s and 1990s demonstrated a growing interest in Vivaldi's vocal music, including both opera and sacred music works. Of special note here is Michael Talbot's study of the sacred music. Establishing a chronology of Vivaldi's works has always been a special issue. Recently, Paul Everett has used special techniques in studying handwriting and music-paper types to develop a method of approximate dating. In 1997 the *Istituto Italiano Antonio Vivaldi* celebrated its 50th anniversary with an international conference that lauded the worldwide collaborative spirit of Vivaldi studies.

In the first major study of Vivaldi's life and works, PINCHERLE (in a condensed English version) focuses on the style and form of Vivaldi's music, primarily through a general examination of the concertos. Pincherle also describes Vivaldi as a virtuoso violinist, his treatment of the orchestra, and the orchestra in Vivaldi's time. Although primarily concerned with Vivaldi as a concerto composer, Pincherle points out the significant parallels in musical substance between his instrumental and dramatic music. He also justly predicts Vivaldi's sacred music finding a widening audience. In seeking to define Vivaldi's style, Pincherle explores Vivaldi's influence on other composers and later generations. Although much of the biographical information is now outdated, all of the subsequent Vivaldi biographies are in part indebted to this book.

KOLNEDER follows the style-analytical model of Pincherle in a full-length book that encompasses several of his separately published writings. Kolneder shares valuable insights on evidence of performance practice from Vivaldi's time, including dynamics, tempo, articulation, bowing, cadenzas, and figured bass. He organizes his description of the concertos according to the designated soloist(s) and includes information on Vivaldi's concertos with wind instruments, as well as some discussion of the sonatas and vocal music. Along with his analysis, Kolneder incorporates vivid reports from Vivaldi's contemporaries. An appendix includes numerous musical examples.

TALBOT's (1978) now classic study of Vivaldi was the first original English-language biography of the composer. The author presents a wealth of information in a concise and highly readable fashion on Vivaldi's career and musical style. In the revised edition (1993), Talbot includes illuminating notes from recent research concerning Vivaldi's biography, new documents and musical sources, and trends in music scholarship. The useful appendices include a catalog of Vivaldi's musical compositions.

TALBOT (1988) is an annotated collection of Vivaldi materials from the 18th through the 20th centuries. It is organized into four main sections. These include sources pertaining to Vivaldi's life and works (letters, manuscripts, books, and articles), sources of Vivaldi's music (catalogs, manuscripts, and editions), iconography, and the current state of Vivaldi research. While mostly suited to the graduate research student, the general index is a useful key to a wide variety of information, contributing much of interest for Vivaldi enthusiasts.

TALBOT (1995) is the first book written exclusively on Vivaldi's sacred music and features much new information on Vivaldi and Venice. While fulfilling its mission in surveying the approximately 50 surviving sacred music works, this elaborate book overflows with the archival treasures and musicological insights that Talbot has accumulated during his years as a leading Vivaldi scholar. He shows that, although Vivaldi's operas may be typical of the 18th-century pan-Italian style, the church music sheds light on a Venetian or Northern Italian practice linked to the local culture and context. He acknowledges that this music is now regarded as the Italian counterpart of the church music of Bach and Handel.

A specialist in Venetian music and cultural history, SELFRIDGE-FIELD includes an excellent chapter on Vivaldi's instrumental music situated within a broader historical context. She points to the significance of the sonata as a vehicle for Vivaldi's creative ingenuity and artistry. Selfridge-Field discusses Vivaldi's experiments with unusual and diverse combinations of instruments. The 1994 edition includes fascinating documentary evidence from her study of contemporary Venetian newsletters (see also her *Pallade Veneta: Writings on Music in Venetian Society 1650–1750*, 1985).

EVERETT attempts to reconcile the popular Vivaldi of *Four Seasons* fame with the "real" Vivaldi, a musician of a considerably broader musical repertoire. This book shows the origins and content of Vivaldi's op. 8 and discusses formal design elements of the solo concerto, including ritornello forms. Everett includes perspectives on the music that draw from his specialized work in dating the manuscripts. He also proposes a connection between the sonnets based on the music to *The Four Seasons* and a pair of poems by the author John Milton.

Prompted by the worldwide popularity of *The Four Seasons*, LANDON, an esteemed Haydn and Mozart scholar, attempts to reveal the secret of Vivaldi's success among young audiences. Written for general readers, this book focuses on selected works considered significant by the author. It relies heavily on compilations from previous biographies but also contains new translations of Vivaldi's letters and other correspondence. It includes Vivaldi's opera production catalog as prepared by Reinhard Strohm and a list of Vivaldi's church music from Talbot. An excellent companion to this book is *Five Centuries of Music in Venice*, by Landon and John Julius Norwich (1991), which contains numerous fine illustrations.

The most recent Vivaldi biography is by HELLER. Along with up-to-date information on the composer gleaned from recent Vivaldi research, it includes an informative chapter on the instrumental music as collected by Vivaldi's violinist-colleague Johann Georg Pisendel and played by the Dresden court orchestra. "The Dresden court was the second most predominant performance venue for Vivaldi, following only the Pietà [in Venice] and its highly praised orchestra." Heller also furthers an understanding of Vivaldi's concerto categories, especially in the realm of the concerto for chamber ensemble and the concerto ripieno. The concerto ripieno, or concerto without soloists, played a significant role in the evolution of the modern symphony. Heller includes selected letters from Vivaldi's correspondence, a chronological list of his operas, and a work list.

FAUN TANENBAUM TIEDGE

W

Wagner, Richard 1813–1883

German composer, poet, and philosopher

1. Biography

Cotterill, Rowland, *Wagner,* Staplehurst: Spellmount, 1996

Deathridge, John, and Carl Dahlhaus, *The New Grove Wagner,* London: Macmillan, and New York: Norton, 1984

Gregor-Dellin, Martin, *Richard Wagner: His Life, His Work, His Century,* translated by J. Maxwell Brownjohn, London: Collins, and San Diego, California: Harcourt Brace Jovanovich, 1983

Gutman, Robert W., *Richard Wagner: The Man, His Mind, and His Music,* New York: Harcourt, Brace and World, and London: Secker and Warburg, 1968

Millington, Barry, *Wagner,* London: Dent, 1984; revised edition, Princeton, New Jersey: Princeton University Press, 1992

Newman, Ernest, *The Life of Richard Wagner,* 4 vols., London: Cassell, and New York: Knopf, 1933–46

Wagner, Richard, *My Life,* translated by Andrew Grey, edited by Mary Whittall, Cambridge: Cambridge University Press, 1983

Westernhagen, Curt von, *Wagner: A Biography,* translated by Mary Whittall, Cambridge: Cambridge University Press, 1978

That Wagner is the most controversial of composers is a now a cliché. Chronicling his life has been correspondingly problematic, and a sobering reminder of the 19th century's long reach into our own time. Wagner and his second wife, Cosima (1837–1930), exercised decided control over a voluminous, self-generated body of documentation. Their propaganda machine, dedicated to creating and preserving an idolatrous Wagnerian mythos, lasted well into the 20th century, culminating in a notorious intimacy with the Third Reich. The earliest biographies are tainted by the insufficient or misleading use of sources, by a covert (or not) mission to propagate a Wagner mystique, or by all of these. Even some comparatively recent works have failed to contend openly with the composer's anti-Semitism.

As the 20th century progressed, authors tended to place their Wagner biographies in relation to their predecessors; as Dahlhaus wrote, "Every book about him has been inspired, not so much by the facts as by an earlier book about those facts." Moreover, the internal issues of Wagner's personality, philosophy, politics, artistic background, and influence are all of such monumental complexity that to examine one area more deeply is inevitably to shortchange another. The provocative facts of Wagner's biography and his uneasy cultural legacies have tended to overwhelm discussion of him as musician. Consequently, his musical achievements, as strange as it may seem, are often inadequately addressed. Millington's book provides the most concise, detached, and up-to-date account, but intensive biographical research on Wagner is probably still best served by an informed survey of a number of sources.

COTTERILL is a short but ambitious book. The author intends a concise synthesis of Wagner's life, works, their intellectual content, and background, boiled down for the educated general reader. A chronological account of the composer's life provides the structure. Accounts of the operas are inserted more or less where they occur in the scheme of things, but this chronological approach causes some organizational trouble when we reach *The Ring, Tristan und Isolde,* and *Der Meistersinger.* Cotterill ends with a succinct essay on Wagner's influence, touching on the composer's complicated relationship with Nietzsche, his influence on successive musicians and writers, and a very brief history of the Bayreuth Festival.

The biographical section of DEATHRIDGE and DAHLHAUS was written by John Deathridge, and the sections on the music were written by Carl Dahlhaus. The original biographical entry in the *New Grove Dictionary of Music and Musicians* (1980) was written by Curt von Westernhagen; Deathridge's is an updated and more detached account. The work is intended as a reference, rather than a literary work, and as such, its aims are completeness and concision, which it certainly achieves. Deathridge's biography is exceptionally well organized and accessible. In Dahlhaus's sections on music and aesthetics, admittedly not a primary concern of those seeking biographical facts, the book transcends the aims of a reference volume. The essays on the operas are essentially condensations of those that appear in Dahlhaus's *Richard Wagner's Music Dramas* (1979); his specific analyses are probably beyond the amateur's grasp. The truly awe-inspiring bibliography still furnishes much more information about sources than all but the most au courant Wagner scholar could ever desire. The volume also includes a comprehensive work list, contributed by Deathridge.

Utilizing archival material that was newly released in the 1970s, GREGOR-DELLIN aims to fill the need for a single-volume, comprehensive biography. The book is structured chronologically and is fundamentally a narrative of the composer's life, with forays into psychology and philosophy. Music is not a primary concern of this biography, and the author does not delve very deeply into Wagner's cultural milieu or its consequences. Despite the transmission of much useful data, the author's pervasive tone of unconcerned geniality flattens the distinctions between great and less-than-great achievements and domesticates much of Wagner's questionable behavior. A comparative reading of this biography with Gutman's will present the reader with almost directly opposing interpretations of Wagner.

GUTMAN's book consists of 17 densely packed chapters, with richly informed and provocative discussions of Wagner's personality, character, and politics situated within a chronological frame. Of the elements enumerated in the title, music is the least prominent, as the author's primary goal is to locate Wagner in the history of ideas. The book's most valuable traits are its unusual attention to the earliest works, as well as the incomplete or lesser-known dramatic projects such as *Die Saraszenin* and *Wieland der Schmied,* and its pursuit of unifying artistic *topoi* from Wagner's earliest works to his mature ones. Its shortcoming is an ultimately wearying tendentiousness that breaks through on nearly every page, although this approach was undoubtedly intended to provide a critical counterpoint to more reverential accounts. The author sometimes enlists relatively trivial evidence in his zeal to authenticate Wagner's character flaws.

MILLINGTON, based on the most recent documentation available at the time, is a concise account of Wagner's life, work, and ideas, taking in most relevant issues and written in an intelligible style. The reader will find an insightful biography, an overview of the composer's musical style, essays on each of the operas, lists of personalia and works (musical and prose), and recent bibliography. Millington's essays on the operas contain some musical analysis with notated examples.

NEWMAN's magisterial four-volume biography was, for most of the last half of the 20th century, the standard English-language work on Wagner. Newman, an English journalist and music critic, wrote the work over 17 crucial years. He began in 1932 with a purpose of rescuing Wagner from virulent anti-German sentiment in England, then proceeded through the years of World War II with the revised mission of rescuing the composer's art from the Third Reich for England and the world. This biography is primarily concerned with demythologizing Wagner and presenting an account of a human being, neither demon nor divinity. Newman also established a tone of neither overlooking nor overplaying the composer's anti-Semitism. The author's own prejudices come into play to some degree in his treatment of Liszt and Nietzsche. Although much older than the most recently accessed documentation, and unable to escape the specific circumstances of its origin, this elegantly written, lively discussion is still greatly valuable. Readers should not be put off by the work's length; Newman is among the most engaging of musical writers.

WAGNER's autobiography was written at the request of his patron and admirer King Ludwig II of Bavaria and leaves off at that monarch's summons in 1864. The text was dictated by Wagner between 1865 and 1880 to his then-mistress, and later his wife, Cosima von Bülow. At the beginning of the dictation process, the two were trying to conceal their affair from Ludwig. The resulting document is very much influenced by these claustrophobic dynamics. The situation probably caused Wagner to minimize his involvement in the Dresden revolt of 1849, for example; his marriage to Minna Planer and his attachment to Mathilde Wesendonck also were downplayed, presumably to preserve illusions held by Cosima and his patron. Wagner's drive to control the image he presented to the world and to posterity was the other distorting influence on the document as biography. Thus, he understates the extent of his musical training, in order to depict himself as a natural, untutored genius, and invents moments of revelatory inspiration to explain the origins of his mature works. Although undependable as a source of factual information, his autobiography is still indispensable to anyone who wants a view of the real Wagner. It is certainly true to Wagner's view of himself, and its intensity, self-aggrandizement, and embellishment of facts were essential to Wagner's personality.

WESTERNHAGEN's study was much anticipated, as it benefited from unprecedented access to such documentation as Cosima Wagner's diaries and Wagner's "Brown Book." In two volumes, with an extensive bibliography, footnotes, a meticulous index, and short, readable chapters, the biography initially appeared to fulfill much of its promise, while provoking critical misgivings about glossing over Wagner's more negative traits. In a devastating review in 1981, however, the English musicologist John Deathridge exposed the author's distortion of source materials, after a close examination of the same sources. Westernhagen, employing a cut-and-paste technique, manipulated his sources to support the invention of a Wagner who was not only oddly philo-Semitic but downright humane and reasonable in his dealings with Minna Wagner, the Wesendonks, King Ludwig II, Hans von Bülow, Nietzsche, Hermann Levi, and others. The discussions of the music are also disappointing, mostly because there is a real lack of substance behind the worshipful tone. Many of the author's other contributions to Wagner scholarship, in the areas of sketch and archival studies, are still of considerable value.

THERESA MUIR

2. Ring Cycle

Abbate, Carolyn, *Unsung Voices: Opera and Musical Narrative in the Nineteenth Century,* Princeton, New Jersey: Princeton University Press, 1991

Cooke, Deryck, *I Saw the World End: A Study of Wagner's Ring,* London: Oxford University Press, 1979

Dahlhaus, Carl, *Richard Wagner's Music Dramas,* translated by Mary Whittall, Cambridge: Cambridge University Press, 1979

DiGaetani, John Louis, editor, *Penetrating Wagner's Ring: An Anthology,* Rutherford, New Jersey: Fairleigh Dickinson University Press, 1978

Donington, Robert, *Wagner's Ring and Its Symbols: The Music and the Myth,* London: Faber, and New York: St. Martin's Press, 1963; 3rd edition, 1974

Newcomb, Anthony, "The Birth of Music out of the Spirit of Drama: An Essay in Wagnerian Formal Analysis," *19th Century Music 5* (1981/82)

Newman, Ernest, *Wagner Nights,* London: Putnam, 1949; as *The Wagner Operas,* New York: Knopf, 1949

Shaw, George Bernard, *The Perfect Wagnerite: A Commentary on the Niblung's Ring,* London: Richards, and New York: Bretano, 1898: 4th edition, London: Constable, 1923; reprint, New York: Dover, 1967

It took Wagner more than a quarter of a century to complete *Der Ring des Nibelungen*—from the earliest prose sketch of *Die Nibelungensage (Mythus)* of 1848 to the composition of the final bars of *Götterdämmerung* in 1874. No other work in the history of music has evoked so many different, and at times contradictory, brilliant interpretations. In his writings, Wagner himself commented on the *Ring* repeatedly, a complication for future scholars. This tetralogy represents the most extensive application of the so-called leitmotivic technique to be found in Wagner's work. Hence, its earliest readings focused on the identification and labeling of the different leitmotivs. Soon, however, interpretations of the work's holistic meaning developed, stemming from Wagner's Schopenhauerian view in which the actions of Wotan (the main god) represent the denial of will. Sociological, psychological, and structuralist readings of the work followed—readings that would evolve into music analysis proper during the 1970s and lead to criticism in the 1990s.

SHAW, a Nobel laureate and one of the most acclaimed playwrights of the 20th century, was the first to interpret the cycle as a parable expressing Wagner's critique of capitalism on the basis of the French philosopher Pierre Proudhon. According to Shaw, the cycle depicts capitalism as the opposite of love, the real fulfillment of human life. Shaw's socio-political interpretation of Siegfried as a revolutionary and of Brünnhilde's love as the redemption of capitalist society is still among the most inspiring readings of the work. This study also includes Shaw's unique relegation of *Götterdämmerung* to the status of an opera rather than a music drama.

NEWMAN's discussion of the *Ring* is a basic study and remains one of the best starting points for someone unfamiliar with the work. He offers a straightforward interpretation of the story and gives detailed synopses of all four parts. These also provide numerous quotations and 198 musical examples—mainly of leitmotifs—whose quite basic harmonic analyses should be treated with care. Newman does not comment on the philosophical, mainly Schopenhauerian, implications of the work. However, his very detailed investigation of the text's development provides interesting insights into the changes Wagner made to the work's dramatic structure over time. This historical perspective alone makes the book worth reading.

DONINGTON's understanding of the *Ring* is informed by Freudian and Jungian psychology. His starting point is Wagner's claim (in his important essay *Oper und Drama* of 1851) that it is the task of an artist "to bring the unconscious part of human nature into consciousness." The entire cycle is thus interpreted as a work of art in which the poetry, myth, characters, and music work as symbols representing the development of the human psyche. The author's interpretation, which includes a table of labeled leitmotivs, is highly original, although he sometimes overlooks some of the connections that link these motives.

DiGAETANI's anthology contains 38 articles grouped according to various aspects of the cycle. These essays include studies of Wagner's theory of opera, interpretations, historical influences, and even aspects of staging and performing this work. Much like Newman's book, this anthology is a good starting point, for the articles are written for a general readership. An advantage of DiGaetani's book is that it contains a study on the sometimes-neglected relationship between Wagner and German nationalism by Frank B. Josserand, and another on the use of Wagner by the Third Reich by George G. Windell.

COOKE's book on the *Ring* remains unfinished and only deals with the texts of *Das Rheingold* and *Die Walküre*. In contrast to Shaw and Donington, whom he criticises strongly, Cooke suggests an interpretation of text and music that uncovers Wagner's own intentions. His claimed objective approach reads *Rheingold* and *Die Walküre* carefully through the sources of northern Germanic mythology that Wagner used. As insightful as his study is, contemporary criticism has demonstrated that interpretations such as Cooke's that are founded on the composer's authority are as ideological as any analytical enterprise.

DAHLHAUS, the most acclaimed figure in modern Wagner scholarship, bases his discussion of the *Ring* on those features that form the poetic conception of music drama. Informed by Wagner's own poetic writings, the author investigates the mythic subject matter, the open dramatic form, the irregular verse rhythm, the dissolution of musical periodic structure, and the extension of leitmotivic technique over the whole work. This important publication is rounded off by a fascinating discussion of the different endings of *Götterdämmerung* that Wagner wrote during the evolution of the work.

NEWCOMB's article is one of the first and foremost Anglo-American attempts to develop new methods of formal musical analysis for Wagner's works. As such, it represents a response to German Wagner scholarship in the 1970s. Arguing against the view that Wagner's works lack form, Newcomb claims that form-defining features (such as tempo, instrumentation, dramatic textual structure, loose periodic structure, musical motives, and especially tonality) are used by Wagner to construct musico-dramatic units. This hypothesis is impressively demonstrated by his analysis of "Fricka's Lament" in *Die Walküre* II, 1, and "Wotan and Erda" in *Siegfried* III, 1.

ABBATE's celebrated book is a study of the conditions required for those instances when instrumental music speaks or narrates through inherent voices. She bases her complex and sophisticated arguments on concepts used in modern literary theory, adjusting the concepts to suit the study of 19th-century orchestral and operatic music. Four chapters are devoted to Wagner's works, the most elucidating of which discusses one of the core scenes of the *Ring*: Wotan's monologue in the second act of *Die Walküre*. This scene is treated as the best example of the *Ring*'s extensive use of narration and retrospection. Abbate demonstrates how the musical narration may speak with and across Wotan's oration. Her study is a landmark in contemporary criticism of both Wagner and narration in music.

ANDREAS BÜCKER

3. Tristan und Isolde

Dahlhaus, Carl, *Richard Wagner's Music Dramas,* translated by Mary Whittall, Cambridge: Cambridge University Press, 1979

Newman, Ernest, *Wagner Nights,* London: Putnam, 1949; as *The Wagner Operas,* New York: Knopf, 1949

Wagner, Richard, *Prelude and Transfiguration, from Tristan und Isolde,* edited by Robert Bailey, New York: Norton, 1985

———, *Tristan und Isolde: Wagner,* London: Calder, and New York: Riverrun Press, 1981

Zuckerman, Elliott, *The First Hundred Years of Wagner's Tristan,* New York: Columbia University Press, 1964

Tristan und Isolde is far more than one of art's most celebrated depictions of romantic love; as a work of music theater, its remarkably integrated structure, continuous texture, and maintenance of musical and dramatic tension over almost unbearably long periods of time, altered composers' and the public's conceptions of the operatic experience. Wagner's experiments in daring, highly chromatic harmonic language strikingly coalesced in this work and became a musical paradigm the influence of which haunted virtually every major composer for nearly a century following its first public performance in 1865. Music critics and scholars were equally challenged by the work. The famous first chord alone has been the focus of fascination and fierce debate. The most significant work on *Tristan,* however, is mostly on a highly technical level and/or in German. There are surprisingly few recent book-length studies in English.

DAHLHAUS is primarily concerned with considering Wagner's works as music drama and exploring how each work affected the evolution of the genre. Dahlhaus first takes up Wagner's extreme compression of the medieval romance he used as his principal source, and the aphoristic nature of the resulting drama. The author then considers Tristan and Isolde's love and the dramatic function of the love potion in Wagner's work as opposed to in the romance. The central part of the chapter is devoted to a brief but intensive discussion of the work as music drama. According to Dahlhaus, the drama encompasses both text and music, and misunderstandings of Wagner's intentions stem from the confusion of the term *drama* with the idea of text alone. The text is not the drama, asserts Dahlhaus; it serves the drama no more or less than does the music. He concludes with a discussion of Wagner's musical procedures, over short then longer time scales, particularly emphasizing the work's integration of motive and harmony.

WAGNER (1981) presents the original libretto and an English translation printed side-by-side, with a numbered thematic guide and several short essays on different aspects of the work, and includes a plot synopsis as well as essays on the music. An essay on staging focuses on Adolphe Appia's innovations, and the German text is briefly introduced. Andrew Porter's performance translation is skillful, but the need to preserve versification drains the force from some passages, particularly Tristan's Act III delirium. An assortment of interesting photographs illustrates the text; unfortunately, in the essay on Appia, there is only one rather blurry picture of his design. The thematic guide is useful for the more musically sophisticated amateur but need not trouble the musical novice, who will find that the guide still offers pithy writing on a difficult subject, as well as good introductions to the background, main issues, and importance of the work.

NEWMAN addresses the canonic works in separate essays; each chapter follows more or less the same format. In the *Tristan und Isolde* chapter, Newman thoroughly introduces Wagner's literary sources, principally the romance by Gottfried von Strassbourg, and considers the romance's medieval milieu. The author surveys certain critical objections to the story, particularly those on moral grounds, and rounds off the introduction by discussing Wagner's composition of the work. Newman, ever the Wagnerian myth-buster, has his own emphatic convictions about Mathilde Wesendonck's role in the work's origins. Finally, the work itself is lucidly discussed, and the musical study is still a fine introduction for the beginner. More sophisticated Wagnerians might find the essay quaintly dependent on leitmotivic interpretation, but reading Newman is a prerequisite for *becoming* a sophisticated Wagnerian.

Bailey's edition of WAGNER's "Prelude and Transfiguration" focuses specifically on the music of the "Prelude and Transfiguration" from *Tristan und Isolde* (Bailey calls the musical selection usually known as *Liebestod* or "Love-Death" by Wagner's own name of *Verklärung* or "Transfiguration"). The edition may pose a problem for the most entry-level operagoers, who are unlikely to be able to negotiate the analytical essays by Schoenberg, Kurth, Lorenz, and Hindemith, among others. These essays, however, along with those by Tovey, Newman, Deryck Cooke, William J. Mitchell, Edward T. Cone, and Milton Babbitt, are classics of musical analysis, which are essential reading for the serious musician or music student. Bailey's own "Analytical Study of the Sketches and Drafts" is also an important contribution to the study of a pivotal work in music history.

ZUCKERMAN is an important work of intellectual history. In his preface, Zuckerman reflects on Friedrich Nietzsche's reactions to *Tristan* and proposes to trace the work's effect in a larger context, which he does in the succeeding six chapters. The author's fundamental premise is a distinction between the cultural phenomenon of Wagnerism and that which he calls "Tristanism." Briefly stated, Wagnerism involves a complex of cultural, aesthetic, and even political convictions and is public in nature, whereas Tristanism is the private, direct response to the music. As Zuckerman writes, "The Wagnerite must learn theories and cultivate habits. The Tristanite has only to be overwhelmed." The six chapters are each devoted to a single concern, and they are organized centrifugally, progressing outward (both chronologically and geographically) from the work's conception and origin. The first two chapters deal with the composition of the work and its consequences among Wagner's immedi-

ate circle. The third chapter takes up Nietzsche and his "classic case of Tristanism," followed by a chapter on the work's Paris reception, which demonstrates the separation between literary "Wagnerians" and musical "Tristanists." The Paris chapter concludes with Debussy's emotional and intellectual struggle with Wagner and *Tristan,* which Zuckerman likens to Nietzsche's reaction to the opera. Chapter 5 considers *Tristan*'s influence among early 20th-century novelists, especially D.H. Lawrence, Gabriele D'Annunzio, and Thomas Mann. The final chapter brings *Tristan* well into the 20th century, with a history of its life in the theater and its wider significance among musicians.

THERESA MUIR

4. Other Operas

Beckett, Lucy, *Richard Wagner: Parsifal,* Cambridge: Cambridge University Press, 1981

Dahlhaus, Carl, *Richard Wagner's Music Dramas,* translated by Mary Whittall, Cambridge: Cambridge University Press, 1979

Deathridge, John, *Wagner's Rienzi: A Reappraisal Based on a Study of the Sketches and Drafts,* Oxford: Clarendon Press, 1977

Newman, Ernest, *Wagner Nights,* London: Putnam, 1949; as *The Wagner Operas,* New York: Knopf, 1949

Wagner, Richard, *Der fliegende Holländer,* London: Calder, and New York: Riverrun Press, 1982

———, *Lohengrin,* London: Calder, and New York: Riverrun Press, 1993

———, *Die Meistersinger von Nürnberg,* London: Calder, and New York: Riverrun Press, 1983

———, *Parsifal,* London: Calder, and New York: Riverrun Press, 1986

Warrack, John, *Richard Wagner: Die Meistersinger von Nürnberg,* Cambridge: Cambridge University Press, 1994

Wagner completed 13 operas, always writing his own librettos as well as the music, seeking an unprecedented synthesis of music and drama. The first operas, *Die Feen* and *Das Liebesverbot,* are considered juvenilia and are almost never performed except as curiosities. Consequently, there is virtually no literature available on these works in English. *Rienzi,* a French-style grand opera of ultra-Wagnerian length, likewise has not assumed a regular place in the operatic repertoire but is more frequently performed than its predecessors. The last ten operas—*Der fliegende Holländer, Tannhäuser, Lohengrin,* the tetralogy *Der Ring des Nibelungen, Tristan und Isolde, Die Meistersinger von Nürnberg,* and *Parsifal*—are considered Wagner's canonical works and represent the attainment of his stylistic aspirations. These operas have remained essential and distinctive elements of the operatic repertoire. Their musical innovations, philosophical and political implications, and rich possibilities of interpretation have made them the subjects of a large and searching literature.

BECKETT is part of the fine series of Cambridge Opera Handbooks, paperback volumes aimed at the serious student or dedicated amateur. These handbooks usually consist of separate chapters devoted to different aspects of the operas: the work's genesis, with literary sources, if applicable; the work's stage history and reception; a plot synopsis; and an analysis of the score. The first chapter of Beckett is an excellent overview of Wagner's literary sources for *Parsifal* and how he created his drama from them. A perceptive musical analysis by Arnold Whittall is aimed at the sophisticated reader and is followed by concise pieces by Beckett on the work's stage history and critical reception. The final chapter, entitled "A Proposed Interpretation," offers Beckett's Christian reading of the work, which breaks away from other critics' more skeptical contemporary commentary on the work. *Parsifal* is so complex, however, that widely divergent readings are both inevitable and desirable.

DAHLHAUS deals with each of Wagner's canonic operas in a compact essay, in which he addresses the concept of music drama and how each work expresses the genre. According to Dahlhaus, the drama encompasses both text and music, and misunderstandings of Wagner's intentions stem from the confusion of the term *drama* with the idea of *text* alone. The text is not the drama, Dahlhaus contends; it serves the drama no more or less than does the music. This book represents Dahlhaus, a musicologist who usually dealt in highly subtle and sophisticated concepts, at his most accessible, but even as such it may make challenging demands on the newcomer.

DEATHRIDGE's study of *Rienzi* is based on his doctoral dissertation. He introduces the book with a consideration of Wagner's own aims for the work and some of its subsequent reception history. The next chapter deals with the prose draft and its origin, organization, and structure, as well as Wagner's literary and philosophical influences. In the central chapter, "Composition of Verse and Music," Deathridge uses extended examples from the sketches and drafts to pursue his central argument: a rebuttal of Hanslick's claim that Wagner developed a "new way" of composing and structuring his theatrical works because *Rienzi*'s traditional grand opera form exposed his musical weaknesses. This study is for the specialist with a particular interest in this work and its place in Wagner's artistic development.

Each of the English National Opera guides contains the original libretto and an English translation printed side-by-side, supplemented by a numbered "Thematic Guide" and as many as four or five short essays on different aspects of the work. The essays are substantial and strike an unusual balance between accessibility and intellectual content. Both the libretto and the essays use the thematic guide's numbering system to refer to specific musical excerpts. The volumes are lavishly illustrated with interesting pictures and photographs from a variety of productions. In WAGNER (1982), John Warrack's essay "Behind the Flying Dutchman" discusses Wagner's affinity for the supernatural, and such influences as Marschner's *Der Vampyr,* Weber's *Euryanthe,* and the stories of E.T.A. Hoffman. Deathridge contributes an essay entitled "An Introduction to the Flying Dutchman," which posits that Wagner moved the story from Scotland to Norway to reflect his own biographical experience of a sea voyage. Deathridge also discusses the function of song (mimetic versus diegetic music) in the opera. Following this essay is a study by William Vaughan on the figure of the Flying Dutchman in legend and literature, Wagner's own notes on the opera overture, and his remarks on performance.

In WAGNER (1993), John Deathridge comments on the plot's personal significance to Wagner, bringing its mythical foundations and medieval symbolism into play with a psychoanalytic interpretation. Thomas S. Grey's "Lohengrin between Grand Opera and Musikdrama" notes the work's grand-opera trappings, "musical colour" (associative keys), and use of reminiscence motifs. Finally, Janet Nelson's investigates the roles and meaning of women in the medieval world. The book also offers the Grimm brothers' "Lohengrin" tale, a thematic guide, and the libretto, translated by Amanda Holden.

In WAGNER (1983) Roland Mathews leads off with an essay on *Die Meistersinger*'s uniqueness as a comedy in Wagner's oeuvre. Arnold Whittall follows with a lucid musical analysis, but the musical novice may find reading it to be laborious, especially flipping back and forth between the text and thematic guide. Last is a provocative essay by Timothy MacFarland, exploring Wagner's conception of late-medieval Nuremberg as an artistic utopia, with some darker social implications.

WAGNER (1986) is distinguished by sensitive essays on the music by Robin Holloway and Carolyn Abbate. Holloway's piece is concerned with the work's distinctive sound world and the elements that unify the immense musical structure. Abbate discusses the relationship of music and words. Although both essays are entirely involved with musical concerns, and refer to the thematic guide, they are not so technical as to put off the listener with a strong aural memory of the music. The piece on dramaturgy by Gerd Rienäcker may prove to be heavier going.

NEWMAN is generally considered a classic among guides to opera, or to any one composer's works. This book established the format the author used in his many subsequent books about operatic repertoire. Wagner's ten canonical works are addressed in separate, extremely detailed essays. Each essay encompasses the dramatic and musical geneses of each work; Wagner's mythical, folkloric, literary, and philosophical sources; the principal musical material; and dramatic plot. The musical and plot discussions are woven together, in keeping with the tight integration of music and plot in the works themselves. Newman further enhances his discussions with his knowledge of Wagner's biography and historical background. Although showing inevitable signs of age, both in its approach to the music and in some research, Newman is still probably the best introduction for the beginner, as well as a useful reference for the serious student.

WARRACK is similar in organization to Beckett. The bulk of the text is by Warrack, with contributing essays by Lucy Beckett and Michael Tanner. Warrack begins with a chapter on the genesis of *Die Meistersinger,* followed by a plot synopsis and a chapter on the history of the Meistersingers in Nuremberg. Beckett's essay investigates how Wagner's reading of Schopenhauer shaped the final product, and Tanner writes about Wagner's transformation of the historical figure of Hans Sachs. Warrack returns with a chapter on the central function of song in the work and concludes with chapters on Sach's famous "Wahn" monologue and the work's stage history. The appendices include the texts of the "Wahn" monologue, Sach's final address, and Wagner's original version of Walther's "Prize Song."

THERESA MUIR

5. Operas: Staging

Appia, Adolphe, *Essays, Scenarios, and Designs,* translated by Walther R. Volbach, edited by Richard C. Beacham, Ann Arbor, Michigan: UMI Press, 1989

————, *Music and the Art of the Theatre,* translated by Robert W. Corrigan and Mary Douglas Dirks, edited by Barnard Hewitt, Coral Gables, Florida: University of Miami Press, 1962

————, *Staging Wagnerian Drama,* translated by Michael Peter Loeffler, Basel: Birkhäuser, 1982

Bauer, Oswald Georg, *Richard Wagner: The Stage Designs and Productions from the Premières to the Present,* New York: Rizzoli, 1982

Burian, Jarka, *Svoboda, Wagner: Josef Svoboda's Scenography for Richard Wagner's Operas,* Middletown, Connecticut: Wesleyan University Press, 1983

Fricke, Richard, *Wagner in Rehearsal 1875–1876: The Diaries of Richard Fricke,* translated by George Fricke, edited by James Deaville and Evan Baker, Stuyvestant, New York: Pendragon Press, 1998

Millington, Barry, and Stewart Spencer, editors, *Wagner in Performance,* New Haven, Connecticut: Yale University Press, 1992

Müller, Ulrich, and Peter Wapnewski, *Wagner Handbook,* translated and edited by John Deathridge, Cambridge, Massachusetts: Harvard University Press, 1992

Petzet, Detta, and Michael Petzet, *Die Richard Wagner-Bühne König Ludwigs II,* Munich: Prestel, 1970

Porges, Heinrich, *Wagner Rehearsing the Ring: An Eyewitness Account of the Stage Rehearsals of the First Bayreuth Festival,* translated by Robert L. Jacobs, Cambridge: Cambridge University Press, 1983

Radice, Mark A., editor, *Opera in Context: Essays on Historical Staging from the Late Renaissance to the Time of Puccini,* Portland, Oregon: Amadeus Press, 1998

Skelton, Geoffrey, *Wagner at Bayreuth: Experiment and Tradition,* London: Barrie and Rockcliff, and New York: Braziller, 1965; revised edition, London: White Lion, 1976

Spotts, Frederic, *Bayreuth: A History of the Wagner Festival,* New Haven, Connecticut: Yale University Press, 1994

Wagner, Richard, *Judaism in Music and Other Essays,* Prose Works, vol. 3: *The Theatre,* translated by William Ashton Ellis, Lincoln: University of Nebraska Press, 1995

Amid the enormous number of books, essays, and articles on Wagner, there are surprisingly few works of quality that objectively discuss the staging of his operas. Too often, an author either has an axe to grind or seeks to propagate a particular political or cultural point of view—particularly the composer's anti-Semitism. The finest overview of the first productions of Wagner is available only in German; there are several publications on these productions in English, but they do not pay attention to the details of staging. Only recently have there appeared several publications that explore some of the more esoteric areas of staging.

In 1895, William Ashton Ellis published his translation of WAGNER's essays "On the Staging of Tannhäuser" and "On the Staging of the Flying Dutchman." Although Ellis attempts to adapt Wagner's often prolix and verbose prose to Victorian-style English, he nonetheless manages to convey Wagner's staging instructions (filled with common sense and still greatly relevant for today) for different parts of the operas. These essays, written in 1852, were the first examination of the staging requirements outside of Wagner's scenic and blocking descriptions published in the vocal and full scores.

Reports of the rehearsals of the first complete *Ring* cycle in Bayreuth for the 1876 festival were published shortly after the festival by PORGES, Wagner's musical assistant. Porges's accounts concentrate primarily on Wagner's musical and vocal interpretations, although the staging is not neglected. In contrast to Porges's sometimes overly reverential writing, FRICKE provides a fresh view as a seasoned professional stage director, grandly recounting in his diaries the trials and tribulations of the entire rehearsal process. The diaries provide great insight into the enormous difficulties of bringing four new productions into life in three intense, pressure-filled months.

Later publications have been hampered by the slavish adherence to the orthodoxy espoused by the Wagner's disciples and his wife, Cosima, in Bayreuth. Thus, writings about different interpretations of Wagner's intentions for the production and staging of his operas have met with fierce resistance opposed to any kind of change. Radical suggestions—such as those of Appia—were curtly rejected. Cosima insisted that Wagner had already stated what was necessary in his own writings and stagings—such as the *Ring* in Bayreuth, or those of *Tristan und Isolde* and *Die Meistersinger von Nürnberg* in Munich—and that there was nothing more to be said. Not until Wieland Wagner—the composer's grandson—revived the Bayreuth Festival in 1951 with his superb and iconoclastic designs for the *Ring* and *Parsifal* was there an open acknowledgment of the influence of Appia.

The finest survey of the first (and subsequent) performances of Wagner's works in Dresden, Munich, and Bayreuth is offered in PETZET and PETZET, which provides a staggering 950 reproductions with copious documentation. Although the fact that the study is written in German may hinder some from understanding much of the text itself, the captions for each reproduction are clear and easy to follow. This book is a model of research, and the reader is afforded the chance to observe the production practices of the 19th century from original sources that are otherwise difficult to find.

The most important works after Petzet and Petzet are those of the Swiss artist and designer Appia. After viewing the iconography of Wagner's original stagings, and those perpetrated by Cosima, one can easily understand the necessity for theatrical reform, particularly for Wagner's work, if the artistic ideals sought by the composer were not to stagnate and become museum pieces. The most accessible of the designer's writings is APPIA (1982) (in an excellent translation by Loeffler, who also provides a fine introductory essay highlighting the primary points). This book, originally published in 1895, is the precursor to the designer's seminal work, APPIA (1962). Both of these monographs are of fundamental importance; not only were the scenic and staging reforms extolled by critics, they also provided the groundwork for stagings in which theatrical lighting became an integral part of the operatic aesthetic. Other important essays appear in APPIA (1989), accompanied by Beacham's informative introductory material.

SKELTON gives a succinct account of Appia's attempt to acquaint Cosima with his work in hopes of integrating it into the festival, and of the refusal of the Bayreuth circle to countenance any changes with Wagner's vision. Skelton also reviews production practices up to 1965. The author enjoyed close proximity to Weiland Wagner, has a sympathetic understanding of Wieland's aesthetics, and aims to challenge past practices while looking toward the future.

BAUER provides an excellent historical overview of the first and more important productions up to 1980. He was press director for the Bayreuth Festival for many years, and in each text accompanying the operas, his commentaries offer a unique perspective on the different productions from all over the world. Each opera is richly illustrated with reproductions of original designs and production photographs. A more succinct version of this work, "Performing History: A Brief Survey"—without illustrations—is published in MÜLLER and WAPNEWSKI.

The best collection of essays dealing with Wagnerian stage design, production, and dramaturgy is found in MILLINGTON and SPENCER. Two essays stand out: Mike Ashman's "Producing Wagner" and Patrick Carnegy's "Designing Wagner" provide lucid overviews of staging practices through the 20th century; their comments (and illustrations) on the productions since Wieland Wagner's death in 1966 are particularly welcome.

Wagnerian production is bound together with the development and the construction of the Bayreuth Festival Theater (Festspielhaus) in 1876. In his contribution to RADICE, Evan Baker ("Richard Wagner and His Search for the Ideal Theatrical Space") surveys the documentation and construction of the theater and subsequent reforms of the theatrical space and auditorium. Some of these changes include the dimming of the auditorium lights during the performance and the lowering of the main curtain to hide all changes of scenery from the view of the audience. All these factors played an enormous role in the first production of the *Ring* in 1876 and especially in the staging of *Parsifal* in 1882. The first production of *Parsifal* with its designs and special effects are discussed in the essay as well.

Josef Svoboda created iconoclastic designs for Wagner at Bayreuth and elsewhere. BURIAN surveys the designer's creations with illustrations and interviews. Analysis is not confined to the designs and dramaturgy alone; the all-important stage machinery—particularly for a production utilizing a revolving platform mounted on a single hydraulic piston—is examined as well.

SPOTTS's contribution is the most recent survey of the Bayreuth Festival and includes some incisive observations. Commentary dealing with the family problems and their relationships to the past—anti-Semitism, Hitler, and the incessant internecine feuding within the festival after its reopening in 1951—does not detract from the summary of production styles over the years.

EVAN BAKER

6. Philosophy

Adorno, Theodor W., *In Search of Wagner*, translated by Rodney Livingstone, London: NLB, 1981

Borchmeyer, Dieter, *Richard Wagner: Theory and Theatre*, translated by Stewart Spencer, Oxford: Clarendon Press, and New York: Oxford University Press, 1991

Deathridge, John, and Carl Dahlhaus, *The New Grove Wagner*, London: Macmillan, and New York: Norton, 1984

Grey, Thomas S., *Wagner's Musical Prose: Texts and Contexts*, Cambridge: Cambridge University Press, 1995

Kropfinger, Klaus, *Wagner and Beethoven*, translated by Peter Palmer, Cambridge: Cambridge University Press, 1991

Nattiez, Jean-Jacques, *Wagner Androgyne: A Study in Interpretation,* translated by Stewart Spencer, Princeton, New Jersey: Princeton University Press, 1993

Stein, Jack Madison, *Richard Wagner and the Synthesis of the Arts,* Detroit, Michigan: Wayne State University Press, 1960

Weiner, Marc A., *Richard Wagner and the Anti-Semitic Imagination,* Lincoln: University of Nebraska Press, 1995

Given Wagner's devotion to the metaphysics of music—an idea whose origins in 18th-century German romanticism did not prevent him from bringing it to magnificent fruition in the otherwise positivist mid-19th century—it is doubtful that his musical works can be properly understood without reference to the role of philosophical speculation in their creation. Of course, his oeuvre does not boast the kind of systematic consistency we would expect from German academic philosophy of the same period; by that standard Wagner was not a philosopher but an artist who used philosophy as a creative aid. Nevertheless, the contradictions for which he is often criticized tend to fade when viewed as products of a dialectical process of reasoning unfamiliar in the English-speaking world. It need not be understood as a crude reversal, for example, that Wagner became a follower of Schopenhauer (who placed music in a superior, indeed unique position among the arts) just after consigning music to the role of a "means" in *Opera and Drama* (1851). But Wagner's artistic vision, like that of many geniuses, did allow him to manipulate his sources and thus find support in unexpected places.

For a pithy, penetrating discussion of Wagner's worldview and its impact on his dramas, no one has surpassed Carl Dahlhaus's writings in DEATHRIDGE and DAHLHAUS. Dahlhaus has a profound knowledge of the cultural and intellectual background, Wagner's biographical history, and the music itself, making him almost uniquely qualified to assess the topic comprehensively. Without the slightest naïveté regarding the composer's personal life, Dahlhaus identifies a "rigorous artistic morality" in the music of Wagner, through which "art usurped the place of religion" by virtue of the experience of transcendent meaning the music gave audiences, and by virtue of its sheer aesthetic power. The difficulties of Dahlhaus's style reflect those of the material and thus may be a precondition of sophisticated thought in this area.

BORCHMEYER comes out of the same scholarly tradition as Dahlhaus, demonstrating a breadth of learning and a subtlety of observation that make short work of crude attacks on Wagner's intellectual integrity. The author approaches the topic of Wagner's reception of Schopenhauer through a study of Nietzsche's volatile writings from before and after his break with Wagnerism, and Borchmeyer argues effectively that Schopenhauerian philosophy provided Wagner with support for musical views that he already held, rather than a completely new

aesthetic. With equally effective discussions of the influence of Goethe (particularly *Faust,* part 2) and the Greeks (above all Aeschylus), this volume's scope matches its depth.

Perhaps the most intellectually formidable Wagner critic of the 20th century, ADORNO treats the composer within a Marxist paradigm that for many discredits this reading at the outset. The question for Adorno is what response Wagner's music offers to the plight of the individual in late capitalist society, in which collective, objective interests inevitably steamroll those of the particular subject. The answer: "Wagner renounces not only the illusory reconciliation [of these interests], but also the attempt to overcome the contradiction"; lacking the courage to face the problem, Wagner covers it up. Adorno's ruthlessly opaque style is designed to resist simplistic interpretation, but it must be considered by those wanting a complete picture of 20th-century Wagner studies.

Less challenging in aim and practice, but accurate as an introduction to Wagner's artistic philosophy, STEIN's work traces the basic trajectory of the topic, from the composer's early involvement with the romanticism of Lessing and the materialism of Feuerbach to the Schopenhauerian reinterpretation of the Greek chorus ventriloquially proposed through Nietzsche. The book works especially well as a survey of Wagner's main rephrasings of his views; the trek through *The Art-Work of the Future, Opera and Drama, Beethoven,* and *The Destiny of Opera* can be arduous, and Stein provides a fine service with his fair, reasonable synopses.

GREY's ambitious work considers the whole of Wagner's sprawling prose output from the standpoint of some of the more mercurial Wagnerian themes: absolute music, the poetic-musical period, endless melody, the symphonic drama, the poetic intent, and so on. By tracing each of these ideas from their historical sources (insofar as these are discernible) through five decades of writings, the author illuminates the contours of Wagner's aesthetic thought in a striking, useful way. Although a turgid style and a tendency toward the speculative sometimes undermine Grey's argument, the connections established among aesthetic, historical, and music-theoretical concerns reward the reader's effort.

In a similar vein, though at once more focused and more freely critical, is the study of Wagnerian androgyny by NATTIEZ. The seduction of a sensational title seems to have won out here; the controlling metaphor invoked by Wagner and analyzed by Nattiez has little to do with androgyny, but refers to male-female sexual union. Nevertheless, beyond the unnecessary repetitions of that word, there are exciting critical insights to be found here—not least the notion that the *Ring of the Nibelung* is held together by multiple narratives of striving to overcome the alienation inherent in sexual individuation (sexual individuation being a particular mode of Schopenhauer's *princip-*

ium individuationis). A complete catalog of Wagner's writings, published as an appendix, makes this book invaluable as a reference work.

In his volume on the composer's reception of Beethoven, KROPFINGER addresses the most influential of Wagner's musical predecessors whose monumental achievement drove Wagner toward his own grandeur. The author wisely extends his topic to Wagner's reception of Beethoven reception itself—in such figures as E.T.A. Hoffmann and A.B. Marx—thus providing a useful contextualization of relevant aesthetic (Beethoven as romantic) and formal (early theories of sonata form and the "symphonic") issues. The observation that Beethoven's musical influence manifested itself more on the "profounder and more interesting" level of construction than on the level of style is worthy and yields enlightening analytical results.

In a controversial, occasionally reckless, but lucid work, WEINER explores the anti-Semitism proclaimed so boldly by the composer himself, yet still so poorly understood as a determining factor in the works themselves. As an entry into the spectrum of encoded anti-Semitic signs ostensibly represented by the Wagnerian dramas, Weiner studies the works' treatment of five focal points of Jewish revulsion: eyes, the voice, odors, feet, and onanism. Weiner's case for a language of commonly understood markers of Jewish identity in 19th-century Germany is strong and benefits from the author's experience with work in other fields, particularly the writings of Sander Gilman. The success rate in analyses of individual passages varies, from an impressive reading of Mime's whines to an absurd "vocal iconography of the onanist" Hagen.

CHARLES YOUMANS

Walton, William 1902–1983

English composer

Craggs, Stewart R., *William Walton: A Source Book,* Aldershot: Scolar Press, and Brookfield, Vermont: Ashgate, 1993

Howes, Frank Stewart, *The Music of William Walton,* 2 vols., London: Oxford University Press, 1942–43; 2nd edition, 2 vols. in 1, 1974

Kennedy, Michael, *Portrait of Walton,* Oxford: Oxford University Press, 1989

Smith, Carolyn J., *William Walton: A Bio-Bibliography,* New York: Greenwood Press, 1988

Tierney, Neil, *William Walton: His Life and Music,* London: Hale, 1984; Dover, New Hampshire: Longwood Press, 1985

Walton, Susana, *William Walton: Behind the Facade,* Oxford: Oxford University Press, 1988

When Sir William Walton died in Italy in 1983, his reputation had moved well beyond that of young iconoclast in the 1920s and 1930s to being one of the most celebrated English composers of the 20th century. At the time of Walton's death, Hugh Ottaway's slim, 24-page biography (life and works), published in 1972, was the only monograph to offer the interested reader even a moderately extended treatment of Walton's life. A natural hesitancy to write about a subject who is still alive probably accounts for the absence of any more comprehensive study prior to 1983. Music specialists and the general audience alike had to rely primarily on article-length studies, reviews of performances and recordings, program notes, and brief discussions within books treating broader topics. Walton's musical output fared slightly better, attracting scholarly attention with Stewart Craggs's chronological thematic catalog and one substantive monograph of musical analysis. The general landscape of Walton scholarship has improved somewhat since 1983; two additional resources for Walton research now complement the considerable detail in the thematic catalog, and three full-length biographies provide a more comprehensive picture of the composer. Interpretive special studies and a scholarly, definitive life-and-works volume would further enhance the mature, balanced, and realistic critical assessment of the composer and his music that is presently emerging.

SMITH's bio-bibliography is a research tool designed for music specialists and general readers alike. The annotated bibliography constitutes the major portion of the book and divides into smaller headings: articles and reviews; books, theses, and dissertations; articles by Walton; and miscellaneous items. Descriptive comments and evaluations accompany each bibliographic entry, helping the reader determine which sources are most useful. Smaller sections in Smith include a brief biography of Walton, an alphabetical list of works and first performances, a discography of sound recordings (in all formats) of the composer's works arranged alphabetically by title, and archival information about collections of Walton manuscripts and personal papers. Smith is a good resource for those who want pertinent information uncluttered with copious detail.

CRAGGS is well known to students of Walton's music because of his pioneering work on the thematic catalog (published 1977, updated 1990). Craggs's newer source book is indispensable for the music specialist in particular because it is nearly encyclopedic in providing information essential to the serious scholar. It begins with a detailed chronology of the composer, outlining the important events in his life. The second and largest section of the book catalogs virtually all known particulars of Walton manuscripts (including unpublished works) and first editions, providing locations, publication dates, and extensive visual and material details for each document. Shorter sections include a listing of collections of Walton's letters and their locations; a list of recordings conducted by the composer, including venues and dates, as well as recordings of interviews he gave and where they can be found; and a selected bibliography of writings relating to Walton, including articles, theses, books, and notes from recordings, organized either by the title of the work discussed or in a general heading at the end. A comprehensive index proves helpful for quick reader referral.

HOWES was the first published monograph on Walton and is, to date, the only extensive analytical study of the composer's music. Apart from an introductory biographical note, the approach is almost purely analytical, discussing, in turn, early works, larger orchestral works, concertos, smaller orchestral works, chamber music and songs, choral works, and *Troilus and Cressida*. Howes presupposes a significant degree of musical knowledge on the part of the reader, making his study intelligible primarily to a musically sophisticated audience. A concluding chapter on aspects of Walton's style forms a kind of summary of the composer's total output, which is relatively small. Howes's analysis focuses primarily on the formal structure of the music; discussion of thematic, harmonic, and rhythmic features relate in turn to the music's formal design. His stated purpose in dissecting these works is to increase cognitive awareness of the musical events and their relationships in the structural design of each piece, which should lead to intelligent criticism and heightened aesthetic appreciation of Walton's musical style—an appropriate objective for Howes, who was a *London Times* music critic for 35 years. Pointing out that Walton "does not give vent to subjective emotion in his music" and is an absolutist, Howes argues incisively that Walton "thinks in themes, textures, and structures," even when working with words, as in vocal music; Walton is most at home, therefore, composing in the larger forms, with relatively few miniatures to his credit. It is difficult to trace influences in his music; the large works seem conditioned only by Walton's own mind, which was uncluttered by extensive formal training or enthusiasm over continental developments and unaffected by the English folk song that cast a spell over so many other English composers of the time.

TIERNEY is the first of the full-length biographies to appear after the composer's death. The book divides into two main sections, the first on Walton's life and the second on his music. Tierney writes warmly of his subject in a style that will readily engage general readers. As the first published biography, the volume fills in many chronological gaps for the first time. Tierney's research is considerable, documented with reference notes. Discussion of Walton's works, which are generically organized into 14 categories, is not so much analytical as descriptive, providing an enthusiastic first encounter with the works in question. A select bibliography may be of interest to the general reader, but it will not prove very helpful to the music specialist.

Four years after Tierney published his biographical study, for which Lady Susana Walton wrote a brief foreword, she published her own biography of her celebrated husband. WALTON, as one would expect, is a highly personal account of the composer's life. The author's recollections of their years together, in particular, resonate with the authentic voice of one who shared them. Lady Walton makes no attempt to provide any critical analysis of the composer's music; her sole purpose seems to be to show what she would like the reader to see of the private man behind the public face. Walton's biography reveals a man of great complexity, capable of considerable shyness, sensitivity, depression, a fiercely competitive spirit, and occasional, surprising verbal bluntness; the study is valuable as an intimate, firsthand account of the composer as artist, husband, and human being.

In 1968 William Walton requested that KENNEDY write the composer's biography, and a contract was signed. Kennedy was determined not to begin while Walton was still alive, so the project was delayed. Kennedy's comprehensive biographical study is the only such book published to date; it is supported by extensive research and documentation. The author deliberately limits discussions of the music to features of particular biographical interest or important stylistic signposts, and he approaches Walton from a more objective point of view than either Tierney or Lady Walton. Kennedy's engaging literary style and sound research make this biography accessible and useful to music specialists and general audiences alike. He is secure enough in his facts to take issue with Lady Walton on occasion. The text of the biography is so dense with quotations from a variety of Walton's correspondence and personal papers that the documents themselves tell much of the story. Kennedy's assessment of Walton is balanced and perceptive, pointing out that the self-critical professionalism that drove the composer to work hard at his craft also limited his output. The author addresses the years Walton lived with Susana on the Italian island of Ischia, the possible reasons for the long self-imposed exile, and the impact it had on his composition (Kennedy titles the penultimate chapter "The Haunted End"). In the end, the author, like others before him, regards Walton as an enigma, arguing that Walton's music ultimately is also an enigma "because it does not tell us the whole truth" about the composer. The same might be said for even the best of these three biographical studies reviewed here.

KATHLEEN E. ROBINSON

Weber, Carl Maria von 1786–1826

German composer, pianist, and conductor

Benedict, Julius, *Carl Maria von Weber,* London: Low, Marston, 1881; reprint, New York: AMS Press, 1980

Henderson, Donald G., and Alice H. Henderson, *Carl Maria von Weber: A Guide to Research,* New York: Garland, 1990

Jähns, Friedrich Wilhelm, *Carl Maria von Weber in seinen Werken: Chronologisch-thematisches Verzeichniss seiner sämmtlichen Compositionen,* Berlin: Lienau, 1871; reprint, 1967

Saunders, William, *Weber,* London: Dent, 1940; reprint, New York, Da Capo Press, 1970

Stebbins, Lucy Poate, and Richard Poate Stebbins, *Enchanted Wanderer: The Life of Carl Maria von Weber,* New York: Putnam, 1940

Tusa, Michael, *Euryanthe and Carl Maria von Weber's Dramaturgy of German Opera,* Oxford: Clarendon Press, and New York: Oxford University Press, 1991

Warrack, John, *Carl Maria von Weber,* London: Hamilton, and New York: Macmillan, 1968; 2nd edition, Cambridge: Cambridge University Press, 1976

Weber, Carl Maria von, *Writings on Music,* translated by Martin Cooper, edited by John Warrack, Cambridge: Cambridge University Press, 1981

Weber, Max Maria, Freiherr von, *Carl Maria von Weber: The Life of an Artist,* 2 vols., translated by J. Palgrave Simpson, London: Chapman and Hall, and Boston: Ditson, 1865; reprint, New York: Greenwood Press, 1969

Carl Maria von Weber is generally regarded as the most important German operatic composer in the generation between Mozart and Wagner and the seminal figure in the development of German romantic opera. Like many other 19th-century composers, Weber was also a prolific writer, and his criticism had wide influence during his lifetime. Equally important was his work as a conductor, especially the nine years he spent as the leader of the German opera in Dresden. Weber achieved his most spectacular success in 1821 with the premiere of his opera, *Der Freischütz.* In this work, Weber combined references to folk music with an innovative, highly dramatic musical style, featuring an expanded harmonic palette and a new interest in orchestral color.

Since the 19th century, most Weber scholarship has been written in German. Weber's colorful life, his many friendships with leaders of the romantic movement in Germany, and the difficult circumstances in which he often worked have made him an appealing biographical subject. Weber has also been of interest to music historians for the ways in which he prefigures certain elements of Wagner's operatic style. Although most of his works have passed out of the repertoire, Weber's efforts to create a "new national opera" retain great historical significance.

HENDERSON and HENDERSON is indispensable to the serious student of Weber's works. The Hendersons have compiled an annotated bibliography of the secondary literature concerning Weber, including books and articles in English, German, French, and other languages. The 883 entries in their book are arranged according to various subjects, including biographical studies, Weber's writings, and the major dramatic works.

Although it is more than a century old, JÄHNS remains an important reference work, which can be extremely helpful even to the reader with a limited knowledge of German. Jähns organizes Weber's works chronologically and includes brief excerpts from all the numbers in the arias. His notes describe the compositional genesis of each work as well as the subsequent cuts, additions, and revisions to which each work was subjected.

The most influential 19th-century work on Carl Maria von Weber is the biography of the composer written by his son, Max Maria von WEBER. A 19th-century English translation of this work was reprinted in 1969 and is still readily available. Max Maria's work is stylish and informative and includes many excerpts from his father's letter and diaries. Creating an "objective" account of his father's life was less important to Max Maria than portraying the composer as a hero of German art who was beleaguered by foreign musicians and the misguided aristocrats who patronized them.

BENEDICT's brief biography of Weber has also been an important source for later writers. Benedict first met Weber when the author was 17 and studied with the composer between 1821 and 1824. His account of Weber's life is less a biography than a description of Benedict's friendship with Weber and his family. Benedict's firsthand accounts of Weber's physical characteristics and way of life are entertaining and picturesque. A sense of a "real personality" emerges from Benedict's work, but later scholars have called some of his observations into question.

Like Benedict's work, the STEBBINS' biography of Weber is more concerned with the details of Weber's life than with a description of his musical style. Each of the chapters in their work has a poetic title (e.g., "Stranger in the Erl-King's Palace") and begins with a poem or short citation from an early German romantic writer. These citations underscore a central theme in the biography, namely, the connections between Weber and the German romantic literary movement. Despite its extensive footnotes and bibliography, the tone of the book is novelistic rather than academic.

SAUNDERS's biography of Weber also appeared in 1940 but is clearly directed at a different audience than the Stebbins' volume. The first eight chapters tell the story of Weber's life but are followed by three chapters that focus exclusively on Weber's musical compositions. It is in these last chapters that Saunders makes his most important contribution to Weber scholarship—they amount to an explication of Weber's musical and dramatic style. The headers at the top of every other page that briefly describe the particular subject that Saunders is addressing make this book especially useful for the reader. Saunders's style is clear and approachable, but his book is also scholarly in tone. He includes not only extensive quotations from Weber's letters and diaries but also musical examples to support his analytical arguments. Saunders's appendices—a calendar of

Weber's life, a catalog of his works, a "personalia" that briefly describes some important people connected with Weber's life, and a bibliography (compiled by Frederick Freedman)—are also helpful.

The most recent and authoritative English-language biography of Weber is that of WARRACK. Like Saunders's work, Warrack's biography is both a narrative of the composer's life and an analysis of his musical style. Warrack takes an interesting structural approach in his book, interweaving chapters on Weber's life with chapters on his music. This structure allows Warrack to highlight the fascinating connections between Weber's biography and his composition. In contrast to earlier biographies, Warrack pays particular attention to the social and cultural milieu in which Weber worked and describes in detail the organizational innovations and new rehearsal techniques that made Weber such a success as a conductor.

Warrack is also the editor of the only English-language collection of WEBER's own writings. This book contains a wide variety of Weber's prose works, including numerous reviews, many of the "musico-dramatic articles" that he published to introduce his own performances, and selections from Weber's hilarious unfinished novel *Ein Tonkunstlers Leben*. Warrack prefaces each selection with one or two paragraphs that provide important and useful background information.

TUSA's goal is not to present a biography of Weber but rather to describe his operatic style through a close analysis of his most ambitious work, *Euryanthe*. Unlike *Der Freischütz*, *Euryanthe* is a through-composed opera, and this composition, Tusa argues, best represents Weber's mature musical dramaturgy. In the first chapters of his book, Tusa provides an excellent account of the circumstances surrounding the premier of *Euryanthe*. He also describes the complicated compositional history of the opera, including the difficult negotiations between Weber and his librettist. Tusa's work is perhaps most significant for the way that it explores the connections between the rhetoric surrounding German opera (made manifest in the writings of Weber himself as well as those of other critics) and the music of *Euryanthe*. His work is clearly directed toward the scholarly community but should be of interest to any serious student of Weber.

STEPHEN MEYER

Webern, Anton 1883–1945

Austrian conductor and composer

Bailey, Kathryn, *The Life of Webern*, Cambridge: Cambridge University Press, 1998

———, *The Twelve-Note Music of Anton Webern: Old Forms in a New Language*, Cambridge: Cambridge University Press, 1991

Bailey, Kathryn, editor, *Webern Studies*, Cambridge: Cambridge University Press, 1996

Eimert, Herbert, and Karlheinz Stockhausen, editors, *Anton Webern*, translated by Leo Black and Eric Smith, Bryn Mawr, Pennsylvania: Presser, and London: Universal Edition, 1958

Hayes, Malcolm, *Anton von Webern*, London: Phaidon Press, 1995

Kolneder, Walter, *Anton Webern: An Introduction to His Works*, translated by Humphrey Searle, Berkeley: University of California Press, and London: Faber, 1968

Moldenhauer, Hans, *Anton von Webern Perspectives*, edited by Demar Irvine, Seattle: University of Washington Press, 1966

Moldenhauer, Hans, and Rosaleen Moldenhauer, *Anton von Webern: A Chronicle of His Life and Work*, London: Gollancz, 1978; New York: Knopf, 1979

Shreffler, Anne C., *Webern and the Lyric Impulse: Songs and Fragments on Poems of Georg Trakl*, Oxford: Clarendon Press, and New York: Oxford University Press, 1994

Webern, Anton, *Letters to Hildegard Jone and Josef Humplik*, edited by Josef Polnauer, translated by Cornelius Cardew, Bryn Mawr, Pennsylvania: Presser, 1967

———, *The Path to the New Music*, edited by Willi Reich, translated by Leo Black, Bryn Mawr, Pennsylvania: Presser, 1963

Wildgans, Friedrich, *Anton Webern*, translated by Edith Temple Roberts and Humphrey Searle, London: Calder and Boyars, 1966; New York: October House, 1967

The Viennese musicologist and composer Anton Webern is best remembered for his use of the 12-tone method of composition, developed by his mentor and colleague Arnold Schoenberg. English publications regarding Webern's life and works have appeared in several distinct phases. The 1955 issue of the contemporary music periodical *Die Reihe* was devoted entirely to Webern and translated into English soon after it first came out, and the articles therein are representative of the earliest phase of Webern scholarship, when the serialist composers of the postwar generation discovered and laid claim to his 12-tone music as the precursor of their own. In the 1960s, several books were published in which the authors reclaimed for Webern's music the traditional values he had himself espoused and began the work of constructing the composer's biography, relying on personal recollections and the limited biographical materials available at the time. Just one full-length study appeared in the next phase of Webern research: the Moldenhauers' comprehensive book based on the nearly exhaustive collection of biographical material the authors had acquired. This volume remains the touchstone of Webern scholarship, but several books published in the 1990s, after the Moldenhauers passed their archives on to publically accessible libraries (primarily the Paul Sacher Foundation in Basel, Switzerland, and the Library of

Congress, Washington, D.C.), have set straight numerous biographical and source manuscript details of the Moldenhauers' account. Recent authors have also sought a more balanced analytical view of Webern's compositional process and aesthetic goals than that found in earlier scholarship raising the question of what his music was—and might have become—if not solely or inevitably 12-tone.

EIMERT and STOCKHAUSEN's essays (originally in the 1955 issue of *Die Reihe*) give readers an idea of how the authors perceived Webern's music when they encountered it for the first time (it had been nearly obscured by the events of World War II). Eimert speaks of the lyrical geometry of the music, with the emphasis on geometry, and yet taken as a whole, his assessment is remarkably apropos of the current scholarly opinion of Webern's compositional aesthetic. The numerous analytical articles that appear in the journal, however, are typical of the mathematical approach to Webern's scores promoted by composers who sought the total organization of music. For the most part, these analyses have only historical value.

WILDGANS, a native of Vienna and acquaintance of Webern, wrote the composer's first full-length biography. Although this account is colored by the author's personal bias and is often factually incomplete or inaccurate, it is engaging for its contemporaneity. The biography also remains valuable for the nuggets of information about the composer's personal life that Wildgans gathered, for example, that Webern discussed new ideas about his compositions with his wife, even though she "lacked artistic and musical education," and that the composer "completely accepted her instincts in taste."

KOLNEDER is the first full-length study of Webern's music, an opus-by-opus descriptive guide, amplified by references to the composer's letters and other contemporary accounts. To counterbalance what he views as the overly cerebral approach of writers in the 1950s, Kolneder emphasizes Webern's links to traditional modes of composition and underscores the expressive, often spiritual character of his music. Despite his conservative leaning, Kolneder's reading of the music is perceptive and at times critical. For example, in discussing the Concerto, op. 24, he states that the listener "will perhaps not escape the impression, which increases with repeated hearings, that monomotivicism is very near to monotony, and that in this work Webern has not always escaped the danger altogether."

WEBERN (1963) had an opportunity to explicate his compositional ideal—"always the same, yet always different"—to a sympathetic, musically literate audience when he delivered his "Path to the New Music" lectures at a private home in 1932 and 1933. His lectures were taken down in shorthand and eventually published in book form (the German edition appeared in 1960), along with the notes of one of his composition students, Willi

Reich, and several of his letters to the same student. Webern's explanation of the 12-tone method of composition is helpful but cryptic and is best read against the background of the creative/scholarly discourse he joins here: Goethe, music theorists such as Heinrich Christoph Koch and A.B. Marx, and early 20th-century modern thinkers such as Adolf Loos and of course, Schoenberg, to identify but a few of the figures to whom Webern refers (largely without acknowledgment).

WEBERN's (1967) letters to his close friends the couple Hildegard Jone (poet) and Josef Humplik (sculptor), together with his letters to Reich published in Webern (1963), offer many revealing details about the composer's conception of his late-period music (basically, opp. 22–31). The overriding theme in these letters is that of unity, particularly between the seen and unseen, known and unknown aspects of art and nature. All of the vocal music from this period utilizes texts by Jone, and in his letters to the her, Webern also speaks of the relationship between words and music.

MOLDENHAUER gave public notice of his acquisition of the Webern estate when he organized the First International Webern Festival in Seattle, Washington, in 1962. Published as a result of this festival, the volume contains a preliminary catalog of Moldenhauer's archive, as well as articles by several scholars who had limited access to the archive at this time and presented their findings at the festival, along with their remarks concerning one or another aspect of Webern's published works. Paul A. Pisk, for example, discusses Webern's early orchestral music, paying special attention to his orchestral piece *Im Sommerwind* (1904), which the Philadelphia Orchestra premiered at the festival. Leland Smith tackles the provocative question of "Composition and Precomposition in the Music of Webern," referring to the composer's sketches to bolster Smith's observation that, in Webern's middle-period works, for instance the Five Canons, op. 16 (1923–24), "the precompositional decisions determined what the standards and process of composition would be. Any notes and rhythms could be used, so long as they made a positive contribution to each work's context," whereas in his later works, "more of the details tended to be controlled by precomposition than were left to free composition. . . . The order, location, and groupings of the notes, as well as the large phrase structure, are highly regulated." Two other noteworthy entries in this book, which by their uniqueness stand unchallenged by subsequent studies, are "Introduction: A Decade Later," Igor Stravinsky's interview with an unnamed faculty member at the University of Washington, in which Stravinsky ruminates on the reception of Webern's music, and Cesar Bresgen's reminiscences of "Webern's Last Months in Mittersill."

The breadth and accuracy of MOLDENHAUER and MOLDENHAUER, the magnum opus written by Hans with the help of his wife (he was nearly blind) after years of delving into the primary source material they had collected, are impressive. The book touches on a far-ranging variety of topics and quotes extensively from Webern's diaries, sketchbooks, and voluminous correspondence, as well as from the written reports and reminiscences of his contemporaries. Chapters are organized by either successive periods of Webern's life or corresponding groups of his compositions, with parenthetical dates after each chapter heading. A detailed index makes it fairly easy to use the book as a reference guide.

HAYES is one of two biographies of Webern published in the 1990s. The author writes in a journalistic style, without notes or extensive bibliography. Thus, although he acknowledges Moldenhauer as his primary source of information, in the few instances where this chronicle differs from Moldenhauer's, one is left to wonder where Hayes has come across his facts. Hayes, for example, reports correctly that Webern's youthful Wagnerian exercise *Siegfrieds Schwert* (1903) was an orchestral arrangement of a ballad written by Martin Plüddemann and not, as Moldenhauer had supposed, Webern's own composition. On the other hand, Hayes's storylike presentation is refreshing for those interested in a nontechnical narrative of the composer's life, and the abundance of photographs reproduced in the book, many of them striking Austrian landscapes taken by Hayes himself, allow readers to catch a glimpse of the mountains and countryside that Webern held so dear.

The second biography published in the 1990s, BAILEY (1998) is well documented and written in a scholarly style, a welcome counterpart to the Moldenhauers' volume. Bailey relies heavily on the composer's diaries and letters but intersperses her summary of their contents with pithy observations about Webern's character and critical comments about his relationship with colleagues, particularly Schoenberg. Bailey departs most significantly from the Moldenhauers' account when she reports on the circumstances of Webern's life during the time of the German takeover of Austria and the details of his death in Mittersill. Especially valuable is her careful analysis of the available evidence concerning the composer's interest in Nazi affairs.

BAILEY (1991) draws on material from Webern's sketchbooks to augment her formal analyses, which, although technical, pose little challenge to musically educated readers. The author's goal is to elucidate the traditional forms that provide the framework for Webern's 12-tone opuses: bipartite, tripartite, sonata, rondo, theme and variation, or some combination thereof. In the sketchbooks, Webern regularly identifies the row forms used throughout each composition, but his disposition of the rows does not always coincide with structural endings and beginnings defined by other musical parameters; thus, although the basic design of each piece in a sense analyzes itself, Bailey does make some critical judgments regarding the subtext or underlying process Webern had

in mind when composing the piece. She also offers some insightful discussion of the place that traditional modes of prolonging musical ideas—antecedent/consequent, development and recapitulation, variation—held in the 12-tone compositional processes of Webern and (with fewer examples given) Schoenberg.

The introduction to BAILEY (1996) gives a brief history of the composer's critical reception and an overview of the articles collected in the book. Bailey herself contributes a detailed examination of Webern's row charts, and Neil Boynton provides a useful update to the bibliography in the Moldenhauers' *Chronicle*. The majority of the articles here are not in such a practical vein, however; they deal in the main with Webern's early works, which until recently had been overshadowed by his mature, 12-tone music. Susanne Rode-Breyman, for example, discusses Webern's youthful settings of poetry by Ferdinand Avenarius. Allen Forte and Robert W. Wason analyze some of Webern's other early songs with an eye to his incipient use of octatonicism and pitch-class motives, respectively. (Along with Wintle's article, mentioned below, these last two are the most technical articles in the book. Readers need to be familiar, in particular, with Forte's set-class theory and George Perle's seminal theoretical study *Serial Composition and Atonality* [1963].) Anne Shreffler and Felix Meyer trace the history of Webern's revisions of one of the few of his works frequently performed in his lifetime, his Four Pieces for Violin and Piano, op. 7 (composed 1910, published 1922); the authors demonstrate how Webern's concern for the comprehensibility of the music led him to lend increasing importance to the clarity of pitch and formal design. Together, these essays on Webern's early compositions point toward two stimulating issues that Derrick Puffett and Christopher Wintle address in other articles: respectively, What can be said about the direction Webern's music might have taken, had he not linked himself up with Schoenberg? and What analytical significance can be drawn from Webern's lifelong penchant for lyrical composition?

Webern's innate lyricism is SHREFFLER's guiding concern in her study of the manuscript sources for the composer's 16 different settings of poetry by Georg Trakl (only seven of these settings stand complete). Webern occupied himself with Trakl's poetry during his so-called middle period, after he had turned his back on tonality but before he took up the 12-tone method. Shreffler skillfully analyzes the composer's sketching routine, going beyond a mere description of the sequence of compositional steps to surmise why and to what effect Webern revised the music as he did. Her conclusion is that, in setting Trakl's poems, Webern increased the complexity of his musical language, making it both more flexible—like the images in Trakl's poems, motives in the songs harbor multiple references—and less developmental/dramatic— the larger shape of the music typically cannot be described in goal-directed terms. Shreffler occasionally borrows terms from Forte's set-class theory, but on the whole, her examples are not too technical for a general musical readership. This excellent study substantially contributes to our understanding of Webern's compositional aesthetic.

DONNA L. LYNN

Weelkes, Thomas ca. 1575–1623

English composer

Brown, David, *Thomas Weelkes: A Biographical and Critical Study,* London: Faber, and New York: Praeger, 1969

Collins, Walter S., "The Reconstruction of the Evening Service for Seven Voices by Thomas Weelkes" in *Five Centuries of Choral Music: Essays in Honor of Howard Swan,* edited by Gordon Paine, Stuyvesant, New York: Pendragon Press, 1988

Kerman, Joseph, *The Elizabethan Madrigal: A Comparative Study,* New York: American Musicological Society, 1962

Le Huray, Peter, *Music and the Reformation in England, 1549–1660,* London: Jenkins, and New York: Oxford University Press, 1967

Long, Kenneth R., *Music of the English Church,* New York: St. Martin's Press, 1971; London: Hodder and Stoughton, 1972

Phillips, Peter, *English Sacred Music: 1549–1649,* Oxford: Gimell, 1991

Teo, Kian-Seng, *Chromaticism in the English Madrigal,* New York: Garland, 1989

As with much of the scholarship on 16th- and 17-century English music, the bulk of research on Thomas Weelkes's life, works, and social circle has appeared in articles published in professional musicological journals. Anyone with more than a passing interest in Weelkes will necessarily have to turn to such articles not only because they offer some of the most current information available, but also because they contain the most in-depth research.

Since Edmund Fellowes published his groundbreaking work in the first half of the 20th century, including *The English Madrigal Composers* (Oxford: Clarendon Press, 1921) and *English Cathedral Music from Edward VI to Edward VII* (London: Methuen, 1941), most scholars have discussed Weelkes in the context of the larger history of English music composed by William Byrd's contemporaries and immediate successors. Except for Walter S. Collins's important dissertation ("The Anthems of Thomas Weelkes," Ph.D. dissertation, University of Michigan, 1960), BROWN is the most exhaustive study of Weelkes's life and works. It is the only source reviewed here to treat all aspects of the composer's life and music comprehensively, and nearly every subsequent discussion of Weelkes cites biographical information taken directly

from this volume, demonstrating its importance and continued value. In addition to the unmatched thoroughness with which the author discusses Weelkes's sacred and secular works—there are separate chapters about each genre—Brown is also the only book to cover Weelkes's instrumental works, to address the thorny question of misattributed works, and to offer an assessment of the composer in light of his output and times. Throughout the text, Brown offers a balanced view of the composer, who was a "major creative mind and one of the most progressive musicians of his time," but who was unfortunately unable to fulfill such high expectations. For anyone wishing to gain more than a summary view of Weelkes as man and composer, Brown is indispensable.

The remaining sources discussed here focus solely on either Weelkes's sacred or secular music. LE HURAY was the first scholar after Fellowes to look carefully at Weelkes's sacred repertoire, and his work remains a useful resource despite its age. Chapter 9, "Thomas Tomkins and his Contemporaries," is necessarily broad, given that it is not a monograph on Weelkes, but Le Huray mentions the salient moments in the most familiar anthems by the composer and includes helpful musical excerpts to illustrate his points. The author emphasizes such important characteristics of Weelkes's work as his technique of recycling material from the beginning of an anthem at later points in the piece, and his tendency to borrow material from one work in another. Unfortunately, this analysis of specific stylistic characteristics does not carry over to Le Huray's discussion of Weelkes's Anglican service music, which is mostly descriptive, covering superficial issues, such as the number of voices used in each service and the status of surviving manuscript parts. (This information has been superceded by Brown.) Le Huray does not attempt to draw any broad conclusions about Weelkes's works or style.

LONG's study of Weelkes is heavily indebted to Fellowes, Collins, and Le Huray (the author admits as much in the preface), and the reader will be hard pressed to find information that is truly new. However, Long's strength resides in his ability to synthesize clearly the characteristics of Weelkes's compositional style. While Le Huray selects important local highlights from representative works, Long offers a more global view, making general observations about Weelkes's sacred style and placing the anthems in the context of works by contemporary English composers. Long's observations are by no means comprehensive, but his analysis will be most useful to inexperienced students who would benefit from a solid understanding of Weelkes's compositional tendencies before tackling a more direct, detailed study of individual anthems. Like Le Huray, Long is not as successful in his coverage of the service music as he is in his analysis of the anthems.

COLLINS's essay on Weelkes's Ninth Service is the only source reviewed here to focus on a single Weelkes composition. Following Brown by almost 20 years, this essay includes important information about published reconstructions of the work—principally that edited by David Wulstan in 1979—that readers will not find elsewhere. Collins begins by offering an overview of Weelkes's service music that is more detailed than any other account except for Brown, including a very helpful general discussion of Weelkes's compositional style as manifested in his services. Collins then investigates nearly every aspect of this service, identifying extant and lost manuscripts and evaluating the need for reconstruction as well as the elements one should consider if undertaking such a project. In the process, the author takes Wulstan to task for his 1979 edition, charging that the editor ignored important manuscript evidence that might significantly change the reconstruction. Collins's protestations are thought-provoking, and scholars or performers interested in this service will want to consider his ideas.

PHILLIPS, the most recently published source mentioned here, divides his discussion of Weelkes's music between two chapters: chapter 3 considers the anthems, along with those of Orlando Gibbons, and chapter 7 explores the service music. The author offers a sentence or two about each extant anthem, but only a few of the compositions receive a more detailed treatment; therefore, one must wade through Phillips's entire discussion to attain a thorough view of Weelkes's style. As he attempts to include every composition in his study, Phillips is forced to choose a single detail of each work for analysis, and his selections result in many curious omissions. His discussion of the service music is only slightly more successful than Le Huray's or Long's. Some specialized musical terms, such as tonic, dominant, tonality, and chordal inversions are used throughout the study, even though in the current world of musicological discourse, such anachronistic language is considered inappropriate for discussions of 16th- and early 17th-century music. Many musical examples are included within the text, but, as with most of the sources mentioned here, a full understanding of Phillips's discussion can only be gained by having a complete score of each work in hand; a fairly broad knowledge of other repertoire of the period is also essential. Readers will find numerous page reference errors in the table of contents; the indices seem to be much more accurate, however.

KERMAN is the first scholar after Fellowes to examine Weelkes's place in the development of the English madrigal and to identify important connections between the composer's style and the Italian madrigal. In this respect, Kerman's work is a pioneering text, which remains one of the few studies on the subject. The author's principal discussion of Weelkes (chapter 6) begins with several general observations about the composer's secular style, followed by a detailed examination of the vocal works found in each of his four published collections (1597, 1598, 1600, and 1608), which initially secured Weelkes's place as one of the preeminent composers of his day. The tone of Kerman's prose is more academic than that found in the other sources discussed here. There are hardly any musical examples to aid the reader, so separate scores at hand are a necessity. While this chapter contains a wealth of information, Kerman fails to connect clearly specific aspects of Weelkes's madrigal style with specific examples from Italianate models. Therefore, if readers hope to gain a deeper understanding of the composer's madrigal style, they will need to read the entire monograph.

TEO's published work stems directly from his doctoral dissertation. Unlike Kerman, he includes numerous musical examples, not only from Weelkes's secular works, but also from compositions by Dowland, Monteverdi, Marenzio, and other contemporary Italian madrigalists that, Teo argues, influenced Weelkes's secular voice. This evidence aids the reader immensely, as the prose is difficult to read, but readers will still need a veritable library of contemporary 16th- and 17th-century scores to be able to follow Teo's entire argument. Although chapter 6 is devoted solely to Weelkes's secular works, students will have to look elsewhere to understand the specialized terminology that is the basis for Teo's argument. The placement of many of the musical examples is awkward, for the music on the page is frequently unrelated to the discussion printed around it. (Each musical excerpt is identified by an example number, but the text does not refer to such identifiers.) Teo's ideas seem interesting, but they are not developed sufficiently. Too often, observations are left without elaboration, leaving the reader uncertain of their global importance, and conclusions are not drawn clearly enough, especially for the nonspecialist. Thus, only the most well-versed reader of the madrigal repertoire and scholarship will be in a position to benefit significantly from Teo's study.

DONNA M. DI GRAZIA

Weill, Kurt 1900–1950

German-born composer

Drew, David, *Kurt Weill: A Handbook,* London: Faber, and Berkeley: University of California Press, 1987

Farneth, David, editor, *Lenya, the Legend: A Pictorial Autobiography,* Woodstock, New York: Overlook Press, 1998

Farneth, David, et al., editors, *A Guide to the Weill-Lenya Research Center,* New York: Kurt Weill Foundation for Music, 1995

Gilliam, Bryan Randolph, editor, *Music and Performance during the Weimar Republic,* Cambridge: Cambridge University Press, 1994

Hinton, Stephen, editor, *Kurt Weill: The Threepenny Opera,* Cambridge: Cambridge University Press, 1990

Kowalke, Kim H., *Kurt Weill in Europe,* Ann Arbor, Michigan: UMI Research Press, 1979

Kowalke, Kim H., editor, *A New Orpheus: Essays on Kurt Weill,* New Haven, Connecticut: Yale University Press, 1986

Kowalke, Kim H., and Horst Edler, editors, *A Stranger Here Myself: Kurt Weill-Studien,* Hildesheim: Olms, 1993

Mercado, Mario R., editor, *Kurt Weill: A Guide to His Works,* New York: Kurt Weill Foundation for Music, and Valley Forge, Pennsylvania: European American Music, 1989; 2d edition, 1994

Nesnow, Adrienne, editor, *The Papers of Kurt Weill and Lotte Lenya: Yale University Music Library, Archival Collection MSS 30,* New Haven, Connecticut: Yale University Music Library, 1984

Sanders, Ronald, *The Days Grow Short: The Life and Music of Kurt Weill,* New York: Holt, Rinehart, and London: Weidenfeld and Nicolson, 1980

Schebera, Jürgen, *Kurt Weill: An Illustrated Life,* translated by Caroline Murphy, New Haven, Connecticut: Yale University Press, 1995

Weill, Kurt, *Speak Low (When You Speak Love): The Letters of Kurt Weill and Lotte Lenya,* edited and translated by Lys Symonette and Kim H. Kowalke, Berkeley: University of California Press, 1996

Although his early instrumental and vocal works evince post-Romantic influences, Kurt Weill established himself as the Weimar Republic's leading theater composer after the 1926 premier of *Der Protagonist,* a one-act opera with libretto by Georg Kaiser. Apparent in the *Zeitopern* (topical operas) that followed were the hallmarks of Weill's mature style: dance idioms associated with jazz, pervasive tonal ambiguity, a blurred duality of high and low idioms, and irony. His short-lived collaboration with Bertolt Brecht produced the memorable full-length opera *Aufstieg und Fall der Studt Mahogonny,* in addition to *Die Dreigroschenoper* (1928). The latter achieved international success with more than 10,000 performances within five years of its premier. Uncomfortable with music's limited role in Brecht's dogmatic dramaturgy, Weill sought collaborations with Caspar Neher (the opera *Die Bürgschaft,* 1931) and Kaiser (the play-with-music *Die Silbersee,* 1932). Weill was a Jew, and after the Nazis branded him a "culture-Bolshevik" and orchestrated propaganda campaigns against his music, he fled Germany in 1933.

After a brief period in France, Weill and his recently divorced wife (they would later remarry each other), Lotte Lenya (1898–1981), emigrated to New York in 1935. Buoyed by his reception and believing that commercial theater in the United States offered many artistic possibilities, Weill quickly established himself as a Broadway composer. Weill's eight completed works for Broadway eschewed the formulaic offerings of Rodgers and Hammerstein and are sui generis, ranging from a spoken play about psychoanalysis in which music articulates the subconscious (*Lady in the Dark,* 1941), to an American opera in which musical diversity characterizes the tenants of a New York brownstone apartment building (*Street Scene,* 1946), to a concept musical in which vaudeville acts interrupt and comment on the chronicle of a marriage (*Love Life,* 1948).

The 1950s rediscovery of Weill's German works was sparked by the off-Broadway production of *The Threepenny Opera* (English translation by Marc Blitzstein). Critics, however, promulgated the "Two Weills": the European talent and the American imposter who squandered his European musical birthright for adoptive status in Shubert Alley. Since the late 1970s, scholars have tended either to regard Weill's bifurcated career and oeuvre as irreparable, reducing the composer to one of music's great might-have-beens; or they have sought to deconstruct the Two Weills as a remnant of high modernism, treating the American works as harbingers of postmodern music-theater with Weill as the prototypical crossover composer. Although the field of Weill studies is burgeoning, it still lacks an authoritative scholarly biography and a critical survey of the entire oeuvre.

First published in German, SCHEBERA's revised and expanded biography comprises the most up-to-date and accurate account of Weill's career. Intended to "help convey a picture of the entire Kurt Weill," the book generally escapes the ideological baggage of the Two Weills. Feasts for the eye, most pages are embellished with photographs and facsimiles—many published here for the first time. The book suffers from a lack of in-depth discussion of the music (save a few manuscript facsimiles, no musical examples are included), and, although Weill's 30-year professional career divides evenly between Europe and the United States, two-thirds of the book's narrative concerns the European period.

SANDERS was hampered in researching his trade biography by the paucity of available primary sources in the mid-1970s (Lenya granted him only a single interview). Basing his narrative almost entirely on secondary sources and oral histories related by Weill's collaborators, associates, and sister-in-law, Sanders's contribution contains some errors of fact and omission and perpetuates popular myths about the composer. Nevertheless, the author's sincere love of the subject shines through in an engagingly written and detailed study of Weill's life and works. This book is far more accurate and less eurocentric than Ronald Taylor's more recent but disappointing biography, *Kurt Weill: Composer in a Divided World* (1991), which should have benefited from complete access to archival holdings.

FARNETH's pictorial autobiography both celebrates the living legend Lotte Lenya became and debunks several of the yarns that she herself concocted. Born Karoline

Blamauer, Lenya, in addition to being Weill's muse and twice his wife, became the indefatigable promoter and protector of his musical legacy, and she was the definitive interpreter of his work. Lavishly accompanied by more than 300 photographs (many in color), the first-person narrative has been culled from Lenya's own autobiographical notes, interviews, and correspondence. The coffee-table book format belies the book's meticulously documented chronology and insights into one of the 20th century's most beguiling personalities.

Symonette and Kowalke have compiled, translated, and annotated the complete WEILL-Lenya correspondence in an elegantly produced and expertly edited volume. The enormous task included decoding the couple's private German expressions that combined Saxonian dialect with Swiss diminutives. The 410 letters, postcards, and telegrams provide psychological insights into the tumultuous and sexually open relationship of two individuals who needed each another on an artistic level. In the editors' assessment, "she gave voice to his music" while "he was giving music to her voice." The reader is afforded a backstage view of both Weimar Germany in the 1920s and Broadway in the period between the Depression and the Cold War. This volume is essential and downright gossipy reading for both the serious student of Weill and the general reader.

Taking David Drew's 1975 suggestion that new approaches to Weill should "start with strictly musical problems and remain close to them," KOWALKE (1979) offers the first book-length study in English devoted to Weill's European works. Originally a doctoral dissertation, this work is divided into three parts: a chronicle of the composer's career, a discussion of his music criticism, and technical analyses of the music. Although the first part has now been superseded by Schebera, the second—including translations of 27 of Weill's more substantial German essays—remains a valuable introduction to the composer's aesthetics. The third part employs a variety of analytical approaches, traces the development of Weill's musical language, and addresses the specialist. The ancillary catalog of Weill's compositions has been superseded by both Drew and Mario Mercado.

By exploring Weill's contribution to *The Threepenny Opera*, HINTON's handbook balances German literature that credits Brecht as primary collaborator. The first of the monograph's three sections, however, is problematic: Brecht's unpublished narration for an unrealized concert version substitutes for a much-needed and sorely missed plot summary. Hinton's two essays on the work's complicated sources and genesis and far-flung performance history, together with Kowalke's detailed chronicle of *Threepenny* in the United States, comprise the second section. The final section reprints important criticism in eight chapters, including essays by Theodor Adorno, Ernst Bloch, and Walter Benjamin translated here into English. Drew's analysis of the score's long-range thematic and motivic connections, Abbott's reconstruction of the Dreigroschen sound, and Hinton's deconstruction of the Marxist critique that "*The Threepenny Opera* owed its success to a misunderstanding" comprise the handbook's most thought-provoking contributions.

The First International Kurt Weill Conference, held at Yale University in 1983, celebrated the opening of two archives dedicated to preserving Weill and Lenya's legacies and spawned the 17 essays contained in KOWALKE (1986). This work begins with a concise history of Weill scholarship and reception and provides helpful synopses of the specialized essays he edited. With only three offerings devoted to Weill in the United States, the collection is heavily weighted toward understanding the aesthetic bases and cultural contexts of Weill's German theater works. For example, Michael Morley seeks to pin down the elusive concept of *Gestus* in parallel settings of a Brecht poem by Eisler and Weill; Hinton plumbs the origin, meaning, and application of the terms *neue Sachlichkeit,* surrealism, and *Gebrauchsmusik;* and John Fuegi bares Brecht's sordid business dealings with Weill. Although some of the essays do not reach the heights to which they aspire, this book remains an important collection.

With its bilingual title and 14 essays evenly divided between German and English, KOWALKE and EDLER's collection goes beyond acknowledging the "forbidding metaphorical gulf that has severed posthumous Weill reception and scholarship" by tackling head-on the Two Weills. Brought together for the 1990 Symposium "Kurt Weill and the Lost Fatherland" (Duisburg, Germany), an international group of scholars addresses with varying methodologies Weill's contentious reception history; student years and lesser-known German works; and first Broadway success, American songs, and activities for the war effort. The two-language format should not intimidate single-language readers: the editors' preface is fully translated; abstracts follow each essay in both languages; and Farneth annotates in English his 167-item Weill bibliography, which spans the decade of the 1980s.

GILLIAM documents the search for a modernist musical aesthetic during the Weimar Republic. The four essays that concern Weill are uniformly excellent and groundbreaking. Gilliam examines how Weill assimilated cinematic techniques or film footage for *Der Protagonist, Royal Palace,* and *Mahagonny Songspiel.* Hinton's study of *Lehrstück* (teaching piece) connects the term's etymology in Christian catechisms and Germany's aesthetic trends with Weill and Brecht's example in this new genre: *Der Jasager.* Revealing that what is assumed to be Brechtian performance practice in Brecht's and Weill's collaborations postdates these works, Kowalke traces the elements of epic dramaturgy and Brecht's transmutable theories in their collaborations. J. Bradford Robinson cogently demonstrates that the media created Germany's Jazz Age, that African-American improvised jazz was virtually unknown in Germany, and that white-American dance music and published jazz manuals informed Weimar composers' music, including Weill's.

DREW's handbook consists of an extended introduction detailing the author's intimate involvement with Weill's music and estate; a chronology of Weill's life; an annotated catalog of works; an outline of unrealized projects; a discussion of Weill and Lenya's Brook House library; and a résumé of lost works. Although resembling at its core a thematic catalog, albeit without musical incipits, the handbook does not aspire to be a neutral musicological document: the specter of the Two Weills hovers over the proceedings. Of inestimable practical assistance to the researcher is the catalog, which has twin purposes: "to list Weill's known works and their constituent elements" and "to locate, list, and describe the extant holographs." As the first and only comprehensive guide to Weill's oeuvre, the handbook is invaluable.

MERCADO's brief guide shares some of the same goals as Drew's lengthy handbook, but the former is intended for performers, conductors, and producers. It aims to provide for each of Weill's works "concise information regarding published editions and performance materials, as well as specifications of cast, instrumentation, and duration." Helpful are the inclusion of voice types required for casting, authorized translations, and tools for negotiating the dense thicket of Weill's publishers. Ancillary materials include a biographical sketch and chronology by Farneth and an essay by Kowalke titled "Hin und Zurück: Kurt Weill Today," which may be the best (and shortest) introduction to the composer's disputed legacy.

Shortly before her death in 1981, Lenya deposited her and Weill's papers at Yale University. Once cataloged, the musical manuscripts, correspondence, photographs, programs, personal documents, scripts, interviews, writings, financial items, and clippings filled 107 boxes and took up nearly 50 linear feet on the shelves of Beinecke Rare Book Library. NESNOW's typescript register, made possible by a National Endowment of the Humanities grant, catalogs the Weill/Lenya Archive by box and folder numbers, in addition to indexing the frame numbers of Weill's musical manuscripts that were microfilmed. Unfortunately, Nesnow's register is not compatible with Drew's handbook because of differing terminology, standards of measurement, and criteria for cataloging. The collection is accessible to researchers Monday through Friday; appointments should be made in advance.

Opened in 1983, the Weill-Lenya Research Center in New York City offers "researchers access to a comprehensive collection of materials that crosses the relevant geographic, political, cultural, and aesthetic divisions so that a more complete understanding of the work of Kurt Weill and Lotte Lenya can emerge." A combination library, manuscript repository, and media center, the Research Center attempts "to acquire original doc-

uments as well as reproductions of materials that are held in repositories or private collections." FARNETH et al. includes an overview of the collection and its arrangement, guidelines for researchers, and descriptions of the Research Center's holdings. The multifarious programs of the Kurt Weill Foundation for Music are also surveyed: the Kurt Weill Edition, copyright administration, grants, the Kurt Weill Prize, and the free Kurt Weill Newsletter.

BRUCE D. MCCLUNG

Wert, Giaches de 1535–1596

Dutch-born composer

Einstein, Alfred, *The Italian Madrigal*, 3 vols., translated by Alexander H. Krappe, et al., Princeton, New Jersey: Princeton University Press, 1949
MacClintock, Carol, *Giaches de Wert, 1535–1596: Life and Works*, N.p.: American Institute of Musicology, 1966
Newcomb, Anthony, *The Madrigal at Ferrara: 1579–1597*, 2 vols., Princeton, New Jersey: Princeton University Press, 1978
Roche, Jerome, *The Madrigal*, London: Hutchinson, and New York: Scribner, 1972; 2nd edition, Oxford: Oxford University Press, 1990
Tomlinson, Gary, *Monteverdi and the End of the Renaissance*, Berkeley: University of California Press, and Oxford: Clarendon Press, 1987

Giaches de Wert was among the last of the Franco-Flemish composers to make Italy his home and the madrigal his genre. He was deeply dedicated to the search for a delicate balance between poetry and music, and between Italian expression and Franco-Flemish construction, and his search resulted in a number of sensitive and elegant solutions to these problems. A representative of the *seconda prattica*, he composed motets and madrigals, which were inspired by his teacher, Cipriano de Rore's emphasis on the careful consideration of text and music. Wert came from the Netherlands, and by 1565 he was named *maestro di cappella* for the ducal chapel of Santa Barbara by the Gonzaga family in Mantua. The proximity of the Mantuan court to Ferrara and Venice, centers in which one could absorb all of the current fashions guiding the madrigal, was a real advantage to the composer. Although he composed a number of sacred works for the chapel, the madrigals reveal his most important contributions to the style of Italian music of the late Renaissance.

The only complete English-language study of Wert's music is by MacCLINTOCK, who has also prepared editions of Wert's works. The author traces Wert's development from his first book of madrigals, published in 1558, through his 11th and final book from 1595, and she credits many of the innovations found in the composer's madrigals to his association with the leading poets of his generation, Tasso and Guarini. Their epic and pastoral poems displaced Petrarch as the primary examples of Italian poetry discussed by the leading intellectual academies of the era, and Wert was inspired by their works to expand the expressive and dramatic possibilities of the madrigal.

Wert's corpus of madrigals provides historical insights into the movement from the madrigal genre exemplified by Rore, which exhibits a delicate bond between text and music, to the early baroque genres of opera and monody, which are characterized by their concern for drama. Studies of Wert's music, however, are overshadowed by those of Monteverdi, who, greatly influenced by Wert, took the madrigal into the baroque era and provided the paradigmatic examples of the new genres of monody and opera. Some analyses of Monteverdi, such as the work of TOMLINSON, include references to Wert's influence. Word painting, melodies composed of wide leaps, and the effective use of a homophonic or *parlando* style are trademarks of Wert's style, and Tomlinson credits these devices as the foundation for Monteverdi's early operatic language.

Extensive discussions of Wert's madrigals can also be found in general histories of the Italian madrigal, such as the monumental study of the genre by EINSTEIN. The author cites Wert's first book of four-part madrigals (1561) as "declamatory melodies in madrigal form, cantatas before the cantatas," supporting the general assessment that Wert was a leader in the movement toward a more dramatic style for the madrigal. Discussions of the composer's works are scattered throughout this three-volume study, which includes full scores for four of Wert's madrigals.

In a concise discussion of Wert's compositional career, ROCHE provides a clear outline of two distinct periods. In the first period, Wert is seen as a successor to Adrian Willaert and Rore, and in the second, he is located among the generation of experimental madrigalists of the late Renaissance, dividing his attention between virtuosic and dramatic possibilities for the genre.

In his regional study of the madrigal, NEWCOMB places Wert within the sphere of his colleagues and competitors in Ferrara and asserts that the composer was in direct contact with Tasso and Guarini. The author presents an extensive comparison of the Mantuan style of Wert to that of Luzzasco Luzzaschi of Ferrara, concluding that Wert was enthusiastic for the newer poetic styles, but he remained heavily under the influence of the older masters Willaert and Rore, always keenly aware of the complex relationship between the poetry he chose and the musical form and syntax ideally required to set those texts. Luzzaschi, like most of the Ferrarese, was excited by the virtuosity of the famous *concerto delle donne*, a group of accomplished women singers for whom many composers, including Wert, wrote madrigals in a new melismatic and soloistic manner. But Luzzaschi, like Wert, was also

interested in the dramatic potential of the madrigal, and Wert derived a dramatic mode of declamation new to the madrigal from Luzzaschi's influence. The *parlando* style found in many of Wert's madrigals would be seen in the next generation within the realm of opera and monody.

SILVIA HERZOG

Wieck, Clara *see* Schumann, Clara

Willaert, Adrian ca. 1490–1562

Belgian?-born composer

Bernstein, Lawrence F., editor, *La Couronne et fleur des chansons a troys,* New York: Broude Trust, 1984

Brown, Howard Mayer, "Words and Music: Willaert, the Chanson, and the Madrigal about 1540," in *Florence and Venice, Comparisons and Relations: Acts of Two Conferences at Villa I Tatti in 1976–77,* 2 vols., edited by Sergio Bertelli et al., Florence: La nuova Italia, 1979–80

Einstein, Alfred, *The Italian Madrigal,* 3 vols., translated by Alexander H. Krappe et al., Princeton, New Jersey: Princeton University Press, 1949

Feldman, Martha, *City Culture and the Madrigal at Venice,* Berkeley: University of California Press, 1995

Zarlino, Gioseffo, *The Art of Counterpoint; Part Three of Le Istitutioni harmoniche, 1558,* translated by Guy A. Marco and Claude V. Palisca, New Haven, Connecticut: Yale University Press, 1968

Adrian Willaert was one of the greatest composers of the mid–16th century. Born in Flanders, educated in Paris, and employed in Italy for most of his long life, he was a truly international composer. He worked in virtually every major genre of the Renaissance era, writing motets, polyphonic Masses and vespers music, Italian madrigals and *canzone villanesche*, French chansons, and instrumental ricercars. His music is notable for its contrapuntal virtuosity, elegance, and restraint, and for its sensitive treatment of Italian, French, and Latin texts.

From 1527 until his death in 1562, Willaert occupied the powerful post of *maestro di cappella* at St. Mark's in Venice. In addition to fulfilling his compositional and administrative responsibilities, he mentored a large group of younger composers (including Nicola Vicentino, Andrea Gabrieli, Costanzo Porta, Girolamo Parabosco, and Gioseffo Zarlino, among others), many of whom became influential composers in their own right. It was those students, and Zarlino in particular, who transmitted Willaert's teachings to future generations of musicians.

ZARLINO invokes Willaert's teachings (in combination with long-standing precepts of music theory and pedagogy) in a four-volume treatise on contemporary musical theory and practice (1558). Part 3 of the treatise, which deals with practical counterpoint, has been of greatest interest to modern readers because it addresses a broad range of topics and provides general advice about polyphonic composition as well as more detailed instructions about specialized contrapuntal devices such as canon, fugue and imitation, and cantus firmus paraphrase. Throughout the volume, Zarlino invokes the teachings and compositions of Willaert when illustrating (and justifying) his (Zarlino's) sometimes controversial point of view. The historical significance of Zarlino's treatise can hardly be overestimated; its precepts were taken up and reworked again and again in later treatises. Such works preserved Willaert's teachings even as his music soon fell out of favor. In fact, by the mid-17th century most of his compositions were virtually unknown, to be revived only in the 20th century by music historians and early music performers.

Until part 3 of Zarlino's treatise was translated in 1968, the major English-language source for information about Willaert was EINSTEIN's classic study. Still highly regarded today for its comprehensive and literate coverage of the Italian madrigal from the 16th century, Einstein remains an excellent starting point for learning more about Willaert. Not only does Einstein examine Willaert's life and Italian compositions (lighter genres as well as madrigals), he also sets the madrigals in a broad historical context by considering the style and structure of madrigal poetry, contemporaneous aesthetic precepts and conceptions of text setting, and Willaert's relationships with patrons and other composers.

Since 1950 a remarkable amount of exciting research on Willaert has been conducted. Most of it, however, has appeared in scholarly articles; to date, there is only one full-length book on the composer, a Dutch monograph by Ignace Bossuyt titled *Adriaan Willaert (ca. 1490–1562): Leven en werk, stijl en genres* (1985). Most of the articles are rather specialized—presenting new facts about Willaert's life, examining the provenance of sources containing his music, or investigating his relationships with individual publishers or patrons. An unusually large body of research has grown up around *Musica nova* (1558), Willaert's most famous publication and one for which many fascinating documents have been uncovered. (Transcriptions of these documents and references to research about them can be found in Richard J. Agee and Jessie Ann Owens, "La stampa della *Musica nova* di Willaert," *Rivista italiana di musicologia* 24 [1989].)

Recent studies of Willaert's music, by contrast, are comparatively rare. One insightful appraisal is BROWN, which contrasts the contrapuntal style and text setting of an early chanson with that of an Italian madrigal from *Musica nova*. The author concludes that Willaert (and the city of Venice) deserves more credit than is usually given for having contributed significantly to the development of the *seconda prattica,* a controversial new style usually associated with Monteverdi and the decades around 1600.

Analyses of Willaert's chansons are found in the historical commentary for BERNSTEIN's edition of *La Couronne et fleur des chansons a troys.* The author's methodological approach is to use evidence from musical sources, compositional modeling, literary trends, and major historical events to corroborate (or to discredit) his own personal observations about musical style. Taking as his sample the 23 chansons that appear in *La Couronne et fleur,* Bernstein delimits three stylistic groups and associates each one with a specific era in Willaert's life: the chansons composed during Willaert's apprenticeship in France (before 1516), which emulate the three-part arrangements so popular in Paris at the time; pieces dating from 1516 to 1528, which vary in style but frequently display Italianate musical characteristics; and a third group written in Italy between 1528 and 1536, which have connections with Renée de France and the d'Este court in Ferrara.

In many ways FELDMAN's treatment of Willaert takes up where Brown leaves off. Adopting a broadly ethnographic approach, Feldman seeks to situate Willaert's madrigals within the culture of mid-16th-century Venice. Her interdisciplinary work addresses a broad range of subjects, in the process providing a great deal of valuable information about Willaert and his madrigals, some of which is new and nearly all of which is newly interpreted. Feldman examines the contents and chronology of Willaert's madrigal publications, his interactions with individual Venetian patrons and academies, and her relationships with students and other protégés, and she presents many detailed (at times technical) analyses of individual madrigals, their poetic texts, and the relationship of the music and text. In addition, she considers at length the historical context, musical style, and historical significance of the madrigals in *Musica nova.*

MICHELE FROMSON

Wolf, Hugo 1860–1903

Austrian composer

Cook, Peter, *Hugo Wolf's Corregidor: A Study of the Opera and Its Origins,* London: Cook, 1976

Newman, Ernest, *Hugo Wolf,* London: Methuen, 1907; New York: Dover, 1966

Ossenkop, David, *Hugo Wolf: A Guide to Research,* New York: Garland, 1988

Pleasants, Henry, editor, *The Music Criticism of Hugo Wolf,* New York: Holmes and Meier, 1978

Sams, Eric, "Hugo Wolf," in *The New Grove Late Romantic Masters,* edited by Deryck Cooke et al., London: Macmillan, and New York: Norton, 1985

————, *The Songs of Hugo Wolf,* London: Methuen, 1961; 2nd edition, London: Eulenburg, 1983

Stein, Deborah J., *Hugo Wolf's Lieder and Extensions of Tonality,* Ann Arbor, Michigan: UMI Research Press, 1985

Walker, Frank, *Hugo Wolf: A Biography,* London: Dent, 1951; New York: Knopf, 1952; 2nd edition, 1968

Wolf, Hugo, *Letters to Melanie Köchert,* edited by Franz Grasberger, translated by Louise McClelland Urban, New York: Schirmer Books, 1991

Youens, Susan, *Hugo Wolf: The Vocal Music,* Princeton, New Jersey: Princeton University Press, 1992

Hugo Wolf enjoyed only limited public and professional recognition during his tragically brief lifetime. However, with each passing decade since the composer's death in 1903, Wolf's stature as a composer has grown. Long considered a "minor figure" because he excelled at writing songs rather than symphonies or operas, and often misunderstood because of his intense, adventurously chromatic musical language, the once-lowly lieder composer now ranks as a full-fledged "Late Romantic Master" alongside Brahms, Bruckner, and Dvořák. Yet, as the 20th century drew to a close, the dearth of English-language literature on Wolf persisted; the ten books described here represent not only the best but also the bulk of what is presently available. Although these books provide a solid foundation for students and professors alike, this topic remains ripe for further endeavor.

NEWMAN, the earliest English monograph on Wolf, continues to be remarkably useful almost a century after it first appeared. Published four years after Wolf's death, the author had limited access to his subject's documentary legacy, a lack that has inevitably undermined the factual reliability of his chronicle. Nevertheless, as long as the reader remembers to verify the particulars, Newman's evaluation of the evidence available to him is admirably well rounded, covering the whole of Wolf's life and all his compositions. The author's discussion of the songs and his chapter detailing Wolf's career as a music critic are especially cogent, insightful introductions to these aspects of Wolf's creativity.

In his thorough and thoughtful biography, WALKER draws the reader completely into the drama of Wolf's life, enriching the tale with copious excerpts from Wolf's diaries and correspondence. The book ranks as a documentary treasure, as many of the sources that Walker consulted were destroyed either during World War II or at the behest of Wolf's surviving family and friends. Chief among the author's discoveries is the revelation of Wolf's long-standing affair with Melanie Köchert, an account that was expunged from the 1951 edition but thankfully restored to the 1968 and later editions. Although Walker admittedly focuses on biographical matters, his discussions of Wolf's music reflect the same high level of discernment and mastery. As impressive today as when it first appeared, Walker's accomplishment has yet to be surpassed by subsequent scholarship.

For the reader who desires a quick biographical and musical survey, SAMS (1985) is both commendable and reliable. Despite the inevitable overlap between this book and his earlier book on Wolf's songs (see below), Sams also incorporates new findings about the composer's syphilitic infection and manic-depressive illness into his penetrating portrait. The connections the author draws between Wolf's maladies and his famously erratic creativity flesh out a suspicion merely hinted at in earlier histories of Wolf's life.

Unfortunately, the zeal that produced three separate English-language Wolf biographies has not been matched by a corresponding enthusiasm to publish translations of primary source material. To date, no complete edition of Wolf's correspondence exists, and of the correspondence that has been published in German, only Grasberger's edition of WOLF's letters to Melanie Köchert has been translated into English. Fortunately, these letters are the most revealing of all the correspondence, offering unparalleled glimpses into the composer's character and personality. PLEASANTS acquaints the English-speaking reader with Wolf in yet another guise: as the opinionated music critic of the *Wiener Salonblatt* from 1884 to 1887. These entertainingly translated reviews conjure up an indelible portrait of the vehement Brahms hater and fanatical Wagner worshipper in the years immediately preceding his artistic maturity.

Readers seeking literature specifically devoted to Wolf's *Lieder* have three exceedingly different monographs to choose from. Of these, SAMS (1961) is not only the earliest study but also the only one that attempts to treat all the songs in the form of an expanded annotated catalog. Although Sams's identification of a "symbolic vocabulary" of motives, keys, and accompanimental patterns in Wolf's *Lieder* remains the author's most noted contribution, his approach seems more sensibly applied as a starting point for analysis than a mature methodology. The other two authors, Stein and Youens, treat a limited selection of songs but succeed in decoding some of the peculiar enigmas of Wolf's style. STEIN is the more theoretical treatment of the two; it requires a familiarity with Schenkerian analysis yet convincingly demonstrates how Wolf formulated a new musical language through exploration of the "plagal domain," third relations, dual tonics, and directional tonality. YOUENS takes a more historical and comparative approach, creating a context for Wolf's achievement as a song composer by comparing his settings of various texts with those of his predecessors and contemporaries. By examining lesser-known components of Wolf's oeuvre, such as his ballads, humorous songs, and operatic experiments, Youens succeeds in enhancing our view of the complex artist.

COOK eschews the more familiar song repertoire in favor of Wolf's obscure and only complete opera, *Der*

Corregidor. The libretto and its sources are fully reproduced in English translation, along with a compendium of Wolf's epistolary comments regarding the work's composition, revision, preparation, and premier. Cook's devotion to the opera becomes especially obvious in the chapter concerning its critical reception, where he does not shrink from exposing the misapprehensions of his peers. Designed, as the author states, "to stimulate interest" in *Der Corregidor,* one hopes that this unique volume never goes out of print.

Finally, for those interested in Wolf research, OSSEN-KOP is indispensable on five counts: for the detailed publication history of Wolf scholarship contained in its introduction, for its annotated bibliography of Wolf literature in all languages, for its indispensable works list, for its survey of Wolf autographs owned by various international libraries, and for the section titled "Directions for Future Research," which lays out territory yet to be explored in the study of this fascinating composer and his extraordinary music.

MARILYN L. MCCOY

Women in Music

Bowers, Jane, and Judith Tick, editors, *Women Making Music: The Western Art Tradition, 1150–1950,* Urbana: University of Illinois Press, 1986

Cook, Susan C., and Judy S. Tsou, editors, *Cecilia Reclaimed: Feminist Perspectives on Gender and Music,* Urbana: University of Illinois Press, 1994

Dahl, Linda, *Stormy Weather: The Music and Lives of a Century of Jazzwomen,* New York: Pantheon Books, 1984

Drinker, Sophie Hutchinson, *Music and Women: The Story of Women in Their Relation to Music,* New York: Coward-McCann, 1948; reprint with new preface and afterword, New York: Feminist Press, 1995

Halstead, Jill, *The Woman Composer: Creativity and the Gendered Politics of Musical Composition,* Aldershot: Ashgate, 1997

Jezic, Diane, *Women Composers: The Lost Tradition Found,* New York: Feminist Press, 1988, 2nd edition, edited by Elizabeth Wood, 1994

Koskoff, Ellen, editor, *Women and Music in Cross-Cultural Perspective,* Westport, Connecticut: Greenwood Press, 1987

McClary, Susan, *Feminine Endings: Music, Gender, and Sexuality,* Minneapolis: University of Minnesota Press, 1991

Neuls-Bates, Carol, editor, *Women in Music: An Anthology of Source Readings from the Middle Ages to the Present,* New York: Harper and Row, 1982; revised edition, Boston: Northeastern University Press, 1996

Pendle, Karin, editor, *Women and Music: A History,* Bloomington: Indiana University Press, 1991

Sadie, Julie Anne, and Rhian Samuel, editors, *The New Grove Dictionary of Women Composers,* London: Macmillan, 1994; as *The Norton/Grove Dictionary of Women Composers,* New York: Norton, 1994

Solie, Ruth, editor, *Musicology and Difference: Gender and Sexuality in Music Scholarship,* Berkeley: University of California Press, 1993

The study of women in music is an astonishingly young discipline. As recently as 1980, the widely-read *New Grove Dictionary of Music and Musicians* contained no entry under this heading. A number of articles concerning individual women appeared in this reference work's 20 volumes, but there was no recognition of women in music as a distinct area of study. This myopia was not unique to the *New Grove Dictionary;* the inclusion of women in the Western musical canon—and works that study that canon—has long been limited. The reasons for omission are complex and controversial, as is—to some extent—the field itself. Are women musicians marginalized by being studied as a separate group? Many women composers, in particular, have expressed a reluctance to be classified by their gender, preferring that they be evaluated solely by their compositions. At the same time, however, numerous scholars have argued that the potential for a fair assessment of any woman's musical accomplishments is limited, thanks to entrenched societal attitudes and (perhaps) subconscious oppression, ignorance of historical achievements, and sometimes overt resistance to reinterpreting the past. The books selected for inclusion in this essay demonstrate the many approaches used by scholars to redress these limitations: they challenge previous perceptions, add to historical knowledge, or reanalyze music itself to see what it has to say about women. Each of these texts helps to illuminate what has been a rather esoteric field of study; if they could be said to have any one unifying theme, it might be their consistent interest in making the invisible visible.

In DRINKER's pioneering study of women's roles in music, the author argues that "healing, religion, and music are the three fields in which woman is preeminently fitted by nature and by experience to express herself and to serve her fellows." She believes that modern women are neglecting their place in ancient creative rituals, allowing themselves to be preempted by men. To support her arguments, Drinker provides one of the earliest historical surveys of the achievements of numerous female composers, including an extensive passage about Hildegard von Bingen.

In the 1980s, scholarship in the field began to burgeon. NEULS-BATES's valuable collection of readings (excerpts from memoirs, diaries, letters, interviews, poetry, articles, and reviews) embraces a wide range of women's musical activities, beginning with a first-century description of women's participation in sacred singing (before they were silenced by the church three centuries later) and ending in the second edition with an interview of musicologist Marcia Citron. It is possible to find many gaps in the anthology's coverage, but it remains an extremely helpful single-volume compilation of sometimes inaccessible information.

JEZIC is a good starting point for those wishing to learn about a selection of women composers. Prompted by dismay about the lack of coverage of women in several leading music history textbooks, Jezic presents essays on 25 composers, spanning a chronological range from Hildegard to Judith Lang Zaimont. Like most of the earlier publications in the field, Jezic's focus is exclusively Western, but her text offers readers a convenient opportunity to explore the sounds of the composers it discusses— Leonarda Publications offers a two-cassette set of companion recordings, featuring 38 compositions discussed in the text.

BOWERS and TICK's collection of 14 essays by eminent historians including Citron, Sadie, and Neuls-Bates provides a series of historical case studies that are partly compensatory (filling in gaps in historical knowledge) and partly analytical, examining women's minority status within music and evaluating how that status has affected their compositional output. Five of the essays focus on individual women, while the other nine examine groups of women in selected time periods. Although the essays are somewhat uneven in answering the sociological questions posed in the book's introduction, they all present new and valuable historical information.

PENDLE's volume of essays, following Bowers and Tick by five years, offers a more continuous historical survey. Written by 15 scholars, the essays vary considerably in style and content; some delve fairly deeply into the music itself (including musical examples), while others are compilations of brief biographical studies. None of the essays is comprehensive, but the book contains several studies of endeavors outside the Western art tradition—"American Popular Music," "African-American Women in Blues and Jazz," "Women in Non-Western Music"—as well as a discussion of women's patronage of music and a brief introduction to the developing field of feminist musical aesthetics.

A welcome addition to the field is SADIE and SAMUEL's reference volume, the last of the subject dictionaries derived from the sixth edition of the *New Grove Dictionary of Music and Musicians*. The connection between this book and the parent volume is "particularly slender," and this new volume corrects many omissions in the older work. Although the 900 composers of art music represented in this dictionary are only a fraction of those contained in Aaron Cohen's earlier reference publication, the *International Encyclopedia of Women Composers* (1987), Sadie and Samuel's volume is generally more scholarly and accurate, containing signed articles. An especially interesting feature is the chronol-

ogy, which lists significant events in the lives of women composers, spanning the seventh century B.C. to 1994.

DAHL's examination of jazzwomen is an early representative of several recent studies that have addressed the role of women in styles outside art music, including rock, pop, soul, jazz, country, and blues. The emphasis in this text is on the biographies of female jazz artists, but Dahl also addresses many of the sociological factors affecting the careers of the musicians she studies. She combines a historical overview of women's participation in jazz with more detailed biographical sketches of selected artists. This text, like most of its counterparts, provides only a limited discussion of the actual music produced by these musicians.

KOSKOFF takes scholarship in a different direction than most of the preceding studies and echoes, in a way, the approach advocated by Drinker. In her introduction to this collection of 15 diverse scholarly essays, Koskoff describes their focus on two questions: "First, to what degree does a society's gender ideology and resulting gender-related behaviors affect its musical thought and practice? And second, how does music function in society to reflect or affect inter-gender relations?" The essays, often based directly on field work, reflect a nicely balanced global distribution. The final essay, by Carol E. Robertson, is a fascinating discussion of how performance functions "as an instrument of power and gender definition."

The ten essays compiled by COOK and TSOU represent the prominent themes of gender studies. In her introduction to the volume, Susan McClary notes that not only do these essays address how misogyny affects musical practice, but they recognize music's "very real power as a cultural medium." Citron contributes an essay titled "Feminist Approaches to Musicology," including an interesting discussion of the myth of universal response. Although the emphasis is once again largely on Western music in this text, the distinction between high-brow and low-brow music is ignored, with female rap artists sharing the pages with 17th-century French women.

Basing her title on traditional musical terminology, which labels weak, off-beat cadences as "feminine endings," McCLARY presents seven essays (some previously published) that challenge conventional readings of and suppositions about music. She explores narratives of violence and misogyny in works that constitute part of the Western canon. In addition, she examines three female musicians with distinctive compositional approaches. Her articulate, engaging writing style—and her freedom in discussing sexual imagery—have made this one of the more controversial and provocative publications connected to the study of women in music.

Similar to the inclusive approach of Cook and Tsou (but focused on art music), SOLIE's collection of essays by 15 scholars requires of the reader a deeper understanding of musical language. Solie calls the text an interrogation rather than an endorsement of difference. The often-contrasting views it contains present a wonderful extension of the title's essential dialectic; McClury, for example, contributes a re-reading of Brahms's Third Symphony, while elsewhere Leo Treitler challenges her approach and even her motivations. Among the rest of the varied and challenging essays, Elizabeth Wood argues that the composer Ethel Smyth reveals her convoluted lesbian relationships via convoluted contrapuntal music, and Carolyn Abbate hypothesizes that metaphorical masks worn in opera allow listeners to assume the opposite gender.

In the most recent publication considered here, HALSTEAD studies factors affecting women composers, asking the specific question, "Why are [they] still such a rarity . . . ?" She includes detailed summaries of brain studies and aptitude measurements, theories about sex differentiation in personality, and evidence from intelligence testing, as well as an examination of the education and social backgrounds of nine British women composers. Feminist scholars might well propose alternative readings to Halstead's cultural analysis, but her text provides many citations of psychological and medical literature not generally addressed in current studies of women in music.

ALYSON MCLAMORE

X

Xenakis, Iannis b. 1922

Greek composer, theorist, and architect

Boris, Mario, *Iannis Xenakis, the Man and His Music,*
London: Boosey and Hawkes, 1967

Matossian, Nouritza, *Iannis Xenakis,* London: Kahn and
Averill, and New York: Taplinger, 1986

Varga. Bálint András, *Conversations with Iannis Xenakis,*
London: Faber, 1996

Xenakis, Iannis, *Formalized Music: Thought and Mathematics
in Composition,* Bloomington: Indiana University, 1971;
revised edition, Stuyvesant, New York: Pendragon Press,
1992

Iannis Xenakis is one of the most independent and influential composers and theorists of Western music in the second half of the 20th century. From 1955, when his orchestral work *Metastasis* played at Donaueschingen and initiated his fame, to the 1970s and 1980s, when the performances of his works seemed to compete in frequency with those of Beethoven's symphonies, hundreds of interviews with Xenakis have appeared in the world press, and an equally large number of articles have been written on the man, his music, and his ideas; most are based on texts written by the composer himself, in French, among which are his book-length publications *Musiques Formelles* (1963) and *Musique-architecture* (1971). A monograph on the composer, *Iannis Xenakis* (1981), written in French by Nouritza Matossian, throws light on the composer's personal life in recent years, citing excerpts from his correspondence with his family as well as among his collaborators. Xenakis's thesis defense for his doctorate appeared, in English, in 1985, under the title *Arts, Sciences/Alloys.*

XENAKIS is a translation of *Musiques Formelles,* much revised by the composer and enlarged with the translations of his articles "Vers une Métamusique" (1967) and "Vers une Philosophie de la Musique" (1968). The term *formalized music* refers to music perceived with mathematical abstraction, capable of being expressed in mathematical formulas. Music, an abstract art, is by virtue of its abstract quality a universal language, but universal appreciation of music is hindered, Xenakis believes, by the divergence of theoretical systems developed within music traditions of the various civilizations during particular phases of evolution, systems that are essential to the study, perception, and understanding of the corresponding music. Xenakis's aim as a theorist is to discover the fundamental and essential rules common to all music and to discern which axioms of the universal language of abstract thinking, mathematics, may express those rules. He proposes three possible categories of musical components: the *outside-time* elements, conceived in graded systems (pitch intervals, degrees of dynamics, duration intervals); their *in-time* succession, that is, the order in which the above elements appear in a piece of music (wherein an interval of a fifth followed by an interval of a fourth, a *ppp* followed by a *mp,* etc., are distinguished from their reverse order); and the *temporal* completion of sound events and their combinations within a composition. By the fundamental operational laws of logic such as those found in algebra, these elements, grouped in sets, may be related to each other. Therefore, algebra and set theory are essential tools for a universal music theory.

Xenakis also reveals here the philosophical and aesthetic ideas behind certain of his works that were landmarks in the development of Western music and describes in detail his compositional process. His works that he termed *stochastic music* are compositions of massive sonic phenomena whose constitution (as well as their temporal form) was created by calculated chance (and not imitated by improvising performers), profiting from the penetration of human thought into chance and disorder and developed in the theory of probability. Xenakis introduces the calculus of probabilities in composition, aiming at the creation of a construction controlled by a minimum of rules. In fact, for Xenakis, mathematics is always the means for the solution of philosophical and aesthetic problems. While recent generations are familiar with most of the mathematical formulas in Xenakis, it is worth remembering that the composer's defense of himself and his application of mathematics to his work was novel when it first appeared. He explicitly relates his attitude to ancient

Greek science and philosophy—which he thoroughly studied—reminding us that the cult of the numbers by the Pythagoreans was initiated in religion. Xenakis's text is illustrated with many examples, the majority of which are not musical examples but graphs, beautiful in appearance and intriguing challenges for listeners.

Despite its concise size, BORIS is a valuable source of information on Xenakis. The main body of the work is an interview with the composer. Xenakis answers questions concerning his life, ideas, and work. It becomes clear how determinant were his years in Greece and his first years in Paris. His involvement in the French Resistance during World War II and his immersion in ancient Greek civilization shaped his character to resist all possible dependencies (physical as well as spiritual) and to aim to unfold creatively all his human capacities. Xenakis is particularly grateful to the *chance* (or fate) that allowed him to encounter such outstanding musicians as Olivier Messiaen and Hermann Scherchen, the two persons that supported him during his first years in Paris.

Boris gives a chronological work list, which is of course incomplete because of the monograph's early appearance; however, for the works included, the author provides instructive explanations concerning the germinating idea behind each work, the mathematical theories applied, and the most characteristic sound formations of the composition. There is also information on the instrumentation, duration, first performance, and publisher for each work.

MATOSSIAN first appeared in French in 1981, and it is the first biography of Xenakis that does not rely solely on the composer's oral testimonies. The volume contains some previously unpublished documents from Xenakis's personal life, such as his correspondence with his wife, Françoise, and his daughter, Makhi, as well as with some of his closest friends and collaborators, such as Hermann Scherchen, who was the first to recognize fully Xenakis's originality (he conducted the world premieres of *Pithoprakta,* 1957, and *Achorripsis,* 1958) and to whom Xenakis felt free to confess every inner thought and sentiment. Matossian also includes fresh information about Xenakis's Greek years and his first years in Paris.

VARGA presents two interviews with Xenakis undertaken in 1980 and 1989. In addition to the information on Xenakis's development as a composer, the book contains some sincere confessions by the composer and reflects the intimacy created by Varga's intelligent, at times even childlike, questions. Varga also provides the most complete catalog of Xenakis's works available in an English-language publication and a short bibliography that includes some important doctoral dissertations on Xenakis.

EKATERINI ROMANOU

Z

Zimbabwe *see* Africa

BOOKLIST INDEX

BOOKLIST INDEX

Books and articles discussed in the entries are listed here by author/editor name. The page numbers refer to the lists themselves, where full publication information is given.

GENERAL INDEX

GENERAL INDEX

Page numbers in **bold** indicate main entries.

a cappella performance, 594
Abbasid era, 442
Abbate, Carolyn, 697, 775, 795
Abbey of Solesmes, 145; *see also* chant
Abbey of St. Victor (Paris), 435, 664
Aboriginal music, 30, 31
Abraham, Gerald, 207, 210, 711
Abraham and Isaac (Stravinsky), 701
Abravanel, Claude, 199
Absalon, fili mi (motet), 366
absolute music, 9, 157, 185; *see also* program
   music
absolute realism, 8
abstract music, 541
Académie Royale de Musique, 405
accademia (ensemble cantata), 126
accented dissonances, 252
accents, organizational role in sequences, 663
acciaccatura, 556
accompaniment, 168, 388; *see also* continuo
accompanying, 554, 645
accordions, 505
acculturation, 228
Acid House music, 610
Acis and Galatea (Handel), 280
Acoustical Society of America, 1
acoustics, **1–2**, 569; baroque trumpet, 56;
   bowed instruments, 336; relation to
   hearing, 321; stringed instruments, 337;
   teaching, 2; violin, 335
Adam, Adolphe, 192
Adams, John, 591
Adams, Sarah, 573
Adirondack mountains, 344
Adler, Guido, 415, 418
Adler, Oskar, 633
Adorno, Theodor W., **2–5**; analysis of Berg,
   78; comparison of Schoenberg and
   Stravinsky, 14; criticism of Weill, 788;
   Mahler Centenary Address, 4;
   minimalism and, 591; views on Wagner,

778; writings on modernism and mass
   culture, 3–4; writings on philosophy of
   music, 11
Adorno scholarship, 4
Adrio, Adam, 153
Ady, Andre, 58
aesthetic autonomy, 483
aesthetics: classical, **5–6**, 552; criteria for
   judgments in, 11; emotional realism, 9;
   Hanslick's views on, 285; idealist
   tradition, 9; of instrumental music, 160;
   medieval, 434–35; modern, **9–14**;
   Nielsen's views on, 494; nineteenth
   century, 8, 67, 160; origin of term, 8;
   Quantz's views on, 550; Renaissance,
   594; research on, 570; romantic, **6–9**,
   613; source readings, 184–85; *see also*
   philosophy of music
aesthetics (by composer): Lutosławski, 408;
   Partch, 541; Puccini, 574; Ravel, 588;
   Saint-Saëns, 624; Satie, 626; Schoenberg,
   635–37; Schumann, 659, 660, 661;
   Thomson, 741–42; Toscanini, 743;
   Webern, 783; Weill, 788
Affaire Fétis, 234
Affaire Weldon, 270
affections, doctrine of, **14–15**
affects, 6
Affektenlehre, 279
Africa, **15–17**
Africaine (Meyerbeer), 440
African-American hymnody, 310
African-American music, in Latin America,
   385
African-American musicians, 555
African-American women, in blues and jazz,
   794
African-Americans, 88, 239, 365
African instruments, 321
African music, 15, 16
African musical instruments, 334

Afro-American Symphony (Still), 694
Agawu, Kofi, 139
Agee, Richard J., 791
aging, relation of music therapy to, 486
Agricola, Alexander, 476
Agricola, Johann Friedrich, 36
Aguado, Dionisio, 332
Ah! troppo è ver (Stradella), 127
Aida (Verdi), 764
airs, *see* songs
Akhenaten, 442
Akhnaten (Glass), 262
Alain, Jehan, 378
Alamo (film score, Tiomkin), 236
Albania, *see* Eastern Europe
Albéniz, Isaac, **17–18**
Albert Herring (Britten), 104
Alberti bass, 468
Albinoni, Tomaso, 163, 164, 256, 556, 681
Albion and Albanius (Dryden), 429
Album für die Jugend (Schumann), 659
Album Leaves (Smetana), 677
Albumleaf (Skryabin), 676
Alceste (Gluck), 265
Aldrich, Elizabeth, 641, 646
Aldwell, Edward, 155
aleatoric music, **18–19**; *see also* Cage, John;
   Lutosławski, Witold
Alexander, Freddie, 364
Alexander's Feast (Handel), 284
"Alexander's Ragtime Band" (Berlin), 81
Alfonso I (of Naples), 343
Alfred (Arne), 429
Alfred (Dvořák), 209
Alia musica, 445
all-female bands, 609
Allgemeine musikalische Zeitung
   (newspaper), 157
allusion, 596, 659, 702
almande (allemande), 187
Almeida, Antonio de, 708

NOTES ON ADVISERS AND CONTRIBUTORS

NOTES ON ADVISERS AND CONTRIBUTORS

Allsen, J. Michael. Lecturer, Department of Music, University of Wisconsin, Whitewater. Contributing Editor to *Current Musicology* (1984–92). Contributor to *New Grove Dictionary of Music and Musicians* (forthcoming edition), *American National Biography, Encyclopedia of Medieval France, Journal of Musicology,* and *Historical Performance.* **Essays:** Du Fay, Guillaume; Dunstaple, John; Motet: Medieval.

Amati-Camperi, Alexandra. Lecturer, Department of Fine and Performing Arts, University of San Francisco, San Francisco, California. Author of *History of Music in Outlines and Tables* (with Mara Parker, 1997) and *Verdelot: Madrigali a Sei Voci* (forthcoming). Contributor to *Proceedings of the International Conference "Cantate Domino," Florence May 1997,* and *Journal of Musicological Research.* **Essays:** Carissimi, Giacomo; Gabrieli, Giovanni; Sonata: Classical.

Antokoletz, Elliott. Professor of Musicology, University of Texas, Austin. Author of *The Music of Béla Bartók* (1984), *Béla Bartók: A Guide to Research* (1988, 1997), and *Twentieth-Century Music* (1997). Editor of *International Journal of Musicology* (1992–) and *Bartók Perspectives* (forthcoming). Contributor to *Studia Musicologica, Tempo, Journal of the American Musicological Society, College Music Symposium, International Journal of Musicology,* and *The Bartók Companion.* Board member, *American Music* (1992–). **Essay:** Bartók, Béla: Works.

Archetto, Maria. Assistant Professor, Division of Humanities, Oxford College of Emory University, Oxford, Georgia. Editor of *Francesco Portinaro: Il terzo libro di Madrigali* and *Francesco Portinaro: Il quarto libro di madrigali.* **Essay:** Cavalieri, Emilo de'.

Attinello, Paul G. Professor, Department of Music, University of Hong Kong. **Essay:** Notation: 20th Century.

Auner, Joseph (adviser). Associate Professor, Department of Music, State University of New York, Stony Brook. Editorial board member, *Journal of the American Musicological Society,* and editor, *Studies in Contemporary Music and Culture.* Contributor to *Schoenberg and His World, Schoenberg, Berg, Weber: A Companion to the Second Viennese School, Constructive Dissonance, Journal of the American Musicological Society,* and *Music Theory Spectrum.*

Bailey, Candace Lee. Associate Professor, Department of Humanities, Louisburg College, Louisburg, North Carolina. Author of *Late-Seventeenth-Century English Keyboard Music: Bodleian Mus. Sch. Ms. D.219 and Christ Church (Oxford) Mus. Ms. 1177* (1997). Contributor to *Early Keyboard Music* and *Tonal Structures in Early Music.* **Essays:** Frescobaldi, Girolamo; Purcell, Henry: Other Works; Theory and Theorists: 17th Century.

Bain, Jennifer. Ph.D. candidate, Department of Music, State University of New York, Stony Brook. **Essays:** Machaut, Guillaume de; Theory and Theorists: 14th Century.

Baker, Evan. Independent scholar. **Essays:** Opera: Set Design; Opera: Staging; Wagner, Richard: Operas: Staging.

Baker, James M. Professor of Music, Brown University, Providence, Rhode Island. Author of *The Music of Alexander Scriabin* (1986). Editor of and contributor to *Music Theory in Concept and Practice* (1997). Editor of *Journal of Music Theory* (1974–75), *Newsletter of the Society for Music Theory* (1987–89), and *Music Theory Spectrum* (1991–94). Contributor to *Music Theory and the Exploration of the Past, Music Analysis, Journal of Music Theory,* and *Music Theory Spectrum.* Board member, *Journal of Music Theory* (1990–). **Essay:** Skryabin, Alexander.

Balensuela, C. Matthew. Assistant Professor, School of Music, DePauw University, Greencastle, Indiana. Author of *Ars cantus mensurabilis mensurata per modos iuris: A New Critical Text and Translation* (1994). Contributor to *Proceedings of the Tenth International Congress of Medieval Canon Law, 12–18 August 1996, The Revised New Grove Dictionary of Music and Musicians*, and *Rivista Internazionale di Dritto Comune*. **Essays:** Notation: To 1600; Theory and Theorists: Early Medieval; Theory and Theorists: 15th Century; Theory and Theorists: 16th Century.

Barz, Gregory F. Assistant Professor, Blair School of Music, Vanderbilt University, Nashville, Tennessee. Editor of and contributor to *Shadows in the Field: New Perspectives for Fieldwork in Ethnomusicology* (1997). Contributor to *Ethnomusicology Online*. **Essays:** Blues; Ethnomusicology: History; Folk Music.

Benson, Mark. Associate Professor of Music, Auburn University, Montgomery, Alabama. Contributor to *Journal of Musicology*. **Essays:** Chamber Music: 19th Century; Gesualdo, Carlo; Instruments: Percussion.

Bergquist, Peter. Professor Emeritus, School of Music, University of Oregon, Eugene. Editor of *Two Motet Cycles for Matins for the Dead*, by Orlando di Lasso (1983), *Seven Penitential Psalms and "Laudate Dominum" by Orlando di Lasso* (1990), *Orlando di Lasso, Sämliche Werke, neue Reihe*, vol. 22–25 (1992–93), *Orlando di Lasso: The Complete Motets* (1995–), and *Orlando di Lasso Studies* (forthcoming). Contributor to *Acta musicologica, Musik in Bayern*, and *Music Forum*. **Essay:** Lasso, Orlando di.

Bisson, Noël. Teaching Fellow and Ph.D. candidate, Harvard University, Cambridge, Massachusetts. Co-author of *Writing about Music* (forthcoming). **Essays:** Tallis, Thomas; Taverner, John.

Black, Brian. Instructor, Department of Music, Vanier College, St. Laurent, Quebec. Contributor to *Schubert durch die Brille*. **Essay:** Schubert, Franz: Chamber Music.

Block, Geoffrey. Professor, School of Music, University of Puget Sound, Tacoma, Washington. Author of *Charles Ives: A Bio-Bibliography* (1988), *Ives: "Concord Sonata"* (1996), and *Enchanted Evenings: The Broadway Musical from "Show Boat" to Sondheim* (1997). Co-editor of *Charles Ives and the Classical Tradition* (1996). Contributor to *Beethoven Essays: Studies in Honor of Elliot Forbes, Musical Quarterly, Opera Quarterly, Beethoven's Compositional Process, Mozart-Jahrbuch, Journal of Musicology, Journal of the Royal Musical Association*, and *Ives Studies*. **Essays:** Beethoven, Ludwig van: Piano Music; Gershwin, George.

Bloom, Peter. Professor of Music, Smith College, Northampton, Massachusetts. Author of *The Life of Berlioz* (1998). Editor of *Berlioz Studies* (1992), *Music in Paris in the Eighteen-Thirties* (1987). Adviser: *The New Berlioz Edition*. Contributor to *Revue de musicologie, Journal of Musicological Research, Cahiers Berlioz, Die Musik in Geschichte und Gegenwart*, and *Musical Quarterly*. **Essay:** Berlioz, Hector: Biography.

Bomberger, E. Douglas. Assistant Professor, Department of Music, University of Hawaii at Manao, Honolulu. Editor of *Brainard's Biographies of American Musicians* (forthcoming). Contributor to *Musical Quarterly, American Music, Notes, Fontes Artis Musicae*, and *Opera in Context: Essays on Historical Staging*. **Essays:** Beach, Mrs. H.H.A. (Amy); Liszt, Franz: Biography.

Brauner, Charles S. (adviser). Professor of Music History and Literature, College of Performing Arts, Roosevelt University, Chicago, Illinois. Editor, with Patricia B. Brauner, of the critical edition of Gioachino Rossini, *Armida*. Contributor to numerous collections and journals, including *Journal of the American Musicological Society, Musical Quarterly*, and *Journal of Musicological Research*.

Brown, A. Peter (adviser). Professor of Musicology, Indiana University, Bloomington. Author of numerous books, including *Performing Haydn's The Creation: Reconstructing the Earliest Renditions* (1986) and *Joseph Haydn's Keyboard Music: Sources and Style* (1986). Contributor to numerous journals and collections, including *Acta musicologica, Haydn Yearbook, Journal of the American Musicological Society*, and *Journal of Musicology*.

Browner, Tara. Assistant Professor, Department of Ethnomusicology, University of California, Los Angeles. Author of *Heartbeat of the People: Music and Dance of the Northern Pow-Wow* (forthcoming). Contributor to *Annual Proceedings of the National Association of Schools of Music, American Music*, and *American Music Center Research Journal*. **Essay:** Native North American Music.

Bryan, Karen. Assistant Professor, School of Music, Arizona State University. Contributor to the *Journal of the Donizetti Society*. **Essay:** Musicology, Traditional.

Buck, Charles. Author of *Robert Schumann and the Stile Antico* (1994). **Essay:** Schumann, Robert: Biography.

Bücker, Andreas. Faculty of Music, Trinity College, Cambridge University. Contributor to *Bamberg Staatsbibliothek Lit. 5*. **Essays:** Theory and Theorists: Ancient; Wagner, Richard: Ring Cycle.

Burdette, Glenn. Editor of *Music Research* Forum (1988–90), *Giovanni Battista Somis: Violin Sonatas, Op. 3* (1999), and *Anthony Philip Heinrich: Funeral Anthems* (1999). Contributor to *Music Research Forum, Tracker,* and *Hymn.* **Essays:** Bach, Johann Sebastian: Keyboard Music; Corelli, Arcangelo.

Burkholder, J. Peter (adviser). Professor of Musicology, Indiana University, Bloomington. Author of *Charles Ives: The Ideas behind the Music* (1985) and *All Made of Tunes: Charles Ives and the Uses of Musical Borrowing* (1995) Editor of *Charles Ives and His World,* co-editor of *Charles Ives and the Classical Tradition.* Contributor to numerous journals, including *Journal of the American Musicological Society, Journal of Musicology, 19th-Century Music, Musical Quarterly, Notes,* and *Music Theory Spectrum.*

Burrows, Donald (adviser). Professor and Head of Music Department, Open University, Milton Keynes. Author of *Handel* (1994), *Handel: Messiah* (1991), and, with Marsha J. Ronish, *A Catalogue of Handel's Musical Autographs* (1994). Editor of *Cambridge Companion to Handel* and numerous critical editions of the music of Handel and Elgar. Contributor to numerous journals.

Caballero, Carlo. Research Associate, University of Colorado. Contributor to *19th-Century Music, Victorian Studies, Regarding Fauré,* and *Music and the Visual Arts.* **Essay:** Fauré, Gabriel.

Cahn, Steven Joel. Assistant Professor of Music Theory, University of Cincinnati, Cincinnati, Ohio. Contributor to *Journal of the Arnold Schoenberg Institute.* **Essay:** Schoenberg, Arnold: Writings.

Calico, Joy Haslam. Assistant Professor of Musicology, Illinois Wesleyan University, Bloomington. Editor of *Bodies of Knowledge: The Sixth Annual Women's Studies Graduate Research Conference Proceedings,* and assistant review editor of *Fontes Artis Musicae.* Contributor to *Music and German National Identity* and *Hanns Eisler: 's muesst dem Himmel Hoellenangst werden.* **Essays:** Henze, Hans Werner; Rorem, Ned.

Carruthers, Glen. Dean, School of Music, Brandon University, Canada. Editor of *A Celebration of Canada's Arts 1930–1970* (1996). Contributor to *Annäherung IX—an sieben Komponistinnen, Canadian University Music Review, Grainger Society Journal, Piano and Keyboard, ARSC Journal, Canadian Music Educator, Clavier, Journal of Musicology,* and *Music Review.* **Essay:** Rachmaninoff, Sergei; Sonata: Romantic.

Cateforis, Theo. Department of Music, State University of New York, Stony Brook. Contributor to *Journal of*

Popular Music Studies and *Musics of Multicultural America* (1997). **Essays:** Rock and Roll: 1980s United States; Rock and Roll: 1980s England.

Champagne, Mario. Independent scholar. **Essays:** Cage, John; Musicology: Gay and Lesbian; Ravel, Maurice.

Chang, Sangtae. Contributor to *In Theory Only* and *Mitteilungen der Paul Sacher Stiftung* (forthcoming). **Essay:** Boulez, Pierre.

Charry, Eric. Associate Professor, Music Department, Wesleyan University. Author of *Mande Music* (forthcoming). Contributor to *The African Diaspora: A Musical Perspective,* edited by Ingrid Monson, *The History of Islam in Africa,* edited by Nehemia Levtzion and Randall Pouwels, *Annual Review of Jazz Studies, Galpin Society Journal,* and *The World of Music.* **Essays:** Africa; Jazz: Free.

Christensen, Thomas. Professor, Department of Music, University of Chicago. Author of *Rameau and Musical Thought in the Enlightenment* (1993). Editor of *Music Theory Spectrum* (1995–1998), *Journal of Music Theory* (1996), and *The Cambridge History of Western Music Theory* (forthcoming). Contributor to *JAMS, Bach Perspectives, Music Theory Spectrum,* and *Journal of Music Theory.* **Essays:** Affections, Doctrine of; Theory and Theorists: General.

Clark, Renée Chérie. Ph.D. candidate, Musicology Division, University of Illinois, Urbana-Champaign. Contributor to *Ralph Vaughan Williams Compendium.* **Essays:** Delius, Frederick; Great Britain: Musical Centers.

Clark, Walter Aaron. Associate Professor, Department of Music and Dance, University of Kansas, Lawrence. Author of *Isaac Albeniz: Portrait of a Romantic* (1998), and *Isaac Albeniz: A Guide to Research* (1998). Contributor to *Latin America: A Panorama, Inter-American Music Review, Revista de Musicología, Musical Quarterly, American Music,* and *Journal of the Lute Society of America.* **Essays:** Albeniz, Isaac; Falla, Manuel de; Flamenco.

Clifton, Keith E. Instructor, Division of Musicology, Northwestern University, Evanston, Illinois. Contributor to *Opera Journal* and *Journal of Singing.* **Essays:** Honegger, Arthur; Poulenc, Francis.

Cochran, Keith Harris. Contributor to *Rivista italiana di musicologia.* **Essays:** Meyerbeer, Giacomo; Spohr, Louis.

Coeyman, Barbara. Visiting Scholar, School of Music, University of Texas, Austin. Editor of *French Opera Facsimiles: Ballet de la Jeunesse* (1996). Contributor to *Early Music, College Music Symposium, Historical*

Performance, Eighteenth-Century Life, Lully Studies, 17th-Century Guide to Performance Practice, Opera in Context, and *Actes du Lully.* **Essays:** Ballet: French; France: Musical Centers; Lully, Jean Baptiste.

Converse, Ralph D. Professor of Theory, Woodwinds and Jazz Studies, Department of Music, Yuba College, Marysville, California. **Essays:** Jazz: Swing; Jazz: West Coast.

Cook, Susan C. (adviser). Professor of Music, School of Music, University of Wisconsin, Madison. Author of *Opera for a New Republic* (1988). Editor of *Cecilia Reclaimed* (1994), and editorial board member for numerous journals, including *American Music, Journal of Musicological Research, Journal of the American Musicological Society, Journal of Popular Music Studies,* and *Women and Music.* Contributor to numerous collections and journals, including *Garland Encyclopedia of World Music* (forthcoming), *Audible Traces, Passion of Music and Dance, Journal of Musicology,* and *American Music.* **Essay:** Tower, Joan.

Coppola, Catherine. Adjunct Assistant Professor, Department of Music, Hunter College of the City University of New York. Contributor to *Text* and *19th-Century Music.* **Essays:** Tchaikovsky, Piotr Ilyich: Ballets.

Cowgill, Rachel. Lecturer in Musicology, Department of Music, University of Huddersfield. Contributor to *Musica Antiqua, Cambridge Opera Journal, Oxford Companion to British Culture, 1776–1832, Oxford Composer Companions: Joseph Hayden, New Dictionary of National Biography, Revised New Grove Dictionary of Music and Musicians,* and *Lives and Works in the Arts.* **Essays:** Burney, Charles; Opera: English.

Cramer, Alfred. Assistant Professor, Department of Music, Pomona College, Claremont, California. Contributor to *Music Theory Spectrum.* **Essay:** Atonality.

Cramer, Eugene Casjen. Professor, Department of Music, University of Calgary, Alberta. Author of *An Introduction to the Study of Music History* (1976; revised as *A Basic Skills Handbook for Music History Students* [1984]), *Officium hebdomadae sanctae: Tomás Luis de Victoria* (1982), and *Tomás Luis de Victoria: A Guide to Research* (1998). Editor of *Music Study at the Graduate Level: Proceedings of the Symposium "The Study of Music, The Pursuit of Advanced Degrees, and the Future"* (1983), and *Teacher of Teachers: Essays in Honour of Lois Choksy* (1998). Contributor to *American Choral Review, NATS Bulletin, Notes, Canadian University Music Review, Muzyka, De Música Hispaña et Aliis,* and *Songs of the Dove and the Nightingale.* **Essay:** Canada.

Crittenden, Camille. Visiting Assistant Professor, Department of Music, Duke University, Durham, North Carolina. Author of *Viennese Musical Life and the Operettas of Johann Strauss* (forthcoming). Contributor to *Die Fledermaus, American Music, Musical Quarterly,* and *Political and Religious Ideas in the Works of Arnold Schoenberg.* **Essays:** Berg, Alban: Biography; Hanslick, Eduard.

Cross, Charlotte M. Contributor to *Current Musicology, The Image of Nature in Literature, the Media, and Society: Proceedings of the Society for the Interdisciplinary Study of Social Imagery, Theoria,* and *Musikleben: Studien zur Musikgeschichte Österreich.* **Essay:** Schoenberg, Arnold: Aesthetics.

Crowe, Barbara J. Professor of Music Therapy, School of Music, Arizona State University, Tempe. Author of *Cost Effective Activity Programs for Older Adults with Dementia* (1995) and *Best Practice in Music Therapy: Utilizing Group Percussion Strategies for Promoting Volunteerism in the Well Older Adult* (1995). Contributor to *Music Therapy from the Client's Perspective, Music Therapy Perspectives Journal, Music: The Ultimate Physician,* and *Arts in Psychotherapy Journal.* **Essay:** Psychology of Music.

Cyr, Mary E. (adviser). Professor and Acting Director, School of Fine Art and Music, University of Guelph. Author of *Performing Baroque Music* (1992). Editor of numerous music editions of the works of Rameau and Martin. Performer on numerous recordings of the works of J.S. Bach and Buxtehude.

Davidian, Teresa. Assistant Professor, Department of Fine Arts and Speech, Tarleton State University, Stephenville, Texas. Contributor to *Theory and Practice, Journal of Musicological Research, St. James International Dictionary of Opera,* and *Cahiers Deloussy.* **Essays:** Crawford, Ruth; Set Theory.

Davis, Mary E. Assistant Professor, Department of Music, Case Western Reserve University, Case Western, Ohio. Contributor to *Musical Quarterly* and *Music and the Condition of Modern Art.* **Essays:** France: General Studies; Nancarrow, Conlon; Satie, Erik.

Desmond, Karen. Department of Music, New York University, New York. **Essays:** Notre Dame Polyphony; Ockeghem, Johannes.

Di Grazia, Donna M. Assistant Professor, Department of Music, Pomona College, Claremont, California. Contributor to *16th-Century Journal, 19th-Century Music, Notes,* and *The Dictionnaire de la musique en France au XIX siècle.* **Essay:** Weelkes, Thomas.

Dirst, Matthew. Assistant Professor of Music, Moores School of Music, University of Houston, Texas. Contributor to *Early Music, American Organist, Predicting the Future and Understanding the Past,* and *French Organ Music from the Revolution to Franck and Widor.* **Essays:** Bach, Johann Sebastian: Cantatas; Bach, Johann Sebastian: Performance Practice; Cantata: German Baroque.

Dragone, Luann. Adjunct Professor, Department of Music, Hofstra University and Manhattan School of Music, New York. Contributor to *Theoria* and *Theory and Practice.* **Essay:** Jazz: Cool.

Dubowchik, Rosemary Thoonen. Department of Music, Southern Connecticut State University, New Haven. Contributor to *Plainsong and Medieval Music.* **Essay:** Chant: Byzantine.

Earp, Lawrence M. (adviser). Professor of Music, School of Music, University of Wisconsin, Madison. Author of *Guillaume de Machaut: A Guide to Research* (1995). Contributor to numerous journals.

Erickson, Raymond. Dean of Arts and Humanities, Queens College of the City University of New York. Author of *DARMS: A Reference Manual* (1976) and *"Musica enchiriadis" and "Scolica enchiriadis"* (1995). Editor of *Schubert's Vienna* (1997). Contributor to *Journal of Music Theory, Computers in the Humanities, Journal of the American Musicological Society, College Music Society Symposium, Computers and Language Research, Quo vadis musica?,* and *Musical Humanism and Its Legacy: Essays in Honor of Claude V. Palisca.* Editorial Board member, *Computers and the Humanities* (1971–76). **Essays:** Ornamentation: Renaissance; Performance Practice: Classical; Performance Practice: Renaissance.

Fader, Don. Stanford University, Stanford, California. Contributor to *Bulletin de l'atelier d'études sur la musique Françoise des XVIIe et XVIIIe sièles* and *Recorder Education Journal.* **Essays:** Cantata: French Baroque; Charpentier, Marc-Antoine; Marais, Marin.

Fairtile, Linda B. Music Specialist, New York Public Library for the Performing Arts. Author of *Giacomo Puccini: A Guide to Research* (1998). Contributor to *Music Library Association Notes, Verdi Newsletter, 19th-Century Music,* and *Verdi's Middle Period.* **Essay:** Toscanini, Arturo.

Farahat, Martha. Adjunct Faculty, School of Music, DePaul University, Chicago. Contributor to *Performance Practice Review* and *Early Music History.* **Essays:** Commedia dell'arte; Instruments: Wind; Mid-

dle East; Ornamentation: Baroque; Performance Practice: Baroque.

Faucett, Bill F. Contributing music critic for *The Palm Beach Post,* Royal Palm Beach, Florida. Author of *George Whitefield Chadwick: His Symphonic Works* (1996) and *George Whitefield Chadwick: A Bio-Bibliography* (1998). Contributor to *Notes* and *Musik in Geschichte und Gegenwart.* **Essays:** Harris, Roy; Sousa, John Philip; Thomson, Virgil.

Feurzeig, Lisa. Assistant Professor of Music, Grand Valley State University, Allendale, Michigan. Editor of *Répertoire Internationale de la Presse Musicale: Eutonia 1829–1833, 1835, 1837* (1990), and *Répertoire Internationale de la Presse Musicale: Die Niederrheinische Musik-Zeitung 1853–1867* (1990). Contributor to *The Dissemination of Music: Five Centuries of European Music Publishing* and *19th-Century Music.* **Essay:** Schubert, Franz: Lieder.

Florea, Luminita. Head of the Department of Rare Books and Manuscripts, Robbins Collection of Roman and Canon Law, University of California, Berkeley. Contributor to *Newz Grove Dictionary of Music and Musicians, Renaissance Quarterly,* and *Tempo.* **Essays:** Marenzio, Luca; Mode: Medieval; Mozart, Wolfgang Amadeus: Keyboard Music.

Flynn, Timothy S. Author of *Early Musical Sources in Non-Musical Microfilm Collections* (forthcoming). Contributor to *Historical Encyclopedia of Chicago Women.* **Essays:** Fétis, François-Joseph; Gounod, Charles; Offenbach, Jacques.

Frantz, Charles Frederick. Adjunct, Department of Music, College of New Jersey, Ewing. Contributor to *Ellipses.* **Essay:** Debussy, Claude: Biography.

Fromson, Michele. Executive Director, Earplay. Editor of *Theory and Practice* (1993–95). Contributor to *New Grove Dictionary of Music, Journal of the American Musicological Society, Theory and Practice,* and *Journal of the Royal Musical Association.* **Essay:** Willaert, Adrian.

Fuller, Sarah (adviser). Associate Professor, Department of Music, State University of New York, Stony Brook. Editorial board member for *Journal of Music Theory* and *Journal of the American Musicological Society.* Contributor to numerous collections and journals, including *Tonal Structures in Early Music,* edited by Cristle Collins Judd, *Journal of the American Musicological Society, Music Theory Spectrum, Journal of Music Theory,* and *Journal of Musicology.*

Gagné, David. Associate Professor, Queens College and Graduate Center, City University of New York. Author of *Analysis of Tonal Music: A Schenkerian Approach* (1998). Editor of *Theory and Practice* (1985–88). Contributor to *Indiana Theory Review, Trends in Schenkerian Research, Music Forum,* and *Schenker Studies.* **Essays:** Mozart, Wolfgang Amadeus: Biography; Mozart, Wolfgang Amadeus: Style.

Gallo, Denise. Instructor, School of Music, Catholic University of America, Washington, D.C. Contributor to *The Rosaleen Moldenhauer Memorial: "Music History from Primary Sources," A Guide to the Moldenhauer Archives, Atti del Convegno internazionale di studi di Giovanni Pacini,* and *Revised New Grove Dictionary of Music and Musicians.* **Essays:** Bellini, Vincenzo; Donizetti, Gaetano; Jazz: Dixieland; Opera: 18th-Century Italian; Opera: 19th-Century Italian.

Garf, Nancy F. Author of *The Role of the Tonic in the First Movement of the Early Symphony* (1994). **Essays:** Babbitt, Milton; Instruments: Harp; Salieri, Antonio; Schubert, Franz: Song Cycles.

Gentry, Theodore L. Contributor to *American Music* and *Opera Quarterly.* **Essay:** Rossini, Gioachino.

Gibbs, Christopher H. Assistant Professor, Department of Music, State University of New York, Buffalo. Editor of *The Cambridge Companion to Schubert.* Contributor to *Schubert-Lexikon, 19th-Century Music, Schubert durch die Brille,* and *Journal of the Arnold Schoenberg Institute.* **Essays:** Reich, Steve; Schubert, Franz: Biography and Social Circle.

Giger, Andreas. Visiting Assistant Professor, Department of Musicology, Indiana University. **Essays:** Korngold, Erich Wolfgang; Verdi, Giuseppe: Operas: Middle Period.

Goldberg, Halina. Assistant Professor, Department of Musiclogy, Indiana University. **Essays:** Chopin, Fryderyk: Biography; Chopin, Fryderyk: Works; Ornamentation: Romantic.

Grave, Floyd K. Associate Professor, Department of Music, Rutgers University, New Brunswick, New Jersey. Author of *Abbé Georg Joseph Vogler: Pièces de Clavecin and 32 Präludien* (1986), *In Praise of Harmony: The Teachings of Abbé Vogler* (with Margaret Grupp Grave, 1988), *Franz Joseph Haydn: A Guide to Research* (with Margaret Grupp Grave, 1990), and *Ballet Music from the Mannheim Court, Part 1* (1996). Contributor to *Journal of the American Musicological Society, Music Theory Spectrum, Music Review, 18th-Century Studies,* and *Journal of Musicology.* Editorial Board member, *Journal of Musicology* (1993–). **Essays:** Haydn, Franz Joseph: Biography; Haydn, Franz Joseph: Chamber Music.

Gray, John Douglas. Instructor, College of Music, University of Colorado, Boulder. Author of *Ars nova* (forthcoming). **Essays:** Ciconia, Johannes; Vitry, Philippe de.

Green, Robert Anthony. Professor, School of Music, Northern Illinois University, DeKalb. Author of *The Hurdy-Gurdy in Eighteen-Century France* (1995). Editor of *Recent Researches in Music of the Baroque Era,* vol. 89 (1998). Contributor to *A Viola da Gamba Miscellany, Early Music, Journal of the Viola da Gamba Society of America,* and *Haydn Yearbook.* **Essays:** Dowland, John; Instruments: Lute and Guitar; Tablatures.

Greenwald, Helen M. Department of Musicology, New England Conservatory of Music, Boston. Contributor to *New Grove Dictionary of Music and Musicians, Journal of the American Musicology Society, ACTA Musicologica, 19th-Century Music,* and *Music and Letters.* **Essay:** Puccini, Giacomo.

Grier, James. Associate Professor, Faculty of Music, University of Western Ontario. Author of *The Critical Editing of Music: History, Theory, and Method* (1996). Contributor to *Journal of the American Musicological Society, Revue D'Histoire des Textes, Speculum, Early Music History,* and *Scriptorium.* **Essay:** Editing.

Haas, David. Associate Professor, School of Music, University of Georgia, Athens. Author of *Leningrad's Modernists: Studies in Composition and Musical Thought* (1998). Contributor to *The Sibelius Companion, Shostakovich in Context, Musical Quarterly,* and *Notes.* **Essays:** Glazunov, Alexander; Shostakovich, Dmitri; Symphony: 19th-Century Russian; Tchaikovsky, Piotr Ilych: Orchestral Music.

Haines, John. Assistant Professor, Department of Music History, Shorter College, Rome, Georgia. Contributor to *Neophilolagus, Ruminatio, Journal of Plainsong and Medieval Music,* and *New Grove Dictionary of Music and Musicians.* **Essay:** Troubadours and Trouvères.

Harley, Maria Anna. Assistant Professor, School of Music, University of Southern California, Los Angeles. Editor of *After Chopin: Essays in Polish Music* (1998), *Polish Music Journal* (1998), and *Gòrecki: An Autumn Portrait* (1998). Contributor to *Muzyka, Contemporary Music Review, Studia Musicologica, American Music, Journal of Musicological Research, Women Composers: Music Through the Ages, Crosscurrents and Counterpoints, Soundscape Yearbook,* and *Lutoskawski Studies.* **Essays:** Górecki, Henryk; Penderecki, Krysztof.

Harris-Warrick, Rebecca. Associate Professor, Department of Music, Cornell University, Ithaca, New York.

Author of *Musical Theatre at the Court of Louis XIV: "Le Marriage de la Grosse Cathos"* (with Carol G. Marsh, 1994). Editor and translator of *Principles of the Harpsichord by Monsieur de Saint Lambert* (1984). Editor of *La Favorite* by Gaetano Donizetti (1997). Contributor to *Early Music, Jean-Baptiste Lully and the Music of the French Baroque, New Grove Dictionary of Opera, Historical Performance, Cambridge Opera Journal,* and *International Encyclopedia of Dance.* **Essay:** Dance: Baroque.

Hart, Brian J. Assistant Professor of Music History, School of Music, Northern Illinois University, DeKalb. Contributor to *Der 'Wagnérisme' in der französischen Musik und Musikkultur (1861–1914), The Symphony from Sammartini to Lutoslawski, vol. 3: The European Symphony, ca 1830–ca. 1930,* and *The Wagnerian Symphony.* **Essays:** Franck, César; Saint-Saëns, Camille.

Harwell Celenza, Anna H. Assistant Professor, School of Music, Michigan State University, East Lansing. Contributor to *Dansk Aarbog for Musikforskning.* **Essays:** Dahlhaus, Carl; Grieg, Edvard; Iconography; Publishing: From 1750; Romantic Music: General Studies; Scandinavia.

Harwood, Gregory W. Associate Professor, Department of Music, Georgia Southern University, Statesboro. Author of *Giuseppe Verdi: A Guide to Research* (1998). Contributor to *19th-Century Music, Opera Journal,* and *Current Musicology.* **Essays:** Schumann, Robert: Chamber Music; Schumann, Robert: Orchestral Music; Schumann, Robert: Piano Music; Verdi, Giuseppe: Biography; Verdi, Giuseppe: Operas: Early Period.

Hayes, Deborah. Professor of Musicology, University of Colorado, Boulder. Author of *Peggy Glanville-Hicks: A Bio-Bibliography* (1990) and *Peter Sculthorpe: A Bio-Bibliography* (1993). Contributor to *Women Composers: Music Through the Ages, Who's Who in Christian History, The Musical Woman, College Music Symposium,* and *Current Musicology.* Editorial Board member, *Journal of the International Alliance for Women in Music* (1993–94). **Essays:** Australia; Sonata: General.

Headlam, Dave. Associate Professor, Department of Music Theory, Eastman School of Music, University of Rochester, Rochester, New York. Author of *The Music of Alban Berg* (1996). Editor of *Music Theory Spectrum* (1999–), *Theory and Practice* (1994–), and *In Theory Only* (1995–). Contributor to *Contemporary Music Review, Music Theory Online, Music Theory Spectrum, International Journal of Musicology, College Music Symposium, Analyzing Rock Music,* and *Concert Music: Rock and Jazz.* **Essays:** Acoustics; Berg, Alban: Other Works.

Heimarck, Brita. Department of Music, Cornell University, Ithaca, New York. **Essays:** Ethnomusicology: Theory and Method; Indonesia.

Herzog, Silvia. Assistant Professor, Musicology, Wichita State University, Wichita, Kansas. Editor of *Ars Lyrica* (1998–). **Essays:** Madrigal: Italy; Publishing: To 1750; Wert, Giaches de.

Heuchemer, Dane. Assistant Professor, Music Department, Kenyon College, Gambier, Ohio. Editor of *Music Research Forum 7* (1992). Contributor to *Music Research Forum.* **Essays:** Gabrieli, Andrea; Monteverdi, Claudio: Sacred Music.

Heyer, John Hajdu. Professor of Music, University of Wisconsin, Whitewater. Editor of *Messe des morts,* by Gilles (critical edition, 1984), *Jean-Baptiste Lully and the Music of the French Baroque: Essays in Honor of James R. Anthony* (also contributor, 1989), and *Notus in Judaea* by Jean-Baptiste Luly (critical edition, 1996). Contributor to *Jean-Baptiste Lully: Actes du colloque/ Kongressbericht Le grand motet français (1663–1792), "Recherches" sur la Musique Française Classique,* and *New Grove Dictionary of Music and Musicians.* **Essays:** Baroque Music: General Studies; Buxtehude, Dietrich.

Hill, Camille Crunelle. Associate Professor, Department of Fine Arts and Humanities, Elizabethtown Community College, Elizabethtown, Kentucky. Contributor to *Messiaen's Language of Mystical Love.* **Essay:** Messiaen, Olivier.

Hisama, Ellie M. Assistant Professor, School of Music, Ohio State University, Columbus. Editor of *Women and Music* (1995–). Associate Editor of *Perspectives of New Music* (1997–). Editorial Board member *American Music* (1997–) and *Journal of Popular Music Studies* (1997–). Contributor to *Popular Music, Journal of Musicology, Concert Music: Rock and Jazz Since 1945, Audible Traces,* and *Reading Pop.* **Essay:** Musicology: Feminist.

Hong, Barbara J. Independent scholar, Kalamazoo, Michigan. Author of *Historical Dictionary of the Music and Musicians of Finland* (with Ruth-Esther Hillila, 1997). Contributor to *Newsletter of the Sibelius Society* and *Danish Yearbook for Musicology.* **Essay:** Sibelius, Jan.

Hooker, Lynn. Graduate student/instructor, Department of Music, University of Chicago; Lecturer, Richard J. Daley College, Chicago. Contributor to *Historical Encyclopedia of Chicago Women.* **Essays:** Bartók, Béla: Biography; Eastern Europe; Kodály, Zoltan.

Horne, William. Associate Professor, College of Music, Loyola University, New Orleans, Louisiana. Contributor to *Musical Quarterly, Brahms als Liedlcomponist,* and *Journal of Musicology.* **Essay:** Brahms, Johannes: Biography.

Houtchens, Alan. Associate Professor, Department of Music and Theater, Texas A&M University, College Station. Editor of *Musica 1558,* by Jan Blahoslav (1991), and *Musika 1561* by Jan Josquin (1991), *Vanda,* by Antonín Dvořák (critical edition, 1999). Contributor to *Journal of Musicology, Rethinking Dvořák: Views from Five Countries, Irish Musical Studies, Janáček and Czech Music, Antonín Dvořák the Dramatist, Dvořák-Studien, Opera Journal, Dvořák in America, 1892–1893,* and *Czech Music.* **Essays:** Dvořák, Antonin: Biography; Dvořák, Antonin: Works; Smetana, Bedřich.

Howe, Sondra Wieland. Independent scholar. Author of *Luther Whiting Mason: International Music Educator* (1997). Editor of *Minnesota Music Education Research Review* (1995 –). Contributor to *Journal of Research in Music Education, Canadian Music Educator, Bulletin of Historical Research in Music Education, Quarterly Journal of Music Learning and Teaching,* and *Bulletin of the Council for Research in Music Education.* Editorial Committee, *Bulletin of Historical Research in Music Education* (1991–). **Essays:** Education: History; Education: Methodologies.

Howell, Standley (adviser). Librarian, Chicago Public Library. Contributor to numerous journals, including *Journal of Musicological Research* and *Journal of the American Musical Instrument Society.*

Hubbert, Julie B. Assistant Professor, Department of Music, University of South Carolina, Columbia. **Essays:** Aesthetics: Romantic; Borrowing; Schumann, Robert: Aesthetics and Writings.

Hung, Eric. Ph.D. candidate in Musicology, Stanford University, Stanford, California. **Essays:** Nielsen, Carl; Romantic Music: Specialized Studies.

Hurley, David Ross. Assistant Professor, Pittsburg State University, Pittsburg, Kansas. Author of *Handel's Music: Compositional Procedures in the Oratorias and Musical Dramas, 1743–1751* (forthcoming). Contributor to *Musical Quarterly, Göttinger Handel Beiträge,* and *The Cambridge Companion to Handel.* **Essay:** Handel, George Frideric: Oratorios.

Jacobson, Daniel. Associate Professor, School of Music, Western Michigan University, Kalamazoo. Author of *A Listener's Introduction to Music* (1991), *The Norton CD-ROM Masterworks* (1996), and *The Genesis and Development of Rock and Roll* (1998). Editor of

Perspectives on the Fine Arts (1993 –). Contributor to *Musicus, Journal of Musicology, Mozart-Jahrbuch, Dvořák in America,* and *Opera Quarterly.* **Essays:** Morley, Thomas; Mozart, Wolfgang Amadeus: Operas; Schubert, Franz: Symphonies.

Joe, Jeongwon. Assistant Professor, Department of Music, University of Nevada, Reno. Editor of *Between Opera and Cinema* (with Rose Theresa, 1999). Contributor to *The Ends of Postmodernism, Music Research Forum,* and *Journal of Musicological Research.* **Essays:** Aleatoric Music; Film Music; Musicology: New Musicology; Opera: 20th Century.

Joyner, David. Professor, College of Music, University of North Texas. **Essay:** Jazz: After 1960.

Karr, John. Instructor, University of Louisville, Louisville, Kentucky. Contributor to *Music Research Forum.* **Essays:** Fauxbourdon; Italy: Music Centers to 1600; Motet: Renaissance.

Katz, Mark. Ph.D. candidate, Department of Music History, University of Michigan, Ann Arbor. Contributor to *International Dictionary of Black Musicians* and *Music and Technology in the Twentieth Century.* **Essays:** Instruments: Strings: Violin; Sound Recording: General.

Kauffman, Deborah. Contributor to *Women Composers: Music Through the Ages, Performance Practice Review, American Music Teacher,* and *Piano and Keyboard.* **Essays:** Convents; Performance Practice: General.

Kearns, Andrew. Furman University, Greenville, South Carolina. Contributor to *Horn Call Annual* and *Journal of Musicological Research.* **Essays:** Classical Music: Specialized Studies; Symphony: 18th-Century German.

Kinder, Keith. Associate Professor, School of Art, Drama and Music, McMaster University, Hamilton, Ontario. Author of *Franz Liszt's Music for Voices and Winds* (1995), *The Wind and Wind-Chorus Music of Anton Bruckner* (forthcoming), and *Best Music for Chorus and Winds* (forthcoming). Contributor to *Liszt Saeculum, Canadian Band Journal, Teaching Music Through Performance in Band,* and *IGEB Kongressbericht Abony/ Ungarn.* **Essays:** Band Music; Bruckner, Anton: Other Works.

Kinderman, William. Professor of Music, University of British Columbia. **Essay:** Beethoven, Ludwig van: Sketches.

King, Richard G. Assistant Professor, School of Music, University of Maryland, College Park. Editor of *Newsletter of the American Handel Society* (1997–). Contributor to *Journal of the Royal Musical Association, Tijdschrift van de Vereniging Voor Nederlandse Muziekgeschiedenis, Notes, Musical Quarterly,* and *Music and Letters.* **Essay:** Handel, George Frideric: Biography.

Kluge, Mark. Independent author. Editor of *Wilhelm Furtwängler Society of America Newsletter* (1992–99). Contributor to *Wilhelm Furtwängler Society of America Newsletter, Maestrino, The Wagnerian Symphony,* and *International Classical Record Collector.* **Essay:** Bruckner, Anton: Symphonies.

Koenig, Laura J. Instructor, Department of Music, University of Alaska, Anchorage. **Essays:** Aesthetics: Classical; Harrison, Lou; Theory and Theorists: 18th Century; Tuning and Temperaments.

Korstvedt, Benjamin M. Author of *Bruchner: Symphony no. 8* (forthcoming). Contributor to *19th Century Music, Musical Quarterly, Chord and Discord,* and *Bruchner Studies.* **Essay:** Bruckner, Anton: Biography.

Kreitner, Kenneth. Associate Professor, Department of Music, University of Memphis, Memphis, Tennessee. Author of *Discoursing Sweet Music: Town Bands and Community Life in Turn-of-the-Century Pennsylvania* (1990) and *Robert Ward: A Bio-Bibliography* (1990). Contributor to *Early Music, Musica Disciplina, Revista de Musicología,* and *Early Music History.* **Essay:** Instruments: Brass.

Krummel, Donald W. (adviser). Professor Emeritus, University of Illinois, Urbana-Champaign. Author of *The Literature of Music Bibliography: An Account of the Writings on the History of Music Printing and Publishing* (1992), *The Memory of Sound: Observations on the History of Music on Paper* (1988), *Bibliographical Handbook of American Music* (1987), and *English Music Printing, 1553–1700* (1975). Editor, with Stanley Sadie, of *Music Printing and Publishing* (1990). Contributor to numerous journals.

Laki, Peter. Program Annotator, Cleveland Orchestra, Cleveland, Ohio. Editor of *Bartók and His World* (1995). Contributor to *MLA Notes, International Journal of Musicology,* and *Musical Quarterly.* **Essay:** Monody.

Lam, Joseph S.C. Associate Professor, Department of Music History and Musicology, School of Music, University of Michigan, Ann Arbor. Author of *State Sacrifices and Music from Ming China (A.D. 1368–1644): Creativity, Orthodoxy and Expressiveness* (1998). Editor of *Themes and Variations: Writings on Music in Honor of Rulan Chao Pian* (1994) and *Journal of the Association for Chinese Music Research* (1998–). Contributor to *Current Musicology, The World of Music, Harmony and*

Counterpoint: Ritual Music in Chinese Context, Yearbook for Traditional Music, and *Journal of Royal Musical Association.* Editorial Board member *Chinoperl* (1996–) and *Ming Studies* (1997–). **Essays:** China; Japan.

Langford, Jeffrey. Director of Doctoral Studies, Manhattan School of Music, New York. Author of *Hector Berlioz: A Guide to Research* (with Jane Denker Graves). Contributor to *Journal of Musicological Research, Verdi Newsletter, Musical Quarterly,* and *Music and Letters.* **Essay:** Berlioz, Hector: Works.

Leclair, Charmaine Fran. Independent scholar. **Essays:** India; Philosophy of Music; Villa Lobos, Heitor.

Lerner, Neil. Assistant Professor, Department of Music, Davidson College, Davidson, North Carolina. Contributor to *Visible Evidence: The Collection* and *Popular Music and Society.* **Essay:** Glass, Philip.

Leve, James. Assistant Professor, Eitchburg State College. **Essays:** Porter, Cole; Rodgers, Richard.

Libin, Kathryn L. Shanks. Visiting Assistant Professor of Music, Vassar College. Editorial board member for *Journal of the American Musical Instrument Society* (1996–). Contributor to *Early Music, Notes, Persuasions, Piano Today,* and *Journal of the American Musical Instrument Society.* **Essays:** Concerto: From 1750; Keyboard Music: Classical.

Lindberg, John E. Associate Professor, Music Department, Mankato State University, Mankato, Minnesota. Author of *Origins and Development of the Sixteenth-Century Tricinium* (1988). Editor of *Concerti Grossi for 2 Violins* by Christoph Graupner (1996) and *Concerto Grosso in B-flat Major for 2 Oboes* by Christoph Graupner (1997). Contributor to *Notes, Fontes artis musicae,* and *American Recorder.* **Essay:** Lied: To 1800.

Lindeman, Stephen. Assistant Professor, School of Music, Brigham Young University, Provo, Utah. Author of *Structural Novelty and Tradition in the Early Romantic Piano Concerto* (1998). Contributor to *Revised New Grove Dictionary of Music and Musicians.* **Essay:** Mendelssohn, Felix.

Lindsey, Roberta. Adjunct Professor, School of Music, Indiana University, Indianapolis. Contributor to *IAWM Journal* and *Ohioana Quarterly.* **Essays:** Barber, Samuel; Copland, Aaron: Works; Hanson, Howard.

Lodato, Suzanne M. Fellow, Society of Fellows in the Humanities, Columbia University, New York. Contributor to *Revised New Grove Dictionary of Music and Musicians, Current Musicology,* and *Proceedings of the*

International Conference "Word and Music Studies: Assessing an Interart Discipline". **Essay:** Reger, Max.

Lopes, Luiz Fernando Vallim. Associate Instructor, Music Department, Indiana University, Bloomington. Contributor to *Resound* and *International Dictionary of Black Composers.* **Essay:** Latin America.

Lorimer, Nancy. Assistant Librarian, Stanford Music Library, Stanford, California. **Essays:** Liturgical Drama; Medieval Music: General Studies; Performance Practice: Medieval.

Lowe, Melanie. Assistant Professor of Musicology, Vanderbilt University, Nashville, Tennessee. **Essays:** Mode: Non-Western; Rock and Roll: 1960s England.

Lowerre, Kathryn. Duke University Medical Center, Durham, North Carolina. Contributor to *Imago Musicae.* **Essays:** Gilbert, William Schwenck, and Sullivan, Arthur; Masque; Purcell, Henry: Dido and Aeneas.

Lynn, Donna L. Independent scholar. Contributor to *Musical Times.* **Essays:** Brahms, Johannes: Chamber Music; Chamber Music: 20th Century; Schoenberg, Arnold: Biography; Schubert, Franz: Piano Music; Webern, Anton.

Magee, Jeffrey. Assistant Professor, Department of Musicology, Indiana University, Bloomington. Editor of *Music of the United States of American* (1993–97). Contributor to *American Music, Journal of the American Musicological Society,* and *Cambridge History of American Music.* **Essays:** Jazz: Bebop; Jazz: Early.

Marissen, Michael. Associate Professor of Music, Swarthmore College, Swarthmore, Pennsylvania. Author of *The Social and Religious Designs of J.S. Bach's Brandenburg Concertos* (1995), *An Introduction to Bach Studies* (with Daniel R. Melamed, 1998), and *Lutheranism, Anti-Judaism, and Bach's St. John Passion* (1998). Editor of *Creative Responses to Bach from Mozart to Hindemith* (1998). Vice President of American Bach Society. Contributor to *Musical Quarterly, Bach,* and *Journal of Musciology.* **Essay:** Bach, Johann Sebastian: Biography (with Daniel R. Melamed).

Marsh, Gordon. Assistant Professor, Department of Fine Arts, Roanoke College, Salem, Virginia. Contributor to *Journal of Musicological Research Volume 12* and *Proceedings from the International Congress for Music.* **Essays:** Aesthetics: Modern; Berio, Luciano; Ligeti, György; Lutosławski, Witold.

Martin, Margot. Department of Fine Arts, El Camino College, Torrance, California. Contributor to *Biblio,*

Notes, and *Consor.* **Essays:** Baroque Music: Specialized Studies; Couperin, François; Instruments: Keyboard: Other Keyboard; Rameau, Jean-Philippe.

Marvin, Roberta M. Associate Professor, School of Music, University of Iowa, Iowa City. Contributor to *Verdi's Middle Period: Source Studies, Analysis and Performance Practice (1849–1859), Irish Music Studies: Maynooth International Musicological Conference: Selected Proceedings , Revista de Musicología,* and *Studi Verdiani.* **Essay:** Verdi, Giuseppe: Operas: Staging.

Mathers, Daniel E. Ph.D. candidate, University of Cincinnati, Cincinnati, Ohio. Assistant Editor of *Theory and Practice* (1991–92). **Essay:** Copland, Aaron: Biography.

Mathiesen, Thomas J. (adviser). David H. Jacobs Distinguished Professor of Music, School of Music, Indiana University, Bloomington. Author of *Apollo's Lyre: Greek Music and Music Theory in Antiquity and the Middle Ages* (1999), *Ancient Greek Music Theory* (1988), and *Aristides Quintilianus on Music* (1983). Editor of *Greek and Latin Music Theory, Festa musicologica: Essays in Honor of George J. Buelow,* and *Thesaurus Musicarum Latinarum.* Contributor to *Journal of Music Theory, Festival Essays for Pauline Alderman,* edited by Burton Karson, *Acta musicologica, Journal of Musicology, Music Theory Spectrum, Indian Theory Review,* and *Musical Humanism and Its Legacy: Essays in Honor of Claude V. Palisca,* edited by B.R. Hanning and N.K. Baker.

Mattis, Olivia. Visiting Assistant Professor of Musicology, Eastman School of Music. Associate editor, *La critique musicale d'Hector Berlioz* (1996), Contributor to *New Grove Dictionary of Music and Musicians* (forthcoming edition), *Electronic Musician, Settling New Scores: Music Manuscripts from the Paul Sacher Foundation,* edited by Felix Meyer, *Lili Boulanger-Tage, Library Chronicle of the University of Texas at Austin, Musical Quarterly, Keyboard,* and *La revue musicale.* **Essays:** 20th-Century Music: General Studies; Varèse, Edgard.

Mayer, Constance. Head of User Services, William and Gayle Cook Music Library, Indiana University, Bloomington. **Essay:** Copyright.

Mayfield, Connie E. Instructor of Music, Kansas City Community College, Kansas City, Kansas. Author of *Theory Essentials* (forthcoming). Editor of *Arnold Bax: Selected Works for Piano* (1986). **Essays:** Electronic Music; Instruments: Electronic; MIDI.

McCachren, Renee. Associate Professor, Department of Music, Catawba College, Salisbury, North Carolina. Associate Editor of *Theoria* (1984–86). Contributor to *Proceedings of the Research Symposium on the Psychol-*

ogy and Acoustics of Music. **Essays:** Beethoven, Ludwig van: Chamber Music; Form: Sonata Form; Keyboard Music: General; Theory and Theorists: 19th Century.

McClellan, Michael E. Assistant Professor, Music Department, Chinese University of Hong Kong. Contributor to *Chimères, Musical Quarterly, Music Research Forum,* and *Cruising the Performative: Interventions into the Representation of Ethnicity, Nationality, and Sexuality.* **Essays:** Castrato; Neoclassicism; Opera: French to 1800; Oratorio: French to 1750; Symphony: 18th-Century French.

mcclung, bruce d. Assistant Professor, Musicology Department, University of Cincinnati, Cincinnati, Ohio. Editor of *Lady in the Dark: A Sourcebook* (1997). Contributor to *A Stranger Here Myself, Playbill,* and *Kurt Weill Newsletter.* **Essay:** Weill, Kurt.

McCoy, Marilyn L. Assistant Archivist, Arnold Schoenberg Institute, University of Southern California, Los Angeles. Co-editor of *Journal of the Arnold Schoenberg Institute* (1994–96). Contributor to *Musik als Text: Bericht des Internationalen Kongress der Gesellschaft der Musikforschung* and *Wien 1897: Kulturgeschichtliches Profil eines Epochenjahres.* **Essays:** Mahler, Gustav: Works; Wolf, Hugo.

McGrade, Michael. Visiting Assistant Professor, Williams College, Williamstown, Massachusetts. Contributor to *Journal of the American Musicological Society* and *Early Music History.* **Essays:** Chant, Ambrosian; Chant; Gregorian; Medieval Music: Specialized Studies; Organum; Sequence.

McLamore, Alyson. Associate Professor, Music Department, California Polytechnic State University, San Luis Obispo. Editor of and contributor to *Musica Franca: Essays in Honor of Frank D'Accone* (1996). Contributor to *Women Composers: Music Through the Ages, Journal of the Music Library Association,* and *The Musical Migration and Ernst Toch.* **Essay:** Women in Music.

Meconi, Honey. Associate Professor, Music School, Rice University, Houston, Texas. Contributor to *Tijdschrift van de Veveniging voor Nederlandse Muziekgeschiedenis, Music in Renaissance Cities and Courts: Studies in Honor of Lewis Lockwood, Journal of the Royal Musical Association, Journal of Musicology,* and *I Tatti Studies: Essays in the Renaissance.* **Essay:** Hildegard von Bingen.

Melamed, Daniel R. Associate Professor, Department of Music, Yale University, New Haven, Connecticut. Author of *J.S. Bach and the German Motet* (1995) and *An Introduction to Bach Studies* (with Michael Marissen, 1998). Editor of *Bach Studies vol. 2 (1995).* **Essays:** Bach, Johann Sebastian: Biography (with Michael Marissen).

Meyer, Stephen. Associate Professor, Syracuse University, Syracuse, New York. Contributor to *Opera Quarterly* and *Opera Journal.* **Essays:** Opera: German to 1800; Opera: 19th-Century German; Weber, Carl Maria von.

Miller, Roark. General Libraries, Emory University, Atlanta, Georgia. Contributor to *Music and Letters* and *Studi musicali.* **Essays:** Caccini, Francesca; Caccini, Giulio; Oratorio: Italian to 1750.

Miller, Stephen R. Assistant Professor, Department of Music, University of The South, Sewanee, Tennessee. Contributor to *Revised New Grove Dictionary of Music and Musicians, Neo-Latin News,* and *Società Italiana di Musicolgia.* **Essay:** Palestrina, Giovanni Pierluigi da.

Miyakawa, Felicia M. Ph.D. candidate, Department of Musicology, Indiana University, Bloomington. **Essays:** Rock and Roll: 1950s United States; Rock and Roll: 1970s United States.

Mockus, Martha. Comparative Studies in Discourse and Society, University of Minnesota. Contributor to *Queering the Pitch: The New Gay and Lesbian Musicology* and *Audible Traces: Gender, Identity, and Music.* **Essay:** Oliveros, Pauline.

Moran, John. Author of *The Cello: A Social History* (forthcoming). Contributor to *Revised New Grove Dictionary of Music and Musicians, Musical Objects,* and *Continuo.* **Essays:** Chamber Music: Baroque; Early Music Movement; Ornamentation: Classsical; Paganini, Niccolò.

Morrison, Julie Dorn. Researcher/Writer, Curriculum Services, Washtenaw Community College, Ann Arbor, Michigan. Contributor to *Opera Quarterly.* **Essays:** Mahler, Gustave: Biography; Quantz, Johann, Joachim.

Morrow, Mary Sue. Associate Professor of Musicology, College-Conservatory of Music, University of Cincinnati, Cincinnati, Ohio. Author of *Concert Life in Haydn's Vienna* (1989) and *German Music Criticism in the Late 18th-Century: Aesthetic Issues in Instrumental Music* (1997). Music editor of *The Eighteenth Century: A Current Bibliography* (1986–89). Contributor to *The Musical Times, Southern Quarterly, 19th-Century Music, Beethoven Journal,* and *Music and Culture in America.* **Essay:** Symphony: 18th-Century Italian.

Moulsdale, Gary. Ph.D. candidate in musicology, Cornell University, Ithaca, New York. **Essay:** Gluck, Christoph Willibald.

Muir, Theresa. Independent musicologist. Contributor to the program book for the Teatro dell' opera, the *Baltimore*

Opera Student Guides, and *Nineteenth-Century British Studies,* vol. 2. **Essays:** Wagner, Richard: Biography; Wagner, Richard: Tristan und Isolde; Wagner, Richard: Other Operas.

Murata, Margaret. Professor, Department of Music, University of California, Irvine. Author of *Operas for the Papal Court, 1631–1668* (1981), and *Strunk's Source Readings in Music History: The Baroque* (rev. ed. 1998). Editor of *Cantatas by Marc'Antonio Pasqualini, 1614–1691.* Contributor to *Revista Italiana di Musicologia, Journal of the American Musicological Society, Analecta Musicologica, Early Music History,* and *Cambridge Opera Journal.* Editorial Board member, *Journal of the Society for 17th-Century Music* (1995–) and Early Music America Performers' Guides (ca. 1992–96). **Essay:** Cantata: Italian Baroque.

Murphy, Sheryl Kathleen. Independent scholar. Author of *The Sacred Music of Gian Francesco de Majo (1732–1770)*(1996). Contributor to *Revised New Grove Dictionary of Music and Musicians.* **Essays:** Hasse, Johann Adolf; Pergolesi, Giovanni Battista; Scarlatti, Alessandro.

Nadeau, Nils. Independent scholar. **Essays:** Chant: Other Western; Rock and Roll: 1960s United States.

Nealon, Michael A. Music Lead Faculty, Department of Humanities and Performing Arts, Lansing Community College, Lansing, Michigan. **Essays:** Instruments: General; Rore, Cipriano de.

Neff, Lyle K. Ph.D. candidate, Musicology Department, School of Music, Indiana University, Bloomington. Contributor to *Biographical Dictionary of Russian/Soviet Composers, Opera Quarterly, Pushkin Review, Bard Yearbook,* and *Revised New Grove Dictionary of Music and Musicians.* **Essay:** Rimsky-Korsakov, Nikolai.

Neff, Teresa M. Lecturer in Music, Tufts University, Medford, Massachusetts. **Essay:** Mattheson, Johann.

Nelson, Bernadette. Research Fellow, Department of Music, University of Hong Kong. Contributor to *Early Music, Musical Times, Leading Notes, Revitsa Portuguesa de Musicologia,* and *Actas del Coloquio Internacional "Fuentes Musicales en la Península Iberica, c. 1250–c. 1500".* **Essay:** Portugal.

Nikitopoulos, Alison Terbell. Instructor, School of Music, Louisiana State University, Baton Rouge. Contributor to *Arrigo Boito.* **Essays:** Libretto; Verdi, Giuseppe: Operas: Late Period.

Nolan, Catherine. Associate Professor, Faculty of Music, University of Western Ontario. Contributor to *Journal of Music Theory, College Music Symposium,* and *Music Theory Spectrum.* Editorial Board member, *Music Theory Online* (1997–99). **Essay:** Theory and Theorists: 20th Century.

Noonan, Timothy. Lecturer, Department of Music, University of Wisconsin, Milwaukee. **Essay:** Boccherini, Luigi.

O'Connell, Jeremy. Graduate student, Department of Music, Cornell University, Ithaca, New York. Contributor to *Revised New Grove Dictionary of Music and Musicians.* **Essays:** Chromaticism; Harmony: Theory.

Ogasapian, John. Professor, Department of Music, University of Massachusetts, Lowell. Author of *Organ Building in New York City, 1700–1900* (1977), *Henry Erben: Portrait of a Nineteenth-Century American Organ Builder* (1980), *Church Organs (1983),* and *English Cathedral Music in New York: Edward Hodges of Trinity Church* (1994). Editor of *Tracker.* Contributor to *Tracker, American Organist, Journal of Church Music, Art of the Organ,* and *Journal of the British Institute for Organ Studies.* **Essay:** Instruments: Keyboard: Organ.

Oldani, Robert William. Professor, School of Music, Arizona State University, Tempe. Author of *Modest Musorgsky and Boris Godunov: Myths, Realities, Reconsiderations* (with Caryl Emerson, 1994). Contributor to *Revised New Grove Dictionary of Music and Musicians, Slavic and Eastern European Arts, History of European Ideas, Opera Quarterly, Musorgskij: L'Opera, Il Pensiero, Musorgsky, In Memorium, 1881–1981,* and *19th-Century Music.* Editorial Board member, *Studies in Russia and Eastern Europe* (1989–) and *Liberal and Fine Arts Review* (1980–84). **Essay:** Mussorgsky, Modest.

Oleskiewicz, Mary. Curator of Musical Instruments, America's Shrine to Music Museum, Vermillion, South Dakota, and Assistant Professor of Music, University of South Dakota, Vermillion. Contributor to *Bach Perspectives, Journal of the American Musical Instrument Society,* and *Scripta Artium.* **Essay:** Instruments: Builders.

Olin, Elinor. Associate Professor, Department of Music, National-Louis University, Evanston, Illinois. Contributor to *19th-Century Music* and *Lyric Opera Season Study Guides.* **Essays:** Chanson; Massenet, Jules.

Olson, Greta J. Associate Professor, Music Department, Chinese University of Hong Kong. **Essays:** Passion Music; Spain: General Studies; Spain: Musical Centers.

Onderdonk, Julian. Visiting Professor of Music, Williams College. Contributor to *Folk Music Journal* and *Vaughan Williams Studies.* **Essay:** Vaughan Williams, Ralph.

Orchard, Joseph. Independent scholar. **Essays:** Chamber Music: Classical; Mozart, Wolfgang Amadeus: Chamber Music.

Orr, N. Lee. Professor of Music, Georgia State University, Atlanta. Author of *The Church Music Handbook* (1991) and *Alfredo Barili and the Rise of Classical Music in Atlanta* (1996). Contributor to *American Organist, Symposium, American Music, Tracker,* and *American Music Research Journal.* Editorial Board member, *19th-Century Studies.* **Essays:** MacDowell, Edward; Psalmody: American.

Ossi, Massimo. Associate Professor of Music, University of Rochester, Rochester, New York. Author of *Divining the Oracle: Aspects of Claudio Monteverdi's Second Practica* (forthcoming). Editor of *17th-Century Music* (1993–97), *Current Musicology* (1985–89), and *Music at the Courts of Italy.* Contributor to *Journal of the American Musicological Society, Music in Renaissance Cities and Courts, Evarini: La Musica, I Musicisti,* and *Opera in Context: Essays on Historical Staging from the Late Renaissance to the Time of Puccini.* **Essays:** Instrumental Music: Renaissance; Monteverdi, Claudio: Biography; Monteverdi, Claudio: Madrigals.

Paige, Diane M. Ph.D. candidate, Department of Music, University of California, Santa Barbara. Contributor to *Musical Quarterly, Czech and Slovak Music Society,* and *Opera Quarterly.* **Essay:** Janáček, Leoš.

Palmer, John R. Freelance musicologist. Author of *Program and Process in the Second Symphony of Gustav Mahler* (1996). **Essay:** Rock and Roll: 1970s England.

Palmer, Robert E. Lecturer, Department of Music, Mason Gross School of the Arts, Rutgers University, New Brunswick, New Jersey. **Essays:** Pertucci, Ottaviano; Renaissance Music: Specialized Studies; Schütz, Heinrich.

Parks, Richard S. Professor, Department of Music Theory and composition, Faculty of Music, University of Western Ontario. Author of *18th-Century Counterpoint and Tonal Structure* (1983) and *The Music of Claude Debussy* (1989). Editor of *Music at The University of Western Ontario* (1991). Contributor to *Debussy in Performance, The Carl Nielsen Companion, Music and Letters, Music Analysis, Journal of Music Theory,* and *Music Theory Spectrum.* **Essays:** Analysis: Atonal; Analysis: General, Debussy, Claude: Works.

Pershing, Drora. Aaron Copland School of Music, Queens College, City University of New York. Contributor to *Journal of the Violin Society of America* and *A New Approach to Sightsinging.* **Essay:** Bach, Johann Sebastian: Orchestral Music.

Platt, Heather. Assistant Professor, School of Music, Ball State University, Munice, Indiana. Editor of *RILM Abstracts of Music Literature* (1986–94) and *Theory and Practice* (1989–91). Contributor to *Brahms Studies, Alban Berg: Music as Encrypted Speech, Fontes Artis Musicae, Journal of Musicology, Fasch und die Musik im Europa des 18. Jahrhunderts, Intégral, Indiana Theory Review,* and *Studien zur Aufführungspraxis und Interpretation der Musik des 18. Jahrhunderts.* **Essays:** Brahms, Johannes: Orchestral Music; Brahms, Johannes: Vocal Music; Lied; 19th Century.

Portowitz, Adena. Lecturer, Department of Musicology, Bar-Ilan University, Ramat-Gan, Israel. Contributor to *Israel Studies in Musicology, Beethoven Journal, Austria 996–1996: Music in a Changing Society,* and *Orbis Musicae.* **Essay:** Mozart, Wolfgang Amadeus: Orchestral Music.

Reich, Nancy B. Author of *Clara Schumann: The Artist and the Woman* (1985). Editor of *Louise Reichardt: Songs* (1981). Contributor to *Women Making Music, 19th-Century Music, Women and Music: A History, Musicology and Difference,* and *Brahms Society Newsletter.* **Essay:** Schumann, Clara.

Reindl, Dawn O'Neal. Ph.D. candidate, Indiana University, Bloomington. **Essays:** Martinů, Bohuslav; Paderewski, Jan Ignaz.

Renwick, William. Associate Professor, School of Art, Drama and Music, McMaster University, Ontario. Author of *Analyzing Fugue: A Schenkerian Approach* (1995) and *The Langloz Manuscript* (1999). Contributor to *Music Theory Spectrum, Music Analysis, Computers in Music Research,* and *Bach Perspectives 4.* **Essays:** Analysis: Schenkerian; Counterpoint; Fugue; Fux, Johann Joseph.

Rio, Robin. Assistant Professor, Music Therapy, Arizona State University, Tempe. Author of *Using Music Therapy for Nursing Home Residents with Severe Dementia: A Training Manual for Caregivers* (forthcoming). Contributor to *Nursing Spectrum.* **Essay:** Music Therapy.

Risinger, Mark. Lecturer, Department of Music, Harvard University, Cambridge, Massachusetts. **Essays:** Handel, George Frideric: Instrumental Music; Manuscript Studies: Baroque; Schumann, Robert: Lieder.

Rivera, Benito (adviser). Professor, Music Theory Department, Indiana University, Bloomington. Translator of Joachim Burmeister, *Musical Poetics* (1993), and Johann Lippius, *Synopsis of New Music* (1977). Author of *German Music Theory in the Early 17th Century: The Treatises of Johannes Lippius* (1980). Contributor to numerous journals.

Rivest, Johanne. Visiting scholar, School of Music, University of Illinois, Urbana. Editor of *Circuit* (1997). Contributor to *Essays in American Music, Circuit*, and *Revue de musique des universités canadiennes*. Editorial Board member, *Les cahiers de la Société québécoise de recherche en musique* (1993–98). **Essay:** Improvisation.

Roberge, Marc-André. Associate Professor, Faculty of Music, Laval University, Quebec. Author of *Ferruccio Busoni: A Bio-Bibliography* (1991). Editor of *Cahiers de L'ARMuQ* (1989–92) and *Revue de Musique des Universités Canadiennes* (1992–). Contributor to *Music Review, Research Chronicle, American Music, Musical Quarterly, Revue of Musicologie, Sorabji: A Critical Celebration* and *Music in Canada/La Musique au Canada: A Collection of Essays*. Editorial Board member *Sonances* (1984–90). **Essay:** Busoni, Ferruccio.

Robinson, Kathleen E. Independent scholar. **Essay:** Walton, William.

Rohling, Geraldine M. Director of Music and Worship, Catholic University of America, Washington, D.C. Contributor to *The "Music" Bruderschaften of Vienna (1288–1783)* and *The Music and Processions of the Corpus Christi Brotherhood at St. Stephan's in Vienna*. **Essays:** Liturgy: Introduction; Liturgy: Divine Office.

Romanou, Ekaterini. Lecturer, Department of Music, University of Athens. Author of *ΕΘΝΙΚΗΣ ΜΟΥΣΙΚΗΣ ΠΕΡΙΗΓΗΣΙΣ 1901–1912* (1996). Editor of *ΜΟΥΣΙΚΟΛΟΓΙΑ* (1985–98). Contributor to *ΜΟΥΣΙΚΟΛΟΓΙΑ, Studies in Easter Chant*, and *Revue de Pedagogie Musicale et Chorégraphique*. **Essays:** Clementi, Muzio; Scarlatti, Domenico; Tchaikovsky, Piotr Ilyich: Biography; Xenakis, Iannis.

Rosenblatt, Jay. Assistant Professor, School of Music, University of Arizona, Tucson. Contributor to *Journal of Musicological Research, Journal of the American Liszt Society, Notes*, and *Pendragon Review*. **Essays:** Liszt, Franz: Orchestral Music; Liszt, Franz: Piano Music.

Saloman, Ora Frishberg. Professor of Music, Bernard M. Baruch College and The Graduate School and University Center, City University of New York. Author of *Beethoven's Symphonies and J.S. Dwight: The Birth of American Music Criticism* (1995). Contributor to *Acta Musicologica, International Review of the Aesthetics and Sociology of Music, Musical Quarterly, Music and the French Revolution, Journal of Musicology, Journal of the Royal Musical Collection*, and *Mainzer Studien zur Musik: Festschrift Walter Wiora zum 90. Geburtstag*. Editorial Board member, *American Music* (1995–97). **Essay:** Criticism: 18th and 19th Centuries.

Saunders, Steven. Associate Professor, Department of Music, Colby College, Waterville, Maine. Author of *The Complete Works of Steven Collins Foster* (1990), *Cross, Sword and Lyre: Sacred Music at the Court of Ferdinand II of Habsburg* (1995), *Fourteen Motets from the Court of Ferdinand II* (1995). Contributor to *Infinite Boundaries, Relazioni musicali tra Italia e Germania, Studien zur Musikwissenschaft, Music and Letters*, and *Journal of the American Musicological Society*. Editorial Board member, *Journal of 17th-Century Music*. **Essay:** Foster, Stephen.

Schenbeck, Lawrence. Associate Professor, Department of Music, Spelman College, Atlanta, Georgia. Author of *Joseph Haydn and the Classical Choral Tradition* (1996). Editor of *Choral Journal* (1996–). Contributor to *American Choral Review, Choral Journal, BACH, Opera Quarterly*, and *Musical Quarterly*. **Essays:** Haydn, Franz Joseph: Sacred Music; Mozart, Leopold; Mozart, Wolfgang Amadeus: Sacred Music.

Schiano, Michael Jude. Assistant Professor of Music Theory, Hartt School, University of Hartford, West Hartford, Connecticut. Contributor to *Notes* and *Revised New Grove Dictionary of Music and Musicians*. **Essays:** Analysis: Serial; Analysis: Tonal; Schoenberg, Arnold: Music.

Schreffler, Anne C. (adviser). Professor, Musikwissenschaftliches Institut, Universität Basel. Author of *Webern and the Lyric Impulse: Songs and Fragments on Poems of Georg Trakl* (1994). Contributor to numerous journals.

Schulenberg, David. Author of *The Instrumental Music of Carl Philipp Emanuel Bach* (1984) and *The Keyboard Music of J.S. Bach* (1992). Editor of *Bach Perspectives*, vol. 4. Contributor to *Current Musicology, Journal of Musicology, Early Music, Musica Disciplina, Journal of Musicological Research, C.P.E. Bach Studies, 18th-Century Keyboard Music*, and *Bach Perspectives*. Editorial Board member, *Journal of the American Musicological Society*. **Essays:** Bach, Carl Philipp Emanuel; Bach, Johann Christian; Continuo; Keyboard Music: Baroque; Keyboard Music: Renaissance.

Sears, Ann. Professor of Music, Wheaton College, Norton, Massachusetts. Review editor of *Sonneck Society for American Music Bulletin* (1995–97) and review editor of *College Music Society Symposium* (1995–). Contributor to *Sonneck Society for American Music Bulletin, Notes, American Music, Black Music Research Journal*, and *Feel the Spirit: Studies in Nineteenth-Century Music*. **Essays:** Haydn, Franz Joseph: Keyboard Music; Joplin, Scott.

Seitz, Elizabeth. Visiting Assistant Professor, Tufts University, Medford, Massachusetts. **Essay:** Stravinsky, Igor: Biography.

Self, Stephen. Professor of Music, Mount Vernon Nazarene College, Mount Vernon, Ohio. Author of *The Si Place Repertoire of 1480–1530* (1996). **Essays:** Cantus Firmus; Lauda; Manuscript Studies: Renaissance.

Sheinbaum, John J. Graduate student, Department of Music, Cornell University, Ithaca, New York. **Essays:** Adorno, Theodor W.; Symphony: 19th-Century German; Symphony: 20th Century.

Sherr, Richard (adviser). Professor of Music, Smith College, Northampton, Massachusetts. Author of *Papal Music Manuscripts in the Late Fifteenth and Early Sixteenth Centuries* (1996), and *Music and Musicians in Renaissance Rome and Other Courts* (1999). Editor of *Papal Music and Musicians in Late Medieval and Renaissance Rome* (1998) and member of the editorial board of the *Journal of the American Musicological Society* (1990–92). Contributor to numerous collections and journals, including *Journal of the American Musicological Society, Musical Quarterly, Renaissance Quarterly, Early Music, Journal of Musicology,* and *Hearing the Motet: Essays on the Motet of the Middle Ages and Renaissance,* edited by Dolores Pesce.

Sherwood, Gayle. Assistant Professor of Musicology, University of Toledo, Toledo, Ohio. Contributor to *Musical Quarterly, Ives Essays,* and *International Dictionary of Black Composers.* **Essays:** Cowell, Henry; Gottschalk, Louis Moreau.

Shinnick, Julia W. Author of *The Manuscript Assisi, Biblioteca del Sacro Convento, Ms. 695: A Codicological and Repertorial Study* (1997). **Essays:** Liturgy: Mass; Luther, Martin; Trope.

Simms, Bryan R. Professor, University of Southern California, Los Angeles. Author of, *Music of the 20th Century: Style and Structure* (1986, 2nd edition, 1996), *The Art of Music: An Introduction* (1993), *Alban Berg: A Guide to Research* (1996), and *The Atonal Music of Arnold Schoenberg, 1908–1923* (1999). Editor of *Journal of Music Theory* (1971–74, 1975–76), *Music Theory Spectrum* (1978–82), *Composers on Modern Musical Culture* (1998), and *Schoenberg, Berg, and Webern: A Companion to the Second Viennese School* (1999). Contributor to *Contructive Dissonance, Cambridge Opera Journal, Models of Analysis: Early 20th-Century Music, Journal of the Arnold Schoenberg Institute,* and *Perspective of New Music.* **Essay:** Berg, Alban: Operas.

Sims, Michael. Managing editor, MIT Press, Cambridge, Massachusetts. **Essays:** Bernstein, Leonard; Ragtime.

Sipe, Thomas. Independent Scholar, Author of *Beethoven: Eroica Symphony* (1998). Contributor to

Beethoven Forum. **Essays:** Beethoven, Ludwig van: Biography; Beethoven, Ludwig van: Influence; Classical Music: General Studies; Hoffmann, E.T.A.; Keyboard Music: Romantic.

Smith, Jeremy L. Assistant Professor, School of Music, State University of New York, Fredonia. Contributor to *MLA Notes* and *Proceedings of the First International Conference on Watermarks.* **Essays:** Byrd, William; Madrigal: England.

Sposato-Allen, Lorraine. Adjunct Professor, Department of Social and Cultural Studies, Floyd College, Rome, Georgia, and Department of Music, State University of West Georgia, Carrollton. **Essay:** Shakespeare and Music.

Sprout, Leslie. Ph.D. candidate, Department of Music, University of California, Berkeley. Contributor to *Repercussions.* **Essays:** Keyboard Music: 20th Century; Milhaud, Darius.

Stayer, Jayme. Assistant Chair, Communications/Humanities, Owens Community College, Toledo, Ohio. Contributor to *Beethoven Journal* and *T.S. Eliot and Music.* **Essays:** Rhetoric; Stravinsky, Igor: Other Music.

Steib, Murray. Assistant Professor, Department of Music, Ball State University, Muncie, Indiana. Contributor to *New Grove Dictionary of Music and Musicians, The Encyclopedia of the Renaissance, Journal of Musicology,* and *Tijdschrift van de Vereniging voor Nederlandse Muziekgeshiedenis.* Editor of critical edition of the music of Martini. **Essay:** Josquin des Prez.

Stempel, Larry. Associate Professor of Music, Department of Art History and Music, Fordham University, New York. Contributor to *Saturday Review, Perspectives of New Music, Musical Quarterly, Schweizerische Musikzeitung, Music Library Association Notes, A New Orpheus: Essays on Kurt Weill, Sennets and Tuckets: A Bernstein Celebration,* and *American Music.* **Essay:** Musical Comedy.

Strader, Nikola D. Lecturer, School of Music, Ohio State University, Columbus. Ohio. **Essays:** Britten, Benjamin: Biography; Britten, Benjamin: Operas; Britten, Benjamin: Other Works.

Strempel, Eileen L. Assistant Professor, Crane School of Music, State University of New York, Potsdam. **Essay:** Song: England.

Suchoff, Benjamin. Adjunct Professor, Department of Ethnomusicology, University of California, Los Angeles. Author of *Guide to Bartók's Mikrokosmos* (1983), *A*

Musician's Guide to Desktop Computing (1994), *Béla Bartók, "Concerto for Orchestra": Understanding Bartók's World* (1995), and *Bartók: The Man as Artist and Folklorist* (1999). Contributor to numerous essay collections and journals. **Essay:** Bartók, Béla: Ethnomusicology.

Sullivan, Todd. Assistant Professor, Department of Music, Indiana State University. **Essays:** Cavalli, Pier Francesco; Obrecht, Jakob; Renaissance Music: General Studies.

Swenson-Eldridge, Joanne E. Assistant Professor, Department of Music, Beloit College, Beloit, Wisconsin. Author of *Charles Hommann: Chamber Music for Strings* (1998). Contributor to *American Music Research Center Journal, American National Biography,* and *Revised New Grove Dictionary of Music and Musicians.* **Essays:** Conductors and Conducting; Dello Joio, Norman; Symphony: General.

Termini, Olga. Professor Emeritus, Music Department, California State University, Los Angeles. Editor of *Drammaturgia Musicale Veneta,* vol. 13 (1986). Contributor to *Festival Essays for Pauline Alderman, Antonio Caldara: Essays on His Life and Times, Liuteria e Musica Strummentale a Brescia, Music in Performance and Society, Music Review, Church Music, Studi musicali, RMA Research Chronicle, Informazioni estudi vivaldiani,* and *Opera Journal.* Editorial Board member, *Journal of the Arnold Schoenberg Institute* (1974–81). **Essays:** Handel, George Frideric: Operas; Monteverdi, Claudio: Operas; Opera: 17th-Century Italian.

Tiedge, Faun Tanenbaum. Professor of Music History and Music Theory, San Francisco Conservatory of Music. Contributor to *New Grove Dictionary of Music and Musicians* (forthcoming edition), *Notes, Informazioni e studi Vivaldiani,* and *Cinquant' anni di produzioni e consumi della musica dell' eta di Vivaldi.* **Essays:** Ballet: Russian; Ballet: United States; Vivaldi, Antonio.

Toft, Robert. Professor, Department of Music History, University of Western Ontario. Author of *Aural Images of Lost Traditions: Sharps and Flats in the Sixteenth Century* (1992), *"Tune thy Musicke to thy Hart:" The Art of Eloquent Singing in England 1597–1622* (1993), and *Expressive Singing in England 1780–1830* (forthcoming). Editor of *Studies in Music from the University of Western Ontario* (1991–98). Contributor to *Tijdschrift van de Vereniging voor Nederlandse Muziekgeschiedenis, Early Music, Music and Letters, Performance Practice Review,* and *Journal of Musicological Research.* **Essays:** Mode: Renaissance; Musica ficta.

Vaughn, Michael. Instructor, Department of Music, National-Louis University, Chicago. **Essays:** Great Britain: General Studies; Oratorio: German to 1750; Psalmody: British; Purcell, Henry: Biography.

Verble, Charles R. Ph.D. candidate, Department of Academic Studies and Composition, Northwestern University, Evanston, Illinois. **Essays:** Beethoven, Ludwig van: Orchestral Music; Haydn, Franz Joseph: Orchestral Music.

Vishio, Anton. Assistant Professor, Music Department, William Paterson University. **Essay:** Serialism.

von der Linn, Michael. Associate Research Scholar, Department of Music, Columbia University, New York. Contributor to *Musical Quarterly* and *Brahms Studies 3.* Editorial Board member, *Current Musicology,* (1992–98). **Essays:** Hindemith, Paul; Ives, Charles: Biography; Ives, Charles: Works.

Wagstaff, Grayson. Professor, School of Music, University of Alabama. Contributor to *Encyclopedia of the Renaissance, Yearbook of the Alamire Foundation, Inter-American Music Review, Musical Quarterly, Notes,* and *New Grove Dictionary of Music and Musicians* (forthcoming edition). **Essay:** Victoria, Tomás Luis de.

Walden, Valerie. Author of *One Hundred Years of Violoncello* (1998). Contributor to *Cambridge Companion to the Cello, Revised New Grove Dictionary of Music and Musicians,* and *The Encyclopaedic Dictionary of the Music of Russia and the Commonwealth of Independent States.* **Essays:** Instruments: Strings: Other Strings; Stradivari, Antonio.

Warfield, Patrick. Associate Instructor, Department of Musicology, Indiana University, Bloomington. **Essays:** Carter, Elliot; Ellington, Edward Kennedy, "Duke".

Warfield, Scott. Visiting Assistant Professor of Music, Centre College, Danville, Kentucky. Contributor to *Richard Strauss Blätter, Kurt Weill Newsletter, Notes, Fontes Artis Musicae,* and *Ars musica Denver.* **Essays:** Berlin, Irving; Elgar, Edward; Kern, Jerome; Still, William Grant.

Wasson, Jeffrey. Professor of Music, Humanities Department, Barat College, Lake Forest, Illinois. Author of *Gregorian Graduals of the First Mode: An Analytical Study and Critical Edition* (1987). Editor of and contributor to *A Compendium of American Musicology: Essays in Memory of John F. Ohl* (1999). Contributor to *Student Musicologist at Minnesota,* and *The Hymnal 1982 Companion.* **Essays:** Dance: Medieval and Renaissance; Dance: Classical; Dance: 19th Century; Dance: 20th Century; Form: General; Manuscript Studies: Medieval; Sweelinck, Jan Pieterszoon.

Wiecki, Ron. Editor, A-R Editions, Madison, Wisconsin. Contributor to *American Music* and *Journal of Band Research*. **Essays:** Instruments: Piano; Partch, Harry; 20th-Century Music: Specialized Studies.

Wile, Kip. Assistant Professor, Department of Music, Sam Houston State University, Huntsville, Texas. **Essay:** Stravinsky, Igor: Ballets.

Wilson Kimber, Marian. Assistant Professor, Department of Music, Cornell College, Mount Vernon, Iowa. Contributor to *Notes, 19th-Century Studies, The Mendelssohn Companion, Mendelssohn and Hensel: Their Music in History,* and *Conference Proceedings of "Ein Rufen nur aus Träumen?" Fanny Hensel, geb. Mendelssohn Bartholdy.* **Essay:** Hensel, Fanny.

Wolf, Edward Christopher. Contributor to *Musical Quarterly, Journal of Research in Music Education, Key Words in Church Music, American Music,* and *American Musical Life in Context and Practice to 1865.* **Essays:** Chorale; Hymn.

Woodside, Mary S. Assistant Professor, School of Fine Art and Music, University of Guelph, Ontario. Contributor to *19th-Century Music, Studies in Music from The University of Western Ontario, Canadian University Music Review, Canadian Slavonic Papers,* and *Canadian Children's Literature.* **Essays:** Glinka, Mikhail; Opera: 19th-Century Russian; Russia; Tchaikovsky, Piotr Ilyich: Operas.

Wright, Lesley A. Associate Professor, Department of Music, University of Hawaii, Honolulu. Editor of *Georges Bizet: Letters in the Nydahl Collection, L'Artésienne Suite No. 1,* and *L'Artésienne Suite No. 2.*

Contributor to *Fu Jen Studies, 19th-Century Music, Journal of Musicological Research, Studies in Music, MGG,* and *English National Opera Guide.* **Essays:** Bizet, Georges; Opera: 19th-Century French.

Youens, Susan (adviser). Professor of Music, Notre Dame University, Notre Dame, Indiana. Author of numerous books, including *Hugo Wolf and His Mörike Songs* (1999), *Schubert, Müller, and Die schöne Müllerin* (1997), *Schubert's Poets and the Making of Lieder* (1996), *Franz Schubert: Die schöne Müllerin* (1992), and *Hugo Wolf: The Vocal Music* (1992). Contributor to numerous collections and journals.

Youmans, Charles. Visiting Assistant Professor of Music, Centre College, Danville, Kentucky. Contributor to *Dialogues and Extensions, Richard Strauss Blätter, 19th-Century Music, Revised New Grove Dictionary of Music and Musicians,* and *Notes.* **Essays:** Strauss, Richard; Wagner, Richard: Philosophy.

Zank, Stephen. Professor, School of Music, University of Illinois at Urbana-Champaign **Essays:** Orchestration; Performance Practice: Romantic.

Zimmerman, Dan. Graduate student, Department of Music, University of Chicago. Contributor to *Journal of Music Theory.* **Essay:** Prokofiev, Sergei.

Zohn, Steven. Assistant Professor, Department of Music History, Boyer College of Music, Temple University, Philadelphia, Pennsylvania. Contributor to *Journal of the Royal Musical Association, Early Music,* and *Johann Friedrich Fasch und sein Wirken für Zerbst.* **Essays:** Bach, Johann Sebastian: Chamber Music; Concerto: Baroque; Sonata: Baroque.